Microsoft®

Second Edition

Microsoft®

ENCYCLOPEDIA of NETWORKING

Mitch Tulloch
Ingrid Tulloch

PUBLISHED BY
Microsoft Press
A Division of Microsoft Corporation
One Microsoft Way
Redmond, Washington 98052-6399

Library of Congress Cataloging-in-Publication Data
Tulloch, Mitch.
Microsoft Encyclopedia of Networking, Second Edition / Mitch Tulloch, Ingrid Tulloch.--2nd ed.
p. cm.
Includes index.
ISBN 0-7356-1378-8
1. Computer networks--Encyclopedias. I. Tulloch, Ingrid. II. Title.

TK5102 .T85 2002
004.6'03--dc21 2002020190

Printed and bound in the United States of America.

1 2 3 4 5 6 7 8 9 QWT 7 6 5 4 3 2

Distributed in Canada by Penguin Books Canada Limited.

A CIP catalogue record for this book is available from the British Library.

Microsoft Press books are available through booksellers and distributors worldwide. For further information about international editions, contact your local Microsoft Corporation office or contact Microsoft Press International directly at fax (425) 936-7329. Visit our Web site at www.microsoft.com/mspress. Send comments to *mspinput@microsoft.com.*

Acquisitions Editor: Juliana Aldous Atkinson
Project Editor: Maureen Williams Zimmerman

Body Part No. X08-22423

Dedicated to our dear friends
Ken and Bonnie Lewis, who have
stuck by us through difficult times

Contents

Alphabetical Reference of Terms

Numbers and Symbols

A

B

C

D

E

F

G

H

I

J

K

L

M

N

O

P

Q

R

S

T

U

V

W

X

Y

Z

Acknowledgments

I would like to welcome and acknowledge my wife, Ingrid Tulloch, as co-author for this second edition of the Microsoft Encyclopedia of Networking. Ingrid is a skilled researcher whose research has contributed extensively to both this edition and the previous one, and I thank Microsoft Press for their willingness to recognize her contribution to this project by adding her name next to mine.

My thanks also to the terrific team at Microsoft Press, including Juliana Aldous (Acquisions Editor) and Maureen Zimmerman (Project Editor), and at nSight, especially Susan McClung (Project Manager), Ari Globerman and John Panzarella (Technical Editors), and Joseph Gustaitis (Copy Editor).

Thanks to David L. Rogelberg and Neil Salkind, my agents at Studio B Literary Agency, and to all the other wonderful people there.

Finally, thanks to my many readers and friends whose suggestions and comments regarding the first edition have been incorporated into this new edition and have helped make it what it is—the BEST networking encyclopedia EVER!

Mitch Tulloch
www.mtit.com

Preface to the Second Edition

Welcome to the second edition of the popular *Microsoft Encyclopedia of Networking*, the premier resource for network architects, system engineers, network administrators, and IT professionals. The purpose of this Preface is to briefly describe the new and exciting changes found in this new edition, which can be summarized by the simple word *more*. Specifically, in this new edition of this encyclopedia you'll find

- **More coverage of key networking concepts and technologies**. We've added hundreds of new articles covering the latest networking technologies, including wireless networking, 3G cellular communication, broadband Internet access, LAN-host integration, network management, network security, network troubleshooting, disaster recovery, enterprise applications, P2P technologies, virus protection, carriers and service providers, and e-business standards and technologies. In addition, coverage of basic networking standards, protocols, architectures, and technologies has been enhanced and extended throughout the work by including new articles on cabling standards, routing protocols, security protocols, signal encoding methods, encryption schemes, component architectures, WAN services, multilayer switching, tape formats, multiplexing methods, remote access, terminal-based computing, Voice over IP, and the organization and operation of the Internet. And that's only scratching the surface!
- **More depth of coverage in key articles**. Essential technologies and standards, such as 802.11b wireless, ATM, Bluetooth, cellular communications, Classless Interdomain Routing, DSL, DNS, Ethernet, frame relay, Gigabit Ethernet, GSM, and ISDN, are covered in much more detail than they were in the first edition. In addition to a brief definition and overview of the subject, longer articles are frequently divided into a number of different subsections for greater clarity and more logical treatment of the subject. Headings for these subsections include Overview, History, Types, Uses, Comparison, Architecture, Implementation, Examples, Advantages and Disadvantages, Issues, Notes, and For More Information.
- **More coverage of key platforms**. Coverage of the Microsoft Windows NT platform and applications has been de-emphasized in this edition to make room for coverage of Windows 2000, Windows XP, and Microsoft's new .NET framework. In addition, increased coverage of popular UNIX platforms and open-source technologies such as Linux and Apache has been included. Overall, this new edition is less Microsoft-centric than the first edition, and instead focuses more on general networking concepts, technologies, and services with fair coverage of competing platforms from many different vendors.
- **Up-to-date coverage of standards, products, and services**. The networking world has changed considerably since the first edition of this encyclopedia came out, with the Application Services Provider marketplace exploding and then imploding, homegrown intranets evolving into powerful Enterprise Knowledge Portals, Token Ring and FDDI going the way of the dinosaur, 3G expectations being replaced by 2.5G realities, XML standards proliferating but failing to displace EDI in the marketplace, and new vendors and service providers appearing, merging, and going bankrupt faster than fruit flies can multiply. As a result of these changes, every article in this work has been thoroughly revised and updated to include the latest and most accurate information possible. In addition, many articles include two special subsections: Marketplace,

which provides a snapshot of vendors and products available at the time of writing; and Prospects, which offers our best prediction of how technologies and services will evolve over the next few years.

- **Expanded cross-references**. The list of cross-references at the end of each article has been greatly expanded to enhance the usefulness of this work as the essential reference guide for networking professionals of all levels, ranging from students pursuing their MCSE to senior network architects with years of field experience.
- **Revised introduction**. The introduction to the book has been revised and updated, and the section called History of Networking has been brought up to date with developments that have taken place since the first edition.

In conclusion, we hope you enjoy using this new edition of the *Microsoft Encyclopedia of Networking* as much as we have enjoyed writing it!

Introduction

Welcome to the second edition of the *Microsoft Encyclopedia of Networking*, a general survey of computer networking concepts, technologies, and services. This work is intended to be a comprehensive, accurate, and up-to-date resource for students, system engineers, network administrators, IT (information technology) implementers, and computing professionals from all walks of life. Before we outline this work's scope and coverage, we will ask a simple question that is surprisingly difficult to answer: what is networking?

What Is Networking?

In the simplest sense, networking means connecting computers so that they can share files, printers, applications, and other computer-related resources. The advantages of networking computers are fairly obvious:

- Users can save their important files and documents on a file server. This is more secure than storing them on workstations because a file server can be backed up in a single operation.
- Users can share a network printer, which costs much less than having a locally attached printer for each user's computer.
- Users can share groupware applications running on application servers, which enables users to share documents, send messages, and collaborate directly.
- The job of administering and securing a company's computer resources is simplified since they are concentrated on a few centralized servers.

The above definition of networking focuses on the basic goals of networking computers together: increased manageability, security, cost-effectiveness, and efficiency over non-networked systems. However, we could also focus our discussion on the different *types* of networks, including

- Personal area networks (PANs), once the stuff of science fiction but rapidly becoming a reality as the mobile knowledge workers of today carry around an array of cell phones, Personal Digital Assistants (PDAs), pagers, and other small devices
- Local area networks (LANs), which can range from a few desktop workstations in a Small Office/Home Office (SOHO) to several thousand workstations and dozens of servers deployed throughout dozens of buildings on a university campus or in an industrial park
- Metropolitan area networks (MANs), which span an urban area and are generally run by telcos and other service providers to provide companies with high-speed connectivity between branch offices and with the Internet
- Wide area networks (WANs), which might take the form of a company's head office linked to a few branch offices or an enterprise spanning several continents with hundreds of offices and subsidiaries
- The Internet, the world's largest network and the "network of networks"

On the other hand, we could also focus on the different networking *architectures* in which these various types of networks can be implemented, including

- Peer-to-peer networking, which might be implemented in a workgroup consisting of computers running Microsoft Windows 98 or Windows 2000 Professional
- Server-based networking, which might be based on the domain model of Windows NT, the domain trees and forests of Active Directory directory

service in Windows 2000, or another architecture such as Novell Directory Services (NDS) for Novell NetWare

- Terminal-based networking, which might be the traditional host-based mainframe environment; the UNIX X Windows environment; the terminal services of Windows NT Server 4 Enterprise Edition; Windows 2000 Advanced Server; or Citrix MetaFrame

Or we could look at the various networking *technologies* used to implement these architectures, including

- LAN technologies such as Ethernet, Token Ring, Fiber Distributed Data Interface (FDDI), Fast Ethernet, Gigabit Ethernet (GbE), and the emerging 10G Ethernet (10GbE)
- WAN technologies such as Integrated Services Digital Network (ISDN), T-carrier leased lines, X.25, frame relay, Asynchronous Transfer Mode (ATM), Synchronous Optical Network (SONET), Digital Subscriber Line (DSL), and metropolitan Ethernet
- Wireless communication technologies such as the wireless LAN (WAN) standards 802.11a and 802.11b, and the consumer wireless technologies HomeRF and Bluetooth
- Cellular communication systems such as Time Division Multiple Access (TDMA), Code Division Multiple Access (CDMA), Global System for Mobile Communications (GSM), and the emerging 3G cellular communication standards

In addition, we could consider the *hardware* used to implement these different networking technologies, including

- LAN devices such as repeaters, concentrators, bridges, hubs, Ethernet switches, and routers
- WAN devices such as modems, ISDN terminal adapters, Channel Service Units (CSUs), Data Service Units (DSUs), packet assembler/disassemblers (PADs), frame relay access devices (FRADs), multiplexers (MUXes), and inverse multiplexers (IMUXes)
- Equipment for organizing, protecting, and troubleshooting LAN and WAN hardware, such as racks, cabinets, surge protectors, line conditioners, uninterruptible power supplies (UPSs), KVM switches, and cable testers
- Cabling technologies such as coaxial cabling, twinax cabling, twisted-pair cabling, fiber-optic cabling, and associated equipment such as connectors, patch panels, wall plates, and splitters
- Unguided media technologies such as infrared communication, wireless cellular networking, and satellite networking, along with their associated hardware
- Data storage technologies such as redundant array of independent disks (RAID), network-attached storage (NAS), and storage area networks (SANs) along with their associated hardware, plus various enabling technologies, including Small Computer System Interface (SCSI) and Fibre Channel

Or we could talk about various technologies that *enhance the reliability, scalability, security, and manageability* of computer networks, including

- Technologies for implementing network security, including firewalls, proxy servers, and virtual private networking (VPN), and such devices as smart cards and firewall appliances
- Technologies for increasing availability and reliability of access to network resources, such as clustering, caching, load balancing, Layer 7 switching, and terminal services
- Network management technologies such as Simple Network Management Protocol (SNMP), Remote Network Monitoring (RMON), Web-Based Enterprise Management (WBEM), Common Information Model (CIM), and Windows Management Instrumentation (WMI)

Returning to a more general level, networking can also be thought of as the various *standards* that underlie the different networking technologies and hardware mentioned above, including

- The Open Systems Interconnection (OSI) networking model from the International Organization for Standardization (ISO)
- The G-series, H-series, I-series, T-series, V-series, and X-series standards from the International Telecommunication Union (ITU)
- Project 802 of the Institute of Electrical and Electronics Engineers (IEEE)
- The Requests for Comment (RFC) series from the Internet Engineering Task Force (IETF)
- Various standards developed by the World Wide Web Consortium (W3C), the Frame Relay Forum, the ATM Forum, the Gigabit Ethernet Alliance, and other standards organizations

Networking *protocols* deserve special attention in any definition of the word *networking*. These protocols include:

- LAN protocols such as NetBEUI, Internetwork Packet Exchange/Sequenced Packet Exchange (IPX/SPX), Transmission Control Protocol/Internet Protocol (TCP/IP), and AppleTalk
- WAN protocols such as Serial Line Internet Protocol (SLIP), Point-to-Point Protocol (PPP), Point-to-Point Tunneling Protocol (PPTP), and Layer 2 Tunneling Protocol (L2TP)
- Protocols developed within mainframe computing environments, such as Systems Network Architecture (SNA), Advanced Program-to-Program Communications (APPC), Synchronous Data Link Control (SDLC), and High-level Data Link Control (HDLC)
- Routing protocols such as the Routing Information Protocol (RIP), Interior Gateway Routing Protocol (IGRP), Open Shortest Path First (OSPF) Protocol, and Border Gateway Protocol (BGP)
- Internet protocols such as the Hypertext Transfer Protocol (HTTP), File Transfer Protocol (FTP), Network News Transfer Protocol (NNTP), and the Domain Name System (DNS)
- Electronic messaging protocols such as X.400, Simple Mail Transfer Protocol (SMTP), Post Office Protocol version 3 (POP3), and Internet Mail Access Protocol version 4 (IMAPv4)
- Directory protocols such as X.500's Directory Access Protocol (DAP) and the Lightweight Directory Access Protocol (LDAP)
- Security protocols such as Password Authentication Protocol (PAP), Challenge Handshake Authentication Protocol (CHAP), Windows NT LAN Manager (NTLM) Authentication, Kerberos, IP Security Protocol (IPsec), Secure Sockets Layer (SSL), and public key cryptography standards and protocols
- Serial interface standards such as RS-232, RS-422/423, RS-485, V.35, and X.21

We could dig still deeper and discuss the *fundamental engineering concepts* that underlie the various networking technologies and services previously discussed, including

- Impedance, attenuation, shielding, near-end crosstalk (NEXT), and other characteristics of cabling and other transmission systems
- Signals and how they can be multiplexed using time-division, frequency-division, statistical, and other multiplexing techniques
- Transmission parameters including bandwidth, throughput, latency, jabber, jitter, backbone, handshaking, hop, dead spots, dark fiber, and late collisions
- Balanced vs. unbalanced signals, baseband vs. broadband transmission, data communications equipment (DCE) vs. data terminal equipment (DTE), circuit switching vs. packet switching, connection-oriented vs. connectionless communication, unicast vs. multicast and broadcast, point-to-point vs. multipoint links, direct sequencing vs. frequency hopping methods, and switched virtual circuit (SVC) vs. permanent virtual circuit (PVC)

We could also talk about the different types of *providers* of networking services, including

- Internet service providers (ISPs), application service providers (ASPs), and integrated communications providers (ICPs)
- Telcos or local exchange carriers (LECs), including both Regional Bell Operating Companies (RBOCs) and competitive local exchange carriers (CLECs), that offer such popular broadband services as Asymmetric Digital Subscriber Line (ADSL) and High-bit-level Digital Subscriber Line (HDSL) through their central office (CO) and local loop connection
- Inter-exchange carriers (IXCs) that provide popular WAN services such as dedicated leased lines and frame relay for the enterprise (large companies)
- Local loop alternatives including cable modems, fixed wireless, and satellite networking companies

We could also list the various *software technologies* vendors have developed that make computer networking both useful and possible, including

- Network operating systems such as Windows, Novell NetWare, UNIX, and Linux
- Specialized operating systems such as Cisco Systems' Internetwork Operating System (IOS), which runs on Cisco routers, and the variant of IOS used on Cisco's Catalyst line of Ethernet switches
- Directory systems such as Microsoft Corporation's domain-based Active Directory, Novell Directory Services (NDS), and various implementations of X.500 and LDAP directory systems
- File systems such as NTFS file system (NTFS) on Windows platforms and distributed file systems such as the Network File System (NFS) developed by Sun Microsystems for the UNIX platform
- Programming languages and architectures for developing distributed computing applications, such as the C/C++ and Java languages, Microsoft's ActiveX and Sun's Jini technologies, component technologies such as Distributed Component Object Model (DCOM) and COM+, interprocess communication (IPC) technologies such as Remote Procedure Calls (RPCs) and named pipes, and Internet standards such as the popular Hypertext Markup Language (HTML) and the Extensible Markup Language (XML) family of standards
- Tools for integrating networking technologies in heterogeneous *environments*, such as Gateway Services for NetWare (GSNW), Services for Macintosh, Services for UNIX on the Windows 2000 platforms, and Microsoft Host Integration Server, all of which provide connectivity with mainframe systems

On an even deeper level, we could focus on the various *administration tools* for managing networking hardware, platforms, services and protocols, including

- The Microsoft Management Console (MMC) and its various snap-ins in the Windows 2000 and Windows .NET Server platforms
- The various ways routers and network appliances can be administered using Telnet, terminal programs, and the universal Web browser interface
- Popular TCP/IP command-line utilities such as arp, ping, ipconfig, traceroute, netstat, nbtstat, finger, and nslookup
- Platform-specific command-line utilities such as various Windows commands used for automating common administration tasks
- Cross-platform scripting languages that can be used for system and network administration, including JavaScript, VBScript, and Perl

We could also look at various *enterprise applications* widely used in networked environments, including

- Enterprise Resource Planning (ERP) and Customer Relationship Management (CRM) platforms
- Enterprise Information Portal (EIP) and Enterprise Knowledge Portal (EKP) platforms
- The Microsoft .NET Enterprise Server family of applications that includes Microsoft Application Center Server, BizTalk Server, Commerce Server,

Exchange Server, Host Integration Server, Internet Security and Acceleration Server, Mobile Information Server, and SQL Server

I think that you can see by now that we could go on and on, slowly unpeeling our answer to the question "What is networking?" like the many layers of an onion. And it is pretty obvious by now that there is more to networking than just hubs and cables! In fact, the field of computer networking today is almost overwhelming in its breadth and complexity, and one could spend a lifetime studying only one small aspect of the subject.

This has not always been the case. Let's take a look now at how the field of computer networking has reached the amazing point where it is today.

The History of Networking

Because networking is such a broad and complex subject, no single event represents its point of origin. However, we can arbitrarily decide on the 1960s as the formative period for the field, since that is when the computer began to affect significantly the lives of ordinary individuals and the day-to-day operation of both business and government.

1960s

In the 1960s computer networking was essentially synonymous with mainframe computing, and the distinction between local and wide area networks did not yet exist. Mainframes were typically "networked" to a series of dumb terminals with serial connections running on RS-232 or some other electrical interface. If a terminal in one city needed to connect with a mainframe in another city, a 300-baud long-haul modem would use the existing analog Public Switched Telephone Network (PSTN) to form the connection. The technology was primitive indeed, but it was an exciting time nevertheless. I remember taking a computer science class in high school toward the end of the decade, and having to take my box of punch cards down to the mainframe terminal at the university and wait in line for the output from the line printer. Alas, poor Fortran, I knew thee well!

To continue the story, the quality and reliability of the PSTN increased significantly in 1962 with the introduction of pulse code modulation (PCM), which converted analog voice signals into digital sequences of bits. A consequent development was the first commercial touch-tone phone, which was introduced in 1962. Before long, digital phone technology became the norm, and DS-0 (Digital Signal Zero) was chosen as the basic 64-kilobit-per-second (Kbps) channel upon which the entire hierarchy of the digital telephone system was built. A later development was a device called a channel bank, which took 24 separate DS-0 channels and combined them together using time-division multiplexing (TDM) into a single 1.544-Mbps channel called DS-1 or T1. (In Europe, 30 DS-0 channels were combined to make E1.) When the backbone of the Bell telephone system finally became fully digital years later, the transmission characteristics improved significantly for both voice and data transmission due to higher quality and less noise associated with Integrated Services Digital Network (ISDN) digital lines, though local loops have remained analog in many places. But that is getting a little ahead of the story.

The first communication satellite, Telstar, was launched in 1962. This technology did not immediately affect the networking world because of the high latency of satellite links compared to undersea cable communications, but it eventually surpassed transoceanic underwater telephone cables (which were first deployed in 1965 and could carry 130 simultaneous conversations) in carrying capacity. In fact, early in 1960 scientists at Bell Laboratories transmitted a communication signal coast-to-coast across the United States by bouncing it off the moon! By 1965 popular commercial communication satellites such as Early Bird were being widely deployed and used.

As an interesting aside, in 1961 the Bell system proposed a new telecommunications service called TELPAK, which it claimed would lead to an "electronic highway" for communication, but it never pursued the idea. Could this have been an early portent of the "information superhighway" of the mid-1990s?

The year 1969 witnessed an event whose full significance was not realized until more than two decades later: namely, the development of the ARPANET packet-switching network. ARPANET was a project of the U.S. Department of Defense's Advanced Research Projects Agency (ARPA), which became DARPA in 1972. Similar efforts were underway in France and the United Kingdom, but it was the U.S. project that eventually evolved into the present-day Internet. (France's MINTEL packet-switching system, which was based on the X.25 protocol and which aimed to bring data networking into every home, did take off in 1984 when the French government started giving away MINTEL terminals; by the early 1990s, more than 20 percent of the country's population was using it.) The original ARPANET network connected computers at Stanford University, the University of California at Los Angeles (UCLA), the University of California at Santa Barbara (UCSB), and the University of Utah, with the first node being installed at UCLA's Network Measurement Center. A year later, Harvard University, the Massachusetts Institute of Technology (MIT), and a few other prominent institutions were added to the network, but few of those involved could imagine that this technical experiment would someday profoundly affect modern society and the way we do business.

The year 1969 also saw the publication of the first Request For Comments (RFC) document, which specified the Network Control Protocol (NCP), the first transport protocol of ARPANET. The informal RFC process evolved into the primary means of directing the evolution of the Internet and is still used today.

That same year, Bell Laboratories developed the UNIX operating system, a multitasking, multiuser network operating system (NOS) that became popular in academic computing environments in the 1970s. A typical UNIX system in 1974 was a PDP-11 minicomputer with dumb terminals attached. In a configuration with 768 kilobytes (KB) of magnetic core memory and a couple of 200-megabyte (MB) hard disks, the cost of such a system would have been around $40,000. I remember working in those days on a PDP-11 in the cyclotron lab of my university's physics department, feeding in bits of punched tape and watching lights flash. It was an incredible experience.

Many important standards for computer systems also evolved during the 1960s. In 1962, IBM introduced the first 8-bit character encoding system, called Extended Binary-Coded Decimal Interchange Code (EBCDIC). A year later the competing American Standard Code for Information Interchange (ASCII) was introduced. ASCII ultimately won out over EBCDIC even though EBCDIC was 8-bit and ASCII was only 7-bit. The American National Standards Institute (ANSI) formally standardized ASCII in 1968. ASCII was first used in serial transmission between mainframe hosts and dumb terminals in mainframe computing environments, but it was eventually extended to all areas of computer and networking technologies.

Other developments in the 1960s included the development in 1964 of IBM's powerful System/360 mainframe computing environment, which was widely implemented in government, university, and corporate computing centers. In 1966, IBM introduced the first disk storage system, which employed 50 metal platters, each of which was 2 feet (0.6 meter) wide and had a storage capacity of 5 MB. IBM created the first floppy disk in 1967. In 1969, Intel Corporation released a RAM chip that stored 1 KB of information, which at the time was an amazing feat of engineering.

1970s

Although the 1960s were the decade of the mainframe, the 1970s gave birth to Ethernet, which today is by far the most popular LAN technology. Ethernet was born in 1973 in Xerox Corporation's research lab in Palo Alto, California. (An earlier experimental network called ALOHAnet was developed in 1970 at the University of Hawaii.) The original Xerox networking system was known as X-wire and worked at 2.94 Mbps. X-wire was experimental and was not used commercially, although a number of Xerox Palo Alto workstations used for word processing were networked together in the White House using X-wire during the Carter administration. In 1979, Digital Equipment Corporation (DEC), Intel, and Xerox formed the DIX consortium and developed the specification for standard 10-Mbps Ethernet, or thicknet, which was published in 1980. This standard was revised and additional features were added in the following decade.

The conversion of the backbone of the Bell telephone system to digital circuitry continued during the 1970s and included the deployment in 1974 of the first digital data service (DDS) circuits (then called the Dataphone Digital Service). DDS formed the basis of the later deployment of ISDN and T1 lines to customer premises, and AT&T installed its first digital switch in 1976.

In wide area networking, a new telecommunications service called X.25 was deployed toward the end of the decade. This new system was packet-switched, in contrast to the circuit-switched PSTN, and later evolved into public X.25 networks such as GTE's Telenet Public Packet Distribution Network (PDN), which later became SprintNet. X.25 was widely deployed in Europe, where it still maintains a large installed base, especially for communications in the banking and financial industry.

In 1970 the Federal Communications Commission (FCC) announced the regulation of the fledgling cable television industry. Cable TV remained primarily a broadcast technology for delivering entertainment to residential homes until the mid-1990s, when technologies began to be developed to enable it to carry broadband services to residential subscribers. Cable modems now compete strongly with Digital Subscriber Line (DSL) as the main two forms of broadband Internet access technologies.

Despite all these technological advances, however, telecommunications services in the 1970s remained unintegrated, with voice, data, and entertainment carried on different media. Voice was carried by telephone, which was still analog at the customer premises; entertainment was broadcast using radio and television technologies; and data was usually carried over RS-232 or Binary Synchronous Communication (BSC) serial connections between dumb terminals and mainframes (or, for remote terminals, long-haul modem connections over analog telephone lines).

The 1970s were also notable for the growth of ARPANET, which grew throughout the decade as additional hosts were added at various universities and government institutions. By 1971 the network had 19 nodes, mostly consisting of a mix of PDP-8, PDP-11, IBM S/360, DEC-10, Honeywell, and other mainframe and minicomputer systems linked together. The initial design of ARPANET called for a maximum of 265 nodes, which seemed like a distant target in the early 1970s. The initial protocol used on this network was NCP, but this was replaced in 1982 by the more powerful TCP/IP protocol suite. In 1975 the administration of ARPANET came under the authority of the Defense Communications Agency.

ARPANET protocols and technologies continued to evolve using the informal RFC process developed in 1969. In 1972 the Telnet protocol was defined in RFC 318, followed by FTP in 1973 (RFC 454). ARPANET became an international network in 1973 when nodes were added at the University College of London in the United Kingdom and at the Royal Radar Establishment in Norway. ARPANET even established an experimental wireless packet-switching radio service in 1977, which two years later became the Packet Radio Network (PRNET).

Meanwhile, in 1974 the first specification for the Transmission Control Protocol (TCP) was published. Progress on the TCP/IP protocols continued through several iterations until the basic TCP/IP architecture was formalized in 1978, but it was not until 1983 that ARPANET started using TCP/IP instead of NCP as its primary networking protocol.

The year 1977 also saw the development of UNIX to UNIX Copy (UUCP), a protocol and tool for sending messages and transferring files on UNIX-based networks. An early version of the USENET news system using UUCP was developed in 1979. (The Network News Transfer Protocol [NNTP] came much later, in 1987.)

In 1979 the first commercial cellular phone system began operation in Japan. This system was analog in nature, used the 800-MHz and 900-MHz frequency bands, and was based on a concept developed in 1947 at Bell Laboratories.

An important standard to emerge in the 1970s was the public-key cryptography scheme developed in 1976 by Whitfield Diffie and Martin Hellman. This scheme underlies the Secure Sockets Layer (SSL) protocol developed by Netscape Communications, which is still the predominant approach for ensuring privacy and integrity of financial and other transactions over the World Wide Web (WWW). Without SSL, popular e-business sites such as Amazon and eBay would have a hard time attracting customers!

Among other miscellaneous developments during this decade, in 1970 IBM researchers invented the relational database, a set of conceptual technologies that has become the foundation of today's distributed application environments. In 1971, IBM demonstrated the first speech recognition technologies—which have since led to those annoying automated call handling systems found in customer service centers! IBM also developed the concept of the virtual machine in 1972 and created the first sealed disk drive (the Winchester) in 1973. In 1974, IBM introduced the Systems Networking Architecture (SNA) for networking its mainframe computing environment. In 1971, Intel released its first microprocessor, a 4-bit processor called the 4004 that ran at a clock speed of 108 kilohertz (kHz), a snail's pace by modern standards but a major development at the time. Another significant event was the launching of the online service CompuServe in 1979, which led to the development of the first online communities.

The first personal computer, the Altair, went on the market as a kit in 1975. The Altair was based on the Intel 8080, an 8-bit processor, and came with 256 bytes of memory, toggle switches, and light-emitting diode (LED) lights. Although the Altair was basically for hobbyists, the Apple II from Apple Computer, which was introduced in 1977, was much more. A typical Apple II system, which was based on the Motorola 6502 8-bit processor, had 4 KB of RAM, a keyboard, a motherboard with expansion slots, built-in BASIC in ROM, and color graphics. The Apple II quickly became the standard desktop system in schools and other educational institutions. A physics classroom I taught in had one all the way into the early 1990s (limited budget!). However, it was not until the introduction of the IBM Personal Computer (PC) in 1981 that the full potential of personal computers began to be realized, especially in businesses.

In 1975, Bill Gates and Paul Allen licensed their BASIC computer programming language to MITS, the Altair's manufacturer. BASIC was the first computer language specifically written for a personal computer. Gates and Allen coined the name "Microsoft" for their business partnership, and they officially registered it as a trademark the following year. Microsoft Corporation went on to license BASIC to other personal computing platforms such as the Commodore PET and the TRS-80. I loved BASIC in those early days, and I still do!

1980s

In the 1980s the growth of client/server LAN architectures continued while that of mainframe computing environments declined. The advent of the IBM PC in 1981 and the standardization and cloning of this architecture led to an explosion of PC-based LANs in businesses and corporations around the world, particularly with the release of the IBM PC AT hardware platform in 1984. The number of PCs in use grew from 2 million in 1981 to 65 million in 1991. Novell, which appeared on the scene in 1983, soon became a major player in file and print servers for LANs with its Novell NetWare platform.

However, the biggest development in the area of LAN networking in the 1980s was the continued evolution and standardization of Ethernet. While the DIX consortium worked on Ethernet standards in the late 1970s, the IEEE with its Project 802 initiative tried working toward a single unified LAN standard. When it became clear that this goal was impossible, Project 802 was divided into a number of separate working groups, with 802.3 focusing on Ethernet, 802.4 on Token Bus, and 802.5 on Token Ring technologies and standards. The work of the 802.3 group resulted in the first Ethernet standard, called 10Base5 or thicknet, which was almost identical to the version developed by DIX. 10Base5 was called thicknet because it used thick coaxial cable, and in 1985 the 802.3 standard was extended to include 10Base2 using thin coaxial cable, commonly called thinnet.

Through most of the 1980s, coaxial cable was the main form of cabling used for implementing Ethernet. A company called SynOptics Communications, however, developed a product called LattisNet that was designed for transmitting 10-Mbps Ethernet over twisted-pair wiring using a star-wired topology that was connected to a central hub or repeater. This wiring was cheaper than coaxial cable and was similar to the wiring used in residential and business telephone wiring systems. LattisNet was such a commercial success that in 1990 the 802.3 committee approved a new standard called 10BaseT for Ethernet that ran over twisted-pair wiring. 10BaseT soon superseded the coaxial forms of Ethernet because of its ease of installation and because its hierarchical star-wired topology was a good match for the architectural topology of multistory buildings.

In other Ethernet developments, fiber-optic cabling, first developed in the early 1970s by Corning, found its first commercial networking application in Ethernet networking in 1984. (The technology itself was standardized as 10BaseFL in the early 1990s.) In 1988 the first fiber-optic transatlantic undersea cable was laid and greatly increased the capacity of transatlantic communication systems.

Ethernet bridges became available in 1984 from DEC and were used both to connect separate Ethernet LANs to make large networks and to reduce traffic bottlenecks on overloaded networks by splitting them into separate segments. Routers could be used for similar purposes, but bridges generally offered better price and performance, as well as less complexity, during the 1980s. Again, market developments preceded standards, as the IEEE 802.1D Bridge Standard, which was initiated in 1987, was not standardized until 1990.

In the UNIX arena, the development of the Network File System (NFS) by Sun Microsystems in 1985 resulted in a proliferation of diskless UNIX workstations having built-in Ethernet interfaces. This development helped drive the demand for Ethernet and accelerated the evolution of Ethernet bridging technologies into today's switched networks. By 1985 the rapidly increasing numbers of UNIX hosts and LANs connected to the ARPANET began to transform it from what had been mainly a network of mainframe and minicomputer systems into something like what it is today. The first UNIX implementation of TCP/IP came in v4.2 of Berkeley's BSD UNIX, from which other vendors such as Sun Microsystems quickly ported their versions of TCP/IP. Although PC-based LANs rapidly grew in popularity in business and corporate settings during the 1980s, UNIX continued to dominate in academic and professional high-end computing environments as the mainframe environment declined.

IBM introduced its Token Ring networking technology in 1985 as an alternative LAN technology to Ethernet. IBM had submitted its technology to the IEEE in 1982 and the 802.5 committee standardized it in 1984. IBM soon supported the integration of Token Ring with its existing SNA networking services and protocols for IBM mainframe computing environments. The initial Token Ring specifications delivered data at 1 Mbps and 4 Mbps, but it dropped the 1-Mbps version in 1989 when it introduced a newer 16-Mbps version. Interestingly, no formal IEEE specification exists for 16-Mbps Token Ring—vendors simply adopted IBM's technology for the product. Efforts were made to develop high-speed Token Ring, but these have finally been abandoned and today Ethernet reigns supreme.

Also in the field of local area networking, in 1982 the American National Standards Institute (ANSI) began standardizing the specifications for Fiber Distributed Data Interface (FDDI). FDDI was designed to be a high-speed (100 Mbps) fiber-optic networking technology for LAN backbones on campuses and industrial parks. The final FDDI specification was completed in 1988, and deployment in campus LAN backbones grew during the late 1980s and the early 1990s. But today FDDI is considered legacy technology and has been superseded in most places by Fast Ethernet and Gigabit Ethernet (GbE).

In 1983 the ISO developed an abstract seven-layer model for networking called the Open Systems Interconnection (OSI) reference model. Although some commercial networking products were developed based on OSI protocols, the standard never really took off, primarily because of the predominance of TCP/IP. Other standards from the ISO and ITU that emerged in the 1980s included the X.400 electronic messaging standards and the X.500 directory recommendations, both of which held sway for a while but have now largely been superseded—X.400 by the Internet's Simple Mail Transfer Protocol (SMTP) and X.500 by Lightweight Directory Access Protocol (LDAP).

A major event in the telecommunications/WAN field in 1984 was the divestiture of AT&T as the result of the seven-year antitrust suit brought against AT&T by the U.S. Justice Department. AT&T's 22 Bell operating companies were formed into 7 new RBOCs (only 4 are left today). This meant the end of the old Bell telephone system, but these RBOCs soon formed the Bellcore telecommunications research establishment to replace the defunct Bell Laboratories. The United States was then divided into Local Access and Transport Areas (LATAs), with intra-LATA communication handled by local exchange carriers (the Bell Operating Companies or BOCs) and inter-LATA communication handled by inter-exchange carriers (IXCs) such as AT&T, MCI, and Sprint Corporation.

The result of the breakup was increased competition, which led to new WAN technologies and generally lower costs. One of the first effects was the offering of T1 services to subscribers in 1984. Until then, this technology had been used only for backbone circuits for long-distance communication. New hardware devices were offered to take advantage of the increased bandwidth, especially high-speed T1 multiplexers, or muxes, that could combine voice and data in a single communication stream. The year 1984 also saw the development of digital Private Branch Exchange (PBX) systems by AT&T, bringing new levels of power and flexibility to corporate subscribers.

The Signaling System #7 (SS7) digital signaling system was deployed within the PSTN in the 1980s, first in Sweden and later in the United States. SS7 made new telephony services available to subscribers, such as caller ID, call blocking, and automatic callback.

The first trials of ISDN, a fully digital telephony technology that runs on existing copper local loop lines, began in Japan in 1983 and in the United States in 1987. All major metropolitan areas in the United States have since been upgraded to make ISDN available to those who want it, but ISDN has not caught on in the United States as a WAN technology as much as it has in Europe.

The 1980s also saw the standardization of SONET technology, a high-speed physical layer (PHY) fiber-optic networking technology developed from time-division multiplexing (TDM) digital telephone system technologies. Before the divestiture of AT&T in 1984, local telephone companies had to interface their own TDM-based digital telephone systems with proprietary TDM schemes of long-distance carriers, and incompatibilities created many problems. This provided the impetus for creating the SONET standard, which was finalized in 1989 through a series of Comité Consultatif International Télégraphique et Téléphonique (CCITT; anglicized as International Telegraph and Telephone Consultative Committee) standards known as G.707, G.608, and G.709. By the mid-1990s almost all long-distance telephone traffic in the United States used SONET on trunk lines as the physical interface.

The 1980s brought the first test implementations of Asynchronous Transfer Mode (ATM) high-speed cell-switching technologies, which could use SONET as the physical interface. Many concepts basic toATM were developed in the early 1980s at the France-Telecom laboratory in Lannion, France, particularly the PRELUDE project, which demonstrated the feasibility of end-to-end ATM networks running at 62 Mbps. The CCITT standardized the 53-byte ATM cell format in 1988, and the new technology was given a further push with the creation of the ATM Forum in 1991. Since then, use of ATM has grown significantly in telecommunications provider networks and has become a high-speed backbone technology in many enterprise-level networks around the world. However, the vision of ATM on users' desktops has not been realized because of the emergence of cheaper Fast Ethernet and GbE LAN technologies and because of the complexity of ATM itself.

The convergence of voice, data, and broadcast information remained a distant vision throughout the 1980s and was even set back because of the proliferation of networking technologies, the competition between cable and broadcast television, and the slow adoption of residential ISDN. New services did appear, however, especially in the area of commercial online services such as America Online (AOL), CompuServe, and Prodigy, which offered consumers e-mail, bulletin board systems (BBSs), and other services.

A significant milestone in the development of the Internet occurred in 1982 when the networking protocol of ARPANET was switched from NCP to TCP/IP. On January 1, 1983, NCP was turned off permanently—anyone who had not migrated to TCP/IP was out of luck. ARPANET, which connected several hundred systems, was split into two parts, ARPANET and MILNET.

The first international use of TCP/IP took place in 1984 at the Conseil Européen pour la Recherche Nucléaire (CERN), a physics research center located in Geneva, Switzerland. TCP/IP was designed to provide a way of networking different computing architectures in heterogeneous networking environments. Such a protocol was badly needed because of the proliferation of vendor-specific networking architectures in the preceding decade, including "homegrown" solutions developed at many government and educational institutions. TCP/IP made it possible to connect diverse architectures such as UNIX workstations, VMS minicomputers, and Cray supercomputers into a single operational network. TCP/IP soon superseded proprietary protocols such as Xerox Network Systems (XNS), ChaosNet, and DECnet. It has since become the de facto standard for internetworking all types of computing systems.

CERN was primarily a research center for high-energy particle physics, but it became an early European pioneer of TCP/IP and by 1990 was the largest subnetwork of the Internet in Europe. In 1989 a CERN researcher named Tim Berners-Lee developed the Hypertext Transfer Protocol (HTTP) that formed the basis of the World Wide Web (WWW). And all of this developed as a sidebar to the real research that was being done at CERN—slamming together protons and electrons at high speeds to see what fragments appeared!

Also important to the development of Internet technologies and protocols was the introduction of the Domain Name System (DNS) in 1984. At that time, ARPANET had more than 1000 nodes and trying to remember their numerical IP addresses was a headache. DNS greatly simplified that process. Two other Internet protocols were introduced soon afterwards: NNTP was developed in 1987, and Internet Relay Chat (IRC) was developed in 1988.

Other systems paralleling ARPANET were developed in the early 1980s, including the research-oriented Computer Science NETwork (CSNET), and the Because It's Time NETwork (BITNET), which connected IBM mainframe computers throughout the educational community and provided e-mail services. Gateways were set up in 1983 to connect CSNET to ARPANET, and BITNET was similarly connected to ARPANET. In 1989, BITNET and CSNET merged into the Corporation for Research and Educational Networking (CREN).

In 1986 the National Science Foundation NETwork (NSFNET) was created. NSFNET networked the five national supercomputing centers together using dedicated 56-Kbps lines. The connection was soon seen as inadequate and was upgraded to 1.544-Mbps T1 lines in 1988. In 1987, NSF and Merit Networks agreed to jointly manage the NSFNET, which had effectively become the backbone of the emerging Internet. By 1989 the Internet had grown to more than 100,000 hosts, and the Internet Engineering Task Force (IETF) was officially created to administer its development. In 1990, NSFNET officially replaced the aging ARPANET and the modern Internet was born, with more than 20 countries connected.

Cisco Systems was one of the first companies in the 1980s to develop and market routers for Internet Protocol (IP) internetworks, a business that today is worth billions of dollars and is a foundation of the Internet. Hewlett-Packard was Cisco's first customer for its routers, which were originally called gateways.

In wireless telecommunications, analog cellular was implemented in Norway and Sweden in 1981. Systems were soon rolled out in France, Germany, and the United Kingdom. The first U.S. commercial cellular phone system, which was named the Advanced Mobile Phone Service (AMPS) and operated in the 800-MHz frequency band, was introduced in 1983. By 1987 the United States had more than 1 million AMPS cellular subscribers, and higher-capacity digital cellular phone technologies were being developed. The Telecommunications Industry Association (TIA) soon developed specifications and standards for digital cellular communication technologies.

A landmark event that was largely responsible for the phenomenal growth in the PC industry (and hence the growth of the client/server model and local area networking) was the release of the first version of Microsoft's text-based, 16-bit MS-DOS operating system in 1981. Microsoft, which had become a privately held corporation with Bill Gates as president and chairman of the board and Paul Allen as executive vice president, licensed MS-DOS version 1 to IBM for its PC. MS-DOS continued to evolve and grow in power and usability until its final version, MS-DOS 6.22, which was released in 1993. (I still carry around a DOS boot disk wherever I go in case I need it—don't you?) Anyway, one year after the first version of MS- DOS was released in 1981, Microsoft had its own fully functional corporate network, the Microsoft Local Area Network (MILAN), which linked a DEC 206, two PDP-11/70s, a VAX 11/250, and a number of MC68000 machines running XENIX. This type of setup was typical of the heterogeneous computer networks that characterized the early 1980s.

In 1983, Microsoft unveiled its strategy to develop a new operating system called Windows with a graphical user interface (GUI). Version 1 of Windows, which shipped in 1985, used a system of tiled windows that allowed users to work with several applications simultaneously by switching between them. Version 2 was released in 1987 and supported overlapping windows as well as expanded memory.

Microsoft launched its SQL Server relational database server software for LANs in 1988. In its current version, SQL Server 2000 is an enterprise-class application that competes with other major database platforms such as Oracle and DB2. IBM and Microsoft jointly released their 32-bit OS/2 operating system in 1987 and released OS/2 1.1 with Presentation Manager a year later.

In miscellaneous developments, IBM researchers developed the Reduced Instruction Set Computing (RISC) processor architecture in 1980. Apple Computer introduced its Macintosh computing platform in 1984 (the successor of its Lisa system), which introduced a windows-based GUI that was the precursor to Windows. Apple also introduced the 3.5-inch floppy disk in 1984. Sony Corporation and Philips developed CD-ROM technology in 1985. (Recordable CD-R technologies were developed in 1991.) IBM released its AS/400 midrange computing system in 1988, which continues to be popular to this day.

1990s

The 1990s were an explosive decade in every aspect of networking, and we can only touch on a few highlights here. Ethernet continued to evolve as a LAN technology and began to eclipse competing technologies such as Token Ring and FDDI. In 1991, Kalpana Corporation began marketing a new form of bridge called a LAN switch, which dedicated the entire bandwidth of a LAN to a single port instead of sharing it among several ports. Later known as Ethernet switches or Layer 2 switches, these devices quickly found a niche in providing dedicated high-throughput links for connecting servers to network backbones. Layer 3 switches soon followed, eventually displacing traditional routers in most areas of enterprise networking except for WAN access. Layer 4 and higher switches are now popular in server farms for load balancing and fault tolerance purposes.

The rapid evolution of the PC computing platform and the rise of bandwidth-hungry applications created a need for something faster than 10-Mbps Ethernet, especially on network backbones. The first full-duplex Ethernet products, offering speeds of 20 Mbps, became available in 1992. In 1995 work began on a standard for full-duplex Ethernet; it was finalized in 1997. A more important development was Grand Junction Networks' commercial Ethernet bus, introduced in 1992, which functioned at 100 Mbps. Spurred by this advance, the 802.3 group produced the 802.3u 100BaseT Fast Ethernet standard for transmission of data at 100 Mbps over both twisted-pair copper wiring and fiber-optic cabling.

Although the jump from 10-Mbps to 100-Mbps Ethernet took almost 15 years, a year after the 100BaseT Fast Ethernet standard was released work began on a 1000-Mbps version of Ethernet popularly known as Gigabit Ethernet (GbE). Fast Ethernet was beginning to be deployed at the desktop, and this was putting enormous strain on the FDDI backbones that were deployed on many commercial and university campuses. FDDI also operated at 100 Mbps (or 200 Mbps if fault tolerance was discarded in favor of carrying traffic on the redundant ring), so a single Fast Ethernet desktop connection could theoretically saturate the capacity of the entire network backbone. Asynchronous Transfer Mode (ATM), a broadband cell-switching technology used primarily in telecommunication/WAN environments, was briefly considered as a possible successor to FDDI for backboning Ethernet networks together, and LAN emulation (LANE) was developed to carry LAN traffic such as Ethernet over ATM. However, ATM is much more complex than Ethernet, and a number of companies saw extending Ethernet speeds to 1000 Mbps as a way to provide network backbones with much greater capacity using technology that most network administrators were already familiar with. As a result, the 802 group called 802.3z developed a GbE standard called 1000BaseX, which it released in 1998. Today GbE is the norm for LAN backbones, and Fast Ethernet is becoming ubiquitous at the desktop level. Work is even underway on extending Ethernet technologies to 10 gigabits per second (Gbps). A competitor of GbE for high-speed collapsed backbone interconnects, called Fibre Channel, was conceived by an ANSI committee in 1988 but is used mainly for storage area networks (SANs).

The 1990s saw huge changes in the landscape of telecommunications providers and their services. “Convergence” became a major buzzword, signifying the combining of voice, data, and broadcast information into a single medium for delivery to businesses and consumers through broadband technologies such as metropolitan Ethernet, Digital Subscriber Line (DSL), and cable modem systems. The cable modem was introduced in 1996, and by the end of the decade broadband residential Internet access through cable television systems had become a strong competitor with telephone-based systems such as Asymmetric Digital Subscriber Line (ADSL) and G.Lite, another variant of DSL.

Also in the 1990s, Voice over IP (VoIP) emerged as the latest “Holy Grail” of networking and communications and promised businesses huge savings by routing voice telephone traffic over existing IP networks. VoIP technology works, but the bugs are still being ironed out and deployments remain slow. Recent developments in VoIP standards, however, may help propel deployment of this technology in coming years.

The first public frame relay packet-switching services were offered in North America in 1992. Companies such as AT&T and Sprint installed a network of frame relay nodes across the United States in major cities, where corporate networks could connect to the service through their local telco. Frame relay began to eat significantly into the deployed base of more expensive dedicated leased lines such as the T1 or E1 lines that businesses used for their WAN solutions, resulting in lower prices for these leased lines and greater flexibility of services. In Europe frame relay has been deployed much more slowly, primarily because of the widespread deployment of packet-switching networks such as X.25.

The Telecommunications Act of 1996 was designed to spur competition in all aspects of the U.S. telecommunications market by allowing the RBOCs access to long-distance services and IXCs access to the local loop. The result has been an explosion in technologies and services offered by new companies called competitive local exchange carriers (CLECs), with mergers and acquisitions changing the nature of the service provider landscape almost daily.

The 1990s saw a veritable explosion in the growth of the Internet and the development of Internet technologies. As mentioned earlier, ARPANET was replaced in 1990 by NSFNET, which by then was commonly called the Internet. At the beginning of the 1990s, the Internet's backbone consisted of 1.544-Mbps T1 lines connecting various institutions, but in 1991 the process of upgrading these lines to 44.735-Mbps T3 circuits began. By the time the Internet Society (ISOC) was chartered in 1992, the Internet had grown to an amazing 1 million hosts on almost 10,000 connected networks. In 1993 the NSF created Internet Network Information Center (InterNIC) as a governing body for DNS. In 1995 the NSF stopped sponsoring the Internet backbone and NSFNET went back to being a research and educational network. Internet traffic in the United States was routed through a series of interconnected commercial network providers.

The first commercial Internet service providers (ISPs) emerged in the early 1990s when the NSF removed its restrictions against commercial traffic on the NSFNET. Among these early ISPs were Performance Systems International (PSI), UUNET, MCI, and Sprintlink. (The first public dial-up ISP was actually The World, with the URL *www.world.std.com.*) In the mid-1990s, commercial online networks such as AOL, CompuServe, and Prodigy provided gateways to the Internet to subscribers. Later in the decade, Internet deployment grew exponentially, with personal Internet accounts proliferating by the tens of millions around the world, new technologies and services developing, and new paradigms evolving for the economy and business. It would take a whole book to talk about all the ways the Internet has changed our lives.

Many Internet technologies and protocols have come and gone quickly. Archie, an FTP search engine developed in 1990, is hardly used today. The WAIS protocol for indexing, storing, and retrieving full-text documents, which was developed in 1991, has been eclipsed by Web search technologies. Gopher, which was created in 1991, grew to a worldwide collection of interconnected file systems, but most Gopher servers have now been turned off. Veronica, the Gopher search tool developed in 1992, is obviously obsolete as well. Jughead later supplemented Veronica but has also become obsolete. (There never was a Betty.)

The most obvious success story among Internet protocols has been HTTP, which, with HTML and the system of URLs for addressing, has formed the basis of the Web. Tim Berners-Lee and his colleagues created the first Web server (whose fully qualified DNS name was info.cern.ch) and Web browser software using the NeXT computing platform that was developed by Apple pioneer Steve Jobs. This software was ported to other platforms, and by the end of the decade more than 6 million registered Web servers were running, with the numbers growing rapidly.

Lynx, a text-based Web browser, was developed in 1992. Mosaic, the first graphical Web browser, was developed in 1993 for the UNIX X Windows platform by Marc Andreessen while he was a student at the National Center for Supercomputing Applications (NCSA). At that time, there were only about 50 known Web servers, and HTTP traffic amounted to only about 0.1 percent of the Internet's traffic. Andreessen left school to start Netscape Communications, which released its first version of Netscape Navigator in 1994. Microsoft Internet Explorer 2 for Windows 95 was released in 1995 and rapidly became Netscape Navigator's main competition. In 1995, Bill Gates announced Microsoft's wide-ranging commitment to support and enhance all aspects of Internet technologies through innovations in the Windows platform, including the popular Internet Explorer Web browser and the Internet Information Server (IIS) Web server platform of Windows NT. Another initiative in this direction was Microsoft's announcement in 1996 of its ActiveX technologies, a set of tools for active content such as animation and multimedia for the Internet and the PC.

In cellular communications technologies, the 1990s were clearly the "digital decade." The work of the TIA resulted in 1991 in the first standard for digital cellular communication, the TDMA Interim Standard 54 (IS-54). Digital cellular was badly needed because the analog cellular subscriber market in the United States had grown to 10 million subscribers in 1992 and 25 million subscribers in 1995. The first tests of this technology, based on Time Division Multiple Access (TDMA) technology, took place in Dallas, Texas, and in Sweden, and were a success. This standard was revised in 1994 as TDMA IS-136, which is commonly referred to as Digital Advanced Mobile Phone Service (D-AMPS).

Meanwhile, two competing digital cellular standards also appeared. The first was the CDMA IS-95 standard for CDMA cellular systems based on spread spectrum technologies, which was first proposed by

QUALCOMM in the late 1980s and was standardized by the TIA as IS-95 in 1993. Standards preceded implementation, however; it was not until 1996 that the first commercial CDMA cellular systems were rolled out.

The second system was the Global System for Mobile Communication (GSM) standard developed in Europe. (GSM originally stood for Groupe Spéciale Mobile.) GSM was first envisioned in the 1980s as part of the movement to unify the European economy, and the European Telecommunications Standards Institute (ETSI) determined the final air interface in 1987. Phase 1 of GSM deployment began in Europe in 1991. Since then, GSM has become the predominant system for cellular communication in over 60 countries in Europe, Asia, Australia, Africa, and South America, with over 135 mobile networks implemented. However, GSM implementation in the United States did not begin until 1995.

In the United States, the FCC began auctioning off portions of the 1900-MHz frequency band in 1994. Thus began the development of the higher-frequency Personal Communications System (PCS) cellular phone technologies, which were first commercially deployed in the United States in 1996.

Establishment of worldwide networking and communication standards continued apace in the 1990s. For example, in 1996 the Unicode character set, a character set that can represent any language of the world in 16-bit characters, was created, and it has since been adopted by all major operating system vendors.

In client/server networking, Novell in 1994 introduced Novell NetWare 4, which included the new Novell Directory Services (NDS), then called NetWare Directory Services. NDS offered a powerful tool for managing hierarchically organized systems of network file and print resources and for managing security elements such as users and groups. NetWare is now in version 6 and NDS is now called Novell eDirectory.

In other developments, the U.S. Air Force launched the twenty-fourth satellite of the Global Positioning System (GPS) constellation in 1994, making possible precise terrestrial positioning using handheld satellite communication systems. RealNetworks released its first software in 1995, the same year that Sun Microsystems announced the Java programming language, which has grown in a few short years to rival C/C++ in popularity for developing distributed applications. Amazon.com was launched in 1995 and has become a colossus of cyberspace retailing in a few short years. Microsoft WebTV (now MSN TV), introduced in 1997, is beginning to make inroads into the residential Internet market.

Finally, the 1990s were, in a very real sense, the decade of Windows. No other technology has had as vast an impact on ordinary computer users as Windows, which brought to homes and workplaces the power of PC computing and the opportunity for client/server computer networking. Version 3 of Windows, which was released in 1990, brought dramatic increases in performance and ease of use over earlier versions, and Windows 3.1, released in 1992, quickly became the standard desktop operating system for both corporate and home users. Windows for Workgroups 3.1 quickly followed that same year. It integrated networking and workgroup functionality directly into the Windows operating system, allowing Windows users to use the corporate computer network for sending e-mail, scheduling meetings, sharing files and printers, and performing other collaborative tasks. In fact, it was Windows for Workgroups that brought the power of computer networks from the back room to users' desktops, allowing them to perform tasks previously possible only for network administrators.

In 1992, Microsoft released the first beta version of its new 32-bit network operating system, Windows NT. In 1993 came MS-DOS 6, as Microsoft continued to support users of text-based computing environments. That was also the year that Windows NT and Windows for Workgroups 3.11 (the final version of 16-bit Windows) were released. In 1995 came the long-awaited release of Windows 95, a fully integrated 32-bit desktop operating system designed to replace MS-DOS, Windows 3.1, and Windows for Workgroups 3.11 as the mainstream desktop operating system for personal computing. Following in 1996 was Windows NT 4, which included enhanced networking services and a new Windows 95–style user interface. Windows 95 was superseded by Windows 98 and later by Windows Millennium Edition (Me).

At the turn of the millennium came the long-anticipated successor to Windows NT, the Windows 2000 family of operating systems, which includes Windows 2000 Professional, Windows 2000 Server, Windows 2000 Advanced Server, and Windows 2000 Datacenter Server. The Windows family has how grown to encompass the full range of networking technologies, from embedded devices and Personal Digital Assistants (PDAs) to desktop and laptop computers to heavy-duty servers running the most advanced, powerful, scalable, business-critical, enterprise-class applications.

2000 and Beyond

It is early in the new millennium—where are we now and where are we going? The first question is relatively easy to answer:

- In the LAN field, Ethernet reigns supreme. Token Ring and FDDI are dead-end technologies, and ATM never caught on.
- Microsoft continues to be by far the dominant player on the desktop, and Windows XP has finally united the separate Windows 95, Windows 98, Windows Me, and Windows NT/2000 code streams into a single platform.
- In the enterprise (large companies), Windows NT and Windows 2000 have proved enormously popular as file, print, and application server platforms. Microsoft Exchange has eclipsed Lotus Notes as the dominant messaging platform, and Microsoft SQL Server is giving Oracle and DB2 a run for their money. IIS and Apache continue to fight it out for Web server supremacy, with each side claiming victory in different market segments. And Linux has established a niche for itself in the enterprise and continues to grow, mostly at the expense of Novell NetWare and UNIX platforms.
- Wireless networking using the 802.11b standard has exploded across the enterprise, but security continues to be a big concern for these networks, as "drive-by hackers" have shown with their laptops and BMWs. Data transmission over cellular communication systems is still incredibly slow in most areas, as 2G technologies are slowly superseded by 2.5G ones.
- Metropolitan Ethernet is the hottest WAN technology, letting companies access GbE services with plug-and-play simplicity. DSL is having trouble establishing itself as a viable enterprise option, mainly due to reliability issues. T1 prices are still ridiculously high, but not likely to change much due to consolidation in the service provider industry. And despite its lack of glamour, frame relay is going strong and still growing in the enterprise WAN.
- The Internet is now the blood and backbone of most businesses, but the number of Internet businesses that failed in the dot-com bust defies description. The Internet access market continues to consolidate, and broadband Internet access is now in the tens of millions of subscribers and rising rapidly. The "Big Three" online portals—MSN, Yahoo!, and AOL—now comprise an estimated 20 percent of all Internet traffic. Apart from eBay and Amazon, the number of truly great e-business success stories is amazingly small.
- B2B (business to business) e-business is on the rise but mostly hidden from view in the form of e-marketplaces for different corporate sectors. And XML, which promised to revolutionize e-business, is still a distant second in popularity to good old EDI.

We could say a lot more, but let's briefly address the questions, "Where are we going? What might the rest of this decade hold as far as the growth and evolution of networking in all its forms?" Here are a few "hedged-bet" predictions for you to consider:

- Will we have 3G wireless broadband connectivity for everyone, everywhere, all the time? Or will most major cellular providers go bankrupt, throwing a monkey wrench into 3G deployments and putting them years behind schedule?
- Will 10 GbE provide users and companies with unparalleled amounts of bandwidth? Or will demand for bandwidth rise even more rapidly than new technologies can accomodate?

- Will P2P file sharing platforms finally bring the Internet (and most enterprises) to its knees? Or will Dense Wavelength Division Multiplexing (DWDM) be a knight in shining armor riding to the rescue?
- Will viruses, worms, Trojans, and other forms of "malware" continue to wreak havoc with the world economy? Or will a solution be found to this growing problem that does not involve disconnecting the network cable from your computer and locking it in your closet?
- Will Bluetooth usher in an exciting high-tech world of bionic humans carrying dozens of spontaneously networked devices all the time? Or will somebody finally invent a single device that does it all?
- And will rapid evolution in computer technologies, programming paradigms, networking architectures, and the Internet make us less human? Or more?

Let the reader decide—we will give you a partial answer when the third edition of this book comes out!

The Scope of This Encyclopedia

Now that you have an idea of what networking is all about and how it has evolved over the years, you probably realize that the scope of this encyclopedia is fairly broad. Most of the information found in this book falls into these categories:

- Information about networking concepts, technologies, standards, and hardware—including such things as Ethernet, Token Ring, bandwidth, latency, hubs, switches, OSI, and X.500.
- Information about the telecommunications industry, including WAN services such as frame relay, leased lines, and ATM. Also included is coverage of various wireless networking and cellular communication technologies.
- Information about the Internet and its standards, protocols, services, architecture, and implementation—including such things as HTTP, SMTP, Web servers, Web browsers, TCP/IP, BGP, and ASP.
- Information about popular software technologies used in developing network-aware solutions, including such platforms as Windows and Linux and such applications as Apache.

Also included in this book are numerous entries from areas that are usually considered peripheral to networking per se, including network-aware programming technologies such as Java and ActiveX and cryptography standards used in networking and communication, such as Advanced Encryption Standard (AES) and Public Key Cryptography Standards (PKCS). Networking professionals and students are likely to encounter many of these terms in their daily work and reading and will benefit from the inclusion of this material.

Finally, since this is the *Microsoft* Encyclopedia of Networking, there is extensive coverage of Microsoft platforms and products, including all versions of Windows, the .NET platform and .NET Server family, services such as TechNet and MSDN, the Microsoft Web site (one of the largest in the world), and Microsoft Corporation itself.

Who This Work Is For

This book will be an invaluable reference and learning tool for all levels of networking professionals, ranging from the seasoned professional with many years of hands-on experience to the individual pursuing an entry-level certification such as CompTIA's Network+. Individuals working toward the popular Microsoft Certified Systems Engineer (MCSE) will find the book particularly helpful in their endeavors.

Many other professionals will also find this work useful, including consultants, IT implementers, sales and marketing people, and the interested lay reader.

How This Work Is Organized

The articles in this work are listed in alphabetical order, of course, and their lengths range from a few paragraphs to several pages. Longer articles are organized for readability into a number of subsections, including Overview, History, Uses, Types, Comparison, Architecture,

Implementation, Examples, Advantages and Disadvantages, Marketplace, Issues, Prospects, and Notes. Figures are included in many articles to help explain key concepts. Most articles end with a section called See Also that has cross-references to related entries elsewhere in the encyclopedia. The section called For More Information provides URLs where you can find further information online.

An effort has been made to minimize technical jargon while maintaining technical accuracy. Coverage has included up-to-the-minute developments at the time of writing, but remember that networking technologies and products change rapidly. Microsoft Press provides short updates and corrections for its books at *www.mspress.microsoft.com/support*, but major updates in material will have to wait until the next edition.

Disclaimer

Information contained in this work has been obtained from sources believed to be reliable. Although the authors and Microsoft Press have made every effort to be accurate, neither the authors nor the publisher assume any liability or responsibility for any inaccuracy or omissions contained in this book, or for any loss or damage arising from the information presented. In other words, the information provided in this book is presented on an "as is" basis. Mention of companies, service providers, vendors, and products in this work are not to be viewed as endorsements by either the authors or by Microsoft.

Comments and Questions

If you have comments, questions, or ideas regarding this encyclopedia, please direct them to Microsoft Press at *MSPInput@microsoft.com* or at the following postal address:

Microsoft Press
Attn: Microsoft Encyclopedia of Networking Editor
One Microsoft Way
Redmond, WA 98052-6399

Please note that product support is not offered through the above addresses.

You can also contact the authors of this work directly through their web site, *www.mtit.com*.

Numbers and Symbols

1Base5

An obsolete 1 megabit per second (Mbps) local area network (LAN) networking technology.

Overview

1Base5 was actually developed after the 10Base5 Standard Ethernet specification was ratified but before the ratification of the 10BaseT standard. It was developed as an initial attempt to deploy computer networking over existing unshielded twisted-pair (UTP) cabling at a time when Ethernet was still based on coaxial cabling. The popular name for 1Base5 networking technologies was StarLAN because it was wired in a hierarchical star topology. When 10BaseT was ratified as an Institute of Electrical and Electronics Engineers (IEEE) standard in 1990, however, StarLAN and similar technologies quickly became obsolete and fell into disuse.

See Also: *10BaseT, Ethernet*

2B+D

Basic Rate Integrated Services Digital Network (ISDN) service, which uses two B channels and one D channel for signaling and communications.

See Also: *Integrated Services Digital Network (ISDN)*

2B1Q

Stands for Two Binary One Quaternary, a physical layer encoding mechanism for translating digital information into electrical signals, standardized by the American National Standards Institute (ANSI) and used in Integrated Services Digital Network (ISDN) networks. In 2B1Q, four electrical amplitude and polarity values are used to represent binary information.

See Also: *line coding*

2G

Stands for second generation and refers to widely deployed cellular communications systems such as Digital Advanced Mobile Phone Service (D-AMPS), Time Division Multiple Access (TDMA), Code Division Multiple Access (CDMA), Global System for Mobile Communications (GSM), and Personal Communication Services (PCS) systems.

See Also: *3G*

2.5G

A label some vendors use to refer to several interim cellular communications systems currently being deployed as a prelude to full third-generation (3G) systems.

Overview

For many cellular systems, upgrading immediately from existing second-generation (2G) systems to full 3G functionality is costly and complex. Furthermore, some vendors question whether there is a need for the high (2 megabits per second) data rates promised by 3G and suggest that lower data rates in the hundreds of kilobits per second (Kbps) are more than sufficient for the majority of current applications. They cannot justify the enormous cost of an upgrade considering the insufficient demand for the type of interactive multimedia communications that 3G will support. Even 2.5G would be a significant leap forward from today's current 2G systems, where typical data rates are a mere 9.6, 14.4, or 19.2 Kbps.

As a result, some cellular service providers have opted to migrate from 2G to 3G in stages by first upgrading their existing Time Division Multiple Access (TDMA) and Code Division Multiple Access (CDMA) networks to interim technologies which offer much higher data transmission rates. These interim 2.5G systems include Enhanced Data Rates for Global Evolution (EDGE), developed by Ericsson, and High Data Rate (HDR), developed by Qualcomm.

For example, some TDMA networks that can carry data at only 19.2 Kbps are being upgraded first to General Packet Radio System (GPRS) overlaid on Global System for Mobile Communications (GSM) to support data transmission at 144 Kbps, and from there to EDGE which supports transmission rates of 384 Kbps. In fact, GPRS is a natural upgrade path for GSM-based systems to support Wireless Application Protocol (WAP)–based data communications easily and inexpensively at speeds from 10s to 100s of Kbps.

Similarly, many CDMA systems carrying data at 14.4 Kbps are being upgraded to intermediate technologies such as HDR before being fully upgraded to Wideband CDMA (W-CDMA) with its 2 megabits-per-second (Mbps) data rate.

In addition to the increased data rates of 2.5G systems compared to 2G (about an order of magnitude faster), another advantage is that 2.5G systems utilize packet-switching technologies that are more efficient in the transmission of IP data over cellular systems as opposed to the circuit-switching technologies in use by existing 2G systems.

Notes

Most 2.5G systems are asymmetric in their transmission speeds, supporting faster downloads than uploads. In this way they bear some similarity to cable modems and Asymmetric Digital Subscriber Line (ADSL).

Some vendors market their 2.5G systems as 3G, but this is a misnomer because they fall short of complying with the International Telecommunication Union (ITU)'s IMT-2000 standard that defines 3G technologies and systems.

See Also: 3G

3G

Stands for third generation, an umbrella name for the latest generation of cellular phone networks capable of high-speed wireless data transmission rates of up to 2 megabits per second (Mbps). 3G technologies are occasionally referred to by the name broadband wireless.

Overview

The history of wireless cellular communications has had three distinct generations since its beginnings in the early 1980s. These generations are typically identified as follows:

- **1G (first generation of cellular communications):** This involved analog transmission of voice only (did not support data) over circuit-switched networks. 1G is represented by legacy systems such as the Advanced Mobile Phone Service (AMPS) introduced by AT&T in the early 1980s and still in use in some parts of North and South America. Other 1G systems included the Extended Total Access Communications System (E-TACS) used in Europe and Asia, the Nordic Mobile Telephone system used in Scandinavia, and the Total Access Communication System (TACS) used in Great Britain, Hong Kong, and Japan. 1G systems transmitted their traffic in clear (unencrypted) form.
- **2G (second generation):** This saw the development of digital cellular systems for transmitting digitally encoded voice and data (though data transmission speeds are limited to about 19.2 kilobits per second [Kbps]). Examples of 2G systems include Digital AMPS (D-AMPS), Time Division Multiple Access (TDMA), Code Division Multiple Access (CDMA), Global System for Mobile Communications (GSM), and Personal Communication Services (PCS) systems. 2G systems are circuit switched and support a variety of extended features such as encryption, Short Message Service (SMS), and fax transmission.
- **3G (third generation):** This was first envisioned by the International Telecommunication Union (ITU) in 1992 and had two aims. The first was to be a truly global digital packet-switched cellular system (as opposed to the circuit-switched 2G systems) for voice and data communications, where users could roam between continents without requiring new phones. The second was to provide consistent high-speed data transmission rates of up to 2 Mbps. Unfortunately, neither of these goals has been completely achieved.

In 1992 the ITU proposed a system called IMT-2000 as the single global 3G-based standard for cellular communications. In 1999 conflicts between carriers, regulators, and vendors in different countries and regions led to a compromise version of the IMT-2000 standard. The agreed-upon standard incorporated a mix of three different proposed versions, two of which use CDMA technologies and the third using TDMA. Existing CDMA providers will find it easier to upgrade to 3G technologies than TDMA providers will.

Types

Qualcomm has proposed a 3G upgrade for its popular 2G system cdmaOne, used throughout much of Asia and North America. The upgrade is called cdma2000 3XMC. It has recently been ratified by the ITU and is expected to provide real data rates of 1.117 Mbps. Other CDMA providers have proposed that an initial upgrade called cdma2000 1XMC be deployed first as an interim "2.5G" cellular system before full deployment of cdma2000 3XMC is achieved. The cdma2000 1XMC technology only supports real data rates of 144 Kbps, although vendor-proprietary extensions have been proposed to extend this.

Another 3G CDMA system similar to cdma2000 3XMC and currently being rolled out in some countries and regions is called Universal Mobile Telecommunications System (UMTS) or Wideband CDMA (W-CDMA) (carriers in Europe prefer the UMTS designation, but those in North America prefer W-CDMA or WCDMA). UMTS is designed to interoperate with existing GSM networks and will provide a natural upgrade path for these networks from 2G to 3G. The first country widely rolling out W-CDMA is Japan, which is using it to replace its Personal Digital Cellular (PDC) system, whose capacity is saturated. Unfortunately, UMTS/W-CDMA cannot be provisioned in the United States because the frequencies this technology requires have already been allocated by the Federal Communications Commission (FCC) for other uses. UTMS/W-CDMA supports wireless data transmission at 2 Mbps. Note, however, that this speed will be achievable for stationary users only—for mobile environments this slows to 384 Kbps and for fast-moving vehicles such as a car on the highway, it is down to 144 Kbps.

Another proposed 3G system based on TDMA instead of CDMA is called EDGE (Enhanced Data Rates for Global Evolution). EDGE is an upgrade to existing General Packet Radio Services (GPRS) systems and supports data rates of 384 Kbps.

Prospects

3G was originally envisioned to become widespread by 2000 (hence the name of the original proposed IMT-2000 system), but these systems are only beginning to be deployed (now pushed back to between 2003 and 2005, depending on the country or region). They provide data rates less than those anticipated, and have developed interoperability problems that may not be easily resolved.

3G technology is also expensive to develop and deploy. In this regard, Europe has a head start on the United States; however, the total cost of deploying 3G throughout the European Union (EU) has been estimated to be as high as $1 trillion. The long-term viability of many European 3G carriers may be affected by the high licensing fees imposed by governments for use of suitable radio spectrum. Most industry watchers expect a shakeout in the next few years, leaving only giants such as Deutsche Telekom, France Telecom, Vodafone, and a few others.

Many countries and regions, including the United Kingdom, Belgium, Germany, and Sweden, hold auctions to parcel off portions of 3G spectrum to the highest bidders. Carriers must quickly recoup these up-front costs to remain viable. Some countries and regions, such as Norway, Finland, France, and Spain, allocate spectrum on a fixed-fee basis to first-comers, but this practice is being challenged in the EU courts as a type of subsidy that is unfair and anticompetitive.

In the United States, AT&T laid out a road map in December 2000 for its deployment of 3G wireless that involves several intermediate steps. First, its existing TDMA network, which carries data at only 19.2 Kbps, will be upgraded to GSM with an overlay of GPRS to support data transmission at 144 Kbps. Then GSM/GPRS will be upgraded to EDGE to support data transmission rates of 384 Kbps. Finally, W-CDMA will be deployed to support data at 2 Mbps. Meanwhile, CDMA carriers such as Sprint Corporation and Verizon Communications are upgrading their systems to cdma2000 and beyond. This split between W-CDMA, supported by AT&T, and cdma2000, supported by Verizon and Sprint, presents some interoperability problems for users in North America, but efforts are underway to resolve these issues.

Ultimately, when 3G systems are fully operational, they will provide mobile users with the equivalent of broadband Internet access, opening up a new world of wireless Web-based services and applications.

Notes

Although 3G wireless systems such as UMTS will be capable of supporting data transmission speeds of 2 Mbps, this will be for stationary clients only, which includes laptop computers equipped such as 3G PC cards. Transmission speeds for mobile clients such as 3G cell phones and handsets will likely top out at 384 Kbps or lower, depending on the environment's reception characteristics.

Because of the high costs and technical challenges associated with rolling out 3G systems, some cellular communications providers are rolling out unofficial "2.5G" systems as a kind of intermediate step along the way to the high-speed data rates of 3G. For more information, see the article "2.5 G" elsewhere in this chapter.

For More Information

An alliance of regulators and vendors committed to remaining neutral in the 3G standards war is the Third Generation Partnership Project, whose site can be found at *www.3gpp.org*.

Details of the ITU's IMT-2000 standard can be found at *www.itu.int/imt2000*.

See Also: *2.5G, cellular communications*

3.1 kHz bearer service

A service provided by some telcos for transmitting data over voice trunk lines.

Overview

When supporting 3.1 kHz bearer service communications, telco switches must have trunk-line echo cancellation turned off because echo cancellation will corrupt data transmissions sent over voice lines. This service is a legacy telecommunications technology that is no longer widely implemented.

Notes

Some carriers call this service data-over-voice (DOV).

4G

An envisioned fourth-generation wireless cellular system to supersede 3G (third-generation) cellular.

Overview

4G is a term sometimes applied to proposed wireless networking systems using Orthogonal Frequency Division Multiplexing (OFDM). OFDM is a modulation scheme theoretically capable of transmitting data at rates of 622 megabits per second (Mbps), which is much higher than the 2 Mbps of the 3G wireless systems that are only now beginning to be deployed. OFDM is currently defined in two implementations, one supported by the Institute of Electrical and Electronics Engineers (IEEE) and the other by the European Telecommunications Standards Institute–Broadband Radio Access Networks (ETSI-BRAN). These two implementations are different in some respects, and efforts are underway by the OFDM Forum to harmonize these systems to reduce the incompatibilities that could result once 4G systems begin to materialize. Apart from these difficulties, 4G wireless networking systems are more of a dream than a reality.

See Also: *3G*

5-4-3 rule

A specification describing limitations on constructing certain kinds of Ethernet networks. The 5-4-3 rule applies specifically to Ethernet networks based on either the thinnet or thicknet cabling option.

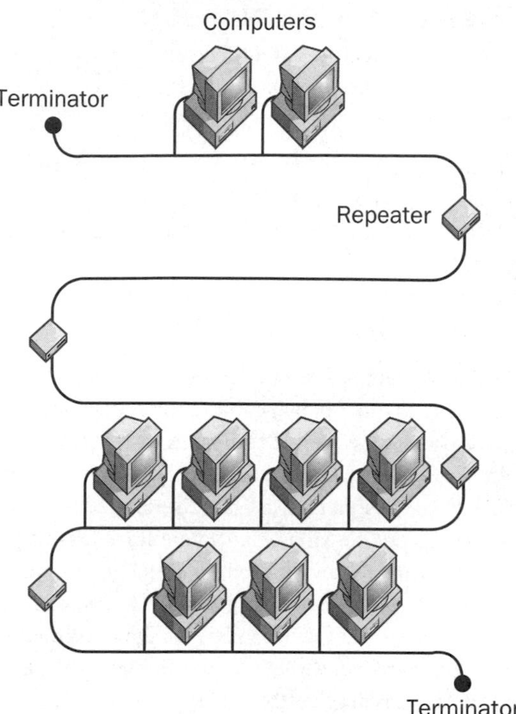

5-4-3 rule. *This rule restricts bus-style Ethernet networks to five total segments, four repeaters, and three populated segments.*

Overview

According to the Ethernet specifications, thinnet (or thicknet) Ethernet network segments can be joined using repeaters to form larger networks, but there are limitations on how you can do this. The maximum number of segments you can join is five. To join these segments, you need to use four repeaters because Ethernet typically uses a bus topology in which all segments are joined linearly. However, in this configuration, no more than three of the segments can actually have computers attached to them, leaving two segments that are used only for extending distances rather than hosting computers. These two unpopulated segments are called inter-repeater links. You should not violate this rule when implementing Ethernet networks; otherwise, unreliable network communications might result.

See Also: *Ethernet*

6bone

A testbed for development of the next generation of the Internet Protocol (IP) protocol, IPv6.

Overview

The 6bone grew out of the IP Next Generation (IPng) project of the Internet Engineering Task Force (IETF) that led to the development of IPv6. It is an informal collaborative project among a number of groups around the world, operating under the oversight of the IETF's Next Generation Transition (NGtrans) Working Group. The 6bone began operation as a virtual network in which IPv6 packets were encapsulated in and tunneled over IPv4, but migration to native IPv6 is underway and should soon be completed.

The 6bone has been playing an important role in testing IPv6 before widespread migration from the current IPv4 (standard IP) networking protocol is recommended for public use. Projects such as FreeNet6, developed by Viagénie, and vendors such as Nortel Networks and 3Com Corporation have provided IPv6 researchers with gateways for tunneling from their IPv6 testbed deployments through the IPv4 Internet and over the 6bone to test and become familiar with the new IPv6 protocol.

For More Information

The official site for the 6bone can be found at *www.6bone.net.* You can also find information there about how to join your network to the 6bone.

If you want to connect an individual workstation to the 6bone, you can use Freenet6, which can be found at *www.freenet6.net.* This site enables IPv6 end stations to connect to the 6bone through IPv4 tunneling over the Internet. You must have a dual IPv4/6 stack to connect. You can download a preliminary IPv6 stack from Microsoft Research at *www.research.Microsoft.com/msripv6.*

See Also: *IPv6*

6to4

A mechanism for connecting networks running IPv6 by tunneling through the IPv4 Internet.

Overview
6to4 was developed as a transitional scheme to support the operation of IPv6 within an IPv4 world until the backbone of the Internet is completely migrated to IPv6. 6to4 works by encapsulating IPv6 packets inside IPv4 packets and transmitting them over the existing IPv4 Internet. In this way, different islands of IPv6 connectivity can be linked across the IPv4 ocean that constitutes the Internet.

A special IPv6 prefix is used to identify an encapsulated 6to4 packet. This header is represented in IPv6 address notation as 2002::/16 and identifies the IPv6 address space specially reserved by IANA for 6to4 tunneling.

For More Information
In order to use 6to4, you must install a dual IPv4/6 protocol stack on your machine. Microsoft is integrating basic support for IPv6 into its Windows XP and Windows .NET Server operating system platforms. You can also download a pre-liminary IPv6 stack from Microsoft Research at *www.research.microsoft.com/msripv6.*

See Also: IPv6

8mm
A format for tape backup developed by Exabyte Corporation.

Overview
8mm is the standard tape format for videotape, and Exabyte developed this format into a tape backup solution to take advantage of this medium's low cost. Typical 8mm tape drives can store up to 40 gigabytes (GB) of data on a tape, and data can be written to tape at speeds in excess of 6 megabytes per second (MBps) using compression or 3 MBps without compression. Exabyte 8mm tape drives are inexpensive, have high performance, and make an attractive tape backup solution for companies developing a disaster recovery plan.

For More Information
See Exabyte online at *www.exabyte.com.*

See Also: tape format

10Base2
An Institute of Electrical and Electronic Engineers (IEEE) standard for implementing 10 megabits per second (Mbps) Ethernet over thin coaxial cabling.

Overview
10Base2 is based on the 802.3 specifications of Project 802 developed by the IEEE. It was ratified as an IEEE standard in 1985 and quickly found its way into corporate networks for small local area networks (LANs) connected to larger 10Base5 backbones.

10Base2 is sometimes referred to as thinnet or thin coax because it uses thin coaxial cabling for connecting stations to form a network (as compared to 10Base5, which uses a thicker form of cabling and hence is called thicknet). The designation 10Base2 is derived from the network's speed (10 Mbps), the signal transmission method (baseband transmission), and the maximum segment length (185 meters, rounded off to 200 with the zeros removed). Another popular nickname for this technology was Cheapernet because thinnet cabling was considerably less costly than thicknet cabling.

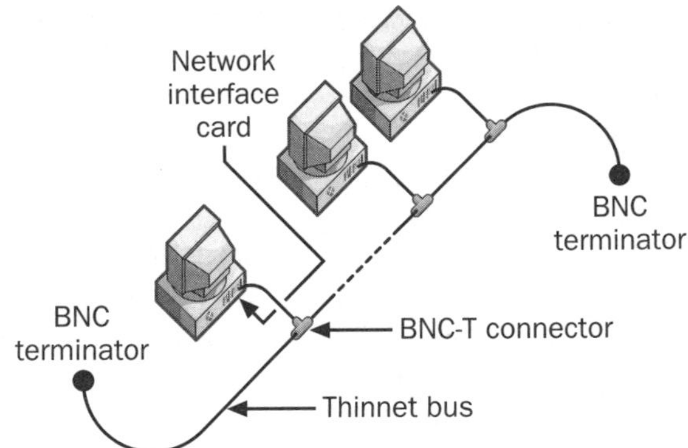

10Base2. *A typical 10Base2 network.*

Implementation
10Base2 networks are wired together using a bus topology, in which individual stations (computers) are connected directly to one long cable. The maximum length of any particular segment of a 10Base2 network is 607 feet (185 meters). If distances longer than this are required, two or more segments must be connected using repeaters. Altogether, a total of five segments can

be connected using four repeaters, as long as only three of the segments have stations (devices) attached to them. This is referred to as the 5-4-3 rule.

A 10Base2 segment should have no more than 30 stations wired to it. The minimum distance between these stations is 1.6 feet (0.5 meters). Stations are attached to the cable using BNC (British Naval Connector or Bayonet-Neill-Concelman) connectors, and the ends of the cabling have BNC cable connectors soldered or crimped to them.

10Base2 supports a maximum theoretical bandwidth of 10 Mbps, but in actuality the presence of collisions reduces this to more like 4 to 6 Mbps.

Notes

10Base2 networks are not deployed much anymore for two reasons. First, because their speed is limited to 10 Mbps, the networks perform poorly in today's bandwidth-hungry, Internet-connected world. Second, 10Base2 networks have a single point of failure—the long, linear bus cable used to connect the stations. A single break or loose connection brings down the entire network, thus every cable segment and station connection must be checked to determine the problem. If you are wiring an office for a small LAN with low bandwidth requirements, use 10BaseT instead, which is easier to manage and troubleshoot. For moderate to high bandwidth requirements, try using Fast Ethernet instead.

The two ends of a 10Base2 bus must be properly terminated. If they are not, signals will bounce and network communication will come to a halt.

See Also: *5-4-3 rule, 10Base5, 10BaseF, 10BaseT, Ethernet*

10Base5

An Institute of Electrical and Electronic Engineers (IEEE) standard for implementing 10 megabits per second (Mbps) Ethernet over coaxial cabling.

Overview

10Base5 is based on the 802.3 specifications of Project 802 developed by the IEEE. It was developed as a standard in the early 1980s and became hugely popular in corporate and campus networks. An earlier form of 10Mbps Ethernet developed by the DIX Consortium was superseded by 10Base5 when the IEEE 802.3 standard was created in 1983.

10Base5 is sometimes referred to as thicknet because it uses thick coaxial cabling for connecting stations to form a network (compared to 10Base2, which uses a thinner form of cable and is hence called thinnet). Another name for 10Base5 is Standard Ethernet because it was the first type of Ethernet to be implemented (it is also sometimes referred to as Original Ethernet, for obvious reasons). The designation 10Base5 is derived from the network's speed (10 Mbps), the signal transmission method (baseband transmission), and the maximum segment length (500 meters).

Implementation

10Base5 networks are wired together in a bus topology—that is, in a linear fashion using one long cable. The maximum length of any particular segment of a 10Base5 network is 1640 feet (500 meters). If distances longer than this are required, two or more segments must be connected using repeaters. Altogether, there can be a total of five segments connected using four repeaters, as long as only three of the segments have stations (computers) attached to them. This is referred to as the 5-4-3 rule.

A 10Base5 segment should have no more than 100 stations wired to it. These stations are not connected directly to the cable as in 10Base2 networks. Instead, a transceiver is attached to the cable, usually using a cable-piercing connector called a vampire tap. From the transceiver, a drop cable is attached, which then connects to the network interface card (NIC) in the computer. The minimum distance between transceivers attached to the cable is 8 feet (2.5 meters), and the maximum length for a drop cable is 164 feet (50 meters). Thicknet cable ends can have N-series connectors soldered or crimped on them for connecting segments together.

10Base5 was often used for backbones for large networks. In a typical configuration, transceivers on the thicknet backbone would attach to repeaters, which would join smaller thinnet segments to the thicknet backbone. In this way a combination of 10Base5 and 10Base2 standards could support sufficient numbers of stations for the needs of a moderately large company.

10Base5 supports a maximum bandwidth of 10 Mbps, but in actual networks, the presence of collisions reduces this to more like 4 to 6 Mbps.

Notes

10Base5 networks are legacy networks that are no longer being deployed, although some companies might choose to maintain existing ones for cost reasons. The complexity and bandwidth limitations of 10Base5 networks render them largely obsolete. If you are wiring an office for a small local area network (LAN) with low bandwidth requirements, use 10BaseT instead. For moderate to high bandwidth requirements, try using Fast Ethernet. If you are implementing a backbone for today's high-speed enterprise networks, Gigabit Ethernet (GbE) is now the preferred technology.

The two ends of a 10Base5 bus must be properly terminated. If they are not, signals will bounce and network communication will come to a halt.

See Also: *5-4-3 rule, 10Base2, 10BaseF, 10BaseT, 802.3, Ethernet, Fast Ethernet*

10BaseF

An Institute of Electrical and Electronic Engineers (IEEE) standard for implementing 10 megabits per second (Mbps) Ethernet over fiber-optic cabling.

Overview

10BaseF is based on the 802.3 specifications of Project 802 developed by the IEEE and differs from other forms of 10-Mbps Ethernet by using fiber-optic cabling instead of copper unshielded twisted-pair (UTP) cabling. The designation 10BaseF is derived from the network's speed (10 Mbps), the signal transmission method (baseband transmission), and the physical media used (fiber-optic cabling).

The 10BaseF standard actually consists of three separate standards describing different media specifications:

- **10BaseFB:** Defines how the synchronous data transmission occurs over the fiber-optic cabling. Using 10BaseFB segments, you can cascade or link synchronous fiber-optic hubs in configurations that are longer than traditional 10BaseT Ethernet networks and contain up to 1024 stations. This standard is more expensive and is not as widely implemented as 10BaseFL.
- **10BaseFL:** Defines the characteristics of the fiber-optic link between the nodes and the hub or concentrator. 10BaseFL replaces the older standard for fiber-optic link segments, Fiber-Optic Inter-Repeater Link (FOIRL) segments, which was developed in the 1980s. 10BaseFL is the most commonly implemented version of 10BaseF.
- **10BaseFP:** Defines the implementation of a star topology that does not use repeaters. 10BaseFP stands for Fiber Passive, and its segments can be only 500 meters (1640 feet) in length with a maximum of 33 stations connected. This standard is rarely used today.

Implementation

10BaseF is similar to 10BaseT in that each station is wired into a hub in a star topology to form the network. The maximum length of any segment of 10BaseF fiber-optic cabling is 6600 feet (2000 meters), compared to the 328 feet (100 meters) supported by 10BaseT, making 10BaseF suitable for long-haul interconnects.

The recommended cabling type for 10BaseF networks is 62.5-micron diameter fiber-optic cabling. This cable can be terminated with either ST connectors or SMA connectors, depending on the vendor and the hub configuration. Two-strand multimode fiber-optic cabling is used, with one strand allotted for transmitting data and the other for receiving data.

Marketplace

Nowadays, 10BaseF is only supported in legacy 10 Mbps Ethernet equipment and has been superseded by 100 Mbps Fast Ethernet in most circumstances for network backbones and interconnects.

Notes

10BaseF is preferable to 10BaseT in environments that are electrically noisy, such as in industrial areas, near elevator shafts, or around other motors or generators.

Fiber-optic cabling is often used for running cables between buildings. Differences in ground potential between the ends of copper cabling can induce voltages that can damage networking equipment if the ends are not grounded properly. Fiber-optic cabling also supports faster speeds than copper UTP cabling and provides a more suitable upgrade option to Fast Ethernet and beyond.

The maximum signal loss or attenuation on a given segment should be no more than 12.5 decibels. Using too many connectors in a segment of fiber-optic cabling can cause the attenuation to exceed this figure, which can lead to signal loss.

See Also: *10Base2, 10Base5, 10BaseT, 802.3, Ethernet*

10BaseT

An Institute of Electrical and Electronic Engineers (IEEE) standard for implementing 10 megabits per second (Mbps) Ethernet over twisted-pair cabling.

Overview

10BaseT is based on the 802.3 specifications of Project 802 developed by the IEEE and is the most popular form of 10-Mbps Ethernet. 10BaseT is deployed over structured cabling systems consisting of unshielded twisted-pair (UTP) cabling used for connecting end stations to centralized hubs to form a network. (Shielded twisted-pair [STP] cabling can also be used, but it never is.) The designation 10BaseT comes from the network's speed (10 Mbps), the signal transmission method (baseband transmission), and the physical medium used for transmission (twisted-pair cabling).

10BaseT became widely popular because of the earlier success of the Public Switched Telephone Network (PSTN), a hierarchical structured-wiring system to which 10BaseT bears many similarities. An advantage of 10BaseT over earlier 10 Mbps Ethernet systems such as 10Base5 and 10Base2 is that it is easier to manage because of the centralization of network traffic in hubs.

Implementation

In10BaseT networks, end stations such as workstations and servers are wired together in a star topology to a central hub. The UTP cabling used for wiring should be Category 3 (Cat3) cabling, Category 4 (Cat4) cabling, or Category 5 (Cat5) cabling, terminated with RJ-45 connectors. Patch panels can be used to organize wiring and provide termination points for cables running to wall plates in work areas. Patch cables then connect each port on the patch panel to the hub. Usually most of the wiring is hidden in a wiring cabinet and arranged on a rack for easy access.

The maximum length of any particular segment of a 10BaseT network is 328 feet (100 meters). In practice this is not a limitation because a survey by AT&T indicated that about 99 percent of desktops in commercial buildings are located within 328 feet (100 meters) of a wiring closet. If distances longer than that are required, two or more segments may be connected using repeaters. The minimum length of any given segment is restricted to 8 feet (2.5 meters).

By using stackable hubs or by cascading regular hubs into a cascaded star topology, you can network large numbers of computers using 10BaseT cable. Although 10BaseT can support up to 1024 nodes, networks with no more than 200 or 300 nodes will yield the best performance by keeping collision domains small. Hubs can be hierarchically arranged to a depth of up to three levels in order to accommodate much larger networks, but performance declines significantly as the number of stations exceeds several hundred.

Notes

Although 10BaseT theoretically supports a maximum bandwidth of 10 Mbps, in actual networks the presence of collisions reduces throughput to about 4 to 6 Mbps.

The maximum length of a 10BaseT cable segment is not a result of the specifications for round-trip communications on an Ethernet network but rather a limitation caused by the relatively low signal strength of 10BaseT systems. With enhanced Category 5 (Cat5e) cabling, you might be able to sustain network communications effectively with cable lengths up to about 490 feet (150 meters), although this is not normally recommended.

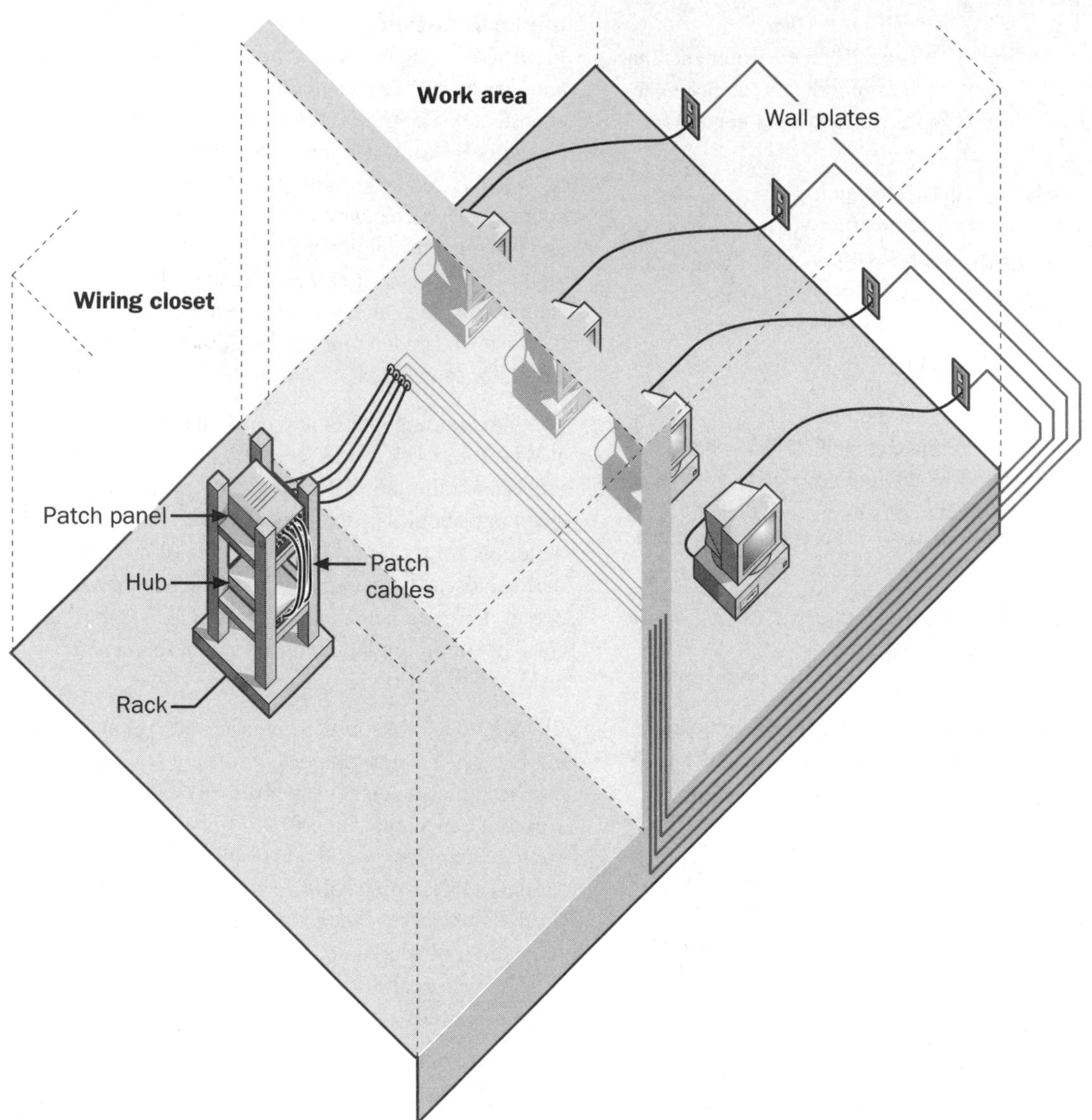

10BaseT. *A typical 10BaseT network.*

When wiring a new 10BaseT network, always use Cat5e cabling. This will make it unnecessary to rewire your network should you decide to upgrade later to Fast Ethernet and beyond.

See Also: *10Base2, 10Base5, 10BaseF, 802.3, Ethernet*

10GbE

An abbreviation for 10G Ethernet.

See: *10G Ethernet*

10G Ethernet

Also known as 10GbE, an emerging form of networking technology based on Ethernet and operating at a speed of 10 gigabits per second (Gbps). 10GbE, which stands for 10 Gigabit Ethernet, is the successor to Gigabit Ethernet (GbE) and will be standardized under the Institute of Electrical and Electronic Engineers (IEEE) 802.3ae working group.

Overview

10GbE is a switched-based technology that has similarities to and differences from earlier versions of Ethernet. It abandons the Carrier-Sense Multiple-Access with Collision Detection (CSMA/CD) Media Access Control (MAC) method of earlier versions, using instead separate send and receive channels. In other words, 10GbE operates only in full-duplex communications mode, similar to GbE and Full-Duplex Fast Ethernet. This does not eliminate contention, however, because 10GbE is designed to interoperate with slower forms of Ethernet where collisions may occur.

10GbE uses the same 48- to 1518-byte frame format as standard 10 megabits per second (Mbps) Ethernet and 100 Mbps Fast Ethernet, abandoning the jumbo frames supported by GbE. And unlike earlier versions of Ethernet, 10GbE operates exclusively over fiber-optic cabling, although efforts are being made to develop a form of 10GbE over copper cabling that can be used over the short distances needed within wiring closets. The maximum range for 10GbE will be 328 to 984 feet (100 to 300 meters) over multimode fiber and 25 miles (40 kilometers) over single-mode fiber. Laser wavelengths of 1310 and 1550 nanometers are used for medium- and long-haul transmission respectively.

Types

The driving force behind the development of 10GbE is twofold:

- Enterprise-level local area networks (LANs) that have deployed core switches with GbE interconnects (and even multiplexed GbE interconnects) are approaching saturation and require the higher backbone speed promised by 10GbE. Many server farms and clusters are being deployed today using 1000BaseT connections to network backbones. As a result, these backbones will soon face saturation unless a technology such as 10GbE can provide the necessary bandwidth to support these GbE farms (the Link Aggregation Control Protocol of 802.3ad only supports up to 8 Gbps aggregated links between switches). The impending arrival of 64-bit PC architectures such as Intel's Itanium also promises to increase the rate at which servers will be able to process data, and new servers are appearing that are able to just saturate a 1 Gbps 1000BaseT NIC. The promise here is that 10GbE will enable network architects to build Ethernet wide area networks (WANs) as easily as they build Ethernet LANs today, without having to learn more complex technologies such as Asynchronous Transfer Mode (ATM) or Synchronous Optical Network (SONET).
- WAN service providers (carriers) see 10GbE as a simpler, less costly replacement for SONET/Synchronous Digital Hierarchy (SDH), and envisage a world of end-to-end Ethernet incorporating both LAN and WAN technologies. Although Ethernet gear only costs about a fifth of what SONET gear costs, incumbent carriers have invested heavily in SONET technologies and ATM, which may affect how quickly they adopt 10GbE. Startup carriers are therefore more likely to jump on the 10GbE bandwagon than existing carriers.

As a result of this twofold need of the carriers (for SONET-compatibility) and enterprise networks (for easy upgrading of core switches from GbE to 10GbE), two different versions of 10GbE are envisioned under the emerging IEEE 802.3ae standard. These versions, listed below, operate differently at the physical layer (PHY):

- **LAN version:** This is essentially just speeded-up GbE and will operate at exactly 10.0 Gbps and use standard Ethernet frames. The primary difference with GbE is that only full-duplex communications will be supported. This version is designed to be an easy upgrade for backbone switches in enterprise LANs.
- **WAN version:** This provides a method of transporting Ethernet frames over SONET/SDH at a speed of 9.58464 Gbps (identical to the current OC-192). This version is designed to maximize compatibility with carrier's existing SONET deployments in their long-haul lines.

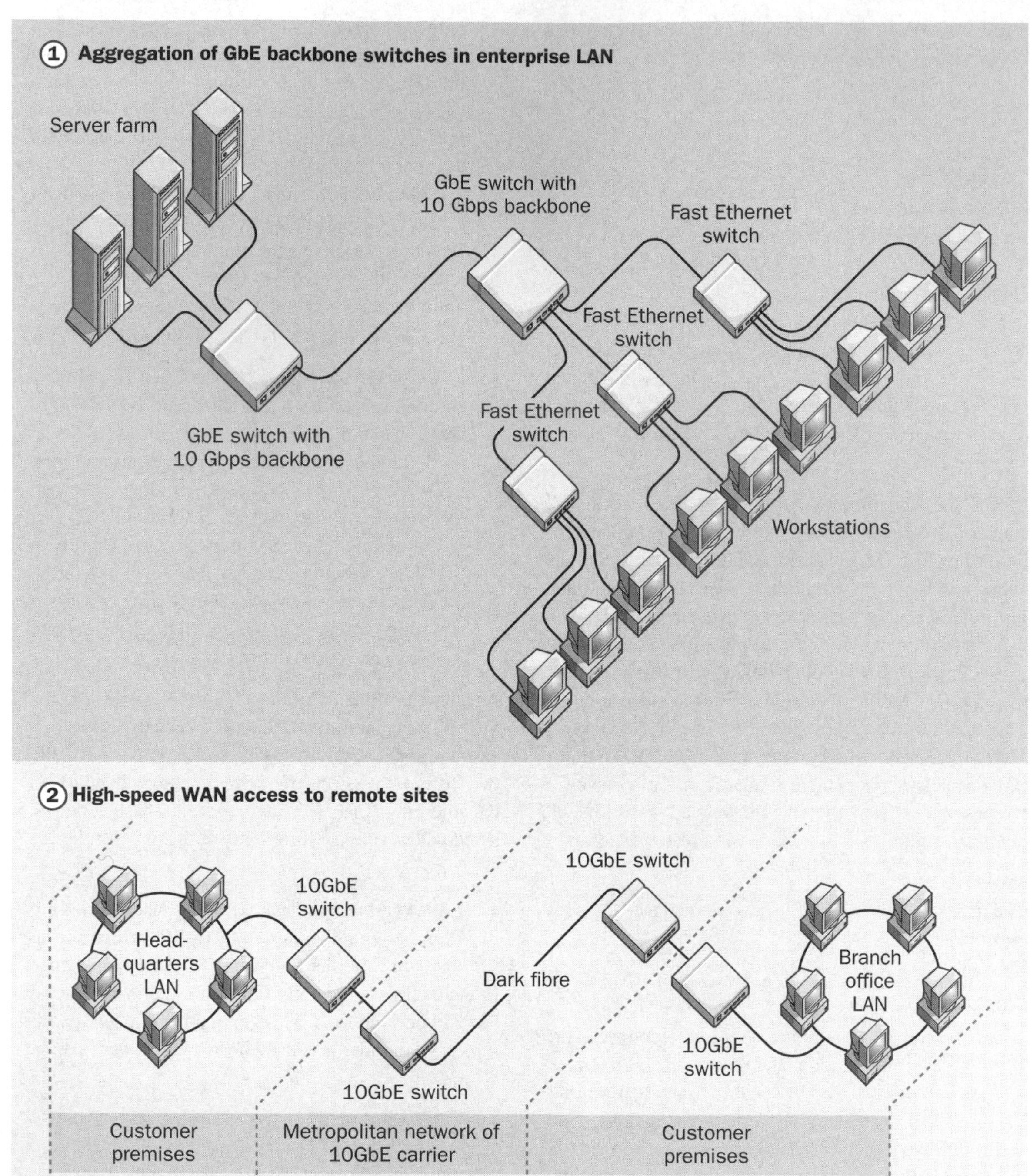

10G Ethernet. *Some scenarios where 10GbE could be deployed.*

Implementation

Some envisioned uses for 10GbE include

- High-speed interconnects between GbE backbone switches in enterprise LANs
- Aggregation of multiple short-haul GbE links and high-speed campus-wide interconnects
- Switched connections to server farms and high-performance clusters

Some telecom carriers plan to replace their SONET/ATM rings with 10GbE in their Metropolitan Area Networks (MANs) to provide high-speed connections in the local loop between Central Offices (COs) and customer premises. These carriers will then be able to provision corporate users with 10GbE Ethernet WAN links to provide end-to-end Ethernet services across the WAN. Because this eliminates the need for costly packet-conversion equipment such as frame relay assembler/disassemblers (FRADs) or ATM access routers at the customer premises, 10GbE WAN services are likely to be much less costly than current T1 and frame relay services. Furthermore, 10GbE has almost no protocol overhead compared to ATM/SONET, which can have as much as 56 percent protocol overhead when implementing Automatic Protection Switching (APS) routines. The desire of carriers to implement 10GbE to save cost is a major force driving vendors to quickly develop 10GbE switching technologies. Due to its distance limitations, however, 10GbE is not expected to replace SONET/SDH for long-haul telecommunications links between cities or continents.

Issues

Most servers are not yet capable of utilizing the full potential of 10GbE because of limitations in processing power and bus speed, though advances in bus, memory, and storage technologies are closing the gap. With standard 1500-byte Ethernet frames being employed, servers would need to be able to process 833,000 frames per second, which is beyond their current limitations. One solution would be to employ Jumbo Frames similar to those used in GbE, but the 802.3ae standard does not cover this feature. The result is that some vendors are starting to implement their own proprietary Jumbo Frame technologies, which raises concerns for future prospects of interoperability between 10GbE equipment from different vendors.

Prospects

Many users are looking forward to the day when carriers can provision their corporate networks with 10GbE. Carriers will likely supply these services using a bandwidth-on-demand model, allowing customers to replace their costly T1 and T3 lines with blocks of purchased bandwidth that can scale in real time to accommodate bursts of traffic. Application Service Providers (ASPs) are also waiting to take advantage of 10GbE to offer outsourced email and workflow applications that will perform as well as LAN-based implementations.

The IEEE published a draft standard (802.3ae) for 10GbE in September 2000, and the final standard is expected to be ratified in 2002. Until then, 10GbE equipment provided by vendors may involve proprietary technologies, and network architects should consider interoperability issues before committing budgets to this emerging technology. Another cost issue to consider is that existing copper and multimode fiber infrastructures would have to be replaced with more costly single-mode fiber if anything more than backbone switch interconnects is considered in a proposed 10GbE deployment.

Some of the vendors developing 10GbE plug-in backplane modules for their carrier-class backbone switches include Nortel Networks, Extreme Networks, and Foundry Networks. Because there is already demand in the corporate WAN market, service providers such as Yipes (*www.yipes.com*) are rapidly rolling out infrastructure to provide 10GbE carrier services in a number of cities across the United States and compete with local telco carriers selling T-carrier and frame relay services.

Notes

10GbE will support Simple Network Management Protocol (SNMP) and (Remote Network Monitoring) RMON at the PHY layer. This will enable carriers to remotely manage provisioned 10GbE services and should be a boon to enterprise network managers as well.

For More Information

You can find the 10 Gigabit Ethernet Alliance (10GEA) at *www.10gea.org*.

Also find out about the IEEE 802.3ae working group at *www.ieee.org*.

See Also: *Ethernet, Fast Ethernet, Gigabit Ethernet (GbE)*

24 x 7

A term implying the uninterrupted running of network services. A 24 x 7 network is a network whose services and resources are available 24 hours a day, seven days a week, with virtually no downtime. A similar term is *24 x 7 x 365*, which implies virtually no downtime during the entire year.

Overview

In today's emerging e-business economy, availability of the network and its resources and applications can make the difference between business success and failure. A variety of technologies can be used to approach the goal of 24 x 7 availability. One of the most successful is clustering, a technology in which an application runs redundantly on multiple servers. When one of the nodes in a cluster fails, the other nodes take on the workload of the failed node so that there's no interruption in service while the failed node is being repaired or replaced. Windows 2000 and .NET Server Advanced Server editions offer clustering services for high-availability line-of-business applications.

Other technologies important to the 24 x 7 goal include fault-tolerant hardware technologies. Examples are hot-swappable components, such as power supplies and hard disks that can be removed and replaced without the system having to power down or reboot. Fault-tolerant storage technologies such as RAID 1 or RAID 5 guard against data loss from disk failure. Cellular phones and pagers also play a role in attaining the 24 x 7 goal, as they allow businesses to keep in touch with administrators and technical support staff around the clock.

Notes

If you are an MIS (Manager of Information Services) or CIO (Chief Information Officer) running an e-business that requires 24 x 7 uptime, it is wise to make sure your network administrators and support staff are adequately compensated—they must work hard to maintain a 24 x 7 networking environment. Also, such people can be difficult to replace, so it is advisable to do what you can to minimize turnover.

See Also: *network management*

64-bit architecture

Any computing hardware based on a processor capable of manipulating 64 bits of information at a time and directly accessing up to 2^{64} bytes (16 exabytes) of different physical memory addresses.

Overview

The PC revolution of the 1990s was based to a large degree upon the x86 processor platform, a series of 32-bit processors developed by Intel Corporation. Compared to their 16-bit predecessors, these new processors could manipulate twice as many bits simultaneously and access up to 4 gigabytes (GB) of directly addressable memory, which provided more than enough processing power and memory space for most PC-based applications.

As the PC platform began to push its way into the high-end server platform previously dominated by Reduced Instruction Set Computing (RISC) processors, the demand for greater power and memory addressability grew. This need has been felt most in the area of enterprise-level database applications, which are processor and memory intensive in their requirements. To address these needs, two leading processor vendors, Intel and AMD, began development of 64-bit processors in the late 1990s.

Comparison

AMD's x86-64 architecture can run today's 32-bit operating systems and applications, but only when running in Legacy mode. Unfortunately, this mode limits addressable memory to 4 GB and provides no processing gain over the present Pentium III platform. In order to run true 64-bit operating systems and applications, the x86-64 architecture must be running in Long mode, which does not support backward compatibility with existing 32-bit applications and operating systems.

In order for Intel's IA-64 architecture to run legacy 32-bit software, an x86 hardware emulation mode is provided. When 32-bit software is run using emulation mode, however, performance is generally slower than that of a typical Pentium III processor.

In order to properly run legacy software on Itanium (or on Sledgehammer running in Long mode) and enable such software to address the full 64-bit address space, the software needs to be recompiled to produce a binary bit-image appropriate to the selected 64-bit platform. Unfortunately, these binary images are different for the two architectures, so either a single architecture will win out or vendors will need to compile two different versions for the two platforms. Until existing software is recompiled, or until 64-bit operating systems and applications are developed from scratch, the usefulness of these two new architectures will be limited as far as the business enterprise is concerned.

Architecture

Intel's new 64-bit Itanium chip uses a radically new architecture called IA-64 that differs in fundamental ways from the x38 architecture used in all of its earlier 32-bit processors, from the 386 through the Pentium III Xeon. Itanium uses a Very Long Instruction Word (VLIW) algorithm that allows it to read strings containing multiple instructions. Using a technique called Explicitly Parallel Instruction Computing (EPIC), Itanium can then execute up to six instructions per clock cycle, which greatly enhances performance over 32-bit processors (not just Intel x86 processors, but also 32-bit RISC and complex instruction set computing [CISC] processors) and eliminates the need for complicated algorithms such as the Out-of-Order Processing implemented in Pentium chips.

Itanium processors are capable of performing 6 billion floating-point operations per second (6 gigaflops) and support up to 512-way symmetric multiprocessing (SMP) for the most transaction-intensive e-commerce and database applications. Itanium uses a new motherboard interface and requires a bus speed of 366 MHz.

AMD's new 64-bit Sledgehammer chip uses an architecture called x86-64 that is a natural evolution from the x86 standard, and AMD's 32-bit Athlon processor. Sledgehammer operates in two modes: long mode, which runs native 64-bit operating systems and applications, and legacy mode, which supports existing 16-bit and 32-bit operating systems and applications. Sledgehammer uses a motherboard with a Plastic Pin Grid Array (PPGA) processor slot and requires a 266 MHz system bus.

Prospects

Both architectures have their camps supporting them. Intel's IA-64 architecture is supported by Microsoft Corporation, Hewlett-Packard, IBM, Compaq Computer Corporation, and others, and is likely to be the platform of choice for users of Microsoft Windows once Microsoft releases its 64-bit version of Windows currently under development. AMD's x86-64 architecture is supported by Sun Microsystems, which has plans to port Solaris (a version of UNIX) to x86-64, and by the Linux community, which is working on a similar port.

Notes

Some software vendors have developed ways of going beyond the hardware limitations of 32-bit processors that limit addressable physical memory to 4 GB. Examples include Microsoft Windows 2000 Advanced Server and Microsoft Windows 2000 Datacenter Server, both of which employ a technique called Physical Address Extension (PAE) to enable them to address 8 GB and 64 GB of memory respectively.

For More Information

More information on these two platforms can be found at *www.intel.com/ebusiness/products/ia64* and *www.amd.com/products/cpg/64bit.*

See Also: *64-bit Windows*

64-bit Windows

A version of Microsoft Windows 2000, Windows XP, and Windows .NET Server designed to operate on computers using Intel's new IA-64 (64-bit) processor architecture.

Overview

64-bit Windows is designed to support today's most processor- and memory-intensive business applications. These applications include e-commerce, data mining, online transaction-processing, high-end graphics, and high-performance multimedia applications. Based on Intel's 64-bit processor architecture called IA-64, which is first realized in the Itanium chip, 64-bit Windows is fully compatible with the Win32 API, allowing developers to develop and compile code for both the 32-bit and 64-bit platforms with equal ease. The main advantage of using a 64-bit processor architecture is that the amount of directly addressable physical memory increases from 64 GB for 32-bit Windows 2000 and Windows .NET Server Datacenter Server to a staggering 16 terabytes (TB) for the new platform. (A terabyte equals 1024 gigabytes.) This means that large databases can be preloaded in-to memory to provide vastly improved data access times, improving the performance and efficiency of enterprise-level applications.

For More Information

For more information on the current state of the 64-bit Windows platform, see *www.microsoft.com/hwdev/64bitwindows/ and www.microsoft.com/windowsxp/pro/techinfo/howitworks/64bit/default.asp.*

See Also: *64-bit architecture, Microsoft Windows*

80/20 rule

A rule of thumb that says that 80 percent of network traffic is local and only 20 percent is destined for remote networks.

Overview

The 80/20 rule was developed in the era of traditional routed Ethernet networks and is now considered a classical description of local area network (LAN) traffic patterns that no longer applies. The main consideration here is the Internet, and corporate use of Internet access means that ever-increasing amounts of remote traffic are being routed through LANs. The 80/20 rule was used in the 1980s to help enterprise network architects plan and design large-scale routed networks.

Notes

Other types of 80/20 rules exist. For example, in programming, the 80/20 rule says that 80 percent of the benefit in coding an application comes from 20 percent of the work involved. In other words, prioritize your development tasks to achieve the most in the time available. The original 80/20 rule seems to have originated with Vilfredo Pareto, an early 20th-century economist who stated that 80 percent of the volume of product produced comes from only 20 percent of the producers who make it. Another modern variant says that 80 percent of your business comes from only 20 percent of your customers, so identify these customers and give them premier service.

See Also: *local area network (LAN)*

100BaseFX

An Institute of Electrical and Electronics Engineers (IEEE) standard for implementing 100 megabits per second (Mbps) Ethernet over fiber-optic cabling.

Overview

100BaseFX is based on the 802.3u standard, which is an extension of the 802.3 standard of Project 802 developed by the IEEE. It's a type of Fast Ethernet that is often used for wiring campus backbones using fiber-optic cabling. The designation 100BaseFX is derived from the network's speed (100 Mbps), the signal transmission method (baseband transmission), and the physical medium used for transmission (fiber-optic cabling).

Implementation

100BaseFX networks are wired together in a star topology using fiber-optic cabling and 100-Mbps fiber-optic hubs or Ethernet switches. 100BaseFX systems may be interconnected with 100BaseTX, 100BaseT4, and 10BaseT systems using auto negotiating hubs and switches with suitable ports. Two-strand fiber-optic cabling is required, and ST, SC, and MIC connectors are all supported. Signaling is at 125 megahertz (MHz), which when combined with the 80 percent efficiency of the 4B5B line coding mechanism used results in an overall transmission speed of 100 Mbps.

The maximum length of any segment of fiber-optic cabling connecting a station (computer) to a hub in 100BaseFX is 1350 feet (412 meters), and not 1480 feet (450 meters) as some sources indicate. The grade of fiber-optic cabling used is usually two-strand multimode fiber-optic cabling, with one strand carrying transmitted data and the other strand receiving data. However, you can also use two-strand single-mode fiber-optic cabling. If multimode fiber-optic cabling is used, the variety used is typically a grade with a 62.5-micron core diameter.

Repeaters can be used to extend the length of cabling and for interfacing between 100BaseFX/TX and 100BaseT4 segments. The maximum allowable distances with repeaters are 2 kilometers using multimode fiber-optic cabling and 10 kilometers using single-mode fiber-optic cabling. Only one or two repeaters can be used per collision domain, depending on whether Class I or Class II repeaters are used.

Notes

100BaseFX and a related standard, 100BaseTX, are sometimes collectively referred to as 100BaseX.

When using 100BaseFX with repeaters for backbone cabling runs, Ethernet switches cannot be more than 1350 feet (412 meters) apart when running in half-duplex mode and 6600 feet (2000 meters) apart when running in full-duplex mode.

See Also: *100BaseT4, 100BaseTX, Fast Ethernet*

100BaseT

Another name for Fast Ethernet and thus for all 100 megabits per second (Mbps) Ethernet varieties. Also sometimes used interchangeably with 100BaseT4.

See: *Fast Ethernet*

100BaseT4

An Institute of Electrical and Electronics Engineers (IEEE) standard for implementing 100 megabits per second (Mbps) Ethernet over twisted-pair cabling.

Overview

100BaseT4 is based on 802.3u, which is an extension of the 802.3 specifications of Project 802 developed by the IEEE. 100BaseT4 is the most commonly used implementation of Fast Ethernet today. The designation 100BaseT4 is derived from the network's speed (100 Mbps), the signal transmission method (baseband transmission), and the physical medium used for transmission (all four pairs of wires in standard twisted-pair cabling). 100BaseT4 is now considered legacy technology and has been largely superseded by 100BaseTX.

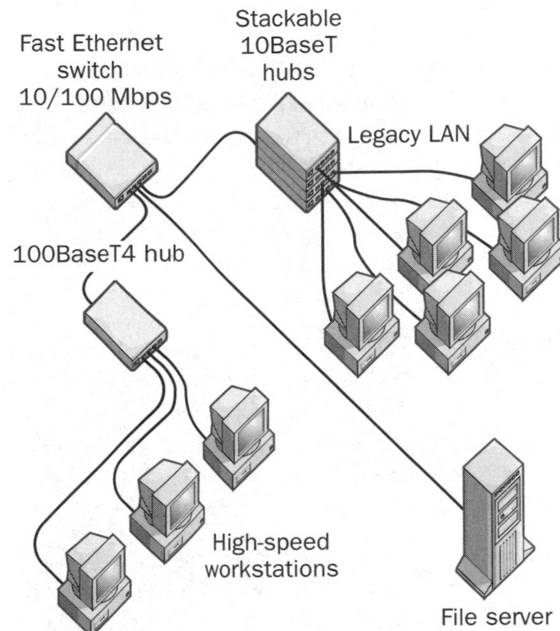

100BaseT4. *A typical 100BaseT4 network.*

Implementation

100BaseT4 networks are wired together in a star topology using unshielded twisted-pair (UTP) cabling and 100-Mbps hubs or Ethernet switches. The UTP cabling involved may be Category 3 (Cat3), Category 4 (Cat4), or Category 5 (Cat5) cabling—with Cat5 cabling and enhanced Category 5 (Cat5e) cabling being the most commonly used solutions nowadays.

100BaseT4 uses all four pairs of wire in standard UTP cabling, for signaling with signaling rates of 25 megahertz (MHz) and an 8B6T line coding mechanism. One pair is used exclusively for transmission and a second pair for reception. The other two pairs are bidirectional and can be used either to transmit or to receive data as required. In this way, three of the four wire pairs are used at any given time to provide half-duplex transmission or reception of signals. Sharing three pairs of wires for data transfer allows 100BaseT4 to make use of lower-grade Cat3 cabling already installed in many older buildings.

The maximum length of any segment of cabling connecting a station (computer) to a hub is 328 feet (100 meters). This ensures that round-trip signaling specifications are met, because violating these specifications can produce late collisions that disrupt network communications. The Electronic Industries Alliance/Telecommunications Industry Association (EIA/TIA)– recommended length of cabling between the station and the wiring closet is only 295 feet (90 meters), allowing up to 32 feet (10 meters) more of cabling for patch cables used to connect patch panels to hubs or switches. The pinning of the RJ-45 connectors used for 100BaseT4 wiring is the same as for 10BaseT wiring.

Notes

Make sure all your cabling, connectors, and patch panels are fully Cat5-compliant. For example, ensure that when UTP cabling is connected to patch panels, wall plates, or connectors, the wires are not untwisted more than half an inch at the termination point.

100BaseT4 hubs and switches are typically available in an autosensing 10/100-Mbps variety for interoperability with older 10BaseT networks and to facilitate an easy upgrade from 10BaseT to 100BaseT.

See Also: *100BaseFX, 100BaseTX, Fast Ethernet*

100BaseTX

An Institute of Electrical and Electronics Engineers (IEEE) standard for implementing 100 megabits per second (Mbps) Ethernet over twisted-pair cabling.

Overview

100BaseTX is based on 802.3u, which is an extension of the 802.3 specifications of Project 802 developed by the IEEE. The designation 100BaseTX is derived from the network's speed (100 Mbps), the signal transmission method (baseband transmission), and the physical medium used for transmission (the same two pairs of wires in standard four-wire twisted-pair cabling that are used for 10BaseT Ethernet).

Implementation

100BaseTX networks are wired together in a star topology using either unshielded twisted-pair (UTP) cabling or data-grade shielded twisted-pair (STP) cabling. If UTP cabling is used (which is the most common scenario), it must be Category 5 (Cat5) cabling or enhanced Category 5 (Cat5e) cabling. Stations are connected together using hubs or switches. Unlike 10BaseT hubs, which can be hierarchically connected up to three levels deep, 100BaseTX hubs can only be connected two layers deep, which imposes additional distance limitations and may necessitate rewiring of existing cabling before upgrading from 10BaseT to 100BaseTX.

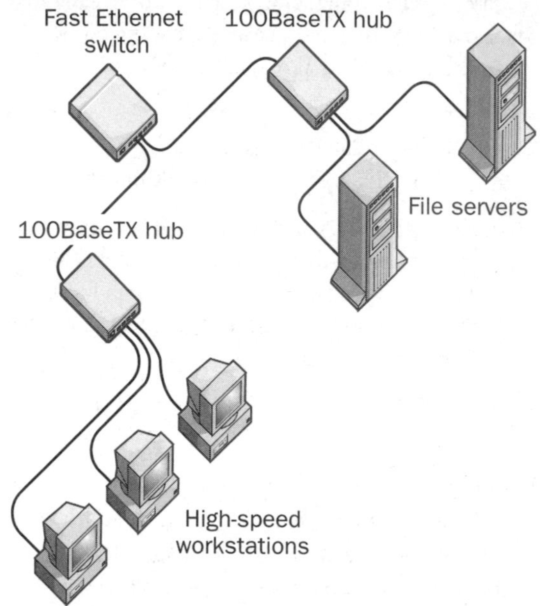

100BaseTX. *A typical 100BaseTX network.*

100BaseTX uses the two pairs of wires in twisted-pair cabling that are used by 10BaseT networks, with one pair of wires used for transmission and the other used for reception. With the appropriate equipment, 100BaseTX is capable of supporting both the familiar half-duplex Ethernet used by 10BaseT and newer full-duplex Ethernet signaling technologies. 100BaseTX employs a signaling rate of 125 megahertz (MHz) for each pair of wires, which, because the 4B5B line coding algorithm used is only 80 percent efficient, translates into a data transmission speed of 100 Mbps.

The maximum length of any segment of cabling connecting a station to a hub is 328 feet (100 meters). This ensures that round-trip signaling specifications are met, because violating these specifications can produce late collisions that disrupt network communications. The pinning of the RJ-45 connectors used for 100BaseTX wiring is the same as for 10BaseT wiring with wires 1 and 2 used for transmission and wires 3 and 6 used for reception. This enables 100BaseTX autosensing hubs and switches to operate in mixed 10/100 Mbps Ethernet networks.

Notes

The maximum distance between 100BaseTX hubs and bridges or switches is 738 feet (225 meters), further than the maximum hub-station distance of only 328 feet (100 meters).

100BaseTX and a related standard, 100BaseFX, are sometimes collectively referred to as 100BaseX.

Although the maximum length of segments joining stations to hubs is 328 feet (100 meters), the Electronic Industries Alliance/Telecommunications Industry Alliance (EIA/TIA) recommends only 295 feet (90 meters) of cabling between the station (computer) and the wiring closet, allowing up to 32 feet (10 meters) more of cabling for patch cables used to connect patch panels to hubs or switches.

Make sure all your cabling, connectors, and patch panels are fully Cat5-compliant. Make sure that when UTP cabling is connected to patch panels, wall plates, or connectors, the wires are not untwisted more than half an inch at the termination point.

See Also: *100BaseFX, 100BaseTX, Fast Ethernet*

100BaseVG

Another name for 100VG-AnyLAN.

See: *100VG-AnyLAN*

100BaseX

An umbrella term that includes 100BaseFX and 100BaseTX Fast Ethernet technologies.

See: *100BaseFX, 100BaseTX, Fast Ethernet*

100VG-AnyLAN

Also called 100BaseVG, a 100 megabits per second (Mbps) networking technology that at one time was a serious alternative to Fast Ethernet, but which now is considered legacy technology.

Overview

100VG-AnyLAN is defined by the 802.12 standard of the Institute of Electrical and Electronics Engineers (IEEE) Project 802. It is a local area network (LAN) communications technology developed by Hewlett-Packard and AT&T around 1994. 100VG-AnyLAN is similar to Fast Ethernet in its speed (100 Mbps) and ability to be deployed in both shared-media (hub-based) and switched implementations. It differs, however, in its media access method, because it uses demand priority instead of the Carrier-Sense Multiple-Access with Collision Detection (CSMA/CD) method used by Ethernet.

Implementation

100VG-AnyLAN networks are wired together in a star topology using unshielded twisted-pair (UTP) cabling, shielded twisted-pair (STP) cabling, or fiber-optic cabling. If UTP cabling is used, it can be Category 3 (Cat3), Category 4 (Cat4), or Category 5 (Cat5) cabling—with Cat5 cabling or enhanced Category 5 (Cat5e) cabling preferred. When using UTP Cat3 or Cat4 cabling, the maximum length of a segment is 100 meters (328 feet). With UTP Cat5 cabling or STP cabling, the maximum length of a segment is 656 feet (200 meters). When using multimode fiber-optic cabling, the maximum length is 6600 feet (2000 meters).

100VG-AnyLAN uses all four pairs of wires in UTP cabling with 25 megahertz (MHz) signaling for each pair. 100VG-AnyLAN uses a special coding scheme called quartet signaling, which makes it possible to transmit data over all four pairs of wires in a UTP cable simultaneously. This means that special 100VG-AnyLan hubs are required to support demand priority media access. Otherwise, the frame format, topology, and other specifications of 100VG-AnyLAN are the same as for Ethernet.

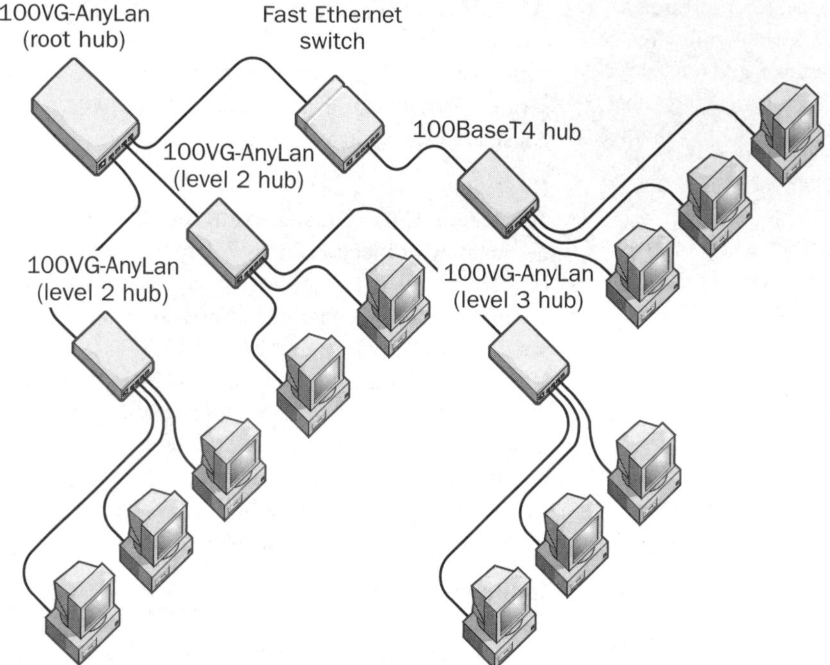

100VG-AnyLAN. *A typical 100VG-AnyLAN network.*

100VG-AnyLAN employs the demand priority Media Access Control (MAC) method specified by the IEEE 802.12 standard. Demand priority means that the central hub controls which station is allowed to transmit data (only one station is allowed to transmit at any given moment). This eliminates the overhead of collisions and means that 100VG-AnyLAN networks have an efficiency of 100 percent compared to the 60-70 percent efficiency of contention-based Fast Ethernet networks. Demand priority works by having the hub poll each station successively in round-robin fashion until a station indicates it has data to transmit, whereupon control is passed temporarily to the transmitting station.

If multiple hubs are used, these are connected hierarchically with the top hub, called the root hub, being the master controller for the network. If a station is connected to a local hub other than the root hub in a large 100VG-AnyLAN network, the local hub detects the station's request to transmit data during regular polling and then forwards this request to the next highest hub in its hierarchy until it reaches the root hub, which communicates with the local hub, telling it when it is allowed to service the station's request. Thus even in a large 100VG-AnyLAN network with a hierarchy of hubs, only one station is allowed to transmit data at any given time. 100VG-AnyLAN supports five levels of hubs in a hierarchy, but performance is best if cascading is limited to only three levels.

Because demand priority is a deterministic rather than contention-based media access method, stations cannot join the network on their own and begin transmitting data. Instead, when a station is first connected, it waits to be polled by the hub and then transmits a training sequence of special frames that enables the station to determine the frame type in use and other network restrictions. This training sequence temporarily suspends polling by the hub, but takes only 5 msec to be completed and so does not seriously disrupt network communications.

Advantages and Disadvantages

100 VG-AnyLAN offers greater efficiency due to elimination of collisions, but another advantage that it has over Fast Ethernet is that it supports both 802.3 Ethernet frames and 802.5 Token Ring frames, although a

single hub cannot support both at the same time (all hubs on any given 100VG-AnyLAN network must be configured to support the same frame type, either 802.3 or 802.5).

Yet another advantage 100VG-AnyLAN has over Ethernet is that it has built-in support for traffic prioritization. Two levels of traffic are recognized by 100VG-AnyLAN hubs: normal priority and high priority. High-priority traffic requests are serviced immediately by the local hub without the need for that hub to first communicate with the network's root hub. All network traffic is then suspended until the high-priority transmission is completed.

Marketplace

Although 100VG-AnyLAN is in some ways a superior technology to Fast Ethernet due to its greater efficiency and inherent support for traffic prioritization, it has not been widely deployed. This is mainly due to limited vendor support, which has kept prices high and made Fast Ethernet more affordable. Furthermore, Fast Ethernet is simpler and is completely compatible with widely deployed 10BaseT Ethernet networks and forms the natural upgrade path for these networks.

See Also: *demand priority, Fast Ethernet*

568-A

A wiring standard for twisted-pair cabling defined by the Telecommunications Industry Association (TIA).

Overview

The 568-A standard was originally intended for analog voice applications but is generally used in data networks as well. The main difference between 568-A and the competing 568-B standard is in the pin layouts for RJ45 jacks, which generally terminate unshielded twisted-pair (UTP) cabling. The pin layout for 568-A wiring is technically referred to as T568A. For a comparison of these two wiring schemes, see the next article, "568-B."

Notes

The T568A wiring scheme is preferred in Canada, although this has been changing recently.

See Also: *568-B, UTP cabling*

568-B

A wiring standard for twisted-pair cabling defined by the Telecommunications Industry Association (TIA).

Overview

The 568-B standard was designed for data transmission over building wires used in computer network and telecommunications systems. It differs from the competing 568-A standard mainly in the pin layouts for the RJ45 jacks that are normally used to terminate unshielded twisted-pair (UTP) cabling. The pin layout for 568-B wiring is technically referred to as T568B, and that for 568-A cabling systems is called T568A. The drawing illustrates these differences between the two wiring systems.

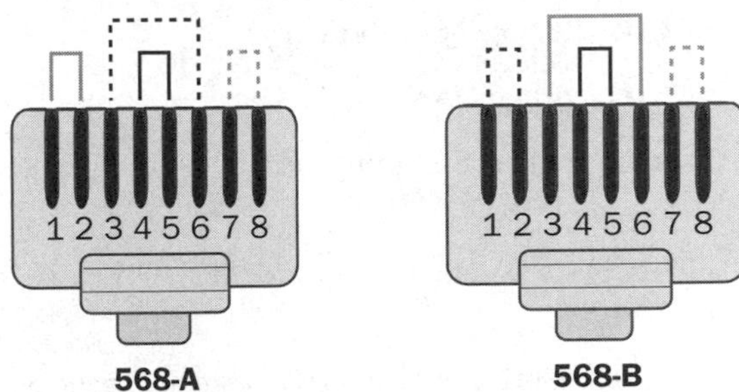

Key		
Pair number	Color	Symbol
1	Blue	—— (solid)
2	Orange	------ (dashed)
3	Green	—— (solid, light)
4	Brown	------ (dashed, light)

568-B. *Comparison of pin layouts in RJ45 connectors between 568-A and 568-B.*

Notes

For 10BaseT and 100BaseT Ethernet networks, only two pairs of wires are used for data transmission, but 1000BaseT Gigabit Ethernet (GbE) uses all four pairs. As a result, running GbE over a cabling infrastructure that contains a mixture of 568-A and 568-B terminations will cause signaling problems that can be hard to troubleshoot.

See Also: *568-A, UTP cabling*

802.1

The Institute of Electrical and Electronics Engineers (IEEE) working group dealing with general local area network/wide area network (LAN/WAN) networking architectures and protocols and their standards.

Overview

This group is responsible for developing standards and recommending practices for LAN architectures, LAN/metropolitan area network (MAN)/WAN internetworking, network management, and all protocol layers above the media access control (MAC) and Logical Link Control (LLC) layers. The three main standards ratified by this group include

- **802.1D:** MAC bridging
- **802.1G:** Remote MAC bridging
- **802.1Q:** Virtual LANs (VLANs)

Some of the projects this group is currently involved in include

- **802.1p:** Prioritization scheme for 802.1Q VLAN traffic
- **802.1s and 802.1w:** Issues relating to the Spanning Tree Algorithm
- **802.1t:** Further MAC bridging issues
- **802.1u and 802.1v:** Issues relating to VLANs and their classification.
- **802.1x:** Port-based network access control

See Also: *media access control method, Project 802, virtual LAN (VLAN)*

802.1p

An Institute of Electrical and Electronics Engineers (IEEE) standard specifying a prioritization scheme for Ethernet networks that support the 802.1Q virtual local area network (VLAN) standard. The 802.1p standard allows a rudimentary form of quality of service/class of service (QoS/CoS) on Layer-2 switched networks.

Overview

One of Ethernet's biggest drawbacks is its lack of an inherent mechanism for prioritizing network traffic. The new 802.1p standard tries to resolve this by making use of three reserved bits in the tags appended to packets by devices that support the 802.1Q VLAN standard. Employing these three bits enables 2^3=8 different priority levels to be assigned to each packet of data, allowing switches and routers to handle these different types of traffic according to preconfigured schemes. The table shows the eight different traffic classes that correspond to priorities 0 (binary 000) through 7 (binary 111) according to IEEE recommendations.

Traffic Classes by Priority

Priority	*Type of Traffic*
0	Standard best-effort LAN traffic (default priority setting)
1	Lowest priority, used primarily for traffic that should not be allowed to affect other forms of traffic, for example, bulk file transfers
2	Unallocated at present
3	Excellent effort—in other words, best-effort delivery for important data
4	Controlled load—supports admission control for mission-critical business traffic
5	Low-priority multimedia traffic with jitter and latency less than 100 ms
6	High-priority multimedia traffic with jitter and latency less than 10 ms
7	Highest priority for traffic that controls the network infrastructure

Marketplace

An example of an Ethernet switch that supports the 802.1p standard is the ProCurve 8000M from Hewlett-Packard. These switches also support 802.1Q, 802.3ad, QoS, and port security.

Notes

Ethernet networks that use Layer 3 switches can implement more sophisticated CoS/QoS schemes such as Differentiated Services (DiffServ) and Integrated Services with resource Reservation Protocol (IntServ/RSVP). For mixed Layer 2/3 networks, the 802.1p standard provides standard mappings between these Layer-3 CoS/QoS mechanisms and the Layer-2 802.1p prioritization scheme.

See Also: *802.1Q, virtual LAN (VLAN)*

802.1Q

An Institute of Electrical and Electronics Engineers (IEEE) standard defining the architecture and operation of virtual local area networks (VLANs).

Overview

The 802.1Q VLAN standard ratified in 1999 allows a tag of 4 bytes to be appended to packets by network hosts and Layer 2/3 switches in Ethernet networks. This tag identifies the VLAN to which the given packet belongs. For a more detailed explanation, see the article "virtual LAN (VLAN)" elsewhere in this book. The 4 bytes of tag information are embedded into the standard Ethernet header by dividing them between the 2-byte tag protocol identifier (TPID) field and the 2-byte tag control information (TCI) field. The TCI field consists of

- **User priority field:** This three-bit field forms the basis of 802.1p traffic prioritization schemes in Level-2 switched networks.
- **Canonical format indicator:** This is a one-bit field that is used to toggle VLAN formats.
- **VLAN Identifier (VID):** This is a 12-bit field that identifies the VLAN to which the packet belongs. Up to 212 (4096) VLANs can be defined.

Marketplace

Many vendors produce Ethernet switches compatible with the 802.1Q standard, although mostly at the high end of their switching gear offerings. At the workgroup level, fewer vendors support this standard in their switches. For example, the low-end Catalyst 2900 switches from Cisco Systems do not support 802.1Q, but Hewlett-Packard's new ProCurve 10/100 stackable switches with Gigabit Ethernet (GbE) backbone transceivers do.

See Also: *802.1p, virtual LAN (VLAN)*

802.2

The Institute of Electrical and Electronics Engineers (IEEE) standards for the Logical Link Control (LLC), defining its operation for all network architectures that follow the Open Systems Interconnection (OSI) model. The physical layer (PHY) and media access control (MAC) layer specifications are specified for a particular technology under the 802 committee that deals with them (for example, 802.3 deals with Ethernet and 802.5 with Token Ring). The IEEE 802.2 working group is no longer active.

See Also: *logical link control (LLC) layer, Project 802*

802.3

The Institute of Electrical and Electronics Engineers (IEEE) working group concerned with Ethernet in its many forms. Although this set of standards is generically referred to as Ethernet, this term is actually a trademarked version of 802.3.

Overview

The 802.3 standards cover those relating to local area networks (LANs) based on Carrier-Sense Multiple-Access with Collision Detection (CSMA/CD) as their Media Access Control (MAC) method, in other words with

- 10 Mbps Ethernet (original 802.3 standard)
- 100 Mbps Fast Ethernet (802.3u)
- 1 Gigabit Ethernet (GbE) (802.3z and 802.3ab)
- 10 Gigabit Ethernet (under development)

Some recently ratified standards of the 802.3 working group include

- **802.3z:** Gigabit Ethernet (1998)
- **802.3ab:** 1000Base-T (GbE over copper) (1999)
- **802.3ac:** Tag switching in virtual local area networks (VLANs) (1998)
- **802.3ad:** Link aggregation (2000)

Some of the projects the 802.3 working group is currently involved with include

- **802.3ae:** 10 Gigabit Ethernet (10GbE)
- **802.3af:** Transmission of electrical power over unshielded twisted pair (UTP) cabling to power Ethernet devices

Notes

802.3 is also used to refer to the frame format used in Ethernet frames. See the article "frame type" elsewhere in this book for more information.

See Also: *Ethernet, frame type, Project 802*

802.3ab

The Institute of Electrical and Electronics Engineers (IEEE) standard for Gigabit Ethernet (GbE) over copper, also known as 1000BaseT or 1000BaseTX. This standard was ratified in June 1999.

See Also: *10BaseT, Gigabit Ethernet (GbE)*

802.3ad

An Institute of Electrical and Electronics Engineers (IEEE) standard for link aggregation of Ethernet switch ports and network interface cards (NICs) to combine multiple data streams into a single large stream.

Overview

Prior to 802.3ad, many vendors of Fast Ethernet and Gigabit Ethernet (GbE) gear developed their own proprietary trunking protocols for aggregating multiple links together into a single higher speed link. Examples include Adaptec's Duralink technology and Cisco Systems' Inter-Switch Link Trunking (ISL) protocol. The 802.3ad standard was developed to promote interoperability between switches from different vendors. The need for such technology is increasingly apparent in a world of streaming media and outsourcing Line of Business (LOB) functions to Application Service Providers (ASPs).

The 802.3ad standard covers all versions of Ethernet (10, 100, and 1000 megabits per second [Mbps]) and enables multiple links of the same or different speeds to be aggregated into a single logical link. For example, two 1-gigabit-per-second (Gbps) GbE ports can be combined to make a single 2-Gbps link, or a 1-Gbps GbE port and a 100-Mbps Fast Ethernet port can be combined to create a single 1100-Mbps link. The maximum bandwidth supported by aggregated 802.3ad links is 8 Gbps—in other words, up to eight full duplex 1-Gbps GbE ports can be combined into a single fat data pipe. The protocol used to accomplish this is called the Link Aggregation Control Protocol (LACP).

Advantages and Disadvantages

The main advantage of 802.3ad is that additional bandwidth for network backbones and connections to server farms can be added incrementally as needed, thus providing greater scalability at minimum cost. The 802.3ad standard includes a mechanism for load balancing traffic across aggregated links. It also supports fault tolerance to handle the failure of any link within an aggregated set of links by automatically rerouting traffic through a different link. This fault-tolerant failover feature makes 802.3ad ideal for mission-critical point-to-point links.

Marketplace

The 802.3ad standard was ratified in July 1999, and 802.3ad-compliant products are just beginning to appear, primarily GbE backbone switches and GbE NICs for high-end server clusters.

See Also: *Gigabit Ethernet (GbE)*

802.3ae

The proposed Institute of Electrical and Electronics Engineers (IEEE) standard for 10 Gigabit Ethernet (10GbE).

See Also: *10G Ethernet*

802.3af

An emerging Institute of Electrical and Electronics Engineers (IEEE) standard that allows data-carrying unshielded twisted pair (UTP) cabling to carry not only data but also electricity for powering Ethernet networking devices.

Overview

Traditionally, in networking devices the wires carrying power to run the device and the wires carrying data to and from the device are kept separate. This is done to isolate the sensitive data-handling electronics from the high power levels required by the device. Many newer network-capable devices such as hubs, Internet Protocol (IP) telephones, and Personal Digital Assistants (PDAs) require only a few watts to operate, and 802.3af promises to simplify the operation of these devices. Instead of separate cables for carrying data and power, 802.3af devices will require only data connections and will receive their power over these connections. The advantage is that fewer cables need to be deployed and used for compliant networking devices, which promises to make Voice over IP (VoIP) telephone equipment as easy to deploy and use as traditional Plain Old Telephone Service (POTS) telephones, which communicate through and are powered by the same RJ-11 outlet found in private homes.

802.3af allows up to 10 watts of power to be carried over Category 3 (Cat3) or Category 5 (Cat5) cabling when running 10BaseT or 100BaseTX Ethernet on the network. The standard provides for the transmission of both AC and DC power as required. To protect non-802.3af devices from damaging power levels that could fry their electronics, the 802.3af standard includes a handshaking protocol to enable 802.3af-compliant devices to be recognized before transmitting power to them.

Marketplace

PowerDsine, Siemens, and Lucent Technologies are vendors that have developed early versions of 802.3af-compliant switches, hubs, and IP telephony equipment. Refer to these vendors' Web sites for the latest information on these products.

Notes

Cisco Systems already has its own proprietary scheme called Inline Power for power transmission over data lines. The Cisco version supports DC power transmission over UTP cabling.

See Also: *Category 5 (Cat5) cabling, Ethernet, UTP cabling*

802.3u

The Institute of Electrical and Electronics Engineers (IEEE) standard for Fast Ethernet that was ratified in 1995. This standard defines the physical layer (PHY) and media access control (MAC) layer specifications for this technology.

See Also: *Fast Ethernet*

802.3z

The Institute of Electrical and Electronics Engineers (IEEE) standard for Gigabit Ethernet (GbE) over fiber, which was ratified in June 1998. This standard defines the physical layer (PHY) and media access control (MAC) layer specifications for this technology.

See Also: *Gigabit Ethernet (GbE)*

802.4

The Institute of Electrical and Electronics Engineers (IEEE) standard for the Token Bus networking architecture. This legacy architecture is now found only in some industrial settings. The IEEE 802.4 working group is no longer active.

See Also: *Project 802*

802.5

The Institute of Electrical and Electronics Engineers (IEEE) standard for the Token Ring networking architecture.

Notes

802.5 is also used to refer to the frame format used in Token Ring frames. See the article "frame type" elsewhere in this book for more information.

For More Information

The Institute of Electrical and Electronics Engineers (IEEE) 802.5 Web site is actually not found at the IEEE Web site (*www.ieee.org*). Instead, it can be found at *www.8025.org*.

See Also: *frame type, Token Ring*

802.6

The Institute of Electrical and Electronics Engineers (IEEE) standard for the Metropolitan Area Networks (MANs). The IEEE 802.6 working group is no longer active.

See Also: *Project 802*

802.7

The Institute of Electrical and Electronics Engineers (IEEE) Broadband Technical Advisory Group (TAG). The IEEE 802.7 working group is no longer active.

See Also: *Project 802*

802.8

The Institute of Electrical and Electronics Engineers (IEEE) Technical Advisory Group (TAG) for developing standards and recommending practices for fiber-optic networking. The IEEE 802.8 working group is no longer active.

See Also: *Project 802*

802.9

The Institute of Electrical and Electronics Engineers (IEEE) standards for isochronous local area networks (LANs) for simultaneous transmission of data and voice/video. The only developed form of this standard is the 802.9a isoEthernet specification.

Overview

Isochronous means "at a precise time," which indicates that 802.9 technologies operate using clocked signals in order to deliver data according to a rigid time schedule. In this fashion 802.9 resembles the Public Switched Telephone Network (PSTN), a circuit-switched network operating at 8 kilohertz (kHz) clocking rate and transmitting one byte every 125 microseconds to produce an overall channel (called a B channel) whose bandwidth is 64 kilobits per second (Kbps).

The isoEthernet standard developed in conjunction with National Semiconductor combines traditional 10BaseT Ethernet data transmission at 10 megabits per second (Mbps) with a separate 6.144 Mbps isochronous data channel for transporting time-sensitive traffic such as voice and video. The isochronous data channel (called the Circuit channel) consists of 96 B-channels of 64 Kbps each. IsoEthernet's total bandwidth, therefore, is 16 Mbps, but this is split between the two types of transmission: data and voice/video. There are also some additional channels (D-, M-, and P-channels) that are used for control and maintenance, but these use only about 200 Kbps of bandwidth. The 10 Mbps of 10BaseT data and 6.144 Mbps of isochronous transmission are carried on the same unshielded twisted pair (UTP) cabling system by incorporating time-division multiplexing (TDM) techniques.

Notes

The IEEE 802.9 working group is no longer active and isoEthernet is now considered a legacy technology.

See Also: *Project 802, time-division multiplexing (TDM)*

802.10

The Institute of Electrical and Electronics Engineers (IEEE) working group for local area network (LAN) security standards. The IEEE 802.10 working group is no longer active.

See Also: *Project 802*

802.11

A set of Institute of Electrical and Electronics Engineers (IEEE) standards for wireless networking designed to do for wireless networking what the 802.3 standards have done for Ethernet: provide clear guidelines for vendors to develop technologies that are standards-based, interoperable, and can operate at different speeds and frequencies and also can use different encoding mechanisms.

Overview

Three standards are currently ratified under 802.11:

- **802.11:** The original wireless networking standard supporting data rates of up to 2 megabits per second (Mbps) and now superseded by 802.11b. This standard was approved in June 1997 and provided for both direct sequence spread spectrum (DSSS) and frequency hopping spread spectrum (FHSS) physical-layer (PHY) transmission methods. 802.11 also supported transmission over infrared, but no products were developed for this method. 802.11 allows data to be transmitted at either 1 Mbps or 2 Mbps, depending on which is the highest rate negotiable in a given configuration of client and access point (the further the distance between them, the lower the possible data rate).

- **802.11b:** A standard for wireless networking supporting data rates of up to 11 Mbps and operating in the unlicensed 2.4 GHz Industrial, Scientific, and Medical (ISM) band. 802.11b transmission is standardized on DSSS.
- **802.11a:** A standard supporting higher data rates of up to 54 Mbps and operating in the 5 GHz UNII (Unlicensed National Information Infrastructure) band. 802.11a transmission is similarly standardized on DSSS.

Of these standards, 802.11b is currently the most widely deployed, with support from over 20 vendors, and 802.11 is considered legacy and is being phased out. Part of the success of 802.11b is due to the successful lobbying of the Wireless Ethernet Compatibility Alliance (WECA), which has helped ensure adherence to standards and interoperability between equipment from different vendors. The 802.11a standard is newer and is seen as the next generation for wireless networking and the natural upgrade path for companies needing its higher data transmission rates.

All these standards use the same Media Access Control (MAC) method, Carrier Sense Multiple Access with Collision Avoidance (CSMA/CA), to allow multiple users to share a single communications channel. Note that this is not the MAC method used by Ethernet (it uses CSMA/CD), so it is a misnomer to call 802.11 technology wireless Ethernet.

Notes

If you upgrade your 802.11 base stations to 802.11b, they will still support legacy 802.11 clients—but only at their maximum data rate of 2 Mbps, which in actual practice is more like 1 Mbps.

For secure wireless transmission, data needs to be encrypted. The most popular solution is Wired Equivalent Privacy (WEP), which now is included as a standard feature with most wireless network interface cards (NICs), PC cards, and access points.

For More Information

You can find information about the Wireless LAN Alliance at *www.alana.com* and the Wireless Ethernet Compatibility Alliance (WECA) at *www.wirelessethernet.org*.

See Also: *802.11a, 802.11b, wireless networking*

802.11a

An Institute of Electrical and Electronics Engineers (IEEE) wireless networking communications standard that supports data transmission rates of up to 54 megabits per second (Mbps). 802.11a is widely seen as the successor to 802.11b.

Overview

The 802.11a standard uses the same Media Access Control (MAC) layer mechanism as the more commonly deployed 802.11b, namely Carrier Sense Multiple Access with Collision Avoidance (CSMA/CA), which allows multiple users to share a single channel at the same time. The encoding scheme used at the physical layer differs, however, because 802.11b uses the same physical-layer (PHY) encoding scheme as Ethernet, but 802.11a uses a different scheme: Coded Orthogonal Frequency Division Multiplexing (COFDM or Coded OFDM).

The frequency bands used by 802.11a also differ from 802.11b, because 802.11b uses the 2.4 GHz Industrial, Scientific, and Medical (ISM) band for its operation, and 802.11a employs portions of the 5 GHz Unlicensed National Information Infrastructure (UNII) band recently allocated by the Federal Communications Commission (FCC).

A single 802.11a communications channel consists of a 20 megahertz (MHz)-wide block of frequencies divided up into 52 subchannels each 300 kilohertz (KHz) wide, 48 of which are used for carrying data, with the remaining 4 subchannels reserved for error correction. By encoding data using 64-level quadrature amplitude modulation (64QAM), a data rate of 1.125 Mbps per subchannel can be achieved, which translates into a maximum overall transmission speed of 48 x 1.125 = 54 Mbps. Due to the limitations of the MAC layer mechanism, however, actual data rates are only about 70 percent of theoretical, so that sustained data rates for 802.11a are rarely above 35 Mbps. Nevertheless, these high attainable speeds are sufficient to enable 802.11a systems to support some types of broadband applications, including Web browsing and multimedia.

The frequencies used by 802.11a cover three 200 MHz blocks of the 5 gigahertz (GHz) band:

- **5.15 to 5.25 GHz:** This band supports five independent channels with a maximum power output of 50 megawatts (mW).
- **5.25 to 5.35 GHz:** This band also supports five independent channels but with a maximum power output of 250 mW for greater distance and penetration of building materials.
- **5.725 to 5.825 GHz:** This upper band is designed for outdoor communications, supports five independent channels, and a maximum power output of 1 watt.

Advantages and Disadvantages

The main advantage of 802.11a over 802.11b is the increased data rate. By way of analogy, 802.11a is to 802.11b as Fast Ethernet is to standard 10 Mbps Ethernet. In fact, both of these standards are sometimes referred to as wireless Ethernet, but this is a misnomer because they use CSMA/CA instead of Ethernet's Carrier-Sense Multiple-Access with Collision Detection (CSMA/CD) mechanism at the MAC layer.

Besides the higher data rates supported by 802.11a as compared to 802.11b, another advantage of 802.11a is that the COFDM encoding mechanism includes greater error correction, which means better recovery from multipath reflection.

Implementation

As a result of these differences in signal encoding mechanisms, 802.11b and 802.11a are incompatible standards. Devices using one standard cannot communicate with devices supporting the other standard. Yet because these two technologies operate at different frequency bands, they can be deployed together and overlap without interference. 802.11b is already widely deployed in many corporate enterprises; the logical migration path to 802.11a is to deploy 802.11a in small pockets where it is most required and gradually extend this as needed.

Marketplace

Two vendors pioneering in 802.11a hardware include Radiata Communications (now owned by Cisco Systems) and Atheros Communications. Both vendors offer devices supporting 6, 12, 24, 36, 48, and 54 Mbps transmission speeds, with different rates being achieved by using different encoding mechanisms. Atheros also supports bonding two channels to achieve a theoretical maximum transmission rate of 108 Mbps, and other vendors are developing proprietary extensions to 802.11a that may boost speeds up to 155 Mbps.

Issues

Because of the higher frequencies used, 802.11a devices are not susceptible to the kind of electromagnetic interference, including interference from microwave ovens and cell phones, that plagues 802.11b devices. However, because of different governmental policies regarding allocation of frequencies in the 5 GHz band, interoperability issues exist for 802.11a technologies used in different parts of the world.

For example, in Europe the upper 100 MHz portion (5.725 to 5.825) is already allocated for other uses, limiting operation of 802.11a gear to only 10 clear channels instead of 15. The 802.11a standard is also incompatible with the competing HiperLAN/2 standard being developed in Europe, which also uses frequencies from the 5 GHz band. In Japan only the lower 100 MHz portion is unallocated, which allows only five channels for 802.11a to work with. Other countries and regions use portions of the 5 GHz spectrum for military or satellite communications purposes, limiting the capability of 802.11a devices within their borders.

See Also: *802.11, 802.11b, wireless networking*

802.11b

An Institute of Electrical and Electronics Engineers (IEEE) wireless networking communications standard that supports data transmission rates of up to 1 megabit per second (Mbps). 802.11b is sometimes called wireless Ethernet, but this is a misnomer because the two technologies use different Media Access Control (MAC) methods.

Overview

The 802.11b standard was developed over a number of years by Lucent Technologies, Intersil Corporation, and other industry partners and ratified as an IEEE standard in 1999. It is the most popular and widely deployed wireless networking standard currently in use, though it may be superseded over the next few years by 802.11a, which supports higher data transmission rates.

802.11b is capable of supporting data transmission rates of 1, 2, 5.5, and 11 Mbps. The actual transmission rate used will depend on the distance between the client adapter (PC card or network interface card [NIC]) and access point (base transmitting station) and upon interference due to obstacles in the transmission path. In general, the further the distance from the base station, the slower the data rate. For directional antennae operating with clear line-of-sight in point-to-point transmission, the top speed of 11 Mbps can be sustained for distances up to about 10 miles (16 km). Within a building using omnidirectional antennae, however, devices may need to be within 100 feet (15 meters) in order to maintain their highest transmission rate. If a device exceeds this range, the transmission rate drops to the progressively lower levels until a sustained transmission rate can be successfully negotiated. Each data rate uses its own characteristic modulation scheme, such as Binary Phase Shift Keying (BPSK) for 1 Mbps transmission, Quadrature Phase Shift Keying (QPSK) for 2 Mbps, and so on.

Although the theoretical top transmission speed for 802.11b is 11 Mbps, in practice the media access control (MAC) layer mechanism (Carrier Sense Multiple Access with Collision Avoidance [CSMA/CA]) and protocol overhead reduce efficiency to 60-70 percent. The result is that data rates of more than 6 Mbps are rarely achieved and 4-5 Mbps is more common. Note that this is the total shared bandwidth for all 802.11b clients within the same service area (serviced by the same set of access points or base stations), so actual throughput may be much less when many clients are active. The 802.11b standard allows multiple users to share a single communications channel at the same time by using the CSMA/CA method as its MAC layer protocol. The 802.11b standard supports Request to Send/Clear to Send (RTS/CTS) as a MAC enhancement for transmission in environments where coverage is distorted by obstacles and interference, but this mechanism adds significant overhead to the protocol, especially during the transmission of small packets.

The drawing shows a typical 802.11b packet. This consists of a 30-byte header containing information for addressing, sequencing, and frame control. This is followed by a data or payload section that may range from zero to 2312 bytes in length, followed by a 4-byte checksum trailer.

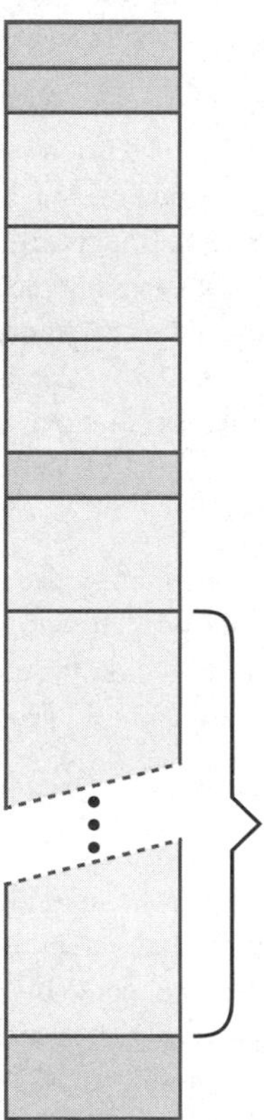

802.11b. *Typical structure of an 802.11b packet.*

As far as frequency and transmission method are concerned, 802.11b employs direct-sequence spread spectrum (DSSS) transmission over an 83-MHz-wide chunk of the unlicensed 2.4 GHz Industrial, Scientific, and Medical (ISM) band of the electromagnetic spectrum, specifically the frequency band from 2.400 to 2.483 GHz. Because this frequency band overlaps with emissions from microwave ovens and some cell phones, proximity of these devices can affect the transmission speed achieved.

Under Federal Communications Commission (FCC) regulations, 802.11b provides 11 separate channels for communications. Theoretically, this means that the total maximum bandwidth for an 802.11b local area network (LAN) utilizing all channels would be 11 x 11 Mbps = 121 Mbps. In practice, due to interference between channels, a given service area can only support three simultaneous channels, which limits total available bandwidth to 3 x 11 = 33 Mbps in theory, or about 14 Mbps in practice once protocol overhead is factored in.

A typical 802.11b wireless LAN segment may support up to 65 different clients, but the contention involved in the CSMA/CA media access method means that one busy client downloading a large file can utilize the segment's entire available bandwidth, leaving the other stations unable to communicate. Adding additional access points to the service area provides fault tolerance and load balancing but does not increase the total available bandwidth.

Implementation

When deciding whether you should immediately deploy 802.11b equipment in your enterprise or wait for the faster 802.11a to gain greater vendor support, you have several issues to consider. Small- and mid-sized companies might find 802.11b a cheap, easy, turnkey solution to deploy and might not need the higher data rates of 802.11a. And although both systems can be deployed in parallel, 802.11b equipment cannot be upgraded to 802.11a. Dual-radio access points are under development, but their deployment is complicated by the two standards' different transmission characteristics. Finally, enterprise architects may want to wait for 802.11a products that are certified by the Wireless Ethernet Compatibility Alliance (WECA) before committing large portions of their budget to a massive rollout of 802.11a.

Marketplace

More than 20 different vendors sell 802.11b-compliant hardware, and the standard's success is evident in the high degree of interoperability between equipment supplied by different vendors. A client network adapter (NIC or PC card) from one vendor is likely to work well with an access point (base station hub) from a different vendor without needing any modifications. Access points from different vendors are less likely to work together, particularly if they need to be configured for roaming users that move from one service area (cell) to another and require seamless networking during the transition. So the best solution is still to purchase all of your 802.11b devices from the same vendor in order to achieve the highest level of interoperability, particularly in large, geographically dispersed deployments with multiple access points spanning multiple subnets.

As a result of increased competition, prices for 802.11b equipment have fallen drastically of late. Client adapters are now available for $99 or less, and access points can be had for under $299. Some popular vendor products include

- **3Com Corporation:** AirConnect PC card and companion AirConnect Wireless Access Point designed for the enterprise, which supports Mobile IP and Microsoft Point-to-Point Encryption
- **Apple Computer:** AirPort client adapter and companion Airport access point, a bargain system designed for Small Office Home Office (SOHO) environments and including Ethernet and V.90 modem support
- **Intel Corporation:** PRO/Wireless LAN PC card and companion PRO/Wireless LAN Access Point, with integrated Web server and 128-bit Wired Equivalent Privacy (WEP) support. Intel also recently acquired Xircom, which makes a wireless Ethernet adapter that is popular with Notebook users and supports 40- and 120-bit WEP.

Issues

While the maximum allowed power output for an 802.11b-compliant device is 1 watt, most 802.11b-compliant NICs and PC cards emit only about 30 milliwatts (mW) to conserve battery life in laptops and avoid excessive heat dissipation. This is generally considered too low to constitute any health hazard to individuals using this equipment—for comparison, a typical cell phone may generate an electromagnetic power output of half a watt or more.

Notes

For an explanation of the different components needed in the deployment of a wireless network and how they operate, see the article "wireless networking" elsewhere in this book.

Do not operate 802.11b devices in an aircraft during flight—turn your device off when boarding. The signals transmitted by your device could adversely affect the aircraft's electronic systems.

Look for the "WiFi" seal of approval on vendor packaging of 802.11b equipment. This designation indicates that the vendor's equipment is approved by WECA as being fully compliant with 802.11b standards.

Wireless networks based on 802.11b can be susceptible to electromagnetic interference produced by microwave ovens, particularly if the clients are located far from the base station. If this occurs, move the oven, move the client adapter, or increase the transmission strength of the access point until you can achieve reliable communications.

To conserve power, especially for 802.11b PC cards in laptops, these client adapters should be set to run in Polled Access Mode (PAM). Clients configured for PAM go to sleep when not communicating with the base station and wake up according to a predefined schedule to check for an inbound Traffic Information Map (TIM) packet from the base station indicating that it has data ready to send the client. PAM typically uses about 10 percent of the power consumed when running in Constant Access Mode (CAM), where the client is always listening.

If your buildings have metal floors, wireless networking using 802.11b systems may not operate beyond 100 feet (30 meters) due to signal absorption. In such buildings you may also require an access point on each floor.

802.11b and Bluetooth devices operate on the same frequencies, so using both systems in the same service area may cause dropouts and transmission errors to occur.

See Also: *802.11, 802.11b, Bluetooth, wireless networking*

802.12

The Institute of Electrical and Electronics Engineers (IEEE) standards outlining the architecture and operation of the Demand Priority Media Access Control (MAC) method. This access method is employed by the legacy 100VG-AnyLAN technology developed in 1994 by Hewlett-Packard and AT&T. The IEEE 802.12 working group is presently in hibernation and is no longer active.

See Also: *100VG-AnyLAN, demand priority, Project 802*

802.13

The Institute of Electrical and Electronics Engineers' (IEEE's) Project 802 includes a number of standards and working groups relating to networking. These standards and working groups currently range from 802.1 through 802.17, but for some reason 802.13 was not used.

See Also: *Project 802*

802.14

The Institute of Electrical and Electronics Engineers (IEEE) working group on cable modems. This working group is no longer active.

See Also: *Project 802*

802.15

A set of standards being developed by the Institute of Electrical and Electronics Engineers (IEEE) for Wireless Personal Area Networks (Wireless PANs or WPANs).

Overview

The 802.15 working group is currently divided into a number of Task Groups (TGs) that are actively working on different aspects of wireless PANs. These TGs include

- **TG1:** This group is working to develop standards for WPANs based on Bluetooth 1.x wireless technologies.
- **TG2:** This group is trying to get 802.15 WPANs to coexist with 802.11 WLANs by overcoming issues

related to electromagnetic interference between the two technologies.

- **TG3:** This group is trying to develop High Rate (HR) WPANs with speeds in excess of 20 megabits per second (Mbps).
- **TG4:** This group deals with developing Low Rate (LR) WPANs with speeds in the range of 10–200 kilobits per second (Kbps). These LR WPANs will be used for things such as home automation, remote control, interactive toys, sensors, and similar systems.

See Also: *Personal Area Network (PAN), Project 802*

802.16

A set of emerging Institute of Electrical and Electronics Engineers (IEEE) standards being developed for fixed broadband wireless networking.

Overview

Broadband wireless, also called Wireless MAN (WMAN), involves wireless high-speed data transmission between fixed points at various frequency bands. In other words, 802.16 is to the metropolitan area network (MAN) what 802.11 is to the local area network (LAN): similar technology but operating at higher speeds and over longer distances. WMAN is the wireless equivalent of broadband wired technologies such as Digital Subscriber Line (DSL).

The IEEE working group on 802.16 is subdivided into a number of Task Groups (TGs) to work at these different frequencies, specifically:

- **TG1:** This group is working on air interfaces in the 10– 66gigahertz (GHz) region of the electromagnetic spectrum.
- **TG2:** This group is working on ensuring coexistence between different wireless broadband access systems.
- **TG3:** This group is working on air interfaces in the 2–11 GHz region of the spectrum.
- **TG4:** This group is working on the Wireless High-Speed Unlicensed Metropolitan Area Network (Wireless HUMAN) standard, which involves transmission in license-exempt portions of the spectrum in the 5– 6GHz range.

See Also: *Project 802*

802.17

The Institute of Electrical and Electronics Engineers (IEEE) working group on Resilient Packet Ring (RPR) technologies.

See Also: *Project 802*

1000BaseCX

An Institute of Electrical and Electronics Engineers (IEEE) standard for implementing 1000 megabits per second (Mbps) Ethernet (that is, Gigabit Ethernet, or GbE) over shielded twisted-pair (STP) cabling.

Overview

The CX in 1000BaseCX stands for short-haul copper and indicates that this version of GbE is intended for short cable runs over copper cabling. 1000BaseCX technologies are in the beginning stages of being widely implemented in enterprise-level networks and are primarily used for collapsed backbones and high-speed interconnects within wiring closets and equipment rooms. 1000BaseCX and other GbE standards are defined in the 802.3z series of standards of Project 802 developed by the IEEE.

Implementation

1000BaseCX is to some degree simply an extension of standard Ethernet technologies to Gigabit-level network speeds. 1000BaseCX is implemented using STP cabling. This STP cabling must be standard 150-ohm balanced cabling and should have a quality slightly better than IBM Type I cabling. Cable segments can have a maximum length of only 82 feet (25 meters).

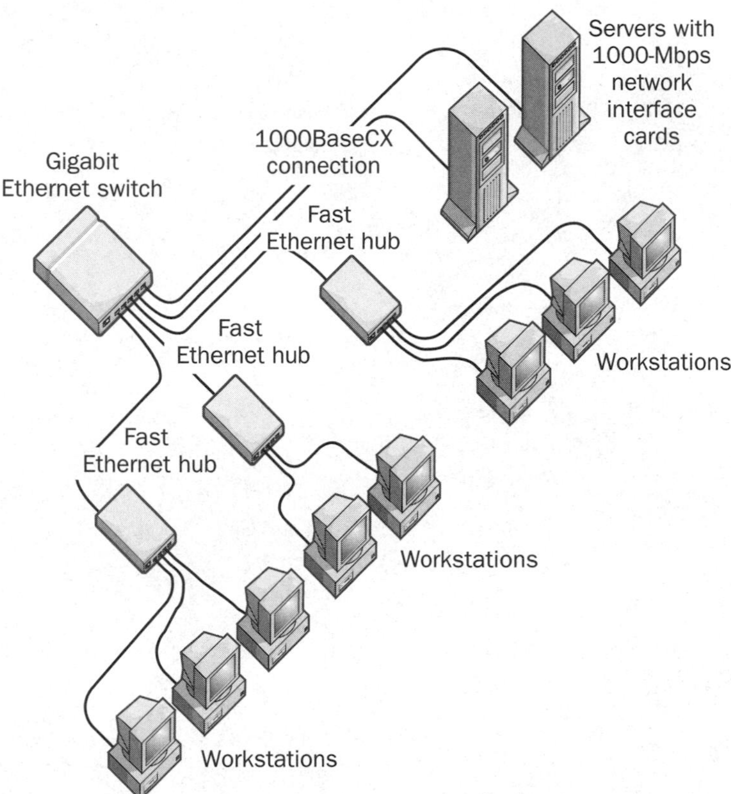

1000BaseCX. *A typical 1000BaseCX network.*

Like other forms of GbE, 1000BaseCX employs 8B/10B coding with a transmission frequency transmission of 1.25 GHz. 1000BaseCX is intended mainly for connecting high-speed hubs, Ethernet switches, and routers together in wiring closets. Common implementations for 1000BaseCX are in switch-switch and switch-server connections, with switch-server connections being the most frequently implemented use for 1000BaseCX.

See Also: *1000BaseLX, 1000BaseSX, 1000BaseT, Gigabit Ethernet (GbE)*

1000BaseLX

An Institute of Electrical and Electronics Engineers (IEEE) standard for implementing 1000 megabits per second (Mbps) Ethernet (that is, Gigabit Ethernet, or GbE) over fiber-optic cabling.

Overview

The *LX* in 1000BaseLX stands for long and indicates that this version of GbE is intended for use with long-wavelength (1300 nm) laser transmissions over long cable runs of fiber-optic cabling. 1000BaseLX technologies are in the beginning stages of being widely implemented in enterprise-level networks and are primarily used for long cable runs between pieces of equipment on a campus or within a building. 1000BaseLX and other GbE standards are defined in the 802.3z standards of Project 802 developed by the IEEE.

Implementation

1000BaseLX can be implemented using either single-mode fiber-optic cabling or multimode fiber-optic cabling. Transmission requires two optical fibers due to the full-duplex operation of 1000BaseLX. Cable segment lengths depend on the cable grade used, as shown in the table on the following page.

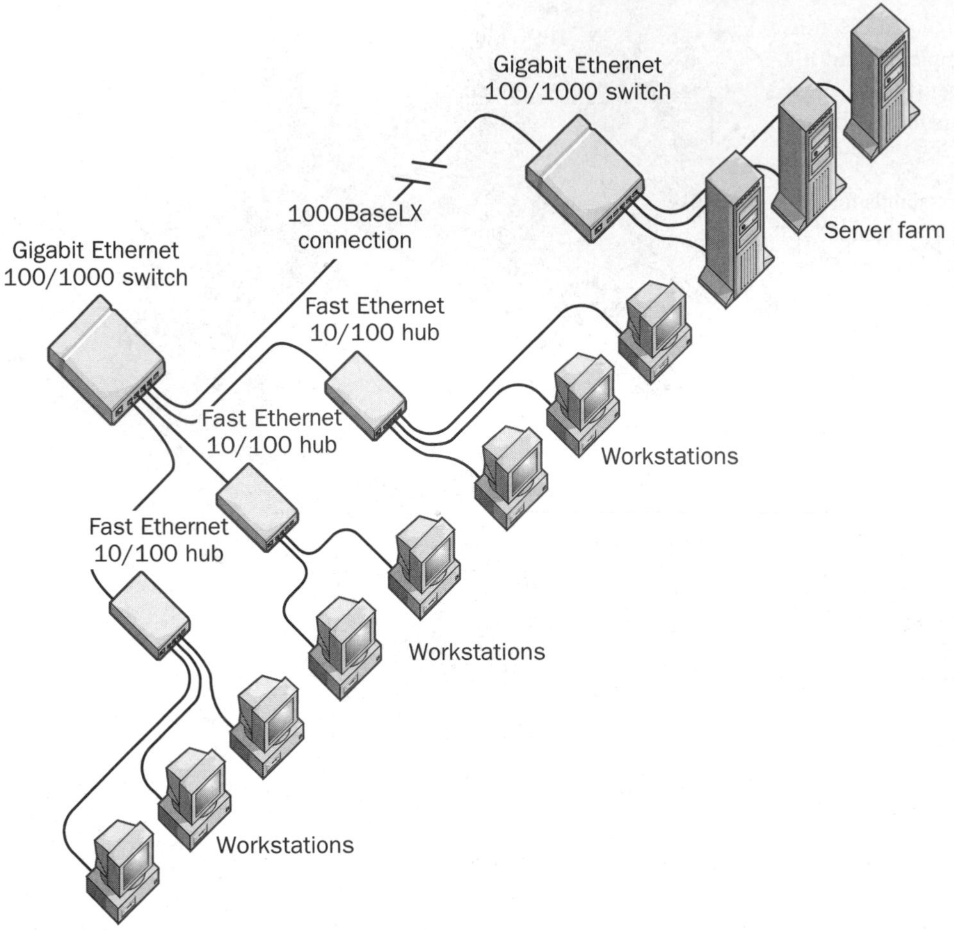

1000BaseLX. *A typical 1000BaseLX network.*

Cable Segment Lengths

Cable Grade	*Maximum Segment Length*
10-micron single-mode fiber	10 kilometers (6.2 miles)
50-micron multimode fiber	550 meters (1800 feet)
62.5-micron multi-mode fiber	440 meters (1440 feet)

1000BaseLX is intended mainly for connecting high-speed hubs, Ethernet switches, and routers together in different wiring closets or buildings using long cabling runs. 1000BaseLX is most commonly implemented in a switch-switch configuration.

Notes

When you use multimode fiber-optic cabling in 1000BaseLX implementations, a condition called differential mode delay (DMD) can sometimes occur. This condition occurs only in cabling of uneven quality, and it leads to signal jitter that can disrupt network communications. To resolve this problem, newer 1000BaseLX transceivers condition the signal to distribute its power equally among all transmission modes of the cable.

See Also: *1000BaseCX, 1000BaseSX, 1000BaseT, Gigabit Ethernet (GbE)*

1000BaseSX

An Institute of Electrical and Electronics Engineers (IEEE) standard for implementing 1000 megabits per second (Mbps) Ethernet (that is, Gigabit Ethernet, or GbE) over fiber-optic cabling.

Overview

The *SX* in 1000BaseSX stands for short and indicates that this version of GbE is intended for use with short-wavelength (850-nanometer) laser transmissions over short cable runs of fiber-optic cabling. 1000BaseSX technologies are in the beginning stages of being widely implemented in enterprise-level networks and are primarily used for shorter cable runs between pieces of equipment within a building.

1000BaseSX is an extension of standard Ethernet technologies to gigabit-level network speeds. 1000BaseSX and other GbE standards are defined in the 802.3z standards of Project 802 developed by the IEEE.

Implementation

1000BaseSX is implemented using only multimode fiber-optic cabling. Cable segment lengths depend on the cable grade used, as shown in the table.

Cable Segment Lengths

Cable Grade	*Maximum Segment Length*
50-micron multimode fiber	500 meters (1640 feet)
62.5-micron multimode fiber	220 meters (720 feet)

1000BaseSX is intended mainly for connecting high-speed hubs, Ethernet switches, and routers together in different wiring closets or buildings using long cabling runs. 1000BaseSX is most commonly implemented in a switch-switch configuration.

Notes

When multimode fiber-optic cabling is used in 1000BaseSX implementations, a condition called differential mode delay (DMD) can sometimes occur. This condition occurs only in cabling of uneven quality, and it leads to signal jitter that can disrupt network communications. To resolve this problem, newer 1000BaseSX transceivers condition the signal to distribute its power equally among all the cable's transmission modes.

See Also: *1000BaseCX, 1000BaseLX, 1000BaseT, Gigabit Ethernet (GbE)*

1000BaseT

An Institute of Electrical and Electronics Engineers (IEEE) standard for a form of Gigabit Ethernet (GbE) involving transmission over copper cabling.

Overview

The *T* in 1000BaseT identifies it as operating over twisted-pair copper cabling and makes it an extension of the traditional 10BaseT and 100BaseT Ethernet technologies for transmission over unshielded twisted-pair (UTP) cabling. 1000BaseT is based on the IEEE 802.3ab standard and is intended to provide the simplest upgrade path for legacy 10BaseT and 100BaseT Ethernet networks.

1000BaseT is implemented using the commonly installed Category 5 (Cat5) cabling or enhanced Category 5 cabling version of UTP cabling. Cable segments for 1000BaseT must have a maximum length of 328 feet (100 meters). Category 6 (Cat6) cabling is expected to provide enhanced transmission characteristics for 1000BaseT networks when it becomes available.

1000BaseT uses all four pairs of wires in standard UTP cabling, as opposed to the two pairs of wires used in 10BaseT and 100BaseT networks. Using all four pairs of wires brings certain problems because of attenuation, crosstalk, and echoes arising from full-duplex transmission over single wires. Full-duplex transmission is used to enable each pair of wires to simultaneously transmit and receive data at a rate of 250 megabits per second (Mbps). The resulting four pairs of wires means that the total data rate is 4 x 250 = 1000 Mbps or 1 Gbps. Although each pair of wires carries data at 250 Mbps, the signaling is only at 125 Mbps. This is accomplished by using five-level pulse amplitude modulation (PAM) as the line coding mechanism, which encodes two bits of information for each signal pulse. The reason for this choice is that Cat5 cabling works well up to 125 megahertz (MHz) in standard installations.

1000 BaseT has been standardized by the IEEE under the 802.3ab specification since June 1999. This specification provides for the implementation of automatic link negotiation so that problems such as crossed cables can be detected and corrected for, that 100 Mbps interface can be detected and accommodated when connected to 1000BaseT ports, and that half-duplex network interface cards (NICs) and hub/switch ports can be recognized and used when detected. The standard also specifies special filters for hybrid circuits used in full-duplex transmission over single wires, a special five-level PAM encoding mechanism instead of binary signals, forward error correction techniques, and pulse shaping technologies to make 1000BaseT a functional and reliable networking technology.

Implementation

One popular use for 1000BaseT (also referred to as GbE over copper) is in wiring closets of enterprise networks. 1000BaseT GbE switches can be used to aggregate Fast Ethernet workgroup switches by first connecting the workgroup switches to 100/1000 Mbps ports on the GbE switches using Cat5 cabling and then uplinking the GbE switches to the network's GbE backbone switches using fiber.

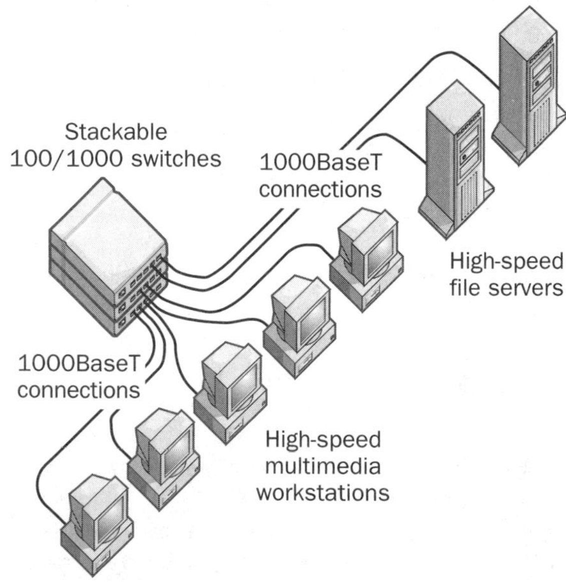

1000BaseT. *A typical 1000BaseT network.*

Another growing use for 1000BaseT GbE switches is for connecting high-performance multimedia workstations and Web server clusters to the network backbone. The main limitation for 1000BaseT workstations is that they must be located within 100 meters of the switch. For interbuilding GbE links you need to use fiber. Note, however, that 1000BaseT only supports cable runs up to 328 feet (100 meters) in length, which means that you may need to modify existing cabling infrastructures in some large buildings when migrating from Fast Ethernet to 1000BaseT. Despite the potential application for supporting high-performance workstations, the most popular uses for 1000BaseT remain for backbone uses such as installing vertical risers between floors and horizontal cable runs between wiring closets, for interconnecting workgroup switches, and for connecting server farms and clusters to backbone switches.

Marketplace

Adapting the Ethernet standard to transmission at rates of 1 Gbps over existing Cat5 wiring means lower costs for companies planning to upgrade their switched backbones from 100 Mbps Fast Ethernet to GbE. A typical 1000BaseSX fiber port costs about 50 percent more than a comparable 1000BaseT copper port, so considerable cost savings can be achieved by implementing GbE over copper instead of fiber. However, copper is more susceptible to noise than fiber for gigabit transmission, and Cat5 cabling must be of the highest standard and deployed according to standards to ensure maximum reliability.

1000BaseT solutions are beginning to be implemented for short, high-speed interconnects within wiring closets in enterprise networks, for consolidating server farms in data centers, and for interconnects in carrier colocation sites. Some also envision using it for connecting high-performance workstations as well. Vendors of 1000BaseT equipment include Cisco Systems, 3Com Corporation, Hewlett-Packard, Asante Technologies, Nortel Communications, Extreme Networks, Intel Corporation, and Foundry Networks. Cisco's Catalyst 6500 for its Catalyst 6506 switch chassis module provides 16 1000BaseT ports and is popular with Internet service providers (ISPs) deployed at carrier colocation sites because of its fault-tolerant load balancing and realtime code upgrade capabilities. Foundry's eight-port 1000BaseT modules for its BigIron 8000 switch chassis is another popular choice with excellent performance.

A number of vendors are also providing 1000BaseT NICs for use in high-speed servers and high-performance networks connected to GbE backbones. These vendors include 3Com, Intel, Sun Microsystems, and SysKonnect. A popular choice in enterprise server farms is the SysKonnect 9822 64-bit 66 MHz PCI card, which comes in single-port and dual-port configurations. Alteon WebSystems also has a 10/100/1000BaseT NIC with support for auto-negotiation and jumbo frames.

Currently 1000BaseT is the fastest growing type of GbE being deployed in enterprise networks, because it leverages the investment of existing Cat5 cabling installations. In the second quarter of 2000, GbE over copper accounted for 25 percent of GbE port sales.

Notes

1000BaseT is also sometimes referred to as 1000BaseTX.

Before installing 1000BaseT switches in a building wired with older Cat5 cabling (as opposed to newer enhanced Category 5 [Cat5e] cabling), be sure to test the cabling using a cable tester to make certain the installation fully complies with IEEE TSB95 field specifications. Common reasons for existing wiring failing to support GbE are crosstalk caused by improper cable termination in punch-down block and wall plates. Hewlett-Packard and Fluke Corporation are two vendors that sell suitable cable test equipment. Also, be sure also to use high-quality Cat5e patch cables for connecting patch panels to switches in wiring closets and for connecting servers or workstations to wall plates in work areas.

See Also: *1000BaseCX, 1000BaseLX, 1000BaseSX, Gigabit Ethernet (GbE)*

1000BaseTX

Another name for 1000BaseT Gigabit Ethernet (GbE) over copper.

See: *1000BaseT*

1000BaseX

A generic designation used to describe all forms of Gigabit Ethernet (GbE), including 1000BaseCX, 1000BaseLX, 1000BaseSX, and 1000BaseT. 1000BaseX actually is the technical designation for the family of physical layer (PHY) technologies used in GbE and evolved directly from the Fiber Channel ANSI94 standards.

See Also: *1000BaseCX, 1000BaseLX, 1000BaseSX, 1000BaseT, Gigabit Ethernet (GbE)*

1394

An Institute of Electrical and Electronics Engineers (IEEE) standard for a high-speed serial transmission technology also known as FireWire (a popular term coined by Apple Computer) and iLink (a Sony Corporation trademark).

See Also: *FireWire*

1822

The original host-to-IMP (interface message processor) interface for the Advanced Research Projects Agency Network (ARPANET), the precursor of the Internet.

See Also: *ARPANET*

3270

An information display protocol for IBM mainframe computers.

Overview

The 3270 protocol is a family of protocols that includes separate specifications for terminal display and printer output. The 3270 protocol enables text-based connection-oriented conversations to take place between centralized mainframe hosts and supported peripherals, including terminals, printers, and controllers. These conversations originally took place over dedicated serial transmission links between the terminal and the mainframe controller. For long-distance computing, transmission over private wide area networks (WANs) such as the IBM Global Network enabled mainframe

COBOL programmers to work from home instead of having to commute to the office.

Private WAN services such as IBM Global Networks have now been dismantled and replaced with the Internet, and Web-based access to mainframe hosts has led to the development of hardware-based and software-based emulators. A 3270 emulator is a device or program that enables a workstation to communicate with a mainframe as if it were a dedicated 3270 terminal. A typical 3270 software emulator might use ActiveX controls or Java applets to display the 3270 terminal interface running within a Web browser window. These controls or applets are downloaded from a Web server acting as an intermediary between the Transmission Control Protocol/Internet Protocol (TCP/IP) local area network (LAN) on which the workstations reside and the mainframe host's Systems Network Architecture (SNA) network. Web-based 3270 emulators are popular in many corporate intranets where they can help leverage the usefulness of legacy mainframes and enable offsite users to access mainframe databases through the Internet.

Notes

You can use Microsoft SNA Server to enable a Windows 2000 or Windows .NET Server network to access a mainframe's hierarchical SNA network. SNA Server accomplishes this by defining and assigning dependent 3270 Logical Units (LUs). SNA Server client software must also be installed on each Windows 2000, Windows XP, or Windows .NET Server client that uses these SNA Server LU services. The SNA Server client software enables communication between 3270 applications on the client and the SNA server that provides a gateway to the mainframe.

The original 3270 protocol transmits streams of clear text information. If you are running terminal emulation software on a remote workstation and accessing the mainframe over the Internet, you need to make sure you are using Secure Sockets Layer (SSL) or some other method of securing your transmission.

See Also: *Web-to-host*

5250

An information display protocol for IBM AS/400 systems.

Overview

The 5250 protocol enables text-based connection-oriented conversations to take place between AS/400 hosts and supporting peripherals, including terminals, printers, and controllers. The 5250 protocol is a family of protocols that includes separate protocols for terminal display and printer output. AS/400 display sessions use 5250 data streams over Advanced Peer-to-Peer Networking (APPN).

Recent years have seen the proliferation of Web-based software for enabling local area network (LAN) workstations to access information on AS/400 hosts. These solutions are called terminal emulators and may be either hardware- or software-based. A typical 5250 emulator is an application that uses ActiveX controls or Java applets to display the 5250 terminal interface running within a Web browser window. Emulation controls or applets are downloaded from a Web server acting as an intermediary between the Transmission Control Protocol/Internet Protocol (TCP/IP) LAN on which the workstations reside and the AS/400 host.

Notes

Printer emulation is the ability to print locally from a workstation running a terminal emulator. In order for 5250 terminal emulators to support printer emulation, they must conform to the TN5250 Telnet protocol. Otherwise, workstations must print to a centralized printer attached to the AS/400.

Microsoft SNA Server supports both 3270 and 5250 sessions between Microsoft Windows clients and IBM mainframes and AS/400 systems.

The 5250 protocol transmits streams of clear text information, so if you are running terminal emulation software on a remote workstation to access your company's AS/400 over the Internet, you need to make sure you are using Secure Sockets Layer (SSL) or some other method for securing your transmission.

See Also: *Web-to-host*

A+ Certification

A certification for computer service technicians from the Computing Technology Industry Association (CompTIA).

Overview

A+ Certification certifies service technicians for competency in troubleshooting, repairing, and installing stand-alone and networked PCs. A+ is an internationally recognized certification that identifies minimum competency for entry-level computer technicians, typically those who have a minimum of six months of practical hands-on and interpersonal support experience. The Association for Services Management International (AFSMI) and a number of prominent hardware and software vendors back the A+ Certification.

A+ Certification was created by CompTIA to benefit all groups involved in the recruiting and hiring process. Specifically, it has the following advantages:

- A+ benefits managers and recruiters by helping them identify trained, competent individuals to fill vacant positions.
- A+ benefits job seekers by identifying skills they need to learn and develop and by providing a recognizable career path for self-advancement and employment.
- A+ benefits educational institutions by providing goals and objectives for developing industry-relevant technical training programs.

The A+ exam consists of two parts: a core section covering general computer hardware and software that is not vendor-specific and a module covering Microsoft operating system technologies for MS-DOS and Microsoft Windows platforms.

For More Information

Find out about the Computer Technology Industry Association at *www.comptia.org.*

A record

A Domain Name System (DNS) record mapping a host name to an Internet Protocol (IP) address.

Overview

Also known as Address records, A records are the most common type of DNS records in name server databases. A records are used to resolve queries where host names need to be translated into IP addresses in order to establish network communications with the target host.

Examples

A typical A record looks like this:

```
MARGE    IN    A    172.16.22.155
```

Here, MARGE is the friendly name of the host, IN indicates the record is part of the Internet family (the default), A indicates the type of resource record (address record), and the IP address for MARGE is last.

See Also: *DNS, resource record (RR)*

A6 record

A Domain Name System (DNS) record for identifying Internet Protocol version 6 (IPv6) hosts on a network.

Overview

The A6 record is used to map a host's name to its 128-bit IPv6 address. To use this record, a host on an IPv6 network can query a name server by specifying the name of a target host, and the name server responds to the query by returning the IPv6 address of the target host. The "A" in A6 stands for address.

Examples

If the name of a host is BART and the IPv6 address is 3dd4:2500:12af:0302:edef:6d52, then the A6 record would be

```
BART     3dd4:2500:12af:0302:edef:6d52
```

Notes

A6 records are supported on BIND version 9.

See Also: *DNS, resource record (RR)*

AAA

Sometimes called triple-A; stands for Authentication, Authorization, and Accounting, a security framework for controlling access to network resources.

Overview

The three components of an AAA system are the following:

- **Authentication:** This is the process by which users are identified as being entitled to access specific network resources.
- **Authorization:** This process determines the level of access a user has to a specific resource.
- **Accounting:** This process determines which resources are being used and who uses them.

An AAA Server is a server providing authentication, authorization, and accounting services for a network. In a typical AAA implementation, users connect to an access server (for example, a Cisco router) using an authentication protocol such as Password Authentication Protocol (PAP) or Challenge Handshake Authentication Protocol (CHAP). The access server then interacts with the AAA server; for instance, Cisco Secure using security protocols such as Kerberos, Remote Authentication Dial-In User Service (RADIUS), or Terminal Access Controller Access Control System (TACACS). Cisco AAA protocols can then be configured on the access server using Internetwork Operating System (IOS) and applied to a particular interface.

See Also: *network security*

AAAA record

Sometimes called quad-A, a Domain Name System (DNS) resource record that helps transition networks from Internet Protocol (IP) to IPv6.

Overview

The Internet Engineering Task Force (IETF) has developed several enhancements to DNS to help network managers migrate their IP networks to IPv6. These enhancements are outlined in RFC 1886. The AAAA record is one such item, and maps a 32-bit IP address to a newer 128-bit IPv6 address.

AAAA records are supported by Berkeley Internet Name Daemon (BIND) 4.9.5 and later. When networks are fully migrated to IPv6, AAAA records can be replaced by A6 records, which are supported in BIND 9.

See Also: *DNS, resource record (RR)*

AAL

Stands for ATM Adaptation Layer, an Asynchronous Transfer Mode (ATM) protocol that performs the functions of the Open Systems Interconnection (OSI) model's Data Link layer.

See: *ATM Adaptation Layer (AAL)*

AATP

Stands for Authorized Academic Training Provider, a Microsoft training program offered to accredited academic institutions.

See: *Authorized Academic Training Provider (AATP)*

Abilene

An advanced high-speed backbone network that was developed to support the Internet2 initiative.

Overview

Abilene was developed through a partnership between Cisco Systems, Nortel Communications, and Quest Communications and is a project of University Corporation for Advanced Internet Development (UCAID). Abilene's goal is to provide an advanced high-speed backbone for research and development testing of advanced applications relating to Internet2 prior to their intended real-world deployment. To this end, Abilene provides a high-speed Synchronous Optical Network (SONET) and Internet Protocol (IP)-over-SONET backbone network that connects gigaPOPs (high-speed regional network aggregation points of presence) scattered around the world. For an administrative fee, universities and other institutions conducting Internet2 research can connect to Internet2 through Abilene's gigaPOPs for research and development purposes.

Abilene is wholly funded by university and corporate agencies affiliated with the Internet2 research project, but Abilene also supports the U.S federal Next Generation Internet (NGI) initiative and connects with the very high performance Backbone Network Service (vBNS) and other federal research networks.

For More Information

Find out more about Abilene at *www.ucaid.org/abilene.*

See Also: *Internet2*

absolute path

The hierarchical path that locates a file or folder in a file system starting from the root.

Overview

A file's absolute path enables that file's location to be precisely specified, independent of where the user's current directory is located. In Microsoft Windows, a file's absolute path is specified starting with a drive letter, followed by the hierarchy of directories in which the file is contained (with each directory separated by a backslash) and concluding with the exact filename. For example, on a computer running Windows Millennium Edition (Me), the absolute path to the executable for the game of Solitaire, which is typically located in the Windows directory on the C drive, would be the following:

```
C:\Windows\sol.exe
```

If the user opens a command prompt and the current directory is C:\Windows, the user can simply type sol.exe to run the Solitaire program. From any other current directory though, the user must either type the absolute path to execute the program, or specify the relative path from the current directory to the executable file.

On UNIX platforms, path names are specified using forward rather than backward slashes and absolute paths do not start with a drive letter. For example, the absolute path to the file script12, located in the /bin subdirectory of the /usr directory, would be

```
/usr/bin/script12
```

See Also: *relative path, Universal Naming Convention (UNC)*

Abstract Syntax Notation One (ASN.1)

A standard from the International Standards Organization (ISO) that provides a mechanism for encoding human-readable symbols into condensed binary form.

Overview

Abstract Syntax Notation One (ASN.1) is a standard with several real-world uses:

- In X.400, it provides a standard way of formatting and encoding X.400-based e-mail messages for transmission over a network.
- In Simple Network Management Protocol (SNMP), the Management Information Base (MIB) is specified in ASN.1 notation.

More generally, ASN.1 is a method of specifying abstract objects that are intended for any form of serial transmission. ASN.1 is also used for defining objects in MIB files for SNMP.

ASN.1 is similar in syntax to a programming language, and it allows the definition of different data types, data structures, arrays, classes, and other structures similar to those found in the C++ programming language. The presentation layer (Layer 6) of the Open Systems Interconnection (OSI) reference model uses ASN.1 as the standard for specifying the syntax of information exchanged between applications at this layer. ASN.1 data types can be either simple or structured. An example of a definition of a simple data type and its value might be

```
EmployeeAddress ::= ISO646STRING    "99
Microsoft Way"
```

A more complex structured data type might be

```
EmployeeRecord ::= SET
{
 name      [0]ISO646STRING  "Bob Smith"
 title     [1]ISO646STRING  "Support Specialist"
 idNumber  [2]INTEGER       "116427"
    }
```

ASN.1 data structures are encoded as octets in hexadecimal notation. These structures are then transmitted over the network as binary information.

Notes

Microsoft Exchange Server uses ASN.1 for its X.400 Connector to provide standards-based connectivity with foreign X.400 messaging systems.

See Also: *Simple Network Management Protocol (SNMP), X.400*

acceptable use policy

A policy created by management to specify acceptable usage for corporate network services as well as the consequences of violating these standards.

Overview

Acceptable use policies have lately become an important feature of corporate IT (information technology) culture for a number of reasons, but mainly because of the widespread implementation of Internet access for desktop users. Management often becomes concerned about the possibilities of employees surfing the Internet for personal use on company time, using company e-mail to send personal messages, sending spam or mail bombs, and so on. Another concern is management's possible legal liability if employees should access illegal or pornographic material on the Internet using their corporate Internet accounts.

Even if a company does not provide desktop Internet access for its employees, it should still have an acceptable use policy governing access to shared network resources such as file servers and color laser printers. To be effective, an acceptable use policy needs to have the following characteristics:

- Acceptable and unacceptable usage must be simply and clearly explained in the policy.
- A graded series of consequences of unacceptable usage must be clearly stated in the policy.
- The policy itself must be clearly visible in employees' work areas.
- Management should regularly call employees' attention to the policy.

In addition, users should be informed if management is utilizing monitoring practices such as logging all employee Internet access or archiving all employee e-mail. Management should consult its legal department in the drafting of an acceptable use policy, and this policy should be reviewed frequently and kept up-to-date as corporate network access evolves.

See Also: *security*

access

Generally, the process of connecting to and using resources on a network.

Overview

To provide a user with access to network resources, permissions must first be granted to the user. For example, if a user is granted the read permission (and only this permission) for a file on the NTFS file system (NTFS), the user is said to have read-only access to the file. An important part of a network administrator's job is to configure appropriate levels of access control—that is, to manage access to network resources such as shared files, printers, and applications so that

- Users who need access to these resources have the appropriate level of access to them
- Users who do not need access to the resources—as well as distrusted users or hackers—are prevented from accessing them

Examples

In Microsoft Windows 2000, when a user or process attempts to access an object such as a file on an NTFS volume, a component of the Windows 2000 operating system called the Security Reference Monitor compares the access token attached to the process with the access control list (ACL) attached to the object. Through this comparison, the Security Reference Monitor determines whether to grant access to the user or process.

See Also: *access control, access control list (ACL), access list, access token*

access control

Any mechanism that controls who can access securable objects and what actions they can perform on them.

Overview

Securable objects are objects whose access can be controlled by an operating system. For example, in Microsoft Windows 2000, Windows XP, and Windows .NET Server, the following are a few of the types of objects that can be secured:

- File system objects such as files and directories
- Service objects (installed services)
- Printer and print server objects
- Registry keys
- Shared directories
- Directory service objects in Active Directory directory service
- Objects exposed to Windows Management Instrumentation (WMI)
- Security provider objects
- Kernel objects such as processes, threads, jobs, semaphores, events, mutexes, named pipes, access tokens, and such

Access control consists of those mechanisms used to control access to the various types of securable objects listed above. In Windows 2000, Windows XP, and Windows .NET Server, access control is performed mainly through the assignment of permissions and rights.

Permissions are assigned to an object to determine who can access that object and at what level. Permissions can be set by an administrator or by the owner of the object. The kind of permission that can be applied depends on the type of object. Some of the objects to which permissions can be applied include

- NTFS file system (NTFS) objects such as files, folders, and volumes
- Local system objects such as processes and programs
- Local or Active Directory objects such as user, group, and printer objects

The issue of inheritance is related to permissions. When permissions are assigned to a folder on an NTFS volume, they are also inherited by default by all existing child folders and files within the folder, and by any new child folders or files created later. Similarly, when permissions are assigned to a container in Active Directory, they are also inherited by default by all existing child objects within the container and by any new child objects created later.

Rights are assigned to user or group accounts to provide them with authorization to perform a specific system task, such as backing up a volume, shutting down the system, or logging on to the console interactively. Rights are most often assigned to groups rather than individual users to simplify administration. Rights can be specified at either the local or domain level.

Another aspect of access control is the issue of *ownership.* When a user creates an object in Active Directory or a file on an NTFS volume, that user becomes the owner of that object or file. The owner has the right to set and modify the permissions of the object. Every object in Active Directory and every file or folder on an NTFS volume has an owner.

One additional aspect of access control is the issue of *auditing.* Files and folders on an NTFS volume can be audited to keep track of failures or successes in accessing them. This can be important in detecting security breaches in your network.

Notes

When assigning permissions to objects in Active Directory, you can assign them either to the object itself (and therefore to all its attributes) or to specific attributes of

the object. For example, you could allow all users to have read access to the Phone Number attribute of users in Active Directory, while granting the clerical group read/write access to that attribute so that they can modify users' phone numbers if necessary.

See Also: *access control list (ACL), auditing, owner, permissions*

access control entry (ACE)

A single entry in an access control list (ACL).

Overview

An access control entry (ACE) is part of an ACL applied to an object, and it contains information that is used to control that object's access. Both discretionary access control lists (DACLs) and system access control lists (SACLs) consist of sequential lists of ACEs. For example, an ACE could specify the access or auditing permissions to an object in Active Directory directory service or on a volume formatted using the NTFS file system (NTFS) for a particular user or group.

ACE

SID 012345
✓ Read
✗ Write
✓ Execute
.
.
.
✗ No Access

Access control entry (ACE). *A simplified example.*

An ACE generally specifies two kinds of information:

- The security identifier (SID) of the security principal (user, group, or computer) to which the ACE applies
- The level of access to the object permitted for that security principal

An access mask specifying the possible permissions that can be assigned to the object is included with each ACE. An ACE can provide one of the following:

- Discretionary access control for explicitly granting or denying access to a specific user or group (AccessAllowed and AccessDenied entries)
- System security access control for generating security audit logs (SystemAudit entry)

See Also: *access control list (ACL), access mask*

access control list (ACL)

Any mechanism for implementing access control on a file system object, directory object, or other operating system object.

Overview

Access control lists (ACLs) are a feature of most operating systems and provide a flexible and granular method for securing different operating system objects. This article will look at two examples of ACL implementations: Microsoft Windows 2000 and Sun Microsystems' Solaris operating system.

ACLs are incorporated into the basic operating system architecture of Windows 2000 and Windows NT operating system platforms and are used to control access to objects in Active Directory directory service as well as files on NTFS file system (NTFS) volumes. An ACL is basically a list attached to an object specifying which security principals (users, groups, computers, and so on) are allowed to access the object and what level of access they are allowed to have.

In Windows 2000, ACLs are more properly called discretionary access control lists (DACLs) because administrators can configure and manage them at their discretion. There's also another type of ACL in Windows called a system access control list (SACL), which is used to control the generation of audit messages when object auditing has been configured on a file system.

In traditional UNIX environments, access to file system objects is controlled using the Chmod (change mode) command, which allows read, write, and execute permissions to be allowed or denied for three different entities: the user (owner), the other users that belong to the same group as the user (group), and every other user on the system (other). This permission-based access control mechanism is extremely limited, and as a result most UNIX systems implement ACLs as an alternative method for securing files and other operating system objects.

Sun's UNIX-based Solaris operating system first implemented ACLs in version 2.5.1. These ACLs can be used to control access to files on various different file systems, including:

- UNIX File System (UFS)
- Network File System (NFS) version 2 and higher
- Loopback File System (LOFS)
- Cache File System (CacheFS)

In Solaris, ACLs can be applied to files, directories, and symbolic links, and default permissions can be defined for directories to give all newly created files in the directory the same ACLs. To set and display access control lists on Solaris, use the setfacl and getfacl commands.

ACLs are also available as third-party software for other UNIX platforms. Other UNIX packages and add-ons may use different commands such as setacl and getacl.

See Also: *access control entry (ACE), discretionary access control list (DACL), system access control list (SACL)*

Accessibility Options

A utility in Control Panel for most versions of Microsoft Windows that allows you to adjust the behavior of the keyboard, mouse, and display to suit the needs of individuals with impaired eyesight, hearing, or motor skills.

Overview

Accessibility Options are part of Microsoft Corporation's initiative to provide access to computer technology to all individuals, regardless of their physical impairments. Settings for Accessibility Options include the following:

- **StickyKeys:** Makes it possible to use a key combination such as Ctrl+Alt+Delete without pressing more than one key at a time
- **FilterKeys:** Makes it more difficult to bounce keys by telling the system to ignore brief or repeated keystrokes
- **ToggleKeys:** Generates sounds when certain toggle keys, such as Caps Lock, are turned on
- **SoundSentry:** Flashes a specified part of the screen when the system generates sounds
- **ShowSounds:** Displays icons or text captions to accompany the sounds that programs generate
- **HighContrast:** Makes reading text easier
- **MouseKeys:** Controls the pointer using the numeric keypad
- **SerialKey:** Enables the use of alternative input devices connected to the computer's serial port instead of the keyboard and mouse

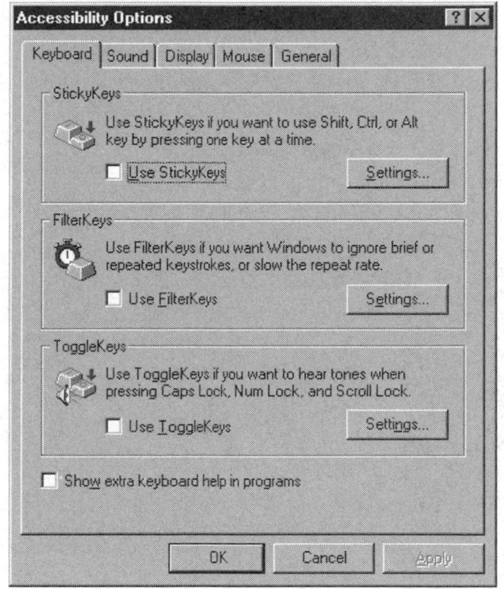

Accessibility Options. *Accessibility Options in Windows 2000.*

Windows includes an additional wizard called the Accessibility Wizard that allows you to configure accessibility options on your computer. Additional accessibility utilities include Magnifier, Narrator, and On-Screen Keyboard.

For More Information

Microsoft product documentation and books from Microsoft Press are available in alternative formats from Recording for the Blind and Dyslexic and the Microsoft Accessibility and Disabilities Group.

You can find out about the Microsoft Accessibility and Disabilities Group at *www.microsoft.com/enable.*

Visit the site of Recording for the Blind and Dyslexic at *www.rfbd.org.*

See Also: *Accessibility Wizard*

Accessibility Wizard

A Microsoft Windows utility for configuring a computer for individuals with impaired visual or motor skills.

Overview

Accessibility Wizard is an alternative to Accessibility Options for configuring computers for individuals with disabilities. To start the Accessibility Wizard, choose Accessories from the Start menu. Then, from the Accessibility program group, choose Accessibility Wizard. Note that in Windows Millennium Edition (Me), you might have to install the Accessibility Tools to gain access to the wizard.

Accessibility Wizard. *The Accessibility Wizard for Windows 98.*

The wizard leads the user through a series of questions concerning his or her disability and configures mouse, keyboard, and display properties to meet that person's particular need. This tool gives administrators the ability to configure workstations for individuals with physical impairments by leading the user through a series of screens that the user can then respond to in real time. Using the Accessibility Wizard is generally more convenient than using the Accessibility Options property sheet to configure accessibility settings. The wizard's final screen lists the accessibility options that have been enabled.

See Also: *Accessibility Options*

access list

A mechanism by which routers can determine which packets should be forwarded and which should be blocked.

Overview

Routers route packets to their destination by examining the destination address of packets received and then determining which port the packet should be forwarded to. However, sometimes packets should not be forwarded to their destinations at all or should be forwarded to different ports using criteria other than a simple destination address. For example, certain incoming packets may constitute a security hazard to the network and should be blocked and dropped. Load balancing may require that packets be distributed across multiple ports in round-robin fashion instead of delivered to a fixed address. And certain types of traffic have high priority and need special handling. Access lists are a mechanism for handling these issues and provide a packet filtering capability that enhances the power and functionality of routers.

An access list is basically an ordered (sequential) series of rules or filters, each of which either permits or denies the flow of packets across an interface depending on the rule's nature and the packet's contents. When a packet arrives at an interface on which an access list has been created and applied, the rules in the list are applied to the packet in order from the top of the list downward. If the packet's contents match the conditions in a rule, that rule is applied and the packet is either forwarded or dropped. If a rule does not apply, the next rule in the list is tried until either a match is found and the packet processed or the end of the list is reached and the packet is finally dropped (in other words, there is an implicit "deny all" at the end of every access list).

You should consider several things when using access lists to filter packets through a router:

- For an access list to function, it must first be created in the router's memory and then explicitly assigned to a router interface.
- When an access list is applied to an interface, the access list's direction must be specified. That is, you must decide whether the access list will be applied to inbound traffic, outbound traffic, or both.
- The order in which the rules are organized within an access list is important. Two access lists with identical rules but in different order can have significantly different effects.
- Each rule either permits a matching packet to be forwarded or denies a packet from being forwarded.
- By default, an access list implicitly denies everything. In other words, when a packet is being processed by an access list, if a match occurs that allows the packet to be forwarded, the packet is allowed to pass across the interface. If no match is found (the contents of the packet do not explicitly match any of the criteria specified in the rules within the access list), the packet is blocked from passing over the interface and is thus dropped by the router.

Examples

The Internetwork Operating System (IOS) by Cisco Systems, the operating system used by all Cisco routers, has commands for creating access lists and applying them to an interface. IOS supports two different types of access lists:

- **Standard:** A standard access list filters packets based only on their source address.
- **Extended:** An extended access list filters packets based both on their source address and on a number of other criteria including destination address, protocol type, traffic priority, and application type.

A simple example of an IOS access list rule that allows traffic from source address 172.16.15.33 to pass across a specified interface would be

```
access-list 1 permit host 172.16.15.33
```

Here the number "1" specifies that this rule is part of the first access list created on the router, and all rules that have this number belong to the same list. Access list numbers identify what kind of access list is used (see the table).

Examples of Different Kinds of IOS Access Lists

Type of Access List	*Range of Access List Numbers*
Standard Internet Protocol (IP)	1–99
Extended IP	100–199
AppleTalk	600–699
Standard Internetwork Packet Exchange (IPX)	800–899
Extended IPX	900-999

To take another example, if your network is class C and has addresses belonging to the 172.16.44.0 network, to allow stations on your network to have unrestricted access to the Internet through your packet-filtering router, you could use the rule

```
access-list 1 permit 172.16.44.0 0.0.0.255
```

Note that 0.0.0.255 is the binary complement of the default subnet mask of your class C network (255.255.255.0).

As a final example, the following access list blocks incoming traffic from the malicious host 133.16.1.11 but allows all other traffic to enter through the router:

```
access-list 1 deny host 133.16.1.11 log
access-list 1 permit any
```

The *log* keyword specifies that all packets dropped from the malicious host will be logged in the router log and can be viewed using the IOS logging console.

IOS access lists can be created using a simple ASCII text editor and transferred to the router using Trivial File Transfer Protocol (TFTP) or some other mechanism. The Interface command is used to apply an access list to an interface once the list has been created, and the Access-group command is used to specify the direction over the interface for which the list applies.

Notes

One limitation of IOS access lists is that if you want to modify a list by removing or changing a statement in the middle of the list, you cannot. Instead you must create a new access list, remove the old one from the interface, and apply the new list to the interface. You can, however, add rules to the bottom of an existing list, if this meets your needs. To get around having to create an access list from scratch when you need to modify a rule, use TFTP to copy the existing router configuration to a text file on a workstation, modify the file, delete the original configuration on the router, and copy the modified configuration onto the router.

IOS version 12 includes a new feature that allows for the creation and application of time-based access lists, which allows different access lists to be applied to routers at different times and days.

Access lists are sometimes called access control lists, but this can be confusing because the term *access control list (ACL)* also refers to a mechanism for securing file system objects and other operating system objects.

The table in this article shows that there can be only 100 possible access lists for each type of access list. In some circumstances (for example, with complex backbone routers) this is not sufficient, and you can use named access lists instead. Named access lists are referenced using an alphanumeric name instead of a number, and you can create as many of them as you need.

Placement is an important issue to consider when applying access lists to ports. Standard access lists should be placed as close as possible to the destination, but enhanced access lists should be placed as close as possible to the source.

See Also: *Internetwork Operating System (IOS), router*

access mask

A double-word value (32-bit entry) contained within each access control entry (ACE) that defines all possible access rights for a particular type of object (file, folder, and so on).

Overview

Microsoft Windows 2000, Windows XP, and Windows .NET Server use access masks that support several types of access rights. Three examples are:

- **Specific access rights:** These access rights include FILE_READ_DATA and FILE_APPEND_DATA, which provide permission to read and write data in a file. Objects can have up to 16 different specific access rights, depending on the object type.
- **Standard access rights:** These apply to all objects and include DELETE, which grants or denies delete access to an object, and WRITE_OWNER, which grants or denies access to the owner security identifier (SID) of an object.
- **Generic access rights:** These map to specific access rights and standard access rights. Each type of securable object maps generic access rights to its own specific and standard access rights. Generic access rights for file objects include FILE_GENERIC_READ, FILE_GENERIC_WRITE, and FILE_GENERIC_EXECUTE. These three types are listed in Windows Explorer in Windows 2000, Windows XP, and Windows .NET Server and in Windows NT Explorer in Windows NT as the special permissions read (R), write (W), and execute (X).

See Also: *access control entry (ACE), access control list (ACL)*

access method

Any method that allows devices to transmit signals over media in a way that ensures that communications can occur between stations.

See: *media access control method*

access mode

A mode of running a console created with the Microsoft Management Console (MMC).

Overview

Different access modes are provided for MMC consoles in order to allow or restrict access to administrative functionality. This enables senior administrators to create custom consoles for junior administrators that have only the functionality needed to perform specified tasks, while preventing them from using functionality that could cause problems if not handled correctly.

Selecting Options from the Console menu configures access modes for MMC consoles. The two modes available for running consoles are

- **Author mode:** This mode grants the user full access to all the functionality of the MMC, including adding snap-ins, removing snap-ins, creating new console windows, and accessing the entire console tree. Only senior administrators should have this access mode.
- **User mode:** This mode does not allow the user to add snap-ins to or remove snap-ins from the console and restricts access to some of the functionality of the MMC, depending on the options selected. For example, by selecting the Limited Access, Single Window option, the MMC displays only a single console window. User mode has three submodes:
  - **Full Access:** This submode allows the user to view the whole console tree but restricts the user from adding new snap-ins or changing the console's properties.
  - **Limited Access, Multiple Window:** This submode allows the user to view portions of the console tree in different windows.
  - **Limited Access, Single Window:** This submode restricts the user to a single console window.

Notes

If an MMC console is set to user mode, you can start it in author mode by running it from the command line with the /a switch. You can also right-click on the console file (*.msc file) in Windows Explorer and use the shortcut menu to start the console in author mode. However, an administrator can also use Group Policy to prevent the user from opening a console in author mode.

See Also: Microsoft Management Console (MMC)

access point (AP)

A device connected to a local area network (LAN) that enables remote wireless stations to communicate with the LAN.

Overview

A wireless networking implementation consists of two parts:

- A wired network such as an Ethernet LAN with an access point attached to it. The access point acts as a bridge between the wired LAN and the remote wireless stations.
- Remote wireless stations with wireless network adapters attached to them.

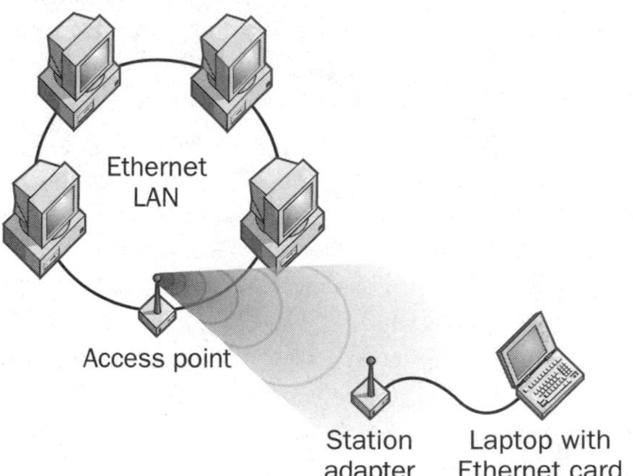

Access point (AP). *How an access point works.*

An access point (AP) is basically a network-capable device containing a transceiver and antenna for transmitting signals to and receiving signals from the remote stations. The access point thus provides a "point of access" to the wired network for the remote stations. The access points allow wireless stations to be quickly and easily connected to a wired LAN.

An example of a remote station might be a laptop computer. The laptop can communicate with the access point using a wireless Personal Computer Memory Card International Association (PCMCIA) card or wireless network interface card (NIC). An alternative is the station adapter, a device that plugs in to the laptop's standard 10BaseT port.

A single AP can generally support 15 to 25 wireless stations while still maintaining optimal data transfer rates. The area covered by a single AP is called a cell. The transceiver within an access point uses spread spectrum transmission, which may be either direct sequencing or frequency hopping. For spread spectrum communication in the 2.4 gigahertz (GHz) frequency band, APs typically support data rates of 1 to 3 megabits per second (Mbps) over distances of up to about 2 miles (3 kilometers).

Marketplace

Most commercial APs consist of a combination of an Ethernet port and a transceiver, which allows the AP to be easily connected into an existing wired LAN for bridging to remote wireless stations. Prices for wireless networking equipment based on the 802.11b standard have fallen dramatically in the last few years. A typical AP can cost as low as $300 or as high as $2,000, while wireless network adapters can be as low as $100 each. Examples of APs for small-office home-office (SOHO) use include the Apple Airport, the D-Link DWL-1000AP, and the Lucent RG-1000, and examples of enterprise-class access points include 3Com's AirConnect Wireless AP, the Cisco AIR-AP341 series, Enterasys's RoamAbout AP 2000, and the Intel PRO/Wireless LAN AP.

The higher-priced APs provide faster speeds, support more users, and include better management features. For coverage of large areas, several APs may be required to create a pattern of overlapping cells—in this case it is best to purchase the more expensive ones because these include features to support remote stations that roam between cells covered by different APs. The more expensive APs also support connection to external antennas for better transmission coverage.

Many APs include other advanced features including Dynamic Host Configuration Protocol (DHCP), network address translation (NAT), and routing functions. These APs fall under the general category of network appliance because of their simplicity and ease of use.

Notes

When purchasing an 802.11b AP, you may want to consider if it can be easily upgraded to the newer 802.11a standard, which uses 5 GHz transmission.

For best coverage within an office environment, mount APs on ceilings. If this is difficult because of lack of electrical outlets, look for APs that can be powered over Category 5 (Cat5) cable.

If multiple APs are used to provide redundant coverage for an area, then they should be connected using a wired LAN. This will provide better performance for stations within the coverage area than having the APs connected as wireless repeaters.

See Also: *802.11b, wireless networking*

access provider

Also known as Internet service provider (ISP), a company that provides individual users and businesses with connectivity to the Internet.

See: *Internet service provider (ISP), xSP*

access token

An object assigned to a user that successfully logs on to a network and that identifies the level of security privileges assigned to that user.

Overview

An access token is like a card key. Your card key will provide you with access to doors that have been configured to grant you permission to open them. The list of card keys that a door will accept is analogous to an access control list (ACL).

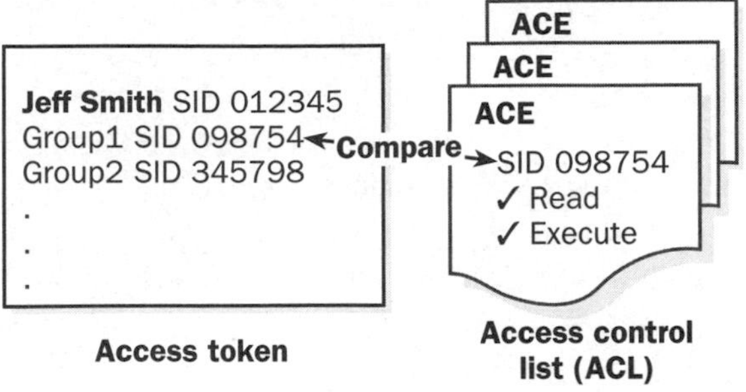

Access token. *A simplified example of an access token at work.*

When you log on to Microsoft Windows NT, Windows XP, Windows 2000, or Windows .NET Server, you are granted an access token that is attached to all your user processes. Your access token contains the security identifier (SID) of your user account and every group to which you belong. When your application tries to access an object such as a file on a volume formatted with the NTFS file system (NTFS), Windows NT, Windows 2000, Windows XP, or Windows .NET Server compares the SIDs in your application's access token to those in the access control entries (ACEs) in the object's ACL. If it finds a match, the system grants access to that object.

See Also: *access control list (ACL)*

account

A set of credentials for gaining access to resources in a network or logging on to a system.

Overview

In a typical network, each user needs an account to access resources on the network, such as shared folders, printers, or applications. Accounts provide a way of identifying users on a network and are the foundation of network security. An administrator or another user with high security privileges typically creates accounts.

Accounts are generally used in server-based networks where a central computer such as a Microsoft Windows 2000 or Windows .NET Server domain controller keeps track of each user's account and grants or denies access to the network based on the credentials entered by the user during the logon process. Accounts are used less frequently in peer-to-peer networks or workgroups because the security requirements are usually much less stringent.

A Windows 2000 or Windows .NET Server network contains various kinds of accounts, including

- **User account:** Identifies users who belong to the domain by storing their names, passwords, the groups they belong to, the permissions they have for accessing system resources, and other personal information
- **Group account:** Identifies a specific group of users and is used to assign them permissions to objects and resources
- **Computer account:** Identifies machines that belong to the domain

See Also: *logon, network security*

account domain

A type of Microsoft Windows NT domain containing accounts for global users and groups.

Overview

Account domains are usually master domains and are typically used in a single or multiple master domain model implementation of Windows NT. The account domain contains user accounts for every user in the enterprise and is usually located at corporate headquarters. Servers and workstations at company branch offices belong to other domains called resource domains. Users at branch offices who want to log on to the network must log on to the account domain, even though their workstations are located within a resource domain.

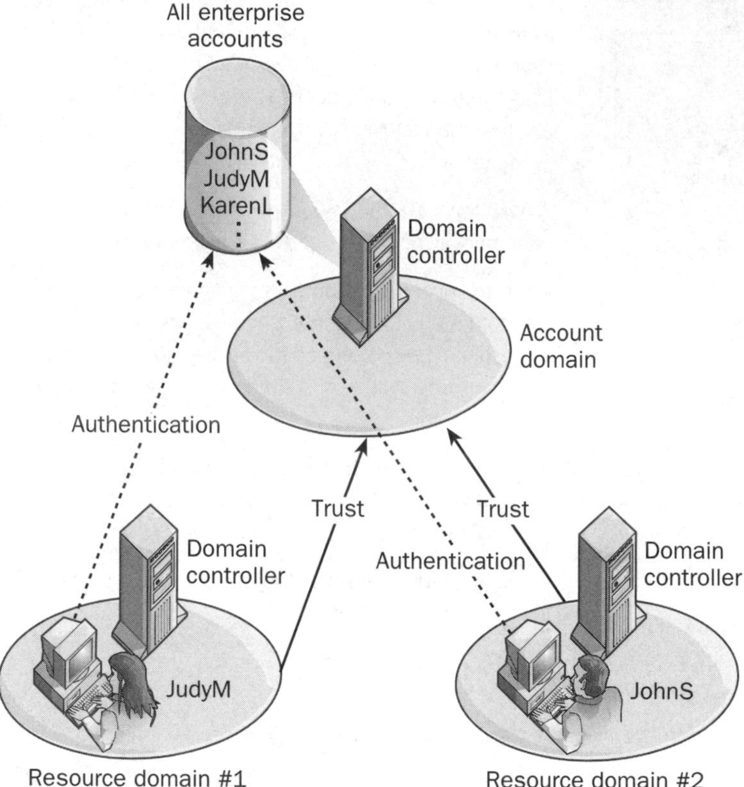

G0AXX06 (was G0Aui06.bmp in 1E)

Account domain. *Account domains in Windows NT.*

For this scenario to work, a trust relationship must be established so that each resource domain trusts the account domain. In this way all user accounts can be centralized in the account domain, which eases account management for administrators located at headquarters.

Account domains simplify account administration by centralizing administration to a single domain.

See Also: *resource domain, trust*

account lockout

A condition in which a user is prevented from logging on to the network.

Overview

If account lockout restrictions are set on a network, a user who fails successively to log on will be locked out of the network after a predetermined number of attempts. For example, if a user forgets the password and repeatedly attempts to log on, the authentication provider (a domain controller on a Microsoft Windows 2000 network) assumes that unauthorized access is being attempted and shuts out the user by locking out the account. The account can either remain locked until an administrator unlocks it or it can be configured to unlock after a specified period of time.

Account lockout restrictions are typically part of the account policy that can be set for domains. Account lockout is used to prevent unauthorized access to the network by preventing distrusted users from attempting to guess a trusted user's password. If you set up account lockout on your network, you will probably also want to configure auditing to record failed logon attempts.

Use account lockout only for high-security networks. In a low-security environment, users can become frustrated if they lock themselves out by mistyping their passwords, and administrators must cope with the additional overhead and bother of unlocking these accounts.

See Also: auditing

account operator

A user who is assigned the responsibility of administering user and group accounts for a network.

Overview

In Microsoft Windows 2000, Windows XP, or Windows .NET Server, if you want to make an individual an account operator, simply make that person a member of the Account Operators group. Account operators can administer accounts only on a domain controller, not on a member server or workstation.

Account operators have the preassigned rights to log on locally to a domain controller and to shut down the system. In addition, account operators have the built-in capacity to create and manage user accounts, global group accounts, and local group accounts, as well as to keep local profiles.

Account operators should be assigned in enterprise-level networking environments only. In small to medium-sized networking environments, creating and configuring user accounts is usually the administrator's responsibility.

See Also: user account

Account Operators group

A built-in security group in Microsoft Windows 2000, Windows XP, and Windows .NET Server where users are account operators.

Overview

Members of the Account Operators group can create, delete, and modify the properties of users, global groups, and local groups. The Account Operators group exists only on domain controllers and has an empty initial membership. The Account Operators group has the following preassigned rights:

- Log on locally
- Shut down the system

Additionally, members of the Account Operators group have the ability to create, delete, and modify user and group accounts using the Active Directory Users and Computers console.

Members of the Account Operators group cannot modify the membership or rights of the following built-in groups:

- Administrators
- Account Operators
- Server Operators
- Print Operators
- Backup Operators

See Also: built-in group

ACE

Stands for access control entry, a single entry in an access control list (ACL).

See: access control entry (ACE)

ACK

Stands for acknowledgment, a transmission from a receiving station to a transmitting station telling it that the transmitted data has been received without errors.

Overview

ACKs play an important role in most network protocols. For example, Transmission Control Protocol (TCP) is a connection-oriented protocol that relies on acknowledgments for successful transmission of data. When a stream of TCP packets is being sent over the network, each packet contains an acknowledgment number indicating the sequence number of the next packet that the receiving station should expect to receive. TCP can use an ACK to acknowledge a series of TCP packets (instead of just a single packet) that have been received. A TCP packet sent as an acknowledgment has its ACK flag set to 1 to indicate that the acknowledgment numbers of the packets received are valid.

During a transmission, if the receiving station determines that the data transmission is late or has not arrived, a negative acknowledgment (NAK) is generated to indicate to the transmitting station that the data should be sent again.

See Also: *Transmission Control Protocol (TCP)*

ACL

Stands for access control list, any mechanism for implementing access control on a file system object, directory object, or other operating system object.

See: *access control list (ACL)*

ACM

Stands for the Association for Computing Machinery, the oldest and largest educational and scientific computing society in the world.

See: *Association for Computing Machinery (ACM)*

ACPI

Stands for Advanced Configuration and Power Interface, a specification for power management of computer hardware.

See: *Advanced Configuration and Power Interface (ACPI)*

ACR

Stands for attenuation to crosstalk ratio, the ratio of the received strength of a signal on a pair of wires (attenuation) to the amount of crosstalk between the wires.

See: *attenuation to crosstalk ratio (ACR)*

Active Desktop

A feature of Microsoft Windows that enables active content from Web sites or channels to be displayed directly on the desktop.

Overview

Active Desktop was first introduced with Microsoft Internet Explorer version 4, and made possible the dynamic downloading and display of content such as graphics, Hypertext Markup Language (HTML) pages, Microsoft ActiveX controls, Java applets, and channels. For example, you could have a stock ticker applet placed directly on your desktop that updates its information continually using a live Internet connection.

Active Desktop integrates the Web and your desktop, allowing you to launch programs, switch between files, and customize your desktop using active Web content. Active Desktop makes your desktop and its folders look and work like the Web, allowing you to browse resources on your computer or local network the same way you browse for content on the World Wide Web. Information about volumes, folders, and files can be displayed as Web pages within folders, and you can move up and down the folder hierarchy using a single click instead of a double click.

Active Desktop is included with Windows 98, Windows Millennium Edition (Me), Windows 2000, Windows XP, and Windows .NET Server and is available for Windows 95 and Windows NT 4 as an option by installing Internet Explorer 4 and the Windows Desktop Update.

The Active Desktop is implemented as an application programming interface (API) called the IActiveDesktop interface, which is part of the Windows Shell API. This interface is designed to allow client programs to manage desktop items and wallpapers on local computers. It also provides methods for adding desktop items (with or without a user interface, allowing the user to decide whether to accept the addition), adding desktop items associated with a Uniform Resource Locator (URL), applying changes by writing settings to the registry, and so on.

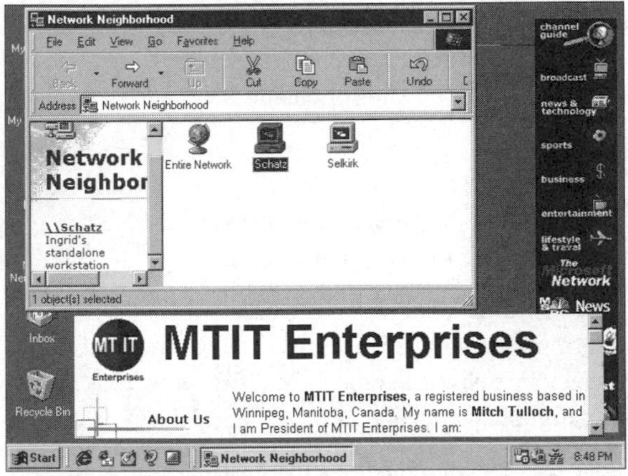

Active Desktop. *Web elements on Active Desktop.*

The Active Desktop consists of two layers:

- **HTML layer:** This is the background layer that hosts active Web content items. The Hypertext Markup Language (HTML) layer has three components: a file named desktop.htm that contains HTML tags for each active Web component on the desktop, an ActiveX control that lets you move or resize components on your desktop, and any other static HTML element you want to display in the background.
- **Icon layer:** This transparent foreground layer integrates a Web-type environment with familiar Windows 95 shell features such as double-clicking, drag-and-drop, file associates, and so on.

Users can add new items to the Active Desktop on their machines by using the display utility in Control Panel (or by right-clicking a blank area of the desktop and choosing Properties from the context menu). Either specify the URL of the object you want to add to your Active Desktop or browse to locate it on your network or on the Internet (if you are connected). Programmers can use the ActiveDesktop interface to write routines that add, remove, or modify items on the Active Desktop. You can also add items to the Active Desktop using a Channel Definition Format (CDF) file.

See Also: *Active Platform*

Active Digital Profile (ADPr)

An Extensible Markup Language (XML) specification for automating the provisioning of IT (information technology) resources.

Overview

XML is becoming the de facto standard for exchange of electronic information, superseding previous standards such as Electronic Data Interchange (EDI). To standardize exchange in different business areas, XML schema are used. Active Digital Profile (ADPr) is a proposed XML schema that allows for the electronic allocation and deployment of IT (information technology) resources such as hardware and software. As an XML schema, ADPr provides a vendor-neutral and platform-independent model for these business processes to take place at a high level.

ADPr is based on software created by Business Layers in conjunction with Novell, CheckPoint Software, and other companies. ADPr has been submitted to the Organization for the Advancement of Structured Information Standards (OASIS) as a proposed XML standard.

See Also: *Organization for the Advancement of Structured Information Systems (OASIS), XML*

Active Directory

The directory service for the Microsoft Windows 2000 and Windows .NET Server network operating systems.

Overview

Active Directory directory service consists of both a database and a service. Active Directory is a database of information about resources on the network, such as computers, users, shared folders, and printers. It is also a service that makes this information available to users and applications.

Active Directory provides the basic features needed for an enterprise-level directory service, including an extensible information source, naming conventions for directory objects, a common set of policies, and tools for administering the service from a single point of access. Administrators can configure Active Directory to control access to network resources by users and applications. Active Directory provides network administrators with centralized administration of all information about resources on the network, and it provides both users and administrators with advanced search capabilities for locating resources on the network.

Information in Active Directory is maintained for each domain on the network. Active Directory database information is stored and maintained on machines called domain controllers. This information is replicated automatically between domain controllers to ensure that every portion of the distributed directory is up to date. By default, the replication of updates to Active Directory occurs automatically every five minutes. Automatic replication of Active Directory information occurs only within the security boundary of a specific domain. Domain controllers in one domain do not automatically replicate with those in another domain.

Architecture

Active Directory's basic element is the object. An object can represent a user, computer, printer, application, file, or another resource on the network. Active Directory objects possess attributes, which are their properties. For example, some user attributes might include first name, last name, e-mail address, and phone number. Some attributes must have mandatory values, and others can be left undefined. A printer's attributes might include its location, its asset number for accounting purposes, its type, and so on. Active Directory also has a set of rules governing which objects can be stored in the directory and which attributes these objects can possess. This set of rules is known as the schema.

A special type of Active Directory object is the organizational unit (OU). An OU is a type of object that can contain other objects. An OU can either contain a specific object, such as a user or an application, or it can contain another OU. Using OUs, you can organize Active Directory into a hierarchical directory of network information based on the X.500 directory recommendations of the International Telecommunication Union (ITU). You can assign users permissions on subtrees of OUs for management and resource access purposes.

Organizational units are contained within domains, which are Active Directory's basic security and organizational structure. Every object in Active Directory must belong to a domain. Domains usually mirror the organizational structure of your enterprise and act as a security boundary in it. For example, privileges granted in one domain are not automatically carried over to another domain. Domains can be joined into larger structures called trees using two-way transitive trusts, and these tree structures can be grouped into forests. Typically one forest is created per enterprise when Active Directory is deployed.

The collection of objects, OUs, domains, trees, and forests represent Active Directory's logical structure. Active Directory's physical structure consists of various layers of programming elements on servers called domain controllers. These programming elements include

- **Directory System Agent (DSA):** The process that provides access to the Active Directory store where directory information is stored on the domain controller's hard drive.
- **Database Layer:** This layer provides a uniform interface for the DSA for accessing the store.
- **Extensible Storage Engine (ESE):** This is a version of the database engine on Microsoft Exchange Server 5.5 and is used to provide access to the Active Directory store, which is capable of storing information about many millions of directory objects.

Above these layers are various interfaces and protocols by which various clients can access Active Directory. These include

- **Lightweight Directory Access Protocol (LDAP):** Supports LDAP clients such as Microsoft Outlook and Active Directory Services Interface (ADSI).
- **Replication transports (REPL):** Supports replication transports such as remote procedure call (RPC) and Simple Mail Transfer Protocol/Internet Protocol (SMTP IP) for Active Directory replication.
- **Security Accounts Manager (SAM):** Supports Windows NT 4 networking application programming interfaces (APIs) and replication with Windows NT backup domain controllers (BDCs).
- **Messaging Application Programming Interface (MAPI):** Supports Outlook and other MAPI-compliant clients.

Other protocols whose implementation is of crucial importance for Active Directory include Domain Name System (DNS) and Transmission Control Protocol/ Internet Protocol (TCP/IP).

Implementation

Before implementing Active Directory in your enterprise, you will need to gather information about your organization's structure because Active Directory usually mirrors this structure in some fashion. A good way to proceed is to use a centralized planning approach with a team consisting of both technical and management representatives. You must develop a naming strategy, plan your domain structure, and consider how you will delegate administrative duties concerning Active Directory. When you delegate administrative control to Active Directory, do so at the OU level instead of at the individual object level. This makes it easier to control portions of the OU hierarchy within Active Directory. In particular, you probably want to delegate control to individuals responsible for creating users, groups, computers, and similar objects.

Consider the speed of the various links between your different geographical locations and how any systems that are not interoperable with Active Directory will be integrated into your new system. You should also profile your user community to determine what sort of domain hierarchy you will be implementing. Also consider integrating your DNS zone information into Active Directory because this will store your DNS zone information in the distributed Active Directory. Plus, it will facilitate and simplify updates of zone information through replication of domain controllers.

An important planning issue is determining where to locate domain controllers and global catalog servers for your enterprise because after Active Directory is installed and configured, the majority of Active Directory traffic is related to Active Directory clients querying Active Directory for information. Directory replication traffic is usually a less important consideration, unless the organization is in a constant state of flux. Placing a domain controller at each site will optimize queries but can increase replication traffic. Nevertheless, placing a domain controller at a site that has users in that domain is usually the best solution. If the domain tree is large, you should not place a global catalog server at each site because this can create a lot of replication traffic. Place global catalog servers only at large regional sites. Remember that replication of modifications made to your Active Directory might take some time to propagate throughout your enterprise. For example, if you create a new user account object, it might be a few minutes before the user can actually log on to the network using the account.

Notes

The default naming convention for objects stored in Active Directory is an Active Directory canonical name of the object. This defines the object's position in a domain tree from left to right, starting with the object's name and delimited by slashes. For example, the User Account JSmith in the Marketing OU of the northwind.microsoft.com domain would have the Active Directory canonical name

```
Jsmith/users/marketing/northwind.microsoft.com
```

Active Directory supports non-DNS naming conventions for interoperability with non-DNS environments. An example is the LDAP naming convention. An LDAP Uniform Resource Locator (URL) is composed of the name of the server with the distinguished name of the object appended to it. Other naming conventions include the following:

- **User principal name:** This convention consists of the user's SAM account name with an object's user principal name suffix appended to it. The user principal name suffix is the name of the domain tree or the name of the domain above the object in the domain tree.
- **Request for Comments (RFC) number 822 name:** This naming convention is essentially the user's e-mail address.
- **Universal Naming Convention (UNC):** This convention can be used for shared resources.

Discretionary access control lists (DACLs) and system access control lists (SACLs) protect Active Directory objects. DACLs and SACLs specify which user or application has permission to access attributes of directory objects and work in a similar fashion to access control lists (ACLs) that are implemented in the version of NTFS file system (NTFS) used in Windows NT 4. DACLs and SACLs can be used to propagate their permissions to connected directory objects. They also provide a simple way for administrators to grant access and usage rights for Active Directory to users and groups.

See Also: *domain (DNS), forest, organizational unit (OU), tree, trust, Windows 2000*

Active Directory Client

Client software running on a machine and enabling it to access information published in Active Directory directory service.

Overview

Microsoft Windows 2000, Windows XP, and Windows .NET Server come with a built-in Active Directory client so that they can participate immediately in an Active Directory–based network. Some other versions of Windows may require an Active Directory client to be installed prior to participating in such a network.

A version of Active Directory Client called the Directory Services client is available for computers running Windows 95 and Windows 98. This client allows them to log on to a Windows 2000 or Windows .NET Server domain and access information published in Active Directory. The Directory Services client can be found in the \clients folder on the Windows 2000 Server compact disc. Microsoft Internet Explorer version 5.0 or later must be installed on the machine running Windows 95 or Windows 98 prior to installing the Directory Services client. A similar client is also available for Windows NT version 4 machines.

See Also: *Active Directory*

Active Directory Domains and Trusts

A management console in Microsoft Windows 2000 and Windows .NET Server that can be used for administering domains and trust relationships.

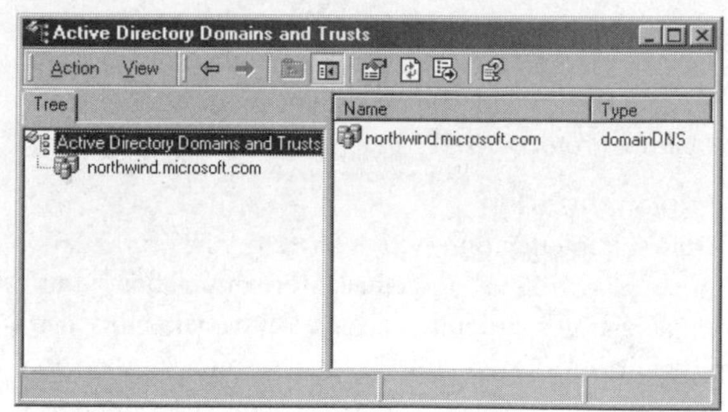

Active Directory Domains and Trusts. *The Active Directory Domains and Trusts console.*

Overview

Active Directory Domains and Trusts provide administrators with a graphical representation of all the domain trees in a domain forest. Using the Active Directory Domains and Trusts, you can perform common administrative tasks such as

- Creating an explicit domain trust and managing existing trust relationships between domains
- Changing the domain mode from mixed mode to native mode
- Adding user principal name suffixes for a forest

Notes

You can also use the Active Directory Domains and Trusts to open Active Directory Users and Computers by right-clicking on a domain and then selecting Manage from the shortcut menu.

See Also: *administrative tools (Windows 2000, Windows XP, and Windows .NET Server)*

Active Directory Installation Wizard

A wizard in Microsoft Windows 2000 Server and Windows .NET Server that installs the Active Directory directory service on a machine.

Overview

Active Directory Installation Wizard promotes member servers or stand-alone servers into domain controllers. You can use Active Directory Installation Wizard to

Active Directory Installation Wizard. *Using the Active Directory Installation Wizard to install Active Directory.*

- Create a new domain controller with a new domain tree
- Create a new domain controller with a new child domain that islocated under a parent domain in an existing domain tree
- Create a replica domain controller for an existing domain

You must be an administrator to run Active Directory Installation Wizard. Start the wizard by running the Dcpromo utility from the command prompt or choose the Run command from the Start menu, enter *dcpromo* in the Run dialog box, and then click OK. This opens the wizard's welcome screen, where you are required to make a number of decisions concerning the following:

- Whether to create a new domain or add a replica domain controller to an existing domain
- If you choose to create a new domain, whether to create a new domain tree or add a child domain to an existing tree
- If you choose to create a new domain tree, whether to create a new domain forest or add the new tree to an existing forest

Names you specify for new or existing domains, domain trees, or domain forests are based on the Domain Name System (DNS) naming system. Other steps in the wizard allow you to specify the path to the Active Directory database, the location of the System Volume (SYSVOL) share, and so on.

Running Active Directory Installation Wizard has the following results:

- The machine on which the wizard is run becomes a domain controller. If it is the first domain controller in your domain, the wizard also creates a new site for that controller. If it is the first domain in your enterprise, it is also the root domain for any domain tree that will be created. You can use the wizard to create the first domain forest in your enterprise, too.
- The first domain controller is also your global catalog server.
- Active Directory files are located in %SystemRoot%\Ntds with the associated log files.
- The shared system volume SYSVOL, which stores scripts used for implementing group policies for your domain, is located in %SystemRoot%\Sysvol.
- A number of default organizational units (OUs) are created, namely the Users, Builtin, Computers, and Domain Controllers.

Notes

You must make sure that DNS is already installed and configured prior to running Active Directory Installation Wizard in order to create the first domain controller for your network. A DNS name will be needed for your new domain controller, and a DNS server must be available on the network during the installation process.

Active Directory files also require an NTFS file system (NTFS) volume, which must be configured as a basic volume. Dynamic volumes cannot be used for Active Directory files. Running the wizard creates a log file in the %SystemRoot%\Debug folder that shows the results of the installation procedure.

If you are creating a new child domain, an available domain controller must be in the existing parent domain. If you are creating a replica domain controller, an available domain controller must be in the target domain.

See Also: *Active Directory, domain controller*

Active Directory schema

The formal term for all object classes that can be stored in Active Directory directory service and all attributes that make up these object classes.

Overview

The schema defines which kinds of objects are permitted to be published in Active Directory and states their possible attributes. The schema consists of two types of objects:

- **Classes:** These objects are predefined collections of attributes. For example, every user account on a network is represented in Active Directory by a User class object.
- **Attributes:** This is the actual information stored in an object. For example, a User class object is composed of attributes such as Name, PhoneNumber, and so on.

Attributes are defined separately from classes. This allows each attribute to be defined only once and then used in many different classes. Class definitions (such as the User class) and attribute definitions (such as the Name attribute) are themselves objects within Active Directory. This means you can manage class and attribute definitions in Active Directory with the same tools you use to manage other objects (user and group accounts, computers, and so on).

The Windows 2000 and Windows .NET Server Active Directory includes a default schema that defines commonly used object classes such as users, groups, computers, domains, organizational units (OUs), and security policies. Active Directory is extensible and can be modified using Active Directory Schema. Specifically, you can modify the schema by

- Defining new object types and their attributes
- Defining new attributes for existing object classes
- Removing attributes from existing object classes
- Removing existing object classes

Some applications such as Microsoft Exchange Server 2000 are also designed to extend the Active Directory schema for application-specific purposes.

Notes

Members of the Schema Admins group, of which the default Administrator account is automatically a member, are the only users who can make changes to the schema. A typical reason for modifying the Active Directory schema might be adding new attributes to an existing User object—for example, a SeniorityLevel attribute.

Before you can use this tool to modify the schema, you must add a registry setting to your machine and specify the one domain controller that can be used to modify the schema for your enterprise. This prevents unauthorized access to the schema and inconsistencies that can occur when the schema is simultaneously modified in more than one place.

Another way of modifying Active Directory schema is to write a script that uses Active Directory Service Interfaces (ADSI) to make calls that modify the schema. This is the best solution if you want to modify the schema for an entire enterprise or if you want to automate modifications to the schema.

Existing object classes and their attributes cannot actually be deleted; they are simply marked "defunct" in Active Directory and can no longer be used.

The schema is located under the rootDSE object, which contains information about the directory and is located at the top of the Lightweight Directory Access Protocol (LDAP) directory naming structure.You can access this object using the LDAP Uniform Resource Locator (URL):

```
LDAP://rootDSE
```

See Also: *Active Directory*

Active Directory Service Interfaces (ADSI)

A set of object-oriented programming interfaces for providing programmatic access to Active Directory objects.

Overview

Active Directory Service Interfaces (ADSI) consist of a set of general interfaces built on the Component Object Model (COM) that lets applications work with various types of directories using a single access method. ADSI works by abstracting the capabilities of directory services

from different network providers to present a single set of interfaces for managing network resources in a distributed computing network. ADSI provides a simple, open, functionally rich, and scriptable method for interfacing with any directory service, independent of the vendor.

Programmers and administrators can use ADSI to create directory-enabled applications using tools such as Microsoft Visual Basic or Microsoft Visual C++. ADSI can be used to create new users and groups, locate and manage printers, and perform other administrative functions on a Windows 2000 or Windows .NET Server network.

ADSI is only a part of a more general Microsoft family of APIs called the Windows Open Directory Services Interfaces (ODSI). Other OSDI interfaces include the Network Provider Interface, Windows Sockets Registration and Resolution (RnR), and RPC OLE DB.

Architecture

ADSI consists of two types of COM objects (directory service leaf objects and directory service container objects) that clients can manipulate with interfaces. ADSI providers are used to implement these objects and their interfaces. Each object in a given namespace is identified using a unique name. For example, file system objects can be specified using their absolute path, and directory objects are usually specified using their X.500 address. However, ADSI is flexible enough to handle any naming system used by third-party vendors' directory service implementations.

Advantages and Disadvantages

Using ADSI for directory access has the following benefits:

- **Open:** ADSI is an open platform for which any directory vendor can develop an ADSI provider.
- **Simple:** ADSI consists of a small collection of easy-to-learn programming interfaces.
- **Extensible:** Independent software vendors (ISVs) and directory service (DS) vendors can enhance ADSI by developing their own objects and functions.
- **Language independence:** ADSI is based on COM and can be used by any programming language that supports COM.
- **DS independence:** ADSI is independent of the DS being used, so developers using ADSI do not have to learn the underlying machinery of the directory they are using ADSI to access.
- **Scriptable:** Automation-compatible languages such as VBScript and Perl can be used to automate directory tasks using ADSI.
- **OLE DB aware:** ADSI can be used to access data sources through OLE DB.

Notes

Windows 2000, Windows XP, and Windows .NET Server contain ADSI providers for accessing the following types of directories:

- Active Directory directory service
- Lightweight Directory Access Protocol (LDAP)
- Novell Directory Services (NDS)
- Windows NT directory services

ADSI supports the LDAP C API defined in Request for Comments (RFC) number 1823, which specifies a low-level interface for C language programming and provides support for the Messaging Application Programming Interface (MAPI) so that legacy MAPI applications will work with Active Directory.

ADSI was formerly known as OLE DS.

See Also: Active Directory, directory

Active Directory Sites and Services

A management console in Microsoft Windows 2000 and Windows .NET Server that can be used for administering sites, domain trees, domain controllers, subnets, and intersite links.

Overview

Using Active Directory Sites and Services, you can perform common administrative tasks such as

- Creating a new site and configuring replication within the site
- Configuring directory service (DS) objects and licensing site settings

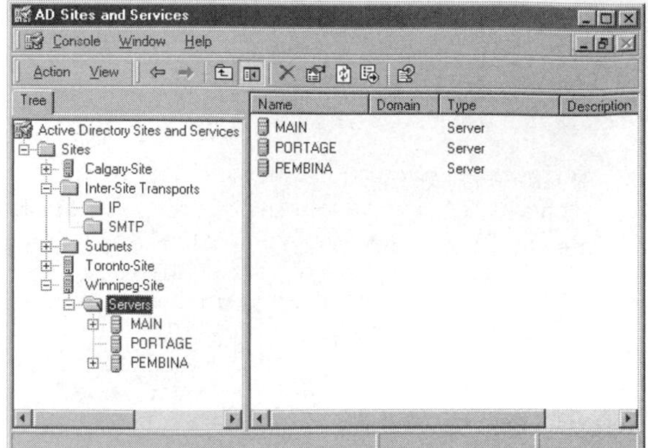

Active Directory Sites and Services. *The Active Directory Sites and Services console.*

- Adding servers, domain controllers, intersite links, and subnets to a site
- Moving and repairing domain controllers
- Delegating control of a site

See Also: *administrative tools (Windows 2000, Windows XP, and Windows .NET Server)*

Active Directory Users and Computers

A management console in Microsoft Windows 2000 and Windows .NET Server that can be used for administering Active Directory objects and information published in the directory.

Overview

Using Active Directory Users and Computers, you can perform common administrative tasks such as

- Creating a new user, group, shared folder, computer, printer, or other resource
- Creating new organizational units (OUs) for organizing directory objects
- Moving directory objects to different OUs
- Deleting objects from the directory
- Displaying and editing the properties of directory objects
- Managing group policies and changing domain controllers

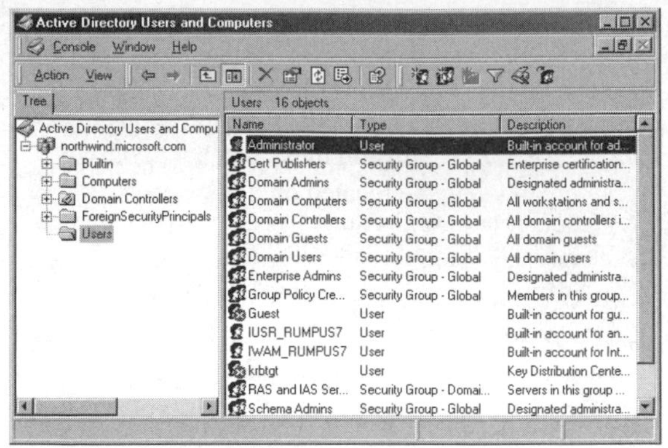

Active Directory Users and Computers. *The Active Directory Users and Computers console.*

- Finding objects within the Active Directory database

Notes

If you want to quickly assign permissions to network resources such as file shares, printers, users, and groups in your enterprise, simply move their associated directory objects to different servers that require the same permissions to the same OU. Objects inherit permissions from their new OU and lose permissions from their old OU. However, permissions assigned directly to an object are moved together with the object.

See Also: *administrative tools (Windows 2000, Windows XP, and Windows .NET Server)*

active hub

A hub that has electronic circuitry to regenerate weak signals.

Overview

Active hubs function as multiport repeaters, allowing computers to be networked together in a star topology. Virtually all hubs sold today are active hubs, so one generally refers to them nowadays simply as hubs.

See Also: *hub, passive hub*

active partition

The partition that contains the boot files for an operating system.

Overview
The active partition is the one from which the operating system boots. On a machine running Microsoft Windows 2000, Windows XP, or Windows .NET Server, the active partition must also be a primary partition and must be located on a basic disk.

Depending on the Microsoft operating system used, you can use any of the following tools to make a partition active:

- The Fdisk utility from the command prompt for MS-DOS and all Microsoft Windows platforms
- The Disk Administrator administrative tool in Windows NT
- The Computer Management administrative console in Windows 2000

Notes
Alpha-based computers running Windows NT have no active partitions. Instead, the boot volume is configured by a manufacturer-supplied configuration program.

See Also: *partition (Active Directory), system partition*

Active Platform
A set of Microsoft technologies for developing applications for the Internet.

Overview
Active Platform is actually an umbrella term for three key Microsoft technologies:

- **Active Desktop:** Integrates the Microsoft Windows desktop with the Internet, providing a seamless connection between local and remote applications and resources. Active Desktop is a core technology of Internet Explorer.
- **Active Server:** The Active Platform component of Microsoft Internet Information Services (IIS) version 5 or later. Using Active Server technologies, core Windows NT services can be extended to the Internet using applications developed with Microsoft Active Server Pages (ASP) technologies.
- **Microsoft ActiveX:** A component software technology based on the Component Object Model (COM). ActiveX allows distributed Web-based applications to be developed in any programming language and then run from within an ActiveX-enabled browser such as Internet Explorer.

Applications developed using Active Platform technologies can be accessed and run from any client platform independent of the operating system, as long as a standard Web browser such as Microsoft Internet Explorer is installed on the client.

See Also: *Active Desktop, Active Server Pages (ASP), ActiveX*

active scripting
Using a scripting language to drive Component Object Model (COM) components.

Overview
Host applications such as Microsoft Internet Information Services (IIS) with Microsoft Active Server Pages (ASP) and Microsoft Internet Explorer have scripting engines for running scripts written in VBScript or JScript. Active scripting engines can be developed for other interpretive scripting languages, such as Perl, to build upon a developer's existing knowledge of these programming platforms. Scripting engines for client software, such as Internet Explorer, are specially designed to eliminate the authoring components that are not needed in a nonauthoring host environment. This makes the client-side scripting engine lightweight, which yields better performance.

In a typical scenario, the host application loads the script document and calls an application programming interface (API) to create a new instance of a scripting engine. The host application feeds the script to the engine and executes the script.

See Also: *Active Server Pages (ASP)*

Active Server Pages (ASP)
An open, compile-free application environment for developing Web applications using Microsoft Internet Information Server (IIS) version 3 and later, including Internet Information Services (IIS) in Windows 2000, Windows XP, and Windows .NET Server.

Overview

Active Server Pages (ASP) can be used to build powerful, distributed Web-based applications that combine Hypertext Markup Language (HTML), script, and Microsoft ActiveX technologies to provide dynamic Web sites. ASP combines the ease of HTML with familiar programming tools such as Microsoft Visual Basic Scripting Edition (VBScript) and Microsoft JScript, along with reusable Component Object Model (COM) components. These components can be used to build powerful, dynamic Web sites. ASP executes on the Web server, and the output returned to the Web browser is a plain HTML file.

Architecture

ASP is implemented in IIS as an Internet Server Application Programming Interface (ISAPI) filter called Asp.dll, which resides in the same memory space as IIS. User requests for ASP pages, which have the suffix .asp appended to them, are processed by the filter which loads the necessary language dynamic-link libraries (DLLs) for interpreting script on the page, executes server-side script on the server, and returns the remaining HTML and client-side script to the browser requesting the page.

ASP pages have the file extension .asp and typically contains a mixture of HTML, scripts, and other components written in any programming language. The scripts can reference components running on either the local server or any other accessible server and can perform actions such as accessing a database, sending e-mail, or processing information in another fashion. The result is then returned by the server to the client as a standard HTML file and displayed in the usual way.

The Asp.dll also includes an object model that encapsulates properties and methods for seven built-in objects: Application, ASPError, ObjectContext, Request, Response, Server, and Session. These objects are available for any .asp page requested. For example, the Response object can be used to control how data is sent to the requesting client.

ASP organizes collections of ASP pages into applications, which are typically groups of files within a given virtual directory and its subdirectories. ASP applications (also known as Web applications) can have global variables and can save state information so that a session can exist across several requested pages in succession. Session-level data is initiated by reference to a file called Global.asa, which is checked whenever a new client makes a request to pages in an ASP application.

Examples

For example, when requested, the following ASP file will return the current time and browser type to the requesting client:

```
<HTML>
<HEAD><TITLE>Sample Web Page</TITLE></HEAD>
<BODY>
The time right now is <% = now %>
Your browser type is <%
=Request.ServerVariables("http_user_agent")
%>
</BODY>
</HTML>
```

You can use ASP to develop Web content that is customized for user preferences and demographics and that uses Microsoft ActiveX Data Objects (ADO) and open database connectivity (ODBC) to provide access to multiple data sources. ASP provides a browser-neutral approach to the design of Web applications where all of the application logic resides on the server.

Notes

Active Server Pages was first introduced as a beta technology code-named "Delani" for the Microsoft Internet Information Server 2 platform.

Unlike the stateless Hypertext Transfer Protocol (HTTP), ASP is a session-based technology. When a user connects to an ASP file on a Web server, a session object is created. After the session expires, the session object is destroyed. The default time-out for ASP applications is 20 minutes, although Outlook Web Access uses a time-out of 60 minutes.

For More Information

To learn more, visit Charles Carroll's ASP site at *www.activeserverpages.com.*

See Also: *Active Platform*

Active Setup

A Microsoft ActiveX engine that can be used to download and install software over the Internet interactively using a Web browser.

Overview

Active Setup makes use of the fact that source files of the application to be installed are partitioned into segments, the traditional cabinet installation files (*.cab files). Active Setup begins by downloading a small, self-extracting setup package to the browser client. This file also collects information about the client's computer to help determine which components already exist on the system and whether the desired application is compatible with the system's configuration. The user specifies a location from which to download the desired application and the types of components to be installed. The application's *.cab files are then downloaded as needed, after which Active Setup is completed and normal installation can continue.

One advantage of Active Setup is that if the download is interrupted, it can be resumed at the interruption point rather than at the beginning.

See Also: *ActiveX*

active volume

The volume in Microsoft Windows 2000, Windows XP, and Windows .NET Server from which a computer boots.

Overview

In Windows 2000, Windows XP, and Windows .NET Server disk terminology, active volumes on dynamic disks are what active partitions are on basic disks. The active volume for a system must be a simple volume; in other words, it cannot be a striped set or mirrored volume.

You can upgrade the basic disk that contains the active partition to a dynamic disk, making it a simple volume that is active, but you cannot mark an existing dynamic volume as the active volume.

See Also: *active partition, dynamic disk*

active window

The particular open window that has the focus on a Microsoft Windows desktop.

Overview

The active window is the window belonging to the application in which the user is currently working. If several windows are open on a user's desktop, only one of these windows can be the active window. A unique color on the active window's title bar distinguishes it from other windows. If the user enters commands or text using the keyboard, these commands or text will be routed to the program displaying the active window. To make a window the active window on the desktop, simply click on it using the mouse, or cycle through the windows on the desktop using Alt+Tab.

Notes

You can capture a bitmap image of the active window to the clipboard by pressing Alt+PrintScreen. Then open Paint, paste the contents of the clipboard into the program, and save it as a *.bmp image.

See Also: *Microsoft Windows*

ActiveX

An umbrella term for Microsoft technology for building lightweight reusable software components.

Overview

The term *ActiveX* was first coined at the Internet Professional Developers Conference (Internet PDC) in 1996 and was based on the conference slogan "Activate the Internet."

Microsoft ActiveX is built on the Component Object Model (COM) and Distributed Component Object Model (DCOM) technologies, which enable software components to interact with each other across a network. ActiveX does not replace object linking and embedding (OLE) but broadens and enlarges it to include the Internet and intranet technologies.

ActiveX is supported by most Microsoft development and productivity applications, including Visual Basic, Visual C++, and Office.

For More Information

Visit the Microsoft COM site at *www.microsoft.com/com.*

See Also: *Component Object Model (COM), OLE*

ActiveX component

A Component Object Model (COM)–based application that allows other applications to use the classes it contains.

Overview

An ActiveX component represents a server application because it can serve other applications that call it. An application that calls an ActiveX component thus functions as a client application. Other names for ActiveX components are ActiveX servers, ActiveX DLLs, and COM components.

You can create ActiveX components using tools from Microsoft Visual Studio such as Microsoft Visual Basic and Microsoft Visual C++.

See Also: ActiveX, COM component object

ActiveX controls

Compiled, reusable software components based on Microsoft Corporation's Component Object Model (COM).

Overview

ActiveX controls can be used as prefabricated components to help developers rapidly build user interfaces for applications. ActiveX controls can draw themselves in their own windows, respond to events such as mouse clicks, and be managed through properties and methods. An ActiveX control cannot run as a stand-alone program but must be loaded into a control container such as Microsoft Visual Basic or Microsoft Internet Explorer.

History

The earliest form of custom controls in the Microsoft Windows platform were Visual Basic Extension (VBX) controls, which were 16-bit dynamic-link libraries (DLLs) in Windows 3.1 that had specific entry points and designed to work with VB forms to provide specific graphical user interface (GUI) functionality. With the introduction of object linking and embedding (OLE), VBX controls were replaced by 32-bit OLE Custom Extension (OCX) controls that supported type libraries and had better C++ support. Unfortunately, OCX controls tended to be bloated because they contained a large number of COM interfaces, whereas the applications calling them may only require a few of these interfaces. This was a particular concern when downloading controls over the Internet, so ActiveX controls, which were basically OCX controls in which the interfaces were optional, were created. ActiveX controls are thus lightweight controls and may even have no interface at all, as in ActiveX Data Objects (ADO).

Uses

ActiveX controls are often used to provide dynamic features for Web pages—for example, a stock ticker control that adds a live stock ticker to a Web page, an advanced user interface navigation tool, and an animation control that adds animation functionality to a page.

ActiveX controls can be embedded into a Hypertext Markup Language (HTML) page by using the HTML <OBJECT> tag. If a user tries to access such a page using a Web browser and the embedded ActiveX control is not installed on the user's system, the control can be automatically downloaded by using the URL specified in the CODEBASE attribute of the <OBJECT> tag. Once the ActiveX control is downloaded and installed on the user's system, the browser will continue to use the cached control until an updated version becomes available on the server.

Here is an example of a typical <OBJECT> tag that includes a CODEBASE attribute:

```
<OBJECT ID="BoomButton" WIDTH=225 HEIGHT=35
CLASSID="clsid:56F1BF40-B2D0-11d0-A6D6-
00AA00A70FC2"
CODEBASE="http://example.microsoft.com/
AControl.cab#Version=1,0,0,1">
</OBJECT>
```

Notes

A malicious ActiveX control can potentially damage software or data on a user's computer. To help users determine whether an ActiveX control is safe to install, Microsoft has developed a code-signing technology called Authenticode, which identifies the creator of a control using a digital signature issued by a well-known security authority such as VeriSign.

ActiveX Data Objects (ADO)

A data access interface developed by Microsoft Corporation and used for communicating with OLE DB-compliant data sources.

Overview

ActiveX Data Objects (ADO) is a high-level object-based interface to OLE DB, in other words, an OLE DB consumer (OLE DB is a generic data access technology from Microsoft). Using ADO and OLE DB, a client application can connect to a variety of data sources using the same programming model. These data sources include relational databases, hierarchical databases, indexed sequential access method (ISAM) databases, and virtually any other kind of data source for which an open database connectivity (ODBC) driver exists. In other words, ADO is intended to be a universal information interface.

In order to communicate with these unique data sources, ADO and OLE DB employ components called OLE DB providers, which are designed for specific data sources. If a native OLE DB provider is not available for a data source, but an ODBC driver is available, it should be possible to access the data source using the ODBC driver and an OLE DB provider designed to communicate with ODBC drivers.

Uses

ADO is supported in a variety of programming environments. For example, ADO can be used in Microsoft Visual C++ and Microsoft Visual Basic to access data in an OLE DB data source such as Microsoft SQL Server. ADO can also be used in conjunction with IIS to create Microsoft Active Server Pages (ASP) applications that access data sources.

In a Web-based environment, ADO is basically a server-based solution for data access. All data operations, such as changes to database records and filtering, must take place on the server. The client can then receive the data but cannot easily manipulate it. For applications in which the client must be able to manipulate the data being accessed, use remote data binding with Remote Data Service (RDS) instead. RDS is a technology that enables the user to manipulate data on the client and have any changes automatically made on the server. Allowing data to be manipulated on the client makes Web applications faster and more responsive.

ADO 2.5 is an integral part of the Microsoft Windows 2000 platform.

Architecture

ADO is based on a collection of Component Object Model (COM) and COM+ interfaces, and its object model is a simple COM-based architecture, which consists of static and dynamic object models. ADO communicates with a database through type libraries. Choosing the right library can significantly improve data access performance. For example, if Microsoft SQL Server is running on the same machine as Microsoft Internet Information Services (IIS), using named pipes can provide better performance than using the Transmission Control Protocol/Internet Protocol (TCP/IP) networking library.

The ADO 2.5 object model includes the following object types: Connection, Command, Errors, Fields, Record, Recordset, Parameters, and Stream.

Notes

Microsoft distributes ADO as part of the Microsoft Data Access Components (MDAC), a package that includes drivers and providers for ADO, OLE DB, and ODBC.

ADO 2.5 can also be used with ExOLEDB to provide access to the Web Storage System on Exchange 2000.

See Also: *ADO+, ADO.NET*

adapter

A device for connecting two different types of electronic hardware without losing information.

Overview

In local area network (LAN) networking, an adapter is a small device with two different connectors that provide data transmission back and forth between two different types of media (cabling). Adapters come in many varieties and are typically specified by stating the two connector types used and whether these connectors are male or female. For example, a DB9(f)-DB25(m) adapter means an adapter with a DB9 female and a DB25 male connector.

Adapters are a necessary part of the network administrator's toolkit because of the large number of connectivity options provided by networking equipment vendors.

Notes

The term *adapter* is also used in a number of different contexts in networking, including the following examples:

- Network interface cards (NICs) are sometimes called network adapter cards because they provide connectivity between computers and network cabling.
- Cigarette lighter adapters can be used to power cellular phones or laptops from an automobile battery.
- Digital phone adapters allow analog modems to be connected directly to Private Branch Exchange (PBX) phone outlets without damage.
- SC/ST adapters provide connectivity between fiber-optic connectors of differing types.

See Also: *connector (device)*

adaptive acceleration

An umbrella name for a group of technologies that expands the capacity of data channels.

Overview

Adaptive acceleration expands the amount of data that can be delivered over a given amount of bandwidth. This boosts network performance and helps overcome bottlenecks due to bandwidth limitations, a condition that affects most Internet service providers (ISPs), application service providers (ASPs), and other types of service providers. While throwing bandwidth at the problem is one way of handling the issue, adaptive acceleration tries to squeeze the best performance out of a fixed amount of bandwidth without dramatically increasing costs.

Adaptive acceleration works by combining several different techniques. These techniques can be incorporated into switching or routing gear or into stand-alone appliances and are targeted particularly towards traffic carried over the Internet. Some of the techniques used in adaptive acceleration include

- **Adaptive packet compression:** This assigns a different data compression algorithm to different types of data. For example, Hypertext Markup Language (HTML) files compress differently from Microsoft Word files, and adaptive packet compression scans packets for different kinds of files and compresses them in the most efficient manner for each type.
- **Selective caching:** This technique makes use of advanced algorithms to determine which files (or portions of files) can benefit most by being cached. For example, an entire Word file might be cached, or only the properties of the file. As another example, a .gif image might be cached, or only its palette.
- **Vertical data analysis:** This technique uses an algorithm that parses the different level protocol headers in packets, compresses it, repackages it, and applies rules to handle it more efficiently. This makes data transfer more efficient and can enhance and prioritize time-sensitive traffic such as voice or video over IP.

See Also: *caching*

Adaptive Differential Pulse-Code Modulation (ADPCM)

A technique for converting analog sound, such as speech, into binary digital information by frequently sampling the sound and expressing its modulation in binary form.

Overview

Adaptive Differential Pulse-Code Modulation (ADPCM) codecs convert analog signals into digital information by quantizing the differences between the actual analog signal and a predicted signal. The result is that analog signals encoded into files using ADPCM have a smaller size than many other formats. ADPCM enables speech information to be compressed into small files for storage and transmission.

Personal Communications Services (PCS) cellular telephony systems use a 32-kilobits per second (Kbps) ADPCM coding system to provide the same quality of voice communication that isavailable in wired telephone networks. This standard was developed by the International Telecommunication Union (ITU) and is known as G.721.

See Also: *modulation*

ADC

Stands for analog-to-digital converter, any device for changing analog signals into digital transmission.

See: *analog-to-digital converter (ADC)*

address book view

A virtual container in Microsoft Exchange that lets Microsoft Exchange Server administrators group recipients according to common attributes.

Overview

Address book views are created automatically when you establish the defining attributes for the address book view. For example, using the Exchange Administrator program, you could create an address book view called By Department and use the Department attribute of the recipients in your Exchange organization to automatically generate various address book view containers called Sales, Marketing, Management, and so on. Each address book view container will contain only those recipients that belong to a specific department.

For instance, when users access the global address list using Microsoft Outlook, these containers will be visible in their address books, along with their recipients. This allows users to more quickly address e-mail to recipients in a particular department instead of scrolling down the entire global address list.

You can also create multilevel address book views. For example, you could create a first level of virtual containers sorted by Country, followed by a second level sorted by State.

Notes

If you use the Exchange Administrator program to move a recipient from one address book view to another, the recipient takes on the defining attributes of the new address book view.

See Also: Exchange Server

address record

A Domain Name System (DNS) record mapping a host name to an Internet Protocol (IP) address.

See: A record

Address Resolution Protocol (ARP)

The Transmission Control Protocol/Internet Protocol (TCP/IP) network layer protocol responsible for resolving Internet Protocol (IP) addresses into Media Access Control (MAC) addresses.

Overview

When a TCP/IP-aware application tries to access another TCP/IP host using its IP address, the destination host's IP address must first be resolved into a MAC address so that the frame can be addressed and placed on the wire and then be recognized by the destination host's network interface card (NIC). This is because NICs operate at the physical layer (Layer 1) and data-link layer (Layer 2) of the Open Systems Interconnection (OSI) reference model and must use physical addresses (such as MAC addresses) instead of logical addresses (such as IP addresses) for network communication.

IP=172.16.8.101
MAC=F0-0D-EE-00-A0-0B
Host #1
Host #2
① ARP Request 172.16.8.101
ARP Reply F0-0D-EE-00-A0-0B ②
③
172.16.8.101=
F0-0D-EE-00-A0-0B
ARP cache of Host #1

Address Resolution Protocol (ARP). *How ARP works.*

Address Resolution Protocol (ARP) broadcasts an ARP request packet that effectively says, "Who has the following IP address?" This broadcast requests the MAC address of the destination host. The destination host then responds with an ARP reply packet containing its own MAC address. The requesting host next temporarily stores the IP-to-MAC-address mapping in its local ARP cache in case this is required again within a short time.

Notes

If the destination host is on a remote network, ARP obtains the MAC address of the local router interface that connects the local network to the remote network.

ARP is defined in RFC 826.

See Also: *Arp command*

ADMD

Stands for Administrative Management Domain; in X.400 messaging, a message-handling system (MHS) that is managed by a registered private agency.

See: *Administrative Management Domain (ADMD)*

ADMIN$

A special administrative share created during installation on computers running Microsoft Windows 2000, Windows XP, and Windows .NET Server and used for remote administration of the computer.

Overview

The Administrators group is assigned full control permissions on the ADMIN$ share on a Windows 2000, Windows XP, or Windows .NET Server system. This allows administrators to access the share and remotely administer the system without needing to know where the system files are stored. Only the Administrators group has access to the ADMIN$ share.

This share's path is always the path to the %SystemRoot% directory (usually C:\Winnt).

See Also: *administrative share*

administrative alert

A pop-up dialog box in Microsoft Windows 2000, Windows XP, and Windows .NET Server that notifies users of problems or issues.

Overview

Administrative alerts are generated by the Alerter service in Windows 2000, Windows XP, and Windows .NET Server. These alerts can be directed towards specified users and computers.

Administrative alerts are typically displayed when problems with security, access, sessions, directory replication, or printing occur or when a server is shut down by an uninterruptible power supply (UPS) device.

See Also: *service*

Administrative Management Domain (ADMD)

In X.400 messaging, a message-handling system (MHS) that ismanaged by a registered private agency.

Overview

Administrative Management Domains (ADMDs) are usually large public telecommunications carriers such as MCI/WorldCom and AT&T. This is in contrast to a Private Management Domain (PRMD), which represents a message-handling system managed by a private corporation. In the X.400 world, PRMDs cannot communicate directly with each other; instead, they must communicate through ADMDs. All the ADMDs in the world therefore form a kind of messaging backbone for global X.400 communication.

Notes

The ADMD is the second field in a typical X.400 originator/recipient (O/R) address and is located right after the country field.

See Also: *X.400*

administrative share

A share created during setup by Microsoft Windows 2000, Windows XP, and Windows .NET Server for system purposes and remote administration.

Overview

Administrative shares end in the "$" character, which makes them hidden shares. You cannot modify the permissions on these shares and you cannot remove the shares.

Some examples of administrative shares include

- **C$, D$, and so on:** The shares used by administrators to connect to the root of each volume on a network server and perform remote administration such as creating and deleting files and folders

- **ADMIN$:** The share name for the %SystemRoot% folder, used by the system during remote administration
- **IPC$:** A share used by interprocess communication (IPC) resources for sharing the named pipe interface, which allows applications running on different computers to communicate over the network
- **PRINT$:** A share used to support shared printers
- **REPL$:** A share used by the Directory Replicator Service that allows directory trees to be exported
- **NETLOGON:** A share used by the NetLogon service that enables the processing of domain requests

See Also: *hidden share*

administrative tools (Windows 2000, Windows XP, and Windows .NET Server)

A program group in Microsoft Windows 2000, Windows XP, and Windows .NET Server containing tools for administering a network based on these versions of Windows.

Overview

Most Windows 2000 administration tools are primarily implemented as preconfigured snap-ins for the Microsoft Management Console (MMC). Such tools are commonly referred to as consoles. Each administrative tool corresponds to an MMC console with a particular snap-in installed.

The set of available tools for a particular machine running Windows 2000, Windows XP, or Windows .NET Server depends on how that machine was installed and configured. Commonly installed tools for Windows 2000 Server, Windows XP, and Windows .NET Server, which can be used for both local and remote administration, include

- Component Services
- Computer Management
- Configure Your Server
- Data Sources (ODBC)
- Distributed File System
- Event Viewer
- Internet Services Manager
- Licensing
- Local Security Policy
- Performance
- Routing and Remote Access
- Server Extensions Administrator
- Services
- Telnet Server Administration

Notes

As an administrator, you can create your own administrative tools by opening a blank MMC console and installing the various snap-ins you need. When you save this tool, it will automatically be saved in the Administrative Tools program group.

See Also: *Windows 2000*

administrative tools (Windows NT)

A program group in Microsoft Windows NT containing tools for administering a Windows NT–based network.

Overview

The basic set of tools for Windows NT Server 4 consists of the following:

- Administrative Wizards
- Backup
- Disk Administrator
- Event Viewer
- License Manager
- Migration Tool for NetWare
- Network Client Administrator
- Performance Monitor
- Routing and Remote Access Admin

- Server Manager
- System Policy Editor
- User Manager for Domains
- Windows NT Diagnostics

You can extend these basic tools by installing additional Windows NT services using the Network utility in Control Panel, which provide the following additional tools:

- DHCP Manager
- DNS Manager
- File Manager
- Network Monitor
- WINS Manager

Notes

You can install a subset of these administrative tools on Windows NT Workstation 4 and a smaller subset on Windows 95 or Windows 98. The files required to install the client-based network administrative tools on Windows NT Workstation 4 and Windows 95 or Windows 98 are available in the \Clients\Srvtools directory on the Windows NT Server 4 compact disc.

See Also: *Windows NT*

administrator

A user who has full rights and permissions to manage any resources on the network.

Overview

The administrator is usually responsible for tasks such as installing, managing, and controlling servers and networking components. Administrators can also modify the properties of user accounts and the membership of groups, create and manage security printers, install printers, share resources, and assign permissions to those resources.

In Microsoft Windows 2000, Windows XP, and Windows .NET Server, the Administrator account is a built-in account whose password is defined during installation. The Administrator account is a member of the Domain Admins group and the Administrators group on the domain controller on which it is defined, and it has full rights and permissions on all user-accessible system resources.

Notes

On a domain controller, the Administrator account is a global user account, while on a stand-alone server or workstation, the Administrator account is a local user account.

You can rename the default Administrator account, but you cannot delete it. If you rename the account, make sure you remember what the new name is!

See Also: *Administrators group*

Administrators group

In Microsoft Windows 2000, Windows XP, and Windows .NET Server, a built-in group whose default membership consists of the Domain Admins group.

Overview

The Administrators group has full rights on all user-accessible processes on a computer running Windows 2000, Windows XP, or Windows .NET Server. For example, on a domain controller, the Administrators group has the right to

- Log on locally
- Access the computer over the network
- Take ownership of files
- Change the system time
- Configure auditing and manage the security log
- Shut down the system
- Back up and restore files and directories
- Force shutdown from a remote system
- Load new device drivers
- Add computers to the domain in Windows NT and Windows 2000

See Also: *administrator, built-in group*

ADO

Stands for ActiveX Data Objects, a data access interface used to communicate with OLE DB–compliant data sources.

See: *ActiveX Data Objects (ADO)*

ADO+

A version of Microsoft ActiveX Data Objects (ADO) for the Microsoft Windows Distributed interNet Applications Architecture (Windows DNA).

Overview

ADO+ is a more scalable, more interoperable, and more strongly typed version of ADO. The programming and object model for ADO+ is radically different from ADO because ADO is designed from the ground up to work with disconnected data sets (ADO included some support for disconnected record sets starting with ADO 2.0). An ADO+ data set is a disconnected in-memory view of a database. Data sets can be created dynamically without any interaction with a database management system (DBMS), so data sets are an evolution of the previous concept of ADO record sets. Data sets can contain any number of tables, and these do not need to correspond to a particular database table or view. ADO+ thus models data, not databases or data providers the way ADO did.

What particularly distinguishes ADO+ is that it utilizes Extensible Markup Language (XML) as its universal format for data transmission. This gives ADO+ its wide interoperability with any platform supporting XML, and receivers no longer need to be COM objects as they were with ADO.

See Also: *ActiveX Data Objects (ADO), Windows Distributed interNet Applications Architecture (Windows DNA)*

ADO.NET

The evolution of Microsoft Corporation's Active X Data Objects (ADO) for its new .NET platform.

Overview

ADO.NET provides the classes necessary to ADO to enable access to Extensible Markup Language (XML) documents and relational data stores. Some of the differences between ADO.NET and ADO are the following:

- While ADO uses the RecordSet object, which looks like a single table, ADO.NET uses the DataSet object, which can contain one or more tables represented by DataTable objects.
- While ADO uses Component Object Model (COM) marshalling to transmit a disconnected record set, ADO.NET transmits a DataSet with an XML file (the XML format places no restrictions on data types and requires no type conversion).
- While ADO has trouble transmitting data through firewalls because firewalls are typically configured to prevent system-level requests such as COM marshalling, ADO.NET can easily transmit data through firewalls because ADO.NET DataSet objects use Hypertext Markup Language (HTML)–based XML, which can pass through firewalls.

See Also: *ActiveX Data Objects (ADO), .NET platform*

ADPCM

Stands for Adaptive Differential Pulse-Code Modulation, a technique for converting analog sound, such as speech, into binary digital information by frequently sampling the sound and expressing its modulation in binary form.

See: *Adaptive Differential Pulse-Code Modulation (ADPCM)*

ADPr

Stands for Active Digital Profile, an Extensible Markup Language (XML) specification for automating the provisioning of IT (information technology) resources.

See: *Active Digital Profile (ADPr)*

ADR

Stands for Advanced Data Recording, a tape backup technology developed by Philips.

See: *Advanced Data Recording (ADR)*

ADSI

Stands for Active Directory Service Interfaces, a set of object-oriented programming interfaces for providing programmatic access to Active Directory objects.

See: *Active Directory Service Interfaces (ADSI)*

ADSL

Stands for Asymmetric Digital Subscriber Line, a form of Digital Subscriber Line (DSL) technology that provides subscribers with high-speed voice and data services over twisted-pair copper phone lines.

See: *Asymmetric Digital Subscriber Line (ADSL)*

ADSL modem

A modem used to terminate an Asymmetric Digital Subscriber Line (ADSL) connection between the customer premises and the ADSL provider.

Overview

ADSL modems are customer premises equipment (CPE) for connecting subscribers to telcos offering ADSL services. ADSL modems are typically used to provide high-speed Internet access for residential and business customers.

ADSL modems operate by dividing the available bandwidth in Plain Old Telephone Service (POTS) telephone lines into separate upstream and downstream channels. This is typically done in one of two ways:

- **Frequency division multiplexing (FDM):** This technique separates upstream and downstream communications into two separate channels with a band of unused frequency between them to prevent crosstalk and reduce interference. If you need to, you can then further divide each of these two channels using time-division multiplexing (TDM).
- **Echo cancellation:** This technique employs overlapping upstream and downstream channels and separates them using V.32/V.34 echo cancellation methods used in modems.

Of these two techniques, echo cancellation offers better utilization of bandwidth but is more complex to implement.

To separate the two data channels from the voice channel used for ordinary telephone communications, ADSL modems include a POTS splitter, a type of filter placed at the carrier side of the modem which splits off the first 4 kilohertz (kHz) of bandwidth and routes it to the telephone. This way, if an ADSL provider goes down and data communications cease, regular POTS telephone service still works at the customer premises.

See Also: *Asymmetric Digital Subscriber Line (ADSL), modem*

Advanced Configuration and Power Interface (ACPI)

A specification for power management of computer hardware.

Overview

Advanced Configuration and Power Interface (ACPI) is an open industry specification that was designed to enable software designers to integrate power management features through all parts of a computer system, including the hardware, the operating system, and application software. ACPI is the successor to the Advanced Power Management (APM) specification and differs by allowing the operating system to control hardware power consumption instead of the basic input/output system (BIOS).

Microsoft Windows 2000, Windows XP, and Windows .NET Server support Advanced Configuration and Power Interface (ACPI), and it enables Windows to handle all the power-management resources for computer subsystems and peripherals. ACPI works with subsystems and peripherals for a wide range of mobile, desktop, and server platforms. ACPI is also the foundation for the OnNow industry initiative that enables computers to start at the touch of the keyboard.

Notes

Your PC must be fully compatible with ACPI for you to use it, regardless of whether your operating system supports it. To find out if your PC supports ACPI, go into the BIOS, look for an ACPI option, and turn it on.

You can also enable ACPI support for Windows 98 by running Setup using the command-line switch Setup /p j. Running Setup in this mode adds the ACPIOption

string value with a value data of 1 to the Windows 98 registry and causes hardware devices to be queried for ACPI support during setup. Note that Windows 98 does not support all ACPI features—Passive Cooling Mode, for example.

For More Information

Find out about ACPI at *www.teleport.com/~acpi.*

Find out about the Microsoft OnNow initiative at *www.microsoft.com/hwdev/onnow.htm.*

See Also: *Advanced Power Management (APM)*

Advanced Data Recording (ADR)

A tape backup technology developed by Philips.

Overview

Advanced Data Recording (ADR) is a technology that writes eight tracks of data simultaneously to a single tape. This gives ADR tape drives a very high throughput. Tapes move slowly in ADR tape drives, which makes for minimal tape wear and quieter operation.

ADR tape drives are available from OnStream and popular models include:

- **ADR30:** Has a capacity of 15 gigabytes (GB) and a transfer rate of 60 megabytes (MB)/min.
- **ADR50:** Has a capacity of 25 GB and a transfer rate of 120 MB per minute.

For More Information

Visit OnStream at *www.onstream.com.*

See Also: *tape format*

Advanced Encryption Standard (AES)

The new U.S. government encryption standard adopted to replace the aging Data Encryption Standard (DES) standard, which no longer offers sufficient security.

Overview

Until recently the U.S. government has used DES as the encryption scheme for security sensitive electronic transmissions. However, a 56-bit DES key was successfully cracked in 1997 using idle processing cycles on thousands of machines distributed across the Internet. Advances in computing in the last few years have made DES even more vulnerable as an encryption mechanism, and as a result an initiative was put forward by the U.S. government to develop a scheme that could not be cracked.

The result of this initiative is the Advanced Encryption Standard (AES), which officially replaced DES in the spring of 2001. AES supports key lengths of 128, 192, and 256 bits, which offers a vast improvement in security over 56-bit DES and even 168-bit Triple DES, in which three DES keys are applied in succession. The National Institute of Standards and Technology (NIST) has calculated that it would take about 149 trillion years to crack an AES-coded message using an algorithm that could crack DES in one second (no such algorithm currently exists), so AES is likely to remain secure for some time to come. Using the maximum level of encryption (256-bit), a cracker would have to generate and test 1.1×10^{77} unique keys in order to crack an AES message, which is currently beyond conception for brute-force computing power.

Architecture

AES is a block cipher, which means that it encrypts data in fixed-length blocks of 128 bits at a time. AES uses the Rijndael algorithm developed by Vincent Rijmen and Joan Daemen. This algorithm was chosen over four competing algorithms because it is easy to implement and is efficient with regard to calculation, making AES suitable for use even in devices such as cell phones and Personal Digital Assistants (PDAs) that have limited processing power. The Rijndael algorithm executes 10 rounds of encryption when using a key length of 128 bits.

Prospects

Although AES has become the official standard for U.S. government encryption, it will continue to coexist with DES and Triple DES for a number of years as hardware and software vendors update their encryption schemes. However, industry is expected to quickly upgrade to AES because DES is no longer secure and Triple DES is inherently slow. AES will also be licensed for commercial use by industry.

Notes

Web browsers, the ubiquitous interface to Web applications, mostly use RC4 encryption. Although the next generation of Web browsers will likely license AES for use, millions of desktop computers are likely to continue to use older browsers for years.

For More Information

Find out more about AES at the site of the National Institute of Standards and Technology at *csrc.nist.gov/encryption/aes.*

See Also: *Data Encryption Standard (DES), encryption*

Advanced Infrared (AIr)

A wireless networking technology for high-speed, low-cost infrared (IR) networking.

Overview

Advanced Infrared (Air) allows ad hoc multipoint wireless peer-to-peer connections to be formed simultaneously between multiple wireless information appliances such as Personal Digital Assistants (PDAs), cellular phones, laptops, and digital cameras. The devices must be within 26 feet (8 meters) of each other to reliably communicate without interference.

AIr ports can receive signals within a 120-degree cone, which means that the ports need not be precisely aimed at each other to achieve reliable transmission.

AIr currently supports data throughput of up to 4 megabits per second (Mbps) for direct line-of-sight communication, but it can interoperate with the existing slower Infrared Data Association (IrDA) 1.1 standard, and it supports the Very Fast Infrared (VFIR) standard currently under development.

IBM developed AIr and was the first vendor to release products based on this standard. IBM is working with the IrDA to standardize the technology.

See Also: *Infrared Data Association (IrDA), infrared transmission*

Advanced Intelligent Tape (AIT)

A tape backup technology developed by Sony Corporation.

Overview

Advanced Intelligent Tape (AIT) is a popular tape backup format that has a native capacity of 25 gigabytes (GB) (uncompressed) per tape and supports transfer speeds of 6 megabits per second (Mbps). AIT supports high data compression rates—typically 2:1 or higher. Access times are low because the tape's spine contains embedded 16-kilobyte (KB) nonvolatile memory chips that store the backup set headers. Thus, when a particular backup set is requested, the tape can spool directly to the required spot without having to search through the data. This results in longer life for the tape. Another feature of AIT is that the heads are self-cleaning and only occasionally require maintenance, which also extends media life.

Sony's AIT tape drives are typically cheaper than Quantum's digital linear tape (DLT) drives, and they have gained a solid foothold in large companies. AIT tape libraries are also available from various vendors for terabyte storage needs.

AIT 2 is a second-generation AIT standard and supports up to 50 GB (uncompressed) per tape, but this can often translate into up to 125 GB compressed. AIT 2 transfer speeds are typically 7 megabytes per second (MBps) or higher. AIT 3 is emerging as the next generation of AIT standards, and it should be competitive with the 100 GB native capacity and 13 MBps transfer rates of the competing Linear Tape Open (LTO) tape backup technology.

See Also: *tape format*

Advanced Mobile Phone Service (AMPS)

The original first-generation (1G) analog cellular phone service. Still used in some parts of North and South America.

Overview

Bell Laboratories invented the technology for Advanced Mobile Phone Service (AMPS) in the 1970s, and AT&T introduced it as a commercial service in

Advanced Mobile Phone Service (AMPS)

1983. AMPS represents the first generation of cellular phone technology widely deployed throughout the United States and was the first fully standardized automatic mobile telephone service in the world. In addition to the United States, AMPS was also deployed in South America, Australia, and China.

AMPS uses frequencies in the 800 megahertz (MHz) band (from 824.04 to 893.7 MHz) of the radio spectrum. AMPS uses Frequency Division Multiple Access (FDMA) to create individual communications channels. FDMA is used to modulate a 3 kilohertz (kHz) voice channel onto a 30 kHz carrier signal using frequency modulation (FM). This creates a series of 30 kHz wide channels for one-way transmission (by contrast, an FM radio station uses a 150 kHz bandwidth channel). Separate channels are used for base station to mobile transmission (forward channels) and mobile station to base transmission (backward channels). In fact, forward channels fall within the range 869.04 to 893.97 MHz and backward channels are found from 824.04 to 848.97 MHz. The 45 MHz between these two bands helps separate forward and reverse transmission and reduces interference and crosstalk.

AMPS can assign only a single subscriber at a time to each channel, so the resulting allocation of bandwidth results in a maximum of 832 simultaneous phone conversations per operator. Because the population of most cities would suggest that 800 simultaneous phone conversations is far from enough, the idea was developed to partition the coverage of cities into a number of small areas called "cells" (this explains the origin of the terms "cellular communications" and "cell phone"). Each base station uses a limited-power transmitter with a directional antenna to provide coverage for a small geographical cell. A typical cell ranges from 1640 feet (500 meters) to 12.5 miles (20 kilometers) in size, depending on whether the coverage is in a densely populated urban area or a sparsely populated rural one.

Because cell phones have limited transmission power, communication is limited to the base station servicing the immediate cell the user is currently in. As a user moves from one cell to another, the signal strength gradually decreases until a threshold limit is reached. Once this threshold is reached, the base station informs the Mobile Telephone Switching Office (MTSO) that the subscriber is leaving the service area of that base station. The MTSO hands off the call to the base station that the subscriber is starting to enter (adjacent cells overlap), which smoothly picks up the call so service is not interrupted. Adjacent cells employ different frequencies to help prevent interference from occurring between them.

Handheld AMPS cellular phones have power levels generally under 0.6 watts with a range of about 5 miles (8 kilometers) from the base station, but power levels in vehicle-mounted phones reach up to 3 watts with a range of 15 miles (24 kilometers). Base stations themselves generally have power levels up to about 1 kilowatt.

Prospects

Because of the need for data transmission and security (encryption), digital cellular phone services such as Time Division Multiple Access (TDMA) and Code Division Multiple Access (CDMA) systems are steadily increasing in popularity as AMPS continues to decline. Nevertheless, market statistics indicate that as recently as 1999 AMPS remained the cellular communications service with the greatest area of coverage across North America. However, the success of AMPS has been its downfall—the limited number of channels per cell means that when too many people subscribe to the service, blocking (the inability to make a call because no channel is available) becomes a problem. Another problem is that when a subscriber roams into a cell where no channels are available, the subscriber's call is dropped (suddenly disconnected without warning).

Notes

Other 1G analog cellular phone systems included Total Access Communication System (TACS) and Extended TACS (E-TACS) used in the United Kingdom and Nordic Mobile Telephone (NMT) used in the Scandinavian countries. AMPS, however, was by far the most popular and widely deployed 1G service.

AMPS can also be used for data transmission, but it is capable of supporting data rates of only about 9.6 kilobits per second (Kbps).

For More Information

Visit the site of the Universal Wireless Communication Consortium at *www.uwcc.org* for information on all types of cellular communications systems.

See Also: *cellular communications, Code Division Multiple Access (CDMA), Digital Advanced Mobile Phone Service (D-AMPS), Global System for Mobile Communications (GSM), Time Division Multiple Access (TDMA)*

Advanced Peer-to-Peer Networking (APPN)

A protocol developed by IBM as the second generation of Systems Network Architecture (SNA).

Overview

Advanced Peer-to-Peer Networking (APPN) is an extension of SNA that was developed for several reasons:

- To enable SNA traffic to flow concurrently with other protocols.
- To provide for prioritization of SNA traffic through it is class-of-service (CoS) features.
- To allow users to establish communication sessions without mainframe involvement.

APPN provides a mechanism for peer-to-peer networking and session establishment between any two logical units (LUs) on an SNA network. APPN provides greater distributed network control than legacy SNA by isolating the effects of single-point failures. It supports the dynamic exchange of information about network topology to facilitate connection, reconfiguration, and route selection. APPN also supports the dynamic definition and automated registration of network resources.

Prospects

APPN was a promising technology that for various reasons ended up failing to make much of an impact on mainframe computing environments. APPN equipment was costly and difficult to manage, and IBM's marketing scheme of requiring third-party developers of APPN hardware and software to contribute royalties from earnings to IBM led to a famous clash between IBM and Cisco Systems in 1994 over this issue. APPN is today considered a legacy technology that is being phased out.

See Also: *Systems Network Architecture (SNA)*

Advanced Power Management (APM)

A legacy specification for power management of computer hardware.

Overview

Advanced Power Management (APM) was the precursor to Advanced Configuration and Power Management (ACPI) and was implemented in versions of Microsoft Windows prior to Windows 2000. APM used the basic input/output system (BIOS) to manage all computer hardware and peripherals. This had several disadvantages that motivated the development of ACPI, namely

- Different hardware platforms from different vendors often used different BIOS chips, which meant that in a large enterprise power management capabilities varied from machine to machine, making troubleshooting more difficult.
- Suspend mode is supported poorly because the BIOS cannot know whether the user or the system initiated the suspend.
- Universal serial bus (USB) and Institute of Electrical and Electronics Engineers (IEEE) 1394 peripherals were not supported by APM.

ACPI addresses these concerns by enabling the operating system to control power to devices, not the BIOS.

Notes

If your machine's BIOS uses APM 1 or 1.1, try to flash upgrade the BIOS to support APM 1.2 if possible to resolve certain issues relating to system instabilities when in standby mode.

Microsoft Windows 2000, Windows XP, and Windows .NET Server support both APM and ACPI, with ACPI being the preferred option. The tool Ampstat.exe in the Support/Tools folder on the Windows 2000 CD can be used to troubleshoot issues relating to APM.

See Also: *Advanced Configuration and Power Interface (ACPI)*

Advanced Program-to-Program Communications (APPC) protocol

A set of protocols developed by IBM that enables transactional programs to communicate with each other.

Overview

The Advanced Program-to-Program Communications (APPC) protocol was originally designed for Systems Network Architecture (SNA) networks and has been implemented in Multiple Virtual Storage (MVS), Operating System/2 (OS/2), Advanced Interactive Executive (AIX), and OS/400. APPC is also supported over Transmission Control Protocol/Internet Protocol (TCP/IP) using IBM's Anynet architecture. APPC was first introduced into the AS/400 series as its native communications platform and was called LU 6.2.

Applications that use APPC to communicate are called transaction programs (TPs) and utilize a package of APPC routines called Common Programming Interface–Communications (CPIC). APPC services are available for applications written in C++, REXX, COBOL, and other languages.

APPC is not a widely deployed platform and is most often employed for its file transfer services.

Notes

Microsoft Host Integration Server provides services necessary for APPC connectivity with AS/400 systems and mainframe hosts.

See Also: *Systems Network Architecture (SNA)*

Advanced Streaming Format (ASF)

A method of streaming data supported by Windows Media Player.

Overview

Advanced Streaming Format (ASF) supports video, audio, images, Uniform Resource Locators (URLs), and scripts. ASF streams can combine different types of data, allowing you to stream presentations involving slides and audio narration. Using the Windows Media Encoder, you can generate live ASF streams that contain audio and video.

You can also use tools provided with Windows Media Encoder to create and store ASF files that you can later stream.

Windows Media Services can deliver ASF streams using either multicasting or unicasting.

Notes

When multicasting an ASF stream, configure Windows Media Services to provide a supplemental unicast source for the stream for any clients that cannot receive multicasts.

Advanced Technology Demonstration Network (ATDnet)

A high-speed test bed network that is part of SuperNet, the cross-country network funded by the Next Generation Internet (NGI) program.

Overview

Advanced Technology Demonstration Network (ATDnet) is deployed in the Washington D.C. area and was developed as a prototype for the next generation of Metropolitan Area Networks (MANs). It is funded by the Defense Advanced Research Projects Agency (DARPA) and serves as an experimental test bed platform for research and development. ATDnet network transport consists of Synchronous Optical Network (SONET) and Asynchronous Transfer Mode (ATM) running over fiber and currently uses a double ring topology that supports 20 gigabits per second (Gbps).

For More Information

You can visit ATDnet at *www.atd.net.*

AES

Stands for Advanced Encryption Standard, the new U.S. government encryption standard adopted in the spring of 2001 to replace the aging Data Encryption Standard (DES) standard, which no longer offers sufficient security.

See: Advanced Encryption Standard (AES)

AFTP

Stands for APPC File Transfer Protocol, a protocol that provides file transfer capabilities for the Advanced Program-to-Program Communications (APPC).

See: APPC File Transfer Protocol (AFTP)

agent

Simple Network Management Protocol (SNMP) client software that runs on a hub, a router, or another networking component.

Overview

Agents collect information about Transmission Control Protocol/Internet Protocol (TCP/IP) statistics and conditions and can supply this information when requested to an SNMP management system. Agents can also alert management systems to errors and other conditions when a trap occurs. SNMP agents are identified by the community to which they belong. By default, SNMP agents listen to TCP port number 161 for SNMP messages and to port number 162 for SNMP traps.

An agent must be installed on each networking component or host that will be managed in an SNMP-managed network. The agent program can then perform operations such as

- Get operations initiated by the SNMP management console for obtaining information about a specific managed object in the host Management Information Base (MIB)
- Get-next operations initiated by the management console to continue traversing the MIB database from the point at which it was accessed by a get operation
- Set operations initiated by the management console to set a value for a managed object (if permissions allow this)
- Trap operations initiated by the managed host itself when an error condition occurs, such as when the computer's disk becomes full

Notes

Windows 98 also includes an SNMP agent conforming to SNMP 1 specifications that lets you monitor remote connections to machines running Windows 98 from an SNMP management console. This agent is implemented as a Win32 service using Windows Sockets over TCP/IP. You can install the Microsoft SNMP agent on Windows 98 using the Network utility in Control Panel.

See Also: *Simple Network Management Protocol (SNMP)*

AGLP

A mnemonic for managing an enterprise-level Microsoft Windows NT network.

Overview

AGLP means that user **A**ccounts are organized by placing them in **G**lobal groups, which are then placed into **L**ocal groups that have appropriate **P**ermissions and rights assigned to them.

In practice, the steps for administering a Windows NT enterprise-level network are the following:

1. Create global user accounts for users in the account domains or master domains.
2. Create global groups in these domains to organize users according to function, location, or some other criteria (or use the Windows NT built-in groups if these suffice).
3. Assign global users to their respective global groups.
4. Determine who needs access to network resources in the resource domains.

5 Create local groups on domain controllers and member servers within the resource domains (or use the Windows NT built-in groups if these suffice).

6 Assign rights and permissions to each local group as desired to provide access to network resources.

7 Place global groups into local groups as desired to provide users with permissions to access resources.

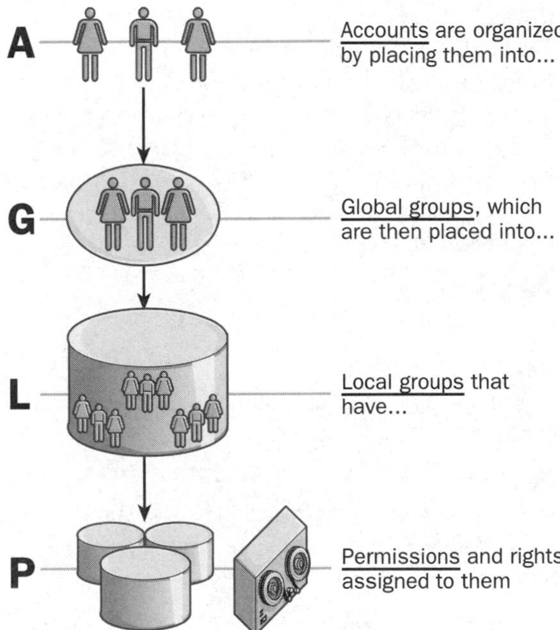
A
Accounts are organized by placing them into...
G
Global groups, which are then placed into...
L
Local groups that have...
P
Permissions and rights assigned to them

***AGLP.** Using AGLP to administering a Windows NT–based network.*

Notes

On Windows 2000– and Windows .NET Server–based networks, the mnemonic is AGDLP because local (L) groups are referred to as domain local (DL) groups. However, because Windows 2000 and Windows .NET Server include an additional type of group (universal groups) and have a more flexible architecture for deployment, these mnemonics do not have as much significance for these versions of Windows as they did for Windows NT.

See Also: *account, group, permissions*

AH

Stands for Authentication Header, a protocol in the IPSec suite of protocols that handles authentication of Internet Protocol (IP) traffic.

See: *Authentication Header (AH)*

AIM

Stands for AOL Instant Messenger, a popular instant messaging service from America Online (AOL).

See: *AOL Instant Messenger (AIM)*

AIr

Stands for Advanced Infrared, a wireless networking technology for high-speed, low-cost infrared (IR) networking.

See: *Advanced Infrared (AIr)*

Air Interface

Generally, the lower levels of the protocol stack in a wireless communications system.

Overview

Different wireless communications systems use different types of air interfaces, but these all generally map well with the Open Systems Interconnection (OSI) model for networking. For example, Personal Communications Service (PCS) cellular service uses a three-level air interface:

- **Physical Layer:** This bottom layer of the interface is responsible for encoding and framing data, interleaving and slotting it into available time slots, and mapping these slots onto a channel for transmission as a burst.
- **Data-link Layer:** This middle layer is responsible for packaging the data, transporting the message to its destination, and performing error correction.
- **Message Layer:** This top layer handles messages transmitted over the air and formats the messages as data elements that are then packaged and transported by the lower levels.

In addition to these three levels, typical wireless messaging systems include higher levels for control purposes, metering, and providing additional services.

See Also: *cellular communications, wireless networking*

AIT

Stands for Advanced Intelligent Tape, a tape backup technology developed by Sony Corporation.

See: *Advanced Intelligent Tape (AIT)*

AIX

A version of the UNIX operating system developed by IBM.

Overview

AIX runs on IBM RS/6000 and systems based on IBM PowerPC processors (a version for Intel Corporation's 64-bit IA-64 processor is also planned). AIX, which stands for Advanced Interactive Executive, was originally based on release 2 of the Unix System V operating system and is compliant with the Unix98 standard. The current release AIX 4.3 is a solid platform for e-business and supports IBM's VisualAge, Java, and C++ developer tools.

Project Monterey is an initiative from IBM for the development of the next version of AIX called AIX 5L. Combining the time-tested reliability of AIX with UnixWare, DYNIX/ptx, and Linux support, AIX 5L promises to make AIX a major contender for high-end 64-bit computing using Intel's 64-bit IA-64 platform.

For More Information

Find out more about AIX at *http://www-1.ibm.com/servers/aix*.

See Also: *UNIX*

Alerter service

A Microsoft Windows 2000, Windows XP, and Windows .NET Server service responsible for sending administrative alerts to users and computers.

Overview

The Alerter service generates an alert when potentially dangerous conditions occur, such as when disk space is running out. You can configure which users or computers receive these alerts by using Server Manager (or by using the Server utility in Control Panel). Pop-up alert messages appear if the administrator is logged on or is at the appropriate computer when the alert occurs. The administrator can then consult the system log for information about what caused the alert.

Notes

The Server service must be running for the Alerter service to function. The Messenger service should also be running on both the sending and receiving computers. Also, restart the Server service and Alerter service on the computer after modifying the list of users and computers to whom alert conditions on that computer should be sent.

See Also: *service*

alias

A form of nickname that identifies a user for e-mail purposes.

Overview

An alias is usually a shortened form of the user's full name, such as the alias JSmith or JeffS for user Jeff Smith.

Aliases are a convenient way of identifying users and form the user-specific portion of an e-mail address. For example, if Jeff Smith belongs to a company whose Domain Name System (DNS) domain on the Internet is northwind.microsoft.com, his e-mail address would be either JSmith@northwind.microsoft.com or, instead, JeffS@northwind.microsoft.com, depending on which alias is selected.

Notes

What if both a Jeff Smith and a Jeff Smythe work at the same company? If JeffS is the alias for the first user, you could use JeffS2 for the second. It all depends on your choice of naming convention.

See Also: *e-mail*

Always On/Dynamic ISDN (AO/DI)

A modified form of Integrated Services Digital Network (ISDN) that supports transmission of data over the ISDN control channel (D channel).

Overview

The ISDN D-channel is always active and is normally used to carry the control information for setting up, managing, and tearing down ISDN B channel connections. Always On/Dynamic ISDN (AO/DI) takes advantages of this by reserving a portion of the D channel's bandwidth for transmitting X.25 packets. This is done by encapsulating X.25 packets within Point-to-Point Protocol (PPP) and allows an X.25 Packet Assembler/Disassembler (PAD) at the subscriber's premises to transmit and receive information through ISDN to the carrier's X.25 network.

The ISDN D channel has a total bandwidth of 16 kilobits per second (Kbps). This is more than enough for carrying ISDN control signals, so in AO/DI 9.6 kbps of this bandwidth is used for X.25 signaling. When an X.25 packet is sent from the customer premises over an ISDN D channel to the telco's central office (CO), a packet handler positioned in front of the carrier's ISDN switch strips off the X.25 packet and relays it to the carrier's X.25 network.

Uses

Although 9.6 Kbps seems like a small amount of useful bandwidth, one use for AO/DI is to provide always-on Internet access to subscribers who can utilize this small bandwidth for practical purposes, such as periodically polling fire alarm sensors over the Internet from a central monitoring station or remotely monitoring electricity and gas meters. From the telco's point of view, the main advantage of AO/DI is to reduce the usage of ISDN B channels, freeing up more circuits and saving costs.

Despite its promised usefulness, real-world deployments of AO/DI are few, primarily due to the communications industry's current focus on developing high-speed broadband access solutions for home and business.

See Also: *Integrated Services Digital Network (ISDN)*

Alpha platform

A computer hardware platform whose processor is based on the Alpha Reduced Instruction Set Computing (RISC) microprocessor architecture originally developed by Digital Equipment Corporation (DEC).

Overview

Alpha-based systems, which are used primarily for high-performance servers and workstations, can run operating systems such as Microsoft Windows NT, Digital UNIX, and OpenVMS. For example, the Alpha 21164 processor was specifically designed for running Windows NT desktop applications and includes a new set of motion video instructions (MVI) for high-performance multimedia applications. The superscalar design of this processor integrates a 16-kilobyte (KB) instruction cache, an 8-KB data cache, and a 96-KB second-level cache and can issue four instructions for each clock cycle. It uses 0.35-micron complementary metal-oxide semiconductor (CMOS)–integrated circuit technology and a fully pipelined 64-bit RISC architecture to provide the highest performance for Windows NT systems. The processor is housed in a 499-pin ceramic package and generates 28 watts of heat and is designed to work with the AlphaPC 164LX motherboard. The latest Alpha chips run at speeds of 833 megahertz (MHz) and higher.

Notes

Windows 2000 does not support the Alpha platform.

For More Information

Visit the Alpha Server home at *www.compaq.com/alphaserver.*

See Also: *x86 platform*

American National Standards Institute (ANSI)

A U.S. standards organization that facilitates and governs the development of standards in many areas, including computing and communication.

Overview

The American National Standards Institute (ANSI) was founded as a private sector voluntary standards association in 1918. It is a nonprofit private association with almost 1,400 member organizations.

ANSI does not create standards itself but oversees groups and organizations in the development of standards. ANSI is a member organization of the International Organization for Standardization (ISO) and provides the charter for the Institute of Electrical and Electronics Engineers (IEEE).

Standards that are approved by ANSI are called ANSI Standards. Examples include the ANSI C/C++ programming language standards, ANSI-89 SQL standards, and ANSI character set. ANSI has approved more than 13,000 standards to date.

Notes

ANSI is also used to refer to the ANSI character set.

For More Information

Visit the American National Standards Institute at *www.ansi.org.*

American Registry for Internet Numbers (ARIN)

A nonprofit organization that administers the registration and allocation of numbers relating to the operation of the Internet in North and South America.

Overview

The American Registry for Internet Numbers (ARIN) was formed in 1997 through the joint efforts of the Internet Assigned Numbers Authority (IANA), the Internet Engineering Task Force (IETF), the National Science Foundation (NFS), and other organizations. ARIN exists primarily to provide a number of critical functions related to the operation of the Internet:

- It oversees the registration and administration of Internet Protocol (IP) addresses. This is probably ARIN's most important function, which it took over from IANA when it was formed in 1997. ARIN works diligently to conserve the pool of available IP addresses and determines the size and scope of blocks of IP addresses granted in response to requests. The careful maintenance of the IP address system is critical to the Internet's health, and ARIN works hard to ensure that the routing tables maintained on the core routers of the Internet remain manageable in size. Internet service providers (ISPs) can contact ARIN to purchase blocks of IP addresses that they can then assign to their customers—ARIN does not supply individual IP addresses directly to individuals (the smallest block available from ARIN is 4096 hosts in scope).
- It is responsible for registration and management of autonomous system numbers (ASNs) to public and enterprise networks.
- It maintains a central routing registry to which network operators can submit and obtain information relating to routing across the Internet.
- It maintains the IN-ADDR-ARPA and IP6.INT inverse mappings for Domain Name System (DNS).

ARIN is actually only one of three Regional Internet Registries (RIRs) that handle the above functions for different parts of the global Internet. ARIN's areas of responsibility are the regions of North and South America, the Caribbean, and sub-Saharan Africa. The other two RIRs are

- **Reseaux IP Europeans (RIPE):** Responsible for Europe, the Middle East, and other parts of Africa.
- **Asia Pacific Network Information Center (APNIC):** Responsible for the Asia/Pacific region.

Notes

ARIN does not handle the registration of domain names but instead manages the underlying IP addresses for which domain names are friendly handles. There are also two delegated name registries within ARIN: the Brazilian Registry (RNP) and the Mexican Registry (NIC-Mexico).

For More Information

You can find ARIN at *www.arin.net.*

See Also: *autonomous system number (ASN), Internet, IP address*

AMP

Stands for asymmetric multiprocessing, a processing architecture in which processes are specifically assigned to different processors.

See: *asymmetric multiprocessing (AMP)*

AMPS

Stands for Advanced Mobile Phone Service, the original first-generation (1G) analog cellular phone service. Still used in some parts of North and South America.

See: *Advanced Mobile Phone Service (AMPS)*

analog

Transmission of electrical signals that vary smoothly with time.

See: *analog transmission*

analog modem

A type of modem used for asynchronous transmission of information over Plain Old Telephone Service (POTS) telephone lines.

Overview

The word *modem* stands for modulator/demodulator, which refers to the fact that modems convert digital transmission signals to analog signals and vice versa. An analog modem performs this modulation, but a digital modem does not perform modulation and simply transports digital signals as they are. In effect the phrase "digital modem" is a misnomer because no modulation occurs, and "analog modem" can simply be termed "modem" instead.

To transmit computer data over a telephone channel, a modem modulates the incoming digital signal received from the computer into an analog signal whose frequency lies within the carrying range of analog phone lines (between 300 hertz [Hz] and 3.3 kilohertz [kHz]). To accomplish this, modulation of the digital signal from the computer with an analog carrier signal is performed. The resulting modulated signal is then transmitted into the local loop and carried over the Public Switched Telephone Network (PSTN) until it arrives at its destination station, where a similar modem demodulates the modulated analog signal into a stream of digital data that the remote computer can understand.

However, this basic modulation/demodulation process over POTS lines can transmit data only at speeds of about 1,200 bits per second (bps). To achieve the much higher speeds of today's modems, advanced technologies must be applied, including echo canceling, training, data compression, and special modulation algorithms such as quadrature amplitude modulation (QAM). Using these technologies, modem speeds of 56 kilobits per second (Kbps) are now common.

Bell Laboratories in the 1960s and 1970s originally formulated modem standards, but after the breakup of Bell Telephone, the task of developing modem standards was taken over by the International Telegraph and Telephone Consultative Committee (CCITT), which is now called the International Telecommunication Union (ITU). According to ITU specifications, modem standards are classified by a series of specifications known as the V series.

See Also: *modem, modulation, V-series*

analog-to-digital converter (ADC)

Any device used for changing analog signals into digital transmission.

Overview

An example of analog-to-digital conversion is recording someone singing onto a CD. The pressure waves in the air produced by the vibration of the person's vocal cords are analog in form and continually vary in strength within a certain range of values. The recording equipment samples this continually varying information at discrete time intervals and converts it to digital form.

Analog-to-digital converters (ADCs) are used in industry to convert environmental variables (temperature, pressure, density, speed, and so on) that vary continuously over time to digital information, which can then be analyzed using computer programs. ADCs are used in analog modems to convert digital signals into audio and vice versa.

See Also: *analog, digital*

analog transmission

Transmission of electrical signals that vary smoothly with time.

Overview

An analog signal can take on any value in a specified range of values as shown in the diagram. A simple example is alternating current (AC), which continually varies between about +110 volts and -110 volts in a sine wave fashion 60 times per second. A more complex example of an analog signal is the time-varying electrical voltage generated when a person speaks into a dynamic microphone or telephone. Analog signals such as telephone speech contain a wealth of detail but are not readily accessible to computers unless they are converted to digital form using a device such as an analog-to-digital converter (ADC). Old-fashioned vinyl records store sound information in the form of a continuously varying analog groove, but modern musical CDs store their information in digital form. Some people claim they can tell the difference between an analog and a digital recording and generally agree that the analog recording sounds "warmer."

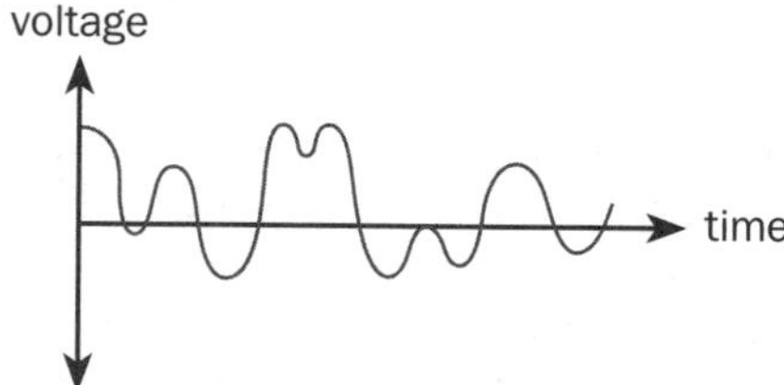

Analog transmission. *Example of an analog transmission.*

Analog signals are usually specified as a continuously varying voltage over time and can be displayed on a device known as an oscilloscope. The maximum voltage displacement of a periodic (repeating) analog signal is called its amplitude, and the shortest distance between crests of a periodic analog wave is called its wavelength.

See Also: *digital transmission*

anchor

In Hypertext Markup Language (HTML), a source or target of a hypertext link.

Overview

Anchors are the key feature of HTML that enables hypertext (linked documents) to be constructed. Without anchor tags, Web pages could not be linked together.

An anchor can be either text or a graphic and is specified using the tag formation <A>…</A>. There are two types of anchor tag. The first type creates a hypertext link that refers to a document. For example, the following HTML element will display the word "contents" as a hyperlink. If the user clicks on the link, the browser will load the contents.htm page specified in this tag:

```
<A HREF="http://www.northwind.microsoft.com/
contents.htm">Contents</A>
```

The second type of anchor tag marks a portion of text as a destination for a hyperlink. You can place the following element at the end of the contents.htm page:

```
<A NAME="bottom">This is the end of the page</A>
```

To load the contents.htm page and jump directly to the bottom of the page, the user needs to click a hyperlink such as this one:

```
<A HREF="http://www.northwind.microsoft.com/
contents.htm#bottom">Contents</A>
```

See Also: *Hypertext Markup Language (HTML)*

announcement

A feature that enables Windows Media Player to receive streaming multimedia information.

Overview

An announcement's function depends on whether the transmission method is multicasting or unicasting. If the transmission method is multicasting, announcements enable Windows Media Player to retrieve the channel file containing channel information. If the transmission method is unicasting, announcements supply the client with information on how to connect to the Windows Media Server.

Announcements, which are used only with Advanced Streaming Format (ASF) transmissions, are text files that have the extension .asx. Once created, an announcement can be distributed to clients by several means: over the Web, through e-mail, or on a network share.

Announcement Manager

A service in Microsoft Windows 98 that automatically runs in the background when you have WebTV for Windows installed on your computer.

Overview

Announcement Manager receives broadcast announcements from TV networks or Web sites that notify your computer about the time and address of the broadcast and which software applications must be running to receive the broadcast. When Announcement Manager receives an announcement, it directs it to the broadcast filters you have configured for your WebTV service. The broadcast filters then determine whether to ignore the broadcast or schedule its reception.

Announcement Manager is part of the Microsoft Broadcast Architecture, a specification for receiving Web information broadcast to your computer through a TV tuner interface.

See Also: *Windows 98*

anonymous access

An authentication scheme in which the user's identity is not verified.

Overview

Anonymous access is one of several authentication protocols supported by Microsoft Internet Information Services (IIS) and is strictly speaking not an authentication scheme at all because the users' credentials are not requested and, if supplied, are ignored. Anonymous access is typically used to allow anonymous users (that is, everyone) to gain access to public content hosted on a Web server. Anonymous access is typically used on low-security public Web sites where the identity of the person visiting the site is not important. By enabling anonymous access to the site, distrusted users from the Internet can access content on the site.

Anonymous access on IIS works by making use of a default anonymous user account called IUSR_machinename. This account is a local user account that iscreated during Setup and is used exclusively to authenticate anonymous users and grant them access to resources on the machine. The IUSR_machinename account requires the Log On Locally system right in order to grant anonymous access to machine resources.

See Also: *authentication protocol*

anonymous user

Any user who attempts to access network resources without providing a username or password.

Overview

Some applications such as Microsoft Internet Information Services (IIS) can be configured to allow anonymous users to access their resources. This allows distrusted users from unsecure networks such as the Internet to access data that ismade available for the public at large.

Access to network resources by anonymous users can be controlled by assigning permissions to a special anonymous user account IUSR_ComputerName. Windows 2000, Windows XP, and Windows .NET Server then provide anonymous users access to resources by impersonating the user utilizing the anonymous user account.

See Also: *anonymous access*

ANSI

Stands for American National Standards Institute, a U.S. standards organization that facilitates and governs the development of standards in many areas, including computing and communication.

See: *American National Standards Institute (ANSI)*

ANSI C/C++

A standard published by the American National Standards Institute (ANSI) for writing C and C++ code.

Overview

Programs written in ANSI C or ANSI C++ are portable to a large number of computing platforms. Most commercial C/C++ programming tools, such as Microsoft Visual C++, contain extensions to ANSI C/C++ that simplify common programming tasks considerably but restrict the portability of the resulting code to different platforms.

You can use Visual C++ to write strict ANSI C/C++ code by following these guidelines:

- Call Win32 application programming interfaces (APIs) directly in your program instead of using the Microsoft Foundation Classes (MFC) libraries.
- Disable the Microsoft extensions to C++ by running Visual C++ using the /Za command-line option.
- Use the isostream and standard template libraries from the ANSI Standard C++ library and the appropriate #include statements in your code.

See Also: *American National Standards Institute (ANSI)*

ANSI character set

An eight-bit character set developed by used by the American National Standards Institute (ANSI).

Overview

The ANSI character set uses 256 characters (numbered 0 through 255). The American Standard Code for Information Exchange (ASCII) character set is a subset of the ANSI character set with characters numbered 32 through 126, each representing a displayable character.

ANSI uses a single byte to represent a character, in contrast to the Unicode standard supported by Microsoft Windows NT, which uses 2 bytes to represent a character. For example, the ANSI character"A" would be represented in hexadecimal notation by the single byte 41h. ANSI's 256-character limit supports only a few international characters, such as accented French and German vowels, but the Unicode's 65,536-character limit supports virtually every alphabet in the world. For example, the Unicode character "A" would be represented in hexadecimal notation by the 2-byte string {41h, 00h}.

The following table shows which Windows environments support ANSI and Unicode for character encoding.

Windows Environments and Character Encoding

ANSI	*Unicode*
16-bit Windows object libraries	32-bit Windows object libraries
Windows 95 and Windows 98 API	Windows NT and Windows 2000 API
	Automation in Windows 95, Windows 98, Windows NT, Windows 2000, Windows XP, and Windows .NET Server

Notes

Some ANSI character codes cannot be displayed by Microsoft Windows applications and are generally displayed as solid blocks in the application interface.

See Also: *American National Standards Institute (ANSI), ASCII*

answer file

A text file that can be used to perform an unattended installation of Microsoft Windows 2000.

Overview

In the answer file you specify in advance the answers to the user prompts that occur during a normal installation. These prompts can include specifications such as what keyboard layout to use, whether the computer should join a domain or belong to a workgroup, what network protocols should be installed, and so on. The answer file is invoked using the /u switch when running the Winnt or Winnt32 setup utility. Answer files can be customized for individual machines by using Uniqueness Database Files (UDFs). The UDFs can be used to specify computer-specific parameters such as the computer name.

A sample answer file Unattend.txt is located in the \I386 folder on the source CD. You can customize this file using Notepad or another text editor to suit your needs.

See Also: *Windows 2000*

antenna

A device used to enhance the transmission and reception of radio signals.

Overview

A full treatment of antenna theory is beyond the scope of this book, and antenna considerations have only become an issue for local area network (LAN) administrators with the recent proliferation of wireless LANs (WLANs), wireless bridges, and wireless cellular data transmission technologies. Just a few issues and developments are considered here.

The first notebook computer to incorporate a built-in factory-installed antenna for wireless networking was the iBook from Apple Computer. The iBook uses the AirPort wireless networking technology, and although the antenna is included, an AirPort add-on card must be purchased to connect the machine to a WLAN. Other vendors such as Dell Computer Corporation have quickly followed Apple's lead in this area. PC board mountable antennae are often flat dielectrically loaded omnidirectional antenna and require no external tuning components.

For a wireless network to be effective, the base station also needs a suitable antenna. The range of antennae available for base stations is large, and the latest ones support multiband operation for the 900-megahertz (MHz) band, 2.4-gigahertz (GHz) Industrial, Scientific, and Medical (ISM) band, and 5-GHz UNI band.

A primary issue regarding antennas for wireless devices is placement. For transmission stations, this means placing antennas as high as possible—on the roof, for example—to ensure the widest possible area of coverage. For end stations, obstacles such as concrete walls and iron girders within buildings can absorb, scatter, and attenuate signals so that practical networking becomes difficult or impossible. To overcome this, more powerful transmissions can be used, but the strength of end-station transmissions are limited for health reasons.

Another issue regards whether unidirectional or omnidirectional antennas are used. For wireless bridges connecting networks in different buildings, unidirectional antennas are used and must be aligned properly with no line-of-sight obstructions. Mobile devices such as laptops, Personal Digital Assistants (PDAs), and cell phones require omnidirectional antennas to function properly, particularly when roaming.

See Also: *wireless networking*

Anycast

A network service for delivering datagrams to any one server belonging to a group of servers on a network.

Overview

Anycast was first proposed in RFC 1546 as a way to direct a network request to the closest (in the network sense of hops) server in a set of mirrored servers for servicing the request. Because fewest hops may not necessarily mean the server that responds best (due to latency, throughput, and host load), other Anycast-related initiatives have arisen in the last few years. These initiatives include Application-Aware Anycast, Global IP-Anycast, Simple Internet Protocol Plus, and others.

AO/DI

Stands for Always On/Dynamic ISDN, a modified form of Integrated Services Digital Network (ISDN) that supports transmission of data over the ISDN control channel (D channel).

See: *Always On/Dynamic ISDN (AO/DI)*

AOL Instant Messenger (AIM)

A popular instant messaging service from America Online (AOL).

Overview

AOL Instant Messenger (AIM) is a free instant messaging service that boasts more than 84 million users worldwide. The service allows users to send messages instantly to other users online, receive alerts and bulletins, have online chat conversations, receive news and other information, share files, and perform other useful activities.

The current version of client software is AIM 4.3, which supports additional features including participating in online games and accessing your buddy list from any computer. AIM is available for various platforms including Microsoft Windows and Windows CE, Mac OS, Linux, and PalmOS. AIM operates using AOL's proprietary AIM Protocol, and AIM competes with other popular Instant Messaging (IM) systems including Microsoft Corporation's MSN Messenger.

For More Information

You can download the current version of AIM from *www.aol.com/aim.*

MSN Messenger can be found at *messenger.msn.com.*

See Also: instant messaging (IM)

AP

Stands for access point, a device connected to a local area network (LAN) that enables remote wireless stations to communicate with the LAN.

See: access point (AP)

Apache

Short for Apache Web server, an open-source Hypertext Transfer Protocol (HTTP) server whose code was developed and is maintained by the Apache Software Foundation.

Overview

Apache started out as a patch for the original National Center for Supercomputing Applications (NCSA) httpd server—hence the new server was "a patchy" server. The NCSA httpd server was stuck at version 1.3 and had some security issues, and so a group of people took the 1.3 code, which was in the public domain, and patched it. The group later rewrote most of the base code from scratch in order to support external modules written in C language.

One of the Apache platform's strengths is its modular design, which consists of a central Apache kernel interacting with various code modules that provide additional functionality. This architecture speeds the development cycle and makes it easy for third-party developers to build custom modules to meet their needs and compile them into the Apache source.

Security is a top priority for administrators who run Web servers, and Apache includes support for a number of advanced security features through various security modules:

- **Access control:** The default security setting for Apache is "deny all," after which selective access can be provided to specific users through the Access.conf file.
- **Authentication:** Apache supports basic authentication using a number of password file formats, starting with /bin/htpasswd. Modules are also available for host-based authentication where access is granted based on Internet Protocol (IP) address and anonymous access using a user's e-mail address as a password.
- **Encryption:** Support for Secure Sockets Layer (SSL) encryption in Apache is provided by freeware packages such as Apache-SSL and mod_ssl, and by commercial packages such as Stronghold from C2Net Software.
- **Logging:** Apache includes support for comprehensive logging of server events. Logs are kept in two files, access_log and error_log.

Apache is one of the most popular Web servers in use, with an estimated more than 6 million Web sites deployed on it. Some market watchers estimate that about 60 percent of all Web servers are running Apache. Apache is widely deployed wherever UNIX is found, including universities and large enterprise networks, and is available for more than a dozen different operating system platforms, including Microsoft Windows.

Notes

The most common vulnerability of Apache servers is running the core process using root privileges. This makes the server vulnerable to what is called a "root exploit," which can allow a malicious remote user to run Common Gateway Interface (CGI) scripts using root privileges. The way to avoid this is to include the following lines in the Httpd.conf configuration file:

```
user  nobody

group nobody
```

For More Information

The Apache Software Foundation can be found at *www.apache.org.*

A good source for timely new and information on the Apache platform is Apache Week (*www.apacheweek.com*).

For information on the Apache conference, see *www.apachecon.org*.

See Also: *open source, UNIX, Web server*

Apache Software Foundation

An open-source community guiding the development of the Apache Web server and other open-source tools and programs.

Overview

The Apache Software Foundation, formerly the Apache Group, is a nonprofit organization that provides legal, organizational, and financial backing toward the development of open-source software projects that use Apache Web server software. Some of the projects the foundation is working on include

- Apache Server
- Apache XML Project-Apache
- Jakarta
- Java-Apache
- mod_perl
- PHP
- Apache Tcl

See Also: *Apache, Apache XML Project, open source*

Apache XML Project

An initiative of the Apache Software Foundation to create open-source tools for developing Extensible Markup Language (XML) business solutions.

Overview

The Apache XML Project is an initiative with three goals:

- Developing tools for creating commercial-class XML-based business solutions that are standards-compliant and follow the open source model.
- Provide helpful feedback to the World Wide Web Consortium (W3C) and other bodies involved in the development of XML standards.
- Provide XML resources for other initiatives of the Apache Software Foundation.

Several commercial companies have contributed technology to this initiative, including Sun Microsystems, IBM, and Lotus Software (formerly Lotus Development Corporation, now part of IBM), and other contributes have come from the Open Source community at large.

Some of the subprojects within this initiative include

- **Cocoon:** XML-based Web publishing using Java.
- **FOP:** Extensible Stylesheet Language (XSL)–formatting objects using Java.
- **Xalan:** XSL Transformation (XSLT) stylesheet processing using Java and C++.
- **Xang:** Dynamic server pages using Java.
- **Xerces:** XML parsing using Java, C++, and Perl.

For More Information

Visit the site of the Apache Software Foundation (*www.apache.org*).

See Also: *Apache Software Foundation, open source*

API

Stands for application programming interface, any collection of programming routines and functions that an application can use to access low-level machine services.

See: *application programming interface (API)*

APIPA

Stands for Automatic Private IP Addressing, a feature of Microsoft Windows 2000, Windows XP, and Windows .NET Server that enables machines to be automatically assigned Internet Protocol (IP) addresses without the use of Dynamic Host Configuration Protocol (DHCP).

See: *Automatic Private IP Addressing (APIPA)*

APM (Advanced Power Management)

Stands for Advanced Power Management, a legacy specification for power management of computer hardware.

See: *Advanced Power Management (APM)*

APM (Application Performance Management)

Stands for Application Performance Management, a set of technologies, business processes, and services for guaranteeing what subscribers experience from service providers.

See: *Application Performance Management (APM)*

APNIC

Stands for Asia Pacific Network Information Center, the counterpart of American Registry for Internet Numbers (ARIN) and the agency responsible for administering the registration and allocation of Internet numbers for the Asia/Pacific region.

See: *Asia Pacific Network Information Center (APNIC)*

APPC

Stands for Advanced Program-to-Program Communications protocol, a set of protocols developed by IBM that enables transactional programs to communicate with each other.

See: *Advanced Program-to-Program Communications (APPC) protocol*

APPC File Transfer Protocol (AFTP)

A protocol that provides file transfer capabilities for the Advanced Program-to-Program Communications (APPC).

Overview

APPC File Transfer Protocol (AFTP) servers are the APPC equivalent of File Transfer Protocol (FTP) servers in the Transmission Control Protocol/Internet Protocol (TCP/IP) world. Microsoft SNA Server can be used to establish AFTP connections to AS/400 or mainframe computers running the APPC applications suite. Users can then utilize standard FTP client software to transfer files between the SNA server and the AS/400 or mainframe host. The optional AFTP service must first be installed on the SNA server. The installation can be configured so that the SNA server performs the function of an FTP-to-AFTP gateway. This will enable standard FTP clients to transfer files to and from the mainframe host.

See Also: *Advanced Program-to-Program Communications (APPC) protocol*

Apple Open Transport

An Apple networking technology for transport-independent networking that ispart of the networking and communication subsystem of the Apple Macintosh operating system.

Overview

Apple Open Transport is designed to make it easy to set up and configure networking on the Macintosh computer and to increase the performance of file, print, and other networking services on a MacOS server. Open Transport provides a consistent interface for configuring network services across supported protocols and a uniform set of application programming interfaces (APIs) for accessing networking and communication services on the Macintosh.

Open Transport enables protocols to be loaded and unloaded on demand, provides a networking naming scheme plus consistent network services over the Transmission Control Protocol/Internet Protocol (TCP/IP) and AppleTalk protocols, and includes support for TCP/IP services such as Dynamic Host Configuration Protocol (DHCP) and Domain Name System (DNS). Open Transport also provides consistent API access to serial communication on the Macintosh, while third-party support is available for Point-to-Point Protocol (PPP), Network Control Protocol over Internetwork Packet Exchange (NCP/IPX), Server Message Block over Transmission Control Protocol (SMB/TCP), NetBIOS, DECnet, LAT, and X.25.

The Open Transport/AppleTalk protocol stack supports both the dynamic self-addressing of traditional AppleTalk clients and newer manually assigned static addressing. The Open Transport/TCP/IP protocol stack supports DHCP, bootstrap protocol (BOOTP), both local hosts files and DNS, Internet Protocol (IP) multicasting, both Ethernet Version 2 and Institute of Electrical and Electronics Engineers (IEEE) 802.3 framing, TCP wildcard source port assignments, Point-to-Point Protocol (PPP) connectivity, IP multihoming, and almost unlimited simultaneous TCP connections (limited only by installed memory and processor power).

Notes

An Apple Macintosh running Open Transport/TCP/IP can function as a DHCP client to a Microsoft Windows NT server running as a DHCP server, but not as a Windows Internet Naming Service (WINS) client.

See Also: *AppleTalk*

AppleShare

The file sharing protocol for AppleTalk networks.

Overview

AppleShare provides the following functions:

- Enables sharing of volumes, folders, and printers
- Provides auditing information on which resources have been accessed
- Supports password-based control of access to shared resources

Notes

By installing Services for Macintosh on a Microsoft Windows 2000 server, the Windows 2000 server can emulate an AppleShare server so that Macintosh clients can access shared resources on the Windows 2000 server.

See Also: *AppleTalk*

AppleShare IP

An Apple networking technology that supports native Transmission Control Protocol/Internet Protocol (TCP/IP) on the Apple Macintosh platform.

Overview

AppleShare IP provides Web, file, print, and e-mail services for departmental and workgroup- level environments. The latest version, AppleShare IP v6.1, features a single integrated administration console for local server management, remote administration using a standard Web browser, IP address filtering, Sherlock searching support, multihosting, Simple Mail Transfer Protocol (SMTP) and point of presence (POP) protocol support, shared Internet Mail Access Protocol (IMAP) folders, Domain Name System (DNS) services, and full compatibility with MacOS 8.5 and higher.

AppleShare IP client software must be installed on Macintosh client machines to enable them to access AppleShare IP services on a server over the network. AppleShare IP supports both Server Message Block (SMB) and File Transfer Protocol (FTP) protocols in addition to AppleShare file sharing, and is compatible with both Macintosh and Microsoft Windows clients.

See Also: *AppleTalk*

applet

A program written using the Java programming language that can be accessed through a Web page and downloaded to the client machine, where it is run within the Web browser window.

Overview

Java applets can be used to add dynamic functionality to static Web pages provided users view these pages with a Java-enabled Web browser.

When an applet is created, its Java statements are compiled into an intermediate pseudo- machine-code language called a bytecode. The bytecode file is stored as a class file on a Web server such as Microsoft Internet Information Services (IIS), and a Web page can reference the class file using an <APPLET> tag. When a Web browser requests the page and encounters the <APPLET> tag, the bytecode in the class file is executed in a Java virtual machine on the browser.

See Also: *Java*

AppleTalk

The original networking protocol for Apple Macintosh networks.

Overview

AppleTalk is a suite of networking protocols that work together to provide file and print sharing services to Macintosh networks. AppleTalk enables users to share folders and printers for access by other network users. AppleTalk is a legacy technology that has been largely replaced by Apple Open Transport, which supports AppleTalk, Transmission Control Protocol/Internet Protocol (TCP/IP), and other popular network protocols.

Architecture

AppleTalk is a workgroup-level networking technology that supports up to 254 network nodes per physical network. AppleTalk can run on top of the legacy LocalTalk data-link protocol, which was built into the Macintosh RS-449/RS-422 serial interface. In the more recent AppleTalk Phase II, the data-link protocols supported include EtherTalk, TokenTalk, and FDDITalk for connectivity with Ethernet, Token Ring, and Fiber Distributed Data Interface (FDDI) networks, respectively.

Addresses of machines on AppleTalk networks are randomly self-assigned when the machine is first attached to the network and then broadcast to ensure they are not already being used. This dynamic addressing feature is based on the AppleTalk Address Resolution Protocol (AARP).

AppleTalk internetworks are logically partitioned into zones whose main function is to make network resources easier for users to access. A *zone* is a logical representation of AppleTalk network nodes that can span multiple physical networks. The mapping between zones and network numbers is maintained by the Zone Information Protocol (ZIP), which creates Zone Information Tables (ZITs) that are stored on AppleTalk routers.

OSI Layer	Protocols			
Application			AppleShare	
Presentation			AppleTalk Filing Protocol (AFP)	
Session	Zone Information Protocol (ZIP)	AppleTalk Session Protocol (ASP)	AppleTalk Data Stream Protocol (ADSP)	Password Authentication Protocol (PAP)
Transport	AppleTalk Echo Protocol (AEP)	Name Binding Protocol (NBP)	AppleTalk Transaction Protocol (ATP)	Routing Table Maintenance Protocol (RTMP)
Network	Datagram Delivery Protocol (DDP)			
Data Link	LocalTalk	EtherTalk	TokenTalk	FDDITalk
Physical	Physical transmission media (coax, twisted-pair, fiber-optic)			

AppleTalk. *The AppleTalk protocol suite.*

appliance

A general term referring to any network-capable or Internet-capable computing device that can be deployed with plug-and-play ease.

Overview

The market for appliances ranges from home users to the largest enterprise. At the small end of the scale are Internet access appliances that allow users to connect home networks to the Internet using dial-up, digital subscriber line (DSL), or cable modem technologies. Many of these Internet access appliances include advanced features such as built-in firewalls, Web-based management consoles, built-in hubs, and so on.

At the larger end are appliances built for large companies and for service providers, for example:

- **Server appliances:** These include Web server appliances running Apache/Linux or IIS/Windows 2000 and file server appliances such as Cobalt's Qube and Compaq NeoServer. Server appliances are typically 1U or 2U rack-mountable devices and can often be set up in minutes or even seconds. These appliance servers fill specific needs for business, and their market is growing rapidly.
- **Storage appliances:** An example here is Novell's Network Attached Storage (NAS), a rack-mountable appliance that provides up to 1 terabyte of storage, supports all major server platforms, and has integrated Novell Directory Services (NDS) eDirectory and ZENworks management applications.

Application Center

One of Microsoft Corporation's new .NET Enterprise Servers, Microsoft Application Center is used for deploying and managing Web applications and Web services.

Overview

Application Center is a platform for deploying and managing high-availability Web applications and Web services. Application Center 2000 is built on the Microsoft Windows 2000 operating system platform and makes managing of clusters of application servers as easy as managing a single server.

Application Center provides simplified application management by allowing administrators to create logical groupings of application components and configuration information. These groupings can be easily managed, regardless of how they are deployed across the cluster, and changes made to one server in a cluster can be automatically applied to other servers. Migration and upgrading of applications can be automated, which simplifies the development cycle as applications are moved from test bed to production phase. Application Center is thus ideal for simplifying the staging and deployment of complex Web-based e-business applications.

Application Center provides built-in support for software scaling to increase the capacity of applications as the business need arises. This is possible through the underlying reliance on clustering technologies in which a group of servers is managed as a single resource, and Application Center simplifies and accelerates the deployment of clusters over traditional clustered server platforms. Application Center also supports load-balancing technologies such as Network Load Balancing (NLB), Component Load Balancing (CLB), and third-party load balancing solutions. With Application Center, your Web applications have no single point-of-failure and consequently high availability and reliability.

Application Center provides the enterprise with mission-critical availability and allows any server in a cluster to be brought down without affecting the integrity or operation of the applications running on the cluster. Application Center includes tools for monitoring cluster health and supports browser-based remote administration. Automated event response allows corrective action to be taken automatically when a component or server fails, without the need for human intervention.

For More Information

You can find out more about Application Center at *www.microsoft.com/applicationcenter.*

See Also: *.NET Enterprise Servers, Web server*

application layer

The top layer (Layer 7) of the Open Systems Interconnection (OSI) reference model for networking.

Overview

The application layer is the layer in which network-aware, user-controlled software is implemented—for example, e-mail, file transfer utilities, and terminal access applications. The application layer represents the window between the user and the network and translates between the user running the application and the presentation layer (Layer 6). In the OSI model the application layer is also responsible for integrating the functionality of different applications together and determining the availability of resources.

Examples of protocols that operate at the application layer include File Transfer Protocol (FTP), Hypertext Transfer Protocol (HTTP), telnet, and similar protocols that can be implemented as utilities the user can interface with.

Notes

Originally the OSI model consisted of two kinds of application layer services with their related protocols:

- **Common Application Service Elements (CASE):** These enable users to initiate or terminate peer (Layer 7 to Layer 7) connections between different machines on the network, enable reliable transfer of information between them, initiate remote operations, and support recovery from failure and rollback steps.
- **Specific Application Service Elements (SASE):** These can include file transfer, message handling, terminal access, and other services that make use of the CASE elements and protocols.

These terms have largely been replaced with the term Application Service Elements (ASE) to describe the elements of the application layer. Note also that in most real-world networking, such as Transmission Control Protocol/Internet Protocol (TCP/IP) networking, these application layer services have no meaning.

See Also: *Open Systems Interconnection (OSI) reference model*

application layer proxy

Any service or server that acts as a proxy for client computer requests at the application's protocols.

Overview

Application layer proxies provide security by hiding internal network addresses from the outside world. An example of an application layer proxy is illustrated in Microsoft Proxy Server. Here the Web Proxy Service is an application layer proxy for the Hypertext Transfer Protocol (HTTP), Secure Hypertext Transfer Protocol (S-HTTP), and File Transfer Protocol (FTP). Microsoft Proxy Server can grant users access to selected application layer protocols and can restrict access to remote Web sites by domain name, Internet Protocol (IP) address, and subnet mask.

Application layer proxies provide more support for the additional capabilities of each protocol than circuit layer proxies do. For example, application layer proxies can support virus scanning. Application layer proxies are also client-neutral and require no special software components or operating system on the client computer to enable the client to communicate with servers on the Internet using the proxy server.

See Also: *proxy server*

application level gateway

A type of firewall that provides application-level control over network traffic.

Overview

Application level gateways examine incoming packets at the application level and use proxies to create secure sessions with hosts on the other side of the firewall. For example, when an external user with a Web browser tries to access the company's internal Web server, the application level gateway runs a proxy application that simulates the internal Web server. A session is established between the remote user and the proxy application, while a separate, independent session is established between the proxy application and the internal Web server. The remote user makes a request to the proxy, the proxy acts as a go-between and obtains the information from the internal web server, and then the proxy returns the result to the remote user.

The advantage of using application level gateways over packet-filtering routers is that although in packet filtering a direct network connection still exists between the remote user and the internal network resource, an application level gateway prevents the remote user from directly accessing the internal network resource. This layer of additional security comes at some cost—namely, that application gateways are generally slower and require a separate proxy application for each internal network service you want to make available through the firewall. These proxy applications are sometimes known as translation agents because they enable an application on one side of the firewall to connect with a similar or complementary application on the other side.

Application gateways are typically used to deny access to the resources of private networks to distrusted users over the Internet. Application level gateways can operate across firewalls or routers using Network Address Translation (NAT), but they must be configured to do so on an application-by-application basis.

See Also: *firewall, network address translation (NAT)*

application log

A Microsoft Windows 2000, Windows XP, and Windows .NET Server log that records events generated by applications running on the system.

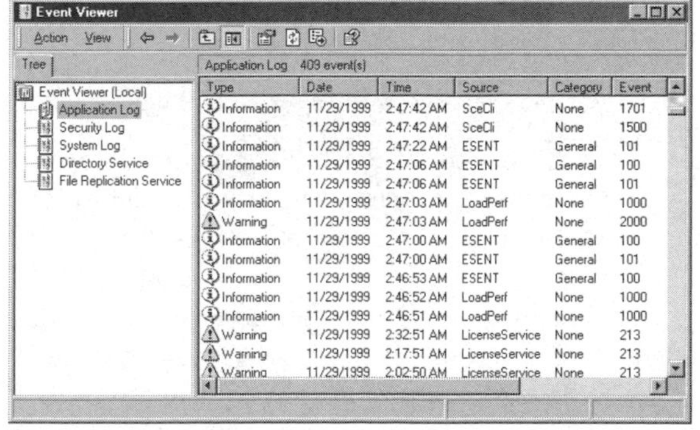

Application log. *Displaying the application log in the Event Viewer console.*

Overview

You can view and manage the application log using Event Viewer, and it can contain three types of events:

- **Error event:** Indicated by a red stop sign and signals a serious condition, such as a failed service
- **Warning event:** Indicated by a yellow warning sign and signals a potentially serious condition, such as low disk space
- **Information event:** Indicated by a blue information sign and signals a noteworthy event, such as a service successfully starting up

Microsoft BackOffice applications typically log events to the application log. Administrators should review the application log regularly to ensure that applications are running properly. The screen capture shows the application log as viewed by the Event Viewer management console for Windows 2000.

See Also: *security log, system log*

Application Performance Management (APM)

A set of technologies, business processes, and services for guaranteeing what subscribers experience from service providers.

Overview

Application Performance Management (APM) carries Service Level Agreements (SLAs) to the next level, providing a model for guaranteeing the end-user experience for customers of application service providers (ASPs). To accomplish this, APM integrates a number of business models and services:

- Traditional help desk services for problem resolution.
- Monitoring of SLAs.
- Network and system management tools working at the application level.
- Professional services to handle serious IT (information technology)–related crises.
- Services for processing management data.
- Support and training services.

A service provider that specializes in APM is sometimes referred to as a management service provider (MSP).

See Also: *application service provider (ASP)*

application programming interface (API)

Any collection of programming routines and functions that an application can use to access low-level machine services.

Overview

When you write applications for a high-level operating system such as Microsoft Windows, you use standard Windows application programming interfaces (APIs) to access standard operating system and networking services and functions. One application can then issue an API call to another application in order to execute that API function. Details of APIs are primarily of interest to developers.

Windows operating systems provide predefined sets of APIs for various purposes, such as Telephony Application Programming Interface (TAPI) for accessing functions related to making voice, data, or fax calls; Messaging Application Programming Interface (MAPI) for messaging functions; and so on.

An example of an API function in Windows NT is NetServerEnum. When a computer on a network issues a net view command to obtain the list of resources or computers that can be accessed using Network Neighborhood or Windows Explorer, the client computer issues a NetServerEnum API call to the Computer Browser service.

Microsoft Windows platforms include two basic sets of APIs:

- **Win16:** These 16-bit APIs were used by Windows 3.1.
- **Win32:** These 32-bit APIs are used on Windows 95, Windows 98, Windows Millennium Edition (Me), Windows NT, Windows 2000, Windows XP, and Windows .NET Server.

Notes

API also represents any set of calling conventions in a programming language that specifies how such a service is invoked through an application. Application programming interfaces (APIs) let C and assembly language routines interact with services and programming tools.

application service provider (ASP)

A general term for a company that offers software services to business customers across the Internet, particularly services involving outsourcing of Web and e-business applications.

Overview

A simple way of understanding the application service provider (ASP) model is to consider an ASP to be a company that hosts software applications for client companies and delivers them using the Internet for a monthly service fee. These applications are typically Web-based applications accessed by clients through a simple Web browser, although other delivery methods may be used, including Windows 2000 Terminal Services and Citrix MetaFrame. Once a client leases an application, the ASP is then responsible for day-to-day administration of the application and for maintenance and upgrades. ASPs may also be responsible for storing client data as well, although companies performing this service are more commonly called Storage Service Providers (SSPs). In contrast with simple Web hosting companies that offer their clients access to database applications and scripting tools but little else, ASPs also host the client's business logic and data at their remote data centers and provide a full range of supporting services to the client.

ASPs generally target one of two different market areas:

- **Vertical-market ASPs:** These target small to medium-sized business (the SMB, or small-to-medium business, segment of the market) by offering them packaged services such as Internet/Intranet hosting, e-mail and workflow applications, and scaled-down Customer Relations Management (CRM) and Enterprise Resource Planning (ERP) applications. Some small companies might not have the resources even to hire a single full-time IT (information technology) person, yet by using an ASP, they can quickly and easily obtain and use the necessary Line-Of-Business (LOB) applications they need to compete in the Internet economy in a cost-effective fashion. ASPs targeting this market tend to offer one-size-fits-all applications based on business logic templates that offer few

customization options. This approach is taken to reduce costs for the ASP and make servicing this market level profitable.

- **Horizontal-market ASPs:** These target enterprise-level customers and offer similar applications but with more customization to fit these customers' needs.

When the ASP craze took off in 1999, most ASPs were dot-com startups targeting the small to mid-sized business market, which was itself growing rapidly due to the dot-com revolution then underway. The ASP revolution was driven largely by the increasing shortage of IT professionals in the marketplace which left hundreds of thousands of IT positions unfilled, the rapid proliferation of new IT technologies based on the Internet, and by the proliferation of dot-com startups that needed to deploy business applications and to deploy them fast in the highly competitive Internet economy of the late 20th century. But with the dot-com crash of 2001 many of the ASPs failed as their market space dried up, and some survivors instead began targeting large enterprises by offering the application customization these businesses required. The attraction of these enterprise-level customers for ASPs is their long-term stability and broad capital base, but such clients tend to be more conservative in their outlook and more cautious about embracing new service models. Meanwhile, large software companies such as Microsoft Corporation and Oracle Corporation began to reposition themselves as service providers instead of software vendors. With their proven track record and large resources, many analysts expect these large companies to dominate the ASP business in a few years, with smaller companies focusing on niche areas where their services can be most effectively marketed. Furthermore, companies such as Microsoft and Oracle are developing a next generation of Web-enabled software that can be easily deployed by new ASP startups without the extensive customization required by the earlier generation of ASP applications. A good example is Microsoft Exchange 2000, which is an ASP-ready platform for providing Web-based messaging and collaborative applications.

When the ASP market was just emerging, the major attraction for customers was saving money. As the market began to mature, other issues became important for customers to consider when shopping for an ASP:

- **Security:** In the beginning, many ASPs failed to address security concerns adequately. This has changed considerably, and the current generation of ASPs offers a full range of authentication and public-key infrastructure (PKI) services, virtual private networks (VPNs), firewall services, virus protection services, and intrusion detection services. Make sure the ASP you select can provide the level of security your company needs for its data.
- **Availability:** Make sure you negotiate a suitable service-level agreement (SLA) with your ASP to ensure that should their services be interrupted or terminated unexpectedly your business will still be able to function. If some of your staff will need to access ASP applications remotely using mobile clients through a VPN, make sure your SLA has a connectivity clause as well.
- **Performance:** Web-based applications mean high-bandwidth requirements for proper performance, both at the client end (usually T-1 or higher connections) and at the ASP's data center. Look for ASPs that colocate their servers at major Internet service providers (ISPs) for best performance and that have multiple redundant connections to the Internet with sufficient bandwidth to support the number of customers they service.
- **Track record:** With many of the first generation ASP startups having failed, companies are developing a "once-bitten, twice-shy" attitude towards outsourcing mission-critical business applications to ASPs. Talk to some of the ASPs larger clients and ask to see their financials to ensure their long-term viability before committing to using their services. When they start up, ASPs typically invest huge amounts of money in data centers, and they need to recover this investment quickly in order to survive. Some tier-1 Internet infrastructure providers offer ASP-level services, and these do not have as much of a capital risk associated with data center buildout as does a startup ASP.

Architecture

The data center is the heart of an ASP. Data centers are often colocated at ISP Points of Presence (POPs) to provide optimal high-speed connections to the backbone of the Internet. Data centers typically contain the following:

- File servers and database servers for storing structured data.
- Directory servers, Domain Name System (DNS) servers, and authentication servers for managing domains.
- Clustered or load-balanced Web servers for hosting Web applications in a redundant fashion.
- Terminal servers for supporting remote administration by customers.
- Storage area networks (SANs) and network attached storage (NAS) for storing data.
- Backup servers for archiving company data.

Advantages and Disadvantages

The advantages for client companies using ASPs are numerous and compelling to the management departments of most companies:

- They do not need to purchase the software themselves, which saves considerably on up-front costs.
- They do not need to hire additional IT staff to deploy and manage the new applications, which means considerable savings on labor costs.
- They can get new LOB applications up and running in a few days or weeks by relying on the expertise and infrastructure of the ASPs they are leasing these applications from.

The disadvantages of using ASPs are also important to consider when you are looking to outsource your LOB applications:

- You lose direct control over your company's software infrastructure and sometimes your data. This may be an issue with companies for which security is a strong concern.
- Many ASPs are new startups that may be acquired in the near future by larger companies or may fail if managed poorly. When your ASP fails, you might be left hanging with no software infrastructure to support your company's operations.

Marketplace

Some of the larger independent ASPs that have established themselves in the marketplace recently include the following:

- USinternetworking (*www.usi.com*)
- Corio (*www.corio.com*)
- Interliant (*www.interliant.com*)

Prospects

Although some industry watchers are predicting that the shakeout in the fledgling ASP industry will continue until only a few major players remain, the ASP model for outsourcing IT services has undeniably changed the IT landscape forever, as companies seek for cost-effective ways to economize on software purchasing by leasing LOB applications instead of purchasing them or developing them in-house.

One sector of the IT economy hit hard by the ASP revolution are the old-guard Independent Software Vendors (ISVs) that have spent years building and enhancing their line of client/server business applications. The Enterprise Resource Planning (ERP) industry has been one of the hardest hit, and established ERP vendors have had to move quickly to Web-enable their products and offer them as services in order to compete with upstart ASPs offering similar services. Some examples of ERP vendors who have repositioned themselves as ASPs include the following:

- SAP, with its SAP Hosting services
- PeopleSoft, with its eCenter
- Oracle, with its Oracle Business Online

Although the first two years of the new millennium have seen the demise of many ASP startups, industry analysts still predict strong growth in the ASP sector. The sector had a total worldwide market value of $300 million in 1999 and some analysts predict this could

grow to as much as $25 billion by 2004. Much of the success or failure of this growth depends on broadband Internet access becoming cheap and ubiquitous at all business levels.

Nevertheless, because things change so fast in the new Internet economy, it is hard to know whether to trust long-term predictions such as these. After all, the ASP market went from infancy to maturity in about a year, so five years seems like a long time to predict its future growth and evolution!

Notes

Other terms used by different vendors to describe the ASP model include hosted applications, e-services, and "software as a service."

For More Information

You can find an ASP to meet your company's needs using the ASP portals WebHarbor (*www.webharbor.com*) and ASPScope (*www.aspscope.com*).

For the latest news on the ASP industry, see ASPNews (*www.aspnews.com*) and ASPPlanet (*www.aspplanet.com*).

An established source of independent information for the ASP community is ASPI, the ASP Industry Consortium (*www.aspindustry.org*). This consortium has taken on the role of policing the rapidly growing ASP market, whose companies range from responsible to vendors of snake oil. ASPI has defined a series of best practices that new ASPs should follow as guidelines for responsible success.

A notable company that provides a meta-infrastructure that enables new ASPs to grow and flourish is Loudcloud (*www.loudcloud.com*), a brainchild of Marc Andreesen of Netscape fame.

See Also: *xSP*

APPN

Stands for Advanced Peer-to-Peer Networking, a protocol developed by IBM as the second generation of Systems Network Architecture (SNA).

See: *Advanced Peer-to-Peer Networking (APPN)*

archive attribute

An attribute of files and folders that isused for managing backups.

Overview

When an archive bit is marked or set for a file by a backup program, it indicates that the file or folder has been backed up. Then, when the backup program is run again, if the archive bit is still set, the file is not backed up because it has not been modified. If the file is modified in the interim, the archive attribute is cleared, indicating that the file needs to be backed up again.

In Microsoft Windows you can also manually set or clear the archive attribute for a file by opening the file's property sheet.

See Also: *backup*

archiving

The process of long-term storage of important data for security and recovery reasons.

Overview

Archived data is usually stored in a compressed format because it is not required frequently. Some of the files that a Microsoft Windows 2000 administrator might consider archiving regularly include

- Event log files for the system, security, and application logs
- Performance monitor files for monitoring trends in memory, disk, processor, and network usage over time
- Log files for applications such as Microsoft Internet Information Services (IIS)

Notes

When you archive event log files, you can save these files in log file format, text file format, or comma-delimited text file format. An event's actual binary data is saved only if you archive it in event log format, but saving the information in a comma-delimited text file format allows you to import these logs into a spreadsheet program to analyze trends.

See Also: *backup, security*

ARCNET

Stands for Attached Resource Computer Network, an early local area network (LAN) architecture.

Overview

ARCNET was developed in 1976 by Datapoint Corporation and became an American National Standards Institute (ANSI) standard in 1982. ARCNET predates Ethernet by several years and can be implemented using a variety of media including RG/62 93-ohm coaxial cabling, RS-485 unshielded twisted-pair cabling, or fiber-optic cabling. ARCNET is a baseband networking technology that is similar to standards for token-passing bus networks running over broadband cabling. ARCNET uses a token-passing bus architecture with nodes forming a logical ring but a physical bus or star pattern. The core of an ARCNET network is a device called an active hub. Each of these hubs can support up to four connected devices. Multiple active hubs can then be interconnected using coaxial cable to support a maximum of 255 stations.

Classic ARCNET carries data at a rate of 2.5 megabits per second (Mbps). On coaxial cable, ARCNET cable runs can be up to 2000 feet (600 meters), but unshielded twisted pair supports distances of 400 feet (120 meters) and fiber-optic cabling distances of 8000 feet (2440 meters). A newer implementation called ARCNET Plus operates at a data rate of 20 Mbps and can support a maximum of 2047 nodes.

Notes

ARCNET is a legacy LAN technology occasionally found in some older networks.

Microsoft Windows 95, Windows 98, and Windows NT all support ARCNET. Sometimes a computer running Windows NT on an ARCNET network will have difficulty communicating with computers running Windows 95 and Windows 98 on the same network. This is because Windows NT uses Raw ARCNET and Windows 95 and Windows 98 use Encapsulated ARCNET. The workaround solution is to install the 16-bit Transmission Control Protocol/Internet Protocol (TCP/IP) stack with Novell Open Data-link Interface (ODI) drivers on the machines running Windows 95 and Windows 98.

ARC path

Stands for Advanced Reduced Instruction Set Computing (RISC) path, a syntax for naming partitions.

Overview

ARC paths are used in the Boot.ini file of Microsoft Windows 2000, Windows XP, and Windows .NET Server. The ARC path specifies the location of the partition that contains the Windows 2000 operating system files. In other words, the ARC path locates the system partition on the machine.

A typical ARC path on a Windows 2000 system might be the following:

```
multi(0)disk(0)rdisk(0)partition(1)\
WINNT="Microsoft Windows 2000 Server"/fastdetect
```

In the above statement:

- Multi(0) indicates that the system is using Integrated Device Electronics (IDE), Enhanced Small Device Interface (ESDI), or Small Computer System Interface (SCSI) drives and that it relies on the computer basic input/output system (BIOS) to load system files using INT 13 BIOS calls. The number in parentheses here should always be 0.
- Disk(0) is always zero when multi() is used; otherwise it refers to the physical disk when scsi() is used instead of multi(). Multi() means that Windows 2000 must use the system BIOS to load system files, and scsi() means that a SCSI device driver must be loaded to access the boot partition.
- Rdisk(0) indicates that the ordinal number for the system disk is 0. This value is usually between 0 and 3.
- Partition(2) indicates the number of the partition where the system files are located.

ARIN

Stands for American Registry for Internet Numbers, a nonprofit organization that administers the registration and allocation of numbers relating to the operation of the Internet in North and South America.

See: *American Registry for Internet Numbers (ARIN)*

ARP

Stands for Address Resolution Protocol, the Transmission Control Protocol/Internet Protocol (TCP/IP) network layer protocol responsible for resolving IP addresses into MAC addresses.

See: *Address Resolution Protocol (ARP)*

ARPANET

Stands for Advanced Research Projects Agency Network, a U.S. Department of Defense project begun in 1969 that was designed to provide high-speed network communication links between supercomputers located at different sites around the country.

Overview

ARPANET was a test bed for the development of the Transmission Control Protocol/Internet Protocol (TCP/IP) protocol suite. The first node on the ARPANET was established in 1969 at UCLA. Soon afterward, more nodes were created at other institutions, including Stanford University and BBN Technologies. The first Request for Comments (RFC) was proposed in the same year by Steve Croker and was entitled "Host Software."

By 1971, ARPANET had grown to over 20 hosts, including MIT, NASA, and the RAND Corporation. The first international nodes were established two years later in Norway and England. In 1983, Military Network (MILNET) was split off from ARPANET, and TCP/IP officially became the standard protocol for ARPANET, at which time ARPANET started to become widely known as the Internet. ARPANET continued to evolve until NSFNET was established in 1986.

ARPANET was finally shut down in 1989.

For More Information

Read about the history of ARPANET at *www.securenet.net/members/shartley/history/arpanet.htm.*

See Also: *Internet*

Arp command

A Transmission Control Protocol/Internet Protocol (TCP/IP) utility for viewing and modifying the local Address Resolution Protocol (ARP) cache, which contains recently resolved MAC addresses of Internet Protocol (IP) hosts on the network.

Overview

When one host on a TCP/IP network wants to communicate with a second host, the first host begins by using the ARP to resolve the IP address of the second host into its associated MAC address. The MAC address is needed for communication to take place over the network.

Typing arp -a displays the MAC addresses of recently resolved IP addresses. A sample display could be

```
Interface: 172.16.8.50
Internet Address     Physical Address    Type
172.16.8.25          00-20-af-b4-a1-4e   dynamic
172.16.8.200         00-40-95-d1-29-6c   static
```

One of these entries is static, meaning the Internet Protocol–to-MAC address mapping has been manually added to the ARP cache using arp –s.

See Also: *Transmission Control Protocol/Internet Protocol (TCP/IP)*

AS

Stands for autonomous system, a group of Internet Protocol (IP) networks administered under a single administrative (routing) policy.

See: *autonomous system (AS)*

AS/400

Stands for Application System/400, a midrange IBM server computing platform for business computing.

Overview

IBM's AS/400 platform is a 64-bit Reduced Instruction Set Computing (RISC) system available in a variety of configurations for different business needs. Until recently seen as a legacy platform similar to mainframes, AS/400 has been revamped in the last few years and is now one of the leading Web application and e-business platforms available for an enterprise.

AS/400 uses the OS/400 operating system but includes support for UNIX through the Portable Application

Solution Environment (PASE). Systems Network Architecture (SNA) support is also available for providing connectivity with IBM mainframe computing environments.

Some of the popular configurations in which AS/400 is offered include

- **AS/400e Model 250:** An entry-level single-processor machine with no support for logical partitioning. Suitable for running packaged Web applications for small businesses.
- **AS/400e Model 820:** A mid-tier four-way symmetric multiprocessing (SMP) server supporting up to 16 gigabytes (GB) of RAM and 4 terabytes of storage.
- **AS/400e Model 840:** Top-of-the-line enterprise-level server for high-transaction, high-volume e-business, supply chain and Enterprise Resource Planning (ERP) applications, supporting up to 24-way SMP, 96 GB of RAM, and up to 18.9 terabytes of storage.

Notes

The newest offerings in IBM's AS/400 line incorporate IBM's new high-performance copper-wired chips.

For More Information

You can find IBM's AS/400 home page at *www-1.ibm.com/servers/eserver/iseries.*

ASCII

Stands for American Standard Code for Information Interchange, a widely accepted system for coding U.S. English text using numeric values.

Overview

The purpose of ASCII is to allow human-readable documents to be stored and processed as binary information by computers. ASCII assigns a unique numeric valuc to each lowercase and uppercase alphabet letter, number, punctuation mark, and to certain other characters. For example, the capital letter"A" has the ASCII code 65 and a blank space has the code 32.

ASCII is a 7-bit character set that isthe same as the first 128 characters (numbers 0 to 127) of the American National Standards Institute (ANSI) character set. The following table shows the various characters in the ASCII character set. The first 32 characters are non-printing control characters that can be executed from the keyboard by using the Control key combined with other keys.

The ASCII Character Set

Char	*Dec*	*Oct*	*Hex*	*Control Key Combination*	*Description*
NUL	0	0	0	^@	Null character
SOH	1	1	1	^A	Start of heading
STX	2	2	2	^B	Start of text
ETX	3	3	3	^C	End of text
EOT	4	4	4	^D	End of transmission
ENQ	5	5	5	^E	Enquiry
ACK	6	6	6	^F	Acknowledge
BEL	7	7	7	^G	Bell
BS	8	10	8	^H	Backspace
HT	9	11	9	^I	Horizontal tab
LF	10	12	a	^J	Line feed
VT	11	13	b	^K	Vertical tab
FF	12	14	c	^L	Form feed
CR	13	15	d	^M	Carriage return
SO	14	16	e	^N	Shift out
SI	15	17	f	^O	Shift in
DLE	16	20	10	^P	Data link escape
DC1	17	21	11	^Q	Device control 1 (XON)
DC2	18	22	12	^R	Device control 2
DC3	19	23	13	^S	Device control 3 (XOFF)
DC4	20	24	14	^T	Device control 4
NAK	21	25	15	^U	Negative acknowledge
SYN	22	26	16	^V	Synchronous idle
ETB	23	27	17	^W	End transmission block
CAN	24	30	17	^X	Cancel line
EM	25	31	19	^Y	End of medium
SUB	26	32	1a	^Z	Substitute
ESC	27	33	1b	^[	Escape

(continued)

The ASCII Character Set *continued*

Char	Dec	Oct	Hex	Control Key Combination	Description
FS	28	34	1c	^\	File separator
GS	29	35	1d	^]	Group separator
RS	30	36	1e	^^	Record separator
US	31	37	1f	^_	Unit separator
SP	32	40	20		Space
!	33	41	21		Exclamation mark
"	34	42	22		Quotation mark
#	35	43	23		Cross hatch
$	36	44	24		Dollar sign
%	37	45	25		Percent sign
&	38	46	26		Ampersand
‘	39	47	27		Apostrophe
(	40	50	28		Opening parenthesis
)	41	51	29		Closing parenthesis
*	42	52	2a		Asterisk
+	43	53	2b		Plus
,	44	54	2c		Comma
-	45	55	2d		Hyphen
.	46	56	2e		Period
/	47	57	2f		Forward slash
0	48	60	30		Zero
1	49	61	31		One
2	50	62	32		Two
3	51	63	33		Three
4	52	64	34		Four
5	53	65	35		Five
6	54	66	36		Six
7	55	67	37		Seven
8	56	70	38		Eight
9	57	71	39		Nine
:	58	72	3a		Colon
;	59	73	3b		Semicolon
<	60	74	3c		Less than sign
=	61	75	3d		Equals sign
>	62	76	3e		Greater than sign
?	63	77	3f		Question mark
@	64	100	40		At sign

(continued)

The ASCII Character Set *continued*

Char	Dec	Oct	Hex	Control Key Combination	Description
A	65	101	41		Uppercase A
B	66	102	42		Uppercase B
C	67	103	43		Uppercase C
D	68	104	44		Uppercase D
E	69	105	45		Uppercase E
F	70	106	46		Uppercase F
G	71	107	47		Uppercase G
H	72	110	48		Uppercase H
I	73	111	49		Uppercase I
J	74	112	4a		Uppercase J
K	75	113	4b		Uppercase K
L	76	114	4c		Uppercase L
M	77	115	4d		Uppercase M
N	78	116	4e		Uppercase N
O	79	117	4f		Uppercase O
P	80	120	50		Uppercase P
Q	81	121	51		Uppercase Q
R	82	122	52		Uppercase R
S	83	123	53		Uppercase S
T	84	124	54		Uppercase T
U	85	125	55		Uppercase U
V	86	126	56		Uppercase V
W	87	127	57		Uppercase W
X	88	130	58		Uppercase X
Y	89	131	59		Uppercase Y
Z	90	132	5a		Uppercase Z
[	91	133	5b		Opening square bracket
\	92	134	5c		Backslash
]	93	135	5d		Closing square bracket
^	94	136	5e		Caret
_	95	137	5f		Underscore
‘	96	140	60		Opening single quote
a	97	141	61		Lowercase a
b	98	142	62		Lowercase b
c	99	143	63		Lowercase c
d	100	144	64		Lowercase d
e	101	145	65		Lowercase e
f	102	146	66		Lowercase f
g	103	147	67		Lowercase g
h	104	150	68		Lowercase h

(continued)

The ASCII Character Set *continued*

Char	Dec	Oct	Hex	Control Key Combination	Description
i	105	151	69		Lowercase i
j	106	152	6a		Lowercase j
k	107	153	6b		Lowercase k
l	108	154	6c		Lowercase l
m	109	155	6d		Lowercase m
n	110	156	6e		Lowercase n
o	111	157	6f		Lowercase o
p	112	160	70		Lowercase p
q	113	161	71		Lowercase q
r	114	162	72		Lowercase r
s	115	163	73		Lowercase s
t	116	164	74		Lowercase t
u	117	165	75		Lowercase u
v	118	166	76		Lowercase v
w	119	167	77		Lowercase w
x	120	170	78		Lowercase x
y	121	171	79		Lowercase y
z	122	172	7a		Lowercase z
{	123	173	7b		Opening curly brace
|	124	174	7c		Vertical line (pipe)
}	125	175	7d		Closing curly brace
~	126	176	7e		Tilde
DEL	127	177	7f		Delete

Notes

When you download files using File Transfer Protocol (FTP), you can choose whether to transfer the files as binary files or text files (ASCII files). Use only the ASCII file setting when downloading plain text files; otherwise, files will not be correctly transferred.

Some people create e-mail signatures for themselves using ASCII text characters, a practice called ASCII art. If you have the time and want to become an expert at this, read thc FAQs (frequently asked questions) on the Web at *non.com/news.answers/ascii-art-faq.html.*

For More Information

There is an online ASCII table at *www.asciitable.com.*

See Also: *Unicode*

ASCII file

A file that contains unformatted American Standard Code for Information Interchange (ASCII) text.

Overview

An ASCII (text) file contains only characters, numbers, punctuation, tabs, and carriage return characters. You can create and edit an ASCII file using Microsoft Notepad. If you save it with the extension .txt, it is usually referred to as a text file, but you can save it with other extensions such as .bat or .cmd for batch files and .ini for initialization files.

Uses

ASCII files are often used for logon scripts and other batch files. Another common use is storing configuration information for operating systems and applications. Microsoft Windows 3.1 platforms used ASCII files for storing system and software configuration settings. These configuration files have the extension .ini and are referred to as INI (initialization) files. More recent Windows operating systems save this information in the registry. Most versions of the UNIX operating system still store their configuration settings in ASCII files.

Because ASCII files contain unformatted text, they can be read and understood by any platform and are useful for sharing information between platforms and between applications. Shared information is often saved in a comma-delimited text file, or .csv file, with the fields separated by commas. Microsoft Exchange Server can export mailbox properties and other information in .csv files, which can then be imported into spreadsheet programs such as Microsoft Excel for manipulation and analysis.

See Also: *ASCII*

ASF

Stands for Advanced Streaming Format, a method of streaming data supported by Windows Media Player.

See: *Advanced Streaming Format (ASF)*

Asia Pacific Network Information Center (APNIC)

A counterpart of the American Registry for Internet Numbers (ARIN), this is the agency responsible for administering the registration and allocation of Internet numbers for the Asia/Pacific region.

Overview

The Asia Pacific Network Information Center (APNIC) is one of the three Regional Internet Registries (RIRs) that provide Internet numbers allocation and registration services to support the operation of the global Internet. These Internet numbers include IPv4 and IPv6 addresses, autonomous system (AS) numbers, and reverse Domain Name System (DNS) delegations. APNIC is responsible for allocation of these numbers for the Asia Pacific region, which comprises 62 different economies.

APNIC is a nonprofit, membership-based organization whose members include National Internet Registries, Internet Service Providers (ISPs), and similar bodies. Membership in APNIC is fee-based.

For More Information

Visit APNIC at *www.apnic.org.*

See Also: *American Registry for Internet Numbers (ARIN)*

ASN

Stands for autonomous system number, a unique number used to identify an autonomous system (AS), that is, a network that can exchange exterior routing information with neighboring networks.

See: *autonomous system number (ASN)*

ASN.1

Stands for Abstract Syntax Notation One, a standard from the International Standards Organization (ISO) that provides a mechanism for encoding human-readable symbols into condensed binary form.

See: *Abstract Syntax Notation One (ASN.1)*

ASP (Active Server Pages)

Stands for Active Server Pages, an open, compile-free application environment for developing Web applications using Microsoft Internet Information Server (IIS) version 3 and later.

See Also: *Active Server Pages (ASP)*

ASP (application service provider)

Stands for application service provider, a company that offers software services to business customers across the Internet, particularly services involving outsourcing of Web and e-business applications.

See Also: *application service provider (ASP)*

ASP.NET

The evolution of Microsoft Corporation's Active Server Pages (ASP) technology for the new .NET platform.

Overview

ASP.NET is an advanced platform for developing Web applications, Web Services, and Web Forms under the Microsoft .NET platform. ASP.NET solutions can be developed using Microsoft Visual Studio .NET and other tools, and ASP.NET supports application authoring in C#, Visual Basic .NET, and other programming languages.

ASP.NET is Microsoft's successor to ASP and ASP+ (Active Server Pages Plus) and is to a large degree backward-compatible with the syntax of these earlier platforms. Unlike ASP and ASP+, however, ASP.NET is a compiled platform rather than an interpreted one, which offers better run-time performance. ASP.NET is also easily factorable so that developers can remove modules that are not required for a particular application, making applications more code-efficient and giving them a smaller footprint.

ASP.NET provides two levels of programming models:

- **Low-level:** ASP.NET provides a programming model similar to Internet Server Application

Programming Interface (ISAPI) but easier to use for rapid development.

- **High-level:** ASP.NET enables the easy building of Web Forms, a high-level programming model for building Web applications.

ASP.NET also supports a number of different authentication schemes including Basic, authentication, Digest authentication, NT Lan Manager (NTLM) authentication, custom cookie-based authentication, and Microsoft Passport authentication.

For More Information

Find out more about ASP.NET at *msdn.microsoft.com/net/aspnet.*

See Also: *Active Server Pages (ASP), .NET platform*

ASR

Stands for Automatic System Recovery, a feature of Microsoft Windows 2000, Windows XP, and Windows .NET Server that allows you to restore your system in the event of hard disk failure or corruption of system files.

See: *Automatic System Recovery (ASR)*

Association for Computing Machinery (ACM)

The oldest and largest educational and scientific computing society in the world.

Overview

The Association for Computing Machinery (ACM) provides a forum for the exchange of information, ideas, and discoveries relating to many aspects of computing. The ACM has a worldwide membership of 80,000 computer professionals representing a wide variety of interests. The ACM sponsors a number of special interest groups (SIGs) that bring together ACM members with shared interests. These SIGs publish technical newsletters, host conferences, and help develop standards.

One SIG of interest to networking professionals is the ACM Special Interest Group on Data Communication (SIGCOMM), which provides a forum for data communication professionals. SIGCOMM focuses on standards for network protocols and architectures. SIGCOMM publishes the ACM/IEEE Transactions on Networking Journal, sponsors conferences, and publishes a quarterly newsletter called the Computer Communication Review (CCR) in conjunction with the Institute of Electrical and Electronics Engineers (IEEE).

For More Information

Find out about the ACM at *www.acm.org* and the SIGCOMM at *www.acm.org/sigcomm.*

Asymmetric Digital Subscriber Line (ADSL)

A form of Digital Subscriber Line (DSL) technology that provides subscribers with high-speed voice and data services over twisted-pair copper phone lines.

Overview

Asymmetric Digital Subscriber Line (ADSL) was developed by Bellcore in 1989 as a means of transmitting digital information over ordinary twisted-pair Plain Old Telephone Service (POTS) telephone lines to subscribers at speeds faster than 1 megabit per second (Mbps). The original vision of ADSL was to provide residential subscribers with high-quality digital multimedia content, particularly Moving Pictures Experts Group (MPEG) movies through Video On Demand (VOD) services. This was intended to allow phone companies to compete with the emerging cable television market for delivering video to residential areas. This goal has since faded, and now the main push for deploying ADSL is residential broadband Internet access.

ADSL specifies how to implement high-speed, full-duplex transmission over the existing twisted-pair copper cabling of POTS. ADSL can be used to simultaneously transmit voice and data over a single telephone line and can be used to provide high-speed Internet access for both homes and businesses. Even should the data link to the Internet go down, POTS voice service would still be available using ADSL.

The *asymmetric* in ADSL refers to the fact that the upstream and downstream transmission rates in ADSL are not equal. Over best-quality copper phone lines, ADSL can achieve upstream speeds of up to 1.5 Mbps and downstream speeds of up to 9 Mbps, usually in a 10:1 ratio. This asymmetry makes ADSL ideal for providing high-speed Internet access to homes and businesses where fast download speeds are more important than upload speeds.

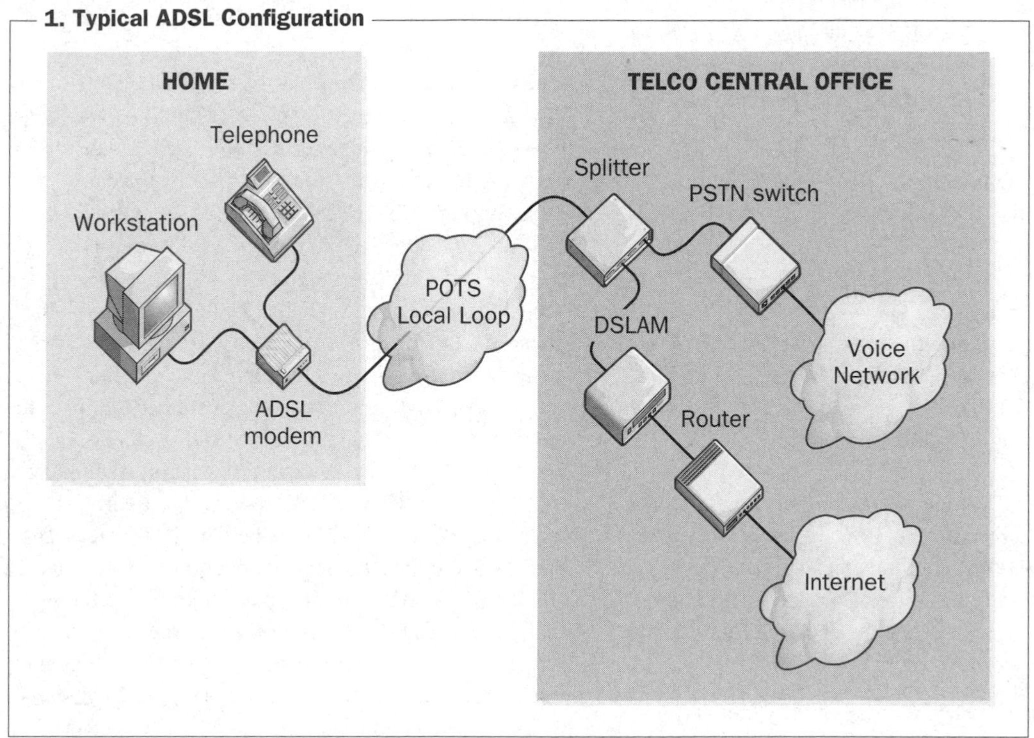

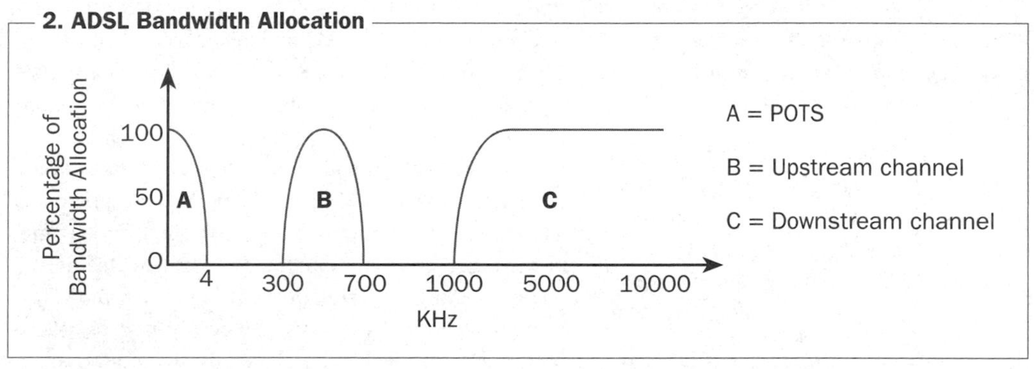

Asymmetric Digital Subscriber Line (ADSL). *Implementing ADSL.*

Asymmetric Digital Subscriber Line (ADSL)

Uses

ADSL has many advantages over standard analog modem access to the Internet, including much higher data rates, instant-on connection, simultaneous transmission of voice and data over a single phone line, and greater security. The negative side of ADSL is the higher equipment cost and the fact that customers must be located within 18,000 feet (5500 meters) of the carrier's CO for ADSL to work. ADSL Internet services typically cost between $40 and $100 per month, depending on the carrier and the area being serviced.

Besides providing residential and business Internet access, ADSL also has other uses, including the following:

- Connectivity with branch offices.
- B2B secure communications (using Point-to-Point Tunneling Protocol [PPTP] or Layer 2 Tunneling Protocol [L2TP]).
- Telecommuting.

An external ADSL modem with support for Network Address Translation (NAT) allows a single modem to connect a network of machines to the Internet using only one carrier-granted Internet Protocol (IP) address. Some ADSL appliances include a built-in Ethernet hub to make this process simpler.

Cable modem technologies are currently competing with ADSL in the residential broadband Internet access, but ADSL offers greater security than cable modems and provides guaranteed bandwidth that shared-network cable modems cannot currently provide.

Implementation

The great advantage of ADSL as a high-speed access service is the ubiquity of the existing twisted-pair POTS wiring system. ADSL providers do not have to build a delivery infrastructure because the wires are already there; they just have to install the switches and modems to make it work.

ADSL uses frequency-division multiplexing (FDM) to separate voice and data into three separate communications channels:

- A baseband voice channel
- An upstream data channel
- A downstream data channel

The range of frequencies used for each channel vary depending on the carrier's particular implementation. Each channel occupies a different portion of the frequency spectrum, as shown in the figure, which illustrates a possible implementation of ADSL. The baseband voice channel is split off from the data channels to guarantee phone services in case the data channel fails. Data transmission rates in the upstream direction range from 128 kilobits per second (Kbps) to 1.54 megabits per second (Mbps), and those in the downstream direction range from 384 Kbps to 7.1 Mbps, depending on the length of the local loop—the distance from the customer premises to the telco's (CO) central office—and the telephone cable's wire gauge. The longer the distance from the customer premises to the CO, the slower the ADSL speed that can be achieved (this feature is why ADSL is referred to as a "best effort" service). ADSL speeds start to drop significantly when the subscriber is beyond 10,000 feet from the CO due to interference, attenuation, and crosstalk, and ADSL becomes almost totally ineffectual beyond 18,000 feet. ADSL speeds also vary depending on the AWG gauge of the twisted-pair telephone wires in the subscriber's local loop and residence, with 24 gauge wire providing better performance than 26 gauge.

In a typical ADSL implementation, an ADSL modem (technically called an ADSL Transmission Unit-Remote, or ATU-R) is used to connect a subscriber's computer or network to a standard analog POTS phone line. The ADSL modem contains a POTS splitter chip that splits the bandwidth of the phone line into a voice and a data channel. The data channel is then split, using a channel separator chip, into a separate upstream and downstream channel, with the downstream channel having the larger portion of allocated bandwidth. The voice band typically uses frequencies from 0 to 3.4 kilohertz (kHz), while the data channels use higher frequencies anywhere from above 26 kHz to beyond 1100 kHz, depending on the carrier's implementation. Carrying capacity depends on the wire's thickness and other line conditions.

At the other end of the subscriber's local loop is another ADSL modem (properly called an ADSL Transmission Unit-Central Office or ATU-C) at the telco's CO. The telco's modem separates the voice signal from the data stream using a splitter and routes voice calls through the POTS system of telco switches, while the data is routed to a Digital Subscriber Line Access Multiplexer (DSLAM) unit. The DSLAM unit combines multiple ADSL lines into a single pipe for transmission over the carrier's fiber-optic Asynchronous Transfer Mode (ATM) backbone network to the Internet or to other DSL provider networks. This process is known as ATM over ADSL.

ADSL can employ several different modulation systems for encoding the data channels:

- Carrierless amplitude/phase (CAP)
- Discrete multitone (DMT)
- Discrete wavelet multitone (DWMT)

For More Information

Find out more about ADSL at the site of the ADSL Forum, *www.adsl.com.*

See Also: *Digital Subscriber Line (DSL), G.Lite*

asymmetric multiprocessing (AMP)

A processing architecture in which processes are specifically assigned to different processors.

Overview

When asymmetric multiprocessing (AMP) is used on a multiprocessor computer (a computer with more than one CPU), each processor is assigned specific tasks to perform. For example, one processor might be dedicated to managing input/output (I/O) requests, another to executing network requests, another to running a user application, and so on.

AMP contrasts with symmetric multiprocessing (SMP), in which the operating system evenly distributes the application load across multiple processors. In SMP, individual processes are not mapped to specific processors but instead are assigned to available processors by the operating system.

Notes

Microsoft Windows 2000 supports SMP but not AMP.

async

Short for asynchronous transmission, a form of data transmission in which the transmitting and receiving stations do not explicitly coordinate their transmissions with each other.

See: *asynchronous transmission*

Asynchronous Transfer Mode (ATM)

A high-speed, broadband transmission data communication technology based on packet switching and multiplexing technologies, and used by telcos, long distance carriers, and campus-wide backbone networks to carry integrated data, voice, and video information.

Overview

Asynchronous Transfer Mode (ATM) technology originated in the late 1970s and early 1980s through research into broadband Integrated Services Digital Network (ISDN) (B-ISDN). Like Internet Protocol (IP), ATM is basically a packet-switching technology, but unlike IP with its variable-length packets,ATM uses fixed-size packets called "cells." The fixed size of an ATM cell makes ATM traffic simple and predictable, and makes it possible for ATM to operate at high speeds.

ATM works primarily at Layer 2 of the Open Systems Interconnection (OSI) reference model and so its operation is independent of the Physical Layer (PHY) transport used. The speeds at which ATM operate depend on the transmission medias being used. The various speeds available include:

- 1.544 megabits per second (Mbps) to 25 Mbps over unshielded twisted-pair (UTP) Category 5 (Cat5) cabling, also known as "ATM to the desktop." This early ATM initiative was derailed by the rapid

advances in Fast Ethernet, which won out over ATM because of its simplicity and lower cost.

- 155 Mbps (OC-3) over either UTP or fiber-optic cabling, used primarily for connecting wiring closets to backbone networks.
- 622 Mbps (OC-12), 2.4 Gbps (OC-48), and 4.8 Gbps (OC-96) over fiber-optic cabling only, used exclusively for ATM core (backbone) networks and Synchronous Optical Network/Synchronous Digital Hierarchy (SONET/SDH) as PHY layer transport.

The *asynchronous* in *ATM* means ATM devices do not send and receive information at fixed speeds or using a timer but instead negotiate transmission speeds based on hardware and information flow reliability. The *transfer mode* in *ATM* refers to the fixed-size cell structure used for packaging information. This cell-based transmission is in contrast to typical local area network (LAN) variable-length packet mechanisms, which means that ATM connections are predictable and can be managed so that no single data type or connection can monopolize the transmission path. As a result, ATM is suitable for transmitting all types of traffic from "bursty" data transmissions to real-time and packaged voice and video playback.

Different "classes of service" are used to accommodate transmission of different traffic types in optimal ways, and ATM optimizes traffic flow performance through these various classes of service, which can be allocated on a per-connection basis by usingATM's Quality of Service (QoS) settings. In this fashion, ATM is different from frame relay, which is essentially a classless service. Note that not all carriers or ATM switching gear support all of these service categories.

The six service categories currently defined forATM defined by the ATM Forum are

- **Constant Bit Rate (CBR):** This level is suitable for applications that require a relatively static amount of bandwidth over the duration of a connection. An example might be network control traffic.
- **Real-time Variable Bit Rate (rt-VBR or VBR-RT):** This level is suitable for real-time applications such as video and voice that are sensitive to delay and use large amounts of bandwidth.
- **Non-real-time Variable Bit Rate (nrt-VBR or VBR-NRT):** This level is suitable for bursty traffic that is not real-time in nature. An example might be data acquisition in experiments or playback of canned video presentations.
- **Unspecified Bit Rate (UBR):** This level is suitable for traffic that is not delay sensitive and non-real-time. Examples might include e-mail and file transfers.
- **Available Bit Rate (ABR):** This level includes a flow-control mechanism and is therefore suitable for non-real-time traffic where the transmission characteristics are subject to change over the life of the connection. An example might be file transfers over a noisy link.
- **Guaranteed Frame Rate (GFR):** This level allows additional bandwidth to be allocated dynamically when needed.

ATM also includes a mechanism for allocating bandwidth dynamically; that is, bandwidth is allocated only in required amounts and the required direction. As a result, when an ATM link is idle, it utilizes no bandwidth, which can result in considerable cost savings depending on the needs of your network. ATM networks use bandwidth at maximum efficiency, while maintaining guaranteed QoS for users and applications that require it.

The evolution of ATM has been guided since 1991 in large measure by the efforts of the ATM Forum. ATM is also based on a group of international signaling and interface standards defined by the International Telecommunication Union (ITU). These standards include the user network interface (UNI) standards that specify how users connect to ATM networks, and the broadband intercarrier interface (B-ICI) and public network-to-network interface (P-NNI) standards for establishing connectivity between different ATM networks.

Uses

ATM was originally envisioned as an end-to-end networking architecture that would supersede Ethernet and Token Ring in enterprise LANs because of its built-in support for QoS. Initial deployments included backbones for enterprise LANs with the vision to carry ATM directly to the desktop, but the rapid evolution, simplicity, and lower cost of Fast Ethernet and, later, Gigabit Ethernet (GbE) have prevented ATM from fulfilling its original vision. Few enterprises deploy new ATM backbones today, and the emergence of 10 Gigabit Ethernet (10 GbE) makes this even more unlikely in the future.

If ATM in the backbone is declining in the enterprise, ATM for WAN access remains relatively strong. GbE backbone switches with core ATM ports can be used to connect enterprise networks to carrier's ATM networks for remote access to branch offices and subsidiaries. Alternatively, an Integrated Access Device (IAD) aggregates network traffic at the customer premises into a single ATM WAN pipe for connection to the carrier.

ATM has been widely adopted in the communications networks of telecommunication carriers (telcos). ATM metropolitan area networks (MANs) are widespread, and ATM is viewed as the de facto technology for long distance fiber-optic communication lines stretching thousands of kilometers across continents.

ATM hardware spans the whole range of networking infrastructure, including ATM backbone switches and edge switches, ATM multiplexers, ATM remote access devices, and ATM network interface cards.

Architecture

ATM uses fixed-size 53-byte cells. Each cell contains 48 bytes of payload (data) and 5 bytes of control and routing information in the header. The 5-byte header provides addressing information for switching the packet to its destination and can be implemented in one of two formats: User to Network Interface (UNI) or Network Node Interface (NNI).

The 48-byte payload section carries the actual information, which can be data, voice, or video. The payload is properly called the user information field. The reason for choosing 48 bytes as the payload size is to compromise between the optimal cell sizes for carrying voice information (32 bytes) and data information (64 bytes).

ATM uses a layered architecture for its protocol stack, similar in some respects to the lower portions of the OSI model. There are three main layers in theATM architecture:

- **ATM Adaptation Layer (AAL):** This is the top layer in ATM and is responsible for guaranteeing service characteristics of transmission and for building different types of data into the 48-byte cell payload. It is called the Adaptation Layer because it adapts the ATM Layer beneath it to the particular services that will be using it. The ATM Adaptation Layer consists of two sublayers, the Convergence Sublayer (CS) and the Segmentation and Reassembly (SAR) sublayer. The ATM Adaptation Layer supports five different AAL protocols from AAL 1 through AAL 5, with the last one being the most widely used. The ATM Adaptation Layer is equivalent to the OSI model's Data Link Layer.
- **ATM Layer:** This middle layer takes the payload formed by the ATM Adaptation Layer and adds the 5-byte header information and routes the packet to its destination.
- **Physical Layer:** This bottom layer defines the electrical characteristics of the network interface and media over which the ATM cell is transmitted and converts the ATM cell into electrical signals. In other words the Physical Layer "puts the bits onto the wire." ATM supports a variety of different PHY level transports, including SONET, SDH, DS3/E3, Fiber Distributed Data Interface (FDDI), and Fibre Channel. The ATM Layer and Physical Layer are together equivalent to the OSI model's Physical layer.

ATM supports a variety of address formats. Public ATM networks implemented by telecommunications carriers use the same 19-byte E.164 addresses used by Narrowband ISDN. Private ATM networks can use three different address formats: Network Service Access Point (NSAP) encapsulated E.164, Data Country Code (DCC), and International Code Designator (ICD).

ATM is generally deployed in a star topology with the ATM switch at the center acting as a concentrator. The advantages of this topology are that troubleshooting is simplified and the network can easily be reconfigured if required. ATM switches can provide bandwidth on demand, and additional connections can be formed with the switch when more bandwidth needs to be added.

ATM is a connection-oriented technology that supports both point-to-point and point-to-multipoint connections, but multipoint connections require multicasting (ATM does not support broadcasts). ATM requires the establishment of a specific network path between two points before data can be transported between them. This path is negotiated by the transmitting station, which specifies the type of connection (service classes discussed above), speed (bandwidth) required, and other attributes.

The paths with which ATM connects end stations are called virtual channels (VCs). Virtual channels consist of one or more physical ATM links connected in a series for transmitting data between remote stations. A VC exists only while data is being transmitted on it, and all cells in a given ATM transmission follow the same VC to ensure reliable data transmission. A virtual path (VP) is a collection of VCs having the same source and destination points that can be used to pool traffic being transmitted to a given destination. The header of an ATM cell contains routing information that defines the VC being used for the connection. This routing information is called the Virtual Path Identifier/Virtual Channel Identifier (VPI/VCI).

VCs and VPs are the basic building blocks ofATM networks and provide end-to-end connections with well-defined end points and traffic routes. VCs may be of two types: permanent virtual circuits (PVCs) and switched virtual circuits (SVCs).ATM can work with either PVCs or SVCs, depending on your wide area network (WAN) traffic needs. PVCs are more commonly used by ATM service provider networks but are less efficient with respect to bandwidth costs.

Typically a subscriber needing an ATM WAN link for their company leases a T1 or T3 line to connect their customer premises equipment (CPE) to the telecommunication carrier's ATM network, but frame relay or SONET can also be used to connect a site to an ATM network. The kind of CPE needed varies with the access method employed—for example, Channel Service Unit (CSU) for T1 line, frame relay access device (FRAD) or router for frame relay, and so on. Large corporate networks using an ATM backbone might use a switch-to-switch connection to the carrier's network instead of CPE.

Advantages and Disadvantages

ATM's two main benefits are its high transmission speeds and its flexible bandwidth-on-demand capability. ATM has the following advantages over competing high-speed networking technologies:

- High-speed, fast-switched integrated data, voice, and video communication that is not bound by the physical or architectural design constraints of traditional LAN networking technologies.
- A standards-based solution formalized by the ITU that allows ATM to easily replace existing telephony network infrastructures. ATM provides a global telephony standard, and more than 70 percent of U.S. telcos have migrated their internal networks to ATM.
- A fixed-length cell-based transmission that is suitable for transport of real-time traffic such as voice and video and which allows high-speed bulk encryption mechanisms to be implemented easily and in an affordable way.
- Interoperability with standard LAN/WAN technologies. ATM networks can be interconnected with Ethernet and token ring LANs using LAN emulation (LANE) services to provide Transmission Control Protocol/Internet Protocol (TCP/IP) over ATM.
- Built-in support for QoS that enables a single ATM network connection to reliably carry voice, data, and video simultaneously and manage bandwidth on a per connection basis depending on the priority of the service required. By assigning a bandwidth profile to an ATM connection, the performance of the connection can be guaranteed.

- A connection-oriented architecture that makes it resistant to the kind of denial of service (DoS) attacks for which Internet Protocol (IP) networks are famous. ATM is a more secure solution than IP for the trust boundary where WAN links are found in enterprise networks.

On the other hand, ATM has some significant disadvantages that have hindered its widespread adoption in enterprise networks:

- ATM switching equipment is more expensive than gear for competing technologies such as GbE.
- ATM is more complex in its architecture and operation than competing technologies. By contrast, GbE is an easy step upwards from Fast Ethernet.
- The ATM vision of integrated voice/video/data throughout the enterprise (a.k.a. "convergence") is not driven by market pressure, so in some ways ATM remains "a solution in search of a problem."
- Support for ATM in the WAN market has also been hindered by the fact that most carriers have not yet deployed switched virtual circuits (SVCs) and instead continue to rely upon static permanent virtual circuits (PVCs), which are less flexible and provide a fixed amount of bandwidth at a relatively high cost. Moving to SVCs would reduce costs for customers by enabling bandwidth-on-demand, but most carriers are reluctant to make the capital outlay for upgrading their switching equipment if the end result is to reduce immediate revenue by lowering costs.

Marketplace

Some of the larger carriers offering ATM services for the WAN/MAN environment include AT&T, Bell Atlantic/GTE, MCI WorldCom/UUNET, Qwest/US WEST, and Sprint. These carriers all offer high-performance services with minimal transit delays, and some of them offer ATM-to–frame relay services as an option as well, allowing multiple remote sites connected by frame relay to have their links aggregated into a single fat ATM pipe.

Marconi is the leading vendor of ATM switching equipment, with a 30 percent share of the market in 1999. Cisco Systems came second with a 25 percent share and has lately been focusing its research and development on packet-over-ATM, the next generation of ATM technologies. Other switch vendors offering ATM modules include Nortel Communications and Enterasys.

The region of the world that currently has the highest investment in ATM technologies is the Asia/Pacific region, where leased lines are expensive and ATM is seen as an affordable solution for the needs of the corporate WAN. By contrast, in North America the cost of leased lines is lower, making carrier-based ATM services unattractive and tending to drive large companies to running ATM over their own private circuits.

Prospects

ATM was once hailed as a revolutionary technology superior to Ethernet and essential for enterprises seeking "convergence," that is, the transmission of voice, video, and data over network backbones. However, its growth in deployment has been hindered by the high cost of ATM equipment and the complexity of implementing and managing it. Meanwhile, bandwidth supported by Ethernet has continued to grow, with the result that few enterprises are contemplating the deployment of new ATM backbones, with most favoring GbE instead. The early dream of corporate ATM networks stretching from the server room to the desktop has all but vanished.

ATM's largest installed base remains in telcos, and ATM or SONET/ATM remains the standard high-speed networking solution for these companies. Most MANs deployed by carriers are still ATM, and attempts by GbE to encroach on this territory have been hindered by the still nascent QoS features currently available for Ethernet. With the advent of 10 GbE, however, the picture may change as new carriers such as Yipes (*www.yipes.com*) move into the MAN space offering enterprises end-to-end Ethernet across the WAN. The long-distance carrier market, however, is destined to remain purely ATM for the foreseeable future, and most Incumbent Local Exchange Carriers (ILECs) have invested too heavily inATM technologies for them to easily make the switch to 10 GbE.

ATM has received a boost in the last couple of years through increasing deployment of business and residential

Digital Subscriber Line (DSL) for providing Internet access to the customer premises. Many local telcos aggregate DSL traffic from subscribers into ATM pipes for transport to their backbone ATM carriers. However, DSL is itself facing stiff competition from cable modem providers, and which technology will win out is unclear.

The greatest threat to ATM's survival in the industry is the development of QoS mechanisms for IP traffic. Standards such as Multiprotocol Label Switching (MPLS) and Differentiated Services (DiffServ) have shown some initial promise but cannot compete at this point with ATM, which is still king of the QoS hill. Solutions such as 10 GbE may succeed by simply throwing bandwidth at the problem, but ultimately incorporating QoS into IP is essential if the vision of enterprise convergence is to be attained.

Notes

A number of different approaches are available for building IP internetworks with ATM backbones. These include

- **Classical IP (CIP):** Based on RFC 1577, this supports only the IP protocol and requires a special Address Resolution Protocol (ARP) Server to handle the broadcasts required to support IP (ATM does not support broadcasts because it is connection-oriented in nature). When CIP is deployed over ATM WAN connections using permanent virtual circuits, it is called CIP over PVC.
- **LANE (LAN Emulation):** Lets you build bridged virtual LAN segments for enabling an ATM network to emulate an Ethernet or Token Ring network. LANE is an early solution developed by the ATM Forum.
- **MPOA (Multiprotocol Over ATM):** Provides a virtual router for creating virtual IP subnets over ATM. MPOA is a more recent initiative of the ATM Forum.
- **MPLA (Multiprotocol Label Switching):** A technology developed by the Internet Engineering Task Force (IETF) for a label-based routing system for carrying IP and other traffic over ATM.

For more information on each of these technologies, see their respective articles elsewhere in this book.

ATM can also be used as the underlying technology for FDDI. Microsoft Windows 2000, Windows XP, and Windows .NET Server support direct connectivity to ATM networks with up to four ATM adapters in a single computer.

For More Information

A good source of information on current developments in ATM technology is the ATM Forum (*www.atmforum.com).*

See Also: *ATM Forum, Gigabit Ethernet (GbE), LAN Emulation (LANE), Multiprotocol Label Switching (MPLS), Multiprotocol over ATM (MPOA), quality of service (QoS)*

asynchronous transmission

A form of data transmission in which the transmitting and receiving stations do not explicitly coordinate their transmissions with each other.

Overview

Asynchronous transmission (async) is used in serial transmission for modems and other telecommunication devices. Data is transmitted as streams of bytes terminated by start and stop bits, and the transmitting station can wait an arbitrary period of time between transmissions. This contrasts with synchronous transmission (sync), in which a timing or clocking mechanism is used to ensure a steady flow of data between the devices.

In asynchronous communication, only about 80 percent of the transmitted bits actually contain data, while the other 20 percent contain signaling information in the form of start and stop bits. Each data frame starts with a start bit and ends with a stop bit, with data bits in between. When the receiving station receives a start bit, it knows that pure data will follow. When it receives a stop bit, it knows the data frame has ended and waits for the next one.

Asynchronous transmission is essentially character-based with additional bits between characters to enable synchronization and error correction. An optional parity bit for error checking can be located immediately before the stop bit in each frame. With parity correction, an 8-bit character requires 3 bits of control information (start, stop, and parity bits), which means an actual overhead of 3/8, or 38 percent.

Asynchronous communication is not synchronized by a timer mechanism or clock, and asynchronous devices are not bound to send or receive information at an exact transmission rate. Instead, the sender and receiver negotiate transmission speeds based on hardware limitations and the need to maintain a reliable flow of information. Asynchronous transmission is mainly suitable for low-speed transmission, but speeds can also be increased by using data compression.

Notes

Cisco routers may use any of four different kinds of async ports:

- RJ-45 jack for standard console and aux ports.
- DB-25 serial connector for Cisco 4000 series routers.
- DB-60 connector, switchable from sync to async using Internetwork Operating System (IOS).
- 68-pin Small Computer System Interface (SCSI) II connector for providing eight serial ports (acts as a serial port concentrator) and typically found on access servers.

See Also: *synchronous transmission*

ATDnet

Stands for Advanced Technology Demonstration Network, a high-speed test bed network that ispart of SuperNet, the cross-country network funded by the Next Generation Internet (NGI) program.

See: *Advanced Technology Demonstration Network (ATDnet)*

ATM

Stands for Asynchronous Transfer Mode, a high-speed, broadband transmission data communication technology based on packet switching and multiplexing technologies, and used by telcos, long distance carriers, and campus-wide backbone networks to carry integrated data, voice, and video information.

See: *Asynchronous Transfer Mode (ATM)*

ATM Adaptation Layer (AAL)

An Asynchronous Transfer Mode (ATM) protocol that performs the functions of the Open Systems Interconnection (OSI) model's Data Link layer.

Overview

The function of the ATM Adaptation Layer (AAL) is to adapt the ATM Layer protocol to high-level networking protocols above it. The AAL consists of two sublayers:

- **Convergence Sublayer (CS):** Top sublayer, responsible for performing functions relating to the class of service specified for the traffic being transported over ATM.
- **Segmentation And Reassembly (SAR):** Bottom sublayer, responsible for breaking up high-level data streams into 48-byte segments for packaging into ATM cells. If there's insufficient data to form a cell, SAR pads the cell to make a full cell.

The ATM Adaptation Layer supports five different AAL protocols from AAL 1 through AAL 5, with the last one being the most widely used.

See Also: *Asynchronous Transfer Mode (ATM)*

ATM Forum

An international not-for-profit organization dedicated to promoting the deployment of Asynchronous Transfer Mode (ATM) products and services.

Overview

The ATM Forum was founded in 1991 by a consortium of four companies (Cisco Systems, Northern Telecom [now Nortel Communications], Sprint Corporation, and Net/Adaptive). The ATM Forum's goal is to help steer the course of the development of ATM standards and technologies with the cooperation of over 600 industry partners (the Forum is itself not a standards body but instead develops specifications and submits them to the International Telecommunication Union [ITU]).

The ATM Forum works by committees, some of which include

- **The Technical Committee:** Works with other standards bodies such as the ITU to develop and evolve ATM standards and ensure interoperability between them. A number of different working groups are under this committee's umbrella.

- **Market Awareness Committees:** Three of these committees cover the North America, Europe, and Asia/Pacific regions.
- **The User Committee:** This consists of ATM users and allows them to provide input to the other committees based on their real-world experience of using ATM.

The ATM Forum also has an Ambassador Program for providing speakers knowledgeable about ATM for conferences and other events. The ATM Forum also has a newsletter called "53 Bytes," which helps keep people informed of developments in the ATM field.

For More Information

The ATM Forum can be found at *www.atmforum.com.*

See Also: *Asynchronous Transfer Mode (ATM)*

ATM over SONET

Also called ATM/SONET, a data transmission technology in which Asynchronous Transfer Mode (ATM) cells are transmitted over Synchronous Optical Network (SONET) circuits.

Overview

ATM over SONET is a technology used by telecommunications carriers when individual circuits have to carry multiple different kinds of traffic such as voice, video, Internet Protocol (IP), and so on. ImplementingATM over SONET adds an additional 5 bytes of overhead to 53-byte ATM cells, so this is done only when necessary. If a SONET circuit carries only one type of traffic—such as IP packets or circuit-switched voice—the ATM layer is not required, thus saving the additional overhead.

ATM over SONET can be implemented either with or without Automatic Protection Switching (APS), the traditional SONET ring-based redundancy technology.

See Also: *Asynchronous Transfer Mode (ATM), Synchronous Optical Network (SONET)*

ATM/SONET

Stands for ATM over SONET, a data transmission technology in which Asynchronous Transfer Mode (ATM) cells are transmitted over Synchronous Optical Network (SONET) circuits.

See Also: *ATM over SONET*

attenuation

The loss of signal strength over long distances when signals travel along cabling.

Overview

Attenuation values for actual cables are measured in units of decibels (dB)—a standard measurement value used in communication for expressing the ratio of two values of voltage, power, or some other signal-related quantity. For example, a drop of 3 dB corresponds to a decrease in signal strength of 50 percent or 2:1, while a drop of 6 dB corresponds to a decrease of 75 percent or 4:1. Attenuation values for cabling media are expressed in units of decibels per 1000 feet, which express the amount of attenuation in decibels for a standard 1000-foot (305-meter) length of cabling composed of that medium.

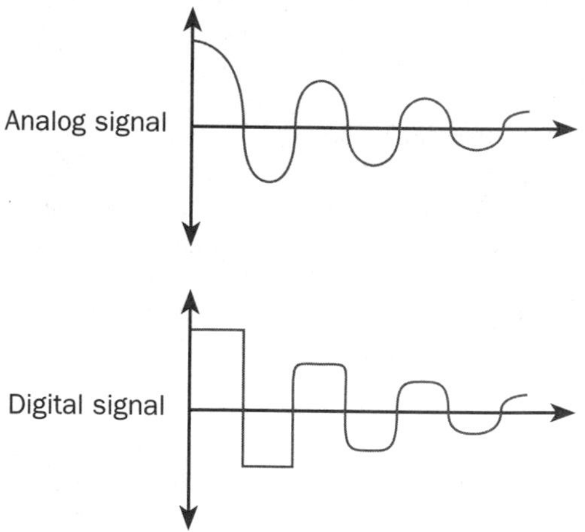

Attenuation. *Attenuation of analog and digital signals.*

Copper cabling has much greater attenuation than fiber-optic cabling, which makes copper suitable only for relatively short cable runs. Typical attenuation values for copper Category 5 (Cat5) cabling vary with frequency and are shown in the following table. Attenuation for lower-grade cable is slightly higher.

Attenuation Values for Copper Cat5 Cabling

Signal Frequency	*Attenuation*
4 megahertz (MHz)	13 dB/1000 feet
10 MHz	20 dB/1000 feet
20 MHz	28 dB/1000 feet
100 MHz	67 dB/1000 feet

Notes

Attenuation is caused by signal absorption, connector loss, and coupling loss. To minimize attenuation, use high-grade cabling such as enhanced category 5 (Cat5e) cabling. Also try to minimize the number of connector devices or couplers, ensuring that these are high-grade components as well. When a signal attenuates a large amount, the receiving device might not be able to detect it or might misinterpret it, therefore causing errors.

attenuation to crosstalk ratio (ACR)

The ratio of the received strength of a signal on a pair of wires to the amount of crosstalk between the wires.

Overview

The attenuation to crosstalk ratio (ACR) is calculated as the difference between the attenuation value and the near-end crosstalk value at a specific frequency. This is because both attenuation and crosstalk are usually expressed in units of decibels for cabling media. The decibel scale is logarithmic in nature, which means that a difference in decibel values corresponds to a ratio of actual signal voltage or power levels.

The higher the ACR for a given cable, the less chance of signal errors. For copper Category 5 (Cat5) cabling, the ACR value is typically about 10 decibels (dB), at a frequency up to about 100 megahertz (MHz). This value decreases slightly with increasing frequency until crosstalk and attenuation values converge, at which point transmission becomes error prone and the cabling ineffective for communication.

See Also: *attenuation, crosstalk*

attrib command

A Microsoft Windows command that can be used to display and modify the attributes of files and directories.

Overview

You can use the attrib command to display and modify the archive, system, hidden, and read-only attributes that can be assigned to files and directories. For example, if you need to manually modify the boot.ini file on a machine running Windows 2000, you can use the attrib command to remove its read-only, hidden, and system attributes.

Examples

```
attrib -r -h -s boot.ini
```

This removes the read-only, hidden, and system attributes from the boot.ini file, allowing you to edit the file manually.

See Also: *attribute (file system)*

attribute (file system)

A type of marker that can be set or cleared for files on a file system such as NTFS file system (NTFS).

Overview

On NTFS, attribute markers determine whether a file is

- Read-only, meaning that it cannot be modified
- Hidden, meaning that the file will not appear when its parent directory is listed at the command line
- System, meaning that the file is a critical operating system file and should not be moved or modified
- Archived, meaning that the file has been backed up
- Encrypted using Microsoft Corporation's Encrypting File System (EFS) (Windows 2000, Windows XP, and Windows .NET Server only)
- Compressed (Windows 2000, Windows XP, and Windows .NET Server only)

To view or modify the attributes of a file, open the file's property sheet and check or clear the appropriate check box.

Notes

The term *attribute* can also refer to other more granular file system information, such as time stamps, file size, or link counts.

See Also: *attrib command*

attribute (Active Directory)

A property of an object in Active Directory directory service.

Overview

Attributes are information relating to objects stored in Active Directory. For example, a user class object is composed of attributes, such as a First Name attribute for a user account object.

Attributes define the actual characteristics of objects in Active Directory. Every class of objects has its own defining set of attributes. Different objects within this class are distinguished by the values of their attributes. Some attributes, such as the First Name attribute for a user account object, must have a value assigned to them when they are created. Other attributes, such as Phone Number, can optionally be left unvalued.

Each attribute in Active Directory is defined only once and can be used for many different object classes. All objects of the same type have the same set of attributes. Different objects of the same type are distinguished by different attribute values. It is therefore the values of the attributes of a particular object that make that object unique in Active Directory.

Attributes are defined in a special portion of Active Directory. An attribute definition includes

- The syntax (type of information) of the attribute, such as integer, date, or string
- Whether the attribute is single-valued or multivalued

Each syntax type is specified by an object identifier, which is a globally unique identifier (GUID) issued by the International Organization for Standardization (ISO). The allowable syntax types for attributes of objects in Active Directory are shown in the following table.

Allowable Syntax Types for Object Attributes

Syntax	*Object Identifier*	*Description*
Undefined	2.5.5.0	Not a legal syntax
Distinguished name	2.5.5.1	The fully qualified name of an object in the directory
Object identifier	2.5.5.2	Identifies an object
Case-sensitive string	2.5.5.3	Differentiates uppercase and lowercase
Case-insensitive string	2.5.5.4	Does not differentiate uppercase and lowercase
Print case string	2.5.5.5	Printable string
Numeric string	2.5.5.6	A sequence of digits
OR name	2.5.5.7	An x400 e-mail address
Boolean	2.5.5.8	TRUE or FALSE
Integer	2.5.5.9	A 32-bit number
Octet string	2.5.5.10	A string of bytes
Time	2.5.5.11	The number of seconds elapsed since 1/1/1970
Unicode	2.5.5.12	Wide string
Address	2.5.5.13	Internal
Distname-address	2.5.5.14	Internal
NT security descriptor	2.5.5.15 66	Microsoft Windows NT Security Descriptor
Large integer	2.5.5.16	A 64-bit number
Security identifier (SID)	2.5.5.17 4	SID

See Also: *Active Directory, Active Directory schema*

ATU-C

Stands for Asymmetric Digital Subscriber Line (ADSL) Transceiver Unit, Central Office end, an ADSL modem that terminates a subscriber's ADSL connection at the ADSL provider's Central Office (CO).

See Also: *Asymmetric Digital Subscriber Line (ADSL)*

ATU-R

Stands for Asymmetric Digital Subscriber Line (ADSL) Transceiver Unit, remote terminal end, an

ADSL modem that terminates a subscriber's ADSL connection at the customer premises.

See Also: *Asymmetric Digital Subscriber Line (ADSL)*

auditing

The process of tracking and monitoring actions performed on servers or networks for security purposes.

Overview

Auditing is an important component of a general security policy for a corporate network. Auditing can be used to detect attempts at unauthorized access to network resources and to track the usage of shared resources. Auditing creates a record of which files have been accessed, who has logged on to the network, who has attempted to use a shared resource, and so on. Specifically, auditing records information in the security log about

- What action was performed
- Who performed the action
- When the action occurred
- Whether the action succeeded or failed

Notes

Microsoft Windows 2000, Windows XP, and Windows .NET Server record two kinds of auditing information in the security log:

- **Success audits:** Symbolized by keys and usually used to track resource usage for capacity and resource planning
- **Failure audits:** Symbolized by padlocks and usually used to monitor network resources for unauthorized access attempts

See Also: *Audit policy, event, security log*

Audit policy

A policy established on a Microsoft Windows 2000 or Windows .NET Server domain that specifies the kinds of security-related events that will be recorded in the security log.

Overview

The following table indicates the kinds of events that can be audited in Windows 2000, WindowsXP, and Windows .NET Server.

Events That Can Be Audited

Type of Event	*Description*
Logon and logoff	Users logging on and off and forming network connections
File and object access	Users accessing a file, folder, or printer on a network
Use of user rights	A right has been exercised—for example, backing up files and directories
User and group management	An account has been modified, created, or deleted
Security policy changes	A change has been made to an Audit policy, a trust relationship, or user rights
Restart, shutdown, and system	The system has been shut down or restarted, or system security has changed
Process tracking	A process has been started or stopped, or some related activity has occurred

Notes

Be careful when enabling auditing for File And Object Access or Process Tracking because logging these events can generate a large amount of overhead on your system, especially when auditing for successes. To audit access to a file, folder, or printer, first enable File And Object Access auditing in your Audit policy, and then access the Security tab on the object's property sheet.

See Also: *auditing, event, security log*

AUI connector

Stands for Attachment Unit Interface connector, a standard 15-pin connector device for thicknet.

Overview

The AUI connector on the free end of a 10Base5 drop cable attaches to the DB15 connector on the network interface card (NIC). The NIC has an AUI port connector for connecting the drop cable. The other end of the drop cable typically connects to a transceiver. The transceiver is then joined to the thicknet cabling using a vampire tap that pierces the cable jacket and insulation to make a connection.

See Also: *connector (device), Ethernet*

Authenticated Users group

A built-in group in Microsoft Windows 2000, Windows XP, and Windows .NET Server for controlling access to resources.

Overview

The Authenticated Users group is similar to the built-in Everyone group, except that anonymous logon users are never members of the Authenticated Users group. The built-in security identifier (SID) for this group is S-1-5-11.

The Authenticated Users group can be used to provide additional security when running Microsoft Internet Information Services (IIS) because the anonymous user account has the ability to enumerate share names and list domain usernames. Using the Authenticated Users group provides an additional layer of security and is one way to restrict access to objects in the file system.

You should generally use the Authenticated Users group instead of the Everyone group if you want to carefully control anonymous access to your network resources.

See Also: *built-in group*

Authentication Header (AH)

A protocol in the IPSec suite of protocols that handles authentication of Internet Protocol (IP) traffic.

Overview

The Authentication Header (AH) header immediately follows the IP header of an IP packet and includes the following fields:

- **Next Header (1 byte):** This field indicates which protocol (Transmission Control Protocol [TCP] or User Datagram Protocol [UDP]) is used in the payload immediately following the AH header.
- **Payload Length (1 byte):** This field indicates the length of the payload following the AH header.
- **Reserved Area (2 bytes):** Not currently used.
- **Security Parameters Index or SPI (4 bytes):** Specifies which security protocols are being used for the transmission of the packet.
- **Sequence Number (4 bytes):** Indicates the position of the packet in the sequence of packets having the same SPI.
- **Authentication Data (variable):** Contains the digital signature for the packet.

Notes

AH usually uses MD5 as its encryption algorithm, but other more secure encryption algorithms can also be used.

See Also: *IPsec*

authentication protocol

Any protocol used for validating the identity of a user to determine whether to grant the user access to resources on a network.

Overview

Authentication protocols can be classified according to how the credentials are passed over the network. Some common kinds of authentication protocols include

- **Anonymous access:** This method is supported by Microsoft Internet Information Services (IIS) and allows anonymous users on the Internet access to Web content on your server.
- **Basic authentication:** This method transmits passwords as clear text and is often used in Unix networks and for File Transfer Protocol (FTP) services. It is also supported by IIS.
- **Digest authentication:** This method hashes (digests) the user's password before transmitting it, making it more secure than Basic authentication. Digest authentication is part of the Hypertext Transfer Protocol (HTTP) 1.1 protocol and is also supported by IIS.
- **Windows NT Challenge/Response:** This is the standard secure authentication method for Windows NT domains. In IIS this protocol is referred to as Integrated Windows authentication. Also called Windows NT Lan Manager or NTLM.

- **Kerberos v5:** This is the standard authentication security protocol for Windows 2000 and Windows .NET Server domains.
- **X.509 Client Certificate authentication:** This is used in conjunction with Secure Sockets Layer (SSL) and digital certificates and is also supported by IIS.

Notes

On a Microsoft Windows NT, Windows 2000, or Windows .NET Server network, authentication can be handled in one of two ways:

- When logging on to a member server or stand-alone workstation, authentication is performed by the member server or workstation itself using its local Security Accounts Manager (SAM) database.
- When logging on to a domain, authentication is performed by a domain controller on the network.

See Also: anonymous access, Basic authentication, Kerberos, Windows NT Challenge/Response Authentication

authentication provider

In Internet Connection Services for Microsoft Remote Access Service (RAS), a database for providing AAA (authentication, access, and accounting) information for the users in a given realm.

Overview

An authentication provider is a server that isused by Internet Authentication Service (IAS) to map a Remote Authentication Dial-In User Service (RADIUS) authentication request to a database containing user credentials. The authentication provider can verify or deny whether the individual exists in the database and return this information to the IAS server.

Choices for authentication providers are

- A Microsoft Windows NT, Windows 2000, or Windows .NET Server domain controller
- A Local Users file on the IAS server
- An open database connectivity (ODBC)–compliant database
- A Microsoft Commercial Internet System (MCIS) membership database

See Also: AAA

Authenticode

A Microsoft security technology that certifies the identity of the publisher of software to ensure the software has not been tampered with.

Overview

To use Authenticode, an Internet software publisher first obtains a digital certificate from a certificate authority (CA). They then use Authenticode signing tools to digitally sign the application.

When a user tries to download the application from the Internet, client-side Authenticode software in Microsoft Windows displays the publisher's certificate information to help the user make a more informed decision about whether to install the software on his or her machine.

Authenticode can be used to sign Microsoft ActiveX controls, .cab files, Java applets, or any other executable files.

See Also: security

Authorized Academic Training Provider (AATP)

A Microsoft training program offered to accredited academic institutions.

Overview

An Authorized Academic Training Provider (AATP) is an educational institution approved for delivery of training on Microsoft platforms and applications. AATPs can include secondary schools, vocational schools, community colleges, and universities. Microsoft Corporation provides participating institutions with tools to facilitate courseware delivery that prepares students for Microsoft Certified Professional (MCP) certifications. This enables schools to serve their communities by educating future employees to fill demands for technically certified computer professionals.

There's no fee for joining the AATP program. Some of the benefits of joining the program include the following:

- A 100-user software license received upon purchase of a Microsoft product—provided the product is the subject of a course being taught that uses a Microsoft Official Curriculum or Microsoft Approved Study Guides. Note that these licenses are for student and instructor use in the classroom only.
- Special academic pricing on Microsoft Official Curriculum and Microsoft Approved Study Guides.
- Online course outlines, evaluation tools, curriculum materials, certification fact sheets, and preparatory exams.
- Access to the private AATP Internet site.

Notes

An organization or institution cannot participate simultaneously in both the AATP and Certified Technical Education Center (CTEC) programs.

For More Information

Find out more about Microsoft's AATP program at *www.microsoft.com/education/aatp/default.asp.*

See Also: *Certified Technical Education Center (CTEC), Microsoft Certified Professional (MCP)*

auto-application

An application that can be automatically started on the user's computer by Microsoft Connection Manager (CM) after a connection is established.

Overview

Auto-applications automatically launch and close upon the start and end of a connection. This lets administrators configure services to trigger when users open their e-mail or Web browser.

You can specify auto-applications using a wizard that allows you to specify the name of the application, command-line switches or parameters, and other information.

An auto-application must be a complete program file. It cannot require other files to work, and it cannot be a self-extracting executable.

AutoComplete

A feature of Microsoft Internet Explorer that attempts to complete a partial Uniform Resource Locator (URL) entered into the browser's Address field.

Overview

When you begin to enter a URL, the AutoComplete function checks the browser's history folder for any URLs that match your partial URL and displays the closest match to what you have entered. This saves users from having to retype long URLs when attempting to revisit a site.

AutoComplete can be viewed as both an accessibility feature and a way to avoid time-wasting mistakes. If the URL that AutoComplete suggests for you is incorrect, just keep typing the URL you want.

AutoComplete is based on the same IntelliSense technology that is implemented in certain features of Microsoft Office, such as the AutoFill feature in Microsoft Excel.

Notes

If you clear your history folder, AutoComplete will not be able to function because it uses URLs stored in that folder. The longer you leave your history folder unemptied, the larger its contents become and the more effectively AutoComplete operates.

See Also: *Internet Explorer*

autodial

A feature of remote access in Microsoft Windows 2000, Windows NT, Windows XP, and Windows .NET Server that maps network resources to phonebook entries.

Overview

When a user or application tries to access a network resource, autodial automatically tries to establish a connection to the resource. To configure autodial in Windows 2000, go to Control Panel in My Computer, and then open Network And Dial-up Connections. Choose Dial-Up Preferences from the Advanced menu. On the Autodial tab, select the check box next to the location where you want to enable autodial, and then click OK. To configure AutoDial in Windows NT, use the User Preferences dialog box for your phonebook entry.

Notes

Certain actions will not trigger autodial. These include

- Pinging an Internet Protocol (IP) address. (Pinging a fully qualified domain name, however, will cause autodial to engage.)
- Using both a dial-up and a local area network (LAN) connection. (AutoDial engages only after an attempt to connect over the LAN has failed.)

See Also: *remote access*

automatic logon

A logon process whereby the user gains access to the network through user credentials previously stored in the registry.

Overview

Automatic logon can be enabled on a machine running Microsoft Windows NT by editing the registry. Use registry editor (Regedit.exe) to open the following key:

```
HKEY_LOCAL_MACHINE
    \Software
        \Microsoft
            \Windows NT
                \CurrentVersion
                    \Winlogon
```

and modify or create the following REG_SZ type values:

- DefaultDomainName
- DefaultUserName
- DefaultPassword
- AutoAdminLogon

Set AutoAdminLogon equal to 1 to enable automatic logon.

You can bypass the automatic logon process by holding down the Shift key upon startup or logoff.

Notes

Use extreme care when making changes to the registry, as improper use of Registry Editor can make your system unbootable.

See Also: *interactive logon*

Automatic Private IP Addressing (APIPA)

A feature of Microsoft Windows 2000, Windows XP, and Windows .NET Server that enables machines to be automatically assigned Internet Protocol (IP) addresses without the use of Dynamic Host Configuration Protocol (DHCP).

Overview

Automatic Private IP Addressing (APIPA) is designed for use on small networks where fewer than 25 machines are deployed. Such networks are too big to easily manage using static (manual) IP addressing and too small to warrant the use of a dedicated DHCP server for automatic IP addressing. APIPA was developed as an alternative to these two addressing methods.

If a Windows 2000, Windows XP, or Windows .NET Server client starts up and is configured for DHCP but finds no DHCP server to lease it an address, APIPA randomly assigns a machine an IP address. This randomly assigned address is in the range 169.254.*x.y*, which is reserved by Microsoft Corporation for this purpose and is not used on the Internet (in case your client has a direct connection to the Internet). A subnet mask of 255.255.0.0 is additionally assigned to the client.

Notes

One disadvantage of using APIPA is that machines whose addresses have been assigned using APIPA periodically poll the network for the presence of a DHCP server. Should a DHCP server be found, the machine yields its APIPA-generated address and leases a new address from the DHCP server. APIPA networks are thus particularly susceptible to interference from rogue DHCP servers, and APIPA should not be used in mission-critical or enterprise networks. You can disable this polling feature, however, by editing the registry.

APIPA is also available on the Windows 98SE platform.

See Also: *Dynamic Host Configuration Protocol (DHCP), IP address*

Automatic System Recovery (ASR)

A feature of Microsoft Windows 2000, Windows XP, and Windows .NET Server that allows you to restore your system in the event of hard disk failure or corruption of system files.

Overview

Automatic System Recovery (ASR) is designed to replace the emergency repair disk (ERD) of Windows NT as the main tool for restoring systems after boot failures. ASR integrates the processes of repair, backup, and restore into a single recovery solution in the event of a disaster.

To use ASR, you must first configure it by running the Disaster Recovery Preparation Wizard, which is part of the Backup utility in Windows 2000, Windows XP, and Windows .NET Server. The resulting ASR disk contains configuration information that will be critical if you need to recover your system as a result of system volume damage or corruption. If you need to reinstall the system software, the ASR disk enables you to bring the system to the same configuration it had before the disaster.

Notes

Always run the Automatic System Recovery Wizard immediately before and after you make any changes to your system configuration using the Disk Management tool. If you do this, you will be able to return your system to the stable configuration that existed prior to your change.

See Also: *Windows 2000*

Automatic Version Synchronization (AVS)

A feature of the Microsoft Internet Explorer Administration Kit (IEAK).

Overview

Automatic Version Synchronization (AVS) runs each time the IEAK administrator runs the IEAK Wizard and checks Microsoft Corporation's Web site for updates to Microsoft Internet Explorer. These updates are automatically downloaded and the administrator can distribute them to users throughout the enterprise.

Automation

A Microsoft technology that enables applications to expose their functionality to other applications.

Overview

Automation, formerly known as OLE Automation, is based on the Component Object Model (COM) and allows run-time binding of components. Automation is used exclusively by scripting languages, such as Microsoft Visual Basic for Applications (VBA), Microsoft Visual Basic Scripting Edition (VBScript), and Microsoft JScript, to access COM components that support Automation. The advantage of Automation is that it allows various languages to access COM components at run time. The drawbacks to Automation are that it is slow and that compile-time data type checking cannot be performed.

An application that exposes its functionality through Automation is called an Automation server. An application that communicates with the server through Automation is called an Automation controller or Automation client.

An Automation server is a COM component that typically implements the IDispatch interface. An Automation controller is a client that communicates with the Automation server, typically using IDispatch. IDispatch is a COM interface that allows a client to indirectly access all of the component's exposed methods and properties. Therefore, IDispatch enables a client to discover and access all a component's various methods and properties at run time through a single interface.

Notes

In the past, Automation required communication using the IDispatch interface. Now the term Automation is more generic and refers to the programmability of an application or component.

See Also: *Automation controller, Automation server*

Automation client

Also called an Automation controller, a client that accesses the functionality of an Automation server.

See: *Automation controller*

Automation controller

A client that accesses the functionality of an Automation server.

Overview

Automation is a way for one application to manipulate the exposed objects (properties and methods) of another application. Automation controllers are client applications that can manipulate the exposed objects of another application called an Automation server. Examples of Automation controllers include Microsoft Word, Microsoft Excel, and Microsoft Visual Basic.

There are two kinds of Automation clients:

- Clients that have static information about the properties and methods of the Automation server bound to them at compile time.
- Clients that dynamically obtain information about the properties and methods of the Automation server at run time. These clients do this by querying the Automation server's IDispatch interface.

See Also: *Automation, Automation server*

Automation server

A Component Object Model (COM) component that exposes its functionality to other applications.

Overview

An example of an Automation server might be a word processing program that can expose its spell-checking functions so that Automation controllers can access them. This allows the functionality of one program (the Automation server) to be used by other programs (the Automation clients or controllers).

An Automation server typically implements the IDispatch interface.

See Also: *Automation, Automation controller*

auto naming

A feature of Microsoft Exchange Server that enables administrators to configure how e-mail aliases and other information are automatically generated when mailboxes are created.

Overview

Using auto naming, you could, for example, automatically generate any of the following e-mail aliases for Jeff Smith's mailbox:

- JSmith
- JeffS
- JS

You could also devise some other custom naming scheme. These e-mail aliases then would be combined with the Domain Name System (DNS) domain name of the Exchange organization to form the user's standard e-mail address. For example, if the domain name of the company is northwind.microsoft.com, JSmith would be combined with it to form the e-mail address JSmith@northwind.microsoft.com.

See Also: *Exchange Server*

autonomous system (AS)

A group of Internet Protocol (IP) networks administered under a single administrative (routing) policy.

Overview

An autonomous system (AS) is part of the routing infrastructure of a large IP internetwork. An AS is essentially a portion of a large internetwork whose routing is administered by a single authority. Typically, this means one AS per enterprise network. An autonomous system can be under the authority of a particular corporation or institution, or it can be defined by the uniform use of a particular routing protocol such as Open Shortest Path First (OSPF).

The Internet is the de facto example of a large IP internetwork divided into different autonomous systems such as AT&T Enhanced Network Services (formerly AT&T CERFnet), SprintLink, AlterNet, and so on. These autonomous systems are connected by the Internet's core routers, which use an exterior routing protocol called Border Gateway Protocol (BGP) for communication among themselves.

Each autonomous system must be identified using a globally unique number called an autonomous system number (ASN). A BGP uses ASNs to avoid routing loops and implement policy-based routing on the Internet backbone. ASNs are required for autonomous systems connected to the Internet, and are obtained from Internet numbers registries such as the American Registry for Internet Numbers (ARIN) and the Asian-Pacific Network Information Center (APNIC). Autonomous systems exchange exterior routing information with one another by using these ASNs to identify themselves to other autonomous systems. Autonomous systems can be further subdivided into routing domains (areas) for more granular routing.

There are three basic types of autonomous systems:

- **Stub AS:** This AS is connected to only one other AS. A corporate network that isconnected to an AS is considered to have the same AS number as the AS it is connected to.
- **Transit AS:** This AS is connected to more than one other AS and can be used for transit traffic between autonomous systems. A Transit AS is usually administered by a large Internet service provider (ISP).
- **Multihomed AS:** This AS is connected to more than one other AS but does not let transit traffic from another AS pass through itself. An example might be a corporate network with several Internet connections to different ISPs.

See Also: *autonomous system number (ASN), Border Gateway Protocol (BGP), routing*

autonomous system number (ASN)

A unique number used to identify an autonomous system (AS), that is, a network that can exchange exterior routing information with neighboring networks.

Overview

Every autonomous system (AS) connected to the global Internet must have a uniquely assigned autonomous system number (ASN). This ASN is required so that your AS can identify itself to other ASs on the Internet and exchange exterior routing information with their routers. ASNs are 16-bit numbers that are assigned to networks by the American Registry for Internet Numbers (ARIN). As of 2000 there were more than 12,000 ASNs assigned to public and enterprise networks, and the number is rising rapidly as more and more enterprises implement multihoming, the use of multiple ISPs for providing Internet access for their networks. To obtain an ASN, contact ARIN and pay the one-time registration fee and the annual maintenance fee. Note that ISPs are not charged the annual maintenance fee for their ASNs.

See Also: *autonomous system (AS), multihoming*

autosensing

Technology by which a local area network (LAN) device can determine the characteristics of an attached device and configure itself accordingly.

Overview

As an example, a port on an autosensing 10/100-Mbps Ethernet switch can automatically detect whether the attached station has a 10-megabits per second (Mbps) or 100-Mbps network interface card (NIC). This is a useful feature that allows a combination of 10BaseT and Fast Ethernet connections in a single LAN.

Often during migration and system upgrades you will find a combination of slower, legacy networking equipment and faster, more modern devices. These devices might need to coexist for months or years, depending on the budget available for upgrades. Using autosensing hubs and switches makes this coexistence cheap and simple and allows a full upgrade to the faster configuration later—without purchasing additional equipment.

See Also: *hub, Ethernet switch*

availability

The degree to which network resources operate without interruptions resulting from scheduled maintenance or unexpected failure.

Overview

Availability has become an important issue in the modern Internet economy in which online electronic businesses are made or broken on the basis of reliable, fault-tolerant technologies.

Clustering is one tool for ensuring continuous uninterrupted 24 x 7 x 365 availability of network resources. Windows 2000, Windows XP, and Windows .NET Server include support for clustering that provides the basic platform for building high-availability e-business and electronic commerce applications that can compete in today's world. Cluster services can automatically detect when an application or server fails and quickly restart it on the surviving cluster node. Users connected to the server will experience only a brief pause in service.

See Also: *24 x 7, clustering*

AVS

Stands for Automatic Version Synchronization, a feature of the Microsoft Internet Explorer Administration Kit (IEAK).

See: *Automatic Version Synchronization (AVS)*

AWG

Stands for American Wire Gauge, a specification for the diameter of conducting wires.

Overview

The higher the AWG number, the thinner the wire. Category 5 (Cat5) cabling is usually AWG 24 wire (0.020 inch or 0.511 millimeter in diameter), while thicknet generally uses AWG 12 wire (0.080 inch or 2.050 millimeters in diameter). Twisted-pair telephone wire at the customer premises is typically 24 or 26 gauge, with 24 giving better performance for high-speed services such as Asymmetric Digital Subscriber Line (ADSL).

The table below shows some of the various AWG gauges for different diameters of wires. Note that the thinner the wire, the higher its electrical resistance and hence the shorter the transmission distance (because resistance varies inversely with thickness).

AWG Gauges for Various Diameters of Wires

AWG Gauge	*Diameter (Inches)*	*Diameter (Millimeters)*
12	0.080	2.050
14	0.064	1.630
16	0.051	1.290
18	0.040	1.020
20	0.032	0.813
22	0.025	0.643
24	0.020	0.511
30	0.010	0.254

AXFR request

A type of Domain Name System (DNS) request in which a secondary DNS server requests the update of information from a master DNS server.

Overview

An AXFR request always results in a full zone transfer. This can take time and use considerable network bandwidth if the zone files are large.

An alternative to AXFR is the incremental zone transfer protocol described in RFC 1995. Incremental zone transfers use an IXFR request and transfer only those portions of the zone file that have been changed.

Incremental zone transfers are supported by the DNS service running on Microsoft Windows 2000 and Windows .NET Server.

See Also: *Domain Name System (DNS)*

B2B

Stands for business-to-business and refers to e-commerce between different companies that have some sort of partnering arrangement, in contrast to B2C, or business-to-consumer, relationships in which individuals or companies purchase the products or services of another company.

Overview

Companies traditionally negotiate special business relationships with other companies that can provide them with the raw materials, tools, and services that they need for the success of their businesses. Such relationships are known as a value chain, which typically includes activities such as obtaining raw materials, processing these materials into finished products, shipping products to distributors, servicing customers, and marketing. To support a value chain, several business activities are essential, including procurement, research and development, manufacturing, and managing of human resources, operations, finances, and customer needs.

B2B is basically the use of the Internet to streamline and automate these business processes to enhance the value chain. This can result in streamlined business-cycle processes that are faster-to-market and in substantial cost savings by eliminating traditional paper-based invoicing and communications used in procurement channels. B2B can benefit companies in many different scenarios, including corporate purchasing, supply chain trading, and direct marketing.

Architecture

The technologies at the heart of B2B are the Internet, virtual private networks (VPNs) and Extensible Markup Language (XML). The Internet now provides a ubiquitous communications infrastructure that allows companies anywhere to connect with each other for exchange of business information. This can be accomplished through a variety of means, including leased lines, xDSL, dial-up modem connections, and wireless satellite links. Just as the existing public switched telephone network (PSTN) catalyzed the explosive growth of fax technology after it was introduced, the Internet is revolutionizing the way business partners communicate to buy and sell goods and services.

VPNs are a popular technology that is widely used to secure communications over the Internet. Without the Internet itself, business partners would have to purchase costly leased lines for secure, reliable electronic communications between them, and many companies still use leased lines to support their Electronic Data Interchange (EDI) platforms. Using VPNs, however, companies can send these communications securely over the public Internet, allowing them to reduce costs by eliminating leased lines in favor of better-positioned technologies such as xDSL.

XML is a third component of most emerging B2B solutions platforms, as it provides a standardized way of encoding business communications for transmission over the Internet.

In addition to these technologies, other elements of successful B2B relationships include establishing credit relationships between companies and building B2B technology into legacy systems.

An emerging standard that may help promote B2B overall is an initiative from Ariba, Microsoft, and IBM called Universal Description, Discovery, and Integration (UDDI). UDDI is a proposed directory service that will make it easier for companies to find business partners that offer specific types of goods and services.

Implementation

You can implement B2B in three basic ways: build a custom solution, buy a packaged solution, or lease services from an online marketplace.

Building a custom B2B solution in conjunction with business partners is an approach that is often taken by large companies that require custom solutions that are integrated deeply into their existing legacy business systems and that have pockets deep enough to implement this type of solution. The disadvantage is the longer time-to-market period required for realizing benefits from this solution, and with the rapidly changing Internet economy this is a concern that needs to be seriously addressed by enterprise e-implementers. B2B solution providers pursuing this market segment are basically pursuing a vertical market in which they will handle a small number of large clients with extensive integration needs.

Buying an off-the-shelf B2B solution is another approach that can take several forms, from purchasing and deploying a software platform for developing B2B solutions such as Microsoft BizTalk Server to hiring a B2B consulting company to implement its own off-the-shelf solution. This approach is often taken by mid-sized companies with reduced capital availability and limited IT (information technology) resources, and especially so by dot-com startups seeking rapid time-to-market. A startup company might outsource all of their procurement needs to a B2B consulting service that will implement a packaged Web-based system for procurement and supply-chain management for them.

Leasing services from an existing B2B exchange is a third solution. Numerous online marketplaces supply B2B services for narrowly targeted market segments such as the food industry and the plastics industry. These B2B exchanges (or online marketplaces) provide packaged B2B solutions that include online catalog publishing services, secure transactions, direct marketing, and related services. An example is the food industry, where a B2B exchange can help grocery store chains manage procurement and speedy delivery of perishable goods.

A B2B exchange with a specific industry focus such as this is often called an Industry-Sponsored Marketplace (ISM), and a B2B solution provider with a more general focus of providing packaged B2B solutions for small-sized or mid-sized companies is generally referred to as a "pure player." These providers are competing in a horizontal market—that is, trying to gain as many customers as they can—and most first-generation B2B marketplaces took this approach to growing their ventures. Many of them provide B2B services on a transaction-fee basis, though there's movement away from this model toward flat-rate pricing that makes B2B costs more predictable for clients.

B2B exchanges come in all flavors, from online shopping portals such as the healthcare industry portal PointStore, to industry-partnered ventures in which several companies form a cooperative exchange such as Hyatt International Corporation and Marriott International's Avendra marketplace for the hospitality industry, to pure-play independent B2B exchanges such as Chemdex for the chemical industry built on B2B software from Commerce One and Ariba. Of these different approaches, the most successful ventures are generally the cooperatives in which the narrow industry focus and high alignment with partner needs generate the best results.

Marketplace

Commerce One and Ariba are two major players in the B2B marketplace arena, and between them they have more than 500 corporate customers. Ariba has partnered with IBM and i2 Technologies to provide software and services, and Commerce One has done the same with SAP AG.

Some of the bigger players in the ISM market include

- **e2Open:** An online marketplace for high technology supported by IBM, Nortel Networks, and others.
- **Altrade:** A B2B exchange developed by Altra Energy Technologies for the energy industry that includes high-profile partners such as Dow Chemical Company and ExxonMobil Corporation and which did over $4 billion in trades in 1999.
- **Covisint:** An online supply-chain procurement marketplace being developed by the Big Three

automakers Ford Motors, General Motors, and DaimlerChrysler.

Companies that provide full-featured packaged B2B platforms include Ironside Technologies, Yantra Corporation, and many others.

Prospects

The future of the emerging B2B market overall is probably bright despite the shakeout of many startups that occurred in 2001. Many early proponents followed the horizontal market strategy of building one-size-fits-all B2B exchanges and then trying to attract customers along the "build it and they will come" paradigm. Unfortunately, most larger companies have legacy business systems that require a great deal of customization to participate effectively in B2B, and, as a result, most public B2B exchanges attracted only small and mid-sized companies whose resources were limited.

The main issues that tend to make many companies slow to jump on the bandwagon of public B2B exchanges are the unpredictable costs of transaction-based fees for involvement in these marketplaces, the complexity of integrating B2B solutions into existing supply chain systems (especially for companies that have progressed little in developing Web-based intranet and extranet solutions for their businesses), and issues relating to branding and customer loyalty that make suppliers reluctant to offer their wares at cut-rate prices in the new online marketplaces. As a result, successful B2B exchanges tend to be those that can build community—that is, a group of buyers and sellers loyal to one another. Private exchanges (those built upon preexisting business relationships) thus tend to fare well but offer few avenues for market growth for suppliers involved, and public exchanges offer a way of helping suppliers find new markets and new customers.

Another issue that has restrained many from the wholesale plunge into B2B is the snake-oil syndrome: new technologies breed startups that offer end-to-end solutions that are ready to implement "yesterday." Due diligence is required of companies contemplating aligning themselves with a B2B solution or platform, and decision-makers should obtain financials and customer testimonials to avoid getting caught in the web of fly-by-night operations that are here today and gone tomorrow.

With the failure of numerous public B2B marketplaces, companies that were early adopters are taking a more cautious view of further involvement, so that while recognizing the need to pursue B2B solutions in order to compete in the future economy, they are now more effectively taking care in investigating the financial viability of exchanges before jumping on board again. Nevertheless, while getting your company involved with a specific B2B provider is a tactical solution that requires good thought and due diligence, getting your company involved generally in B2B solutions is a strategic requirement for any company that hopes to survive in the Internet economy that is here and yet to come.

Notes

Microsoft Corporation has its own internal B2B solution called the Microsoft Market, which allows employees to quickly and easily procure goods and services from a wide variety of partner businesses. Microsoft Market has enabled Microsoft to lower average procurement costs by more than 90 percent.

Many B2B marketplaces provide procurement services based on either forward (sell-side) auctions which benefit suppliers or reverse (buy-side) auctions in which buyers submit a Request for Quotation (RFQ) and wait for the lowest bid to come in from suppliers. These services have not been as successful as anticipated, however, mainly because companies generally negotiate trusted long-term contractual business relationships with partners rather than just bid for the best-priced solution.

See Also: *BizTalk Server 2000, Commerce Server 2000, Digital Subscriber Line (DSL), electronic data interchange (EDI), Microsoft Market, Universal Description, Discovery, and Integration (UDDI), virtual private network (VPN)*

B2C

Stands for business-to-consumer, relationships in which individuals or companies purchase the products or services of another company.

See: B2B

backbone

The portion of a network that ties different departmental networks into a single whole.

Overview

Backbones are primarily used in medium to large networks, such as those occupying a building or a group of buildings on a campus. The backbone carries the bulk of the network traffic and must be designed accordingly. Backbone designs generally fall into two basic categories:

- **Distributed backbone:** Refers to using cabling to join different departmental networks in a bus topology or mesh topology. This cabling is referred to as backbone cabling, and it connects the hubs, switches, or routers of each network into a single whole. In a typical scenario, each floor or building might have a local area network (LAN) and wiring closet containing, among other things, a main hub or router. Backbone cabling is then run between floors or buildings, connecting the main hub or router for each department into a bus-style network (see illustration).
- **Collapsed backbone:** Refers to using cabling to directly join each departmental network's main hub or router using backbone cabling to a central hub, switch, or router in a star topology (see illustration). The central unit is often referred to as the collapsed backbone, although this term properly describes the entire configuration. The central unit can be located in the building's main equipment room or, in a campus scenario, in the IS (Information Services) department's building.

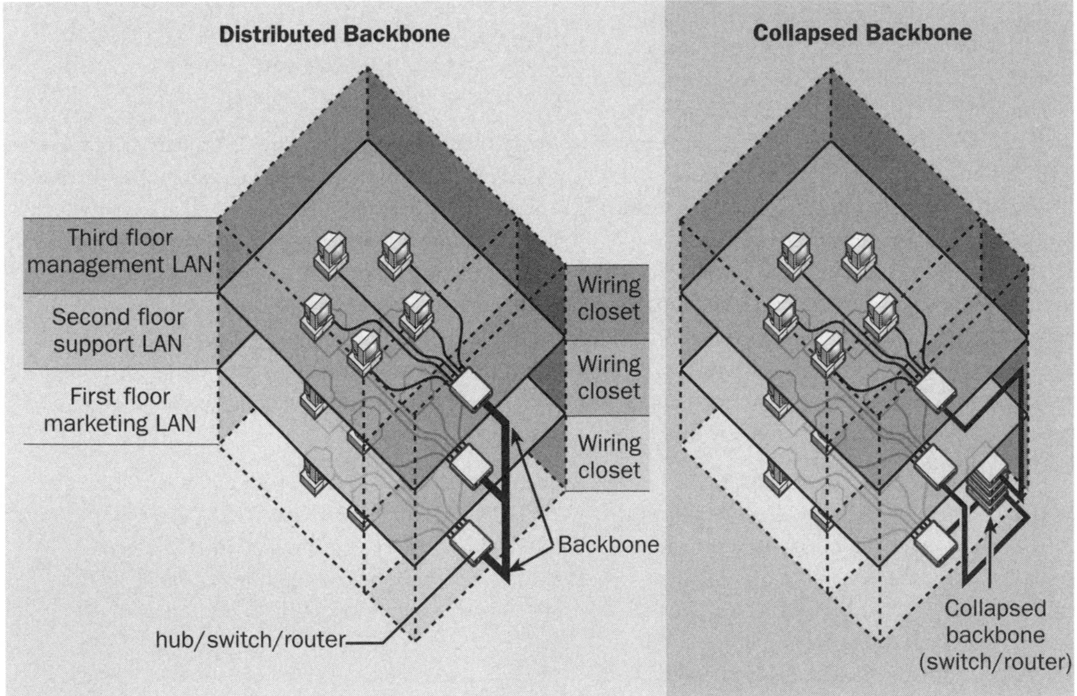

Backbone. *Two basic types of network backbone: distributed and collapsed.*

Distributed backbones generally have a greater degree of fault tolerance than collapsed ones, because the collapsed backbone unit forms a single point of failure. However, collapsed backbones usually have better traffic flow than distributed backbones because of the underlying star topology. Collapsed backbones generally offer better performance because of the reduced number of hops that traffic must make when passing between departmental LANs. Collapsed backbones are also easier to manage because they bring all the backbone switching and routing equipment into a single room or building. Collapsed backbones are used frequently for connecting departmental LANs within a single building, but less often for connecting building LANs across a campus network because of the increased distances and cabling costs.

Backbone cabling should have the highest bandwidth of any cabling in your network, since backbones are used to join together hubs, switches, and routers, linking departmental LANs or subnetworks into building-wide or campus-wide internetworks. In buildings, backbone cabling often refers to the vertical cabling running through the risers or elevator shafts that connects the hubs and switches in each floor's wiring closet. Depending on performance requirements, anticipated growth, and cost, any of the following might be suitable for backbone cabling:

- Category 5 (Cat5) unshielded twisted pair (UTP) cable
- Type 1A shielded twisted pair (STP) cable
- Thinnet coaxial cabling
- Multimode fiber-optic cabling
- Single-mode fiber-optic cabling

Notes

The term *backbone* is also used to refer to the collection of networking components (cabling, hubs, switches, and routers) that form the supporting network into which workgroup and departmental LANs are connected. A mesh topology is often used for network backbones to provide fault tolerance for critical high-speed data paths.

You should put considerable thought and planning into the design and implementation of your network's backbone, because the overall performance of networking services is largely dependent on the backbone's bandwidth and reliability. Design your backbone with network expansion in mind. Planning for growth is especially important if the cost of cable reinstallation is high. Fiber-optic cabling is preferred for most network backbones because of its high bandwidth, security, and resistance to electromagnetic interference.

See Also: *collapsed backbone*

backboning

Sending messages between similar messaging systems by using an intermediate messaging system of a different type.

Overview

A simple backboning example is the connecting of two or more Lotus cc:Mail postoffices using a Microsoft Exchange Server organization as the messaging backbone. By installing the cc:Mail Connector on Exchange Server, messaging connectivity can be established with connected cc:Mail postoffices. Messages can then be routed from one postoffice through the Exchange organization to other postoffices on the network.

Another example of backboning is connecting different sites in an Exchange Server organization using a public or private messaging network. Here are two possible scenarios:

- Using Simple Mail Transfer Protocol (SMTP) hosts on the Internet to connect Exchange sites.
- Using a public or private X.400 messaging system for connecting Exchange sites using the X.400 Connector.

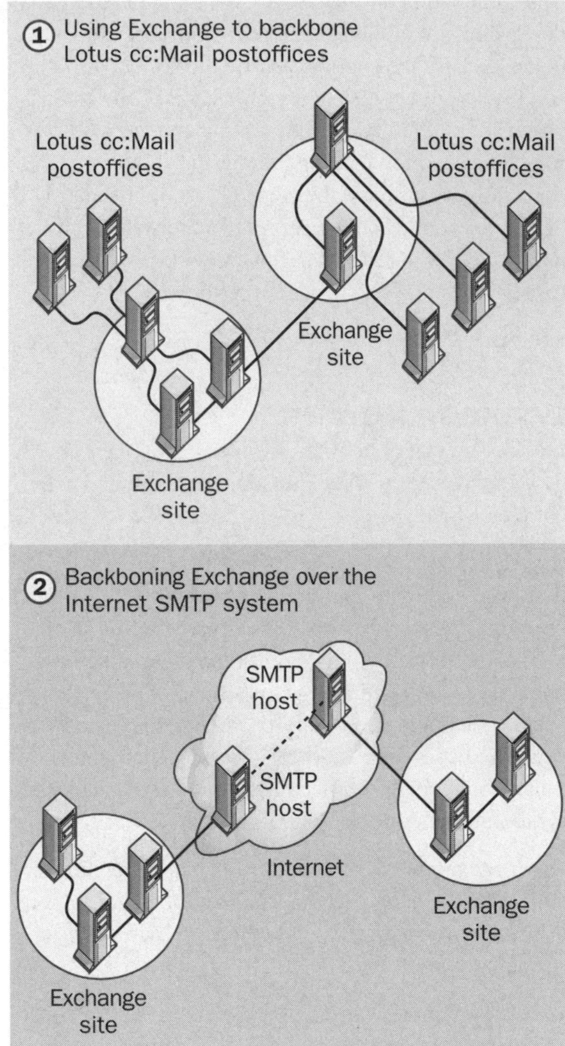

***Backboning.** Connecting similar messaging systems by backboning over a different messaging system.*

When using a public messaging backbone (or a private one owned by a different company) for connecting your Exchange sites, you should consider the following:

- Installing and configuring appropriate messaging connectors on suitable messaging bridgehead servers
- Establishing and maintaining directory replication between Exchange sites
- Handling background traffic from other users of the backbone
- Tuning messaging performance to optimize use of the backbone
- Implementing a suitable topology for the messaging backbone

For very large Exchange organizations, use a hub and spoke topology instead of a mesh topology. Hub and spoke topologies have less redundancy and fault tolerance, but mesh topologies have routing tables that grow exponentially with the number of sites involved. Mesh topologies for large organizations can lead to routing tables that are so large they degrade the performance of the message transfer agents, even on high-performance servers.

Notes

The term *backboning* is sometimes used to describe the core messaging paths set up for a large Exchange organization, regardless of whether messaging systems other than Exchange are involved.

See Also: *Exchange Server*

background

A context for running applications or services on a computer.

Overview

A program that runs in the background is unnoticed while the user performs another task on a different program in the foreground. For example, a spreadsheet that calculates data could be hidden and running in the background while the user types a letter using a word processor program running in the foreground. If the user switches from the letter to the spreadsheet, the roles of the two programs become reversed.

Operating systems usually assign fewer CPU resources to background programs than to foreground ones. In Microsoft Windows 2000, Windows XP, and Windows .NET Server, the System utility in Control Panel offers you several Performance options on the Advanced tab for optimizing performance between background and foreground tasks:

- **Applications:** Provides more CPU resources to the foreground program and allocates short, variable quanta to running applications
- **Background Services:** Divides CPU resources equally among the foreground program and any running background programs and allocates long, fixed-length quanta to applications

In addition, you can tune or enhance performance by modifying the total paging file size on all drives.

BackOffice

A suite of integrated server products from Microsoft Corporation.

Overview

The Microsoft BackOffice suite of server products is built upon the foundation of the Microsoft Windows 2000 Server and Advanced Server platform and provides a scalable, reliable solution for the needs of departments, branch offices, and medium-sized businesses. BackOffice is provided in an integrated package called BackOffice Server 2000, which provides tools for building directory, networking, messaging, Web services, database, proxy and firewall services, and Systems Network Architecture (SNA) host integration infrastructures.

BackOffice Server 2000 includes the following Microsoft server products:

- Windows 2000 Server or Advanced Server with Service Pack 1
- Exchange Server 2000
- SQL Server 2000
- Systems Management Server 2
- Internet Security and Acceleration Server 2000
- Host Integration Server 2000

In addition, BackOffice Server 2000 offers a host of additional tools for deploying and managing BackOffice components such as BackOffice Server management consoles, various wizards, reporting tools, and Microsoft FrontPage and Microsoft Outlook client software. For additional information on each of the server applications listed above, see their respective articles elsewhere in this book.

For More Information

Visit the BackOffice site at *www.microsoft.com/backoffice.*

See Also: *Small Business Server*

BackOffice Server

A suite of integrated server products from Microsoft Corporation.

See: *BackOffice*

Back Orifice

A remote administration tool for Microsoft Windows developed by the hacker group Cult of the Dead Cow.

Overview

Back Orifice was first released for the Microsoft Windows NT platform in 1997 by Cult of the Dead Cow (CDC), a professed hacker group. Although the tool is basically a form of Trojan horse that can be used to gain control of a target machine, it is also a full-featured remote administration system for computers that run Windows NT and Windows 2000.

Back Orifice consists of two parts:

- **Server component:** This is a small-footprint application that can be installed in a stealthy fashion on target systems and can also attach itself to any Windows executable on the target machine or run as a separate service using any name designed. The server runs invisibly in the background and is not visible to users logged on to the target machine even in the task list or close-program dialog box.
- **Client component:** This application is used by the administrator (or hacker) to control the remote Windows 2000 computer. The client component can be used either in graphical user interface (GUI) or command-line mode and can be used to send commands to the server component to perform directory listings, copy or delete files, display or kill running processes,

log all keystrokes entered at the remote machine's console, reboot or lock the system, edit the registry, and perform other actions. By default the client sends commands to the server through User Datagram Protocol (UDP) port 31337 but can be configured to use any available UDP port instead.

Back Orifice is a powerful remote administration tool, but because of its stealth features it is also a serious threat to systems running Windows NT and Windows 2000. Administrators who are concerned about this threat should consult article Q237280 in the Knowledge Base on Microsoft TechNet, which explains how to detect when the server component of Back Orifice is present on a system and how to remove it.

For More Information

You can find Back Orifice 2000 at *www.cultdeadcow.com.* Microsoft TechNet can be found at *www.microsoft.com/technet.*

See Also: *virus*

backup

The process of making reliable copies of important data so that the data can be recovered in the event of a disaster.

Overview

Performing regular backups is perhaps the system or network administrator's least glamorous but most important task. Data loss on a corporate network can occur for various reasons, including

- Disk failures caused by hardware failure, power outages, or improper use
- Network problems leading to lost packets that are not acknowledged because of router congestion or other situations
- Virus infection, resulting in corrupted files
- Sabotage by hackers or disgruntled employees, resulting in erased data
- Theft of hardware from the premises

In each of these scenarios, having reliable backups of your company data is essential to recover from the disaster and continue normal business functioning.

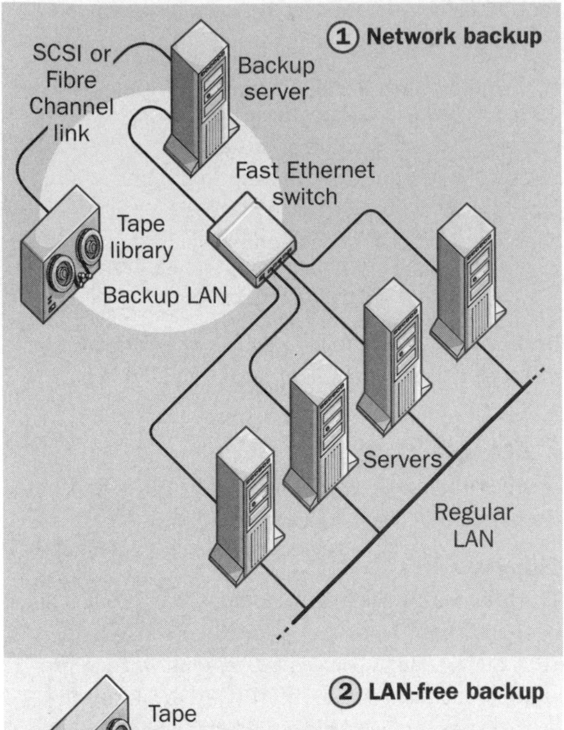

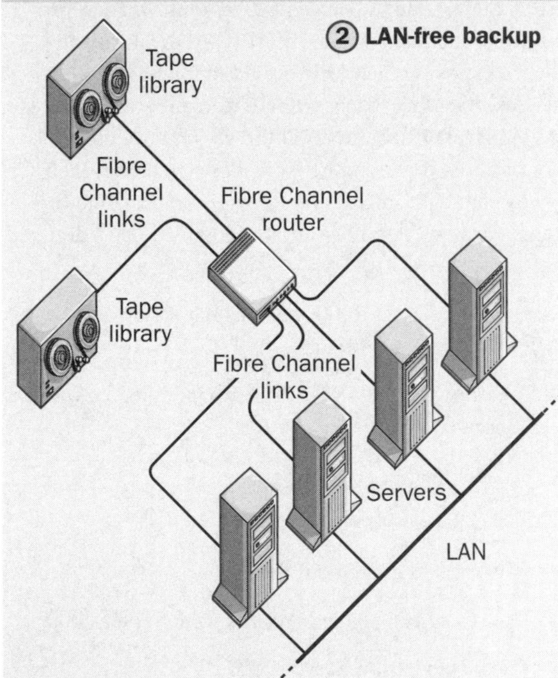

Backup. *Network and LAN-free backup scenarios in the enterprise.*

At the enterprise level, backups can be performed using a variety of technologies, each of which have their own advantages. These technologies are a blend of backup device hardware and how these devices are implemented. The next section of this article looks at a few common scenarios. First, backup solutions can be characterized by the devices used to store the backed-up data. These devices can include

- **Tape drives:** A tape drive is a device that stores data on magnetic tape. Many kinds of tape drives and tape formats are supported by different vendors, and these are discussed more fully in the articles "tape drive" and "tape format" elsewhere in this book. Generally speaking, however, tape drives have capacities in the tens of gigabytes range and are suitable for backing up data from individual servers or small groups of servers.
- **Tape libraries:** A tape library consists of a set of tape drives, a large collection of tapes, and a robotic mechanism for loading and unloading tapes into drives. Tape libraries are common in large companies and can typically store several terabytes (one terabyte equals 1000 gigabytes) of data from groups of servers. For more information, see the article "tape library" elsewhere in this book.
- **Optical drives:** Another medium for backing up data is optical drives, which range from simple CD-R/W drives to DVD-W drives and libraries containing many such drives. Optical drives are not as common as tape drives and libraries.
- **Storage appliances:** These are generally rack-mountable black-box solutions in which the underlying operation is not important. Storage appliances are generally used for live data storage but can also be used for small-scale backup purposes.
- **Storage Area Networks (SANs):** While SANs are primarily used for live storage of data, they can also be used for archiving backup data. See the article "storage area network (SAN)" elsewhere in this book for more information.

Besides these different backup devices, there are also various ways of implementing them for backing up data from network servers:

- **Server-based backups:** In this scenario each server that holds valuable data has a tape drive directly attached to it, usually through a Small Computer System Interface (SCSI) connection. The disadvantage of this scenario is that it scales poorly for large companies—administrators would need to run around each morning to collect tapes from drives scattered all over the network.
- **Network backups:** This is the most common scenario in most large companies. In a typical network backup scenario, a group of servers on a local area network (LAN) are connected using a second network interface card (NIC) in each server to a separate LAN dedicated for backup purposes. This dedicated backup LAN is concentrated using a Fast or Gigabit Ethernet Switch, which is also connected to a dedicated server called the backup server. The backup server has special software running on it that initiates and manages the job of backing up data on the production servers. The backup server itself is then connected by SCSI or FiberChannel to a tape library (see illustration).
- **LAN-free backup:** This is a simplified form of network backup in which there's no second backup LAN. Instead, fiber channel cards are added to servers needing to be backed up and these are connected using fiber-optic cabling to a fiber-channel router, which then forwards the information directly over Fibre Channel links to tape libraries (see illustration). LAN-free backup is an emerging approach that is gaining in popularity due to its simplicity and high performance.
- **Serverless backups:** This is a further refinement of LAN-free backups that takes the actual task of processing the backup from the servers and moves it to a Fibre Channel switch or router used to connect the servers to the tape libraries. This can provide significant relief to the servers since generating backups is a processor-intensive and memory-intensive job that limits other functions they can perform while the backup is occurring. Serverless backup solutions are just emerging in the marketplace.
- **Storage over IP:** This technology backs up data from network servers directly to backup devices such as tape libraries and SANs using only an Ethernet

network. No backup server is required to convert the data from Ethernet frames for transmission over SCSI or Fibre Channel connections to the backup device. Storage over IP is an emerging technology that promises to have a large impact on the backup market, and it is discussed further in the article "storage over IP" elsewhere in this book.

- **Internet backups:** Backups can also be outsourced over the Internet to a Storage Service Provider (SSP) that is responsible for managing actual backup hardware and securely storing your data. For more information on this, see the article "televaulting" elsewhere in this book.

Finally, a third component of a backup system is the backup software itself. Some of the more popular backup software products used in the enterprise include

- ArcServeIT from Computer Associates
- Backup Exec and NetBackup from VERITAS Software Corporation
- Legato NetWorker from Legato Systems
- Storage Manager from Tivoli Systems
- Backup Express from Syncsort
- Hiback and Hibars from Hicomp Software Systems

Implementation

Instituting a regular backup plan is one of the main components of a company's disaster recovery policy (see the article "disaster recovery" elsewhere in this book for more information), and the importance of doing so cannot be stressed enough. To guard against these unexpected losses of data—or rather, to prepare for them, since they are, to a certain extent, inevitable—establish a disaster recovery policy that includes a reliable backup plan. In today's business world, where data is the lifeblood of the enterprise, a comprehensive plan is essential. The following steps are recommended when creating such a plan:

- Decide what kind of backup storage devices to use. Options range from small digital audio tape (DAT) drive units capable of backing up several gigabytes of data to large automated tape libraries capable of handling terabytes of centralized data storage. Other backup options include optical storage libraries and removable disks such as Iomega's Zip drive disks or Imation SuperDisk disks.
- Decide whether to back up servers with dedicated, locally connected storage devices or over the network to centralized backup libraries. Network backup systems suffer from a single point of failure (the network itself) but are simpler to administer than a multitude of individual backup units.
- Decide whether individual users' workstations should also be backed up. A more cost-effective option is to educate users to always save their work on a network share located on a server that is regularly backed up.
- Decide how to secure the storage of backup tapes and other media. Will duplicate copies be stored both on-site (for easy access if a restore is needed) and off-site (in case the company's building burns down)? Make sure the storage facilities are climate-controlled and secure.
- Decide what kind of backup strategy to employ. A backup strategy is a combination of a backup schedule and various backup types, including normal, copy, incremental, differential, and daily copy backup types. Also consider whether you will verify all tapes immediately after each backup is performed. For further information, see the articles "backup strategy" and "backup type" elsewhere in this chapter.
- Assign various aspects of the backup procedure to the responsible party. One option some companies now use is to back up data over the Internet to a third-party backup service provider that stores and maintains the backed-up data. This method involves issues of trust and of the Internet connection as a point of failure.
- Test backups periodically to ensure that they are actually readable. Nothing is worse than thinking you have a backup when in fact it is unreadable.

Notes

To enable administrators to perform regular backups, Microsoft Corporation includes backup utilities with all versions of Microsoft Windows, such as the Backup tool in Windows XP.

See Also: *backup strategy, backup type, storage over IP, storage service provider (SSP), tape drive, tape format, tape library*

backup agent

A service that can be installed on a computer to allow files and folders stored on the computer to be backed up remotely over the network.

Overview

Backup agents enable backups to be performed across an entire network from a centralized location. In networks that utilize this type of storage retention architecture, where a backup agent is installed on each server, files are backed up over the network to a central storage location, which in enterprise environments is usually a tape library or some type of Network Attached Storage (NAS). This approach to backups makes it easier to manage enterprise storage requirements even for large scale corporate networks and Internet service providers (ISPs).

Backup agents are specific to the type of backup software being used and are usually supplied with that software when you purchase it from a vendor. Once an agent is installed on a computer, you can back it up over the network as easily as if a tape drive were connected directly to the computer.

See Also: *backup*

backup browser

A Windows 2000, Windows XP, and Windows .NET Server computer that participates in the Computer Browser service.

Overview

A backup browser is a computer that obtains a copy of the browse list from the master browser. The browse list contains information about which shared resources are available to client machines on the network and about which domains are on the network. Backup browsers automatically contact the master browser every 12 minutes to request a copy of the browse list. If the contact is successful, the master browser issues the list to the backup browser. If the backup browser cannot contact the master browser, it starts a browser election to force a new master browser to be selected.

Once the backup browser has obtained the browse list, it caches the list and distributes it to any client that requests it. To request the browse list from a backup browser, a client calls the NetServerEnum application programming interface (API) on the backup browser.

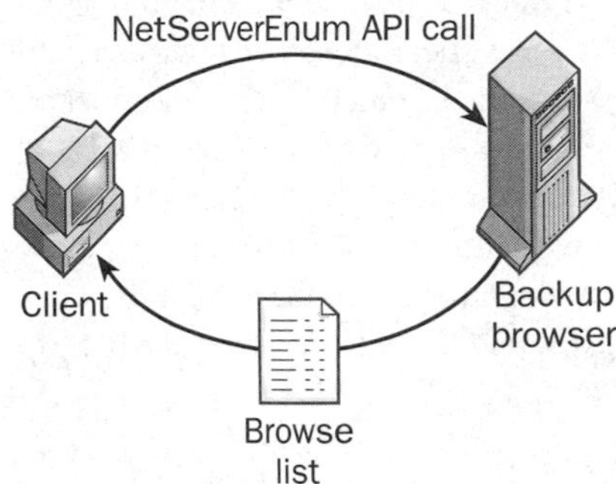

Backup browser. *How a client obtains the browse list from a backup browser.*

Notes

There will be one backup browser for every 32 systems in a given domain or workgroup on the network. The Computer Browser service determines the number of backup browsers necessary to ensure that clients can have efficient access to network resources.

See Also: *Computer Browser service, domain master browser, master browser*

backup catalog

A representation of the results of performing a backup of servers on a network.

Overview

Backup software, such as the Backup tool in Microsoft Windows 2000, Windows XP, and Windows .NET Server, creates catalogs so that the location and properties of backed-up files are documented and can be found easily when a restore needs to be performed. Windows 2000, Windows XP, and Windows .NET Server Backup stores its catalogs on the backup storage media themselves. These catalogs are then loaded into memory when the program is run. Catalogs can also be saved to disk and printed for documentation purposes.

Windows 2000, Windows XP, and Windows .NET Server Backup creates two different types of backup catalogs:

- **Tape catalog:** Lists the details of all backup sets that have been stored on the tape. If a backup operation spans several tapes, the tape catalog is located on the last tape of the series, because it is created at the end of the backup operation.
- **Backup set catalog:** Lists the details of files and folders included in a specific backup set. A backup set catalog is saved at the end of each backup set on the tape. This catalog is used by the Windows 2000, Windows XP, and Windows .NET Server Backup program to store a summary of the file and directory information for the backup set, the number of tapes in the backup set, and the date on which the backup was performed.

See Also: *backup set*

backup domain controller (BDC)

A Microsoft Windows NT domain controller containing a read-only copy of the Security Accounts Manager (SAM) database.

Overview

On the Windows NT platform, the only writable copy of the SAM database is located on the primary domain controller (PDC). In addition to this PDC, a Windows NT domain can have zero or more backup domain controllers (BDCs) as well. These BDCs are used to provide load balancing and redundancy for network authentication. These BDCs periodically undergo directory synchronization with the PDC by retrieving a copy of the directory database from the PDC.

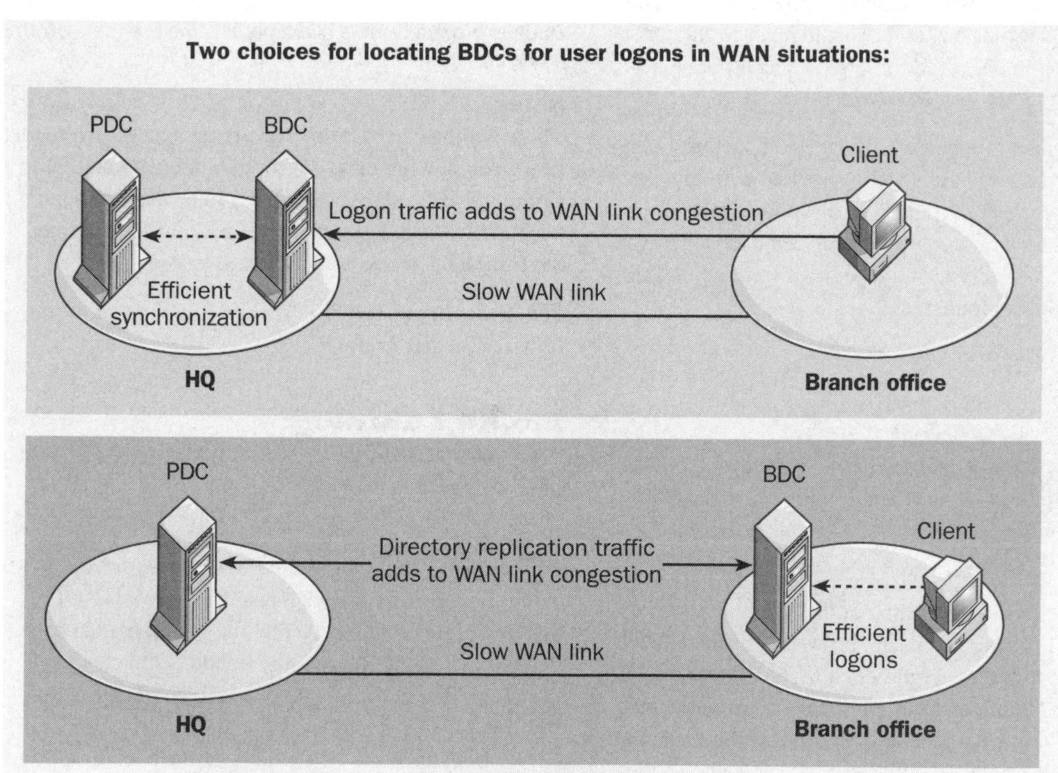

Backup domain controller (BDC). *Different ways to deploy a BDC over a WAN link.*

Every Windows NT network should have at least one BDC for fault tolerance. If the PDC fails, the BDC can be promoted to take its place. One BDC can support approximately 2000 users on a network, but many factors can affect this figure.

Note that a BDC can perform logon validation and authentication as a PDC can, but it cannot manage accounts—for example, it cannot change user passwords.

Implementation

The placement of BDCs in wide area networks (WANs) that are based on Windows NT is an important issue. In a master domain model scenario, user accounts are centralized in a master domain located at company headquarters, but users and shared network resources are distributed in resource domains located at branch offices in different locations. The users in this scenario must log on to the master domain in order to access resources in the enterprise. There are two ways of facilitating this:

- Locate all BDCs belonging to the master domain at headquarters. Unfortunately, when users at the branch offices want to log on, they will have to use the relatively slow WAN link to do so. The additional logon traffic can cause congestion on the WAN link, particularly at certain times of the day.
- Locate one or more BDCs belonging to the master domain at each branch office (resource domain). This will facilitate logons by users located at branch offices, since they can log on to one of these BDCs locally instead of being validated over the relatively slow WAN link by a domain controller at headquarters. However, directory replication traffic between the BDCs located at the branch offices and the PDC at headquarters can cause congestion over the WAN links. To make directory synchronization more efficient over the WAN link, registry parameters such as ReplicationGovernor and ChangeLogSize can be adjusted and batch files can be scheduled using the at command to configure different replication rates at different times of the day.

See Also: *domain controller, primary domain controller (PDC)*

Backup Operator

In Microsoft Windows 2000, Windows XP, and Windows .NET Server, a user who is assigned the responsibility of backing up and restoring servers on a network.

Overview

To make an individual a Backup Operator, simply make him a member of the Backup Operators group. Backup Operators can exist on Windows NT domain controllers, on member servers, and on workstations. In Windows 2000, Windows XP, and Windows .NET Server, Backup Operators are members who have a similar function and belong to the built-in group called the Backup Operators built-in group.

Backup Operators have the preassigned right to log on locally to a computer and to back up and restore files and directories on the system. Backup Operators also have the right to shut down the system. Backup Operators do not need permissions assigned to them in order to back up a particular file or directory—they have a broad system right to do so.

Notes

Backup Operators should be assigned only in enterprise-level networking environments. In small to medium-sized networking environments, backing up and restoring servers is usually the responsibility of the administrator.

See Also: *Backup Operators built-in group, built-in group*

Backup Operators built-in group

In Microsoft Windows 2000, Windows XP, and Windows .NET Server, a built-in group for containing users who need privileges to back up servers on the network.

Overview

Backup Operators is a built-in group existing on all Windows 2000–, Windows XP–, and Windows .NET Server–based servers and workstations. The Backup Operators built-in group is a local group with the following preassigned rights:

- Log on locally
- Back up files and directories
- Restore files and directories
- Shut down the system

Notes

If you want a user to be able to back up files and directories on any domain controller in a domain, place the user in the Backup Operators group on any domain controller. Since all domain controllers share the same directory database, the user will be a member of the Backup Operators built-in group for all domain controllers. However, if you want a user to be able to back up a member server, place the user in the Backup Operators built-in group that is a local group on that particular member server.

See Also: *built-in group*

backup set

A collection of files and folders on a backup media that were saved in a single Microsoft Windows 2000, Windows XP, and Windows .NET Server Backup operation.

Overview

There are several options for creating backup sets in Windows 2000, Windows XP, and Windows .NET Server:

- Multiple backup sets can be saved on a single backup tape by appending each new set to the last one.
- A backup set can span multiple tapes if you have a large quantity of information to back up.
- Tapes can be overwritten so that a new backup set replaces the old one.

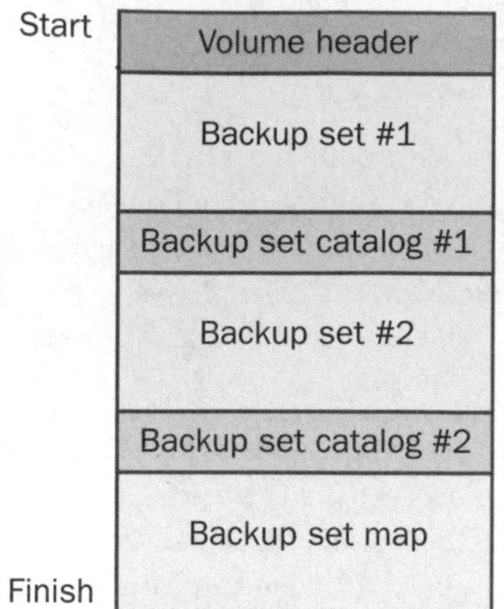

Backup set. *A representation of a backup set.*

Windows 2000, Windows XP, and Windows .NET Server Backup creates a backup set catalog for each backup set. This catalog lists the various files and directories that have been backed up, and you can use it for restoring individual files or directories or print it for documentation purposes. The backup set catalog is saved at the end of each backup set on the tape. A backup set map at the end of the tape locates all backup sets on the tape.

Notes

A copy of the local system's registry can also be included in the backup set for a Windows 2000, Windows XP, and Windows .NET Server system. Backup sets are described with friendly names that can be up to 32 characters long.

See Also: *backup catalog*

backup strategy

A plan for performing backups to ensure against data loss.

Overview

Successful backup strategies take the following issues into account:

- The various backup types that can be performed
- The need to archive tapes for long-term data security
- The time needed to perform backups and restores

- The cost of tapes
- The cost of losing data

There's no one right way to implement a backup strategy for resources on a network of computers. To select the best backup strategy for your network, you must consider each of the items in the preceding list and balance them against one another. Your strategy should be simple, efficient, and reliable. The following table shows some examples of backup strategies:

Possible Backup Strategies

Backup Strategy	*Advantages*	*Disadvantages*
Normal backups Monday through Friday.	Most secure—every tape contains all backed up files	Longest time to back up
Normal backup Monday; differential backups Tuesday through Friday.	Less time to restore	More time to back up
Normal backup Monday; incremental backups Tuesday through Friday.	Less time to back up	More time to restore
Use a separate tape for each weekday and archive Monday's full backup tape weekly or monthly.	Less chance of data loss	Higher cost, since more tapes are needed
Use the same tape for each weekday and archive the tape each week or month.	Cheaper—only one tape required per week or month	Greater chance of data loss, since using only one tape

See Also: *backup, backup type*

backup type

A particular method for performing a backup of files and directories.

Overview

Each type of backup has a different function in an overall backup plan. Most network backup software (such as Microsoft Windows 2000, Windows XP, and Windows .NET Server Backup) supports five backup methods:

- **Normal backup:** Backs up volumes, folders, and files that have been specified by the administrator. Normal backups are the fastest and easiest to restore. Normal backups are sometimes referred to as "full backups." Use a normal backup when you want to ensure that all your critical system and data files are backed up in a single operation. If your backup cycle consists only of normal backups and you need to perform a restore, you need to use only the most recent normal backup to do so.
- **Copy backup:** Primarily used to produce an additional copy of a backup—for example, a copy to send to the accounting department for monthly archiving and reporting. While a copy backup backs up the same files as a normal backup, there is a difference between the two operations. Performing a normal backup clears the archive bit on each backed-up file and marks them as having been backed up. A copy backup, however, does not modify the archive bit on the files backed up. In other words, you can perform a copy backup at any time in a backup cycle without interrupting the cycle in any way—the copy backup is distinct from the backup cycle and is not required when a restore is performed from the cycle's set of tapes.
- **Incremental backup:** Backs up only files that have been created or modified since the last normal or incremental backup. Files that are backed up in an incremental backup have their archive attributes cleared in order to indicate that they have been backed up. Using a combination of normal and incremental backups takes less time and uses less storage space than performing only normal backups. However, if you need to perform a restore, you typically need to use the normal backup plus every incremental backup from the current backup cycle to do so.
- **Differential backup:** Copies those files that have been created or changed since the last normal or incremental backup. Files that are backed up by a

differential backup do not have their archive attributes cleared, which means that these files will be backed up again in any succeeding differential backups. Differential backups are cumulative with regard to changes—that is, each differential backup in a given backup cycle contains all the files from the last differential backup, plus any files that have been modified since the last differential backup. Thus, if you need to perform a restore, you will typically need to use only the normal backup and the most recent differential backup from the current backup cycle to do so.

- **Daily copy backup:** Copies all files that have been modified on the day the daily copy backup is performed. This method is sometimes used to make a copy of all files a user worked on in a day so that he or she can take them home to work on. Like a copy backup, the daily copy backup does not modify the archive bit of the files backed up; therefore, the daily copy backup does not interrupt the backup cycle in any way.

Notes

Different types of backup operations have different effects on the archive attributes of the files and directories they back up. A backup operation marks the archive attribute by clearing it to indicate that the file has been backed up. If the file is later modified in some way, its archive attribute is set (unmarked). The following table shows what each type of backup operation does to the archive attribute.

Effects of Backup Operations on the Archive Attribute

Backup Type	*Archive Attribute*
Normal	Cleared
Copy	No effect
Incremental	Cleared
Differential	No effect
Daily copy	No effect

See Also: *backup, backup strategy*

Backup Wizard

A wizard that is part of the Microsoft Windows 2000, Windows XP, and Windows .NET Server Backup tool.

Overview

You can use the Backup Wizard to configure, schedule, and execute a backup. The Backup Wizard starts by letting you choose among the following:

- Backing up all files on the computer on which it is running.
- Backing up files and folders that you specify. These files and folders can be either on the local computer or on any shared location on the network.
- Backing up Active Directory directory service information and the registry on the computer on which the wizard is running. Active Directory can be backed up only on a domain controller.

The wizard then leads you through the process of specifying a backup location and other advanced backup options, such as verification, compression, and remote storage. You can also schedule a backup job to run unattended at a later time when users have stopped working and all files are closed.

See Also: *backup*

BACP

Stands for Bandwidth Allocation Control Protocol, an enhanced version of Bandwidth Allocation Protocol (BAP), a protocol that manages bandwidth for Multilink Point-to-Point Protocol (MPPP) connections.

See: *Bandwidth Allocation Control Protocol (BACP)*

balanced line

An electrical cable consisting of pairs of conductors that have identical electrical characteristics with respect to each other and with respect to ground.

Overview

In a balanced line, both of the two wires are carrying current at any given instant. However, at any particular moment, the directions of the current in the wires are opposite each other. This condition is also described by saying that the currents in the wires are 180 degrees out of phase with each other at any given moment.

Both wires have voltages that are above ground potential, but the potentials of the wires are different with respect to ground, resulting in a flow of current. The wire pair is twisted in order to ensure that the electromagnetic radiation produced by both wires is effectively canceled out, reducing the overall electromagnetic interference (EMI) produced by the wires and reducing their sensitivity to induced currents from external sources of EMI.

The most common example in computer networking is the twisted-pair cabling used in 10BaseT Ethernet networks.

Notes

A balun can be used to connect a balanced line to an unbalanced line.

See Also: *balun, unbalanced line*

balun

Stands for balanced unbalanced, a device used to connect balanced lines and unbalanced lines.

Overview

Balanced and unbalanced lines have different electrical characteristics that prevent them from simply being connected to each other. A balun matches these different characteristics by providing impedance transformation between the two different lines.

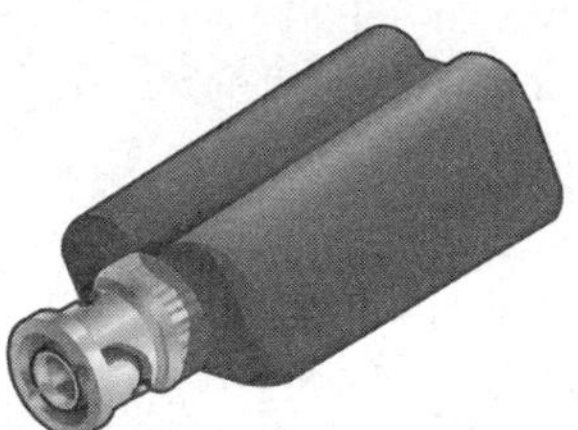

Balun. *An example of a coxial-to-twisted-pair balun.*

Baluns can be used for various types of connections between different wiring systems:

- **Twisted-pair cabling to coaxial cabling:** Typically used for connecting 10BaseT networks with 3270 equipment running on coax or twinax networks
- **Twisted-pair cabling to Token Ring cabling:** Used for matching Token Ring Type 1 cabling to standard unshielded twisted-pair (UTP) cabling to connect 10BaseT or faster hubs or adapters with RJ-45 ports into a Token Ring network
- **Asynchronous Transfer Mode (ATM) cabling to Token Ring cabling:** Used for connecting Token Ring networks to high-speed ATM hubs in campus backbone networks

See Also: *balanced line, unbalanced line*

bandwidth

The information-carrying capacity of a signal or technology.

Overview

By definition, bandwidth equals the difference between the highest and lowest frequencies in a given range of frequencies. For example, if the lowest and highest frequencies a telephone line can carry are 300 hertz (Hz) and 3300 Hz, the bandwidth of the telephone line is 3300 – 300 = 3000 Hz, or 3 kilohertz (kHz).

The above definition of bandwidth applies to any signaling system, analog or digital. With digital systems such as computer data networks, the term *bandwidth* is often used to describe the capacity of a communication channel for carrying signals. The greater the bandwidth, the more data can be transferred in a given time. Since bandwidth is here synonymous with information, and digital information is conveyed in bits (1=on and 0=off), bandwidth for such systems is usually expressed in bits per second (bps) or some multiple thereof (including Kbps, Mbps, Gbps, and Tbps). This rate of flow of information in bits per second is more properly termed "throughput," but bandwidth is the usual expression used in popular literature.

Shannon's Law can be used to determine the information-carrying capacity of a transmission channel as follows:

(Throughput in bps) = (Bandwidth in Hz) x log2 [1 + R]

where

R = (Signal power in Watts) / (Noise power in Watts)

This formula is only approximate since it does not take into account the medium's transmission properties and other considerations. The significant thing to notice, however, is that as noise (due to crosstalk, interference, or some other source) increases, the channel's capacity to carry information decreases.

For fiber-optic cabling, the bandwidth is usually expressed in units of MHz-km. For example, a cable rated at 500 MHz-km could carry 500 Mbps of data a distance of 1 kilometer (km), 250 Mbps of data a distance of 2 kilometers, 100 Mbps of data a distance of 5 kilometers, and so on. A similar explanation holds for measurements in units of MHz-miles.

Notes

Adequate bandwidth is a prerequisite for reliable communications, and ensuring sufficient bandwidth in today's Internet economy often drives upgrades for enterprise networks. When a new bandwidth need arises, such as deployment of streaming media across a network, the obvious solution may seem to be to "throw bandwidth at the problem," that is, to spend money on upgrading the network infrastructure from Ethernet to Fast Ethernet to Gigabit Ethernet (GbE) and beyond. This is really only one solution—another, sometimes better, approach is to implement Quality of Service (QoS) mechanisms to prioritize traffic so that certain forms of traffic receive preferential transport over less important forms. QoS is an elegant solution that sidesteps the brute-force approach of simply adding more bandwidth, but QoS can be difficult to configure and manage. Although Asynchronous Transport Mode (ATM) networks have the advantage of having QoS built into their operational fabric, the far more common Ethernet networks require new protocols such as DiffServ and Resource Reservation Setup Protocol (RSVP) to be implemented to support even rudimentary QoS features. And with the rapidly dropping prices of GbE switching gear and the appearance of 10 GbE on the horizon, simply adding more bandwidth when it is needed is still the most common solution for most large companies.

See Also: *quality of service (QoS), signaling*

Bandwidth Allocation Control Protocol (BACP)

An enhanced version of Bandwidth Allocation Protocol (BAP), a protocol that manages bandwidth for Multilink Point-to-Point Protocol (MPPP) connections.

Overview

Although BAP dynamically controls how bandwidth can be allocated for Multilink Point-to-Point Protocol (MPPP) connections, a condition can sometimes occur in which both hosts at the two ends of a MPPP connection try to add or remove an additional link at the same time. The Bandwidth Allocation Control Protocol (BACP) is an enhanced version of BAP that is designed to handle such a scenario. It does this by establishing ahead of time which MPPP host is the favored peer, that is, the one whose BAP request will be honored in case of a collision of two requests.

See Also: *Bandwidth Allocation Protocol (BAP), Multilink Point-to-Point Protocol (MPPP)*

Bandwidth Allocation Protocol (BAP)

An offshoot of Multilink Point-to-Point Protocol (MPPP) that allows new links to be added or removed dynamically when needed.

Overview

The Bandwidth Allocation Protocol (BAP) dynamically controls how bandwidth can be allocated for multilink connections using the Point-to-Point Protocol (PPP). BAP makes multilink remote access (RAS) connections more efficient by allocating lines only as required, thus eliminating wasted bandwidth. This can be especially useful if the telecommunications carrier provisioning the PPP connection charges by the amount of bandwidth being utilized by the customer.

BAP allows the administrator to configure the PPP server to specify which particular MPPP lines can be added or dropped. The administrator also specifies which bandwidth thresholds must be crossed before additional lines are added or existing ones are dropped. BAP is especially useful over Integrated Services Digital Network (ISDN) connections, because these dial-up services can almost instantly add or drop lines.

Notes

BAP is included in Microsoft Windows 2000 and Windows .NET Server as an enhancement to the Routing and Remote Access Service (RRAS) of Windows NT 4. BAP is outlined in detail in RFC 2125.

See Also: *Bandwidth Allocation Protocol (BAP), Multilink Point-to-Point Protocol (MPPP)*

bandwidth on demand

Any networking or telecommunications technology that provides both a permanent, dedicated connection and the capability of quickly increasing bandwidth when needed by users.

Overview

Many telecommunications devices incorporate bandwidth-on-demand features of various types. For example, some Integrated Services Digital Network (ISDN) devices used for Basic Rate Interface ISDN (BRI-ISDN) can be configured to use the second ISDN B channel only when the utilization of the first channel exceeds a certain threshold. If this threshold is exceeded for a specified period of time, the second B channel automatically opens up to facilitate and speed data transfer. Once the data rate has dropped below the threshold, the second B channel shuts down until it is needed again. The ISDN technology for accomplishing this combining of channels is called bonding. Many Asynchronous Transfer Mode (ATM) products also support various bandwidth-on-demand features.

Bandwidth-on-demand technologies are typically used in bursty networking situations in which high transmission speeds and capacities are required for transporting video, voice, and data on common networking circuits. Bandwidth-on-demand configurations often involve a mix of leased-line services and circuit-switched telecommunications services, and they can save users money by opening additional circuits only on an as-needed basis. Networks that make use of bandwidth on demand can be designed to supply additional bandwidth under conditions such as

- Exceeding a specified threshold of network traffic
- Scheduling for expected peak periods of the day
- Failover in case the permanent link goes down

See Also: *Asynchronous Transfer Mode (ATM), bandwidth, Integrated Services Digital Network (ISDN)*

bandwidth throttling

Generally, any networking technology that controls the amount of network bandwidth used by servers, applications, or network communication paths.

Overview

In the context of Microsoft Internet Information Services (IIS), for example, bandwidth throttling is a technique for controlling the amount of network bandwidth used by individual Web sites hosted on the server. You can use bandwidth throttling to prevent hits on a popular site from overwhelming the server and preventing other sites hosted on the server from being accessed by clients.

For example, if five Web sites are being hosted on a single machine running IIS but one of them is extremely popular, the other sites might get starved for bandwidth and users might have difficulty connecting to them. In order to rectify this situation, a specific maximum bandwidth level can be allocated to the popular site with the Internet Services Manager snap-in used for administering IIS using the Microsoft Management Console (MMC). If this maximum bandwidth is exceeded, no further connections to that site are allowed until the bandwidth utilization level drops below the threshold. This allows the unallocated bandwidth to be shared among the remaining less popular sites so that users can connect to them.

See Also: *bandwidth, Internet Information Services (IIS)*

B

Banyan VINES

Stands for Banyan Virtual Integrated Network Service (VINES), a legacy network operating system (NOS) for building enterprise-level networks.

Overview

VINES was originally based on a proprietary family of protocols that was derived from the Xerox Network Systems (XNS) protocol. VINES uses a client/server distributed networking architecture for allowing clients to access network resources on servers over the network. VINES includes such features as

- Basic file and print sharing
- A distributed directory service called StreetTalk for managing networks
- Support for the Transmission Control Protocol/ Internet Protocol (TCP/IP) protocol
- Graphical administration tools
- Support for Simple Network Management Protocol (SNMP) management

VINES includes clients for MS-DOS, OS/2, Microsoft Windows, and Macintosh platforms as well as optional applications for integrating Windows NT, AppleTalk, Novell, and UNIX networks into existing VINES-based networks.

VINES is built on a client/server model in which clients can make requests for services from servers on the network. The VINES protocol stack consists of five basic layers that map to the seven-layer Open Systems Interconnection (OSI) reference model as follows:

- **Physical and data-link layers:** VINES can operate over Ethernet, Token Ring, X.25, and other types of networking architectures.
- **Network layer:** The main protocol here is the VINES Internetwork Protocol (VIP), which is similar in function to the IP of the TCP/IP protocol suite. VIP encapsulates data and addresses it using a 48-bit address that contains a 32-bit network number and a 16-bit host number. Dynamic address assignment and address resolution are performed using VINES servers, which are referred to as service nodes. VINES clients obtain their addresses dynamically from the nearest server on the network. Multihomed servers function as routers, and routing tables are maintained by periodic announcements from clients and servers. Other network layer protocols include an Address Resolution Protocol (ARP), an Internet Control Protocol (ICP), and a Routing Table Protocol (RTP).
- **Transport layer:** For reliable delivery of data using acknowledgments and sequence numbers, VINES uses its Reliable Message Service. Another service, the Unreliable Datagram Service, supports only best-effort delivery of packets. Finally the Data Stream Service can be used to transmit large amounts of data using virtual circuits with flow-control mechanisms.
- **Session and presentation layers:** VINES implements the standard remote procedure call (RPC) mechanism for enabling communication between VINES client and server components on different stations on the network.
- **Application layer:** VINES supports standard file and print services, directory services (StreetTalk), and a number of other application layer services and protocols.

Notes

When connecting Windows 95 or Windows 98 clients to a VINES-based network, use the 32-bit client for Windows that comes with VINES instead of the 16-bit VINES client included with Windows 95 and Windows 98.

For More Information

Visit the Banyan home page at *www.banyan.com.*

BAP

Stands for Bandwidth Allocation Protocol, an offshoot of Multilink Point to Point Protocol (MPPP) that allows new links to be added or removed dynamically when needed.

See: *Bandwidth Allocation Protocol (BAP)*

baseband transmission

A signaling technology that sends digital signals over a single frequency as discrete electrical pulses.

Overview

The entire bandwidth of a baseband system carries only one data signal and is generally less than the amount of bandwidth available on a broadband transmission system. The baseband signal is bidirectional so that a baseband system can transmit and receive signals simultaneously.

Baseband signals can be regenerated using repeaters in order to travel longer distances before weakening and becoming unusable because of attenuation. Baseband transmission technologies do not use modulation but often use time-division multiplexing (TDM) to accommodate multiple channels over a single baseband transmission line.

Common local area network (LAN) networking technologies such as Ethernet use baseband transmission technology. All stations on a baseband network share the same transmission medium, and they use the entire bandwidth of that medium for transmission. As a result, only one device on a baseband network can transmit at a given instant, resulting in the need for a media access control method to handle contention.

See Also: *broadband transmission, Ethernet*

baseline

A set of data that indicates normal usage of monitored network resources.

Overview

You can use the Microsoft Windows 2000, Windows XP, or Windows .NET Server Performance console to collect data for the present performance of your network to establish a baseline. Then, if you upgrade hardware or add new users, you can measure the network's performance again and compared it with the baseline to determine trends, identify bottlenecks, and measure capacity.

Creating a baseline for server and network activity begins with the process of identifying which server and network resources should be systematically measured. Generally, you always want to measure at least the following four resources: memory, processor, disk, and network subsystems. Using the Performance console, you should collect data for the objects shown in the following table.

Resources and Corresponding Performance Objects to Monitor Performance

Resource	*Objects to Collect*
Memory	Memory, cache
Processor	Processor, system, server work queues
Disk	Logical disk, physical disk
Network	Server, network interface, network segment

These performance objects should be regularly captured for a period of time in order to collect the data needed to establish the baseline. Generally, you should append each log file collected to a master log file using relogging. Focus on periods of peak server and network activity and collect at least a week of measurements to establish your baseline.

Notes

If you want to collect disk subsystem data, first enable disk objects using the Diskperf command. Make sure you use a computer that is not being monitored to create your measurement baseline log files so that the activity of the computer doing the monitoring will not affect the data being collected.

Basic authentication

Also called cleartext or plaintext authentication, an authentication scheme that passes a user's credentials over a network in unencrypted form.

Overview

Basic authentication is defined as part of the Hypertext Transfer Protocol (HTTP) version 1 specification in RFC2617. It is not a secure authentication scheme, since anyone who can intercept network traffic and read it using a protocol analyzer can obtain the user's credentials. Although it is sometimes called cleartext authentication, Basic authentication actually encodes a user's credentials using a well-known public encoding algorithm known as Uuencoding or Base64. Because the algorithm for this encoding method is so well known, however, it is easy to decode encoded text and extract a user's credentials from a Basic authentication session.

Implementation

Basic authentication is one of several authentication schemes available on Microsoft Internet Information Services (IIS) for the Microsoft Windows 2000, Windows XP, and Windows .NET Server platforms. When a user tries to access content on a Web site hosted on IIS and the site implements Basic authentication, a dialog box appears on the user's browser asking for the user's credentials (username and password). The credentials are passed to IIS in the headers of the HTTP GET request, and are compared either to credentials in Active Directory directory service (if implemented) or to the Security Accounts Manager (SAM) database (on a workgroup server). If Active Directory is used, the user's User Principal Name (UPN) can be utilized for authentication purposes. Users who need to be able to access IIS using Basic authentication require the Log On Locally system right (although this can be changed using Active Directory Services Interface, abbreviated ADSI).

The problem with employing Basic authentication is that it is inherently insecure because of the cleartext transmission of the user's password. However, IIS does allow Basic authentication to be implemented with Secure Sockets Layer (SSL) encryption, in which case an encrypted session is first established for the user after which the user's credentials are passed to IIS in encrypted form.

The plus side of Basic authentication is that it can be performed through a firewall or proxy server (Integrated Windows authentication or Windows NTLM cannot work in this case).

Notes

Basic authentication is often used in a UNIX environment for authenticating remote HTTP users.

If you employ Basic authentication with IIS, make sure you also use the NTFS file system (NTFS) to secure access to files on your system.

See Also: *authentication protocol*

basic disk

In Microsoft Windows 2000, Windows XP, and Windows .NET Server, a physical disk that can contain primary partitions, extended partitions, and logical drives.

Overview

Basic disks can be accessed by MS-DOS and legacy Windows platforms and are backward-compatible with these platforms for multiboot systems. Basic disks can also contain volumes created using Windows NT version 4 or earlier, such as spanned volumes (volume sets), striped volumes (stripe sets), mirrored volumes (mirror sets), and RAID 5 volumes (stripe sets with parity).

Basic disks are the default type of disk in Windows 2000 and Windows XP. All disks are basic disks unless you convert them to dynamic disks. Basic disks can have two kinds of partitions:

- **Primary partitions:** Basic disks support up to four primary partitions, only one of which can be marked as active.
- **Extended partitions:** Basic disks support only one extended partition, which can be further subdivided into logical drives or logical volumes.

Notes

You can create only basic volumes on basic disks. You cannot create new simple, spanned, striped, mirrored, or RAID 5 volumes on basic disks.

See Also: *basic volume, dynamic disk*

Basic Rate Interface ISDN (BRI-ISDN)

The slower version of Integrated Services Digital Network (ISDN) communications (the faster being Primary Rate Interface ISDN, abbreviated as PRI-ISDN).

Overview

Basic Rate Interface ISDN (BRI-ISDN, or simply BRI) communications links consist of two B channels and one D channel. The B channels carry the voice or data between the customer premises and the telco central office (CO), and the D channel (control channel) is used for establishing connections and signaling various conditions. BRI is often referred to as 2B+D because of the channels that it employs.

Since the bandwidth of each B channel is 64 kilobits per second (Kbps), the total bandwidth of BRI is twice that, or 128 Kbps. This bandwidth can be used as two separate communication links of 64 Kbps each (for example one for voice and the other for data), or it can be combined into a single 128-Kbps communication link using a technique called bonding. The bandwidth of the D channel is 16 Kbps.

Implementation

BRI connections at customer premises can be connected directly to a switch at the CO, an ISDN call controller that is linked to the CO, an ISDN Private Branch Exchange (PBX), or some other signaling and communication equipment.

If you plan to order a router or access server that supports BRI, make sure you find out from your telco of what kind of ISDN interface is used at your customer premises. The two most common interfaces are the U interface and the S/T interface, and they physically appear the same. Many ISDN access devices support both kinds of interfaces, but check to make sure first.

See Also: *bonding, Integrated Services Digital Network (ISDN), Primary Rate Interface ISDN (PRI-ISDN)*

basic volume

A type of volume in Microsoft Windows 2000, Windows XP, and Windows .NET Server that is compatible with earlier Windows operating systems.

Overview

A basic volume can be created only on a basic disk and can be

- A primary partition, extended partition, or logical drive that was created using the Disk Management portion of the Computer Management tool
- A volume set, mirror set, stripe set, or stripe set with parity that was created using Windows NT version 4 or earlier

See Also: *basic disk, dynamic volume*

bastion host

A network server that is hardened against attack from the outside world.

Overview

Bastion hosts are servers exposed to the outside world and fortified to protect them from attack by hackers. Bastion hosts usually reside on the edge of your corporate network where it connects to the Internet, and often within a specific area called the perimeter network, also known as the DMZ (demilitarized zone), which forms a kind of transition network between your corporate network and the public Internet.

There are many different kinds of bastion hosts:

- **Sacrificial hosts:** These are hosts whose security being compromised is not an issue of great importance. Examples might be a public Web server exposed only to the Internet and not to the corporate side of the perimeter network, or a test server running new applications whose security configuration is still under development, or a dummy host to distract attackers away from the real prize.
- **External service hosts:** These are servers that are primarily exposed to the Internet and may include mail servers, Web servers, and news servers. These hosts are sometimes called primary bastion hosts.
- **Internal service hosts:** These are servers that are primarily exposed to the corporate network and

may include name servers and logon servers. These hosts are sometimes called secondary bastion hosts.

- **Nonrouting multihomed hosts:** These are servers connected to both the internal and external networks but are configured to prevent routing between the two networks. It is essential to verify with this type of host that routing is in fact disabled.

Managing a bastion host involves several activities:

- The initial configuration of the host is important and usually involves removing unnecessary applications, disabling unnecessary services, and removing unnecessary user accounts from the host. In this sense, a bastion host can be thought of as a stripped-down server with limited but highly specific functionality. The motto "keep it simple" is a good rule of thumb when configuring a bastion host—the simpler the server's configuration, the easier it is to monitor and troubleshoot.
- The implementation of a firewall is an essential step in securing a bastion host. The firewall may reside on the host itself or on some other server within the perimeter network, or it may be a multistage firewall residing on several hosts.
- Monitoring the bastion host once it is configured is essential to determine whether it has been attacked and whether any damage has occurred that might compromise the network. Network security is not a one-time affair but an ongoing commitment that involves auditing, performance monitoring, traffic capture and analysis, logging, and reporting.

Finally, it is essential to accept the fact that bastion hosts are likely to be compromised as new operating system and application bugs are reported and fixes issued by vendors. As a result, never put anything on a bastion host that you would mind losing or which is not available somewhere else. Accept the worst—your host will be compromised someday.

Notes

Some additional tips on deploying bastion hosts:

- Use older, slower machines for bastion hosts if possible because they are less attractive targets for attack by hackers, and, if compromised, are less useful for executing code that can be used to attack the internal network.
- Use the operating system platform you are most familiar with for your bastion hosts, as you need an intimate knowledge of the platform's services to be able to harden them against attack.
- Place bastion hosts on a separate network from the internal corporate one, usually the DMZ or some other perimeter network.
- Make sure you physically secure the bastion hosts as well—hardening a host and then leaving it an unlocked basement room does not make sense.
- Remove all user accounts from bastion hosts except a dedicated administrator account that is protected by a strong password. Use a machine-specific administrator account rather than a domain administrator account if possible.
- Keep abreast of all releases of service packs and patches for the operating system deployed on your bastion host and apply these when required.

See Also: *firewall, network security*

batch commands

A special set of commands generally found only in batch files.

Overview

Although batch files can essentially contain any commands that can be executed at the command line, a special set of batch commands enable special actions to be performed such as jumps, terminal echoing, and conditional processing.

The table on the following page lists special batch commands that are found only in batch files. These commands are all supported by Microsoft Windows 2000, Windows XP, and Windows .NET Server, but earlier versions of Windows might support only a subset of them.

Batch File Commands

Command	*Description*
Call	Calls one batch program from another while allowing the calling program to continue running
Echo	Toggles command-echoing on or off
Endlocal	Restores environment variables set by a Setlocal command
For	Used to run a specified command for each file in a set of files
Goto	Jumps to a specific line that is labeled in a batch file
If	Used to perform conditional processing of commands
Pause	Suspends processing of the batch file and waits for the user to respond
Rem	Used to insert remarks (comments) in a batch file for documentation purposes
Setlocal	Initiates localization of environment variables in a batch file
Shift	Used to change the position of replaceable parameters in a batch file

See Also: *batch file, Windows commands*

batch file

Also called a batch program, an ASCII file containing a series of commands.

Overview

The commands within a batch file are executed sequentially when the file is invoked. Generally, any command that can be entered at the command line can be used within a batch file as well. You can execute batch files either at the command prompt, by associating a shortcut with them and double-clicking on the shortcut, or by invoking them in a logon script or through some other script or program.

Batch files are traditionally identified using the extension .bat or .cmd. Batch files trace their origins back to MS-DOS, with the Autoexec.bat file being the best-known example. While batch files are still used by many administrators for logon scripts, the advent of the Windows Script Host (WSH) in Microsoft Windows 98, Windows NT Option Pack, Windows 2000, Windows XP, and Windows .NET Server allows more powerful administrative scripts to now be written using higher-level scripting languages such as Microsoft Visual Basic Scripting Edition (VBScript) and JavaScript. As a consequence of the WSH, the old paradigm of batch files may finally be about to disappear.

Examples

Batch files are used primarily to simplify the execution of routine or repetitive administrative tasks such as mapping drives, synchronizing system clocks, or performing backups. For example, on a Windows NT–based network, to control the rate at which directory information is replicated between a backup domain controller (BDC) and a primary domain controller (PDC), you can create a batch file that will change the value of the ReplicationGovernor parameter on the BDC. To do this, first create a script that has the full path to this parameter in the registry along with the value you want to assign to it and then create the following simple batch file:

```
regini <Script_Name>
net stop netlogon
net start netlogon
```

Two different scripts and batch files can be created for different times of the day, and the At command can be used to schedule the execution of each batch file at the appropriate time. This illustration is especially useful if directory replication must occur over a slow wide area network (WAN) link, and you can use it to ensure that most replication traffic occurs during off hours.

See Also: *batch commands, scripting, Windows Script Host (WSH)*

bCentral

An initiative from Microsoft Corporation to help small businesses get online by providing them with subscription-based services, tips and advice, technology consultants, and other aids.

B

Overview

Microsoft bCentral is designed to help small businesses get online so they can increase sales, improve their market share, and provide better services to customers. The bCentral initiative is an integral part of Microsoft's .NET strategy of providing software as a service to consumers and businesses.

Services available from bCentral include

- Web site hosting packages that range from basic sites to full e-mail services, online advertising, e-commerce, and e-mail newsletters.
- Tools and services for advertising your online business, including search engine submission tools, opportunities to advertise on larger well-known sites, and e-mail newsletters for building customer communities.
- Back-end business support, from online services for managing your customers and tracking sales leads to secure accounting services for managing your business's finances.

In addition, bCentral services are available to any computer having a Web browser and an Internet connection, so you can manage your online business from anywhere using a laptop computer. Partnerships with companies such as Office Depot provide value-added services such as purchasing office equipment and supplies over the Internet from any location. Many bCentral services have free 30-day trial periods that allow businesses to test these services. Finally, bCentral helps you sell your company's products and services at MSN eShop and through an online auction site developed by Microsoft Corporation and FairMarket.

For More Information

You can find bCentral at *www.bcentral.com.*

B channel

Stands for Bearer channel, a circuit-switched channel for carrying voice or data in Integrated Services Digital Network (ISDN) services.

Overview

Such channels are called Bearer channels because they "bear," or carry, the actual information being communicated between the customer premises and the telco's central office (CO). B channels are standard, bidirectional, digital telephone channels that can carry digital information at a rate of 64 kilobits per second (Kbps). Users with greater bandwidth needs can combine several B channels into larger data-carrying pipes. The two most common configurations are

- **2B+D:** Combines two B channels to form a single data pipe with a total bandwidth of 128 Kbps
- **23B+D:** Combines 23 B channels to form a high-speed data pipe equivalent to a T1 line with a total bandwidth of 1.438 megabits per second (Mbps)

Notes

B channels carry voice or data only, not signaling information. D channels carry information for establishment and control of ISDN connections.

See Also: *802.10, Integrated Services Digital Network (ISDN)*

BDC

Stands for backup domain controller, a Microsoft Windows NT domain controller containing a read-only copy of the Security Accounts Manager (SAM) database.

See: *backup domain controller (BDC)*

beaconing

A technique used on token-passing networks for monitoring the status of the token-passing process.

Overview

Beaconing is used in Token Ring and Fiber Distributed Data Interface (FDDI) networks to ensure that token passing is functioning properly. On a token-passing network such as FDDI, every station is responsible for monitoring the status of the token-passing process. If a station detects that a fault has occurred, it starts placing beacons onto the ring. When the next station on the ring detects a beacon, it in turn starts placing beacons on the ring and the first station stops transmitting them. This process will continue until the station immediately upstream of the fault location is the only station sending beacons.

Beaconing enables administrators to quickly locate the fault and repair it. Once the fault is fixed, the station emitting the beacon detects its own beacon returning to it after traveling around the ring, and the station stops beaconing.

See Also: *Fiber Distributed Data Interface (FDDI), Token Ring*

BEEP

Stands for Blocks Extensible Exchange Protocol, an emerging framework to replace Hypertext Transfer Protocol (HTTP) for transport of Extensible Markup Language (XML)–based information over the Internet.

See: *Blocks Extensible Exchange Protocol (BEEP)*

benchmarking

Any systematic method for performing comparative measurements of computer hardware, operating systems, and their components and subsystems.

Overview

Benchmarking began as system attempts to compare the speed and power of hardware, operating systems, and applications that had similar functions. For example, an early comparison between Microsoft Word and Corel WordPerfect might have been to compare how quickly both applications could spell-check the same 100-page document. In the early days, vendors themselves often performed benchmarking to highlight the superior performance of their products in the marketplace.

To elevate benchmarking to something more consistent and reliable, independent nonprofit organizations have been formed to benchmark certain aspects of system and application behavior. Two of these organizations have achieved a high degree of credibility in the industry, namely Standard Performance Evaluation Corporation (SPEC) and the Transaction Processing Performance Council (TPC).

SPEC's goal is to establish a suite of standardized benchmarks for comparing the performance of computer systems. SPEC licenses its tools for use by vendors, who can publish and report the results on SPEC's Web site. An example is the SPEC CPU2000 benchmark for comparing performance of CPU subsystems, which replaces the popular, but now retired, SPEC CPU95 benchmark.

TPC's goal is to develop standard benchmarking tools and procedures for comparing transactional processing between different database products. A transaction is a form of business action performed by a computer system—for example, an online purchase or sale. Database transactions include inventory control, books, account updates, and similar procedures. TPC benchmarks such as TPC-C for Online Transactional Processing (OLTP) and TCP-W for Web-based e-commerce transactions attempt to mirror real-world transaction processing to compare the performance of database systems from different vendors.

Another popular set of benchmarks are those of media company ZDNet, which has developed its set of Winbench and Winstone benchmarks for comparison of business and consumer computer systems and peripherals.

The main difficulty with most benchmarking systems is interpreting them. While trying to mirror real-world effects, benchmarks nevertheless operate under idealized conditions in which certain variables are controlled and others are changed to study the results. The challenge continues to be to develop reliable independent benchmarks that will test significant components of complex real-world systems while maintaining fairness and vendor-neutrality.

For More Information

You can find SPEC at *www.spec.org*. TPC can be found at *www.tpc.org*. ZDNet can be found at *www.zdnet.com*.

B

BeOS

Stands for Be Operating System, an operating system especially developed as a high-performance platform for multimedia applications.

Overview

BeOS was developed by Be, a company founded in 1991 by Jean-Louis Gassée, a former president of Apple Computer's product division. The first version of BeOS became available in 1995, and the current release is version 5.

BeOS is a preemptive multitasking operating system that incorporates pervasive multithreading in which every application has at least two threads, one for application logic and one for the user interface. BeOS also supports eight-way symmetric multiprocessing (SMP). BeOS also includes a 64-bit journaling file system that supports 18 petabytes of direct storage, protected memory, and a Portable Operating System Interface for UNIX (POSIX)-compliant subsystem.

BeOS has an object-oriented set of application programming interfaces (APIs) that are optimized for real-time digital multimedia and communication functions. Because of this, BeOS is sometimes called a "media OS" to emphasize its high-performance multimedia capabilities.

BeOS runs on Intel-based platforms and certain PowerPC-based hardware, and it includes basic Transmission Control Protocol/Internet Protocol (TCP/IP) support and services. On a PowerPC, you can even run the MacOS as a shell within the BeOS desktop interface.

A lightweight version of BeOS called BeIA (Be Internet Appliance) is also being developed for Internet appliances and similar devices.

For More Information

Visit the Be home page at *www.be.com.*

BER

Stands for Bit Error Rate, a measurement of the reliability of a networking architecture or device.

See: *Bit Error Rate (BER)*

Berkeley Internet Name Domain (BIND)

A popular software tool for administering and maintaining the Domain Name System (DNS) on UNIX platforms.

Overview

Berkeley Internet Name Domain (BIND) was originally written for 4.3BSD UNIX and replaced an earlier domain naming system called JEEVES. BIND is now maintained by the Internet Software Consortium (ISC) and its current major version is BIND 9.

Because most versions of UNIX include some sort of BIND with their distributions and a majority of Internet Service Providers (ISPs) still use the UNIX platform for much of their operations, BIND is still the most popular DNS server on the Internet. BIND is also freely distributed by the ISC and is available for AIX, HP-UX, Irix, Solaris, SunOS, and other operating systems such as Linux and Windows NT.

Notes

The DNS Server services of Microsoft Windows 2000 and Windows .NET Server are Request for Comments (RFC)–compliant implementations of DNS and are fully compatible with BIND. Active Directory directory service can also use BIND as its DNS naming service, provided BIND 8.1.2 or later is used. If you choose to use BIND with Active Directory, make sure you disable name checking on your BIND server because Active Directory uses the underscore character in its SRV records and BIND name checking flags this character as an illegal character.

For More Information

Visit the Internet Software Consortium at *www.isc.org.*

See Also: *Active Directory, Domain Name System (DNS), Internet, UNIX*

BERT

Stands for Bit/Block Error Rate Tester, a device used to troubleshoot serial lines.

See: *Bit/Block Error Rate Tester (BERT)*

best effort

Used to describe network communications in which delivery of data is not guaranteed.

Overview

Routable internetworking protocols such as Internet Protocol (IP) and Internetwork Packet Exchange (IPX) use best effort delivery based on datagrams. In other words, delivery of data by these protocols is not guaranteed. The reason is that these protocols are connectionless in operation, and acknowledgements are not returned as they pass from one hop to the next across a routed internetwork.

An example where communications may fail is what is called a "black hole." In this situation, a failed router drops packets it is supposed to forward, and the station from which the packets originated is unaware that these packets never reached their destination.

See Also: *black hole, Internet Protocol (IP), routing*

BGP

Stands for Border Gateway Protocol, an exterior routing protocol used on the Internet to provide loop-free routing between different autonomous systems (ASs).

See: *Border Gateway Protocol (BGP)*

Binary Runtime Environment for Wireless (BREW)

A platform from QUALCOMM for developing applications for cellular communications systems.

Overview

Binary Runtime Environment for Wireless (BREW) was developed by QUALCOMM as an alternative to Java 2 Micro Edition (J2ME) from Sun Microsystems. Although both platforms enable downloading of applications over wireless phones, BREW has been designed from the ground up to work effectively in the cellular environment and J2ME is a general-purpose developer environment for small devices. BREW's main disadvantage is that it was designed with QUALCOMM's Code Division Multiple Access (CDMA) cellular technology in mind, but J2ME is device- and technology-independent.

A number of companies have committed to building products and services that use BREW, including Wireless Knowledge and Visto Corp.

For More Information

Find out more about BREW at QUALCOMM's Web site at *www.qualcomm.com/brew.*

See Also: *cellular communications*

Binary Tulloch Transport Protocol (BTTP)

A draft specification for a routing protocol to save the Internet from its projected meltdown on or around April 1, 2003.

Overview

Because of the proliferation of Autonomous System Numbers (ASNs) used to identify internetworks connected to the Internet and due to the limited pool of possible ASNs, which is quickly drying up, analysts predict that no more ASNs will be available on or around April 1, 2003. At that point the Internet is expected to collapse.

A proposed solution soon to be presented to the Internet Engineering Task Force (IETF) is the Binary Tulloch Transport Protocol (BTTP). BTTP addresses the underlying issue of ASNs running out by assigning a binary flag (1=on and 0=off) to each ASN, allowing half the ASNs connected to the Internet to be temporarily revoked while the other half remain available at any given time. The protocol switches ASNs between these two states at a frequency of 1000 times per second; in other words, autonomous systems are online one millisecond and off the next, effectively reducing the size of the Internet by half at any given moment and thus giving room for several more years of expansion and growth of the Internet before the problem becomes critical again. Since the average latency for establishing Internet connections is around 20 milliseconds for wired connections (and several hundred milliseconds for satellite links), this is clearly sufficient time for connections to be established with Internet hosts whose networks are rapidly switching on and off.

For More Information

You can find out more about BTTP and its creator, Mitch Tulloch, at *www.mtit.com.*

BIND

Stands for Berkeley Internet Name Domain, a popular software tool for administering and maintaining the Domain Name System (DNS) on UNIX platforms.

See: *Berkeley Internet Name Domain (BIND)*

bindery

In Novell's NetWare version 3.*x* and earlier networking operating systems, the database containing network security information (such as users, groups, and rights) for a particular server.

Overview

Each NetWare 3.*x* server has its own bindery for controlling access to that server's file and print resources. In version 4.*x* and later, the bindery is replaced by the Novell Directory Services (NDS), although 4.*x* servers are also capable of running in bindery emulation mode.

Microsoft's optional Microsoft Windows 2000 Server service Gateway Services for NetWare (GSNW) can be used to implement gateways to resources located on NetWare file and print servers that are using bindery security. This allows Windows users to access volumes, directories, and print queues on NetWare servers without requiring NetWare client software to be installed on them. Client Services for NetWare (CSNW) can also be installed on client machines running Windows 2000 Professional and Windows XP to enable them to directly access bindery-based NetWare 2.*x*, 3.*x*, or 4.*x* servers that are running in bindery emulation mode.

See Also: *Client Services for NetWare (CSNW), Gateway Service for NetWare (GSNW), Novell Directory Services (NDS)*

bindings

A mechanism for linking the various components of an operating system that make network communications possible.

Overview

Bindings link together network interface card (NIC) drivers, network protocols (such as Transmission Control Protocol/Internet Protocol [TCP/IP]), and networking services (such as Workstation service). Microsoft Windows 2000, Windows XP, and Windows .NET Server let you optimize network communication by selectively enabling, disabling, and modifying the order of the bindings between these different networking components. Windows 2000, Windows XP, and Windows .NET Server support Network Driver Interface Specification (NDIS) version 5, which allows multiple protocols to be independently bound to multiple NICs.

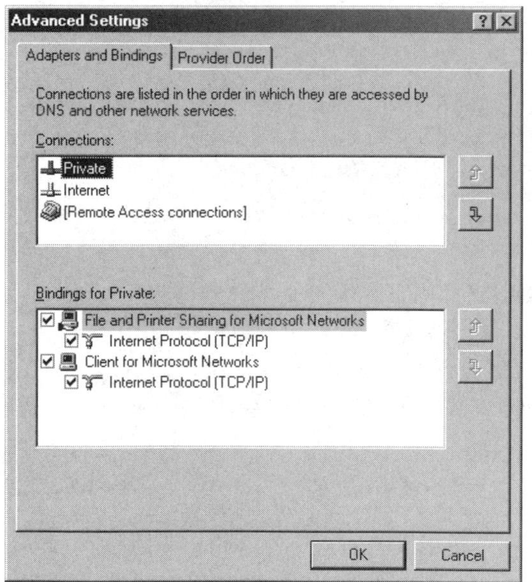

Binding. *Configuring bindings in Windows 2000.*

To configure bindings for Windows 2000, choose Advanced Settings from the Advanced menu of the Network And Dial-Up Connections window, which is accessed from Control Panel. In this way bindings can be easily enabled, disabled, or reordered. To optimize network performance, disable any unnecessary bindings on your workstations.

See Also: *network driver interface specification (NDIS)*

biometric authentication

Any authentication scheme that uses an aspect of a person's physical body or behavior to verify that person's identity.

Overview

Biometric authentication (or biometric identification) has been employed for years for entry-access control of high-security environments such as military compounds and virology laboratories, but only recently have commercial products become available for securing computer networks. Biometric authentication mechanisms take many forms, including

- Fingerprint or thumbprint identification devices
- Face-recognition systems (measure dimensions of prominent facial features)
- Iris-scanning devices (retina scanners are much more rare and expensive)
- Voice-print identification systems (usually a sound card, microphone, and software)
- Biometric trackballs and mice (measures vein patterns, creases on the palm, or density of fatty tissue using infrared lasers)

Some biometric authentication systems measure behavior patterns instead of physical features. An example is BioPassword from Net Nanny Software International, which requires a user to enter a password on a keyboard and then compares the way the user typed the password with information stored in a database.

Biometric authentication systems must be designed carefully in order for them to be truly secure. For example, a simple voice-print authentication system could be fooled by using a tape recording of the user's voice. To guard against this, these systems commonly ask the user to speak a randomly generated series of words into the microphone, which renders such tape recordings useless.

Biometrics will probably soon make their way into the wireless arena as well. Cellular communications vendor Nokia has prototyped a biometric-enabled cell phone, which would make stealing such a phone useless. The main barrier against this development is cost—cell phones are mass-produced cheaply and even a biometric component costing $10 per phone could break the cost model.

Another general barrier to all forms of biometric authentication systems are privacy issues regarding having digital information about your physical makeup stored on a device that could be stolen or misused. Despite these concerns, the biometrics market in 1999 was $166 million and is rising rapidly.

Notes

When implementing biometric authentication systems, be sure to consider fallback authentication options should the biometric device fail. Costs of purchasing and deploying such systems across an enterprise may also be considerable, and help desk departments might find it more time-consuming to troubleshoot a faulty sound card of a voice-print authentication system than simply resetting a user's traditional text-based password.

See Also: *network security*

B-ISDN

Stands for broadband ISDN, the broadband transmission counterpart of Integrated Services Digital Network (ISDN).

See: *broadband ISDN (B-ISDN)*

Bit/Block Error Rate Tester (BERT)

A device used to troubleshoot serial lines.

Overview

A Bit/Block Error Rate Tester (BERT) is a kind of cable tester specially designed for testing serial lines. BERTs can be connected to serial ports on PCs, routers, and other devices to provide a visual indication of the condition of the serial interface.

A typical BERT is a small box with a 25-pin serial connector and 25 light-emitting diodes (LEDs), one for each lead of the interface. A quick visual inspection can provide information about whether data is being reliably transmitted across the interface. You can also use jumpers to make or break specific leads to see the effect—this simulates the effect of crossed wires and can be used to detect such wires in miswired serial cables or connectors.

See Also: *test equipment*

Bit Error Rate (BER)

A measurement of the reliability of a networking architecture or device.

Overview

Bit Error Rate (BER) is expressed in terms of probability of a bit of data being lost while being transported over a network or processed by a device. As an example, standard (10 megabits per second [Mbps]) Ethernet over copper specifies a maximum BER of 10^{-8}, which means only 1 out of every 100,000,000 (100 million) bits transported can be allowed to be lost. This is actually a worst-case scenario, however, as actual Ethernet networks generally have a BER of 10^{-11} or better, meaning that only 1 out of every 100,000,000,000 (100 billion) bits is lost. Fast Ethernet and Gigabit Ethernet (GbE) have BERs an order of magnitude smaller.

An associated measure for Ethernet reliability is Frame Loss Rate (FLR), which for Ethernet networks is typically 10^{-7}, or 1 frame lost in every 10,000,000 (10 million) frames transported. Lost frames are handled by higher-level layers of the Open Systems Interconnection (OSI) model and are ignored by the Data Link Layer.

See Also: *Ethernet*

bits per second (bps)

A unit used for measuring the speed of transmission of data on a network of computers.

Overview

Bits per second, or bps, represents the rate at which information is being sent or received. A bit is a single unit of digital information, represented by either a 1 or a 0. The total number of bits per second that can be transmitted over a network link describes the bandwidth or throughput of that link.

Because most network communication takes place at thousands or millions of bits per second, the following related units are commonly used:

- Kbps = kilobits per second (10^3 bps)
- Mbps = megabits per second (10^6 bps)
- Gbps = gigabits per second (10^9 bps)

See Also: *bandwidth*

BizTalk

An initiative from Microsoft Corporation to standardize the exchange of electronic documents between businesses.

Overview

Businesses exchange information for various reasons:

- Product invoicing and delivery
- Supply-chain management
- Electronic catalogs and ordering systems

BizTalk is designed to standardize these processes using Extensible Markup Language (XML) as a foundation for creating a standard "electronic envelope" for exchanging electronic documents between businesses.

BizTalk actually consists of four interlocking facets:

- **BizTalk Framework:** A framework for developing XML schemas to serve different sectors of business and industry. BizTalk Framework provides a set of rules and a collection of base XML tags for building new schema for B2B e-commerce. These tags provide the "envelope" that ensures electronic documents reach their intended recipient. See the article "BizTalk Framework" later in this chapter for more information.

- **BizTalk server:** Any software that can read and process documents formatted according to the BizTalk Framework is called a BizTalk server. BizTalk servers can be third-party applications developed using any programming language and running on any operating system platform and can be designed for either front-end or back-end exchanges of B2B documents.
- **BizTalk Server 2000:** Microsoft's own version of a BizTalk server, which runs on the Windows 2000 platform and provides orchestration of business processes and XML document exchange. BizTalk Server 2000 can transmit XML and Simple Object Access Protocol (SOAP)–based messages over a variety of transports including Hypertext Transfer Protocol (HTTP), Simple Mail Transfer Protocol (SMTP), and others.
- **BizTalk.org:** A site devoted to the support and proliferation of BizTalk.

For More Information

Visit the BizTalk resource site at *www.biztalk.org.*

See Also: *B2B, BizTalk Framework, BizTalk Server 2000, XML*

BizTalk Framework

A specification describing the architecture of BizTalk messages.

Overview

BizTalk Framework is part of the BizTalk initiative from Microsoft Corporation to facilitate the exchange of electronic documents and orchestration of business processes between trading partners, supply-chain partners, and other business partners. BizTalk Framework is designed to be the underlying document standard for B2B e-commerce and is based on the standard Extensible Markup Language (XML) specification.

Architecture

When two businesses in a B2B relationship need to exchange information electronically, the first step is to decide on a common XML schema to use that both can understand. A schema defines the type of content being transmitted and the structure of the document containing it. Microsoft has established the site *www.biztalk.org* as a resource site for businesses to develop and publish BizTalk schemas for their industry sectors.

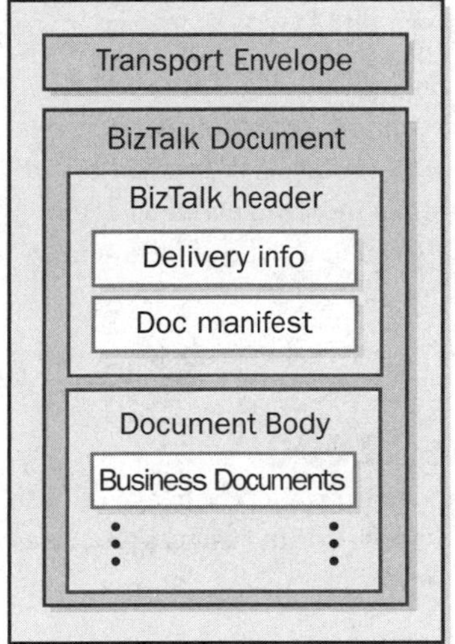

BizTalk Framework. *Format for a BizTalk Message.*

A BizTalk message consists of two parts: the Transport Envelope and the BizTalk Document.

The Transport Envelope specifies the transport protocol used to deliver the message. BizTalk Server 2000, Microsoft's own implementation of a platform for building BizTalk solutions, supports a number of different transports, including

- Hypertext Transport Protocol (HTTP)
- HTTP over Secure Sockets Layer (SSL), or HTTPS

B

- Simple Mail Transfer Protocol (SMTP)
- File Transfer Protocol (FTP)
- Microsoft Message Queue Server (MSMQ)
- Application Integration Components (COM building blocks)
- Fax

The other portion of a BizTalk message, the BizTalk Document itself, consists of the following parts:

- **BizTalk Header:** Specifies the source address, destination address, subject, transmission time and date, and document manifest describing the type of document being transmitted (such as invoice, purchase order, or service request).
- **Document Body:** Contains the actual business documents formatted in XML using the agreed-upon schema. If the manifest indicates an invoice, the body describes things such as type of item sent, quantity, payment requested, and sales tax.

See Also: *BizTalk, BizTalk Server 2000, XML*

BizTalk Server 2000

Microsoft Corporation's platform for exchange of business documents and orchestration of business processes using the BizTalk Framework.

Overview

BizTalk Server 2000 is one of the new Microsoft Windows 2000 Server applications. BizTalk Server 2000 is used for building B2B e-commerce through using Extensible Markup Language (XML) to deliver business documents such as sales orders, invoices, and service requests. BizTalk Server 2000 can transmit both XML and Simple Object Access Protocol (SOAP)–based messages. It can use a variety of transports for accomplishing this, including Hypertext Transport Protocol (HTTP), Simple Mail Transfer Protocol (SMTP), File Transfer Protocol (FTP), and others.

For More Information

Find out more about BizTalk Server 2000 at *www.microsoft.com/biztalk.*

See Also: *BizTalk, BizTalk Framework, XML*

Blackcomb

Microsoft Corporation's code name for its upcoming successor to the Windows .NET Server family of operating system platforms.

Overview

"Blackcomb" is planned for release sometime after the release of Windows .NET Server, which had the code name "Whistler." "Blackcomb" will be the first fully .NET version of Microsoft Windows and will be an integral platform for developing and deploying Microsoft's .NET vision of software-as-services.

At this point, little is known about "Blackcomb," but at the Windows Hardware Engineering Conference (WinHEC) in March 2001, Microsoft unveiled some of its intended features, including

- New services for Application Service Providers (ASPs) to deploy and manage .NET Web services running on Blackcomb.
- Dynamic partitioning of servers for greater reliability in mission-critical scenarios.
- Greater communications capabilities and an enhanced user interface.

Notes

Whistler and Blackcomb are two ski resorts in British Columbia, Canada, only a few hours away from Microsoft's headquarters at Redmond, Washington.

For More Information

Find out about the latest developments with the Microsoft Windows series of operating system platforms at *www.microsoft.com/windows.*

See Also: *Microsoft Windows*

black hole

A network condition in routed internetworks where packets are dropped without any explanation to the transmitting host.

Overview

A black hole is generally caused by a router that goes down and whose absence from the network is not detected by other routers. Packets that are forwarded to the black hole are dropped—that is, they never reach their destination and give no indication to the stations sending them of the situation—therefore, the data is lost. Normally, a router will issue an "ICMP Destination Unreachable" message when it cannot forward a packet. However, with a black hole, these messages are not generated, so the transmitting host does not know that data is being permanently lost.

If static routing is being used, a black hole persists until the affected router is brought back on line or until other static routers have their routing tables reconfigured to take the downed router into account. If dynamic routing is used, other routers soon detect the presence of the black hole and adjust their routing tables accordingly to favor other paths.

Black holes can also originate when routers that are active nevertheless drop certain packets for specific reasons. An example is when the Path Maximum Transmit Unit (PMTU) is configured for a router so that it discards Internet Protocol (IP) packets that need to be fragmented in order to be forwarded. If a PMTU router is not configured to also forward indications of dropped packets to transmitting hosts (and by default they are not so configured), then the network problems they produce can be difficult to detect since some (smaller) packets get through successfully while other (larger) packets mysteriously disappear.

The reason, of course, why this condition is known as a "black hole" is its parallel with black holes in Einstein's theory of General Relativity. Einstein's black holes are collapsed stars that swallow everything and from which not even light can return.

See Also: *routing*

BLEC

Stands for Building-centric Local Exchange Carriers, a telecommunications carrier focused on the Multitenant Unit (MTU) market.

See: *Building-centric Local Exchange Carrier (BLEC)*

block coding

An encoding scheme whereby groups of data bits are encoded into a larger number of code bits.

Overview

A variety of block codes are used for encoding transmissions for networking and telecommunications systems. Examples of some common ones include

- **4B/5B:** This packages four bits of data into five code bits and is used by 100 megabits per second (Mbps) Ethernet and Fiber Distributed Data Interface (FDDI).
- **8B/6T:** This packages eight bits of data into six ternary (base-three) code symbols and is used by 100BaseT4 Ethernet.
- **5B/6B:** This packages five bits of data into six code bits and is used by 100VG-AnyLAN.

The reasons for making the "code space" larger than the "bit space" in these encoding schemes are to allow for additional data characteristics to be included in transmissions and to make room for control signals to manage the flow of data or check for error conditions.

See Also: *line coding*

Blocks Extensible Exchange Protocol (BEEP)

An emerging framework to replace Hypertext Transport Protocol (HTTP) for transport of Extensible Markup Language (XML)–based information over the Internet.

Overview

Blocks Extensible Exchange Protocol (BEEP) is a proposed framework for a protocol that would run on top of Transmission Control Protocol (TCP) as an alternative to HTTP. It is designed to facilitate the exchange of

XML-framed information for a variety of uses, including file transfer, instant messaging (IM), and network management.

BEEP has been proposed because HTTP was not originally intended for XML data transport and performs poorly when performing this function. BEEP uses a peer-to-peer (P2P) architecture instead of the client-server one used by HTTP. In a typical scenario, BEEP first establishes a connection between two hosts on a network. The hosts alternate between client and server roles to allow two-way communications between them over a channel. Hosts can choose either to push or pull data between themselves. An advantage of BEEP is that unlike HTTP, a single BEEP connection can open multiple channels for exchange of XML data, which means, for instance, that files could be transferred through one channel while an IM chat session occurs on another.

The BEEP framework also includes a toolkit for rapid development of custom application protocols that would run on top of BEEP to efficiently handle specific types of communications tasks. In effect, BEEP would provide reusable code that would greatly facilitate the development of such special-purpose protocols.

BEEP is being presented as a draft standard to the Internet Engineering Task Force (IETF) for consideration, and the framework is outlined by RFCs 3080 and 3081. BEEP's development has been spearheaded by the company Invisible Worlds.

Notes

BEEP was formerly known by the acronym BXXP.

For More Information

Visit Invisible Worlds at *www.invisibleworlds.com.*

See Also: *Hypertext Transfer Protocol (HTTP), XML*

blue screen

In Microsoft Windows platforms, a blue screen on a user's monitor indicates that something has gone seriously wrong with the system.

Overview

In Windows 2000, Windows XP, and Windows .NET Server, blue screens are normally called stop screens. A stop screen contains complex information that qualified support technicians can use to diagnose the problem. A reboot might get the system going again, but the stop screen might reappear if the problem is not resolved. The problem causing the stop screen to appear can be either hardware-related or software-related, but the stop screen itself is generated by the operating system in response to the underlying problem.

In Windows 95 and Windows 98, the blue-colored screen normally appears when parity errors or memory violations occur. Parity errors can indicate that your system random access memory (RAM) has mismatched single inline memory modules (SIMMs) on your motherboard—for example, RAM with different speeds or a mix of parity and nonparity RAM. Also, systems from some manufacturers require special proprietary RAM in order to function. You should consult the documentation from your computer's manufacturer or your RAM's manufacturer to ensure that you have the correct type of RAM in each slot. The Windows 98 blue screen requests that you either shut down the offending application or restart your system using Ctrl+Alt+Delete.

Bluetooth

An evolving specification for short-range wireless transmission between small portable devices in a Personal Area Network (PAN).

Overview

Bluetooth is a wireless networking technology that promises to provide a simple, low-cost method of linking together cellular phones with headsets, Personal Digital Assistants (PDAs) with printers, and similar ad hoc associations between devices in a PAN. A PAN is essentially a network of portable devices carried by a user or devices within which a user comes into close proximity by movement. The vision of Bluetooth actually extends beyond personal data networking to a nirvana world of wireless devices that includes milk containers that signal refrigerators when they are almost empty, whereupon the refrigerator orders more milk using an Internet connection.

Needless to say, not everyone expects (or even wants) this brave new world to happen!

Original work on the Bluetooth specification dates back to 1994 when cellular phone manufacturer Ericsson first outlined the technology. The original intention was to provide a way to connect wireless headsets with cellular phones, but the Bluetooth specification has evolved far past this initial goal. In 1998 a consortium called the Bluetooth Special Interest Group (SIG) was created, and it published its first specification in 1999. The original members included Ericsson, its rival Nokia, and other industry leaders such as IBM, Intel Corporation, and Toshiba Corporation. This consortium has grown to include over 2000 different vendors, and the current Bluetooth specification is version 1.1.

The success of the Bluetooth SIG is based largely on the fact that companies that join must grant a royalty-free license to all other members of the alliance for any Bluetooth-related technology they develop. The SIG's main purpose is to develop specifications for real-world interoperable Bluetooth products—it is not a standards body, and the intention is that any specifications developed by the SIG will be passed on to the Institute of Electrical and Electronics Engineers (IEEE) for final standardization.

Because of the original vision of Bluetooth for small handheld devices, a consistent goal of the Bluetooth SIG has been to develop Bluetooth technology that can be implemented on a single chip. Much success has been achieved in that respect, with chip prices in large lots coming down to the $4 range.

Architecture

Bluetooth is based on baseband FM transmission using frequencies between 2.4 and 2.4835 gigahertz (GHz) within the unlicensed 2.4-GHz Industrial, Scientific, and Medical (ISM) band. Bluetooth divides this band of frequencies into 79 separate channels, and transmission uses a frequency-hopping scheme to hop between channels randomly at a rate of 1,600 hops per second. The result is that a different frequency is used to transmit each packet of a Bluetooth transmission. The advantage of such aggressive frequency-hopping is to provide smooth operation by minimizing the effects of fading due to reflecting obstacles and overcoming noise due to electromagnetic interference (EMI) generated by microwave ovens and other devices. Bluetooth also uses short packets and fast acknowledgments to increase reliability and employs forward error correction to reduce the effects of random noise.

Bluetooth's data transmission rate is 1 megabit per second (Mbps), but with protocol overhead the resultant practical maximum transmission rate is more like 780 kilobits per second (Kbps) or lower. Bluetooth uses a shared-media transmission scheme similar to Ethernet in which only one device in a group of connected devices can transmit at any one time, and duplex transmission is simulated through time-division multiplexing of simplex transmissions. The result is that a PAN with many Bluetooth devices will perform more poorly than one with only a few devices, but this is not considered a serious disadvantage since the specification was designed to be a lightweight one from the beginning.

Given its aim of supporting devices in PANs, Bluetooth is a low-power technology with a maximum range of transmission of 33 feet (10 meters). Bluetooth's automatic power adaptation adjusts transmission power to the minimum needed for reliable transmission in any given situation to enhance battery life in portable devices.

The Bluetooth protocol suite is centralized around the Logical Link Control and Adaptation Protocol (L2CAP). This protocol supports two data transmission modes:

- Asynchronous packet-switched communications with simplex speeds of 721 Kbps in the forward direction and 57.6 Kbps in the reverse.
- Synchronous circuit-switched communications for duplex communications over three 128 Kbps channels for a total bandwidth of 432.6 Kbps in each direction.

The Application Layer of the Bluetooth protocol suite is implemented as a series of "profiles" representing operating parameters for different kinds of uses of Bluetooth. Currently, 13 different application layer profiles have been developed under the specification, and Bluetooth systems are required only to implement a

B

core subset of these together with other profiles needed for their operation.

Other Bluetooth protocols include the Link Manager Protocol (LMP), which manages device authentication for forming new connections, and the Service Discovery Protocol (SDP), which maintains the browse list of accessible devices.

Security is built into Bluetooth at the data-link level and provides the following services:

- **Authentication:** Bluetooth has built-in device authentication, while user authentication needs to be implemented at the application level. Once a device has been authenticated, it is then considered "trusted" by all other devices in the ad hoc PAN.
- **Authorization:** This is used to control which services are accessible from which devices. For example, a Bluetooth-enabled PDA is authorized to print to a similarly enabled printer but not to a Bluetooth cell phone.
- **Encryption:** Bluetooth includes support for 128-bit encryption. In addition, the frequency-hopping transmission scheme employed by Bluetooth helps guard against eavesdropping by unauthorized users.

Implementation

Bluetooth supports concurrent connections among up to eight devices, forming what is called a piconet. Each device in a piconet is temporarily assigned a unique 3-bit MAC address for the duration of the connection. A master/slave relationship exists between one device and all other devices in the piconet for the duration of the connection. The purpose of this is for establishing clocking to synchronize devices for using the hopping sequence. In all other respects, the devices operate as peers during a connection.

Unconnected Bluetooth devices are always on in a standby mode where they listen for connection attempts every 1.28 seconds on each of 32 preassigned hopping frequencies. Once a compatible device is found, link setup and authentication is then performed using the Link Manager Protocol (LMP), which uses the link controller services built into the Bluetooth chip. Connections between Bluetooth devices can be either point-to-point or point-to-multipoint, and groups of piconets can be joined together into larger associations called scatternets, with each piconet within a scatternet having a uniquely different hopping sequence.

Marketplace

The Bluetooth marketplace is still in its infancy, but some of the highlights are as follows:

- Bluecore, the first working Bluetooth chip, was developed by British startup Cambridge Silicon Radio. This was incorporated into the first commercial Bluetooth product, a Bluetooth-capable CompactFlash expansion card named Bluecore CF+, which was developed by California-based Socket Communications for the Microsoft Windows CE platform of portable devices. Since then other Bluetooth chips have been developed by major players such as Ericsson, Intel Corporation, and Motorola.
- RocketChips (*www.rocketchips.com*) has developed a vision for integrating Bluetooth onto CPU chips within PCs; in other words, a no-chip solution instead of the usual single-chip solution. If this vision is implemented, Bluetooth could become as ubiquitous as the PC.
- Red-M (*www.red-m.com*) has developed a complete Bluetooth solution including access server, access point, and PC cards for clients.
- Ensure Technologies has developed a Bluetooth security card that users wear and that can automatically unlock their PCs when they come near them.
- Major vendors developing Bluetooth PC cards include Toshiba, Compaq, Hewlett-Packard, and others. Motorola is producing a PC combo card with a V.90 modem and a Bluetooth chip combined.
- IBM is currently licensing Bluetooth device driver software for the Linux platform and plans similar software for Microsoft Windows platforms. IBM has also prototyped a Bluetooth-enabled PDA called WatchPad that a user wears on the wrist like an ordinary watch.

- 3Com Corporation and Extended Systems are planning on delivering a set of management tools, protocol stacks, and software development kits (SDKs) for developing Bluetooth-based solutions for the Microsoft Windows platform.
- Palm plans on integrating support for Bluetooth in its next version of the PalmOS.
- Intesil Corporation is working on dual 802.11b/Bluetooth chipsets for overcoming issues relating to interference between the two wireless networking technologies.
- Ericsson, the initial force behind Bluetooth's development, has released Bluetooth adapters for some of its cellular phone models that enable wireless connectivity between phone and headset.

The Bluetooth SIG holds a yearly conference called Unplugfest where old and new vendors of Bluetooth products meet to test interoperability between their different implementations of the specifications. Because of the specification's evolving nature, early-to-market products based on the 1.0 specification may have compatibility issues with products based upon the newer 1.1 standard.

Issues

Using the ISM band for Bluetooth communications has been problematic. The ISM band is supposedly reserved worldwide for unlicensed communications, but governments in some countries and regions have licensed portions of this band for specific uses. The problem is of special concern in Spain and France, which have only a narrow portion of the band available, and the Bluetooth specifications have been massaged to produce a special version of the specification technically able to function under these restrictions, but legal restrictions prohibit its use in these two countries to prevent the jamming of other services. The reason this is such an issue is that, due to the multiplication of different specifications, Bluetooth cellular phones will not be able to easily function throughout Europe as originally envisioned by Ericsson.

Another issue is that not only is the ISM band also used by other wireless networking technologies such as 802.11b and HomeRF, but it is also used for non-networking applications such as garage door openers, microwave ovens, cordless telephones, telco local loop systems, baby monitors, medical scanners, and various other business and consumer devices. By using an aggressive frequency-hopping scheme, Bluetooth is fairly resistant to interference from these different systems, but that very fact means that Bluetooth easily interferes with the operation of these other systems. Tests have shown, in fact, that communications over 802.11b wireless networks can be degraded and even disrupted by nearby Bluetooth devices. The result has been that large companies that rely heavily on 802.11b wireless networks have instituted policies to ban Bluetooth devices from the premises.

Besides the threat to 802.11b local area networks (LANs), Bluetooth poses dilemmas for other industries as well. The airline industry has voiced particular concern that Bluetooth devices carried by different passengers might detect each other during a flight, turn themselves on, and generate transmissions that could disrupt an aircraft's sensitive navigation equipment. The Bluetooth SIG is attempting to allay these concerns through further refinement of the specifications.

Prospects

Despite issues relating to interference with 802.11b wireless local area networks (WLANs) and whether ad hoc always-on wireless networking is desirable or even safe, Bluetooth has a great deal of momentum from industry and products are likely to be widely available soon. In addition to consumer-oriented applications for PANs and wireless public access kiosks, Bluetooth may also find some place in the enterprise as a cable-replacement technology.

Only time will tell, however, whether a Bluetooth-enabled can of beer will someday communicate with a similarly enabled refrigerator to ask it to lower the temperature for just the right taste.

Notes

The goals of Bluetooth and 802.11b are different: although 802.11b was specifically developed mainly for laptop computers as a wireless replacement for wired Ethernet LANs, Bluetooth is optimized for

B

forming short-range ad hoc networks for connecting smaller portable devices such as cell phones and PDAs. The implementations of these technologies, although confined to the same ISM frequency band, are also different: Bluetooth uses frequency-hopping, but 802.11b uses spread-spectrum transmission.

The interesting name "Bluetooth" comes from Harald Bluetooth, the Viking who in the 10th century unified Norway and Denmark.

Bluetooth also supports voice transmission that use up to three concurrent synchronous 64-Kbps voice-only channels or one channel that simultaneously supports both asynchronous data and synchronous voice transmission. The voice channels use the continuous variable-slope delta modulation-coding scheme.

A competing technology for PANs besides Bluetooth is the Infrared Data Association (IrDA) protocol, but while IrDA devices require line-of-site communication, Bluetooth devices overcome this restriction. IrDA does have certain advantages however, including much greater data transmission rates.

For More Information

You can find the Bluetooth SIG at *www.bluetooth.com.*

See Also: *802.11b, 802.15, Infrared Data Association (IrDA), Personal Area Network (PAN), piconet, wireless networking*

BNC connector

A group of connectors used for joining thinnet cable segments together and for connecting thinnet cabling to 10Base2 network cards.

Overview

BNC connectors are used on 10Base2 (thinnet) Ethernet networks and use a twist-and-lock mechanism that provides a secure connection between network cabling and components. The male connector has a center pin with a rotating ring with projections that mate with the female connector.

The various types of BNC connectors include the following:

- **BNC cable connector:** Soldered or crimped to the ends of a thinnet cable
- **BNC T-connector:** Used to connect a network interface card (NIC) to a thinnet cable segment
- **BNC barrel connector:** Used to connect two pieces of thinnet cable
- **BNC terminator:** Provides a 50-ohm termination for the free end of a thinnet cable

Notes

Several possibilities are usually suggested as to the origin of the term *BNC*:

- British Naval Connector
- Bayonet Nut Connector
- Bayonet-Neill-Concelman (probably the correct explanation since the connector was named after Neill and Concelman, its two creators)

For situations where large mechanical loads may affect cabling, a threaded form of the connector is available called TNC.

See Also: *connector (device), terminator*

B-node

A NetBIOS name resolution method used by Microsoft Windows NT in which broadcast messages are used for name registration and resolution.

Overview

Name resolution is the process of converting the name of a host on the network into a network address (such as an Internet Protocol [IP] address). Name resolution must be performed in order to establish communication over a Windows NT network. B-node is one of four basic methods supported by Windows NT for resolving NetBIOS host names—that is, computer names—into IP addresses.

If a computer running Windows NT is configured as a B-node machine, it always uses broadcasts to resolve names of other hosts on the network. For example, if a B-node machine wants to communicate with another machine with the NetBIOS name SERVER7 (for example, if it wants to connect to a shared resource on SERVER7), the B-node machine broadcasts a packet containing a NetBIOS name query request. If SERVER7 receives the packet, it responds by returning a frame containing its IP address. If SERVER7 is off line or fails to return a response, the B-node client will be unable to establish a connection with SERVER7.

As a name resolution method, B-node is flawed in two ways:

- Since broadcast packets are used, B-node consumes network bandwidth and can degrade overall network communication in a busy network.
- Since routers are usually configured to not forward broadcast packets, B-node clients can resolve only the NetBIOS names of hosts on the client's local subnet.

A better approach to NetBIOS name resolution on Windows NT networks is to configure clients as H-node machines and use a Windows Internet Naming Service (WINS) server. H-node is a NetBIOS name resolution method that combines B-node and P-node.

Notes

On Windows 2000 and Windows .NET Server networks, the Domain Name System (DNS) is the preferred name resolution scheme, and NETBIOS can be disabled when there are no longer any downlevel Windows NT machines left after an upgrade is complete. Note, however, that Windows 2000, Windows XP, and Windows .NET Server systems based on the Active Directory directory service must be configured with the IP address of a WINS server in order to communicate with any Windows-based systems that are not Active Directory–based, including other Windows 2000, Windows XP, and Windows .NET Server systems.

See Also: *H-node, M-node, NetBIOS name resolution, P-node*

bonding

A term used to describe a variety of different technologies for aggregating multiple wide area network (WAN) links together to form a single fatter pipe.

Overview

In Integrated Services Digital Network (ISDN) and T-carrier transmission technologies, bonding provides a way of combining multiple DS0 channels from different circuits into a single, faster data transmission channel. This is accomplished using inverse multiplexing technologies together with special techniques for resolving the timing differences found among groups of different circuits.

ISDN Bonding is typically found in Basic Rate Interface ISDN (BRI-ISDN) where it is used to combine the two 64-kilobits-per-second (Kbps) B channels into a single 128-Kbps data transmission channel. Several different bonding protocols can be implemented for BRI-ISDN services, a common one being Multilink PPP (MPPP), which is used for asynchronous bonding.

Bonding must be supported by the ISDN devices at both ends of the ISDN link. Typically, one of the B channels is designated as responsible for initiating the bonding process. Many ISDN terminal adapters can override bonding when the user wants to place a regular Plain Old Telephone Service (POTS) phone call. For example, you might be using ISDN for high-speed Internet access with both B channels bonded to give you 128-Kbps (or 14-kilobyte-per-second [KBps]) access. Then, if you suddenly pick up a phone connected to the terminal adapter's POTS jack, bonding stops and the second B channel is freed up for the phone call. Once the call is complete, bonding will resume.

Another WAN technology that uses bonding is digital subscriber line (DSL). By configuring the DSL Access Multiplexer (DSLAM) at the service provider's central office (CO), hardware bonding can be implemented to link multiple DSL connections into a single high-bandwidth pipe.

An alternative to hardware bonding for DSL is customer premises equipment (CPE) bonding in which Multilink PPP is used to aggregate multiple DSL circuits at the customer premises instead of the DSLAM. This newer form of bonding has the advantage of being easier to deploy and configure than hardware bonding, which often requires costly upgrades of DSLAMs. A market example is Netopia, a DSL service provider that offers bonding of up to four Internet Digital Subscriber Line (IDSL) lines.

DSL bonding has several advantages:

- Customers requiring greater bandwidth than can be afforded by a single DSL link can use bonding to deploy better than T1 services for much less the cost of a T1 line.
- Customers who are too far from their telco CO can use bonding to boost DSL carrying capacity to typical DSL speeds at twice the normal distance from customer premises to CO. For example, Netopia's IDSL bonding can provide up to 576 Kbps at distances up to 35,900 feet (10,940 meters) from the CO, which is almost double the normal DSL limiting distance of 18,000 feet (5500 meters).

See Also: *Digital Subscriber Line (DSL), Integrated Services Digital Network (ISDN), Multilink Point-to-Point Protocol (MPPP)*

boot

A term used to refer to the process of starting a computer, as in the phrase, "Please boot the computer."

Overview

The term *boot* also refers specifically to the series of steps by which a computer locates and loads the operating system once the power is turned on. This series of steps is usually referred to as the boot sequence or boot process, and it depends on both the type of operating system installed on the machine and the type of hardware platform (for example, x86 platform or Alpha platform).

The term *warm boot* refers to resetting the system or rebooting using Ctrl+Alt+Delete. The power to the system is not interrupted during a warm boot, but the boot process starts again from the beginning using the system basic input/output system (BIOS).

The term *cold boot* refers to shutting down a computer and actually turning off the power source and then turning it back on. Cold boots are sometimes necessary after installing or configuring some legacy hardware devices to ensure that the devices are properly initialized. For example, if you change the configuration parameters of an internal modem, you sometimes need to cold boot your system for these changes to take effect.

See Also: *boot files, boot process*

boot files

Files needed to boot an operating system on a computer.

Overview

Every operating system has its own set of boot files needed to locate, load, and initialize the operating system during the boot sequence. For example, MS-DOS and Windows 3.*x* use the hidden files Io.sys and Msdos.sys and the file Command.com. Configuration information stored in the text files Config.sys and Autoexec.bat is also used during the process.

On Windows 95, Windows 98, and Windows Millennium Edition (Me), the files used for booting are Io.sys, Msdos.sys, and Win.com, with the files Config.sys and Autoexec.bat used optionally to support legacy hardware.

The files needed to boot Windows NT vary depending on whether the x86 or Alpha processor platform is used.

The files needed to boot Windows 2000, Windows XP, and Windows .NET Server (and Windows NT on x86) include the following:

- Boot.ini
- Bootsect.dos
- Hal.dll
- Ntdetect.com
- Ntbootdd.sys
- Ntldr
- Ntoskrnl.exe

The Windows 2000, Windows XP, and Windows .NET Server boot process also makes use of other files, including device drivers and the system hive.

See Also: *boot, boot process*

B

Boot.ini

A file used to create the boot loader menu in Windows 2000, Windows XP, and Windows .NET Server.

Overview

Boot.ini is a hidden, read-only text file on the root of the system partition of a Microsoft Windows 2000, Windows XP, or Windows .NET Server machine. The boot loader menu is used on dual-boot and multiboot systems to select which operating system (Windows 2000 or some other operating system) to boot. The Boot.ini file creates this menu, which normally is only displayed if more than one operating system is installed on the machine.

Examples

A typical Boot.ini file for a default Windows 2000 installation might look like this:

```
[boot loader]
timeout=30
default=multi(0)disk(0)rdisk(0)partition(1)\
WINNT
[operating systems]
multi(0)disk(0)rdisk(0)partition(1)\
WINNT="Microsoft Windows 2000 Professional"
/fastdetect
```

You can see a close correspondence between the appearance of the Boot.ini file and the boot loader menu, which the Ntldr program creates during the Windows NT boot sequence.

A Boot.ini file for a dual-boot system configured to boot to either Windows 2000 or Windows 98 usually looks like this:

```
[boot loader]
timeout=30
default=multi(0)disk(0)rdisk(0)partition(1)\
WINNT
[operating systems]
multi(0)disk(0)rdisk(0)partition(1)\
WINNT="Microsoft Windows 2000 Professional"
/fastdetect
C:\="Microsoft Windows"
```

The last line of the file is the same for booting to any MS-DOS–based operating system, including Windows 95, Windows 98, and Windows Millennium Edition (Me).

See Also: *boot, boot files, boot loader menu, boot process*

boot loader menu

A menu that appears when you boot a Microsoft Windows 2000, Windows XP, or Windows .NET Server computer configured for dual-boot or multiboot operation with other operating systems.

Overview

The boot loader menu appears during the boot loader phase of Windows NT startup, and it is displayed by the Windows 2000, Windows XP, and Windows .NET Server loader program called Ntldr. The boot loader menu allows you to select the particular operating system you want to run on a dual-boot or multiboot system and to use optional boot-time switches for booting Windows 2000, Windows XP, and Windows .NET Server in various enhanced ways or for troubleshooting purposes. The table summarizes some of the more commonly used boot-time switches used in Boot.ini.

Some Common Boot-Time Switches Used in Boot.ini

Switch	*Description*
/3GB	Used only with Windows 2000 Advanced Server to increase user address space from 2 gigabytes (GB) to 3 GB
/basevideo	Starts Windows 2000 using generic Video Graphics Adapter (VGA) video
/bootlog	Creates a log, called Ntbtlog.txt, of steps in the boot process
/fastdetect	Skips enumeration of serial and parallel devices during the boot process (included by default)
/numproc=	Specifies the number of CPUs to use on a symmetric multiprocessing (SMP) system
/sos	Lists the device drivers marked to load at boot time and displays other information

B

Notes

The boot loader menu is created by the Boot.ini file. This file can be edited using a text editor such as Notepad, but this should be done with care as mistakes could render your system unbootable.

See Also: *boot, boot files, Boot.ini, boot process*

BOOTP

Stands for bootstrap protocol, a Transmission Control Protocol/Internet Protocol (TCP/IP) protocol and service that allows diskless workstations to obtain their IP address, other TCP/IP configuration information, and their boot image file from a bootstrap protocol (BOOTP) server.

See: *bootstrap protocol (BOOTP)*

boot partition

The partition of a disk on which Microsoft Windows 2000, Windows XP, or Windows .NET Server installs its core operating system files.

Overview

The core operating system files for Windows 2000, Windows XP, and Windows .NET Server are typically stored in \Winnt and its subdirectories. The \Winnt directory and its system files are located on what is referred to as the boot partition (by a strange choice of terminology, the boot files in Windows 2000, Windows XP, and Windows .NET Server are stored on the system partition).

The choice of which partition is to be the boot partition is made during installation of Windows 2000, Windows XP, and Windows .NET Server and cannot be changed afterward. An important consideration when installing Windows 2000, Windows XP, and Windows .NET Server is designating a boot partition that has sufficient free space to contain the various operating system files together with all the optional and future components such as device drivers.

Notes

The boot partition can be the same as or different from the system partition.

See Also: *boot process, system partition*

boot process

The series of steps that occurs when an operating system boots on a machine.

Overview

Each operating system has its own particular boot sequence and uses its own specific set of boot files. Knowledge of the boot sequence for a particular operating system can aid in troubleshooting problems booting a machine on which that operating system is installed. For example, from messages displayed during the boot process, a technician can often determine whether a particular boot file is missing or corrupt.

The following is a brief summary of the boot sequence for the Microsoft Windows 2000 operating system (the Windows XP and Windows .NET Server boot sequences are similar). Note that the actual boot process involves more than 100 different steps and that this description gives only an overview of the process.

- **Preboot:** The boot process can take place only because during installation Windows 2000 Setup writes boot code (a short series of executable instructions) on the master boot record (MBR) located on the first sector of the first hard disk. The MBR also contains the partition table identifying which partition is the active (bootable) partition that contains the operating system boot files. Setup also creates a file called Boot.ini that is used to display a boot loader menu on systems configured for dual-booting or multibooting to Windows 2000 and other operating systems.
- **Ntldr:** When a Windows 2000 system is powered on, the basic input/output system (BIOS) reads the MBR into memory and transfers control to the MBR, which then finds, loads, and executes Ntldr, a key Windows 2000 executable boot file. When

Ntldr starts, the processor is still running in 16-bit real mode, and the first thing Ntldr does is switch the processor to 32-bit protected mode. Ntldr then creates page tables and enables paging. At this point, if the boot or system drive is on a Small Computer System Interface (SCSI) drive, Ntldr loads Ntbootdd.sys, which functions as a device driver for the drive. Once this stage is passed, Ntldr clears the screen and if the system is configured for multiboot operation, it then displays the boot loader menu generated using Boot.ini (this menu is not displayed if the only operating system installed is Windows 2000 itself). Assuming single-boot mode, Ntldr then locates the system directory (usually \Winnt), clears the screen again, displays the "Starting Windows" progress bar, and begins loading additional files including the kernel (Ntoskrnl.exe); and the hardware abstraction layer, or HAL (Hal.dll), reads the SYSTEM hive to determine which other device drivers to load, loads and initializes the file system and device drivers needed, and various other tasks. Then Ntldr calls Ntoskrnl.exe for the next stage of the boot process.

- **Ntoskrnl.exe:** The operating system kernel Ntoskrnl.exe performs a two-phase initialization that consists of more than 30 different steps that are too involved to explain here. As these steps are performed, the Starting Windows progress bar moves toward 100 percent, at which time the Session Manager subsystem (Smss) is initialized.
- **Smss:** The role of Smss is to create the user-mode environment that provides the graphical user interface (GUI) by which the user completes the boot process and accesses the system. Smss performs a whole series of steps ending in its main thread waiting for the Winlogon process to generate the logon dialog box.
- **Logon:** Once the logon dialog box is generated, the user enters the necessary credentials, is authenticated, and the desktop user interface appears. The boot process is now complete.

See Also: *boot, boot files*

Bootsect.dos

A boot file in Microsoft Windows 2000, Windows XP, and Windows .NET Server used to support dual-boot scenarios with MS-DOS–based operating systems such as Windows Millennium Edition (Me).

Overview

When the boot loader menu appears during the boot process on a dual-boot Windows 2000, Windows XP, or Windows .NET Server machine, the user selects the operating system to boot. If an MS-DOS–based operating system such as Windows 95, Windows 98, or Windows Me is selected, the Ntldr program immediately switches the processor back to 16-bit real mode and then loads Bootsect.dos and turns control of the boot process over to it. Bootsect.dos then continues with an MS-DOS-specific boot process leading to initialization of the selected operating system.

Bootsect.dos contains the location of the partition boot sector that existed on the partition prior to the installation of Windows 2000, Windows XP, or Windows .NET Server. Thus, Bootsect.dos enables the system to locate and load the alternate operating system. Bootsect.dos is not loaded during a normal boot of the Windows 2000, Windows XP, or Windows .NET Server operating system.

See Also: *boot files, boot process*

bootstrap protocol (BOOTP)

A Transmission Control Protocol/Internet Protocol (TCP/IP) protocol and service that allows diskless workstations to obtain their IP address, other TCP/IP configuration information, and their boot image file from a bootstrap protocol (BOOTP) server.

Overview

The network interface card (NIC) on these diskless workstations contains a programmable read-only memory (PROM) chip containing code necessary to initialize the client.

When a bootstrap protocol (BOOTP) client is started, it has no IP address, so it broadcasts a message containing its MAC address onto the network. This message is called a "BOOTP request," and it is picked up by the

B

BOOTP server, which replies to the client with the following information that the client needs:

- The client's IP address, subnet mask, and default gateway address
- The IP address and host name of the BOOTP server
- The IP address of the server that has the boot image, which the client needs to load its operating system

When the client receives this information from the BOOTP server, it configures and initializes its TCP/IP protocol stack, and then connects to the server on which the boot image is shared. The client loads the boot image and uses this information to load and start its operating system.

BOOTP is defined in RFCs 951 and 1084. The Dynamic Host Configuration Protocol (DHCP) was developed as an extension of BOOTP.

Notes

The term *bootstrap protocol* (or *boot protocol*) comes from the idea of lifting yourself up by your own bootstraps—something that is obviously difficult to do. In other words, how does a client machine start up when it initially has neither an IP address nor an operating system? BOOTP makes this difficult task possible.

Most UNIX servers support diskless workstations using the BOOTP protocol. BOOTP is implemented on UNIX servers using the bootpd daemon. Certain aspects of BOOTP are supported by Microsoft Windows 2000, Windows XP, and Windows .NET Server, but the protocol is rarely used in Windows networks.

See Also: *Dynamic Host Configuration Protocol (DHCP)*

boot volume

In Microsoft Windows 2000, Windows XP, and Windows .NET Server, the volume that has the operating system files.

Overview

The boot volume can be the same as or different from the system volume, and it can be formatted in either NTFS file system (NTFS) or file allocation table (FAT). The term *volume* indicates that we are referring here to dynamic storage, which enables volumes to be created and managed. By contrast, basic storage enables the creation and management of partitions instead.

See Also: *boot partition*

Border Gateway Protocol (BGP)

An exterior gateway protocol (EGP) used on the Internet to provide loop-free routing between different autonomous systems (ASs).

Overview

The Internet consists of large, independently administered networks called ASs connected by routers to form a single, enormous internetwork. ASs themselves are smaller internetworks and contain routers that exchange routing information with each other using various interior gateway protocols (IGPs) such as Routing Information Protocol (RIP) and Interior Gateway Routing Protocol (IGRP). These IGPs do not scale well enough to handle exchange of routing information between the border routers that join various ASs together, however, and for such purposes exterior gateway protocols (EGPs) are used, the de facto standard EGP for the Internet being the Border Gateway Protocol (BGP).

Like RIP and IGRP, BGP is based on the distance vector routing algorithm (or more specifically on a variant called path-vector), which enables groups of routers to share their routing information in a highly efficient and scalable manner. The routing information BGP exchanges between boundary routers is called Network Layer Reachability Information (NLRI), and specifies which other AS's data can be forwarded to from the local AS and the most efficient routes (best path) for doing this. BGP also can ensure against routing loops occurring.

BGP was developed in 1982 as the successor to EGP and was formalized in RFCs 827 and 904. Since then it has gone through several versions, with the current version being BGP 4, specified by RFC 1771. BGP 4 includes a number of enhancements over earlier versions, including support for

- Route and path aggregation
- Route, path, and community filtering
- Routing policies
- Advertising Internet Protocol (IP) prefixes
- Classless Interdomain Routing (CIDR)

Architecture

BGP is a connection-oriented protocol that runs on top of Transmission Control Protocol (TCP) to provide reliable transport of routing updates. TCP port 179 is used for forming connections between BGP-enabled routers, and incremental updates to routing tables only are transmitted, which makes BGP efficient in terms of bandwidth utilization (other distance-vector routing protocols exchange entire routing tables at regular intervals, which makes them scale poorly to internetworks the size of the Internet).

To use BGP, your internetwork must first be assigned an Autonomous System Number (ASN). You can get one by contacting your regional Internet registry, such as the American Registry for Internet Numbers (ARIN) for North and South America, Reseaux IP Européens (RIPE) for Europe, or the Asian-Pacific Network Information Center (APNIC) for Asia. ASNs for public internetworks are assigned from the range 1 through 64511.

BGP-speaking routers within an AS establish peering relationships with each other to form a loop-free routing mesh. The first update between two peers includes all known routes on the network, while succeeding updates are incremental.

Implementation

BGP needs to be implemented only in very large internetworks. When smaller internetworks using IGRP grow to the point that IGRP performs poorly, BGP can be used to partition the internetwork into two autonomous systems for better routing performance.

Another situation where you might implement BGP is if your corporate internetwork is multihomed, that is, has several dedicated connections to the Internet using different Internet service providers (ISPs). In this case, you can use BGP to balance the load between the Internet connections and provide redundancy.

Finally, if your corporate internetwork is being used as a transit network to connect other networks to the Internet, you need to employ BGP.

If you plan to implement BGP, make sure your router is powerful enough to handle it, especially if your internetwork will be directly connected to a regional ISP's network.

Notes

There are actually two flavors of BGP, though this distinction is not widely used in the literature:

- **EBGP (Exterior BGP):** The form used for communication between different ASs for BGP-enabled routers. This is also simply known as BGP and is the version described in this article.
- **IBGP (Interior BGP):** The form used for communication within an AS for BGP-enabled routers.

See Also: *autonomous system (AS), exterior gateway protocol (EGP), routing protocol*

border router

A router that connects two different autonomous systems (ASs).

Overview

The Internet consists of a collection of thousands of different independently administered large internetworks called ASs. Border routers are high-speed backbone routers that connect these different internetworks.

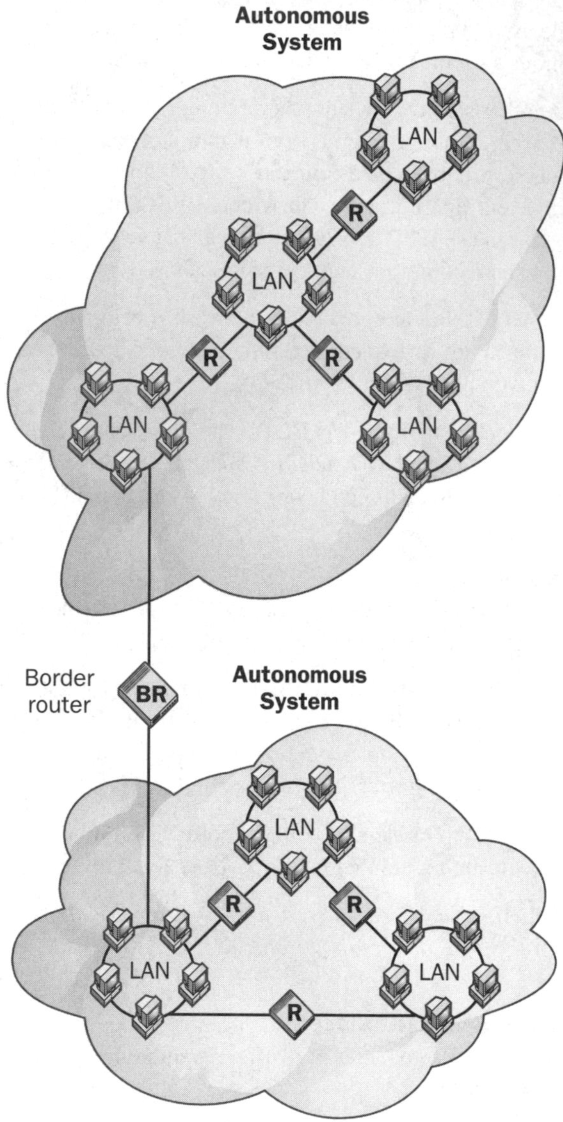

Border router. *Using a border router to connect two autonomous systems.*

Border routers use the Border Gateway Protocol (BGP) as the routing protocol for exchanging route information between them. Since the routing tables for border routers are large and rapidly growing as the Internet itself expands and evolves, border routers need to be high-performance, with at least 64 kilobytes (KB) of memory to hold these routing tables. Without these border routers and BGP, the Internet would be limited to a much smaller size than it is.

See Also: *autonomous system (AS), Border Gateway Protocol (BGP), Internet, router*

bottleneck

A situation that occurs when computer and network systems and components are unable to meet the demand placed upon them by real-world situations.

Overview

A bottleneck is essentially the particular network component or server subsystem that is causing the problem. For example, if users on a Microsoft Windows 2000–based network are complaining that it takes too long to log on when they arrive at the office in the morning, the bottleneck and its potential resolution might be

- Not enough domain controllers to handle logon requests (A solution: add more domain controllers)
- The domain controller does not have enough memory to process large numbers of simultaneous logons (A solution: add more random access memory [RAM])
- Network bandwidth is saturated in the morning with directory replication traffic (A solution: reschedule directory replication or upgrade to 100 megabits per second (Mbps) Ethernet)

The etymological reason for describing each of the above situations as a "bottleneck" is that a bottle's thinnest point is its neck and hence the neck controls the flow of liquid should the bottle be inverted. In the same way, the performance of an application running on a computer system can be limited by the amount of physical memory, read/write speed of the disk subsystem, throughput of the network interface card, speed of the CPU, and other parameters—any of these components (or several of them) could be a bottleneck that prevents the application from performing as desired. Or more generally, the performance of a browser accessing Web content on a corporate Intranet could be affected by overworked name servers for Domain Name System (DNS) name resolution, an insufficient number of domain controllers to handle authentication requests, slow or faulty routers joining subnets within an internetwork, misconfigured firewalls, and a host of other issues that could represent bottlenecks.

Notes

Troubleshooting bottlenecks is the science (sometimes the art) of identifying, isolating, and correcting issues that limit application performance. Valuable tools for ferreting out bottlenecks in Windows 2000–, Windows XP–, and Windows .NET Server–based networks are the Performance console, one of the administrative tools in Windows 2000, Windows XP, and Windows .NET Server, and Task Manager. For system performance, there are four main types of bottlenecks:

- **Processor bottlenecks:** If a CPU's utilization is constantly running near 100 percent when a certain application is running, it might indicate a processor bottleneck, in which case the application is said to be processor-bound. Upgrading to a faster processor or adding a second processor to a multiprocessor-capable motherboard might correct the problem.
- **Memory bottlenecks:** These bottlenecks arise when the system has insufficient RAM, which generally results in excessive paging and overall poor performance. Adding more RAM is often the simplest and cheapest solution to improve performance of most computer systems.
- **Disk bottlenecks:** Sometimes the hard disk subsystem cannot keep up with read/write requests generated by an application. In such a case the application is said to be disk-bound, and upgrading to a faster disk subsystem, implementing disk striping, or using a storage area network (SAN) can improve performance. Often, however, when disk activity is consistently too high, this simply indicates excessive paging caused by insufficient RAM. In this situation, what appears at first to be a disk bottleneck is actually one of memory instead.
- **Network bottleneck:** With today's Gigabit Ethernet (GbE) networks, older servers simply cannot pipe data fast enough from their system bus into their GbE network cards to get it onto the network. What seems to be a network bottleneck here is really caused by the inadequate speed of the system bus, and upgrading the motherboard is the only real option. True network bottlenecks are more difficult to find and may result from misconfigured routers, network cards running in promiscuous mode, excessive broadcast overhead from using too many protocols on the network, poor planning of network topologies, and many other issues.

bounce

An effect that happens to signals on a bus topology network when the ends of the bus are improperly terminated or unterminated.

Overview

A signal that is placed on a bus that is unterminated will continue to reflect from the end of the bus until that signal is attenuated by the impedance of the cable. Another situation that can cause signals to bounce is a break in the cable, which essentially creates two unterminated ends for the two segments.

The effect of signal bounce on baseband networks such as Ethernet is serious, since the transceivers on the network interface cards (NICs) attached to the bus interpret the problem as a collision and stop transmitting. This collision occurs because the signal is colliding with its own reflection. Once the proper termination is applied to the bus, network communication can resume.

See Also: *terminator*

bps

Stands for bits per second, a unit used for measuring the speed of transmission of data on a network of computers.

See: *bits per second (bps)*

B

breakout box

A troubleshooting tool used to determine the wiring of an RS-232 interface on a networking device or computer.

Overview

A breakout box can be inserted between two RS-232 devices to determine which wires are active. Breakout boxes are useful in troubleshooting RS-232 connection problems resulting from a manufacturer's device not using standard pinning.

Breakout boxes are specific examples of a more general category of network testing equipment called "status monitors." Status monitors are available for testing a variety of serial interfaces, including RS-232, RS-449, V.35, and X.21. They generally come with a variety of connectors and are quick and easy to use for isolating problems with serial transmission connections in networking, telecommunications, and industrial settings.

See Also: *serial transmission*

BREW

Stands for Binary Runtime Environment for Wireless, a platform from QUALCOMM for developing applications for cellular communications systems.

See: *Binary Runtime Environment for Wireless (BREW)*

bridge

A networking component used either to extend or to segment networks.

Overview

Bridges work at the data-link layer of the Open Systems Interconnection (OSI) model of networking. They can be used to

- Segment networks into smaller collision domains
- Join dissimilar media such as unshielded twisted-pair (UTP) cabling and fiber-optic cabling
- Join together different network architectures such as Token Ring and Ethernet (called a translation bridge)

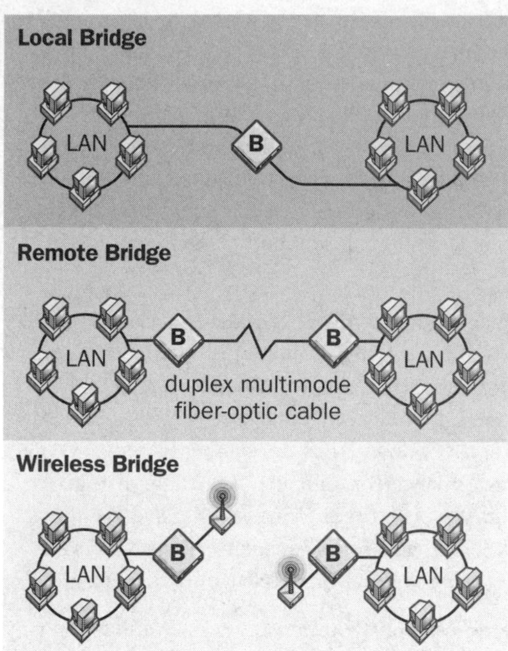

Bridge. *The three basic types of bridge.*

Bridges regenerate signals but do not perform any protocol conversion, so the same networking protocol (such as Transmission Control Protocol/Internet Protocol [TCP/IP]) must be running on both network segments connected to the bridge. Bridges can also support Simple Network Management Protocol (SNMP), and they can have other diagnostic features.

Bridges come in three basic types:

- **Local bridges:** Directly connect local area networks (LANs) (called a transparent bridge for Ethernet networks and a source-routed bridge for Token Ring networks)
- **Remote bridges:** Can be used to create a wide area network (WAN) link between two LANs
- **Wireless bridges:** Can be used to join LANs or connect remote stations to LANs without wiring between them

Architecture

Bridges operate by sensing the source MAC addresses of the transmitting nodes on the network and automatically building an internal routing table. This table is used to determine which connected segment to route packets to, and it provides the filtering capability that bridges are known for.

If the bridge knows which segment a packet is intended for, it forwards the packet directly to that segment. If the bridge does not recognize the packet's destination address, it forwards the packet to all connected segments except the one it originated on. And if the destination address is in the same segment as the source address, the bridge drops the packet.

Bridges also forward broadcast packets to all segments except the originating one.

Advantages and Disadvantages

Bridges are less expensive than routers and can easily be used to add more stations to a network. They are transparent to high-level protocols and can even be used with nonroutable protocols that routers cannot handle.

Bridges have the disadvantages, however, of increasing the chance of broadcast storms occurring on a network and are not as efficient in larger networks as routers are.

Implementation

Use bridges to reduce network congestion and improve performance by segmenting busy Ethernet networks into smaller collision domains. You can also use bridges to connect segments more efficiently than repeaters and to join dissimilar networks such as Ethernet and Token Ring. Remote bridges can be used to create WAN links.

A poorly placed bridge can actually worsen network performance. For example, if you use a bridge to divide users who belong to the same department and frequently communicate with one another over the network, this might actually slow down communication among users by creating a bottleneck. It is better to use bridges to join together separate departmental LANs on which intradepartmental traffic is greater than interdepartmental traffic.

When using bridges to connect networks, make sure that only one path leads to any destination node on the network; otherwise, frames could become locked in loops and circle the network endlessly, causing a network storm.

Notes

Switches and bridges function similarly, but although switches can have many ports, bridges only have two.

See Also: remote bridge, wireless networking

bridgehead server

A server that acts as an endpoint of communications with another site.

Overview

In Microsoft terminology, bridgehead servers occur in several contexts. For example, in Microsoft Exchange Server, a bridgehead server in one site is responsible for routing messages through a connector to a similar server in a different site. More generally, in Microsoft Windows 2000 and Windows .NET Server, a bridgehead server is a domain controller that replicates Active Directory directory service information with domain controllers in other sites. The first domain controller in each site assumes the role of Inter-Site Topology Generator and determines which domain controllers in the site will be selected as bridgehead servers.

BRI-ISDN

Stands for Basic Rate Interface ISDN, the slower version of Integrated Services Digital Network (ISDN) communications (the faster being Primary Rate Interface [PRI]-ISDN).

See: Basic Rate Interface ISDN (BRI-ISDN)

broadband

A signaling technology that sends signals simultaneously over a range of different frequencies as electromagnetic waves. The opposite of baseband.

See: broadband transmission

B

broadband Internet access

Generally refers to various technologies such as digital subscriber line (DSL) and cable modems that provide high-speed Internet access for residential and business customers.

Overview

The growth and evolution of the Internet and World Wide Web over the last 10 years has seen simple text-based Web pages become replaced with media-rich content that includes graphic files, sound clips, Shockwave animations, and streaming media. In addition text-based Simple Mail Transfer Protocol (SMTP) e-mail has become heavy with large attachments including Microsoft Word files, spreadsheets, images, and other content. These changes in content forms require high-bandwidth Internet connections, and traditional dial-up modem connections (even 56K) feel inadequate to many users.

As a result, the broadband Internet access market has taken off in the last couple of years, with widespread deployment of cable modem and DSL connections now in the millions. In addition, for remote locations, companies such as StarBand Communications and Digistar provide satellite-based broadband Internet access with download speeds in the 2-megabit-per-second (Mbps) range (for more on satellite-based broadband, see the article "broadband wireless communications" elsewhere in this chapter).

The two most commonly deployed broadband Internet access solutions are cable modems and variants of DSL. Cable modems are a low-cost solution that is easier to deploy than DSL, but they are generally only available in residential markets where the cabling infrastructure has already been widely deployed. DSL is a more complex solution offered by telcos but has the advantage that connections are dedicated rather than shared: a DSL connection offers guaranteed bandwidth, while the effective bandwidth for a cable modem connection depends on the number of users to which it is deployed in a given area (cable modem users are essentially connected in a LAN and so share the available bandwidth of the LAN).

Speed is the main benefit of various broadband Internet access technologies, and a comparison is useful:

- **Copper DSL:** Running various flavors of DSL such as Asymmetric Digital Subscriber Line (ADSL) and Symmetric Digital Subscriber Line (SDSL) over the copper local loop to subscribers can offer speeds of up to 8 Mbps, but download speeds of 1 or 2 Mbps are more common (upload speeds may be less).
- **Fiber DSL:** By running fiber to the curb, significantly higher DSL speeds of up to 60 Mbps or higher can be achieved, but the cost is high due to the need to deploy a new fiber infrastructure. This is an attractive solution for businesses, however, especially where telcos are rolling out such infrastructures.
- **Cable modem:** Typical cable modem speeds are between 2 and 6 Mbps, but effective speeds may be much less for users due to the shared-bandwidth nature of this solution.

Uses

In addition to providing the ability to surf the Web at high speeds or send Christmas card images through e-mail, broadband Internet access is seen by increasing numbers of companies as an idea solution for supporting the remote workforce of home-based telecommuters. By using a cable modem or DSL connection and setting up a Virtual Private Network (VPN) connection using Microsoft Windows 2000, Windows XP, and Windows .NET Server, or some other platform, employees can work from home across secure connections to their company intranet.

Large companies that choose DSL or other broadband solutions as replacements for or backups to existing leased-line wide area network (WAN) links need to consider things such as service level agreements (SLAs), Quality of Service (QoS) guarantees (usually nonexistent for DSL), the number of Internet Protocol (IP) addresses that can be provided with the connection (usually under 150 for DSL), deployment times (usually weeks, but sometimes months), and business pricing (which is significantly more than residential pricing).

Advantages and Disadvantages

One important limitation of DSL as a broadband Internet access solution is that it is only viable within a small distance from the telco's central office (CO). This distance is typically about 18,000 feet (5500 meters) for the most popular implementation of DSL; that is, ADSL. Cable modem provisioning does not suffer from this distance limitation, but its deployment is limited to areas where the necessary cabling infrastructure is already present, which excludes most business and industrial parks.

Cable modems also have the additional advantage of being simpler to implement than DSL, which often requires professional installation services. On the other hand, DSL is intrinsically more secure than cable modems since DSL connections are dedicated—it is just your customer premises and the DSL provider on the network. With cable modems, all users in a given service area are on a shared LAN, and if your connection is not secured using a firewall, then other users in your neighborhood may be able to view and access shared files on your system.

Marketplace

Copper DSL is available from most telcos and carriers, including Sprint Corporation, Covad Communications Company, the various "baby Bells," and many others. Fiber DSL is being piloted by Pacific Bell Telephone Company and others.

Most cable companies provide cable modem access now, with AT&T being a major player in this market.

Prospects

While broadband Internet access services are becoming more and more widely deployed in the United States, the marketplace tends to be fractured, and solutions and equipment from one vendor often have interoperability issues with those from other vendors. This is especially the case with broadband wireless technologies.

One country that is taking a more aggressive approach to broadband is Japan. While the Japanese economy largely missed out on the narrowband Internet and PC revolution of the 1990s, the country is making strong efforts to become the world leader in implementing broadband Internet technologies, with companies such as Sony taking the lead.

See Also: *broadband transmission, broadband wireless communications, cable modem, Digital Subscriber Line (DSL), Internet access, xDSL*

broadband ISDN (B-ISDN)

The broadband transmission counterpart of Integrated Services Digital Network (ISDN).

Overview

Broadband ISDN (B-ISDN) encompasses a set of International Telecommunication Union (ITU) standards and services designed to provide an integrated digital network for audio, video, and data transmission. Instead of using the copper media used in ordinary ISDN, broadband ISDN uses fiber-optic and radio media.

Broadband ISDN is designed to use the cell-switching transport technology of Asynchronous Transfer Mode (ATM) together with the underlying physical transport mechanisms of Synchronous Optical Network (SONET). Broadband ISDN standards and technologies were intended to provide high-speed digital connectivity for homes and businesses, but the technology was never widely deployed and has been superseded by Digital Subscriber Line (DSL) and other high-speed telco services.

See Also: *Digital Subscriber Line (DSL)*

broadband transmission

A signaling technology that sends signals simultaneously over a range of different frequencies as electromagnetic waves. The opposite of baseband transmission.

Overview

Broadband transmissions are divided into multiple bands or channels by multiplexers using a multiplexing scheme such as frequency-division multiplexing (FDM). Each channel has a carrier frequency that is modulated to carry the signal from a given source. At the receiving station, multiplexers separate the various signals. Guard bands are used to prevent interference among channels.

Broadband signals are unidirectional—traveling in only one direction at a time—so a broadband system can generally either transmit or receive but cannot do both simultaneously. Broadband signals can be regenerated using amplifiers in order to travel longer distances before becoming attenuated.

Uses

Broadband transmission is typically used for environments in which video, audio, and data need to be transmitted simultaneously. Cable television systems are based on broadband transmission technologies, as are satellite-based television services. Examples of broadband services in the computer networking arena include T-carrier services, Asynchronous Transfer Mode (ATM), and the various flavors of Digital Subscriber Line (DSL).

See Also: *Asynchronous Transfer Mode (ATM), baseband transmission, broadband Internet access, broadband wireless communications, Digital Subscriber Line (DSL), T-carrier*

broadband wireless communications

Generally refers to high-speed wireless communications systems where data rates are approximately 1 megabit per second (Mbps) or higher.

Overview

Broadband wireless (or wireless broadband) is an emerging high-speed communications technology that is being largely driven by the Internet access market. Broadband wireless systems achieve data rates comparable to Digital Subscriber Line (DSL) or cable modems and can be used in environments where these technologies are unavailable or difficult to deploy, such as isolated rural areas. And like DSL and similar technologies, broadband wireless is an always-on solution that provides fast access to the Internet and can be used in other corporate wide area network (WAN) scenarios as well.

Broadband wireless basically comes in three forms: fixed wireless, mobile wireless, and satellite-based.

Fixed broadband wireless is a technology that is gaining significant market share at all levels, from small businesses to the enterprise. In a typical fixed wireless scenario, a business requiring high-speed Internet access or a WAN connection deploys a broadband radio transmitter/receiver with a fixed unidirectional dish or horn antenna pointed toward the service provider's antenna. A clear line of sight is required between the customer premises antenna and the provider's antenna, which generally means customers deploy their antenna on their rooftop and providers deploy antennas on high towers, skyscrapers, or nearby mountains. Fixed wireless broadband can be based on various different technologies including Local Multipoint Distribution System (LMDS), Multichannel Multipoint Distribution System (MMDS), and others. Fixed broadband wireless communications systems are based on spread-spectrum communications technologies and may use frequencies from the Industrial, Scientific, and Medical (ISM) band's 2.5 GHz range up to millimeter wavelengths in the 66 gigahertz (GHz) range. Dedicated point-to-point microwave links can offer data transmission speeds of 10 Mbps or higher, but speeds of 1 or 2 Mbps are more common.

Mobile broadband wireless solutions are still in planning stages in most countries and regions, with Europe and Asia in the lead with planned rollouts of 3G cellular technologies such as Wideband Code Division Multiple Access (WCDMA) and Universal Mobile Telecommunication System (UMTS). Nevertheless, widespread deployment of these technologies probably will not happen until 2005 or later.

Mobile broadband services are also expected to provide significantly slower speeds than fixed solutions. For example a WCDMA system that provides 2 Mbps for fixed transmission can only support 384 Kbps for mobile (walking) transmission when handoffs are required, and may go as low as 144 Kbps for highway travel.

Satellite-based broadband wireless solutions generally offer speeds of around 2 Mbps, are easy to deploy, and are rapidly becoming more widely available. An in-depth discussion of how this technology works can be found in the article "satellite networking" elsewhere in this book.

Uses

Companies may implement broadband wireless in a variety of scenarios:

- Fixed broadband wireless is often used for providing high-speed Internet access, for streaming video broadcasting from remote locations, and for backup links to leased-lines used for WAN links between branch offices.
- Mobile broadband wireless, when deployed, will probably be used for high-speed Internet access for cell phones, Personal Digital Assistants (PDAs), and other hand-held information appliances.
- Satellite-based broadband wireless is primarily intended to replace enterprise WAN links and for providing high-speed Internet access in remote locations.

Advantages and Disadvantages

A primary advantage of broadband wireless over competing wired broadband technologies such as DSL or cable modems is their ease of setup and the speed at which they can be deployed. Industry reports indicate that DSL services sometimes take weeks to set up, but fixed broadband wireless solutions typically take only a day or two. In the rapidly evolving Internet economy where time-to-market is critical for new startups, deployment speed is a factor that has influenced many new companies in adopting broadband wireless solutions. In addition, many large companies are turning to broadband wireless to replace or provide backup for expensive leased lines such as T1 or E1 at a fraction of the cost of these lines. Some broadband wireless carriers are also looking at providing value-added services such as Voice over IP (VoIP) in the near future as part of their integrated package of services. Broadband wireless systems are also relatively secure because most are based on spread-spectrum wireless communications technologies, which means that signals are scrambled across a large number of frequencies, making it difficult to eavesdrop (a firewall is nevertheless recommended when implementing broadband wireless as this is an always-on solution). Finally, broadband wireless is often the only solution for customers in remote areas requiring broadband Internet access or WAN links.

Besides the line-of-site limitation, broadband wireless does have other disadvantages that need to be considered before deployment. High-frequency broadband wireless platforms such as LMDS are more easily influenced by environmental factors such as weather than systems that use the low-frequency ISM or other low-frequency bands, and that can be a consideration in certain locations. Satellite-based broadband services have a latency on the order of several hundred milliseconds (compared with under 20 msec for most wired land-based systems), which is fine for corporate data transmission but annoying to users for Web browsing.

Marketplace

In the fixed wireless broadband marketplace, many carriers and service providers are starting to provision broadband wireless for business and enterprise customers. Sprint Broadband Direct provisions 2 Mbps MMDS services, typically in a matter of days. MCI WorldCom is also making significant inroads into the MMDS market. Players in the higher-frequency LMDS market include Teligent, NextLink Communications, WinStar Communications, and others. AT&T is, of course, also a major player in the fixed wireless broadband market.

In the mobile wireless broadband market, the emerging players are currently Ericsson and Nokia, with their pre–third generation (3G) broadband cellular initiatives known as 2.5G.

In the satellite-based broadband wireless market, major players include DirecPC and StarBand Communications, both of which offer nationwide coverage. Tachyon also provides 2 Mbps service across the United States.

Notes

The Institute of Electrical and Electronics Engineers (IEEE) is standardizing fixed broadband wireless technologies under the new 802.16 group of standards.

See Also: *802.16, broadband transmission, Digital Subscriber Line (DSL), Internet access, Local Multipoint Distribution Service (LMDS), Multipoint Multichannel Distribution Service (MMDS)*

B

broadcast domain

The collection of all stations on a network that can receive broadcast messages from any station among them.

Overview

Broadcast domains and collision domains are two different things:

- **Broadcast domains:** These are defined by broadcasting only as all those stations that can receive a broadcast.
- **Collision domains:** These are defined by any type of transmission, including unicasting, multicasting, and broadcasting.

Examples of broadcast domains include

- All stations connected to a given group of hubs or switches
- All stations on an internetwork whose routers are configured to forward broadcasts (not a desirable configuration)
- All stations in a given virtual local area network (VLAN) configured on a group of Ethernet switches.

Notes

Bridges used to segment Ethernet networks divide collision domains but do not divide broadcast domains.

See Also: *collision domain*

broadcast frame

In Ethernet networks, a frame broadcast to every station on the network.

Overview

An Ethernet media access control (MAC)–layer broadcast frame has a hexadecimal MAC address of FF-FF-FF-FF-FF-FF. This hexadecimal address is equivalent to 48 binary "ones." The meaning of this address in Ethernet is simply that this frame is intended to be received and processed by every connected node on the network.

Broadcast frames are typically generated when network services make announcements of their presence and availability to other hosts on the network. Too many broadcast frames on a network can degrade communication between nodes on the network.

Notes

In routed internetworks, routers are usually configured not to forward broadcast frames to other subnets. The reason is to prevent broadcast storms in one subnet from overwhelming hosts in other connected subnets. As a result of this limitation, however, broadcast frames used as service announcements are usually limited in scope to the local subnet on which the host providing the services is located.

See Also: *broadcasting, broadcast packet, broadcast storm, directed frame, frame*

broadcasting

A network communications method in which a packet or frame is sent simultaneously to all stations on the network.

Overview

Broadcasts take place when broadcast frames (or packets) are sent out over the network. These frames contain a special address that instructs every station on the network to accept and process the frame's contents.

Broadcasts have various functions on a network, including

- Announcing the availability of network services
- Resolving host names into addresses
- Troubleshooting and testing network connectivity

Examples of Internet Protocol (IP) services that employ broadcasts include

- Address Resolution Protocol (ARP)
- Dynamic Host Configuration Protocol (DHCP)
- Domain Name System (DNS)
- NETBIOS

Broadcasts are usually not an efficient use of network bandwidth, since only one or a few network stations might actually be interested in the information being broadcast. For this reason, directed frames (or packets) are used for most network communication, which involves targeting a packet directly for the intended station. (All other stations ignore the directed packet.) Another alternative is multicasting, which involves a form of limited broadcast to a select group of hosts.

Notes

Certain network conditions, such as certain types of device failure, can generate large numbers of unwanted broadcasts. These broadcast storms can sometimes bring down a network if the condition is not resolved.

Applications that are poorly designed may sometimes employ unnecessary amounts of broadcasting, with resulting degradation of overall network services.

See Also: *broadcast frame, broadcast packet, multicasting, unicasting*

broadcast packet

In Internet Protocol (IP) networks, an IP packet broadcast to every host on the network.

Overview

Broadcasts can be used in any type of IP network, including class A, B, C, D, and E networks. The actual broadcast address depends on the class of network under consideration. For example:

- For a class A network 27.0.0.0 the address for a broadcast packet would be 27.255.255.255.
- For a class B network 139.65.0.0 the broadcast address is 139.65.255.255.
- For a class C network 207.17.125.0 the broadcast address is 207.17.125.255.

The general broadcast address 255.255.255.255 is called a local area network (LAN) broadcast and can be routed to every host on an internetwork if routers are allowed to forward broadcasts. A faulty device that produces excessive 255.255.255.255 packets is said to be "flooding" the internetwork with broadcasts, and this can lead to a condition called a "broadcast storm."

The common denominator in these examples is 255, which is the decimal representation of the binary octet 11111111. Thus, the LAN broadcast address 255.255.255.255 in binary notation is a series of 32 binary "ones."

See Also: *broadcasting, broadcast frame, broadcast storm, directed packet, packet*

broadcast storm

A network condition in which so many broadcasts are occurring that normal communication between hosts is disrupted.

Overview

Broadcast storms commonly occur on Ethernet networks where baseband transmission technologies allow only one station to transmit at a time. The presence of broadcast storms often indicates that a networking component is malfunctioning and is continually sending out broadcast messages. A typical situation might be a failed transceiver on a network interface card (NIC) that is continually sending out a stream of binary "ones."

During a broadcast storm, the wire is continually busy and no other station is able to transmit information over the network. As a result, a broadcast storm essentially brings down the network. Since routers often are not configured to forward broadcast frames between subnets, broadcast storms usually are confined to a single subnet (configuring routers to forward broadcasts is thus a bad idea as a broadcast storm in one subnet could bring down the entire internetwork).

Broadcast storms might also indicate that your network's bandwidth is nearly saturated and needs to be upgraded.

See Also: *broadcasting*

B

brouter

Any network device having the capabilities of both a bridge and a router.

Overview

Usually, a brouter acts as a router for one protocol (for example, Transmission Control Protocol/Internet Protocol [TCP/IP]) and a bridge for all other protocols (for example, Internetwork Packet Exchange/Sequenced Packet Exchange [IPX/SPX]). Network services often send their announcements over every protocol on the network, which generates additional traffic and makes it generally disadvantageous to run more than one protocol on a single network.

Brouters are not common anymore, however, and the solution adopted by most network designers nowadays is to use a single protocol for all network communication on the main portion of the network, with gateways connecting to segments running other protocols. The protocol of choice for most internetworking today is TCP/IP.

See Also: *bridge, router*

browse list

The list of available shared network resources on a Microsoft Windows network.

Overview

The browse list is maintained and distributed by the Computer Browser service. The browse list contains a list of all available domains, workgroups, and servers on the network. This list is then distributed to clients who desire to connect to shared resources on the network so that they can locate and connect to these resources.

Essentially, when you are browsing Network Neighborhood in Windows NT or My Network Places in Windows 2000, Windows XP, or Windows .NET Server, you are looking at a representation of the browse list for your locally accessible network.

Notes

The browse list is maintained by the master browser computer, but clients that need it obtain it from backup browsers on the network.

If a server or domain is not heard from by the master browser after three announcement periods (amounting to approximately 45 minutes), the server or domain is removed from the browse list.

See Also: *Computer Browser service, election*

browser (Computer Browser service)

Any Microsoft Windows machine that is running the Computer Browser service and participates in updating and maintaining the browse list of shared resources available on the network.

See: *Computer Browser service*

browser (Web browser)

A client application that supports Hypertext Transfer Protocol (HTTP), the language of the World Wide Web.

See: *Hypertext Transfer Protocol (HTTP), Web browser*

browsing

Generally, the process of exploring the shared resources available on a network or the Web content available on the Internet.

Overview

You can browse for shared resources on a Microsoft Windows network using Windows Explorer, My Network Places, and other tools. Browsing a Windows network is made possible by the Computer Browser service, which keeps track of all shared resources on a Windows NT network and communicates this information to clients when they need to access a resource. The Computer Browser service is at the core of the ability to locate shared file and printer resources on a network and maintains the browse list, the list of available shared resources.

Regarding the Internet, the term *browsing* refers to the process of using a Web browser such as Microsoft Internet Explorer, Netscape Navigator, or Opera Software's Opera to view and download Web pages from the Internet. The origin of the term probably stems from the idea of reading magazines, in which you pick up one magazine and skim through its contents, then go to another magazine, and so on. On the Internet, it is even easier. You do not have to "pick up" anything; you simply keep clicking the links.

See Also: *Computer Browser service, Web browser*

BSD

Stands for Berkeley Software Distribution, a family of UNIX operating systems.

Overview

BSD UNIX was developed in the 1970s at the University of California at Berkeley, which licensed the UNIX operating system from AT&T and then made a number of modifications and enhancements, including many common UNIX features such as the vi editor, the C shell, and Transmission Control Protocol/Internet Protocol (TCP/IP) networking.

BSD UNIX and its offshoots constitute one of the two most popular families of UNIX in use today, the other family being UNIX System V and its offshoots. BSD UNIX formed the basis of the SunOS from Sun Microsystems, but Sun later combined features of both BSD and System V into their popular Solaris operating system. BSD UNIX is older than Linux but has not attracted as much attention as Linux has lately.

The major flavors of BSD UNIX popular today include

- **FreeBSD:** A free version of BSD UNIX available for the Intel x86, DEC Alpha, and PC-98 architectures. FreeBSD is the most popular of the BSDs and has a large and active developer community. FreeBSD has been popular with many Internet service providers (ISPs) as the base platform for their Web and mail servers. The current release of FreeBSD is version 4.3.
- **OpenBSD:** A popular version that stresses security with integrated cryptography and support for SSH1 and SSH2. The current release of this operating system is OpenBSD 2.9, and it is also available for free.
- **NetBSD:** Another free version of BSD UNIX that has been incorporated as the base operating system of a number of commercial products. The current release is NetBSD 1.5.1.

Notes

The commercial version BSDi is now known as iXsystems and is licensed by Wind River Systems.

For More Information

For a general overview of BSD flavors, see *www.bsd.org.* FreeBSD can be found at *www.freebsd.org.* OpenBSD can be downloaded from *www.openbsd.org.* NetBSD can be found at *www.netbsd.org.*

See Also: *UNIX*

BSP

Stands for business service provider, an application service provider (ASP) that offers a wide range of online business services that include not just Web hosting and e-commerce services typical of ASPs but also customer relations management, desktop maintenance support, system integration and consulting services, and other value-added business services.

See Also: *application service provider (ASP), xSP*

building-block services

A component of Microsoft Corporation's .NET platform that provides core Extensible Markup Language (XML) Web services.

Overview

Building-block services provide consistency and ease of use across services and applications developed for the .NET platform. These services are used to move the control of data from applications to the users who use these applications and ensure that user content forms the basis of all transactions.

Microsoft is developing a number of different building-block services to empower developers for rapid development of .NET Web services. Examples of these include services for

- User identification (for example, Microsoft Passport)
- User preference management
- Message delivery
- Calendar management
- File storage

B

While Microsoft is developing the core set of .NET services, third-party partners will develop additional services to build in enhanced functionality to .NET applications and services.

See Also: *.NET platform*

Building-centric Local Exchange Carrier (BLEC)

A telecommunications carrier focused on the Multitenant Unit (MTU) market.

Overview

With the increasing deregulation of the U.S. telecommunications industry over the last decades, several different types of local exchange carriers (LECs) have emerged in the marketplace, including Incumbent Local Exchange Carriers (ILECs) and Competitive Local Exchange Carriers (CLECs). The latest of these is the Building-centric Local Exchange Carrier (BLEC), which represents a carrier focused on providing broadband telco services within multitenant units (MTUs). An MTU is essentially a building or group of buildings that primarily host small and medium-sized businesses with between 10 and 200 employees. Examples of business environments serviced by BLECs include office skyscrapers, industrial parks, and hotels. Some BLECs also target residential apartment blocks and malls as well. By targeting MTUs, BLECs are essentially focusing on a market that ILECs have generally neglected (ILECs have historically focused on the large-enterprise and individual consumer markets instead). The requirements of BLEC clients are usually diverse, and typically include Internet Protocol (IP) data, Web hosting, e-mail, and Internet access, which BLECs offer as value-added data services to traditional voice telephone connectivity.

BLECs can typically be grouped into two categories:

- Those focused on retail services to end-user business clients.
- Those focused on the wholesale end of purchasing broadband access for MTUs from inter-exchange carriers (IXCs) who provision these wholesale services. Note that some IXCs themselves are getting into the MTU market by deploying high-speed metropolitan area networks (MANs) to service such customers and are in effect competitors to BLECs.

Implementation

Typically a single business client within an MTU cannot justify the cost of having a leased line such as T1 deployed to service its needs. That is where BLECs come in, however—they provision such services for all clients within a given MTU.

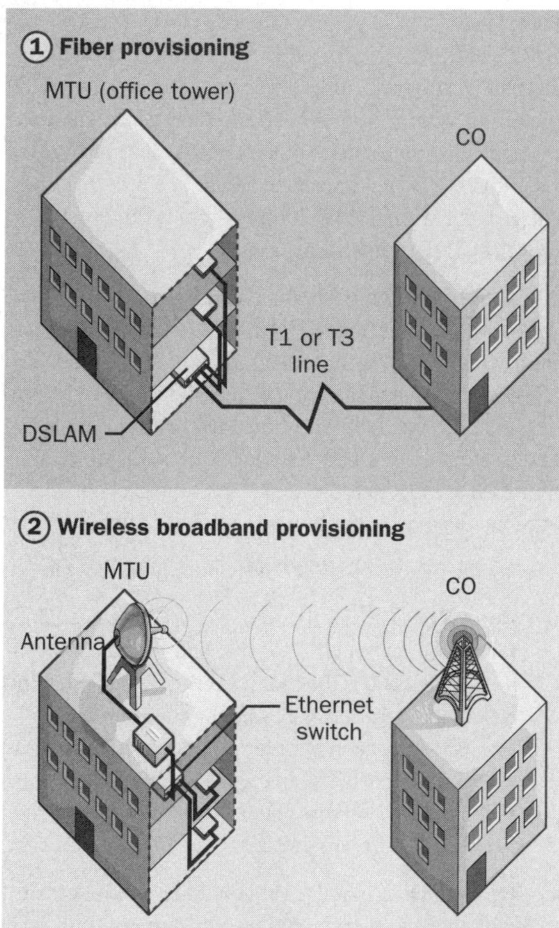

Building-centric Local Exchange Carrier (BLEC). *How a BLEC provisions customers with broadband services.*

Typically, a BLEC first has to provide new fiber to an MTU to provide clients with high-speed services brokered from larger LECs and IXCs. This first step is necessary because the majority of large office buildings in the United States do not currently have fiber-optic cabling deployed to them. Once fiber has been laid by the BLEC from the building to the central office (CO) of the LEC or IXC from which the BLEC obtains wholesale broadband provisioning, the BLEC then purchases T1 or T3 services from the LEC or IXC to run over the fiber. Switching gear (usually a DSLAM, an Asynchronous Transfer Mode [ATM] access switch, or some form of high-speed Ethernet switch) is then deployed by the BLEC in the basement of the MTU to provide broadband services to clients throughout the building. This arrangement is preferable to co-locating such equipment at LECs and IXCs and often give BLECs a competitive edge in the speed at which new services can be deployed and problems troubleshot.

Another technology option for BLECs is fixed broadband wireless, which bypasses the initial step of laying fiber to the building. This is often a method for cost-effective provisioning of broadband services for MTUs that is easy to implement rapidly and is often the only solution when the MTU is too far from a central office (CO) for DSL or T-carrier services to be effective.

To provision either of these scenarios, BLECs first have to negotiate right-of-way through revenue-sharing agreements with building owners to gain access to basement wiring closets or deploy rooftop antennas, and this is usually factored into the price for services offered by BLECs to tenants.

Marketplace

Some of the major players among BLECs include Broadband Office, which has right-of-way to a large portion of U.S. commercial office space; Comactive, which is an offshoot of Intermedia Communications; and many others.

Prospects

With increasing deregulation of the telecommunications industries, BLECs find themselves squeezed by rising customer expectations on the one hand, high levees from building owners for fiber and rooftop right-of-way on another hand, and direct competition from CLECs, ILECs, and IXCs higher up on the carrier feeding chain. Customers owning multiple MTUs desire simultaneous rollout regardless of the up-front costs to BLECs for servicing smaller premises. Some building owners (usually real estate companies) are also consider deploying their own broadband switching gear instead of partnering with BLECs to do so and thus bypass BLECs entirely by going to LECs and IXCs directly. Future rulings of the Federal Communications Commission (FCC) might also affect how this all works out in the marketplace.

Notes

Another common name for BLECs is Multitenant Broadband Service Providers (MBSPs).

See Also: *broadband Internet access, broadband wireless communications, carrier, inter-exchange carrier (IXC), local exchange carrier (LEC), multitenant unit (MTU)*

built-in account

In Microsoft Windows 2000, Windows XP, and Windows .NET Server, a type of user account that is created during installation.

Overview

All computers running Windows 2000, Windows XP, and Windows .NET Server, have two built-in user accounts:

- **Administrator account:** Used to provide administrative access to all features of the operating system
- **Guest account:** Intended to provide occasional users with access to network resources

Depending on whether the computer is a domain controller, a member server, or a workstation, built-in accounts will be either local user accounts or global user accounts. A built-in account on a domain controller is a global user account that exists everywhere within the domain. Users can log on to any machine in the domain using such an account, which provides administrators with the capability of administering a Windows 2000–based network from anywhere on the network. On a member server or workstation, the Administrator and Guest accounts are local user accounts and exist only on those machines.

Notes

Rename the Administrator built-in user account to make it more secure.

See Also: *built-in group*

built-in domain local group

In Microsoft Windows 2000, Windows XP, and Windows .NET Server, a domain local group created during installation that has preassigned rights and permissions. Built-in local groups are used to simplify the administrative task of assigning users and groups rights to perform system tasks and permissions to access network resources. Some of these groups include

- **Users:** Contains the Domain Users global group and is used to assign rights and permissions to all ordinary users.
- **Administrators:** Contains the Domain Admins global group and the Administrator account created during setup.
- **Guests:** Contains the Domain Guests global group.
- **Power Users:** Members have the right to share folders and printers.
- **Backup Operators:** Members have the right to back up and restore servers.
- **Account Operators:** Members have the right to administer accounts.
- **Server Operators:** Members have the right to administer servers.
- **Print Operators:** Members have the right to administer printers.

See Also: *built-in global group*

built-in global group

A type of global group created during installation of Active Directory directory service.

Overview

Built-in global groups are created in order to organize common groups of users for administrative purposes. These built-in global groups are created within either Active Directory (when implemented) or in the Security Accounts Manager (SAM) database (for stand-alone servers). The four types of built-in global groups are

- **Domain Admins:** Initially, this group contains only the Administrator account that was created during setup. Only people with administrative responsibilities should be assigned to this group.
- **Domain Guests:** This group contains the Guest account and is designed for organizing temporary users of network resources and granting them access.
- **Domain Users:** When a new user account is created, it is automatically added to this group, whose function is to collect all ordinary users for the purpose of assigning them permissions to resources on the network.
- **Enterprise Admins:** This group contains users who are assigned administrative rights over the entire network. The Enterprise Admins global group should be added to the Administrators domain local group in each of your network's domains. By default, the Administrator account is a member of the Enterprise Admins group.

See Also: *built-in group, built-in domain local group*

built-in group

In Microsoft Windows 2000 and Windows .NET Server, a type of group created during installation to simplify the delegation and assignment of common administrative tasks.

Overview

Built-in groups have preassigned sets of user rights, and some also have preassigned members.

Windows 2000 and Windows .NET Server contain three kinds of built-in groups:

- **Built-in domain local groups:** These are used to assign predefined sets of rights and permissions to users and groups of users, and they exist on all computers running Windows 2000 and Windows .NET Server.

- **Built-in global groups:** These groups are used to automatically organize users into common groups for administrative purposes, and they exist only on Windows 2000 and Windows .NET Server domain controllers.
- **Built-in identities:** These are used by the operating system to automatically group users for system purposes, and they exist on all computers running Windows 2000 and Windows .NET Server.

Notes

You cannot rename or delete a built-in group, and you cannot change the membership of a built-in identity.

See Also: *built-in global group, built-in domain local group*

built-in identities

In Microsoft Windows 2000, Windows XP, and Windows .NET Server, a term used to refer to what were known in Windows NT as system groups.

Overview

Built-in identities can represent different subsets of users in different situations, and they do not have a specific membership that administrators can modify. However, you can assign built-in identities rights and permissions for accessing resources or performing system tasks. Examples of built-in identities include

- **Everyone:** Represents all users who can be, or are, on the network, whether from trusted or distrusted domains.
- **Network:** Represents all users who can access, or are accessing, network resources over the network. It does not include users logged on locally to a machine and accessing those resources locally.
- **Interactive:** Represents all users who can be, or are, currently logged on locally to a computer to access local resources on it. It does not include users who can access, or are accessing, network resources over the network.

See Also: *built-in group*

burst

A condition in which network activity rises suddenly for a short period of time.

Overview

A burst is a transient elevation in network activity, and a network on which a lot of bursts occur is said to be bursty. Bursty networks have different bandwidth requirements than networks on which the traffic is steady, and they need to be designed accordingly. For example, a network on which large video files are frequently transmitted tends to be bursty in its traffic flow.

Bursts can be indicative of a sudden increase in demand for network resources, or they can indicate hardware or software problems. Some networking components are capable of briefly sending data at speeds greater than normal transmission speeds; this is referred to as "operating in burst mode."

A good first step in accommodating bursty conditions is to use Ethernet switches instead of hubs for concentrating your network connections.

bus

A linear circuit path that can be used to connect multiple devices for exchange of data.

Overview

The idea of a bus in computer networking technology is analogous to that of a bus as a means of transportation: a bus travels over a fixed route across a city, carrying people and stopping at various points for people to get on or off. In the same way, computers and networks use buses to transport data from one device to another. The point on a bus where a device can be connected is generally called a slot.

Buses generally fall in three categories: system buses, peripheral buses, and network buses (or bus topology networks).

System buses are internal to computer systems and are used to carry data between the processor, chipset, memory, disk subsystem, video subsystem, and peripheral cards such as network adapters and sound cards. Examples of different types of system buses include

- **Processor bus:** This transports data between the CPU (central processing unit) and the chipset.
- **Memory bus:** This transport data between the memory subsystem, CPU, and chipset.
- **I/O bus:** This transports data between the CPU, chipset, memory subsystem, and internally attached peripherals such as network adapters, video adapters, and disk controllers.
- **Cache bus:** This transports data between the CPU and the L2 cache (present only in sixth-generation processors such as the Pentium III).

When the term *bus* is used in conjunction with computer systems, it is commonly interpreted as meaning input/output (I/O) bus. The I/O bus has gone through many changes over the years, including the following:

- **Industry Standard Architecture (ISA) bus:** The 8-bit ISA bus was developed by IBM in 1981 for the original IBM PC. A 16-bit version was then developed in 1984 for the newer IBMAT. Some desktop systems still include an ISA bus and slots for backward compatibility of legacy peripheral devices, but the presence of an ISA bus is problematic because it does not support plug and play (PnP).
- **VESA Local Bus (VLB):** This was used by some 486 systems but had the disadvantage that the bus was essentially an extension of the CPU's leads, which resulted in poor performance.
- **Peripheral Component Interconnect (PCI) bus:** This is the most common form of I/O bus in use today, and it comes in both 32-bit (PCI 2.0) and 64-bit (PCI 2.1) versions.

Peripheral buses are buses whose primary use is for connecting peripherals to computer systems or network switches. Examples of this type include Small Computer System Interface (SCSI) and Fibre Channel.

Network buses (or bus topology networks) represent any form of network in which devices are connected together in linear fashion. Examples include 10Base2 and 10Base5 Ethernet and Token Bus networks, all three of which are obsolete. Most networks today are based on a star topology, which is easier to manage than bus topology because of its centralized nature.

Prospects

The state of system bus technology is currently in flux. Whereas previously networks could not keep up with their servers, now the server has become the bottleneck: a Peripheral Component Interface (PCI) local bus has a difficult time performing I/O fast enough to fully utilize a Gigabit Ethernet (GbE) network connection. The result has been various industry initiatives to speed up the I/O bus to match rapidly growing network capacity (10 GbE is now on the horizon). Another source of pressure has been the increasing need for modern servers to be able to rapidly access large amounts of database storage, sometimes in the terabyte range.

Some of the newer industry initiatives for evolving system buses include

- **PCI-X (or PCIx) bus:** This proposed next-generation PCI bus will have a theoretical data transfer rate of 1 gigabit per second (Gbps), based on a clock speed of 133 megahertz (MHz), and is backward-compatible with existing PCI peripherals. A draft standard for PCIx was produced in 1999.
- **Infiniband:** Unlike legacy bus systems (including PCI), which are shared-bus systems in which connected devices must contend with each other for the right to transmit data, Infiniband is a switched-bus fabric that is capable of data transfer rates of 6 Gbps or higher and is supported by industry heavyweights such as IBM and Intel Corporation.
- **Ethernet:** Since high-speed switched Ethernet performs so well in the network, why not use it for I/O within computer systems? This is the thinking of Performance Technologies, which has joined with other manufacturers in proposing a new form of PCI bus called cPCI based on switched Ethernet technologies that provides 2 Gbps of dedicated bandwidth per slot.

Other proposals include using high-speed SCSI technologies (such as Ultra160 SCSI) and FiberChannel for internal system buses, but these initiatives have not gained much momentum.

Notes

A bus and a port are both similar in that they transport data between devices, but although a port can be used only to connect two devices, a bus can connect three or more devices.

See Also: 10Base2, 10Base5, Fibre Channel, Infiniband (IB), Small Computer System Interface (SCSI)

business logic

That portion of an application that reflects the actual way the enterprise does business.

Overview

Business logic is a term used in writing applications for Microsoft Transaction Server (MTS) using reusable COM+ components. These components represent a combination of logon verifications, policies, database lookups, validation edits, and other processes that constitute how business is done in the enterprise. An application's business logic specifies how the component's programming logic reflects the actual way the enterprise does business. Business logic enables consistent and logical processing of business data.

A representation of a real-world component of the enterprise's business is called a "business object." Examples of business objects include customers, orders, products, invoices, and anything else that can be encapsulated in an application's business logic and manipulated by its users.

business-to-business

Also known as B2B, e-commerce between different companies that have a partnering arrangement.

See: B2B

business-to-consumer

Also known as B2C, a relationship in which individuals or companies purchase the services of another company.

See: B2B

bus topology

A networking topology that connects networking components along a single cable or that uses a series of cable segments that are connected linearly.

Overview

A network that uses a bus topology is referred to as a "bus network." Bus networks were the original form of Ethernet networks, using the 10Base5 cabling standard. Bus topology is used for

- Small workgroup local area networks (LANs) whose computers are connected using a thinnet cable
- Trunk cables connecting hubs or switches of departmental LANs to form a larger LAN
- Backboning, by joining switches and routers to form campus-wide networks

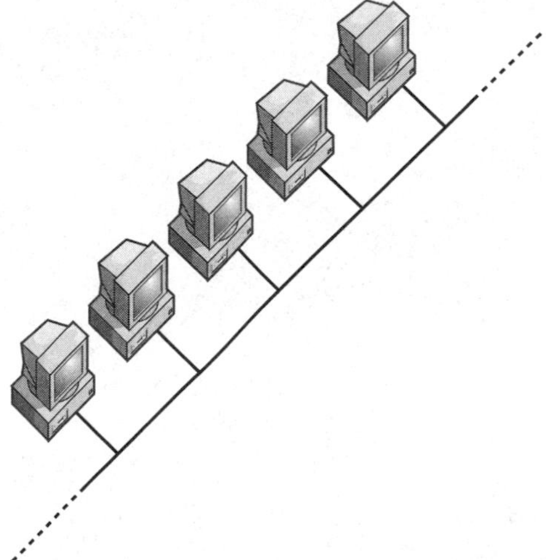

Bus topology. *A simple example of a bus topology network.*

Bus topology is the cheapest way of connecting computers to form a workgroup or departmental LAN, but it has the disadvantage that a single loose connection or cable break can bring down the entire LAN.

Notes

A hub or concentrator on an Ethernet network is really a collapsed bus topology. Physically, the network appears to be wired in a star topology, but internally the hub contains a collapsed bus, creating a configuration called a star-wired bus. However, in this case, a failure in one of the cables does not affect the remaining network.

Communication problems on bus networks might indicate that the bus ends are improperly terminated. A break in the cable will produce a similar result, since the ends of the break are not terminated. Use a cable tester to determine the problem's nature and location.

See Also: *mesh topology, ring topology, star topology*

C++

The most widely used object-oriented programming language.

Overview

C++ is the standard programming language used for developing tools and applications for high-speed networking. This is because it is a compiled language whose object code is essentially native assembly language and hence runs extremely fast. For example, a form handler written for a Hypertext Markup Language (HTML) form that runs on a UNIX Apache Web server will run much faster if it is written in a compiled language such as C or C++ than if it is written in an interpretive language such as Perl or Microsoft Visual Basic, Scripting Edition (VBScript).

High-performance Internet Server API (ISAPI) applications and dynamic-link libraries (DLLs) written for Microsoft Internet Information Services (IIS) generally perform best when written in C++. Powerful distributed Web-based applications for the Internet can be developed using a combination of Active Server Pages (ASP) scripts in VBScript or JScript, with Microsoft ActiveX components and ISAPI dynamic-link libraries (DLLs) written in C++ using Microsoft Visual C++.

C++ programs for Windows network operating system platforms can be developed using a variety of tools:

- Traditional C++ development tools using editors, compilers, and debuggers support low-level application programming interface (API) access, Microsoft Foundation Classes (MFC), software development kits (SDKs), and other supporting elements.
- Rapid application development (RAD) tools provide integrated development environments (IDEs) that focus on providing developers with ease-of-use features.
- Component deployment tools take a component-based approach to generating and reusing C++ code for building distributed and multitier applications.

C++ is based on the earlier C language that is used for developing applications, including Win32 applications for Microsoft Windows platforms. The standard form of C++ is called ANSI C++ and is defined by the American National Standards Institute (ANSI).

Notes

Microsoft Visual C++ combines the best features of these various classes of tools. It is an excellent choice for developing large-scale distributed networking applications based on the C++ language and Microsoft Corporation's own specific extensions to ANSI C++ that are designed for the Win32 platform.

See Also: *C#*

C#

Pronounced "C sharp," a programming language developed by Microsoft Corporation for its new .NET platform.

Overview

C# is an offshoot of C and C++ that is designed for rapid development of Web services for Microsoft's new .NET platform. C# is derived from C++ and has much of the power of C++ while improving on it in many respects from the point of view of the developer who needs to rapidly create and deploy applications in the e-economy.

The main weaknesses of C++ as a development environment are its complicated code-compile-debug development cycle, its potential of creating memory leaks that are difficult to troubleshoot, and the requirement of having applications explicitly manage memory resources. C# is similar to the Java platform developed by Sun Microsystems in that memory resources and garbage collection (object lifetime management) are automatically handled by the language itself, freeing developers to work on creating applications instead of being bothered by handling these intricate details. C# also simplifies access to external objects and simplifies the object creation process compared with C++. And although C++ applications require frequent use of include files to allow access to system services, in C# these services are transparently wrapped in objects. Like Java, C# thus relieves programmers of much of the chore of object and memory management, speeding up the development cycle in the process.

On the other hand, C# is unlike Java in that it maintains powerful features such as pointers, passing arguments through reference, overloading operators, and manually allocating memory. These features, basic to C++, are included in C# to provide programmers with the functionality should they need it, but they are deemphasized in C# compared to their common use in C++. For example, when pointers are used in C#, they need to be tagged in a section of code marked as "unsafe," making it easier to troubleshoot difficulties that may arise from their misapplication. Furthermore, C# has the advantage over Java of providing direct access to native Microsoft Windows services, and C# is easier to learn than Java for C++ programmers because its syntax is derived from and is similar to C++, whereas the syntax for Java has many differences from C++ that make it difficult for C++ programmers to use easily.

It is relatively simple to port existing C++ programs to C# (by contrast, it is much more difficult to port such applications to Java). The main disadvantage of C# as a development environment is a weakness shared with Java: unlike C++, which compiles programs into native machine code, C# compiles programs into an intermediate bytecode called intermediate language (IL) that is then interpreted by the .NET runtime. This means C# shares a performance hit similar to Java, which is also an interpreted platform. C++ will still be used for writing code modules where the best performance possible is required (such as device drivers), but C# performs sufficiently well on today's hardware platforms to be used as a primarily development platform. And because C# executes on the .NET runtime, it shares the interoperability features of this runtime, which allows modules written in C# to communicate with code written using other programming languages.

Microsoft plans to submit the C# language to the standards board of the European Computer Manufacturers Association (ECMA). The ECMA will then manage the language as a standard, which means that third parties wanting to use C# to develop applications will not be required to pay licensing fees to Microsoft. This will keep the cost of development tools and applications development low.

Notes

The Object Management Group (OMG), the creators of Common Object Request Broker Architecture (CORBA), is developing a language mapping for C# to enable it to communicate through CORBA with applications written in other languages such as C, C++, Cobol, Java, Python, and Ada.

See Also: *C++, .NET platform*

C2

A security standard for computer systems established by the National Computer Security Center (NCSC).

Overview

The NCSC is a U.S. government agency responsible for evaluating the security of software products. The C2 security standard is defined in the Trusted Computer Systems Evaluation Criteria (TCSEC) manual (or Orange Book) published by the NCSC.

The NCSC rated Microsoft's Windows NT 3.5 (with Service Pack 3) C2-compliant. The C2 designation assures that the base operating system satisfies a number of important security criteria. This designation also represents an independent, unbiased evaluation of the system architecture's security with regard to the government's operating and implementation standards. Windows 2000 also supports C2, but is still undergoing the NCSC evaluation process.

A C2 rating does not indicate that a system is free of security bugs; instead, this rating certifies that the computer system's underlying architecture is suitable for high-security environments in specific networking configurations. It is incorrect to say that Windows NT is C2-certified or runs in C2 mode. Only a complete computer system (including hardware) can be rated C2. A rating of C2 means that in a particular implementation, in a particular networking environment and configuration, using specific hardware and software, a computer network using a Windows NT operating system can apply for, and might receive, C2 certification.

According to the Orange Book, in a C-level system, the security policy must be based on what is known as Discretionary Access Control (DAC), which essentially means that users of the system can own objects (such as files and directories) and can control access to these objects by other users. A user who establishes control over an object is responsible for granting or denying all access rights to that object. In other words, the owner of an object grants or denies users access to the object at his or her discretion. This is in contrast to a B-level system, in which Mandatory Access Control (MAC) specifies that all objects have security levels that are defined independent of the object's owner.

For More Information

Visit the NCSC at *www.radium.ncsc.mil.*

See Also: security

CA

Stands for certificate authority, any entity (individual, department, company, or organization) that issues digital certificates to verify the identity of users, applications, or organizations.

See: certificate authority (CA)

cabinet

An enclosure with a built-in rack for holding and organizing patch panels, switches, hubs, routers, servers, and any other networking equipment within a wiring closet.

Overview

Cabinets can be wall-mounted or freestanding, come in various heights, and are usually standardized for 19-inch-wide shelving and paneling. They generally come in 83-inch and 48-inch heights, although many vendors offer custom-designed cabinets. The reason for standardizing the width to 19 inches (18.31 inches to be precise) is that hubs, switches, routers, and other networking devices are produced in this width so that they can be organized in racks and cabinets designed for this purpose. Cabinets come with a variety of accessories for organizing cables, power strips, and other equipment. Because heat can accumulate in cabinets, they usually include vented walls and have an exhaust fan on top. A cabinet will often have a locking front panel made of clear plastic so that status lights on equipment are easily visible. Shelves can be fixed, mounted, or sliding to enable easy access to the sides and backs of equipment.

Cabinet. *A typical cabinet for mounting networking and telecommunications equipment.*

Notes

When should you choose a cabinet instead of a rack? Choose a cabinet for equipment that is exposed to user traffic, and then you can lock equipment away when the room itself is not locked. Cabinets are also best for expensive networking equipment that you do not want anyone but authorized administrators to touch. Cabinets with filter fans installed can protect equipment in environments where dust is a problem. Use filler panels to enclose areas of the cabinet that are not occupied by equipment.

See Also: *premise cabling, rack*

cabinet file

A file with the extension .cab that stores compressed files, usually for distributing software on Microsoft platforms.

Overview

Cabinet files can contain multiple files in a compressed state, or a single compressed file can be spread over several cabinet files. During installation of software, the setup program decompresses the cabinet files and copies the resulting files to the user's system.

Cabinet files can be digitally signed using a Microsoft technology called Authenticode. This allows setup files to be downloaded safely over distrusted networks such as the Internet. Cabinet files are compressed using a compression algorithm called MSZIP, which is based on the Lempel-Ziv algorithm.

Notes

Cabinet files in Microsoft Windows 95 were located in the Win95 directory on the source CD, and most were represented as a series of large files with names such as Win95_1.cab and Win95_2.cab. Windows 98 uses a different naming convention and names many of its smaller cabinet files by function rather than by the order in which they are used during setup. Naming by function makes the extraction of files easier, which in turn makes the setup process smoother.

In Windows 95, if you want to extract specific operating system files from a cabinet file (for example, to replace a missing or corrupt file), you have to use the command-line utility called extract. Using Windows 98 and later versions, you can simply double-click on a cabinet file using Windows Explorer to view its contents in a new window, double-click on the specific file you want to extract, and specify the destination folder to send it to. You can also use the System File Checker tool to extract files without knowing which specific cabinet file they are located in.

See Also: *Authenticode*

cable modem

A device that allows your computer to access the Internet through dedicated broadband transmission networking services by means of your home cable TV (CATV) connection.

Overview

Cable modems modulate and demodulate analog signals like regular modems, but for transmission over broadband video services instead of telephone voice services. A cable modem can be internal or external and can interface with the coaxial cable connection at the user's end and the Cable Modem Termination System (CMTS) at the cable provider's head office.

Cable modem and Asymmetric Digital Subscriber Line (ADSL) are competing technologies for bringing high-speed broadband Internet services to homes and businesses. Cable modems offer downstream speeds of 10 megabits per second (Mbps) and higher, but competing technologies, lack of standards, and implementation costs have slowed widespread deployment and use of this technology.

There are two basic types of cable modem services:

- **One-way cable modems:** These are used by unidirectional cable service providers. Most cable TV services are designed to carry information in one direction only—from the broadcaster to the customer premises. With one-way cable modems, the customer uses a regular telephone modem to send information to the cable company but uses the cable TV system with cable mode to receive signals from the company. The telephone modem handles all upstream communication, and the cable modem handles all downstream communication. One-way cable modems are typically cards installed inside a subscriber's computer.

- **Two-way cable modems:** These require that the broadcasting cable company has converted its cabling and repeater infrastructure for bidirectional communication. Two-way cable modems are typically external devices connected to a network interface card (NIC) that is installed in the subscriber's computer. The cable modem is used for both upstream and downstream communication in this configuration. Most cable companies currently have initiatives under way to make such a conversion, but it requires a large capital investment. Therefore, it will be several years before these systems become widely available.

Implementation

In a typical one-way cable modem implementation, the CMTS uses separate subsystems for upstream and downstream connections that terminate at a router. The downstream subsystem is designed for converting incoming Internet Protocol (IP) traffic into radio frequency broadband signals that are broadcast using a broadband network hub (BNH) over cable TV wiring to local groups of connected subscribers. The upstream subsystem usually consists of banks of ordinary telephone modems to allow for easy expansion of services to additional subscribers. The router is used to route network traffic between clients and local content servers hosted by the cable provider, and to the Internet.

Downstream traffic is typically modulated using 64 or 256 Quadrature Amplitude Modulation (QAM) and can achieve speeds of 27 Mbps or higher. Upstream traffic is encoded using 16 QAM or Quadrature Phase Shift Keying (QPSK) and typically ranges from 320 kilobits per second (Kbps) to several Mbps.

Marketplace

Excite@Home was an early player in the cable modem marketplace, and many local cable companies followed offering high-speed Internet access to their cable TV subscribers. Consolidation in the industry has led to the emergence of several major players, including AT&T Broadband and AOL/Time Warner.

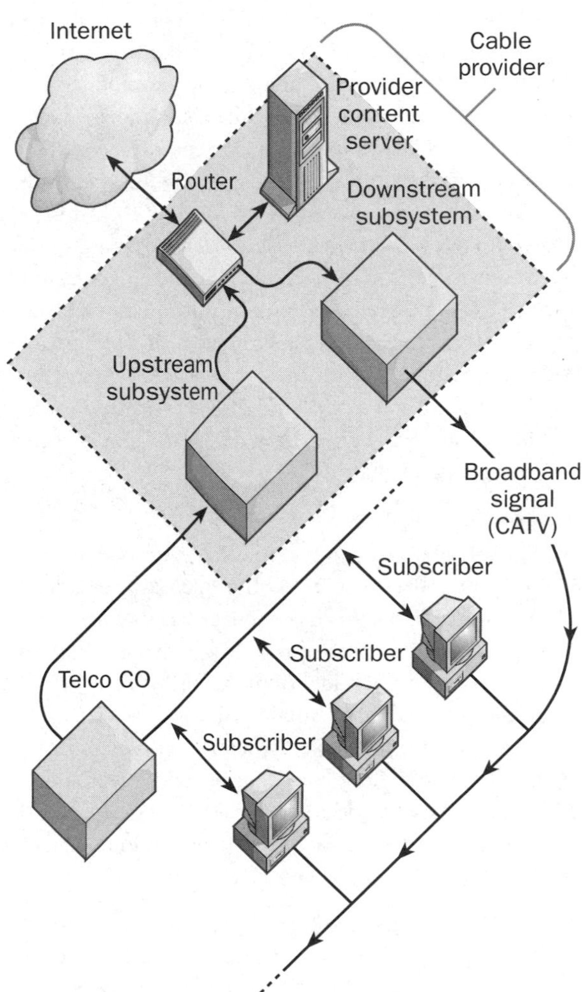

Cable modem. *A one-way cable modem service.*

Cable modem Internet access costs around $40 a month in most locations but, because their operation depends on the wiring infrastructure of cable TV systems, cable modems are almost exclusively offered for residential customers and home-based businesses. Some cable modem providers such as Cox Communications also compete with telcos by offering voice as well as data services.

The cable modem market is growing more rapidly than the Digital Subscriber Line (DSL) market, its main competitor. This is happening despite the security and bandwidth issues associated with cable modems (see below), and is driven largely by the complexity of DSL compared to the simplicity of cable modems and by the fact that cable modems are not limited by the 3-mile (4.8-kilometer) distance restriction that governs how far a DSL customer can be from the DSL provider's central office (CO). A Federal Communications Commission (FCC) survey found that cable modem subscribers in the United States grew from just over 100,000 in 1998 to almost 1 million in 1999. In 2000 worldwide cable modem usage was estimated at over 6 million subscribers, almost twice that of DSL.

Issues

Most cable television companies have jumped on the cable modem bandwagon to offer Internet access for their customers, but this has not been without problems. Existing tree-and-branch coaxial systems were built for one-way transmission and often require expensive upgrades to make them suitable for two-way data transmission. Some of the steps typically involved in the upgrade are upgrading core distribution networks to fiber (creating a hybrid fiber-coax network) and troubleshooting ingress noise due to poor shielding and loose connectors.

Many cable operators, although they support multi-megabit upstream data speeds, have instead restricted upstream speeds to 128 Kbps or lower to help prevent customers from running rogue Web servers on their network in violation of their customer agreements. Also, all subscribers in a one-way cable modem local service area are essentially on a local area network (LAN) and, if they have a packet sniffer, they can see one another. If you are using a one-way cable modem with Microsoft Windows on your computer, you should disable file and print sharing so that other users in your local service area cannot see your system or access resources on it. The cable modem industry itself has proposed a solution to the security issue through an initiative called Data Over Cable Service Interface Specification (DOCSIS) that specifies encryption of all cable modem traffic using 56-bit Data Encryption Standard (DES), although DES is no longer secure.

Furthermore, although in theory a cable modem might support downstream transmission speeds of 10 Mbps or higher, in practice downstreams may be significantly less than 1 Mbps. This is because all cable modems serviced by a given neighborhood Cable Modem Termination System (CMTS) are essentially on a LAN and share the available bandwidth. Thus, the more modems deployed in a given neighborhood, the slower the system performs for Internet access, especially when some users are downloading large files or streaming media (a common occurrence among cable modem users). In this respect DSL has an advantage because it is a secure, private connection directly to the Internet.

Notes

If you have a one-way cable modem installed on a computer running Microsoft Windows 2000, Windows XP, or Windows .NET Server and it is not working properly, you might have IP Auto-Configuration Addressing enabled, causing an addressing problem that prevents packets from being routed successfully to your machine. Also, try checking with your cable service provider to determine whether you have correctly configured the line-in frequency, line-out phone number, and proxy server address.

For More Information

Visit Cablemodems.com at *www.cablemodems.com.*

See Also: *Asymmetric Digital Subscriber Line (ADSL), broadband Internet access, Data Over Cable Interface Specification (DOCSIS), modem*

cable run

A length of installed cable connecting two network components that are not in immediate proximity to one another.

Overview

Laying cable runs is the main work of installing premise cabling in a customer premises. Types of cable runs include

- **Horizontal cable:** Runs through building plenums (the space between the floor and the ceiling) and false ceilings, connecting wiring closets together and connecting patch panels to wall plates

- **Vertical cable:** Runs through vertical building rises, connecting wiring closets on each floor with the building's main equipment room

Different grades of cabling must be used for different runs to ensure compliance with building codes and safety standards. Examples include polyvinyl chloride (PVC) cabling and plenum cabling. The Electronic Industries Association/Telecommunications Industry Association (EIA/TIA) wiring standards specify guidelines for using cable types and grades.

Notes

Cables connecting computers to patch panels (drop cables) and connecting patch panels with hubs and switches (patch cables) are not generally referred to as cable runs because they are not permanently installed and are usually quite short. The term *cable run* generally applies to cables that run from the patch panels in a wiring closet to other parts of the building.

When installing horizontal or vertical cable runs, use the highest grade that your budget will allow in order to accommodate future upgrades of your network's speed and bandwidth. Use the enhanced Category 5 (Cat5e) cabling—which is a variety of unshielded twisted-pair (UTP) cabling—for all copper cabling installations. If you can, install parallel vertical runs of fiber-optic cabling with copper cabling in vertical rises to allow for future expansion of your network backbone. Installing two cables at once saves costs later, even if you need only the copper cabling now.

See Also: cabling, premise cabling

cable tester

Any device for measuring the integrity and transmission characteristics of cabling.

Overview

Cable testers perform various functions to test network cabling for compliance with cabling standards developed by bodies such as the Telecommunications Industry Association (TIA), the International Organization for Standardization (ISO), and the International Electrotechnical Commission (IEC). Cable testers are useful to local area network (LAN) administrators, cable installers, and field service providers for testing and certifying cabling installations as compliant with these standards.

Cable tester. *A handheld cable tester.*

Cable testers come in a variety of forms, ranging from handheld to briefcase size. They are generally divided between those used for testing fiber-optic cabling and those used for testing copper cabling. Different testers have different capabilities, but their general function is to measure various electrical characteristics across different ranges of frequencies. Testers will typically measure some or all of the following parameters at various frequencies from 100 megahertz (MHz) to 350 MHz and beyond:

- Attenuation, which is the decibel decrease in signal strength as a signal propagates through a physical medium
- Impedance, which is the resistance to the flow of alternating current
- Noise, indicated by the floor values for randomly generated electrical signals

C

- Near-end crosstalk (NEXT), which is a decibel measurement of crosstalk taken at the end where a signal is injected
- Attenuation to crosstalk ratio (ACR), which is the decibel difference between NEXT and attenuation values
- PowerSum NEXT, which measures the crosstalk between a single pair of wires and all other pairs in the cable
- The distance to a short or unterminated cable end, used for link-testing the continuity of circuits

Uses

Cable testers are particularly important for testing Category 5 (Cat5) and enhanced Category 5 (Cat5e) structured wiring deployments to see if they will properly support Gigabit Ethernet (GbE) networking. GbE pushes unshielded twisted-pair (UTP) cabling to its limits and requires top-quality properly installed cabling to operate as expected. Particularly in older buildings with existing Cat5 wiring, use a cable tester to measure such parameters as cross-talk and NEXT to determine if packet loss will occur over portions of the network. Particularly vulnerable portions include cable termination at RJ-45 wall jacks and at patch panels inside wiring closets. Poor quality patch cables between workstations and wall jacks are a common problem, as are patch panel connections that have been untwisted beyond the specified limits.

Marketplace

A number of vendors produce different kinds of test equipment for cable testing. Two of the top vendors of such equipment include Fluke Corporation, which offers a wide range of cable testers, and Hewlett-Packard.

Today's cable testers can perform comprehensive and programmable sets of autotests for a variety of cable types. A good cable tester can tell you at the push of a button whether installed wiring can support different kinds of networking architectures—such as coax, 10BaseT, 100BaseT, 100BaseVG, and Token Ring. Cable testers can also store measurements taken so that they can be analyzed separately afterward.

The most accurate types of cable testers for UTP cabling are those that can test and certify Category 5 (Cat5) cabling to Level II TSB-67 compliance and support the Institute of Electrical and Electronics Engineers (IEEE) TSB95 field testing specifications. An all-in-one cable tester is an invaluable tool and a good investment for the network administrator. It can make up for its cost in higher network availability.

Notes

Use a fiber-optic tester and an optoelectronic light source to test both ends of a new spool of fiber-optic cabling before beginning an installation with this cable. A good fiber-optic cable test should give you not only a pass/fail analysis of an installed cabling setup, but also quantitative values of the optical link capabilities of your wiring configuration.

See Also: *cabling, network troubleshooting, test equipment*

cabling

Any wires used for connecting computers and networking devices together to enable them to communicate.

Overview

Cabling constitutes the passive portion of any computer network—the active portion consists of the servers, workstations, switches, routers, and other components. Good cabling provides the foundation for creating reliable local area networks (LANs). Cabling is also used for connecting LANs into wide area networks (WANs). Network administrators are usually involved in the deployment of LAN cabling, but WAN cabling is usually the responsibility of the telecommunications carriers whose services are being leased.

Two basic types of cabling are used in LAN networking environments:

- **Copper cabling:** This type consists of insulated copper conductors that transmit signals using electrical voltages and currents. Copper cabling can be

either coaxial cabling (such as thinnet or thicknet) that is used mainly in industrial environments, or the more commonly employed twisted-pair cabling. Twisted-pair cabling comes as either unshielded twisted-pair (UTP) cabling (commonly used in Ethernet or Fast Ethernet environments) or the less common shielded twisted-pair (STP) cabling (employed for token ring networks and sometimes for Gigabit Ethernet [GbE] installations). Copper cabling is mainly used for shorter cable runs such as horizontal cable runs between wiring closets and wall plates in work areas, for patch cables, and for equipment interconnects.

- **Fiber-optic cabling:** This type is made of glass strands that transmit signals as light waves or pulses. Fiber-optic cabling can be either single-mode, which is used for the longest cable runs, or multimode, which has a much higher carrying capacity. Fiber-optic cabling is generally used for backbone cable runs such as vertical rises in buildings and building-to-building interconnects on a campus, for high-speed interconnects between networking devices in a wiring closet, and for connections to high-speed servers and workstations.

Implementation

The process of installing cabling in a building for purposes of computer networking is called establishing premise wiring. Unfortunately, cabling is only as good as the way it is deployed and only as good as the connectors and other elements that help make a computer network. Poor quality cabling, improperly installed cabling, or cheap wall plates and patch panels can make a cabling system perform more poorly than expected, particularly at GbE speeds.

The Telecommunications Industry Association (TIA) and the Electronic Industries Alliance (EIA) have defined a series of standards on the required electrical characteristics of commercial cabling for computer networking and also standards for the proper layout and organization of premise cabling. These standards are called the EIA/TIA wiring standards. The EIA/TIA-568A Commercial Building Telecommunication Cabling Standard specifies standards for each of the following:

- Establishing wiring closets on each floor of the building to contain rack-mounted equipment such as hubs, switches, and patch panels
- Running vertical backbone plenum cabling through building risers and building plenums, for connecting wiring closets to the main equipment room
- Running horizontal polyvinyl chloride (PVC) cabling for each floor through false ceilings
- Connecting the patch panels in the wiring closet to wall plates in computer work areas

Cabling installed in a building must also meet all legal requirements, including federal and local building regulations for fire safety. Do not attempt to wire a building unless you are fully familiar with the regulations.

Choosing the right kind of cabling at the beginning of an installation can save considerable expense when you later upgrade networking equipment for higher transmission speeds. Some tips for successfully outsourcing cabling installations for computer networks in buildings include

- Hiring a qualified cabling consultant to review the scope and details of your plans and procedures. Hire cabling consultants who either have vendor certification (if you are using "channel cabling," that is, all the cabling components are being purchased from a single vendor) or an independent consultant affiliated with BICSI.
- Ensure that if you outsource your cabling installation that the company you hire is properly licensed and insured for such work.

If you plan to lay cable yourself for your building, here are a few more guidelines:

- Use no more than 30 to 40 pounds of pull when pulling cabling through a conduit or a plenum.
- Do not excessively bend wiring (especially fiber-optic cabling), and be sure not to untwist UTP wires more than specifications allow.

C

- Make sure data wiring and power cables are at least 6 inches (15 centimeters) apart, and, if they need to cross each other, they do this at a 90 degree angle.

Notes

Specialized cables—such as serial, parallel, or Small Computer System Interface (SCSI) cables—are used to connect peripherals and therefore do not serve the same purpose as the cables just discussed. Serial cables and other special purpose cables are generally very short and are not permanently installed.

Note that not all networks use physical cabling. Wireless networks can use infrared, microwave, radio, or some other form of electromagnetic radiation to allow networking components to communicate with each other. A cabled network is sometimes referred to as a wireline network, as opposed to a wireless network.

For More Information

Look at *www.cablingstandards.com*. You can also visit the BICSI Web site at *www.bicsi.org*.

See Also: *copper cabling, fiber-optic cabling, premise cabling*

CA certificate

Also called a root certification, a digital certificate that can be used to verify the identity of the certificate authority (CA) itself.

Overview

The CA certificate contains the identification information and public key for the certificate authority it identifies. A certificate authority that is part of a hierarchical public key infrastructure (PKI) receives its CA certificate from the CA directly above it in the hierarchy. A root CA at the top of a PKI hierarchy must self-sign its own certificate, in effect certifying itself.

The CA certificate plays an important part in the workings of the Secure Sockets Layer (SSL) protocol. The CA's public key, contained in the CA certificate, is used to validate all other digital certificates that have been issued by that CA for entities (individuals, systems, companies, and organizations). When an entity such as a Web browser (perhaps Microsoft Internet Explorer) or a Web server (perhaps Microsoft Internet Information Services) requests a digital certificate from a CA, the CA certificate identifies the CA that issues the certificate.

This CA certificate is downloaded from a shared storage location at the certificate authority and installed onto the Web server or browser. Later, when the Web browser tries to access the Web server using the SSL protocol, the Web browser uses the CA certificate to validate the Web server's certificate. Similarly, the server can use the CA certificate to validate the browser client's certificate, if it has one.

Notes

The digital CA certificate for a CA must be kept in a location that is readily available for all servers and clients that will access it and install it on their Web browser or Web server. From this location, Web servers and Web clients that need to use the SSL protocol must obtain and install the CA certificate in their certificate stores. On Microsoft Certificate Server, this location is the default Web location http://Server_Name/certsrv, where Server Name is the name of the Microsoft Windows NT server on which Microsoft Certificate Server is installed.

Internet Explorer comes with the CA certificates of a number of certificate authorities preinstalled. These root certificates enable Internet Explorer to be used for functions such as SSL authentication and sending secure e-mail. If you want to use the services of a CA that does not have its CA root certificate installed in Internet Explorer, you can visit that CA's Web site to find instructions on how to obtain its root certificate. Administrators can also use the Internet Explorer Administration Kit (IEAK) for importing and installing root certificates on Web browsers prior to installation on client machines.

See Also: *certificate authority (CA), client certificate, digital certificate*

caching

Generally, any mechanism for storing frequently needed information in accessible memory so that it can be quickly retrieved. This article focuses on caching as the temporary storage of Web content to enable faster access by users.

Overview

While caching in general has been around a long time and has been implemented in various ways in computer systems and networks (see Notes at the end of this article), caching of Web content has exploded over the last few years into a big industry. In the context of the Internet, caching means the copying of Web content to storage locations near the client so that the client's Web browser can more quickly access the information. Caching speeds up accessing Web content and makes better use of available bandwidth (especially important when the Internet is accessed over slow and costly wide area network [WAN] connections).

While the emergence of broadband Internet access may seem to sidestep the need for caching, this is not really so. Most analysts agree that with the Internet, providing faster access simply drives up demand further and raises expectations, leading to even greater traffic congestion and frustration for users. The solution to bogged-down Internet access is caching.

Implementation

Caching can be implemented in a variety of ways using different systems. The simplest arrangement is deploying cache servers on the network. A cache server is used to speed corporate access to Web content on the Internet by caching the Web pages that users most frequently request. Cache servers reduce network traffic and speed up access to frequently requested content by caching such content. If a user requests a page that has recently been cached, the page will be retrieved from the cache server instead of from the Internet. Pages are held in the cache until they expire.

The cache server locates the content closer to the users who need it than the Web servers that contain the original version of this content. In general, the closer the cache to the user, the faster the response time the user will experience when trying to access this content in a browser. In the enterprise, cache servers are typically deployed at the edge of the corporate network, thus reducing overall WAN link traffic and congestion and saving money. Many firewalls and proxy servers include some form of content caching. Although firewalls and proxy servers are mainly concerned with securing access between a private corporate network and an distrusted public network such as the Internet, including cache server functionality in these products enhances their overall performance.

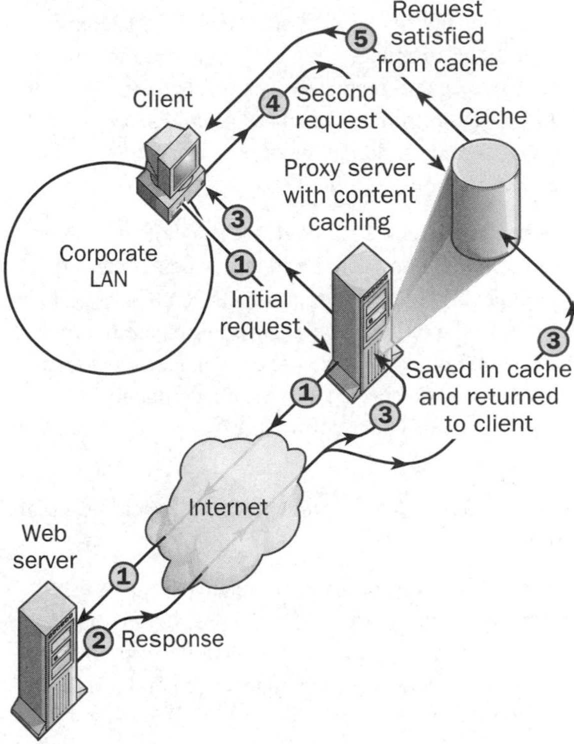

Caching. *How a simple cache server can improve access time for clients.*

Caching servers are also useful in situations where a sudden increase in Web traffic is anticipated, as when a major sports or fashion event will be covered on the Web. In this case, simply throwing bandwidth at the problem of Internet traffic congestions is not a viable solution because increased bandwidth simply leads to increased demand from users. Instead, by preloading content from Web servers to caching servers, users will not overwhelm the Web servers on the day of the event and be disappointed. This use for caching servers is sometimes called "dealing with flash crowd control" or the "instant popularity problem." By using a network of cache servers in such situations and configuring replication appropriately between them, supply can be scaled for demand at virtually any level.

Dedicated cache servers are also used in high-traffic situations within the Internet backbone itself to reduce congestion on the backbone. Caching servers are often located at Internet service providers (ISPs) and Network Access Points (NAPs) for improving the overall performance and responsiveness of the Internet. This can be used to reduce the effect of bottlenecks on ISP networks and to reduce the cost of local ISPs buying bandwidth from regional ISPs.

Cache servers can even be deployed at the customer premises and configured with preloaded content to speed access to corporate intranets. Such a scenario is similar to the built-in content caching capability of Web browsers, but in this case the content is cached locally on a machine separate from the client machine to improve performance even more.

Types

As far as administrators are concerned, caching servers come in two basic types:

- **Caching appliances:** These are preconfigured servers with preloaded caching software that can easily be dropped into the network by simply connecting them to a backbone switch and turning them on.
- **Caching software:** This includes software from different vendors that can be loaded onto servers and deployed as needed within the network by the administrator. Caching software is especially targeted toward the needs of the corporate enterprise for improving remote access to corporate intranets.

In addition, from the user's perspective, cache servers can be implemented in different ways:

- **Transparent caching:** Here cache servers filter Internet Protocol (IP) traffic to find out which Web pages are most requested in order to determine which pages should be cached and for how long. Transparent cache servers require no special modification or configuration of the client in order to operate, but the cache server itself must be placed at the edge of the WAN, typically by connecting it to a Layer 4 switch orWAN access router so that every request sent by a client is examined by the cache server first before routing it over the Internet to its intended destination.
- **Proxy caching:** Here the administrator configures the client browsers to send their requests forWeb content directly to the cache servers., If these cannot respond to the request (for example, if the page has not been cached or has expired from the cache), the cache server refers the client to the actual Web server hosting the content. This option requires more configuration but gives administrators greater control over what content users can access and provides an extra layer of security.
- **Reverse proxy caching:** Here a group of cache servers typically serves as a front-end to the Web server on the Internet, which hides behind them. User requests go directly to the cache servers, which appear as Web servers to the client. Reverse proxy caching is typically used to deal with flash crowd control discussed earlier.

Cache servers also determine whether to flush content from their cache in different ways:

- **Active caching:** Here the cache server uses intelligent heuristics to determine how long to keep a page in the cache before marking it expired. Many factors can be taken into account, including the requesting IP address, the hit statistics for the page, and how long the page has been cached.
- **Passive caching:** When a client requests a page from the cache, the cache server issues an HTTP GET IF MODIFIED command to the originating Web server to determine if the cache contains the latest version of the page. If not, the cache requests the current version and then forwards this to the client. If the cache does hold the current version, this is returned immediately to the client. The main disadvantage of passive caching is that it introduces the extra step of having the cache server contact the Web server each time a client requests a page, which, unless the cache server is close (in a network sense) to the Web server,

will have the opposite effect from what caching was intended to do—it will slow down the response time instead of speeding it up.

- **Forced caching:** In this case the cache server is preloaded with content that users are expected to frequently access. Forced caching is typically used for improving access to corporate intranets for remote users.

Marketplace

The caching industry has exploded over the last few years, driven by the tremendous growth of the Internet and the demand of users for fast performance in accessing Web sites. In the arena of general caching software, the top players include Microsoft Corporation's Internet Acceleration and Security Server (IAS Server), the successor to Microsoft Proxy Server; Novell's Internet Caching System; and several UNIX-based solutions.

In the arena of prepackaged caching appliances, offerings are available from Dell Computer Corporation's (PowerApp.cache), Compaq (TaskSmart), Cobalt Networks (Qube), Network Appliance (NetCache), and many others. Caching appliances range from those targeted for corporate intranets to powerful caching solutions for ISPs and telecoms.

A number of pure-play caching vendors have had a large impact on the caching market. Some of the big players here include Inktomi Corporation, CacheFlow, and Network Appliance. Inktomi offers routers and load balancers from Alteon WebSystems and Foundry Networks bundled together with Inktomi's Traffic Server caching software. Cisco Systems and Lucent Technologies also offer high-end caching appliances with proprietary operating system kernels tuned for top performance in this application.

A relatively new approach is called predictive client-side caching and involves configuring a plug-in for client browsers that determines what kinds of content the client accesses and then attempts to preload such content during idle times so that when the client requests it the content is already in the browser cache. Blueflame, a product from Fireclick, is one example of predictive client-side caching technology. Fireclick also has a hosted version of this application called Netflame. Packeteer has a product called AppCelera Internet Content Accelerator (ICX) that boosts performance by adapting requested content to the type of browser requesting it and by compressing content to make better utilization of available bandwidth.

Issues

Caching of dynamic Web content presents an ever-greater challenge as more and more Web sites move away from static informational content to deploying database-driven e-commerce Web applications. Dynamic Web pages are generated from databases in response to user queries and often include some form of personalization as well. Dynamic content cannot be cached the way static content can, but a number of vendors have come up with various methods for improving the performance of dynamic Web applications by using caching. For example, the components of a Web application can be cached for reuse across multiple user sessions. Another approach is to dynamically monitor the configuration of Web applications to better manage stale cache content. Vendors of dynamic caching systems include Xcache Technologies, Chutney Technologies, and SpiderSoftware. NetScaler offers a caching device that routes requests for static content to traditional cache servers while multiplexing requests for dynamic content over persistent connections with Web servers to improve performance.

Notes

Caching in a general sense is used in various ways by operating systems, applications, and network devices to improve performance by providing temporary storage of information that needs to be quickly accessed. Some common examples include

- The file system cache for the Microsoft Windows 2000 operating system, which speeds up file access from hard disk drives
- Offline Files in Windows 2000, which allows users to browse network file system content when disconnected from the network
- Domain Name System (DNS) cache for caching recently resolved host names on a name server, which speeds up the resolution of host names for the DNS on the Internet

- Address Resolution Protocol (ARP) cache on a host connected to an IP internetwork, which is used for caching IP addresses that have recently been resolved into MAC addresses, thus speeding up network communications between hosts
- Microsoft Internet Security and Acceleration (ISA) Server, which allows Web content obtained from the Internet to be cached locally for faster access and reduction of WAN link congestion
- Caching of open database connectivity (ODBC) connections for improved access to Microsoft SQL Server databases for Active Server Pages (ASP) applications written for Microsoft Internet Information Services (IIS)

For More Information

Find out more about caching technologies at these sites: *www.caching.com* and *www.web-caching.com.*

See Also: *Content Delivery Provider (CDP), Web server*

Caching Array Routing Protocol (CARP)

A protocol developed by Microsoft Corporation that allows multiple proxy servers to be arrayed as a single logical cache for distributed content caching.

Overview

Caching Array Routing Protocol (CARP) is implemented as a series of algorithms that are applied on top of Hypertext Transfer Protocol (HTTP). CARP allows a Web browser or downstream proxy server to determine exactly where in the proxy array the information for a requested Uniform Resource Locator (URL) is stored.

CARP enables proxy servers to be tracked through an array membership list that is automatically updated using a Time to Live (TTL) countdown function. This function regularly checks for active proxy servers in the array. CARP uses hash functions and combines the hash value of each requested URL with each proxy server. The URL/proxy server hash with the highest value becomes the owner of the information cached. This results in a deterministic location for all cached information in the array, which enables a Web browser or downstream proxy server to know exactly where a requested URL is locally stored or where it will be located after it has been cached. The hash functions result in cached information being statistically distributed (load balanced) across the array. Using hashing means that massive location tables for cached information need not be maintained—the Web browser simply runs the same hashing function on the object to locate where it is cached.

Advantages and Disadvantages

CARP provides two main benefits:

- It saves network bandwidth by avoiding the query messaging between proxy servers that occurs with conventional Internet Cache Protocol (ICP) networks.
- It eliminates the duplication of content that occurs when proxy servers are grouped in arrays, resulting in faster response times and more efficient use of server resources.

See Also: *caching, proxy server*

caching-only name server

A name server in the Domain Name System (DNS) that can resolve name lookup requests but does not maintain its own local DNS database or zone file of resource records.

Overview

Caching-only name servers do not have their own DNS databases. Instead, they resolve name lookup requests from resolvers by making iterative queries to other name servers. When the responses to these queries are received, the caching-only name server caches them, in case another resolver issues the same request within a short period of time.

A caching-only name server is not authoritative for any particular DNS domain. It can look up names that are inside or outside its own zone.

Notes

Caching-only name servers are not the only kind of name server that performs caching of resolved queries. For example, primary name servers also cache name lookups that they perform. This caching generally improves the primary name server's response to name lookup requests from resolvers. Caching-only name servers are distinguished by the fact that they perform only one function: issuing iterative queries to other name servers and then caching the results.

Caching-only name servers provide support for primary and secondary name servers in environments where name lookup traffic is heavy. Using caching-only name servers where possible also reduces the overhead of zone transfers between name servers on a network.

See Also: *Domain Name System (DNS), name server*

caching service provider (CSP)

A company that maintains caching servers that speed the transfer of information across the Internet's infrastructure and offers managed access to these servers for a fee.

Overview

Many companies think that if they host their Web site at an Internet service provider (ISP) or at a major Web hosting company, the site will always be accessible from anywhere on the Internet, but this is not necessarily true. Traffic congestion can cause access to a Web server to be slow and unreliable from various parts of the Internet at various times of the day, and equipment failures (such as routes going down at Internet peering points) can make a server completely inaccessible to certain portions of the Internet until the problem is fixed. ("Peering" means two ISPs or other providers passing traffic between each other's customers.)

One solution is to mirror (replicate) your Web server at various points around the globe so that a copy of your site is relatively close to any location on the Internet. For companies with a global presence, this is a fairly simple solution to implement, but most companies do not have the presence or the resources to implement global mirroring. A better solution might be to use the services of a caching service provider (CSP), which maintains cached copies of your Web site at various points in the Internet's infrastructure and provides tools for managing and load balancing the content to handle traffic spikes that occur at certain times of the day or year.

CSPs maintain data centers around the world with caching server farms that have high-speed connections to the Internet's backbone. These caching servers are usually designed to cache Web content and often support features such as content management and proxying. Caching servers can also be used within the corporate network to speed access to large, distributed corporate intranets.

See Also: *caching*

CAL

Stands for client access license, a license that grants a client machine access to a Microsoft BackOffice product running on a network of computers.

See: *client access license (CAL)*

callback

A security feature for remote access servers.

Overview

Callback provides an extra layer of security for users dialing in to a remote access server. When callback is configured, the client software dials in to a remote access server and has the user's credentials authenticated. The remote access server then disconnects the client and calls the client back at a previously specified phone number. Callback might be configured in the following ways:

- To ensure that the user matches his or her credentials by verifying the telephone location
- For accounting reasons—for example, to charge the phone bill to the remote access server instead of to the client

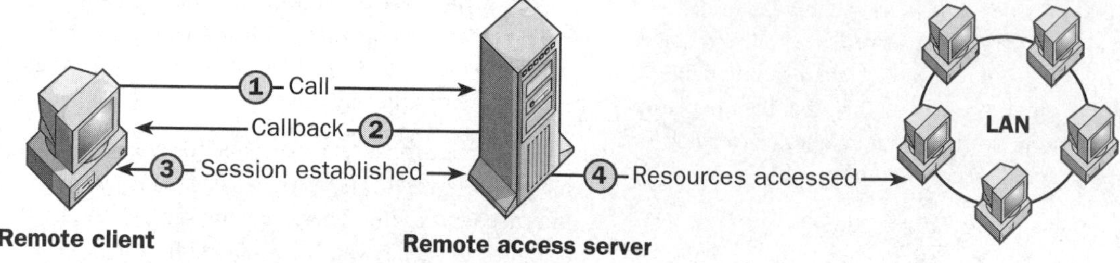

Callback. *How callback is used in remote access.*

Callback is an optional feature supported by the Routing and Remote Access service of Microsoft Windows 2000 and Windows .NET Server. Note that in Windows 2000 and Windows .NET Server, the phone number specified for callback is called the Caller ID number.

See Also: *remote access*

Callback Control Protocol (CBCP)

A protocol that enables callback for establishing Point-to-Point Protocol (PPP) connections.

Overview

The Callback Control Protocol (CBCP) is part of Microsoft Corporation's implementation of the Point-to-Point Protocol (PPP). CBCP makes it possible for a PPP server to call back the remote dial-in client to complete initiation of a PPP dial-up session. Callback is a useful security feature for ensuring that dial-in clients are authentic.

Implementation

The CBCP is used during the third phase of establishing a PPP connection. After the PPP link is established using the Link Control Protocol (LCP) and the user's credentials are authenticated using Microsoft Challenge Handshake Authentication Protocol (MS-CHAP) or some other authentication protocol supported by the client, the network access server (NAS) at the PPP service provider can optionally initiate a PPP callback control phase, provided that callback is configured on the server. The NAS and the PPP clients both disconnect from the PPP link, and the NAS calls the client back using the specified callback phone number. If the client responds, the link is reestablished; no further authentication is needed, and compatible network protocols are negotiated so that data transmission can begin.

See Also: *Point-to-Point Protocol (PPP)*

campus area network (CAN)

A group of connected local area networks (LANs) on a campus.

Overview

A campus area network (CAN) is intermediate in size between a LAN, which typically resides in a single room or building, and a metropolitan area network (MAN), which spans a city or metropolitan area. CANs exist on university campuses, in industrial parks, and in similar collections of buildings under a single administrative authority.

Implementation

CANs are typically built in hierarchical fashion starting from the top or inside with a core network (usually a collapsed backbone), a distribution network (routers or switches in different buildings), an access network (a collection of hubs and switches within wiring closets on each floor of the buildings), and finally end-user stations.

See Also: *local area network (LAN), metropolitan area network (MAN), Personal Area Network (PAN), wide area network (WAN)*

CAN

Stands for campus area network, a group of connected local area networks (LANs) on a campus.

See: *campus area network (CAN)*

CAP

Stands for carrierless amplitude and phase modulation, a line coding scheme in which data is modulated using a single carrier frequency.

See: *carrierless amplitude and phase modulation (CAP)*

capture

A collection of frames gathered from network traffic by a sniffer.

Overview

You can use packet-sniffing software such as Microsoft Network Monitor (which is included in Microsoft Systems Management Server and in a simplified form in Microsoft Windows 2000, Windows XP, and Windows .NET Server) for capturing all kinds of traffic on the network. This captured traffic is displayed in the capture window as a variety of statistics and details about the nature of the traffic. Additional windows can display details about individual packets that have been captured.

Capturing network traffic is a common troubleshooting technique on enterprise-level networks. Captures can show whether services such as Dynamic Host Configuration Protocol (DHCP), Windows Internet Name Service (WINS), Domain Name System (DNS), and other common network services are performing properly. Captures can also isolate servers that are generating excessive network traffic because of failed hardware. Captures can even be used to detect unauthorized traffic initiated by hackers and disgruntled employees and to profile network traffic for planning purposes.

See Also: *capture window, sniffing*

capture window

In Microsoft Network Monitor, the window that displays the statistics about the frames being captured on a network.

Overview

The capture window displays four kinds of real-time statistics concerning the traffic that an administrator captures using Network Monitor:

- **Graph statistics:** A graphical representation of current network activity that shows the percent of network utilization, frames captured per second, bytes captured per second, and broadcasts or multicasts captured per second
- **Session statistics:** Information about current sessions between computers on the network, showing which hosts have sent packets to each other
- **Station statistics:** Information about various stations involved in sending or receiving packets, showing how many of each type of packet they have sent or received
- **Total statistics:** Summary statistics about network activity since the capture began, including the number of frames, bytes, and frames dropped during the capture

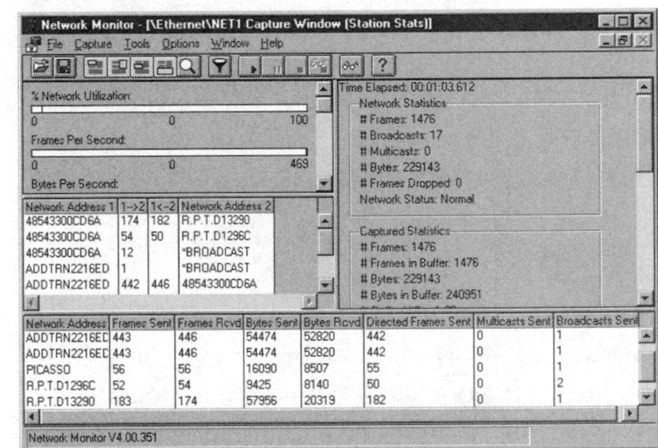

Capture window. *The capture window in Network Monitor, which is included with Microsoft Systems Management Server.*

You can toggle these various windowpanes on and off during a capture to focus on statistics of interest.

See Also: *capture, sniffing*

Carnivore

An Internet surveillance system developed by the FBI (Federal Bureau of Investigation).

C

Overview

Carnivore was designed to help the FBI collect evidence to convict terrorists, drug smugglers, and hackers. Carnivore is a self-contained "black-box" Internet Protocol (IP) traffic filtering system that sniffs network traffic to find e-mail and other traffic that contains evidence of criminal activity.

Implementation

To use Carnivore, the FBI first obtains a court order to capture specific types of Internet traffic that may contain evidence of criminal wrongdoing by parties under consideration. The FBI then brings the Carnivore system to an Internet service provider (ISP) and connects the system to the backbone switches of the ISP's network. Carnivore then monitors all traffic through the ISP, capturing only such traffic as matches the filter conditions established in the court order (this is called minimization—Carnivore does not snoop all traffic indiscriminately). For example, Carnivore might filter all messages coming from or going to a specific IP address block or having a certain keyword in the Subject line.

See Also: *sniffing, security*

CARP

Stands for Caching Array Routing Protocol, a protocol developed by Microsoft Corporation that allows multiple proxy servers to be arrayed as a single logical cache for distributed content caching.

See: *Caching Array Routing Protocol (CARP)*

carrier

A company that provides various kinds of telecommunication services to its customers.

Overview

A carrier provisions telecommunication services to the customer premises. These services include voice transmission, data transmission over analog modems, Integrated Services Digital Network (ISDN), digital subscriber line (DSL), frame relay, and anything else the carrier's equipment supports. There are two basic kinds of carriers: LECs and IXCs.

A local exchange carrier (LEC) is a company that provides access to both local and long-distance telephone services through the local loop connecting the telco's central office (CO) with the customer premises. In the United States, LECs are typically one of two kinds:

- Local phone companies, now usually called Incumbent Local Exchange Carriers (ILECs) but sometimes called Regional Bell Operating Companies (RBOCs).
- Competitive Local Exchange Carriers (CLECs), a new breed of LEC that has arisen in response to the Telecommunications Act of 1996. CLECs that offer primarily DSL voice/data services are often called DSL carriers.

An inter-exchange carrier (IXC), on the other hand, is a company that provides long-distance services only. IXCs own their own telecommunication facilities and provide long-distance services between LECs located in different toll-free areas. The big three in the IXC arena in order of size are AT&T, MCI WorldCom, and Sprint Corporation.

All long-haul carriers in the United States use Synchronous Optical Network (SONET) or ATM (Asynchronous Transfer Mode)/SONET as their backbone transport, and most local telcos use ATM in their own backbone networks also. Some LECs are also deploying Gigabit Ethernet (GbE) as an alternative to ATM for metropolitan area networks (MANs) that can bring GbE ports directly to the edge of corporate networks, providing end-to-end Ethernet connectivity for corporate wide area networks (WANs).

Outside the United States, most carriers use Synchronous Digital Hierarchy (SDH), essentially a variant of SONET.

Implementation

Almost all carriers rely on ATM as their underlying backbone transport and use this backbone to provision local and long-distance voice services, Internet access over DSL, leased-line WAN links, and other services. A large portion of the backbone of most long-haul carriers is currently at or near OC-48, providing maximum throughput of 2.488 gigabits per second (Gbps), but these backbone fiber connections are constantly being upgraded to support higher speeds such as OC-192 and OC-768.

Carriers usually house their high-speed switching equipment in large buildings called colocation centers. These centers have this name because under the Telecommunications Act of 1996, competitive local exchange carriers (CLECs) are allowed to lease space within carrier facilities for locating their own switching equipment. Another name for these centers is "data centers," and they are usually huge nondescript buildings that typically occupy hundreds of thousands of square feet. Sometimes several floors of existing buildings are used for data centers, but the trend is to build new centers to ensure that the highest standards of fire safety and security are used.

Marketplace

The global carrier market has become complex over the last decade, with traditional incumbent telcos in the United States and Post, Telegraph, and Telephone (PTT) companies in Europe being challenged on all sides by newcomers to the game. International carriers can be classified in different types, including

- **Incumbents:** These are traditional or established carriers such as public telephone companies, long distance companies, and PTTs in Europe.
- **Cross-border infrastructure owners:** These are companies that own the international lines carrying voice and data between countries, regions, and continents.
- **Resellers:** This includes companies reselling both local loop and long haul services purchased wholesale from other carriers.

To complicate things further, many large national carriers are constantly making efforts to expand into the international market by acquiring, or merging with, other carriers, upgrading their core equipment to provision new high-speed data services, while relegating some existing services to the legacy domain and trying to cope with the ever-exploding amounts of Internet bandwidth demanded by their customers. Because of the state of flux of the global telecommunications carrier market, the enterprise architect's dream of simple, seamless, global WAN connectivity remains a complicated reality of tariffs, interoperability issues, and politics.

See Also: *Competitive Local Exchange Carrier (CLEC), Incumbent Local Exchange Carrier (ILEC), inter-exchange carrier (IXC), local exchange carrier (LEC), telecommunications services*

carrierless amplitude and phase modulation (CAP)

A line coding scheme in which data is modulated using a single carrier frequency.

Overview

Carrierless amplitude and phase modulation (CAP) is used for transmission of voice information over a phone line. The transmission is considered "carrierless" because the carrier is suppressed before transmission and is reconstructed at the receiver. CAP is algorithmically similar to the quadrature amplitude modulation (QAM) line coding scheme, which encodes bits as discrete phase and amplitude changes, but it has different transmission characteristics.

Notes

Some competitive local exchange carriers (CLECs) deploy Asymmetric Digital Subscriber Line (ADSL) using CAP as the encoding method, but results of some independent tests suggest that CAP-encoded ADSL lines might cause spectral interference with proximate T1 lines and Integrated Services Digital Network (ISDN) circuits, resulting in bit errors that can reduce throughput. However, these tests might be misleading because of the limited number of ADSL circuits currently deployed by CLECs. Check with your carrier before signing up for ADSL services to get the latest information about this issue.

Such interference is not a problem with symmetric digital subscriber line (SDSL) technologies, which use the 2B1Q encoding scheme. Furthermore, ADSL deployed by incumbent local exchange carriers (ILECs) uses discrete multitone (DMT) technology, which does not produce the same degree of spectral interference as CAP.

Competitive local exchange carriers generally do not use DMT for ADSL because they must deal with the copper local loop, which effectively supports DMT only about half the time but can support CAP about 85 percent of the time. Furthermore, DMT has been adopted as the standard for ADSL by both the American National Standards Institute (ANSI) and the International Telecommunication Union (ITU).

See Also: *line coding*

Carrier Sense Multiple Access with Collision Avoidance (CSMA/CA)

The media access control method used by AppleTalk.

Overview

Carrier Sense Multiple Access with Collision Avoidance (CDMA/CA) is a type of media access control method for placing signals on baseband transmission networks. Because baseband networks can carry only one data signal at a time, there must be some way of controlling which station has access to the media at any given time. CSMA/CA is one such control method.

Uses

CSMA/CA is the standard access method for AppleTalk networks based on LocalTalk. LocalTalk is a legacy network media technology that specifies the proprietary cabling components of the original AppleTalk networking architecture. LocalTalk uses a bus topology or tree topology that supports up to 32 stations on a network.

Implementation

In networking technologies that use CSMA/CA as their access method, stations announce their intention to transmit before they actually transmit their data onto the network media. Each station "listens" constantly to the wire for these announcements, and if it hears one, it avoids transmitting its own data. In other words, on a CSMA/CA network, stations try to avoid collisions with signals generated from other stations. The extra signaling generated by CSMA/CA makes it a slower access method than the Carrier Sense Multiple Access with Collision Detection (CSMA/CD) method used in Ethernet networking.

See Also: *AppleTalk, Carrier Sense Multiple Access with Collision Detection (CSMA/CD), Ethernet, media access control method*

Carrier Sense Multiple Access with Collision Detection (CSMA/CD)

The media access control method used by Ethernet.

Overview

Carrier Sense Multiple Access with Collision Detection (CSMA/CD) is a type of media access control method developed by Xerox Corporation in the 1970s for placing signals on baseband transmission networks. Because baseband networks can carry only one data signal at a time, there must be some way of controlling which station has access to the media at any given time. CSMA/CD is one such control method.

Implementation

In networking technologies that use CSMA/CD as their access method, a station first "listens" to the network media to make sure there is no signal already present from another station before it tries to place its own signal on the media. If a carrier signal is detected on the media, which indicates that a station is currently transmitting a signal, no other station can initiate a transmission until the carrier stops. If no carrier is detected, any station can transmit a signal.

If two stations listen to the wire and detect no carrier signal, they may both decide to send signals simultaneously. If this happens, a collision occurs between the two signals generated. Next, both stations detect the collision and stop transmitting their signals immediately, sending out a jamming signal that informs all other stations on the network that a collision has occurred and that they should not transmit. Meanwhile, the two stations whose signals created the collision cease transmitting and wait random intervals of time (usually a few milliseconds) before attempting to retransmit.

Issues

CSMA/CD is known as a contention method because computers contend for the chance to transmit data onto the network media. CSMA/CD is the standard access method for Ethernet networks. This method has two main drawbacks:

- Only a relatively small number of computers can exist within any one collision domain. More computers will produce more collisions and slow overall network traffic.
- CSMA/CD is not reliable beyond a distance of 1.5 miles (2.5 kilometers) because of signal attenuation.

Notes

The designation CSMA/CD derives from the following:

- CS means that stations first **s**ense a **c**arrier present on the media before transmitting their own signals.
- MA means that **m**ultiple stations can **a**ccess the network media.
- CD means that if a **c**ollision is **d**etected because of multiple simultaneous transmission of signals, the stations that are transmitting signals stop, and then retransmit a short time later.

See Also: *Carrier Sense Multiple Access with Collision Avoidance (CSMA/CA), Ethernet, media access control method*

carrier signal

An alternating electromagnetic signal with a steady frequency upon which information is superimposed by some form of modulation.

Overview

The specific frequency at which a carrier signal runs is called the carrier frequency and is measured in hertz (Hz). The modulation of the carrier signal enables information such as voice or data traffic to be integrated into the carrier signal. The carrier signal thus "carries" the voice or data information using modulation technologies.

The type of modulation used in digital communication systems depends on whether the underlying carrier signal is analog or digital. For example, in digital radio or microwave communication, some form of digital-analog modulation, such as frequency-shift keying (FSK), is used to impose the digital (binary) information on the analog carrier wave. On the other hand, in Ethernet networking, a digital-digital encoding scheme called Manchester coding is used to enable the digital signal to carry binary 1s and 0s.

In Ethernet networks, the carrier signal plays an important role in the media access control method that Ethernet uses, namely the Carrier Sense Multiple Access with Collision Detection (CSMA/CD) method.

See Also: *Carrier Sense Multiple Access with Collision Detection (CSMA/CD)*

cascaded star topology

A layered form of star topology.

See Also: *star topology*

cascading style sheets (CSS)

A method for giving Web developers more control over how the pages of a Web site will look when displayed on a Web browser.

Overview

Cascading style sheets (CSS) is a standard from the World Wide Web Consortium (W3C) that gives Web developers control over design elements such as fonts and font sizes and allows two-dimensional overlapping and exact positioning of page elements. The CSS standard also makes it easier to globally change the style and appearance of a Web site without having to change elements on every page.

Implementation

Hypertext Markup Language (HTML) was designed for logical communication of linked information without much regard for its style or format, and it was not designed to provide a high degree of control over how that information is laid out on a page. Using CSS, a Web developer can control the appearance of an entire Web site, or a portion of it, using a single HTML page

C

called a style sheet. The genius of CSS is that it separates the content of the page (formatted in HTML) from the page layout (defined in the style sheet using CSS).

Style sheets define the functions of different HTML tags on your site's Web pages and allow you to make global changes to your site's style by changing a single entry on a style sheet. Web pages then link to style sheets using a <LINK> tag.

For example, you can use a style sheet to define the <H1> tag as representing green, 18-point, Arial font text, and you can then apply this style to the entire site or a portion of it. Cascading style sheets involve the operation of several levels of style sheets that provide control over how an element on an HTML document is placed. CSS applies these settings in the following order:

- The STYLE attribute in the object's tag
- The STYLE element between the <TITLE> and <BODY> tags that specifies the style sheet to be used
- The settings of the browser accessing the page and its default style sheet

Issues

The main factor that has prevented CSS from being widely implemented on most Web sites is that neither Microsoft Internet Explorer nor Netscape Navigator fully supports all aspects of the CSS standard. Thus, a CSS-enabled site may look one way in Internet Explorer and another way in Netscape, and neither may be what the site designer intended. One Web browser that fully implements the CSS standard is Opera, developed by Hakon Lie, who has been involved in the W3C.

For More Information

You can find the W3C standard for CSS version 2 at *www.w3c.org/Style*.

See Also: *Hypertext Markup Language (HTML)*

Cat5 cabling

Stands for Category 5 cabling, the most common grade of unshielded twisted-pair (UTP) cabling used for structured wiring in commercial buildings.

See: *Category 5 (Cat5) cabling*

Cat5e cabling

Stands for enhanced Category 5, a form of Category 5 (Cat5) cabling that supports higher speeds.

See: *enhanced Category 5 (Cat5e) cabling*

Cat6 cabling

Stands for Category 6 cabling, the proposed next step up from enhanced Category 5 (Cat5e) cabling.

See: *Category 6 (Cat6) cabling*

Cat7 cabling

Stands for Category 7 cabling, a still-hypothetical next step up from the proposed Category 6 (Cat6) cabling.

See: *Category 7 (Cat7) cabling*

catalog

The top-level organizational structure for the Indexing service in Microsoft Windows 2000, Windows XP, and Windows .NET Server.

Overview

The catalog contains the master index and other persistent indexes. The Index Server catalog is located by default in the directory %systemdrive%\inetpub\catalog.wci, but this can be overridden during installation. The maximum size of the catalog for Index Server is 40 percent of the size of the documents being indexed (the corpus), so it is important when installing Index Server to locate the catalog on a drive with sufficient free space. For example, if you will be indexing 10 gigabytes (GB) of documents, you will need about 4 GB of space for locating your catalog.

Notes

An Indexing service query can span only one catalog at a time, so do not create multiple catalogs unless you want to completely separate the indexing of their documents—for example, if you are hosting Web sites for multiple companies on your server.

If you are hosting more than one virtual server on a Microsoft Internet Information Services (IIS) machine, and these virtual servers represent different companies, you might want to create multiple catalogs for the Indexing service, one for each virtual server. Each catalog will then be used for indexing a specific virtual server, and queries based on a catalog will return only results for content on the associated virtual server.

Category 1 (Cat1) cabling

The lowest grade of unshielded twisted-pair (UTP) cabling.

Overview

Category 1 (Cat1) cabling was designed to support analog voice communication only. Cat1 cabling was used prior to 1983 for wiring installations of analog telephone systems, otherwise known as the Plain Old Telephone Service (POTS). The electrical characteristics of Cat1 cabling make it unsuitable for computer networking purposes, and it is never installed as premise wiring for structured cabling installations. Instead, all premise wiring should use either Category 3 (Cat3) cabling, Category 4 (Cat4) cabling, or Category 5 (Cat5) cabling, with Cat5 or enhanced Category 5 (Cat5e) cabling preferred for all new installations.

See Also: *cabling, premise cabling, structured wiring*

Category 2 (Cat2) cabling

The second-lowest grade of unshielded twisted-pair (UTP) cabling.

Overview

Category 2 (Cat2) cabling was designed to support digital voice and data communication. Cat2 cabling was capable of data transmissions up to 4 megabits per second (Mbps). It was used primarily in the installation of premise wiring for legacy Token Ring networks from IBM. The electrical characteristics of Cat2 cabling make it unsuitable for most networking purposes today, thus it is no longer installed as premise wiring. Instead, all premise wiring today should use only Category 3 (Cat3) cabling, Category 4 (Cat4) cabling, or Category 5 (Cat5) cabling, with Cat5 or enhanced Category 5 (Cat5e) cabling preferred for all new installations.

See Also: *cabling, premise cabling, structured wiring*

Category 3 (Cat3) cabling

The third-lowest grade of unshielded twisted-pair (UTP) cabling.

Overview

Category 3 (Cat3) cabling was designed to support digital voice and data communication at speeds up to 10 megabits per second (Mbps). It uses 24-gauge copper wires in a configuration of four twisted-pairs enclosed in a protective insulating sheath. Cat3 cabling is the lowest grade of UTP cabling that can support standard 10BaseT types of Ethernet networks and was often used for legacy 4-Mbps Token Ring installations.

Cat3 cabling still has a significant installed base in older buildings, and for basic 10BaseT Ethernet purposes, it is often cheaper to use existing Cat3 cabling than to upgrade to Category 5 (Cat5). Installing higher-grade cabling for backbone cabling in vertical rises and elevator shafts can extend the life of work areas that still use Cat3 cabling. However, if greater speeds are required at users' workstations, the best solution is to rewire the work areas using Cat5 cabling or enhanced Category 5 (Cat5e) cabling.

The following table summarizes the electrical characteristics of Cat3 cabling at different frequencies, which correspond to different data transmission speeds. Note that attenuation increases with frequency, while near-end crosstalk (NEXT) decreases.

Cat3 Cabling Characteristics

Characteristic	*Value at 10 MHz*	*Value at 16 MHz*
Attenuation	27 decibels (dB)/ 1000 feet	36 dB/1000 feet
NEXT	26 dB/1000 feet	23 dB/1000 feet
Resistance	28.6 ohms/1000 feet	28.6 ohms/1000 feet
Impedance	100 ohms (± 15%)	100 ohms (± 15%)
Capacitance	18 pF/feet	18 pF/feet

See Also: *cabling, Category 5 (Cat5) cabling, enhanced Category 5 (Cat5e) cabling, premise cabling, structured wiring*

Category 4 (Cat4) cabling

The grade of unshielded twisted-pair (UTP) cabling just below standard Category 5 (Cat5) cabling.

Overview

Category 4 (Cat4) cabling was designed to support digital voice and data communication at speeds up to 16 megabits per second (Mbps). It uses 22-gauge or 24-gauge copper wires in a configuration of four twisted-pairs enclosed in a protective insulating sheath. Cat4 cabling can support standard 10BaseT types of Ethernet networks. It was also commonly used in older 16-Mbps Token Ring installations.

Cat4 cabling still has some installed base in older buildings where it is often cheaper to use the existing cabling than to upgrade to newer grades. Installing higher-grade cabling for backbone cabling in vertical rises and elevator shafts can extend the life of work areas that still use Cat4 cabling. However, if greater speeds are required at users' workstations, the best solution is to rewire the work areas using Cat5 cabling or enhanced Category 5 (Cat5e) cabling.

The following table summarizes the electrical characteristics of Cat4 cabling at different frequencies, which correspond to different data transmission speeds. Note that attenuation increases with frequency, while near-end crosstalk (NEXT) decreases.

Cat4 Cabling Characteristics

Characteristic	*Value at 10 MHz*	*Value at 20 MHz*
Attenuation	20 decibels (dB)/ 1000 feet	31 dB/1000 feet
NEXT	41 dB/1000 feet	36 dB/1000 feet
Resistance	28.6 ohms/1000 feet	28.6 ohms/1000 feet
Impedance	100 ohms (± 15%)	100 ohms (± 15%)
Capacitance	18 pF/feet	18 pF/feet

See Also: *cabling, Category 5 (Cat5) cabling, enhanced Category 5 (Cat5e) cabling, premise cabling, structured wiring*

Category 5 (Cat5) cabling

The most common grade of unshielded twisted-pair (UTP) cabling used for structured wiring in commercial buildings.

Overview

Category 5 (Cat5) cabling was designed to support digital voice and data communication at speeds up to 100 megabits per second (Mbps). It uses 22-gauge or 24-gauge copper wires in a configuration of four twisted-pairs enclosed in a protective insulating sheath. It is still the highest official grade of UTP cabling currently recognized by the Electronic Industries Alliance (EIA) and Telecommunications Industry Association (TIA), although proposals have been made for higher Category 6 (Cat6) and Category 7 (Cat7) grades.

Cat5 cabling is the standard grade of UTP cabling for common networking architectures including 10BaseT Ethernet, Fast Ethernet, and 1000BaseT Gigabit Ethernet (GbE) over copper. Cat5 cabling typically makes up over 80 percent of the wiring in today's corporate network. Its continuing popularity in high-speed networks is because fiber-optic cabling is still about twice as expensive to deploy as Cat5 cabling. Because of its superior electrical characteristics, Cat5 cabling is recommended for all new structured wiring installations as well as for upgrading existing premise wiring to support higher-speed networks.

The following table summarizes the electrical characteristics of Cat5 cabling at different frequencies, which correspond to different data transmission speeds. Note that attenuation increases with frequency, while near-end crosstalk (NEXT) decreases.

Cat5 Cabling Characteristics

Characteristic	*Value at 10 MHz*	*Value at 100 MHz*
Attenuation	20 decibels (dB)/ 1000 feet	22 dB/1000 feet
NEXT	47 dB/1000 feet	32.3 dB/1000 feet
Resistance	28.6 ohms/1000 feet	28.6 ohms/1000 feet
Impedance	100 ohms (± 15%)	100 ohms (± 15%)
Capacitance	18 pF/feet	18 pF/feet
Structural return loss	16 dB	16 dB
Delay skew	45 nanoseconds (ns)/100 meters	45 ns/100 meters

Marketplace

There are a vast number of different brands of Cat5 cabling on the market today. One estimate is that there are over 150 different vendors of such cabling. Not all Cat5 cabling is alike, and before undertaking a costly large-scale deployment of structured wiring, the enterprise architect should carefully investigate and compare the different brands.

Notes

For typical installations of Ethernet and Fast Ethernet, Cat5 cables in work areas should be no more than 300 feet (90 meters) long, and Cat5 patch cords should be no longer than 33 feet (10 meters). Check the Ethernet specifications for exact lengths permitted.

Many vendors offer an enhanced Cat5 (Cat5e) cabling grade with electrical characteristics exceeding those of standard Cat5. Cat5e cabling typically supports data transmission up to frequencies of 350 MHz, and new standards are under development to allow even higher data transmission frequencies. Cat5e networking is recommended for Gigabit Ethernet (GbE) over copper, but properly installed Cat5 cabling should work in most GbE setups. For best performance of GbE networks, however, use Cat5e or Cat 6 cabling whenever possible.

There is widespread agreement that Cat5 cabling will not be able to support networks beyond GbE, such as the 10 GbE architecture currently under development. Such ultra-high speed networks will likely work only with fiber and will not support copper.

See Also: *cabling, enhanced Category 5 (Cat5e) cabling, premise cabling, structured wiring*

Category 6 (Cat6) cabling

The proposed next step up from enhanced Category 5 cabling (Cat5e).

Overview

Category 6 (Cat6) is a proposed Electronic Industries Association/Telecommunications Industry Association (EIA/TIA) cabling standard that represents the next step up from Cat5 and Cat5e cabling. The following table shows the current draft standard for Cat6 cabling characteristics.

Proposed Cat6 Cabling Characteristics

Characteristic	*Value at 250 MHz*
Attenuation	19.9 decibels (dB)/1000 feet
NEXT	44.3 dB/1000 feet
Impedance	100 ohms (± 15%)
Return loss	20.1 dB
Delay skew	45 nanoseconds (ns)/100 meters
PS-NEXT	42.3 dB

Implementation

Great care must be taken when installing Cat6 cabling in order to have it achieve its design goals because poorly installed Cat6 cabling may offer only Cat5 performance. To get best performance out of Cat6 cabling for high-speed networking, be sure to follow the following guidelines:

- Buy cabling that has a definite spline separating the cables to reduce crosstalk.
- Make sure twists in wires are kept flush with connections at all termination blocks to avoid return-loss issues.
- Liberally use a hook and loop fastener, such as Velcro, to prevent cable from becoming excessively crimped.

Issues

Despite the formation in 1999 of a TIA task force to develop an official standard for a proposed Cat6 cabling, this unshielded twisted-pair (UTP) cabling standard remains to be ratified. The inherent engineering difficulties of standardizing cabling transmission characteristics for transmissions at 250 MHz and above, coupled with the fact that many cabling vendors have released their own "Category 6 or better" cabling, has led to some confusion in the marketplace. A factor that has slowed the development of Cat6 standards was the successful implementation of 1000BaseT Gigabit Ethernet (GbE) over Cat5 cabling, which relaxed the immediate need for a higher Cat6 class of cable and slowed the momentum of the Cat6 standards process. Cat6 thus currently appears as a solution in search of a problem, and the emergence of 10 Gigabit Ethernet (10 GbE) may have little impact on this situation because 10 GbE is envisioned as a fiber-only architecture.

At present Cat6 cabling solutions are essentially "channel solutions," meaning that their successful implementation depends on purchasing cabling components (such as cabling, patch panels, jacks, and wall plates) from a single vendor. Until an official Cat6 standard emerges, networking architects are recommended to use such channel solutions from a singling cabling vendor. In fact, some believe that "mix and match" cabling solutions for Cat6 will never be achieved due to the careful tuning of components that must be performed to make such systems work.

Notes

Existing cable testing equipment will not be able to evaluate Cat6 cabling because Cat6 not only includes additional parameters that must be measured but also specifies at least 10 dB greater precision in measuring existing cabling transmission characteristics over that achieved by Cat5e test equipment.

Some experts believe that it may be possible in the future to run 10 gigabits per second (Gbps) over Cat6 cabling at distances up to 330 feet (100 meters). If this is the case, then Cat6 cabling may well serve as an alternate infrastructure solution to fiber for the emerging 10 GbE standard. Such uses of Cat6 cabling are likely to be restricted to niche applications such as switch-switch and switch-server interconnects and within some types of storage area networks (SANs).

Another name for the proposed Cat6 cabling standard is Class E.

See Also: *10GbE, cabling, enhanced Category 5 (Cat5e) cabling, premise cabling, structured wiring*

Category 7 (Cat7) cabling

A still-hypothetical next step up from the proposed Category 6 (Cat6) cabling.

Overview

There is as yet no official Telecommunications Industry Association (TIA) standard for unshielded twisted-pair (UTP) cabling above Cat6, and Cat6 itself is still under consideration and has not been ratified as a standard. Nevertheless, many cabling vendors are offering "Category 7 cabling solutions" that exceed the specifications of Cat6. Such marketing should be taken with a grain of salt, as they do not represent true Cat7 standards, but such "channel solutions" involving cabling system elements purchased from a single vendor can provide significantly better performance than standard enhanced Category 5 (Cat5e) cabling. It is likely that when a true Cat7 standard emerges, it may require the replacement of the ubiquitous RJ-45 connector, which is a weak point in the transmission architecture for UTP cabling. Unfortunately, this means that existing networking equipment such as switches and routers may not be able to support Cat7.

While the Electronic Industries Association/Telecommunications Industry Association (EIA/TIA) has currently abandoned efforts to standardize Cat7, standards efforts are underway on the international scene through the efforts of the International Standards Organization (ISO) and International Electrotechnical Commission (IEC).

Notes

Another name for proposed Cat7 cabling is Class F cabling.

See Also: *cabling, Category 6 (Cat6) cabling, premise cabling, structured wiring*

CBCP

Stands for Callback Control Protocol, a protocol that enables callback for establishing Point-to-Point Protocol (PPP) connections.

See: *Callback Control Protocol (CBCP)*

CBQ

Stands for class-based queuing, an emerging technology for WAN traffic management.

See: *class-based queuing (CBQ)*

CBT

Stands for Core-Based Trees, a multicast routing protocol.

See: *Core-Based Trees (CBT)*

CDDI

Stands for Copper Distributed Data Interface, a form of Fiber Distributed Data Interface (FDDI) deployed over copper cabling instead of fiber.

See: *Copper Distributed Data Interface (CDDI)*

CDE

Stands for Common Desktop Environment, a graphical user interface (GUI) or desktop environment developed for UNIX systems.

See: *Common Desktop Environment (CDE)*

CDF

Stands for Channel Definition Format, an open standard created by Microsoft Corporation for Microsoft Internet Explorer version 4 (and proposed as a standard to the World Wide Web Consortium) that defines a "smart pull" technology for webcasting information to users' desktops.

See: *Channel Definition Format (CDF)*

CDF file

Text files used for creating Active Channels, Active Desktop items, and channel screen savers for managed webcasting of content to users' desktops.

Overview

CDF files are based on the Channel Definition Format (CDF) standard. CDF files provide a mechanism for allowing users to select the content they want to download from a Web site, and they let administrators schedule content for delivery to users' desktops.

CDF files are used to convert existing Web sites into Active Channels without the need to change the existing site in any way. You simply create a CDF file using a text editor such as Microsoft Notepad and include it in your site. This will allow the content of the site to be webcast to users' browsers. The CDF file must be saved with the extension .cdf, and a link on your site should point to this file so that users can subscribe to the channel.

A typical CDF file defines a channel hierarchy for the different Web sites making up the Active Channel. This channel hierarchy contains a table of contents for webcasting the content and consists of a top-level channel, subchannels, and actual content items (Web pages). The simplest format for a CDF file is a list of Uniform Resource Locators (URLs) that point to specific Web pages in the site. More advanced CDF files can contain information such as the following:

- A map of the hierarchical structure of the URLs in the Web site
- Logical groupings of different content items within a site that can differ from the observable link structure of the site itself
- The title of each referenced Web page and a brief abstract of its contents
- Information controlling the scheduling of content updates

The syntax of advanced CDF file items is based on the Extensible Markup Language (XML), an open specification that provides extensibility to standard Hypertext Markup Language (HTML) files. More than one CDF file can be created for a site, allowing users to subscribe to information in different fashions. For example, a news site can have separate CDF files for news, sports, and weather subscriptions.

Notes

For specific information on the syntax of CDF files and how to create them, refer to the Microsoft Internet Client software development kit (SDK).

Channels in Active Channel enable personalized delivery of Web content using Web applications designed for Internet Information Service (IIS) for Windows 2000. Active Server Pages (ASP) can be used for dynamically generating personalized CDF files for users. Cookies can also be used for dynamically generating customized CDF files for users. These CDF files can be customized on the basis of preferences that a user specifies on an HTML form prior to subscribing to the channel.

See Also: *Channel Definition Format (CDF)*

CDFS

Stands for CD-ROM File System, a file system designed for read-only CD-ROM media.

See: *CD-ROM File System (CDFS)*

CDMA

Stands for Code Division Multiple Access, a second-generation (2G) digital cellular phone technology that uses spread-spectrum techniques, popular in the United States and some other parts of the world.

See: *Code Division Multiple Access (CDMA)*

CDMA2000

A proposed third-generation (3G) upgrade for existing Code Division Multiple Access (CDMA) cellular telephone systems.

Overview

CDMA2000 was developed by the Telecommunications Industry Association (TIA) and is part of the International Mobile Telecommunications 2000 (IMT-2000) initiative of the International Telecommunication Union (ITU). CDMA2000 will boost the bandwidth of existing cdmaOne cellular systems to 2 megabits per second (Mbps), making global broadband wireless communications a reality.

Because the proposed CDMA2000 upgrade includes only a small portion of the overall wireless communication market, the IMT-2000 initiative also includes proposed upgrades to Time Division Multiple Access (TDMA) systems such as Global System for Mobile Communications (GSM). A competing upgrade for TDMA systems is General Packet Radio Service (GPRS), which is closer to implementation than CDMA2000 and might therefore win more initial support than CDMA2000.

The term *CDMA2000 1x* is commonly used to describe various interim CDMA2000 systems that use existing IS-95a base stations to provide 2.5G cellular services. CDMA2000 1*x* systems expect to achieve data transmission speeds of between 144 kilobits per second (Kbps) and 307 Kbps and are therefore classed as 2.5G cellular services instead of the much faster 3G services envisioned by IMT-2000. The proposed 3G system Wideband CDMA (W-CDMA) is comparable to CDMA2000 2*x*, meaning the 3G version of CDMA2000.

The CDMA Development Group is also promoting a different CDMA2000 upgrade called High Data Rate (HDR) CDMA2000 1*x*. This platform is based on the American National Standards Institute (ANSI) IS-95c standard and is viewed as an alternative upgrade path from CDMAone toward 3G. It involves a hardware upgrade using chipsets produced by QUALCOMM (the originators of CDMA) and may provide data speeds up to 2.4 Mbps, even better than the 2 Mbps speeds anticipated by W-CDMA. In some respects HDR may be superior to W-CDMA, the 3G version of CDMA being proposed by the ITU in its IMT-2000 initiative. Specifically, while W-CDMA is expected to provide 2 Mbps service only for stationary users, and much slower speeds for mobile and roaming users, HDR is intended to provide the same 2.4 Mbps speed for all users whether mobile or stationary. However, W-CDMA has the advantage of being a proposed standard for implementing compatible systems throughout the world. Only time will tell which system achieves market dominance.

For More Information

Visit the CDMA Development Group at *www.cdg.org.*

See Also: *3G, cellular communications, cdmaOne, Code Division Multiple Access (CDMA)*

cdmaOne

The commercial name for the Code Division Multiple Access (CDMA) cellular communications system used in North America and parts of Asia.

See: *Code Division Multiple Access (CDMA)*

CDN

Stands for content delivery network, a method for efficiently pushing out content over the Internet to users.

See: *content delivery network (CDN)*

CDO

Stands for Collaboration Data Objects, a collection of Component Object Model (COM) objects that allow developers to create Microsoft Internet Information Services (IIS) Web applications that send and receive electronic mail.

See: *Collaboration Data Objects (CDO)*

CDP

Stands for Content Delivery Provider, a company that builds and operates a content delivery network (CDN).

See: *content delivery network (CDN)*

CDPD

Stands for Cellular Digital Packet Data, a type of packet-switched data transmission network operating as an overlay for a cellular communications system.

See: *Cellular Digital Packet Data (CDPD)*

CD-ROM File System (CDFS)

A file system designed for read-only CD-ROM media.

Overview

CD-ROM File System (CDFS) is an International Organization for Standardization (ISO) standard (ISO 9660) for a read-only formatting standard for CD-ROM media. CDFS provides the same kind of file and directory management for CD-ROM devices that the file allocation table (FAT) and NTFS file systems (NTFS) do for hard disks.

CDFS is implemented on the Microsoft Windows 95, Windows 98, Windows Millennium Edition (Me), Windows NT, Windows 2000, Windows XP, and Windows .NET Server platforms. On 32-bit Windows systems, CDFS uses a 32-bit protected-mode driver that replaces the 16-bit real-mode Microsoft CD-ROM Extension (MSCDEX) driver that was used in the legacy 16-bit Windows and MS-DOS operating system platforms. In Windows 95 and Windows 98, the file system driver that supports CDFS is called Cdfs.vxd, and in Windows NT, Windows 2000, Windows XP, and Windows .NET Server, it is called Cdfs.sys.

CDFS is optimized for reading compact discs that have a standard data block size of 2048 bytes (2 KB). The Microsoft implementation of CDFS includes a dynamic, protected-mode cache pool for caching CD-ROM data to improve read performance. This allows CDFS to read ahead to ensure that playback of multimedia content from CDs is smooth and seamless. On Windows 95 OEM Service Release 2 (OSR2), Windows 98, Windows Me, Windows NT, Windows 2000, Windows XP, and Windows .NET Server platforms, CDFS includes a number of enhancements over the original version of CDFS for Windows 95, such as

- CD-XA support for optimized reading of Moving Picture Experts Group (MPEG) video CDs having larger block sizes of 2352 bytes.
- Auto-Run, which allows applications on CDs to start immediately when the CD is inserted into the drive. To do this, the operating system reads the Autorun.inf file that is stored in the root of the directory structure on the CD.

CDFS does have several limitations compared to disk file systems such as FAT and NTFS, namely:

- Names for files and directories can be no longer than 32 characters
- Directories can be nested only eight levels deep

CDFS is now considered a legacy format and is being replaced by the industry-standard Universal Disk Format (UDF), the new standard for read-only disk media.

Notes

Using Services for Macintosh, you can create an Apple Macintosh–accessible volume on a CDFS volume by following the same steps you would use to make an NTFS volume accessible to Macintosh clients. Of course, the CDFS volume has one difference: it is read-only.

See Also: *file system, Universal Disk Format (UDF)*

CDSL

Stands for Consumer DSL, a broadband transmission technology based on Digital Subscriber Line (DSL) technology.

See: *Consumer DSL (CDSL)*

cell (ATM)

A 53-byte packet of data, the standard packet size used by Asynchronous Transfer Mode (ATM) communication technologies.

Overview

Cells are to ATM technologies what frames are to Ethernet networking. In other words, they form the smallest element of data for transmission over the network.

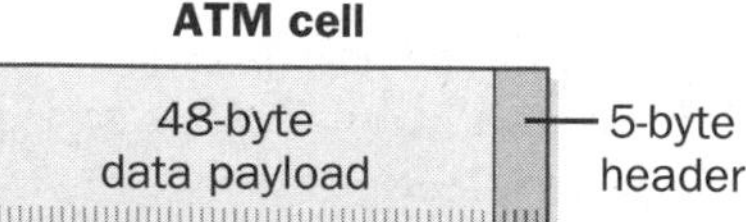

Cell in ATM. *Details of an ATM cell.*

ATM cells are standardized at a fixed-length size of 53 bytes to enable faster switching than is possible on networks using variable-packet sizes (such as Ethernet). It is much easier to design a device to quickly switch a fixed-length packet than to design a device to switch a variable-length packet. (Switching a fixed-length packet is easier because the device knows in advance the packet's exact length and can anticipate the exact moment at which the last portion of the packet will be received. With variable-length packets, the device must examine each packet for length information.) Using fixed-length cells also makes it possible to control and allocate ATM bandwidth more effectively, making support for different quality of service (QoS) levels for ATM possible.

The functions of information stored in the 5-byte header of an ATM cell include the following:

- Providing information about the physical layer transmission method being used
- Providing flow control to enable a steady flow of cell traffic and to reduce cell jitter
- Specifying virtual path or channel identification numbers so that multiplexed cells belonging to the same ATM connection can be distinguished from cells belonging to other ATM connections and cells can be switched to their intended destination
- Specifying the nature of the payload contained in the cell—that is, whether it contains actual user data or ATM cell-management information
- Specifying the priority of the cell to determine whether the cell can be dropped in congested traffic conditions
- Providing error checking by means of an 8-bit field containing cyclical redundancy check (CRC) information for the header itself

Two kinds of header formats are used in ATM cells:

- **User-Network Interface (UNI) format:** Used for communication between end nodes and an ATM network

- **Network-Node Interface (NNI) format:** Used within the ATM network itself after the cell has been multiplexed for transmission over its virtual path

Notes

Why a 48-byte data payload for ATM cells? This is the result of a trade-off between larger 64-byte payloads that contain more data but take longer to package and unpackage— and are therefore not suitable for real-time transmissions such as voice or multimedia—and shorter 32-byte payloads that provide better real-time transmission but are inefficient for larger amounts of data. By compromising at a 48-byte payload size, ATM has good transmission capabilities for both voice and data communication, providing efficient packet transfer with low latency.

See Also: Asynchronous Transfer Mode (ATM)

cell (cellular communications)

In wireless communication technologies, the geographical region that is covered by a transmission facility.

Overview

The term **cell** is most often used in reference to cellular phone technology, but it can also be used in reference to the coverage areas for transmission of cordless telephones, satellite transmissions, wireless local area networks (LANs), packet radio, and paging technologies.

Cells range in size from a few dozen feet to thousands of miles in diameter, depending on the technology being used, the power of the transmission station, and the terrain topography. The following table summarizes typical cell size ranges for different wireless communication technologies. These figures are only approximate because wireless technologies are constantly evolving.

Satellite-based systems have by far the largest cell sizes and are rapidly increasing in popularity. Cellular phone technologies in rural areas typically use cells with a radius of 6 to 30 miles (10 to 50 kilometers), while cells in urban areas range in size from 0.6 to 6 miles (1 to 10 kilometers). For highly dense urban areas, cell sizes as small as 330 feet (100 meters) can be used, especially in high-tier Personal Communications Devices (PCD) cellular technologies.

Cell Radius Measures by Technology

Wireless Technology	*Cell Radius*
Wireless LANs	10 to 100 meters
Cellular telephone	0.1 to 50 kilometers
PCD	0.1 to 1 kilometer
Satellite-based	1000 kilometers or more

Notes

When a mobile caller using a cell phone passes from one cell to another, the cellular phone system transfers the call to the system servicing the adjacent cell, a process called roaming.

See Also: cellular communications, wireless networking

Cellular Digital Packet Data (CDPD)

A type of packet-switched data transmission network operating as an overlay for a cellular communications system.

Overview

Cellular Digital Packet Data (CDPD) is a specification for overlaying digital data transmissions on the existing circuit-switched Advanced Mobile Phone Service (AMPS) analog cellular phone service. CDPD was developed by IBM together with a consortium of Regional Bell Operating Companies and other organizations to leverage the existing installed base of AMPS cellular equipment in the United States to provide low-cost, packet-switched data services. CDPD was first offered in 1994 by Bell Atlantic Mobile.

Uses

CDPD is typically used to provide wireless access to public packet-switched networks such as the Internet so that mobile users can access their e-mail and other services. Multiple users can share the same channel; the user's modem determines which packets are destined for the user's machine. CDPD also supports IP multi-

casting and is an open standard based on the Open Systems Interconnection (OSI) reference model for networking.

Architecture

CDPD makes use of idle times between calls in cellular phone network channels for interleaving packets of digital data. In other words, CDPD makes use of the "bursty" nature of typical voice transmission on the AMPS cellular system. Voice communication has gaps or pauses where packet data can be inserted and transmitted without interfering with the communication taking place between customers.

CDPD uses the Reed-Solomon forward-error-correcting code to encode each block or burst of data sent, and includes built-in RC4 encryption to ensure security and privacy of the transmitted data. CDPD is also based on the industry standard Internet Protocol (IP), allowing data to be transmitted to and from the Internet.

Although CDPD supports data transmission rates of 19.2 kilobits per second (Kbps) and higher, actual data throughput is usually around 9.6 Kbps. This is because of the large overhead added by CDPD to each data block transmitted. This overhead is designed to ensure that communications are reliable and to maintain synchronization between the modems at each end of the transmission. In addition, a color code is added to every data block to detect interference resulting from transmissions on the same channel from neighboring cell sites.

Implementation

A typical implementation of CDPD consists of three components:

- **Mobile-End System (M-ES):** A user device such as a laptop equipped with a cellular modem. This system communicates in full-duplex mode with a Mobile Data Base Station (MDBS) using the Digital Sense Multiple Access protocol, which prevents collisions of data streams from multiple Mobile-End Systems.
- **Mobile Data Base Station (MDBS):** A telco device for receiving and transmitting CDPD data.
- **Mobile Data Intermediate System (MDIS):** Provides the central control for a CDPD network.

Marketplace

In the United States, the main providers of CDPD services are AT&T Wireless and Verizon Wireless. CDPD is also supported by several carriers in Canada and by AirData in New Zealand. CDPD is not widely deployed as a cellular data transmission technology, and coverage in the United States is spotty even in urban areas.

For More Information

You can find the CDPD Forum at *www.cdpd.org.*

See Also: *cellular communications, wireless networking*

cellular communications

A group of technologies that support roaming cell-based wireless communications.

Overview

Common to all forms of cellular communications is the concept of the cell. Instead of using one extremely powerful transmission to provide coverage for a geographical area (for example, a city, state, region, or country), the area is divided into a series of overlapping smaller areas called cells. Each cell has a relatively low-power base station that provides coverage for users within that cell, and when a user moves (roams) from one cell to another, the first base station seamlessly hands off servicing of the user to the second base station and the user experiences no interruption in communication.

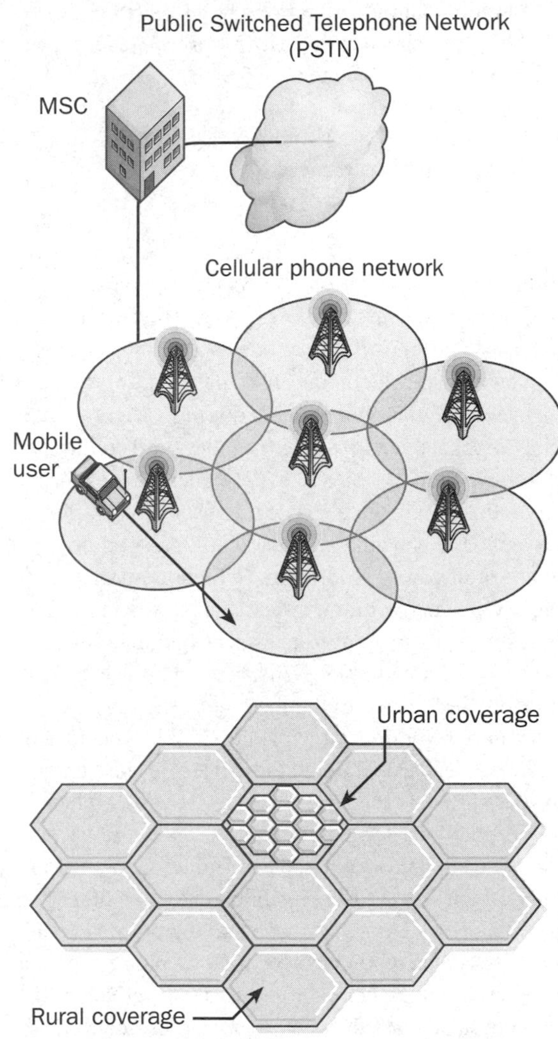

Cellular communications. *How a cellular phone system works.*

Dividing the coverage area into many cells makes cellular communications systems more complicated than systems that use a single high-powered base station. Complex functions such as call setup and tear down, call authorization, call handoff, routing of call traffic, and call billing must operate seamlessly as users move between cells, and they require complex technology to implement. These functions are provided by connecting groups of base stations to a mobile switching center (MSC), which coordinates the activities of the base stations and connects them to the Public Switched Telephone Network (PSTN) so wireless users can call wireline users and vice versa.

Communications channels also need to be allocated to cells in such a way that no two adjacent cells use the same set of channels. This is necessary to ensure that signals from one base station do not interfere with those from base stations in adjacent cells. Repeating patterns of cells are used to optimize coverage of an area while maintaining the maximum number of available channels per cell. For example, in a typical cellular system, if you travel in a straight line every third cell utilizes the same set of frequencies.

Cells can also vary considerably in size. Because each cell can only support a certain number of users, cells in dense urban areas are much smaller than those in sparsely inhabited rural areas, and when population increases cells may need to be split to continue to provide adequate coverage. All this makes cellular communications complicated to implement, which explains why the technology took so many years to be widely deployed after the it was first conceived. The main advantage of such systems, however, is that, because cells are relatively small, the mobile client (cell phone or other device) does not need to be very powerful, which saves considerably on the size and the cost of the phone and has helped propel the widespread use and popularity of these systems.

History

The concept of a cellular phone system originated in 1947 at AT&T Bell Laboratories. AT&T first proposed a commercial cellular system to the Federal Communications Commission (FCC) in the late 1960s, and the FCC allocated the necessary frequency spectrum in 1974. A demonstration system was tested in Chicago in 1978, but the first actual cellular system was deployed in Japan in 1979 by the Nippon Telephone and Telegraph Company. This was followed by Europe in 1981, and finally in 1983 AT&T began deploying Advanced Mobile Phone Service (AMPS), the first nationwide cellular system in the United States.

C

AMPS was a first-generation (1G) analog cellular phone system that used frequency modulation for voice transmission and frequency-shift keying (FSK) for transmission of signaling information. AMPS uses channels within the 800 megahertz (MHz) frequency band of the electromagnetic spectrum, and channel access is provided by using Frequency Division Multiple Access (FDMA) as the media access method. AMPS achieved widespread implementation across the United States in the 1980s and is still widely used.

Another wave of cellular communications systems was developed in the 1990s and is still widely deployed. These second-generation (2G) systems differ from AMPS in being digital rather than analog in nature, and they can support not just voice but also data transmission, typically at 9.6 to 19.2 kilobits per second (Kbps). Several competing digital cellular systems have evolved and have become widely deployed:

- **Time Division Multiple Access (TDMA):** The main TDMA system deployed in the United States is AT&T Wireless Services, a subsidiary of AT&T. This TDMA system operates in the same 800 MHz frequency band as AMPS and is sometimes referred to as either Digital AMPS (D-AMPS) or North American TDMA (NA-TDMA).
- **Code Division Multiple Access (CDMA):** CDMA was developed by QUALCOMM, and its cdmaOne system is the most popular digital cellular system in North America. Other CDMA carriers include Bell Mobility, Sprint Corporation, and Verizon Communications. CDMA is more complex than TDMA, but it is more efficient in its utilization of the frequency spectrum.
- **Global System for Mobile Communications (GSM):** This system is based on TDMA and is the most popular digital cellular phone technology in Europe and much of Asia. GSM can operate in the 900, 1800, or 1900 MHz frequency bands. There are only a few GSM carriers in the United States, and they cover only a small portion of the market. An example is VoiceStream Wireless Corporation.
- **Personal Communications Services (PCS):** These systems can be TDMA-based or CDMA-based and operate in the higher 1900 MHz frequency band using smaller cell sizes than 800 MHz cellular systems. Sprint PCS, for example, is based on CDMA technology.

Issues

A major concern that has been receiving media attention lately is the safety of using cellular phones. While most agree that using a cellular phone while driving can increase the chances of an accident (and some civic and municipal governing bodies have passed laws regulating use of cellular phones while driving), scientists continue to debate whether other health hazards might be associated with the long-term use of cell phones. A particular concern is the possible link between cell phone use and brain cancer, particularly among children whose brains are still forming. Cell phones transmit microwave energy through their antennas, and microwaves have a known heating effect (think of a microwave oven, for example). When a cell phone is held next to the ear, some of the microwave energy penetrates into the brain, and while the FCC has mandated emission standards for cellular phones to keep these emissions below dangerous levels, some researchers believe that long-term exposure to even low-level microwave radiation may be harmful to the brain and other organs, particularly in children. On the other hand, many researchers believe that there is no conclusive link between brain cancer and cell-phone use, and in general such associations between cancer and environment factors are difficult to prove (consider how long it took to resolve the controversy over whether cigarettes caused lung cancer). The American Medical Association and other bodies continue to call for further study of these issues, but it will likely take years for studies to produce any significant results. Some governing bodies are already taking steps, however, such as the United Kingdom, which has mandated that mobile telephone handsets must now come with leaflets warning of potential health risks to children who use these devices over a prolonged period.

Impact

Cellular communications have revolutionized business and personal communications worldwide. About one-third of Americans now own cell phones, and this is growing at an annual rate of 25 percent. Use of cell phones in Europe and Asia is even higher on a percentage basis, and some analysts predict that by 2005 there will be more than 1.25 billion cell phones and other cellular communications devices used around the world.

Cell phones have helped catalyze the e-business revolution by providing employees with 24x7 connectivity with the office—something desirable from a management point of view but debatable in terms of the quality of life for workers. Using data-enabled cell phones and wireless Personal Digital Assistants (PDAs), workers can perform tasks such as sending and receiving e-mail, checking inventory and ordering products, reboot servers, and perform other essential tasks to keep an e-business operating. Nonbusiness uses of data-enabled cell phones including browsing the Web, checking weather reports, downloading news headlines, confirming airline reservations, checking stock quotations, and many other uses. Although many of these uses are exciting, most data operations are still tedious over slow 2G cellular systems, and the real promise of cellular Internet access will not be realized until 3G comes into full operation in the latter part of this decade.

Prospects

The current 2G cellular systems will be replaced over the next few years by broadband cellular systems that support much higher rates of data transmission than can now be achieved. Proposed 3G systems will support data transmission as fast as 2 megabits per second (Mbps) and include

- **Wideband CDMA (W-CDMA):** This system has the support of the International Telecommunication Union (ITU) as the upgrade for TDMA-based systems such as GSM, offers data rates of up to 2 Mbps, and is expected to become widely deployed in Europe and Asia.
- **CDMA2000:** This system has been proposed by QUALCOMM as the upgrade for CDMA systems, has the support of the ITU as an alternative to W-CDMA, offers data rates of up to 2 Mbps, and is expected to become widely deployed in North America.
- **Enhanced Data rates for Global Evolution (EDGE):** This system is a proposed upgrade by AT&T for its North American TDMA system but offers data rates of only 384 Kbps.

Because 3G technologies are not expected to be deployed until 2003 (or more likely 2005), some carriers are implementing interim 2.5G systems to provide increased data rates over 2G until 3G becomes a reality. Some 2.5G systems starting to be deployed include

- **CDMA2000 1X:** This system developed by QUALCOMM supports data transmission at 307 Kbps, and is an interim step toward the 3G version CDMA2000 (sometimes called CDMA2000 2X).
- **General Packet Radio Service (GPRS):** This system upgrades AT&T's existing TDMA system to support data rates of 115 Kbps and is an interim step toward EDGE.

For More Information

For the latest news about the cellular industry, visit the Cellular Telecommunications & Internet Association's (CTIA) World of Wireless at *www.wow-com.com.*

See Also: *2G, 2.5G, 3G, broadband wireless communications, CDMA2000, Code Division Multiple Access (CDMA), Enhanced Data Rates for Global Evolution (EDGE), General Packet Radio Service (GPRS), Global System for Mobile Communications (GSM), Personal Communications Services (PCS), Time Division Multiple Access (TDMA), wireless networking*

central office (CO)

A telco switching facility.

Overview

The central office (CO) provides access to the Plain Old Telephone Service (POTS), leased lines, and other services that a telco offers its customers in a given geographical area (usually a dozen square miles or so).

The CO contains the Class 5 switching equipment that connects telephone subscribers to both local and long-distance phone services. A telco typically has one CO servicing several dozen square miles in urban areas, so in large cities there may be many COs for each telco.

A typical CO may look like a fortress built to withstand an earthquake or any other natural disaster. Building standards for COs are high because of the importance of the communications infrastructure to a nation's economic health and safety. Banks of batteries and diesel generators provide backup power in case of blackouts so that phone communication will not be disrupted.

Multitudes of twisted-pair copper telephone lines from customer premises usually enter the building through the underground cable vault. These twisted-pair lines are grouped into bundles of thousands of lines, forming large cables 3 to 4 inches (7.5 to 10 centimeters) in diameter. The cables have grounding mesh to provide a drain for unwanted electrical surges and tough polyvinyl chloride (PVC) insulating jackets that are pressurized to prevent water from seeping in at cable junctions. Steel racks organize these cables as they enter the cable vault.

From the vault, the cables snake their way to the main cross-connect grid. It is in these steel-frame grids that all the individual twisted-pairs fan out and connect through feeders to the main switching equipment. The importance of the feeders is that they allow any incoming twisted-pair line to connect to virtually any switching bank. This makes it possible for customers to move to a different part of the city and maintain their old telephone number at their new location. It also allows for redundancy: if a switch fails, a CO technician can rewire the feeder blocks quickly and easily. The main switches are then used to route calls to other local subscribers or to a long-distance telecommunications carrier such as AT&T or MCI WorldCom. In the United States, these Class 5 telephone switches are usually Basic-5ESS switches, also called AT&T basic rate switches.

Subscribers are connected to their local CO through a segment of wiring called the local loop. This wiring is typically copper, but telcos lay fiber to the building for customers requiring high-speed services not supported by copper lines.

Finally, a telco may have dozens of COs in a dense urban area, all interconnected using cross-links and redundant switches. Each CO services subscribers within a specific geographical area and manages voice and data traffic in that area. When a call is made from a customer over the local loop to the CO, the call is either switched to another circuit within the same exchange (for local calls) or switched to a trunk line joining the CO to a CO belonging to a different company, typically a long-haul carrier such as Sprint or AT&T. For business customers needing multiple telephone lines at their location, the carrier typically deploys a private branch exchange (PBX) at the customer premises.

Notes

Not all of a telco's switching and telecommunications equipment is located at a central office. There are recent trends where telcos have pushed out their ATM switching gear to within 500 feet (150 meters) of residential neighborhoods in pursuit of better-quality Digital Subscriber Line (DSL) connections. These remote stations shorten the copper DSL connections between customer premises and the provider's switching gear, and the remote Asynchronous Transfer Mode (ATM) concentrators are then connected to the COs using fiber.

In countries and regions other than the United States, a CO is often referred to as a public exchange.

See Also: *telco*

Centrex

An acronym for **Centr**al Office **Ex**change Service, a business telephone service provided by telcos.

Overview

By using a Centrex instead of a Private Branch Exchange (PBX), a business can eliminate the necessity of having its own dedicated switching facilities at its customer premises. Centrex also eliminates the need for customers to upgrade to expensive new telephones because existing telephone lines and touch tone phones can be used with it. This frees the customer from the need to invest in the cost and management of customer premises equipment (CPE).

Centrex services partition the switching capabilities of the telco's central office (CO) equipment and allow a portion of these capabilities to be dedicated to a particular customer. In essence, the business customer is leasing dedicated switching facilities at the CO to enable a large number of employee telephones to be routed through a few telephone lines. All routing of calls to individual employee telephones takes place using the Centrex. Configuration changes can be performed at the CO instead of requiring technicians to visit the customer premises. This can save the cost of installing a local PBX at the customer premises.

Centrex can handle advanced communication features such as internal call handling, inbound and outbound call handling, and multiparty calling. Each individual connected can have customized calling features just as they can with a PBX. Maintenance is entirely the responsibility of the telco central office, which provides around-the-clock support.

Notes

Some carriers such as Pacific Bell Telephone Company also offer Integrated Services Digital Network (ISDN) as a Centrex service in addition to standard business ISDN lines.

See Also: *central office (CO), Private Branch Exchange (PBX), telco*

certificate

Also called digital certificate, a technology for verifying the identity of the user or service you are communicating with.

See: *digital certificate*

certificate authority (CA)

Any entity (individual, department, company, or organization) that issues digital certificates to verify the identity of users, applications, or organizations.

Overview

Before issuing a digital certificate to someone, the certificate authority (CA) must verify the user's identity according to a strictly established policy, which can involve face-to-face communication, examination of a driver's license with photograph, or another method of establishing a user's identity. When the user's identity has been verified, the certificate is issued to the user. This certificate can then be presented by the user as a "digital driver's license" to identify himself or herself during network transactions.

CAs can be trusted third parties such as the private companies VeriSign, CyberTrust, and Nortel Networks; or they can be established within your own organization using Microsoft Certificate Server. CAs can be standalone authorities with their own self-signed certificates (that is, they validate their own identity as a root CA), or they can be part of a hierarchy in which each CA is certified by the trusted CA above it (up to a root CA, which must always be self-certified).

For digital certificates to work as an identification scheme, both client and server programs must trust the CA. In other words, when a client program presents a certificate to a server program, the server program must be able to validate that the certificate was issued by a valid and trusted CA. Certificate authorities also maintain a certificate revocation list (CRL) of revoked certificates. Certificates issued by CAs expire after a specified period of time.

CAs are necessary for the functioning of a public key infrastructure (PKI), which is essential to the widespread acceptance and success of any public key cryptography system. Microsoft Windows 2000 and Windows .NET Server can use standard X.509 digital certificates to authenticate connections across unsecured networks such as the Internet and to provide single sign-on using smart card authentication systems.

For More Information

Visit VeriSign, Inc. at *www.verisign.com.*

See Also: *digital certificate, public key infrastructure (PKI)*

C

certificate mapping

A feature of Microsoft Internet Information Server (IIS) version 4 and Internet Information Services (IIS) version 5 (for Windows 2000) and later that allows mapping between user accounts and digital certificates.

Overview

Certificate mapping is useful when an organization issues client certificates to users. Client certificates are digital certificates that verify the identity of client software (Web browsers) belonging to users. Client certificates are often used in situations in which mobile clients using laptops require secure access to a corporate intranet site.

Before users can be granted remote access to the corporate intranet, they must be authenticated by the Web server they are connecting to. IIS supports four kinds of Web authentication mechanisms:

- **Anonymous access:** Allows anonymous users access to Web sites—such as public sites on the Internet.
- **Basic authentication:** Passes a user's credentials over the network as clear text. Although this mechanism is not very secure, it has the advantage of being able to work through a firewall or a proxy server.
- **Microsoft Windows NT Challenge/Response Authentication** (called Integrated Windows Authentication in Windows 2000): A secure authentication method that does not actually pass the user's credentials over the network but uses a cryptographic exchange instead. The only Web browser that supports this authentication method is Microsoft Internet Explorer. This method cannot work through a firewall or a proxy server.
- **Certificate mapping:** Uses the Secure Sockets Layer (SSL) protocol to authenticate users by examining the contents of their client certificate in order to log them on to the network without requiring them to enter their credentials.

Client certificates provide verification of identity, but certificate mapping associates a user's account with the user's client certificate and permits the user to log on to the network. The user typically utilizes a Web browser with SSL protocol to connect to a secure company Web site. The company Web server checks the Web browser's client certificate. If the certificate is valid, the user is automatically logged on using his or her user account without ever having to enter credentials and can access whatever intranet resources for which the account has permissions.

IIS allows two kinds of client certificate mappings:

- One-to-one mappings between user accounts and client certificates on the user's browser. This type of mapping is typically used to allow users secure access to corporate intranet resources—for example, to view or modify their employee information.
- Many-to-one mappings can map several client certificates to a single user account. Many-to-one mappings have the advantage of permitting administrators to allow multiple certificates to be used to grant users access to the corporate intranet utilizing a single Windows account. For example, you can set a rule that maps all certificates issued by the CA of an agency that provides your company with temps to a single Windows account.

Notes

Certificate mapping is also supported by Active Directory directory service in Microsoft Windows 2000, Windows XP, and Windows .NET Server operating systems. You can use the Active Directory Users and Computers administrative tool for this purpose.

See Also: *digital certificate*

certificate request

A file containing an entity's identification information and public key that is submitted to a certificate authority (CA) in order to obtain a digital certificate.

Overview

A certificate request is a text file encoded using Base64 encoding. This text file is generated by an application in response to the entity's request for a key pair and digital certificate. The entity here refers to the individual, system, company, or organization requesting the certificate. The certificate request is then submitted to a CA to obtain a digital certificate for the entity.

The Key Manager utility in Internet Services Manager (the utility used to manage Microsoft Internet Information Services) can be used to generate a key pair and a standard public key cryptography standards (PKCS) #10 format certificate request file. The certificate request file is a simple text file that can be viewed with Microsoft Notepad. If this file is submitted to a public certificate authority, such as VeriSign, or to the company's own certificate authority, such as Microsoft Certificate Server, a standard X.509 format digital certificate will be granted in return.

See Also: *digital certificate, public key infrastructure (PKI)*

certificate revocation list (CRL)

A list, maintained by a certificate authority (CA), of digital certificates that have been issued and later revoked.

Overview

A certificate revocation list (CRL) is similar to lists of revoked credit card numbers that credit card companies used to give to vendors. The certificate authority makes the CRL publicly available so that users can determine the validity of any digital certificate presented to them.

Creating and maintaining a CRL is an essential ingredient in running a public key infrastructure (PKI) to support public key cryptography systems. Microsoft Certificate Server includes a Web-based utility called the Certificate Administration Log Utility that can be used to revoke certificates and maintain a CRL.

See Also: *digital certificate, public key infrastructure (PKI)*

Certified Technical Education Center (CTEC)

An education-delivery company, such as a school or training center, that is qualified by Microsoft Corporation for the delivery of Microsoft Official Curriculum (MOC) courseware.

Overview

Certified Technical Education Centers (CTECs) are one of Microsoft's main channels for training on Microsoft products and technologies. CTECs can deliver training in a variety of forms, including instructor-led, self-paced, customized, and online training. CTECs are one of the ways that Microsoft contributes to solutions addressing the shortage of skilled IT professionals worldwide.

Network professionals who want to become familiar with Microsoft operating systems, applications, and development platforms can take MOC courses offered by CTECs at various locations around the world. Microsoft CTECs are also a source for the best in self-paced training materials on Microsoft products and services.

For More Information

Visit the Microsoft CTEC site at *www.microsoft.com/ctec*.

See Also: *Authorized Academic Training Provider (AATP)*

CGI

Stands for Common Gateway Interface, a mechanism by which a Web browser can request a Web server to execute an application.

See: *Common Gateway Interface (CGI)*

Challenge Handshake Authentication Protocol (CHAP)

A standard form of challenge/response authentication protocol.

Overview

Challenge Handshake Authentication Protocol (CHAP) is a standard authentication protocol defined in RFC 1994. CHAP is one of several authentication schemes used by the Point-to-Point Protocol (PPP), a serial transmission protocol for wide area network (WAN) connections. Other authentication schemes supported by PPP include Password Authentication Protocol (PAP), Shiva Password Authentication Protocol (SPAP), and

C

Microsoft Challenge Handshake Authentication Protocol (MS-CHAP). PAP is a widely implemented authentication protocol, but CHAP is more secure than PAP because CHAP encrypts the transmitted password and PAP does not. SPAP and MS-CHAP are vendor-specific implementations.

CHAP is an encrypted authentication scheme in which the unencrypted password is not transmitted over the network. A typical CHAP session during the PPP authentication process works something like this:

- The client connects to a network access server (NAS) and requests authentication.
- The server challenges the client by sending a session ID and an arbitrary string.
- The client uses the MD5 one-way hashing algorithm and sends the server the username, along with an encrypted form of the server's challenge, session ID, and client password.
- A session is established between the client and the server.

To guard against replay attacks, the challenge string is chosen arbitrarily for each authentication attempt. To protect against remote client impersonation, CHAP sends repeated, random interval challenges to the client to maintain the session.

Notes

CHAP is supported by the Routing and Remote Access (RRAS) service of Windows 2000 and Windows .NET Server as a way to allow non-Microsoft clients to dial in and receive authentication for a Remote Access Server (RAS) session, and to allow Microsoft RAS clients to connect to any industry-standard PPP server.

With Cisco routers, CHAP repeatedly challenges the connecting host every two minutes after the connection is established. This helps to prevent session hijacking by hackers on the network.

See Also: *authentication provider, challenge/response, Microsoft Challenge Handshake Authentication Protocol (MS-CHAP), Password Authentication Protocol (PAP), Point-to-Point Protocol (PPP)*

challenge/response

A mechanism for securely authenticating users over a network.

Overview

Challenge/response provides a way of employing user credentials to negotiate a connection over a network without actually passing these credentials over the network. Challenge/response forms the basis of the Integrated Windows authentication method supported by Internet Information Services (IIS) on Microsoft Windows 2000, Windows XP, and Windows .NET Server (Integrated Windows authentication was previously called Windows NT Challenge/Response authentication in Internet Information Server [IIS] on Windows NT).

Implementation

The basic steps of challenge/response are straightforward and independent of the actual platform they are implemented on. Here are the steps in a typical challenge/response authentication session:

- The client contacts the server to access a resource on the server.
- The server requests the client to authenticate itself and sends the "challenge," a randomly generated string, to the client.
- The client hashes the challenge string together with the client's password using a predetermined hashing algorithm. The result of this hash is called the "response."
- The client sends the response to the server, together with the client's name.
- The server meanwhile has performed the identical hashing operation as the client has, using the client's credentials, which are securely stored ahead of time in the server's security database.
- When the server receives the client's hash, it compares this with its own hash. If the hashes are identical, the client's identity is authenticated and the client is allowed to access the desired resource.

See Also: *authentication protocol, hashing algorithm, Integrated Windows Authentication*

Change and Configuration Management

A set of features in Microsoft Windows 2000, Windows XP, and Windows .NET Server for managing user settings and installing applications.

Overview

Change and Configuration Management is included in Windows 2000, Windows XP, and Windows .NET Server to provide support for tasks such as

- Installing initial operating systems on new computers
- Managing deployment of software on computers
- Managing user desktop configuration settings and user personal folders

Change and Configuration Management is an umbrella term for two underlying Microsoft technologies that make these things possible. These two technologies are

- **Intellimirror:** Enables management of user preferences, user documents, and software installation and maintenance.
- **Remote Operating System (OS) Installation:** Uses Remote Installation Services (RIS) to install Windows 2000, Windows XP, and Windows .NET Server on remote machines.

See Also: *IntelliMirror*

channel (Active Channel)

The delivery method in Active Channel, a technology for Microsoft Internet Explorer that allows Web content to be "webcast" to users.

Overview

Channels deliver content to users' Web browsers. The content is displayed as ordinary Web pages and can be viewed off line. Channels are delivered to users by way of Microsoft Corporation's Channel Definition Format (CDF) technology. Channels can contain Hypertext Markup Language (HTML); Microsoft ActiveX controls; Microsoft Visual Basic, Scripting Edition (VBScript); Java applets; and other dynamic Web elements. The channels that a user has subscribed to are listed as part of his or her channel bar.

See Also: *Channel Definition Format (CDF)*

channel bank

A telecommunications device that consolidates multiple Digital Signal Zero (DS0) channels into a larger single digital transmission.

Overview

Channel banks usually combine 24 different voice and data 64 kilobits per second (Kbps) DS0 channels into a single 1.544 megabits per second (Mbps) DS1 channel, though some channel banks are capable of combining up to 96 DS0 channels into a 6.312 Mbps DS2 channel. The channel bank combines the individual DS0 signals using a technique called multiplexing, which allows multiple signals to be combined for transmission over a single line. The resulting multiplexed digital signal can then be sent over a T1 line to the telco.

A channel bank interfaces with the wires of the local loop connection that carry the phone signals from the customer premises to the telco's central office (CO). In a typical business scenario, the channel bank would be connected to the front end of an analog Private Branch Exchange (PBX) to support multiple telephones within the company. The channel bank also includes circuits for converting the analog voice signals into digital data signals, usually using pulse code modulation (PCM). The resulting modulated digital signal conforms to the standard 64-Kbps DS0 format. The digital signals can then be routed through the digital switching backbone of the Public Switched Telephone Network (PSTN) as necessary.

Channel banks are typically located at the telco's CO and support the digital switching functions of the PSTN. However, channel bank equipment can also be installed at customer premises for larger enterprises.

Notes

Channel banks are becoming obsolete as older analog PBXs are being replaced by digital PBXs. When a digital PBX is used, the PBX can be connected directly to

C

the T1 line using a Channel Service Unit (CSU), making a channel bank unnecessary.

See Also: Channel Service Unit (CSU), DS-0, multiplexer (MUX), Private Branch Exchange (PBX), pulse code modulation (PCM), T1

channel bar

A component of Microsoft Internet Explorer version 4 and later that displays the available user-subscribed Active Channels.

Overview

Active Channels provide a way of webcasting information to subscribers using Microsoft Corporation's Channel Definition Format (CDF) technology. When Internet Explorer is first installed on a user's machine, a selection of preloaded channels is stored in the channel bar according to the country or region preference the user specified during installation. These channels are stored by default in C:\Windows\Favorites\Channels on a computer running Microsoft Windows 95 or Windows 98 and in C:\Winnt\Profiles\<user>\Favorites\Channels on a computer running Windows NT, Windows 2000, Windows XP, or Windows .NET Server. When a user subscribes to a channel, a small red gleam appears next to the icon representing the channel. This gleam indicates that new content has been downloaded and is available for browsing.

Notes

Administrators who plan to deliver and install Internet Explorer on users' machines can use the Internet Explorer Administration Kit (IEAK) to customize the users' set of startup channels. Administrators can thus use the channel bar to deliver important information to users through the company's intranet site.

See Also: Channel Definition Format (CDF)

Channel Definition Format (CDF)

An open standard created by Microsoft Corporation for Microsoft Internet Explorer version 4 (and proposed as a standard to the World Wide Web Consortium [W3C]) that defines a "smart pull" technology for webcasting information to users' desktops.

Overview

Based on the Extensible Markup Language (XML), Channel Definition Format (CDF) lets administrators create Active Channels for delivery of content through the user's Web browser and Active Desktop elements and channel screen savers for delivery directly to the user's desktop. Channel content can be personalized, and delivery can be scheduled according to users' needs and preferences. Using CDF also reduces server load and allows delivery of just the needed content, instead of requiring users to download large quantities of unnecessary content.

Consider the delivery of Web content to the user's browser using Active Channels. A Web site can be made into an Active Channel through the addition of a CDF file, a simple text file formatted using XML. It forms a kind of table of contents of the logical subset of the Web site that comprises the Active Channel. A link is then created to the CDF file on the Web site. The user clicks the link to subscribe to the Active Channel and download the CDF file. The Active Channel then appears on the channel bar on the user's desktop. The content for the channel is downloaded to a cache on the user's system. Channel updates are accomplished by scheduled Web crawls, using either the publisher's predefined schedule or a user's customized one. Users can also receive updates to channels by e-mail.

Some of the advantages of using CDF for the distribution of Web information to users include

- **Simplicity:** Turning an existing Web site into a channel merely involves creating a CDF file with a text editor and creating a hyperlink to this file.
- **Structure:** CDF describes how to logically group information in a hierarchical structure, independent of the content format.
- **Personalization:** Standard Hypertext Transfer Protocol (HTTP) cookies can be used to deliver personalized information to users.
- **Administrator control:** The administrator can control how much of the site can be downloaded by users.

- **User control:** The user can use CDF to specify which portions of a site to download to his or her browser, instead of pulling a lot of content off the site and hoping that it contains the needed information.

Notes

CDF is not true webcasting in the sense of Internet Protocol (IP) multicasting because it is a "pull" technology. True webcasting is supported by Microsoft Windows Media Player for delivery of content using IP multicasting.

channel (Microsoft Windows Media Player)

In Microsoft Windows Media Player, a mechanism that supplies clients with information needed to receive and render Advanced Streaming Format (ASF) streams.

Overview

A Windows Media Player channel specifies the multicast address and port number the clients should listen to in order to receive the stream. The channel also specifies the data types and formats in the stream, enabling the client to correctly render the stream. Windows Media Player saves channel information as files with the extension .nsc. A Windows Media Player channel is analogous to a television channel or a radio frequency: if a Windows Media Player client is tuned to a channel at the right time, the client receives streaming information sent by the Windows Media Player server.

Windows Media Player channels also support additional features, such as

- **Roll over to unicast:** If clients cannot receive a multicast, you can configure the channel so that they automatically receive a unicast of the same program.
- **Stream distribution:** On corporate Transmission Control Protocol/Internet Protocol (TCP/IP) networks whose routers do not support multicasting, one Windows Media Player server can distribute a stream to other Windows Media Player servers that are each located on separate local area network (LAN) segments. These secondary servers can then multicast to clients on their own LAN segment.

Channel Service Unit (CSU)

A device that is used to connect a synchronous digital telecommunications line to a computer network.

Overview

Channel Service Units (CSUs) are used to link local area networks (LANs) into a wide area network (WAN) using telecommunications carrier services such as Digital Data Services (DDS), T-carrier services such as a T1 line, and frame relay links.

The function of a CSU is to terminate the carrier's digital line at the customer premises. It also provides signal amplification and allows the carrier to perform remote loopback testing to monitor and troubleshoot the integrity of the line. Some CSUs also support Simple Network Management Protocol (SNMP) features that allow the unit to be monitored by the service provider.

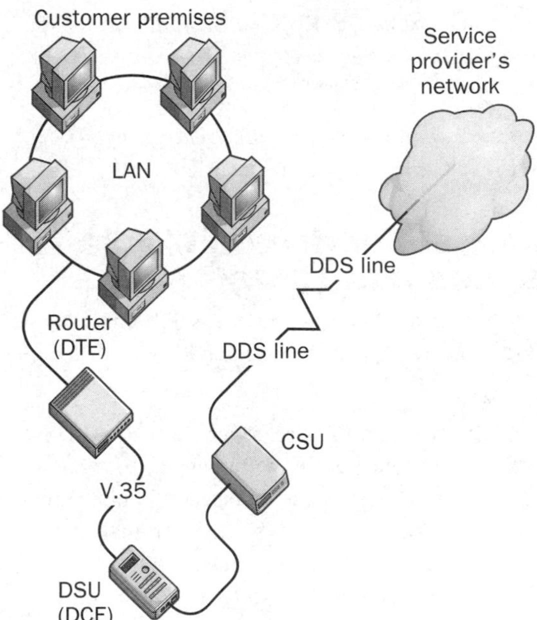

Channel Service Unit (CSU). *Using a CSU in a WAN link.*

CSUs are always used together with Data Service Units (DSUs), which convert signals from data terminal equipment (DTE) such as a router, switch, multiplexer (MUX), or dedicated server on the LAN to a signaling format suitable for transmission over the line.

C

Implementation

The service provider interface of the CSU terminates at the telco's digital line where it enters the customer premises. The other interface of the CSU then connects to a DSU, and then the DSU connects with data terminal equipment (DTE) on the LAN (a router, switch, or other LAN device). The DTE is typically an RS-232 or a V.35 serial transmission interface.

Typically, the telecommunications service provider will lease the CSU to the customer, having preconfigured it for the type of digital line to be supported. CSUs usually come in a dual Channel Service Unit/Data Service Unit (CSU/DSU) package that drops into the edge of the network to provide WAN link connectivity. Dedicated stand-alone CSUs are typically used only for interfacing with installed customer premises telecommunications equipment that contains integrated DSUs. This installed equipment could be a channel bank, Private Branch Exchange (PBX), T1 multiplexer, or some other device. Some access routers have built-in CSU/DSUs as well.

See Also: *Channel Service Unit/Data Service Unit (CSU/DSU), Data Service Unit (DSU)*

Channel Service Unit/Data Service Unit (CSU/DSU)

A device that combines the functions of both a Channel Service Unit (CSU) and a Data Service Unit (DSU).

Overview

Channel Service Unit/Data Service Units (CSU/DSUs) are placed between the telephone company network and the customer network at the demarcation point and are the local interfaces between the data terminal equipment (DTE) at the customer premises and the telco's digital communications line (such as a T1 line).

CSU/DSUs package digital data into a format suitable for the particular digital transmission line they are servicing and buffer and rate-adapt digital signals going to and from the telephone company network. CSU/DSUs ensure that data frames are properly formed and timed for the telephone company network and provide a protective barrier to electrical disturbances that can harm customer premises equipment (CPE).

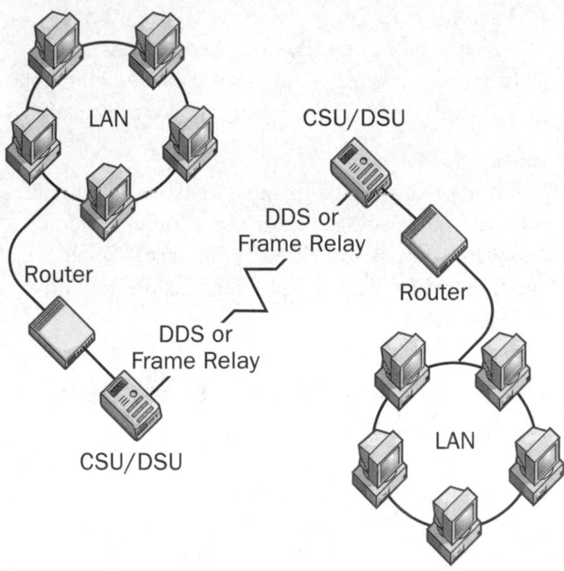

Channel Service Unit/Data Service Unit (CSU/DSU). *Using a CSU/DSU to connect two local area networks (LANs) over a wide area network (WAN) link*

Implementation

CSU/DSUs essentially function as the digital counterpart to analog modems. They are typically external units that look similar to an external modem, but they can also come in sizes that can be mounted in a rack. Unlike analog modems, CSU/DSUs do not perform signal conversion because the signal at both ends is already digital.

Digital lines usually terminate at customer premises with four-wire connections having various connector types, including RJ-45, four-screw terminal blocks, and M-block connectors (used for V.35 interfaces). The four-wire connection is joined to the appropriate connector on the CSU/DSU. The CSU/DSU typically adjusts itself to the line speed of the digital data service (DDS) line using an autosensing feature. The customer's CSU/DSU then connects directly to the customer's router and from there connects to the customer's network.

At the other end of the DDS line at the central office (CO), the telco has a similar CSU that interfaces with a multiplexer to feed into the carrier's backbone network.

Notes

When purchasing CSU/DSUs, consider first the traffic requirements of your wide area network (WAN) link and make sure they support the full range of data rates for the DDS lines you plan to use (56 K, 64 K, or T1 speed).

See Also: *Channel Service Unit (CSU), Data Service Unit (DSU)*

CHAP

Stands for Challenge Handshake Authentication Protocol, a standard form of challenge/response authentication protocol.

See: *Challenge Handshake Authentication Protocol (CHAP)*

child domain

A domain in a Microsoft Windows 2000 or Windows .NET Server domain tree whose Domain Name System (DNS) name is a subdomain of the parent domain.

Overview

As an example, if the name of the parent or company domain is microsoft.com, some typical names of child domains might include dev.microsoft.com, marketing.microsoft.com, and support.microsoft.com.

You can create new child domains using the Active Directory Installation Wizard. You must create a child domain in an existing domain tree, because creating a new tree automatically creates a new parent domain. A two-way transitive trust exists between a parent domain and its child domains.

See Also: *Active Directory, domain tree*

CICS

Stands for Customer Information Control System, the multipurpose transaction monitor for IBM mainframe computing environments.

See: *Customer Information Control System (CICS)*

CIDR

Stands for classless interdomain routing, an alternative way of classifying Internet Protocol (IP) addresses from the traditional class A-E system. Also called supernetting.

See: *classless interdomain routing (CIDR)*

CIFS

Stands for Common Internet File System, a public version of the Server Message Block (SMB) file-sharing protocol that has been tuned for use over the Internet.

See: *Common Internet File System (CIFS)*

CIM

Stands for Common Information Model, a schema for defining manageable network objects.

See: *Common Information Model (CIM)*

CIM Object Manager (CIMOM)

Part of the Microsoft Windows Management Information (WMI) architecture.

Overview

CIM Object Manager (CIMOM) functions as a broker for object requests within the WMI architecture. CIMOM supplies the required interfaces between management applications (WMI consumers) and a managed physical or logical network object (WMI providers).

CIMOM abstracts management information from a variety of different providers, including the Win32 programming interfaces for Windows applications and the Simple Network Management Protocol (SNMP) for managed network devices. CIMOM then employs the WMI application programming interface (API) to present the gathered information in a consistent fashion to the network management application.

A network management application can register with CIMOM in order to receive notifications when specific network events occur, such as a full disk or a saturated network path. If such a condition arises, the WMI provider for the managed device or application sends a notification to CIMOM, which notifies the registered management application of the condition.

See Also: *Common Information Model (CIM), Windows Management Instrumentation (WMI)*

CIMOM

Stands for CIM Object Manager, part of the Microsoft Windows Management Information (WMI) architecture.

See: *CIM Object Manager (CIMOM)*

CIP

Stands for Classical IP, a method for running Internet Protocol (IP) packets over Asynchronous Transfer Mode (ATM) networks.

See: *Classical IP (CIP)*

CIR

Stands for Committed Information Rate, a way of guaranteeing bandwidth in frame relay services.

See: *Committed Information Rate (CIR)*

circuit

A path between two points over which an electrical signal can pass.

Overview

In telecommunications, a circuit is a path over which voice, data, or other analog or digital signals can pass. A physical circuit is a collection of wires or cables that are connected with switches or other devices; it can be thought of as a straight line between the two endpoints.

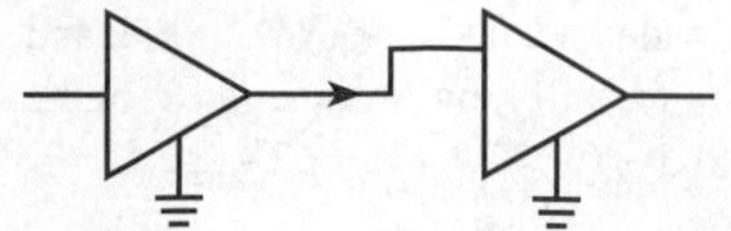

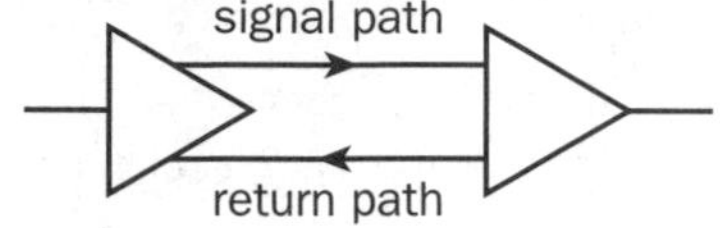

Circuit. *Two basic types of circuits.*

For an electrical signal to actually flow between two points in a circuit, the circuit must be closed—that is, there must be a return path for the current. Two basic types of circuits are used in serial transmission for telecommunications technologies:

- Balanced circuits, such as those based on the RS-422 interface, use a separate signal path and return path, with two separate wires.
- Unbalanced circuits, such as those based on the RS-232 interface, use a single signal path, adding ground to complete the circuit.

Balanced circuits typically support higher data transmission rates because the are less susceptible to noise caused by electromagnetic interference (EMI) than unbalanced circuits.

Notes

A typical serial interface such as RS-232 includes specifications for a number of different types of circuits, including data circuits, control circuits, timing circuits, secondary circuits, and ground connections.

See Also: *circuit-switched services, virtual circuit*

circuit layer proxy

Any service or server that provides proxy services using a specially installed component on the client computer to form a circuit between the proxy server and the client computer.

Overview

Microsoft Proxy Server is a product that combines firewall and proxy server functions and has two services for providing circuit-level proxy functions:

- **Winsock Proxy Service:** This enables Microsoft Windows Sockets clients such as Microsoft Windows Media Player, RealAudio, and Internet Relay Chat (IRC) to function as if they are directly connected to the Internet. The Winsock Proxy Service provides Windows NT Challenge/Response Authentication with clients, regardless of whether the clients support it, and supports Windows Sockets version 1.1–compatible applications on computers running Windows. The Winsock Proxy Service can control access by port number, protocol, and user or group. Ports can be enabled or disabled for specific users or groups, and the list of users that can initiate outbound connections on a given port can differ from the list of users that can listen for inbound connections on that port.
- **SOCKS Proxy Service:** This includes support for the SOCKS 4.3a protocol. The SOCKS Proxy Service provides support for Macintosh-based and UNIX-based client computers, while the Winsock Proxy Service supports only Windows-based computers. SOCKS uses Transmission Control Protocol (TCP) and can be used to control access to the Telnet, File Transfer Protocol (FTP), Gopher, and Hypertext Transfer Protocol (HTTP) protocols. The SOCKS Proxy Service does not support RealAudio, streaming video, or Windows Media Player clients.

Notes

Circuit layer proxies support a wider variety of protocols than application layer proxies.

See Also: *application layer proxy*

circuit-level gateway

A type of firewall that provides session-level control over network traffic.

Overview

Similar in operation to packet filtering routers, circuit-level gateways operate at a higher layer of the Open Systems Interconnection (OSI) reference model protocol stack. Circuit-level gateways are host-based and reside on individual clients and servers inside the network, rather than on a dedicated machine as they do with other types of firewalls. Circuit-level gateways examine incoming Internet Protocol (IP) packets at the session level—Transmission Control Protocol (TCP) or User Datagram Protocol (UDP)—and act as relays by handing off incoming packets to other hosts. Circuit-level gateways are rarely used as a stand-alone firewall solution; instead, they are typically used in combination with application layer proxy services and packet filtering features in dedicated firewall applications.

Microsoft Proxy Server combines the features of packet filtering, circuit-level gateways, and application layer proxy to provide a full firewall solution for protecting your corporate network. Proxy Server supports both the SOCKS protocol, which provides nontransparent circuit-level gateway security, and the Winsock Proxy, which provides transparent circuit-level gateway security.

See Also: *firewall, proxy server*

circuit-switched services

A term describing any telecommunications service that provides switched connections between a telco and their customers.

Overview

Circuit switching is the oldest form of digital communications used by telecommunications carriers. Circuit-switched telecommunications services can be provided to businesses by both local telcos and long-distance carriers. The Public Switched Telephone Network

C

(PSTN) is the classic example of a circuit-switched service (even its earlier analog form as the Plain Old Telephone System [POTS], it was also circuit-switched in operation). Another common example, often used for wide area network (WAN) connectivity between companies and remote branch offices, is Integrated Services Digital Network (ISDN).

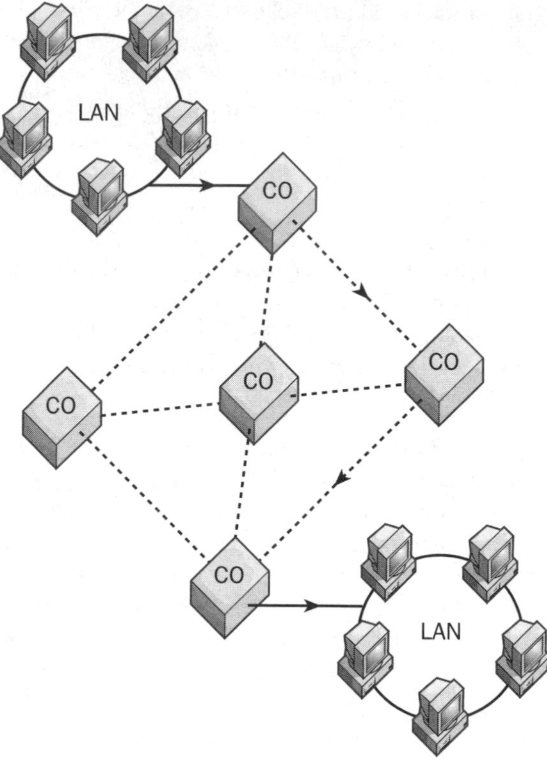

Circuit-switched services. *How typical circuit-switched services work.*

Circuit-switched services are generally more suitable than packet-switched services for real-time transport of delay-sensitive traffic such as voice and video. This is because, after the circuit has been set up for a given connection, traffic is routed with minimal delay to its destination. Circuit-switched services offer guaranteed delivery and differentiated services that are only beginning to be offered by packet-switched services such as Ethernet that carry best-effort Internet Protocol (IP) traffic.

Uses

In the enterprise, circuit-switched services are often used as backup lines for more expensive leased lines. For example, if your more expensive T1 line fails, you can switch to a dial-up ISDN line (if it comes from a different provider). When using circuit-switched services, it is a good idea to monitor their usage because when a certain usage level is reached, leased lines may become economically preferable. Leased lines such as T1 lines use dedicated switches that are set up in a permanent configuration for as long as the customer leases the services.

Implementation

With circuit-switched services, a new switched circuit must be established each time one local area network (LAN) attempts to connect to a remote LAN. Circuit-switched services are temporary circuits only, and when the connection is terminated the circuits are torn down. Different switches can be used for each connection established, depending on availability and traffic, so the quality of services can vary between connections.

Typically, your corporate LAN is connected to these services through bridges, routers, modems, terminal adapters, or other equipment, depending on the type of service being offered. At the other end of the connection is the telco central office (CO), which sets up switches on demand to connect you to your remote branch office LAN. When you disconnect theWAN link, the switches are freed up for other purposes.

Advantages and Disadvantages

One advantage of circuit-switched services is that they are generally less expensive than leased lines. This is because switches are not dedicated to your network as leased lines are, and can therefore be used for other purposes when you are not using them. The cost for circuit-switched services is usually based on usage.

Another advantage of circuit-switched services is that you are not restricted to a single destination as you are with leased lines; you can dial up any destination that supports services similar to yours.

A disadvantage with circuit-switched services is that they are usually dial-up in nature, and a dial-up connection takes time to be established. This connection time varies with the technology used. For example, analog modems might take 10 to 20 seconds to establish a connection, and an ISDN terminal adapter might take only 1 to 2 seconds. This latency interval tends to make circuit-switched lines unsuitable for dedicated services, such as those used for connecting company Web servers to the Internet.

Another disadvantage of circuit-switched services is that the quality can differ substantially between connections, because each circuit is a temporary connection that can exist along different paths, switches, and communication devices.

See Also: *Integrated Services Digital Network (ISDN), leased line, Multiprotocol Label Switching (MPLS), packet-switching services, T1*

circular logging

A feature of Microsoft Exchange Server whereby transaction logs can be overwritten when full. Circular logging lowers disk space usage but reduces the chances of successfully recovering from a system crash.

Overview

Exchange Server databases, such as the directory database and information store, maintain special log files called transaction log files. These log files improve the performance and fault tolerance of the databases, and help track and maintain changes made to them. Transactions are immediately written both to the log files and to memory, and only afterward to the database files. Transaction logs are normally kept on a different drive from the database files to ensure fault tolerance in case of a disaster that causes data loss, such as a crashed disk or a power failure.

When circular logging is enabled, only a few transaction log files are maintained, and these are overwritten when they become full. This prevents log files from continually building up, which saves disk space. However, circular logging has the disadvantage of allowing you to perform only full backups, rather than incremental or differential ones, because you can restore information only up to the last full backup.

Notes

Do not use circular logging if data recoverability is of high importance to your mail system, which is almost always the case with e-mail. Circular logging is enabled by default. You should always disable it and ensure that you have enough free disk space to hold the transaction files. The only reasons you might want to enable circular logging would be if you run low on disk space or if your server is being used for noncritical data only, such as a public news server.

class

More precisely called "object class," a logical grouping of objects within Active Directory directory service in Microsoft Windows 2000 and Windows .NET Server.

Overview

Objects are organized within Active Directory by their classes. Examples of object classes can include users, groups, computers, domains, and organizational units (OUs). Each class of objects has its own defining properties or attributes, as laid out in the Active Directory schema. Grouping objects logically into classes makes it easier to find and access these resources on the network.

Active Directory comes with predefined object classes. You can create additional classes or modify existing ones using the Active Directory schema.

See Also: *Active Directory, object (Active Directory)*

Class A

A type of Internet Protocol (IP) network where the first octet of IP addresses ranges between 0 and 126 inclusive.

Overview

Class A networks were originally intended for very large internetworks. Using the default class A subnet mask of 255.0.0.0, each class A network can support a maximum of 16,777,214 individual hosts with unique IP addresses—large enough for the largest of enterprise networks. However, there are no longer any Class A networks available since all 125 of them were assigned

C

in the 1980s to large corporate customers, organizations, and the military. None of these organizations actually has networks large enough to require the full 16 million host addresses provided by their Class A addresses, so classless interdomain routing (CIDR) was developed by the Internet Engineering Task Force (IETF) to allow unused Class A addresses to be reassigned to other users.

Notes

For a huge private network not directly connected to the Internet or hidden behind a firewall using Network Address Translation (NAT), the Internet Assigned Numbers Authority (IANA) recommends using Class A addresses whose first octet is 10. This provides millions of possible host addresses ranging from 10.0.0.1 to 10.255.255.254.

The Class A address 127.0.0.1 is reserved for loopback and represents the local host being used.

See Also: *Class B, Class C, Class D, Class E, classful domain, classless domain, classless interdomain routing (CIDR), IP address*

Class B

A type of Internet Protocol (IP) network where the first octet of IP addresses ranges between 128 and 191 inclusive.

Overview

Class B networks were originally intended for large internetworks. Using the default Class B subnet mask of 255.255.0.0, each Class B network can support up to 65,534 individual hosts with unique IP addresses—large enough for the largest of enterprise networks. There are 65,536 possible Class B networks that can be assigned, and in the early days of internetworking a number of these network IDs were assigned to large corporations and to the military by the Internet Assigned Numbers Authority (IANA). Today it is virtually impossible to obtain a class B network ID.

Notes

For a large private network not directly connected to the Internet or hidden behind a firewall using Network Address Translation (NAT), IANA recommends using Class B addresses whose first two octets range from 172.16 to 172.31. This provides many thousands of host addresses ranging from 172.16.0.1 through 172.31.255.254 and up to 16 different subnets if required.

See Also: *Class A, Class C, Class D, Class E, classful domain, classless domain, IP address*

class-based queuing (CBQ)

An emerging technology for wide area network (WAN) traffic management.

Overview

Traditionally, WAN traffic for different classes of service (CoS) have been managed using router-based schemes that provide best-effort control of bandwidth allocation. For example, a router might be configured to allow no more than 20 percent of available bandwidth for streaming video. Such a bandwidth allocation is relative (percentage) rather than absolute (bps) in nature, which does not give much granularity for control of traffic, particularly mission-critical network traffic.

Class-based queuing (CBQ) is an emerging technology for WAN access routers that allows network managers to classify traffic types into a hierarchy of classes and then assign absolute bandwidth allocations to each type. For example, CBQ could first be used to divide traffic types according to different kinds of business applications and then to create a second level classifying traffic according to the department using the application. The customer relationship management (CRM) software used by the marketing department could then be assured a given minimum bandwidth.

Implementation

CBQ operates at Level 2 (the network layer) for IP traffic and works with any IP protocol including Transmission Control Protocol (TCP), User Datagram Protocol (UDP), or Internet Control Message Protocol (ICMP). To implement CBQ in a corporate WAN setting, a CBQ-capable access router would be inserted at the WAN edge of each corporate local area network (LAN) and configured with suitable classes to control allocation of bandwidth for WAN traffic. CBQ classes are implemented on routers by using policies.

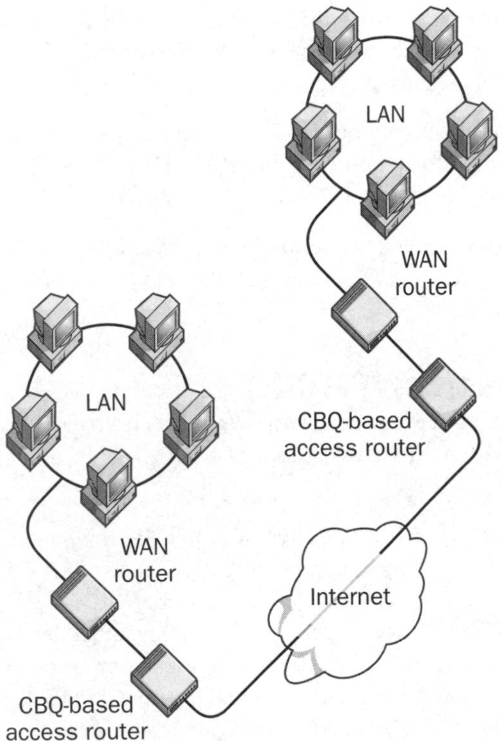

Class-based queuing (CBQ). *Implementing CBQ on a WAN.*

See Also: *wide area network (WAN)*

Class C

A type of Internet Protocol (IP) network where the first octet of IP addresses ranges between 192 and 223 inclusive.

Overview

Class C networks were originally intended for small internetworks. Using the default Class C subnet mask of 255.255.255.0, each Class C network can support up to 254 individual hosts with unique IP addresses. There are 16,777,216 possible Class C networks that can be assigned, and it is relatively easy to obtain a Class C network ID from your Internet Service Provider (ISP) should your company require it.

Notes

For a small private network not directly connected to the Internet or hidden behind a firewall using Network Address Translation (NAT), the Internet Assigned Numbers Authority (IANA) recommends using Class C addresses whose first three octets range from 192.168.0 through 192.168.255. This provides thousands of host addresses ranging from 192.168.0.1 through 192.168.255.254 and up to 256 different subnets if required.

See Also: *Class A, Class C, Class D, Class E, classful domain, classless domain, IP address*

Class D

A type of Internet Protocol (IP) network where the first octet of IP addresses ranges between 224 and 239 inclusive.

Overview

Class D addresses are used exclusively for multicasting purposes. Most Class D addresses whose first octet is 224 are reserved for special purposes, as shown in the table. For multicasting within a private network not directly connected to the Internet or hidden behind a firewall using Network Address Translation (NAT), the Internet Assigned Numbers Authority (IANA) recommends using Class D addresses whose first octet is 239. For multicasting over the Internet you must first obtain a multicast address from IANA.

Examples of Some Reserved Class D Addresses with First Octet 224.

Address	*Reserved for*
224.0.0.1	Multicasting to all hosts on the local subnet
224.0.0.2	Multicasting to all routers on the local subnet
224.0.0.4	Multicasting to all Distance Vector Multicast Routing Protocol (DVMRP) routers
224.0.0.5	Multicasting to all Multicast Open Shortest Path First (MOSPF) routers
224.0.0.9	Multicasting to all Routing Internet Protocol version 2 (RIPv2) routers
224.0.0.10	Multicasting to all Interior Gateway Routing Protocol (IGRP) routers
224.0.18.255	Dow Jones multicasting service

See Also: *Class A, Class B, Class C, Class E, classful domain, classless domain, IP address*

C

Class E

A type of Internet Protocol (IP) network where the first octet of IP addresses ranges between 240 and 255 inclusive.

Overview

Class E addresses are reserved for research and experimental purposes, and are not used in ordinary computer networking. Class E addresses have a first octet that ranges from 240 to 255. The only Class E address commonly used is 255.255.255.255, which represents a local area network (LAN) broadcast.

See Also: *Class A, Class B, Class C, Class D, classful domain, classless domain, IP address*

classful domain

An Internet Protocol (IP) network that uses a default subnet mask.

Overview

A classful domain is an IP network that contains only the single default subnet. All hosts on the network are therefore in the same broadcast domain. For example, a network that is using a Class A address such as 10.0.0.0 and the default subnet mask 255.0.0.0 is a classful domain. The same would be true of a network using a Class B address such as 172.11.0.0 with subnet mask 255.255.0.0 and a network using a Class C address such as 192.16.33.0 with subnet mask 255.255.255.0—all three of these are examples of classful domains and are networks with only one subnet and therefore one broadcast domain.

Generally speaking, classful domains are not the way to go as they are very busy places with respect to traffic and may be susceptible to broadcast storms. Large networks are thus subnetted into a group of subnets forming what is called a classless domain.

See Also: *classless domain, IP address, subnetting*

classful routing protocol

A routing protocol for classful networks.

Overview

Classful routing protocols require that all Internet Protocol (IP) addresses on a network have the same subnet mask. For example, if a Class B network ID of 172.24.0.0 is subnetted into several subnets such as 172.24.1.0, 172.24.2.0, and 172.24.3.0, then classful routing requires that all these subnets have the same subnet mask. The reason for this limitation is that when routers using classful routing protocols exchange routing table updates with one another, the subnet mask is not included in the updates.

Examples of common classful routing protocols include Routing Information Protocol (RIP) versions 1 and 2, and Interior Gateway Routing Protocol (IGRP).

See Also: *Interior Gateway Routing Protocol (IGRP), routing, Routing Information Protocol (RIP), routing protocol*

Classical IP (CIP)

A method for running Internet Protocol (IP) over Asynchronous Transfer Mode (ATM).

Overview

Classical IP (CIP) is an alternative to LAN Emulation (LANE) as a way of transporting IP packets over Asynchronous Transfer Mode (ATM) networks. CIP is based on RFC 1577 and supports only IP and no other network protocols (LANE can also be used to transport multiprotocol traffic such as IP and Internetwork Packet Exchange [IPX] over ATM). CIP has a number of benefits that make it an attractive solution in many situations:

- CIP is fast—speeds of 25 megabits per second (Mbps), 155 Mbps, 625Mbps, and 2.4 gigabits per second (Gbps) are supported, making it competitive with Fast Ethernet and Gigabit Ethernet (GbE) as a network transport.
- CIP is a circuit-switched technology that provides full bandwidth to each station on the network.
- CIP is simpler to implement, manage, and troubleshoot than LANE and utilizes fewer ATM resources (virtual circuits).
- CIP utilizes bandwidth effectively by eliminating broadcast traffic (as described later).

Implementation

CIP groups IP hosts together into groupings called logical IP subnets (LISs). Each LIS has an Address

Resolution Protocol (ARP) server to support IP broadcasts. Because broadcasts are essential to IP for the operation of the ARP, CIP implements a device called an ARP server to eliminate the need for these broadcasts. This is necessary because ATM in itself does not support broadcasts. When an IP host appears on a CIP network, it first registers itself with the ARP server so that IP communications can take place.

When an IP host needs to communicate with a target host on the network, it passes the IP address of the target host to the ARP server in the LIS, which returns the ATM address of the target host. To make this possible, the ARP server must be preconfigured with mappings of the IP and ATM addresses of each IP host in the LIS. When the host knows the target host's ATM address, a switched virtual circuit (SVC) can be established between the two hosts and IP packets can be transmitted to the target host.

An alternative implementation of CIP is called CIP over PVC (permanent virtual circuit). This is used primarily for wide area network (WAN) connections that are always on.

See Also: *Asynchronous Transfer Mode (ATM), LAN Emulation (LANE)*

Classic desktop

A way of displaying the desktop and its contents that was first used in Microsoft Windows 95.

Overview

The Classic desktop presents users with a graphical user interface (GUI) that allows icons, shortcuts, files, and folders to be placed on it. These desktop items provide a simple way for users to launch and access frequently used programs and network resources. The Start menu provides another tool for launching programs and accessing resources. The taskbar displays the programs currently running and the Windows-to-network resources that are open.

The choice of GUI for users' client computers can make a big difference in employee productivity. The following are two factors involved in determining whether network administrators should maintain the Classic desktop or upgrade to the newer Active Desktop included with Microsoft Internet Explorer beginning with version 4:

- The cost of introducing users to the new desktop paradigm
- The necessity for tight integration among the desktop, the corporate network, and the Internet

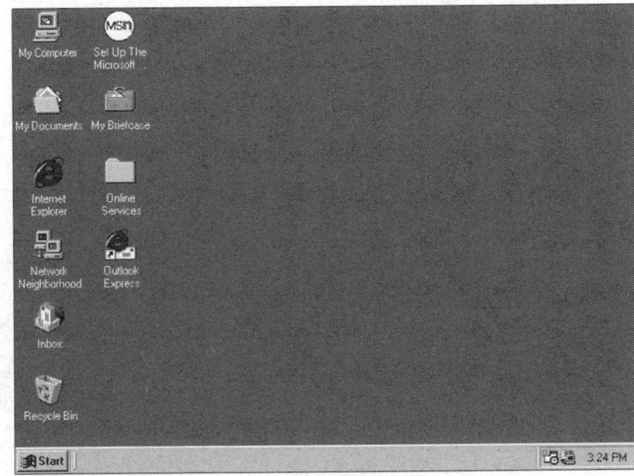

Classic desktop. *The Classic desktop, first used in Windows 95.*

classless domain

An Internet Protocol (IP) network that uses a variable-bit subnet mask.

Overview

A classful domain is an IP network that uses a default subnet mask such as 255.0.0.0 for Class A networks, 255.255.0.0 for Class B, or 255.255.255.0 for Class C. Classful domains thus have only one subnet and one broadcast domain. By contrast, a classless domain is an IP network that uses a variable-bit subnet mask (VBSM), also called a classless subnet mask, to divide the network into two or more subnets, each of which represents a different broadcast domain.

Classless domains are generally built using routers. Each subnet within a classless domain constitutes a unique broadcast domain and collision domain, which generally improves performance over using a single broadcast and collision domain. Switches operate at the

C

data-link layer and can partition a network into different collision domains, but they do not create different broadcast domains.

See Also: *classful domain, IP address, subnetting*

classless interdomain routing (CIDR)

Also called supernetting, an alternative way of classifying Internet Protocol (IP) addresses from the traditional Class A-E system.

Overview

Classless interdomain routing (CIDR) is a more efficient routing mechanism than the original method of segregating network IP addresses into classes named Class A, B, and C. The trouble with the old system is that it leaves too many unused IP addresses. For example, while Class A networks support large numbers of network nodes, there are not enough Class A networks to go around and none of the owners of these networks make anywhere near full use of the large number of IP addresses available to them. As a result, large numbers of Class A (and Class B) IP addresses go unused, and CIDR was developed as a way of reclaiming those IP addresses for allocation elsewhere. Similarly, while many Class C network IDs are available, many companies require more than the 254 IP addresses available on a Class C network, but not nearly as many as the 65,534 IP addresses available on any Class B network.

History

In the late 1980s, prescient architects of the Internet foresaw that the standard Class A-E method for assigning IP addresses would eventually fail and that the routing tables used by the core routers of the Internet's backbones would eventually grow unmanageably large. The class system provides for a huge number of IP addresses, but for only about 2 million different IP networks. As the number of networks attached to the Internet grew exponentially, a time was anticipated when there would be no more network numbers left to assign for new Class B and C networks (all Class A networks were assigned early on).

In the early 1990s the Internet Engineering Task Force (IETF) produced a group of Requests for Comments (RFCs), namely RFCs 1517 to 1520, that brought a way out of the dilemma. These RFCs formed the basis of CIDR and provided a way of not only reducing the growing load on the Internet's core routing tables (another result of the Internet's rapid growth) but also of reusing unused IP addresses to make about 8 million additional IP networks of Class C size available for assignment to other companies and organizations.

Uses

CIDR is used primarily by routers and gateways on the backbone of the Internet for routing packets across the Internet. CIDR is not used much in private networks because most networks are hidden behind firewalls and can use any arbitrary block of IP addresses, such as the 10.*x.y.z* block allocated by Internet Network Information Center (InterNIC) for general, private use. Instead, CIDR comes into its own on the Internet backbone to facilitate routing and ensure the continued functioning of the Internet. However, CIDR is viewed only as a workaround to the issues of insufficient numbers of IP networks available for allocation and maintaining the routing tables of backbone routers at workable sizes. Most Internet architects see IPv6 as the real solution to these issues and expect the need to change over to this system of addressing in the next few years.

Implementation

CIDR replaces the old class method of allocating 8, 16, or 24 bits to the network ID, and instead allows any number of contiguous bits in the IP address to be allocated as the network ID. For example, if a company needs a few thousand IP addresses for its network, it can allocate 11 or 12 bits of the address for the network ID instead of 8 bits for a Class C (which would not work because you would need to use several Class C networks) or 16 bits for Class B (which is wasteful).

CIDR assigns a numerical prefix to each IP address. For example, a typical destination IP address using CIDR might be 177.67.5.44/13 (the last part being pronounced "slash thirteen"). The suffix /13 indicates that the first 13 bits of the IP address identify the network, while the remaining 32–13 = 19 bits identify the host. In subnetting notation, the CIDR address 177.67.5.44/13 would be equivalent to the combination of IP address 177.67.5.44 and subnet mask 255.255.128.0 (see the following table). As another example, in CIDR notation an old style class B network 132.16.0.0 with default subnet mask 255.255.0.0 would be represented simply as 132.16/16.

The prefix helps to identify the Internet destination gateway or group of gateways to which the packet will be forwarded. Prefixes vary in size, with longer prefixes indicating more specific destinations. Routers use the longest possible prefix in their routing tables when determining how to forward each packet. CIDR enables packets to be sent to groups of networks instead of to individual networks, which considerably simplifies the complex routing tables of the Internet's backbone routers. The table shows the different CIDR values and their subnet mask equivalents.

CIDR Values and Their Subnet Mask Equivalents

Class	*CIDR Value*	*Subnet Mask*
Class A	/8	255.0.0.0
	/9	255.128.0.0
	/10	255.192.0.0
	/11	255.224.0.0
	/12	255.240.0.0
	/13	255.248.0.0
	/14	255.252.0.0
	/15	255.254.0.0
	/16	255.255.0.0
Class B	/17	255.255.128.0
	/18	255.255.192.0
	/19	255.255.224.0
	/20	255.255.240.0
	/21	255.255.248.0
	/22	255.255.252.0
	/23	255.255.254.0
	/24	255.255.255.0
Class C	/25	255.255.255.128
	/26	255.255.255.192
	/27	255.255.255.224
	/28	255.255.255.240
	/29	255.255.255.248
	/30	255.255.255.252
	/31	255.255.255.254
	/32	255.255.255.255

Notes

There might seem to be an alternate solution for avoiding the waste of IP addresses from Class A and Class B networks. Consider, for example, a company with a network of 5,000 nodes. Assigning a single Class B network ID such as 166.33.0.0 to the network would provide 65,534 possible IP addresses for hosts, which is far too many—60,534 addresses would remain unused. A solution to this might seem to be assigning the company a contiguous set of 20 Class C network IDs. Because each Class C address provides 254 possible host addresses, 20 contiguous Class C network Ids, such as 198.15.1.0 through 198.15.20.0, would provide 20 x 254 = 5080 possible IP addresses, which is just right, plus a few to spare.

Using this technique does eliminate the wasting of IP addresses, but it creates a new problem: to handle routing between your corporate network and the Internet, you need to add 20 new entries to the routing tables on Internet routers, one entry for each network ID you are using. Following this method quickly overwhelms the routers that form the Internet's backbone because as their routing tables grow their performance slows down. CIDR was devised to address this very issue by decreasing the number of entries required in the Internet's routing tables. CIDR does this by supernetting the 20 Class C networks above into a single supernet, which needs only one entry in the routing tables.

See Also: *Internet, IP address, IPv6, routing*

classless routing protocol

A routing protocol for classless networks.

Overview

Classless routing protocols allow different portions of an Internet Protocol (IP) network to use different subnet masks for the same network ID. Then, when routers using classless routing protocols exchange routing table updates with one another, the subnet mask is included in each update. Thus, given a single IP network ID, variable length subnet masking (VLSM) may be used to create different subnets having different subnet masks. Classless routing protocols also help conserve network resources by using route summarization.

C

Examples of common classless routing protocols include Border Gateway Protocol (BGP), Enhanced Interior Gateway Routing Protocol (EIGRP), and Open Shortest Path First (OSPF).

See Also: *Border Gateway Protocol (BGP), Enhanced Interior Gateway Routing Protocol (EIGRP), Open Shortest Path First (OSPF), routing, routing protocol*

CLB

Stands for Component Load Balancing, a Microsoft clustering technology supported by Microsoft Windows 2000 Server and Windows .NET Server and provided by Microsoft Application Center 2000.

See: *Component Load Balancing (CLB)*

cleartext

The process of sending data over a network in an unencrypted form.

Overview

By using a packet sniffer or software such as Network Monitor, anyone who can capture cleartext packets can read the information within them. Cleartext authentication methods are sometimes the best choice in a heterogeneous network environment where users running different operating system platforms need to access resources on network servers. For example, UNIX clients that need to access a Microsoft Internet Information Services (IIS) machine using a Web browser will need to be authenticated using a cleartext method called Basic Authentication.

Notes

Basic Authentication is usually described as cleartext authentication, but in actuality Basic Authentication weakly encrypts data using the well-known Uuencoding algorithm. This algorithm is in the public domain and can easily be decrypted by knowledgeable users.

The standard AppleTalk protocol uses clear-text authentication for allowing Apple Macintosh clients to access shared folders on Macintosh file servers using AppleShare.

See Also: *Basic authentication*

cleartext authentication

Also called Basic authentication, an authentication scheme that passes a user's credentials over a network in encrypted form.

See: *Basic authentication*

ClearType

A new display technology from Microsoft Corporation designed for liquid crystal display (LCD) displays.

Overview

Microsoft ClearType is intended to provide more readable displays on LCD screens for laptops, tablet PCs, and Pocket PCs. ClearType does this by a process known as sub-pixel rendering, which triples the perceived number of pixels for vertical screen resolution (horizontal resolution remains unchanged). The results are easier-to-read text that appears more like a page out of a book than text displayed on a screen. ClearType was designed with Microsoft Reader in mind, a technology developed by Microsoft for eBooks.

ClearType technology was developed by Microsoft Research, but a similar subpixel rendering concept was developed in the 1970s by Steve Gibson for the Apple II platform. ClearType support will be included in all future releases of Microsoft Windows and Microsoft Office.

For More Information

You can find out more about ClearType at *research.microsoft.com.*

CLEC

Stands for Competitive Local Exchange Carrier, a telco that competes with existing incumbent telcos under the terms of the Telecommunications Act of 1996.

See: *Competitive Local Exchange Carrier (CLEC)*

client

A workstation or computer, usually belonging to a single user, as opposed to a server, which is shared by many users.

Overview

Planning the hardware, software, configuration, deployment, and maintenance of clients is as important to the network administrator as the other server-related activities.

Choice of a client operating system depends on various considerations. For example, in determining whether to install Microsoft Windows Millennium Edition (Me), Windows 2000 Professional, or Windows XP Professional on client computers, users should consider the following:

- Both client operating systems, in conjunction with Microsoft Internet Explorer versions 5 and later, offer the same desktop configuration options, similar utilities, and similar support for features such as user profiles, hardware profiles, and system policies.
- Windows 2000 Professional or Windows XP Professional will provide client machines with better performance, greater reliability, and more robust security, but they have higher hardware requirements than Windows Millennium Edition (Me).
- Windows Me supports a broader range of devices and legacy software applications, and includes power-management support—making it a better solution for mobile users.

Notes

In configuring clients to operate on a network, appropriate software must be installed on each client to allow it to access servers on the network. For example, to access Windows 2000 servers, client machines require Microsoft client software such as Client for Microsoft Networks. To access Novell NetWare servers, client machines require NetWare-compatible clients, such as Client for NetWare Networks.

See Also: *client/server, server*

client access license (CAL)

A license that grants a client machine access to a Microsoft BackOffice product running on a network of computers.

Overview

Every client computer on a network, regardless of whether it is running a Microsoft or non-Microsoft operating system, requires a client access license (CAL) if it will be accessing any of the following Microsoft Windows NT, Windows 2000, Windows XP, or Windows .NET Server services:

- File services, for accessing shared files and folders on a server
- Print services, for accessing shared network printers
- Remote Access Service (RAS) or Routing and Remote Access Service (RRAS)
- File and Print Services for NetWare (FPNW)
- File and Print Services for Macintosh (FSM)
- Microsoft Transaction Server (MTS) and Microsoft Message Queue (MSMQ) Server access
- Windows NT Terminal Server functionality

Client access licenses can operate in one of two modes:

- Per Server licensing, which is based on concurrency of access to network resources
- Per Seat licensing, which is the more commonly implemented solution and is supported by all BackOffice applications

See Also: *license*

client certificate

A digital certificate obtained for a client application (such as a Web browser) that can be used by the client to digitally sign data it transmits.

Overview

Client certificates can be used to enable client machine authentication for the purpose of secure communication over the Internet using the Secure Sockets Layer (SSL) protocol.

C

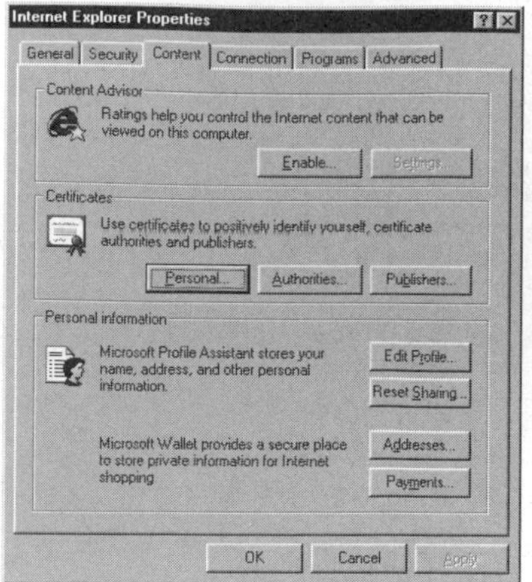

Client certificate. *Importing a client certificate in the Internet Explorer Properties dialog box.*

A client obtains a certificate from a certificate authority (CA) by submitting a certificate request file. The CA responds by issuing a client certificate, which contains the client's identification information in encrypted form, along with the client's public key. The client certificate must then be installed on the client's Web browser. Microsoft Internet Explorer can import client certificates into the browser's certificate store using the Personal button on the Content tab of the Internet Options dialog box. Administrators can also use the Internet Explorer Administration Kit (IEAK) for preconfiguring client certificates prior to installation on user computers.

In SSL communication, a Web server can validate the identity of a client using the certificate installed on the client. With Microsoft Internet Information Server (IIS) version 4, client certificates can be mapped to Microsoft Windows NT user accounts by way of a process called certificate mapping. (Windows 2000, Windows XP, and Windows .NET Server support a similar feature in their Internet Information Services.) Certificate mapping makes it easier for administrators to control access to content located on the Web server.

Notes

Use client certificates when it is important for servers to validate the identity of clients—for example, when your enterprise includes mobile users with laptops who need to remotely and securely access the company's intranet server using Internet Explorer.

See Also: *digital certificate, public key cryptography*

Client for Microsoft Networks

A networking component in Microsoft Windows 95, Windows 98, Windows Millennium Edition (Me), Windows 2000, Windows XP, and Windows .NET Server that makes it possible to access file and print services on all of the above versions of Windows, as well as Windows NT, Windows for Workgroups, and LAN Manager dedicated servers and peer servers.

Overview

Client for Microsoft Networks works with any combination of NetBEUI, IPX/SPX-Compatible Protocol, and Transmission Control Protocol/Internet Protocol (TCP/IP) protocols. Client for Microsoft Networks cannot be used for accessing non-Microsoft servers such as Novell NetWare servers. You must install Client for NetWare Networks to access these servers. Windows 95 and Windows 98 allow you to install more than one client at a time to access different kinds of servers on the network.

Use the Network utility in Control Panel to install Client for Microsoft Networks on a computer running Windows 95 or Windows 98. Then use the property sheet of Client for Microsoft Networks to configure the computer to either participate in a workgroup or log on to a Windows NT, Windows 2000, or Windows .NET Server domain.

Notes

In Windows NT, the equivalent component is called the Workstation service, but in Windows 2000, Windows XP, and Windows .NET Server, the component is Client for Microsoft Networks, as in Windows 95 and Windows 98.

Client for NetWare Networks

In Microsoft Windows 95, Windows 98, Windows Millennium Edition (Me), Windows 2000, Windows XP, and Windows .NET Server, a networking component that makes it possible to access file and print services on Novell NetWare servers.

C

Overview

Client for NetWare Networks requires that the IPX/SPX-Compatible Protocol be installed. Client for NetWare Networks cannot be used for accessing Microsoft servers such as Windows NT, Windows 2000, and Windows .NET Server. You must install Client for Microsoft Networks to access these servers. Windows 95 and Windows 98 allow you to install more than one client at a time to access different kinds of servers on the network.

Use the Network utility in Control Panel to install Client for NetWare Networks on a computer running Windows 95 or Windows 98. Then use the property sheet of Client for NetWare Networks to configure the preferred NetWare server, to select the first drive letter to use for mapping network drives from NetWare command-line utilities, and to enable processing of logon scripts on the preferred server.

Notes

Client for NetWare Networks can connect to NetWare 3 and earlier servers, or NetWare 4 servers running in bindery emulation mode. If you want to use Client for NetWare Networks to connect to a NetWare 4 server running Novell Directory Services (NDS), you must also install Service for NetWare Directory Services on the Windows 95 or Windows 98 client. This service is available with Windows 95 OSR2 or Service Pack 1 for Windows 95, and is included with Windows 98.

Before installing Client for NetWare Networks on a computer running Windows 95 or Windows 98, make sure you remove any real-mode NetWare requestor software running on the machine, such as NETX (the NetWare 3.*x* client shell) or VLM (the NetWare 4.*x* client shell).

client installation point

A shared directory on a network file server to which users on your network can connect to install client software locally on their client computers.

Overview

Creating a client installation is the first step in preparing to install software over the network. To create a client installation point, create a directory on a server and share the folder with full permissions for administrators and read-only permissions for ordinary users. Either copy the installation files for the software from the CD to the shared directory, or run the setup program using a special switch to copy the files so that they can be used for network installation—for example, to uncompress the cabinet files on the CD. Users can then connect to the shared directory, run the setup program, and complete the installation process.

client/server

A paradigm for deploying two-tiered distributed applications.

Overview

In the client/server model, an application is split into a front-end client component and a back-end server component. The front-end client part of the application runs on a workstation and receives data that is input by the user. The client component prepares the data for the server by preprocessing it in some fashion, and then sends the processed information to the server, usually in the form of a request for some service. The back-end server component receives the client's request, processes it, and returns information to the client. The client receives the information returned from the server and presents it to the user by way of its user interface. Usually most of the processing is done at the back end (server end) where database servers, messaging servers, file servers, and other resources are located.

An example of a simple client/server application is a Web application that is designed for Microsoft Internet Information Services (IIS) using a combination of server-side Active Server Pages (ASP) programming and client-side scripting. The ASP scripts run on the Web server, while the client-side scripts run on the client Web browser.

See Also: *distributed application*

C

Client Services for NetWare (CSNW)

A Microsoft Windows 2000, Windows XP, and Windows .NET Server service that provides Windows clients with access to Novell NetWare file, print, and directory services.

Overview

Client Services for NetWare (CSNW) is an optional service that can be installed on Windows 2000, Windows XP, and Windows .NET Server machines to enable them to directly connect to file and print resources on Novell NetWare servers. In other words, CSNW is a Microsoft version of the NetWare redirector for Windows 2000, Windows XP, and Windows .NET Server.

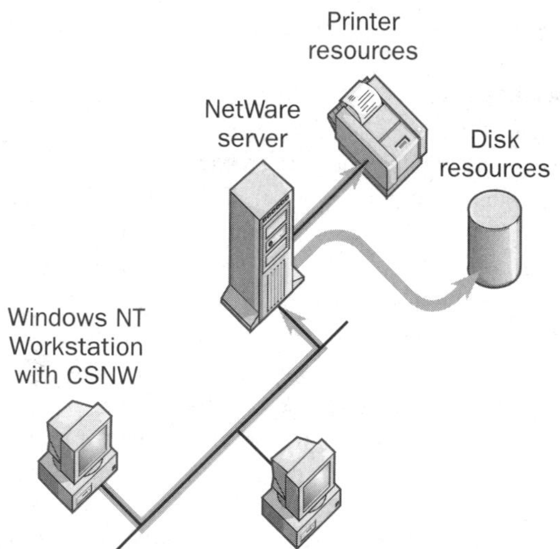

Client Services for NetWare (CSNW). *How CSNW works.*

CSNW is a full-featured, 32-bit client for NetWare networks that can be installed on Windows 2000 Professional or Windows XP Professional by using the Network and Dial-Up Connections utility in Control Panel. If you are connecting to a NetWare 3.12 or earlier server, you must specify a preferred NetWare server for access to its bindery. If you are connecting to NetWare 4, specify the Novell Directory Services (NDS) tree and default context. CSNW supports browsing NDS trees, but it does not support administration of NDS trees.

CSNW supports connections to servers running version 2, 3, or 4 of NetWare, including both bindery emulation and NDS on NetWare 4. CSNW includes support for NetWare Core Protocol (NCP), Large Internet Protocol (LIP), and Long filenames (LFNs). Additional options are included for printing and login script support. CSNW requires installation of the NWLink protocol, but if it is not installed already, it will be added automatically when you install CSNW on a machine.

Notes

On a machine running Windows 2000 Server, NetWare connectivity is provided by Gateway Services for NetWare (GSNW). Use CSNW to provide your Windows 2000 Professional or Windows XP Professional clients with dedicated access to Novell NetWare servers; use GSNW only to provide occasional access to NetWare servers from Windows 2000 Professional or Windows XP Professional clients.

An alternative to using CSNW on Windows 2000 Professional machines is to use the Novell Client for Windows 2000.

See Also: *bindery, Gateway Service for NetWare (GSNW), Novell Directory Services (NDS), NWLink*

cloud

In networking, any part of the network whose data transmission paths are unpredictable and vary from session to session.

Overview

Clouds are often used in networking diagrams to represent packet-switching services. In these services, a packet sent from one node to another follows an unpredictable path because, at any given moment, different routers or other devices can be used to forward the packet toward its destination. The Internet is an example of a packet-switching cloud for Transmission Control Protocol/Internet Protocol (TCP/IP) networking because data sent between two points can travel over many possible paths. This is why the Internet is graphically represented as a cloud in drawings of wide area networks (WANs). Other examples of packet-switching services include frame relay and X.25 networks.

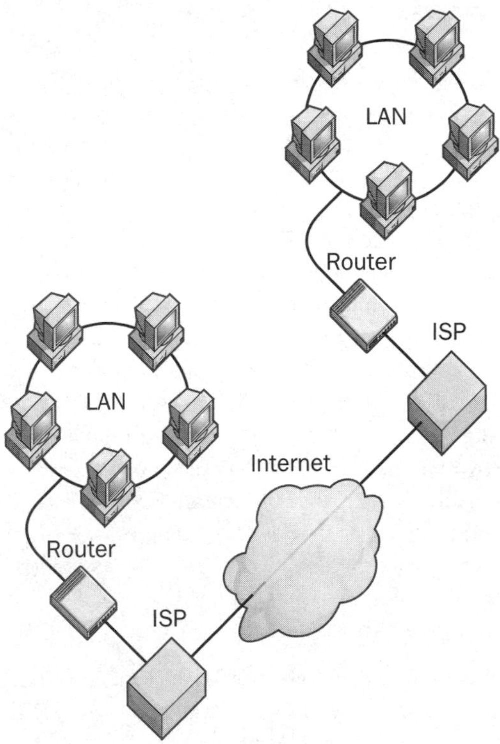

***Cloud.** The Internet depicted as a cloud of paths and connections.*

Circuit-switched services are often represented as clouds as well. In circuit-switched services, communication switches at various telco and carrier central offices (COs) and switching facilities are temporarily used for establishing circuits between two communicating nodes. Each time communication is terminated and reestablished, different sets of switches can be used.

***See Also:** telecommunications services*

cluster

A group of two or more nodes within a system supporting clustering.

Overview

When a client on a network tries to access shared resources or applications on a cluster, the cluster appears to the client as a single node or server instead of the group of nodes or servers it really is.

In the Cluster service of Microsoft Windows 2000 and Windows .NET Server Enterprise Server and Datacenter Server, each node in a cluster is a completely independent computer system that must be running Windows 2000 Enterprise Server. Typically, such nodes are connected by a shared storage bus such as an external Small Computer System Interface (SCSI) disk subsystem or RAID array.

***See Also:** clustering*

cluster-aware application

An application that can run on a node of a cluster and can be managed as a cluster resource.

Overview

In the Cluster service on Microsoft Windows 2000 or Windows .NET Server Enterprise Server and Datacenter Server editions, a cluster-aware application is one that can run on a node of a cluster and can be managed as a cluster resource. Cluster-aware applications can be written to access the Windows 2000, or Windows .NET Server Cluster service by using its cluster application programming interface (API). Cluster-aware applications also implement the extension dynamic-link libraries (DLLs) of Cluster Administrator, which allow them to be managed using Cluster Administrator. These features allow developers to write high-scalability applications that can operate across the different nodes in a cluster.

A cluster-aware application is one that is aware of the fact that it is running on a cluster and can make use of the scalability, load balancing, and failover aspects of clustering to provide high availability for mission-critical business environments. Cluster-aware applications include database applications such as Microsoft SQL Server, messaging applications such as Microsoft Exchange Server, and Web applications for running on Web servers such as Microsoft Internet Information Services (IIS).

***See Also:** clustering*

clustering

Any technology that enables two or more servers to appear to clients as a single system.

C

Overview

A cluster consists of a group of computers functioning together as a unit, running a common set of applications, and presenting a single image to client systems. Clustering can be implemented in various ways, but its basic goals are to provide businesses with high availability, high reliability, and high scalability solutions for mission critical business operations.

Clustering solutions generally come in two basic types:

- **Stateful clustering:** The goal of this type of clustering is to provide high availability and high reliability for fast, uninterrupted service in high-demand environments that can tolerate minimal downtime (stateful clustering is not designed to scale applications out to handle more users—this is the purpose of stateless clustering discussed next). Stateful clustering works by connecting independent computer systems into a single entity called a cluster, with each system within the cluster being called a node. Generally some multiple of two is used as the number of nodes within a cluster, for example, 2, 4, 8, 16, or 32 nodes. The different nodes within a cluster are usually connected using a shared disk subsystem which typically consists of a hard disk system or RAID-5 array connected to each node using a fast Small Computer System Interface (SCSI) bus or fiber channel connection. The result is a cluster of computer systems that acts and functions as if it were a single system. In stateful clustering, the nodes within a cluster generally share the workload, and when one node fails its workload fails over (transfers to) another node in the cluster with no interruption of services from the user's perspective. When the failed node comes back online, the workload fails back to this node and normal operation of the cluster resumes. Failover in stateful clustering systems can be implemented in different ways, and this is discussed below. An example of a platform supporting stateful clustering is the Cluster service of Microsoft Windows 2000 Enterprise Server and Datacenter Server. Another name for stateful clustering is shared storage or shared something clustering.
- **Stateless clustering:** The goal of this type of clustering is to provide high availability and high reliability by enabling administrators to scale out applications to meet increased demand as the number of users and traffic generated increase. Stateless clustering uses a group of nodes (servers) that are not connected in any way apart from the underlying network connectivity. No failover occurs between nodes when a node in the cluster fails. Instead, some form of load balancing is used to share the workload between the different nodes, and if one node fails the other nodes pick up the extra workload with no interruption of services. Stateless clustering is supported by three Microsoft products: Network Load Balancing (NLB), Component Load Balancing (CLB), and Application Center 2000. Another name for stateless clustering is shared-nothing clustering, and SQL Server 2000 supports a form of shared-nothing clustering known as Federated Server Groups.

Stateful clustering solutions themselves generally fall into three different categories, depending on if and how failover occurs between different nodes:

- **Active/active clustering:** This type of clustering makes the most efficient use of system resources because there are no redundant nodes: all nodes run active processes. If one node of a cluster fails, other nodes take on the failed cluster's workload. The latency for failover in this scenario is typically 15 to 150 seconds, depending on the hardware/software configuration. Active/active clustering is supported by the Cluster service of Microsoft Windows 2000 Enterprise Server and Datacenter Server, and by the Cluster service of Windows .NET Server (discussed later in this article).
- **Active/standby clustering:** Nodes are paired within a cluster, with one node designated to take over should another node fail. If an active node fails, a standby node assumes its workload. Latency for failover is also 15 to 150 seconds. Active/standby clustering is a more expensive solution than active/active because the standby node is essentially doing nothing unless the active node fails.

- **Fault-tolerant clustering:** Nodes are paired within a cluster, and all nodes perform all tasks simultaneously. This is an expensive solution from a hardware point of view, but latency for failover is reduced to a second or less.

Marketplace

Many different clustering solutions are in the marketplace, but this article focuses on four different clustering technologies delivered by Microsoft platforms and products, namely:

- Windows clustering, previously known as Microsoft Cluster Services (MCSC)
- Network Load Balancing (NLB)
- Application Center 2000
- Component Load Balancing (CLB)

You can find additional information in separate articles on each of these four solutions.

Windows clustering is a feature of Microsoft Windows 2000 Advanced Server and Datacenter Server and of Windows .NET Server. Windows clustering is probably Microsoft's best-known clustering platform and was originally developed for Microsoft Windows NT Server Enterprise Edition where it was code-named Wolfpack during its development. Windows clustering is a stateful clustering solution that enables system architects to create clusters from groups of independent computer systems and to run and manage cluster-aware applications. Using Windows clustering, you can build two-way clusters (that is, clusters with only two nodes) on Windows 2000 and Windows .NET Server Enterprise Server edition or four-way clusters on Windows 2000 and Windows .NET Server Datacenter Server edition (Windows NT Server Enterprise Edition supported only two-way clustering). In Windows clustering a cluster connects nodes together using a shared file system and clusters can utilize active/active clustering for maximum reliability and availability. Windows clustering makes an excellent choice for clustering database and messaging applications for enterprises.

Network Load Balancing (NLB) is a stateless clustering solution included with Windows 2000 and Windows .NET Server Enterprise Server and Datacenter Server editions, and it was formerly called Windows Load Balancing Services (WLBS) on the Windows NT Server 4 platform. NLB provides load balancing of Internet Protocol (IP) traffic to up to 32 independent network nodes (servers) and is typically used to build farms of Web servers or Exchange 2000 Outlook Web Access (OWA) servers for large enterprises. When one node in an NLB cluster goes down, the load is simply redistributed to the remaining nodes.

Application Center 2000 is a part of Microsoft Corporation's .NET Server family, and is a stateless clustering platform designed to provide a single point of management for farms of Web servers. Appcenter is typically used in conjunction with NLB and CLB to provide high availibity, high reliability clustering that can scale out to large numbers of users. Appcenter manages a collection of servers in a Web farm as a single entity and can be used to create new clusters, join servers to existing cluster, remove nodes from clusters, deploy applications and application components to different nodes within a cluster, move components between nodes of a cluster, monitor the performance of a cluster, and manage load balancing of network connections to cluster nodes and COM+ components within a cluster-aware application.

Component Load Balancing (CLB) is supported by all versions of Windows 2000 Server and is used to provide load balancing of COM+ objects across distributed applications deployed on up to 16 nodes (servers). CLB is a stateless clustering solution that requires no special hardware but needs Microsoft Application Center 2000 in order to operate.

See Also: *Application Center, cluster, cluster-aware application, Component Load Balancing (CLB)*

CMAK

Stands for Connection Manager Administration Kit, a wizard-based tool for creating custom connectivity solutions, and a component of Internet Connection Services for Microsoft Remote Access Service (RAS).

See: *Connection Manager Administration Kit (CMAK)*

C

CMP cabling

A grade of cabling that is resistant to combustion.

See Also: *plenum cabling*

CN

Stands for connected network; in Microsoft Message Queue (MSMQ) Server terminology, a name for a collection of computers in which any two computers can directly communicate.

See: *connected network (CN)*

CNAME record

Stands for Canonical Name record, a Domain Name System (DNS) resource record for assigning an alias to a host.

Overview

A CNAME record is used to map an alias to the canonical name (true name) of a host on the Internet or a private Internet Protocol (IP) internetwork. The CNAME record thus lets you use more than one name to refer to a single host on the network. If a name server is queried by a resolver to look up a host and the queried name is an alias in a CNAME record, the name server replaces the alias name with the canonical name of the host being looked up and then looks up the address of the canonical name.

Examples

Here is an address record for the host named server12 in the microsoft.com Internet domain. This record has the IP address 172.16.8.5, followed by a CNAME record indicating that the name bobby (or the fully qualified domain name bobby.microsoft.com) is an alias for the same host:

```
server12.microsoft.com  IN  A  172.16.8.55
bobby                   IN  CNAME  server12
```

Uses

CNAME records are generally used to hide the true names of important servers on your network from the outside world.

CNRP

Stands for Common Name Resolution Protocol, a proposed Internet Engineering Task Force (IETF) standard for a protocol to replace Uniform Resource Locators (URLs) with a simpler, more natural scheme for navigating the Web.

See: *Common Name Resolution Protocol (CNRP)*

CO

Stands for central office, a telco switching facility.

See: *central office (CO)*

coax

Short for coaxial cabling, a legacy form of network cabling.

See: *coaxial cabling*

coaxial cabling

A legacy form of network cabling.

Overview

Coaxial cabling (or simply coax) is a form of network cabling that was used in legacy 10Base2 and 10Base5 Ethernet networks. The name *coax* comes from its two-conductor construction in which the conductors run concentrically with each other along the axis of the cable. Coaxial cabling in local area networks (LANs) has been largely replaced by twisted-pair cabling (structured wiring installations) within buildings, and by fiber-optic cabling for high-speed network backbones.

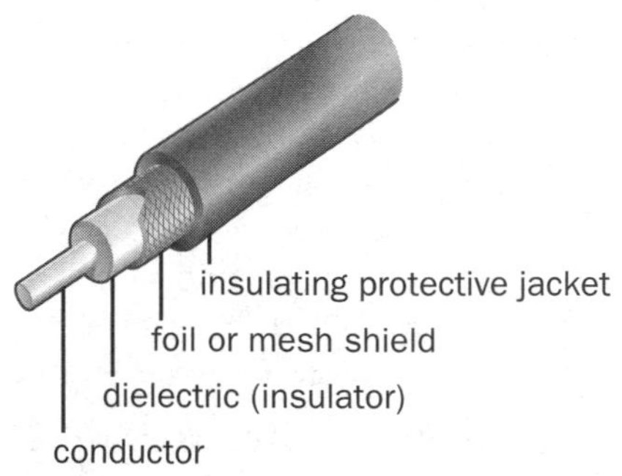

Coaxial cabling. *Typical coax cabling.*

Coaxial cabling generally consists of a solid copper core for carrying the signal, covered with successive layers of inner insulation, aluminum foil, a copper braided mesh, and outer protective insulation. A solid conductor provides better conductivity than a stranded one, but is less flexible and more difficult to install. The insulation is usually polyvinyl chloride (PVC) or a non-stick coating; the aluminum foil and copper mesh provide shielding for the inner copper core. The mesh also provides the point of grounding for the cable to complete the circuit.

Types

Coaxial cabling comes in various types and grades. The most common are the following:

- Thicknet cabling, which is an earlier form of cabling used for legacy 10Base5 Ethernet backbone installations. This cabling is generally yellow and is referred to as RG-8 or N-series cabling. Strictly speaking, only cabling labeled as IEEE 802.3 cabling is true thicknet cabling.
- Thinnet coaxial cabling, which is used in 10Base2 networks for small Ethernet installations. This grade of coaxial cabling is generally designated as RG-58A/U cabling, which has a stranded conductor and a 53-ohm impedance. This kind of cabling uses bayonet Neill-Concelman (BNC) connectors for connecting to other networking components, and must have terminators at free ends to prevent signal bounce.
- ARCNET cabling, which uses thin coaxial cabling called RG-62 cabling with an impedance of 93 ohms.
- RG-59 cabling, which is used for cable television (CATV) connections.

In addition, a number of special types of coaxial cabling are sometimes used for certain networking purposes. An example is twinax cabling, which consists of two conductors first enclosed in their own insulation and then enclosed in a single copper mesh and insulating jacket. Twinax is used in legacy IBM networks for connecting AS/400 systems to 5250 terminals. Other more exotic varieties include triax, quadrax, and ribbon types of coaxial cables.

Notes

Coaxial cabling is often used in heavy industrial environments where motors and generators produce a lot of electromagnetic interference (EMI), and where more expensive fiber-optic cabling is unnecessary because of the slow data rates needed. Coaxial cabling is also used frequently in IBM mainframe and minicomputer environments. A device called a splitter can be used to fork one coaxial cable into two—for example, when connecting two 3270 terminals to one IBM mainframe system. A splitter is used at either end of the connection so that the signals for both terminals can be sent over a single coaxial cable. Coax multiplexers can be used to connect eight or more terminals to a single controller.

See Also: *cabling, fiber-optic cabling, twinax cabling, twisted-pair cabling*

codec

Short for **co**mpressor/**dec**ompressor, an encoding algorithm used for recording digital audio or video.

Overview

A codec compresses transmitted data at the sending end and decompresses it at the receiving end. Microsoft Windows Media Player uses different codecs to provide streaming multimedia information over a Transmission Control Protocol/Internet Protocol (TCP/IP) network such as the Internet. Windows Media Player provides a number of different codecs for different purposes. You can select a codec to give you the audio or image quality and image size that you want for your transmission.

Code Division Multiple Access (CDMA)

A second-generation (2G) digital cellular phone technology popular in the United States and parts of Asia.

Overview

Code Division Multiple Access (CDMA) can be used to refer both to a type of digital cellular phone system and to the specific media access method used by this kind of cellular system. CDMA was developed by QUALCOMM in 1993, and it was adopted and ratified by the Telecommunications Industry Association (TIA) as part of their Interim Standard 95, specifically as TIA standard IS-95a.

CDMA supports combined voice and data over a single channel and supports circuit-switched data transmission at a rate of 14.4 kilobits per second (Kbps), although in practice speeds are more typically around 13 Kbps. Speeds up to 19.2 Kbps are also possible by using special error detection and correction techniques.

Architecture

CDMA uses the spread spectrum wireless networking technology—first developed for military communication systems in the 1940s because it spreads its transmission over a large bandwidth, making it difficult to jam. Instead of dividing the available radio spectrum into a series of discrete channels using the older Time Division Multiple Access (TDMA) media access method, a CDMA channel occupies the entire available frequency band. In other words, all CDMA users on a given network utilize the same frequency band.

What enables users to share the same spectrum is that CDMA assigns a special digital code sequence to each user. Users thus share time and frequency resources on the available bandwidth, and their individual communications are channeled using these codes. The code tag identifies the conversation to the transmission station and enables multiple users to simultaneously access the network and divide its frequency resources between them—hence the name Code-Division Multiple Access.

Without knowledge of a conversation's code tag, eavesdropping on CDMA conversations is difficult, making CDMA a more secure cellular phone technology than the Advanced Mobile Phone Service (AMPS) still used widely in the United States. CDMA also has a much higher call capacity than AMPS and is comparable to the Global System for Mobile Communications (GSM) standard for cellular communication used in Europe. The disadvantage is that CDMA is more complex to implement than TDMA digital cellular technologies.

Marketplace

The main CDMA-based system in the market today is QUALCOMM's cdmaOne, the operation of which is now supervised by the CDMA Development Group and independent organization. The cdmaOne system uses 64 different codes called Walsh sequences, and in theory thus supports up to 64 concurrent users talking over a single 1.25-megahertz (MHz)-wide channel. In practice, however, this works out to more like 20 concurrent users, especially when data transmissions are included. The cdmaOne system has approximately 30 million users in the United States and Asia, with its competitors being Global System for Mobile Communications (GSM), which has 150 million users worldwide; Digital Advanced Mobile Phone Service (D-AMPS), with 15 million users in the United States; and Personal Digital Cellular (PDC), with 45 million users in Japan.

A special upgrade to cdmaOne called IS-95b provides improved data speeds of up to 115 Kbps, though real speeds are usually more like 64 Kbps (the version of IS-95b in Japan and Korea supports packet-switched data rates of only 64 Kbps). Further proposed 2.5G and third-generation (3G) improvements fall under the umbrella name of CDMA2000, and the CDMA technology itself forms the basis of much of the proposed IMT-2000 standard for 3G cellular communications from the International Telecommunication Union (ITU).

Another cellular system in the United States based on CDMA technologies is Sprint PCS from Sprint Corporation, which operates at a higher frequency band than cdmaOne but uses CDMA as its media access control method.

Notes

CDMA does not assign specific frequencies to each user as do other competing systems. Instead, CDMA uses a unique technique where every channel uses the entire available spectrum. CDMA was developed and first used by the military during World War II by the English to thwart German attempts at jamming transmissions. The Allies utilized CDMA to transmit over different frequencies, instead of one, which made it extremely difficult for the Germans to pick up entire signals.

For More Information

You can find the CDMA Development Group at *www.cdg.org*. QUALCOMM is at *www.qualcomm.com*.

See Also: *2G, 2.5G, 3G, Advanced Mobile Phone Service (AMPS), CDMA2000, cellular communications, Global System for Mobile Communications (GSM), Time Division Multiple Access (TDMA)*

Coded Orthogonal Frequency Division Multiplexing (COFDM)

A technique for enhancing the speed of wireless networking.

Overview

Coded Orthogonal Frequency Division Multiplexing (COFDM) is employed by the 802.11a wireless networking standard as a way to work around the difficulty of radio frequency (RF) interference caused by scattering and reflection off of buildings, walls, and similar objects. The problem with wireless networking, as opposed to wireline (wired) networking, is that although wireline networks usually have a single path between different stations, wireless communication is often multipath. As the figure shows, a signal can travel between a wireless client and a base station along different paths due to reflection of RF signals off walls and other objects. The result is that when the signal arrives it is spread out in time. If the time over which a signal can be spread out by interference (the delay spread) is less than the time between individual packet transmissions (the symbol rate), then the receiver can still be processing one packet while the next one arrives, creating a problem.

COFDM works around this problem not only by slowing down the symbol rate (the rate of packet transmission) but also by cramming as much information as possible into each packet. COFDM thus transmits data in a massively parallel fashion, ensuring that each symbol can be processed in a time less than the delay spread between divergent signal paths. Each symbol transmitted is proceeded and followed by a cyclic prefix called a guard interval, which helps give the baseband processor time to receive and process the information. Additional error-correcting information is encoded to help reduce the effects of interference.

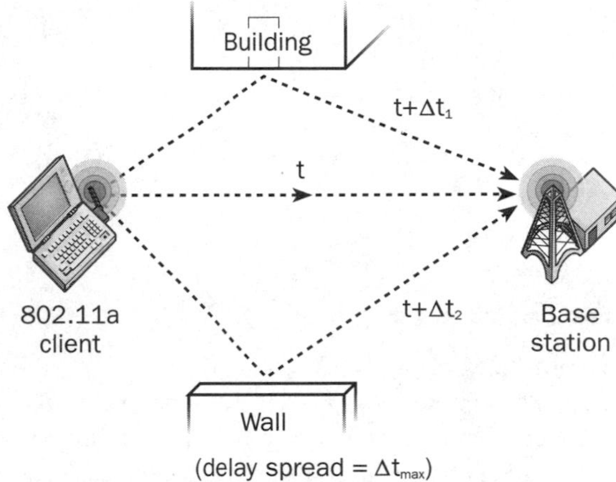

Coded Orthogonal Frequency Division Multiplexing (COFDM). *COFDM helps overcome the delay spread caused when signals are reflected off of interfering objects.*

Using COFDM, wireless networks based on 802.11a can break through their current speeds of 10 to 20 megabits per second (Mbps) to achieve speeds of 155 Mbps or even higher.

See Also: *802.11a, wireless networking*

code-operated switch

A switch with a combination of input and output ports, the connections between which can be remotely reconfigured by commands entered into a computer.

Overview

Code-operated switches are useful in environments where remote switching is needed for file-sharing or monitoring purposes. For example, you could use an RS-232 serial code-operated switch to remotely switch between pieces of data terminal equipment (DTE), such as servers or routers for running diagnostics from a remote console.

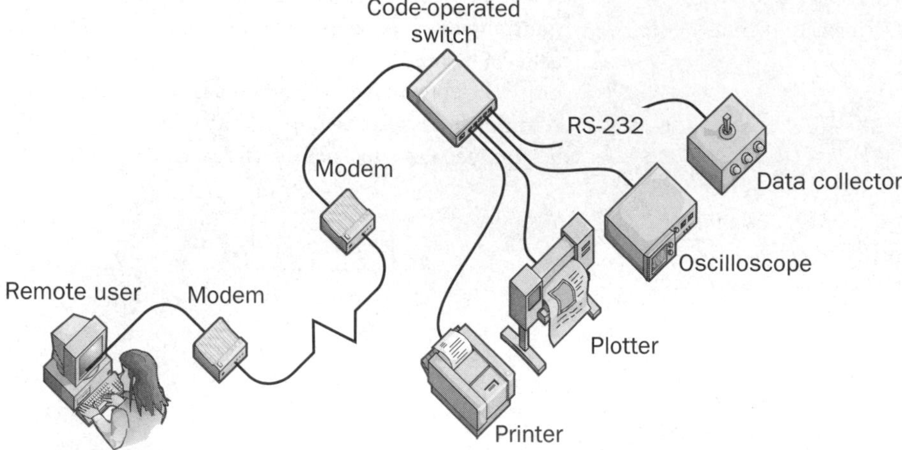

Code-operated switch.

Implementation

Internal dual inline package (DIP) switches are usually used to configure the code-operated switch so that a different arming character can be used to trigger each connected device. The code-operated switch then examines the incoming data stream for these special text-string codes in order to determine to which device it should route data. An example might be the remote switching between printers. A remote computer could send an embedded switching character to specify which printer connected to the code-operated switch should be used for printing the data.

A remote user can connect to the company network using a modem that interfaces with a code-operated switch, and then use the switch to control a variety of serial-controlled devices in an industrial environment, such as a group of laboratory instruments. Code-operated switches are available from different vendors in configurations supporting up to 64 different serial devices from one remote connection.

Besides embedding switching characters in the data stream, embedded control characters can also be used to directly control the code-operated switch.

See Also: *switch*

COFDM

Stands for Coded Orthogonal Frequency Division Multiplexing, a technique for enhancing the speed of wireless networking.

See: *Coded Orthogonal Frequency Division Multiplexing (COFDM)*

cold boot

Restarting the computer by turning the power switch off and then on, or by shutting down the computer, turning it off, and then turning it on again.

Overview

If you perform the first type of rebooting, open files will not be properly closed and data can be lost. However, this method ensures that memory is cleared and devices are properly reset. An example might be when you reconfigure the settings of a legacy modem using the modem utility in Control Panel. You might find that you must cold boot your machine in order for the new configuration settings to fully take effect.

See Also: *boot*

Cold Fusion

A popular tool for developing dynamic Web applications.

Overview

Cold Fusion from Allaire Corporation lets developers rapidly create and deploy dynamic Web applications that can access information from databases and other data sources. Cold Fusion uses a set of proprietary tags that are similar to Hypertext Markup Language (HTML) tags. The resemblance to HTML tags makes Cold Fusion a comfortable platform for experienced HTML users to develop database-driven applications that can be accessed from Web browsers. Cold Fusion is available for both UNIX and Microsoft Windows platforms, and it is an alternative to Microsoft Corporation's Active Server Pages (ASP) technology for developing dynamic Web applications.

For More Information

Find out more about Cold Fusion at *www.allaire.com.*

See Also: *Active Server Pages (ASP)*

Collaboration Data Objects (CDO)

A collection of Component Object Model (COM) objects that allow developers to create Microsoft Internet Information Services (IIS) Web applications that send and receive electronic mail.

Overview

Collaboration Data Objects (CDO) is a Microsoft object library that provides messaging capability for applications written in Microsoft Visual Basic, Microsoft Visual C++, and Win32 Virtual Machine for Java. CDO provides distributed Web applications with a standard way to quickly and easily create, send, post, receive, read, and manipulate messages using interfaces based on standard Internet protocols such as Simple Mail Transfer Protocol (SMTP), Network News Transfer Protocol (NNTP), and Multipurpose Internet Mail Extensions (MIME).

CDO was formerly known as Active Messaging, and on the Microsoft Windows NT platform was called Collaboration Data Objects for Windows NT Server (CDONTS). CDONTS actually provides a subset of CDO functionality that includes messaging services but omits the calendaring and workflow functions that CDO on Microsoft Exchange 2000 provides.

CDO 2 is included with IIS in Windows 2000, Windows XP, and Windows .NET Server to support the built-in SMTP and NNTP services. CDO 2 does not support mailboxes, but it does support protocol events to enable programmers to write routines that respond to incoming messages and process outgoing messages. Developing mail-enabled applications using CDO is easier and faster than building custom Common Gateway Interface (CGI) mail programs, and CDO applications have more flexibility than typical CGI applications.

CDO is also a powerful development tool for Exchange Server 2000 and is the premier application programming interface (API) for building collaborative solutions using Exchange. CDO in Exchange 2000 consists of three components:

- **CDO for Exchange 2000:** Used for building collaborative solutions that make use of e-mail, contact management, and scheduling.
- **CDO Workflow Objects for Exchange:** Used to build workflow and routing applications.
- **CDO for Exchange Management:** Used for creating and managing mailboxes and recipients.

Notes

For security reasons, scripts running on Microsoft Internet Explorer cannot access CDO.

See Also: *Exchange Server, Internet Information Services (IIS)*

collapsed backbone

An enterprise networking methodology in which the network backbone consists of a single device.

Overview

In a traditional network, local area networks (LANs) are multipoint connections connected using a backbone cable. For example, in a building, a fiber-optic backbone might run from floor to floor and connect with a hub in a wiring closet on each floor. In contrast, collapsed

C

backbones make use of centralized switches, which provide virtual point-to-point connections for LAN connections. These switches are located in the same place as the network servers—in fact it was the move toward centralized location of network servers that helped drive the development of collapsed backbones.

In a typical collapsed backbone scenario, instead of having a hub for each floor located in that floor's wiring closet, a set of stackable Ethernet switches would be located in the equipment room in the basement, with individual cables running from this closet through vertical rises to wiring closets on each floor where hubs distribute connections to stations in work areas.

Advantages and Disadvantages

The advantages of using a collapsed backbone are that they eliminate the costs of backbone cabling installation, they require fewer devices, their equipment administration is more centralized, and they offer higher available bandwidth for each station. The disadvantages are that collapsed backbones generally are not feasible for use in more than one building, they require more cabling, they use more expensive devices, and they have a more limited distance capability.

See Also: *backbone, network*

collision

A condition that occurs when two or more computers on a network try to transmit signals over the same wire at the same time.

Overview

Collisions are inevitable on a network as long as there is more than one computer on the network. Handling collisions is one of the main functions of a network access method. For example, in Ethernet networks, collisions often occur when two or more stations attempt to place frames on the wire at the same time. To handle this situation, Ethernet uses the access method called Carrier Sense Multiple Access with Collision Detection (CSMA/CD).

When a station begins transmitting a signal and detects a collision, the station stops transmitting and issues a jam signal to tell the other station that a collision has occurred. Both stations then stop transmitting and wait a random length of time before retransmitting their signals. The amount of time the stations wait before retransmitting increases with the number of collisions occurring on the network.

See Also: *Carrier Sense Multiple Access with Collision Detection (CSMA/CD), collision domain, Ethernet*

collision domain

An area of a network where signals transmitted by different stations with that area can collide.

Overview

In Carrier Sense Multiple Access with Collision Detection (CSMA/CD) networks such as Ethernet, a collision can occur if two computers on the network attempt to transmit signals at the same time. When a collision occurs, the network is momentarily offline and no computers can communicate on it.

The larger the collision domain of an Ethernet network, the more computers present and the higher the probability of collisions occurring and negatively affecting network performance. When collision domains become too large, so many collisions occur that network communications become possible. As a result, it is important to segment Ethernet networks to keep collision domains small enough that the effect of collisions is minimized on the network.

Segmenting a collision domain can be accomplished using bridges, switches, routers, and other devices. For example, if two Ethernet hubs are connected directly to a third hub, the resulting local area network (LAN) is still only a single collision domain because only hub connections are used between segments of the network. But if the two hubs are directly connected to an Ethernet switch, you have two collision domains because the switch enables the two networks to function independently. Routers also segment networks into broadcast domains to prevent the occurrence of broadcast storms.

See Also: *broadcast domain, broadcast storm, Carrier Sense Multiple Access with Collision Detection (CSMA/CD), collision, Ethernet*

COM

Stands for Component Object Model, an object-based software architecture developed by Microsoft Corporation that allows applications to be built from binary software components.

See: *Component Object Model (COM)*

COM+

An extension of Microsoft Corporation's Component Object Model (COM).

Overview

COM was originally designed for building component-based applications to run on single systems. Distributed COM (DCOM) was an evolution of COM that enabled COM components to reside on different machines and communicate with each other over the network. COM+ takes DCOM a step further by providing services and features that enable large, distributed, multitier applications to be built for enterprise-wide systems and the Internet.

COM+ is part of the Microsoft Windows Distributed Network Architecture (DNA) programming paradigm. The COM+ that is supported by the Microsoft Windows 2000, Windows XP, and Windows .NET Server operating system platforms is basically COM plus Microsoft Transaction Server (MTS) and Microsoft Message Queue Server (MSMQ), minus some legacy COM functionality no longer needed. Some of the enhancements of COM found in COM+ include the following:

- Dynamic load balancing, which distributes client requests across multiple equivalent COM components
- Registration of COM+ objects that is cached in memory to speed up the process of locating and instantiating components
- In-memory database (IMDB), which provides quicker data access to applications by lowering overhead
- Publish and subscribe services, which provide an event mechanism enabling multiple clients to subscribe to published events and send notification to subscribers when events are fired
- Integration of Microsoft Message Queue Server (MSMQ) to support queued asynchronous calls issued to COM components, which let clients invoke methods on COM components using an asynchronous model for increased reliability over poor network connections and in disconnected usage scenarios
- Integration of Microsoft Transaction Server (MTS) into COM, which supports attribute-based programming, improvements in transactions, security and administration services, and improved interoperability with other transaction environments through support for the Transaction Internet Protocol (TIP)
- Inclusion of basic COM services in the COM+ runtime to simplify and speed up application development.

See Also: *Component Object Model (COM), Distributed Component Object Model (DCOM)*

COM component object

A compiled software component based on Microsoft Corporation's Component Object Model (COM) technology.

Overview

COM components generally refer to the physical files that contain the classes that define COM objects. COM components also include additional code, such as code to register the component in the registry and code for loading the component.

COM components can be written in many languages using tools such as Microsoft Visual Basic, Microsoft Visual J++, Microsoft Visual C++, and Microsoft Visual FoxPro. COM components that support Automation can be called by scripting languages such as Microsoft Visual Basic, Scripting Edition (VBScript) or Microsoft JScript.

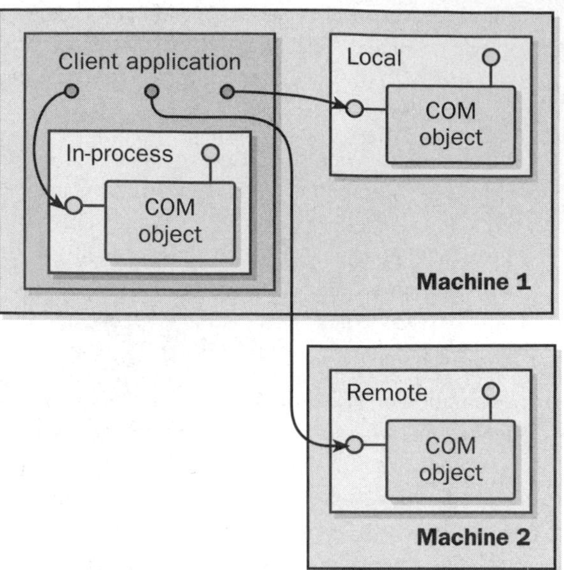

COM component object. *In-process, local, and remote COM components.*

COM components can be run on an application server, a Web server, a Microsoft Transaction Server (MTS), or a client. COM components can be stand-alone applications or reusable software components, and they make the development of Web applications comparable to the development of system applications.

COM components interact with each other and with user applications in a client/server fashion. The client therefore uses the functionality of the server component by creating instances of classes that the server component provides and calling their properties and methods.

COM components can be designed to run in three different modes:

- **In-process:** The component executes in the calling application's process space.
- **Local:** The component executes in its own process space.
- **Remote:** The component executes in a process space on another machine.

An in-process COM component has the extension .ocx or .dll, while an out-of-process COM component (one running outside the calling application process) has the extension .exe. COM components can run on another machine in a manner transparent to the calling application by using the Distributed Component Object Model (DCOM).

When developing applications based on COM components, use in-process components to optimize the speed of object access but use out-of-process components to maximize thread safety.

See Also: *Component Object Model (COM)*

command

A method by which actions can be performed on a computer running Microsoft Windows by typing text into a command prompt window. The commands that are available depend on which version of Windows is used.

Overview

Examples of commands common to most Windows platforms include the Attrib command, Cacls command, Copy command, Dir command, and Diskcopy command. In addition to these Windows commands, some special commands are available only when certain networking services or protocols are installed. For example, if Transmission Control Protocol/Internet Protocol (TCP/IP) is installed on a computer running Windows, a number of TCP/IP commands are available, including the Arp command, Ping, Tracert, and Nbtstat.

Commands are useful for administering different aspects of a system or network using a command-line interface, such as a telnet connection or a command prompt. Commands are also often used in writing batch files that can perform a group of operations on a system or network service. You can run such a batch file directly, or you can schedule its operation for a predetermined time.

Finally, many Windows programs can be started in different ways from the command prompt using optional switches. For example, Windows Explorer can be run by typing explorer.exe from the command prompt. These programs are normally run using a graphical user interface (GUI), are started by desktop shortcuts, and are not usually referred to as commands.

See Also: *UNIX commands, Windows commands*

command interpreter

The underlying service or daemon that supports a command-line interface.

Overview

The command interpreter is a system process that allows users to type text commands into the command line or command prompt and execute them to perform various routines and manage system and networking resources. Traditional UNIX systems make heavy use of the command line, while MS-DOS, the legacy Microsoft operating system, is basically a command shell for running text-based commands to control operating system processes.

On Microsoft Windows 2000, Windows XP, or Windows .NET Server systems, users can open a command prompt window to issue text-based commands to the underlying command interpreter Cmd.exe. These text-based Windows commands represent only a subset of the full functionality of the GUI-based administration tools available on the Windows 2000, Windows XP, and Windows .NET Server platforms.

The command interpreter is sometimes referred to as the operating system shell, especially on UNIX platforms. Entering a command into the command interpreter is referred to as "working at the command line."

See Also: *command line, command prompt*

command line

A general name for any user interface that allows text-based commands to be entered and executed on a system. The term *command line* is popular in UNIX environments, but Microsoft Windows systems use *command prompt* to mean essentially the same thing.

See Also: *command interpreter, command prompt*

command prompt

A Microsoft Windows application that allows text-based Windows commands to be entered and executed.

Overview

The Windows command prompt provides a command-line interface (CLI) similar to those provided by UNIX systems. The command prompt can be used for running operating system tasks, configuring networking services, and even accessing resources and applications over the network. Many common administrative tasks can be performed from the command prompt, although the command prompt itself provides a more complex and less intuitive interface than the usual desktop graphical user interface (GUI) of Windows operating systems. However, administrators who have spent significant time working in UNIX networking environments often find the command prompt a more familiar paradigm for administering a Windows-based network.

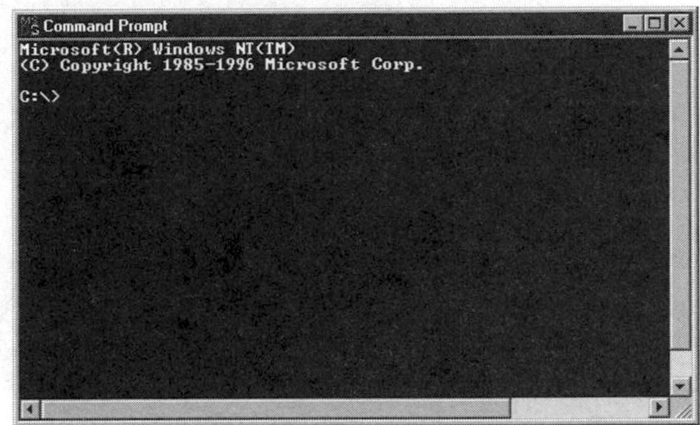

Command prompt. *The command prompt in Windows 2000.*

Notes

In Windows 2000, Windows XP, and Windows .NET Server, the command prompt application is Cmd.exe, located in the %SystemRoot%\system32 folder. In Windows Millennium Edition (Me), it is called the MS-DOS prompt, has the executable filename Command.com, and is in the \Windows folder. The Windows 2000, Windows XP, and Windows .NET Server versions can be configured using the Console utility in Control Panel.

For security reasons, should you wish as an administrator to disable the command prompt on a Windows 2000, Windows XP, or Windows .NET Server machine, you can accomplish this by either renaming Cmd.exe to something only you yourself are aware of, set NTFS file system (NTFS) permissions so that only Administrators can access it, or (not recommended) delete Cmd.exe entirely from the system.

See Also: *command interpreter*

C

Commerce Server 2000

Microsoft Corporation's platform for building and managing e-commerce solutions.

Overview

Commerce Server 2000 reduces the time it takes to develop and deploy complex e-commerce solutions. Commerce Server is based on Microsoft Site Server version 3 Commerce Edition (SSCE), and it builds on the strength of this earlier product. Commerce Server is part of the Microsoft Windows .NET Server family.

Commerce Server provides core services for managing your e-commerce site, including

- **Profile system:** Used to profile and manage customers and trading partners
- **Product catalog system:** Lets you manage millions of different products and find them quickly
- **Targeting system:** Lets you target customers with personalize one-on-one marketing
- **Business processing pipelines system:** Lets you customize your products to meet your customers' needs

In addition to these services, Commerce Server includes administration and development tools for building and managing your site, sample e-commerce sites you can use as templates and models, a data-warehousing decision-making system, help-desk customer support functionality, and much more.

For More Information

Find out more at *www.microsoft.com/commerceserver/.*

See Also: *.NET platform*

commercial service provider (CSP)

Internet service providers (ISPs), online service providers, telephone and cable network operators, and other companies.

Overview

CSPs provide software services such as community access to mail, news, chat, and conferencing services. By utilizing these services of a CSP, customers do not have to acquire licenses for the software the CSP provides.

See Also: *xSP*

Committed Information Rate (CIR)

A way of guaranteeing bandwidth in frame relay services.

Overview

Committed Information Rate (CIR) provides a way of guaranteeing minimum bandwidth for frame relay customers. Because customers on a frame relay network share the network, it is possible that service providers might oversubscribe the service—with the result that some customers receive insufficient bandwidth. Another situation where this can be a problem is if many customers try to access the frame relay network at the same time.

CIR guarantees that data throughput on frame relay connections will not drop below a previously agreed-upon contractual lower limit. However, CIR does permit short bursts of traffic to occupy greater amounts of bandwidth.

See Also: *frame relay*

Common Desktop Environment (CDE)

A graphical user interface (GUI) or desktop environment developed for UNIX systems.

Overview

Common Desktop Environment (CDE) was developed by IBM, Sun Microsystems, and Hewlett-Packard under the Common Open Software Environment (COSE) initiative. CDE is a paradigm that is widely used in the UNIX industry. CDE is based on various industry standards including the X Window System (X11) release 5, X/OPEN, OSF/Motif 1.2, and others.

CDE is designed to provide UNIX users with a simple and consistent desktop interface that includes

- Standard Windows-management features

- File-system browsing tools supporting multiple views
- Customizable user interface–management tools for changing backdrops, mouse and keyboard settings, and screen savers
- Extensive and easily accessed online help features
- Multiple workspaces for increasing available desktop area

See Also: *UNIX, X Window System*

Common Gateway Interface (CGI)

A mechanism by which a Web browser can request a Web server to execute an external application.

Overview

Common Gateway Interface (CGI) was developed in the UNIX networking environment to allow Web browsers to execute "gateway" applications on Web servers. These gateway programs are typically written either in a compiled language such as C or in an interpreted language such as Perl. CGI allows Web servers to run scripts or programs on the server and send the output to the client Web browser, thus turning the Web into a platform for running dynamic applications instead of merely presenting static information to clients.

Architecture

CGI programs are called "gateway" programs because the Web server passes the CGI request to the external program, which then runs as a separate process to process the input data, generate the results, and pass these results back to the Web server, which then returns them properly formatted in Hypertext Markup Language (HTML) to the client.

The main disadvantage of CGI is that each request must spawn a new CGI process and that, after the request is satisfied, the process is killed. Thus a Web server experiencing multiple simultaneous requests from clients will spawn multiple copies of the gateway process, each of which consumes memory and processing overhead. The fact that processes are terminated at the end of each request limits CGI to single-step Web applications and requires much ingenuity to handle data across a multistep user session.

Examples

CGI applications are often used as form handlers for Web forms, and are executed using a <FORM> tag embedded in the form document. When a Web client such as Microsoft Internet Explorer submits a form or otherwise passes information to a Web server using CGI, the Web server receives the information from the client and passes it to the gateway program for processing. The gateway program then returns the result of the processing to the server, which returns it to the Web browser as an HTML page. Here's a simple example:

```
<FORM METHOD=POST ACTION=
"http://www.northwind.microsoft.com/cgi-bin/
results.pl">
```

In this example, the Perl script results.pl in the cgi-bin directory functions as the form handler for processing the information submitted using the form.

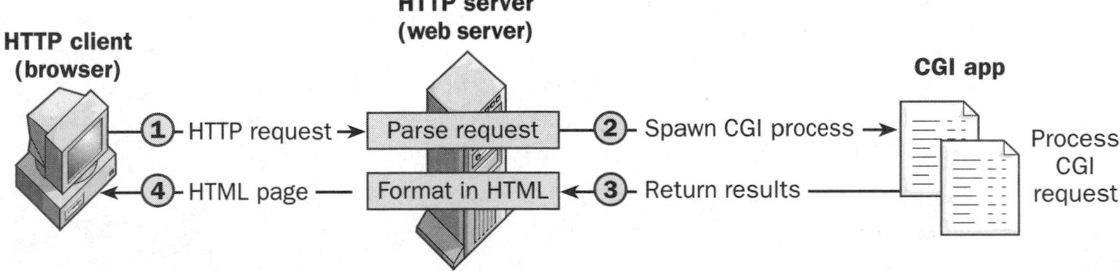

Common Gateway Interface (CGI). *How CGI works.*

C

Notes

Although CGI was developed for UNIX-based systems, it is supported by most Web servers, including Microsoft Internet Information Services (IIS). Microsoft Internet Server API (ISAPI) is a set of server extensions for IIS that functions similarly to those of CGI but uses fewer resources. The main difference is that with CGI the system creates a unique process for every CGI request, but ISAPI extensions do not require separate processes. This makes ISAPI applications generally more responsive than CGI applications.

See Also: *Internet Server API (ISAPI), UNIX, Web server*

Common Information Model (CIM)

A schema for defining manageable network objects.

Overview

The Common Information Model (CIM) defines a set of schema for describing information collected for network and systems management purposes. CIM was developed by the Distributed Management Task Force (DMTF), formerly named the Desktop Management Task Force, as an extensible, object-oriented schema for managing information collected from computers, networking devices, protocols, and applications.

CIM supports management of two types of objects:

- **Hardware objects:** This includes router interfaces and disks.
- **Software objects:** This includes applications, application components, and services.

Another way of defining the different types of information that can be described by CIM is as follows:

- **Static information:** Examples include the capacity of a hard drive on a desktop computer or the specific applications installed on a server.
- **Dynamic information:** Examples include the current bandwidth being used on a port on a switch or router.

Uses

CIM is similar to the Simple Network Management Protocol (SNMP) and Desktop Management Interface (DMI) standards. However, unlike SNMP and DMI, CIM is able to manage the widest possible range of hardware and software systems. CIM also shows the relationships between the different hardware and software components of an enterprise network more completely, making it easier to troubleshoot complex distributed systems and applications.

CIM information that is collected can be shared between systems on a peer-to-peer basis. This information sharing allows network devices to not only be managed from a centralized management console but also to talk to one another to resolve problems as they arise.

CIM was designed by the DMTF to operate together with their Web-Based Enterprise Management (WBEM) initiative to provide a broad WBEM/CIM framework for managing resources across a network.

Architecture

CIM is based on an object-oriented programming model that allows inheritance to be used to grant subclasses the characteristics of their parent classes. CIM classes have the properties, methods, and associations typical of object classes. CIM supports both physical and logical objects and models these objects for purposes of network management applications. CIM is also extensible and allows vendors to define the features of their products using inherited subclasses. The fact that these subclasses are inherited from standard parent classes ensures that data collected from different vendors' systems will be compatible with the CIM standard.

CIM consists of two parts: a language definition specifying the constructs and methods that can be used to model network and system resources, and a set of schema that describes how specific types of resources will be represented.

CIM supports three kinds of schema:

- **Core schema:** These define general areas of network and system management, and core CIM classes are platform-independent.
- **Common schema:** These define specific areas of management.
- **Extension schema:** These define the management of vendor-specific technologies.

Notes

Microsoft Systems Management Server (SMS) 2 is capable of collecting CIM data from managed systems and exporting this data to other enterprise management applications, such as NetView from Tivoli Systems and Unicenter from Computer Associates.

See Also: *Distributed Management Task Force (DMTF), Web-Based Enterprise Management (WBEM)*

Common Internet File System (CIFS)

A public version of the Server Message Block (SMB) file-sharing protocol that has been tuned for use over the Internet.

Overview

Common Internet File System (CIFS) is a remote file system access protocol that enables groups of users to collaborate and share documents over the Internet or within corporate intranets. CIFS is an open, cross-platform technology that is based on the native file-sharing protocols of Microsoft Windows platforms. It is supported by other platforms such as UNIX.

CIFS has been viewed as a possible replacement for both the File Transfer Protocol (FTP) and the Network File System (NFS) file system protocols. CIFS supports encrypted passwords and Unicode filenames, and it can be used to mount a remote file system as a directory or drive on the local machine. CIFS also includes features not supported by NFS, including write-ahead and native support for locks. Microsoft Corporation's Distributed file system (Dfs) is covered as part of the CIFS specification.

Microsoft has submitted CIFS to the Internet Engineering Task Force (IETF). CIFS client and server software is available for the Windows 2000 operating system platform.

See Also: *Server Message Block (SMB)*

Common Name Resolution Protocol (CNRP)

A proposed Internet Engineering Task Force (IETF) standard for a protocol to replace Uniform Resource Locators (URLs) with a simpler, more natural scheme for navigating the Web.

Overview

The existing Internet naming systems (domain names and URLs) are not particularly user friendly, as anyone knows who has ever picked up the phone and heard someone ask, "What is the URL for [name of Web page]?" After tediously repeating a long string of characters and slashes, you begin to wish the Internet community could come up with something different.

Enter the proposed Common Name Resolution Protocol (CNRP), an initiative of Network Solutions, AT&T, and other companies. Using CNRP, users could enter the name of a company into their browsers to reach the company home page, then enter a product name to reach the page for a particular product, and enter "2000 Sales Figures" to retrieve a document with these figures. Areas where CNRP might excel include government and public information portals and corporate intranets. Wireless Internet access may also benefit by eliminating the need to enter long, complex URLs on small keypads in order to access specific content on the Internet.

Architecture

CNRP basically runs on top of Hypertext Transfer Protocol (HTTP) as an Extensible Markup Language (XML)–encoded service. A user could enter "Go:2000 Sales Figures" into the browser's address bar, and the browser would encode this request in XML and forward it to a CNRP name server. The name server would then return the URL of the requested page to the browser, which would then request the actual content from where it is located on the Internet or corporate intranet.

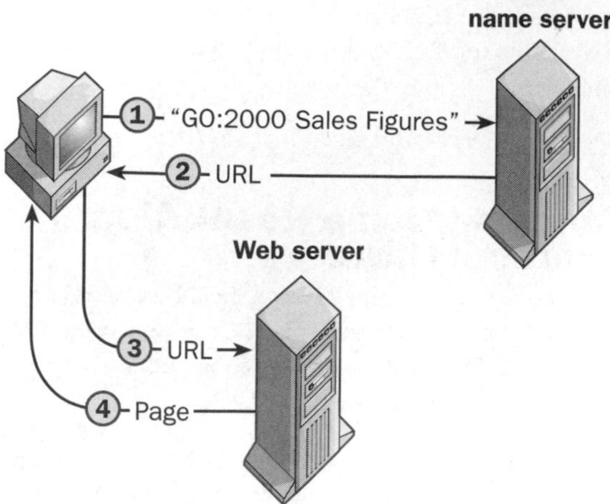

Common Name Resolution Protocol (CNRP). *How the CNRP works.*

Current Web browsers do not support CNRP, and until they do, users who want to use this service will have to download a plug-in for their browser to provide this functionality. Network Solutions offers a free, downloadable CNRP plug-in, as do several other vendors. Whether CNRP will become widely used will depend largely on social inertia (most people are used to URLs despite being fed up with them) and on whether CNRP is natively supported by the next release of Microsoft Internet Explorer and other Web browsers.

See Also: *Uniform Resource Locator (URL)*

Common Object Request Broker Architecture (CORBA)

A component architecture that specifies technologies for creating, distributing, and managing component programming objects over a network.

Overview

Common Object Request Broker Architecture (CORBA) was developed by the Object Management Group and its member companies and was designed to provide interoperability between applications in heterogeneous distributed environments.

In a CORBA environment, programs request services through an object request broker (ORB), which allows components of distributed applications to find each other and communicate without knowing where applications are located on the network or what kind of interface they use. ORBs are the middleware that enable client and server programs to establish sessions with each other, independent of their location on the network or their programming interface.

The process of a client invoking a call to an application programming interface (API) on a server object is transparent. The client issues the call, which is intercepted by the ORB. The ORB takes the call and is responsible for locating a server object that is able to implement the request. When it has located such an object, the ORB invokes the object's method and passes it any parameters submitted by the client. The results are then returned to the client. ORBs communicate among themselves using the General Inter-ORB Protocol (GIOP) or the Internet Inter-ORB Protocol (IIOP) so that any ORB can fulfill any client request on the network.

Uses

CORBA is primarily used in the UNIX world as an underlying architecture for developing distributed applications. CORBA is not natively supported by Microsoft Windows, which uses its own distributed object management architecture called Distributed Component Object Model (DCOM). The OMG has indicated, though, that it plans to include support for Microsoft's new C# programming language in CORBA, which should promote interoperability between UNIX applications using CORBA and Web services developed under Microsoft Corporation's new .NET platform.

For More Information

Find out more about CORBA from the Object Management Group at *www.omg.org.*

See Also: *C#, Distributed Component Object Model (DCOM), .NET platform, UNIX*

C

community

A group of hosts managed by Simple Network Management Protocol (SNMP) running SNMP agents.

Overview

Communities provide a simple way of partitioning and securing a network for SNMP management. SNMP agents and management systems use community names as the mechanism for authenticating SNMP messages. All SNMP agents belonging to the same community share the same community name, which functions as a kind of shared password for those agents so that they can be recognized by the SNMP management program and other agents. SNMP messages sent by SNMP management systems to a specific community are accepted only by hosts configured to belong to that community. If an SNMP agent program receives an SNMP message with a community name that it is not configured to recognize, it typically drops the message and sends a trap message to the SNMP management program indicating that a message was not authenticated on that machine.

Notes

An agent can be a member of one or more communities. By default, all agents belong to the public community. If all community names including public names are removed from an SNMP-managed host, the host will accept all SNMP messages sent to it.

See Also: *agent, Simple Network Management Protocol (SNMP)*

Competitive Local Exchange Carrier (CLEC)

A telco that competes with incumbent telcos under the terms of the Telecommunications Act of 1996.

Overview

Before 1996, the U.S. telecommunications market was dominated by a small group of telcos called Incumbent Local Exchange Carriers (ILECs) or Regional Bell Operating Companies (RBOCs) and a group of long-distance carriers or inter-exchange carriers (IXCs). The Telecommunications Act of 1996 was designed to open things up by allowing new companies to compete with the established ones in both the local and long-distance markets.

Competitive Local Exchange Carriers (CLECs) generally compete with ILECs for provisioning the local loop market, but unlike ILECs, which focus more on residential and large enterprise customers, many CLECs have targeted the small to mid-sized business market that has traditionally been poorly served by ILECs. CLECs generally offer high-speed data services and often focus on specific niche services such as Digital Subscriber Line (DSL)—these are often known instead as DSL providers—but many CLECs also offer a much wider spectrum of services including voice (local and long-distance), high-speed Internet access (using DSL), virtual private networks (VPNs), and business-to-business data links.

CLECs come in many types and range from smaller start-ups that piggyback on ILECs and purchase services wholesale from them for reselling purposes, to larger start-ups building out new fiber from their own switching centers, to large IXCs such as AT&T (which acquired Teleport, a pioneering CLEC) and MCI WorldCom (which bought MFS, another pioneer CLEC) competing in the local telco market.

Like ILECs, CLECs are generally concerned about provisioning buildings, not individual users. However, some CLECs are also getting into the Building Local Exchange Carrier (BLEC) markets by offering to-the-desktop services for building-out wiring and deploying services not just to buildings but also within them.

Advantages and Disadvantages

One of the advantages that CLECs have over traditional ILECs is that, instead of competing directly with ILECs by building switching centers, building out wiring to customer premises, and purchasing expensive Class 5 telephone switches to handle all-important voice traffic, they can save implementation costs considerably by colocating their switching equipment at ILEC COs, sharing the existing local loop infrastructure owned by ILECs, and focusing on purchasing more modern, less expensive switching gear dedicated to specific uses such as DSL. Using less expensive and more modern equipment theoretically means the CLEC can offer its services at a discount compared to the ILEC, but CLECs also have to pay the ILECs for the right to use their services, including line provisioning and maintenance, switching interconnects, and colocation services.

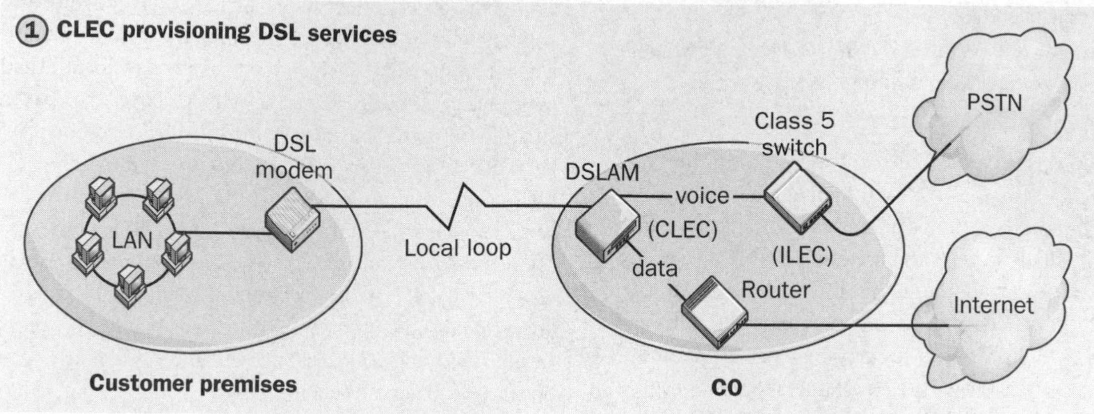

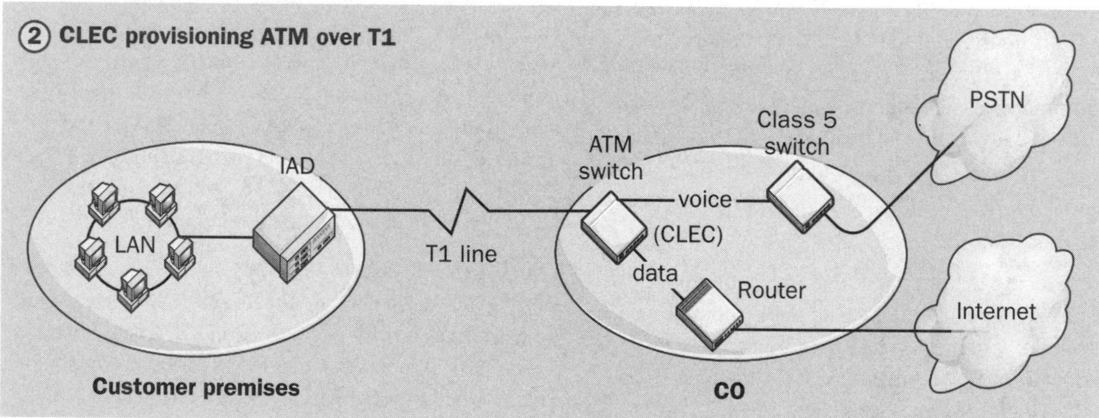

Competitive Local Exchange Carrier (CLEC). *Two ways CLECs can provision customers with voice and data services.*

On the other hand, contracting CLECs to provision telecommunication services for your company instead of ILECs has an element of risk. This is evidenced by the changing nature of the CLEC market, in which some startups have failed and others have been acquired, and by litigation initiated by some CLECs against ILECs. An example is Pronto, a project of mega-bell SBC Communications, which is building out thousands of neighborhood DSL remote terminals to shorten customer DSL connections, thereby improving DSL reliability and data rates. CLECs that want to provide their own DSL services to the same customers have complained to the Federal Communications Commission (FCC) that Pronto cuts them out of the loop because they cannot service Pronto customers using DSLAMs colocated at SBC's COs. Other RBOCs are contemplating similar projects, which could undercut the operations of many CLECs.

Implementation

Because the ILECs own the infrastructure of the last-mile (local loop) wiring serving residential and business markets in the United States, the Telecommunications Act required ILECs to open up use of the local loop to CLECs, allow CLECs to colocate their equipment at the ILEC central offices (COs), and allow CLECs to lease use of the local loop from the ILECs that provision it. CLECs can architect to provision services in many ways, two of which are shown in the diagram.

The top part of the diagram shows a DSL modem at the customer premises that connects the customer's local area network (LAN) over the local loop to a DSL Access Multiplexer (DSLAM) colocated by the CLEC at the CO of the customer's incumbent telco. The CLEC's DSLAM is connected to the ILEC's switching backbone to provide the customer with voice and data services. Such an arrangement is typical of a CLEC that functions as a DSL provider.

The bottom part shows an Integrated Access Device (IAD) at the customer premises. The IAD converts the Internet Protocol (IP) packets of the customer's Ethernet LAN to Asynchronous Transfer Mode (ATM) cells for transmission over the T1 line to an ATM switch colocated by the CLEC at the ILEC's CO. In this case, the ILEC is responsible for provisioning the T1 for the CLEC and acts as a wholesaler of T1 services toward the ILEC. The CLEC's ATM switch then filters the voice and data traffic from the customer. The voice traffic is routed either to the ILEC's telephone switch or directly to an IXC, while the data traffic is routed to an ISP for Internet access or to an IXC for long-haul wide area network (WAN) connections to branch offices.

Marketplace

The CLEC landscape is constantly changing, but some of the bigger players include Covad Communications Company (*www.covad.com*), Intermedia Communications (*www.intermedia.com*), Cogent Communications (*www.cogentco.com*), and others. Despite these big players and the large number of smaller CLECs on the market, analysts estimate that CLECs currently have less than 10 percent of the local telecom market, with more than 90 percent still in the hands of the incumbent ILEC/RBOCs.

CLECs that provision DSL services typically pay RBOCs about $15 to $25 per month to use their local loop connection for deploying such services, the cost of which must be recovered when they resell such services to businesses and consumers, typically at $40 to $60 per month. A newer technology called line sharing may lower the cost for CLECs to lease lines from ILECs, and the savings might be passed on to consumers.

Prospects

Times have gotten tough in the telecommunications industry in general at the start of the new millennium. After the dot-com crash of 2000, sources of venture capital for new telecom startups has dried up, leaving some CLECs in financial difficulty (the same difficulties are faced by 3G wireless vendors and other segments of the telecom sector). Although a few CLECs have failed and others have been acquired, there were still about 200 different CLECs in the marketplace in 2001, with a market capitalization of about $6 billion.

One aim of the Telecommunications Act of 1996 was to open the doors for cable TV companies and utilities to begin competing with ILECs for residential and business voice and data services. When the act was passed, these companies were slow to build out these services, and a diverse host of CLECs appeared to compete in the residential, office, and metropolitan marketplaces. Now, however, cable companies and utilities are beginning to deploy high-speed data services in large rollouts, and so now many CLECs face competition on two fronts instead of from just the ILECs. Finally, FCC rulings have begun to come down on the side of large carriers, which may squeeze many smaller startups out of the marketplace or lead to their being acquired by big carriers such as AT&T and SBC.

The shakeout in the CLEC market and its uncertain future makes it advisable for businesses to use due diligence in investigating the financially viability of CLECs before deploying mission-critical WAN services just to save costs over similar services offered by RBOCs. Many enterprise network architects believe that leasing reliable services for WAN and Internet access from large RBOCs is more important than saving a few dollars by using CLECs. On the other hand, some e-commerce companies have chosen to go with CLECs because they can typically provision services much faster than traditional RBOCs. CLECs that are building out their own infrastructure (own their own fiber) are probably more likely to succeed in the long term. Enterprise network architects should also consider purchasing redundant services from different carriers to provide fault-tolerance for their WAN connections, but they should realize that as the CLEC market consolidates, their options may narrow.

For More Information

You can find industry news on CLECs at *www.clec.com* and *www.clec-planet.com*. A current list of CLECs can be found at *www.dslreports.com/clecs*.

See Also: *carrier, Digital Subscriber Line (DSL), Incumbent Local Exchange Carrier (ILEC), inter-exchange carrier (IXC), line sharing, local loop, Regional Bell Operating Company (RBOC), telco*

C

complete trust model

A domain model in Microsoft Windows NT in which every domain trusts every other domain with two-way trusts.

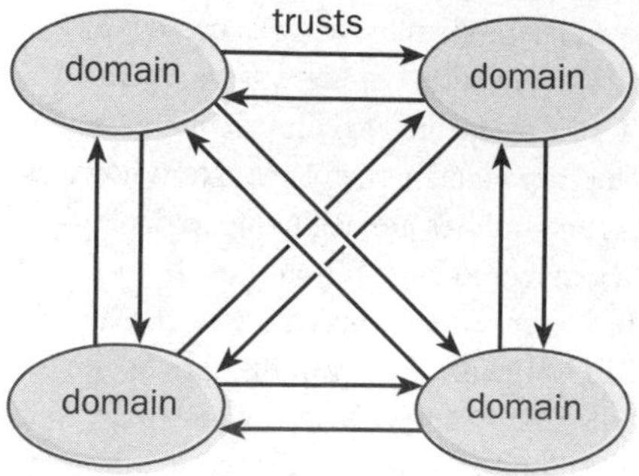

Complete trust model. *Shown for Windows NT.*

Overview

The complete trust model is rarely implemented in Windows NT–based networks unless the motivation for using Windows NT is being driven from the bottom up. For example, if a number of individual departments start implementing domains, the company might soon find itself implementing the complete trust model in order to make administration of these domains more efficient. This model also might be used in a situation in which two companies using Windows NT merge into a single company. Because of the large number of trusts in a complete trust model, there are additional security concerns about who is able to administer what. The following table outlines the pros and cons of using this domain model.

Advantages and Disadvantages of Using the Complete Trust Model

Advantages	*Disadvantages*
Scalable to any number of user accounts.	Complex to set up and administer.
Suitable for merging companies or organizations with no central MIS department.	Multiple local groups must be created in each resource domain.

Notes

When you upgrade a Windows NT network based on the complete trust model to a Windows 2000 or Windows .NET Server network, you can maintain the relative independence of each domain by migrating each domain to be the root domain of a domain tree. Each domain tree would have a single domain, namely the root domain. Two-way transitive trusts can then be established between the trees to form a domain forest.

See Also: *multiple master domain model, single domain model, single master domain model*

Component Load Balancing (CLB)

A Microsoft clustering technology supported by Microsoft Windows 2000 and Windows .NET Server Server and provided by Microsoft Application Center 2000.

Overview

Component Load Balancing (CLB) is a Microsoft clustering solution that is designed to increase the availability and reliability of distributed applications developed using Microsoft COM+ technologies. A CLB cluster consists of a group of up to 16 nodes (servers) running a distributed COM+ application whose components are distributed across the cluster. A CLB cluster is connected together by a network and is managed by Application Center 2000. When one node in a CLB cluster fails, its workload is distributed to the remaining nodes and the COM+ application keeps running.

Implementation

CLB is usually used in conjunction with other forms of clustering such as Network Load Balancing (NLB) and Microsoft Cluster Services (MCSC) for Microsoft Windows 2000 and Windows .NET Server Enterprise Server edition. This scenario is often used for farms of Web servers running mission-critical Web applications. Typically, NLB is used to handle load balancing of Web servers at the front-end, while CLB load balances COM+ application logic in the middle tier and MCSC provides clustering for back-end database servers. Application Center 2000 is then used to manage the CLB middle tier of the Web farm.

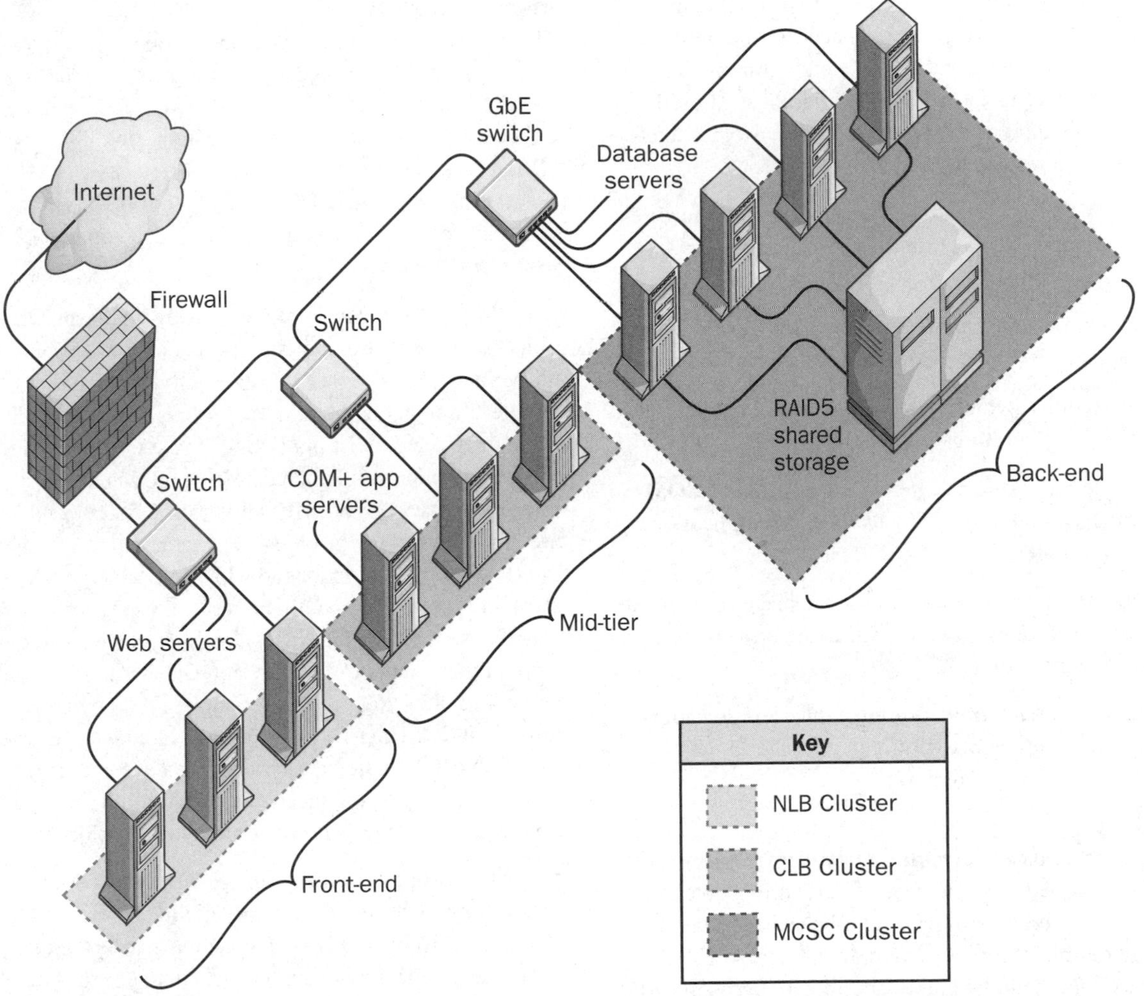

Component Load Balancing (CLB). *Using CLB to provide high reliability and availability for distributed COM+ applications.*

To distribute the load across the nodes of the CLB cluster, CLB uses round-robin techniques and polling algorithms based on server response time. Because CLB uses frequent polling, be sure to implement your CLB cluster on a fast network (100 megabits per second [Mbps] or faster).

See Also: *Application Center, clustering*

Component Object Model (COM)

An object-based programming architecture developed by Microsoft Corporation that allows applications to be built from binary software components.

Overview

Component Object Model (COM) is both a set of specifications for building application components and a group of underlying services for supporting these components. COM defines a standard method for building components and specifies what these components will

C

look like at the binary level. Because it is a binary standard, COM is language-neutral and COM components can be written using a variety of programming languages including C++, Visual Basic, Java, COBOL, SmallTalk, and other languages. COM also has the following features:

- Support for object-oriented programming features including encapsulation, inheritance, and polymorphism.
- Location transparency, which allows COM components to be moved from one system to another.
- Portability, which lets you port COM applications to other operating system platforms.
- Code reuse, the result of encapsulation of COM functionality and a way to speed up application development.
- Loose coupling, which lets you replace components with new ones that have similar interfaces for accessing them.
- Stable version transitioning, which lets you upgrade some components within an application without breaking the application.

History

Microsoft released an earlier technology, Object Linking and Embedding (OLE), in 1991. OLE enabled functionality from one application to be embedded into another application. For example, a Microsoft Excel spreadsheet could be embedded into a Microsoft Word document and still maintain its spreadsheet functionality. OLE used an underlying technology called Dynamic Data Exchange (DDE) that was complicated in its operation.

In 1995, OLE 2 was released, which replaced DDE with COM as an underlying architecture for OLE. It was soon realized that COM had more uses than embedding one document within another, and COM became the fundamental technology while OLE withdrew to the background. COM has continued to evolve, and its present version is called COM+, which is discussed in a separate article in this chapter.

Implementation

The basic unit of COM is the COM component object, a binary programming object that complies with the COM standards. COM objects can be implemented as either executable (.exe) files or dynamic-link libraries (DLLs) and can function in one of two roles: COM servers (providers) and COM clients (consumers). COM servers and clients interact with each other by using COM interfaces.

A COM interface is a set of methods by which a COM object exposes its functionality to other COM objects. COM interfaces allow COM objects to invoke one another through the methods and properties residing in these interfaces. COM interfaces consist of groups of related functions implemented by the COM class. An interface is basically a table of pointers to functions that are implemented by the object. The table represents the interface, and the functions to which the table points represent the methods of that interface. COM objects can expose multiple interfaces. Each interface has its own unique interface ID (IID), and COM interfaces begin with the letter "I." For example, IUnknown is an important COM interface that must be included in every COM object. IUnknown provides reference counting and interface querying mechanisms and allows navigation to all other interfaces exposed by COM objects.

When COM-based applications are written, COM components are identified by globally unique identifiers (GUIDs), a 16-byte (128-bit) alphanumeric string that is uniquely generated using the current data and time and other information. COM component objects must be registered in order for location transparency to work. You can manually register a COM component object using Regsrv32.exe and other tools.

COM also includes a set of COM services implemented as Win32 library routines (DLLs). These DLLs are used to create new instances of COM components, find and keep track of the location of COM component objects, and perform remote procedure calls (RPCs) for communicating between component objects.

Notes

An alternate component object technology found primarily in the UNIX world is Common Object Request Broker Architecture (CORBA).

For More Information

Learn more about COM at the Microsoft COM site at *www.microsoft.com/com.*

See Also: *ActiveX, COM+, COM component object, Distributed Component Object Model (DCOM), globally unique identifier (GUID), object linking and embedding (OLE)*

CompTIA

Stands for Computing Technology Industry Association, a computer industry trade association formed in 1982.

See: *Computing Technology Industry Association (CompTIA)*

computer account

An account in the Active Directory directory service of Microsoft Windows 2000 and Windows .NET Server that signifies that a particular computer is a part of a Windows 2000 or Windows .NET Server domain.

Overview

Windows 2000 and Windows .NET Server domain controllers can store three types of accounts: user accounts, group accounts, and computer accounts. Windows 2000 and Windows .NET Server use computer accounts to determine whether a particular system that a user is employing to attempt to log on to the network is part of the domain. When the NetLogon service running on a client computer connects to the NetLogon service on a domain controller in order to authenticate a user, the NetLogon services challenge each other to determine whether they both have valid computer accounts. This allows a secure communication channel to be established for logon purposes.

In order for a Windows 2000, Windows XP, or Windows .NET Server machine to join a domain, the machine must have a computer account created for it in Active Directory. There are two ways to create this account:

- Use Active Directory Users and Computers in Windows 2000 and Windows .NET Server to create a computer account for the machine, and then have the machine join the domain.
- Use an administrator account to create a computer account while installing Windows 2000, Windows XP, or Windows .NET Server on the machine.

Notes

Machines running Windows 95, Windows 98, and Windows Millennium Edition (Me) can participate in domain authentication, but they do not have computer accounts in Active Directory. This is why the logon box for a Windows 95 or Windows 98 machine has a hard-coded domain name and can log on to only one domain.

If you reinstall Windows 2000 on a machine, you must delete the old computer account and create a new computer account, even if the machine has the same name as before.

See Also: *account*

Computer Browser service

In Microsoft Windows 2000, Windows XP, or Windows .NET Server, a service responsible for enabling the browsing of network resources using Network Neighborhood and Windows Explorer.

Overview

The Computer Browser service simplifies the user task of locating and accessing network resources by eliminating the need for users to remember Universal Naming Convention (UNC) paths or other network syntax and by eliminating the need for all computers on the network to maintain their own list of all available network resources.

The Computer Browser service maintains a distributed series of lists called browse lists that contain information about shared resources available on the network.

Different computers on the network have different roles. These computers include the following:

- **Domain master browser:** Collects and maintains the master browse list for the domain, and synchronizes this list with other domain master browsers in different domains. In a Windows NT network, the domain master browser must be the Primary Domain Controller (PDC).
- **Master browser:** Collects and maintains the master browse list for the domain and distributes this list to backup browsers in the domain. This can be a computer running Windows 2000, Windows XP, Windows .NET Server, Windows NT, Windows 95, Windows 98, or Windows for Workgroups.
- **Backup browser:** Maintains copies of the browse list received from the master browsers and distributes this list to any network client requesting a network resource. This can be a computer running Windows 2000, Windows XP, Windows .NET Server, Windows NT, Windows 95, Windows 98, or Windows for Workgroups.
- **Potential browser:** Any computer on the network configured so that it can assume the role of a master browser or backup browser if required. This can be a computer running Windows 2000, Windows XP, Windows .NET Server, Windows NT, Windows 95, Windows 98, or Windows for Workgroups.
- **Nonbrowser:** Any computer that cannot be a browser but can share resources with the network.

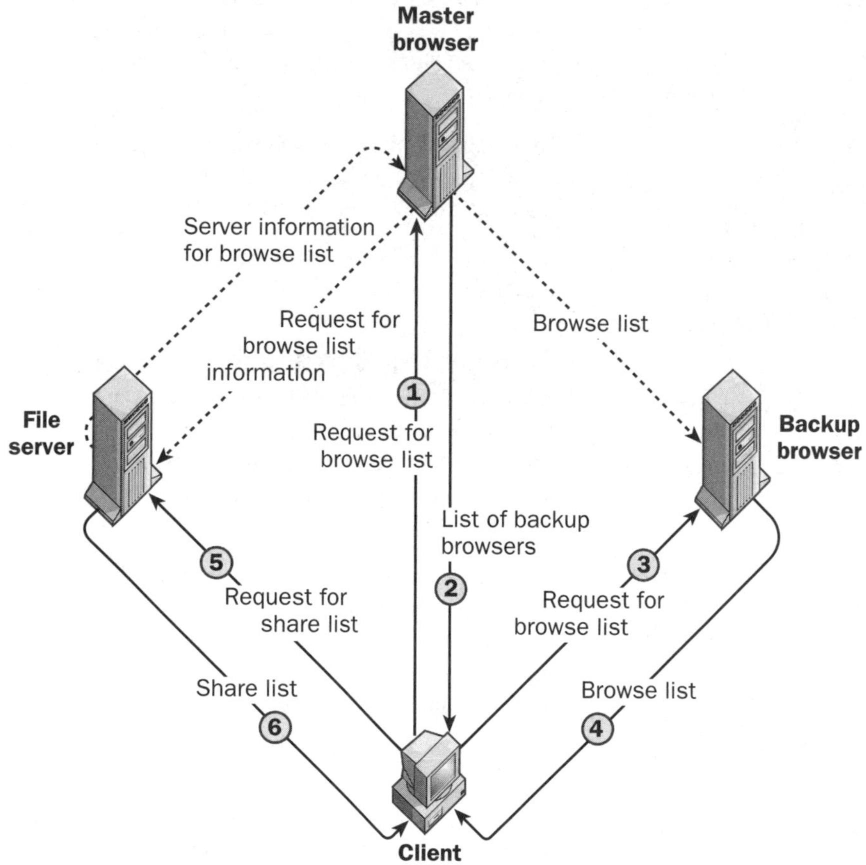

Computer Browser service. *How the Computer Browser service works.*

When a client tries to access a shared resource on the network, such as a shared folder on a file server, it first contacts the master browser for a list of backup browsers. Then it contacts a backup browser for a copy of the browse list. When the client has the browse list, it contacts the file server for a list of shares, and then connects to the desired share.

Notes

The Workstation service and Server service must be started for the Computer Browser service to function.

See Also: *browse list, browsing*

Computer Management

A Microsoft Windows 2000, Windows XP, and Windows .NET Server management console that provides a single integrated desktop tool for managing local and remote machines.

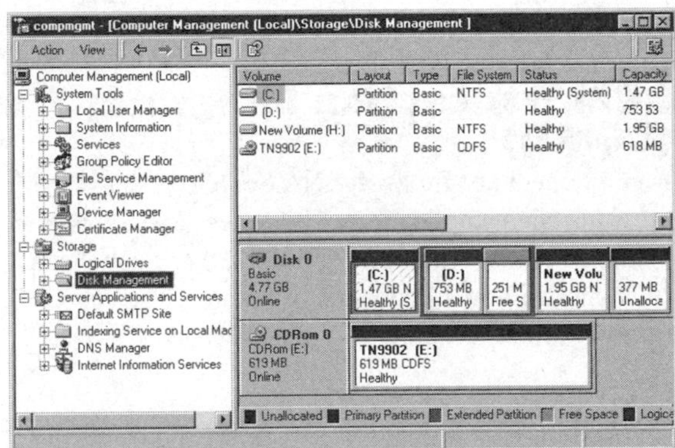

Computer Management. *A typical Computer Management console.*

Overview

Computer Management combines a number of administrative utilities from Windows NT with additional Windows 2000, Windows XP, and Windows .NET Server tools to provide an easy way of viewing and managing properties of any computer running Windows 2000, Windows XP, or Windows .NET Server on the network. Using Computer Management, an administrator can perform the following actions on local and remote machines:

- Create and manage shares
- Display a list of connected users
- Manage services such as Dynamic Host Configuration Protocol (DHCP) and Domain Name System (DNS)
- Start and stop system services
- Configure properties of storage devices
- Monitor system events and application errors
- Display device settings and add new device drivers

To use Computer Management for modifying administrative settings, you must be a member of the Administrators group.

See Also: *Microsoft Management Console (MMC)*

computer name

For computers running Microsoft Windows, a name that identifies a computer on the network.

Overview

Computer names can be up to 15 characters in length. In Windows NT, Windows 95, and Windows 98, you specify a computer's name using the Network utility in Control Panel. (In Windows 2000, Windows XP, and Windows .NET Server, use the Network Identification tab of the System utility in Control Panel.) The computer must be restarted if its name is changed. This name is used by services that perform NetBIOS name resolution on the network, such as the Windows Internet Name Service (WINS). Computer names provide a friendly way of accessing network resources without having to remember complex numerical addresses such as IP addresses.

A hidden 16th character is appended to the computer name to form the NetBIOS name for NetBIOS-aware networking services on the machine. Each NetBIOS-aware service has a different NetBIOS name, some of which are based on the name of the computer and others of which are based on the name of the domain in which the computer resides.

Notes

Give friendly names, derived from some common source such as *A Midsummer Night's Dream*, to groups of computers offering related services. For example, you could call your servers Puck, Oberon, and Titania. This makes it easy to remember that these computers all belong to the same group.

C

computer-telephony integration (CTI)

A general term describing the integration of computer and telephone technologies.

Overview

By joining computer systems with switched telephone services, users can access advanced functions such as automatic incoming call routing, call display, and power dialing. For example, a computer can use computer-telephony integration (CTI) to issue commands to a telephone switch to control call routing of calls.

CTI applications generally fall into one of two categories:

- **Call-control applications:** Allow computers to dial numbers, establish conference calls, and other functions. The computer essentially replaces the touch-tone telephone keypad.
- **Media-processing applications**: Deal with more complex issues, such as voice recognition, speech synthesis, and converting fax messages to e-mail. These applications pursue the goal of completely integrated unified messaging in which voice, fax, e-mail, and video conferencing features are combined.

CTI is made possible on Microsoft Windows platforms by operating system application programming interfaces (APIs) such as Microsoft Corporation's Telephony Application Programming Interface (TAPI). The range of products and technologies that support CTI continues to evolve. Cross-platform, vendor-neutral standards have not yet been established.

Computing Technology Industry Association (CompTIA)

A computer industry trade association formed in 1982.

Overview

The Computing Technology Industry Association (CompTIA) currently has more than 7500 members. CompTIA membership includes resellers, value-added resellers (VARs), distributors, manufacturers, and training companies in the United States and Canada. The goals of CompTIA are to foster professional competence and business ethics among its members and throughout the computer industry. CompTIA provides its members with educational opportunities, a professional network, and a forum for the development of ethical, professional, and business standards in the computing industry. A number of committees meet to consider issues such as software licensing and electronic warranty forms.

For More Information

Visit the CompTIA online at *www.comptia.org.*

COMTI

Stands for COM Transaction Integrator, a component of Microsoft SNA Server version 4 that provides client applications with access to two popular mainframe transaction processing (TP) environments, Customer Information Control System (CICS) and Information Management System (IMS).

See: *COM Transaction Integrator (COMTI)*

COM Transaction Integrator (COMTI)

A component of Microsoft SNA Server version 4 that provides client applications with access to two popular mainframe transaction processing (TP) environments, Customer Information Control System (CICS) and Information Management System (IMS).

Overview

COM Transaction Integrator (COMTI) works in conjunction with Microsoft Transaction Server (MTS), making CICS and IMS programs appear as MTS components that can be used with other MTS components to build distributed applications. COMTI includes both a Microsoft Windows NT Server run-time environment and a development tool called Component Builder, which can import mainframe COBOL code and automatically generate an object compatible with MTS. This lets developers program in the visual, object-oriented environments they are accustomed to, allowing them access to host transactions without needing to learn the intricacies of Systems Network Architecture (SNA).

See Also: *SNA Server, Systems Network Architecture (SNA)*

concurrency

A term referring to the simultaneous access to a network resource by more than one client.

Overview

Concurrency is an important issue in the licensing of a server operating system or application. For example, the Per Server licensing mode for Microsoft Windows NT Server is based on concurrency. If you purchase 10 client access licenses (CALs) for your Windows NT Server, a maximum of 10 concurrent connections can legally be formed with that server for accessing network resources.

Notes

Some products, such as Microsoft Outlook 98, do not support concurrent access. In other words, you cannot install a central copy of Outlook 98 on a server and have thin clients run this program from the centralized location. Instead, you must install one copy of Outlook 98 on each client that needs to run it.

connected network (CN)

In Microsoft Message Queue (MSMQ) Server terminology, a name for a collection of computers in which any two computers can directly communicate.

Overview

Computers in the same connected network must be running the same network protocol. A connected network (CN) is essentially a label describing how MSMQ servers are related in an enterprise. CNs are logical groupings of computers that can communicate directly using MSMQ messages. When you install an MSMQ server, you specify a connected network for each network address on the server.

When you specify connected networks for your MSMQ enterprise, it is a good idea to use meaningful labels so that administrators can easily select a connected network from a list when they need to override the default connected network settings.

connection

A link between two computers for the purpose of exchanging information.

Overview

An example would be a Microsoft Windows NT Workstation, Windows 95, or Windows 98 client computer accessing a shared folder or printer on a Windows 2000 server. The term *connection* is also used to describe the establishment of communication over a WAN link, as in using a dial-up connection over a modem.

When a client computer tries to connect to a server, the success or failure of the attempt can depend upon whether

- The server has shared the resource that the client wants to connect to
- The client has been properly authenticated or has permission to access the resource
- The client is properly licensed to connect to the server, and free licenses are available

See Also: *client access license (CAL), license*

connectionless protocol

Any transport layer protocol that relies on broadcast packets instead of directed packets.

Overview

Connectionless protocols can only offer "best-effort" delivery and cannot guarantee that packets will arrive in the correct order or even at all. Connectionless protocols cannot guarantee delivery of packets. Instead, reliability of packets is handled by the application itself or some higher layer of the protocol stack.

An example of a connectionless protocol is the User Datagram Protocol (UDP), which is part of the Transmission Control Protocol/Internet Protocol (TCP/IP) protocol suite. UDP provides connectionless services for delivering small packets of information commonly called datagrams. Another connectionless transport layer protocol is the Appletalk Transaction Protocol (ATP), part of the AppleTalk suite of protocols.

Notes

The term *connectionless* is also used to describe any delivery mechanism where complete addressing information (the address of the source and the address of the destination) is included in every packet. Packets are

C

then placed on the network and are delivered to their destination independently, sometimes taking different routes and arriving in a mixed-up order that needs to be sorted out using packet numbers.

In this more general context, we can also examine protocols at other layers such as the network layer and data link layer. Most local area network (LAN) protocols at these layers are connectionless. For example, at the network layer we have IP, Internetwork Packet Exchange (IPX), Datagram Delivery Protocol (DDP), which is part of the legacy AppleTalk protocol suite, and DECnet Routing Protocol (DRP), which is part of the legacy DECnet protocol suite, all connectionless. At the datalink layer we have Ethernet, Token Ring, Fiber Distributed Data Interface (FDDI), and others, again all connectionless. An example of a data-link layer protocol that is connection-oriented instead of connectionless is Asynchronous Transfer Mode (ATM).

See Also: *connection-oriented protocol, protocol*

Connection Manager Administration Kit (CMAK)

A wizard-based tool for creating custom connectivity solutions, and a component of Internet Connection Services for Microsoft Remote Access Service (RAS).

Overview

The Connection Manager Administration Kit (CMAK) is used to customize the Microsoft Connection Manager (CM) client component. Internet service providers (ISPs) can use this tool to customize dial-up installation packages for their customers. Customization features include

- Animated logon screen, which can include a custom logo
- Desktop icons
- The language the dialer displays to the customer
- Support numbers and help files
- Various connect actions that the dialer performs when dialing, such as shutting down applications or downloading files

connection-oriented protocol

Any transport layer protocol that establishes a connection first in order to reliably send packets over the network.

Overview

Connection-oriented protocols guarantee delivery of packets by making use of acknowledgments and retransmission of data. Connection-oriented protocols are used primarily for reliable delivery of large packets of data, as opposed to the unreliable connectionless protocols that are used to deliver small datagrams.

An example of a connection-oriented protocol is TCP, which is part of the Transmission Control Protocol/Internet Protocol (TCP/IP) protocol suite. The TCP protocol uses a TCP three-way handshake to establish a connection between two hosts on a network. During session establishment, the hosts negotiate the TCP window size, segment size, and other information needed to ensure reliable and efficient communication. A TCP connection is terminated using a similar handshake procedure. Another example of a connection-oriented transport layer protocol is Sequenced Packet Exchange (SPX), part of the NetWare suite of protocols. The legacy network service provider (NSP) protocol of the DECnet suite of protocols is also a connection-oriented transport layer protocol.

Notes

At lower Open Systems Interconnection (OSI) levels such as the network layer and data link layer, most local area network (LAN) protocols are connectionless instead of connection-oriented. Asynchronous Transfer Mode (ATM) is an exception and is connection-oriented. In ATM a virtual circuit (data pathway) is first established prior to sending any data. Instead of addressing data packets (actually cells) with source and destination addresses as in a connectionless protocol, ATM assigns the circuit number to the cells to ensure they reach their destination. Because circuit numbers are much smaller than network addresses, connectionless protocols such asATM have less overhead than connection-oriented protocols such as IP or Ethernet.

See Also: *connectionless protocol, protocol*

connection pooling

A technique for optimizing Active Server Pages (ASP) applications running on Microsoft Internet Information Server (IIS) version 4 and Internet Information Services (IIS).

Overview

Connection pooling allows more efficient implementation when connecting ASP front-end applications to a back-end database. Connection pooling involves the pooling of open database connectivity (ODBC) connections to reduce the frequency at which ODBC connections need to be opened and closed on heavily accessed servers. Connection pooling improves ASP performance for ODBC-enabled Web applications and provides a graceful way to manage connection timeouts.

To use ODBC connection pooling on IIS, perform the following steps:

1. Configure the database driver using ODBC in Control Panel.
2. Enable connection pooling in the Microsoft Windows NT registry.
3. Open individual connections in your Microsoft ActiveX Data Objects (ADO) code right before data access is needed for an ASP page and release connections as soon as the data has been accessed.

When connection pooling is enabled, the ODBC driver will check the connection pool for idle connections it can reuse before creating a new connection in response to an ODBC request. When connections are released, they are returned to the connection pool instead of being closed.

Notes

You can control the amount of time an idle connection remains in the pool using the CPTimeout registry setting, which has a default setting of 60 seconds.

See Also: *Active Server Pages (ASP)*

connectivity server

A computer running Microsoft Exchange Server that is dedicated for routing messages to other sites and foreign mail systems using Exchange connectors.

Overview

Large companies often require servers that are dedicated to message routing because of the high volume of message traffic they experience. In a typical high-volume site configuration, one server might be optimized as a home server for users' mailboxes, another server for dedicated public-folder replica hosting, and a third for providing dedicated messaging connectivity with other sites and foreign messaging systems. A connectivity server can have one or more connectors installed on it to provide connectivity with Exchange sites, Simple Mail Transfer Protocol (SMTP) hosts, X.400 messaging systems, or Microsoft Mail postoffices. The more connectors you have on a server, the greater its hardware requirements become.

Notes

On Exchange 5.5 systems, run the Performance Optimizer wizard after you have installed your connectors on the Exchange server. This will allow your server to take maximum advantage of its particular hardware configuration.

connector (device)

A device that terminates a segment of cabling or provides a point of entry for networking devices such as computers, hubs, and routers.

Overview

Connectors can be distinguished according to their physical appearance and mating properties, such as jacks and plugs (male connectors) or sockets and ports (female connectors). They can also be distinguished by their different pinning configurations, such as DB9 and DB15 connectors, which have 9 and 15 pins, respectively. In addition, connectors are distinguished by the kind of electrical interfaces they support. Examples of different types of connectors include

- Connectors for serial interfaces, such as RS-232 and V.35
- Ethernet connectors, such as RJ-45 and bayonet Neill-Concelman (BNC) connectors
- Fiber-optic cabling connectors, such as SC and ST connectors

C

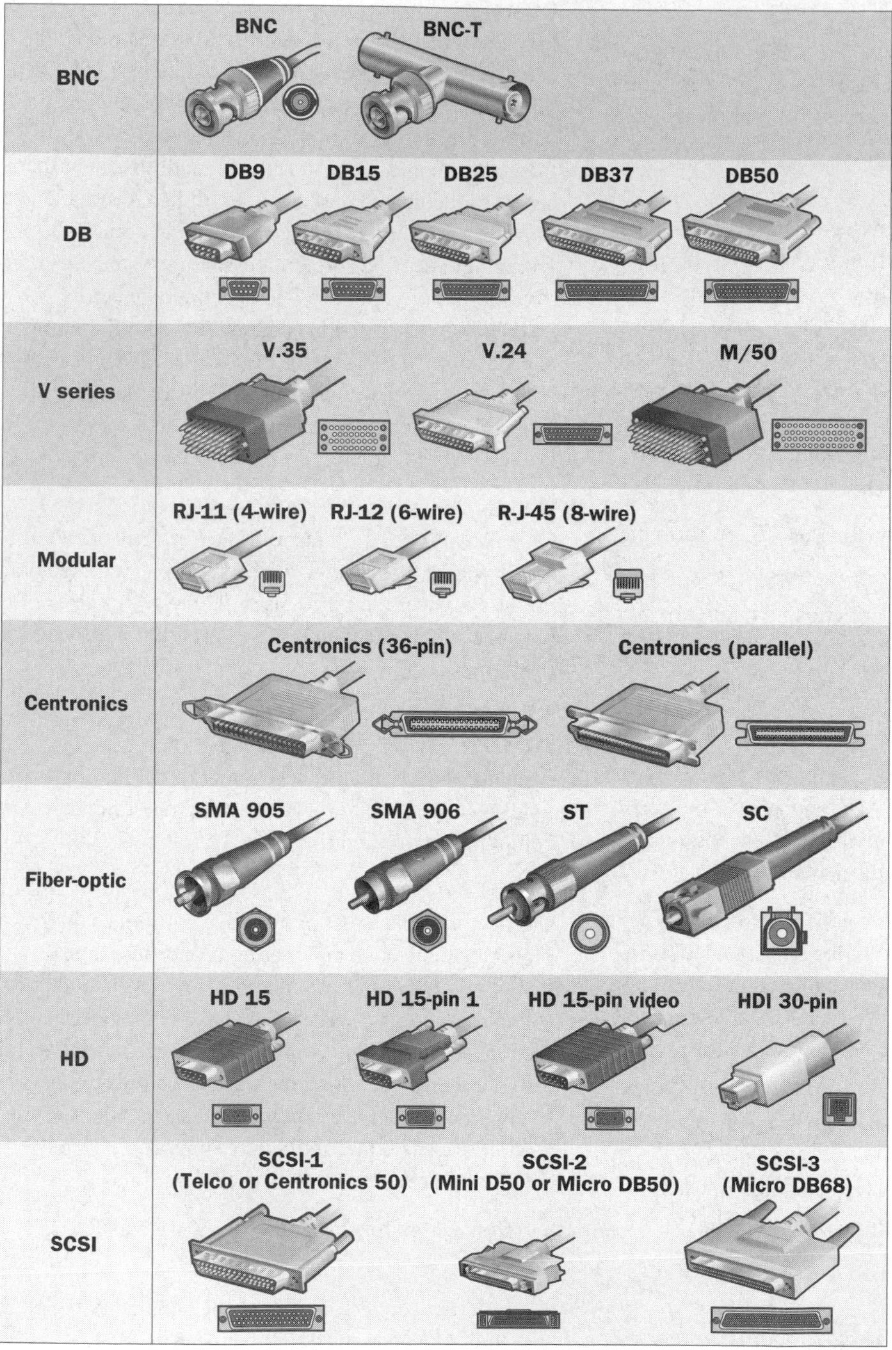

Connector (device). *Common networking and telecommunications connectors.*

A single connector may be used for a variety of purposes and different interfaces. For example, the DB-60 connector supports any of the following interfaces: V.35, X.21, EIA-530, EIA/TIA-232, and EIA/TIA-449. So you cannot always tell from the appearance of a connector what its function is—it depends on the interface it implements.

There are literally dozens of types of connectors used in networking, and the networking professional needs to be familiar with many of them. The illustration shows some of the common connector types used in different aspects of networking and telecommunications. Many of these connectors are discussed in separate articles elsewhere in this book.

Connector for Lotus cc:Mail

A component of Microsoft Exchange Server 5.5 that enables message transfer and directory synchronization between Exchange Server and Lotus cc:Mail systems.

Overview

Lotus cc:Mail uses a shared-file messaging architecture similar to that of Microsoft Mail. The Connector for Lotus cc:Mail is implemented as a Microsoft Windows NT service on Exchange Server and supports the following functions:

- Message transfer between Exchange Server and cc:Mail messaging systems
- Synchronization of directory information between Exchange Server and cc:Mail servers

Only one Connector for Lotus cc:Mail can be installed on a given computer running Exchange Server, and that connector can connect to only one cc:Mail postoffice. However, multiple computers running Exchange Server can each have a cc:Mail connector installed in order to connect to multiple postoffices throughout a cc:Mail messaging system. The Lotus cc:Mail programs export.exe and import.exe must be installed on the computer running Exchange Server for connectivity to be established.

The Connector for Lotus cc:Mail can be used to provide connectivity with database versions 6 or 8 cc:Mail postoffices.

Connector for Lotus Notes

A component of Microsoft Exchange Server 5.5 that enables message transfers and directory synchronization between Exchange Server and Lotus Notes systems.

Overview

The Connector for Lotus Notes allows either single or multiple Lotus Notes servers to be accessed from a single machine running Exchange Server. The Connector for Lotus Notes is implemented as a Microsoft Windows NT service on Exchange Server and supports

- Message transfer between Exchange Server and Lotus Notes
- Synchronization of directory information between Exchange Server and Lotus Notes

The Connector for Lotus Notes also converts message content to Rich Text Format (RTF) and converts Object Linking and Embedding (OLE) objects on Exchange Server to Lotus Doclinks objects.

The Connector for Lotus Notes supports Lotus Notes 3.*x* and Lotus Notes/Domino 4.*x*.

Notes

Be sure to install the Lotus Notes client on the computer running Exchange Server prior to attempting to install the Connector for Lotus Notes on the machine. The connector needs this client to log on to the Lotus Notes mail server. If you have trouble establishing connectivity, check that the connector has a valid Lotus Notes ID and that this ID has the appropriate permissions needed to access the databases on the machine running Lotus Notes.

connector (Microsoft Exchange)

A component of Microsoft Exchange Server 5.5 used to connect Exchange sites or to connect an Exchange organization to foreign mail systems.

Overview

Connectors are components of Exchange that can be used to route messages over a messaging system.

Connectors are implemented on Exchange as Microsoft Windows NT services and can be stopped and started using the Services utility in Control Panel.

Various types of connectors can be installed on Exchange, including the following:

- **Site Connector:** Used for establishing high-speed messaging links between different sites in an Exchange organization
- **X.400 Connector:** Used for establishing connectivity with a foreign X.400 messaging system such as those found in different parts of Europe
- **Dynamic RAS Connector:** Used for establishing dial-up connectivity between sites in an Exchange organization
- **Internet Mail Service:** Used for establishing connectivity with the Internet's Simple Mail Transfer Protocol (SMTP) messaging system
- **Microsoft Mail Connector:** Used for establishing messaging connectivity with legacy Microsoft Mail networks
- **Connector for Lotus cc:Mail:** Used for establishing connectivity with a foreign cc:Mail system
- **Connector for Lotus Notes:** Used for establishing connectivity with a Lotus Notes network

See Also: *Connector for Lotus cc:Mail, Connector for Lotus Notes*

Consumer DSL (CDSL)

A broadband transmission technology based on Digital Subscriber Line (DSL) technologies.

Overview

Consumer DSL (CDSL) was developed by Rockwell and is a slower technology than the more common DSL variant called Asymmetric Digital Subscriber Line (ADSL). CDSL provides data rates of about 1 megabit per second (Mbps) downstream (about 128 kilobits per second [Kbps] upstream) to the customer premises over standard Plain Old Telephone Service (POTS) local loop wiring. However, CDSL has the advantage of not requiring installation of a splitter at the customer premises. CDSL can operate only at distances of up to 18,000 feet (5500 meters) from the telco's central office (CO).

See Also: *Digital Subscriber Line (DSL)*

container (Active Directory)

In Microsoft Windows 2000 and Windows .NET Server, an object in Active Directory directory service that can contain other objects.

Overview

Examples of containers include organizational units (OUs), domains, and local networks. Domains are the core containers for organizing the structure of Active Directory. The other kinds of objects in Active Directory are leaf objects, which cannot contain other objects.

Objects created in a container inherit the discretionary access control list (DACL) of the container itself. In other words, a child object obtains its permissions from its parent object by inheritance.

Notes

Groups are not containers; they are security principals.

See Also: *Active Directory*

container (Microsoft Management Console)

In Microsoft Management Console (MMC), any node in a console tree to which other nodes can be added.

Overview

The usual icon for a container in MMC is the folder icon. The highest-level container in a console is the console root node. Beneath this node in the hierarchy are the top-level nodes for individual snap-ins that have been installed. Administrators who are creating new MMC consoles can create additional containers (folders) for organizing their console trees as desired.

See Also: *Microsoft Management Console (MMC)*

container (NTFS)

In NTFS file system (NTFS), a file system object (such as a directory) that can contain other objects (such as files).

C

Overview

Objects created in a container inherit the access control list (ACL) of the container itself. In other words, a child object obtains its permissions from its parent object by inheritance. For example, if a directory on an NTFS volume has read permission assigned to the Everyone group, any new file that you create or save in the directory will inherit the same permission. Using containers therefore simplifies the assignment of permissions to objects in the file system.

See Also: NTFS file system (NTFS)

Content Advisor

A feature of Microsoft Internet Explorer that allows you to control user access to Web sites based on the content ratings of the sites.

Overview

The Internet provides individuals with access to a wide variety of information, but some of this information might be unsuitable for certain viewers. For example, parents are often concerned about their children being exposed to violent or sexually explicit material on the Internet.

Content Advisor lets you control the kind of Internet content that can be accessed using Internet Explorer. This is a useful feature in corporate networks that have high-speed connectivity to the Internet because it can be used to discourage improper use of Web browsers on employee machines, thus helping to implement a company's acceptable use policy for the Internet. With Content Advisor, you can specify ratings settings to indicate acceptable levels of content to view with regard to sex, nudity, violence, and offensive language, and you can password-protect these settings.

Notes

Content Advisor functions properly only with Web sites that are rated.

Content Analyzer

A tool included with Microsoft Site Server and Microsoft Site Server Express that lets Web server administrators perform content analysis and link management of Web sites.

Overview

Content Analyzer can visually display the structure and integrity of a site in the form of a diagram called a Web map. Web maps allow administrators to visually examine a site's structure and quickly identify problems, such as loops and broken links. Web maps display various Web content items using different icons and can use a variety of colors to convey different kinds of information. You can also use Content Analyzer to search Web maps for various kinds of information using predefined Quick Searches. When you find an item of interest on a Web map, you can open your Web page editing tool directly from the Web map. You can also export Web map information into a database or spreadsheet file for further analysis.

Content Analyzer can also generate predefined site reports you can use to identify broken links and analyze the structure of Web sites. These site reports can be generated in Hypertext Markup Language (HTML) format for easy reading and evaluation and can identify changes to the content of a site, broken links, and other information.

content caching

A feature of a proxy server such as Microsoft Proxy Server.

Overview

Content caching allows a proxy server to cache the results of a client request. The next time a client requests the same content, it is retrieved from the cache to improve performance. Content remains in the cache for a predetermined period of time, or until the cache becomes full and old content is moved to allow new content to be cached.

Microsoft Proxy Server makes use of distributed caching, which lets content caching take place closer to users and allows caching activity to be load-balanced across several Proxy Servers for scalability and fault tolerance. For example, within corporate intranets, caching can be moved toward the branch office and workgroup levels of the organization. For Internet service providers (ISPs), caching can be moved toward regional points of presence (POPs). Distributed caching is particularly effective for solving network bandwidth problems associated with Internet push technologies.

Microsoft Proxy Server's distributed caching can be implemented in two ways:

- **Array-based caching:** In this approach, an array or group of proxy servers works together and is administered as a single, logical entity. A cache array provides load balancing, fault tolerance, scalability, and ease of administration. Cache arrays can provide a higher cache hit rate than an individual proxy server because of the larger size of the virtual cache.
- **Hierarchical caching:** In this approach, you arrange proxy servers in a hierarchy by branch office or department. Requests from clients are then forwarded up the hierarchy until the requested object is found in a proxy server's cache.

See Also: proxy server

content delivery network (CDN)

A method for efficiently pushing out content over the Internet to users.

Overview

The idea of content delivery networks originated as the next evolutionary step up from caching ofWeb content on the Internet. Like caching, the idea of CDN is to deliver content to users over the Internet as efficiently and quickly as possible. CDN takes caching a step further by actively pushing content out rather than passively caching frequently-requested content. A company that builds and operates a CDN is sometimes called a Content Delivery Provider (CDP).

Akamai Technologies developed the first CDN solution to efficiently deliver streaming media content over the Internet. Akamai accomplished this through alliances with regional Internet service providers (ISPs) for hosting their caching servers around the globe and setting up their own advanced Web hosting centers. Akamai then used forward-proxy caching servers at their hosting centers to push content out to caching servers at the edges of the Internet, allowing users around the globe to access streaming media presentations from nearby caching servers instead of from centralized streaming media servers many network hops away. The result was a system with better performance than existing implementations of streaming media.

CDNs are now used not just for streaming media but for supporting a wide variety of different kinds of content delivered over the Internet including static and dynamic Web content, video-on-demand, and other services.

Implementation

There are many ways to implement a CDN, and the technology continues to evolve rapidly. A simple example would be a CDP that hosts content for a company on Web and media servers in its data center and then uses a private network to push this content out to caching servers colocated at points of presence (POPs) of regional ISPs located near the company's customers. The private network could be a satellite link, leased lines, private backbone networks (such as those owned by AT&T Wireless), or a leased portion of Internet backbone bandwidth (usually an expensive solution). Private peering arrangements between ISPs and the CDP enable the CDN to work. Personalization servers keep track of user personalization data for customers in different regions.

The resulting CDN can be envisioned as a "content island" within the ocean representing the Internet—only subscribers on this island can make use of the CDN to improve access to hosted content. With many CDNs in existence around the globe and run by different CDPs, interoperability between them becomes an issue—what if a subscriber of one CDN wants to access content in a different CDN?To solve this problem, the Content Bridge is a vendor consortium of CDNs and CDPs whose aim is to move toward developing new protocols to enable interoperability between different CDNs so that a subscriber of one CDN can access content from the network of a different CDN. The Internet Engineering Task Force (IETF) is also working on a number of draft protocols to support interoperability between different CDNs.

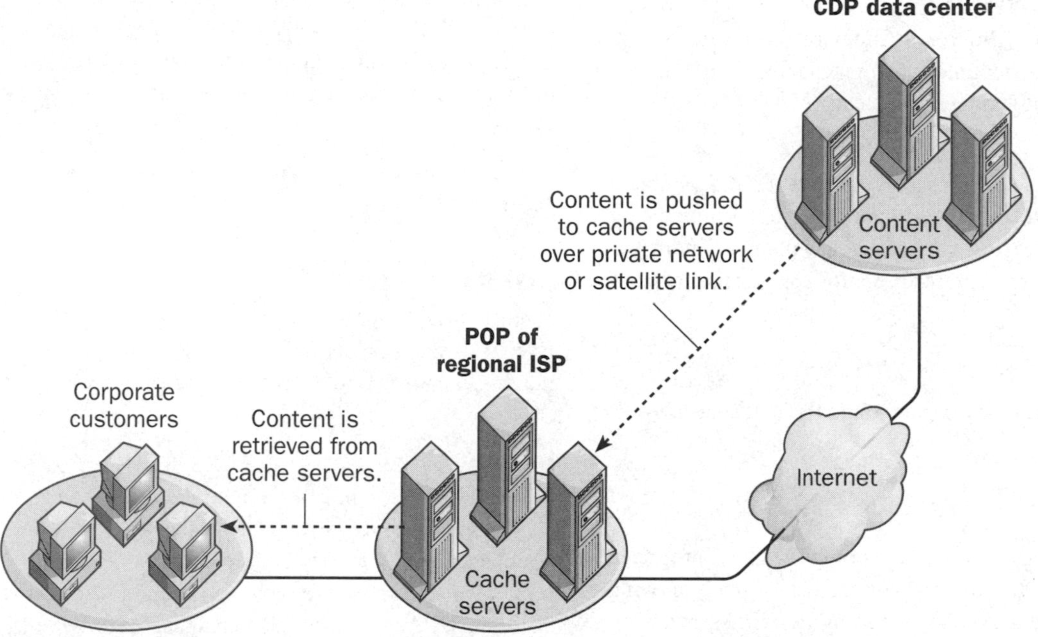

Content delivery network (CDN). *A simple example of how a CDN works.*

Marketplace

Since Akamai blazed the path, a plethora of new CDNs have arisen and are vying for market dominance. These include

- CDNs built by private companies such as Yahoo! that have put together their own custom CDNs using technologies from vendors such as Cisco Systems.
- Companies such as Inktomi Corporation, CacheFlow, and Network Appliance that create hardware and software tools that can be used to build custom CDNs.
- Pure-play CDPs who build virtual CDNs by leasing bandwidth needed to push out their content to cache servers from bandwidth providers (BPs) such as Exodus Communications and Globix Corporation.

Despite the proliferation of CDN vendors and solution providers, Akamai and Inktomi, two early comers to the market, have established their platforms as cornerstone solutions for many large ISPs and enterprise customers. Akamai has more than 4000 caching servers distributed at POPs in over 50 countries. Other prominent players include new companies such as Digital Island. Existing networking companies are also releasing CDN solutions to the marketplace, though, including Cisco and Lucent Technologies.

A number of vendors are offering turnkey CDN solutions that can be easily implemented to improve content hosting performance for corporate intranets, ISPs, carriers, and others who need it. A leading vendor of CDN-in-a-box solutions is EdgeStream.

See Also: *caching*

Content Delivery Provider (CDP)

A company that builds and operates a content delivery network (CDN).

See: *content delivery network (CDN)*

content filter

A component of Microsoft Indexing service that can read a specific document format and turn it into a stream of text characters.

Overview

Content filters are an essential part of the indexing process on Indexing service because they determine which types of documents can be read and indexed. Indexing service includes content filters for popular file formats such as

- ASCII text
- Hypertext Markup Language (HTML) pages
- Microsoft Word documents
- Microsoft Excel spreadsheets

In addition, many third-party companies have produced content filters for their own document formats, allowing these documents to be indexed by Indexing service when their content filters have been installed. Content filters also handle the presence of embedded objects in documents and recognize when a language shift occurs in a multilingual document.

contention

A condition that occurs when two or more stations on a network try to access the network medium simultaneously. In other words, the stations are contending for control of the medium.

Overview

There are different ways of resolving contention issues on a network. One way is to use a single station as the master or primary station that controls all communication on the network. Other devices on the network function as slave, or secondary, stations. The entire system is known as a master-slave system. The master station normally functions in transmit mode, while the slave stations operate in receive mode. The master station tells individual slave stations when they should switch to transmit mode in order to transmit information over the network. This kind of scenario is used in networks based on IBM's Systems Network Architecture (SNA).

In Ethernet networks, the Carrier Sense Multiple Access with Collision Detection (CSMA/CD) method is used to resolve contention on the network by allowing collisions to occur, and then resolving them successfully.

See Also: Carrier Sense Multiple Access with Collision Detection (CSMA/CD)

content rating

A mechanism for preventing users of Microsoft Internet Explorer from viewing Web sites that contain objectionable language, violence, nudity, or sexually explicit content.

Overview

These ratings are configured on the Web server on a site-by-site basis. Ratings for each category have been established at four levels of acceptable use. The Webmaster who creates the site can then include information about the levels of objectionable language, violence, nudity, or sexually explicit content present on their site. Content ratings are defined by the Recreational Software Advisory Council (RSAC). The user can configure her browser to a specified accessibility level for each type of content by using the Content Advisor feature of Internet Explorer.

For More Information

RSAC can be found at *www.rsac.org.*

control message

A command sent from one Usenet host to another.

Overview

Control messages are defined in the Network News Transfer Protocol (NNTP) specifications. Control messages can be issued by Usenet hosts to perform actions such as

- Creating a new newsgroup on the host
- Deleting a newsgroup
- Canceling messages that have already been posted

Control messages are simple text commands. You can troubleshoot a Usenet host by using telnet to connect to port 119 and manually typing various control messages and examining their results.

See Also: *Network News Transfer Protocol (NNTP), Usenet*

Control Panel

A Microsoft Windows feature consisting of a number of utilities for configuring hardware devices and operating system services.

Overview

The following table shows some of the more common Control Panel utilities in Windows 95, Windows 98, Windows NT, Windows 2000, Windows XP, and Windows .NET Server and briefly describes their function. Note that some utilities are named differently in the various Windows versions, such as 32-bit ODBC for Windows NT and ODBC (32 bit) for Windows 95 or 98; these utilities are listed separately here. Note also that some Control Panel utilities are present only when additional Windows components have been installed. For example, the GSNW utility is present only when Gateway Services for NetWare has been installed. Finally, installing additional third-party software can add new utilities to Control Panel associated with that software.

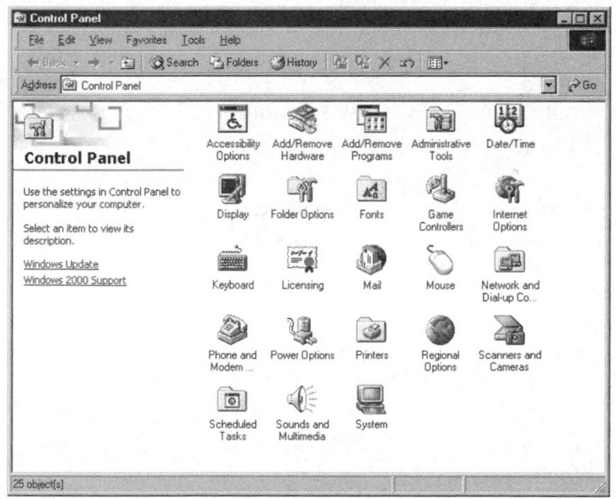

Control Panel. *Windows 2000 Control Panel.*

Common Control Panel Utilities

Control Panel Utility	*Function*	*Windows 95 and 98*	*Windows NT*	*Windows 2000*	*Windows XP and .NET Server*
32-bit ODBC	Database connectivity		x	x	x
Accessibility Options	Help for visually or motor-impaired individuals	x		x	x
Add New Hardware	Hardware installation wizard	x			
Add/Remove Hardware	Hardware installation wizard			x	x
Add/Remove Programs	Installs new software or Windows components	x	x	x	x
Administrative Tools	Shortcut to Administrative Tools program group			x	x
Console	Command prompt window		x		
Date/Time	Date, time, time zone	x	x	x	x
Desktop Themes	Configures appearance of desktop	x			
Devices	Startup profiles for hardware devices		x		
Dial-Up Monitor	Monitors RAS connections		x		
Display	Screen and desktop settings	x	x	x	x
Folder Options	Enables Active Desktop and determines how folders are displayed			x	x
Fonts	Installs new fonts	x	x	x	x
Game Controllers	Configures joysticks	x		x	x
GSNW	Gateway Services for NetWare		x	x	x
Internet	Internet Explorer options	x	x		

(continued)

C

Common Control Panel Utilities *continued*

Control Panel Utility	*Function*	*Windows 95 and 98*	*Windows NT*	*Windows 2000*	*Windows XP and .NET Server*
Internet Options	Internet Explorer options			x	x
Keyboard	Style and response rate	x	x	x	x
Licensing	Changes licensing mode and configures replication		x	x	x
MacFile	Services for Macintosh		x		
Mail	Messaging profiles	x	x	x	x
Message Queuing	Configuration options for Microsoft Message Queue Server			x	x
Modems	Modem settings	x	x		
Mouse	Mouse settings	x	x	x	x
Multimedia	Audio/video settings	x	x		
Network	Networking clients, services, protocols, and adapters	x	x		
Network and Dial-up Connections	Creates and configures network connections			x	x
ODBC (32-bit)	Database connectivity	x			
Passwords	Configures passwords, enables remote administration, and enables user profiles	x			
PC Card	Settings for Personal Computer Memory Card International Association (PCMCIA) cards	x	x	x	x
Phone and Modem	Modem and TAPI location settings			x	x
Ports	COM port settings		x		

(continued)

Common Control Panel Utilities *continued*

Control Panel Utility	*Function*	*Windows 95 and 98*	*Windows NT*	*Windows 2000*	*Windows XP and .NET Server*
Power Management	Advanced power management settings	x		x	x
Power Options	Advanced power management settings			x	x
Printers	Adds printer wizard and manages printers	x	x	x	x
Regional Options	Currency and other settings for countries and regions			x	x
Regional Settings	Currency and other settings for countries and regions	x	x		
Scanners and Cameras	Configures these devices			x	x
Scheduled Tasks	Schedule system management tasks			x	x
SCSI Adapters	SCSI device settings		x		
Server	Server role		x		
Services	Starting and stopping services		x		
Sounds	System sounds	x	x		
Sounds and Multimedia	Audio/visual hardware/software and system sounds			x	x
System	Boot, file system, profiles, devices, environment, network identification, and other functions (depending on the version of Windows)	x	x	x	x
Tape Devices	Tape drive settings		x		
Telephony	TAPI location settings	x	x		
UPS	Uninterruptible Power Supply settings		x		
Users	User profiles	x			

control set

Refers to a set of registry keys in Microsoft Windows 2000, Windows XP, and Windows .NET Server that contain configuration information used for system startup.

Overview

Control sets define certain aspects of the Windows 2000, Windows XP, and Windows .NET Server boot process to allow Windows 2000, Windows XP, and Windows .NET Server to boot up successfully. Up to four control set subkeys are located under the HKEY_LOCAL_MACHINE\SYSTEM registry key, including the following:

- ControlSet001, ControlSet002, and so on, which represent backup copies of control sets that successfully started the system.
- CurrentControlSet, which refers to the control set that was used to successfully boot the system under its current configuration. The key here is a pointer to one of the ControlSet00x registry keys.

The Select registry key found under HKEY_LOCAL_MACHINES\SYSTEM identifies which of the control set keys corresponds to the current, default, failed, and Last Known Good configurations. If the current control set cannot start the system, you can press the Spacebar when indicated during the boot process to select the last known good configuration, which is the last control set that worked for sure.

See Also: *registry*

convergence

The process of updating routing tables after a change in the routing topology of an internetwork.

Overview

When a change occurs in the routing infrastructure of an internetwork, information concerning the change needs to be replicated to all routers that need to know about it. The process by which all routers gradually become aware of the change that occurred is called convergence.

Examples of occurrences that affect the routing infrastructure of an internetwork include adding a new router to the network, having an existing router fail on the network, and adding a new route to the routing table of a router on the network. When any of these situations arise, the routing protocol used to provide communications between the routers on your network is used to communicate these changes to all the routers that need to be aware of them. It typically takes time (from minutes to hours) for such changes to propagate completely through the internetwork's routing infrastructure, and as routers become updated with the new routing information, the network is said to "converge" toward its final state.

Convergence is important—if it does not occur fully, some routes may be unavailable on the network, making some parts of the network inaccessible. Furthermore, some packets may end up disappearing into "black holes" instead of arriving at their destination.

Notes

A more popular usage of the term *convergence* is to describe the merging of voice, data, and video services for transmission over a single network.

See Also: *black hole, internetwork, routing*

cookie

A small text file that the Web server saves the Web browser during a Hypertext Transfer Protocol (HTTP) session.

Overview

Cookies were originally intended to enable session state information to be maintained for Web applications across multiple HTTP requests. However, most commercial Web sites also use cookies to record information about the client's usage patterns, including the date and time the client visited the site, which pages were accessed, and Web browser preferences. Other uses for cookies include providing custom or personalized pages for users visiting Web sites, targeting advertising to users according to the pattern of their previous visits to a site, and enabling online shopping carts to function.

Cookies use the storage system of the client for saving this information instead of storing it on the server. Because the vast number of clients might visit the site only once, it would be inefficient to dedicate a large portion of server storage to tracking anonymous clients who might never return. Furthermore, client preferences (such as IP address) might change between sessions, especially for dial-up clients, so servers would have no way of recognizing clients if cookie information were saved on the server. Cookies therefore provide a way for the server to recognize that the client previously visited the site and record what the client did during previous visits, allowing the server to customize the HTTP session to meet the needs of the client (or the needs of the site's advertisers!).

Cookies are harmless text files and cannot be used to transmit a virus to the client. Cookies are simply passive holders of information; they cannot be used by hackers and other unauthorized users to "get" information off your computer such as your e-mail address. Nevertheless, most Web browsers, such as Microsoft Internet Explorer, have an optional setting that allows users to reject cookies. However, rejecting cookies can result in poorer browsing experiences on sites that are cookie-dependent. You can also delete any cookies on a computer running Microsoft Windows by deleting the contents of the Cookies subdirectory within the user profile directory on your hard drive (do not delete the directory itself, however!)

Notes

Web applications written using Microsoft Active Server Pages (ASP) technology can use cookies for maintaining session state information.

Shareware sites offer a variety of third-party browser plug-ins for managing or disabling cookies.

See Also: *Hypertext Transfer Protocol (HTTP), Web browser, Web server*

copper cabling

One of the two basic types of physical cabling media (the other being glass, or fiber-optic, cabling).

Overview

Copper cabling is cheap and flexible, but it is susceptible to electromagnetic interference (EMI), has limited range because of attenuation, and generates electromagnetic radiation that can be intercepted by nearby equipment. The types of copper cabling commonly used in networking include

- Twisted-pair cabling, such as unshielded twisted-pair (UTP) cabling and shielded twisted-pair (STP) cabling
- Coaxial cabling, such as thinnet and thicknet

For more information on these types of copper cabling, refer to their individual entries in this book.

Implementation

UTP cabling of Category 5 (Cat5) grade is the most commonly used copper cabling in networking environments today. Cat5 cabling comes in either solid core or stranded cabling. Solid core cabling is stiffer, but it has better conductivity and less attenuation, and it is simpler to terminate than stranded cabling. Stranded cabling is more flexible and easier to work with than solid cabling, and it is more resistant to breaking or fracturing. Use solid core UTP cabling for fixed horizontal cable runs, cross-connects, and backbone cabling; use stranded UTP cabling for locations where equipment is frequently moved, for short cable runs between computers and wall plates, or as patch cables in the wiring closet.

See Also: *cabling, coaxial cabling, fiber-optic cabling, unshielded twisted-pair (UTP) cabling*

Copper Distributed Data Interface (CDDI)

A form of Fiber Distributed Data Interface (FDDI) deployed over copper cabling instead of fiber.

Overview

Copper Distributed Data Interface (CDDI) can send data over unshielded twisted-pair (UTP) cabling at 100 megabits per second (Mbps), but cable lengths are limited to about 330 feet (100 meters). The architecture and operation are similar to FDDI, but CDDI is not as commonly implemented as FDDI (and because FDDI is usually considered a legacy networking architecture now, CDDI is also likely to fade away quickly.

If cost is an issue, CDDI offers an alternative to FDDI. CDDI still provides a 100-Mbps network with redundancy, but at reduced cost because copper cabling is cheaper than fiber-optic cabling. Note that CDDI does not provide the security that FDDI does: copper cabling can be tapped, but fiber-optic cabling cannot.

See Also: *Fiber Distributed Data Interface (FDDI)*

copy backup

A backup type in which all the selected files and folders are backed up, but the archive attribute is not marked for each file and folder.

Overview

Copy backups (or simply copies) do not interrupt the normal backup schedule because they do not change the state of the archive bit on files being backed up. Copy backups are typically used to produce additional copies of backup tapes. Copy backups might be used for

- Archiving information in a different location
- Generating tapes of month-end financials, which can then be given to the accounting department
- Providing branch offices with copies of information on file servers

See Also: *backup, backup type*

copying files

Making a replica of files.

Overview

On Microsoft Windows platforms, files can be copied using a graphical user interface (GUI) tool such as Windows Explorer or from the command prompt using the copy command. Some inheritance issues are associated with copying files on Windows NT, Windows 2000, Windows XP, and Windows .NET Server platforms that use the NTFS file system (NTFS). Specifically, copying a file within or between different NTFS volumes causes the file to inherit the permissions of the folder into which it is copied. For example, if a file on the NTFS drive C has read permission for everyone and it is copied to a directory on the NTFS drive D, which has change permission for everyone, the copy of the file inherits the change permission from the directory it is moved to.

See Also: *moving files*

CORBA

Stands for Common Object Request Broker Architecture, a component architecture that specifies technologies for creating, distributing, and managing component programming objects over a network.

See: *Common Object Request Broker Architecture (CORBA)*

Core-Based Trees (CBT)

A multicast routing protocol.

Overview

Internet Protocol (IP) multicasting relies on the spanning tree algorithm to ensure delivery of information to intended recipients. Spanning-tree technologies can be implemented in two basic ways:

- **Dense mode:** Used for Webcasting and other large-scale multicast events.
- **Sparse mode:** Used for delivering multicast information to specific, small pockets of users on a large internetwork.

Core-Based Trees (CBT) is one of two sparse-mode protocols commonly used, the other being Protocol Independent Multicast Sparse Mode (PIM-SM).

Architecture

CBT works by having a single core router create a single multicast routing tree, regardless of the multicast transmission's source. Then, when a multicast client wants to register to receive a multicast transmission, the client contacts the nearest upstream multicast router by sending an Internet Group Membership Protocol (IGMP) packet to the router. If the member router is already receiving the multicast transmission, it registers the client and forwards the transmission to the client. If the router is not receiving the transmission, it contacts the next router upstream, and this continues until, if necessary, the core router is reached. The core router then adds the member routers to the multicast group and forwards the transmission to the member router, which then passes it to the client.

See Also: *dense mode, multicasting, Protocol Independent Multicast-Sparse Mode (PIM-SM), routing, sparse mode*

counter

An aspect of an object in Performance for which usage statistics can be collected.

Overview

Performance is a Microsoft Windows 2000, Windows XP, and Windows .NET Server administrative console for monitoring system resources. It can be used to collect status information about various objects. For example, if the object Processor is being studied, the Performance Monitor collects information on all counters that belong to this object. This includes counters such as

- **% User Time:** The percentage of the time the processor is in user mode executing a nonidle thread
- **% Privileged Time:** The percentage of the time the processor is in kernel mode executing a nonidle thread
- **Interrupts/sec:** The number of device interrupts a processor receives per second

If the machine is a multiprocessor system, each instance of each counter can be monitored. Performance Monitor counters are usually one of two types:

- Instantaneous counters, which display the most recent value of a measurement— for example, Processor: % Processor Time
- Average counters, which display the average of the last two measured values— for example, LogicalDisk: Avg. Disk Bytes/Read

country code

A two-letter code identifying top-level domains for countries and regions in the Domain Name System (DNS).

Overview

Country codes are a way of geographically identifying a domain name as belonging to a particular country or region. They are an alternative to the more commonly used organizational codes such as .com, .org, and .net. This table lists the various country codes in the DNS system.

Country Codes

Code	*Country/Region*	*Code*	*Country/Region*
ad	Andorra	ca	Canada
ae	United Arab Emirates	cc	Cocos (Keeling Islands)
af	Afghanistan	cf	Central African Republic
ag	Antigua and Barbuda	cg	Congo (Congo Republic)
ai	Anguilla	ch	Switzerland
al	Albania	ci	Cote d'Ivoire
am	Armenia	ck	Cook Islands
an	Netherlands Antilles	cl	Chile
ao	Angola	cm	Cameroon
aq	Antarctica	cn	China
ar	Argentina	co	Colombia
as	American Samoa	cr	Costa Rica
at	Austria	cu	Cuba
au	Australia	cv	Cape Verde
aw	Aruba	cx	Christmas Island
az	Azerbaijan	cy	Cyprus
ba	Bosnia and Herzegovina	cz	Czech Republic
bb	Barbados	de	Germany
bd	Bangladesh	dj	Djibouti
be	Belgium	dk	Denmark
bf	Burkina Faso	dm	Dominica
bg	Bulgaria	do	Dominican Republic
bh	Bahrain	dz	Algeria
bi	Burundi	ec	Ecuador
bj	Benin	ee	Estonia
bm	Bermuda	eg	Egypt
bn	Brunei Darussalam	eh	Western Sahara
bo	Bolivia	er	Eritrea
br	Brazil	es	Spain
bs	Bahamas	et	Ethiopia
bt	Bhutan	fi	Finland
bv	Bouvet Island	fj	Fiji Islands
bw	Botswana	fk	Falkland Islands (Islas Malvinas)
by	Belarus	fm	Micronesia
bz	Belize	fo	Faroe Islands

(continued)

C

Country Codes *continued*

Code	Country/Region	Code	Country/Region
fr	France	jp	Japan
fx	France (Metropolitan)	ke	Kenya
ga	Gabon	kg	Kyrgyzstan
gd	Grenada	kh	Cambodia
ge	Georgia	ki	Kiribati
gf	French Guiana	km	Comoros
gh	Ghana	kn	Saint Kitts and Nevis
gi	Gibraltar	kp	Korea (North)
gl	Greenland	kr	Korea (South)
gm	Gambia	kw	Kuwait
gn	Guinea	ky	Cayman Islands
gp	Guadeloupe	kz	Kazakhstan
gq	Equatorial Guinea	la	Laos
gr	Greece	lb	Lebanon
gs	South Georgia and South Sandwich Islands	lc	Saint Lucia
gt	Guatemala	li	Liechtenstein
gu	Guam	lk	Sri Lanka
gw	Guinea-Bissau	lr	Liberia
gy	Guyana	ls	Lesotho
hk	Hong Kong SAR	lt	Lithuania
hm	Heard and McDonald Islands	lu	Luxembourg
hn	Honduras	lv	Latvia
hr	Croatia (Hrvatska)	ly	Libya
ht	Haiti	ma	Morocco
hu	Hungary	mc	Monaco
id	Indonesia	md	Moldova
ie	Ireland	mg	Madagascar
il	Israel	mh	Marshall Islands
in	India	mk	Macedonia, Former Yugoslav Republic of
io	British Indian Ocean Territory	ml	Mali
iq	Iraq	mm	Myanmar
ir	Iran	mn	Mongolia
is	Iceland	mo	Macau SAR
it	Italy	mp	Northern Mariana Islands
jm	Jamaica	mq	Martinique
jo	Jordan	mr	Mauritania

(continued)

Country Codes *continued*

Code	Country/Region	Code	Country/Region
ms	Montserrat	ru	Russian Federation
mt	Malta	rw	Rwanda
mu	Mauritius	sa	Saudi Arabia
mv	Maldives	sb	Solomon Islands
mw	Malawi	sc	Seychelles
mx	Mexico	sd	Sudan
my	Malaysia	se	Sweden
mz	Mozambique	sg	Singapore
na	Namibia	sh	St. Helena
nc	New Caledonia	si	Slovenia
ne	Niger	sj	Svalbard and Jan Mayen Islands
nf	Norfolk Island	sk	Slovak Republic
ng	Nigeria	sl	Sierra Leone
ni	Nicaragua	sm	San Marino
nl	Netherlands	sn	Senegal
no	Norway	so	Somalia
np	Nepal	sr	Suriname
nr	Nauru	st	Sao Tome and Principe
nu	Niue	sv	El Salvador
nz	New Zealand	sy	Syria
om	Oman	sz	Swaziland
pa	Panama	tc	Turks and Caicos Islands
pe	Peru	td	Chad
pf	French Polynesia	tf	French Southern Territories
pg	Papua New Guinea	tg	Togo
ph	Philippines	th	Thailand
pk	Pakistan	tj	Tajikistan
pl	Poland	tk	Tokelau
pm	St. Pierre and Miquelon	tm	Turkmenistan
pn	Pitcairn	tn	Tunisia
pr	Puerto Rico	to	Tonga
pt	Portugal	tp	East Timor
pw	Palau	tr	Turkey
py	Paraguay	tt	Trinidad and Tobago
qa	Qatar	tv	Tuvalu
re	Reunion	tw	Taiwan
ro	Romania	tz	Tanzania

(continued)

C

Country Codes *continued*

Code	*Country/Region*	*Code*	*Country/Region*
ua	Ukraine	vi	Virgin Islands (US)
ug	Uganda	vn	Viet Nam
uk	United Kingdom	vu	Vanuatu
um	US Minor Outlying Islands	wf	Wallis and Futuna Islands
us	United States	ws	Samoa
uy	Uruguay	ye	Yemen
uz	Uzbekistan	yt	Mayotte
va	Vatican City State	yu	Yugoslavia
vc	Saint Vincent and The Grenadines	za	South Africa
ve	Venezuela	zm	Zambia
vg	Virgin Islands (British)	zr	Congo (Democratic Republic of Congo)
		zw	Zimbabwe

coupler

A small device for connecting two cables to make a longer cable, sometimes called an inline coupler.

Overview

Inline couplers do not provide any amplification or signal boost, and can cause attenuation and signal degradation unless they are of high quality. One example would be a small box that accepts two Category 5 (Cat5) cables with RJ-45 connectors and links them to form a longer cable. Another example would be the BNC barrel connector for joining two lengths of thinnet cabling. A third example would be a coupler with two RJ-11 connectors for joining two phone lines.

Coupler. *A Category 5 UTP (unshielded twisted-pair) coupler.*

The term *coupler* is also used to refer to modular connectors that can snap into customizable patch panels to allow different kinds of cabling to be mixed in one patch panel.

CPE

Stands for customer premises equipment (CPE), telecommunications equipment that is installed at the customer's location.

See: *customer premises equipment (CPE)*

CRC

Stands for cyclical redundancy check, an error-checking technique for ensuring packets are successfully delivered over a network

See: *cyclical redundancy check (CRC)*

Creator Owner

A Microsoft Windows 2000, Windows XP, or Windows .NET Server built-in identity that is used as a security context for running services and operating system functions.

Overview

The membership of the Creator Owner system group cannot be modified directly. The Creator Owner system group includes only the user who created or took ownership of a network resource and is functionally equivalent to that user's primary group. The Creator Owner system group has full permissions on the resource, but the rights of the Creator Owner system group cannot be modified. Whoever creates a file system object or print job becomes the Creator Owner of that object or job.

See Also: *built-in identities*

credentials

Information required from users who want to log on to a network and access its resources.

Overview

Credentials, which are formed by combining a user's username and password, identify users so that they can be authenticated by the network security provider. Credentials for access to one network do not guarantee access to another network.

In networks that are based on Microsoft Windows NT, Windows 2000, and Windows .NET Server, computers called domain controllers are responsible for authentication of user's credentials. In addition, trust relationships can be established between Windows NT domains to allow user's credentials to be authenticated from anywhere in the enterprise. Windows NT, Windows 2000, Windows XP, and Windows .NET Server support single-user logon, which allows a user to use a single set of credentials for accessing resources anywhere on a network.

See Also: *authentication protocol, password, username*

crimper

A cabling installation tool used for attaching connectors to cabling.

Overview

Crimpers are used to terminate cables by applying appropriate pressure to contacts within a connector so that it remains physically attached to the cable without soldering. A crimper is an essential component of a network administrator's toolkit. Crimpers can include built-in strippers for removing the outer insulation from a cable. They can include a set of dies for crimping different kinds of connectors, or they can be specialized for a single type of termination. Crimpers are most often used for terminating Category 5 (Cat5) unshielded twisted-pair (UTP) cabling with RJ-45 connectors. A good crimper should be made of heavy-duty metal and be able to cut, strip, and terminate a cable easily.

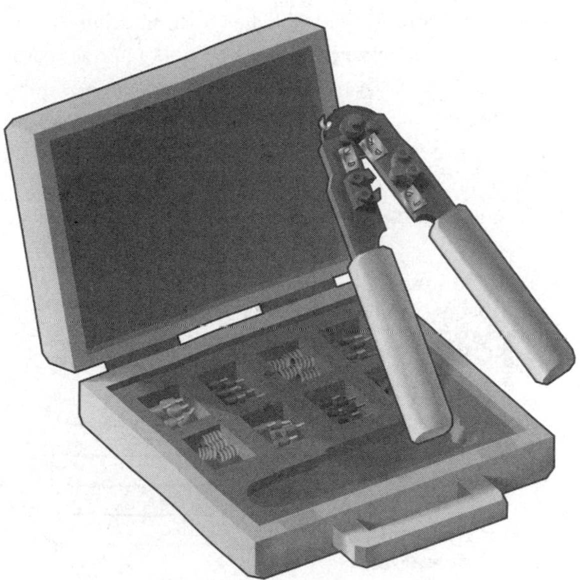

Crimper. *A crimper with connector set.*

See Also: *cabling, connector (device)*

CRL

Stands for certificate revocation list, a list, maintained by a certificate authority (CA), of digital certificates that have been issued and then later revoked.

See: *certificate revocation list (CRL)*

CRM

Stands for Customer Relations Management, a type of business application used to manage business-to-consumer (B2C) connections

See: *Customer Relationship Management (CRM)*

crossover cable

Twisted-pair cabling with the send and receive pairs of wires crossed.

Overview

Crossover cables are primarily used for connecting hubs to each other. In addition, a small, two-station local area network (LAN) can be established by connecting two computers together with 10BaseT network interface cards (NICs) and a crossover cable. This configuration is often utilized when one computer is used to test the networking functions of another because it allows the computer being tested to be isolated from the network. The illustration shows the pinning configuration of a crossover cable.

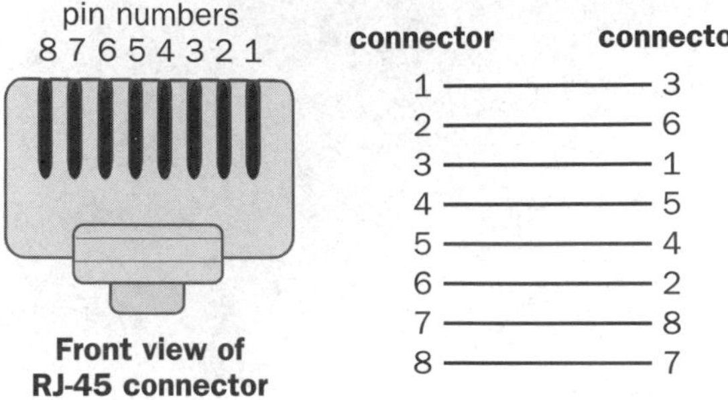

Crossover cable. *Pinning for a crossover cable.*

See Also: *cabling, twisted-pair cabling*

crosstalk

A form of interference in which signals in one cable induce electromagnetic interference (EMI) in an adjacent cable.

Overview

The ability of a cable to reject crosstalk in Ethernet networks is usually measured using a scale called near-end crosstalk (NEXT). NEXT is expressed in decibels (dB), and the higher the NEXT rating of a cable, the greater its ability to reject crosstalk. A more complex scale called Power Sum NEXT (PS NEXT) is used to quantify crosstalk in high-speed Asynchronous Transfer Mode (ATM) and Gigabit Ethernet (GbE) networks.

The twisting in twisted-pair cabling reduces the amount of crosstalk that occurs, and crosstalk can be further reduced by shielding cables or physically separating them. Crosstalk is a feature of copper cables only—fiber-optic cables do not experience crosstalk. Crosstalk can be a problem for unshielded twisted-pair (UTP) cabling. To minimize crosstalk, make sure that

- You do not untwist or sharply bend the UTP cabling
- The cable ends connected to a patch panel or wall plate are untwisted no more than 0.5 inch (1.3 centimeters)

See Also: *cabling, near-end crosstalk (NEXT)*

CryptoAPI

A core component of the latest versions of Microsoft Windows that provides application programming interfaces (APIs) for cryptographic security services that provide secure channels and code signing for communication between applications.

Overview

CryptoAPI provides a set of standard Win32 libraries for managing cryptographic functions using a single consistent interface independent of the underlying cryptographic algorithms and ciphers. CryptoAPI interfaces with modules called cryptographic service providers (CSPs), such as the Microsoft RSA Base Cryptographic Provider, to provide cryptography functions such as hashing, data encryption and decryption, key generation and exchange, digital signature issuance and verification, and so forth.

CryptoAPI is natively supported by the latest versions of Windows NT, Windows 98, Windows 2000, Windows XP, and Windows .NET Server. Microsoft Internet Explorer version 4 provides CryptoAPI support for Windows 95. The current version of CryptoAPI is version 2.

See Also: *cryptography*

Cryptographic Message Syntax Standard

A standard that defines the general syntax for data that includes cryptographic features such as digital signatures, encryption, and certificate chains.

Overview

Cryptographic Message Syntax Standard, also known as PKCS #7, specifies the format in which the data is signed and encrypted, and the types of encryption algorithms used.

Data encrypted according to the PKCS #7 standard can have multiple digital certificates attached, including certificate revocation lists (CRLs). Certificates include information concerning the issuer and serial number of the public key of the signer so that the recipient can decrypt the message.

See Also: *cryptography, digital certificate, encryption*

cryptography

In networking and telecommunications, the process of securely transmitting data over a network in such a way that if the data is intercepted, it cannot be read by unauthorized users.

Overview

Cryptography involves two complementary processes:

- **Encryption:** The process of taking data and modifying it so that it cannot be read by distrusted users.
- **Decryption:** The process of taking encrypted data and rendering it readable for trusted users.

Encryption and decryption are performed using algorithms and keys. An algorithm, a series of mathematical steps that scrambles data, is the underlying mathematical process behind encryption. There are a variety of cryptographic algorithms that have been developed based on different mathematical processes.

Some algorithms result in stronger encryption than others—the stronger the algorithm, the more difficult the encrypted data is to crack. For example, Network and Dial-up Connections in Microsoft Windows 2000 supports standard 40-bit RAS RC4 encryption, but if you are located in the United States or Canada, you can get a stronger 128-bit version. Similar versions are offered for Windows NT.

Encryption algorithms involve mathematical values called keys. Earlier cryptography systems were secret key encryption systems in which only the hosts involved in transmitting and receiving the encrypted transmission knew the key. This key had to somehow be transported securely to anyone needing to decrypt a message. This was the main disadvantage with secret key cryptosystems.

Most cryptography today involves a process called public key encryption, which uses two different keys:

- A public key that is distributed to any user (or to any client program) requesting it
- A private key that is known only to the owner (or the owner's client program)

To send an encrypted message, the sender uses his or her private key to encrypt the data, and the recipient uses the sender's public key to decrypt it. Similarly, the recipient can return a response to the original sender by using the sender's public key to encrypt the response, and the original sender uses his or her private key to decrypt it.

See Also: *digital certificate, public key cryptography*

CSMA/CA

Stands for Carrier Sense Multiple Access with Collision Avoidance, the media access control method used by AppleTalk.

See: *Carrier Sense Multiple Access with Collision Avoidance (CSMA/CA)*

CSMA/CD

Stands for Carrier Sense Multiple Access with Collision Detection, the media access control method used by half-duplex Ethernet networks.

See: *Carrier Sense Multiple Access with Collision Detection (CSMA/CD)*

CSNW

Stands for Client Services for NetWare, a Windows 2000, Windows XP, and Windows .NET Server service that provides Microsoft Windows clients with access to Novell NetWare file, print, and directory services.

See: *Client Services for NetWare (CSNW)*

CSP (caching service provider)

Stands for caching service provider, a company that maintains caching servers that speed the transfer of information across the Internet's infrastructure and offers managed access to these servers for a fee.

See: *caching service provider (CSP)*

C

CSP (commercial service provider)

Stands for commercial service provider, typically Internet service providers (ISPs), online service providers, telephone and cable network operators, and other companies.

See: *commercial service provider (CSP)*

CSS

Stands for cascading style sheets, a method for giving Web developers more control over how the pages of a Web site will look when displayed ona Web browser.

See: *cascading style sheets (CSS)*

CSU

Stands for Channel Service Unit, a device that is used to connect a synchronous digital telecommunications line to a computer network.

See: *Channel Service Unit (CSU)*

CSU/DSU

Stands for Channel Service Unit/Data Service Unit, a device that combines the functions of both a Channel Service Unit (CSU) and a Data Service Unit (DSU).

See: *Channel Service Unit/Data Service Unit (CSU/DSU)*

.csv file

A text file having the extension .csv, which contains fields of data separated by commas and a carriage return/linefeed at the end of each record. The extension .csv stands for comma-separated values.

Overview

These files are often used as a standard format for importing and exporting information between applications. For example, in Microsoft Exchange Server you can modify the properties of a group of mailboxes by exporting the properties of the mailboxes to a .csv file, opening this file as a spreadsheet in Microsoft Excel, modifying the properties using string functions and search/replace, exporting the information back into another .csv file, and then importing the modified file back into Exchange. Many applications can export log files or other information as .csv files. These files can then be imported into a spreadsheet or database program where they can be subjected to further inspection and analysis. Graphics and charts can also be generated from the imported information.

CTEC

Stands for Certified Technical Education Center, an education-delivery company such as a school or training center that is been qualified by Microsoft Corporation for the delivery of Microsoft Official Curriculum (MOC) courseware.

See: *Certified Technical Education Center (CTEC)*

CTI

Stands for computer-telephony integration, a general term describing the integration of computer and telephone technologies.

See: *computer-telephony integration (CTI)*

Ctrl+Alt+Delete

A control sequence that has different effects depending upon the operating system involved.

Overview

Holding down the Control, Alt, and Delete keys simultaneously produces the following results (depending upon the operating system being used):

- **MS-DOS:** Restarts the computer.
- **16-bit Microsoft Windows, Windows 95, and Windows 98:** Shows running tasks and allows you to terminate a task. A second Ctrl+Alt+Delete will restart the computer.
- **Windows NT:** Brings up the Windows NT Security dialog box.
- **Windows 2000:** Brings up the Windows Security dialog box.
- **Windows XP and Windows .NET Server:** Brings up the Windows Security dialog box.

See Also: *secure attention sequence (SAS)*

custom authentication

Any user-created method for authentication of clients on a network.

Overview

Microsoft Internet Information Services (IIS) lets you create custom authentication schemes to control access to Web content. These can be implemented using several different technologies, including Active Server Pages (ASP), Internet Server API (ISAPI) authentication filters, or Common Gateway Interface (CGI) applications. For example, using any of these technologies, you can create an authentication scheme to

- Perform a search of a client's credentials in a custom user database
- Examine a client's digital certificate to determine whether to allow access
- Use cookies or some other mechanism to establish whether the client should be authenticated

See Also: *authentication protocol*

Customer Information Control System (CICS)

Customer Information Control System (CICS) enables transaction-based applications to operate on IBM mainframe systems. More than half of all mainframes running today still use some CICS applications. Traditionally CICS-based applications are accessed using legacy IBM 3270 text-based terminals, but newer products allow CICS transactions to be wrapped in Hypertext Markup Language (HTML) for access by Web browsers. One such product is Shadow AutoHTML for CICS/TS from Neon Systems, which also supports Open Database Connectivity (ODBC) interfaces for CICS applications.

For More Information

Find Neon Systems at *www.neonsys.com.*

See Also: *Systems Network Architecture (SNA)*

customer premises

A general term referring to your local company's networking environment.

Overview

The term *customer premises* is typically used by service providers who provide leased or contractual services to help you implement and support your network. For example, a cabling company would install cabling at your customer premises and call this installation "premise wiring." A telecommunications company might send a representative to a customer premises in order to install a Channel Service Unit/Data Service Unit (CSU/DSU) or other device in the wiring closet to enable wide area network (WAN) communication. Typically, your company is responsible for the physical security of such installed equipment, but the actual configuration and monitoring of the equipment often takes place at the telco's central office (CO).

See Also: *customer premises equipment (CPE), enterprise resource planning (ERP)*

customer premises equipment (CPE)

Telecommunications equipment that is installed at the customer's location.

Overview

Customer premises equipment (CPE) is installed to terminate wide area network (WAN) links and local loop connections between the customer and the carrier's central office (CO) and to route traffic between the customer premises and the carrier from which telecommunications services are leased. Common examples of customer premises equipment include telephones, modems, Channel Service Unit/Data Service Units (CSU/DSUs), Private Branch Exchanges (PBXs), and Integrated Access Devices (IADs) routers.

Generally, the telecommunications service provider is responsible for configuring and monitoring the equipment, which is purchased or leased by the customer from the carrier. For example, when installing a CSU/DSU as a termination for a T1 line, the configuration of the CSU/DSU is likely to have been done previously by the service provider. The carrier then uses Simple Network Management Protocol (SNMP) and loopback monitoring to determine, from its central office, whether the remotely installed equipment is functioning correctly.

Alternatively, customers may purchase or lease their own CPE from third-party vendors. In this case the customer is usually responsible for configuring and monitoring the equipment. In general, cost/benefit is usually on the side of leasing CPE from the provisioning carrier because the cost of replacing defective or failed equipment or upgrading equipment to support enhanced services is the burden of the carrier.

See Also: *carrier, customer premises, local loop, telecommunications services, wide area network (WAN)*

Customer Relationship Management (CRM)

A type of business application used to manage business-to-consumer (B2C) connections.

Overview

Customer Relationship Management (CRM) software is used to manage mission-critical business information concerning the direct relationship between a business and its clients. CRM enables business users to quickly and easily access up-to-date information concerning client accounts, and it provides the tools for managing and growing a company's relationship with its customers. CRM software enables a business to manage leads, distribute timely information to customers, and coordinate a multitude of other customer-centric activities.

Marketplace

Some of the bigger players among CRM vendors include Onyx Technology, Pivotal Software, and Siebel Systems. CRM software takes a variety of forms depending on whether it is being implemented in small, mid-sized, or enterprise-level businesses. Some CRM vendors build their products around customer databases, while newer players and CRM startups often use the application service provider (ASP) model for outsourcing CRM needs.

The worldwide market revenue for all forms of CRM software and services was estimated at over $10 billion in 2000 and may reach $25 billion by 2003, according to some analysts.

Notes

A recent offshoot of CRM is partner relationship management (PRM), which helps companies to manage the more indirect relationship they have with business channels and supply chain partners, among others. Besides the big CRM players, a number of emerging pure-play PRM vendors are attracting market share. These include Allegis, ChannelWave, and many others.

See Also: *B2B, enterprise resource planning (ERP)*

custom recipient

A recipient in Microsoft Exchange Server that does not reside in the Exchange organization.

Overview

When creating a custom recipient, you specify the e-mail address of the remote user first, and then configure the properties of the recipient. An example of a custom recipient is the Simple Mail Transfer Protocol (SMTP) address of a user on the Internet.

Custom recipients are often created on Exchange servers to place frequently used foreign addresses in the global address book so that users do not have to specify the recipient's e-mail address manually or maintain their own personal address books. Custom recipients can be used for various other purposes in Exchange, such as to enable a user's Internet mail to be forwarded to his or her Exchange mailbox.

cyclical redundancy check (CRC)

An error-checking technique for ensuring that packets are successfully delivered over a network.

Overview

A cyclical redundancy check (CRC) is a number that is mathematically calculated for a packet by its source computer and then recalculated by the destination computer. If the original and recalculated versions at the destination computer differ, the packet is corrupt and needs to be resent or ignored.

The mathematical procedure for performing a CRC is specified by the International Telecommunication Union (ITU) and involves applying a 16-bit polynomial to the data being transmitted by the packet for packets of 4 KB of data or less, or a 32-bit polynomial for packets larger than 4 KB. The results of this calculation are appended to the packet as a trailer. The receiving station applies the same polynomial to the data and compares the results to the trailer appended to the packet. Implementations of Ethernet use 32-bit polynomials to calculate their CRC.

D

DAB

Stands for Digital Audio Broadcasting, a specification for broadband digital radio.

See: *Digital Audio Broadcasting (DAB)*

DACL

Stands for discretionary access control list, an access control list (ACL) that can be configured by administrators.

See: *discretionary access control list (DACL)*

daemon

The UNIX equivalent of a Microsoft Windows 2000, Windows XP, or Windows .NET Server service.

Overview

A daemon is a program associated with the UNIX operating system that runs in the background and performs some task without instigation from the user. An example of a daemon is the telnet daemon, which runs continuously in the background, waiting for a connection request from a telnet client. The telnet daemon facilitates the remote connection and makes it possible for the user to control the machine.

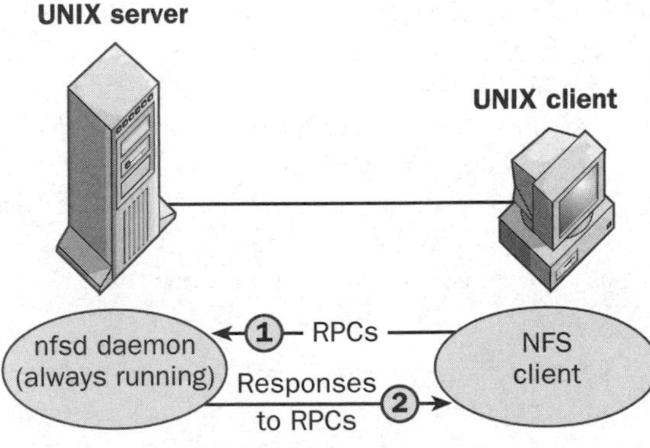

Daemon. *How the nfsd daemon works.*

Another example is the HTTPd daemon for the Apache Web server, which waits for Hypertext Transfer Protocol (HTTP) requests from Web browser clients and fulfills them.

A third example of a daemon is the nfsd daemon, which supports the remote file access aspect of the Network File System (NFS) in a UNIX environment. The nfsd daemon runs in the background on UNIX servers, waiting for remote procedure calls (RPCs) from NFS clients.

Daemons typically use RPCs for communication with clients. Because NFS is implemented as daemon processes at the user level instead of at the kernel level, NFS is thread-safe for execution, allowing multiple NFS processes to run as independent threads of execution.

Notes

The Microsoft equivalent of daemon is service. For example, the Workstation service of Windows 2000 would be known in UNIX as a daemon instead of a service.

See Also: *service*

daily copy

A type of tape backup in which only files and folders that have changed on that day are backed up.

Overview

When a daily copy is performed during a backup, files and folders modified on that day are backed up but their archive attribute is not marked.

Daily copies are not a common type of backup operation. They are typically used only if a user wants to take home copies of the files she has been working on during the day. Few administrators would be willing to schedule and run the system backup software just to make copies of these files, so users taking advantage of this backup type usually have a locally attached backup device along with a similar device attached to their systems at home.

Daily copy backups are likely to be performed on media such as Iomega Zip or Jaz disks rather than on tape.

Notes

Daily copy backups are supported by the Microsoft Windows 2000 Backup utility.

See Also: *backup, backup type*

D-AMPS

Stands for Digital Advanced Mobile Phone Service, the digital version of the Advanced Mobile Phone Service (AMPS) cellular communications system.

See: *Digital Advanced Mobile Phone Service (D-AMPS)*

DAO

Stands for Data Access Objects, a Microsoft technology that enables you to use a programming language to access and manipulate data stored in both local and remote databases.

See: *Data Access Objects (DAO)*

DAP

Stands for Directory Access Protocol, a protocol for accessing information in a directory service based on the X.500 recommendations.

See: *Directory Access Protocol (DAP)*

dark fiber

Any fiber-optic cabling or fiber device such as a repeater that is installed but not currently in use.

Overview

When no light is being transmitted through fiber-optic cabling, it is called dark fiber since it is, in effect, dark. When a carrier or cabling company first provisions fiber, it is called dark fiber. Then once all the components of the system are installed, including connectors, amplifiers, repeaters, switches, routers, and such, the light can be turned on and the fiber is no longer dark. Dark fiber is thus simply unused fiber or fiber that is not yet ready to be used.

Before dark fiber is activated, the system is usually tested using an optical time domain reflectometer (which measures and analyzes a fiber link) and other measuring devices to determine whether the system has integrity, and to measure its bandwidth and attenuation parameters.

Implementation

When an enterprise needs a fiber connection for wide area usage, it can take three possible approaches:

- **Lay their own fiber:** This is an expensive solution, not only because large amounts of fiber may be required, but also because expertise in fiber-optic cabling technologies is needed and is often in short supply. Right of way must also often be purchased in order to lay the fiber, and this is often difficult or downright impossible. Only the largest enterprises can afford this approach, and it is rarely implemented beyond campus networks.
- **Lease dark fiber:** This involves paying a telecommunications carrier for one or more strands of fiber-optic cabling from the carrier's own system. Companies that want to maintain total control of their wide area network (WAN) links can choose this route. They first lease dark fiber from a carrier, and then install switches and repeaters to build their own long-haul fiber-optic network. Leasing dark fiber was a popular solution for many enterprises in the 1990s, especially for financial institutions that required the highest level of privacy and security for their WANs. Also, in the 1990s carrier networks were almost exclusively Asynchronous Transfer Mode/Synchronous Optical Network (ATM/SONET)–based, and the WAN services they offered were expensive; enterprises saw leasing dark fiber as a way of controlling costs and simplifying their WANs.
- **Leasing managed wavelength services:** With the advent of dense wavelength division multiplexing

(DWDM) on carrier networks at the end of the 1990s, the carrying capacity of carrier networks increased dramatically. This, and the emergence of new carriers such as Metropolitan Gigabit Ethernet providers, drove down the cost of carrier WAN services, making leasing WAN services more cost attractive to some enterprises than leasing their own dark fiber. New providers called managed wavelength services providers quickly arose as resellers of fiber capacity from traditional carriers. Some of these managed wavelength services providers include 360networks, Global Crossing, Level 3, Metromedia, XO Communications, and others. AT&T also directly leases managed wavelength services up to 2.4 gigabits per second (Gbps) to large companies.

Notes

Although the term *dark fiber* at first sounds like there is a problem in the fiber-optic cabling system, this is not the case. However, various problems can occur in a fiber-optic cabling system that can cause it to remain dark once the system is turned on. These can include the following:

- Microfractures in the glass core or cladding caused by improper installation techniques, such as excessive bending or stretching of a segment of cable
- Improper terminations for the fiber or loose connectors
- Malfunctioning repeaters

See Also: *dense wavelength division multiplexing (DWDM), fiber-optic cabling*

Data Access Objects (DAO)

A Microsoft technology that enables you to use a programming language to access and manipulate data stored in both local and remote databases.

Overview

Data Access Objects (DAO) lets you access and manage databases, along with their structure and objects, by providing a framework called an object model that uses code to create and manipulate different kinds of databases.

DAO supports two different interfaces, which are known as workspaces:

- **ODBCDirect workspace:** This lets you can access database servers such as Microsoft SQL Server through open database connectivity (ODBC). This workspace lets you execute queries or stored procedures against a database server, perform batch updates, and execute asynchronous queries. ODBCDirect makes it possible for you to take advantage of Remote Data Objects (RDO) technology in your DAO code.
- **Microsoft Jet workspace:** This lets you access databases based on Jet technology or on installable indexed sequential access method (ISAM) data sources in other formats such as Paradox, dBase, and Btrieve. You use this workspace to access a single database, such as a .mdb database from Microsoft Access, or to join together data originating from several different database formats.

Prospects

DAO and RDO are both available now, but these technologies are being superseded by Microsoft ActiveX Data Objects (ADO) and Remote Data Service (RDS). All these components can be found in the Microsoft Data Access Software Development Kit.

See Also: *ActiveX Data Objects (ADO), open database connectivity (ODBC)*

data alarm

A device for alerting network administrators to network problems relating to serial transmission.

Overview

Data alarms typically monitor serial lines such as RS-232 connections for the presence or absence of certain signals. For example, you can monitor the connection between a print server and its attached printer or between an access server and a modem or a Channel Service Unit/Data Service Unit (CSU/DSU).

D

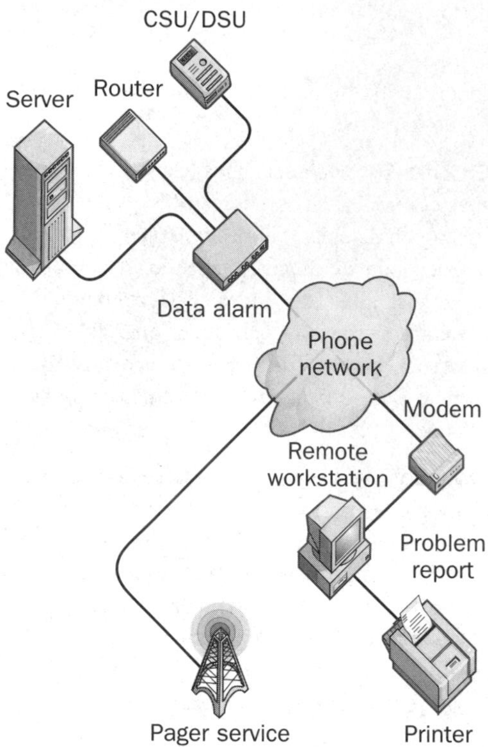

Data alarm. *Implementing a data alarm for alerting administrators to problems with serial links.*

A data alarm can be a simple device that monitors one serial line for the presence or absence of data. If the data flow stops, a flashing LED or audible alarm signals the problem to the administrator. More complex data alarms can support multiple serial lines or other serial interfaces such as RS-449 and V.35, can have programmable functions and menu-driven commands, and can monitor other devices, such as Time to Live (TTL) devices. These more complex devices can be configured to dial a remote station when a problem arises and to generate a report of the condition or even activate an alphanumeric pager.

Notes

Some vendors use the term *data alarm* to describe a device that senses network problems associated with the flow of data in other networks such as Ethernet.

See Also: *network management*

database

In its simplest form, a file used to store records of information, with each record containing multiple data fields. More generally, any application used to manage structured information.

Overview

Databases are an essential component of every business, representing the back-end of a company's information structure. Databases are used to store a broad range of information including inventory, customer contacts, sales records and invoices, catalogs, and so on. Without databases, modern businesses could not operate with the scope and range that they have, as they would be overwhelmed with information they could not manage.

Databases allow information to be stored, updated, manipulated, and queried. Sales figures for a given month can be extracted from a database using a standard programming language for building queries called Structured Query Language (SQL), versions of which are built into products from every database vendor.

Implementation

The most popular type of database is the relational database, in which the records are stored in tables that are related to each other using primary and foreign keys. A primary key is the field in each record that uniquely defines the record. (For example, a part number might be used as the primary key in a table that holds the price of each item a company sells.) A foreign key is a field in another table that matches the first table's primary key, creating a relationship between the two. An application for creating and managing relational databases is called a relational database management system (RDBMS).

Records are like the rows of a table. Each record is a collection of information about some physical system or logical object. Field names are like the column names of a table. Each field name represents a property or attribute of the system or object. Databases are widely used by businesses for storing information about inventory, orders, shipping, accounting, and so forth.

Microsoft SQL Server is Microsoft Corporation's enterprise-level RDBMS. SQL Server databases are stored on devices. Each computer running SQL Server has four system databases plus one or more user databases installed on it. The system databases are as follows:

- The master database, which is used for tracking system-wide information.
- The tempdb database, which is used for temporary working storage and sort operations.
- The model database, which is a template for creating new databases.
- The msdb database, which is used to store system data and transaction logs and to support the SQL Server Agent service and its scheduling information. The msdb database is stored on two devices, the Msdbdata system device and the Msdblog system device.

Marketplace

Major players in the enterprise database market include Microsoft Corporation with its SQL Server, Oracle Corporation with its Oracle 9i, IBM with its DB2, and others. These database products frequently compete for mindshare in the enterprise arena by surpassing each other in TCP-C benchmark figures.

Competing with these major players are open-source databases such as MySQL from NuSphere Corporation and PostgreSQL from Great Bridge, which run on the Linux and Berkeley Software Distribution (BSD) platforms and build upon the stability of those platforms.

Given the ubiquity and importance of databases to business, a wide spectrum of tools is available for planning, implementing, managing, tuning, monitoring, and troubleshooting database platforms. For example, pocketDBA has a module for the wireless Palm OS handheld device which allows an administer to remotely monitor and manage Oracle databases using a Palm. Similar applications will soon be available for the PocketPC platform as well.

Notes

The term *database* can have different meanings for different vendors. In Oracle products, for example, *database* refers to the entire Oracle DBMS environment. In SQL Server, databases provide a logical separation of data, applications, and security mechanisms, but in Oracle this separation is achieved using *tablespaces*.

See Also: *SQL Server*

database owner (DBO)

In Microsoft SQL Server, the user account that created the database and is responsible for managing administrative tasks related to the database.

Overview

Each SQL Server database is considered to be a self-contained administrative domain and is assigned a database owner (DBO) who is responsible for managing the permissions for the database and performing tasks such as backing up and restoring the database's information. The DBO also applies to any database object, including tables, indexes, views, functions, or stored procedures.

Essentially, the DBO can do anything within the database. By default, the SA (system administrator) account is also a DBO account for any database on a computer running SQL Server. The DBO has full permissions inside a database that it owns.

Notes

To avoid the complexity of managing separate DBO accounts for each SQL Server database, you might want to perform all administration tasks—both server-wide and specific to the database—using only the SA account.

See Also: *SQL Server*

data communications equipment (DCE)

Any device that supports data transmission over a serial telecommunications link.

Overview

Typically, data communications equipment (DCE) refers to analog and digital modems, Integrated Services Digital Network (ISDN) terminal adapters, Channel Service Units (CSU), multiplexers, and similar devices. The purpose of a DCE is to provide termination for the telecommunications link and to provide an interface for connecting data terminal equipment (DTE) to the link.

The term *DCE* specifically refers to serial transmission, which generally occurs over links such as a local loop Plain Old Telephone Service (POTS) connection, an ISDN line, or a T1 line. An example of a DCE is an analog modem, which provides a connection between a computer (the DTE) and the local loop POTS phone line (the serial transmission line). A DCE accepts a stream of serial data from a DTE and converts it to a form that is suitable for the particular transmission line medium being used. The DCE also works in reverse, converting data from the transmission line to a form the DTE can use.

D

On a Cisco router, the DCE interface is typically an RJ-45 jack on the back of the router.

See Also: *data terminal equipment (DTE), Integrated Services Digital Network (ISDN), serial transmission, T-carrier*

Data Encryption Standard (DES)

The former U.S. government standard for encryption, now replaced by Advanced Encryption Standard (AES).

Overview

In 1972 the National Bureau of Standards called for proposals for an encryption standard to enable secure transmission of government documents by electronic means. IBM responded to the call with a 128-bit key algorithm called Lucifer, which was accepted in 1976, reduced to 56-bit key length, renamed Data Encryption Algorithm (DEA), and then further developed by the National Security Agency (NSA). In 1977, DEA was officially adopted as the Data Encryption Standard (DES) and became the official encryption standard of the U.S. government. DES is formally defined by Federal Information Processing Standard FIPS 46-1.

Implementation

DES is a symmetric encryption scheme in which both the sender and the receiver need to know the secret key in order to communicate securely. DES is based on a 56-bit key (actually a 64-bit key with 8 parity bits stripped off) that allows for approximately 7.2×10^{16} possible keys. When a message is to be encrypted using DES, one of the available keys is chosen and applied in 16 rounds of permutations and substitutions to each 64-bit block of data in the message. Because DES encrypts information 64 bits at a time, it is known as a block cipher.

Issues

DES was originally designed for hardware encryption (dedicated devices that encrypt information at high speeds). The newer AES standard is more flexible in its application, and performs well in a variety of different environments from small-footprint devices such as smart cards to ordinary desktop computers running standard operating systems.

While the large number of keys available makes DES fairly secure, it was known early on that DES was crackable in theory. In 1997, Whitfield Diffie and Martin Hellman (developers of Diffie-Hellman public key encryption) proposed a DES cracking machine that could in principle be built with existing hardware at a cost of about $20 million. Then in 1997 a DES key was successfully cracked using the idle processing cycles of 14,000 computers cooperating over the Internet. The next year a DES cracking machine costing only $210,000 was created by the Electronic Frontier Foundation (EFF). The EFF machine was capable of cracking a DES key in about four days. Despite these accomplishments, DES is still viewed in practice as a secure encryption algorithm because so far no other method for cracking DES keys than simple brute force (trying every possible key) has been found.

Notes

A more secure variant of DES, Triple DES, encrypts each message using three different 56-bit keys in succession. Triple DES thus extends the DES key to 168 bits in length, providing for a total of approximately 6.2×10^{57} different keys. Unfortunately Triple DES is a relatively slow encryption mechanism that is not suitable for some situations, such as cell phones having limited processing power.

Another symmetric encryption scheme is IDEA (International Data Encryption Algorithm), which uses a 128-bit key and performs 8 cipher rounds on 64 bit blocks of information. Other symmetric encryption schemes include Blowfish, CAST, RC2, RC4, and others. The most common examples of asymmetric encryption schemes are Diffie-Hellman and Rivest-Shamir-Adleman encryption (RSA).

See Also: *Advanced Encryption Standard (AES), encryption*

datagram

A term sometimes used as a synonym for packet, but most often meaning a packet that is sent across a network using connectionless services, where the delivery does not depend on the maintenance of specific connections between computers.

Overview

Networking protocol suites such as Transmission Control Protocol/Internet Protocol (TCP/IP) generally support both connection-oriented and connectionless delivery services. In TCP/IP, the Transmission Control Protocol (TCP) is responsible for providing connection-oriented services that guarantee delivery of Internet Protocol (IP) packets. On the other hand, the User Datagram Protocol (UDP) handles connectionless services that guarantee only "best-effort" delivery of datagrams. For networking services that use connectionless datagrams, higher-layer protocols must ensure delivery. Datagrams are generally small packets sent over the network to perform functions such as announcements.

See Also: *connectionless protocol, connection-oriented protocol, packet, Transmission Control Protocol/Internet Protocol (TCP/IP), User Datagram Protocol (UDP)*

data integrity

The correctness and consistency of data stored in a database.

Overview

Maintaining integrity is essential, because a database is only useful if its contents can be retrieved and manipulated as expected. For example, without data integrity, data could be input into the system and then be inaccessible. Data integrity must be enforced on the database server. The following items are among those that should be verified:

- Individual field contents during insertion, updating, or deletion of data
- The values of one field relative to another (especially for primary keys) and of data in one table relative to another (especially for foreign keys)
- Successful completion of database transactions

Database systems employ many features to ensure data integrity. For example, Microsoft SQL Server 7 makes use of data types, constraints, rules, defaults, declarative referential integrity (DRI), stored procedures, and triggers. All these play a role in keeping the integrity of the database intact.

See Also: *database, SQL Server*

data isolator

A device that protects serial equipment from voltage surges.

Overview

If two pieces of data terminal equipment (DTE) are connected by a long serial line, voltage differences with respect to ground between the devices can cause surges over the line that can damage the devices. This can be a problem in a mainframe environment when you connect terminals to asynchronous mainframe hosts using long RS-232 cables. The problem is especially troublesome when the cabling has to run outdoors between buildings or when nearby generators or other equipment induce voltages.

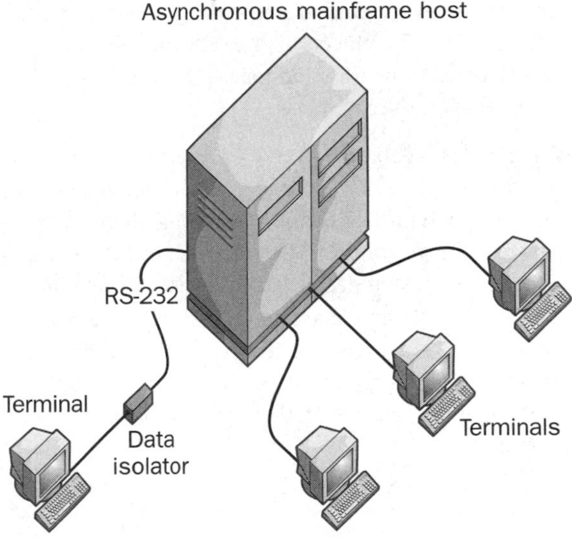

Data isolator. *Using a data isolator.*

The solution to these problems is to insert a data isolator between the mainframe host and the terminal. This isolator provides electrical isolation between the two devices, somewhat like an opto isolator for fiber-optic cabling. Data isolators typically use transformers to electrically isolate the two connected circuits from voltage surges. Data isolators can support high data transfer speeds, and they come with a variety of interfaces, such as RS-232, RS-422, and Time to Live (TTL) connections.

See Also: *data terminal equipment (DTE), serial transmission*

data line protector

A device that provides surge protection for network cables carrying data.

Overview

Data line protectors prevent voltage spikes and surges from damaging costly hubs, switches, routers, and other devices. They are essentially surge protectors that are placed inline between stations on the network and concentrating hubs or other devices in the wiring closet. Data line protectors are available from different vendors for virtually every kind of networking connection, including RJ-45 connections for Ethernet networks, RJ-11 connections for telephone lines, and RS-232 connections for serial lines.

You connect a data line protector directly to one of the two connected devices, and then you attach the ground wire to a good ground connection so that there will be a path for voltage surges to flow down. For Ethernet networks using unshielded twisted-pair (UTP) cabling, data line protectors are available with multiple ports that are attached directly to the hub or the switch. Additional 10BaseT surge protectors can also be installed directly on the stations on the network for more protection.

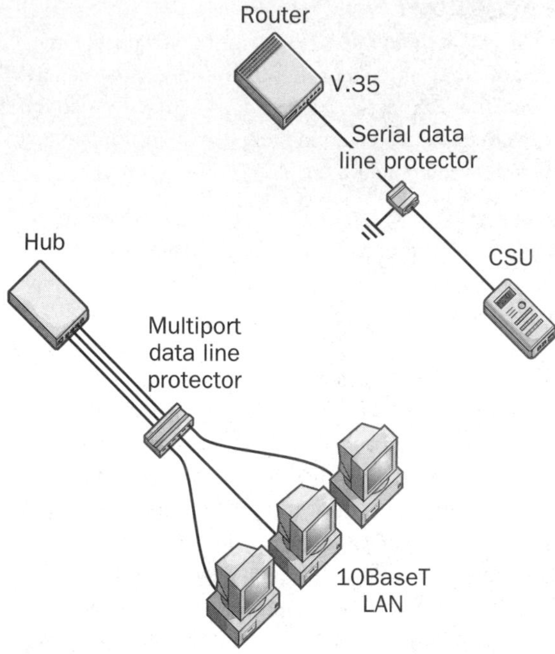

Data line protector. *Using a data line protector.*

Notes

Most newer hubs, switches, routers, and other networking devices include built-in data line protection circuitry, which eliminates the need for additional data line protectors.

See Also: *Ethernet*

Data Link Control (DLC)

Generally, the services that the data-link layer of the Open Systems Interconnection (OSI) reference model provides to adjacent layers of the OSI protocol stack. Specifically, Data Link Control (DLC) is a specialized network protocol.

Overview

The DLC protocol is used primarily for two purposes:

- To provide connectivity with IBM mainframe or AS/400 environments, such as Systems Network Architecture (SNA), which are configured to run

DLC. DLC complements SNA because SNA operates only at higher levels of the OSI model.

- To provide connectivity for network print devices (such as certain Hewlett-Packard printers that have their own network cards and are connected directly to the network).

DLC is not used as a network protocol in the usual sense of enabling communication among computers on the network. It is not used by the redirector by the Microsoft Windows 2000 operating system and so cannot be used for session-level communication over a network. DLC is not routable; it is designed only to give devices direct access to the data-link layer. DLC is supported by most Windows operating systems, including Windows 95, Windows 98, Windows Millennium Edition (Me), Windows NT, and Windows 2000. DLC is no longer supported on Windows XP and Windows .NET Server. Windows 95 OSR2 includes both a 16-bit and a 32-bit version of DLC.

Implementation

To use DLC on Windows 2000 to connect to a Hewlett-Packard network print device, perform the following steps:

1. Connect the printer to the network, and run the self-test routine to obtain the printer's MAC address. Also, think of a friendly name for the printer.
2. Install the DLC protocol on the Windows NT or Windows 2000 server that will be used as a print server for the network print device. (Use the Network utility or the Windows 2000 Network and Dial-Up Connections utility in Control Panel.)
3. Run the Add Printer Wizard on the print server, choosing My Computer, Add Port, Hewlett-Packard Network Port, and New Port. Enter the friendly name for the printer, and select its MAC address from the list (or type it if the print device is offline). In Windows 2000, run the Add Printer Wizard, then right-click on the printer in the Printers folder and choose Properties. In the Property sheet for the printer, click the Ports tab, click Add Port, select Hewlett-Packard Network Port, and then click New Port. Enter the friendly name for the printer and select its MAC address from the list (or type it if the print device is offline).

See Also: *data-link layer, Open Systems Interconnection (OSI) reference model, printing terminology*

data-link layer

Layer 2 of the Open Systems Interconnection (OSI) reference model.

Overview

The data-link layer converts frames of data into raw bits for the physical layer and is responsible for framing, flow control, error correction, and retransmission of frames. media access control (MAC) addresses are used at this layer, and bridges and network interface cards (NICs) operate at this layer.

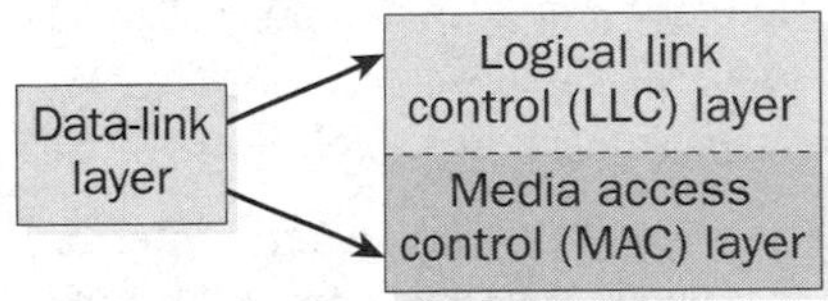

Data-link layer. *Two sub-layers of the data link layer.*

The data-link layer establishes and maintains the data link for the network layer above it. It ensures that data is transferred reliably between two stations on the network. It is responsible for packaging data from higher levels into frames, which are basically constructs containing data, a header, and a trailer.

Uses

A variety of network protocols can be implemented at the data-link layer. These differ depending on whether you are establishing local area network (LAN) or wide area network (WAN) connections between stations. Data-link protocols are responsible for functions such as addressing, frame delimiting and sequencing, error detection and recovery, and flow control.

Examples of data-link protocols for local area networking include the following:

- IEEE 802.3, which provides the Carrier Sense Multiple Access with Collision Detection (CSMA/CD) access method for baseband Ethernet networks

- IEEE 802.5, which provides the token-passing access method for baseband token ring implementations

For WANs, data-link layer protocols encapsulate LAN traffic into frames suitable for transmission over WAN links. Common data-link encapsulation methods for WAN transmission include the following:

- Point-to-point technologies such as Point-to-Point Protocol (PPP) and High-level Data Link Control (HDLC) protocol
- Multipoint technologies such as frame relay, Asynchronous Transfer Mode (ATM), Switched Multimegabit Data Services (SMDS), and X.25

Implementation

For LANs, the Project 802 standards of the Institute of Electrical and Electronics Engineers (IEEE) separate the data-link layer into two sublayers. The reason for doing this is to make it simpler for network equipment vendors to develop drivers for data-link layer services. The two sublayers of the data-link layer are the following:

- **Logical link control (LLC) layer:** This is the upper of the two layers, which is responsible for flow control, error correction, and resequencing functions for connection-oriented communication, but which also supports connectionless communication. Programming of the LLC layer is generally done by software vendors.
- **Media access control (MAC) layer:** This is the lower of the two layers, which is responsible for providing a method for stations to gain access to the medium. Programming of the MAC layer is generally done by manufacturers of network cards and similar devices.

See Also: *Carrier Sense Multiple Access with Collision Avoidance (CSMA/CA), High-level Data Link Control (HDLC), Open Systems Interconnection (OSI) reference model, Point-to-Point Protocol (PPP)*

Data Manipulation Language (DML)

A subset of Structured Query Language (SQL).

Overview

Generally speaking, the term *Data Manipulation Language (DML)* can apply to any nonprocedural computer language designed specifically for the manipulation of structured data. In common use, DML refers to a subset of SQL commands used specifically for manipulating data in a database. The four SQL commands that comprise DML are

- **SELECT:** Lets you retrieve rows from tables
- **INSERT:** Lets you add rows to tables
- **DELETE:** Lets you remove rows from tables
- **UPDATE:** Lets you modify rows in tables

See Also: *Structured Query Language (SQL)*

Data Over Cable Interface Specification (DOCSIS)

A specification defining standards for implementation of cable modem systems.

Overview

Data Over Cable Interface Specification (DOCSIS) is a set of standards developed by CableLabs together with a consortium of cable system vendors and operators to promote interoperability between different cable modem systems. The DOCSIS standards focus on the interaction between equipment at cable providers and their customers.

DOCSIS is also a certification issued by CableLabs to cable modem system vendors meeting DOCSIS specifications and requirements. CableLabs is responsible for certifying DOCSIS-compliant cable modems and related equipment.

Architecture

In its original and widely implemented version, DOCSIS 1 provides a specification for transmission of a single stream of data from a Cable Modem Termination System (CMTS) router at the provider, through a distribution system of more routers, to a cable modem at the customer premises. The cable modem data stream defined by DOCSIS is a best-effort shared-media system that uses contention on upstream traffic and has limited support for class of service (CoS) differentiation between different types of traffic. DOCSIS defines the physical and data-link layers for cable modem systems and solves the problem of eavesdropping due to the shared nature of the network by supporting 56-bit Data Encryption Standard (DES) encryptions of all cable modem traffic.

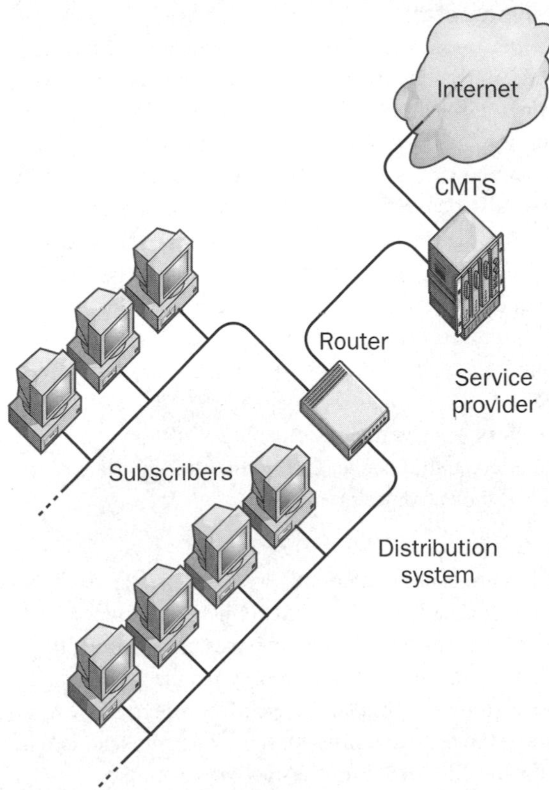

Data Over Cable Interface Specification (DOCSIS). *How DOCSIS works.*

DOCSIS 1 specifies the characteristics of upstream and downstream transmission as follows:

- **Downstream:** Data rates of 27 to 36 megabits per second (Mbps) using frequencies between 50 and 750 megahertz (MHz)
- **Upstream:** Data rates of 320 kilobits per second (Kbps) and 10 Mbps using frequencies between 5 and 42 MHz

A newer version of the specification, DOCSIS 1.1, has a number of enhancements over the original DOCSIS standard, specifically

- **Multiple data streams:** DOCSIS 1.1 supports creating multiple data streams from CMTS to customer premises. Each application can be assigned its own data stream and priority using multiprotocol label switching (MPLS) or Diffserv, and providers can assign service level agreements (SLAs) to business customers to guarantee bandwidth for each stream.
- **Classification of traffic:** Different forms of traffic can now be mapped to specific service flows according to their content. Thus a specific Web application could be assigned a specific service flow to ensure adequate class of service for that application. Service flows themselves can be preconfigured or can be dynamically established and torn down.
- **Network access:** Access to the network can be scheduled using several different schemes including real-time polling, non-real-time polling, and constant bit rate (CBR). This provides better performance for applications that perform poorly on the simple, contention-based shared network defined in DOCSIS 1.
- **Packet fragmentation:** Large packets can be fragmented to provide better quality of service (QoS) for applications such as Voice over IP (VoIP) that require low latency.

See Also: *cable modem*

Data Provider

A tool that simplifies data access to different kinds of data sources such as relational databases.

Overview

Also known as the OLE DB Provider for AS/400 and Virtual Storage Access Method (VSAM), Data Provider is included with Microsoft SNA Server version 4. It gives Web applications written with Microsoft Active Server Pages (ASP) technology the ability to access record-level mainframe AS/400 and VSAM file systems.

Using Data Provider, you can write applications that access legacy file data on mainframes and minicomputers running Systems Network Architecture (SNA). You can also directly access AS/400 file structures and

VSAM data sets using the IBM DDM protocol native to many IBM host systems without needing to install additional Microsoft software on the host system. You can also integrate unstructured legacy file data on host systems with data stored in a Microsoft Windows 2000 networking environment.

See Also: *Systems Network Architecture (SNA)*

Data Service Unit (DSU)

A digital communication device that works with a Channel Service Unit (CSU) to connect a local area network (LAN) to a telecommunications carrier service.

Overview

Data Service Units (DSUs) provide a modem-like interface between data terminal equipment (DTE) such as a router and the CSU connected to the digital service line. DSUs also serve to electrically isolate the telco's digital telecommunication line from the networking equipment at the customer premises. While the CSU connects to the termination point of the carrier's digital line at the customer premises, the DSU connects to the access device (typically a router) at the border of the customer's LAN.

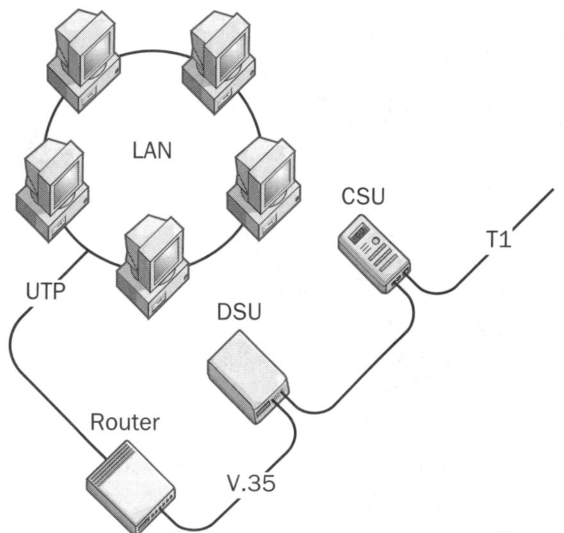

Data Service Unit (DSU). *Using a DSU.*

Implementation

As an example, in T1 transmission technologies, the DSU converts network data frames that are received from the router's RS-232, RS-449, or V.35 serial transmission interface into the standard DSX framing format, encoding scheme, and voltages of the T1 line. The DSU also converts the unipolar networking signal into a bipolar signal suitable for transmission over the digital line. The DSU is also responsible for handling signal regeneration and for controlling timing errors for transmission over the T1 line. DSUs usually provide other functions such as line conditioning of the T1 line, as well as remote diagnostic capabilities such as Simple Network Management Protocol (SNMP), which allows the telco central office (CO) to monitor the state of the line at the customer premises.

Notes

DSUs are usually integrated with CSUs to create a single device called a CSU/DSU (Channel Service Unit/ Data Service Unit). If these devices are separate, the telco usually supplies and configures the CSU, while the customer supplies the DSU. If the devices are combined, the telco usually supplies, configures, and maintains the CSU/DSU for the customer premises.

The DSUs (or CSU/DSUs) at either end of a digital data transmission line should be from the same manufacturer. If they are not, they might not communicate with each other correctly because different vendors employ different multiplexing and diagnostic technologies that are often incompatible with those of other vendors.

See Also: *Channel Service Unit (CSU), Channel Service Unit/Data Service Unit (CSU/DSU), T-carrier*

data source name (DSN)

A unique name used to create a data connection to a database using open database connectivity (ODBC).

Overview

Data source names (DSNs) are used by applications that need to access or manage data in its associated database. All ODBC connections require that a DSN be configured to support the connection. When a client application wants to access an ODBC-compliant database, it references the database using the DSN.

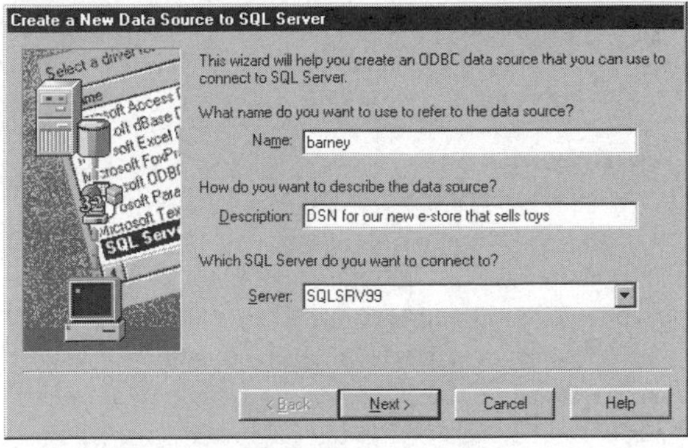

Data source name (DSN). *Configuring a DSN.*

You can configure a DSN for an ODBC-compliant database using the Microsoft Windows 2000, Windows XP, or Windows .NET Server Administrative Tools\Data Sources (ODBC) utility in Control Panel. You can create three kinds of DSNs:

- **User DSN:** This is visible only to the user who creates it and can be used only on the current machine.
- **System DSN:** This is visible to all users on the machine and is also accessible to Windows NT, Windows 2000, Windows XP, or Windows .NET Server services. A system DSN is stored in the registry.
- **File DSN:** This can be shared by users who have the same ODBC drivers installed. A file DSN is stored in a file.

Notes

When you design Web applications that use Microsoft ActiveX Data Objects (ADO) for accessing database information, be sure to use either a file DSN or a system DSN because ADO does not work with user DSNs.

See Also: *open database connectivity (ODBC)*

Data Space Transfer Protocol (DSTP)

A protocol for accessing large amounts of information stored in distributed locations.

Overview

The Data Space Transfer Protocol (DSTP) is a new protocol designed to transport gigabits of information at high speeds around the globe. DSTP finds typical applications in international research projects between different universities where large amounts of data are generated and need to be shared and analyzed. Typical applications include human genome analysis and particle physics.

Implementation

DSTP is derived from Network News Transfer Protocol (NNTP) and uses a similar stream architecture augmented by a command set similar to Simple Mail Transfer Protocol (SMTP). DTSP enables information stored in different formats on servers in different locations to be indexed and retrieved in the form of a database file consisting of rows and columns. Indexing and retrieval is facilitated using a key called a Universal Correlation Key (UCK), which is used to create an Extensible Markup Language (XML) index file by tagging columns in databases.

DSTP is capable of transferring multiple flat-file databases simultaneously at high speeds.

For More Information

Find out more about DSTP at *www.www.ncdm.uic.edu/dstp.*

See Also: *Network News Transfer Protocol (NNTP), Simple Mail Transfer Protocol (SMTP)*

data tap

A type of networking device that you can use to monitor the flow of data in serial lines.

Overview

Data taps provide an easy way to connect monitoring equipment such as data scopes to serial interfaces such as RS-232. These serial connections are used for a variety of networking purposes, including connecting data terminal equipment (DTE) such as servers and routers to data communications equipment (DCE), such as modems, and CSU/DSUs (Channel Service Unit/Data Service Units) for implementing wide area networks (WANs); connecting dumb terminals to asynchronous mainframe hosts; and connecting servers to plotters and other serial devices. Data taps generally display network traffic in binary, hexadecimal, or character format and are used for troubleshooting various kinds of network connections.

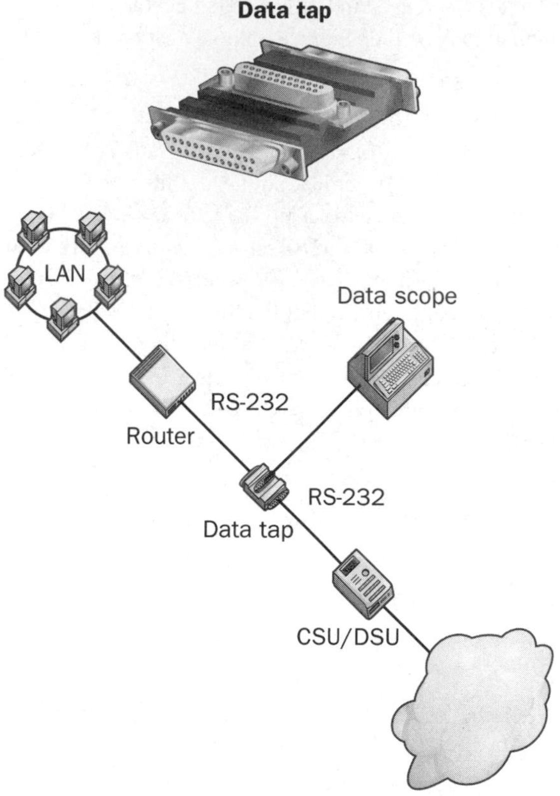

Data tap. *Using a data tap to troubleshoot a serial connection.*

A data tap is essentially a three-way connector in which the third connector interfaces with the test equipment. For RS-232 serial lines, data taps come in a variety of configurations, with mixtures of male and female DB-9 and DB-25 connectors.

See Also: *serial transmission*

data terminal equipment (DTE)

Any device that is a source of data transmission over a serial telecommunications link.

Overview

The term *data terminal equipment (DTE)* specifically refers to a device that uses serial transmission such as the transmissions involving the serial port of a computer. Most serial interface devices contain a chip called a universal asynchronous receiver-transmitter (UART) that can translate the synchronous parallel data transmission that occurs within the computer's system bus into an asynchronous serial transmission for communication through the serial port. The UART also performs other functions in a DTE, including the following:

- **Error detection:** Ensures that data arrives at its destination uncorrupted
- **Clocking:** Ensures that data is sent at the correct rate in order to be received at its destination

Typically, data terminal equipment (DTE) can be a computer, a terminal, a router, an access server, or some similar device. The earliest form of DTE was the teletype machine.

Implementation

To connect a DTE to a telecommunications link, you use data communications equipment (DCE). The DCE provides termination for the telecommunications link and an interface for connecting the DTE to the link. In other words, the DCE connects to the carrier's phone line and the DTE connects to the customer's network or system. The DTE and DCE are then joined together using a serial cable. Typical serial interfaces for DCE-to-DTE connections include RS-232, RS-449, RS-530, X.21, V.35, and HSSI.

An example of a DCE would be an analog modem, which can be used for connecting a DTE such as the serial port on a computer or router to the local loop connection of the Plain Old Telephone Service (POTS).

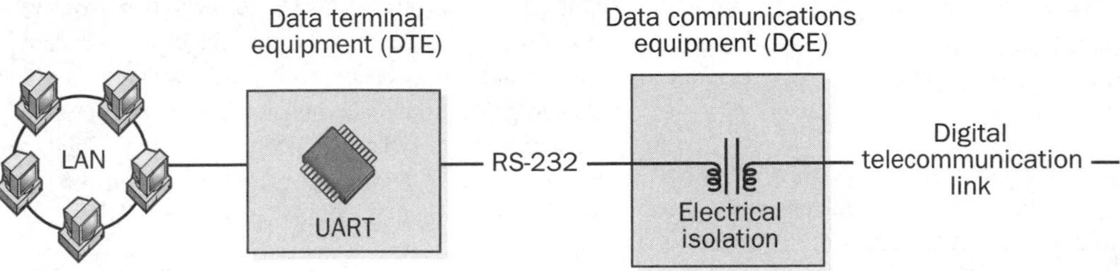

Data terminal equipment (DTE). *Example of DTE.*

While the usual configuration is to connect DTE with DCE, there are situations where DTE may need to be connected to DTE, for example when a computer needs to be connected to a router using a serial interface. In this situation a null modem cable is required.

See Also: *data communications equipment (DCE), serial transmission*

DAWS

Stands for Digital Advanced Wireless System, a proposed standard for a multimegabit packet-switching radio network from the European Telecommunications Standards Institute (ETSI).

See: *Digital Advanced Wireless System (DAWS)*

DB connector

A common family of connectors used for connecting data terminal equipment (DTE).

Overview

The letters *DB* stand for *data bus* and are followed by a number that indicates the number of lines or pins in the connector. DB connectors were formerly called D-series connectors. DB connectors can be used for either serial or parallel connections between devices.

Common members of the DB family include the following:

- **DB-9:** A 9-pin serial connector for connecting modems, serial printers, mouse devices, and so on
- **DB-15:** A 15-pin connector for connecting such devices as Macintosh monitors and network interface cards (NICs) for 10Base5 drop cables
- **DB-25:** A 25-pin connector for connecting Macintosh Small Computer System Interface (SCSI) devices, modems, serial printers, parallel cables, and switch boxes, among other equipment
- **DB-37:** A 37-pin connector for connecting such devices as routers and Channel Service Units (CSUs)
- **DB-60:** A 60-pin connector for connecting such devices as Cisco routers

See Also: *connector (device), data terminal equipment (DTE)*

DBO

Stands for database owner, the user account in Microsoft SQL Server that created the database and is responsible for managing administrative tasks related to the database. The DBO also owns any database object, including tables, indexes, views, functions, or stored procedures.

See: *database owner (DBO)*

DCE

Stands for data communications equipment, which refers to any device that supports data transmission over a serial telecommunications link.

See: *data communications equipment (DCE)*

D channel

One of two channels used in Integrated Services Digital Network (ISDN).

Overview

An ISDN D-channel is a circuit-switched channel that carries signaling information between the customer premises termination and the central office (CO) of the telecommunications service provider, or telco. The letter *D* here stands for *data* or *delta*. The D channel is used to signal the telco CO when connections need to be created or terminated. The D channel is thus a control channel for ISDN call setup and tear down.

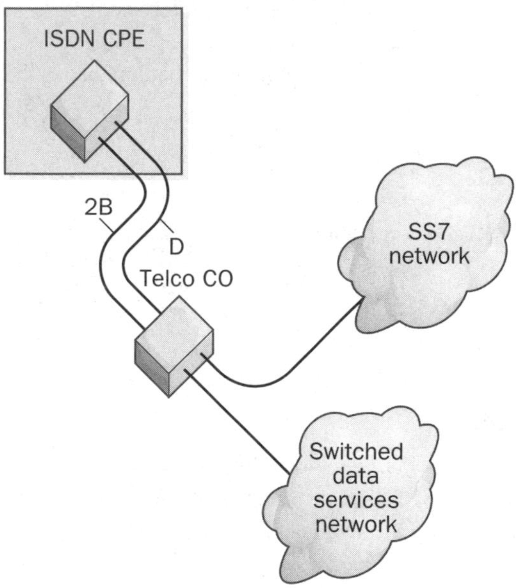

D channel. *How the D channel works.*

The D channel forms the "D" part of a 2B+D Basic Rate Interface ISDN (BRI-ISDN) line and carries signaling information at a rate of 16 kilobits per second (Kbps). On a 23B+D Primary Rate Interface ISDN (PRI-ISDN) line, the D channel carries signaling information at the faster rate of 64 Kbps.

Implementation

D channel communication uses a completely separate out-of-band communication network called the Signaling System 7 (SS7) network, as shown in the illustration. This telco network is dedicated solely to servicing system functions that are overhead as far as voice or data communication is concerned. The SS7 network on which D channel communication takes place makes possible the low latency of dial-up ISDN connections, which are typically 1 or 2 seconds (compared to a latency of 15 to 30 seconds for analog phone connections).

The data-link layer of the D channel is defined by the Q.921 standard and uses LAPD (Link Access Protocol, D-channel) for full-duplex, synchronous, serial communications. The physical layer of the D channel is no different from that of the B channel.

Notes

In ISDN voice communication, D channels are also used to activate special calling features such as line call forwarding and caller ID.

See Also: *B channel, Integrated Services Digital Network (ISDN), Link Access Protocol, D-channel (LAPD), out-of-band (OOB) signaling*

DCOM

Stands for Distributed Component Object Model, a Microsoft programming technology for developing distributed applications.

See: *Distributed Component Object Model (DCOM)*

DCOM Configuration Tool

A Microsoft Windows NT, Windows 2000, Windows XP, Windows .NET Server, and Windows 98 utility used to configure 32-bit Windows applications for Distributed Component Object Model (DCOM) communication between components of distributed applications on a network.

Overview

You can use the DCOM Configuration Tool to configure DCOM applications to run across computers on a network. Computers can be configured to operate as DCOM clients (making calls to DCOM servers), DCOM servers, or both. Using this tool, you can configure the locations of components of distributed applications and the security settings for those components.

Implementation

To start the tool, choose Run from the Start menu, and then type **dcomcnfg**. To use the tool to configure a distributed application, you must specify the security and location properties of both the calling client application and the responding server application. For the client application, you specify the location of the server application that will be called by the client. For the server application, you select a user account that will have permission to start the application and the user accounts that will run it.

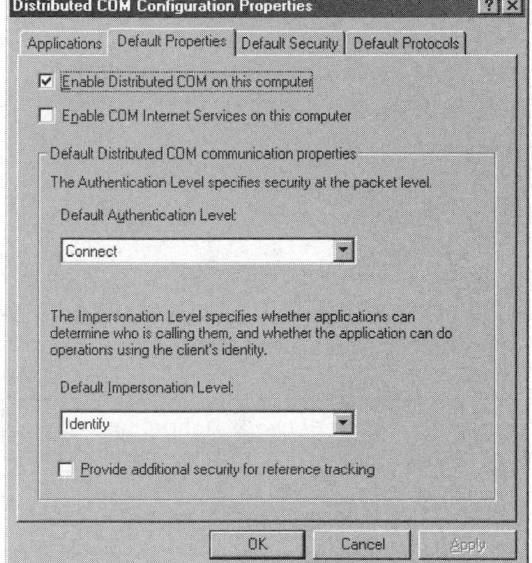

DCOM Configuration Tool. *Using the DCOM Configuration Tool.*

Notes

Before you can use the DCOM Configuration Tool on Windows 98, you must be sure that user-level security is being used.

See Also: *Distributed Component Object Model (DCOM)*

DDNS

Stands for Dynamic DNS, a new feature of the Domain Name System (DNS) that enables DNS clients to automatically register their DNS names with name servers.

See: *dynamic DNS (DDNS)*

DDoS

Stands for Distributed Denial of Service, a form of Denial of Service (DoS) attack that employs a large number of intermediate hosts to multiply the effect of the attack.

See: *Distributed Denial of Service (DDoS)*

DDR (Demand-Dial Routing)

Stands for Demand-Dial Routing, a method of forwarding packets on request across a Point-to-Point Protocol (PPP) wide area network (WAN) link.

See: *Demand-Dial Routing (DDR)*

DDR (Dial-on-Demand Routing)

Stands for Dial-on-Demand Routing, a method for connecting two remote networks together using Integrated Services Digital Network (ISDN) and dial-up Public Switched Telephone Network (PSTN) connections.

See: *Dial-on-Demand Routing (DDR)*

DDS (digital data service)

Stands for digital data service, a family of leased line data communication technologies that provides a dedicated synchronous transmission connection at speeds of 56 kilobits per second (Kbps).

See: *digital data service (DDS)*

DDS (Digital Data Storage)

Stands for Digital Data Storage, a tape backup technology that evolved from Digital Audio Tape (DAT) technologies.

See: *Digital Data Storage (DDS)*

dead spot

In wireless networking, a location within the coverage area where a signal is not received.

Overview

Dead spots are typically caused by physical barriers (such as buildings or concrete structures) that absorb or reflect radio or microwave frequencies. The receiving station must relocate or the barrier must be moved if the station is to receive a signal. Dead spots can also be caused by high levels of electromagnetic interference (EMI) from heavy machinery (such as motors and generators) or broad-spectrum sources of radiation (such as microwave ovens). In these cases, too, the solution is to relocate the receiver or eliminate the source of interference.

See Also: *wireless networking*

decibel

A mathematical way of representing power ratios.

Overview

A decibel (dB) is the ratio of two values that measure signal strength, such as voltage, current, or power. This ratio is expressed using base 10 logarithms. In mathematical terms, this means that the decibel is defined as follows, where P1 and P2 are the power (signal strength) measurements:

$dB = 10 \log_{10} (P1/P2)$

Uses

In computer networking and telecommunications, decibels are the units used for measuring signal loss within a circuit. Decibels are also used in network cabling systems for measuring signal losses. In addition, quantities such as attenuation and near-end crosstalk (NEXT) for fiber-optic cabling are expressed in units that contain decibels. In this scenario, P1 is the strength of the signal when it enters the cabling system, and P2 is its strength at some later point, after it has traversed segments of cable, repeaters, connectors, and other cabling system components. The following table shows signal strength ratios expressed both as ratios and as decibels for conversion purposes.

Signal Strength Ratios

Signal Strength Ratio (P1:P2)	*Decibels (dB)*
1:1 (no signal loss)	0 dB
2:1 (50 percent signal loss)	-3 dB
4:1 (75 percent signal loss)	-6 dB
10:1 (90 percent signal loss)	-10 dB
100:1 (99 percent signal loss)	-20 dB
1000:1 (99.9 percent signal loss)	-30 dB

Notes

The Category 5 (Cat5) cabling version of unshielded twisted-pair (UTP) cabling has an attenuation rating of 30 dB/1000 feet. This means that after traveling 1000 feet (304 meters) along a UTP cable, the electrical strength of the signal typically diminishes by 99.9 percent and is only 0.1 percent of its original strength at the far end of the cable.

See Also: *cabling, fiber-optic cabling, unshielded twisted-pair (UTP) cabling*

DECnet

A protocol suite developed by Digital Equipment Corporation (DEC).

Overview

DECnet was originally designed in 1975 to allow PDP-11 minicomputers to communicate with each other. DECnet conforms to the Digital Network Architecture (DNA) developed by DEC, which maps to the seven-layer Open Systems Interconnection (OSI) reference model for networking protocols.

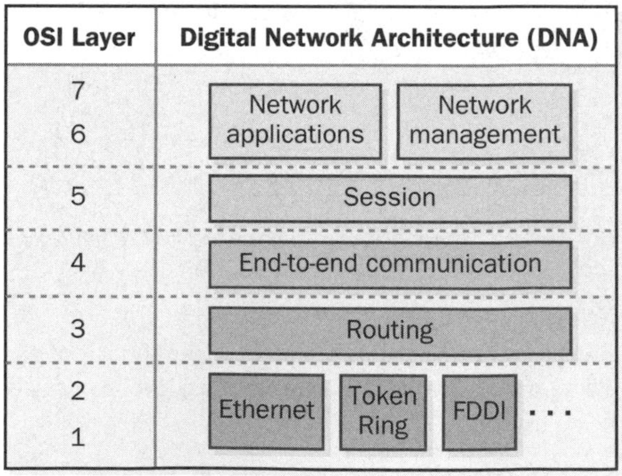

OSI Layer	Digital Network Architecture (DNA)
7, 6	Network applications; Network management
5	Session
4	End-to-end communication
3	Routing
2, 1	Ethernet; Token Ring; FDDI; . . .

DECnet. *Overview of DECnet.*

DECnet is essentially a peer-to-peer networking protocol for all DEC networking environments. DECnet supports various media and link-layer technologies, including Ethernet, Token Ring, and Fiber Distributed

Data Interface (FDDI). The current release of DECnet is called Phase V, but DECnet is essentially a legacy protocol that is rarely used nowadays.

dedicated line

Any telecommunications line that is continuously available for the subscriber with little or no latency.

Overview

Dedicated lines are also referred to as leased lines, since businesses lease these lines from telcos so that they can have continuous, uninterrupted communication with branch offices and with the Internet. The opposite of a dedicated line is a dial-up line, which costs less because it is used intermittently and requires fewer telco resources. However, dial-up lines suffer from the delaying effects of latency as well as less available bandwidth. Dial-up lines are generally local loop Plain Old Telephone Service (POTS) connections that use modems and provide backup services for more expensive leased lines. Dedicated lines, on the other hand, use specially conditioned phone lines and are allocated to the subscriber's private domain with dedicated switching circuits. By contrast, circuits for dial-up lines are shared with all other subscribers in the Public Switched Telephone Network (PSTN) domain.

Dedicated lines can be either point-to-point or multipoint communication paths. They are generally synchronous digital communication lines, and are terminated with one of the following serial interfaces: RS-232, RS-449, RS-530, X.21, V.35, or HSSI.

Advantages and Disadvantages

The main advantages of dedicated lines are the following:

- They involve minimal connection delays and minimal latency for establishing communication.
- They provide a consistent level of service.
- They are always available without any busy signals.

The main disadvantage of dedicated lines is that they cost more than dial-up lines.

See Also: *dial-up line, leased line, T-carrier*

Dedicated Token Ring (DTR)

A high-speed Token Ring networking technology.

Overview

Dedicated Token Ring (DTR) is an extension of 802.5 Token Ring technologies developed as an evolutionary upgrade to higher speeds for Token Ring users. It defines a set of signaling protocols and topologies that are backward-compatible with standard Token Ring networking.

DTR uses the same 802.5 frame format as standard Token Ring and supports full-duplex communications using the Transmit Intermediate (TXI) protocol to allow simultaneous transmission and reception of frames by stations.

DTR uses special concentrators to create high-speed ring topology networks. A traditional Token Ring Multistation Access Unit (MAU) can be joined to a DTR concentrator to enable 802.5 stations to communicate over the high-speed ring.

Prospects

Although DTR began development in 1995, it has fallen into eclipse in recent years along with standard Token Ring technologies due to the continued evolution of Ethernet into its Fast Ethernet and Gigabit Ethernet (GbE) varieties.

See Also: *802.5, Multistation Access Unit (MAU or MSAU), Token Ring*

default gateway

An address in a routing table to which packets are forwarded when there is no specific route for forwarding them to their destination.

Overview

In an internetwork, a given subnet might have several router interfaces that connect it to other, remote subnets. One of these router interfaces is usually selected as the default gateway of the local subnet. When a host on the network wants to send a packet to a destination subnet, it consults its internal routing table to determine whether it knows which router to forward the packet to in order to have it reach the destination subnet. If the routing table does not contain any routing information about the destination subnet, the packet is forwarded to the default gateway (one of the routers with an interface on the local subnet). The host assumes that the default gateway knows what to do with any packets that the host itself does not know how to forward.

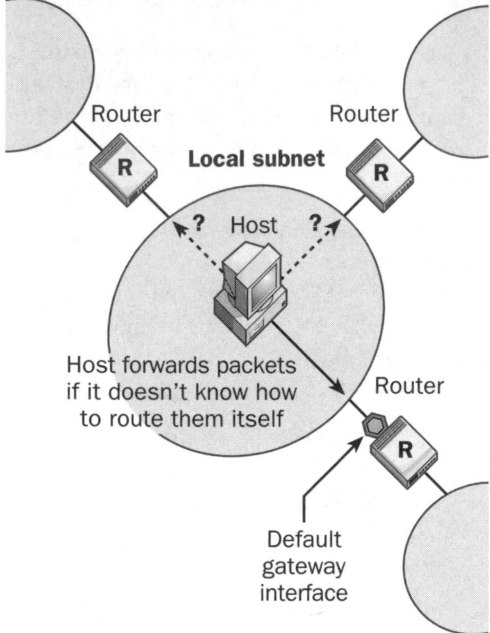

Default gateway. *How a default gateway works.*

When configuring a client machine on a TCP/IP internetwork, the client must know the Internet Protocol (IP) address of the default gateway for its network. On Microsoft Windows NT, Windows 95, and Windows 98 clients, you configure this information on the TCP/IP property sheet for the client. The property to configure is known as the Default Gateway Address. In Windows 2000, Windows XP, and Windows .NET Server, you can have a default gateway assigned automatically using Dynamic Host Configuration Protocol (DHCP).

See Also: *IP address, routing table*

Defense Messaging System (DMS)

A global messaging system for the U.S. Department of Defense (DoD).

Overview

The Defense Messaging System (DMS) is a program established by the U.S. Undersecretary of Defense (Acquisition) to develop an integrated, global messaging system for transferring classified and unclassified data. The Defense Messaging System (DMS) will replace the existing Automatic Digital Network (AUTODIN) system currently in use by the U.S. Department of Defense.

Microsoft Exchange DMS, a version of Microsoft Exchange Server, complies with the DMS specification. It is suited for government agencies that are required to use DMS-compliant products and for companies that do defense business with the U.S. government. Exchange DMS technology can be purchased only through Lockheed Martin Federal Systems.

See Also: *Exchange Server*

defragmentation

The process of reorganizing information written on disk drives to make reading the information more efficient.

Overview

When files on disk drives are frequently written, copied, moved, and deleted, the information stored on the drive tends to become fragmented over time. Instead of storing a file across several contiguous (successive) sectors of the drive, files tend to become split up into discontiguous (disconnected) portions scattered all over the drive. Then when the file needs to be accessed again, the drive heads need to skip around a lot to find and read the successive portions of the file, which is a slower process than if the file was located in only one continuous section of the drive. Fragmented drives thus perform more poorly for disk reads (and writes) than drives that are not significantly fragmented. And the more often files are modified on a drive, the more fragmented it tends to become and the more poorly it performs (you can hear the sound of a fragmented drive "thrashing" as it reads files while loading programs and data into memory).

To improve performance of a fragmented drive, the drive should be defragmented. A defragmentation tool is an application that reads portions of fragmented files, copies them to memory, erases them from the disk, and then copies them back to the disk in successive sectors or clusters for better performance. Defragmentation can be performed on files, free space, or both for best performance, and should be done regularly on all computers and particularly those (such as file servers) that experience a lot of disk reads and writes.

Marketplace

Studies by industry analysts have estimated that as much as $50 billion per year is being lost by businesses simply by failing to defragment computers regularly on their networks. While best gains are achieved by defragmenting servers regularly (performance gains of 10 percent to 20 percent are typical), workstations also perform better when periodically defragmented. In spite of these estimates, the present penetration of network defragmentation software in enterprise environments is currently less than 15 percent, so much work remains to be done alerting IT (information technology) administrators to the problem.

While Windows 2000 and other operating systems have their own built-in defragmentation tools, several third-party vendors offer defragmentation tools that are more powerful and manageable and allow an administrator to centrally configure and schedule defragmentation of computers across a network. Some of the more popular tools include Diskeeper from Executive Software (Windows 2000 includes a "light" version of this tool that lacks scheduling capability), PerfectDisk from Raxco Software, and Norton Speed Disk from Symantec Corporation.

delegation

A feature of Microsoft Windows 2000 and the Windows .NET Server family that simplifies the administration of Active Directory directory service.

Overview

Delegation is a process for simplifying the assignment of permissions and rights to an object, container, or subtree of containers or organizational units (OUs) within Active Directory. These permissions and rights can be assigned for the following purposes:

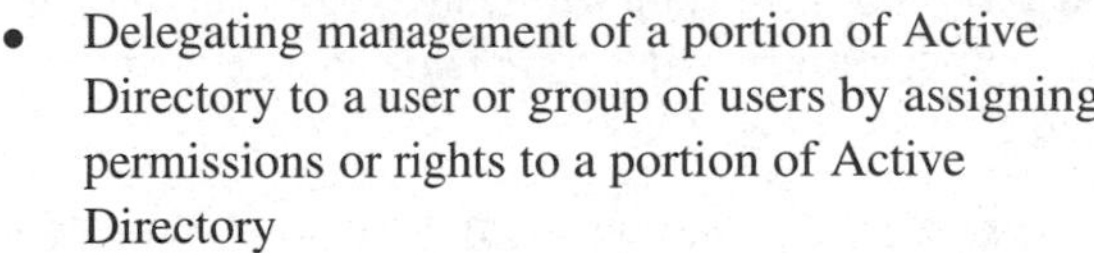

- Delegating management of a portion of Active Directory to a user or group of users by assigning permissions or rights to a portion of Active Directory
- Protecting a portion of Active Directory from unauthorized access by denying permissions or rights to a portion of Active Directory

Using delegation, the network administrator can distribute the job of managing an Active Directory enterprise-level implementation among a group of individuals, each with the appropriate permissions and rights to manage her or his portion of the directory. For example, users can be granted permissions and rights on the Users container so that they can create new users or modify the attributes of existing ones. In this fashion, the network administrator can be relieved of the tiresome duty of creating and configuring new user accounts by delegating the job to a junior administrator. Delegation is designed to relieve the network administrator of the burden of managing the entire Active Directory and is an important security management feature in Windows 2000 and Windows .NET Server.

You can perform delegation using the Delegation of Control Wizard, which is part of the Active Directory Users and Computers administrative tool, and you can use it to delegate administration of portions of Active Directory to other administrators and users.

Delegation is part of the security framework of Active Directory. Along with other features such as the discretionary access control list (DACL), inheritance, and trust relationships, it enables Active Directory to be administered securely, protected from unauthorized access.

D

Notes

Always delegate administrative control at the level of OUs, not at the level of individual objects. This allows you to better manage access to Active Directory because OUs are used to organize objects in the directory. One good idea is to delegate authority to those who are responsible for creating users, groups, computers, and other objects that commonly change in an enterprise.

Always assign permissions to groups instead of to individual users. Groups can be nested within one another and, together with inheritance of permissions, they provide a powerful tool for organizing the administration of Active Directory.

See Also: *Active Directory, Delegation of Control Wizard, permissions*

Delegation of Control Wizard

A wizard that you can run using the Active Directory Users and Computers administrative tool for networks in Microsoft Windows 2000 and the Windows .NET Server family.

Overview

The Delegation of Control Wizard facilitates delegating control of different portions of Active Directory directory service to other administrators and users. The wizard simplifies the process by allowing only the administrator to assign permissions at the level of organizational units (OUs). Assigning permissions to OUs rather than to particular directory objects ultimately simplifies the Active Directory administrator's work.

To start the wizard, open the Active Directory Users and Computers tool, select the OU for which you want to delegate control, and on the Action menu, choose Delegate Control. Specify the users or groups to whom you want to delegate control, the subset of object types in the OU for which this should take place, and the kinds of permissions you want to assign.

See Also: *Active Directory, delegation, permissions*

Demand-Dial Routing (DDR)

A method for forwarding packets on request across a Point-to-Point Protocol (PPP) wide area network (WAN) link.

Overview

Demand-Dial Routing (DDR) is a technology in Microsoft Windows 2000 and the Windows .NET Server family that uses PPP links to create on-demand connections for transferring packets to remote networks. DDR works with a variety of dial-up technologies, including Public Switched Telephone Network (PSTN), Integrated Services Digital Network (ISDN), and X.25.

DDR is used to connect networks and uses Windows 2000 and Windows .NET Server's Routing and Remote Access Service (RRAS). DDR links are represented by RRAS as demand-dial interfaces and can be either persistent or on-demand and either one-way or two-way initiated. DDR is different from remote access—in remote access a single user connects to a remote network, but in DDR two networks connect. Like remote access connections, however, DDR connections can use the same security and encryption mechanisms, be implemented using remote access policies, support Remote Authentication Dial-In User Service (RADIUS) authentication, and use advanced PPP features such as Multilink PPP (MPPP), Microsoft Point-to-Point Compression (MPPC), and Bandwidth Allocation Protocol (BAP).

Notes

Demand-Dial Routing (DDR) is not the same as Dial-on Demand Routing (DDR), a Cisco router technology for connectivity-on-demand between Cisco routers.

See Also: *Point-to-Point Protocol (PPP)*

demand priority

The media access control method used by 100VG-AnyLan networks.

Overview

100VG-AnyLan is a high-speed networking architecture developed by Hewlett-Packard and based on the Institute of Electrical and Electronics Engineers (IEEE) standard 802.12. Demand priority is the method by which stations on a 100VG-AnyLan network gain access to the wire for transmitting data.

Implementation

A 100VG-AnyLan network based on the demand priority access method consists of end nodes (stations), repeaters (hubs), switches, routers, bridges, and other networking devices. A typical 100VG-AnyLan network consists of a number of stations plugged into a cascading star topology of repeaters (hubs). Because of timing, a maximum of five levels of cascading of the physical wiring is permitted. Hubs are connected using uplink ports. Each hub is aware only of the stations directly connected to it and any hubs that are uplinked from it.

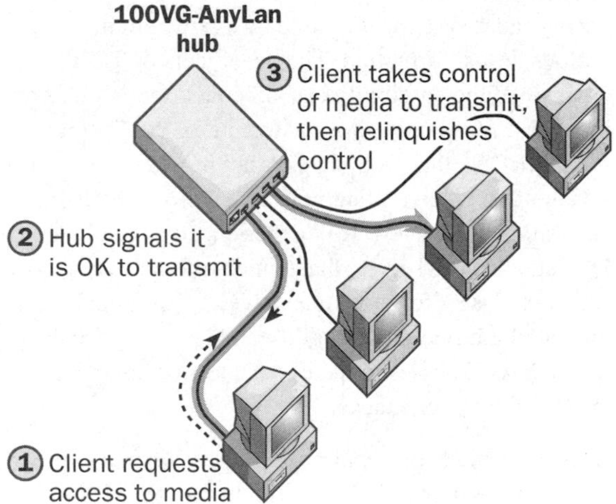
100VG-AnyLan hub
3 Client takes control of media to transmit, then relinquishes control
2 Hub signals it is OK to transmit
1 Client requests access to media

Demand priority. *How the demand priority media access method works.*

The key feature of the demand priority access method, as shown on the illustration, is that the 100VG-AnyLan hubs control which computers are allowed to transmit signals on the network at any given moment. Hubs can be thought of as servers and end nodes as computers (clients). With demand priority, a client (a computer with a 100VG-AnyLan network interface card installed in it) must first request access to the network media (cabling) before transmitting data. The server (hub) processes this request and decides whether to allow the client access to the media. If the hub decides to grant the client access to the wire, it sends the client a signal informing it of this decision. The client then takes over control of the media and transmits its data.

Demand priority is considered a contention method, but it operates differently from the Carrier Sense Multiple Access with Collision Detection (CSMA/CD) access method used in Ethernet networks. Cables in a 100VG-AnyLan network are capable of transmitting and receiving data at the same time using all four pairs of twisted-pair cabling in a quartet signaling method. Each pair of wires in a twisted-pair cable transmits and receives data at 25 megahertz (MHz), for a total bandwidth of 100 MHz. All contention on the network occurs at the hub. If two computers attempt to transmit signals at the same time, the hubs can either choose between the two signals based on priority or alternate between them if the priorities are equal. The hubs can do this because demand priority provides mechanisms for prioritizing transmission of different data types. Computers in demand priority networks can simultaneously transmit and receive data, and they do not need to listen to the network because the hubs control access to the wire.

See Also: *100VG-AnyLAN, Carrier Sense Multiple Access with Collision Detection (CSMA/CD), media access control method*

demarc

The point in a carrier's wide area network (WAN) service at which the customer's responsibility for line management ends and the carrier's responsibility begins.

Overview

Demarc is short for *demarcation point* and indicates the point at which the carrier assumes responsibility for troubleshooting the WAN connection. For example, if a carrier provides the customer with a Channel Service Unit/Data Service Unit (CSU/DSU) for a leased line, the CSU/DSU is included within the carrier's responsibility and the demarc point is the serial interface on the CSU/DSU to which the customer's router is connected. If the demarc point instead is the RJ-48 connector that terminates the leased line at the customer premises, then the customer is responsible for managing and troubleshooting (and possibly also providing) the CSU/DSU that connects to this connector.

See Also: *telecommunications services*

demilitarized zone (DMZ)

Also called a perimeter network, a security network at the boundary between a corporate local area network (LAN) and the Internet.

See: *perimeter network*

DEN

Stands for Directory Enabled Network, an initiative toward a platform-independent specification for storing information about network applications, devices, and users in a directory.

See: *Directory Enabled Network (DEN),*

denial of service (DoS)

Any attack conducted against a system that tries to prevent legitimate users from accessing it.

Overview

Denial of service (DoS) refers to a broad family of different methods that hackers use to try to prevent legitimate users from accessing Web servers, mail servers, networks, and other systems. DoS attacks exploit weaknesses inherent in the Transmission Control Protocol/Internet Protocol (TCP/IP) suite, bugs in operating systems and applications, and holes in firewalls and other security devices. Over the last half dozen years, holes have been discovered in Apache, Berkeley Internet Name Domain (BIND), Sendmail, Internet Information Services (IIS), Common Gateway Interface (CGI), Simple Network Management Protocol (SNMP), and other systems that make them vulnerable to DoS attacks. Vendors of these systems have issued patches to guard against these attacks, but new ones are often being discovered.

Generally speaking, DoS attacks occur when a malicious user consumes so many resources on a remote network or system that none are left for legitimate users who need them. The resources attacked might include processors, disk space, memory, network connections, modems, and telephone lines. In a way, a DoS attack is like driving an extra-wide truck down a freeway—the truck blocks legitimate traffic from getting through to its destination.

Another general goal of DoS attacks is to disable critical services on a machine. Once these services are disabled, requests from legitimate users cannot be serviced until the machine is rebooted. For example, if an attacker can send malformed packets to a Web server to shut down its Hypertext Transfer Protocol (HTTP) service, the attacker has succeeded in denying access to the server by its real clients.

History

DoS attacks are not new in theory—a similar technique, jamming, was used during World War II to render enemy radar systems unusable by overwhelming them with useless information. The developers of TCP/IP envisioned the possibility of DoS attacks early on as an inevitable result of the open nature of TCP/IP, but it was not until 1996 that DoS attacks caught widespread public attention when an Internet service provider (ISP) called PANIX in New York experienced a sustained DoS attack on its servers that denied Internet services to legitimate users for more than a week. This attack demonstrated the Internet's fragility and led many vendors to patch weaknesses in their products that could be exploited by DoS attacks.

DoS again made the front page in 1999 when a number of U.S. government Web sites (including the FBI's Web site) were attacked by disgruntled hackers as retaliation for an FBI crackdown on some of their members.

More recently, a new and deadlier type of attack called Distributed Denial of Service (DDoS) made headlines in February 2000 when a young Canadian nicknamed Mafiaboy allegedly denied service for several hours to a number of major commercial Web sites, including Yahoo!, eBay, Amazon.com, Buy.com, E-Trade.com, ZDNet, and CNN.com. Also in 2000, a coordinated Distributed Denial of Service (DdoS) attack was launched against the Internet's Internet Relay Chat (IRC) system, crippling the system for several weeks.

The Internet Engineering Task Force (IETF) is currently working on a new Internet protocol called ICMP Traceback Messages that, if implemented widely, would allow networks experiencing DoS attacks to better determine the source of the attacks. Until then, network managers and system administrators need to be vigilant in applying the latest patches to systems and monitoring their networks for evidence of intrusion and DoS attacks.

Types

There are a number of different types of DoS attacks. Some of these are described in some detail below, but others are mentioned only briefly.

- **Synchronous idle character (SYN) flooding:** This famous attack exploits weaknesses in the three-way handshaking protocol of TCP. Typically, SYN flooding is used to render a Web server's networking services unavailable. SYN flooding is a type of attack in which TCP connection request packets (SYN packets) are sent in large numbers to a Web server. These packets use a false or "spoofed" source IP address to hide the attacker to fool the server into sending responses to a nonexistent client. SYN packets are used to place the TCP ports in the SYN_RECEIVED, or "half-open," state on the Web server and then do nothing with them until they time out. If enough of these ports are half-opened, the server cannot handle requests from normal clients until the unused ports expire. Unfortunately, it takes time for the half-opened ports to time out because when a SYN packet is received, the server generates a SYN-ACK packet to acknowledge the request and then waits for a final ACK from the requester before fully opening the port for a communication session. (This is called a TCP three-way handshake.) However, that final ACK is not received because the source address in the SYN packet was spoofed. The SYN-ACK packet is thus retransmitted several times at increasingly longer time intervals until, after a total time of 189 seconds (in the implementation of TCP/IP on Microsoft Windows platforms), the server finally gives up and closes the half-open port. For that time period, the requested port is unavailable to perform any other services.
- **Ping of Death:** This type of attack floods a machine or network with malformed Packet Internet Groper (PING) packets to crash remote systems. Many operating systems are vulnerable to this type of attack, as are some routers and network printers. Check with your vendor for any patches that have been released to deal with this type of attack. Also be sure to configure your routers not to allow broadcasts to pass into your network from outside.
- **Smurf attack:** This variant of the Ping of Death employs an intermediate network to send broadcast pings to tie up a system. A broadcast ping is an Internet Control Message Packet (ICMP) directed to a subnet broadcast address and is received by all hosts on the subnet. The source address of the broadcast ping is spoofed to appear as the address of the machine being targeted. The effect is for the targeted system to receive a flood of ICMP Echo response packets, depending on how many intermediate systems are employed. For more information, see the article "Distributed Denial of Service (DDoS)" elsewhere in this chapter.
- **Overlapping fragment attack:** This attack fragments packets into small pieces and then reassembles them starting from the middle of a packet instead of the beginning. The resulting bad packets are held in the receiving system's buffer until the system's memory resources are full, causing the machine to hang up.
- **Address Resolution Protocol (ARP) cache poisoning:** This attack preloads false information into a system's ARP cache, preventing it from communicating over the network with other systems.
- **Domain Name System (DNS) cache poisoning:** This attack fills the cache on name servers with name lookup information about nonexistent hosts, causing legitimate name lookup requests to be dropped. Upgrading to the latest version of BIND solves this problem.
- **User Datagram Protocol (UDP) attack:** This attack causes two systems to send a continuous flood of UDP packets to each other, preventing legitimate network communications from being able to occur.

- **Mail bombs:** This type of attack tries to overwhelm mail servers by sending them large amounts of useless messages. Mail filters are the usual method for dealing with such attacks.

Notes

If users try to connect to an IIS Web server and receive error messages such as "The connection has been reset by the remote host," a SYN attack might be under way on your machine. (When the maximum number of TCP ports are in use [open or half-open] on a machine, the machine usually responds to any further connection attempts with a reset.)

To determine whether such an attack is in progress, type netstat -n -p tcp at the command prompt to see whether there are a large number of ports in the half-open SYN_RECEIVED state. If so, try using a network protocol analyzer such as Network Monitor to further examine the situation. You might need to contact your ISP to investigate the problem more closely.

If your server is under a heavy SYN attack, one fix you can try on Windows NT platforms running Microsoft IIS is to decrease the default timeout for terminating half-open TCP connections. Open the TcpMaxConnectResponseRetransmissions parameter in the registry and set it to 3, 2, or even 1 to reduce the timeout to 45, 21, or 9 seconds, respectively. However, if you set this parameter too low, legitimate connections might experience timeouts. Windows 2000 and Windows NT 4 Service Pack 3 have corrected this problem. A fix is available for Windows NT version 3.51 from Microsoft Corporation.

If your Cisco router is experiencing a SYN attack, use the TCP Intercept feature to validate incoming TCP connection requests to counter the flood.

For More Information

Visit these Web sites for useful information about DoS issues: CERT Coordination Center at *www.cert.org,* SANS Institute at *www.sans.org,* International Computer Security Association at *www.icsa.net,* FBI National Infrastructure Protection Center at *www.nipc.gov,* and Forum of Incident Response and Security Teams at *www.first.org.*

See Also: *Distributed Denial of Service (DDoS), hacking, security, spoofing*

dense mode

One of two forms of the spanning tree algorithm used in multicasting.

Overview

While sparse mode routing is designed to be efficient in routing multicast packets to clusters of hosts across a network, dense mode is intended for large-scale multicasting where hosts are spread out across every corner of the network. Dense mode thus assumes that hosts are densely concentrated in large subnets. An example of a situation where dense mode multicasting is required would be a large-scale webcast of a corporate presentation or sports event.

Implementation

Dense mode multicasting creates multiple routing trees, one for each multicast group. Dense mode multicasting floods the network with multicast packets and so assumes that a large amount of bandwidth is available for transmission. Packets are multicast to every area of the network, and then the unneeded branches of the routing tree are pruned for more efficiency.

Dense mode multicasting can employ several different routing protocols to handle the flow:

- Distance Vector Multicast Routing Protocol (DVMRP)
- Multicast Open Shortest Path First (MOSPF)
- Protocol Independent Multicast Dense Mode (PIM-DM)

See Also: *Distance Vector Multicast Routing Protocol (DVMRP), multicasting, Multicast Open Shortest Path First (MOSPF), Protocol Independent Multicast-Dense Mode (PIM-DM), routing protocol, spanning tree algorithm (STA), sparse mode*

dense wavelength division multiplexing (DWDM)

A multiplexing technology for achieving extremely high data rates over fiber-optic cabling.

Overview

Also known sometimes as simply wavelength division multiplexing (WDM), dense wavelength division multiplexing (DWDM) modulates multiple data channels into optical signals that have different frequencies and then multiplexes these signals into a single stream of light that is sent over a fiber-optic cable. Each optical signal has its own frequency, so up to 160 separate data streams can be transmitted simultaneously over the fiber using only eight different light wavelengths. In addition, each data stream can employ its own transmission format or protocol. This means that, using DWDM, you can combine Synchronous Optical Network (SONET), Asynchronous Transfer Mode (ATM), Transmission Control Protocol/Internet Protocol (TCP/IP), and other transmissions and send them simultaneously over a single fiber. At the other end, a multiplexer demultiplexes the signals and distributes them to their various data channels.

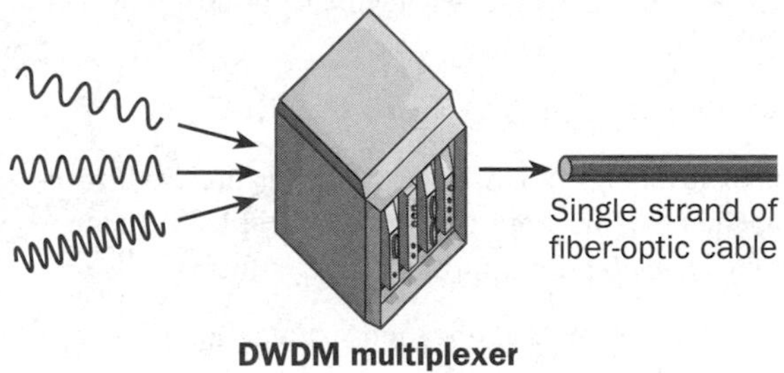

Dense wavelength division multiplexing (DWDM). *How DWDM is implemented.*

Marketplace

Many networking vendors now offer switching equipment that supports DWDM. Big players in this area include Lucent Technologies and Nortel Networks, with numerous smaller players being attracted to the market.

An example of a DWDM deployment is AT&T, which has implemented DWDM switching equipment through much of its long-haul backbone network to carry up to 80 different channels per strand of fiber, and is planning to upgrade this soon to 160 and eventually 320 channels per fiber. This managed DWDM service from AT&T is called Ultravailable Broadband Network, and it can provide 2.4 gigabits per second (Gbps) of bandwidth for metropolitan-area connections where it is available. AT&T targets mainly large enterprises that enter into long-term contracts for these services.

Prospects

DWDM is rapidly replacing time-division multiplexing (TDM) as the standard transmission method for long-haul high-speed fiber-optic carrier links. The main deployment issue for many carriers is cost: devices that support DWDM are more expensive because the laser light sources for generating signals over fiber must be extremely stable. The benefits are so great, however, that many carriers are moving toward implementing it on their backbone networks, particularly long-distance carriers (inter-exchange carriers, or IXCs) who see the greatest benefit/cost ratio in deploying it. DWDM is less likely to be used by competitive telcos (competitive local exchange carriers or CLECs) or baby bells (regional bell operating companies, or RBOCs) for their access networks because of the cost of upgrading equipment to support DWDM compared to simply laying additional fiber to meet their needs.

A newer all-optical switching technology called lambda switching has recently evolved from DWDM and promises significant advantages over traditional DWDM. As a result of these developments, some carriers are holding back on further DWDM deployments while they wait for the new technology to mature.

See Also: *fiber-optic cabling, lambda switching, time-division multiplexing (TDM)*

DES

Stands for Data Encryption Standard, the former U.S. government standard for encryption. It now has been replaced by Advanced Encryption Standard (AES).

See: *Data Encryption Standard (DES)*

desktop

The graphical user interface (GUI) for Microsoft Windows 95, Windows 98, Windows NT version 4, Windows 2000, Windows XP, and Windows .NET Server operating system platforms.

Overview

The desktop is the user's on-screen work area; its various icons and menus are arranged as if on top of a physical desk. Users can place items on the desktop, drag them around, move them into folders, and start and stop tasks using simple mouse actions such as clicking, double-clicking, dragging, and right-clicking.

When the Active Desktop feature of many of these platforms is selected, Web browser functions also appear on the desktop. Users can browse local and network file system objects along with content on the Internet using a familiar Web browser paradigm. Active Web content can be placed directly on the desktop and updated automatically.

See Also: *Active Desktop*

Desktop Management Interface (DMI)

A standard for managing desktop systems developed by the Desktop Management Task Force (DMTF), now the Distributed Management Task Force.

Overview

Desktop Management Interface (DMI) was designed to allow information to be automatically collected from system components such as network interface cards (NICs), hard disks, video cards, operating systems, and applications that comply with the DMI standard. DMI was designed to be operating system-independent and protocol-independent and was designed for use on local systems that do not have a network installed.

Implementation

DMI by itself does not specify a protocol for managing systems over the network. Instead, DMI must use an existing network management protocol such as Simple Network Management Protocol (SNMP) to send and receive information over the network. DMI is in fact similar in design to SNMP. Each component to be managed must have a Management Information Format (MIF) file that specifies the location of the component, name of vendor and model, firmware revision number, interrupt request line (IRQ), input/output (I/O) port address, and so on. MIF files are formatted as structured ASCII flat-file databases; the Desktop Management Task Force has defined several standard MIFs, including the Desktop System MIF file, the Adapter Card MIF file, and the Printer MIF file.

DMI service layer software running on the desktop collects information from DMI-enabled components and stores this information in the appropriate MIF file. The service layer thus acts as an intermediary between the DMI-enabled components and the DMI management application, and it coordinates shared access to the various MIFs installed on the desktop system. DMI management applications can then query the service layer on the desktop to obtain the various system components and applications from these MIF files. The service layer allows the management layer to interact with the MIFs by using commands such as

- **Get:** Obtains information from a MIF
- **Event:** Alerts the management application when certain events occur
- **Set:** Modifies the contents of a MIF

One advantage of DMI over SNMP is that DMI management applications can access MIF files even when they have no prior information about them.

DMI management applications include Intel Corporation's LANDesk and Microsoft Systems Management Server (SMS). SMS 1.2 uses standard DMI 4.5 MIF files to expose inventory data for systems it manages and then stores this information in a Microsoft SQL Server database.

Prospects

DMI is now considered a legacy specification, and the newer Web-Based Enterprise Management (WBEM) initiative from the DMTF has largely replaced it. WBEM specifies a Common Information Model (CIM) as a common abstraction layer for unifying the various existing data providers for system and network management, including DMI and SNMP. Microsoft Corporation has implemented WBEM into the Windows 2000, Windows XP, and Windows .NET Server family operating systems as Windows Management Instrumentation (WMI) and in Microsoft System Management Server 2.

See Also: *Common Information Model (CIM), Distributed Management Task Force (DMTF), Web-Based Enterprise Management (WBEM), Windows Management Instrumentation (WMI)*

destination address

The address to which a frame or packet of data is sent over a network.

Overview

The destination address is used by hosts on the network to determine whether the packet or frame is intended for them or for other hosts. The destination address is also used by routers to determine how to forward the packet or frame through an internetwork. The destination address can be one of the following:

- **Physical address:** For example, the media access control (MAC) address of an Ethernet frame
- **Logical address:** For example, the Internet Protocol (IP) address of an IP packet

Destination addresses can be either specific or general. Specific addresses point to a specific host on the network. A general address points the packet or frame to all hosts on the network or multicasts it to a specific multicast group of hosts on the network.

You can see the destination address of a packet or frame by using a network sniffer device such as Network Monitor, a tool included with Microsoft Systems Management Server (SMS). Network Monitor displays destination addresses in both ASCII and hexadecimal form.

Notes

The other kind of address in a packet or frame is the source address. This is the address of the host from which the packet originates (unless the source address is being spoofed).

See Also: *source address*

device

Generally, any hardware component that can be driven by software. In Microsoft SQL Server, a file used to store databases.

Overview

In Microsoft Windows 2000, Windows XP, and Windows .NET Server, you can manage devices and their drivers using Device Manager, which you access through the System utility in Control Panel. In Windows NT, you can view, enable, disable, stop, and start devices using the Devices utility in Control Panel. You can also install and uninstall devices and update device drivers in Device Manager.

In Microsoft SQL Server, a device is a file used to store SQL Server databases. Multiple SQL Server databases can be stored on a single device, and a single database can span multiple devices.

The master system device contains four databases:

- The master system database, which is used for tracking system-wide information
- The tempdb system database, which is used for temporary storage purposes
- The model system database, which is a template for generating new databases
- The msdb database, which is used by SQL Server Agent for scheduling alerts and jobs, and recording operators

Dfs

Stands for distributed file system, a network file system that makes many shares on different file servers look like a single hierarchy of shares on a single file server.

See: *Distributed file system (Dfs)*

DHCP

Stands for Dynamic Host Configuration Protocol, a protocol that enables the dynamic configuration Internet Protocol (IP) address information for hosts on an internetwork.

See: *Dynamic Host Configuration Protocol (DHCP)*

D

DHCP client

Software running on an Internet Protocol (IP) host that enables the host to have its IP address information dynamically assigned using Dynamic Host Configuration Protocol (DHCP).

Overview

The term *DHCP client* can also describe the software component on a computer that is capable of interacting with a DHCP server to lease an IP address.

Microsoft Windows comes with DHCP client software that you can configure when you install the TCP/IP protocol suite. This software allows a machine to immediately take its place in TCP/IP internetworks using DHCP. Other operating systems might require that the DHCP client software be installed and configured separately.

Microsoft operating systems that can function as DHCP clients include the following:

- Windows .NET Server
- Windows XP
- Windows 2000
- Windows NT
- Windows 98
- Windows 95
- Windows for Workgroups with the Microsoft TCP/IP-32 add-on installed
- Network Client 3 for MS-DOS
- LAN Manager 2.2c

Notes

On machines running Windows 2000, Windows XP, and Windows .NET Server, the DHCP client is DNS-aware and uses dynamic update for registering addresses, which allows the IP address and fully qualified domain name (FQDN) of client machines to be assigned and supported together.

Windows NT, Windows 95, and Windows 98 clients can release and renew their IP address leases using the ipconfig command. This command can also be useful for resolving IP address conflicts or for troubleshooting DHCP clients and servers.

See Also: *DHCP server, Dynamic Host Configuration Protocol (DHCP)*

DHCP client reservation

A process for configuring a Dynamic Host Configuration Protocol (DHCP) server so that a particular host on the network always leases the same Internet Protocol (IP) address.

Overview

You can create a client reservation on a DHCP server if you want the server to always assign the same IP address to a specific machine on the network. You might do this to assign IP addresses to servers on the network because the IP addresses of servers should not change. (If they do, client machines might have difficulty connecting with them.) An alternative and more common way to assign a client reservation to a server is to manually assign a static IP address to the server.

On Microsoft Windows 2000– and Windows .NET Server–based networks you can create DHCP client reservations using the DHCP console, and in Windows NT you use DHCP Manager. Enter the media access control (MAC) address as the client's unique identifier. When the client with that address contacts the DHCP server to request an IP address, the server leases the reserved address to the client.

See Also: *DHCP console*

DHCP Client service

The service in Microsoft Windows 2000, Windows XP, Windows .NET Server, and Windows NT that implements the client component of the Dynamic Host Configuration Protocol (DHCP) on workstations and servers.

Overview

You can use the DHCP Client service to obtain Internet Protocol (IP) addresses and other Transmission Control Protocol/Internet Protocol (TCP/IP) configuration information from a DHCP server (such as a Windows 2000 or Windows NT server running the DHCP Server service).

Microsoft Windows includes support for DHCP and provides client software that lets you manage a machine's IP address over a network. This software runs as a service under Windows 2000, Windows XP, Windows .NET Server, and Windows NT. DHCP simplifies the administration and management of IP addresses for machines on a TCP/IP network.

See Also: *DHCP Server service, Dynamic Host Configuration Protocol (DHCP)*

DHCP console

A Microsoft Windows 2000 and Windows .NET Server administrative tool for managing the DHCP Server service on Windows 2000 Server and Windows .NET Server.

Overview

The DHCP console is the main tool used for managing and configuring all aspects of the Dynamic Host Configuration Protocol (DHCP) on a Windows 2000– and Windows .NET Server–based network and is implemented as a snap-in for the Microsoft Management Console (MMC).

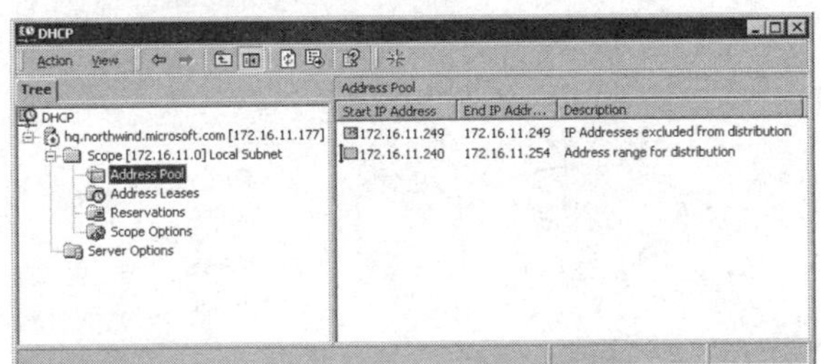

DHCP console. *The DHCP console for Windows 2000 Server.*

You can use the DHCP console for the following standard DHCP administration tasks:

- Creating a scope of Internet Protocol (IP) addresses to lease to DHCP clients
- Creating a set of scope options, which are passed on to clients
- Configuring the lease duration for IP addresses leased to clients
- Viewing and terminating active leases on a network
- Creating reservations for servers that need specific IP addresses
- Monitoring DHCP statistics

The DHCP console also includes the following advanced features, which are new to Windows 2000 and are also included with Windows .NET Server:

- Automatic detection of rogue DHCP servers on the network
- Automatic self-assignment of temporary IP addresses to clients if a lease cannot be obtained from a DHCP server
- New DHCP options for multicast groups (class D IP addresses), superscopes for grouping together DHCP scopes for management purposes, and other vendor-specific functions
- Integration of DHCP and Domain Name System (DNS), allowing clients to use dynamic update to update their host names to IP address mappings in DNS server zone files

See Also: *Dynamic Host Configuration Protocol (DHCP)*

DHCP lease

The duration for which a Dynamic Host Configuration Protocol (DHCP) server lends an IP address to a DHCP client.

Overview

You can configure the lease duration using the Microsoft Windows NT administrative tool DHCP Manager or the Windows 2000 or Windows .NET Server console snap-in. If your Transmission Control Protocol/Internet Protocol (TCP/IP) network configuration does not change often or if you have more than enough IP addresses in your assigned IP address pool, you can increase the DHCP lease considerably beyond its default value of three days. However, if your network configuration changes frequently or if you have a limited pool of IP addresses that is almost used up, keep the reservation period short—perhaps one day. The reason is that if the pool of available IP addresses is used up, machines that are added or moved might be unable to obtain an IP address from a DHCP server and thus will be unable to participate in network communication.

See Also: *DHCP console*

DHCP options

Additional Internet Protocol (IP) address settings that a Dynamic Host Configuration Protocol (DHCP) server passes to DHCP clients.

Overview

When a DHCP client requests an IP address from a DHCP server, the server sends the client at least an IP address and a subnet mask value. Additional information can be sent to clients if you configure various DHCP options. You can assign these options globally to all DHCP clients, to clients belonging to a particular scope, or to an individual host on the network.

You can configure a number of different DHCP options using the Microsoft Windows 2000 or Windows .NET Server snap-in DHCP console, but the options listed in the following table are the ones most commonly used by Microsoft DHCP clients. In Windows 2000– and Windows .NET Server–based networks, options 3, 6, and 15 are commonly used.

DHCP Options

Number	*Option*	*What It Configures*
003	Router	Default gateway IP address
006	DNS Servers	IP addresses of DNS servers
015	DNS Domain Name	Parent domain of associated DNS servers
044	NetBIOS over TCP/IP Name Server	IP addresses of Windows Internet Name Service (WINS) server
046	NetBIOS over TCP/IP Node Type	Method of NetBIOS name resolution to be used by the client
047	NetBIOS over TCP/IP Scope	Restricts NetBIOS clients to communication with clients that have the same scope ID

See Also: *DHCP console*

DHCP relay agent

A host that enables a Dynamic Host Configuration Protocol (DHCP) server to lease addresses to hosts on a different subnet than the one the server is on.

Overview

DHCP relay agents make it unnecessary to maintain a separate DHCP server on every subnet in an internetwork. Without DHCP agents, every subnet on an internetwork would need at least one DHCP server to provide address leases to hosts on that subnet. With DHCP agents, you can manage with only a single DHCP server for your entire internetwork (though two are recommended in case of failure).

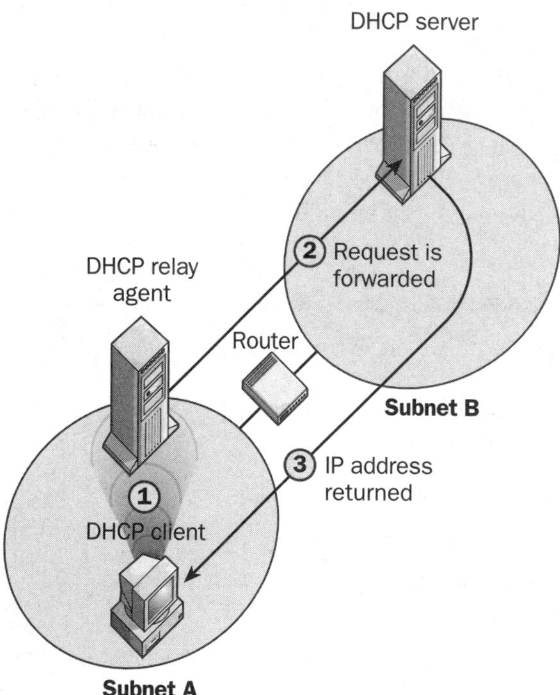

DHCP relay agent. *How a DHCP relay agent works.*

Implementation

The DHCP relay agent is a machine with the DHCP Relay Agent service installed and configured to forward DHCP requests to a DHCP server on a different subnet (as shown in the illustration). The process happens as follows:

1. A DHCP client on the subnet where the DHCP relay agent is configured broadcasts a request for a lease from a DHCP server.

2 Since there is no DHCP server on the client's subnet, the DHCP relay agent picks up the client's request and forwards it directly to the DHCP server on another subnet.

3 The DHCP server responds to the request by offering a lease directly to the client.

Notes

You can configure Microsoft Windows NT, Windows 2000 and Windows .NET Server machines to operate as DHCP relay agents. To configure a machine running Windows NT Server as a DHCP relay agent, you must do the following steps:

1. Install the DHCP Relay Agent service using the Services tab of the Network utility in Control Panel.
2. Configure the DHCP server that the agent will pass requests to. Do this on the DHCP Relay tab of the Microsoft TCP/IP Properties sheet of the TCP/IP protocol.

To configure a Windows 2000 server as a DHCP relay agent, follow these steps:

1. Open the Routing and Remote Access console from the Administrative Tools program group.
2. Expand the server node to display General beneath IP Routing in the console tree.
3. Right-click General, and select New Routing Protocol from the context menu.
4. Specify DHCP Relay Agent in the New Routing Protocol dialog box, and click OK.
5. Open the property sheet for DHCP Relay Agent under IP Routing in the console tree, specify the IP address of the DHCP server to which lease requests should be relayed, and click OK.
6. Right-click DHCP Relay Agent in the console tree, and select New Interface to specify a router interface on which relay will be enabled.

See Also: *Dynamic Host Configuration Protocol (DHCP)*

DHCP scope

A range of Internet Protocol (IP) addresses that a Dynamic Host Configuration Protocol (DHCP) server can lease out to DHCP clients.

Overview

You configure the DHCP scope using the Microsoft Windows NT administrative tool DHCP Manager or the Windows 2000 and Windows .NET Server snap-in DHCP console. The IP addresses are leased for a specific Time to Live (TTL), usually three days. Information about scopes and leased IP addresses is stored in the DHCP database on the DHCP server. The values for IP address scopes created on DHCP servers must be taken from the available pool of IP addresses allocated to the network. Errors in configuring the DHCP scope are a common reason for problems in establishing communication on Transmission Control Protocol/Internet Protocol (TCP/IP) networks.

Notes

If non-DHCP clients have static IP addresses that fall within the range of the server's DHCP scope, these static IP addresses must be excluded from the scope. Otherwise, two hosts might end up with the same IP address, one assigned statically and the other assigned dynamically, resulting in neither host being able to communicate on the network.

See Also: *DHCP console*

DHCP server

A server that dynamically allocates Internet Protocol (IP) addresses to client machines using the Dynamic Host Configuration Protocol (DHCP).

Overview

DHCP servers perform the server-side operation of the DHCP protocol. The DHCP server is responsible for answering requests from DHCP clients and leasing IP addresses to these clients.

DHCP servers should have static IP addresses. A DHCP server gives DHCP clients at least two pieces of Transmission Control Protocol/Internet Protocol (TCP/IP) configuration information: the client's IP address and the subnet mask. Additional TCP/IP settings can be passed to the client as DHCP options.

D

Implementation

To have Microsoft Windows 2000 or Windows .NET Server function as a DHCP server, install the DHCP Server service and manage it using the DHCP console snap-in for the Microsoft Management Console (MMC). To have Windows NT Server function as a DHCP server, install the DHCP Server service and configure it using the administrative tool DHCP Manager. Note that a DHCP server should generally not be a DHCP client—that is, it should have a static IP address.

Notes

If hosts on a TCP/IP network are randomly losing connectivity with the network one by one, the DHCP server might be down and unable to renew leases for IP addresses obtained by the clients. Without a valid IP address leased to them, DHCP clients cannot communicate over the network.

See Also: *DHCP client, DHCP Server service, Dynamic Host Configuration Protocol (DHCP)*

DHCP Server service

The service in Microsoft Windows 2000, Windows .NET Server, and Windows NT that implements the server component of the Dynamic Host Configuration Protocol (DHCP) on Windows 2000, Windows .NET Server, or Windows NT Server.

Overview

The DHCP Server service is an optional networking component that can be installed on

- Windows NT Server by using the Network utility in Control Panel, selecting the Services tab, and adding the Microsoft DHCP Server service. When this service is installed on a machine running Windows NT Server, the administrative tool DHCP Manager is also installed.
- Windows 2000 Server and Windows .NET Server by using the Add/Remove Programs utility in Control Panel, selecting Add/Remove Windows Components, and selecting Dynamic Host Configuration Protocol (DHCP) from Networking Services. When this service is installed on a machine running Windows 2000 Server or Windows .NET Server, the DHCP console administrative tool is implemented as a snap-in for the Microsoft Management Console (MMC).

Notes

The DHCP Server service should generally be installed only on a machine that has a manually assigned static IP address.

See Also: *Dynamic Host Configuration Protocol (DHCP)*

DHTML

Stands for Dynamic HTML, a proposed World Wide Web Consortium (W3C) standard developed by Microsoft Corporation for creating interactive multimedia Web content.

See: *Dynamic HTML (DHTML)*

Dial-on-Demand Routing (DDR)

A method for connecting two remote networks together using Integrated Services Digital Network (ISDN) and dial-up Public Switched Telephone Network (PSTN) connections.

Overview

Dial-on-Demand Routing (DDR) is a procedure used in Cisco routers to connect two remote networks only when there is traffic to forward between them. DDR uses circuit-switched dial-up connections that must first be established for communications to take place and that are torn down when communications are finished. DDR is not the same as remote access: in remote access a computer connects with a remote network, but in DDR two networks are being connected together using routers.

DDR is a way of minimizing costs over wide area network (WAN) links. DDR is only active when data needs to be sent to the remote network, and this is generally cheaper than having a dedicated or leased line connecting the networks that is on all the time.

Implementation

DDR is typically implemented using ISDN for backup WAN connections when the primary WAN link is a dedicated T1 line. DDR allows ISDN calls to be placed to one or more remote networks as required. These calls typically take less than 5 seconds to connect and begin transferring data. During the connection phase a switched circuit must be established between the networks. After the call is finished, this circuit is torn down after a prespecified idle time period has elapsed to save money. Since different circuits may be used for each DDR session, the quality of the connection can vary from session to session.

When used with ISDN, DDR allows different service types to be assigned to different kinds of traffic. Only traffic classified as "interesting" causes a dial-up session to be initiated—all other traffic is ignored by the DDR-capable router. A typical scenario might be to use DDR to connect when Simple Mail Transfer Protocol (SMTP) mail needs to be forwarded to a remote network. On a Cisco router you use the dialer-list command from the Internetwork Operating System (IOS) command set to specify which kinds of traffic are "interesting" from the standpoint of DDR. For IOS 11 and higher, DDR supports a number of different protocols including Internet Protocol (IP), Internetwork Packet Exchange (IPX), and Appletalk.

When implementing DDR for a WAN link, make sure you configure static routes to your remote network. Using dynamic routing will generate routing table advertisements that may trigger unwanted DDR sessions.

Notes

Dial-on Demand Routing (DDR) is different from Demand-Dial Routing (DDR), a Microsoft technology for forwarding packets on request across a Point-to-Point Protocol (PPP) WAN link.

See Also: *Integrated Services Digital Network (ISDN), routing*

dial-up line

Any telecommunications link that is serviced by a modem.

Overview

Dial-up lines are ordinary phone lines used for voice communication, but dedicated or leased lines are digital lines with dedicated circuits. Dial-up lines are generally much less expensive to use, but they have less available bandwidth.

Companies often use dial-up lines for occasional, low-bandwidth usage (such as remote access networking) or as a backup for more costly dedicated lines. Dial-up lines are shared with all subscribers in the Public Switched Telephone Network (PSTN) domain, while dedicated or leased lines are allocated solely to the subscriber's private telecommunications domain.

Besides dial-up lines using analog modems over local loop connections, there are also some digital services that can be dial up (instead of dedicated) in nature. These services include

- ISDN (Integrated Services Digital Network)
- X.25

See Also: *dedicated line*

DID

Stands for direct inward dialing, a service provided by a local exchange carrier (LEC) to a corporate client.

See: *direct inward dialing (DID)*

differential backup

A backup type in which the only files and folders that are backed up are those that have changed since the last normal backup occurred.

Overview

Unlike an incremental backup, a differential backup does not clear the archive attribute for each file and folder. You can use differential backups in conjunction with normal backups to simplify and speed up the process. If a normal backup is done on a particular day of the week, differential backups can be performed on the remaining days of the week to back up the files that have changed since the first day of the schedule. Differential backups are faster than normal backups and use less tape or other storage media.

Notes

Differential backups are cumulative (unlike incremental backups), so when you need to do a restore, you need only the normal backup and the most recent differential backup. Differential backups take longer to complete than incremental backups, but you can restore data from them faster.

See Also: *backup type, incremental backup*

Differentiated Services (DS)

A system for service classification of network traffic.

Overview

Differentiated Services (DS) was developed by the diff-serv working group of the Internet Engineering Task Force (IETF) as a framework for standardizing service classification mechanisms. DS manages network traffic based on the forwarding behaviors of packets instead of by traffic priority or application. DS is rule-based and can be used for policy-based traffic management.

Implementation

DS works by packaging Differentiated Services Code Point (DSCP) information within standard Internet Protocol (IP) headers. This DSCP information specifies the level of service required for the packet, and supports up to 64 different traffic forwarding behaviors. DSCP maps a particular packet to a packet hop behavior (PHB) applied by a policy to a DS-compliant router.

See Also: *quality of service (QoS)*

Diffie-Hellman (DH)

An encryption scheme used in public key cryptography.

Overview

Diffie-Hellman (DH) is an asymmetric encryption scheme that uses a key pair consisting of different public and private keys. The private key is used to encrypt the message, and the public key is used to decrypt it. DH also specifies a key exchange mechanism that allows private keys to be used over the Internet.

Another asymmetric encryption algorithm is RSA, developed by Ron Rivest, Adi Shamir, and Leonard Adleman. Asymmetric encryption schemes typically have much larger keys than symmetric schemes such as DES (Data Encryption Standard). A key for an asymmetric scheme is typically 10^{24} bits or larger. Asymmetric encryption schemes form the basis of the Secure Sockets Layer (SSL) protocol used on the Internet.

See Also: *Data Encryption Standard (DES), public key cryptography*

digital

Transmission of signals that vary discretely with time.

See Also: *digital transmission*

Digital Advanced Mobile Phone Service (D-AMPS)

The digital version of the Advanced Mobile Phone Service (AMPS) cellular communications system.

Overview

AMPS is the oldest cellular phone system still widely deployed. It is an analog system operating in the 800 megahertz (MHz) band and is based on the EIA-533 standard.

Digital Advanced Mobile Phone Service (D-AMPS) is the digital version of AMPS and is based on the IS-54 standard. D-AMPS has been around since 1992, and it builds on the large installed base of AMPS cellular network installations. D-AMPS is used in North and South America and in parts of Asia and the Pacific region. The technical name for D-AMPS is Time Division Multiple Access/IS-136.

Implementation

D-AMPS uses the same 800 Mhz frequency band as AMPS, specifically frequencies between 824 and 891 MHz (although a dual-band 800/1900 MHz system has also been implemented). D-AMPS also uses 30-kilohertz (kHz) channels as AMPS does, but whereas AMPS can carry only one conversation per channel, D-AMPS can carry between three and six conversations. As a result, D-AMPS extends the capacity of AMPS from 50 conversations per cell to up to 300 conversations per cell, making D-AMPS more efficient in bandwidth utilization than AMPS.

While AMPS transmits information continuously, D-AMPS transmits in bursts over a time-shared system based on Time Division Multiple Access (TDMA) technology as the media access method. D-AMPS is more immune to interference from noise than AMPS and can be scrambled to make it more secure (AMPS is very easy to eavesdrop on).

D-AMPS is cheaper and easier to implement than other digital cellular systems such as Code Division Multiple Access (CDMA), but its transmissions are not as secure as CDMA. D-AMPS represents a simpler upgrade path from AMPS than Global System for Mobile Communications (GSM), which also uses TDMA technology but does so in an incompatible format.

See Also: *Advanced Mobile Phone Service (AMPS), cellular communications, Code Division Multiple Access (CDMA), Global System for Mobile Communications (GSM), Time Division Multiple Access (TDMA)*

Digital Advanced Wireless System (DAWS)

A proposed standard for a multimegabit packet-switching radio network from the European Telecommunications Standards Institute (ETSI).

Overview

The Digital Advanced Wireless System (DAWS) will be compatible with the existing packet radio system called the Terrestrial Trunked Radio (Tetra), which enables terminals to communicate directly with each other in regions without cellular coverage.

DAWS is being developed in response to the rapid deployment of Global System for Mobile Communications (GSM) wireless cellular communication systems and the increasing demand for high-speed wireless mobile data services in response to the phenomenal growth of the Internet in recent years. The ultimate goal of the DAWS effort is to provide mobile wireless Asynchronous Transfer Mode (ATM) data communication services with full-terminal mobility over wide areas of roaming. ATM has been selected by ETSI as the technology of choice for the backbone of the future envisaged European Information Infrastructure (EII).

DAWS will be designed to support applications that require data rates in excess of the 2-megabit-per-second (Mbps) rate supported by the International Mobile Telecommunications-2000 (IMT-2000) standards, with eventual planned support for full ATM rates of 155 Mbps envisioned. Examples include wireless networking, Internet browsing, video conferencing, file transfer, and Voice over IP (VoIP).

See Also: *Global System for Mobile Communications (GSM), International Mobile Telecommunications-2000 (IMT-2000), Terrestrial Trunked Radio (Tetra)*

Digital Audio Broadcasting (DAB)

A specification for broadband digital radio.

Overview

Digital Audio Broadcasting (DAB) is a specification for broadband transmission of digital information at speeds up to 2.4 megabits per second (Mbps). DAB is designed for transmission of digital audio and is envisioned as a replacement for existing analog AM/FM radio systems. DAB is a European specification only; however, a similar (but not interoperable) specification called IBOC (In Band, On Channel) is being developed in the United States.

Uses

Although DAB is intended mainly for audio broadcasting and is regulated as such, the possibility of it supporting digital data broadcasts, and even Internet access, are currently being explored. Since digital audio only requires 56 kilobits per second (Kbps), DAB's 2.4 Mbps bandwidth leaves lots of room for broadcasting location-based information such as weather reports, traffic information, airline arrivals and departures, stock quotes, and so on.

Britain leads the world in DAB deployment, with five channels already allocated to the BBC. Other European countries and regions are following with their own deployments. Psion has introduced a DAB receiver that plugs into the USB port of a PC to provide users with reception of DAB broadcasts, and other vendors are developing similar devices.

Although DAB is a broadcast (one-way) service, some carriers are envisioning using DAB to provide users with high-speed Internet access by using conventional or wireless modems for the upstream connection and DAB for downstream.

Prospects

DAB may gain the advantage over 2.5G and third-generation (3G) cellular systems such as General Packet Radio Services (GPRS) and Universal Mobile Telecommunications System (UMTS) by being first-to-market with high-speed location-based digital broadcast services. Spectrum licenses for DAB have cost only a small fraction of what carriers have bid for 3G licenses, allowing DAB providers more liquidity for rolling out deployments rapidly.

See Also: *2.5G, 3G*

digital certificate

A technology similar to an identification card that can be used for verifying the identity of a user or service you are communicating with electronically.

Overview

Digital certificates are entities issued by certificate authorities (CAs), public or private organizations that manage a public key infrastructure (PKI). Digital certificates are the networking equivalent of driver's licenses, and they go hand in hand with encryption to ensure that communication is secure. Digital certificates verify the authenticity of the holder, and they can also indicate the holder's privileges and roles within secure communication. They can be used like driver's licenses for identification purposes or like bank cards (together with a password) to perform financial transactions in e-commerce and online banking. Digital certificates enable various rights, permissions, and limitations to be applied to their holders for various kinds of trusted communication purposes such as purchasing, government banking, benefits, and voting rights. The main function of a digital certificate is to associate a specific user with his public/private key pair.

Implementation

A digital certificate consists of data that definitively identifies an entity (an individual, a system, a company, or an organization). Digital certificates are issued by and digitally signed with the digital signature of the CA (once the CA has verified the identity of the applying entity). In addition to identification data, the digital certificate contains a serial number, a copy of the certificate holder's public key, the identity and digital signature of the issuing CA, and an expiration date. The CA also maintains a copy of the user's public key in its centralized certificate storage facility.

Digital certificates are formatted according to an International Organization for Standardization (ISO) standard called X.509 v3. The X.509 standard specifies that a digital certificate must contain the following information fields:

- Version number
- Certificate serial number
- Signature algorithm ID used
- Name of certificate issuer
- Validity period (for certificate expiration)
- Subject name (name of certificate owner)
- Public key information for subject
- Unique identifier of certificate issuer
- Unique identifier of subject
- Extensions
- Digital signature for all the above fields

Uses

Digital certificates and public key cryptography are used in the popular Secure Sockets Layer (SSL) protocol, which provides secure transactions over the Internet. Several types of digital certificates are involved in this process, including

- CA certificate, which identifies the certificate authority, such as those based on Microsoft Certificate Server, and is used by Web browsers and Web servers to validate client and server certificates
- Server certificate, which identifies a Web server such as Microsoft Internet Information Services (IIS)
- Client certificate, which identifies a Web browser such as Microsoft Internet Explorer

Notes

A digital certificate is not the same as a digital signature. A digital certificate is a file that certifies the owner's identity, contains the owner's public key, and can be used to support encrypted communication. The purpose of a digital certificate is to certify that the user has the right to use the public/private key pair that has been issued by the CA. A digital signature, on the other hand, contains identity information along with the message or document itself (which has been hashed using the private key of the sender), and it confirms the identity of the sender and ensures that the content of the message has not been modified in transit.

In other words, to send an encrypted transmission, a user signs the message with a digital signature. But in order to be able to do this at all, the user must first be issued a key pair and its associated digital certificate.

See Also: *certificate authority (CA), digital signature, public key cryptography*

digital dashboard

A technology based on Microsoft Office for customizing a user's interface to contain information from multiple data sources.

Overview

Digital dashboards allow users to consolidate business information from different sources such as personal folders, team folders, databases, messaging systems, Web sites, and so on. They provide a single, customizable user interface that helps users sift through and organize the mass of information crying for their attention in today's busy office environment.

Digital dashboards are designed to make knowledge workers more productive and help facilitate collaboration between teams of individuals. They are easy to build and customize and are based on standard Microsoft technologies, with Microsoft Outlook at the center of things.

Implementation

A digital dashboard in its simplest sense is a dynamic Web page displayed in Outlook. Outlook is the messaging and collaboration component of Office and acts as the infrastructure on which digital dashboards are constructed. Using Office Web Components (OWCs), developers can build systems that can allow documents, messages, spreadsheets, databases, and charts to be generated and published from back-end systems and displayed through digital dashboards. Typical back-end systems that can support digital dashboards include Microsoft Exchange Server, which lets users create and share team folders for collaboration purposes, and Microsoft SQL Server, an online analytical processing (OLAP) repository for storing and analyzing business data.

For More Information

You can download the Digital Dashboard Starter Kit from *www.microsoft.com/business.*

See Also: *Exchange Server, Outlook, SQL Server*

digital data service (DDS)

A family of leased line data communication technologies that provides a dedicated synchronous transmission connection at speeds of 56 kilobits per second (Kbps).

Overview

DDS was originally a trademark for an AT&T all-digital service running at 56 Kbps, but it has evolved into a general descriptor for a variety of digital services offered by different carriers under various names. Digital data service (DDS) is available in both a dial-up version called Switched 56 and a dedicated leased line service for continuous connections. The dial-up version can serve as a backup for the dedicated version. The more common dedicated version are lines with negligible connection establishment latency; they are always on and never busy.

Implementation

Typically, DDS uses four wires to support digital transmission speeds of 56 Kbps, but it is actually a 64-Kbps circuit that uses 8 Kbps for sending signaling information. Some vendors provide a variant of DDS with a data transmission rate of a full 64 Kbps—this service is sometimes called Clear 64.

D

To use DDS services for wide area network (WAN) connectivity, route packets from your local area network (LAN) through a bridge or a router, which is connected by means of a V.35 or RS-232 serial interface to a Channel Service Unit/Data Service Unit (CSU/DSU). The CSU/DSU is connected to the four-wire termination of the DDS line by means of an M-block connector, a screw terminal block, or some other connection mechanism. The Channel Service Unit (CSU) converts the data signal into a bipolar signal suitable for transmission over the telecommunications link. The DDS lines themselves use four wires and support speeds of 64 Kbps, but 8 Kbps of bandwidth is usually reserved for signaling, so the actual data throughput is usually only 56 Kbps.

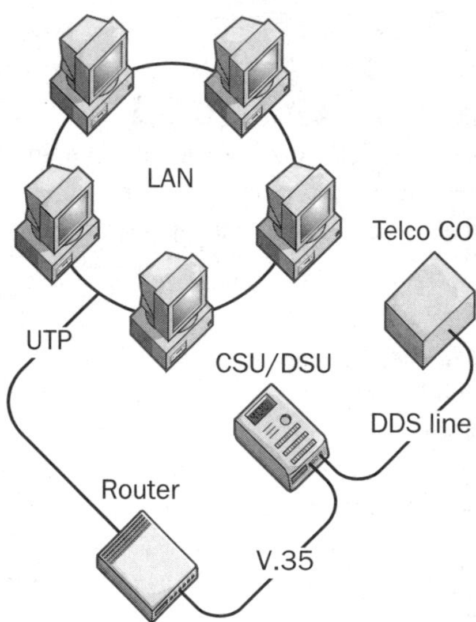

Digital data service (DDS). *Implementing DDS.*

(DDS is only one example of a type of digital line; others include Integrated Services Digital Network (ISDN) and T1. DDS can be used in either multipoint or point-to-point communications and requires dedicated digital lines. DDS lines can also be used to connect buildings on a campus, usually with a maximum distance of about 3 miles (5 kilometers).

Notes

Another name for DDS is Dataphone Digital Service.

See Also: *Switched 56, telecommunications services*

Digital Data Storage (DDS)

A tape backup technology that evolved from Digital Audio Tape (DAT) technologies.

Overview

Digital Data Storage (DDS) is a tape backup technology broadly used in all levels of businesses. DDS provides high capacity and performance at a relatively low cost. Although commonly called DAT instead of DDS, this is a misnomer and refers only to the type of tape employed.

Implementation

DDS records information on tapes using a helical scan method similar to that used in VCRs. Tracks are laid down at an angle in sweeps across the width of the tape, which allows DDS tape drives to operate at slower speeds than parallel-scan drives. The result of lower tape speeds is less wear and tear on both the tape and the drive.

DDS tape drives use a Small Computer System Interface (SCSI) interface to connect to backup servers. Most DDS tape drives are capable of simultaneous reading and writing of information.

DDS comes in different flavors that determine capacity and backup speed. For example, DDS-2 supports backup of 4 gigabytes (GB) of data at a transfer rate of 46 megabytes (MB) per minute, and DDS-3 lets you back up 12 GB at 70 MB per minute. Higher levels, such as DDS-4, exist for large enterprise networks. These storage figures are for uncompressed data (double them for compressed data).

DDS tapes are cheap (usually costing under $10), which means that DDS is best used when your company's tape rotation scheme demands that a large number of tapes be used. DDS is a good solution for small to mid-sized companies implementing their first tape backup solution because it is inexpensive, easy to use, and performs well. The price of DDS tape drives starts at around $1,000.

See Also: *tape format*

digital line

An umbrella term for various kinds of digital telecommunications services.

Overview

The distinguishing feature of a digital line is that it is digital from end to end and does not employ any kind of analog modem technologies. As a result, digital lines have higher traffic-carrying capacities, less noise, and better error-handling features than analog lines. The term *digital line* can refer to circuits based on the following:

- Digital data service (DDS)
- Integrated Services Digital Network (ISDN)
- T-carrier services such as T1 lines, fractional T1, and T3
- Switched 56 services

See Also: *digital data service (DDS), Integrated Services Digital Network (ISDN), Switched 56, T-carrier*

Digital Linear Tape (DLT)

A tape backup technology.

Overview

Digital Linear Tape (DLT) was developed in 1991 by Conner (later acquired by Quantum Corporation) as a tape backup solution for large companies. DLT tape drives can typically back up information at rates as high as 300 megabytes (MB) per minute. DLT tape drives typically cost $10,000 or more and are available in robotic tape libraries as well as standard single-tape units. DLT was designed as an enterprise backup solution and is comparable to Exabyte Corporation's 8mm format in that respect.

Implementation

DLT is a channelized tape backup technology that allows multiple channels to be backed up simultaneously in parallel on a single tape. A DLT drive's tape head is stationary and has multiple read/write channels on it. As a result, DLT can back up information much more quickly than many other types of tape backup technologies such as 8mm or Digital Data Storage (DDS).

An example is Quantum's DLT 7000 series, which supports backup of 35 gigabytes (GB) uncompressed (70 GB compressed) at transfer speeds up to 5 MBps.

Notes

Quantum has recently developed an upgrade to DLT called SuperDLT, which competes with linear tape open (LTO) tape drive technology in speed and storage capacity.

See Also: *tape format*

digital modem

Any type of modem used for synchronous transmission of data over circuit-switched digital lines.

Overview

Unlike analog modems, which convert analog signals into digital ones using analog-to-digital converter (ADC) technologies, digital modems operate on end-to-end digital services.

A common example of a digital modem is an Integrated Services Digital Network (ISDN) terminal adapter, which uses advanced digital modulation techniques for changing data frames from a network into a format suitable for transmission over a digital line such as an ISDN line. Terminal adapters are thus basically data framing devices, rather than signal modulators such as analog modems, so in some sense the term *digital modem* is a misnomer because no modulation actually occurs.

See Also: *Integrated Services Digital Network (ISDN)*

digital nervous system

A paradigm created by Microsoft Corporation for electronic connectivity between businesses.

Overview

A digital nervous system enables businesses to create efficient, integrated systems that are easy to use and manage. The digital nervous system can be viewed as the next evolutionary phase of the Information Age.

The idea of this business paradigm is that businesses connect to each other in a way that is similar to the organization of a living organism. Digital information—

whether it is text, graphics, audio, or video—flows between businesses much as electrical impulses flow between parts of the body. A stimulus of information entering one business that is generated by another business produces a response. The greater the complexity and the more interconnected the nervous system, the higher the organism—and the same applies to business. Greater interflow of digital information can lead to the evolution of new forms of doing business. The Internet and its related paradigms "intranet" and "extranet" serve as examples of this evolution. These concepts grew naturally—almost organically—from the complex interconnectedness fostered by advances in software and networking.

For More Information

You can visit the Digital Nervous System site at *www.microsoft.com/dns.*

Digital Signal Zero

More usually known simply as DS-0, a transmission standard for digital telecommunications having a transmission rate of 64 kilobits per second (Kbps) and intended to carry one voice channel.

See: *DS-0*

digital signature

An electronic signature that you can use to validate the identity of the sender of a digital transmission.

Overview

Digital signatures can be used to sign a document being transmitted by electronic means such as e-mail. Digital signatures validate the identity of the sender and ensure that the document they are attached to has not been altered by unauthorized parties during the transmission.

Uses

Digital signatures are mainly intended for signing documents that have a relatively short lifespan of no more than a few years. Examples include business contracts, invoices, and similar documents. They are not generally suited for documents requiring long-term archiving, such as medical or financial documents, because advances in cryptography might render them insecure within the next decade or so. If you use digital signatures for documents that have to be archived for the long term, you need to also include a verification trail of how the documents are transmitted and stored. This evidentiary trail might be necessary should the authenticity of these signatures ever be challenged in court.

Implementation

Digital signatures are based on public key cryptography. In order for digital signatures to work, the sender must have both a digital certificate and a key pair issued by a certificate authority (CA) such as VeriSign.

A digital signature for a particular document is created by first performing a mathematical hash of the document. A hash is an iterative cryptographic process that employs a complex one-way mathematical function. To create digital signatures, a special hash called SHA-1 (Secure Hash Algorithm-1) is employed, and the end result of this process is a 160-bit text file called a message digest (MD). The MD is then encrypted using the sender's private key to create the digital signature, and the resulting signature is then attached to the document, which is then transmitted to its intended recipient. Note that each digital signature is unique and depends on the document being transmitted.

When the recipient receives the signed message, the same hash is performed on the received document to create a new message digest. The sender's public key is then applied to the MD, and the result is compared with the signature of the received message to determine whether the message is from its expressed recipient and whether it is intact or has been tampered with during transmission.

Marketplace

The complexity of public key cryptography and the wide variety of CAs in the marketplace have slowed the general adoption of digital signatures for sender verification purposes. In 2000, however, the U.S. government passed legislation called Esign (the Electronic Signatures in Global and National Commerce Act) that should speed widespread adoption of digital signatures. Esign basically makes digital signatures carry the same weight in law as regular signatures.

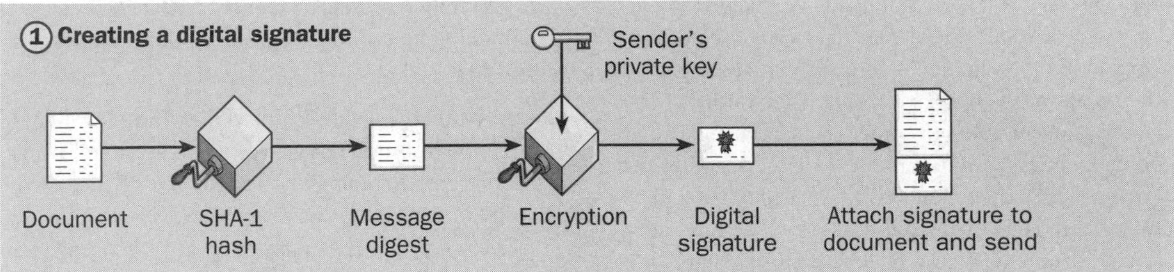

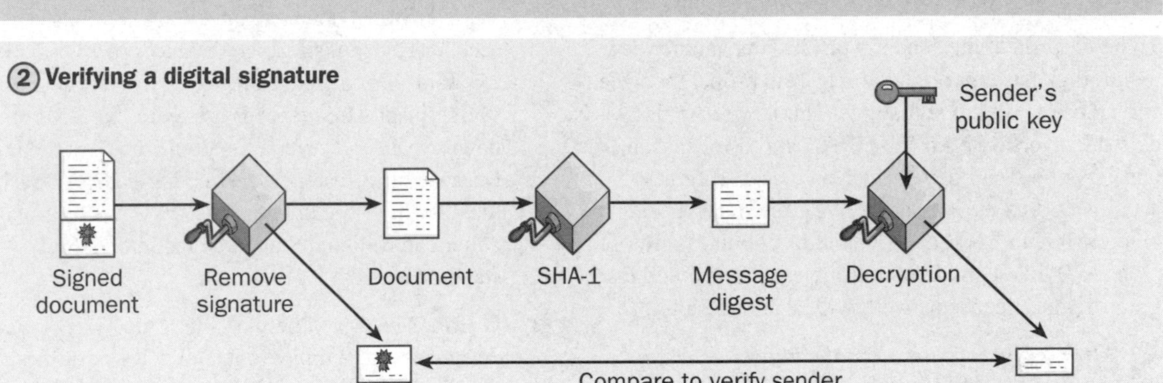

Digital signature. *How a digital signature is created and verified.*

As a result of Esign, several vendors have started offering turnkey solutions for signing electronic documents that are designed to be as easy to use as sealing and stamping an envelope. Examples of such vendors include Digital Applications International, Silanis Technology, and signOnline. The first of these vendors to receive approval from a government agency was Silanis, whose Approvelt software was approved by the Food and Drug Administration (FDA) for government use.

A second group of vendors to emerge as a result of Esign consists of consulting companies whose products and services are designed to help large enterprises integrate digital signatures into their business processes. These vendors include Digital Signature Trust, NewRiver, Entrust Technologies, ValiCert, and DataCert.com.

A recent development that might lead to much wider use of digital signatures for signing documents is the implementation of public key infrastructure (PKI) technology by the United States Postal Service (USPS). In 2001, the USPS announced NetPost.Certified, a service that uses an electronic postmark based on digital signatures and stored on smart cards to guarantee the identity and integrity of electronic transmissions. NetPost.Certified is currently available only when one of the parties involved (sender or receiver) is the U.S government (where it should help streamline government by reducing the vast amount of paperwork needed for traditional document processing), but in a few years it is expected that the service will become more widely deployed in business use for signing contracts, deeds, affidavits, and other legal documents. The first U.S. government agency to use NetPost.Certified is the Social Security Administration, which uses it for vital statistics collections.

Issues

The weakest point in the digital signature process is making sure that the sender's private key is secure. The private key is normally stored on the hard disk of the sender's machine and is secured using a secret PIN (personal identification number) code known only to the sender. Because of its location on the hard drive, however, the private key is often vulnerable to hackers who break into networks to collect such information. Should hackers obtain a copy of your private key and somehow guess or determine your PIN code, they can sign electronic documents using your identity, and unless there is an evidential trail to the contrary, these signed documents would be legally enforceable.

To better protect the sender's private key, another new technology has emerged that may help propel the widespread use of digital signatures. This new technology is called Universal Serial Bus (USB) crypto-tokens, and it consists of a small device such as a smart card that securely stores the sender's private key in a medium inaccessible to hackers (you could, of course, still lose your USB token and land in trouble, but you could lose your driver's license as well, with similar results).

See Also: *cryptography, digital certificate, message digest (MD) algorithms, public key cryptography*

Digital Subscriber Line (DSL)

A group of broadband telecommunications technologies supported over copper local loop connections.

Overview

Digital Subscriber Line (DSL) was originally designed to provide high-speed data and video-on-demand services to subscribers. DSL is an always-on service such as Integrated Services Digital Network (ISDN) but works at much faster speeds compared to T1 (and even T3) leased lines for a fraction of the cost.

DSL uses the same underlying PHY layer as ISDN Basic Rate Interface (BRI) and is basically a form of modem technology that specifies a signaling process for high-speed, end-to-end digital transmission over the existing copper twisted-pair wiring of the local loop. DSL accomplishes this feat by using advanced signal processing and digital modulation techniques. DSL uses digital modems in which the digital signals are not converted to analog or vice versa; instead, the signals remain digital for the complete communication path from the customer premises to the telco's central office (CO).

DSL actually represents a family of related services commonly referred to as "*x*DSL," which includes the following:

- **Asymmetric Digital Subscriber Line (ADSL):** This flavor of DSL is asymmetric in nature, with different upstream (customer to carrier) and downstream (carrier to customer) speeds. ADSL theoretically supports data rates of up to 6.1 megabits per second (Mbps) downstream and 640 kilobits per second (Kbps) upstream at distances of 18,500 feet (5340 meters) from the telco CO. In practice, however, typical ADSL speeds are more like 1 Mbps downstream and several hundred Kbps upstream. Because of its faster downstream speeds, ADSL is ideal for high-speed Internet access. ADSL is an American National Standards Institute (ANSI) standard called T1.413.
- **G.Lite:** This is a variety of ADSL that was designed to be simpler to install at the customer's premises than regular ADSL (an external ADSL modem is used, and a splitter is not required at the customer's premises). G.Lite is an International Telecommunication Union (ITU) standard called G.992.2 and is sometimes called DSL Lite or ADSL Lite. Transmission rates for G.Lite range from 1.544 to 6 Mbps downstream and 128 to 384 Kbps upstream. GLite is growing in popularity as a "plug and play" form of DSL that customers can install themselves using DSL modems provided by providers. The disadvantage is that G.Lite generally has to be deployed using a second phone line because it provides unacceptable performance for voice transmission.
- **Rate-adjusted Digital Subscriber Line (RADSL):** This is a form of ADSL that dynamically negotiates the best possible speed based on changing line conditions. Speeds for RADSL are comparable to those for ADSL.
- **ISDN Digital Subscriber Line (IDSL):** This is essentially ISDN with no voice service, only data. IDSL provides 144 Kbps throughput in both directions, and unlike ISDN, it is always on and has no need for call setup.

- **High-bit-rate Digital Subscriber Line (HDSL):** This flavor supports high-speed, full-duplex communications over four-wire telephone lines at distances up to 12,000 feet (3650 meters) from a telco CO. HDSL provides equal upstream and downstream speeds of up to 1.544 Mbps, equal to a T1 line in throughput (it usually requires a conditioned line such as a T1 line as well). HDSL is usually deployed using bridges or routers instead of modems, and is best suited for wide area network (WAN) links.
- **Symmetric Digital Subscriber Line (SDSL):** This is a two-wire variety of HDSL that is the same in every respect except that it is half-duplex instead of full-duplex. Another name for this service is HDSL II.
- **Very-high-rate Digital Subscriber Line (VDSL):** This form of ADSL supports speeds of up to 54 Mbps upstream and 2.3 Mbps upstream over short distances of up to 1000 feet (305 meters). At longer distances the speed drops rapidly, and VDSL can rarely be provisioned beyond 4500 feet (1,370 meters) from the CO. VDSL is currently vendor-specific technology that has not been standardized, and because of its high speed and short distances, it is essentially a solution in search of a problem.

Uses

In the last few years, the use of DSL for residential broadband Internet access has skyrocketed, and DSL is currently the main competition for cable modem services to provide such services. DSL also can deliver other services to homes and businesses, including digital TV and Voice over DSL (VoDSL).

Another common use of DSL is for telecommuting (working remotely from home). DSL modems provide a cheap and easy way of gaining high-speed access to corporate intranets for telecommuters. DSL offers good security, performance, and reliability for telecommuters, but its distance limitation means that they must reside in metropolitan areas.

Many small to mid-sized businesses look on DSL as a replacement for aging 56 Kbps synchronous lines, ISDN lines, frame relay, and other traditional WAN services. DSL provides much higher bandwidth than these services, typically at half the cost or less. For example, although a T-1 line might cost more than $1,000 a month, HDSL can provide similar throughput for less than $400 a month.

Implementation

DSL can be deployed in different ways depending on the flavor being used. In ADSL, for example, an ADSL modem and a signal splitter are installed at the customer's premises and connected to the copper phone line. The splitter separates voice and data signals so that a single phone line can carry both voice and data. At the telco's CO, a Digital Subscriber Line Access Multiplexer (DSLAM) connects subscribers to a high-speed Asynchronous Transfer Mode (ATM) backbone, which typically uses a permanent virtual circuit (PVC) connection to an ISP for Internet access.

DSL modems can use a variety of signal coding methods, including carrierless amplitude and phase modulation (CAP) or discrete multitone (DMT) technology modulation, depending on the vendor's implementation, with CAP currently being the most popular modulation scheme used. DSL modems are simple Layer-2 devices that generally have few security features, lack remote management capability, and are intended for connecting a single computer to the Internet. For connecting an office LAN, a DSL router with built-in firewall and Network Address Translation (NAT) support is used instead of a DSL modem. All customer premises equipment (CPE) DSL devices are technically called ADSL Transmission Unit-Remote (ATU-R), and DSLAMs and similar DSL equipment at telco COs are known as ADSL Transmission Unit-Central office (ATU-C).

Advantages and Disadvantages

The main advantage DSL has over cable modem technology for delivering high-speed Internet access is that DSL uses ordinary phone lines to accomplish this, and such phone lines are everywhere. By contrast, cable TV,

D

the service on which cable modem Internet access rides, has been widely deployed in residential areas but is rare in business districts and industrial parks. As a result, DSL has the advantage of having a ready-made wiring infrastructure, while cable companies have to invest money and effort to build their infrastructure out to business customers.

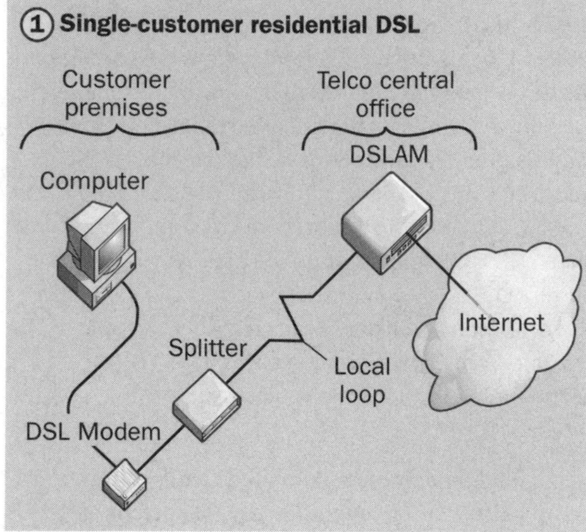

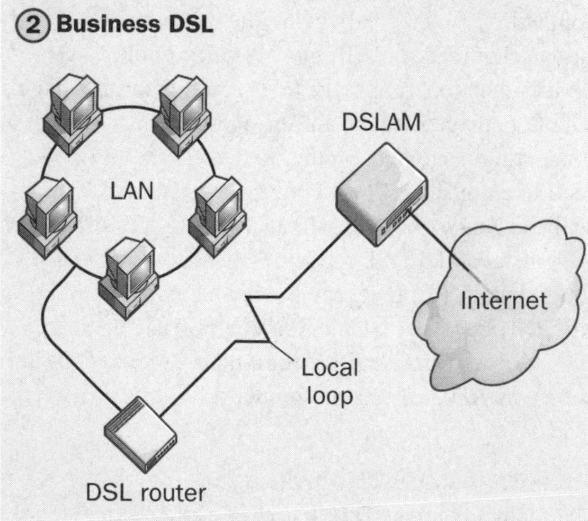

Digital Subscriber Line (DSL). *Implementing DSL for residential and business customers.*

DSL is also inherently more secure than cable modem services and offers better throughput guarantees. This is because each DSL connection between subscriber and telco CO is a dedicated connection. By comparison, all cable modem users in a given neighborhood essentially operate as a shared local area network (LAN). As a result, cable modem users can often see each other's computers on the network, and the more cable modem users simultaneously accessing the Internet in a given neighborhood, the slower the download speed everyone will experience. By contrast, DSL line speeds are independent of other users and depend only on the distance from the CO and the backbone capacity of the carrier's connection to the Internet.

For businesses, DSL can provide wide area network (WAN) links that are faster and cost less than traditional WAN services such as Frame Relay and ISDN. Unlike ISDN and modem-based services, DSL is an always-on technology as well.

DSL does have several disadvantages, however, the most important being its distance limitations. DSL typically cannot be deployed beyond 18,500 feet (5340 meters) from a CO, and even within this distance, the farther the subscriber is from the CO, the worse the connection and slower the speed. DSL is thus restricted mainly to dense urban areas and is often not an option in rural areas. Using remote DSL access terminals, however, some regional bell operating companies (RBOCs) are pushing DSL farther out from the CO (see Issues below).

Another issue is that DSL may be impossible to deploy over older portions of the PSTN. This is because load coils and bridged taps often prevent DSL signals from passing between the customer's premises and the telco CO. Load coils are induction coils that shift frequencies upward for voice transmission to compensate for unwanted wire capacitance, and unfortunately this often shifts voice transmission into the frequency band used by DSL, causing interference. Bridged taps are a shortcut method for telcos to provide local loop phone services to customers without actually running dedicated

lines to those customers. Instead, an existing local loop line is tapped somewhere in the middle to run a line to a second customer. Too many such taps cause excessive echoes that can create noise that interferes with DSL signals. Finally, if a telco has fiber deployed anywhere along a local loop, DSL cannot be provisioned since it works only over copper and not over fiber (see Issues below).

DSL is also more difficult to provision than cable modem services. This is because to provision DSL typically requires the cooperation of three different companies: the DSL provider, which deploys the connection at the customer premises, the RBOC or inter-exchange carrier (IXC) from which the DSL provider purchases wholesale DSL services to retail to customers, and the ISP, which provides the actual connection to the Internet. As a result of this complexity, DSL provisioning can sometimes take weeks or even months, and when a connection goes down, finger-pointing among the different players can sometimes make for slow resolution of problems.

Finally, for business purposes traditional leased lines have a much better track record of reliability than DSL because of the aforementioned lack of cooperation among the DSL provider, RBOC, and ISP. T-1 lines are generally provisioned by a single company (the RBOC), which makes problems easier and quicker to troubleshoot. Medium and large companies often consider DSL an option for backup WAN services, but many are reluctant to make DSL their front-tier WAN service, despite the cost savings they can achieve by replacing their T-1 and fractional T-1 lines with DSL connections.

Marketplace

While most RBOCs offer DSL services, several independent DSL providers have recently appeared. However, some of these have failed or been acquired by RBOCs during the dot-com shakeout of 2000. Some of the larger players that remain in the pure-play DSL arena include Covad Communications Company, EarthLink, and Rhythms NetConnections. These providers are often classified as competitive local exchange carriers (CLECs), though their services are generally limited to DSL. Other names sometimes used to describe them include competitive DSL providers and DSL local exchange carriers (DLECs).

DSL providers generally offer high-speed residential Internet access for service charges in the range of $40 to $60 a month. Business customers generally pay up to 10 times more, primarily because of additional services supported, such as providing access to multiple users on a LAN, managed firewalls, service level agreements (SLAs), and top-tier customer support.

Some DSL providers offer a service called bonding, which allows two or more DSL connections to be combined into a higher throughput connection. In a typical bonding scenario, two or four 144 Kbps IDSL lines are connected to a DSL router and combined using MLPPP (Multilink PPP) into a single 576 Kbps connection. Bonding-enabled DSL routers are much cheaper to deploy at the customer premises than a DSLAM, which can accomplish the same thing but has greater space requirements.

Issues

A major issue that has hindered the widespread use of DSL is that different DSL vendors use proprietary solutions that make equipment from one vendor incompatible with that from another. This situation is particularly aggravating for businesses with offices scattered around geographically, as each office may use different equipment provided by different DSL providers or RBOCs. To overcome this issue, the OpenDSL initiative has been formed by 3Com Corporation, Cisco Systems, SBC Communications, Qwest Communications, and others. The goal of OpenDSL is to standardize all aspects of DSL the same way the Data Over Cable Service Interface Specification (DOCSIS) has done with cable modem technologies. Widespread acceptance of OpenDSL will likely drive DSL deployment further, especially in the business marketplace, but it is likely to take a few years for RBOCs and Competitive Local Exchange Carriers (CLECs) to replace their proprietary DSL systems with the new standard.

Although DSL appears to provide guaranteed throughput due to its dedicated connection (as opposed to shared-LAN cable modem services, where throughput decreases for each user as more users come online), such guarantees may not take into account the back-end configuration at the telco CO. For example, the DSLAM at the CO may become a bottleneck when multiple DSL subscribers all try to simultaneously download large files from the Internet. Even if the DSLAMs can scale to meet demand, the DSL provider's connection to the ISP can also be a bottleneck, particularly if the DSLAM is not colocated at the ISP's point of presence (POP). Business customers should be certain that the DSL provider they are considering working with has adequate DSL equipment at the CO end of the connection to guarantee the level of service they desire.

In an attempt to overcome DSL's distance limitation of 5.6 kilometers (3 miles) from the telco CO, some RBOCs have begun deploying remote DSL access terminals that are located within that distance of potential subscribers while being connected to the CO using fiber. This configuration allows RBOCs to push DSL out to remote neighborhoods to gain additional customers but has provoked a reaction from some pure-play DSL providers as it makes their own deployments difficult or impossible. This is because the fiber between the remote terminal and the CO makes it impossible for the DSL provider to provision DSL to customers directly from the CO (DSL cannot be provisioned over fiber). Furthermore, these remote terminals are often installed inside digital loop carrier (DLC) systems, small boxes deployed by RBOCs in neighborhoods, and these DLCs may not have sufficient space within them for DSL providers to deploy their own equipment to provision their own pushed-out DSL services (even if there is sufficient space, this means another costly expense for cash-strapped DSL providers). An example of this is Project Pronto, being deployed by SBC Communications, an RBOC. DSL remote terminals are sold by Alcatel, Lucent Technologies, and other vendors.

Prospects

Prospects are uncertain for some pure-play DSL providers. This is because the success of their DSL deployments depends on cooperation with both the RBOCs from which they lease local loop access and the ISPs they partner with to provide their DSL customers with Internet access. Nevertheless, DSL providers remain a popular choice for business customers seeking DSL services, mainly because such providers generally offer better service than some traditional RBOCs that have not yet adjusted to the new economy way of doing business. Pure-play DSL providers can also provide nationwide coverage compared to the regional coverage of most RBOCs, and this appeals to companies that have branch offices scattered geographically, but such rollouts are complicated by the fact that the DSL provider has to work with multiple RBOCs and ISPs to make everything work properly for such customers.

RBOCs, however, often have the advantage of having deeper pockets, which may give them a competitive edge in the long run over many competitive DSL providers. Furthermore, some larger RBOCs such as SBC Communications and Qwest are planning nationwide rollouts of DSL through partnerships and mergers with other providers.

An emerging technology that may help competitive DSL providers grow market share is line sharing. This technology lets a CLEC provision DSL to a customer over the same local loop connection that the RBOC uses to provide the customer with voice telephone service. In this way the DSL provider does not have to roll out a second phone line to the customer, which often takes weeks because it must be done in cooperation with the RBOC.

Notes

If you are using a DSL connection to the Internet, check with your DSL provider before you try to use it to deploy a public Web server, or else you might find your DSL service unexpectedly cut off once they discover what you are doing.

For More Information

You can find DSL news at *www.dslreports.com.* The DSL Forum Web site can be found at *www.adsl.com.*

See Also: *Asymmetric Digital Subscriber Line (ADSL), cable modem, G.Lite, High-bit-rate Digital Subscriber Line (HDSL), ISDN Digital Subscriber Line (IDSL), line sharing, Rate-Adjusted Digital Subscriber Line (RADSL), Symmetric Digital Subscriber Line (SDSL), Very-high-rate Digital Subscriber Line (VDSL)*

Digital Subscriber Line Access Multiplexer (DSLAM)

The DSL termination device at a telco central office (CO).

Overview

The Digital Subscriber Line Access Multiplexer (DSLAM) is an Asynchronous Transfer Mode (ATM) access device installed at the CO of a DSL provider. DSL lines coming from multiple subscribers terminate at the DSLAM and are multiplexed together to ride on the provider's ATM backbone, typically through a permanent virtual circuit (PVC) to an Internet service provider (ISP) to provide customers with Internet access.

A typical DSLAM can aggregate up to 100 DSL customer connections. Multiple DSLAMs are required for larger numbers of subscribers. DSLAMs usually have minimal support for quality of service (QoS) as they are often required to split off voice traffic from Internet Protocol (IP) data, and voice traffic is delay-sensitive in nature. Since DSLAMs usually package IP traffic into ATM cells, they cannot distinguish between different kinds of IP traffic to provide different levels of service to these different types of traffic. For service to customers who need to transport both voice and data traffic, telcos must set up a different PVC for each type of traffic and for each customer, which means that managing and configuring DSLAMs is a lot of work for a DSL provider that is rolling out thousands of DSL lines to customers. For example, if 50 customers need both voice and data DSL services, then 100 PVCs will need to be configured.

DSLAMs usually support only one kind of DSL service, but now reaching the market are newer DSLAMs are that support multiple services (including Asymmetric Digital Subscriber Line [ADSL], ISDN Digital Subscriber Line [IDSL], and Very-high-rate Digital Subscriber Line [VDSL]) across thousands of ports in a single device. These new DSLAMs have greater QoS support to enable them to carry Voice over DSL (VoDSL) services in addition to traditional wide area network (WAN) and Internet access services. Some new DSLAMs also act as concentrators, allowing traffic to be aggregated according to type. Thus if 50 customers require both voice and data DSL services, only two PVCs need to be configured, one for voice traffic and the other for data.

Marketplace

Some of the vendors offering state-of-the-art DSLAM equipment include Nortel Networks, Lucent Technologies, Paradyne, and Copper Mountain.

See Also: *Asynchronous Transfer Mode (ATM), Digital Subscriber Line (DSL), multiplexing, telco*

digital transmission

Transmission of signals that vary discretely with time.

Overview

Digital transmission signals vary between two discrete values of some physical quantity, one value representing the binary number 0 and the other representing 1. With copper cabling, the variable quantity is typically the voltage or the electrical potential. With fiber-optic cabling or wireless communication, variation in intensity or some other physical quantity is used. Digital signals use discrete values for the transmission of binary information over a communication medium such as a network cable or a telecommunications link. On a serial transmission line, a digital signal is transmitted 1 bit at a time.

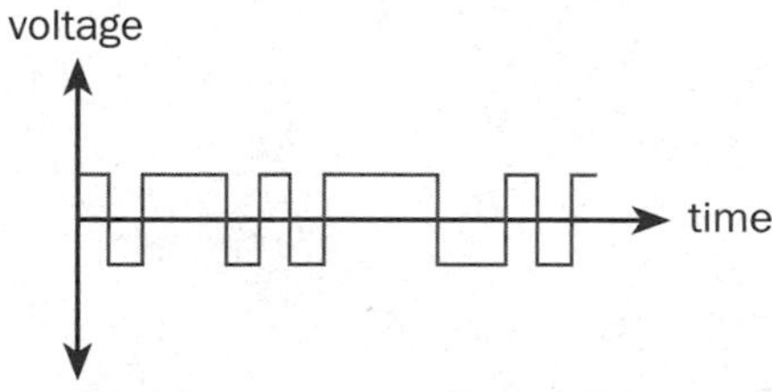

Digital transmission.

The opposite of digital transmission is analog transmission, in which information is transmitted as a continuously varying quantity. An analog signal might be converted to a digital signal using an analog-to-digital converter (ADC) and vice versa using a digital-to-analog converter (DAC). ADCs use a method called "quantization" to convert a varying AC voltage to a stepped digital one.

See Also: *analog*

DIME

Stands for Direct Internet Message Encapsulation, a protocol for encapsulating attachments to Simple Object Access Protocol (SOAP) routing protocol messages.

See: *Direct Internet Message Encapsulation (DIME)*

direct burial fiber-optic cabling

Fiber-optic cable designed for burial.

Overview

Direct burial fiber-optic cable typically consists of multiple fiber-optic cables bundled together and enclosed in a protective sheath. Direct burial fiber-optic cabling is designed to be buried in trenches and contains a gel filling that protects the individual fibers from temperature and moisture variations. A strip of strengthening material runs axially down the cable to prevent excessive bending, which can fracture the individual fibers. Direct burial cabling can have steel-armor construction with heavy waterproof polyethylene jackets and can contain either multimode or single-mode fiber-optic strands.

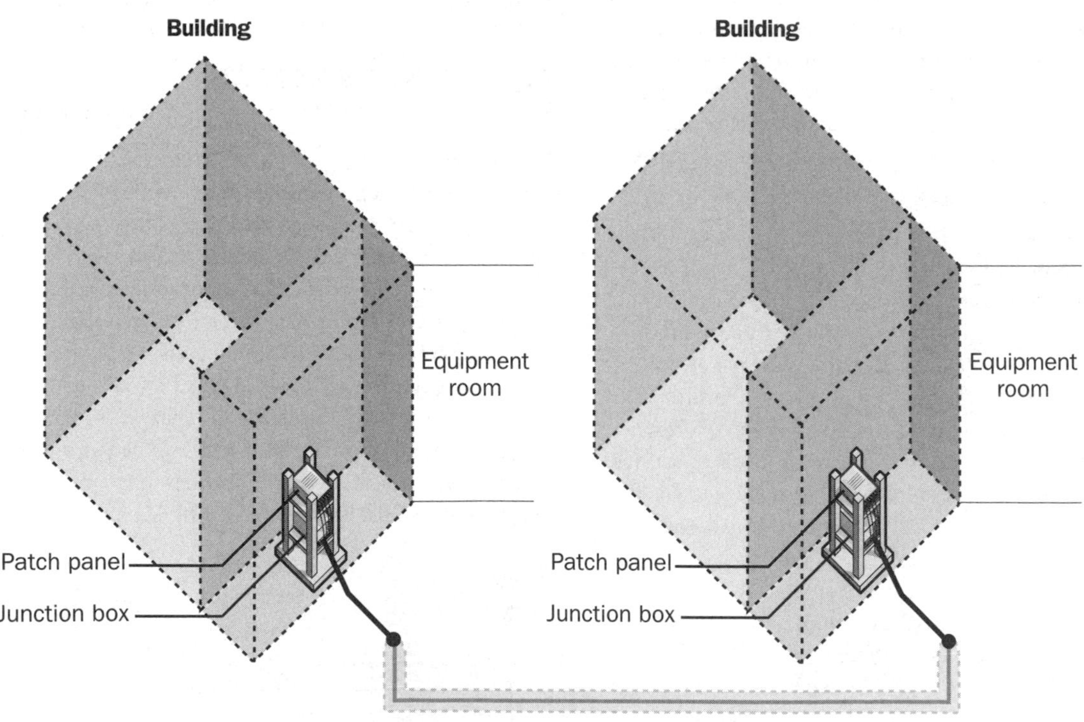

Direct burial fiber-optic cabling. *Deploying direct burial fiber-optic cable to connect networks in different buildings.*

Uses

Direct burial cabling is more cost-effective than single-fiber cabling for long outdoor cable runs between buildings or across a campus because it allows for future bandwidth upgrades.

See Also: *fiber-optic cabling*

Direct Cable Connection

A Microsoft Windows tool that facilitates file transfers between two non-networked computers.

Overview

Direct Cable Connection can be used on Windows 95, Windows 98, Windows 2000, Windows XP, and Windows .NET Server to establish a temporary network connection for the purpose of transferring files between machines. Direct Cable Connection is implemented using a serial null-modem cable or a standard parallel cable. One computer must be designated as the host (the server) and the other as the guest (the client). The desired resources must be shared on the host computer, and Dial-Up Networking must be installed on the guest computer.

If desired, the host computer can also act as a router that allows the guest computer to access resources on other computers on the host computer's network.

See Also: *null modem cable*

directed frame

A frame that is being sent by one station to a specific destination station on the network.

Overview

On an Ethernet network, a directed frame is one that uses the hexadecimal MAC address of a specific target machine on the network as its destination address. The directed frame is picked up by the target machine and is ignored by all other machines on the network.

Directed frames are used for most network communication because they are the most efficient type of frame for communication. However, some services, such as network announcements, require that all stations on the network receive a frame. To send a frame to all stations on the network, you use a broadcast frame instead of a directed frame.

See Also: *broadcast frame, broadcast packet, directed packet*

directed packet

An Internet Protocol (IP) packet that is being sent by one host on a Transmission Control Protocol/Internet Protocol (TCP/IP) network to a specific destination host on the network.

Overview

A directed packet contains the IP address of a specific target host on the network as its destination address. The directed packet is picked up by the target host and is ignored by all other hosts on the network.

Directed packets are used for most network communication on a TCP/IP network because they are the most efficient method for communication. However, some services, such as network announcements, require that all hosts on the network receive a packet. To send a packet to all stations on the network, you use a broadcast packet instead of a directed packet.

See Also: *broadcast frame, broadcast packet, directed frame*

Direct Internet Message Encapsulation (DIME)

A protocol for encapsulating attachments to Simple Object Access Protocol (SOAP) routing protocol messages.

Overview

Direct Internet Message Encapsulation (DIME) is a protocol for encapsulating multiple payloads of arbitrary type and size for transmission in a single message construct. DIME is lightweight in nature and encapsulates binary information for transmission within SOAP messages. Since SOAP is based on Extensible Markup Language (XML), DIME performs a similar function to what Muiltipurpose Internet Mail Extensions (MIME) does for Simple Mail Transfer Protocol (SMTP) messages: provide a method for encoding binary attachments into text. The difference between DIME and MIME is that DIME is much simpler and faster to parse than MIME.

DIME can be used to encapsulate any binary information, including image files, XML data, and so on. DIME allows multiple logically connected records to be aggregated into a single message. DIME does not specify the type of messages being sent and can be used over any connection-oriented or virtual logical circuit.

Implementation

The DIME encapsulation format specifies only three additional pieces of information for each payload: the length of the payload in bytes, the type of payload (to allow routing of messages according to application type), and a payload identifier, which is basically a globally unique identifier (GUID).

See Also: *Simple Object Access Protocol (SOAP), XML*

direct inward dialing (DID)

A service provided by a local exchange carrier (LEC) to a corporate client.

Overview

Direct inward dialing (DID) uses a Private Branch Exchange (PBX) that allows outside callers to dial individuals within the company directly. Typically, the LEC allocates a block of phone numbers to the company, usually differing only in the last two, three, or four digits. For example, a company with 50 employees who each need a separate phone number could be assigned the numbers 555-1201 through 555-1250. Outside callers could dial the employees directly using these numbers, which are routed through perhaps only eight trunk lines that service the PBX, supporting a maximum of eight simultaneous calls. Inbound calls are routed by the PBX to the appropriate extension.

See Also: *local exchange carrier (LEC), Private Branch Exchange (PBX)*

directory

A tool designed to provide a single source for locating, organizing, and managing network resources within an enterprise.

Overview

Directories are used in enterprise networks to organize network resources so that they can easily be found and managed. These network resources typically include computers, disk volumes, folders, files, printers, users, groups, and other types of objects. Directories are typically used for one of two general purposes:

- **Internal directory:** These are directories used within the corporate network for publishing information about users and resources within the enterprise. A company's internal directory may be accessible to employees when they are outside the company network using a secure connection such as a virtual private network (VPN) connection, but it is not accessible to non-employees.
- **External directory:** These are directories typically located on servers in the perimiter network or demilitarized zone (DMZ) at the boundary between the corporate local area network (LAN) and the public Internet. External directories are typically made available to customers, clients, and business partners to provide them with selected business information such as catalogs and so on.

Network operating systems (NOSs) typically have their own directories built into them. This NOS directory functions much like the yellow pages of a phone book. For example, if you look up the word *printers*, you will find a list of available printers and information for accessing them. Examples of NOS directories include Windows NT Directory Services (NTDS) for Windows NT, Active Directory for Windows 2000, and Novell Directory Services (NDS) for Novell NetWare version 4 and higher.

Many applications use their own proprietary directories. An example is Microsoft Exchange 5.5, which uses a proprietary Exchange directory service based on the Microsoft Jet database. The more recent Exchange 2000 instead uses the Active Directory directory service of Windows 2000 for storing its hierarchy of information concerning Exchange directory objects.

An international standard has long existed for how directory services should operate and directory databases be structured. This standard, called X.500, was developed by the International Organization for

Standardization/International Electrotechnical Commission (ISO/IEC) in the 1980s. The X.500 standard specifies a protocol called Directory Access Protocol (DAP) that enables users and applications to search and modify an X.500 directory. Because DAP is complex and difficult to implement, a simpler protocol called Lightweight Directory Access Protocol (LDAP) was developed later on and has become the de facto standard for directory protocols. Active Directory, the directory service used by Windows 2000 and Windows .NET Server, is LDAP-compliant.

To function at the enterprise level, a directory should have the following essential characteristics:

- It should be scalable, so that it can grow to accommodate information and provide services as the enterprise itself grows.
- It should be extensible and have a schema that can be modified by adding new classes, objects, and attributes.
- It should provide simple ways of finding directory objects
- It should be possible to administer it from a single point on the network.

Active Directory for Windows 2000 and Windows .NET Server satisfies all these conditions.

Implementation

A directory typically consists of the following two components:

- **Directory database:** A hierarchical database structure that contains the actual information about the resources on the network.
- **Directory service:** Software that allows you to search for and locate information stored in the directory database.

In addition to these two components, consideration must be given to where the directory database is stored. This database is typically located on directory servers that are located at different points on the network. The database can be stored in the following ways on these servers:

- **Distributed:** In this scenario each directory server contains only a portion of the directory database for which it is authoritative. An example of a distributed directory service is the Domain Name System (DNS) found on the Internet.
- **Single-master:** Here one directory server contains a writeable master copy of the database, while all other directory servers contain read-only copies of this database. When changes need to be made to the directory, they are made first to the master server and then later copied to the other servers on the network. An example where this is used is in a Windows NT domain.
- **Multimaster:** Here each directory contains a writeable copy of the entire directory database. Modifications may be made to any directory server on the network, and these modifications are then automatically propagated by means of directory replication to all other servers on the network. An example of a multimaster directory is Windows 2000's Active Directory.

Marketplace

While Active Directory and NDS are the most popular general NOS directory products, there are also third-party directories that the enterprise architect may consider. One of the most popular of these is iPlanet's Directory Server, an LDAP server that is highly optimized for rapidly performing LDAP queries. Another is Novell's eDirectory, which is NDS uncoupled from the Novell NetWare NOS and made available for other platforms. Still another LDAP-compliant directory on the market is InJoin from Critical Path. Other popular directory vendors include Oracle Corporation and Innosoft International.

Some factors to consider when evaluating directory software for purchase for the enterprise environment include

- **Security:** Access to the directory can be managed by access lists and by policies. Some vendors provide additional tools for managing directory security. Examples of such vendors include Netegrity and Oblix.

D

- **Access method:** Nowadays everything needs to be Web-enabled, and information within an enterprise directory should be accessible by issuing LDAP queries over Hypertext Transfer Protocol (HTTP) through a simple Web browser.
- **Management tools:** Directories that can be managed using LDAP/HTTP are a distinct advantage over others where remote administration is concerned.
- **Namespace design:** Most general-purpose NOS directories map a company's geographical structure to its directory namespace. This may be the simplest and most logical thing to do, but whether it is most efficient for LDAP searching is something that you should consider before implementing the directory. For a company that has already implemented its directory but has trouble searching it efficiently, a product called RadiantOne from Radiant Logic can help by mapping a virtual LDAP namespace over the top of the existing namespace to speed search queries and maintain directory independence when the network configuration is changed.

Issues

The main issue confronting the enterprise concerning directories is interoperability. A large enterprise typically has many different directories implemented at various levels of its network, and consolidating all these directories into a single directory through migration is often impractical from the point of view of cost (large enterprises tend to be heterogeneous in many ways and for many reasons).

To allow directories from different vendors to share information with one another, a number of metadirectory products has appeared in the marketplace. Examples of metadirectory software include Microsoft Metadirectory Services (MMS) and Novell's DirXML.

Another issue regarding interoperability between directories is that the LDAP standard has certain limitations that require directory vendors to add their own proprietary extensions to LDAP if they want to give their LDAP directory products greater functionality. Thus even different LDAP-compliant directories from different vendors might not be able to interoperate to a desired degree. To solve this problem, an XML language called Directory Service Markup Language (DSML) is being developed to better allow different directories to communicate with one another. Other related initiatives include Simple Object Access Protocol (SOAP) and the Universal Description, Discovery, and Integration (UDDI) specification.

Finally, it must be mentioned that simply implementing a directory will not necessarily save costs for an enterprise or make the lives of administrators easier. Directories can be complex to implement, especially if legacy information needs to be migrated to them. Also, tools for managing directories can be difficult to use and require extensive training. As a result of such complexity, industry analysts estimated that as of 2000 less than 35 percent of all companies were using LDAP directories.

See Also: *Active Directory, Directory Access Protocol (DAP), directory database, directory replication (Windows 2000 and Windows .NET Server), Directory Service Markup Language (DSML), Lightweight Directory Access Protocol (LDAP), metadirectory, Novell Directory Services (NDS), Simple Object Access Protocol (SOAP), Universal Description, Discovery, and Integration (UDDI), Windows NT Directory Services (NTDS), X.500*

Directory Access Protocol (DAP)

A protocol for accessing information in a directory service based on the X.500 recommendations.

Overview

The Directory Access Protocol (DAP) specifies how an X.500 Directory User Agent (DUA) communicates with a Directory System Agent (DSA) to issue a query. Using DAP, users can view, modify, delete, and search for information stored in the X.500 directory if they have suitable access permissions.

DAP is a complex protocol with a lot of overhead, which makes it generally unsuitable for implementations in a Microsoft Windows environment. A simpler version called Lightweight Directory Access Protocol (LDAP) is growing in popularity and can be used to access and update directory information in X.500 directories. LDAP is more suitable than DAP for implementation on the Internet and has mostly superseded DAP as an access protocol for X.500-based directories (which are now often called LDAP directories).

See Also: *directory, Lightweight Directory Access Protocol (LDAP), X.500*

directory database

The central store of directory information on a network.

Overview

The directory database is one of two components of a typical directory application, the other being the directory service, which allows the directory database to be searched and modified.

In Microsoft Windows NT, Windows 2000, and Windows .NET Server, the directory database resides on the domain controllers, which manage all security-related aspects of the network. In Windows NT, the directory database is generally called the Security Accounts Manager (SAM) database. In Windows 2000 and Windows .NET Server, the directory database is the database component of Active Directory directory service.

Both the SAM database and the Active Directory directory service store information about objects on the network. The SAM is limited to storing information about users, groups, and computers that participate in the domain and security policy information such as password expiration policies and audit policies. The SAM stores its information in a privileged area of the registry. The practical upper limit for a SAM database is 40 megabytes (MB), which corresponds to approximately 26,000 user and computer accounts. If an enterprise has more than 26,000 users, the Windows NT directory database can be partitioned (split) into two or more portions and trust relationships can be configured according to a multiple master domain model.

Active Directory is considerably more flexible and powerful than the Windows NT SAM. Active Directory scales upward to tens of millions of objects, and these objects may be users, groups, computers, printers, shares, and many other forms of information.

See Also: *Active Directory, directory, directory replication (Windows 2000 and Windows .NET Server), Security Account Manager (SAM) database*

Directory Enabled Network (DEN)

An initiative toward a platform-independent specification for storing information about network applications, devices, and users in a directory.

Overview

Directory Enabled Network (DEN) was started by Microsoft Corporation and Cisco Systems in 1997 with the goal of developing standards for directory-based management of network resources. DEN is a policy-based mechanism that binds a user's name and network access profile to a policy. This procedure maps users to network services to make a more intelligent network that can better manage its resources, especially bandwidth. User rights on the network and bandwidth allocation can then be assigned to the user by using the profile.

DEN's goal is to unify the disparate network management platforms in existence today to provide a single, directory-based, cross-platform specification for the development of standard network management systems. The DEN initiative is now managed by the Distributed Management Task Force (DTMF) and is open to network device vendors, Internet service providers (ISPs), independent software vendors (ISVs), carriers, and others who might be interested.

Prospects

DEN has not materialized as fast as many had hoped, but the Desktop Management Task Force (DMTF) is still guiding it toward final release within the next few years. Part of this is because one of the major driving forces initially behind DEN was the hope of managing quality of service (QoS) policies using directories. This would allow bandwidth to be allocated to users and applications more easily. The pressure to do this has lessened in the last few years, however, as bandwidth costs continue to drop, especially with the emergence of Gigabit Ethernet (GbE). As a result, QoS issues can be sidestepped in many situations simply by overprovisioning bandwidth. Furthermore, simple Internet Protocol (IP) QoS techniques such as 802.1p have lessened the need for more complex directory-based QoS schemes.

Technical issues have also hindered the development of DEN as a real-life specification. One recent step forward involved the mapping of Common Information Model (CIM) schema to Lightweight Directory Access Protocol (LDAP) so that CIM object information could be stored and accessed in LDAP-compliant directories such as Microsoft's Active Directory directory service.

See Also: *Active Directory, Common Information Model (CIM), directory, Distributed Management Task Force (DMTF), Lightweight Directory Access Protocol (LDAP)*

directory export

The process of exporting information from a directory to another application.

Overview

An example of directory export can be found in Microsoft Exchange Server, which supports the exporting of information about recipients stored in its directory database. This information can be exported to a comma-delimited text file (.csv file), edited, and then imported into another system.

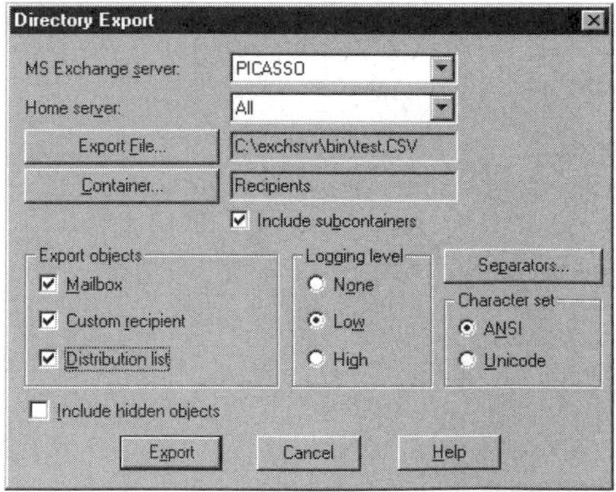

Directory export. *Configuring directory export for Exchange Server.*

For example, you can import recipient information into a spreadsheet to print it out. Or you can export the information into a spreadsheet, use spreadsheet functions to mass-modify certain fields, and then use directory import for re-importing the modified account information back into Exchange. Using directory export/import is in fact the usual method in Exchange for modifying the properties of a large number of recipients at one time.

See Also: *directory, directory import, Exchange Server*

directory hierarchy

The hierarchy of objects in a directory.

Overview

Directories typically store information about the objects they manage in a hierarchical fashion. As an example we can consider the containers and leaf objects in a Microsoft Exchange Server directory, which is displayed and configured using the Exchange Administrator program. This hierarchy is based on the directory recommendations given by X.500.

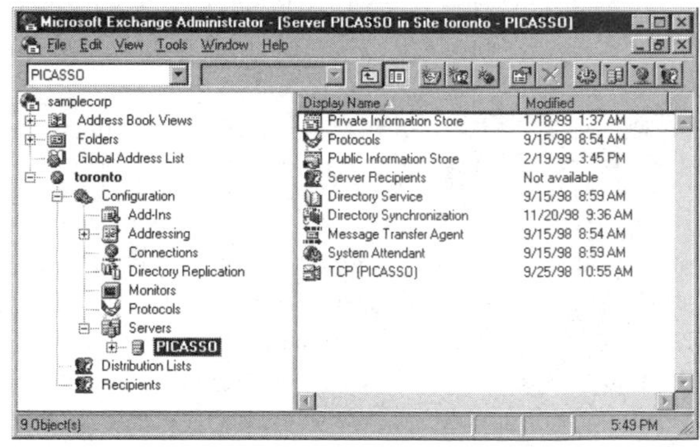

Directory hierarchy.

The Exchange directory hierarchy begins at a root object called the Organization container, and then branches down into sites, servers, connectors, recipients, and other objects. To configure any object in the directory hierarchy, you use its property sheet.

Objects in the directory hierarchy of Exchange come in two types:

- **Containers:** These can contain other directory objects. Containers usually also have configurable properties.

- **Leaf objects:** These are end nodes in the directory tree and whose properties can be configured using their property sheets.

See Also: *directory, Exchange Server, X.500*

directory import

The process of importing information into a directory from another application.

Overview

An example of directory import can be seen in Microsoft Exchange. Here the information to be imported must be in a format that the importing system can understand, usually a delimited text file such as a .csv file. Microsoft Exchange Server allows recipient information to be imported into its directory database and allows recipients exported from other mail systems to be imported into Exchange. For example, you can use the Exchange Migration Wizard to extract mailbox information from a foreign mail system into a .csv file. You can then import this information into a spreadsheet program such as Microsoft Excel, modify it as needed, and import it into Exchange to create new mailboxes in your organization for users of the foreign mail system who are migrating to Exchange.

See Also: *directory, directory export*

directory replication (Windows 2000 and Windows .NET Server)

A process that ensures that all directory servers contain identical copies of the directory database.

Overview

In a typical implementation of a directory, the directory database is replicated to a number of servers called directory servers. These servers are located at different points around the network to provide accessible points for clients needing to search the directory for resources on the network.

Implementation

As an example of the directory replication process, consider the Active Directory directory service in Microsoft Windows 2000 or Windows .NET Server, which stores copies of the directory database on machines called domain controllers. In Windows 2000, directory replication is thus the process of replicating Active Directory updates to all the domain controllers on the network. Directory replication ensures that users have access to resources on the network by ensuring that information about users, groups, computers, file shares, printers, and other directory objects is current on all domain controllers in the network.

Directory replication of Active Directory on a Microsoft Windows 2000– or Windows .NET Server–based network takes place in two ways, depending on whether the participating domain controllers are in the same site.

- **Intrasite:** Within a site, intrasite replication between domain controllers uses remote procedure calls (RPCs) by means of a dynamically allocated port number. This replication takes place automatically every five minutes. Domain controllers within a site exchange update information in a ring fashion, from one domain controller to another. This ring topology is established by a process called the Knowledge Consistency Checker (KCC) and ensures a minimum of two replication paths between each pair of domain controllers and a maximum replication hop count of three to support efficient replication and fault tolerance.
- **Intersite:** Between sites, intersite replication can use RPCs if the local area network (LAN) or wide area network (WAN) connection supports them or some other method, such as Simple Mail Transfer Protocol (SMTP) e-mail messages. Intersite replication uses a compressed format for more efficient use of slow WAN links and is easier to schedule and manage than intrasite replication. To take advantage of the greater flexibility of intersite replication and to use it instead of intrasite replication, configure your domain controllers to belong to more than one physical site.

See Also: *Active Directory, directory, directory database*

directory replication (Windows NT)

In Microsoft Windows NT, the replication of a tree of folders from one server to another using the Directory Replicator Service.

Overview

The Directory Replicator service is a Windows NT service for replicating files and folders over the network. The Directory Replicator Service simplifies the task of updating key network configuration files needed by all users, such as system policies and logon scripts. You can also use directory replication to load balance between multiple servers when a large number of users need access to specific files or folders.

You can perform directory replication in Windows NT to create and manage identical directory structures on different Windows NT servers and workstations. When a change is made to the master directory structure, such as modification of a file or addition of a directory, that change is replicated to the other computers. One use for directory replication is to provide a means for load balancing file system information across several servers. This allows more clients to efficiently access the data stored in the replicated directory structure because identical data is stored on different machines. For example, you might replicate a database of customer information across several servers in your network to provide easier access. You can also use directory replication to copy logon scripts from a primary domain controller (PDC) to a set of backup domain controllers (BDCs). You can configure replication to occur between different computers in a domain or from one domain to another.

Implementation

The Directory Replicator Service replicates files from an export computer to an import computer. The export computer must be running the Windows NT Server operating system, but the import computer can run Windows NT Server, Windows NT Workstation, or LAN Manager for OS/2 servers.

The export server is the computer that contains the master copy of the directory tree to be replicated. This export server must be a machine running Windows NT Server. The computers that will replicate with the export server are called import servers. Import servers can be machines running Windows NT Server, Windows NT Workstation, or LAN Manager Server.

Prior to configuring directory replication, you must create a new user account as a security context within which the replicator service will run. This account should have a password that never expires and should be a member of the Replicator, Domain Users, and Backup Operators groups. The account should be accessible from both export and import machines. Use the Services utility in Control Panel to configure the Directory Replicator Service to start automatically upon system startup and to use your new account for logging on.

Server Manager is the administrative tool used for configuring replication in Windows NT. You can configure replication to occur either immediately after a change is made to the directory structure or after a stabilization period. When configuring replication, you select one of the following options:

- Replicate the entire subtree of directories and files beneath a specific directory on the export server.
- Replicate only specific files contained in the subtree by applying locks to its directories and files to prevent them from being exported.

By default, the export directory in which the master copy of the replicated data is contained is located in the path %SystemRoot%\system32\repl\export. The default path to which the directory structure is imported on the import server is %SystemRoot%\system32\repl\import.

Notes

Do not use directory replication as a substitute for a regular program of tape backups. The Directory Replicator Service can create a lot of network traffic and should not be used for backing up data across a network. If the data you are replicating contains large files that change frequently, replication traffic can cause network congestion unless you watch it carefully. Be especially careful when you replicate directory structures over slower wide area network (WAN) links to avoid congestion that interferes with other essential forms of traffic such as logon traffic.

The Directory Replicator Service on Windows NT can export only one directory tree from a given export server. It is a good idea to leave the default export location as it is and move the directory structure and information you want to replicate to this default export location. This allows you to also replicate logon scripts because by default these are located on a PDC in the location %SystemRoot%\system32\repl\export\scripts and on a BDC in the location %SystemRoot%\system32\repl\import.

Since these script directories are located within the default export and import paths, they can be replicated along with other data.

directory service log

A log that contains events written by the Active Directory directory service on machines running Microsoft Windows 2000 or Windows .NET Server.

Overview

The directory service log exists only on domain controllers because these are the only computers that have copies of Active Directory. The directory service log contains events such as informational, warning, and error events concerning operations that have been performed on or by Active Directory. These events reveal the state of Active Directory and can be used for diagnostic and troubleshooting purposes.

Information in the directory service log can be displayed using Event Viewer, a Windows 2000 and Windows .NET Server administrative tool that runs as a snap-in for the Microsoft Management Console (MMC). Event Viewer for Windows 2000 and Windows .NET Server supports a number of different kinds of logs in addition to the three supported in the Windows NT version of Event Viewer, namely, the system log, security log, and application log. The actual types of event logs available in Windows 2000 and Windows .NET Server Event Viewer depend on which optional networking components are installed on the machine.

See Also: *Active Directory*

Directory Service Manager for NetWare (DSMN)

An optional Windows 2000 utility for managing directory information stored on NetWare servers.

Overview

Directory Service Manager for NetWare (DSMN) enables Windows 2000 domain controllers to manage account information on NetWare 2.*x*, 3.*x*, and 4.*x* servers. It does this by copying NetWare account information to the primary domain controller (PDC) and then propagating changes back to the bindery on the NetWare servers. DSMN also synchronizes accounts across all NetWare servers allowing users to access any NetWare server using a single logon username. DSMN does not come with Windows 2000 but can be ordered separately from your Microsoft value-added reseller (VAR).

Notes

DSMN supports NetWare 4.*x* servers only when they are running in bindery emulation mode, not in Novell Directory Services (NDS) mode.

See Also: *Novell Directory Services (NDS)*

Directory Service Markup Language (DSML)

A specification based on XML (Extensible Markup Language) that enables different directory applications to share information.

Overview

Directory Service Markup Language (DSML) is a markup language (such as Hypertext Markup Language [HTML]) whose function is to allow directory information to be represented using XML. Its purpose in doing this is to make XML the common language for exchange of information between different directory systems.

DSML is an open specification, and its membership includes Microsoft, IBM, Novell, and Oracle. A draft standard is being developed by the Organization for the Advancement of Structured Information Standards (OASIS).

Implementation

DSML is essentially a set of extensions to XML that is expressed as a schema. The DSML schema for XML provides mechanisms for accessing information in directories even if the actual format of the data is unknown. Using a set of tags specific to directory services, DSML allows information in one proprietary directory to be exchanged with another proprietary directory without the need to pay attention to the mechanics happening underneath or how the directories operate.

The original DSML 1 specification was limited to specifying how to use XML to describe a directory's contents. The newer DSML 2 specification adds standard mechanisms for using XML to locate, access, and manipulate information stored in directories. Using DSML 2, developers will be able to build transactional applications that use XML to find and modify objects stored in a directory, regardless of the vendor from which the directory is obtained.

Notes

A related initiative is the Directory Interoperability Forum (DIF), whose aim is to establish a standard that will enable use of the Lightweight Directory Access Protocol (LDAP) for performing data queries across multiple directories. DSML and DIF are separate initiatives, but they might eventually merge or be subsumed within a wider objective.

For More Information

You can find out more about DSML at *www.dsml.org.*

See Also: *directory, XML*

Directory Service Migration Tool (DSMigrate)

A tool for migrating information from Novell NetWare networks to Microsoft Windows 2000.

Overview

Directory Service Migration Tool (DSMigrate) is a tool that you can use to migrate NetWare users, groups, files, and permissions to Active Directory directory service. DSMigrate can migrate both bindery-based NetWare 3.*x* servers and Novell Directory Services (NDS)–based NetWare 4.*x* and 5.*x* servers to Windows 2000.

DSMigrate lets you perform a test migration to assess any difficulties that might occur before you perform your final migration. DSMigrate is one of the NetWare tools included with Windows 2000.

See Also: *bindery, Novell Directory Services (NDS)*

directory synchronization (Microsoft Mail)

The process by which information stored in Microsoft Mail 3.*x* mail systems is replicated between postoffices.

Overview

There is only one directory server postoffice in a Microsoft Mail 3.*x* mail system; other postoffices that participate in directory synchronization are called requestor postoffices. Requestor postoffices send their address list updates to the directory server postoffice, which then sends cumulative changes back to the requestor postoffice. Directory synchronization also ensures that the global address list is updated.

When migrating legacy MS Mail systems to Microsoft Exchange Server, establishing directory synchronization between the old MS Mail directory and the new Exchange directory is a typical step in the process. To make this possible, Microsoft Exchange includes a dirsync component that emulates the MS Mail directory until the old directory information can be entirely migrated to the new system.

See Also: *Exchange Server*

directory synchronization (Windows NT)

The process of directory synchronization within a Microsoft Windows NT domain.

Overview

Directory synchronization is the process whereby the domain directory databases of backup domain controllers (BDCs) in a Microsoft Windows NT domain are synchronized with the master directory database on the primary domain controller (PDC). Accurate and reliable directory synchronization is the foundation for effective operation of Windows NT Directory Services (NTDS).

In Windows 2000 and Windows .NET Server, this process of replicating directory information between domain controllers is called directory replication.

Notes

If directory synchronization must be performed over slow wide area network (WAN) links, you can adjust some registry parameters to make directory synchronization more efficient and prevent it from consuming excessive bandwidth.

See Also: *directory replication (Windows NT), domain controller, Windows NT Directory Services (NTDS)*

Direct Sequence Spread Spectrum (DSSS)

A combination of two transmission technologies (direct sequencing and spread spectrum) used in wireless networking and cellular communications.

Overview

Direct Sequence Spread Spectrum (DSSS) is the most popular transmission scheme used in wireless networking and is widely deployed in cellular communications systems also. DSSS is the basis of the 802.11b wireless local area network (LAN) standard used around the world.

Implementation

DSSS transmits data 1 bit at a time. Each bit is processed by modulating it against a pattern called a chipping sequence. For example, in 802.11b the chipping sequence is an 11-bit binary sequence 10110111000 called the Barker code. This sequence is chosen as it has certain mathematical properties that make it suitable for modulation of radio waves. The sequence is exclusively ORd (XORd) with each bit of the data stream, which has the effect of multiplying the number of bits transmitted by a factor of 11 (each 11-bit transmission is called a "chip" and represents only a single bit of actual data). While this seems wasteful in terms of bandwidth, it has the advantage that if some of the transmitted bits are lost, the original data stream can still be reliably reconstructed by processing the remaining information. This feature, in addition to spread spectrum transmission, which sends the data over multiple frequencies simultaneously, makes DSSS strongly resistant to interference due to extraneous radio sources, multipath reflection, and atmospheric conditions.

See Also: *802.11b, cellular communications, direct sequencing, spread spectrum, wireless networking*

direct sequencing

A transmission method used for wireless networking.

Overview

Direct sequencing systems transmit data one bit at a time. Each bit of data is then transmitted simultaneously over a range of frequencies.

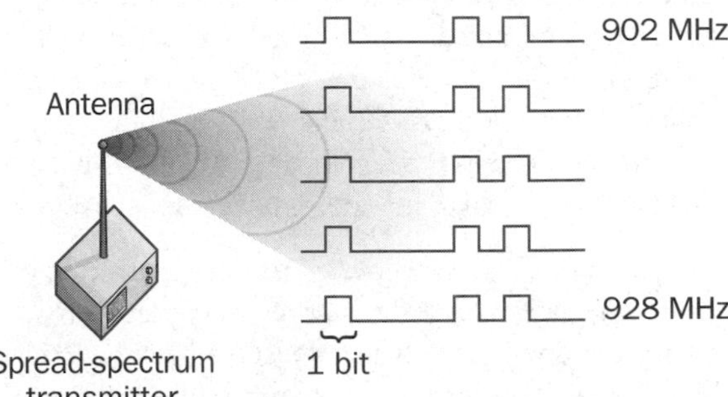

Direct sequencing. *How direct sequencing works.*

Direct sequencing is usually used in conjunction with spread spectrum, a transmission method where the data transmitted is spread over multiple frequencies to reduce signal loss due to noise and interference. The transmitter feeds each bit of the data stream into a signal spreader that multiplies the input, creating a wideband signal. The wideband signal is then amplified and broadcast by using an antenna.

Uses

Direct sequencing can be used for both wireless local area network (LAN) connections and as part of a cellular telephone system. Direct sequencing has a faster theoretical maximum data transmission rate than frequency hopping, another wireless transmission method, but in practice both methods provide similar throughput for wireless transmission of data because of protocol overhead in typical wireless communication systems.

See Also: *Direct Sequence Spread Spectrum (DSSS), frequency hopping, spread spectrum, wireless networking*

disaster recovery

The process of recovering IT (information technology) operations after a failure or disaster.

D

Overview

Because IT is the lifeblood of today's e-business economy, it is essential to be able to recover IT operations quickly after a disaster. An IT disaster can be something as small as a failed disk drive within a server or something as big as a data center burning to the ground. Other common examples of disasters include power failures, destruction due to viruses, theft, sabotage, accidental commands issued by administrators that result in files being deleted or modified, earthquakes, insurrections, and so on. Being prepared for eventualities such as these is the responsibility of IT management and is critical to the success of modern businesses.

The key to successful recovery from these situations is a comprehensive, tested disaster recovery plan. This is a business plan that involves not just redundant hardware but personnel, procedures, responsibilities, and issues of legal liability.

Implementation

The first step in such a plan involves risk assessment to determine which components are most vulnerable and how the company can function in response to loss of data or critical IT services. It is also important to determine what is acceptable to management in terms of a recovery window—many businesses today would suffer significant loss if it should take more than a day or two to recover from failed systems.

Disaster recovery plans can be implemented in different ways depending on the size and needs of the company involved. Three common approaches to implementing disaster recovery plans are traditional tape backup, e-vaulting, and mirroring.

The traditional approach of small to mid-sized businesses to disaster recovery is to create full backups to tape daily and archive these tapes off-site in secure locations. Most computer systems in businesses use this method, primarily due to its low cost and its well-known procedures. However, tape backups must be verified, and test restores must be performed periodically to ensure that this system is in fact working. Furthermore, businesses must realize that it typically takes up to 48 hours to restore a failed disk or system from tape backup, a recovery window that may be unacceptable from an e-business standpoint.

E-vaulting (or electronic vaulting or data vaulting) takes a different approach. Instead of archiving data to tape, it is sent over high-speed leased lines or Internet connections to a remote data center for safe storage. E-vaulting makes it possible to do more frequent backups and rapid restores, but the weak link is the wide area network (WAN) connection, for if that goes down, a restore might be difficult or impossible.

To make e-vaulting more effective, companies sometimes arrange for backup servers to be running at the remote site and back up data directly to those servers. Then if a failure occurs with the company's main servers, control can be switched over to the backup servers and business can continue without interruption. The problem is that having duplicate systems in place is an expensive proposition and complex to manage, and companies often try to save money by placing older hardware at the remote site. When disaster strikes, this hardware may not be able to perform as hoped and business will go down.

Another version of e-vaulting involves using a mobile data center (a network in a moving van) at the remote site. When disaster strikes the primary site, the mobile data center can be brought on location and managed by your staff.

Regardless of which form of e-vaulting is used, the main disadvantage in the eyes of most companies is the cost, which is typically many times that of using traditional tape backup solutions.

Extending the idea of e-vaulting is a method called mirroring, in which identical hardware is placed at a remote site and data is kept synchronized between servers in the primary and remote site. This is a costly solution both from the point of view of the redundant hardware required and the throughput needed for WAN links, but the restore window is typically under an hour when disaster strikes, so it is a good option from the perspective of e-businesses. Financial institutions such as banks and credit unions often employ this solution to ensure maximum availability and reliability for customer access to accounts.

Marketplace

While smaller companies tend to manage their own tape backup and e-vaulting solutions in-house, large enterprises generally outsource their disaster recovery needs, particularly if mainframe systems and AS/400s are involved. Three companies handle the lion's share of disaster recovery business at the enterprise level: Comdisco Continuity Services, SunGard Recovery Services, and IBM's Business Continuity Recovery Services (BCRS).

E-vaulting companies abound and their range of services varies greatly. One example of such a company is Imation, which offers its LiveVault services for small and medium-sized companies.

Businesses that host their business services with Web hosting companies often make use of disaster recovery services provided by these services. An example is Exodus Communications, which provides mirroring services for customers at remote data centers.

See Also: backup, tape format

discrete multitone (DMT)

A line coding technique used in Asymmetric Digital Subscriber Line (ADSL).

Overview

Discrete multitone (DMT) describes a specification for the physical layer transport for ADSL and is an efficient mechanism for transmitting data at high speeds at frequencies above the voice cutoff on ordinary copper phone lines. DMT offers good performance and resistance to crosstalk and electromagnetic interference, and it can be used to dynamically adapt data flow to line conditions. DMT is the most popular ADSL line coding scheme in use today.

History

DMT was developed by Bellcore in 1987 as a line coding scheme of Asymmetric Digital Subscriber Line (ADSL) services. DMT evolved from V.34 modem technology and was first commercially implemented in ADSL modem technology by Amati Corporation. At the time, DMT was one of several line coding schemes that had been proposed by carriers offering ADSL services. Another competing scheme used was carrierless amplitude phase modulation (CAP), which is based on quadrature amplitude modulation (QAM). But while CAP was more widely deployed initially in ADSL rollouts, DMT was adopted by standards bodies in the United States and Europe and is supported by the International Telecommunication Union (ITU).

Implementation

CAP employs a band of frequencies from 40 kilohertz (KHz) to 1.1 megahertz (MHz), well above the 4 KHz cutoff for voice transmission over the copper local loop. CAP divides this band into 4 KHz wide channels, with each channel being modulated independently and all of them simultaneously carrying data in parallel. An ADSL modem that uses CAP can thus be thought of as a collection of hundreds of tiny modems operating in parallel.

Each CAP channel can carry up to 15 bits/symbol/hertz (Hz) of information, using QAM as a modulation scheme (actual throughput per channel may be less due to electromagnetic interference and other conditions). Upstream transmission uses 25 channels giving a maximum throughput of

25 channels x 15 bits/symbol/Hz x 4 KHz = 1.5 Mbps

while downstream uses 249 channels giving a maximum throughput of

249 channels x 15 bits/symbol/Hz x 4 KHz = 14.9 Mbps

See Also: Asymmetric Digital Subscriber Line (ADSL), line coding, modulation

discretionary access control list (DACL)

An access control list (ACL) that can be configured by administrators.

Overview

In Microsoft Windows 2000, Windows XP, Windows .NET Server, and Windows NT, a discretionary access control list (DACL) is an internal list attached to a file or folder on a volume formatted using the NTFS file system (NTFS). The administrator can configure the DACL, and it specifies which users and groups can perform different actions on the file or folder. In Windows 2000, Windows XP, and Windows .NET Server, DACLs can also be attached to objects in Active Directory directory service to specify which users and groups can access the object and what kinds of operations they can perform on the object.

Implementation

In Windows 2000 and Windows .NET Server, each object in Active Directory or file on a local NTFS volume has an attribute called Security Descriptor that stores information about the following:

- The object's owner (the security identifier or the owner) and the groups to which the owner belongs
- The DACL of the object, which lists the security principals (users, groups, and computers) that have access to the object and their level of access
- The system access control list (SACL), which lists the security principals that should trigger audit events when accessing the list

The DACL for an object specifies the list of users and groups who are authorized to access the object and also what levels of access they have. The kinds of access that can be assigned to an object depend on the type of object under consideration. For example, a file object can have read access assigned to a user but a printer object cannot. (You cannot read a printer!)

The DACL for an object consists of a list of access control entries (ACEs). A given ACE applies to a class of objects, an object, or an attribute of an object. Each ACE specifies the security identifier (SID) of the security principal to which the ACE applies, as well as the level of access to the object permitted for the security principal. For example, a user or group might have permission to modify all or some of the attributes of the object, or might not even have permission to be aware of the object's existence. In common parlance, DACLs are sometimes simply referred to as access control lists or ACLs, although this is not strictly correct.

Notes

The owner of an object always has permission to modify its DACL by granting permissions to other users and groups.

See Also: *access control, access control entry (ACE), access control list (ACL), system access control list (SACL)*

disk duplexing

Disk mirroring using separate disk controllers.

Overview

Disk duplexing is a fault-tolerant disk technology that is essentially the same as disk mirroring, except that a separate disk drive controller is used for each mirrored drive. Disk duplexing thus provides two levels of fault tolerance:

- If one drive fails, the other contains a mirrored copy of the data.
- If one controller fails, the other controller continues to function.

Advantages and Disadvantages

Besides the additional level of fault tolerance, disk duplexing also provides slightly better read and write performance than disk mirroring because the two controllers provide two separate channels for data transmission. The down side is that disk duplexing is more expensive than disk mirroring since an extra controller card is required.

Microsoft Windows 2000, Windows XP, Windows .NET Server, and Windows NT Server support disk duplexing. You establish disk duplexing on Windows NT systems at the partition level and on Windows 2000, Windows XP, and Windows .NET Server at the volume level. In terms of system recovery and management, there is no difference between disk mirroring and disk duplexing.

See Also: *disk mirroring, fault tolerance, redundant array of independent disks (RAID)*

disk imaging

A method for creating an exact duplicate of the software installed on a computer system.

Overview

Disk imaging (also called cloning) is frequently used in enterprise environments as a way of rapidly deploying workstations (and occasionally servers) on a network. The first step in disk imaging is to create the reference system, a computer that has its operating system and applications installed and configured exactly as desired. A snapshot or image of this system is then taken using disk imaging software, and the image is stored on a server on the network. Agent software is then used to boot fresh systems (that is, computers with no operating system installed), connect to the server, download the image, and recreate it bit for bit on the new systems. The resulting systems are exact duplicates of the reference system.

Advantages and Disadvantages

Disk imaging is a much faster way of installing operating systems and applications on machines than the traditional methods of running setup programs. A traditional installation of an operating system and suite of applications might take hours—disk imaging often takes only a few minutes.

The downside of the process is that disk imaging is usually successful only when the cloned machines have the exact same hardware configuration as the reference machine. Nevertheless, disk imaging is a speedy and easy way to roll out large numbers of identical workstations and has become widely popular among enterprise administrators.

One further issue that must be considered is licensing—before using disk imaging to roll out a network, make sure that the operating system vendor supports this operation and that it does not violate your licensing agreement.

Marketplace

One of the earliest and still popular disk imaging applications is Ghost from Symantec Corp. In fact, disk imaging is often referred to as "ghosting" in reference to this product's impact on the industry. Other popular tools include ImageCast IC3 from Innovative Software, DriveImage from PowerQuest Corporation, and RapiDeploy from Altiris.

See Also: *network management, storage*

disk mirroring

A fault-tolerant disk technology that employs two drives having identical information on them instead of just one.

Overview

In disk mirroring, both drives are controlled by the same disk controller, and when data is written to the controller, it is copied to both drives. Disk mirroring thus provides a measures of fault tolerance for disk subsystems, since if one drive in the mirror set fails, the other contains an up-to-date copy of all the data and can immediately take over without interruption of services.

Advantages and Disadvantages

In addition to fault tolerance, disk mirroring also provides better write performance than RAID-5 systems. On the other hand, disk mirroring read performance is worse than RAID-5 (though better than for a single disk).

Microsoft Windows 2000, Windows XP, Windows .NET Server, and Windows NT Server support disk mirroring. You establish disk mirroring on Windows NT systems at the partition level and on Windows 2000, Windows XP, and Windows .NET Server at the volume level. A more fault-tolerant form of disk mirroring is disk duplexing, which is discussed in its own article elswhere in the book.

See Also: *disk duplexing, fault tolerance, redundant array of independent disks (RAID)*

Diskperf command

A Microsoft Windows NT, Windows 2000, Windows XP, and Windows .NET Server command for starting and stopping disk performance counters for Performance Monitor (System Monitor in Windows 2000, Windows XP, and Windows .NET Server).

Overview

Counters for the objects Logical Disk (partition) and Physical Disk (drive) are disabled by default because a performance hit of a few percent can occur if they are enabled. You must run the Diskperf command prior to monitoring disk activity with Performance Monitor. On some disk subsystems, enabling these counters might produce a small decrease in system performance, so you should disable them when monitoring of the system is completed. You must reboot the system after running Diskperf.

Diskperf –n sets the system to not use any disk performance counters.

For the full syntax of this command, type **diskperf /?** on the command line.

See Also: *Windows commands*

disk quotas

A mechanism for managing how much data users can store on disks.

Overview

Disk quotas are a feature of Microsoft Windows 2000, Windows XP, and Windows .NET Server that administrators can use to track and control disk usage on a per-user basis for each NTFS file system (NTFS) volume that the user stores data on. Support for disk quotas is built into the new version of NTFS on Windows 2000, Windows XP, and Windows .NET Server.

Disk quotas are tracked independently for each NTFS volume even if several volumes are on the same physical disk. For purposes of managing disk quotas for users, disk space usage is based on file and folder ownership. Windows 2000, Windows XP, and Windows .NET Server ignore compression when it calculates how much disk space a user is utilizing. Whatever is unallocated in a user's disk quota is reported as free space for applications that allow the user to access disk space.

Depending on how disk quotas are configured, when a user exceeds the specified disk limit, one of two things can occur:

- An event is logged to the system log.
- Disk access is blocked and an event is logged. The user is presented with an "insufficient disk space" error.

Implementation

To use disk quotas on an NTFS volume, you must first enable this feature when the volume is created and before any users have access to it. Typically, you will begin by setting more restrictive settings for all users, and then relax these settings for users who need more disk space or work with large files.

To enable disk quotas, set quota limits, and specify what happens when users exceed their quotas, use the Quota tab on the property sheet for an NTFS volume. To configure disk quotas for users, you essentially specify two values:

- **Quota limit:** How much disk space the user is allowed to use
- **Quota threshold:** The conditions under which an event should be logged to indicate that the user is nearing his or her quota limit

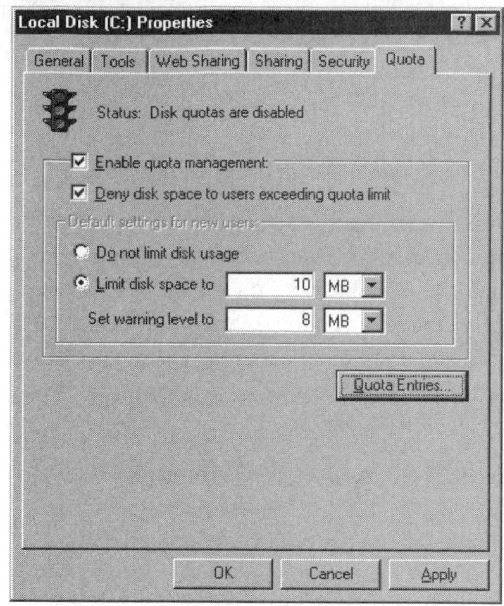

Disk quotas. *Configuring disk quotas in Windows 2000.*

For example, if the quota limit for a user is set to 10 megabytes (MB) while the quota threshold is specified as 8 MB, an event is logged when the user stores more than 8 MB of data on the volume, and the user is prevented from storing more than 10 MB of data on the volume.

To view the status of disk quotas on an NTFS volume for which this feature has been enabled, open the volume's property sheet and examine the traffic light icon. The light is

- Red if quotas are disabled
- Yellow if the NTFS file system is recalculating the status of quota compliance
- Green if quotas are enabled

If you want to track disk usage by user but do not want to deny users access to a volume, you can enable disk quotas but specify that users can exceed their disk quota limit. Note also that enabling disk quotas incurs slight overhead in file system performance.

See Also: *NTFS file system (NTFS), storage*

disk status

Information about whether a disk is healthy or has a problem.

Overview

In Microsoft Windows 2000, Windows XP, and Windows .NET Server, disk status is displayed in the Disk Management portion of the Computer Management console. The Status column shows the status indicators according to the following table. The letter *B* here indicates that the status indicator can apply to basic disks, and *D* indicates dynamic disks.

Disk Status

Disk Status	*Description/Prescription*
Online (BD)	The disk is accessible. There are no problems.
Online—Errors (D)	I/O errors detected. Try reactivating the disk to see whether the errors are transient.
Offline (D)	The disk is not accessible and might be corrupted, disconnected, or powered down. Try reactivating the disk, and check the cables and the controller.
Foreign (D)	The disk has been moved to this machine from another computer running Windows 2000 (same for Windows XP and Windows .NET Server). You must import the foreign disk before you can use it.
Unreadable (BD)	The disk is not accessible and might be corrupted, have I/O errors, or hardware failure. Try rescanning the disk or rebooting the system to see whether it recovers.
Unrecognized	The disk type is unknown, and the disk is probably from a different operating system, such as UNIX.
No Media	The drive is either a CD-ROM drive or some type of removable drive and has no media in it.

See Also: *storage*

Distance Vector Multicast Routing Protocol (DVMRP)

A multicast routing protocol based on the spanning tree algorithm.

Overview

Distance Vector Multicast Routing Protocol (DVMRP) is one of three routing protocols used for multicast routing, the other two being Protocol Independent Multicast Dense Mode (PIM-DM) and Multicast Open Shortest Path First (MOSPF). DVMRP is used for dense mode multicasting where the hosts receiving the multicast are densely congregated in large pockets of the network. DVMRP assumes that all hosts on connected subnets want to receive the multicast. A typical scenario where DVMRP might be used would be for webcasting sports events, concerts, or corporate presentations.

Implementation

DVMRP floods the network with multicast packets to try to get information out as rapidly as possible to the furthest corner of the network. DVMRP assumes that there is sufficient bandwidth to support this operation. Once a multicast session is established, DVMRP then prunes the routing tree by cutting off multicasts to routers whose connected networks have no hosts receiving them. If a router determines using Internet Group Membership Protocol (IGMP) that no downstream hosts or routers require the multicast transmission, it contacts the upstream DVMRP router and asks to be removed from its list for the multicast session.

DVMRP routers check their routing tables frequently to determine the optimal route to nearby DVMRP routers. DVMRP uses broadcasts to keep routing tables up to date, which tends to consume a lot of network bandwidth. As a result, DVMRP should only be implemented on connections that have sufficiently high bandwidth to support it.

See Also: *dense mode, Multicast Open Shortest Path First (MOSPF), multicasting, Protocol Independent Multicast-Dense Mode (PIM-DM), routing protocol*

D

distance vector routing algorithm

A routing algorithm used by certain types of routing protocols.

Overview

Also called the Bellman-Ford algorithm after its originators, the distance vector routing is an algorithm designed to enable routers to maintain up-to-date information in their routing tables. The main alternative to distance vector routing is link state routing, which is discussed in its own article elswhere in this book.

Implementation

Using the distance vector method, each router on the internetwork maintains a routing table that contains one entry for each possible remote subnet on the network. To do this, each router periodically advertises its routing table information to routers in adjacent subnets. Each routing advertisement contains the following information about each route in that routing table:

- The metric (hop count) for the route, which indicates the distance to the remote subnet
- The vector (direction) in which the route is located

These router advertisements are performed independently by all routers (that is, no synchronization exists between advertisements made by different routers). In addition, routers receiving advertisements do not generate acknowledgments, which reduces the overhead of routing protocol traffic.

Routers select the route with the lowest cost to each possible destination and add this to their own routing tables. Routers in adjacent subnets then propagate this information to more distant subnets hop by hop until information from all routers has spread throughout the entire internetwork and convergence (agreement between routing tables on all routers in the internetwork) is attained. The end result is that each router on the network is aware of all remote subnets on the network and has information concerning the shortest path to get to each remote subnet.

Uses

The Routing Information Protocol (RIP), which is supported by Microsoft Windows 2000, Windows XP, and Windows .NET Server, is one example of a dynamic routing protocol that uses the distance vector routing algorithm. Other examples are described in the article "distance vector routing protocol" elsewhere in this chapter.

Advantages and Disadvantages

Distance vector routing protocols (that is, protocols based on the distance vector routing algorithm) are generally simpler to understand and easier to configure than link state routing algorithm protocols. To configure a router that supports distance vector routing, you basically connect the interfaces to the various subnets and turn the router on. The router automatically discovers its neighbors, which add the new router to their routing tables as required.

The main disadvantage of the distance vector routing algorithm is that changes are propagated very slowly throughout a large internetwork because all routing tables must be recalculated. This is called the Slow Convergence Problem. When convergence is slow, it is possible that routing loops can temporarily form, which forward packets to black holes on the network, causing information to be lost. Most distance vector routing protocols implement use a technique such as the split horizon method to ensure that the chances of routing loops being formed are extremely small.

Another disadvantage of distance vector routing is that routing tables can become extremely large, making distance vector routing protocols unsuitable for large internetworks, and that route advertising generates a large amount of traffic overhead.

As a result of these issues, distance vector routing is generally best used in internetworks having 50 routers or fewer and in which the largest distance between two subnets is less than 16 hops. Despite these limitations, distance vector routing protocols are more popular than link state routing protocols, mainly because they are easier to set up and maintain (everything is automatic) and because their CPU processing requirements are small, which allows such protocols to be implemented on low-end and mid-end routers.

See Also: *distance vector routing protocol, link state routing algorithm, routing protocol*

distance vector routing protocol

Any routing protocol that is based on the distance vector routing algorithm.

Overview

The most popular routing protocols based on the distance vector routing protocol are

- **RIPv1 (Routing Information Protocol version 1):** This is a classful routing protocol that is suitable for small to mid-sized internetworks. RIPv1 supports both Internet Protocol (IP) and Internetwork Packet Exchange (IPX) routing.
- **RIPv2:** This is a newer version of RIP that supports variable length subnet masks (VLSMs).
- **IGRP (Interior Gateway Routing Protocol):** This is an interior gateway protocol (IGP) that uses a combination of different metrics for more efficient routing. IGRP was designed by Cisco Systems and is a proprietary routing protocol.
- **RTMP (Routing Table Maintenance Protocol):** This routing protocol is used in AppleTalk networks.

Advantages and Disadvantages

Distance vector routing protocols have some advantages over link state routing protocols: they are easier to configure and manage and their router advertisements are easier to understand and troubleshoot. On the other hand, distance vector routing protocols often have much larger routing tables, greater overhead of router traffic, long convergence times, and they scale poorly. As a result, they are most often used for small to mid-sized internetworks.

See Also: *distance vector routing algorithm, Interior Gateway Routing Protocol (IGRP), link state routing algorithm, Routing Information Protocol (RIP), routing protocol*

distinguished name (DN)

A method for uniquely naming objects within a directory.

Overview

Distinguished names (DNs) are part of the X.500 directory specifications and are used for locating and accessing objects using the Lightweight Directory Access Protocol (LDAP), and directories based on the X.500 or LDAP specifications are hierarchical in structure. For example, in an LDAP directory, the root or top node is a container that contains child nodes that can be either leaf nodes (end nodes) or containers themselves. An object that is a leaf node has a common name (CN) that identifies it, but this common name is not necessarily unique. By including with the common name the names of the root node (o node) and any containers and subcontainers (ou nodes) along the branch to the leaf node, a unique name can be constructed for the leaf node. This unique name is called the DN and is unique to the entire directory.

The DN for an object is thus formed by concatenation of the common name or relative distinguished name (RDN) of the object together with the names of each ancestor of the object all the way to the root object of the directory. As a result, if an object is renamed or moved to another container within a directory, its DN changes. Since this is undesirable from the point of view of applications accessing a directory, real-life directories such as Microsoft Corporation's Active Directory directory service use an internal naming scheme for objects that is invariant under object renames and moves (Active Directory uses globally unique identifiers [GUIDs] for internally naming objects).

Examples

DNs are one of the addressing formats for objects within Active Directory in Microsoft Windows 2000. In Active Directory, every object in the directory requires a unique name. Several kinds of names can be used to define a specific object in Active Directory, including

- **Distinguished name (DN):** This specifies the complete path to the object through the hierarchy of containers.
- **Relative distinguished name (RDN):** This is the portion of the distinguished name that is an attribute of the object itself.

- **User principal name (UPN):** This is the name used when a user logs on to the network.

For example, let's consider a User object within Active Directory. A User object is an example of a leaf object because it cannot contain other objects. User objects such as Jeff Smith are identified using CNs. A container is a directory object that can contain other objects. In Active Directory, containers are referred to as organizational units (OUs) because they are used to organize other objects into hierarchies of containers. For example, the user Jeff Smith would typically be contained within the Users container. At the top of the container hierarchy are the containers that represent different components of the domain itself. These components are called domain components (DCs). For example, if user Jeff Smith exists in the microsoft.com domain, the DN for this user is represented by the path DC=com,DC=microsoft,OU=Users,CN=Jeff Smith.

In Microsoft Exchange Server 5.5, which used its own proprietary directory instead of Active Directory, DNs were also used to identify recipients. Exchange automatically creates a DN for every recipient object in its directory database, including objects such as mailboxes, distribution lists, and public folders. For example, if a user Jeff Smith has a mailbox named JeffS located on an Exchange server in Redmond at the organization Microsoft, the DN for this user would be represented internally as O=Microsoft,OU=Redmond,CN=Recipients,CN=JeffS.

The Message Transfer Agent (MTA) uses a recipient's DN to determine how to route messages to that recipient within an Exchange organization.

See Also: *Active Directory, globally unique identifier (GUID), Lightweight Directory Access Protocol (LDAP), X.500*

distributed application

An application consisting of two or more parts that run on different machines but act together seamlessly.

Overview

In the simplest example of a distributed application, the user interface portion runs on a client machine while the processor- or storage-intensive portion runs on a server. This type of distributed application is called a client/server application. Examples of client/server applications include the following:

- Microsoft Exchange Server (back end) as a mail server with users running Microsoft Outlook (front end) on their client machines
- Microsoft Access (front end) as an interface for accessing database information stored in Microsoft SQL Server (back end)
- A Web application written using Active Server Pages (ASP) for Internet Information Services (IIS) (back end) that is accessed from a client machine running Microsoft Internet Explorer (front end)

In a more complex scenario, three tiers are used to create a distributed application. The back end may be an SQL database containing customer or sales information. The front end might be a simple Web browser, used by the employee to request sales information from the database. The middle tier of the distributed application would be the Web application running on an IIS machine.

See Also: *client/server, distributed computing*

Distributed Component Object Model (DCOM)

A Microsoft programming technology for developing distributed applications.

Overview

Distributed Component Object Model (DCOM) is a Microsoft technology developed in 1996 for component-based development of software that is network-aware. Using DCOM, developers can create network-aware applications using Component Object Model (COM) components. DCOM works under various network transports, including Transmission Control Protocol/Internet Protocol (TCP/IP), and is basically a set of extensions to COM. DCOM is the preferred method for building client/server applications in Windows 2000, Windows XP, and Windows .NET Server, and it was formerly known as Network OLE.

Implementation

DCOM functions as a client/server protocol that provides distributed network services to COM, allowing DCOM-enabled software components to communicate over a network in a similar fashion to the method by which COM components communicate among themselves on a single machine. DCOM client objects make requests for services from DCOM server objects on different machines on the network using a standard set of interfaces.

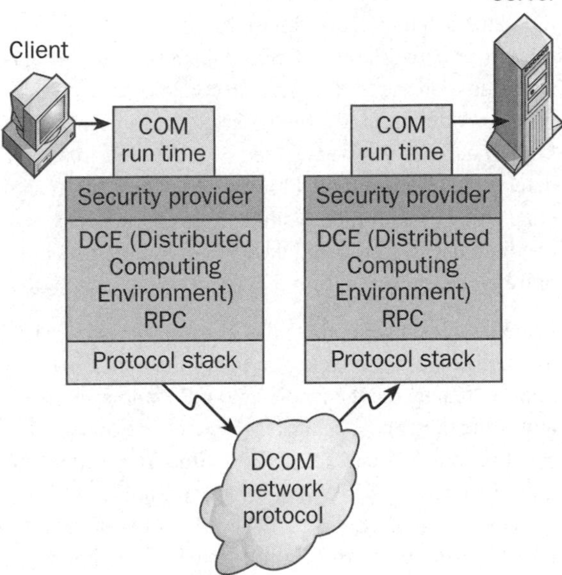

Distributed Component Object Model (DCOM). *How DCOM works.*

The client object cannot call the server object directly. Instead, the operating system intercepts the DCOM request and uses interprocess communication mechanisms such as remote procedure calls (RPCs) to provide a transparent communication mechanism between the client and server objects. The COM run time provides the necessary object-oriented services to the client and server objects. The COM run time also uses the security provider and RPCs to create network frames that conform to the DCOM standard.

In Microsoft Windows 2000, DCOM requests are sent using RPCs. Windows 2000 use security features such as permissions to enable software components to securely and reliably communicate over the network.

See Also: *client/server, Component Object Model (COM), distributed application*

distributed computing

A programming model that distributes processing across a network.

Overview

The architecture of programming applications has gone through several evolutionary steps over the last few decades. The original mainframe computing model had all the processing done centrally on the mainframe, with dumb terminals used for input and displaying results. The next evolutionary step was client/server computing where the client and server shared different aspects of the processing. Applications had to be specially tailored to take advantage of the client/server processing model. Recently a three-tier model has become dominant, which augments the client/server paradigm with a middle tier that encapsulates business logic in programming constructs.

The next evolutionary step in business computing is the distributed computing model. In distributed computing, there is no single centralized server. Instead, network communications are used to connect servers, clients, handheld devices, and other smart devices into a processing fabric. The different components of this fabric may be scattered widely across a network.

Microsoft Corporation's new .NET platform is designed to maximize processing gains through implementing a distributed computing model for building Web services and applications. Distributed computing is poised to revolutionize business services and how they are developed, and .NET supports peer-to-peer (P2P) computing as one manifestation of its distributed computing model.

See Also: *client/server, .NET platform, peer-to-peer network*

Distributed Denial of Service (DDoS)

A type of denial of service (DoS) attack that employs a large number of intermediate hosts to multiply the effect of the attack.

Overview

Although a DoS attack typically uses the attacker's machine or group of machines to launch it, a DDoS attack uses unwitting third-party hosts instead. The result can be devastating if hundreds—or thousands—of machines are involved.

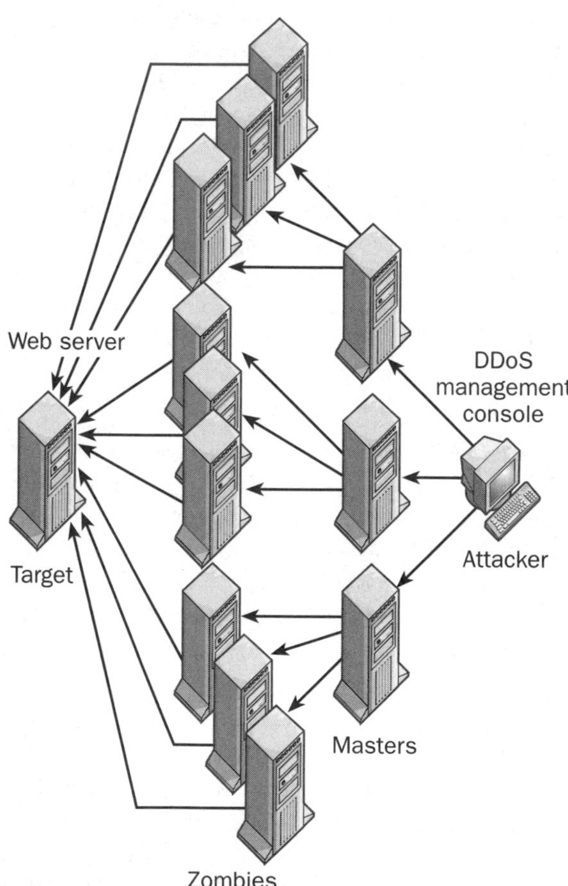

Distributed Denial of Service (DDoS). *How a DDoS attack works.*

To launch a DDoS attack against a specific Web server, an attacker first finds a vulnerable network and installs DDoS tools on hundreds or even thousands of hosts on that network. Common tools used include Tribe Flood-Net (TFN), TFN2K, trinoo, Stacheldraht, and many others easily downloaded from locations on the Internet. These compromised hosts become "zombies" under the attacker's control (other terms used to describe them include agents, daemons, or DDoS servers). Linux and Solaris systems have been the most popular systems exploited as zombies so far. A good indicator that an attacker might be trying to compromise your network by installing DDoS tools on hosts is a sudden increase in Rcp (remote copy protocol) traffic, which is often used to install these tools remotely. This kind of activity can be detected by a network intrusion detection system (firewall logs are less help, as attackers usually compromise a single host on the network and then use Rcp to install the tools on other hosts internally on the network from that point on).

Once the intermediate network is compromised and tools installed, the attacker launches the attack using a remote management console, and the zombies then attack the target host using a DoS attack method such as synchronous idle character (SYN) flooding, User Datagram Protocol (UDP) flooding, a smurf attack, or Internet Control Message Protocol (ICMP) flooding. The attack is usually overwhelming, usually bringing down the targeted server and often saturating the target's network so that other servers on the network are unable to communicate as well. Address spoofing is used to make it difficult to trace the machines launching the attack, and even if these zombies are identified, it is usually even more difficult to trace the single machine from which the attacker is managing the attack. An even more insidious version of DDoS makes it even harder to track the attacker by employing another layer of intermediate machines called masters, which are controlled by the attacker's management console and which themselves control the zombies. A master is typically the first host compromised on an intermediate network, and a full-scale DDoS attack may employ dozens of

intermediate networks, each with their own master and hundreds of zombies.

Prospects

The most famous DDoS attack was instituted by Mafiaboy, a Canadian teenager who allegedly brought down a number of major Web sites for hours in February 2000, including Amazon.com, Buy.com, CNN.com, eBay, E-Trade.com, Yahoo!, and ZDNet. The attack was performed using tools that are easily downloadable from a number of sites on the Internet.

There is still no simple solution for protecting sites against DDoS attacks. The main problem is the large number of networks connected to the Internet that are poorly secured and are open to exploitation for using their machines as zombies for launching DDoS attacks on other, better-secured sites. Lack of vigilance on the part of the administrators of these vulnerable networks thus affects the success of everyone's sites on the Internet. Omissions such as allowing directed inbound broadcasts to networks and failing to implement ingress and egress filtering properly on routers on a network's border are typical mistakes by administrators that render corporate networks vulnerable to hijacking for performing DDoS attacks.

One step forward was the establishment in 2001 of the Information Technology Information Sharing and Analysis Center (ITISAC) by the U.S. Department of Commerce. ITISAC is designed to help companies share information about DDoS attacks to better defend against them. Another issue is the impending prospect of organizations being held liable for their poorly secured corporate networks should hackers establish zombies on these networks and use them to launch DDoS attacks against other sites. The Internet Engineering Task Force (IETF) is also involved and has established a working group RFC 2267+ to help strategize on the best way to deal with DDoS attacks. Despite these initiatives, the Internet remains vulnerable to such attacks and will likely continue to be so for the immediate future.

See Also: *denial of service (DoS), hacking, network security*

Distributed file system (Dfs)

A network file system that makes many shares on different file servers look like a single hierarchy of shares on a single file server.

Overview

Distributed file system (Dfs) is a feature of the Microsoft Windows 2000 and Windows .NET Server operating systems and a separately available add-on for the Windows NT operating system. Dfs allows file servers and network shares to be logically organized into a single Dfs directory tree. This simplifies management of network resources and makes it easier for users to locate and access network resources. From the user's perspective, Dfs makes it appear that there is only one server containing a hierarchical tree of resources, while in fact these resources might be distributed across multiple servers in different locations.

Dfs simplifies directory browsing, offers search tools that simplify locating network resources, and offers administrative tools for building and managing Dfs directory trees. It also eliminates the need for Windows 95, Windows 98, or Windows NT Workstation clients to form multiple persistent network connections because users require only one persistent connection to the directory tree.

Implementation

In the Windows 2000 and Windows .NET Server implementation, you first open the Dfs snap-in for Microsoft Management Console (MMC) to create a Dfs root node. You can then create Dfs child nodes under the root node. Each child represents a shared folder that can be located anywhere on the network. When users want to access a resource on the network, they navigate through the Dfs tree and do not need to know the particular server the resource is located on. Users must have Dfs client software installed on their machines. Dfs client software is included with Windows 2000, Windows XP, Windows .NET Server, Windows NT, and Windows 98. An optional Dfs client can be downloaded for Windows 95 from the Microsoft Web site.

You can configure Dfs to operate in two ways:

- **Stand-alone Dfs:** This type of Dfs stores the description of the Dfs file system topology on a single computer. If that computer fails, the entire Dfs system goes down, although users can still access resources the traditional way using mapped network drives or Universal Naming Convention (UNC) paths if they know which servers these resources are stored on and the names of the shares.

- **Fault-tolerant Dfs:** This type of Dfs stores the Dfs topology information in Active Directory directory service on Windows 2000 and Windows .NET Server domain controllers. This configuration is better for fault tolerance and file replication.

Notes

If a server containing Dfs shares fails, you can simply move the files to another machine, create new shares, and map the existing Dfs child nodes to the new shares. Your users will not even know that anything has changed. If you assign a user permission to access a shared folder, that person automatically has permission to access it through the Dfs tree as well.

See Also: *file system, storage*

Distributed Management Task Force (DMTF)

An industry consortium that develops specifications for cross-platform management standards.

Overview

The Distributed Management Task Force (DMTF) is a consortium of industry players that are developing specifications and standards for managing disparate systems using a common and ubiquitous tool, the Web browser. The DMTF was formerly known as the Desktop Management Task Force, and it has the support of most major networking and operating system vendors.

The DMTF has been working on several initiatives since its inception in 1996:

- **Web-Based Enterprise Management (WBEM):** A set of standards for developing systems to manage networks and systems using simple Web browsers.
- **Common Information Model (CIM):** A set of schema for describing information collected for network and systems management purposes.
- **Directory Enabled Networking (DEN):** A specification for how to store network and systems management information in a directory.

A complementary set of standards for cross-platform network and system administration is being developed by the Internet Engineering Task Force's (IETF) Policy Framework Working Group.

Notes

Windows Management Interface (WMI) is Microsoft Corporation's implementation of the DMTF'S WBEM architecture. WMI is a core feature of the Microsoft Windows 2000, Windows XP, and Windows .NET Server operating system platforms.

For More Information

You can find the DMTF at *www.dmtf.org.*

See Also: *browser (Web browser), Common Information Model (CIM), Directory Enabled Network (DEN), network management, Web-Based Enterprise Management (WBEM), Windows Management Instrumentation (WMI)*

distribution box

A fixed or freestanding miniature patch panel in an enclosure.

Overview

Typically, horizontal cable runs are connected to the punchdown blocks within the distribution box, and drop cables are plugged into the RJ-45 ports of the box. You can thus use distribution boxes to provide central cabling points away from walls. Stations can then be plugged and unplugged from an accessible location in the work area instead of from the back of the workstations (after you bend down and crawl behind the machine) or from the land drops in the wall (which are often hidden behind desks or other obstacles).

Uses

Use distribution boxes for classrooms and work areas in which computers frequently need to be moved around and rearranged.

See Also: *patch cable, patch panel*

distribution group

One of two types of groups within Active Directory directory service in Microsoft Windows 2000, the other type being security groups.

Overview

While security groups can be listed in discretionary access control lists (DACLs) for controlling access to resources or sending e-mail to users, distribution groups can be used only for e-mail purposes. By sending e-mail to a distribution group, you send e-mail to every member of that group.

Distribution groups can be converted to security groups and vice versa as long as the domain is in native mode. You cannot perform conversion if the domain is in mixed mode.

See Also: *group, security group*

distribution list

A grouping of recipients in Microsoft Exchange Server that you can use to send a single message to multiple users simultaneously.

Overview

When a message is sent to a distribution list, it is sent to all recipients on the list. Distribution lists provide a convenient way of performing mass mailings to users. For example, a marketing department might create several hundred custom recipients for regular customers outside the Exchange organization. These custom recipients can then be included as members within a single distribution list. When the department wants to send e-mail to its customers announcing new products or services, the e-mail can be sent to the distribution list. A computer running Exchange Server (configured to expand distribution lists) makes sure that each custom recipient receives a copy of the message.

distribution server

A server that contains the source files for a software product and that is used to perform remote installations.

Overview

As an example, if you want to perform remote installations of Microsoft Windows 2000 Professional on client machines, you can copy the I386 folder from the CD onto a folder called NTWKS on your file server, and then share this folder. Windows NT Workstation clients can then connect to this share and run the Setup program to upgrade their systems to Windows 2000 Professional.

Notes

When you copy files from the CD to a folder on the server, use the Xcopy command or, if you are using Windows Explorer, be sure to first choose Options from the View menu and select Show All Files. Otherwise, some hidden files will not be copied, and installation will fail.

DLC

Generally refers to the services that the data-link layer of the Open Systems Interconnection (OSI) reference model provides to adjacent layers of the OSI protocol stack. Specifically, a Data Link Control (DLC) is a specialized network protocol.

See: *Data Link Control (DLC)*

DLL

Stands for dynamic-link library, a file containing executable routines that can be loaded on demand by an application.

See: *dynamic-link library (DLL)*

DLT

Stands for Digital Linear Tape, a tape backup technology.

See: *Digital Linear Tape (DLT)*

DMI

Stands for Desktop Management Interface, a standard for managing desktop systems developed by the Desktop Management Task Force (DMTF), now the Distributed Management Task Force.

See: *Desktop Management Interface (DMI)*

DML

Stands for Data Manipulation Language, a subset of Structured Query Language (SQL)

See: *Data Manipulation Language (DML)*

D

DMS

Stands for Defense Messaging System, a global messaging system for the U.S. Department of Defense (DoD).

See: *Defense Messaging System (DMS)*

DMT

Stands for discrete multitone, a line coding technique used in Asymmetric Digital Subscriber Line (ADSL).

See: *discrete multitone (DMT)*

DMTF

Stands for Distributed Management Task Force, an industry consortium that develops specifications for cross-platform management standards.

See: *Distributed Management Task Force (DMTF)*

DMZ

Stands for demilitarized zone, a former name for perimeter network, a security network at the boundary between a corporate local area network (LAN) and the Internet.

See: *perimeter network*

DN

Stands for distinguished name, a method for uniquely naming objects within a directory.

See: *distinguished name (DN)*

DNA

Short for Windows DNA, an application development model from Microsoft Corporation for highly adaptable business solutions that use Microsoft's digital nervous system paradigm.

See: *Windows Distributed interNet Applications Architecture (Windows DNA)*

DNS

Stands for Domain Name System, a hierarchical naming system for identifying Transmission Control Protocol/Internet Protocol (TCP/IP) hosts on the Internet.

See: *Domain Name System (DNS)*

DNS client

A client machine configured to send name resolution queries to a name server.

Overview

A Domain Name System (DNS) client is also called a resolver because it uses name servers to resolve a remote host's name into its Internet Protocol (IP) address. To accomplish this, it sends such a request to a name server (a DNS server), which then returns the IP address of the remote host.

DNS client software is built into operating systems that support TCP/IP to enable client machines to issue DNS queries to name servers. For example, on Microsoft Windows platforms, the DNS client software makes possible the use of DNS names for browsing the Internet using Microsoft Internet Explorer.

In Windows operating systems, you must configure the IP address of the DNS server in the client's TCP/IP property sheet in order for the DNS client software to work properly. With dial-up networking connections to the Internet, this information can be communicated to the client machine during negotiation of the Point-to-Point Protocol (PPP) connection with the Internet service provider (ISP).

See: *Domain Name System (DNS), name server*

DNS console

A snap-in for the Microsoft Management Console (MMC) in Microsoft Windows 2000 and Windows .NET Server that enables administrators to manage Windows 2000 Servers and Windows .NET Server running as Domain Name System (DNS) servers.

Overview

You can use the DNS console to

- Create and maintain the DNS database of host name to Internet Protocol (IP) address mappings
- Create and manage zones of authority
- Create start of authority (SOA), name server (NS), address (A), CNAME, and other resource records in the DNS database
- View DNS server statistics

- Control how zones are stored and replicated between DNS servers
- Configure how DNS servers will process DNS queries and handle dynamic updates
- Configure security for specific zones and resource records

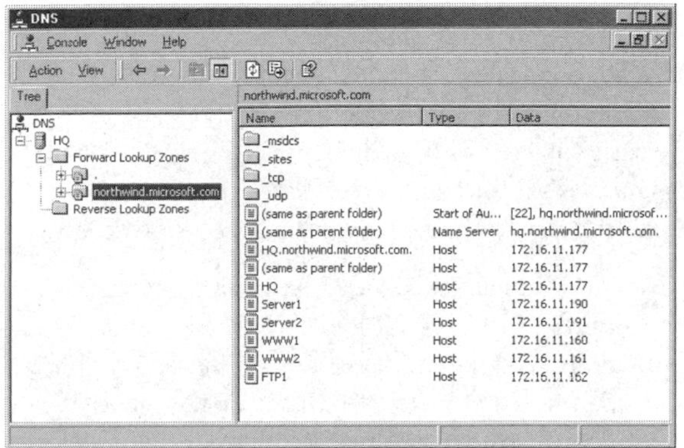

DNS console. *The DNS console in Windows 2000.*

Notes

Windows 2000 Server and Windows .NET Server include a new command-line utility, Dnscmd, which can be used for managing certain aspects of DNS servers. This utility can be run from the command prompt or scripted into batch files to automate certain aspects of DNS administration. To use this command, you must install the Windows 2000 Support Tools from the \Support\Tools folder on the Windows 2000 product CD (Windows .NET Server also supports Dnscmd and is also part of the Windows .NET Server Support Tools). Type **dnscmd /?** to see the syntax for this command.

See Also: *Domain Name System (DNS), DNS server, Microsoft Management Console (MMC)*

DNS database

The collection of database files, or zone files, and associated files that contain resource records for a domain.

Overview

Zone files are stored on a name server and are used to provide name resolution in response to name lookup requests. On Berkeley Internet Name Domain (BIND) name servers and Microsoft Windows NT Domain Name System (DNS) servers, these DNS database files are stored as flat-file database (text) files, that is, simple ASCII files.

On a Windows NT server with the Microsoft DNS Service installed, DNS database files are located in the \System32\DNS directory. The DNS database files in this directory are

- The zone file, which has the extension .dns and contains the resource records that the DNS server manages
- The reverse lookup file, which resolves Internet Protocol (IP) addresses into host names
- The cache file, which has the names and IP addresses of the root name servers for DNS
- The boot file, which is used for startup configuration of the DNS server and is needed only for resolving the names of hosts that are located outside the zones for which the DNS server is authoritative

On a Windows 2000 or Windows .NET Server DNS server, DNS database information can be either stored in the preceding standard text files or can be integrated into Active Directory directory service, depending on how DNS is installed and configured on the machine. Using Active Directory for storing DNS database information has the benefits of Active Directory's enhanced security features and multimaster replication, providing faster and more efficient replication of DNS zone information than using standard DNS text files.

See Also: *Active Directory, Domain Name System (DNS), zone*

DNS namespace

The collection of domains, subdomains, and fully qualified domain names (FQDNs) within the Domain Name System (DNS).

Overview

DNS uses a namespace that is hierarchical in structure and is stored as a distributed database on servers called name servers. The term *namespace* can have two meanings:

- The abstract space of FQDNs that are used to identify hosts on the Internet or on a private corporate TCP/IP internetwork

- The physical space of DNS database files (zone files) that exist on name servers and that actually define or contain the abstract DNS namespace

D

Notes

Active Directory directory service in Microsoft Windows 2000 and Windows .NET Server requires that a DNS namespace be configured in a domain-based implementation of Windows 2000 or Windows .NET Server in an enterprise.

See Also: *Domain Name System (DNS), fully qualified domain name (FQDN), name server*

DNS query

A request to a name server for name lookup.

Overview

DNS queries can occur two ways:

- Between resolvers and name servers
- Between name servers and other name servers

Queries can be answered by the queried name server from its local Domain Name System (DNS) database, from previously cached query results, or by a referral to another name server.

The three basic kinds of DNS queries are recursive queries, iterative queries, and inverse queries. For more information on these types of DNS queries, see their respective entries in this book.

See Also: *Domain Name System (DNS), host name resolution, inverse query, iterative query, recursive query*

DNSSEC

Stands for DNS Security Extensions, an enhancement of the Domain Name System (DNS) that supports cryptographic authentication of domain names.

See: *DNS Security Extensions (DNSSEC)*

DNS Security Extensions (DNSSEC)

An enhancement of the Domain Name System (DNS) that supports cryptographic authentication of domain names.

Overview

DNS Security Extensions (DNSSEC) uses public-key encryption and digital signatures to enable name servers to verify the identity of domain names. DNSSEC is a set of enhancements to existing name servers that will allow users to be certain that the Web site they are seeing in response to looking up a URL is in fact the one they desired and not some other "spoofed" site.

History

DNS has long been viewed in many quarters as the weak link in the Internet's chain of protocols. DNS's lack of security makes spoofing domain names easy, allowing malicious users to hijack Web traffic and redirect it to sites different from the ones users intended to access.

The most famous incident of Web site spoofing occurred in 1997. An IT (information technology) consultant in Washington State named Eugene Kashpureff set up servers to hijack Web traffic on the Internet and redirect it away from Network Solution's InterNIC name servers to his own name servers, dubbed AlterNIC. As a result, a large segment of legitimate traffic on the Internet was disrupted for about a week, with significant financial loss to many involved.

Many other Web site spoofing incidents have occurred since then, highlighting the fundamental weakness with the security of DNS and driving forward the search for solutions that culminated in RFC 2535, which defines DNSSEC.

Implementation

DNSSEC works by enabling name servers to verify the information they exchange with each other using public key cryptography and digital signatures. Typically, a user enters a URL into his or her Web browser to access a site on the Internet. The browser's Hypertext Transfer Protocol (HTTP) GET request is forwarded to the local name server, which is either a corporate name server in a large enterprise or a name server at a small to medium-sized company's Internet service provider (ISP). This local name server then contacts a root name server to locate a name server authoritative for the top-level domain listed in the URL, which then directs the local name server to the name server authoritative for the second-level domain in the URL, and so on until the Internet Protocol (IP) address of the desired Web site can be looked up and communications established. The role of DNSSEC in all this is that when these exchanges are going on between name servers, digital signatures are issued and verified at each stage to verify that the responses are being received from the actual name servers rather than spoofing name servers.

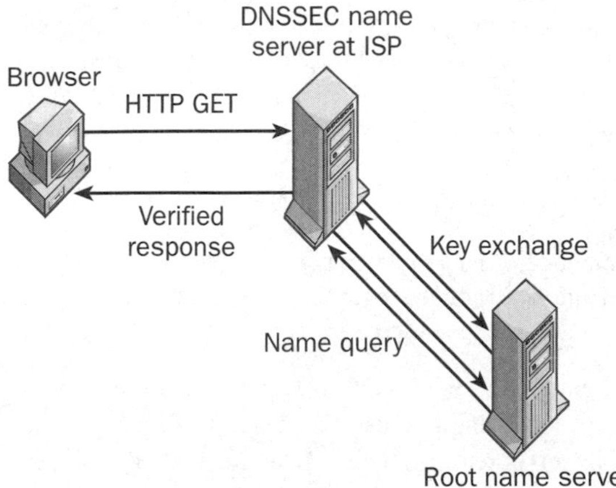

DNS Security Extensions (DNSSEC). *How DNSSEC works.*

DNSSEC works at both the zone and resource record levels to secure DNS information. DNSSEC requires several new resource records in name server databases:

- **SIG:** This resource record supplies digital signatures signed with private keys to encrypt resource record information.
- **PUB:** This resource record supplies the necessary public keys to decrypt encrypted resource record information.
- **NXT:** This resource record determines which records are mapped to which names.

Marketplace

The first DNS name server software to support DNSSEC is also the most popular in the Internet community, the Berkeley Internet Name Domain (BIND). DNSSEC is included in BIND 9, the latest release of the name server software, and is being packaged with most major UNIX operating systems including those from Sun Microsystems, Hewlett-Packard, and Red Hat Linux. The funding for developing DNSSEC for BIND 9 was provided by the U.S. Defense Information Systems Agency (DISA) and the work was done by NAI Labs and the Internet Software Consortium (ISC).

Although larger enterprises will likely move quickly to upgrade their name servers to support DNSSEC, smaller businesses may balk at the expense involved, particularly in the management of DNSSEC name servers. To meet this need, companies such as Nominum and UltraDNS Corporation are planning to offer outsourced DNSSEC services to such businesses.

Issues

A number of issues may delay the full-scale deployment of DNSSEC on name servers all across the Internet (DNSSEC must be widely deployed for it to work reliably):

- DNSSEC has greater processor and memory requirements than standard DNS in order to support the additional load of issuing and managing digital certificates and cryptographic keys.
- DNSSEC utilizes greater network bandwidth for its communications, both with DNS clients (resolvers) and with other name servers.
- DNSSEC is more complicated to install and maintain than standard DNS, particularly because of the key management issues involved.
- The root name servers of the Internet must be upgraded first for DNSSEC to properly operate, and this requires political decisiveness on the part of the Internet Corporation for Assigned Names and Numbers (ICANN), the agency that runs most of these servers.
- Regional and local ISPs must upgrade their name servers next in order for DNSSEC to succeed, and this involves additional costs due to hardware and management overhead that some ISPs may feel reluctant to commit.
- Finally, name servers have traditionally been managed on an " If it ain't broke, don't fix it" basis, where network administrators are reluctant to upgrade a server that is critical for the successful operation of a dot-com enterprise.

Despite all of these issues, there is still tremendous pressure for DNSSEC to go ahead, and it is likely to be fully deployed across the Internet in the next few years.

Prospects

DNSSEC is seen by many as an essential upgrade for the Internet's DNS infrastructure. Governments, B2B exchanges, financial servers, and others are likely to be early adopters of this technology. The U.S. military is already taking steps to implement DNSSEC by enhancing existing BIND 8 name servers with additional software to make the .mil top-level domain more secure.

See Also: *Berkeley Internet Name Domain (BIND), Domain Name System (DNS), name server*

DNS server

A server that is used to resolve host names or fully qualified domain names (FQDNs) into Internet Protocol (IP) addresses on a TCP/IP network.

Overview

A Domain Name System (DNS) server, which is also called a name server, accomplishes name resolution by accepting DNS queries from DNS clients (called resolvers) and by performing DNS queries among other DNS servers, depending on how the servers have been configured.

The most common type of name server in use on the Internet is the Berkeley Internet Name Domain (BIND) name server, which runs on the UNIX operating system. For Windows 2000 and Windows .NET Server deployments using Active Directory directory service, Microsoft Windows 2000 Server and Windows .NET Server can function as a DNS server and are managed using an administrative tool, DNS console, which is a snap-in for the Microsoft Management Console (MMC). Windows 2000 and Windows .NET Server DNS servers include advanced capabilities such as dynamic update, which allows DNS servers to update their DNS database files automatically using Dynamic Host Configuration Protocol (DHCP). Another feature of Windows 2000 and Windows .NET Server is tight integration of DNS and Active Directory. For example, when a Windows 2000, Windows XP, or Windows .NET Server client needs to locate a Windows 2000 or Windows .NET Server domain controller, the NetLogon service uses the DNS server's support for the SRV resource record to allow registration of domain controllers in the local DNS namespace.

Notes

DNS servers can provide a simple means of load balancing connections to heavily used file or application servers such as Internet Information Services (IIS). The method is called Round Robin DNS, and it works as its name implies. Say you have three Web servers hosting identical content and you want to load balance incoming Hypertext Transfer Protocol (HTTP) requests across these servers. You can create three A records in the DNS zone file, each with the same host name but different IP addresses, one IP address for each Web server, as shown in this example:

```
www.northwind.microsoft.com          172.16.8.33
www.northwind.microsoft.com          172.16.8.34
www.northwind.microsoft.com          172.16.8.35
```

When a DNS client requests resolution of the name www.northwind.microsoft.com into its IP address, the DNS server returns all three IP addresses (.33, .34, .35), and the client chooses the first address (.33) and sends the HTTP request to the Web server associated with this address. The next time the DNS server receives the same name resolution request, it rotates the IP addresses in round-robin fashion (.34, .35, .33) and returns them to the client. The client picks the first address, which is now .34. This way, each DNS name resolution returns a different IP address, and the load is balanced between the Web servers.

The drawback to using Round Robin DNS is that if a server fails, DNS will continue to return the address of the failed server.

See Also: *Berkeley Internet Name Domain (BIND), Domain Name System (DNS)*

DOCSIS

Stands for Data Over Cable Interface Specification, a specification defining standards for implementation of cable modem systems.

See: *Data Over Cable Interface Specification (DOCSIS)*

Document Object Model (DOM)

A set of programming interfaces for developing and managing Extensible Markup Language (XML) documents.

Overview

Document Object Model (DOM) has been a major driving force behind the development and proliferation of XML tools and standards. This is because DOM provides programmers with standard application programming interfaces (APIs) for representing and manipulating XML data. XML parsers based on DOM are widely implemented in Web browsers and other Web client tools, and the evolution of DOM is in large part driving the development of these tools.

DOM is a recommendation of the World Wide Web Consortium (W3C), and in its original version, it lets programmers model the data hierarchy of XML documents as objects that can be manipulated in Java, JavaScript, C++, and other languages. Using these and other languages, programmers can write scripts and applications that can dynamically modify the content, style, and structure of XML documents.

DOM was originally targeted toward small XML documents that could be loaded in entirety into memory and manipulated using repetitive operations. Because XML documents can be relatively large, a newer version called DOM 2 has been developed that includes a number of new features not supported by the original DOM, including support for

- Programmatically loading and saving XML documents
- Searching APIs for programmatic querying of properties and data in XML documents
- Programmatic implementation of custom namespaces for combining XML from different sources
- Programmatic management of cascading style sheets (CSS 1 and 2)

The W3C DOM Working Group is currently at work on DOM 3.

Marketplace

Support for DOM is included in products from many vendors of XML products, including Microsoft Corporation, Oracle Corporation, IBM, SoftQuad, and others. Microsoft Internet Explorer 5.5 also supports key aspects of DOM 2, including APIs for custom namespaces and cascading style sheets.

See Also: *World Wide Web Consortium (W3C), XML*

document type definition (DTD)

A file that defines the allowed structure of an Extensible Markup Language (XML) document.

Overview

Document type definitions (DTDs) are used in XML to specify the structure of documents. For example, Hypertext Markup Language (HTML) documents are defined by the HTML DTD, which is implemented in Web browsers such as Microsoft Internet Explorer and Web page editing software such as Microsoft FrontPage. The DTD specifies which kinds of tags are mandatory and which are optional, and also the range of allowed values for each type of tag.

DTD originated as part of the Standard Generalized Markups Language (SGML) specification developed by the International Standards Organization (ISO) in the 1980s. DTD is now a basic part of the XML specification.

Implementation

DTDs are implemented as plain-text files. They use a highly condensed language or syntax, which is very concise and can be parsed rapidly and efficiently. Schemas are another feature of XML and provide functionality similar to DTDs. The main difference is that schemas are more verbose than DTDs since they are written in XML instead of the more concise (but less readable) DTD language.

See Also: *Hypertext Markup Language (HTML), XML*

DoD model

A networking model developed by the U.S. Department of Defense (DoD).

D

Overview

The DoD model was developed in the 1970s as the networking model for the Transmission Control Protocol/Internet Protocol (TCP/IP), which was first deployed by in the ARPANET project and is now the worldwide de facto standard for the Internet. The DoD model is older than the seven-layer Open Systems Interconnection (OSI) model, which was developed in the 1980s by the International Organization for Standardization (ISO) to provide a more detailed framework for developing network protocols.

Architecture

The DoD model consists of four layers. These layers map loosely to the seven-layer OSI model in the fashion described below. Describing the DoD layers from the top down, they are

- **Application/Process Layer:** Also called simply Application Layer, this layer covers the functions of the top three layers of the OSI model. TCP/IP protocols at this layer include Hypertext Transfer Protocol (HTTP), File Transfer Protocol (FTP), Simple Mail Transfer Protocol (SMTP), Simple Network Management Protocol (SNMP), and many others.
- **Host-to-Host Layer:** Also called the Transport Layer, this layer functions similarly to the OSI model Transport layer. Protocols at this layer include Transmission Control Protocol (TCP) and User Datagram Protocol (UDP).
- **Internetworking Layer:** This layer functions similarly to the OSI model Network Layer. Protocols at this layer include Internet Protocol (IP), Internet Control Message Protocol (ICMP), Internet Group Membership Protocol (IGMP), and Address Resolution Protocol (ARP).
- **Network Interface Layer:** This layer functions similarly to the OSI model Data Link and Physical layers. There are no TCP/IP protocols at this layer. Instead, TCP/IP runs over standard networking architectures such as Ethernet and Token Ring, which are defined at this layer.

See Also: *OSI model, Transmission Control Protocol/Internet Protocol (TCP/IP)*

DOM

Stands for Document Object Model, a set of programming interfaces for developing and managing Extensible Markup Language (XML) documents.

See: *Document Object Model (DOM)*

Domain Admins

A built-in group on Microsoft Windows NT, Windows 2000, and Windows .NET Server networks for users who need administrator-level access to systems.

Overview

The Domain Admins group simplifies administration of users on the network. It is a global group and does not have any preassigned system rights. The initial membership of the group is the sole user account called Administrator. Other user accounts that are added to this group gain rights and privileges equivalent to those of the Administrator account and can perform actions similar to those of the Administrator account. All network administrators in a given domain should be members of this group.

Notes

On Windows 2000– and Windows .NET Server–based networks, the Domain Admins group is created by default in the Users organizational unit (OU) within Active Directory directory service.

See Also: *built-in group*

domain blocking

The ability to block traffic from a specific Domain Name System (DNS) domain.

Overview

Domain blocking is a security technology used in Microsoft Internet Information Server (IIS) Web servers to protect them from undesirable traffic. It was first introduced with IIS4.

Domain blocking allows IIS administrators to grant or deny access to content on the server based on a client's Internet Protocol (IP) address, subnet, or Internet domain name. This is a useful security feature for protecting machines running Internet Information Server from repeated attack by hackers. Domain blocking can be applied at various levels, including the following:

- All virtual servers on the machine (master level)
- A specific virtual server
- A specific virtual directory
- A specific file

See Also: *domain name, IP address, subnet*

domain controller

A server running Microsoft Windows NT, Windows 2000, or Windows .NET Server that manages security for the domain.

Overview

Users and computers that need to obtain access to network resources within the domain must be authenticated by a domain controller in the domain. Windows NT domain controllers are the foundation of Windows NT Directory Services (NTDS), and Windows 2000 and Windows .NET Server domain controllers are based on Active Directory directory service.

In a Windows NT–based network, the domain controllers form a hierarchy. There are two types of Windows NT domain controller:

- **Primary domain controller (PDC):** This contains a writeable master copy of the domain directory database. A domain can have only one PDC, which is at the top of the domain controller hierarchy. All changes to directory information (such as user accounts or passwords) must be made on the PDC.
- **Backup domain controller (BDC):** This contains read-only replicas of the domain directory database stored on the PDC. There can be zero or more BDCs per domain. BDCs provide redundancy and load balancing for the domain. Periodically, the BDCs in a domain undergo directory synchronization with the PDC to ensure that the BDCs contain an accurate copy of the domain directory database. This replication ensures the proper functioning of the NTDS.

A Windows 2000 or Windows .NET Server domain controller is any Windows 2000 server or Windows .NET Server with the optional Active Directory installed. Windows 2000 and Windows .NET Server domain controllers contain a complete, writeable copy of the Active Directory information for the domain in which they are installed. Run the Active Directory Installation Wizard to promote any Windows 2000 or Windows .NET Server member server to the role of a domain controller. A domain controller manages information in the Active Directory database and enables users to log on to the domain, be authenticated for accessing resources in the domain, and search the directory for information about users and network resources. A Windows 2000 or Windows .NET Server domain controller contains a writeable copy of the domain directory database.

Unlike in a Windows NT–based network, where domain controllers are in a hierarchy, all domain controllers in a Windows 2000– or Windows .NET Server–based network are equal, and changes to the domain directory database can be made at any domain controller. Replication of directory information between Windows 2000 and Windows .NET Server domain controllers follows a multimaster model. In this configuration, each domain controller acts as a peer to all other domain controllers. In other words, there are no primary or backup domain controllers in Windows 2000 or Windows .NET Server, only domain controllers.

Although most domain controller options (sending and receiving updates that add, move, copy, and delete objects from the directory) are multimaster in nature, a few domain controller operations function on only certain domain controllers. These special functions are called flexible single-master operations (FSMO) and perform functions such as modifying the schema, assigning pools of relative identifiers to other domain controllers within a domain, emulating a Windows NT PDC for downlevel compatibility with Windows NT domain controllers, updating security identifiers and distinguished names in cross-domain objects when such an object is moved or deleted, and ensuring that all domain names within a forest are unique.

Uses

An important issue regarding domain controllers in Windows 2000– and Windows .NET Server–based networks is where to place them. After an administrator implements Active Directory and populates its initial information, most Active Directory–related traffic will come from users querying for network resources. The key to optimizing user queries is in how you locate the domain controllers and the global catalog servers on your network. Placing a domain controller at each physical site optimizes query traffic but increases replication traffic between sites. Nevertheless, the best configuration is usually to place at least one domain controller at each site with a significant number of users and computers.

In a pure Windows 2000 networking environment, all domain controllers can be configured to run in native mode. If you have a mix of Windows NT 4 and Windows 2000 domain controllers, the Windows 2000 domain controllers must be configured to run in mixed mode.

Notes

To upgrade a Windows NT–based network to Windows 2000, upgrade the PDC first. This allows the domain to immediately join a domain tree, and administrators can administer the domain using the administrative tools of Windows 2000 and create and configure objects in Active Directory.

If you need to move a Windows NT domain controller to a new domain, you must reinstall Windows NT. Domain controllers cannot migrate from one domain to another because when you create a domain, a unique security identifier (SID) is created to identify the domain, and domain controllers have this SID hard-coded into their domain directory database.

You can use the administrative tool Active Directory Users and Computers to convert a Windows 2000 domain controller from mixed mode to native mode. However, domain controllers running in native mode cannot be changed to mixed mode. If you create a new domain controller for an existing Windows 2000 domain, this new domain controller is referred to as a replica domain controller. Replica domain controllers are typically created to provide fault tolerance and better support for users who access resources over the network.

See Also: *Active Directory, domain modes, flexible single-master operation (FSMO)*

domain (DNS)

A collection of related hosts in the hierarchical Domain Name System (DNS).

Overview

Domains are the building blocks of DNS. A domain consists of a group of nodes in the DNS namespace that have the same domain name. Domains are organized hierarchically in the DNS namespace, with the topmost domain called the root domain.

DNS domains can be classified as one of the following:

- A parent domain, which contains other domains. An example of a parent domain is microsoft.com.
- A child domain, or subdomain, which is contained within a parent domain. Examples of child domains in the microsoft.com parent domain are northwind.microsoft.com and marketing.microsoft.com.

Domain names can include only the characters a–z, A–Z, and 0–9, the dash (-), and the period. A name that completely identifies a host in the DNS namespace is called a fully qualified domain name (FQDN).

See Also: *Domain Name System (DNS)*

domain forest

Also called simply a forest, a logical structure formed by combining two or more Microsoft Windows 2000 or Windows .NET Server domain trees.

Overview

Forests provide a way of administering enterprise networks for a company whose subsidiaries each manage their own network users and resources. For example, a company called Contoso, Ltd. might have a domain tree with the root domain contoso.com, and a subsidiary company called Fabrikam, Inc. might have a domain tree with the root domain fabrikam.com. Note that these two companies do not share a contiguous portion of the DNS namespace; this is typical of trees in a forest. The two companies might want to administer their own users and resources but make those resources available to each other's users. They can combine the two domain trees into a forest by establishing a two-way transitive trust between the root domains of the two trees.

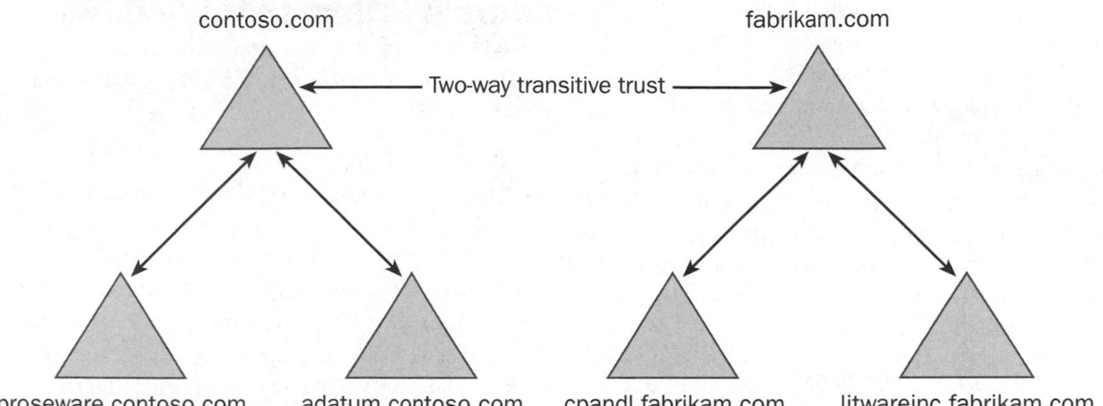

Domain forest. *Example of a domain forest.*

All trees in a forest must share a common directory schema and global catalog. The global catalog holds information about all objects in all domains of the forest and acts as an index of all users and resources for all domains in the forest. By searching the global catalog, a user in one domain can locate resources anywhere in the forest. The global catalog contains only a subset of the attributes of each object. This ensures fast searches for users trying to locate network resources.

See Also: *domain (Microsoft Windows), domain tree*

Domain Guests

A built-in group on Microsoft Windows 2000 and Windows .NET Server networks.

Overview

The Domain Guests group simplifies administration of users on the network. It is a global group and does not have any pre-assigned system rights. The initial membership of the Domain Guests group is the sole user account called Guest. Other user accounts that are added to this group gain the rights and privileges equivalent to those of the Guest account and can perform actions similar to those of the Guest account. Domain Guests are typically users who are given occasional, temporary access to network resources.

Notes

The Domain Guests group is created by default in the Users organizational unit (OU) within Active Directory directory service. Normally, the only member of this group is the Guest account, but when Internet Information Services (IIS) is installed, additional guest accounts are created for use by IIS.

See Also: *built-in group*

domain local group

A type of group in a Microsoft Windows 2000– or Windows .NET Server–based network.

Overview

Windows 2000 and Windows .NET Server use groups to organize users or computer objects for administrative purposes. Groups can have different scopes, or levels of functionality. The scope of a group can be a single domain, a group of domains connected by trust relationships, or the entire network.

Domain local groups are Windows 2000 and Windows .NET Server groups whose scope is restricted to the specific domain in which they are defined. Domain local groups are used to provide users with access to network resources and to assign permissions to control access to these resources. Domain local groups have open mem bership, which means that you can add members from any domain to them.

To use a domain local group, you first determine which users have similar job responsibilities in your enterprise. Then you identify a common set of network resources in a domain that these users might need to access. Next, you create a domain local group for the users and assign the group appropriate permissions to the network resources. This procedure is called A-G-DL-P (access, group, domain local, permissions), which is a variation of the AGLP administration paradigm used in Windows NT–based networks.

Notes

If network resources within a domain are used only within the domain, you can group users in the domain using domain local groups. If your scope of resource usage is several domains linked by trust relationships, use global groups instead. If your network is a pure Windows 2000– or Windows .NET Server–based network and your domain controllers are running in native mode, you can use universal groups as well.

See Also: *global group, universal group*

domain master browser

A role of a browser computer on a Microsoft Windows–based network.

Overview

Domain master browser is one of the browser roles for the computer browser service on Windows networks. A domain master browser must be a machine running Windows NT, Windows 2000, or Windows .NET Server.

The role of the domain master browser is to collect the master list of available network resources in the domain. The domain master browser then distributes this list to master browsers on each subnet. If the domain has only one subnet, the domain master browser is also the master browser for that subnet.

Notes

A Windows NT domain has only one domain master browser, which is always the primary domain controller (PDC).

See Also: *Computer Browser service*

domain (Microsoft Windows)

A model developed by Microsoft Corporation for grouping computers together for administrative and security purposes.

Overview

Computers on a Microsoft Windows NT, Windows 2000, or Windows .NET Server network that are in the same domain share a common directory database of security information such as user accounts, passwords, and password policies. Domains can span geographical boundaries and networks; an enterprise can have branches in several continents with all machines belonging to a single domain. Alternatively, a single network or location can have multiple domains installed, with or without trust relationships between them.

Domain-based networks have the following features:

- **Centralized administration:** The entire network can be administered from a single location.
- **Single-user logon:** Users need only one user account to access any workstation on the network.
- **Universal resource access:** Users can access any network resource for which they have the appropriate permissions.

Implementation

Domains can contain different types of computers, that is, computers performing various different roles. Typically, the following kinds of computers are members of the domain:

- **Domain controllers:** These computers maintain the database of directory information for the domain. In Windows NT, this database is called the Security Accounts Manager (SAM) database, while in Windows 2000 and Windows .NET Server, this information is stored in Active Directory directory service. Domain controllers periodically exchange directory information using directory replication so that the information in any given domain controller is kept up to date. (If the information stored in a domain controller is out of date, users might have trouble logging on with that particular domain controller or finding recently shared resources on the network.)

- **Member servers:** These are stand-alone servers typically used for file and print services, Web services, or running applications such as Microsoft SQL Server. Member servers cannot authenticate users as domain controllers can.
- **Workstations or client computers:** These participate in the security policies of the domain and are members of the domain, but they are used as desktop machines for users instead of as network servers.

A Windows NT or Windows 2000 network can be installed as either a domain or a workgroup. The domain model is preferable because it allows computers to share a common security policy and a common domain directory database. Machines running Windows Millennium Edition (Me), Windows 98, Windows 95, and legacy 16-bit Windows machines can also participate in domain security on Windows NT and Windows 2000 networks but are not considered full members of the domain because they have no computer accounts within the domain directory database.

A Windows NT domain requires only one primary domain controller (PDC) and can have a number of backup domain controllers (BDCs). By creating a PDC, you create a new domain. Windows NT member servers and workstations can join a domain. Other systems, such as computers running Windows 95 and Windows 98, can participate in a domain but are not considered members of the domain because they have no computer accounts in the domain directory database.

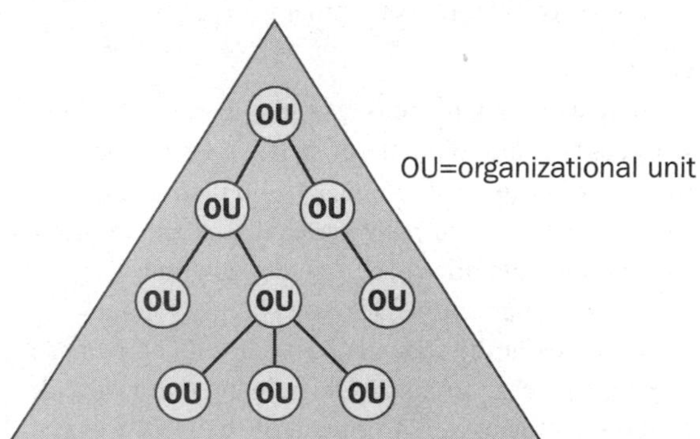

Domain (Microsoft Windows). *This illustration shows a Windows 2000 domain.*

Windows 2000 domains use peer domain controllers, which are all equal in status. In Windows 2000, domains are core entities within Active Directory and act as a boundary for network security and for the replication of directory information over the network. If you establish a security policy in one domain, the settings, rights, and discretionary access control lists (DACLs) of that policy are limited to that domain. Domains are also the fundamental containers for all network objects within them. Domains contain users, groups, computers, and other directory objects. These objects can be grouped together using a hierarchy of organizational units (OUs).

See Also: *Active Directory, domain controller, domain (DNS), workgroup*

D

domain model

A model for building an enterprise-level network using Microsoft Windows NT or Windows 2000 domains.

Overview

Windows NT uses domain models for building enterprise networks radically different from those used by Windows 2000 and Windows .NET Server. In Windows NT networks, four main domain models can be implemented:

- **Single domain model:** This model keeps all of the machines in the network in a single domain and is usually implemented in smaller companies
- **Single master domain model:** This model separates resource domains from a master or accounts domain and is suitable for companies with a hierarchical organizational structure
- **Multiple master domain model:** This model uses multiple accounts or master domains and is suitable for large organizations that span different countries, regions, or continents
- **Complete trust model:** This model is used by very decentralized organizations or during the transition period when two companies merge

Because of their two-way transitive trusts between domains, Windows 2000 and Windows .NET Server are capable of building more flexible domain structures than Windows NT. In addition to the single domain model above, Windows 2000 and Windows .NET Server domains can be linked together hierarchically in domain trees, and domain trees can be joined at their roots to form domain forests.

D

Windows NT, Windows 2000, and Windows .NET Server can be scaled for implementation in enterprise-level businesses that support thousands of users and cover geographically diverse regions, with Windows 2000 and Windows .NET Server being the more scalable platforms. Choosing the correct domain model for implementing your network can greatly simplify administration of your network.

See Also: *domain (Microsoft Windows), domain tree, forest*

domain modes

A mode of operation for domain controllers in Microsoft Windows 2000– and Windows .NET Server–based networks.

Overview

Windows 2000 and Windows .NET Server domain controllers are computers that contain a writeable copy of Active Directory directory service. You can convert a Windows 2000– or Windows .NET Server–based server to a domain controller by running the Active Directory Installation Wizard on that machine. You can run Windows 2000 or Windows .NET Server domain controllers in either of two modes (though .NET Server introduces a new mode called "Windows .NET version 2002," which is exclusively for .NET Server–based networks):

- **Mixed mode:** This mode provides backward compatibility with Windows NT domain controllers (downlevel domain controllers). This mode supports networks with a mixture of Windows 2000, Windows .NET Server and Windows NT domain controllers and allows them to interoperate. Multimaster replication cannot be used in mixed-mode environments.
- **Native mode:** This mode interoperates only with other Windows 2000 or Windows .NET Server domain controllers. Native mode should be used when there are no longer any downlevel domain controllers on the network.

Notes

By default, Active Directory is installed on a Windows 2000 server or Windows .NET Server in mixed mode. You can change a domain controller from mixed mode to native mode, but not vice versa. Use the administrative tool Active Directory Users and Computers to perform the change.

See Also: *Active Directory, domain controller, mixed mode, native mode*

domain name

A name for a domain within the Domain Name System (DNS).

Overview

Domain names are used by companies and organizations to provide a uniform naming scheme for hosts on their Transmission Control Protocol/Internet Protocol (TCP/IP) internetworks and for providing friendly names for Web servers, mail servers, and other servers that are exposed to the Internet.

Domain names must be registered with a domain name registry before they can be used. Formerly this meant registering with the Internet Network Information Center (InterNIC), and later on Network Solutions. Today a number of different domain name registrars exist, each of which must be accredited by the Internet Corporation for Assigned Names and Numbers (ICANN) in order to operate. ICANN is the ultimate controlling organization for domain names and determines both generic and country-specific top-level domains (TLDs).

Uses

Owning a domain name is essential in today's business world as the dot-com enterprise becomes the standard model for business. A company's domain name typically reflects the company's trademark name or logo—for example, the microsoft.com domain owned by Microsoft Corporation. Because company names can be registered at the state or federal level, companies in different states or countries might want to register identical domain names. Unfortunately, the DNS was not established with consideration of these trademark issues, and the courtroom has become a common arena for resolving domain name ownership disputes.

The most popular domain names that companies register are the .com domain names. These were originally intended for commercial enterprises only, but they are also used by individuals, nonprofit organizations, and other entities that want to establish a clear presence on the Internet. About 75 percent of all registered domain names belong to the .com top-level domain. As of 2000, there were about 15 million registered domain names worldwide, and this figure is climbing rapidly.

Prospects

The Internet and its Domain Name System were developed in the United States, and the fact that the Internet is now a worldwide entity has put new pressures on DNS. Countries and regions have pressed for modifications to DNS to allow domain names to be registered in languages other than English, including languages that do not use Roman alphabet characters, such as Chinese. The IETF has established an Internationalized Domain Name (IDN) working group to develop such a system, which is likely to be based on the Unicode standard for internationalization of alphabets. The goal is to implement non-English DNS with minimal modifications to existing DNS itself.

ICANN is also in the process of creating additional top-level domains as alternatives for companies that are unable to register suitable .com domain names and for other purposes such as personal home pages. For the latest developments in this regard, see the ICANN Web site at *www.icann.org*.

Notes

In an interesting development, a commercial company called New.net has created its own new set of TLDs and is selling domain names based on them without the ICANN's approval. This is probably an attempt to apply market pressure to what is often perceived as ICANN's slow, politically based decision-making process of creating new TLDs. New.net is collaborating with commercial DNS provider UltraDNS to provide support for these new TLDs on name servers. To do this, Internet service providers (ISPs) install special software on their own name servers that allows client lookups for these new TLDs to be forwarded directly to UltraDNS's name servers. Users whose ISPs do have such software installed on their name servers can download a free plug-in from New.net to allow them to access sites using these TLDs.

For More Information

You can find a list of ICANN-accredited domain name registrars at *www.ispworld.com/isp/ICANN.htm.*

See Also: *Domain Name System (DNS), fully qualified domain name (FQDN), top-level domain (TLD)*

Domain Name System (DNS)

A hierarchical naming system for identifying Transmission Control Protocol/Internet Protocol (TCP/IP) hosts on the Internet.

Overview

The Domain Name System (DNS) is a distributed, hierarchical system that provides

- A method for identifying hosts on the Internet using alphanumeric "friendly" names called fully qualified domain names (FQDNs) instead of using difficult to remember numeric Internet Protocol (IP) addresses
- A distributed mechanism for storing and maintaining a database of the FQDNs and their associated IP addresses for all hosts on the Internet
- A method for locating hosts on the Internet by resolving their FQDN into their associated IP address so that network communication can be initiated with the host

History

Until 1983 the Internet computers used locally stored Hosts files to perform name resolution. Hosts files are text files that are basically lists of FQDNs and their associated IP addresses for remote hosts that the local host may need to communicate with. With the rapid growth of the Internet, however, updating these Hosts files became an unmanageable chore—each machine had to have its own local Hosts file that needed to be kept up to date, and whenever a host was added to the Internet or removed from it, the Hosts file needed an appropriate modification.

To solve this problem, the hierarchical DNS naming system was invented in 1984 and name servers were deployed across the Internet. The original RFCs 882 and 883 that defined DNS have since been replaced by RFCs 1034 and 1035, and additional RFCs have been added for additional features added to DNS.

Today DNS functions like a backbone for the Internet—without DNS, network communications over the Internet would not be possible.

D

Uses

Although the primary use of DNS is as the naming system for the Internet, large private TCP/IP internetworks sometimes used DNS internally with their own private name servers. This practice is rare now, however, as most private networks are now connected to the Internet.

DNS is essential to the operation of Active Directory directory service in Windows 2000 and Windows .NET Server. Active Directory uses the DNS as its naming system for Windows 2000 and Windows .NET Server hosts, and DNS servers provide name resolution services to enable network communications to take place on a Windows 2000– or Windows .NET Server–based network.

Not all name servers support the necessary DNS features that Active Directory requires. In order to implement Active Directory, name servers must support SRV records described in RFC 2052bis (SRV records enable Windows 2000 and Windows .NET Server clients, including Windows XP, to locate a domain controller for network authentication purposes). In addition, the following advanced DNS features are recommended for name servers that will support Active Directory:

- DNS dynamic updates described in RFC 2136.
- DNS change notification described in RFC 1996.
- Incremental zone transfer (IXFR) described in RFC 1995.

Windows 2000 and Windows .NET Server DNS service supports all of the above features by default. If you want to use Berkeley Internet Name Domain (BIND) name servers to support an Active Directory implementation, you must use at least BIND 8.1.2 and preferably BIND 8.2 or higher. Make sure you also disable name checking so your BIND name servers will ignore the illegal underscore character used by Active Directory's version of DNS.

Note that in BIND, name servers zone information is stored in text files. In Windows 2000 and Windows .NET Server, zone information can be stored either in text files or stored in and replicated using Active Directory.

Implementation

For DNS to work, four elements are required:

- A naming system that uniquely assigns each host on the Internet a DNS name.
- Name servers that keep track of the DNS namespace (collection of DNS names).
- Resolvers that can query the name servers asking what IP address corresponds to a particular DNS name.
- A way of assigning domain names to companies and organizations that have networks that need to be connected to the Internet.

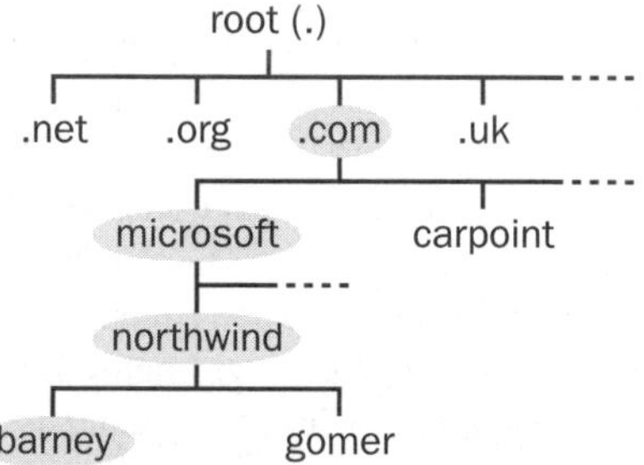

Domain Name System (DNS). *The hierarchical structure of DNS.*

The DNS naming system assigns a unique name to each TCP/IP host on the Internet. Here the word host typically refers to servers, workstations, routers, TCP/IP printers, and similar devices. This unique name for a host is called the fully qualified domain name (FQDN) of the host.

The DNS namespace is defined as the collection of all FQDNs for all hosts on the Internet. This DNS namespace is hierarchical in structure, beginning with the root domain, which branches to top-level domains, then second-level domains, and so on to the individual host name. The FQDN barney.northwind.microsoft.com can be broken down as follows:

- **Host name:** barney
- **Third-level domain:** northwind (stands for Northwind Traders Ltd., a fictitious Microsoft subsidiary)
- **Second-level domain:** microsoft (Microsoft Corporation)
- **Top-level domain:** com (commercial domain)

The root domain has a null label and is not expressed in the FQDN.

The DNS namespace is stored as a distributed database on name servers located at various points on the Internet. Each name server on the Internet is responsible for a subset of the DNS namespace known as a zone. Each zone can consist of one or more domains and subdomains over which the zone is said to be authoritative.

The most important name servers on the Internet are the dozen or so root name servers, which are responsible for maintaining the infrastructure of the domain name system. These root name servers are maintained mostly by the Internet Network Information Center (InterNIC) and by U.S. military agencies (because the Internet evolved from the ARPANET project of the U.S. Defense Department in the 1970s).

Name servers typically store their DNS information in text files called zone files, which consist of a series of resource records (but Microsoft Windows 2000 and Windows .NET Server can do this differently, as discussed later in this article). There are many types of resource records, but the most common type is the A (address) record, which maps the host name or FQDN of a single host to its IP address.

The main function of a name server is to answer queries from DNS clients called resolvers. A resolver contacts a name server, asking it for the IP address associated with a given host name or FQDN. The name server then replies to the resolver with the IP address of the host or contacts a different name server for this information if it is unable to provide it itself.

All name servers can answer queries from resolvers or forward these queries to other name servers. However, name servers also function in four specific roles within the Domain Name System:

- **Primary name server:** This type of name server stores the master copy of the zone file for the zones that the name server has authority over
- **Secondary name server:** This type obtains its zone files by means of a zone transfer from a master name server
- **Master name server:** This type of name server is capable of providing zone information to secondary name servers
- **Caching-only name server:** This type contains no zone information of its own but can cache names resolved by other name servers and then use this cached information to respond to subsequent name lookups

Finally, companies and organizations can obtain domain names for their networks from domain name registrars. These registrars are accredited by the Internet Corporation for Assigned Names and Numbers (ICANN), which used to maintain the DNS system itself until recently.

Marketplace

Most ISPs run their own name servers (usually BIND) and implement registered DNS domains for a small fee to allow companies to run Web servers and mail servers accessible to the Internet. A new type of player is the pure-play DNS service provider, which runs its own dedicated DNS name servers and provides managed, high-availability DNS services to companies for a monthly service charge. Once such company is UltraDNS, which uses a network of redundant DNS servers for failover support and locates these servers near the Internet's backbone for best performance.

Issues

Security is the most important issue regarding DNS. Since DNS was designed to be completely open (any host on the Internet may query any name server), it is inherently insecure and open to attack. The most important type of attack is the denial of service (DoS) attack, which floods a name server with so many false DNS queries that it is unable to respond to real queries. Access to a company's Web server can be completely stopped through DoS attacks on name servers.

Since DNS is critical to the operation of the Internet, it is also viewed sometimes as a prize target by hackers seeking to disrupt the Internet's operation (actually these are more like anarchists than hackers, since a true hacker needs DNS in order to intrude into networks connected to the Internet). BIND name servers, which are the primary form of name server used on the Internet, have had a number of well-publicized vulnerabilities discovered in recent years, and an essential task of Internet service providers (ISPs) is keeping up with patches for their BIND name servers to protect them against attack.

D

Prospects

DNS will continue to play an essential role for the Internet, but with the transition to the new IPv6 addressing scheme, DNS needs a few modifications. The most important modifications are the inclusion of two new resource record types:

- **A6 record:** This is the counterpart for the A (address) record for IPv4 and maps a host name or FQDN to its IPv6 address to support name lookups.
- **DNAME:** This is the IPv6 counterpart of the CNAME record in IPv4.

In addition, reverse name resolution using PTR (pointer) records is different in IPv6 DNS. Specifically, while IPv4 DNS uses the in-addr.arpa domain for such reverse name resolution, IPv6 DNS uses a new domain called IP6.INT.

Finally, during the transition between IPv4 to IPv6 both versions of DNS will need to be supported (probably for many years), and to make this possible, the AAAA record was created to enable IPv4 name servers to provide IPv6 addresses to resolvers performing name lookups.

AAAA records are supported by BIND 8.1 and higher, while IPv6 DNS is supported by BIND 9.

Notes

On smaller TCP/IP networks, Hosts files can be used instead of DNS to support name lookups, while on legacy Windows NT–based networks, Windows Internet Name Service (WINS) provided NetBIOS name resolution as an alternative to DNS. WINS is also supported by Windows 2000 and Windows .NET Server but only for downlevel compatibility with Windows NT in networks that have not been fully upgraded from Windows NT to Windows 2000 or Windows .NET Server.

Windows 2000 and Windows .NET Server also use other naming conventions besides DNS. For example, to locate objects within Active Directory, the following naming conventions can be used:

- The Lightweight Directory Access Protocol (LDAP) naming convention of distinguished names and relative distinguished names (RDNs). This includes LDAP Uniform Resource Locators (URLs).
- User principal names for identifying users and groups.
- Security Accounts Manager (SAM) account names for user accounts.
- Universal Naming Convention (UNC) paths for shared network resources.

See Also: *domain (DNS), domain name, fully qualified domain name (FQDN), hosts file, name server, resource record (RR), root name server, zone*

domain tree

A hierarchical grouping of Microsoft Windows 2000 or Windows .NET Server domains.

Overview

Domain trees are created by adding one or more child domains to an existing parent domain. Domain trees are used to make a domain's network resources globally available to users in other domains.

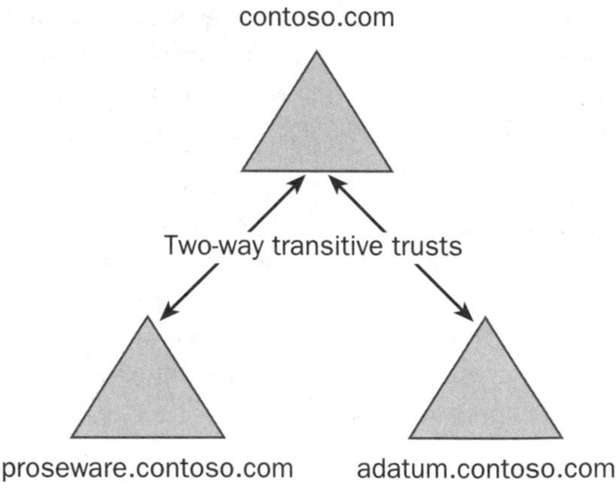

Domain tree. *Example of a domain tree.*

In a domain tree, all domains share their resources and security information to act as a single administrative unit. A user who logs on anywhere in a domain tree can access file, printer, and other shared resources anywhere in the tree if he or she has appropriate permissions. A domain tree has only one Active Directory, but each domain controller in a tree maintains only the portion of Active Directory directory service that represents the objects in that particular domain.

Domains in a domain tree are joined using two-way transitive trusts. These trusts enable each domain in the tree to trust the authority of every other domain in the tree for user authentication. This means that when a domain joins a domain tree, it automatically trusts every domain in the tree.

For child domains to be part of a domain tree, they must share a contiguous namespace with the parent domain. The namespace of a Windows 2000 or Windows .NET Server domain is based on the Domain Name System (DNS) naming scheme. For example, in the illustration, the child domains proseware.contoso.com and adatum.contoso.com share the same namespace as the parent domain contoso.com. In this example, contoso.com is also the name of the root domain—the highest-level parent domain in the tree. The root domain must be created first in a tree.

All domains in a domain tree have their directory information combined into a single directory: Active Directory. Each domain provides a portion of its directory information to an index on the domain controllers. By searching this index, users can locate and access shared resources, applications, and even users anywhere in the domain tree.

Notes

Two or more domain trees that do not share a contiguous namespace can be combined into a domain forest.

See Also: *Active Directory, domain (Microsoft Windows), domain forest, namespace*

domain user account

One of two types of user accounts available on a Microsoft Windows 2000– or Windows .NET Server–based network.

Overview

User accounts enable users to log on to domains or computers and access any resources in the domain for which they have appropriate permissions. This is in contrast to local user accounts, which are used only for logging on to a specific machine (such as a member server) and accessing resources on that machine.

Domain user accounts are created in Active Directory directory service and stored in organizational units (OUs). Domain user account information is replicated to all domain controllers in a domain using directory replication. This replication enables the user to quickly and easily log on from any part of the domain.

You create domain user accounts using the administrative tool called Active Directory Users and Computers, a snap-in for the Microsoft Management Console (MMC). You can create domain user accounts in the default Users OU or in any other OU that you have created in Active Directory.

Notes

Windows 2000 and Windows .NET Server also include a number of built-in accounts that simplify the task of administering users on a network. The two built-in user accounts are the Administrator and Guest accounts.

Domain Users

A built-in group on Microsoft Windows NT, Windows 2000, and Windows .NET Server networks.

Overview

The Domain Users group simplifies administration of users on the network. It is a global group and does not have any preassigned system rights. Its initial membership is empty until ordinary network users are created for the domain. User accounts that are added to this group gain the rights and privileges that are assigned to ordinary users in the network, such as the right to log on over the network. All ordinary users on the network should be members of this group.

Notes

On Windows 2000– and Windows .NET Server–based networks, the Domain Users group is created by default in the Users organizational unit (OU) within Active Directory.

See Also: *built-in group*

DoS

Stands for Denial of Service, any attack conducted against a system that tries to prevent legitimate users from accessing the system.

See: *denial of service (DoS)*

D

DOS

Stands for Disk Operating System, which is short for Microsoft Disk Operating System (MS-DOS), the venerable operating system created by Microsoft Corporation for the first IBM personal computer in 1981.

See: *MS-DOS*

down

The state of a network when some or all network communications are disrupted.

Overview

Common reasons for networks being down include

- Loose connectors on cables
- Breaks or shorts in cables
- Failed networking components

Indications that the network might be down include

- Users complain that they cannot log on to the network or access certain network resources.
- Alarm systems in Simple Network Management Protocol (SNMP) management software start sending administrative alerts or e-mail to administrators.
- The uninterruptible power supply (UPS) unit in the wiring closet generates its annoying high-pitched tone.

See Also: *network troubleshooting*

drain wire

An uninsulated wire included in shielded cabling that runs the length of some coaxial cabling or shielded twisted-pair (STP) cabling.

Overview

The drain wire makes contact with the foil sleeve or mesh along the wire. The externally exposed portion of the drain wire should be connected to a secure ground connection. This ensures that the wire is properly grounded and that the shielding in the wire operates effectively. It also helps to maintain the two ends of the wire at the same voltage with respect to ground. If voltage differences form between the ends of a network cable, they can lead to a sudden voltage surge or discharge that can damage attached networking devices.

See Also: *coaxial cabling, shielded twisted-pair (STP) cabling*

drop

Another name for a wall plate or some other receptacle for connecting workstations to a local area network (LAN).

Overview

For example, a network administrator might say, "This room has 24 drops, and 6 are still available." This means that there are 24 wall plate connections on the walls of the room, and 18 of them have drop cables attached to them to connect them to computers in the room. The other end of the drops usually terminates at a patch panel in the wiring closet. Another name for a drop is a *LAN drop*.

See Also: *premise cabling, wall plate*

drop cable

In Standard Ethernet networks, a cable connecting a computer's network interface card (NIC) to a transceiver attached to a thicknet cable.

Overview

In Standard Ethernet networks, a drop cable is also called a transceiver cable. More generally, a drop cable is any short cable connecting a computer's NIC to a wall plate. Drop cables allow computers to be easily disconnected and reconnected from the network so that you can move them around in the room. Drop cables are generally needed because horizontal cabling connecting patch panels in wiring closets terminates at wall plates in the work areas, but computers in the work areas are distributed throughout the entire room. In a more permanent networking configuration, wall plates might be located on floors and very short drop cables might be used to connect the computers to the network.

See Also: *Ethernet*

Dr. Watson

A Microsoft Windows utility that intercepts software faults and provides the user with information on which software faulted and why the fault occurred.

Overview

In earlier versions of Windows, this information was terse and cryptic, but it was greatly expanded and reorganized in the version of Dr. Watson included with Windows 98, as shown in the screen capture. However, this information is usually not helpful to the person running the software. Dr. Watson is primarily of interest to the providers of the software to determine what caused the software to crash. A piece of software that frequently generates Dr. Watson messages can be considered buggy, and you should contact your software vendor for a fix or a replacement.

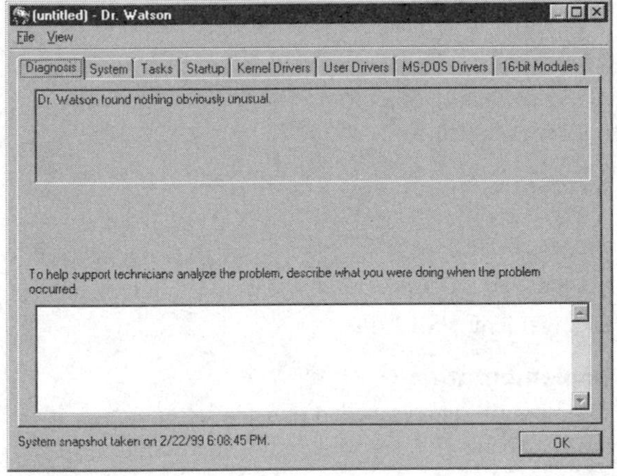

Dr. Watson. *A report generated by Dr. Watson.*

DS

Stands for Differentiated Services, a system for service classification of network traffic.

See: Differentiated Services (DS)

DS-0

Also known as DS0, stands for Digital Signal Zero, a transmission standard for digital telecommunications.

Overview

DS-0 defines a transmission rate of 64 Kbps and can carry either a single voice channel or data. Telecommunication carriers transmit digital signals in multiples of DS-0 called DS-1, DS-2, and so on. These multiples differ depending on whether you are dealing with the T-carrier system of North America or the E-carrier system of Europe and other continents. The following table lists the common DS-series transmission rates and their T-series or E-series equivalents (when defined). For example, you can see that a T1 data transmission is equivalent to 24 DS-0 transmissions multiplexed together and can transmit data at a rate of 1.544 Mbps.

DS-Series Transmission Rates

DS Type	*Multiple of DS0*	*Data Rate*	*T-Series*	*E-Series*
DS0	1	64 Kbps	N/A	N/A
DS1	24	1.544 Mbps	T1	N/A
N/A	32	2.048 Mbps	N/A	E1
DS1C	48	3.152 Mbps	N/A	N/A
DS2	96	6.312 Mbps	T2	N/A
N/A	128	8.448 Mbps	N/A	E2
N/A	512	34.368 Mbps	N/A	E3
DS3	672	44.736 Mbps	T3	N/A
N/A	2048	139.264 Mbps	N/A	E4
DS4	4032	274.176 Mbps	N/A	N/A
N/A	8192	565.148 Mbps	N/A	E5

DS-1

Also known as DS1, a transmission standard for digital telecommunications.

Overview

A DS-1 circuit consists of 24 DS-0 circuits multiplexed together into a circuit. The bandwidth of a DS-1 circuit is 1.544 Mbps, and a common name for such an arrangement is a T1 line. DS-1 is also a typical signaling rate for frame relay links.

Implementation

DS-1 circuits can be implemented singly or multiplexed together to form fatter pipes for carrying data faster. Multiple DS-1 circuits can be bonded together to create NxDS-1 circuits. Here N can be from 2 up to 8, providing a maximum throughput of 12 Mbps. In this arrangement, the first DS-1 circuit is the one responsible for managing the link, and if this circuit goes down the entire link fails.

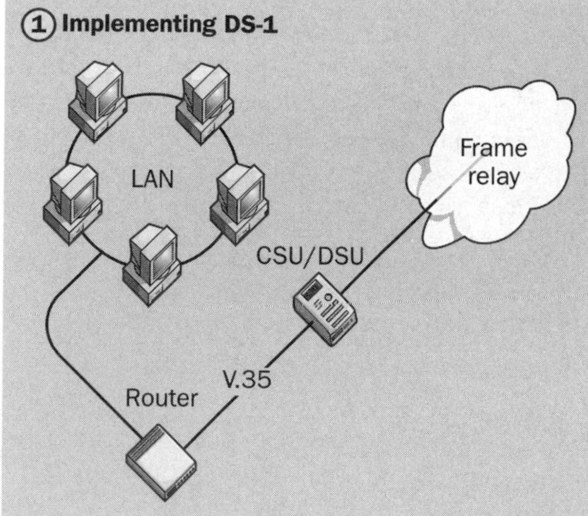

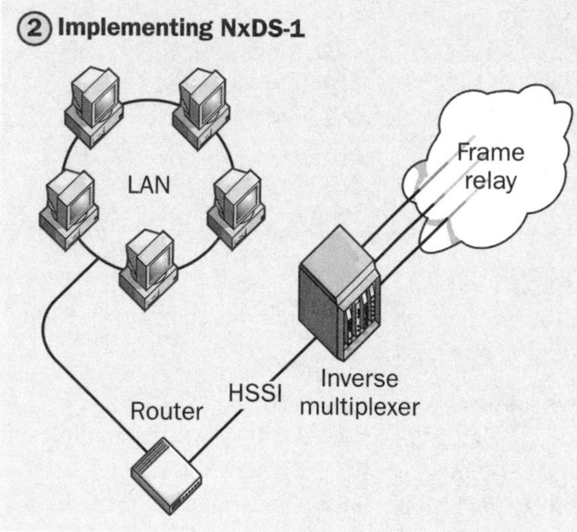

DS-1. *Implementing DS-1 and NxDS-1 on a Frame Relay network.*

NxDS-1 is typically used when you do not expect your data requirements to radically increase for several years. If you are expecting much faster growth in data rates, consider moving to DS-3 or fractional DS-3 instead of NxDS-1.

Issues

When you want to upgrade form DS-1 to NxDS-1, you typically need to give up your old DS-1 circuits and obtain all new ones. This is because carriers terminate single and multiplexed DS-1 circuits differently at their end. Furthermore, it is a good idea to upgrade to the highest value of N you might require immediately because adding additional DS-1 circuits later could cause problems if these circuits follow different paths and experience different latencies at the multiplexor.

You may also need to upgrade your router if you move from DS-1 to NxDS-1. This is because the V.35 interface on most Cisco routers only supports speeds up to 3 Mbps, which corresponds to 2xDS-1. For higher speeds, obtain a router with High Speed Serial Interface (HSSI).

See Also: *DS-0, DS-3, frame relay, High-Speed Serial Interface (HSSI), T1, V.35*

DS-3

Also known as DS3, a transmission standard for digital telecommunications.

Overview

A DS-3 circuit consists of 672 DS-0 circuits multiplexed together into a circuit. The bandwidth of a DS-3 circuit is 44.736 Mbps, and a common name for such an arrangement is a T3 line.

Implementation

DS-3 circuits are typically connected to enterprise local area networks (LANs) using an Asynchronous Transfer Mode (ATM) switch. DS-3 is rarely available for frame relay links and is usually reserved for dedicated leased lines only.

DS-3 is usually available in several forms:

- **Channelized DS-3:** This consists of multiplexed DS-1 lines that terminate at the customer premises at a device called an M13 (DS-1 to DS-3 multiplexor). You can implement from 1 to 28 DS-1 circuits in channelized DS-3, which is cost-efficient because you pay only for what you need.
- **Fractional DS-3:** This is similar to channelized DS-3 but lets you add or remove bandwidth in 3-Mbps chunks (equivalent to a pair of DS-1 circuits).
- **Full DS-3:** In this scenario an M13 is not required, and the coax cable at the demarc point where the circuit enters the customer's wiring closet is simply connected directly to the router (only the most powerful routers support this arrangement).

Notes

Most companies do not have a need for DS-3, and a slower (and cheaper) alternative is NxDS-1, which uses multiplexed DS-1 circuits.

See Also: *DS-0, DS-1, frame relay*

DSL

Stands for Digital Subscriber Line, a group of broadband telecommunications technologies supported over copper local loop connections.

See: *Digital Subscriber Line (DSL)*

DSLAM

Stands for Digital Subscriber Line Access Multiplexer, the DSL termination device at a telco central office (CO).

See: *Digital Subscriber Line Access Multiplexer (DSLAM)*

DSMigrate

Stands for Directory Service Migration Tool, a tool for migrating information from Novell NetWare networks to Microsoft Windows 2000.

See: *Directory Service Migration Tool (DSMigrate)*

DSML

Stands for Directory Service Markup Language, a specification based on Extensible Markup Language (XML) that enables different directory applications to share information.

See: *Directory Service Markup Language (DSML)*

DSMN

Stands for Directory Service Manager for NetWare, an optional Microsoft Windows 2000 utility for managing directory information stored on NetWare servers.

See: *Directory Service Manager for NetWare (DSMN)*

DSN

Stands for data source name, a unique name used to create a data connection to a database using open database connectivity (ODBC).

See: *data source name (DSN)*

DSSS

Stands for Direct Sequence Spread Spectrum, a combination of two transmission technologies, direct sequencing and spread spectrum, used in wireless networking and cellular communications.

See: *Direct Sequence Spread Spectrum (DSSS)*

DSTP

Stands for Data Space Transfer Protocol, a new protocol for rapidly transporting large amounts of information.

See: *Data Space Transfer Protocol (DSTP)*

DSU

Stands for Data Service Unit, a digital communication device that works with a Channel Service Unit (CSU) to connect a local area network (LAN) to a telecommunications carrier service.

See: *Data Service Unit (DSU)*

DTD

Stands for document type definition, a file that defines the allowed structure of an Extensible Markup Language (XML) document.

See: *document type definition (DTD)*

DTE

Stands for data terminal equipment, any device that is a source of data transmission over a serial telecommunications link.

See: *data terminal equipment (DTE)*

D

DTMF

Stands for Dual Tone Multiple Frequency, the audio signaling method used by Touch-Tone phones.

See: *Dual Tone Multiple Frequency (DTMF)*

DTR

Stands for Dedicated Token Ring, a high-speed Token Ring networking technology.

See: *Dedicated Token Ring (DTR)*

dual boot

A computer that can boot one of several operating systems by means of a startup menu.

Overview

An example of a dual boot configuration is a machine on which Windows 98 and then Windows 2000 has been installed. The user can utilize the Windows NT boot loader menu to choose which operating system to run at startup.

Windows 2000, Windows XP, and Windows .NET Server support dual booting with other operating systems, but this is neither recommended nor supported by Microsoft Corporation. Dual boot systems are typically used in hobbyist and test networks in which a variety of operating systems are used to test different networking functions or when the number of available machines is fewer than needed to perform the tasks.

Notes

The Windows 2000, Windows XP, and Windows .NET Server boot loader menus can include up to 10 operating systems.

See Also: *boot*

Dual Tone Multiple Frequency (DTMF)

The audio signaling method used by Touch-Tone phones.

Overview

Each DTMF signal generated by pressing a key on a Touch-Tone phone generates two simultaneous audible tones of different frequencies, as shown in the table below. The advantage of this scheme is that faster and better accuracy of tone recognition (and hence recognition of what number is dialed) is achieved than if single tones were used.

Frequencies of DTMF Signals

	697 Hz	*770 Hz*	*852 Hz*	*941 Hz*
1209 Hz	1	4	7	*
1336 Hz	2	5	8	0
1477 Hz	3	6	9	#

DTMF was developed by AT&T; the term Touch-Tone was originally an AT&T trademark.

Uses

Microsoft Corporation's Telephony Application Programming Interface (TAPI) can recognize and interpret Dual Tone Multiple Frequency (DTMF) signals, allowing Microsoft Windows–based applications to integrate with telephony. Some networking vendors also supply hardware devices called DTMF/ASCII converters, which convert DTMF tones directly into different ASCII characters, which can then be fed as input into a program that routes telephone calls accordingly.

See Also: *Telephony Application Programming Interface (TAPI)*

duplex

A telecommunications term referring to bidirectional communication.

Overview

In full-duplex communication, both stations send and receive at the same time, and usually two communication channels are required. However, you can also achieve full-duplex communication using a multiplexing technique whereby signals traveling in different directions are placed into different time slots. The disadvantage of this technique is that it cuts the overall possible transmission speed by half.

In half-duplex communication, only one station can transmit at any given time while the other station receives the transmission. The opposite of duplex communication is simplex communication, which can occur only in one direction.

DVMRP

Stands for Distance Vector Multicast Routing Protocol, a multicast routing protocol based on the spanning tree algorithm.

See: *Distance Vector Multicast Routing Protocol (DVMRP)*

DWDM

Stands for dense wavelength division multiplexing, a multiplexing technology for achieving extremely high data rates over fiber-optic cabling.

See: *dense wavelength division multiplexing (DWDM)*

dynamic disk

In Microsoft Windows 2000, Windows XP, and Windows .NET Server, a new kind of disk management technology for hard disks.

Overview

Dynamic disks are different from basic disks, which are disk systems that function similarly to earlier versions of Windows (basic disks are also supported by Windows 2000, Windows XP, and Windows .NET Server). Dynamic disks support advanced features such as online management, disk reconfiguration, and fault tolerance.

While basic disks are divided into partitions, a dynamic disk is divided into volumes. A simple volume consists of one or more regions of space on a dynamic disk (these regions need not be contiguous). Although a multidisk system using basic disks has a single partition table describing the data structure of all disks on the system, things are different with dynamic disks. When a system contains multiple dynamic disks, each dynamic disk reserves 1 MB of space at the end of the drive, and this space stores configuration information concerning all of the disks in the system. This provides a measure of fault-tolerance, for if one disk fails the configuration information is not lost concerning the other disks in the system.

When changes are made to a dynamic disk, such as extending a volume to add more space for storage, no reboot is required for the changes to take effect (basic disks must be rebooted when changes are made). You can also use dynamic disks in hot-swappable systems to add or remove drives without requiring a reboot.

Uses

Dynamic disks are intended for use on servers where high-availability and fault tolerance are essential. Workstations gain little by using dynamic instead of basic disks, and dynamic disks are not supported on laptops since they would bring no benefit there.

Dynamic disks are not supported by removable drives such as Zip and Jaz drives, USB and firewire drives, SyQuest drives, and so on.

Dynamic disks also cannot be used on dual-boot systems, as earlier versions of Windows cannot recognize them even if they are formatted using FAT or FAT32.

Implementation

You create and manage dynamic disks in three ways:

- Use the Disk Management console to convert an existing basic disk to a dynamic one.
- Add a new drive to a system and configure it as a new dynamic disk.
- Import a dynamic disk from a different Windows 2000, Windows XP, or Windows .NET Server system into your own system.

Note that the only way to convert a dynamic disk back to a basic disk is to back up all your information, reinitialize the disk by creating partitions, and restore.

See Also: *basic disk, partition (disk), storage, volume*

dynamic DNS (DDNS)

A feature of the Domain Name System (DNS) that enables DNS clients to automatically register their DNS names with name servers.

Overview

Ordinary DNS must be administered manually, with administrators typically making changes directly to zone files on name servers. Information in zone files needs to be updated whenever a new host appears on the network or a host leaves, so the more the network changes, the more work this entails for DNS administrators. Once a zone file is updated on a name server, the updated information is then propagated to other name servers by zone transfers, which are typically scheduled to occur periodically.

Dynamic DNS (DDNS) lets changes to zone files to be made automatically instead of manually, saving DNS administrators the labor-intensive work of maintaining up-to-date zone information concerning all hosts on their network. To accomplish this, DDNS uses a process called dynamic updates outlined in RFC 2136.

Uses

DDNS in Microsoft Windows 2000, Windows XP, and Windows .NET Server is used in two scenarios:

- **Registration of DHCP clients:** When DDNS is enabled and used in conjunction with DHCP, Windows 2000, Windows XP, and Windows .NET Server machines that initialize on the network dynamically acquire an Internet Protocol (IP) address and then automatically register their DNS name and IP address with the DNS server by adding an A record for the client to the name server's zone file.
- **Registration of domain controllers**. When a domain controller boots up for the first time, it registers an SRV record with the DNS server. This SRV record is needed by DNS clients so they can locate the domain controller in order to log on to the network.

Implementation

DDNS is supported by the Windows 2000 and Windows .NET Server implementation of DNS and greatly simplifies the administration of DNS zone information in Windows 2000 and Windows .NET Server networks. DDNS is recommended for Windows 2000– and Windows .NET Server–based networks because Active Directory directory service uses DNS as its name locator service for locating hosts on the network and DDNS also reduces the chances of error that occur when DNS is administered manually.

Dynamic update lies at the heart of Active Directory because domain names in Windows 2000 and Windows .NET Server are also DNS names. For example, northwind.microsoft.com can be both a legal DNS name and the name of a Windows 2000 domain. When DNS is integrated with Active Directory and configured for dynamic updates, the root zone and forward lookup zones are created and configured automatically for each domain, but administrators must enable and manage reverse lookup zones.

DDNS is similar to ordinary DNS in that zone update operations occur using primary or master servers only. DDNS, however, allows primary servers to receive updates initialed by a specified list of "authorized servers," which can include secondary zone servers, domain controllers, and other servers that perform name registration services, such as Windows Internet Name Service (WINS) or DHCP servers.

Most name servers on the Internet either do not yet support or are configured not to support DDNS because of the extra security issues involved when using it. DDNS is currently most popular in corporate networks using Windows 2000 and Active Directory.

Notes

You can use the DNS Manager snap-in for the Microsoft Management Console (MMC) to enable Active Directory integration on an existing DNS server. The zone file information will be written into Active Directory.

Note that by default DDNS on Windows 2000 and Windows .NET Server does not automatically scavenge (purge) old resource records for clients no longer on the network—you need to manually enable and schedule scavenging.

See Also: *Active Directory, Domain Name System (DNS), name server, zone*

Dynamic Host Configuration Protocol (DHCP)

A protocol that enables the dynamic configuration Internet Protocol (IP) address information for hosts on an internetwork.

Overview

Dynamic Host Configuration Protocol (DHCP) is an extension of the bootstrap protocol (BOOTP). DHCP is implemented as a client-server protocol that uses DHCP servers and DHCP clients.

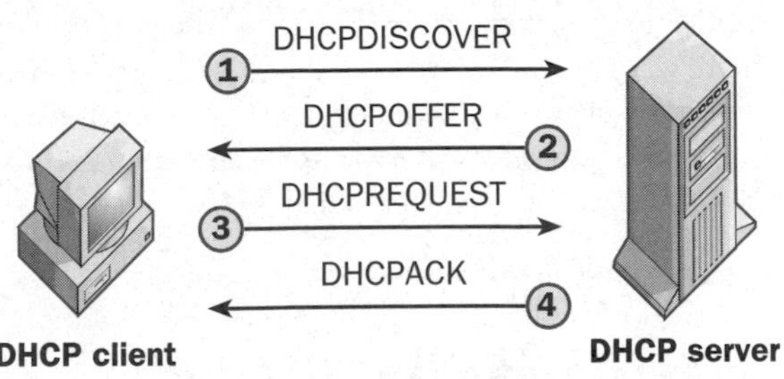

Dynamic Host Configuration Protocol (DHCP). *How a DHCP client leases an IP address from a DHCP server.*

A DHCP server is a machine that runs a service that can lease out IP addresses and other Transmission Control Protocol/Internet Protocol (TCP/IP) information to any DHCP client that requests them. For example, on Microsoft Windows 2000 servers, you can install the Microsoft DHCP Server service to perform this function. The DHCP server typically has a pool of IP addresses that it is allowed to distribute to clients, and these clients lease an IP address from the pool for a specific period of time, usually several days. Once the lease is ready to expire, the client contacts the server to arrange for renewal.

DHCP clients are client machines that run special DHCP client software enabling them to communicate with DHCP servers. All versions of Windows include DHCP client software, which is installed when the TCP/IP protocol stack is installed on the machine.

DHCP clients obtain a DHCP lease for an IP address, a subnet mask, and various DHCP options from DHCP servers in a four-step process:

1. **DHCPDISCOVER:** The client broadcasts a request for a DHCP server.
2. **DHCPOFFER:** DHCP servers on the network offer an address to the client.
3. **DHCPREQUEST:** The client broadcasts a request to lease an address from one of the offering DHCP servers.
4. **DHCPACK:** The DHCP server that the client responds to acknowledges the client, assigns it any configured DHCP options, and updates its DHCP database. The client then initializes and binds its TCP/IP protocol stack and can begin network communication.

DHCP lease renewal consists only of steps 3 and 4, and renewal requests are made when 50 percent of the DHCP lease time has expired.

Implementation

When you implement DHCP on a network, you should consider the following:

- DHCP servers do not share their database of leased IP addresses, so if your network has more than one DHCP server, be sure that their DHCP scopes do not overlap.
- Assign DHCP options to the DHCP server if clients need them.
- Assign static IP addresses to non-DHCP clients, and exclude these addresses from the scope on the DHCP server if necessary.
- Assign static IP addresses to all servers on your network or assign them DHCP client reservations on the DHCP server to ensure that they always lease the same IP address.
- Configure DHCP relay agents if one DHCP server must serve hosts on several subnets.

Marketplace

Although network operating system platforms such as Microsoft Windows 2000 and Novell NetWare include their own DHCP services, enterprise network architects may also want to consider self-contained DHCP applications from third-party vendors as well. Some of these third-party DHCP products include additional features such as query and reporting tools that make them attractive to use in an enterprise environment. Some examples of such products include Shadow Ipserver from Network TeleSystems (recently acquired by Efficient Networks), IP AddressWorks from Process Software, NetID from Nortel Networks, network Registrar from Cisco Systems, and Meta IP from CheckPoint Software Technologies.

For More Information

Find out more about DHCP at *www.dhcp.org.*

See Also: *BOOTP, Domain Name System (DNS), IP address*

Dynamic HTML (DHTML)

A proposed World Wide Web Consortium (W3C) standard developed by Microsoft Corporation for creating interactive multimedia Web content.

Overview

Developers can use Dynamic HTML to make Web pages look and behave more like typical desktop applications. Dynamic HTML supports features such as

- Document Object Model (DOM), a standard whereby every element of a Web page is exposed for scripting. Each element on a Hypertext Markup Language (HTML) page can function as an object that can be modified using scripts and other programs. For example, Dynamic HTML can make the appearance of an object on a Web page change during an onmouseover or onclick event.
- Cascading Style Sheets (CSS) positioning, which allows HTML content developers to control the style and layout of objects on a Web page using style sheets. These style sheets can then be cascaded to define different levels of precedence.
- Dynamic Content and Dynamic Styles, which HTML content developers can use to dynamically change the content or style of every HTML element on a Web page based on mouse events or other forms of user interaction.
- Data Binding, which integrates data with HTML elements. For example, table rows can be automatically generated from data records and data-bound fields.

See Also: *cascading style sheets (CSS), Document Object Model (DOM)*

dynamic-link library (DLL)

A file containing executable routines that can be loaded on demand by an application.

Overview

Dynamic-link libraries (DLLs) offer the advantage of providing standard services for many different calling applications, and they simplify and modularize application development by providing component–based services. DLLs are loaded into RAM only when needed by the calling application, which reduces the memory requirements of large applications. DLLs are files that have the extension .dll.

See Also: *application programming interface (API)*

dynamic packet filtering

The process of filtering packets according to real-time criteria.

Overview

Dynamic packet filtering is a feature of firewalls, routers, and proxy servers such as Microsoft Proxy Server. Using dynamic packet filtering, a system can

- Determine dynamically whether to accept a packet from the Internet while minimizing the number of exposed ports in both directions and the length of time the port is open to the Internet
- Drop all packets on an external interface by default

Implementation

In Microsoft Proxy Server, dynamic packet filtering involves two components:

- **Packet Filter Driver:** This component talks directly to the external network interface
- **Packet Filter Manager:** This component provides the high-level interface for interaction between Proxy Server services and the driver

In a typical scenario, a client with the Winsock Proxy client might attempt to connect to an Internet server using Telnet. The Winsock Proxy client intercepts the Telnet connection request and remotes the request to the Winsock Proxy server, which verifies that the client has proper Microsoft Windows NT permissions to use Telnet to access servers on the Internet and opens a local socket. The Winsock Proxy server then informs the Packet Filter Manager that an outbound connection request from the socket to a remote Telnet service has been approved, and the Packet Filter Manager orders the Packet Filter Driver to open the socket and the

Winsock Proxy server to start a Telnet session on behalf of the client. When the Winsock Proxy determines that the client has closed the Telnet session, it tells the Packet Filter Manager to close the socket and thus blocks any further packets from the remote system.

See Also: *firewall, packet filtering, proxy server, router*

dynamic routing

A routing mechanism for dynamically exchanging routing information among routers on an internetwork.

Overview

Dynamic routing operates using a dynamic routing protocol, such as Routing Information Protocol (RIP) or Open Shortest Path First (OSPF) Protocol. Routers that use dynamic routing are sometimes called dynamic routers.

For dynamic routing to work, the routing protocol must be installed on each router in the internetwork. The routing table of one router is manually seeded with routing information for the first hop, and then the routing protocol takes over and dynamically builds the routing table for each router. Dynamic routers periodically exchange their routing information so that if the network is reconfigured or a router goes down, the routing tables of each router are automatically modified accordingly.

Advantages and Disadvantages

Dynamic routers are much simpler to administer than static routers, but they are sometimes less secure because routing protocol information can be spoofed. If the network is reconfigured or a router goes down, it takes a certain period of time for this information to propagate between the various routers on the network. This router reconfiguration process is usually referred to as convergence. However, getting a dynamic router up and running is often as simple as connecting the interfaces and turning it on—routes are discovered automatically by communications with other routers on the network. Dynamic routers are also fault-tolerant, for when a router fails the other routers soon learn about it and adjust their routing tables accordingly to maintain communications across the network.

Using dynamic routing protocols also creates additional network traffic due to routing table updates and exchanges, and different dynamic routing protocols offer their own advantages and disadvantages in this regard.

Dynamic routers cannot exchange information with static routers. To configure static and dynamic routers to work together on the same internetwork, you must add manual routes to the routing tables of both types of routers.

Notes

You can configure a multihomed Microsoft Windows 2000 or Windows .NET Server server as a dynamic RIP router by selecting Enable IP Forwarding on the Routing tab of the Transmission Control Protocol/Internet Protocol (TCP/IP) property sheet and then using the Services tab of the Network property sheet to add the RIP for Internet Protocol (IP) service to the server. Another example of a dynamic router is a multihomed computer running Windows 2000 Server with Routing and Remote Access Service (RRAS) and either RIP or OSPF configured.

See Also: *router, routing table, static routing*

dynamic routing protocol

A protocol that enables dynamic routing to be used to simplify management of a routed network.

Overview

If we focus on Internet Protocol (IP) routing, which is the standard for the Internet and most corporate networks, several kinds of dynamic routing protocols can be deployed. These routing protocols can be classified in a hierarchical scheme as shown in the illustration.

First, dynamic routing protocols can be one of two types:

- **Interior Gateway Protocols (IGPs):** These are used to manage routing within autonomous systems (ASs). IGPs are further classified below.
- **Exterior Gateway Protocols (EGPs):** These are used to manage routing between different ASs. The de facto example of an EGP is the Border Gateway Protocol (BGP) used on the Internet.

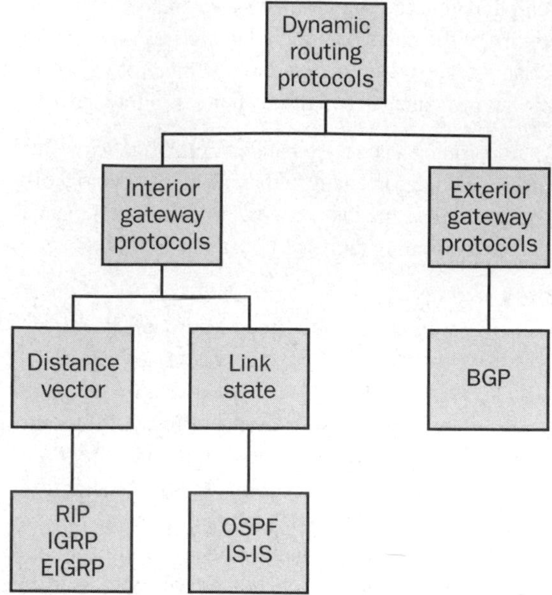

Dynamic routing protocol. *Classification of popular dynamic routing protocols.*

IGPs can be further classified according to the type of algorithm used to build and distributed routing table information. Specifically, IGPs can employ the

- **Distance vector routing algorithm:** Examples of dynamic routing protocols that use this algorithm include Routing Information Protocol (RIP), Interior Gateway Routing Protocol (IGRP), and Enhanced Interior Gateway Routing Protocol (EIGRP).
- **Link state routing algorithm:** Examples of dynamic routing protocols that use this algorithm include Open Shortest Path First (OSPF) and Integrated System to Integrated System (IS-IS).

See Also: *autonomous system (AS), Border Gateway Protocol (BGP), distance vector routing algorithm, Enhanced Interior Gateway Routing Protocol (EIGRP), exterior gateway protocol (EGP), interior gateway protocol (IGP), Interior Gateway Routing Protocol (IGRP), link state routing algorithm, Open Shortest Path First (OSPF), Routing Information Protocol (RIP)*

dynamic volume

In Microsoft Windows 2000, Windows XP, or Windows .NET Server, a volume created on a dynamic disk.

Overview

Windows 2000, Windows XP, and Windows .NET Server support several kinds of dynamic volumes including

- **Simple volumes:** These consist of onc or more regions of contiguous space on a single drive.
- **Spanned volumes:** These consist of one or more regions of contiguous space from two or more drives.
- **Striped volumes:** RAID 0 or disk striping using dynamic disks.
- **Mirrored volumes:** RAID 1 or disk mirroring using dynamic disks.
- **RAID 5 volumes:** Disk striping with parity using dynamic disks.

You can create dynamic volumes using the Disk Management portion of the Computer Management administrative tool. You can create dynamic volumes only on dynamic disks.

See Also: *basic disk, basic volume, dynamic disk, RAID, storage, volume*

E

EAP

Stands for Extensible Authentication Protocol, a security enhancement of Point-to-Point Protocol (PPP).

See: *Extensible Authentication Protocol (EAP)*

EBGP

Stands for Exterior Border Gateway Protocol, the version of Border Gateway Protocol (BGP) used for exchanging routing information between different autonomous systems.

See: *Exterior Border Gateway Protocol (EBGP)*

e-business

Refers generally to the process of using the Internet for conducting key activities of your business.

In the new Internet economy two terms are generally confused:

- **e-commerce:** This refers specifically to the process of buying and selling goods and services over the Internet.
- **e-business:** This more general term may include e-commerce activity, but also includes using the Internet for additional core business processes, including management of supply-line services, customer relations, and human resources.

E-commerce is generally B2C (business-to-consumer) in orientation, but e-business includes B2B (business-to-business) activities that join separate businesses entities over the Internet into value chains using negotiated agreements. In an e-business scenario, the basic activities of business (including invoicing, transactions, and procurement) are all performed electronically over the Internet. Technologies such as Electronic Data Interchange (EDI) and Extensible Markup Language (XML) are employed to facilitate the exchange of information between business partners. Because the Internet is a public network, security is a high priority for e-business, and technologies such as virtual private networks (VPNs) and Internet Protocol Security (IPsec) are used to ensure the privacy, integrity, and authenticity of electronic business transactions.

In addition to businesses forming their own private negotiated business arrangements, a large number of public and private e-business marketplaces have emerged in the last few years to facilitate B2B relationships. An example is the Microsoft Market, which is Microsoft Corporation's internal Web-based procurement system.

For companies migrating from the old brick-and-mortar model to the new e-business model, there are many advantages incurred in the move. These include lowered procurement costs, shorter business cycles, more efficient customer service, and new kinds of sales opportunities.

See Also: *B2B, electronic data interchange (EDI), XML*

ebXML

Stands for Electronic Business Extensible Markup Language, an XML standard that allows businesses to locate each other on the Internet, form partnerships, and exchange business information.

See: *Electronic Business Extensible Markup Language (ebXML)*

E-carrier

The digital telecommunications services backbone system of Europe, a format standardized by the International Telecommunication Union (ITU).

Overview

The E-carrier service rates are specified by the organization CEPT (Conférence Européenne des Administration des Postes et des Télécommunications, or European

Conference of Postal and Telecommunications Administrations). The most popular of these services, E1, is also the slowest. E1 transmits data at speeds of up to 2.048 megabits per second (Mbps) over two pairs of twisted wires. It consists of 32 separate 64-kilobits-per-second (Kbps) DS-0 channels multiplexed together, each of which can carry either a voice conversation or a stream of data. E1 is sometimes referred to as 2-Meg.

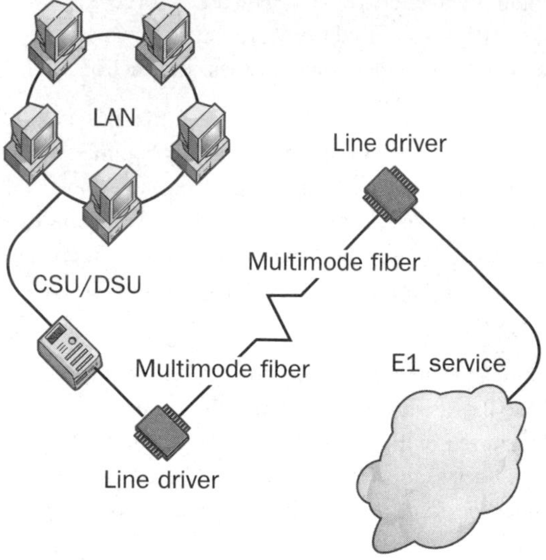

E-carrier. *Connecting to an E-carrier service.*

E-carrier transmissions are graded E1, E2, and so on, in order of increasing transmission speeds. These different service grades are multiples of the basic DS-0 data transmission rate, similar to the T-carrier system of North American telecommunications carriers. The E-carrier transmission rates are shown in the table included in the article "DS-0" elsewhere in this book. E-carrier lines use 8 bits per channel for encoding signals and do not rob bits for control signals as T-carrier lines do.

E-carrier services were developed in the 1970s and became widely available in the 1980s. E-carrier services can be used for wide area network (WAN) connections, for high-speed Internet connections, for private videoconferencing services, and for public frame relay services. E-carrier services are generally available wherever the parallel T-carrier services are not.

Notes

If the E1 service entering your customer premises needs to connect directly to a different building, you have two options. First, you could have the service provider extend the E1 line to the other building, thus moving the demarcation point (termination point) of the line. This could be costly, however. A simpler solution might be to connect the E1 line to a fiber-optic line driver, install a fiber-optic cable from the line driver to a similar driver in the other building, and then connect the remote line driver to your E1 equipment (see diagram).

See Also: *T-carrier*

EDGAR

Stands for Electronic Data Gathering, Analysis, and Retrieval, an online document management system used by the U.S. Securities and Exchange Commission (SEC).

Overview

EDGAR is an online service with two main functions:

- To provide corporations with an electronic method for filing public disclosures such as quarterly earnings statements, annual reports, and so on. This is the "private" side of EDGAR, and companies currently file this information by means of the Web, through virtual private network connections (VPN) or through dial-up modem connections.
- To provide a clearinghouse that allows individuals and organizations to view archived reports of publicly traded companies. This is the "public" side of EDGAR, which receives almost 1 million visitors daily.

EDGAR was upgraded in 2000 from its older OS/2 system to Microsoft Windows NT, and the SEC is looking into ways to use Extensible Markup Language (XML) to help EDGAR submissions search for information in its vast database more easily.

For More Information

Visit the SEC at *www.sec.gov.*

EDGE

Stands for Enhanced Data Rates for Global Evolution, a third-generation (3G) upgrade for General Packet Radio Service (GPRS).

See: *Enhanced Data Rates for Global Evolution (EDGE)*

edge router

A device in an Asynchronous Transfer Mode (ATM) network that routes data between an ATM backbone network and local area networks (LANs).

Overview

Edge routers can be used to translate Ethernet or Token Ring data for transmission over ATM backbones. This allows ATM to be used as a backbone for connecting multiple LANs into a metropolitan area network (MAN) or wide area network (WAN).

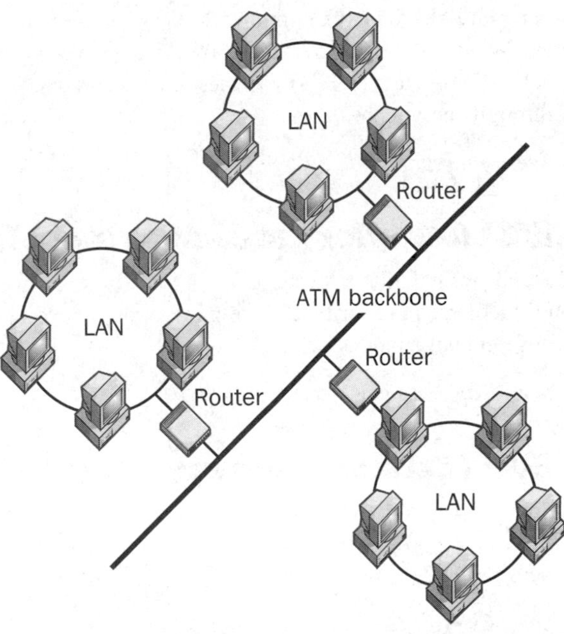

Edge router. *Using an edge router to connect LANs to an ATM backbone.*

An alternative and more commonly used configuration is to connect LAN networking equipment directly to ATM backbone switches, which provide points of contact with an ATM provider's backbone network.

An edge router can function as an ATM switch and provide routing capabilities for LAN networking protocols—all in one hybrid device.

See Also: *Asynchronous Transfer Mode (ATM), backbone*

EDI

Stands for electronic data interchange, the industry standard format for exchanging business information electronically.

See: *electronic data interchange (EDI)*

eDirectory

The latest version of Novell Directory Services (NDS).

Overview

Novell eDirectory is the new name for NDS version 8.*x* and emphasizes the enhanced Internet functionality of NDS. Novell eDirectory is a key part of Novell's "One Net" strategy and includes the following enhancements over previous versions of NDS:

- Native support for Lightweight Directory Access Protocol version (3LDAPv3) and LDAP Data Interchange Format (LDIP)
- An internal schema that more closely conforms to the LDAPv3 standard than earlier versions
- Support for enhanced Domain Name System (DNS) naming conventions
- Extensible support for management using the ConsoleOne utility
- Increased scalability to support more than a billion objects per directory tree

Novell eDirectory is available for the Novell NetWare, Microsoft Windows NT, Windows 2000, UNIX, AIX, Compaq Tru64 UNIX, Solaris, and Linux platforms. The current version is eDirectory 8.5.

See Also: *directory*

E

effective permissions

In Microsoft Windows 2000, Windows XP, and Windows .NET Server, the cumulative permissions a user has for accessing a resource based on a user's individual permissions, group permissions, and group membership.

Overview

The effective permissions a user experiences in trying to access a file or folder depend on the various permissions granted to the user expressly or by virtue of membership in a particular group. When a permissions conflict exists between one group and another, or between the user and a group, rules are applied that resolve the issue.

In networks based on Windows 2000, Windows XP, and Windows .NET Server, calculation of effective permissions can be determined using three simple rules:

First, if a user belongs to two (or more) groups, and these groups have different NTFS file system (NTFS) standard file permissions on a given file, the user's ability to access the file both locally and over the network is determined as follows: the effective NTFS permission is the least restrictive (most permissive) NTFS standard permission. For example,

```
read (NTFS) + change (NTFS) = change (NTFS)
```

The exception to this is that the no-access permission overrides all other permissions. For example,

```
read (NTFS) + no access (NTFS) = no access (NTFS)
```

Second, if a user belongs to two (or more) groups, and these groups have different shared folder permissions on a given shared folder, the user's ability to access the shared folder over the network is determined as follows: the effective shared folder permission is the least restrictive (most permissive) shared folder permission. For example,

```
read (shared folder) + change (shared folder)
= change (shared folder)
```

The exception to this is that the no-access permission overrides all other permissions. For example,

```
read (shared folder) + no access (shared
folder) = no access (shared folder)
```

Third, when a user attempts to access a folder or file over a network that has both NTFS permissions (the first example) and shared folder permissions (the second example) configured on it, the effective permission is the most restrictive (least permissive) permission. For example,

```
read (NTFS) + change (shared folder)
= read (combined)
```

See Also: *NTFS permissions (Windows 2000, Windows XP, and Windows .NET Server), shared folder permissions*

EFI

Stands for Extensible Firmware Interface, a firmware standard for 64-bit Intel processors.

See: *Extensible Firmware Interface (EFI)*

EFS

A feature of Microsoft Windows 2000, Windows XP, and Windows .NET Server that allows files stored on NTFS file system (NTFS) volumes to be secured through encryption.

See: *Encrypting File System (EFS)*

EGP (exterior gateway protocol)

Stands for exterior gateway protocol, any routing protocol used to distribute routing information among different autonomous systems.

See: *exterior gateway protocol (EGP)*

EGP (Exterior Gateway Protocol)

Stands for Exterior Gateway Protocol, the original exterior routing protocol used to connect autonomous systems on the Internet.

See: *Exterior Gateway Protocol (EGP)*

EIA

Stands for Electronic Industries Alliance, the main trade organization representing the U.S. high-tech community.

See: *Electronic Industries Alliance (EIA)*

EIA/TIA wiring standards

Standards for commercial and telecommunications wiring developed by the Electronic Industries Alliance (EIA) and Telecommunications Industry Association (TIA).

Overview

The EIA/TIA wiring standards actually comprise a group of standards covering different aspects of premise cabling and other wiring practices. These standards include

- **EIA/TIA 570:** Residential/Light Commercial Wiring Standard
- **EIA/TIA 568A:** Commercial Building Telecommunications Cabling Standard
- **EIA/TIA 569:** Commercial Building Standard for Telecommunications Pathways and Spaces
- **EIA/TIA 606:** Design Guideline for Administration of Telecommunications Infrastructure in Commercial Buildings
- **EIA/TIA 607:** Commercial Building Grounding and Bonding Requirements for Telecommunications

When installing wiring for your network, be sure to follow the EIA/TIA standards to ensure that your network functions as expected and that it complies with all local and state building codes and regulations.

The EIA/TIA wiring standards are also supported by the American National Standards Institute (ANSI).

For More Information

Visit the Electronic Industries Alliance (EIA) at *www.eia.org and the* Telecommunications Industry Association (TIA) at *www.tiaonline.org.*

See Also: *premise cabling, structured wiring*

EIGRP

Stands for Enhanced Interior Gateway Routing Protocol, a popular interior routing protocol developed by Cisco Systems.

See: *Enhanced Interior Gateway Routing Protocol (EIGRP)*

EIP

Stands for Enterprise Information Portal, a business software system used to provide a single point of access to information stored in different corporate databases.

See: *Enterprise Information Portal (EIP)*

EJB

Stands for Enterprise Java Beans, a Java-based technology from Sun Microsystems for building transactional e-commerce systems.

See: *Enterprise Java Beans (EJB)*

EKP

Stands for Enterprise Knowledge Portal, a business software system that couples knowledge management tools with an Enterprise Information Portal (EIP) to provide a powerful way of handling the flood of information that characterizes large businesses today.

See: *Enterprise Knowledge Portal (EKP)*

election

The process of selecting a new master browser from a Microsoft Windows network's potential browsers.

Overview

If a client machine cannot locate a master browser on the network in Windows NT, Windows 2000, Windows XP, or Windows .NET Server, it initiates an election to select a new master browser. Elections ensure that a master browser is always available on the network, since the absence of a master browser means that clients will be unable to locate and access network resources such as shared files and folders.

If a client machine cannot locate a master browser on the network, it broadcasts an election datagram. When a machine that is a potential browser receives this datagram, it examines the election criteria in the datagram. If its election criteria are better than those of the datagram's sender, the potential browser broadcasts its own election datagram and an election is declared to be in progress. The election criteria for becoming a master browser include many factors, such as the machine's operating system, version, and role. Eventually, one potential browser prevails over other machines on the network because it has superior election criteria, and the election ends.

E

Notes

Elections also occur when domain controllers are restarted.

See Also: *browsing, Computer Browser service*

electromagnetic interference (EMI)

Electrical noise induced in cabling by the presence of nearby electrical equipment such as motors, air conditioners, fluorescent lights, and power lines.

Overview

Electromagnetic interference (EMI) can interfere with the transmission of signals and render network communications unreliable or impossible. EMI is only a problem if copper cabling is used-fiber-optic cabling is immune to sources of EMI.

EMI is caused when the changing electromagnetic fields generated by one cable induce extraneous currents or interference in adjacent or nearby cables. EMI in copper cabling can be reduced to acceptable levels by

- Avoiding bunching of unshielded cabling
- Keeping all cabling away from power cords and transformers
- Using shielded twisted-pair (STP) cabling instead of unshielded twisted-pair (UTP) cabling
- Enclosing cabling in external mesh or wire shielding
- Properly grounding electrical equipment and external shielding
- Taking care not to excessively untwist the terminating ends of twisted-pair cabling

EMI can be a greater concern in heavy industrial settings where high voltages and equipment, such as motors and generators, produce high levels of electrical noise. Using coaxial cabling in these settings affords greater resistance to the effects of EMI than using twisted-pair cabling. Fiber-optic cabling is an even better solution in heavy industrial settings because it is wholly resistant to EMI. (Changing electromagnetic fields has no effect on the light waves traveling along a glass fiber.)

See Also: *cabling, noise, signal*

Electronic Business Extensible Markup Language (ebXML)

An Extensible Markup Language (XML) standard that allows businesses to locate each other on the Internet, form partnerships, and exchange business information.

Overview

The ebXML standard specifies protocols and mechanisms that allow businesses to use the Internet and XML to create and centrally store business profiles of their companies, find other companies providing desired types of business services, enter into partnership agreements, and collaborate through electronic document exchange such as invoicing, receipts, shipping notices, and so on. The ebXML standard is designed to promote electronic business between companies of any size located anywhere in the world using a common infrastructure (the Internet) and a common language for sharing structured information (XML).

The ebXML standard provides open specifications for how companies define their business processes, create and register company profiles and business processes, enter into trading agreements, and exchange business information using XML messages. Businesses can use ebXML to exchange business information with each other without being concerned about the structure of the underlying data processes of other partners in the process.

The ebXML standard is an initiative of the Organization for the Advancement of Structured Information and Standards (OASIS) and a United Nations (UN) standards body called UN/CEFACT (United Nations Center for Trade Facilitation and Electronic Business). Development of the ebXML standard began in 1999 with the backing and support of IBM, Sun Microsystems, BEA Systems, Commerce One, and a number of other companies.

Implementation

The ebXML standard specifies a set of protocols for packaging business information as high-level messages and routing them to required destinations. Any kind of business transactional message can be encapsulated by ebXML, including electronic data exchange (EDI) X12 messages, EDIFACT messages, XML messages, or some proprietary transactional message schemes.

The ebXML protocol suite is modular in architecture and consists of several protocols that enable encapsulation, transport, and routing of XML messages. To help promote uniform standards in the B2B arena and prevent fracturing of the market, the ebXML group has agreed not to compete with the developers of Simple Object Access Protocol (SOAP), but instead to incorporate SOAP 1.1 as its underlying protocol for enabling remote activation of software components over the Internet. SOAP 1.1 was developed by Microsoft in conjunction with IBM.

For More Information

Visit the ebXML initiative at *www.ebxml.org.*

See Also: Simple Object Access Protocol (SOAP), XML

Electronic Data Gathering, Analysis, and Retrieval

An online document management system used by the U.S. Securities and Exchange Commission (SEC), better known by its acronym, EDGAR.

See: EDGAR

electronic data interchange (EDI)

The industry standard format for exchanging business information electronically.

Overview

Electronic data interchange (EDI) is a well-established standard by which companies can exchange business data and perform financial transactions using electronic means. EDI is commonly used by large companies to link their financial systems to supply-chain partners to automate and speed procurement for assembly line processing. Some analysts estimate there are more than 300,000 companies worldwide using some form of EDI to streamline their procurement processes.

EDI is a compact format that allows information to be structured in a way that it can easily mapped to traditional business forms such as invoices, purchase orders, receipts, and so on. EDI is used mostly by large companies that process high volumes of business transactions, and it can save these companies considerable costs by greatly reducing paperwork, mail, and fax charges.

History

EDI was born in the 1970s when large companies such as Kmart Corporation and Sears, Roebuck, and Company saw the need for a standard way of exchanging business information with trading and supply-chain partners. Developing custom solutions for electronic business document exchange was costly, so the Data Interchange Standards Association (DISA) was formed, consisting of government, transportation, and private sector companies, to address this issue. In 1979, EDI was approved as an American National Standards Institute (ANSI) standard called X.12. The X.12 standard defines the data dictionary used by EDI for formatting messages for standard communications between business partners. Other standards competing with EDI for electronic exchange of business documents were concurrently developed, but by the mid-1980s, X12 had become a widely recognized standard and EDI began to be widely deployed, especially in large companies.

Architecture

The basic unit of an EDI transmission is the message, which consists of a transaction set with a header and footer attached. An EDI message adheres to a standard format called the Electronic Data Interchange for Administration, Commerce, and Transport (EDIFACT) protocol.

An EDI transaction set is roughly equivalent to a typical business form, such as a purchase order, and consists of data segments, each containing various fields delimited by some character. These fields represent individual elements of the business transaction, such as company name, account number, quantity, and so on; they are formatted according to a standard code. This code is then implemented as a map between your business application's data fields and the type of EDI standard appropriate to the transaction performed.

EDI transactions are typically processed in batch form. Some forms of interactive EDI have emerged, but the basic architecture of EDI was designed around the concept of mainframe batch processing.

Implementation

EDI-enabled systems communicate through translation software that formats the data into standard EDI encoding format. This information is then exchanged using one of several methods:

- Using a dedicated leased line between the business partners. This method is expensive but is often employed by large enterprises that have high volumes of EDI transactions to process.
- Using a dial-up modem connection between business partners. This method saves costs by using EDI's strength batch-processing strength. Transactions can be queued and then sent as a batch job over a dial-up connection to save money. Small to medium-sized supply-chain partners often use this method to exchange business information with a large company purchasing their goods or services.
- Through an external third-party value-added network (VAN) service provider that acts as a clearinghouse for EDI transactions. The VAN processes EDI messages and routes them to the appropriate electronic mailbox for the destination business partner, who can then retrieve the EDI messages from the mailbox and process the transactions using business applications. The VAN is responsible for message routing, delivery, security, auditing, and archiving. This approach has grown in popularity over the last decade and is probably the most popular EDI implementation in use today.

A newer method used by small suppliers to exchange EDI information with large manufacturers is Web-enabled EDI. Typically, a VAN will offer a Web forms front end that the supplier can use to submit invoices and issue receipts to the purchasing company. This saves suppliers considerable costs over having to build EDI into the back end of their business processes but involves additional expenditure of manual labor in entering data into the forms. Nevertheless, this is a popular scheme that has become widely implemented in some sectors.

Advantages and Disadvantages

Besides its entrenched usage in the big business marketplace, particularly in government, manufacturing, transport, and warehouse sales, EDI has other advantages over such emerging technologies as Extensible Markup Language (XML). For one thing, EDI messages are compact, using a highly condensed format that makes them difficult to read. XML messages, by comparison, are plain text and tend to be much larger than EDI messages. As a result, small businesses that use dial-up connections for exchanging business information with their purchasers and suppliers can save online costs using EDI compared to XML. Because EDI mainly uses leased lines, the technology is intrinsically more secure than a technology such as XML that uses an insecure public network such as the Internet. However, by employing virtual private network (VPN) technology for tunneling over the Internet, the level of security in using XML has been made comparable to that of EDI.

While the costs of implementing EDI or leasing VAN services might at first glance seem higher than XML, this is not actually true because XML is not yet an established standard for communication of business transactions. In particular, XML has the same hidden costs as EDI due to the expense of building either system into a company's back-end business processes, which usually requires much customized programming and tinkering.

EDI's disadvantages are more perception than reality. That EDI is difficult to implement is acknowledged, but so is any translation system that must be deeply integrated into the back end of a company's business software, and nowadays EDI-enabled Enterprise Resource Planning (ERP) and customer relationship management CRM systems are commonly available, as are tools for helping developers custom-build EDI into existing business processes. Another perceived disadvantage of EDI is that it is complex and difficult to learn, but most EDI programmers would disagree with this assessment.

Marketplace

Some of the bigger VANs in the EDI marketplace include GE Information Services and IBM's Advantis. General Electric also offers a Web-based EDI service called GE TradeWeb, which provides companies with browser-based access to a library of EDI-enabled Web forms and an EDI mailbox for exchanging transactions with their business partners. Another player in this market is Sterling Commerce with its Gentran Web Suite, which uses Microsoft ActiveX technologies.

For the foreseeable future, both EDI and XML are expected to coexist, and as a result efforts are under way by both standards bodies and vendors to harmonize the two. Vitria Technology offers a kind of universal translation system for changing EDI information into XML and vice versa. General Electric is implementing the XMLSolutions Business Integration Platform to streamline its online procurement system. Another player in this hybrid EDI/XML service provider market is Paper-Free Systems, now acquired by Sybase.

Prospects

Some analysts view the emergence of XML as a threat to the very existence of EDI, supposedly relegating EDI to the arena of legacy systems. This is hardly the case, and most of the electronic business world still gets by using EDI. However, XML has some advantages over EDI; namely, it is more flexible, easier to work with, and more open in its specifications. On the other hand, just as there are different flavors of EDI that hinder interoperability, XML itself has more than 100 different variants, and it might take an initiative such as ebXML (Electronic Business Extensible Markup Language) to bring order to the XML chaos and make XML a truly viable alternative to EDI.

Most large companies are somewhat reluctant to migrate wholesale form EDI to XML. Besides the considerable investment they have already made in EDI systems and the "if it ain't broke, don't fix it" attitude that results, a big concern is the reliability of using XML for exchange of business information over the Internet. Because large businesses usually implement EDI using leased lines, carriers can provide these companies with service-level agreements (SLAs) guaranteeing minimal downtime. The Internet is another factor, however, and it is hard to guarantee bandwidth and availability for information transmitted over the Internet. For batch processing of EDI transactions this is not a big issue, but for companies with delay-sensitive assembly-line processes that use real-time EDI for procurement of direct materials, the XML/Internet combination does not offer the same guarantees as the leased-line/VAN implementations of EDI. As a result, large companies that depend on EDI have been reluctant to open their supply chains to replace EDI with XML, and many are taking a wait-and-see attitude, believing that if they fall behind in the short run they can always use their deep pockets to catch up in the long run.

For More Information

Visit the Data Interchange Standards Association (DISA) at *www.disa.org*.

See Also: *B2B, e-business, XML*

Electronic Industries Alliance (EIA)

The main trade organization representing the U.S. high-tech community.

Overview

The Electronic Industries Alliance (EIA) was founded in 1924 as the Radio Manufacturers Association. The EIA plays an important role in enabling U.S. electronics producers to be competitive by developing technical standards, hosting trade shows and seminars, performing market analyses, and facilitating relations with the government. The EIA represents a broad spectrum of U.S. electronics manufacturing interests.

The EIA is organized along the lines of specific electronic products and markets, with each sector, group, or division having its own board of directors and its own agenda for enhancing competitiveness. Major divisions include the components, consumer electronics, electronic information, industrial electronics, government, and telecommunications divisions.

An important computer networking function of the EIA is the series of standards for residential and commercial network cabling that are collectively known as the EIA/TIA wiring standards. Individuals and companies installing cabling for computer networks must follow these standards to meet government legal and safety requirements.

For More Information

Visit the Electronic Industries Alliance (EIA) at *www.eia.org*.

electronic tape vaulting

The practice of backing up data directly to a remote backup facility.

Overview

Classic backup procedures involve backing up data regularly to network tape drives and libraries. In addition, daily copy backups are made of critical business data on servers and these tapes are taken off-site to a secure storage facility. When a disaster occurs, recovery using these off-site daily copies typically takes 48 to 72 hours because the hardware failure must be repaired or the server replaced, the operating system installed, and tapes shipped in from the off-site storage location. Some data is typically lost permanently under this scenario because the tapes are written only once a day but business transactions take place continually.

Electronic tape vaulting, or e-vaulting, is a technique that helps make recovery times faster and restores more up-to-date. In a typical scenario, e-vaulting supplements an existing backup plan similar to the one described above. Information written to local storage on servers is also transmitted over the network through a wide area network (WAN) link to a remote e-vaulting site, where it is written to tape. Data can be e-vaulted periodically (once an hour, for example), or even continuously as each transaction occurs. This transactional information, coupled with traditional daily copy backups, allows databases and other business information to be restored with little or no data loss.

Marketplace

Large enterprises have been using e-vaulting for some time, but recently with the proliferation of storage service providers (SSPs) even small to medium-sized businesses can lease e-vaulting services from a provider. An example of such a service is provided by CNT, a specialist in storage area networking and other storage technologies, and Iron Mountain, a global leader in records management services. Using UltraNet, CNT's storage networking solution, a company can e-vault information incrementally to Iron Mountain's tape vaulting sites.

Notes

E-vaulting can also be used to back up data directly to mirror servers running at remote locations controlled either by the company itself or by storage service providers. This form of e-vaulting is more properly called mirroring.

See Also: *backup, disaster recovery, mirroring*

e-mail

Stands for electronic mail; any system for electronically sending and receiving messages.

Overview

E-mail is arguably the technology that has had the greatest impact on how companies conduct businesses in modern times. E-mail has become the lifeblood of business, with some analysts estimating that fully one-third of all business-related information resides on mail servers, users' personal folders, and mail archiving systems.

E-mail is used for virtually every type of business communication, including marketing, invoicing, and customer service. E-mail saves businesses millions of dollars through the elimination of costly paper contracts, invoices, and receipts. E-mail also costs businesses millions of dollars in wasted time dealing with spam (unsolicited commercial e-mail) and undoing the effects of e-mail viruses. Despite these negative aspects, however, most companies would be at a standstill if their e-mail systems went down.

Estimates suggest that the number of commercial and private e-mail mailboxes globally was more than 500 million in 1999 and may well top 1 billion by the end of 2002. With the advent of wireless messaging, this figure may increase much more rapidly in the next few years. E-mail today is what the telephone was at the beginning of the century—a technology that shaped the evolution of business and commerce worldwide.

History

While e-mail had its roots in the early 1970s with the UNIX community and ARPANET, the first widely-used commercial e-mail system was the IBM mainframe host-based system called PROFS. Early e-mail systems were purely text-based and were expensive to deploy and complex to maintain, but they had an immediate impact on business.

With the move from mainframe systems to a client/server environment in the 1980s, a new breed of e-mail system arose called workgroup mail or LAN mail. Notable products in this area included Microsoft Mail, Lotus cc:Mail, and Novell GroupWise. Over time, these were replaced with collaborative systems that allowed users to exchange not only messages but also schedule and task information. Popular examples of these third-generation systems included Microsoft Exchange and Lotus Notes.

While these developments were occurring, efforts were under way to develop global standards for electronic messaging. These efforts resulted in two main systems: Simple Mail Transfer Protocol (SMTP), developed by the Internet community, and X.400, developed by the International Telecommunication Union (ITU). X.400 rapidly became a popular messaging format that is still used in parts of Europe, but SMTP mail, which was developed in the United States as part of the ARPANET project, eventually superseded X.400 and now enjoys worldwide popularity and acceptance as the universal e-mail system. Messaging and collaboration platforms, such as Microsoft Exchange, now support SMTP by default.

Implementation

Early local area network (LAN) mail systems such as Microsoft Mail and Lotus cc:Mail were essentially passive systems where the mail server was nothing more than a set of folders for containing users' mail. It was up to the mail client to deliver messages to the server and retrieve waiting messages. All processing was thus done by the client, which would periodically poll the server to see if any mail was waiting for it to download. These systems were cheap and easily set up and maintained, but they scaled poorly and had difficulty supporting more than a few hundred users effectively.

The next evolution of e-mail was client/server messaging. Here the passive mail server was replaced by an active server that contacted the client when mail was ready to be picked up. This push model of message delivery was more effective than the old pull model of constant server polling by the client, and it also made messaging more secure. In a client/server system, the client and the server both share the processing and transport of messages.

The X.400 messaging standards introduced a set of standard terminology and concepts into the messaging arena. The most notable of these new terms was MTA (message transport agent or mail transport agent), which was responsible for routing, or forwarding, messages across the network to its destination mail server. A complex messaging system would have a number of MTAs handling mail delivery. In the UNIX world where SMTP mail was born, a popular MTA was developed called Sendmail, which is still widely used on the Internet. Early UNIX mail clients such as Pine and Elm soon became popular, especially at universities and among government researchers. To augment the functionality of SMTP mail, a number of other Internet mail protocols were developed, including Post Office Protocol (POP) and Internet Message Access Protocol (IMAP), which enabled individual mailboxes to be assigned to users, and Multipurpose Internet Mail Extensions (MIME), which made it possible for text-based e-mail to contain binary information such as multimedia files and executables. SMTP itself was extended through SMTP Service Extensions and e-mail was made secure with such new technologies as Pretty Good Privacy (PGP) and Secure MIME (S/MIME).

Marketplace

For corporate messaging and collaboration, the market leader today is probably Microsoft Exchange 2000, a powerful platform that supports a host of features and can be deployed in a wide range of environments, from workgroups to enterprises to service providers. On the Internet, however, Sendmail is still the most popular program for forwarding SMTP mail.

Web-based e-mail allows users to access their personal mailboxes from anywhere on the Internet using a PC with a Web browser and a modem. Microsoft Exchange

2000 Server includes a feature called Outlook Web Access (OWA) that supports this kind of e-mail, as do Lotus iNotes R5, Novell GroupWise 5.5e, Imail Server from Ipswitch, and InScribe Internet Messaging Server Web Mail from Critical Path.

In the wireless messaging arena, a major player is Research In Motion (RIM) with its BlackBerry messaging system. The BlackBerry server application works with Microsoft Exchange or Lotus Notes mail servers and allows messages to be relayed to BlackBerry handheld devices. This allows mobile professionals such as IT (information technology) administrators, to be alerted when systems go down, and it is a more effective way of communicating than using simple pagers. BlackBerry is also a very secure messaging platform because it uses Triple Data Encryption Standard (Triple DES) for encrypting all transmissions.

Service providers, too, now offer various commercial e-mail services to businesses. For businesses that need to send out mass mailings and do not want to overwhelm their mail servers with these duties, companies such as BoldFish offer server software that simplifies the creation and transmission of large volumes of e-mail. Businesses can also outsource this activity to service providers.

Issues

The greatest obstacle to wider use of e-mail in business has been security. Traditionally, SMTP mail has been transmitted in clear text across the Internet, a notoriously unsafe place for such an action to be performed. The slow evolution toward universally trusted public key infrastructure (PKI) systems has hindered the widespread deployment of encrypted messaging and has led to other solutions such as PGP being adopted by some businesses in the meantime. Another solution called Privacy Enhanced Mail (PEM) was developed by the Internet Engineering Task Force (IETF) and is commercially offered by vendors such as RSA Data Security and Trusted Information Systems.

Besides the encryption issue, the last few years have seen the proliferation of what many thought could never occur: e-mail viruses. Some of these viruses have wreaked terrific havoc on corporate and commercial messaging systems around the world. The first such instance was the Internet worm developed by Robert Morris in 1988, which took advantage of a weakness in Sendmail to bring down 6,000 SMTP mail servers around the globe in only 24 hours. More recent examples include the Melissa and LoveLetter viruses, which exploited enhanced collaboration features of Microsoft Outlook to crash mail servers at major Internet service providers (ISPs) and large corporations.

The growing trend toward Hypertext Markup Language (HTML) mail instead of plaintext messaging has also had its associated issues. For example, some marketing companies now send out their HTML messages with a tiny 1-pixel scripted image called a bug in them. The result is that when a user opens the message to read it in his mail program, information such as his Internet Protocol (IP) address and Web site visiting habits is collected from his machine and transmitted to the company. Some companies deal with such issues by simply disabling HTML mail altogether or preventing scripts from running on mail clients, but this seriously hinders the collaborative power of modern mail applications.

Prospects

E-mail continues to gain ground in the business world through such innovative technologies as Web-based messaging, which allows a user to access his personal mailbox from any Internet-enabled PC that has a Web browser on it, and wireless messaging, the "next big thing," is starting to make big inroads in the enterprise through BlackBerry and Personal Digital Assistants (PDAs) Palm and PocketPC.

On the other hand, the next big thing may be the legal issues associated with the growing mountain of old e-mail residing on mail servers in back rooms of corporate networks. In regulated industries such as banking and securities trading, the law requires that all documents relating to business activity be retained for a number of years. Companies often archive old mail in user folders to file servers, but this makes it difficult to search for specific messages when required. In several instances, companies that were sued have been forced to settle because it was simply not cost-feasible for them to search through hundreds of millions of old e-mail messages for documentation that could have won their case. It is important for companies to develop digital records management policies that articulate how old e-mail should be handled and to enforce these policies to limit their legal liability when challenged in court.

Even from a business point of view, having so much critical information stored in nonrelational database management system (RDBMS) systems such as mail servers means that executives and management sometimes lack the information necessary to make truly informed decisions. The emergence of Enterprise Knowledge Portals (EKPs) is one bright spot here, as these systems are designed in part to help tap the unrealized potential of business information stored in old e-mail.

See Also: *ESMTP, Exchange Server, Internet Mail Access Protocol version 4 (IMAP4), Multipurpose Internet Mail Extensions (MIME), Post Office Protocol version 3 (POP3), Pretty Good Privacy (PGP), Privacy Enhanced Mail (PEM), Secure/Multipurpose Internet Mail Extensions (S/MIME), Simple Mail Transfer Protocol (SMTP), X.400*

e-mail address

Any address that ensures that an e-mail message reaches its intended recipient.

Overview

An e-mail address must contain sufficient information so that the message can be routed to its specific recipient. There are various kinds of e-mail address formats depending on the e-mail system in use. Address formats typically include at least two parts:

- **User portion:** This indicates the name or alias of the user to whom the mail is directed.
- **Routing portion:** This indicates the information needed to route the message to the particular mail system where the user's mailbox resides.

The following table shows some examples of e-mail address formats.

E-Mail Address Formats

Type of Address	*Example*
SMTP (Internet)	JeffS@Northwind.Microsoft.com
Microsoft Mail	Northwind/MICROSOFT/JEFFS
Lotus cc:Mail	JeffS at Northwind
X.400	C=US;a=SPRINT;p=Microsoft; o=Northwind;s=JeffS

E

embedded system

Any type of small-footprint specialized computer system used in industrial, commercial, and consumer applications.

Overview

An embedded system is essentially a way of making ordinary industrial and consumer devices "smart" by embedding computer technology in them. An embedded system typically consists of a single microprocessor, a small amount of memory, a specialized operating system, and applications. These applications are used to control and manage certain functions of the device that contains the embedded system. Typical uses for embedded systems are control and monitoring of industrial machinery and automated management of plant and assembly line operations.

Embedded systems typically have limited processing power and task-specific applications that are used to control and manage larger systems. They may be responsive to environmental or user-controlled conditions and may operate alone or be networked to other systems by wireline or wireless networks, including the Internet.

Examples of embedded systems abound, including

- Industrial sensors and control equipment
- Automobile antilock brake systems
- Automobile Global Positioning Systems (GPSs)
- DVD and VCR players
- Digital cameras
- Microwave ovens

Some analysts estimate there are over 5 billion embedded systems in operation today in industrial, commercial, and consumer devices.

Marketplace

In the 1980s and 1990s, most embedded systems were variants on the 8086 and 8088 processors and used DOS as their operating system platform. In recent years the market has opened up, and a number of vendors are competing in the embedded operating systems marketplace. Big players include

- Microsoft Corporation, with its Windows CE and Embedded NT operating systems platforms. Microsoft's embedded operating systems have the advantages of having mature integrated development environments (IDEs) that allow developers to quickly create and deploy applications for embedded systems, and support Transmission Control Protocol/Internet Protocol (TCP/IP) networking, Internet, and wireless networking application programming interfaces (APIs) for building distributed networks of smart devices.
- Sun Microsystems, with its Java 2 Micro Edition (J2ME). J2ME exploits the ease of development of the Java platform and has a moderate memory footprint (128 kilobytes [kB] or higher). Third-party vendor Metrowerks has an IDE for J2ME called CodeWarrior that allows embedded J2ME applications to be developed rapidly and easily. Because of the sandbox implementation of the Java VM, however, J2ME is considered by some analysts to be unsuitable for time-sensitive deterministic embedded systems such as microprocessor control systems for spacecraft or automobiles.
- Red Hat Linux, with its Linux for Embedded Developers, offers the advantages of Linux's stability and small-footprint operation (32 KB or more).
- Wind River Systems, whose VxWorks embedded operating system has been used in devices as diverse as digital cameras, Hewlett-Packard printers, and the Mars Lander space vehicle built for the National Aeronautics and Space Administration (NASA).

Prospects

An impetus has been given to the embedded systems market in recent times through the widespread availability of the Internet. Most analysts expect that the greatest growth of embedded systems in the next few years will be in the area of small Internet appliances such as Web-enabled Personal Digital Assistants (PDAs) and cell phones. The continuing advancements in processor technology that have led to continually more powerful chips for continually lower prices have also provided impetus to the growth of the embedded sector.

For More Information

Visit Microsoft's embedded systems site at *www.microsoft.com/embedded.*

See Also: *Java, Linux, Windows CE*

Emergency Management Services (EMS)

A feature of the Microsoft Windows .NET Server family that allows servers to run in headless operation.

Overview

Traditionally, UNIX enterprise systems have been configurable for headless operation—that is, running servers without a keyboard, mouse, or video card. Such headless servers are typically used for greater security and are run behind closed doors. Administrators manage these systems by using Telnet to connect to them over the network and issue administrative commands.

Windows .NET Server supports headless operation through its Emergency Management Services (EMS) feature. EMS allows a Windows .NET server to be run in headless mode and managed using a Telnet-based administration console. All management instructions are sent to the headless server using text-based commands.

Implementation

To implement a headless server, you must first enable EMS on the server, either through selecting this option during setup or by configuring the boot loader file afterward. A null modem is then used to connect the headless system through its serial port to VT100 terminal emulation software on a client machine. If the hardware supports it, the VT100 client can also manage the headless server through the universal serial bus (USB) port or over an Ethernet network using an RJ-45 jack.

Notes

To run Windows .NET Server in headless mode, the system's basic input/output system (BIOS) must allow operation without a video card, keyboard, or mouse.

See Also: *Telnet, terminal emulator, Windows .NET Server*

emergency repair disk (ERD)

A Microsoft Windows 2000 recovery tool for repairing missing or corrupt files and restoring the registry.

Overview

In Windows NT, the emergency repair disk (ERD) was a valuable recovery tool for restoring the registry or replacing boot files on a corrupted system. The Windows NT ERD contained compressed versions of registry hive, default user profile, setup.log, and other system configuration files, and it could be created from the command line using the Rdisk command.

In Windows 2000, the ERD is a little different. Instead of containing registry hives, it contains only boot files and some pointers to operating system files. When a Windows 2000 system is first installed, the registry hives are backed up to \Winnt\repair directory. Also, the ERD is created by selecting an option in the Windows 2000 Backup tool. When the Backup tool is used to back up the registry, this backup is placed in \Winnt\repair\regback.

You can use the ERD to restore a corrupted master boot record (MBR), restore missing or corrupted boot files such as Ntldr, or restore the registry from backup. However, when ERD is used to restore the registry, it does so from \Winnt\repair instead of \Winnt\repair\regback, using the pristine form of the registry that is backed during the initial installation. For more fine-grained control of restoring the registry, use the new Recovery Console tool of Windows 2000 instead of the ERD.

Having a current copy of the ERD for each server on your network is a critical part of preparing for disaster recovery. Always create a new ERD after installing new services or software or upgrading hardware or device drivers on a system.

Uses

To perform a system recovery on a machine running Windows 2000, try booting to Safe Mode first by pressing the F8 function key during startup. If this fails or if the system cannot be repaired, boot the system using the four boot floppies, select the Repair option by pressing the R key when prompted, and then either use the ERD to attempt a repair or press C to open the Recovery Console. The Recovery Console is a powerful command-line interface to the operating system designed for use only by advanced administrators.

Notes

If you cannot find your four Windows 2000 boot floppies, insert the Windows 2000 compact disc and a blank floppy into any machine running MS-DOS or Windows, click Start, select Run, and enter the following path into the Run box:

```
<cdrom_drive>\bootdisk\makeboot a:
```

In Windows XP and Windows .NET Server, ERD is being replaced by a feature called Automated System Recovery (ASR).

See Also: *Automatic System Recovery (ASR)*

emergency startup disk

A floppy disk created during the setup process for Microsoft Windows 98 and Windows Millennium Edition (Me) that can be used to troubleshoot boot problems.

Overview

The emergency startup disk contains files necessary to load a command-line version of Windows, plus other useful system-recovery utilities, including a real-mode registry editor. When you insert an emergency startup disk into your computer and reboot, the computer starts from the disk instead of from the hard drive.

Having a current copy of the emergency startup disk for each machine running Windows 98 or Windows Me on your network helps with disaster recovery if these machines fail to boot properly. You should create a new emergency startup disk whenever you make a configuration change to a machine running Windows—for example, when you install new hardware or update device drivers.

E

EMI

Stands for electromagnetic interference, electrical noise induced in cabling by the presence of nearby electrical equipment such as motors, air conditioners, fluorescent lights, and power lines.

See: *electromagnetic interference (EMI)*

EMS

Stands for Emergency Management Services, a feature of the Windows .NET Server family that allows a server to run in headless operation.

See: *Emergency Management Services (EMS)*

emulation

Any process by which one device mimics the functions of another device.

Overview

In computer networks, emulation usually refers to protocol conversion, a process by which a device that understands one protocol can speak with a device that understands a different, incompatible protocol. The environment in which emulation is chiefly used is mainframe computing, where asynchronous terminal emulators are used to emulate and replace more expensive synchronous terminals. For example, a PC with a modem and VT100 terminal emulation software can replace a synchronous VT100 terminal, eliminating the need for a dedicated serial connection between the mainframe and the terminal.

Common types of mainframe terminal emulators include

- **3270:** The 3270 synchronous protocol is used by IBM mainframe hosts that use the Systems Network Architecture (SNA).
- **5250:** The 5250 synchronous protocol is used in the IBM S-series mainframe environment and in AS/400 midframe environments.

See Also: *3270, 5250*

Encapsulating Security Payload (ESP)

A protocol in the IPsec suite of protocols that handles encryption.

Overview

IPsec is actually a suite of protocols that consists of two main protocols:

- **Authentication Header (AH):** This protocol ensures that IPsec packets have not been altered during transmission and to verify the sender's identity. AH is included in IPsec to provide authenticity.
- **Encapsulating Security Payload (ESP):** This protocol ensures that IPsec packets cannot be read except by their intended recipients. ESP is included in IPsec to provide privacy.

ESP is generally used in conjunction with AH to provide maximum security and integrity for IPsec transmissions. However, either ESP or AH can be used alone if sufficient for the intended purposes.

By default, ESP uses the symmetric encryption algorithm Data Encryption Standard (DES) to encrypt the payload of an IPsec packet. ESP can also be configured to use Triple DES, depending upon encryption export restrictions of the business involved.

See Also: *Authentication Header (AH), Internet Protocol Security (IPsec)*

encapsulation

Generally, the process of enclosing one type of data packet using another type of data packet.

Overview

Encapsulation occurs when a lower-layer protocol receives data from a higher-layer protocol and then places the data into the data portion of its packet format. Encapsulation at the lowest levels of the Open Systems

Interconnection (OSI) reference model is usually referred to as framing. Examples of different types of encapsulation include

- An Ethernet frame that encapsulates an Internet Protocol (IP) packet, which itself encapsulates a Transmission Control Protocol (TCP) packet, which then encapsulates the actual data being transmitted over the network
- An Ethernet frame encapsulated in an Asynchronous Transfer Mode (ATM) frame for transmission over an ATM backbone

The data-link layer (Layer 2) of the OSI networking model is responsible for encapsulating or framing data for transmission over the physical medium. In local area network (LAN) technologies, this is usually Carrier Sense Multiple Access with Collision Detection (CSMA/CD) for Ethernet networks. For wide area network (WAN) technologies, the data-link protocols used depend on whether the communications are point-to-point or multipoint:

- For point-to-point communications, possible WAN data-link protocols include Point-to-Point Protocol (PPP) and High-level Data Link Control (HDLC) protocol.
- For multipoint communications, possible WAN data-link protocols include frame relay, ATM, Switched Multimegabit Data Services (SMDS), and X.25.

See Also: *frame, Open Systems Interconnection (OSI) reference model*

Encrypting File System (EFS)

A feature of Microsoft Windows 2000, Windows XP, and Windows .NET Server that allows files stored on NTFS file system (NTFS) volumes to be secured through encryption.

Overview

Encrypting File System (EFS) is designed to protect data on NTFS volumes from local access by unauthorized user EFS which does not work onFAT orFAT32 volumes encrypts information in files at the bit level so that if a hard drive is stolen from a user's system and placed in another system, the information on the drive will be unreadable. In this way, EFS ensures the privacy of a user's information stored on disk and finds particular application with systems vulnerable to theft, such as laptop computers.

EFS is integrated in the NTFS used by Windows 2000, Windows XP, and Windows .NET Server; it is not available for older forms of NTFS, such as the one used in Windows NT 4. EFS operates transparently from the point of view of users: files are automatically encrypted when they are created or moved to encrypted folders and are automatically decrypted when the user needs to access the information stored within them.

EFS also includes a Data Recovery System that employs a trusted recovery agent (usually the Administrator account) that can decrypt any user's encrypted files in an emergency.

The following EFS features have been added to Windows XP Professional and Windows .NET Server editions:

- Additional users can be authorized to access encrypted files.
- Offline files can now be encrypted.
- Data recovery agents are recommended options.
- The Triple-DES encryption algorithm can be used to replace DESX.
- A password reset disk can be used to safely reset a user's password.
- Encrypted files can be stored in Web folders.

Implementation

EFS employs a combination of private and public key cryptography schemes. When EFS receives a request to encrypt a file, a secret (private) key is automatically generated in the form of a random number string. This secret key is called the File Encryption Key (FEK) and is generated using a modified version of the Data Encryption Standard (DES). The FEK itself is secured by encrypting it using the user's private key—a public/private key pair is automatically generated for each user and stored in Active Directory directory service. The encrypted FEK is stored on disk with the user's encrypted files.

The advantage of using this combination of two encryption schemes is that the faster symmetric encryption scheme is used for actual encryption and decryption of file data and the slower public key scheme is used only to protect the user's own private key from theft and misuse. Although EFS employs public key encryption, it does not require a certificate authority (CA) to issue public/private key pairs. Instead, EFS automatically generates these key pairs for individual users and for trusted recovery agents.

Notes

If you are working with applications that create temporary files, you might want to enable encryption at the folder level instead of the file level to guard against unauthorized access to your temporary files. With folder-level encryption, all files in the folder are encrypted.

See Also: *encryption, encryption algorithm*

encryption

The process of rendering information unreadable to all but the intended recipients, who have the ability to decrypt it.

Overview

Cryptography is the science of creating workable procedures for encrypting and decrypting messages. Encrypting messages and transmissions ensures their

- **Privacy:** No one can read an encrypted message other than its intended recipients.
- **Integrity:** An encrypted messages that is intercepted in transit and modified generally becomes garbage when received by its intended recipient—a simple test of whether the message has been tampered with.
- **Authenticity:** A good encryption scheme will help you verify that the message was indeed sent by the person it says it is from by authenticating the identity of the sender.

Cryptography's goal is to ensure that an encrypted message intercepted by a distrusted user cannot be decrypted in a feasible amount of time. Encryption is synonymous with cryptography and has been the basis of all secure communications since ancient times. With the rapid growth in recent years of the Internet as the de facto medium for businesses and consumers to exchange information, encryption has taken on new importance resulting in an explosion of cryptographic technologies and standards has resulted.

Uses

Symmetric key encryption is widely used for securing digital transmission of information. For example, the DES encryption scheme used by the U.S. government since 1974 is a symmetric key encryption algorithm, as is its recent successor, the Advanced Encryption Standard (AES). Symmetric key encryption is also employed in the Windows NT LAN Manager (NTLM) authentication scheme of Microsoft Windows NT and in Kerberos, the default authentication scheme of Microsoft Windows 2000, Windows XP, and Windows .NET Server.

Asymmetric or public key encryption, on the other hand, is widely used on the Internet in the form of the SSL protocol discussed previously. Public key encryption was developed by Whitefield Diffie and Martin Hellman in 1976, and it was made popular by Phil Zimmerman with his Pretty Good Privacy (PGP) encryption scheme for e-mail messaging, which was first released in 1991.

Asymmetric encryption is much slower than symmetric encryption, so many encryption technologies use a combination of the two. In SSL, for example, asymmetric encryption is used during SSL session initialization to securely exchange a secret key between users so that the remaining encryption performed during the session is done using the much faster symmetric encryption scheme.

Implementation

The basic element that makes possible both encryption and decryption is the key. A key is typically a numeric value that is employed in a mathematical procedure called an encryption algorithm to convert ordinary text (plaintext) into encrypted text (ciphertext) and vice versa (encryption algorithms are discussed separately in the corresponding article in this chapter). The number of keys used and the details of how they are employed distinguishes two basic types of encryption, namely symmetric and asymmetric (public) key encryption.

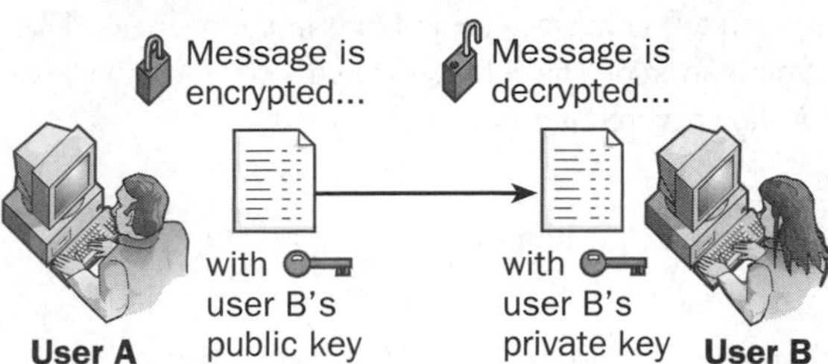

Encryption. *The public key encryption method.*

Symmetric key encryption uses a secret key known only to the sender and the recipient of the message (and perhaps to others whom they trust). The secret key is used to encrypt the message when it is sent and to decrypt it when it is received. The actual encryption process involves mathematically combining (hashing or transforming) the message and the key in some complex fashion that is virtually impossible to undo unless the recipient also has the key. Symmetric key encryption is very secure, but suffers from one problem—if you want to send a message to someone who does not have your key, you must also find a way to securely transmit a copy of the key. This difficulty makes symmetric key encryption generally unworkable for electronic communication over a network or telecommunications service, except where only the original sender and recipient will need the key. For example, symmetric key encryption works in cellular phone communication when only the subscriber and the service provider need a copy of the user's key. Symmetric key encryption is the oldest form of encryption, dating from at least Roman times.

Asymmetric or public key encryption is a newer method that is becoming widely used in many computer networking and telecommunications systems. For example, public key encryption is employed by the Secure Sockets Layer (SSL) protocol used for transmitting sensitive information such as credit card numbers over the Internet. SSL establishes a secure communications session over the Internet by using public key encryption, which provides every participating user with a public key and a private key. Users are the only ones who know their private keys, whereas their public keys are generally available to anyone who wants them. Remember that if a message is encrypted with a user's public key, it can be decrypted only with the same user's private key, and vice versa.

For example, in public key encryption, if user A wanted to send an encrypted message to user B, it would typically work like this:

1. User A requests user B's public key or obtains this key from a certificate authority (CA) that both users trust.
2. User A encrypts his message using user B's public key and sends the encrypted message to user B.
3. User B receives the encrypted message from user A and decrypts it with user B's private key.

The preceding approach outlines the steps used for encrypting and decrypting the actual message being transmitted during a secure communication session. A different approach, called a digital signature, is used to confirm the sender's authenticity and the message's integrity. Digital signatures are encrypted in a reverse fashion to the message itself. Specifically, if user A wants to send his digital signature to user B, then

1. User A creates a hash of his message using a hashing algorithm. This hash forms the basis of the digital signature, which user A then encrypts using his own private key.
2. User A appends the encrypted digital signature and his own public key to the message, which is then encrypted using user B's public key.
3. User B receives the message and attachments, decrypts its contents using her own private key, and uses user A's public key to decrypt the digital signature that he attached to the message. User B then generates a hash of the received message and compares this to the digital signature that user A sent. If the two are identical, it is unlikely that the message has been tampered with in transit.

Issues

Export of encryption technology is controlled by U.S. law. Certain encryption schemes can be exported only to trusted nations and might require a government review before such export is allowed.

E

See Also: *Advanced Encryption Standard (AES), Data Encryption Standard (DES), encryption algorithm, Pretty Good Privacy (PGP), public key cryptography, Secure Sockets Layer (SSL)*

encryption algorithm

A mathematical procedure for encrypting data using a key.

Overview

Encryption algorithms form the basis by which encryption can take place and are fundamental to cryptography. Encryption algorithms generally use some kind of mathematical key (chosen from a large set of available keys) to transform plaintext (the data being encrypted) into ciphertext (the resulting encrypted data). An encryption algorithm must be reversible so that the recipient can use another mathematical key to decrypt the data. A good encryption algorithm should be difficult to decrypt if you do not know the decrypting key, and the only method that should be possible to force decryption should be the brute force method of simply trying every possible decryption key (in other words, there must be no shortcuts or back doors for decryption). If an encryption algorithm is really good, it would take massively parallel computers centuries, or even eons, of intense processing, trying all possible keys, to decrypt a single message if they do not know the specific decryption key.

Implementation

Encryption algorithms typically perform their encryption process on multibyte segments of data instead of on one byte at a time. Such an algorithm is known as a block cipher because it encrypts data one block at a time. For example, the Data Encryption Standard (DES) algorithm, a 56-bit key algorithm used for many years by the U.S. government, encrypts data 64 bytes at a time.

Encryption algorithms employ mathematical procedures called hash functions, which are repeatedly applied to plaintext to scramble it into ciphertext. The combination of a hash function and a key form the basis for the encryption process.

Examples

Encryption algorithms are of two basic types: symmetric and asymmetric.

Symmetric algorithms employ the same key, called a secret key, for both encryption and decryption of a message. This process is also known as asymmetric or secret key cryptography. Examples of symmetric algorithms include

- **DES:** This uses a 56-bit key and was the U.S. government standard for encryption until 2001, when it was replaced by the Advanced Encryption Standard (AES). DES is no longer considered secure and was first cracked in 1997.
- **AES:** This can use keys up to 256 bits in length, and it has replaced DES as the official U.S. government encryption standard.

Asymmetric algorithms employ a different key for encrypting and decrypting data. The two keys are mathematically related and are called a key pair, with the private key used for encrypting the message and the public key used for decrypting it. Examples of asymmetric algorithms include

- **Diffie-Hellman:** Developed by Whitefield Diffie and Martin Hellman in 1976, this is the original public key encryption algorithm and is used in the Secure Sockets Layer (SSL) protocol on the Internet for securely exchanging secret keys between remote systems.
- **Rivest-Shamir-Adelman (RSA):** Developed in 1997 by the Ron Rivest, Adi Shamir, and Leonard Adelman, this algorithm can be used both for encryption and secure authentication. It is used in SSL, Transport Layer Security (TLS), and IPsec communications in virtual private networks (VPNs) and over the Internet.

See Also: *Advanced Encryption Standard (AES), Data Encryption Standard (DES), encryption, public key cryptography*

End-User License Agreement (EULA)

A type of contract between a computer software publisher and the purchaser of the software that outlines the various rights granted to the purchaser for legal use of the software.

Overview

The End-User License Agreement (EULA) for a software product is usually found on a separate piece of paper accompanying the product, inside the front cover of the user manual, or onscreen prior to installing the software. You should read and become familiar with the terms of your EULA for the software you purchase. Failure to follow the terms of the EULA might expose you or your company to prosecution for software piracy.

You can access the EULA for Microsoft Windows Millennium Edition (Me) by opening the text file License.txt. It is located in the \Windows folder. In Windows 2000, Windows XP, and Windows .NET Server, the file is called eula.txt and is located in the \System32 folder.

For More Information

Visit Microsoft Corporation's antipiracy site at *www.microsoft.com/piracy.*

See Also: *license*

enhanced Category 5 (Cat5e) cabling

Also known simply as Cat5e, a recently ratified standard for structured local area network (LAN) wiring.

Overview

Enhanced Category 5 (Cat5e) cabling is the only ratified cabling standard that is capable of supporting transmission speeds faster that 100 megabits per second (Mbps), although Category 6 (Cat6) and Category 7 (Cat7) specifications have been proposed. Supporting frequencies up to 350 megahertz (MHz) or higher, Cat5e cabling is typically four-pair solid conductor 24-gauge unshielded twisted-pair (UTP) cabling that has a low capacitance in the range of 13 to 14 pF/foot, as compared with regular Category 5 (Cat5) cabling that has a capacitance of around 17 pF/feet. The impedance of Cat5e cabling is 100 ohms, the same as for regular Cat5 cable.

Other specifications of Cat5e include

- Attenuation less than 22 decibels (dB) at 100 MHz (same as Cat5)
- Near-end crosstalk (NEXT) less than 35.3 dB (3 dB higher than Cat5)
- Power-sum NEXT (PS-NEXT) less than 32.3 dB (unspecified for Cat5)
- Return loss less than 20.1 dB (unspecified for Cat5)

Uses

The electrical characteristics of Cat5e cabling make it the recommended type of cabling for most new installations of structured wiring, especially companies planning an eventual migration from Fast Ethernet to 1000BaseTX Gigabit Ethernet (GbE). Cat5e cabling can be used for Ethernet, Integrated Services Digital Network (ISDN) wiring, and 155-Mbps Asynchronous Transfer Mode (ATM) networks.

If you plan to use Cat5e cabling in your network, you should ensure that all your other wiring components match these specifications. This means purchasing and installing enhanced Cat5 patch panels, wall plates, and other components. Also, be sure to strictly follow wiring guidelines because improper installation of Cat5e cabling will result in loss of potential bandwidth. The real key to operating a successful high-speed UTP wiring system is careful installation.

See Also: *cabling, Category 5 (Cat5) cabling, premise cabling, structured wiring*

Enhanced Data Rates for Global Evolution (EDGE)

A third-generation (3G) upgrade for the 2.5G General Packet Radio Service (GPRS).

Overview

Enhanced Data Rates for Global Evolution (EDGE) was designed as a way of easily upgrading certain second-generation (2G) cellular systems to 3G systems with little additional cost. EDGE can be used to upgrade both Time-Division Multiple Access (TDMA) systems such as AT&T Wireless and Global System for Mobile Communications (GSM), which are also based on TDMA

E

 Enhanced Interior Gateway Routing Protocol (EIGRP)

technologies. EDGE cannot be used to upgrade Code-Division Multiple Access (CDMA) systems. The official 3G upgrade for CDMA systems is instead the International Telecommunication Union's (ITU) Wideband CDMA (W-CDMA) standard. EDGE is designed to provide mobile users with wireless roaming data services of up to 400 kilobits per second (Kbps).

EDGE comes in two flavors:

- **Enhanced Circuit-Switched Data (ECSD):** This is EDGE technology applied to circuit-switched GSM systems, which provide direct connection to the Public Switched Telephone Network (PSTN) backbone.
- **Enhanced GPRS (EGPRS):** This is EDGE technology applied to packet-switched General Packet Radio Services (GPRS) systems, which routes Internet Protocol (IP) packets over the Internet.

Implementation

EDGE works by modifying the physical layer of GSM and GPRS to increase data transmission rates threefold. This is accomplished by replacing the Gaussian Minimum Shift Keying (GMSK) encoding mechanism of GSM and GPRS, which only allows one bit of information to be encoded per symbol, to 8-bit Phase Shift Keying (8-PSK), which encodes 3 bits per symbol. The result is that the theoretical transmission speed of GPRS is raised from 171 Kbps to 513 Kbps, with similar effect for GSM (these theoretical speeds are not realized in practice due to bandwidth being used for error correction).

Above the physical layer, EDGE uses the same technologies as GSM and GPRS. Existing GSM and GPRS cellular networks are easy to upgrade to EDGE, because the same equipment can be used for both the older 2G services and the newer 3G EDGE (though some hardware and software upgrades are required). In addition, costs remain low because no additional frequency licenses are required for EDGE. Although the 400-Kbps data rates offered by EDGE fall short of the envisioned 2-megabit-per-second (Mbps) speeds for 3G cellular systems, EDGE has been ratified as an official 3G system by the ITU in its IMT-2000 specifications.

Marketplace

In North America, EDGE will soon be deployed by AT&T, the major Time Division Multiple Access (TDMA) cellular provider. This will be done in stages, first by upgrading the TDMA system to GSM together with an overlay of GPRS to support data rates of 144 Kbps. The GSM/GPRS system will then be upgraded to EDGE to provide data rates of 384 Kbps. Further 3G upgrades are likely down the road, pushing speeds to 2 Mbps.

Prospects

Although EDGE is an official standard, it is not likely to be supported in many areas outside North America because most other countries having 2G TDMA systems are likely to upgrade them to W-CDMA instead, which is incompatible with EDGE.

See Also: *2G, 2.5G, 3G, General Packet Radio Service (GPRS), Global System for Mobile Communications (GSM), Time Division Multiple Access (TDMA)*

Enhanced Interior Gateway Routing Protocol (EIGRP)

A popular interior routing protocol developed by Cisco Systems.

Overview

Enhanced Interior Gateway Routing Protocol (EIGRP) is a proprietary interior routing protocol developed by Cisco to overcome certain weaknesses of IGRP (Interior Gateway Routing Protocol), an earlier proprietary routing protocol also developed by Cisco. EIGRP is a reliable, efficient dynamic routing protocol that converges quickly and avoids routing loops. EIGRP is intended for classless routing within an autonomous system (AS) and provides a way for routers within an AS to exchange routing table information with each other.

EIGRP is a hybrid protocol that employs features of both distance vector and link state routing protocols. EIGRP is similar to IGRP in several ways:

- EIGRP is a classless interior routing protocol used inside an autonomous system.
- EIGRP uses a distance vector algorithm for calculating route metrics based on link characteristics instead of hops.

- Metrics can be based on values of bandwidth, route latency, reliability, and load.

But EIGRP also differs from IGRP in many ways, and most of these differences involve the incorporation of features common to link state routing protocols. For example:

- EIGRP includes a mechanism for automatically discovering neighboring routers using HELLO packets and downloading necessary routing information from these neighbors.
- Instead of using periodic broadcasts of entire routing tables, which consumes valuable network bandwidth, EIGRP sends out only incremental updates for routing tables and only when a change in the tables requires such updates.
- Routing table information is contained within a topology database similar to that used by link state routing protocols. Only information about adjacent routers is kept in the database, not the routing table for the entire network. This helps keep the topology database small and efficient for fast routing and helps an EIGRP router to recover quickly after a failure.

Other features of EIGRP include

- **Diffusing Update Algorithm (DUAL):** This complex routing algorithm that is similar to Dijkstra's algorithm provides fast convergence and avoids routing loops.
- **Reliable Transport Protocol (RTP):** This protocol guarantees delivery of EIGRP packets to neighboring routers.
- **Protocol-dependent modules:** This feature allows an EIGRP router to support multiple network protocols including Internet Protocol (IP), Internetwork Packet Exchange (IPX), and AppleTalk.
- **MD5 authentication:** Each EIGRP packet contains an MD5 checksum to secure routing communications from outside monitoring.

Notes

Although EIGRP and IGRP share some characteristics and can work together, they are essentially different protocols (by contrast, RIPv2 is simply Routing Information Protocol [RIP] with a few added features). EIGRP can also work seamlessly with IGRP to allow routing information to be shared across boundaries of autonomous systems, which simplifies the setup and configuration of EIGRP routers considerably.

See Also: *autonomous system (AS), classless routing protocol, dynamic routing protocol, Interior Gateway Routing Protocol (IGRP), routing protocol*

E

enterprise

A large, geographically distributed company with a high number of users.

Overview

In a computer networking context, an enterprise-level network of computers refers to the network belonging to an enterprise; that is, a network that typically consists of thousands of computers distributed across several geographically remote locations and connected by wide area network (WAN) links.

Enterprise-level networks generally use Transmission Control Protocol/Internet Protocol (TCP/IP) and are divided into a number of smaller networks called subnets, which are linked by routers. Enterprise-level networks are often heterogeneous networks consisting of different protocols and operating systems such as Microsoft Windows NT, Windows 2000, Windows XP, Windows .NET Server, Novell NetWare, and varieties of UNIX, all interoperating to various degrees. Enterprise-level networks can include legacy mainframe and minicomputer systems as well.

This mixture of systems and protocols can make it challenging to administer and manage an enterprise-level network and offers a strong argument for upgrading legacy systems to newer, standardized ones. Companies can save considerable costs in the long run by upgrading their networks to secure, reliable, scalable network operating systems such as Windows NT, Windows 2000, Windows XP, or Windows .NET Server. The initial cost of upgrades and training are quickly recouped through lower maintenance and administration costs, the result of migrating an enterprise's heterogeneous combination of systems and protocols to a homogeneous network consisting of computers running Windows NT, Windows 2000, Windows XP, or Windows .NET Server and running TCP/IP.

Enterprise Admins

A built-in group for the Microsoft Windows 2000 and Windows .NET Server operating system platforms.

Overview

Enterprise Admins is one of four global groups that Windows 2000 and Windows .NET Server create by default to help administrators organize users in their network. The other three groups are Domain Users, Domain Guests, and Domain Admins.

Although Domain Admins are users who can perform administrative tasks on any computer belonging to the domain, the Enterprise Admins group is intended to have an even larger scope. Enterprise Admins must be able to perform administrative tasks on any computer in the enterprise.

A Windows 2000– or Windows .NET Server–based enterprise can consist of a number of domains interconnected in a domain tree, or even several domain trees connected into a domain forest. Enterprise Admins can administer the entire network for the enterprise.

Just as with the Domain Admins group, the Enterprise Admins group has one initial member: the Administrator user account that belongs to the domain. The Enterprise Admins group exists only in the root domain of the forest.

See Also: *built-in group*

Enterprise Information Portal (EIP)

A business software system used to provide a single point of access to information stored in different corporate databases.

Overview

Enterprise Information Portals (EIPs) are an evolution of corporate intranets that apply portal technologies to help manage the flood of information that fuels business. Although the intranet revolutionized the way businesses handled information by providing a standard interface (the Web browser) for accessing such information, portals provide other tools such as user profiles, personalization services, workgroup and collaboration tools, automatic indexing, and push/pull information delivery that help manage large amounts of information residing in the diverse data sources of a typical enterprise.

EIPs are simply a wedding of these two technologies, turning corporate intranets into collaborative tools that deliver personalized business information to users as they need it. EIPs generally focus on managing structured information found in databases of two common types of business applications: enterprise resource planning (ERP) and customer relationship management (CRM) applications. EIPs excel in helping users identify, analyze, and present useful information mined from diverse databases used by businesses, and are in many ways simply an extension of data warehousing (DW) and data mining (DM) technologies with an additional emphasis on integrated content management (CM) technologies. EIPs generally excel in bringing together data found in structured data sources such as structured query language (SQL)– and open database connectivity (ODBC)–compliant databases. A further evolution of these systems called Enterprise Knowledge Portals (EKPs) can also mine unstructured sources such as e-mail message repositories and document management systems.

Marketplace

Many new players have appeared since the EIP market exploded in 1999. Some of the early pioneers that have gained significant market share with their packaged EIP offerings include HummingBird International, Epicentric, and Plumtree Software. Some examples of popular EIP offerings in the marketplace include Brio.Portal from Brio Technology, Corporate Portal from Plumtree, DataChannel server from DataChannel, Freedom from InfoImage, iPlanet Portal server from Sun-Netscape Alliance, and many others.

Major operating system and business applications vendors such as IBM, Oracle Corporation, Microsoft

Corporation, and Sun Microsystems also offer suites of business applications that can be used to help build EIP solutions for corporate customers. Some EIP applications are more focused on providing corporate users with workgroup tools for collaborative use, and others focus more on enabling decision-makers in a company to access the information they need to map their company's future.

Prospects

The EIP market, which started in 1998, has grown to a multibillion-dollar industry and is expected to rival the traditional ERP and CRM markets in the next few years in scope and deployment.

See Also: *Enterprise Knowledge Portal (EKP), enterprise resource planning (ERP), intranet, portal*

Enterprise Java Beans (EJB)

A Java-based technology from Sun Microsystems for building e-commerce systems.

Overview

Enterprise Java Beans (EJB) is a set of Java specifications that can be used for building Web-based distributed transactional applications typical of e-commerce and e-business solutions. EJB is a core component of Java 2 Enterprise Edition (J2EE) and works with Java Server Pages (JSP) technologies to provide tools for developers to meet the needs of businesses in today's Internet economy. EJB is particularly popular in the UNIX environment as an alternative to Common Gateway Interface (CGI) solutions based on PERL and C/C++, but EJB applications can run on any Java-supporting platform, including Linux, Solaris, AIX, Windows NT and Windows 2000.

EJB was developed under the umbrella of the Java Community Process, and its current version 1.1 is being revised toward version 2.

Implementation

EJB is implemented as an object-oriented component programming model based on the Java programming language. As a result, EJB is a platform-independent and vendor-neutral solution for building transactional applications. EJB supports both stateful and stateless transactions through its different types of session beans. It can be used to build scalable, distributed applications that run on farms of application servers, and its component-based technology speeds and simplifies the development process to gain better time-to-market advantage.

EJB operates as a server-side component technology. It includes a number of services that make it easy for developers to write middleware supporting distributed transactional processing over the Internet. These services include database connectivity, support for distributed transactions, and security functions.

Marketplace

IBM and Inprise/Borland Corporation both offer EJB server platforms for building e-business solutions. Another company that is a popular player in this market is BEA Systems. The open-source movement is contributing its own EJB server platform, called jBoss, as well.

See Also: *Java*

Enterprise Knowledge Portal (EKP)

A business software system that couples knowledge management tools with an Enterprise Information Portal (EIP) to provide a powerful way of handling the flood of information that characterizes large businesses today.

Overview

Information is at the center of today's business, but this information is typically stored in diverse places, such as:

- **Structured data sources:** This includes information in enterprise resource planning (ERP), customer relations management (CRM), and various structured query language (SQL) and open database connectivity (ODBC) databases scattered on servers throughout an enterprise.
- **Unstructured data sources:** This includes e-mail, scheduling, and journaling information stored on mail servers and groupware servers, document management systems that include file servers and document archive systems, and Web-based information repositories such as intranets, extranets, and public Web sites.

- **Legacy data sources:** This covers all forms of data stored on legacy systems such as IBM mainframe and AS/400 systems.

Enterprise Knowledge Portals (EKPs) are systems that gather all these sources of information and allow corporate users to locate, analyze, deliver, and present personalized information through a single point of access. Using the simple Web browser as the universal front end for these systems, users can pull useful information from these sources to help them make informed business decisions or have this information pushed out to them on a regular basis using automatic search engines that parse the data sources using intelligent criteria to determine what users might need. User profiles allow EKPs to personalize the information delivered to users to present what they need, when they need it, and how they need it.

Implementation

EKPs work by combining two technologies:

- **Enterprise Information Portals (EIPs):** These systems are essentially portals to corporate intranets and provide features such as user profiles, personalization services, single sign-on, customizable interface, automatic indexing, and push/pull delivery of information to basic Web-based intranet systems.
- **Knowledge Management (KM):** These tools enable useful information to be combined and mined from sources as diverse as SQL databases, Word documents, spreadsheets, slide-show presentations, text files, and e-mail repositories.

By combining these two kinds of tools, EKP allows information of every form within a company to be unlocked and made available for making informed business decisions.

Advantages and Disadvantages

Although an EKP's advantages are clear in that it provides a unified single point of access to a company's varied sources of business information, the disadvantages are also clear, in that EKP systems are costly to set up and complex to implement. In particular, building an EKP into a company's varied sources of data could require months, or even years, to implement fully, with much of that time spent on custom development work. On the other hand, once these systems are fully implemented, they are easy to maintain and they bring significant long-term cost savings by enabling faster, more informed decision-making and improved communications among corporate users.

Marketplace

A number of companies are offering turnkey EKP solutions that can fit the needs of medium-sized companies without much development work. Portal-in-a-Box from Autonomy Corporation is one example of a turnkey EKP system that automatically classifies, links, and personalizes information and then delivers it to users as they need it.

Big players such as Lotus Development Corporation and OpenText Corporation also offer EKP systems that focus more on the collaborative aspect of business decision-making. And major business application vendors such as Microsoft Corporation, IBM, Sun Microsystems, and Oracle Corporation offer their own suites of applications that can be used to build EKP systems for large enterprises.

See Also: *Enterprise Information Portal (EIP), enterprise resource planning (ERP), intranet, portal*

enterprise resource planning (ERP)

A term describing software systems for managing a broad scope of an enterprise's business functions.

Overview

Enterprise resource planning (ERP) includes tasks such as planning, purchasing, tracking orders, supplying customers, managing inventory, servicing customer requests, producing financial reports, and bookkeeping. ERP software is modular software designed to integrate these various business functions and simplify their management.

ERP software typically consists of an integrated suite of tools for performing standard line-of-business functions such as payroll, accounting, inventory management, and order entry. ERP software is used in transportation and automotive businesses, industrial environments, and other large industrial settings. ERP software lets these businesses manage diverse business resources across the enterprise to plan more effectively for growth and expansion.

History

ERP has its roots in the software-controlled inventory control systems developed and used by large companies in the 1960s. These systems evolved in the 1970s to include scheduling features for automating procurement for assembly-line systems and were then called Material Requirement Planning (MRP) systems. During the 1980s, MRP systems continued to evolve to include distribution and shop floor control and management capabilities and became known as Manufacturing Resources Planning (MRP-II) systems. In the 1990s, these systems were further extended to include the full gamut of business functions, including project planning, engineering, finance, and human resources. The term *enterprise resource planning* emerged at this time to represent the wider scope of these large software systems.

Marketplace

The three big players in the traditional ERP marketplace are Oracle Corporation, PeopleSoft, and SAP. The biggest of these vendors is Germany's SAP AG, which has an estimated 35 percent share of the ERP market, mainly with its SAP R/3 suite of ERP applications. Another big player is Baan, which has both a traditional ERP offering and an initiative to integrate Extensible Markup Language (XML)– ERP platform through their Baan OpenWorld Integration Framework.

Traditional ERP systems are expensive and often take years to implement fully for large enterprises. In the last few years, a flood of new companies entered the marketplace offering applications that would provide Web-based front ends for traditional ERP software to Internet-enable this software for simplifying enterprise business management. One example of this is the Online Information System (OIS) from Impress Software, which uses the application programming interfaces (APIs) from the big three ERP software vendors to provide businesses access to their SAP R/3 manufacturing systems and other enterprise applications over the Internet. OIS has support for both XML and electronic data interchange (EDI) information exchange, and it is available for diverse platforms, including Windows NT, UNIX, and Linux.

With the proliferation of third-party solutions, the big three have also moved recently to Internet-enable their traditional ERP offerings to make them more competitive. An example is mySAP from SAP AG, which integrates customer relations management (CRM) functions with ERP and provides a portal front end. Although previously most ERP deployments were performed by consulting companies, the Big Three have moved recently to offer their professional services.

Prospects

The most obvious trend in the ERP market is the continuing effort to fully Internet-enable ERP systems and processes. Although early attempts at this represented no more than embedding legacy client ERP interfaces within Web browsers, ERP systems continue to evolve to make their Web-based interface friendlier and easier to use.

ERP was more than a $20-billion market in 2000 and is expected to grow over the next few years. A large portion of this represents planning, consulting, licensing, and maintenance fees for such systems. One recent development is Enterprise Information Portals (EIPs), which provide a new and innovative way of managing the flood of business data that traditional ERP applications expose. EIPs integrate the functions of ERP, CRM, and SCM (supply-chain management) systems into a single Web-based system. Many analysts believe that traditional ERP implementations are on their way out and more sophisticated and powerful EIP systems will grow rapidly, but because of the huge investment most large enterprises have put into ERP systems and the ongoing costs of maintaining them, ERP is likely to be with us for many years.

See Also: *Enterprise Information Portal (EIP)*

enterprise server

A designated server running Microsoft Windows NT, Windows 2000, or Windows .NET Server in an enterprise, which is used as a central repository for software

E

licensing information regarding Windows NT, Windows 2000, Windows .NET Server, and Microsoft BackOffice.

Overview

In Windows NT networks an enterprise server is typically a primary domain controller (PDC), yet can also be a stand-alone server that is not part of any domain in the enterprise. All PDCs in the enterprise replicate their licensing information with the enterprise server, so the enterprise server contains a master database of this information. If there is only one domain in the enterprise, the PDC for that domain is the master licensing server. If there are several domains, each domain's PDC keeps track of licenses for that domain, and all PDCs then replicate their licensing information to the specifically designated enterprise server. Stand-alone member servers that are not part of any domain also must replicate their licensing information with the enterprise server.

They can be more than one enterprise server in an enterprise, but it is simplest to have only one because enterprise servers cannot replicate with each other.

See Also: *license*

environmental subsystems

Components of Microsoft Windows NT, Windows 2000, Windows XP, and Windows .NET Server that support the running of applications from different operating system architectures.

Overview

Environmental subsystems provide the necessary "environment" in which these applications can run. They are an essential part of the Windows NT operating system that enables cross-platform support for applications written for different operating systems. Windows NT, Windows 2000, Windows XP, and Windows .NET Server include the following environmental subsystems:

- Win32 subsystem for running 32-bit Windows applications
- OS/2 subsystem for running OS/2 1.X character-based applications (does not support the OS/2 Presentation Manager GUI or Warp versions)
- POSIX subsystem for running POSIX.1-compliant applications

Notes

MS-DOS–based applications run on Windows NT, Windows 2000, Windows XP, and Windows .NET Server in the context of a Win32 application called a Virtual DOS Machine (VDM) that emulates an MS-DOS environment.

environment variables

String variables containing information that an operating system uses to control services and applications.

Overview

Environment variables have been used in Microsoft operating systems since MS-DOS, where the PATH and TEMP variables used in the Autoexec.bat file were early examples. Microsoft Windows NT, Windows 2000, Windows XP, and Windows .NET Server offer a far more extensive selection of environment variables, including the following types:

- System (predefined) environment variables such as USERNAME, USERDOMAIN, WINDIR, and HOMEPATH. These variables are set on the system no matter who logs on and cannot be changed by any user. They specify particular parameters pertaining to the system itself, such as the location of the operating system files. They can be used in logon scripts because they are always present when any user logs on.
- User (user-defined) environment variables, such as the path to application files. User environment variables take precedence over system environment variables when the two conflict.
- Autoexec.bat environment variables, such as those used in path statements.

You can view and specify environment variables in Windows NT, Windows 2000, Windows XP, and Windows .NET Server by using the System utility in Control Panel. Environment variables may be used in logon scripts by enclosing them within percent symbols; for example, %USERNAME% contains the currently logged-on user name.

Notes

The System utility in Control Panel shows only a portion of the system environment variables defined on a system running Windows NT, Windows 2000, Windows XP, or Windows .NET Server.

ERD

Stands for emergency repair disk, a Microsoft Windows 2000 recovery tool for repairing missing or corrupt files and restoring the registry.

See: *emergency repair disk (ERD)*

ERP

Stands for enterprise resource planning, software systems for managing a broad scope of business functions for an enterprise.

See: *enterprise resource planning (ERP)*

ESMTP

Stands for SMTP Service Extensions, a set of extensions to the Simple Mail Transfer Protocol (SMTP) protocol.

Overview

ESMTP provides a series of enhancements to SMTP, including authentication between SMTP hosts, the ability to resume a connection that is interrupted without having to begin all over again (called checkpointing), and the ability to transmit multiple SMTP messages at once (called pipelining).

The ESMTP standard is defined in RFC 1869.

Implementation

ESMTP works by enabling the receiving host in an SMTP transmission to inform the sending host of what extensions it supports. Instead of beginning the session with the HELO command, the receiving host issues the EHLO command. If the sending host accepts this command, the receiving host then sends it a list of SMTP extensions it understands, and the sending host then knows which SMTP extensions it can use to communicate with the receiving host.

Implementing ESMTP requires no modification of the SMTP configuration of either the client or the mail server. Most modern SMTP mail systems, including Microsoft Exchange, support ESMTP.

See Also: *Simple Mail Transfer Protocol (SMTP)*

ESP

Stands for Encapsulating Security Payload, a protocol in the IPsec suite of protocols that handles encryption.

See: *Encapsulating Security Payload (ESP)*

EtherLEC

A Competitive Local Exchange Carrier (CLEC) offering metropolitan optical Ethernet services to businesses.

See: *metropolitan Ethernet*

Ethernet

The most popular network architecture for local area networks (LANs).

Overview

Ethernet is a baseband networking technology that sends its signals serially 1 bit at a time. In its most basic form, Ethernet operates in half-duplex mode, in which a station can either transmit or receive but cannot do both simultaneously. Another form of Ethernet is full-duplex Ethernet, which uses two pairs of wires with Ethernet switches to allow stations to send and receive data simultaneously without collisions.

Ethernet specifications define the functions that occur at the physical layer and data-link layer of the Open Systems Interconnection (OSI) reference model and package data into frames for transmission on the wire. It is available in three speeds:

- 10 megabits per second (Mbps), which is simply called Ethernet
- 100 Mbps, which is called Fast Ethernet
- 1000 Mbps or 1 gigabit per second (Gbps), which is called Gigabit Ethernet (GbE)

Because of its simplicity and reliability, Ethernet is by far the most popular networking architecture used today.

E

History

Ethernet was originally developed by Xerox Corporation in the 1970s and was proposed as a standard by Xerox, Digital Equipment Corporation (DEC), and Intel Corporation in 1980. A separate standardization process for Ethernet technologies was established in 1985 in the Institute of Electrical and Electronics Engineers (IEEE) 802.3 standard known as Project 802. The IEEE standard was then adopted by the International Organization for Standardization (ISO), making it a worldwide standard for networking.

Ethernet in its original form, called Standard Ethernet (or 10Base5 or thicknet), was first commercially available in 1981 and standardized as 10Base5 in 1984. A version running on thinner coaxial cable called thinnet (or 10Base2) emerged in 1985 for workgroup LAN deployments, while thicknet remained the providence of campus backbones. The first commercial Ethernet bridges also appeared about 1985.

The next major advance was deploying Ethernet over unshielded twisted-pair (UTP) cabling. This occurred in 1990 with the standardization of 10BaseT Ethernet. A fiber version called 10BaseF was developed in 1993 but never really caught on as advances in technology allowed the speed of Ethernet to be increased tenfold two years later with the development of Fast Ethernet or 100BaseT. Meanwhile, in 1992 the first commercial full-duplex Ethernet products appeared in the marketplace.

The next advance was another tenfold increase in speed to 1000 Mbps or 1 Gbps. This was standardized in 1998 as GbE or 1000BaseX, which initially ran only over fiber but was extended in 1999 to run over copper as well in the form 1000BaseT.

Other significant advances in Ethernet technologies in the last decade include

- **Auto-negotiation:** This was developed in 1996 to support hybrid 10/100 Mbps Ethernet gear and has been extended to 10/100/1000 Mbps as well.
- **Ethernet switching:** The first Layer-2 switches became available in 1992, and VLAN (virtual LAN) features were added in 1998.

Architecture

Ethernet uses the Carrier Sense Multiple Access with Collision Detection (CSMA/CD) media-access control method for determining which station can transmit at a given time over the shared medium. In an Ethernet network, each station (computer) listens to the network and transmits data only if no other station is using the network. If the wire is free of signals, any station can contend (try to take control of) the network to transmit a signal. Ethernet networks are thus based on the concept of contention and operate on a first-come, first-served basis, rather than relying on a master station that controls when other stations can transmit. If two stations try to transmit data at the same time, a collision occurs, and both stations stop transmitting. They wait a random interval of time (measured in milliseconds) and then try again. The more stations on an Ethernet network, the higher the number of collisions, and the worse the network's performance. Typical performance of a 10-Mbps Ethernet network with 100 stations will support a bandwidth of only about 40 to 60 percent of the expected value of 10 Mbps. One way of solving the collision problem is to use Ethernet switches to segment an Ethernet network into smaller-collision domains.

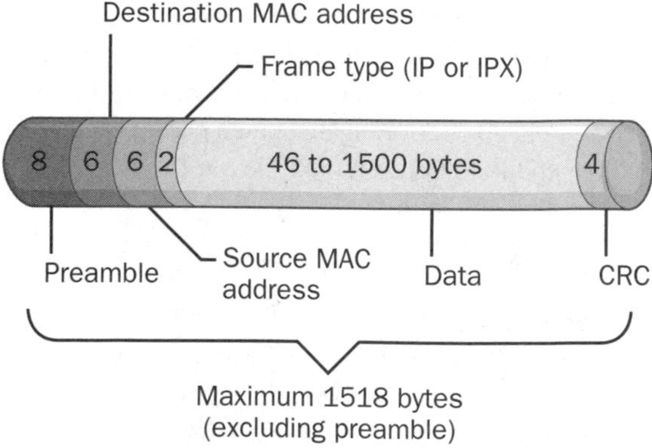

Ethernet. *The Ethernet II frame format.*

Ethernet stations transmit data over the wire in packages called frames. An Ethernet frame has a minimum size of 64 bytes and a maximum size of 1518 bytes. A total of 18 bytes are used for information such as source and destination addresses, network protocol being used, and other frame overhead. Thus, the maximum payload size (amount of data carried) for an Ethernet frame is

1500 bytes. Ethernet packages data into a frame by four different Ethernet encapsulation methods:

- Ethernet II, used for Transmission Control Protocol/Internet Protocol (TCP/IP)
- Ethernet 802.3, called Raw 802.3 in Novell networking and used for connectivity with NetWare 3.11 and earlier
- Ethernet 802.2, also called Ethernet 802.3/802.2 without subnetwork access protocol (SNAP) and used for connectivity with NetWare 3.12 and later
- Ethernet SNAP, also called Ethernet 802.3/802.2 with SNAP and created for compatibility with Macintosh and TCP/IP systems

Implementation

Ethernet can use virtually any physical networking topology and cabling system (medium). Although a star topology (stations that are wired in a star-like configuration to a central hub) is often used from the physical point of view, all Ethernet networks are logical bus-topology networks at heart. One station places a signal on the bus, and that signal travels to every other station along the bus.

Ethernet is available in three speeds and can be further differentiated by media and other considerations, as shown in the table.

Ethernet Speeds, Types, Standards, and Specs

Speed	*Type of Ethernet*	*IEEE Standards*	*IEEE Specs*
10 Mbps	Ethernet	10Base2 10Base5 10BaseF 10BaseT	802.3
100 Mbps	Fast Ethernet	100BaseFX 100BaseT 100BaseT4 100BaseTX	802.3u
1000 Mbps or 1 Gbps	GbE	1000BaseCX 1000BaseLX 1000BaseSX 1000BaseT	802.3z

Ethernet media specifications such as 10BaseT may seem strange and obscure but can be easily interpreted. For example, 10BaseT means **10**-Mbps baseband transmission over Twisted-pair cabling media.

Prospects

The prospects for the continuing evolution of Ethernet look strong. On the horizon is 10 GbE (10 Gbps Ethernet), which will probably become the next upgrade for enterprise network backbones. Another advance is the recent incorporation of Quality of Service (QoS) features into Ethernet using the 802.1p standard, making Ethernet more suitable for carrying delay-sensitive traffic such as voice an area that until now has been dominated by Asynchronous Transfer Mode (ATM).

Optical Ethernet is a new development that sees carriers such as Yipes extend high-speed Ethernet metropolitan area network (MAN) and wide area network (WAN) connections to businesses in metropolitan areas, eliminating the need for costly Ethernet-to-ATM/Synchronous Optical Network (SONET) access devices and turning corporate WANs into large Ethernet local area networks (LANs).

Another amazing development is that Ethernet is being considered in some quarters as a bus technology to replace PCI for computer system buses. One company involved in this development is Performance Technologies.

Where Ethernet will finally hit the wall and be replaced by some other technology is anyone's guess. In the past 20 years, Ethernet has delivered all but knockout blows to its competitors in the LAN arena, including Token Ring, Fiber Distributed Data Interface (FDDI), and ATM. Whether it can do the same in the WAN arena reamins still in question, but it is bound to be an exciting fight.

Notes

The various Ethernet framing formats are incompatible, so if you have a heterogeneous Ethernet network, you must specify the correct frame type to allow machines running Microsoft Windows NT to see your Novell NetWare servers. Windows NT allows you to select Auto Detect from the Frame Type drop-down list on the NWLink IPX/SPX-Compatible Transport protocol configuration property sheet if you do not know what frame type your NetWare servers are using. (In Windows 2000, Windows XP, and Windows .NET Server, select the check box next to Auto Frame

Type Detection in the NWLink IPX/SPX/NetBIOS-Compatible Transport protocol configuration property sheet.) You might also need to configure your routers for the proper frame type. Older Cisco routers running Internetwork Operating System (IOS) version 10 or earlier do not support Ethernet 802.3/802.2 with SNAP.

The table shows some troubleshooting tips for Ethernet media problems.

Troubleshooting Tips for Ethernet Media Problems

Problem	*Suggestion*
No link integrity	Check that you have not mismatched 10BaseT and 100BaseT (or 100BaseTX and 100BaseT4) cables, hubs, or network interface cards; that ensure no crossover cables are used for station-to-hub cable connections.
Too much noise	Check for damaged cables; ensure you are using Category 5 (Cat5) cabling (or enhanced Cat5 [Cat5e] cabling for 100BaseT) and that all your cabling interface components (patch panels, wall plates, terminal blocks, and so on) are Cat5 certified.
Too many collisions (greater than 0.1 percent of total frames on the network)	Check for unterminated cables using a time-domain reflectometer; use a protocol analyzer to look for a jabbering transceiver (a network interface card that is continually broadcasting); and ensure that cables exceed the maximum specified length.

For More Information

Visit Charles Spurgeon's Ethernet Web site at *www.ots.utexas.edu/ethernet.*

See Also: *10Base2, 10Base5, 10BaseF, 10BaseT, 10G Ethernet, 100BaseFX, 100BaseT, 100BaseT4, 100BaseTX, 1000BaseCX, 1000BaseLX, 1000BaseSX, 1000BaseT, Ethernet switch, Fast Ethernet, Gigabit Ethernet (GbE)*

Ethernet address

A unique 6-byte (48-bit) address that is usually permanently burned into a network interface card (NIC) or other physical-layer networking device and that uniquely identifies the device on an Ethernet-based network.

See: *MAC address*

Ethernet Industrial Protocol (Ethernet/IP)

A new standard that allows Ethernet and Transmission Control Protocol/Internet Protocol (TCP/IP) to be used for automation networks within industrial plants.

Overview

The Ethernet Industrial Protocol (Ethernet/IP) was developed by the Open DeviceNet Vendor Association, spearheaded by Rockwell Automation. Ethernet/IP is designed to allow commodity Ethernet equipment and TCP/IP software to be used for connecting industrial controllers and automation devices on factory floors. For example, using Ethernet/IP, a programmable logic controller and sensor can be used to remotely control an assembly-line robot tool using IP running over a switched Ethernet network. Other devices that might be used on an Ethernet/IP network include bar-code readers, automated weigh scales, stepping motors, and so on. More generally, Ethernet/IP can be used to tie in a company's industrial control network with its corporate business network, thus automating the exchange of information between inventory control systems and shipping systems for assembly-line processes.

Ethernet/IP is designed to replace an existing industrial controller network protocol called ControlNet, which was developed some years ago by Rockwell Automation and has found widespread acceptance in robotic and industrial environments.

Implementation

Ethernet/IP works by encapsulating messages from two industrial automation protocols, ControlNet and DeviceNet. Ethernet/IP employs the same application layer protocol as these two protocols, namely Control and Information Protocol (CIP). The CIP protocol runs on top of the network layer protocols TCP (used for explicit messaging between controllers and devices) and User Datagram Protocol (UDP) (used for implicit messaging). Ethernet/IP supports both real-time and asynchronous messaging as well as client/server and peer-to-peer messaging.

Ethernet/IP is usually implemented as a switched Ethernet fabric using full-duplex communications. This is necessary because the latency caused by contention in traditional Ethernet networks can have a detrimental effect on time-sensitive industrial assembly-line processes.

Advantages and Disadvantages

The advantage of Ethernet/IP over traditional automation networks is that cost savings can be achieved by running both the corporate network and the automation network using the same technology, namely Ethernet. Ethernet/IP allows control messages to be delivered across a plant floor using off-the-shelf Ethernet gear and without the need to develop custom Ethernet-to-ControlNet gateways. This helps industrial businesses leverage Ethernet's low cost, proven operation, and high bandwidth.

Special training in automation protocols is not required, and only one set of gear needs to be deployed and kept in stock.

Marketplace

Some of the bigger vendors that offer Ethernet/IP-enabled controllers and interfaces are Rockwell, MicroLogix Information Systems, and FLEX I/O.

For More Information

Visit the Open DeviceNet Vendor Association at *www.odva.org.*

See Also: *Ethernet*

Ethernet/IP

Stands for Ethernet Industrial Protocol, a new standard that allows Ethernet and Transmission Control Protocol/Internet Protocol (TCP/IP) to be used for automation networks within industrial plants.

See: *Ethernet Industrial Protocol (Ethernet/IP)*

Ethernet switch

A multiport device based on bridging technologies that is mainly used to segment Ethernet networks.

Overview

Often simply called switches (when referring implicitly to Ethernet networking), these devices are used to enhance the performance of Ethernet networks. An Ethernet switch basically resembles a hub, and consists of a box with a number of RJ-45 jacks on the front to provide ports for network connections. Inside, however, are advanced electronics that generally make switches more costly than hubs.

In a hub, a packet entering one port is regenerated and forwarded to every other port. While the packet is being forwarded, no other port can receive packets, so a hub can be thought of as a shared-media device in which all ports are connected using a shared bus. If a collision occurs on a hub-based Ethernet network, no port on the hub can receive traffic until the collision is resolved. The set of stations connected to a hub is thus called a collision domain. On the average, if a 10-megabits-per-second (Mbps) Ethernet hub has 10 ports, each port effectively gets one-tenth of the total bandwidth, or 1 Mbps. In reality this can be much worse, however, for a single station actively transferring files can consume a large percentage of the available 10 Mbps bandwidth of the hub, leaving other stations starved for bandwidth for their communications. Hub-based Ethernet networks are thus based on contention in which every station must fight for its share of bandwidth.

If you connect several hubs and their networks by uplinking them to a main hub, the situation only gets worse because the new larger network remains a single collision domain. With the increased number of nodes on the network, however, more collisions are likely to occur and network traffic congestion can result, slowing the network to a crawl.

The solution to this congestion problem is to strategically use Ethernet switches in place of, or in addition to, hubs. When a packet enters a port of an Ethernet switch, the switch looks at the frame's destination address, compares it to a table of address-to-port mappings maintained internally by the switch, internally establishes a temporary internal logical connection between the incoming port where the packet arrived and the outgoing port where the packet is destined, and forwards the packet along this internal connection to its destination. Only the port where the packet arrived and the destination port are involved in this process; all other ports on the switch have no part in the connection.

The result of this process is that each port on the switch corresponds to an individual collision domain, and network congestion is therefore avoided. Thus, if a 10-Mbps Ethernet switch has 10 ports, each port effectively gets the entire bandwidth of 10 Mbps, and to an incoming packet the switch's port appears to provide a dedicated connection to the destination node on the network.

In other words, replacing switches with hubs does not add bandwidth to your network. Instead, it reduces the size of collision domains to allow bandwidth to be used more efficiently. If 12 stations are connected to a 12-port 10 Mbps hub, the maximum bandwidth any one station can theoretically use is 10 Mbps, but if a station were actually using this much bandwidth, all remaining stations connected to the hub (except for the station being communicated with) would have zero bandwidth available to them. If a 12-port, 10 Mbps switch were used instead of the hub, however, all 12 stations could participate in 10 Mbps conversations simultaneously, which means the switching fabric supports 12 ports = 6 communications x 2 ports/communication = 6 x 10 Mbps = 60 Mbps throughput. However, the total bandwidth available to any one station is still only 10 Mbps, no more than for the hub. The difference is that this 10 Mbps bandwidth is guaranteed to be always available for each station!

Architecture

A basic Ethernet switch operates at Layer 2 (the data link layer) of the Open Systems Interconnection (OSI) model. Like a bridge, an Ethernet switch is a smart device that can learn the media access control (MAC) address of each connected station by listening to network traffic. The switch builds an internal table listing the MAC address of each port and consults this table when it needs to forward incoming packets.

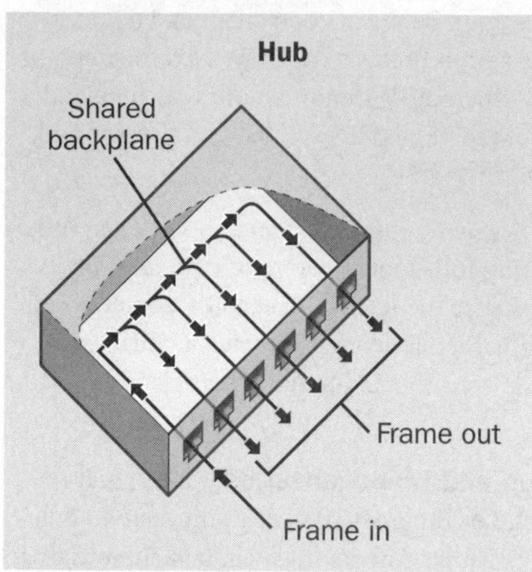

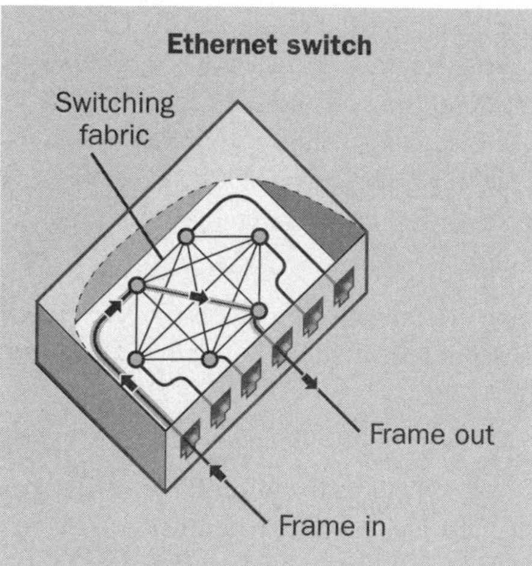

Ethernet switch. *Comparison between how a hub and an Ethernet switch work.*

When an Ethernet frame arrives at a port, the destination MAC address is read from the first 64 bits of the frame. This destination address is then found in the switch's internal address table to determine the correct destination port for the frame. Once this is determined, the switching fabric (a mesh-like connection) inside the switch establishes a temporary logical connection between the incoming and destination ports, forwards the frame, and then tears down the connection. Ethernet switches are also capable of establishing multiple internal logical connections simultaneously between different pairs of ports. The result is that each port receives the switch's full dedicated bandwidth at all times, giving Ethernet switches intrinsically much more bandwidth than shared hubs.

The actual mechanism by which switching (the forwarding of the packet between the ports) occurs divides Ethernet switches into two general device classes:

- **Store-and-forward switches:** This type waits until the entire incoming frame arrives, buffers the frame, reads the destination address from the buffered frame, performs cyclical redundancy check (CRC) error checking to verify that the frame is valid, and either forwards the frame to the destination port using the switching fabric or drops the frame if it represents a runt, jabber, or some other invalid frame. Store-and-forward is the same method by which most bridges work. The advantages of this method are that bad frames are eliminated and collisions are handled well, while the disadvantage is that it suffers from high latency (delay) because the frame must be entirely read and buffered before being processed. Nevertheless, most switches used today are of the store-and-forward type, and Transmission Control Protocol/Internet Protocol (TCP/IP) is generally well able to handle any additional latency that arises in networks due to use of these switches.
- **Cut-through switches:** This type reads the frame as it comes into the receiving port, and after the source and destination addresses are read from the first 64 bits, the switch then checks the internal address table and immediately forwards the frame to the correct destination port. Error checking is not performed by cut-through switches, since to perform this check the CRC byte would have to be read first, and this is located at the end of the frame. As a result of not performing error checking, cut-through switches reduce latency and accelerate performance over store-and-forward switches, but the result is that collisions can affect overall communications and bad frames are passed rather than dropped. The earliest Ethernet switches were of the cut-through type and found particular application in NetWare 3.*x* networks where Internetwork Packet Exchange/Sequenced Packet Exchange (IPX/SPX) was less tolerant to delay than Internet Protocol (IP). Limitations in bridging electronics also made cut-through switching appealing in the earliest implementations, but advances in electronics have made store-and-forward switching more appealing. The first commercial Ethernet switches were cut-through switches developed in 1990 by Kalpana, which is now a subsidiary of Cisco Systems.

E

Implementation

Ethernet switching (or switched Ethernet) can be implemented in various ways depending on the OSI layers at which the switches operate. These include

- **Layer-2 switch:** This basic Ethernet switch operates at the OSI data-link layer (Layer 2) and is based on bridging technologies as explained above. Layer-2 switches establish logical connections between ports based on MAC addresses and are generally used for segmenting an existing network into smaller collision domains to improve performance.
- **Layer-3 switch:** This type operates at the OSI network layer (or Layer 3) and is based on routing technologies. Layer-3 switches establish logical connections between ports based on network addresses such as IP addresses. You can use Layer-3 switches instead of routers for connecting different networks into an internetwork, and they generally perform better than routers due to their enhanced electronics. Layer-3 switches are sometimes called routing switches, multilayer switches, or sometimes simply routers.
- **Layer-4 switch:** This is basically an enhanced Layer-3 switch that has the additional capability of examining the source and destination ports of Transmission Control Protocol (TCP) and User Datagram Protocol (UDP) connections and making forwarding decisions based on this information. They are called Layer-4 switches because they examine OSI transport layer (Layer 4) information within frames and determine how to forward the frames based on this information.

- **Layer-7 switch:** In this type of device the entire frame is unpackaged to determine OSI application layer (Layer 7) information such as what application layer protocol is being used, such as Hypertext Transfer Protocol (HTTP) or File Transfer Protocol (FTP). Frames can then be forwarded or dropped based on this information.
- **Multilayer switch:** This is simply a switch that uses unpackaged frame information from several OSI layers to determine how to forward frames. For example, most Layer-4 switches are actually Layer-3/4 switches since they operate at both layers.

Ethernet switches are also distinguished in other ways, such as by the number of ports they have, whether they operate in half-duplex or full-duplex mode, their transmission speed (for example, 10 Mbps, 1/100 Mbps, or 100/1000 Mbps), ports for connectivity with high-speed Fiber Distributed Data Interface (FDDI) backbones, and so on. Advanced features can include Simple Network Management Protocol (SNMP), out-of-band management (OBM), and custom packet filtering.

Uses

Ethernet switches have two basic uses: segmenting networks to improve performance and interconnecting networks of different speeds. The most common use is network segmentation, and introducing Ethernet switches will provide the most obvious benefit for parts of your network where the most contention occurs. For example, if you have several heavily used servers on the same hub-based local area network (LAN) as clients, the clients have to contend for use of the servers and the result is poor performance. To improve things, segment your LAN into several collision domains, one for each hub and one for each group of clients, as shown in the figure. Now several clients can connect to different servers simultaneously and receive the full throughput of those servers. A good rule of thumb for deciding whether to use switches to segment your existing network is that switches can improve your network's performance if the current network utilization level is higher than 35 percent or if collisions are running at more than 10 percent.

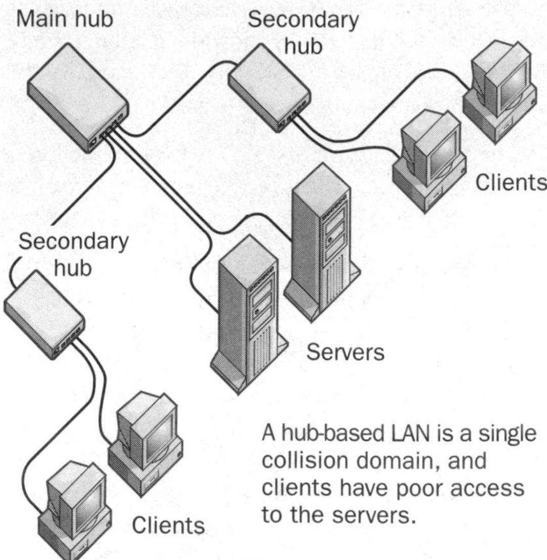

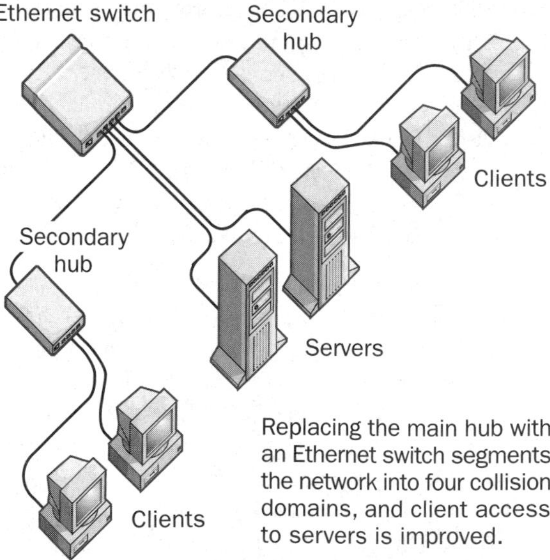

Ethernet switch. *Improving performance of a hub-based LAN by using an Ethernet switch.*

The second main use for switches is to connect fast workgroup hubs to slower hubs on a network. Again, the main hub is replaced by an Ethernet switch, typically 10/100 or 100/1000 Mbps, and the performance of stations on the fast hub is no longer hindered by the presence of the slower parts of the network. Another related use for Ethernet switches is to connect 100-Mbps Ethernet "islands" to an existing 10-Mbps Ethernet LAN. Simply use a 10/100-Mbps Ethernet switch with two ports to connect them. You can also connect two LANs several kilometers apart by using two Ethernet switches, both having one 100BaseT port and one 100BaseFX port. Connect the switches to the LANs, and then connect a fiber-optic cable between the FX ports.

If users in a department have high bandwidth needs, such as those running computer-aided design (CAD) or multimedia applications, consider replacing their workgroup hub with an Ethernet switch, or if the number of users is small, connect their stations directly to the main Ethernet switch.

When purchasing Ethernet switches, make sure they have Remote Monitoring (RMON) agents built into each port, which will considerably ease remote network troubleshooting.

Marketplace

Ethernet switches are made all shapes and sizes from dozens of different vendors. They vary from small 12-port 10/100 workgroup switches to modular 1 Gbps backbone switches supporting Asynchronous Transfer Mode (ATM) and Synchronous Optical Network (SONET) connectivity. Probably the most popular 10/100 Ethernet switches are those of the Cisco Catalyst 3500 Series XL, which by some counts are deployed twice as often as any other type of similar switch from other vendors. A popular enterprise switch used for collapsed backbones is the Big Iron 4000 switch from Foundry Networks. Another widely deployed backbone switch is the Hewlett-Packard 9304.

Issues

Although Ethernet switches relieve traffic congestion by segmenting collision domains, they do have some disadvantages:

- They are generally several times more expensive than hubs of the same speed.
- Networks involving switches are more difficult to monitor and troubleshoot.

Ethernet switches should generally be implemented judiciously within Ethernet networks. Simply replacing every hub with a switch is an unnecessary expense that brings negligible performance enhancement over just replacing a few key hubs with switches.

See Also: *Ethernet, hub*

ETRN

Stands for Extended Turn, an enhancement for Simple Mail Transfer Protocol (SMTP) to enable SMTP hosts to initiate mail transfers with one another.

See: *Extended Turn (ETRN)*

EULA

A type of contract between a computer software publisher and the purchaser of the software that outlines the various rights granted to the purchaser for the legal use of the software.

See: *End-User License Agreement (EULA)*

e-vaulting

Stands for electronic tape vaulting, the practice of backing up data directly to a remote backup facility.

See: *electronic tape vaulting*

event

Any operating system or software condition that is logged by the Event Logging service of Microsoft Windows 2000, Windows XP, and Windows .NET Server.

Overview

You can view events by using the administrative tool called Event Viewer. There are five basic types of events:

- **Errors:** These events represent a significant problem that can lead to loss of data or functionality in the operating system, such as failure of a service to start upon reboot. The corresponding symbol in the system or application log is a red stop sign.
- **Warnings:** These events indicate some impending problem such as low remaining disk space. The

corresponding symbol in the system or application log is an exclamation point superimposed on a yellow circle.

- **Information:** These events indicate that a significant system operation has successfully occurred for example, a service has started. The corresponding symbol in the system or application log is an information sign—that is, the letter *i* superimposed on a blue circle.
- **Successes:** These events are recorded only in the security log and represent auditing information concerning the successful completion of attempts to access secured resources, such as when a user logs on to the network.
- **Failures:** These events are recorded only in the security log and represent auditing information concerning failed attempts to access secured resources, such as when a user attempts to access a shared folder and fails.

Everyone group

A system group existing on all Microsoft Windows NT, Windows 2000, Windows XP, and Windows .NET Server servers and workstations.

Overview

The Everyone group is one of seven (additional new groups exist on Windows XP and Windows .NET Server) built-in system groups that are defined on networks based on the Windows 2000, Windows XP, and Windows .NET Server operating system and includes all local and remote users. This includes users from distrusted domains and non-Windows networks. By default, the Everyone system group has the sole preassigned system right "Access this computer from network." You can grant additional rights to this group if desired. You cannot modify the membership of system groups such as the Everyone group directly.

Notes

When you share a folder on a server running Windows 2000 or Windows .NET Server, or on a workstation running Windows XP, full control permission is initially assigned to the Everyone group. It is advisable to remove this group and assign appropriate permissions to other groups, such as Administrators and Users.

Be careful about assigning additional permissions to the Everyone group. If you allow users who do not have valid user accounts to access the network using the Guest account, they will gain any permissions and rights assigned to the Everyone group.

See Also: *built-in group, special identity*

Exchange Server

Microsoft Exchange Server 2000 is Microsoft Corporation's premier messaging and collaboration solutions-building platform for Windows 2000. Exchange 2000 is part of the Microsoft BackOffice suite of server applications. Exchange Server is designed for mission-critical enterprise-level messaging solutions and includes such features as

- Intelligent message rerouting
- Transaction-based directory services
- Fault-tolerant message store
- Built-in server and link monitoring tools
- Connectors and gateways for connectivity with foreign mail systems

Exchange 2000 can coexist with most popular and legacy mail systems and can be used for messaging connectivity with the following:

- Microsoft Mail
- Internet mail (Simple Mail Transfer Protocol [SMTP])
- X.400
- Lotus cc:Mail
- IBM PROFS and SNADS

Exchange 2000 supports all key industry messaging standards, including:

- Internet messaging standards such as SMTP, Post Office Protocol 3 (POP3), Internet Message Access Protocol 4 (IMAP4), Lightweight Directory Access

Protocol (LDAP), Hypertext Transfer Protocol (HTTP), Network News Transfer Protocol (NNTP), Secure Sockets Layers (SSL), Multipurpose Internet Mail Extensions (MIME), and Secure/Multipurpose Internet Mail Extensions (S/MIME)

- X.400 messaging standards
- Microsoft's Messaging Application Programming Interface (MAPI)

The Microsoft Outlook 2000 client software, part of the Microsoft Office 2000 suite of business productivity tools, complements Exchange Server by providing users with a full desktop information-management tool for managing messages, appointments, tasks, and contacts. Although the preferred client for Exchange 2000 is Outlook 2000, Exchange clients are available for all the popular operating systems, including MS-DOS, Windows 3.*x*, Windows 95, Windows 98, Windows NT, Windows 2000, Apple Macintosh, UNIX, and OS/2. Note that the features supported by different clients vary with the platform used.

History

Exchange 4 replaced Microsoft Mail 3.51 in 1996 as Microsoft's client/server messaging and collaboration system. Exchange 4 employed an X.500-based directory and natively supported the SMTP, MIME, MAPI, and X.400 messaging standards, with X.400 being the underlying message transport protocol. In 1997, Exchange 5 was released, which supported additional Internet standards such as POP3 for mailbox access, NNTP for Usenet newsgroups, LDAP for X.500 directory access, HTTP and HTML for Web browser access, and SSL for secure authentication and encryption. Later in 1997 Exchange Server 5.5 added support for Microsoft Cluster Server, IMAP4 and S/MIME protocols, Key Management services, Virtual Organizations, and unlimited message store size.

Exchange 2000 was a radical departure from early versions because it eliminated the proprietary Exchange directory and instead tightly integrated Exchange with Windows 2000's Active Directory directory service. Exchange 2000 includes the Web Storage System, which provides a hierarchical data storage mechanism that incorporates Extensible Markup Language (XML) as part of its specification. Exchange 2000 also tightly integrates with Internet Information Services (IIS), Microsoft's Web services platform and uses IIS as its Internet messaging protocol handler. Exchange 2000 is available in several editions and can be deployed in various ways, including as a messaging system for small companies, a platform for building collaborative workflow applications for large enterprises, Internet mail servers for Internet service providers (ISPs), and hosted messaging and collaboration services offered by Application Service Providers (ASPs).

For More Information

Find our more about Exchange 2000 at *www.microsoft.com/exchange.*

See Also: *BackOffice, e-mail*

experience

A modern term used to describe applications that have an interface designed for the user.

Overview

The term *experience* has recently come into common use in programming parlance to describe any application that has a customizable user interface. Developers who work on client software are thus "developing experiences" for the users of their software.

The term *experience* is also used in the discussion of Microsoft Corporation's .NET platform to mean the delivery of integrated functionality to users through Web services. The .NET platform is designed to allow developers to build compelling user experiences that will provide sets of targeted functionality to bring about the next phase of the Internet's evolution. Some of the pieces already in place to provide this experience include

- bCentral, a resource for small businesses
- MSN (the Microsoft Network), targeted for consumers
- Microsoft Office, aimed at knowledge works
- Visual Studio.NET, targeted for developers

Notes

The term *user experience* is also commonly used to describe the visual appearance and interactivity of software for the Apple Macintosh platform, particularly Aqua in Mac OS X.

E

See Also: *.NET platform*

extended partition

A physical disk partition on which a series of logical drives can be created.

Overview

You can create an extended partition on a disk to overcome the limitation of having only four partitions per disk. Information about the various partitions on a disk is stored in a structure called the partition table. The partition table is 64 bytes in size and is located on cylinder 0, head 0, sector 1 of your hard drive, in the same sector as the Master Boot Record. The partition table has the same format no matter what operating system is used on the disk. Up to four partitions can be created on a disk, but only one partition can be extended per disk. In Microsoft Windows 2000, Windows XP, and Windows .NET Server, you can create an extended partition using Disk Management console. For earlier Windows platforms, use the fdisk utility.

Notes

In Windows 2000 and Windows XP, and Windows .NET Server, extended partitions can be created only on basic disks.

See Also: *partition (disk)*

Extended Turn (ETRN)

An enhancement for Simple Mail Transfer Protocol (SMTP) to enable SMTP hosts to initiate mail transfers with one another.

Overview

SMTP hosts were originally envisioned as machines that always had to be connected to the Internet using dedicated connections such as leased lines. In this scenario, when a host must send mail to another host on the Internet, it simply does so, assuming the other host is there and is listening to receive any mail forwarded to it. With the advent of companies wanting to connect their SMTP hosts to the Internet using dial-up connections to save money over leased lines, some mechanism had to be developed to allow a host to tell other hosts that it was online and ready to receive mail. Extended Turn (ETRN) was developed for this purpose. For example, a company may configure its SMTP host to dial up to the company's Internet service provider (ISP) and issue an ERTN command to the ISP's remote host to deliver mail queued on the remote host.

Issues

ERTN is a stopgap solution that was added to SMTP to work around the problem described above. ERTN has several disadvantages, including its complexity to configure and its requirement for a permanent Internet Protocol (IP) address for the dial-up server. A much better solution for downloading corporate mail from an ISP's SMTP host is to use a Post Office Protocol 3 (POP3) server instead.

See Also: *Post Office Protocol version 3 (POP3), Simple Mail Transfer Protocol (SMTP)*

extender

A general name for a class of networking devices that extend the distances over which stations (computers) can typically be connected to concentrators such as hubs and switches.

Overview

An example of an extender is a 10BaseT extender for Ethernet networks. In 10BaseT networks, stations should be located no more than 328 feet (100 meters) from a hub, but by using an extender, you can increase this to about 600 feet (183 meters). A 10BaseT extender can thus be used for connecting a remote station, such as a station located in a nearby building, to the network. Extenders are essentially a simplified form of bridge designed to support only a few remote stations. They must be installed in pairs, one at the remote location and one at the main network. Some extenders can be used to carry network data over installed phone lines, connecting remote stations without installing additional network cabling.

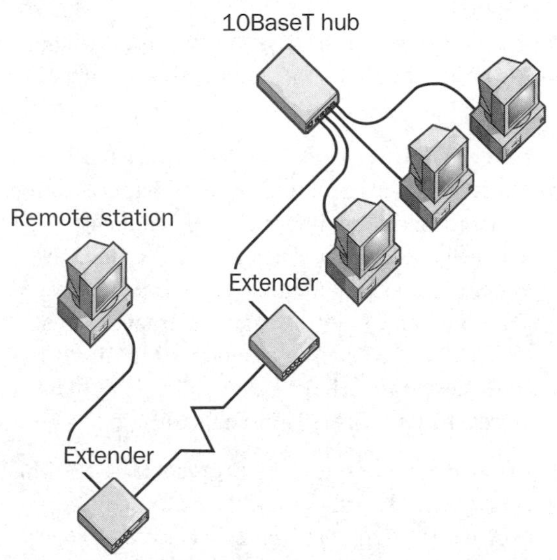

Extender. *Using an extender to join a remote station to a local area network (LAN).*

Extenders are also available for increasing the maximum connection distance for other data transmission technologies such as the Small Computer System Interface (SCSI) bus. A normal SCSI bus is limited to about 20 feet (6 meters), but a fiber-optic SCSI extender can increase this distance to 0.6 mile (1 kilometer) or more using duplex fiber-optic cable. You can use parallel extenders for directly connecting to printers located in a different building. You can use serial extenders to connect computers to remote RS-232 serial test equipment located in laboratories in different buildings.

Extensible Authentication Protocol (EAP)

A security enhancement of Point-to-Point Protocol (PPP).

Overview

Extensible Authentication Protocol (EAP) is an extension to PPP specified in RFC 2284. EAP allows for an arbitrary authentication method to be negotiated during initialization of a PPP session. This is accomplished during the Link Control Protocol (LCP) negotiation portion of the PPP session establishment sequence. EAP allows third-party security products to be used to provide additional security to PPP sessions using special application programming interfaces (APIs) built into operating systems whose implementation of PPP supports EAP.

EAP is designed to make remote access and virtual private network (VPN) communications more secure by allowing any kind of authentication to be used, including

- Smart cards such as Fortezza, SecurID, and other token technologies.
- MD5-CHAP, which provides 128-bit encryption during authentication.
- Kerberos authentication, the standard authentication method for Windows 2000, Windows XP, and Windows .NET Server.
- Transport Layer Security (TLS), which is implemented in Web browsers, smart cards, biometric authentication devices, and so on.

In Microsoft Windows 2000 and Windows .NET Server, EAP is supported by both the Routing and Remote Access Service (RRAS) and Internet Security and Acceleration (IAS) services and by dial-up networking (DUN). Each type of EAP authentication method allowed is implemented through specific plug-in modules designated dynamic-link libraries (DLLs) on both the client and the server. So if you purchase a smart card system from a vendor for use with Windows 2000 or Windows .NET Server remote access, you run the vendor's Setup program on both your DUN client and Remote Access Service (RAS) server to install the necessary EAP DLLs.

See Also: *Point-to-Point Protocol (PPP)*

Extensible Firmware Interface (EFI)

A new firmware standard for 64-bit Intel processors.

Overview

Extensible Firmware Interface (EFI) is a new standard for the firmware that is used to boot PCs using Intel Corporation's new 64-bit Itanium processor family. EFI is required for all Itanium-based systems that will run

Microsoft's new 64-bit Windows platform because these systems cannot boot using the basic input/output system (BIOS) or System Abstraction Layer (SAL) alone. EFI will be supported in all 64-bit versions of Microsoft Windows.

E

For More Information

See *www.microsoft.com/hwdev/EFI.*

See Also: *64-bit architecture, 64-bit Windows*

Extensible Markup Language (XML)

A meta-language used as a universal standard for electronic data exchange.

See: *XML*

extension cable

A cable used to extend a length of cabling.

Overview

Extension cables are available in all types with various connector devices and can be used to extend serial lines, parallel lines, network cables, power cables, and other cords.

Extending a cable using an extension cable is not always a good idea because the additional interface introduced by the connection usually results in some signal loss. Furthermore, extending network cables can cause problems if the new, longer cable exceeds the maximum length of the specifications for that type of network. For example, extending unshielded twisted-pair (UTP) cabling beyond 328 feet (100 meters) in a 10BaseT Ethernet network can result in unreliable communication between hosts on the network.

Exterior Border Gateway Protocol (EBGP)

The version of Border Gateway Protocol (BGP) used for exchanging routing information between different autonomous systems.

Overview

There are two versions of BGP, the classless dynamic routing protocol used on the Internet. These versions are

- **Exterior Border Gateway Protocol (EBGP):** This is an exterior routing protocol that is used for exchanging routing information dynamically between border routers connecting autonomous systems (ASs) on the Internet or in a large private Transmission Control Protocol/Internet Protocol (TCP/IP) internetwork. When referring simply to BGP, the variant EBGP is always implied. In other words, EBGP is usually just called BGP.
- **Interior Border Gateway Protocol (IBGP):** This is an interior routing protocol that is used for exchanging routing information between routers within an AS.

See Also: *autonomous system (AS), Border Gateway Protocol (BGP), classless routing protocol, dynamic routing*

exterior gateway protocol (EGP)

Any routing protocol used to distribute routing information between autonomous systems.

Overview

Also known as exterior routing protocols, exterior gateway protocols (EGPs) specify how different autonomous systems (ASs) within large Transmission Control Protocol/Internet Protocol (TCP/IP) internetworks such as the Internet communicate with each other to exchange routing information. EGPs facilitate the exchange of inter-autonomous-system routing information between different autonomous systems, independent of which interior gateway protocols (IGPs) are used within these autonomous systems.

There are two EGPs for IP internetworks:

- **Exterior Gateway Protocol (EGP):** This is the original EGP developed in the early days of the Internet to facilitate the Internet's growth. Note the confusing use of the term *Exterior Gateway Protocol (EGP)* here—EGP stands both for the general category of inter-AS routing protocols and also for the first actual protocol developed within this category. In other words, EGP is one of two examples of an EGP! For more information, see the second article titled "Exterior Gateway Protocol (EGP)," which is the next entry in this chapter.

- **Border Gateway Protocol (BGP):** This is a newer EGP that has replaced the Exterior Gateway Protocol for inter-AS communication on the Internet.

See Also: *autonomous system (AS), Border Gateway Protocol (BGP), dynamic routing, Exterior Gateway Protocol (EGP), interior gateway protocol (IGP), Internet, routing protocol*

Exterior Gateway Protocol (EGP)

The original exterior routing protocol used to connect autonomous systems on the Internet.

Overview

Exterior Gateway Protocol (EGP) was the original interdomain routing protocol developed for communicating routing information between autonomous systems on the Internet. In fact, the idea of autonomous systems was developed in conjunction with EGP.

EGP was developed in 1982 for the ARPANET, the precursor to the Internet, and was conceived at a time when the Internet was envisioned as a single core network to which various other networks were connected. The developers of the Internet saw early on that scaling problems would occur as the Internet grew in size and complexity, and so the idea of apportioning the Internet into separate sections called autonomous systems (ASs), each under someone else's authority, was developed. Large private internetworks connected to the Internet were assigned autonomous system numbers (ASNs), and the core network itself was divided into several ASs.

To facilitate exchange of routing information between routers connecting these different networks, the concept of dynamic routing was introduced and two kinds of dynamic routing protocols were developed:

- **Interior gateway protocols (IGPs):** These are used for routing within an AS and are thus intra-AS routing protocols. IGPs allow the routers within an AS to exchange routing table information with each other dynamically. Examples of IGPs include Routing Information Protocol (RIP) and Open Shortest Path First (OSPF).
- **Exterior gateway protocols (EGPs).** These are used for routing between different ASs and are thus inter-AS or interdomain routing protocols. EGPs allow routers on the borders between different ASs to exchange routing table information with each dynamically. Examples of EGPs include Exterior Routing Protocol (EGP), from which the more general category EGP was later derived, and Border Gateway Protocol (BGP), the EGP commonly in use on the Internet today.

Implementation

Exterior Gateway Protocol, as defined in RFC 904, is based on the distance vector routing algorithm, but has the limitation that it only maintains information about a single route between two different ASs. EGP thus assumes that only a single path exists between any two ASs within the Internet, a condition that was seen early on as unrealistic. EGP also does not indicate the cost of the route between two ASs, only whether the route is reachable or unreachable. Furthermore, EGP supported only classless routing, and when it was implemented it was already obvious that the class A/B/C system of allocating Internet addresses would soon exhaust available addresses. As the Internet grew it became more complex in its structure as multipath connections between ASs began to develop. EGP's weakness was quickly realized and BGP was developed to replace it. BGP also supports Classless Interdomain Routing (CIDR), which superseded the Internet's earlier classful routing system.

Today EGP is considered a legacy routing protocol and is no longer used on the public Internet, although it is probably still used in some large private Internet Protocol (IP) internetworks that have seen no real need for upgrading to BGP. Interestingly enough, as of 2001 EGP was still being used for MILNET, the public portion of the U.S. Defense Data Network.

See Also: *autonomous system (AS), autonomous system number (ASN), Border Gateway Protocol (BGP), classless interdomain routing (CIDR), dynamic routing protocol, Exterior Gateway Protocol (EGP), interior gateway protocol (IGP), Internet, Open Shortest Path First (OSPF), Routing Information Protocol (RIP), routing protocol*

exterior routing protocol

Another name for an Exterior Gateway Protocol (EGP), any routing protocol used to distribute routing information between autonomous systems.

See: *Exterior Gateway Protocol (EGP)*

extranet

A private Transmission Control Protocol/Internet Protocol (TCP/IP) network that securely shares information using Hypertext Transfer Protocol (HTTP) and other Internet protocols with business partners.

Overview

An extranet is basically a corporate intranet that is securely exposed over the Internet to specific groups that need access to it. Extranets are powerful tools because they let businesses share resources on their private networks over the Internet with suppliers, vendors, business partners, and wholesale customers. Extranets are typically used for supporting real-time supply chains, for enabling business partners to work together, and to share information such as catalogs with customers. Extranets basically comprise the B2B (business-to-business) portion of an e-business system, and building an extranet is an essential step for companies who want to compete in today's Internet economy.

Implementation

Extranets built on the corporate intranet model follow the client/server paradigm, with Web servers such as Microsoft Internet Information Services (IIS) functioning as the server, and Web browsers such as Microsoft Internet Explorer functioning as the client. Other extranet models exist, however, such as a peer-to-peer business connection for electronic data interchange (EDI). Peer-to-peer extranets between business partners typically use virtual private networks (VPNs) to establish secure, encrypted communication over the unsecured Internet for the transmission of sensitive business information, such as EDI between partners, or between headquarters and branch offices. These extranets act as dedicated gateways between business partners and generally do not allow private access to individual users. Peer-to-peer extranets can use Internet Protocol Security (IPsec) with a public key infrastructure (PKI) to provide IP-based authentication and encrypted transmission of information.

Client/server extranets have different requirements, however, because individual users must be authenticated before receiving secure, encrypted access to company resources. Instead of authenticating on the basis of IP addresses as in peer-to-peer extranets, users must be authenticated using user accounts or digital certificates mapped to accounts. Client/server extranets might support HTTP access only or might allow other client/server applications to run. Encryption for HTTP access is performed using the Secure Sockets Layer (SSL) protocol.

Although a basic extranet can be built easily by scripting a Web server to run as a front end for a corporate database, real-world extranets are often more complex. The difficult part is to build the extranet back into the back-end database systems and other sources of business information that business partners need to access. Virtual Private Network (VPN) and firewall technologies are commonly used to provide secure access between different partners over the Internet, and Extensible Markup Language (XML) is emerging as an essential tool for structuring business information for exchange between partners. Extranets also often need to be coupled with directory services for managing access to information through policy-based mechanisms.

Advantages and Disadvantages

The power of the extranet is that it leverages the Internet's existing technology to increase the power, flexibility, and competitiveness of businesses using well-known and easily used tools such as Web servers and Web browsers. Extranets also save companies money by allowing them to establish business-to-business connectivity over the Internet instead of using expensive dedicated leased lines. Extranets can also save money by reducing phone and fax costs.

Marketplace

A new breed of policy-based access management tools has emerged for providing the infrastructure needed to build large directory-enabled extranets. Two popular products in this arena are GetAccess from enCommerce and SiteMinder from Netegrity. The Microsoft BizTalk framework and its associated server platform is seen as a key player in the emerging XML-ization of business extranets and other B2B services.

See Also: *electronic data interchange (EDI)*

F

failback

In clustering technology, the action of moving resources back to a failed node or primary node (a computer in a cluster) once it has been recovered. This action can take place manually or automatically depending on how the cluster is configured.

Overview

Suppose you have a cluster that has two nodes, each containing different resources. If Node A experiences failure, failover occurs and the workload of Node A (its set of resources) is transferred to Node B. When Node A reboots, it checks with Node B to see which resources are running on Node B and discovers that some of these cluster groups would "prefer" to reside on Node A. At this point failback will occur if the cluster is configured to failback automatically if the primary node recovers. The preferred groups are then moved from Node B back to Node A. Failback might be configured to occur immediately or at a scheduled time if access to resources is low.

Notes

Failback is sometimes known as "rebalancing the workload."

See Also: clustering, failover

failover

Any technology that allows one device to take over for a similar device that has failed.

Overview

An example of a typical failover system would be a failover cluster. Failover is also often used to ensure that a break in a communication line does not cause a break in communication between networked systems.

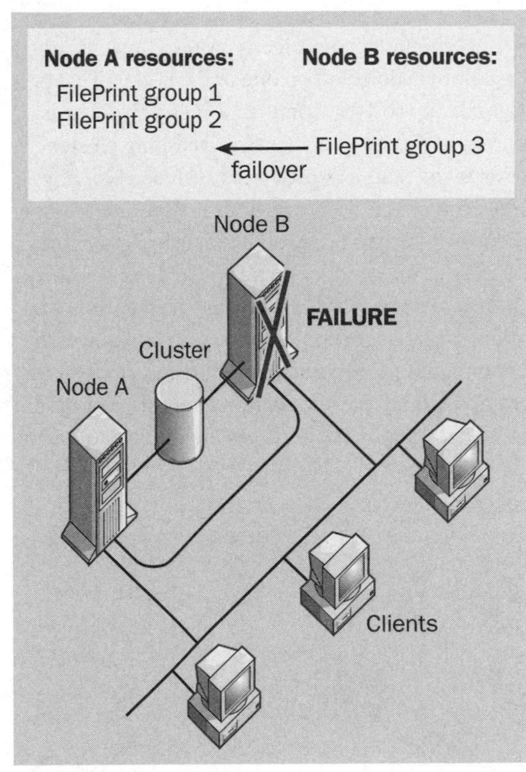

Failover. *How failover works.*

Suppose you have a cluster that has two nodes, each containing different resources. If Node B experiences failure, failover occurs and the workload of Node B (its set of resources) is transferred to Node A. In Microsoft Corporation's clustering services (Microsoft Cluster Server for Microsoft Windows NT 4 Enterprise Edition and the Cluster service for Windows 2000 Enterprise Server and Datacenter Server and Windows .NET Server Enterprise Server and Datacenter Server), the cluster resources (network applications, data files, and other tools installed on the nodes of the cluster) provide services to clients on the network. A resource can be hosted on only one node at any given time, but by using the Cluster Administrator program, you can configure the resource to failover to the second node if the first node fails. This causes the resource and its operation to move from one node to the other if a failure of one node occurs.

Failover is initiated automatically by the Cluster service when a failure is detected on one of the nodes. This process can take up to 10 seconds to initiate. Failover is transparent to the users if they are accessing cluster resources using stateless protocols such as Hypertext Transfer Protocol (HTTP) and does not require any special client software to be installed on users' machines. If a client is connected using a tool such as Windows Explorer, it will be notified that the connection is unavailable. The user should abort, retry, or cancel the connection attempt. (To connect to the resource on the failover node, retry the connection attempt.) For other Cluster service applications, users might have to log on again to the resource.

Notes

Microsoft's clustering services support failover at the level of virtual servers, which means items such as Web sites, print queues, file shares, and applications can be protected from system failure.

See Also: clustering

fallback switch

A class of switches used to provide failover support for critical network communication lines.

Overview

Fallback switches are an essential component of a fault-tolerant network system with resources that must have a high availability. In such a scenario, resources can be connected to your network using two circuits:

- A primary line that normally provides access to the resource
- A secondary line to which the fallback switch reroutes the moment the primary line fails

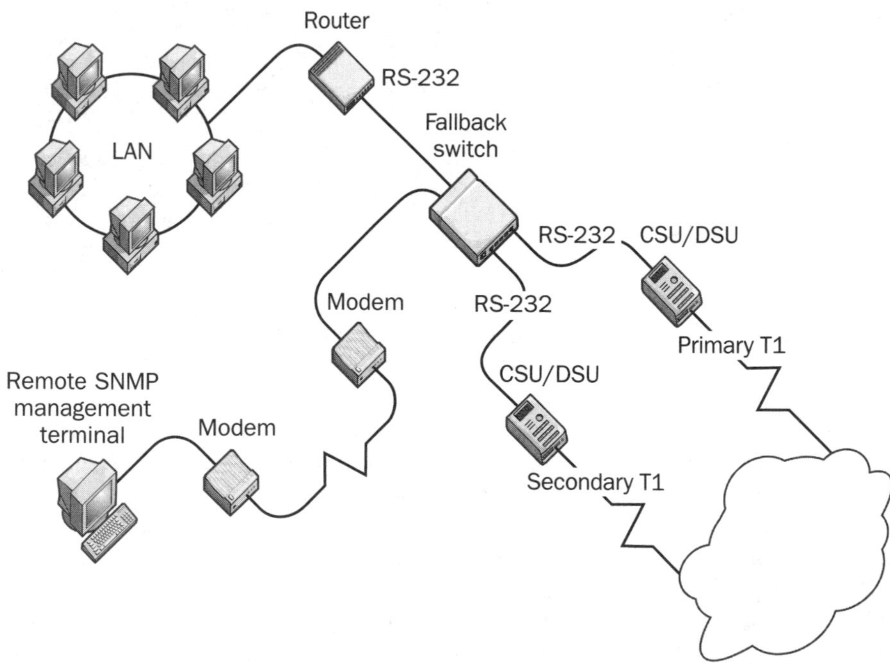

Fallback switch. *Using a fallback switch.*

Uses

Fallback switches can also be used to provide fault tolerance for a high-speed backbone for Fast Ethernet, Fiber Distributed Data Interface (FDDI), or Asynchronous Transfer Mode (ATM) networking. For example, you can use fallback switches to run two multimode fiber-optic cables between a pair of Ethernet switches, instead of having only one cable connecting them. If one fiber-optic cable goes dark, the fallback switch immediately detects the problem and switches over to the backup cable.

Fallback switches that can be managed using Simple Network Management Protocol (SNMP) management consoles are very useful. For example, you could use a remote SNMP terminal to cause a fallback switch to change from a primary to a secondary line if you need to take the primary line down for maintenance. Ganged fallback switches can be used to control multiple serial or local area network (LAN) devices simultaneously. For example, you could schedule a ganged switch to switch over from a set of primary Web servers to a backup Web server every night during a period of low traffic while maintenance or backups are performed on the primary servers. Be sure to use a fallback switch with some form of password protection on its SNMP management functions.

Examples

An example of a resource requiring high availability is a high-speed T1 line that is used by remote clients for accessing a corporate intranet. If the primary T1 line goes down, there must be a backup line that provides instant, transparent failover support for clients. The solution is to use two T1 lines connected to a fallback switch by a serial interface such as RS-232 or V.35. The fallback switch detects a failure the moment the primary line goes down and can perform a remedial action such as

- Automatically switching over to the backup line
- Sounding an audible alarm to notify administrators
- Generating an alert to an SNMP management console

FAQ

Stands for frequently asked questions, a list of commonly asked questions and their answers.

See: *frequently asked questions (FAQ)*

Fast Ethernet

A set of Ethernet standards for 100-megabit-per-second (Mbps) data transmission.

Overview

Ratified as the IEEE 802.3u specification in 1995, Fast Ethernet is an evolution of regular 10 Mbps Ethernet that transmits data at 10 times the speed of standard Ethernet. Fast Ethernet uses the same contention-based media access control method (Carrier Sense Multiple Access with Collision Detection, or CSMA/CD) and the same framing format as standard Ethernet. It also runs over the same structured wiring systems as well, including twisted pair and fiber-optic cabling, with the exception that there is no shared media (physical bus) cabling option as in 10Base2 and 10Base5 Ethernet.

Fast Ethernet is actually a group of standards collectively known as 100BaseT. Like the various 10 Mbps forms of Ethernet, Fast Ethernet also comes in full- and half-duplex varieties and can be implemented as shared media using hubs or in switched networks.

Uses

Fast Ethernet is used mainly for switch uplinks and interconnects for high-speed backbones, switch connections to high-speed servers in server farms, and islands of high-performance workstations running bandwidth-intensive software such as computer-aided design (CAD) or multimedia applications.

Fast Ethernet switches can also be used for segmenting your network to reduce bottlenecks caused by users trying to access key servers on the network. Simply connect each 10/100 autosensing hub to a Fast Ethernet switch, and connect the servers directly to the switch.

Architecture

Fast Ethernet increases its speed tenfold over standard Ethernet by decreasing the bit time (the time duration of each transmitted bit) by a factor of 10. This allows Fast Ethernet to maintain all of the main characteristics of 10 Mbps Ethernet and be compatible with 10 Mbps Ethernet to allow mixed networks of 10 and 100 Mbps segments to coexist. The Fast Ethernet specifications also include a mechanism for autonegotiation of frame speed called autosensing, which lets vendors build dual 10/100-Mbps hubs, switches, and bridges for easily incorporating Fast Ethernet into legacy 10 Mbps Ethernet networks.

Implementation

Fast Ethernet can be implemented in four different media (cabling) formats, which are collected under the umbrella designation of 100BaseT. These four formats are

- **100BaseTX:** This is the most popular implementation of Fast Ethernet. 100BaseTX uses two pairs of wires in Category 5 (Cat5) unshielded twisted-pair (UTP) cabling (the same cabling as the popular but lower-speed 10BaseT variety of Ethernet). 100BaseTX also supports w-pair shielded twisted-pair (STP) cabling as well, but this is rarely used and is available in both half-duplex and full-duplex signaling.
- **100BaseFX:** This form can use duplex (two-strand) 50 or 62.5 micron multimode fiber-optic cable or 9 micron single mode cabling, typically terminated with ST connectors. It is used mainly for backbone wiring such as switch-switch connections and is available in both half-duplex and full-duplex signaling.
- **100BaseT4:** This form uses all four pairs of wires in twisted-pair cabling and enables Fast Ethernet to be used over inexpensive Category 3 (Cat3) UTP cabling. 100BaseT4 supports half-duplex signaling only.
- **100BaseT2:** This form uses two pairs of wires in either Cat3, Category 4 (Cat4), or Cat5 UTP cabling and supports both half- and full-duplex signaling. This option was developed by the Institute of Electrical and Electronics Engineers (IEEE) but was never implemented in commercial Fast Ethernet equipment.

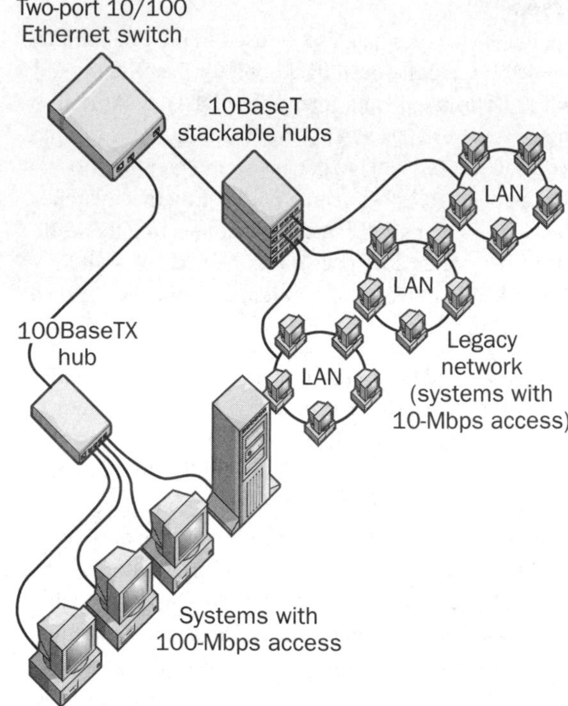

Fast Ethernet. *Fast Ethernet island connected to legacy 10BaseT network.*

Repeaters (hubs) for Fast Ethernet networks come in two varieties:

- **Class I repeaters:** Perform internal signal translation that introduces slight propagation delays but allows different types of Fast Ethernet media, such as 100BaseTX and 100BaseFX, to be connected. You can use only one Class I repeater per Fast Ethernet segment.
- **Class II repeaters:** Take incoming signals and repeat them immediately (without translation) to all outgoing ports, thus minimizing port latency. Class II repeaters require that all ports connect to the same media, such as 100BaseTX. You can use up to two Class II repeaters per Fast Ethernet segment.

For 100BaseTX, attached stations cannot be more than 328 feet (100 meters) from a hub or repeater (same as 10BaseT) with the maximum network diameter being 690 feet (210 meters), compared to 1640 feet (500 meters) for 10BaseT. 100BaseFX supports longer distances up to 1.25 miles (2 kilometers). In reality, building Fast Ethernet networks is a trifle more complex because the distance limitations of different media options often depend on the class of repeaters used and whether station-hub or hub-hub connections are under consideration.

There are also nonstandard vendor-specific external transceivers available that allow Fast Ethernet to be extended over long-haul multimode fiber for distances as long as 62 miles (100 kilometers).

Advantages and Disadvantages

Switching to Fast Ethernet is probably the easiest and cheapest way of upgrading your network to meet increasing bandwidth needs. The advantages of upgrading 10 Mbps Ethernet networks to Fast Ethernet include the following:

- Fast Ethernet integrates easily into existing 10 Mbps Ethernet networks without requiring reinvestment in new network-management and troubleshooting software.
- Fast Ethernet is based on the same simple technology as standard 10 Mbps Ethernet, which makes equipment cheap and easy to produce and reduces the amount of training needed to implement it.
- Fast Ethernet can carry voice, data, and video at 100 Mbps, which is 10 times faster than traditional 10 Mbps Ethernet.
- Fast Ethernet can operate over the same installed media used for a traditional 10 Mbps Ethernet network.
- The network can be migrated slowly to Fast Ethernet by using autosensing 10/100 hubs and network interface cards (NICs).

These advantages have made Fast Ethernet the natural successor to standard 10 Mbps Ethernet and have led to the eclipse of competing high-speed networking technologies such as Fast Token Ring and Fiber Distributed Data Interface (FDDI).

Marketplace

The list of vendors offering Fast Ethernet equipment is too long to mention here. One example of the technology's popularity is that every version of Cisco Catalyst switch available supports Fast Ethernet.

Analysts estimate that more than 100 million Fast Ethernet ports were shipped in 2000, a figure that is expected to double by 2004. Price per port has dropped to below $100, making Fast Ethernet an attractive and affordable option for small and mid-sized businesses that need to upgrade their networks. Despite the current market excitement over Gigabit Ethernet (GbE) and the predicted arrival of 10 GbE, Fast Ethernet is likely to remain the primary networking technology for corporate networks for at least the next five years.

Notes

An alternative to Fast Ethernet developed by Hewlett-Packard is 100VG-AnyLAN, also called 100BaseVG and standardized as IEEE 802.12. 100VG-AnyLAN is a 100 Mbps transmission technology that uses a media access control technology called demand priority that Hewlett-Packard originally developed for transporting both Ethernet and Token Ring frames. 100VG-AnyLAN is now considered a legacy technology compared to Fast Ethernet.

See Also: *100BaseFX, 100BaseT4, 100BaseTX, 100VG-AnyLAN, Ethernet, Gigabit Ethernet (GbE)*

FAT

Stands for file allocation table; specifically, a table maintained on a hard disk by MS-DOS and Microsoft Windows operating systems that acts as a table of contents, showing where directories and files are stored on the disk. By extension, the acronym FAT is also used to refer to the file system itself for MS-DOS and Windows platforms.

See: *file allocation table (FAT)*

F

F

FAT32

An enhanced version of a file allocation table (FAT), supported by Microsoft Windows 95 OSR2, Windows 98, Windows Millennium Edition (Me), Windows 2000, Windows XP, and Windows .NET Server.

Overview

FAT32 theoretically supports drives of up to 2 terabytes (2048 gigabytes [GB]) in size, although for Windows 2000, Windows XP, and Windows .NET Server the actual size limit is 32 GB. If the installation partition is smaller than 2 GB, it will automatically be formatted using FAT. If the installation partition size is equal to or greater than 2 GB, it will automatically be formatted as FAT32.

FAT32 uses a smaller cluster size than FAT so is more efficient at utilizing disk space on large volumes (those greater than 512 megabytes [MB] in size) than FAT. The savings in disk space using FAT32 instead of FAT for large volumes is typically 20 to 30 percent. The following two tables show the difference in cluster sizes between the original FAT and FAT32.

FAT Cluster Sizes

Drive Size	*FAT Cluster Size*
0 MB–32 MB	512 bytes
33 MB–64 MB	1 kilobyte (KB)
65 MB–128 MB	2 KB
129 MB–256 MB	4 KB
257 MB–512 MB	8 KB
513 MB–1024 MB	16 KB
1025 MB–2048 MB	32 KB

FAT32 Cluster Sizes

Drive Size	*FAT32 Cluster Size*
260 MB–8 GB	4 KB
9 GB–16 GB	8 KB
17 GB–32 GB	16 KB
More than 32 GB	32 KB

Notes

Using FAT32 (or FAT) with the Windows 2000, Windows XP, and Windows .NET Server operating system platforms is not recommended because it does not offer the security features that are provided by the NTFS file system (NTFS). FAT32 also does not support disk compression. The only time you'd use FAT32 with Windows 2000, Windows XP, or Windows .NET Server is in a dual-boot situation, which Microsoft Corporation does not recommend. Note that in a dual-boot system, FAT32 volumes cannot be accessed by any operating systems other than Windows 95 OSR2, Windows 98, Windows 2000, Windows XP, or Windows .NET Server. For dual-boot with Windows 95, Windows 98, or Windows NT, drive C must be a FAT partition.

Remember, a client that connects over the network to a shared folder in Windows 2000, Windows XP, or Windows .NET Server can access files in that folder regardless of whether the folder is stored on an NTFS, FAT, or FAT32 volume—provided the client has the appropriate permissions to do so.

See Also: *file allocation table (FAT), NTFS file system (NTFS)*

FAT volume

A partition on a physical disk formatted using the file allocation table (FAT) file system.

Overview

FAT volumes can be used to share folders for users to access over the network, but they lack the advanced security control and auditing features of NTFS file system (NTFS) volumes. The maximum file partition size is 4 gigabytes (GB) in Microsoft Windows NT and 2 GB in MS-DOS, Windows 3.*x*, Windows 95, and Windows 98. Windows 2000, Windows XP, and Windows .NET Server will actually format a partition as FAT32 if the partition is larger than 2 GB.

Notes

Be sure to regularly defragment heavily used FAT volumes because the FAT file system can easily become fragmented when files are deleted and created. Use FAT volumes instead of NTFS volumes when you want to dual-boot Windows NT, Windows 2000, Windows XP, or Windows .NET Server systems with earlier MS-DOS, Windows 3.*x*, Windows 95, or Windows 98 systems.

See Also: *file allocation table (FAT), NTFS file system (NTFS)*

fault tolerance

Any mechanism or technology that allows a computer or operating system to recover from a failure.

Overview

In fault-tolerant systems, the data remains available when one component of the system fails. Here are some examples of fault-tolerant systems:

- Transactional log files that protect the Microsoft Windows registry and allow recovery of hives
- Redundant array of independent disks (RAID)-5 disk systems that protect against data loss
- Uninterruptible power supply (UPS) to protect the system against primary power failure

Notes

Just because your system is fault tolerant does not mean you are fully prepared for disaster. You still need to perform regular backups of important data. For example, a RAID-5 disk system will protect against data loss if one disk drive fails, but not if two or more drives fail simultaneously.

See Also: *disaster recovery, redundant array of independent disks (RAID)*

FCC

Stands for Federal Communications Commission, a U.S. government agency regulating all aspects of telecommunications.

See: *Federal Communications Commission (FCC)*

FDDI

Stands for Fiber Distributed Data Interface, a high-speed network technology used mainly for campus backbones.

See: *Fiber Distributed Data Interface (FDDI)*

FDDI token passing

The token-passing access method for Fiber Distributed Data Interface (FDDI) networking.

Overview

The token-passing method used by FDDI is generally similar to the token-passing definition outlined in the IEEE 802.5 specification for Token Ring networks. However, in an FDDI ring, each host holds the token for a predetermined amount of time and can transmit as many frames as it can produce during this time. When the time interval expires, the host must release the token for the next host on the ring to use. This differs from the IEEE 802.5 specification in that many frames from each host can exist on the ring at the same time, instead of only one frame per host, as is the case in Token Ring networks. This allows FDDI networks to support higher data traffic rates than Token Ring networks and makes FDDI more suitable for network backbones.

See Also: *Fiber Distributed Data Interface (FDDI), Token Ring*

FDM

Stands for frequency-division multiplexing, a signal transmission technology in which multiple signals can simultaneously be transmitted over the same line or channel.

See: *frequency-division multiplexing (FDM)*

FDMA

Stands for Frequency Division Multiple Access, the signal multiplexing technology used in the Advanced Mobile Phone Service (AMPS) analog version of cellular phone technology.

See: *Frequency Division Multiple Access (FDMA)*

Federal Communications Commission (FCC)

A U.S. government agency regulating all aspects of telecommunications.

Overview

The Federal Communications Commission (FCC) was established under the Communications Act of 1934 as an independent federal regulatory agency. Among other responsibilities, the FCC licenses portions of the electromagnetic spectrum for communication technologies such as cellular phones and wireless networking. For example, in 1994 the FCC auctioned off portions of the 1900-megahertz (MHz) radio wave section of the electromagnetic spectrum to enable companies to deploy Personal Communications Services (PCS) technologies for cellular communication. FCC auctions are intended to increase the number of cellular phone providers in the United States, foster growth and competition in the telecommunications industry, and raise money for the U.S. government treasury.

F

One role of the FCC is to implement communication legislation passed by Congress. The Telecommunications Act of 1996 represents the first major overhaul of the laws regarding telecommunications in more than 60 years. The FCC is tasked with enforcing this legislation, which is designed to open up competition in the telecommunications arena to foster innovation and economic progress.

For More Information

Visit the FCC at *www.fcc.gov.*

Federal Information Processing Standard (FIPS)

Any standard ratified by the National Institute of Standards and Technology (NIST).

Overview

NIST is a U.S. government organization responsible for developing standards in industry and commerce. Federal Information Processing Standard (FIPS) standards are one aspect of the work of NIST and represent standards relating to computing, networking, cryptography, and related subjects.

An example of a FIPS standard is FIPS-140, the "Security Requirements for Cryptographic Modules" standard whose compliance is required by the U.S. government by vendors developing hardware and software platforms for sensitive (but not classified) cryptographic purposes. Microsoft Windows 2000, Windows XP, and Windows .NET Server cryptographic services are FIPS 140-1 Level 1 compliant.

Notes

Another recent FIPS standard is the Advanced Encryption Standard (AES) that officially replaced the aging Data Encryption Standard (DES) in 2001.

For More Information

You can find FIPS publications at *www.itl.nist.gov/fipspubs.*

See Also: *cryptography, encryption, National Institute of Standards and Technology (NIST)*

FHSS

Stands for Frequency Hopping Spread Spectrum, any type of wireless communications system based on frequency hopping.

See: *Frequency Hopping Spread Spectrum (FHSS)*

Fiber Distributed Data Interface (FDDI)

A high-speed networking technology used mainly for campus backbones.

Overview

Fiber Distributed Data Interface (FDDI) was developed in the early 1980s as a high-speed networking technology for processor-to-processor communications. It was the first local area network/metropolitan area network (LAN/MAN) networking technology that could support data transmission speeds of 100 megabits per second (Mbps). (Until 1993, its only competitor was 16 Mbps Token Ring, a much slower technology.) Although developed originally for the host interconnection environment, FDDI quickly evolved into a popular technology for building high-speed distributed backbones for campus-wide networks and reached its peak of popularity in the mid-1990s.

FDDI transmits data at 100 Mbps over fiber-optic cabling (either single-mode or multimode) configured in a dual physical ring topology. The dual ring topology provides redundancy since the secondary ring is used as a standby for the primary ring. By utilizing the secondary ring for traffic instead of redundancy, FDDI is also capable of transporting data at 200 Mbps. There is also a version of FDDI called Copper Distributed Data Interface (CDDI) that is implemented using copper cabling instead of fiber-optic cabling, but this is not as popular as the fiber version.

FDDI is standardized by the X3T9 committee of the American National Standards Institute (ANSI) and is an International Organization for Standardization (ISO) standard.

Architecture

FDDI uses a token-passing technology similar to that of Institute of Electrical and Electronics Engineers (IEEE) 802.5 Token Ring networks. FDDI stations generate a three-octet token that controls the sequence in which other stations will gain access to the wire. The token passes around the ring, moving from one node to the next. When a station wants to transmit information, it captures the token, transmits as many frames of information as it wants within the specified access period and releases the token (this feature of transmitting multiple data frames per token capture is known as a timed token or capacity allocation scheme and differentiates it from the priority mechanism used in IEEE 802.5 Token Ring). Each node on the ring checks each and every frame to see if it is the frame's intended recipient, and the recipient node reads the information from the frame. When a frame completes its travel around the ring and returns to its originating node, the frame is stripped from the ring.

FDDI is a connectionless networking architecture that supports both asynchronous and synchronous transmission. FDDI packages data in frames that use 48-bit addressing similar to MAC addressing for Ethernet. The frame size for an FDDI frame can range from 32 to 4400 bytes. FDDI frames can encapsulate local area network (LAN) traffic such as Internet Protocol (IP) packets for transmission over FDDI backbones. Different FDDI implementations use one of three possible framing formats:

- **FDDI-raw:** Supported by Cisco routers running Internetwork Operating System (IOS) versions 11.1.*x* and later, and by some third-party vendors
- **FDDI with LLC:** Supported by IOS versions 10.0 and earlier
- **FDDI with LLC and SNAP:** Default format for encapsulating Internetwork Packet Exchange (IPX) packets on FDDI

Implementation

FDDI is usually implemented as a dual token-passing ring that uses a physical and logical ring topology for campus-wide backbone networks or a physical ring but logical star topology for FDDI LANs within a building. An FDDI dual ring consists of a primary and secondary ring operating in a counter-rotating fashion. While the primary ring always carries data, the secondary ring is usually reserved as a backup in case the primary ring goes down. This scheme provides FDDI with the degree of fault tolerance valuable for mission-critical network backbones. In the event of a failure on the primary ring, FDDI automatically reconfigures itself to use the secondary ring, as shown in the illustration. Faults can be located and repaired using a fault isolation technique called beaconing.

FDDI can also be implemented in a form where the secondary ring also carries data, but in the opposite direction from the primary ring. This configuration extends the maximum potential bandwidth of FDDI to 200 Mbps.

Nodes (or stations) on an FDDI backbone can connect to either one or both rings depending on the media interface connector (MIC) employed. These nodes may be directly attached computer systems, concentrators (similar to Token Ring Multistation Access Units [MAUs]), or bridges and switches for connecting FDDI to other LAN/WAN architectures. The two ways of attaching nodes to an FDDI backbone are

- **Dual-Attached Stations (DAS):** Also called Class A stations, these devices connect to both rings using dual fiber-optic connectors. The A port is the point at which the primary ring enters and the secondary ring leaves, and the B port is the reverse. Dual-attached stations use both rings, with the secondary ring serving as a backup for the primary. Dual-attached FDDI is used primarily for network backbones that require fault tolerance. Single-attached stations can be connected to dual-attached FDDI backbones using a dual-attached device called a concentrator or multiplexer.

F

Fiber Distributed Data Interface (FDDI)

- **Single-Attached Stations (SAS):** Also called Class B stations, these devices connect to either the primary or secondary ring using S ports. Single-attached FDDI uses only the primary ring and is not as commonly deployed for network backbones as dual-attached FDDI. Single-attached stations are used primarily to connect Ethernet LANs or individual servers to FDDI backbones.

F

FDDI supports up to 500 nodes in its normal dual-ring configuration with distances up to 1.25 miles (2 kilometers) between adjacent nodes. The maximum circumference for an FDDI ring is 62.5 miles (100 kilometers) (or 125 miles/200 kilometers for both rings combined), and there must be a repeater every 1.25 miles (2 kilometers) or less. Bridges or routers are used to connect the FDDI backbone network to Ethernet or Token Ring departmental LANs.

Prospects

In the late 1980s and early 1990s, FDDI was the most popular networking technology for building distributed high-speed campus backbones. Asynchronous Transfer Mode (ATM) was its only competition, but ATM's complexity resulted in slow adoption and relegation of this technology mainly to telecommunication carrier networks.

When Fast Ethernet emerged in 1993, it competed with FDDI with respect to speed but could not do so with respect to distance. Nevertheless, FDDI lost some ground to Fast Ethernet, mainly because Fast Ethernet could be deployed in a switched full-duplex form to build collapsed backbones, a new network backbone architecture that competed with FDDI's distributed backbone architecture. The result was that the market for FDDI technology peaked in 1995 and has been declining ever since.

With the emergence of Gigabit Ethernet (GbE) in 1997, however, the death knell for FDDI began to sound. Switched full-duplex GbE could replace legacy FDDI backbones in campus networks and provide speed increases of tenfold to better carry escalating network traffic.

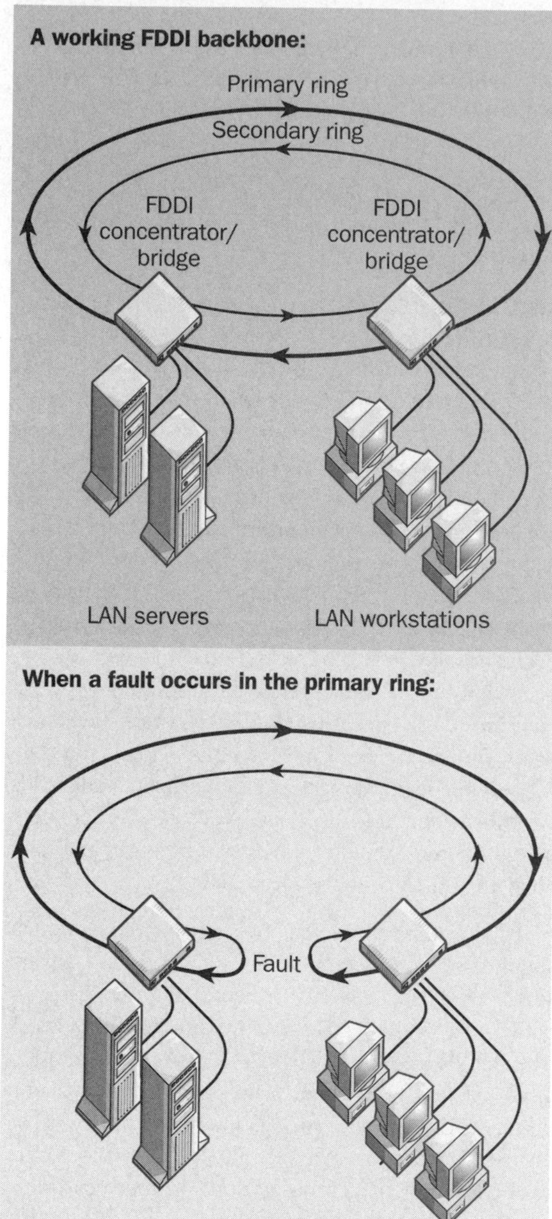

Fiber Distributed Data Interface (FDDI). *Fault-tolerant operation of dual-ring FDDI.*

The final blow came in early 2001, when manufacturers of chips used in FDDI transceivers closed shop and stopped producing, which means that once the current supply of vendor's FDDI equipment is sold, no more will be manufactured. Because of these market developments, most large enterprises using FDDI have begun or already completed migrating their network backbones from FDDI to GbE. Although FDDI is a stable technology that has proved reliable in the enterprise, the impending unavailability of replacement equipment makes migration to GbE advisable.

Notes

When bridging between Ethernet LANs and FDDI backbones, be aware that there are two types of bridges:

- **Encapsulating bridges:** Encapsulate Ethernet frames into FDDI frames
- **Translating bridges:** Translate source and distention MAC addresses into FDDI addresses

Deploying these two FDDI bridging technologies together can result in incompatibilities. For example, although Cisco FDDI bridges can generally interoperate with translating bridges from other vendors, their encapsulation method is proprietary and usually will not work with encapsulating bridges from other vendors. Both types of bridging methods are commonly used in FDDI networks.

The following table shows some troubleshooting tips for FDDI networks.

FDDI Troubleshooting

Problem	*Suggestions*
FDDI ring is not functioning.	Check the status of the router's FDDI interface, making sure the interface and line protocol are up. Try pinging a remote router. Check the physical connections of the cable; use an optical time domain reflectometer to test for problems.
Signal is degraded.	Check whether the upstream FDDI neighbor has failed and the bypass switch has been activated.

See Also: *Asynchronous Transfer Mode (ATM), fiber-optic cabling, Gigabit Ethernet (GbE), Token Ring*

fiber exhaust

A term referring to the potential saturation of the fiber-optic backbone of the Internet due to the exponentially increasing demand for Internet services.

Overview

As high-speed residential Internet access using cable modems and Asymmetric Digital Subscriber Line (ADSL) technology becomes more and more widely deployed, this creates stress on the capacity of the Internet's backbone for carrying all this additional traffic. Another factor contributing to fiber exhaust is the move within the corporate arena toward new high-bandwidth services such as Internet Protocol (IP) telephony and video multicasting technologies delivered over the Internet. Some analysts foresee conditions arising within the next few years that could cause significant degradation in the performance of the Internet due to the proliferation of these services.

Strategies that telecommunications carriers can use to prevent fiber exhaust from occurring include

- Creating additional high-speed, fiber-optic backbone lines for the Internet by laying down more fiber
- Using dense wavelength division multiplexing (DWDM) technologies to enable existing fiber backbones to carry additional traffic
- Upgrading existing time-division multiplexing (TDM) fiber backbones to higher bit rates

See Also: *Internet*

fiber-optic cabling

A glass cabling media that sends network signals using light.

Overview

Fiber-optic cabling (or simply fiber) is the main alternative to copper cabling for building wired computer networks (a network build using wires is called a wireline network, as opposed to a wireless network that transmits data using radio transceivers). Fiber-optic cabling has higher bandwidth capacity than copper cabling and is used mainly for high-speed networking such as Asynchronous Transfer Mode (ATM) and Gigabit Ethernet

(GbE) backbone networks, long cable runs between buildings, and switched connections to high-speed server farms and high-performance workstations.

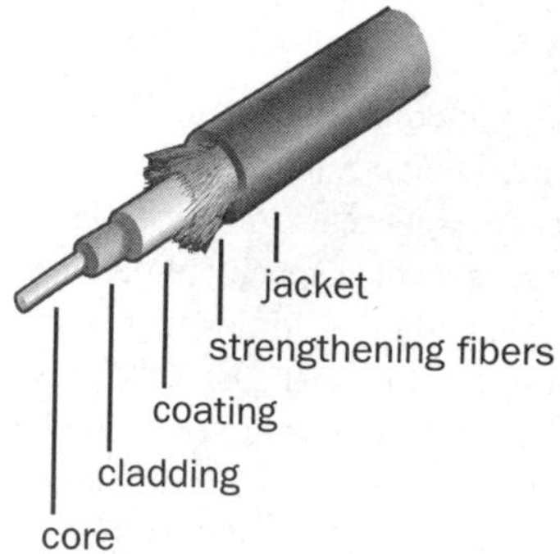

Fiber-optic cabling. *Composition of fiber-optic cabling.*

As shown in the illustration, fiber-optic cabling consists of a glass core between 5 and 100 microns in diameter (for comparison, a sheet of paper is about 25 microns thick and a human hair about 75 microns thick). This glass core is the signal-carrying medium of the cable, and its extreme purity and transparency allow light to travel along it for many miles before being attenuated.

The glass core is surrounded by a thin layer of pure silica called cladding, which prevents light from escaping from the core by a process called total internal reflection. Surrounding the cladding are protective layers of acrylic plastic coating that give the cable stiffness to prevent it from being excessively bent (bending a fiber-optic cable too much can cause the glass core to fracture), Kevlar fibers for providing additional strength to resist stretching during installation, and a waterproof protective polyvinyl chloride (PVC) jacket that is usually colored a distinctive orange.

Fiber optic-capable networking components such as network interface cards, bridges, switches, and routers convert electrical signals into light pulses for transmission over fiber-optic cables. These light pulses are generated using either light-emitting diode (LED) or laser-emitting diodes and associated electronic circuitry.

The bandwidth of a fiber-optic cable depends on the distance (length of the cable) as well as the frequency used for transmitting the signal. Fiber bandwidth is usually expressed in frequency-distance form—for example, in megahertz-kilometers, or MHz-km. In other words, a 500-MHz-km fiber-optic cable can transmit a signal a distance of 5 kilometers at a frequency of 100 MHz (5 x 100 = 500), or a distance of 50 kilometers at a frequency of 10 MHz (50 x 10 = 500). In other words, there is an inverse relationship between frequency and distance for transmission over fiber-optic cables—the higher the frequency, the shorter the distance supported.

Uses

Fiber-optic cabling is often used for campus-wide backbones, long cabling runs between buildings, and local area network (LAN) connections to heavily used servers or high-speed workstations. Fiber is still not used extensively at the LAN level because it is more expensive and more difficult to install than copper cabling, but the gain in capacity to support future network upgrades often compensates for the increased installation costs.

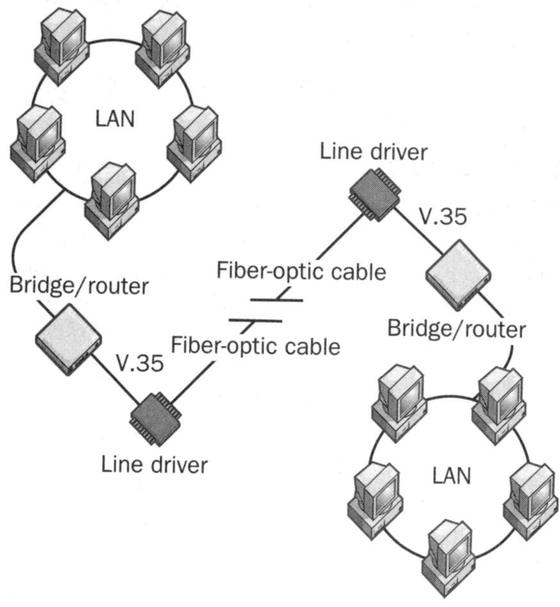

Fiber-optic cabling. *Connecting two local area networks (LANs) using fiber-optic cabling.*

fiber-optic cabling

Multimode fiber of 62.5 micron diameter is the main type of fiber used for GbE networking. This is because 62.5 micron multimode fiber is also the standard for widely deployed 10BaseF Ethernet and 100BaseFX Fast Ethernet (and also FDDI) networks. This type of fiber supports distances up to 1800 feet (550 meters), making it suitable for building GbE backbones within buildings. If gigabit transmission over longer distances is required, 50 micron multimode fiber can be used instead, but this reduces flexibility since this type cannot be used for slower Ethernet networks. For really long GbE fiber connections, such as between buildings on a campus or across a metropolitan area network (MAN), single-mode fiber must be used.

Fiber is used also in heavy industrial environments where machinery can cause high levels of electromagnetic interference (EMI). Long-distance telecommunications carriers such as Sprint Corporation, MCI Worldcom, and AT&T also use fiber-optic cabling extensively for their long-haul (long-distance) telecommunications trunk lines.

Different styles of fiber-optic cabling exist, depending on the intended use. Examples include the following:

- **Duplex multimode cable:** With 62.5-micron core and 125-micron cladding, this is the most common general purpose cable type for most networking environments that require fiber-optic cabling. These cables usually come already terminated with pairs of connectors attached at each end, but you can also buy the cabling in bulk form where you can separate the two cables for termination purposes just as you can with an appliance power cord.
- **Breakout style cable:** This style of cabling contains multiple individual simplex fibers that are stranded around a central strengthening member. It is used for work-area connections and does not require patch panels.
- **Distribution style cable:** This style of cabling contains multiple individual simplex color-coded fibers that are stranded around a central strengthening member. It is often used in backbone applications that require multiple fiber connections.
- **Steel-reinforced cable:** This type of cabling uses a corrugated steel inner tube for protecting cable that needs to be buried or run outdoors.

Fiber-optic cabling is also available for purchase in bulk for those who want the challenge of terminating it themselves, but most customers buy standard or custom preterminated cables from suppliers. These cables can be simplex or duplex; they can be single-mode or multimode (multimode is most common); and they can be terminated with ST-ST, ST-SC, SC-SC, or SMA connectors.

Implementation

There are two basic types of fiber-optic cabling:

- **Single-mode fiber-optic cabling:** Has a narrow core (typically 7.1, 8.5, or 9 microns in diameter) that allows only one signal (light beam) to be sent or received at a time. Single-mode fiber-optic cabling uses laser-emitting diodes operating at frequencies between 1270 and 1355 nanometers (in the infrared range) to transmit signals over distances up to about 30 miles (50 kilometers) before dispersion will distort signals. Single-mode fiber is therefore ideal for long cable runs (up to 50 times farther than for multimode fiber-optic cabling).
- **Multimode fiber-optic cabling**: Has a thicker core (50, 62.5, or 100 microns in diameter) with sufficient width to allow multiple signals (light beams) to be transmitted simultaneously with each signal following a different path or mode through the fiber. Light-emitting diodes are used to transmit signals operating at frequencies between 770 and 860 nanometers (the near infrared) over distances up to about 3000 feet (900 meters) (longer cable runs can distort signals through modal dispersion). The thicker the glass core, the shorter the distance signals can be carried over the cable before dispersion causes signals to be degraded.

There are also two different types of multimode fiber:

- **Step-index multimode fiber:** The less costly variety of multimode fiber, it uses a wide core with a uniform index of refraction, causing the light beams to reflect in mirror fashion off the core's inside surface by the process of total internal reflection.

F

Because light can take many different paths down the cable and each path takes a different amount of time, signal distortion can result when step-index fiber is used for long cable runs, so use this type only for short cable runs.

- **Graded-index multimode fiber:** The more expensive type of multimode fiber, it uses a core made of multiple concentric layers of glass, each having a lower index of refraction than the layer it contains. In graded-index fiber, light beams follow curved paths and all rays reach the end of the fiber simultaneously, reducing the signal distortion that occurs in step-index fiber when long cable runs are used.

Connectors for fiber-optic cabling come in several varieties, including SC, ST, and SMA connectors. ST connectors have a wider installed base, but SC connectors are more versatile and more popular and are used in 100BaseFX, GbE, and Fibre Channel deployments. SMA connectors are sometimes used but do not conform to Electronic Industries Association/Telecommunication Industry Association (EIA/TIA) wiring standards. A newer type of connector is the MT-RJ, which has a snap latch fastener similar to an RJ-45 plug to simplify reconfiguring fiber networks from patch panels. Other connectors have appeared on the horizon for special purpose usage, but how popular these will become remains to be seen.

All forms of networking components are available in fiber-capable forms, including network cards, hubs, bridges, switches, and routers. Also available are line drivers, devices that enable you to extend or interconnect LANs in either point-to-point or multipoint configurations. Line drivers for fiber-optic cabling are available for synchronous or asynchronous transmission as well as for single-mode or multimode fiber.

Advantages and Disadvantages

Fiber-optic cabling has many advantages over copper cabling, including the following:

- Data transmission rates of up to 100 gigabits per second (Gbps) and higher are supported (copper transmission currently maxes out around 5 Gbps).
- Bit error rate (BER) for fiber is about 10^{-10} compared to 10^{-6} for copper, making fiber a much more reliable transmission media than copper.
- Low attenuation, allowing signals to be sent over distances measured in miles instead of feet.
- Less than 10 percent the weight of equivalent copper cabling.
- Immunity to crosstalk and noise caused by electromagnetic interference (EMI).
- Prevention of ground loops by electronically isolating transmitting and receiving stations.
- Greater signal security because signals cannot be picked up by electromagnetic induction as they can from copper cabling. Fiber must be tapped (physically opened) in order to eavesdrop on the transmission.

Prospects

Although copper has sufficed in many instances as LAN speeds have increased from 10 Mbps standard Ethernet to 1 Gbps GbE, it is not likely to be able to support speeds beyond 4 to 5 Gbps. The impending 10 GbE specification will likely be a fiber-only specification, and as a result, copper will probably be considered legacy technology in 5 to 10 years.

Although many have argued that fiber is prohibitively expensive for workgroup LAN deployments, recent case studies have suggested that this is not the case. The cost of laying fiber in a structured wiring scenario is only 10 to 20 percent higher than laying copper, and fiber network interface cards (NICs) for PCs are nearing prices of equivalent RJ-45 NICs. In structured wiring, however, laying fiber everywhere allows you to eliminate the traditional wiring closet on each floor and connect floors directly through patch panels and vertical rises to the main equipment room. This means you need far fewer switches and routers in a fiber-based structured wiring deployment than in a copper one. For example, ComputerWorld magazine reported that when George Washington University wired their 80-building campus using fiber, only 11 wiring closets were needed compared with an estimated 160 that would have been required had copper been used. The savings in equipment costs for new installations make fiber a logical choice over copper and also lay the groundwork for future upgrades when faster networking technologies become available. Enterprise network architects would do well to always seriously consider using fiber for both new deployments and when networks are being upgraded.

Another impetus toward the long-awaited goal of fiber to the desktop is technological improvements in fiber-optic cabling and connectors. Some new fiber-optic cabling is so flexible that it can be tied in a knot without fracturing the core, making installation simpler and less worrisome. New and simpler connectors such as the LC connector from Lucent Technologies, Fiber Jack from Panduit Corporation, and VF-45 from 3M Corporation, Corning, and Siemens make fiber installation and configuration a simple plug-and-play process, with some of these connectors rivaling RJ-45 in size.

Notes

Be careful not to stress fiber-optic cabling unduly during installation. The maximum acceptable bend radius is usually 10 times the diameter of the cable, or about 1.2 inches (3 centimeters). Use an optical time domain reflectometer (OTDR) to test for faults after installation. Loss of signal, or attenuation, in fiber-optic cables can be caused by absorption (no medium is completely transparent to light), cable microbending (especially in single-mode fiber if it is not installed correctly), connector loss because of poor splicing or poorly installed or misaligned connectors, or coupling loss at the transmitter or receiver.

For safety, never look down a fiber-optic cable connected to your network because the invisible laser light can injure your retinas. When splicing connectors onto fiber, be careful to avoid getting shards of glass in your eyes or on your hands—use double-sided tape to clean the connection and remove loose shards and always wear protective goggles.

For More Information

Find out what's happening in the fiber market at *www.fiberopticsonline.com.*

See Also: *copper cabling, dark fiber, SC/ST connectors, time domain reflectometry (TDR)*

fiber to the curb (FTTC)

The laying of fiber-optic cabling by telcos to the customer premises.

Overview

Fiber to the curb (FTTC) is viewed by telcos as the successor to the copper local loop and will allow high speed broadband voice, video, and data services to be delivered directly to the subscriber on all-fiber lines without requiring conversion to electrical signals for transmission over copper. FTTC is thus envisioned by telcos as the replacement for the aging Plain Old Telephone System (POTS).

Other versions of the acronym include

- **FTTB:** Fiber to the building, used to describe commercial (as opposed to residential) upgrades of the copper local loop.
- **FTTN:** Fiber to the neighborhood, used to describe laying fiber from the telco central office (CO) to distribution boxes in neighborhoods.

Prospects

FTTC has been talked about by telcos for years, but it has not been deployed much for two reasons:

- The cost of building an entirely new cabling system to replace the existing copper one is extremely high.
- Technologies such as Asymmetric Digital Subscriber Line (ADSL) have allowed telcos to deliver high-speed data services and Internet connections to subscribers using existing copper local loop lines, and demand for ADSL has not yet been saturated.

A recent change in this situation is Project Pronto, an FTTN deployment underway by SBC Communications (a Regional Bell Operating Company [RBOC]). Project Pronto is designed to bring ADSL to areas that are currently too far away from COs for this to be possible, and it involves replacing copper subloops with fiber that runs directly from COs to remote terminals in distant neighborhoods. Some other RBOCs are also pursuing similar projects, so the era of FTTC may in fact be only a few years away, at least in metropolitan areas of the United States.

See Also: *Asymmetric Digital Subscriber Line (ADSL), fiber-optic cabling, local loop, telco*

Fibre Channel

A high-speed networking technology mainly used for connecting storage devices to computer networks.

Overview

Fibre Channel is a gigabit networking technology developed in the late 1980s for connecting peripheral storage systems to mainframe hosts over long distances. The Fibre Channel specification was defined in 1994 by American National Standards Institute (ANSI) standard X3.230.

Fibre Channel typically provides data transfer at 1000 megabits per second (Mbps) or higher and is envisioned as the successor to Small Computer System Interface (SCSI) for connecting storage peripherals to computer systems and networks. Enterprise-level data storage technologies can benefit from Fibre Channel because the traditional SCSI interface has become a bottleneck in high-speed server-to-disk operations. Fibre Channel eliminates the limitations of bandwidth, distance, and scalability that are related to the SCSI standard and is becoming the industry standard for enterprise-level storage solutions involving high-performance redundant array of independent disks (RAID) arrays and storage area networks (SANs).

A simple Fibre Channel implementation could use a stackable hub or switch to connect a server or mainframe host to an external Fibre Channel RAID storage system using 100-Mbps redundant loops and hot-swappable disks. Servers can also use SCSI over Fibre Channel for connecting to legacy storage systems, and Fibre Channel can also carry Transmission Control Protocol/Internet Protocol (TCP/IP) and video traffic for server-to-server connections and high speed workstation connections in computer-aided design/computer-aided engineering (CAD/CAE) or multimedia environments.

Uses

Although Fibre Channel is viewed as the future replacement for the SCSI standard for connecting servers to external data storage units such as external hardware RAID arrays, it can also be used as a transport for high-speed data and video transmission over networks where Fibre Channel competes with other high-speed networking technologies, such as Gigabit Ethernet (GbE) and Asynchronous Transfer Mode (ATM).

Architecture

Fibre Channel is built in a layered architecture that has five layers:

- **FC-0:** This is the lowest layer or physical interface and defines the optical and electrical characteristics and media options for deployment.
- **FC-1:** This layer is responsible for signal encoding and link control. Fibre Channel uses an 8B/10B encoding scheme that packages 8 bits of data into 10 symbols for transmission, which results in 25 percent protocol overhead (for example, 125 megahertz [MHz] signaling can only transmit data at 100 Mbps). Commands can be sent over a Fibre Channel network by prefixing them with a special character called K28.5.
- **FC-2:** This layer is responsible for framing, flow control, and class of service. Fibre Channel frames are 2,148 bytes long, of which 2,112 bytes constitute payload. Fibre Channel currently supports five different service classes, only three of which are commonly implemented, namely, Class 1 (circuit-switched), Class 2 (connectionless frame-switched), and Class 3 (connectionless point-to-multipoint).
- **FC-3:** This layer is open for specifying various advanced services that might be needed.
- **FC-4:** This is the top layer and is responsible for interoperability with other protocols such as Internet Protocol (IP) and SCSI-3.

Fibre Channel is a serial transmission scheme (like SCSI) and supports various transmission speeds, including 133 Mbps, 266 Mbps, 532 Mbps, and 1.0625 gigabits per second (Gbps). The last speed is most commonly used, and with 8B/10B line coding results in data rates of 100 megabytes (MBps), or 200 MBps in full duplex mode). There are plans to increase speeds to 4 Gbps as well.

Implementation

Despite its name, Fibre Channel can operate over both fiber-optic and copper cabling depending on how it is implemented, with fiber being the norm. Fiber links can be 6.2 miles (10 kilometers) or longer using single-mode fiber or up to 1640 feet (500 meters) on multi-mode fiber. Copper links are used mainly for short interconnects and are limited to 100 feet (30 meters) in length.

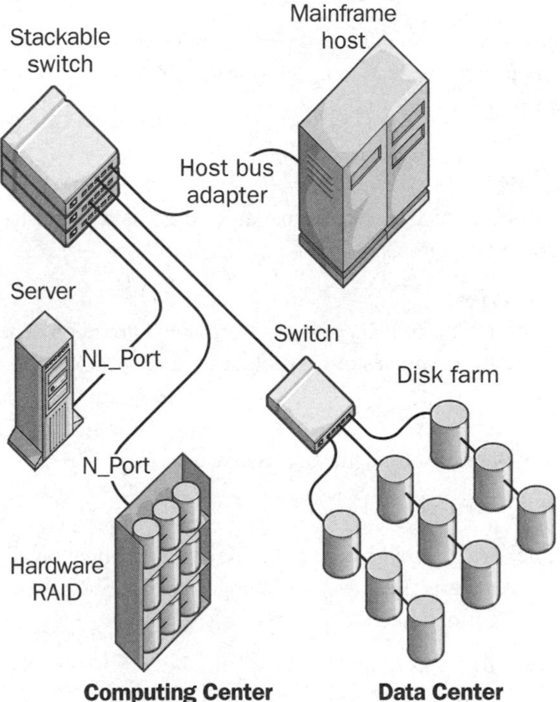

Fibre Channel. *An example of using Fibre Channel to connect network storage systems to computer systems.*

Fibre Channel signaling is performed by special transceivers. A Fibre Channel transceiver is more commonly known as a gigabit interface converter (GBIC), and GBICs can be found in Fibre Channel hubs, switches, and interface cards.

Fibre Channel can be deployed in three different network topologies:

- **Point-to-point:** This involves a dedicated link between only two devices such as two servers, a server and a disk storage system, a router/switch and a SAN, and so on.
- **Arbitrated loop:** This implementation, commonly called Fibre Channel Arbitrated Loop (FC-AL), uses a shared media approach to allow multiple devices to be connected together. It is the most common implementation method for Fibre Channel networks because of its flexibility and efficient use of bandwidth. A special process called arbitration determines which node has control of the media at any moment and is allowed to transmit. The logical topology is a daisy-chained system of loops similar to Fiber Distributed Data Interface (FDDI) and Token Ring architectures, but the actual physical topology is more commonly a hierarchical system of hubs and switches similar to Ethernet. Arbitrated loops can support hundreds of attached devices, but the more devices there are the less average bandwidth available to each device.
- **Switched fabric:** This involves using Fibre Channel switches to provide 100 Mbps switched connections to all connected devices through virtual point-to-point connections. Fully meshed topologies are supported for complete redundancy, and any number of devices can be connected to the fabric. Switched fabrics can theoretically support up to 15 million attached devices (unique addresses), but in practice the limit is about 1000. A downside of this approach is the additional latency caused by the need for virtual connections to be established and torn down frequently.

Advantages and Disadvantages

Fibre Channel's strengths include its protocol-independent transport service (in contrast to GbE's frame format, which extends from the desktop to the network backbone) and its guaranteed delivery service (included in Class 4 Fibre Channel, which makes it competitive with ATM's Quality of Service features). Also, although GbE is limited to general networking transport solutions and ATM is limited to networking and video transport, Fibre Channel can carry both network and

F

video traffic, connect computer systems and networks to network storage devices, and it can be used in high-performance clustering technology.

The main disadvantages are that Fibre Channel equipment is generally expensive, the technology is complex (compared to Ethernet), equipment from different vendors often suffers from interoperability problems, and native file sharing support is not provided.

F

Prospects

Interoperability issues between vendor implementations of Fibre Channel have been one factor slowing general adoption of the technology, but new specifications were released in 2000 to help make Fibre Channel equipment from different vendors work as simply as plug and play. The two most important of these new specifications are Direct Access File Specification (DAFS) and Fabric Shortest Path First (FSPF).

More seriously, Fibre Channel faces stiff competition from emerging new storage-over-IP network technologies including Service Specific Connection Oriented Protocol (SSCOP) from SAN Ltd., SCSI over TCP/IP from IBM and Cisco Systems, EtherStorage from Adaptec, and especially 10 GbE. This is somewhat ironic as the underlying physical layer technologies of GbE were in fact borrowed from the FC-0 and FC-1 layers of the earlier Fibre Channel standard!

These emerging storage-over-IP technologies promise several advantages over Fibre Channel, including more familiar underlying technology (Ethernet), better latency, lower packet loss, and transmission over longer distances. The industry debate is sometimes hot, from Fibre Channel proponents envisioning Fibre Channel being used for general local area network (LAN) transport to 10 GbE proponents declaring Fibre Channel as dead as FDDI.

But things are constantly changing in the networking world, and Fibre Channel may be down but not out. A new contender in the arena is Fibre Channel Over IP (FCOP), a scheme proposed by Lucent Technologies and other vendors. FCOP encapsulates Fibre Channel frames in IP packets to allow them to be carried over GbE or even long-haul ATM/Synchronous Optical Network (SONET) trunk lines, making FCOP a technology that could extend Fibre Channel links to transcontinental distances. Using FCOP, for example, a SAN in New York can be connected to a corporate network in California over anATM/SONET wide area network (WAN) link. A similar standard called Fibre Channel Backbone has also been proposed as a possible ANSI standard. We will have to wait until the dust clears on this one!

For More Information

Visit the Fibre Channel Industry Association at *www.fibrechannel.com.*

See Also: *10G Ethernet, Gigabit Ethernet (GbE), Small Computer System Interface (SCSI), storage over IP*

file

Information assigned a name and stored on a disk or some other media.

Overview

Files are the primary unit of information stored on disk systems. Examples of files include

- Executable files (programs)
- Data files (documents, databases)
- Web pages (HTML files)

Files are generally stored in a file system, which provides a hierarchical way of saving, locating, and accessing information.

See Also: *file system*

file allocation table (FAT)

Specifically, a table maintained on a hard disk by MS-DOS and Microsoft Windows operating systems that acts as a table of contents, showing where directories and files are stored on the disk. By extension, the acronym FAT is also used to refer to the file system itself for MS-DOS and Windows platforms.

Overview

On Microsoft operating system platforms, when we refer to the file allocation table (FAT) file system, we often simply call it the FAT. The FAT is widely supported by all Windows platforms and can be installed on partitions of up to 2 gigabytes (GB) in size on Windows 95 and Windows 98, and on partitions of up to 4 GB on Windows NT. In Windows 2000, Windows XP, and Windows .NET Server, if the partition size is greater that 2 GB, it will automatically be formatted as FAT32. The FAT is often used in dual-boot scenarios or when the security and reliability of the NTFS file system (NTFS) is not required.

The FAT file system is based on the FAT, a structure that maps the locations of the clusters in which files and folders are stored on the disk. The FAT records the location of each cluster that makes up a given file and the sequence in which it is stored. This is necessary because files usually are not stored in a contiguous location on a hard disk because of the presence of disk fragmentation caused by the creation and deletion of files on the disk. For each file on a FAT volume, the FAT contains the entry point for the allocation unit in which the first segment of the file is stored, followed by a series of links called the allocation chain. The allocation chain indicates where succeeding segments of the file are located and is then terminated by an end-of-file (EOF) marker.

Two copies of the FAT are kept in fixed locations on the disk to provide redundancy. A disk formatted with the FAT file system is said to be a FAT volume. The sizes of the individual clusters in which file information is stored on a FAT volume depend on the size of the partition or logical drive formatted using FAT, as shown in the following table. For compatibility reasons, these cluster sizes are the same whether the FAT volume is on an MS-DOS or Windows platform. In the table, you will see that on small FAT partitions (under 15 megabytes [MB] in size) a special 12-bit FAT file system is used instead of the usual 16-bit FAT.

FAT Information for Different Volume Sizes

Drive Size	*FAT Type*	*Sectors/ Cluster*	*Cluster Size*
0 MB–15 MB	12-bit	8	4 kilobytes (KB)
16 MB–127 MB	16-bit	4	2 KB
128 MB–255 MB	16-bit	8	4 KB
256 MB–511 MB	16-bit	16	8 KB
512 MB–1023 MB	16-bit	32	16 KB
1024 MB–2047 MB	16-bit	64	32 KB
2048 MB–4095 MB	16-bit	128	64 KB

Different versions of Windows support different file systems. The original release of Windows 95 supports only FAT, but Windows 95 OSR2 and Windows 98 support FAT and FAT32. FAT32 is a newer 32-bit version of FAT that was first included with the OSR2 release of Windows 95. The original version of FAT is 16-bit and is sometimes referred to as FAT16. Windows NT supports both FAT and NTFS, but not FAT32. Windows 2000, Windows XP, and Windows .NET Server support FAT, FAT32, and NTFS. Possible advantages of using FAT volumes with Windows NT, Windows 2000, Windows XP, and Windows .NET Server include the following:

- **Multiboot capability:** If you need to dual boot between Windows 95 or Windows 98 and Windows NT, use FAT instead of NTFS because Windows 95 and Windows 98 cannot read or recognize NTFS volumes.
- **Efficiency on small partitions:** FAT requires less overhead than NTFS and is more efficient on smaller volumes (those under 400 MB in size).

Notes

The root directory on a FAT volume has a fixed size and can contain only a limited number of entries.

See Also: *FAT32, file system, NTFS file system (NTFS)*

File and Printer Sharing for Microsoft Networks

A Microsoft Windows networking component that allows computers running Windows to share folders and printers so that other clients can access them.

Overview

File and Printer Sharing for Microsoft Networks uses the Server Message Block (SMB) file sharing protocol and is compatible with clients such as

- Computers running Windows have Client for Microsoft Networks installed
- Windows NT, Windows 2000, Windows XP, and Windows .NET Server
- Windows for Workgroups
- LAN Manager

Use the Network utility in Control Panel to install Client for Microsoft Networks on a computer running Windows 95 or Windows 98.

Notes

You cannot install File and Printer Sharing for Microsoft Networks if File and Printer Sharing for NetWare Networks is already installed.

F

See Also: *File and Printer Sharing for NetWare Networks*

File and Printer Sharing for NetWare Networks

A Microsoft Windows networking component that allows computers running Windows to share folders and printers so that they can be accessed by Novell NetWare clients and by computers running Windows with Client for NetWare Networks.

Overview

Use the Network utility in Control Panel to install File and Printer Sharing for NetWare Networks on most versions of Windows. Installing File and Printer Sharing for NetWare Networks automatically installs the NWLink Internetwork Packet Exchange/Sequenced Packet Exchange (IPX/SPX)-Compatible Transport protocol and Client for NetWare Networks, if these have not already been installed. A bindery-based NetWare server must also be available as a network security provider because File and Printer Sharing for NetWare Networks does not support NetWare servers running Novell Directory Services (NDS).

Notes

You cannot install File and Printer Sharing for NetWare Networks if File and Printer Sharing for Microsoft Networks is already installed.

See Also: *File and Printer Sharing for Microsoft Networks*

File and Print Services for Macintosh (FSM)

A Microsoft Windows 2000 service that provides Apple Macintosh users with access to files stored on NTFS file system (NTFS) volumes on Windows 2000 file servers.

Overview

File and Print Services for Macintosh (FSM) is the Windows 2000 counterpart to Services for Macintosh on machines running Windows NT. FSM lets PC and Apple Macintosh clients share files and printers. With FSM on a server running Windows 2000, Macintosh client machines need nothing more than the Macintosh operating system software installed to access resources on the server.

FSM integrates the following three services:

- **File Services for Macintosh:** Also called MacFile, this service lets Macintosh clients access files stored on the server running Windows 2000. Use MacFile to specify a directory on an NTFS volume as a Macintosh-accessible volume.
- **Print Services for Macintosh:** This service lets Macintosh clients print to printers connected to the server running Windows 2000 and spools print jobs for AppleTalk printers such as the LaserWriter.
- **AppleTalk protocol:** This service can be installed on the server running Windows 2000 to enable it to function as an AppleTalk router.

Once FSM is installed on your server, you can make directories available as Macintosh volumes by using the Shared Folders node in the System Tools folder of the Computer Management tool.

Notes

You can install an optional authentication module for Macintosh clients so that they can securely log on to Windows 2000–based servers running FSM.

See Also: *AppleTalk*

File and Print Services for NetWare (FPNW)

A Microsoft Windows NT and Windows 2000 add-on utility for providing Internetwork Packet Exchange (IPX) file and print services to NetWare clients.

Overview

File and Print Services for NetWare (FPNW) enables a server running Windows NT or Windows 2000 to perform the following functions:

- Allow legacy NetWare 3.*x* IPX client machines to access resources on a server running Microsoft Windows NT
- Share directories and printers on a server running Windows NT so that NetWare 3.*x* clients can access them
- Manage NetWare 3.*x* printers from a server running Windows NT, making these printers also available to Microsoft clients

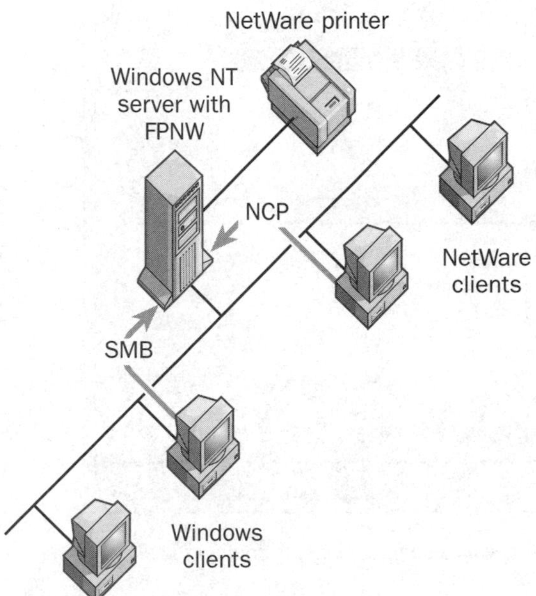

File and Print Services for NetWare (FPNW). *How FPNW works.*

Implementation

FPNW accomplishes these functions by mimicking the functionality of a NetWare 3.12 file and print server and providing file and print services directly to NetWare and compatible client computers. A server running Windows NT or Windows 2000 using FPNW appears to NetWare client machines as if it were really a NetWare server, and clients can access volumes, files, and printers just as they would on a NetWare server. Accounts for NetWare client users are stored in the Security Accounts Manager (SAM) database, instead of requiring maintenance in a separate NetWare server. The FPNW server supports both the Server Message Block (SMB) protocol for Windows client connections and the NetWare Core Protocol (NCP) for NetWare client connections. FPNW requires that the NWLink IPX/SPX-Compatible Transport protocol be installed on the server.

FPNW supports NetWare functions such as user-account creation, remote administration, secure logins, and print queue management. However, it does not support NetWare functions such as user disk volume restrictions or inherited rights masks.

Notes

FPNW is not included with Windows NT or Windows 2000, but you can obtain it as a separate utility from your Microsoft value-added reseller (VAR). FPNW can be installed only on server machines, not on workstations. The directory that will be used as a NetWare SYS volume should be on an NTFS file system (NTFS) partition.

file extension

In Microsoft operating systems, a string appended to a filename, consisting of a period followed by three alphanumeric characters.

Overview

File extensions usually identify the application that can open or run them. For example, text files end with the extension .txt and are opened with Microsoft Notepad. Other common file extensions include the following:

- .doc for Microsoft Word documents
- .exe for executable files
- .htm for Web pages created in Hypertext Markup Language (HTML)
- .gif for GIF 87/89 format images, commonly used on the Internet

File extension. Viewing file extension mappings.

Associations between different file extensions and the programs used to open them are stored in the registry. Sometimes you might need to modify or remove a registered file extension. For example, if two different applications save files using the same file extension, you can easily modify file extensions in Microsoft Windows by using Windows Explorer. Just select Options from the View menu to open the Options dialog box, and select the FileTypes dialog box. Create, remove, or edit file extensions as desired. Be aware that using this tool might negatively affect the ability of applications on your system to function, so modify extensions with care. In Windows 2000, Windows XP, and Windows .NET Server, you can do the same by selecting Folder Options from the Tools menu.

file permissions

A method for controlling access to files stored on NTFS file system (NTFS) volumes in systems running Microsoft Windows 2000 and Windows XP.

Overview

File permissions govern access to files on an NTFS volume, and folder permissions govern access to folders on an NTFS volume. There are five standard file permissions on NTFS volumes for computers running Windows 2000, Windows XP, and Windows .NET Server: Full Control, Modify, Read & Execute, Read, and Write. For any given file on an NTFS volume, each of these file permissions can be allowed or denied for a specific user or group by using the Security tab of the file's property sheet in Windows Explorer (see the illustration).

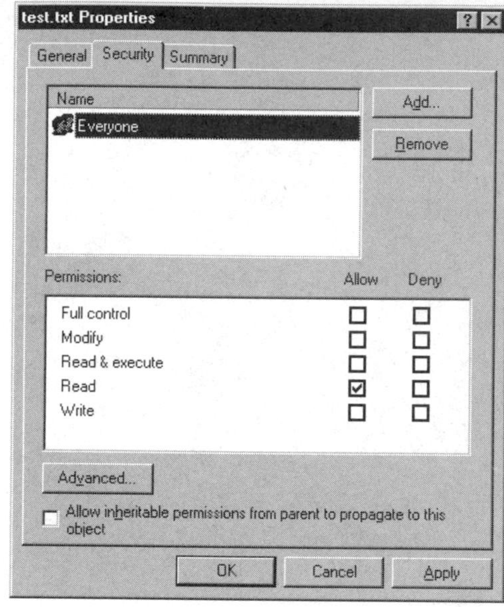

File permissions. *Viewing and configuring file permissions in Windows 2000.*

Each of these five standard file permissions is made up of a subset of the individual or special file permissions that are available on NTFS volumes on machines running Windows 2000, Windows XP, and Windows .NET Server. The following table lists the various special file permissions and how they are combined to form the five different standard file permissions.

Special File Permissions

Special Permissions	*Full Control*	*Modify*	*Read & Execute*	*Read*	*Write*
Execute File	x	x	x		
Read Data	x	x	x	x	
Read Attributes	x	x	x	x	
Read Extended Attributes	x	x	x	x	
Create Files/Write Data	x	x			x
Append Data	x	x			x
Write Attributes	x	x			x
Write Extended Attributes	x	x			x
Delete Subfolders and Files	x				
Delete	x	x			
Read Permissions	x	x	x	x	x
Change Permissions	x				
Take Ownership	x				
Synchronize	x	x	x	x	x

See Also: *folder permissions*

file system

Any technology for organizing, storing, and locating data on a system or network.

Overview

The file system for a computing platform defines the method by which the operating system stores, locates, and accesses files on its hard disk subsystem. File systems usually have a hierarchical structure consisting of a series of nested directories for storing files. Each directory can contain files, other subdirectories, or both. The top of the file system is called the root, and the various directories are its branches. The file system thus forms a tree.

File systems include conventions for the type and the maximum number of characters that can be used to name a file. A file can be located in the file system by specifying its absolute path—that is, its path starting from the root and traversing through the directory structure until the file is reached. Using graphical user interface (GUI) or command-line tools, files can be located, copied, moved, and deleted. Microsoft Windows Explorer is an example of a GUI tool that shows the hierarchical structure of the file system on a Windows-based machine. File systems can incorporate technologies for marking files with attributes such as hidden and read-only. Some file systems allow you to compress files, and some allow you to specify file system quotas for users.

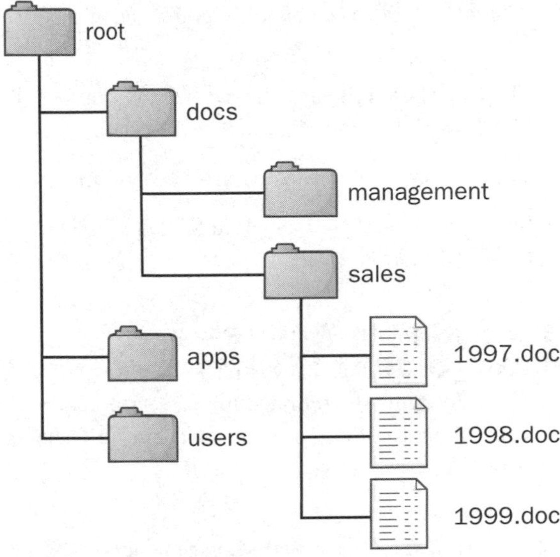

File system. *A hierarchical file system.*

Types

File systems can generally be classified into two types, depending on where the stored resources are located:

- **Local file systems:** These systems are part of the operating system and manage locally attached storage devices such as disk drives and removable drives. Portions of local file systems can be shared to allow users on the network to access specific files, but users generally need to know the name or location of the share in order to access it.
- **Distributed file systems:** These systems are used to combine shared portions of local file systems on many different machines into a single network-wide hierarchical file system. Distributed file systems allow shared network resources located all over the network to appear as though they are located on a single "superserver," and they simplify the process of users locating and accessing shared network resources.

Examples

Examples of common file systems include the following:

- The file allocation table (FAT) file system for MS-DOS–based and Windows-based computers
- The NTFS file system (NTFS) for Windows NT, Windows 2000, Windows XP, and Windows .NET Server
- The Distributed file system (Dfs) for Windows NT, Windows 2000, and Windows .NET Server
- The standard hierarchical UNIX file system
- Sun's distributed Network File System (NFS) for UNIX platforms

File-Transfer Access and Management (FTAM)

The Open Systems Interconnection (OSI) reference model counterpart of the Internet standard File Transfer Protocol (FTP).

Overview

The File-Transfer Access and Management (FTAM) protocol is an OSI application layer (Layer 7) protocol that specifies a standard mechanism for access and management of a distributed network file system. FTAM enables users to

- Access file stores both locally and remotely, making FTAM a distributed file access protocol more similar to Gopher in this regard than to FTP
- Integrate management of both local and remote file stores, including the ability to manipulate both files and their attributes
- Access file stores on different kinds of machines that have different types of file systems
- Transfer files both synchronously and asynchronously

The FTAM model defines the architecture of a hierarchical virtual file store in terms of file structure, file attributes, and the kinds of operations that can be performed on files and their attributes. The FTAM standard does not specify the actual user interface for file access and management, simply the system's underlying architecture. Vendors are left free to create their own user interfaces to FTAM file systems or use existing interfaces for their vendor-specific file systems. Some third-party vendors have developed FTAM-based products for Microsoft Windows NT and other operating systems, but like many aspects of the OSI model, FTAM has not caught on the way Internet protocols such as FTP have, mainly because of its complexity.

See Also: *Open Systems Interconnection (OSI) reference model*

File Transfer Protocol (FTP)

An application-level protocol that can be used for transferring files between hosts on a Transmission Control Protocol/Internet Protocol (TCP/IP) network.

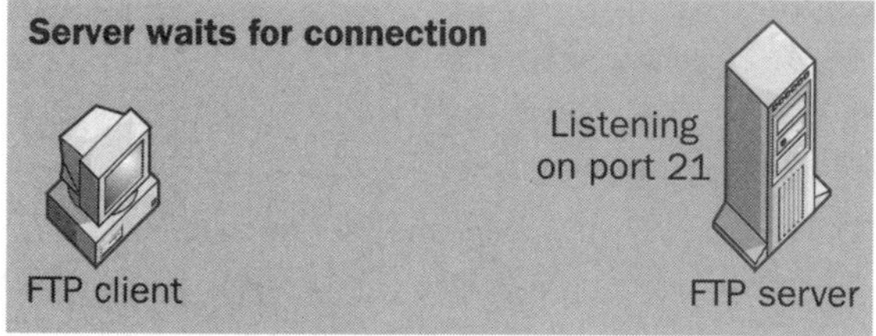

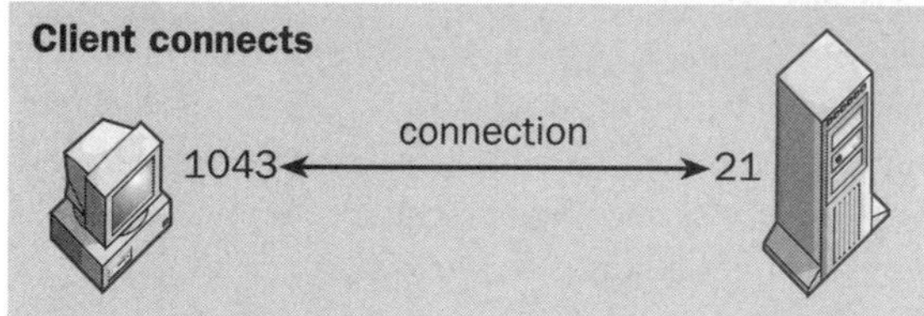

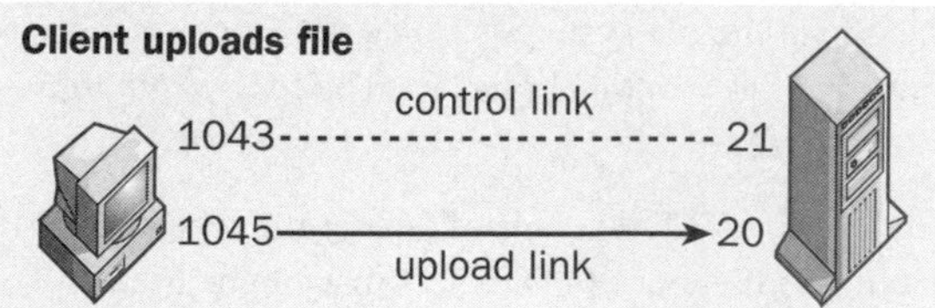

File Transfer Protocol (FTP). *How FTP works.*

Overview

File Transfer Protocol (FTP) is one of the earliest Internet protocols, and it is still used for uploading and downloading files between clients and servers. An FTP client is an application that can issue FTP commands to an FTP server, and an FTP server is a service or daemon running on a server that responds to FTP commands from a client. FTP commands can be used to change directories, change transfer modes between binary and ASCII, upload files, and download files.

Implementation

FTP uses TCP for reliable network communication by establishing a session before initiating data transfer. TCP port number 21 on the FTP server listens for connection attempts from an FTP client and is used as a control port for establishing a connection between the client and server, for allowing the client to send an FTP command to the server, and for returning the server's response to the command. Once a control connection has been established, the server opens port number 20 to form a new connection with the client for transferring the actual data during uploads and downloads.

Notes

Internet Information Services (IIS) supports virtual servers and virtual directories using FTP. You can view the status of open ports on IIS using the netstat command. If an FTP client has trouble accessing information on IIS, try changing the directory listing style for the FTP service on IIS. FTP supports only Basic Authentication or anonymous access for authentication schemes and does not support the more secure Microsoft Windows NT Challenge/Response Authentication method.

See Also: *Internet Information Services (IIS), Transmission Control Protocol/Internet Protocol (TCP/IP)*

Find

A dialog box in Microsoft Windows 2000, Windows XP, and Windows .NET Server that lets you locate objects in Active Directory directory service.

Overview

The Find dialog box allows you to query the global catalog server for objects such as users, groups, computers, shared folders, printers, and other objects in Active Directory.

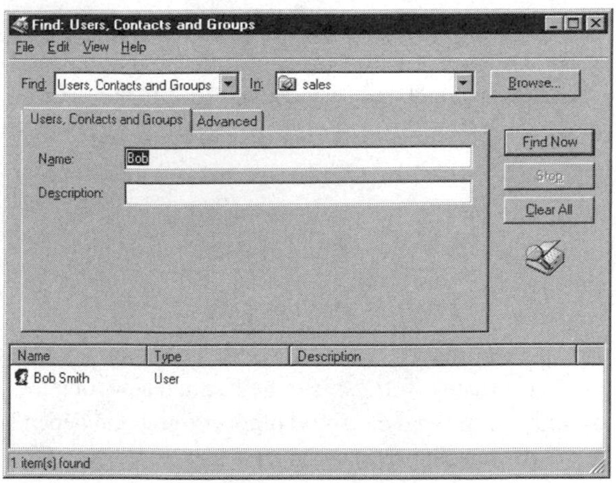

Find. *Using Find in Active Directory Users And Computers.*

To use the Find dialog box, open a console with the snap-in for Active Directory Users And Computers installed, right-click on a container or organizational unit, and select Find from the shortcut menu. Then specify what kinds of objects you want to search for within Active Directory, such as

- Users, contacts, and groups
- Computers
- Printers
- Shared folders
- Directory folders
- Routers
- Custom search

Next, specify whether you want to search the entire Active Directory, a particular domain, or a particular organizational unit (OU). Finally, specify the query parameters associated with the type of object you are looking for. For example, if you are looking for users, contacts, or groups, you can specify the name of the object, its description, or specific attributes of the object, such as home phone or e-mail address.

Notes

If you are performing a search based on an attribute of an object, you must specify a value for this attribute.

finger

A Transmission Control Protocol/Internet Protocol (TCP/IP) protocol and service for viewing information about a user.

Overview

For a user on the client machine to be able to "finger" someone using finger client software, the finger daemon (service) must be running on the remote system being queried. Then if you finger a user's e-mail address, the result returned to you typically includes the user's username, full name, whether and how long the user has been logged on, and other information depending on the configuration of the finger service you are querying.

Microsoft Corporation's implementation of TCP/IP on Microsoft Windows 2000, Windows XP, and Windows .NET Server has finger client software but no finger service. In other words, you can run the finger client on a machine running Windows 2000, Windows XP, or Windows .NET Server that is connected to the Internet in order to obtain results from a UNIX server at an Internet service provider (ISP) running the finger daemon. For example, typing the command **finger jsmith@ s12.microsoft.com** displays information about user Jeff Smith on a server called s12.microsoft.com.

If an ISP makes its finger daemon publicly available on the Internet, it is commonly referred to as a finger gateway.

Notes

Finger is more of a security risk than a useful service in most cases and is not widely implemented anymore. A related service that also is not used much these days is whois.

For More Information

Visit Finger Lookup, a popular Internet finger gateway, at *alabanza.com/kabacoff/Inter-Links/cgi/finger.cgi.*

See Also: *Transmission Control Protocol/Internet Protocol (TCP/IP)*

FIPS

Stands for Federal Information Processing Standard, any standard ratified by the National Institute of Standards and Technology (NIST)

See: *Federal Information Processing Standard (FIPS)*

firewall

Any system or device that allows safe network traffic to pass while restricting or denying unsafe traffic.

Overview

Firewalls are usually dedicated machines running at the gateway point between your local network and the outside world and are used to control who has access to your private corporate network from the outside—for example, over the Internet. More generally, a firewall is any system that controls communication between two networks. In today's networking environment in which corporate networks are connected to the Internet—inviting hackers to attempt unauthorized access to valuable business information—a corporate firewall is essential.

A firewall is an essential component of a company's security policy and is one of the primary means for enforcing that policy. A firewall acts as a kind of police officer to monitor, control, arrest, and incarcerate malicious traffic, logging all questionable traffic to allow the administrator to determine the cause or source of the attack.

Types

A corporate firewall can either be a dedicated machine such as a packet filtering router or a rack mountable firewall appliance or firewall software that the administrator must install on a dual-home hardened system. Both approaches are popular and each has its advantages and disadvantages.

A personal firewall is a firewall used to protect a single machine, typically a home user connected to the Internet using dial-up, Asymmetric Digital Subscriber Line (ADSL), or cable modem connections. The personal firewall marketplace has exploded in the last few years as broadband Internet access services have become widely deployed. Personal firewalls are usually implemented as software to be installed on users' machines, but the first personal firewall that was offered in appliance form was Firebox from WatchGuard Technologies in 1997. Personal firewalls also come preinstalled on some ADSL and cable modem routers to protect home users and Small Office/Home Office (SOHO) networks.

An offshoot of personal firewalls is the agent-based firewall. Agent-based firewalls are installed on every machine on a network, but their configuration is managed remotely using policies configured on a central policy server. At the enterprise level, this scenario is called a distributed firewall, and it is becoming a popular approach to secure servers on a network. The advantage here is that servers can be protected not just from hackers on the Internet but also from malicious users inside the corporate network. The agent also serves as an extra level of protection if the regular network firewall has been compromised. Another name for this approach is host-resident firewall, since it involves moving firewall security from the network's perimeter to the hosts themselves, a process that scales much better as perimeter traffic increases.

A new type of firewall is a combination of virtual private networking (VPN) and firewall software. This combination can be used for different purposes from enabling mobile users to connect securely to a corporate intranet over the Internet (using VPN and firewall software installed on their laptops) to enabling e-commerce sites to provide their users with secure access to their services (using rack-mounted VPN/Firewall appliances). In general, the firewall software is placed in front of (nearer the Internet) than the VPN software to simplify configuration. The main problem with this combination is that the VPN slows down access through the firewall, so a method of implementing this combination that is growing more popular is using dedicated high-performance VPN/Firewall appliances.

Finally, a different approach to implementing firewalls is outsourcing your firewall services to a Managed Firewall Service Provider (MFSP). This is becoming a popular alternative for small to mid-sized companies that cannot afford to hire trained security experts to configure, monitor, and maintain a firewall. Some analysts expect this segment of the market to grow to $1.5 billion by the end of 2002.

Architecture

In its simplest form, a firewall is a router (or dual-homed computer with two network interface cards) that filters incoming network packets. This configuration is usually called a packet-filtering router. By comparing the source addresses of these packets with an access list specifying the firewall's security policy, the router determines whether to forward the packets to their intended destinations or stop them. The firewall can simply examine the Internet Protocol (IP) address or domain name from which the packet was sent and determine whether to allow or deny the traffic. To specify a list of IP addresses which the router will permit or deny, an access control list (ACL) or access list (AL) is configured on the router. The router can filter both inbound and outbound packets.

A related form of firewall is the network-level firewall because it operates at the network layer of the Open Systems Interconnection (OSI) reference model for networking. Network-level firewalls are transparent to users and use routing technology to determine which packets are allowed to pass and which will be denied access to the private network. Network-level routers can be configured to block certain types of IP traffic while permitting others to pass. Usually this is done by disabling or enabling different Transmission Control Protocol (TCP) and User Datagram Protocol (UDP) ports on the firewall system. For example, TCP port 25 is usually left open to permit Simple Mail Transfer Protocol (SMTP) mail to travel between the private corporate network and the Internet, while other ports (such as port 23 for Telnet) might be disabled to prevent Internet users from accessing other services on corporate network servers. The difficulty with this approach is that the size of the access list for the firewall can become huge if a large number of domains or ports are blocked and a large number of exceptions are configured, and a large access list can slow down the router. Another difficulty is that some ports are dynamically assigned at random to certain services (such as remote procedure call services) on startup, so it is more difficult to configure firewalls to control access to these ports using static access lists. Network-level firewalls are sometimes known as screening routers since they screen different types of traffic, and they are usually combined with packet-filtering using access lists for better security.

Routers that employ stateful filtering maintain an internal table of allowed TCP connections and only allow incoming connections to be established if they conform to this table. Stateful filtering is an alternative to access lists and is often used to control outbound traffic and reduce the size of access lists.

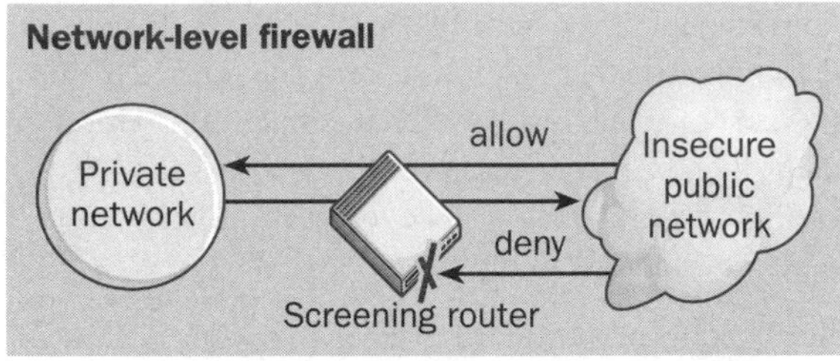

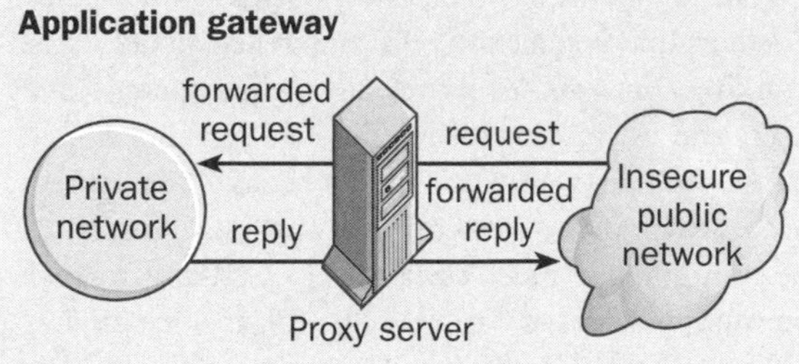

Firewall. *Two basic types of firewalls.*

Another type of firewall is the circuit-level gateway, which is usually implemented as part of a proxy server. Circuit-level gateways essentially operate at a higher level of the OSI model protocol stack than network-level firewalls do. With a circuit-level gateway, connections with the private network are hidden from the remote user. The remote user connects with the firewall, and the firewall forms a separate connection with the network resource being accessed after changing the IP address of the packets being transmitted in either direction through the firewall using a process called Network Address Translation (NAT). The result is a sort of virtual circuit between the remote user and the network resource. This is a safer configuration than a packet-filtering router because the external user never sees the IP address of the internal network in the packets he or she receives, only the IP address of the firewall. A popular protocol for circuit-level gateways is the SOCKS v5 protocol. Circuit-layer gateways are typically used in conjunction with packet-filtering and network-layer protection.

Another more advanced type of firewall is the application gateway, which is also usually included in a proxy server. Application gateways do not allow any packets to pass directly between the two networks they connect. Instead, proxy applications running on the firewall computer forward requests to services on the private network and then forward responses to the originators on the unsecured public network. Application gateways generally authenticate a user's credentials before allowing access to the network, and they use auditing and logging mechanisms as part of their security policy. Application gateways generally require lots of configuration by users to enable their client machines to function properly, but they are more granular in their configurability than network-level firewalls. For example, if a File Transfer Protocol (FTP) proxy is configured on an application gateway, it can be configured to allow some FTP commands but deny others. You could also configure an SMTP proxy on an application gateway that would accept mail from the outside (without revealing internal e-mail addresses) and then forward the mail to the internal mail server. However, because of the additional processing overhead, application gateways have greater hardware requirements and are generally slower than other types of firewalls.

Other advanced features used by firewalls include

- **Execution control lists (ECLs):** These are like access lists but instead control which applications can be executed over the firewall.
- **Intrusion Detection Systems (IDSs):** Usually separate systems from firewalls but sometimes packaged with them, IDSs complement a regular firewall by allowing administrators not just to

prevent intrusion into their private networks but also to detect and analyze the source of this intrusion.

Implementation

Before looking at implementing firewalls, it is a good idea to first review some firewall terminology:

- **Host:** Any computer attached to your network.
- **Bastion host:** A host directly exposed to the Internet. Bastion hosts need to be "hardened" to make them more secure by removing nonessential services and software. Web servers and mail servers are two examples of common types of bastion hosts.
- **Perimeter network:** An extra network located between your corporate network and the Internet. Also called a DMZ, which stands for demilitarized zone.

The simplest way of implementing a firewall is to use a packet-filtering router with port screening at the junction between your private network and the Internet. All traffic flows through this point, and the router handles the entire job of securing your network from attack.

For more extensive protection than a simple packet-filtering router, install circuit-level or application-gateway firewall software on a dual-homed hardened system and use it in place of (or in addition to) the dedicated router.

A screened-host firewall allows a bastion host located on the private network to be accessed from the Internet while preventing other hosts from being compromised. This is perhaps less secure than locating the bastion host outside the private network, but it allows easier access to the bastion host for configuration and maintenance.

A screened subnet architecture employs an intermediate network (the perimeter network) between the private and public networks, each of which are connected to the perimeter network using a separate screening router. One or more bastion hosts are then located on the perimeter network. For greater protection, the perimeter network may be split into two segments using another router or a dual-homed host running firewall software.

Still another configuration makes each bastion host dual-homed, with one interface of each bastion host connected to the perimeter network segment adjacent to the Internet and the other interface connected to the perimeter network segment adjacent to the private network. You can make the topology even more complex by having separate perimeter networks for each bastion host, and so on.

Advantages and Disadvantages

Although firewalls are essential for networks connected to the Internet, a firewall is only as effective as its configuration. A misconfigured firewall is worse than no firewall at all since it provides the user with a false sense of security that the network is protected. In other words, firewalls cannot configure themselves and are only as smart as the administrators configuring them.

Another misconception is that a carefully configured firewall is all your network needs to be safe from attack. This is hardly the case. Network security begins with the development of a comprehensive security policy on paper and is implemented using a variety of systems and services including firewalls, perimeter networks, antivirus software, an intrusion detection system (IDS), and good network management practices. In addition, administrators need to be on top of possible new threats by subscribing to security newsletters, watching for notices of bugs and fixes from operating system and application vendors, reviewing firewall logs regularly, and educating users about the practices of safe computing.

Marketplace

For the corporate segment of the market, firewall products range from dedicated routers to software to install on hardened dual-homed hosts. A popular dedicated router firewall product is the PIX firewall service from Cisco Systems, included with IOS 11.2 and higher as the Cisco Firewall Feature Set. PIX comes in different flavors depending on whether the need is enterprise or Small Office/Home Office (SOHO) protection, and by some analysts' estimates is used by half of all large companies.

In the enterprise software firewall market, popular products include Firewall-1 from CheckPoint Software Technologies, Microsoft Proxy Server from Microsoft Corporation, and many others. The new Microsoft Internet Security and Acceleration (ISA) Server integrates firewall and Web caching functionality and supports policy-based security.

F

In the personal firewall arena, some popular products include BlackICE Defender from Network Ice Corporation, Norton Personal Firewall from Symantec Corporation, eSafe from Aladdin Networks, ZoneAlarm from Zone Labs, Secure Desktop from Sybergen Networks, McAfee Personal Firewall from Network Associates, CyberArmor from InfoExpress, and PC Firewall from ConSeal. In general, personal firewalls come with a standardized default configuration that provides a basic level of security, but remember that firewalls are only as smart as the person who configures them. Personal firewalls are also not a substitute for antivirus software and are usually ineffective in dealing with Trojan horses.

Distributed firewalls are popular in corporate environments and are typically used to protect critical servers using firewall agents that are remotely managed from a central policy server. Examples in this market include CyberArmor Enterprise Personal Firewall from Info Express and McAfee Active Virus Defense Suite from Network Associates.

Several vendors offer combinations of firewall and VPN software that can be used to provide secure remote access to corporate networks. Examples include VPN-1 Gateway (a combination of Firewall-1 and VPN-1) from CheckPoint Software, Raptor Firewall with PowerVPN from Symantec, GuardianPro with Guardian IPSec VPN from NetGuard, and eTrust Firewall with eTrust VPN from Computer Associates.

In the VPN/Firewall appliance arena, Cobalt Networks and Axent Technologies have teamed up to provide a 1U-high rack-mountable VPN/Firewall appliance called VelociRaptor that is based on the Linux operating system. Gigabit products in this market include Cisco's PIX 535 firewall and NetScreen-1000ES from NetScreen Technologies, both of which support Triple DES encryption for greater security (although using 3DES slows down performance to about 600 megabits per second [Mbps]).

In the outsourced managed firewall services sector, two popular providers include DefendNet Solutions, whose DefendNet Enterprise solution uses CheckPoint Software's Firewall-1 product and targets companies with more than 250 users, and RIPTech, whose sentry monitoring system works with several popular firewalls including PIX, Raptor, and Firewall-1. Another managed firewall service provider is NetSolve.

Notes

TruSecure, in conjunction with ICSA Labs, acts as an independent standards body that certifies firewall products and provides a number of resources on their Web site relating to firewalls and network security. See *www.icsalabs.com* for more information.

The best way to begin configuring a packet-filtering firewall is to block all packets at first and then start allowing access to the internal network on a case-by-case basis. Make sure that internal network addresses do not cross the firewall to the outside world and do not store sensitive data on the machine running the firewall software itself. Treat your firewall machine as expendable—the worst possibility should be a hacker's damage to the firewall; this would simply leave your private network securely disconnected from the outside world. You can disable all unnecessary network services on your firewall machine to protect the firewall itself from attack.

If you are concerned only about controlling outgoing access from your network and your users do not need to be able to remotely access your network over the Internet, a packet-filtering router or circuit-level gateway type of firewall is probably sufficient. For users who frequently need to remotely access your network, however, an application gateway is generally best.

See Also: *appliance, network security, proxy server, router*

FireWire

A name trademarked by Apple Computer for the IEEE 1394 High Performance Serial Bus.

Overview

FireWire (or IEEE 1394 or simply 1394) is a serial transmission specification originally proposed by Apple for connecting high-speed peripherals to computers at speeds of up to 393 megabits per second (Mbps). FireWire supports hot-swapping of peripherals with up to 63 peripherals connected to a single FireWire bus. In addition, up to 1023 buses can be interconnected to form a vast array of peripherals if needed.

FireWire features simple plug-in connectors using thin serial cables that can be hot-plugged without interfering with your system's operation. FireWire connectors are based on the Nintendo Game Boy connector.

The main competitor for PC peripheral interconnection is Universal Serial Bus (USB). Although USB is targeted mainly toward computer peripherals running at speeds up to 12 Mbps, FireWire supports much higher speeds and can transport both asynchronous data and video streams and isochronous streams.

Other vendors have their own trademarked names for IEE 1394, including Sony Corporation with its popular i.Link technology.

Implementation

FireWire as defined in IEEE 1394 uses 64-bit device addresses. FireWire cables use two twisted-pair wires for data transmission and two wires for power. FireWire includes two different serial interfaces:

- **Backplane interface:** Runs at speeds between 12.5, 25, and 50 Mbps for bus connections within a computer system
- **Point-to-point interface:** Runs at speeds of 98.304 Mbps (S100 specification), 196.608 Mbps (S200), and 393.216 Mbps (S400) for connecting devices to computers using serial cables

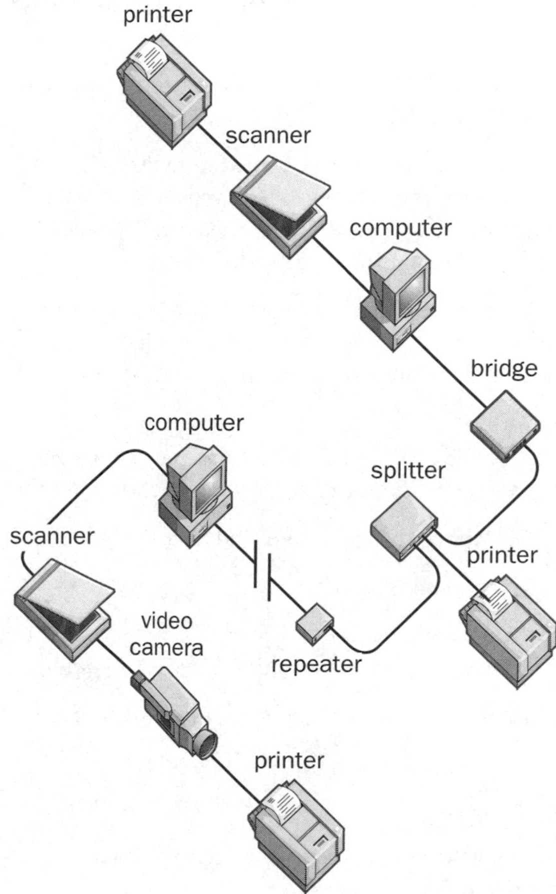

FireWire. *Connecting peripherals using FireWire.*

The topology of a typical FireWire implementation can be complex, but it is typically a hierarchical or tree topology consisting of various IEEE 1394 components. More complex topologies, including several computers sharing portions of the peripheral network, are also possible. The illustration shows how you can use FireWire. The four types of components you can use in a FireWire implementation are

- **Devices:** Typically have 3 ports but can have up to 27 ports and can be daisy-chained up to 16 devices
- **Splitters:** Provide extra IEEE 1394 ports if needed to accommodate the number and arrangement of devices used

- **Repeaters:** Overcome distance limitations in IEEE 1394 cables
- **Bridges:** Isolate traffic within a specific portion of an IEEE 1394 bus

FireWire connections have a maximum distance of 15 feet (4.5 meters), but up to 16 components can be daisy-chained to a maximum distance of 236 feet (72 meters) without using repeaters.

FireWire is supported by the Microsoft Windows 98, Windows 2000, and Windows XP operating systems, along with the universal serial bus (USB) specification.

Notes

Windows 98 resets the FireWire bus and assigns new physical addresses to IEEE 1394 devices when

- Devices are added or removed from the bus
- The system is rebooted

For More Information

Visit the 1394 Trade Association at *www.1394ta.org.*

See Also: *serial transmission, universal serial bus (USB)*

flapping

A problem condition that can occur with dynamic routers on large internetworks.

Overview

When a router is flapping (called a flapping router), it broadcasts routing table updates that alternate between two different routes to a host. For example, the flapping router might indicate during the first broadcast that route A is the best route to a given host, indicate during the second broadcast that route B is the best route, indicate during the following broadcast that route A is best, and so on. Flapping routers thus generate unnecessary routing traffic over the network. This generally happens when a router is unnecessarily configured to load balance between paths with equal hop counts. To determine whether a router is flapping, use a network packet sniffer.

See Also: *router*

flexible single-master operation (FSMO)

A unique set of single-master roles for domain controllers in Microsoft Windows 2000 and Windows .NET Server networks.

Overview

Although domain controllers in a Windows 2000 or Windows .NET Server network mainly function in multimaster mode in which all of them are peers, a few special domain controllers in an Active Directory directory service forest have special roles and execute these in single-master mode. These special roles are known as flexible single-master operation (FSMO) or "fizmo" roles, and there are five of them:

- **Schema Operations Master:** There is only one of these domain controllers in the entire forest, and it is the only one that can be used to create new classes or attributes for the forest schema.
- **Domain Naming Master:** There is only one of these domain controllers in the entire forest, and it manages the names of every domain within the forest and is the only domain controller that can add or remove domains to the forest.
- **PDC Emulator or PDC Operations Master:** There is one of these domain controllers in each domain, and it is used to provide backward compatibility for downlevel Windows NT backup domain controllers (BDCs) within a mixed-mode network.
- **RID Master:** There is one of these in each domain, and it manages the assignment of domain-wide security IDs (SIDs).
- **Infrastructure Master:** There is one of these in each domain, and it updates the SIDs and distinguished names (DNs) in cross-domain references to objects.

See Also: *Active Directory, domain controller*

flooding

Generally, a condition where a network is being bombarded by packets. In routing technologies, a method by which routers communicate to exchange routing table updates.

Overview

Flooding is a mechanism used by dynamic routers for exchanging routing table information with one another across an internetwork. When a router's routing table has changed, it typically floods the network with update messages to alert other routers to modify their tables too. This information is flooded so that every possible recipient router on the internetwork is notified.

The update packets broadcast by the first router are specially formed so that they are received by each subnet only once (otherwise the network could become truly flooded with such broadcasts and communications would be brought to a standstill).

See Also: *dynamic routing, routing protocol*

flow control

The mechanism by which one asynchronous device controls the rate at which it receives data from another asynchronous device.

Overview

One common type of device where flow control is implemented is the modem, the most ubiquitous of asynchronous communications devices. Flow control is also used to describe data rate control mechanisms between other devices, such as computers and attached printers, or between Channel Service Unit/Data Service Units (CSU/DSUs) and routers.

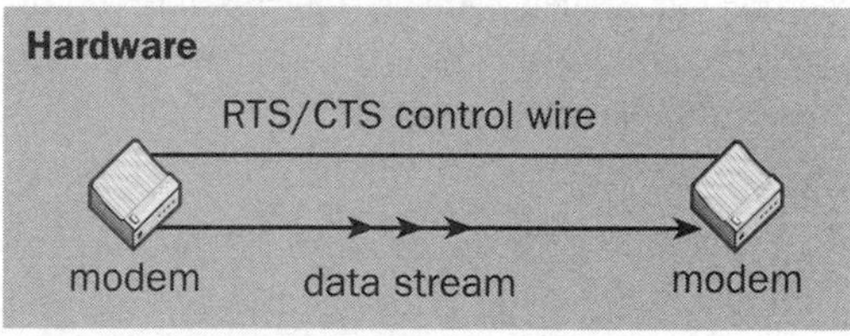

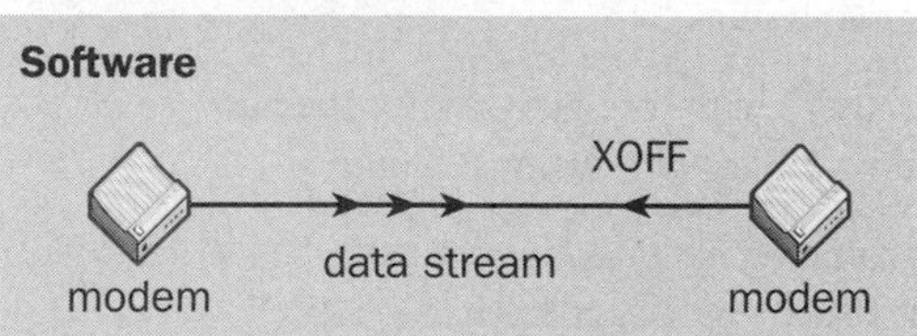

Flow control. *Different types of flow control between modems.*

Flow control is sometimes equated with handshaking, but the term *handshaking* specifically refers to flow control negotiations that take place at the beginning of a communication session, although the term *flow control* also can apply to data transmission management during an active communication session.

In asynchronous communications technologies, two basic types of flow control exist:

- **Hardware flow control:** Also known as RTS/CTS (Request To Send/Clear To Send) control, this method uses special dedicated pinning on cables to leave flow control to the modem itself. In other words, a separate hard-wired signal link (wire) that does not carry data is used to enable one modem to send stop and start messages to the other modem by raising or lowering voltage levels on this wire. Hardware flow control is used with high-speed modems that can compress data and is usually the default setting for Microsoft Windows-based software, such as HyperTerminal, that uses modems.
- **Software flow control:** Also known as XON/XOFF control, this method uses special data characters (usually Ctrl+S to stop transmission, and Ctrl+Q to resume) sent within the data stream itself to enable a local modem to signal a remote modem to stop transmitting data so that the local modem can catch up.

Software flow control is slower and less reliable than hardware flow control because a user, program, or line noise might inadvertently generate a stop signal for the remote modem. In addition, software flow control is used only for transmitting ASCII text information, not for binary data files, because the binary data might contain the Ctrl+S stop character and cause the remote modem to stop transmitting data.

See Also: *asynchronous transmission, modem*

folder permissions

A method for controlling access to folders and their files stored on NTFS file system (NTFS) volumes in systems running Microsoft Windows 2000, Windows XP, or Windows .NET Server.

Overview

Folder permissions govern access to folders on an NTFS volume, and file permissions govern access to files on an NTFS volume. NTFS volumes for computers running Windows 2000, Windows XP, or Windows .NET Server have six standard folder permissions: Full Control, Modify, Read & Execute, List Folder Contents, Read, and Write.

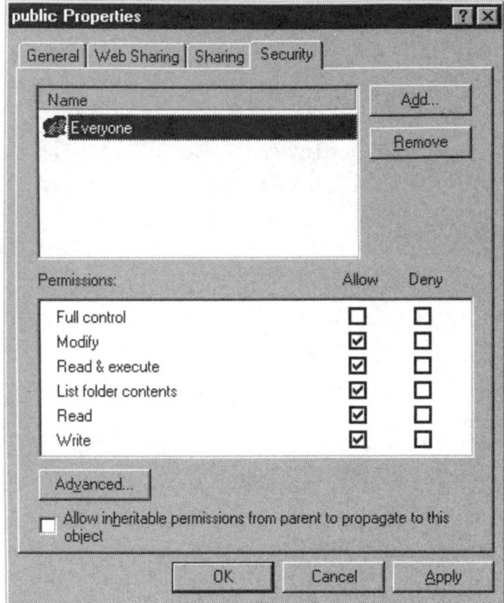

Folder permissions. *Configuring folder permissions in Windows 2000.*

For any given folder on an NTFS volume, each of these folder permissions can be allowed or denied for a specific user or group by using the Security tab of the folder's property sheet in Windows Explorer (see the illustration).

Each of these six standard folder permissions is made up of a subset of the individual or special permissions that are available on NTFS volumes on machines running Windows 2000, Windows XP, or Windows .NET Server. The following table lists the various special permissions and how they are combined to form the six different folder permissions.

Special Folder Permissions

Special Permissions	*Full Control*	*Modify*	*Read & Execute*	*List Folder*	*Read*	*Write*
Traverse Folder	x	x	x	x		
List Folder	x	x	x	x	x	
Read Attributes	x	x	x	x	x	
Read Extended Attributes	x	x	x	x	x	
Create Files	x	x				x
Create Folders	x	x				x
Write Attributes	x	x				x
Write Extended Attributes	x	x				x
Delete Subfolders And Files	x					
Delete	x	x				
Read Permissions	x	x	x	x	x	
Change Permissions	x					
Take Ownership	x					

Notes

The List Folder Contents and the Read & Execute Folder permissions have the same special permissions. However, Read & Execute permission is inherited by both files and folders, but List Folder Contents permission is inherited only by folders.

See Also: file permissions

foreign host

In a Microsoft implementation of Transmission Control Protocol/Internet Protocol (TCP/IP), any host that uses a non-Microsoft operating system.

Overview

Examples of foreign hosts on Microsoft IP internetworks might be OS/2 workstations, Solaris servers, and VMS mainframes.

Connectivity with foreign hosts for the purpose of transferring files with the host requires

- A common networking protocol, such as TCP/IP or Internetwork Packet Exchange (IPX)

- A common file-sharing protocol, such as Server Message Block (SMB) or Network File System (NFS)

See Also: *Transmission Control Protocol/Internet Protocol (TCP/IP)*

foreign mail system

A mail system that belongs to a different company than your own and that might also be of a different type.

Overview

In Microsoft messaging terminology, the term *foreign mail system* usually refers to a mail system other than Microsoft Exchange Server. An example of a foreign mail system could be a public X.400 messaging system in Europe or the Internet's Simple Mail Transfer Protocol (SMTP) mail system. You can establish connectivity between an Exchange organization and a foreign mail system by installing and configuring an appropriate connector on an Exchange server in your organization. Examples include

- Using the Internet Mail Service to connect an Exchange organization to the SMTP mail system on the Internet
- Using the X.400 Connector to connect an Exchange organization to a public X.400 messaging network such as those common in Europe

See Also: *Exchange Server, X.400*

forest

Also called a domain forest, a logical structure formed by combining two or more Microsoft Windows 2000 or Windows .NET Server Active Directory directory service trees. The trees within a forest are usually organized as peers and are connected by two-way transitive trust relationships that span across the root domains of each tree. All trees within a forest share a common schema and Global Catalog.

See: *domain forest*

form

A feature of Hypertext Markup Language (HTML) that allows users to submit information to Web servers using Web browsers.

Overview

A form is a portion of a Web page that presents a series of fields for the Web browser user to complete, along with a Submit button to send the data to the Web server for processing. Forms are often used in Web sites for guest books, registration, and similar purposes. If you create an HTML form, you must create a corresponding form handler—an application that accepts the data from the form and processes it accordingly. Form handlers are typically written in Perl and implemented as Common Gateway Interface (CGI) scripts on UNIX Web server platforms such as Apache. On Internet Information Services (IIS), form handlers can be Internet Server API (ISAPI) applications written in C or Active Server Pages (ASP) scripts written in Microsoft Visual Basic, Scripting Edition (VBScript).

See Also: *Hypertext Markup Language (HTML)*

forwarder

A name server configured to perform iterative queries with other name servers on the Internet.

Overview

If one of your name servers is configured as a forwarder, all off-site queries for resolving Domain Name System (DNS) names are first sent to the forwarder. The forwarder then performs an iterative query with an off-site name server located at your Internet service provider (ISP) to resolve the query. The results of the query are cached by the forwarder. This caching of name query results by the forwarder speeds later name query requests and reduces traffic between your network and the ISP.

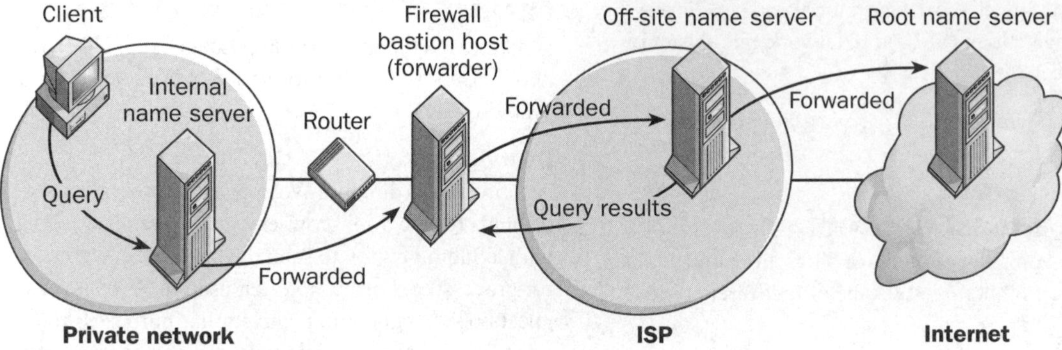

Forwarder. *How a forwarder resolves a DNS name lookup.*

Uses

Forwarders are useful for reducing name resolution traffic and speeding Domain Name System (DNS) name queries for large private Transmission Control Protocol/Internet Protocol (TCP/IP) internetworks that are connected to the Internet. They are also used to resolve name queries when a firewall between your network and the Internet prevents clients in your network from directly querying name servers located at your ISP or elsewhere on the Internet. In this case, a typical location for the forwarder is on the bastion host. (The bastion host is the host running the proxy server or application layer gateway application.)

See Also: *Domain Name System (DNS), name server*

FORTEZZA

A card-based system of cryptographic authentication.

Overview

FORTEZZA was developed by the National Security Agency (NSA) as a way of providing secure authentication to computer systems and services. FORTEZZA functions similarly to smart cards but has greater processing power and memory. The format for a FORTEZZA card is industry-standard Personal Computer Memory Card International Association (PCMCIA) interface, commonly used in laptop computers.

FORTEZZA cards are token-based authentication systems that are tamper-resistant and that protect the data stored on them using cryptography. FORTEZZA is supported by Microsoft Internet Explorer in Microsoft Windows 2000 and Windows XP to control secure Web communications.

You can obtain FORTEZZA card systems from a variety of vendors approved by the NSA. One such vendor is Litronic, which offers a variety of FORTEZZA products and services.

See Also: *cryptography, encryption, smart card*

FPNW

Stands for File and Print Services for NetWare, a Microsoft Windows NT and Windows 2000 add-on utility for providing Internetwork Packet Exchange (IPX) file and print services to NetWare clients.

See: *File and Print Services for NetWare (FPNW)*

FQDN

Stands for fully qualified domain name; in the Domain Name System (DNS), a dotted name that fully identifies a Transmission Control Protocol/Internet Protocol (TCP/IP) host on the Internet.

See: *fully qualified domain name (FQDN)*

fractional T1

A T-carrier digital circuit with a speed of less than 1.544 megabits per second (Mbps).

Overview

A fractional T1 line is a T1 line, leased by a T-carrier service provider to a customer, that carries only a fraction of the regular T1 bandwidth of 1.544 Mbps. Regular T1 lines consist of 24 DS0 channels multiplexed together, but fractional T1 lines consist of fewer than 24 channels. Fractional T1 lines typically consist of a combination of nailed-up channels and switched channels. The technology of fractional T-carrier services is the same as that of regular T-carrier services; the extra channels are simply unused. Customers might want to lease fractional T1 services when they do not require the entire bandwidth (or cost) of a regular T1 line.

See Also: *T-carrier*

FRAD

Stands for Frame Relay Access Device, a telecommunications device that enables a customer site to be connected to a telco's frame relay services.

See: *Frame Relay Access Device (FRAD)*

frame

A segment of data transmitted over a network or telecommunications link.

Overview

Frames are assembled and generated by the data-link layer and physical layer of the Open Systems Interconnection (OSI) reference model. This assembly process is called framing. In other words, packets from the network layer are encapsulated by the data-link layer into frames. Data segments generated by higher layers of the OSI model are generally referred to as packets, but the term *packet* is also sometimes used to include frames.

Architecture

A frame generally consists of a header with preamble (start of frame flag), destination and source addresses, data payload, and usually some form of error-checking information. Frames can be fixed-length or variable-length and have addressing information for multipoint connections or no addressing information for point-to-point connections. They can also have error correction, as in X.25, or no error correction, as in frame relay.

The format in which data frames are constructed depends on the particular data-link layer protocol being used. Thus, we can speak of Ethernet frames, Integrated Services Digital Network (ISDN) frames, X.25 frames, frame relay frames, and so on. Each particular local area network (LAN) or wide area network (WAN) data-link protocol has its own method of framing data for transmission over the network or telecommunications line.

See Also: *Ethernet, frame relay, Integrated Services Digital Network (ISDN), X.25*

frame relay

A high-speed packet-switching service offered by telcos and long-distance carriers and used primarily for corporate wide area network (WAN) links.

Overview

Frame relay technology is a packet-switching service with transmission speeds ranging from 56 kilobits per second (Kbps) for DS-0 or ISDN, to 1.544 Mbps for DS-1 or T1, and even sometimes to 45 Mbps for DS-3 or T3. Frame relay is independent of network-level protocols and can thus carry network traffic of all types, including Transmission Control Protocol/Internet Protocol (TCP/IP), Internetwork Packet Exchange/Sequenced Packet Exchange (IPX/SPX), AppleTalk, DECnet, and Systems Network Architecture (SNA).

Frame relay offers both guaranteed bandwidth necessary for most client/server communications and also accommodates "bursty" traffic when demand for bandwidth suddenly increases, as when a file transfer occurs. Because of these features, frame relay has been a popular solution in the enterprise to connect remote branch offices over frame relay WAN links to corporate headquarters.

Frame relay services are available from all major carriers and Regional Bell Operating Companies (RBOCs).

History

The standardization process for frame relay began in the late 1980s, but it was not until the start of the 1990s that commercial frame relay services began to be available from major telecommunications carriers. The impetus for frame relay originally came from Integrated Services Digital Network (ISDN) technologies—in fact the data-link layer of frame relay is Link Access Protocol-D (LAPD) and is borrowed directly from ISDN.

Frame relay is similar in operation to X.25, an earlier CCITT packet-switching technology from which it also evolved. Frame relay, however, is a more streamlined protocol that has lower latency and thus better performance than X.25. This improvement is possible because frame relay is transmitted over digital lines as opposed to analog lines for X.25. Since analog lines are "noisy," X.25 required additional protocol overhead for handling error correction and retransmission of bad packets. By contrast, the digital lines used by frame relay have very little noise, with the result that the error correction and retransmission functions can be moved from the protocol itself to the end stations. This results in much lower latency and hence faster transmission in frame relay than in X.25. Frame relay also does not support the hop-by-hop flow control functions that X.25 supports, which further streamlines the operation of frame relay.

Frame relay services were first offered in 1992 as a faster alternative to X.25 by AT&T, Sprint, and other long-distance carriers. These carriers established POPs (points of presence) major metropolitan locations to provide a means of connecting customers to frame relay services. Frame relay is now a popular solution for building corporate WANs and is available from Incumbent Local Exchange Carrier (ILECs), Competitive Local Exchange Carrier (CLECs), RBOCs, and European Post, Telephone, and Telegraph (PTT) companies all around the world.

Uses

Frame relay is primarily used for connecting corporate local area networks (LANs) into a WAN. In the early 1990s, WAN links were mainly used for batch transfers between remote offices and mainframes at corporate headquarters. For this scenario, frame relay was ideal since companies only accrued charges when the service was actually being used—in between batch transfers, no charges were incurred. With the rise of client/server computing, frame relay remained the best alternative to more expensive leased lines for WAN links between remote offices, and frame relay is today the most popular and widely deployed carrier service for such WAN links.

Most corporate frame relay WAN links use T1 circuits and carry data at rates between 64 kilobytes per second (Kbps) and 1.544 Mbps, with 256 and 512 Kbps being typical values. Until a few years ago, these values sufficed for most remote branch connectivity solutions, but with the explosion of the Internet the bandwidth requirements for corporate WAN links have risen. There are a number of solutions for providing frame relay links beyond T1 speeds (1.5434 Mbps), including

- **Bonding:** This method allows a maximum of two T1 circuits to be joined together to provide 3 Mbps throughput.
- **Multiplexing:** This method allows many DS-1 (another name for T1) circuits to be joined together to provide NxDS-1 frame relay at speeds from 3 Mbps upward. In this scenario the first DS-1 circuit functions as the management circuit for the entire multiplexed group of circuits—if this circuit goes down, connections are broken. Routers with V.35 interfaces support multiplexing of up to about 6 DS-1 circuits, beyond that routers having a faster High-Speed Serial Interface (HSSI) are required.
- **Channelized DS-3:** Multiplexing a large number of DS-1 circuits can be costly. Instead, a single DS-3 (that is T-3) circuit can be "channelized" to provide fractional DS-3—that is, only a portion of the 45 Mbps that a full DS-3 circuit can provide. Implementing channelized DS-3 for frame relay usually requires specialized equipment such as an M13 (DS-1 to DS-3 multiplexer).

- **Full DS-3:** This is the heavy hitter of frame relay services and involves deploying a T-3 circuit to connect a "big iron" frame relay router at your Customer Premises Equipment (CPE) to the carrier. Only a few carriers provide full DS-3 frame relay services.

Architecture

Frame relay is a connection-oriented service similar to X.25 and Asynchronous Transfer Mode (ATM). Frame relay differs from X.25 mainly in eliminating the complex layer-3 error detection and retransmission mechanisms of X.25. Frame relay is thus a simple layer-2 or data-link layer technology that is simple, fast, and independent of higher protocol layers. Although X.25 defines explicit processes for error correction, acknowledgements, packet sequencing, and so forth, in frame relay these functions are handled by the frame relay devices themselves, giving frame relay connections a much lower latency than X.25 connections. In fact, the protocol overhead for frame relay is only about 2 percent compared to almost 50 percent for X.25.

Frame relay is sometimes classified as an "unreliable" service because it performs no error checking or retransmission—if frames become corrupted or delayed by network congestion, they are silently dropped. To make frame relay a reliable service is the responsibility of the frame relay equipment at the ends of the connection, which performs error checking and retransmission and provides flow control.

A carrier's frame relay network is typically depicted as a "cloud" of connections. This cloud is better known as a Frame Relay Bearer Service (FRBS) and physically consists of the collection of ATM/ Synchronous Optical Network (SONET) trunk lines and switches owned by the carrier. As in other packet-switching networks, frame relay operates by packaging network data into "packets" and tagging each packet with address information (discussed below). In frame relay these packets are called frames and are variable length in nature with payload up to 4 kilobytes (KB), making them especially suitable for carrying network traffic such as Internet Protocol (IP) traffic since entire IP packets can be packaged within individual frames without the need to fragment the packets.

Once frames are transmitted onto the FRBS, they are relayed through the switching nodes that make up the FRBS. Instead of relaying each frame individually, frame relay uses virtual circuits (VCs) that act as logical paths through the carrier cloud. These virtual circuits can be either switched virtual circuits (SVCs) that are set up and torn down on a call-by-call basis or permanent virtual circuits (PVCs) that are established in advance. PVCs are generally preferred because they provide a more reliable grade of service for the customer. PVCs provide dedicated point-to-point connections between local and remote customer premises through the cloud. The particular virtual circuit to which a frame belongs is determined by the frame's address information or Data Link Connection Identifier (DLCI), a 10-bit binary value that identifies the frame to the carrier switches within the FRBS. The DLCI is a logical value that uniquely identifies the two end points of the virtual circuit.

Frame relay lets you establish multiple PVCs (and hence multiple logical WAN links) over one physical frame relay connection using statistical time-division multiplexing (STDM). You manage frame relay PVCs using the Local Management Interface (LMI) protocol, which provides features for verifying link integrity and managing the status of PVCs. Frame relay PVCs provide customers with services similar to those of dedicated leased lines such as T1 lines, but since frame relay PVCs are software-implemented instead of hardware-implemented on carrier switches, frame relay is faster and easier to provision and costs less than leased lines.

There are two ways of connecting to a frame relay network:

- **UNI:** Stands for User-Network Interface, this is a signaling method for connecting data terminal equipment (DTE) to an FRBS.
- **NNI:** Stands for Network-Network Interface, this is a signaling method for connecting trunk lines together from two different FRBSs (clouds belonging to different carriers).

Frame relay provides customers with a predefined level of service called the Committed Information Rate (CIR) that is agreed upon by the carrier and customer in advance. CIR is a negotiated level of service you purchase from the carrier that specifies the guaranteed minimum throughput for your frame relay connection. CIR acts as a kind of bandwidth throttling mechanism that facilitates the use of shared frame relay circuits by different users and prevents carriers from oversubscribing their services. Frame relay also allows temporary bursts of traffic to greatly exceed the CIR, thus providing bandwidth-on-demand for customer applications that require it. Bursts of traffic above the CIR are generally short (less than two seconds in duration) and are possible only during off-peak utilization times. When access to the service provider's frame relay network is heavy, your maximum bandwidth will generally be your CIR. Traffic above a higher service level called the Committed Burst Rate (CBR) is flagged as expendable and is dropped if the network is too busy to carry it.

Frame relay is capable of encapsulating IP traffic for transmission over a FRBS. The encapsulation of IP packets by frame relay frames is performed using the High-level Data Link Control (HDLC) protocol described in RFC 2427.

Implementation

The physical layer or Layer 1 for frame relay is the same as ISDN and T-carrier services, and as a result end stations are typically connected to a carrier's frame relay services using T1 or T3 circuits. Frame relay connections can thus be established using any customer premises equipment (CPE) that supports T-carrier services, including many bridges, routers, and switches. Alternatively, a dedicated frame relay device called a FRAD (Frame Relay Access Device) can be installed at the customer premises to connect the customer's network to an Edge Switch (ES) on the carrier side. Most frame relay–capable routers can be configured to operate either as customer-side or carrier-side equipment, but carriers themselves use special "big iron" routers and switches for establishing their cloud of frame relay circuits.

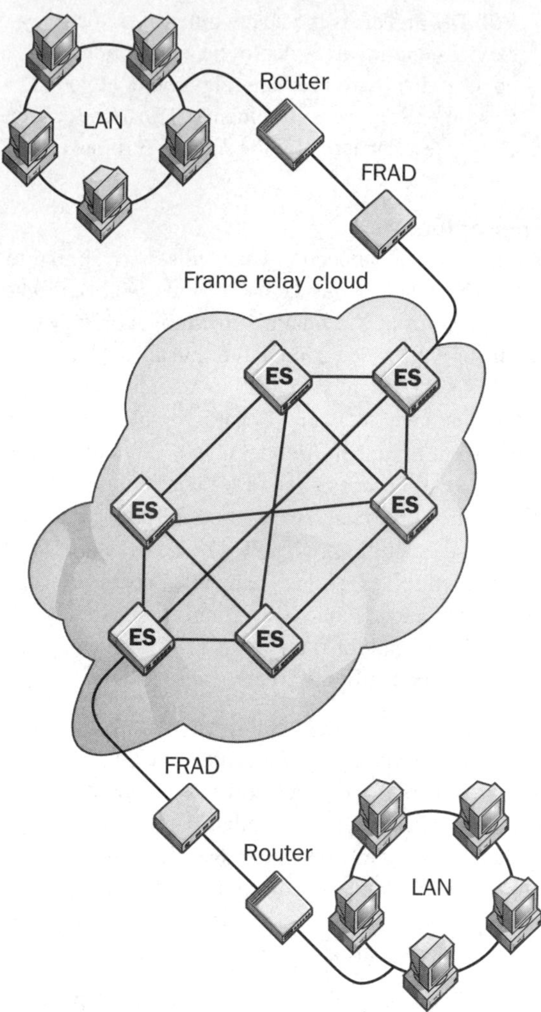

Frame relay. *A typical frame relay WAN link.*

To set up WAN links between several of your company's locations using frame relay, you typically lease the following services and equipment for each location:

- A FRAD or some other device, such as a Cisco router, that is capable of supporting frame relay connections. The FRAD at your customer premises is the data terminal equipment (DTE) side of the connection, and the frame relay/ATM switch at the telco end represents the data circuit-terminating equipment (DCE) end of the connection. Your CPE FRAD is usually connected to your network's backbone switch or router using an RS232, V.35, or X.21 serial interface.

- A T1 circuit to connect the FRAD to the carrier network. Even though you may only want to provision a 256 Kbps frame relay link, most carriers require you to purchase a full 1.544 Mbps T1 circuit to do this instead of a fractional T1 circuit.
- The required number of virtual circuits to support the number of WAN links you need and the speeds they require. Although frame relay intrinsically supports SVCs, few carriers offer this option because it is more expensive and complicated to implement and more complex for billing purposes than PVCs. A single frame relay physical port can have multiple PVCs configured on it.
- The CIR required for each of yourWAN links to guarantee the necessary bandwidth for your applications to function optimally over these links. Choose a CIR that is just sufficient to handle your needs to minimize costs, because the higher the CIR, the greater the cost.

If you have more than two remote networks to connect using frame relay WAN links, you have to decide on the topology you want the carrier to provide for you. Frame relay implementations usually follow one of two networking topologies:

- **Fully meshed topology:** In this implementation, each remote location with a FRAD is connected to every other location with a FRAD using PVCs to form a fully meshed multipoint WAN. When an update is transmitted to one device, it is seen by every other device as well. The advantages of this configuration are the redundancy provided within a multipoint mesh network and that the entire frame relay network can be treated as a single data-link connection. The disadvantage is that the number of PVCs needed grows exponentially with the number of locations, and frame relay carriers usually charge per PVC. So this is not really a good solution for more than three remote locations.
- **Partially meshed topology:** This implementation uses a hub-and-spoke topology in which FRADs at branch offices (spokes) are connected by point-to-point connections to the FRAD at the head office (hub). There is no redundancy in this scenario, so typically redundancy is added by providing backup dial-up ISDN links between branch offices and headquarters in case a frame relay link goes down. This scenario must be carefully implemented to avoid split-horizon problems (routing loops).

F

Advantages and Disadvantages

Frame relay has several advantages over X.25 that has led to the almost complete demise of the earlier technology and its being superseded in the 1990s by frame relay. These advantages include low protocol overhead, low latency, and easy integration with ATM. Originally, when frame relay was developed in 1992, some observers thought that it would soon be superseded by Switched Multimegabit Data Services (SMDS), a packet-switched service that operates at faster speeds than frame relay and does not use PVCs. But apart from MCI Worldcom, few other carriers decided to provision SMDS and instead offer ATM as their top-speed WAN service. If we think of X.25 as the first generation of wide-area packet-switching carrier services, then frame relay is second generation (2G) and ATM is third generation (3G). Although many industry observers expected frame relay itself to be superseded by ATM for WAN connections, this has not occurred, mainly due to the complexity of implementingATM. Frame relay has also superseded Digital Data Services (DDS), another early WAN service provided by carriers in the early 1990s.

Frame relay also has advantages over dedicated leased line services such as ISDN and T-carrier services. In general, frame relay is less than half the cost of leased lines of equivalent throughput, and, unlike some leased line services, frame relay's cost is independent of distance. Frame relay PVCs are also easier to provision and can be configured more quickly than ISDN or T1 lines. Because frame relay provides bandwidth-on-demand and is charged the same way as regular long-distance services (that is, by usage), using it forWAN links can result in considerable cost savings over leased lines, which rack up charges even when not in use. Finally, frame relay only requires a single router or FRAD at each remote site, even in a fully redundant mesh topology, but deploying multiple leased lines at a site requires additional CPE for each line, incurring further cost and adding management headaches.

The many advantages of frame relay ensure its continued survival in the jungle of today's WAN marketplace. Frame relay is simple in concept and in implementation, has established itself as a reliable solution, has an easy-to-understand pricing structure, is cheaper than other comparable services, supports up to 1024 virtual circuits per WAN to meet the needs of even the largest enterprise, is offered by carriers around the world, and has the intrinsic security of point-to-point connections. The only real challenge to its dominance in the WAN is from upstart Digital Subscriber Line (DSL) coupled with IP VPN (virtual private network) technology, which is discussed later in this article.

Marketplace

The three largest providers of nationwide frame relay services in the United States are the Big Three long distance carriers—AT&T, Sprint Corporation, and MCI Worldcom. Sprint, in fact, was the first carrier to offer CIR for its frame relay subscribers, something that is now universally available. AT&T and Sprint between them have more than 1500 POPs nationwide, which provide good coverage for large enterprises using frame relay for their WAN service. Various RBOCs such as BellSouth Corporation, Bell Atlantic/GTE, and Qwest/US West also provide frame relay services, but with fewer POPs and covering specific geographical regions. Other providers of frame relay services include CLECs such as Intermedia Communications and WinStar Communications.

Although most carriers offer DS-1 frame relay services with CIR up to 1.544 Mbps, enterprises that need higher speeds for frame relay WAN links are more limited in their choice of providers. BellSouth now offers an NxDS-1 frame relay service called Subrate T3 that lets customers choose various frame relay rates between 2xT1 bonding (3 Mbps) and full T3 (45 Mbps). Instead of using a traditional conditioned copper T1 circuit at the customer premises, customers implementing this new service use a fiber T3 circuit, which allows them to upgrade to full T3 if eventually required. A few other carriers offer similar NxDS-1 frame relay services and fewer still offer full DS-3 frame relay. For the few customers requiring speeds higher than DS-3 (45 Mbps) for WAN connectivity, ATM can be used instead of frame relay. If a company has a mix of frame relay and ATM in its WAN, it must choose one of two methods for making these technologies interoperate: FRF.5, which tunnels frame relay over ATM, or FRF.8, which translates frame relay frames into ATM cells. An alternative to ATM for high-speed WAN connectivity that is just starting to emerge is Optical Ethernet, offered by carriers such as Yipes, which can provide Gigabit Ethernet (GbE) to the door WAN services. This is an attractive development that may shake the market up considerably in the next few years, but frame relay and ATM still reign supreme in the international arena and for long-haul WAN links.

The prohibitive costs of building a fully meshed frame relay topology for companies with multiple locations has recently been surmounted by a new service offered from AT&T called IP-enabled Frame Relay (IPFR) and a similar service from MCI WorldCom called Business Class IP. In these new scenarios, each branch office is connected to the carrier's frame relay cloud using a single PVC as in a normal hub-and-spoke implementation. However, each frame is tagged using Cisco Systems' proprietary Multi-Protocol Label Switching (MPLS) technology, which allows traffic to be routed across the cloud using destination IP addresses instead of virtual circuit identifiers. The result is the equivalent of a VPN in an IP network. In a hub-and-spoke network, each frame is first sent to the head office FRAD and then forwarded to the appropriate branch office LAN; in the MPLS scenario, however, frames can be routed directly to their destination LAN. All the switching is done by the carrier's core network (usuallyATM), which relieves the FRADs of the additional processing they would otherwise need to do in a normal full-mesh network with multiple PVCs at each site.

Although frame relay supports the capability of billing customers according to usage, most providers bill at flat rates based on the number of frame relay ports, number of virtual circuits, and CIR.

Prospects

Frame relay, despite rumors to the contrary, is still on the rise. Industry analysts predict the frame relay market will be $6 billion in 2002, and this is expected to double over the next five years.

Although costs for leased lines in North America have fallen somewhat in recent years, frame relay still provides equivalent services for WAN connectivity for about half the cost as leased lines. In Europe, prices for leased lines have fallen much more sharply than in the United States, and frame relay is considered to be on a par with leased lines there. In the Asia/Pacific region, however, leased lines are still expensive and most companies use frame relay for linking their regional offices to U.S. offices.

The biggest challenge to frame relay is DSL services now being offered by telcos. DSL can provide frame relay speeds for rock-bottom costs of $50 a month or less. However, DSL is not seen yet to have the same reliability as frame relay, and although widely deployed for residential Internet access, it is not seen by most enterprises as ready for prime-time WAN links that carry mission-critical business traffic. Most DSL deployments involve the cooperation of several parties including CLECs, ILECs, and Internet service providers (ISPs). As a result, when DSL goes wrong, it can take weeks or even months to troubleshoot, with everyone pointing fingers at one another. With frame relay, however, the customer only needs to deal with one provider, or two if User-to-Network Implementation (UNI) services are provided since Network-to-Network Implementation (NNI) services are provisioned directly from the carrier. This makes both provisioning and troubleshooting of frame relay links a snap compared to DSL. Another advantage of frame relay in the WAN is security—frame relay links are point-to-point connections that cannot be hijacked or pirated. By contrast, for companies to use DSL in the WAN, they need to deploy a VPN over the connection to make it secure. Because of all these issues, frame relay is expected to remain a strong player in the corporate WAN marketplace for the next 5 to 10 years until an alternative technology such as DSL makes a compelling case for enterprises to migrate.

Being a packet-switching service, frame relay is inherently poor at carrying delay-sensitive traffic such as voice and video (frame relay was originally designed for carrying data only). Nevertheless, recent advances have led to the provisioning of Voice over Frame Relay (VoFR) services by some carriers, and it remains to be seen how these services will evolve in the marketplace.

Notes

The following table shows some possible strategies for troubleshooting frame relay links in different kinds of situations.

Troubleshooting Frame Relay Links

Problem	*Suggestions*
Frame relay link is down (connections fail)	Check cabling and connections, make sure you are using a data terminal equipment (DTE) cable, try connecting the cable to a different port, or try a different cable. Make sure you are using Internet Engineering Task Force (IETF) encapsulating if mixing frame relay devices from different vendors.
Cannot ping remote router	Check the status of PVC; contact carrier if this is down. Check the router's access list, disable access list, and retry. Make sure you are using IETF encapsulating if mixing frame relay devices from different vendors. Check the configuration of the frame relay address map.
Cannot ping device on remote network	Try pinging local router's frame relay address; check that a default gateway is specified. Check for split horizon conditions in a hub-and-spoke frame relay implementation.

For More Information

Visit the Frame Relay Forum at *www.frforum.com.*

See Also: *Asynchronous Transfer Mode (ATM), DS-0, DS-1, DS-3, Frame Relay Access Device (FRAD), Integrated Services Digital Network (ISDN), Switched Multimegabit Data Services (SMDS), T-carrier, wide area network (WAN), X.25*

F

Frame Relay Access Device (FRAD)

A telecommunications device that enables a customer site to be connected to a telco's frame relay services.

Overview

A Frame Relay Access Device (FRAD) is a device that accepts data packets from the customer's network and encapsulates them into a format acceptable for transmission over a T-carrier circuit to a telco's frame relay network. Some FRADs can also statistically multiplex several frame relay virtual circuits (logical data streams) into a single physical communication circuit to support fully meshed frame relay wide area networks (WANs). Statistical multiplexing enables FRADs to provide customers with greater flexibility in bandwidth use, in contrast to time-division multiplexing (TDM) techniques, which ensure a full level of service for each data stream, even when they carry no data. For example, if two data streams are multiplexed using TDM, frames from the two streams will alternate to form the single serial data link. If one of these streams has no data, empty frames will still be sent, resulting in a poor utilization of bandwidth. In statistical multiplexing, the multiplexed data stream contains only frames from data streams that are carrying data, and the higher the data transmission rate of a stream, the greater the number of frames that are multiplexed into the serial data link.

Implementation

A FRAD is typically connected to a bridge, router, or switch attached to your network backbone (some FRADs also have built-in switching and routing capabilities, too). The FRAD accepts network packets, buffers and frames them, and then transmits them over a T1 or T3 circuit to an Asynchronous Transfer Mode (ATM)/frame relay switch at the telco central office (CO).

The FRAD at the customer premises end is the data terminal equipment (DTE) end of the WAN link and typically connects to a router or switch on the customer's backbone network using a serial interface such as RS-232, X.21, or V.35. The switch at the CO end represents the data circuit-terminating equipment (DCE) end of the link and often interfaces directly to the telco's ATM trunk line network.

Some bridges and routers, such as many of those from Cisco Systems, have built-in FRAD technology and need to be connected only to a CSU/DSU (Channel Service Unit/Data Service Unit) through a V.35 or other serial transmission cable to provide customers with an all-in-one frame relay access solution for wide area networking. Use a bridge if you want an easy way to connect a branch office using frame relay. Use a router if you want to control traffic flow or reroute failed connections.

Marketplace

FRADs come in all shapes and sizes from networking vendors and often are described as switches, routers, or access devices instead of FRADs. The reason is that these devices tend to be able to perform several functions, and different vendors classify these functions differently.

Two popular FRADs in enterprise networks are the Netperformer SDM-8200 from ACT Networks and Cisco's 2600 series routers. 3Com Corporation, Openroute Networks, Motorola ING, Fastcomm Communications, IBM, Alcatel, and many other vendors also sell FRADs.

Notes

Sometimes called a Frame Relay Assembler/Disassembler.

See Also: *Asynchronous Transfer Mode (ATM), data communications equipment (DCE), data terminal equipment (DTE), frame relay*

frame relay cloud

The totality of frame relay circuits within a telecommunication carrier's frame relay network.

Overview

A carrier's frame relay network is commonly known as a frame relay cloud, but the more technically correct term is Frame Relay Bearer Service (FRBS). Typically, a frame relay cloud is a collection of packet-switching devices owned by the carrier and used as a shared public network for backboning wide area network (WAN) traffic for private customers. Frame relay clouds can also consist of frame relay circuits owned by private networking consortiums. The frame relay network is described as a "cloud" because of the large number of interconnections between the various edge switches, usually forming a fully connected mesh topology. In frame relay services, each frame of information contains the routing information needed to enable the frame to be routed to its destination through the cloud.

See Also: frame relay

frame tagging

A method developed by Cisco Systems for building multiswitch virtual local area networks (VLANs).

Overview

A VLAN consists of a collection of ports on an Ethernet switch that acts as if it were a separate LAN from the remaining ports. In other words, you can segment a network into several VLANs using only one Ethernet switch to create smaller broadcast domains.

Frame tagging is a mechanism developed by Cisco to identify which VLAN a packet belongs to. Frame tagging encapsulates a packet into a frame containing the VLAN ID of the packet. When a tagged packet leaves the switch and arrives at another switch, the second switch can determine which VLAN the packet belongs to and switch it accordingly. The result is that frame tagging can be used to build VLANs that span more than one switch, and the process is scalable to the enterprise level.

Frame tagging is implemented in Cisco Catalyst switches and is widely used for building enterprise VLANs.

See Also: Ethernet switch, virtual LAN (VLAN)

frame type

Specifies the data format for frames when using the NWLink IPX/SPX-Compatible Transport on machines running Microsoft Windows 2000, Windows XP, and Windows .NET Server.

Overview

Two machines on a network using NWLink must be using the same frame type to communicate. NWLink on Windows 2000, Windows XP, and Windows .NET Server can listen to Internetwork Packet Exchange/ Sequenced Packet Exchange (IPX/SPX) traffic on the network and automatically configure itself to use the network frame type, which is usually

- 802.3 for NetWare 2.2 through 3.11
- 802.2 for NetWare 3.12 and later

The following table shows the frame types supported by NWLink.

Supported NWLink Frame Types

Network Topology	*Frame Types Supported*				
	Ethernet II	802.2	802.3	SNAP	802.5
Ethernet	x	x	x	x	
Token Ring				x	x
FDDI		x		x	

Notes

NWLink on Windows 2000 Server and Windows .NET Server lets you configure multiple frame types if needed, but if multiple frame types are detected where one of them is 802.2, then the 802.2 frame type will be selected by default. NWLink on Windows 2000 Professional and Windows XP Professional can be configured for multiple frame types only by editing the registry.

See Also: NWLink IPX/SPX-Compatible Transport (NWLink)

Free Space Optics (FSO)

The transmission of data through free space using lasers.

Overview

Free Space Optics (FSO) was conceived 20 years ago when fiber-optic technology was still in its infancy. The promise of FSO has only begun to be commercially realized, however, in the last couple of years.

FSO sends data using modulated laser beams through the air without wires or cables. It can be used to connect networks together and to link networks to high-speed wide area network (WAN) services provided by carriers. It can work with any networking architecture but is most commonly used to transport Internet Protocol (IP) packets. It is fundamentally similar to microwave communications but operates in the terahertz frequency range of infrared and visible light.

Implementation

FSO is a line-of-site (LOS) technology that supports point-to-point, multipoint, and fully meshed networking topologies. Point-to-point connections enable data to be carried up to gigabit speeds over distances of several miles. Multipoint connections tend to be lower in speed, but fully meshed topologies can provide a measure of fault tolerance and resiliency in case of link failure.

F

Advantages and Disadvantages

The main advantage of FSO over traditional fiber networking is that it is cheaper and easier to deploy. The cost of laying new fiber from a telco central office (CO) to a customer's building can run in the hundreds of thousands of dollars, and it takes weeks or months to be provisioned. By contrast, a point-to-point FSO link can be established between two buildings in a matter of days and for a fraction of the cost.

Since FSO operates in an unregulated portion of the frequency band, no additional licensing costs are required to implement the technology. This cost savings can be passed down to customers, making FSO an attractive alternative to fiber. A factor in favor of FSO deployment is that some analysts estimate that 90 percent of buildings in the United States do not yet have fiber deployed to them by carriers.

On the negative side, FSO has some issues associated with its deployment and usage. Since it is a line of sight technology, interference from buildings, airplanes, birds, and weather can interrupt service, reducing FSO's reliability to well under the 99.999 percent rating of conventional fiber-based carrier services. Often the best solution for FSO providers is to establish a backup network to handle these situations, and a typical such network would be a set of point-to-point microwave links (microwaves can be affected by rain but are impervious to the fog and pollution that can interfere with FSO transmissions).

Another issue is that the buildings on which FSO transceivers are mounted tend to sway in the wind and even change size and shape with the seasons, making it complex to align FSO transmissions accurately. Obtaining rooftop right-of-way to deploy FSO equipment often proves costly, but some vendors have reacted by producing transceivers that can be mounted inside offices and transmit their laser beams through windows.

There is also the issue of public perception of safety hazards associated with FSO, namely of having invisible laser beams running all over the place. Although FSO transceivers typically generate less intensity than a laser pointer, safety is still considered an issue of public import and the U.S. Food and Drug Administration (FDA) will probably set specific guidelines in this area.

Marketplace

The number of vendors and service providers offering FSO has been exploding recently. Some of the vendors offering FSO equipment include AirFiber, LightPointe, Terabeam Corporation, and many others.

Service providers Tellaire and Broadband Highway also offer metropolitan area networking (MAN) services in a number of major cities across the United States.

See Also: *fiber-optic cabling*

Frequency Division Multiple Access (FDMA)

The signal multiplexing technology used in the AMPS (Advanced Mobile Phone Service) cellular phone system.

Overview

Frequency Division Multiple Access (FDMA) is one of three methods used for allocating channels to users over the shared wireless communications medium in cellular phone communication; the others are Time Division Multiple Access (TDMA) and Code Division Multiple Access (CDMA). FDMA is the oldest of these methods and is used in the analog AMPS cellular phone system still widely deployed throughout the United States and some other parts of the world. FDMA is also used by traditional AM and FM radio bands to allow broadcast by individual stations and by the CT2 communications system used for cordless telephone systems.

Implementation

FDMA is based on frequency-division multiplexing (FDM) and is implemented at the media access control (MAC) layer of the data-link layer in the Open Systems Interconnection (OSI) reference model. One way to understand FDMA is to imagine different people in the same room communicating in voices with different pitches, some high and some low; they'd all be able to talk simultaneously and (more or less) understand one another.

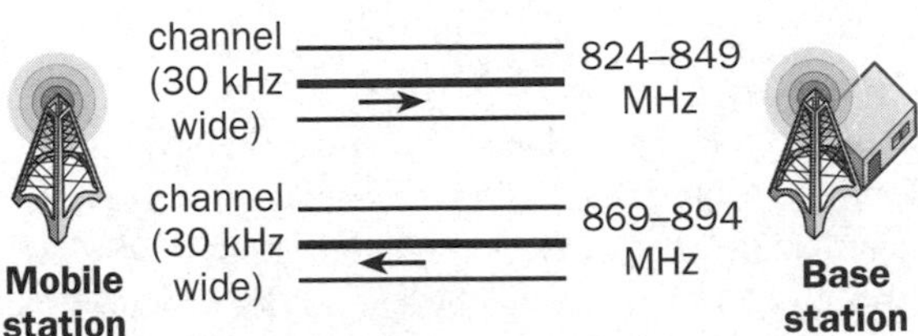

Frequency Division Multiple Access (FDMA). *How FDMA works.*

In the AMPS cellular system that is based on FDMA, each user is assigned a specific channel (frequency band) in the allotted electromagnetic spectrum, and during a call that user is the only one who has the right to access the specific band. These frequency bands are allocated from the electromagnetic spectrum as follows:

- **Transmission by mobile station:** 824 megahertz (MHz) to 849 MHz
- **Transmission by base station:** 869 MHz to 894 MHz

Two different frequency bands are used to allow full-duplex communication between base and mobile stations. Both of these bands are then divided into discrete channels that are 30 kilohertz (kHz) wide in bandwidth.

Advantages and Disadvantages

One disadvantage of FDMA is that only one subscriber can be assigned at a time to a particular channel within a cell. Once the channel is allocated, it remains the possession of the subscriber until the call is terminated or the subscriber roams outside the cell.

See Also: *cellular communications, Code Division Multiple Access (CDMA), frequency-division multiplexing (FDM), Time Division Multiple Access (TDMA)*

frequency-division multiplexing (FDM)

A signal transmission technology in which multiple signals can simultaneously be transmitted over the same line or channel.

Overview

Frequency-division multiplexing (FDM) can be used in both wired and wireless networking for transmitting large amounts of data at high speeds. FDM is the simplest and oldest form of multiplexing in wireless networking technology.

FDM involves simultaneously transmitting multiple signals on different frequencies. These different frequencies, called channels, share nonoverlapping portions of the total frequency band being used. Signals from different data sources are fed into a multiplexer that modulates each signal and transmits them at different frequencies. These signals are then transmitted over the wire or through wireless communication and are separated at the destination into individual data signals using a demultiplexer.

Uses

FDM is used in a number of popular technologies including cable television (primarily within Hybrid Fiber Coaxial [HFC] cable systems), microwave and satellite networking, and in the older Advanced Mobile Phone Service (AMPS) cellular phone system.

See Also: *Frequency Hopping Spread Spectrum (FHSS), multiplexing, time-division multiplexing (TDM)*

frequency hopping

A spread-spectrum transmission technology for wireless networking.

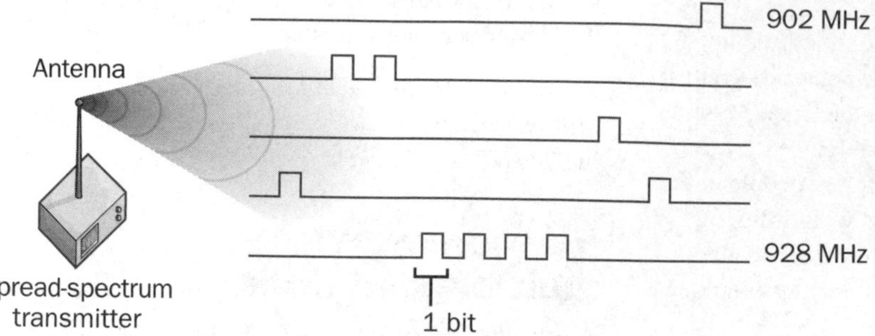

Frequency hopping. *How frequency hopping works.*

Overview

Spread-spectrum wireless technologies trade throughput for increased reliability and were originally developed by the U.S. military to provide communication that could not easily be jammed. Frequency hopping transmitters take the incoming data stream and segment it into multibit packets. These packets are then transmitted sequentially in a pseudo-random manner over the various frequency channels within the spread-spectrum band being used. In other words, the frequency of the carrier signal keeps hopping around. Synchronization between the master transmitter and slave devices is achieved by modulating the center or carrier frequency of the communication band according to a preset algorithm. Both the mobile and the base station know the modulation algorithm, which enables them to keep in communication with each other. For increased security, the modulation algorithm can be dynamically modified.

Frequency hopping is employed in cellular communications systems and some wireless networking systems. It is also used in BluetoothPAN (personal area network) technologies.

See Also: *Bluetooth, direct sequencing, Frequency Hopping Spread Spectrum (FHSS), spread spectrum*

Frequency Hopping Spread Spectrum (FHSS)

Any type of wireless communications system based on frequency hopping.

Overview

Frequency Hopping Spread Spectrum (FHSS) is the earliest secure transmission mechanism used for the physical layer of wireless communications. FHSS was conceived as a technology by actress Hedy Lamarr and composer George Antheil during World War II and became popular as a secure communications system that was resistant to eavesdropping.

Implementation

FHSS employs a narrowband carrier and divides communications up into a number of discrete channels. Information is transmitted in a series of short bursts that hop from one frequency to another. To a non-FHSS receiver, the transmission seems to be random bursts of noise. To make FHSS work, both the transmitter and receiver are programmed with the same hopping sequence and are synchronized with each other so that the receiver always knows what frequency the transmitter is going to hop to next. If interference is encountered on a channel, the transmission for that channel is discarded and retransmitted on the next hop, making FHSS an efficient means of communication in noisy environments.

Uses

FHSS is one of the three PHY layer technologies defined by the 802.11 wireless networking standard, the others being Direct Sequence Spread Spectrum (DSSS) and infrared. Although early 802.11 radio equipment employed FHSS, the newer 802.11b standard does not support FHSS and uses DSSS instead.

Another technology that uses FHSS is Bluetooth, a short-range wireless networking technology for building personal area networks (PANs).

See Also: *Bluetooth, Direct Sequence Spread Spectrum (DSSS), spread spectrum, wireless networking*

frequently asked questions (FAQ)

A list of commonly asked questions and their answers.

Overview

Frequently asked questions (FAQ) are usually developed for beginners in a given subject to reduce the amount of customer technical support required. They are often available for computer products and services on company and organization Web sites on the Internet, as well as for many different Usenet newsgroups. Some Microsoft software documentation also includes FAQs to provide quick answers to commonly asked questions about the software. To ease your customer support requirements, create simple and highly usable FAQ for your clients.

FSM

Stands for File and Print Services for Macintosh, a Microsoft Windows 2000 service that provides Macintosh users with access to files stored on NTFS volumes on Windows 2000 file servers.

See: *File and Print Services for Macintosh (FSM)*

FSMO

Stands for flexible single-master operation, a unique set of single-master roles for domain controllers in Windows 2000 and Windows .NET Server networks.

See: *flexible single-master operation (FSMO)*

FSO

Stands for Free Space Optics, the transmission of data through free space using lasers.

See: *Free Space Optics (FSO)*

FTAM

Stands for File-Transfer Access and Management, the Open Systems Interconnection (OSI) reference model counterpart of the Internet standard File Transfer Protocol (FTP).

See: *File-Transfer Access and Management (FTAM)*

FTP

Stands for File Transfer Protocol, an application-level protocol that can be used for transferring files between hosts on a Transmission Control Protocol/Internet Protocol (TCP/IP) network.

See: *File Transfer Protocol (FTP)*

FTP service

A Microsoft Windows NT service on servers running Microsoft Internet Information Server, or a Windows 2000, Windows XP, or Windows .NET Server service on servers running Internet Information Services (IIS).

Overview

The FTP service supports the Internet standard File Transfer Protocol (FTP) and allows users to upload and download files between FTP clients and FTP servers. IIS FTP servers support only anonymous authentication or Basic Authentication. When an FTP client attempts to connect to an FTP server configured to use Basic Authentication, the user's name and password are transmitted as clear text over the network, which is insecure. The best way to secure FTP services is to enable anonymous authentication on all FTP servers, which requires users to log on with the username "anonymous." (They can enter anything for the password, but the FTP server's welcome message usually requests politely that they use their e-mail address as their password for logging purposes.) You should configure the FTP service on IIS to allow only anonymous logons to prevent users from passing their credentials over the network. Then simply avoid storing critical information on your FTP servers and use them for access to public information only.

You will probably also want to configure your FTP servers to allow only downloads and prohibit all uploads. If your corporate users must upload files remotely using FTP, you can create an FTP drop box for them. An FTP drop box is a folder on an NTFS volume, configured as a virtual directory that has write permission on it but not read permission. In other words, users can upload files to the directory but cannot read what has already been uploaded.

F

FTTC

Stands for fiber to the curb, the laying of fiber-optic cabling by telcos to the customer premises.

See: *fiber to the curb (FTTC)*

full backup

Commonly called a normal backup in Microsoft terminology, a backup type in which an entire volume or system is backed up.

See: *normal backup*

full-duplex

A mode of communication in which data is simultaneously transmitted and received between stations.

Overview

Full-duplex communication is twice as fast as half-duplex communication and typically uses two separate pairs of wires (or two channels for wireless networking) for supporting simultaneous transmission and reception by a host. An alternative arrangement is to use some multiplexing technique, such as time-division multiplexing (TDM), to interleave transmission and reception on a single channel. This does not produce true full-duplex communication, but to an ordinary user it might appear to do so if the interleaving process is fast enough.

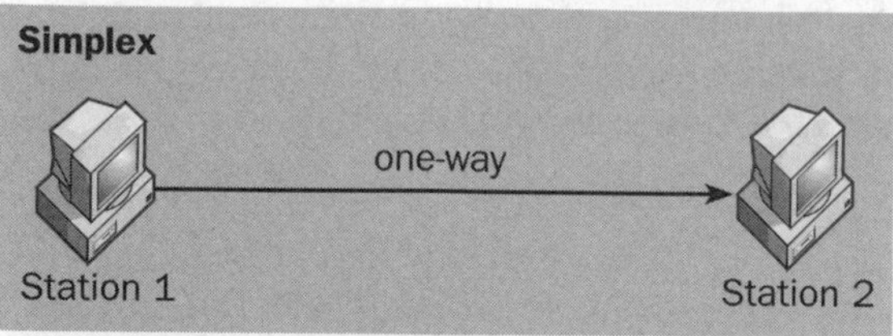

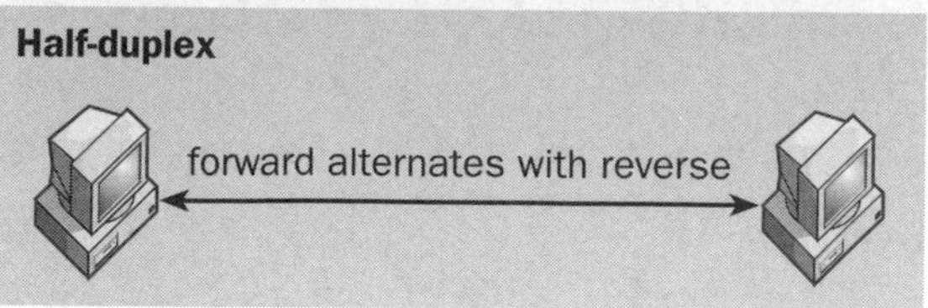

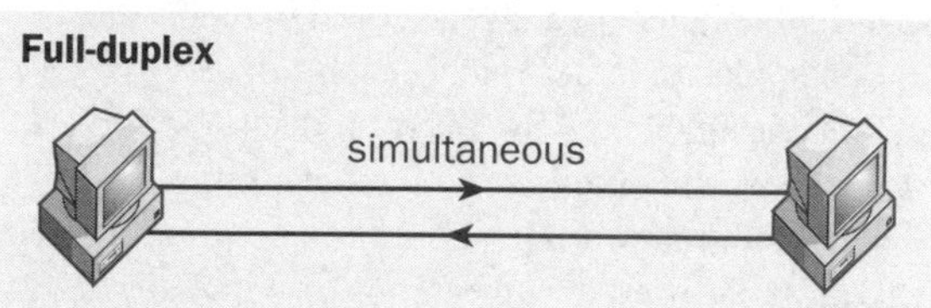

Full-duplex. *Full duplex communications compared to simplex and half-duplex.*

Examples of full-duplex communication include cellular telephone technologies and full-duplex Ethernet. Examples of half-duplex communication are walkie-talkies, CB radios, and standard Ethernet networks. Examples of simplex communication technology include satellite broadcasting and cable TV broadcasting.

See Also: *full-duplex Ethernet, half-duplex, signaling, time-division multiplexing (TDM)*

full-duplex Ethernet

A form of Ethernet that supports full-duplex communication between stations on the network.

Overview

Full-duplex Ethernet lets stations send and receive data simultaneously, thus giving it twice the maximum throughput of traditional forms of Ethernet. Full-duplex Ethernet uses two wires for sending and receiving data simultaneously.

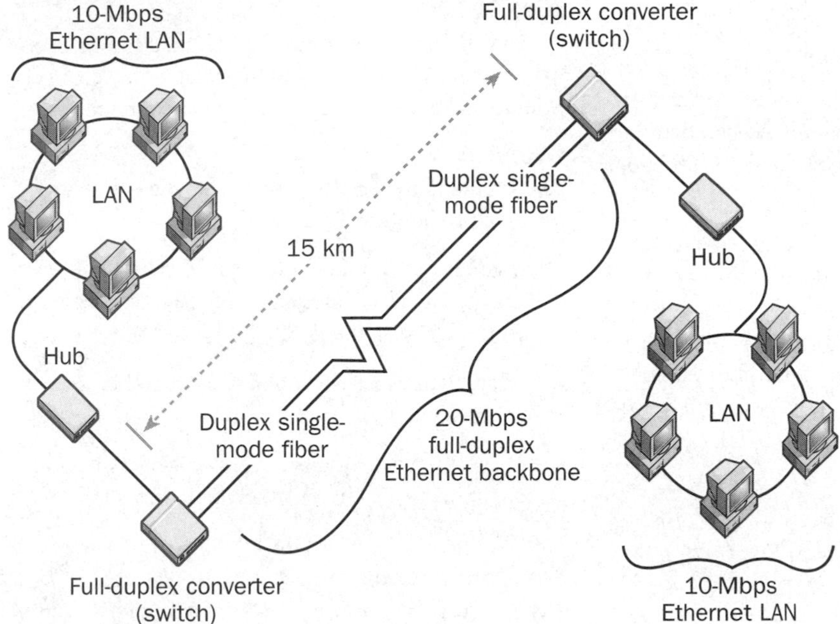

Full-duplex Ethernet. *Using full-duplex Ethernet to connect local area networks (LANs) using long-haul fiber.*

Full-duplex Ethernet does not use the traditional Carrier Sense Multiple Access with Collision Detection (CSMA/CD) media access control method of traditional half-duplex Ethernet since collisions cannot occur on a full-duplex, point-to-point link between two stations. Instead, full-duplex Ethernet uses dedicated point-to-point connections between stations where collisions cannot occur. To implement these point-to-point connections, you must use Ethernet switches instead of traditional hubs or repeaters since hubs are shared media devices and cannot provide dedicated connections.

Using switches means that full-duplex Ethernet avoids the collisions that can degrade the performance of standard half-duplex Ethernet. In theory, a full-duplex connection on a 100 megabits per second (Mbps) Fast Ethernet network has a maximum speed of 200 Mbps. In reality, however, full-duplex Ethernet tends to achieve only a 20 to 60 percent higher throughput than regular half-duplex Ethernet.

The table below shows which varieties of Ethernet support both half-duplex and full-duplex signaling and which are restricted to half-duplexing only.

Ethernet Media Options Supporting Full-Duplex Signaling

Media specification	*Full-Duplex Supported*
10Base2	
10Base5	
10BaseT	X
10BaseFL	X
10BaseFB	
10BaseFP	
100BaseTX	X
100BaseT2	X
100BaseT4	
100BaseFX	X
1000BaseCX	X
1000BaseLX	X
1000BaseSX	X
1000BaseTX	X

Uses

Because the distance limitations between two stations in full-duplex Ethernet depend only on the strength of the transceivers with respect to the medium used, station-to-station distances for full-duplex Ethernet connections can be much greater than for traditional Ethernet networks. For 100-Mbps full-duplex links, this is generally around 1.25 miles (2 kilometers) over fiber-optic cabling but using vendor-specific nonstandard repeaters, this can be extended to 62.5 miles (100 kilometers) or more.

You can also use 10-Mbps full-duplex Ethernet to connect two 10BaseT Ethernet networks over duplex single-mode fiber-optic cabling at distances of up to 15 kilometers. To do this, use a pair of half-to-full duplex converters at either end of the fiber-optic line. These converters should always be used in pairs, and they typically have an attachment unit interface (AUI) port that accepts the fiber-optic transceiver.

See Also: *Carrier Sense Multiple Access with Collision Detection (CSMA/CD), Ethernet, Fast Ethernet, full-duplex, half-duplex*

fully qualified domain name (FQDN)

In the Domain Name System (DNS), a dotted name that fully identifies a Transmission Control Protocol/Internet Protocol (TCP/IP) host on the Internet.

Overview

A fully qualified domain name (FQDN) of a host consists of its host name together with its domain name and any names of subdomains in which the host resides, all of which are separated by periods. FQDNs are used in Uniform Resource Locators (URLs) for accessing Web pages on the Internet and provide an absolute path through the DNS namespace to the target host on which the Web page resides. They are also sometimes called absolute domain names.

Examples

For the host having the FQDN

```
server7.microsoft.com
```

the host name is server7 and the domain is microsoft.com.

See Also: *domain name, Domain Name System (DNS)*

Fusion

An annual business symposium designed for the business experts and managers in the Microsoft Certified Solution Provider (MCSP) worldwide community.

Overview

The general purpose of Microsoft Fusion is to enable solution providers to

- Share information on the latest Microsoft Corporation products, technologies, and sales strategies from experts in the field
- Share their experiences and tips with other industry experts and peers
- Discover new methods for growing a business by capitalizing on Microsoft technologies and resources

For More Information

Visit Microsoft Fusion at *events.microsoft.com/events/fusion.*

G

G.703

A digital signaling specification from the International Telecommunication Union (ITU).

Overview

G.703 is an ITU recommendation for interfacing DCE (data communications equipment) with digital high-speed synchronous communication services. The G.703 interface covers signaling speeds from 64 kilobits per second (Kbps) to 2.048 megabits per second (Mbps) over a four-wire physical interface. G.703 also supports special data recover features that make it suitable for high-speed serial communications.

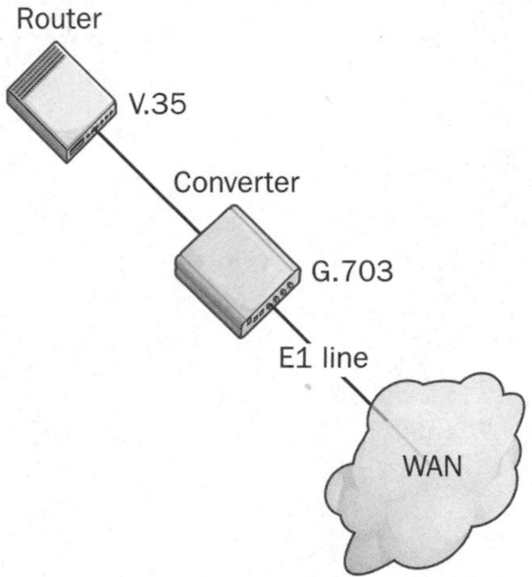

G.703. *Using a G.703 converter to interface a router to an E1 circuit.*

Although G.703 has been updated to include support for U.S. standard T-carrier service speeds, such as T1 transmission at 1.544 Mbps, it's not widely used in North America and is found mainly in Europe. Private Branch Exchange (PBX) systems often use 64-Kbps leased lines using the G.703 standard, as do E-carrier services such as E1 communication links. Some U.S. vendors sell converters for connecting synchronous V.35, RS-449, RS-232, or X.21 interfaces to G.703 in order to sell their switching equipment in Europe. G.703 converters are also used to interface digital microwave and satellite communication channels and for translating between 56 and 64 Kbps speeds for different serial interfaces. G.703 optical converters can handle speeds of 45 Mbps (E3) and higher.

See Also: *data communications equipment (DCE), serial transmission*

gateway

A term used to describe a variety of networking technologies that enable communication between different networking architectures and protocols.

Overview

Gateways generally operate at the higher levels of the Open Systems Interconnection (OSI) reference model for networking. They are commonly used to provide connectivity between two different protocol stacks that might be running on different systems. Examples include the following:

- E-mail gateways—for example, a gateway that receives Simple Mail Transfer Protocol (SMTP) e-mail, translates it into a standard X.400 format, and forwards it to its destination
- Gateway Service for NetWare (GSNW), which enables a machine running Microsoft Windows NT Server, or Windows 2000 Server to be a gateway for Windows clients so that they can access file and print resources on a NetWare server
- Gateways between a Systems Network Architecture (SNA) host and computers on a Transmission

Control Protocol/Internet Protocol (TCP/IP) network, such as the one provided by Microsoft SNA Server

- A packet assembler/disassembler (PAD) that provides connectivity between a local area network (LAN) and an X.25 packet-switching network

A gateway is usually a dedicated device or a set of services running on a dedicated computer. Gateways are essentially devices that direct network traffic in some fashion and translate that information.

G

See Also: *network*

Gateway Service for NetWare (GSNW)

A feature of Microsoft Windows 2000 Server that allows Windows clients access to NetWare servers.

Overview

When Gateway Service for NetWare (GSNW) is installed and configured on a machine running Windows 2000 Server, the server can act as a gateway to enable Windows clients to access file, print, and directory resources on Novell NetWare servers. The process is totally transparent to the users on the Windows client machines—to them the resources appear to be located on the Windows 2000 server itself instead of the NetWare server.

GSNW can perform gateway functions for all versions of Microsoft Windows client operating systems, including Windows for Workgroups, Windows 95, Windows 98, Windows Millennium Edition (Me), Windows NT Workstation, Windows 2000 Professional, and Windows XP. GSNW can provide gateway access for Windows clients to bindery-based NetWare 2.*x* and 3.*x* servers and to NetWare 4.*x* servers running either NDS (Novell Directory Services) or in bindery emulation mode. A Windows 2000 server that has GSNW installed also must have the NWLink protocol loaded. This protocol, which is an Internetwork Packet Exchange/Sequenced Packet Exchange (IPX/SPX)–Compatible Transport, makes it possible for the Windows 2000 server to communicate with the NetWare server. If it is not already installed, NWLink will install automatically on the Windows 2000 server when you install GSNW.

Implementation

To prepare the NetWare server for the gateway, you must create a group and a user account as follows:

- Create a group called Ntgateway on the NetWare server and give it the necessary rights for accessing the resources you want to make available on the server.
- Create a user account on the NetWare server and give it the necessary rights for accessing the resources you want to make available on the server. Make this user account a member of the Ntgateway group.

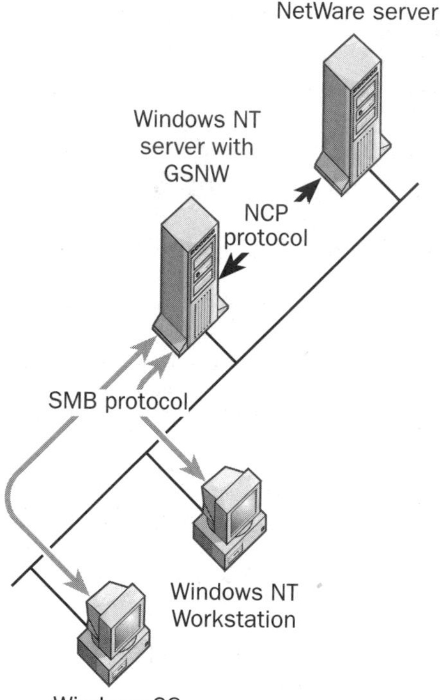

Gateway Service for NetWare (GSNW). *How GSNW provides Microsoft Windows clients with access to file and print resources on a Novell NetWare server.*

GSNW will use this user account for creating a connection to the NetWare server. The connection will appear on the server running Windows 2000 as a redirected drive that can be shared, as if it were a resource located on the Windows 2000 server. Windows clients can then connect to the shared resource by browsing My Network Places, by mapping a drive using Windows

Explorer, or by using the net use command. From the perspective of Windows clients on the network, the shared resources they access appear to reside on the Windows 2000 server. In actuality, the GSNW service on the server is performing protocol conversion between the Server Message Block (SMB) protocol, which the Windows clients understand, and the NetWare Core Protocol (NCP), which the NetWare file server uses.

After GSNW is installed, the first time you log on to the server for connectivity to a NetWare 4.*x* server using NDS, you are prompted to specify a default tree and context for connecting to the NetWare server. If the NetWare server is running in bindery-emulation mode or is an earlier 2.*x* or 3.*x* server, you must specify a preferred server when you log on. You can also configure these settings using the GSNW utility in Control Panel.

Uses

Because GSNW must process all requests directed through the gateway and perform protocol conversion between SMB and NCP, access is slower than if the clients actually had NetWare client software installed and could directly access the NetWare server. You should use GSNW only for occasional or temporary access to NetWare servers by Windows clients—for example, during a process of migrating NetWare servers to Windows 2000. When Windows clients need frequent access to resources on NetWare servers, as in a heterogeneous networking environment, install Client Services for NetWare (CSNW) instead of GSNW on Windows 2000 client machines to allow them direct access to resources on NetWare servers. On other versions of Windows, you can install Client for NetWare Networks to achieve the same result.

Notes

Both GSNW and CSNW are also available on the Windows NT platform.

See Also: *Client Services for NetWare (CSNW), File and Print Services for NetWare (FPNW), NetWare protocols*

GbE

Stands for Gigabit Ethernet, a form of Ethernet that operates at 1 gigabit per second (Gbps).

See: *Gigabit Ethernet (GbE)*

GBIC

Stands for Gigabit Interface Converter, a modular transceiver for Fibre Channel switches and other gigabit networking devices.

See: *Gigabit Interface Converter (GBIC)*

gender changer

An adapter with two connectors of the same type and gender.

Overview

A gender changer enables you to change the gender of the connector to which it is joined. For example, you could change the gender of a cable connector from male (with pins) to female (with sockets) or vice versa. This is typically done to allow two male or female cable ends to be joined together to form a longer cable or to allow equipment to be connected to a cable with the wrong gender.

Gender changers come in a variety of types and are specified by the connector type and gender involved. An example would be a V.35 to V.35 male/male gender changer, which can be used to connect twoV.35 serial cables (or one cable and a Channel Service Unit/Data Service Unit [CSU/DSU]) that terminate with female connectors.

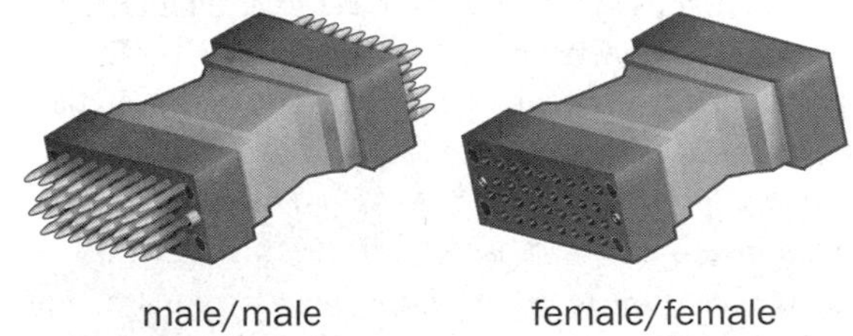

Gender changer. *Examples of V.35 gender changers.*

G

Some gender changers can also act as adapters for different data interfaces. For example, a V.35 to RS-232 male/male gender changer can be used to connect a V.35 connection on a CSU/DSU to a router using an RS-232 serial cable. Be sure that the pinning for such a gender changer is suitable for the type of equipment you want to connect because different pinnings might exist when different serial interfaces are connected.

See Also: *Channel Service Unit/Data Service Unit (CSU/DSU), RS-232, V.35*

G

General Packet Radio Service (GPRS)

A 2.5G upgrade to existing Time Division Multiple Access (TDMA) cellular communications systems.

Overview

General Packet Radio Service (GPRS) was designed as an upgrade for existing second-generation (2G) cellular systems such as Global System for Mobile Communications (GSM) and other TDMA systems such asAT&T Wireless. GPRS is a packet-switching overlay that can support Internet Protocol (IP) data transmission at speeds up to 171 kilobits per second (Kbps), which is more than 10 times faster than currently supported data rates for these systems (data transmission on current GSM systems is typically 9.6 Kbps). In practice, however, the maximum data rates are usually more like 52 Kbps downstream and 13 Kbps upstream. This is because of the overhead of combining channels together, throttling of bandwidth by providers to enable more users to share channels, and the power limitations of handsets at the subscriber end.

GPRS will provide the first global high-speed mobile IP communications system and is intended as an interim solution until broadband third-generation (3G) cellular systems can be fully deployed. Using GPRS, a cellular phone can access Internet services by means of Wireless Application Protocol (WAP). WAP provides a richer format for information exchange than the existing Short Message Service (SMS), which is limited to a maximum of 160 characters per transmission. With its higher data rates, GPRS makes possible the kinds of wireless applications and services that simply have not been feasible on existing GSM and TDMA systems. Possible uses for GPRS include wireless mobile Web browsing, discussion groups, chat services, mobile commerce, and home automation through wireless remote control.

The GPRS standard 03.60 was developed by the European Telecommunications Standards Institute (ETSI). Trials of GPRS began in 1999, and the first commercial rollouts appeared in 2000. A number of European and Asian countries and regions are piloting GPRS systems and thus have an edge over the United States in the arena of wireless communication systems running at more than 20 Kbps.

Uses

Besides cellular phones, GPRS can be implemented in a wide variety of devices, including PCMCIA modems for laptops, expansion modules for Personal Digital Assistants (PDAs) and handheld computers. Research in Motion (RIM), makers of the popular BlackBerry handheld e-mail devices, is working with Microcell Telecommunications, a GSM provider, to use GPRS as a transport for its wireless messaging system.

Architecture

Most existing 2G cellular systems are circuit-switched services in which a dedicated connection must be established in order for communications to take place. As long as the session lasts, the subscriber owns the channel and is billed for its usage even if no data is being sent. By contrast, packet-switching is a more efficient technology because it allows several users to share a channel. No actual connection needs to be established in order to send data—from the point of view of the subscriber the system is "always on" and ready to transmit. And instead of billing for connection time, subscribers are billed according to the amount of data they transmit and receive instead.

GPRS uses the same underlying TDMA time slot architecture as GSM, but instead of assigning only a single time slot to each user for transmission or reception, it can multiplex up to eight slots (the maximum for a TDMA frame) to give a maximum possible data transmission rate of 171 Kbps. In most implementations, however, three or four slots can are multiplexed for downstream transmission and only one for upstream, which makes practical transmission speeds much slower (but still better than GSM alone).

When a GPRS user wants to send data, the handset finds the first available time slot and sends the first chunk of data, sending more chunks as further slots become available. In this respect, GPRS operates like an Ethernet network—the more users sharing the system, the less bandwidth available for each user to transmit or receive data. Collisions do not occur, however, since time-division multiplexing (TDM) prevents contention from occurring.

GPRS was designed to transport both IP and X.25 packet data, but all current implementations use IP to provide connectivity with the Internet. To provide this connectivity, a GPRS mobile phone needs an IP address, which can be either statically or dynamically assigned. All existing application-layer Internet protocols can run over GPRS, including Hypertext Transfer Protocol (HTTP), File Transfer Protocol (FTP), Simple Mail Transfer Protocol (SMTP), and so on. Most GPRS systems use WAP as their application layer protocol, however, because it is more efficient for devices with limited memory and small displays.

Implementation

Implementation of GPRS requires that existing TDMA hardware be upgraded, including handsets and base stations. In addition to the base stations and mobile switching centers of existing TDMA networks, GPRS adds two additional components:

- **Serving GPRS Support Node (SGSN):** This transmits and receives IP packets to mobile stations through the existing base stations, and exchanges these packets with the Gateway GPRS Support Node (GGSN) using a special tunneling protocol called GPRS Tunneling Protocol (GTP).
- **Gateway GPRS Support Node (GGSN):** This acts as a gateway between the SGSN and the Internet, forwarding packets between them.

GPRS handsets are similar to GSM handsets, and they require a Subscriber Identity Module (SID), a form of smart card containing the subscriber's ID, billing address, private key, and other information. GPRS supports several security schemes including Password Authentication Protocol (PAP), Challenge Handshake Authentication Protocol (CHAP), Secure Sockets Layer (SSL), and IPsec.

It is probable that GPRS upgrades will be easiest for carriers whose networks operate in the 1800-megahertz (MHz) or 1900-MHz frequency bands, because they usually have sufficient unused capacity to implement channel aggregation without having to upgrade their bearer equipment. Upgrading to GPRS is more expensive for carriers operating in the 800-MHz or 900-MHz bands because of the near-full capacity of those bands.

Another cost involved in the GPRS upgrade process is that of replacing the circuit-switched core network connecting existing base stations with an IP-based backbone network for interfacing between the wireless system and the Internet. You can create an interface between a GPRS network and an IP network by using a GGSN. You can also use GGSNs to connect GPRS networks with legacy X.25 packet-switching networks.

Prospects

GPRS is viewed as an interim solution to give mobile users a measure of access to the Internet. The GSM Alliance, representing 400 GSM providers and their 250 million subscribers worldwide, is a driving force behind the move toward upgrading existing GSM systems to GPRS. As an example, AT&T Wireless plans to migrate its existing TDMA system (a 2G system based on IS-136) in several stages over the next few years, starting first with GPRS, a 2.5G upgrade, then Enhanced Data Rates for Global Evolution (EDGE), an IMT-2000 3G upgrade to GPRS, and finally to Universal Mobile Telecommunications System (UMTS) which will support 3G speeds of 2 megabits per second (Mbps).

In late 2000, a large cellular operator in Hong Kong SAR called Pacific Century CyberWorks (PCCW) launched a 20 kilobits per second (Kbps) GSM-based GPRS overlay, which, in order to access, subscribers need to upgrade their handsets to Motorola P7389i.

Other GSM operators around the world are involved in similar upgrades, with GPRS handsets becoming available from Nokia and other vendors. Lucent Technologies and Sun Microsystems are also working together to provide a platform for GSM upgrades to GPRS.

Notes

EDGE is almost identical to GPRS, the main difference being that EDGE uses a more efficient encoding scheme (8-bit phase shift keying or 8-PSK) which encodes three bits per symbol instead of the Gaussian phase shift keying (GMSK) mechanism of GSM (and also GPRS) that encodes only one bit per symbol. The result is that EDGE theoretically supports data transmission rates up to 513 Kbps, three times the maximum possible for GPRS. Real speeds for EDGE systems will be much lower, however, due to protocol overhead, error correction, and bandwidth throttling by providers. Although EDGE speeds are lower than the 2 Mbps limit intended for 3G systems by the IMT-2000 recommendations from the International Telecommunication Union (ITU), EDGE is still classified under IMT-2000 as a 3G system.

GPRS cannot be used to easily upgrade existing Code Division Multiple Access (CDMA) cellular systems, which are widely in use throughout North America and some other parts of the world. These systems are expected to migrate to Wideband CDMA (W-CDMA) instead, a 3G recommendation from the ITU that offers speeds up to 2 Mbps.

See Also: *2G, 2.5G, 3G, cellular communications, Code Division Multiple Access (CDMA), Enhanced Data Rates for Global Evolution (EDGE), Global System for Mobile Communications (GSM), Time Division Multiple Access (TDMA), Wideband Code Division Multiple Access (W-CDMA)*

Gigabit Ethernet (GbE)

A form of Ethernet that operates at 1 gigabit per second (Gbps).

Overview

Gigabit Ethernet (GbE) is an evolution of standard Ethernet technologies that supports the transmission of data at 1 gigabit per second (Gbps) or 1000 megabits per second (Mbps) over both fiber-optic cabling and copper twisted-pair cabling. GbE was developed to solve the problem of increasing congestion on local area network (LAN) backbones currently running Fast Ethernet, Fiber Distributed Data Interface (FDDI), and Asynchronous Transfer Mode (ATM). Because of its simplicity and throughput, GbE has become the dominant LAN backbone technology, relegating the slower FDDI to the legacy arena and pushing the complicated ATM back into the wide area network (WAN) environment where it originated. Because of its close similarities to other forms of Ethernet, GbE provides a smooth upgrade path from 10 megabits per second (Mbps) Ethernet and 100 Mbps Fast Ethernet.

The Gigabit Ethernet Alliance is an open forum that promotes cooperation and industry standards for GbE. The Alliance includes a number of prominent companies, including Cisco Systems, Intel Corporation, Sun Microsystems, Nortel Networks, and 3Com Corporation. GbE is standardized by the IEEE specifications 802.3z in 1998 and 802.3ab in 1999.

Uses

GbE's main application is for building high-speed backbones for LANs and campus networks. An example would be for high-speed switch-switch connections where you might connect two 100 Mbps switches with 1 Gbps uplinks to create Fast Ethernet islands joined by a GbE backbone. Alternatively, you could connect several 10/100 switches to one 100/1000 switch. For collapsed backbones, 1000BaseT copper interconnects are sufficient to join switches together, but for campus-wide distributed backbones, 1000BaseLX running over single-mode fiber supports the long distances needed to build such infrastructure. The problem is that many existing FDDI campus backbones use multimode fiber, and GbE does not operate over long distances on this type of fiber. This usually necessitates pulling new fiber to replace existing multimode fiber campus backbones with single-mode fiber to enable GbE to run over these backbones. Single-mode fiber is more expensive than the multimode type, and pulling fiber is an expensive process itself, so these costs generally add a significant amount to the process of converting legacy FDDI campus backbones to newer GbE ones. On the other hand, upgrading switched Fast Ethernet backbones in small and mid-sized companies to GbE may simply be overkill. Overprovisioning of GbE is common by system integrators, and it provides small gains over existing Fast Ethernet networks with considerable added cost.

GbE is also finding an increasing place in server-switch connections for joining server farms to high-speed backbones. This configuration can theoretically provide users with 1-Gbps access to application or file servers, but there are limitations at present. The problem is that even with newer 1 Gbps network interface cards, most servers still cannot make full use of a gigabit link to a GbE switch. Various factors are at work here, including the existing 64-bit Peripheral Component Interconnect (PCI) bus being too slow to pump data out at gigabit speeds (the upcoming PCI-X standard may help here), hard disk subsystems being unable to keep up with the flow of data to and from the server (even 10,000 RPM hard disks cannot read/write at gigabit speeds), and the Transmission Control Protocol/Internet Protocol (TCP/IP) stacks of operating systems being unable to handle gigabit data transfer rates (though Microsoft Windows 2000 is a considerable improvement in this area over Windows NT). The bottom line is that aggregating two or three Fast Ethernet links is currently sufficient for handling data transfer to most Wintel servers and is a cheaper solution than adding a Gigabit network interface card (NIC) and connecting it to a Gigabit switch. This will probably change around 2002 as 64-bit Windows running on Itanium chips may finally perform to the point of needing a second Gigabit NIC to handle throughput, but keep your eyes on developments in hard disk technologies as their performance is usually the limiting factor or bottleneck in keeping file servers from pumping data at gigabit speeds.

Gigabit-to-the-desktop is a vision of deploying GbE end-to-end across a network, and involves installing 1 Gbps NICs into high-performance workstations to provide them with incredibly fast access to network servers. This is still more a dream than a reality, though, because such workstations suffer from the same limitations that were described for servers above, and even more so. The result is that deploying GbE end-to-end across a network generally results in only a marginal improvement over Fast Ethernet in applications performance and greatly complicates the already difficult task of troubleshooting high-speed switched networks. In the old days of shared Ethernet networks, a "sniffer" could be connected to the main hub and traffic on the entire LAN could be analyzed—capturing and analyzing traffic on a switched LAN is much more complicated, and protocol analyzers operating at gigabit speeds are expensive. In any case, gigabit-to-the-desktop is still several years from everyday reality, and most desktop applications can achieve sufficient bandwidth using only Fast Ethernet.

Another hindrance to completely migrating a network's infrastructure from Fast Ethernet to GbE over copper (1000BaseTX) is cabling. Although GbE can theoretically run over existing Category 5 (Cat5) cabling, such cabling usually has not been installed with the care and precision needed to support gigabit signaling speeds. Also, GbE over copper requires the use of all four pairs of wires, whereas some flavors of Fast Ethernet only needed two pairs of wires. As a result, corporate networks often need considerable rewiring to support GbE, and even new deployments using enhanced Category 5 (Cat5e) or Category 6 (Cat6) wiring require exceptional care in how they are installed to ensure that GbE will perform as expected.

Architecture

Like earlier forms of Ethernet, the GbE standards specify only the physical (PHY) layer and data-link layer of network operation and support any protocols running at higher levels. This means that upgrading from Ethernet or Fast Ethernet to GbE is relatively straightforward and only involves insuring that GbE supports the cabling media, cable lengths, and cabling topology. No changes need to be made to higher-layer protocols such as TCP/IP during such an upgrade (although sometimes such network layer protocols can be "tuned" to provide better performance in a GbE environment).

GbE uses the same connectionless datagram delivery services as earlier forms of Ethernet. It uses the same frame format as other forms of Ethernet and likewise supports both unicast, multicast, and broadcast frames. It can operate in both shared (half-duplex) and switched

Gigabit Ethernet (GbE)

(full-duplex) modes. GbE employs a line coding scheme called 8B/10B that packs 8 bits (1 byte) of data into 10 baud (symbols) for transmission, a system known as 1000BaseX. This means that in order to achieve a data transmission rate of 1 Gbps, a signaling frequency of 1.25 GHz is required. The 8B/10B encoding scheme for GbE was borrowed from Fibre Channel technologies. GbE actually borrows most of the characteristics of its PHY and data-link layers from the Fibre Channel's FC-0 and FC-1 sublayers, with the exception of using a signaling rate of 1.250 Gbaud instead of Fibre Channel's 1.0625 Gbaud.

G

GbE uses the same standard 802.3 framing structure as standard Ethernet, with frames between 64 and 1514 bytes in length and using the same 48-bit MAC addresses (jumbo frames up to 9000 bytes are also supported). It also supports the same Carrier Sense Multiple Access with Collision Detection (CSMA/CD) media access method supported by earlier versions of half-duplex Ethernet. To achieve the tenfold speed increase of GbE over Fast Ethernet while maintaining support for reasonably large networks, GbE makes some changes to the Ethernet MAC algorithm and how CSMA/CD operates. These changes are necessary because reducing the transmission time for a frame by a factor of 10 on an Ethernet network normally means that the size of the network (maximum distance between stations) would also decrease by the same factor.

One of the media access control (MAC) layer modifications introduced by GbE is called carrier extension, which involves extending the length of the carrier and slot times to pack out all frames to a minimum carrier length of 512 bytes to ensure that collisions can be properly detected and recovered from. In other words, the smallest possible frame (64 bytes) would have its carrier signal extended until it appears to the physical layer as 512 bytes in length. This is different from merely padding a 64-byte frame with an additional 448 bytes of junk to produce a 512-byte frame—instead, the carrier signal is extended for a time equivalent to 448 additional bytes, but the frame still appears to be 64 bytes in length from the point of view of layers above the MAC layer. As a result, if the frame is bridged from a GbE to a Fast Ethernet network segment, for example, the frame remains 64 bytes in length on the Fast Ethernet segment, instead of 512 bytes if the frame were merely padded. Another MAC layer modification in GbE is support for frame bursting, which allows multiple short frames to be grouped in a way that it allows a station to take temporary control of the wire to send out a number of small packets in succession, arbitrating the signal for the channel only once. This second feature is optional but results in better performance in many situations.

Both of these modifications are done to enable shared half-duplex implementations of GbE to support a network diameter of up to 655 feet (200 meters), instead of the inadequately small 65.5-foot (20-meter) wide network that would result if CSMA/CD were implemented without these modifications. When implementing switched full-duplex GbE, CSMA/CD is not used and these issues are irrelevant because no collisions can occur.

GbE also supports several schemes for autonegotiation, allowing hubs, switches, routers, and NICs capable of supporting 100/1000 Mbps or even 10/100/1000 Mbps speeds.

Implementation

GbE can be implemented in four different PHY layer options, all of which support both half-duplex and full-duplex operation:

- **1000BaseCX:** Uses 150-ohm balanced twinax cabling or shielded twisted-pair (STP) cabling with a maximum link length of 82 feet (25 meters). This version is designed primarily for device clustering and is not much used.
- **1000BaseLX:** Uses both long wavelength transmissions over single-mode fiber-optic cabling supporting distances of 3 miles (5000 meters) over 10 micron fiber and also short wavelength transmissions over multimode fiber supporting distances of 1640 feet (550 meters) over both 62.5 and 50 micron fiber. The single-mode version is used mainly for long cable runs; for example, to connect LANs across a campus.

Gigabit Ethernet (GbE)

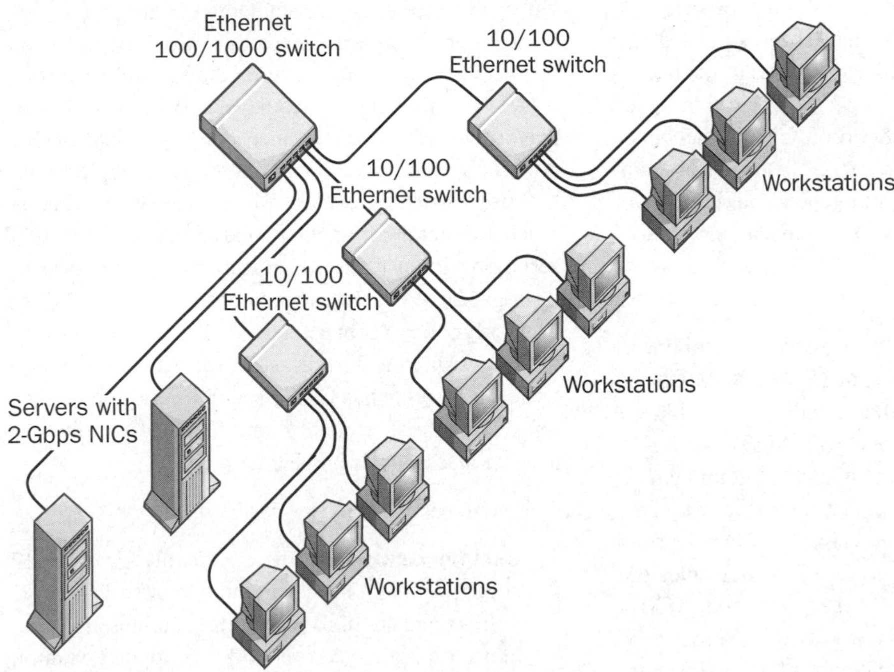

Gigabit Ethernet. *Simple example of using a 100/1000 Mbps GbE switch.*

- **1000BaseSX:** Uses short wavelength transmissions over multimode fiber-optic cabling. This version is used mainly for short cable runs of up to 1805 feet/550 meters (over 50-micron fiber) or 900 feet/275 meters (over 62.5-micron fiber) and is intended for connecting workgroup switches in a building to a GbE backbone switch.
- **1000BaseTX or 1000BaseT:** Uses twisted-pair Cat5 cabling (all four pairs of wires are needed) with a maximum link length of 328 feet (100 meters), giving a maximum network diameter of 655 feet (200 meters). It is intended mainly for connecting high-speed servers to GbE switches and for switch-switch interconnects in collapsed backbones.

Note that the distances specified above are for full-duplex operation only, because they are the inherent or physical distance limitations of the media for Gigahertz signaling. For half-duplex networks, the distance restrictions are more severe and depend on the round-trip propagation delay supported by the MAC signaling method. For example, the maximum supported link length for 1000BaseLX and 1000BaseSX is only 364 feet (111 meters), well below the physical signaling distances supported by fiber medium.

Shared (half-duplex) implementations of GbE support only two simple topologies: a point-to-point connection between two stations and a star-wired topology with a hub (repeater) at the center, typically with 8, 12, or 24 ports on a hub. Cascaded hub topologies are not supported by shared GbE LANs, though some manufacturers sell stackable hubs whose backplanes can be connected to form a single collision domain. As a result of these topology restrictions, switched (full-duplex) implementations are much more common in real-world networks, and they support virtually any topology you can imagine as long as the length restrictions outlined above are adhered to (there are even ways around these length restrictions at times, as will be mentioned later).

Advantages and Disadvantages

Compared to other network backbone technologies, GbE has a number of distinct advantages. The most obvious advantage over FDDI is the superior speed offered by GbE. The result is that GbE has pushed FDDI from the corporate mainstay it was in the mid-1990s to being legacy technology today that most enterprises are phasing out. Most corporate FDDI network backbones have now migrated to GbE, and the remaining ones are not likely to last beyond a couple of years as chip manufacturers for FDDI equipment stopped producing as of 2001.

GbE also has several advantages over ATM that make it the current favorite for enterprise network backbones. Most ATM backbones operate at 155 or 625 Mbps and fall short of the 1 Gbps for shared half-duplex GbE and 2 Gbps of switched full-duplex GbE. ATM is also more expensive and difficult to deploy and maintain than GbE. Most network architects can transition from Fast Ethernet to GbE technologies as easily as they previously moved from 10BaseT to Fast Ethernet, since the technologies are so similar. On the other hand, ATM still holds the superior hand in the WAN where it can run over Synchronous Optical Network (SONET) for thousands of miles and for delay-sensitive applications such as voice and multimedia where GbE still falls short, although new quality of service (QoS) mechanisms for Ethernet, such as DiffServ and 802.1p VLAN tagging, may help narrow the gap.

Upgrading a Fast Ethernet backbone switch to a GbE 100/1000-Mbps switch is straightforward and will enable you to connect high-speed server farms using GbE NICs. Benefits include increased throughput and performance, more network segments, more bandwidth per segment, and more nodes per segment.

Marketplace

The growth of GbE market in the last few years has been impressive, with GbE port module shipments reaching 4 million in 2000, a quarter of which were 1000BaseTX copper ports. For comparison, however, these port figures only represent 3 percent of the total market for all forms of Ethernet, but the figures for GbE are more than doubling each year.

GbE hubs (repeaters) are not common, but GbE switches and routers are made by a wide variety of vendors. A popular example is the Catalyst 3500 series of switches from Cisco, which have a 10 Gbps backplane that provides high performance, come in 12 and 24 GbE port configurations, and support both full-duplex and half-duplex operation even over copper. 3Com's SuperStack 3 switches are another good choice, with the 4900 series providing 12 copper or fiber gigabit ports for aggregation of Fast Ethernet workgroups. A typical scenario might be to connect a dozen 3300 series 10/100 switches using gigabit fiber uplinks to a core 4900 switch. Enterasys has GbE through its entire product line of switches and routers, and Foundry gigabit products are also popular in the enterprise.

GbE switches come in two basic types:

- **Backbone switches:** These generally have 8 or 12 copper or fiber GbE ports and one or two GbE uplinks and are used for building collapsed backbones for high-speed networks. A popular example is the 12-port AT-9006LX switch from Allied Telesyn International, which has a lower per-port price than many comparable switches. Other popular backbone switches for mid-sized networks include the Intel 480T, the Catalyst 4908 from Cisco, and the Summit5i from Extreme Networks.
- **Workgroup switches:** These can have 8, 2, 24, or even 48 Fast Ethernet 10/100 ports and up to four GbE uplinks, and they are used for building Fast Ethernet islands by uplinking many Fast Ethernet switches to a single workgroup switch. Galileo Technologies has managed to cram 48 autosensing 10/100 ports and two GbE uplinks into a 1U rack-mountable device, which is quite an engineering feat.

In the distributed backbone market, the 1805-foot (550-meter) limitation for GbE over multimode fiber can be overcome by a GbE extender such as Allied Telesyn's AT-EX1001SC/GM1, which allows GbE to run over multimode fiber to a distance of 1.25 miles (2 kilometers). Campuses needing to upgrade their old FDDI-based distributed backbones to GbE can save money by using extenders like these instead of replacing existing multimode fiber with single-mode fiber.

Finally, network analyzers for troubleshooting GbE networks are available from Agilent Technologies (a spinoff from Hewlett-Packard), Network Associates, and Fluke Networks.

Prospects

GbE is here to stay. Most new enterprise networks being deployed these days are implemented with GbE backbones instead of FDDI or ATM (Fast Ethernet is still used for backbones in small to mid-sized companies). The only thing that can probably dethrone GbE is the emerging 10 GbE standard, an even faster version of Ethernet that finally discards the inefficient CSMA/CD media access method, operates instead only in switched full-duplex mode, and supports up to 40 kilometers (25 miles) using single-mode fiber. Meanwhile, prices per 1 Gbps port for GbE switches continue to fall, and even though the industry average was around $1,000 per port at the end of 2000, there were some vendors offering switches with prices as low as $300 per port. It will not be long until the price per port drops to the point where network architects may as well buy GbE switches instead of Fast Ethernet ones even if they achieve no immediate performance gains.

Another emerging use for GbE is as a transport for moving data between servers and storage area networks (SANs). GbE SANs encapsulate Small Computer System Interface (SCSI) traffic within Internet Protocol (IP) packets, making it possible to greatly extend the 165-foot (50-meter) limitation of SCSI and to locate SANs at remote data centers.

Gigabit in the metropolitan area network (MAN) is the latest development and provides an attractive alternative to telco T-carrier services to enterprises needing high-speed WAN connections. For more information on this exciting new technology, see the article "metropolitan Ethernet" elsewhere in this book.

Notes

By employing jumbo frames up to 9000 bytes in length, performance of gigabit server-switch connections can generally be improved significantly, provided the hard disk bottleneck has not been reached.

For More Information

You can visit the Gigabit Ethernet Alliance at *www.gigabit-ethernet.org.*

See Also: *1000BaseCX, 1000BaseLX, 1000BaseSX, 1000BaseTX, Carrier Sense Multiple Access with Collision Detection (CSMA/CD), Ethernet, Ethernet switch, Fast Ethernet, Fibre Channel, jumbo frames, MAC address, metropolitan Ethernet*

G

Gigabit Interface Converter (GBIC)

A modular transceiver for Fibre Channel switches and other devices.

Overview

Gigabit Interface Converters (GBICs) provide network architects with flexibility in choosing different media options for gigabit-speed switches. They support a variety of different cabling options, including unshielded twisted-pair (UTP) and single-mode or multimode fiber-optic and copper Fibre Channel cabling. By simply plugging the appropriate GBIC module into a port on a Fibre Channel or Gigabit Ethernet (GbE) switch, a different media option can be easily configured for that port, providing flexibility for configuring switches according to need. This is accomplished by having the GBIC convert the signals in the connected media (for example, light signals on a fiber-optic cable) into electrical signals compatible with the 1000BaseX port on the switch. GBICs can also regenerate signals, allowing transmission to occur over distances of 62 miles (100 kilometers) or greater over long-haul single-mode fiber.

Marketplace

An example is 1000BaseT GBIC from Cisco Systems, which can be used to provide flexibility in cabling options for Cisco Catalyst 2900 and 3500 Series XL GbE switches. Cisco 1000BaseT GBICs come in a wide variety of transceiver configurations that support copper, long-haul and short-haul fiber, and backplane interconnects for stacking switches. They are also hot-swappable, allowing cabling to be switched to different types on the fly in a simple plug-and-play fashion.

See Also: *Ethernet switch, Fibre Channel, Gigabit Ethernet (GbE)*

G.Lite

A splitterless version of Asymmetric Digital Subscriber Line (ADSL).

G

Overview

G.Lite is a form of ADSL that is targeted mainly for the residential Internet access market. G.Lite is easy to install—so easy that a home user can perform the installation, eliminating the need for a "truck roll" (technician visit) from the telco to the subscriber. This saves the telco considerable costs and allows them to pass this saving on to the subscriber. G.Lite was partly developed as a response to the challenge presented by cable modem technology, where subscribers can usually perform the installations themselves. G.Lite is intended to be a "plug and play" version of Digital Subscriber Line (DSL).

Like other forms of DSL, G.Lite connections are "always on"—once you turn your computer on, the connection is active and you can send or receive e-mail or browse the Web without having to dial up a connection. G.Lite is slower than regular ADSL and supports maximum downstream transmission of 1.536 megabits per second (Mbps) and upstream 384 kilobits per second (Kbps), depending on the implementation.

G.Lite is sometimes called DSL Lite or Universal ADSL, but the International Telecommunication Union (ITU) has endorsed the term *G.Lite* as official nomenclature for this technology under the G.992.2 standard. Commercial rollouts of G.Lite began in 1999, and the service is gaining popularity among DSL providers.

Implementation

G.Lite is sometimes referred to as splitterless ADSL because a splitter is not required at the customer premises to separate the voice and data signals being carried over the phone line. This is different from ordinary ADSL, which uses a splitter to separate the baseband analog Plain Old Telephone Service (POTS) voice channel from the upstream and downstream DSL simplex bearer signals. The splitter protects the ADSL signal from variations in impedance of the POTS signal and from dial tones and other forms of interference. Likewise, the splitter protects the POTS signal from interference due to intermodulation of the ADSL tones. In ordinary ADSL, a splitter must be installed at both the customer premises and the telco's central office (CO). G.Lite gets around the need for a splitter at the customer premises by incorporating a number of advanced signal processing techniques that help keep the bit error rate (BER) within reasonable tolerances. These advanced techniques include forward error correction, trellis encoding, and interleaving.

To use G.Lite, the customer obtains a G.Lite modem from the DSL provider and simply connects it to her computer and phone line. No second phone line or other form of rewiring of the customer premises is required, since G.Lite uses the existing local loop connection to the customer premises. Customers can make phone calls or send faxes while connected to the Internet over their G.Lite connection.

Notes

The quality of a G.Lite connection to your home can suffer if you have a large number of RJ-11 phone jacks installed. This is because each phone jack acts as a bridged tap that is run off the main phone line as a parallel connection. Signals traveling along your phone line can reflect off these jacks and affect the overall reliability of your G.Lite connection. Also, the farther your home is from the telco CO, the less bandwidth might be available for your G.Lite connection.

See Also: *Asymmetric Digital Subscriber Line (ADSL), Digital Subscriber Line (DSL)*

Global.asa

A file that contains global information for Active Server Pages (ASP) applications.

Overview

The Global.asa file is used to manage functions common to all users of an ASP application. Specifically, a Global.asa file includes

- Four event procedures common to all users of an ASP application, namely Application_OnStart, Application_OnEnd, Session_OnStart, and Session_OnEnd.
- Object declarations (using <OBJECT> tags) for defining application-level and session-level objects, variables, and event handlers.
- Type library declarations for COM components used by the application.

Global.asa files should not generate or contain any content that is visible to a client Web browser—Asp.dll will simply ignore any Hypertext Markup Language (HTML) placed in the Global.asa file. Furthermore, you can have only one Global.asa file per ASP application, and the file must be located in the root virtual directory of the application.

Notes

If your Global.asa file generates an error, you should ensure that any object declarations within the file have application-level or session-level scope, that any script in the file is enclosed within <SCRIPT> tags, and that any <OBJECT> tags are placed outside of <SCRIPT> tags.

See Also: Active Server Pages (ASP)

global catalog

A Microsoft Windows 2000 or Windows .NET Server domain controller that contains a read-only, partial replica of information from all domains in a forest.

Overview

The global catalog resides on a selected group of domain controllers in your Windows 2000 or Windows .NET Server enterprise called global catalog servers. The global catalog is automatically created the first time you run the Active Directory Installation Wizard and is installed on the first domain controller in the root domain by default. Other domain controllers must then be manually designated as global catalog servers by using the administrative tool Active Directory Sites and Services. The Active Directory directory service replication process then automatically maintains the contents of each global catalog server.

In a geographically distributed enterprise, each physical site should have at least one domain controller to speed network traffic. Most Active Directory–related traffic is the result of queries on Active Directory, so the domain controller for small sites should also be configured as a global catalog server. This will reduce traffic over wide area network (WAN) links to other sites by allowing the global catalog server to locally resolve queries for information on directory objects from other domains.

Every Active Directory object in the entire enterprise is represented in the global catalog, but only a subset of the attributes of each object is stored in the catalog. The properties represented are those most likely to be used as search attributes, such as the user's first or last name. However, administrators can specify storing additional object attributes in the catalog if desired. You can modify which attributes are represented for objects in the global catalog by editing the schema of Active Directory, but you must do so with care.

Uses

The global catalog enables users to easily locate objects in any domain with maximum speed and minimum network traffic. In effect, the global catalog acts as a kind of index for looking up objects stored in Active Directory anywhere on your network. Having the global catalog store only a subset of an object's attributes in Active Directory improves the response time for performing search queries on Active Directory. You can search the global catalog for Active Directory objects by using the Find dialog box in Active Directory Users and Computers. Note that the global catalog also includes the access permissions for directory objects, so if you search for an object and it does not show up, you probably do not have permission to access the object.

The global catalog also has another important function—in native-mode domains, users require access to a global catalog server in order to log on to the domain. If no global catalog server is in the local site, a global catalog server in a remote site may be used. If all global catalog servers are down in a native mode domain, users can only log on using their cached user credentials. An exception to this is that members of the Domain Admins group can log on to native domains even when no global catalog server is available.

See Also: *Active Directory, domain (DNS), domain controller, global catalog server*

G

global catalog server

A Microsoft Windows 2000 or Windows .NET Server domain controller that contains a copy of the global catalog.

Overview

Global catalog servers let users search for objects located anywhere in a forest and enable users to log on to the domain in native-mode networks. Information stored on global catalog servers is updated each time Active Directory directory service performs its directory replication process.

Global catalog servers should be located appropriately so that queries on Active Directory can be performed effectively. Ideally, you should have at least one global catalog server in each site within the enterprise. However, in a multidomain environment, the replication traffic generated by maintaining these servers can be a burden on overall network traffic, especially if slow wide area network (WAN) links are involved. In this case, consider placing your global catalog servers as follows:

- Place several global catalog servers in each major site where large numbers of users and resources can be found.
- Place a global catalog server at each small site where there are significant numbers of users and resources or where the WAN connection to major sites is slow.

See Also: *global catalog*

global group

A type of security group in Microsoft Windows NT, Windows 2000, and Windows .NET Server.

Overview

In Windows NT, global groups are used to simplify administration of user accounts by organizing them into groups. For example, you can use them to group users by function (such as the Accountants global group), by location (such as the Third-Floor global group), or by some other criteria. By contrast, local groups are designed to provide users with permissions for accessing network resources and rights for performing system tasks.

Global groups can contain only global user accounts from their own domain. They cannot contain global user accounts from other domains, nor can they contain other groups. Global groups are created on domain controllers and are stored within the Security Accounts Manager (SAM) database.

In Windows 2000 and Windows .NET Server mixed-mode domains, global groups operate much the same as in Windows NT, and they can be granted permissions on resources in any domain in the current forest. In native mode, however, global groups can contain both user accounts and global groups from the same domain.

See Also: *AGLP, group, local group*

global load balancer

A hardware-based or software-based solution that can direct requests for Web content to multiple geographical locations where the content is stored.

Overview

An example of using global load balancers might be for an e-business that has many data centers scattered around the world to use global load balancers to direct Web customers' traffic to centers that can provide the fastest response time for each customer's location. If a data center goes down as a result of a power outage or some other condition, traffic to that site can be transparently redirected to other sites. The overall effect of implementing global load balancers in an e-business enterprise is an increase in reliability and performance from the customer's point of view.

Implementation

Global load balancers essentially act as intelligent Domain Name System (DNS) name servers, performing name lookups for Uniform Resource Locators (URLs) and directing requests to the most appropriate Internet Protocol (IP) addresses. The five criteria listed below are typically used to determine which address to forward a request to. (Note that not all global load balancers support all of five of these criteria.)

- Proximity of the site to the client, usually measured in router hops and established by using the Border Gateway Protocol (BGP), Internet Control Message Protocol (ICMP), or User Datagram Protocol (UDP)
- Latency (the overall response time of the site), which is usually determined by pinging the site and calculating the delay
- Server load (how busy the site is and how much capacity the server has for responding to clients)
- Server health (whether the site is up and what its CPU and connection load are)
- Packet loss (the average quality of the Transmission Control Protocol [TCP] connection to the site), which is established by using ping

Of course, the DNS standard itself has built-in load balancing in the form of round-robin DNS. If multiple IP addresses are mapped to the same domain name, clients requesting the domain are directed to each IP address in a round-robin fashion. However, this rudimentary load-balancing scheme does not take into account such factors as which IP address belongs to the nearest host, the relative capability of the hosts to respond to requests, the availability of hosts, and so on. This is where global load balancers come in—they take over the role of authoritative name server for a company's domain.

Global load balancers come in three varieties:

- Layer 4 switches or routers with built-in support for global load balancing. Many Layer 4 switches and routers support some form of local load balancing, and software upgrades might be available that add such support. These switches tend to perform faster than appliances or software because they use hardware for packet forwarding and use software for routing purposes only. However, they also tend to be the most expensive solution.
- Network appliances, which are essentially self-contained, stripped-down servers running global load-balancing software on top of operating systems optimized for this particular function.
- Software that can run on standard servers running Microsoft Windows 2000, Windows NT, or UNIX that enables the servers to function as global load balancers. If you use this solution, be sure that your server is dedicated to running this software and does not run any other applications.

Global load balancers talk only to the local DNS server configured for the client, not to the client itself. This works well, except when mobile users travel to other cities and use their laptops to try to access the site. In this situation, if the client is still using a preconfigured DNS server at the home location, the global load balancer thinks that the client is still there as well. Also, once a DNS-based global load balancer has directed a client to the appropriate site or server, it is no longer involved in the client's session and cannot tell whether the server goes down or whether some problem occurs with the connection.

For this reason, some global load balancers also use Hypertext Transfer Protocol (HTTP) redirects to masquerade as the target site and redirect HTTP requests to different servers. The client actually talks to the load balancer itself, and performance is faster than using DNS because fewer TCP connections are required. If the client's connection to the server is interrupted, the global load balancer can redirect the client to a different server with minimal interruption. The downside of using HTTP redirects is that they work only with HTTP and not with other Internet protocols, such as File Transfer Protocol (FTP) or Network News Transfer Protocol (NNTP), or with streaming multimedia. This can be a limitation if your e-business delivers this type of content to the customer.

Other mechanisms can be used to perform global load balancing, including cookie-based and proprietary schemes. Windows NT 4, Enterprise Edition, provides a load-balancing service called Windows NT Load Balancing Service (WLBS). This IP load-balancing service employs a fully distributed clustering design that is ideal for creating highly available and scalable IP-based services such as Web, virtual private networking (VPN), streaming media, and proxy services.

G

See Also: Domain Name System (DNS), Hypertext Transfer Protocol (HTTP), Uniform Resource Locator (URL)

globally unique identifier (GUID)

In Microsoft Corporation operating system platforms and programming, a 128-bit value based on time and space that can be used to uniquely identify a component.

Overview

Globally unique identifiers (GUIDs) are employed by the Component Object Model (COM) to uniquely identify classes and interfaces so that naming conflicts will not occur. A GUID is virtually guaranteed to be unique across all systems at any time. For example, every object, class, and attribute in Active Directory directory service is assigned a unique GUID when it is created. The GUID of an entity in Active Directory never changes, even if the entity itself is renamed or moved to another location. The GUID acts as a kind of permanent name for the entity within the directory to ensure that it can be positively identified when needed.

Microsoft BackOffice products such as Exchange Server and SQL Server also use GUIDs to uniquely tag objects. For example, the information store in Exchange Server has a base GUID that is used to generate individual GUIDs for all messages, attachments, and folder contents kept in the store. If you restore the information store from a backup, you need to run the command isinteg-patch before restarting the information store to change the base GUID. Running this patch ensures that new objects created in the information store do not accidentally end up with GUIDs that are identical to those of objects already existing in the information store. This could cause inconsistencies in the information store database.

Notes

You can also manually generate GUIDs for components using the console-based Uuidgen utility or the Microsoft Windows–based Guidgen utility in Microsoft Visual C++.

See Also: Active Directory, Component Object Model (COM)

Global System for Mobile Communications (GSM)

A second-generation (2G) digital cellular communications technology popular in Europe, Asia, and other parts of the world.

Overview

Global System for Mobile Communications (GSM) is the only truly worldwide cellular communications system. More than 400 different GSM carriers have implemented GSM systems in more than 200 countries and regions, and there are more than 250 million subscribers worldwide (all other cellular systems combined account for only 150 million subscribers worldwide).

GSM cellular supports voice communications rivaling the analog Advanced Mobile Phone Service (AMPS) system in speech quality. GSM also supports other services, including

- Group 3 fax (ITU recommendation T.30)
- Circuit-switched and packet data communications at speeds up to 14.4 kilobits per second (Kbps)
- Short Message Service (SMS), a two-way paging service that supports store-and-forward delivery of short text messages up to 160 characters in length.

GSM also supports other services including caller ID, call waiting, call forwarding, and conference calling.

GSM operates in different frequency bands and is described by different names depending on the band used, including the following:

- **GSM 900 or simply GSM:** This is the original GSM system that began operation in 1992.
- **GSM 1800 or PCN (Personal Communications Network):** This is a high-frequency version of GSM found in parts of Europe and gradually becoming the standard there.
- **GSM 1900 or PCS (Personal Communications System):** This is the counterpart of GSM 1800 in the United States and Canada.

History

GSM began as an initiative of the Conference of European Posts and Telegraphs (CEPT) to develop a pan-European digital communications system that would allow users to roam between different countries and regions with no interruption in service. Work on the new standard was begun in 1982 by a body called Groupe Spéciale Mobile, which gave the technology its acronym, GSM (later on GSM was changed to mean Global System for Mobile Telecommunications). GSM standards development was turned over to the European Telecommunications Standards Institute (TESI) in 1989.

GSM was deployed in several phases, starting with GSM Phase 1, which was first commercially deployed in 1991 and which supported call forwarding, global roaming, call barring, and similar features. These initial 900-megahertz (MHz) GSM systems spread rapidly to 22 different countries and regions by 1993. GSM Phase 2 added additional features such as short message service, call holding, call waiting, caller ID, multiparty calling supporting up to five parties per call, and mobile fax and data services. GSM Phase 2+ deployments currently underway include support for data transmission at 64 Kbps and higher, packet radio, virtual private networks, enhancements to the Subscriber Identity Module (SIM) card, higher spectral efficiency, integration with satellite links, and even GSM services in the local loop.

Architecture

GSM uses a combination of Frequency Division Multiple Access (FDMA) and Time Division Multiple Access (TDMA) media access control methods to provide full-duplex communication. In the 862-to-960-MHz World Association of Radio Communications (WARC) portion of the electromagnetic spectrum, GSM communicates using two separate frequency bands:

- The 890- to 915-MHz band for mobile-to-base (uplink) communication
- The 935- to 960-MHz band for base-to-mobile (downlink) communication

Carrier signals are spaced 200 kilohertz (kHz) apart within these bands based on frequency-division multiplexing (FDM) to provide 124 pairs of superchannels (carriers). Each superchannel is then subdivided using time-division multiplexing (TDM) into eight traffic channels (time slots), some of which are used as communications channels and others as control channels. Each communications channel carries either digitized voice at 13 Kbps or data at either 9.6 or 14.4 Kbps. Altogether GSM provides 992 full-duplex channels for voice communication. By comparison AMPS cellular systems, which also use TDMA, employ three time slots instead of eight.

A single GSM time slot can carry a payload of 156 bits and is 0.577 microseconds in duration, a time interval called the burst period. This suggests that the total data carrying capacity of GSM could theoretically be 33.8 Kbps, but much of this is used for protocol and error correction overhead, reducing the maximum possible data transmission rate to only 14.4 Kbps. The short duration of a GSM time slot also restricts the maximum distance at which a GSM phone can communicate with its base station to about 22 miles (35 kilometers) regardless of the power used.

Power classes for GSM mobile units range from 0.8 through 2.0 watts transmission power for handsets to 8 through 20 watts for vehicle-mounted units. Approximately half of a GSM transmission consists of overhead for signaling, such as synchronization and error handling. Such high overhead is typical in cellular phone systems and is necessary—not so much because of external interference of buildings and other structures, but because of internal interference due to crosstalk between channels and across cell boundaries.

G

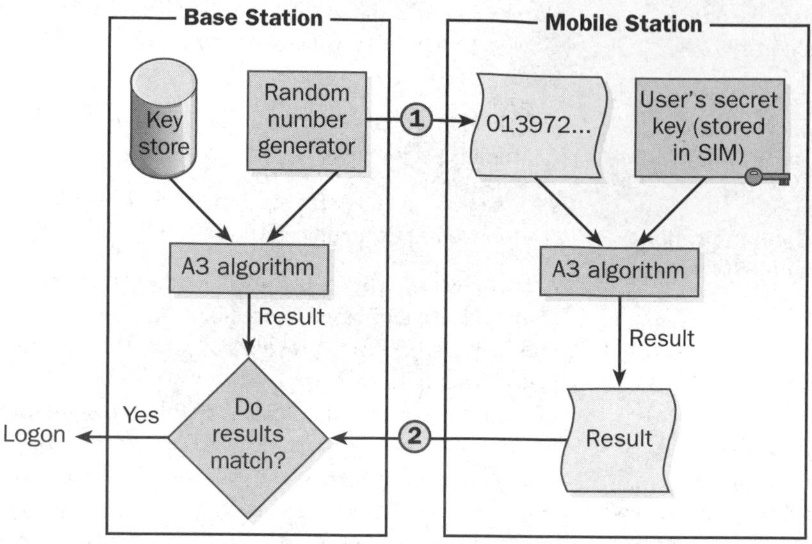

Global System for Mobile Communications (GSM). *The authentication process for GSM.*

Implementation

A basic GSM communications system consists of three parts:

- **Mobile station (MS):** This is a cellular phone or vehicle-mounted phone used for sending and receiving calls. The MS also contains the user's SIM, a small "smart card" about the size of a postage stamp that is issued when a user subscribes to a GSM service. The SIM contains a unique number called an International Mobile Subscriber Identity (IMSI) that uniquely identifies the MS, the user's private key for encrypting transmissions, and billing information, such as the subscriber's address. The MS itself is uniquely identified by a number called an International Mobile Equipment Identity (IMEI), and the IMEI and IMSI are independent of each other. When a user moves from his home location to one where a different GSM system is used, the user can simply remove the SIM from his own GSM phone and install it in a GSM phone rented from a service in that location.
- **Base station subsystem (BSS):** This is a fixed radio transmitter that provides coverage for a specific cell and handles call setup and tear down for mobile stations in the area.
- **Mobile switching center (MSC):** This is a switching center that coordinates the operation of all BSSs in its coverage area, coordinates billing for subscribers, handles roaming and handoffs between cells, and provides gateway connectivity with the Public Switched Telephone Service (PSTN) or Post, Telephone, and Telegraph (PTT) land-based telephone system.

GSM communications are secured by employing key-based encryption for authentication traffic (and optionally for data transfer as well). The diagram shows the process that occurs when a mobile user wants to place a call. When the user dials a number, the mobile unit connects with the base station requesting authorization. The base station generates a random number and transmits it to the mobile unit, which then combines the random number with the owner's secret key stored in the phone's SIM by using a secret ciphering algorithm called A3. The result of this process is transmitted to the base station. Meanwhile, the base station, which has the private keys for all its subscribers stored in a database, follows the same steps, using the A3 algorithm to combine the generated random number with the caller's private key. The result is compared with the result transmitted by the user. If the two results agree, the user is logged on to the system. Encryption of message traffic is similar to encrypted authentication, except that each transmitted frame is encrypted using a different random number. This makes encrypted GSM messages extremely difficult to crack, so much so that some countries and regions prohibit GSM providers from encrypting user messages!

Marketplace

Although GSM is the dominant cellular communications system in Europe and a major player in other parts of the world, such as Asia and the Pacific Rim, it ranks a distant third in North America behind the popular Code Division Multiple Access (CDMA) digital cellular systems such as Sprint PCS and behind Time Division Multiple Access (TDMA) systems best represented by AT&T Wireless Services and SBC Communications. This is changing, however, as U.S. GSM carriers such as VoiceStream Wireless Corporation (now owned by Deutsche Telekom) expand their coverage across areas connecting urban centers, especially in California, the Eastern seaboard states, Florida and the South, and the Texas-Minneapolis corridor.

With interoperability between these competing systems being a major issue for U.S. subscribers needing to travel abroad, QUALCOMM, the company behind CDMA cellular systems, has announced it plans to develop a chip that will enable cellular phones to work with both CDMA and GSM systems.

Prospects

GSM has fared well as a global standard communications technology apart from garnering little support in the United States. Initiatives are underway to enhance this 2G system into one capable of carrying data at speeds of 64 Kbps and higher. Two such upgrades are the General Packet Radio Service (GPRS) and High Speed Circuit Switched Data (HSCSD), both of which operate by multiplexing GSM's existing TDM slots. These 2.5G initiatives are stepping stones toward the next generation high-speed third-generation (3G) broadband cellular systems that are just beginning to appear in parts of the world.

Notes

GSM has a counterpart service called Digital Communication Service (DCS) that works in essentially the same way as GSM, except at a higher 1.8-gigahertz (GHz) frequency band. DCS provides a total of 2992 channels for voice communication. One advantage DCS has over GSM is that it uses much lower power levels for mobile units, ranging from 0.25 to 1.0 watts transmission power.

For More Information

Visit the GSM Association at *www.gsmworld.com.*

See Also: *2G, 2.5G, 3G, Advanced Mobile Phone Service (AMPS), cellular communications, Code Division Multiple Access (CDMA), General Packet Radio Service (GPRS), High-Speed Circuit Switched Data (HSCSD), Time Division Multiple Access (TDMA)*

global user account

A Microsoft Windows NT account that has a domain-wide scope.

Overview

In Windows NT, global user accounts are stored in the Security Accounts Manager (SAM) database on domain controllers. You can create them using User Manager for Domains, a Windows NT administrative tool. Global accounts allow users to take full advantage of the Windows NT Directory Services (NTDS). Users who have global accounts can access resources anywhere in the domain, provided they have permissions for those resources.

The other type of user account in Windows, the local user account, exists only within the directory database of the machine on which it is created. Use only global accounts for users when implementing Windows NT domains as your security model. User Manager for Domains creates global accounts by default.

Notes

In Windows 2000 and Windows .NET Server, global user accounts are instead called domain user accounts and they are managed using the Active Directory Users and Computers snap-in for the Microsoft Management Console (MMC).

See Also: *local user account, user account*

GNOME

Stands for GNU Object Modeling Environment, a graphical desktop for UNIX and Linux platforms.

See: *GNU Object Modeling Environment (GNOME)*

GNU General Public License (GPL)

The open source licensing scheme of the Free Software Foundation (FSF).

G

Overview

The GNU Project was started in 1984 with the aim of developing a UNIX-like operating system that could be freely distributed. The acronym GNU itself recursively stands for GNU's Not UNIX (recursion is a feature of the UNIX operating system). The GNU General Public License (GPL) allows developers to freely copy and make changes to software as long as they provide the source code freely upon request and do not add any additional copyright restrictions to the modified software.

GPL is the licensing scheme used in all distributions of Linux, the popular free operating system developed by Linus Torvalds. The GNU gcc compiler is also the only C compiler that can be used to compile the Linux kernel. GPL forms the basis for licensing much of the free software that drives the Internet. GPL has also been chosen by Sun Microsystems as the licensing scheme for its free StarOffice suite of business applications.

See Also: *Linux, UNIX*

GNU Object Modeling Environment (GNOME)

A graphical desktop for UNIX and Linux platforms.

Overview

GNU Object Modeling Environment (GNOME) is an open-source graphical user interface (GUI) developed by the GNOME Foundation under the GNU General Public License (GPL) licensing scheme. The GNOME Foundation was modeled after the Apache Foundation and includes such members as the Free Software Foundations (the originators of GPL), IBM, Hewlett-Packard, Compaq Computer Corporation, Sun Microsystems, Red Hat, and many others.

GNOME's purpose is to make UNIX and Linux platforms easier to use. GNOME is a highly configurable windows–based user environment that includes a desktop with application icons, a status panel, a set of tools, and other elements. The GNOME session manager allows a user's desktop settings to be maintained across user sessions.

Prospects

A competing open-source alternative to GNOME is the K Desktop Environment (KDE) developed under the auspices of the KDE League. KDE has many supporters, but GNOME is backed by industry heavyweights and has been selected by Hewlett-Packard as the standard graphical user interface for HP-UX and by Sun as the GUI for Solaris.

For More Information

You can visit the GNOME Developer's Site at *developer.gnome.org.*

See Also: *GNU General Public License (GPL), K Desktop Environment (KDE), Linux, UNIX*

Gopher

A legacy Internet protocol used for distributed storage of documents.

Overview

Gopher is similar to another Internet protocol, File Transfer Protocol (FTP), because it remotely accesses files over a Transmission Control Protocol/Internet Protocol (TCP/IP) internetwork such as the Internet. But although an FTP site exists on only one server and there can be many different FTP sites, there's really only one distributed Gopher file system. The Gopher file system is a single collection of all Gopher servers in the world (although private Gopher subnetworks could also exist).

Gopher was popular in the late 1980s and early 1990s as a mechanism for storing and disseminating information across the Internet, especially for libraries and universities, but it has fallen out of favor because of the rising popularity of the World Wide Web (WWW). Not many Gopher servers still work, and most of them are not regularly updated with new information.

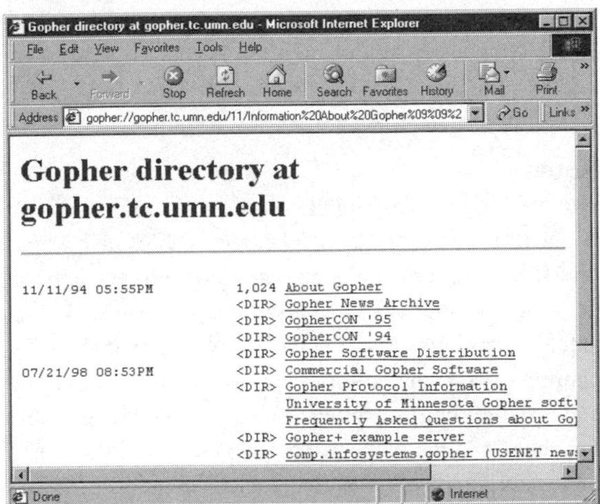

Gopher. *The simple interface of the legacy Gopher protocol.*

Implementation

Any Gopher server can act as a logical root of the hierarchical Gopher distributed file system. To access a file or document, a person using a Gopher client (a standard Web browser such as Microsoft Internet Explorer will do) types the Uniform Resource Locator (URL) of an accessible Gopher server. For example, *gopher://gopher.tc.umn.edu* takes the user to a Gopher server for the University of Minnesota (where Gopher originated). The Gopher file system is presented as a series of folders, each of which can contain

- Additional folders
- Individual documents
- Links to other Gopher servers (displayed as folders)

Users then work their way down the "gopher hole" (to use the metaphor) until they locate the document they want, and then they display or download it. They can also use a search tool developed at the University of Nevada called Veronica (Very Easy Rodent-Oriented Netwide Index to Computerized Archives) to perform keyword searches to locate documents on the worldwide Gopher network.

See Also: *Uniform Resource Locator (URL), World Wide Web (WWW)*

GPL

Stands for GNU General Public License, the open source licensing scheme of the Free Software Foundation.

See: *GNU General Public License (GPL)*

GPRS

Stands for General Packet Radio Service, a 2.5G upgrade to second-generation (2G) Time Division Multiple Access (TDMA) cellular communications systems.

See: *General Packet Radio Service (GPRS)*

grep

Stands for global regular expression print, a powerful UNIX command.

Overview

Grep lets you search a file or multiple files for a specific pattern or string of characters and, if desired, replace it with a different string. Grep is also useful for searching for specific entries in text files such as log files, UNIX system error logs, or C program code files.

You can use wildcards and other meta-characters to perform complex search and replace operations with grep. The output of grep is a display of each line of the file that contains the desired character string.

Examples

Typing **grep 'a[b-f]' log.txt** searches the text file called log.txt for any lines that contain the character *a* immediately followed by *b*, *c*, *d*, *e*, or *f*.

Notes

Shareware versions of the grep utility are available from third-party vendors for Microsoft Windows platforms. Grep can also be combined with other UNIX commands in scripts that can perform more complex search functions. For example, you can pipe the output of a verbose command into grep to display a more selective form of output.

See Also: *UNIX*

ground loop

A condition created when two or more parts of a network are grounded at separate points, causing a voltage difference between connected networking components.

Overview

Voltage differences between different parts of a computer network typically occur because of nonuniformities in the electrical characteristics of the grounding at different locations. For example, consider two computers that are located some distance apart and are connected by coaxial cabling. Each device is also connected to the earth by the ground wire of its AC power cable, but the two devices are plugged into different power outlets. These power outlets are connected to different parts of your building's electrical distribution system, and these different parts are under different loads (have different currents being drawn from them by different configurations of devices). Thus they provide slightly different voltages.

You might also find slight differences in the ground potential at the two locations. These voltage differences can cause currents to be induced through the shielding of the network cabling, and these currents can be large because of the cable's low resistance. Large pulses of current can occur when other devices on the power circuits are switched on or off abruptly. This situation can be potentially damaging to sensitive networking components and might cause them to reset or lock up.

Implementation

You can prevent ground loops in two main ways:

- By using nonconducting fiber-optic cabling instead of copper cabling, especially for longer cable runs
- By employing opto isolators or isolation transformers to break electrical connections between networking components

One might think that you could eliminate ground loops entirely by not grounding networking equipment, but this is wrong for several reasons. Ground connections are essential for electrical equipment to ensure their safety in the case of a short, and all electrical equipment should be properly grounded to ensure against shock hazard. Grounding also reduces noise due to electromagnetic interference (EMI) that can affect the performance of hubs, switches, and cables. Noise can result in corrupted packets leading to retransmissions that eat up network bandwidth, and grounding equipment properly can reduce such noise and boost throughput.

Notes

Ground loops are especially problematic with serial connections such as RS-232 because cables using this interface have a second signal ground path between the devices. Ground loops can also be a problem with shielded cabling such as shielded twisted-pair (STP) cabling or coaxial cabling. These loops will occur if the cable's shielding is grounded by a direct connection to the chassis of the devices, because this provides a second ground path between the devices in addition to that produced by the ground portion of the AC power connection. The resulting current loops can build up until they are potentially damaging to the connected equipment. To prevent such damage, the shielding in a shielded cable should be grounded only at one end of its connection. Finally, when grounding a metal rack or cabinet that houses networking equipment, you should ground it using the same AC power cable ground connection that you used for the equipment itself. Note that ground loops are not a significant problem with unshielded twisted-pair (UTP) cabling because the wiring is transformer-isolated in the hub and network interface card (NIC) connections.

See Also: *opto isolator*

group

A collection of user accounts.

Overview

Groups simplify the task of network administration by allowing administrators to group similar user accounts together in order to grant them similar rights and permissions. In Microsoft Windows 2000 and Windows .NET Server, there are two types of groups:

- **Security groups:** Can contain members and can be granted permissions in order to control user access to network resources. Security groups can contain users, other groups, and even computers.
- **Distribution groups:** Used for nonsecurity functions, such as grouping users together to send mass

e-mail. Unlike security groups, these groups cannot be used to control user access to network resources.

In Windows NT there is only one type of group, which is equivalent to security groups in Windows 2000 and Windows .NET Server.

Implementation

In Windows 2000 and Windows .NET Server, you create groups using the Active Directory Users and Computers console, and these are stored as group objects within Active Directory directory service. In Windows NT, you create groups using User Manager for Domains, and they are stored in the Security Accounts Manager (SAM) database. Users can belong to multiple groups at the same time. A group does not actually contain its member user accounts; it is merely a list of user accounts.

The scope of a group is the portion of the network where the group can be granted rights and permissions. For example, a group whose scope is global can be granted permissions to resources in its own domain and to resources in trusting domains. On the other hand, a group whose scope is local can be granted permissions to resources only on the machine where it was created. In Windows 2000 and Windows .NET Server, there are three levels of scope for security groups:

- **Universal groups:** Can contain members from any domain and can be granted permissions to resources in any domain in the current domain forest. Universal groups can contain user accounts, global groups, and universal groups from any domain in the current forest. Note that you can create universal groups only when the domain is in native mode and not in mixed mode.
- **Global groups:** Can contain members only from their own domain but can be granted permissions to resources in any trusting domain. When the domain is in native mode, global groups can contain user accounts and global groups from the same domain. When the domain is in mixed mode, these groups can contain only user accounts.
- **Domain local groups:** Can contain members from any domain but can be granted permissions only to resources in their own domain. However, unlike the local groups of Windows NT, a domain local group can be granted permissions to resources on all servers (both the domain controllers and member servers) in its domain. When the domain is in mixed mode, domain local groups can contain user accounts and global groups from any domain in the forest. When the domain is in native mode, they can also contain domain local groups from their own domain and universal groups from any domain in the forest.

On Windows 2000 and Windows .NET Server member servers and client computers and Windows XP machines, you can also create a fourth scope of group called a local group, one that exists only within the local security database of the machine on which it is created. Local groups in Windows 2000, Windows .NET Server, and Windows XP are similar to local groups in Windows NT. They can contain user accounts that are local to the machine and user accounts and global groups from their own domain. A local group can be granted permissions only to resources on the machine where it was created. You use Local Users and Groups, a snap-in for Microsoft Management Console (MMC), to create local groups on a machine.

Windows NT groups have only two levels of scope:

- **Global groups:** A global group can be granted permissions to resources in its own domain and to resources in trusting domains. A global group can contain user accounts only from its own domain. Global groups are created on Windows NT domain controllers and exist in the domain directory database.
- **Local groups:** A local group created with Windows NT Workstation can be granted permissions only to resources on the machine where it was created. A local group created with Windows NT Server (on a domain controller) can be granted permissions only to resources on the domain controllers of its own domain. A local group can contain user accounts and global groups both from its own domain and from trusted domains. Network administrators of enterprise-level Windows NT networks can use a resource-access strategy called AGLP (Accounts are organized by placing them in Global groups, which are then placed in Local groups that have appropriate Permissions and rights assigned to them) to plan and implement local groups in their network.

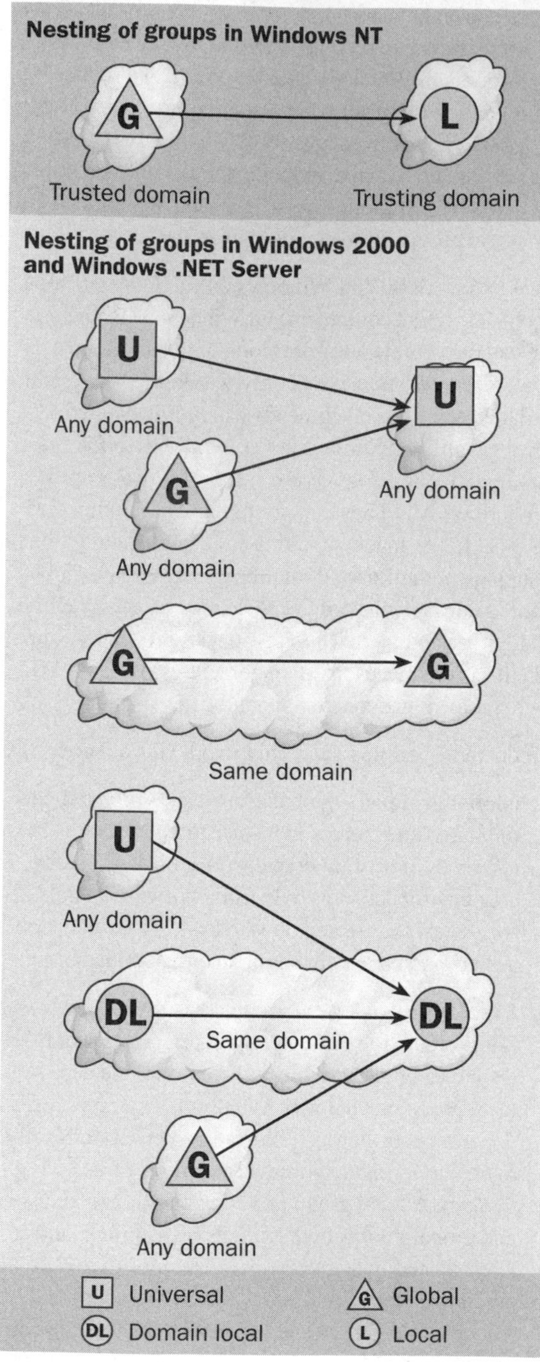

Group. *Nesting of groups in Windows NT and in Windows 2000 and Windows .NET Server.*

In Windows 2000 and Windows .NET Server, you can change the scope of a group if you want (you cannot do this in Windows NT). For example,

- Global groups that are not members of other global groups can be converted to universal groups.
- Domain local groups that do not contain other domain local groups can be converted to universal groups. Do this if you want to enable users in other domains to access resources that have been made accessible to the domain local group under consideration.

Groups can also be nested by adding groups to other groups, with certain restrictions. For example, in Windows NT a local group can contain global groups (but not other local groups) as members, but a global group can contain only users as members, not other global or local groups. With Windows 2000 and Windows .NET Server, the nesting of groups is more complicated, as shown in the diagram. Furthermore, when running Windows 2000 or Windows .NET Server in native mode, you can nest groups inside groups to any level, although nesting to one level is the recommended practice for effective administration.

Notes

If your Windows 2000 or Windows .NET Server network has a single domain, use global groups and domain local groups to grant permissions to network resources. Create global groups according to function, add users to the global groups, create domain local groups according to groups of common resources, assign permissions to the domain local groups, and finally, place the global groups in the appropriate domain local groups. If you have a domain tree, use global and universal groups instead in a similar administrative approach.

On high-speed Windows 2000 and Windows .NET Server networks, using only universal groups simplifies network administration. But if you have slower wide area network (WAN) links within your enterprise, using global and domain local groups can reduce the size of the global catalog at each site and significantly reduce the WAN traffic required to keep the global catalog current. Using global and domain local groups further reduces WAN traffic by reducing the size of users' security tokens.

See Also: *domain local group, global group, local group, universal group*

group account

Another name for a group, a collection of user accounts.

See: *group*

Group Policy

A feature of Microsoft Windows 2000, Windows XP, and Windows .NET Server that simplifies management of user and computer settings.

Overview

Group Policy enables administrators of Windows 2000 and Windows .NET Server networks to define policies that manage the environment of users and computers. A typical use for group policies is to enforce a written company policy across all users in a specific site or domain. Group policies can used to simultaneously configure the desktop working environments for different groups of users, but they have many other uses as well. For example, group policies can be used to do the following:

- Manage applications—for example, by configuring policies to allow users to install applications published in Active Directory directory service or to automatically install or upgrade applications on their machines
- Redirect folders from the Documents and Settings folder on a user's local machine to a share on the network
- Assign scripts for startup, shutdown, logon, and logoff events
- Manage security—for example, to control users' access to files and folders, control user logon rights, and configure account lockout restrictions
- Manage software—for example, to configure user profiles such as desktop settings, Start menu, and other common settings

Implementation

Group policies can be assigned to domains, sites, or organizational units (OUs) and apply to all Active Directory objects (users, computers, printers, and so on) within these containers. To assign a group policy, first use the Group Policy snap-in for the Microsoft Management Console (MMC) to create a Group Policy object (GPO) and configure its settings, and then assign the GPO to the appropriate container. An object may have several GPOs influencing it (for example, one GPO assigned to the OU containing the object and another to the domain containing the OU). If this is the case, a conflict may occur, and then the last setting applied wins. Group policies are applied to users when they log on and to computers when they boot up. Users are subject to both GPO settings that apply to them as users and to GPO settings that apply to the computer at which they are working.

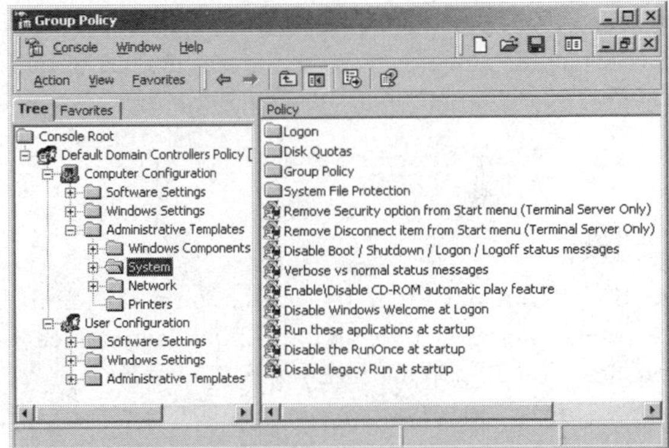

Group Policy. *Using the Group Policy console to configure a Group Policy Object (GPO).*

GPOs are really abstractions whose contents are stored in two different locations:

- **Group Policy Container (GPC):** This is a container within the Active Directory database on domain controllers that contains information about the globally unique identifier (GUID), version number, permissions, and inheritance of the GPO.
- **Group Policy Template (GPT):** This is a folder within the SYSVOL volume on domain controllers. It contains the actual GPO settings themselves and is identified by the GUID of the GPO.

Every Windows 2000 or Windows .NET Server domain has a default GPO that applies to all users and computers in the domain. Computers that are moved to a different domain lose the GPO of their original domain and have the GPO of their new domain applied to them. The default GPO for a domain is the only GPO on which you can configure password restrictions, lockout restrictions, Kerberos, the Encrypting File System (EFS), and Internet Protocol (IP) security settings.

Notes

You cannot use Group Policy for Windows 2000 or Windows .NET Server to configure group policies for downlevel Windows NT, Windows 95, or Windows 98 clients. Instead, use System Policy Editor, a Windows NT tool that stores policy settings in a file called ntconfig.pol that modifies a portion of the Windows NT registry.

FullArmor offers a tool called FAZAM 2000 that simplifies the planning, deployment, and management of group policies. You can find more info at *www.fullarmor.com.*

See Also: *Active Directory, domain controller*

GSM

Stands for Global System for Mobile Communications, a second-generation (2G) digital cellular communications technology popular in Europe, Asia, and other parts of the world.

See: *Global System for Mobile Communications (GSM)*

GSNW

Stands for Gateway Services for NetWare, a feature of Windows 2000 Server that allows Windows clients access to NetWare file, print, and directory services.

See: *Gateway Service for NetWare (GSNW)*

Guest account

A built-in account in Microsoft Windows 2000, Windows XP, and Windows .NET Server used for guest access to network resources.

Overview

The Guest account is intended for occasional users who need temporary access to resources on the network. It is disabled by default and can be enabled using User Manager for Domains. The Guest user account is a member of the Domain Guests global group and is assigned a null password during installation.

The Guest account is a domain user account on a domain controller. On a member server or workstation, however, there's a separate Guest local user account.

You should not enable the Guest account unless you are sure you will need it. You should also make sure that all your shared resources have correct permissions assigned to them because enabling the Guest account otherwise could pose a security risk.

See Also: *Guests group*

Guests group

A built-in group in the Microsoft Windows 2000, Windows XP, and Windows .NET Server operating systems whose members can be assigned guest access to network access.

Overview

The Guests group is a domain local group whose initial membership is the built-in Guest domain user account. If a member server or workstation joins a domain, the global group called Domain Guests is added to the local Guests group.

The Guests group has no preassigned rights or permissions. You can assign any network resource permissions to this group in order to grant temporary or guest users the access they require. Members of the Guests group do not have the right to make permanent changes to their desktop settings.

See Also: *built-in group, Guest account*

GUID

Stands for globally unique identifier; in Microsoft operating system platforms and programming, a 128-bit value based on time and space that can be used to uniquely identify a component.

See: *globally unique identifier (GUID)*

H.323

A videoconferencing standard developed by the International Telecommunication Union (ITU).

Overview

H.323 is a comprehensive suite of protocols for voice, video, and data communications between computers, terminals, network devices, and network services. H.323 is designed to enable users to make point-to-point multimedia phone calls over connectionless packet-switching networks such as private Internet Protocol (IP) internetworks and the Internet. H.323 was designed to replace the earlier H.320 standard that ran over circuit-switched services such as Integrated Services Digital Network (ISDN) telephone systems.

H.323 is widely supported by manufacturers of videoconferencing equipment, Voice over IP (VoIP) equipment, and Internet telephony software and devices. Any hardware or software system that supports the H.323 standard can communicate easily with any other H.323 system. With ordinary telephone communications, you can purchase a telephone from any vendor, plug it into your phone system, and the equipment works and interoperates with other devices already on the system. The idea behind H.323 is to make multimedia communications over the Internet easy to set up and use.

Architecture

The H.323 protocol stack performs various functions related to establishing and maintaining real-time communications over voice, video, and data. H.323 does not represent a single standard, but rather an umbrella of many other ITU standards. The H.323 protocol stack includes more than two dozen G-level, H-level, and T-level protocols, including

- H.323 Conference Manager, which manages the establishment of multimedia conferencing connections
- The H.245 protocol, which controls communication with data terminal equipment (DTE)
- The H.225 protocol, which performs synchronization and framing mechanisms for multimedia data streams
- The T.120 protocol, which provides support for real-time, multipoint data communication

H.323 also specifies standard codecs for audio (G.723) and for video (H.263) that enable H.323 products to send and receive voice and video images. Specifically, H.323 defines standards for data codecs for audio transmission rates of 14.4 kilobits per second (Kbps) or faster, and video transmission rates of 28.8 Kbps or faster. H.323 recognizes the T.120 protocol for data conferencing and provides a set of standards-based conferencing features for audio and video conferencing.

Implementation

An H.323 network consists of four different types of entities:

- **Terminals:** These are the client end points for multimedia communications. An example would be an H.323-enabled Internet phone or PC.
- **Gateways:** These provide connectivity between H.323 networks and other communications services such as the circuit-switched Public Switched Telephone Network (PSTN).
- **Gatekeepers:** These provide services for call set up and tear down, and registering H.323 terminals for communications.
- **Multipoint control units (MCUs):** These support three-way and higher multipoint communications between terminals.

Marketplace

Many vendors provide H.323 videoconferencing systems and appliances. Examples include Polycom's

ViewStation MP, a popular system in many enterprise environments. Other vendors include Sony Corporation with its Contact system (which also works over ISDN) and VCON's MC6000 that is multicast-capable.

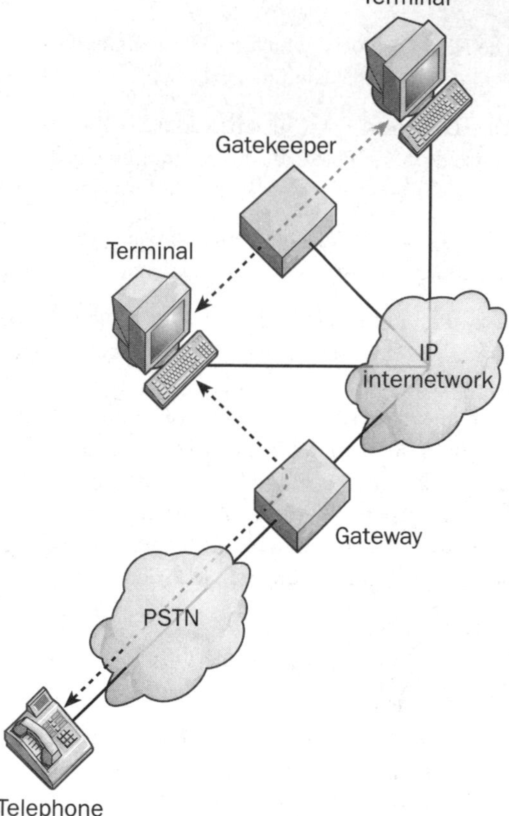

H.323. *Components of an H.323 network.*

PC-based H.323 collaboration software products include PictureTel Corporation's 900 Series appliances, which support both H.323 and H.320 communications; VCOM's MC8000; Intel Corporation's TeamStation; and VTEL Corporation's SmartStation.

Prospects

H.323 was extolled by industry in the 1990s but is now beginning to be considered legacy technology, suitable mainly for migrating legacy telephony systems to VoIP and for interoperating with legacy Private Branch Exchanges (PBXs). The problem is that H.323 was designed with videoconferencing strictly in mind and is not flexible enough to support a full range of VoIP features.

A newer protocol proposed by the Internet Engineering Task Force (IETF) is Session Initiation Protocol (SIP), which is seen in some quarters as preferable for newer VoIP deployments. SIP is designed from the ground up to support IP and is slimmer and more flexible than H.323, a protocol known to have excessive overhead.

Notes

The OpenH323 Project is an initiative of Equivalence Pty Ltd. to develop an open-source version of the H.323 protocol suite licensed under Mozilla Public License (MPL).

See Also: *session initiation protocol (SIP), T.120, Voice over IP (VoIP)*

H.323 gateway

A service that allows you to connect an H.323-based communication system on the Internet to a telephony system.

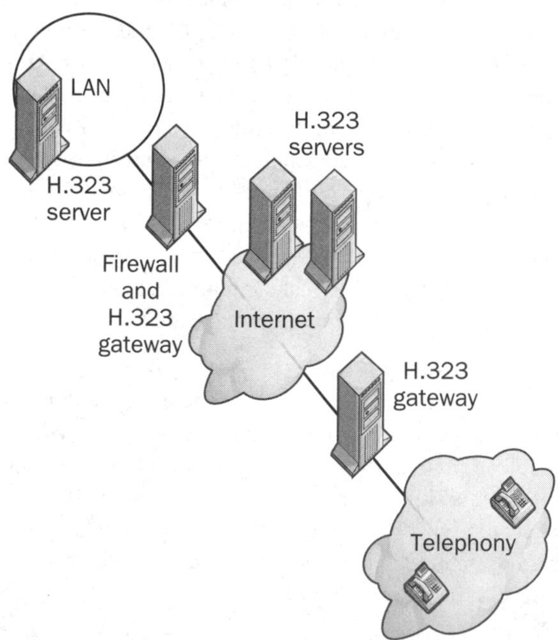

H.323 gateway. *Making a phone call using an H.323 gateway.*

Overview

You can use H.323 gateways to connect corporate networks to telephony systems for supporting integrated audio and video conferencing. For example, you can use an H.323 gateway to place a Microsoft NetMeeting call to someone's telephone. The Uniform Resource Locator (URL) format for doing so is "callto:<address>", in which <address> is the fully qualified domain name (FQDN), Internet Protocol (IP) address, or e-mail address of the person you are calling. You can use this URL as a link on a Web page or enter it directly in the address box of your Web browser.

NetMeeting does not include any H.323 gateway software, but third-party gateways are supported.

See Also: *gateway, H.323*

hacking

The action of trying to compromise the security of a computer system or network.

Overview

In the 1980s the term *hacker* was used to describe curious programmers who enjoyed getting into the nuts and bolts of how computer systems worked, usually UNIX systems and Transmission Control Protocol/Internet Protocol (TCP/IP) networks. In the 1990s hacking emerged as a malicious pursuit with the goal of stealing information, crashing systems, bringing down networks, and interfering with the daily activities of businesses and governments worldwide.

Various kinds of activities constitute hacking, but their overall similarity is that they are performed with malicious intent and without the knowledge or permission of the systems being hacked. Some of the different types of activities that hackers perform include

- **Footprinting:** The initial stage of a hacker's activities involves getting as much background information about the target system or network as possible. For example, a list of Internet Protocol (IP) addresses could be obtained through a simple whois query or by zone transfers from Domain Name System (DNS) servers.
- **Scanning:** Uses such tools as ping, traceroute, and netstat to identify the topology of a network and the types of hosts it contains. Port scanning involves testing hosts for open ports through which the attacker can gain access. Some common ports to scan include port 23 (telnet), 512 (rexec), and 513 (rlogin).
- **Enumeration:** The process by which hackers determine valid user accounts, names of shared resources, versions of installed applications, and other information.
- **Sniffing:** Using widely available tools, hackers can quietly capture traffic between clients and servers in order to obtain credentials and other useful information for breaking into systems.
- **Diffing:** This involves comparing two files for differences, and it is typically used to try to extract encrypted passwords from database files in which they are stored. Once extracted, these encrypted passwords can be subjected to dictionary and brute force attacks to try to crack them.
- **Back doors:** Software manufacturers sometimes leave secret user accounts created in their products so administrators have a "back door" to get in if they lock themselves out by invalidating their account. Hackers test commercial software to try to find such back doors. Also, once hackers have compromised a system, they generally try to create a back door for themselves on the system in case they are discovered and locked out.
- **Wardialing:** Using automated dialing software and modems to try to find entry points to remote networks.
- **Script Kiddies:** Novice hackers who employ scripts and other tools written by experienced hackers to test systems for vulnerabilities and launch automated attacks.
- **Social engineering:** A potentially devastating form of attack in which the hacker enters the building posing as a system administrator, repair person, or other trusted individual and gains unauthorized access to network resources. This takes more guts than the usual forms of hacking, though!

Types

Hacker attacks fall under a number of different categories, including the following:

- **Denial of Service (DoS):** Blocks access by legitimate users to a system or network by using up all available resources. Examples include LAND attacks, SYN flooding, Smurf attacks, and Teardrop attacks. The first famous DoS attack was the Internet Worm created by Robert Morris in 1988. Another notable attack was developed by Kevin Mitnick in 1995 to exploit weaknesses in the Internet Control Message Protocol (ICMP) and Transmission Control Protocol (TCP) protocols that had long been recognized in academic circles but had never been deliberately exploited.
- **Distributed Denial of Service (DDoS):** Employs large numbers of compromised intermediate machines called zombies to launch an overwhelming attack against a system or network. In February 2000, DDoS attacks were launched against a number of high-profile Web sites, including Yahoo!, and brought down these sites for several hours.
- **Elevation of privileges:** The goal is to enable the attacker to elevate his privilege level for accessing system resources from anonymous user to root (administrator), if possible.
- **Buffer overflow:** Flaws in software may cause systems to crash when invalid data is submitted through Uniform Resource Locators (URLs), Web forms, and other user interfaces. Besides crashing systems, buffer overflows can sometimes give hackers the ability to execute arbitrary code on the systems affected.
- **Spoofing:** Assuming the identity of a trusted user or of another system in order to gain access to a resource.
- **Session hijacking:** This involves taking the place of the client in an existing client/server connection such as a TCP connection. Session hijacking is a form of the man-in-the-middle attack.

Notes

The Openhack Project was developed by eWeek Labs to help publicize the issues around hacking of business networks. The project challenged people to try deliberately attacking a test bed network, and the results of these attempts were published to help educate people on how hackers perform their attacks.

For More Information

Visit the Microsoft Security site at *www.microsoft.com/security.*

See Also: *denial of service (DoS), security*

Hailstorm

An emerging platform for development of Internet-based services from Microsoft Corporation based on its new .NET platform.

Overview

In many ways, Microsoft Hailstorm represents the next evolutionary stage of the Internet. Hailstorm is a user-centric architecture based on Microsoft's .NET platform and on the open standards Extensible Markup Language (XML), Simple Object Access Protocol (SOAP), and Universal Description and Discovery Interface (UDDI).

Hailstorm provides users with a standard set of Web services that enables users to collaborate and participate in business transactions seamlessly and transparently. Hailstorm places control squarely in the user's court—data is not shared unless users explicitly grant their consent to do so. This makes Hailstorm a secure platform for 21st-century business communications in the Internet economy.

Initial support for Hailstorm is included in Microsoft's Windows XP, Office XP, and Xbox platforms. Hailstorm transforms MSN Messenger into an enterprise and consumer development platform for building advanced user experiences that leverage the power of Internet-based instant messaging.

Architecture

Hailstorm services are designed to allow users to access their data from a variety of platforms, including traditional PCs, Tablet PCs, handheld Personal Digital Assistants (PDAs), mobile phones, and other Web appliances. User data is stored in a distributed fashion and can be securely accessed from any device and any location with the user's consent.

Users and applications access Hailstorm services through end points, which may be applications, devices, or services. With a user's consent, Hailstorm automatically connects end points to widely distributed Web services to perform transactions desired by the user. Hailstorm services are XML-enabled Web services running on the .NET platform and are built upon the foundation service Microsoft Passport, which provides security and authentication to perform transactions. Other parts of a user's experience supported by Hailstorm's Web services include profile information, location information, and calendar information. The table lists the initial set of core Web services to be included in Hailstorm.

Initial Set of Web Services Included in Microsoft Hailstorm

Service	*Description*
myAddress	User's address
myApplication Settings	User's application settings
myCalendar	User's time and task management information
myContacts	User's list of contacts
myDevices	Settings and capabilities of user's devices
myDocuments	Location for storing user's personal files
myFavorite WebSites	User's favorite Uniform Resource Locators (URLs)
myInbox	User's inbox for e-mail and voice mail
myLocation	User's geographical location
myNotifications	User's subscriptions and notifications
myProfile	User's personal profile information such as nickname, birth date, etc.
myServices	Services provided to user by Hailstorm
myUsage	User's usage of Hailstorm services
MyWallet	Receipts, coupons, and payment instruments for user's transactions

For More Information

Find out more about Hailstorm at *www.microsoft.com/hailstorm.*

See Also: *.NET platform*

HAL

Stands for hardware abstraction layer, a thin layer of software at the base of the Microsoft Windows 2000, Windows XP, and Windows .NET Server operating systems that provides portability between different machine architectures and processor platforms.

See: *hardware abstraction layer (HAL)*

half-duplex

A mode of communication where at any given moment data can be either transmitted or received but cannot be transmitted and received simultaneously.

Overview

The simplest example of half-duplex communications is using a walkie-talkie: you have to press a button to talk and release the button to listen. When two people use walkie-talkies to communicate, at any given moment only one of them can talk while the other listens. If both try to talk simultaneously, a collision occurs and neither hears what the other says.

Communication through traditional hub-based Ethernet networks is another example of half-duplex communications. When one station on an Ethernet network transmits, the other stations detect the carrier signal and listen instead of transmitting themselves. If two stations transmit signals simultaneously, a collision occurs and both stations stop transmitting and wait random intervals of time before retransmitting.

By contrast, full-duplex communication enables stations to transmit and receive signals simultaneously, with the advantage of providing twice the bandwidth of equivalent half-duplex technologies. However, full-duplex requires two communication channels to achieve these results—one to transmit and one to receive signals. Hub-based Ethernet networks can only be used for half-duplex communications—for full-duplex Ethernet, you need switches instead of hubs.

A third mode of communications is called simplex, which involves transmission in one direction only, with one station transmitting signals and the other receiving them. A television broadcast is a simple example of simplex communications.

See Also: *Ethernet, full-duplex, simplex*

HAN

Stands for home area network, a network of several computers at a user's home.

See: *home area network (HAN)*

handheld

Generally used to refer to Personal Digital Assistants (PDAs) and other computers that can be held in the palm of the hand.

Overview

In the late 1990s the handheld market became popular among consumers for managing contacts, appointments, and other personal information. At the end of the decade, the issue arose as to which of the two common platforms, Palm and Microsoft Windows CE, would dominate in the enterprise market. The outcome is still uncertain. Palm has the advantage of a large installed base, a wide range of third-party applications, and support by such popular wireless services as AvantGo. The new PocketPC platform has made the Windows CE operating system competitive with the PalmOS by providing interoperability with Windows-based services, and pocket versions of Microsoft Office applications, Microsoft Internet Explorer. At the end of 2000, analysts reported that Palm held three-quarters of the handheld market share and Windows CE held only 18 percent, but the Windows CE has been gaining market share steadily.

A newcomer to the handheld market is the Linux PDA, represented by Agenda Computing's VR3. It is too soon to say what impact porting Linux to the handheld platform will have on market leaders Palm and PocketPC.

Handheld Device Markup Language (HDML)

A markup language loosely modeled on Hypertext Markup Language (HTML) and optimized for providing Internet access to cell phones and other handheld devices.

Overview

Handheld Device Markup Language (HDML) was developed by Unwired Planet (now Phone.com) to enable mobile communications devices such as cell phones and Personal Digital Assistants (PDAs) to access content on the Internet. Such devices usually have limited size displays (typically four lines by 20 characters or smaller) and limited processing power that make them require that information they download from the Internet be specially formatted to meet these requirements.

HDML is not intended as a means of delivering standard HTML-formatted Web content to such devices—most standard Web pages simply cannot be reformatted to fit on devices with such small display areas. HDML is not a subset or scaled-down version of HTML but an entirely new markup language specifically designed from the ground up for these devices.

HDML can be used to deliver a broad range of time-sensitive information to handheld wireless devices, including appointments, weather information, stock quotes, telephone directory white pages, inventory, catalog pricing, and similar business and commercial information. Scripts can be developed to extract this kind of information from the databases in which it resides and format it into HDML cards in much the same way that Perl can be used to write scripts to access database information stored on UNIX servers or that Active Server Pages (ASP) can be used to build Web-based applications that connect to Structured Query Language (SQL) databases.

HDML is an open standard guided and licensed by Phone.com. The current version of this technology is HDML 2.

Implementation

HDML provides a way to format information for delivery to handheld wireless devices that support packet-switched Internet Protocol (IP) services instead of traditional circuit-switched cellular services. HDML uses the same Hypertext Transfer Protocol (HTTP) as its application layer protocol, just as HTML does. The difference is that an HDML/HTTP system uses three components (client, server, and gateway) instead of the traditional two (client and server) used by HTML/HTTP.

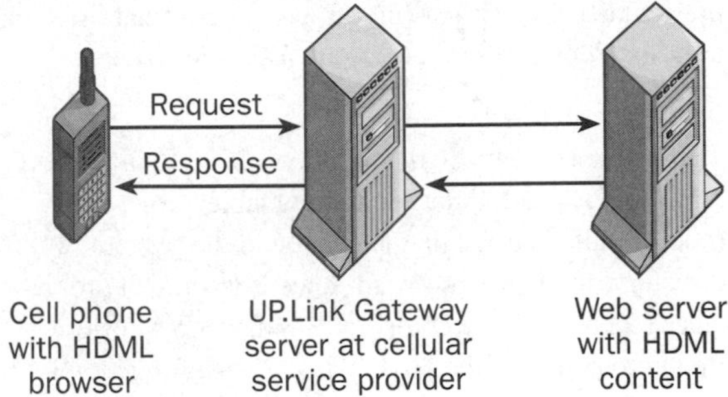

Handheld Device Markup Language (HDML). *How an HDML communications system works.*

When a user with an HDML-enabled client device (a device running an HDML browser) wants to access HDML-formatted content on a Web server, the client device communicates over the provider's cellular network with a special gateway server called an UP.Link Gateway. This gateway server then "gates" the user's request over a Transmission Control Protocol/Internet Protocol (TCP/IP) wireline connection to the Web server. The Web server responds with the requested content that is then "gated" back to the client over the cellular network.

HDML uses a navigation model that is based on a filing card metaphor. Cards of HDML-formatted information are grouped into "activities," which facilitates the development of HDML-based applications. The user can enter information and share it among cards using variables, and the user can parameterize cards so that a family of cards differing only in the value of a variable can be stored more efficiently in the limited-size cache of these devices. You can use variables to create forms for entering information in HDML applications. HDML currently does not support scripting, branching, or conditional statements.

Marketplace

HDML is currently used by more than 80 cellular and mobile carriers in the United States, including AT&T, Ameritech, and Bell Atlantic. Some analysts estimate that more than 90 percent of Internet-enabled phones sold in the United States support HDML and include Phone.com's HDML browser. Outside the United States, the competing Wireless Markup Language/ Wireless Application Protocol (WML/WAP) combination is more popular (WAP shares many of the features of HDML and was developed from HDML).

Prospects

WAP is currently gaining popularity at the expense of HDML and may eventually replace it. One indication of this is Nokia and Ericsson, which are two major players in the world cellular market and which provide WAP-enabled phones. Nokia is even giving away the source code for its WAP browser to promote this standard. Meanwhile, enterprises that want to deploy mobile clients with Internet access have to support two interoperable solutions, HDML and WAP.

See Also: *Hypertext Markup Language (HTML), Hypertext Transfer Protocol (HTTP), Wireless Application Protocol (WAP), Wireless Markup Language (WML)*

handshaking

The process that establishes communication between two telecommunications devices.

Overview

When two computers first connect with each other through modems, the handshaking process determines which protocols, speeds, compression, and error-correction schemes will be used during the communication session. Handshaking is necessary at the start of each session because typically the modems differ in their vendor, model, or hardware/software configuration. The handshake ensures that communication is possible despite these differences.

The term *handshaking* arises from the analogy of two people meeting to conduct business. They first shake hands to greet each other, announcing their names, titles, and intentions. They might also "size each other up" to determine the other person's capacities and capabilities.

During the handshaking process, both modems send the other a series of control signals and respond to each other's signals. Handshaking is also referred to as "flow control" because the process establishes the ground rules for managing the flow of data between the two devices. Some of the parameters that the modems need to negotiate are

- The maximum transmission speed, taking into consideration the speed of both modems and the quality of the transmission
- The length of the line delay to apply echo cancellation
- The communication protocol

Modern modems transmit the control signals in full-duplex mode over the RS-232 interface that connects them to the computers.

See Also: *flow control, modem*

hardware abstraction layer (HAL)

A thin layer of software at the base of the Microsoft Windows 2000, Windows XP, and Windows .NET Server operating systems that provides portability between different machine architectures and processor platforms.

Overview

The hardware abstraction layer (HAL) hides hardware differences from the operating system so that uniform code can be used for all hardware. The HAL thus offers a uniform interface between the underlying hardware and the higher layers of the operating system. All underlying hardware looks the same to the Windows 2000, Windows XP, and Windows .NET Server operating systems because they "see" the hardware through the filtered glasses of the HAL.

The HAL is located at the base of the Executive Services, and it encapsulates most hardware-specific functions that are performed by the operating system. If another portion of the operating system wants to access a hardware device, it must refer its request to the HAL. The HAL handles all communication between the kernel of the operating system and the hardware, particularly those regarding processor commands, system interrupts, and input/output (I/O) interfaces.

Implementation

The HAL is implemented in Windows 2000, Windows XP, and Windows .NET Server as a loadable kernel mode module called hal.dll that is located in the System32 directory. If a hardware vendor needs to protect proprietary technology, the company can develop a custom implementation of the HAL. This means, for example, that different processor configurations such as multiprocessor machines might use different HAL drivers.

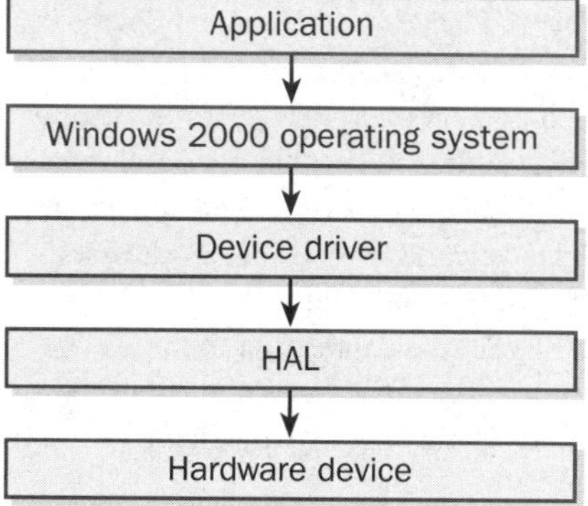

Hardware Abstraction Layer (HAL). *How a Windows 2000 application communicates with hardware through the HAL.*

Usually, what happens when Windows 2000, Windows XP, or Windows .NET Server want to access a hardware device is that the operating system issues a command to the appropriate device driver, which then talks to the HAL, which talks directly to the hardware.

Using the wrong HAL driver can result in degraded system performance since all hardware calls made by the operating system go through the HAL. Contact your vendor to make sure that you have the correct HAL for your system. To check which HAL is installed on your system, open the Setup.log file found in the \Winnt\Repair directory and examine the filename after the equal sign. The following table shows a list of HALs that can be installed from the Windows 2000, Windows XP, and Windows .NET Server compact disc.

HALs Found on the Windows 2000, Windows XP, and Windows .NET Server Compact Disc

File name	*Description*
hal.dll	Used for standard PCs
halacpi.dll	Used for PCs supporting Advanced Configuration and Power Interface (ACPI)
halapic.dll	Used for PCs supporting Advanced Programmable Interrupt Controller (APIC)
hapaacpi.dll	Used for PCs supporting both ACPI and APIC
halmps.dll	Used for multiprocessor PCs
halmacpi.dll	Used for multiprocessor PCs that support ACPI
halsp.dll	Used for Compaq SystemPro servers

For More Information

Find out about the HAL Development Kit at *www.microsoft.com/DDK/halkit.*

See Also: *Windows 2000, Windows .NET Server, Windows XP*

hardware address

Also called a MAC address, a unique 6-byte (48-bit) address that is usually permanently burned into a network interface card (NIC) or other physical-layer networking device and uniquely identifies the device on an Ethernet-based network.

See: *MAC address*

Hardware Compatibility List (HCL)

A list of hardware that is compatible with a Microsoft Windows operating system product.

Overview

The Hardware Compatibility List (HCL) for a Microsoft Windows platform defines all supported hardware, including computer systems as well as individual hardware components such as video cards, motherboards, and sound cards. When in doubt, you should consult the HCL before installing an operating system on a nonstandard or customized machine or installing new hardware into a system with an existing operating system. Using components not included on the HCL can lead to installation failures or system instabilities. Microsoft has determined that drivers for hardware devices listed on the HCL are compatible with that version of Windows; Microsoft supports only these drivers.

If you use drivers for devices that are not on the HCL, you might not be entitled to Microsoft product support for your system configuration. If you must use non-HCL devices, contact the device's manufacturer to see whether a supported driver exists for the particular Windows operating system you are using. If you contact Microsoft Product Support Services (PSS) about a problem and the support engineer determines that a hardware device in your system is not on the HCL, you will likely incur a charge for the call even if the problem cannot be resolved.

Notes

You can usually find the HCL for a particular Windows operating system on its distribution CD. (The file might be called hcl.txt.) A more up-to-date version of the HCL for all Windows operating system platforms is available on the Web at the HCL site listed in the "For More Information" section of this entry.

For More Information

You can visit Microsoft Product Support Services at *www.microsoft.com/support.* You can look at the Microsoft HCL site at *www.microsoft.com/hwtest/hcl.*

hardware profile

Information about the configuration of devices and services that are used to boot an operating system into a certain configuration.

Overview

A hardware profile tells the operating system which devices are present when the computer boots.

You can create several different hardware profiles on Microsoft Windows operating systems and select the one you want to use at boot time. For example, if

Windows 2000 is installed on a laptop computer, you can create two hardware profiles for that computer:

- One profile for when the computer is docked and connected to the network. (The profile will contain configuration information for the network adapter.)
- Another profile for when the computer is undocked and used in the field. (The profile will contain no configuration information about networking.)

When the laptop is booted, you select the appropriate hardware profile from a menu generated by the operating system.

Notes

Hardware profiles are usually not necessary for plug-and-play laptops running Windows 2000, Windows XP, or Windows .NET Server. These computers can recognize when new hardware becomes available (for example, by docking) and automatically configure themselves.

hashing algorithm

A mathematical procedure for randomizing (hashing) information to make it more secure in transmission.

Overview

Hasting algorithms take information and scramble it repeatedly to create a fixed-length string of numbers and characters called a hash. A good hashing algorithm has the following characteristic: if you apply a hashing algorithm to some data and then change only a few bits in the data and apply the algorithm again, the two resulting hashes will differ in almost every bit.

Hashing algorithms are used extensively in cryptography for encrypting keys or messages. Examples of popular cryptographic hashing algorithms include MD2, MD4, MD5, and SHA-1. Message Digest 5 (MD5) uses a 128-bit hash, and Secure Hash Algorithm (SHA) uses a 60-bit hash. The more bits in a hash, the greater the security of the encryption process.

Hashing is also used in some database technology for creating indexes of items in a database. Hashes of database objects are generally smaller than the objects themselves, so they can be indexed and searched more quickly. You can generate unique hashes of fixed length for each database record, creating a hash table that you can use for quick searches for records.

See Also: *cryptography, encryption*

HBA

Stands for host bus adapter, a device that converts Peripheral Component Interconnect (PCI) bus signals into Small Computer System Interface (SCSI) or Fibre Channel format.

See: *host bus adapter (HBA)*

H channel

A designation for groups of channels on Basic Rate Interface ISDN (BRI-ISDN) services.

Overview

H channel standards are defined by the International Telecommunication Union (ITU) and are composed of different combinations of Integrated Services Digital Network (ISDN) B channels. The most common configurations are as follows:

- **H0 channel:** This consists of six B channels multiplexed to provide a data transmission speed of 384 kilobits per second (Kbps). This service is sometimes called ISDN H0 or switched 384.
- **H11 channel:** This consists of 24 B channels to provide 1536 kilobits per second (Kbps) of bandwidth. This is sometimes called ISDN H11 or switched 1536.
- **H12 channel:** This consists of 30 B channels to provide 1920 Kbps of bandwidth. This is sometimes called ISDN H12 or switched 1920.

See Also: *B channel, Integrated Services Digital Network (ISDN)*

HCL

Stands for Hardware Compatibility List, a list of hardware that is compatible with a Microsoft Windows operating system product.

See: *Hardware Compatibility List (HCL)*

HDLC

Stands for High-level Data Link Control, an encapsulation protocol for point-to-point serial wide area network (WAN) links.

See: *High-level Data Link Control (HDLC)*

HDML

Stands for Handheld Device Markup Language, a markup language loosely modeled on Hypertext Markup Language (HTML) and optimized for providing Internet access to cell phones and other handheld devices.

See: *Handheld Device Markup Language (HDML)*

HDSL

Stands for High-bit-rate Digital Subscriber Line, a form of Digital Subscriber Line (DSL) technology that provides T-1 speeds in both directions.

See: *High-bit-rate Digital Subscriber Line (HDSL)*

header

The initial portion of a packet or a frame.

Overview

The header typically contains control information such as addressing, routing, and protocol version. The format of this information depends on the protocol being used. For example, an Internet Protocol (IP) header contains information about the version of the IP protocol, the length of the header, the type of service used, the packet's Time to Live (TTL), the source and destination address, and other data. Headers are used to control the flow of packets through the network or over the communication link.

The end of a frame sometimes has a smaller structure called a footer or trailer, but this usually contains only error-checking information. Control information is always placed in the header because this is the first portion of the packet or frame that is read by a networking device such as a switch or a router.

See Also: *frame, packet*

heartbeat

A polling feature of cluster servers.

Overview

An internal communications interface in Microsoft Cluster Server (MSCS) in Microsoft Windows NT Server, Enterprise Edition, and in the Cluster service in Windows 2000 Advanced Server and Windows .NET Enterprise Server, the heartbeat continuously provides interserver communication between cluster nodes in a cluster. One function of the heartbeat is to generate a message that the Cluster service running on one node regularly sends to the Cluster service on the other node to detect a failure within the cluster. Nodes in a cluster communicate status information with each other through the heartbeat using MSCS or the Cluster service. These messages appear as network traffic between the two nodes in the cluster on the dedicated network connection between the nodes, which is called the private network of the cluster. The primary heartbeat network interface is usually a crossover network cable directly attached between cluster nodes or in a private network. If the heartbeat is lost over the private connection, Cluster Server reverts to a public network or alternate connection for its heartbeat and other Cluster service traffic. You can configure the polling interval for the heartbeat using Cluster Administrator.

See Also: *clustering*

Help

Any of several systems of online help for Microsoft Corporation products.

Overview

The type of help features available depends on the nature of the product, the date of release, and the context in which it is invoked. Examples of help functions include the following:

- **Help:** Choose Help from the Start menu in Microsoft Windows 95, Windows 98, Windows NT, Windows 2000, Windows XP, and Windows .NET Server to open a Help Topics window (in Windows XP and Windows .NET Server, the window is called "Help And Support Center"). The window has three tabs: Contents (to browse the help database using a hierarchical set of book icons), Index (to type the topic you want help on and then display the appropriate entry), and Find (named Search in Windows 98 and Windows 2000, to conduct a full-text keyword search of the help database). Windows 2000 includes a fourth tab, Favorites, that lets you save links to Help topics.

In Windows XP and Windows .NET Server, Help has an entirely new look and setup. It now resembles Internet Explorer and offers many new features and customized user options. For example, the mechanism to search Microsoft Online has been integrated into the main search engine.

H

- **What's This?:** To find information about a setting in a dialog box or property sheet, right-click the item and choose What's This? from the context menu, or click the question mark button at the top right of the dialog box.
- **F1 key:** To get context-sensitive help at any point, press the F1 function key.
- **Browser-based help:** In Windows 2000, online help is provided through a new interface called Online Support and Information, which is accessible in Windows 2000 Help by selecting Web Help. The interface displays a new page within Windows 2000 Help that provides links to various Windows 2000 online support Web pages, including a new Windows 2000 Resource Kits Web page.
- **Books Online:** Many Microsoft products have additional user manuals in an online format that you can access from the Start menu.

heterogeneous network

A network that uses multiple network architectures and operating systems.

Overview

An example of a heterogeneous network at the hardware level is a combination of Ethernet and Token Ring local area networks (LANs) connected with a Fiber Distributed Data Interface (FDDI) backbone. An example at the network operating system (NOS) level is a server room in which some machines are running Microsoft Windows NT, others are running UNIX, and still others are running Novell NetWare. An example at the application level is a messaging system that includes Microsoft Exchange Server, Novell GroupWise, UNIX Sendmail, and IBM PROFS mail systems.

Heterogeneous networks are generally more complex to administer than homogeneous networks. Most networks are heterogeneous because they evolve over time. Most startup companies cannot afford to buy a completely homogeneous, state-of-the-art network platform, and even if they could, it would soon become out of date. One advantage of deliberately maintaining a heterogeneous network is that customers can use any product they choose instead of being locked into a single vendor's system. Networking and operating system choices can be made on a "best-served" basis instead of an "only buy from us" approach.

See Also: *homogeneous network*

hidden share

A share not visible when users browse the network for resources.

Overview

In Microsoft Windows operating systems, a share with a dollar sign ($) appended to the share name. Hidden shares are accessible on the network using Universal Naming Convention (UNC) paths or mapped network drives, but only if the user knows that they are present and knows their exact name. These shares do not show up in My Network Places or Windows Explorer or when you use the net view command. Users are unaware of their presence unless they are specifically informed.

It is a good idea not to acquaint ordinary users with hidden shares, because they might create such shares on their workstations if appropriate file and print services are installed. This can lead to secret, uncontrolled publishing of information within the company, which is usually against company policy.

Windows 2000, Windows XP, and Windows .NET Server also create certain hidden shares during the installation process that the operating system uses for specific purposes. These hidden shares are called administrative shares; permissions on them should not be modified.

See Also: *share*

Hierarchical Storage Management (HSM)

A data storage system for archiving infrequently needed data while still making it easily available.

Overview

A Hierarchical Storage Management (HSM) system is a way of providing users with seemingly endless amounts of storage space. This is accomplished by moving much of the data from hard disks to an archival storage system, such as an optical drive or tape library. Pointers are created on the hard disks indicating where the archived data is located. Users who need access to data need only request it from the disk, and if the requested data has been archived, the pointers allow the data to be found and returned to the user. The whole process is transparent from the user's viewpoint—all the data appears to be stored on the hard disks.

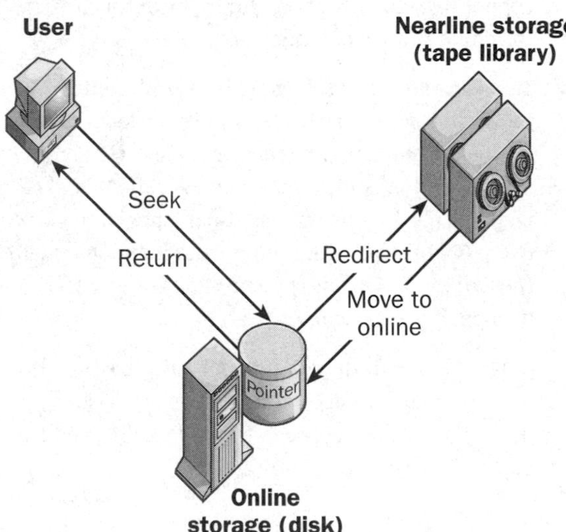

Hierarchical Storage Management (HSM). *How an HSM system works.*

Implementation

HSM defines two types of storage:

- **Online storage:** This is storage immediately accessible to users, typically hard disks on servers. Online storage is relatively expensive and provides almost instantaneous seek/return of requested data. In Microsoft terminology this form of storage is called local storage.
- **Nearline storage:** This is storage on archival media such as tape or optical disk and employs automated seek/return technologies such as robotic tape libraries. Nearline storage is cheaper than online storage but is slower in its ability to return requested data. In Microsoft parlance, this type of storage is known as remote storage.

Note that nearline storage differs from offline storage, which uses removable archive media (usually tape) that needs to be manually inserted in order to access information stored on the media. For HSM to work, the archival storage system employed must be automated or nearline in operation.

In HSM, when an online storage system approaches full capacity, HSM automatically starts to archive files, directories, or whole volumes to nearline storage. The particular data archived depends on the policies configured for HSM's operation, which typically initiate file archiving based on how frequently files have been accessed or when they have last been accessed. The archiving process happens automatically, and files moved from online storage are replaced with pointers to their nearline location. When a user tries to access a file stored nearline, the file is moved to online storage where the user can read it (the user cannot read nearline storage directly).

Marketplace

HSM systems have been around for some time in the UNIX world as third-party add-ons developed by different vendors for enterprise environments. Microsoft now includes an integrated HSM system in its Microsoft Windows 2000 Server platform called Remote Storage Service (RSS), which can archive data to Small Computer System Interface (SCSI) tape libraries using 4mm, 8mm, and digital linear tape (DLT) tape formats (quarter-inch cartridge [QIC] tapes and optical disk libraries are not supported). RSS works by using a new feature of NTFS version 5 called reparse points, which are similar to pointers used by UNIX file systems.

Issues

Traditional HSM loses its usefulness when used to archive large files such as video feeds and database files. This is because users sometimes need to access only a portion of such a file, but in order for them to access it, the entire file must be fetched from nearline storage and moved to online storage, a process that can take excessive time (for example, retrieving a 2 gigabyte (GB) file from a DLT tape library could take five minutes or more). A recent solution to this problem is the implementation of file segmentation to HSM systems. Using file segmentation, large files are broken up into smaller segments for archiving and retrieval, and when a part of a file is modified, only the segment modified needs to be rearchived. File segmentation can be implemented on UNIX-based HSM systems by employing a segmentation attribute—setting this attribute causes a file, directory, or volume to be broken into segments when moved to nearline storage, with pointers to each segment created on the online storage where the object previously resided. The whole process is again transparent to the user and typically reduces seek/return time for portions of large files to seconds instead of minutes.

Notes

Note that HSM systems such as Microsoft's RSS are not a substitute for regular tape backups. HSM will not archive critical operating system and application files, so regular backups are still necessary when using such systems.

See Also: *storage, tape format, tape library*

High-bit-rate Digital Subscriber Line (HDSL)

A form of Digital Subscriber Line (DSL) technology that supports high-speed symmetric data transmission.

Overview

High-bit-rate Digital Subscriber Line (HDSL) can be used to transmit data over existing copper local loop connections at T1 or E1 speeds. It is used to transport data only (HDSL signals overlap the voice portion of the Plain Old Telephone Service [POTS] spectrum and therefore cannot carry voice) and is generally used in wide area networking (WAN) scenarios. The maximum distance for HDSL transmission is typically 15,000 feet (4500 meters) when running over unconditioned copper twisted-pair telephone wiring. Some providers, however, claim that their devices support twice this distance. This maximum distance from the telco's central office (CO) to an HDSL customer's premises is sometimes called the Carrier Service Area (CSA).

HDSL was the earliest symmetric version of DSL to be widely implemented and was designed in the early 1990s as an alternative to traditional T-1 services. T1 lines originally required intermediate repeaters to be installed every 6000 feet (1830 meters) between termination points in order to ensure the signal strength necessary to transport data at such high speeds. HDSL was developed by Bellcore as a repeaterless form of T1 that would save the cost of installing repeaters and speed deployment of T1 lines for customers.

HDSL comes in various formats, including the following:

- 668-kilobit-per-second (Kbps) full-duplex transmission over a single unconditioned, unshielded copper twisted-pair phone line. This is an early form that is not used much anymore.
- 1.544-megabit-per-second (Mbps) full-duplex transmission (T1 speed) over unconditioned, unshielded copper twisted-pair cables. This is the most common configuration and is called Dual-Duplex HDSL. It uses twisted-pair phone lines with two pairs of wires (four wires) within the line, with full-duplex 784-Kbps transmission taking place over each pair of wires.
- 2.048-Mbps full-duplex transmission (E1 speed) over two or three unconditioned copper twisted-pair lines. This is the European form of HDSL, and two pairs is the usual form nowadays.

Implementation

The main different between HDSL and the original T1 specification is the line coding scheme employed. T1 lines originally used bipolar alternate mark inversion (AMI) for signal encoding, which has a spectral efficiency of only 1 bit/baud (in other words, to transmit one bit of data requires one symbol or character). By contrast, HDSL employs 2B1Q (2 Binary 1 Quaternary) line coding, which transmits information at 2 bits/baud (2B1Q is also the encoding scheme for Integrated Services Digital Network [ISDN]). Each pair of copper phone wires in an

HDSL implementation carry data at 784 Kbps over unconditioned lines without the need of repeaters. Two pairs of copper wires thus provide a throughput of 1.536 Mbps, which is the same as regular T1.

In a typical scenario, a line driver called an HTU-R terminates the lines at the customer premises end through a serial connection to a router that provides connectivity for the customer's local area network (LAN). At the telco end, a similar line driver called an HTU-C terminates the other end and provides a connection to the digital cross connect (DCC) that routes signals to trunk lines between central offices (COs). A group of HTU-Cs are typically combined in a rack to service more customers.

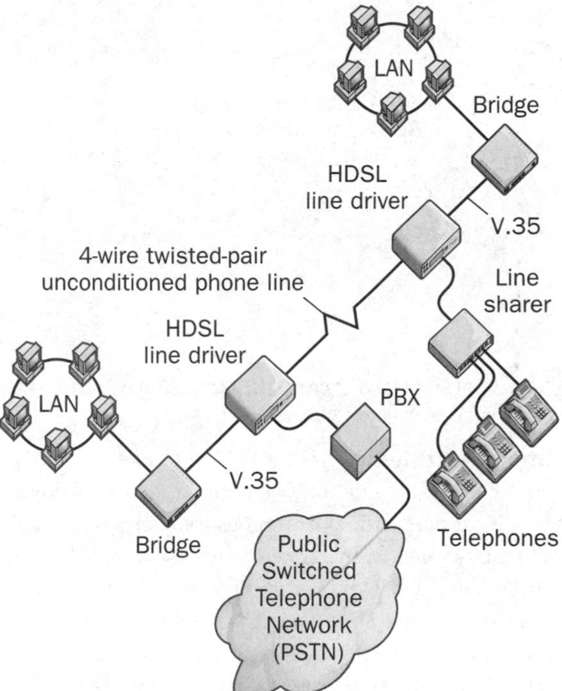

High-bit-rate Digital Subscriber Line (HDSL). *Some possible deployment scenarios for HDSL.*

Uses

Because it is a high-speed symmetrical service, HDSL is typically used to provide dedicated WAN links for enterprises. Many telcos now offer HDSL instead of traditional T1 lines because of reduced deployment costs associated with this repeaterless technology. An enterprise customer wanting to run a public Web server at her company site might use HDSL to provide a high-bandwidth connection between the server and the Internet.

HDSL can also be used for connecting bridges, routers, and telephone equipment such as Private Branch Exchanges (PBXs) over a campus using HDSL line drivers with built-in Channel Service Unit/Data Service Unit (CSU/DSU) functionality. It can also be used to build private data telecommunications networks, connections between points of presence (POPs), and other telecommunications services. You can use HDSL to connect campus networks and phone equipment at T1 speeds without the need for costly fiber-optic cabling. HDSL line drivers or line terminals generally support a variety of data interfaces, includingV.35, G.703, and 10BaseT connections. They are configurable for Nx64 Kbps transmission speeds and sometimes include bridge or router functionality for framing of High-level Data Link Control (HDLC), Point-to-Point Protocol (PPP), Internet Protocol (IP), and other protocols. They can be used for LAN-LAN connections and for connecting LANs to frame relay networks or the Internet.

HDSL can also be used for other purposes such as videoconferencing, telecommuting, and shared Internet access for connecting business networks to the Internet. HDSL is not used for residential Internet access—Asymmetric Digital Subscriber Line (ADSL) is commonly used there instead. ADSL is able to provide line sharing (combined voice/data services over a single pair of copper lines), but HDSL carries only data and requires two pairs of lines.

Prospects

A newer form of HDSL called HDSL2 works similarly to HDSL but requires only one pair of copper lines in order to operate. HDSL2 is standardized by the International Telecommunication Union (ITU) as G.991.1 and by the American National Standards Institute (ANSI) as T1E1.4.

See Also: *Digital Subscriber Line (DSL), T-carrier*

H

High-level Data Link Control (HDLC)

An encapsulation protocol for point-to-point wide area network (WAN) links.

Overview

High-level Data Link Control (HDLC) is a data-link layer protocol for synchronous communication over serial links. HDLC was developed in the 1970s by IBM as an offshoot of the Synchronous Data Link Control (SDLC) protocol for their Systems Network Architecture (SNA) mainframe computing environment. It was later standardized by the International Organization for Standardization (ISO) as a standard Open Systems Interconnection (OSI) Layer-2 protocol.

H

Architecture

HDLC is called an encapsulation protocol because it encapsulates bit stream data into fixed-length frames for transmission over synchronous serial lines. HDLC is a bit-stream protocol (bit streams are streams of data not broken into individual characters) that uses a 32-bit checksum for error correction and supports full-duplex communication. HDLC frames consist of a special flag byte (01111110) followed by address and control information, data bits, and a cyclic redundancy check (CRC) byte. A control field at the start of a frame is used for establishing and terminating data link connections. As a data-link protocol, HDLC is responsible for ensuring that data is received intact, without errors, and in the proper sequence. HDLC also supports flow-control mechanisms for managing synchronous data streams. HDLC also supports multiple protocols but does not include any mechanisms for authentication (since authentication is not really needed in dedicated point-to-point communications).

An HDLC link typically consists of a primary station and a secondary station, with the primary station issuing the commands and the secondary station issuing the responses. HDLC is used mainly for point-to-point communication, in contrast to otherWAN transports such as Asynchronous Transfer Mode (ATM), frame relay, and X.25, which can be used for both point-to-point and point-to-multipoint communication. Because HDLC is used mainly in point-to-point communication, it does not need to have addressing implemented at the data-link layer because the local and remote stations are connected directly. In this configuration, either one station is the primary and the other the secondary (unbalanced point-to-point link) or both stations function in a primary/secondary capacity (balanced point-to-point link). You can also use HDLC in a more complex configuration in which one primary links to several secondaries (unbalanced multipoint configuration), but this is not common.

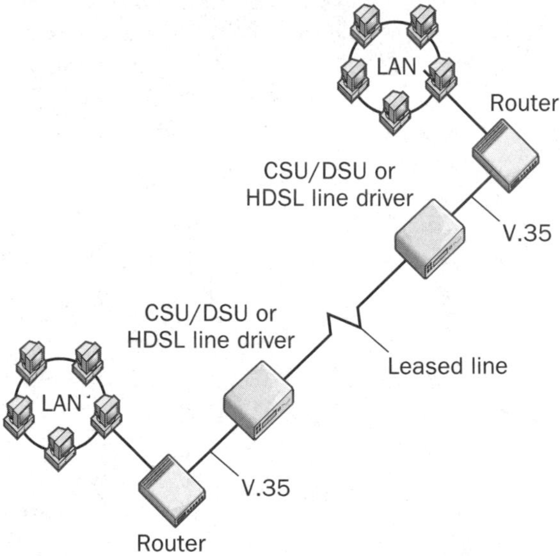

High-level Data Link Control (HDLC). *Using HDLC for WAN communications over a leased line.*

Implementation

HDLC is the default encapsulation protocol employed by Cisco routers for synchronous transmission over serial links such as Integrated Services Digital Network (ISDN) and T-1 lines. For point-to-point communications over a leased line using Cisco routers at both ends, HDLC is a good choice. A typical leased-line configuration uses Channel Service Unit/Data Service Units (CSU/DSUs) to terminate the ends of the leased line, with Cisco routers connecting the CSU/DSUs to the two networks. The CSU/DSUs are nowadays often integrated into the routers for simplicity.

Issues

When HDLC was first developed, vendors made their own modifications to the protocol, with the result that versions of HDLC from different vendors cannot interoperate with each other. This was the driving force behind the development by the Internet Engineering Task Force (IETF) of Point-to-Point Protocol (PPP), a newer encapsulation protocol that has largely replaced HDLC in WAN environments. PPP supports both synchronous and asynchronous communications and has a standard implementation by every vendor to ensure interoperability between networking equipment from different vendors. Both PPP and Link Access Protocol, Balanced (LAPB), the data-link protocol for X.25, evolved from HDLC and were built upon its foundation.

Notes

A version of HDLC known as Normal Response Mode (NRM) HDLC is basically the same thing as Synchronous Data Link Control (SDLC), a protocol developed by IBM as a replacement for its BiSync protocol.

See Also: *Channel Service Unit/Data Service Unit (CSU/DSU), leased line, Open Systems Interconnection (OSI) reference model, Point-to-Point Protocol (PPP), Synchronous Data Link Control (SDLC), wide area network (WAN), X.25*

High Performance File System (HPFS)

A file system designed for version 1.2 of the Microsoft/ IBM OS/2 operating system as a successor to the file allocation table (FAT) file system used by MS-DOS.

Overview

High-Performance File System (HPFS) improves on the performance of the FAT file system for MS-DOS in the following ways:

- It locates file directory and allocation information in close physical proximity to the files themselves on the hard disk. (The FAT file system locates the root directory and allocation information on the outermost cylinders of the drive.)
- It has a more robust and efficient file system tree structure than FAT, so you can locate directories more quickly.
- It has multiple asynchronous read/write threads.
- It uses sector-based allocation instead of the more space-wasting, cluster-based allocation used by FAT.
- It uses large file cache sizes and lazy-writes.

Other features of HPFS that were considered advanced at the time of its development included the following:

- Long filenames—up to 256 characters in length. These long filenames are case preserving but not case sensitive. MS-DOS applications can still access HPFS volumes either over the network to an OS/2 LAN Manager server or from inside an MS-DOS compatibility box on an OS/2 workstation.
- Extended attributes—a series of name/value pairs associated with each directory or file. These extended attributes can be 64 kilobytes (KB) in size and support advanced kinds of search queries, such as by file type, version number, subject, or comments.
- Support for extended character sets.
- Maximum 64-gigabyte (GB) drive size. (The practical limit is 16 GB, however.)

Notes

HPFS is supported by Microsoft Windows NT version 3.51 but not by the Windows NT 4, Windows 2000, Windows XP, or Windows .NET Server operating systems, which use the more advanced NTFS file system (NTFS). HPFS was designed to function as an Installable File System (IFS), which is implemented as a dynamic-link library (DLL) that hooks into the file system component of the operating system kernel. In Windows NT 3.51, you configured HPFS through an IFS= line in the config.sys file. The CD file system (CDFS) was also designed to support IFS.

See Also: *file allocation table (FAT), file system, NTFS file system (NTFS)*

High-Performance Parallel Interface (HIPPI)

A gigabit networking technology for point-to-point communications.

Overview

High-Performance Parallel Interface (HIPPI) is an American National Standards Institute (ANSI) standard for point-to-point networking at gigabit speeds. HIPPI was developed in the 1980s as a technology for

H

interconnecting supercomputers, mainframes, and their storage devices. Fibre Channel is the closest networking technology to HIPPI in terms of its use and capabilities and is more widely used than HIPPI.

Uses

While HIPPI is comparable in speed to Gigabit Ethernet (GbE), it is not widely used in general networking applications since it is basically a connection-oriented technology suitable for point-to-point communications due to latency involved in negotiating connections. HIPPI also lacks the multicasting capability provided by Internet Protocol (IP)–based GbE. HIPPI is mostly deployed in a few high-speed research projects by universities and for high-speed data collection in specialized scientific experiments, one of the most notable being at the European Center for Particle Physics (CERN), the world's largest particle physics facility.

Implementation

HIPPI operates at the physical and data-link layers to provide connection-oriented communications between two points. HIPPI can operate at either 800 megabits per second (Mbps) or 1.6 gigabits per second (Gbps), and it has a simple flow control command set that can establish or tear down a connection in under a microsecond using a HIPPI switch. There is also a new standard called HIPPI-6400 that supports speeds up to 6.4 Gbps for distances up to 164 feet (50 meters) over twisted pair copper and up to 0.62 miles (1 kilometer) over fiber-optic cabling.

In its original format, HIPPI was a parallel transmission technology that used 50-pair shielded twisted-pair (STP) copper cabling for transmission of 800 Mbps over a distance of up to 82 feet (25 meters). Because longer parallel cables are impractical, a newer version called Serial HIPPI was developed in 1997 that encoded HIPPI's parallel bit stream into a single serial bit stream over fiber-optic cabling. For 800 Mbps transmission, the signaling rate is 1.2 Gbaud and two fibers are used, one for simplex transmission in each direction, giving full-duplex communications. For 1.6 Gbps transmission, four fibers are used. The maximum distances over which Serial HIPPI can operate are:

- 0.62 miles (1 kilometer) over multimode fiber
- 6.2 miles (10 kilometers) over single-mode fiber

Marketplace

Vendors of HIPPI equipment include Ascend, Cray Research, GigaLabs, Hewlett-Packard Company, IBM, and Silicon Graphics, Inc. (SGI). Products offered include adapter boards and interfaces, frame buffers, storage devices, tape servers, switches and routers, cables, and test equipment.

For More Information

Find out more about HIPPI standards activities at *www.hippi.org.*

See Also: *Fibre Channel, Gigabit Ethernet (GbE)*

High-Speed Circuit Switched Data (HSCSD)

An interim upgrade for Global System for Mobile Communications (GSM) cellular communications systems.

Overview

High-Speed Circuit Switched Data (HSCSD) is the first upgrade available for GSM that boosts GSM's data-carrying capacity above its current maximum of 14.4 kilobits per second (Kbps). HSCSD is a pre-2.5G upgrade for GSM that has been deployed by a few carriers in lieu of General Packet Radio Service (GPRS), a 2.5G upgrade for GSM and other Time Division Multiple Access (TDMA) cellular systems that is just beginning to be widely deployed. Unlike GPRS, which requires that existing base station hardware be upgraded, HSCSD is a software-only upgrade and is easily implemented.

Implementation

HSCSD works by aggregating together groups of GSM time slots. Each GSM frame consists of eight time slots, each of which can provide up to 14.4 Kbps throughput for data transmission. HSCSD uses one slot for upstream communications and aggregates four slots for downstream communications. HSCSD is thus an asymmetrical data transmission technology that supports speeds of 14.4 Kbps upstream and 57.6 Kbps downstream. However, the overhead required by slot aggregation usually results in downstream bandwidth of only 28.8 Kbps instead of the theoretical 57.6 Kbps.

HSCSD supports two different transmission modes:

- **Transparent mode:** Offers a fixed bit rate for data transmission
- **Nontransparent mode:** Provides a variable bit rate

Prospects

HSCSD test deployments began in 1999. Some GSM operators that have upgraded their networks to HSCSD include Sonera in Finland and SingTel in Singapore. The majority of operators are upgrading directly to GPRS, however, and HSCSD is likely to be eclipsed quickly. This may be unfortunate, because HSCSD's circuit-switched transmission method has advantages over packet-switched GPRS in such applications as digital video, where low latency and guaranteed quality of service (QoS) are important.

See Also: *General Packet Radio Service (GPRS), Global System for Mobile Communications (GSM), Time Division Multiple Access (TDMA)*

High-Speed Serial Interface (HSSI)

A serial interface that supports speeds up to 52 megabits per second (Mbps).

Overview

High-Speed Serial Interface (HSSI) is defined by the standard EIA 612/613. HSSI supports serial transmission at speeds much higher than those supported by traditional serial interfaces such as RS-232 and V.35. At a top speed of 52 Mbps, HSSI is capable of supporting

- Synchronous Optical Network (SONET) transmission at 51.82 Mbps
- T3 lines at 45 Mbps
- E3 lines at 34 Mbps

Uses

HSSI is typically used to connect access servers and routers to T3 circuits for enterprise wide area network (WAN) connectivity. Top-end Cisco routers support HSSI through installable HSSI Interface Processor (HIP) cards that provide one HSSI port per router. HSSI is necessary for companies that want to deploy T3 WAN services such as DS-3 frame relay links because slower V.35 and RS-232 serial interfaces cannot operate at such speeds.

Notes

HSSI uses a 50-pin Centronics connector similar to a Small Computer System Interface (SCSI) connector, but you cannot use a SCSI cable to connect a HSSI router to a Data Service Unit (DSU)—you have to use a special HSSI cable instead.

See Also: *router, RS-232, serial transmission, T-carrier, V.35*

High-Speed Token Ring (HSTR)

A high-speed version of Token Ring that never got off the ground.

Overview

High-Speed Token Ring (HSTR) was a development project of the High-Speed Token Ring Alliance, which consisted ofToken Ring hardware vendors IBM, Olicom, and Madge Networks. HSTR was initially intended as a 100 megabits per second (Mbps) version of 802.5 Token Ring networking architecture that would provide a logical upgrade for existing 4 and 16 Mbps Token Ring networks. Speeds up to 1 gigabit per second (Gbps) were envisioned as being possible down the line.

Unfortunately, customer interest in HSTR waned with the rapid development of Fast Ethernet and Gigabit Ethernet (GbE) technologies, and in 1998 IBM withdrew from the alliance and the effort collapsed. The effective result is that Ethernet has finally won the local area network (LAN) wars with Token Ring and Fiber Distributed Data Interface (FDDI) networking architectures, and these two architectures are now considered legacy technologies that have no real future.

See Also: *802.5, Ethernet, Fast Ethernet, Fiber Distributed Data Interface (FDDI), Gigabit Ethernet (GbE), Token Ring*

HiperLAN/2

An emerging high-speed wireless networking standard.

Overview

HiperLAN/2 is a global standard for broadband wireless networking developed by the Broadband Radio Access Networks (BRAN) group of the European Telecommunications Standards Institute (ETSI). HiperLAN/2 is designed to be an extension of Asynchronous Transfer

Mode (ATM) technology to the wireless networking arena and is expected to be ratified as a standard sometime in 2002. HiperLAN/2 is an alternative to the existing 802.11a high-speed wireless networking standard developed by the Institute of Electrical and Electronics Engineers (IEEE) and is intended as a worldwide wireless networking platform that is interoperable with ATM, third-generation (3G) cellular systems, and 1394 (Firewire) systems.

Adoption of HiperLAN/2 standards is being driven by the HiperLAN2 Global Forum (H2GF), an open industry forum launched in 1999 and whose founding members were Bosch, Dell Computer Corporation, Ericsson, Nokia, Telia, and Texas Instruments. Two other HiperLAN standards being promoted include

- **HiperAccess:** A standard for fixed outdoor use and for providing access to wireline networks
- **HiperLink:** A standard for building indoor radio backbones

Architecture

HiperLAN/2 provides raw data transfer speeds of up to 54 megabits per second (Mbps), which corresponds to roughly 20 Mbps actual sustained throughput. Instead of operating in the slower, crowded 2.5 gigahertz (GHz) Industrial, Scientific, and Medical (ISM) frequency band, HiperLAN/2 uses the higher 5 GHz frequency band for greater throughput. Actual frequencies used depend on the country in which the technology is deployed, for example:

- **United States:** 5.15–5.35 and 5.725–5.825 GHz
- **Europe:** 5.15–5.35 and 5.470–5.725 GHz
- **Japan:** 5.15–5.35 GHz currently proposed for an alternate standard similar to HiperLAN/2

HiperLAN/2 shares some similarities with the IEEE's 802.11n and 802.11a wireless networking standards, especially at the physical (PHY) layer. Specifically, both technologies use channels 20 megahertz (MHz) wide and employ orthogonal frequency division multiplexing (OFDM) at the PHY layer to support high data transfer rates. In HiperLAN/2, however, these 20 MHz channels are shared using Time Division Multiple Access (TDMA) at the media access control (MAC) layer, instead of the Carrier Sense Multiple Access with Collision Avoidance (CSMA/CA) MAC employed by 802.11a. This makes HiperLAN/2 more like ATM than Ethernet in its operation, and, in fact, HiperLAN/2 supports Quality of Service (QoS) features similar to those found in ATM, something 802.11 does not.

Prospects

HiperLAN/2's QoS features make it an attractive solution for wireless transport of multimedia and video. The main issue with the technology, however, is its use of the 5 GHz frequency spectrum, which conflicts with the Federal Communication Commission's (FCC) spectrum allocation in the United States. This means that HiperLAN/2 is likely to be much more popular in Europe, where it was developed, than in the United States (HiperLAN/2 is accepted everywhere except Japan). Furthermore, 802.11a has the advantage of being first to market and is already beginning to be widely deployed, which may make it prevail over HiperLAN/2. Large enterprises may find it easier to deploy 802.11a globally throughout their offices than to try to support two different technologies.

A company called Atheros Communications has proposed a standard called 5-UP (5 GHz Unified Protocol) that would enable HiperLAn/2 and 802.11a technologies to interoperate. The 5-UP standard has been submitted to the IEEE for consideration.

See Also: *802.11a, Asynchronous Transfer Mode (ATM), Carrier Sense Multiple Access with Collision Avoidance (CSMA/CA), Orthogonal Frequency Division Multiplexing (OFDM), quality of service (QoS), Time Division Multiple Access (TDMA), wireless networking*

HIPPI

Stands for High-Performance Parallel Interface, a gigabit networking technology for point-to-point communications.

See: *High-Performance Parallel Interface (HIPPI)*

History

A folder in Microsoft Internet Explorer that contains shortcuts to Web pages that you have recently browsed.

Overview

The History folder makes it simple to return to sites that you have recently visited but have not been designated as Favorites. By clicking the History button on the Internet Explorer toolbar, you can view the contents of the History folder and revisit any of the links. You can configure how many days items should be kept in the folder, and you can delete the files manually if desired. Using the offline browsing feature of Internet Explorer, you can browse the History folder while you are disconnected from the Internet.

hive

A physical file containing part of the registry in Microsoft Windows.

Overview

Hives are opposed to subtrees, which are logical sections of the registry. The term *hive* is loosely connected with the idea of the cellular structure of a beehive.

Hives consist of a discrete collection of keys and subkeys that have a root at the top of the registry. Five of these hives are located in the folder %SystemRoot%\system32\config; the sixth hive (Ntuser.dat), which contains user profile information, is stored on machines running Windows NT in the folder %SystemRoot%\Profiles\username. On machines running Windows 2000, Windows XP, or Windows .NET Server, it is stored in the folder

- %SystemRoot%\Documents and Settings\username if this is a new Windows 2000, Windows XP, or Windows .NET Server installation or an upgrade from Windows 95 or Windows 98
- %SystemRoot%\Profiles\username if this is an upgrade from Windows NT to Windows 2000, Windows XP, or Windows .NET Server

Each hive has an associated transactional .log file that logs all modifications made to the registry and provides fault tolerance. Each hive file also has a .sav file, which is a backup copy of the hive file. The functions of the hives and the logical key they map to are indicated in the following table.

Windows NT Hives

Hive	*Key*	*Function*
Default	HKEY_USERS\DEFAULT	Contains the default system profile used when the logon screen is displayed.
SAM	HKEY_LOCAL_MACHINE\SAM	Contains information for the Security Account Manager (SAM). This hive cannot be viewed with the registry editor and must be accessed using specific application programming interfaces (APIs).
Security	HKEY_LOCAL_MACHINE\SECURITY	Contains the computer's security policy information. This hive also cannot be viewed with the registry editor and must be accessed using specific APIs.
Software	HKEY_LOCAL_MACHINE\SOFTWARE	Contains global configuration information for installed software.
System	HKEY_LOCAL_MACHINE\SYSTEM and HKEY_CURRENT_CONFIG	Contains configuration information for installed hardware devices and services.
Ntuser.dat	HKEY_CURRENT_USER	Contains user-specific configuration settings for the user who is currently logged on interactively.

See Also: *registry*

H-node

A NetBIOS name resolution method used for name registration and resolution.

Overview

H-node is a type of NetBIOS over Transmission Control Protocol/Internet Protocol (TCP/IP) node defined in RFCs 1001 and 1002. It's supported by Microsoft Windows NT, Windows 2000, Windows XP, and Windows .NET Server. H-node is also one of four basic methods for resolving NetBIOS host names (computer names) into Internet Protocol (IP) addresses. Name resolution is the process of converting the name of a host on the network into a network address, such as an IP address. Name resolution must be performed to establish communication over a network.

Implementation

When a computer running Windows NT, Windows 2000, Windows XP, or Windows .NET Server is configured as an H-node machine, it first tries to use a NetBIOS name server to resolve names of other hosts on the network; this is the way a P-node machine functions. A server running Windows NT, Windows 2000, Windows XP, or Windows .NET Server with the Windows Internet Name Service (WINS) configured on it is the typical example of a NetBIOS name server. If name resolution fails this way (for example, if all WINS servers are down), an H-node machine tries to use broadcasts to resolve the names of the hosts; this is the way a B-node machine functions. H-node is thus a combination of P-node and B-node (in that order), which explains the origin of the term *H-node*: *H* stands for hybrid.

If no WINS server is on a network, machines running Windows NT, Windows 2000, Windows XP, and Windows .NET Server automatically configure themselves as B-nodes. If at least one WINS server is on the network, however, the systems default to H-node.

See Also: *B-node, M-node, NetBIOS name resolution, P-node*

home area network (HAN)

A network of several computers at a user's home.

Overview

With the rapid growth in the PC market, an estimated 20 percent of homes in the United States that have one PC have at least one additional PC. As a result, ordinary PC users are becoming interested in networking their home PCs to use them for purposes such as

- Dedicating one PC to the role of a file server
- Sharing a printer among multiple PCs
- Installing a home Web server connected to the Internet by means of a cable modem
- Playing network games with family and friends
- Using networked PCs to prepare for certifications such as Microsoft Certified Systems Engineer (MCSE)

Implementation

A variety of different technologies can be used for deploying home area networks (HANs). Examples include the following:

- **Ethernet:** Basic Ethernet networking kits are available from most computer vendors and home/office supply stores. These kits are reasonably easy to set up and provide 10-megabit-per-second (Mbps) throughput. The main disadvantage is that these kits require that users have enough computer expertise to be able to install a network interface card (NIC) inside the machine and load the appropriate drivers. Then there's also the issue of laying the cabling so that people do not trip over the cable or wear it away by walking on it. Make sure you purchase 10BaseT kits that contain a hub, NICs, and cables instead of older 10Base5 kits that use bulkier coaxial cable.
- **Power line networking:** This technology allows computers in different parts of the house to communicate using installed power wiring and AC outlets. Implementations range from special AC port interface cards that need to be installed in machines to plug-and-play adapters that connect to a machine's parallel (LPT) port. This technology's main disadvantage is that it is relatively slow—most devices support speeds of 2 Mbps or less at present.
- **Phone line networking:** This technology leverages your installed telephone wiring infrastructure and RJ-11 phone line jacks to connect computers to form a network. Unfortunately, it only works if

these jacks have been properly installed with wires connected correctly, which is not always the case. Phone line networking typically supports Ethernet speeds of about 1 Mbps and is available for Peripheral Component Interconnect (PCI), pulse code modulation (PCM), and universal serial bus (USB) format. Initiatives from the Home Phone Networking Alliance (HomePNA) aim at increasing speeds to 10 Mbps and higher. Phone line networking works by utilizing frequencies above 2 megahertz (MHz), well beyond the range of both voice communications and Asymmetric Digital Subscriber Line (ADSL).

- **Wireless networking:** Kits for building simple wireless networks are more expensive than other forms of home networking technologies but have the advantage of greater flexibility in deployment. These range from expensive 802.11b kits that contain transceivers for PCs and a central access point and support speeds up to 11 Mbps, to consumer products running in the Industrial, Scientific, and Medical (ISM) range of the frequency spectrum and supporting speeds of about 1.5 Mbps.
- **Infrared (IR) networking:** This technology is generally used only to connect peripherals to PCs in the same room and requires clear line-of-site for communications.

Marketplace

The number of vendors offering Ethernet kits for home networking is legion. Vendors for phone line networking kits include 3Com Corporation and Intel Corporation. In the wireless networking market, Proxim offers a product called Symphony that uses PCI or PCM cards with antennae attached and no central access point. Intel also offers a popular wireless solution called AnyPoint that features plug-and-play USB connectivity.

See Also: 10BaseT, 802.11b, Ethernet

home folder

Also called home directory, a user's private folder for storing personal files.

Overview

Home folders for users are usually centrally located on a network server for the following reasons:

- To ensure that their contents are backed up regularly
- To make home folders available from any computer on the network
- To make home folders available from any client operating system

In Microsoft Windows 2000 and Windows XP, home folders are not part of the user profile of roaming users, so they must be specified. Use the Active Directory Users and Computers console to assign home folder locations. Open the property sheet for the user and specify the location of the user's home folder on the Profile tab.

HomeRF

A wireless networking specification targeted toward consumers.

Overview

HomeRF is a wireless networking technology that supports both voice and data transmission. HomeRF is designed for consumer applications such as wireless home networks, communication between Personal Digital Assistants (PDAs) and laptops, and similar uses.

HomeRF is based on a specification called RangeLan2 developed by Proxim. It operates in the same 2.4 gigahertz (GHz) unlicensed Industrial, Scientific, and Medical (ISM) band of the electromagnetic spectrum used by 802.11b and Bluetooth wireless networking technologies and by such devices as microwave ovens. HomeRF is less costly than these competing technologies due to the simplicity of its design and operation.

Implementation

The original HomeRF specification supports networking of PCs and other devices at data transfer rates up to 1.6 megabits per second (Mbps). In April 2001 the HomeRF Working Group released the HomeRF 2 specification, which boosts speeds to 10 Mbps. The

Working Group aims at releasing a HomeRF 3 standard in 2002 that will push data rates up to 22 Mbps.

In contrast to the competing 802.11 wireless networking technologies that use direct sequence spread spectrum (DSSS) radio transmission, HomeRF instead employs frequency hopping spread spectrum (FHSS) transmission. FHSS employs a signal that "hops" over a number of different frequencies to find one that is clear for transmission and provides better resistance to electromagnetic interference (EMI) than DSSS. Voice transmission is supported using time division multiple access (TDMA), but data uses Carrier Sense Multiple Access with Collision Avoidance (CSMA/CA).

H

HomeRF is deployed by using a central device called a home gateway, which enables communications between various types of devices including PCs, display pads, Web appliances, PDAs, stereos, home automation devices, and cordless phones. HomeRF uses a new protocol called Shared Wireless Access Protocol (SWAP) to enable its home networking features. Using SWAP, a user can do such things as

- Network a variety of different devices together into an integrated home networking environment
- Share files, printers, and Internet connections among devices on a home network
- Control PCs, home automation, and other devices from handsets and cordless phones

Marketplace

HomeRF products are available from a number of vendors, including Cayman Systems, Compaq Computer Corporation, Intel Corporation, Motorola, and Proxim. Intel's AnyPoint wireless networking platform supports HomeRF networking and is a popular choice.

Issues

Proponents of 802.11 have criticized HomeRF because it can potentially interfere with 802.11-based wireless communications. To a DSSS 802.11 receiver, FHSS signals produced by a HomeRF transmitter appear as random noise that can disrupt communications channels. Proponents of HomeRF often respond by saying that their product is targeted to a different market, the home networking market, than is 802.11, which is aimed mainly at the enterprise. They also point out that HomeRF fills a niche for combined data-voice wireless networking that 802.11, which is strictly data-oriented, has not filled. The Federal Communications Commission (FCC) has tried to resolve these concerns by limiting HomeRF hardware to power transmission under 125 milliwatts. This limits the range of HomeRF transmission to about 150 feet (45 meters) and makes it less likely to interfere with a neighboring 802.11 network.

Market prospects for HomeRF look good, but it has to play catch up to 802.11, which already has a large installed base worldwide. Intel is one company that already has home network products available in the consumer market that are based on the HomeRF standard.

For More Information

Visit the HomeRF Working Group at *www.homerf.org.*

See Also: *802.11, Bluetooth, wireless networking*

homogeneous network

A network that uses a single network architecture and operating system.

Overview

Homogeneous networks are the simplest networks to administer, but most corporate networks are heterogeneous networks for the following reasons:

- Budgets are limited, so it is not always possible to upgrade an older heterogeneous network into a newer homogeneous one unless the ultimate cost savings can be justified to management.
- Products continually evolve, so what might be a state-of-the-art network operating system today will be a second-class system tomorrow.
- Management and user expectations and needs evolve, so upgrading a second-class system might

not be as appropriate as replacing it entirely with something newer.

- Decision making involves politics, and different groups might press for purchasing software that they are more comfortable with instead of making prudent long-term decisions.

A simple example of a homogenous network would be an Ethernet local area network (LAN) in which all machines are running Microsoft Windows 2000.

Another example would be an enterprise-level messaging system based solely on Microsoft Exchange Server with no other mail systems used.

See Also: *heterogeneous network*

honey pot

A dummy server used to distract hackers from real targets.

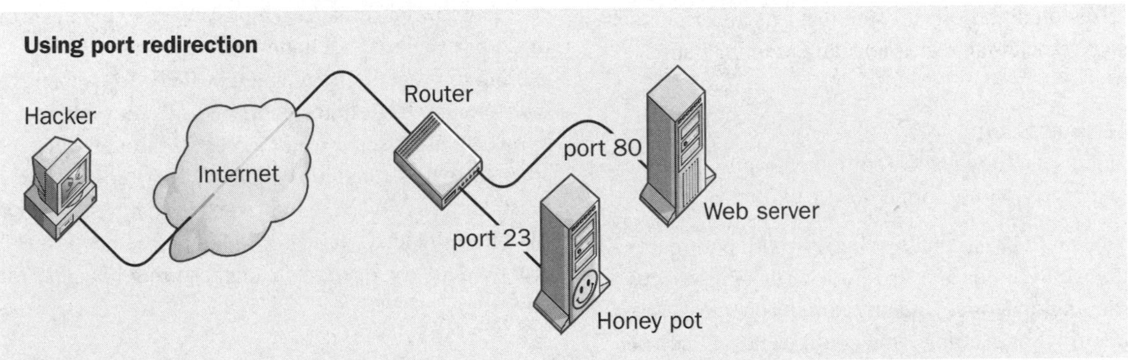

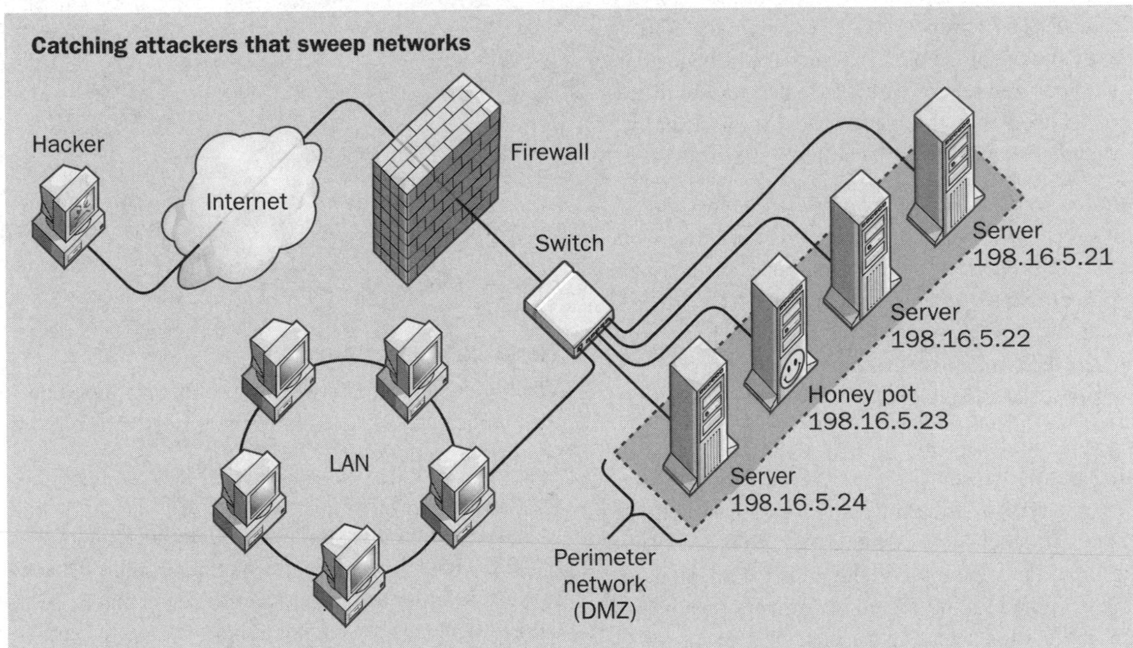

Honey pot. *Two ways of setting up honey pots to attract and catch hackers.*

Overview

A honey pot emulates a real server, with the goal of drawing hackers away from your actual production servers. For example, you could set up a dummy Web server, mail server, or authentication server as a honey pot. Honey pots should include

- Data that makes them attractive to a hacker. Typically, this could be a small sampling of real data, such as authentic Web pages or a few real user accounts (without their passwords, of course!).
- Intrusion detection software that logs all suspicious activity with the server and alerts administrators to it.

H

Implementation

There are several ways to deploy honey pots on the perimeter of your corporate network:

- You could use a router or firewall with port redirection configured to make it look as though services running on a honey pot are running on a real server instead. For example, you could set up a honey pot for a Web server, leaving only Transmission Control Protocol (TCP) port 80 (HTTP) open on the Web server and opening port 23 (Telnet) on the honey pot. Using port redirection, it looks to the attacker like port 23 is open on the Web server, but this actually redirects the attacker to the honey pot instead.
- Alternatively, to deal with attackers who sweep entire ranges of Internet Protocol (IP) addresses for vulnerabilities, you could set up a honey pot among a group of real servers having sequential IP addresses. When the attacker scans the network, the honey pot detects the scan and warns an administrator that a possible attack is underway.

Honey pots require resources to be dedicated to them and are essentially useless unless you have the time and personnel to analyze their intrusion logs and respond to their alerts. In other words, a honey pot that is set up and then ignored is worse than no honey pot at all. Honey pots are designed to provide administrators with information not just for detecting attacks, but also for tracking down those performing the attacks, but this requires skill and time to accomplish.

See Also: *firewall, router, security*

hood

Sometimes called a boot, the protective enclosure at the ends of cabling that houses the pins.

Overview

The hood protects the contacts between the cable's wires and the pins in the enclosed connector. The term *hood* is usually applied to serial cables for serial transmission interfaces such as RS-232 and V.35. The RJ-45 termination of unshielded twisted-pair (UTP) cabling and the SC termination of fiber-optic cabling are simply called connectors or jacks. Hoods are generally made of metal or plastic. Metal hoods are used on shielded cabling to provide shielding against electromagnetic interference (EMI) at the cable ends. Removable metal hoods are also used for running cable through tight spaces, such as conduits, or for repinning connections. Plastic hoods, which are less expensive, are used primarily on unshielded cabling. Molded plastic hoods are also used to provide durable, tamper-proof housings for pins.

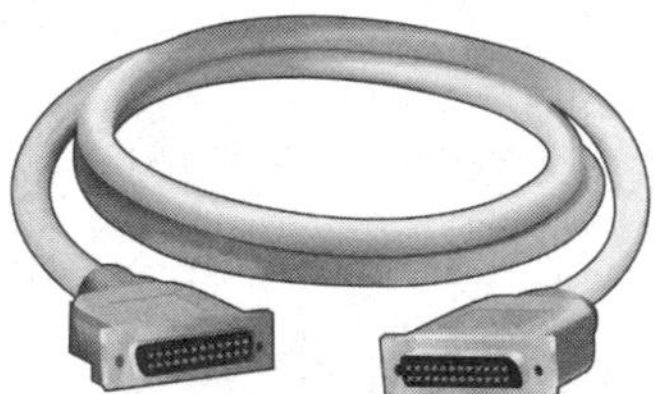

Hood. *An example of a hood.*

hop count

The logical distance between two networks based on the number of routers that must be traversed by packets sent between them.

Overview

In Transmission Control Protocol/Internet Protocol (TCP/IP) internetworking, the number of hops between two hosts would be the number of routers that an Internet Protocol (IP) packet would have to pass through in order to reach its destination.

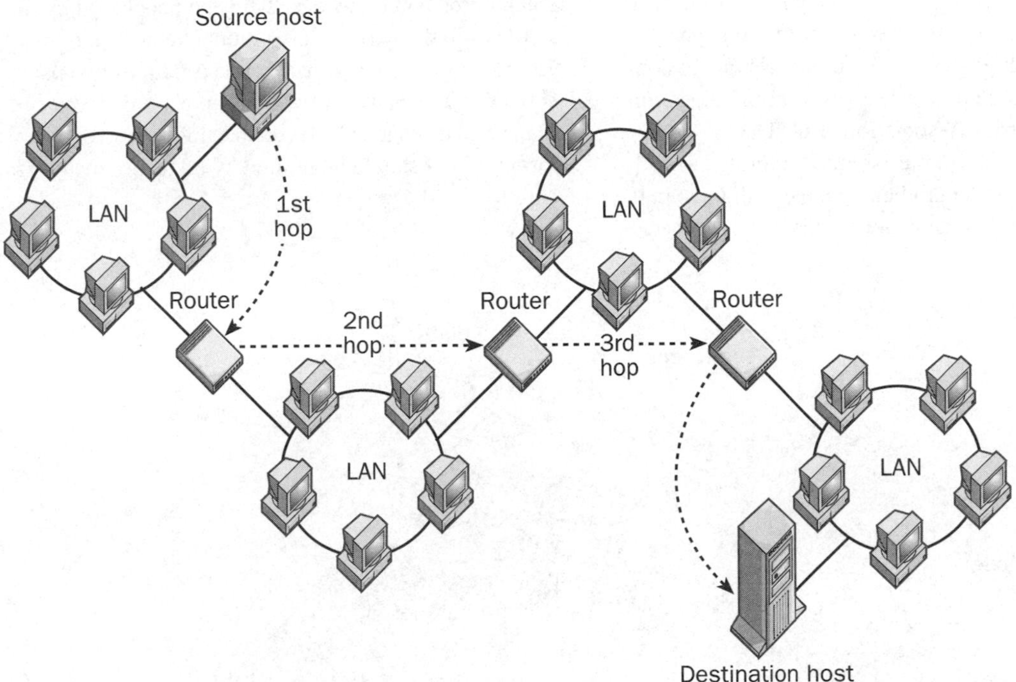

Hop count. *Two hosts that are three hops apart on an internetwork.*

The illustration shows a network path that is three hops long. As the packet travels from source to destination, the packet's header maintains information about the "hop count" (the number of hops traversed). This information is stored as a Time to Live (TTL) parameter within each packet that typically starts with a value of 128 and is decremented by 1 at each router (that is, after each hop). If router congestion delays the packet at a router, the TTL might be decremented by more than 1 to indicate this. If the TTL is decremented to 0 before the packet reaches its ultimate destination, the next router drops the packet and retransmission is required from the source host.

Uses

Hop counts are used by dynamic routers to determine the best route for forwarding data across a large internetwork. The route that has the smallest total number of hops is generally the best route for sending the data. Hop counts are also used to prevent packets from endlessly circulating around an internetwork by having packets dropped (discarded) once they reach a certain maximum hop count (that is, once the TTL decrements to zero).

Notes

In Microsoft Windows 2000, you can use the tracert command to watch the hop count decrease as an IP packet traverses an internetwork toward its destination.

See Also: *routing*

horizontal cabling

In premise cabling, any cabling that is used to connect a floor's wiring closet to wall plates in the work areas to provide local area network (LAN) drops for connecting users' computers to the network.

Overview

Horizontal cabling is usually installed in a star topology that connects each work area to the wiring closet, as shown in the illustration. Four-pair 100-ohm unshielded twisted-pair (UTP) cabling (Category 5 [Cat5] cabling or enhanced Category 5 [Cat5e] cabling) is usually recommended for new installations because it supports both voice and high-speed data transmission. To comply with Electronic Industries Association/Telecommunications Industries Association (EIA/TIA) wiring standards, individual cables should be limited to 295 feet (90 meters) in length between the wall plate in the work area and the patch panels in the wiring closet. Patch cords for connecting the patch panel to hubs and switches in the wiring closet should be no longer than 23 feet (7 meters) total, with a maximum of two patch cords per line, neither of which can exceed 19.7 feet (6 meters) in length. Cables connecting users' computers to wall plates should be limited to 9.8 feet (3 meters) in length.

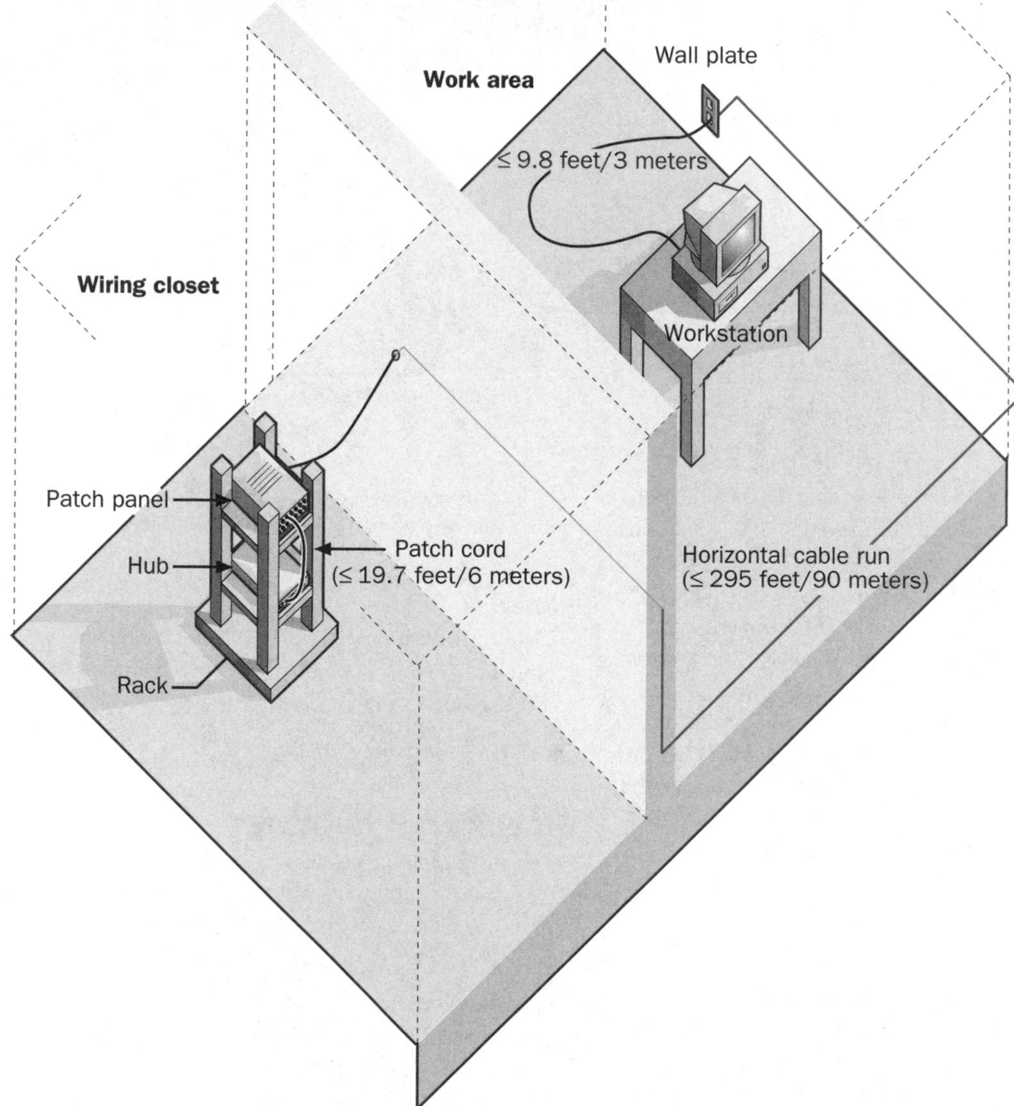

Horizontal cabling. *Deploying horizontal cabling to connect a work area to a wiring closet on the same floor.*

Horizontal cabling is most easily installed during construction or renovation of the building because proper installation might require opening false ceilings or walls. If this is not feasible, installing external cable trays and conduits might be the best solution because loose cables on the floor pose a hazard and should be avoided at all costs.

Notes

Avoid installing cables near motors, generators, transformers, or power lines in order to minimize electromagnetic interference (EMI). Keep cables away from photocopying machines and elevators because these machines generate a lot of EMI. If you anticipate increased bandwidth needs in the near future, use multimode fiber-optic cabling instead of unshielded twisted pair (UTP) cabling for horizontal cabling. You probably want to install two four-pair UTP cables in each work area, one for voice and the other for data transmission. Be sure to use the right kind of wall plates (RJ-11 for voice and RJ-45 for data).

See Also: *cabling, premise cabling, structured wiring*

host

Any device on a Transmission Control Protocol/Internet Protocol (TCP/IP) network that has an Internet Protocol (IP) address.

Overview

Examples of hosts include servers, workstations, network-interface print devices, and routers. The terms *node* and *host* are often used interchangeably in this regard. Sometimes the term *host* specifically means a device on a TCP/IP network that can both receive data and initiate contact with other devices. For example, a computer configured as a Simple Mail Transfer Protocol (SMTP) host receives e-mail messages and forwards them to their destination.

Notes

In mainframe computing environments, a host is a mainframe computer that is accessed by users through remote terminals.

See Also: *IP address, Transmission Control Protocol/Internet Protocol (TCP/IP)*

host bus adapter (HBA)

A device that converts Peripheral Component Interconnect (PCI) bus signals into Small Computer System Interface (SCSI) or Fibre Channel format.

Overview

Host bus adapters (HBAs) have traditionally been SCSI-based devices used in Storage Area Networks (SANs). They are also used in Fibre Channel SANs to provide connectivity with Gigabit Ethernet (GbE) networks. The Storage Network Industry Association is developing a proposed set of standard application programming interfaces (APIs) for HBAs to ensure interoperability between products from different vendors. With the emergence of the new Infiniband bus standard, things are likely to change and host bus adapters may decline in importance.

Marketplace

A number of vendors produce host bus adapters for storage networking, including Emulex Corporation, whose LightPulse and Giganet Fibre Channel PCI host bus adapter is a popular choice for enterprise SANs. One new development in this market is the recent marriage of high-speed switching technology with host bus adapters, represented by companies such as Qlogic Corporation.

See Also: *Fibre Channel, Infiniband (IB), storage area network (SAN)*

Host Data Replicator

A Microsoft Corporation database replication tool that copies data from legacy DB2 database tables on an IBM mainframe to Microsoft SQL Server database tables.

Overview

The Host Data Replicator consists of a data replicator service implemented as a service in Microsoft Windows NT and Windows 2000 plus an administrative tool called the Data Replication Manager. The Host Data Replicator performs the replication by taking a snapshot of the entire source table. It then either copies the entire snapshot to the target database table, overwriting any records in the existing target table, or appends the information to the target table, depending on how it is configured. The Host Data Replicator can also replicate SQL Server tables back to a DB2 database. The Host Data Replicator can copy data either on demand or according to a predefined schedule.

The Host Data Replicator is supported by Microsoft SNA Server version 3 and later and Microsoft SQL Server version 6.5 and later.

host header names

A feature of Hypertext Transfer Protocol version 1 (HTTP/1.1) that enables multiple Web sites to be hosted on the same Web server.

H

Overview

Host headers are supported by Microsoft Internet Information Services (IIS) and allow multiple Web sites having the same Internet Protocol (IP) address and HTTP port number to be hosted on the same Web server. Web browsers such as Microsoft Internet Explorer also support host header names and can access such IIS Web sites seamlessly. Web browsers that support host header names include Internet Explorer 3 and later or Netscape Navigator 3 and later.

Implementation

To configure multiple Web sites on an IIS server to share one IP address and use host header names for client access to them, perform the following steps:

1. Open the property sheet for each virtual server in Internet Services Manager.
2. Select the Web Site tab and specify the IP address and port number (usually port 80), or select All Unassigned if your server has only one IP address.
3. Click the Advanced button, select the identity you want to use from the Multiple Identities For This Web Site list, and add a host header name. Note that each identity can have only one host header name, but each virtual server can have multiple identities.
4. Register the host header name with your Domain Name System (DNS) server or Internet service provider (ISP).

Once the IIS server and DNS name resolution environments are configured properly, a Web browser that supports host header names, such as Internet Explorer 4 and later, can use these names to access different virtual servers that have the same IP address and port number and are located on the same machine running IIS. The browser makes an HTTP 1.1–compliant GET request, which contains in its header the host header name being requested.

Notes

IIS 4 and later also support host header names for older noncompliant browsers through the mechanism of cookies. For very old browsers that do not support cookies, a tool in the IIS Resource Kit called the Cookie Munger enables these browsers to access such sites on IIS 4 as well.

Do not create host header names for the Default Web Site because this might affect other services installed on the server that expect the Default Web Site to have no host header names.

See Also: *Hypertext Transfer Protocol (HTTP), IP address, Web server*

host ID

The portion of an Internet Protocol (IP) address that uniquely identifies a host on a given Transmission Control Protocol/Internet Protocol (TCP/IP) network.

Overview

You can determine the host ID from a host's IP address by logically NANDing the binary form of the IP address with the binary form of the subnet mask for the network. The remaining part of an IP address is the network ID, which specifies the network to which the host belongs.

For example, if a host has an IP address of 172.16.8.55 on a network with a subnet mask of 255.255.0.0 (the default subnet mask), the host ID is 0.0.8.55 or simply 8.55. The host ID uniquely identifies the host but only within the boundary of the network ID for the network on which the host is installed.

See Also: *IP address, network ID*

Host Integration Server

Microsoft Corporation's gateway and application integration platform.

Overview

Microsoft Host Integration Server 2000 is the successor to Microsoft's previous BackOffice gateway platform, SNA Server. Host Integration Server is part of the new .NET Enterprise Server platform and provides access to applications and data stores on IBM mainframe and AS/400 platforms. Host Integration Server supports network interoperability between Microsoft Windows 2000 client/server networks and Systems Network Architecture (SNA)-based mainframe computing platforms. Host Integration Server helps enterprises maximize their existing investments in legacy mainframe systems while leveraging the power of the Windows 2000 Server platform.

Features of Host Integration Server include

- Enterprise scalability with support for up to 30,000 simultaneous host sessions per server
- Load balancing and hot failover for mission-critical reliability
- Seamless access by clients to host-based file, print, and application services
- Industry-standard clients plus Web-deployable 3270 and 5250 clients based on Microsoft ActiveX technology
- Turnkey gateway solutions for host-to-Internet and host-to-intranet connectivity
- Support for Microsoft Message Queue (MSMQ) and COM+ object-oriented development
- Drag-and-drop integration between Microsoft Transaction Server and IBM's CICS and IMS transactional development environments
- Object-oriented access to DB2 and flat file databases on hosts
- Support for virtual private networking (VPN) and single sign-on
- Integration with Microsoft SQL Server 2000, BizTalk Server 2000, and Commerce Server 2000

For More Information

Find out more about Host Integration Server at *www.microsoft.com/hiserver.*

See Also: *.NET Enterprise Servers*

host name

An alias given to a computer on a Transmission Control Protocol/Internet Protocol (TCP/IP) network to identify it on the network.

Overview

Host names are a friendlier way of identifying TCP/IP hosts than Internet Protocol (IP) addresses. Host names can be resolved into IP addresses by host name resolution using either a Domain Name System (DNS) server or the hosts file. Host names can include the characters a–z, A–Z, 0–9, period, and dash (-). To ensure full compatibility with DNS, do not use any other special characters in host names.

Notes

To find out the host name of a computer running any version of Microsoft Windows, type Hostname at the command prompt.

See Also: *Domain Name System (DNS), host name resolution, hosts file*

host name resolution

The process by which a host determines the Internet Protocol (IP) address of another host on a Transmission Control Protocol/Internet Protocol (TCP/IP) network given its host name or fully qualified domain name (FQDN).

Overview

Suppose you go to the command prompt of a machine running Microsoft Windows 2000 and type **ping** followed by a host name or FQDN of another host on the network. The host name or FQDN of the target host must first be resolved into its IP address before the TCP/IP utility ping can occur. This process is called host name resolution.

A number of different methods can be used to perform host name resolution. The following table shows the order in which these are attempted on a Microsoft network. The methods are tried in succession until the host name is resolved into its IP address or until name resolution finally fails. Some methods will not be available—for example, if there is no Domain Name System (DNS) server or NetBIOS Name Server (NBNS) on the network.

Host Name Resolution Methods in the Order Applied

Host Name Resolution Methods	*Comments*
Check whether the target host is the local host.	The local host knows its own host name!
Check local hosts file.	This check is performed only if a hosts file has been configured.
Contact DNS server.	This check is performed only if the DNS tab of the TCP/IP property sheet has a DNS server specified on it. The local host tries again at intervals of 5, 10, 20, and 40 seconds.
Check local NetBIOS name cache. (Unique to Microsoft networks.)	The cache contains recently resolved NetBIOS names. (On Microsoft networks, NetBIOS names and host names are usually the same.)
Contact NBNS. (Unique to Microsoft networks.)	This check is performed if NBNS has been configured by creating a Windows Internet Name Service (WINS) record within the DNS database. On a Microsoft network, this is usually a WINS server. The local host tries three times to contact the WINS server and then tries the secondary WINS server three times.
Perform local broadcast. (Unique to Microsoft networks.)	Local host broadcasts a NetBIOS name query request packet three times.
Check local lmhosts file. (Unique to Microsoft networks.)	This check is performed if a lmhosts file has been configured.

If all methods fail, an error message states that the computer could not be found on the network.

Notes

There is a separate series of steps for attempting to resolve NetBIOS names on a network that uses WINS. For more information, see the entry "NetBIOS name resolution" elsewhere in this book.

See Also: *Domain Name System (DNS), host name*

host routing

The routing process that occurs when a host (computer) on a network forwards a packet to a destination host on the network.

Overview

Host routing is different from router routing, which is what happens when a router receives a packet that needs to be forwarded to a destination host. Host routing essentially involves a simple decision: should the packet be forwarded directly to its destination host, or should it be forwarded to a router? The host makes this decision by comparing the packet's destination address with entries in its internal routing table.

To perform host routing, the host must first obtain the internetwork address of the destination host using some form of name resolution. For example, in order for a host to forward a packet to a remote host called northwind.microsoft.com, it could first use the Domain Name System (DNS) to obtain the Internet Protocol (IP) address of the remote host. The host then compares this address with entries in its internal routing table to determine whether the destination has a local or remote network address. If the address is a local network address, the host forwards the packet directly to its destination using the physical layer or physical address of the remote host. This process is known as direct delivery. On Transmission Control Protocol/Internet Protocol (TCP/IP) networks, the physical address of a host is its MAC address, which is obtained by using the Address Resolution Protocol (ARP).

If, however, the host determines that the destination host has a remote network address (that is, the destination host is on a different network than the sending host), the host forwards the packet to a nearby router after first obtaining the physical address of the near-side interface of the router. This process is known as indirect delivery. It is the router's responsibility to ensure that the packet is forwarded toward its destination, although in a typical internetwork the destination might be several hops away, in which case the router's responsibility extends only to the next hop on the path.

See Also: *Address Resolution Protocol (ARP), Domain Name System (DNS), hop count, IP address, router, routing*

hosts file

A text file that provides a local method for name resolution of Internet Protocol (IP) hosts.

Overview

A hosts file can be used to resolve a host name or fully qualified domain name (FQDN) into its associated IP address. Hosts files are a local alternative to using distributed Domain Name System (DNS) name servers for performing name resolution on Transmission Control Protocol/Internet Protocol (TCP/IP) networks. Hosts files are used mainly on small networks where maintaining a DNS server is impractical or as a backup in case no name servers are available to perform name lookups.

History

Hosts files predated the DNS as a name resolution method. During the 1970s, when the ARPANET, the Internet's precursor, consisted of only a few hundred different hosts, using hosts files was a relatively painless way of enabling name resolution to be performed. When someone added a new host to the network, they would e-mail the Network Information Center (NIC), which would update the information in their master hosts file stored on a server called SRI-NIC. Users around the ARPANET typically checked this server a few times each week to see if an updated hosts file was updated and if so would download it to their own hosts using File Transfer Protocol (FTP).

When the ARPANET migrated to TCP/IP in the early 1980s, the number of hosts exploded and a new method of name resolution had to be found. This new method had to overcome the problems with hosts: it scaled poorly, had no automated process for registering new hosts, and had no way of pushing out updates from the master hosts file server. The result was the development of DNS, a distributed name resolution service that is still in use and forms the backbone of communications on the Internet.

Implementation

Hosts files consist of a series of FQDN-to-IP address mappings, one per line. Each line in the hosts file contains the IP address of a host followed by the FQDN of the host, followed by an optional comment prefixed with a pound sign (#). Hosts files should contain mappings for hosts on both local and remote networks. Mappings can consist of an IP address and one or more host names (aliases). If you are using hosts files to resolve host names on a network, each computer on the network should have a hosts file.

On a UNIX system, the hosts table is found in /etc/hosts, and on Microsoft Windows 2000, Windows XP, and Windows .NET Server systems, it is located in the %SystemRoot%\system32\ drivers\etc\Hosts directory.

Notes

Although DNS has largely eliminated the need for maintaining hosts files, they are still useful in two scenarios:

- On small TCP/IP networks not connected to the Internet, it may be easier to maintain a hosts file than to run a DNS server.
- Hosts files can be used as a backup in case DNS goes down. Typically, you would keep the hosts file small in this case, adding only entries for your servers and for gateways to remote networks, plus a line for localhost, which maps to 127.0.0.1, the loopback address for testing IP communications.

Notes

Place the host names that need to be most frequently resolved near the top of the hosts file because the file is parsed linearly from the beginning.

See Also: *lmhosts file, Networks file, protocol file, services file*

hot

An adjective referring to actions that can be performed on systems or hardware devices while the power for the device is still turned on or while the device still has a live network connection or telecommunications link.

Overview

"Hot" networking and system technologies are used in

- Fault-tolerant disk drive systems such as redundant array of independent disks (RAID) systems
- Redundant power supply systems
- Modular Ethernet switches and routers
- Redundant high-speed data communication links

Examples of disk storage systems that use "hot" technologies include the following:

- **Hot-rebuild system:** A drive subsystem that can automatically rebuild its original drive configuration after drive failure
- **Hot-spare system:** A drive subsystem that has additional unused drives that can be called into action when drive failure occurs
- **Hot-swap system:** A drive subsystem in which drives are mounted on trays and can be removed and replaced without shutting down the system

For example, when you buy a hardware RAID unit, you might want to be sure that it has hot-rebuild, hot-spare, and hot-swap capabilities.

hotfix

A fix for a bug in an application or operating system.

Overview

Hotfix is a term used by Microsoft Corporation to describe a software patch issued to correct a problem with a version of Microsoft Windows or a Microsoft application. For the BackOffice platform, hotfixes are now called Quick Fix Engineering (QFE).

Generally, you should apply a hotfix (QFE) only if you are experiencing a problem related to an issue the hotfix is designed to correct. In other words, if you are not experiencing the problem described in the documentation for a hotfix, it is generally best to wait for the next release of a service pack (a group of hotfixes applied in one shot) instead of applying the hotfix individually. This is especially true of hotfixes that have not been "regression tested," that is, whose interaction with other software is currently uncertain.

Some hotfixes are made available publicly through Microsoft's File Transfer Protocol (FTP) site. Others are only available from Microsoft Product Support Services (PSS) and require a support agreement to be in place before downloading them.

For More Information

You can find current hotfixes for Microsoft products at *ftp.microsoft.com.*

See Also: *service pack*

Hot Standby Router Protocol (HSRP)

A proprietary Cisco technology for implementing fault-tolerant routing.

Overview

Hot Standby Router Protocol (HSRP) was developed by Cisco Systems as a way of providing fault tolerance for routed internetworks. Normally, when a router goes down, routing protocols communicate this fact to all the routers on the network, which then reconfigure their routing tables to select alternate routes to avoid the downed router. The problem is that the process of convergence, the updating of all routing tables on the network, is slow and can take some time to complete. HSRP was designed to work around this problem of slow convergence by allowing a standby router take over from a router that has gone down and fill its role in a manner completely transparent to hosts on the network.

HSRP is outlined in RFC 2281 but is a proprietary standard and not an Internet Engineering Task Force (IETF) standard. The IETF has proposed its own vendor-independent fault-tolerant routing technology called Virtual Router Redundancy Protocol (VRRP), which is documented in RFC 2338.

Implementation

HSRP works by creating virtual groups that consist of two routers, an active router and a standby router. HSRP creates one virtual router in place of each pair of actual routers, and hosts need only to have their gateway address pointed to the virtual router. When a host forwards an Internet Protocol (IP) packet to its default gateway (the virtual router), it is actually handled by the active router. Should the active router go down, the standby router steps in and continues to forward packets it receives. To IP hosts on the network, the virtual router acts as a real router and everything works transparently whether the active or standby router actually does the forwarding.

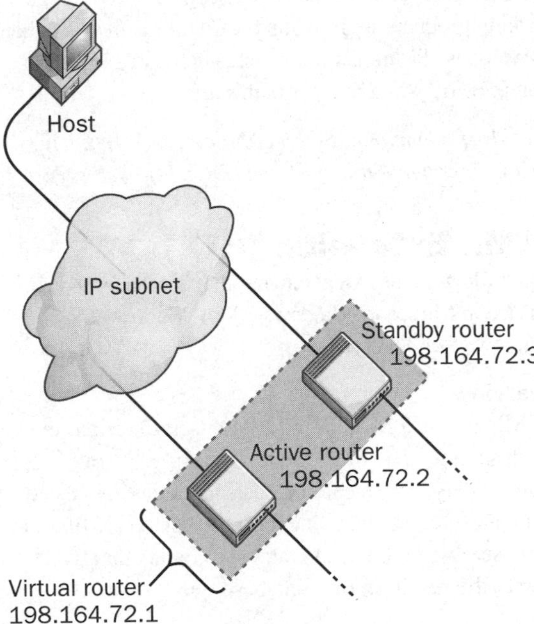

Hot Standby Router Protocol (HSRP). *How HSRP works.*

HSRP allows for complex arrangements of virtual routers. For example, actual routers can belong to more than one virtual group, and there can be up to 255 virtual groups on the network. HSRP can also be used to provide backup default gateways for hosts capable of addressing only a single default gateway.

See Also: *default gateway, router, routing*

HPFS

Stands for High Performance File System, a file system designed for version 1.2 of the Microsoft/IBM OS/2 operating system as a successor to the file allocation table (FAT) file system used by MS-DOS.

See: *High Performance File System (HPFS)*

HP-UX

Hewlett-Packard's version of the UNIX operating system platform.

Overview

HP-UX is the only version of UNIX that supports application development on UNIX, Linux, and Microsoft Windows platforms. The most recent version HP-UX 11i includes such features as

- Support for 4 gigabytes (GB) of addressable RAM
- Integrated Apache Web server software
- Lightweight Directory Access Protocol (LDAP)–compliant Internet directory services
- Inktomi Internet caching software
- Ultraseek search engine from Infoseek
- Linux application programming interfaces (APIs) and GNU's Not UNIX (GNU) tools
- Nokia Wireless Application Protocol (WAP) server software
- Internet load balancing software from Resonate

For More Information

Visit Hewlett-Packard online at *www.hp.com.*

See Also: *Linux, UNIX*

HSCSD

Stands for High-Speed Circuit Switched Data, an interim upgrade for Global System for Mobile Communications (GSM) cellular communications systems.

See: *High-Speed Circuit Switched Data (HSCSD)*

HSM

Stands for Hierarchical Storage Management, a data storage system for archiving infrequently needed data while still making it easily available.

See: *Hierarchical Storage Management (HSM)*

HSRP

Stands for Hot Standby Router Protocol, a proprietary Cisco protocol for implementing fault-tolerant routing.

See: *Hot Standby Router Protocol (HSRP)*

HSSI

Stands for High-Speed Serial Interface, a serial interface that supports speeds up to 52 megabits per second (Mbps).

See: *High-Speed Serial Interface (HSSI)*

HSTR

Stands for High-Speed Token Ring, a 100 megabits per second (Mbps) version of Token Ring that never got off the ground.

See: *High-Speed Token Ring (HSTR)*

HTML

Stands for Hypertext Markup Language, a formatting or markup language used to create documents for the World Wide Web (WWW).

See: *Hypertext Markup Language (HTML)*

HTMLA

Stands for HTML-based administration, a method for remotely administering Microsoft Internet Information Services (IIS) Web servers.

See: *HTML-based administration (HTMLA)*

HTML-based administration (HTMLA)

A method for remotely administering Microsoft Internet Information Services (IIS) Web servers.

Overview

HTML-based administration (HTMLA) allows administrators to manage IIS Web servers using a standard Web browser such as Microsoft Internet Explorer as the client-side interface. IIS supports administration using HTMLA from any Web browser that supports the use of frames and JScript.

HTMLA is based on Microsoft Corporation's Component Object Model (COM) and Distributed Component Object Model (DCOM) programming architectures. The purpose of HTMLA is to simplify remote management of network resources and services by requiring that client machines used for remote administration of Web servers need only be running a standard Web browser. Most of today's networking products are moving toward one form or another of Web-based administration, and Microsoft's HTMLA feature of IIS was a pioneer in this area.

See Also: *Component Object Model (COM), Distributed Component Object Model (DCOM), Web server*

HTML Extension (HTX)

A text file with the extension .htx that is used by Indexing Service in Microsoft Windows 2000, Windows XP, and Windows .NET Server.

Overview

HTML Extension (HTX) files are used to format the result set issued by Index Server in response to a catalog search query. These catalog search queries are issued using an Internet Data Query (IDQ) file. HTX files are also used by the Internet Database Connector (IDC) to format the result set of a database query.

The .htx file formats the result set of a query into a Hypertext Markup Language (HTML) page that the user who issued the query can read and understand. The .htx file acts as a template for formatting the result set and consists of HTML statements with additional tags and specific read-only variables such as

- CiMatchedRecordCount, which contains the number of records that match the query
- CiRecordsPerPage, which indicates the number of records on the next page

- CiContainsFirstRecord, which is 1 if the page contains the first record of query results and 0 otherwise

HTTP

Stands for Hypertext Transfer Protocol, a protocol that defines how Web browsers communicate and download information from Web servers.

See: *Hypertext Transfer Protocol (HTTP)*

HTTP Keep-Alives

An enhanced version of Hypertext Transfer Protocol (HTTP)–persistent connections supported by Microsoft Internet Information Services (IIS).

Overview

HTTP Keep-Alives allow a client Web browser to keep connections open with the Web server instead of closing them after the request has been answered and reopening them for each new Hypertext Transfer Protocol (HTTP) request, which consumes system resources. For this feature to work, however, both the client Web browser and the Web server must support HTTP Keep-Alives. Web browsers that support this feature include Microsoft Internet Explorer version 2 and later and Netscape Navigator 2 and later.

Notes

HTTP Keep-Alives are enabled by default in IIS. They are not the same as Transmission Control Protocol (TCP) Keep-Alives, which are periodic packets sent between machines to determine whether an idle connection is still active.

HTTPS

A secure version of Hypertext Transfer Protocol (HTTP).

Overview

Hypertext Transfer Protocol Secure (HTTPS) is essentially a combination of HTTP and the Secure Sockets Layer (SSL) protocol, and the designation *HTTPS* comes from the combination of the words *HTTP* and *secure*. HTTPS was originally developed by Netscape to enable the secure transmission of Web content over the Internet.

HTTPS is based on a public key cryptography system and allows information transmitted over the Internet to be encrypted for greater security. To run HTTPS on a Web server, you must first install a digital certificate on the server. Web browsers then connect to the server by providing a Uniform Resource Locator (URL) that begins with the prefix https:// rather than http://, which is usually used. HTTPS uses the TCP well-known port number 443 instead of port 80, which is used by standard HTTP.

Notes

Note that HTTPS is not the same as Secure Hypertext Transfer Protocol (S-HTTP), another protocol for secure HTTP transmission.

See Also: *Hypertext Transfer Protocol (HTTP), Secure Sockets Layer (SSL)*

HTTP status codes

Codes that Hypertext Transfer Protocol (HTTP) servers return in response to requests from HTTP clients.

Overview

HTTP status codes are three-digit codes that Web servers return in response to HTTP requests from clients. They are also known as HTTP error codes because most of them signify that some sort of error has occurred. An HTTP status code is one of the first pieces of information returned by a Web server in response to a request from a Web browser, and it informs the browser of the status of the request—whether the request was successful or not, and if not, why. When the server cannot satisfy the client's request for some reason, a status code is returned to the client, which displays it for purposes of troubleshooting the problem. The client typically displays a message along with the status code to help the user understand the nature of the problem.

HTTP status codes are grouped into different categories by their first digit, as shown in the table on the following page.

HTTP Status Codes by Category

Status Code	*Category*	*Description*
1*xx*	Informational	An acknowledgement message from the server.
2*xx*	Success	The requested action was understood and completed.
3*xx*	Redirection	Further action must be taken to fulfill the request.
4*xx*	Client error	The request could not be performed because of client error.
5*xx*	Server error	The request could not be performed because of server error.

Examples

Some common status codes that are fairly self-explanatory include the following:

- 200 OK (not seen by the client)
- 301 Moved Permanently
- 400 Bad Request
- 401 Unauthorized
- 403 Forbidden
- 404 File Not Found
- 500 Internal Server Error

Notes

Web servers running Microsoft Internet Information Services (IIS) allow administrators to create customized HTTP status code pages that can be considerably more informative to users than traditional status codes such as "403 Forbidden."

See Also: *Hypertext Transfer Protocol (HTTP), Web server*

HTX

Stands for HTML Extension, a text file with the extension .htx that is used by Indexing Service in Windows 2000, Windows XP, and Windows .NET Server.

See: *HTML Extension (HTX)*

hub

A device used to connect shared Ethernet segments into a single local area network (LAN).

Overview

Hubs are the foundation of traditional 10/100BaseT shared Ethernet networks. They can be used to connect several dozen computers together to form a workgroup LAN, or they can be cascaded to create larger LANs of up to a hundred computers or more. Hubs typically have 4, 8, 12, or 24 ports for connecting stations using unshielded twisted pair (UTP) cabling terminated with RJ-45 connectors.

When a hub receives a signal from a station connected to a port, it repeats the signals to all other stations connected to the hub's ports (hence the alternative name "multiport repeater" is sometimes used to describe a hub). From a logical cabling point of view, stations wired into a hub form a star topology with the hub at the center and the stations at the points of the star. The physical topology of a hub, however, is bus topology, and all stations connected to a hub share the same bus connection.

Hubs were originally passive devices that simply repeated signals, but today's hubs are active hubs in which the signal received from one port is regenerated (amplified) and retransmitted to the other ports on the hub. Hubs typically have one or more uplink ports that are used for connecting the hub to other hubs in a cascaded star topology. You connect an uplink port on one hub to a regular port on another hub using a standard UTP cable. Alternatively, you can connect two hubs using the uplink ports by using a crossover cable.

Hubs generally have light-emitting diode (LED) indicator lights to indicate the status of each port, link status, collisions, and other information. Hubs with several different types of LAN connectors such as RJ-45, BNC, and AUI are commonly called combo hubs.

Types

There are numerous types of hubs for various specialized uses. These include the following:

- **Minihubs:** These typically have only four to eight ports and are used for quick or temporary LAN extensions. Minihubs can be as small as a cigarette pack and are often used for home area networks (HANs).

Stackable Hubs

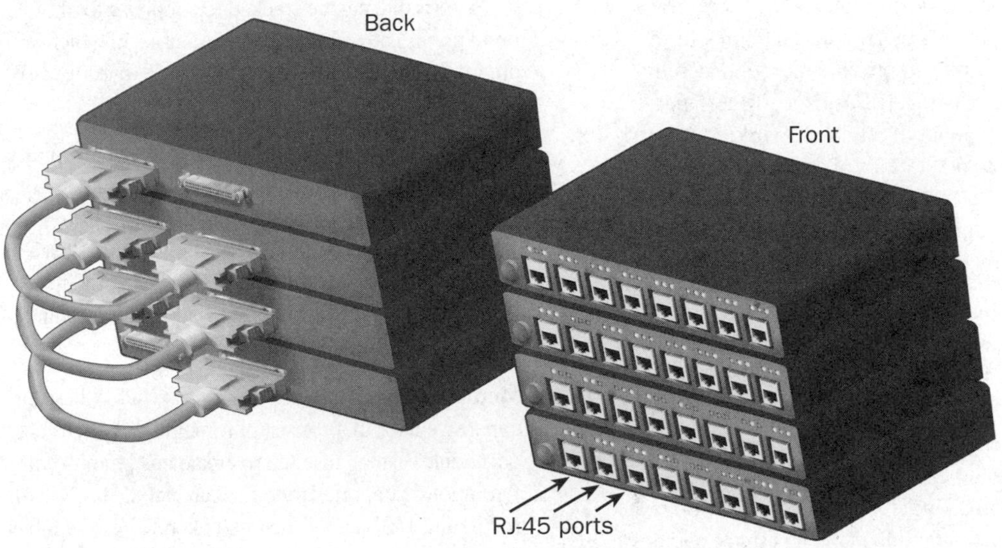

Using Hubs

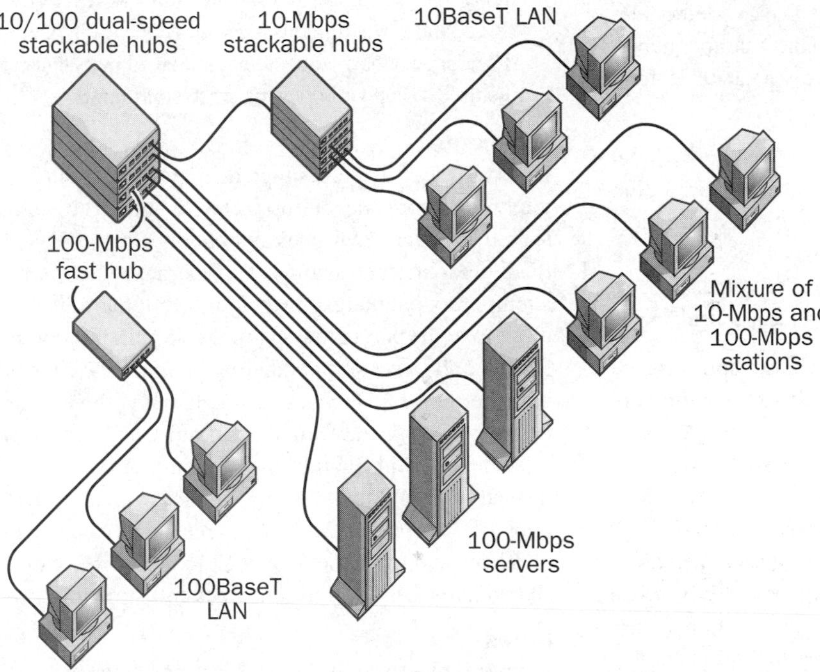

Hub. *Stackable hubs and a diagram of hubs at work.*

- **Workgroup hubs:** These are the basic building blocks for creating workgroup LANs. Workgroup hubs typically have 8 or 16 ports on them, plus a BNC or an AUI port to provide more connectivity options within existing 10Base2 or 10Base5 networks. A hub is generally termed a workgroup hub if it supports up to 50 stations, a departmental hub if it supports up to 250 stations, and an enterprise hub if it supports more than 250 stations. Stackable hubs can also be used to provide these various capabilities.
- **Stackable hubs:** These hubs are modular in design and can be mounted in racks and cabinets within the wiring closet. The backplanes of stackable hubs can be connected together using special ribbon or DB-50 cables. Stackable hubs are available in configurations of 8, 16, and 24 ports and can be stacked to effectively form a single hub with 48, 72, 144, or more ports. Stackable hubs take less space and are easier to manage than regular workgroup hubs. Most stackable hubs also have an uplink switch that can be used to convert one of the ports into an additional uplink port, allowing you to connect another hub directly to the port. The opposite of a stackable hub is a simple stand-alone hub.
- **Intelligent hubs:** Also called managed hubs, these can be remotely managed and monitored using Simple Network Management Protocol (SNMP). Special connectors on the back of advanced hubs might provide features such as an RS-232 serial interface for connecting to an SNMP management console.
- **Dual-speed hubs:** These have autosensing ports that support combinations of both 100-megabit-per-second (Mbps) Fast Ethernet connections and 10-Mbps traditional Ethernet connections. Each port senses the speed of the attached station and configures itself to function at the appropriate speed. Advanced dual-speed hubs often contain internal Ethernet switch circuitry that segments the 10-Mbps and 100-Mbps connections into separate collision domains and forwards data between the domains to improve overall performance. These advanced hubs are sometimes called master hubs, and only one of these is required in a mixed 10/100-Mbps LAN.

  Dual-speed hubs are typically stackable hubs with 8 or 16 ports that can be stacked to support a total of 32 or 48 ports. They are useful in situations in which you are gradually migrating from 10BaseT to 100BaseT.
- **Fast Ethernet hubs:** These have 100-Mbps ports only for creating 100BaseT LANs. They are usually stackable hubs with advanced SNMP management functions, and they may also have built-in Ethernet switching functions. Often you can mix 100BaseTX and 100BaseT4 hubs in a stack that supports up to 144 stations, including fiber-optic ports for connecting to a high-speed fiber-optic backbone.
- **Modular hubs:** Also called enterprise hubs, these are expensive hubs that consist of a chassis in which cards or modules can be inserted to create custom hub configurations. Supported modules can include LAN cards for 10 and 100BaseT Ethernet, Token Ring, and Fiber Distributed Data Interface (FDDI); and wide area network (WAN) modules can include cards for frame relay, Integrated Services Digital Network (ISDN), X.25, and Asynchronous Transfer Mode (ATM). Enterprise hubs are intelligent, managed hubs that can be used to build complex network configurations.

Prospects

Hubs have largely been supplanted by switches in today's enterprise-level Ethernet networks. Although a shared hub receives frames and blindly forwards them to all other attached stations, an Ethernet switch forms a temporary internal pathway to transmit the frame directly to the port belonging to the destination station. Shared hubs were still popular in the mid-1990s when price per port for switches was high, but with switch prices now comparable to those of hubs, any new enterprise deployment should consist mainly of switches instead of hubs. About the only remaining places where hubs can sensibly be deployed are in small workgroup scenarios and for home networks. In most other cases shared hubs usually represent a bad investment.

Notes

A device called a wiring concentrator or Multistation Access Unit (MAU) is similar to a hub but is used in Token Ring networks. Another device called a patch panel is used to organize UTP cabling in structured wiring implementations. Do not confuse either of these devices with a hub.

See Also: *10BaseT, 100BaseT, Ethernet, Ethernet switch*

HybridAuth

An authentication protocol proposed by the Internet Engineering Task Force (IETF) for Virtual Private Networking (VPN).

Overview

To deploy a secure VPN, companies must implement a public key infrastructure (PKI) for issuing and managing digital certificates. But deploying a PKI is complex, and the IETF has proposed a new protocol called HybridAuth to simplify the process.

The HybridAuth protocol is an extension to the Internet Key Exchange (IKE) protocol that defines how a user's credentials are exchanged over secure IPsec tunnels. IKE supports tunneling of two forms of authentication: digital certificates and preshared keys. HybridAuth enables digital certificates to be used asymmetrically between users and authentication servers and is simpler to deploy than a full-scale PKI solution.

See Also: *digital certificate, public key infrastructure (PKI), virtual private network (VPN)*

HyperTerminal

A communication utility included with Microsoft Windows that provides terminal access to remote computers using a modem.

Overview

HyperTerminal can be used to send and receive files between a local and remote computer over a modem and to connect to remote computer bulletin board systems. Network administrators can also use HyperTerminal to remotely connect to routers, switches, and other devices that support VT100 terminal emulation, and to enter text commands for configuring the device.

If you want to access files and printers on a remote computer running Windows 2000, Windows XP, or Windows .NET Server using a modem, use Network and Dial-Up Connections instead of HyperTerminal.

See Also: *router*

Hypertext Markup Language (HTML)

A formatting or markup language used to create documents for the World Wide Web (WWW).

Overview

Hypertext Markup Language (HTML) is the standard formatting language used to publish information on Web servers for delivery to Web browsers over the Internet. HTML allows linked sets of documents (that is, hypertext) to be created, stored, and accessed from Web servers using Uniform Resource Locators (URLs). HTML is simple to learn and was a key enabler in the explosion of the Internet in the 1990s.

History

HTML was created together with Hypertext Transfer Protocol (HTTP) in 1991 by Tim Berners-Lee as a means of disseminating information more easily among physicists and other scientists at CERN, the European Laboratory for Particle Physics. HTML was designed as a simplified version of Standardized Generalized Markup Language (SGML), a much more complicated formatting language that was developed previously but never widely implemented. HTML was created by combining the concept of hypertext, a concept created in the 1940s for linking documents together, with URLs, a method of uniquely naming hypertext documents so they could be easily accessed regardless of which servers they reside on. HTTP provides the additional protocol for communications between clients (called HTTP clients or Web browsers) and the servers (called Web servers or HTTP servers) on which HTML documents are stored.

In 1993, Marc Andreesen developed Mosaic at the National Center for Supercomputing Applications (NCSA). Mosaic was the first Web browser that supported documents containing both text and graphics (previous Web browsers supported only text documents). Andreesen left the NCSA to cofound Netscape Communications (now just Netscape), which produced the popular Netscape Navigator browser. Meanwhile, Microsoft Corporation licensed code from Mosaic through the commercial outlet Spyglass and developed its own popular browser, Microsoft Internet Explorer. Both Netscape and Microsoft pushed the evolution of HTML by introducing their own proprietary extension tags, the first being the

H

<font> tag from Netscape. The result was that HTML rapidly developed through several versions, including

- **HTML 2:** This was defined by RFC 1866 in 1995 and included various additional tags developed by Netscape and Microsoft.
- **HTTP 3.2:** Developed in 1996, this included support for tables, text flow around images, and other features.
- **HTTP 4:** Developed in 1997, this included support for style sheets that made <font> and other tags unnecessary (although they are still supported for backward compatibility).

H

To steer the evolution of HTML and prevent different vendor-specific versions from emerging, Berners-Lee formed the World Wide Web Consortium (W3C) in 1994. HTML 3.2 was the first version of HTML standardized by the W3C. Current work on HTML by the W3C involves development of the XHTML standard, a version of HTML written as an Extensible Markup Language (XML) application instead of an SGML one. The complementary HTTP protocol is standardized by a different group from the W3C, namely the Internet Engineering Task Force (IETF).

HTML has gone through several versions since it was created. At the time of this writing, the current version is HTML 4. The original HTML did not provide much control over how documents were formatted—that is, how objects such as text and graphics were laid out on a page. Its original set of tags was quite limited and was intended primarily for linking documents using hyperlinks to form hypertext. As the Web grew in popularity, however, first Netscape and then Microsoft introduced their own proprietary HTML tags to provide Web developers with more control over document formatting, thus increasing the pace at which the W3C developed the HTML standard. HTML 4 includes standards for creating cascading style sheets, which provides powerful formatting capabilities for precise placement of objects on a Web page.

Implementation

HTML in its simplest form uses tags to format ASCII text documents. These tags then indicate text that should be displayed as boldface, italic, bulleted, hyperlinked, and centered. HTML tags usually come in pairs, can be nested, can contain additional attributes, and are used to "mark up" the text. For example, the text "Save 50%" can be displayed on Web browsers in boldface by marking it up using the <STRONG> tag (which means "turn on the bold style") and the </STRONG> tag (which means "turn off the bold style"). The resulting HTML would look like this:

```
<STRONG>Save 50%</STRONG>
```

HTML pages can be created using a broad range of tools from simple text editors such as Notepad to advanced publishing tools such as Microsoft FrontPage. HTML pages are saved as files with the extension .htm or .html to indicate they contain HTML text. Once created, HTML pages can be stored on Web servers such as Microsoft Windows 2000 servers running Microsoft Internet Information Services (IIS). When a Web browser such as Internet Explorer downloads an HTML page from a Web server, it interprets the tags and displays the document with the appropriate formatting.

Advantages and Disadvantages

The main advantage of HTML is its simplicity—a child can learn enough HTML to create a simple Web page. Because HTML was originally intended for exchanging information between scientists, support for formatting documents was initially limited. As the Web became more popular, new tags were introduced which made snazzy-looking documents possible. Together with style sheets, HTML documents can now be as complex in their formatting as documents produced for desktop publishing.

The main disadvantages of HTML are that it cannot easily create data hierarchies or structures, has a fixed set of tags, and cannot communicate information about the document's content, only its format. As a result, a richer language called XML has been created to allow self-describing structured documents to be created. While HTML is designed for document presentation, XML is primarily designed to facilitate the exchange of hierarchically structured information, such as between businesses in a supply chain.

Prospects

Due to its simplicity, HTML will probably live on and not be replaced by the more powerful and complex XML. Several offshoots of HTML have been developed for mobile communications platforms that use devices whose display is too small to show traditional HTML pages. Some examples of these new platforms include

- Handheld Device Markup Language (HDML), developed by Phone.com
- Wireless Markup Language (WML), developed for use with the Wireless Application Protocol (WAP)
- cHTML, a subset of HTML developed for the I-mode cellular service of NTT DoCoMo in Japan

For More Information

You can see the W3C's HTML 4 Specification at *www.w3c.org/TR/REC-html40.*

See Also: Handheld Device Markup Language (HDML), Hypertext Transfer Protocol (HTTP), Internet Engineering Task Force (IETF), Uniform Resource Locator (URL), Wireless Markup Language (WML), World Wide Web (WWW), World Wide Web Consortium (W3C), XML

Hypertext Transfer Protocol (HTTP)

A protocol that defines how Web browsers download information from Web servers.

Overview

Hypertext Transfer Protocol (HTTP) is an application-level Transmission Control Protocol/Internet Protocol (TCP/IP) protocol first developed in 1990 as HTTP/0.9 and later standardized in 1996 by RFC 1945 as HTTP/1. The current version number for the protocol is HTTP/1.1 as defined by RFC 2616.

HTTP specifies the syntax for communication between HTTP clients and servers, which are defined as follows:

- **HTTP clients:** The most common example of an HTTP client is the Web browser, such as Microsoft Internet Explorer or Netscape Navigator, but any Web-enabled application can function as an HTTP client to request information from HTTP servers.
- **HTTP servers:** These are more informally known as Web servers, any servers that can communicate by means of HTTP with a client such as a Web browser. Examples of popular Web servers include Microsoft Internet Information Services (IIS) and Apache, the Open Source Web server.

Implementation

HTTP is implemented as a stateless request/response protocol. That is, clients make requests to servers, which then respond to the client. The HTTP protocol is called "stateless" because each request/response session is independent.

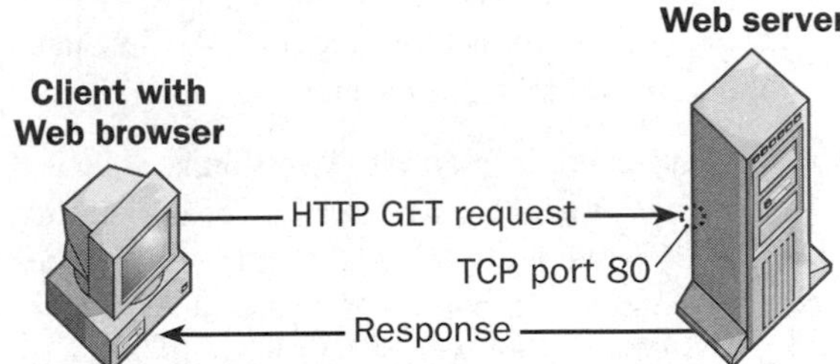

Hypertext Transfer Protocol (HTTP). *How a typical HTTP session works.*

An HTTP request consists of a message containing a request method, the file requested, and information about the client's capabilities. The request message consists of a series of headers encoded in plain text. The request method identifies the nature of the request and can be any of the following (not all methods may be supported by a particular HTTP server):

- **CONNECT:** Used by proxies for tunneling, for example, with Secure Sockets Layer (SSL) protocol
- **DELETE:** Deletes a file on the server
- **GET:** Requests a file from the server
- **HEAD:** Requests information concerning a file from the server (similar to GET, but the file itself is not returned in the response)
- **OPTIONS:** Requests information about the server's capabilities

- **POST:** Sends data to the server for processing, typically used with Hypertext Markup Language (HTML) forms
- **PUT:** Uploads a file to the server
- **TRACE:** Requests a loopback of the request message

An HTTP response may be either

- The information requested, encoded as a series of headers and an optional message body

or

- An error code indicating why the requested action could not be performed (see the article HTTP Status Codes elsewhere in this chapter)

The simplest example of an HTTP session is a client requesting a Web page from the server. The client sends an HTTP GET request over port 80 to the server. Other ports may be used, but port 80 is the default TCP port for HTTP requests, and Web servers typically listen to port 80 for such requests in order to fill them. When the server receives the request, it parses the headers and determines which file to return to the client. The file is then encoded using the appropriate Multipurpose Internet Mail Extensions (MIME) format and gets returned as a message body with a series of headers attached. The client receives the message, parses the headers, extracts the file from the message body, and displays the downloaded Web page.

In the HTTP/1 protocol, each request requires a separate TCP connection to be initiated and torn down afterward. This is slow—a Web page that has five images in it would need to be accessed using six requests, one for the text and one for each embedded image. As a result, a newer version, HTTP/1.1, was developed that allows a persistent TCP connection to be maintained so that many HTTP requests can be issued using it. This new feature is called HTTP Keep-Alives. Other features of HTTP/1.1 include

- Buffering of multiple HTTP GET requests into a single HTTP GET request
- Pipelining of multiple Internet Protocol (IP) packets to the server without waiting for the server to respond to each packet
- Support for caching of HTTP requests, proxies, and virtual hosts
- Host headers, a feature that enables a single Web server to host multiple Web sites using a single IP address

Notes

IIS supports the HTTP/1.1 version of HTTP.

HTTP's stateless nature makes it difficult to build Web applications that remember client requests across sessions. A common way of working around this issue is to use cookies, small files placed on the client by the server to store information across multiple sessions.

Do not confuse HTTP with HTML! HTTP is the protocol through which Web servers communicate with Web browsers. It is a control language for passing commands between clients and servers. HTML is Hypertext Markup Language, the language for constructing Web pages (the actual content passed from Web servers to Web clients in an HTTP request).

For More Information

Find out more about HTTP at the World Wide Web Consortium (W3C) Web site (*www.w3.org*).

See Also: *browser (Web browser), cookie, HTTP Keep-Alives, HTTP status codes, Web server*

I2O

Stands for Intelligent Input/Output (I2O), a hardware architecture developed by a consortium led by Intel that improves the input/output (I/O) performance of systems by relieving the CPU of interrupt-intensive I/O tasks.

See: *Intelligent Input/Output (I2O)*

IAB

Stands for Internet Architecture Board (IAB), a technical advisory group for the Internet Society (ISOC).

See: *Internet Architecture Board (IAB)*

IAD

Stands for Integrated Access Device, a wide area network (WAN) access device for consolidating voice and data, usually over Asynchronous Transfer Mode (ATM) circuits.

See: *Integrated Access Device (IAD)*

IANA

Stands for Internet Assigned Numbers Authority, the organization that coordinates the assignment of unique Internet Protocol (IP) parameters such as the IP address space and the Domain Name System (DNS).

See: *Internet Assigned Numbers Authority (IANA)*

IB

Stands for Infiniband, an emerging high-performance input/output (I/O) architecture.

See: *Infiniband (IB)*

IBGP

Stands for Interior Border Gateway Protocol, the version of Border Gateway Protocol (BGP) used for exchanging routing information within the same autonomous system (AS).

See: *Interior Border Gateway Protocol (IBGP)*

ICA

Stands for Independent Computing Architecture, a general-purpose presentation services protocol developed by Citrix Systems.

See: *Independent Computing Architecture (ICA)*

iCal

An Internet Engineering Task Force (IETF) standard for exchange of calendaring information.

Overview

The iCal standard defines a uniform data format for exchanging scheduling information. The intention is for iCal to be used by Internet-based applications so users can exchange information about meetings, appointments, and other events. The iCal standard replaces an earlier initiative called vCal or vCalendar.

The iCal standard is supported by Microsoft Outlook, the premier messaging and collaboration client from Microsoft. Specifically, Outlook uses a portion of iCal called iCalendar, together with an Outlook feature called Internet Free/Busy (IFB), to allow Outlook clients to exchange scheduling information over the Internet.

See Also: *vCard*

ICANN

Stands for Internet Corporation for Assigned Names and Numbers, a nonprofit corporation that has taken over some of the functions of the Internet Assigned Numbers Authority (IANA).

See: Internet Corporation for Assigned Names and Numbers (ICANN)

ICF

Stands for Internet Connection Firewall, a new integrated firewall application featured in Windows XP and Windows .NET Server.

See: Internet Connection Firewall (ICF)

ICMP

Stands for Internet Control Message Protocol, a Transmission Control Protocol/Internet Protocol (TCP/IP) network layer protocol used for various purposes.

See: Internet Control Message Protocol (ICMP)

ICMP Traceback Messages

An emerging standard from the Internet Engineering Task Force (IETF) for combating distributed denial of service (DDoS) attacks.

Overview

One of the Internet's greatest vulnerabilities is its exposure to DDoS, a form of attack in which hackers commandeer a large number of machines and turn them into "zombies" that are then used to attack Web servers with a flood of Internet Control Message Protocol (ICMP) packets. The source of these packets is difficult to track down because the packets contain spoofed Internet Protocol (IP) source addresses, making it difficult for administrators whose machines are under attack to trace the origin of these attacks. ICMP Traceback Messages, also known by the nickname itrace, is a protocol being developed by the IETF to make such tracking down possible.

Implementation

The itrace protocol is implemented on border and backbone routers deployed at Internet service providers (ISPs). Routers enabled with itrace occasionally tag regular IP packet traffic forwarded by routers with itrace messages. Typically, out of every 20,000 IP packets forwarded by a router, only one will have an itrace message attached to it. As a result, itrace has a negligible impact on network and router performance.

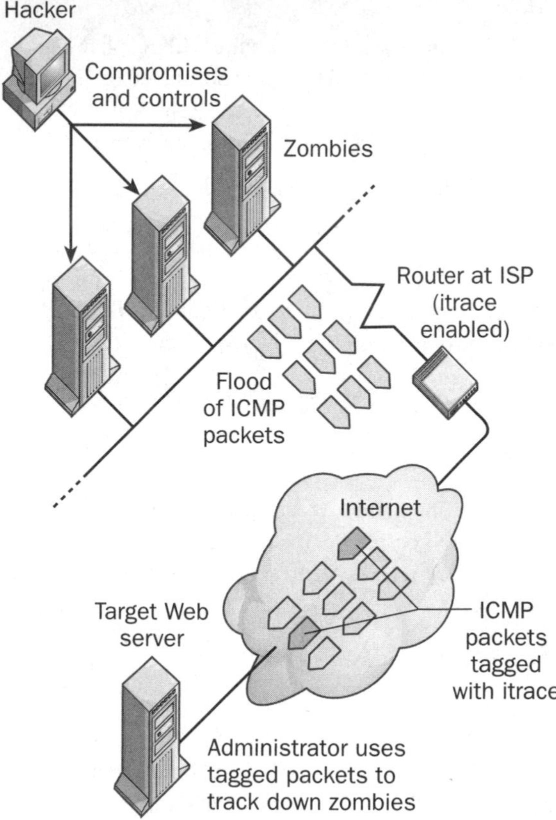

ICMP Traceback Messages. *How ICMP Traceback Messages can be used to track down the source of a DDoS attack.*

When a DDoS attack is underway, a flood of ICMP packets arrives at the target host. A small number (0.002 percent) of these packets will have itrace messages attached, and these messages can be used with a little ingenuity to trace the ICMP packets back to their sources on zombie machines, regardless of whether the source IP address of the packets is spoofed or not. Once the zombies can be identified, the administrator of the network on which they are located can be contacted to stop the attack and try to determine how their network was originally compromised. Note that itrace by itself can be used only to identify the zombies, not the hacker who originally compromised these machines.

To prevent hackers from spoofing the itrace messages themselves, a public key infrastructure (PKI) must guarantee the identity of the messages. This requirement, together with the cost of upgrading ISP routers, makes it probable that it may take a year or so after the ICMP Traceback Messages standard is ratified before it is widely deployed on key routers around the Internet. And for itrace to be effective in defeating DDoS attacks, it must be implemented on edge and backbone routers all over the Internet.

See Also: *Distributed Denial of Service (DDoS), hacking, Internet Control Message Protocol (ICMP), Internet service provider (ISP), router*

ICP (integrated communications provider)

Stands for integrated communications provider, a telecommunications service provider that offers one-stop shopping for voice and data telecommunications through a single integrated architecture.

See: *integrated communications provider (ICP)*

ICP (Internet Cache Protocol)

Stands for Internet Cache Protocol, a protocol that enables arrays of proxy servers to work together over a network.

See: *Internet Cache Protocol (ICP)*

ICQ

A popular Internet conferencing (chat) protocol.

Overview

ICQ is a proprietary protocol developed by Mirabilis and is similar to IRC (Internet Relay Chat). It enables users to locate other ICQ users on the Internet and communicate with them in real time. ICQ, which homophonically stands for "I seek you," lets you search for users currently online on ICQ networks and alerts you when friends go online. You can use ICQ to send real-time messages to other users, have group chat sessions, send e-mail, transfer files and URLs, play games, and perform other functions. ICQ can even function as a universal platform for launching any peer-to-peer application, such as Microsoft NetMeeting.

When you install ICQ and begin the registration process, you are connected to an ICQ server that belongs to a network of such servers distributed across the Internet. During registration, you are given a unique number called an ICQ#, which identifies you to all other users on the ICQ network. You use your ICQ# to register your presence with the ICQ network when you go online and start ICQ and to allow other ICQ users to recognize when you are online so that they can contact you. You can specify a list of ICQ friends, and an ICQ server will alert you when any of these friends go online.

For More Information

Visit ICQ Inc. at *www.icq.com.*

See Also: *instant messaging (IM), Internet Relay Chat (IRC)*

IDS

Stands for intrusion detection system, any system used to detect attacks on a host or network.

See: *intrusion detection system (IDS)*

IDSL

Stands for ISDN Digital Subscriber Line, a hybrid of Integrated Services Digital Network (ISDN) and Digital Subscriber Line (DSL) technologies.

See: *ISDN Digital Subscriber Line (IDSL)*

IE

Stands for Internet Explorer, Microsoft Corporation's integrated suite of client-side Internet software, which is included with all current versions of Microsoft Windows.

See: *Internet Explorer*

IEAK

Stands for Internet Explorer Administration Kit, a tool for customizing and deploying Microsoft Internet Explorer throughout an enterprise.

See: *Internet Explorer Administration Kit (IEAK)*

IEEE

Stands for Institute of Electrical and Electronics Engineers, a worldwide nonprofit association of technical professionals.

See: *Institute of Electrical and Electronics Engineers (IEEE)*

IEEE 488

A parallel interface standardized by the Institute of Electrical and Electronics Engineers (IEEE).

Overview

Also known as the General-Purpose Interface Bus (GPIB), the IEEE 488 parallel interface was developed by Hewlett-Packard and is used mainly for connecting computers to measurement sensors and test equipment for automatic data acquisition in a laboratory or industrial setting. Examples of such equipment include signal generators, frequency counters, voltmeters, and temperature sensors.

Architecture

IEEE 488 supports high-speed parallel communication using a 24-pin connector. An IEEE 488 cable generally has eight single wires for data transfer, eight twisted-pairs for interface handshaking and management, and a drain (ground) wire, all enclosed in an insulating protective jacket. This configuration provides eight bidirectional channels for transmitting 1 byte (8 bits) of information at a time, at a maximum bus speed of 1 megabit per second (Mbps) using tristate drivers.

The IEEE 488 standard lets you chain together up to 15 devices for a total length of 20 meters (66 feet), with no more than three connectors stacked and no more than 2 meters (6.5 feet) between adjacent devices. The master device acts as a controller that determines which device can transmit data over the bus at any given time, while the other devices are placed in standby mode. Only one device can transmit signals on the bus at any given time, but multiple devices can receive those signals.

Notes

If your industrial environment is dusty or has high levels of electromagnetic interference (EMI) from motors, generators, or other heavy equipment, you can obtain special shielding covers to protect your IEEE 488 connectors. You can also use switchboxes to alternate several industrial sensors on a single IEEE 488 cable.

IEEE 802 standards

Also called Project 802, an ongoing project of the Institute of Electrical and Electronics Engineers (IEEE) for defining local area network (LAN) and wide area network (WAN) standards and technologies.

See: *Project 802*

IEEE 1284

A high-speed bidirectional parallel interface standardized by the Institute of Electrical and Electronics Engineers (IEEE).

Overview

IEEE 1284 enables bidirectional communication between computers and attached printers and enables computers to spool jobs to printers at more than 10 times the speed of a traditional parallel port interface. Also called Enhanced Parallel Port (EPP), IEEE 1284 is compatible with the Centronics interface standard used for connecting parallel port printers to computers. This bidirectional communication allows the print device to return information to the computer that queried it for hardware information. This information can include device ID value, printer memory, installed fonts, and other information that the printer driver on the server can use to install and configure the printer. Bidirectional communication also allows the print device to send status messages (such as an "out of paper" message) to the server.

Architecture

IEEE 1284 specifies two electrical interfaces:

- Level I interface, which functions at a lower speed and provides only reverse-mode capabilities
- Level II interface, which functions at a higher speed and provides bidirectional communication

The connectors for the IEEE 1284 interface also come in various types:

- Type A connectors, which are standard 25-pin DB25 connectors
- Type B connectors, which are 36-pin centerline Champ connectors with bale locks to hold the cable in place for physical security
- Type C connectors, which are 36-pin centerline miniconnectors with clips for physical security

Implementation

Microsoft Windows 2000 can detect plug-and-play print devices by communicating with them using IEEE 1284. To make bidirectional printing work, you need

- A print device such as a laser printer that supports bidirectional printing.
- A correctly configured parallel port on the connected computer or print server. For example, if the parallel port is configured as AT-compatible, change it to PS/2 mode.
- An IEEE 1284–compliant cable having a DB25 male connector on one end and a Centronics 36 male connector on the other. IEEE 1284 cables are commonly used for connecting laser printers, scanners, tape drives, and portable storage devices (such as Iomega Zip drives) to a computer. An IEEE 1284 cable typically has "IEEE 1284" printed on its insulating jacket.

Notes

You can also obtain cables for converting the IEEE 1284 parallel interface to the universal serial bus (USB) interface to connect print devices with a Centronics connector to a computer with a USB connector. Special signal-powered IEEE 1284 cables can allow printers to be located up to 100 feet (30 meters) from the connected computer and still maintain reliable communication. Adapters are available for connecting 36-pin and DB25 connectors.

IEEE 1394

Better known by its trademarked name "FireWire," a serial interface for connecting high-speed peripherals to computers.

See: *FireWire*

IETF

Stands for Internet Engineering Task Force, an international community of networking engineers, network administrators, researchers, and vendors whose goal is to ensure the smooth operation and evolution of the Internet.

See: *Internet Engineering Task Force (IETF)*

iFS

Stands for Internet File System, a technology developed by Oracle Corporation for sharing data over the Internet.

See: *Internet File System (iFS)*

IGMP

Stands for Internet Group Management Protocol, a Transmission Control Protocol/Internet Protocol (TCP/IP) network layer protocol used for informing routers of the availability of multicast groups on the network.

See: *Internet Group Management Protocol (IGMP)*

IGP

Stands for interior gateway protocol, any routing protocol used to distribute routing information within an autonomous system.

See: *interior gateway protocol (IGP)*

IGRP

Stands for Interior Gateway Routing Protocol, an interior gateway protocol (IGP) developed by Cisco Systems.

See: *Interior Gateway Routing Protocol (IGRP)*

IIOP

Stands for Internet Inter-Orb Protocol, a CORBA (Common Object Request Broker Architecture) technology for distributed computing over the Internet.

See: *Internet Inter-Orb Protocol (IIOP)*

I

IIS

Stands for Internet Information Services, a Microsoft Windows service that provides support for application-layer Internet protocols.

See: *Internet Information Services (IIS)*

IIS Object Cache

A cache maintained by Microsoft Internet Information Services (IIS).

Overview

The IIS Object Cache stores file objects that are frequently requested by the World Wide Web (WWW), File Transfer Protocol (FTP), and Simple Mail Transfer Protocol (SMTP) services and by Active Server Pages (ASP) applications. The IIS Object Cache contains handles for open file objects, directory listings, and other frequently used file system objects. The cache runs within the main inetinfo.exe process and provides improved performance for IIS services and ASP applications.

Notes

For performance reasons, you should keep the IIS Object Cache in the working set of the IIS process in RAM. Be sure that you have sufficient RAM to do this. If you do not have enough RAM, the IIS Object Cache will be paged to disk and performance will be impaired. You can observe the performance of the cache by using Performance Monitor. Look for counters relating to cache hits and cache misses for each IIS service.

See Also: *Internet Information Services (IIS)*

IISP

Stands for Interim Interswitch Signaling Protocol, an Asynchronous Transfer Mode (ATM) protocol that enables cells to be routed over a switched virtual network (SVC).

See: *Interim Interswitch Signaling Protocol (IISP)*

IKE

Stands for Internet Key Exchange, a protocol for managing keys in public key cryptography systems.

See: *Internet Key Exchange (IKE)*

IL

Stands for Intermediate Language, an intermediate byte code used by Microsoft Corporation's new .NET platform.

See: *Intermediate Language (IL)*

ILEC

Stands for Incumbent Local Exchange Carrier, another name for local telephone companies or telcos.

See: *Incumbent Local Exchange Carrier (ILEC)*

ILS

Stands for Internet Locator Service, a Lightweight Directory Access Protocol (LDAP) directory service that enables Microsoft NetMeeting users to locate and contact other users for conferencing and collaboration over the Internet.

See: *Internet Locator Service (ILS)*

IM

Stands for instant messaging, a service that supports real-time call-based communications over the Internet.

See: *instant messaging (IM)*

IMA

Stands for Inverse Multiplexing over ATM, a high-speed Asynchronous Transfer Mode (ATM) technology.

See: *Inverse Multiplexing over ATM (IMA)*

IMAP4

Stands for Internet Mail Access Protocol version 4, a standard protocol for storage and retrieval of e-mail messages.

See: *Internet Mail Access Protocol version 4 (IMAP4)*

i-mode

A popular mobile communications service in Japan.

Overview

The i-mode service is currently the largest national packet-switched cellular service in the world. By the end of 2000 there were more than 10 million subscribers to this service and thousands of third-party applications and services developed for it. The i-mode service is a 2.5G cellular service operated by NTT DoCoMo and represents a model that's being considered by some providers that are currently implementing General Packet Radio Service (GPRS), such as Pacific Century CyberWorks (PCCW), a mobile services provider in Hong Kong SAR.

See Also: *2.5G, cellular communications*

impedance

In engineering, the measure of resistance to the flow of electric current.

Overview

Impedance to signal flow within a transmission line has three components: a resistive component, a capacitative component, and an inductive component. The value for each component varies with the frequency of the current, which means that the overall impedance of a transmission line also varies with frequency. A perfect transmission would have an impedance that does not change with frequency.

Characteristic impedance is the measure of resistance of a transmission line (such as a cable) calculated with the assumption that the cable is of infinite length. It is represented by the symbol Z_0. Each type of network cabling has its own characteristic impedance. Twisted-pair cabling can have a relatively constant impedance by virtue of its design and dimensional characteristics. The Electronic Industries Association/Telecommunications Industries Association (EIA/TIA) wiring standards, specifically EIA/TIA 568-A (Commercial Building Telecommunications Cabling Standard), mandate that Category 5 (Cat5) cabling should have an impedance of 100 ohms, plus or minus 15 percent, up to a frequency of 100 megahertz (MHz). It is important that cabling meet these standards because networking equipment, such as hubs, switches, and routers, is designed to match this impedance value. If wiring with a different impedance is used with such equipment, reflections of signals can occur that can distort signals, create signal loss, and degrade network communications—or even render them impossible.

Notes

Impedance is an issue only with copper cabling and is not a relevant physical characteristic for fiber-optic cabling.

See Also: *cabling*

impersonation

A security mechanism for client/server communication.

Overview

In Microsoft Windows 2000, Windows XP, and the Windows .NET Server family, impersonation is a method that a server uses to determine whether a client has sufficient rights to access a resource.

Impersonation involves temporarily altering the server's security context so that it matches that of the client. When the client attempts a connection to a resource on the server, it tells the server the impersonation level that the server can use to service the client's request. The client can offer four impersonation levels:

- **Anonymous:** The server does not receive any information about the client's security context.
- **Identification:** The server can authenticate the client but cannot use the client's security context for performing access checks.
- **Impersonation:** The server can both authenticate the client and use the client's security context to perform access checks.
- **Delegation:** The server authenticates the client and passes the client's security context to a remote server on the client's behalf. Delegation is not supported by the NTLM authentication method of Windows NT Server, but delegation is supported by the Kerberos authentication method of Windows 2000, Windows XP, and Windows .NET Server.

Examples

An example of impersonation occurs when anonymous access is enabled on a Web site hosted on Internet Information Services (IIS). Anonymous access uses the IUSR_ComputerName anonymous account on the IIS server, which is by default part of the Guests local group. If an IIS machine receives a Hypertext Transfer Protocol (HTTP) request from a remote Web browser, IIS impersonates the IUSR_ComputerName account so that it can allow the remote client to access the requested files or run the requested application. This prevents access to system files on the IIS machine by the remote client.

IMT-2000

Stands for International Mobile Telecommunications-2000, an initiative of the International Telecommunication Union (ITU) to create a global standard for third-generation (3G) wireless data networks.

See: *International Mobile Telecommunications-2000 (IMT-2000)*

IMUX

Stands for inverse multiplexer, a device that can perform inverse multiplexing of digital telecommunication channels.

See: *inverse multiplexer (IMUX)*

in-addr.arpa

A special domain in the Domain Name System (DNS) that is used for inverse queries.

Overview

The in-addr.arpa domain contains nodes whose names are based on Internet Protocol (IP) addresses with octets in the reverse order. For example, a host with the IP address 172.16.8.44 would be represented in the in-addr.arpa domain by 44.8.16.172.in-addr.arpa. Resource records for the in-addr.arpa domain are called pointer (PTR) records and are contained within a type of zone file called a reverse lookup file. Using the in-addr.arpa domain, a resolver can submit a request to a name server to resolve an IP address into its corresponding fully qualified domain name (FQDN).

See Also: *Domain Name System (DNS)*

in-band signaling

A method of transmitting control information through the same circuit or line that carries data.

Overview

Generally, any signaling transmission that takes place within a range of frequencies that is normally used only for data transmission is known as in-band signaling. Instead of using separate control and data channels, control information is transmitted using a portion of the data channel. If a separate control channel is used instead, the approach is called out-of-band signaling.

Implementation

As an example, in-band signaling is used in switched 56 services, in which a 64-kilobit-per-second (Kbps) digital communication link has 8 Kbps set aside for control signaling. This is sometimes referred to as "robbed-bit signaling" because the 8-Kbps bandwidth is "robbed" from the data channel for handling control functions such as wide area network (WAN) link synchronization. T1 lines that use switched channels also use in-band signaling techniques.

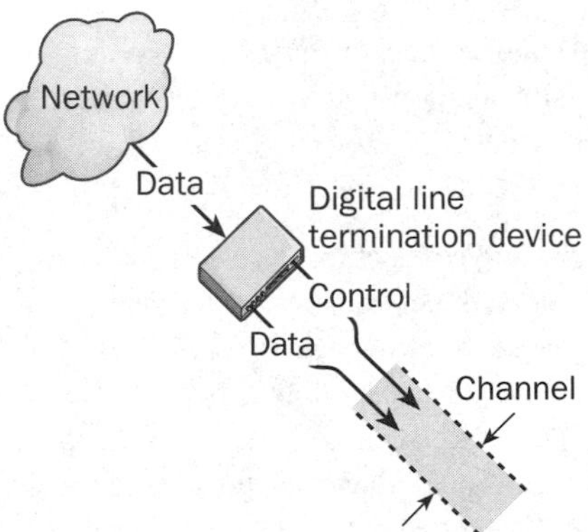

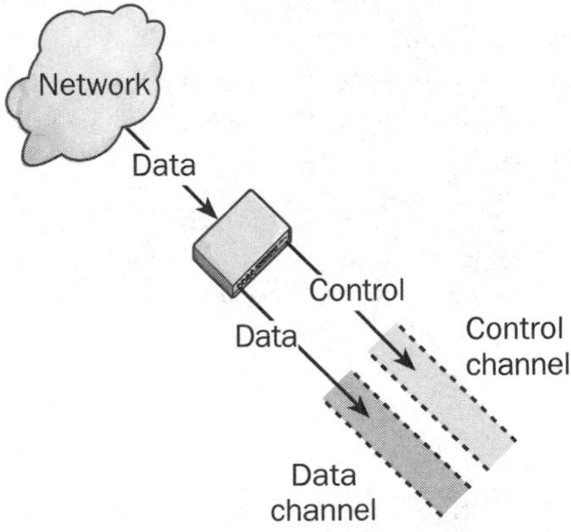

In-band signaling. *Comparison with out-of-band signaling.*

See Also: *out-of-band (OOB) signaling*

incremental backup

A form of partial backup used in between normal backups during a backup cycle.

Overview

In an incremental backup, only those files and folders that have changed since the last normal backup are backed up. The archive attribute is also marked for each file and folder backed up.

Incremental backups are typically used in conjunction with normal backups to simplify and speed up the overall backup process. If you do a normal backup on one particular day of the week, you can perform incremental backups on the remaining days to back up only the files that have changed during each day of the backup schedule. Incremental backups are faster than normal backups and use less tape.

Notes

Incremental backups are not cumulative, as differential backups are, so when you need to perform a restore, you need the normal backup and all incremental backups since the normal backup was done. Incremental backups are faster to perform but take longer to restore.

See Also: *backup type, differential backup*

incremental zone transfer

A method of updating zone information between name servers in the Domain Name System (DNS).

Overview

Incremental zone transfer is a more efficient method of propagating zone updates than the earlier standard DNS method of transferring the entire zone file using the AXFR request. Incremental zone transfer is defined in RFC 1995 and uses the IXFR request to transfer only the minimal information needed to keep the DNS servers within a given zone of authority in synchronization.

In incremental zone transfer, every primary or master DNS server maintains a full copy of the up-to-date zone file plus an additional version history that records any changes to resource records that occurred during recent updates of the zone file. When a secondary DNS server makes an IXFR request to a primary or master DNS server, the master server compares the zone version number of the secondary server's zone to its own current version number. The zone version number is the serial number stored in the start of authority (SOA) record of the DNS server. If the master server has a newer version number and incremental zone transfers are supported, the master server sends to the secondary server only those changes to resource records that have occurred in the time interval between the two version numbers. If the version numbers of the master and secondary servers match, no zone transfer takes place. And if incremental zone transfer is not supported, the normal full zone transfer takes place instead.

Notes

Incremental zone transfers are supported as part of the dynamic update features of Microsoft Windows 2000 and Windows .NET Server.

See Also: *Domain Name System (DNS), zone transfer*

Incumbent Local Exchange Carrier (ILEC)

Another name for local telephone companies or telcos.

Overview

Incumbent Local Exchange Carriers (ILECs) include

- Regional Bell Operating Companies (RBOCs), holding companies for about two dozen telephone companies that were created by the divestiture of AT&T in 1984.
- Other smaller independent telephone companies, especially in rural areas

The name *Incumbent Local Exchange Carrier* basically means that ILECs are

- **Incumbent:** They are the ones who own and control the local loop wiring infrastructure that provides telephone services to customers in their particular area.
- **Local:** They service specific regions of the United States, in contrast to inter-exchange carriers (IXCs), which provide long-distance services from coast to coast.
- **Exchange:** They provide telephone exchange services through their central office (CO) switching facilities, enabling customers to dial and make calls.
- **Carriers:** They "carry" phone line signals and generally provide a wide range of telecommunication services as well.

In contrast, Competitive Local Exchange Carriers (CLECs) are companies that either

- Lease local loop services from ILECs to provide customers with such services as Digital Subscriber Line (DSL), T-carrier, and frame relay (DSL is the most popular CLEC offering), or
- Provide their own connection to customers, typically fiber-optic connections for businesses in dense urban areas to provide such services as Voice over IP (VoIP) and Metropolitan Ethernet. Cable TV (CATV) operators generally are not referred to as CLECs even though they may provide services such as Internet access that "compete" with other Local Exchange Carriers (LECs).

Prospects

Despite the Telecommunications Act of 1996, which was intended to open up the telecom market by giving IXCs and CLECs access to ILEC's local loop wiring, the process has been far from smooth. Analysts have often seen ILECs as reactionary dinosaurs compared to the cutting-edge technologies offered by CLECs. For example, ILECs have not followed through on decades-old promises of replacing the existing copper loop wiring infrastructure with fiber-optic cabling to provide "fiber to the curb" services for business and residential customers. In addition, since the Telecommunications Act some ILECs have been slow in opening up their local loop networks to competitors, resulting in legal challenges that have led in some cases to Federal Communications Commission (FCC) rulings and penalties.

With the collapse of the dot-com bubble in 2001, however, investment in CLECs has declined precipitously, driving many out of the market and forcing others to merge or to be acquired by ILECs and IXCs. The result after five years is that the ILECs have had time to consolidate their positions as regulated monopolies and have begun modernizing their networks to provide high-demand services such as Asymmetric Digital Subscriber Line (ADSL) services for Internet access and High-bit-rate Digital Subscriber Line (HDSL) for enterprise wide area network (WAN) connectivity. ILECs are now offering broadband telecommunication services through Digital Subscriber Line (DSL) over the copper local loop.

Notes

Enterprise network architects looking for telecommunication carriers they can use to build reliable, fault-tolerant WANs should carefully investigate the current offerings before jumping in and making commitments. Wherever possible, each branch of a large enterprise should employ two LECs instead of one to provide redundancy for its WAN connection, but make sure that each LEC uses a different point of presence (POP). For example, if you use the services of an ILEC and a CLEC, make sure the CLEC is not simply reselling services from the same ILEC using the same POP, which would nullify the redundancy of the arrangement. If buying WAN services, such as frame relay, from an IXC, be sure to also consider incorporating a redundant arrangement from another IXC or RBOC to protect your investment.

If you want to provision your company with DSL services, you typically have to go through a CLEC because ILECs are effectively regulated monopolies and usually are not allowed to act as Internet service providers (ISPs). This double provisioning makes DSL services more complex to deploy and troubleshoot because you have to deal with two companies instead of one (although the CLEC will usually be your front-end contact in the matter).

See Also: Competitive Local Exchange Carrier (CLEC), inter-exchange carrier (IXC), local exchange carrier (LEC), Regional Bell Operating Company (RBOC)

Independent Computing Architecture (ICA)

An architecture for server-based computing from Citrix Systems.

Overview

Independent Computing Architecture (ICA) is similar to Microsoft Corporation's RDP (Remote Desktop Protocol) and the X Windows System from Sun Microsystems and X/Open in that it provides

- A centralized multiuser operating system that allows remote users to log on and run applications on the server from thin clients such as terminals and appliances.
- A presentation services protocol that displays a desktop generated by the server on the client.

Implementation

ICA enables the user interface of an application to run with minimal consumption of resources on a client device while the actual application logic executes on an ICA-enabled server (sometimes called a terminal server). The only data transferred over the network between the server and the client device are the user interface, keystrokes, and mouse movements. This results in minimal resource requirements for the client, allowing the use of a "thin client." An ICA presentation only requires about 5 Kbps throughput each direction, so ICA clients can access ICA servers over a wide variety of connections, including 14.4 Kbps and higher modems, ISDN terminal adapters, wireless 802.11b LANs, and traditional Ethernet local area networks (LANs).

ICA provides location independence because it runs the server operating system and application programs at a centralized location while displaying the user interface on supporting clients anywhere on the network. The ICA presentation services protocol also runs over most industry-standard networking protocols including Transmission Control Protocol/Internet Protocol (TCP/IP), NetBEUI, and Internetwork Packet Exchange/Sequenced Packet Exchange (IPX/SPX). ICA also runs over encapsulation transports such as Point-to-Point Protocol (PPP) on top of wide area network (WAN) transport protocols such as Integrated Services Digital Network (ISDN), frame relay, and Asynchronous Transfer Mode (ATM).

ICA also supports browser-based access, enabling applications to be launched from Web pages and making ICA a platform-independent solution. ICA also supports shadowing, which enables administrators to remotely take over control of thin clients for troubleshooting or instructional purposes.

Marketplace

Citrix makes a product called Metaframe that can be installed on different Microsoft Windows server platforms to allow ICA clients to access these servers. In the arena of thin clients, the first ICA appliance to reach the market was the Winterm 1200LE from Wyse Technology, which uses embedded BSD UNIX.

See Also: *Remote Desktop Protocol (RDP), terminal, terminal server*

index

In relational database terminology, a database object that enables efficient and rapid access to data in the rows of a table using key values.

Overview

Indexes are created on columns in a database table and provide a way to logically order rows in a database table. Because databases without indexes take much longer to query, planning and implementing indexes comprise an essential part of database design. Indexes can also be used to enforce the uniqueness of rows in a database table by building the index on a key value.

Notes

Although using indexes generally speeds queries, it is not a good idea to have an index for every column because building the index takes time and requires additional disk space, plus modifying the contents of the database causes modifications to the index. You should only create indexes for the following:

- Primary and foreign keys
- Data on which you frequently issue search queries
- Columns that are often retrieved in a sorted order or are used in joins

See Also: *database, join, key (database)*

Infiniband (IB)

An emerging high-performance input/output (I/O) architecture.

Overview

Infiniband (IB) is a new I/O architecture designed for connecting high-performance servers with distributed storage systems such as Storage Area Networks (SANs). IB is designed to overcome the limitations of the standard Peripheral Component Interconnect (PCI) system bus, which is often a bottleneck in enterprise computing systems as far as storage is concerned. The 32-bit 33 megahertz (MHz) PCI bus and its faster 64-bit 133 MHz PCI-X bus are system buses that are capable of transporting data at speeds up to 1 gigabit per second (Gbps). Unfortunately, this means that for high-performance servers using Gigabit Ethernet (GbE) network interface cards (NICs), the entire throughput of the bus could be eaten up by the NIC alone, leaving insufficient bandwidth for moving data between disk storage and RAM. In contrast, IB will offer bus speeds of 10 Gbps or more, sufficient for most current situations.

Another limitation of PCI and PCI-X is that they are shared-bus architectures in which attached devices contend for use of the bus (similar to half-duplex Ethernet). In contrast, IB is a switched architecture that provides each attached device the maximum possible bandwidth and high scalability. IB is not intended to replace PCI/PCI-X but rather to complement these architectures in high-end servers and network storage systems.

History

IB emerged from two earlier competing architectures: Next Generation I/O (NGIO) and Future I/O. These technologies were similar but were supported by different industry coalitions. In 1999, these coalitions joined forces to forge a new System I/O standard, which was renamed IB or Infiniband Architecture (IBA). The IB

Infiniband (IB)

standards are steered by the Infiniband Trade Association, whose members include Compaq Computer Corporation, Dell Computer Corporation, Hewlett-Packard, IBM, Intel Corporation, Microsoft Corporation, and Sun Microsystems.

Implementation

IB employs a switched point-to-point architecture. Virtual channels are used for establishing communications between different IB-capable devices connected to an IB switch, and multiple channels can be established between two devices to provide fault tolerance in communications. Devices are connected to switches using channel adapters, of which there are two types:

- **Host channel adapter (HCA):** This is used within hosts (servers) to connect processors and memory with external storage systems and network connections. The HCA connects to the server's memory controller, which controls access to the PCI/PCI-X system bus, the processors, and memory.
- **Target channel adapter (TCA):** This is used to connect devices that provide a network service, such as a JBOD (just a bunch of disks) storage farm, a Small Computer System Interface (SCSI) drive array, a Fibre Channel Storage Area Network (SAN), or a local area network (LAN) connection.

IB currently runs only over fiber-optic cabling, although proposals have been made for running it over specialized copper cabling (not standard Category 5 cabling).

Marketplace

The first company to release a commercial product based on the IB 1 standard was the startup Mellanox Technologies, which produced switches and adapters in its InfiniBridge line of products. Since then a number of vendors have started to release similar products, and a flood of Infiniband products is expected to hit the market sometime in 2002.

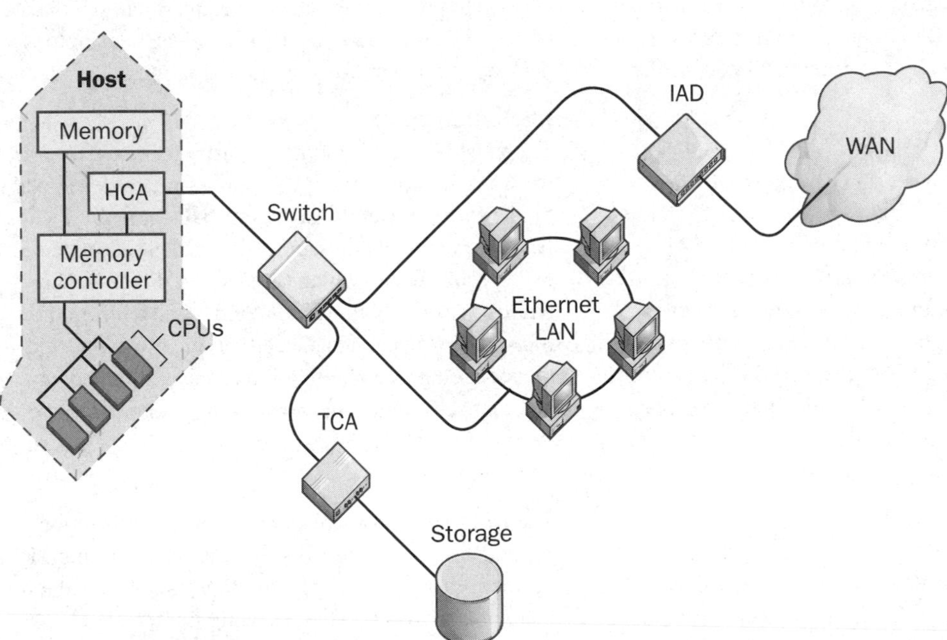

Infiniband (IB). *A simple example of using the IB architecture in enterprise computing.*

Prospects

The main competitor for IB is Fibre Channel, which already has a head start through a large installed base in enterprise SANs. Although IB was developed mainly as an I/O bus for distributed storage, it can also be used for creating server clusters and to interface directly with LAN switches and wide area network (WAN) access devices. The advantage in speed that IB has over Fibre Channel may also be eroded as efforts are made to push Fibre Channel speeds to 10 Gbps. The biggest advantage IB has is probably its current wide support among major vendors. The next few years will decide which architecture wins out.

See Also: *Fibre Channel, storage, storage area network (SAN)*

Infrared Data Association (IrDA)

An international consortium of hardware and software manufacturers that creates and promotes interoperable solutions for infrared (IR) data networking for computer networks, communication, and other networking applications.

Overview

The Infrared Data Association (IrDA), which was formed in 1993, has more than 150 members from hardware, software, and communication sectors. It has developed and agreed on standard formats for communication between computers and infrared devices to ensure interoperability between different systems, platforms, and devices. The IrDA also schedules meetings, conferences, and other events relating to infrared networking technologies. IrDA standards include the IrDA Data and IrDA Control infrared communication standards.

Notes

The IrDA standards have not been as widely implemented as had been hoped, mainly because infrared communication is essentially a line-of-sight (LOS) communications technology that is suited only to stationary users and devices. Some analysts believe the emergence of Bluetooth wireless networking technologies may eventually relegate IrDA to legacy technology, but this remains to be seen.

For More Information

Visit the IrDA at *www.irda.org.*

See Also: *infrared transmission, IrDA Control, IrDA Data*

infrared transmission

The transmission of data or voice information over infrared (IR) light.

Overview

IR light is beyond the red end of the visible spectrum. Wavelengths in the range of 770 to 1400 nanometers (nm) are called the near infrared region of the electromagnetic spectrum, and longer wavelengths are called the far infrared. In computer networking, IR is often used to connect laptops or Personal Digital Assistants (PDAs) to peripherals (such as printers) without the use of wires. IR is also frequently used to connect laptops to desktop computers for synchronizing files.

Implementation

The most popular computer industry standard for infrared transmission is the IrDA Data standard developed by the Infrared Data Association (IrDA). In a typical IrDA scenario, IR communication makes use of devices called transducers, which consist of a driver and an emitter that can both transmit and receive infrared transmissions. The transducer is typically connected to an encoder/decoder that interfaces with the computer or peripheral's universal asynchronous receiver-transmitter (UART) for asynchronous serial transmission between the devices.

The IrDA Data protocol suite initiates a connection using the discovery functions of the Infrared Link Management Protocol (IrLMP) and then establishes the primary and secondary stations using the Infrared Link Access Protocol (IrLAP). The secondary station then adjusts its data speed to match the primary station and establishes a serial communication link.

Advantages and Disadvantages

The main disadvantages of IrDA devices are that they have severe distance limitations and require a direct line of sight between devices in order to communicate. Furthermore, outdoor communications can be adversely affected by fog and other bad weather conditions. The main advantage, of course, is that communications can be established without the bother of having to deploy wiring or cables, which makes IR mainly useful for transient (short time period) connections in a mobile or changing environment.

See Also: *Infrared Data Association (IrDA)*

infrastructure

A term that refers to the collection of hardware and cabling that makes network communications possible in an enterprise.

Overview

In computer networking and telecommunications, infrastructure generally consists of two aspects:

- **Passive portion:** The cabling and other wiring used to connect hardware devices. This also includes passive devices such as patch panels, connectors, and other devices. If wiring is mainly Category 5 (Cat5) or higher twisted pair copper cabling, the hierarchical structure of such wiring is typically referred to as structured wiring or structured cabling.
- **Active portion:** Hardware devices such as hubs, switches, routers, and other networking devices. If the enterprise is geographically distributed across multiple locations, then wide area network (WAN) access devices and carrier services may also be considered part of the company's infrastructure.

Marketplace

The infrastructure market is mainly dominated by large players. Examples include

- **Cisco Systems:** Holds a large share of the networking hardware market at three levels: service providers (such as Internet service providers [ISPs] and telcos), enterprise (large companies), and commercial (small and mid-sized companies). Popular vendor for switches, routers, integrated access devices (IADs), and other hardware.
- **Juniper Networks:** Popular switch/router vendor at the service provider level, with roughly one-third of this market.
- **Nortel Networks:** Top vendor in the optical networking market, and a major Voice over IP (VoIP) vendor through partnership with Cable & Wireless.
- **IBM:** Popular vendor in the Web-to-host networking environment.
- **EMC Corporation:** Heavyweight in the network storage arena, with 35 percent of the market. The network storage market, including both Storage Area Network (SAN) and network attached storage (NAS) approaches, is the fastest growing segment of the enterprise infrastructure market.

Other popular infrastructure vendors include Enterasys Networks, Lucent Technologies, and many others.

Prospects

One recent development is the emergence of online superstores where enterprise customers can purchase infrastructure products. Examples of these include Buy.com and cdw.com. Another development is online IT (information technology) exchanges, where infrastructure products and services can be purchased and provisioned. Examples here include Cymerc Exchange (switches and routers), Simplexity (telecom services), ITParade.com (refurbished equipment), and Tek-Sell.com (online auctions of IT equipment).

See Also: *router, structured wiring, switch*

inheritance

The process of child objects acquiring the security settings of parent objects.

Overview

In Microsoft Windows 2000, Windows XP, and the Windows .NET Server family, inheritance is a feature that allows the access control entry (ACE) for an object whose security settings are being configured to be propagated to other objects that are beneath it in the file system

or directory hierarchy. Inheritance simplifies the administration of hierarchical file systems and directories by allowing administrators to configure ACEs globally and then modify them on an exception basis, rather than configure ACEs individually for each object in the system.

In Windows NT, inheritance is used in the NTFS file system for propagating the permissions assigned to a folder to the files and folders within that folder. In Windows 2000, inheritance also applies to the Active Directory directory service and allows permissions assigned to a container or an organizational unit (OU) within Active Directory to be propagated further down the directory tree. Inheritance also appears in other directory-based systems such as Microsoft Exchange Server, in which Exchange administrative permissions assigned to a container in the Exchange directory that is based on the Lightweight Directory Access Protocol (LDAP) can be applied to leaf objects and other containers within that container.

See Also: *delegation, discretionary access control list (DACL), permissions*

INI files

Text files used in legacy versions of Microsoft Windows.

Overview

Windows 3.1 and Windows for Workgroups stored configuration information about hardware, devices, and services in text files called INI (initialization) files. These files, which have the extension .ini, included

- WIN.INI, which stores information about the desktop environment, fonts, and printers, as well as other settings
- SYSTEM.INI, which stores boot settings and information specific to running in Standard and 386 Enhanced modes
- CONTROL.INI, which maintains the Windows color schemes
- PROGMAN.INI, which stores information about program groups
- WINFILE.INI, which stores status information for File Manager

In addition, individual applications often created their own INI files during installation to store application-specific settings.

In later versions of Windows, including Windows 95, Windows 98, Windows Millennium Edition (Me), Windows NT, and Windows 2000, INI files are replaced by the registry, a hierarchical structure used to store all system and application configuration settings. Nevertheless, INI files are still included in these operating systems to provide backward compatibility for running 16-bit Windows programs because such programs were designed to save their settings in INI files and cannot access the registry.

See Also: *Microsoft Windows, registry*

instance

A particular occurrence of a System Monitor counter in Microsoft Windows 2000, Windows XP, and the Windows .NET Server family.

Overview

As an example, if the %Privileged Time counter is being monitored for the Processor object on a symmetric multiprocessing (SMP) machine with four processors, individual instances of that counter are instances 0, 1, 2, and 3. By using instances, you can monitor the performance of processes, threads, and devices on a per-instance basis for detailed understanding of their resource use on a machine. Individual instances of a given counter can be displayed in the usual way using charts and graphs.

instant messaging (IM)

A service that supports real-time, call-based communications over the Internet.

Overview

The basic idea of instant messaging (IM) started in the early days of networked UNIX environments, where users who were logged on to the network could use UNIX commands such as Talk, Write, and Finger to determine who else was logged on and to send them short text messages. However, IM now generally refers to a set of technologies popularized by America Online (AOL), Microsoft Corporation, and other companies.

Types

The two most widely used IM services today are AOL Instant Messenger (AIM), developed by AOL, and ICQ ("I seek you"), developed by Mirabilis and now owned by AOL. Together, both services are used by more than 100 million people worldwide, and they support text-based messaging, voice, and file sharing/transfer. Other systems include Yahoo Messenger from Yahoo!, MSN Messenger from MSN (Microsoft Network), and Odigo from Odigo.

Implementation

Using AOL's AIM system as an example, AOL users can send instant messages to other AOL users online by using AIM client software. To use AIM messaging, an AOL user first signs on at an AIM central server, indicating that he or she is online and can receive instant messages from other users. The central server records the user's Internet Protocol (IP) address for that session. (The user's IP address is assigned by Dynamic Host Configuration Protocol [DHCP] and can vary from session to session.) Other users can then send instant messages to that user through the server. The user's AIM client sends the server a copy of the user's "buddy list" (a list of other users that he or she frequently exchanges messages with), and the server responds by telling the user which buddies are currently online and can receive messages. The user can select a buddy from the list and submit a message to the server, which forwards the message to the buddy.

Advantages and Disadvantages

IM exploded in popularity as a consumer-oriented service that allowed people to keep in touch with each other while surfing the Internet. The advantages of IM are similar to those of the telephone: simplicity and immediacy. IM is even more immediate than e-mail and include a wider range of communication methods, including voice, text, and file sharing. Since it uses the Internet as its carrier service, IM is effectively free for people already subscribed to an Internet service provider (ISP).

From a corporate perspective, though, some analysts see some disadvantages of IM, whose constant requests for communications can interfere with work even more than the telephone. Furthermore, as IM moves toward multimedia services, such communications can quickly swallow up network bandwidth in the enterprise. Policies also need to be in place and enforced to ensure that IM solutions are not misused, especially if they are outsourced to public service providers such as AOL or MSN. Another big concern about IM by corporate customers is security, as sensitive business information may be sent over the Internet through IM. Some vendors, however, are working to address this issue by encrypting IM communications. Finally, the main problem with all current IM systems is lack of interoperability between systems from different vendors. While AIM is the most widely used system, it is a proprietary system that AOL has not opened up to competing systems. This lack of ubiquity has hindered IM from being as widely useful as the telephone system, and attempts to develop vendor-independent standards for IM have so far been unsuccessful (see Prospects, later in this article).

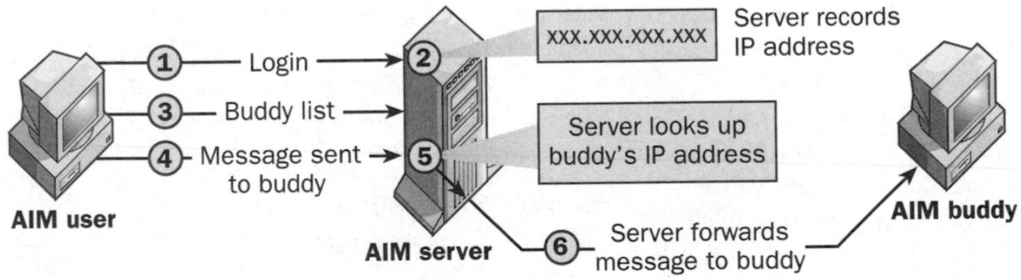

Instant messaging. *The instant messaging system used by AOL.*

Marketplace

Many enterprises are looking to set up their own IM solutions in order to better control with whom users are able to communicate. Packaged IM solutions are available from numerous vendors, including the IM features of Microsoft Exchange Server 2000, Lotus SameTime messaging for their Lotus Notes Domino platform, and Novell's instantme 2 secure IM platform. Other vendors have developed IM systems targeted directly for enterprise and not consumer use, including Planet Exchange with their Web-based IM system, NetLert from SoftBase Systems, and Interactive Messaging from 2WAY Corporation.

Prospects

Although IM is widely deployed as a consumer service, it has become attractive to businesses in the last few years. Analysts estimate that by 2002 almost half of Fortune 1000 companies will have either deployed corporate IM solutions in their enterprise or will outsource IM to existing service providers such as Microsoft or AOL. The next big thing will likely be mobile IM that allows users to send instant messages to each other over cellular phones and Personal Digital Assistants (PDAs). The Short Message Service (SMS) widely deployed among Global System for Mobile Communications (GSM) cellular systems in Europe is a first step in this direction and has proved enormously popular—and a revenue booster as well for cellular providers, since users are usually billed by the number of SMS messages sent. Evolution to multimedia IM such as that now available on the Internet is hampered, however, by the slowness of migrations of existing second-generation (2G) cellular systems to 2.5G and third-generation (3G) wireless.

The lack of a universal open standard for IM has resulted in a balkanization of the IM landscape and has prevented it from becoming as universal as the telephone. In 2000 the Internet Engineering Task Force (IETF) attempted to develop such a standard, called Instant Messaging and Presence Protocol (IMPP), and narrowed it down to three candidates: Instant Messaging Extensible Protocol (IMXP), Simple Instant Messaging Protocol (SIMP), and Instant Messaging and Presence using SIP (IMPSIP). This effort failed to produce an agreement, but other efforts toward a universal IM system continue, including the activities of the IMUnified coalition, which includes Microsoft, Yahoo!, and Tribal Voice. The IMUnified specification provides functional interoperability between popular proprietary IM systems but requires users to first sign up for accounts on those systems. Another approach to the problem of IM interoperability is Aimster, the peer-to-peer file-sharing program that has been updated to support buddy lists from such multiple IM systems as those of AOL, MSN, and Yahoo! The real solution to this problem, though, and the one that will eventually transform IM into an essential business tool for the enterprise, must come from the development of vendor-neutral IM specifications from standards bodies such as the IETF.

See Also: *AOL Instant Messenger (AIM), ICQ, Short Message Service (SMS)*

Institute of Electrical and Electronics Engineers (IEEE)

A worldwide nonprofit association of technical professionals.

Overview

The Institute of Electrical and Electronics Engineers (IEEE) promotes the development of standards and acts as a catalyst for new technology in all aspects of the engineering industry, including computer networking, telecommunications, electric power, aerospace, and consumer electronics. The IEEE has more than 365,000 individual members in 150 countries and regions. Its activities include standards committees, technical publishing, and conferences.

A major contribution of the IEEE in the field of computer networking is Project 802, a collection of standards for local area network (LAN) architectures, protocols, and technologies. These standards continue to evolve under the auspices of various IEEE working groups and committees.

For More Information

Visit the IEEE at *www.ieee.org.*

See Also: *Project 802*

Integrated Access Device (IAD)

A wide area network (WAN) access device for consolidating voice and data, usually over Asynchronous Transfer Mode (ATM) circuits.

Overview

Integrated Access Devices (IADs) are a type of WAN access device used for connecting corporate networks and voice telephone systems into wide area networks. A typical IAD can consolidate voice traffic, both analog and ISDN (Integrated Services Digital Network, together with Ethernet local area network (LAN) traffic, for transmission over frame relay or T1 links onto carrier ATM backbone networks. These different types of traffic are aggregated by the IAD into a single traffic flow for transmission over a single WAN link (access circuit). The advantages of IADs are that by integrating multiple WAN functions into a single box, costs are reduced through the elimination of redundant equipment and the traditional truck roll for carrier installation. Also, precious rack space in telecommunications closets can be saved by replacing multiple devices with a single integrated device. IADs provide a simple, cost-effective alternative to other WAN access devices, such as enterprise switches and WAN edge switches. They do not represent new WAN technology but rather an integration of existing technology into a single, easily managed device.

Implementation

IADs combine voice and LAN data traffic into a single data stream through Time Division Multiplexing (TDM) or some other scheme. IADs usually reside at the customer premises and can easily be connected to Private Branch Exchanges (PBXs) and Ethernet backbone switches. IADs are often supplied preconfigured by telecommunications carriers such as Competitive Local Exchange Carriers (CLECs) and Regional Bell Operating Companies (RBOCs).

The simplest form of IAD is essentially just a traffic aggregator, combining several data streams into one for transmission over frame relay, T-carrier, or Digital Subscriber Line (DSL) carrier services. Enhanced IADs include such features as Dynamic Host Configuration Protocol (DHCP), network address translation (NAT), integrated firewall, voice mail, multiprotocol routing, and many other features. High-end IADs are mainly ATM-based and support voice packetization for dynamic bandwidth allocation.

Marketplace

IADs first appeared on the market in 1998 and were expensive and aimed mainly at high-end enterprise customers. Since then, prices have fallen so that units under $2,000 are now available for small and mid-sized businesses. Some popular vendors of IADs include Cabletron Systems with its SmartSwitch 15000, Mariposa with its ATX series of ATM IADs, and offerings from Accelerated Networks, Lucent Technologies, Memotec Communications, Sonoma Systems, and many others.

See Also: *Asynchronous Transfer Mode (ATM), Competitive Local Exchange Carrier (CLEC), Integrated Services Digital Network (ISDN), Regional Bell Operating Company (RBOC), wide area network (WAN)*

integrated communications provider (ICP)

A telecommunications service provider that offers one-stop shopping for voice and data telecommunications through a single integrated architecture.

Overview

The main difference between an integrated communications provider (ICP) and a traditional carrier such as a Regional Bell Operating Company (RBOC), Competitive Local Exchange Carrier (CLEC), or Incumbent Local Exchange Carrier (ILEC) is that the ICP generally installs a single, all-in-one integrated access device (IAD) at the customer premises that enables voice and data traffic to be serviced over a single line. This provides for easier management than using multiple lines with different technologies and devices. The IAD typically connects to the provider by using Asynchronous Transfer Mode (ATM) over a single T1 line or Digital Subscriber Line (DSL) circuit at the local loop. (About 80 percent of the customer cost for ICP services is for the ICP's rental of local loop access from an RBOC). At the provider end, ICPs often build their own integrated ATM backbone networks so that they can better control the services they offer.

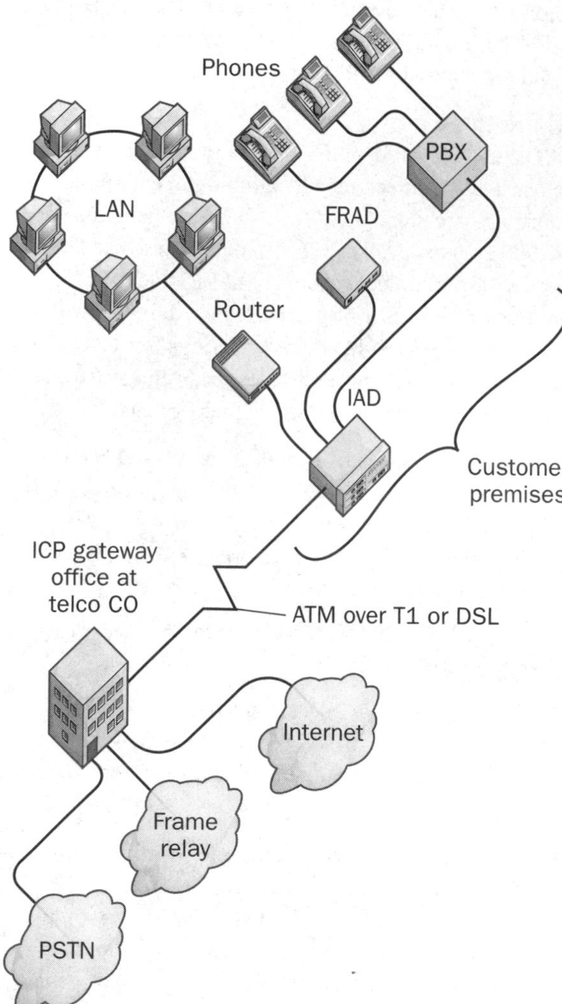

Integrated communications provider (ICP). *How an ICP provisions telecommunication services using an integrated access device (IAD).*

Advantages and Disadvantages

Using an ICP can save companies a considerable amount of money compared to leasing the services separately from traditional carriers. However, although the cost of using an ICP might be less than that of using an RBOC or a CLEC, the ICP might not offer some services, such as toll-free long distance and DSL services. You should also be sure that you understand how the various services are billed before you sign a contract.

Some ICPs use time-division multiplexing (TDM) to allow a single T1 line to carry voice, data, and video over 24 DS0 (Digital Signal Zero) channels. In this scenario, you might be paying for bandwidth that you are not using because TDM dedicates slots of bandwidth to services whether or not data is being carried in these slots. You can generally get better value from ICPs that use ATM circuits between the subscriber and provider because ATM can use statistical multiplexing, which allocates bandwidth dynamically between voice and data. However, the disadvantage of the ATM approach is that if the line goes down, all voice and data transmission is interrupted, while with the TDM approach, customers might still have access to analog phone lines if such lines are used.

Marketplace

The landscape for ICPs is in a state of flux, but players include CTC Communications, e.spire Communications, GST Telecommunications, ICG Telecommunications, Intermedia Communications, and many others.

See Also: *Competitive Local Exchange Carrier (CLEC), Incumbent Local Exchange Carrier (ILEC), Integrated Access Device (IAD), Regional Bell Operating Company (RBOC)*

Integrated Services Digital Network (ISDN)

A digital communication service provided by telephone companies (telcos).

Overview

Integrated Services Digital Network (ISDN) is an end-to-end digital telephone and telecommunications service provided by telcos to subscribers who request it. ISDN is a dial-on-demand (dial-up) service that has fast call setup and low latency. It is a circuit-switched service that can be used in both point-to-point and multipoint connections.

ISDN can be used to carry high-quality voice, data, and video transmissions. To do this, ISDN employs the existing widely deployed copper local loop wiring of the Public Switched Telephone Network (PSTN).

ISDN was developed in the 1970s by Bell Laboratories and standardized in the 1980s by the Comité Consultatif International Télégraphique et Téléphonique (CCITT), a precursor to the ITU (International Telecommunication Union). ISDN was originally envisioned as a digital replacement for the analog Plain Old Telephone System (POTS) and is available around the world with slight differences in architecture and operation.

Types

ISDN is available in a number of different interfaces (flavors) with the two most common being

- **Basic Rate Interface (BRI):** This uses two 64-kilobit-per-second (Kbps) B channels and one 16-Kbps D channel and is thus often referred to as 2B+D (B and D channels are explained later in this article). BRI can support combined voice and data with a maximum data transfer rate of 128 Kbps.
- **Primary Rate Interface (PRI):** This combines 23 64-Kbps B channels with one 64-Kbps D channel and is often referred to as 23B+D. PRI supports maximum data transfer rates up to the DS1 rate of 1.536 megabits per second (Mbps). PRI is generally used to provide the underlying transport for T1 lines.

Within PRI, however, there are also several ways in which ISDN B channels can be bundled together. These bundlings are called H-series configurations and common examples include

- **H0:** Combines 6 B channels for 384 Kbps throughput, equivalent to a fractional T1 line (fT1).
- **H11:** Combines 24 B channels for 1.536 Mbps throughput, equivalent to a T1 line.
- **H12:** Combines 30 B channels for 1.92 Mbps throughput, equivalent to an E1 line (used in Europe).

Another form of ISDN is known as Multirate ISDN, which allows subscribers to specify the bandwidth they need on a per-call basis in increments of 64 Kbps.

Comparison

Since ISDN is a dial-on-demand service, it has similarities to dial-up connections using analog modems. Both analog modem and ISDN use the same copper local loop and PSTN to allow connections to be established with distant stations. Both also require a call to be made before a connection can be established. With analog modems, this may take 15 to 30 seconds, but with ISDN, it is typically only 1 or 2 seconds. But although analog modems operate in an asynchronous fashion, ISDN uses a synchronous connection. And although analog modems transmit their control information (used for call setup and tear-down) in-band, ISDN uses out-of-band signal management with a separate channel called the D channel.

Uses

Because of its dial-on-demand nature, ISDN charges are typically based on a fixed monthly service fee plus usage charges. ISDN is thus ideal for applications where a dedicated (always-on) leased line is unnecessary and would be too costly. ISDN used to be popular with enterprise networks in the 1980s for connecting remote branch offices to company headquarters using ISDN wide area network (WAN) links. These remote offices would transfer their accumulated transactions several times a day over the WAN link for batch processing on mainframes located at headquarters. With the decline of the mainframe computing environment and the rise of client/server computing, however, many enterprises migrated their slow dial-up ISDN links to fast always-on T1 lines. ISDN remained popular with enterprise networks, however, as backup lines in case their dedicated T1 lines go down.

Architecture

The ISDN standards from the ITU define several different series of ISDN protocols, for example:

- **E-series:** These protocols define the addressing and telephone numbering system used by ISDN.
- **I-series:** These protocols cover the basic concepts of ISDN, including definition of the Basic Rate Interface (BRI) and Primary Rate Interface (PRI) interfaces.

- **Q-series:** These protocols describe how ISDN calls are set up and torn down and how switching occurs in an ISDN system.

ISDN uses a layered protocol architecture similar to the Open Systems Interconnection (OSI) model. The physical layer signaling is specific to ISDN and is the same for both B and D channels. For data transmission, ISDN uses a framing (encapsulation) format called V.120, which is the international standard for synchronous ISDN data stream framing. ISDN frames are 48 bits long and are transmitted at 4,000 frames per second. Each ISDN frame contains two 8-bit slots for the Bl channel and two 8-bit slots for the B2 channel, which alternate with each other and with one 1-bit D channel slot after each B channel slot using Time Division Multiplexing (TDM). Each B channel thus provides a data transfer rate of 2 x 8 bits x 4000 hertz (Hz) = 64 Kbps, while the D channel has a bandwidth of 4 x 1 bits x 4000 Hz = 16 Kbps. The remainder of the frame is used for line balancing, echo detection, activation, and padding.

Above the physical layer lies the data-link layer, which employs Link Access Protocol – D channel (LAPD) for flow control and signaling management. LAPD is derived from and is similar to the earlier High-level Data Link Protocol (HDLC) and Link Access Protocol – B channel (LAPB) used by X.25.

Above the data-link layer is the network layer, which employs ISDN-specific I-series protocols for such functions as call setup, establishment, and teardown, and for establishing point-to-point or multipoint circuit-switched or packet-switched connections between call endpoints.

As mentioned previously, there are two different types of ISDN channels:

- **B (bearer) channels:** These are full-duplex bearer (that is, carrying or "bearing" data) channels used for carrying either voice or data at 64 Kbps. The data transmission can be either circuit-switched (telco) or packet-switched (such as X.25) services. Each B channel can function as a completely separate connection, but you can also use a protocol called BONDING to dynamically combine the two B channels of BRI by using inverse multiplexing to produce a single 128-Kbps data channel.
- **D (delta) channels:** These are full-duplex 16 Kbps control channels for setting up connections and for other signaling purposes. For example, ISDN voice communication uses D channels to implement special services such as call forwarding and call display. The D channel uses a completely separate telco communication network called the Signaling System 7 (SS7). This out-of-band telco network is used exclusively for system overhead signaling for ISDN and digital data service (DDS) services, and it makes possible the low latency of ISDN dial-up connections. For example, it takes only 1 to 2 seconds for an ISDN dial-up connection to be established, compared to 15 to 30 seconds for a typical analog modem. D channels can also be used to connect ISDN subscribers to an X.25 network in a flavor of ISDN called Always-On Dynamic ISDN (AO/DI).

Implementation

Provisioning ISDN at a customer premises basically involves two steps:

- Installing and configuring ISDN customer premises equipment (CPE) at the subscriber's location. The installation procedure involves setting up and testing the ISDN equipment and configuring the service profile identifier (SPID), which effectively represents the "phone number" of the subscriber's ISDN setup. CPE for ISDN is further discussed later in this article.
- Changing the subscriber's connection type at the telco central office (CO) from POTS to ISDN. This basically means disconnecting wires from an analog POTS switch to a digital ISDN switch at the CO. In North America, these ISDN CO switches are typically either 4ESS or 5ESS switches produced by AT&T or DMS-100 switches from Northern Telecom (now Nortel). Other types of switches are used in different parts of the world.

Two ways to connect to ISDN customer premises equipment

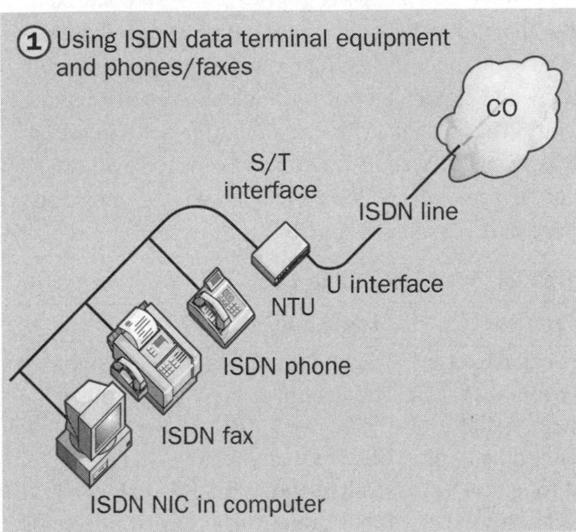

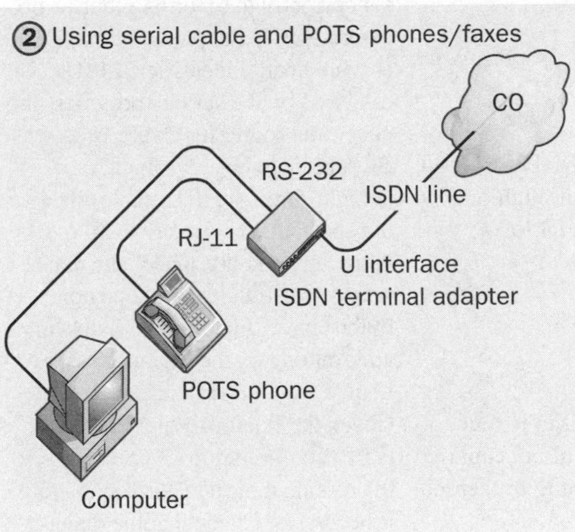

Integrated Services Digital Network (ISDN). *Some examples of how to implement ISDN.*

The method of connecting CPE to the termination point of an ISDN line at the customer premises depends on the type of equipment you want to connect and which part of the world in which you are located (we will focus here on North American ISDN). The simplest case is if you are connecting "native" ISDN equipment such as an ISDN phone, which is referred to as Terminal Equipment type 1 (TE1), to your ISDN line. A bit more complicated is connecting non-ISDN equipment (known as Terminal Equipment type 2, or TE2) such as computers or routers—here you need to use an intermediary device called a Terminal Adapter (TA). The terminal adapter is usually connected to the TE2 using a serial interface such as RS-232 or V.35. ISDN terminal adapters can be external boxes, cards you plug into a computer's motherboard, or modules you drop into the chassis of a router or integrated access device (IAD). ISDN terminal adapters are sometimes called ISDN modems, but they are not really modems because ISDN is an end-to-end digital communication service and no analog-to-digital signal modulation occurs within an ISDN setup.

The function of Terminal Equipment such as TE1 and TE2 described above is to convert signals received from CPE into BRI or PRI framing format. But to transmit these frames over the ISDN line, they need to be translated into electric signals that can be physically carried over the line. This translation is accomplished by means of a Network Termination Unit (NTU), which again comes in two types: NT1 devices that provide basic ISDN connectivity and NT2 devices used mainly for digital Private Branch Exchange (PBX) connections.

How all these different types of equipment are connected is determined by what are called ISDN interfaces, specifically:

- **R interface:** Specifies how non-ISDN CPE (TE2), such as standard analog telephones, are connected to an ISDN terminal adapter (TA).
- **S interface:** Specifies how ISDN CPE (TE1), such as an ISDN phone, ISDN PBX, or ISDN TA, is connected to ISDN network termination equipment (NTU).
- **T interface:** Specifies how NT1 connects with NT2 (this sometimes combined together as NT1/NT2 equipment, supporting what is called the S/T interface).

Integrated Services Digital Network (ISDN)

- **U interface:** Specifies how NTU connects to the local loop wiring.

Advantages and Disadvantages

For WAN links, ISDN has a couple of advantages over leased lines and analog modems:

- It is cheaper than leased lines such as T1 lines.
- It has faster call setup than analog modem dial-up connections.

On the downside, ISDN subscribers must be located within 3.5 miles (5.5 kilometers) of a telco CO or from a remote ISDN terminal, which means that ISDN is not always available, especially in rural areas. Also, in today's client/server and Internet networking environments, ISDN may provide insufficient bandwidth and excessive network latency to support today's distributed processing environments. As a result, some industry analysts have begun chanting an "ISDN is dead" mantra, but see the following Prospects section.

Prospects

Although ISDN BRI services may be relegated by the advent of Digital Subscriber Line (DSL) to backup WAN links for offices relying on DSL or T1 as their primary data link, ISDN PRI services are actually thriving worldwide. This is because PRI is an ideal platform for Internet service providers (ISPs) to use for connecting their banks of dial-up analog modems to the PSTN, and with the phenomenal growth of the Internet in the last few years, ISPs are buying up PRI at unprecedented rates. Another popular use for PRI is in corporate environments where it is used to connect digital PBXs at the customer premises to the PSTN. This is a more expensive arrangement than using analog trunk lines for this purpose (compare $1,000 to $2,000 a month for PRI to $50 to $100 a month for trunk lines), but it provides advanced features supported by digital telephones and native data transport at high speeds. So ISDN is definitely not dead as far as the new millennium is concerned, although the BRI version may be fading in usefulness in the enterprise.

Notes

Plug your ISDN network termination unit (NTU) into an uninterruptible power supply (UPS) so that you can use the phone during a power failure and so that your WAN link does not go down. If you have a large company and expect a lot of local telephone calls within your organization, you can sometimes obtain a Centrex ISDN service in which local calls have no usage charges. Microsoft Windows operating systems also have built-in support for ISDN.

Tips for Troubleshooting ISDN

Problem	*Suggestions*
ISDN router or terminal adapter fails to dial	Check the cabling, the line signal, and the dialer map on the router.
Dial fails to go through on a BRI line	Be sure that you are using a straight-through RJ-45 cable. Check other cables, make sure the speed is set correctly to 56 or 64 Kbps as necessary, verify the phone number and service profile identifier (SPID) assigned by the service provider, and check the router hardware.
Dial fails to go through on a PRI line	Be sure that you are using a straight-through DB15 cable and that the speed is set correctly to 56 or 64 Kbps as necessary. Check the dialer map on the router, the phone number of the remote PRI, and the status lights and framing on the Channel Service Unit (CSU). Power-cycle the CSU.
Dial is successful but cannot ping the remote router	Check the Point-to-Point Protocol (PPP) configuration (if used). Check the routing table and add a static route if necessary. Check that the dialer map has the correct remote router specified, and have the telco check the remote router configuration.

See Also: *Always On/Dynamic ISDN (AO/DI), B channel, bonding, BRI-ISDN, D channel, ISDN fallback adapter, ISDN router, ISDN terminal adapter, modem, PRI-ISDN, Public Switched Telephone Network (PSTN), T-carrier, time-division multiplexing (TDM), wide area network (WAN)*

Integrated Windows Authentication

A superset of Microsoft Windows NT Challenge/Response (NTLM) authentication.

Overview

Windows NT Challenge/Response authentication (also called NT LAN Manager or NTLM authentication) was the default authentication protocol used by all versions of Microsoft Windows prior to Windows 2000. The Windows 2000 platform now uses the Kerberos V5 authentication by default, which is faster and more secure than NTLM and authenticates both the client and the server (NTLM authenticates only the client). In Windows 2000, NTLM is retained for backward compatibility with earlier versions of Windows.

Integrated Windows Authentication was introduced in Windows 2000 as an enhanced version of NTLM that is backward-compatible with earlier versions of NTLM. The only difference in the new version is that IIS 5, the version of Internet Information Services (IIS) in Windows 2000, sends both an NTLM header and a Negotiate header to requesting clients using Microsoft Internet Explorer 5 or higher. In earlier versions of Windows, Microsoft Internet Information Server (IIS), and Internet Explorer, NTLM headers are used only, and not Negotiate headers.

See Also: *authentication protocol, Internet Information Services (IIS), Kerberos, Windows NT Challenge/Response Authentication*

Intel-based platform

A computer platform whose processor is based on the Intel 386 architecture microprocessor.

See: *x86 platform*

intelligent hub

A hub that can be remotely managed using Simple Network Management Protocol (SNMP) or some other management protocol.

Overview

An intelligent hub contains an SNMP Management Information Base (MIB) that specifies which hub functions can be managed and which conditions can be monitored. Examples include

- Setting alerts on problem conditions such as excessive collisions
- Isolating and disconnecting problem computers
- Providing network statistics to remote management consoles

Intelligent hubs are usually managed using in-band signaling methods, but they usually offer out-of-band management functions as well, such as being managed by a remote Telnet connection. Modular hubs often have SNMP modules that can be installed in the hub chassis to provide remote manageability and monitoring.

See Also: *hub, in-band signaling, Management Information Base (MIB), out-of-band (OOB) signaling, out-of-band management (OBM), Simple Network Management Protocol (SNMP), Telnet*

Intelligent Input/Output (I2O)

A hardware architecture developed by a consortium led by Intel that improves the input/output (I/O) performance of systems by relieving the central processing unit (CPU) of interrupt-intensive I/O tasks.

Overview

Intelligent Input/Output (I2O) makes use of a separate I2O processor such as the Intel i960 series of processors. This enables the CPU to offload interrupts received from peripherals to the I2O processor for handling. This scheme can improve the performance of servers by as much as 30 percent.

I2O also provides a way of standardizing I/O device drivers across different operating systems and hardware platforms. I2O standardizes device drivers by dividing them into two components:

- **Hardware Device Module (HDM):** This component directly interfaces with the peripheral being managed.

I

- **Operating System Service Module (OSM):** This component interfaces with the operating system on the machine.

In addition, an intermediate layer between the HDM and OSM provides independence between them by providing standard communication mechanisms that allow any HDM for any peripheral to interoperate with any OSM for any operating system.

Notes

The Microsoft Windows 2000, Windows XP, and Windows .NET operating systems support I2O.

I

IntelliMirror

A set of management technologies native to Microsoft Windows 2000, Windows XP, and the Windows .NET Server family that simplifies the task of configuring and maintaining applications, settings, and data at the client and server level.

Overview

IntelliMirror provides a distributed replication service that lets clients and servers "intelligently mirror" and share information stored on local and distributed file systems. IntelliMirror mirrors the workstation environment on the network server so that the environment can be easily managed. IntelliMirror also offers full roaming support by allowing a user to log on to any client machine and access his or her software, settings, and data. IntelliMirror is designed to simplify network administration and eliminate the need for administrators to "visit" desktop clients to upgrade operating systems and applications.

IntelliMirror is a combination of several features of Windows 2000 and depends on various aspects of the operating system's architecture, including Active Directory directory service, Group Policy, and various services. IntelliMirror's Change and Configuration Management (CCM) features are provided in three ways:

- **User data management:** Data can follow users wherever they roam on the network and even be available when the user is offline.
- **User settings management:** Enables administrators to use Group Policy to restrict and customize a user's desktop working environment, including which software applications the user is allowed to use.
- **Software installation and maintenance:** Allows software applications to be installed either by assigning them (the first time the user clicks on the application shortcut in the Start menu, the application is downloaded and installed on his machine) or publishing them in Active Directory (the user employs Add/Remove Programs in Control Panel to install the software).

IntelliMirror can also use Remote Installation Services (RIS) to enable authorized clients to download fully configured operating systems, applications, and data from remote servers, thus performing unattended installations on the clients.

IntelliMirror technologies significantly reduce the total cost of ownership (TCO) of PC-based networks.

See Also: *Active Directory, Group Policy*

Interactive

A built-in identity in Microsoft Windows 2000, Windows XP, and Windows .NET Server.

Overview

The Interactive built-in identity includes any user who has successfully logged on to the console of the local machine. The operating system uses this identity to enable the user to access resources on the machine. The name *Interactive* stems from the idea that the user who belongs to this group is "interacting" with the local computer through the console.

As with all built-in identities, administrators cannot directly modify the membership or assigned rights of the Interactive identity.

See Also: *built-in identities*

interactive logon

Logging on to a network through a local machine.

Overview

Interactive logon is a process whereby a user gains access to a network by entering credentials in response to a dialog box displayed on the local machine. This is in contrast to a remote logon, which occurs when a user who is already logged on locally tries to make a network connection to a remote computer—for example, using the Net Use command at the command prompt. Interactive logons are supported by all versions of Microsoft Windows.

In a Windows 2000 or Windows .NET network, the information that the user must specify during an interactive logon depends on the network's security model, as described in the following table. After successfully logging on interactively, the user is granted an access token that is assigned to the initial process created for her.

Required Logon Information for Security Models

Security Model	*What the User Must Specify*
Workgroup	Username and password
Domain	Username and password
Domain with a trust relationship trusting other domains	Username, password, and domain

Notes

When trust relationships are configured between Windows 2000 or Windows .NET Server domains, the interactive logon dialog box for Windows 2000 and Windows XP clients allows the user to select a logon domain—that is, the domain in which the user's user account is located. In contrast, the earlier Windows 98 and Windows Millennium Edition (Me) logon domains are hard-coded using Client for Microsoft Networks and offer only one domain to choose from at logon time.

See Also: *logon*

inter-exchange carrier (IXC)

A telecommunications carrier that provides long-distance services.

Overview

IXCs own or share the various high-bandwidth, fiber-optic trunk lines that cross different geographic areas and provide high-speed switched digital services for voice, data, and video communication. About 90 percent of the U.S. long-distance communication market is controlled by the Big Three IXCs: AT&T, MCI/WorldCom, and Sprint Corporation. These companies provide services such as long-distance telephone services, frame relay, virtual private networking (VPN), T-1 and T-3 lines, ATM (Asynchronous Transfer Mode) backbone services, and even Internet access.

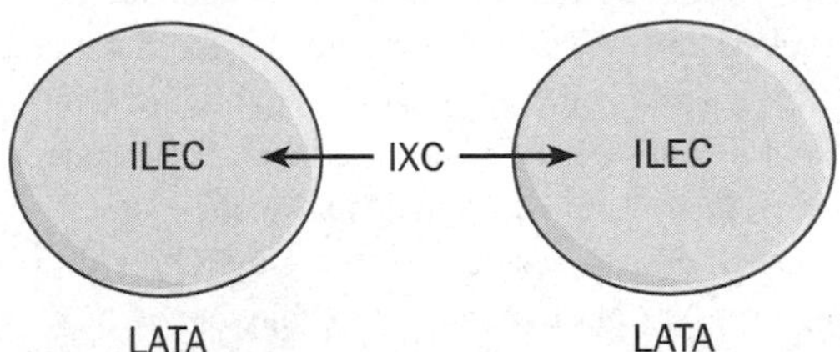

Inter-exchange carrier (IXC). *Traditional relationship between IXCs and Incumbent Local Exchange Carriers (ILECs). This landscape is evolving as a result of the Telecommunications Act of 1996.*

While IXCs dominate the long-distance market, the local telephone companies (telcos) provide subscribers in their particular geographical service areas, called Local Access and Transport Areas (LATAs), with the actual local loop wiring that makes all telephony-based services possible. In other words, the telcos are dependent upon the IXCs for long-distance services, but the IXCs need the telcos' local loop in order to provide their services to customers. Each telco offers services only in their own specific LATA, but IXCs provide services connecting different LATAs. Telcos themselves are properly known as Local Exchange Carriers (LECs) and come in two varieties:

- **ILECs (Incumbent Local Exchange Carriers):** These include the Regional Bell Operating Companies (RBOCs) and rural telcos.
- **CLECs (Competitive Local Exchange Carriers):** These include Digital Subscriber Line (DSL) providers, Metropolitan Ethernet providers, and other kinds of carriers.

IXCs provide their own services through one of two methods:

- Colocating their equipment and sharing point of presence (POP) facilities at telco central offices (COs)

- Building their own POP facilities

Either way, IXCs need to share access with the local loop wiring owned by ILECs. This is facilitated by the government overseeing ILECs as regulated monopolies in their service areas.

Prospects

The Telecommunications Act of 1996 has opened up the market so that LECs can compete in long-distance markets by leasing services from IXCs, and IXCs can compete in local markets by leasing local loop connections from LECs. Some companies have also gained access to each other's services by merging. Other emerging competitors for IXCs are cable television companies, who have customer premises installations in most U.S. residences and who are upgrading their networks for bidirectional communication.

See Also: *Competitive Local Exchange Carrier (CLEC), Incumbent Local Exchange Carrier (ILEC), Local Access and Transport Area (LATA), local exchange carrier (LEC), Regional Bell Operating Company (RBOC)*

interface

In networking and telecommunication, a mechanism for communicating between two devices.

Overview

An interface specifies the nature of the boundary between two devices and determines the procedures and protocols that make it possible for the devices to exchange data.

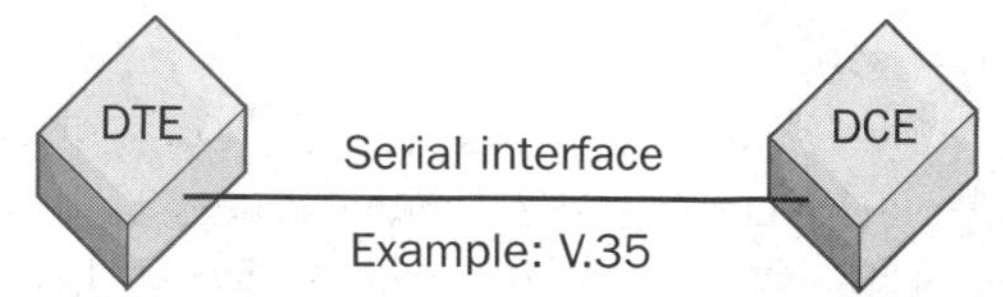

Interface. *An example of an interface between data terminal equipment (DTE) and data communications equipment (DCE) devices.*

The most common type of interface in networking and telecommunication is the serial interface. A serial interface is one that transfers data one bit at a time between two devices. Serial interfaces are commonly used for connecting data terminal equipment (DTE), such as computers or routers, to data communications equipment (DCE), such as modems or Channel Service Unit/Data Service Units (CSU/DSUs). The most common type of serial interface is the RS-232 interface found on the back of most computers and used to connect modems. The following table shows other common examples of serial interfaces.

Types of Serial Interfaces

Serial Interface	*Description*
RS-232	A common interface for communication over unbalanced lines. Uses DB-9 or DB-25 connectors.
RS-422/485	For communication over balanced lines. More suitable than RS-232 for environments with significant electromagnetic interference (EMI) or with DB-9 or DB-37 connectors.
V.35	A high-speed serial interface for data transmission at 48 Kbps. Combines balanced lines with unbalanced lines and is used in Integrated Services Digital Network (ISDN) and frame relay connections. Uses a 24-pin block connector.
X.21	A high-speed serial interface that uses the International Telecommunication Union (ITU) standard for connecting DCE and DTE for synchronous communication. Uses a DB-15 connector.

Another type of interface is the parallel interface, which transfers data several bits at a time, usually one or more bytes at a time. The most common parallel interface is the one used for connecting printers to computers, which uses a female DB-25 or 36-pin Centronics connector.

Note that the type of interface a device uses is related to the kind of connector or cable used to connect to the device, but not in a one-to-one fashion. For example, you could say that a device has an RS-232 serial interface, but it is incorrect to say that you use an RS-232 connector or an RS-232 cable to connect to that device. RS-232 specifies the interface, but several cabling options can support it, such as a cable terminated with a DB-9 or a DB-25 male connector.

Notes

The term *interface* is also used in routing terminology, in which it describes the connection between a router and an attached network. In routing terminology, an interface is a remote network that can be reached from the local network. A router interface is said to be active if it provides connectivity with the remove network or inactive if connectivity is not possible at the time.

The term *interface* is also used in Microsoft Component Object Model (COM) programming to represent pointers through which clients invoke methods of COM objects. From the perspective of a client application, a COM object appears as a set of interfaces.

See Also: *connector (device), routing, RS-232, serial transmission, V.35*

interface card

A card you plug into a computer's motherboard to provide connectivity between the main system bus and an external serial or parallel bus.

Overview

Computers usually come with installed serial/parallel interface cards for connecting modems, printers, and other devices to your system, but in certain situations you might want to purchase a separate interface card. These situations include

- When you have an older computer whose serial interface card cannot support the newer fast 56-kilobit-per-second (Kbps) V.90 modems or whose parallel interface card cannot support IEEE 1284 bidirectional print devices such as the newer Hewlett Packard LaserJet print devices
- When you need a different serial interface such as RS-422/485 to connect your machine to special networking or industrial measurement equipment

Many different kinds of interface cards are available, including the following:

- RS-232 high-speed serial input/output (I/O) cards with 16550 universal asynchronous receiver-transmitter (UART) chips for connecting to high-speed modems and Integrated Services Digital Network (ISDN) terminal adapters. These cards can be either Industry Standard Architecture (ISA) or Peripheral Component Interconnect (PCI) bus cards and can support transfer speeds of up to 460.8 Kbps—much higher than the 115.2-Kbps rate supported by standard RS-232 interfaces.
- Enhanced Capabilities Port (ECP)/Enhanced Parallel Port (EPP) high-speed parallel I/O cards that support up to 2.5-megabit-per-second (Mbps) transfer speeds.
- RS-422/485 interface cards for connecting to industrial sensor and measuring equipment. These cards can support up to 31 separate devices that can be located up to 4000 feet (1220 meters) from the computer. Data transfer speeds are up to 460.8 Kbps.

See Also: *interface, RS-232, serial transmission*

interface converter

Any device that converts one interface to another.

Overview

Interface converters are generally stand-alone, powered devices for midline use or rack-mounted devices for use in wiring closets. There are interface converters for serial and parallel interfaces, asynchronous and synchronous communication, half-duplex and full-duplex communication, single-node and host converters, copper and fiber-optic converters, AC-powered or interface-powered devices, and other devices. Examples of interface converters include the following:

- RS-232 to RS-422 serial interface converters for directly connecting the RS-232 serial interface of a computer to an RS-422 programmable logic controller for synchronous data transmission. If handshaking is required, you should use an RS-232 to RS-422/449 serial interface converter instead.

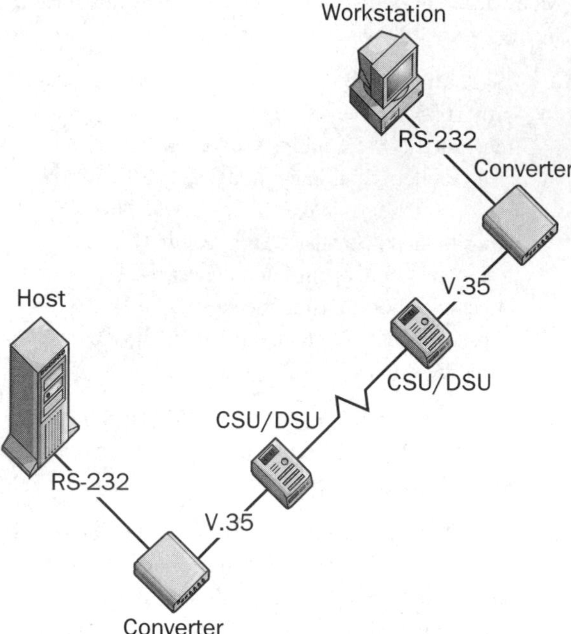

Interface converter. *Using an interface converter to convert between an RS-232 interface and a V.35 interface.*

- RS-232 to RS-422/485 serial interface converters that allow RS-422/485 data collection equipment or industrial measurement devices to be connected to a computer using its built-in RS-232 serial interface. Alternatively, you can install an interface card in the computer to allow it to connect directly with the RS-422/485 device.
- RS-232 to V.35 serial interface converters for connecting RS-232 devices toV.35 lines.
- V.35 to G.703 or X.21 serial interface connectors for use in Europe.
- Small Computer System Interface (SCSI) to parallel converter for connecting SCSI peripherals to an Enhanced Capabilities Port (ECP)/Enhanced Parallel Port (EPP) parallel port.

See Also: *interface, RS-232, Small Computer System Interface (SCSI), V.35*

interference

Also called electromagnetic interference (EMI), electrical noise induced in cabling by nearby electrical equipment, such as motors, air conditioners, fluorescent lights, and power lines.

See: *electromagnetic interference (EMI)*

Interim Interswitch Signaling Protocol (IISP)

An Asynchronous Transfer Mode (ATM) protocol that enables cells to be routed over a switched virtual circuit (SVC).

Overview

The Interim Interswitch Signaling Protocol (IISP) is essentially a form of static routing for ATM networks. Normally, ATM is a connection-oriented architecture in which a switched connection is first established between the transmitting and receiving node, after which cells are delivered across that connection. When IISP is used, the result is more like Internet Protocol (IP) internetworks, where packets can be routed to their destination addresses by various paths.

IISP was created in 1994 and is an extension to the ATM UNI (user-to-network interface) specification.

Architecture

To use IISP, the ATM carrier network must employ switched virtual circuits (SVCs). Unfortunately most ATM carriers currently support only permanent virtual circuits (PVCs), as they are cheaper and easier to implement, which means that IISP is not a widely available solution for enterprises needing to route data over ATM carrier backbone networks.

IISP routes cells based on their 20-octet network service access point (NSAP) address. IISP employs channels 32 to 255 of virtual path identifier (VPI) zero. These channels function as trunk lines for routed transport of cells over ATM networks.

Notes

An alternative to IISP for routing cells over ATM backbone networks is to use Private Network-to-Network Interface (PNNI) protocol. You can combine both IISP and PNNI with multiprotocol label switching (MPLS) for enhanced functionality and performance.

See Also: *Asynchronous Transfer Mode (ATM)*

Interior Border Gateway Protocol (IBGP)

The version of Border Gateway Protocol (BGP) used for exchanging routing information within the same autonomous system (AS).

Overview

There are two versions of BGP, the classless dynamic routing protocol used on the Internet. These versions are

- **Exterior Border Gateway Protocol (EBGP):** This exterior routing protocol is used for exchanging routing information dynamically between border routers connecting different ASs on the Internet or in a large private Transmission Control Protocol/Internet Protocol (TCP/IP) internetwork. When referring simply to BGP, the variant EBGP is always implied. In other words, EBGP is usually just called BGP.
- **Interior Border Gateway Protocol (IBGP):** This interior routing protocol is used for exchanging routing information between routers within an AS. IBGP is less "chatty" than EBGP and does not communicate route information as frequently. Unlike EBGP, all IBGP routers within a particular AS must be configured as peers.

See Also: *autonomous system (AS), Border Gateway Protocol (BGP), classless routing protocol, dynamic routing*

interior gateway protocol (IGP)

Any routing protocol used to distribute routing information within an autonomous system (AS).

Overview

Also known as interior routing protocols, interior gateway protocols (IGPs) specify how routers within an AS exchange routing information with other routers within the same AS. This is in contrast to exterior gateway protocols (EGPs), which facilitate the exchange of routing information between routers in different ASs.

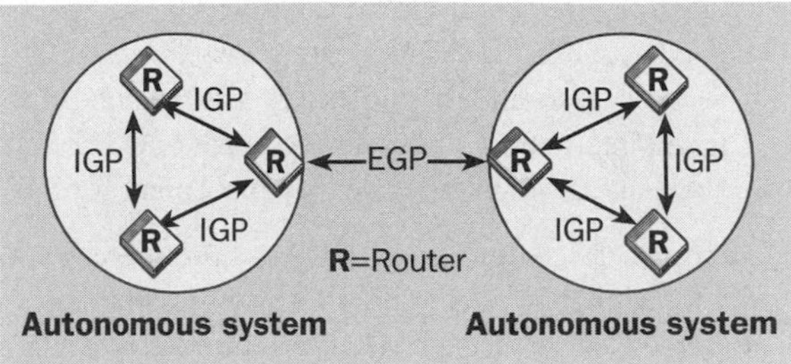

Interior gateway protocol (IGP). *A network using IGP to route information within an autonomous system and exterior gateway protocol (EGP) to route information between autonomous systems.*

Examples of IGPs include

- **Routing Information Protocol (RIP):** This is a popular protocol for small to medium-sized internetworks and is based on the distance-vector routing algorithm.
- **Open Shortest Path First (OSPF) Protocol:** This is used mainly on medium-sized to large-sized internetworks and is based on the link-state routing algorithm.
- **Interior Gateway Routing Protocol (IGRP):** This is a proprietary distance-vector routing protocol developed by Cisco Systems.

See Also: *autonomous system (AS), dynamic routing protocol, exterior gateway protocol (EGP), Internet, routing protocol*

Interior Gateway Routing Protocol (IGRP)

An interior gateway protocol (IGP) developed by Cisco Systems.

Overview

Interior Gateway Routing Protocol (IGRP) is a proprietary classful interior routing protocol that was developed by Cisco for two reasons:

- Routing Information Protocol (RIP) was widely deployed but had several deficiencies, including a simplistic metric that did not mirror real-world network topologies and a limitation in maximum hop count to 15 hops.

- Open Shortest Path First (OSPF) was being developed by the Internet Engineering Task Force (IETF) as a successor to RIP and as a routing protocol for larger internetworks, but development of OSPF was slow and the market needed a replacement for RIP.

As a result, Cisco developed IGRP as a proprietary protocol for exchange of routing information within an autonomous system (AS). IGRP was tuned to provide optimal routes to ensure that communications within a network would be minimally disrupted should a router go down. IGMP is a stable protocol capable of supporting very large networks, supports up to 255 hops (100 by default), has fast convergence, provides rudimentary load balancing between parallel routes, and prevents routing loops from occurring.

Architecture

IGRP is based on the same distance-vector routing algorithm used by RIP. In this algorithm a router uses IGRP to exchange routing table updates with adjacent (neighboring) routers only. In contrast to the simple metric of RIP, which forwards packets over the route having the least number of hops, IGRP uses a complicated formula to determine the best route to select, basing the decision on link characteristics that mirror the network's real topology and traffic flow. These factors include

- The time it would take a packet to reach its destination when the network is quiet (no traffic)
- The amount of bandwidth currently being used by each route (varies with time)
- The bandwidth of the slowest hop over the route
- The reliability of the route

IGRP routing updates are issued every 90 seconds, compared to every 30 seconds for RIP. In addition, IGRP routing updates are issued in a compressed form that requires fewer packets per update than RIP.

In addition, IGRP makes use of the following features to provide efficient routing:

- **Hold-down:** Prevents a route that has previously gone bad from being reinstated as a valid route
- **Split horizon:** Prevents routing loops from occurring between two routers
- **Poison reverse update:** Reduces the chance of routing loops occurring between three or more routers

Notes

Enhanced IGRP (EIGRP) is another proprietary interior routing protocol developed by Cisco. Despite the similarity in their names, EIGRP is a very different protocol from IGRP.

See Also: *dynamic routing protocol, Enhanced Interior Gateway Routing Protocol (EIGRP), interior gateway protocol (IGP), interior routing protocol, Routing Information Protocol (RIP)*

interior routing protocol

Another name for an interior gateway protocol (IGP), any routing protocol used to distribute routing information within an autonomous system (AS).

See: *interior gateway protocol (IGP)*

intermediary device

Any networking device positioned between a remote access server (RAS) and a remote client.

Overview

Intermediary devices are third-party devices for performing security-related tasks such as authentication, encryption, and other functions. An intermediary device such as a security host is typically positioned between the RAS server and the modem pool. Remote clients connecting to the modem pool must be authenticated by the security host before they can establish a connection with the RAS server. The security host thus provides an extra layer of security for remote access to the network. The security host might prompt the user for credentials, or the user might be required to use a security card to gain access to the network. Once you have configured the RAS server to work with intermediary devices such as third-party security hosts, you must then configure the client to work with the device. You can typically do this by activating terminal mode on the client so that it can respond to the special prompts issued by the device.

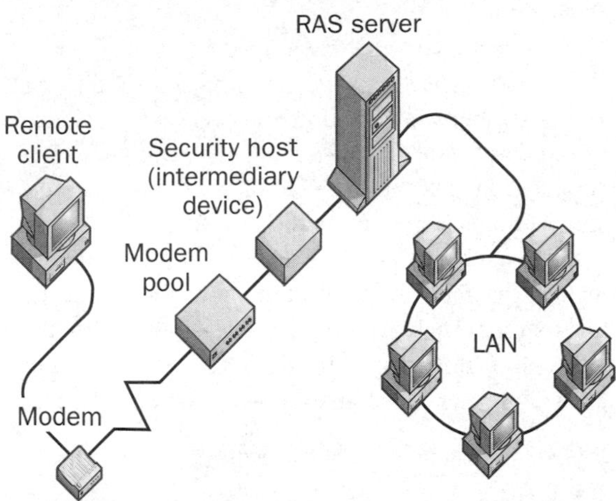

Intermediary device. *A security host as an intermediary device between an RAS server and a client.*

Notes

Microsoft Windows 2000 and the Windows .NET Server family support intermediary devices for its Routing and Remote Access Services (RRAS).

See Also: *remote access*

Intermediate Language (IL)

An intermediate byte code used by the Windows .NET platform.

Overview

Microsoft Corporation's new .NET platform is a language-independent programming framework for developing secure, scalable Web services. Applications and services can be developed for the .NET platform using a variety of programming languages, including Visual Basic (VB), C++, and Microsoft's new C# language. When compiled on the .NET platform, these languages all produce an architecture-independent intermediate byte code called Intermediate Language (IL). Code written in different languages can be mixed easily since they share the same architecture and data types—all compiled code is in the form of .NET objects.

See Also: *.NET platform*

International Mobile Telecommunications-2000 (IMT-2000)

An International Telecommunication Union (ITU) initiative to create a global standard for third-generation (3G) mobile communication networks.

Overview

The International Mobile Telecommunications-2000 (IMT-2000) initiative has its roots in 3G wireless research undertaken by the ITU in 1986. The goal of the initiative is to establish global mobile communication standards that support voice messaging services integrated with existing Public Switched Telephone Network (PSTN) services, integrated multipoint paging and dispatch services, and high speed data transmission at rates of up to 2 megabits per second (Mbps) for both packet-switched and circuit-switched communications (see table).

Proposed Data Rates for IMT-2000 Communications Systems

Mobility	*Minimum Data Rate*
Fixed	2 Mbps
Pedestrian	384 kilobits per second (Kbps)
Vehicular	144 Kbps

Because of differences in how the spectrum is regulated in different countries and regions and because of the fundamental inoperability between the two major types of cellular communication technologies—Time Division Multiple Access (TDMA) and Code Division Multiple Access (CDMA)—the ITU realizes that the initiative probably will not be able to unify worldwide mobile communication into a single global standard. As a result, the original IMT-2000 initiative has evolved somewhat to support several proposed standards, including the following:

- **Universal Mobile Telecommunications System (UMTS):** A standard for 3G wireless networks proposed by the European Telecommunications Standards Institute (ETSI)
- **Universal Wireless Communications (UWC-136):** A standard for 3G wireless networks proposed by the Telecommunications Industry Association (TIA)

- **CDMA2000:** A proposed hardware upgrade to the existing Code Division Multiple Access (CDMA) cellular phone systems used in the United States and in some parts of Asia
- **W-CDMA:** A proposed upgrade to Global System for Mobile Communications (GSM) networks that provides an alternative air interface to CDMA2000 for upgraded CDMA systems in Europe and Japan

The upgrade for CDMA bearers will be simpler and will move them directly from the current IS-95a standard called cdmaOne (the brand name used by the vendor consortium called the CDMA Development Group for existing data transmission at 16 Kbps) to the proposed CDMA2000. The upgrade for TDMA bearers may take several different paths—for example, from TDMA to General Packet Radio Service (GPRS) to Enhanced Data Rates for Global Evolution (EDGE) to UMTS. Some industry watchers predict that GPRS and IMT-2000 will be widely adopted worldwide in the next five years, which will give Europe and Asia an edge in high-speed wireless data communication over the United States, where as many as five competing systems might be deployed widely.

Notes

Note that the *2000* in the term *International Mobile Telecommunications-2000* refers to the transmission speed (approximately 2000 Kbps), not the final deployment date (which is likely to be around 2005).

For More Information

Find out more about IMT-2000 at *www.itu.int/imt.*

See Also: CDMA2000, Universal Mobile Telecommunications System (UMTS), Universal Wireless Communications (UWC-136)

International Organization for Standardization (ISO)

A nongovernmental organization based in Geneva, Switzerland, that has representatives from about 130 countries and regions and is responsible for developing a variety of international standards in science and engineering.

Overview

The International Organization for Standardization (ISO), established in 1947, runs almost 3000 different working groups and committees covering a broad range of standards issues. The ISO's goals are to develop cooperation in scientific, technological, intellectual, and economic activities and to facilitate the international exchange of goods and services. The ISO includes member agencies in more than 30 countries and regions. These member agencies include the American National Standards Institute (ANSI) and the European Computer Manufacturers Association (ECMA).

ISO standards include the following:

- Open Systems Interconnection (OSI) reference model for networking
- ISO/IEC SQL-92 standard for the transact-SQL language
- ISO codes for photographic film speeds
- ISO 9000 framework for business-management and quality-assurance standards
- ISO 216 international standard paper sizes
- Standards for telephone and bank cards
- ISO international country codes and currency codes

Notes

If you work with enterprise directory services, you might need to contact the ISO someday. For instance, if you plan to modify the schema of Active Directory directory service for Microsoft Windows 2000 and create new classes or attributes, you must obtain a unique object identifier for your enterprise to ensure that your new classes and attributes do not conflict with those defined by other directory services. This is especially important in a heterogeneous networking environment with multiple interoperating directory services such as Active Directory, Novell Directory Services (NDS), an X.500-based directory service, or Simple Network Management Protocol (SNMP). You can contact the ISO to receive an object identifier for your organization and then subdivide your object identifier space as you desire and assign object identifiers to your new classes and attributes.

For More Information

Visit the ISO at *www.iso.ch.*

See Also: *Active Directory, Novell Directory Services (NDS), Simple Network Management Protocol (SNMP), X.500*

International Telecommunication Union (ITU)

An international organization headquartered in Geneva, Switzerland, that coordinates global telecommunications networks and services with governments and the private sector.

Overview

Known until 1993 as the International Telegraph and Telephone Consultative Committee, also known by its French name, Comité Consultatif International Télégraphique et Téléphonique (CCITT), the International Telecommunication Union (ITU) is responsible for a number of important international networking and communication standards, including the following X series and V series standards:

- V.35 serial interface standard
- V.90 56-Kbps modem standard
- X.25 packet-switching network standard
- X.400 message-handling system (MHS) standard
- X.435 standard for electronic data interchange (EDI) over X.400
- X.500 directory service recommendations
- X.509 digital certificate and authentication standard
- Standards for Standardized Generalized Markup Language (SGML), the precursor to Extensible Markup Language (XML)

The ITU also hosts important study groups, meetings, and conferences and is a leading publisher of information on telecommunications technology and standards. The section of the ITU that is concerned with developing international standards for telecommunications is called the ITU Telecommunications Standardization Sector, or ITU-T.

For More Information

Visit the ITU at *www.itu.int.*

See Also: *American National Standards Institute (ANSI), V.35, V.90, X.25, X.400, X.500*

Internet

The global public Transmission Control Protocol/ Internet Protocol (TCP/IP) internetwork.

Overview

The Internet has evolved in a single decade from an academic network to the backbone of today's economy. The Internet is synonymous in most people's minds with the World Wide Web (WWW) and has displaced most other early Internet protocols apart from Simple Mail Transfer Protocol (SMTP) and File Transfer Protocol (FTP).

The Internet is not owned by any one government, organization, or company. Nevertheless, various administrative bodies oversee different aspects of the Internet's operation. These groups include the following:

- Internet Society (ISOC), which coordinates a number of other bodies and gives them advice and direction.
- Internet Architecture Board (IAB), which is responsible to the ISOC and oversees the Internet's architecture.
- Internet Engineering Task Force (IETF), which is responsible to the IAB and develops Internet protocols that define such applications as the TCP/IP protocol suite and the Domain Name System (DNS).
- Internet Assigned Numbers Authority (IANA), which is responsible for coordinating the registration of DNS names and assigning Internet Protocol (IP) addresses. Many of the functions of IANA have

been replaced recently by a new body called the Internet Corporation for Assigned Names and Numbers (ICANN).

History

The Internet originated with the ARPANET project of the U.S. Department of Defense in the early 1970s. The original purpose of ARPANET was to create a wide area network (WAN) that would allow researchers at various defense and civilian research agencies to communicate with each other and to collaborate on projects. ARPANET originally consisted of a few hundred IP hosts joined together at several locations across the country.

When ARPANET grew larger and an increasing number of civilian agencies such as universities and networking companies wanted access to it, administration of the network was given to the National Science Foundation (NSF). The NSF then linked five national supercomputing centers together across the country using TCP/IP running over dedicated 56-kilobits-per-second (Kbps) links. This was essentially the birth of the public Internet as we know it. As more and more universities and private individuals became connected to this network, the NSF realized it had to upgrade the network to handle the new traffic. So in 1987 the NSF awarded a contract to Merit network, which in conjunction with MCI and IBM linked together 13 sites totaling 170 local area networks (LANs) using 1.544 megabit-per-second (Mbps) T1 lines. A year later the NSF terminated the original 56-Kbps backbone.

A few years later, traffic on the network had increased to such an extent that a further upgrade was needed. This was performed by Advanced Network and Services (ANS), a spin-off of the earlier Merit/MCI/IBM coalition. In 1990 the backbone was upgraded to T3 lines (45 Mbps) connecting 16 sites representing 3500 LANs. At this point, several other companies tried to get into the act. Alternet (now UUNET) and PSI created the Commercial Internet Exchange (CIX), which began as an alternative network but which soon was connected into the NSF backbone.

Then a company called MFS began to set up fiber-optic ring networks called Metropolitan Area Ethernets (MAEs). These MAEs were connected to the Internet backbone in metropolitan areas. These soon became obvious places for companies to connect their corporate networks to the Internet, and MAE soon stood for Metropolitan Area Exchange instead. The first such exchange was called MAE-East, which is still operational and is located in Washington, D.C. Other MAEs include MAE-West in San Jose, California, and MAE-LA in Los Angeles.

By 1993 the NSF had decided to stop funding and managing the Internet backbone and to turn this job over to private operators. To facilitate this, the NSF established several network access points (NAPs) where backbone networks of these private operators could connect to the NSF's network. There are now several dozen NAPs in the United States (and many others around the world) and these include both the original MAEs and newer ones created by the NSF and by private companies. Finally, in 1995 NSF turned off its network and the Internet was reborn as a "core" of NAPs that are connected and owned by such companies as AT&T, Cable and Wireless, Genuity (formerly part of GTE Corporation), PSINet, Sprint Corporation, Qwest Communications International, and UUNET. Today, these NAPs are connected by fast OC-12, OC-48, and OC-192 connections, and traffic at the Internet's core is estimated by analysts as costing about $800 per megabit per second per month.

Architecture

From a network architecture point of view, the Internet's architecture is amazingly simple: the Internet can be viewed as a collection of thousands of large privately managed networks called Autonomous Systems (ASs). Each AS has a number (Autonomous System Number, or ASN) to identify it to other ASs. Different ASs are joined in a loose mesh configuration using powerful border routers that exchange routing information with each other using Border Gateway Protocol (BGP). IP packets traverse the Internet by being forwarded by these border routers and by routers within the ASs themselves. A typical request for a Web page from somewhere else in the world might result in your request making 15 or more hops across routers on the Internet.

For More Information

You can find interesting and useful information about the Internet at the following sites: *www.netsizer.com*, *www.isc.org*, and *www.cyberatlas.internet.com*.

See Also: *autonomous system (AS), autonomous system number (ASN), Border Gateway Protocol (BGP), Internet2, Internet access, Internet Architecture Board (IAB), Internet Assigned Numbers Authority (IANA), Internet Corporation for Assigned Names and Numbers (ICANN), Internet Engineering Task Force (IETF), Internet service provider (ISP), Internet Society (ISOC)*

Internet2

A project of the University Corporation for Advanced Internet Development (UCAID) to develop a high-speed network for research and collaboration and for developing innovative applications for education.

Overview

The Internet2 project is supported by more than 150 universities in the United States and is designed to create a leading-edge network for developing and testing new Internet applications for researchers. Its members consist of a collection of national, regional, and campus organizations whose networks are linked by new technologies and common research goals. Internet2 is not a successor to the present Internet, but rather new technologies to be used as part of the Internet. Internet2 is being developed by a consortium of institutions working to improve on existing Internet technologies. The knowledge and new technologies developed using Internet2 will be made available to the broader Internet community as they emerge.

Some of the potential benefits of new Internet technologies include advances in areas such as telemedicine, digital libraries, and virtual laboratories. Internet2 will also provide researchers with a test bed for developing new networking technologies, such as the following:

- Broadband networking
- Quality of service (QoS) networking technologies
- IPv6, the new 128-bit version of the Internet protocol
- Multicasting technologies

Notes

Other groups are working toward similar goals in cooperation with Internet2. Examples include the federally led Next Generation Internet (NGI) initiative, the National Science Foundation's High Performance Connections program, and the MCI/WorldCom vBNS network service.

Europe's version of the Internet2 is called GEANT and is intended as a backbone network joining 30 countries and regions together using 2.5-gigabit-per-second (Gbps) links for the purposes of academic research and industry collaboration.

For More Information

Visit the Internet2 site at *www.internet2.edu.*

Internet access

The process of connecting subscribers to Internet service providers (ISPs).

Overview

In the early 1990s, the ways in which businesses and consumers could connect to the Internet were limited, slow, and costly. These technologies included dial-up modems, Integrated Services Digital Network (ISDN) connections, and expensive leased lines such as T1 lines. By the end of the decade, the landscape had changed, however, and broadband Internet access technologies had become widespread, at least in dense urban areas. These new methods for providing Internet access to subscribers include:

- **Asymmetric Digital Subscriber Line (ADSL):** Provides downstream speeds up to about 10 megabits per second (Mbps)—upstream speeds are less—

over dedicated connections at about $50 a month. The main disadvantage is that it is available only within a few miles from the telco central office (CO).

- **Cable modem:** Provides symmetric speeds of up to 10 Mbps in theory, but because the system is a shared network, typical speeds are more like 1 Mbps. Cable modem access is widely available in residential areas but difficult to obtain in business and industrial parks.
- **Fixed wireless:** Provides downstream speeds typically of only a few hundred kilobits per second and has limited availability but can be deployed in locations too distant for ADSL or cable modems to function.

See Also: *Asymmetric Digital Subscriber Line (ADSL), cable modem, Integrated Services Digital Network (ISDN), T-carrier, wireless networking*

Internet Architecture Board (IAB)

A technical advisory group for the Internet Society (ISOC).

Overview

The Internet Architecture Board (IAB) was established in 1983 for the purpose of providing oversight for the development of Internet protocols and standards. It consists of 13 volunteer members, 6 of whom are nominated by the Internet Engineering Task Force (IETF) and approved by the ISOC. IAB members are part-time volunteers who provide the IETF community with advice and support. The IAB's functions include the following:

- Overseeing the evolution of the Internet's architecture and protocols from a long-term, strategic level. The most important of these issues is to ensure the continued scaling of the Internet's core services and protocols.
- Overseeing the process for developing Internet standards and for managing and publishing the Request for Comments (RFC) series of standards documents.
- Providing guidance to the ISOC on technical and procedural matters relating to the Internet.
- Selecting and appointing the chair of the IETF and candidates for the Internet Engineering Steering Group (IESG), which is responsible for the day-to-day operation of the IETF, and the Internet Assigned Numbers Authority (IANA), most of whose functions are now replaced by the Internet Corporation for Assigned Names and Numbers (ICANN).

For More Information

Visit the IAB at *www.iab.org.*

See Also: *Internet Assigned Numbers Authority (IANA), Internet Corporation for Assigned Names and Numbers (ICANN), Internet Engineering Task Force (IETF), Internet Society (ISOC)*

Internet Assigned Numbers Authority (IANA)

The organization that coordinates the assignment of unique Internet protocol parameters such as the Internet Protocol (IP) address space and the Domain Name System (DNS).

Overview

The Internet Assigned Numbers Authority (IANA) operates under the auspices of the Internet Society (ISOC) and is considered part of the Internet Architecture Board (IAB). IANA is the ultimate authority for managing the root name servers that maintain the central database of information for the DNS. IANA also controls the assignment of Transmission Control Protocol/Internet Protocol (TCP/IP) protocol identifiers such as IP addresses and the numbers for autonomous systems (ASs) on the Internet.

IANA delegates authority to other organizations and companies to grant users unique IP address blocks and register DNS domain names. IANA delegates these responsibilities to three regional bodies:

- The American Registry for Internet Numbers (ARIN), which manages North America, South America, and sub-Saharan Africa

- Réseaux IP Européens (RIPE), which manages Europe and North Africa
- The Asia Pacific Network Information Center (APNIC), which manages Asia and Australia

IANA is funded by the U.S. government. A new international nonprofit organization called the Internet Corporation for Assigned Names and Numbers (ICANN) has taken over the responsibilities of IANA because of the Internet's increasingly international and commercial nature.

Notes

Actual registration of IP addresses and DNS names is performed by network information centers, which in the United States include:

- Various accredited domain name registrars, which have replaced Internet Network Information Center (InterNIC) as the authorities for registering the .com, .org, .net, .gov, and .edu top-level domains
- The U.S. Domain Registration Service, which administers the .us top-level domain
- The U.S. Department of Defense Network Information Center, which manages the .mil top-level domain
- The .int top-level domain registry in Marina del Rey, California

For More Information

Visit IANA at *www.iana.org*.

See Also: *American Registry for Internet Numbers (ARIN), Asia Pacific Network Information Center (APNIC), Domain Name System (DNS), Internet Architecture Board (IAB), Internet Society (ISOC), RIPE*

Internet Cache Protocol (ICP)

A protocol that enables arrays of proxy servers to work together over a network.

Overview

The Internet Cache Protocol (ICP) was developed to allow individual proxy servers to query neighboring proxy servers to try to locate cached copies of requested objects. If these queries fail, the object is requested from the Internet. ICP has some inherent drawbacks:

- ICP arrays use queries to determine the location of cached information, a process that generates additional network traffic.
- ICP arrays have negative scalability—the more proxy servers in the array, the more query traffic is generated.
- ICP arrays tend to become highly redundant, with each cache containing similar information (the URLs of the most frequently visited sites).

Microsoft Corporation's solution to these problems is the Caching Array Routing Protocol (CARP), which it developed for its Microsoft Proxy Server version 2.

See Also: *Caching Array Routing Protocol (CARP), proxy server*

Internet Connection Firewall (ICF)

A new firewall feature of Windows XP and the Windows .NET Server family.

Overview

Internet Connection Firewall (ICF) is a software-based firewall application that is used to set restrictions on what type of network traffic or information is allowed to communicate between your home or small office network and the Internet. ICF is similar to a "stateful" firewall in that it monitors all aspects of the communications that cross its path and inspects the source and destination address of each message that it handles. Communications that originate from a source outside the ICF computer are dropped by the firewall unless an entry for the type of traffic being received is designated to allow passage. No notifications are created; ICF simply discards unsolicited communications, which prevents common hacking attempts such as port scanning. A security log can be created to allow viewing of the activity that ICF tracks.

See Also: *firewall, network security*

Internet Control Message Protocol (ICMP)

A Transmission Control Protocol/Internet Protocol (TCP/IP) network layer protocol used for various purposes.

Overview

The Internet Control Message Protocol (ICMP) is a simple TCP/IP protocol that operates at the network layer, the same layer at which Internet Protocol (IP) functions. Unlike IP, whose main function is to enable datagrams to be sent and received, ICMP has more restricted functions, including

- Testing of TCP/IP connectivity with remote hosts to make sure they are alive (using ping)
- Issuing simple control requests to routers and other hosts
- Reporting error conditions from routers and other hosts

In effect, ICMP complements IP by providing control messages and reporting errors on behalf of IP. ICMP is defined in RFCs 792 and 1700.

Architecture

ICMP messages are encapsulated in IP datagrams for transmission over a network. ICMP packets are thus connectionless and do not provide for guaranteed message delivery. ICMP supports broadcast traffic, but unlike both Transmission Control Protocol (TCP) and User Datagram Protocol (UDP), which operate at the higher Internet layer, ICMP does not use port numbers.

The function of an ICMP message is determined by the first 2 bytes of its message header. Some of the more common types of ICMP packets are

- **Echo Reply (ICMP type 0):** The Ping command uses this packet type to test TCP/IP connectivity.
- **Destination Unreachable (ICMP type 3):** Indicates that the destination network, host, or port cannot be reached.
- **Source Quench (ICMP type 4):** Routers send this packet type when they cannot process IP traffic as fast as it is sent. A Source Quench message essentially means "Slow down!" A Microsoft Windows NT or Windows 2000 host can respond to a Source Quench message by slowing down its rate of data transmission.
- **Redirect Message (ICMP type 5):** Used to redirect the host to a different network path. This message essentially tells the router to override the entry in its internal routing table for this packet.
- **Echo Request (ICMP type 8):** The Ping command uses this packet type to test TCP/IP connectivity.
- **Router Advertisement (ICMP type 9):** Sent at random intervals in response to an ICMP Router Solicitation request.
- **Router Solicitation (ICMP type 10):** Sent by routers to request router advertisement updates.
- **Time Exceeded (ICMP type 11):** Indicates that the Time to Live (TTL) has been exceeded because of too many hops. The Tracert command uses this message to test a series of routers between the local and remote hosts.
- **Parameter Problem (ICMP type 12):** Indicates an error processing the header of an IP packet.

Issues

Because of its broadcast nature, ICMP has been open to exploitation as a means of network attack. Many types of denial of service (DoS) attacks are based upon ICMP, including the Smurf attack, Tribe Flood Network (TFN) attack, Loki, and WinFreeze. For example, ICMP redirects can modify a router's routing table, so sometimes hackers try to subvert routers by issuing forged ICMP redirects in order to perform a DoS attack. ICMP redirects are usually sent by routers only if all the following conditions occur:

- The router is configured to generate ICMP redirects.
- The incoming router interface for the packet is the same as the outgoing router interface.

- The subnet of the source IP address is identical to the next-hop IP address.
- The IP datagram is not source routed.

See Also: *denial of service (DoS), hacking, Internet Protocol (IP), Transmission Control Protocol (TCP), Transmission Control Protocol/Internet Protocol (TCP/IP), User Datagram Protocol (UDP)*

Internet Corporation for Assigned Names and Numbers (ICANN)

A nonprofit corporation that has taken over some of the functions of IANA (Internet Assigned Numbers Authority).

Overview

The Internet Corporation for Assigned Names and Numbers (ICANN) is responsible for

- Allocating portions of the Internet Protocol (IP) address space
- Managing the Domain Name System (DNS), including developing new top-level domains and managing root name servers
- Assigning Internet Protocol (IP) parameters

Until recently, a U.S. company, Network Solutions, exclusively managed the registration of domain names and maintained the DNS database. With the emergence of ICANN, however, these processes have been opened up to allow competition in the DNS registration arena through establishing guidelines for determining the following:

- Who can function as a domain name registry
- Policies on fees and privacy rights for domain name registries
- How disputes will be resolved between domain name registries
- What new top-level domain names will be allowed

Prospects

The transition from IANA to ICANN has not been entirely smooth. Some members of the international Internet community still see ICANN as largely dominated by U.S. government and corporate interests and would like to see a more radical redesign of the DNS to make it more international and to help reduce the tide of trademark litigation regarding domain names.

For More Information

Visit ICANN at *www.icann.org.*

See Also: *Domain Name System (DNS), Internet Assigned Numbers Authority (IANA)*

Internet Engineering Task Force (IETF)

An international community of networking engineers, network administrators, researchers, and vendors whose goal is to ensure the smooth operation and evolution of the Internet.

Overview

The Internet Engineering Task Force (IETF) receives its charter from the Internet Society (ISOC), and its daily operations are overseen by the Internet Architecture Board (IAB). The work of the IETF is performed by a number of working groups who are dedicated to such aspects of the Internet as routing, operations and management, transport, security, applications, and user services. These working groups interact primarily through mailing lists and are managed by area directors who belong to the Internet Engineering Steering Group (IESG). Some working groups develop extensions and newer versions of familiar protocols such as Hypertext Transfer Protocol (HTTP), Lightweight Directory Access Protocol (LDAP), Network News Transfer Protocol (NNTP), Point-to-Point Protocol (PPP), and Simple Network Management Protocol (SNMP). Others develop new protocols such as the Common Indexing Protocol, Internet Open Trading Protocol, and the Internet Printing Protocol.

The working groups produce documents called Internet Drafts, which have a life span of six months, after

which they must be deleted, updated, or established as a Request for Comments (RFC) document.

For More Information

Visit the IETF at *www.ietf.org.*

See Also: *Internet Architecture Board (IAB), Internet Society (ISOC), Request for Comments (RFC)*

Internet Explorer

Microsoft Corporation's integrated suite of client-side Internet software, which is included with all current versions of Microsoft Windows.

Overview

Microsoft Internet Explorer has evolved from a simple Web browser to a full-featured suite of Internet tools. It provides access not only to information on Web sites on corporate intranets and the Internet but also to file system resources on the local machine and to shared folders on the network. When deployed using the Internet Explorer Administration Kit (IEAK), the following optional components can be installed or upgraded in addition to the basic Web browser:

- Microsoft Outlook Express
- Microsoft NetMeeting
- Microsoft FrontPage Express
- Microsoft Chat
- Web Publishing Wizard
- Connection Wizard

Features of Internet Explorer 5 and later include

- Support for the latest Internet standards and scripting languages, including Hypertext Markup Language (HTML) version 4; Microsoft Visual Basic, Scripting Edition (VBScript); JScript; ActiveX; Java; and Dynamic HTML
- Split-screen Search, History, Channel, and Favorites Explorer bars that can be toggled on and off
- Security zones for dividing intranets and the Internet into safe and unsafe regions with their own security settings
- Authenticode 2 code-signing technology that enables users to check the digital certificate of downloaded code before installing it on their system
- Offline browsing, which enables users to access Web content in their History or Subscribed Content folders when they are not connected to the Internet
- Scheduled, unattended dial-up for obtaining Web content from subscribed sites to view offline later
- Autocompletion of Uniform Resource Locators (URLs) typed into the address bar using Microsoft IntelliSense technology
- Dynamic HTML behaviors that allow Dynamic HTML functionality to be extended through hosted components
- Development enhancements that allow users to set the properties of items based on the value of an expression
- Enhancements to tables that allow users to create fixed-layout tables and collapsible borders
- Accessibility enhancements

For More Information

You can visit the Internet Explorer home page at *www.microsoft.com/windows/ie.*

See Also: *Internet Explorer Administration Kit (IEAK), Web browser*

Internet Explorer Administration Kit (IEAK)

A tool for customizing and deploying Microsoft Internet Explorer throughout an enterprise.

Overview

Some of the features of the Internet Explorer Administration Kit (IEAK) include

- IEAK Configuration Wizard, which is used to download, configure, and package Internet Explorer components for distribution to users in the enterprise.

- Automatic Version Synchronization (AVS) for notifying administrators when software updates for Internet Explorer 4 are available. Administrators can download these updates and distribute them to users.
- Profile Manager for centrally managing user desktop settings after deployment of Internet Explorer 4.
- Wizard-based configuration for determining which portions of Internet Explorer 4 will be deployed and how they will be configured.

The IEAK also supports deployment methods such as Microsoft Systems Management Server (SMS), e-mail, Web sites, floppy disks, and CDs.

Implementation

You first decide how you want to distribute your custom package for Internet Explorer: CD, floppy disks, or an Internet Uniform Resource Locator (URL) for users to download the package. You use the IEAK Configuration Wizard to build custom packages that include Internet Explorer, its related components, and up to 10 other custom components.

Once you create your package, you can distribute it using the appropriate method for the type of package: locate it on an Internet or file server or give users copies of CDs or floppy disks. Users can then run the Setup program to install Internet Explorer and the additional components on their systems. You can also use the IEAK Configuration Wizard to do the following:

- Create silent installation packages that do not allow users to change the configuration settings you have specified
- Create branded packages that customize users' browsers using a company-specific logo, title bar text, toolbar background bitmap image, or channel title bar for Internet Explorer
- Create packages with preconfigured browser settings such as a Start page, Search page, Support page, default favorites, Welcome page, desktop wallpaper, Active Channels, and proxy settings

See Also: *Internet Explorer*

Internet File System (iFS)

A technology developed by Oracle Corporation for sharing data over the Internet.

Overview

Oracle's Internet File System (iFS) leverages Extensible Markup Language (XML) to enable applications, services, and users to share data easily using standard Internet protocols. The iFS is included in the Oracle 9i database platform and provides a repository for all types of information including Web documents, e-mail messages, and other files. Using iFS, you can easily move data between Web applications and Oracle databases.

The iFS supports a number of standard Internet protocols, including

- Hypertext Transfer Protocol (HTTP)
- Web-based Distributed Authoring and Versioning (WebDAV)
- File Transfer Protocol (FTP)
- Simple Mail Transfer Protocol (SMTP)

The iFS also supports Server Message Block (SMB) protocol, the native file sharing protocol of the Microsoft Windows platform.

See Also: *File Transfer Protocol (FTP), Hypertext Transfer Protocol (HTTP), Simple Mail Transfer Protocol (SMTP), XML*

Internet Group Management Protocol (IGMP)

A Transmission Control Protocol/Internet Protocol (TCP/IP) network layer protocol used for informing routers of the availability of multicast groups on the network.

Overview

The Internet Group Management Protocol (IGMP) is used in a multicasting environment to exchange information on the status of membership in multicast groups between routers on the network. Once a router becomes aware that there are hosts on a locally attached network that are members of a particular multicast group, it advertises this information using IGMP to other routers on the internetwork so that multicast messages are forwarded to the appropriate routers. IGMP is thus used to maintain the group membership on a local subnet for an Internet Protocol (IP) multicast.

Architecture

There are two versions of IGMP: IGMPv1 and the newer IGMPv2. IGMPv1 is defined in RFC 1112 and supports only two types of IGMP messages:

- **Host membership report:** Hosts send this type of message to inform local routers that the host wishes to receive multicast IP traffic addressed to a specific group address.
- **Host membership query:** Routers send this message to poll a local area network (LAN) segment in order to determine if any hosts on the segment are listening for multicast traffic.

IGMPv2 is defined in RFC 2236 and includes several new message types, including

- **Leave group:** Used by a host to inform a router that it is the last member to leave a multicast group (so that the router knows it no longer needs to forward IP multicasts to that subnet).
- **Group-specific query:** Similar to the IGMP Host membership query, except that it checks for membership in a specific multicast group.
- **Multicast querier election:** This allows a single router to be selected for issuing IGMP Host membership query messages to a particular network segment.

IGMPv2 is fully backward-compatible with IGMPv1.

Implementation

Operation of IGMP is best illustrated with a simple example. To join a multicast group, a host must report its request for membership to nearby routers. These routers periodically poll the hosts in their locally attached networks to check on their membership status. When a host first joins a multicast group, it sends an IGMP Host Membership Report to the multicast address 244.0.0.1. The message contains the multicast address that identifies the group it wants to join. Routers connected to that host's local network then advertise to other routers throughout the internetwork that the particular network has hosts belonging to that multicast group. The routers poll the hosts regularly by sending IGMP Host Membership Query messages to determine whether any of them are still members of that group. If no hosts on the network belong to that group any longer, the router stops advertising the information to other routers on the internetwork so that multicast messages directed to that group are no longer forwarded to it.

Notes

IGMP is used by the Routing and Remote Access Service (RRAS) of Microsoft Windows 2000 for IP multicasting. IGMP is also used in Windows NT by the Windows Internet Naming Service (WINS)—at startup a WINS server sends IGMP packets to the multicast address 224.0.1.24 to seek out possible WINS replication partners on the network.

See Also: Internet Protocol (IP), multicasting, Transmission Control Protocol/Internet Protocol (TCP/IP)

Internet guest account

A user account in Microsoft Windows 2000, Windows XP, and the Windows .NET Server family used by Microsoft Internet Information Services (IIS).

Overview

The Internet guest account on Windows 2000 is usually an account named IUSR_ComputerName, where ComputerName is the name of the Windows 2000 server on which IIS is installed. The account is used to allow anonymous access to World Wide Web (WWW) and File Transfer Protocol (FTP) sites on IIS. The IUSR_ComputerName account is given a randomly assigned password and is made a member of the Guests local group. The account is also granted the sole system right "log on locally" so that when users on the Internet try to anonymously access a WWW or FTP site on IIS, they are authenticated as if they had logged on locally to the system console (instead of being authenticated as normal network users). This secures the computer against unauthorized network access. Once a user is authenticated as an anonymous user, he or she transparently uses the IUSR_ComputerName account to gain access to files on the WWW or FTP sites of interest.

The IUSR_ComputerName account is automatically included in the built-in Guests local group on the server on which IIS is installed, so be sure to review the permissions and rights that you have granted to the Guests group.

See Also: *Internet Information Services (IIS)*

Internet Information Services (IIS)

A Microsoft Windows service that provides support for application-layer Internet protocols.

Overview

Internet Information Services (IIS) enables Windows 2000 servers to function in the roles of Web servers, File Transfer Protocol (FTP) servers, Network News Transfer Protocol (NNTP) servers, and similar Internet and intranet servers. IIS is also a foundational component for a wide variety of other Microsoft server platforms, including Microsoft Exchange Server 2000, Microsoft Sharepoint Server, and other Microsoft .NET Enterprise Servers.

IIS was first released for Windows NT 3.51 as version 1. The highest version available for the Windows NT platform is version 4.01, which was included as part of the Windows NT Option Pack. On Windows 2000, the version of IIS is 5, but on Windows XP, it is 5.1 and on Windows .NET Server, it is 6.

All current versions of IIS support the following features:

- Fully integrated with Windows NT security and the version of NTFS file system (NTFS) used in Windows NT
- Full support for version 1.1 of Hypertext Transfer Protocol (HTTP)
- Support for File Transfer Protocol (FTP)
- Limited support for Simple Mail Transfer Protocol (SMTP)
- Support for Network News Transfer Protocol (NNTP)
- Support for advanced security using the Secure Sockets Layer (SSL) and related protocols
- Provides a platform for deploying scalable Web server applications using Active Server Pages (ASP); Internet Server API (ISAPI); Common Gateway Interface (CGI); Microsoft Visual Basic, Scripting Edition (VBScript); JScript; and other installable scripting languages, such as Perl
- Allows Web applications to be run as isolated processes in separate memory spaces to prevent one application crash from affecting other applications
- Integrates with Microsoft Transaction Server (MTS) and Microsoft Message Queue (MSMQ) Server for deploying transaction-based Web applications
- Can be managed using the Microsoft Management Console (MMC), through a standard Web browser such as Microsoft Internet Explorer, or by running administrative scripts using the Windows Scripting Host (WSH)
- Includes domain blocking for granting/denying access on the basis of IP address or domain
- Allows IIS activity to be logged in various formats, including IIS, World Wide Web Consortium (W3C), National Computer Security Association (NCSA), and open database connectivity (ODBC) logging
- Allows Web site operators to be assigned for limited administration of each Web site
- Bandwidth throttling to prevent one Web site from monopolizing a server's available bandwidth

Notes

The acronym *IIS* also stands for "Internet Information Server," the forerunner of this feature in the Windows NT platform.

See Also: *Active Server Pages (ASP), Common Gateway Interface (CGI), File Transfer Protocol (FTP), Hypertext Transfer Protocol (HTTP), Internet Server API (ISAPI), Network News Transfer Protocol (NNTP), Secure Sockets Layer (SSL), Simple Mail Transfer Protocol (SMTP), Web server*

Internet Inter-Orb Protocol (IIOP)

A Common Object Request Broker Architecture (CORBA) technology for distributed computing over the Internet.

Overview

CORBA is a technology for building object-oriented distributed applications. A CORBA application consists of objects that communicate with each other using orbs (object request brokers). The Internet Inter-Orb Protocol (IIOP) is an extension for CORBA that allows orbs to communicate with each other over the Internet.

IIOP uses Transmission Control Protocol (TCP) as its underlying network transport. IIOP supports bidirectional communications once a TCP session has been established. IIOP also supports callbacks to allow separate connections for client and server communications.

IIOP does not have a standard well-known TCP port number—instead, different orbs each have their own predefined port numbers. Some orbs also support dynamic allocation of port numbers, and some other orbs do not support IIOP at all.

IIOP does not include built-in authentication and encryption features. Instead, CORBA applications are responsible for secure communications using IIOP. An enhanced version of IIOP does exist, however, called IIOPS, standing for IIOP SSL and using the standard Secure Sockets Layer (SSL) protocol for secure communications over the Internet.

See Also: *Common Object Request Broker Architecture (CORBA), Secure Sockets Layer (SSL)*

Internet Key Exchange (IKE)

A protocol for managing keys in public key cryptography systems.

Overview

Internet Key Exchange (IKE) is used by the Internet Protocol Security (IPsec) protocol for generating and exchanging keys to enable secure IP network communications. IKE defines the procedures involved in the exchange of credentials necessary for establishing secure communications sessions. When IKE is used with IPsec, network authentication can employ either digital certificates or preshared keys. Preshared keys are used where the number of users is small, and digital certificates can scale effectively to the enterprise level. When digital certificates are used, however, IPsec must be rolled out in conjunction with a full public key infrastructure (PKI) to support the generation and management of such certificates.

The Internet Engineering Task Force (IETF) has recently developed several extensions to IKE to simplify how IPsec authentication is performed:

- **Hybrid Auth:** This uses tunneling to send client credentials to a central security server, which responds by returning a digital certificate to the client.
- **Xauth:** This is similar to Hybrid Auth, but the digital certificate resides on the client instead of the server.

See Also: *Internet Protocol Security (IPsec), public key infrastructure (PKI),*

Internet Locator Service (ILS)

A Lightweight Directory Access Protocol (LDAP) directory service that enables Microsoft NetMeeting users to locate and contact other users for conferencing and collaboration over the Internet.

Overview

Microsoft Commercial Internet System (MCIS) has an Internet Locator Service (ILS) that functions as a memory-resident database for storing dynamic directory information about NetMeeting users. This information, which includes a user's name, company, and Internet Protocol (IP) address, is stored in an Active Directory Global Catalog and can be accessed by any LDAP client, such as

NetMeeting. Clients periodically refresh the information in the ILS database. Users can access the ILS using LDAP to place a call to other NetMeeting users and to determine which NetMeeting users are currently logged on to the ILS. Using Active Server Pages (ASP), you can design a customizable Web interface that displays who is currently online and allows users to search for other users and initiate NetMeeting sessions with them.

Notes

ILS replaces the earlier User Locator Service (ULS) technology.

See Also: *Lightweight Directory Access Protocol (LDAP)*

Internet Mail Access Protocol version 4 (IMAP4)

A standard protocol for storage and retrieval of e-mail messages.

Overview

Simple Mail Transport Protocol (SMTP) provides the underlying message transport mechanism for sending e-mail messages over the Internet, but it does not provide any facility for storing and retrieving those messages. In order to communicate, SMTP hosts must be continuously connected to one another, but for ordinary users this is not always the case.

Internet Mail Access Protocol version 4 (IMAP4) complements SMTP by providing a mechanism for holding received messages in receptacles called mailboxes. An IMAP4 server stores messages received by each user in a personal mailbox until the user can connect to the server to download and read them. To do this, the user requires an IMAP4-capable mail client such as Microsoft Outlook or Microsoft Outlook Express.

IMAP4 provides functions similar to an earlier protocol called Post Office Protocol version 3 (POP3), but it includes a number of features that were not supported by POP3. Specifically, IMAP4 allows users to

- Access multiple folders, including public folders
- Create hierarchies of folders for storing messages
- Leave messages on the server after reading them so that they can access the messages again from another location
- Search a mailbox for a specific message to download
- Flag messages as read
- Selectively download portions of messages or attachments only
- Review the headers of messages before downloading them

Implementation

To retrieve a message from an IMAP4 server, an IMAP4 client first establishes a Transmission Control Protocol (TCP) session using TCP port 143. The client then identifies itself to the server and issues a series of IMAP4 commands:

- **LIST:** Retrieves a list of folders in the client's mailbox
- **SELECT:** Selects a particular folder to access its messages
- **FETCH:** Retrieves individual messages
- **LOGOUT:** Ends the IMAP4 session

To troubleshoot problems with remote IMAP4 servers, use Telnet to connect to port 143. Then try issuing various IMAP4 commands such as the ones described in this entry and examine the results.

Advantages and Disadvantages

Because IMAP4 clients can allow read messages to remain on the IMAP4 server, IMAP4 is especially useful for mobile users who dial up and access their mail from multiple locations. The downside is that IMAP4 servers require more resources than POP3 servers because users tend to leave large numbers of messages on the server. IMAP4 also is not as widely supported by Internet service providers (ISPs) as POP3.

Notes

IMAP4 is supported by Microsoft Exchange Server.

See Also: *e-mail, Post Office Protocol version 3 (POP3), Simple Mail Transfer Protocol (SMTP)*

Internet Printing Protocol (IPP)

A method for printing over the Internet.

Overview

The Internet Printing Protocol (IPP) is a standard method for printing files over Internet Protocol (IP) networks and is defined in RFCs 2565 through 2569 and RFC 2639. Using IPP, a user can specify a Uniform Resource Locator (URL) to print to instead of a Universal Naming Convention (UNC) path for the target print device.

Microsoft Windows 2000 supports using IPP to print to Microsoft Windows 2000 print servers running Microsoft Internet Information Services (IIS). Internet printers are represented in Active Directory directory service as printer objects and can be accessed by HTTP/1.1-compatible browsers such as Internet Explorer 4 or higher. IPP print commands run on top of text-based HTTP messages, which itself runs on top of IP.

IPP is a standards-based vendor neutral solution that allows any compatible client to print to any IPP-enabled print server. IPP is also extensible to allow notifications for blocking and job status.

See Also: printing terminology, Universal Naming Convention (UNC)

Internet Protocol (IP)

The network layer protocol used by Transmission Control Protocol/Internet Protocol (TCP/IP) for addressing and routing packets of data between hosts.

Overview

The Internet Protocol (IP) is one of the key protocols within the TCP/IP protocol suite. IP packets carry the actual data being sent across the network from one point to another. IP is a connectionless protocol that provides best-effort delivery of data. IP does not guarantee delivery of data; instead, the responsibility for guaranteeing delivery and sending acknowledgments lies with the higher-level transport layer protocol called Transmission Control Protocol (TCP).

Architecture

The diagram shows an IP packet's structure. Some of the more important header fields in the IP packet structure include

- **Source IP address:** The IP address of the host transmitting the packet.
- **Destination IP address:** The IP address of the host to which the packet is being sent, a multicast group address, or the broadcast IP address 255.255.255.255.
- **Header checksum:** A mathematical computation used for verifying that the packet received is intact.
- **Time to Live (TTL):** The number of router hops that the packet can make before being discarded.
- **Fragment offset:** The position of the fragment if the original IP packet has been fragmented (for example, by a router). This information enables the original packet to be reconstructed.

IP Packet Structure	Bytes
Version	$\frac{1}{2}$
Header length	$\frac{1}{2}$
Type of service	1
Total length	2
Identifier	2
Flags	$\frac{3}{8}$
Fragment offset	$1\frac{5}{8}$
Time to Live (TTL)	1
Protocol	1
Header checksum	2
Source IP address	4
Destination IP address	4
Options and padding	4
Data	varies

Internet Protocol (IP). *The structure of an IP packet.*

Implementation

IP packets are usually moved across a routed TCP/IP internetwork in the following fashion:

- If IP determines that the destination IP address is a local address, it transmits the packet directly to the destination host.
- If IP determines that the destination IP address is a remote address, it examines the local routing table for a route to the destination host. If a route is found, it is used; if no route is found, IP forwards the packet to the default gateway. In either case, the packet destined for a remote address is usually sent to a router.
- At the router, the TTL is decreased by 1 or more (depending on network congestion), and the packet might be fragmented into smaller packets if necessary. The router then determines whether to forward the packet to one of the router's local network interfaces or to another router. This process repeats until the packet arrives at the destination host or has its TTL decremented to zero and is discarded by a router.

See Also: *host, internetwork, routing, Transmission Control Protocol (TCP), Transmission Control Protocol/Internet Protocol (TCP/IP)*

Internet protocols

Application-layer Transmission Control Protocol/Internet Protocol (TCP/IP) protocols commonly used on the Internet.

Overview

The following table shows some of the standard Internet protocols in use today. Some of these protocols, such as Gopher, have declined in popularity and are now considered legacy protocols. To access a protocol such as Hypertext Transfer Protocol (HTTP) with a Web browser such as Microsoft Internet Explorer, you would use a Uniform Resource Locator (URL) beginning with http://.

Standard Internet Protocols

Protocol	*Protocol Name*	*Description*
http	Hypertext Transfer Protocol	Used for Web pages that contain text, graphics, sound, and other digital information stored on a Web server on the World Wide Web
ftp	File Transfer Protocol	Transfers files between two computers over the Internet
gopher	Gopher protocol	Displays information stored on a network of Gopher servers
wais	WAIS protocol	Used for accessing a Wide Area Information Servers database
file	File protocol	Opens a file on a local hard disk or a network share
https	Hypertext Transfer Protocol Secure	Establishes an encrypted HTTP connection using the Secure Sockets Layer (SSL) protocol
mailto	MailTo protocol	Starts a Simple Mail Transfer Protocol (SMTP) e-mail program to send a message to the specified Internet e-mail address
news	News protocol	Opens a Network News Transfer Protocol (NNTP) newsreader and the specified Usenet newsgroup
nntp	Network News Transfer Protocol	Performs the same function as the News protocol
midi	Musical Instrument Digital Interface (MIDI) protocol	Plays MIDI sequencer files if the computer has a sound card
telnet	Telnet protocol	Starts a Telnet terminal emulation program
rlogin	Rlogin protocol	Starts an Rlogin terminal emulation program

(continued)

Standard Internet Protocols *continued*

Protocol	*Protocol Name*	*Description*
tn3270	TN3270 protocol	Starts a TN3270 terminal emulation program
pnm	RealAudio protocol	Plays RealAudio streaming audio from a RealAudio server
mms	Microsoft Media Server (MMS) protocol	Plays .asf streams from a Microsoft Streaming Media server

Internet Protocol Security (IPsec)

A protocol for secure transmission over Transmission Control Protocol/Internet Protocol (TCP/IP).

Overview

Internet Protocol Security (IPsec) defines an end-to-end model for data encryption and integrity implemented at the Internet Protocol (IP) level. "End-to-end" means only that the hosts at the two endpoints of an IPsec session need to be IPsec-enabled; intermediate hosts only need to support TCP/IP communications. IPsec can be used to encrypt transmission of data and ensure that the data originated from the sender and was not modified in transit.

IPsec is frequently used to send information securely over the public Internet through a virtual private network (VPN). IPsec is an Internet Engineering Task Force (IETF) standard and is implemented in Microsoft Windows 2000, Windows XP, and the Windows .NET Server family.

Architecture

IPsec is a Layer-3 TCP/IP protocol that is managed by security policies installed on each machine and by an encryption scheme negotiated between the sender and the receiver. Devices and software configured to support IPsec can use either public key encryption using keys supplied by certificate authorities (CAs) or preshared keys for private encryption.

IPsec implements encryption and data integrity through two additional security protocols, which can be used either separately or together. These protocols are

- **Authentication Header (AH) protocol:** Provides user authentication and protection from replay attacks and supports data authentication and integrity functions. AH enables the recipient to be sure of the sender's identity and that the data has not been modified during transmission. AH does not provide any encryption of the data itself. AH information is embedded in the IP packet's header and can be used alone or with the Encapsulating Security Payload (ESP) protocol. AH is defined in RFC 2402.
- **Encapsulating Security Payload (ESP) protocol:** Encapsulates and encrypts user data to provide full data confidentiality. ESP also includes optional authentication and protections from replay attacks and can be used either by itself or with AH. ESP information is also embedded in the IP packet's header. ESP is defined in RFC 2406.

To establish a security association (secure communication session) between two computers, a protocol framework called ISAKMP/Oakley can also be used. ISAKMP/Oakley includes a set of cryptographic algorithms and is extensible, supporting user-defined encryption algorithms. During the negotiation process, agreement is reached on the authentication and security methods to be used, and a shared key is generated for data encryption.

Implementation

IPsec security policies can be configured to meet the needs of securing users, sites, applications, or the enterprise in general. These security policies consist of a collection of filters with associated behaviors. When the IP address, port number, and protocol of an IP packet match a particular filter, the corresponding behavior is applied to the packet. In Windows 2000, for example, IPsec security policies are created and assigned at the domain level or for individual hosts using the IPsec Management snap-in for the Microsoft Management

Console (MMC). IPsec policies consist of rules that specify the security requirements for different forms of communication. These rules are used to initiate and control secure communication based on the nature of the IP traffic, the source of the traffic, and its destination. These rules specify authentication and negotiation methods, tunneling attributes, and connection types.

Advantages and Disadvantages

IPsec implements security differently from such tunneling protocols as Point-to-Point Tunneling Protocol (PPTP) and Layer 2 Tunneling Protocol (L2TP), which create secure tunnels and operate at the OSI data-link layer (Layer 2). Instead, IPsec secures information at the packet level and operates at the OSI network layer (Layer 3). IPsec also supports only IP traffic, which limits its use in some enterprise environments. PPTP and L2TP, by contrast, support any network protocol including TCP/IP, Internetwork Packet Exchange/ Sequenced Packet Exchange (IPX/SPX), or NetBEUI.

Although the restriction to IP traffic is somewhat of a disadvantage, IPsec does have two significant advantages over tunneling protocols:

- Application-layer TCP/IP protocols such as Hypertext Transfer Protocol (HTTP) that reside above IPsec can take full advantage of the security offered by IPsec.
- Security policies for configuring IPsec make the protocol more powerful and flexible than tunneling protocols.

See Also: *data-link layer, Internet Protocol (IP), Layer 2 Tunneling Protocol (L2TP), network layer, Point-to-Point Tunneling Protocol (PPTP), Transmission Control Protocol/Internet Protocol (TCP/IP)*

Internet Relay Chat (IRC)

A text-based Internet conferencing protocol.

Overview

Internet Relay Chat (IRC) is a technology that can be used to send real-time, text-based messages over the Internet. IRC is a client/server technology in which users employ IRC client software to connect to an IRC server or hub. Clients can then connect to an existing chat group (also called chat room or channel) and type messages to other users currently in that group. Chat groups are identified using a pound sign (#) prefix. Messages are transmitted in real time and can appear character by character on the recipients' client software if the person sending the message types slowly enough. Depending on how the chat server is configured, users might be able to create their own chat rooms and hold private discussions. Some chat servers require that you register once to obtain a unique nickname, but others allow you to select a nickname for the current session only. Some Web sites also offer Web-based interfaces to their chat servers.

The network of IRC servers on the Internet is known as Undernet. These servers are generally owned and operated by Internet service providers (ISPs) that provide a free IRC environment to online users. The IRC protocol is defined in RFC 1459.

Prospects

In late 2000, the Undernet network was crippled by a lengthy Distributed Denial of Service (DDoS) attack that prevented IRC users from using the network and created havoc for ISPs hosting Undernet servers. The attack graphically illustrated the Internet's current vulnerability to DDoS attacks and has called into question the long-term viability of Undernet and IRC unless changes are made to the Internet's basic architecture to protect it from such attacks.

Notes

Microsoft Exchange Server includes an IRC-based chat service that you can use to set up public or private IRC sites.

For More Information

Find out more about IRC at *www.irc.net.*

See Also: *Distributed Denial of Service (DDoS), ICQ, instant messaging (IM)*

Internet Research Task Force (IRTF)

An umbrella organization for a number of long-term research groups that focus on standards for Internet protocols, architecture, applications, and technologies.

Overview

The Internet Research Task Force (IRTF) is overseen by the Internet Architecture Board (IAB) and includes research groups such as

- The End-to-End (E2E) group, which is concerned with end-to-end services and protocols implemented in hosts
- The Information Infrastructure Architecture group, which works to articulate a common information infrastructure for the Internet to support greater interoperability between applications
- The Internet Resource Directory group, which develops models for resource description on the Internet, including mechanisms for querying, indexing, and retrieval
- The Network Management group, which is concerned with issues relating to the management of the Internet from the perspectives of high-level management domains and customer-oriented services
- The Services Management group, which is concerned with the convergence of networking technologies relating to the Internet

For More Information

Visit the IRTF at *www.irtf.org.*

See Also: *Internet Architecture Board (IAB)*

Internet Security and Acceleration Server (ISA Server)

Microsoft Corporation's firewall, proxy, and Web-caching platform.

Overview

Microsoft Internet Security and Acceleration Server (ISA Server) 2000 replaces and extends its earlier Proxy Server 2 platform that was part of the BackOffice suite of server applications. ISA Server belongs to Microsoft's new .NET Enterprise Server platform and is designed to meet the security needs of Internet-based businesses. ISA Server provides

- A full-featured firewall set that includes stateful inspection, integrated intrusion detection, integrated virtual private network (VPN) support, and broad application support for circuit-level proxies.
- Web caching technology to speed the retrieval of frequently used Web content, saving valuable network bandwidth.
- Policy-based management for traffic management that can be scheduled and configured at the user, group, site, application, or content type level.

For More Information

Learn more about ISA Server at *www.microsoft.com/isa.*

See Also: *firewall, .NET Enterprise Servers, proxy server*

Internet Server API (ISAPI)

A set of standard application programming interfaces (APIs) for developing extensions to Microsoft Internet Information Services (IIS).

Overview

Internet Server API (ISAPI) provides Web developers with a powerful way to extend the functionality of IIS. ISAPI provides developers with low-level access to all Microsoft Win32 API functions, and ISAPI applications often have better performance than applications written using Active Server Pages (ASP) or Common Gateway Interface (CGI) . But as ISAPI dynamic-link libraries (DLLs) are generally written in a high-level programming language such as C or C++, ISAPI applications are usually more difficult to develop than ASP-based or CGI-based solutions and often do not scale as well.

There are two basic kinds of ISAPI DLLs, which have different uses on IIS:

- **ISAPI extensions:** Run-time DLLs that can run either in process or out of process on IIS. ISAPI extensions provide extended functionality to IIS.
- **ISAPI filters:** Used to preprocess packets of data before they enter or leave the IIS main process. An example of an ISAPI filter is the Secure Sockets Layer (SSL) protocol component on IIS 4.

Notes

You can create ISAPI extensions easily using the ISAPI Extension Wizard in Microsoft Visual C++.

See Also: *Active Server Pages (ASP), Common Gateway Interface (CGI), dynamic-link library (DLL), Internet Information Services (IIS), ISAPI extension, ISAPI filter*

Internet service provider (ISP)

A company that provides Internet access to consumers, businesses, or both.

Overview

Internet service providers (ISPs) come in various shapes and sizes, from volunteer-run freenets to local, regional, and national service providers such as AT&T WorldNet. ISPs can provide a wide range of services, including

- Dial-up Internet access
- Broadband Internet access—Digital Subscriber Line (DSL) or cable modem
- Leased lines and other wide area network (WAN) services.
- Web hosting services
- E-mail services
- Virtual private networking (VPN)

Types

ISPs can be classified into different types according to their size, service area, and particular business orientation. For example,

- **National:** These are often owned by or partnered with inter-exchange carriers (IXCs) to offer services across the country. Examples include AT&T WorldNet, EarthLink, Genuity, MSN, PSI-net, Sprint, UUNET, and Verizon.
- **Regional:** These offer services in specific regions of the country and are often owned by or partnered with Regional Bell Operating Companies (RBOCs) or Incumbent Local Exchange Carriers (ILECs). Examples are Ameritech and BellSouth.
- **B2B:** These focus exclusively on the business-to-business market. Examples include GNS from AT&T and Gridnet from UUNET.

Implementation

Choosing an ISP for your enterprise or business is a process you should approach carefully. If your enterprise spans several locations, you need to consider your ISP as part of your network infrastructure, especially if you are using VPN. Be sure to ask potential ISPs questions about

- The capacity their backbone can handle and who owns it. OC-12 and OC-48 backbones are common, and OC-192 backbones are beginning to be deployed by large national carriers (the first ISP to deploy OC-192 was AT&T).
- Whether they employ redundant backbone connections to upstream providers and what sort of peering arrangements (public or private) they have with these providers. Most large ISPs use private peering arrangements to connect to similar ISPs, but small ISPs generally have to lease wholesale services from upstream ISPs.
- Whether they offer colocation for running your own Web servers at their point of presence (POP).
- Which advanced features (such as VPN and VoIP) they offer.
- What level of reliability or SLA (service level agreement) they offer.

Examples

One example of a national (Tier 1) ISP is UUNET (*www.uu.net*), which merged with MCI/WorldCom, an IXC. UUNET offers a wide range of services, including dial-up, Integrated Services Digital Network (ISDN), frame relay, Asynchronous Transfer Mode (ATM) access, leased lines, DSL, fast wireless Internet access, and more. UUNET's backbone stretches from North America to Europe and the Asia/Pacific region. Peering in the United States takes place at eight different network access points (NAPs), including MAE-East and MAE-West. All UUNET POPs have redundant links to their backbone.

Notes

If you are a consumer looking for an ISP in your area, try TheList (*www.thelist.com*).

See Also: *infrastructure, Internet, Internet access*

Internet Society (ISOC)

A professional society founded in 1992 that provides leadership for the development and evolution of the Internet.

Overview

The Internet Society (ISOC) comprises over 150 individual organizations, including government agencies and private companies, and is an umbrella organization for other Internet groups, including the Internet Engineering Task Force (IETF) and the Internet Architecture Board (IAB). The ISOC has more than 6,000 individual members in over 100 countries and regions. It is governed by a board of trustees elected from its membership. The ISOC hosts conferences and issues publications related to the development and management of the Internet. The ISOC has taken the lead in promoting the formation of a nonprofit constituency for the new Internet Corporation for Assigned Names and Numbers (ICANN), which oversees the Internet Domain Name System (DNS). The ISOC essentially functions as a legal umbrella for the standardization processes managed by the IETF and the IAB.

For More Information

Visit ISOC at *www.isoc.org*.

See Also: *Internet, Internet Architecture Board (IAB), Internet Corporation for Assigned Names and Numbers (ICANN), Internet Engineering Task Force (IETF)*

internetwork

A network, usually Transmission Control Protocol/Internet Protocol (TCP/IP), consisting of multiple networks joined by routers.

Overview

More generally, an internetwork is any network consisting of smaller networks joined in any fashion using bridges, switches, routers, and other devices. For example, an Internet Protocol (IP) internetwork could consist of a mix of Microsoft Windows NT or Windows 2000 and UNIX machines distributed over different subnets connected with standard IP routers from Cisco Systems or another vendor. An Internetwork Packet Exchange (IPX) internetwork could be a set of networks using Novell NetWare clients and servers running IPX that are connected using IPX-enabled routers.

Internetworking is the process of planning, implementing, and maintaining an internetwork. For IP internetworks, this involves such tasks as

- Determining which IP address classes and network IDs to use
- Dividing the internetwork into different subnets using a custom subnet mask
- Managing host IP address information using the Dynamic Host Configuration Protocol (DHCP)
- Configuring dynamic routers for efficient exchange of routing information
- Acquiring tools and skills for troubleshooting internetwork problems

Internetwork Operating System (IOS)

The operating system developed by Cisco Systems for its line of routers and access servers to provide a standard way to configure these devices.

Overview

Internetwork Operating System (IOS) is a text-based operating system that users access using a command-line interface (CLI) called EXEC. In this way IOS is similar to UNIX, but IOS commands are specific to

Internetwork Operating System (IOS)

router configuration and management functions instead of file system management and input/output (I/O). While IOS was originally designed as a monolithic, "router-centric" operating system, it has evolved into a modular operating system composed of different subsystems that can easily be upgraded and that support more complex distributed networking functions. The most recent release of Cisco IOS at the time of writing is IOS 12.2, which has support for IPv6 built into it across the board.

Note that the operating system used on Cisco Catalyst switches is somewhat different from the version used on routers and is referred to either as Catalyst IOS or Catalyst Operating System (COS) in various literature.

Implementation

IOS is typically stored as a system image within a router's flash memory. The startup configuration file called Startup-config is stored in nonvolatile RAM, and the router's actual operating configuration (its routing tables, queues, and other elements) is stored in ordinary RAM. Cisco routers can typically run in three different operating environments:

- **ROM monitor:** Also called the bootstrap program, this environment is accessed through the console port. The ROM monitor initiates the bootstrap process and can be used to run diagnostics, recover lost passwords, and recover from system failures.
- **Boot ROM:** This environment is used mainly to upgrade to new versions of IOS by loading a new image of IOS into flash memory.
- **Cisco IOS:** This is the normal operating environment, in which you can enter commands to configure and troubleshoot your router's operation. For example, you can enter the Show Version command to determine which version of IOS your router is running.

The normal IOS operating environment itself can run in four different modes:

- **User EXEC mode:** This mode is enabled by default when you connect to a router using a command-line console (for example, using a Telnet connection). Using EXEC, the IOS system command interpreter, you can type commands using a command-line interface. User EXEC mode supports a subset of IOS commands for performing basic actions such as configuring terminal settings, running tests, and displaying configuration information.
- **Privileged EXEC mode:** This mode lets you do everything you can do in User EXEC mode and more, including running the Setup command to enter configuration information, running the configure command to modify configuration information, and running the debug command to display event messages. Enter Privileged EXEC mode by typing the enable command.
- **Configuration mode:** This mode lets you configure your router's settings. You enter this mode by typing the configure terminal command.
- **Setup mode:** This mode is used to create new configuration files that enable features such as addressing, routing, and security.

Notes

You can quickly tell which command mode of IOS you are running by looking at your command prompt. The table shows the various IOS command modes and their prompts.

IOS Command Modes

Prompt	*IOS Mode*
Router>	User EXEC
Router#	Privileged EXEC
Router(config)#	Configuration
(A series of dialog box prompts)	Setup

You access most router functions by using EXEC mode, either User to view information in read-only format or Privileged to modify and configure router settings. User and Privileged modes also support different subsets of the IOS command set. Note that Privileged EXEC mode should always be password-protected because it lets you reconfigure key operating system parameters.

Do not run the debug command when you are connected to the network unless it is absolutely necessary because this increases the load on the processor. Type a question mark (?) at a prompt to determine which commands are available in the currently enabled IOS mode.

There are typically three ways you can connect to a router and issue IOS commands:

- **Console:** By connecting the serial port of a nearby PC to the router using a Cisco console cable, you can run IOS commands on the router using a terminal program such as Microsoft HyperTerminal on the PC.
- **Modem:** For routers in remote locations, you can use a modem to connect the router to the telephone system, allowing administrators to remotely dial-in and run IOS commands using a PC similarly equipped with a modem.
- **Telnet:** If the router has connectivity with a network, a user anywhere in the network can connect to the router and run IOS commands using Telnet.

For More Information

Find out more about Cisco IOS at *www.cisco.com/warp/public/732*.

See Also: *command line, router*

Internetwork Packet Exchange (IPX)

A NetWare protocol used for routing packets across an internetwork.

Overview

Internetwork Packet Exchange (IPX) is a network layer protocol that provides connectionless datagram services for Ethernet, Token Ring, and other common data-link layer protocols. IPX is the commonly used local area network (LAN) protocol on legacy NetWare 3.*x* and 4.*x* LANs but has now been replaced with native Transmission Control Protocol/Internet Protocol (TCP/IP) in NetWare 5.*x* and later.

Architecture

IPX packets use 32-bit (4-byte) network numbers to uniquely identify each data link (connected network) in an IPX internetwork. The administrator of each network assigns these network numbers, which must be unique for each connected network; all nodes on a connected network must have the same network number. Nodes discover their network number by communicating with routers attached to the local network. Routers use these network numbers to route IPX packets from one network to another within an internetwork. IPX is thus a routable protocol. The structure of an IPX packet is shown in the diagram.

IPX Packet Structure	Bytes
Checksum	2
Length	2
Transport control (hop count)	1
Packet type	1
Destination network	4
Destination node	6
Destination socket	2
Source network	4
Source node	6
Source socket	2
Data	varies

Internetwork Packet Exchange (IPX). *The structure of an IPX packet.*

IPX also uses 48-bit (6-byte) addresses for each node within a given network. An entire IPX network address is thus 4 + 6 = 10 bytes long. IPX packets are assigned a 16-bit (2-byte) socket number to identify the networking service they are communicating with—for example, Network Control Protocol (NCP), Service Advertising Protocol (SAP), or Routing Information Protocol (RIP). Thus, the following 12-byte triple completely identifies the networking service that a packet is communicating for:

```
{network number, node address, socket number}
```

When an IPX client is booted on a NetWare internetwork using IPX-enabled routers, the client broadcasts a

Get Nearest Server (GSN) request message to its locally connected network in order to locate the nearest NetWare server. If a NetWare server cannot be located on the connected network, the router informs the client of the nearest available server based on the cost of the connection. The router is familiar with this information because NetWare servers using IPX periodically notify the network of their presence using SAP, which allows IPX routers to construct server tables based on SAP numbers.

IPX is a connectionless protocol that works at the network layer of the Open Systems Interconnection (OSI) reference model, and IPX packets are connectionless datagrams. To function within connected networks, IPX works with a transport layer protocol called the Sequenced Packet Exchange (SPX) protocol. SPX is responsible for generating acknowledgments for IPX packets received over the network to ensure that no packets were lost during transport.

Notes

On Ethernet networks, NetWare clients and servers can communicate with each other using IPX only if they use compatible frame types (encapsulation formats). The terminology used to describe these frame types depends on whether you are discussing Novell NetWare clients and servers or IPX-enabled routers from Cisco Systems. The following table illustrates these differences.

Frame Type Terminology

Common Terminology	*Novell Terminology*	*Cisco Terminology*
Ethernet	Ethernet_II	arpa
raw	Ethernet_802.3	novell-ether
802.3	Ethernet_802.2	sap
snap	Ethernet_SNAP	snap

Ethernet_II is the default frame type for NetWare version 3.*x* and earlier, but NetWare 4.*x* uses the Ethernet_802.2 frame type.

See Also: *NetWare protocols*

interprocess communication (IPC)

A mechanism for establishing a connection between processes running on two computers or on a single multitasking computer to allow data to flow between those processes.

Overview

Interprocess communication (IPC) mechanisms are commonly used in client/server environments and are supported to various degrees by the different Microsoft Windows operating systems. An IPC generally consists of two components:

- An application programming interface (API) that defines the standard set of functions that can be called when software tries to use an IPC.
- A protocol that specifies the format in which the information is transmitted using the IPC. When IPCs are passed over the network, the format specified is the format of the packet or frame transmitted between the computers.

The following table lists some IPC mechanisms and the platforms that support them.

Built-in Support for IPC Mechanisms on Various Windows Platforms

Process	*Windows NT*	*Windows 95*	*Windows 98*	*Windows 2000*
Named pipes	x	x	x	x
Mailslots	x	x	x	x
NetBIOS	x	x	x	x
Windows Sockets	x	x	x	x
Remote procedure call (RPC)	x	x	x	x
Network Dynamic Data Exchange (NetDDE)	x	x	x	x
Distributed Component Object Model (DCOM)	x		x	x

Inter-Switch Link (ISL)

A Cisco technology that is used for frame tagging.

Overview

Inter-Switch Link (ISL) was developed by Cisco Systems to enable a single physical Ethernet interface to support multiple logical Virtual LAN (VLAN) interfaces. A device using ISL thus appears on the network as if it had multiple physical network interfaces present instead of one.

ISL works by tagging Ethernet frames with the logical VLAN address to which each frame belongs. This technique is more generally known as frame tagging. ISL is implemented in modules for Cisco Catalyst switches and also for special network interface cards (NICs) used in routers and high-performance servers.

Prospects

ISL is widely used in the enterprise but represents a proprietary Cisco solution. The Institute of Electrical and Electronics Engineers (IEEE) is developing a vendor-neutral standard for frame tagging called 802.1Q, but it may take time for this standard to replace ISL due to its large installed base.

See Also: *802.1Q, Ethernet, frame tagging, virtual LAN (VLAN)*

intranet

A private Transmission Control Protocol/Internet Protocol (TCP/IP) internetwork within an organization that uses Internet technologies such as Web servers and Web browsers for sharing information and collaborating.

Overview

Intranets can be used to publish company policies and newsletters, provide sales and marketing staff with product information, provide technical support and tutorials, and just about anything else you can think of that fits within the standard Web server/Web browser environment.

Microsoft Internet Information Services (IIS), with its support for Active Server Pages (ASP), is an ideal platform for building intranet applications that can be accessed using a standard Web browser such as Microsoft Internet Explorer.

See Also: *Internet, Internet Information Services (IIS), Web server*

intrusion detection system (IDS)

Any system used to detect attacks on a host or network.

Overview

Intrusion detection systems (IDSs) can detect, log, report, and even respond to a wide variety of attempts to compromise a network's security. IDSs range from simple tools such as network sniffers and application logs to complex, distributed systems costing thousands of dollars. They can be implemented as software installed on computers, blades inserted into enterprise Ethernet switches, or dedicated network appliances.

An IDS is an essential component of a network security policy and is complementary to a firewall—a firewall prevents certain kinds of intrusion, but an IDS detects what gets through the firewall. An IDS is not a "silver bullet" that solves all network security issues—a poorly implemented or unmonitored IDS is worse than no IDS at all because it provides a false sense of security. The reports generated by an IDS are typically 90 percent false positives and usually require human intelligence to distinguish the real attacks from the false ones.

There are two basic types of IDS:

- **Network IDS (NIDS):** These are systems that capture network traffic and analyze it looking for evidence of attacks. NIDS generally determines which traffic is hostile on the basis of predefined rules or signatures. These signatures must be kept up to date by downloading new versions from the vendor to ensure that NIDS continues to be effective in patrolling the network. NIDS are operating-system independent and can be implemented without modifying your network's infrastructure. On the downside, they increase network traffic, thus consuming valuable bandwidth, and are difficult to implement in a switched environment.

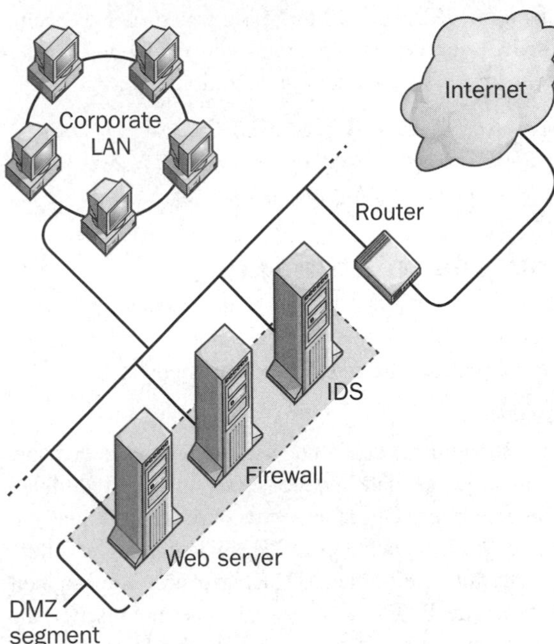

Intrusion detection system. *An example of how a network intrusion detection system might be implemented.*

- **Host-based IDS:** These are applications installed on critical hosts such as Web servers that monitor such things as Transmission Control Protocol (TCP) sessions, port activity, file integrity, and log files. Host-based IDSs are platform-specific solutions that must be installed on any servers considered in danger of attack.

This distinction between the two types of IDS is beginning to be blurred as vendors combine aspects of both types into newer IDS applications and appliances. Vendors are also beginning to add "intelligent" pattern-recognition functionality into their IDSs to enable them to detect attacks for which no signatures currently exist. The use of artificial intelligence (AI) in IDS systems is probably the big goal in the network security field for the next decade.

Implementation

This example deals with the implementation of a NIDS. A typical NIDS consists of two components:

- **Sensors:** These capture network traffic on various segments and forward it to the management station.
- **Management station:** This receives reports from sensors of possible intrusions and then logs the information in a database, generates reports for human inspection, notifies administrators of the occurrence, and (if configured to do so) shuns harmful traffic.

To detect intrusion at the perimeter of a network connected to the Internet, a sensor would typically be deployed in the perimeter network (otherwise known as a demilitarized zone [DMZ]) where the firewall is located.

Marketplace

The IDS market has exploded over the last few years, with the result that IDS has often become a buzzword that vendors use to market products that have little IDS functionality. Examples of host-based IDS include Intruder Alert from Axent Technologies, Dragon Squire from Enterasys Networks, Kane Security Enterprise from Intrusion.com, and RealSecure OS Sensor from Internet Security Systems. Popular network IDSs include NetProwler from Axent Technologies, Cisco Secure IDS from Cisco Systems (available as both a stand-alone appliance and as a module for Cisco Catalyst 6000 series switches), eTrust Intrusion Detection from Computer Associates, Armor from nCircle Network Security, BlackICE Sentry from Network Ice Corporation, and NFR from Network Flight Recorder. Some popular free UNIX-based IDS tools include Shadow, Snort, and Pakemon.

Issues

One of the main difficulties in deploying NIDS is that most enterprise networks are now switch-based instead of hub-based. All stations connected to a hub share the same broadcast and collision domain, and by connecting a NIDS sensor to a hub, traffic to and from every station can be easily monitored. Ethernet switches are different, however—each attached station forms its own private segment and to monitor traffic effectively would, in theory, require a NIDS sensor for each port.

One workaround for this problem is to use port mirroring (spanning) to copy portions of traffic from each port on the switch to a mirror port to which the sensor can then be attached. The problem with doing this, however, is that it adds an extra processing load to the switch and is difficult to implement in full-duplex configurations. Cisco solves this problem in its Catalyst 6000 series of enterprise switches by providing its Cisco Secure IDS product as a blade that can be installed in the switch to monitor traffic directly on the backplane. By configuring access control lists (ACLs), administrators can then pull up different kinds of traffic such as Hypertext Transfer Protocol (HTTP) to get more targeted information about possible intrusions. Another solution is provided by Shomiti Systems, which sells "taps" that let you unobtrusively listen in to traffic on any 10/100 Mbps Ethernet link and copy traffic to a second switch to which IDS sensors are attached. This way, no extra processing burden is placed on the network's backbone switches.

See Also: *firewall, network security*

inverse multiplexer (IMUX)

A device that can perform inverse multiplexing of digital telecommunication channels.

Overview

A typical inverse multiplexer (IMUX) might be capable of inverse multiplexing together four Basic Rate Interface ISDN (BRI-ISDN) lines, two T1 lines, or four T1 lines to provide a throughput of 512 kilobits per second (Kbps), 3.088 megabits per second (Mbps), or 6.176 Mbps, respectively. This saves the expense of having to purchase or lease equipment to individually terminate each Integrated Services Digital Network (ISDN) or T1 line, and it provides an efficient way to increase wide area network (WAN) speed for high-bandwidth uses such as videoconferencing, T1 backup, or large file transfers. IMUXes can include built-in Channel Service Unit/Data Service Unit (CSU/DSU) functionality, they have a 34-pin built-in V.35 LAN (data) interface, and they have an RJ-45 or DB25 connector for the line interface. They often feature load-sharing functions so that if one ISDN or T1 line goes down, no delays occur. IMUXes usually include diagnostic and loopback functions for both local and remote troubleshooting.

See Also: *Channel Service Unit/Data Service Unit (CSU/DSU), Integrated Services Digital Network (ISDN), inverse multiplexing, T-carrier*

inverse multiplexing

A way of combining the bandwidths of a number of digital network or telecommunication lines into a single virtual pathway for high-speed communication.

Overview

Inverse multiplexing can be used to aggregate the bandwidth of digital data service (DDS), switched 56, Integrated Services Digital Network (ISDN), or T1 and higher T-carrier services into a single high-bandwidth data terminal equipment (DTE) interface. You can then connect this DTE interface to customer premises equipment such as routers or Channel Service Unit/Data Service Units (CSU/DSUs), which are connected to the customer's network.

Inverse multiplexing is the opposite of multiplexing, which combines data transmissions from multiple pieces of DTE into a single digital communication channel.

Implementation

By connecting a device called an inverse multiplexer, or IMUX, to the termination points of several leased digital lines, you can use inverse multiplexing to create a single virtual connection with a bandwidth equal to the sum of the bandwidths of the individual lines. To implement this, for example, with ISDN, an IMUX is required at both the customer premises and the telco central office (CO). When several ISDN subchannels are multiplexed into a single high-speed channel, a connection is initiated when the customer's IMUX dials a number to establish a connection with the CO IMUX. Once a single ISDN subchannel is established, the customer IMUX dials the remaining numbers and establishes the additional ISDN subchannels. Once all the subchannels are up, a protocol called BONDING establishes synchronization between the two stations using a handshaking mechanism to resolve any delays between the subchannels. These delays are primarily the result of the different circuit-switched communication subchannels having physical paths of different lengths, even though they have the same two endpoints. The bonding protocols also ensure that data sent over each subchannel arrives at its destination in the correct order.

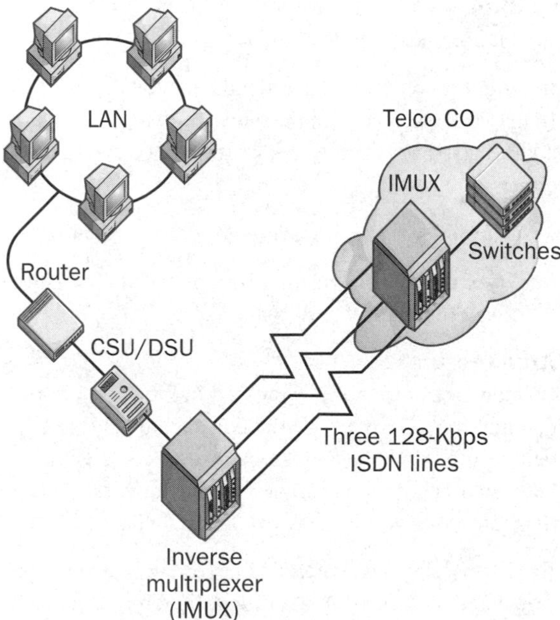

Inverse multiplexing. *A simple example of using inverse multiplexing to provide a high-bandwidth wide area network (WAN) connection to a corporate network.*

Advantages and Disadvantages

The main advantage of inverse multiplexing is that it is often less expensive to lease several low-speed digital lines and inverse multiplex them together than to lease a single high-speed digital line with the same aggregate bandwidth. Inverse multiplexing is also useful in areas where high-speed digital services such as T1 are not readily available.

See Also: *multiplexing*

Inverse Multiplexing over ATM (IMA)

A high-speed Asynchronous Transfer Mode (ATM) technology.

Overview

Enterprises that need to connect theirATM backbones by means of wide area network (WAN) links to interexchange carriers (IXCs) such as AT&T, Sprint, and MCI/Worldcom have traditionally been limited to two main options:

- **T1 lines:** These operate at 1.544 megabits per second (Mbps), well below the speed of even a traditional 10 Mbps Ethernet LAN.
- **T3 lines:** These offer higher speeds of 44.736 Mbps, close to the range of 100 Mbps Fast Ethernet, but at a much higher cost than T1 lines.

Inverse Multiplexing over ATM (IMA) bridges the gap between these two solutions by allowing multiple T1 lines carrying ATM to be aggregated for transmission over a fractional T3 circuit. IMA is a good solution for enterprises needing ATM WAN connectivity faster than T1 but at costs much lower than T3.

See Also: *Asynchronous Transfer Mode (ATM), inverse multiplexing*

inverse query

A Domain Name System (DNS) query in which a resolver contacts a name server to perform a reverse name lookup, requesting a host name for a given Internet Protocol (IP) address.

Overview

An inverse query is a process whereby given a host's fully qualified domain name (FQDN), the host's IP address is looked up. This is the opposite of the usual DNS query where a FQDN is resolved into its associated IP address. Because of the hierarchical structure of the namespace of the DNS, inverse queries normally have to search all domains to resolve the IP address. To circumvent this, a special domain called in-addr.arpa exists for reverse name lookups. The nodes in this domain are named after the IP addresses of hosts but with the octets in reverse order to facilitate searching. However, inverse queries can take place only on the name server queried and cannot be forwarded to another name server. Because individual name servers manage only a small portion of the entire DNS namespace, there is no guarantee that a given inverse query issued against a specific name server will meet with a successful response.

Notes

Most names used on Internet servers are configured for reverse name lookups to avoid the extra overhead required. However, if you need to use the DNS troubleshooting utility Nslookup, you should configure the in-addr.arpa domain on name servers to support inverse queries. Otherwise, there is no need to configure this inverse domain.

See Also: in-addr.arpa, iterative query, recursive query

IOS

Stands for Internetwork Operating System, the operating system developed by Cisco Systems for its line of routers and access servers to provide a standard way to configure and administer these devices.

See: Internetwork Operating System (IOS)

IP

Stands for Internet Protocol, the network layer protocol used by Transmission Control Protocol/Internet Protocol (TCP/IP) for addressing and routing packets of data between hosts.

See: Internet Protocol (IP)

IP address

In IPv4, a 32-bit logical address for a host on an Internet Protocol (IP) network; in IPv6, IP addresses are 64 bits in length.

Overview

IP addresses allow packets to be routed over an IP network. Each IP packet has a header that contains the IP address of the source host that transmitted the packet and the destination host to which the packet is being sent. IP addresses can be one of three types:

- **Unicast:** This type forwards the packet to a single target host (one-to-one forwarding).
- **Multicast:** This type forwards the packet to all hosts that have joined a multicast group (one-to-many forwarding).
- **Broadcast:** This type forwards the packet to all hosts on a subnet or network (one-to-all forwarding).

In order for communication to take place reliably on an IP network, each host on the network needs a unique IP address assigned to it. IP addresses can be assigned either

- **Manually:** By using static IP addressing, or
- **Dynamically:** By using Dynamic Host Configuration Protocol (DHCP)

Architecture

IP addresses are usually expressed in four-octet, dotted-decimal form—w.x.y.z—in which each octet ranges in value from 0 to 255 (with some restrictions). The IP address of a host is partitioned by the network's subnet mask into two parts, a network ID and a host ID.

IP addresses belong to certain classes according to their first octet, as defined in the following table. The actual distinguishing feature of each class is the pattern of high-order bits in the first octet, but it is easier to remember these classes by their first octet decimal numbers. IP addresses whose first octet is 127 represent the loopback address and are used for troubleshooting purposes only, and cannot be assigned to hosts.

IP Address Classes

IP Address Class	*Possible First Octet*	*Used For*
Class A	1–126	Very large networks
Class B	128–191	Medium to large networks
Class C	192–223	Small networks
Class D	224–239	Multicasting
Class E	240–255	Reserved (experimental)

Networks that are directly connected to the Internet must have their IP addresses assigned by the Internet Network Information Center (InterNIC) or some other authority. Businesses usually obtain these addresses through their local Internet service provider (ISP). However, firewall and proxy server combinations, which are popular on today's networks, hide a network's IP addresses from other hosts on the Internet. These private networks can use any IP addresses they choose, although InterNIC recommends the following IP address blocks for private networks:

- **Class A networks:** 10.x.y.z
- **Class B networks:** 172.16.y.z through 172.31.y.z
- **Class C networks:** 192.168.0.z through 192.168.255.z

Note

Note the following considerations for valid IP addressing:

- The network ID cannot be 127.
- The network ID and host ID cannot both be 255.
- The network ID and host ID cannot both be 0.
- The host ID must be unique for a given network ID.

See Also: *Class A, Class B, Class C, Class D, Class E, Internet Protocol (IP), subnet mask, subnetting*

IP/ATM

Also called IP over ATM, a method for enabling Transmission Control Protocol/Internet Protocol (TCP/IP) networks to access Asynchronous Transfer Mode (ATM) networks.

Overview

The traditional way of connecting TCP/IP and ATM networks is to run LAN Emulation (LANE) services on the ATM network. IP/ATM is an alternative to LANE and allows TCP/IP networks to directly use ATM networks and take advantage of ATM's Quality of Service (QoS) features. IP/ATM is faster than LANE and is supported by Microsoft Windows 2000.

Implementation

IP/ATM is implemented as a client/server architecture that includes

- IP/ATM servers that include two components: ATM address resolution protocol (ARP) servers and multicast address resolution server (MARS). IP/ATM servers can reside either on anATM switch or on a Windows 2000 server.
- IP/ATM clients, which support both static and dynamic IP addressing.

See Also: *Asynchronous Transfer Mode (ATM), LAN Emulation (LANE), Transmission Control Protocol/ Internet Protocol (TCP/IP)*

I

IPC

Stands for interprocess communication, a mechanism for establishing a connection between processes running on two computers or on a single multitasking computer to allow data to flow between those processes.

See: *interprocess communication (IPC)*

Ipconfig

A utility for displaying the Internet Protocol (IP) configuration settings of a network interface.

Overview

The Ipconfig command is often one of the first commands you use to check the status of the connection when you experience communication problems on a Transmission Control Protocol/Internet Protocol (TCP/ IP) network. When you type **ipconfig** at a Microsoft Windows 2000 command prompt, the following information is displayed for each network interface card (NIC):

- IP address
- Subnet mask
- Default gateway

You can display additional information, including the host name, physical address, and Dynamic Host

Configuration Protocol (DHCP), Windows Internet Name Service (WINS), and Domain Name System (DNS) configuration, using ipconfig /all. You can release and renew IP addresses obtained by DHCP using ipconfig /release and ipconfig /renew.

See Also: *default gateway, IP address, subnet mask*

IP Fax

Transmission of fax information over Internet Protocol (IP) networks.

Overview

Fax is a popular method of communications in large enterprises—analysts estimate that almost half of enterprise telephone charges come from faxing. IP Fax is a standard method for formatting fax images into frames for transmission over IP networks. IP Fax can save enterprises considerable costs in long-distance charges by routing faxes over either private IP wide area network (WAN) links or over the public Internet.

Implementation

IP Fax employs the T.37 protocol from the International Telecommunication Union (ITU), which is based on RFCs 2301 and 2305 from the Internet Engineering Task Force (IETF). This protocol implements a store-and-forward method for formatting and transmitting fax information over IP networks. Typically, a user will send a fax from her computer directly to a local fax server, which formats the information using the T.37 protocol. The fax server then sends the information as IP traffic over the private IP network or Internet to a remote fax server near the customer location. The remote fax server unpackages the information and reconstructs the fax and then transmits the fax over the Public Switched Telephone Network (PSTN) as a local call to the intended recipient of the fax. In this way, long-distance charges between the sender and recipient are avoided.

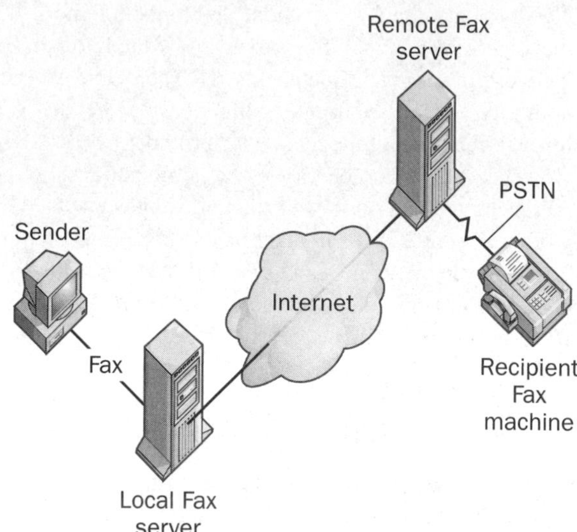

IP Fax. *How IP Fax is implemented.*

The general concept of transmitting faxes over IP networks is not new, but earlier solutions had used proprietary routing methods developed by different vendors. IP Fax is expected to promote interoperability between equipment from different fax vendors by providing a standards-based solution to the problem.

See Also: *Internet Protocol (IP)*

IPng

Stands for IP Next Generation, an early name for IPv6, next generation Internet Protocol (IP) addressing scheme for Transmission Control Protocol/Internet Protocol (TCP/IP) networks.

See: *IPv6*

IP over ATM

Also called IP/ATM, a method for enabling Transmission Control Protocol/Internet Protocol (TCP/IP) networks to access Asynchronous Transfer Mode (ATM) networks.

See: *IP/ATM*

IPP

Stands for Internet Printing Protocol, a method for printing over the Internet.

See: *Internet Printing Protocol (IPP)*

IP PBX

A private branch exchange (PBX) that uses an Internet Protocol (IP) network as its transport.

Overview

IP PBXs are alternatives to traditional telecom PBXs. They use IP networks for all or part of their transport of call information. IP PBXs come in two main types:

- Those that transport call information over the local area network (LAN) and employ special IP telephones and fax machines that plug directly into LAN drops in work areas.
- Those that employ IP networks (either dedicated leased lines or over the Internet) to connect branch offices but transport calls to work areas using conventional telephone lines.

Advantages and Disadvantages

IP PBXs are generally cheap compared to traditional PBXs and can save corporate clients from costly service contracts with telcos. They allow voice, fax, and data to be carried over a single wiring infrastructure (the network) instead of requiring an additional wiring infrastructure (telephone wiring). Finally, IP PBXs provide more flexibility than traditional PBXs by supporting Voice over IP (VoIP) and other options.

On the downside, the quality of IP PBXs and the range of features offered, particularly for voice, is often less than that of traditional PBXs. Furthermore, most IP PBXs support only a few hundred users, whereas traditional PBXs can support tens of thousands of users (at a price, of course).

Marketplace

A number of vendors produce IP PBX equipment, including Cisco Systems, 3Com Corporation, Vertical Networks, Shoreline Communications, Sphere Communications, Siemens, and many others. IP Exchange Systems from Lucent Technologies is a popular full-featured high-end IP PBX solution for the enterprise. Cisco's AVVID platform is an enterprise-level IP PBX system that's been around since 1999. A popular IP PBX in the small to mid-size business market is 3Com's NBX 100, and 3Com has over half the share of this market, followed by Vertical Networks and Cisco.

Traditional PBX vendors such as Nortel Networks offer a competing solution to IP PBXs in the form ofVoIP gateways that connect with installed traditional PBXs to provide similar services to IP PBXs.

A new offering in the market is the IP Centrex, which is basically outsourcing IP PBX services to a service provider. IP Centrex may appeal to small and mid-sized businesses whose traditional Centrex systems are aging. IP Centrex services are offered from MCI/WorldCom and others.

See Also: *Private Branch Exchange (PBX), Voice over IP (VoIP)*

IPsec

Stands for Internet Protocol Security, a protocol for secure transmission over Transmission Control Protocol/Internet Protocol (TCP/IP).

See: *Internet Protocol Security (IPsec)*

IP storage

A generic name for any method of sending block data over Internet Protocol (IP) networks.

Overview

IP storage is an emerging family of technologies that has great promise. The purpose of these technologies is to enable Ethernet local area networks (LANs) running IP to be directly connected to Storage Area Networks (SANs). IP storage is expected to simplify the management of distributed network storage systems in the enterprise. Another generic name for these technologies is storage-over-IP.

Two approaches to IP storage being considered by the Internet Engineering Task Force (IETF) are

- Encapsulation of Fibre Channel control codes in IP packets for communication between Fibre Channel SANs.
- Transport of native Small Computer System Interface (SCSI) commands over IP. This technology is generally known as iSCSI.

See Also: *Fibre Channel, iSCSI, storage*

IP telephony

An umbrella term for technologies that allow the transmission of voice and video over Transmission Control Protocol/Internet Protocol (TCP/IP) internetworks instead of the traditional Public Switched Telephone Network (PSTN).

Overview

The advantage of IP telephony is that it allows voice communication to be closely integrated with data transmission over corporate networks and allows long-distance communication to be established over the Internet instead of through private long-distance carriers such as Sprint and MCI/WorldCom. The primary difficulty with IP telephony is that the existing Internet Protocol (IP) internetwork is connectionless and suffers from latency that can cause annoying glitches (pauses) in voice and video transmission over IP packets. This happens because TCP/IP was not originally designed as a connection-oriented service capable of specific levels of quality of service (QoS), whereas the PSTN, with its circuit-switched connections, provides just that.

Marketplace

Many vendors have produced platforms and software for IP telephony, but the technology is still in its growth stage and standards are not clearly established yet. The biggest push in recent years has been by the interexchange carriers (IXCs)AT&T and MCI/WorldCom, who have made large overtures into the Voice over IP (VoIP) marketplace. IP private branch exchanges (PBXs) have proven popular among small and mid-sized businesses, with offerings from 3Com Corporation, Cisco Systems, and others.

See Also: *H.323, Voice over IP (VoIP)*

IPv4

The current version of Internet Protocol (IP).

Overview

IPv6 employs a 32-bit IP addressing scheme that is used on Transmission Control Protocol/Internet Protocol (TCP/IP) networks worldwide. Because the number of hosts connecting to the Internet has skyrocketed in recent years, however, unique IP addresses are running out. A new scheme called IPv6 has been proposed and is currently under review by the Internet community. However, with most corporate networks now hiding their networks behind firewalls, the pressure to move to IPv6 has lessened because companies can choose any network ID they want for their private network. The only assigned IP addresses they require from their Internet service provider (ISP) are for the public interfaces on their firewall machines. At this point, IPv4 seems to be firmly entrenched in the networking world for at least the next few years.

See Also: *Internet Protocol (IP), IPv6*

IPv6

The next generation Internet Protocol (IP) addressing scheme for Transmission Control Protocol/Internet Protocol (TCP/IP) networks.

Overview

IPv6 was developed to replace the current IPv4 scheme that has been running out of available addresses due to the explosion of the Internet. The features of IPv6 include

- 128-bit IP addresses to solve the problem of the available IP address pool being depleted
- A simplified header format to reduce network overhead and improve performance
- Support for preallocation of network resources to enable time-dependent services such as voice and video to receive guaranteed bandwidth and quality of service (QoS)

- Extensibility to account for future growth and evolution of Internet technologies and standards
- Built-in support for Internet Protocol Security (IPsec) and DiffServ

IPv6 is also sometimes referred to as IPng, which stands for "IP Next Generation." A network called the 6Bone was set up in 1995 as a test bed for IPv6 and to investigate how the Internet can be migrated from IPv4 to IPv6.

Prospects

Japan has been in the forefront of implementing IPv6 as a real-world networking protocol, with products by Hitachi, Fujitsu, and others reaching the marketplace in early 2001. In fact, the first Internet service provider (ISP) to offer support for Ipv6 was Japan's NTT telecommunications company. Cisco Systems fully incorporated IPv6 into its IOS operating system in the recent upgrade version 12.2. Microsoft Windows XP also includes built-in support for IPv6, and a downloadable IPv6 stack is available for Windows 2000 as well. All these developments will likely propel IPv6 to the forefront in the next few years, except for one important factor: the inertia of the corporate networking world. The cost of upgrading corporate networks from IPv4 to IPv6 will be high and may bring no immediate benefits. Consequently, many companies may put upgrading on the back burner for several years.

The proliferation of wireless Internet appliances is expected to put pressure on migration to IPv6 since traditional IPv4 will be hard-pressed to fill the need for addressing large numbers of such devices. For once, it may be consumers, and not the enterprise, who drive the evolution of the Internet's core protocols forward.

See Also: *Internet Protocol (IP)*

IPX

Stands for Internetwork Packet Exchange, a NetWare protocol used for routing packets across an internetwork.

See: *Internetwork Packet Exchange (IPX)*

IPX/SPX-Compatible Protocol

Microsoft Corporation's version of the Novell NetWare IPX/SPX (Internetwork Packet Exchange/Sequenced Packet Exchange) protocol.

Overview

Using IPX/SPX and Client for NetWare Networks, clients running Microsoft Windows can access shared resources on NetWare servers directly, as long as they have appropriate permissions and rights. IPX/SPX-Compatible Protocol can be used to access Windows 2000 servers running File and Printer Sharing for NetWare Networks. IPX/SPX-Compatible Protocol supports the 32-bit Windows Sockets 1.1 and NetBIOS over Internetwork Packet Exchange (IPX) programming interfaces. In Windows 2000, this protocol is commonly referred to as NWLink.

Notes

Although the Windows 95 and Windows 98 user interfaces allow you to configure multiple bindings for IPX/SPX-Compatible Protocol to multiple network interface cards (NICs), only the first binding is actually used. You cannot use IPX/SPX-Compatible Protocol for connecting to NetWare over an ARCNET network; you must install real-mode IPX drivers instead.

IPX/SPX-Compatible Protocol is set by default to autodetect the frame type used on a NetWare network. If no frame type is detected, the default 802.2 type is used. If multiple frame types are detected, the predominant one is selected.

See Also: *Internetwork Packet Exchange (IPX), NetWare protocols*

IRC

Stands for Internet Relay Chat, a text-based Internet conferencing protocol.

See: *Internet Relay Chat (IRC)*

IrDA

Stands for Infrared Data Association, an international consortium of hardware and software manufacturers that creates and promotes interoperable solutions for infrared (IR) data networking for computer networks, communication, and other networking applications.

See: *Infrared Data Association (IrDA)*

IrDA Control

A specification developed in 1998 by the Infrared Data Association (IrDA) for communication over infrared (IR) light between in-room cordless peripheral devices and a host computer.

Overview

IrDA Control is implemented using a suite of protocols that peripherals such as keyboards, joysticks, mouse devices, and other pointing devices can use for communicating with their host computer. IrDA Control includes the following protocols:

- **IrDA Control PHY (physical) layer:** This provides for data transmission that is bidirectional and error-correcting over IR light at speeds of up to 75 Kbps over distances of up to 5 meters (16 feet).
- **IrDA Control MAC (media access control) layer:** This enables host devices to communicate with multiple IrDA Control peripherals and up to eight peripherals simultaneously. IrDA Control MAC offers a fast response time by using a polling interval of 13.8 microseconds) and supports the dynamic assignment and reuse of addresses assigned to peripheral devices.
- **IrDA Control LLC (logical link control) layer:** This ensures proper sequencing of data and handles retransmissions when errors occur.

See Also: *Infrared Data Association (IrDA), IrDA Data*

IrDA Data

A specification developed by the Infrared Data Association (IrDA) in 1994 for two-way point-to-point communication over infrared (IR) light at speeds of up to 4 megabits per second (Mbps).

Overview

IrDA Data is implemented using a suite of protocols that can be used for communication between palm computers, digital cameras, cellular phones, and other devices. IrDA Data includes the following protocols:

- **IrDA Data PHY (physical) layer:** This provides low-level continuous bidirectional error-correcting operation from 9600 bits per second (bps) up to 4 Mbps over distances of at least 3.3 feet (1 meter). Specifically, asynchronous serial transmission is supported between 9600 bps and 115.2 kilobits per second (Kbps), synchronous serial transmission at 1.152 Mbps, and synchronous communication at 4 Mbps.
- **IrDA Data Infrared Link Access Protocol (IrLAP):** This is a serial link protocol adapted by the IrDA for infrared serial communication from the High-level Data Link Control (HDLC) protocol. IrLAP provides a single serial connection between two IrDA devices and manages the device-to-device discovery, connection, and reliable data transfer functions.
- **IrDA Data Infrared Link Management Protocol (IrLMP):** This is used for link control and multiplexing of IrDA devices. IrLMP allows multiple IrDA devices to communicate over a single infrared link and provides for protocol and service discovery through the Information Access Service (IAS).

In addition to the three mandatory IrDA Data protocols described, a number of optional protocols are available that support flow control, port emulation, object exchange services, image exchange, interfacing with telephony devices, and infrared wireless access to local area networks (LANs).

See Also: *Infrared Data Association (IrDA), IrDA Control*

Irix

A flavor of the UNIX operating system developed by Silicon Graphics, Inc. (SGI).

Overview

Irix was developed by SGI for their high-end graphics workstations and servers and has been an important factor in the company's success in the imaging and animation market. SGI workstations running Irix are used for creating film and TV animation, medical image processing, and for visualization of scientific concepts such as molecular structures and weather patterns. Irix is a version of UNIX that is tuned specifically for such applications and supports multiprocessing of up to 512 CPUs, up to 1 terabyte of RAM, and high-performance input/output (I/O) throughput. The current version of the platform is Irix 6.5.

Irix was designed to run on MIPS (millions of instructions per second) processors, which these days are slower than their Intel counterparts, bringing the long-term viability of Irix into question. With the broad base of installed SGI workstations and servers, however, SGI is likely to continue to support and develop Irix in the near future, even as it expands its hardware platform to support Microsoft Windows and Linux.

See Also: *Linux, Microsoft Windows, UNIX*

IRTF

Stands for Internet Research Task Force, an umbrella organization for several long-term research groups that focus on standards for Internet protocols, architecture, applications, and technologies.

See: *Internet Research Task Force (IRTF)*

ISAPI

Stands for Internet Server API, a set of standard application programming interfaces (APIs) for developing extensions to Microsoft Internet Information Services (IIS).

See: *Internet Server API (ISAPI)*

ISAPI extension

A dynamic-link library (DLL) that runs in the same address space as the Web server running Microsoft Internet Information Services (IIS) and can access all available resources on the Web server.

Overview

You can use ISAPI extensions wherever you might use Common Gateway Interface (CGI) applications, such as for a form handler for Hypertext Markup Language (HTML) forms. An ISAPI extension is generally called in a manner similar to calling a CGI application. For example, the following Uniform Resource Locator (URL) invokes the extension TEST.DLL on the Web site *www.northwind.microsoft.com* and passes it the parameters Value1 and Value2: *www.northwind.microsoft.com/isapie/TEST.DLL?Value1&Value2*.

ISAPI extensions can run either in process or out of process on IIS. Extensions are generally loaded on demand the first time a user requests them and remain in memory until the service is stopped.

See Also: *Common Gateway Interface (CGI), dynamic-link library (DLL), Internet Information Services (IIS), Internet Server API (ISAPI), ISAPI filter*

ISAPI filter

A dynamic-link library (DLL) that is loaded into Microsoft Internet Information Services (IIS) when it starts and that remains in memory until it stops.

Overview

ISAPI filters provide Web servers such as IIS with the ability to preprocess or postprocess information sent between the client and server, and they have no equivalent in the Common Gateway Interface (CGI) scheme. ISAPI filters receive special filter event notifications and respond based on these notifications. You use ISAPI filters for such tasks as custom authentication, encryption, and compression schemes or for updating logging statistics on the Web server. ISAPI filters are generally called for every Uniform Resource Locator (URL) that the Web server processes instead of being explicitly invoked by a URL, as are ISAPI extensions.

Custom ISAPI filters can be designed by third-party developers for such tasks as

- Custom authentication
- Data encryption
- Data compression
- Filtering
- Traffic analysis

See Also: *Common Gateway Interface (CGI), dynamic-link library (DLL), Internet Information Services (IIS), Internet Server API (ISAPI), ISAPI extension*

ISA Server

Stands for Internet Security and Acceleration Server, Microsoft Corporation's firewall, proxy, and Web-caching platform.

See: *Internet Security and Acceleration Server (ISA Server)*

iSCSI

An emerging standard for transfer of Small Computer System Interface (SCSI) commands and data over Internet Protocol (IP) networks.

Overview

Traditional SCSI is limited in distance to several meters and is thus suitable only for local storage systems and shared storage in clusters. The goal of iSCSI is to remove these distance limitations by enabling SCSI commands and data to be sent between hosts and storage units over a standard IP network.

The iSCSI standard is expected to be a popular IP storage technology in the next few years, propelled on the backs of Gigabit Ethernet (GbE) and the emerging 10 GbE standard.

Implementation

Consider the example of a client trying to remotely access data from a remote storage system such as a SCSI array over a network. With iSCSI, the client simply issues the request in the form of SCSI commands as if to a local SCSI drive. The operating system or dedicated iSCSI card then packages these SCSI commands into a stream of bytes separated by iSCSI headers. The byte stream is broken up into IP packets and transmitted over the network to the remote storage array. Once received by the array, the packets are reassembled into the byte stream and the iSCSI headers are parsed to produce a series of SCSI commands, which are then issued to the local SCSI storage system. The data is then retrieved from the storage system and returned to the client.

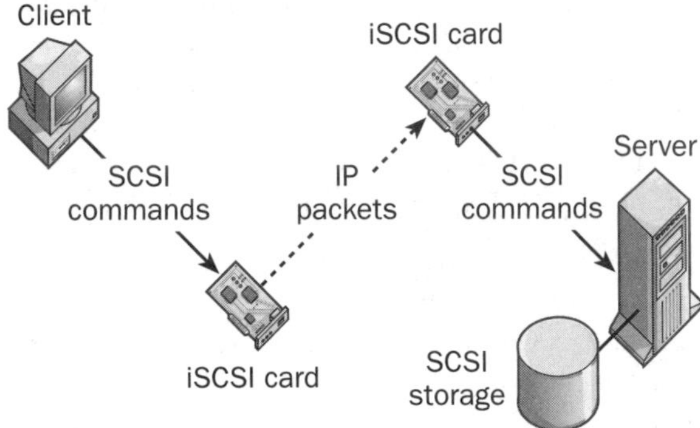

iSCSI. *How iSCSI allows clients to remotely access storage over an IP network.*

Marketplace

A number of vendors produce products and appliances based on the iSCSI standard. One example is the TotalStorage IP storage family of iSCSI storage appliances from IBM. These appliances are designed for workgroups and departments that need turnkey network storage solutions. The future of iSCSI looks good, as it is backed by such major players as Adaptec, Cisco Systems, Hewlett-Packard Company, IBM, Quantum Corporation, and SANgate Systems.

See Also: *IP storage, Small Computer System Interface (SCSI), storage*

ISDN

Stands for Integrated Services Digital Network, a digital communication service provided by telephone companies (telcos).

See: *Integrated Services Digital Network (ISDN)*

ISDN Digital Subscriber Line (IDSL)

A hybrid of Integrated Services Digital Network (ISDN) and Digital Subscriber Line (DSL) technologies.

Overview

ISDN Digital Subscriber Line (IDSL) is a form of DSL that is based on ISDN signal coding. IDSL transports data bidirectionally at a speed of 144 kilobits per second (Kbps), which is 16 Kbps more than normal ISDN. IDSL can be deployed at distances up to 6.8 miles (11 kilometers) from a telco central office (CO).

Unlike other forms of DSL that use the Public Switched Telephone Network (PSTN) as their underlying transport, IDSL uses the digital ISDN system. But unlike normal ISDN, there is no call delay setup in IDSL—it is an "always-on" service.

Prospects

Due to its slow speed compared to other forms of DSL, IDSL has not been widely deployed by telecommunication carriers to date, but a recent development called IDSL bonding may change this. Using IDSL bonding, up to four 144 Kbps IDSL links can be aggregated together using Multilink Point-to-Point Protocol (MPPP) into a respectable fat pipe of 576 Kbps. And because it supports distances up to 6.8 miles (11 kilometers) from a CO, IDSL provides an important option for customers too far from telco COs for Asymmetric Digital Subscriber Line (ADSL) or High-bit-rate Digital Subscriber Line (HDSL) to be deployed for wide area network (WAN) or Internet access. Netopia was the first DSL provider to commercially offer bonded IDSL services to its customers.

See Also: *Asymmetric Digital Subscriber Line (ADSL), Digital Subscriber Line (DSL), High-bit-rate Digital Subscriber Line (HDSL), Integrated Services Digital Network (ISDN)*

ISDN fallback adapter

A device that allows you to use an Integrated Services Digital Network (ISDN) line as a back up for a digital data service (DDS) line.

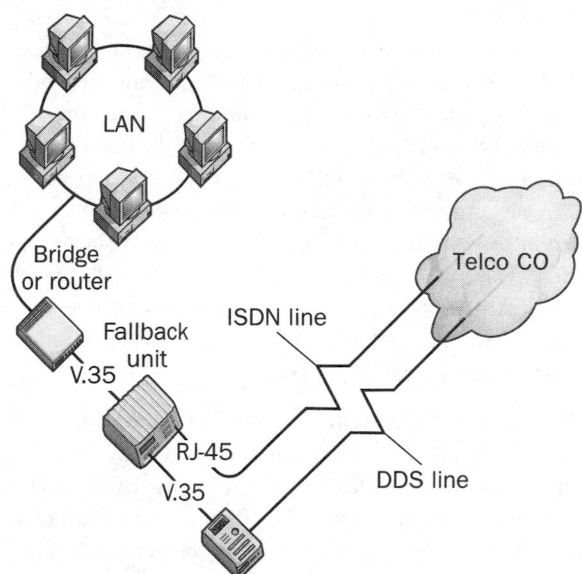

ISDN fallback adapter. *Using an ISDN fallback adapter to provide a backup for a DDS line.*

Overview

ISDN fallback adapters typically have built-in ISDN terminal adapter functionality and can sometimes provide backup support for multiple DDS lines. The fallback and restore settings are configurable using a built-in or serial-connected terminal interface.

To use a fallback adapter, you connect it to the ISDN line with the RJ-45 connector and to the local area network (LAN) bridge or router and the DDS CSU/DSUs (Channel Service Unit/Data Service Units) using the V.35 or RS-232 serial interfaces. When the DDS line fails, the ISDN fallback adapter automatically kicks in the ISDN line to maintain wide area network (WAN) connectivity.

See Also: *Channel Service Unit/Data Service Unit (CSU/DSU), digital data service (DDS), Integrated Services Digital Network (ISDN), RS-232, V.35*

ISDN router

A router with built-in hardware for connecting directly to Integrated Services Digital Network (ISDN) lines.

Overview

ISDN routers—also called ISDN access routers because they provide direct connectivity to a wide area network (WAN) connection—are a popular way of providing SOHOs (Small Office/Home Offices) with 128-Kbps dial-up ISDN connectivity to the Internet or to a remote private corporate network through the industry-standard Point-to-Point Protocol (PPP). They typically support up to 10 users in a small workgroup Ethernet local area network (LAN) and might provide some firewall, network address translation (NAT), or Dynamic Host Configuration Protocol (DHCP) support.

ISDN routers include RJ-11 jacks for connecting several analog phones, fax machines, or other devices for simultaneous voice/fax/data connectivity. Built-in data compression can increase the effective bandwidth by a factor of 5 or higher. Some ISDN routers include built-in hubs for quick connectivity. Many are manageable using a remote Telnet connection or through Simple Network Management Protocol (SNMP).

See Also: *Dynamic Host Configuration Protocol (DHCP), Integrated Services Digital Network (ISDN), network address translation (NAT), Point-to-Point Protocol (PPP), router, Simple Network Management Protocol (SNMP)*

ISDN terminal adapter

A device used at the customer premises to terminate an Integrated Services Digital Network (ISDN) line and connect it to an analog telephone, computer, or local area network (LAN).

Overview

You must employ ISDN terminal adapters when you do not have telephone, computing, or networking equipment that are ISDN-ready. Another name for ISDN terminal adapters is *ISDN modems*, but this is a misnomer, since no modulation/demodulation is performed by the device.

ISDN terminal adapters can be stand-alone AC powered devices or interface cards that you install on your computer. They can provide 128-kilobit-per-second (Kbps) throughput using the Bandwidth On Demand Interoperability Group (bonding) protocol for high-speed Internet and wide area network (WAN) connectivity, with higher effective data transfer rates using built-in data compression. ISDN terminal adapters are dial-up and do not provide an "always on" network connection, but their latency time interval for establishing a connection is typically small (1 to 3 seconds). To save costs, you can usually also configure an idle timer for dropping idle connections.

When you buy ISDN terminal adapters, be sure that they support the ISDN standard used by your telco. Such standards can include the National ISDN-1, ISDN-2, and ISDN-3 standards for AT&T, Northern Telecom, and Siemens. An ISDN terminal adapter with automatic service profile identifier (SPID) detection generally works with most ISDN installations.

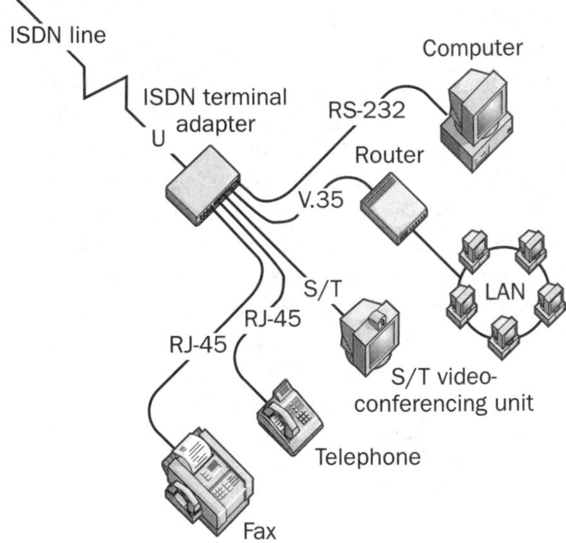

ISDN terminal adapter. *Using an ISDN terminal adapter.*

Implementation

A terminal adapter typically connects to the U interface of the ISDN line at the customer premises using an RJ-45 connector and provides electrical termination for this line. The other interface on the terminal adapter is typically an RS-232, RS-366, RS-530, or V.35 serial interface such as DB25, or a 34-pin connector for connecting the terminal adapter to a bridge, router, or computer at the customer premises. Terminal adapters can include several RJ-11 connectors for connecting an analog telephone or a fax machine so that you can transfer data, talk on the phone, and fax documents simultaneously over one ISDN line. Some newer terminal adapters have an S/T interface for connecting to an S/T videoconferencing unit.

Notes

If you need more speed than ISDN but cannot afford to upgrade to T1 lines, try using an inverse multiplexer (IMUX) to combine several ISDN lines into one high-speed data pipe.

See Also: *Integrated Services Digital Network (ISDN), inverse multiplexer (IMUX)*

ISL

Stands for Inter-Switch Link, a Cisco Systems technology that is used for frame tagging.

See: *Inter-Switch Link (ISL)*

ISM

Stands for the Industrial, Scientific, and Medical band of the electromagnetic spectrum.

Overview

The ISM band consists of 83 megahertz (MHz) of spectrum at the 2.4 gigahertz (GHz) range that is freely available to anyone who wants to use it.

The ISM band is used by common wireless technologies including cordless phones, microwave ovens, wireless local area networks (LANs) such as 802.11b, and emerging technologies such as Bluetooth and HomeRF. Many of these devices interfere with each other, so as a result, the ISM band has grown "crowded" in recent years. To alleviate this congestion, the Federal Communications Commission (FCC) has allocated another similar portion of spectrum called the UNII band, which provides 300 MHz of spectrum within the 5 GHz range. The UNII band is used by the newer 802.11a wireless networking standard.

Notes

The reason for selecting 2.4 GHz for the ISM band is that the resonant frequency of water molecules is about 2450 MHz, which means this is the optimal frequency for microwave ovens to work.

See Also: *802.11a, 802.11b, Bluetooth, Federal Communications Commission (FCC), wireless networking*

ISO

Stands for International Organization for Standardization, a nongovernmental organization based in Geneva, Switzerland, that has representatives from about 130 countries and regions and is responsible for developing a variety of international standards in science and engineering.

See: *International Organization for Standardization (ISO)*

ISOC

Stands for Internet Society, a professional society founded in 1992 that provides leadership for the development and evolution of the Internet.

See: *Internet Society (ISOC)*

isoEthernet

Stands for isochronous Ethernet, an offshoot of 10BaseT Ethernet.

Overview

IsoEthernet was developed in 1992 by National Semiconductor and was standardized by the Institute of Electrical and Electronics Engineers (IEEE) as 802.9a. IsoEthernet follows the cabling specifications of 10BaseT Ethernet but is capable of dedicating some circuits for transport of latency-sensitive multimedia traffic.

The signaling layer of isoEthernet is based on Integrated Services Digital Network (ISDN) protocols instead of those of standard Ethernet.

IsoEthernet never caught on with the industry, mainly because the problem it attacked (the issue of latency for time-sensitive traffic) has been largely solved by Fast Ethernet and Gigabit Ethernet (GbE)—in other words, by simply throwing bandwidth at the problem. IsoEthernet is thus now seen as a legacy networking architecture and is virtually gone from the enterprise scene.

See Also: *10BaseT, Ethernet, Fast Ethernet, Gigabit Ethernet (GbE), Integrated Services Digital Network (ISDN)*

ISP

Stands for Internet service provider, a company that provides Internet access to consumers, businesses, or both.

See: *Internet service provider (ISP)*

iterative query

A Domain Name System (DNS) query in which a name server contacts a second name server to perform a name lookup.

Overview

In a typical Internet name lookup (such as the URL *www.fabrikam.microsoft.com*), a resolver sends a recursive query to a locally accessible name server such as a name server maintained by your local Internet service provider (ISP). If the local name server cannot resolve the name because it is outside of its zone of authority and it is configured as a forwarder, the server performs an iterative query to a root name server, which responds with the Internet Protocol (IP) address of a name server whose zone of authority includes the desired top-level domain (.com). The local name server then performs an iterative query with this top-level name server, which responds with the IP address of a second-level name server whose zone of authority includes the desired second-level domain (expedia.com). The local name server contacts this second-level name server and resolves the fully qualified domain name (FQDN) into its IP address or returns an error if the query cannot be resolved.

See Also: *inverse query, recursive query*

itrace

Code name for ICMP Traceback Messages, an emerging standard from the Internet Engineering Task Force (IETF) for combating distributed denial of service (DDoS) attacks.

See: *ICMP Traceback Messages*

ITU

Stands for International Telecommunication Union, an international organization headquartered in Geneva, Switzerland, that coordinates global telecommunications networks and services with governments and the private sector.

See: *International Telecommunication Union (ITU)*

IXC

Stands for inter-exchange carrier, a telecommunications carrier that provides long-distance services.

See: *inter-exchange carrier (IXC)*

jabber

Random, malformed frames of data that are sent continuously by failed circuitry in a networking component.

Overview

A network interface card (NIC) or other device that is jabbering generates a continuous stream of unwanted signals that can disrupt communication between other devices on the network. This is especially common on Ethernet networks, in which each device must compete for use of the line using the Carrier Sense Multiple Access with Collision Detection (CSMA/CD) contention protocol. When a NIC jabbers on an Ethernet network, all network communication might cease until the offending NIC is replaced. Other causes of jabbering on a network include loose cabling or a poorly grounded cable (for shielded cabling).

Jabbering can also occur in Fast Ethernet networks, in which a combination of 100BaseT4 and 100BaseTX cabling schemes are employed in one network. The continuously generated idle stream signal of the TX network can appear to the T4 network as jabber and can bring down the entire network. This should not be a problem if all network devices implement autonegotiation in an IEEE-compliant fashion. In addition, Fast Ethernet repeaters generally implement jabber control by automatically disconnecting any port that transmits information in streams longer than 40 kilobits (Kb).

The term *jabber* is also used in the Institute of Electrical and Electronic Engineers (IEEE) 802.3 specification for any frame of data that exceeds the maximum frame length for that specification. For Ethernet networks, the maximum frame length is 1518 bytes (18 bytes of overhead and 1500 bytes of payload). A frame longer than 1518 bytes is often called a jabber frame. Another name for jabber is *long packet error*.

Notes

A frame shorter than 64 bytes on an Ethernet network is called a runt frame.

See Also: *Carrier Sense Multiple Access with Collision Detection (CSMA/CD), Ethernet, Fast Ethernet, frame*

J

jack

A receptacle into which you can insert a connector or plug to form a connection.

Overview

The best example of a jack in computer networking is the standard RJ-45 jack in which a connector (plug) on the end of a Category 5 (Cat5) cable can be inserted. RJ-45 jacks are typically built into Ethernet networking devices such as hubs, switches, and routers, but some devices also allow modular jacks to be inserted and removed in order to support other kinds of connectors. Patch panels and wall plates are other examples of items that may either be hardwired with RJ-45 jacks or allow modular jacks to be inserted into them for greater flexibility.

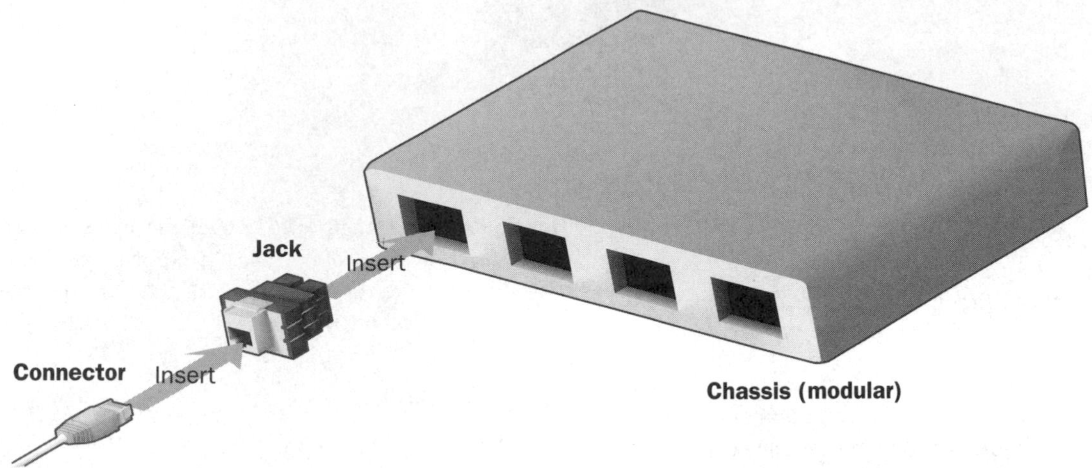

Jack. *Example of a modular RJ-45 jack.*

Notes

The terms *connector, jack,* and *plug* have some overlap and are often used interchangeably. Some vendors use *plug* to refer to the male connector and *jack* to refer to the female, but others use the terms *male jacks* and *female jacks*.

See Also: *cabling, Category 5 (Cat5) cabling, Ethernet*

jacket

The outer covering of cabling that protects it from physical damage.

Overview

A cable's jacket protects the wiring from various kinds of damage, including damage caused by

- Exposure to sun, heat, moisture, dust, and chemicals
- Contact with sharp edges of walls, furniture, or plenum ducts (such as ventilation ducts); by mechanical vibrations; or by mechanical stresses introduced during the cable installation process

The jacket is usually made of an insulating material, although its primary purpose is not insulation. (This function is provided by the insulation of individual wires within the jacket.) Common materials used for cable jackets include the following:

- **Polyvinyl chloride (PVC):** This is the most common material used for cable jackets. PVC is a tough, fire-resistant material formed from resins and plastics that can withstand a wide range of temperatures. PVC cables are typically used in vertical rises, but they should not be used in plenums because PVC gives off toxic fumes when burned.
- **Kynar plastic (polyvinylidene fluoride):** This material has good fire-retardant qualities, which makes it suitable for installation in plenums, but it is several times more costly than PVC.
- **Flamarrest:** This chloride compound has high fire retardance and is suitable for plenum installations.
- **Neoprene:** This dark-colored plastic is resistant to moisture and does not degrade in sunlight. It is a good choice for use in outdoor cable runs.
- **Polyethylene:** This soft, moisture-resistant plastic has poor fire retardance and is suitable only for outdoor cable runs.

See Also: *cabling*

jam signal

A signal sent by a device on an Ethernet network to indicate that a collision has occurred on the network.

Overview

Collisions occur on Ethernet networks because access to media (usually a cable) is based on contention—that is, stations on the network transmit on a first-come, first-served basis. If two stations attempt to take control of the medium at the same time and begin transmitting, both stations will detect each other's signal and realize that a collision has occurred. The two stations then issue a jam signal, which notifies all other stations on the network of the collision. They all must wait a short period of time before attempting to transmit again. The length of time is random for each station so that the retransmissions will not cause more collisions. The jam signal sent by one transmitting station must start with a 62-bit pattern of alternating 0s and 1s, followed by a 32-bit sequence that provides a dummy checksum value for the other transmitting station. This 32-bit sequence cannot be equal to the cyclical redundancy check (CRC) value for the frame preceding the jam.

See Also: *Carrier Sense Multiple Access with Collision Detection (CSMA/CD), collision, Ethernet,*

Java

An object-oriented programming language developed by Sun Microsystems.

Overview

Java was designed to reduce the amount of time needed to build robust, scalable object-oriented applications. Java is a powerful object-oriented programming (OOP) platform like C and C++, but it has several advantages over these languages, including

- **Portability:** Java is an interpreted language that runs on any platform for which the interpreter, the Java Virtual Machine (JVM), is available. This currently includes virtually every major operating system platform, including various flavors of UNIX, Linux, Microsoft Windows, and the Mac OS. The original Java mantra, "Write once, run anywhere," stressed the language's platform-independence and code portability.
- **Reliability:** Certain advanced features of C/C++ such as pointers have been eliminated in Java to reduce the likelihood of hard-to-trace errors from creeping into complex programs. Java also includes new features such as automatic garbage collection to simplify the complex programming task of reserving and releasing memory.
- **Security:** Java uses a "sandbox" model that implements security by running small, downloadable client-side programs called "applets" within a protected area of memory. This prevents hostile applets from adversely affecting users' systems and makes Java an ideal platform for developing dynamic Web applications that run within a user's Web browser.
- **Easy to learn:** Java's syntax is not too different from C/C++, making it relatively easy for developers experienced in these platforms to move to Java.

History

Version 1 of Sun's Java Developer Kit (JDK) was released in 1995 at the company's SunWorld conference. Although a full-featured programming language, this initial release was especially popular with Web developers, who used Java to build applets that could be embedded in Hypertext Markup Language (HTML) pages to enhance the user experience by providing interactive content. With the release of JDK 1.1 in 1997, Sun added support for database connectivity and other features that made Java a more powerful and attractive programming environment for developing server-side applications.

JDK 1.2 was released in 1999, and incorporated the Java Foundation Classes (JFC) into Java's core run-time libraries. JDK 1.2 also provided a number of other enhancements that made Java a more scalable and secure platform. As a result of these improvements, Sun renamed the platform Java2 with this release of the JDK. Later in 1999, Sun made the Java2 platform available to developers in three versions: Java2 Standard Edition (J2SE), Java2 Enterprise Edition (J2EE), and Java2 Micro Edition (J2ME). These editions are discussed in the Implementation section of this article.

The current release of Java is the JDK 1.3 version of Java2. The Java specification is currently controlled by Sun through its Java Community Process (JCP) initiative.

Uses

Although Java was originally designed for developing full-fledged enterprise applications, much of its initial appeal came from its ability to create applets that could be downloaded from Web sites by browsers. These applets would then run on the browser to provide interactive elements such as advanced user interfaces and exciting display elements such as rotating ad banners and animated stock tickers.

As Java has grown to include more enterprise features such as database connectivity and server-side execution elements, it has evolved into a popular platform for the development of commercial e-business applications that is widely used in today's enterprise and business world.

Architecture

When you write an application (or applet) in Java, the Java compiler takes your source code (which is usually saved with the extension .java) and compiles it into something called bytecode. Bytecode is not true machine code—it is a set of generic instructions that are not specific to any particular hardware platform or operating system. Bytecode files generally have the extension .class and are referred to as class files. The following is a simple example of a Java application called HelloThere.java:

```
Class HelloThere {
  Public static void main (String args[]) {
    System.out.println("Hello there");
  }
}
```

The HelloThere.java program defines a new class called HelloThere and contains only one method: main(). When this program is compiled into the class file HelloThere.class and then run, it displays the text "Hello there" on the screen (the standard output device).

To run the application (class file), you must have a bytecode interpreter called a Java Virtual Machine (JVM) on the system. The JVM reads your application's bytecode and executes it by converting each bytecode instruction into a machine-native instruction or set of instructions. This translation process takes place regardless of whether the particular piece of bytecode has been previously executed. If the application is an applet, the Web browser that accesses it must have a JVM installed. The use of a bytecode interpreter instead of a "true" compiler, which generates platform-specific machine code, means that applications written in Java are often slower than those written in C or C++, but the ease of development and portability of code offset these disadvantages in most cases. To obtain additional functionality, you can link native code to Java applications.

The JVM has special security features built into it to ensure that any malicious Java applet downloaded from the Internet cannot perform any harmful actions on the user's system. In this sense, you can consider the JVM running in the Web browser a "sandbox" that allows the applet to execute safely while preventing access to certain items, such as the client machine's file system.

Implementation

The Java2 specification is currently available from Sun in three different developer platforms:

- **Java2 Standard Edition (J2SE):** This includes the standard java.* packages, the Java Foundation Classes (JFC), the Abstract Window Toolkit (AWT) application programming interfaces (APIs) used for developing graphical user interfaces (GUIs), and other basic elements of the Java platform. J2SE is intended primarily as a platform for developing applets for Web sites.
- **Java2 Enterprise Edition (J2EE):** This edition has pushed Java into the forefront of enterprise application development by providing advanced features for development of server-side applications. J2EE includes advanced Java components such as Enterprise JavaBeans (EJB), Java Database Connectivity (JDBC), Java Server Pages (JSP), Java Servlets, and more. Some of these components of Java are further discussed later in this article.
- **Java2 Micro Edition (J2ME):** This version has a small footprint designed for developing applications for devices having limited processing power, memory, and display capability. Examples of devices where J2ME can be used include cell phones, Personal Digital Assistants (PDAs), pagers, smart cards, and embedded systems such as industrial control systems and intelligent sensors.

Some other key Java terminology includes the following:

- **Enterprise JavaBeans (EJB):** A component architecture for developing transactional server-side Java applications. EJBs can be either self-contained programs or small portions of programs and can be used as building blocks for building more complex Java applications. EJB is currently in version 1.1 (the EJB 2 specification is being developed) and is the Java counterpart of the Microsoft technology called Component Object Model (COM).
- **Java Foundation Classes (JFC):** Also known as Swing, these classes are building blocks for creating interfaces for Java applications.
- **Java Database Connectivity (JDBC):** This component provides standard APIs for connecting Structured Query Language (SQL) databases to Java applications. JDBC is currently in version 2 and is the counterpart of the Microsoft technology known as Open Database Connectivity (ODBC).

Marketplace

Java2 Micro Edition (J2ME) is emerging as a popular platform for developing distributed applications for the next generation of third-generation (3G) cellular communication systems. A consortium of over 20 industry partners, including Sun, Ericsson, Motorola, Nokia, and Siemens, has developed the Mobile Internet Device (MID) profile, a platform for developing interactive mobile services that is based on J2ME. The J2ME platform complements the existing Wireless Application Protocol (WAP) platform and usesWAP as its underlying transport mechanism. Motorola's iDEN handset was the first commercially available mobile device compliant with the J2ME specification. A popular platform for creating J2EE applications is Code Warrior from Metrowerks.

Java in the enterprise has recently been furthered by Sun's new Java Web Start (JWS) platform. JWS simplifies the deployment of applications developed with Java 2 Enterprise Edition (J2EE) to network clients. This is done packaging all the various components of a Java application into a Java Archive (JAR) file, which can be downloaded and installed on client machines through a simple click of a link on a Web page. JWS also automates the process of upgrading Java applications on client machines, lowering the costs of deploying and managing Java desktop applications across an enterprise.

Prospects

Java has established itself in the enterprise market and is widely used for developing server-side applications for e-business. The Java community includes more than 2.5 million developers, a tribute to the platform's ease of use and reliability. On the client side, however, the original expectation of Java transforming the Internet through dynamic interactive content has faded somewhat. The biggest prospect for Java's future is likely to be in the embedded device field, where it competes with platforms such as Wireless Markup Language, QUALCOMM's Binary Runtime Environment for Wireless (BREW), and Microsoft Corporation's Windows CE. In the near future, Java is likely to find its main competition to be Microsoft's new .NET platform with its powerful C# programming language.

For More Information

Visit Sun Microsystems Java site at *java.sun.com.*

See Also: *C#, Java Database Connectivity (JDBC), Java Server Pages (JSP), .NET platform*

Java Database Connectivity (JDBC)

A data access interface developed by Sun Microsystems that allows Java applications to access information stored in databases.

Overview

The Java Database Connectivity (JDBC) application programming interface (API) is a standard component of Java 2 Enterprise Edition (J2EE) development platform. The JDBC API specifies a set of Java classes that represent database connections, Structured Query Language (SQL) queries and their result sets, and other objects associated with accessing databases. Multiple drivers for JDBC exist that allow access to different database formats, and the JDBC drivers themselves can be implemented either within applets or as native methods on the operating system. JDBC also supports drivers that act as a bridge between Open Database Connectivity (ODBC) and JDBC. This type of driver

J

translates JDBC function calls into native ODBC calls, but this bridge cannot be run by distrusted applets within a Web browser environment.

Notes

JDBC is to the Java platform what ODBC is to Microsoft Windows.

See Also: *application programming interface (API), Java, open database connectivity (ODBC), Structured Query Language (SQL)*

Java Online Analytical Processing (JOLAP)

A Java-based interface for online analytical processing (OLAP) databases.

J

Overview

Java Online Analytical Processing (JOLAP) provides an interface for accessing, storing, and managing metadata stored in OLAP databases. JOLAP is intended to provide a uniform, platform-independent method for allowing clients to interact with OLAP servers. Just as the Java Database Connectivity (JDBC) specification allows data stored in relational databases to be accessed using Java, JOLAP provides similar functionality for accessing metadata stored in OLAP systems.

The JOLAP specification is an initiative of a company called Hyperion and is backed by an industry consortium that includes IBM, Oracle Corporation, and Sun Microsystems.

Notes

Microsoft Corporation's own specification for accessing OLAP systems is known as OLE DB.

See Also: *OLE DB, online analytical processing (OLAP)*

JavaScript

A scripting language developed for the Web by Netscape.

Overview

JavaScript is a cross-platform, object-based scripting language that is similar to C but much simpler in syntax. JavaScript was developed by Netscape Communications (now just Netscape) and built into the Netscape Navigator Web browser version 2 and later. JavaScript enables Web developers to produce Web pages with dynamic functionality such as animated graphics, browser detection, cookies, scrolling text, form handlers, and authentication without needing to write or invoke Common Gateway Interface (CGI) applications. JavaScript can be used to develop both client and server applications, but it is usually run on the client Web browser.

The European Computer Manufacturers Association (ECMA) based its ECMA-262 standard upon both Netscape's JavaScript 1.1 and Microsoft's JScript 2 scripting languages. This ECMA-standardized scripting language is known as ECMAScript, and JavaScript 1.5 fully complies with the ECMA 262 standard.

Examples

JavaScript scripts are placed in standard Hypertext Markup Language (HTML) files using special tags. Here is a simple example:

```
<HTML>
<HEAD><TITLE>Javascript Test</TITLE></HEAD>
<BODY>
<H1>Knock Knock</H1>
<SCRIPT LANGUAGE="JavaScript">
alert("Who's there?");
</SCRIPT>
</BODY>
</HTML>
```

The <SCRIPT> and </SCRIPT> tags identify and contain the actual JavaScript script. When this page is loaded into a Web browser such as Netscape Navigator version 3, the browser reads the script and interprets it, causing an alert dialog box to be displayed with the message "JavaScript Alert: Who's there?" and an OK button that closes the dialog box when clicked.

Notes

JavaScript is not the same as Java, which is an object-oriented programming language. A syntactically similar scripting language called JScript is supported on Microsoft Internet Explorer.

See Also: *Java, JScript, scripting*

Java Server Pages (JSP)

A technology from Sun Microsystems for creating dynamic Web applications.

Overview

Java Server Pages (JSP) is a Java-based technology that is part of the Java 2 Enterprise Edition (J2EE) specification from Sun Microsystems. JSP can be used to write server-side Web applications that dynamically generate Hypertext Markup Language (HTML) pages when accessed through a Web browser. Like the underlying Java programming environment on which it is based, JSP is a platform-independent, vendor-neutral development architecture that provides full access to Java's features, including standard Java APIs, Java servlets, and Java Database Connectivity (JDBC).

JSP also complements another Java server-side Web programming architecture called Java Servlets. Using JSP, you can include portions of Java code within an HTML page to call external Java components from the page. Java supports both tag-based programming similar to that used by Macromedia's Cold Fusion platform and embedded script blocks such as those used by Microsoft Corporation's Active Server Pages (ASP) platform.

Architecture

JSP separates the presentation (the display of HTML pages) layer from the business logic layer, simplifying the process of creating portable, scalable Web-based applications. JSP has a simple syntax that can be used to write applications that run on Web servers and dynamically generate Web content in response to requests from Web browsers. An example of a simple "Hello World" application written in JSP might be as follows:

```
<HTML>
<HEAD><TITLE>Sample JSP Application</TITLE>
</HEAD>
<BODY>
<%
String guest = request.getParameter("name");
if (guest == null) guest = "World";
%>
Hello <%= guest %>
</BODY>
</HTML>
```

In this example, a form on a Web page could request the user to input his or her name, which would then be passed as a parameter to the JSP application on the Web server. For example, if the user's name is Mary and the form uses the GET method, the Name parameter would be passed to the JSP application (which might be called Hello.jsp) by appending it to the URL, for example:

```
http://www.microsoft.com/JSPtest/
Hello.jsp?name=Mary
```

The client-side browser would then display a simple dynamically generated Web page that says "Hello Mary." If the user instead submitted the form without specifying a name, the browser would display simply "Hello World."

Marketplace

JSP has established itself as a popular platform for developing dynamic Web applications. As a server-side development platform, JSP competes in the commercial and enterprise environments with many similar platforms, including Macromedia's Cold Fusion, Personal Home Pages (PHP), the CGI/PERL combination popular in the UNIX world, and Microsoft Corporation's ASP platform.

For developers who want to create JSP applications, a variety of integrated development environments (IDEs) is available, including JRun and DreamWeaver UltraDev from Macromedia, and WebGain Studio from WebGain.

See Also: *Active Server Pages (ASP), Hypertext Markup Language (HTML), Java*

JBOD

Stands for "just a bunch of disks" and refers to an unstructured high-capacity disk-storage system.

Overview

A JBOD is essentially just an array of disks connected to a common backplane and arranged within an enclosure. The disks within the JBOD are usually controlled by an attached server called the host server, which may manage them as independent volumes or combine them into logical volumes in any way desired. JBODs are used anywhere a large amount of storage capacity is required but do not provide the fault tolerance of redundant array of independent disks (RAID) systems.

JBODs are more difficult to manage than Storage Area Networks (SANs) and Network Attached Storage (NAS) systems. As they rapidly expand their network, companies often implement JBODs without planning, creating storage management headaches for administrators. On the plus side, JBODs are cheaper to implement than SANs and can quickly provide additional network storage when needed.

Architecture

There is no one standard JBOD architecture. In its simplest form, a JBOD can be constructed by chaining together a series of external Small Computer System Interface (SCSI) disk drives, removable Jaz drives, optical drives, or any mixture of drives. In enterprise environments, Fibre Channel JBODs are more common; they generally have dual-loop DB9 copper interfaces and can be connected easily to a Fibre Channel hub or switch to provide additional network storage. Fibre Channel JBODs typically range from small 8-disk enclosures to large rackmount form factors that include several hot-swappable modules, each of which may contain 20 or more disks.

See Also: *Fibre Channel, network attached storage (NAS), Small Computer System Interface (SCSI), storage, storage area network (SAN)*

JDBC

Stands for Java Database Connectivity, a data access interface developed by Sun Microsystems that allows Java applications to access information stored in databases.

See: *Java Database Connectivity (JDBC)*

Jet

Stands for Joint Engine Technology, a database engine technology used in various Microsoft products.

See: *Joint Engine Technology (Jet)*

Jini

An on-demand networking architecture developed by Sun Microsystems.

Overview

Jini is designed to provide a simple way of spontaneously creating networks without the need to install drivers or configure network parameters. It provides an underlying infrastructure that allows a wide range of devices to connect to one another as needed to perform specific tasks. Jini devices can automatically discover, recognize, and form federations or communities with one another spontaneously without user intervention. Jini devices are always on and establish impromptu networks as needed. Jini can be implemented on a wide range of devices, including not only computing platforms such as PCs, Personal Digital Assistants (PDAs), and cell phones, but also VCRs and DVD players, stereo systems, copiers, thermostats, and security systems.

Jini is based on Java technology from Sun and can be implemented on any device running the Java Virtual Machine (VM). Java is the key enabler of Jini technology, and, like Java, is a fundamental component of the Sun Open Network Environment (Sun ONE) initiative.

Architecture

Jini's basic underlying architecture involves two components:

- **Services:** These are Jini-enabled devices that can provide resources to other Jini-enabled devices and can include core system services such as Java's VM, JavaBeans component technology, Java Naming and Directory Interface (JNDI), Java's Remote Method Invocation (RMI), and other services. Jini also supports other services, including a discovery and join-in protocol to enable clients to locate Jini services, distributed security services to manage user rights and privileges, database services, distributed garbage collection, and more.
- **Clients:** These are Jini-enabled devices that can find, request, and lease services from other Jini-enabled devices. Clients lease services for a specific task and for a limited time until the task is completed and then release the resource for other clients to use.

Jini uses a distributed architecture in which no single central server is needed. Jini devices can federate to form spontaneous communities without the need to have a central PC controlling them. For example, a Jini-enabled PDA and cell phone could communicate with each other when the user accesses the cell phone to dial a phone number. The cell phone could automatically network with the PDA using Jini to look up the phone number.

For More Information

Find out more about Jini at *www.sun.com/jini.*

See Also: Java

jitter

Distortion in transmission that occurs when a signal drifts from its reference position.

Overview

Jitter is inherent in all forms of communication because of the finite response time of electrical circuitry to the rise and fall of signal voltages. An ideal digital signal would have instantaneous rises and falls in voltages and would appear as a square wave on an oscilloscope. The actual output of a digital signaling device has finite rise and fall times and appears rounded when displayed on the oscilloscope, which can result in phase variation that causes loss of synchronization between communicating devices.

Jitter can also be caused by variations in the timing or the phase of the signal in an analog or digital transmission line. In this instance, jitter can be caused by poor connectors, malfunctioning repeaters, transient problems in switches, and variations in transmission characteristics of cabling. Jitter typically results in a loss of data because of synchronization problems between the transmitting stations, especially in high-speed transmissions. The goal in designing a transmission device is to ensure that the jitter remains within a range that is too small to cause appreciable data loss.

Jitter is different from a related concept called delay. Delay is the amount of time for a signal to reach its destination, but jitter represents unevenness in delay. For example, when you download a file from the Internet using File Transfer Protocol (FTP), the delay between transmission of packets from the FTP server to the client is typically several hundred milliseconds, but, due to jitter in the connection, the first half of the file may download much more quickly than the last half.

Jitter is particularly annoying in multimedia communications involving audio or video streaming. Jitter can render a communication unintelligible, and it can cause dropouts unless buffering is used to prevent them. Buffering introduces delay, however, and although this may be acceptable in one-way streaming transmission, it is unacceptable in two-way communications.

See Also: noise, latency, signal

join

A database operation that allows you to retrieve and modify data from more than one table at a time using a single Structured Query Language (SQL) SELECT statement.

Overview

You can use the Microsoft Query Analyzer tool for Microsoft SQL Server to graphically create joins for transact-SQL queries that join two or more tables or join a table to itself. Joins are a necessity because a single table might not provide all the information you want to retrieve about a specific database entity. By connecting tables using joins, you can retrieve information that resides in more than one table in a single operation.

You can create three kinds of joins:

- **Inner joins:** Connect two tables to form a result set that contains only the matching rows that satisfy the join condition. Inner joins can be equijoins or natural joins.
- **Cross or unrestricted joins:** Produce a result set that contains all combinations of all rows from the tables that are joined. A cross join between a table of 5 rows and another table of 4 rows creates a result set of 20 rows.
- **Outer joins:** Maintain information that does not match the join condition. For example, a left outer join contains at least all rows from the first table.

Notes

There are two kinds of syntax for creating joins, ANSI join syntax and SQL Server join syntax. You can use only one of these types of syntax in a given SELECT statement.

See Also: *database, Structured Query Language (SQL)*

Joint Engine Technology (Jet)

A database engine technology used in various Microsoft products.

Overview

Jet is an advanced 32-bit multithreaded database engine developed by Microsoft Corporation in 1992. The Jet database engine is employed in several Microsoft products, including Microsoft Exchange, Microsoft Access, Microsoft Visual Basic, and Active Directory directory service for Microsoft Windows 2000. The Jet engine is not available as a separate product.

Architecture

The Jet database engine employs transaction logs to track and maintain information and provide fault tolerance. Native Jet database files usually have the extension .mdb. Jet databases can be accessed using Data Access Objects (DAO) and open database connectivity (ODBC). DAO provides the Component Object Model (COM) interface for accessing indexed sequential access method (ISAM) databases such as Microsoft FoxPro, dBASE, or Paradox through Jet. Jet databases are best accessed through DAO (rather than ODBC) because they expose only a limited amount of functionality to ODBC drivers. Jet cannot use ODBC to build queries that use server-side cursors, and it has limited capability for stored procedures and multiple result sets.

See Also: *Component Object Model (COM), Data Access Objects (DAO), Exchange Server, open database connectivity (ODBC)*

JOLAP

Stands for Java Online Analytical Processing or Java OLAP, a Java-based interface for OLAP databases.

See: *Java Online Analytical Processing (JOLAP)*

JScript

Microsoft Corporation's implementation of the ECMA-Script standard.

Overview

JScript is an interpreted object-based Web scripting language originally developed as Microsoft's counterpart to Netscape's JavaScript scripting language. JScript was designed to allow Web developers to easily add dynamic, interactive content to static Hypertext Markup Language (HTML) pages.

JScript is a superset of the ECMA-262 specification, a standard for cross-platform, vendor-neutral scripting languages developed by the European Computer Manufacturers Association (ECMA). JScript complies with the ECMAScript standard and includes advanced features that make it a powerful scripting tool for the Microsoft Windows platform. In particular, JScript allows Component Object Model (COM) objects such as ActiveX controls to be called from within scripts and executed using the Windows Scripting Host (WSH), enabling the full power of the Windows operating system to be accessed.

Architecture

JScript is an interpreted programming language that is executed at run time. JScript files use the extension .js to identify themselves to WSH for execution. JScript supports standard programming elements such as statements, variables, constants, operators, conditionals, loops, functions, and arrays. It also supports a limited number of objects and methods. JScript supports six different data types including the variant data types. The language is thus loosely typed, meaning you do not have to declare a variable's data type before you use the variable. JScript has limited file input/output (I/O) features.

You can execute scripts written in JScript in several ways:

- By double-clicking on a shortcut to a .js file and executing them directly using the WSH
- By running them from the command line using the WSH
- By embedding them into HTML pages using <SCRIPT> tags

In the third scenario above, JScript is typically used to add functionality to HTML files stored on a Web server. When a Web browser such as Microsoft Internet Explorer accesses a page containing an embedded block of JScript script, it downloads the block of script and executes it locally on the client machine. Internet Explorer can do this because it has a built-in scripting engine that can understand and interpret scripts written in JScript and Microsoft Visual Basic, Scripting Edition (VBScript).

Examples

The following is a simple example of an embedded script written in JScript. The script is embedded in an HTML page between the <SCRIPT> and </SCRIPT> tags and displays a confirm message box when the user opens the file using Internet Explorer. When the user makes a selection, the remaining portion of the page loads.

```
<HTML>
<BODY>
<H1>Welcome to our restaurant!</H1>
<HR>
<SCRIPT>
var testing=window.confirm("Click OK for food,
Cancel for drink.");
if (testing) {
    window.alert("Hot dog");
} else window.alert("Beer");
</SCRIPT>
<H1>Thanks for coming!</H1>
</BODY>
</HTML>
```

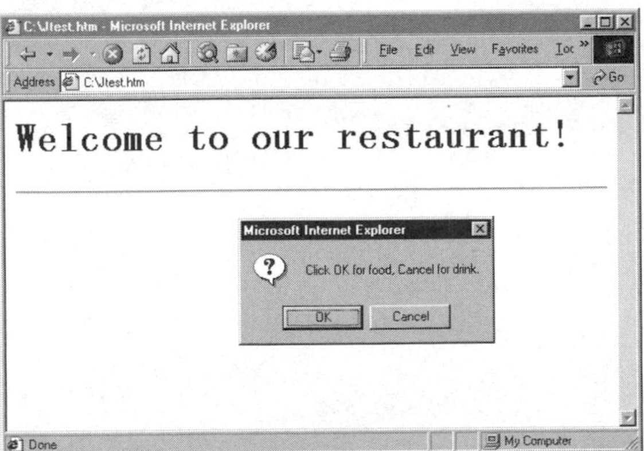

JScript. *A dialog box created using JScript.*

Notes

Unlike its cousin VBScript, JScript is a case-sensitive language.

For More Information

Visit the Microsoft Windows Script Technologies site at *msdn.microsoft.com/scripting.*

You can find the ECMA-262 specification at *www.ecma.ch/stand/ecma-262.htm.*

See Also: *JavaScript, scripting, Windows Script Host (WSH)*

JSP

Stands for Java Server Pages, a technology from Sun Microsystems for creating dynamic Web applications.

See: *Java Server Pages (JSP)*

jumbo frames

A feature of Gigabit Ethernet (GbE) that allows frames up to 9 kilobytes (KB) in size.

Overview

Standard 10Base5 Ethernet, created in the early 1980s, supports frames up to 1.5 KB in length. This standard has been supported by all subsequent versions of Ethernet, including 10BaseT Ethernet, Fast Ethernet, and GbE. Unfortunately, for the speeds of 1 gigabit per second (Gbps) supported by GbE, these standard frames become inefficient, and better performance can be achieved at these speeds by using larger frames. Consequently, the designers of the 802.3z GbE standard included support for jumbo frames as an option for gigabit networking.

Implementation

Jumbo frames can have payloads up to 9 KB in length and can result in much higher network utilizations for activities such as file transfers, where utilization of over 80 percent is achievable when using jumbo frames compared to typically under 20 percent when using standard Ethernet frames. Unfortunately, using jumbo frames adds issues of interoperability for enterprise networks, as these frames are not supported by slower 10 and 100 megabits per second (Mbps) versions of Ethernet. Since performing Layer-2 fragmentation and reassembly of jumbo frames is not a desirable solution, two standard methods are generally employed to incorporate GbE jumbo frames into typical enterprise networks:

- Dedicating all downstream traffic on specific ports of core GbE switches to devices supporting jumbo frames, such as GbE workgroup switches or server-switch interconnects
- Employing 802.1q virtual LANs (VLANs) to logically segregate those portions of the network that use jumbo and standard Ethernet frames

While Internet Protocol (IP) can intrinsically support frames of even larger size up to 64 KB (and IPv6 can support frames up to 4 gigabytes [GB] in length!) and using such monster frames could make gigabit networking even more efficient, there is an inherent obstacle to using such large frames. Ethernet uses a 32-bit cyclical redundancy check (CRC) at the end of each frame, and this error correction method is only efficient for frames up to about 12,000 bytes in length. The reason for choosing 9 KB as the maximum length for jumbo frames is to ensure the efficiency of such error correction while making possible the transmission of 8-KB Network File System (NFS) datagrams without the need of fragmentation.

Marketplace

The use of jumbo frames is increasing in enterprise networking environments. Vendors such as Nortel Networks offer autonegotiating 10/100/1000BaseT network interface cards (NICs) that feature support for jumbo frames to make implementing this feature in the enterprise easier.

See Also: *802.3z, Ethernet, Fast Ethernet, frame, Gigabit Ethernet (GbE)*

JXTA

A peer-to-peer (P2P) networking initiative from Sun Microsystems.

Overview

Project JXTA (pronounced "juxta") is an outgrowth of work by Sun to extend and standardize P2P technology in computer networking. The JXTA architecture is designed to support heterogeneous systems and platforms from all levels, from enterprise servers to handheld personal devices. JXTA is designed to simplify P2P networking by providing a set of general, open protocols for communications between different kinds of devices including PCs, Personal Digital Assistants (PDAs), cell phones, and other devices. The aim of Project JXTA is to explore and advance the new paradigm of distributed computing popularized by the P2P movement.

JXTA is part of the Sun Open Network Environment (Sun ONE) initiative that includes the companion technologies Java and Jini. JXTA technology is licensed from Sun under the Sun Project JXTA Software License, which is based on version 1.1 of the open-source Apache Software License.

For More Information

Find out more about JXTA at *www.jxta.org.*

See Also: *Java, Jini*

KCC

Stands for Knowledge Consistency Checker, a feature of the Active Directory directory service that ensures that directory replication properly takes place.

See: *Knowledge Consistency Checker (KCC)*

KDE

Stands for K Desktop Environment, a graphical user interface for Linux.

See: *K Desktop Environment (KDE)*

K Desktop Environment (KDE)

A graphical user interface (GUI) for Linux.

Overview

K Desktop Environment (KDE) provides users with an integrated, graphical, open-source working environment suitable for Linux workstations. KDE is comparable in many ways to the power and functionality of the Microsoft Windows and Mac OS user interfaces. The latest version, KDE2, incorporates a number of applications and utilities that include

- **Konqueror:** A combination file manager and Web browser that features a two-pane tree-and-view similar to Windows Explorer on the Windows platform.
- **Koffice:** A suite of office productivity tools that includes word processing, spreadsheet, presentation, and drawing applications.

Prospects

Although Linux has established itself in the server side of the enterprise market, it has made little headway until now on the desktop. The KDE Project's aim is to promote the use of Linux in the desktop environment in particular. KDE is one of two main GUI environments for Linux, the other being Gnu Object Modeling Environment (GNOME). KDE currently has about 70 percent of the Linux market, and the KDE League is an industry consortium dedicated to promoting KDE on the Linux desktop.

For More Information

Find out more about KDE at *www.kde.org.*

See Also: *GNU Object Modeling Environment (GNOME), Linux*

keepalives

A feature of Hypertext Transfer Protocol (HTTP) version 1.1 that minimizes the number of connections that Web browsers need to make to access content on Web servers.

Overview

When a Web browser that supports keepalives (such as Microsoft Internet Explorer 4 or higher) makes an HTTP GET request to a Web server that supports keepalives (such as Microsoft Internet Information Services [IIS]), the Web browser includes a new "Connection: Keep-Alive" header in the list of HTTP headers that it sends to the Web server in the request. The Web server responds by giving the client the file it requested (usually a Hypertext Markup Language [HTML] page or an image file). After the server sends the file to the client, instead of closing the Transmission Control Protocol/Internet Protocol (TCP/IP) socket, it keeps the socket open for a period of time in case the client wants to download additional files. A typical Web page might include a dozen images, and normally up to four sockets are kept open for transferring files between the client and the server.

Keepalives, which are also known as persistent connections, are supported by both Microsoft Internet Information Services (IIS) and Internet Explorer. Note that keepalives do not work unless both the Web browser and the Web server support them.

Notes

The term *keepalives* also refers to special packets used to keep a TCP connection open on a TCP/IP internetwork.

See Also: *Hypertext Transfer Protocol (HTTP), Internet Explorer, Internet Information Services (IIS)*

Kerberos

A security protocol used for securing access to network services.

Overview

Kerberos was developed in the early 1980s at the Massachusetts Institute of Technology (MIT) by Project Athena, the same group responsible for the X Windows system for the UNIX platform. Kerberos is based on the Data Encryption Standard (DES) and uses security tickets to manage the authentication of users and applications on a network. The Kerberos protocol is defined by RFC 1510 and the security tickets it employs are covered by RFC 1964. The current version of Kerberos (Kerberos v5, or version 5) was developed in 1993.

Kerberos has been used in the UNIX world for some time, and Kerberos v5 is the default authentication protocol used by the Microsoft Windows 2000 network operating system platform. Kerberos is a powerful authentication method that allows mutual authentication of both client and server during an authentication session. This is unlike the earlier Windows NT LAN Manager (NTLM) authentication protocol used on the Windows NT platform. NTLM authenticated clients only; Kerberos is thus more secure, as it authenticates both the client and the server.

Kerberos is a strong authentication protocol suited for implementation in a distributed processing environment. Kerberos also supports delegation, in which one machine can contact another machine on behalf of a client request for authentication. Kerberos shifts the processing load for authentication from the server to the client, making it an efficient authentication method for large enterprises. Kerberos is also a cross-platform standard and can be implemented in heterogeneous networks where multiple operating system platforms are present.

Architecture

Kerberos is named after the mythical three-headed dog (Kerberos in Greek mythology, Cerberus in Roman mythology) that guarded the gates of Hades. This name was chosen because Kerberos requires three different entities to be present in order to operate:

- **Kerberos clients:** These are users, applications, or machines that need to be authenticated in order to access network resources.
- **Network servers:** These are Kerberos-enabled servers hosting the network resources that the Kerberos clients want to access.
- **Key Distribution Center (KDC):** This is a special server that's trusted by both Kerberos clients and network servers and is responsible for issuing Kerberos tickets to clients.

Kerberos uses a ticket-based method for granting a user access to a network service. When a Kerberos-enabled client wants to request a network service (such as network logon) from a Kerberos-enabled server, the client must first contact an authentication server (AS) to receive a ticket and an encryption key. The encryption key, called the session key, is generated using symmetric key encryption and is used to unlock communication between the client and the server and thereby authenticate that communication. The initial ticket, often called the ticket-granting ticket (TGT), contains a copy of the session key and an identity, which is a randomly generated number. The AS passes the TGT and the identity back to the client, which stores the ticket in its ticket cache. When the client wants to access a particular service, it sends the ticket to a ticket-granting server (TGS). (The TGS and AS are usually the same machine.) The TGS gives the client a ticket that securely identifies the client to the service it's requesting. Finally, the client presents the ticket to the network service it's trying to access and is granted access to the resource as many times as desired until the ticket expires. When the client sends a ticket, the ticket is always accompanied by an authenticator message that's encrypted with the session key. This authenticator includes a time stamp, which is used to ensure that the ticket is legitimate.

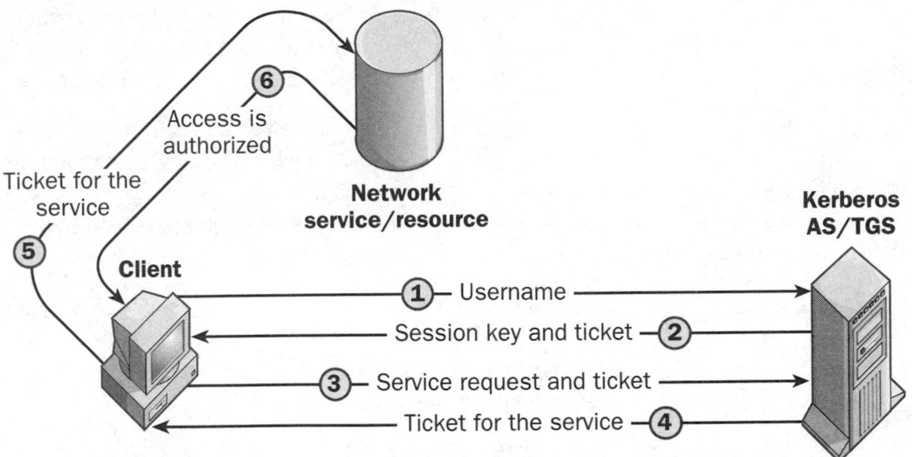

Kerberos. *The Kerberos v5 protocol defines the steps a client must take to be authenticated for gaining access to network services or resources.*

Implementation

In the Windows 2000 implementation of Kerberos, each domain controller has the Kerberos v5 service running on it. Kerberos client software is also built into each server and workstation running Windows 2000. The Kerberos service maintains encrypted user passwords and identities in the Active Directory directory service database. When a user logs on to a domain controller, the initial Kerberos authentication enables the user to access available resources anywhere in the enterprise because authentication credentials issued by the Kerberos services of one domain are accepted by all domains within a domain tree or a domain forest.

The Kerberos service issues an initial ticket for the logon domain when a user logs on to a Windows 2000 workstation. Any server running Windows 2000 can then validate the client's ticket without having to contact the domain Kerberos service. It can do this because servers running Windows 2000 share the encryption key that the Kerberos service uses to encrypt tickets. This encryption key is called the server key.

If a Windows 2000 client in one domain requests access to a resource in a remote domain that's part of the same domain tree or forest, the Kerberos service in the local domain issues a referral ticket that the client presents to the Kerberos service in the remote domain. The Kerberos service in the remote domain then issues an initial ticket that's valid for its own domain and identifies the domain. Using this ticket, the client can then access resources in the remote domain.

See Also: *authentication protocol, Data Encryption Standard (DES), Windows NT Challenge/Response Authentication*

kernel

The core of an operating system.

Overview

In most operating systems, the kernel is the part that is responsible for low-level (essential) activities such as multitasking, scheduling processes and threads, handling interrupts from devices, memory management, error handling, and managing input/output (I/O) operations. The kernel interfaces with other components of the operating system through system calls, which provide a standard interface to kernel functions. The kernel runs within protected mode memory in order to ensure the operating system's stability.

The term *kernel* is more often used in a UNIX environment and is contrasted with the term *shell*, which describes the outer portion of the operating system that is exposed to the user and provides a user interface for entering commands and receiving output. In Microsoft Windows operating systems, the shell is known as the desktop.

Architecture

The Windows 2000 kernel uses a microkernel architecture. This means that the kernel is a small component with limited functionality that loads other components such as drivers and services into memory only as required to complete requested system tasks. By contrast, a kernel constructed using a monolithic architecture has device drivers and services built right into it (Berkeley Software Distribution [BSD] UNIX follows this architecture).

The kernel for Windows 2000, Windows XP, and Windows .NET Server, called Ntoskrnl.exe, is located in the \Winnt\System32 directory in Windows 2000 and the \Windows\System32 directory in Windows XP and Windows .NET Server. It runs in nonpageable memory, which means that it's always resident in memory. The kernel is responsible for thread scheduling and dispatching threads to processors on a symmetric multiprocessing (SMP) platform. The kernel code itself is not preemptive—that is, no other thread or process can preempt the kernel's operations. Each thread is assigned a priority level from 0 to 31 by the kernel, as follows:

- Levels 0 through 15 indicate dynamic priority and are assigned to application and user threads.
- Levels 16 through 31 indicate real-time priority and are assigned only to key operating system threads.

The kernel adjusts priority levels for threads to ensure that no thread is starved and that each receives proper attention, with threads having a higher priority level getting the greater share of processor resources.

The kernel does its job by managing two classes of objects:

- Control objects, which control the operation of the kernel and include processes, interrupts, asynchronous procedure calls, and profiles
- Dispatcher objects, which manage thread dispatching and synchronization and include events, threads, timers, semaphores, mutants, and mutexes

The kernel communicates with the hardware abstraction layer (HAL) to interact with hardware and communicates with the Executive and its components for higher-level operating system functions. The kernel loads when the screen turns blue during the boot process.

Another example of a microkernel architecture is found in the Linux operating system, which uses device drivers that can be loaded into memory and unloaded from memory as required.

Notes

In Windows 95 and Windows 98, the kernel file is Kernel32.dll, and it's located in the \Windows\System directory. If the kernel is corrupt or missing, you can expand the file from the distribution CD and replace the damaged or missing file on your hard disk (as long as you can access that drive in a way that does not involve this file, such as through MS-DOS).

See Also: *desktop, hardware abstraction layer (HAL), kernel mode, shell*

kernel mode

A privileged mode of operation in which processes can execute within the Microsoft Windows 2000 operating system.

Overview

Kernel mode processes include components of the operating system that directly manage resources on the computer, such as the following:

- Windows 2000 executive, which contains operating system modules that manage objects, processes, security, memory, and devices
- The kernel, which manages core operating system services
- The hardware abstraction layer (HAL), which isolates operating system code from hardware differences

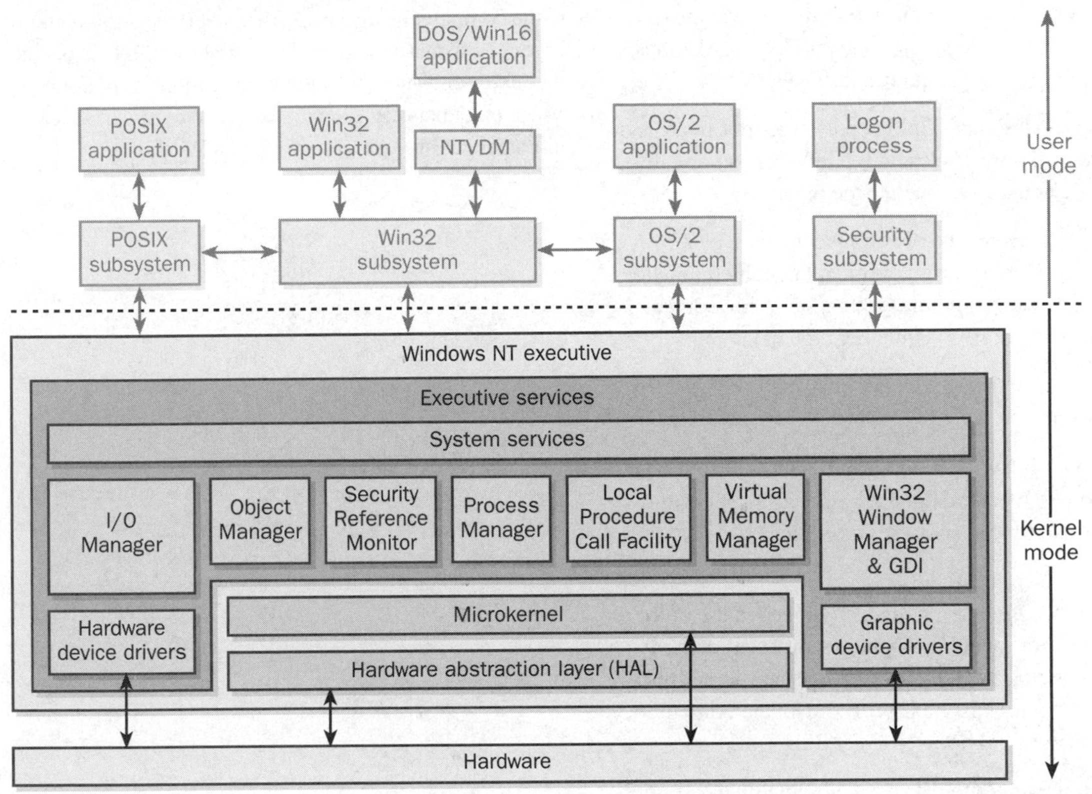

Kernel mode. *Kernel mode of the Windows 2000 operating system architecture.*

Notes

Kernel mode is also known as supervisor mode, protected mode, or Ring 0.

See Also: user mode

keyboard emulator

A device that can be plugged into the keyboard port of a server to emulate the presence of a connected keyboard.

Overview

When a power outage causes the server to reboot, the server detects the presence of a keyboard and the reboot is allowed to occur. This is important when administrators are off site when servers need to be rebooted, because computers normally do not boot unless a keyboard is attached.

A keyboard emulator is used as a security device when the presence of an attached keyboard is not desirable, such as when the servers are in an unlocked room or can be tampered with in some other fashion. By removing the keyboard and installing a keyboard emulator, you can prevent unauthorized users from attempting a local logon to a server.

Keyboard Video Mouse (KVM) switch

A device that allows several computers to be controlled from a single keyboard, mouse, and monitor.

Overview

Keyboard Video Mouse (KVM) switches are typically employed in the enterprise to managed server farms, which are collections of rack-mounted servers grouped together for various purposes. They are also used in help desk environments and in data centers where large numbers of computers need to be centrally managed by a few people.

Using a KVM switch to control multiple computers has several advantages over using a separate keyboard, mouse, and monitor for each machine, specifically:

- Savings on the cost of additional keyboards, mice, and monitors. This includes both purchase costs and the cost of electricity to operate the monitors.
- Lessening the chance of equipment failure by reducing the amount of heat generated through elimination of unnecessary monitors (and thus also lowering air conditioning costs in equipment rooms).
- Preventing equipment clutter in already crowded server rooms.

KVMs typically support two, four, eight, or more computers and can often be daisy-chained to support hundreds—or even thousands—of computers.

Types

The simplest KVMs are manual switches that employ push buttons for switching between different computers. These analog switches are cheap, but the peripherals tend to become unsynchronized with the computers, often requiring a reboot to correct things.

More commonly, commercial KVMs employ electronics to switch between different machines, typically by using keyboard shortcuts or through an on-screen menu. The menu may also include some form of password protection for each computer and a master password that grants access to all computers attached to the switch. The switch is typically connected to the keyboard, mouse, and video ports on the computers using proprietary cables purchased with the switch. A single keyboard, mouse, and monitor are then connected to the switch to control the various machines. KVM switches generally send analog signals all the time to all connected computers in order to give each computer the illusion that it has a directly connected keyboard, monitor, and mouse. Keyboard signals are most important, for Intel PCs in particular require a keyboard signal in order to reboot.

Sometimes the computers that need to be controlled are located in another part of the building in a special "clean room" or other secure location. In this case, use an analog KVM switch with a built-in video extender, which amplifies the video signal so that the monitor can be connected to the computer using a cable that's 500 feet (150 meters) or longer. You actually need two video extenders, one at the server end and one at the remote monitor station. Video extenders can often be connected using a single interconnect line of Category 5 (Cat5) cabling.

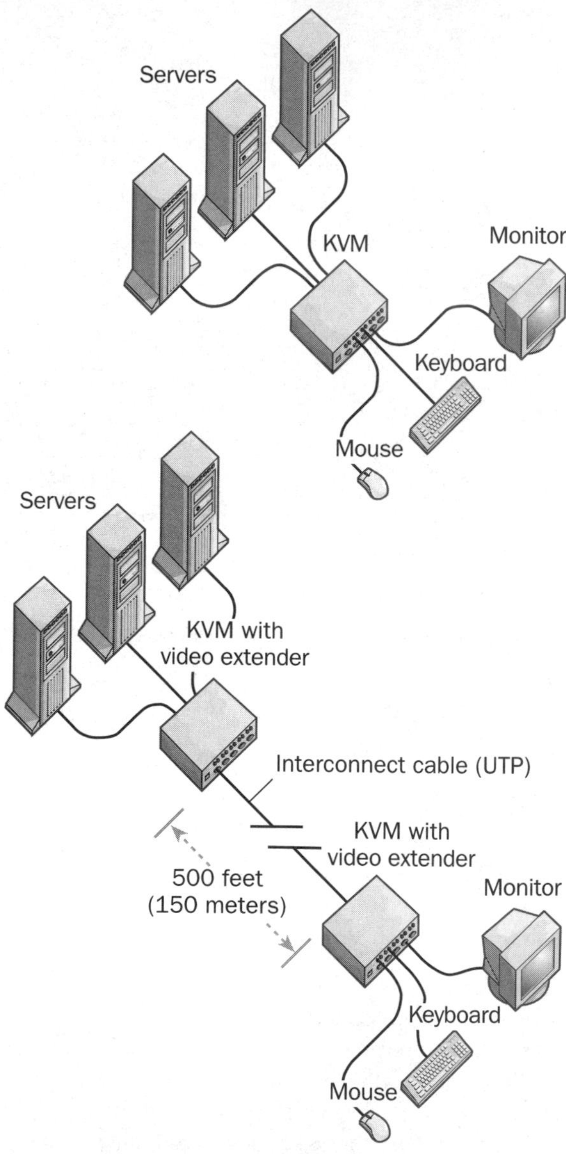

Keyboard Video Mouse (KVM) switch. *Using a KVM switch to control several servers from a single keyboard, monitor, and mouse.*

Marketplace

A number of companies make KVM switches for various markets from small businesses to enterprise data centers. Some popular vendors include Avocent Corporation, Black Box Corporation, Rose Electronics, and Tron International.

A recent development is the digital KVM switch, whose operation resembles remote control software such as pcAnywhere but allows you to manage servers running any operating system. Digital KVM switches work by converting analog keyboard, video, and mouse signals into digital signals, which are then packaged in Internet Protocol (IP) packets and transmitted over a network. They can be used to control hundreds of computers at different locations and can even operate over the Internet. Instead of controlling the computers from a keyboard/mouse/monitor combination, they are instead controlled from a central management workstation that has special software installed on it.

When deploying a digital KVM switch, the management workstation controls the remote servers over a standard Ethernet local area network (LAN) or wide area network (WAN) connection, which can be configured in either of two ways:

- **In-band management:** This method employs the existing LAN on which the servers reside for sending control signals to the servers. The disadvantage of this method is that if the network goes down, you have no way of controlling the servers.
- **Out-of-band management:** This method employs a separate maintenance LAN for controlling the servers. The advantage here is that you can manage the servers even when the regular LAN or WAN connection is down, but the disadvantage is that you have to deploy a separate Cat5 wiring infrastructure to make this possible, which can incur considerable extra cost.

The first commercially available digital KVM switch was the DS1800 from Avocent. This market is likely to grow over the next several years, driven by demand mainly from Internet data centers and e-commerce companies.

See Also: *out-of-band management (OBM), switch*

key (cryptography)

A mathematical value used in cryptography for encrypting and signing messages.

Overview

The degree of security of a key depends on the type of mathematical algorithm used with the cryptosystem and the length of the key. Most cryptography algorithms employ transformations that use prime numbers and congruency. Key lengths typically range from 40 bits for the RC2 and RC4 cryptography algorithms to 512 bits for RSA public key systems.

The number of keys used depends on the kind of cryptographic system being employed. In secret (or symmetric) key cryptography, both the sender and the recipient use the same key for encrypting and decrypting messages. By contrast, public key cryptography employs a key pair that consists of the private and public keys of the message sender. In a public key system, these keys are usually obtained from a certificate authority (CA). This is accomplished by having the user submit a key request file, such as one generated by the Key Manager component of Microsoft Internet Information Services (IIS).

See Also: *encryption, key pair, public key cryptography*

key (database)

A column or group of columns used to uniquely identify records in a table of a relational database.

Overview

Two main types of keys are used in relational databases such as Microsoft SQL Server:

- **Primary keys:** These are columns or groups of columns that uniquely identify the rows of a table. Each row has a unique value in the primary key column or columns. Each table in a relational database should have one and only one primary key, and primary keys cannot allow nulls (NN), duplicates (ND), or no changes (NC).
- **Foreign keys:** These are columns or groups of columns in one table that match the primary key of a different table. Foreign keys are used to define relationships between tables and to enforce referential integrity in a database by ensuring that each value in the foreign key column is actually a valid entry in the primary key column of another table.

Note that a column in a database table can be both a primary key for its own table and a foreign key for a different table.

See Also: *database*

key management

A method for managing private keys within a public key infrastructure (PKI).

Overview

Key management is an essential function of any PKI system. This is because private keys issued to users must be kept secure and confidential to protect the PKI system's integrity. Should a user's private key be compromised, various consequences could result, depending on the privileges of the user within the enterprise, including the following:

- The user's reputation could be damaged by an impersonator sending harassing mail signed with the user's private key.
- Data could be stolen or other damage could be done if the user has high-level privileges on the network.
- Agreements could be signed without proper consent should the user have signing authority using his private key.

Implementation

The essential requirement for securely managing users' private keys is to make sure that these keys are stored in only one location and that no copies exist anywhere else. While many PKI implementations are software-based systems in which keys are stored on computers' hard disks, a better solution is hardware-based key management. A good example of this is smart cards, which you can use to store a single existing copy of a user's private key in a tamper-proof format. Besides secure key storage, another important aspect of key management is secure delivery of generated keys to their users.

See Also: *key (cryptography), public key cryptography, public key infrastructure (PKI), smart card*

key pair

A pair of keys generated for an individual, system, or organization within a public key cryptography system.

Overview

Public key systems always generate keys in pairs that consist of a private and a public key. The private key belongs to the user alone and must be kept secret and carefully guarded. Should a user's private key be compromised, it must immediately be revoked. Otherwise, the user's identity could be forged for e-mail, document signing, and other purposes, damaging the user's reputation and hurting the company.

By contrast, a user's public key is available to anyone who requests it. If a message is encrypted with someone's private key, it can be decrypted by the message recipient using the sender's public key. This is possible because each pair of private and public keys is bound together by a specific mathematical relationship.

See Also: *encryption, key (cryptography), public key cryptography*

key (registry)

An entity within the Microsoft Windows registry that can contain subkeys and values.

Overview

Registry keys are used to name and identify collections of registry values and to organize the registry into a hierarchical structure. Registry keys are thus analogous to directories in a file system; in fact, keys are displayed as folders by the Registry Editor just as directories are displayed in Windows Explorer.

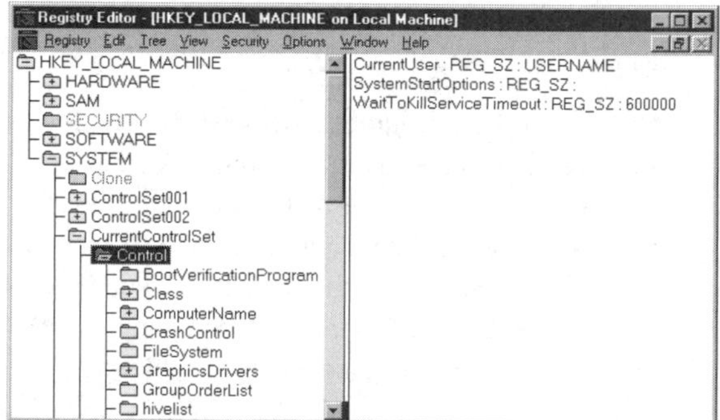

Key (registry). *The Control key as displayed by the Windows 2000 Registry Editor (Regedt32.exe).*

The screen capture shows the Control key being displayed, which contains value entries (in the right pane) and subkeys (the series of items under it in the left pane). The Control key itself is a subkey of the CurrentControlSet key.

See Also: *hive, registry*

KM

Stands for knowledge management, a business strategy for using software to make all the knowledge contained in an enterprise easily accessible.

See: *knowledge management (KM)*

Knowledge Consistency Checker (KCC)

A feature of Active Directory directory service that ensures that directory replication takes place properly.

Overview

The Knowledge Consistency Checker (KCC) is an Active Directory process running on each domain controller within a Microsoft Windows 2000 network. The KCC generates a map of the replication topology for the network, enabling domain controllers to find and replicate with each other efficiently in order to ensure that information within Active Directory is up-to-date everywhere throughout the enterprise.

Implementation

The KCC is implemented as a dynamic-link library (DLL) that runs in the background every 15 minutes to generate and maintain the replication topology. Should a domain controller become unavailable for any reason, the KCC detects this change and modifies the topology to ensure that replication still takes place effectively and all domain controllers in the forest are properly synchronized.

The KCC manages the replication topology by creating connection objects between domain controllers. Replication topology is established at two different levels: forest-wide and domain-wide. Although the KCC runs automatically in the background and has no user interface, you can manually force the KCC to update the replication topology by using the Active Directory Sites and Services console. You might do this, for example, when you take down a DC for maintenance.

See Also: *Active Directory, Active Directory Sites and Services, directory replication (Windows 2000 and Windows .NET Server), domain controller*

knowledge management (KM)

A business strategy for using software to make all the knowledge contained in an enterprise easily accessible.

Overview

Knowledge management (KM) is used to refer both to a business goal and to various software applications used to reach this goal. KM's goal is to provide mechanisms for searching, retrieving, and analyzing all the different kinds of information found in today's commercial enterprise. These sources of information can include relational databases, file servers, e-mail servers, intranet and corporate Web sites, Enterprise Resource Planning (ERP) applications, Customer Relationship Management (CRM) applications, and other repositories of business information.

The first applications that performed limited KM functions were corporate portals, which focused mainly on consolidating databases, documents, and Web pages to make them easily accessible. Over the last few years, these portals have evolved into a new type of tool, the Enterprise Information Portal (EIP), which provides access to information stored in ERP and CRM systems. EIPs, however, have difficulty managing unstructured data such as documents stored on file servers and e-mail servers. As a result, a new type of portal has evolved called the Enterprise Knowledge Portal (EKP), which not only can consolidate information from both structured and unstructured sources but also can employ user profiles to dynamically push data to users who need it. EKPs employ Business Intelligence (BI) software that can turn raw corporate data into helpful knowledge upon which companies can base business decisions.

See Also: *Enterprise Information Portal (EIP), Enterprise Knowledge Portal (EKP), enterprise resource planning (ERP), intranet, portal, Web server*

KVM switch

Stands for Keyboard Video Mouse switch, a device that allows several computers to be controlled from a single keyboard, mouse, and monitor.

See: *Keyboard Video Mouse (KVM) switch*

L2CAP

Stands for Logical Link Control and Adaptation Layer Protocol, the data-link layer protocol for Bluetooth wireless networking.

See: *Logical Link Control and Adaptation Layer Protocol (L2CAP)*

L2F

Stands for Layer 2 Forwarding, a media-independent tunneling protocol developed by Cisco Systems.

See: *Layer 2 Forwarding (L2F)*

L2TP

Stands for Layer 2 Tunneling Protocol, a wide area network (WAN) protocol used for virtual private networking (VPN).

See: *Layer 2 Tunneling Protocol (L2TP)*

L2TP/IPsec

Stands for Layer 2 Tunneling Protocol (L2TP) over Internet Protocol Security (IPsec), which is the normal way of using L2TP for creating secure virtual private networks (VPNs).

See: *Layer 2 Tunneling Protocol (L2TP)*

LADC

Stands for Local Area Data Channel, a telco service for transmitting data using line drivers.

See: *Local Area Data Channel (LADC)*

lambda switching

An emerging optical switching technology.

Overview

Lambda switching is an emerging technology that represents the next stage in the development of high-speed switched optical networks. Lambda switching uses a combination of dense wavelength division multiplexing (DWDM), multiprotocol label switching (MPLS), and Resource Reservation Protocol (RSVP) to automatically connect the endpoints of an optical networking system without the setup and configuration required by DWDM by itself. Light paths between endpoints can be established on an ad hoc basis, providing better mechanisms for managing traffic flows through fiber-optic networks.

Like DWDM, lambda switching is likely to find its place of deployment mainly in long-haul fiber managed by inter-exchange carriers (IXCs). Several vendors are developing lambda switching equipment called optical cross connects (OCXs), with AT&T being one major player in this arena. Deployment of lambda switching technologies should eventually provide bandwidth on demand for the enterprise wide area network (WAN) and should speed up the provisioning process of OC-48 and higher WAN links.

See Also: *dense wavelength division multiplexing (DWDM), inter-exchange carrier (IXC), Multiprotocol Label Switching (MPLS), Resource Reservation Protocol (RSVP)*

LAN

Stands for local area network, typically a group of computers located in the same room, on the same floor, or in the same building, that are connected to form a single network.

See: *local area network (LAN)*

LANE

Stands for LAN Emulation, a technology that enables local area network (LAN) traffic such as Ethernet frames to be carried over an Asynchronous Transfer Mode (ATM) network.

See: LAN Emulation (LANE)

LAN Emulation (LANE)

A technology that enables local area network (LAN) traffic such as Ethernet frames to be carried over an Asynchronous Transfer Mode (ATM) network.

Overview

LAN Emulation (LANE) was designed to allow connectionless traffic on Ethernet networks to be transported over connection-oriented ATM backbones. LANE accomplishes this by fragmenting and encapsulating variable-length Ethernet frames into fixed-length ATM cells and by configuring mappings between ATM and Ethernet addresses. Using LANE, you can use ATM as a backbone transport for connecting widely separated Ethernet LANs. Since LANE operates at the data-link layer, it can use ATM to connect LANs using any network-layer protocol, such as Internet Protocol (IP) and Internetwork Packet Exchange (IPX). LANE can also be used for connecting Token Ring networks using an ATM backbone.

Implementation

LANE is implemented utilizing Emulated LANs (ELANs), which are essentially subsets of an ATM cloud in which all stations see each other as neighbors as if they were on the same LAN. An ELAN is thus a kind of "virtual" LAN, but do not confuse LANE ELANs with Virtual LANs (VLANs) in Ethernet switching—they are two different technologies. Stations on an ELAN are known in LANE terminology as LAN Emulation Clients (LECs) and can include servers with special ATM network interface cards (NICs), Ethernet switches such as Cisco Catalyst switches, or routers such as Cisco 7000 series routers. Two LECs on the same ELAN can communicate with each other using LANE, but LECs on different ELANs must communicate through a router.

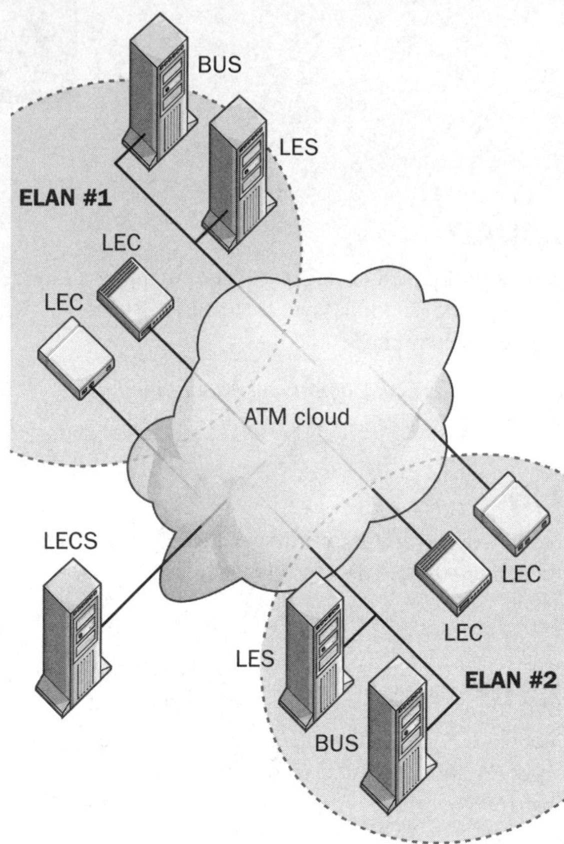

LAN Emulation (LANE). *The architecture of a simple LANE implementation.*

To implement LANE on a combined ATM and Ethernet network, several special components must be present:

- **LAN Emulation Server (LES):** This component maintains a list of media access control (MAC)-to-ATM address mappings for LECs on the particular ELAN it manages. In other words, an LES maps ATM endpoint addresses (which are 20-byte network service access point or Network Service Access Protocol [NSAP] addresses) to non-ATM endpoint Ethernet MAC addresses. The LES is connected to the LECs on the ELAN it manages using a point-to-multipoint ATM virtual circuit (VC).
- **LAN Emulation Configuration Server (LECS):** This component tells new LECs that appear on the

network how to find the LES for their particular ELAN. A typical LANE deployment will have one LECS for the entire ATM cloud and as many LESs as the cloud is divided into ELANs.

- **Broadcast and Unknown Server (BUS):** Since ATM is a connection-oriented technology that does not inherently support broadcasts, some way of implementing broadcasts is required for interoperability with Ethernet. The BUS accomplishes this, and there is one BUS for each ELAN to handle broadcasts from LECs on that ELAN.

A basic LANE communication session between two LECs on an ELAN takes place something like this: when LEC#1 wants to communicate with LEC#2, it first contacts the LES for that ELAN and requests the ATM address that corresponds to the MAC address of LEC#2. The LES responds to the request, and LEC#1 then establishes an ATM virtual circuit with LEC#2 and begins to transmit.

Prospects

Just as ATM is a technology that never really established itself in the LAN and has largely been superseded by Fast Ethernet and Gigabit Ethernet (GbE), so also LANE is no longer widely used in enterprise networking. Part of this is due to ATM's complexity, but another reason has been limitations with LANE itself. The main problem is the lack of redundancy in LANE, where a single LECS for the ATM cloud and a single LES and BUS for each ELAN make for single points of failure. To resolve this, a new version of LANE called LANE2 has been developed that supports the following enhanced features:

- Multiple LECS per ATM cloud, using a single master LECS that communicates with multiple slave LECS using a new protocol called LANE Network-to-Network Interface (LNNI).

- Redundant LESs and BUSs on each ELAN. In LANE2, when a LEC tries to contact a LES or BUS and fails, it contacts the LECS again to find another LES or BUS to service its needs.

Notes

Microsoft Windows 2000 supports LANE and comes with a LEC that is installed automatically if an ATM network adapter is detected during startup.

See Also: *Asynchronous Transfer Mode (ATM), Ethernet, MAC address*

LAN-host integration

The integration of local area network (LAN)-based networks that use protocols such as Transmission Control Protocol/Internet Protocol (TCP/IP) or Internetwork Packet Exchange/Sequenced Packet Exchange (IPX/SPX) with host systems such as IBM mainframes and AS/400 systems that use Systems Network Architecture (SNA).

Overview

SNA-based networks originally developed separately from LANs, and as a result both architectures have unique adapters, cabling, and networking protocols. Today's LANs are typically built around the Ethernet networking architecture, use TCP/IP as their networking protocol, and run over structured cabling using Category 5 (Cat5) unshielded twisted-pair (UTP) cabling. LANs can be joined together into wide area networks (WANs) using routers, which provide access to telco communications networks. By contrast, SNA networks typically employ mainframe host systems with front-end controllers connected over serial links to remote terminals. As a result of these two different architectures, many large companies have developed a two-tier network, consisting of a traditional LAN-based Ethernet network and an entirely separate SNA host-based network. However, because of the cost of maintaining separate networks, many have merged their SNA-only networks with non-SNA networks.

Early attempts at LAN-host integration involved directly connecting PC computers to IBM host systems using SNA hardware adapters and SNA protocols across a dedicated SNA network. Each PC was connected to a local IBM control unit such as an IBM 3174 or IBM 5294 using coaxial or twinax cabling. Standards were developed to allow SNA and non-SNA protocols to share the same network, but networking engineers soon found that mixing SNA and TCP/IP was like mixing oil and water, especially with regard to WAN connections, in which Data Link Control (DLC) timeouts and other difficulties made network management complex.

One solution is to install a TCP/IP protocol stack on the mainframe host, but this often results in degradation of host performance and additional challenges in terms of IP address administration. A more workable solution is the LAN-to-SNA gateway. The gateway computer lets desktop PCs access applications and data on the mainframe host using traditional LAN protocols. TCP/IP is used to connect the desktop PC and the SNA gateway, and SNA is used to connect the SNA gateway and the mainframe host. This LAN-to-SNA gateway solution has become the de facto standard for providing host access to LAN-based PCs. An example of an SNA gateway application is Microsoft Host Integration Server, which provides LAN-to-SNA gateway services over a variety of network protocols that include NetBIOS Enhanced User Interface (NetBEUI), TCP/IP, IPX/SPX, Banyan VINES, and AppleTalk.

See Also: *Host Integration Server, Systems Network Architecture (SNA)*

LAN security switch

A manual switch that can be used to physically disconnect two or more local area network (LAN) segments.

Overview

LAN security switches are typically utilized in high-security networking environments that must meet the highest government or military security standards. For example, a network supervisor can use a LAN switch at the end of the day to physically disconnect a portion of the network that includes servers that store sensitive data, thus preventing users from accessing the servers during off hours. This is generally more convenient and safer than going into the server room and unplugging connectors from a hub.

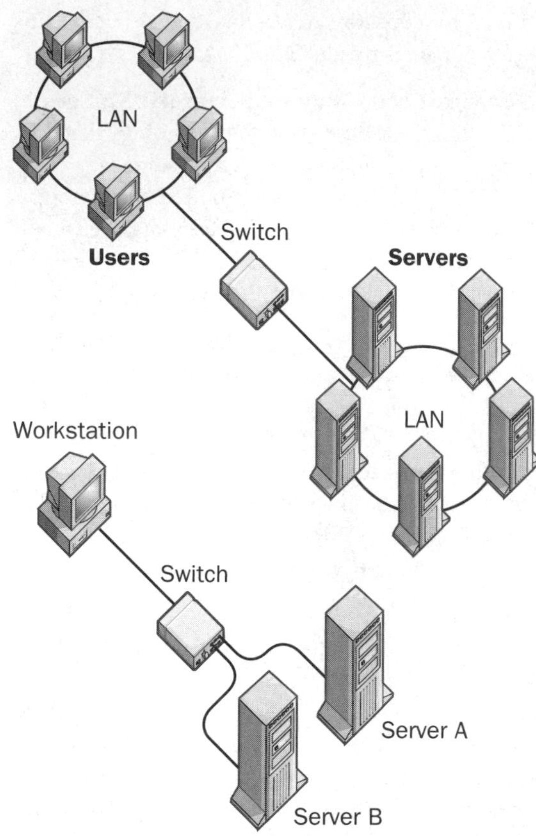

LAN security switch. *Two ways of using a LAN security switch.*

LAN security switches are available for both copper cabling and fiber-optic cabling. A fiber-optic LAN security switch has a small mirror inside that rotates when you manually flip a switch or rotate a dial to open or close the connection.

LAN security switches work by creating a physical break in a circuit, thus preventing the flow of data between connected LAN segments. LAN security switches must be operated manually—you cannot operate them remotely using electronic means.

See Also: *network security*

LAN segment

A physical portion of a local area network (LAN), usually separated from other portions by bridges or routers.

Overview

LANs such as Ethernet networks are often "segmented" using bridges in order to improve network performance. Segmentation improves performance by reducing the number of stations in each segment that must compete with one another for access to the network. Bridges are generally used for segmenting smaller LANs because they are cheaper than routers and require no special configuration. Bridges are smart devices that build media access control (MAC)-level routing tables that forward network traffic on the basis of each frame's destination MAC address. If a frame's destination address is a machine in the local LAN segment, bridges attached to that segment will not allow the frame to pass; this reduces unneeded network traffic in other segments attached to the bridge. In a typical scenario, you would place a bridge between your department or workgroup hub and the main network backbone to improve traffic on your local LAN segment.

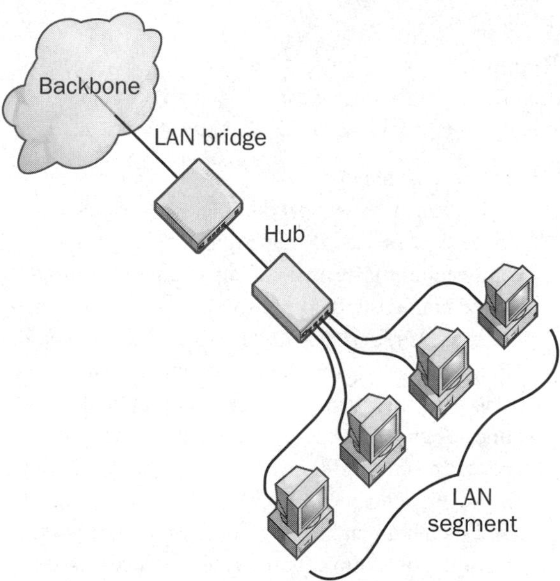

LAN segment. *Segmenting a LAN using a bridge.*

See Also: *bridge, Ethernet, router*

LAN switch

Another name for Ethernet switch, a multiport device based on bridging technologies that is used mainly to segment Ethernet networks.

See: *Ethernet switch*

LAPD

Stands for Link Access Protocol, D-channel, the data-link layer protocol for Integrated Services Digital Network (ISDN).

See: *Link Access Protocol, D-channel (LAPD)*

Last Known Good configuration

The current configuration information for drivers and services when a user successfully logs on to a Microsoft Windows 2000 or Windows NT system.

Overview

In Windows 2000, the configuration information from the last successful logon is copied to the LastKnownGood control set in the registry. You can then use this configuration to recover your system if later on you find that you cannot log on to the system. This may occur, for example, if you add or upgrade a driver that is incorrect for your particular hardware configuration. If you modify your system and are unable to log on again, you can restart your system, press F8 at the beginning of the boot process in Windows 2000, and follow the prompts to select Last Known Good configuration to reset the Windows configuration information for your system.

See Also: *boot, logon*

LATA

Stands for Local Access and Transport Area, service boundaries for local exchange carriers (LECs).

See: *Local Access and Transport Area (LATA)*

late collision

A collision on an Ethernet network that is detected late in the transmission of the packet.

Overview

Signals on a network cable do not travel instantaneously from point to point; they travel at a fixed speed, which is near the speed of light on copper cabling. If segments of an Ethernet network are too long, collisions can occur that are not properly detected by the stations on the network. This can result in lost or corrupted data, and it can degrade network performance.

Collisions themselves are natural and inevitable on an Ethernet network and occur when two stations transmit their signals simultaneously or almost simultaneously. When two transmitting stations detect a collision (the concurrent signal from the other transmitting station), they both stop their transmission and wait a random time interval before attempting retransmission. The Ethernet standard, however, specifies that if a station on the network is able to transmit 64 bytes or more before another signal is detected, the first station is considered to be "in control" of the wire and can continue to transmit the remainder of its frame, while the second station must stop transmitting and wait. If the distance between two transmitting stations exceeds Ethernet specifications, the stations might not become aware soon enough that another station already has control of the wire. The resulting collision is called a late collision, and results in a data packet that is more than 64 bytes in length (which in itself is allowable) but which contains cyclical redundancy check (CRC) errors. Transmission errors and unreliable communication between the stations are the result.

Late collisions can result from defective Ethernet transceivers, having too many repeaters between stations, or exceeding Ethernet specifications for maximum node-to-node distances.

See Also: *collision, Ethernet*

latency

The delay that occurs when a packet or signal is transmitted over a communications system.

Overview

Latency is the amount of time it takes for information to travel between two stations on a network. A network with high latency causes users to experience unpredictable delays in transmission of voice, data, and video signals. This can lead to awkward conversations and time-outs in data transmissions that can cripple network performance. Latency is usually measured in milliseconds (msec) for computer networking and telecommunications systems.

Latency can be a serious issue, especially in voice communications where delays of more than about 250 msec make conversations awkward by creating pauses that cause parties to interrupt one another when speaking (The G.114 recommendation from the International Telecommunication Union [ITU] specifies that round-trip latency in a voice communications system should be less than 300 msec). Similar latency in multimedia transmission can be compensated for by buffering. Latency in data transmission is less serious, although excessive latency can result in Transmission Control Protocol (TCP) connections being closed and retransmissions occurring, which slows down overall network performance.

Types

Latency is an inevitable aspect of any communications system and generally has several possible causes:

- Intrinsic latency in a transmission is caused by the finite transmission speed of electrical signals through wires (or of light signals through fiber-optic cabling). Intrinsic latency cannot be eliminated but is usually quite small in a local area network (LAN) and usually less than a microsecond. In a wide area network (WAN), intrinsic latency is also generally small when transcontinental trunk lines or undersea cables are used and is usually between 10 and 100 msec. For satellite WAN links, however, latency can be 500 msec or even higher, and such high latency can sometimes be frustrating for users of satellite-based Internet access systems.
- Latency is also introduced into a communications path by devices used to switch or modulate signals.

The amount of latency varies greatly with the type of device. For example, the latency for a bridge (the time delay between the moment when the packet enters one port of the bridge and the moment when it leaves another port) is usually between 5 and 50 microseconds (a microsecond is one-thousandth of a millisecond). By contrast, the latency that is usually introduced into a network by routers and gateways that process packets and perform protocol conversion is usually an order of magnitude higher. Latency for signals passing through analog modems is typically about 150 msec due to signal modulation, compression, and error correction processes. See the table below for a comparison of latency introduced into communications paths by different kinds of networking and communications devices.

- Devices that establish a connection can introduce even greater amounts of latency into a communications channel. Integrated Services Digital Network (ISDN) terminal adapters typically take 1 to 2 seconds to establish a connection, but it can take as much as 15 to 30 seconds to establish an analog modem connection. The term *latency*, however, is sometimes restricted to delay over a preestablished communications channel, in which case these scenarios would not normally be identified as latency.

Typical Latency Introduced into Signal Paths by Networking Devices

Device	*Typical Latency*
Network interface card	< 5 msec
Asymmetric Digital Subscriber Line (ADSL) modem	5–10 msec
Plain Old Telephone Service (POTS) landline	< 20 msec
Integrated Services Digital Network (ISDN) terminal adapter	20–30 msec
V.90 analog modem	~ 150 msec
Global System for Mobile Communications (GSM) cellular	~ 150 msec
Voice over IP (VoIP) system	80–500 msec

Notes

Latency for bridges and LAN switches can actually be broken down into two types:

- **Bit-forwarding devices:** Latency here is measured from the moment the first bit of an incoming frame arrives at one port to the moment the first bit of an outgoing frame departs at another port.
- **Store and forward devices:** Latency for these devices is measured from the moment the last bit of an incoming frame arrives at one port to the moment the first bit of an outgoing port departs at another port.

For more information on these types of latency, see RFC 1242 (*www.faqs.org/rfcs/rfcs1242.html*).

See Also: *bridge, Ethernet switch, jitter, local area network (LAN), noise, router, signal, wide area network (WAN)*

Layer 2 Forwarding (L2F)

A media-independent tunneling protocol developed by Cisco Systems.

Overview

Layer 2 Forwarding (L2F) can be used to create virtual private networks (VPNs) that tunnel information securely over public networks such as the Internet using wide area network (WAN) data-link protocols such as Point-to-Point Protocol (PPP) or Serial Line Internet Protocol (SLIP). L2F supports such features as Remote Authentication Dial-In User Service (RADIUS), dynamic allocation of addresses, and quality of service (QoS).

L2F has been superseded by the newer Layer 2 Tunneling Protocol (L2TP), an Internet Engineering Task Force (IETF) standard that provides a vendor-neutral tunneling solution for virtual private networking. L2TP is an extension of PPP and supports the best features of the Point-to-Point Tunneling Protocol (PPTP) and the L2F protocol.

Implementation

As an example, when PPP is used with L2F, PPP provides the connection between a dial-up client and the network access server (NAS) that receives the call. A PPP connection initiated by a client terminates at a NAS located at a PPP service provider, usually an Internet service provider (ISP). L2F allows the connection's termination point to be extended beyond the NAS to a remote destination node, so the client's connection

L

appears to be directly to the remote node instead of to the NAS. The function of the NAS in L2F is simply to project or forward PPP frames from the client to the remote node. This remote node is called a home gateway in Cisco's Internetwork Operating System (IOS) networking terminology.

See Also: *Layer 2 Tunneling Protocol (L2TP), Point-to-Point Protocol (PPP), Point-to-Point Tunneling Protocol (PPTP), virtual private network (VPN)*

Layer 2 switch

An Ethernet switch that forwards frames according to Layer-2 addresses.

Overview

Layer 2 switches operate at the data-link layer (Layer 2) of the Open Systems Interconnection (OSI) reference model. Layer 2 switches are essentially multiport bridges that forward frames based on their destination MAC address without any concern for the actual network protocol being used. Layer 2 switches operate near wire speed and have very low latency compared to Layer 3 devices such as routers.

Layer 2 switching originated in the 1980s with vendors such as Kalpana, which was acquired by Cisco Systems. Although originally developed for a variety of local area network (LAN) architectures including Ethernet, Token Ring, and Fiber Distributed Data Interface (FDDI), by far the most widespread use of these switches is in switched Ethernet, Fast Ethernet, and Gigabit Ethernet (GbE) networks. Layer 2 switches have displaced bridges, hubs, and routers in much of today's enterprise network.

Uses

There are two main kinds of Layer 2 switches, and each type is optimized for its own particular role in the network. These types are

- **Segmentation switches:** These are used to segment large networks into collections of smaller collision domains to reduce congestion and improve network performance. Routers have traditionally been used for segmenting enterprise networks, but Layer 2 switches are cheaper than routers, easier to deploy and manage, and have lower latency. As a result, most large companies have replaced much of their router infrastructure with Layer 2 switches, relegating routers mainly to the role of wide area network (WAN) access devices. In addition to segmenting large networks, such Layer 2 switches are also used to connect LANs across a campus network and to build collapsed backbone networks together with their more powerful cousins, Layer 3 switches.
- **Workgroup switches:** These are used to provide high-throughput switched connections to servers and high-performance workstations. A typical workgroup switch would have 12 or 24 autosensing 10/100 megabits per second (Mbps) or 100/1000 Mbps ports with one or more gigabit uplink ports for connection to the LAN backbone. Hubs have traditionally been used for concentrating servers and workstations into workgroups, but hubs use a shared-media approach that cannot match switches in throughput and latency. As a result of falling port prices in Layer 2 switches, most large companies have migrated their legacy hub infrastructure to Layer 2 switches.

Implementation

Layer 2 switches can generally be installed transparently into networks with no configuration required unless virtual LANs (VLANs) are needed. When Layer 2 switches first appeared, the mantra "switch when you can, route when you must" was promoted (this originated with Synoptics, which later became Bay Networks and has now been acquired by Nortel Networks).

Once installed, a Layer 2 switch dynamically learns about connected hosts and networks by examining the source addresses of frames it receives. The switch continually builds a cache or database of mappings between each port on the switch and the various MAC addresses of hosts and networks connected to that port. Then, when a frame arrives at a given switch port, the switch reads the destination MAC address and forwards the frame to the switch port to which the destination host or network is connected. If the frame's destination address is unfamiliar or if it is a broadcast frame, the switch forwards the frame to all of its ports except the port through which the frame originally entered.

If a Layer 2 switch has ports of different media types (for example, Ethernet and FDDI), frame forwarding is complicated. Frames that must be forwarded to destination ports having different media types must first be reformatted at Layer 1 (the PHY or physical layer) before being forwarded to their destination ports.

Layer 2 switches avoid routing loops by implementing a method first used in bridged networks, namely, the spanning tree protocol. This protocol works automatically to ensure that frames are not endlessly switched around in loops, which would make other network communications impossible.

Advantages and Disadvantages

Advantages of Layer 2 switches over traditional hubs and routers include higher throughput, lower latency, cheaper cost per port, and easier management. Disadvantages of such switches include the danger of broadcast storms and greater complexity in troubleshooting network problems (traditional packet sniffers work on shared media LANs where they can monitor traffic simultaneously from large numbers of stations). A broadcast storm occurs when broadcasts become so common that other forms of network communication are prevented. Broadcasts typically occur due to network advertisements from servers, routers, and other devices. Because Layer 2 switches (and bridges) allow broadcasts to pass, a network built entirely of Layer 2 switches represents a single broadcast domain. When the number of stations in a broadcast domain reaches several hundred, broadcast storms are likely to occur. Layer 2 switches by themselves therefore do not represent a scalable solution for building large enterprise networks. You can solve this broadcast problem in several ways:

- By combining newer Layer 2 switches with traditional routers in the network infrastructure. This brings some of the benefits of switches but leaves some of the problems relating to routers such as cost, and latency, and throughput.
- By configuring separate VLANs for ports or groups of ports on each Layer 2 switch. VLANs let you logically segment the network independently from its physical topology. This approach is functionally equivalent to flattening the network into a number of smaller broadcast domains, and it works well with traditional enterprise networks that followed the 80/20 rule of network traffic distribution. But with the ubiquity of Internet-related technologies in today's network, the pattern of network traffic has shifted to become more like 20/80 (20 percent of traffic is local and 80 percent travels along the backbone), and VLANs do not work well in such a situation, as the optimal network configuration becomes using a single VLAN again—which takes us back to the broadcast storm problem! Another issue with VLANs is that most approaches to creating them are vendor specific, and until the new 802.1Q VLAN standard becomes widely supported, VLANs will be difficult to implement unless all Layer 2 switches are obtained from a single vendor. Finally, VLANs make troubleshooting switched Ethernet networks even harder.
- By building collapsed network backbones using a combination of Layer 2 (bridging) switches with Layer 3 (routing) switches or by using switches combining Layer 2/3 functionality (called multiplayer switches). This is the most popular solution in today's enterprise—see the article "Layer 3 switch" elsewhere in this book for more information.

See Also: *bridge, Ethernet switch, Layer 3 switch, Layer 4 switch, Layer 7 switch, Open Systems Interconnection (OSI) reference model*

Layer 2 Tunneling Protocol (L2TP)

A wide area networking (WAN) protocol used for virtual private networking.

Overview

The Layer 2 Tunneling Protocol (L2TP) was developed as a vendor-neutral tunneling protocol that supersedes proprietary tunneling protocols such as Microsoft Corporation's Point-to-Point Tunneling Protocol (PPTP) and Cisco Systems' Layer 2 Forwarding (L2F) protocol. L2TP can be used to encapsulate Point-to-Point Protocol (PPP) frames for transmission over a variety of network transports, including Transmission Control Protocol/Internet Protocol (TCP/IP), X.25, frame relay,

L

and Asynchronous Transfer Mode (ATM). L2TP is an Internet Engineering Task Force (IETF) standard defined in RFC 2661 and is typically used for creating virtual private networks (VPNs) to securely tunnel network traffic over the Internet and other public data networks.

L2TP supports the same authentication options supported by PPP, including Password Authentication Protocol (PAP), Challenge Handshake Authentication Protocol (CHAP), and Microsoft Challenge Handshake Authentication Protocol (MS-CHAP). L2TP is not a secure protocol in itself, however, for although secure authentication is supported, data encryption is not. As a result, L2TP is usually combined with Internet Protocol Security (IPsec), a Layer 3 protocol that performs encryption to ensure data integrity during transmission. This combination is sometimes referred to as L2TP over IPsec or L2TP/IPsec, but since this form is almost always used, it is more common to simply refer to the combination as L2TP.

L2TP is supported by both Cisco access routers and by the Routing and Remote Access Service (RRAS) of Microsoft Windows 2000.

Comparison

Both L2TP and PPTP are commonly used tunneling protocols in virtual private networking. L2TP has some advantages over PPTP, however:

- Although PPTP can only be used to create IP tunnels, L2TP supports a much wider variety of WAN transports, including X.25, frame relay, and ATM.
- Although PPTP supports only one tunnel between two endpoints, L2TP supports multiple tunnels between two points, each of which can have its own quality of service (QoS) level defined.
- L2TP has less overhead because L2TP headers are only 4 bytes in length and are compressed and PPTP uses uncompressed 6-byte headers.
- L2TP can also support multilink configurations in which each link terminates at a different L2TP server at the service provider. This provides more flexibility than Multilink PPP (MPPP), in which all the links from the customer premises must terminate at the same MPPP server at the service provider.

The main disadvantage of L2TP compared to PPTP is that it requires more processing power due to its use of compression and IPsec encryption.

L2TP is also a significant improvement over Cisco's earlier L2F tunneling protocol. Some of the differences between L2TP and L2F include

- Although L2F has no defined client, L2TP uses a well-defined client.
- Although L2F functions in compulsory tunnels only, L2TP can also use voluntary tunnels.
- L2TP provides additional features, such as flow control and Attribute Value Pair (AVP) hiding, which are not supported by L2F.

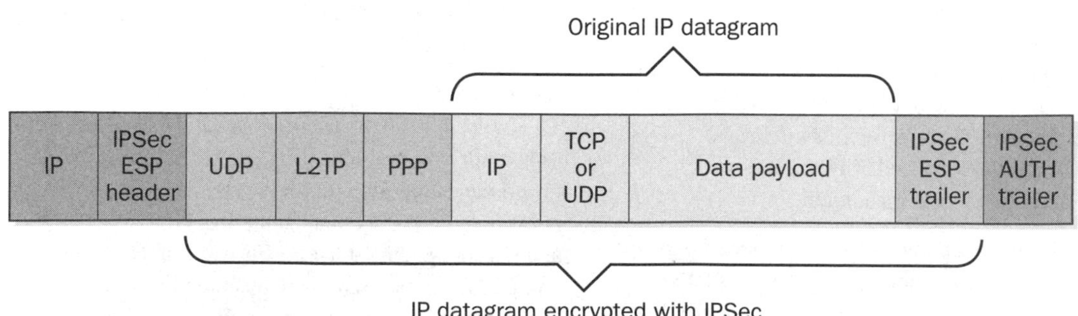

Layer 2 Tunneling Protocol (L2TP). *How L2TP is used to encapsulate an IP datagram.*

Architecture

As its name suggests, L2TP operates at Layer 2 of the Open Systems Interconnection (OSI) reference model. When used on IP networks, L2TP uses User Datagram Protocol (UDP) datagrams on port 1701 for both the establishment and management of tunnels and for data transmission. In other words, L2TP transmits its control information using in-band signaling through the same tunnel that data is transmitted over. To transmit data, an IP packet is first wrapped in a PPP frame, which is then encapsulated into a UDP datagram. An L2TP header is then added for transmission over the WAN. In a typical VPN, IPsec is then used to add security by encrypting the data and adding an additional header and trailer to the L2TP frame.

Implementation

Implementing L2TP requires an L2TP client and an L2TP server that both support IPsec. A VPN constructed using L2TP can be initiated in two ways:

- The client can initiate the tunnel in a similar fashion to PPTP tunnels. For example, Windows 2000 clients can initiate L2TP tunnels and connect with routers that support L2TP, such as Cisco routers. In a typical scenario, a dial-up tunnel is initiated by a client who connects with a network access server (NAS) at the client's telco central office (CO) or Internet service provider (ISP). The NAS performs the server-side function of PPP termination and acts as the receiver of incoming connections. In some implementations, the NAS is referred to as an L2TP access concentrator (LAC). The LAC then forwards its L2TP traffic to a remote node called an L2TP network server (LNS).
- A NAS can initiate the tunnel, enabling telcos and ISPs to provide corporate customers with complete VPN solutions. In this scenario, the remote client acts as the LNS.

See Also: *Internet Protocol Security (IPsec), Layer 2 Forwarding (L2F), Multilink Point-to-Point Protocol (MPPP), Point-to-Point Protocol (PPP), Point-to-Point Tunneling Protocol (PPTP), User Datagram Protocol (UDP), virtual private network (VPN)*

Layer 3 switch

An Ethernet switch that forwards frames according to Layer 3 addresses.

Overview

Layer 3 switches operate at the network layer (Layer 3) of the Open Systems Interconnection (OSI) reference model. Layer 3 switches have many of the characteristics of traditional routers and forward datagrams based on their network layer addresses. For example, on a Transmission Control Protocol/Internet Protocol (TCP/IP) network, Layer 3 switches forward IP packets based on their destination IP addresses, but on a legacy Internetwork Packet Exchange/Sequenced Packet Exchange (IPX/SPX) network, they forward IPX packets based on their destination IPX addresses.

Layer 3 switching originated in the early 1990s and was developed mainly in response to scaling problems with Layer 2 switches and the difficulty traditional routers had with keeping up with backbone traffic flows. 3Com Corporation pioneered the development of Layer 3 switching by incorporating routing functions in some of its Layer 2 switches in 1992. These early switches were mainly software-based and were superseded in the mid-1990s by hardware-based switches such as the popular CoreBuilder 3500 and 9000 series of switches, which employed application specific integrated circuits (ASICs) dedicated to high-speed bridging and routing functions.

Layer 3 switches are currently available from a wide variety of vendors for Ethernet, Fast Ethernet, and Gigabit Ethernet (GbE) networks. Layer 3 switches are also available for other networking architectures, including Token Ring, Fiber Distributed Data Interface (FDDI), and Asynchronous Transfer Mode (ATM), but these are not as common as Ethernet switches.

Uses

Using a combination of Layer 2 and Layer 3 switches, you can easily build and operate highly scalable collapsed backbones for enterprise-level networks. Due to their routing functionality, Layer 3 switches have largely replaced traditional routers in campus backbones and other large networks, relegating the router mainly to the role today of wide area network (WAN) access device.

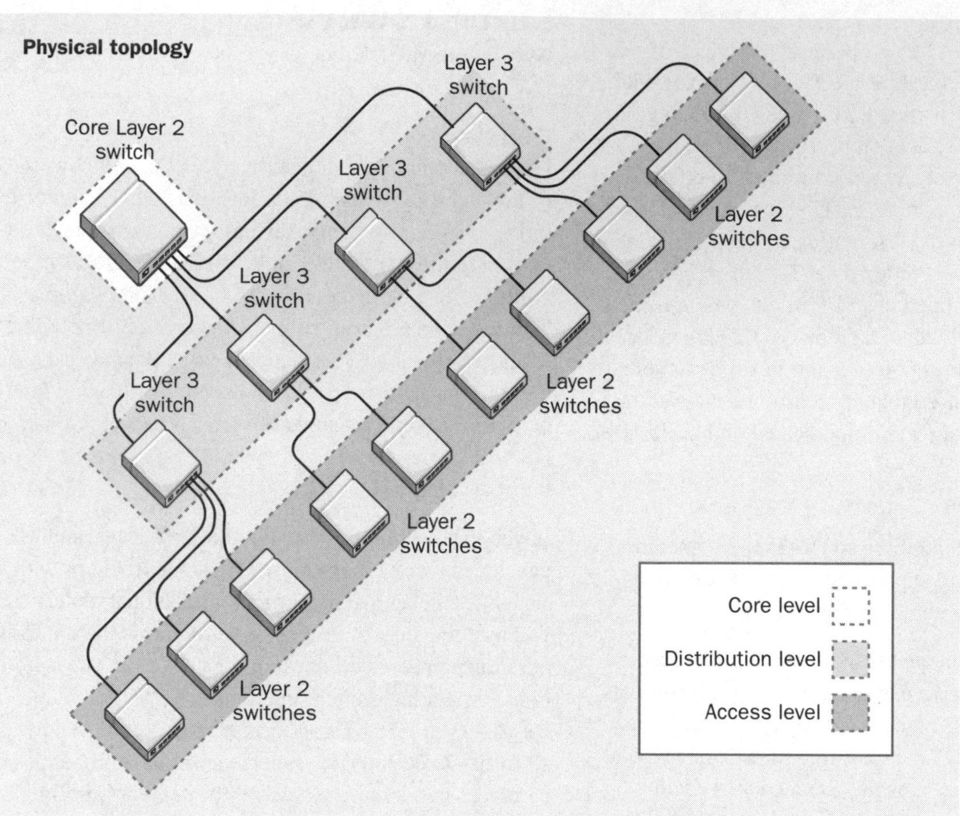

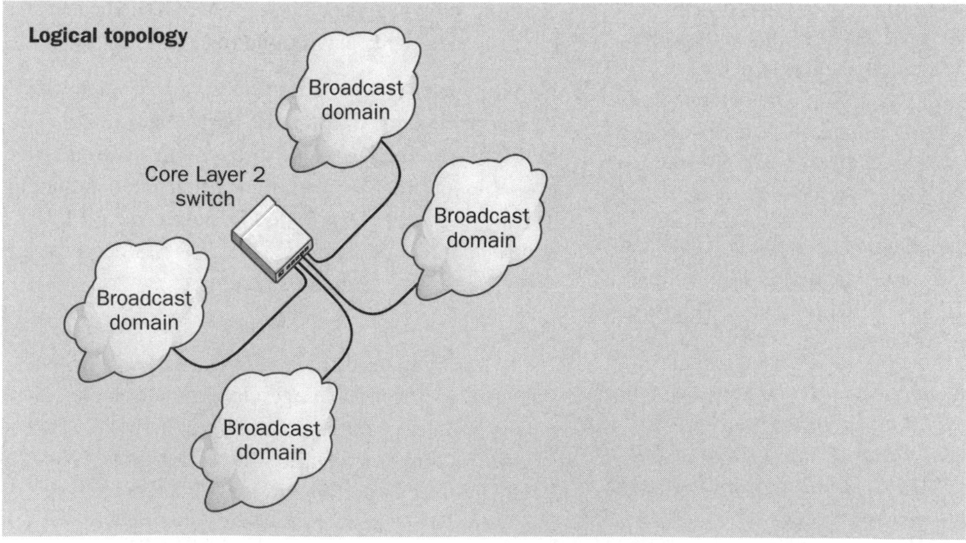

Layer 3 switch. *Building a switched network backbone using Layer 2 and Layer 3 switches.*

A typical switched network backbone is built in a hierarchical fashion in several levels using a combination of Layer 2 and Layer 3 switches. At the periphery of the network is the access level, which uses multiple Layer 2 switches to provide connection points for workgroup collections of servers and workstations. These Layer 2 switches represent collision domains but pass broadcasts; consequently, to prevent broadcast storms from occurring they need to be consolidated using Layer 3 switches. These Layer 3 switches represent the distribution level of the network, as they are used to distribute traffic to different access points for workgroup connections. Layer 3 switches represent broadcast domains, and the number of connected devices downstream from each switch must be small enough to prevent broadcast storms from occurring (a good rule of thumb is a maximum of 2000 connected devices). Finally, these Layer 3 switches at the distribution level are connected using high-speed Layer 2 switches, which form the network's core level. The network's hierarchical physical structure is thus equivalent to a logical star network with multiple broadcast domains connected using one or more Layer 2 switches (see diagram on the previous page).

If you are migrating a legacy routed network to a modern switched one, you can also simply deploy a Layer 3 switch anywhere in your network a traditional router is used.

Implementation

This discussion will focus on Layer 3 switching in TCP/IP running on Ethernet, where the primary Layer 3 protocol is IP. Layer 3 switches essentially do the same thing traditional routers do—route (forward) packets to their destination based on their Layer 3 address (see the table for a comparison of routers and Layer 3 switches). However, traditional routers really perform two different functions:

- **Route calculation:** This is the process of building routing tables and usually takes place dynamically using a routing protocol such as Routing Information Protocol (RIP) or Open Shortest Path First (OSPF).
- **Packet forwarding:** This involves examining a packet's destination IP, looking up this address in the routing table, and determining which port (connected network) to forward the packet to so that it can eventually reach its destination.

The difficulty with traditional routers is that they are software-based devices that are slow and unable to keep up with today's gigabit speed networks. Vendors have found different ways around this problem, all of which generally fall under the umbrella name of Layer 3 switching. Some of the common solutions are

- **Wirespeed routers:** This involves replacing traditional software-based routing technology with hardware-based routing by using specialized ASICs developed specifically to perform route calculation and packet forwarding. In other words, a wirespeed router is simply a router that performs its routing functions using preprogrammed hardware instead of installable routing software. Wirespeed routers are typically an order of magnitude or more faster than traditional software routers and can keep up with gigabit data flows and route millions of packets per second. Another name for these devices is Packet-by-Packet Layer 3 (PPL3) switches since they individually examine and forward each packet in a train of packets. The name *switch* is really a misnomer in this case—these devices are actually routers, not switches.
- **Cut-through switches:** These devices operate on the principle of "Route once, switch many" and work by separating the two functions of traditional routers: calculating routes and forwarding frames to their destination. When a train of packets (a data stream or communications flow between two hosts or networks) reaches a port on a cut-through switch, the switch examines the train's first packet, reads the destination IP address, looks up the best route to the destination in its routing table, and determines which port to forward the packet to. The device then switches the entire series of packets in the train to the outgoing port without examining any further packets in the train. In other words, routing is performed on the first packet of the train, and

L

switching is performed on the remaining packets. Switching means that an internal logical circuit is set up between the incoming and outgoing ports on the switch. Since switching is much faster than routing, cut-through switches perform significantly better than routers while accomplishing the same function: forwarding packets on the basis of their destination IP addresses.

Within the realm of cut-through switches, there are also many differences in operation depending on vendors. For example, some cut-through switches operate similarly to bridges in the sense that they dynamically learn the addresses of attached hosts and networks by "listening" to traffic. The difference is that instead of learning the Layer 2 (MAC) addresses of devices attached to each port, as bridges and Layer 2 switches do, these Layer 3 switches learn the Layer 3 (IP) addresses of connected devices instead. Such Layer 3 "learning" switches build their routing tables dynamically by listening to traffic on their ports, but they cannot exchange this information with similar switches the way routers do using routing protocols. The main use for this type of switch is to "front-end" for traditional routers. For example, if a packet arrives at the switch and the switch does not know what to do with it, the switch simply forwards the packet to the router for handling. Traditional routers are also still needed for routing legacy protocols such as DECnet and AppleTalk and for providing access to the WAN.

By contrast, some cut-through switches perform virtually all the functions that a traditional router performs, such as using the packet's checksum to verify its integrity, updating the packet's Time to Live (TTL) information after each hop, processing any option information in the packet's header, and sharing their routing table information with similar switches using a standard routing protocol, such as RIP or OSPF, so that they become aware of the network's overall topology. In short, they are identical to routers except that they route only the first packet of any train and switch the remainder to improve performance.

A common feature of Layer 3 switches is their support for Layer 2 switching or frame forwarding. This combination is called either a Layer 2/3 switch, a multiplayer switch, a routing switch, or simply a Layer 3 switch. These devices are becoming so common in the enterprise that many networking professionals simply call them switches, without any further qualifier.

Deploying Layer 3 switches in a network is usually as easy as doing so with Layer 2 switches, which are essentially plug-and-play in their simplicity, and it is much simpler than configuring a router. As a result, Layer 3 switches are rapidly displacing traditional routers in the enterprise, except in the role of WAN access devices where routers still predominate. Layer 3 switches are generally easy to manage also, and they typically support Simple Network Management Protocol (SNMP) and Remote Monitoring (RMON) management protocols.

Traditional Router vs. Layer 3 Switch

Feature	*Router*	*Layer 3 Switch*
Local area network (LAN) protocols supported	IP, IPX, AppleTalk	IP, IPX, AppleTalk
Packet-forwarding method	Software-based	Hardware-based
Throughput	Lower	Higher
Definition of subnet	Per port	Per Layer 2 switching domain
Support for policy-based routing	Less	More
Relationship with bridges	Peer	Layered
Cost	Higher	Lower

Marketplace

Layer 3 switches are typically sold in two configurations: fixed and modular. Fixed switches are simpler and cheaper and usually have 8, 12, or 24 autosensing 10/100 megabits per second (Mbps) or 10/100/1000 Mbps Ethernet ports. Modular switches are more complex and costly and typically consist of a chassis that supports various kinds of modules, each providing one or more ports of Ethernet, FDDI, Token Ring, or ATM connectivity.

Popular Layer 3 switches include offerings from large vendors, such as Cisco's popular Catalyst series of routing switches, and switches from second-tier vendors such as Allied Telesyn International, Asante Technologies, D-Link Systems, Hewlett-Packard, Network Peripherals, and many others. For core switching in network backbones, popular Layer 3 switches that are widely used in enterprise networks include the Catalyst 5000 and 6000 series of switches from Cisco, BigIron 4000 switches from Foundry Networks, BlackDiamond from Extreme Networks, Passport 8600 from Nortel Networks, and the SmartSwitch Router from Enterasys Networks.

Prospects

The growth of Layer 3 switches (and all types of LAN switches) is one of the most significant trends in the networking market. While overall sales of 10 Mbps Ethernet switches peaked in 1998 with 23 million ports sold, sales of Fast Ethernet and GbE switches continue to rise steadily. Sales of Fast Ethernet switches amounted to over 88 million ports sold in 2000 and are increasing at more than 33 percent a year. GbE switches sold almost 6 million ports in 2000 but are expected by some analysts to increase at a rate of more than 200 percent for the next few years. Sales of traditional routers would be expected to suffer in this market as enterprises migrate their router-based infrastructures to switched backbones, but router sales actually continue to increase, driven largely by the growth of the Internet and the needs of large Internet service providers (ISPs) for such devices and their enduring use as WAN access devices. Nevertheless, the days of routed networks are fading and the switch has risen to the dominant position in the infrastructure of enterprise networks, largely replacing traditional hubs, bridges, and routers.

See Also: *Ethernet switch, Layer 2 switch, Layer 4 switch, Layer 7 switch, Open Systems Interconnection (OSI) reference model, router*

Layer 4 switch

An Ethernet switch that forwards frames according to Layer 4 header information.

Overview

Layer 4 switches operate at the transport layer (Layer 4) of the Open Systems Interconnection (OSI) reference model. Layer 4 switches are capable of examining frames and reading their Layer 4 header information, such as Transmission Control Protocol (TCP) and User Datagram Protocol (UDP) port numbers, and then forwarding packets based on this information. In Transmission Control Protocol/Internet Protocol (TCP/IP), these port numbers are used to identify different applications—for example, Hypertext Transfer Protocol (HTTP) typically uses port 80 and Simple Mail Transfer Protocol (SMTP) typically uses port 25. By being able to switch packets according to port numbers, Layer 4 switches are thus able to prioritize the flow of IP traffic according to application. For example, to prioritize HTTP traffic, a Layer 4 switch would be configured to allocate greater bandwidth to IP packets where the Layer 4 header indicates TCP port number 80. Alternatively, a Layer 4 switch could be configured to block or restrict traffic over certain ports, fulfilling the role of a firewall. The key difference between Layer 4 switches and switches that operate at Layer 2 or Layer 3 is that Layer 4 switches provide the ability to prioritize traffic according to application.

Uses

Layer 4 switches are not intended to replace Layer 2 and Layer 3 switches as the basic building blocks of collapsed backbones in enterprise networks. Instead, they can be selectively deployed in the distribution level of the network (see the article "Layer 3 switch" elsewhere in this book) to add traffic prioritization and firewall services for the network when these features are needed or desired.

Implementation

Layer 4 switches typically perform bridging (forwarding by Layer 2 or MAC addresses) and routing (forwarding by Layer 3 or IP addresses) also. In other words, a typical Layer 4 switch is really a multilayer switch or Layer 2/3/4 switch. Alternatively, Layer 3 switches are sometimes marketed as featuring additional Layer 4 switching capabilities. Layer 4 switches thus need to be able to store a large number of mappings for each switch port, namely

- MAC addresses for each connected device
- IP addresses for each connected device
- Multiple port numbers for each connected device

As a result, Layer 4 switches require a great deal of processing power and memory and are more expensive than their Layer 2/3 cousins. Because of their ability to switch according to port numbers, Layer 4 switches enable multiple logical network connections to be established for each path to a device having a Layer 3 address. The combination of a Layer 3 address, such as an IP address and a port number, is usually called a socket, and a train of frames all having the same socket information is referred to as a flow. Most Layer 4 switches can enforce Layer 3 traffic flows on a policy basis, making management of complex traffic flows simple to implement.

L

Marketplace

Vendors of Layer 4 switches include Cisco Systems, with its Catalyst series of switches; Extreme Networks, with its Summit series; 3Com Corporation, with its CoreBuilder series; and companies such as Alteon WebSystems (acquired by Nortel Networks in 2000), F5 Networks, Foundry Networks, and Radware.

See Also: *bridge, Ethernet switch, Layer 2 switch, Layer 3 switch, Layer 7 switch, Open Systems Interconnection (OSI) reference model, router*

Layer 4+ switch

An Ethernet switch that forwards frames according to header information found in Layer 4 and higher.

Overview

Layer 4+ switches combine bridging (Layer 2), routing (Layer 3), and port mapping (Layer 4) with functionality derived from layers higher than 4 of the Open Systems Interconnection (OSI) reference model. What this usually means in reality is that they can use Layer 7 (application layer) information found in packet headers and make routing decisions based upon this information. Hence Layer 4+ switches are effectively just Layer 7 switches with a different name. For more information, see the article "Layer 7 switch" below.

See Also: *bridge, Ethernet switch, Layer 2 switch, Layer 3 switch, Layer 4 switch, Layer 7 switch, Open Systems Interconnection (OSI) reference model, router*

Layer 7 switch

Also called Layer 4+ or Layer 4/7 switch, an Ethernet switch that forwards frames according to Layer 4 header information.

Overview

Layer 7 switches operate at the application layer (Layer 7) of the Open Systems Interconnection (OSI) reference model. In this respect, they fill a niche in e-business networks that Layer 4 switches cannot. Considering Hypertext Transport Protocol (HTTP) traffic or Web traffic as an example, Layer 4 switches can use port numbers to distinguish Web traffic from other types of Internet traffic such as Simple Mail Transport Protocol (SMTP) traffic, but they cannot distinguish static HTTP traffic (which can be cached) from dynamic traffic (which is not easily cached). When Layer 4 switches are used to front-end a Web server farm, the result is that all forms of HTTP traffic get cached, which is wasteful and adds unnecessary latency to dynamic Web applications.

Enter Layer 7 switches, which can examine Layer 7 HTTP headers in detail and route traffic according to request type, Uniform Resource Locators (URLs), cookies, and other information. Layer 7 switches are thus capable of switching Web traffic to different servers according to URLs requested (called URL switching), caching different types of traffic differently (cache switching), and directing traffic to different servers in the farm to distribute the load (load balancing) or to servers hosting different types of content (content distribution). As a result, Layer 7 switches are variously marketed by different vendors under names such as Web switches, Web content switches, URL switches, and load balancers.

Uses

Layer 7 switches need be deployed only sparingly in an enterprise. A typical use for such a switch is to act as a front-end for a group of Web servers in a server farm used to support an e-commerce application. The Layer 7 switch provides a single Internet Protocol (IP) address for users to access over the Internet using their browsers, making the server farm appear to the user as a single Web server. The Layer 7 switch typically interfaces with a router that provides connectivity to the Internet (see diagram).

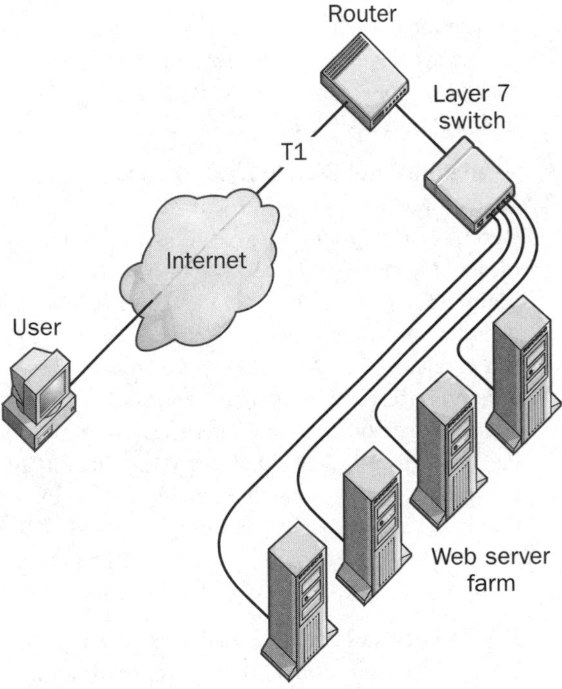

Layer 7 switch. *Using a Layer 7 switch to front-end a Web server farm.*

Marketplace

Most Layer 7 switches are special purpose devices dedicated to managing HTTP traffic more effectively for e-commerce systems—true Layer 7 switches that are fully configurable for any form of application traffic are rare. A Web content switch should typically support such additional features as application redirection, content-intelligent switching, local and global load balancing, packet filtering, quality of service (QoS) traffic routing, and Secure Sockets Layer (SSL) acceleration.

Popular makers of Layer 7 switches include Alteon WebSystems (acquired by Nortel Networks in 2000) with its Alteon 184 switch, ArrowPoint Communications (acquired by Cisco Systems) with its CS-800 switch, Foundry Networks with its ServerIronXL switch, F5 Networks with its Big-IP series of switches, and Intel Corporation with its NetStructure E-Commerce Director switches. Some vendors also claim that their Layer 2, 3, or 4 switches include limited Layer 7 switching capabilities, so the marketplace can be confusing to the newcomer.

Prospects

An emerging use for Layer 7 switches is to provide QoS for Voice over IP (VoIP) systems and load balancing for IP Private Branch Exchange (PBX) equipment. These switches use Layer 7 information in IP headers to identify packets containing H.323 and Session Initiation Protocol (SIP) voice traffic as payload and help to prioritize the forwarding of these packets in such a way as to provide better quality voice communications over IP networks. Two examples of such switches are AppSwitch from Top Layer Networks and a VoIP module for Web Server Director from Radware.

See Also: bridge, Ethernet switch, Layer 2 switch, Layer 3 switch, Layer 4 switch, Open Systems Interconnection (OSI) reference model, router, Voice over IP (VoIP)

LCP

Stands for Link Control Protocol, the portion of Point-to-Point Protocol (PPP) responsible for link management.

See: Link Control Protocol (LCP)

LDAP

Stands for Lightweight Directory Access Protocol, a standard protocol for accessing information in a directory.

See: Lightweight Directory Access Protocol (LDAP)

leased line

A permanent link leased from a telecommunications carrier.

Overview

Leased lines are dedicated point-to-point circuits that are installed between a customer premises and a telco central office (CO). Examples of leased line services include switched 56, T1, fractional T1, and T3 lines. Integrated Service Digital Network (ISDN) is also sometimes considered a leased line service, but ISDN is really a dial-up service unlike always-on T-carrier services. These services are provisioned, installed, and leased from a telecommunications carrier such as a local exchange carrier (LEC) or inter-exchange carrier (IXC).

Uses

Leased lines have been around since the 1980s and have long been the primary means for enterprises to connect their remote offices in a wide area network (WAN). In a traditional WAN the larger branch offices would be connected to headquarters by T1 or fractional T1 lines, sometimes with ISDN lines as backup, and smaller branch offices would get by with dial-up modem connections used for nightly transfers of batch jobs. With the explosion of the Internet in the 1990s, this picture has changed, and the rapid rise of WAN traffic has driven large companies to find solutions other than deploying additional expensive leased lines.

The main alternatives to leased lines during the 1990s included frame relay and Asynchronous Transfer Mode (ATM) circuits, but these technologies are complex and expensive to deploy and have not gained the same popularity in the enterprise as leased lines. Recently, Digital Subscriber Line (DSL) has emerged as a promising alternative to leased lines. By combining a DSL connection to the Internet with virtual private networking (VPN) technology, corporate networks can tunnel through the public Internet to connect securely with remote offices and mobile workers.

In the age of the Internet and e-commerce, leased lines are finding other popular uses:

- Providing reliable high-speed Internet access for corporate networks.
- Connecting e-businesses with hosting centers that host their e-commerce Web sites.

Advantages and Disadvantages

Leased lines have several advantages over competing WAN technologies:

- **Security:** Leased lines are dedicated point-to-point links between the customer premises and the telco, and are therefore difficult to eavesdrop on. By contrast, a VPN over DSL solution has to employ encryption to ensure data security and integrity, and holes have sometimes been found in encryption schemes—for example, in the Point-to-Point Tunneling Protocol (PPTP).
- **Availability and Reliability:** Leased lines have been around for a long time and are well understood. As a result, they are easy to set up and troubleshoot, and they provide virtually 100 percent uptime. Frame relay and ATM are more complex, and there have been well-publicized failures of the frame relay and ATM backbones of some of the largest carriers in recent years. And since a VPN over DSL solution uses the Internet as its transport, the reliability of a link depends on the reliability of the Internet itself—something that is open to question in the age of massive Distributed Denial of Service (DDoS) attacks and Internet backbone congestion.
- **Low latency and jitter:** Leased lines offer virtually latency-free connections, suitable for transmission of data, voice, and multimedia. By contrast, a VPN over DSL solution employs Internet Protocol (IP), which can have significant latency and jitter that can adversely affect both voice and multimedia communications.

By contrast, the main disadvantage of leased lines is their cost, which has remained high over the last decade. For example, a T1 line can cost well over $1,000 a month compared to perhaps $50 to $100 per month for a faster DSL connection. Despite these huge costs, leased lines still remain the most popular way for enterprises to connect their remote offices in a WAN, primarily because of their high reliability. For mission-critical or time-sensitive traffic, leased lines still rule—for less critical traffic, VPN over DSL is a good solution, however.

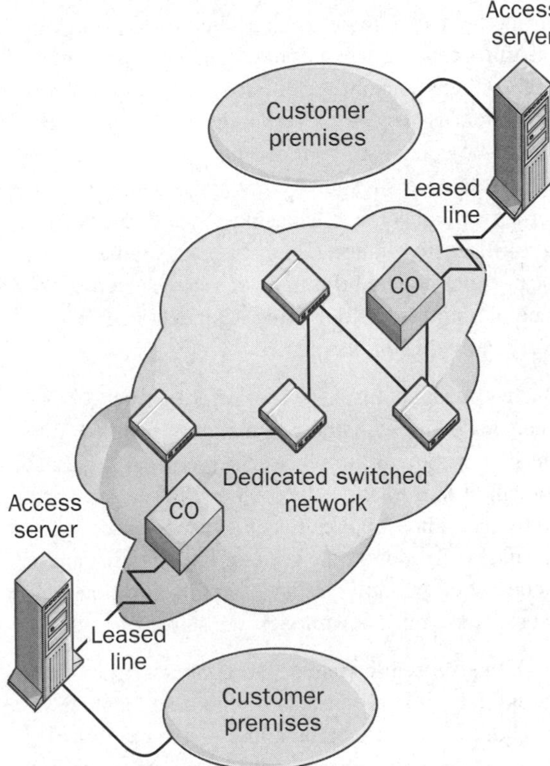

Leased line. *How a leased line is provisioned.*

Implementation

Provisioning a leased line involves steps at both the customer premises and telco ends:

- **Customer premises:** Special equipment is required to connect the customer's local area network (LAN) to the line termination point at the customer premises. This is typically either a combination of router and channel service unit/data service unit (CSU/DSU) or an access server (also called integrated access device, or IAD) that combines the functionality of a router and a CSU/DSU into a single device.
- **Telco CO:** The telecommunications carrier dedicates certain switches in its switching fabric to set up a permanent circuit between the local and remote customer premises. Data then flows along a single permanent path between the two locations.

Marketplace

Leased lines are generally available from both LECs and IXCs. Provisioning and service quality vary greatly but in general are good for large Regional Bell Operating Companies (RBOCs) such as BellSouth Corporation. IXCs such as AT&T and Sprint are logical choices for large enterprises wanting to deploy leased lines across the United States, but these carriers rely on LECs for the actual provisioning at the local loop level, and this introduces a second tier into the service end, which can sometimes cause delays and difficulties. For enterprises having a global presence in several countries and regions around the world, the largest player in the leased line market is Concert, a joint venture ofAT&T and British Telecom (BT).

Charges for a leased line are typically based on the distance of the line and not on the bandwidth used—usually you pay for the available bandwidth even if you do not use it all. Actual provisioning of a leased line from time of order to deployment typically takes four to eight weeks, depending on demand.

See Also: *Asynchronous Transfer Mode (ATM), central office (CO), circuit-switched services, customer premises, Digital Subscriber Line (DSL), frame relay, Integrated Services Digital Network (ISDN), inter-exchange carrier (IXC), local exchange carrier (LEC), T-carrier, virtual private network (VPN), wide area network (WAN)*

LEC

Stands for local exchange carrier, any telco in the United States that provides telephone and telecommunication services for subscribers within a geographic region.

See: *local exchange carrier (LEC)*

license

A legal authorization to use software in a given networking scenario.

Overview

Purchasing most business software typically involves two steps:

- Purchasing media containing the installation files from which the software can be installed on your computers.
- Determining how your software will be used and how many users will use it, and then purchasing licenses to use the software legally in the manner you have chosen.

Licensing is a complex issue and varies from vendor to vendor and across product lines, but it is important to take licensing into account in the planning stage before purchasing software, as the cost of licenses can add significantly to the overall deployment cost.

History

Early licensing programs for commercial software usually used a per-server basis—that is, licenses were applied to the client instead of the server. A single per-server license authorized a single client connection to the server for file, print, or whatever server services were being licensed. Per-server licensing meant that administrators had to determine the maximum number of users who might want to access the server simultaneously and to purchase sufficient per-server licenses to ensure that licensing requirements were being met. The main problem with per-server licensing was that it did not scale well from a financial perspective. For example, if no more than five users were expected to access a file server at any given time, five per-server licenses would need to be purchased at a cost of *x* dollars. If two more file servers were added to the company network, 3 x 5 = 15 licenses would be required (five for each server), at a total licensing cost now of 3*x* dollars.

Per-seat licensing was developed to address the scalability issue of per-server licensing. With per-seat licensing, the client machines are licensed, rather than the servers (although the servers usually require additional licenses of their own). Each client machine requires only a single per-seat license to authorize it to access any server on the network. Per-seat licensing scales better than per-server licensing, and it is simple to calculate—a company requires as many per-seat licenses as it has client machines or users.

Prospects

With the widespread penetration into business networks of Internet technologies such as the World Wide Web, existing licensing schemes have begun to show signs of strain. Client machines are no longer simply desktop computers used by employees—they might also include users who connect to your company Web site over the Internet to access resources on your network. Both the per-server and per-seat licensing schemes break down here—licensing Internet applications would logically mean either buying billions of per-server licenses for each of your servers or buying a per-seat license for every individual on the planet!

One way around this issue is to offer Internet services freely to clients, with no licensing costs involved. While this may work with simple Web servers that serve static content, it fails to solve the problem that arises when Web servers host applications that access back-end databases. To address the issue of how Internet and e-commerce technologies are affecting traditional licensing systems, new models are starting to evolve:

- **Usage-based licensing:** Administrators pay licensing fees monthly instead of one-time fees. These monthly fees are based either on the number of users or on the number of transactions performed against the vendor's applications.
- **Leasing applications:** Instead of buying shrink-wrapped software and installing it on company servers, companies lease the e-commerce applications and services they need from application service providers (ASPs) and pay a flat monthly fee along with a surcharge based on usage.
- **Value-based licensing:** This scenario envisions licensing fees calculated on actual business results related to using the software—for example, based on number of units sold and number of solid sales leads generated.

The advantage of these new licensing paradigms are that licensing costs can be drastically reduced by basing costs upon actual rather than expected maximum usage—in other words, you pay only for what you use. The downside is that these schemes are more difficult to plan from an accounting perspective and make the IT (information technology) budgeting process more complex.

For More Information

For current information about Microsoft licensing practices, visit *www.microsoft.com/licensing*.

Lightweight Directory Access Protocol (LDAP)

A standard protocol for accessing information in a directory.

Overview

The Lightweight Directory Access Protocol (LDAP) defines processes by which a client can connect to an X.500-compliant or LDAP-compliant directory service to add, delete, modify, or search for information, provided the client has sufficient access rights to the directory. For example, a user could use an LDAP client to query a directory server on her network for information about specific users, computers, departments, or any other information stored in the directory.

The term *LDAP* can mean three different things, depending on the context:

- **LDAP data format:** This defines the manner in which information is stored and recalled in an LDAP-compliant directory. This is called the LDAP Data Interchange Format (LDIF).
- **LDAP protocol:** This defines the processes that are involved when an LDAP client and LDAP server interact with each other—for example, when a client queries a server for some information.
- **LDAP API:** This is a set of application programming interfaces (APIs) that defines how applications can programmatically interact with LDAP servers.

LDAP was developed by the Internet Engineering Task Force (IETF) and its current version, LDAPv3, is defined in RFC 2251. LDAP is designed to run over Transmission Control Protocol/Internet Protocol (TCP/IP) and is a subset of Directory Access Protocol (DAP), part of the X.500 recommendations from the International Telecommunication Union (ITU).

History

Directories store information in a hierarchical fashion. The first attempt at defining a directory standard that could scale to global proportions was X.500, which was developed by the ITU in a series of recommendations spanning 1984 to 1994. Unfortunately, these recommendations were so complex that they were seen as too difficult to implement on most computing systems of that era. For example, the Directory Access Protocol (DAP), a part of X.500 that defined how X.500 clients would communicate with X.500 directory services, was so complex that its footprint would be too large and too slow to implement on a standard PC workstation. As a result of these problems with X.500, a process was launched to develop a simpler directory standard that would be easy to implement on PCs while remaining fully backward-compatible with X.500. The result of this development process was an open standard called LDAP.

Initial work on the LDAP standard and the first LDAP-compliant server, called SLAPD, was developed by researchers at the University of Michigan in conjunction with PSINet and the ISODE Consortium. LDAP began as a simple replacement for DAP that was intended to work with X.500 directory services—it was not intended to define a separate standard for directory services themselves. Version 2 of LDAP, defined in RFC 1777, took things a step further by divorcing LDAP from the X.500 standard proper, and it allowed for the development of stand-alone LDAP directory servers to replace the more complex directory service agents (DSAs) of a full X.500 directory service. LDAPv2 directory servers were stand-alone in the sense that they could not perform referrals. For example, if a client queried an LDAPv2 server for information that the server did not possess, the server would return a negative response to the client and would not be able to refer the client to other LDAPv2 servers that might have the information. This limitation severely affected the scalability of LDAPv2 directory service systems.

To overcome the scalability issues and other limitations of LDAPv2, a new version, LDAPv3, was developed by the Internet Engineering Task Force (IETF) in 1997 and was standardized as RFC 2251. LDAPv3 is the version of LDAP widely used in today's directory products, including Microsoft's Active Directory directory service, and it is a superset of LDAPv2 that remains backward-compatible with DAP and X.500. LDAPv3 has the following enhancements over earlier versions:

- **Internationalization:** Support for Unicode instead of the American National Standards Institute (ANSI) used in previous versions.
- **Referrals:** An LDAP server that cannot answer a client's query can refer the client to a different LDAP server that knows the answer. This makes LDAPv3 a highly scalable standard that can be used in large enterprises.
- **Security:** LDAPv3 supports both Transport Layer Security (TLS) and Kerberos security protocols.
- **Extended operations:** LDAPv3 is extensible and supports extended searching operations.

Advantages and Disadvantages

Some of the qualities of LDAP that have enabled it to gain widespread popularity include

- **Open:** LDAP is an open standard running on TCP/IP that specifies a protocol for communication between LDAP clients and servers but leaves implementation details for servers up to the vendors themselves, who develop various LDAP products.
- **Secure:** LDAP supports various kinds of security to preserve the integrity of directory data on a network.
- **Extensible:** The LDAP schema can be extended by defining new classes of objects and attributes to support applications that need these.
- **Programmable:** LDAP employs a standard set of APIs written in C/C++ and defined by RFC 1832. These APIs specify how LDAP client applications can programmatically query and obtain information from LDAP servers.
- **Scalable:** LDAPv3 supports referrals that allow LDAP directory services to scale easily to millions of objects for enterprise deployments.

Architecture

To understand how LDAP works, you need to know its terminology first. A good way of understanding LDAP terminology is to compare it with terminology for relational databases. Despite the similarities between these two systems, LDAP is not intended to replace relational databases because it lacks features such as locking, transactional processing, reporting, and efficient storage of binary large objects (BLOBs). The following are the basic LDAP terms and concepts:

- **Object:** Also called entries, objects are anything about which you want to store data in the directory. Objects are typically users, groups, computers, printers, organizational units, and domains. Objects are for LDAP what records are for a relational database.
- **Attribute:** Information about an object. For example, a user object might have attributes such as last name, first name, address, phone number, and e-mail address. An attribute can sometimes have more than one value—for example, a user might have several e-mail addresses. Attributes are for LDAP what fields are for relational databases. An LDAP server stores the values of an object's attributes in name/value pairs.
- **Classes:** Define what attributes go with what objects. Classes are for LDAP what tables are for relational databases—but unlike tables, classes are extensible and allow additional attributes to be defined for objects as required.
- **Schema:** The collection of classes and attributes used for a particular implementation of an LDAP directory service. LDAP schemas are extensible and allow new classes and attributes to be defined as required. Schemas have no counterpart in relational database terminology.

Lightweight Directory Access Protocol (LDAP)

- **Directory information tree (DIT):** The tree of objects stored within an LDAP directory.
- **Directory service agent (DSA):** An LDAP directory server.
- **Distinguished name (DN):** A unique name identifying an object within an LDAP directory.
- **Namespace:** The collection of possible names for objects within a specific LDAP directory.
- **Organizational unit (OU):** Containers within a namespace. OUs can contain leaf objects and other OUs. OUs are typically departments within a company, regions within a geographical area, and so on.
- **Domain:** Top-level names within a namespace. Domains can contain OUs and leaf objects, and they are typically names of things such as companies and countries.
- **Leaf object:** Any LDAP object that is not a domain or an OU. Examples of leaf objects include individual users, computers, and printers.

LDAP operates as a client/server protocol in which an LDAP client connects to an LDAP server over TCP port 389, issues a query, receives a response, and disconnects from the server. LDAP clients on LDAP servers can perform six operations:

- Binding (authenticating)
- Searching (querying)
- Adding an entry
- Modifying an entry
- Removing an entry
- Comparing entries

LDAP servers can perform three additional operations among themselves:

- Referral
- Replication
- Encryption

Examples

To understand LDAP naming conventions, the distinguished name (DN) for the object representing user Jeff Smith within Active Directory (Microsoft's implementation of an LDAP server) might be:

```
DC=com,DC=Microsoft,OU=Users,CN=Jeff Smith
```

You can read this as

```
Domain = com

Domain = Microsoft

Organizational unit (OU) = Users container

Common Name (CN) of user-type leaf object =
Jeff Smith
```

LDAP Uniform Resource Locators (URLs) are another naming convention that can be used to allow LDAP clients to access objects in an LDAP directory. An LDAP URL is formed by appending the distinguished name of the directory object to the fully qualified DNS domain name (FQDN) of the server containing the LDAP directory. The LDAP URL for referencing the above object would thus be

LDAP://Server7.Microsoft.com/CN=Jeff Smith/OU=Users/DC=Microsoft/DC=com

Marketplace

According to analysts, as of 2000, there were about 1.6 million LDAP servers deployed in enterprises worldwide. This figure is expected to grow to more than 4 million by 2003. The more popular LDAP products on the market include

- Active Directory, Microsoft's LDAP-compliant server that is part of the Microsoft Windows 2000 operating system platform
- iPlanet, formerly Netscape's Directory Server
- eDirectory, Novell's latest version of Novell Directory Services (NDS)
- eTrust, an X.500 directory with LDAP interface from Computer Associates

- Oracle Internet Directory, an LDAP directory built upon the Oracle database platform
- IDDS and Directory Portal, from Innosoft International and Sun Microsystems
- DirX, from Siemens
- Global Directory Server, from Critical Path

There is also an open source LDAP directory called OpenLDAP that is based on the University of Michigan's SLAPD server.

Notes

In Windows 2000, the standard C/C++ LDAP APIs of RFC 1823 are implemented in a library called Wldap32.dll. Applications can programmatically query Active Directory using either Active Directory Services Interface (ADSI), which is implemented as a Component Object Model (COM) interface that is layered on top of the LDAP library, or by employing the LDAP APIs directly.

L

See Also: *Active Directory, directory, Directory Access Protocol (DAP), distinguished name (DN), Uniform Resource Locator (URL), X.500*

Linear Tape Open (LTO)

A high-capacity tape backup technology.

Overview

Linear Tape Open (LTO) was developed in 1998 by a consortium that includes Hewlett-Packard, IBM, and Seagate Technology. LTO is intended to be an open, multivendor tape architecture comparable in speed and capacity to the more proprietary SuperDLT architecture developed by Quantum Corporation. LTO is intended for heterogeneous enterprise networking environments and has been implemented in both stand-alone tape drives and robotic tape libraries.

Architecture

LTO has a native data capacity of up to 100 gigabytes (GB) per tape uncompressed or 200 GB compressed with a standard 2:1 compression ratio. Using a standard single-reel drive architecture, LTO supports data transfer rates of 10–20 megabytes (MB)/sec uncompressed or 20–40 MB/sec compressed. LTO can also be implemented as a dual-reel system that offers the advantage of fast restores—data that is required can be usually retrieved from tape in less than 10 seconds.

Marketplace

More than 30 different storage vendors have licensed the LTO tape format for implementation in their tape backup products. The first vendor to ship an LTO tape library was Exabyte Corporation with their 110L tape library, which has since been replaced by the 221L tape library.

See Also: *backup, tape format*

line booster

A device for connecting peripherals to computers when distances are longer than cabling normally supports.

Overview

Line boosters work by regenerating or boosting the signal strength so you can use longer cables than specifications usually allow. Because the signal strength in a serial or parallel transmission line decreases with the length of the cable being used, line boosters are sometimes needed to connect peripherals to computers when the distances involved exceed normal cabling capabilities.

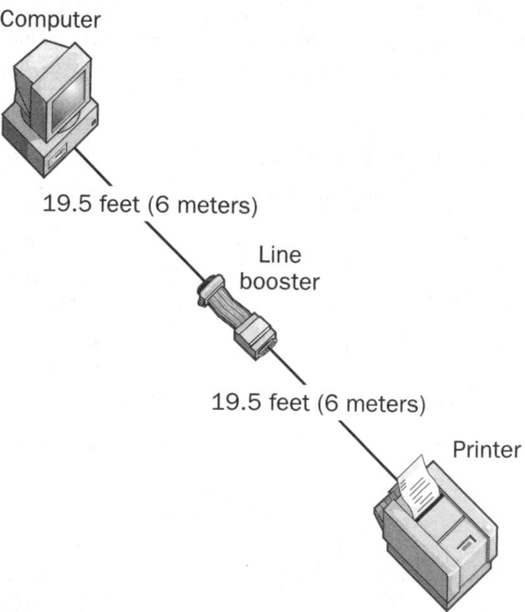

Line booster. *Using a line booster to connect a computer to a printer.*

For example, a typical line booster used with a serial RS-232 interface can generally double the distance over which an attached peripheral can transmit, increasing the limit from 49 feet (15 meters) to 98 feet (30 meters). For parallel printers, line boosters can typically increase allowed distances from 19.5 feet (6 meters) to 40 feet (12 meters).

Notes

When deploying line boosters, be sure to install them at the midway point between the computer and the peripheral, not at one end of the connection.

See Also: RS-232, serial transmission

line coding

Any algorithm for transforming binary information into discrete (digital) signals.

Overview

A line coding mechanism specifies a mathematical relationship between the binary information in a bitstream of data and the square-wave signal variations on the medium the signals are transmitted over. For copper wires, these signals are expressed as time-varying voltages, but on fiber-optic cabling, they are transmitted as discrete light pulses.

Types

Many types of line coding mechanisms are used in computer networking and telecommunication technologies. Some of these schemes are simple to encode and decode but unreliable in their transmission, and others are reliable even in the presence of external noise but require CPU-intensive processing to encode. Selecting the right line coding scheme for a particular technology requires a good understanding of information theory, electromagnetic theory, and engineering.

Encoding schemes are classified into two basic categories: digital signal codes and block codes. Digital signal codes specify the details of how the voltages (or light intensities) vary with time in copper (or fiber-optic) cabling. Common digital signal codes include

- **NRZ:** This stands for Non-Return to Zero and simply means that the discrete electrical signals (or light pulses) use two different voltages (or intensities) but not zero voltage (or intensity). NRZ is employed in serial interfaces such as RS-232 and by many of the block coding schemes described below, including those for Integrated Services Digital Network (ISDN), Fast Ethernet, and Gigabit Ethernet (GbE). NRZ requires that signal pulses all have equal duration with no gaps between them and that the transmitter and receiver be synchronized in order to communicate with each other.
- **NRZI:** This stands for Non-Return to Zero Inverted and uses a transition (either low-high or high-low) to indicate a binary 1, while a lack of transition indicates a zero. This scheme is more reliable than NRZ and requires less power to transmit.
- **Bipolar-AMI:** In this scheme, both a positive and negative pulse represents binary 1 and no pulse indicates a zero. Unlike NRZ and NRZI, there is no DC component to the signal. Bipolar-AMI is easy to synchronize between the transmitter and receiver and a lost pulse can be easily recovered. On the other hand, it requires more power to transmit than NRZ/NRZI.
- **Pseudoternary:** This is just the opposite of Bipolar-AMI and has the same advantages and disadvantages.
- **Manchester encoding:**. This scheme is the one used by standard 10 megabits per second (Mbps) Ethernet. In Manchester encoding, a low-high transition in the middle of a pulse interval represents binary 1 and a high-low transition represents binary zero. This kind of digital signal encoding scheme is known as a biphase scheme and has the advantage that no prior synchronization between transmitter and receiver is required, as in NRZ/NRZI. Manchester encoding is an inefficient scheme that encodes one bit of information into two baud or code bits, but this "wastefulness" actually makes Manchester simple to encode and decode and thus easy to implement in electronic devices. (An encoding scheme that is more efficient in converting bits to baud is said to be "rich," but the downside is that the richer the encoding scheme, the more complex

and processor-intensive the actual encoding mechanism becomes.)

- **Differential Manchester encoding:** This is an offshoot of Manchester encoding in which either a high-low or low-high transition at the start of a pulse indicates binary 1 and no transition indicates binary 0.

By contrast to the digital signal codes above, the following line coding schemes are sometimes called block codings. This is because their purpose is to transform a block of data (collection of bits from a bitstream) into a block of electrical or light pulses. Some common examples of these encoding schemes include

- **4B/5B:** This scheme is used by the 100BaseX form of Fast Ethernet. The name *4B/5B* stands for "4 binary, 5 baud" and indicates in shorthand that four bits of data require five baud or code bits for transmission. The 4B/5B scheme is thus (5-4)/4 = 25% wasteful in terms of bandwidth compared to the (2-1)/1 = 100% wastefulness of Manchester encoding. Another way of describing it is to say that 4B/5B has a coding efficiency of 5/4 = 1.25 baud/bit. The 4B/5B scheme is also used by the Fiber Distributed Data Interface (FDDI) network architecture.
- **5B/6B:** This scheme is used by 100VG-AnyLAN and has a coding efficiency of 1.2 baud/bit.
- **8B/6T:** This scheme is used by the 100BaseT4 form of Fast Ethernet. The name *8B/6T* stands for "8 binary, 6 ternary" and indicates that eight bits of data require six ternary or three-level signals for transmission. By contrast, 4B/5B uses two-level signals in which there are only two voltages, not three, for each signal pulse. The 8B/6T scheme has a coding efficiency of 0.75 baud/bit, which means that more than one bit is crammed into each signal pulse.
- **PAM 5x5:** This is used by 100BaseT2 Fast Ethernet and encodes 4 bits of data into a two-dimensional 5x5 = 25 code point space. This scheme has a coding efficiency of 0.50 baud/bit.
- **8B/10B:** This scheme is used by GbE and Fibre Channel and is patented by IBM. The coding efficiency is 1.25 baud/bit.
- **2B1Q:** This stands for "2 binary, 1 quaternary" and is used by the U interface of the Basic Rate Interface ISDN (BRI-ISDN) flavor of ISDN. The U interface is located at the line termination point at the customer premises, where a two-wire metallic cable terminates with an RJ-11 jack. The 2B1Q encoding scheme is actually used only in the United States, as European ISDN uses a different 4 binary, 3 ternary (4B3T) for BRI-ISDN.
- **B8ZS:** This stands for Bipolar with 8 Zero Substitution and is used by the U interface of the Primary Rate Interface ISDN (PRI-ISDN) flavor of ISDN. The B8ZS encoding scheme is actually used only in the United States, as European ISDN uses a different High Density Bipolar 3 (HDB3) for PRI-ISDN.

Ordinary Binary Transmission

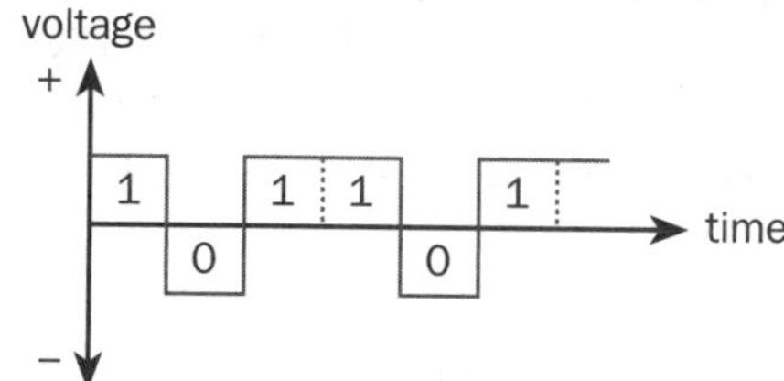

2B1Q Coding

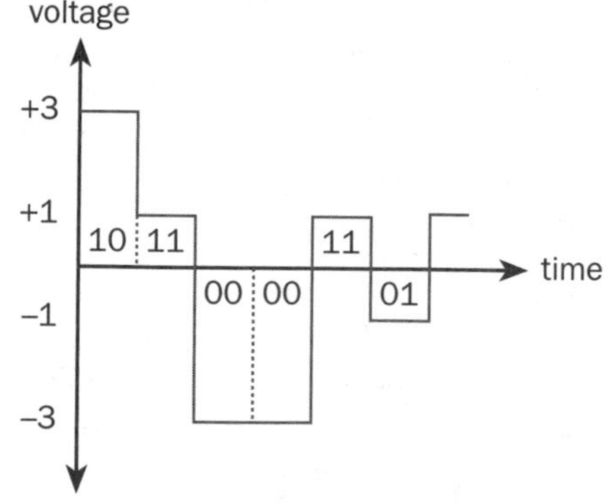

Line coding. *How the 2B1Q line coding scheme works.*

Other schemes include Discrete Multitone (DMT), Carrierless Amplitude/Phase (CAP) modulation, and Quadrature Amplitude Modulation (QAM), all of which are used in various implementations of Asymmetric Digital Subscriber Line (ADSL) communications.

Examples

This example briefly considers one line coding scheme in more detail, namely BRI-ISDN's 2B1Q scheme.

In this scheme, a block of two binary bits can represent four different values: 00, 01, 10, and 11. These four values are mapped to one quaternary value, which is encoded using four different voltages. The first bit represents a positive or negative voltage, and the second bit represents either 1-volt or 3-volt line potential. The following table lists the four possible combinations. The result of using 2B1Q line coding for BRI-ISDN is that a single electrical pulse represents two binary bits instead of one binary bit. This effectively doubles the possible bandwidth of the communication channel, as shown in the illustration on the previous page.

Binary Data and Corresponding Voltage Level for 2B1Q Line Coding

Binary Data Represented	*Voltage of Electrical Pulse*
00	-3
01	-1
10	+3
11	+1

See Also: *100VG-AnyLAN, Asymmetric Digital Subscriber Line (ADSL), Ethernet, Fast Ethernet, Fiber Distributed Data Interface (FDDI), Fibre Channel, Gigabit Ethernet (GbE), Integrated Services Digital Network (ISDN), Manchester coding, signal*

line conditioner

Any device that is used to prevent undesirable electrical signals from damaging computer, networking, or telecommunication equipment and to guard against data loss due to electrical noise, sags, and surges.

Overview

Line conditioners contain circuitry that enables them to filter out noise caused by electromagnetic interference (EMI) and other sources. They typically contain isolation transformers that electrically isolate the circuitry from unwanted DC voltages, impedance-matching circuitry for reducing unwanted signal reflections, and surge suppressors to guard against high-voltage surges (6000 volts or more) caused by lightning strikes and power failures. Line conditioners can also correct sags (drops) in voltages caused by momentary brownouts, but they are not meant to replace or supply power during a power loss. They often include fault indicators and audible alarms.

Line conditioners also ensure that a transmission's signal parameters remain within specifications for the medium or interface being used, even over excessively long or noisy transmission lines. By maintaining signal integrity, line conditioners can thus allow communication devices to function at higher throughput rates than would normally be supported and ensure data integrity over noisy lines. Another common name for line conditioners is line shapers.

Uses

You typically use line conditioners in the following places:

- In power supplies and in uninterruptible power supply (UPS) systems (power conditioners) to protect computers and networking devices from AC surges coming through power lines.
- In local area networks (LANs) to protect hubs, routers, and other networking equipment from EMI and unwanted noise coming through the networking cables and to maintain the integrity of network data signals.
- In offices to protect modems, telephones, fax machines, and other equipment by filtering out electrical surges in phone lines and to reduce noise so that the devices can operate at their nominal throughput speeds.
- In wide area network (WAN) links for protecting Channel Service Unit/Data Service Units (CSU/DSUs) and access servers connected to Integrated Services Digital Network (ISDN), T1, and other copper telecommunication lines against EMI surges. T1 lines must have line conditioners at regular intervals to ensure the integrity of the signal transmitted over the line.

- With high-speed analog modems to enable them to function at their maximum transmission speeds over noisy telephone lines in the local loop.

See Also: *electromagnetic interference (EMI), Integrated Services Digital Network (ISDN), line filter, local loop, modem, T-carrier, uninterruptible power supply (UPS)*

line driver

Any device used to extend the distance over which a signal may be transmitted over a copper or fiber-optic cable.

Overview

A line driver is essentially a combination of a signal converter and an amplifier. The signal converter performs line conditioning, and the amplifier increases the signal strength.

Line drivers allow signals to be carried over a longer distance than the media or transmission interface normally allows. Line drivers are typically used to extend the maximum distance of serial communication protocols such as RS-232, V.35, X.21, and G.703 and can provide either synchronous or asynchronous communication in various vendor implementations.

Uses

A common type of line driver often used in mainframe computing environments is the RS-232 line driver. This device is used to extend the distance over which dumb terminals can be connected to mainframe computers located in different parts of a building or in different buildings on a campus. RS-232 line drivers support synchronous transmission of data over installed four-wire telephone cabling or fiber-optic cabling and are typically deployed on existing twisted-pair phone lines within a building or on custom-installed fiber-optic lines laid between buildings. These line drivers can extend the maximum distance of RS-232 serial transmission from 49 feet (15 meters) to several miles or more.

Another common use for line drivers is in Asymmetric Digital Subscriber Line (ADSL) and T-1 circuits between a customer and a telco central office (CO).

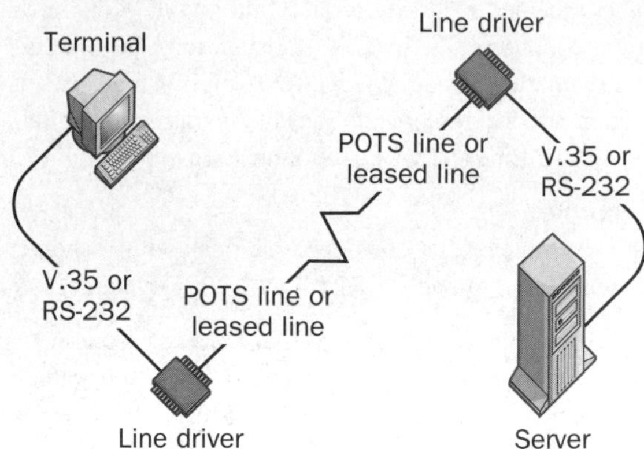

Line driver. *Using a line driver to connect a remote terminal to a server.*

Implementation

Line drivers are always used in pairs. One line driver is placed at the local site and is connected to the client or terminal, and the other is located at the remote site and is connected to the server or mainframe. For intrabuilding connections using line drivers, copper unshielded twisted-pair cabling or the installed telephone lines are typically used. For inter-building connections, fiber-optic cabling is preferred.

Line drivers are available for almost every kind of communication mode, from 19.2-kilobit-per-second (Kbps) RS-232 serial line drivers over 3.5 miles (6 kilometers) to 2-megabits per second (Mbps) single-mode fiber-optic line drivers over 11 miles (18 kilometers). Line drivers can also be used to extend parallel transmission of data from about 20 feet (6 meters) to several miles.

When you use line drivers, be aware that your maximum bandwidth and transmission distance are inversely related—that is, the longer the line, the less bandwidth you have. Considerations for purchasing a line driver include whether it supports full-duplex or half-duplex communication, 2-wire or 4-wire cabling options, and what kinds of connectors are used. Line drivers for customer premises generally are cheaper and have a smaller footprint than those used by service providers such as telcos at the COs.

Notes

For connecting data terminal equipment (DTE) such as two computers, you should use a modem eliminator instead.

See Also: *Asymmetric Digital Subscriber Line (ADSL), modem eliminator, RS-232, T-carrier*

line filter

A device used to suppress noise in a transmission line or cable, caused by electromagnetic interference (EMI).

Overview

EMI is produced by nearby power lines, motors, generators, and other sources. EMI can introduce noise into a transmission line or cable that can degrade a signal's quality or even make communication impossible. By inserting a line filter at the appropriate point, you can suppress the noise and potentially improve transmission speeds.

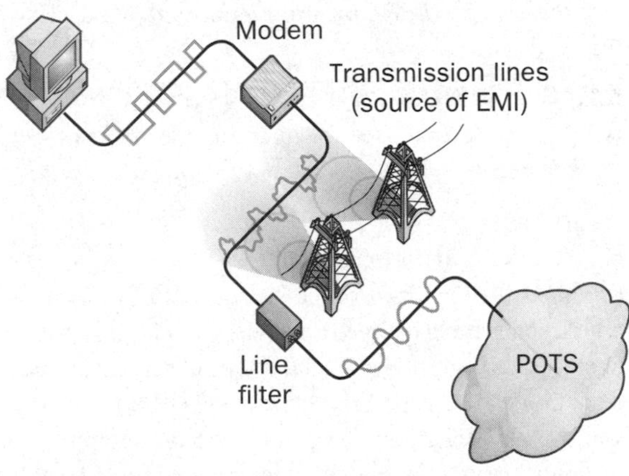

Line filter. *Using a line filter to screen out EMI.*

Line filters are sometimes needed in homes or small businesses that use modems to connect to the Internet through a dial-up connection over the local loop. High-speed V.90 modems sometimes have difficulty attaining their top data transfer speeds because of ambient line noise caused by nearby sources of EMI. By placing a line filter at the customer premises between the modem and the Plain Old Telephone Service (POTS) connection, you can filter out noise, which could improve modem speeds.

Notes

Before installing a line filter, you should use a radio frequency (RF) spectral analyzer to determine the general frequency of the source of EMI so that you can choose an appropriate line filter. Line filters typically filter out one of the following frequency ranges: low frequency (LF), high frequency (HF), very high frequency (VHF), or ultra high frequency (UHF) signals.

See Also: *electromagnetic interference (EMI), line conditioner, modem, Plain Old Telephone Service (POTS)*

Line Printer Daemon (LPD)

The UNIX daemon (background service) used for spooling print jobs.

Overview

Line Printer Daemon (LPD) is a daemon that resides on UNIX print servers. Its function is to simply wait and receive any print jobs submitted from clients using the Line Printer Remote (LPR) protocol. When LPD receives a job, it temporarily stores the job in the print queue, a file system subdirectory. There the job sits waiting to be serviced by LPD. When a print device becomes available, LPD retrieves the job from the queue and sends it to the device for printing.

UNIX sends print jobs to printers as raw data streams—for example, as a Postscript file and does not use print drivers the way Microsoft Windows does. However, sometimes print job formatting is required—for example, when you want to send a plain text file to a postscript printer. In this case, a printer filter is used to properly format the job so the output will not look garbled. Printer filters are specified in a UNIX system file called Printcap.

To view the status of jobs currently waiting in the queue, use the Line Printer Queue (LPQ) utility.

Implementation

Both Windows NT and Windows 2000 support UNIX LPD printing, although it is implemented differently on each platform.

Windows NT Server has an optional LPD service that you configure by installing the Microsoft TCP/IP Printing service. This service enables computers running UNIX to send print jobs to the Windows NT server by using the standard UNIX LPR command. Windows NT servers can also use LPR to submit print jobs to either a Windows NT server running LPD or a UNIX LPD print server. The Microsoft TCP/IP Printing service thus provides printing interoperability between the UNIX and Windows platforms for heterogeneous network environments.

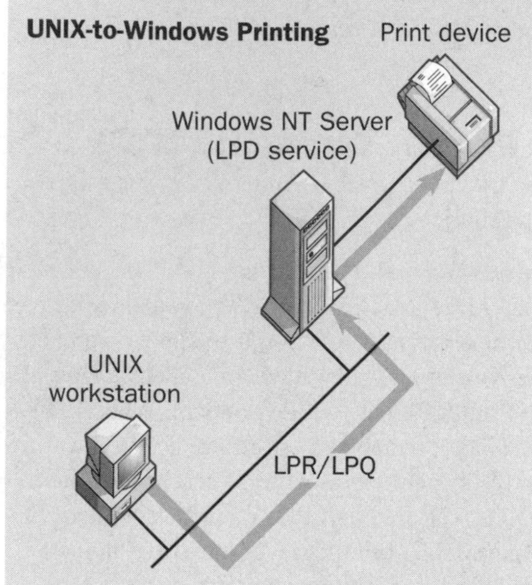

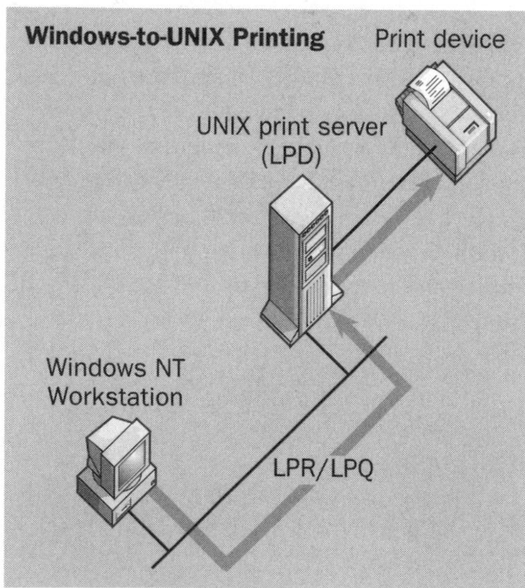

Line Printer Daemon (LPD). *How UNIX-to-Windows and Windows-to-UNIX printing work.*

To support UNIX printing services, Windows 2000 Server and Windows .NET Server employ Microsoft Print Services for UNIX, which provides both LPD and LPR services through two services:

- **LPDSVC:** Runs on the Windows 2000 and Windows .NET Server print servers and receives print jobs from native LPR utilities running on UNIX workstations
- **LPRMON:** Runs on the Windows 2000 and Windows .NET Server print servers and forwards print jobs to native LPD processes running on UNIX computers with attached printers

The startup configuration for the LPD service on Windows 2000 and Windows .NET Server is set to Manual by default and should be changed to Automatic if this feature is used.

See Also: *daemon, Line Printer Queue (LPQ), Line Printer Remote (LPR), printing terminology, UNIX*

Line Printer Queue (LPQ)

A UNIX command used for querying the status of a print queue.

Overview

On the UNIX platform, print jobs are submitted to print servers using the Line Printer Remote (LPR) command, which sends them to the print queue to wait for spooling to an available print device. UNIX print servers employ a daemon called Line Printer Daemon (LPD), which waits in the background for print jobs to be submitted to the queue from LPR clients. It is often useful to be able to examine the queue to determine which jobs are still waiting for spooling—the LPQ command does just that. You can use the LPQ command on a UNIX platform to determine

- What jobs are waiting for spooling in the print queue
- Who submitted these jobs to the print server
- Which print device each job is destined for

Examples

The LPQ command displays a list of files on the server that are waiting to be printed, along with associated information. For example, the lpq -S Foxhound -P Laser12 command might be used to display the status of the print queue called Laser12 on a UNIX print server named Foxhound. Alternatively, Foxhound might be a Microsoft Windows NT server with the Microsoft TCP/IP Printing service installed, or a Windows 2000 server with Microsoft Print Services for UNIX installed. Both of these Windows platforms support UNIX LPD printing as an optional feature.

See Also: daemon, Line Printer Daemon (LPD), Line Printer Remote (LPR), printing terminology, UNIX

Line Printer Remote (LPR)

A UNIX networks command used to submit print jobs to print servers.

Overview

Line Printer Remote (LPR) is the standard protocol for submitting print jobs to print servers. On the UNIX platform, print servers use the Line Printer Daemon (LPD), a service that runs in the background waiting for print jobs to be received. When LPD receives a job, it temporarily places it in a queue. When a print device becomes available, the job is spooled or moved from the queue to the print device for printing. Note that files to be printed using LPR must be either text files or files specially formatted for the printer being used (for example, a PostScript file for a PostScript printer).

LPR is a Transmission Control Protocol/Internet Protocol (TCP/IP) protocol defined in RFC 1179 and is implemented on all UNIX platforms and on Linux. Microsoft Windows NT and Windows 2000 can also use LPR by installing optional components to support UNIX printing. In UNIX implementations, LPR connections (both inbound and outbound) are formed only on TCP ports 721 through 731. On Windows 2000 and on Windows NT 4 service pack 3 or later, however, LPR may use any port in the range 512 through 1023.

Examples

To print the file Readme.txt using the print queue called Laser12 on an LPD print server named Lazyboy, you would use the command lpr -S Lazyboy -P Laser12 readme.txt.

See Also: daemon, Line Printer Daemon (LPD), Line Printer Queue (LPQ), printing terminology, UNIX

line sharer

Any device that allows multiple devices to share the same communications line.

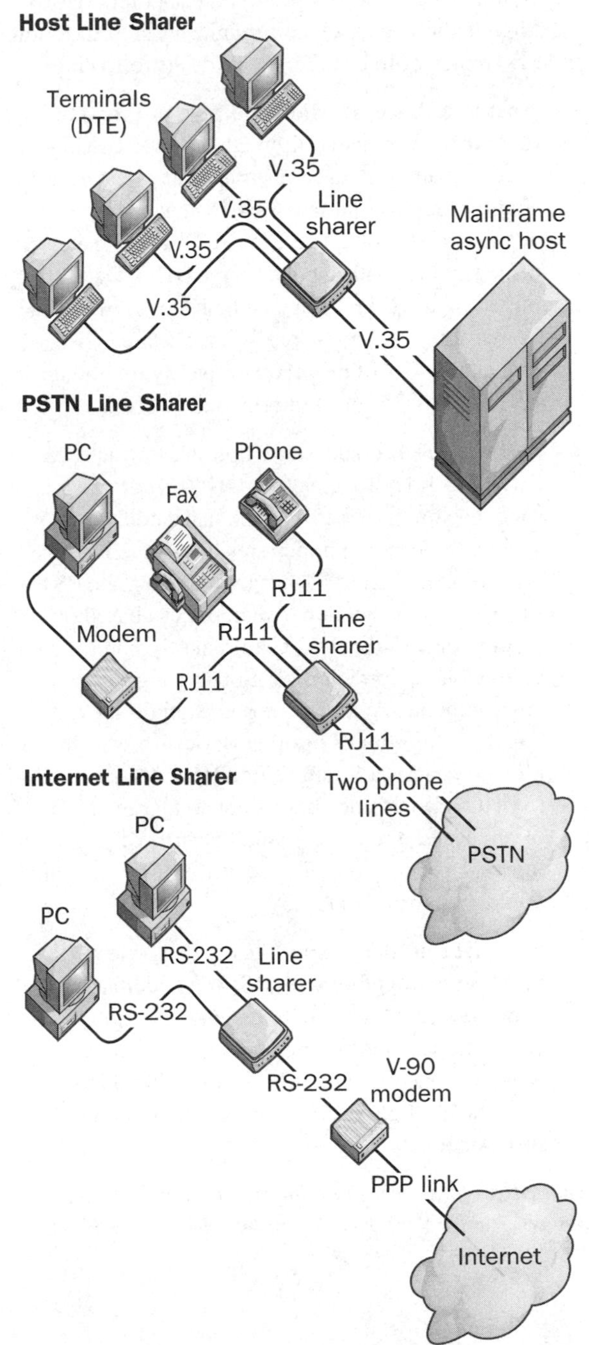

Line sharer. *Three varieties of line sharer.*

Overview

Many different types of devices function as line sharers. These vary from those used in mainframe computing environments to customer premises equipment (CPE) used in telephony and telecommunications. Some common examples of line sharers include the following:

- **Host line sharers:** Allow multiple terminals or other data terminal equipment (DTE) to be connected to an asynchronous mainframe host over a single, shared serial transmission line using V.35 adapters and cable. You can use host line sharers primarily to broadcast data to the DTEs. Data transmitted by the DTEs can also be buffered in the line sharer until the line is free and the data can be sent to the host. Host line sharers typically use either RS-232 or V.35 serial interface connections.
- **PSTN line sharers:** Allow multiple Public Switched Telephone Network (PSTN) devices, such as phones, fax machines, and modems, to share one or more phone lines by using RJ11 connectors and adapters. You can often program PSTN line sharers to switch between devices based on calling tones, so that you can remotely control data collection equipment over modems in industrial environments. A small line sharer might let you connect four phones or other devices to two shared phone lines for a Small Office/Home Office (SOHO). Other line sharers connect large numbers of phones to a relatively small number of phone lines on a first-come, first-served basis in modem-pooling environments.
- **Internet line sharers:** Typically stand-alone devices that together with RS-232 modem adapters allow several PCs to share one modem for dial-up connection to the Internet. Internet line sharers typically use one Internet Protocol (IP) address to allow multiple users to browse the Internet simultaneously.

See Also: *data terminal equipment (DTE), Internet access, Public Switched Telephone Network (PSTN), RS-232, V.35*

line sharing

An emerging telco technology for speeding up Digital Subscriber Line (DSL) provisioning.

Overview

In the aftermath of the Telecommunications Act of 1996, new companies known as Competitive Local Exchange Carriers (CLECs) have entered the marketplace. These CLECs frequently focus on provisioning DSL services to residential customers requiring high speed Internet access and to business customers as an alternative wide area network (WAN) technology to traditional (and expensive) leased lines. Because Incumbent Local Exchange Carriers (ILECs) such as Regional Bell Operating Companies (RBOCs) actually own the local loop wiring that enters homes and offices, however, CLECs have been forced to either resell DSL services from ILECs (the ILEC provisions the line for DSL) or request that the ILEC lay down an additional separate line to provision DSL to the customer.

Line sharing is an emerging approach that speeds up the provisioning process without incurring the cost of additional lines or leasing DSL from ILECs. In a line sharing scenario, a splitter is installed at the customer premises end of the existing local loop connection and at the telco central office (CO), separating DSL data transmission from voice traffic. In other words, both voice and DSL are carried on the same existing telephone line, but each is managed by a different carrier: DSL service by the CLEC and voice by the ILEC. No disruption in phone service occurs, and the cost to the ILEC is negligible, while the CLEC saves costs that can be passed on to the consumers.

Prospects

Line sharing is expected to breathe new life into the beleaguered CLEC marketplace and to allow for more aggressive rollouts of DSL to bring broadband Internet access to customers who need it. Several CLECs and ILECs have already formed agreements to implement this technology, and state regulators are holding hearings to set appropriate pricing policies.

See Also: *Competitive Local Exchange Carrier (CLEC), Digital Subscriber Line (DSL), local* *exchange carrier (LEC), Regional Bell Operating Company (RBOC), wide area network (WAN)*

Link Access Protocol, D-channel (LAPD)

The data-link layer protocol for D channel communications in Integrated Services Digital Network (ISDN).

Overview

ISDN uses two separate channels for communication: a D channel for signaling and control and one or more B channels for data transfer. As shown in the table, these different channels use different protocols at the data-link and network layers of the Open Systems Interconnection (OSI) reference model. Link Access Protocol, D-channel (LAPD) is the data-link protocol for the D channel and is defined by the Q.921 specification from the International Telecommunication Union (ITU).

ISDN Protocols for Bottom Three OSI Layers

OSI Layer	*B Channel*	*D Channel*
Physical layer	ITU's I.430 (Basic Rate Interface, BRI) or I.431 (Primary Rate Interface, PRI)	ITU's I.430 (BRI) or I.431 (PRI)
Data-link layer	High-level Data Link Control/Point-to-Point Protocol (HDLC)/PPP)	LAPD (Q.921)
Network layer	Internet Protocol/ Internetwork Packet Exchange (IP/IPX)	Q.931

Architecture

LAPD provides full-duplex transmission over synchronous serial links and supports both point-to-point and point-to-multipoint communications links. LAPD also supports multiplexing of multiple logical channels over a single physical D channel.

LAPD frames always begin with a standard flag (binary 01111110) to identify the start of the frame. This is followed by a 2-byte address that identifies the ISDN device transmitting the frame, a 1-byte or 2-byte control field, variable-length octet-aligned data payload, and a 2-byte frame check sequence (FCS).

See Also: *data-link layer, D channel, full-duplex, Integrated Services Digital Network (ISDN), multiplexing, Open Systems Interconnection (OSI) reference model, serial transmission, synchronous transmission*

link aggregation

Any technology for combining multiple physical data links into a single logical link.

Overview

Link aggregation occurs at Layer 2 (the data-link layer) of the Open Systems Interconnection (OSI) reference model. The basic idea is to combine two or more data-link connections into a single fat logical connection. An aggregated link has several advantages over a single physical link:

- **Scalability:** If demand for bandwidth increases, another physical link can simply be added to the logical bundle. Likewise, if demand for bandwidth decreases, a physical link can be deallocated from the aggregation and assigned elsewhere as needed.
- **Fault tolerance:** If one physical link goes down in a logical bundle, there is no interruption in transmission, just a reduction in allowed bandwidth. Link aggregation is also a useful way of implementing redundancy on point-to-point connections.
- **Load balancing:** Links from several sources can be load balanced by combining them into a single logical pipe.

Link aggregation is also known sometimes as port aggregation or trunking in vendor literature.

Uses

Link aggregation has two main uses in the enterprise:

- Increasing throughput of switch-switch connections in collapsed backbones.
- Combining data streams from multiple network interface cards (NICs) on a multihomed server into a single logical network connection.

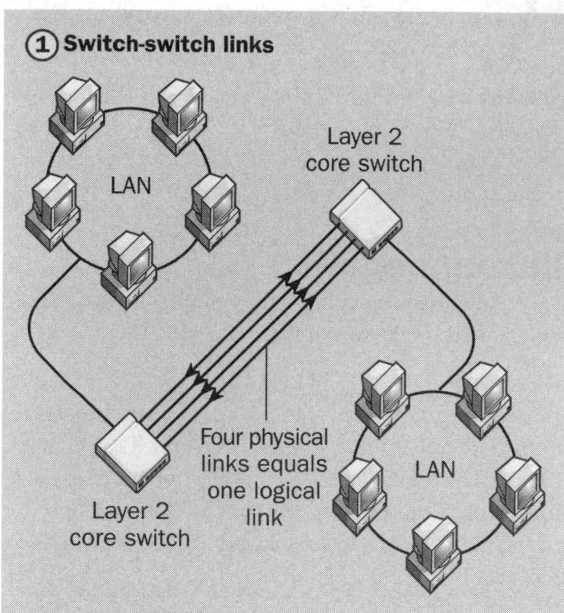

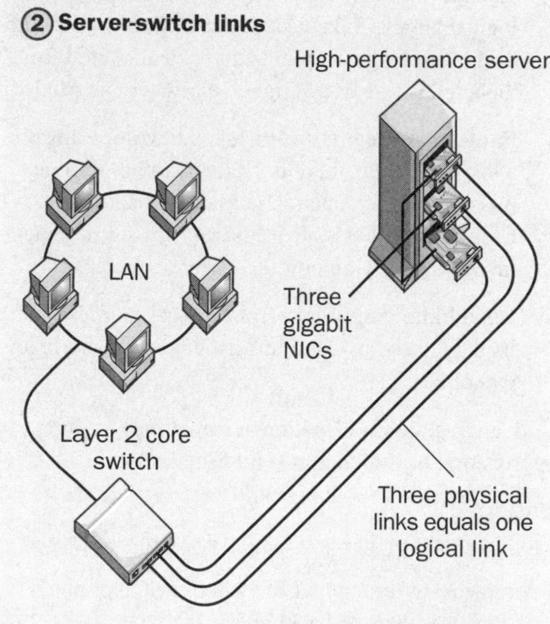

Link aggregation. *Two uses for link aggregation in the enterprise.*

Implementation

Early implementations of link (or port) aggregation were vendor-specific technologies that required solutions to be built and deployed using technologies from a single source. Examples of proprietary Layer 2 link aggregation technologies include

- Cisco Systems' proprietary Fast EtherChannel (FEC) and Giga EtherChannel (GEC) technologies, which enable up to four full-duplex Fast Ethernet or Gigabit Ethernet (GbE) links to be combined into a single logical link having throughputs of 800 megabits per second (Mbps) or 8 gigabits per second (Gbps). FEC and GEC employ Cisco's proprietary Port Aggregation Protocol (PagP) to automate the process of discovering and configuring link aggregation.
- Cisco's proprietary Inter-Switch Link (ISL) trunking technology, which allows link aggregation across Cisco Catalyst switches.
- Adaptec's proprietary Duralink port aggregation technology.

Prospects

Proprietary link aggregation technologies and interoperability problems are soon to be a thing of the past as vendors implement the new Institute of Electrical and Electronics Engineers (IEEE) 802.3ad standard, which defines a vendor-neutral approach to port aggregation. As more vendors implement this new standard in switching and NIC technologies, enterprise network architects will be able to aggregate links across equipment from different vendors.

See Also: *802.3ab, data-link layer, Ethernet switch, Fast Ethernet, Gigabit Ethernet (GbE)*

Link Control Protocol (LCP)

The portion of Point-to-Point Protocol (PPP) responsible for link management.

Overview

The Link Control Protocol (LCP) operates at the data-link layer (Layer 2) of the Open Systems Interconnection (OSI) reference model and is responsible for opening and closing PPP connections and negotiating their configuration.

During session establishment, LCP establishes the link, configures PPP options, and tests the quality of the line connection between the PPP client and PPP server.

Architecture

During the negotiation phase, LCP handles four main functions: authentication, callback, compression, and multilink establishment. After a PPP link has been established at the physical layer and a modulation method selected, the client must then be authenticated. Different authentication protocols are supported for satisfying the security needs of different networking environments. LCP can negotiate the following authentication protocols:

- **Password Authentication Protocol (PAP):** Transmits passwords in clear text using a two-way handshake
- **Shiva PAP (SPAP):** A vendor-specific implementation of PAP
- **Challenge Handshake Authentication Protocol (CHAP):** Passes a password hash using a three-way handshake and is more secure than PAP or SPAP
- **Microsoft Challenge Handshake Authentication Protocol (MS-CHAP):** Microsoft Corporation's implementation of CHAP, which is more secure than regular CHAP

Once an authentication method has been negotiated that is understood by both the PPP client and server and the client has been successfully authenticated by the server, the next phase is callback. This phase is optional and allows the client to request that the server hang up and call it back to ensure greater security or to reverse billing charges. After callback is complete, the next phase is compression. This phase is also optional and a variety of different compression algorithms are supported, including Predictor, Stacker, Microsoft Point-to-Point Compression (MPPC), and Transmission Control Protocol (TCP) header compression. The final phase of LCP is aggregation of multiple PPP links using Multilink PPP (MPPP). This last phase is also optional.

See Also: *Challenge Handshake Authentication Protocol (CHAP), Multilink Point-to-Point Protocol (MPPP), Password Authentication Protocol (PAP), Point-to-Point Protocol (PPP)*

link state routing algorithm

An algorithm for dynamic routing that was designed to address scalability limitations of distance-vector routing protocols.

Overview

The first dynamic routing protocols were based on the distance-vector routing algorithm, which required that routers periodically advertise their routing tables to neighboring routers. Routing protocols such as Routing Information Protocol (RIP) that are based on the distance-vector algorithm suffer from two main problems: large amounts of routing updates, which consume valuable network traffic, and slow convergence, which results in an inability to scale to large internetworks.

As a result of these problems, the link state routing algorithm was developed. Routing protocols that use link state include

- **Open Shortest Path First (OSPF):** This is the main link state protocol in use today and can be used to build large IP internetworks.
- **NetWare Link Services Protocol (NLSP):** This is a legacy protocol used on Internetwork Packet Exchange (IPX) networks but not much used anymore.
- **Intermediate System to Intermediate System (IS-IS):** This is not much used anymore.

Architecture

Link state routers advertise changes in network topology to other routers using link state packets (LSPs). The router advertises these LSPs only when changes occur in the network—for example, a router going down or a new router being brought up. When a network change occurs, LSPs are sent to all routers everywhere on the network, not just to neighboring routers as in distance-vector routing.

Using the LSPs a router receives from other routers on the network, link state routers use the Shortest Path First (SPF) algorithm to construct a logical tree that represents the topology of the entire network based on the local router as the root of the tree. The router then uses this tree to calculate the optimal paths to different parts of the network and populates routes in its internal routing table with this information. Every link state router on a network thus knows the exact router topology of the entire network.

Comparison of Link State and Distance Vector Routing Protocols

Link State	*Distance Vector*
Fast convergence	Slow convergence
Highly scalable	Small to mid-sized networks only
Broadcasts entire routing table	Broadcasts link status information
Sends updates periodically	Sends updates only when a change occurs to the network
Views network from perspective of itself	Views network from perspective of neighbors
Calculates optical routes based on lowest metric	Calculates optimal routes based on least cost factors, including hops, segment speeds, and traffic flow patterns

L

Advantages and Disadvantages

Link state routing protocols have several advantages over distance-vector protocols:

- Faster convergence
- Better scalability
- Less traffic due to router updates

On the other hand, there are some issues with link state protocols:

- They are more processor-intensive and memory-intensive in their operation, hence routers using link state are usually more expensive.
- They are more complex to configure than distance-vector routing protocols.
- When several link state routers start up, there can be a large amount of network traffic associated with router discovery, a problem called link state flooding. This can temporarily saturate the network and make other communications impossible.
- If LSPs are not synchronized properly, it is possible for routers to acquire wrong or incomplete link state information, causing black holes and other routing problems. Most link state routers now use time stamps and sequence numbers to ensure that convergence occurs properly.

Notes

Link state routing protocols are classless routing protocols, a feature that enhances their scalability by allowing discontiguous subnets and variable length subnet masks (VLSMs) to be employed to reduce the amount of interrouter traffic propagated on the network.

See Also: *distance vector routing algorithm, dynamic routing protocol, NetWare protocols, Open Shortest Path First (OSPF), Routing Information Protocol (RIP), routing protocol*

Linux

An open-source UNIX-like operating system.

Overview

Linux is a Portable Operating System Interface for UNIX (POSIX)–compliant operating system that is freely available from numerous sites on the Internet. Linux is available on a large number of hardware platforms including Intel, Alpha, MIPS, PowerPC, Sparc, and even IBM S/390 mainframe. Linux provides a multiuser multitasking operating system environment that supports symmetric multiprocessing (SMP) and clustering. The platform supports a wide range of file systems and standard architecture features such as interprocess communications (IPCs), remote procedures calls (RPCs), and dynamic and shared libraries.

History

Linux was developed in 1991 by Linus Torvalds, a student at the University of Helsinki in Finland. The platform's name is a contraction of Linus and UNIX and reflects the similarity between Linux and the UNIX operating system. Unlike UNIX, however, Linux was released under the GNU Public License (GPL) as open source software whose underlying code base is shared openly. Under this license, others can share in the Linux development process, and a whole community has arisen whose job is to refine and evolve Linux into a better and more powerful platform. Development of the standard Linux kernel development tree, however, is still controlled by Torvalds himself.

The first distribution of Linux to appear was Slackware, which became available in 1993. A distribution is typically a package that contains the Linux kernel and supporting modules, the GNU C/C++ compiler, Xfree86, or some other freeware version of the X Windows graphical interface, the Apache web server, various applications and tools, an installer, and source code for everything. Version 1 of the Linux kernel appeared in 1994. Since that time, the kernel has gone through several revisions and now stands at version 2.4.

Uses

Linux has found a niche in many companies for specific server-based needs, including Web servers, mail gateways, file servers, and Domain Name System (DNS) name servers. Although the fact that Linux is free would seem to make it an appealing solution for companies wanting to build out their server infrastructure while saving money, many companies have been reluctant until recently to embrace Linux in their mission-critical operations. Reasons for this reluctance have included the lack of a single company responsible for the platform's development and support, as well as the fact that trained Linux professionals are in high demand and are thus difficult and expensive to hire. Recently, however, Linux has consolidated its toehold in large companies through developments such as the appearance of easy-to-install Linux distributions such as Red Hat and Caldera, and through system management software that allows large numbers of Linux servers to be remotely managed from a central console. For example, companies such as Google.com have successfully deployed up to 5000 Linux servers to provide Internet services. Although the low cost of Linux distributions would seem an inducement to deploying Linux in a corporate environment, most IT (information technology) departments carefully weigh this against the cost of supporting and administering a Linux environment before choosing to deploy Linux servers.

Linux on the desktop is less visible in the enterprise than Linux on the server end. Reasons for this include a lack of device drivers (improved universal serial bus [USB] support is provided in current release 2.4 of the Linux kernel), lack of support for running widely used business applications such as Microsoft Office (even though Win4Lin from NeTraverse allows you to run a Microsoft Windows 98 emulator on a Linux box and the StarOffice suite from Sun Microsystems is also available for Linux), lack of implementers and administrators skilled in the Linux platform, limited support from commercial vendors (even though Red Hat has set an example of how a vendor can base a business on services and support of the Linux platform), and the slow desktop upgrade cycle of large IT departments. Some analysts estimate that Linux had less than 2 percent of the client operating system market in 2000, though it has passed the Apple Macintosh platform and now holds second place behind the dominant desktop platform, Microsoft Windows. Corel Corporation's departure from the Linux desktop market was probably another setback to Linux on the desktop; the fact that there are two competing Linux desktop environments, K Desktop Environment (KDE) and GNU Network Object Model Environment (GNOME), may be another.

Another tree of Linux platform development targets the embedded device space, where Linux's small footprint is an advantage. For example, Red Hat has developed a set of Linux APIs called EL/IX that can run Linux and applications having 32 kilobytes (KB) memory.

Architecture

The core of the Linux operating system is the kernel. Linux is built on a modular (as opposed to monolithic) kernel architecture, which enables custom kernels to be built using subsystem modules, device drivers, and protocol stacks. The Linux kernel follows two different development trees:

- **Odd-numbered versions:** Kernel builds having odd numbers such as 2.1, 2.3, and so on are development (experimental) builds. These are used for trying out new features of Linux and are generally not recommended for use in production systems.
- **Even-numbered builds:** These are builds intended for production systems and are tested until they are believed to be stable. Recent examples include versions 2.2 and 2.4.

Features of the most recent Linux kernel (version 2.4) include

- Improved symmetric multiprocessing (SMP) that supports up to 32 processors on Intel x86 servers and scales better than previous kernel versions
- Up to 64 gigabytes (GB) of addressable physical memory
- Support for large file systems up to terabytes of stored data
- Kernel-level Web daemon called kHTTPd that provides high-performance delivery of static Web pages
- Support for Intel's 64-bit Itanium (IA-64) processor architecture
- Support for Network File System (NFS) version 3
- Logical Volume Manager (LVM) that improves how files and volumes are handled
- Improved USB support

Marketplace

Although the core Linux platform is freely available for download from various places on the Internet, Linux is also available as commercial Linux distributions from a number of companies, including Red Hat, Caldera International, SuSE, Turbolinux, Debian, and many others. Some distributions include special tools or other "value-adds" to meet specific needs of enterprise users. For example, Turbolinux includes its TurboCluster tools for building clustering solutions, Red Hat Linux includes Red Hat PowerTools to enable administrators to remotely manage servers, and VALinux Systems provides vendor-neutral turnkey Linux systems. Both the Red Hat and Helixcode distributions have proved popular for deploying Linux on the desktop.

A thin-client version of Linux is also available from Neoware Systems and is designed for use in devices such as firewall appliances, smart card readers, and cash registers. This platform is called NeoLinux and is a customized version of Red Hat Linux. Korea's LG Electronics has a Linux tablet PC called Digital iPad, and Linux Personal Digital Assistants (PDAs) are also available. Linux also forms the basis for a number of server appliance platforms, such as the 1U rack-mountable Qube2 and RaQ 4r server appliances from Cobalt Networks. Preconfigured Linux servers are available from Penguin Computing and also from large vendors such as Compaq Computer Corporation and Dell Computer Corporation.

Linux on the mainframe is one new development that has given Linux greater credibility as an enterprise-class operating system. IBM's S/390 platform can run thousands of Linux virtual machines (VMs) on a single mainframe and provides significant cost savings over running Linux on thousands of separate PCs instead. A side effect of this is that stodgy old mainframes are now viewed as a cutting-edge platform for application development, giving a boost to the badly sagging mainframe market.

The most popular server-side applications for the Linux platform are probably the Apache Web server (still used by more than half of all public Web sites) and Samba, a program than enables a Linux server to provide file and print services to other platforms such as Windows and Apple Macintosh. Popular open-source network monitoring tools for Linux include NetSaint and Multi-Router Traffic Grapher (MRTG). Caldera International has released a systems management platform called Volution that allows secure remote administration of thousands of Linux servers and desktops. Volution employs a standard Web browser interface; uses a Lightweight Directory Access Protocol (LDAP)-compliant directory service for storing system object information; provides remote installation, inventory, and monitoring services; and supports policy-based and profile-based management similar to Microsoft's Active Directory directory service and Novell's ZENworks platforms.

Prospects

Some of the largest players in the enterprise computing market have embraced Linux to various degrees. Examples include IBM, Oracle Corporation, Sun Microsystems, Hewlett-Packard, and others. IBM has ported their DB2 Universal Database, WebSphere Application

Server e-commerce platform, and Lotus Notes groupware to Linux. Hewlett-Packard has done many Linux deployments, including running SAP AG's Enterprise Resource Planning (ERP) software on Linux. Compaq, Dell, and Hewlett-Packard all offer pre-installed Linux systems for customers who request it. And Oracle has ported its Oracle 8i database platform to Linux.

IBM's commitment to supporting the Linux platform is probably the biggest development in the Linux story. IBM has demonstrated a 512-node cluster running Linux at the Albuquerque High Performance Computing Center in New Mexico and has built in support for Linux using the SuSE distribution across its full range of computing platforms, from PC servers to its S/390 and zSeries mainframes.

Linux's most significant impact on the enterprise networking scene will probably be the displacement of most versions of the UNIX operating system by Linux. Industry analysts indicate that Linux is already outselling all versions of UNIX combined. Although Windows has firmly established itself as the market leader in application server platforms and is indisputably king of the desktop, Linux is likely to establish itself and remain the number two player in the server arena due to its entrenched use in specific niches of enterprise networking such as DNS name servers, public Web servers, and a few other popular applications.

Notes

An application that runs on one Linux distribution may not automatically run on another, as there are small differences between where different distributions store key system files and other issues. The Linux Development Platform Specification (LDPS) developed by the Linux Standard Base (LSB) project is expected to reduce these interoperability problems by ensuring that an application developed for one distribution runs on others.

The U.S. government, through the National Security Agency (NSA), is also developing a hardened version of Linux called Security-Enhanced Linux. This version will include mandatory access controls for type enforcement and role-based access.

For More Information

A good general source of Linux information is Linux Online at *www.linux.org.* Advanced Linux users can visit Linux Journal at *www.linuxjournal.com.* A popular event for Linux users is LinuxWorld, found at *www.linuxworldexpo.com.*

See Also: *Apache, GNU General Public License (GPL), GNU Object Modeling Environment (GNOME), K Desktop Environment (KDE), open source, POSIX, UNIX*

list server

A program that allows people to subscribe to an e-mail mailing list.

Overview

Organizations typically set up list servers for facilitating the discussion of marketing issues, asking and receiving answers from technical support, announcing new products and services, disseminating tips and tricks for using software, and similar activities. To use a list, users must first subscribe to the list using a special e-mail command, although nowadays many lists also have Web interfaces for doing things such as subscribing, unsubscribing, posting messages, and receiving help. Once a user successfully subscribes to the list, the user generally receives a copy of every message posted to the list, and every message the user posts is distributed to all members of the list. Other common list options include receiving daily collections of messages compacted into a single message and accessing archives of old messages.

Marketplace

Two common list server programs are Listserv and Majordomo. Of these, Listserv is the older and was originally developed for the BITNET/EARN network.

Notes

Do not subscribe to too many mailing lists, because the e-mail traffic might clog up your mailbox.

For More Information

Search CataList, the official catalog of LISTSERV lists at *www.lsoft.com/catalist.html.*

LLC layer

Stands for logical link control layer, a sublayer of the data-link layer in the Open Systems Interconnection (OSI) reference model.

See: *logical link control (LLC) layer*

LMDS

Stands for Local Multipoint Distribution Service, an emerging broadband wireless service with speeds up to 155 megabits per second (Mbps).

See: *Local Multipoint Distribution Service (LMDS)*

lmhosts file

A file used to resolve NetBIOS computer names into Internet Protocol (IP) addresses.

Overview

Lmhosts is a text file that provides a local method for name resolution of remote NetBIOS names into their respective IP addresses on a Transmission Control Protocol/Internet Protocol (TCP/IP) network. Using lmhosts files is an alternative to using WINS servers for name resolution on Microsoft Windows–based networks. Using a WINS server is generally preferable because it reduces administrative overhead.

The lmhosts file contains mappings for hosts on remote networks only. Mappings are not required for hosts on local networks because these can be resolved using broadcasts. If you are using lmhosts files to resolve NetBIOS names on a network, each computer on the network should have an lmhosts file.

Examples

Each line in the lmhosts file contains the IP address of a NetBIOS computer on the network, followed by the NetBIOS name of the computer. The computer name can be followed by optional prefixes that identify domains and domain controllers and allow entries to be loaded into the NetBIOS name cache at startup. Comments are prefixed with the pound sign (#). Here is an example taken from the sample lmhosts file included with Windows 98:

```
102.54.94.97    rhino      #PRE  #DOM:networking
#net group's DC
102.54.94.123   popular    #PRE  #source server
102.54.94.117   localsrv   #PRE  #needed for
                                 the include
```

You can find the lmhosts file in the %SystemRoot%\system32\drivers\etc directory in Windows NT, Windows 2000, Windows XP, Windows .NET Server, and in the \Windows directory in Windows 95 and Windows 98.

Notes

Place the NetBIOS names that need to be resolved most frequently near the top of the lmhosts file because the file is parsed linearly from the beginning.

See Also: *hosts file, Networks file, protocol file, services file*

load balancing

The process of distributing client connections across multiple servers.

Overview

Load balancing is a technique used to increase the reliability of server-based computing. In a typical load balancing scenario, incoming client requests are redirected to different servers on a server farm. The way in which redirection occurs varies with product and implementation, as in the following examples:

- **Round robin:** This method passes each incoming request to the next server in a series. When the final server is reached, the next request is passed to the first server of the series. Each server in a round-robin load balancing scenario receives an equal number of client connections averaged over time.
- **Weighted:** This form of load balancing employs a cost metric to determine how many client connections to direct to each server. For example, if server A has weight 10 and server B has weight 5, twice as many incoming requests will be redirected to server A than server B.
- **Least connected:** In this scenario, incoming requests are forwarded to the server that currently has the fewest number of connections.
- **Fastest:** Here requests are simply directed to the server that responds the quickest.

Uses

The primary use for load balancing in today's networks is in Web server farms. Load balancing increases the reliability of these farms for e-commerce applications by ensuring that user demand can be accommodated for and failure of any one server will not affect the application's overall functioning. The following figure illustrates a typical implementation of Web farm load balancing using a hardware load-balancing device such as Cisco LocalDirector (described later in this article).

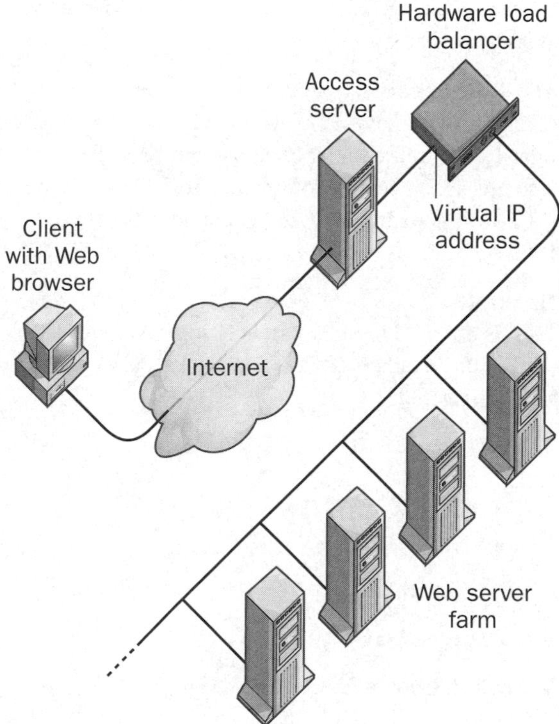

Load balancing. *Using load balancing to increase reliability of a Web server farm.*

The biggest issue with Web server load balancing is ensuring that applications that employ persistent connections (a session that spans multiple Hypertext Transfer Protocol [HTTP] requests) work properly. Most modern Web server load balancers accomplish this by using sticky sessions, in which a request that is part of a session already opened is directed to the server in the farm that previously serviced it.

Other newer approaches to Web server load balancing on the market today include

- **Layer 4 load balancing:** Uses Layer 4 switches to ensure persistent HTTP connections are maintained between a client and a server having a specific Internet Protocol (IP) address and port.
- **Layer 5 (or Layer 4/5 or Layer 4/7) load balancing:** Similar to Layer 4 load balancing but includes the capability of differentiating traffic on the basis of Uniform Resource Locators (URLs), not just IP addresses and ports. This approach is sometimes called URL parsing, Web directing, and a dozen other vendor-specific names.

Implementation

The oldest form of load balancing is called Round Robin DNS and takes advantage of a feature of Domain Name System (DNS) name server that allows it to map multiple IP addresses to a single fully qualified domain name (FQDN). The main problem with this approach is that the name server directs clients to different servers without any regard to the availability of those servers. For example, if a server in the farm suddenly goes down, the name server has no way of knowing this and continues to redirect client requests to that server as it goes through the round-robin procedure. Because of this weakness, round-robin load balancing is seldom used anymore.

Hardware-based load balancers are more popular and are typically routers or switches that use application-specific integrated circuits (ASICs) to distribute load quickly and effectively to hundreds or even thousands of connected servers. In a typical scenario, a hardware load balancer will be assigned a "virtual" IP address while the real IP addresses of servers in the farm are hidden behind the load balancer. To the outside world, the farm of servers appears as a single server with a single IP address, the address of the load balancer. Hardware-based load balancers are expensive but provide best performance, and analysts estimate that they own over 60 percent of the load balancer market. Some newer hardware load balancers are better classified as network appliances than switches or routers due to their packaged functionality and ease of use.

Software-based load balancers are rising in popularity and consist of a load-balancing application that is installed on a standard PC or UNIX host. Software-based load balancers are slower than hardware-based ones and typically support only a few dozen servers, but they are cheaper and are an attractive solution for many e-businesses.

Marketplace

The first and still most popular hardware-based load balancer is the LocalDirector from Cisco Systems. LocalDirector sits in front of your server farm and bridges incoming traffic between the external network and the local area network (LAN) segment on which the servers all reside. If you need to load balance servers from several different sites or local area network (LAN) segments, you can use LocalDirector in conjunction with another Cisco product, DistributedDirector, to accomplish this. Other examples of hardware load balancers include ServerIron from Foundry Networks, BIG/ip and Edge-FX Local Cache Cluster from F5 Networks, and products from Alteon WebSystems (acquired by Nortel Networks in 2000), ArrowPoint Communications (now part of Cisco), Coyote Point Systems, and many others.

A popular software-based load balancing solution is Microsoft Corporation's network Load Balancing Service (NLBS), a feature that comes with Microsoft Windows 2000 Advanced Server and replaces the Windows Load Balancing Service (WLBS) of Windows NT 4 Enterprise Edition. NLBS can load balance up to 32 servers and provides basic load balancing functionality at a price anyone can afford (it is free with the Windows 2000 Advanced Server operating system). Other examples of software load balancers include WebSphere from IBM, WSD Pro from Radware, and Central Dispatch/Global Dispatch from Resonate.

See Also: *Domain Name System (DNS), Layer 4 switch, Layer 7 switch, name server, router*

Local Access and Transport Area (LATA)

Service boundaries for local exchange carriers (LECs).

Overview

When the divestiture of AT&T occurred in 1984, 197 separate LATAs were created to specify the service boundaries for different LECs. These LATAs are identified by three-digit numbers that are different from area codes and do not necessarily match the same geographical areas as these codes. Calls made within a LATA are handled by the LEC administering the LATA and are typically local calls but may be long distance if the LATA spans a large enough region. Calls made between LATAs are always long-distance calls and are handled by inter-exchange carriers (ICXs) such as AT&T, MCI/Worldcom, and Sprint Corporation.

The Telecommunications Act of 1996 made some changes to this landscape by allowing LECs to handle inter-LATA traffic under certain conditions. The act also gives the Federal Communications Commission (FCC) full jurisdiction over the boundaries between LATAs.

Examples

LATAs are used in other parts of North America as well. Some examples of LATAs and their associated numbers include

- New York Metro (132)
- San Francisco (722)
- Los Angeles (730)
- Puerto Rico (820)
- Mexico (838)
- British Columbia, Canada (886)

See Also: *inter-exchange carrier (IXC), local exchange carrier (LEC)*

local address

An Internet Protocol (IP) address on the local subnet.

Overview

A host that is located on the same subnet is said to have a local address (with respect to the particular host under consideration). A host with a local address can be reached without the need to traverse any routers. By contrast, a remote address is an address of a host located on a different subnet. To communicate with a host having a remote address, IP packets must be routed across subnet boundaries by routers or Layer 3 switches.

Examples

As an example of a local address, consider a Transmission Control Protocol/Internet Protocol (TCP/IP) network with the following subnetting scheme:

- Network ID = 181.55.0.0
- Subnet Mask = 181.255.240.0

Using the above class B network and custom subnet mask, there will be 16 different subnets of 4094 hosts each, specifically

- Subnet 1 has hosts 181.55.0.1 through 181.55.15.254.
- Subnet 2 has hosts 181.55.16.1 through 181.55.31.254.
- Subnet 3 has hosts 181.55.32.1 through 181.55.47.254.

...

- Subnet 16 has hosts 181.55.240.1 through 181.55.255.254.

Now consider the following three hosts on the network:

- Host A = 181.55.22.147
- Host B = 181.55.28.12
- Host C = 181.55.43.6

From the point of view of Host A, which is located on Subnet 2:

- Host B is located on the local subnet (Subnet 2), so Host B's address is local to Host A.
- Host C is located on a remote subnet (Subnet 3), so Host C's address is remote to Host A.

See Also: *Internet Protocol (IP), IP address, routing, subnetting*

Local Area Data Channel (LADC)

A telco service for transmitting data using line drivers.

Overview

Also called telco restricted lines, Local Area Data Channel (LDAC) conforms to the Bell 43401 standard published by AT&T and basically specifies DC continuity. This means that metallic (copper) conductors must be used, typically the unshielded twisted-pair (UTP) cabling employed for phone lines. The LADC standard also indicates that these lines must also be unloaded—that is, without terminators, loading coils, or protection circuitry that can add to the inductance of the line and thus distort signals.

LADC lines are available to distances of 3 miles (5 kilometers) from the telco's central office (CO). The longer the distance for a line, the lower the carrying bandwidth supported.

See Also: *central office (CO), unshielded twisted-pair (UTP) cabling*

local area network (LAN)

Typically, a group of computers located in the same room, on the same floor, or in the same building that are connected to form a single network.

Overview

Local area networks (LANs) are the simplest forms of computer networks and enable groups of users to share storage devices, printers, applications, data, and other resources on the network. LANs are typically limited to a single location but can sometimes span several buildings or even a campus. The collection of cabling and networking devices used to build a LAN is known as its infrastructure.

LANs do not contain any telecommunications circuits such as phone lines in the infrastructure—if they do, they are properly called wide area networks (WANs) instead. LANs come in all shapes and sizes, including

- **Workgroup LANs:** Typically a group of workstations deployed in a single room or on a single floor.

- **Shared LANs:** These use legacy hubs and bridges to connect stations.
- **Switched LANs:** These use Ethernet switches to connect stations and have largely displaced shared LANs in the enterprise.
- **Campus LANs:** These LANs span several buildings across a few miles and usually consist of smaller workgroup LANs connected by routers or Layer 3 switches.

Implementation

Building a LAN from a group of stand-alone computers requires the assembly and configuration of a number of components:

- **Network architecture:** The vast majority of today's LANs are of the Ethernet type, usually 10BaseT or Fast Ethernet.
- **Cabling:** This is used to join the computers so they can communicate with one another. The most common type of cabling used in LANs is Category 5 (Cat5) unshielded twisted-pair (UTP) cabling. This cabling is typically installed in a topology called structured wiring, which is essentially a hierarchical or cascaded star topology employing hubs, switches, and routers.
- **Network protocol:** To communicate on a network, computers must speak a common "language" or protocol, the most popular of which is Transmission Control Protocol/Internet Protocol (TCP/IP), which is necessary for Internet connectivity.
- **Network-aware operating system:** This must be installed on the computers to enable them to share their resources with other computers (thus acting as a server) and access resources on other computers (acting as a client). The choice of operating system depends on whether the network will be a peer-to-peer network or a server-based network. Microsoft Windows 98 or Windows Millenium Edition (Me) is a good choice for small peer-to-peer workgroup LANs, while Windows 2000 offers the security and scalability needed to support a larger server-based network.
- **Network interface card (NIC):** This must be installed in each computer in an available slot on the motherboard, together with a software driver, to control the card's functions. The network cabling is then connected to the NIC in each computer to form the actual network.

See Also: *bridge, cabling, Category 5 (Cat5) cabling, Ethernet switch, hub, infrastructure, NetBEUI, network, protocol, router, server, Transmission Control Protocol/Internet Protocol (TCP/IP), unshielded twisted-pair (UTP) cabling, wide area network (WAN)*

local exchange carrier (LEC)

A telco in the United States that provides telephone and telecommunication services for subscribers within a geographic region.

Overview

Traditionally, the *local exchange* part of the term *local exchange carrier* is another word for the telco's central office (CO), and the *carrier* part means they are the company that "carries" telephone and data traffic for their customers. In other words, your local exchange carrier (LEC) is simply the company that sends you a telephone bill each month. The LEC owns the local loop wiring between their CO and their subscribers' premises, and these premises are in a geographic area known as the Local Access and Transport Area (LATA). Any calls that take place within a given LATA are considered local calls and are billed accordingly. A single LEC may have control over the local loop in one or more LATAs.

The largest LECs came into existence with the breakup of AT&T in the early 1980s, which led to the formation of a number of independent Regional Bell Operating Companies (RBOCs). However, a number of smaller, independent LECs in the United States, especially in rural areas, were never part of the Bell system.

LECs directly handle traffic, including both local and long distance types, only within their area of jurisdiction. For subscribers of one LEC to communicate with those in a different LEC, long-distance carriers called inter-exchange carriers (IXCs) are used. In the United

States, the "Big Three" IXCs are Sprint Corporation, AT&T, and MCI/WorldCom.

Types

Several different types of LECs are in the marketplace today:

- **Incumbent Local Exchange Carriers (ILECs):** These include the RBOCs that came into existence through the AT&T divestiture, plus various independent telcos such as Verizon Communications. They are called "incumbent" because they own the local loop wiring in their service areas.
- **Competitive Local Exchange Carriers (CLECs):** These arose as a result of the Telecommunications Act of 1996 and include mainly resellers of voice and Digital Subscriber Line (DSL) services. Some CLECs provide services regionally, but others, such as Intermedia Communications, have become a national presence or transformed themselves into other types of service providers.
- **Building Local Exchange Carriers (BLECs):** These are essentially offshoot CLECs that focus on provisioning voice and data services to office towers, hotels, industrial parks, and so on.

Prospects

The Telecommunications Act of 1996 changed the landscape of the telephone system in the United States by allowing LECs to compete in the deregulated long-distance market and by allowing IXCs to provide services directly to customer premises through mergers, acquisitions, and new technologies. Before 1996, each LEC was essentially an incumbent LEC (ILEC) that was the sole provider of telephone services to subscribers in its geographical region. The Telecommunications Act allowed new companies to become competitive LECs (CLECs) that could compete directly with ILECs in their areas of jurisdiction by mandating the leasing or purchasing of local loop and switching services from the ILECs or installing their own separate distribution and switching systems. LECs have an advantage over IXCs, however, in that they already own a right-of-access to customer premises, but IXCs have an advantage in that they are larger, more highly capitalized companies that can afford to invest heavily in new technologies and services or even acquire LECs outright.

The landscape is still changing after six years, but it appears to many analysts that the Telecommunications Act has largely failed to deliver on its promise of opening up more competition in the telephone and telecommunications industry. Many CLECs, particularly those that specialized in offering digital subscriber line (DSL) services, went out of business during the dot-com bust of 2001. Meanwhile, RBOCs, traditionally viewed as dinosaurs when it comes to implementing technological innovation, have modernized their services and consolidated their positions in the local loop. And the "Big Three" IXCs remain just three, with little expectation of things changing in that arena.

See Also: *central office (CO), Competitive Local Exchange Carrier (CLEC), Incumbent Local Exchange Carrier (ILEC), inter-exchange carrier (IXC), Local Access and Transport Area (LATA), Regional Bell Operating Company (RBOC), telco*

local group

A type of group that exists only on the Microsoft Windows 2000 computer on which it is created.

Overview

Local groups reside within the local security database of the computer on which they are created. Local groups are intended for use only on Windows 2000 computers that are not part of a domain and are used for granting users who are interactively logged on to the computer access to resources on that computer. Local groups can contain only local user accounts from the same machine. You create local groups on a stand-alone Windows 2000 machine using the Local Users and Groups console.

Notes

Another type of Windows 2000 group called domain local groups have a domain-wide scope and can be used to provide users with access to resources located anywhere in a domain.

See Also: *AGLP, built-in group, global group, group*

localhost

The friendly name used in the HOSTS file for the loopback address, a special Internet Protocol (IP) address used to test the protocol stack on a host.

See: *loopback address*

local loop

The portion of the telephone system that connects a subscriber to the nearest telco central office (CO).

Overview

The wiring used in the local loop is typically unshielded twisted-pair (UTP) four-wire copper cabling terminated at RJ-11 jacks in the customer premises. With traditional Public Switched Telephone Network (PSTN) lines that use analog transmission, the maximum distance allowed between the customer premises and the CO is about 3 miles (5 kilometers). In many urban and commercial areas, the local loop has been upgraded to Integrated Services Digital Network (ISDN), which employs the same wiring but provides all-digital transmission for better voice and data connections. Local loop wiring can also carry a combination of voice and data at high speeds using various forms of Digital Subscriber Line (DSL) technologies.

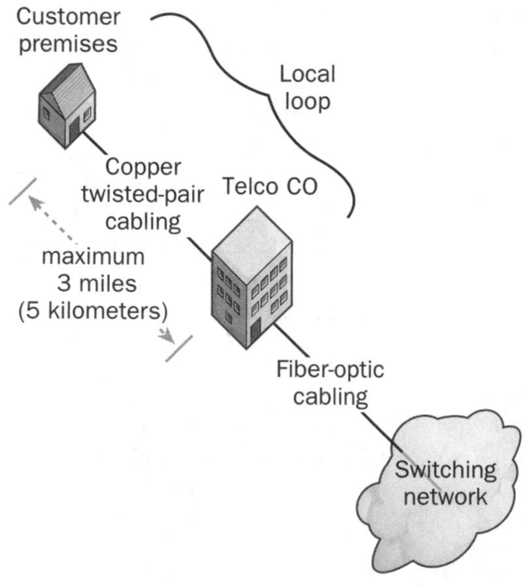

Local loop. *The local loop wiring between a telco CO and the customer premises.*

Prospects

In many respects, the local loop represents the bottleneck in providing subscribers with high speed voice, data, multimedia, and Internet access services. This is because of two issues:

- The copper nature of the local loop wiring makes it much less efficient than fiber-optic cabling at carrying large amounts of information.
- The local loop wiring is owned by the Incumbent Local Exchange Carrier (ILEC) in your area, typically a Regional Bell Operating Company (RBOC). This legislated monopoly means that the main competition for providing customers with broadband services generally has to come from technologies other than traditional copper local loop wiring. Furthermore, because of their monopoly, RBOCs have generally been slow to bring about promised innovation such as fiber to the curb (FTTC), which was promised decades ago but never delivered.

For residential customers, the main competition for the traditional copper local loop consists of cable modem and satellite dish systems. For business customers, cable modems are generally not an option due to the lack of cable television infrastructure in industrial parks and office towers. Instead, business customers have other alternatives, such as Local Multipoint Distribution System (LMDS), a fixed wireless broadband service, and optical Ethernet, which involves provisioning fiber to office towers in dense urban areas.

See Also: *analog transmission, central office (CO), Digital Subscriber Line (DSL), digital transmission, fiber to the curb (FTTC), Incumbent Local Exchange Carrier (ILEC), Integrated Services Digital Network (ISDN), Local Multipoint Distribution Service (LMDS), optical Ethernet, Public Switched Telephone Network (PSTN), Regional Bell Operating Company (RBOC), telco, unshielded twisted-pair (UTP) cabling*

Local Multipoint Distribution Service (LMDS)

An emerging wireless broadband technology operating in the millimeter band of the electromagnetic spectrum.

Overview

Local Multipoint Distribution Service (LMDS) is a new wireless telecommunications technology that can simultaneously carry voice, data, and multimedia at speeds as high as 155 megabits per second (Mbps). LMDS is primarily targeted toward the business market and is designed to help alleviate the bottleneck of the telco local loop. LMDS is simple to deploy and relatively inexpensive, and it provides businesses with speeds higher than those of Digital Subscriber Line (DSL) technologies. It can also be deployed where cable modem infrastructures generally do not exist, such as industrial parks and office towers.

Implementation

LMDS is a cellular communications system in which coverage areas are typically 2.5 to 6 miles (4 to 10 kilometers) in diameter. Each cell is served by one or more LMDS transmitters. A transceiver is deployed with a fixed antenna at the customer premises, usually on a rooftop or other high location (LMDS does not support mobile users and does not support roaming between cells).

LMDS operates in the millimeter range at frequencies between 27.5 and 31.3 gigahertz (GHz). Transmissions in this range require precise line of sight between transmitter and station and are strongly affected by reflections of walls and other surfaces. Since frequencies used by LMDS are those at which water molecules absorb energy (which is how a microwave oven works), rain and moisture can absorb and scatter LMDS transmissions, causing dropouts. Deploying multiple transmitters per coverage area may lessen this effect, however.

LMDS can operate in two configurations:

- **Point-to-multipoint (PMP):** This is the usual way of deploying LMDS and uses a single base station transmitter or "hub" broadcasting to multiple fixed end stations. Range is typically less than 6 miles (10 kilometers) for this configuration.
- **Point-to-Point (PTP):** This is used to connect two LMDS stations and can sustain longer distances up to about 12 miles (19 kilometers).

Prospects

Trial deployments of LMDS are currently underway. The technology is expected to be deployed mainly in dense urban areas by implementing wireless rings to serve a region of customers. The main issue with LMDS is that communications are easily affected by moisture and bad weather, but efforts are underway to work around these problems. Some companies that have licensed LMDS frequencies include Advanced Radio Telecom Corporation, NextLink Communications, Teligent, and WinStar Communications.

See Also: *cellular communications, Digital Subscriber Line (DSL), local loop*

local network

The network on which your computer resides, as opposed to a remote network.

Overview

The local network consists of all computers having the same network number as your machine. For example, on a Transmission Control Protocol/Internet Protocol (TCP/IP) network, if your computer is assigned the IP address 208.16.8.25, then your network ID number is 208.16.8.0, and your local network would consist of all computers having the same network ID number. Each computer on a network has the same network ID number but a different host ID to distinguish it from other hosts on the local network. In the above example, your host ID would be .25 and host IDs for other hosts on your local network might be .26, .27, and so on. The IP address of a host is a combination of the host ID and network ID. For example, if your network ID is 208.16.8.0 and your host ID is .25, your IP address would be 208.16.8.25.

The term *local network* is also used in another context to describe hosts that are on the same physical LAN segment, such as all the hosts connected to the same hub in an Ethernet network. The usage of the term is sometimes vague, and you must determine its meaning from the context in which it is used.

See Also: *IP address, network, subnet, Transmission Control Protocol/Internet Protocol (TCP/IP)*

LocalSystem

A built-in identity in Microsoft Windows 2000 that provides a security context for running operating system tasks.

Overview

The LocalSystem account is a special identity built into the Windows 2000 operating system. LocalSystem has the attributes of a user account but has special privileges:

- It is an implicit member of the Administrators group
- It has full permissions on every operating system object
- It can take ownership of any object
- It has the system right "act as part of the operating system"

LocalSystem is used as a security context for running operating system services. The LocalSystem account can run these services whether or not any user is interactively logged on to the machine.

Notes

The System account on the Windows NT platform was also used as a security context for running services, but it could only do so for individual computers. In other words, if you had five Windows NT computers on a network, there were five System accounts present, one on each computer. The System account on one computer could not be used as a security context for running services on a different computer. This scenario has changed in Windows 2000 and Windows .NET Server, where the LocalSystem account has forest-wide applicability.

See Also: *built-in identities*

LocalTalk

A legacy networking protocol for the Apple platform.

Overview

LocalTalk was originally called AppleBus and operated over serial connections at a speed of 230.4 kilobits per second (Kbps). A LocalTalk segment could have a maximum of only 32 nodes, and network addresses were assigned dynamically using AppleTalk Address Resolution Protocol (AARP). LocalTalk was strictly a Layer 2 protocol only—higher layer functions had to be managed by the operating system itself. LocalTalk is a legacy protocol that was later replaced by AppleTalk, initially in a configuration called AppleTalk over LocalTalk and later AppleTalk Phase II.

See Also: *AppleTalk*

local user account

A user account that exists only on the local machine on which it is defined.

Overview

In Microsoft Windows NT–based networks, a local user account is a user account that resides in the local security database of a particular Windows NT member server or workstation. When a user has a local account on a computer, the user can log on to the computer interactively. In a Windows NT–based network based on the workgroup security model, all user accounts are local user accounts and are created using the administrative tool called User Manager, the version of User Manager for Domains that is installed on stand-alone Windows NT member servers and workstations. In a Windows NT–based network that is based on the domain security model, new user accounts that are created using User Manager for Domains are by default global user accounts that are valid everywhere in the domain and are stored in the Security Accounts Manager (SAM) database on domain controllers. However, in a domain, you can also create a local account with User Manager for Domains by clicking the Account button in the New User dialog box and specifying Local Account as the Account Type. This is generally not recommended because local user accounts are not valid throughout the domain and are valid only for logging on interactively to the computer on which they are created.

In a Windows 2000–based or Windows .NET Server–based network, a local user account is one of three types of user accounts, the others being domain user accounts and built-in accounts. Local user accounts enable users to log on interactively to stand-alone Windows 2000 and Windows .NET servers or client computers in a workgroup and access system resources on the machine for which they have suitable permissions. Domain user accounts allow users to log on to a domain and access resources anywhere in the domain. Local user accounts are created using the Local Users and Groups tool, which is implemented as a snap-in for Microsoft Management Console (MMC). Local user accounts are stored in the local security database on the machine on which they are created, but domain user accounts are created in Active Directory directory service and stored in organizational units (OUs).

See Also: *Active Directory, built-in account, domain user account, global user account*

local user profile

A user profile stored locally on a computer.

Overview

In Microsoft Windows 2000, Windows NT, Windows XP, and Windows .NET Server, a local profile is created for a user the first time the user successfully logs on to his or her computer. If the user does not have a preconfigured roaming user profile at the time of the first logon, Windows 2000 copies the default user profile to the new local user profile folder.

Local profiles are created for all users who interactively log on to computers running Windows 2000 so that they can access their own personal settings on that machine. Each user who logs on to a machine thus has his or her own local profile stored on the machine. Local profiles are stored in the folder Documents and Settings. Each user's profile is stored in a subfolder that is named after the user's username and contains the user's personal settings. The personal settings include both the appearance of the desktop and Start menu and the user's network connections (such as mapped drives). Even if users have a roaming profile that allows them to log on from any machine in the network and obtain their personal settings, each machine also stores a local copy of their profiles in case the network is down when they try to log on.

See Also: *roaming user profile, user profile*

Local Users and Groups

A Microsoft Windows 2000 administrative tool for managing local user and group accounts on a standalone server or workstation.

Overview

Local Users and Groups is available on member servers running Windows 2000 Server and client computers running Windows 2000 Professional that you can use to create and manage local user accounts and local groups on the machine. Local Users and Groups is implemented as a snap-in for Microsoft Management Console (MMC), like other Windows 2000 administrative tools. You can use Local Users and Groups only if a workgroup security model is being used for your network. In a workgroup, each computer manages its own security and maintains its own local security database of account information. If your network uses a domain security model, all user accounts for the domain are stored in the Active Directory database, which contains a distributed domain directory database maintained by domain controllers on your network. You cannot install Local Users and Groups on domain controllers; on these machines, you should use Active Directory Users and Computers for creating domain user accounts.

See Also: *Active Directory, Active Directory Users and Computers, Microsoft Management Console (MMC)*

locking

A mechanism that protects data in a database from being overwritten.

Overview

Locking is a mechanism used to protects a database against data loss when users simultaneously attempt to modify the same database object. Locking synchronizes users' access to the database and prevents concurrent data manipulation problems to ensure that data remains consistent and query results are correct.

Locking provides concurrency in a multiuser environment—that is, it enables multiple clients to simultaneously access and modify a database without the danger of the data becoming corrupted. If one user locks a portion of the database to view or modify data, that data cannot be accessed or modified by any other user until the first user's updates have been committed.

Examples

The Microsoft SQL Server relational database platform employs multigranular locking, in which each database

resource is locked at a level appropriate for that kind of resource. The following table shows the various database resources that can be locked in SQL Server, in order of decreasing granularity. This range of granularity allows a balance between concurrency (the ability of multiple clients to simultaneously access a database) and performance (speed). For example, highly granular locking such as row-level locking allows more concurrency (different users can simultaneously modify different rows in the same database table), but this increases system overhead because the server must manage more locks.

Database Resources That SQL Server Can Lock

Locked Resource	*Description*
DB	Locks the entire database
Table	Locks an entire database table, including its data and indexes
Extent	Locks a contiguous group of eight data pages or eight index pages
Page	Locks individual 8-kilobyte (KB) data pages or index pages
Key	Locks a row within an index
RID (row identifier)	Locks individual rows in a table

SQL Server uses a number of resource lock modes that specify how concurrent transactions can access different database resources. These include the following:

- **Shared locks:** Allow concurrent transactions to read data—for example, by using transact-SQL SELECT statements. Shared locks allow concurrent reads but lock the resource against modification until the reads are completed. After the data is read, the lock is removed unless a repeatable read is being performed.
- **Exclusive locks:** Lock data so that it can be modified—for example, by using INSERT, DELETE, or UPDATE statements. No other reads or modifications can be performed on the resource while it is exclusively locked.

Other locking modes include update locks, bulk update locks, and intent locks.

See Also: *database, Structured Query Language (SQL)*

log

Any file that contains records corresponding to application or operating system events or conditions, usually arranged sequentially by time.

Overview

Log files are usually delimited text files (such as .csv files) in which each line represents a transaction or logged event, with individual data fields separated by delimiting characters such as commas. Delimited text files can be imported into spreadsheet programs such as Microsoft Excel, database programs such as Microsoft Access, and report and analysis tools such as Crystal Reports for further analysis and graphical display of trends and usage patterns. Relogging is the process of taking a log file and sampling it at larger time intervals to reduce the size of the file for archiving purposes while maintaining the overall trend of data within the log.

Numerous processes within the Microsoft Windows operating systems and the Microsoft BackOffice applications maintain logs. Some log functions include the following:

- Keeping track of transactions performed on an information store or database (as in Microsoft SQL Server or Microsoft Exchange Server)
- Monitoring server or network performance over time when Performance Monitor is used on a Windows NT–based, Windows 2000–based, Windows XP–based, or Windows .NET Server–based network
- Recording details of visitors to Web sites when you use Internet Information Services (IIS)
- Recording the details of modem commands or Point-to-Point Protocol (PPP) transmissions when you use Network and Dial-up Connections to connect to an Internet service provider (ISP)

Regular inspection of log files is often an important component of insuring the security of a software platform or application.

See Also: *security*

Logical Link Control and Adaptation Layer Protocol (L2CAP)

The data-link layer protocol for Bluetooth wireless networking.

Overview

The Logical Link Control and Adaptation Layer Protocol (L2CAP) resides over the Baseband layer, which is the physical (PHY) layer mechanism for Bluetooth communications. L2CAP enables logical channels to be established between different Bluetooth devices. L2CAP identifies different devices using channel identifiers (CIDs), which are also used for sending control information (for example, the L2CAP signaling channel is designated as CID 0x0001).

L2CAP provides both connection-oriented and connectionless services at the data-link layer, provides segmentation and reassembly, and supports protocol multiplexing. L2CAP packages real-time data streams into packets that can be up to 64 kilobytes (KB) in length and employ a little endian byte ordering.

See Also: *Bluetooth*

logical link control (LLC) layer

A sublayer of the data-link layer in the Open Systems Interconnection (OSI) reference model.

Overview

For local area network (LAN) data-link protocols such as Ethernet, the data-link layer is divided into an upper layer called the logical link control (LLC) layer and a lower layer called the media access control (MAC) layer. The MAC layer coordinates access to the physical layer according to a media access control method, which for standard Ethernet is the Carrier Sense Multiple Access with Collision Detection (CSMA/CD) scheme. The MAC layer thus provides services to the LLC layer so that protocol data units can be transferred to the medium without any concern about the broadcast, framing, addressing, or error-detection schemes used. The LLC uses the MAC services to provide two types of data-link operations to the network layer above it: LLC1 for connectionless and LLC2 for connection-oriented data-link communication services (known as Type 1 and Type 2, respectively). These LLC services are grouped into two classes:

- **Class 1 services:** Connectionless services used by applications that do not require error detection or flow control.
- **Class 2 services:** Either connectionless (Type 1) or balanced-mode connection-oriented (Type 2) data transfer services. The LLC provides the error detection and recovery, flow control, and resequencing services needed for connection-oriented data transfer.

Notes

The LLC protocol is based on the earlier High-level Data Link Control (HDLC) protocol. The term *LLC* sometimes refers to the IEEE 802.2 protocol itself, which is the most common LAN protocol implemented at the LLC layer.

See Also: *Carrier Sense Multiple Access with Collision Detection (CSMA/CD), Ethernet, High-level Data Link Control (HDLC), media access control (MAC) layer, Open Systems Interconnection (OSI) reference model*

logoff

The process by which users notify their network's security authority (for example, domain controllers on a Microsoft Windows 2000 network) that they are terminating their session on the network. Users should always log off their computers when they are finished for the day to prevent unauthorized access to the network through their computers by others who might use the building at night. If, as an administrator, you find that users do not log off their computers, configure logon hours restrictions to forcibly disconnect users after work hours. You can also check whether your password policy is too strict, which might encourage users to stay logged on to avoid having to reenter a complex password each time they return to their stations.

Notes

If you are leaving your desk for only a short time, you can lock a machine running Windows 2000, Windows XP, or Windows .NET Server instead of

logging off. You do this by pressing Ctrl+Alt+Delete followed by Lock Computer. You can unlock your workstation by pressing Ctrl+Alt+Delete again and reentering username and password. This approach is faster than logging off and allows applications such as your e-mail program to continue running in the background.

See Also: *Active Directory, logon*

logon

The process by which a user's credentials are verified by a network security authority so that the user can be granted access to resources on the local machine or network.

Overview

There are two basic types of logons:

- **Interactive logons:** Occurs when a user sit at the console of his local computer and enters credentials (usually username and password) in the logon dialog box.
- **Remote logons:** Occurs when a user has already logged on interactively to a machine but wants to establish a network connection with a remote computer. For example, if the user tries to map a drive letter to a shared folder on the remote computer, a remote logon must take place during the process so that the remote computer can be sure that the user has the right to perform the action.

When a user attempts an interactive logon on a local computer, the user's credentials are verified by a security authority. On Microsoft Windows networks, this security authority may be

- **The local machine itself:** This scenario typically occurs on computers that are configured to belong to a workgroup rather than a domain. In the workgroup security model, each machine maintains its own separate list of valid user accounts in its own local security database. For example, when a user performs an interactive logon to a stand-alone machine running Windows 2000, the machine itself validates the user's credentials.
- **A designated machine or group of machines on the network:** For example, on a Windows 2000–based network that has Active Directory directory service installed, special Windows 2000 servers called domain controllers store and maintain information about valid user accounts for all users on the network. These domain controllers are then used for validating users' logon attempts. When the user tries to log on interactively to his or her local machine, the machine forwards the user's credentials to a nearby domain controller using a mechanism called pass-through authentication. The domain controller authenticates the credentials and then builds and returns an access token to the user, granting that user suitable levels of access to resources on the network.

Notes

Windows 2000 includes a feature called Run As that lets an administrator temporarily log on to a client machine without requiring that the user first log off from his machine. This feature is useful, for example, if an administrator needs to install an application or troubleshoot some problem while at the user's machine.

See Also: *logoff*

logon script

A batch file that automatically runs on a user's client machine every time the user logs on to the network.

Overview

Logon scripts allow administrators to run a special series of commands each time a user logs on to her machine. These commands can perform functions such as

- Configuring the desktop working environment for the user
- Configuring legacy network clients and launching network connections
- Automatically launching certain applications the user will need
- Communicating a "message of the day" and other information to users

On the Microsoft Windows 2000 and Windows .NET Server platforms, logon scripts are primarily used for configuring legacy Windows clients and non-Windows clients that belong to a Windows 2000 network. On a pure Windows 2000 network, logon scripts are rarely needed because Windows 2000 employs Intellimirror technologies for performing tasks such as configuring the user's desktop, synchronizing home folders, and establishing network and printer connections.

Examples

On Windows NT networks, however, logon scripts still perform many useful functions. A typical Windows NT logon script might contain a series of Net.exe commands that synchronize the client computer's clock with a particular server, ensure that mapped network drives are available, restore printer connections, and perform other actions to configure the user's work environment.

The following simple script runs when a Windows client logs on to a Windows NT Primary Domain Controller (PDC). The script synchronizes the workstation's clock with the server, maps the drive letter K to a share on the server, and then exits.

```
net time \\pdc /set /yes >nul
net use k: \\pdc\home
exit
```

See Also: *IntelliMirror, scripting*

long packet error

A random, malformed frame of data that is sent continuously by failed circuitry in a networking component. Better known as jabber.

See: *jabber*

Long Reach Ethernet (LRE)

A new technology from Cisco Systems that supports Ethernet over older telephone wiring.

Overview

Provisioning new high-speed data services to multitenant units (MTUs) such as office towers and hotels can be complex and expensive. In-building digital subscriber line (DSL) is one solution, but this approach can be expensive due to costs of installing Digital Subscriber Line Access Multiplexer (DSLAM) equipment at the customer premises. DSL is also complex to provision because it involves Asynchronous Transfer Mode (ATM) technology and generally ties customers in to a single service provider, their Incumbent Local Exchange Carrier (ILEC). Fixed wireless services are another approach, but these services are currently limited to a few dense urban locations.

To open up the last mile marketplace, Cisco has developed a new technology called Long Reach Ethernet (LRE). This system provides customers with the plug-and-play simplicity of Ethernet running over existing in-building telephone wiring. In addition, LRE can be used to simultaneously carry voice, data, and video traffic over a single wiring infrastructure, and it can simultaneously support Plain Old Telephone System (POTS) analog voice, Integrated Services Digital Network (ISDN), and even asymmetric digital subscriber line (ADSL).

LRE supports data transmission at speeds between 5 and 15 megabits per second (Mbps). It can run over distances as long as 4970 feet (1515 meters), which is considerably greater than the 330 feet (100 meters) that can be achieved using standard 10 Mbps Ethernet. LRE thus allows Ethernet to be deployed in scenarios where previously it could not be used due to distance limitations and nonstandard wiring. LRE also saves money by eliminating the need to deploy a separate networking infrastructure by laying twisted pair or fiber-optic cabling throughout a building.

Implementation

LRE operates over existing telephone wiring and does not require deploying a parallel Category 5 (Cat5) cabling infrastructure or laying fiber. LRE makes use of several Cisco products working together, including

- **Cisco Catalyst 2900 LRE XL switches:** These are available in either 12-port or 24-port configurations.

- **Cisco 575 LRE Customer Premises Equipment (CPE):** These devices have an RJ-11 port for connecting to phone lines and an RJ-45 port for connecting to a computer or network.
- **Cisco LRE 48 POTS Splitters:** These are installed at the customer's private branch exchange (PBX) and allow coexistence of voice and data traffic on the telephone lines.

See Also: *Asymmetric Digital Subscriber Line (ADSL), Asynchronous Transfer Mode (ATM), Digital Subscriber Line (DSL), Digital Subscriber Line Access Multiplexer (DSLAM), Ethernet, Incumbent Local Exchange Carrier (ILEC), Integrated Services Digital Network (ISDN), Plain Old Telephone Service (POTS)*

loop

In routing terminology, a route that causes packets to be forwarded until they time out.

Overview

A routing loop—a packet that enters a loop circle endlessly until its Time to Live (TTL) value decrements to zero and it is dropped by a router interface—is an undesirable thing. Routing loops result in dropped packets and retransmissions and waste network bandwidth.

Early routing protocols such as the Exterior Gateway Protocol (EGP) lacked the intelligence to detect and eliminate loops from their routing topologies. For this reason, EGP was eventually replaced with a superior routing protocol called Border Gateway Protocol (BGP), which guaranteed loop-free forwarding of packets between autonomous systems (ASs) in an Internet Protocol (IP) internetwork. All routing protocols today include mechanisms for detecting and eliminating loops, which is essential in a strongly meshed network topology such as that of the Internet.

See Also: *Border Gateway Protocol (BGP), Exterior Gateway Protocol (EGP), routing*

loopback

A test circuit that goes from one device to another and back again.

Overview

Loopback tests are used to check line integrity and the proper functioning of customer premises equipment and to diagnose and troubleshoot problems with telecommunications equipment. Loopback tests can be performed by wide area network (WAN) access devices such as Channel Service Unit/Data Service Units (CSU/DSUs) and routers to place calls to themselves over a WAN to test the WAN link's integrity.

Implementation

In loopback testing, a test signal is typically sent from a service provider's central office (CO) to the customer premises and is returned or echoed by the customer premises equipment (CPE) back to the service provider. If the loopback signal fails to return, the WAN link is down and must be repaired. If the signal returns, the device compares the original signal with the returned one; any discrepancies can be used to troubleshoot communication problems.

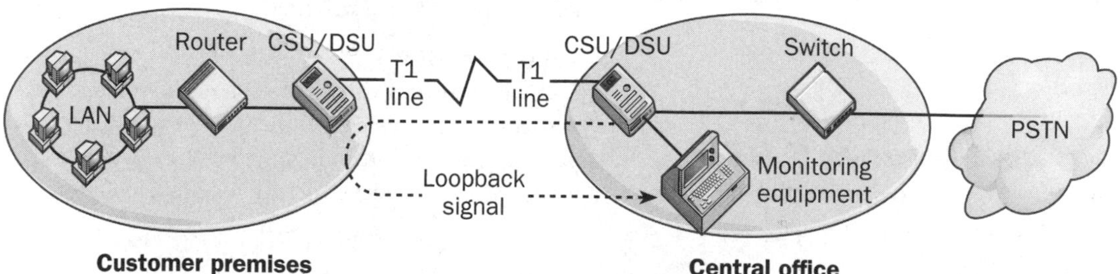

Loopback. *An example of how loopback testing can be used to verify the integrity of a telecommunications link.*

Examples

One place where loopback testing is valuable is for testing Integrated Services Digital Network (ISDN) lines. If the Service Profile Identifiers (SPIDs) and ISDN directory numbers have been configured for your ISDN interface, a loopback test will determine whether

- You can connect with your provider's ISDN exchange. If not, you might have a cable or interface problem.
- Your ISDN numbers are correctly assigned.
- You have caller ID or other advanced ISDN services on your line.

Another type of loopback test is called a local loopback test. This is often used with WAN access devices to test networking connectivity with locally attached network devices. You can also implement a local loopback test by having network application software place a call to the WAN access equipment and having the equipment return an echo to the application.

See Also: *Channel Service Unit/Data Service Unit (CSU/DSU), customer premises equipment (CPE), Integrated Services Digital Network (ISDN), router*

loopback address

A special Internet Protocol (IP) address used to test the protocol stack on a host.

Overview

In Transmission Control Protocol/Internet Protocol (TCP/IP) networking, the loopback address is the special IP address 127.0.0.1. The loopback address can be used to test the protocol stack on a host even when the host is not connected to a network. For example, to test whether TCP/IP is installed and configured correctly on a machine running Microsoft Windows, type **ping 127.0.0.1** at the command prompt. Alternately, you can type the command **ping localhost** to achieve the same result since the Hosts file on a Windows machine resolves the friendly name localhost into the IP address 172.0.0.1. Finally, you can even ping any legal IP address of the form 127.x.y.z to test your TCP/IP protocol stack. If this test produces an error, either your network interface card (NIC) is incorrectly configured or your protocol stack is corrupt. If the configuration looks correct, try removing and reinstalling TCP/IP on your machine to fix the problem. If that fails, try reinstalling the driver for your NIC or replacing the NIC.

See Also: *hosts file, IP address, ping, Transmission Control Protocol/Internet Protocol (TCP/IP)*

LPD

Stands for Line Printer Daemon, the UNIX daemon used for spooling print jobs.

See: *Line Printer Daemon (LPD)*

LPQ

Stands for Line Printer Queue, a UNIX command used for querying the status of a print queue.

See: *Line Printer Queue (LPQ)*

LPR

Stands for Line Printer Remote, a UNIX network command used to submit print jobs to print servers.

See: *Line Printer Remote (LPR)*

LRE

Stands for Long Reach Ethernet, a new technology from Cisco Systems that supports Ethernet over older telephone wiring.

See: *Long Reach Ethernet (LRE)*

LTO

Stands for Linear Tape Open, a high-capacity tape backup technology.

See: *Linear Tape Open (LTO)*

MAC address

A Layer 2 address for a network node.

Overview

On an Ethernet network, a MAC address is a unique 6-byte (48-bit) address that identifies a computer, router interface, or other node on the network. The *MAC* in the term *MAC address* stands for media access control, a sublayer of the Layer 2 or data-link layer of the Open Systems Interconnection (OSI) reference model for networking. MAC addresses are sometimes called Ethernet addresses, hardware addresses, or physical addresses.

MAC addresses enable devices on a network to communicate with each other. On an Ethernet network, for example, each frame contains a source MAC address and destination MAC address in its header information. Devices such as bridges and Layer 2 switches examine the source MAC address of every frame received and then use these MAC addresses to dynamically build internal routing tables for directing further traffic. They then use these tables to forward future frames received to the specific port or network segment on which the station having that particular destination MAC address resides.

Implementation

On a computer, the MAC address is assigned to the network interface card (NIC) that is used to connect the computer to the network. The MAC address is typically hard-coded into the card's read-only memory (ROM). Some cards come with a software utility that you can use to change the card's MAC address, but this is generally not a good idea. If you accidentally configure two network cards on your network to have the same MAC address, address conflict problems will result and the computers will not be able to communicate on the network. Token Ring cards, however, actually require you to assign a unique MAC address to them before they will work.

The uniqueness of MAC addresses for network devices is ensured by the Institute of Electrical and Electronics Engineers (IEEE), which allocates vendors of networking devices specific blocks of MAC addresses. The first 3 bytes (24 bits) represent the manufacturer of the card, and the last 3 bytes (24 bits) identify the particular card from that manufacturer. Each group of 3 bytes can be represented by 6 hexadecimal digits, forming a 12-digit hexadecimal number that represents the entire MAC address. Examples of manufacturer 6-digit numbers include the following:

- 00000C (Cisco Systems)
- 00001D (Cabletron Systems)
- 0004AC (IBM)
- 0020AF (3Com Corporation)
- 00C0A8 (GVC Corporation)
- 080007 (Apple Computer)
- 080009 (Hewlett-Packard Company)

In order for computers to communicate on a network, frames must be addressed using Layer 2 or MAC addresses. To simplify network communications, however, computers are given Layer 3 addresses instead, which in Transmission Control Protocol/Internet Protocol (TCP/IP) consist of IP addresses. A TCP/IP protocol called Address Resolution Protocol (ARP) is then used to translate Layer 3 addresses into Layer 2 addresses.

Notes

To determine the MAC address of your computer's NIC, use the following commands:

- Type **ipconfig /all** at the command prompt in Microsoft Windows 2000, Windows NT, Windows XP, and Windows .NET Server.
- Enter **winipcfg** at the Run box in Windows 95 or Windows 98.

See Also: *Address Resolution Protocol (ARP), Ethernet, frame, IP address, media access control (MAC) layer, Open Systems Interconnection (OSI) reference model*

Macintosh

A personal computing platform from Apple Computer.

Overview

The Apple Macintosh platform incorporates both a hardware platform and an operating system called MacOS. The original Macintosh hardware platform employed the 680x0 series of microprocessors from Motorola and now uses the Reduced Instruction Set Computing (RISC)-based PowerPC processor developed jointly by Apple, IBM, and Motorola.

M

The MacOS operating system incorporated a number of innovations into personal computing, including a graphical user interface (GUI) with resizable windows, a mouse, icons for applications, and common activities such as creating Notes and deleting files to the Trashcan. Many of these innovations had been developed earlier by the Stanford Research Institute and the Xerox Palo Alto Research Center (XeroxPARC) and were later licensed by Apple for use by Microsoft Corporation in its Microsoft Windows operating system platform.

History

The Macintosh was first released by Apple in 1984 and quickly became popular with high-end personal computer users. Starting from version 1 in 1984, the MacOS operating system has continued to evolve, as MacOS 8 introduced a new look for the desktop in 1997 and MacOS 9 made significant enhancements in the file system in 1999. The new MacOS X, released in 2001, marked a significant departure from earlier operating system versions by basing the kernel upon a free version of UNIX.

Uses

The Macintosh platform has established a niche for itself in a number of industry sectors, including desktop publishing, graphics, and animation. It is also popular among university professionals. While holding a much smaller share of the market than Microsoft Windows, the Macintosh is a popular alternative desktop platform, but it has made few inroads into the server marketplace. Popular Macintosh platforms include the iMac, iBook, and Power Macintosh versions.

Notes

Using Services for Macintosh, an optional feature of Microsoft Windows 2000, Macintoshes and Intel-based computers can operate together on the same network. Services for Macintosh enables Windows 2000 servers to support Macintosh client machines by emulating an AppleShare server and to provide Macintosh clients with file and print sharing service and AppleTalk routing capability. AppleShare is a file-sharing protocol that is a part of AppleTalk, a suite of networking protocols developed by Apple for its Macintosh computing platform.

For More Information

Visit Apple at *www.apple.com.*

See Also: *Apple Open Transport, AppleShare, AppleShare IP, AppleTalk, UNIX, Windows 2000*

MAC layer

Stands for media access control layer, a sublayer of the data-link layer.

See: *media access control (MAC) layer*

MADCAP

Stands for Multicast Address Dynamic Client Allocation Protocol, an extension to the Dynamic Host Configuration Protocol (DHCP) for dynamic assignment of multicast addresses.

See: *Multicast Address Dynamic Client Allocation Protocol (MADCAP)*

mail client

Software that provides users with an interface for creating, sending, receiving, viewing, and storing e-mail messages.

Overview

Most electronic messaging systems are client/server based, in which users send and receive messages using mail clients and mail servers are used to store and forward mail between users. An example of a client/server messaging system is the combination of Microsoft Exchange Server, a powerful platform for messaging and collaboration, and Microsoft Outlook, the premier messaging client from Microsoft Corporation.

Other popular mail clients include

- Microsoft Outlook Express, a free mail and news client included with Microsoft Windows platforms
- Eudora, developed by QUALCOMM, which is available in a full professional version and a shareware version
- Netscape Messenger, which is part of the Netscape Communicator suite of Internet tools
- Pine and Elm, which are command-line mail clients used in UNIX environments

See Also: *e-mail, Exchange Server, mail system, Simple Mail Transfer Protocol (SMTP)*

mailslot

An interprocess communication (IPC) mechanism.

Overview

Mailslots provide connectionless, datagram-based one-to-one or one-to-many communication between processes on different computers running versions of Microsoft Windows. Mailslots are implemented in Microsoft Windows as file system drivers and, therefore,

- Are opened by requests made from the redirector
- Take full advantage of the features of file system drivers, such as security and validation

Mailslots are similar to named pipes, another interprocess communication mechanism. Although named pipes support only point-to-point, bidirectional communications, mailslots support point-to-multipoint, unidirectional communications.

Uses

Mailslots were originally developed for Microsoft OS/2 LAN Manager and have been maintained in later versions of Microsoft Windows for purposes of backward compatibility. They are usually used for broadcast purposes, such as service announcements in the Computer Browser service on Windows 2000 and for the WinPopUp messaging tool in Windows 95 and Windows 98.

See Also: *interprocess communication (IPC), named pipe, point-to-multipoint, point-to-point*

mail system

Any set of applications used to support e-mail messaging between a group of users within an organization or between users in different organizations.

Overview

E-mail has become as indispensable to modern business as the telephone or fax machine. To implement e-mail within a company, you need to deploy the elements of a mail system. A typical mail system has two basic components:

- **Client software:** Employed by users for composing, sending, receiving, and viewing messages
- **Server software:** Used for storing and transporting messages across a network or telecommunications system

Architecture

Mail systems generally employ one of two kinds of architecture:

- **Shared-file mail systems:** Here the client software initiates and maintains all messaging activity. The server is essentially a passive file server and is usually called a postoffice. The client regularly polls the postoffice for new messages that have arrived for the user, and if they are found, the client downloads and displays them for the user to read. An example of a shared-file mail system is Microsoft Mail 3.*x*. Advantages of shared-mail systems include low server-end requirements and simple

M

maintenance. Disadvantages include limited security, high processing load for the client, and poor scalability.

- **Client/server mail systems:** Here the mail server and client share the task of processing messages. An example of a client/server mail system is the Microsoft Exchange Server/Microsoft Outlook combination. Advantages of client/server mail systems include lower network traffic, scalability, and security. The main disadvantage is that they require more powerful servers than shared-file mail systems do.

Mail systems can also be distinguished by the address formats they employ. Examples of mail address formats include industry-standard formats such as the Simple Mail Transfer Protocol (SMTP) used on the Internet and the Originator/Recipient (O/R) format developed by the International Telecommunication Union (ITU) for its X.400 messaging standards. Examples of proprietary address formats include the Microsoft Mail version 3.*x* format and the Lotus cc:Mail format. The following table illustrates examples of these different address formats.

Examples of Address Formats Used in Electronic Messaging

Address Format	*Example*
SMTP	mitch@northwind.microsoft.com
X.400 O/R	C=US;a=Sprint;p=microsoft; o=northwind;s=Tulloch;g=Mitch;
Microsoft Mail	microsoft/northwind/mitch
cc:Mail	Tulloch, Mitch at northwind

Marketplace

The most popular mail system used in the corporate world today is Microsoft Corporation's Exchange Server platform, which can be deployed with a variety of clients, including

- **Microsoft Outlook:** A full-featured messaging, scheduling, and collaboration client
- **Microsoft Outlook Express:** A lightweight mail and news client included free with Microsoft Windows versions
- **Outlook Web Access (OWA):** A Web application for Microsoft Exchange Server that allows users to access their mail using a Web browser such as Microsoft Internet Explorer

Exchange Server provides a comprehensive messaging solution that supports

- Internet standard Simple Mail Transport Protocol (SMTP) messaging
- Connectivity with legacy mail systems such as Microsoft Mail and IBM PROFS/SNADS
- Connectivity with foreign mail systems such as Lotus cc:Mail, Novell GroupWise, and X.400 messaging systems

Exchange can be deployed as a messaging backbone within a heterogeneous mail system environment and also includes a Migration Wizard that lets you migrate users and mailboxes from legacy and foreign mail systems to Exchange. Consolidation of multiple disparate mail systems into a single messaging system through migration can both simplify administration and reduce costs.

See Also: *e-mail, Exchange Server, Simple Mail Transfer Protocol (SMTP), X.400*

mainframe

A general term for a high-level, typically large computer that is capable of performing demanding computational tasks.

Overview

Mainframes were the original computing platform developed at the dawn of the computer age in the 1950s and 1960s. Mainframe computers typically operated as centralized computing systems in which dumb terminals were attached through serial connections to a central mainframe computer. Users entered text-based commands into these terminals, and the terminal forwarded the commands to the mainframe, where all the processing was performed. The results of the processing were returned to the terminal and displayed. Modern mainframes typically offer standard 3270 or 5250 terminal communication and also support connections to "smart terminals"—desktop computers that are connected to the mainframe but also have their own computing power.

Mainframe computing established itself in government, industry, and large enterprises as the standard platform for information processing. Purchasing and running mainframes involved considerable expense and required specially trained personnel, so generally only the largest companies and organizations purchased them. Smaller businesses could access mainframe services by submitting batch jobs through remote terminals and paying the company owning the mainframe for processing cycles used.

Vendors of mainframes include IBM, Unisys Corporation, and Hitachi Data Systems, with IBM being the dominant player in today's marketplace. The most widely used mainframe platform is IBM's S/390 system, and a popular midframe platform is IBM's AS/400 system.

Prospects

Mainframe computing went into eclipse in the 1980s and 1990s with the emergence of the PC and client/server computing paradigm, but in recent years, mainframes have been making a comeback as a platform for running Web applications. Many corporations have repurposed older mainframes as Web application platforms, and modern mainframes can run thousands of UNIX or Linux "virtual servers" simultaneously on one physical machine. Once relegated to the role of legacy platform, "big-iron" mainframes are now viewed as fashionable platforms for e-commerce and other Internet-related business paradigms.

Despite the rapid evolution of computing over the last two decades, much of the information processing performed in the government, financial, and industrial sectors still employs traditional mainframes running large COBOL applications to perform functions such as records processing, accounting, and payroll functions.

Notes

Microsoft Host Integration Server can be used as a gateway to provide users on Microsoft Windows networks with access to data stored on IBM S/390 mainframes and AS/400 midframe systems.

For More Information

Learn about the IBM S/390 platform at *www.ibm.com/servers/s390/pes.*

See Also: *3270, 5250, Host Integration Server, terminal*

MAN

Stands for metropolitan area network, which traditionally represents a network spanning a metropolitan area.

See: *metropolitan area network (MAN)*

Management Information Base (MIB)

A database of information about a device that is managed using Simple Network Management Protocol (SNMP).

Overview

A Management Information Base (MIB) is a collection of information about managed devices, such as computers, hubs, routers, and switches. MIBs store information about the configuration of these networking components, such as the version of the software running on the component, the Internet Protocol (IP) address assigned to a port or interface, and the amount of available disk space for storage. MIBs thus function as a kind of directory containing information about network settings and resources on managed devices.

Architecture

The SMNP data within an MIB is organized in hierarchical fashion in the form of a tree. The structure of the MIB tree is defined by a number of Internet Engineering Task Force (IETF) standards, including RFCs 1155, 1213, 1514, and 1759.

The generalized MIB tree contains several kinds of branches:

- Public branches that are defined by RFCs and are the same for all SNMP managed devices
- Private branches that are defined by the companies and organizations to which these branches are assigned

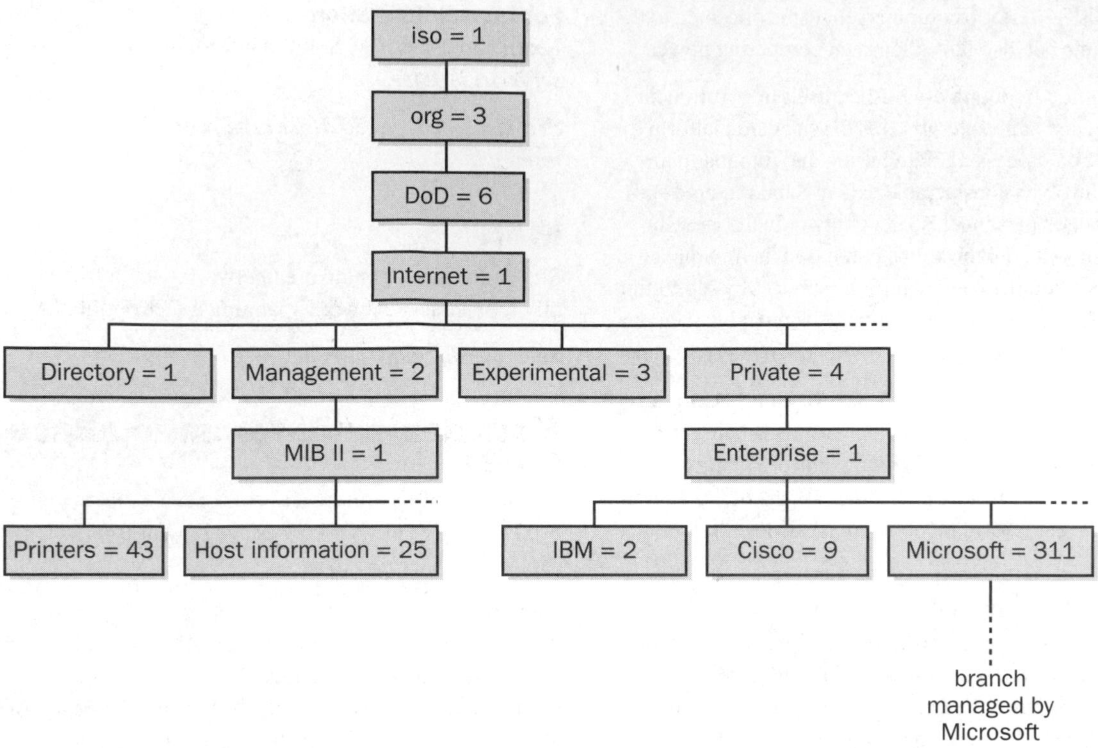

M

Management Information Base (MIB). *The general structure of the SNMP MIB hierarchy.*

The diagram illustrates the general structure of the MIB tree, which consists of a number of objects represented in ASN.1 notation. Note that a managed device will typically contain only the portion of the entire MIB tree that is relevant to its particular operation. The root of the MIB tree is International Organization for Standardization (iso), followed by Organization (org), Department of Defense (dod), and then Internet (internet). The main public branch is then Management (mgmt), which defines network management parameters common to devices from all vendors. Underneath mgmt is MIB-II (mib-2), and beneath this are branches for common management functions such as system management, host resources, interfaces, and printers. For example, in the diagram we see that the root of the MIB branch that contains objects for SNMP manageable printers is called Printer. In MIB notation, this object is uniquely defined by the text string

```
.iso.org.dod.internet.mgmt.mib-2.printer
```

Alternatively, MIB objects are also assigned a numerical label (called an object identifier or OID) that provides a more compact representation of these objects than text strings can provide. Using the numerical values in the diagram, the root Printer object would be uniquely described by

.1.3.6.1.2.1.43

The Private branch of the MIB tree contains branches for large companies and organizations. These are organized under an object called Enterprise, and each vendor has a root branch node under this object. For example, IBM's root branch node is ibm (2), Cisco Systems is cisco (9), Sun Microsystems is sun (42), Microsoft LAN Manager MIB II is lanman (77), and Microsoft Corporation is microsoft (311). Vendors can apply to the Internet Assigned Numbers Authority (IANA) to have specific MIB numbers reserved for their enterprise. Each company or organization has complete authority over what objects will be created within their own branch of the MIB tree and what OIDs will be assigned to each object. All MIB objects must comply with a common definition of SNMP information called Structure of Management Information (SMI), which defines the various data types allowed.

Using Microsoft (.1.3.6.1.4.1.311) as an example of an enterprise, various MIB branches are defined under its root node, as seen here:

.1.3.6.1.4.1.311.1.3 for Dynamic Host Configuration Protocol (DHCP)

.1.3.6.1.4.1.311.1.7.2 for File Transfer Protocol (FTP)

.1.3.5.1.4.1.311.1.7.3 for Hypertext Transfer Protocol (HTTP)

and so on.

Implementation

MIBs are incorporated into special software called SNMP agents that run on SNMP-manageable devices. This is done by using MIB files, which are plain text files constructed using a special format. Once these MIB objects are compiled by the agent software, the device can be managed using a network management system that supports SNMP. You can use SNMP commands to retrieve the value of a MIB object or, in some cases, to change the object's value.

For More Information

Try out the MIB Browser at *www.ibr.cs.tu-bs.de/cgi-bin/sbrowser.cgi.*

See Also: *network management, Simple Network Management Protocol (SNMP)*

Management Information Format (MIF)

A standard format for describing hardware and software management information.

Overview

The MIF format and Desktop Management Interface (DMI) specification were developed by the Distributed Management Task Force (DMTF), an organization composed of computer industry leaders whose aim is to lead the development, adoption, and unification of standards for managing systems. MIF can be used in conjunction with DMI to manage networked PCs using systems management software such as Microsoft Systems Management Server (SMS).

Implementation

The MIF database on a computer system is implemented as a collection of plain text files called MIF files. MIF files are text files that are supplied with each manageable hardware or software component installed on the system and that contain information about the attributes of that component. These MIF files provide system management software with configuration information concerning the various hardware and software components on the system. A program called a DMI Service Provider that runs locally and is resident on the system being managed collects and manages the information from MIF files and delivers it to the central management station. You can retrieve and display the information in the MIF database using any standard management interface (MI) utility.

Notes

Microsoft SMS uses six types of MIF files for collecting and storing information in the SMS database:

- PersonalComputer (.mif)
- SMSEvent (.emf)
- UserGroup (.umf)
- JobDetails (.jmf)
- PackageLocation (.pmf)
- CustomArchitecture (.mif)

SMS can also use MIF files to add information to the SMS database about objects such as routers with custom architectures. Note that MIF files differ slightly in syntax between SMS 2 and the earlier SMS 1.2.

See Also: *Desktop Management Interface (DMI), Distributed Management Task Force (DMTF), Systems Management Server (SMS)*

Management Service Provider (MSP)

A company that manages the IT (information technology) infrastructure for other businesses.

Overview

Management Service Providers (MSPs) are a new breed of service provider that evolved out of the changing application service provider (ASP) marketplace. MSPs offer outsourced IT services that can include

- Managing desktop computers and their applications
- Monitoring and troubleshooting servers and their applications
- Managing network infrastructure devices such as routers and switches
- Managing network security and virus protection

MSPs are particularly appealing to startups, small and mid-sized businesses, and e-commerce companies where rapid time-to-market is essential and where the hiring or training of staff with the required expertise may be too expensive. Instead of purchasing expensive and complex systems management platforms such as HP Openview and IBM Tivoli, outsourcing system and network management tasks to an MSP is a viable option for companies that lack the capital resources or personnel to implement these systems. In addition, MSPs can keep rapidly evolving high-tech companies from being caught in the trap of technological obsolescence by obviating the need to lock in to management systems that may become legacy platforms.

MSPs are part of an evolving breed of xSPs that include ASPs and storage service providers (SSPs). MSPs generally provide their services to client companies on a subscription basis, helping smaller companies avoid the high capital outlay of running their own IT department. MSPs differ from ASPs, whose primary aim is servicing end users on behalf of companies—MSPs instead provide high-level services to businesses and IT departments.

Marketplace

The MSP marketplace is new and evolving rapidly, but some of the players that have made names for themselves include InteQ Corporation, Luminate (now part of EMC Corporation), Manage.Com, Nuclio Corporation, SilverBack Technologies, and Triactive.

For More Information

To learn more about the MSP marketplace and where it is headed, you can visit the MSP Association online at *www.mspassociation.org.*

See Also: *application service provider (ASP), storage service provider (SSP), xSP*

Manchester coding

A line coding mechanism used in 10 megabit per second (Mbps) versions of Ethernet.

Overview

Manchester encoding is the technology used since 1979 to convert information into electrical signals for all versions of 10 Mbps Ethernet, including 10Base2, 10Base5, and 10BaseT.

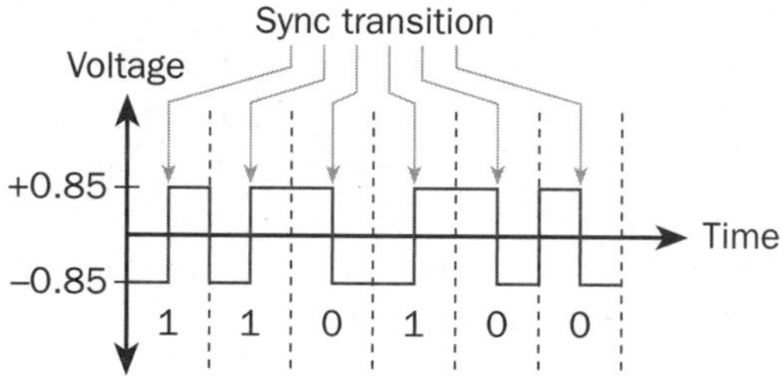

Manchester coding. *Example of how Manchester coding works for standard Ethernet.*

Manchester coding employs a two-state transition of line voltage to represent one bit of information. In other words, two baud (voltage changes) are used for one bit (piece of information). A binary 0 is represented by a transition from high to low voltage in the time set for transmitting one bit (that is, one "bit time"), while a binary 1 is represented by a transition from low voltage to high. For Ethernet networks, the high voltage is typically +0.85 volts and the low is typically -0.85 volts, making each voltage transition equal to 1.7 volts. This also results in Manchester encoding being balanced for DC operation, which enables signals to pass through devices such as transformers without being corrupted.

Manchester coding enables data to be transmitted between two stations without the need for an extra clocking signal to synchronize communications between the stations. This is possible because voltage transitions take place in the middle of each bit transmission interval, which establishes a timing pattern between stations. The mid-interval voltage changes thus allow the sending and receiving stations to maintain proper synchronization with each other in order to ensure the integrity of the transmission. Because of the extra transition per bit that is used for clocking purposes, Manchester coding is only 50 percent efficient—for example, a 20-megahertz (MHz) bandwidth is required to produce a 10-Mbps data transmission rate.

Advantages and Disadvantages

Manchester encoding has the advantage of being relatively easy to encode (or decode) information. Manchester encoding was selected as the line-coding mechanism for 10 Mbps Ethernet simply because in those days network devices such as hubs, bridges, and network interface cards (NICs) had limited processing capabilities and could easily support Manchester. Another factor in this choice was that coaxial cabling, the original media format used by Ethernet, had a high bandwidth capability and could easily support the 20 MHz signaling required to transmit Ethernet frames at 10 Mbps.

Because Manchester is a relatively wasteful encoding scheme, and with advances in processor power for network devices, newer flavors of Ethernet such as Fast Ethernet and Gigabit Ethernet (GbE) do not employ Manchester.

Notes

Another version of this line coding mechanism called differential Manchester encoding represents binary 0 by a voltage transition at the start of the bit-interval, and binary 1 by no transition at the start of the bit-interval. In both cases, a transition takes place in the middle of the interval for synchronization purposes. Differential Manchester encoding is used for IEEE 802.5 Token Ring networking.

mandatory user profile

A roaming user profile in Microsoft Windows 2000 and Windows .NET Server that the user cannot modify.

Overview

Mandatory user profiles are typically configured by administrators who want to prevent users from modifying their desktops so that administrators can reduce the time they spend troubleshooting modifications or enforcing uniformity because of company policies. Mandatory profiles can also be used for several users who require the same desktop configuration. The administrator can create a mandatory profile and use it for the entire group of users. Changing the mandatory user profile once affects all of the users assigned to it. This simplifies the administrator's job when desktops require upgrading or additional applications.

Because a mandatory user profile is a type of roaming user profile and is therefore stored on a network server, users can access their personal desktop settings from any machine on the network. Mandatory user profiles are configured as read-only, however, so that users cannot permanently change their desktop settings. They can reconfigure their desktop for the duration of the current logon session, but once they log off, their changes are lost.

Implementation

To change a roaming user profile into a mandatory one, simply place the user's roaming profile on the file server where user profiles are stored and rename Ntuser.dat to Ntuser.man. This makes the roaming user profile read-only from the user's perspective.

Notes

Windows 95 and Windows 98 also support mandatory user profiles in conjunction with networks based on Windows NT or Windows 2000.

See Also: *local user profile, roaming user profile, user profile*

manual switch

Any manually operated (as opposed to electronically operated) switch used for switching between peripherals or other network devices.

Overview

Manual switches generally cost less than electronic switches that have similar features and capabilities. They are available in a variety of configurations for different kinds of uses and typically have rotary switches on the front and connectors on the back. These connectors could be standard DB9, DB15, RJ-11, RJ-45, RS-232, V.35, BNC, or Centronics connectors.

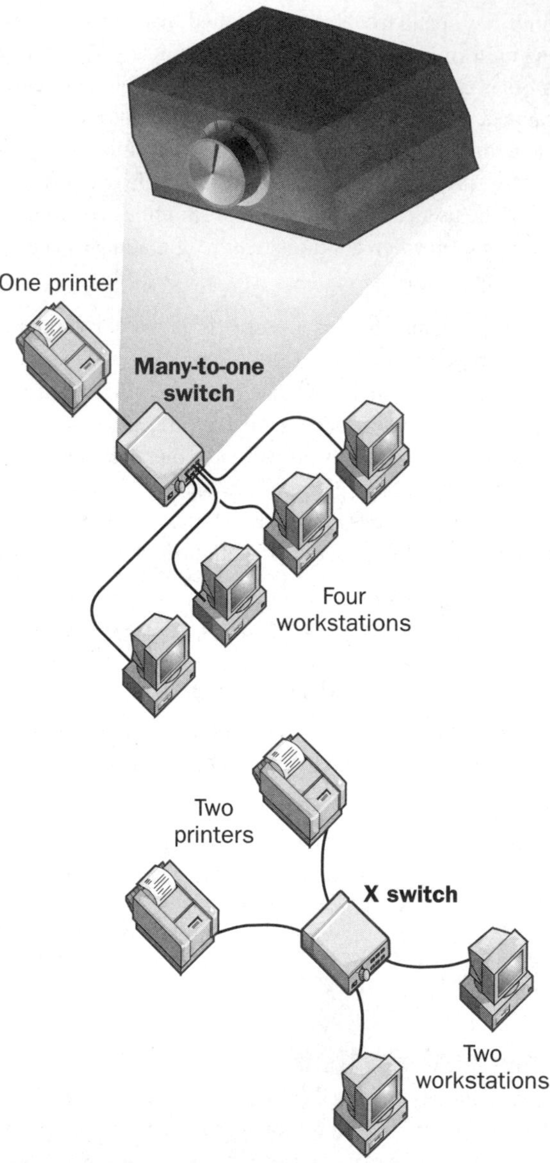

Manual switch. *Two manual switch configurations: a many-to-one switch and an X switch.*

Manual switches are typically used in high-security environments in which a user can access a device only by physically switching to it. Some manual switches include key locks that control access.

Types

Examples of different types of manual switches include the following:

- **Stand-alone manual switches:** Generally small boxes with a rotary switch on the front and a set of connectors on the back. They can be used for switching connections between printers, monitors, keyboards, and other devices.
- **Rack-mounted manual switches:** Standard 19-inch (48-centimeter)-wide rack-mounted boxes, typically with a number of rotary switches on the front and connectors on the back. These are used more rarely and essentially combine a number of stand-alone switches into one rack-mounted box.
- **Many-to-one switches:** Allow several users to share one device or allow one user to access different devices. For example, a user can use a many-to-one switch to manually switch between a color laser printer and a black-and-white printer. Or an administrator can manually switch a server from a primary 10BaseT Ethernet network to a secondary network. These switches are typically either two-to-one or four-to-one switches.
- **X switches:** Allow several users to share several devices in different configurations. These switches are typically two-to-two switches.
- **Dual switches:** Allow you to switch two connectors at once.

See Also: *switch*

MAPI

Stands for Microsoft Application Programming Interface, a Microsoft technology that allows developers to use the Windows messaging subsystem for writing messaging applications.

See: *Messaging Application Programming Interface (MAPI)*

mapped network drive

A shared folder on a network that has been associated with an available drive letter on a local PC.

Overview

A mapped network drive enables a shared folder on a remote computer to behave as a logical drive on the local computer. Mapped drives can be created in all versions of Microsoft Windows, typically using procedures such as the following:

- Right-click on My Computer, Network Neighborhood, or My Network Places (depending on your version of Windows) on the desktop and select Map Network Drive from the shortcut menu. Choose an available drive letter, enter the Universal Naming Convention (UNC) path to the shared folder, and specify credentials to gain access to the shared folder.
- Click the Map Network Drive button on the toolbar in Windows Explorer and continue as described in the first procedure.
- From a command prompt, use the Net Use command.

Notes

An alternative way of accessing a shared folder on a network server is using the Run command. This method does not require you to use an available drive letter as mapping a drive does. Simply choose Run from the Start menu, and then type the UNC path to the network share you want to access.

See Also: Universal Naming Convention (UNC)

markup language

A language used to add information or provide additional meaning to a document.

Overview

Markup languages typically consist of a set of symbols called markup and a set of syntax rules defining how markup should be used. There are generally four types of markup:

- **Functional:** Markup that adds new functionality to a document, such as embedding images or hyperlinks
- **Semantic:** Markup that describes the document's content, such as the title or purpose of the document
- **Structural:** Markup that defines how a document is structured, such as headings, paragraphs, and lists
- **Stylistic:** Markup that adds style formatting to the document, such as words in bold or italic

History

Markup languages first appeared in the computing world in the 1960s. Soon afterward, attempts were made to unify different types of markup languages, an effort that led in 1986 to the Standardized Generalized Markup Language (SGML) becoming established as an International Organization for Standardization (ISO) standard called ISO 8879. In 1991 SGML was used by Tim Berners-Lee to create a simple markup language called Hypertext Markup Language (HTML) that could be used with the newly developed Hypertext Transfer Protocol (HTTP) to deliver hypertext (linked content) over the Internet. Limitations in HTML led the World Wide Web Consortium (W3C) to propose the new Extensible Markup Language (XML) in the late 1990s. XML is rapidly headed toward becoming the standard language for communicating information over the Internet.

M

Types

The three kinds of markup language described above have similarities and differences, such as the following:

- **SGML:** This is a complex language that was never implemented with any success in the computing field. SGML documents are difficult to interpret and require the use of a document type definition (DTD), which specifies the syntax rules by which SGML documents are created. SGML instead evolved to become a metalanguage used to define other markup languages, for example, HTML, which is considered an SGML application.
- **HTML:** This language has become more wildly popular than anyone could have imagined and is the foundation for most of the e-commerce and e-business done today. HTML lets you create

simple Web pages for communicating information and, in its basic essence, is so simple anyone can learn to use it. Most Web pages are created using special HTML editors instead, however, rather than requiring that HTML tags (markup) be added manually to plain text documents. The main drawbacks to HTML that led to the search for a replacement (later found in XML) are the limitations of the fixed tag set used by HTML, the fact that HTML can only be used to present information rather than to communicate the meaning of a document, and that data hierarchies are not supported (HTML is flat).

- **XML:** This markup language is basically a bare-bones version of SGML (the DTD for XML is only about 20 percent the size of that for SGML). XML has the expected advantages over HTML that a successor would be expected to have, namely, support for creating user-defined tags, ability to describe both the presentation and meaning of a document, and support for data hierarchies.

M

See Also: *document type definition (DTD), Hypertext Markup Language (HTML), Hypertext Transfer Protocol (HTTP), International Organization for Standardization (ISO), World Wide Web Consortium (W3C), XML*

master boot record (MBR)

A key data structure on a hard disk.

Overview

The master boot record (MBR) performs an essential role on a hard-disk system of a computer: when a computer boots up, the basic input/output system (BIOS) executes a small portion of code residing in the MBR. This code scans the partition table (found within the MBR) to determine which is the active partition, then scans the active partition to locate the boot sector on this partition, loads the code it found in this boot sector into RAM (random access memory), and then transfers control to this resident code to continue execution or the boot process.

Sometimes the MBR for a disk system can become corrupt—for example, when a system is invaded by an MBR virus. In this case, when you try to boot your system, you may see one of the following messages:

- Error loading operating system
- Invalid partition table
- Missing operating system

In Microsoft Windows 2000 and Windows .NET Server, you can sometimes repair corruption of the MBR by using the Recovery Console's Fixmbr command.

master browser

A Microsoft Windows 2000 computer that participates in the Computer Browser service.

Overview

The master browser collects and maintains a list of available servers that have shared network resources in its domain. This list, known as the browse list, is created when individual servers announce their presence on the network by sending a server announcement to the master browser.

The master browser also collects and maintains a list of all Windows 2000 domains on the network. If the domain of a master browser spans several subnets, the master browser maintains only the browse list for its own subnet and one master browser will exist for each subnet in the domain.

Backup browsers obtain a copy of the browse list from the master browser. Backup browsers automatically contact the master browser every 15 minutes to request a copy of both the browse list and a list of domains on the network. The backup browser caches this list and distributes it to any client on the network that requests it.

The master browser for a domain is usually the first domain controller installed in that domain.

See Also: *backup browser, Computer Browser service, domain master browser*

master domain

In Microsoft Windows NT–based networks, a trusted domain that contains user accounts for the enterprise.

Overview

Master domains are used in enterprise-level implementations of Windows NT to allow user accounts to be centralized and managed in one domain. The master domain is typically found at the company headquarters, while resource domains are implemented at branch offices. A trust relationship is established between the resource domains and the master domains, in which each resource domain trusts the master domain. Users who log on to their computers at headquarters automatically log on to the master domain to validate their credentials. Users at branch offices can log on to either their local resource domain or the trusted master domain, but they must choose the master domain because all user account information resides there. In a wide area network (WAN), one or more backup domain controllers (BDCs) belonging to the master domain are installed at each branch office to facilitate local logons and to prevent logon traffic from being routed over slow WAN links to headquarters.

Notes

Many companies use the Windows NT master domain model to administer users and groups in master domains and resources in second-tier (or resource) domains. Because the majority of reasons to use the Windows NT master domain model disappear when domains are migrated to Active Directory directory service in Windows 2000 and a domain tree is established, these companies might choose to dissolve existing second-tier domains into organizational units (OUs) in the master domains.

See Also: *Active Directory, domain (Microsoft Windows), organizational unit (OU), resource domain, trust*

master index

The final version of an index generated by Microsoft Indexing Service.

Overview

The indexing process first creates word lists, which are merged into shadow indexes and then become one master index. Unlike word lists, which reside in volatile memory, the shadow indexes and the master index are persistent indexes that are stored on disk. The process by which shadow indexes are combined into a master index is called a master merge. A master merge combines multiple shadow indexes with any old master index to create a new master index. The new master index is the most efficient form for the index of a corpus of documents being indexed by the Indexing Service.

The master index stores the indexing data in a highly compressed format in a structure called the catalog. The compressed nature of the master index provides the most efficient data structure for storing information and for issuing queries against the corpus, but the process of generating a master index is resource intensive and is generally performed by the Indexing Service when load on the server is low. However, the administrator can also force a merge to update the master index after new documents are added to the corpus being indexed.

See Also: *catalog*

master name server

A name server in the Domain Name System (DNS) that has authority over a given zone.

Overview

A master name server can be either a primary name server or a secondary name server. If it is a secondary name server, the master name server must obtain its own resource records from another master name server. If it is a primary name server, it contains the master copy of the resource records for its zone of authority.

Master name servers provide read-only copies of their DNS database to secondary name servers. A secondary name server must obtain and update its resource records from a master name server. The process by which these records are obtained and updated between name servers is called a zone transfer.

Notes

When you configure zone transfers between name servers, be sure that the start of authority (SOA) record for the secondary name server is correctly configured with the name of the master name server from which it will obtain its resource records. No configuration is required with the master name server itself.

See Also: *caching-only name server, Domain Name System (DNS), name server, primary name server, secondary name server*

master station

Any network device that controls the operation of other network devices.

Overview

The term *master station* is typically used in mainframe/terminal networking. For example, in a point-to-point connection between an IBM controller and a 3270 terminal, the controller is the master station while the terminal is a slave station. Or, in a multipoint circuit, one of the devices might function as a master station while all the rest are slaves.

Typically, the master station polls all the slave stations regularly in order to determine whether a slave wants to initiate communication with the master. This is different from a peer multipoint circuit such as an Ethernet network, where each station contends for control of the media.

Notes

Another scenario where the term *master station* sometimes is used is in Token Ring networks, where one of the devices can function as a master station and be responsible for detecting and replacing tokens lost by other stations.

See Also: *3270, Ethernet, mainframe, terminal, Token Ring*

matrix switch

A multiport switch that supports any-to-any connectivity.

Overview

The term *matrix switch* originates from a mathematical structure called a matrix, which is a two-dimensional structure with N rows and M columns representing N times M values. Likewise, a matrix switch with N input ports and M output ports has N x M switching possibilities. Typical configurations for these switches include 4 x 4 and 4 x 8 matrix switches, in which any input device can be connected to any output device by operating the switch.

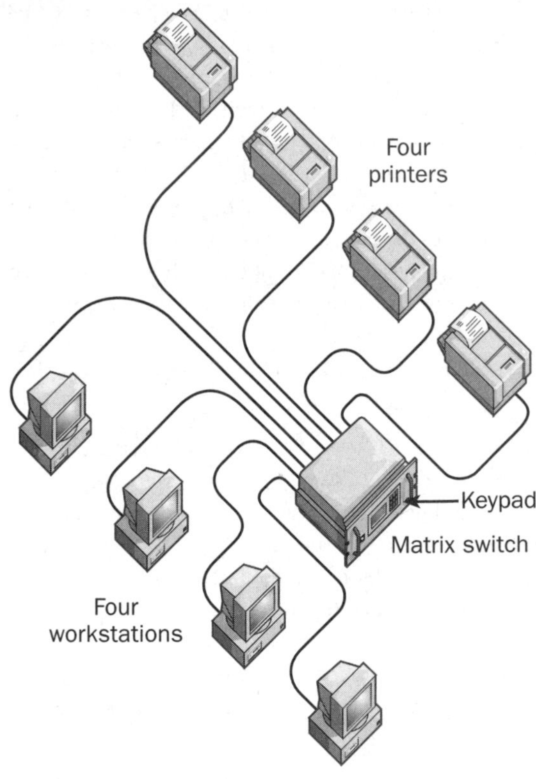

Matrix switch. *Using a matrix switch to connect four printers to four computers.*

Types

A typical matrix switch would be an electronic switch that has multiple ports and that can be controlled using a keypad or some other front-panel interface on the switch. Another type of switch called a code-operated switch is basically a switch that can be operated using character codes embedded in the data stream sent from user workstations. Code-operated matrix switches can thus be operated remotely from computer terminals by entering ASCII commands into a text window.

Uses

Matrix switches are typically used in serial connections such as RS-232 to allow multiple computers to share a group of peripherals such as printers, modems, and other devices. A high-end matrix switch may consist of a chassis into which ports can be added as required to support different interfaces and may be packaged either as a desktop unit or a standard 19-inch (48-centimeter) rackmount enclosure.

A popular use of matrix switches is for Keyboard Video Mouse (KVM) switches, which incorporate matrix switching technology to allow multiple computers to access multiple monitors, keyboards, and mice simultaneously. Although low-end KVM switches may allow a single keyboard, monitor, and mouse to be switched between two, four, or eight different computers, higher-end KVM switches are essentially matrix switches that allow X keyboard/monitor/mouse combinations to actively control Y different computers, with high-end configurations supporting up to 128 computers and 128 different users. Examples of vendors providing KVM matrix switches include ITM Components, Network Technologies, and Lightwave Communications.

Also available are matrix switches that support Small Computer System Interface (SCSI) and parallel communications interfaces. For example, a 4 x 2 SCSI matrix switch could allow two hosts (computers) to switch between four different SCSI drive systems (such as redundant array of independent disks [RAID] arrays). SCSI matrix switches generally allow multiple hosts to access multiple drive systems concurrently, subject to an overall maximum throughput and to the 15 device SCSI limit. An example of a vendor of SCSI matrix switches is Avax International, which provides a modular SCSI matrix switch that can be customized for different host/device combinations.

Notes

The term *matrix switching* also describes the switching technology at the center of an Asynchronous Transfer Mode (ATM) network that functions by supplying needed bandwidth for end-to-end sessions. ATM matrix switching avoids contention by end stations on the network.

See Also: *code-operated switch, Keyboard Video Mouse (KVM) switch, parallel transmission, RS-232, serial transmission, Small Computer System Interface (SCSI), switch*

MAU

Stands for Multistation Access Unit, a wiring concentrator (passive hub) used in Token Ring networks.

See: *Multistation Access Unit (MAU or MSAU)*

MBone

An experimental portion of the Internet that is used to test multicasting technology.

Overview

The MBone platform was established to test and develop technology and software for multicasting audio and video information over the Internet. Although the MBone came into existence in 1992, Internet Protocol (IP) multicasting actually dates back to 1988, when the first multicast tunnel was established between Stanford University and BBN Technologies (now part of Verizon Communications). The MBone initially joined together 40 academic and research networks in four different countries but expanded rapidly to include thousands of networks in dozens of countries and regions.

The MBone is essentially a virtual multicasting network lying on top of the Internet and implemented using routers configured to support IP multicast transmission. These multicast-enabled routers can forward IP packets through nonmulticast routers using tunneling technologies that encapsulate multicast IP packets into unicast packets that the routers can understand. MBone IP addresses used for multicasting of audio and video information have been allocated by the Internet

Assigned Numbers Authority (IANA) as those in the range 224.2.y.z, which is a subset of the class D group of IP addresses ranging from 224.0.0.0 to 239.255.255.255.

Notes

The name *MBone* was selected because the network represents a multicast backbone; that is, a backbone network for multicasting.

See Also: *Internet, multicasting*

MBR

Stands for master boot record, a key data structure on a hard disk.

See: *master boot record (MBR)*

MBS

Stands for Mobile Broadband System, a proposed fourth-generation (4G) mobile cellular communication system.

See: *Mobile Broadband System (MBS)*

MBSP

Stands for Multitenant Broadband Service Provider, another name for a building-centric local exchange carrier, a telecommunications carrier focused on the Multitenant Unit (MTU) market.

See: *Multitenant Broadband Service Provider (MBSP)*

MCP

Stands for Microsoft Certified Professional, a family of technical certifications relating to proficiency in working with Microsoft products.

See: *Microsoft Certified Professional (MCP)*

MCS

Stands for Microsoft Consulting Services, a service from Microsoft Corporation that provides direct assistance to large enterprises for the planning, deployment, and support of solutions based on Microsoft technologies.

See: *Microsoft Consulting Services (MCS)*

MDA

Stands for media-dependent adapter, a standard for modular Ethernet switches.

See: *media-dependent adapter (MDA)*

MDAC

Stands for Microsoft Data Access Components, a set of Microsoft technologies that provide access to information stored in a broad range of data sources.

See: *Microsoft Data Access Components (MDAC)*

MDHCP

Stands for Multicast Dynamic Host Configuration Protocol, the former name for what is now called Multicast Address Dynamic Client Allocation Protocol (MADCAP).

See: *Multicast Address Dynamic Client Allocation Protocol (MADCAP)*

media

Anything over which signals can be transported.

Overview

In computer networking, the term *media* refers generally to the types of cabling over which data is transmitted. Types of cabling for networking and telecommunications include copper cabling and fiber-optic cabling. Copper cabling generally comes in two main forms:

- **Coaxial cabling:** Used mainly in industrial settings because of its resistance to interference.
- **Twisted-pair cabling:** The main kind of cabling used in most networks today. Popular forms include Category 5 (Cat5) and enhanced Category 5 (Cat5e) forms of unshielded twisted-pair (UTP) cabling. Shielded twisted-pair (STP) cabling is used mainly in electrically noisy environments.

Fiber-optic cabling is used mainly in campus backbones and for long-haul telecommunications. At one time, it was expected that fiber would supplant copper, but improvements in switching technologies has enabled copper-based networks to support gigabit speeds and higher.

Another type of media is not really media at all: wireless networking. This type of networking transports signals through empty space using radio and microwave frequency electromagnetic radiation traveling at the speed of light. Although most wireless networking signals travel near the Earth's surface and hence go through air, this air is not considered a medium—electromagnetic waves do not require a medium in which to travel. Wireless networking is sometimes said to employ "unguided media" in contrast to the "guided media" provided by wires and cables. Another way of saying this is to contrast "wireline" (guided) networks with wireless (unguided) ones.

Notes

Another common use of the term *media* is to refer to a combination of cabling and topology used for different types of Ethernet networks. Thus, for example, 10BaseT refers to a star topology using unshielded twisted-pair (UTP) cabling, and 10Base2 refers to a bus topology using thinnet cabling. You can loosely refer to these examples as 10BaseT and 10Base2 Ethernet media.

See Also: *cabling, coaxial cabling, fiber-optic cabling, twisted-pair cabling, wireless networking*

media access control (MAC) layer

A sublayer of the data-link layer.

Overview

The Project 802 specifications of the Institute of Electrical and Electronics Engineers (IEEE) subdivide the data-link layer (Layer 2) of the Open Systems Interconnection (OSI) reference model into two sublayers:

- **Logical link control (LLC) layer:** This is the top sublayer and interfaces with the network layer (Layer 3) above it.
- **Media access control (MAC) layer:** This is the bottom sublayer and interfaces with the physical layer (Layer 1) below it.

The function of the MAC layer is to decide which station on the network is allowed to use the media at any given moment. The MAC layer is therefore responsible for implementing the particular media access control method on a network and thus distinguishes different networking architectures such as Ethernet and Token Ring. The table illustrates the different types of MAC layers defined by Project 802.

MAC Layers Defined by Project 802

Project 802 Committee	*Type of LAN*	*Channel Management Algorithms Defined*
802.3	Carrier Sense Multiple Access with Collision Detection (CSMA/CD)	Binary backoff after collision detection, framing, error detection
802.4	Token bus LAN	Token passing, priority scheme, framing, error detection
802.5	Token ring LAN	Token passing, priority scheme, framing, error detection

As part of the OSI protocol stack, the MAC layer receives framed data from the LLC layer immediately above it, which is media independent, and reframes the data, adding a source and destination physical address or MAC address to the frame for transmission on the medium. The MAC layer is also responsible for making sure that data is delivered without errors to layers above it.

See Also: *802.3, 802.4, 802.5, Carrier Sense Multiple Access with Collision Detection (CSMA/CD), data-link layer, Ethernet, Institute of Electrical and Electronics Engineers (IEEE), logical link control (LLC) layer, media access control method, Open Systems Interconnection (OSI) reference model, Project 802, Token Ring*

media access control method

Any method for allowing multiple stations to transmit signals over a network without conflict.

Overview

If two computers simultaneously place signals on a network cable, a collision can occur. Collisions can result in data being lost or corrupted. The solution is to provide a media access control method for the network. Media access control methods act as traffic lights by permitting the smooth flow of traffic on a network and either prevent collisions entirely or provide a graceful way of dealing with them when they occur.

Media access control methods are implemented at Layer 2, the data-link layer, of the Open Systems Interconnection (OSI) reference model. Specifically, media access control methods are the responsibility of the media access control (MAC) layer, one of two sublayers of the data-link layer. Four main media access control methods are used in local area networks (LANs):

- **Carrier Sense Multiple Access with Collision Detection (CSMA/CD):** Used in half-duplex Ethernet (full-duplex Ethernet uses switched instead of shared media and hence does not require a media access control method). CSMA/CD is the most commonly used media access control method used in LANs, reflecting the dominance of Ethernet over other forms of LAN architectures. CSMA/CD is defined by the 802.3 committee of Project 802 of the Institute of Electrical and Electronic Engineers (IEEE).
- **Carrier Sense Multiple Access with Collision Avoidance (CSMA/CA)**: Used in legacy AppleTalk networking and in some forms of wireless networking, such as 802.11a and 802.11b. CSMA is defined for AppleTalk by IEEE 802.3 and for wireless networking by IEEE 802.11.
- **Token passing:** Used in Token Ring and Fiber Distributed Data Interface (FDDI) networking. Token Ring employs a token passing method defined by IEEE 802.5, but FDDI uses a different method defined by the American National Standards Institute (ANSI).
- **Demand priority:** Used in 100VG-AnyLAN networking and defined by IEEE 802.12.

Implementation

In real-life networking devices such as network interface cards, switches, and routers, media access control methods are implemented using a MAC algorithm. Although the algorithms for Ethernet and Token Ring networks are publicly defined by the IEEE standards described above, those used in full-duplex Ethernet are usually patented by the companies that developed them and are hard-coded into application-specific integrated circuits (ASICs) to achieve the best possible performance. For example, in full-duplex Fast Ethernet and Gigabit Ethernet (GbE) networking, the most popular MAC layer is that designed by Alcatel, from which most switch and router vendors lease their MAC technology. The Alcatel MAC is used in more than half of all GbE ports on the market today and in more than 80 percent of all Fast Ethernet ports. Network engineers should note that mixing switching equipment from vendors that use different MACs can sometimes lead to interoperability problems.

See Also: *802.3, 802.4, 802.5, 802.11a, 802.11b, 802.12, AppleTalk, Carrier Sense Multiple Access with Collision Avoidance (CSMA/CA), Carrier Sense Multiple Access with Collision Detection (CSMA/CD), demand priority, Fiber Distributed Data Interface (FDDI), Institute of Electrical and Electronics Engineers (IEEE), media access control (MAC) layer, Project 802, Token Ring*

media converter

A device that connects two different networking media.

Overview

Media converters are commonly used for Ethernet networks where each type of Ethernet has different specifications for the media that can be used. For example, 10Base2 and 10Base5 use different media types (thinnet and thicknet cabling, respectively) and 10BaseT employs unshielded twisted-pair (UTP) cabling. Media converters allow these different types of cabling to be joined together transparently.

Implementation

Media converters come in many types, with many different kinds of connectors. They range from simple two-port small boxes for connecting two different cables to expensive rack-mounted chassis units with 8 or 16 modular ports that support a wide range of configuration options. Some media converters also include bridging functionality and can be deployed wherever bridges or switches are used.

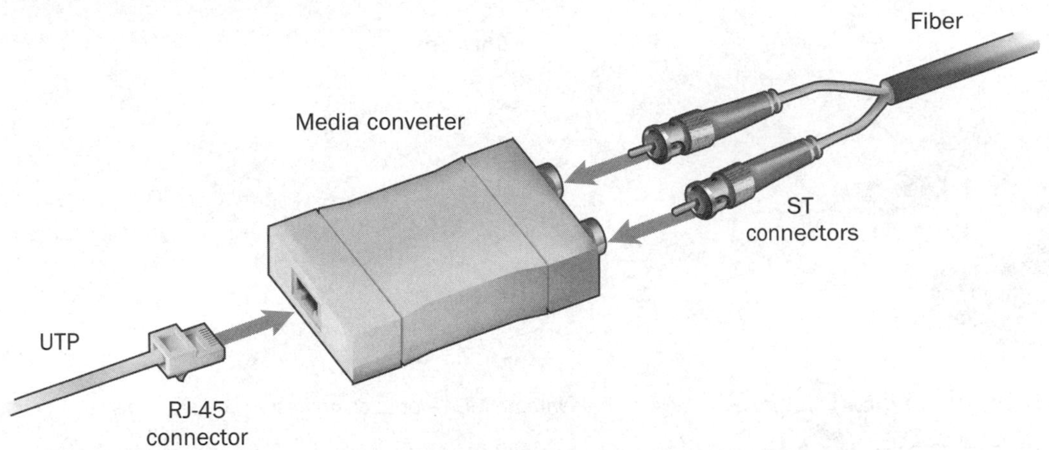

Media converter. *Using a media converter to connect unshielded twisted pair (UTP) and fiber optic cabling.*

Uses

Common uses of media converters in networks include

- Connecting two different wiring systems, such as 100BaseTX and 100BaseFX, without adding to the repeater count for your network
- Connecting two 10BaseT or 100BaseTX networks in different buildings using fiber-optic cabling runs as long as 9.3 miles (15 kilometers)
- Connecting a 100Base2 thinnet Ethernet segment to an RJ-45 port on a 10/100-Mbps hub
- Integrating a mix of cabling, including UTP cabling, thinnet, thicknet, and fiber-optic cabling

Media converters can often be valuable for companies that have a legacy thicknet or thinnet Ethernet local area network (LAN) but want to take advantage of Fast Ethernet switching technology. Instead of rewiring your entire LAN to unshielded twisted-pair (UTP) cabling, which is the standard cabling type for 100BaseT Ethernet, you can utilize some of your existing cabling by connecting your coaxial cabling to a media converter and then connecting the media converter to the Ethernet switch using UTP patch cables.

Media converters are also commonly used to join copper LANs together using long runs of fiber. Canoga Perkins Corporation offers its EdgeAccess Gigabit Ethernet Media Converter for connecting Gigabit Ethernet (GbE) backbone switches using fiber-optic cabling. Products such as this can be used to build custom metropolitan area networks (MANs) using dark fiber leased from telcos and are often used by service providers that are building metropolitan Ethernet backbone networks.

See Also: *10Base2, 10Base5, 10BaseT, 100BaseT, coaxial cabling, Ethernet, Fast Ethernet, fiber-optic cabling, Gigabit Ethernet (GbE), metropolitan Ethernet, thicknet, thinnet, unshielded twisted-pair (UTP) cabling*

media-dependent adapter (MDA)

A standard for modular Ethernet switches.

Overview

Ethernet switches come in two types:

- **Fixed**: These switches are self-contained units that generally provide a fixed number of ports for unshielded twisted-pair (UTP) cabling or fiber-optic cabling.
- **Modular**: These switches can be customized to support different numbers of UTP and fiber ports as needed.

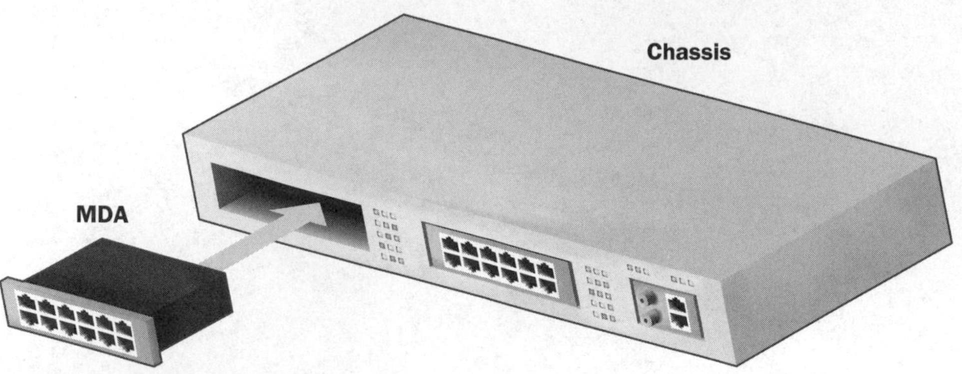

Media-dependent adapter (MDA). *Inserting an MDA module into an MDA slot to customize a modular Ethernet switch.*

Modular Ethernet switches generally consist of a chassis with two to four media-dependent adapter (MDA) slots on the front panel. To customize these switches for your network, you simply insert MDA modules into the slots to provide the media configuration you require. A single MDA module might provide one of the following typical port configurations:

- Eight 100/10BaseT ports or 1000/100/10BaseT ports
- Two 100BaseTX or 100BaseFX ports
- A single Fiber Distributed Data Interface (FDDI) double-ring connection

By selecting and inserting different MDAs into a modular Ethernet switch, you can quickly reconfigure complex networks. Bridging between the different types of media is performed internally by the chassis circuitry inside the switch.

See Also: *10BaseT, 100BaseFX, 100BaseT, 100BaseTX, Ethernet, Fiber Distributed Data Interface (FDDI), fiber-optic cabling, unshielded twisted-pair (UTP) cabling*

Megaco

An emerging framework for connecting voice, fax, and videoconferencing systems to packet-switching networks.

Overview

Megaco is a standard developed jointly by the International Telecommunication Union (ITU) and the Internet Engineering Task Force (IETF). Megaco is designed to support convergence of telephone and data services and is especially targeted toward the Internet Protocol (IP) telephony sector to ensure interoperability between gateways and controllers supplied by different vendors. The name Megaco is short for Media Gateway Control, and the ITU standard for this framework is H.248.

Architecture

Integrating circuit-switched systems such as the Public Switched Telephone Network (PSTN) and packet-switched systems such as the Internet are complicated by the fact that the PSTN actually consists of two separate networks:

- **Traffic network:** The network that actually transports voice and data traffic between callers.
- **Signaling network:** The network responsible for control functions such as call setup and tear down. The signaling network for the PSTN is known as Signaling System 7 (SS7).

In a typical IP telephony system, the IP network interfaces with the two PSTN networks using two different kinds of devices:

- **Media gateway (MG):** Enables data on the PSTN to be converted into IP packets for transmission over the Internet and vice versa. The MG interfaces the IP network with the traffic portion of the PSTN, and MGs communicate with each other using protocols such as Real Time Protocol (RTP).

- **Media gateway controller (MGC):** Enables control signals on the PSTN to be converted into IP packets for transmission over the Internet and vice versa. The MGC interfaces the IP network with the SS7, and MGCs communicate with each other using protocols such as H.323 or Session Initiation Protocol (SIP). MGCs are sometimes known as softswitches or call agents.

Megaco's role in the IP telephony framework is to provide a standard protocol for communication between MGs and MGCs. Megaco allows MGCs to control MGs and enables the remote control of connection-aware devices across signaling domains. Megaco can be implemented on a wide range of devices, including

- Digital Subscriber Line Access Multiplexers (DSLAMs)
- Optical cross-connects in telecom switching centers
- Routers that support Multiprotocol Label Switching (MPLS)
- Voice over IP (VoIP) gateways

Prospects

Megaco is intended as an industry standard, vendor-independent protocol for MG/MGC communication and is expected to displace the proprietary Media Gateway Control Protocol (MGCP) defined in RFC 2705, which has established itself as a de facto standard but which lacks some of Megaco's advanced capabilities, such as peer-to-peer device control (MGCP supports only master/slave control). Megaco also replaces earlier protocols, including Internet Protocol Device Control (IPDC) and Simple Gateway Control Protocol (SGCP).

See Also: *Digital Subscriber Line Access Multiplexer (DSLAM), H.323, IP telephony, Multiprotocol Label Switching (MPLS), Public Switched Telephone Network (PSTN), Voice over IP (VoIP)*

member server

A server that does not perform logon authentication.

Overview

In Microsoft Windows 2000–based networks, a member server is any server that is not a domain controller. A member server, therefore, does not contain a copy of Active Directory directory service. Member servers do participate in domain security, however, by allowing folders and other resources on them to be shared with permissions assigned to different users and groups. However, member servers cannot be used to authenticate the credentials of users so they can log on to the network—domain controllers are required to perform this action.

Member servers are usually used for dedicated network purposes such as the following:

- File and print servers
- Application servers
- Database servers
- Web servers
- Mail servers

Notes

In Windows 2000, you can change a member server into a domain controller by running the Active Directory Installation Wizard.

See Also: *Active Directory, domain controller*

mesh topology

A network topology that has redundant data paths between nodes.

Overview

A mesh network (a network that has a mesh topology) is any network in which information typically has more than one route it can take between any two end stations. Meshed topologies are commonly used in backbone networks to provide fault tolerance—if a wire, hub, switch, or other component fails, data can always reach its destination by traveling along an alternate path. Meshed networks are common in older, routed Internet Protocol (IP) internetworks and prevent the failure of a single router from bringing down a portion of the network.

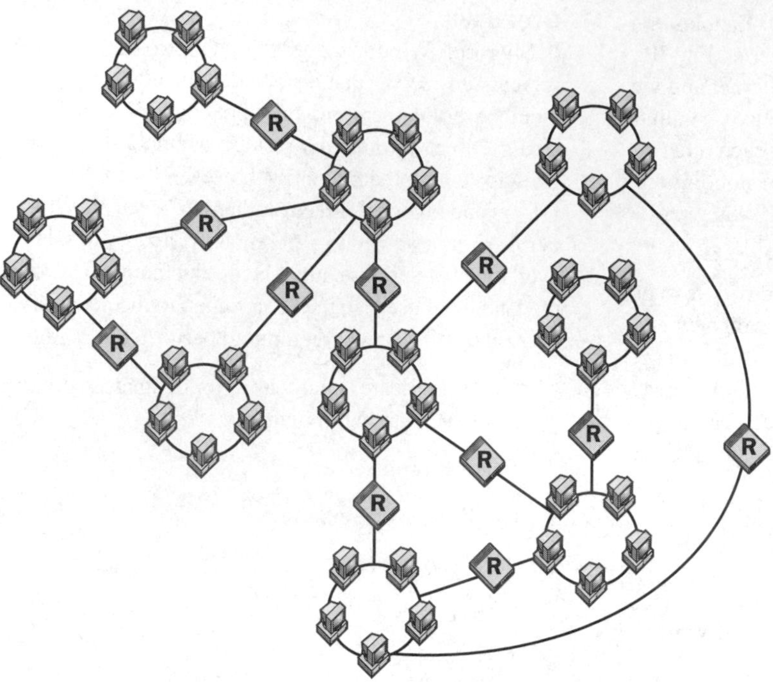

Mesh topology. Example of mesh topology for a routed internetwork.

There are two basic types of mesh networks:

- **Fully meshed:** This type of network provides a direct link between every pair of nodes on the network. Full mesh topologies have the highest possible level of fault tolerance, but when used in routed internetworks, they increase the computational strain on dynamic routers for calculating their routing tables. A full mesh network with N routers would in fact have N! (N factorial) paths (1 x 2 x 3 x . . . x N) to calculate, and N! increases very rapidly with N.
- **Partially meshed:** This type of network is more common than the fully meshed type and includes a certain number of redundant data paths to provide some degree of fault tolerance to the network.

See Also: *bus topology, fault tolerance, internetwork, ring topology, router, star topology*

message

Information sent between two entities.

Overview

The common definition of a message in computer networking is a communication sent by one user to another user by means of an e-mail system such as the Simple Mail Transfer Protocol (SMTP) mail system that is used on the Internet. More generally in computer networking, a message is any grouping of information at the application layer (Layer 7) of the Open Systems Interconnection (OSI) reference model that is exchanged between applications for various purposes. These Layer 7 messages can contain control information or report errors, or they can support the running of a network-aware application in some other fashion.

In Microsoft Message Queuing (MSMQ) terminology, a message is a unit of information or data that is sent between two applications, usually hosted on different computers on a network.

See Also: *application layer, e-mail, Internet, Open Systems Interconnection (OSI) reference model, Simple Mail Transfer Protocol (SMTP)*

message digest (MD) algorithms

A series of hashing algorithms used in cryptography.

Overview

Message digest (MD) algorithms are commonly used in cryptography to generate digital signatures for ensuring the integrity and authenticity of encrypted messages. The term *message digest* refers to a short string or hash value of fixed length that is computed from the longer variable-length message being hashed by the algorithm.

Types

The important message digest algorithms include MD2, MD4, and MD5, all of which produce a 128-bit hash value. The details of these different algorithms are as follows:

- **MD2:** Developed in 1989 for 8-bit encoders. It pads the message to be encoded until it is a multiple of 16 bytes in length, appends a 16-byte checksum, and computes the hash.
- **MD4:** Developed in 1990 for 32-bit encoders. It pads the message to be encoded until it is 56 bytes short of being a multiple of 512 bytes, appends an 8-byte message length value, and iteratively hashes the message in three rounds. MD4 can be broken fairly easily in a dedicated cryptographic attempt. It is implemented in the Microsoft Challenge Handshake Authentication Protocol (MS-CHAP) supported by the Remote Access Service (RAS) on Microsoft Windows NT.
- **MD5:** Developed in 1991 for 32-bit encoders. It is an extension of MD4 and uses four rounds of hashing instead of three. It is fairly difficult to crack. Windows NT RAS Client supports MD5-CHAP for connecting to third-party Point-to-Point Protocol (PPP) servers supporting MD5 authentication, but Windows NT RAS Server does not. However, Service Pack 3 for Windows NT provides limited support for MD5-CHAP PPP authentication. Microsoft Windows 2000 Routing and Remote Access Service (RRAS) supports MD5.

See Also: *cryptography, digital signature, encryption, hashing algorithm, Microsoft Challenge Handshake Authentication Protocol (MS-CHAP), Point-to-Point Protocol (PPP)*

Message Tracking Query Protocol (MTQP)

An emerging protocol for tracking e-mail messages over the Internet.

Overview

Message Tracking Query Protocol (MTQP) is a proposed standard from the Internet Engineering Task Force (IETF) to enable administrators to track the route that Simple Mail Transport Protocol (SMTP) messages take as they travel across the Internet. MTQP enables a message's sender to determine the specific host and router hops taken by SMTP messages, regardless of whether they reach their destination or not. MTQP thus provides the capability for determining whether messages have actually reached their intended recipients or where along the way they may have been prevented from reaching their destination.

MTQP solves a problem inherent with SMTP: the current best-effort delivery model of this protocol means that there is no guarantee that messages will reach their recipients and no way of knowing if they are delayed or lost. In this respect, X.400 messaging systems based on the X.400 recommendations developed in the 1980s by the International Telecommunication Union (ITU) have had a distinct advantage over SMTP, namely, messaging accountability. This accountability enables X.400 systems to be used for important purposes such as sending contracts and other legal documents—if the message is not received, the sender knows it and can act accordingly. As a result, X.400 continues to be used in situations where message integrity is vital, as in certain international and government organizations such as the North Atlantic Treaty Organization (NATO). Until now, however, SMTP lacked the essential accountability to make it a suitable medium for transmission of this kind of information. With a combination of MTQP, encryption, and digital signatures, the Internet might soon become the de facto medium for secure electronic transmission of legal information such as contracts, agreements, invoices, and bank statements.

MTQP was designed with input from AT&T Labs, MessagingDirect (now part of ACI Worldwide), and the Sendmail Consortium. The protocol operates in conjunction with SMTP Service Extensions (ESMTP), enabling the exact path that a message takes as it travels between hosts and across routers over the Internet.

Prospects

MTQP will be supported by upcoming versions of Sendmail and will likely be supported by other Internet mail platforms as well. MTQP's full value will only be realized, however, if it becomes widely implemented across the Internet and by major Internet service providers (ISPs). However, MTQP can be implemented on a limited basis between companies that frequently exchange e-mail and can alert them to problems with their messaging communications.

See Also: *ESMTP, Internet Engineering Task Force (IETF), Simple Mail Transfer Protocol (SMTP), X.400*

Messaging Application Programming Interface (MAPI)

A Microsoft technology that allows developers to use the Windows messaging subsystem for writing messaging applications.

M

Overview

The Messaging Application Programming Interface (MAPI) provides a generic programming interface for making Windows applications mail-enabled and standardizes how messages are handled by messaging applications. MAPI also provides a general messaging subsystem built into the Windows operating system that can function with any message transport mechanism. The messaging subsystem is thus similar to the printing subsystem that allows Windows to interface with any kind of print device and perform standard printing functions.

Implementation

MAPI is a kind of middleman between the messaging application running on the computer and the underlying messaging services. The client interface for accessing these services through MAPI is the same whether the services are local area network (LAN)-based messaging services, e-mail services, fax services, or any other messaging service. MAPI allows standard function calls to access general messaging functions such as sending, receiving, and reading messages in a uniform fashion regardless of the messaging subsystem used. MAPI provides two sets of interfaces: the client-side application programming interfaces (APIs) called by the messaging application, and the service-provider interfaces that the Windows messaging subsystem uses to connect with different messaging-handling systems.

Microsoft Outlook is an example of a MAPI-enabled client, and Microsoft Exchange Server supports MAPI messaging.

See Also: *application programming interface (API), Exchange Server, Outlook*

metabase

A database for storing configuration settings for Microsoft Internet Information Services (IIS).

Overview

The metabase is a hierarchical, memory-resident database that is used to store IIS configuration information. Prior to version 4 of IIS, such information was stored mainly in the Microsoft Windows NT registry. The metabase was introduced in IIS 4 as a more flexible and expandable repository than the registry, and being memory-resident, it also provides better performance than the disk-based registry. Some settings for IIS are still stored in the registry, however, for backward compatibility with older versions of IIS.

The metabase is stored as the file Metabase.bin in the \WINNT\system32\inetsrv directory on a Windows 2000 machine running IIS.

Notes

The Microsoft Internet Information Server Resource Kit includes a number of administrative scripts that you can use to back up and restore the metabase.

See Also: *Internet Information Services (IIS), registry*

metadirectory

A tool for combining diverse data sources into a single directory.

Overview

One of the realities of enterprise networks is heterogeneity, and this is particularly apparent in where and how an enterprise stores its data. A large enterprise might have several directory services such as Microsoft Active Directory directory service, Novell Directory Services (NDS) eDirectory, a homegrown Lightweight Directory Access Protocol (LDAP) directory, user account directories such as those found in Microsoft Windows NT and Novell NetWare, database platforms such as Oracle and Microsoft SQL Server, and messaging applications such as Lotus cc:Notes and Microsoft Exchange Server 5.5 that use their own proprietary directories. The task of a metadirectory is to integrate these various data sources into a single hierarchical directory that can be managed and queried as easily as if a single directory service were used across the enterprise.

Implementation

A metadirectory is really an integration strategy rather than a specific set of tools. Important decisions have to be made when thinking about integrating disparate directories together in the enterprise. For example, will one directory be chosen as the master and all others be slaves with respect to it? If this is the case, the directory chosen must be sufficiently scalable, robust, and extensible to enable it to integrate with all the other kinds of directories in the enterprise. In some situations, it may make sense for several directories to operate as masters with respect to different kinds of information. At other times, tools may be selected to enable several directories to operate as peers with each other, but this is rarer.

Another important question to decide is the level of integration to be achieved. For example, will updates be propagated across different directories or will queries simply be distributed across them instead? This question boils down to two basic ways of implementing integration of different directories: synchronization and brokering.

- **Synchronization:** In this approach, information that is updated on one directory is propagated to other directories or, more likely, to the master directory for the enterprise. The master directory, in this case, maintains an up-to-date repository of all the information stored in the various directories of the enterprise, and queries are issued against this master directory when information is required rather than querying individual directories. Metadirectory tools are used to enable the slave directories to talk to the master and to ensure that the slaves are properly synchronized with the master at all times. The master directory, in this case, becomes the authoritative information source for the enterprise. The downside of this approach is that the master directory becomes a single point of failure for information retrieval within the enterprise. This approach also has the tendency to make the master directory unwieldy due to the large amount of information it needs to store.
- **Brokering:** This approach avoids the issue of updating disparate directories with each other by allowing one directory to proxy requests to another directory. In this case, each directory maintains its own island of information, and queries issued against the master directory are forwarded to the appropriate slave directories for answering using metadirectory brokering tools. The slave directories then return their results to the master, which returns them to the client making the request. The advantage of this approach is that each directory can be kept small. The disadvantage is that querying can be slower due to the proxied requests that have to be issued.

Marketplace

Microsoft MetaDirectory Services (MMS) from Microsoft Corporation is a metadirectory product originally developed by Zoomit Corporation that can be used for integrating different directories together. MMS uses a core metadirectory service called Metaverse that communicates with other directories such as Microsoft Active Directory using management agents. MMS agents are available for a wide range of enterprise applications, including enterprise resource planning (ERP) and customer relationship management (CRM) applications from different vendors.

Another metadirectory product is Novell's new DirXML platform, which uses XML-based connectors to integrate Novell eDirectory to directory services from other vendors and to various messaging platforms. Connectors will be available for a wide range of enterprise applications, including those from SAP and PeopleSoft, X.500 directory services, and databases that support the Open Database Connectivity (ODBC) and Java Database Connectivity (JDBC) platforms.

Prospects

Although LDAP has securely replaced the complex and unwieldy X.500 directory recommendations from the International Telecommunication Union (ITU), the emergence of Extensible Markup Language (XML) has complicated the directory landscape somewhat. Most commercial directories, such as Microsoft Active Directory and Novell eDirectory, are LDAP-compliant and support LDAP application programming interfaces (APIs) that make it fairly simple to enable these directories to communicate with each other. Other applications that have non-LDAP data stores can often be integrated with LDAP directories by writing custom middleware that translates application-specific APIs into LDAP APIs. With the emergence of XML, however, new strategies are being tried for storing enterprise information, and an initiative called Directory Services Markup Language (DSML) is being developed to further support the integration of vendor-specific directories. Enterprises should not view metadirectories as a panacea for directory interoperability problems but as a workaround for lack of planning and unstructured growth of enterprise information sources, and these products are sometimes little more than veiled attempts by vendors to persuade customers to migrate to the vendor's own directory platform.

See Also: *Active Directory, directory, Directory Service Markup Language (DSML), Java Database Connectivity (JDBC), Lightweight Directory Access Protocol (LDAP), Novell Directory Services (NDS), open database connectivity (ODBC), X.500, XML*

metasearching

Integrating multiple search engines into a single search entity.

Overview

Search engines such as Google, AltaVista, and Yahoo! are popular tools for users to find helpful information on the Internet. Metasearching simply means integrating several of these tools using a single search interface. Metasearching can employ several architectures:

- **Metasearch servers:** Web sites to which users submit their search requests and which then proxy user requests to traditional search engines such as Google and AltaVista. The replies from these search engines are then consolidated by the metasearch server and returned to the user as a single result set. Examples of sites that use this approach include Metacrawler, the first metasearch engine and now owned by Go2Net; SavvySearch, now owned by CNET Networks and available from Search.com; Dogpile, which displays result sets for each search engine used separately; and Profusion, which allows you to select which traditional search engines to proxy your requests to.
- **Metasearch utilities:** Applications that run on the client and generally offer additional features such as sorting, highlighting, and automatic downloading of results pages. Examples of metasearch utilities include Copernic, available for both the Microsoft Windows and Apple Macintosh platforms; BullsEye, a popular Windows application from Intelliseek; and Sherlock, a metasearch utility integrated into the Macintosh operating system in versions 8.5 and later.

See Also: *Internet*

metropolitan area network (MAN)

Traditionally, a network spanning a metropolitan area.

Overview

Metropolitan area network (MAN) is a concept that can mean several things depending on the context. For example, a MAN could be

- A telco service that provides data transport across an urban area using ATM over SONET technology.
- Several local area networks (LANs) connected across an urban area using a high-speed fiber-optic backbone.
- Several connected networks within a city, forming a citywide network for a specific government organization or corporation.
- Any network bigger than a LAN but smaller than a wide area network (WAN).
- Any network that spans more than a single building.
- A Distributed Queue Dual Bus architecture network based on the IEEE 802.6 standard of Project 802 (this is the formal definition of a MAN, but it is now obsolete).

The first definition on this list is the one most familiar to enterprise network architects. To build a WAN consisting of LANs in different geographic locations, enterprises lease MAN services from their local telco. These MAN services thus enable LANs to be joined together into a WAN, and the MAN thus functions as the demarcation point between LAN and WAN. Common MAN services offered by telcos include Integrated Services Digital Network (ISDN), T1 and T3 lines, and Digital Subscriber Line (DSL) services. Enterprises typically interface their LANs with the telco MAN by deploying an access device (also called a WAN switch or access multiplexer) in the basement of their equipment room. The access device then aggregates company LAN traffic and backhauls it from the customer premises to the Point of Presence (POP) of the telco, where it typically traverses the metropolitan area over a dual SONET ring.

Prospects

A new development is the emergence of metropolitan Ethernet service providers, which compete with traditional telcos for hauling data traffic by building their own fiber MANs and provisioning fiber to businesses in downtown areas. Metropolitan Ethernet is cheaper than traditional telco WAN services that rely on ATM over SONET, is easier to deploy and manage, and is fast becoming a viable alternative for the MAN demarcation point between LAN and WAN.

See Also: *ATM over SONET, local area network (LAN), metropolitan Ethernet, wide area network (WAN)*

metropolitan Ethernet

A service that uses Gigabit Ethernet (GbE) to provision metropolitan areas with high-speed data services.

Overview

Metropolitan Ethernet represents a new kind of data service now offered in many dense urban areas. Traditionally wide area network (WAN) and metropolitan area network (MAN) services have been provisioned by telcos, particularly by Incumbent Local Exchange Carriers (ILECs) that own the local loop telephone wiring connecting customer premises to their services. Telecommunication services offered by telcos have included dial-up Internet access, Integrated Services Digital Network (ISDN), T1 and fractional T1 lines, and recently Digital Subscriber Line (DSL). The monopoly enjoyed by telcos as a result of local loop ownership has enabled them to maintain high prices for many of these services. For example, a T1 line typically costs around $1,000 a month and provides only 1.5 megabits per second (Mbps) bandwidth, but a T3 line offers a much higher bandwidth of 45 Mbps but at a correspondingly higher price of tens of thousands of dollars per month, which is beyond the budget of most businesses except the largest enterprises and large service providers. DSL is a relatively new technology that offers multimegabit data speeds, and competition with cable modem technologies has kept DSL prices low for residential customers, but the absence of cable television infrastructure buildout in business parks and downtown areas has meant that DSL prices for business customers can be kept artificially high.

M

The result of all this is that the MAN has become the bottleneck between the corporate local area network (LAN) and the WAN. Although LAN speeds have risen to 100 Mbps Fast Ethernet and higher and WAN speeds within the Synchronous Optical Network (SONET) backbones of carriers is also 100 Mbps or higher, companies trying to join their LANs into a WAN using traditional T1 lines find that these lines have become the bottleneck in the equation and that upgrading to T3 is too costly a solution.

Enter the metropolitan (or metro) Ethernet service providers, companies who are building their own separate MANs to compete with the existing SONET rings owned by telcos. These new service providers are building their MANs using GbE switching gear, laying their own fiber backbones in dense urban areas to connect their points of presence (POPs) with industrial parks, campuses, and downtown multitenant units (MTUs). The demarcation point at the customer premises now becomes as simple as an RJ-45 connection, and customers can simply use a Category 5 (Cat5) patch cord to connect their Ethernet LAN to their carrier's GbE backbone to build a WAN or receive high-speed Internet access. Other services supported by some metro Ethernet providers include high-speed connectivity to storage area networks (SANs), Web and application server hosting, and multicast Internet Protocol (IP) video services.

Implementation

Metro Ethernet is made possible by the use of new carrier-class GbE switches that can be deployed at either the service provider's POP or the basement of the customer's MTU, depending on the scenario. At the provider's end, these switches interface with telco SONET rings to provide connectivity for long-distance WAN links; within a downtown area of a city, however, the metro Ethernet provider maintains end-to-end Ethernet connectivity for customers without the need of telco SONET services.

Metro Ethernet service providers may either lay their own fiber downtown or lease dark fiber from other carriers. To get the most out of this fiber, providers are starting to employ Wavelength Division Multiplexing (WDM), which enables as many as eight full-duplex GbE channels to run over a single fiber pair. Dense Wavelength Division Multiplexing (DWDM) offers the potential of squeezing even greater bandwidth out of individual fiber strands.

With GbE now supporting distances up to 150 miles (240 kilometers) over single-mode fiber, metro Ethernet can be deployed across even the largest cities to provide a high-speed alternative to SONET for data transport. The emergence of 10 Gigabit Ethernet (10 GbE) promises to provide even greater capacity for this service.

Advantages and Disadvantages

Metro Ethernet offers a number of advantages over traditional SONET rings for building WANs:

- **Simplicity:** The fact that Ethernet is running on both sides of the access device at the customer premises makes installation, configuration, and management of WAN links easier.
- **Cost:** Metro Ethernet connections are typically only 25 to 50 percent of the cost of traditional telco data services, even taking into account the cost of laying new fiber. The cost of GbE switching equipment used for WAN access to metro Ethernet services is about a tenth the prices of traditional ATM over SONET access devices, which adds up to another cost savings for metro Ethernet over telco WAN services. Finally, GbE is a well-known technology to LAN administrators, and so the cost of hiring or training IT (information technology) people skilled in ATM over SONET technologies is eliminated, which further reduces the cost.
- **Scalability:** Metro Ethernet is typically provisioned in 1 Mbps increments up to 1 gigabit per second (Gbps), with prices scaled accordingly. Although upgrading a traditional T1 line to T3 can take weeks, increasing bandwidth on a metro Ethernet connection usually takes only a few hours. Some service providers even offer customers a Web interface from which they can provision additional bandwidth for themselves as required.

- **Manageability:** Metro Ethernet simplifies the task of data management by enabling packets to be processed at Layers 3 through 7 of the Open Systems Interconnection (OSI) reference model. This contrasts with SONET, where it is difficult to process packets on the backbone.
- **Fault-tolerance:** Traditional dual SONET rings deployed by telcos offer fault-tolerance that GbE networks do not intrinsically possess. By combining GbE with Dense Wavelength Division Multiplexing (DWDM), however, SONET's dual-ring architecture can be imitated to provide a robust, fault-tolerant backbone comparable to SONET.

The main disadvantage of metro Ethernet is availability: for the foreseeable future, this service will probably be available only in the downtown sections of large urban areas. Another disadvantage is that although dual SONET rings deployed by telcos are self-healing (typically in less than 50 milliseconds), GbE networks do not have such built-in recoverability features. Furthermore, while ATM over SONET is a cell-based connection-oriented technology that is optimized for voice but can also carry data easily, Ethernet is a connectionless packet-switched technology that suffers unpredictable delay and jitter, factors that have little effect on data traffic but which make it difficult to transport voice traffic (unless bandwidth is far below saturation point). Finally, SONET networks traditionally offer five-nines (99.999 percent) uptime, which is typically an order of magnitude better than the best metro Ethernet networks available today.

Marketplace

Metro Ethernet service providers offer a wide range of services from LAN-LAN interconnection within urban areas to high-speed Internet access and even Voice over IP (VoIP) services. They can provision a single fiber link to an MTU in such a way that each client within the building has its own secure connection and is billed separately according to usage. Popular service providers in the metro Ethernet marketplace include Yipes Communications, Telseon, FiberCity Networks, Cogent Communications, Everest Broadband Networks, IntelliSpace, XO Communications, and many others. Although some of these providers offer services only in a few urban centers, many of them are scaling out to offer services nationally in large cities across the United States. Some metro Ethernet service providers specialize only in high-speed Internet access or WAN connectivity, but others offer a full range of services comparable to telcos.

Carrier-class GbE switches for metro Ethernet rollouts are now available from a number of vendors, including Extreme Networks, Foundry Networks, Cisco Systems, Nortel Networks, and Riverstone Networks.

Prospects

Just as GbE has won out over competing LAN backbone technologies such as Fiber Distributed Data Interface (FDDI) and Asynchronous Transfer Mode (ATM), the same thing may happen in the WAN, at least for data services. ATM over SONET still offers a much higher Quality of Service (QoS) for voice communications, but the simplicity and price advantages of end-to-end Ethernet in the WAN make it the leading technology as far as data services are concerned. Unfortunately, metro Ethernet is likely to remain exactly that—Ethernet restricted to metropolitan areas where dense clusters of MTUs make laying fiber a cost-effective decision for service providers. Metro Ethernet is unlikely to be available in the foreseeable future in smaller urban or rural areas, which must continue to rely on telco services as their only option. Nevertheless, metro Ethernet is having a profound impact on the enterprise WAN cost model and may even eat into the traditional voice market of telcos as VoIP technologies become more standardized and widely deployed.

See Also: *Asynchronous Transfer Mode (ATM), ATM over SONET, dense wavelength division multiplexing (DWDM), Digital Subscriber Line (DSL), Fiber Distributed Data Interface (FDDI), Gigabit Ethernet (GbE), Incumbent Local Exchange Carrier (ILEC), Integrated Services Digital Network (ISDN), local area network (LAN), metropolitan area network (MAN), storage area network (SAN), Synchronous Optical Network (SONET), T-carrier, Voice over IP (VoIP), wide area network (WAN)*

M

MExE

Stands for Mobile Execution Environment, an emerging standard for running Java applications on mobile phones.

See: *Mobile Execution Environment (MExE)*

MFC

Stands for Microsoft Foundation Classes, a set of object-oriented interfaces to the Microsoft Windows application programming interface (API).

See: *Microsoft Foundation Classes (MFC)*

MFR

Stands for Multilink Frame Relay, a new frame relay aggregation technology.

See: *Multilink Frame Relay (MFR)*

M

MIB

Stands for Management Information Base, a database of information about a device that is managed by using the Simple Network Management Protocol (SNMP).

See: *Management Information Base (MIB)*

microkernel

An operating system architecture in which the kernel is a small component with limited functionality that loads other components such as drivers and services into memory only as required to complete requested system tasks.

See: *kernel*

Microsoft Certified Partner

An independent company that partners with Microsoft Corporation to provide IT (information technology) services to corporate, government, and small business customers.

Overview

The Microsoft Certified Partner Program is a partnership between Microsoft and independent companies where Microsoft provides IT services and products that enable these companies to provide solutions for their clients based on leading-edge Microsoft technologies. The program is global in scope and is the primary channel by which Microsoft solutions are provided. The Microsoft Certified Partner Program evolved primarily from the Microsoft Certified Solution Provider program formed in 1992, and it has over 31,000 partners worldwide.

Microsoft Certified Partners receive numerous benefits to help them deliver Microsoft solutions, including licenses for internal and marketing use of Microsoft products, access to prerelease software information and program codes, sales and marketing resources, technical training and support, and direct support from Microsoft staff. Partners participate in joint marketing ventures and receive valuable customer referrals.

The Microsoft Certified Partner Program has two levels of membership:

- **Member:** Companies that receive useful technical, marketing, and sales information, and also licenses for Microsoft products for internal testing and development purposes.
- **Gold:** Companies that have demonstrated a high level of proficiency in building solutions using Microsoft technologies within one or more solutions areas, including enterprise systems, support centers, e-commerce, and Application Service Provider (ASP) services.

For More Information

Find out more about the Microsoft Certified Partner program at *www.microsoft.com/certpartner.*

Microsoft Certified Professional (MCP)

A family of technical certifications relating to proficiency in working with Microsoft products.

Overview

Microsoft Certified Professionals (MCPs) are individuals who have demonstrated in-depth knowledge of specific Microsoft operating system and application platforms. Different Microsoft certifications relate to different areas of expertise, knowledge, and skill. The various types of technical certifications offered by Microsoft Corporation can be summarized as follows:

- **System Engineering:** Directed toward professionals who install, administer, and troubleshoot networks based on Microsoft operating systems. Certifications in this family range from the basic Microsoft Certified Professional (MCP) designation, which signifies that the holder has demonstrated proficiency by passing an exam in at least one Microsoft operating system, to the prestigious Microsoft Certified System Engineer (MCSE) designation, which requires the candidate to pass five core exams and two elective exams. The MCSE designation is used in the IT (information technology) industry as a benchmark for identifying individuals who have proficiency in skills related to occupations such as systems engineers, technical support engineers, systems analysts, network analysts, and technical consultants. A typical MCSE has expertise in Microsoft Windows 2000 (or Windows .NET Server) and in one or more Microsoft BackOffice (or Microsoft .NET Server) application platforms.
- **Solutions Development:** Directed toward professionals who design, build, and implement solutions using Microsoft application development technologies such as Visual Basic, Visual C++, C#, and other Microsoft programming platforms. Certifications in this family range from the basic MCP designation, which signifies that the holder has demonstrated proficiency by passing an exam in at least one Microsoft application development platform, to the Microsoft Certified Solution Developer (MCSD) designation, which requires the candidate to pass three core exams and one elective exam. The MCSD designation is used to identify individuals whose proficiency relates to occupations such as software engineers, software applications engineers, software developers, and technical consultants.
- **Database Administration:** Directed toward professionals who deploy, administer, and troubleshoot solutions using Microsoft database technologies based on Microsoft SQL Server. Certifications in this family range from the basic MCP designation, which signifies that the holder has demonstrated proficiency by passing at least one exam related to Microsoft database technologies, to the Microsoft Certified Database Administrator (MCDA) designation, which requires the candidate to pass three core exams and one elective exam. The MCDA designation is used to identify individuals whose proficiency relates to occupations such as database administrator, database analysts, and database developers.

A fourth area of Microsoft professional certification is the Microsoft Certified Trainer (MCT) designation, which is used to identify individuals qualified to deliver technical training in Microsoft platforms and applications using Microsoft Official Curriculum (MOC) courseware at a Microsoft-authorized training center.

Employers can use Microsoft certifications for screening candidates for technical positions in their IT departments, and current employees can be encouraged to achieve this designation as part of their career advancement path. Certifications are achieved by passing exams administered by independent organizations such as Sylvan Prometric and Virtual University Enterprises, which together have more than 1400 testing centers worldwide.

Notes

Microsoft also has a nontechnical certification for users, including the Microsoft Office User Specialist (MOUS) certification.

For More Information

You can find out about Microsoft certification at *www.microsoft.com/trainingandservices.*

See Also: *Microsoft Office User Specialist (MOUS), Microsoft Official Curriculum (MOC)*

Microsoft Challenge Handshake Authentication Protocol (MS-CHAP)

An encrypted authentication scheme for Point-to-Point Protocol (PPP) sessions.

Overview

Microsoft Challenge Handshake Authentication Protocol (MS-CHAP) is Microsoft Corporation's version of the Internet standard Challenge Handshake Authentication Protocol (CHAP) defined in RFC 1994. Remote access servers use MS-CHAP to encrypt authentication sessions with remote access clients. Although CHAP requires the plaintext version of the remote user's password to be available on the access server for comparison purposes, MS-CHAP requires only the MD4 hash of the user's password to be available. The user's password information is thus stored in encrypted form on the access server, which makes MS-CHAP more secure than CHAP. MS-CHAP also differs from CHAP in that it employs a challenge/response packet format specifically designed for Windows platforms.

M

There are two different versions of MS-CHAP:

- **MS-CHAPv1:** Used by Microsoft Windows NT 4.0. Supports one-way authentication of remote clients by access servers.
- **MS-CHAPv2:** Used in Microsoft Windows 2000 or later. Supports mutual authentication of both the remote client and the access server to guard against server impersonation. MS-CHAPv2 also includes the following new features:
  - Unique cryptographic keys are generated each time the user connects. These keys are based on a hash of the user's password and the arbitrary challenge string generated during the authentication session.
  - Separate keys are employed for data transmission and reception rather than the single key used in MS-CHAPv1.
  - LAN Manager encoding is no longer supported.

Implementation

Use of MS-CHAP is negotiated during the Link Control Protocol (LCP) portion of the PPP authentication process. Once the remote client requests authentication from the access server and negotiates MS-CHAP, the authentication process is encrypted in three steps:

1. The access server sends the remote client a Challenge message consisting of a session ID and an arbitrary challenge string.
2. The client sends the server a Response message consisting of the username (in plaintext), a hash of the challenge string, the session ID, and a one-way MD4 hash of the user's password.
3. The server generates a duplicate version of the hash of the user's password and compares this with the Response message received from the client. If these match, the client is authenticated and the PPP session is initiated.

See Also: *Challenge Handshake Authentication Protocol (CHAP), Link Control Protocol (LCP), Point-to-Point Protocol (PPP), remote access*

microsoft.com

The Web site for Microsoft Corporation, the worldwide leader in software for business and personal computing.

Overview

Microsoft's Web site is one of the largest and most complex in the world, as might be expected for a company having over 48,000 employees in over 60 regional offices worldwide. The *microsoft.com* site is also the main resource for those who use Microsoft products, including consumers, businesses, consultants, system integrators, and software developers. The staffs of IT (information technology) departments, sales and marketing, help desk, and business implementers can find useful information on *microsoft.com* about planning, designing, deploying, managing, maintaining, and troubleshooting solutions built using Microsoft products, platforms, and technologies.

Despite the size and complexity of the site, *microsoft.com* is actually amazingly simple to navigate! Nevertheless, finding information on a site as large as this is sometimes difficult, as many important Uniform Resource Locators (URLs) are not found on the site's home page. This article is designed to simplify this process of finding useful information for networking professionals by providing a summary of links to valuable information found on Microsoft's Web site. The URLs listed here are mostly top-level URLs that are unlikely to change frequently (many have remained the same for several years), and even if the site managers change them, these URLs are likely to be redirected automatically to the updated information. The URLs in the main table below are listed in short form as relative URLs; for example, */windows* is short for *www.microsoft.com/windows*.

Note that a few URLs listed below are redirections to other Microsoft Web sites, such as the Microsoft Developer Network (MSDN) site at *msdn.microsoft.com*. And information about Microsoft's suite of developer products is actually found on the MSDN site rather than on the main *www.microsoft.com* site. For example, the site for Microsoft Visual Studio is found at *msdn.microsoft.com/vstudio* instead of *www.microsoft.com/vstudio*, but the latter URL actually redirects you to the former.

Essential Links for Networking Professionals on Microsoft.com

Relative URL	*Information on . . .*
/backofficeserver	Microsoft BackOffice Server home
/backstage	Inside view of microsoft.com operations
/billgates	Bill Gates's home page
/business	Microsoft business products and services
/catalog	Catalog of all Microsoft products
/certpartner	Microsoft Certified Partners home
/college	Microsoft jobs for college students
/ddk	Microsoft Windows Driver Development Kits
/directx	Microsoft DirectX home
/diversity	Microsoft Diversity home

(continued)

Essential Links for Networking Professionals on Microsoft.com *continued*

Relative URL	*Information on . . .*
/downloads	Microsoft download center (redirection)
/ebooks	Microsoft eBooks home
/education	Microsoft education home
/embedded	Windows Embedded home (redirection)
/enable	Microsoft accessibility information
/games	Microsoft games official Web site
/giving	Microsoft giving programs
/hcl	Hardware compatibility list (HCL) for Microsoft products
/hwdev	Windows driver and hardware development site
/insider	Microsoft consumer products and services
/jobs	Jobs at Microsoft
/kids	Free stuff and special offers for kids
/mac	Mactopia, Microsoft products for Macintosh
/mba	Microsoft jobs for MBAs
/mindshare	Mindshare User Group Support Program
/mobile	Mobile Devices and Pocket PC home
/mscorp	Corporate information about Microsoft
/msft	Microsoft investor relations
/museum	Microsoft museum online
/net	Microsoft .NET platform home
/office	Microsoft Office main site (see Note 1 later in this article)
/partner	Microsoft for partners home
/piracy	Microsoft anti-piracy home
/presspass	Microsoft news and press releases
/reader	Microsoft Reader with ClearType
/security	Microsoft security home
/seminar	Microsoft Multimedia Central

(continued)

M

Essential Links for Networking Professionals on Microsoft.com *continued*

Relative URL	*Information on . . .*
/servers	Microsoft .NET Enterprise Servers (see Note 2 later in this article)
/serviceproviders	Microsoft service providers home
/support	Product support home (redirection)
/technet	Microsoft TechNet home for IT professionals
/trainingandservices	Microsoft training and certification home
/usability	Participate in product evaluations
/vstudio	Redirection to Microsoft Visual Studio .NET site on MSDN (see Note 3 later in this article)
/windows	Microsoft Windows main site (see Note 4 later in this article)
/winlogo	Microsoft Windows logo program
/worldwide	Microsoft worldwide information

The following table lists some other useful URLs in the microsoft.com domain; these, however, begin with a host prefix different from the usual *www.* prefix. Each of these sites represents a wealth of information useful to IT professionals.

Some Other Sites in the Microsoft.com Domain

URL	*Description*
communities.microsoft.com/home/	Microsoft newsgroups, technical chats, and user groups
dgl.microsoft.com	Microsoft Office Design Gallery Live (redirection)
office.microsoft.com	Office Update home
mcsp.microsoft.com/home	Microsoft Certified Partner home
mcspreferral.microsoft.com	Find a Microsoft Certified Partner
msdn.microsoft.com	Microsoft Developer Network home

(continued)

Some Other Sites in the Microsoft.com Domain *continued*

URL	*Description*
msdnisv.microsoft.com	Microsoft Business Connection for Partners
msevents.microsoft.com	Search for Microsoft events (redirection)
mspress.microsoft.com	Microsoft Press
murl.microsoft.com	Multi-University Research Laboratory
research.microsoft.com	Microsoft Research (MSR) home
search.microsoft.com	Search for info on microsoft.com (redirection)
shop.microsoft.com	Shop online at Microsoft
support.microsoft.com/directory	Microsoft product support home
support.microsoft.com/search	Microsoft Knowledge Base (KB)
terraserver.microsoft.com	Microsoft Terraserver (redirection)
windowsupdate.microsoft.com	Windows Update home

Finally, here are some interesting and useful URLs to Web sites that are managed by or connected with Microsoft but are not part of the microsoft.com domain.

Some Microsoft Sites Outside the Microsoft.com Domain

URL	*Description*
bcentral.com	Microsoft small business resource center
expedia.com	Expedia.com home
hotmail.com	Hotmail
msn.com	MSN
msnbc.com	MSNBC home
passport.com	Microsoft Passport home (redirection)
webtv.com	MSN TV Service
windowslogo.com	Windows Logo Program (redirection)
windowsmedia.com	MSN site for music, radio, video, and more

Notes

1 URLs for specific components of Microsoft Office are usually easy to guess. For example, to find the page for Microsoft Word, use *www.microsoft.com/office/word*, and to find the page for Microsoft Excel, use *www.microsoft.com/office/excel*. This does not always work, however; for instance, *www.microsoft.com/frontpage* for the Microsoft FrontPage home.

2 Although the URL *www.microsoft.com/servers* provides a starting point for information about any of Microsoft's .NET Enterprise Servers, you can usually reach the page for a specific server by using the name of the server in the URL. For example, to find information on Microsoft Application Center 2000, use *www.microsoft.com/applicationcenter*; for information on Microsoft BizTalk Server 2000, use *www.microsoft.com/biztalk*; and so on. Sometimes the URL can be a little more cryptic, as in *www.microsoft.com/isaserver* for Microsoft Internet Security and Acceleration Server 2000. And sometimes the URL requires a specific page, such as *www.microsoft.com/sharepoint/portalserver.asp,* for Microsoft SharePoint Portal Server, although in this case there is a link from the default page *www.microsoft.com/sharepoint* to the main SharePoint Portal Server page.

3 URLs for specific components of Microsoft Visual Studio are sometimes easy to guess. For example, the main page for Microsoft Visual Basic is *msdn.microsoft.com/vbasic*, but the page for Microsoft Visual C++ is *msdn.microsoft.com/visualc* instead. Do not forget to use *msdn* instead of *www* as the first portion of a URL for a developer product.

4 URLs for versions of Microsoft Windows are usually obvious; for example, *www.microsoft.com/windowsxp* for Windows XP, *www.microsoft.com/windows2000/* for Windows 2000, and so on. This pattern breaks, however, with Windows CE, where the URL is instead *www.microsoft.com/windows/embedded/ce*.

See Also: *Microsoft Corporation, Microsoft Developer Network (MSDN), TechNet*

Microsoft Consulting Services (MCS)

A service from Microsoft Corporation that provides direct assistance to large enterprises for planning, deploying, and supporting solutions based on Microsoft technologies.

Overview

Microsoft Consulting Services (MCS), in over 100 offices worldwide, has around 4000 Microsoft experts who can provide consulting services to help enterprises improve productivity, establish a competitive advantage, and make the most of their IT (information technology) investment. MCS offers a full range of programs, including enterprise application planning, distributed network architecture computing, e-commerce solutions, and more. Services offered by MCS include

- **Microsoft Consulting Services:** Integrated consulting and support services that includes on-site technical consulting and the support offered previously by Microsoft Product Support Services (PSS).
- **Microsoft Solutions Framework (MSF):** Provides training on how to plan, build, and deploy enterprise level solutions using Microsoft technologies.
- **Microsoft Operations Framework (MOF):** Provides self-paced training and reference materials addressing best practices for managing the people, processes, and technologies of the IT life cycle.
- **Microsoft Technology Centers (MTC):** Allow IT staff to work directly with Microsoft experts and partners in centers across North America.

For More Information

Visit *www.microsoft.com/business/services/mcs.asp*.

See Also: *Microsoft Operations Framework (MOF), Microsoft Solutions Framework (MSF), Microsoft Technology Center (MTC)*

Microsoft Corporation

The worldwide leader in software for business and personal computing.

Overview

Microsoft Corporation is organized around seven core groups focusing on different aspects of product services:

- **Microsoft Research (MSR):** Focuses on devising innovative ways of making computers easier to use, developing the software design process, designing software for the next generation of hardware, and advancing the mathematical underpinnings of computer science.
- **MSN & Personal Services Business Group:** Concentrates on programming, development, and worldwide sales and marketing for MSN and other services efforts, including MSN eShop, MSN Carpoint, MSN HomeAdvisor, MSNBC, *Slate*, and MSNTV.
- **Operations Group:** Responsible for overall business planning and managing business operations. Its functions include corporate finance, administration, human resources, and IT (information technology).
- **Personal Services Group (PSG):** Encompasses Microsoft's Personal .NET initiative, the Services Platform division, the Mobility group, the MSN Internet Access and Consumer Devices group, and the User Interface Platform division. This group's specialty is making it easy for consumers and businesses to deliver software as a service on a variety of platforms.
- **Platforms Group:** Includes the .NET Enterprise Server group, the Developer Tools division, and the Windows Digital Media division. The group's focus is on continuing to develop the Windows platform by making storage, communication, notification, and sharing services a natural extension of the Windows experience.
- **Productivity and Business Services Group:** Includes the Emerging Technologies group, the Business Tools division, and the Business Applications group, which includes bCentral and Great Plains. The group's goal is to develop and drive Microsoft's broad vision for productivity and business process applications and services.
- **Worldwide Sales, Marketing, and Services Group:** Includes Microsoft Product Support Services, the Network Solutions group, the Enterprise Partner group, the Central Marketing Organization and Microsoft's major business-sales regions worldwide. The group's focus is on integrating the activities of Microsoft's sales and service partners with the needs of Microsoft customers around the world.

The current business leadership team for Microsoft includes

- Bill Gates, Chairman and Chief Software Architect
- Steve Ballmer, Chief Executive Officer
- Rick Belluzzo, President and Chief Operating Officer
- plus many key vice presidents covering different platform and service areas

Microsoft is headquartered in a large campus located in Redmond, Washington. The main campus consists of 40 buildings that provide more than 4 million square feet (371,500 square meters) of office space. Microsoft employs more than 48,000 people worldwide, with almost half of these working in Washington State. Almost half of Microsoft's employees are involved in research and development, and most of the rest are in sales and marketing, with a small percentage in corporate operations and administration. The average age of a Microsoft employee is 34.3 years, and men outnumber women by almost three to one.

Microsoft operates subsidiary offices in more than 60 foreign countries and regions; more than half of Microsoft's revenue comes from these offices. Microsoft's net revenue for the fiscal year ending in June 2001 was $25.3 billion, with a net profit of $7.35 billion. Microsoft is traded on the Nasdaq using the symbol MSFT and has the largest capitalization of any corporation in the world.

History

September 2000 marked the 25th anniversary of Microsoft Corporation, and much has happened in those 25 years. In 1975, the personal computer (PC) was basically a toy for hobbyists, but today it represents the ubiquitous tool of business and consumers. Microsoft and its founder Bill Gates have played a major role in the evolution of the PC into what it has become. By striving to produce innovative products and services to meet customers' evolving needs, Microsoft seeks to realize its vision of "empowering people through great software—anytime, anyplace, and on any device."

Microsoft was founded as a partnership on April 4, 1975, by William H. Gates III and Paul G. Allen. Microsoft began its operations in Albuquerque, New Mexico, and earned only $16,005 in its first year of business. The company soon moved to the Seattle area, and by 1978 its sales had passed the $1 million mark. The company was incorporated on June 25, 1981, as Microsoft Corporation. Microsoft became a publicly traded company in 1986 at $21 per share.

In 1981, IBM decided to bundle Microsoft's MS-DOS operating system with the IBM PC. Microsoft continued to work with IBM throughout the 1980s to develop a successor to MS-DOS called OS/2 but abandoned this relationship in 1990. Meanwhile, Microsoft was developing its own graphical operating system called Microsoft Windows, the first version of which appeared in 1985. Version 3 of Windows was released in 1990, and in 1991 Windows 3.1 became the standard desktop operating system for PCs everywhere. Since then, Microsoft has released a series of successors to Windows 3.1, including the popular Windows 95, Windows 98, and Windows Millennium Edition (Me) platforms for consumers and the Windows NT and Windows 2000 platforms for businesses. The latest versions of Windows, Windows XP and the Windows .NET Server family, offer state-of-the-art technology and performance for business and consumer computing platforms.

In 1989, Microsoft launched its first version of Office, a suite of desktop business productivity software applications. Office has evolved to its present version, Office XP, a powerful suite of tools for business workflow and productivity. Microsoft Office has become the leading office productivity suite used in the workplace today, just as Microsoft Windows has become the dominant desktop operating system.

In 1993, Microsoft released the first version of its 32-bit business computing platform, Windows NT. This operating system soon became the foundation for a suite of server business applications developed by Microsoft and integrated into a single platform called Microsoft BackOffice. The BackOffice suite of server applications included Microsoft Exchange, which has become the leading enterprise messaging and collaboration platform, and Microsoft SQL Server, which is on its way to becoming the leading database platform for business knowledge management solutions. In 2000 a new vision was articulated by Microsoft for the enterprise to succeed BackOffice. This new vision of software as services is based on Microsoft's .NET family of server products and is the major focus of Microsoft research and development at the start of the new millennium.

Notes

Corporate contact information for Microsoft is

Microsoft Corporation
One Microsoft Way
Redmond, WA 98052-6399
USA
Tel: (425) 882-8080
E-fax: (425) 706-7329

For More Information

To find out more about Microsoft and Microsoft products, visit *www.microsoft.com.*

See Also: *BackOffice, microsoft.com, Microsoft Windows, .NET platform*

Microsoft Data Access Components (MDAC)

A set of Microsoft technologies that provide access to information stored in a broad range of data sources.

Overview

Microsoft Data Access Components (MDAC) include the following:

- **ActiveX Data Objects (ADO):** A simplified interface to OLE DB
- **OLE DB:** A low-level interface to multiple types of data sources, including relational databases, ISAM, spreadsheets, and delimited text files
- **Open database connectivity (ODBC):** A standard interface to relational data sources

Developers can use MDAC components for building distributed Web applications and e-commerce solutions.

See Also: *ActiveX Data Objects (ADO), OLE DB, open database connectivity (ODBC)*

Microsoft Developer Network (MSDN)

Microsoft Corporation's portal and support program for its developer community.

M

Overview

Microsoft Developer Network (MSDN) provides developers who work with Microsoft programming platforms with tools, information, training, and events to help them develop applications for Microsoft Windows platforms. The core of the MSDN program is the MSDN Web site, which provides developers with

- Timely information about Microsoft products and technologies
- MDSN Library, a vast collection of technical information and sample code
- Code Center, an online repository of useful code for Microsoft programming technologies
- Downloadable tools and service packs
- *MSDN Magazine*, helping developers keep up with current trends and developments in Microsoft technologies
- A variety of featured columns and news items on different subjects important to developers
- An online community of newsgroups, technical chats, and user groups
- Information about training, seminars, and special events

MSDN also offers paid subscriptions of various levels, providing developers through monthly CD shipments with news, product documentation, code samples, technical articles, and software for various Microsoft platforms, applications, and programming tools. Developers can also receive regular updates of information on the MSDN site by subscribing to MSDN Flash, a semimonthly e-mail newsletter with news, event listings, and important announcements.

For More Information

Visit MSDN online at *msdn.microsoft.com.*

See Also: *microsoft.com, TechNet*

Microsoft Disk Operating System (MS-DOS)

An operating system created by Microsoft Corporation in 1981 for the first IBM personal computer (PC).

Overview

Microsoft Disk Operating System (usually known only by its acronym, MS-DOS) was a 16-bit operating system that used a text-based command-line interface (CLI) for executing commands. The DOS part of MS-DOS indicates that the operating system is disk-based—that is, the operating code resides on a disk (initially a floppy disk and later the hard disk). MS-DOS revolutionized the nascent PC market by providing users with low-level access to operating system functions such as managing disk storage and memory resources, creating directories and manipulating files, and creating batch files for automating tasks. MS-DOS was so popular that other vendors soon produced their own versions of DOS, including IBM's PC-DOS and Novell's DR-DOS.

History

MS-DOS evolved rapidly and went through a number of revisions that added greater functionality and power to the basic operating system. Its final version, MS-DOS 6.22, was so stable and reliable that even though it had already been superseded for several years by Microsoft Windows 3.1, Microsoft's popular graphical operating system, in the late 1990s some companies could still be found running MS-DOS—some examples being conservative companies such as banks and other financial institutions.

Few companies still run MS-DOS today, however, as Microsoft Windows 2000 provides similar levels of stability and reliability, plus the ease of use of a graphical user interface (GUI) coupled with the processing power and storage capacity of modern Intel-based hardware platforms. Computer technicians still occasionally use MS-DOS, however, mainly in the form of MS-DOS boot disks for repairing problem systems.

History of MS-DOS Versions

Version	*Release Date*	*Features*
1	August 1981	Designed for the IBM PC, the initial version was distributed on a single 160-kilobyte (KB) floppy disk and ran in 8 KB of RAM.
1.1	May 1982	Support was added for double-sided 320-KB disks.
2	March 1983	Designed for the IBM PC/XT, this version added support for hard disks, hierarchical directories, background printing, and third-party device drivers.
2.1	October 1983	Designed for the short-lived IBM PCjr.
3	August 1984	Designed for the new IBM PC/AT, this version added support for 1.2-megabyte (MB) floppy disks and hard drives larger than 10 MB.
3.1	March 1985	Added support for networking and file sharing.
3.2	January 1986	Added support for the new 3.5-inch floppy disks.
3.3	April 1987	Designed for the IBM PS/2, this version added commands and support for international versions.
4.01	February 1988	This version added the Mem command, the MS-DOS shell, and support for hard drives larger than 32 MB.
5	May 1991	For this version, the MS-DOS shell was redesigned, task-swapping was added, and more extensive help, undelete, unformat, and memory-management tools were added.
6	March 1993	Added the MemMaker utility, real-time disk compression, multiple boot configurations, and antivirus and backup utilities.
6.2	October 1993	Added Scandisk for low-level disk checking.
6.22	February 1994	Added DriveSpace disk compression.

Architecture

MS-DOS commands come in two types:

- **Built-in commands:** Embedded in the MS-DOS command interpreter Command.com. Examples include Dir, Copy, and Date.
- **External commands:** MS-DOS utilities that reside as separate files. Examples include Doskey, Edit, and Smartdrv.

M

```
C:\DOS>dir s*

 Volume in drive C is MS-DOS_6
 Volume Serial Number is 2565-9A28
 Directory of C:\DOS

SCANDISK EXE     124,262 05-31-94  6:22a
SCANDISK INI       6,920 05-31-94  6:22a
SETUP    EXE      72,842 05-31-94  6:22a
SYS      COM       9,432 05-31-94  6:22a
SETVER   EXE      12,015 05-31-94  6:22a
SHARE    EXE      10,912 05-31-94  6:22a
SIZER    EXE       7,169 05-31-94  6:22a
SMARTDRV EXE      45,145 05-31-94  6:22a
SMARTMON EXE      28,672 05-31-94  6:22a
SMARTMON HLP      10,727 05-31-94  6:22a
SORT     EXE       6,938 05-31-94  6:22a
SUBST    EXE      18,526 05-31-94  6:22a
     12 file(s)      353,560 bytes
                 423,239,680 bytes free
```

MS-DOS. *Example of running Dir, an MS-DOS command.*

The core of the MS-DOS operating system consists of three primary files in the root of the system partition:

- **Io.sys:** Controls the boot process and contains basic input/output (I/O) drivers.
- **Msdos.sys:** Operating system kernel. Applications request operating system services through Msdos.sys, which translates them into actions that can be performed by Io.sys and device drivers.
- **Command.com:** Command interpreter, which provides a user interface for executing MS-DOS commands.

In addition, two other text files help control the MS-DOS boot process:

- **Config.sys:** Contains commands that configure hardware components such as memory, keyboard, mouse, and printer
- **Autoexec.bat:** Contains startup commands that configure your prompt and path and run memory-resident programs such as Doskey and Smartdrv

The remaining external MS-DOS commands and utilities are by default found in the directory C:\DOS.

Notes

You can add networking functionality to MS-DOS by using the Microsoft Network Client 3 for MS-DOS add-on. You can create installation disks for this software using the Network Client Administrator tool in Microsoft Windows NT.

See Also: *Microsoft Windows*

Microsoft Foundation Classes (MFC)

A set of object-oriented interfaces to the Microsoft Windows application programming interface (API).

Overview

Microsoft Foundation Classes (MFC) include classes, global functions, global variables, and macros that provide a framework for developing applications for Windows platforms. MFC encapsulates much of the Windows API by providing classes that represent key Windows objects, such as windows, controls, dialog boxes, brushes, and fonts. Programmers can develop Windows-based applications by using a combination of C++ code and MFC instead of calling Windows API functions directly. Many MFC class member functions actually call the encapsulated Windows API functions. Note that you cannot call MFC class member functions directly—you have to instantiate the class first.

Architecture

The majority of the MFC are derived by inheritance from the root class named CObject. CObject provides support for serializing data and obtaining run-time class information, although you do not need to derive new classes from CObject if you do not need these capabilities. Other classes in MFC include the following:

- MFC application architecture classes, which supply common functionality to most applications and create the framework for an application. The AppWizard uses these classes to create new applications.
- Windows, dialog, and control classes for creating and managing windows.
- Drawing and printing classes for encapsulating device contexts for graphical output and creating drawing tools such as brushes, palettes, and bitmaps.
- Data type, array, list, and map classes for handling data of various types.

M

- File and database classes for storing and retrieving files in databases or on disks. These include classes for file input/output (I/O), Data Access Objects (DAO), ActiveX Data Objects (ADO), and open database connectivity (ODBC).
- Internet and networking classes for exchanging information between computers and over the Internet. These include classes for Windows Sockets and Internet Server API (ISAPI).
- OLE classes for creating compound documents and OLE objects, using Automation, creating ActiveX controls, and other functions.
- Debugging and exception classes for error handling and debugging applications.

See Also: *ActiveX, application programming interface (API), Data Access Objects (DAO), open database connectivity (ODBC)*

Microsoft Management Console (MMC)

A tool and software framework for administering systems running Microsoft Windows 2000 or later.

Overview

The Microsoft Management Console (MMC) was first included with Microsoft Windows NT Option Pack to provide an integrated management framework for a wide range of administrative tasks. The MMC later became the standard administrative interface for managing the Microsoft Windows 2000 operating system and server applications such as Microsoft Exchange Server and Microsoft SQL Server.

MMC offers the following features:

- **Customization:** Administrators can create an MMC tool that contains the exact functionality they need.
- **Integration:** MMC integrates all management capability into a single common framework, making it easier to learn and perform network administration.
- **Flexibility:** Third-party companies can create their own snap-ins to further extend the capabilities of MMC.

Windows 2000 and later versions include a number of preconfigured consoles known as administrative tools. These tools are used for performing specific administrative tasks, and you can access them using the Administrative Tools shortcut in the Programs group of the Start menu.

Implementation

By itself, the MMC does not provide any system or network management capability. Instead, it provides an environment in which administrative tools called snap-ins can be run. A snap-in is a software component that provides some system or network management capability for administrators to perform standard tasks.

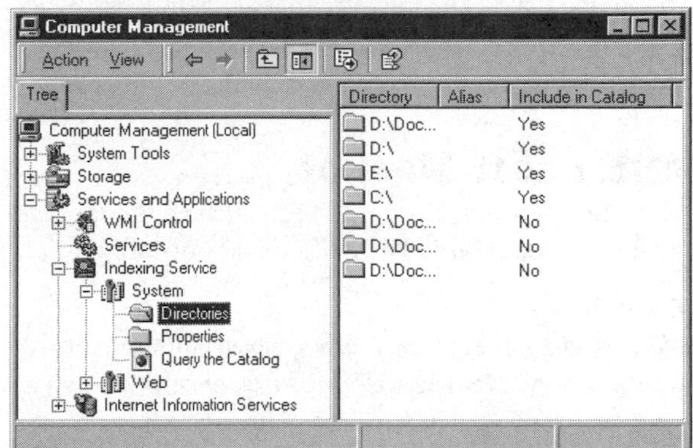

MMC console. *Computer Management, an example of an MMC console.*

When one or more snap-ins have been added to a blank console, the configuration can be saved as an .msc file and then shared with other administrators by e-mail or by sharing it on a file server. The MMC also supports deregulation of different levels of management capability to other administrators. For example, an administrator might

- Create a specific console for a specific administrative task. An administrator can thus create a custom administrative tool that is not cluttered with unnecessary functionality and provides just enough functionality to perform the task at hand.
- Create a console for unifying a set of different administrative tasks. An administrator can thus create a single console with which all common

administrative tasks can be performed instead of switching between different tools for different tasks.

- Create a read-only console that could be distributed to junior administrators so they can use only the functionality added to the console.

The MMC user interface presents a hierarchical view of your network resources in a two-pane view similar to that of Windows Explorer. The left pane (the Scope pane) shows a hierarchical view of the administrative namespace of manageable nodes (network objects), while the right pane (Results pane) shows the contents, services, or configuration items of the selected node in the Scope pane. You perform management tasks by using the menu or toolbars, opening property sheets for nodes, and accessing Web pages in the Results pane.

Microsoft Market

A business-to-business (B2B) procurement system created and used internally by Microsoft Corporation.

Overview

Microsoft Market is an Internet-based procurement system developed by Microsoft to streamline operations with its supply-chain partners. Although Microsoft Market is used internally by Microsoft and is not open to the public, it is an excellent example of how B2B systems using the Internet can reduce the cost of doing business with a company's business partners.

Before deploying Microsoft Market, Microsoft's procurement costs typically were $60 per transaction. With Microsoft Market implemented, this overhead fell to less than $5 per transaction. Using Microsoft Market, purchases of goods and services from partners and vendors can be performed using a standard Web browser interface. Microsoft Market has helped Microsoft lower its procurement costs and speed up its business cycle; it has also reduced sales and marketing costs and has created new sales opportunities and improved customer service. Microsoft Market puts Microsoft in the forefront of companies implementing B2B Internet technologies in streamlining business process to gain a competitive advantage in the marketplace.

See Also: *B2B, e-business*

Microsoft Office User Specialist (MOUS)

A Microsoft certification for users of Microsoft Office.

Overview

The Microsoft Office User Specialist (MOUS) certification enables individuals to demonstrate their in-depth knowledge of the Office suite of business productivity tools. The MOUS certification can be used for skills assessment to help them find the qualified knowledge workers they need for business success.

Depending on the version of Office considered, the MOUS program provides different levels of certification to help identify proficient, expert, and master levels of competency in using the product. MOUS certification is also available for Microsoft Project 2000.

For More Information

Find out more about MOUS at *www.microsoft.com/trainingandservices.*

See Also: *Microsoft Certified Professional (MCP)*

Microsoft Official Curriculum (MOC)

Courseware developed by Microsoft Corporation for training in Microsoft products and technologies.

Overview

Microsoft Official Curriculum (MOC) courseware is designed to provide comprehensive training in Microsoft products to IT (information technology) professionals who develop, implement, administer, and support business solutions based on Microsoft platforms, applications, and tools. MOC courseware are available for the full range of Microsoft products, including all versions of Microsoft Windows, the .NET Enterprise Server family, and Microsoft programming platforms. MOCs are available in different forms, including

- Instructor-led courseware designed for use at Microsoft Certified Technical Education Centers (CTECs) and taught by Microsoft Certified Trainers (MCTs).
- Self-paced training kits available through Microsoft Press.

- Online courseware.

MOCs are the standard means for IT professionals to prepare for exams leading to Microsoft Certified Professional (MCP) certifications.

For More Information

Find out more about MOCs at *www.microsoft.com/trainingandservices.*

See Also: *Certified Technical Education Center (CTEC), Microsoft Certified Professional (MCP)*

Microsoft Operations Framework (MOF)

A service by Microsoft Corporation that provides technical guidance on Microsoft technologies to large enterprises.

Overview

Microsoft Operations Framework (MOF) is part of the Microsoft Consulting Services (MCS) program and is designed to help enterprises achieve mission-critical reliability, availability, supportability, and manageability in their use of Microsoft products and technologies. MOF provides various tools to enterprises, including assessment tools, best practices, case studies, operations guides, support tools, templates, and white papers. Issues covered in these resources address the people, process, technology, and management issues that arise in large, heterogeneous IT (information technology) environments. MOF also provides structured support programs and other services that can enhance the capabilities of your in-house IT operations.

For More Information

Learn about MOF at *www.microsoft.com/business/services/mcsmof.asp.*

See Also: *Microsoft Consulting Services (MCS)*

Microsoft RAS Protocol

A legacy remote access protocol from Microsoft Corporation.

Overview

Microsoft RAS Protocol is a remote access protocol developed for Microsoft Windows for Workgroups 3.11 and Windows NT 3.1 as an alternative to Serial Line Internet Protocol (SLIP) that was in common use at that time on the UNIX platform. Microsoft RAS Protocol enables legacy Windows for Workgroups and Windows NT clients to dial in and connect to a remote access server (RAS) using the NetBIOS Enhanced User Interface (NetBEUI) protocol. Once the remote client establishes a connection, the remote access server acts as a NetBIOS gateway to enable the client to access other servers on the network using NetBEUI, NetBIOS over Internetwork Packet Exchange (IPX), or NetBIOS over Transmission Control Protocol/Internet Protocol (TCP/IP).

Microsoft RAS protocol is supported by later versions of Windows only for purposes of backward compatibility. You need RAS Protocol only if you are connecting to a Microsoft Windows remote access server from legacy Windows clients running Windows for Workgroups 3.11 or Windows NT 3.1. Apart from this usage, Microsoft RAS Protocol has been entirely superseded by the Point-to-Point Protocol (PPP), the industry-standard protocol for remote access.

See Also: *NetBEUI, NetBIOS, Point-to-Point Protocol (PPP), Serial Line Internet Protocol (SLIP), UNIX*

Microsoft Research (MSR)

A branch of Microsoft Corporation concerned with advanced research in computer science and technologies.

Overview

Microsoft Research (MSR) pursues research in a variety of different technologies that are viewed as having the potential to change the face of computing over the next decade. These technologies include artificial intelligence (AI), computer vision, speech processing, quantum computing, and advances in operating systems and programming language and tools that will make computers friendlier and easier to use.

MSR was founded in 1991 and was the first research laboratory for basic computer science established by any software company. MSR currently has over 600 researchers operating in four different laboratories around the world:

- Redmond, Washington
- San Francisco, California
- Cambridge, United Kingdom
- Beijing, China

For More Information

Visit MSR at *www.research.microsoft.com.*

Microsoft Solutions Framework (MSF)

A Microsoft Corporation training program for large companies that provides guidance on planning, building, and deploying solutions based on Microsoft products and technologies.

Overview

Microsoft Solutions Framework (MSF) addresses training in the areas of enterprise application development, architecture design, component design, and deployment of infrastructure. MSF training is based on best practices from real-life consulting done by Microsoft Consulting Services (MCS), Microsoft Certified Partners, and others who develop Microsoft solutions for business needs. The MSF program is offered to enterprises through MCS.

MSF is based on a series of guidelines-based models, including

- **Application Model:** Provides guidelines for software design and development to improve development, maintenance, and support.
- **Design Process Model:** Provides guidelines for project design based on a flexible, user-centric continuum and using a three-phase approach of conceptual, logical, and physical design.
- **Enterprise Architecture Model:** Provides guidelines for building enterprise architecture through versioned releases to shorten the enterprise architecture planning cycle.
- **Process Model:** Provides guidelines for structuring projects to improve project control, shorten delivery time, and minimize risk.
- **Risk Management Model:** Provides guidelines for assessment, prioritization, and risk management for projects.
- **Team Model:** Provides guidelines for organizing teams by project to improve internal teamwork.

For More Information

Visit *www.microsoft.com/business/services/mcsmsf.asp.*

See Also: *Microsoft Certified Partner, Microsoft Consulting Services (MCS)*

Microsoft Technology Center (MTC)

A state-of-the-art training center for learning about Microsoft technologies and solutions.

Overview

Microsoft Technology Centers (MTCs) are laboratories where enterprise IT (information technology) staff can work side by side with Microsoft experts and partners to design, develop, and test solutions based on Microsoft applications and platforms. MTCs are located in various cities across North America and offer a broad range of facilities, programs, and expertise for developing technology solutions for specific business needs. MTCs also offer boot camps to provide environments for rapid learning of state-of-the-art Microsoft technologies and solutions such as BizTalk and the .NET framework. MTCs are available to enterprises through Microsoft Consulting Services (MCS).

For More Information

Visit *www.microsoft.com/business/services/mtc.asp.*

See Also: *Microsoft Consulting Services (MCS)*

Microsoft Windows

Microsoft Corporation's flagship operating system platform.

Overview

Microsoft Windows is a family of operating systems that lie at the core of Microsoft's strategy to make PCs easier to use, reduce the cost of PC ownership, advance the PC platform in the enterprise, and integrate PCs with the Internet.

Windows operating systems evolved in the 1990s from the earlier MS-DOS, Microsoft's powerful text-based disk operating system for personal computers. The first versions of Windows were 16-bit operating systems that essentially ran on top of MS-DOS and provided an easy-to-use graphical user interface (GUI) that made computers easier to learn and use. These 16-bit versions included Windows 3.1 and Windows for Workgroups 3.11, the network-aware version of Window 3.1. In the middle of the decade, Microsoft released a new version of Windows called Windows 95, a desktop operating system that included a new and more powerful GUI, support for preemptive multitasking, and enhanced management of system resources. Windows 95 evolved into Windows 98 and then Windows Millennium Edition (Windows Me).

Meanwhile, Microsoft also developed a fully 32-bit operating system called Windows NT. This new operating system was more powerful, robust, and secure than the Windows 95/98/Me family and was intended for business users instead of consumers. Although Windows NT 3.51 was based on the Windows 3.1 GUI, the popular Windows NT 4 employed a GUI similar to Windows 95. Windows NT 4 was offered in a variety of flavors targeted at the desktop, local area network (LAN) server, and enterprise server operating system markets.

As the decade concluded, Windows NT was superseded by the powerful Windows 2000 family of operating systems, which offered great stability and powerful features foundational for building strategic e-business solutions for the enterprise. Most recently, two new Windows platforms have evolved:

- **Windows XP:** A completely new 32-bit desktop operating system that removes all remaining vestiges of MS-DOS and comes in two flavors: Windows XP Home Edition for home users and Windows XP Professional for corporate use. Windows XP is the natural desktop upgrade path for Windows 95/98/Me, Windows NT 4 Workstation, and Windows 2000 Professional.
- **Windows .NET Server family:** The next evolution of the Windows 2000 Server family of operating systems.

A separate evolutionary path for Windows has produced the Windows CE 3 operating system, a lightweight version of Windows designed for handheld PCs and appliances. Windows NT Embedded, another flavor of Windows, is a low-footprint version designed for industrial control systems and other devices with limited processing and memory.

The table below lists the current versions of Windows. For more information about particular versions, see the corresponding entries in Chapter W of this book.

Current Microsoft Windows Operating Systems

Version	*Description*
Windows .NET Server	Comes in Standard, Enterprise, Datacenter, and Web Server versions and is the successor to the Windows 2000 family of business operating systems
Windows XP	Comes in Professional and Home Edition and is the successor to both the Windows Me and Windows 2000 Professional lines of business and consumer Windows desktop operating systems
Windows 2000	Comes in Professional, Server, Advanced Server, and Datacenter Server versions and is the successor to the Windows NT 4 family of business operating systems
Windows Me	Successor to Windows 95 and Windows 98 consumer Windows desktop operating systems
Windows CE	Lightweight version of Windows designed for handheld computing devices and computer appliances
Windows NT Embedded	Small-footprint version of Windows NT designed for industrial control systems and small devices

For More Information

Visit the Windows home at *www.microsoft.com/windows.*

See Also: *Windows 3.1, Windows 95, Windows 98, Windows 2000, Windows CE, Windows Me (Windows Millennium Edition), Windows .NET Server, Windows NT, Windows XP*

M

middleware

Application logic between the client and data sources.

Overview

The concept of middleware emerged in the mid-1990s as a solution to scalability problems inherent in the traditional two-tier client/server computing paradigm. In a typical business computing system, client machines access information stored on back-end database servers for accessing inventory, sales, invoicing, and other business information. The scalability issue arises as databases grow in size and complexity—then the problem becomes where to implement the application logic for best performance. Choosing a "fat client" approach moves more of the processing load to the client, but the result is that whenever the business application is upgraded or patched, new software needs to be installed on every client across the enterprise. Another approach is to move application logic to the database servers by using centrally stored procedures, but this increases the processing load on the servers considerably.

A third approach is to use middleware, which represents a third tier of software stored on a special server separate from the client and the database server. Employing middleware means that thin clients can be used rather than fat ones, that desktop systems do not need to be updated as frequently, and that some of the processing load is siphoned off from the database servers. When application logic needs to be updated, it can be done quickly and easily on the servers running the middleware. The result of proper implementation of middleware in the enterprise is greater scalability and better performance of line-of-business applications that use database technologies, such as Enterprise Resource Planning (ERP) and Customer Relations Management (CRM) applications.

Middleware technologies are also used in other scenarios. For example, cellular systems can allow mobile users to access company intranets using personal digital assistants (PDAs) and other devices. This is generally done by implementing a middleware server that connects the mobile devices to the database servers. An example of such a middleware application is Microsoft Mobile Information Server, one of the new .NET Enterprise Servers from Microsoft Corporation. Another type of middleware system is a wireless e-mail gateway that connects mobile users with handheld devices such as Research In Motion's Blackberry with Internet mail hosts. Such middleware servers are often available from vendors as either installable applications or as self-hosted (stand-alone) appliances.

As enterprise systems grow more complex, three-tiered systems often grow into *n*-tiered systems that employ several levels of middleware. The principles are still the same, though: improving performance and scalability by isolating application logic from both the client and the database server.

Notes

The term *middleware* is sometimes used in other contexts. For example, it can refer to the various technologies and protocols used to connect the clients with the back-end servers. These technologies can include remote procedure calls (RPCs), synchronous transactions, asynchronous message passing mechanisms, and distributed object oriented programming technologies such as Microsoft's Distributed Component Object Model (DCOM), Sun Microsystems' JavaBeans, and The OpenGroup's Common Object Request Broker Architecture (CORBA).

See Also: *client/server, Common Object Request Broker Architecture (CORBA), Customer Relationship Management (CRM), Distributed Component Object Model (DCOM), enterprise resource planning (ERP), Java, Mobile Information Server, remote procedure call (RPC)*

MIF

Stands for Management Information Format (MIF), a standard format for describing hardware and software management information.

See: *Management Information Format (MIF)*

Millennium

An advanced distributed computing architecture being developed by Microsoft Research.

Overview

Millennium is a radically new vision for distributed computing in which the automatic distribution of application processing is the norm rather than the exception. The Millennium paradigm assumes that all applications are intrinsically distributed across the network rather than locally centralized on servers. Millennium is based on an advanced network-aware operating system than can dynamically distribute processing tasks and manage resources across the network. Millennium is based on four key concepts:

- **Abstract distribution of tasks:** The network automatically distributes tasks for execution to different processing nodes. Programmers do not need to worry about how network resources are managed for the applications they develop.
- **Abstract locality:** Applications do not need to know where they reside or are executed. Resources for applications are automatically located by the network and assigned as needed.
- **Automatic performance tuning:** The network dynamically monitors and adjusts how and where processing tasks are distributed in order to optimize application performance.
- **Dynamic resource management:** Hardware and software resources are automatically enlisted and bound to application processes at runtime and released when no longer required.

One of the Millennium prototype projects is called Coign, which supports the self-configuration and self-tuning of Component Object Model (COM) objects across a network. Coign supports the dynamic partitioning of applications to improve performance and simplify the management of distributed applications.

For More Information

Find out more at *www.research.microsoft.com/sn/millennium.*

See Also: *Component Object Model (COM), Jini, Microsoft Research (MSR)*

MIME

Stands for Multipurpose Internet Mail Extensions, extensions to Simple Mail Transport Protocol (SMTP) that allow multipart and binary messages to be sent using e-mail.

See: *Multipurpose Internet Mail Extensions (MIME)*

mirrored volume

A type of fault tolerance supported by Microsoft Windows 2000 and Windows .NET Server.

Overview

In Microsoft Windows 2000 and Windows .NET Server, a mirrored volume is a type of volume created with Disk Management that duplicates data on two separate physical disks. This provides a measure of fault tolerance, for if one physical disk fails, the data is still accessible from the second disk.

In Windows 2000 and Windows .NET Server, mirrored volumes cannot be extended and they must be created on dynamic disks. Although mirrored volumes perform read operations more slowly than RAID 5 volumes, they do execute write operations more quickly.

Notes

The Windows NT equivalent of a mirrored volume was called a mirror set.

See Also: *dynamic volume, mirroring, mirror set, redundant array of independent disks (RAID)*

mirroring

Maintaining an identical copy of an information store or disk system for fault tolerance purposes.

Overview

Mirroring is one of several different strategies for integrating fault tolerance into storage systems. Using mirroring, two identical copies of mission critical data are maintained, and if the primary system goes down, the secondary system can be brought online quickly with little or no loss of data. Mirroring can be implemented at various levels from disk mirroring (two identical disk drives within a server) to server mirroring (two identical servers having the same data and running at different locations) to mirroring of enterprise storage solutions such as storage area networks (SANs). Mirroring at higher levels is commonly used in financial institutions such as banks and brokerages to ensure speedy recovery in the event of a disaster.

Mirroring is not a replacement for tape backup systems; instead, it complements the standard backup cycle by providing additional redundancy and fault tolerance. Mirroring of enterprise servers is a popular solution in high availability environments because the recovery window (the time to bring a mirrored system online after a disaster) is typically less than an hour, while the time to restore a system completely from backup sets may be 24 to 48 hours. Mirroring does have the disadvantage of being expensive compared to tape backup, since duplicate storage systems are required to implement it.

Implementation

Mirroring can implemented using several techniques:

- **Symmetric mirroring:** Usually simply called mirroring, symmetric mirroring involves real-time replication of information using a transaction model to ensure the mirrors are identical at all times. In symmetric mirroring, data is written nearly simultaneously to both the primary and secondary mirrored systems. An example of symmetric mirroring is disk mirroring in Microsoft Windows 2000, which mirrors two volumes to provide fault tolerance for high-availability servers. In addition, symmetric mirroring can also be performed across a wide area network (WAN) between two network storage systems, a setup that requires a reliable, high-speed, low-latency WAN link such as Metropolitan Ethernet for best performance.
- **Asymmetric mirroring:** Also known as shadowing, asymmetric mirroring complements symmetric mirroring and generally employs three identical storage systems. In a typical scenario, systems 1 and 2 are colocated at your customer premises and symmetrically mirror each other. Systems 2 and 3 asymmetrically mirror each other, with system 3 being located at a secure remote location. Local data is always current on both mirrors, while the remote mirror is slightly out of sync by a time period called the "mirror gap." The result is that if both local mirrors go down and the remote mirror is brought online, some transactions will inevitably be lost. The advantage is that theWAN link to the remote site does not have to be an expensive high-speed link as in remote symmetric mirroring, but can instead be a cheaper low-bandwidth link such as frame relay or Integrated Services Digital Network (ISDN). The remote storage system may even be managed by a separate company such as a storage service provider (SSP), eliminating the cost overhead of needing to purchase three identical storage systems.

See Also: backup, electronic tape vaulting, fault tolerance, frame relay, Integrated Services Digital Network (ISDN), metropolitan Ethernet, mirrored volume, storage, storage area network (SAN), storage service provider (SSP), wide area network (WAN)

mirror set

A type of fault tolerance supported by Microsoft Windows NT.

Overview

Mirroring is the process whereby data is written simultaneously to two disks, making one disk drive an exact mirror image of the other. This form of fault tolerance technology is properly known as RAID-1 but is called a mirror set in Windows NT (Windows 2000 calls this same configuration a mirrored volume).

The duplication of disk information in a mirror set provides the system with data redundancy, for if one half of the mirror set fails, the system can continue to operate using the duplicate of the failed disk. In Windows NT, mirror sets are commonly used to provide fault tolerance for the system and boot partitions. You can use Disk Administrator, the administrative tool in Windows NT, to create, break, and reestablish mirror sets. In Windows 2000, the corresponding administrative tool is called Disk Management.

For read operations, mirror sets are slower than other redundant array of independent disks (RAID) configurations such as stripe sets with parity, but on the other hand they are faster for write operations.

See Also: *fault tolerance, mirrored volume, mirroring, redundant array of independent disks (RAID)*

mixed mode

A mode of running Microsoft Windows 2000 domain controllers.

Overview

When Windows 2000 domain controllers are running in mixed mode, they are backward compatible with domain controllers running the Windows NT operating system. This is because Windows 2000 domain controllers running in mixed mode use Windows NT LAN Manager (NTLM) as their authentication protocol instead of Kerberos, which allows Active Directory directory service to communicate with downlevel Windows NT domain controllers.

Mixed mode has the following special considerations:

- It does not support the use of universal groups.
- It does not support unlimited nesting of groups—you can only add global groups to domain local groups with one level of nesting.
- It does not support policy-based management of remote access servers.
- Multimaster replication does not function between uplevel and downlevel domain controllers—downlevel Windows NT domain controllers replicate updates from the PDC to the backup domain controllers (BDCs) in the usual way.
- Some advanced management options for Windows 2000 domain controllers are not available for downlevel Windows NT domain controllers.

Implementation

Mixed mode is designed to be used mainly as a temporary solution during the process of migrating a Windows NT–based network to a Windows 2000–based one. Once the migration is complete, you can switch your Windows 2000 domain controllers from mixed mode to native mode. Note that this is a process that can be performed only once—you cannot change native mode domain controllers back to mixed mode.

Windows 2000 domain controllers are installed in mixed mode by default when you run the Active Directory Installation Wizard to upgrade a member server to a domain controller. To change domain controllers from mixed mode to native mode, use the Active Directory Users and Computers console. During a migration from Windows NT to Windows 2000, after you have upgraded all your downlevel domain controllers to Windows 2000 you should change your domain to native mode in order to take advantage of Windows 2000's special features, such as multimaster replication, nesting of groups, and universal groups. If you are deploying a pure Windows 2000–based network, however, you should configure your domain controllers to run in native mode from the start.

See Also: *Active Directory, Active Directory Users and Computers, domain controller, domain modes, Kerberos, native mode, universal group, Windows NT LAN Manager Authentication*

M

MLP

Stands for Multilink Point-to-Point Protocol, a wide area network (WAN) protocol for aggregating multiple Point-to-Point Protocol (PPP) connections.

See: *Multilink Point-to-Point Protocol (MPPP)*

MLS

Stands for Multilayer Switching, a LAN switching term that can have several meanings.

See: *Multilayer Switching (MLS)*

MMC

Stands for Microsoft Management Console, a tool and software framework for administering systems running Microsoft Windows 2000 or later.

See: *Microsoft Management Console (MMC)*

MMDS

Stands for Multipoint Multichannel Distribution Service, a fixed wireless broadband networking architecture.

See: *Multipoint Multichannel Distribution Service (MMDS)*

M-node

A NetBIOS name resolution method used by Microsoft Windows NT.

Overview

Name resolution is the process of converting the name of a host on the network into a network address (such as an Internet Protocol [IP] address). Name resolution must be performed in order to establish communication over a Windows NT network. M-node is one of four basic methods supported by Windows NT for resolving NetBIOS host names—that is, computer names—into IP addresses.

If a computer running Windows NT is configured as an M-node machine, it first tries to use broadcasts to resolve the names of the hosts, similar to a B-node machine. If name resolution fails this way (for example, if broadcasts are stopped by routers from reaching computers on other subnets), Windows NT tries to use a NetBIOS name server to resolve names of other hosts on the network, similar to a P-node machine. A Windows NT server with the Windows Internet Naming Service (WINS) configured on it is a typical example of a NetBIOS name server. The *M* in the term *M-node* stands for *mixed*, as M-node is a mixture of B-node and P-node, in that order.

Notes

M-node is defined in RFCs 1001 and 1002.

See Also: *B-node, H-node, NetBIOS name resolution, P-node*

Mobile Broadband System (MBS)

A proposed fourth-generation (4G) mobile cellular communication system.

Overview

The Mobile Broadband System (MBS) is a project of the Research and Technology Development in Advanced Communications Technologies in Europe (RACE) program. MBS is designed to extend mobile communications to support broadband communication at multimegabit data transmission rates of up to 155 megabits per second (Mbps). MBS is seen as a key enabler for transmission of multimedia video and audio content on cellular communications systems.

MBS is basically a wireless extension to broadband ISDN (B-ISDN), a technology that has been talked about for many years and is still in the developmental stage. The underlying transport used in MBS is Asynchronous Transfer Mode (ATM), and the proposed MBS standard from the International Telecommunication Union (ITU) is intended to fully integrate MBS with the ATM-based Integrated Broadband Communications Network (IBCN), also proposed for Europe.

See Also: *Asynchronous Transfer Mode (ATM), broadband ISDN (B-ISDN), cellular communications, International Telecommunication Union (ITU)*

Mobile Execution Environment (MExE)

An emerging standard for running Java applications on mobile phones.

Overview

Mobile Execution Environment (MExE) is a proposal of the European Telecommunications Standards Institute (ETSI) to enable mobile devices with limited processing power such as cell phones and personal digital assistants (PDAs) to run Java applications. Using MExE, for example, a mobile knowledge worker could easily access enterprise applications using his cell phone.

MExE is designed to reduce the footprint required for running Java on small mobile devices. This is done by partly compiling client-side Java applications on middleware servers, thus reducing the processing and memory requirements needed to run a full Java interpreter on these mobile devices. Wireless Application Protocol (WAP) is then used as a transport for delivery of information to the mobile devices.

See Also: *cellular communications, Java, Wireless Application Protocol (WAP)*

Mobile Information Server

Microsoft Corporation's .NET Enterprise Server for enabling wireless access to enterprise data.

Overview

Microsoft Mobile Information 2001 Server provides enterprises with a platform for allowing users to access data stored on corporate intranets and database servers from mobile devices such as cell phones and wireless personal digital assistants (PDAs). Mobile Information Server thus extends the reach of .NET enterprise applications by bringing content to the mobile knowledge worker. Using Mobile Information Server, people can have access to corporate e-mail, calendars, contacts lists, tasks, and any other desired information.

Mobile Information Server includes two components:

- A server application that acts as middleware between back-end .NET Enterprise Servers such as Microsoft Exchange 2000 Server and Microsoft SQL Server
- A client application called Microsoft Outlook Mobile Access that provides a Web-based portal to information residing on these servers

Mobile Information Server offers an extensible architecture that supports connectors for allowing mobile users to access information stored on any type of data server or information store. Mobile Information Server supports end-to-end security, load balancing and clustering, and content replication and delivery.

For More Information

Find out more at *www.microsoft.com/miserver.*

See Also: *cellular communications, Exchange Server, middleware, .NET Enterprise Servers, SQL Server*

Mobile Services Initiative (M-Services)

A proposed set of standards for broadband cellular Internet access.

Overview

Mobile Services Initiative (M-Services) is designed to speed the deployment of broadband cellular Internet access. The aim is to bring standards and consistency by providing guidelines for graphical displays on cellular handsets, transmission schemes for accessing music and video, and other functions. M-Services is designed to overcome some of the problems inherent in Wireless Application Protocol (WAP), the first generation of cellular Internet access technologies. WAP is generally viewed as too slow and complex for mobile platforms, and application development for this platform has tended to result in a variety of proprietary extensions.

M-Services focuses on providing guidelines for application development on General Packet Radio Services (GPRS), a 2.5G upgrade to existing second-generation (2G) Global System for Mobile Communications (GSM) cellular systems used widely in Europe and becoming more popular in North America. GPRS is viewed as a stepping stone to true third-generation (3G) broadband mobile communications systems, which are now not likely to be widely deployed until 2005.

M-Services is supported by the GSM Association, by manufacturers of mobile technologies such as Ericsson, Motorola, and Nokia, and by mobile operators such as France Telecom and Telecom Italia Mobile.

See Also: *2.5G, 3G, cellular communications, General Packet Radio Service (GPRS), Global System for Mobile Communications (GSM), Wireless Application Protocol (WAP)*

Mobile Transport Serving Office (MTSO)

A component of a cellular communications system.

Overview

In a cellular communications system, the region where coverage is desired is broken up into a series of small overlapping areas called cells. Each cell is serviced by a base station, which has a transceiver (transmitter/receiver) for sending and receiving calls with mobile users in that area. For communications to take place, however, frequencies or time slots (depending on the cellular technology used) must be allocated without conflict to users in different cells, a function performed by a central station called a Mobile Transport Serving

Office (MTSO). The MTSO thus coordinates the activities of the different transceivers within a given region and provides a land-based (wireline) link between these transceivers and the telco central office (CO) for connection to the Public Switched Telephone Network (PSTN). Connections between base stations and the MTSO, and between the CO and the MTSO, are usually made using telco trunk lines.

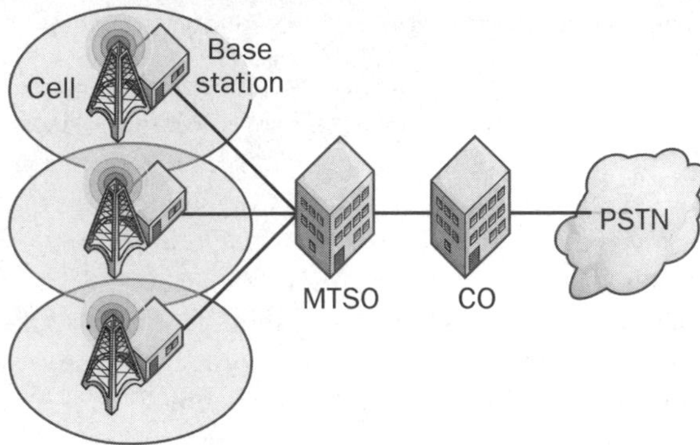

Mobile Transport Serving Office (MTSO). *How the MTSO connects a cellular communications system to the Public Switched Telephone Network (PSTN).*

See Also: *cellular communications, central office (CO), Public Switched Telephone Network (PSTN), telco*

MOC

Stands for Microsoft Official Curriculum, courseware developed by Microsoft Corporation for training in Microsoft products and technologies.

See: *Microsoft Official Curriculum (MOC)*

modem

A device that enables digital data transmission to be transmitted over telecommunications lines.

Overview

The term *modem*, which stands for modulator/demodulator, generally refers to analog modems, data communications equipment (DCE) that converts the digital signals used by data terminal equipment (DTE) such as computers into analog sound waves that can be transmitted over the analog local loop portion of the Public Switched Telephone Network (PSTN). Analog modems generally have two interfaces: an RS-232 serial transmission interface for connecting to the DTE, which is usually a computer; and an RJ-11 telephone interface for connecting to a standard four-wire PSTN telephone jack.

Analog modems are popular and come in various types:

- Internal modems, which are installed as interface cards inside the computer and might use some of the machine's CPU (central processing unit) processing power for functions such as encoding and data compression. One popular type of internal modem is the soft modem, an inexpensive modem that utilizes some of the processing power of the computer's CPU to operate.
- External modems, which are generally more expensive and connect to the serial port on the computer using a DB9 or DB25 connector. External modems are useful when several users need to share a modem.
- Personal Computer Memory Card International Association (PCMCIA) modems, which are credit-card-sized modems for laptop computers used by mobile workers. PCMCIA soft modems are also available.
- Voice/data/fax modems, which can be used for file transfer, sending and receiving faxes, and voice mail using associated software. These are available in internal, external, and PCMCIA formats.

Another kind of modem is the digital modem, one example of which is the Integrated Services Digital Network (ISDN) terminal adapter. Although a digital modem does not convert digital signals into analog and vice versa, a form of modulation called line coding does take place. Line coding is used to modulate the digital signals from the DTE, which is typically a switch or router connecting to a local area network (LAN), into digital signals that can be transmitted over the specially conditioned ISDN telephone. Other popular types of digital modems include cable modems and Digital Subscriber Line (DSL) modems. Digital modems use a variety of serial interfaces, including RS-232, RS-449, V.35, X.21, and High Speed Serial Interface (HSSI).

See Also: *analog modem, cable modem, data communications equipment (DCE), data terminal equipment (DTE), digital modem, Digital Subscriber Line (DSL), Integrated Services Digital Network (ISDN), ISDN terminal adapter, Public Switched Telephone Network (PSTN), RS-232, serial transmission*

modem eliminator

A device for connecting two pieces of data terminal equipment (DTE).

Overview

Modem eliminators provide an easy way to connect two pieces of DTE without a modem. Modem eliminators accomplish this by simulating a synchronous transmission data link through generating timing and handshaking signals. Modem eliminators can use a variety of serial interfaces, including RS-232, RS-422/485, RS-530, V.25, or X.21, and can operate at speeds of up to 2.048 megabits per second (Mbps).

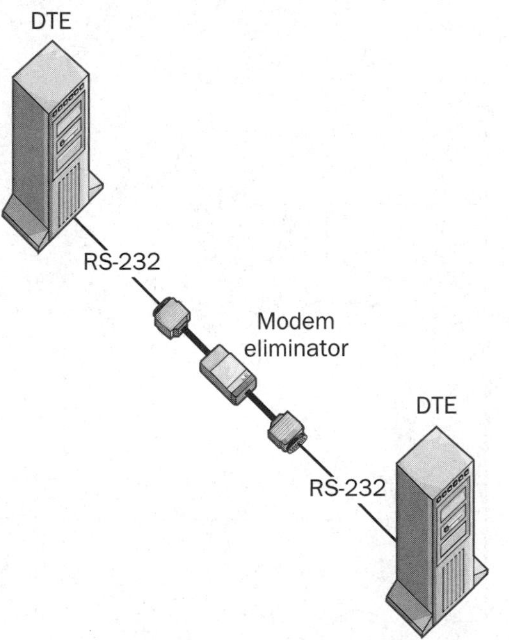

Modem eliminator. *Using a modem eliminator to connect two DTE over a serial link.*

Modem eliminators are similar to line drivers, but modem eliminators simply connect two pieces of DTE and line drivers connect DTE to data communications equipment (DCE). Also, line drivers regenerate signals and thus extend the maximum possible distance, but modem eliminators do not. Finally, line drivers are used in pairs (one at each end of the line), and modem eliminators are used singly and are placed at the midpoint between the two devices being connected.

See Also: *data communications equipment (DCE), data terminal equipment (DTE), line driver, modem, serial transmission*

modem sharing

Any method for sharing a modem among several computers.

Overview

Modem sharing is an inexpensive method for small networks to share a single Internet or remote access connection. For example, in a Small Office/Home Office (SOHO) environment, a cable modem or Digital Subscriber Line (DSL) modem can be used to share a single high-speed Internet connection among several users. Another scenario is in remote branch offices where a single shared modem can be used for occasional remote access connectivity over a wide area network (WAN) link to the head office.

Modem sharing can be implemented in two ways:

- **Hardware-based:** Hubs and routers that have built-in 56K, DSL, or Integrated Services Digital Line (IDSN) modems often have modem sharing capability. In this scenario, you simply plug your phone line into a hub or a router, and then use a Category 5 (Cat5) patch cord to connect the hub or router to your local area network (LAN) hub or switch, and computers on your network transparently have access to the external network. In another approach, you can use a broadband router to connect your LAN to your DSL or cable modem to provide high-speed Internet access to users on your network.
- **Software-based:** By connecting a modem to one machine on the network and installing modem

sharing software on that machine, other machines on that network gain access to the external connection through that machine. Microsoft Corporation includes modem sharing software called Internet Connection Sharing with its Windows Millennium Edition (Me), Windows 2000, and Windows XP operating system platforms. Third-party modem sharing software is also available from a variety of vendors. The main disadvantage of the software-based approach to modem sharing is that if the computer having the modem goes down, other computers on the network cannot use the modem.

Marketplace

Modem sharing hardware for DSL and cable Internet services are becoming popular. Some examples of broadband routers from different vendors include the ZyXEL Prestige 310, Netopia 9100, and WatchGuard SOHO.

Notes

If you use modem sharing to provide your network with high-speed connectivity to the Internet, be sure to use a firewall to secure your network against outside intrusion. If you use Windows 2000, another good step is to turn off Internet File Sharing.

See Also: *broadband Internet access, cable modem, Digital Subscriber Line (DSL), hub, Integrated Services Digital Network (ISDN), modem, router*

modulation

Converting analog signals into digital signals (the reverse process is called demodulation).

Overview

Modulation is the process by which digital information is encoded into analog electrical signals for transmission over a medium. Digital information is usually binary information, as represented by a series of 1s and 0s, and must be converted into analog electrical signals (voltages) for transmission over wires (or into light waves for transmission over fiber-optic cabling).

Modulation is often confused with signal encoding or line coding, as these processes are inherently similar. However, for transmission using modems over the Public Switched Telephone Network (PSTN) lines, the process is generally called modulation, but for transmission over digital lines such as T1, frame relay, and Integrated Services Digital Network (ISDN) lines, the term *encoding* or *line coding* is usually used instead. Some reference works tend to blur this distinction, however, and there is usually some overlap between the concepts.

Types

Modulation forms the basis of the digital-to-analog converter (DAC) component of a standard analog modem. Modulation in modems allows digital binary information to be received from a serial interface on a computer and modulated into sound waves for transmission over the voice-grade PSTN.

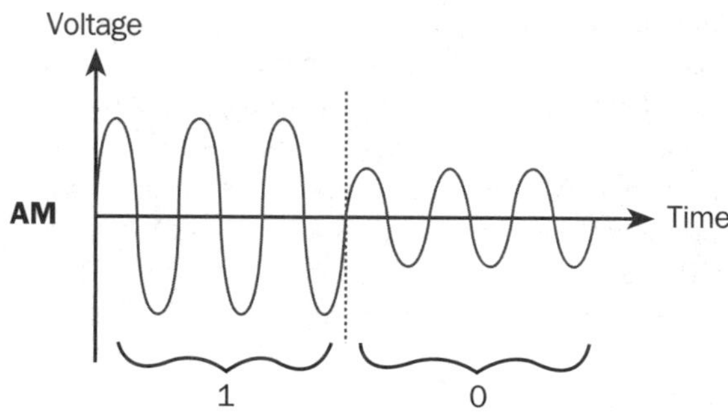

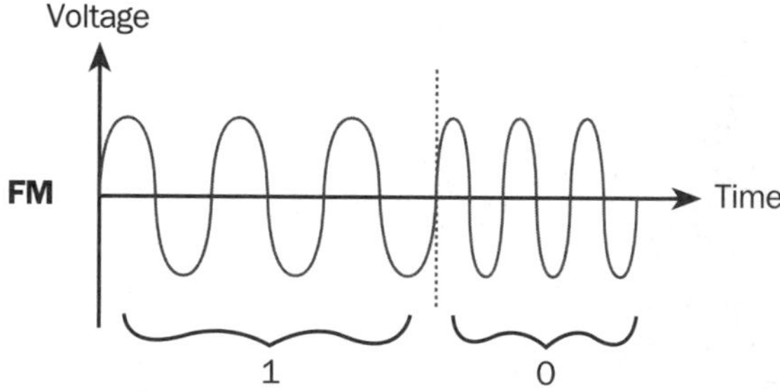

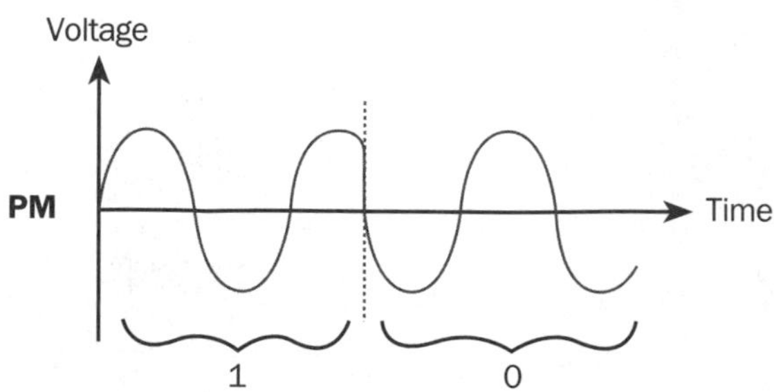

Modulation. *Examples of different types of modulation.*

Common types of signal modulation that are used for converting digital to analog signals include

- **Amplitude modulation (AM):** Carries information by modulating the amplitude (voltage) of the carrier signal. Different amplitudes represent different information values. For example, an amplitude of 3 volts might represent a 1, while an amplitude of 1 volt represents a 0.
- **Frequency modulation (FM):** Carries information by modulating the frequency of the carrier signal. Different frequencies represent different information values. For example, a frequency of F might represent a 1, while a frequency of 2F represents a 0.
- **Frequency-shift keying (FSK):** A form of frequency modulation scheme in modem technologies is called in which four frequencies within the PSTN 3-kilohertz (kHz) line bandwidth are used for transmission and reception of binary data, as shown in the following table:

Frequencies Used in FSK Modulation

FSK Frequency	*Meaning*
1070 Hz	Transmitted binary 1
1270 Hz	Transmitted binary 0
2025 Hz	Received binary 0
2225 Hz	Received binary 1

- **Phase modulation (PM):** Carries information by modulating the phase of the carrier signal. Different phases represent different information values. For example, a phase of 0° might represent a 1, while a phase of 180° represents a 0.
- **Differential phase-shift keying (DPSK):** A form of phase modulation used in modem technologies in which relative phase changes instead of absolute phase values are used to represent encoded binary information.
- **Quadrature amplitude modulation (QAM):** A combination of amplitude and phase modulation which allows the encoding of pairs of binary values to be represented as different phase values, as shown in the following table:

QAM Encoding of Binary Value Pairs

QAM Phase Value	*Binary Information Represented*
45° phase shift	11
135° phase shift	10
225° phase shift	01
315° phase shift	00

- **Trellis encoding:** A form of differential phase-shift keying in which a 32-bit constellation of different state symbols for more efficient encoding of information and greater immunity to electromagnetic interference (EMI).

Notes

For modulation (line coding) over digital transmission lines, various techniques can be employed, depending on the networking technology under consideration. These include

- Manchester coding used for standard 10 megabits per second (Mbps) Ethernet networks.
- Carrierless amplitude and phase (CAP) modulation used in older Digital Subscriber Line (DSL) technologies.
- Discrete multitone (DMT) modulation standardized for use in Asymmetric Digital Subscriber Line (ADSL) by the American National Standards Institute (ANSI) and for DSL-Lite by the International Telecommunication Union (ITU).
- Discrete wavelet multitone (DWMT) modulation, used for Very high-rate Digital Subscriber Line (VDSL).

See Also: *Asymmetric Digital Subscriber Line (ADSL), Digital Subscriber Line (DSL), electromagnetic interference (EMI), line coding, modem, Public Switched Telephone Network (PSTN), signal, Very-high-rate Digital Subscriber Line (VDSL)*

M

MOF

Stands for Microsoft Operations Framework, a service from Microsoft Corporation that provides technical guidance on Microsoft technologies to large enterprises.

See: *Microsoft Operations Framework (MOF)*

MOSPF

Stands for Multicast Open Shortest Path First, a dense mode multicast routing protocol.

See: *Multicast Open Shortest Path First (MOSPF)*

MOUS

Stands for Microsoft Office User Specialist, a Microsoft certification for users of Microsoft Office.

See: *Microsoft Office User Specialist (MOUS)*

moving files

Changing the directory in which a file is stored.

M

Overview

On Microsoft Windows platforms, files can be moved using a graphical user interface (GUI) tool such as Windows Explorer or from the command prompt using the Move command. Some inheritance issues are associated with moving files on Windows NT and Windows 2000 platforms that use the NTFS file system (NTFS). In particular, the effect of moving a file depends on whether the file is moved within a volume or to a different volume:

- If you move a file within an NTFS volume, it retains its original permissions.
- If you move a file between volumes, it inherits the permissions of the folder it is moved to.

Notes

If you move an object within Active Directory directory service on a Windows 2000–based network, the object loses any permissions that were assigned to the organizational unit (OU) in which it resided and inherits the permissions assigned to the OU to which it is moved. Also, any permissions that were explicitly assigned to the object remain in effect after the object is moved. For example, you might move an object in Active Directory if a user has changed departments and you have to move the user object from the Sales OU to the Marketing OU. Use the Active Directory Users and Computers snap-in for Microsoft Management Console (MMC) to move objects in Active Directory.

See Also: *copying files*

Mozilla

An open-source Web browser.

Overview

Mozilla is an open-source project aimed at developing a free, standards-based Web browser. Mozilla is based on Netscape Navigator, a popular Web browser platform developed by Netscape in the mid-1990s which was itself based on the earlier NCSA Mosaic browser. Mozilla will run on a variety of operating system platforms, including Microsoft Windows, Apple Macintosh, and Linux. The development of the Mozilla browser is being coordinated by Mozilla.org, an open-source organization.

For More Information

Visit *mozilla.org* for details on Mozilla.

See Also: *Internet Explorer, open source, Web browser*

MP

Stands for Multilink Point-to-Point Protocol, a wide area network (WAN) protocol for aggregating multiple Point-to-Point Protocol (PPP) connections.

See: *Multilink Point-to-Point Protocol (MPPP)*

MPLS

Stands for Multiprotocol Label Switching, a protocol for efficiently routing traffic across a large Internet Protocol (IP) network such as the Internet.

See: *Multiprotocol Label Switching (MPLS)*

MPOA

Stands for Multiprotocol over ATM, a method for forwarding Internet Protocol (IP) packets over Asynchronous Transfer Mode (ATM) networks.

See: *Multiprotocol over ATM (MPOA)*

MPPP

Stands for Multilink Point-to-Point Protocol, a wide area network (WAN) protocol for aggregating multiple Point-to-Point Protocol (PPP) connections.

See: *Multilink Point-to-Point Protocol (MPPP)*

MSAU

Another acronym that stands for Multistation Access Unit, a wiring concentrator (passive hub) used in Token Ring networks. An alternative to MAU, the most common acronym for this term.

See: *Multistation Access Unit (MAU or MSAU)*

MS-CHAP

Stands for Microsoft Challenge Handshake Authentication Protocol, an encrypted authentication scheme for Point-to-Point Protocol (PPP) sessions.

See: *Microsoft Challenge Handshake Authentication Protocol (MS-CHAP)*

MSDN

Stands for Microsoft Developer Network, Microsoft Corporation's portal and support program for their developer community.

See: *Microsoft Developer Network (MSDN)*

MS-DOS

Stands for Microsoft Disk Operating System, an operating system created by Microsoft Corporation in 1981 for the first IBM personal computer (PC).

See: *Microsoft Disk Operating System (MS-DOS)*

MS-DOS mode

An operating system mode for some versions of Microsoft Windows that is compatible with running MS-DOS applications.

Overview

MS-DOS mode is a special operating system mode in Windows 95, Windows 98, and Windows Millennium Edition (Me) that allows applications to access hardware directly. This functionality is sometimes needed in order to run older MS-DOS applications (especially games) on these versions of Windows. You can also use MS-DOS mode when you have to run stubborn MS-DOS programs that will not run within an MS-DOS window on these versions of Windows 95.

To switch to MS-DOS mode from Windows, choose Shutdown from the Start menu, and then choose Restart In MS-DOS Mode. The Windows graphical user interface (GUI) vanishes, leaving only an MS-DOS prompt, which allows you to run a single MS-DOS-based application. A stub of the Windows operating system remains in memory and restores the Windows GUI when you type **exit** at the MS-DOS prompt.

See Also: *Microsoft Disk Operating System (MS-DOS), Microsoft Windows*

M-Services

Stands for Mobile Services Initiative, a proposed set of standards for broadband cellular Internet access.

See: *Mobile Services Initiative (M-Services)*

MSP

Stands for Management Service Provider, a company that manages the information technology (IT) infrastructure for other businesses.

See: *Management Service Provider (MSP)*

MSF

Stands for Microsoft Solutions Framework, a training program developed by Microsoft Corporation for large enterprises that provides guidance on planning, building, and deploying solutions based on Microsoft products and technologies.

See: *Microsoft Solutions Framework (MSF)*

MSR

Stands for Microsoft Research, a branch of Microsoft Corporation concerned with advanced research in computer science and technologies.

See: *Microsoft Research (MSR)*

MTC

Stands for Microsoft Technology Center, a state-of-the-art training center for learning about Microsoft technologies and solutions.

See: *Microsoft Technology Center (MTC)*

MTQP

Stands for Message Tracking Query Protocol, an emerging protocol for tracking e-mail messages over the Internet.

See: *Message Tracking Query Protocol (MTQP)*

MTSO

Stands for Mobile Transport Serving Office, a component of a cellular communications system.

See: *Mobile Transport Serving Office (MTSO)*

MTU

Stands for multitenant unit, a building with many tenants, such as a skyscraper.

See: *multitenant unit (MTU)*

Multicast Address Dynamic Client Allocation Protocol (MADCAP)

An extension to the Dynamic Host Configuration Protocol (DHCP) for dynamic assignment of multicast addresses.

Overview

MADCAP is an extension to DHCP that offers dynamic assignment and configuration of Internet Protocol (IP) multicast addresses on Transmission Control Protocol/Internet Protocol (TCP/IP) networks. The MADCAP extensions to DHCP are described in RFC 2131, which makes the earlier RFC 1541 obsolete. MADCAP is supported by the Microsoft Windows 2000 operating system platform.

Implementation

In the Windows 2000 and Windows .NET Server implementations, MADCAP allows DHCP servers to include class D multicast IP addresses in separate DHCP scopes. These class D addresses can range from 224.0.0.0 through 239.255.255.255, although some class D addresses are permanently reserved for specific multicast groups and others can be assigned as desired. MADCAP dynamically assigns available class D addresses to clients who need to temporarily join a multicast group in order to receive a multicast transmission. The DHCP clients must also support MADCAP in order to request and receive multicast addresses from the MADCAP service (client machines running Windows 2000 and Windows .NET Server also support MADCAP).

MADCAP operates separately from DHCP, and a client that has an IP address from a DHCP server (or has a static IP address that has been manually assigned to it) can request from the MADCAP service an additional multicast address so that it can receive a multicast transmission over the network. A client can lease only one unicast address, but it can request and obtain multiple multicast addresses and belong to multiple multicast groups simultaneously.

Notes

If a client does not support MADCAP, it cannot request addresses from the MADCAP service, but it might be able run multicast-enabled applications such as Windows Media Player to receive multicast transmissions over a network.

MADCAP was formerly known as the Multicast Dynamic Host Configuration Protocol (MDHCP).

See Also: *Dynamic Host Configuration Protocol (DHCP), multicasting, unicasting*

Multicast Dynamic Host Configuration Protocol (MDHCP)

The former name for what is now called Multicast Address Dynamic Client Allocation Protocol (MADCAP).

See: *Multicast Address Dynamic Client Allocation Protocol (MADCAP)*

multicasting

Also called IP multicasting, a method for sending one Internet Protocol (IP) packet simultaneously to multiple hosts.

Overview

Most communications between two hosts on an IP network are performed using one of two methods:

- **Unicasting:** One host transmits a packet directly to another host on the network. Unicasting is the main method for transmitting data from one host to another over an IP network. Unicasting is essentially a point-to-point form of communication—unless network interfaces are operating in promiscuous mode for troubleshooting purposes, a unicast packet is received only by the host it is specifically addressed to.
- **Broadcasting:** One host transmits a packet to all other hosts on the network. Broadcasting is used primarily for service announcements and for address registration and resolution and is not generally used for host-host communications. Broadcast packets are sent to a special broadcast address that informs every host on the network to receive and process the packet.

Unfortunately, neither of these two IP transport methods is suited to a rapidly growing segment of Internet traffic—multimedia presentations and videoconferencing. For example, consider one host transmitting an audio or video stream and 10 hosts that want to receive this stream. If unicasting were used, the sending host would need to transmit 10 separate IP packets, one for each receiving host. As the number of receiving hosts scales upward, this scenario rapidly results in saturation of network bandwidth. On the other hand, if broadcasting were used by the sending host, then only one IP packet (a broadcast packet) would need to be transmitted, not just the 10 hosts but all hosts on the network would receive and process the packet. The result is that network hosts would incur unnecessary processing, which is clearly also an undesirable situation.

The solution to this is multicasting—the sending host transmits a single IP packet with a specific multicast address, and the 10 hosts simply need to be configured to listen for packets targeted to that address to receive the transmission. Multicasting is thus a point-to-multipoint IP communication mechanism that operates in a connectionless mode—hosts receive multicast transmissions by "tuning in" to them, a process similar to tuning in to a radio station. Multicasting is supported by Ethernet, Token Ring, Fiber Distributed Data Interface (FDDI), and Asynchronous Transfer Mode (ATM) networking architectures.

Architecture

IP multicast addresses (also known as group addresses) are IP addresses belonging to class D, and therefore fall within the range 224.0.0.0 through 239.255.255.255. IP multicast addresses thus have their four high-order bits set to 1110 when viewed in binary notation. In Classless Inter-Domain Routing (CIDR) notation, the block of IP multicast addresses is expressed as 224.0.0.0/4.

Multicast addresses come in two types:

- **Permanent:** Addresses that are reserved for special uses, such as host and router announcements. A multicast group based on one of these addresses can have any number of hosts within it, including zero hosts. In other words, when the last host leaves a permanent multicast group, the group continues to exist even though it has no members. Permanent addresses are defined either in Requests for Comment (RFCs) defining IP multicasting standards, such as RFC 1112, or they can be reserved by the Internet Assigned Numbers Authority (IANA) for specific uses. Examples of such uses include topology and gateway discovery for multicast routing protocols, and group membership registration and reporting. The following table shows some common reserved multicast addresses and their uses. All multicast addresses within the range 224.0.0.0 through 224.0.0.255 are reserved for special use, although some of these addresses have not had their uses specifically assigned yet. Addresses within this range are reserved for local subnet use only and are not forwarded to other subnets by routers, regardless of the time-to-live (TTL) in the packet headers. Addresses that fall within the range 239.0.0.0 through 239.255.255.255 are similarly reserved. Some addresses in the 224.0.1.0 through 224.0.1.255 are also reserved, and, unlike other permanent addresses, these can be forwarded by routers. Additional addresses are also reserved for vendor-specific and service provider-specific multicast transmissions.

Examples of Reserved IP Multicast Addresses

Address	*Description*
224.0.0.0	Base address (not used)
224.0.0.1	All hosts on the local subnet
224.0.0.2	All routers on the local subnet
224.0.0.5	All Open Shortest Path First (OSPF) version 2 routers on the network
224.0.0.6	Designated Open Shortest Path First (OSPF) version 2 routers on the network
224.0.0.9	Routing Information Protocol (RIP) version 2 group address
224.0.0.18	Internet Group Management Protocol (IGMP) group address
224.0.1.1	Network Time Protocol (NTP)
224.0.1.24	WINS server group address
224.0.1.75	Session Initiation Protocol (SIP) group address
224.0.12.0 to 224.0.12.63	Used by MSNBC
224.0.18.0 to 224.0.18.255	Used by Dow Jones

- **Transient:** Addresses that are used to define multicast groups formed for specific multicast transmissions such as a videoconferencing session. Each transient address specifies a multicast group, and once the last host has left this group, the group ceases to exist and the address is released for other uses. Addresses for transient multicast groups are chosen from the range 224.0.1.0 through 238.255.255.255, as all other class D addresses are reserved as described previously.

IP hosts can support multicasts at one of three levels:

- **Level 0:** Cannot send or receive multicast traffic
- **Level 1:** Can send but not receive multicast traffic
- **Level 2:** Can send and receive multicast traffic

Microsoft Windows 2000 supports Level 2 multicast functionality for all forms of IP traffic.

Implementation

Membership in a multicast group is dynamic—hosts can join or leave a group as they choose. To join a multicast group, a host sends a message to the all hosts multicast group 224.0.0.1. This informs routers on the local subnet that the host wants to join a specific multicast group. Routers then periodically send queries to the same multicast group to ensure hosts are still interested in belonging to multicast groups. Hosts can belong to more than one multicast group simultaneously, and multicast groups can span multiple subnets.

When the host wants to leave a group, it sends a message to the All Routers multicast group 224.0.0.2. These messages between hosts and routers are sent using the Internet Group Management Protocol (IGMP).

Routers must be multicast-enabled to support multicasting. Multicast routers communicate using multicast routing protocols such as Multicast Open Shortest Path First (MOSPF) and Protocol Independent Multicast (PIM).

For More Information

Visit the IP Multicast Initiative at *www.ipmulticast.com.*

See Also: *broadcasting, Class D, classless interdomain routing (CIDR), Internet Group Management Protocol (IGMP), Internet Protocol (IP), IP address, multicast routing, multicast routing protocol, router, unicasting*

Multicast Open Shortest Path First (MOSPF)

A dense mode multicast routing protocol.

Overview

Multicast Open Shortest Path First (MOSPF) is a protocol that allows multicast-enabled routers to communicate with each other in order to build multicast forwarding tables. These tables contain trees of information specifying which subnets have hosts that belong to different multicast groups. This allows hosts belonging to a specific group to receive multicast transmissions directed toward that group.

MOSPF is designed to be used within a single routing domain or autonomous system (AS). Although it is classified as a dense mode multicast routing protocol, MOSPF does not work well for networks that have large numbers of active multicast groups due to the large amount of overhead involved in recalculating distribution trees when multicast groups are added or removed from the network. Performance is best for MOSPF when only a few multicast groups are active, and, as a result, MOSPF is not widely used for multicasting over the Internet.

MOSPF is based on the unicast Open Shortest Path First (OSPF) routing protocol and is defined in RFC 1584. Cisco routers do not support MOSPF.

See Also: *autonomous system (AS), multicasting, multicast routing, multicast routing protocol, Open Shortest Path First (OSPF)*

multicast routing

Routing of multicast packets across an internetwork from the sending host to the receiving group of hosts.

Overview

Ordinary routing is unicast routing—that is, the routing of unicast packets. Unicast routing involves forwarding Internet Protocol (IP) packets from the sending host to a specific, globally unique receiving host. Routing involves forwarding the packet across multiple subnets to its final destination, the number of subnets crossed being the number of hops required for the packet to reach its destination. From the point of view of unicasting, subnets are well-defined entities connected by routes.

Multicast routing is different: multicast packets are forwarded to multicast-enabled routers and these routers are responsible for ensuring that hosts belonging to the multicast group specified by the destination address receive the transmitted packet. Group members may be located in a single subnet or in many different subnets and may be concentrated either in a small portion of the larger internetwork or scattered all over the place. To ensure that multicast packets are not forwarded to subnets where no interested hosts reside and to ensure that they are forwarded from routers on noninterested subnets to other routers further downstream, multicast routing protocols are used to allow multicast-enabled routers to communicate with each other and exchange information.

Information about which subnets interested hosts reside on is maintained in multicast forwarding tables stored on multicast-enabled routers. An entry in this table indicates that there is at least one interested host (a host belonging to the multicast group to which the transmission is directed) in the subnet mapped to that entry. Multicast routing protocols generally store their multicast forwarding tables as hierarchical structures called multicast trees. A tree defines the distribution of multicast packets from the sending host to all receiving hosts within its multicast group. Mulitcast trees are created and maintained by processes known as grafting and pruning and can be either source trees which find the shortest path from the sending host to each potential receiving host, or shared trees which merge source trees into a single tree for each specific group. Multicast traffic is prevented from being sent to subnets where no interested hosts reside by a process known as scooping.

See Also: *multicasting, multicast routing protocol, routing, unicasting*

multicast routing protocol

Any protocol used for communication between multicast-enabled routers.

Overview

Multicasting on an Internet Protocol (IP) internetwork relies on special multicast-enabled routers. These

M

routers enable hosts to register themselves for sending or receiving multicast transmissions. Multicast routers communicate with each other using multicast routing protocols in order to create multicast forwarding tables (multicast trees) that ensure that each host that joins a multicast group receives the transmission directed toward that group.

Types

There are two basic kinds of multicast routing protocols:

- **Dense mode:** Protocols used when large numbers of hosts grouped together in dense clusters need to receive multicast traffic. Dense mode protocols need a large amount of network bandwidth in order to operate because they periodically flood the network with multicast traffic. Examples of dense mode multicast routing protocols include
    - **Distance Vector Multicast Routing Protocol (DVMRP):** An early protocol based on Routing Information Protocol (RIP) and now rarely used. It is defined in RFC 1075.
    - **Multicast Open Shortest Path First (MOSPF):** A protocol based on the unicast Open Shortest Path First (OSPF) routing protocol. MOSPF is designed for use within a single autonomous system (AS) and is defined in RFC 1584.
    - **Protocol Independent Multicast-Dense Mode (PIM-DM):** Similar to DVMRP but uses a unicast routing protocol for building its multicast trees.
- **Sparse mode:** Protocols used when smaller numbers of hosts are widely scattered over the network. Sparse mode protocols utilize less bandwidth than dense mode ones, and they build multicast trees by joining branches to the main distribution tree. Examples of sparse mode multicast routing protocols include
    - **Protocol Independent Multicast-Sparse Mode (PIM-SM):** Similar to PIM-DM but optimized for sparse multicasting environments.
    - **Core-Based Trees (CBT):** Creates a single distribution tree for each multicast group. CBT is defined in RFC 2201.

See Also: *Core-Based Trees (CBT), Distance Vector Multicast Routing Protocol (DVMRP), multicasting, Multicast Open Shortest Path First (MOSPF), multicast routing, Protocol Independent Multicast-Dense Mode (PIM-DM), Protocol Independent Multicast-Sparse Mode (PIM-SM), routing protocol*

multihoming

The process of having more than one network interface on a device.

Overview

Networking devices that have more than one interface are called multihomed devices. A router is a good example of a multihomed device because it has several network interfaces, each usually connected to a different subnet.

Computers can also be multihomed by giving them multiple interfaces to a network. This is true even if the computer has only a single physical interface (network interface card, or NIC). For example, Microsoft Windows 2000 allows you to assign more than one Internet Protocol (IP) address to a single physical interface, resulting in multiple virtual interfaces and making the machine a multihomed host. When a computer is connected to both a local area network (LAN) using a NIC and the Internet using a dial-up connection, this can also be considered multihoming since the dial-up connection is also an interface (a wide area network [WAN] interface typically running Point-to-Point Protocol [PPP]), though the term multihoming is not always used in this scenario.

The most common way of multihoming a computer, however, is to install two or more physical interfaces (NICs) and assign separate IP addresses to each NIC. Windows 2000 supports all of these methods of multihoming. Note that the first method of using multiple virtual interfaces is sometimes called multinetting and is considered by some not to be true multihoming.

Uses

Multihoming has a number of possible uses:

- For turning a computer into a router. If you install multiple NICs in a Windows 2000 server computer, the machine can be used as a router on an IP internetwork. The Routing and Remote Access Service (RRAS) of Windows 2000 makes this scenario possible. If you enable Routing Information Protocol (RIP) on the computer, it can function as a dynamic router that can exchange routing table information with other RIP-enabled routers. Or if you do not enable RIP, the computer can function as a static router, in which case you would manually configure the server's routing table from the command prompt using the Route command.
- For increasing the bandwidth to critical servers by enabling them to connect to several networks simultaneously or to the same network using multiple interfaces having different IP address.
- For connecting Dynamic Host Configuration Protocol (DHCP) servers to several subnets simultaneously for dynamic IP address allocation to hosts.
- For connecting a privileged host to both a low-security LAN and a restricted high-security LAN.

Issues

Some issues can arise with multihomed hosts:

- **Multiple default gateways:** If you multihome a computer with two or more physical interfaces that are not aware of each other's presence and then assign different default gateway addresses to each interface, network communications problems can arise. To solve this, use only a single default gateway and assign the corresponding address to the interface carrying more traffic.
- **Remote access:** A typical remote access server has both a local area network (LAN) interface and a wide area network (WAN) interface. You should generally use static routing between these two interfaces to avoid routing problems.

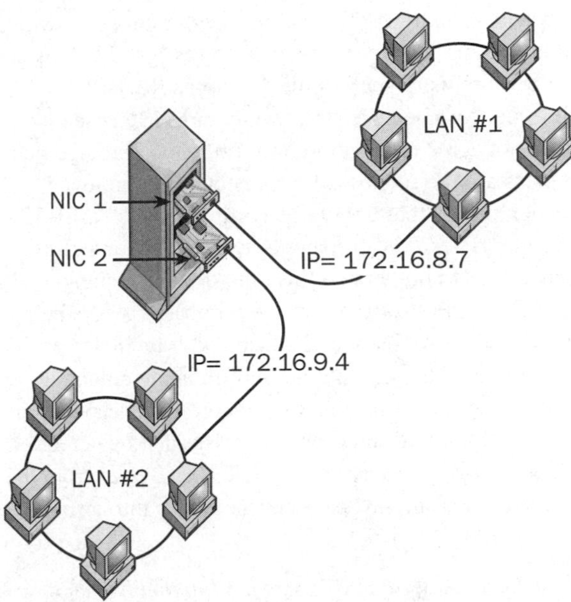

Multihoming. *A multihomed server with two interfaces.*

Notes

The term *multihoming* is also used in a different sense in the modern enterprise: using several Internet Service Providers (ISPs) to connect your network to the Internet. A typical multihoming scenario would see two leased lines joining your network to the Internet. Each line is leased from a different ISP, and one line is used to bring IP traffic into your network while the other is used to carry traffic out of the network. The motive for this kind of multihoming is to ensure redundant connection for enterprise data centers to the high-speed backbone of the Internet through different points of presence (POPs) belonging to different carriers. This is desirable for companies that view the Internet as a mission-critical resource and cannot afford any downtime.

To implement Internet multihoming in this way generally requires high-end routers and an understanding of complex protocols, such as Border Gateway Protocol (BGP), that are used on the Internet's backbone. Often, the challenge in this scenario is to get the different ISPs to cooperate with one another to ensure your network does not have IP address space problems. This is

M

because a multihomed network needs to have its own autonomous system number (ASN) assigned to it by an Internet registry such as the American Registry for Internet Numbers (ARIN). Many large ISPs usually will not agree to this kind of multihoming arrangement unless a minimum of a T3 connection is employed, which means that only large companies such as IBM, Hewlett-Packard Company, Amazon.com, and eBay can afford to implement this kind of multihoming. Nevertheless, the steady rise in the number of ASNs being allocated by ARIN over the last few years indicates the rise in popularity of Internet multihoming among large enterprises and e-business companies. A cheaper alternative to multihoming for enterprises that need redundancy is simply to lease several T1 or T3 lines from the same carrier and inverse multiplex them into a single connection.

See Also: *American Registry for Internet Numbers (ARIN), autonomous system number (ASN), Border Gateway Protocol (BGP), Dynamic Host Configuration Protocol (DHCP), interface, inverse multiplexing, network interface card (NIC), router*

M

Multilayer Switching (MLS)

A local area network (LAN) switching term that can have several meanings.

Overview

The term *Multilayer Switching (MLS)* can have several meanings within the context of LAN switching. Specifically, it can refer to

- The ability of a LAN switch to mimic the functions of a router. In other words, the term can be synonymous with Layer 3 switching.
- A switch that can operate at multiple layers of the Open Systems Interconnection (OSI) reference model. For example, a multilayer switch could bridge at Layer 2, route at Layer 3, and screen ports at Layer 4.
- A Cisco LAN switching architecture that allows switches and routers to work together within the high-speed core of an enterprise network. The MLS architecture is built using several components, including a Multilayer Switching Switch Engine (MLS-SE), Multilayer Switching Route Processor (MLS-RP), and Multilayer Switching Protocol (MLSP) from Cisco Systems.

See Also: *Ethernet switch, Layer 2 switch, Layer 3 switch, Layer 4 switch, Open Systems Interconnection (OSI) reference model, router*

Multilink Frame Relay (MFR)

A new frame relay aggregation technology.

Overview

Multilink Frame Relay (MFR) is a new standard from the Frame Relay Forum that allows multiple frame relay links to be aggregated using inverse multiplexing. The goal of MFR is to make frame relay an attractive technology in the market niche between T1 and T3 lines. Enterprises using multiplexed T1 lines that require more bandwidth often balk at the cost of upgrading to T3, which offers speeds of 45 megabits per second (Mbps) compared to T1's 1.5 Mbps. MFR is designed to provide a lower-cost option that can provide bandwidth intermediate between T1 and T3.

Implementation

MFR is implemented at the service provider end using MFR-enabled carrier-class frame relay switches and at the customer premises end using MFR-enabled Integrated Access Devices (IADs). Multilink Point-to-Point Protocol (MPPP) service providers include competitive local exchange carriers (CLECs), building local exchange carriers (BLECs), and large Internet service providers (ISPs). Service providers generally target midsize businesses and multitenant units (MTUs) for deploying MFR.

MFR is often used in conjunction with MPPP, a wide area network (WAN) protocol that allows scalable bandwidth allocation using dynamic bonding of multiple Point-to-Point Protocol (PPP) links. MPPP devices can aggregate up to 128 separate frame relay links into a single logical pipe, with individual links ranging from DS-0 to T1.

See Also: *Building-centric Local Exchange Carrier (BLEC), Competitive Local Exchange Carrier (CLEC), DS-0, frame relay, Integrated Access Device (IAD), Internet service provider (ISP), Multilink Point-to-Point Protocol (MPPP), multitenant unit (MTU), Point-to-Point Protocol (PPP), T-carrier*

Multilink Point-to-Point Protocol (MPPP)

A wide area network(WAN) protocol for aggregating multiple Point-to-Point Protocol (PPP) connections.

Overview

Multilink Point-to-Point Protocol (MPPP) can be used to bundle together multiple physical PPP links into a single logical link. This is accomplished by using inverse multiplexing on each end of the link, at both the customer premises, and at the service provider (for an MPPP connection to be established, both ends of the connection must support MPPP). MPPP's purpose is usually to provide greater bandwidth for a WAN connection than a single PPP link can provide, but since MPPP is a dynamic process, it can also be used to better utilize bandwidth and even load-balance between connections. The advantages of using MPPP on WAN links include increased bandwidth, dynamic bandwidth allocation, reduced latency, and fault tolerance. MPPP's main disadvantage is that it is difficult to support callback for remote access servers.

MPPP is an extension to the industry-standard PPP and is defined in RFC 1990. MPPP is supported by most access servers and routers and also by the Microsoft Windows 2000 operating system. Multilink Point-to-Point Protocol is variously abbreviated as MPPP, MP, or MLP, and is abbreviated occasionally (and wrongly) as MPP or even MLPPP. Sometimes it is simply called Multilink Protocol for short!

Uses

A popular use of MPPP is in Integrated Services Digital Network (ISDN) networking where it can be used to either bond (combine) the two 64-kilobits per second (Kbps) B channels of an ISDN-BRI interface into a single 128-Kbps logical channel or aggregate two or more BRI interfaces together for even greater throughput.

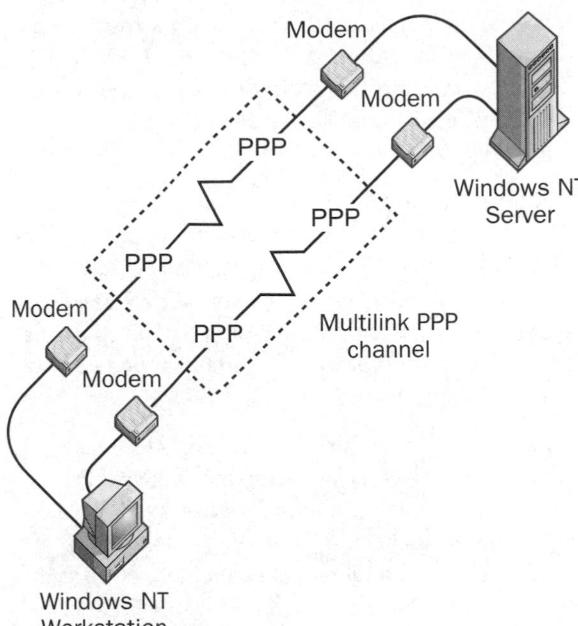

Multilink Point-to-Point Protocol (MPPP). *Using MPPP to bond two PPP links together.*

MPPP was the first industry-standard nonproprietary method for ISDN bonding, and as a result, it is popular where ISDN technologies are still used. Because MPPP is a dynamic protocol, it can also be used to dynamically bring online the second B channel whenever the bandwidth of a single channel is insufficient and then dynamically release the second channel when it is no longer required. This is done by configuring a traffic threshold above which the second channel will automatically be activated. MPPP is supported by most ISDN terminal adapters.

A newer use of MPPP is in ISDN Digital Subscriber Line (IDSL), a form of Digital Subscriber Line (DSL) technology based on ISDN signal coding. By installing an MPPP-enabled IDSL router at the customer premises and a similar router at the service provider's point of presence (POP), up to four 144 kilobits per second

M

(Kbps) IDSL links can be multiplexed into a single 576 Kbps link. MPPP IDSL is a technology pioneered by Netopia and is intended mainly for corporate WAN use and not for residential Internet access. Using MPPP IDSL eliminates the need for installing a costly Digital Subscriber Line Access Multiplexer (DSLAM) at the customer premises and is ideal for environments such as remote telco terminals that are too limited in size to house DSLAMs.

Implementation

MPPP can be implemented over a variety of interfaces, including asynchronous dial-up modem connections, Integrated Services Digital Network (ISDN), and even synchronous connections. MPPP is negotiated during the Link Control Protocol (LCP) portion of a PPP authentication session.

MPPP defines procedures for splitting a PPP data stream into packets, sequencing the packets into time slots, transmitting them over a logical data link, and reassembling them at the receiving station. MPPP works by inverse multiplexing data frames from multiple client PPP connections into a single PPP link, and then demultiplexing the link to recreate the individual connections at the service provider's router.

MPPP supports two kinds of PPP authentication: Challenge Handshake Authentication Protocol (CHAP) and Password Authentication Protocol (PAP).

Notes

A proprietary extension to MPPP supported by some vendors is called Multichassis Multilink Point-to-Point Protocol (MMP), which allows MPPP connections to be aggregated across multiple routers and network access servers (NASs) in a way that is transparent to the dial-up MPPP client. In other words, the client initiates an MPPP session but is actually connected to several MMP-enabled NASs at the ISP instead of only one NAS, as in the usual scenario. MMP enables the data stream to be split, sequenced, and recombined at several different points to provide a single logical connection between the client and the ISP.

Another proprietary extension to MPPP is called Multichannel PPP (MPP), which in addition to inverse multiplexing of PPP links also supports session and bandwidth management functions, including the dynamic addition or removal of channels without the need to reinitialize the link. Both the client and the server must support MPP for this to work.

See Also: *Challenge Handshake Authentication Protocol (CHAP), Digital Subscriber Line (DSL), Digital Subscriber Line Access Multiplexer (DSLAM), Integrated Services Digital Network (ISDN), inverse multiplexing, ISDN Digital Subscriber Line (IDSL), ISDN fallback adapter, Link Control Protocol (LCP), Password Authentication Protocol (PAP), Point-to-Point Protocol (PPP), wide area network (WAN)*

multimaster replication

Replication between peers.

Overview

Replication is an important aspect of many kinds of network services. For example, in network directory services, replication ensures that each directory server has an up-to-date version of directory information for the network. Replication between directory servers can take place in two ways: master/slave and multimaster replication.

In master/slave replication, the master server maintains the master copy of directory information and replicates this information with slave servers through periodic updates. Directory information can usually only be modified directly on the master server—slave servers usually have read-only versions of directory information. Master/slave replication is reliable but scales poorly and has a single point of failure—should the master server go down, the directory cannot be updated unless a slave server is promoted to the role of master. Master/slave replication is used by the Windows NT Directory Services (NTDS) of the Microsoft Windows NT 4.0 operating system, where master servers are called primary domain controllers (PDCs) and slaves are backup domain controllers (BDCs). In Windows NT, directory information is stored on domain controllers in the Security Account Manager (SAM) database, and although the PDC for each domain has a writable copy of the SAM database, the BDCs for that domain have read-only copies of the database.

In multimaster replication, however, there is no master directory server—all directory servers are peers of one another. Multimaster replication scales well and has no single point of failure, but it must be implemented properly using time stamping of updates and time synchronization between servers to ensure that replication occurs properly if collisions are to be avoided. A collision occurs when an object in Active Directory directory service has the same attribute modified almost simultaneously on two different domain controllers, and collisions are resolved using timestamps as a tie-breaking mechanism. Active Directory in Microsoft Windows 2000 uses multimaster replication to replicate directory information between all domain controllers in a domain. Multimaster replication, in fact, means that all domain controllers are "master" domain controllers—in other words, applications and users having sufficient privileges can update directory information on these servers directly.

The advantages of the multimaster replication method supported by Windows 2000 over the PDC/BDC master/slave replication method of Windows NT include the following:

- You can make updates to Active Directory as long as any domain controller is functioning on the network.
- When domain controllers are distributed at all sites, you can make updates to Active Directory anywhere on the network with a local domain controller, even when wide area network (WAN) links to other sites are down.

See Also: *Active Directory, directory*

multimode fiber-optic cabling

A type of fiber-optic cabling that can carry multiple signals simultaneously.

Overview

Multimode fiber-optic cabling allows large amounts of information to be transmitted over a single strand of fiber. This is accomplished by transmitting multiple light signals simultaneously through specially constructed fiber. This enables multimode fiber to sustain a much greater bandwidth than single-mode fiber, a type of fiber that supports only one light signal at a time.

The disadvantage of multimode cabling is that multimode transmission is more complex and incurs greater risk of signal loss. As a result, multimode fiber runs cannot be as long as single-mode fiber, which can carry signals for several kilometers without degradation. So although multimode fiber can carry many times more bandwidth than single-mode fiber, single-mode fiber can generally carry signals up to 50 times farther than multimode.

Implementation

Multimode fiber is fiber-optic cabling that has a glass core whose index of refraction varies in a specific fashion with the distance from the core axis. This variation in index of refraction is done to ensure that multiple separate light signals can be effectively transported down the fiber without interference or signal loss. The variation is implemented in one of two ways:

- **Step-index:** Here light rays reflect off the inner surface of the core by a mechanism called total internal reflection. By varying the angle at which the rays are incident on the inner surface of the core, different light paths can be transmitted down the fiber to carry additional light signals, thus increasing the bandwidth capacity of the fiber. In long step-index fiber runs, however, these light paths can get out of step with each other at the far end of the fiber and thus degrade overall signal quality. Step-index fiber is cheaper than graded-index fiber and should be used only for shorter cable runs or where less bandwidth is required.
- **Graded-index:** Here the core consists of concentric layers of homogeneous material, each successive layer having a lower index of refraction than the layer that it envelops. In this type of fiber, the rays of light travel along curved paths and all arrive in step with each other at the far end of the fiber, which means that graded-index fiber runs can be longer than step-index ones.

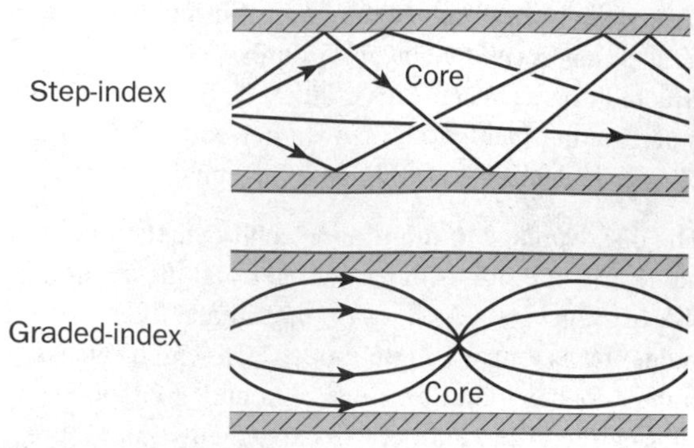

Multimode fiber-optic cabling. *How light travels along two kinds of multimode fiber.*

Multimode fiber is available with different core diameters, typically 50, 62.5, and 100 microns. Line drivers transmitting signals through multimode cables generally use light-emitting diodes (LEDs) to generate their signals.

Uses

Because of the length restrictions for multimode fiber, this type of cabling is generally restricted in use to small cable runs such as switch-switch and switch-server links and backbone connections within buildings (intrabuilding connections). Single-mode fiber is necessary for long cable runs such as inter-building connections and distributed campus backbones.

Multimode cable lengths are restricted to various distances depending on the networking technology used. For example, in Gigabit Ethernet (GbE), multimode fiber of the 50 and 62.5 micron size are supported (62.5 is preferred) with maximum cable run lengths supported being 1800 feet (550 meters). If this limit is exceeded, the light traveling along different paths through the fiber can produce a condition called modal dispersion, which results in parts of the signal arriving at unexpected times at the end station. This condition can quickly degrade the signal's quality, causing it to be unrecognizable so that communication is impossible. Note that older forms of Ethernet such as 10BaseT and Fast Ethernet support multimode links up to 6600 feet (2000 meters) in length due to their slower signaling speed.

See Also: *cabling, Ethernet, Fast Ethernet, fiber-optic cabling, Gigabit Ethernet (GbE), single-mode fiber-optic cabling*

M

multiple master domain model

A strategy for deploying large networks based on Microsoft Windows NT.

Overview

The multiple master domain model represents a Windows NT domain model in which all user and group accounts for the enterprise reside in two or more account domains that trust one another using two-way trusts. Network resources for the enterprise reside in separate resource domains, and each resource domain trusts every account domain in the enterprise. The goal of this structure is to ensure that users anywhere in the enterprise can access network resources anywhere in the enterprise provided they have suitable permissions.

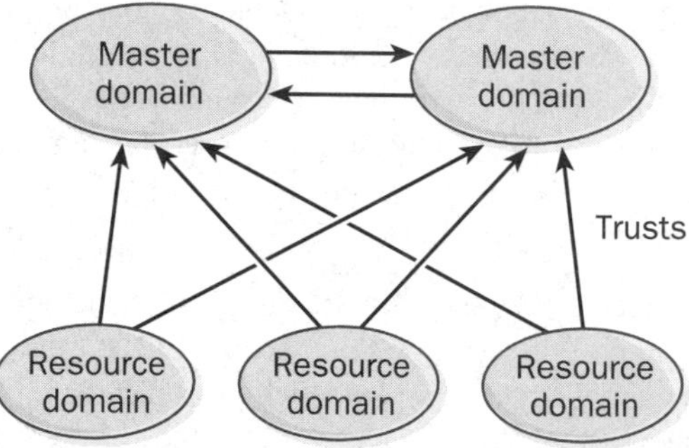

Multiple master domain model. *Using the multiple master domain model to deploy Windows NT for a large enterprise.*

Large enterprises may use the multiple master domain model either because of limitations on the recommended number of users in a Windows NT domain (about 20,000) or because their company is spread across several geographically separate locations.

Advantages and Disadvantages

The advantages of the multiple master domain model are that it is scalable to any number of user accounts and that resource domains in this model manage their own resources. Among the disadvantages are the fact that the master domain model is complex to set up and administer and that multiple local groups must be created in each resource domain.

Notes

Enterprises can simplify network administration considerably by upgrading their large Windows NT–based networks to Windows 2000. Windows 2000 overcomes the limitations of Windows NT's multiple master domain model by supporting the storage of up to 10 million objects in Active Directory directory service and by allowing a single domain to be partitioned into multiple sites with intersite directory replication traffic being scheduled for times of low wide area network (WAN) usage. As a result, it is often the best approach and a relatively straightforward process to consolidate a large Windows NT–based network having multiple master domains and resource domains into a single large Windows 2000 domain having multiple sites. In this approach you can mirror the administrative structure of your former network by creating a hierarchy of organizational units (OUs) within Active Directory and assigning suitable permissions for these OUs to users and groups.

If you want to maintain the existing administrative structure of your company more closely, however, you can take a different approach in your migration. You can migrate each Windows NT master or resource domain to a distinct Windows 2000 domain. Here each master domain would become the root of a domain tree, and the resource domains that trusted them become child domains joined by two-way transitive trusts to their parent domain. This results in one new domain tree for each former master domain. You then establish two-way transitive trusts between the root domains of each tree, forming a domain forest. All users in your enterprise thus gain access to resources anywhere on the network.

See Also: *Active Directory, complete trust model, master domain, organizational unit (OU), single domain model*

Multiple Virtual Storage (MVS)

A legacy IBM mainframe operating system.

Overview

Multiple Virtual Storage (MVS) was originally developed for the System/360 series of IBM mainframes. The name comes from the fact that MVS uses virtual memory (storage) for sharing memory among multiple applications.

MVS is still used on many legacy mainframes found in government, finance, and industry for running accounting and payroll systems, large databases, and other legacy applications. MVS is mainly used to run applications written in COBOL, but it supports other languages, including FORTRAN, PL/1, and CICS.

MVS has been supplanted by the OS/390 operating system, which runs on IBM's System/390 mainframe models.

See Also: *mainframe*

multiplexer (MUX)

A device that combines multiple data streams into a single stream.

Overview

Multiplexers (MUXes) are used in wide area networks (WANs) to make optimum use of available bandwidth in leased lines. A multiplexer allows data streams from several pieces of data terminal equipment (DTE) to be multiplexed (combined) into a single stream that can be transmitted over the leased line. In addition, multiplexers allow leased lines to carry voice, video, and data traffic simultaneously.

An inverse multiplexer, or IMUX, takes a single input data channel from a DTE, such as a router, and spreads it to several digital transmission lines. A demultiplexer is simply a MUX at the remote end of a multiplexed communication system. A modular MUX allows you to expand your wide area network (WAN) link as your network grows by adding modules to provide additional V.35, RS-232, or RS-530 input ports.

Implementation

Multiplexers can save companies costs by eliminating the need for extra line termination devices such as Channel Service Unit/Data Service Units (CSU/DSUs). For example, a T1 MUX typically has several V.35 interfaces that can accept incoming data from switches or routers connected to your local area networks (LANs), plus a DSX-1 interface for connecting to a channel bank or private branch exchange (PBX) system. The MUX takes this serial data input and voice input and multiplexes them together into a single data stream using an integrated CSU/DSU and then transmits this stream over the T1 line, letting you use your

T1 line for voice and data combined. You can use a similar device to multiplex data and voice for transmission over a public frame relay carrier network.

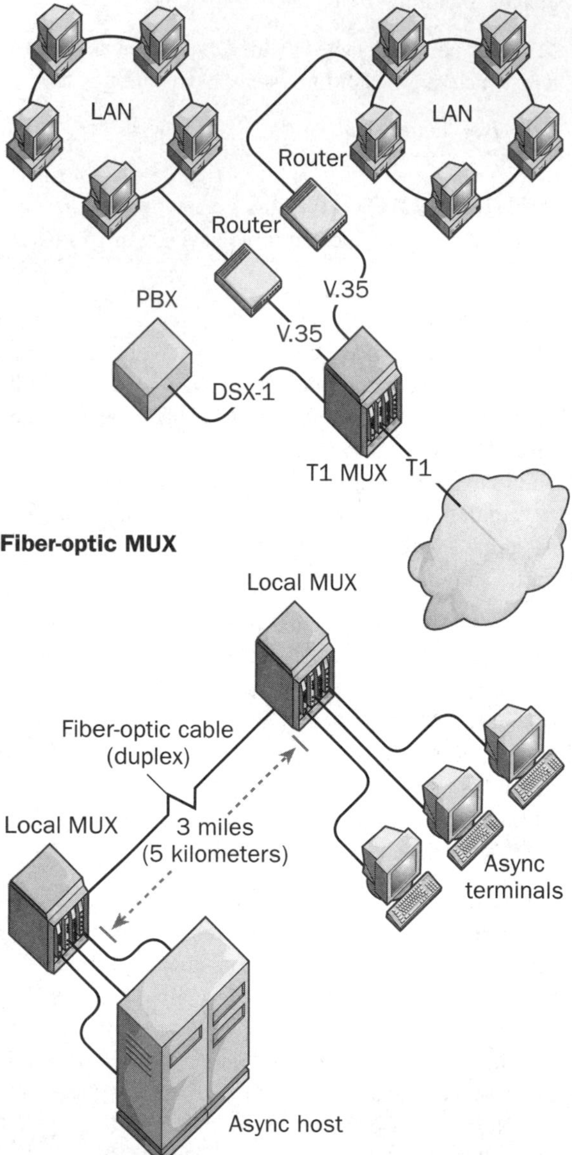

Multiplexer (MUX). *Examples of using a T1 multiplexer and a fiber-optic MUX.*

These T1 MUXes often offer advanced management functions. For example, a T1 MUX can usually be remotely managed using the Simple Network Management Protocol (SNMP), and it can be configured to send a trap to an SNMP management console whenever a problem occurs with the MUX. Some MUXes are also used in mainframe environments for connecting remote terminals to async hosts without the need for individual cabling to each terminal. These kinds of MUXes are generally used in pairs and utilize time-division multiplexing (TDM). Examples include the following:

- Fiber-optic MUXes for combining several sync or async data channels onto one duplex fiber-optic cable. A typical fiber-optic MUX might have 12 or 24 RS-232 input ports and support speeds in excess of 115.2 kilobits per second (Kbps) per channel. These MUXes are typically used in pairs to connect remote terminals to an async mainframe host across a campus environment and are often referred to as short-haul or local MUXes.
- Twisted-pair MUXes for multiplexing several RS-232 serial channels over installed RJ-11 wiring to save costs.
- Coax MUXes for connecting several 3270 terminals to an IBM controller in order to reduce the costs of cabling.

Another type of multiplexer is the Ethernet MUX, which can multiplex signals from several ports from an Ethernet switch and transmit the multiplexed signal over a single fiber-optic cable at distances up to 1.25 miles (2 kilometers). Ethernet MUXes are also typically used in pairs.

See Also: *Channel Service Unit/Data Service Unit (CSU/DSU), data terminal equipment (DTE), inverse multiplexing, multiplexing, Simple Network Management Protocol (SNMP), T1, T-carrier*

multiplexing

Combining multiple data streams into a single stream.

Overview

Multiplexing is used in networking and telecommunications to aggregate data streams from different sources into a single channel, typically for transmission over a wide area network (WAN) connection. For example, signals from several data terminal equipment (DTE) can be combined into a single signal using a multiplexer and transmitted over a leased line such as a T1 line. For information to be transmitted successfully, the leased line must have a bandwidth equal to or greater than the combined bandwidth of the signals from the various DTE.

Implementation

Several methods of multiplexing signals are commonly used in telecommunications and networking. Each method is suited to a specific form of communication. Some more common methods used include

- **Frequency-division multiplexing (FDM):** This method is used to multiplex analog signals. In this scenario, the total bandwidth of the carrier signal is subdivided into a series of channels having different frequencies.
- **Time-division multiplexing (TDM):** This is a common method for multiplexing digital signals used, for example, in T1 lines. Data from different bitstreams are placed in alternating fashion in different time slots in the carrier signal. One time slot is assigned to each incoming stream of data. The problem with this method is that if one source of data has nothing to transmit, the time slot for that source will not be used and the associated bandwidth will be wasted. TDM is suitable mainly for applications that transmit data in real time, such as voice, video, or multimedia transmissions. This is because TDM has predictable latency and can thus provide guaranteed levels of Quality of Service (QoS) for transmissions.
- **Statistical multiplexing (SM):** Also called statistical packet multiplexing (SPM) or statistical time division multiplexing (STDM), this method is similar to TDM but can reassign time slots to different sources when they are not needed. Statistical multiplexing thus makes better use of available bandwidth than TDM and is useful mainly for transmissions that have unpredictable latency, such as Internet Protocol (IP) transmissions. Statistical multiplexing is used in WAN technologies such as frame relay and Asynchronous Transfer Mode (ATM).
- **Dense wavelength division multiplexing (DWDM):** A multiplexing technology used in high-speed fiber-optic backbone networks. DWDM sends multiple bitstreams through a single strand of fiber using a different color (wavelength) of laser light for each stream. DWDM is emerging as the technology of choice for telcos and other carriers who need to enhance the carrying capacity of their trunk lines and backbone networks.

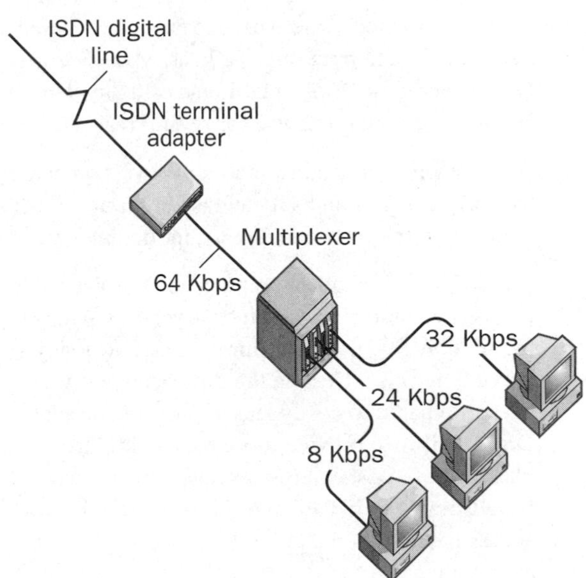

Multiplexing. *How multiplexing combines multiple physical data links into a single logical connection.*

See Also: *Asynchronous Transfer Mode (ATM), dense wavelength division multiplexing (DWDM), frame relay, frequency-division multiplexing (FDM), inverse multiplexing, leased line, multiplexer (MUX), statistical multiplexing (STM), time-division multiplexing (TDM)*

multipoint

Short for point-to-multipoint, communication from a single sending station to multiple receiving stations.

See: *point-to-multipoint*

Multipoint Multichannel Distribution Service (MMDS)

A fixed wireless broadband networking architecture.

Overview

Also known as fixed wireless, Multipoint Multichannel Distribution Service (MMDS) is a new broadband wireless service designed to compete with Digital Subscriber Line (DSL) and cable modem technologies. It can be used to provide enterprise with high-speed wireless wide area network (WAN) connections and for high-speed Internet access.

MMDS is a serious contender in the enterprise WAN arena and is a low-cost alternative to expensive leased lines such as T1 and fractional T1 lines. MMDS is generally considered superior to DSL and cable modem technologies for enterprise use for several reasons:

- It can be provisioned in a matter of days, compared to the weeks or months it can take to set up a DSL connection (or even frame relay, for that matter).
- It is stable and reliable compared to DSL and cable modem technologies, which have yet to provide the required 99.999 percent uptime needed by today's wired enterprise. Despite the dirt-cheap cost of DSL compared to costly leased lines and despite DSL's ability to provide more bandwidth than leased lines, most enterprises have stayed away from using DSL in their WAN links and for Internet access because of the reliability issues still associated with it.
- It can be provisioned without the need to install additional wiring, which is a costly expenditure in older buildings.

Implementation

MMDS operates in the 2.1, 2.5, and 2.7 gigahertz (GHz) portions of the electromagnetic spectrum. Typical speeds for MMDS are 384 kilobits per second (Kbps) to 1 megabit per second (Mbps) for downstream transmission and 384 Kbps to 512 Kbps upstream.

In a typical MMDS scenario, a base station with antenna is set up at a high location (building rooftop or hill) in or near an urban area. The base station provides coverage for customer sites within a 22-mile (35-kilometer) radius. Customer sites must have a clear line of sight with the base station's antenna in order for MMDS to work properly.

Marketplace

Currently, the two major players in the MMDS arena are Sprint Corporation and MCI/Worldcom, two interexchange carriers (IXCs). MMDS is being rolled out by these companies in major urban areas around the United States. A major producer of MMDS equipment is Vyyo Wireless Systems.

Prospects

The main issue with MMDS is the clear line of sight (LoS) requirement for transmission. One way of working around this is to implement orthogonal frequency division multiplexing (OFDM) on MMDS, which helps overcome the LoS, reach, and antenna size issues relating to MMDS.

See Also: *broadband Internet access, cable modem, Digital Subscriber Line (DSL), frame relay, Orthogonal Frequency Division Multiplexing (OFDM), T-carrier, wide area network (WAN), wireless networking*

multiport repeater

An older name for a hub, a device used to connect shared Ethernet segments into a single LAN.

See: *hub*

Multiprotocol Label Switching (MPLS)

A protocol for efficiently routing traffic across a large Internet Protocol (IP) network such as the Internet.

Overview

Multiprotocol Label Switching (MPLS) is an emerging standard from the Internet Engineering Task Force (IETF) designed for implementation on high-speed backbone routers in large IP networks such as the Internet. MPLS is an outgrowth of several proprietary vendor-based solutions to the problem of routing traffic through high-speed switched backbones. The most prominent of these proprietary solutions is the tag switching technology developed by Cisco Systems, from which much of MPLS was derived. Other companies whose technologies have contributed to the development of MPLS include Ipsilon Networks (now part of Nokia), Cascade Communications, 3Com Corporation, IBM, and Cabletron Systems.

MPLS is designed to bring some of the advantages of circuit-switched networks to switched IP networks. These advantages include predictable delay and latency, the ability to reserve bandwidth, and different levels of Quality of Service (QoS).

Implementation

The name MPLS defines two aspects of this protocol:

- **Multiprotocol (MP):** MPLS can work with any network transport. Although it is intended mainly for IP, it can work with Asynchronous Transfer Mode (ATM), IP over ATM, frame relay, and other transports.
- **Label Switching (LS):** MPLS works by attaching labels to packets, uniquely identifying the data flow or path that packet takes across a routed network such as the Internet.

An MPLS label is simply a four-octet binary number. The first 20 bits of the label uniquely identify the Forwarding Equivalence Class (FEC) to which the packet belongs, while the remaining bits specify the time to live of the packet and other information. Each data flow through the internetwork is mapped to an FEC—in other words, all packets belonging to the same FEC are handled similarly by MPLS-enabled routers. Multiple labels can be attached to each packet, which enables MPLS to support features such as tunneling and even stacked tunnels. A sequence of labels or a label stack is called a Label-Switched Path (LSP).

MPLS-enabled routers are called Label Switching Routers (LSRs), and for MPLS to work properly it must be supported by routers all across the internetwork. LSRs forward packets by examining their LSP and switching them accordingly, a process that can be much faster than traditional IP routing. Packets are introduced into an MPLS domain using a Label Edge Router (LER) connected to both the local network and the backbone network. Once the packet is on the backbone, it is label-switched to the LER adjacent to the destination network, at which point it is routed using traditional IP routing to its final destination. LSRs communicate with each other using the Label Distribution Protocol (LDP) to let each other know what labels they are assigning to different traffic flows.

Uses

Because MPLS is a complex protocol, it is unlikely to be used extensively in the enterprise. Instead, service providers and telcos are likely to deploy MPLS on their ATM backbones to increase the efficiency with which they carry IP traffic. MPLS offers an alternative to permanent virtual circuits (PVCs) commonly used in telco ATM networks. Using MPLS, ATM switches become routers that can dynamically switch traffic to their destination, taking the advantage of multiple redundant nondedicated paths to their destination.

When service providers offer customers MPLS on their WAN links, a number of features can be implemented at the IP level by the customer instead of having to implement them at the ATM level by the carrier. These features include the ability to perform traffic engineering, support for multiple independent private data streams over a single WAN connection, implementing bandwidth reservation and Quality of Service (QoS), and more.

An example of MPLS deployment at the telco level is AT&T, which has deployed MPLS running on Cisco switches on its frame relay backbone network for more efficient transport of IP traffic over that network. MPLS is used to define different Classes of Services (CoS) and supports virtual private networking (VPN). Another example of how MPLS can be used is demonstrated by CoSine, which combines MPLS with Internet Protocol Security (IPsec) for secure tunneling and virtual routing.

MPLS is also expected to find application in pure optical backbone networks, an emerging technology driven mainly by the demand for greater capacity for Internet backbone traffic.

See Also: *Asynchronous Transfer Mode (ATM), frame relay, Internet Protocol (IP), quality of service (QoS), routing*

Multiprotocol over ATM (MPOA)

A method for forwarding Internet Protocol (IP) packets over Asynchronous Transfer Mode (ATM).

Overview

Multiprotocol over ATM (MPOA) defines a standard for forwarding Layer 3 packets (such as IP packets) over ATM backbones. MPOA is intended to support any Layer 3 network transport, but IP is the main transport used with MPOA due to its ubiquitous use in the enterprise and on the Internet. The MPOA standard is being guided by the ATM Forum.

MPOA can be used to establish connections between different IP subnets using an ATM backbone. This contracts with LAN Emulation (LANE), another IP over ATM technology (and a technology from which MPOA was derived), which is used mainly to support IP communications within a subnet. Neither MPOA nor LANE are suitable for transmission of IP traffic over wide area network (WAN) connections, however, due to the large number of ATM virtual circuits (VCs) required—nine for each pair of hosts communicating using MPOA. MPOA can also be used to connect virtual LANs (VLANs) in a switched backbone network.

Architecture

The MPOA architecture involves MPOA Servers (MPSs), also called route servers, which operate as virtual routers to switch IP packets across the ATM network. Each subnet requires one or more route servers, and IP traffic is bridged from the sending host to a route server, switched across one or more additional route servers, and then bridged directly to its destination. These route servers have intelligence that enables them to track the overall topology of theATM network and enable IP traffic to be switched across shortcut paths between end nodes on the network. The result is low latency and delay and greater Quality of Service (QoS) for IP traffic. This architecture enables MPOA to provide the "route once, switch many" functionality needed in the core switching backbone of today's high-speed networks.

See Also: *Asynchronous Transfer Mode (ATM), Internet Protocol (IP), quality of service (QoS), routing, virtual circuit, virtual LAN (VLAN)*

Multipurpose Internet Mail Extensions (MIME)

Extensions to Simple Mail Transport Protocol (SMTP) that allow multipart and binary messages to be sent using e-mail.

Overview

SMTP, the popular e-mail system used on the Internet, is defined in RFC 822 as a mechanism for forwarding simple text-based messages between hosts. An SMTP message consists of a single text file encoded in 7-bit ASCII format with headers attached. SMTP uses these headers to determine how the message is forwarded by SMTP hosts along the route to its destination.

Early on, two limitations of SMTP became apparent to users of the system:

- SMTP could only be used to send text messages, and some mechanism was needed to support sending other types of files, including word-processing documents, images, video clips, and other binary information.
- An SMTP message body could only have one part—it would be nice if multiple files could be embedded in, or attached to, a single message body.

Multipurpose Internet Mail Extensions (MIME) were developed to address these two concerns. MIME does not replace SMTP but simply extends it to include support for multipart message bodies and non-ASCII message content. MIME is defined in RFC 1521, and various MIME types are defined in later RFCs.

Implementation

MIME adds two additional types of headers for SMTP messages. These headers are

- **Content-Type:** Specifies the various kinds of content carried by SMTP messages
- **Content-Transfer-Encoding:** Specifies the various methods by which SMTP message content is encoded

RFC 1521 defines seven basic message content types that can be specified in the Content-Type header of SMTP messages. Each content type can have several subtypes to further specify the type of information carried by SMTP messages. Although RFC 1521 defined some of these subtypes, succeeding RFCs have defined many more subtypes. The main MIME content types are

- **Text:** Subtypes include plain, richtext, html, and other
- **Application:** Subtypes include octet-stream (8-bit chunks of binary data), Postscript (for Postscript printing), msword (for Microsoft Word documents), and almost a hundred others
- **Image:** Subtypes include gif, jpeg, tiff, and others
- **Audio:** Subtypes include basic and others
- **Video:** Subtypes include mpeg, quicktime, and others
- **Message:** Subtypes include rfc822 (a standard RFC 822 SMTP text message), http (for Hypertext Transfer Protocol [HTTP] traffic), and others
- **Multipart:** Subtypes include mixed (each part of the message body can have a different content type), alternative, parallel, digest, encrypted, and others

RFC 1521 also defines six basic data encoding methods that can be specified in the Content-Transfer-Encoding headers of SMTP messages. These are 7bit (ASCII text with line lengths less than 1000 characters), 8bit, binary, quoted-printable, base64 (Uuencoded data), and x-token. Later RFCs have defined other MIME encoding methods.

See Also: *e-mail, Simple Mail Transfer Protocol (SMTP)*

multiservice switch

A switch that can route packets and switch cells.

Overview

Multilevel switches are generally high-end switches that can support both Asynchronous Transfer Mode (ATM) circuit-switching and frame relay packet switching in a single chassis. Multilevel switches have been responsible in part for a rising interest in ATM backboning as a result of evolution in frame relay technologies such as Multilink Frame Relay (MFR).

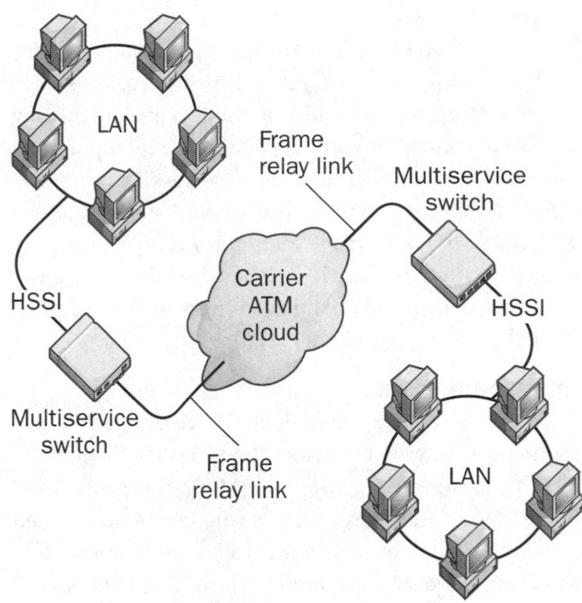

Multiservice switch. *A wide area network (WAN) built using multiservice switches.*

In a typical wide area network (WAN) scenario, frame relay might be used at the edge of corporate local area networks (LANs) at the ingress and egress points, connecting the LANs using carrier ATM services as the internetwork backbone technology.

Multiservice switches conform to two frame relay specifications:

- **FRF.5:** Frame Relay Permanent Virtual Circuit to ATM
- **FRF.8:** Frame Relay Permanent Virtual Circuit to ATM Service Internetworking

See Also: *Asynchronous Transfer Mode (ATM), circuit-switched services, frame relay, Multilink Frame Relay (MFR), packet switching*

Multistation Access Unit (MAU or MSAU)

A wiring concentrator (passive hub) used in Token Ring networks.

Multistation Access Unit (MAU or MSAU)

Overview

Multistation Access Units (MAUs) are the core wiring components for building Token Ring networks. MAUs direct traffic from one station to the next around the ring of a Token Ring network. While the logical topology (electrical path) of a Token Ring network is a ring, the physical topology (wiring) is actually a star topology with the MAU at the center and the stations connected in a star pattern to the MAU. The MAU thus concentrates the wiring and contains circuitry that makes the logical star network operate as a physical ring.

Implementation

A typical MAU is a stand-alone device or a rack-mounted device that provides 8 or 16 ports for connecting stations to the ring. The MAU also generally includes two additional ports: a ring-out connector and a ring-in connector. These ports are used to connect MAUs together to form larger Token Ring networks. For example, a larger network can be constructed by joining several MAUs to form a larger ring by connecting the ring-out connector of one MAU to the ring-in connector of another and continuing to connect until the ring-out of the last MAU in a series is connected to the ring-in of the first to complete the loop. Using this method, you can connect up to 33 MAUs into a large Token Ring network. Some MAUs include ring-in/out connectors for both copper cabling (RJ-45 connectors) and fiber-optic cabling (typically ST connectors).

When interconnecting MAUs to form large Token Ring networks, use MAUs that have automatic loopback functions on their ring-in/out ports. If a break in the ring should then occur between two MAUs, the break is automatically detected and traffic is rerouted along a preconfigured backup path.

MAUs often support both 4 megabits per second (Mbps) and 16 Mbps Token Ring signaling. Note, however, that a common way to bring down a Token Ring network is to connect a Token Ring station that has the wrong speed for the given network—for example, connecting a 4-Mbps station to a 16-Mbps network. This speed mismatch causes beaconing that brings down the network. A smart MAU can detect a mismatched station and lock out the station before a problem can occur.

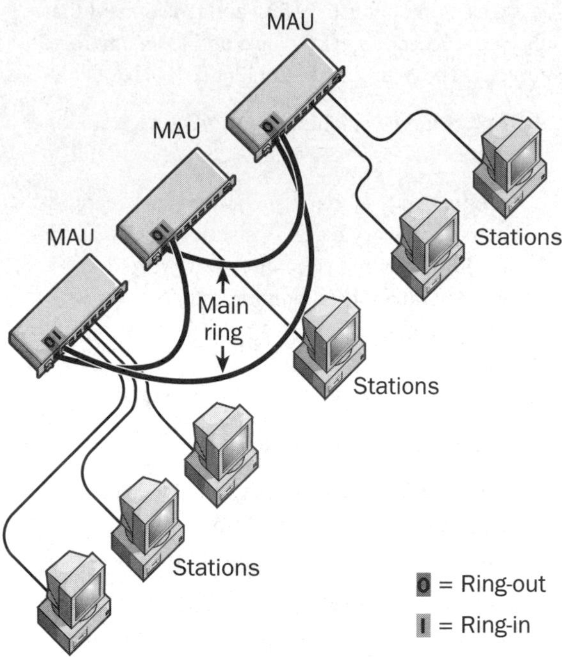

Multistation Access Unit (MAU). *Connecting several MAUs together to create a large Token Ring network.*

MAU connections typically use either proprietary IBM universal data connectors for IBM Type 3 cabling (Type 1 Token Ring) or RJ-45 lobe connectors for 100-ohm shielded twisted-pair (STP) cabling (Type 3 Token Ring). MAUs also usually include circuitry that provides fault tolerance so that if a station fails or is disconnected from the MAU Token Ring, traffic can still continue unaffected around the ring. If you need to locate Token Ring stations at distances greater than 328 feet (100 meters) from a MAU, you can use stand-alone repeaters or a powered (active) MAU that has built-in repeaters to support greater lobe distances.

Other types of MAUs include

- **Modular MAU:** Lets you add different connector or repeater modules for greater flexibility of network design
- **Stackable MAU:** Lets you easily create large Token Ring networks with up to 256 stations

- **Manageable MAU:** Includes modules that support Simple Network Management Protocol (SNMP) management through in-band or out-of-band connections
- **Active MAU:** Regenerates signals at each port in order to reduce jitter and extend signaling distances beyond recommended specifications

Notes

The acronym *MAU* also stands for Medium Access Unit or Media Attachment Unit, a term that refers to the circuitry in an Ethernet hub, Ethernet switch, or Ethernet network interface card (NIC) that enables the correct form of electrical or optical connection to be established with the particular type of media being used. This type of MAU, also known as a transceiver, detects the carrier signal and data signals on the media, notes when collisions between signals occur, and forwards this information to the remaining circuitry for processing. To distinguish the two different meanings of the acronym "MAU," the acronym *MSAU* is sometimes used to refer specifically to a Multistation Access Unit, as used in Token Ring networking.

See Also: *hub, loopback, shielded twisted-pair (STP) cabling, Simple Network Management Protocol (SNMP), Token Ring*

multitasking

Running two or more programs simultaneously.

Overview

From the point of view of the user, multitasking makes programs appear to be executing at the same time, but from the operating system's point of view, one of two things might be happening:

- **On multiprocessor machines:** Here each processor might be running a separate program simultaneously. This is true multitasking, which can only take place on machines with more than one processor and with operating systems that support multiple processors.
- **On single-processor machines:** Here the operating system time-slices between applications so that each application receives a small portion of time to run before giving this privilege to another application.

Types

There are two basic types of multiprocessing on machines that run versions of the Windows operating system:

- **Preemptive multitasking:** The operating system decides which thread or process is allowed to run at any specific time. Windows 95, Windows 98, and Windows NT support this form of multitasking.
- **Cooperative multitasking:** Each application is responsible for voluntarily relinquishing control to other applications. Windows 3.*x* supports this form of multitasking.

Notes

Windows 2000 supports symmetric multiprocessing (SMP) on multiprocessor machines, whereby the Windows 2000 kernel lets processors share memory and assign ready threads to the next available processor. This SMP support ensures that no processor is ever idle or running a low-priority thread when a high-priority thread is waiting. Windows 2000 also supports soft affinity, whereby a thread tries to run on the same processor it last ran on, all things being equal. You can even use Task Manager to assign a specific process to a particular processor, a feature called processor affinity.

See Also: *asymmetric multiprocessing (AMP)*

Multitenant Broadband Service Provider (MBSP)

Another name for a building-centric local exchange carrier, a telecommunications carrier focused on the Multitenant Unit (MTU) market.

See: *Building-centric Local Exchange Carrier (BLEC)*

multitenant unit (MTU)

A building with many tenants, such as a skyscraper.

Overview

Multitenant units are generally large office buildings in dense urban areas, but the term can also include apartment complexes, hotels, industrial parks, and other large buildings and complexes. The MTU market is one that is rapidly growing in importance as far as telcos and other carriers are concerned—estimates indicate there are about 120,000 MTUs in the United States, and many of these MTUs host businesses that are eager for broadband data services. Traditional incumbent local exchange carriers (ILECs) have been slow to provision broadband services such as Digital Subscriber Line (DSL) for this market segment, and, as a result, many competitive local exchange carriers (CLECs) are targeting them. These carriers targeting MTUs for broadband services are generally called Multitenant Broadband Service Providers (MBSPs) or building-centric local exchange carriers (BLECs).

See Also: *broadband Internet access, Building-centric Local Exchange Carrier (BLEC), Competitive Local Exchange Carrier (CLEC), Digital Subscriber Line (DSL), Incumbent Local Exchange Carrier (ILEC)*

MUX

Stands for multiplexer, a device that combines multiple data streams into a single stream.

See: *multiplexer (MUX)*

MVS

Stands for Multiple Virtual Storage, a legacy IBM mainframe operating system.

See: *Multiple Virtual Storage (MVS)*

MX record

A Domain Name System (DNS) record identifying Simple Mail Transfer Protocol (SMTP) hosts.

Overview

MX records specify the DNS name and Internet Protocol (IP) address of a host that can forward e-mail for a given domain. (The acronym *MX* stands for mail exchange.) MX records are required for SMTP hosts to enable them to forward SMTP mail over the Internet.

Examples

An MX record specifying that incoming mail directed toward the microsoft.com domain should be forwarded to the SMTP host called mail.microsoft.com might be expressed as

```
microsoft.com.  IN  MX  0
mail.microsoft.com.
```

Here the number 0 is the preference value that specifies the priority of the SMTP host. This is used if more than one SMTP mail exchanger exists for a given domain.

See Also: *Domain Name System (DNS), resource record (RR)*

My Computer

A desktop icon in Microsoft Windows that enables users to browse resources on their computer.

Overview

The My Computer icon provides a view that is different but complementary to Windows Explorer's view of system and network resources. My Computer gives users a simple way to view the resources on their computer. With Active Desktop installed, however, My Computer has an optional interface that supports browsing resources using a Web browser format.

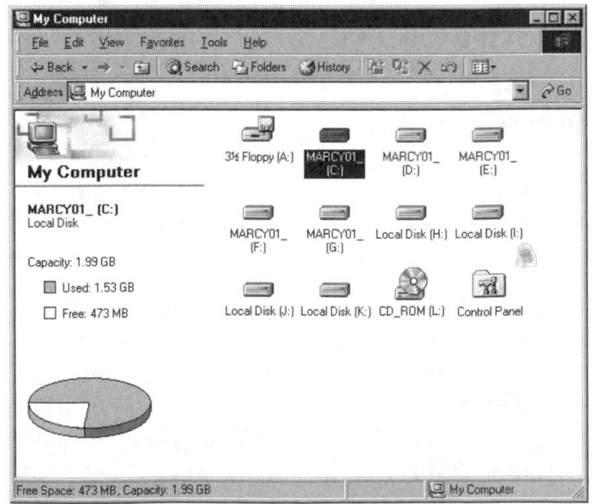

My Computer. *Typical contents of My Computer.*

See Also: *My Documents, My Network Places*

My Documents

A folder in Microsoft Windows that gives users a convenient location for storing their documents.

Overview

My Documents is the default location where applications such as Microsoft Office save the files you create. The desktop icon for My Documents is a folder containing a sheet of paper. My Documents is also part of the user profile on a machine running Windows 2000, Windows XP, and Windows .NET Server, and you can redirect (change) the location of the target folder for My Documents by right-clicking on My Documents and selecting Properties. For example, you could modify My Documents to point to a network share where the user's documents can be safely stored and regularly backed up. Users should generally be instructed to always save their personal documents in their My Documents folder even if their applications do not automatically do so.

See Also: My Computer, My Network Places

My Network Places

A desktop icon in Microsoft Windows 2000, Windows XP, and Windows .NET Server that displays various aspects of the network your computer resides on.

Overview

My Network Places can be used to browse resources on the network. When you open My Network Places, it may contain

- **Add Network Place:** Starts the Add Network Place Wizard. You use the wizard to create shortcuts to network resources such as shared folders, printers, and File Transfer Protocol (FTP) sites.
- **Entire Network:** Contains links to all computers on your network.
- **Microsoft Windows Network:** Included in Entire Network and provides access to computers belonging to Windows 2000 and Windows NT domains and workgroups.
- **Directory:** Included in Entire Network and provides access to information on users, groups, and computers stored in Active Directory directory service on domain controllers.
- **Computers Near Me:** Shows all computers in your local domain or workgroup.
- **Network shortcuts:** These point to shared network resources that you have created using the Add Network Place Wizard.

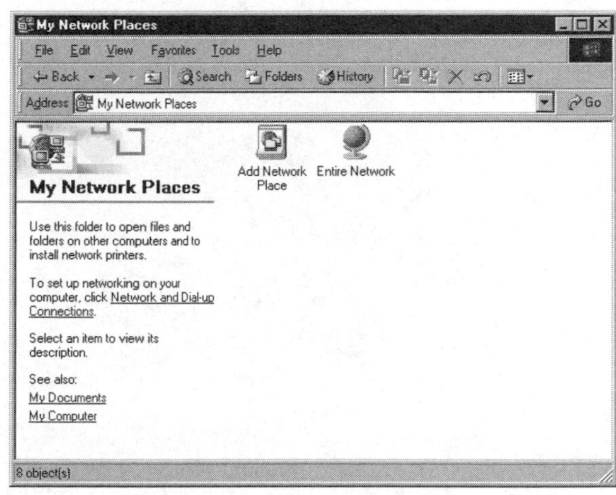

My Network Places. *Typical contents of My Network Places.*

Note also that if you right-click My Network Places and choose Properties, you can open your Network Connections folder, which displays the types of connections that your computer has with local area networks (LANs) or the Internet and allows you to configure these connections.

Nagle's algorithm

A Transmission Control Protocol (TCP) algorithm for controlling traffic congestion on a network.

Overview

Nagle's algorithm increases the efficiency of routers by reducing the latency of the routing process. This is accomplished by limiting the transmission of small Internet Protocol (IP) datagrams and by controlling the size of the TCP sending window. Nagle's algorithm is crucial in enabling IP networks to efficiently support applications such as Telnet that communicate using large numbers of small datagrams.

Nagle's algorithm is defined in RFC 896 and is implemented in common TCP/IP protocol stacks, including that of Microsoft Windows operating systems. Proposals have been put forth for improving the algorithm because it does not produce optimal results with certain kinds of TCP/IP interactions, such as those based on Hypertext Transfer Protocol (HTTP) version 1.1.

Implementation

To understand how the algorithm works, consider a Telnet client communicating with a Telnet server. When a user types a single character into the Telnet client window, TCP normally packages the character and sends it to the server as a very small IP packet. It would be highly inefficient if every character typed into a Telnet window were sent as such a packet, as this would flood the network with small packets. Using Nagle's algorithm, however, what actually happens is that when the user types the next character, one of two things occurs:

- If an acknowledgment has already been received for the first packet sent, TCP packages the second character into a second small packet and sends it immediately to prevent delay.
- If an acknowledgment has not been received for the first packet, TCP buffers the second character, then the third, and so on, until the acknowledgment is received or the buffer has reached a certain size, triggering TCP to package the buffered characters and send them. This process of buffering the TCP send buffer is sometimes called "nagling."

The other part of Nagle's algorithm addresses the problem of a network system getting bogged down when a large datagram is sent over and over again because it takes too long to fill a sending window (the receiving buffer) with the data from the datagram. According to the algorithm, when a client receives a message that datagrams are being dropped because of congestion at a particular host, the client responds by temporarily acting as if the host's window size has been reduced. This "throttles back" the amount of information sent to the host and enables the host to catch up.

See Also: *Hypertext Transfer Protocol (HTTP), Internet Protocol (IP), Telnet, Transmission Control Protocol (TCP)*

named pipe

A legacy interprocess communication (IPC) mechanism.

Overview

Named pipes are a client/server communication mechanism that provides reliable, connection-oriented, two-way communication between processes running on different computers. A named pipe is essentially a portion of memory reserved for one process to pass information to another.

Developed originally for Microsoft OS/2 LAN Manager and maintained as a feature in later versions of Microsoft Windows for backward compatibility, named pipes provide guaranteed delivery of data between computers for distributed applications in a client/server environment. They provide a reliable, one-to-one, bidirectional, connection-oriented form of communication between a client process running on one machine and a server process (service) running on a different machine. Named pipes are implemented as file system drivers and therefore are opened by requests made from the redirector. They take full advantage of the features of file system drivers, such as security and validation.

Examples of situations where named pipes are still used include

- WinLogon process of Windows NT Server
- Client/server applications designed on older versions of Microsoft SQL Server
- Windows 98 and Windows Millennium Edition (Me), which support client-side named pipes but not server-side named pipes

Notes

Named pipes consume more server-side memory than other IPC mechanisms (such as Windows Sockets) and generate a bit more network traffic.

N

See Also: *interprocess communication (IPC)*

name lookup

Resolving a fully qualified domain name (FQDN) into its associated Internet Protocol (IP) address.

Overview

In the Domain Name System (DNS), name resolution is the process of a resolver (DNS client) sending a request to a name server (DNS server). The resolver sends the name server the host name of an IP host on the network, and the name server returns the host's IP address. The name server is thus said to "resolve" the name of the host into its associated IP address.

The query sent by the resolver to the name server is most often a recursive query, which returns either the expected IP address or an error. This type of query makes it possible for a name server to forward the request on to other name servers if it cannot resolve the name and then return the result of that request to the resolver. If the queried name server is configured to forward requests, it can perform an iterative query, querying several name servers in succession until it resolves the name or runs out of name servers to query.

See Also: *Domain Name System (DNS), fully qualified domain name (FQDN), host name resolution, name server*

name resolution

The process of resolving the name of a host on a network into its associated network address.

Overview

Name resolution plays an important part of network communication because the logical names of hosts on the network must be resolved into their network addresses before actual communication can take place between them.

Transmission Control Protocol/Internet Protocol (TCP/IP) networks running Microsoft Windows operating systems support two basic name resolution methods:

- **NetBIOS name resolution:** Used to resolve NetBIOS names into IP addresses. Performed by using broadcasts or by querying a Windows Internet Name Service (WINS) server. NetBIOS name resolution was used in Microsoft Windows NT and is supported by Windows 2000, Windows XP, and Windows .NET Server for backward compatibility purposes only.
- **Host name resolution:** Used to resolve fully qualified domain names (FQDNs) in the Domain Name System (DNS) into IP addresses. Performed either by using a local Hosts file on the machine or by querying a name server.

Notes

Once the name of a host has been resolved into its associated IP address, a TCP/IP protocol called Address Resolution Protocol (ARP) is then used on Ethernet networks to resolve the host's IP address into its associated physical layer address (MAC address). Once ARP has completed this task, frames can then be placed on the wire with the destination MAC addresses embedded in their frame headers.

See Also: *Address Resolution Protocol (ARP), Domain Name System (DNS), Ethernet, frame, fully qualified domain name (FQDN), host name resolution, hosts file, MAC address, name server, NetBIOS name resolution, Transmission Control Protocol/Internet Protocol (TCP/IP), Windows Internet Name Service (WINS)*

name server

A host used to resolve fully qualified domain names (FQDNs) into their associated Internet Protocol (IP) addresses.

Overview

Name servers are hosts on the Internet (or on large IP internetworks) that can be used to resolve host names into IP addresses, a process known as a name lookup. Name servers are an essential part of the Domain Name System (DNS). Because of name servers, when you want to access or reference a host on a TCP/IP network, you can use its friendly DNS name instead of its IP address, which is generally harder to remember.

The distributed system of name servers positioned at various locations around the Internet makes it possible to share the load of name resolution among many such servers instead of relying on a single server. Just imagine if one machine had to track the name of every host on the Internet—not only would its hardware requirements be astronomical, but it also would represent a single point of failure for the entire Internet economy!

Implementation

DNS operates as a client/server-based system, with name servers forming the server part and resolvers forming the client part. Each name server has authority over a portion of DNS namespace known as a zone, which means that the name server can resolve name lookups for hosts located within that zone. A resolver sends a name lookup request to a name server by passing it the DNS name of a host on the network. The name server performs name resolution by determining the IP address that corresponds to the requested host's name. Name servers can also refer such queries to other name servers if they cannot answer them themselves, so a typical name lookup from a resolver might involve obtaining responses from several name servers in sequence.

Each zone has one name server called the master name server that is authoritative over hosts located in the zone. In addition, name servers can be classified on the basis of how they store zone information:

- **Primary name servers:** These name servers keep a local file of the information relating to their zone. This local file or DNS database contains resource records, which are mappings of host names to IP addresses for hosts in that zone. A DNS administrator must generally create and maintain the DNS database manually on a primary name server, although with dynamic DNS (DDNS), hosts can automatically register this information with name servers. Microsoft Windows 2000 and Windows .NET Server support DDNS.
- **Secondary name servers:** These name servers obtain their database of resource records from a master name server, which can be either a primary name server or another secondary name server. The process by which the DNS database is transferred from a master name server to a secondary name server is known as zone transfer. Secondary name servers are provided mainly for fault tolerance and load balancing.

See Also: *Domain Name System (DNS), dynamic DNS (DDNS), fault tolerance, load balancing, master name server, primary name server, resolver, secondary name server, zone, zone transfer*

namespace

An abstract space of names of nodes on a network.

Overview

The term *namespace* can be thought of as "the space of all names" for the particular type of network naming system under consideration. A simple example is Internet Protocol (IP) address space, the space of all possible IP addresses. This space is divided into class A, class B, and so on, which represent disjoint subgroups of the IP address space. Generally, every node on a Transmission Control Protocol/Internet Protocol (TCP/IP) network, internetwork, or the Internet must occupy a unique point in IP address space—that is, it must have a unique IP address. This ensures that a packet addressed to a particular node (such as a computer, network printer, or router interface) can be directed to the node using its IP address as the destination address. If two nodes on a network were to have the same IP address number, a packet intended for one might end up at the other. One exception to this is multicasting, in which a packet is sent to a group of hosts simultaneously and ignored by all other hosts. Another exception is when you have a private network connected to the Internet through a firewall that uses network address translation (NAT) to hide the addresses of hosts on the private network from hosts on the Internet. In this case, if no direct communication is expected between nodes in the two networks (except through the firewall), nodes in the private network can be assigned arbitrary IP addresses, such as 10.*x.y.z*, and two or more private networks can use the same addressing scheme without fear of confusion or lost packets.

Examples

Some other common examples of namespaces include the Domain Name System (DNS) namespace used on the Internet, the NetBIOS namespace used in legacy Microsoft Windows NT networks, and the LDAP namespace used by Active Directory. Unlike the space of IP addresses described above which is essentially flat, DNS namespace is hierarchical in nature and highly scalable. It also has the advantage of being a logical naming scheme that is easily remembered, in contrast to a physical naming scheme such as an IP address, which is hard to memorize and which is bound to the particular network structure being used. The root of the DNS namespace branches out to a relatively small number of top-level domains such as .com, .org, and .edu. Organizations, companies, and individuals can register a domain name in one of these domains and then subdivide their branch of the DNS namespace as they desire. For example, a company named Northwind Traders might register the domain name northwindtraders.com and then create three new subdomains under it named sales.northwindtraders.com, support.northwindtraders.com, and hq.northwindtraders.com. Specific servers and router interfaces exposed to the Internet might then be given specific DNS addresses to uniquely identify them in the DNS namespace. An address in the DNS namespace, called a fully qualified domain name (FQDN), maps to a unique node on the Internet. An example might be widgets.support.northwindtraders.com, which might map to the address 10.15.6.133. Names of domains, subdomains, and individual hosts are maintained on name servers located at various points across the Internet or within large private internetworks. If you want to locate a particular node in the DNS namespace, you query a name server. The process of locating a particular DNS node and resolving its FQDN into its associated IP address is called host name resolution.

The NetBIOS namespace used in Windows NT–based networks (and supported by Windows 2000 and Windows XP for backward compatibility) is simply the space of all NetBIOS names (computer names) of Microsoft Windows machines on the network. Unlike the hierarchical tree structure of the DNS namespace, the NetBIOS namespace is flat and is managed using the Windows Internet Name Service (WINS), which runs on WINS servers in the network. Because the NetBIOS namespace is flat, it is not as highly scalable as DNS. For example, say that you query a name server to resolve an FQDN such as widgets.support.northwindtraders.com into its associated IP address. The name server might first have to find another name server that is authoritative in the northwindtraders.com domain. Next, the name server must find a name server that is authoritative in the support.northwindtraders.com subdomain whose database contains a record for the widgets.support.northwindtraders.com host. Finally, the name server must resolve the information in the record into an IP address. The whole process might take only several referrals and a short inspection of a relatively small database of resource records because each name server on the Internet is authoritative over only a small portion of the DNS namespace. Once you locate the correct name server through a series of hierarchical queries, the final name lookup deals with only a small number of records. The NetBIOS namespace is different, however, because each WINS server maintains a database of records for all NetBIOS names on the network. So if you were to use WINS to manage a network the size of the Internet with its millions of hosts, each WINS server would have a flat-file database containing millions of records, which would need to be searched from top to bottom each time a query was issued against it.

An additional example of a namespace is the hierarchy of distinguished names (DNs) used to identify objects in a directory based on the Lightweight Directory Access Protocol (LDAP). The LDAP namespace is closely tied to the DNS namespace of the Internet, as the top-level LDAP containers are simply top-level domain names. The Active Directory directory service of Windows 2000 is based on LDAP and uses DNs to name objects stored within its directory.

Notes

Because of the flexibility and scalability of DNS and its association with the Internet, DNS is the primary naming system used by Windows 2000. Support for WINS is included only for backward compatibility with downlevel Windows NT stations and legacy Windows stations. Active Directory in Windows 2000 and Windows .NET Server uses DNS as the service for name resolution (for locating users, groups, computers, shared folders, printers, and other objects on the network). The namespace of Active Directory represents a bounded area within which the DNS name of the root of Active Directory is translated to all the objects within the directory. Within Active Directory, a domain tree represents a contiguous namespace of connected objects, but a domain forest is a disjointed namespace formed from two or more domain trees. Companies that have Windows 2000– or Windows .NET Server–based networks can use the same DNS namespace for both internal and external network connections, or they can use separate DNS names for the network from an internal or an external perspective.

See Also: *Active Directory, domain (DNS), Domain Name System (DNS), fully qualified domain name (FQDN), host name resolution, IP address, Lightweight Directory Access Protocol (LDAP), NetBIOS, NetBIOS name resolution, network address translation (NAT), Windows Internet Name Service (WINS)*

naming context

A contiguous subtree or branch of Active Directory directory service namespace.

Overview

Naming contexts are used in Microsoft Windows 2000 and Windows .NET Server to partition the Active Directory namespace into sections, each with its own security boundary. Naming contexts are used during the process of directory replication to form the basic unit of the replication process. During multimaster replication of Active Directory, any naming context that has been updated is replicated to other domain controllers. For example, if the schema is modified on one domain controller, the schema naming context is replicated to all other domain controllers in Active Directory and also to the global catalog server. Only those portions of the naming context that have changed are actually replicated.

Active Directory always includes at least three naming contexts:

- **Configuration:** Contains information about sites, services, partitions, and the Active Directory schema
- **Domain naming:** Contains information relating to directory data for the domain in which the Active Directory domain controller resides
- **Schema:** Contains the schema information that defines the classes, objects, and attributes used in Active Directory

See Also: *Active Directory, directory replication (Windows 2000 and Windows .NET Server), namespace, schema*

naming convention

A rule for ensuring that users have their own unique username.

Overview

A simple and consistent naming convention for users on a network is an important part of network administration. Examples of naming conventions applied to the user Jeff Smith might include the following:

- **Jsmith:** Here the first letter of the user's first name is concatenated with the user's full last name
- **Jeffs:** Here the user's first name is concatenated with the first letter of the user's last name

N

Two users on a network might have the same first or last name, so your naming convention should include a rule to break ties. For example, if Jeff Smith is "jsmith," James Smith might be "jsmith2." You might also want to establish a rule for easily identifying temporary employees, such as "T-jsmith" or "jsmith(temp)."

Notes

On Microsoft Windows 2000–based networks, usernames of domain user accounts must be unique within the given organizational unit (OU) in which they are created in the Active Directory database. Usernames can be more than 20 characters long, but only the first 20 characters are used as logon credentials.

See Also: *Active Directory, domain (DNS), organizational unit (OU), user account*

NAP

Stands for Network Access Point, a point where Internet traffic is exchanged between Internet service providers (ISPs).

See: *Network Access Point (NAP)*

NAPT

Stands for network address port translation, a form of network address translation (NAT) in which both Internet Protocol (IP) addresses and port numbers are translated.

See: *network address translation (NAT)*

NAS (network access server)

Stands for network access server, the server at the Internet service provider (ISP) end of a dial-up connection.

See: *network access server (NAS)*

NAS (network attached storage)

Stands for network attached storage, a storage appliance that attaches directly to the network.

See: *network attached storage (NAS)*

NAT

Stands for network address translation, a method of substituting one Internet Protocol (IP) address for another.

See: *network address translation (NAT)*

National Electric Code (NEC)

A series of specifications for protecting commercial and residential buildings from electrical hazards.

Overview

The National Electric Code is published by the National Fire Protection Association (NFPA), an international organization that advocates standards for fire safety and related issues. The NEC is one of hundreds of standards documents produced by the NFPA. The NEC, which is NFPA standard number 70, deals with how to properly install and maintain electrical and electronic equipment in order to minimize fire hazards. In the area of computer networking, the NEC covers the proper installation and construction of copper cabling, fiber-optic cabling, and other network infrastructure. The NEC also covers issues relating to the powering of network devices, such as proper grounding.

The NEC is legally enforced in every state in the United States and in a number of other countries and regions. Most U.S. municipalities have adopted NEC recommendations in local building codes. Testing of electrical equipment for compliance with NEC standards is performed by Underwriters Laboratories (UL).

For More Information

Visit the NFPA at *www.nfpa.org.*

See Also: *cabling, infrastructure*

National Institute of Standards and Technology (NIST)

A U.S. government organization that provides services and programs to help U.S. industries commercialize new technologies and compete internationally.

Overview

National Institute of Standards and Technology (NIST) certification identifies technologies as meeting federal government requirements. For example, in the area of relational database management systems (RDBMSs), NIST administers a test named Federal Information Processing Standard (FIPS) 127-2. FIPS 127-2 is based on the broader American National Standards Institute (ANSI) SQL92 standard, which ensures portability across heterogeneous RDBMSs by establishing a common set of structured query language (SQL) commands. There is no higher standard for SQL database languages than FIPS 127-2. Microsoft SQL Server 6.5 was the first RDBMS to pass the NIST version 5.1 validation tests for Entry Level FIPS 127-2, as it fully complied with both the ANSI SQL92 standard and the FIPS standards.

The following table shows some of the FIPS cryptography standards developed by NIST. One action of NIST that has had wide impact on the cryptography field is the contest recently hosted by NIST to find a successor to the Data Encryption Standard (DES), which has been shown to be no longer secure. NIST selected the Rijndael algorithm developed by Belgian cryptographers as the replacement for DES and as the basis of NIST's new Advanced Encryption Standard (AES).

Some Cryptography Standards from NIST

Standard	*Description*
FIPS 46-3	Data Encryption Standard (DES) and Triple DES
FIPS 81	DES Modes of Operation
FIPS 180-1	Secure Hash Standard (SHS)
FIPS 186-2	Digital Signature Standard (DSS)

For More Information

Visit NIST online at *www.nist.gov.*

See Also: *Advanced Encryption Standard (AES), cryptography, Data Encryption Standard (DES), encryption, Structured Query Language (SQL)*

native mode

A mode for running Microsoft Windows 2000 and Windows .NET Server domain controllers.

Overview

Windows 2000 domain controllers operate in mixed mode by default. Mixed mode allows Windows 2000 and Windows NT to interoperate, which is essential during the migration of a Windows NT–based network to Windows 2000. If your migration is complete, however, or if you have a pure Windows 2000 network, then you should switch your domain controllers to native mode. Domain controllers running in native mode can only be used to authenticate users on a pure Windows 2000–based network.

Native mode gives you more options than mixed mode about types of groups. Specifically, you can use universal groups and you can nest groups to any degree. Running in mixed mode means that universal groups are not available, and you can nest global groups only in domain local groups and only to one level of nesting.

Windows 2000 domain controllers running in native mode are incompatible with Windows NT domain controllers, and if you want to use native mode, all domain controllers must be running Windows 2000 and must be configured to run in native mode, but member servers and client workstations can still run either Windows 2000 or Windows NT.

To change domain controllers from mixed mode to native mode, use the administrative tool Active Directory Domains and Trusts. Note that if you change a domain controller to native mode, you cannot change it back to mixed mode, so do not make the change until all your domain controllers are running Windows 2000.

Notes

Windows .NET Server domain controllers can operate in one of three available modes: Windows 2000 mixed, the default; Windows 2000 native; and Windows .NET. The first mode is used for the greatest degree of backward compatibility, at the cost of new functionality. The second mode provides some enhanced functionality but remains limited. Windows .NET mode does not allow for backward compatibility with former OS domain controllers, but it provides functionality that can be found only in this latest version of Active Directory. Domain functional levels can be raised from lower to higher, but once they are, the backward compatibility with domain controllers of a former OS is eliminated.

See Also: *domain controller, domain modes, native mode, universal group*

NBF

Stands for NetBEUI Frame, an enhanced version of NetBIOS Extended User Interface (NetBEUI) supported by Microsoft Windows NT.

See: *NetBEUI Frame (NBF)*

NBNS

Stands for NetBIOS Name Server, a server responsible for maintaining a list of mappings between NetBIOS computer names and network addresses for a network that uses NetBIOS as its naming service.

See: *NetBIOS Name Server (NBNS)*

Nbtstat

A Transmission Control Protocol/Internet Protocol (TCP/IP) command that displays current connections and statistics using NetBIOS over TCP/IP (NBT).

Overview

Nbtstat can be run from the Microsoft Windows 2000 command prompt to view NBT statistics for the local computer and to display the status of TCP/IP connections on the computer. This is useful for troubleshooting certain NetBIOS name resolution problems.

You can also use Nbtstat to

- Preload #PRE entries in the Lmhosts file into the NetBIOS name cache, which contains NetBIOS name to IP address mappings for other hosts on the network
- View the NetBIOS name and NetBIOS scope ID of the machine

Examples

Some examples of using Nbtstat include

- **Nbtstat -n**, which shows the NetBIOS names of the host that have been registered on the system
- **Nbtstat -c,** which displays the current contents of the NetBIOS name cache
- **Nbtstat -a** *ComputerName*, which displays the local NetBIOS name table on the computer named *ComputerName* and also its MAC address

See Also: *NetBIOS, NetBIOS over TCP/IP (NetBT), Transmission Control Protocol/Internet Protocol (TCP/IP)*

NCP (NetWare Core Protocol)

Stands for NetWare Core Protocol, a legacy NetWare protocol.

See: *NetWare Core Protocol (NCP)*

NCP (Network Control Protocol)

Stands for Network Control Protocol, the portion of Point-to-Point Protocol (PPP) responsible for encapsulating network layer protocols.

See: *Network Control Protocol (NCP)*

NDIS

Stands for network driver interface specification, a specification for network driver architecture.

See: *network driver interface specification (NDIS)*

NDS

Stands for Novell Directory Services, the directory services platform from Novell Networks.

See: *Novell Directory Services (NDS)*

near-end crosstalk (NEXT)

A measurement of the ability of network cabling to reject crosstalk.

Overview

Crosstalk is an undesirable condition in which the signals traveling through adjacent pairs of wire in twisted-pair cabling interfere with each other. Near-end crosstalk (NEXT) measures the ability of a cable to reject crosstalk between pairs of wire at the near end of the circuit. The pair causing the interference is called the "disturbing pair," and the pair experiencing the interference is the "disturbed pair." Channel NEXT is the NEXT value measured between one wire pair and another in the same cable; it is measured at both ends of the wire.

The NEXT value for a given cable type is typically expressed in decibels (dB) per 1000 feet and varies with the frequency of transmission. The higher the NEXT value, the greater the cable's ability to reject crosstalk at its local connection. For example, the specifications for Category 5 (Cat5) cabling include the minimum NEXT values shown in the following table. Note that the NEXT value generally decreases with increasing frequency, indicating increasing interference due to crosstalk at higher frequencies.

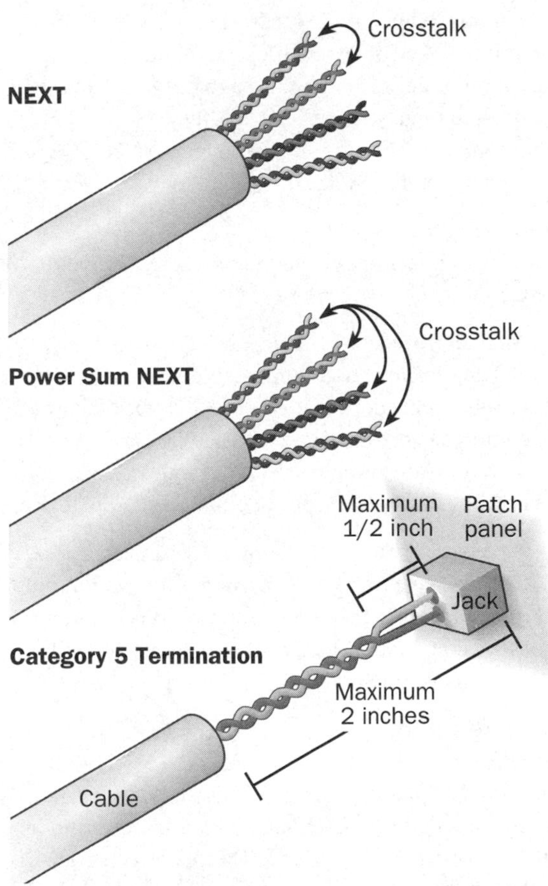

Near-end crosstalk (NEXT). *Different types of NEXT.*

Desired Data Rate and the Cable's Minimum NEXT Value

Frequency	*Minimum NEXT Value*
4 megahertz (MHz)	53 dB/1000 feet
10 MHz	47 dB/1000 feet
20 MHz	42 dB/1000 feet
1000 MHz	32 dB/1000 feet

Types

The various types of NEXT that can be measured are as follows:

- **Pair-to-Pair NEXT:** NEXT between adjacent pairs of wire in a twisted-pair cable. A typical four-pair (eight-wire) unshielded twisted-pair (UTP) cable has six possible values for pair-to-pair NEXT, which are then averaged. This simple measurement is not adequate, however, because every pair of wire generates crosstalk with every other pair in the cable.
- **Power Sum NEXT (PS NEXT):** A more rigorous way of rating a cable's crosstalk that measures the total amount of crosstalk between one wire pair and all its neighboring pairs in the same cable. PS NEXT is particularly important for cabling used in high-speed networks such as Gigabit Ethernet (GbE) and Asynchronous Transfer Mode (ATM) networks.
- **Far-End Crosstalk (FEXT):** A measurement of how the far end of one wire pair affects the near end of another pair.

Notes

To minimize NEXT in installations of Cat5 cabling, do not expose more than 2 inches (6 centimeters) of wire pairs at the termination point of the cable (the patch panel, wall plate, or RJ-45 connector). Also, do not untwist the wire pairs more than 0.5 inches (1.27 centimeters).

See Also: *cabling*

NEC

Stands for National Electric Code, a series of specifications for protecting commercial and residential buildings from electrical hazards.

See: *National Electric Code (NEC)*

.NET

Stands for Microsoft .NET platform, Microsoft Corporation's new Extensible Markup Language (XML) Web services platform for building integrated service-oriented applications to meet the needs of today's Internet businesses.

See: *.NET platform*

NetBEUI

Stands for NetBIOS Extended User Interface, a networking protocol developed by IBM and Microsoft Corporation.

See: *NetBIOS Extended User Interface (NetBEUI)*

NetBEUI Frame (NBF)

An enhanced version of NetBIOS Extended User Interface (NetBEUI) supported by Microsoft Windows NT.

Overview

Some of the enhancements and special features of NetBEUI Frame (NBF) include

- Support for network driver interface specification (NDIS) version 3 for full 32-bit asynchronous transport layer communication using the transport driver interface (TDI) layer as a NetBIOS emulator
- Support for automatic memory tuning through dynamic memory allocation
- Support for dial-up clients through the Remote Access Service (RAS)
- An extension of NetBEUI's limit of 256 concurrent NetBIOS sessions to more than 1000 sessions

Notes

Although NetBEUI is essentially a nonroutable protocol, NBF supports Token Ring Source Routing on IBM Token Ring networks.

See Also: *NetBIOS, NetBIOS Extended User Interface (NetBEUI), network driver interface specification (NDIS)*

N

NetBIOS

A legacy protocol for network communications.

Overview

NetBIOS, which stands for Network Basic Input/Output System (though no one calls it that anymore), is a specification originally created by Sytec for IBM in the early 1980s. NetBIOS was originally designed to enable personal computers to communicate with mainframes running Systems Network Architecture (SNA). It was later adopted by Microsoft Corporation for its LAN Manager platform to enable distributed applications to access network services running on different machines independent of the transport protocol used.

NetBIOS is defined in RFCs 1001, 1002, and 1088. The original NetBIOS specification could support a maximum of only 72 nodes, though this was later extended to thousands of hosts through various enhancements. The current version of the NetBIOS specification is NetBIOS 3.

Architecture

From an architectural viewpoint, NetBIOS defines two things:

- An interprocess communication (IPC) mechanism and application programming interface (API) that allows applications that are NetBIOS-enabled to communicate remotely over a network and request services from lower levels of the protocol stack. This is the primary and original definition of NetBIOS.
- A network protocol operating at the session and transport layers of the Open Systems Interconnection (OSI) reference model that supports functions such as session establishment and termination as well as name registration, renewal, and resolution.

Implementation

NetBIOS formed an essential part of the Microsoft Windows NT platform. Each Windows NT machine required a unique NetBIOS name in order to communicate on a network. These NetBIOS names consisted of 15 characters plus a 16th character that is reserved to identify various network services to the operating system. Also, depending on the underlying network protocol over which it is running, NetBIOS on Windows NT could take different forms. The following table lists some common network protocols and the form that NetBIOS takes over each protocol.

Examples of NetBIOS Protocol Stacks

Network Protocol	*Name When Combined with NetBIOS*
NetBEUI	NBF (NetBEUI Frame protocol)
NWLink IPX/SPX-Compatible Transport	NWLink NetBIOS
TCP/IP	NetBT (NetBIOS over TCP/IP)

Issues

NetBIOS has been superseded in Windows 2000, Windows XP, and Windows .NET Server by the industry-standard Domain Name System (DNS), which is used for naming hosts and for name resolution (Windows NT also supported DNS but did not require it). Support for NetBIOS is still included, however, in Windows 2000, Windows XP, and Windows .NET Server to ensure backward compatibility with Windows NT, Windows 95, Windows 98, and Windows Millennium Edition (Me) computers. There are several instances where incompatibilities between the two naming systems can arise, however:

- In Windows 2000, Windows XP, and Windows .NET Server, host names can be 64 characters long, but NetBIOS names can only be 15 characters long. If host names are longer than 15 characters, they are truncated, which can lead to collisions.
- DNS names can use hyphens but not underscores to represent spaces, although NetBIOS names have traditionally used underscores for such purposes. Since the Windows 2000 and Windows .NET Server versions of DNS support Unicode characters, this is not really an issue unless support for downlevel name servers is required.

Another problem with leaving NetBIOS enabled on Windows 2000, Windows XP, and Windows .NET Server networks is that NetBIOS is not intrinsically secure. Using the Nbtstat command, for example, a user can easily find out the name, MAC address, services running, and other information about hosts on a network that supports NetBIOS. As a result, once a migration to Windows 2000 or later is complete, NetBIOS should be disabled if it is no longer required for communications with machines using earlier versions of Windows.

See Also: *application programming interface (API), Domain Name System (DNS), interprocess communication (IPC), Nbtstat, NetBIOS name, NetBIOS name resolution, NetBIOS Name Server (NBNS), NetBIOS over TCP/IP (NetBT), NetBIOS over TCP/IP node types, Open Systems Interconnection (OSI) reference model, Windows Internet Name Service (WINS)*

NetBIOS Extended User Interface (NetBEUI)

A networking protocol developed by IBM and Microsoft Corporation.

Overview

NetBIOS Extended User Interface (NetBEUI) is an extension of the NetBIOS specification that functions as a network protocol for workgroup-size local area networks (LANs) having up to 200 stations. This is because NetBEUI relies more heavily on broadcast packets than do protocols such as Transmission Control Protocol/Internet Protocol (TCP/IP) and NWLink Internetwork Packet Exchange/Sequenced Packet Exchange (IPX/SPX)-Compatible Transport protocols, which can support much larger networks. Because NetBEUI has a single-part naming scheme, it is also a nonroutable protocol and therefore generally unsuitable for wide area networks (WANs).

NetBEUI is a fast and efficient protocol with low overhead. NetBEUI is self-tuning and implements flow control and error detection. It also defines a framing mechanism at the transport layer and implements the Logical Link Control version 2 (LLC2) protocol of the Open Systems Interconnection (OSI) reference model.

NetBEUI supports two types of network communications:

- **Connection-oriented:** Used, for example, when mapping drives using the Net Use command and starting services remotely using the Net Start command

- **Connectionless:** Used, for example, when sending datagrams, registering NetBIOS names, and performing NetBIOS name resolution

Implementation

NetBEUI was developed in 1985 and was implemented as the main networking protocol for the Microsoft LAN Manager and Microsoft Windows for Workgroups operating system platforms. NetBEUI is supported by most Windows platforms for backward compatibility. The implementation of NetBEUI on Windows NT is properly known as NetBEUI Frame (NBF) protocol.

See Also: *NetBEUI Frame (NBF), NetBIOS, NetBIOS name resolution, Open Systems Interconnection (OSI) reference model, routing*

NetBIOS name

A 16-byte name for a node on a network supporting the NetBIOS specification.

Overview

NetBIOS names are a friendly way of identifying computers on a network that supports the NetBIOS specification. This is because alphanumeric names are easier for users to remember than network numbers, such as dotted Internet Protocol (IP) addresses. In Microsoft Windows NT, for example, NetBIOS names are used to identify individual machines and also the various networking services running on each machine. Each service that is NetBIOS-enabled requires a unique NetBIOS name to identify it on the network in order for other computers to access those services on the machine.

The NetBIOS name (computer name) for a Windows NT machine is assigned to it during installation and can be up to 15 characters long. A 16th character is then suffixed to the computer name (or domain name or current user name) to identify the particular network service being referenced. For example, the 16th character identifying the Messenger service is 03h in hexadecimal form, so on a computer named SERVER12 the Messenger service would be uniquely identified on the network by NetBIOS as SERVER12[03h].

NetBIOS names are also distinguished by whether they are

- A unique name, which applies to a single IP address
- A group name, which applies to a subnet group of IP addresses
- A multihomed name, which applies to a multicast group of IP addresses

The following table shows some of the more common suffixes that constitute the hidden 16th character of a NetBIOS name and the networking service with which they are associated.

Common Suffixes for NetBIOS Names

Suffix (Hex)	*First 15 Characters*	*Networking Service*
00	Computer name	Workstation service
00	Domain name	Domain name
03	Computer name	Messenger service
03	User name	Messenger service
06	Computer name	RAS Server service
20	Computer name	File Server service
21	Computer name	RAS Client service
1B	Domain name	Domain master browser
1C	Domain name	Domain controllers
1D	Domain name	Master browser
1E	Domain name	Browser service election

Notes

To view the NetBIOS names registered for your computer, use the Nbtstat command. NetBIOS names are also supported by Windows 2000, Windows XP, and Windows .NET Server, but only for interoperability with some Windows NT machines, as they use the Domain Name System (DNS) instead for naming hosts and name resolution on a network.

See Also: *Domain Name System (DNS), Nbtstat, NetBIOS, NetBIOS name resolution, Windows NT*

NetBIOS name resolution

Resolving a computer's NetBIOS name into its corresponding Internet Protocol (IP) address.

Overview

NetBIOS over TCP/IP (NetBT) enables hosts on a Microsoft Windows NT–based network to communicate with each other. This is accomplished by resolving the NetBIOS name of a target host into its associated IP address, a process called NetBIOS name resolution. Once the host's name has been resolved, address resolution protocol (ARP) is then used to further resolve the host's IP address into its corresponding physical layer address (MAC address). Then once the host's physical address is known, frames can be placed on the wire and directed to this address.

The following describes the main NetBIOS over TCP/IP (NetBT) naming functions in detail:

- **NetBIOS name discovery:** NetBT hosts that want to communicate with similar hosts must issue a NetBIOS name query request to resolve the NetBIOS name of the target server into its IP address.
- **NetBIOS name registration:** NetBT hosts must register their NetBIOS name when they are initialized on a network to ensure that no duplicate names are on the network. NetBIOS name registration can be done either by broadcasts or by directed packets sent to a WINS server. Either or both methods can be used in either order, depending on the NetBT node type of the host.
- **NetBIOS name release:** NetBT hosts must release their NetBIOS names when they are shut down or when a particular NetBIOS-enabled service is stopped on the server. This enables another host to use the released name. NetBIOS name release can be done by broadcasts or by directed packets sent to a WINS server. Either or both methods can be used in either order, depending on the NetBT node type of the host.

Implementation

A number of different methods are used to perform NetBIOS name resolution. The following table shows the order in which these are attempted when the Windows NT machines on the network are configured as H-node machines (see the article called "NetBIOS over TCP/IP node types" elsewhere in this book). In a typical scenario where one Windows NT machine tries to establish communication with another, each name resolution method in the table is successively tried until either the target NetBIOS name is resolved into its associated IP address or the name resolution process fails. Note that some methods may not be available—for example, if there is no NetBIOS Name Server (NBNS) or DNS server on the network then these name resolution methods cannot be employed.

NetBIOS Name Resolution Methods in Order Attempted on Windows NT–Based Networks

Method	*Comments*
Check local NetBIOS name cache	The cache contains recently resolved NetBIOS names.
Contact NBNS	This method works only if NBNS is configured. The name server is usually a Windows Internet Name Service (WINS) server on a Microsoft network. The requestor tries three times to contact the name server and then tries to contact a secondary WINS server three times (if configured with secondary servers).
Perform local broadcast	The requestor broadcasts a NetBIOS name query request packet. The requestor tries three times before giving an error.
Check local Lmhosts file (Unique to Microsoft networks. If all methods fail, an error message states that the computer could not be found on the network.)	The requestor checks if an Lmhosts file exists.
Check local Hosts file (Unique to Microsoft networks. If all methods fail, an error message states that the computer could not be found on the network.)	On Windows NT the requestor checks the Hosts file if Enable DNS For Windows Resolution is selected on the WINS Address tab of the Transmission Control Protocol/Internet Protocol (TCP/IP) property sheet. This option is not available for Windows 2000 and later versions.
Contact DNS server (Unique to Microsoft networks. If all methods fail, an error message states that the computer could not be found on the network.)	The requestor contacts the DNS server if Enable DNS For Windows Resolution is selected on the WINS Address tab of the TCP/IP property sheet and the DNS tab has a DNS server specified on it. The requestor also tries 5, 10, 20, and 40 seconds later.

N

Examples

An example of when NetBIOS name resolution is used is when you go to the command prompt of a Windows machine and type **net use** followed by the NetBIOS name of the remote host in order to map a drive to a network share, for example, **net use x: \\server7\pub**. In order for this command to be fulfilled, the NetBIOS name of the remote host must first be resolved into its IP address so that it can be contacted on the network, and this is done using NetBIOS name resolution.

Notes

Note that NetBIOS name resolution is not confined only to TCP/IP networks—on Internetwork Packet Exchange/Sequenced Packet Exchange (IPX/SPX) networks, NetBIOS over IPX (NBIPX) resolves NetBIOS names to IPX addresses.

NetBIOS names are also supported by Windows 2000, Windows XP, and Windows .NET Server, but only for interoperability with some Windows NT machines. Windows 2000, Windows XP, and Windows .NET Server use the Domain Name System (DNS) instead for naming hosts and name resolution on a network. Note that a different series of steps is used to resolve host names on a network that uses the Domain Name System (DNS)—this process is usually called host name resolution.

See Also: *Domain Name System (DNS), host name resolution, MAC address, Nbtstat, NetBIOS, NetBIOS name, NetBIOS Name Server (NBNS), NetBIOS over TCP/IP (NetBT), NetBIOS over TCP/IP node types, Net commands*

NetBIOS Name Server (NBNS)

A server responsible for maintaining a list of mappings between NetBIOS computer names and network addresses for a network that uses NetBIOS as its naming service.

Overview

On networks that support NetBIOS (such as Microsoft Windows NT–based networks), NetBIOS name servers (NBNSs) are employed to register NetBIOS names and perform NetBIOS name resolution. Normally, when computers boot up on such a network, they register themselves with the NBNS by providing it with their computer names and network addresses. Then, when one computer needs to communicate with another, the first computer queries the NBNS for the network address of the remote computer.

NBNSs operate in a NetBIOS over TCP/IP (NetBT) mode called p-node, which is defined in RFCs 1001 and 1002. On a Windows NT–based network, you can configure a Windows NT server to assume the role of an NBNS by installing and configuring the Windows Internet Naming Service (WINS) on the machine. WINS servers can also be used on Windows 2000–based networks, but only for communication with some Windows NT computers—the main naming scheme for Windows 2000 networks is the Domain Name System (DNS).

Notes

On networks too small to justify using an NBNS, NetBIOS names can also be resolved by using broadcasts, but this wastes more network bandwidth than using a dedicated NBNS. On such small networks, using Lmhosts files may be preferable to deploying an NBNS.

See Also: *Domain Name System (DNS), NetBIOS, NetBIOS name, NetBIOS name resolution, NetBIOS over TCP/IP (NetBT), NetBIOS over TCP/IP node types, Windows Internet Name Service (WINS)*

NetBIOS over TCP/IP (NetBT)

NetBIOS session-layer protocol running over Transmission Control Protocol/Internet Protocol (TCP/IP).

Overview

NetBIOS over TCP/IP (NetBT) provides NetBIOS session management and naming functions such as NetBIOS name discovery, resolution, renewal, and release. In order to utilize NetBT effectively, a

NetBIOS name server (NBNS) is required to centrally manage name processes, such as NetBIOS name registration. Using the Windows Internet Naming Service (WINS), a Windows NT server can fill the role of such an NBNS and facilitate network communications on a routed TCP/IP internetwork. WINS servers are essential on such internetworks to enable the NetBIOS client/server interface to function since broadcast-based name registrations are not normally forwarded by routers to remote subnets.

Notes

In Windows NT, the Server, Workstation, NetLogon, Browser, and Messenger services interact with NetBT using the Transport Driver Interface (TDI).

See Also: *NetBIOS, NetBIOS name, NetBIOS name resolution, NetBIOS Name Server (NBNS), NetBIOS over TCP/IP node types, Windows Internet Name Service (WINS)*

NetBIOS over TCP/IP node types

Different ways of configuring NetBIOS-enabled nodes to perform naming functions.

Overview

The NetBIOS node type of a computer supporting NetBIOS (such as a Microsoft Windows NT machine) determines exactly how NetBIOS naming functions such as name discovery, registration, and release are implemented by that machine. In particular, such naming functions can be performed by broadcast, by a NetBIOS Name Server (NBNS), or by both methods attempted in either order. The NetBIOS node type thus specifies both which methods are used and the order in which they are used.

The common NetBIOS over TCP/IP node types are listed in the following table.

NetBIOS over TCP/IP Node Types

Node Type	*Method (in the Order Applied)*	*Comments*
B-node (broadcast)	Broadcast only	Uses NetBIOS name queries for name registration and name resolution. Typically not forwarded by routers, so limited to local subnet. Can create excessive traffic in large networks.
P-node (peer-to-peer)	NBNS only	Uses NBNS, which is a single point of failure for NetBIOS naming functions.
M-node (mixed)	Broadcast NBNS	A combination of B-node and P-node. Uses broadcast by default. If unable to resolve, uses NBNS.
H-node (hybrid)	NBNS Broadcast	A combination of P-node and B-node. Uses NBNS by default. Default node type for Microsoft clients if an NBNS is configured on the network.
Microsoft enhanced B-node	NetBIOS name cache Broadcast Lmhosts file	An enhanced broadcast that utilizes the Lmhosts file. Default node type for Microsoft clients if no NBNS is configured on the network.

See Also: *NetBIOS, NetBIOS name, NetBIOS name resolution, NetBIOS Name Server (NBNS), NetBIOS over TCP/IP (NetBT), Windows Internet Name Service (WINS)*

NetBIOS scope ID

A character string appended to a NetBIOS name of a host that identifies the host as belonging to a specific group.

Overview

On Microsoft Windows NT–based networks you can use NetBIOS scope IDs to segment the flat NetBIOS namespace into a series of smaller subspaces. Two hosts can then communicate only if they have the same NetBIOS scope ID and thus belong to the same subspace. The total length of a NetBIOS name plus scope ID cannot exceed 256 characters. Note that the topology of NetBIOS subspaces does not have to match the physical topology of the network or the logical topology of subnets on a Transmission Control Protocol/Internet Protocol (TCP/IP) internetwork.

Uses

You might configure NetBIOS scope IDs if you wanted to isolate a particular subset of computers on your network from the rest of the network and allow them to communicate only among themselves. To configure a NetBIOS scope ID on a computer running Windows NT, use the WINS Address tab of the TCP/IP property sheet. In Windows 2000, you must manually modify an entry in the registry to accomplish this.

Notes

N

Actually using NetBIOS scope IDs is not recommended. For example, if trust relationships are configured between several Windows NT domains, using NetBIOS scope IDs can break the effect of these trust relationships by preventing pass-through authentication between trusted domain controllers that have different scope IDs. Furthermore, in a single-domain environment, if the scope ID of a workstation is different from that of the domain controllers, users will not be able to log on to the network at that workstation.

See Also: domain (DNS), NetBIOS, NetBIOS name

NetBT

Stands for NetBIOS over TCP/IP, the NetBIOS session-layer protocol running over Transmission Control Protocol/Internet Protocol (TCP/IP).

See: NetBIOS over TCP/IP (NetBT)

Net commands

A family of commands that can be utilized at the Microsoft Windows command prompt for managing certain aspects of networking.

Overview

These commands are summarized in the following tables. For more information about a specific command (such as net accounts), type **net accounts /?** or **net help accounts** at the command prompt. For additional information on the Net commands for Windows NT, Windows 2000, Windows XP, and Windows .NET Server, refer to Windows Help.

Net Commands for Windows NT, Windows 2000, Windows XP, and Windows .NET Server Platforms

Command	*Description*
Net Accounts	Update the accounts database, modify account and password settings, or display account information
Net Computer	Add or remove computers from the domain
Net Config	Display or change the setting for the Server or Workstation service
Net Continue	Restart a paused Windows service
Net File	Display a list of open shared files and file locks; this command can be used to close a shared file and remove a file lock
Net Group	Add, modify, delete, or display global group account information in the domain directory database
Net Help	Obtain a list of net commands or get help for a specific net command
Net Helpmsg	Obtain further information about Windows network messages
Net Localgroup	Add, modify, delete, or display local group account information in the local or domain directory database
Net Name	Add, delete, or display the names or aliases that the Messenger service recognizes as representing your computer
Net Pause	Pause a Windows service to allow users to disconnect before stopping it

(continued)

Net Commands for Windows NT, Windows 2000, Windows XP, and Windows .NET Server Platforms *continued*

Command	*Description*
Net Print	Display and manage jobs in a print queue
Net Send	Send a message to a user or computer over the network
Net Session	Display the list of currently connected sessions on the local computer
Net Share	Create, delete, or display shared resources
Net Start	Display a list of running services or start a specific stopped service
Net Statistics	Display statistics about the Server and Workstation services
Net Stop	Stop a specified Windows service that is currently running
Net Time	Synchronize the computer's clock with that of another computer or domain or display the time for a computer or domain
Net Use	Connect or disconnect to shared resources or display information about connections
Net User	Add, modify, delete, or display user account information in the local or domain directory database
Net View	Display a list of computers in the domain or display the shared resources available on a specific computer

Net Commands for Windows 95, Windows 98, and Windows Millennium Edition (Me) Platforms

Command	*Description*
Net Config	Display current computer settings
Net Diag	Run the Microsoft Network Diagnostic program to display diagnostic information about a computer
Net Help	Obtain a list of net commands or get help for a specific net command or error message
Net Init	Load protocol and network-adapter drivers without binding them to Protocol Manager

(continued)

Net Commands for Windows 95, Windows 98, and Windows Millennium Edition (Me) Platforms *continued*

Command	*Description*
Net Logoff	Break connections to network resources
Net Logon	Log on to a domain
Net Password	Change logon password
Net Print	Display and manage jobs in a print queue
Net Start	Start services
Net Stop	Stop services
Net Time	Synchronize the computer's clock with that of another computer or workgroup or display the time for a computer or workgroup
Net Use	Connect or disconnect to shared resources or display information about connections
Net Ver	Display information about workgroup redirector
Net View	Display a list of computers in the workgroup or display the shared resources available on a specific computer

Notes

Some of these commands produce more than one screen of output at the command prompt. To prevent information from scrolling off the screen, pipe the output through More—for example, type **net help accounts | more.**

See Also: command prompt

.NET Enterprise Servers

A set of servers that facilitate the deployment, implementation, and management of the Web services foundational to the Microsoft .NET platform.

Overview

The .NET Enterprise Servers include

- **Application Center 2000:** Used for deploying and managing Web services and applications across the enterprise
- **BizTalk Server 2000:** Uses Extensible Markup Language (XML) and Simple Object Access Protocol (SOAP) to enable the exchange of information between business partners

N

- **Commerce Server 2000:** Facilitates the development of Web applications for e-commerce
- **Content Management Server 2001:** Facilitates simplified management, rapid deployment, and personalization of Web content on intranets or extranets
- **Exchange Server 2000:** Provides the underlying support for messaging and for building collaborative Web-based workflow applications
- **Host Integration Server 2000:** Enables access to data stores on mainframe computing platforms
- **Internet Security and Acceleration Server 2000:** Enhances enterprise security through firewall and Web caching services
- **Mobile Information Server 2001:** Enables wireless access to enterprise data from mobile clients
- **SharePoint Portal Server:** Provides the ability to create intranet portals which facilitate the sharing of information stored in a variety of formats across the enterprise
- **SQL Server 2000:** Standard platform for relational data storage that supports XML-based access to data

N

For More Information

Find out more about Microsoft's .NET Enterprise Servers at *www.microsoft.com/servers*.

See Also: *Application Center, BizTalk Server 2000, Commerce Server 2000, Exchange Server, Host Integration Server, Internet Security and Acceleration Server (ISA Server), Mobile Information Server, .NET platform, SQL Server*

.NET experience

A term representing a user's interaction with Web services based upon the Microsoft .NET platform.

Overview

The term *experience* is often used in modern-day programming parlance to describe the interaction between the user and the user interface for an application. A .NET experience is similar to user interaction with traditional client/server applications, but with several enhancements. Specifically, .NET experiences are

- **Location-independent:** .NET experiences can be accessed both offline (for example, at home from a PC) or online (for example, from a cell phone or wireless Personal Digital Assistant [PDA]).
- **Personalized:** .NET experiences store user profile information that simplifies user interaction regardless of the device being used or services being accessed.
- **Targeted:** A single .NET experience can manifest itself differently to the user depending on whether the user is employing a PC, cell phone, Pocket PC, Tablet PC, game console, or some other smart device.

See Also: *.NET platform*

.NET Framework

A developer environment for building, deploying, and running Web services and applications. The .NET Framework is a key piece of Microsoft's .NET platform.

Overview

The .NET Framework comprises three pieces:

- **Common Language Runtime (CLR):** Supports the execution of code written in any programming language (the .NET Framework is language-neutral).
- **Framework Classes:** Self-contained classes that do not require separate type libraries.
- **ASP.NET and ADO.NET:** The .NET versions of ASP+ and ADO+. ASP.NET provides programming models for building Web Forms and Web Services. ADO.NET provides classes for accessing Extensible Markup Language (XML) documents in relational data stores.

The .NET Framework is designed to run on a variety of platforms, including Microsoft Windows 95, Windows 98, Windows NT 4, Windows Millennium Edition (Me), Windows 2000, Windows XP, and Windows .NET Server. There is also a version called the .NET

Compact Framework that is designed to run on Windows CE, and embedded Windows to support key .NET functionality on cell phones, Personal Digital Assistants (PDAs), Tablet PCs, and other smart devices.

Notes

Developers can use the .NET Framework to create and deploy not only XML-based .NET Web services but also traditional COM+ applications. The .NET Framework resembles Windows Distributed interNet Applications Architecture (Windows DNA) in some ways, but it employs a more loosely coupled distributed component architecture.

See Also: *ADO.NET, ASP.NET, .NET platform*

NetLogon Share

An administrative share used by Microsoft Windows NT domain controllers.

Overview

The NetLogon share maps to the %SystemRoot%\system32\repl\import\scripts directory and is used for the following purposes:

- Storing logon scripts (for example, Logon.bat).
- Storing system policies (Ntconfig.pol or Config.pol files).
- Storing a default user profile for users (which must be stored in a subdirectory called Default User). If a user without a local profile on his or her workstation or a server-based roaming profile logs on, the default user profile is used instead.

When a client is authenticated on a Windows NT domain, the final step in the logon process involves connecting to the NetLogon share and downloading or applying any of the items in the preceding list.

See Also: *domain controller, Windows NT*

.NET platform

Microsoft Corporation's new Extensible Markup Language (XML) Web services platform for building integrated service-oriented applications to meet the needs of today's Internet businesses.

Overview

Microsoft .NET aims to leverage several important technology shifts in today's economy:

- The increasing availability of low-cost broadband Internet access for home and business, which makes delivery of fat content such as streaming video a practical reality.
- The proliferation of new computing platforms such as handheld Personal Digital Assistants (PDAs), Tablet PCs, portable MPEG (Moving Pictures Experts Group) players, and Web-enabled cell phones, which are making the computing experience ever more pervasive in today's society.

The .NET platform is designed to help developers build distributed applications that leverage the power of Web for a wide variety of end-user devices. To facilitate this, the .NET platform consists of five components:

- **Tools for developers:** Microsoft Visual Studio .NET, the latest incarnation of Microsoft's popular developer platform, provides language-independent tools and an integrated development environment for programmers to create both.NET experiences for end-user devices and the underlying Web services that provide the foundation for the realization of these experiences. Also key to developers is the .NET Framework, which provides the programming interfaces used for developing the Web services that are at the heart of the .NET vision. The foundation of these new tools is XML, an open standard created and managed by the World Wide Web Consortium (W3C) that is used to facilitate sharing of data and integration of software across different platforms. Other standards supported by .NET include Simple Object Access Protocol (SOAP) and Universal Description, Discovery, and Integration (UDDI) protocols.
- **.NET Enterprise Servers:** The essential underpinning for the .NET platform. These servers, including the Microsoft Windows .NET Server, are designed to aggregate, integrate, and deliver .NETWeb services, providing a consistent and compelling user experience across all levels of devices. The .NET Enterprise Servers include familiar ones such as Exchange Server

N

2000 and SQL Server 2000, which have been partially XML-enabled and provide the underlying "plumbing" for Web services to function. Other .NET servers, such as Application Center 2000 and BizTalk Server 2000, carry this aggregation and integration of Web services to a higher level using special languages such as XLANG and SOAP.

- **Building block services:** These services are designed to ensure that the .NET end-user experience is simple, consistent, and compelling. Building block services perform functions such as managing identities, providing notifications, and providing schematized storage that are necessary to enable the user experience to be consistent across different services, applications, devices, and platforms. Microsoft Corporation is developing a core set of building block services, but many more will be developed by third-party partners for corporate use.
- **Devices:** An important part of the .NET vision is that Microsoft is developing client and device software that can bring the rich .NET experience to users through a variety of smart devices such as Web-enabled cell phones, Pocket PCs, Tablet PCs, and other devices. Microsoft is developing .NET device software for a number of platforms, including Windows XP, Windows 2000, Windows Millennium Edition (Me), Windows CE, and embedded Windows.
- **User Experiences:** Microsoft aims to provide a powerful and compelling user experience through .NET. These experiences will leverage the flexibility of XML Web services together with the power of broadband business, residential, and wireless Internet access to provide a user experience that is secure, simple, consistent, and personalized.

For More Information

Microsoft expresses the heart of its .NET vision at *www.microsoft.com/net.*

See Also: *ASP.NET, building-block services, .NET Enterprise Servers, .NET experience, .NET Framework, XML*

netstat

A Transmission Control Protocol/Internet Protocol (TCP/IP) command that displays current TCP/IP connectivity status and statistics.

Overview

Netstat can be run from the Microsoft Windows 2000 command prompt to view current TCP/IP protocol statistics and connections for the local computer. You can also use it to view statistics on a per-protocol basis for Transmission Control Protocol (TCP), User Datagram Protocol (UDP), Internet Protocol (IP), and Internet Control Message Protocol (ICMP).

In particular, netstat provides information on

- IP addresses and port numbers of TCP/IP connections, including client and server connections. Either host names or IP addresses can be displayed.
- Ethernet statistics, including bytes sent and received, directed and broadcast frames sent and received, discards, and errors.
- The routing table for the local machine.

Examples

To display all connections and listening ports for both TCP and UDP, type **netstat –a** at the command prompt.

See Also: *Transmission Control Protocol/Internet Protocol (TCP/IP)*

NetWare

The popular network operating system from Novell Networks.

Overview

Novell NetWare is a network operating system developed in the early 1980s that has been widely used in local area networks (LANs). It began as a platform for LAN-based file and print services and has evolved into a platform suitable for enterprise networking and e-commerce. The current version of NetWare is 6.

History

NetWare initially became popular in its NetWare 2.*x* and 3.*x* versions, which proved remarkably stable and easy to administer using text-based menu-driven MS-DOS–based utilities such as Syscon, Filer, Fconsole, Pconsole, and Monitor. Security on these platforms was based on the NetWare bindery, and networking was supported by a proprietary suite of protocols based on Internetwork Packet Exchange/ Sequential Packet Exchange (IPX/SPX) developed by Novell.

NetWare 4 provided a more scalable solution for the enterprise by introducing Novell Directory Services (NDS), a hierarchical directory service that replaced the bindery of earlier versions. NDS enabled users and applications to easily locate and access shared resources anywhere on a Novell network regardless of their location. NetWare 4 supported single-network logon, in which users log on once to the NDS tree, are authenticated, and can then find and access all resources on the network for which they have appropriate permissions. NetWare 4 also supported industry-standard Internet Protocol (IP) by encapsulating IP datagrams within IPX packets. The Windows-based administration tool Nwadmin also replaced most of the menu-driven MS-DOS–based administration tools and enabled managing a NetWare 4-based network from a single console.

NetWare 5 included support for native IP, replacing the legacy IPX/SPX used in earlier versions, plus related Internet protocols such as Dynamic Host Configuration Protocol (DHCP) and Domain Name System (DNS). NetWare 5 also included a new multiprocessing kernel with support for virtual memory.

The latest version, NetWare 6, includes a number of enhancements, including Internet file and printing services, 32-way symmetric multiprocessing (SMP), and 32-way clustering support.

Notes

Microsoft Windows 2000 includes a number of protocols and services that support interoperability between Microsoft Windows and Novell NetWare platforms, and migration from NetWare to Windows 2000. These tools include

- NWLink IPX/SPX-Compatible Transport
- Gateway Service for NetWare (GSNW)
- Client Services for NetWare (CSNW)
- File and Print Services for NetWare (FPNW)
- Migration Tool for NetWare

For More Information

Visit Novell online at *www.novell.com.*

See Also: *Client Services for NetWare (CSNW), File and Print Services for NetWare (FPNW), Gateway Service for NetWare (GSNW), Internet Protocol (IP), NetWare protocols, Novell Directory Services (NDS)*

NetWare Core Protocol (NCP)

A legacy NetWare protocol.

Overview

NetWare Core Protocol (NCP) operates at the presentation layer protocol of the Open Systems Interconnection (OSI) reference model. NCP enables sharing of file and print services on legacy NetWare 2.*x* and 3.*x* platforms and performs various other accounting and security functions.

NCP functions by using information learned through Service Advertising Protocol (SAP) broadcasts. It employs Internetwork Packet Exchange (IPX) as its underlying transport and requires acknowledgment of every packet transmitted.

NCP is the analog of Server Message Block (SMB), a protocol used for similar purposes in Microsoft Windows platforms.

See Also: *Internetwork Packet Exchange (IPX), NetWare protocols, Open Systems Interconnection (OSI) reference model, Server Message Block (SMB)*

NetWare Directory Services (NDS)

Old name for Novell Directory Services, the directory services platform from Novell Networks.

See: *Novell Directory Services (NDS)*

N

NetWare protocols

A suite of protocols developed for legacy versions of Novell NetWare.

Overview

The networking architecture of NetWare evolved from the earlier Xerox Network System (XNS) created in the late 1970s. NetWare 2.*x* and 3.*x* used a proprietary suite of networking protocols that mapped to the upper five layers of the Open Systems Interconnection (OSI) reference model. The more important NetWare protocols included

- **Internetwork Packet Exchange (IPX):** A network layer protocol used to route packets across a network. IPX is a connectionless protocol that identifies nodes on a network using a two-part address. The host portion of an IPX address is just the MAC address of the network interface on the host, and the network portion of the address is arbitrarily assigned by the administrator to uniquely identify each portion of the network. IPX also performs encapsulation for the data-link layer using one of four schemes: 802.2 (Novell proprietary), 802.3 (IEEE), Ethernet II, and Subnetwork Access Protocol (SNAP). IPX is the analog of Internet Protocol (IP), part of the Transmission Control Protocol/Internet Protocol (TCP/IP) suite.
- **Sequenced Packet Exchange (SPX):** A transport layer protocol that ensures reliable delivery of data. SPX performs functions such as delivering acknowledgments of successful delivery and performing error checking. SPX is the analog of Transmission Control Protocol (TCP/IP), also part of TCP/IP.
- **NetBIOS:** A session layer protocol that performs name registration and discovery functions and supports interoperability with other NetBIOS-enabled operating systems, such as Microsoft Windows NT.
- **NetWare Core Protocol (NCP):** A presentation layer protocol that enables sharing of file and print services and performs accounting and security functions. NCP uses information learned through SAP broadcasts and employs IPX as its underlying transport. NCP is the analog of Server Message Block (SMB), a protocol used in Microsoft Windows platforms.
- **Service Advertising Protocol (SAP):** Enables NetWare servers to advertise themselves and their shared resources as present on the network in a fashion similar to the Computer Browser services of the Windows platform. This enables NetWare clients to find and access resources on these servers. SAP employs broadcasts issued every 60 seconds. In versions 4 and higher of NetWare, SAP is no longer required and is replaced by Novell Directory Services (NDS).
- **Get Nearest Server (GNS):** A protocol used when a NetWare client boots to locate NetWare servers on the local network.

There are also several routing protocols specific to legacy versions of NetWare. These routing protocols are used for communication between routers, in contrast to the above protocols, which are used for communication between hosts. Examples of NetWare routing protocols include

- **Novell Routing Information Protocol (IPX RIP):** This is a distance vector routing protocol that is a close analog of Internet Protocol Routing Information Protocol (IP RIP), usually just called Routing Information Protocol (RIP).
- **NetWare Link Services Protocol (NLSP):** This is a link state routing protocol derived from the Intermediate System to Intermediate System (IS-IS) routing protocol, and was developed in response to the lack of scalability of IPX RIP to large internetworks.
- **Enhanced Interior Gateway Routing Protocol (EIGRP):** This protocol supports both IPX and IP.

Notes

In addition to these original NetWare protocols, NetWare version 4 also supports Internet Protocol (IP) encapsulation of IPX/SPX packets, which means that IPX datagrams can be encapsulated within User Datagram Protocol (UDP) packets for transmission over TCP/IP internetworks. NetWare 5 and later now have native support for IP, and SAP has been replaced by Service Location Protocol (SLP), which uses IP as its underlying transport.

See Also: *Enhanced Interior Gateway Routing Protocol (EIGRP), Internetwork Packet Exchange (IPX), MAC address, NetBIOS, NetWare, NetWare Core Protocol (NCP), Open Systems Interconnection (OSI) refer-*

ence model, routing, Routing Information Protocol (RIP), Service Advertising Protocol (SAP), Transmission Control Protocol/Internet Protocol (TCP/IP), User Datagram Protocol (UDP)

network

A group of computers that can communicate with one another.

Overview

Networks harness the power of computers by allowing them to work together. By creating a network, users can share resources with one another and send messages to one another. Networks also allow applications to be distributed across multiple computers. Networks provide applications and users with many benefits over standalone (independent) computers, including

- Distributed processing capability
- Enhanced storage capability
- Centralized management of security and access to resources
- Greater scalability, robustness, and redundancy

For computers to be connected into a network, they require three things:

- **Network client:** Software running on the computer that makes the computer network-aware (able to be networked to other computers and to communicate with them). Operating systems such as Microsoft Windows are sometimes called network operating systems because they have built-in network client software and are thus intrinsically network-aware. Older operating systems such as Microsoft Disk Operating System (MS-DOS) were not networkable by themselves and required additional software such as the Microsoft Network Client 3 for MS-DOS in order to communicate on a network.
- **Network interface card (NIC):** A card inserted into a slot on the computer's motherboard. The card provides a physical connection and the necessary electronics in order for a network cable to be connected to the computer. Other forms of NICs include Personal Computer Memory Card International Association (PCMCIA) cards for laptop computers and wireless access cards for wireless networking.
- **Network protocol suite:** A collection of protocols that control the exact steps which computers use when communicating over a network. An example is the Transmission Control Protocol/Internet Protocol (TCP/IP) suite, which includes Internet Protocol (IP), Transmission Control Protocol (TCP), Address Resolution Protocol (ARP), and Hypertext Transfer Protocol (HTTP). Each protocol within a network protocol suite has a specific function to support communication between computers on a network.

In addition to cables, NICs, and computers, most modern networks also require some kind of dedicated networking device in order to concentrate (join together) the cabling into an actual network. These devices fall into two general categories:

- **LAN devices:** Used to build local area networks (LANs) and include hubs, bridges, routers, and switches.
- **WAN devices:** Used to connect LANs using wide area network (WAN) services from a telecommunications service provider. Examples include routers, access servers, channel service unit/data service units (CSU/DSUs), multiplexers, Frame Relay Access Devices (FRADs), analog modems, Integrated Services Digital Network (ISDN) terminal adapters, and a host of other devices depending on the telecom service employed.

Together with the cabling, these LAN and WAN devices constitute the infrastructure of a company's network.

Types

Networks can be classified in many ways. For example, they can be distinguished according to

- **Administration:** Networks can be private networks (owned and operated by a company or organization) or public networks (shared or leased to companies by a service provider). The Internet is a collection of public networks connected together and running the TCP/IP protocol suite. Not all public networks are part of the Internet, however—for example, AT&T's Frame Relay network is a telecommunications network that companies can lease and use to connect networks located in geographically separated regions.

- **Architecture:** This describes the way signals are transmitted across the network. Examples of common network architectures include Ethernet (including Fast Ethernet and Gigabit Ethernet), Token Ring, Fiber Distributed Data Interface (FDDI), Asynchronous Transfer Mode (ATM), and even serial transmission using RS-232, V.35, and other interfaces.
- **Physical size:** Depending on the number of computers involved and the location of these machines, networks can be variously labeled as local area networks (LANs), campus area networks (CANs), metropolitan area networks (MANs), or wide area networks (WANs). LANs and CANs are usually owned and managed by a single company or organization, MANs are typically owned and managed by telcos and other service providers and leased to companies to connect their LANs, and WANs typically consist of LANs owned and operated by one or more organizations and connected using leased services owned by another organization.
- **Protocol:** Networks use a variety of different protocols, that is, methods for packaging information into frames, packets, or cells for transmission across a network. Common examples of networking protocols include TCP/IP, Internetwork Packet Exchange/ Sequential Packet Exchange (IPX/SPX), and Systems Network Architecture (SNA).
- **Security:** Networks vary depending on how clients are authenticated and how resources are secured. Two common ways of implementing this include the workgroup, where every computer controls its own security, and the domain, where a special server called a domain controller manages security for the entire network. Both the workgroup and the domain model are supported by Windows 2000, Windows XP, and Windows .NET Server.
- **Topology:** The term *topology* refers to the manner and complexity of interconnections between computers on a network. Possible network topologies include the bus topology, star topology, ring topology, and mesh topology. Networks can also be described as either flat (using one of the topologies listed previously) or hierarchical (using combinations of different topologies or multiple levels of a single topology).
- **Media:** Computers can be physically connected together in various ways including using coaxial cabling, twisted-pair cabling, and fiber-optic cabling. Computers can also be networked without wires, an approach called wireless networking.

Notes

In TCP/IP networking, the term *network* is sometimes used to refer specifically to a group of hosts having the same network ID. Several such networks can then be connected using routers to form a larger network called an internetwork. Individual networks within an internetwork are usually referred to as subnets or subnetworks.

See Also: *analog modem, Asynchronous Transfer Mode (ATM), backbone, bridge, bus topology, cabling, campus area network (CAN), coaxial cabling, domain controller, domain (DNS), Ethernet, Ethernet switch, Fast Ethernet, Fiber Distributed Data Interface (FDDI), fiber-optic cabling, Gigabit Ethernet (GbE), hub, infrastructure, Internet, internetwork, ISDN terminal adapter, local area network (LAN), mesh topology, metropolitan area network (MAN), multiplexer (MUX), network architecture, network client, network design, network ID, network management, network operating system (NOS), network troubleshooting, ring topology, router, serial transmission, star topology, subnet, Systems Network Architecture (SNA), Token Ring, Transmission Control Protocol/Internet Protocol (TCP/IP), twisted-pair cabling, wide area network (WAN), wireless networking, workgroup*

N

Network Access Point (NAP)

A point where Internet traffic is exchanged between Internet service providers (ISPs).

Overview

Network Access Points (NAPs) are points where sections of the Internet's high-speed backbone are connected together in order to exchange traffic between ISPs—typically, this means connections between Tier 1 ISPs (large backbone providers) and Tier 2 ISPs (regional providers). Since the global portion of the Internet's backbone consists of long-haul fiber-optic cabling and high-speed Asynchronous Transfer Mode (ATM) switching equipment owned and is operated by inter-exchange carriers (IXCs) such as AT&T, Sprint Corporation, and MCI WorldCom, such NAPs are usually located where these carriers interconnect their long-haul lines together, and they contain high-speed switching facilities for transferring traffic from one carrier's lines to another's.

In the Internet's early days, the National Science Foundation established four different NAPs in Chicago, New York, San Francisco, and Washington, D.C. With the growth of the Internet and the changing landscape of telecommunication companies, many more NAPs have been created. These include the well-known "MAE West" in San Jose, California, and "MAE East" in Washington, D.C., both of which are operated by MCI WorldCom.

To lessen the traffic burden on the Internet's backbone, major ISPs can connect their services directly to a NAP in the form of a "peering arrangement," whereby traffic that needs to move between two ISPs connected to the same NAP can move directly from one ISP to the other instead of having to traverse the Internet's backbone.

See Also: inter-exchange carrier (IXC), Internet service provider (ISP)

network access server (NAS)

The server at the Internet service provider (ISP) end of a dial-up connection.

Overview

The term *network access server (NAS)* is a general name for the server at an ISP that supports Point-to-Point Protocol (PPP) connections for dial-up clients. The NAS is typically responsible for authenticating the dial-up client's credentials and negotiating flow control and error correction. The NAS is often a general-purpose server running special software such as Microsoft Windows 2000's Internet Connection Services. Alternatively, a NAS may be a standard router that supports PPP.

The NAS can sometimes also be used to establish tunnels through the Internet for virtual private networking (VPN), for example, by using Point-to-Point Tunneling Protocol (PPTP).

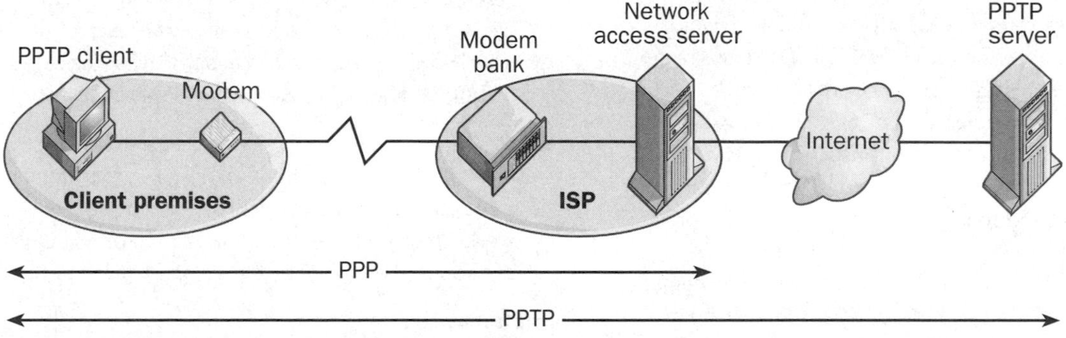

Network access server (NAS). *How a NAS works.*

Another name for a NAS is a point of presence (POP) server.

See Also: *Internet service provider (ISP), Point-to-Point Protocol (PPP), Point-to-Point Tunneling Protocol (PPTP), router, virtual private network (VPN)*

network adapter card

Usually called network interface card, a device that allows a computer to communicate on a network.

See: *network interface card (NIC)*

network address translation (NAT)

A method of substituting one Internet Protocol (IP) address for another.

Overview

Network address translation (NAT) is a mechanism for translating the IP addresses of hosts on one network into IP addresses belonging to a different network. NAT is usually used at the boundary of two networks, especially where a private network such as a corporate network meets a public network such as the Internet.

The motivation behind the creation of NAT is that the number of available global (public) registered IP addresses on the Internet is rapidly being depleted. NAT works around this problem by

- **Address reuse:** NAT allows multiple private networks to use the same network IDs (same range of IP addresses). Private networks (networks not directly connected to the Internet) can use any range of IP addresses but usually employ those addresses specially reserved by the Internet Assigned Numbers Authority (IANA) for private network usage, such as 10.0.0.0 through 10.255.255.255 (or 10/8 in classless interdomain routing [CDIR] notation), 172.16.0.0 through 172.32.255.255 (or 172.16/12), and 192.168.0.0 through 192.168.255.255 (or 192.168/16). Addresses in this range are designated by IANA as nonroutable addresses, and networks using these addresses cannot directly connect to the Internet using a router. Instead, they need a router or access device that supports NAT so that these nonroutable addresses can be translated into public addresses for routing over the Internet.
- **Address multiplexing:** NAT allows IP addresses of multiple hosts on a private network to be exposed to the Internet as a single public IP address. This allows the addresses of hosts on a private network to be hidden from the outside world, improving security on the network. Address multiplexing is sometimes referred to as network address port translation (NAPT).

NAT is defined in RFC 1631, and the IP addresses reserved by IANA for use on private networks is defined in RFC 1918.

Uses

NAT has several uses in enterprise networks:

- NAT allows corporate networks using RFC 1918 private network addresses to access the Internet through NAT-enabled routers and access servers. NAT also enables older enterprises that deployed addresses noncompliant with RFC 1918 to connect to the Internet.
- NAT allows corporate networks to hide the address topology of their networks from the Internet. NAT is not a replacement for firewalls, though, as in itself it performs no address or port filtering, just translation. In fact, NAT is usually available as an additional feature on most firewall products today.
- Often two private networks need to join together as a result of a merger. If both networks are using the same RFC 1918 addresses, NAT enables the networks to be united without the needed of readdressing one of them.

Implementation

In a typical NAT scenario, a NAT-enabled router connects an internal corporate network with the Internet. The internal network has multiple IP hosts using private

N

network IP addresses, while the router has a similar private IP address on its near-side (internal) interface and a public (global) address on its far-side (internal) interface. NAT operates by examining traffic that passes through the router and building a table that maps the connections between hosts inside the network and hosts outside on the Internet. For each connection the table contains

- Original IP address and port number of source address
- Original IP address and port number of destination address
- Translated IP address and port number of source address
- Translated IP address and port number of destination address
- Transmission Control Protocol (TCP) and Internet Control Message Protocol (ICMP) sequence numbers

All packets that enter the network through the router have their addresses translated, and all packets leaving the network have their addresses translated back again.

Implementing NAT on a router or firewall thus involves creating and configuring a NAT table containing these private/public IP address mappings. These address mappings can either be

- **Manually created:** A static NAT table essentially consists of a series of manually created NAT rules that specify how IP addresses will be translated. Static NAT mappings are always one-to-one mappings between actual and translated addresses. For example, a typical static NAT rule might be equivalent to the statement, "Translate all IP addresses belonging to the network 176.43.8.*z* to IP addresses in the form 145.5.133.*z* with the subnet mask 255.255.255.0 used for both networks." This rule results in the address 176.43.8.1 being mapped to 145.5.133.1, 176.43.8.2 being mapped to 145.5.133.2, and so on. This approach can be used, for example, when corporate networks with conflicting addresses need to be merged into one network. Static mappings are not very useful, however, for connections between private networks and the Internet due to the large number of possible connections to Internet hosts, which can make the NAT table grow excessively large thus degrading router performance.

or

- **Dynamically assigned:** NAT-enabled routers can often dynamically allocate IP addresses to hosts on the private network by selecting addresses drawn from a specified pool. Dynamic NAT mappings are also one-to-one mappings between actual and translated addresses. This process is similar to Dynamic Host Configuration Protocol (DHCP) and can be done either randomly or, more usually, on a round-robin basis. Each time a connection is formed between the external and internal networks, NAT assigns a different IP address from the pool to the internal host being connected to and address information in packets is modified accordingly.

Another popular form of dynamic NAT is called address overloading, masquerading, port address translation (PAT), or network address port translation (NAPT). In this situation all the IP addresses of the internal private network are hidden to outsiders, who can access only the single IP address of the interface exposed to the public network. Address overloading thus employs many-to-one mappings of IP addresses and is used when the number of internal addresses is greater than the available number of global addresses. Address overloading differs from standard NAT in that port numbers are also translated, not just IP addresses. For example, it is possible to multiplex many TCP connections through a single global IP address by assigning each connection a different port number. These numbers might be chosen, for example, from the range 61,000 through 65,096, which would allow up to 4096 simultaneous TCP connections through a single overloaded IP address. Address overloading is often used by firewalls and sometimes for load balancing Web servers.

Advantages and Disadvantages

NAT provides corporate networks with portability by eliminating the need for an organization to obtain globally unique IP addresses from its Internet service provider (ISP). Should an organization using global addresses need to change providers, this usually means obtaining new global addresses from the new provider and reconfiguring the network accordingly. With NAT, a company can use RFC 1918 private addresses for hosts on its corporate network, regardless of which ISP it is connected to the Internet through. And when changing ISPs, the only reconfiguration that would be required would be on the external interface of the company's router or firewall, which would need a new global address obtained from the new provider.

NAT also reduces cost for large corporate networks that need to connect to the Internet. This is because without NAT you would need to purchase a large block of unique IP addresses from your ISP in order to connect your network with the Internet, and such address blocks are sometimes scarce and therefore costly. Using NAT, however, only the far side (public interface) of your router or firewall needs a unique global IP address obtained from your ISP—within your network you can use RFC 1918 addresses because your private network is securely hidden from the outside world behind your NAT-enabled router firewall. And RFC 1918 addressing provides companies with access to address blocks as large as Class A (the 10/8 block) that can support millions of different hosts. Try obtaining a Class A from an ISP today if you think you need one—all Class A addresses have been assigned years ago, and only a few Class B addresses are still available.

NAT also helps to conserve the available pool of IPv4 addresses for the Internet, thus postponing the day when networks will need to be migrated to IPv6, a process that may be costly for large enterprises and will require considerable training of network professionals in use of the new protocol.

NAT's main disadvantage is that some protocols (and hence the applications that use them) simply do not work when IP addresses are translated. This particularly applies to protocols that involve

- **Encryption:** NAT does not work with protocols that use encryption schemes, and it can interfere with authentication systems that employ encryption as well. The main way of working around this issue with IPsec, a popular IP encryption protocol, is to use a router that supports both NAT and virtual private networking (VPN) to tunnel IPsec-encrypted packets through unencrypted IP packets that can be translated using NAT, but this is a complicated workaround that increases the router's processing load (and therefore the cost).
- **Embedded addresses:** NAT does not work with protocols that embed address and port information within the data portion of packets in a nonpredictable fashion.

The following table lists some of the protocols that have no trouble working with NAT, that can work with NAT as long as NAT devices are specially configured to support them, and that cannot easily work with NAT.

Support for NAT by Popular Internet Protocols

Work with NAT by Default	*Can Be Configured To Work with NAT*	*Cannot Easily Work with NAT*
Hyptertext Transfer Protocol (HTTP)	Domain Name System (DNS) name resolution	Boot Protocol (BOOTP)
Network File System (NFS)	File Transfer Protocol (FTP)	IPsec
Network Time Protocol (NTP)	H.323	Kerberos
Rlogin	Internet Control Message Protobol (ICMP)	Novell Directory Services (NDS) zone transfers
Telnet	IP multicast	Routing table updates
Trivial File Transfer Protocol (TFTP)	NetBIOS over TCP/IP (NetBT)	Simple Network Management Protocol (SNMP)

Another disadvantage of NAT is that end-to-end connectivity is effectively lost, which makes it more difficult to troubleshoot routing issues. Also, more costly routers may be required due to the additional processing overhead incurred by NAT. This processing overhead can introduce additional latency into internetworks using NAT-enabled routers, which can degrade time-sensitive applications such as Voice over IP (VoIP) and streaming multimedia presentations.

Marketplace

Many routers and access servers support NAT. In particular, Cisco System routers running Cisco's Internetwork Operating System (IOS) versions 11.2 and higher support NAT.

Microsoft Windows 2000 supports two ways of translating IP addresses for connecting a private network with the Internet:

- **Internet Connection Sharing (ICS):** Intended for small office/home office (SOHO) environments to provide access to the Internet through a designated Windows 2000, Windows XP, or Windows .NET Server computer. ICS automatically allocates addresses for internal hosts and only supports one interface to the internal network.
- **Routing and Remote Access Service (RRAS):** Provides a robust solution for larger corporate networks to access the Internet through multiple interfaces and using an addressing scheme chosen by the administrator. Windows 2000 or Windows .NET Server computers using the NAT feature of RRAS also function as DNS and Windows Internet Name Service (WINS) proxies for their connected subnets.

Prospects

NAT is essentially a workaround to extend the viability of the current IPv4 system by reducing the number of unique IP addresses required for connectivity to the Internet. NAT is viewed as a temporary solution until existing IPv4 networks can be fully migrated to the new IPv6 standard. However, the security advantages of using NAT-enabled firewalls has actually revitalized IPv4 to an extent and hence made migration to IPv6 seem less urgent to many network architects. Thus, while the Internet community presses for migration to IPv6, most large enterprises are content to use NAT and avoid the costs associated with a mass upgrade to the newer IPv6 protocol.

On the other hand, the proliferation of small mobile networked devices such as Web-enabled cell phones and Personal Digital Assistants (PDAs) may provide the impetus needed to push the wider networking community toward IPv6. The current IPv4 system lacks sufficient available addresses to support the millions of Internet-enabled mobile devices just over the horizon, and some countries such as Japan are already starting to roll out IPv6 on these devices. Workarounds such as NAT may still be in use for years, however, and gateways can be deployed for converting IPv6 to IPv4 addresses within the mixed IPv6/4 environment that is likely to characterize the global Internet of the next decade.

See Also: *classless interdomain routing (CIDR), Dynamic Host Configuration Protocol (DHCP), firewall, Internet, IP address, IPsec, routing, virtual private network (VPN)*

network architecture

Method used for packaging information for transmission over a network.

Overview

The term *network architecture* is used to describe the signaling, media access control method, and types of cabling for a particular type of computer network. Network architectures are different for local area networks (LANs), wide area networks (WANs), and networks that use terminals to connect to mainframes. Some common examples of LAN network architectures include

- **Ethernet:** This is by far the most popular LAN network architecture in use today. Ethernet, together with Fast Ethernet and Gigabit Ethernet (GbE), forms the basis of all types of business networks from the small office/home office (SOHO) to the enterprise.
- **Token Ring:** This architecture was developed by IBM and can support speeds of 4 and 16 megabits per second (Mbps). In the mid-1990s work was going on to push Token Ring to speeds up of 100 Mbps and higher, but these have been largely abandoned as Fast Ethernet and GbE have displaced Token Ring in most enterprises.
- **Fiber Distributed Data Interface (FDDI):** This architecture runs over fiber-optic cabling and was widely used in the late 1980s and early 1990s for backbones in campus area networks (CANs). It has largely been replaced by Fast Ethernet and GbE.

- **Asynchronous Transfer Mode (ATM):** This technology was envisioned as the successor to both Ethernet and FDDI, but its complexity and high cost have resulted in it being restricted to backbones in large enterprises. If current trends continue, GbE and the emerging 10G Ethernet standard are likely to displace ATM. ATM still retains a strong hold in the telcom market, however, where it is widely implemented in telco switching centers and for long-haul communications between inter-exchange carriers (IXCs).

Examples of LAN architectures that were once popular but are now rarely used include

- **ARCNET:** A legacy LAN architecture that was developed by Datapoint Corporation for small bus topology networks. It has almost disappeared, having been replaced by Ethernet.
- **100VG-AnyLAN:** A legacy architecture that was developed by AT&T and Hewlett-Packard and which has been largely replaced by Fast Ethernet and GbE.

The following are also sometimes considered LAN architectures, but they are really protocol suites that run on top of architectures such as Ethernet and Token Ring:

- **AppleTalk:** A legacy architecture developed by Apple Computer for its Macintosh platform that is essentially a protocol suite that can run on top of Ethernet, Token Ring, or FDDI networks. AppleTalk has largely been replaced by Transmission Control Protocol/Internet Protocol (TCP/IP) running on Ethernet.
- **Banyan VINES:** A legacy set of network protocols and applications developed by Banyan (now called ePresence) that runs on top of Ethernet and Token Ring.

See Also: *10G Ethernet, 100VG-AnyLAN, AppleTalk, ARCNET, Asynchronous Transfer Mode (ATM), backbone, cabling, campus area network (CAN), Ethernet, Fast Ethernet, Fiber Distributed Data Interface (FDDI), Gigabit Ethernet (GbE), inter-exchange carrier (IXC), local area network (LAN), media access control method, network, protocol, signaling, telco, Token Ring, topology, Transmission Control Protocol/ Internet Protocol (TCP/IP), wide area network (WAN)*

N

network attached storage (NAS)

A storage appliance that attaches directly to the network.

Overview

Traditional file servers use bus-attached disk storage and tend to be processor-bound machines unless unnecessary services and applications are disabled on the machine. Network attached storage (NAS) devices are essentially dedicated file servers that do nothing else. They are generally rack-mounted boxes containing a processor, memory, a Fast Ethernet or Gigabit Ethernet (GbE) network interface card (NIC), and disk drives either in the form of "just a bunch of disks" (JBOD) or a RAID 5 array for fault tolerance. NAS devices usually run an embedded operating system that is optimized for the sole task of rapid serving of files to clients on an Internet Protocol (IP) network.

Using a NAS device is typically as simple as plugging it in and connecting it to the network. Client machines on the network see the NAS device as just another file server. Management of NAS devices may be through a Web interface or from a management console that supports Simple Network Management Protocol (SNMP).

Storage capacity for NAS devices range from hundreds of gigabytes (GB) for those designed for the small to mid-sized business market to large boxes supporting multiterabyte (TB) storage for the large corporation.

Advantages and Disadvantages

NAS devices are generally more efficient file servers than traditional network file servers that use bus-attached storage. They are usually cheap, easy to set up, reliable, and they may sometimes be expandable to meet your growing storage demands. NAS devices typically support a wide range of clients including Microsoft Windows, Apple Macintosh, UNIX, and Linux. They are not as flexible as their larger cousin, storage area networks (SANs), which can be repartitioned when necessary, but they are much easier to manage. Some NAS devices also support advanced features such as load balancing, clustering, remote mirroring, and snapshot fault tolerance.

Marketplace

Vendors of NAS devices for the small office/home office (SOHO) and mid-sized businesses include Compaq Computer Corporation, Dell Computer, Hewlett-Packard, Maxtor Corporation, Network Appliance, Quantum Corporation, Snap Appliances, and Sun Microsystems. In the enterprise arena, EMC Corporation, Network Appliance, and Procom Enterprises are popular enterprise NAS vendors.

See Also: *Fast Ethernet, Gigabit Ethernet (GbE), network interface card (NIC), RAID, Simple Network Management Protocol (SNMP), storage, storage area network (SAN)*

network client

Software that makes a computer network-aware.

Overview

Network client software typically runs on a client computer, a desktop computer (workstation) used by one or more users. The purpose of network client software is to enable the client computer to communicate with other computers called servers in order to access network resources (applications, files, or services) located on these servers.

Without the appropriate client software, a workstation cannot access resources on a network server. For example, a Microsoft Windows client can access resources on a Windows-based server easily, but in order for the Windows client to access resources on a Novell NetWare server the client computer needs special NetWare-aware network client software installed on it.

Windows 2000, Windows XP, and Windows .NET Server include the following network clients:

- **Client for Microsoft Networks:** Enables the computer to participate in a Windows-based network and access resources on servers running different versions of Windows
- **Client Service for NetWare (CSNW):** Enables the computer to directly access resources on Novell NetWare servers

Note that in some Windows operating systems such as Windows 95, Windows 98, and Windows Millennium Edition (Me), the NetWare client is called Client for NetWare Networks instead of Client Service for NetWare. Some versions of Windows also include clients for legacy networks such as Banyan VINES.

See Also: *Client for Microsoft Networks, Client for NetWare Networks, Client Services for NetWare (CSNW), Microsoft Windows, NetWare, network, network operating system (NOS)*

Network Client 3 for MS-DOS

An add-on for Microsoft Disk Operating System (MS-DOS) that makes it a network-aware operating system.

Overview

Network Client enables MS-DOS–based workstations to access resources (such as shared folders, printers, and applications) on a Microsoft network using text-based Net commands. Using Network Client, an MS-DOS–based workstation can participate in either workgroups or domains.

Network Client must be installed on a machine that already has MS-DOS installed on it (you can create installation disks for Network Client using the Windows NT administrative tool called Network Client Administrator). Network Client has only limited support for Transmission Control Protocol/Internet Protocol (TCP/IP), but it does support the Dynamic Host Configuration Protocol (DHCP), Windows Internet Name Service (WINS), and Domain Name System (DNS).

Notes

If you cannot remember the syntax for Network Client commands when you use the MS-DOS command prompt, type **net** to load and open the Network Client pop-up command interface.

See Also: *Domain Name System (DNS), Dynamic Host Configuration Protocol (DHCP), Microsoft Disk Operating System (MS-DOS), Net commands, network, network client, Transmission Control Protocol/Internet Protocol (TCP/IP), Windows Internet Name Service (WINS)*

Network Control Protocol (NCP)

The portion of Point-to-Point Protocol (PPP) responsible for encapsulating network layer protocols.

Overview

Establishing communications between a PPP client and a PPP server involves several stages. The first step in establishing a PPP session is negotiating the actual connection. This is performed using Link Control Protocol (LCP), a PPP data-link layer protocol that is used for authenticating the client and performing callback, compression, and establishing a multilink connection if required. Once LCP has done its job, Network Control Protocol (NCP), another PPP data-link protocol that is actually a family of protocols, takes over to perform two functions:

- **Negotiating network layer attributes:** This involves selecting a network layer protocol understood by both the PPP client and server.
- **Encapsulating the network layer protocol:** This involves selecting the appropriate NCP protocol to encapsulate network layer packets for transmission over the connection. The table shows some of the common NCP protocols used for different network-layer protocols.

N

NCP Protocols for PPP

Network Layer Protocol	*NCP Protocol*	*Request For Comments (RFC)*
Internet Protocol (IP)	Internet Protocol Control Protocol (IPCP)	1332
Internetwork Packet Exchange (IPX)	Internetwork Packet Exchange Control Protocol (IPXCP)	1552
AppleTalk	AppleTalk Control Protocol (ATCP)	1378
IPv6	IPv6 Control Protocol (IPV6CP)	2023

See Also: Link Control Protocol (LCP), Point-to-Point Protocol (PPP)

network design

The science (or art) of designing a properly functioning network.

Overview

Designing networks that can efficiently transport traffic in expected ways can be a challenge. The performance, reliability, scalability, and manageability of a network depend on a variety of factors, including

- **Bandwidth:** Dealing with traffic congestion on a network is important to ensure that applications function smoothly and that users are happy. Solutions include simply throwing bandwidth at the problem (for example, replacing Ethernet with Fast Ethernet), replacing shared media devices (hubs) with switches (local area network [LAN] or Ethernet switches), and implementing Quality of Service (QoS) to better manage existing bandwidth. An issue related to bandwidth is how that bandwidth is distributed across a network. In the 1980s most enterprise networks were designed with the 80/20 rule in mind, which said that you could expect 80 percent of network traffic to be local (within a workgroup or department) but 20 percent of the traffic would need to be carried over the backbone to remote locations. With the rapid growth of the Internet, however, and the fact that it has become an essential element of enterprise networks, the 80/20 rule has shifted to more like a 20/80 rule, especially for networks that need to support multimedia applications such as streaming audio and video presentations or Voice over IP (VoIP).
- **Fault tolerance:** Networks that run mission-critical business applications need some degree of fault tolerance so they can continue operation in the event of a problem. Solutions can include using routed networks with mesh topologies that provide alternate routes, multihoming a corporate network by connecting it to several Internet service providers (ISPs), and using a dual-ring architecture as in Fiber Distributed Data Interface (FDDI).
- **Geography:** Networks that span a continent are designed and built differently from those that occupy only a single office. Wide area networks (WANs) not

only use different technologies than LANs but also involve leasing telecommunications services from telcos and other service providers, distributing network administration among regional offices, and dealing with legal and political issues.

- **Simplicity:** Managing a heterogeneous network consisting of multiple network architectures and protocols can be a headache, but it is also a reality that most large enterprises grow their network in an organic fashion over a period of years. As new networking technologies are added, existing ones are maintained as legacy services to reduce the up-front cost of migrating architectures, services, and data. The result is anything but simple, so anything a network manager can do to reduce the complexity of an enterprise network should be done. The most important thing to do, of course, is to plan each modification of the network carefully.

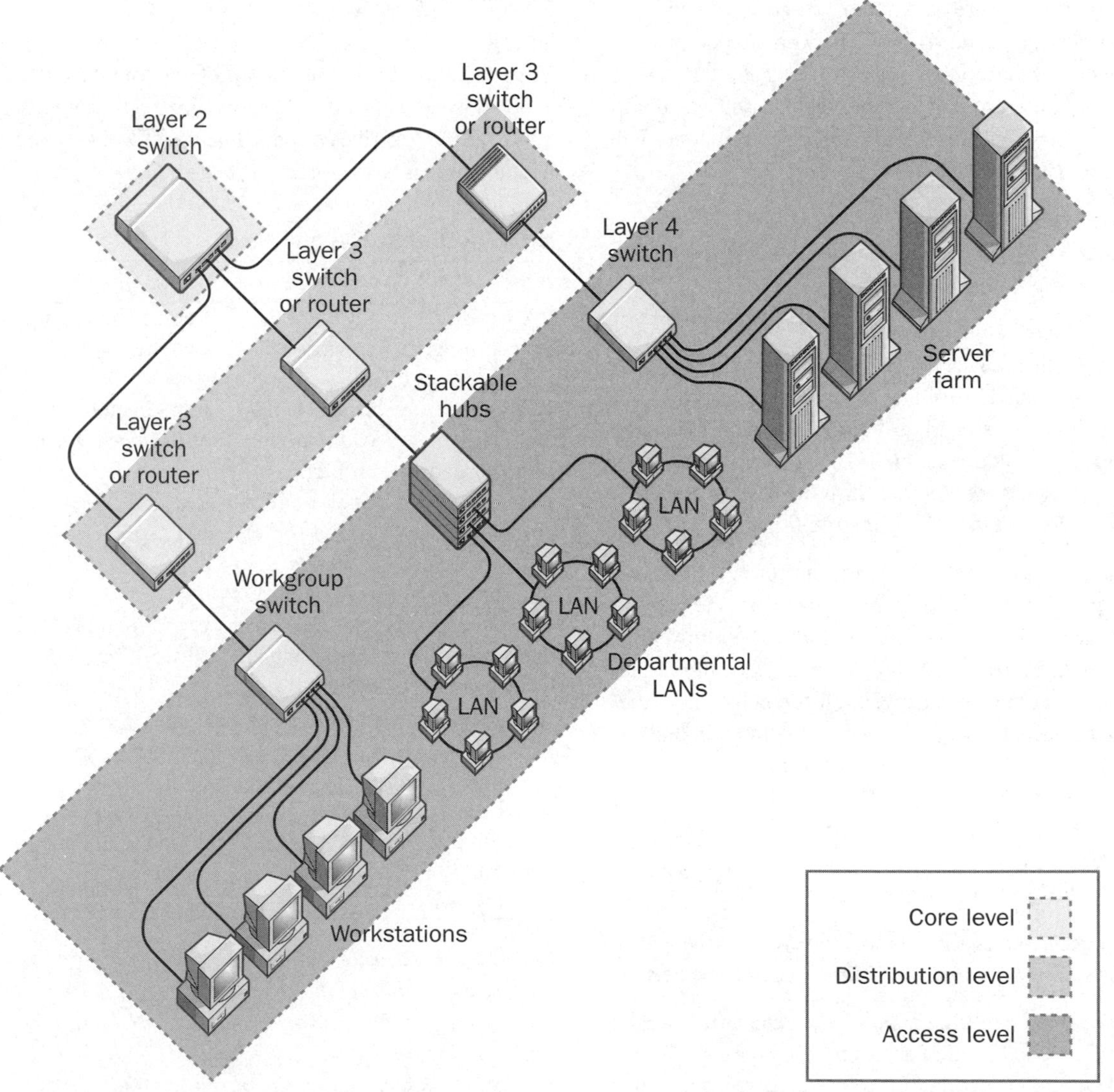

Network design. *Typical hierarchical design of an enterprise network.*

- **Size:** Flat networks may suffice for small businesses, but in enterprises where thousands of machines need to be networked, a hierarchical network is more scalable and manageable.
- **Standards:** Using protocols and equipment that conform to internationally recognized standards can be a lifesaver in network design. Although networking devices can initially be purchased from a single vendor to eliminate interoperability issues, the vendor you purchased from might not be around several years later when you want to expand your network. Purchasing standards-based networking equipment ensures (usually) that when you later add devices from a different (but also standards-based) vendor to your existing network, no interoperability issues will arise to haunt you.

Architecture

A typical enterprise network today uses a hierarchical design having three levels:

- **Core level:** This is the network's backbone, and it carries the greatest load of traffic. The network's core can be located in a single equipment room (collapsed backbone) or spread throughout a building or campus (distributed backbone). The core connects the switches and routers that form the basis of the next level of the network, the distribution level.
- **Distribution level:** This is the portion of the network responsible for moving traffic from one site (or department or workgroup or floor or building) to another. Traffic control features are typically implemented at this level as well. Different blocks of the distribution level are connected by the core, and the distribution level delivers traffic to end users through the access level. Each block of the distribution level (called switch block) defines a separate broadcast domain, typically serving no more than 2000 hosts to ensure good performance.
- **Access level:** This portion of the network provides users' client machines with direct access to the network.

The specific networking technologies and infrastructure used within each level of an enterprise network vary as well. The main function of the core is to transport traffic quickly, and, as a result, large Layer 2 backbone switches are typically used at this level. Many enterprises employ a dual core with redundant switches to ensure that critical backbone traffic is carried uninterrupted. The distribution level of older enterprise networks employed routers for routing traffic to and from the core, but modern networks tend to use Layer 3 switches instead. The access level uses hubs or Layer 2 workgroup switches if greater carrying capacity is required for multimedia desktop applications. The switches for the access and distribution layers are often combined in the form of switch blocks as mentioned above.

Notes

To get an idea of how the science of network design has evolved over the last decade, consider the following table, which describes a typical network problem and how to solve it based on late 1980s and late 1990s network design principles.

Network Design: Old and New

Issue	*Old Approach*	*New Approach*
LAN traffic is becoming congested	Segment the network	Replace hubs with switches
Real-time applications perform poorly	Throw bandwidth at the problem	Implement Quality of Service (QoS)
Network is complex, heterogeneous, and multiprotocol	Use a combination of routers, switches, and load balancers	Use multilayer switches
Remote users need access to the network	Use expensive leased lines for branch offices and slow dial-up for mobile users	Use virtual private networking (VPN) over the Internet
WAN traffic is becoming congested	Lease a bigger WAN pipe	Use a content delivery network (CDN) or redirect traffic to local caching devices

See Also: *80/20 rule, backbone, Ethernet, Ethernet switch, Fast Ethernet, hub, infrastructure, Layer 2 switch, Layer 3 switch, local area network (LAN), multihoming, Multilayer Switching (MLS), network, network architecture, quality of service (QoS), router, routing, wide area network (WAN)*

network driver interface specification (NDIS)

A specification for network driver architecture.

Overview

Network driver interface specification (NDIS) simplifies the process of writing drivers for network interface cards (NICs) by enabling them to interact transparently with different transport protocols such as Transmission Control Protocol/Internet Protocol (TCP/IP), Internetwork Packet Exchange/Sequential Packet Exchange (IPX/SPX), and NetBIOS Extended User Interface (NetBEUI). NDIS is also a library of routines (a "wrapper") that is implemented in Microsoft Windows 2000, Windows XP, and Windows .NET Server as the driver Ndis.sys, which provides a uniform programming interface between NIC drivers and network protocols.

NDIS Versions

Version	*Platform*	*16- or 32-bit*	*Features*
2	Windows for Workgroups and OS/2	16	Real mode; each NIC must have its own driver.
3	Windows NT 3.5*x*	32	Unlimited number of NICs can be bound to an unlimited number of protocols.
3.1	Windows 95	32	A superset of NDIS 3 with plug and play functionality and support for minidrivers. Windows 95 supports up to four NICs in a computer.
4	Windows NT 4	32	Unlimited number of NICs can be bound to an unlimited number of protocols. Also allows capturing of all frames on local network segment without the need to switch the NIC to promiscuous mode.
5	Windows 98, Windows Me, Windows 2000, Windows XP, Windows .NET Server	32	Adds support for connection-oriented networks such as Integrated Services Digital Network (ISDN) or Asynchronous Transfer Mode (ATM), including support for multiple virtual circuits on one network adapter.

NDIS was developed jointly by Microsoft Corporation and 3Com Corporation in 1989 and has gone through a series of revisions, as shown in the above table. The most recent versions allow one NIC to be bound to many protocols (which is ideal for heterogeneous networks) and one protocol to run on a system with multiple NICs (which helps increase network bandwidth for heavily used servers).

See Also: *NetBIOS Extended User Interface (NetBEUI), network interface card (NIC), Transmission Control Protocol/Internet Protocol (TCP/IP)*

Network File System (NFS)

A suite of protocols for accessing file systems across a network.

Overview

Network File System (NFS) is a distributed file system developed by Sun Microsystems in the early 1980s that has become the de facto standard in distributing file systems. NFS was designed to enable the exporting of files system across heterogeneous networks comprising multiple operating systems and platforms. NFS technology has been licensed to over 200 vendors and implementations have been made available for a wide variety of platforms including UNIX, Linux, Microsoft Windows, and mainframe environments.

NFS allows clients to locate and access files stored on remote servers. The original NFS specification was designed for local area network (LAN) use and was not optimized for wide area network (WAN) connections, but the current version NFS 3 performs well in the WAN as well as the LAN. The features of NFS 3 include

- Support for terabyte-size files using 64-bit file size indicators (previous versions supported files up to 4 gigabytes in size).
- Maximum packet size of 64 kilobytes (earlier versions supported only 8 KB packet size).
- Choice of User Datagram Protocol (UDP) or Transmission Control Protocol (TCP) for NFS network transport (earlier versions supported only UDP, which performed poorly over a WAN).
- Support for caching of client requests by the server.

The original NFS specification is defined in RFC 1094 and the current NFS 3 version is defined in RFC 1813.

Implementation

NFS uses a layered protocol architecture that maps to the seven layers of the Open Systems Interconnection (OSI) reference model as shown in the following table.

N

NFS Protocol Suite

OSI Layer	*NFS Protocol*
Physical	Any (Ethernet common)
Data link	Same as Physical
Network	Internet Protocol (IP)
Transport	User Datagram Protocol (UDP) and Transmission Control Protocol (TCP)
Session	Remote Procedure Call (RPC) protocol
Presentation	External Data Representation (XDR) protocol
Application	Network File System (NFS) and Network Information System (NIS)

NFS is implemented as a client/server system that uses special NFS servers and NFS client software running on workstations. These servers use NFS to export (make available) their file system to machines running NFS clients—to the client machine the exported file system appears as part of its own local file system. NFS typically uses remote procedure calls (RPCs) running over User Datagram Protocol (UDP) on server port 2049 for stateless communication between clients and file servers on the network. NFS clients (client machines running NFS client software) import remote file systems from NFS servers, while the NFS servers export local file systems to clients. Machines running the NFS client can connect to NFS servers and read, modify, copy, move, or delete files on the server using RPC requests such as READ, WRITE, CREATE, and MKDIR. To the user accessing the remote file system from the client, the files appear to be stored locally on his or her system. Before a user can access files within the directory structure on the local UNIX file system of the NFS server, the administrator must generally mount the portions of the local UNIX file system that will be made accessible to clients and assign appropriate user privileges.

Marketplace

Although NFS is widely used on UNIX platforms, another file sharing protocol called Server Message Block (SMB) is common on Windows platforms. Windows 2000 and Windows .NET Server support NFS in Services For Unix (SFU) version 2, and products such as Samba implement SMB on UNIX platforms. Interoperability between SMB and NFS is thus available both ways for integrating Windows and UNIX platforms for common file sharing purposes. A wide variety of third-party products are also available that implement NFS on the Windows platform, including ChameleonNFS from NetManage, NFS Maestro from Hummingbird International, and many others.

See Also: Internet Protocol (IP), Linux, Microsoft Windows, Network Information System (NIS), remote procedure call (RPC), Server Message Block (SMB), Transmission Control Protocol (TCP), UNIX, User Datagram Protocol (UDP)

network ID

The portion of an Internet Protocol (IP) address that identifies the subnet on which the host resides.

Overview

The IP address of a host consists of two parts: the network ID and the host ID. The network ID portion of an

IP address uniquely identifies the host's local subnet. By contrast, the host ID portion of the IP address identifies the host within its local subnet. Together, the host ID and network ID uniquely identify the host on an internetwork.

Examples

The network ID is found by logically ANDing the binary form of the IP address with the binary form of the subnet mask for the network. For example, if a host has an IP address of 172.16.8.55 on a network with a subnet mask of 255.255.0.0 (the default subnet mask), the network ID of the host is 172.16.0.0, or simply 172.16, as it comprises the first 16 bits of the 32-bit address.

See Also: *host ID, Internet Protocol (IP), IP address, subnet*

Network Information System (NIS)

A protocol used for naming and directory services on UNIX platforms.

Overview

Network Information System (NIS) functions as a kind of telephone book for locating resources on a Transmission Control Protocol/Internet Protocol (TCP/IP) network. In fact, the original name for NIS was "Yellow Pages (YP)." NIS enables users and applications distributed across a network to locate and access files and applications anywhere in the network by accessing a central NIS server. The kinds of information typically provided by NIS servers include password files, host tables, and e-mail aliases.

NIS operates using broadcasts, and on most UNIX platforms, NIS clients communicate with NIS servers using remote procedure calls (RPCs) running over User Datagram Protocol (UDP).

The original NIS was not secure and NIS servers were often targeted in attacks on UNIX networks. A newer version developed by Sun Microsystems called NIS+ includes additional security features, but it has gained only limited popularity in the marketplace.

See Also: *remote procedure call (RPC), UNIX, User Datagram Protocol (UDP)*

network interface card (NIC)

Also called network adapter card or network card, a device that allows a computer to communicate on a network.

Overview

Network interface cards (NICs) are typically adapter cards that plug into a slot on the a computer's motherboard, but they also come in Personal Computer Memory Card International Association (PCMCIA) card format for laptop computers and as cards or external devices for wireless networking. A wide variety of devices for home networking also perform the same general function of a NIC, including devices that plug into Universal Serial Bus (USB), parallel, or serial ports and transmit network signals over twisted pair wiring, telephone lines, or even electrical lines in a home. This article focuses, however, on the use of NICs in servers in enterprise environments, particularly in Gigabit Ethernet (GbE) networking.

Types

NICs are typically

- **Media-specific:** UTP and fiber-optic cabling are the two most common options. Some older combo cards support both thinnet and UTP.
- **Network architecture-specific:** Ethernet, Token Ring, and Fiber Distributed Data Interface (FDDI) each use their own distinctive type of NIC.

NICs for Ethernet networks are available in various speeds including 10 megabits per second (Mbps) for Ethernet, autosensing 10/100 Mbps for Fast Ethernet, and autosensing 10/100/1000 Mbps for GbE. These autosensing NICs determine the highest network speed supported by hubs and switches on the network and configure themselves accordingly.

Implementation

NICs are available for all common system bus types, including Industry Standard Architecture (ISA), Extended Industry Standard Architecture (EISA), Micro Channel Architecture, and Peripheral Component Interconnect (PCI). PCI cards are available in 32-bit and 64-bit form and give the best performance. In addition, PCI NICs are plug and play and hence easy to install and configure, in comparison to legacy NICs that require manual configuration of interrupt request (IRQ) and base I/O port settings.

A NIC's role is to convert the parallel stream of data on a computer's bus to serial form for transmission over the medium joining computers together on the network. This medium is typically either Category 5 (Cat 5) or enhanced Category 5 (Cat 5e) unshielded twisted-pair (UTP) cabling, fiber-optic cabling, or in the case of wireless networking, free space. The computer can communicate with the NIC using several methods, including memory-mapped I/O, direct memory access (DMA), or shared memory. A parallel stream of data is sent to the card and buffered in on-card memory before being packaged into discrete frames for transmission over the network. Framing adds headers and trailers to the data, which contains addressing, clocking, and error-checking information. The frames are then converted to electrical voltage pulses that drive an electrical signal over the wire (for copper wiring), modulated light pulses (for fiber-optic cabling), or microwaves (for wireless networking). The NIC on the receiving computer processes the signal in the reverse order, converting the signal first into a bit stream of frames and then into a parallel data stream for the receiving computer's bus. Some of the above functions are built into the NIC's firmware, and the remainder are implemented by the NIC driver software installed on the computer.

Marketplace

The largest producer of enterprise NICs overall is 3Com Corporation, while the top producer of GbE NICs is Intel Corporation, which has almost half of the enterprise market in this arena. 3Com is in second place in the GbE NIC market after its recent acquisition of Alteon Web Systems' GbE adapter technology. Asanté Technologies rocked the market in 2000 with its introduction of a copper-based 1000BaseT NIC that sold for around $150—half the price of other vendors at the time. The copper GbE NIC market has steadily grown against the fiber GbE NIC market, and by the end of 2000, half of all GbE NICs shipped were copper 1000BaseT NICs.

Choosing the right NIC for a high-performance server is a crucial consideration in enterprise computing and e-commerce, as an inferior NIC can easily become a bottleneck for accessing network services. Some GbE NICs support advanced features such as onboard Internet Protocol Security (IPsec) processing to offload workload from the server. Certain NICs from 3Com fall into this category. Other smaller vendors have produced high-performance NICs with specialized features, such as Akamba Corporation's technology that allows for NICs used in Web servers to process Hypertext Transfer Protocol (HTTP) traffic, and Alacritech's technology for implementing a server's TCP stack in hardware on the NIC.

See Also: *Category 5 (Cat5) cabling, enhanced Category 5 (Cat5e) cabling, Ethernet, Fast Ethernet, Fiber Distributed Data Interface (FDDI), fiber-optic cabling, frame, Gigabit Ethernet (GbE), serial transmission, Token Ring, universal serial bus (USB), unshielded twisted-pair (UTP) cabling, wireless networking*

network layer

Layer 3 of the Open Systems Interconnection (OSI) reference model.

Overview

When two hosts on a network need to communicate, the network layer is responsible for determining a suitable path across the network, usually through some form of route calculation. The network layer thus enables hosts on a network to establish communications with each other. The network layer is also responsible for

- Logical addressing of packets so they can be routed over the network to their intended destination
- Fragmenting packets that are too large to be forwarded by router interfaces into sequences of smaller packets
- Reassembly of sequences of packets into their original order
- Performing congestion control

Types

Network layer protocols may be either connectionless or connection-oriented in operation. Examples of connectionless network-layer protocols include

- **Internet Protocol (IP):** The network layer protocol used on the Internet
- **Internetwork Packet Exchange (IPX):** A legacy NetWare protocol

The above protocols employ the transport layer protocols Transmission Control Protocol (TCP) and Sequential Packet Exchange (SPX), respectively, to ensure reliable communications by fragmenting and reassembling packets and requesting retransmissions when required.

Examples of connection-oriented network layer protocols include X.25 and Logical Link Control Type 2 (LLC-Type 2).

Protocols that enable routers to exchange information to create network topology maps also work at the network layer. Examples of such network layer routing protocols include Routing Information Protocol (RIP), Open Shortest Path First (OSPF), Interior Gateway Routing Protocol (IGRP), Enhanced Interior Gateway Routing Protocol (EIGRP), and Border Gateway Protocol (BGP).

See Also: *Border Gateway Protocol (BGP), Enhanced Interior Gateway Routing Protocol (EIGRP), Interior Gateway Routing Protocol (IGRP), Internet Protocol (IP), Internetwork Packet Exchange (IPX), NetWare protocols, Open Shortest Path First (OSPF), Open Systems Interconnection (OSI) reference model, Routing Information Protocol (RIP), transport layer, X.25*

network management

Managing a network's hardware, applications, and performance.

Overview

Network management is a broad term describing platforms and applications that can manage the various devices and software that constitute a network. This includes such general tasks as

- Monitoring, measuring, and optimizing the performance of routers, switches, access servers, multiplexers, Web servers, mail servers, and other network devices and hardware.
- Detecting, diagnosing, repairing, working around, and predicting the likelihood of failures and other problems.
- Installing, upgrading, patching, distributing, configuring, managing, monitoring, and troubleshooting operating systems and applications on servers, desktop workstations, routers, and other hardware. This is often called desktop or systems management.

Network management may also involve

- Mapping the topology of a network in real time through autodiscovery and graphically displaying this information in useful form to administrators.
- Maintaining a central inventory database describing all devices, operating systems, and software on the network and how they are configured. When a change is made to the configuration of a device or application, the database is updated with the information automatically.
- Setting alarms and establishing automated responses to various alert conditions when they arise. These alerts may relate to device failure, traffic bottlenecks, server overload, and other problems.
- Remotely adding, removing, or rearranging local area network (LAN) and wide area network (WAN) links, a process called configuration management.
- Monitoring a network against intrusion by hackers and other attacks.
- Taking remote control of systems to manage, repair, or troubleshoot them.
- Monitoring service level agreements with vendors and service providers.
- Using artificial intelligence to determine the root cause of network failure and perform needed fixes automatically.
- Generating real-time and cumulative logs and reports of network performance, traffic flow, server load, and other information. These can be for auditing, management, planning, troubleshooting, or provisioning purposes.

N

- Managing different aspects of a network from workstations, using standard Web browsers, and even using wireless Personal Digital Assistants (PDAs).
- Perform policy-based management of network resources and traffic prioritization, a rapidly emerging new area in network management.

Implementation

Most network management platforms employ a combination of proprietary solutions and standards-based usage of Simple Network Management Protocol (SNMP) and its cousin Remote Monitoring (RMON). Other standards from the Distributed Management Task Force (DMTF) and Internet Engineering Task Force (IETF) are important also, particularly Web-Based Enterprise Management (WBEM) and the emerging Policy Framework and SNMPConf initiatives. Network management platforms support these existing and emerging standards to various degrees.

Network management can be accomplished in several ways:

- **Using prepackaged tools included with network operating systems such as Microsoft Windows and UNIX:** For example, Windows 2000 includes administrative tools such as Performance Monitor, Network Monitor, Computer Management, and other utilities that can be used to remotely monitor, manage, and troubleshoot server and network problems. Command-line tools such as Ping, Ipconfig, Tracert/Traceroute, Netstat, Nslookup, and others are also available on both Microsoft and UNIX platforms for configuring and troubleshooting Transmission Control Protocol/Internet Protocol (TCP/IP) networks. Trivial File Transfer Protocol (TFTP) and Telnet are often used for remote management of Cisco routers and other networking equipment from a command-line interface.
- **Using enterprise network management frameworks:** These are suites of tools integrated to various degrees that enable (or promise to enable) administrators to remotely manage all aspects of a diverse, heterogeneous network from a central administrator console. Many of these systems began in the 1980s as organic collections of tools united by a common user interface (admin console) and back-end database (for storing network configuration information). They were large, complex, expensive, and difficult to implement, often requiring a great deal of customization to work properly and never quite living up to their marketed goals. Such systems were targeted mainly to large enterprises having deep pockets and have found wide acceptance in such environments to this day. This failure to fulfill customer expectations was partly a result of the rapid pace of technological evolution in operating system and networking technologies, with the result that vendors of such network management systems had difficulty keeping up with the pace of change in these technologies. Many of these systems have now evolved into one-size-fits-all packaged management systems that are easier to deploy and use but which are more limited in their goals. Some framework vendors have also made their systems extensible to allow third-party point products to fill gaps in their framework products. Popular examples of these types of frameworks are listed below in the section entitled "Marketplace."
- **Using loose collections of freeware and open source network management tools:** Network administrators of small to mid-sized companies often create their own custom toolkit of useful management tools and utilities developed in-house or downloaded from the Internet and used for monitoring, configuring, and troubleshooting networks and servers. Using such diverse collections of tools, however, requires a high level of understanding of how networks actually work and how they ought to work and requires the discipline of implementing proper procedures and processes for maximum benefit.
- **Outsourcing network management needs:** Small companies often benefit from outsourcing all of their network management needs to a network/systems integrator, who often can remotely manage network performance and troubleshoot server problems by means of the Internet using browser-based tools. Larger companies may outsource only specific portions of their management needs, such as allowing telcos to remotely monitor the channel service unit/data

service units (CSU/DSUs) and T1 multiplexers that they lease to the customers. Outsourcing is a viable option for companies that do not have the resources to hire their own qualified network personnel.

Whatever the approach used for managing networks, most companies do not make this a high enough priority or allocate sufficient resources (in terms of both staff and money) to this aspect of their business as they do for their deployments of enterprise resource planning (ERP) and customer relationship management (CRM) software. If a company's customer and product data and communication/collaboration abilities are important and must be safeguarded and maintained at all costs, then safeguarding and maintaining the network on which information is stored and over which it travels should be an equally high priority, whatever the cost.

Marketplace

Network management frameworks for enterprise use are available from both traditional vendors and newer startups. Traditional vendors include Tivoli/IBM, Hewlett-Packard, Computer Associates, BMC Software, and several others. Tivoli Enterprise is a suite of platforms and tools providing desktop, network, storage, security, service, Web, and performance management. Tivoli products are available for a wide range of network operating systems, including Microsoft Windows, UNIX, and IBM's OS/390 mainframe platform. Tivoli even has a product line supporting end-to-end management of retail solutions that include point-of-sale terminals and automated teller machines (ATMs). They also have one for managing Personal Digital Assistants (PDAs), a rapidly growing concern in the enterprise environment. Tivoli software is used by 96 percent of Fortune 500 companies and is probably the most widely used management framework in enterprise environments. IBM's earlier NetView management platform is also integrated into the Tivoli line of products.

Another popular framework product is HP OpenView from Hewlett-Packard. Sun Microsystems also offers a management platform called Sun NetManager for their SunOS and Solaris machines. VERITAS Software Corporation is another contender in the enterprise arena with their Veritas NerveCenter—other vendors include Aprisma, NextPoint Networks, Lucent Technologies, and others. Finally, Microsoft has Microsoft Operations Manager (MOM) that provides enterprise-class event and application monitoring for the Windows 2000 and Windows .NET Server operating systems, and .NET Server application platforms.

Microsoft Systems Management Server is popular in the enterprise as a server, desktop, and applications management system. So is LANDesk Management Suite from Intel Corporation and Unicenter TNG from Computer Associates. Windows 2000 also supports a number of networking application programming interfaces (APIs) that allow information about network resources to be programmatically accessed, and some Active Directory Services Interface (ADSI) interfaces also provide similar functionality for script access.

Some vendors of point products that fill specific gaps in the management functionality of framework platforms include Concord Communications, Micromuse, RiverSoft Technologies, Tavve Software, and many others. A good example is CiscoWorks, which can be installed as an add-in for popular management frameworks such as HP OpenView and Sun NetManager. A number of startups provide point products providing root-cause analysis, automated event correlation, and other features previously lacking in big-name framework products. These startups include Evidian, Oxydian, Magnum Technologies, and many others.

Policy-based management tools include Cisco QoS Policy Manager from Cisco Systems and Orchestream Enterprise Edition from Orchestream. Application monitoring and performance tools include EcoSCOPE from Compuware Corporation, NextPoint S^3 from NextPoint Networks, eHealth from Concord Communications, VitalSuite from Lucent Technologies, and many others. The most popular remote control software used in enterprise systems management is undoubtedly PCAnywhere from Symantec Corporation. The Terminal Services component of Windows 2000, Windows XP, and Windows .NET Server offers out-of-the-box remote control functionality for these operating systems. Citrix RMS from Citrix Systems is another network management tool that includes remote control.

Network probes are growing in popularity as weapons in the network manager's arsenal. These probes are small SNMP-enabled devices that can be plugged into a WAN demarcation point or LAN segment to monitor network traffic and collect statistics for network management stations.

Management of Linux systems can be easily performed using Volution, a platform from Caldera International designed for large enterprises, application service providers (ASPs), Internet service providers (ISPs), and similar companies that may use large numbers of Linux machines. Volution is based on Red Hat Package Manager (RPM) technology and supports a number of major Linux distributions. Also in the open source arena, an initiative called OpenNMS was acquired by Atipa Technologies and rebranded as the Bluebird network management platform. Bluebird is available under the open-source license.

For More Information

A good overview on network management standards and free software can be found at *www.simpleweb.org.*

See Also: *Distributed Management Task Force (DMTF), Internet Engineering Task Force (IETF), network, network probe, network troubleshooting, Remote Network Monitoring (RMON), Simple Network Management Protocol (SNMP), Telnet, topology, Transmission Control Protocol/Internet Protocol (TCP/IP), Web-Based Enterprise Management (WBEM)*

Network Monitor

A software-based protocol analyzer included with Microsoft Windows 2000 and Windows .NET Server.

Overview

Network Monitor is a useful tool for troubleshooting network problems at the data-link, network, transport, and higher layers of the Open Systems Interconnection (OSI) reference model. You can use Network Monitor to

- Capture data frames from a connected network
- Display, filter, edit, and retransmit frames on the network
- Monitor and display protocol statistics
- Examine individual captured frames in detail

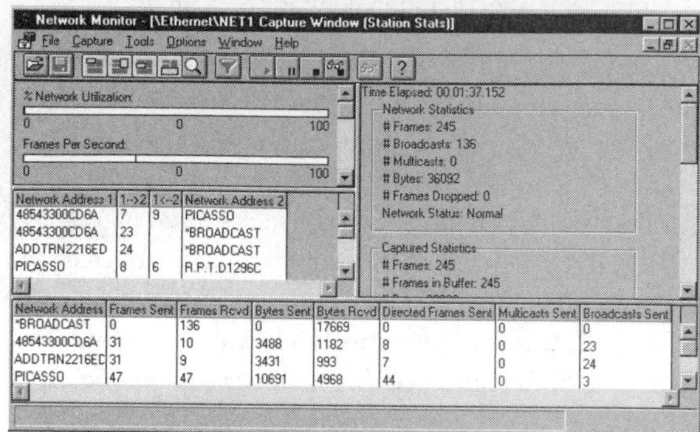

Network Monitor. *Example of a trace in Network Monitor.*

Notes

The version of Network Monitor included with Windows NT, Windows 2000, and Windows .NET Server is a simplified version that lacks some of the features in the full version included with Microsoft Systems Management Server (SMS). In particular, the simplified version can perform only local capturing of data to and from the computer running Network Monitor.

See Also: *network troubleshooting, Open Systems Interconnection (OSI) reference model, Systems Management Server (SMS)*

Network News Transfer Protocol (NNTP)

The Internet protocol for Usenet newsgroups.

Overview

Network News Transfer Protocol (NNTP) is an Internet standard protocol that governs the interaction between NNTP servers (news servers) and NNTP clients (news readers). NNTP is the underlying protocol on which the Usenet news system popular on the Internet. NNTP connections between clients and servers and between servers and servers use Transmission Control Protocol (TCP) for reliable, guaranteed packet delivery.

NNTP is defined in RFC 977.

Implementation

NNTP is both a client/server protocol and a server/server protocol. NNTP supports a set of simple text commands that:

- Enable NNTP clients such as Microsoft Outlook Express to connect to NNTP servers on TCP port 119 and download a list of newsgroups, read the messages in a newsgroup, and post a reply or a new message to a newsgroup.
- Enable NNTP servers to replicate newsgroups and their content among each other. This replication process between NNTP servers (or NNTP hosts, as they are often called) forms the basis of the worldwide news system called Usenet.

NNTP client commands include the following:

- **LIST:** To obtain a list of newsgroups available on the server
- **GROUP:** To select a specific newsgroup
- **ARTICLE:** To display a selected message
- **POST:** To post a new message or reply to an existing one

NNTP clients connecting to NNTP servers sometimes require authentication before their NNTP commands are accepted.

See Also: *Internet, newsfeed, newsgroup, Transmission Control Protocol (TCP)*

network numbers

Numbers assigned to subnets on a legacy Internetwork Packet Exchange/Sequential Packet Exchange (IPX/SPX) internetwork.

Overview

Network numbers uniquely identify portions of the network on an IPX/SPX internetwork. Network numbers must typically be manually assigned to hosts by the administrator to ensure proper network communication.

When using the NWLink IPX/SPX-Compatible Transport protocol on Microsoft Windows 2000, Windows XP, or Windows .NET Server networks, you must configure two different network numbers to ensure proper network communication:

- The IPX network number (also known as the external network number), a unique number assigned to all computers on the same network segment that are using the same NWLink frame type. In Windows 2000, Windows XP, and Windows .NET Server, you configure this number by accessing the NWLink IPX/SPX/NetBIOS Compatible Transport Protocol property sheet, selecting Manual Frame Type Detection, clicking Add, and entering the number.
- The virtual network number (also known as the internal network number), a unique number assigned to a machine that enables it to be used in a multiple network environment. This number is hexadecimal 0 by default; in Windows 2000, Windows XP, and Windows .NET Server, you can configure it by specifying it on the NWLink IPX/SPX/NetBIOS Compatible Transport Protocol property sheet.

To view the network number of a computer running Windows 2000, type **ipxroute config** at the command prompt.

Notes

When using the Transmission Control Protocol/Internet Protocol (TCP/IP), network numbers are instead called network IDs.

See Also: *internetwork, network ID, NWLink IPX/SPX-Compatible Transport (NWLink)*

network operating system (NOS)

An operating system that is network-aware.

Overview

Network operating systems (NOSs) are used to build local area networks (LANs) that can be used for

- Authenticating users who want to access the network for greater security
- Enabling users to share files and printers and exchange messages for performing collaborative work

- Centralizing administration of multiple computers to a single management console
- Running distributed applications that share processing on multiple computers

Marketplace

Examples of popular NOSs include

- Microsoft Windows 2000
- Novell NetWare
- Various flavors of UNIX
- Linux

Internetwork Operating System (IOS) from Cisco Systems is an example of a NOS that runs not on computers but on internetworking devices such as routers.

See Also: *Internetwork Operating System (IOS), Linux, local area network (LAN), NetWare, UNIX, Windows 2000*

network probe

A device for collecting network statistics.

N

Overview

Network probes are generally small devices that can be plugged into various points of a network to collect statistics and forward them to a network management station. These statistics then allow you to perform traffic analysis and identify trends so you can plan proper upgrades and identify problems.

Implementation

Network probes are a complement to existing network monitoring functionality based on Simple Network Management Protocol (SNMP) and Remote Monitoring (RMON) and are built in to today's intelligent network hubs, switches, and routers. Different probes are available that collect different kinds of information in various levels of detail, store this information in memory, and forward it to troubleshooting tools and management systems. Probes are available for different kinds of network architectures ranging from Ethernet to Asynchronous Transfer Mode (ATM) and from local area network (LAN) to wide area network (WAN) usage. LAN probes can usually be attached anywhere in a network or plugged into a port on an Ethernet switch. WAN probes are usually best located at the demarc point, the location where the physical circuit for the WAN link first enters the network—in other words, before the channel service unit/data service unit (CSU/DSU) when using leased lines such as T-carrier circuits.

See Also: *Asynchronous Transfer Mode (ATM), Channel Service Unit/Data Service Unit (CSU/DSU), Ethernet, Ethernet switch, local area network (LAN), network, network troubleshooting, Remote Network Monitoring (RMON), Simple Network Management Protocol (SNMP), T-carrier, wide area network (WAN)*

network protocol

A Layer 3 (network layer) of the Open Systems Interconnection (OSI) reference model for networking.

Overview

Common network protocols include the following:

- **Internet Protocol (IP):** Part of the Transmission Control Protocol/Internet Protocol (TCP/IP) protocol suite for connectivity with the Internet
- **Internetwork Packet Exchange (IPX):** A legacy Novell NetWare protocol.
- **NetBEUI:** A protocol developed from NetBIOS that functions at both the network and transport layers

Microsoft Corporation's 32-bit Windows operating systems are implemented in a layered fashion that allows multiple network protocols to be bound to multiple network interface cards (NICs) and allows multiple network clients and services to access these protocols. Windows computers can thus establish connectivity and interoperability with non-Microsoft operating system platforms such as UNIX and Novell NetWare.

See Also: *Internet Protocol (IP), Internetwork Packet Exchange (IPX), NetBEUI, network layer, Open Systems Interconnection (OSI) reference model*

network security

The methods used to protect a network from hostile attack.

Overview

Network security is not only a broad topic but also an essential one for today's network administrator. Attempts to intrude, disrupt, and deface business and corporate networks has never been higher, facilitated in part by the ubiquitous presence of the Internet and broadband Internet access. The vulnerability of today's networks to security attacks is compounded by lack of awareness by corporate management, overworked IT (information technology) staff, rapid software upgrade cycles that encourage the release of buggy software, widespread availability on the Internet of easy-to-use hacking and cracking tools, and vulnerabilities in the underlying Transmission Control Protocol/Internet Protocol (TCP/IP) itself, the networking protocol used by the Internet.

Some of the risks faced by networks today include

- Denial of service (DoS) attacks that tie up a network's resources so that legitimate users cannot gain access to them
- Trojan horse programs that install back doors to allow valuable network credentials to be stolen and misused or that install remote control programs that provide intruders with full access to network resources
- Viruses that invade networks through e-mail attachments and wreak havoc with important files
- Network operating systems and applications whose default configurations are insecure and permit a wide range of attacks to be performed
- Public Web sites that expose credit card information stored in databases through buffer overflows and script issues
- Wireless networks with weak or no encryption that can be accessed easily by anyone driving by with a wireless-enabled laptop

Some of the tools and techniques network administrators can use to secure their networks include

- **Physical security:** Simply locking the server room is a step that should not be overlooked. Users should also be taught not to write down their passwords on slips of paper taped under their keyboards and to be alert for malicious social engineering and persons calling and posing as network administrators and asking for passwords to fix alleged network problems.
- **Virus protection:** Subscribing to a virus protection service is essential for hosts connected to the Internet.
- **Authentication:** Properly configuring authentication methods are a necessary step to ensure against unauthorized logons. For high-security environments users can be provided with smart cards and other authentication tokens. Biometrics can also be employed if required, enabling users to be authenticated using fingerprint or retina scanners.
- **Access control:** Properly securing resources with suitable permissions is a necessary step to ensure against unauthorized resource access. Periodic auditing of access controls is also important.
- **Auditing:** Periodic auditing of security logs is essential, as even intelligent risk-analysis systems may miss certain kinds of attacks.
- **Encryption:** Using a protocol such as Internet Protocol Security (IPsec) can ensure the integrity and privacy of data transmitted over the network, and other protocols such as Pretty Good Privacy (PGP) can be used to secure e-mail.
- **Firewalls:** This is an essential tool for securing the perimeter of a network connected to the Internet, but firewalls must be properly configured and maintained and their logs should be periodically reviewed.
- **Remote access:** Remote access systems can be made more secure by implementing callback and other features. If the Internet is used for remote access, virtual private networks (VPNs) can employ IPsec for greater security.
- **Intrusion detection:** Installing an intrusion detection system (IDS) is becoming an essential part of corporate network security. Usually, the more intelligence these systems have the better, but they cannot replace the intelligence of the network administrator.

- **Patches:** Operating systems and applications are frequently found to be buggy or insecure, and vendors issue fixes to address these problems. Keeping up to date regarding available patches and applying them in timely fashion is essential for today's network administrators. Web servers are especially viewed as targets by attackers, and they require considerable attention to maintain security and protect against newly discovered vulnerabilities.
- **Backups and fault tolerance:** Every system is liable to be breached at some point, so having redundant hot standby systems is important in mission-critical e-commerce systems, and regular backups that are periodically restored for testing purposes are often the last line of defense against attackers damaging corporate databases.
- **Security policy:** Developing, internally publishing, monitoring, and enforcing a corporate security policy is a vital step in securing your network.
- **Training:** Making sure that IT staff are trained in using security tools is essential unless network operations are outsourced to other companies.

For More Information

Visit the SANS Institute at *www.sans.org*. Visit the CERT Coordination Center at *www.cert.org*.

See Also: *access control, auditing, authentication protocol, backup, biometric authentication, denial of service (DoS), disaster recovery, encryption, fault tolerance, firewall, hacking, Internet Protocol Security (IPsec), intrusion detection system (IDS), remote access, virtual private network (VPN), virus*

network service type

The way that a network appears to end nodes communicating over it.

Overview

There are two different ways to consider the service method employed for host-host communications on a network: connection method and delivery method. These methods are provided through the operation of the lower three layers of the Open Systems Interconnection (OSI) reference model; namely, the network, data link, and physical layers. Delivery methods may be either

- **Reliable:** Packets are delivered in the correct order without loss or duplication.

or

- **Best effort:** Also called the datagram method, packets (datagrams) may be delivered out of order with possible duplication or lost packets. With best effort delivery, the transport layer (Layer 4 of the OSI model) is usually responsible to ensure out of sequence packets are reordered, duplicate packets are ignored, and lost packets are retransmitted.

From the point of view of network connectivity, there are also two kinds of network services:

- **Connectionless:** Each packet is transmitted independently and contains the full source and destination address of the hosts communicating. No session establishment is required before communications can begin—the transmitting host simply starts sending packets to the destination, hoping higher layer protocols will ensure that delivery is achieved.
- **Connection-oriented:** Also called the virtual circuit (VC) method, this method involves first establishing a communication session between two hosts before transmitting data. Once a session has been established, it is usually assigned some kind of session identifier in place of full source/destination addressing, and all data packets transmitted include this identifier and are routed or switched similarly.

See Also: *connectionless protocol, connection-oriented protocol, Open Systems Interconnection (OSI) reference model, virtual circuit*

Networks file

A text file that provides a local method of resolving network names into their network IDs on a Transmission Control Protocol/Internet Protocol (TCP/IP) network.

Overview

The entries in the networks file are friendly names for TCP/IP networks; they can be used in TCP/IP commands such as the route command and for TCP/IP network management.

The networks file is at the following location on computers running Microsoft Windows:

- **Windows NT, Windows 2000, Windows XP, and Windows .NET Server:** %SystemRoot%\system32\drivers\etc
- **Windows 95 and Windows 98:** \Windows

Examples

Each line in the networks file contains a friendly network name for the network, followed by the IP address of the network and an optional comment prefixed with a pound sign (#). The following example is from the sample networks file included with Windows 95 and Windows 98:

```
loopback      127
campus        284.122.107
london        284.122.108
```

See Also: *hosts file, lmhosts file, protocol file, services file*

Network Termination Unit (NTU)

A telecommunications device used in Integrated Services Digital Network (ISDN) networking.

Overview

The Network Termination Unit (NTU) allows customer premises equipment to be connected to the switching equipment at the telco's central office (CO). ISDN customer premises equipment, such as routers and ISDN phones, usually have an ISDN S/T interface, while the ISDN termination at the customer end of the local loop usually has a U interface using an RJ-45 connector. The NTU converts the U termination of the ISDN line to one or more standard coding S/T interfaces that are suitable for connecting digital ISDN-ready phones, routers, and other devices to an ISDN line.

NTUs work differently from ISDN terminal adapters, which allow you to connect analog telephones, faxes, and similar equipment to your ISDN line. NTUs typically support either point-to-point or multipoint connections over distances of up to 3.4 miles (5.4 kilometers) on 26 AWG copper twisted-pair cabling. Some newer ISDN-enabled devices have a built-in U interface, making an NTU unnecessary.

The following table shows the differences between the Basic Rate ISDN U and S/T interfaces.

Basic Rate ISDN U Interfaces vs. Basic Rate ISDN S/T Interfaces

Property	*U Interface*	*S/T Interface*
Number of wires	2	4
Connector	RJ-45	RJ-45
Zero-to-peak voltage	2.5 V	0.75 V
Line coding	2B1Q (or 4B3T in Europe)	ASI (Alternate Space Inversion)

See Also: *Integrated Services Digital Network (ISDN), ISDN terminal adapter*

Network Time Protocol (NTP)

An Internet protocol for synchronizing computer clocks to an accurate reference clock.

Overview

Network Time Protocol (NTP) is used to synchronize computers with a remote reference system such as a cesium atomic clock. Synchronization of computers on a network is important for distributed applications, directory services, mail services, and other network services to work reliably. NTP solves this problem by providing a hierarchical series of time servers from which other computers can obtain the exact time, typically within an accuracy of several milliseconds. NTP time servers use Universal Time Coordinated (UTC), a global standard time that is independent of time zones.

NTP is defined in RFC 1305 and is supported by most UNIX platforms. A simplified version of NTP called Simple Network Time Protocol (SNTP) is also widely used and is supported by Microsoft Windows 2000, Windows XP, and Windows .NET Server.

Architecture

Master clocks are located at the U.S. Naval Observatories in Washington, D.C., and Colorado Springs, Colorado. These clocks are highly accurate atomic clocks that lose less than a second in a thousand years. Stratum 1 NTP servers obtain their time from direct connections to these master clocks. Stratum 2 servers obtain their time from stratum 1 servers and can provide time synchronization for computers on a network.

See Also: *UNIX, Windows 2000*

network transmission method

The way in which information transmitted over a network is received.

Overview

There are three basic types or models of how network transmissions are performed:

- **Unicasting:** One host transmits to another host. An example is Transmission Control Protocol (TCP), part of the Transmission Control Protocol/Internet Protocol (TCP/IP) suite. Unicasting is the main transmission method used for sending data over a network.
- **Broadcasting:** One host transmits to all hosts. An example is Address Resolution Protocol (ARP), used by TCP/IP networks running on Ethernet to resolve Layer 3 (network layer) Internet Protocol (IP) addresses into their associated Layer 2 (data link layer) MAC addresses. Broadcasts are often employed on networks for advertisements, announcements, name registrations, and other purposes.
- **Multicasting:** One host transmits to a select group of hosts. Multicasting is often used for delivery of streaming audio or video across an IP network.

Notes

A broadcast's scope depends on the aspect of the network under consideration. For example, on IP networks a broadcast is delivered to all hosts on the local subnet, but on Ethernet networks a broadcast is sent to all hosts within a given broadcast domain.

See Also: *Address Resolution Protocol (ARP), broadcast domain, broadcasting, data-link layer, Ethernet, MAC address, multicasting, subnet, Transmission Control Protocol (TCP), Transmission Control Protocol/Internet Protocol (TCP/IP), unicasting*

network troubleshooting

The process of identifying and fixing network communication problems.

Overview

Computer networks are complex entities, and problems can arise on many levels that can prevent network communications from working. Network troubleshooting involves tools and procedures for identifying, locating, repairing, and maintaining networks so they can perform as expected.

Network administrators have a variety of weapons in their arsenal for troubleshooting different types of network problems, including

- **Physical-layer tools:** The physical layer (Layer 1) of the Open Systems Interconnection (OSI) reference model is the layer responsible for signaling, that is, for placing voltages on the wire or light pulses within fiber-optic cabling. Cable testers and time domain reflectometers (TDRs) are the main tools used for diagnosing and locating cable breaks, fractures, and loose connections.
- **Higher-layer tools:** For troubleshooting at the data link, network, transport, and higher layers of the OSI model, protocol analyzers are the primary tool. Protocol analyzers sniff (capture) network traffic and use various degrees of intelligence to interpret the nature of this traffic and any underlying problems that may be present. They range from software that can be installed on standard PCs that have network interface cards (NICs) that support promiscuous mode, to stand-alone devices ranging from handheld to briefcase size.
- **Integrated analyzers:** These tools package cable testers and TDRs with protocol analyzers to provide an integrated platform for troubleshooting a wide range of network problems.
- **Network probes:** Also called Remote Network Monitoring (RMON) probes, these are generally small devices that can be plugged into a network or into switch ports to capture and buffer traffic statistics for forwarding to a network analyzer or network management system. Network probes

N

facilitate troubleshooting of switched networks, an area in which traditional network analyzers designed for shared networks are less effective.

Marketplace

The market leader in network test equipment is Fluke Corporation, whose LANMeter line of protocol analyzers are widely used in enterprise environments. Fluke's new OptiView Integrated Network Analyzer takes this a step forward by providing an integrated network test device for troubleshooting cabling issues, performing protocol analysis, and capturing RMON statistics at speeds up to the gigabit per second range and using intelligence to present information to users in an understandable format.

Other vendors of network test equipment include 3Com Corporation, Agilent Technologies, Datacom Textron, Microtest, NetScout Systems, Network Associates/ Sniffer Technologies, Network Instruments, Nortel Networks, and WildPackets.

Notes

Some general tips on diagnosing and resolving network problems include

- Determining whether the problem affects a single user, group of users, or all users on the network
- Establishing whether the problem is continuous, periodic, or intermittent
- Checking for loose, sharply bent, or damaged cabling
- Swapping hardware such as cabling, network interface cards (NICs), hubs, and switches to see the effect
- Using Transmission Control Protocol/Internet Protocol (TCP/IP) troubleshooting commands such as ping and tracert

See Also: *cable tester, network, network interface card (NIC), network probe, Open Systems Interconnection (OSI) reference model, ping, Remote Network Monitoring (RMON), time domain reflectometry (TDR), tracert*

network utilization

The percentage of available bandwidth being used in a network.

Overview

For Ethernet networks, a network utilization of 40 to 60 percent is normally the maximum. Higher utilization than this typically results in excessive collisions and retransmissions. Another word that describes network utilization is *throughput,* which is typically measured in megabits per second (Mbps) or megabytes per second (MBps).

See Also: *Ethernet, network*

newsfeed

Replication of Network News Transfer Protocol (NNTP) newsgroup listings and content.

Overview

Newsfeeds are an essential part of the architecture of NNTP. Newsfeeds enable news servers belonging to the Internet's Usenet system to exchange lists of newsgroups and messages with one another.

Newsfeeds come in two types:

- **Push feed:** Initiated by the remote host. This type is usually used when the newsfeed is very large.
- **Pull feed:** Initiated by the local host. This type gives the local host more control over what to download.

The host that provides the newsfeed is called the inbound host; the host that receives the newsfeed is called the outbound host.

See Also: *Internet, Network News Transfer Protocol (NNTP)*

newsgroup

A group of related messages on a Network News Transfer Protocol (NNTP) host.

Overview

Newsgroups generally contain postings on a particular topic, although they are often a prime target for spammers who post unsolicited advertisements. Newsgroups are defined hierarchically using a dotted notation. An

N

example of a newsgroup is alt.books.computing, which is an "alternative" group that discusses books about computing. The dotted notation of the newsgroup name emphasizes the hierarchical structure of the Usenet system of newsgroups. For example,

- alt is the root of the hierarchy of alternative newsgroups.
- alt.books refers to either a newsgroup on alternative books or a collection of such newsgroups.
- alt.books.cooking refers to either a newsgroup on alternative cookbooks or to a collection of such newsgroups.

Newsgroups can be either moderated or unmoderated. In moderated newsgroups, all messages posted to the newsgroup are first sent to the newsgroup moderator, who accepts or rejects messages depending on their relevance to the group's focus. Unmoderated groups are generally a free-for-all, although politeness dictates that users post only messages related to the newsgroup's focus.

Notes

When you first join a newsgroup, it's a good idea to "lurk" in the background for a while and read the postings to understand the focus and tone of the group. Posting off the topic or at too low a level in an advanced group can cause a "newbie" to get "flamed" (bombarded with offensive mail).

See Also: *Internet, Network News Transfer Protocol (NNTP)*

NEXT

Stands for near-end crosstalk, a measurement of the ability of network cabling to reject crosstalk.

See: *near-end crosstalk (NEXT)*

Next Generation I/O (NGIO)

A specification designed to replace the Peripheral Component Interconnect (PCI) system bus.

Overview

With today's Pentium III processors and high-speed hard disks, the PCI bus is rapidly becoming the bottleneck that limits the performance of high-speed data center servers. The PCI bus is limited to about 500 megabits per second (Mbps) of shared throughput. It lacks an error-detection mechanism and has relatively high latency. Next Generation I/O (NGIO) is intended to overcome these limitations. It uses a channel-based architecture that supports full-duplex transmission speeds of up to 2.5 gigabits per second (Gbps).

The NGIO Forum recently combined its efforts with a group called Future I/O, which was promoting a different standard. The combined standard will be called System I/O; its development group is headed by Intel Corporation and IBM and includes Microsoft Corporation, Sun Microsystems, Hewlett-Packard, and Dell Computer Corporation. System I/O will use a channel-based I/O architecture instead of a bus architecture and will use from 1 to 12 wires, each having a throughput of 2.5 Gbps. The channel-based architecture will allow different channels to carry different information to different components simultaneously, which will be a great improvement over parallel-transmission bus technologies. System I/O will also fully support hot-swapping of components.

For More Information

Visit the NGIO Forum at *www.ngioforum.org.*

NFS

Stands for Network File System, a suite of protocols for accessing file systems across a network.

See: *Network File System (NFS)*

NGIO

Stands for Next Generation I/O, a specification designed to replace the Peripheral Component Interconnect (PCI) system bus.

See: *Next Generation I/O (NGIO)*

NIC

Stands for network interface card, a device that allows a computer to communicate on a network.

See: *network interface card (NIC)*

NIS

Stands for Network Information System, a protocol used for naming and directory services on UNIX platforms.

See: *Network Information System (NIS)*

NIST

Stands for National Institute of Standards and Technology, a U.S. government organization that provides services and programs to help U.S. industries commercialize new technologies and compete internationally.

See: *National Institute of Standards and Technology (NIST)*

NNTP

Stands for Network News Transfer Protocol, the Internet protocol for Usenet newsgroups.

See: *Network News Transfer Protocol (NNTP)*

node

A general term for a device on a network that has a specific physical or logical address.

Overview

Nodes on a network can be computers, repeaters, bridges, or other devices on a network that can transmit, receive, or process signals. Another name for a node, especially on Ethernet networks, is a *station.*

Other common meanings of the term *node* include

- A domain or subdomain in the namespace of the Domain Name System (DNS)
- An object in the console hierarchy of Microsoft Management Console (MMC)
- In clustering terminology, a machine that is a member of a cluster

See Also: *clustering, Ethernet, network*

noise

Random disturbances in a transmission.

Overview

In computer networking, noise is undesirable random electrical transmission that is generated by networking components such as network interface cards (NICs) or induced in cabling by proximity to electrical equipment that generates electromagnetic interference (EMI). Noise is generated by all electrical and electronic devices, including motors, fluorescent lamps, power lines, and office equipment, and it can interfere with the transmission of signals on a network. The better the signal-to-noise ratio of an electrical transmission system, the greater the throughput of information on the system.

Noise can usually be reduced (but never entirely eliminated) by using higher-quality components, lowering the temperature of components, or using shielded cabling. Be sure to locate sensitive networking components and cabling away from heavy machinery, generators, motors, and other equipment that can generate a lot of EMI. Also be sure to terminate cables properly at patch panels and wall plates to minimize noise due to crosstalk.

See Also: *cabling, crosstalk, electromagnetic interference (EMI), network interface card (NIC), signal*

normal backup

A type of backup in which all the selected files and folders are backed up.

Overview

Also known as full backup, normal backups are the most secure way of backing up files and folders to tape. In a normal backup, the archive attribute is marked for each file and folder that is backed up. If the file is later modified, the archive attribute is cleared, indicating that the file needs to be backed up again. Normal backups are the safest form of backup but take the longest and use the most tape. They are also the easiest form of backup to perform a restore from, because you generally need only one tape to perform the restore (unless the amount of information to be backed up exceeds the capacity of the tape).

Notes

A good backup plan consists of at least one normal backup each week, with either incremental or differential backups during the rest of the week.

See Also: *backup, backup type*

NOS

Stands for network operating system, an operating system that is network-aware.

See: network operating system (NOS)

Novell Directory Services (NDS)

The directory services platform from Novell Networks.

Overview

Novell Directory Services (NDS) is a distributed network directory service platform for managing network resources such as users, groups, servers, shares, printers, and applications. NDS was introduced in 1993 with version 4 of the Novell NetWare operating system. Eventually, NDS was ported to other platforms, ranging from Sun Microsystems' Solaris platform to IBM S/390 mainframes. NDS is widely used in enterprise environments and is the main competitor for the Active Directory directory service of Microsoft Windows 2000 and Windows .NET Server.

Implementation

N

NDS is loosely modeled after the X.500 specification from the International Telecommunication Union (ITU). The foundation of NDS is the directory tree, which provides a hierarchical view of all network resources. Resources in the network can be grouped logically according to their location, function, or the structure of the company. Objects in the tree can be either containers or leaf objects, with the root container being the name of the company or organization. Containers can be considered branches and can hold leaf objects or other containers. When a user is assigned access rights to a container, these rights flow down into any subcontainers within the container. Trees, subtrees, and containers can also be renamed and merged.

You can implement NDS directories as a distributed database that is partitioned among multiple NDS servers on the network to provide fault tolerance and load balancing. As a result, no single server contains or is responsible for the entire directory. The NDS servers replicate with each other to ensure that each server contains an up-to-date version of the directory for the portion of the directory that the server is responsible for. To locate an object such as a user, a group, a shared directory, or a printer on the network, an NDS client can access the directory on any NDS server.

Notes

NDS was originally called NetWare Directory Services, since it was tightly coupled to the Novell NetWare operating system. The latest version of NDS is now called Novell eDirectory.

See Also: *Active Directory, directory, eDirectory, X.500*

Nslookup

A utility for diagnosing problems with name servers.

Overview

Nslookup is a Transmission Control Protocol/Internet Protocol (TCP/IP) command-line utility for troubleshooting name servers that are part of the Domain Name System (DNS). Nslookup can be used to manually display resource records contained in the zone files of name servers. Nslookup is supported by the Microsoft Windows NT, Windows 2000, Windows XP, and Windows .NET Server operating systems.

Examples

Nslookup can operate in either interactive or noninteractive (batch) mode. You enter interactive mode by typing **nslookup** at the command prompt. Once in the interactive running state, you could type **ls -d microsoft.com,** for example, to list all the resource records for the microsoft.com domain that are stored in the DNS database of the name server being queried.

See Also: *Domain Name System (DNS), name server, Transmission Control Protocol/Internet Protocol (TCP/IP)*

NS record

A Domain Name System (DNS) record that identifies a secondary name server for a zone.

Overview

For each zone in the DNS namespace there are typically one or more name servers that can be used to resolve the names of hosts in that zone into their associated Internet Protocol (IP) addresses. The master name server for a zone (the name server that is authoritative for that zone) is listed in the SOA record that defines the zone's characteristics. Secondary name servers for the zone are identified by one or more NS records, one for each secondary name server in the zone. Each NS record also requires a matching A record that resolves the fully qualified domain name (FQDN) of the secondary name server into its associated IP address.

NS records are also used to specify primary name servers for delegated zones. The full syntax for the NS record is found in RFC 1035.

Examples

Here is a typical example of an NS record:

```
microsoft.com.   IN   NS   ns2.microsoft.com.
```

In this example, hosts within the microsoft.com domain can be resolved using the name server called ns2. In this example IN stands for Internet and NS stands for name server.

See Also: *A record, Domain Name System (DNS), fully qualified domain name (FQDN), name server, SOA record*

NTFS

Stands for NTFS file system, the file system of Microsoft Windows NT, Windows 2000, Windows XP, and Windows .NET Server.

See: *NTFS file system (NTFS)*

NTFS file system (NTFS)

The file system of Microsoft Windows NT, Windows 2000, Windows XP, and Windows .NET Server.

Overview

NTFS file system (NTFS) is an advanced, high-performance file system designed for use with the Windows NT and supported by Windows 2000 and later. NTFS provides better performance and reliability than the file allocation table (FAT) file system first developed for the Microsoft Disk Operating System (MS-DOS) and used in earlier versions of Windows. NTFS also supports security features for data access control and ownership privileges that make it suitable for corporate file and application servers. The following table shows a comparison between the features of NTFS and FAT.

NTFS Compared with FAT

Feature	*NTFS*	*FAT*
Local security	x	
File-level access permissions	x	
Automatic recoverability using lazy writes and transaction logging	x	Lazy writes only
File-level compression	x	
POSIX-compliant	x	
Supports Services for Macintosh	x	
Dual boot with Windows 95 and Windows 98		x
Maximum volume size	2^{64} = 32 exabytes (theoretical) 2^{41} = 2 terabytes (practical)	2^{32} = 4 gigabytes (GB)
Optimal volume size	Less efficient for volumes under ~50 megabytes (MB)	Less efficient for volumes over ~500 MB

Windows 2000, Windows XP, and Windows .NET Server support a new version of NTFS called NTFS5 that includes additional features not supported by the earlier NTFS4 of Windows NT. These features provide greater manageability and enhanced security and include

- **Multiple data streams:** Allow libraries of files to be defined as alternate streams.
- **Reparse points:** Alter the way in which NTFS resolves path names.
- **Change journal:** Provides a persistent log of all changes made to files on the volume.

N

- **Encryption:** Allows data to be stored in encrypted form using the Encrypting File System (EFS).
- **Sparse file support:** Allows programs to create very large files while consuming disk space only as needed.
- **Disk quotas:** Allow administrators to control how much disk space users have access to.
- **FAT32:** Supports an enhanced version of FAT first included with the OSR2 version of Windows 95. FAT32 supports larger disk partitions than FAT.
- **Universal Disk Format (UDF):** The replacement for the earlier Compact Disk File System (CDFS). UDF is an international standard (ISO-13346) that supports both CD-ROM and DVD-ROM drives.

Architecture

Like FAT, NTFS uses the cluster as the fundamental unit of disk space allocation. The default size of the clusters for an NTFS volume depends on the size of the volume, as shown in the table. When you create a new NTFS volume by formatting a disk partition with NTFS, the master file table (MFT), which contains information concerning all the files and folders stored on the volume, is created. The MFT is located on the disk immediately after the partition boot sector, which contains the BIOS parameter block and the code that enables the operating system to find and load the startup files. After the MFT comes NTFS system files, which help implement NTFS by storing information such as the contents of the volume, volume name and version, table of attribute names and numbers, a list of transaction steps used for NTFS recoverability, and the root folder. After the NTFS system files is the file area where user data can be stored. The total overhead of the MFT and NTFS system files is about 1 MB.

Partition boot sector	Master file table (MFT)	NTFS system files	File area

NTFS file system (NTFS). *Structure of an NTFS volume.*

Default Cluster Sizes for NTFS

Volume Size	*Sectors/ Cluster*	*Cluster Size*
512 MB or less	1	512 bytes
513 KB–1024 MB	2	1 kilobyte (KB)
1025 MB–2048 MB	4	2 KB
2049 MB–4096 MB	8	4 KB
4097 MB–8192 MB	16	8 KB
8193 MB–16384 MB	32	16 KB
16385 MB–32768 MB	64	32 KB
32769 MB or more	128	64 KB

Notes

Note that Windows NT 4 systems must be running Service Pack 4 or later to read basic volumes formatted using the Windows 2000 version of NTFS. Also, because of the different disk structures, Windows NT 4 disk utilities such as Autochk and Chkdsk will not work on Windows 2000, Windows XP, or Windows .NET Server NTFS volumes. Because of these incompatibilities, Microsoft Corporation does not recommend dual booting between Windows NT 4 and Windows 2000.

See Also: file allocation table (FAT), file system

NTFS permissions (Windows 2000, Windows XP, and Windows .NET Server)

A set of permissions used in Microsoft Windows 2000, Windows XP, and Windows .NET Server to secure folders and files located on an NTFS file system (NTFS) partition or volume.

Overview

NTFS permissions provide security for both local and network access to the file system. They are different from shared folder permissions, which can be applied only to folders and which secure the file system for network access only, not for local access.

NTFS permissions in Windows 2000 differ depending on whether they are applied to files or to folders. The five standard file permissions and six standard folder permissions are listed in the following tables. These standard file and folder permissions are actually composed of various groupings of the 18 different special permissions—for more information, see the "NTFS special permissions (Windows 2000, Windows XP, and Windows .NET Server)" article elsewhere in this book. These groupings simplify the job of securing files and folders on NTFS file system partitions and volumes.

Standard NTFS File Permissions in Windows 2000, Windows XP, and Windows .NET Server

File Permission	*User Access Granted*
Read	Open the file and view its permissions, attributes, and ownership
Write	Modify the file, modify its attributes, and view its permissions, attributes, and ownership
Read & Execute	Delete the file and do everything Read permission allows
Modify	Delete the file and do everything Read & Execute and Write permissions allow
Full Control	Take ownership, modify permissions, and do everything Modify permission allows

Standard NTFS Folder Permissions in Windows 2000, Windows XP, and Windows .NET Server

Folder Permission	*User Access Granted*
Read	View contents of folder and view its permissions, attributes, and ownership
Write	Create new files and folders in the folder, modify its attributes, and view its permissions, attributes, and ownership
List Folder Contents	View contents of folder
Read & Execute	View subfolders within the folder and do everything Read and List Folder Contents permissions allow
Modify	Delete the folder and do everything Read & Execute and Write permissions allow
Full Control	Take ownership, modify permissions, and do everything Modify permission allows

To use these standard permissions to secure a file or folder, you must be the object's owner, have full control of the object, or be a member of the Administrators system group. You must explicitly assign a permission to a file or folder for the permission to be granted. If no permission is specified for a given user or group, the user or group has no access to the file or folder. When you explicitly assign a permission, you can choose to either allow or deny that permission.

When you create a file or folder on an NTFS file system volume, it inherits the permissions of its parent folder or volume. When you assign a permission to a parent folder or volume, you have the option of propagating that permission to all of its child folders and files.

The following rules apply to assigning permissions for files and folders on NTFS file system volumes:

- If a user belongs to two or more groups and the groups have different permissions on a given folder, the user's effective permission is the least restrictive of the permissions. For example, if a user has Read permission on a file and a group the user belongs to has Modify permission, the user's effective permission is Modify, which is the least restrictive of the two.
- A permission explicitly denied overrides a similar permission explicitly allowed. For example, if a user has Read permission on a file and a group the user belongs to has been denied Read permission, the user cannot open and read the file.
- A permission for a file overrides a similar permission for the folder containing the file. For example, if a user has Modify permission on a file and Read permission on the folder containing the file, the user can open, read, edit, and save changes to the file.

Notes

The differences between NTFS standard permissions for the Windows 2000, Windows XP, and Windows .NET Server operating systems and those for Windows NT include the following:

- Windows 2000, Windows XP, and Windows .NET Server have six folder permissions; Windows NT has seven.

- Windows 2000, Windows XP, and Windows .NET Server have five file permissions; Windows NT has four.
- In Windows 2000, Windows XP, and Windows .NET Server, you can explicitly grant or explicitly deny any standard file or folder permission. In Windows NT, you can only explicitly grant a permission (but you can explicitly grant no access as a permission).

When you format a partition or volume using NTFS, the Everyone system group is automatically assigned full control permission for the root of the volume. Any new files or folders you create on the volume inherit this permission. Be aware that leaving full control for everyone might create a security risk; you should replace it with more suitable permissions such as full control for the Authenticated Users special identity.

See Also: *NTFS permissions (Windows NT), NTFS special permissions (Windows 2000, Windows XP, and Windows .NET Server), NTFS special permissions (Windows NT)*

NTFS permissions (Windows NT)

A set of permissions used in Microsoft Windows NT to secure folders and files on an NTFS file system (NTFS) partition.

Overview

NTFS permissions provide security for both local and network access to the file system. They are different from shared folder permissions, which can be applied only to folders and which secure the file system for network access only, not for local access.

NTFS permissions in Windows NT differ depending on whether they are applied to files or to folders. The four standard file permissions and seven standard folder permissions are listed in the following tables. These standard file and folder permissions are actually composed of various groupings of six NTFS special permissions:

- Read (R)
- Write (W)
- Execute (X)
- Delete (D)
- Change Permission (P)
- Take Ownership (O)

For more information on these special permissions, see the "NTFS special permissions (Windows NT)" article elsewhere in this book.

Standard NTFS File Permissions in Windows NT

File Permission	*Special Permissions*
Full Control	RWXDPO
Change	RWXD
Read	RX
No Access	None

Standard NTFS Folder Permissions in Windows NT

Folder Permission	*Special Permissions for Folders*	*Special Permissions for Files in a Folder*
Full Control	RWXDPO	RWXDPO
Change	RWXD	RWXD
Add & Read	RWX	RX
Add	WX	Unspecified
Read	RX	RX
List	RX	Unspecified
No Access	None	None

To use these standard permissions to secure a file or folder, you must be the object's owner, have full control of the object, or be a member of the Administrators system group. You must explicitly assign a permission to a file or folder for the permission to be granted. If no permission is specified for a given user or group, the user or group has no access to the file or folder.

When you create a file or folder on an NTFS file system partition, it inherits the permissions of its parent folder or partition. When you assign a permission to a parent folder or partition, you have the option of propagating that permission to all of its child folders and files.

The following rules apply to assigning permissions for files and folders on NTFS file system volumes:

- If a user belongs to two or more groups and the groups have different permissions in a given folder, the user's effective permission is the least restrictive of the permissions. For example, if a user has Read permission on a file and a group the user belongs to has Change permission, the user's effective permission is Change, which is the less restrictive of the two.

- The No Access permission overrides all other permissions. For example, if a user has Read permission on a file and a group the user belongs to has No Access permission, the user cannot open and read the file.
- A permission for a file overrides a similar permission for the folder containing the file. For example, if a user has Change permission on a file and Read permission on the folder containing the file, the user can open, read, edit, and save changes to the file.

Notes

For a description of the differences between NTFS standard permissions for Windows 2000 and for Windows NT, see the "NTFS permissions (Windows 2000)" article elsewhere in this book.

In most cases NTFS standard permissions are sufficient for controlling access to a file or folder. If standard permissions are not sufficiently granular for your purposes, you can use NTFS special permissions.

See Also: *NTFS permissions (Windows 2000, Windows XP, and Windows .NET Server), NTFS special permissions (Windows 2000, Windows XP, and Windows .NET Server), NTFS special permissions (Windows NT)*

NTFS special permissions (Windows 2000, Windows XP, and Windows .NET Server)

Individual permissions granted or denied when NTFS file system (NTFS) standard permissions are not sufficiently granular for specific security purposes.

Overview

NTFS special permissions available depend on whether you are securing files or folders. In both cases, 14 special permissions are available; 10 of these are common to the two scenarios. The following tables list the various NTFS special permissions available in Microsoft Windows 2000, Windows XP, and Windows .NET Server.

NTFS Special Permissions for Both Files and Folders in Windows 2000, Windows XP, and Windows .NET Server

Special Permission	*User Access Granted*
Read Attributes	View the attributes (including read-only, hidden, system, and archive) of the file or folder
Read Extended Attributes	View custom attributes that can be defined by certain applications for the file or folder
Write Attributes	Modify the attributes of the file or folder
Write Extended Attributes	Modify custom attributes that can be defined by certain applications for the file or folder
Delete Subfolders And Files	Delete subfolders or files
Delete	Delete the file or folder; however, even if this permission is denied on a file, you can delete it if its parent folder has been granted Delete Subfolders And Files permission
Read Permissions	View the permissions on the file or folder
Change Permissions	Modify the permissions on the file or folder
Take Ownership	Take ownership of the file or folder
Synchronize	Lets threads in multithreaded programs wait on the file or folder handle and synchronize with another thread that signals it

NTFS Special Permissions Only for Files in Windows 2000, Windows XP, and Windows .NET Server

Special Permission	*User Access Granted*
Execute File	Execute the file
Read Data	Read the file
Write Data	Modify the file
Append Data	Append to the file (but not modify existing data)

N

NTFS Special Permissions for Folders in Windows 2000, Windows XP, and Windows .NET Server

Special Permission	*User Access Granted*
Traverse Folder	Drill down to other files and folders in the folder even if you have no permissions on intermediate subfolders
List Folder	View the names of subfolders and files in the folder
Create Files	Create files in the folder
Create Folders	Create subfolders within the folder

You can grant or deny special permissions by using the Advanced button on the Security tab of a file's or folder's property sheet. You can select different combinations of special permissions to create custom sets of permissions for special purposes. In most cases, however, it is simplest to use NTFS standard permissions for securing files and folders. If you use special permissions, there is a lot of flexibility in how you can apply them, especially if you are applying them to a folder. For example, you can apply a custom set of special permissions to

N

- The selected folder only
- The selected folder, its subfolders, and files
- The selected folder and its subfolders only
- The selected folder and its files only
- Subfolders and files of the selected folder but not the folder itself
- Subfolders of the selected folder but not the folder itself
- Files in the selected folder but not the folder itself

To use special permissions you must be the object's owner, have full control of the object, or be a member of the Administrators group.

Notes

In Windows XP and Windows .NET Server, the Full Control permission is listed in the Special Permissions screen. When selected, Full Control gives the user all special permissions that apply to the file or folder.

There are significant differences between NTFS special permissions for Windows 2000, Windows XP, and Windows .NET Server and those for Windows NT. The most obvious difference is that in Windows 2000, Windows XP, and Windows .NET Server, you can assign any of 14 special permissions, but in Windows NT you have 6 special permissions to choose from: Read (R), Write (W), Execute (X), Delete (D), Change Permission (P), and Take Ownership (O). The reason for this difference is that in Windows NT much of the machinery of NTFS is hidden from the user interface, but in Windows 2000, Windows XP, and Windows .NET Server, this machinery is exposed in the user interface.

See Also: *NTFS permissions (Windows 2000, Windows XP, and Windows .NET Server), NTFS permissions (Windows NT), NTFS special permissions (Windows NT)*

NTFS special permissions (Windows NT)

Individual permissions granted or denied when NTFS file system (NTFS) standard permissions are not sufficiently granular for specific security purposes.

Overview

The special permissions available are the same whether you are securing files or folders, with the exception that when you secure a directory you have the additional option of leaving access unspecified instead of assigning a specific set of special permissions. In both cases, six special permissions are available; these are listed in the following table.

NTFS Special Permissions in Windows NT

Special Permission	*Symbol*	*User Access When Applied to Files*	*User Access When Applied to Folders*
Read	R	View file owner and permissions Read the file	View contents of the folder View folder attributes View folder owner and permissions

(continued)

NTFS Special Permissions in Windows NT *continued*

Special Permission	*Symbol*	*User Access When Applied to Files*	*User Access When Applied to Folders*
Write	W	View file owner and permissions Modify file attributes Edit the file	Add files to the folder Add sub-folders Modify folder attributes View folder owner and permissions
Execute	X	View file owner and permissions Modify file attributes Run the executable file	View folder attributes Browse folder hierarchy View folder owner and permissions
Delete	D	Delete the file	Delete the folder
Change Permission	P	Change file permissions	Change folder permissions
Take Ownership	O	Take ownership of the file	Take ownership of the folder

By selecting different combinations of special permissions, you can create custom sets of permissions for special purposes. In most cases, however, NTFS standard permissions are sufficient for securing files and folders. To use special permissions, you must be the object's owner, have full control of the object, or be a member of the Administrators system group. For information on which sets of special permissions comprise the various standard permissions, see the "NTFS permissions (Windows NT)" article elsewhere in this book.

Notes

For a description of the differences between NTFS special permissions for Microsoft Windows NT and for Microsoft Windows 2000, see the "NTFS special permissions (Windows 2000, Windows XP, and Windows .NET Server)" article elsewhere in this book.

See Also: *NTFS permissions (Windows 2000, Windows XP, and Windows .NET Server), NTFS permissions (Windows NT), NTFS special permissions (Windows 2000, Windows XP, and Windows .NET Server)*

NTLM protocol

Another name for Windows NT Challenge/Response Authentication, an authentication scheme used in Microsoft Windows NT–based networks.

See: *Windows NT Challenge/Response Authentication*

NTP

Stands for Network Time Protocol, an Internet protocol for synchronizing computer clocks to an accurate reference clock.

See: *Network Time Protocol (NTP)*

NTU

Stands for Network Termination Unit, a telecommunications device used in Integrated Services Digital Network (ISDN) networking.

See: *Network Termination Unit (NTU)*

NTVDM

Stands for NT Virtual DOS Machine, an MS-DOS environment simulator in Windows NT.

See: *NT Virtual DOS Machine (NTVDM)*

NT Virtual DOS Machine (NTVDM)

An MS-DOS environment simulator in Microsoft Windows NT.

Overview

NT Virtual DOS Machine (NTVDM) is a single-threaded Win32 application that simulates an MS-DOS environment on Microsoft Windows NT, Windows 2000, Windows XP, and Windows .NET Server. The

NTVDM enables the system to properly run MS-DOS and Windows 3.*x* applications. Each MS-DOS–based application running on Windows NT requires its own NT Virtual DOS Machine (NTVDM). As a result, if an MS-DOS–based application fails while running on Windows NT, it does not affect other MS-DOS-based applications.

You can customize the NTVDM for an MS-DOS–based application by right-clicking on the application's executable file and choosing Properties. The settings you can configure are similar to those available in the Windows 3.*x* tool PIF Editor.

See Also: *Microsoft Disk Operating System (MS-DOS), Windows NT*

null modem cable

A serial cable with cross-pinning that is used for file transfers and for other specialized communication between computers.

Overview

Null modem cables, also known as file transfer cables, are used to directly connect two computers for transferring files between them—for example, by using the Direct Cable Connection accessory of Microsoft Windows 95 and Windows 98. Note that parallel data-transfer cables achieve faster data transfer rates for file transfer than serial null modem cables.

The most common form of null modem cable is based on the RS-232 serial transmission interface specifications. Pins 2 and 3 are crossed in a null modem cable to allow you to directly link two RS-232 serial ports on different computers. Other pins can also be crossed depending on the intended purpose of the cable. The most common forms of termination for these cables are DB9 and DB25 connectors.

Serial RS-232 null modem cables support distances of up to about 50 feet (15 meters) and can be used for any communication for which a direct DTE-to-DTE connection or DCE-to-DCE connection is required. If longer distances are needed in serial communication, you can use a line driver to amplify the signal up to several kilometers. A cable connecting two pieces of data terminal equipment (DTE) is specifically called a null modem cable, but a cable connecting two pieces of data communications equipment (DCE) is usually called a tail-circuit cable and has a different cross-pinning. You can obtain null modem cables for other serial interfaces such as V.35 and those with special types of pinning.

Notes

Use a shielded null modem cable to extend distances up to 98 feet (30 meters) without using line drivers.

See Also: *data communications equipment (DCE), data terminal equipment (DTE), RS-232, serial transmission*

NWLink

Stands for NWLink IPX/SPX-Compatible Transport, Microsoft Corporation's version of Novell's legacy Internetwork Packet Exchange/Sequential Packet Exchange (IPX/SPX).

See: *NWLink IPX/SPX-Compatible Transport (NWLink)*

NWLink IPX/SPX-Compatible Transport (NWLink)

Microsoft Corporation's version of Novell's legacy Internetwork Packet Exchange/Sequential Packet Exchange (IPX/SPX).

Overview

IPX/SPX is a legacy networking protocol used in Novell NetWare 2.*x* and 3.*x*. NWLink IPX/SPX-Compatible Transport (NWLink) is Microsoft's 32-bit version of this protocol for the Microsoft Windows NT, Windows 2000, Windows XP, and Windows .NET Server platforms.

NWLink supports the following features:

- Compliance with network driver interface specification (NDIS) 4 on Windows NT and NDIS 5 on Windows 2000, Windows XP, and Windows .NET Server.
- Support for NetBIOS over NWLink (NWLink NetBIOS)

- Support for the following interprocess communications (IPC) mechanisms: Windows Sockets, named pipes, and remote procedure calls (RPCs)

Uses

NWLink can be used on Microsoft platforms when

- Microsoft clients such as Windows NT Workstation, Windows 2000 Professional and Windows XP Professional require access to NetWare file, print, and application servers. These clients can access NetWare servers either directly using Client Services for NetWare (CSNW) or through a gateway server running Gateway Service for NetWare (GSNW).
- NetWare clients need access to servers running Windows NT, Windows 2000, and Windows .NET Server. NetWare clients can access file and print services directly on Windows servers using File and Print Services for NetWare (FPNW).

Notes

If a Windows NT, Windows 2000, Windows XP, or Windows .NET server or client with NWLink installed is unable to communicate with NetWare clients or servers, check the properties of NWLink to make sure you are using the same frame type as the machines running NetWare. Note that you must also specify IPX/SPX network numbers when configuring NWLink.

See Also: *Client Services for NetWare (CSNW), File and Print Services for NetWare (FPNW), Gateway Service for NetWare (GSNW), NetBIOS, NetWare, network driver interface specification (NDIS)*

OASIS

Stands for Organization for the Advancement of Structured Information Systems, a nonprofit consortium that promotes Extensible Markup Language (XML) standards.

See: *Organization for the Advancement of Structured Information Systems (OASIS)*

object (Active Directory)

An element of Active Directory directory service that represents a network resource.

Overview

Some common types of objects in Active Directory include

- **Users:** Required for users to log on to the network.
- **Groups:** Collections of user accounts, computers, or other groups created for organizational purposes or for assigning permissions to shared resources.
- **Computers:** Represent machines that belong to the domain.
- **Shared folders:** Pointers to shared folders on a server on the network. If you create a shared folder on a computer running Microsoft Windows 2000, an associated shared folder object is automatically created in Active Directory.
- **Printers:** Pointers to printers on the network. If you create a network printer on a machine running Windows 2000, an associated printer object is automatically created in Active Directory.

Objects have attributes that define and describe them. For example, the attributes of a user object might include the user's name, e-mail address, and phone number. All objects of the same type or class have the same set of attributes, but they are distinguished from each other by having different values for at least one of these attributes. Some attributes are required to have values (such as the First Name attribute of a user object), but other attributes can be optional (such as Telephone Number).

You can group objects by placing them into container objects (containers) such as the following:

- **Domains:** The fundamental units of Active Directory that share common administration, security, and replication requirements. Domains can also be grouped into domain trees and forests to reflect an enterprise's administrative structure.
- **Organizational units (OUs):** Container objects that are used to organize other directory objects. OUs are part of the hierarchical structure of Active Directory, and allow objects are grouped according to common functions and purposes to simplify network administration. The hierarchical grouping of objects and OUs also simplifies the process of searching Active Directory for information about network resources.

Access to an object in Active Directory is based on the object's discretionary access control lists (DACLs), which list the users and groups authorized to access the object and their access levels. You can group objects with similar security requirements into OUs to simplify assignment of permissions to the objects and to facilitate administration and control of network resources. You can assign permissions to objects by using Active Directory Users and Computers, a snap-in for Microsoft Management Console (MMC).

Objects can be referenced by name by using

- **Distinguished names:** Analogous to absolute paths of objects within a file system. The distinguished name of an object specifies complete information about the object's location within Active Directory and includes the domain name, names of OUs that it belongs to, and the name of the object itself. Each object in Active Directory must have a unique distinguished name.

- **Relative distinguished names:** Analogous to relative paths of objects in the current directory of a file system. The relative distinguished name of an object is the portion of the distinguished name that is unique to the object. Any two objects in the same OU need to have unique, differing relative distinguished names.

Notes

When you use Active Directory Users and Computers to view the property sheet for an object, the Security tab, which displays the Active Directory permissions assigned to that object, is usually not visible. Choose Advanced Features from the View menu to make this tab visible.

If you have resources such as shared folders or printers on computers that are not running Windows 2000 or Windows .NET Server, you must manually publish information about these resources in Active Directory if you want users to be able to locate and access them through Active Directory. You do this by adding the appropriate type of object for that resource to Active Directory and having it point to where the resource is located on the network.

When you create a new Active Directory object, you usually use a wizard to specify values for the important attributes of the object. You can specify other attributes after the object is created by opening the property sheet for that object.

See Also: *Active Directory, organizational unit (OU)*

object identifier (OID)

A numeric value that universally identifies data and syntax elements for certain distributed systems.

Overview

Object identifiers (OIDs) are employed in distributed systems such as X.500 and Lightweight Directory Access Protocol (LDAP) directories, Simple Network Management Protocol (SNMP) management systems, Open Systems Interconnection (OSI) applications, and so on. In the directory arena, for example, OIDs are used to identify the various classes and attributes used by Microsoft Active Directory for Windows 2000 and by Novell Directory Services (NDS).

OIDs are assigned by organizations that are recognized as issuing authorities, such as the International Organization for Standardization (ISO), which also maintains a complete list of the world's various issuing authorities. In the United States, for example, the issuing authority is the American National Standards Institute (ANSI).

Examples

In Microsoft's Active Directory directory service, for example, OIDs are used as globally unique identifiers for object classes and attributes. OIDs ensure that when Active Directory is integrated with other directory systems, no conflicts occur, as each attribute and class in Active Directory has an OID that is globally unique. The OID for a class or attribute remains unchanged even when the distinguished name of a directory object is modified because of system configuration changes.

OIDs are expressed in dotted numeric form using an explicitly defined hierarchy of possible values. For example, the OID 1.2.840.113556.1.5.4 represents the Builtin-Domain class of objects within Active Directory. You can determine this by parsing the OID tree as follows:

```
1           ISO
2           ANSI
840         United States
113556      Microsoft
1           Active Directory Service
5           Classes
4           Builtin-Domain
```

An example of an object identifier for a different U.S. company might be 1.2.840.105670, where 1.2.840 is assigned to U.S. companies and 105670 is the number assigned to the specific company. Once your company has an object identifier, you can extend it by appending dotted decimal portions. So if 1.2.840.105670 represents Northwind Traders, 1.2.840.105670.27 might represent the Sales division, 1.2.840.105670.33 might represent the Support division, and so on. Further levels of subdivision are also possible.

Notes

If you want to use Active Directory Schema Manager to create a new class of objects or a new attribute in Active Directory, you should first obtain an object identifier for your organization from ANSI, ISO, or some other issuing authority.

See Also: *Active Directory, American National Standards Institute (ANSI), directory, International Organization for Standardization (ISO), Lightweight Directory Access Protocol (LDAP), Management Information Base (MIB), Novell Directory Services (NDS), Simple Network Management Protocol (SNMP), X.500*

object linking and embedding (OLE)

A low-level object-oriented technology that was the precursor of the Component Object Model (COM).

Overview

Object linking and embedding (OLE) was an early Microsoft technology for programmatically providing services to applications to support the creation of compound documents. For example, using OLE, you could insert bitmap images, sound clips, spreadsheet files, and other objects into Microsoft Word documents.

The term *object linking and embedding* comes from the two possible ways in which OLE enabled the creation of compound documents, specifically:

- Linking adds a link in a document that points to source data stored somewhere else. Linked objects are stored in the document as a path to the original linked data, usually a separate file from the container document.
- Embedding, on the other hand, adds one document directly to the other. Embedded objects are stored with the document that contains them.

History

The meaning of the term *OLE* has shifted somewhat since Microsoft Corporation first introduced it in 1991. Version 1 of OLE, referred to as OLE 1, was Microsoft's first mechanism for creating compound documents. OLE 2, the second version of OLE, improved on OLE 1 and expanded the support for creating more complex compound documents. OLE 2 was based on a new model known as the Component Object Model (COM). Microsoft began to recognize that OLE 2 could be used to solve other software problems and that it could be applied to other areas of software development. Microsoft saw OLE 2 as an expandable architecture to create software and, as such, decided to drop the version number. Microsoft also reduced the name from *object linking and embedding (OLE)* to just *OLE*, with no spell-out. At that time, OLE referred to any technology based on COM. In 1996, Microsoft introduced the term *ActiveX* which initially referred using to COM-based technologies on the Internet, but ActiveX also overlapped with OLE. Soon, OLE technologies were being referred to as *ActiveX technologies*. At that time, Microsoft decided to change the name *OLE* back to its original name, *object linking and embedding (OLE)*, and once again use it to refer to technologies for creating compound documents and the linking and embedding of objects.

Architecture

An OLE application can be one or both of the following:

- **OLE server application:** Used to create objects that will be contained in compound documents. A server application can create OLE components that can be placed in documents created by OLE container applications.
- **OLE container application:** Used to create the actual compound documents. A container application can create documents that can contain and display OLE components using OLE.

OLE container documents support in-place activation, which allows users to activate an embedded OLE component from within the container document. Activating the component changes the container application's user interface to include features that allow users to directly edit the component from within the container document.

See Also: *ActiveX, Component Object Model (COM)*

object (programming)

A construct containing data as well as methods (functions for manipulating the construct's data).

Overview

Object-oriented programming (OOP) focuses on objects instead of functions for manipulating separate data entities. The "blueprint" for an object is a class; a specific object is an "instance" of a class that you access using its associated methods. New classes can be derived from more general classes through a procedure called inheritance. The derived class contains all the methods and data of the original class, which can simplify programming.

See Also: *C++*

OBM

Stands for out-of-band management, remotely managing networking and telecommunications equipment using out-of-band (OOB) signaling.

See: *out-of-band management (OBM)*

OCSP

Stands for online certificate status protocol, an emerging specification for validating digital certificates.

See: *Online Certificate Status Protocol (OCSP)*

OC-x

Stands for optical carrier level, a measure of Synchronous Optical Network (SONET) capacity.

See: *optical carrier (OC-x) level*

ODBC

Stands for open database connectivity, a standard method of accessing data stored in relational databases and other structured data sources.

See: *open database connectivity (ODBC)*

ODI

Stands for Open Data-link Interface, a legacy network protocol software interface used by early versions of Novell NetWare.

See: *Open Data-link Interface (ODI)*

OFDM

Stands for orthogonal frequency division multiplexing, an emerging technology for achieving higher data rates in wireless communications.

See: *Orthogonal Frequency Division Multiplexing (OFDM)*

offline browsing

A feature of Microsoft Internet Explorer that allows users to browse cached or subscribed Web content when they are not connected to the Internet.

Overview

Offline browsing is an easy way to browse Web content on a laptop when an Internet connection is not available. Users can surf their history folder to view recently accessed Uniform Resource Locators (URLs). If users click on an unsaved link, they are notified that they are working offline and are asked whether they would like to connect to the Internet to access the resource.

When you add a Web page to your Favorites list, you can specify that the page be available for offline browsing, indicate how deep you want to be able to browse the page's links offline, and specify how you want to keep the offline content up to date. To view the site offline later, you can

- Choose Synchronize from the Favorites menu to manually synchronize offline content

- Choose Work Offline from the File menu to switch to offline browsing mode
- Select the item from your Favorites list

To leave Work Offline mode, choose Work Offline from the File menu.

See Also: *Internet Explorer*

Offline Files

A feature of Windows 2000, Windows XP, and Windows .NET Server that lets you continue working with shared network resources after you disconnect from the network.

Overview

Shared files and folders from any computer that supports Server Message Block (SMB)–based file and print sharing, such as those running Windows .NET Server, Windows XP, Windows 2000, Windows NT 4, Windows 98, or Windows Millennium Edition (Me), can be made available for offline use by Windows 2000 or Windows XP clients. These clients that are configured to use offline folders can cache the network resources in a local folder. When disconnected from the network, the client can continue working normally on the cached files. The client can then synchronize the contents of the cache with the network share when the connection is restored.

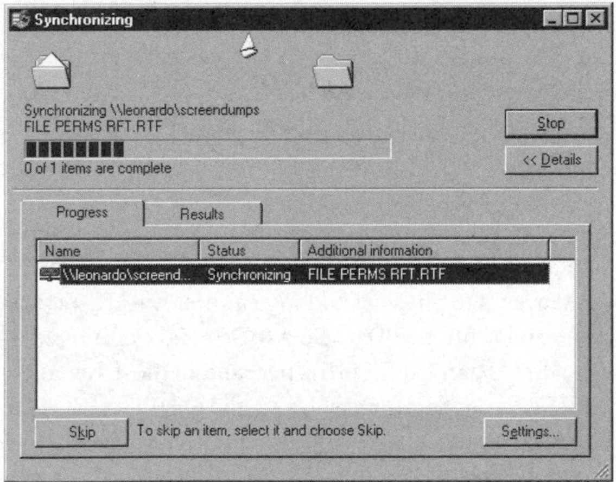

Offline Files in Windows 2000. *Synchronizing with a network share using Offline Files in Windows 2000.*

To enable offline file support on a computer running Windows 2000 or Windows XP, open My Computer and choose Folder Options from the Tools menu. Select the Offline Files tab and check Enable Offline Files. Specify synchronization options, a cache size, and additional advanced options. To make a share on the network available for offline use, select the share in My Computer (where it might appear as a mapped network drive) or My Network Places (where it will appear as a network share) and choose Make Available Offline from the File menu. The contents of the network share will be copied to the local computer's cache in a process known as synchronizing. You can specify additional synchronization settings by selecting Settings in the Synchronizing dialog box.

OID

Stands for object identifier, a numeric value that universally identifies data and syntax elements for certain distributed systems.

See: *object identifier (OID)*

OLAP

Stands for online analytical processing, a technology that allows users to perform sophisticated data analysis on typically large amounts of enterprise data to gain insight on the information it contains.

See: *online analytical processing (OLAP)*

OLE

Stands for object linking and embedding, a low-level object-oriented technology that was the precursor of the Component Object Model (COM).

See: *object linking and embedding (OLE)*

OLE DB

A Microsoft technology for universal data access.

Overview

Based on Component Object Model (COM) technologies, OLE DB represents a specification for developing extensible COM interfaces designed to provide applications with uniform methods of accessing data from diverse data sources that can include

- Mainframe databases, including IBM's Information Management System (IMS) and DB2
- Relational databases, including Microsoft SQL Server and Oracle
- Desktop databases, including Microsoft Access, Microsoft FoxPro, and Paradox
- Other data sources, including file systems, spreadsheets, text files, and e-mail message repositories

OLE DB is a key element in Microsoft Corporation's Universal Data Access (UDA) initiative and facilitates the development of applications that combine various types of queries from diverse data sources. OLE DB is the successor to Microsoft's earlier data access technology, Open Database Connectivity (ODBC), which was limited mainly to relational databases and was based on C/C++ application programming interfaces (APIs) instead of COM.

A related technology called ActiveX Data Objects (ADO) provides a simplified front-end for OLE DB that enables access to diverse data sources through OLE DB using scripting languages such as VBScript and JScript.

Architecture

OLE DB works by enabling COM interfaces to be defined that can encapsulate various types of database functionality such as record containers, query processors, and transaction coordinators. The architecture of OLE DB has three parts:

- **Data source:** This can be any structured or unstructured source of data, including ODBC-compliant databases, legacy mainframe systems, file systems, or other data source for which an OLE DB provider can be constructed.
- **OLE DB provider:** A set of COM components designed to extract data requested by an OLE DB consumer from the data source associated with the provider and to return it to the client in tabular format. Each type of data source requires its own special provider in order for clients to be able to access the data using OLE DB. OLE DB providers are available for the full range of data sources, including SQL Server, Microsoft Jet databases, Oracle, and many other common types of data sources. There is also a generic OLE DB provider for standard ODBC-compliant databases.
- **OLE DB consumer:** Represents the client application that needs to access data from the data source. Because of the standard set of interfaces used in OLE DB providers, any consumer is able to access data from any provider. Furthermore, because providers are COM objects, consumers can access them using any programming language, including C++, Microsoft Visual Basic, and Java.

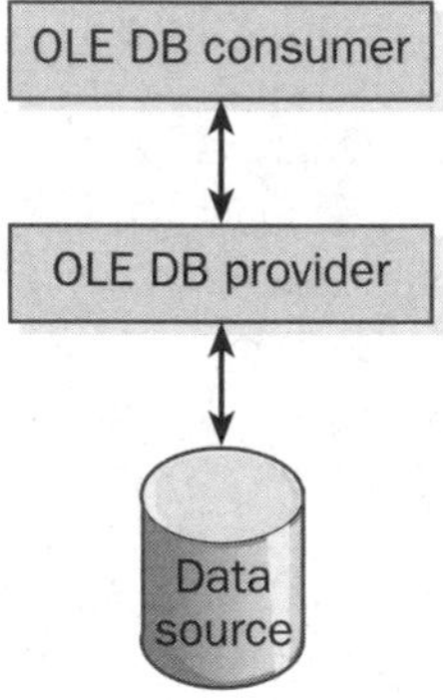

OLE DB. *The architecture of an OLE DB system.*

Examples

As an example of an OLE DB provider, the OLE DB Provider for AS/400 and VSAM enables record-level access to mainframe Virtual Storage Access Method (VSAM) files and to the AS/400 native file system. The OLE DB Provider for AS/400 and VSAM is included with Microsoft Host Integration Server. You use the OLE DB Provider for AS/400 and VSAM to develop applications for discrete data access and for record-level access to physical and logical files on AS/400 systems, in Partitioned Data Sets (PDS) and Partitioned Data Set Extended (PDSE) files, and in most versions of VSAM on mainframes. Using the OLE DB Provider for AS/400 and VSAM, programmers can access mainframe VSAM or AS/400 data using Microsoft's object-based OLE DB data access technology. Programmers can thus access source data from host systems without having to learn about Systems Network Architecture (SNA) or host applications programming. The OLE DB Provider for AS/400 and VSAM facilitates a broad range of data access, from individual records to complete files. Using ActiveX Data Objects (ADO), you can develop web-to-host integration solutions using programming languages such as Microsoft Visual Basic or scripting languages such as Microsoft Visual Basic, Scripting Edition (VBScript), and Microsoft JScript.

Marketplace

OLE DB is the dominant data access technology on the Microsoft Windows platform and is widely used in Online Analytical Processing (OLAP) systems that employ a variety of popular database platforms, including Oracle, DB2, and SQL Server. A competitor to OLE DB is the Java OLAP (JOLAP) initiative, developed by Sun Microsystems, Oracle Corporation, IBM, and Hyperion Solutions Corporation. JOLAP is a specification for creating Java-based interfaces for universal data access, and JOLAP parallels OLE DB in the same way that Java Database Connectivity (JDBC) parallels ODBC.

Notes

The name OLE DB for this technology can be confusing for two reasons:

- OLE stands for "object linking and embedding," a legacy technology that was the precursor to COM.
- DB suggests "database," but OLE DB works with any kind of data source and is not limited to relational database systems.

See Also: *ActiveX Data Objects (ADO), Component Object Model (COM), database, Java Database Connectivity (JDBC), Java Online Analytical Processing (JOLAP), online analytical processing (OLAP), open database connectivity (ODBC)*

OLE DB for OLAP

A set of Component Object Model (COM) interfaces and objects that extends OLE DB to allow access to information stored in multidimensional information sources.

Overview

OLE DB for OLAP is included in OLE DB 2 and leverages the OLE DB architecture to enable online analytical processing (OLAP) functions for COM-based applications.

See Also: *Component Object Model (COM), OLE DB*

online analytical processing (OLAP)

A technology that allows users to perform sophisticated data analysis on typically large amounts of enterprise data to gain insight on the information it contains.

Overview

Examples of OLAP analysis include financial modeling, budget forecasting, production planning, and determining broad sales and distribution trends. A query issued in an online analytical processing (OLAP) system could be, "What would be the effect on sales over the next three quarters if the cost of widgets went up 5 percent while sales dropped 15 percent?" OLAP systems primarily focus on queries that ask "What if . . . ?" In other words, OLAP systems are designed for making predictions, modeling scenarios, and supporting decision-making.

The database for an OLAP system is typically structured to allow for efficient retrieval of information. The database can be a data warehouse. A data warehouse is a database that contains static data on a particular subject, drawn from various sources. Queries issued against data warehouses tend to focus on queries that ask "What was . . . ?" or "Who did . . . ?" and are useful for analyzing past sales and growth figures. For example, "What were the total sales for the five largest subsidiaries in the first two quarters of last year?" OLAP systems and data warehouses thus constitute two complementary tools for analyzing and interpreting business data in order to make intelligent decisions.

An OLAP system is typically based on a multidimensional model, which allows users to select, explore, and view the data easily. An OLAP system generally provides the technology for creating and managing the databases. An OLAP system can have tools to discover relationships between data items by comparing the results of various OLAP queries.

Microsoft SQL Server includes tools for data warehousing and online analytical processing, including Data Transformation Services (DTS) Designer and SQL Server OLAP Services (now called Analysis Services). You can use DTS Designer to specify the workflow steps and transactions for combining multiple heterogeneous data sources into a data warehouse. You can then use OLAP Services to analyze the data, preaggregate data into multidimensional cubes for frequently asked queries, model data, create new views, and perform ad hoc sets of calculations.

For More Information

Visit the OLAP Council at *www.olapcouncil.org.*

See Also: *database*

Online Certificate Status Protocol (OCSP)

An emerging specification for validating digital certificates.

Overview

Traditional public key infrastructure (PKI) systems allow recipients of digitally signed documents to check the validity of digital certificates through comparison with a certificate revocation list (CRL), a list of invalid or expired certificates. This has several disadvantages:

O

- It places the burden of processing on the client, and for large CRLs, this can consume a lot of time.
- CRLs are typically updated every few days, so a client could receive a document with a compromised certificate and not be able to know it.

As a result of these problems, widespread adoption of digital signatures and certificates in business-to-business (B2B) e-commerce transactions has been slow. To overcome this, the Internet Engineering Task Force (IETF) has developed the Online Certificate Status Protocol (OCSP) specification to speed the process of validating certificates and shift the burden of processing away from the client.

Implementation

OCSP is implemented using strategically placed special servers called responders that maintain up-to-date CRL information. These responders are linked together using OCSP to ensure that they all share common CRL information. When a B2B trading partner sends a client a digitally signed document over the Internet, the client verifies the validity of the certificate by formatting a special request and submitting it to a responder. The responder either issues an authoritative reply such as GOOD, REVOKED, or UNKNOWN, or forwards the request to the trading partner's responder or to a third-party responder for validation.

See Also: *B2B, digital certificate, digital signature, public key infrastructure (PKI)*

OnNow

A power-management design initiative from Microsoft Corporation.

Overview

OnNow combines innovations in PC hardware and software to produce a computer that is always on but appears to be off and that responds immediately when a user or application makes a request. For example, an incoming telephone call could wake the computer and start a Telephony Application Programming Interface (TAPI)–enabled application. OnNow is designed to make personal computers function like appliances in the sense that they respond instantly to user action instead of requiring a warm-up period or boot process. OnNow is based on the Advanced Configuration and Power Interface (ACPI) specification developed by Intel Corporation, Microsoft, and Toshiba Corporation.

The power management functions of Microsoft Windows 2000, Windows XP, and Windows .NET Server, as well as those of Windows 98 and Windows Millennium Edition (Me), conform to the OnNow specifications. Instead of having the system basic input/output system (BIOS) control the power state of the system devices and peripherals, OnNow lets the operating system control it. The operating system can place various devices in a sleep state to conserve power and wake them to full power instantly when a user or application issues a request. For OnNow to function as designed, the system must have peripherals and applications that support OnNow power-management functions and the system BIOS must support ACPI.

For More Information

Find out more at *www.microsoft.com/hwdev/onnow.*

See Also: *Advanced Configuration and Power Interface (ACPI)*

OOB

Stands for out-of-band signaling, any transmission technology in which signaling is separate from the data being transmitted.

See: *out-of-band (OOB) signaling*

OpenBSD

A free version of UNIX.

Overview

OpenBSD is based on the BSD 4.4 operating system and is maintained and supported by a large community of developers. Theo de Raadt, a computer science graduate of the University of Calgary in Alberta, Canada, heads the OpenBSD project. OpenBSD is viewed as one of the most secure UNIX platforms available; even its default installation is fairly hacker-proof. OpenBSD includes support for the Kerberos IV security protocol and Internet Protocol Security (IPsec). OpenBSD also supports binary emulation of most software written for other popular UNIX flavors, such as HP-UX, SunOS, Solaris (SVR4), Linux, and FreeBSD. The current release of the OpenBSD software is version 2.5.

For More Information

Find out more about OpenBSD at *www.openbsd.org.*

See Also: *UNIX*

open database connectivity (ODBC)

A standard method of accessing data stored in relational databases and other structured data sources.

Overview

Microsoft open database connectivity (ODBC) is a database access technology that specifies a series of C/C++ application programming interfaces (APIs) that enable Microsoft Windows–based applications to access data stored in ODBC-compliant databases. ODBC thus defines a call-level interface that lets applications access data in any data source by using a suitable ODBC driver. Therefore, the ODBC APIs allow applications to be written independently of the specific database management systems (DBMSs) that contain their source data.

ODBC was originally a specification developed by an industry consortium called X/Open, which is now known as the Open Group. ODBC defines a call-level interface for implementing queries using structured query language (SQL).

Implementation

The main components of ODBC are

- **ODBC API:** A set of function calls, error codes, and SQL syntax that defines how data in a DBMS is accessed.
- **ODBC database drivers:** Dynamic-link libraries (DLLs) that can process ODBC function calls for specific DBMSs. ODBC drivers translate application calls to ODBC into calls that the specific DBMS can respond to.
- **ODBC Driver Manager:** Loads the ODBC drivers that an application needs.

ODBC uses database drivers to link applications to any ODBC-compliant DBMS. ODBC database drivers are available for more than 50 popular DBMSs, including Microsoft SQL Server, Microsoft Access, Microsoft FoxPro, Microsoft Excel, Paradox, dBASE, and delimited text files. With ODBC, applications are not tied to proprietary vendor APIs and can run independently of the underlying data communication protocols. Data can be sent and received in a format suitable for the application instead of being tailored for a vendor-specific DBMS.

Prospects

Microsoft ODBC was designed for the Windows platform. ODBC is implemented as a set of C/C++ function calls and is thus not easily accessed by other languages, such as Microsoft Visual Basic or Sun Microsystems'

Java language. ODBC is considered a legacy technology and has been superseded largely by OLE DB, Microsoft's COM-based specification for enabling universal data access using any programming language. The parallel to ODBC on the Java platform is Java Database Connectivity (JDBC).

See Also: *Component Object Model (COM), dynamic-link library (DLL), OLE DB, Java Database Connectivity (JDBC), Structured Query Language (SQL)*

Open Data-link Interface (ODI)

A legacy network protocol software interface used by early versions of Novell NetWare.

Overview

Novell and Apple Computer developed the ODI specification for defining the communication mechanism between network interface card (NIC) drivers and network protocols. Open Data-link Interface (ODI) is a legacy standard that was defined primarily for the Internetwork Packet Exchange (IPX) protocol on Novell NetWare 2.*x* and 3.*x* networks. ODI allows multiple NICs to be bound to multiple protocols.

Microsoft's NWLink IPX/SPX-Compatible Transport supports ODI for backward compatibility, but ODI has been superseded on Microsoft platforms by the network driver interface specification (NDIS).

See Also: *Internetwork Packet Exchange (IPX), NetWare, network driver interface specification (NDIS), network interface card (NIC)*

O

Open Shortest Path First (OSPF)

A popular link state dynamic routing protocol for large Internet Protocol (IP) networks.

Overview

Open Shortest Path First (OSPF) is a routing protocol that enables routers on an IP internetwork to dynamically share their routing table information with each other. The Internet Engineering Task Force (IETF) designed OSPF in the 1980s as a replacement for the earlier Routing Information Protocol (RIP), which scaled poorly for large internetworks.

OSPF is an interior gateway protocol (IGP) used for routing traffic within an autonomous system (AS), which is a large IP network managed by a single authority. Since IGPs such as OSPF are used within (not between) autonomous systems, they are sometimes called intra-AS routing protocols (as opposed to inter-AS routing protocols). OSPF is an open standard developed by the IETF, in contrast to Interior Gateway Routing Protocol (IGRP) and Enhanced Interior Gateway Routing Protocol (EIGRP), which are both vendor-specific IGPs developed by Cisco Systems.

OSPF was originally defined in RFC 1131, but this version of the protocol was experimental and not widely deployed. OSPFv2 is defined in RFC 2328 and is the most widely deployed version of OSPF in use today. The IETF has recently developed OSPFv3, which improves on earlier versions by supporting any network layer protocol (not just IP), streamlines link state advertisements, enhances security, and supports Internet Protocol version 6 (IPv6).

Uses

OSPF is widely used in two areas of networking:

- Enterprise-level private IP internetworks, including networks that span several countries, regions, or even continents. OSPF works well in a wide area network (WAN) environment because it updates routing tables only when necessary. Although RIP is still used for some small and mid-sized networks, OSPF has become the de facto IGP for large IP networks and is generally used wherever an internetwork contains about 50 or more routers.
- The Internet, the collection of publicly accessible IP internetworks and backbones connecting them.

OSPF is supported by the Internetwork Operating System (IOS) used by Cisco routers, and by the Routing and Remote Access Service (RRAS) of Microsoft Windows 2000 and Windows .NET Server.

Architecture

Dynamic routing protocols work by enabling routers to exchange routing table information with each other automatically without administrative intervention. OSPF excels in both the way it stores routing table information and in how it keeps this information current. OSPF is a link state routing protocol, which means that OSPF routers store information about the "state of the link" between the local router and other routers. OSPF stores this information in a link state database, which essentially stores a topological map of all routers in the same administrative portion of the internetwork. This may either be all routers within the autonomous system, or, if the AS is subdivided into different areas, all routers within the local area. Each OSPF router stores this link state database information in the form of a tree whose root is centered on the local router itself.

To construct the link state database, each interface of every OSPF router is assigned a cost value. This cost is generally inversely proportional to the bandwidth of the link the interface is connected to, although different cost values can be assigned as desired to shape the flow of traffic through the network. These cost values are then used to create the metrics for different routes within routing tables, with the route having the least cost being the preferred one.

Once the link state database has been constructed, OSPF routers can then use the Shortest Path First (SPF) algorithm (also called Dijkstra's algorithm) to compute the shortest path between any two subnets in the AS or area. Thus, when traffic needs to be routed from one point of the internetwork to another, the router calculates the optimal path from the link state database and forwards packets accordingly. The SPF algorithm enables routing information to be quickly recalculated if routers go down, a feature called Fast Convergence. The algorithm also ensures that routing loops do not occur.

OSPF routers communicate with each other using HELLO packets, which are sent periodically every 10 to 15 seconds and basically tell other OSPF routers that the sending router is still alive. If an OSPF router does not receive a HELLO packet from another router within an expected time, it assumes that the other router is down and that the link state database is no longer accurate. The router then floods the network with link state advertisements (LSAs) that are picked up by other OSPF routers, and a recalculation of the link state database for all routers is initiated. This recalculation process generally converges quickly, depending on the size of the internetwork and the number of routers used. LSAs contain information about incremental changes to network topology and therefore are efficient in terms of bandwidth usage. LSAs can be secured by either password protection or MD5 checksums.

Implementation

The reason OSPF scales well for large internetworks is because it is hierarchical in design. OSPF allows large autonomous systems to be further subdivided into multiple areas. OSPF routers within an area only need to know about other routers within their own area, not outside their area, and all OSPF routers within a given area share the same link state database. This keeps the routing tables small enough to prevent processing bottlenecks from occurring. OSPF areas within an AS are designated by unique 32-bit identifiers and typically have no more than about 30 or 40 routers within them.

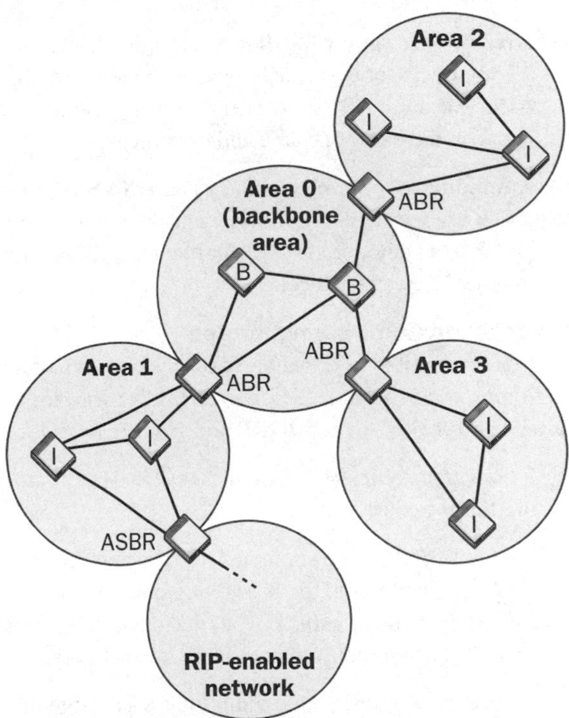

Open Shortest Path First (OSPF). *An example of an internetwork using OSPF, showing different types of OSPF routers.*

O

If an AS is subdivided into multiple OSPF areas, one of these areas must be a specially designated area called the backbone area, which has the identifier 0 (zero). Every other area within an AS must be directly connected to the backbone area in hub-and-spoke fashion, and adjacent areas communicate with each other directly between their backbones.

To support this hierarchical router topology, OSPF routers can be designated to operate in one of four different roles:

- **Internal router (I):** A router whose interfaces are all within the same area (the area where the router resides). Internal routers are used for routing traffic within the area, and their routing tables contain information only about all other internal routers in that area.
- **Backbone router (B):** A router that has at least one interface connected to the backbone area. Backbone routers are used for routing traffic within the backbone area.
- **Area border router (ABR):** A router that has multiple interfaces, one of which must be connected to the backbone area. ABRs are used for routing traffic between the backbone area and other areas.
- **Autonomous system boundary router (ASBR):** A router used to connect an autonomous system running OSPF to an autonomous system running a different interior gateway protocol.

Advantages and Disadvantages

OSPF has a number of advantages over earlier dynamic routing protocols such as RIP and over other interior gateway protocols such as IGRP and EIGRP, namely:

- It converges quickly and minimizes the risk of routing loops occurring.
- It allows routes to be summarized, reducing the size of routing tables and the processing power needed for routers to use it. This is what makes OSPF highly scalable and suitable for very large internetworks.
- It utilizes very little bandwidth unless a change in network topology has occurred. This is different from RIP routers, which periodically broadcast their entire routing table to neighbors. By contrast, OSPF transmits only incremental changes to network topology.
- It optimizes use of network bandwidth through multicasting instead of broadcasting.
- It supports variable-length subnet masking (VLSM) for classless routing.
- It is flexible and allows administrators to configure routers so that specific routes are preferred over others. This makes OSPF networks fault-tolerant because they can automatically reroute traffic when a link goes down.

Notes

When you design an OSPF-based internetwork, you should work from the top down—that is, you should first plan your autonomous system and how it will interact with other autonomous systems, and then you should subdivide the autonomous system into areas and then into individual networks. Try to map your IP address space and subnets to this hierarchy of areas and networks and assign each area a small set of network IDs that can be summarized as a small series of routes. Be sure that areas connect to each other through your high-speed backbone area and not directly to each other. (In other words, avoid back doors.) Specify cost values that relate to the amount of traffic and each router's hardware characteristics.

See Also: *autonomous system (AS), distance vector routing algorithm, dynamic routing protocol, Enhanced Interior Gateway Routing Protocol (EIGRP), interior gateway protocol (IGP), Interior Gateway Routing Protocol (IGRP), IPv6, Internetwork Operating System (IOS), link state routing algorithm, Routing Information Protocol (RIP), routing protocol, variable-length subnet mask (VLSM)*

open source

A philosophy of software development that makes application code freely available.

Overview

Open source is a philosophy of application development that allows code to be read, redistributed, and modified based on the GNU Public License (GPL) formula. The term *open source* also refers to a loosely organized community of developers dedicated to producing quality software and making it available free or at minimal cost.

Although the open-source operating system called Linux has recently garnered the majority of media attention for this movement, the underlying ideas of open-source software development go back more than 20 years to the early days of the Internet. The development of the BSD UNIX variants FreeBSD, OpenBSD, and NetBSD was a pioneering effort in opening up the UNIX platform for development. From this effort emerged the "hacker" culture of the 1980s (the term *hacker* originally meant someone who tinkered with software to make it better, not someone who maliciously tried to break into systems). The overriding philosophy of software development within the hacker community was originally that software must be free (without cost to its users), but this sharply ideological attitude alienated many in the corporate world and slowed their acceptance of software developed by the hacker community.

In 1998 the term *open source* was coined to replace the confrontational *free software* label and promote acceptance of this philosophy in the corporate arena. The result has been an acceleration of interest in open-source applications and development by enterprises over the last few years, pushed along by large investments in Linux and other open-source technologies by companies such as IBM, Sun Microsystems, Compaq Computer Corporation, and others. The result is that today many open-source applications are packaged and sold by commercial software vendors. These vendors also provide technical support and customization services for their open-source packages, a critical factor in helping open-source software gain acceptance in the corporate world.

Marketplace

Some of the more popular open-source applications and platforms include

- **Linux:** UNIX-like operating system gaining popularity in enterprise networks, especially at the server end in niche applications such as Web servers, mail servers, and storage appliances. A popular form of Linux is available from Red Hat.
- **Apache:** Popular Web server software that runs on UNIX and Linux platforms.
- **Sendmail:** Simple Mail Transport Protocol (SMTP) server software popular on the Internet.
- **PHP:** Programming language for developing Web applications for the Apache/Linux platform.
- **Samba:** Popular application that enables Linux file servers to run Server Message Block (SMB) protocol so they can interoperate with Microsoft Windows-based servers and clients.
- **MySQL:** Structured query language (SQL) database application available from AbriaSoft Company and Nusphere Corporation.
- **Bluebird:** Open-source network management platform project originally called OpenNMS and acquired by Atipa Technologies.

For More Information

Visit the Open Source Initiative (OSI) at *www.opensource.org.*

See Also: *Apache, GNU General Public License (GPL), Linux, UNIX*

O

Open Systems Interconnection (OSI) reference model

An architectural model for computer networking developed by the International Organization for Standardization (ISO).

Overview

The ISO began work on the Open Systems Interconnection (OSI) model in 1974 to address the problem that the various networking systems being developed at that time could not communicate with each other. The OSI model was intended as a reference model to which vendor-specific networking systems could be compared so that interoperability solutions could be developed. The OSI model was thus intended to allow heterogeneous systems to communicate easily with each other in an open, standardized fashion and to provide a basis for developing standardized network protocols.

Uses

The primary use for the OSI model is as a starting point for understanding how real-world networking protocols work. In other words, the OSI model is a "reference model" to which such protocols as Transmission Control Protocol/Internet Protocol (TCP/IP), DECnet, and Systems Network Architecture (SNA) can be compared. These real world-protocols generally map only loosely to the OSI reference model, however, and usually omit some of the functions, or even levels, of the OSI model. TCP/IP, for example, maps to only four levels of the OSI model—namely, the physical, network, transport, and application layers.

Another popular use of the OSI model is to simplify the process of troubleshooting networking problems. The basic idea is that upper layer protocol functions cannot work unless all lower layer functions first work properly. This means that when you troubleshoot a network problem, you should generally begin with lower-layer issues (addressing such questions as "Is the cable connected?" and "Does the network card have an IP address configured?") before progressing to testing upper layer issues ("Is the httpd daemon running on the Web server?" or "Are the routing tables up to date?"). As such, the OSI model can probably be said to be the networking professional's fundamental troubleshooting tool, as it guides the whole troubleshooting process.

O

Architecture

The premise behind the OSI model is that communication between hosts on a computer network is too complex a phenomena to be understood as a unity and that it can best be understood by breaking it down into simpler components. The ISO adopted a layered approach in which the OSI model was divided into seven logical layers. Each layer deals with a certain aspect of communications, and upper layers utilize the functions of lower layers to make network communications possible.

You can think of each layer as being logically connected to the same layer on a different computer on the network. For example, the application layer on one machine communicates with the application layer on another machine. But this communication is logical only; physical communication occurs when packets of data are sent down from the application layer of the transmitting computer, encapsulated with header information by each lower layer, and then put on the wire at the transmitting computer's physical layer. After traveling along the wire, the packets are picked up by the receiving computer's physical layer, passed up the seven layers while each layer strips off its associated header information, and then passed to the receiving computer's application layer, where the receiving application can process the data.

The first table lists the seven layers of the OSI model, starting with the lowest layers and working upward, and provides a brief description of the communications functions that operate at each level. The second table provides examples of networking protocols that operate at each layer of the OSI model.

Description of Layers of OSI Model

Layer	*Description*
Physical	Defines network transmission media, signaling methods, bit synchronization, architecture (such as Ethernet or Token Ring), and cabling topologies. Defines how network interface cards (NICs) interact with the media (cabling).
Data-link	Specifies how data bits are grouped into frames, and specifies frame formats. Responsible for error correction, flow control, hardware addressing (such as MAC addresses), and how devices such as hubs, bridges, repeaters, and Layer 2 switches operate. The Project 802 specifications divide this layer into two sublayers, the logical link control (LLC) layer and the media access control (MAC) layer.
Network	Defines logical host addresses such as IP addresses, creates packet headers, and routes packets across an internetwork using routers and Layer 3 switches. Strips the headers from the packets at the receiving end.
Transport	Sequences packets so that they can be reassembled at the destination in the proper order. Generates acknowledgments and retransmits packets. Assembles packets after they are received.

(continued)

Description of Layers of OSI Model *continued*

Layer	*Description*
Session	Defines how connections can be established, maintained, and terminated. Also performs name resolution functions.
Presentation	Translates data to be transmitted by applications into a format suitable for transport over the network. Redirector software, such as the Workstation service for Microsoft Windows NT, is located at this level. Network shells are also defined at this layer.
Application	Connects user applications with network functionality, controls how applications access the network, and generates error messages. Protocols at this level include HTTP, FTP, SMTP, and NFS.

Examples of Network Protocols Operating at Each Layer of OSI Model

Layer	*Protocols*
Physical	802.3, 802.5, 10BaseX, 100baseX, 1000BaseX, RS-232, V.35, HSSI, FDDI, PPP, DSL, ISDN, Frame Relay, ATM
Data-link	HDLC, SDLC, LAP, LAPB, AAL, SLIP, PPTP, L2F, L2TP, ARP, RARP
Network	IP, ICMP, IGMP, BOOTP, DHCP, IPX, NetBIOS, NetBEUI, APPN, IS-IS, IGRP, EIGRP, BGP, OSPF
Transport	TCP, UDP, SPX, RAS, ATP, NBP, ASP, DVMRP, RTP
Session	LDAP, DNS, RPC, PAP, SSL, TLS
Presentation	ASN.1, LU6.2, Postscript, 3270 Data Stream
Application	HTTP, SMTP, FTP, POP3, IMAP4, Telnet, SNMP, TFTP, RLOGIN, SMB, NLP, NDS, SAP, NCP, X-Windows

Implementation

Although some vendors attempted to develop networking protocols fully compliant with the OSI model, these attempts by and large failed for several reasons:

- **Complexity:** The OSI model was overly complex and its use of seven layers created unnecessary overhead in processing information for transmission on a network. Also, some communications functions, such as connectionless communication, were relatively neglected by the OSI model, while others, such as error correction and flow control, were repeated at several layers in redundant fashion.
- **Closed standards process:** The ISO standards process was relatively closed compared with the open standards process that the Internet Engineering Task Force (IETF) used to develop the TCP/IP suite of protocols. As a result, development of TCP/IP was fast while development of OSI protocols was slow, with the result that TCP/IP established itself long before OSI protocols could gain significant market foothold.

The U.S. government originally tried to require compliance with the OSI reference model for U.S. government networking solutions in the late 1980s by implementing standards called Government Open Systems Interconnection Profiles (GOSIPs). This effort was abandoned in 1995, however, and today virtually no real-world implementations of OSI model protocols exist outside of Europe, and only a few European governments still use OSI model protocols in specialized systems. Instead, the TCP/IP protocol suite has become the de facto world standard for computer networking.

See Also: *application layer, data-link layer, International Organization for Standardization (ISO), Internet Engineering Task Force (IETF), network layer, physical layer, presentation layer, session layer, Transmission Control Protocol/Internet Protocol (TCP/IP), transport layer*

optical carrier (OC-x) level

A measure of Synchronous Optical Network (SONET) capacity.

Overview

The optical carrier (OC-x) levels represent a set of signaling rates for SONET transmission over fiber-optic cabling. The basic unit is OC-1, which represents an aggregation of 810 DS-0 circuits, each having a capacity of 64 kilobits per second (Kbps), resulting in a total OC-1 capacity of 51.84 megabits per second (Mbps). In

SONET transmission, however, 30 of these DS-0 circuits are required for protocol overhead, making the actual data throughput of OC-1 only 50.112 Mbps. A single OC-1 circuit is roughly equivalent to a T3 circuit in the telco T-carrier system. Higher data transmission rates (such as OC-3 and OC-12) are simply multiplexed OC-1 circuits—for instance, OC-3 is three times faster than OC-1. The table shows the common OC-x transmission rates used in carrier-class SONET circuits.

Much of the SONET fiber used in the backbone of the Internet still runs at OC-48, although inter-exchange carriers (IXCs) and other carriers are upgrading to higher speeds. AT&T was the first IXC to deploy an OC-192 trunk from coast to coast across the United States, and UUNET, Genuity, and Cable and Wireless also have OC-192 links deployed.

Common Optical Carrier Levels

Level	*Line Rate*	*Payload Rate*
OC-1	51.840 Mbps	50.112 Mbps
OC-3	155.520 Mbps	150.336 Mbps
OC-12	622.080 Mbps	601.344 Mbps
OC-24	1.244160 Gbps	1.202688 Gbps
OC-48	2.488320 Gbps	2.405376 Gbps
OC-96	4.976640 Gbps	4.810752 Gbps
OC-192	9.953280 Gbps	9.621504 Gbps

O

Notes

OC-x levels also apply to Asynchronous Transfer Mode (ATM) networks. For wireline communications, electrical levels called Synchronous Transport Signal (STS) correspond directly to SONET optical carrier levels. For example, the OC-3 rate for SONET corresponds to the STS-3 rate for electrical transmission.

See Also: inter-exchange carrier (IXC), Internet, Synchronous Optical Network (SONET), T-carrier

optical Ethernet

More commonly called metropolitan Ethernet, the process of using Gigabit Ethernet to provision metropolitan areas with high-speed data services.

See: metropolitan Ethernet

optical networking

End-to end networking without conversion of electrical signals into optical and back again.

Overview

Traditional optical networks use fiber-optic backbones in local area networks (LANs) or long-haul fiber in wide area networks (WANs). Such networks are not "optical," however, as only a portion of the network (backbone or WAN link) employs light signals traveling over fiber-optic cabling, while the remainder of these networks involves electrical signals traveling over copper cabling. The main reason that all-optical networks have not yet become commonplace is that routing and switching functions have traditionally been implemented at the electrical level, as there has been no easy way to switch light signals themselves. As a result, traditional networks employ devices that transform electrical signals into optical ones and back again.

This situation, however, is just beginning to change as new technologies are being developed to create all-optical switches and routers. Companies in the forefront of research in this area include Cisco Systems, Nortel Networks, Lucent Technologies, and several startups. Some of the technologies being developed include switches that route light signals of a given wavelength using

- **Tiny adjustable mirrors:** An example of a product using this technology is the Lambda router from Lucent Technologies. Because this technology employs mechanical parts, however, industry analysts do not view it as especially promising.
- **Tiny bubbles in a heated liquid:** These bubbles can be used to divert light signals in response to changing temperature conditions. Agilent Technologies is one company that has worked on this approach, which can form the switching fabric of all-optical mesh networks.
- **Thermo-optic gateways:** This uses narrow silica waveguides whose transmission properties change with temperature to allow light paths to be switched on and off in milliseconds. A start-up called Lynx Photonic Networks is using this approach to develop all-optical switches.

Uses
Initial uses for optical switches and routers are likely to be in carrier-class switching equipment used by service providers and telcos. Some analysts expect such equipment to become widely available about 2005. Enterprise networks may also want to deploy such equipment in their high-speed switched backbones, but this will not likely become popular until several years later due to initial costs of such equipment. Eventually all-optical mesh networks may displace traditional Synchronous Optical Network (SONET) ring architectures in the metropolitan area network (MAN) arena and in cross-connects for long-haul circuits. SONET was originally designed to support time-sensitive voice traffic and is not efficient for carrying packetized data. About half of the capacity of SONET rings in the MAN environment is currently used for data, but the proportion of data to voice traffic is rising rapidly, a critical factor in driving research and development into new optical switching technologies.

Notes
The term *optical networking* is sometimes incorrectly used to refer to either metropolitan Ethernet (also called optical Ethernet) or lambda switching technologies.

See Also: *fiber-optic cabling, lambda switching, metropolitan Ethernet, Synchronous Optical Network (SONET)*

opto isolator
A device for electrically isolating networking components that are joined by long runs of copper cabling.

Overview
Opto isolators are commonly used in RS-232 serial connections between mainframe hosts and terminals connected by long cables. Opto isolation is typically built into line drivers for serial communication, so separate opto isolators are not required. Opto isolators also prevent ground loops from damaging networking components.

Implementation
When a network component or cable transmitting a signal is connected to one port on an opto isolator, the signal is converted briefly into light and then back into an electrical signal before exiting through the other port on the opto isolator. This brief metamorphosis from electric current into light and back again breaks the electrical connection between the two ports of the device, allowing the signal (alternating current) to flow but preventing direct current from flowing along the cable.

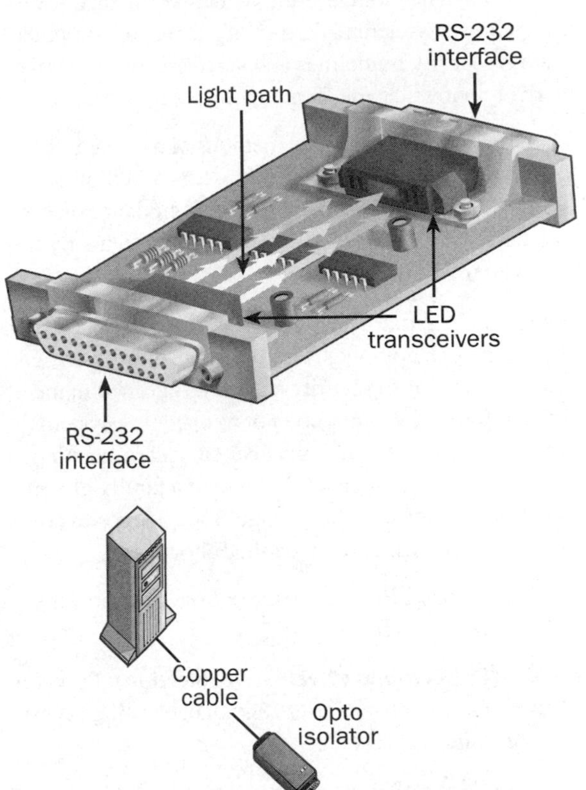

Opto isolator. *Using an opto isolator to eliminate ground loops.*

See Also: *ground loop, RS-232, serial transmission*

Orange Book
Another name for the publication Trusted Computer Systems Evaluation Criteria (TCSEC), published by the National Computer Security Center (NCSC) of the U.S. Department of Defense (DoD).

Overview

Orange Book standards are used to evaluate the security of both stand-alone and network operating systems (NOSs). The current version of this publication dates from 1985. The Orange Book, which was named for its orange cover, is actually a part of a series of computer system security guidelines and standards that are collectively known as the Rainbow Series.

The Orange Book provides methods of assessing the security of a specific computer system, and it offers hardware and software manufacturers guidance on how to create products that can be certified as secure by the U.S. government and military.

For example, Microsoft Windows NT Server in certain configurations complies with the C2 (Controlled Access Protection) security standards outlined in the Orange Book. C2 is applied not to operating systems but to specifically tested physical computers running those operating systems. C2 is one of a family of security designations that the Orange Book applies to computer systems, which include the following:

- **D (Minimal Protection):** For systems that were evaluated but failed.
- **C1 (Discretionary Security Protection):** Provides separation between users and data by using access controls.
- **C2 (Controlled Access Protection):** Adds user accountability to C1 in the form of logons, auditing, and other features.
- **B1 (Labeled Security Protection):** Builds on C2 by including informal written security policies, data labeling, and mandatory access control.
- **B2 (Structured Protection):** Builds on B1 by including formal written security policies, separation of critical and noncritical elements, and protection against covert entry.
- **B3 (Security Domains):** Builds on B2 by including reference monitoring of all object access to ensure security, a designated security administrator, and system recovery procedures.
- **A1 (Verified Design):** The same as B3, except security is verified by both testing and analysis of formal design. An A1 system is considered impenetrable to hostile attack.

organizational unit (OU)

A container object used in Microsoft Active Directory directory service to group together other objects within a domain.

Overview

Organizational units (OUs) are logical groupings of resources within a domain. An OU can contain a variety of objects, including users, groups, computers, printers, or even other OUs. OUs are essential to the scalability of Active Directory as they allow objects in a domain to be hierarchically organized in tree-like structures for easier administration. OUs thus simplify the management of Active Directory domains by allowing different administrative tasks to be delegated to different people.

OUs are often used to duplicate the organizational structure of the company within Active Directory. For example, a company might have OUs named Dev, Marketing, and Sales that represent the network resources of these three departments. OUs can also be assigned according to geographical criteria (NewYork, Los Angeles, and Detroit, for example) or by administrative function (Accounts, Shares, and Printers).

If several domains are connected into a domain tree, each domain can have its own specifically designed hierarchy of OUs. The structures of domains within a domain tree are independent of one another. However, an OU can contain objects only from its own domain, not from any other domain within a domain tree.

Implementation

When you run the Active Directory Installation Wizard to install Active Directory on a member server running Windows 2000 (thus turning the member server into a domain controller), a hierarchy of default OUs is created. This default hierarchy helps you begin administering Active Directory. It consists of the following default OUs, which you can display by using Active Directory

Users and Computers, a snap-in for Microsoft Management Console (MMC):

- **Builtin:** Includes built-in security groups such as Administrators and Account Operators
- **Computers:** Includes other computers in the domain
- **Users:** Includes domain user objects
- **Domain Controllers:** Includes the domain controllers in the domain

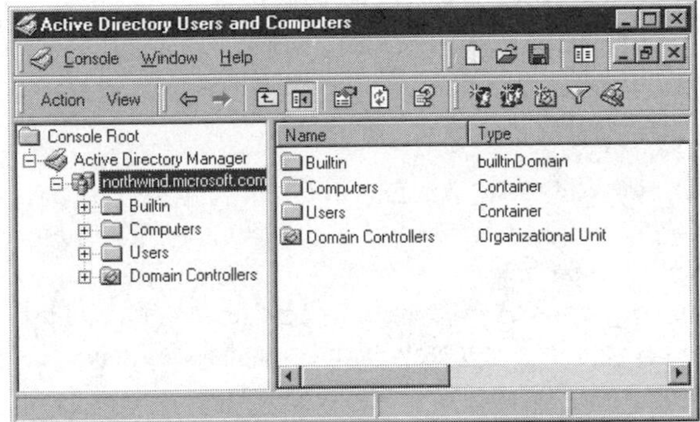

Organizational unit (OU). *The Domain Controllers OU in a domain.*

OUs are displayed in Windows 2000 administrative consoles as folders, much like the folders in a file system that store individual files. You can create OUs for groups of users who will be assigned similar permissions to network resources. You can also create separate OUs for permanent and temporary employees. You can group shared folders and printers with similar security requirements into OUs.

You should create OUs that are stable and will not change frequently, and you should avoid making the hierarchy of OUs too complicated. In a multidomain scenario with a domain tree, it is usually a good idea to make first-level OUs the same for all domains to provide consistency for the company's network resources. First-level OUs typically represent the following:

- Different geographical locations, such as countries, regions, or continents, or different functional locations, such as headquarters and branch offices. This is usually the best way to define first-level OUs.
- Different types of network resources, such as users, printers, and computers. This simplifies resource administration but might lead to too many first-level OUs.
- Different business units, such as Sales, Support, and Management. Keep it flexible and broad enough so that if your company reorganizes, you will not have to re-create everything.
- Projects and cost centers.
- When creating a hierarchy of OUs, you should generally keep the entire structure of OUs fairly shallow—no more than two or three levels—to ensure good performance when users query Active Directory. A maximum of 10 levels of OUs is recommended.

When migrating from Windows NT to Windows 2000, you can also create OUs to replace resource domains, which are used in Windows NT to simplify and centralize administration of network resources. You can also create domain trees with separate domains for resources. You should create new domains instead of OUs if you want to implement different security policies in different locations or branches of your company or in an extremely large enterprise. Otherwise, it is simpler to create only one domain and organize resources and administrative tasks using OUs within that domain.

OUs are useful in facilitating the administration of Active Directory and therefore the administration of resources on the network itself. Administrators use OUs to organize users and resources on the network and to delegate administrative and other rights and permissions to users and groups. The administrator has full access rights on all objects in the directory and can assign permissions to various subtrees of OUs for appropriate users and groups. For any OU, the administrator can delegate either of the following rights to specific users and groups:

- **Complete administrative control:** Full control over all objects in the OU
- **Limited administrative control:** The ability to modify only certain aspects of objects contained in the OU

Access to objects in Active Directory is based on discretionary access control lists (DACLs), which offer a security model similar to that used in the NTFS file system. Because objects with similar security requirements are grouped into an OU, permissions assigned to the OU are inherited by all objects in the OU. You assign permissions to OUs and other objects by using Active Directory Users and Computers.

Notes

OUs are not part of the namespace of a company, which in Windows 2000 is based on the Domain Name System (DNS). In other words, you can identify a Windows 2000 domain by using a DNS name such as northwind.microsoft.com, but you cannot identify OUs within the domain by using DNS names. However, you can specify OUs by using Lightweight Directory Access Protocol (LDAP) names.

See Also: *Active Directory, Active Directory Users and Computers, domain (DNS), Domain Name System (DNS), domain tree, Lightweight Directory Access Protocol (LDAP), object (Active Directory)*

Organization for the Advancement of Structured Information Systems (OASIS)

A nonprofit consortium that promotes Extensible Markup Language (XML) standards.

O

Overview

The Organization for the Advancement of Structured Information Systems (OASIS) is a vendor-neutral international organization that strives to develop and promote standards for structured information systems. OASIS was originally formed in 1993 as SGML Open and initially focused on the Standardized Generalized Markup Language (SGML). The name was changed to OASIS in 1998 to reflect the changed focus on XML-based standards and solutions. OASIS acts as a clearinghouse for standards and information concerning structured information systems and helps vendors design products that comply with open XML-based standards.

Together with the United Nations/CEFACT body, OASIS has been active in the development of the Electronic Business Extensible Markup Language (ebXML) standard, a new XML standard for simplifying the exchange of information between business partners to promote e-commerce. OASIS also sponsors the XML.ORG site as a reliable source of information regarding XML standards.

For More Information

Visit OASIS at *www.oasis-open.org.*

See Also: *Electronic Business Extensible Markup Language (ebXML), XML*

Orthogonal Frequency Division Multiplexing (OFDM)

An emerging technology for achieving higher data rates in wireless communications.

Overview

Orthogonal Frequency Division Multiplexing (OFDM) is an emerging signal modulation technology for high-speed communications. While OFDM can be employed in both wireless and wireline communication systems, the technology is mainly being developed to enhance transmission speeds of cellular communications systems beyond the range of emerging third-generation (3G) systems. Other improvements that OFDM provides include overcoming line-of-site (LOS) communications problems, extending the range and subscriber coverage areas of cellular communication systems, and overcoming antenna size issues relating to fixed wireless communications.

Prospects

Current work on OFDM involves harmonizing competing standards developed by the Institute of Electrical and Electronic Engineers (IEEE) and the European Telecommunications Standards Institute-Broadband Radio Access Networks (ETSI-BRAN) standards bodies. Practical OFDM systems are under development by AT&T and others for future fourth-generation (4G) cellular communication systems. Another example is Flarion Technologies, a spin-off from Lucent Technologies, which is developing an OFDM signal-processing scheme called Flash OFDM.

See Also: *3G, cellular communications, wireless networking*

OS/2

A network operating system from IBM.

Overview

OS/2 is a 32-bit operating system that was originally developed by IBM and Microsoft Corporation as a replacement for the 16-bit text-based Microsoft Disk Operating System (MS-DOS). After Microsoft left the project to focus on its own Microsoft Windows operating system, IBM continued to develop OS/2, which is now called OS/2 Warp and includes both server and desktop versions.

IBM's current line of OS/2 software includes the OS/2 Warp Server, the OS/2 Advanced Warp Server, and the OS/2 Warp 4 client. OS/2 Warp in its various forms is a 32-bit preemptive multitasking operating system that supports application, file and print, groupware, and Web server configurations as well as desktop workstations. OS/2 Warp Server includes symmetric multiprocessing support and clustering technologies for high-availability server environments. OS/2 Warp Server supports most common networking protocols and all types of clients, including Microsoft Windows, Apple Macintosh, and AIX clients.

For More Information

Visit OS/2 Warp online at *www.software.ibm.com/os/warp.*

See Also: *Microsoft Windows, network operating system (NOS)*

OSI model

Stands for Open Systems Interconnection model, a reference model for computer networking developed by the International Organization for Standardization (ISO).

See: *Open Systems Interconnection (OSI) reference model*

OSPF

Stands for Open Shortest Path First, a popular link state dynamic routing protocol for large Internet Protocol (IP) networks.

See: *Open Shortest Path First (OSPF)*

OS X

A new operating system for the Apple Macintosh computing platform.

Overview

Mac OS X represents a radical departure from earlier versions of the Mac OS. Unlike earlier versions, the OS X kernel called Mach is based on a version of the UNIX operating system called BSD 4.4. This radical departure allows the Macintosh platform to marry its advanced graphical user interface and multimedia features with the stability and reliability of the well-tested UNIX platform.

Other enhancements in Mac OS X include

- Apple Computer's new Quartz 2-D imaging technology
- 3-D imaging based on the OpenGL standard
- Integrated QuickTime technology
- Adobe Portable Document Format (PDF) printing technology
- A powerful new graphical user interface called Aqua

See Also: *Macintosh, UNIX*

O

OU

Stands for organizational unit, a container object used in Active Directory directory service to group together other objects within a domain.

See: *organizational unit (OU)*

Outlook

Microsoft Corporation's premier mail client and full-featured desktop information-management application.

Overview

Microsoft Outlook, which is part of the Microsoft Office suite, enables users to manage their messages, appointments, contacts, tasks, and activities. It also integrates with other Office applications at the front end and with Microsoft Exchange at the back end to enable users to collaborate using e-mail, calendar, contact lists, task lists, journals, and notes. Outlook is a full Messaging Application Programming Interface (MAPI) client and interoperates with all e-mail systems that support MAPI.

Outlook can be run as a stand-alone application or as part of the Office suite. Outlook's advanced features include the following:

- Support for MAPI, Post Office Protocol version 3 (POP3), Internet Mail Access Protocol version 4 (IMAP4), and Hypertext Transfer Protocol (HTTP)
- A common user interface with other Office components
- AutoNameCheck, message tracking, message recall, embedded hyperlinks, and other e-mail enhancements
- Enhancements to calendar and scheduling functions to facilitate processing of meeting requests, tracking attendees, and configuring the duration of appointments
- Simplified tracking of "to do" lists using task requests, task tracking, status reports, and task categorizations
- Custom Outlook forms for creating custom collaboration applications

For More Information

You can find out more about Microsoft Outlook at *www.microsoft.com/outlook.*

See Also: *e-mail*

Outlook Express

A basic Internet mail and news client included with Microsoft Internet Explorer version 4 and later.

Overview

Microsoft Outlook Express replaces the older Microsoft Internet Mail and News client included with Internet Explorer 3 and includes the following features:

- Customizable three-pane view that shows folders, messages, and message content
- WYSIWYG editing of Hypertext Markup Language (HTML) messages
- Support for Internet standard protocols, including Simple Mail Transfer Protocol (SMTP), Post Office Protocol version 3 (POP3), Internet Mail Access Protocol version 4 (IMAP4), Lightweight Directory Access Protocol (LDAP), and Network News Transfer Protocol (NNTP)
- Support for multiple Internet service provider (ISP) accounts so that users can receive mail from multiple e-mail accounts and download all messages into the same Inbox
- Integration with Internet Explorer security zones
- Automatic name resolution (matching address book entries to a typed username)
- Stationery templates for adding a personal touch to messages
- Enhanced Inbox rules for filtering incoming mail

out-of-band management (OBM)

Remotely managing telecommunications equipment using out-of-band (OOB) signaling.

Overview

Out-of-band management (OBM) is a popular method of remotely managing the wide area network (WAN) telecommunications components. OBM manages devices "outside of the normally used bandwidth," in other words, using a separate communications link than the one being used for data transmission. These out-of-band (OOB) links are typically secondary serial communication links. WAN devices typically managed using OOB include routers, switches, access servers, multiplexers, and Channel Service Unit/Data Service Units (CSU/DSUs). Devices that can be managed out of band usually have an RS-232 port or some other kind of serial interface for remote control of their functions.

OBM offers several advantages over in-band management systems such as Simple Network Management Protocol (SNMP) management systems. For one thing, OBM is more secure than in-band management since it typically uses a dedicated serial link for management purposes, Also, SNMP employs the network itself for communication, so if the WAN link goes down, the remote station cannot use SNMP to determine the problem because SNMP functions only if the WAN link is working. OBM is often used as a backup system for in-band SNMP management, when the devices have limited SNMP support, or when the cost of an SNMP management system cannot be justified. You can often manage a device in-band by using a remote Telnet client for entering the same commands that are used in OBM.

Implementation

In a typical OBM setup, a remote PC is connected by a modem through a phone line to a code-operated switch located at the office local area network (LAN). This switch controls networking and telecommunication devices such as routers, bridges, switches, CSUs, and even power supplies through their RS-232 serial connections. Alternatively, the modem might be connected directly to a remote modem connected to the device being managed. In either case, the result is a separate low-cost dial-up circuit connecting the administrator and the network devices that is independent of the main network connection, which is usually a more expensive T1 or other leased line. The administrator can thus access the WAN device from a remote location even when the WAN link itself is down, and can troubleshoot the problem from off-site. OBM also allows administrators to access and configure WAN devices without disturbing the WAN link itself.

You could use OBM functions on a power supply to remotely reboot or reset your network devices when they go down. You can use out-of-band switches to select different serial interfaces remotely over a modem by issuing simple ASCII commands to different devices. You can even use OBM to remotely configure and control devices on your network. OBM devices are a useful part of a network disaster recovery plan.

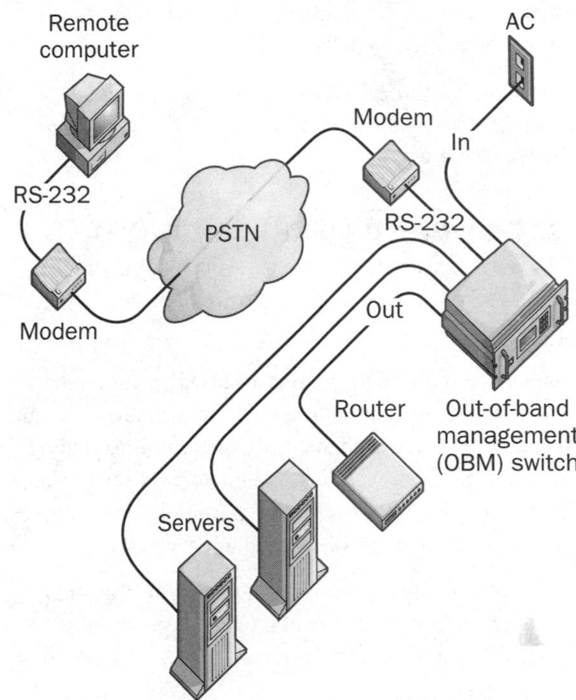

Out-of-band management (OBM). *Managing WAN hardware out-of-band.*

For networking devices that you can configure and troubleshoot using out-of-band connections, you usually perform management tasks by connecting to a serial port (also called the setup port or configuration port) either locally with a cable or remotely through a modem. You usually use text-based commands from a terminal emulator program such as Windows HyperTerminal, which can emulate a VT100 terminal. You can often control access using passwords for extra security.

You can often use out-of-band transmission so that a device that enters a problem state calls an administrator's pager through a modem. The administrator can then dial in to the device remotely and correct the problem. Some network devices include built-in modems and data switches for remote OBM.

OBM is also used in other areas—for example, servers are often built with OBM capabilities and when they enter a problem state can also take advantage of an OOB connection to deliver an alert.

See Also: *out-of-band (OOB) signaling, Simple Network Management Protocol (SNMP), wide area network (WAN)*

out-of-band (OOB) signaling

Any transmission technology in which signaling is separate from the data being transmitted.

Overview

Out-of-band (OOB) signaling uses one or more channels for transmitting data or voice information and one special out-of-band channel for performing signaling functions such as establishing and terminating the communication link, controlling flow, or transmitting error information. The out-of-band channel can be

- A physically separate set of wires (such as pins 4 and 5 of an RS-232 cable, which perform flow control functions and do not carry data)
- A multiplexed system in which bandwidth is divided into two or more channels within the same set of wires such as Integrated Services Digital Network (ISDN), in which the two B channels and one D channel are multiplexed onto the same set of wires)

The opposite of out-of-band is in-band, in which signaling information is sent over the same channel as the data transmission. Out-of-band transmission is usually considered a better choice than in-band transmission for the following reasons:

- None of the valuable data bandwidth is used for signaling.
- The data stream is not interrupted with signaling information.
- The signaling information cannot be disrupted by the noise created by the data transmission.
- Data transmission characters cannot accidentally (or purposefully) initiate control actions.

Notes

Out-of-band circuits are often used for out-of-band management (OBM) of wide area network (WAN) devices. These are usually physically separate dial-up lines.

See Also: *in-band signaling, out-of-band management (OBM)*

outsourcing

Contracting business functions to external companies.

Overview

Outsourcing of IT (information technology) needs has been an increasing trend in recent years, but such outsourcing is not new. Broadly speaking, for the first few decades of the computing era outsourcing reigned supreme as companies either leased mainframe technology and staff or bought time-sharing services from mainframe computing centers. The client/server revolution of the 1980s then saw the rise of in-house IT departments as large companies sought to gain strategic control of their own IT services and smaller companies tended to rely more on outsourcing deployment and troubleshooting services to consultants and system integrators. In the late 1990s, however, the pendulum began to swing back toward outsourcing a larger share of IT functions. This happened for several reasons:

- Time-to-market has become critical in the accelerating Internet economy, and startup companies often gain a significant edge in this respect by outsourcing their system management and application needs to a new breed of Application Service Providers (ASPs) and Management Service Providers (MSPs).
- The Internet itself has become a key enabler for outsourcing network, desktop, and application management through new browser-based management platforms. The Internet has also realized the virtual enterprise in which companies can manage contract IT staff in remote locations in order to fulfill application development, technical training, and help desk needs that are difficult or expensive to achieve locally.

- The difficulty of recruiting and hiring experienced IT professionals and the cost of retaining them has made outsourcing of many IT functions an attractive solution for many companies.

Today, common outsourced IT functions and services include application hosting, messaging, disaster recovery, enterprise resources planning (ERP), customer relationship management (CRM), supply-chain logistics management, and help desk functions.

Marketplace

The big three companies in the enterprise IT outsourcing arena are EDS, Computer Sciences Corporation, and IBM Global Services. These companies together service the largest share of the corporate outsourcing market, but dozens of ASPs and other service providers have arisen in the last few years to compete in this arena. In 2000, the total IT outsourcing market was estimated at over $100 billion and was growing at over 10 percent a year.

See Also: *application service provider (ASP), Customer Relationship Management (CRM), enterprise resource planning (ERP), Management Service Provider (MSP)*

owner

The user ultimately responsible for the permissions assigned to a file, usually the creator of the file.

Overview

In the NTFS file system, for example, a file stored on an NTFS volume always has an owner. Ownership creates a trail of accountability for actions performed on the file. By default, a file's owner has permission to modify the object's discretionary access control list (DACL) by granting users and groups permissions for various objects.

The ownership of a file on an NTFS volume can be changed in two ways:

- The user who owns the file, or any user who has full control permission on the file, can grant the NTFS take ownership permission to another user, thus allowing that user to take ownership of the file by using the file's Security property sheet. Users can be allowed to take ownership of a file they do not own, but ownership cannot be assigned to them by other users (even the original owner or an administrator).
- Members of the Administrators group can always take ownership of any file by using the Security property sheet. When an administrator takes ownership of a file, the Administrators group, and not the individual administrator, becomes the file's owner.

Notes

In the Microsoft Windows 2000 and Microsoft .NET Server operating systems, objects in Active Directory directory service also have owners. The user who creates an object in Active Directory becomes the object's owner. The owner controls the permissions for the object and its attributes. Ownership of an object in Active Directory can be changed in ways similar to those for a file on an NTFS volume.

See Also: *NTFS file system (NTFS)*

O

P2P

Applications that enable computers to function as both clients and servers.

Overview

Although the acronym *P2P* officially stands for "peer-to-peer," the acronym has taken on a somewhat different meaning than the earlier concept of peer-to-peer networking that evolved in the 1980s. The original idea referred to networks that were too small to warrant having dedicated servers, hence client machines could share files with one another to facilitate collaboration between users. Such peer-to-peer networks became popular with the release of Microsoft Windows for Workgroups (WFW). A key characteristic of such networks was that security was distributed—that is, there was no central authentication server to manage logon security and access control. As such, peer networking is suitable only for low security environments. Microsoft Corporation developed Windows NT to provide centralized security for such networks, turning them into domain-based networks instead of peer-to-peer ones.

The concept of peer networking has evolved in the last few years, however, to include a whole range of powerful applications that allow client computers to share resources while bypassing servers. This new concept is today called P2P and was popularized by the music sharing service called Napster, which at its peak had over 20 million users worldwide. An essential ingredient in the popularity of the P2P model is the ubiquity of the Internet. However, P2P is also making inroads into traditional enterprise corporate networks as well.

Uses

Some of the emerging uses for P2P applications and platforms include

- **File sharing:** P2P allows clients to share files with one another without using network servers. Napster is the classic example here, but today's P2P platforms can share any kind of file, including text files and documents, multimedia files, virus definition files, and software patches and updates.
- **Shared processing:** This enables multiple client machines to share the processing load for certain tasks, reducing pressure on network servers. A good example here is the Search for Extra-Terrestrial Intelligence (SETI) at Home Project developed by the University of California at Berkeley. SETI at Home has more than 2 million registered users who have downloaded P2P software and use it to help search radio telescope signal archives for messages that extraterrestrials might be sending from other star systems. Another classic example in this category is Intel Corporation, which has saved $500 million over 10 years by using a P2P program called Netbatch to harness the processing power of thousands of workstations for the job of chip design.
- **Automatic software distribution:** Many enterprises have expressed interest in P2P as a vehicle for distributing software such as virus updates and system patches across the network. One company that pioneered in this direction is myCIO.com (now McAfee AsaP), which developed antivirus definition distribution software that employs token-based authentication to ensure secure distribution of updates.
- **B2B collaboration:** P2P provides new mechanisms for businesses to interact online to integrate supply-chain processes and foster a collaborative business environment. An example of such an application is Mangomind from Mangosoft, which provides a secure real-time Internet-based file-sharing service along the P2P model. Consilient is another company with P2P platforms for B2B linkage.

Marketplace

P2P file sharing services are popular on the Internet. Napster was the pioneer here, and newer alternatives include BearShare, Gnutella, LimeWire, and ToadNode. In the enterprise arena, secure P2P file sharing platforms are also appearing from such vendors as NextPage, Tacit Knowledge Systems, OpenCola, 3Path, and Groove Networks. Many of these platforms can not only share files but also deliver messages, distribute Web content, locate content of interest automatically using rules-based procedures, and perform other functions.

In the area of distributed processing, a P2P application called WebProc from Datasynapse securely allows unused cycles of client machines to be used for complex processing tasks, offloading some of the processing burden from network servers. Porivo Technologies has a similar product called Peer, implemented as a Java-based application, and Entropia has a similar product.

Other emerging P2P vendors include AgentWare, with its P2P platform for managing web sites, portals, and B2B e-commerce; WorldStreet Corporation with P2P software for online brokerages and investment institutions; and Porivo Technologies with Web performance testing software.

Prospects

Early use of Napster and similar P2P file sharing applications by users on corporate networks caused headaches for IT (information technology) managers, as these applications tended to eat up available bandwidth and thus deny access to legitimate network services. This initially created a bias against P2P platforms in the enterprise that still remains in some measure today. Other reasons network administrators have been reluctant to utilize P2P in the enterprise are the lack of standards and because P2P applications bypass centralized server-based network security. Nevertheless, interest in P2P continues to grow in the enterprise.

Major industry players Intel Corporation, Hewlett-Packard, and others have established the P2P Working Group to steer the development of P2P standards, especially in the area of security. The Working Group's efforts are directed toward making P2P a more secure platform for use in the enterprise. Microsoft's .NET platform and Sun Microsystems' JXTA also represent exciting initiatives that will enable secure, enterprise-class P2P applications to be developed for enterprise use.

See Also: *B2B, JXTA, .NET platform, peer-to-peer network*

P3P

Stands for Platform for Privacy Preferences, a standard specifying how Web sites communicate their privacy policy to visitors.

See: *Platform for Privacy Preferences (P3P)*

package

In Microsoft Systems Management Server (SMS), an object that defines software to the SMS system.

Overview

Packages store information about software so that various components of the software can be identified as a group. You use SMS to install a package on client computers, share the package so that it can be run from network servers, and maintain inventory information about the package. You can create packages for all types of software, including Microsoft, third-party, and in-house applications; data files; batch files; and scripts.

A package contains a definition of the files that make up the software, plus other configuration and identification information. You create packages using the Systems Management Server Administrator program. Packages are stored in the SMS database at your site and at all subsites. After you create a package, you must also create a job that can be used to install the package on clients or share the package on servers.

You use a package server—a type of server in an SMS implementation—to install and maintain packages. There are two kinds of package servers:

- **Source servers:** These contain the original source files for software to be distributed.
- **Distribution servers:** These store and distribute the package files.

Notes

If you want to perform software inventory, you need not explicitly create a job for this purpose. When you define the inventory properties for a package, SMS automatically creates a system job to update the SMS inventory components. This allows SMS to maintain inventory information on the package.

See Also: *Systems Management Server (SMS)*

packet

The fundamental unit of information transmitted over a packet-switched network or digital communication link.

Overview

A packet is essentially a chunk of information sent over a network. For example, to transfer a file from one host to another on the Internet using the File Transfer Protocol (FTP), the file is first broken down into a series of chunks of data that are packaged into units called "packets." These packets have a header added to the beginning of the packet that contains control information concerning the packet type, the source address, and the packet's destination address. They may also contain error-checking information, often as a trailer (footer) added to the end of the packet. Packets have a logical structure based on the particular type of protocol used, but the general structure of a packet always includes a header followed by a payload (data) and an optional trailer. Packets can also have different sizes and structures depending on the underlying network architecture.

A packet might also be called a datagram, a frame, or a cell, depending on the type of networking under consideration. However, from the perspective of the Open Systems Interconnection (OSI) reference model, the terms *packet* and *frame* have precise definitions and are considered different entities. From the OSI perspective, a packet is an electronic envelope containing information formed in one of the layers from Layer 3 through Layer 7 of the OSI model, but a frame is an electronic envelope of information that includes the packet as well as other information from all seven layers of the OSI model.

See Also: *frame, Open Systems Interconnection (OSI) reference model, packet switching, packet-switching services*

packet assembler/ disassembler (PAD)

A device that connects computers and other networking equipment to an X.25 packet-switched network.

Overview

Packet assembler/disassemblers (PADs) are telecommunications devices that break down binary data streams into individual packets suitable for asynchronous transmission over X.25 networks. PADs also format packets by adding suitable headers to enable the packets to reach their destination. When receiving data, a PAD also accepts packets from the network and translates (reassembles) them into a data stream that the computer can understand. The PAD's function is thus to assemble data such as strings of characters into packets to transmit over the X.25 network to the remote host and to disassemble packets that are received.

PADs were originally developed to enable remote dumb terminals to communicate over X.25 networks with mainframe computers. They were needed because such terminals lacked the processing capability to implement the X.25 protocol on them directly. The PAD thus acted as an intermediary between the terminal and the mainframe and buffered data received from the terminal and assembled or disassembled it into X.25 packets depending on whether it was transmitting or receiving.

Although early PADs required external data communications equipment (DCE), most PADs now have integrated DCE to allow them to be directly connected to asynchronous data terminal equipment (DTE) such as terminals, computers, routers, and access servers.

Implementation

When one computer on an X.25 network wants to communicate with another computer in a remote location, the first computer sends a signal to its attached PAD requesting a connection to the remote computer. The remote computer responds by either accepting the request and initiating full-duplex communication or rejecting the request. Either computer can then terminate the link at any time. Note that this communication link is for data only—X.25 does not support voice transmission. Note also that PADs are DCEs, and even though they are located at the customer premises, they are actually considered nodes on the X.25 network and are therefore drawn within the cloud in the diagram.

When PADs are used for providing remote access through dumb terminals over X.25 to mainframe or minicomputer hosts, the terminals require PADs but the mainframe hosts do not—they are directly connected to the X.25 network. To configure the PAD, the administrator must specify a number of PAD parameters such as echo control, data forwarding, break signals, line folding, and binary speed. The PAD parameters (usually 22 for each terminal that the PAD services) are defined by an International Telecommunication Union (ITU) protocol called X.3. Communication between terminals and PADs is governed by the protocol X.28, and communication between the PAD and the remote host is governed by X.29.

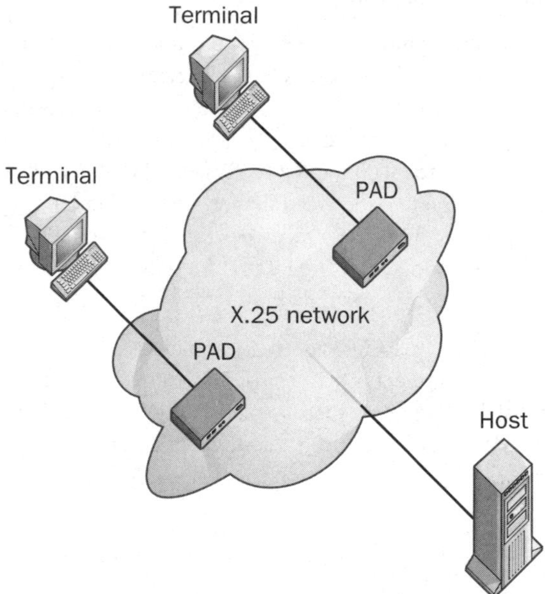

Packet assembler/disassembler (PAD). *Using PADs to connect dumb terminals to a mainframe host.*

PADs come in different configurations. Some PADs support eight or more asynchronous DTE connections and have multiple DCE interfaces for maximum configurability. Typically, you connect your asynchronous hosts (computers) to the PAD using RJ-45 connectors on twisted-pair cabling. The PAD then connects to a Channel Service Unit/Data Service Unit (CSU/DSU), which interfaces with the X.25 connection using a serial interface such as RS-232 or V.35. Some PADs now have integrated CSU/DSU functionality to allow them to be directly connected to the X.25 networks using serial interfaces. Some PADs even support both X.25 and frame relay and can thus be used to ease the migration path from older X.25 to newer frame relay services.

Notes

The Routing and Remote Access Service (RRAS) on Microsoft Windows 2000 and Windows .NET Server support PADs and other ways of connecting to X.25 networks, such as X.25 smart cards and special modems for dialing up X.25 carriers such as SprintNet and Infonet.

See Also: *Channel Service Unit/Data Service Unit (CSU/DSU), data communications equipment (DCE), data terminal equipment (DTE), frame relay, International Telecommunication Union (ITU), packet switching, packet-switching services, RS-232, serial transmission, terminal, V.35, X.25*

packet filtering

Controlling a flow of packets based on information contained within the packets.

Overview

Packet filtering is simply a way of controlling traffic on a packet-switched network such as the Internet. Filtering can be performed on packet attributes such as source address, destination address, packet type, packet length, and source and destination port numbers.

Most routers support some degree of packet filtering capability that enables these routers to provide firewall capabilities for protecting a network from unauthorized traffic. Such routers are often called packet-filtering routers or screening routers. Note, however, that implementing packet filtering on a traditional hardware router can cause a performance degradation of about 30 percent on the router's ability to handle network traffic.

Administrators can create rules or policies on screening routers for filtering out unwanted packets and can arrange these rules in the most efficient order. Using these rules, different actions can then be performed on each individual packet that arrives at the router. For example, a packet arriving at the router may be forwarded to its destination, dropped (ignored), or rejected (an error message is returned to the sender). Also, the router may log the event or send an alert to notify the administrator if configured. More sophisticated routers can also

- Modify the contents of the packet—for example, to perform Network Address Translation (NAT).
- Route the packet to a different destination than intended—for example, in load balancing a connection.

Some routers and firewalls can actually ping the source address of each packet to ensure that addresses local to the company network are coming from inside the network and are not being spoofed by a hacker outside the network.

Implementation

Packet filtering can be implemented on screening routers and firewall appliances in two basic ways: static filtering and dynamic filtering.

- **Static packet filtering:** This provides limited security by configuring selected ports as either permanently open or permanently closed. For example, to deny outside packets access to a company intranet server on port 80 (the standard port number for the Hypertext Transfer Protocol, or HTTP) you could configure the router or firewall to block all incoming packets directed toward port 80.
- **Dynamic packet filtering:** Also called stateful packet filtering, this provides enhanced security by allowing selected ports to be opened at the start of a legitimate session and then closed at the end of the session to secure the port against attempts at unauthorized access.

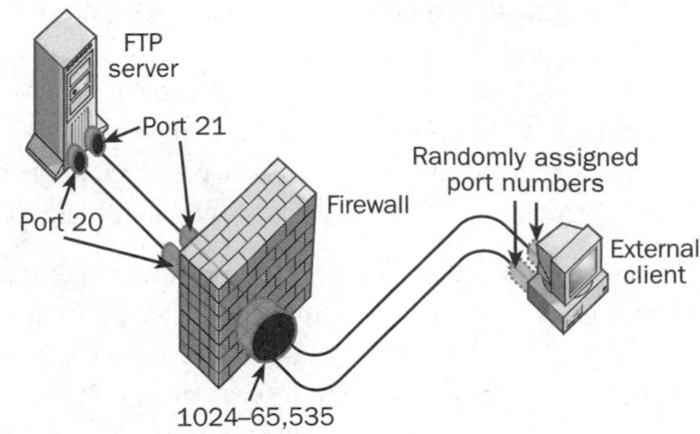

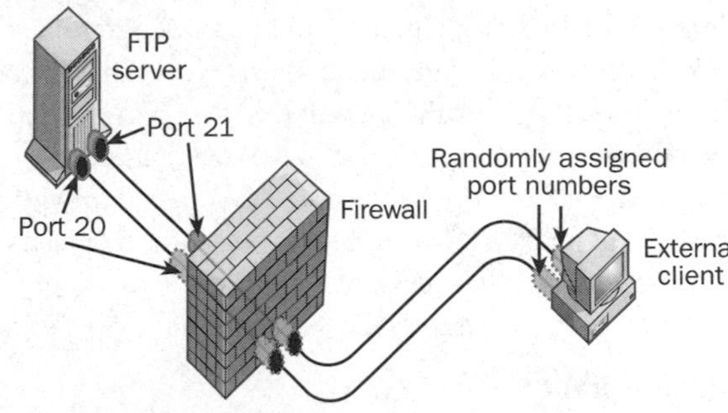

Packet filtering. *Two forms of packet filtering.*

Dynamic packet filtering is particularly useful for protocols that allocate ports dynamically—for example, with the File Transfer Protocol (FTP). If you want to grant outside users secure access to an FTP server behind the firewall (within the corporate network), you need to consider the following:

- Port 21 (the FTP control port) needs to be left permanently open so that the FTP server can "listen" for connection attempts from outside clients. A static filtering rule can accomplish this.

P

- Port 20 (the FTP data port) needs to be opened only when data will be uploaded to or downloaded from the FTP server. With static filtering this port would have to be configured as permanently open, which could provide a door for hacking attempts. Dynamic filtering allows this port to be opened at the start of an FTP session and then closed at the end of the session.

Then, in order to establish an FTP connection with the client, the FTP server randomly assigns two port numbers in the range 1024 through 65,535 to the client, one for the control connection and one to transfer data. Because these ports are assigned randomly, there is no way to predict which ports above 1024 must be able to be opened by the firewall. With static filtering, you would therefore have to leave all ports above 1024 permanently open if you wanted to allow FTP access through the firewall, which would be a real security risk. With dynamic filtering, however, you can configure rules on the firewall that will read the packets issued by the server, dynamically open the two randomly assigned ports to allow a session to be opened, monitor the flow of packets to ensure that no unauthorized users attempt to hijack the session, and close the randomly assigned ports when the FTP session ends.

Marketplace

Most traditional hardware routers today support various degrees of packet filtering functions. Packet filtering can be configured on Cisco routers using Cisco Internetwork Operating System (IOS) commands.

An alternative to using screening routers is using a dedicated server with Microsoft Internet Security and Acceleration (ISA) Server installed. ISA Server includes dynamic packet filtering among its various other security features. If packet filtering is enabled, all incoming and outgoing packets are rejected unless an exception is explicitly created that allows them to pass. Packet filters can be enabled on ISA Server only if the machine has an external network interface, such as one connected to a distrusted network such as the Internet. ISA Server includes a number of predefined filters that you can use to quickly configure exceptions for common protocols when securing your network to the Internet. ISA Server also supports domain filters for allowing or denying access to Hypertext Transfer Protocol (HTTP) or File Transfer Protocol (FTP) services based on the source Internet Protocol (IP) address or Domain Name System (DNS) domain name. ISA Server can issue alerts to inform you when packets are rejected or illegal packets are detected. It will also keep a log of alerts that occur for analysis and record keeping.

See Also: *Domain Name System (DNS), File Transfer Protocol (FTP), firewall, Hypertext Transfer Protocol (HTTP), Internet Security and Acceleration Server (ISA Server), Internetwork Operating System (IOS), IP address, packet, port, router*

packet forwarding

Accepting a packet and transmitting it to its destination.

Overview

A router receives packets from hosts on one attached network and either forwards them to hosts on another attached network or forwards them to another router for further forwarding to a more distant network.

The exact way in which a packet is forwarded is typically based on a comparison of the packet's destination address with the routing table stored in the router. Each act of forwarding performed by a router is called a hop across the internetwork.

See Also: *hop count, packet, router*

packet switching

A form of communication in which data is broken into small packets that are forwarded individually across a network to their destination.

Overview

Packet switching allows data to be broken down and sent over computer networks and telecommunications services in short bursts called packets that contain sequence numbers so that they can be reassembled at the destination. These packets typically travel over a network or telecom "cloud" that contains routers or switches that examine and route packets from one such device to another, causing the packets to "hop" from switch to switch or router to router. Individual packets belonging to the same communication session might be switched over several different paths, depending on factors such as traffic congestion and switch availability at any given moment. Once the packets reach their destination, they are reassembled into a bit-stream to enable reliable communications to occur.

Types

Packet switching is the transmission method used for most computer networks because the data transported by these networks is fundamentally bursty in character and can tolerate latency (due to lost or dropped packets). In other words, the transmission bandwidth needed varies greatly in time, from relatively low traffic due to background services such as name resolution services, to periods of high bandwidth usage during activities such as file transfer. This contrasts with voice or video communication, in which a steady stream of information must be transmitted in order to maintain transmission quality and in which latency must remain minimized to preserve intelligibility.

The Internet is the prime example of a packet-switched network based on the Transmission Control Protocol/ Internet Protocol (TCP/IP). A series of routers located at various points on the Internet's backbone forwards each packet received on the basis of destination address until the packet reaches its ultimate destination. TCP/IP is considered a connectionless packet-switching service because TCP connections are not kept open after data transmission is complete.

X.25 public data networks are another form of packet-switching service, in which packets (or more properly, frames) formatted with the High-level Data Link Control (HDLC) protocol are routed between different X.25 end stations using packet switches maintained by X.25 service providers. Unlike TCP/IP, X.25 is considered a connection-oriented packet-switching protocol because it is possible to establish permanent virtual circuits (PVCs) that keep the logical connection open even when no data is being sent. However, X.25 can be configured for connectionless communication by using switched virtual circuits (SVCs). An X.25 packet-switched network typically has a higher and more predictable latency (about 0.6 seconds between end stations) than a TCP/IP internetwork. This is primarily because X.25 packet switches use a store-and-forward mechanism to buffer data for transmission bursts, which introduces additional latency in communication. In addition, X.25 uses error checking between each node on the transmission path, while TCP/IP uses only end-to-end error checking.

Frame relay (formerly called "fast packet switching") is another connection-oriented packet-switching service that gives better performance than X.25. It does this by switching packets immediately instead of using the store-and-forward mechanism of X.25 networks. Frame relay also eliminates flow control and error checking to speed up transmission. This is possible because frame relay networks use modern digital telephone lines, which are intrinsically much more reliable than the older analog phone lines on which much of the X.25 public network still depends. Frame relay supports only connection-oriented PVCs for its underlying switching architecture.

Finally, Asynchronous Transfer Mode (ATM) is yet another packet-switching service in which small fixed-length packets called cells are switched between points on a network.

Comparison

Packet switching is different from circuit switching, in which switches are configured in a fixed state for the duration of the session so that the route the data takes is fixed. A network that is circuit-switched requires a dedicated switched communication path for each communication even if its full bandwidth is not being used. In packet switching, bandwidth can be used when available for more efficient transmission. Circuit switching is generally used in telephone systems, and packet switching is used for computer networks. Digital cellular phone services were originally circuit-switched as well, but most cellular systems are now packet-switched networks to achieve greater efficiency in data transmission.

Another difference between packet switching and circuit switching is that circuits must first be established before any data is sent, and this generally involves a certain amount of setup time. During this process, the request for a circuit connection must pass through the circuit-switched network, resources must be reserved for the connection, and a signal must be returned to the initiating station when the circuit is established and data transmission can begin. Circuit-switched networks are thus useful only when the duration of the data transmission is much longer than the setup time involved in establishing the circuit. With packet switching, data can be sent at the start of transmission, which is better suited to the bursty, irregular nature of short network transmissions over a computer network or WAN link. Packet switching is thus a connectionless service in which it is unnecessary to establish a communications line (circuit) before sending a transmission.

See Also: *Asynchronous Transfer Mode (ATM), circuit-switched services, connectionless protocol, connection-oriented protocol, frame relay, Internet, latency, packet, packet-switching services, permanent virtual circuit (PVC), routing, switched virtual circuit (SVC), Transmission Control Protocol/Internet Protocol (TCP/IP), X.25*

packet-switching services

P

Telecommunications services provided by telcos for building wide area networks (WANs).

Overview

Packet-switching services are services that route customer traffic over telco packet-switching networks. Such services may include frame relay, X.25, Asynchronous Transfer Mode (ATM), or Switched Multimegabit Data Services (SMDS).

Packet-switching services are only one form of WAN service offered by telcos to enable enterprises to connect remote offices. The main alternative to packet-switched services are circuit-switched services such as T-carrier leased lines, which tend to be much more costly because they require dedicated telco switches instead of routing traffic over a public packet-switching network.

Implementation

In a typical scenario, the customer's local network is typically connected through routers, bridges, Frame Relay Access Devices (FRADs), or other devices to a telco's central office (CO). These customer premises equipment (CPE) either have built-in technology for connecting directly to packet-switching services or use intermediary devices such as Channel Service Unit/Data Service Unit (CSU/DSU) devices. The packet-switching CPE then takes network frames and "packages" them into packets suitable for the specific type of packet-switching service being used. The packaging process varies with the particular service used, but it basically consists of breaking down network frames into relatively small individual packets of data and tagging the packets with the destination address of the remote node to which the packet is directed. Each end node (local network access device) connected to the cloud has a Layer 2, or data-link layer, address that is known to every other end node. These addresses are used to route packet data between individual nodes on the WAN or to broadcast packets to all nodes when needed. Other information is also tagged onto the packets for error correction and other purposes, depending on the service used. The packets are usually small to lessen the load on the switching devices and to enable quick retransmission when transmission errors occur.

Packets are individually placed onto the carrier's packet-switched network and switched from circuit to circuit until they reach their destination. Two packets forming part of the same network message might take entirely different routes to reach their destination node—it depends on the best route available at any given moment, as determined by the packet-switching services themselves. This is different from circuit-switched networks, in which all packets are sent over the same switched circuits for the duration of the connection. At the destination, the packets are reassembled into network frames and delivered to the remote network, where they are routed to their destination.

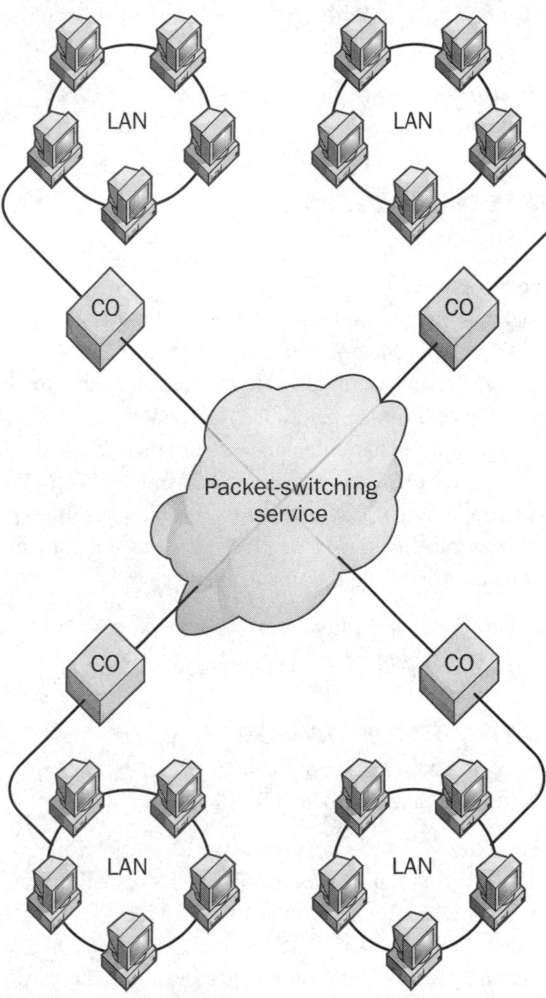

Packet-switching services. *How packet-switching services connect LANs into a WAN.*

In networking diagrams, a public packet-switched network is typically depicted as a cloud because the details of the switches and connections are not of interest to the customer—they are the responsibility of the carrier or carriers providing the services.

Advantages and Disadvantages

Advantages of packet-switching services include the following:

- Customers are not restricted to a single destination, as with point-to-point connections using leased lines.
- Packets can be routed to any destination that supports similar services, so businesses are not tied to a particular carrier or telco.
- Packet-switched networks have low latency and are suitable for hosting dedicated services such as company Web servers if the connection has sufficient bandwidth.
- Customers usually pay monthly rates plus additional charges based on bandwidth use, which means that the primary charges are on a per-transaction basis. The less you use the service, the less you pay.

The main disadvantage of packet-switching services is that they are shared services rather than dedicated ones, although today's telco services offer service level agreements (SLAs) and quality of service (QoS) to guarantee minimum bandwidth for greater reliability.

Notes

If virtual private network (VPN) technologies are employed, the public Internet can also be used as a packet-switching service for multipoint WAN connections, something that is rapidly growing in popularity due to the ubiquity and low cost of Internet access.

See Also: *Asynchronous Transfer Mode (ATM), bridge, Channel Service Unit/Data Service Unit (CSU/DSU), circuit-switched services, customer premises equipment (CPE), frame relay, Frame Relay Access Device (FRAD), leased line, packet, packet switching, quality of service (QoS), router, Switched Multimegabit Data Services (SMDS), T-carrier, telco, virtual private network (VPN), wide area network (WAN), X.25*

PAD

Stands for packet assembler/disassembler, a device that connects computers and other networking equipment to an X.25 packet-switched network.

See: *packet assembler/ disassembler (PAD)*

P

PAN

Stands for Personal Area Network, a network that surrounds and travels with an individual.

See: *Personal Area Network (PAN)*

PAP

Stands for Password Authentication Protocol, an authentication protocol supported by Point-to-Point Protocol (PPP).

See: *Password Authentication Protocol (PAP)*

parallel transmission

A form of signal transmission that sends multiple bits simultaneously over a cable.

Overview

Although a serial interface such as RS-232 transfers only 1 bit of data at a time, parallel interfaces typically transfer 8 bits (1 byte) of data at a time. Parallel interfaces are used mainly to connect printers, hard disks, and other peripherals to computers. A typical parallel interface for a computer uses a port that accepts a female DB25 connector. The parallel interface for a printer often uses a 36-pin Centronics connector.

For the DB25 connector, all 25 of the leads must be working for parallel transmission to function. In contrast, serial interfaces, which sometimes also use DB25 connectors, require only three active leads to transmit data. The parallel 25-pin connector has 17 leads for carrying signals and 8 leads for grounding. Of the 17 leads, 8 are used for data bit signals, 5 for status signals, and 4 for handshaking. Typical throughput of a parallel interface is 16 kilobits per second (Kbps) or 128 Kbps. Parallel communication is usually limited to cables of up to 20 feet (6 meters), but devices can be used to boost signals for longer distances.

Notes

A new type of parallel interface, conforming to the IEEE 1284 standard, supports bidirectional parallel communication at speeds of up to 1 megabit per second (MBps) over distances of up to 33 feet (10 meters). Parallel ports that support this standard are referred to as Enhanced Parallel Ports (EPPs) or Extended Capabilities Ports (ECPs).

See Also: *connector (device), IEEE 1284, RS-232, serial transmission*

parent domain

A domain that contains other subdomains.

Overview

A parent domain is a domain that has subdomains (or child domains) under it within a domain tree. The Domain Name System (DNS) name of the parent domain forms the basis of the names for the subdomains. For example, the parent domain named microsoft.com could include three child domains named dev.microsoft.com, marketing.microsoft.com, and support.microsoft.com. A two-way transitive trust exists between a parent domain and its associated child domains.

See Also: *Active Directory, domain (Microsoft Windows), domain tree*

parity information

Redundant information associated with any block of information that provides fault tolerance.

Overview

Parity information for a block of data is typically calculated from the data itself and can be used to reconstruct the data in the event of data loss or link failure. One place that parity information is used is in RAID-5 volumes. These volumes stripe data and parity information across a set of physical disks in such a way that for each stripe one disk contains the parity information while the other disks contain the data being stored. Each stripe uses a different (rotating) disk for storing its parity data.

The parity information for the stripe is created using an exclusive OR (Boolean XOR) operation on the data in the stripe. As a simple example, suppose that the block of binary data 10011 is to be written to a stripe on a RAID-5 volume that comprises six physical disks. Bit "1" is written to the first disk, bit "0" to the second disk, bit "0" to the third disk, and so on. The sixth, or parity, disk in the stripe contains the parity bit:

```
1 XOR 0 XOR 0 XOR 1 XOR 1 = 1
```

If the first disk fails so that the "1" bit stored on it is lost, the missing bit can be mathematically reconstructed using the remaining data bits and the parity bit for the stripe as follows:

```
? XOR (0 XOR 0 XOR 1 XOR 1) = 1
? XOR 0 = 1
Therefore ? = 1
```

See Also: *fault tolerance, redundant array of independent disks (RAID)*

partition (Active Directory)

A logical divider for organization information in Active Directory directory service in Microsoft Windows 2000.

Overview

Partitions divide Active Directory into separate sections and enable it to store large numbers of objects in a distributed directory over the network. They also allow Active Directory to scale to millions of objects. A partition functions as a physical storage container for a portion of the directory data for an organization. Each domain's directory information is stored in a separate partition and is identified using the distinguished name of the domain. The global catalog server can find an object in Active Directory by using the object's distinguished name (DN), which can be used to identify a replica of a partition that contains the object.

See Also: *Active Directory, distinguished name (DN), global catalog server*

partition (disk)

A portion of a physical disk that functions like a completely separate physical disk.

Overview

Partitions allow physical disks to function as multiple separate storage units for isolating operating systems from applications data on a single-boot system or for isolating operating systems from one another on a multiboot system.

Disks can have two types of partitions:

- **Primary partitions:** You can install a bootable operating system along with its associated file system on primary partitions. A physical disk can have up to four primary partitions.
- **Extended partitions:** A series of logical drives can be created on extended partitions. You can create an extended partition on a disk to overcome the limitation of four primary partitions per disk.

Notes

You can create partitions by using the Fdisk command in MS-DOS and all versions of Microsoft Windows, by using Disk Administrator in Windows NT, or by using the Disk Management tool in Windows 2000, Windows XP, and Windows .NET Server. Using the Fdisk command, you can create one primary partition and one extended partition. Disk Administrator can create up to four primary partitions or three primary and one extended partition. In Disk Management on Windows 2000, Windows XP, and Windows .NET Server, you can create partitions only on basic disks, not on dynamic disks (volumes are created on dynamic disks instead of partitions).

See Also: *basic disk, dynamic disk*

passive hub

Another name for a patch panel, a rack-mounted panel with a series of connectors that provides a branching-out point for network cabling to leave the wiring closet and make horizontal runs to wall plates in the work areas.

See: *patch panel*

P

passive optical network (PON)

A technology for bypassing the bottleneck of the local loop.

Overview

Traditional telco data services have been limited by the technology of the local loop, the "last mile" of copper wiring connecting businesses to the Public Switched Telephone Network (PSTN). This copper wiring means that data rates delivered to customers are far below the speeds at which data is transported in the core of telco networks. A passive optical network (PON) provides a way of working around this bottleneck that analysts estimate affects three-quarters of all businesses in the United States.

Implementation

Instead of deploying a full "fiber-to-the-curb" buildout with its high cost and complexity, a PON connects an optical access switch (OAS) or optical line terminal (OLT) located at the telco central office (CO) using a single strand of fiber-optic cabling to a passive optical splitter or coupler located in the neighborhood of a group of customers. The fiber connecting the CO to the splitter is passive—that is, it has no active components such as repeaters or optical amplifiers. Instead, a high-power laser is used to ensure that signals maintain strength over the trunk length, which is typically limited to 12 miles (19 kilometers). Multiple splitters can be deployed on a single fiber, up to a maximum of 32 splitters, and these may be configured in various ways to create star or ring networks as needed and support both permanent virtual circuits (PVCs) and switched virtual circuits (SVCs).

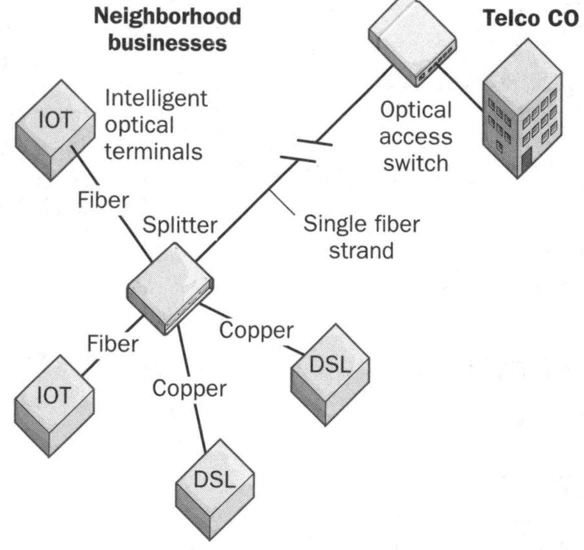

Passive optical network. *Provisioning business customers with high-speed data services using a PON.*

Customers can then be connected to splitters in their neighborhood either by deploying intelligent optical terminals (IOTs) or optical network units (ONUs) located at the customer premises and connecting them to the splitters using fiber-optic cabling (if it has been deployed to the customer premises) or by using existing copper local loop cabling running high-speed Digital Subscriber Line (DSL) technologies. The result is that high-speed data services can be more easily and efficiently provisioned to customers without the need to lay a lot of fiber.

PONs multiplex data at the splitters using either time-division multiplexing (TDM) for downstream traffic or time division multiple access (TDMA) for upstream. Two speed configurations are common: 155 megabits per second (Mbps) in both directions or asymmetric 622 Mbps downstream and 155 Mbps upstream. Some faster speeds have been achieved in test bed environments, such as OC-48 PONS running at 2.48 gigabits per second (Gbps).

Advantages and Disadvantages

PONs help telcos offer high-speed services to more customers without the cost of building out excessive amounts of neighborhood fiber structure. The downside is that they are shared, rather than dedicated, services, but by overlaying dense wavelength division multiplexing (DWDM) on PONs, telcos can provide users with individual lambdas simulating dedicated links. Such services, however, are likely to be several years away.

Marketplace

Several startups have reached market with PON switches, including Quantum Bridge and Terawave Communications. This market is likely to explode in the next few years as real-life PON rollouts accelerate.

For More Information

Visit the Full Service Access Network coalition at *www.fsanet.net.*

See Also: *central office (CO), Digital Subscriber Line (DSL), fiber-optic cabling, fiber to the curb (FTTC), permanent virtual circuit (PVC), Public Switched Telephone Network (PSTN), switched virtual circuit (SVC), telco, Time Division Multiple Access (TDMA), time-division multiplexing (TDM)*

passive termination

A terminator such as a resistor that absorbs signal energy and prevents signal bounce.

Overview

Passive termination is generally used in bus topology networks such as legacy 10Base2 and 10Base5 Ethernet networks. Termination is not required in star topology networks because the central concentrator (hub) provides the termination for each signal path. Ring topology networks such as Token Ring also do not require termination points because the signal path has no beginning or end.

Passive termination is also used in some forms of Small Computer System Interface (SCSI) systems for terminating a chain of SCSI devices. Active termination, which involves electronically canceling the signal incident on the end of a transmission system, is generally more expensive than passive termination but more efficient.

See Also: *10Base2, 10Base5, bus topology, Ethernet, hub, Small Computer System Interface (SCSI), star topology, Token Ring*

pass-through authentication

In Microsoft Windows NT–based networks, a method of performing authentication to a domain controller that resides in a trusted domain.

Overview

Pass-through authentication enables users to log on to computers in domains in which they do not have a valid user account. Users in a multidomain Windows NT–based network can thus access resources anywhere in the enterprise for which they have suitable permissions.

Consider the example of an enterprise consisting of three domains—two resource domains (the trusting domains) in which network resources such as shared folders or printers reside, and a master domain (the trusted domain) in which all user accounts are defined. The resource domains trust the master domain using Windows NT one-way nontransitive trusts. When a user attempts to log on to a computer in a resource domain, pass-through authentication takes place in one of two ways:

- When the user first logs on to the computer, the domain controller in the resource domain passes the user's credentials to the domain controller in the master domain. The user is authenticated, and the user's security identifier (SID) and group membership are returned to the domain controller in the resource domain.
- If the user tries to access a shared folder or printer in the other resource domain, the user's credentials are passed to the domain controller in the master domain in order to be authenticated for resource access.

Notes

Windows 2000 and Windows .NET Server networks employing Active Directory directory service and running in native mode use the Kerberos authentication protocol to authenticate across domain boundaries.

See Also: *Active Directory, domain (Microsoft Windows), Kerberos, trust*

password

A secure identifier that enables a user to access a secured resource.

Overview

Passwords are a part of a user's credentials, which include, at a minimum, the username and password. In a multidomain Microsoft Windows 2000–based enterprise, these credentials also include the user's domain. Passwords are generally known only to users themselves and possibly to members of the Administrators or Account Operators group on Windows 2000–based networks. Users can use their password to log on to the network and access resources for which they have permission. If a user forgets his or her password, the user cannot log on to the network unless the user contacts the administrator and requests that the password be reset.

Notes

When establishing a password policy for your company, you should determine

- Who will control passwords—the administrators or the users. Giving users control over their own passwords makes them completely responsible for their systems and personal data. You can configure Windows NT, Windows 2000, Windows XP, and

Windows .NET Server so that the first time users log on to the network they must change their initial password to one that only they know. This is usually the best solution.

- How complex passwords should be and how often they should be changed. If you make passwords too complex, such as random scrambles of letters, numbers, and symbols, the network might be less secure instead of more secure because users are likely to write down a difficult-to-remember password and tape it under their keyboard or in some other handy location. Also, if passwords must be changed frequently, users will typically make simple changes such as adding an incremental number to the end of each new password. The best policy is usually to require a password of six to eight characters that does not change and to teach users to select passwords that do not include family names, addresses, postal codes, or other easily obtainable personal information. Passwords should usually be simple combinations of letters and numbers, such as "blue144" or "max13one."

See Also: *username*

Password Authentication Protocol (PAP)

An authentication protocol supported by Point-to-Point Protocol (PPP).

Overview

Password Authentication Protocol (PAP) is a clear-text authentication scheme employed in PPP wide area network (WAN) links. PAP is not a secure form of authentication because the user's credentials are passed over the link in unencrypted form. For this reason, Challenge Handshake Authentication Protocol (CHAP) or some other authentication protocol is preferable if the remote PPP client supports it. If the password of a remote client using PAP has been compromised, the authentication server can be attacked using replay attacks or remote client impersonation.

PAP is outlined in RFC 1334.

Implementation

PAP uses a two-way handshake to perform authentication. Once the PPP link is established using the Link Control Protocol (LCP), the PPP client sends a username and password to the PPP server. The server uses its own authentication scheme and user database to authenticate the user, and if the authentication is successful, the server sends an acknowledgment to the client.

PAP is typically used only if the remote access server and the remote client cannot negotiate any higher form of authentication. The remote client initiates the PAP session when it attempts to connect to the PPP server or router. PAP merely identifies the client to the PPP server; the server then authenticates the client based on whatever authentication scheme and user database are implemented on the server.

See Also: *Challenge Handshake Authentication Protocol (CHAP), Link Control Protocol (LCP), Point-to-Point Protocol (PPP), wide area network (WAN)*

PASTE

Stands for Provider Architecture for Differentiated Services and Traffic Engineering, an emerging standard for Internet service billing and traffic delivery.

See: *Provider Architecture for Differentiated Services and Traffic Engineering (PASTE)*

PAT

Stands for port address translation, another name for network address port translation, a form of network address translation (NAT) in which both Internet Protocol (IP) addresses and port numbers are translated.

See: *network address translation (NAT)*

patch cable

A short cable for connecting networking devices.

Overview

Patch cables are usually unshielded twisted-pair (UTP) cabling terminated at both ends with RJ-45 connectors. Cable vendors usually supply patch cables in fixed lengths such as 1, 3, 6, 10, 25, 50, and 100 feet, and also in custom lengths. Patch cables usually come in various colors, which can be helpful in organizing the cabling joining devices on your equipment racks and avoiding "spaghetti." A common use for patch cables is to connect a port on a patch panel to a port on a hub or a switch.

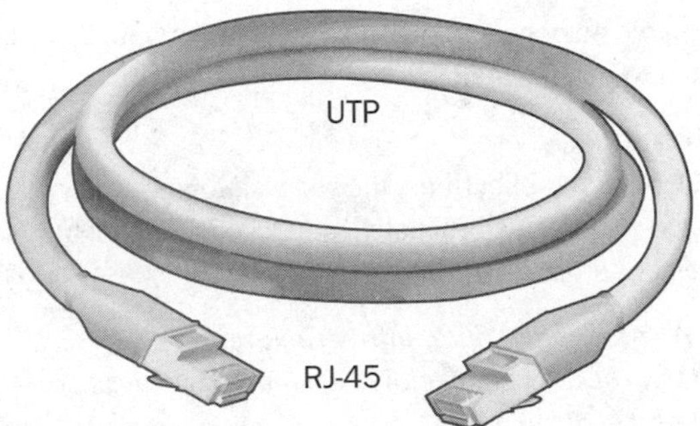

Patch cable. *An example of a patch cable.*

Types

Always use patch cables that meet the requirements of your networking equipment and wiring infrastructure. Category 5 (Cat5) patch cables, which are certified to 100 megahertz (MHz), or enhanced Category 5 (Cat5e) patch cables, which are certified to 350 MHz and higher, are generally recommended for most modern structured wiring installations. Cat5 UTP patch cables should generally be no longer than 33 feet (10 meters).

Using patch cables with molded boots can help prevent kinks from forming and thus prevent pins from becoming bent through rough handling. Molded boots can also reduce the amount of crosstalk in the cable and allow it to perform at higher frequencies.

Be sure to purchase the correct type of patch cable according to its usage. For example:

- The wiring type (pinning) of the cable should match that of your installed premise cabling. Pinning types include TSB 568A, TSB 568B, and USOC, which are described in the table.
- Use straight-pinning or crossover cabling depending on the types of devices you are connecting. Crossover cabling, which has the send and receive wire pairs switched, is used primarily for connecting legacy hubs.

Color Codes by Cable Type

UTP Pinning Type	*Pinning for Each Wire Pair*
568A	Blue 4 and 5
	Orange 3 and 6
	Green 1 and 2
	Brown 7 and 8
568B	Blue 4 and 5
	Orange 1 and 2
	Green 3 and 6
	Brown 7 and 8
USOC	Blue 4 and 5
	Orange 3 and 6
	Green 2 and 7
	Brown 1 and 8

See Also: *Category 5 (Cat5) cabling, crossover cable, crosstalk, enhanced Category 5 (Cat5e) cabling, infrastructure, premise cabling, RJ connectors, structured wiring, unshielded twisted-pair (UTP) cabling*

patch panel

A panel for connecting cabling in a structured wiring infrastructure.

Overview

Patch panels are usually standard 19-inch-wide panels for mounting in equipment racks in wiring closets. A typical patch panel is a rack-mounted panel with a series of RJ-45 jacks that provides a branching-out point for network cabling to leave the wiring closet and make horizontal runs to wall plates in the work areas. They typically contain between 16 and 96 ports for connecting to hubs and switches using patch cables.

Patch panels are mainly used to organize wiring and to avoid "spaghetti." The horizontal cables running from the wiring closet to the wall plates are usually connected to the back of the patch panel, and the patch cords connecting to the hubs and switches plug into the front of the patch panel. The back of the patch panel is a form of punchdown block—wires are not soldered but punched down using a sharp tool called a punchdown block tool. Although an older name for a patch panel is "passive hub," a patch panel is a "hub" only in the sense that it is a physical device in which wires are concentrated—patch panels themselves cannot be used to network computers. All true hubs used in networking are active hubs, which are powered devices that regenerate signals coming into one port for transmission through other ports on the hub.

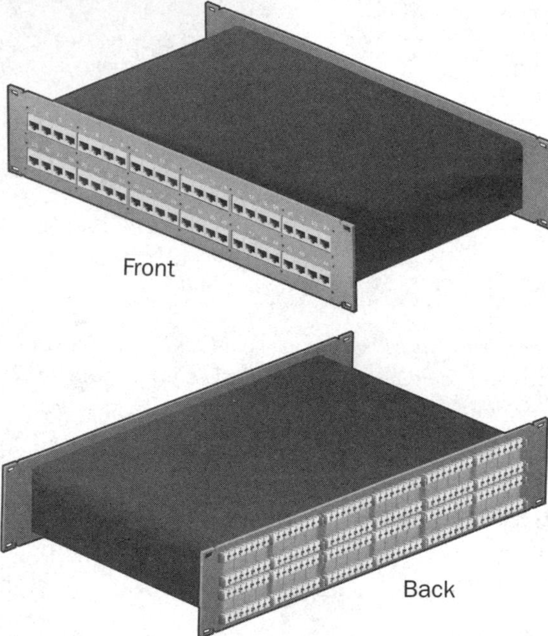

Patch panel. *Example of a patch panel.*

Types

Modular patch panels allow the greatest flexibility of configuration by allowing different kinds of jacks (RJ-45 or fiber-optic connectors) to be installed as needed.

Although front-access patch panels are the easiest to install in cramped conditions, you can use hinged or folding patch panels as a convenient alternative to full-size, rack-mounted patch panels.

There are a few things you should be aware of when selecting patch panels:

- Be sure that your patch panels are Category 5 (Cat5)–approved if you plan to upgrade your network.
- Do not remove excessive amounts of cable jacket when you terminate Cat5 cables to terminal blocks.
- Purchase patch panels with built-in surge protection to protect expensive Ethernet switches.

Use cable managers to organize and support cables connected to patch panels.

Notes

In telephony applications, the termination point for twisted-pair wiring is usually called a punchdown block instead of a patch panel.

See Also: *cabling, hub, infrastructure, premise cabling, rack, RJ connectors, structured wiring, switch, wall plate, wiring closet*

path

The route that a user or application follows to locate a file in a file system, an object in a directory, a server on a network, or some other kind of resource in a hierarchical system.

Overview

A path to an object can be one of the following:

- **Absolute path:** This starts from the root of the file system or directory.
- **Relative path:** This starts from the user's current directory or location.

Examples

On a system running Microsoft Windows, the absolute path to a file is expressed using backslashes, as follows:

```
C:\Windows\Profiles\Administrator\User.dat
```

If the current directory is C:\Windows\Profiles, the relative path to the same file is as follows:

```
\Administrator\User.dat
```

To access files in shared folders on a Windows network, you can use the Universal Naming Convention (UNC) path:

```
\\server16\pub\readme.txt
```

On UNIX platforms, forward slashes are used instead of backslashes, as in this example:

```
/user/bin/blah.gz
```

To request a Web page on the Internet, you specify the page's Uniform Resource Locator (URL), which is essentially the path to the page in the hierarchical Domain Name System (DNS), as follows: *http://www.microsoft.com/support/FAQ.htm*

See Also: *Domain Name System (DNS), Uniform Resource Locator (URL), Universal Naming Convention (UNC)*

pathping

A utility that combines features of ping and tracert.

Overview

Pathping is a Transmission Control Protocol/Internet Protocol (TCP/IP) troubleshooting tool that was introduced in Microsoft Windows 2000 and is included in both Windows XP and Windows .NET Server. You can use pathping to discover the route to a remote host such as tracert (or the UNIX traceroute). It then pings the remote host for a period of time and collects statistics and reports them.

Examples

The following example pathpings a router on the Internet from a remote location:

```
C:\>pathping core2-toronto12-pos10-1.in.
bellnexxia.net

Tracing route to
core2-toronto12-pos10-1.in.bellnexxia.net
[206.108.97.29] over a maximum of 30 hops:

  0  mtit44 [216.130.91.131]

  1  wnpgas06.mts.net [216.130.90.1]

  2  216.130.90.7

  3  wnpgbr01-g11-102.mts.net [205.200.28.82]

  4  dis4-winnipeg32-pos11-0.in.bellnexxia.net
[206.108.110.5]

  5  core2-winnipeg32-pos6-2.in.bellnexxia.net
[206.108.102.129]

  6  core2-toronto12-pos10-1.in.bellnexxia.net
[206.108.97.29]

Computing statistics for 150 seconds...

          Source to Here  This Node/Link
Hop  RTT Lost/Sent=Pct  Lost/Sent=Pct  Address
  0                     babel33 [216.129.43.88]

                          0/ 100 = 0%

  1  191ms 0/ 100=0%     0/ 100 = 0%
wnpgas06.mts.net [216.130.90.1]

                          0/ 100 = 0%

  2  190ms 0/ 100=0%  0/100=0%  216.130.90.7

                          0/ 100 = 0%

  3  204ms 0/ 100=0%  0/
100=0%  wnpgbr01-g11-102.mts.net
[205.200.28.82]

                          0/ 100 = 0%

  4  225ms 0/ 100=0%  0/
100=0%  dis4-winnipeg32-pos11-0.in.bellnexxia.
net [206.108.110.5]

                          0/ 100 = 0%

  5  225ms 0/ 100=0%  0/
100=0%  core2-winnipeg32-pos6-2.in.bellnexxia.
net [206.108.102.129]

                          0/ 100 = 0%

  6  230ms 0/ 100=0%  0/
100=0%  core2-toronto12-pos10-1.in.bellnexxia.
net [206.108.97.29]

Trace complete.
```

See Also: *ping, tracert, Transmission Control Protocol/Internet Protocol (TCP/IP)*

P

PBX

Stands for Private Branch Exchange, a telephone switch at the customer premises that supports multiple independent telephone extensions.

See: *Private Branch Exchange (PBX)*

PCM

Stands for pulse code modulation. a common method used by telcos for converting analog signals into digital.

See: *pulse code modulation (PCM)*

PCS

Stands for Personal Communications Services, a general term for digital cellular phone technologies.

See: *Personal Communications Services (PCS)*

PCT

Stands for Private Communication Technology, an encryption protocol similar to Secure Sockets Layer (SSL).

See: *Private Communication Technology (PCT)*

PDA

Stands for Personal Digital Assistant, a handheld computer used mainly as a personal information manager (PIM) and messaging device.

See: *Personal Digital Assistant (PDA)*

PDC

Stands for primary domain controller, a Microsoft Windows NT domain controller that contains the master copy of the Security Accounts Manager (SAM) database.

See: *primary domain controller (PDC)*

peer server

A computer that functions as a server for a group of users in a peer-to-peer network.

Overview

For example, in a small office with only five users running Microsoft Windows XP, you can set aside an additional machine running Windows XP as a peer server for storing company files. You should use peer servers only in small networks with no great need for security. Security on peer servers is limited to share-level security, which allows only three kinds of access:

- Read-only access based on a password
- Full-control access based on a password
- A combination of the above, based on two separate passwords

If security is an issue, consider using a dedicated server running Windows 2000 or Windows .NET Server.

See Also: *peer-to-peer network*

peer-to-peer network

A network in which the computers are managed independently of one another and have equal rights for initiating communication with each other, sharing resources, and validating users.

Overview

A peer-to-peer network usually has no special server for authenticating users. Each computer manages its own security, so a separate user account might need to be created for each computer that a user needs to access. Users usually store files on their own computers and are responsible for ensuring that those files are appropriately backed up. In a peer-to-peer network, each computer typically runs both client and server software and can be used to make resources available to other users or to access shared resources on the network.

Peer-to-peer networks are simple to set up and are often ideal for small businesses that have fewer than 10 computers and that cannot afford a server-based solution. The disadvantages of peer-to-peer networks are poor security and lack of centralized file storage and backup facilities.

See Also: *server-based network*

PEM

Stands for Privacy Enhanced Mail, a specification for encrypting and securing e-mail.

See: Privacy Enhanced Mail (PEM)

perimeter network

A security network at the boundary between a corporate local area network (LAN) and the Internet.

Overview

The perimeter network is an important part of the security framework of any corporate enterprise. The perimeter network is designed to protect servers on the corporate network from attack by malicious users on the Internet. Formerly known as a demilitarized zone (DMZ), the term *perimeter network* emphasizes the location of this security network as standing between the corporate LAN and the Internet.

Implementation

The perimeter network is implemented using a corporate firewall at the border of the corporate LAN. In a typical configuration, such a firewall has three network interfaces:

- **Internet:** The interface exposed to the external, unsecure public network called the Internet.
- **Intranet:** The interface connected to the corporate LAN where vulnerable servers reside.
- **Perimeter network:** The interface connected to the separate network called the perimeter network or demilitarized zone (DMZ). This interface is on the same side of the firewall as the Internet interface, making servers on the perimeter network available to users on the Internet.

The perimeter network typically contains the following kinds of servers:

- **Proxy servers:** These provide secure access for external users to information stored on intranet servers on the corporate LAN.
- **Web servers:** These are public web servers accessible to everyone on the Internet.

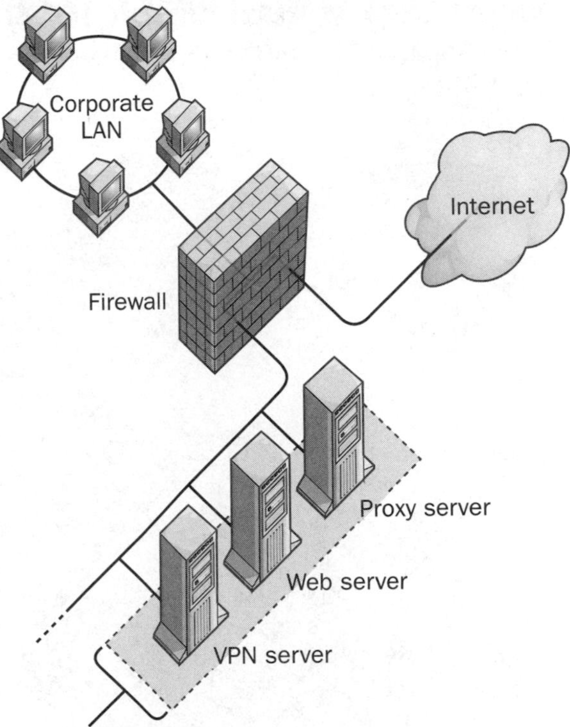

Perimeter network. *How a perimeter network is implemented.*

- **Virtual private network (VPN) servers:** These are remote access and authentication servers that allow company employees to securely access servers on their corporate LAN from outside the LAN over the Internet.

In addition, the perimeter network may contain routers, switches, and other devices to enable it to function as desired.

See Also: firewall, network security, proxy server, virtual private network (VPN)

Perl

Stands for Practical Extraction and Reporting Language, an interpreted scripting language used for Web applications.

See: Practical Extraction and Reporting Language (Perl)

P

permanent virtual circuit (PVC)

A dedicated circuit between two nodes in a circuit-switched network.

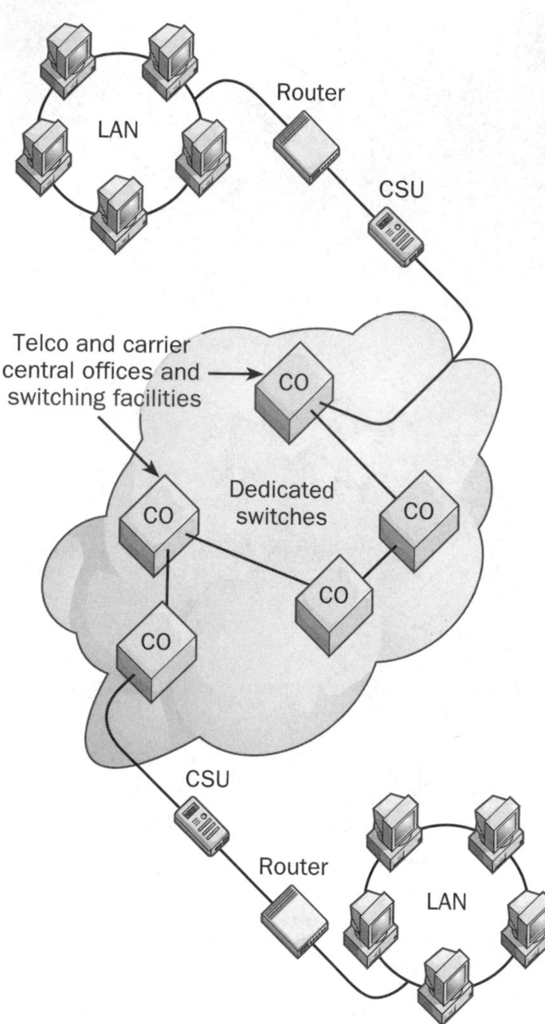

Permanent virtual circuit (PVC). *How a PVC can be established between two LANs to form a WAN.*

Overview

Permanent virtual circuits (PVCs) are typically used in frame relay networking to establish permanent, dedicated links between remote stations or networks. The effect is similar to that of a leased line, but it has added flexibility because fault tolerance can be built into the circuit. For example, BellSouth Corporation offers a frame relay service called Intelligent PVCs that are continually monitored so that should a PVC fail, the switches in the frame relay cloud automatically reconfigure to reroute the customer's traffic over a different circuit.

PVCs are best for wide area network (WAN) links that carry steady, high volumes of network traffic. PVCs offer guaranteed bandwidth and extremely low latency for establishing a connection. Also, because the switching pathway is permanent, the quality of the connection does not vary with time. The result is more reliable service than switched virtual circuits (SVCs). However, PVCs are more expensive than SVCs because telco resources are dedicated to the customer and cannot be used for other purposes. Furthermore, with a PVC you pay for the bandwidth whether or not you use it; with SVCs, the amount you pay depends on how much bandwidth you use.

Implementation

To provision a PVC for a customer, switches are first set up and configured by the telco or carrier to provide a permanent, point-to-point connection between the two nodes. These circuits are called permanent because the telco dedicates specific resources (switches) to your company—they cannot be used by anyone else as long as you lease the service. The switches are called "virtual" because the customer does not have a physical wire connecting two networks but rather a logical connection between switches configured by the telco's management software. In fact, the customer does not even need to know how the circuit is set up.

See Also: *frame relay, frame relay cloud, switched virtual circuit (SVC), virtual circuit*

permissions

Authorization to access or perform an operation on a specific object.

Overview

Permissions are settings that you establish for a network resource to control which users and groups can access the resource and what degree of access they have. Permissions are implemented at several levels in Microsoft

Windows by using discretionary access control lists (DACLs), which are attached to the object they control.

Permissions can be granted to objects by their owners and by anyone to whom owners delegate this ability. Permissions can be used to both grant and deny access to objects—permissions that are not explicitly granted are implicitly denied.

Examples

Examples of permission types on the Windows platform include the following:

- **Shared folder permissions:** Can be applied to shared folders on Windows systems to control access to network shares by users
- **NTFS permissions:** Can be applied to files and folders on NTFS volumes for both local and network control of access to the resources
- **Print permissions:** Can be assigned to printers to control who can manage printers, manage documents, or print documents
- **Active Directory permissions:** Can be assigned to objects within Active Directory directory service of Windows 2000 or Windows .NET Server using Active Directory Users and Computers
- **Public folder permissions:** Can be assigned using Microsoft Outlook to files in public folders to control who can read, edit, or delete those files

See Also: *access control, Active Directory, discretionary access control list (DACL), NTFS permissions (Windows 2000, Windows XP, and Windows .NET Server), NTFS permissions (Windows NT), print permissions, shared folder permissions*

persistent connection

A network connection that is opened for communications to take place and then kept open in case it is needed again.

Overview

One place persistent connections are employed is with the Windows Internet Name Service (WINS) on the Microsoft Windows 2000 platform. Windows 2000 WINS replication partners maintain persistent connections among themselves so that replication can be initiated at any time without the network traffic overhead associated with establishing new connections. This means that WINS databases are updated immediately and shared network resources are always available.

On the other hand, in the earlier version of WINS for Windows NT Server replication partners had to open a new connection between each other every time WINS replication was initiated. As a result, most administrators of large networks configured WINS replication to occur at certain time intervals or after a certain number of updates to the WINS database had accumulated. Because of delays in updating WINS databases on WINS servers, clients sometimes could not access shared network resources.

See Also: *Windows Internet Name Service (WINS)*

Personal Area Network (PAN)

A network that surrounds and travels with an individual.

Overview

The idea of a Personal Area Network (PAN) sounds a lot like science fiction, but with the proliferation of mobile devices such as cell phones, laptops, pagers, and Personal Digital Assistants (PDAs) carried by many knowledge workers today, the day of the PAN may at last be at hand. The enabling technology for PANs may be Bluetooth, a wireless communication technology for small, ad-hoc networks. Using Bluetooth, a "PAN-wired" individual could walk to the front door of an office building and the door would open automatically as the building security network detects and communicates with information stored in the user's PDA. As this person walks up to the soft drink machine, his or her PAN could notify the machine to issue a favorite drink and automatically debit the cost from his or her account. PAN enthusiasts have envisioned other futuristic scenarios, but they are probably still light years away for most of us!

See Also: *Bluetooth*

Personal Communications Services (PCS)

A general term for digital cellular phone technologies.

Overview

Personal Communications Services (PCS) technologies were first developed in the early 1990s because the existing Advanced Mobile Phone Service (AMPS) technologies were running out of available bandwidth in the electromagnetic frequency spectrum. PCS systems are end-to-end digital in nature and are more secure than analog cellular systems. PCS networks can be used for voice, fax, and data applications such as e-mail and file transfers. PCS systems were originally circuit-switched, although most are now being migrated to packet-switched networks.

Some of the standards and technologies that developed from the PCS initiatives include the following:

- **Time Division Multiple Access (TDMA):** These digital cellular systems are based on the TDMA IS-136 standard. TDMA divides frequency bands into time slots and then multiplexes user conversations within these slots. TDMA operates in both the 800-megahertz (MHz) and 1900-MHz frequency bands, but only frequencies at 1900 MHz are specifically referred to as PCS, and those in the 800-MHz range are referred to as cellular.
- **Code Division Multiple Access (CDMA):** These digital cellular systems are based on the CDMA IS-95 standard, which was developed by QUALCOMM. CDMA uses spread-spectrum transmission technologies and assigns codes to individual users transmitting within the same broad frequency spectrum. CDMA operates at both the 800-MHz and 1900-MHz frequencies, but only frequencies at 1900 MHz are specifically referred to as PCS, while those in the 800-MHz range are referred to as cellular.
- **Global System for Mobile Communications (GSM):** These digital cellular systems are based on the GSM 1900 standard. GSM is based on TDMA technologies and divides frequency bands into time slots. GSM has the advantage of supporting roaming between Europe and North America. GSM operates in the 1900-MHz frequency range (or the 1800-MHz range in Europe).

Types

PCS systems and services can also be classified as follows:

- **Narrowband PCS:** Uses the 900-MHz portion of the electromagnetic spectrum, specifically the frequency bands 901–902, 930–931, and 940–941 MHz. Narrowband PCS is used for wireless telephony, wireless data transmission, voice message paging and text-based paging, and other services.
- **Broadband PCS:** A newer technology that uses the 2-gigahertz (GHz) portion of the electromagnetic spectrum, specifically the frequency band from 1850 to 1990 MHz, with the exception of a 20-MHz band reserved for unlicensed voice and data services. Broadband PCS with its greater bandwidth allocation is used or intended for wireless telephony, high-speed wireless data transmission, portable facsimile transmission, wireless Personal Digital Assistants (PDAs), and wireless video telephony services.

See Also: *Advanced Mobile Phone Service (AMPS), broadband transmission, cellular communications, circuit-switched services, Code Division Multiple Access (CDMA), Global System for Mobile Communications (GSM), packet-switching services, Time Division Multiple Access (TDMA)*

Personal Digital Assistant (PDA)

A handheld computer used mainly as a personal information manager (PIM) and messaging device.

Overview

Personal Digital Assistants (PDAs) are generally used for personal and business functions such as keeping track of appointments, sending and receiving e-mail, browsing the Internet, composing memos, performing spreadsheet calculations, managing contact lists, online banking, and viewing stock quotes. A typical PDA has a small grayscale or color liquid crystal display (LCD) with either a small keyboard or a pen-based user interface for entering data. Information can be exchanged with a desktop or laptop PC by using a docking cradle connected to the computer using a serial port, Universal Serial Bus (USB) port, or infrared (IR) communication port, depending on the make and model. The processing power of a typical PDA is similar to that of a 386 processor, and its memory is typically limited to about 16 megabytes. Many PDAs also support standard or even wireless modems for sending and receiving e-mail or accessing specialized Internet content.

Marketplace

One of the earliest PDAs was the Apple Newton, a device whose reach was beyond the technology of its time (it was too large and heavy). Most PDAs today run one of two operating systems:

- **Palm OS:** This is used by the Palm Pilot and Handspring Visor line of PDAs. Palm OS is the most widely-used PDA platform with about 70 percent of the market share, with particular focus on the business executive and consumer markets. The current version of this platform is Palm OS 4.
- **Pocket PC:** This is a version of Microsoft Windows CE used by the Compaq iPaq and Hewlett-Packard Jornada series of PDAs. The Pocket PC platform is rapidly growing in popularity, especially in the large corporation, where it integrates well with Windows-based networks since the Pocket PC includes scaled-down versions of many popular Microsoft software products. The current version of this platform is Pocket PC 2002.

Because PDA management is becoming an increasingly important job for network administrators, a number of vendors have introduced platforms for managing large numbers of PDAs in the enterprise. Examples include two products from TRG (now called HandEra):

- InstallPro Application Guard, which lets administrators deploy applications to Palm OS PDAs.
- ImagePro Deployment Manager, which lets you create an image of a PDA's contents for backup or deployment purposes.

The eventual success of PDAs in the enterprise depends largely upon these new management platforms.

See Also: *universal serial bus (USB)*

PGP

Stands for Pretty Good Privacy, a popular scheme for encrypting e-mail for secure messaging.

See: *Pretty Good Privacy (PGP)*

PHP

A popular server-side scripting language.

Overview

PHP is a scripting language used to create dynamic Web applications. It is an open-source platform and is available for a wide range of operating systems including Linux, versions of UNIX, and Microsoft Windows.

PHP is similar to C language in syntax and to Perl in its support for regular expressions. PHP has capabilities similar to other popular Web scripting languages, including Microsoft Corporation's Active Server Pages (ASP), Sun Microsystems' Java Server Pages (JSP), and Allaire Corporation's ColdFusion. When used on the Apache web server platform, PHP can be built as a binary module and run as a Common Gateway Interface (CGI) application. PHP includes support for Open Database Connectivity (ODBC) databases and can be interfaced with external libraries to extend its functionality.

Notes

The acronym *PHP* originally meant "personal home pages," but the product quickly outgrew this name. The acronym now officially means "PHP: Hypertext Preprocessor," a recursive definition in the style of GNU's not UNIX (GNU).

See Also: *Active Server Pages (ASP), Common Gateway Interface (CGI), Java Server Pages (JSP), open database connectivity (ODBC), Practical Extraction and Reporting Language (Perl), scripting*

P

physical address

Another name for MAC address, a Layer 2 address for a network node.

See: MAC address

physical layer

Layer 1 (or the PHY layer) of the Open Systems Interconnection (OSI) reference model.

Overview

The physical layer is the bottom layer of the seven-layer OSI networking architecture model. It establishes the physical interface and mechanisms for placing a raw stream of bits onto the wire. It defines the voltage, current, modulation, bit synchronization, connection activation and deactivation, and various electrical characteristics for the transmission media (such as unshielded or shielded twisted-pair cabling, coaxial cabling, and fiber-optic cabling). Protocols at the PHY layer include IEEE 802.3, RS-232C, and X.21. Repeaters, transceivers, network interface cards (NICs), and cabling all operate at the PHY level.

See Also: cabling, Open Systems Interconnection (OSI) reference model, network interface card (NIC), protocol, repeater

piconet

The basic building block of Bluetooth wireless networks.

Overview

A piconet is a small network running Bluetooth that has eight or fewer devices on it. Piconets can also be connected to form larger networks called scatternets, but it is unlikely that individual users will often carry more than eight Bluetooth-enabled devices on their person at any given time!

Piconets are not the same as Personal Area Networks (PANs). A PAN may be constructed from one or more separate piconets, but generally devices that need to communicate frequently with each other (such as a cell phone and a head set) should be on the same piconet.

See Also: Bluetooth, Personal Area Network (PAN)

PIM-DM

Stands for Protocol Independent Multicast-Dense Mode, a dense mode multicast routing protocol.

See: Protocol Independent Multicast-Dense Mode (PIM-DM)

PIM-SM

Stands for Protocol Independent Multicast-Sparse Mode, a sparse mode multicast routing protocol.

See: Protocol Independent Multicast-Sparse Mode (PIM-SM)

ping

A utility that verifies the integrity of a network connection.

Overview

The Ping command is one of the first commands to use when troubleshooting communication problems on a Transmission Control Protocol/Internet Protocol (TCP/IP) network. To use ping, you open a command line window and type **ping** followed by either the IP address or the fully qualified domain name (FQDN) of the host for which you want to test network connectivity. Internet Control Message Protocol (ICMP) echo packets are then transmitted to the host, and if connectivity is working, an equal number of echo replies are received. The replies show the packet size in bytes, response time in milliseconds, and Time to Live (TTL) of the echo reply. The TTL is decremented for each hop along the way and indicates the number of routers (hops) passed through along the network path.

The usual procedure for using ping to troubleshoot communications on a TCP/IP network is as follows:

1. Verify that TCP/IP is installed and running by pinging the local loopback address using **ping 127.0.0.1**.
2. Ping your own IP address and host name.
3. Ping the IP address of the default gateway for your local network.
4. Ping the IP address of a host on a remote network.

If all of these steps produce the expected results, TCP/IP is installed and running properly on your network. If you can ping a host's IP address but not its fully qualified domain name (FQDN), you probably have a name resolution problem. Check your Domain Name System (DNS) configuration and make sure that the DNS server is running, or check your Hosts file if it is implemented.

Notes

Although ping stands for Packet Internet Groper, it is almost never referred to by that name anymore.

See Also: *default gateway, Domain Name System (DNS), fully qualified domain name (FQDN), host, Internet Control Message Protocol (ICMP), loopback address, pathping, tracert, Transmission Control Protocol/Internet Protocol (TCP/IP)*

PKCS

Stands for Public Key Cryptography Standards, a set of standards for cryptography.

See: *Public Key Cryptography Standards (PKCS)*

PKCS #7

Also called the Cryptographic Message Syntax Standard, a cryptographic standard from RSA Security for the exchange of digital certificates in public key cryptography.

Overview

PKCS #7 specifies the syntax of digital certificates and other encrypted information—specifically, the method by which data is encrypted and digitally signed, as well as the algorithms involved. When you use PKCS #7 to digitally sign data, the result includes the signing certificates, a list of relevant certificate revocation lists, and any other certificates in the certification path. If you use PKCS #7 to encrypt data, it usually includes references to the issuer and the serial number of the certificate that is associated with the public key that can be used to decrypt the encrypted data.

PKCS #7 also supports additional features such as

- Recursion, in which a digital envelope is enclosed in a digital envelope, which is enclosed in another digital envelope, and so on
- Time-stamping of encrypted messages and digital signatures
- Counter-signatures and user-defined attributes

Implementation

PKCS #7 can be used to encrypt two types of data:

- **Base data:** Data that has not been encrypted and contains no cryptographic enhancements such as hashes or digital signatures.
- **Enhanced data:** Data that is encrypted or contains cryptographic enhancements or both. Enhanced content encapsulates one form of content within another.

A variety of content types are defined by the PKCS #7 standard, including the following:

- **Data:** String of bytes or octets.
- **Signed data:** Data along with an encrypted message digest. A message digest is the value produced when a hashing algorithm is applied to data. (The terms *digest* and *hash* are synonymous.) The recipient uses the message digest to confirm that the original message was not tampered with during transit and to validate the identity of the sender.
- **Enveloped data:** Encrypted data plus the public key that can decrypt the data. You use this method to keep the contents of the message secret from all but trusted recipients.
- **Signed-and-enveloped data:** Encrypted content with its public key and doubly encrypted message digest.
- **Digested data:** Data plus a message digest.
- **Encrypted data alone:** The public key for decrypting the data must be transmitted by some other mechanism in this case.

See Also: *digital certificate, encryption, Public Key Cryptography Standards (PKCS)*

P

PKCS #12

A cryptographic standard for the exchange of digital certificates.

Overview

PKCS #12 is an industry-standard format for the transfer, backup, and restoration of digital certificates and their associated public or private keys used in public key cryptography. PKCS #12 is the export format that is usually used to export a digital certificate with its private key, because exposing a user's private key using a less secure method of export poses a security risk. PKCS #12 is used to export certificates to other computers, to removable media for backup purposes, or to smart cards to enable smart card authentication schemes.

See Also: *digital certificate, encryption, public key cryptography, Public Key Cryptography Standards (PKCS)*

PKI

Stands for public key infrastructure, an infrastructure to enable the use of public key cryptography in a corporate or public setting.

See: *public key infrastructure (PKI)*

Plain Old Telephone Service (POTS)

The basic analog telecommunications service provided by a local telco.

Overview

Plain Old Telephone Service (POTS) is an inexpensive circuit-switched service originally designed for voice communications and supporting data transfer speeds up to 56 kilobits per second (Kbps). POTS was originally the only type of telephone service available, and most residential customers still use it today. Since 1972, however, the old analog POTS is gradually migrating toward an all-digital Integrated Services Digital Network (ISDN) infrastructure, starting mainly with trunk lines and business connections. The combination of the old analog POTS with the newer ISDN infrastructure is commonly called the Public Switched Telephone Network (PSTN).

Architecture

Starting from your home or customer premises, POTS uses a copper twisted-pair cable that eventually terminates at your local telco's central office (CO). Send and receive functions are shared over both wires of the two-wire cable. The connection between the customer premises and the CO forms what is known as the local loop. The CO is a facility with switches that can connect you to another local subscriber, to another CO, or to a long-distance provider, depending on whether your call is local or long distance.

Although POTS is basically an analog service in the local loop and is thus designed for voice traffic, it can also transport data traffic by using a modem to convert analog signals into digital and back again.

See Also: *central office (CO), Integrated Services Digital Network (ISDN), modem, Public Switched Telephone Network (PSTN), telco*

Platform for Privacy Preferences (P3P)

A standard specifying how Web sites communicate their privacy policy to visitors.

Overview

Platform for Privacy Preferences (P3P) is a project of the World Wide Web Consortium (W3C), whose goal is to give Internet users greater control over the privacy of their personal and financial information. Major industry players such as Microsoft Corporation, IBM, America Online, and AT&T have committed to implementing P3P on their sites. Internet Explorer 6, which comes with Windows XP and Windows .NET Server, is P3P-enabled.

P3P is an ongoing initiative to develop standards to ensure the privacy of e-commerce and other transactions over the Internet. The initial version 1 of P3P ensures that users who visit P3P-compliant Web sites will be presented with the site's privacy policy so they can decide whether to give their personal information to the site when doing business or shopping on the Internet. P3P is designed to make corporate privacy policies more accessible to users, instead of requiring users to dig through complex Web sites to find them buried somewhere.

Implementation

P3P specifies a standard format for companies to create machine-readable versions of their privacy policies. When P3P is implemented on a Web site, a user visiting the site will automatically download the company's policy the first time he or she visits the site. Using client-side P3P software, the policy is then displayed on the user's machine along with options about what kind of privacy level the user wants to establish with the site. Once user has selected the privacy level, the next time the user visits the site the policy is automatically downloaded, compared to user settings, and the required degree of privacy is enforced.

Server-side P3P software translates document-based privacy policies into a standardized Extensible Markup Language (XML) format. Client-side P3P software may be integrated into Web browsers, downloaded as a plug in, or built into various applications such as financial applications.

Issues

P3P is an evolving standard. The initial version, P3P 1, has several weaknesses, namely:

- There is no provision to ensure that personal information collected by companies will not be used against the user's wishes. In other words, companies may falsify their privacy policies in order to trick users into submitting their personal data. P3P 1 is thus essentially an "honor system" that still requires users to trust the companies they transact with, but it does make the company's privacy policy more visible so the user can take legal action if the policy has been misrepresented.
- There is no restriction on any interorganizational transfer of user data that may occur during or after an online transaction. For example, the policy does not restrict what the company does with regard to interaction with credit institutions during payment of a transaction.

For More Information

Visit the W3C's P3P site at *www.w3c.org/p3p*.

See Also: *Internet, World Wide Web Consortium (W3C), XML*

plenum cabling

Cabling used for long cable runs within a building.

Overview

Also known as CMP cabling, plenum cabling is a grade of cabling that is resistant to combustion and is used for horizontal cable runs in building plenums and vertical rises such as elevator shafts. A plenum is a horizontal space within a building that houses building components and allows the movement of air. False ceilings are not considered plenums.

Plenum cabling is less flexible and costlier than polyvinyl chloride (PVC) cabling. The external insulating jacket of plenum cabling is usually a fluoropolymer such as Teflon FEP.

See Also: *cabling, polyvinyl chloride (PVC) cabling, premise cabling*

Plug and Play (PnP)

A design philosophy and set of specifications for PC architectures that enables computer hardware, peripherals, device drivers, and operating systems to be easily reconfigured with minimal user understanding and intervention.

Overview

Plug and Play (PnP) frees users from having to manually configure devices and device drivers when they add or remove peripherals from computer systems. For example, to configure a non-PnP sound card, a user typically has to manually change jumpers or dual inline package (DIP) switches on the sound card itself, a task that is often difficult for the inexperienced user. With PnP, you simply plug in the device and follow a series of prompts (if any are necessary) to configure the appropriate drivers for your device.

Implementation

A true PnP system consists of the following three elements:

- A PnP operating system such as Microsoft Windows 2000 or Windows XP.
- A PnP system basic input/output system (BIOS) that supports Advanced Power Management (APM)

or Advanced Configuration for Power Interface (ACPI), automatic configuration of boot and motherboard devices, hot docking, and other features.

- PnP system buses such as Peripheral Component Interconnect (PCI) or universal serial bus (USB) and PnP peripheral devices (internal or external) and their associated drivers. PnP peripheral devices include universal serial bus (USB), Institute of Electrical and Electronics Engineers (IEEE) 1394, Small Computer System Interface (SCSI), Personal Computer Memory Card International Association (PCMCIA), and PCI devices. Industry Standard Architecture (ISA), Extended Industry Standard Architecture (EISA), and Video Electronics Standards Association (VESA) devices are not fully PnP. Other PnP devices include Integrated Device Electronics (IDE) controllers, Enhanced Capabilities Port (ECP) parallel ports, and video adapters.

If a system does not support all three of these features, it is not truly PnP, although it might have some limited PnP support. In a completely PnP system, these features work together to automatically enumerate (identify) new devices installed in or connected to the system, determine their resource requirements, establish a system configuration that can support these requirements without device conflicts, program the devices as necessary and load their device drivers, and notify the user of the changes to the system's configuration.

When you add a new hardware device to a PnP system, the Add New Hardware Wizard starts and installs the necessary drivers for the hardware. The wizard selects suitable hardware resources for the device, which might include an interrupt request (IRQ) line, input/output (I/O) address, direct memory access (DMA) channel, and memory range. If the system cannot properly detect the hardware, you can manually run the Add New Hardware Wizard to configure the hardware.

Notes

When using PnP to install new devices on Microsoft Windows platforms, be sure that the new device is attached to the computer and is turned on before you run the Add New Hardware Wizard.

See Also: *Advanced Configuration and Power Interface (ACPI), Advanced Power Management (APM)*

P-node

A NetBIOS name resolution method used for name registration and resolution.

Overview

P-node is a type of NetBIOS over Transmission Control Protocol/Internet Protocol (TCP/IP) node and is defined in RFCs 1001 and 1002. P-node is supported by computers running Microsoft Windows and is one of four basic methods supported by Windows NT for resolving NetBIOS host names (that is, computer names) into IP addresses. Name resolution is the process of converting the name of a host on the network into a network address (such as an IP address).

Implementation

If a computer running Windows is configured as a P-node machine, it does not use broadcasts to resolve the names of the hosts. Instead, it tries to query a NetBIOS name server to resolve names of other hosts on the network. The advantage of doing this is that name resolution can function across large internetworks consisting of IP subnets connected with routers since routers normally block broadcasts but will forward packets directed toward a specific name server. An example of a NetBIOS name server on a Microsoft Windows network is a Windows NT, Windows 2000, or Windows .NET Server machine running the Windows Internet Name Service (WINS). If the WINS server is unavailable to the client issuing the query, the requested name cannot be resolved into its associated IP address. Furthermore, each client must be configured with the IP address of the WINS server in order for P-node name resolution to work. For this reason, M-node or H-node methods are usually preferred; they can use both broadcasts and directed traffic to resolve NetBIOS names of hosts.

See Also: *B-node, H-node, M-node, NetBIOS name resolution*

PnP

Stands for Plug and Play, a design philosophy and set of specifications for PC architectures that enables computer hardware, peripherals, device drivers, and operating systems to be easily reconfigured with minimal user understanding and intervention.

See: *Plug and Play (PnP)*

pointer (PTR) record

A resource record for reverse name resolution.

Overview

Pointer (PTR) records associate an Internet Protocol (IP) address with a host name in the in-addr.arpa domain. They are used for reverse name lookups to provide host name to IP address mappings.

Examples

Here is an example of a PTR record:

```
1.141.205.202.in-addr.arpa     IN     PTR
server9.microsoft.com.
```

In this PTR record, the IP address 202.205.141.1 is mapped to the host Server9 within the microsoft.com domain. Note that the host's IP address appears in the reverse order in the in-addr.arpa domain.

See Also: *Domain Name System (DNS), resource record (RR)*

point of presence (POP)

A carrier facility that provides an access point for telecommunication services.

Overview

The term *point of presence (POP)* generally refers to a data center to which users can connect in order to access dial-up, leased line, and other telecommunication services. The following can all be considered POPs:

- The central office (CO) for a telco
- The modem bank or switching facility at an Internet service provider (ISP)
- A metropolitan area exchange (MAE) or network access point (NAP) where several ISP backbones connect
- A base station for a cellular communication system

An ISP's POP, for example, would be a facility that housed call aggregators, modem banks, routers, and high-speed Asynchronous Transfer Mode (ATM) switches. Such a POP generally has one or more unique IP addresses plus a pool of assignable IP addresses for its permanent and dial-up clients. The actual POP for an ISP might be colocated within the telecommunications facility of a telco or a long-distance carrier. The ISP rents or leases space in the facility to install the routers and access servers that provide Internet connectivity for clients and for the equipment that provides the ISP with a high-speed T1 or T3 connection to the Internet's backbone.

See Also: *Asynchronous Transfer Mode (ATM), central office (CO), Internet, Internet service provider (ISP), Network Access Point (NAP)*

point-to-multipoint

Communication from a single sending station to multiple receiving stations.

Overview

A point-to-multipoint (or multipoint) wide area network (WAN) consists of three or more end nodes interconnected using a packet-switching telecommunications service. A number of Layer 2, or data-link layer, protocols support multipoint WANs, including frame relay, Switched Multimegabit Data Services (SMDS), Asynchronous Transfer Mode (ATM), and X.25 packet-switched networks.

The opposite of point-to-multipoint is point-to-point communications.

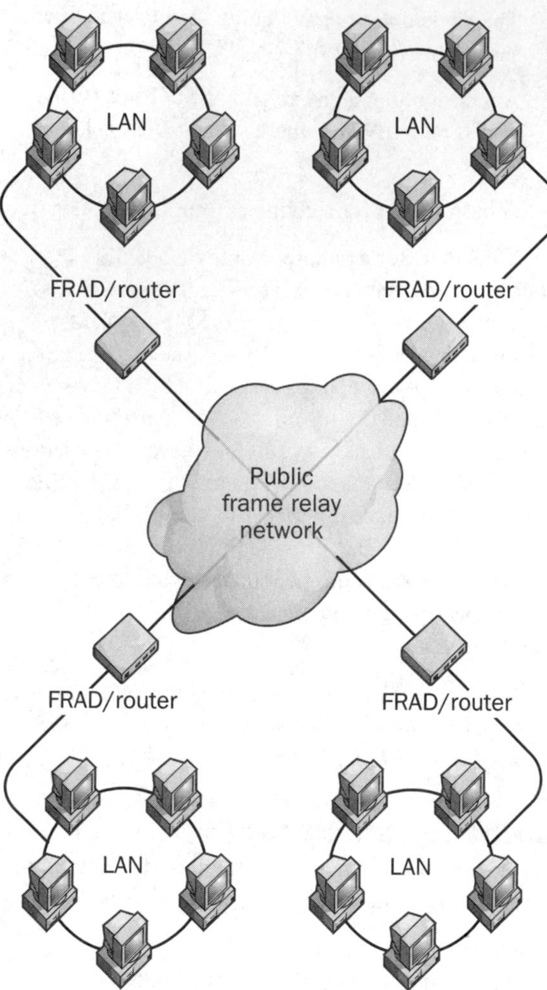

Point-to-multipoint. *Connecting LANs using a multipoint frame relay service.*

A public or private frame relay network can be used to connect multiple networks into a multipoint WAN configuration, as shown in the diagram. Each end node is configured with a unique data-link address, which allows any node on the WAN to communicate with any other node.

See Also: *Asynchronous Transfer Mode (ATM), frame relay, point-to-point, Switched Multimegabit Data Services (SMDS), wide area network (WAN), X.25*

point-to-point

Communication from a single sending station to a single receiving station.

Overview

A point-to-point connection may be a serial link, a dial-up modem connection, a leased line such as a T1 line, or an Integrated Services Digital Network (ISDN) connection. Consider a leased line, for example, which can be used to create a wide area network (WAN) by linking together two end nodes on different local area networks (LANs). In a typical configuration, a router is connected using a serial transmission interface such as V.35 to a Channel Service Unit (CSU) at the customer premises. The CSU provides the interface between the router and the telco's leased line. An identical setup is configured at the remote customer premises.

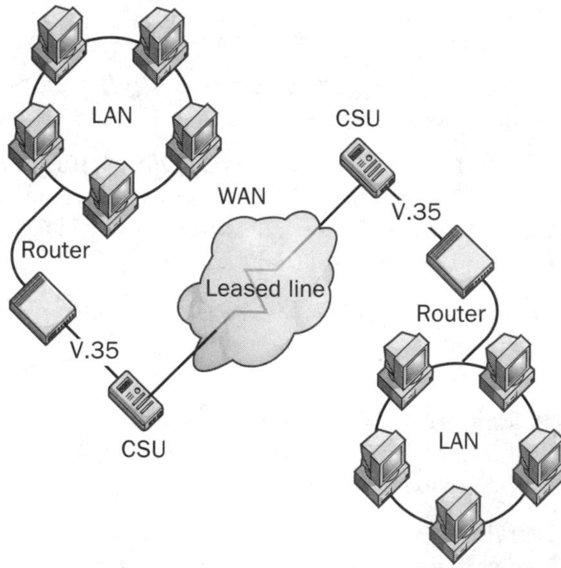

Point-to-point. *Implementing a point-to-point WAN connection.*

Such point-to-point WAN links typically use either High-level Data Link Control (HDLC) for synchronous connections using Cisco routers or Point-to-Point Protocol (PPP) for asynchronous or synchronous communications linking equipment from different vendors. PPP is usually used in heterogeneous networking environments in which the routing and access equipment comes from different vendors, and HDLC tends to be used in homogeneous networking environments in which the routers and access equipment run only Cisco Systems' Internetwork Operating System (IOS) software. One of the derivatives of these protocols, such as Point-to-Point Tunneling Protocol (PPTP), may also be used as the data-link layer protocol for encapsulating local network traffic into frames for transmission over the WAN link.

Note that because there are only two end nodes in a point-to-point WAN link, addressing need not be provided for the end nodes at the data-link layer.

The opposite of point-to-point is point-to-multipoint communications.

Notes

The term *point-to-point* is also used more generally. For example, the configuration of a terminal connected to a minicomputer using two short-haul asynchronous modems is referred to as a point-to-point connection.

See Also: *Channel Service Unit (CSU), data-link layer, High-level Data Link Control (HDLC), Integrated Services Digital Network (ISDN), Internetwork Operating System (IOS), leased line, point-to-multipoint, Point-to-Point Protocol (PPP), Point-to-Point Tunneling Protocol (PPTP), T-carrier, V.35*

Point-to-Point Protocol (PPP)

A popular wide area network (WAN) encapsulation protocol.

Overview

Point-to-Point Protocol (PPP) is an industry standard data-link layer protocol developed in the early 1990s in response to problems associated with Serial Line Internet Protocol (SLIP), which supported only static Internet Protocol (IP) addressing for clients. PPP is superior to the older SLIP in that it is much faster, it offers error correction and dynamic negotiation of sessions without user intervention, and it can support multiple network protocols simultaneously.

PPP provides reliable delivery of packets over both asynchronous and synchronous serial communications links. PPP works with a wide variety of network protocols by encapsulating and compressing them for efficient delivery over WAN connections. Because of its flexibility, PPP allows WAN devices from different vendors to interoperate.

PPP is also the basis of Point-to-Point Tunneling Protocol (PPTP) and Layer 2 Tunneling Protocol (L2TP), which can be used to create virtual private networks (VPNs). All versions of Microsoft Windows support PPP.

PPP is defined in RFCs 1661 and 1662.

Architecture

PPP encapsulation is based on the High-level Data Link Control (HDLC) derived from the mainframe environment. It supports a wide variety of network layer protocols, including IP, Internetwork Packet Exchange (IPX), NetBEUI, and AppleTalk. Once encapsulated, PPP frames can then be transmitted over serial transmission lines such as Public Switched Telephone Network (PSTN), Integrated Services Digital Network (ISDN), or over packet-switched networks such as X.25.

PPP includes two additional subprotocols:

- **Link Control Protocol (LCP):** This is an extensible protocol for establishing, tearing down, and testing data-link WAN connections.
- **Network Control Protocol (NCP):** This is a family of protocols used for establishing and configuring PPP communication using the different network protocols listed above.

PPP supports a wide range of authentication protocols, including

- Password Authentication Protocol (PAP)
- Challenge/Handshake Authentication Protocol (CHAP)
- Microsoft Challenge/Handshake Authentication Protocol (MS-CHAP)
- Shiva Password Authentication Protocol (SPAP)

Implementation

A typical dial-up session using PPP is completely automated and requires no real-time user input. It has four stages:

- **Link establishment:** PPP uses LCP to establish and maintain a PPP link over a serial transmission line. LCP frames are sent over the data link to test its integrity and establish the link.
- **User authentication:** PPP uses one of several authentication protocols, including PAP, CHAP, and Microsoft Challenge Handshake Authentication Protocol (MS-CHAP).
- **Callback:** PPP Callback Control (Microsoft's implementation of PPP) uses Callback Control Protocol (CBCP) if it is configured.
- **Configuration:** NCPs are used to establish network connections, perform compression and encryption, and lease IP addresses using Dynamic Host Configuration Protocol (DHCP), among other functions. NCP frames are sent over the link to establish a network connection between the PPP server and the remote PPP client.

Notes

If you can connect to a remote PPP server but you cannot ping the remote server, try turning off IP header compression. If that does not work, try logging all PPP communication and examining it later for troubleshooting purposes.

See Also: *asynchronous transmission, Challenge Handshake Authentication Protocol (CHAP), data-link layer, High-level Data Link Control (HDLC), Integrated Services Digital Network (ISDN), Internet Protocol (IP), Layer 2 Tunneling Protocol (L2TP), Link Control Protocol (LCP), Microsoft Challenge Handshake Authentication Protocol (MS-CHAP), Multilink Point-to-Point Protocol (MPPP), Network Control Protocol (NCP), Password Authentication Protocol (PAP), Point-to-Point Tunneling Protocol (PPTP), Public Switched Telephone Network (PSTN), Serial Line Internet Protocol (SLIP), serial transmission, synchronous transmission, wide area network (WAN), X.25*

Point-to-Point Tunneling Protocol (PPTP)

An encapsulation protocol for virtual private networking (VPN).

Overview

Point-to-Point Tunneling Protocol (PPTP) is a data-link layer protocol based on the Internet standard Point-to-Point Protocol (PPP). PPTP was developed by Microsoft Corporation to enable network traffic to be encapsulated and sent over an unsecured public Internet Protocol (IP) network such as the Internet. PPTP does this through the creation of virtual private networks (VPNs), which securely tunnel network traffic through the Internet. Remote users can use PPTP to securely access resources on their corporate network over the Internet instead of having to use direct modem connections or costly leased lines.

PPTP is defined in RFC 2637.

Architecture

PPTP is an extension of PPP that is based on standard PPP negotiation, authentication, and encryption schemes. PPTP can encapsulate any form of network traffic including IP, Internetwork Packet Exchange (IPX), or NetBIOS Enhanced User Interface (NetBEUI) packets, and then create a "tunnel" for secure communication across a wide area network (WAN) link. This tunnel is responsible for authentication and data encryption and makes it safe to transmit data over unsecured networks.

PPTP supports two types of tunneling:

- **Voluntary tunneling:** Initiated by the PPTP client, which includes all versions of Microsoft Windows. This type of tunneling does not require support from an Internet service provider (ISP) or network devices such as bridges.
- **Compulsory tunneling:** Initiated by the PPTP server on the corporate network or at the ISP. This type of tunneling must be supported by network access servers (NASs) or routers.

Notes

Because PPTP supports multiple network protocols, including IP, IPX, and NetBEUI, two computers can establish a tunnel over the Internet only if they are running the same network protocol. To troubleshoot PPTP over a TCP/IP connection, use ping to determine whether you are connected to your PPTP server. Also be sure that you have trusted credentials in the domain of the PPTP server, and be sure that you do not have an active Winsock Proxy client that might be redirecting PPTP packets to a proxy server instead of to your VPN.

See Also: *data-link layer, Internet Protocol (IP), Internetwork Packet Exchange (IPX), NetBIOS Extended User Interface (NetBEUI), Point-to-Point Protocol (PPP), tunneling, virtual private network (VPN), wide area network (WAN)*

polyvinyl chloride (PVC) cabling

A grade of network cabling that uses polyvinyl chloride (PVC) plastic for its outer protective insulating jacket.

Overview

PVC cabling is cheap and flexible but gives off dangerous gases during combustion. PVC cabling is usually used to connect wall plates to computers. Building codes usually require that plenum cabling be used instead of PVC cabling for horizontal runs from wiring closets to wall plates.

Both coaxial and twisted-pair cabling are generally available in either PVC or plenum-grade jackets.

See Also: *cabling, plenum cabling, premise cabling*

PON

Stands for passive optical network, a technology for bypassing the bottleneck of the local loop.

See: *passive optical network (PON)*

POP

Stands for point of presence, a carrier facility that provides an access point for telecommunications services.

See: *point of presence (POP)*

POP3

Stands for Post Office Protocol version 3, an Internet standard protocol for storing and retrieving e-mail.

See: *Post Office Protocol version 3 (POP3)*

port

An endpoint of a connection between two Internet Protocol (IP) hosts.

Overview

Ports identify the applications and services that use connections in Transmission Control Protocol/Internet Protocol (TCP/IP) networks. A port thus identifies a unique process for which a server can provide a service or by which a client can access a service. Ports are identified by two-byte numbers called port numbers and are classified as either TCP ports or User Datagram Protocol (UDP) ports, depending on the type of service being supported.

Notes

In computer terminology, the term *port* represents a connector for attaching cables or peripherals to the computer—for example, a parallel port for connecting a printer to a computer or a serial port for connecting a serial mouse or modem to a computer. Connectors on networking components, such hubs or routers, are also sometimes called ports, although a better term for such a connector on a router would be an *interface*.

See Also: *port number, Transmission Control Protocol (TCP), Transmission Control Protocol/Internet Protocol (TCP/IP), User Datagram Protocol (UDP)*

portal

A general name for a wide range of platforms and services ranging from Internet search engines to systems for managing corporate data.

Overview

The term *portal* means doorway and refers to any application or service that provides easy access to useful information or data. The term was first applied to public Web sites such as Yahoo! that provided visitors with a directory of useful and interesting sites on the Internet along with an associated search engine. Today such

Internet portals offer a much wider range of services, including instant messaging, managing personal contacts and calendars, online shopping and bill payment, customized information about your local news, sports, and weather, and customized personal pages. A number of Internet portals exist, but the "big three" are MSN, Yahoo!, and America Online (AOL).

In the enterprise arena, the portal concept evolved from the earlier concept of intranets, or internal corporate Web sites. Enterprise portals focus more on knowledge management (KM), which deals with making readily available all the various sources of knowledge in an enterprise. Several kinds of enterprise portals have evolved in the last few years, including

- **Enterprise Information Portal (EIP):** Provides front-end access to business data stored in different applications and repositories
- **Enterprise Knowledge Portal (EKP):** Includes functionality of EIPs and provides virtual workspaces for collaboration and file sharing

Marketplace

Some examples of popular portal products for the enterprise include Brio.Portal from Brio Technology, Corporate Portal from Plumtree Software, DataChannel Server from DataChannel, Epicentric Portal Server from Epicentric, Decision Portal from InfoImage, iPlanet Portal Server from Sun-Netscape Alliance, Oracle9iAS from Oracle Corporation, SharePoint Portal Server from Microsoft Corporation, and many others.

See Also: *Enterprise Information Portal (EIP), Enterprise Knowledge Portal (EKP), intranet, knowledge management (KM)*

port number

A 16-bit (2-byte) positive integer used to identify a port on a Transmission Control Protocol/Internet Protocol (TCP/IP) network.

Overview

Ports can be assigned numbers ranging from 0 to 65,536. The number assigned to a port identifies the network service or process supported by the port. For example, the File Transfer Protocol (FTP) uses TCP port 20 for transferring data and port 21 for sending control messages. Transmission Control Protocol (TCP) and User Datagram Protocol (UDP) ports are considered distinct.

There are three main types of ports according to their numbering:

- **Well-known ports:** These originally ranged from 0 to 255 but were later expanded to cover 0 through 1023. Well-known port numbers always represent the same network services and are assigned by the Internet Assigned Numbers Authority (IANA). Some of these numbers are currently unassigned and are reserved for future use. For example, FTP uses the well-known port numbers 20 and 21 as discussed above. For a list of well-known port numbers see the article "well-known port numbers" elsewhere in this book.
- **Registered ports:** These are ports used by different vendors to support their operating systems and applications. Registered ports are acknowledged and listed by IANA but are not considered permanently allocated, so other vendors may use the same port numbers provided they anticipate no interoperability issues. Registered ports range from 1024 through 49,151 and overlap with the numbers of dynamically assigned ports below. Examples of registered ports on the Microsoft Windows platform include TCP/UDP port 1512 for the Windows Internet Name Service (WINS) and UDP port 2504 for the Network Load Balancing service.
- **Dynamically assigned ports:** These are ports that an operating system or application assigns to service client requests as needed. Dynamic ports are allocated from the range 1024 through 65,536 and can be released and reassigned as needed.

See Also: *Internet Assigned Numbers Authority (IANA), port, Transmission Control Protocol (TCP), Transmission Control Protocol/Internet Protocol (TCP/IP), User Datagram Protocol (UDP), well-known port numbers*

POSIX

A set of standards for cross-platform implementations of UNIX.

Overview

POSIX is a standard UNIX operating system interface and environment developed by the Institute of Electrical and Electronics Engineers (IEEE) that supports portability of applications at the source code level. POSIX arose because different vendors were producing different "flavors" of UNIX and code written for one flavor would not run on another unless it was modified appropriately. The solution was to develop a standard in which code could be portable between all UNIX flavors, so that a POSIX call in one program would work on any other POSIX-compliant system.

Because of vendor-specific enhancements most UNIX systems are not 100 percent POSIX-compliant. The POSIX.1 standard defines the portability of C language code by specifying a standard application programming interface (API). Microsoft Windows NT, Windows 2000, and the 32-bit versions of Windows XP and Windows .NET Server are fully compliant with the POSIX.1 standard, which means that their POSIX subsystem can run native C language code written to the POSIX.1 standard. Windows NT does not support other POSIX standards.

POSIX Standards

Standard	*Description*
POSIX.1	Specifies the base system interfaces for C language programming
POSIX.2	Specifies standards for shells and system utilities plus additional C language interfaces
POSIX.3	Specifies methods for testing conformance to POSIX
POSIX.4	Adds real-time extensions to POSIX.1
POSIX.5	Extends POSIX.1 to the Ada programming language
POSIX.9	Extends POSIX.1 to the FORTRAN77 language

Notes

Note that POSIX originally stood for Portable Operating System Interface for UNIX, but no one actually refers to it this way anymore.

See Also: *UNIX*

POST

Stands for power-on self test, a special set of initialization routines stored in read-only memory (ROM) that run whenever a PC is booted.

See: *power-on self test (POST)*

postoffice

The central message store in a legacy Microsoft Mail messaging system.

Overview

The postoffice consists of a series of message storage directories on the Microsoft Mail file server. The postoffice stores information such as user ID, password, user preferences, message folders, mail messages, and attachments. The postoffice is a passive file system; no active software runs on it. The International Telecommunication Union (ITU) refers to this component of a mail system as the "message store."

See Also: *e-mail, International Telecommunication Union (ITU)*

Post Office Protocol version 3 (POP3)

An Internet standard protocol for storing and retrieving e-mail.

Overview

Simple Mail Transfer Protocol (SMTP) provides the underlying transport mechanism for sending e-mail messages over the Internet, but it does not provide any facility for storing and retrieving messages. SMTP hosts must be continuously connected to one another, but most users do not have a dedicated connection to the Internet.

Post Office Protocol version 3 (POP3) solves this problem by providing mechanisms for storing messages sent to each user and received from SMTP hosts in a receptacle called a mailbox. A POP3 server such as Microsoft Exchange Server stores messages for each user until the user connects to download and read them using a POP3 client such as Microsoft Outlook. After a POP3 client reads a message in the user's mailbox on a POP3 server, the message is deleted from the mailbox on the server. Primarily for this reason, POP3 is slowly giving way to a newer protocol called Internet Mail Access Protocol version 4 (IMAP4), which can retain read mail on the server and thus offers better support for mobile users.

Implementation

To retrieve a message from a POP3 server, a POP3 client establishes a Transmission Control Protocol (TCP) session using TCP port 110, identifies itself to the server, and then issues a series of POP3 commands:

- **Stat:** Asks the server for the number of messages waiting to be retrieved
- **List:** Determines the size of each message to be retrieved
- **Retr:** Retrieves individual messages
- **Quit:** Ends the POP3 session

To troubleshoot problems with remote POP3 servers, use Telnet to connect to port 110 and examine the results as you try issuing various POP3 commands such as the ones just described.

See Also: *e-mail, Internet Mail Access Protocol version 4 (IMAP4), port number, Simple Mail Transfer Protocol (SMTP), Telnet, Transmission Control Protocol (TCP)*

POTS

Stands for Plain Old Telephone Service, the basic analog telecommunications service provided by a local telco.

See: *Plain Old Telephone Service (POTS)*

power-on self test (POST)

A special set of initialization routines stored in read-only memory (ROM) that run whenever a PC is booted.

Overview

The power-on self test (POST) is designed to test whether system components are functioning properly before attempting to boot the operating system, and checks such things as the RAM, keyboard, and disk drives. If a problem is detected during the POST, the system typically emits a series of beeps and displays a corresponding error message giving some indication of the problem. Specific problems are indicated by different numbers of beeps, but the interpretation of these varies depending on the BIOS used.

On Pentium III systems that use the popular AMI WinBIOS, use the following table to interpret the number of beeps in order to troubleshoot the problem.

POST Beep Codes for AMI WinBIOS

Number of Beeps	*Problem*	*Resolution*
1, 2, or 3	Memory error	Check speed and voltage of dual inline memory modules (DIMMs), try reseating DIMMs, or replace DIMMs
4	Timer error	Replace motherboard
5	CPU error	Try replacing CPU, or replace motherboard
6	Gate A20 error	Try reseating keyboard controller chip, try replacing keyboard controller chip, or replace motherboard
7	Interrupt error	Replace motherboard
8	Video memory error	Try reseating the video RAM (VRAM), try replacing the VRAM, or replace video card
9	BIOS ROM error	Replace BIOS ROM chip

Power Users group

A built-in group in Microsoft Windows 2000, Windows NT 4, Windows XP, and Windows .NET Server.

Overview

The Power Users group is a local group that exists only on stand-alone servers and client machines. The initial membership of this group is empty. Generally speaking, a power user is a person who is familiar with the advanced features of a program's user interface.

The Power Users group has preassigned rights including the following:

- Log on locally
- Access this computer from the network
- Change the system time
- Shut down the system

Power users also have the right to share and manage local disk resources and printers and to create and modify local user accounts on the local machine.

See Also: *built-in group*

PPP

Stands for Point-to-Point Protocol, a popular wide area networking (WAN) encapsulation protocol.

See: *Point-to-Point Protocol (PPP)*

PPP Multilink

Another name for Multilink Point-to-Point Protocol, a wide area network (WAN) protocol for aggregating multiple Point-to-Point Protocol (PPP) connections.

See: *Multilink Point-to-Point Protocol (MPPP)*

PPTP

Stands for Point-to-Point Tunneling Protocol, an encapsulation protocol for virtual private networking (VPN).

See: *Point-to-Point Tunneling Protocol (PPTP)*

Practical Extraction and Reporting Language (Perl)

An interpreted scripting language used for Web applications.

Overview

Practical Extraction and Reporting Language (Perl) is often used on UNIX platforms to develop Common Gateway Interface (CGI) programs to add dynamic functionality to Web sites—for example, input handlers for Hypertext Markup Language (HTML) forms on Web sites running on Apache web servers. Perl's unique capabilities revolve mainly around its powerful string manipulation capabilities. However, because Perl is an interpreted scripting language, applications that are written in Perl are easy to develop and test but tend to run more slowly than if they were compiled programs written in C or some other high-level programming language.

The current version of Perl is version 6.

Notes

You can use Microsoft Corporation's Windows Script Host (WSH) to run administrative scripts written in Perl by installing a third-party ActiveX scripting engine for Perl. Administrators from UNIX backgrounds can do this to leverage their knowledge of Perl to administer Microsoft Windows 2000.

For More Information

Find out more about Perl at *www.perl.com.*

See Also: *Apache, Common Gateway Interface (CGI), Hypertext Markup Language (HTML), scripting, UNIX, Windows Script Host (WSH)*

premise cabling

The entire wiring system in a building.

Overview

Premise wiring for a building includes the cabling, power lines, wiring closets, distribution centers, wall plates, and fixtures needed to build out a wiring infrastructure. Premise cabling should be installed according to the Electronic Industries Alliance and Telecommunications Industry Association (EIA/TIA) wiring standards and must comply with all state and municipal building codes and requirements.

Implementation

In most computer networking installations today, the premise wiring system is a hierarchical system based on the star topology, starting with the equipment room (main cross-connect) that houses the main telecommunications equipment for the particular building, including servers, Private Branch Exchanges (PBXs), and routers. The equipment room contains the facilities for telecommunications signals to enter and leave the building. It can be one room or several rooms on different floors, depending on the building layout and administrative considerations.

From the equipment room, a vertical backbone cable runs up the building riser or elevator shaft, connecting the equipment room with wiring closets (intermediate cross-connects) on each floor. Additional backbone cabling runs horizontally to secondary wiring closets (horizontal cross-connects) if necessary. No further cross-connects should be used; in other words, the hierarchy should be no more than three cross-connects deep.

The wiring closets contain cabinets or racks with patch panels and a variety of networking equipment such as hubs, switches, and routers. Horizontal wiring runs from the patch panels through wall and ceiling spaces to wall plates and distribution boxes to form local area network (LAN) drops in the work areas where computers are set up. Patch cables or drop cables then connect computers in the work area to the wall plates or other distribution boxes.

See Also: *cabinet, cabling, infrastructure, patch cable, patch panel, rack, star topology, structured wiring, wall plate, wiring closet*

presentation layer

Layer 6 of the seven-layer Open Systems Interconnection (OSI) reference model.

Overview

The presentation layer structures data that is passed down from the application layer into a format suitable for network transmission. This layer is responsible for data encryption, data compression, character set conversion, interpretation of graphics commands, and other functions. The network redirector also functions at this layer.

Transmission Control Protocol/Internet Protocol (TCP/IP) and other common network protocols do not use a separate presentation layer protocol. The presentation layer is thus an abstraction in real-world networking.

See Also: *Open Systems Interconnection (OSI) reference model*

Pretty Good Privacy (PGP)

A popular scheme for encrypting e-mail for secure messaging.

Overview

Pretty Good Privacy (PGP) is a digital signature and encryption scheme developed by Phil Zimmermann in 1991 for secure exchange of e-mail and attached documents. You can use Pretty Good Privacy (PGP) to encrypt e-mail messages so that no one but the intended recipient can read them and to digitally sign messages so that the recipient can be sure of the identity of the sender and that the message has not been tampered with during transit.

Implementation

PGP generally uses the Rivest-Shamir-Adleman (RSA) or Diffie-Hellman public key cryptography algorithm and supports 128-bit keys. When you send a digital signature, a hashing algorithm generates a hash from the username and other information, which is then encrypted using the sender's private key. The hashing algorithm is MD5 when you use RSA and SHA-1 when you use Diffie-Hellman. As in a typical public key cryptography system, the recipient uses the sender's public key to decrypt the signature and verify the sender's identity. The sender's public key is retrieved by the recipient from a public PGP key management server such as the one maintained by certificate servers at Network Associates Technology.

Prospects

PGP is popular in the Internet community but does not scale well for corporate enterprise applications because its key management facilities are implemented as a distributed "web of trust" rather than the usual hierarchical certificate authority (CA) scheme of a traditional public key infrastructure (PKI) needed for Privacy Enhanced Mail (PEM). However, the complexity and cost of rolling out a large-scale PKI has turned many enterprises away from this technology in search of simpler and cheaper schemes such as PGP, so the outlook for PGP in the enterprise still remains to be seen.

In 1997, Zimmermann sold the rights to PGP technology to NAI, which currently offers both a commercial version and a freeware version to customers. NAI also provides the necessary PKI infrastructure and CA for free PGP users, which currently number more than a million. Zimmerman, meanwhile, has joined Hush Communications in developing encryption software based on the Open PGP standard from the Internet Engineering Task Force (IETF). In contrast to traditional PGP that requires special software to be installed on each client, the new version from Hush delivers the private key for authenticated user using a Java applet running in the user's Web browser. This allows PGP to be used on machines without dedicated PGP client software installed, an advantage for mobile users.

For More Information

You can get PGP at *www.nai.com.*

See Also: *certificate authority (CA), e-mail, encryption, Privacy Enhanced Mail (PEM), public key infrastructure (PKI)*

PRI-ISDN

Stands for Primary Rate Interface ISDN, a high-speed version of Integrated Services Digital Network (ISDN).

See: *Primary Rate Interface ISDN (PRI-ISDN)*

primary domain controller (PDC)

A Microsoft Windows NT domain controller that contains the master copy of the SAM database.

Overview

A Windows NT domain has one primary domain controller (PDC), which periodically undergoes directory synchronization to copy its directory database to back up domain controllers in the domain. The primary domain controller (PDC) must be the first computer installed in a domain and defines the domain. The PDC contains the master copy of the SAM database, but backup domain controllers (BDCs) contain read-only versions of this database.

If a PDC needs to be taken offline for maintenance or repair or if it unexpectedly goes down, a BDC can be promoted to the role of PDC. This is necessary because BDCs contain read-only copies of the domain directory database, so user accounts cannot be modified and passwords cannot be changed unless there is a PDC on the network.

See Also: *backup domain controller (BDC), domain controller, SAM database*

primary name server

A name server that maintains its own local database of resource records.

Overview

A primary name server has a master copy of resource records for each zone over which it has authority. In the Berkeley Internet Name Domain (BIND) implementation of DNS, these resource records are stored locally on the name server in the form of a text file called the zone file. All changes to the resource records for a zone must be made on the primary name server.

Secondary name servers obtain their resource records from master name servers, which can be either primary name servers or other secondary name servers. The usual configuration when name servers are used within a Transmission Control Protocol/Internet Protocol (TCP/IP) internetwork for name resolution is one primary and one secondary name server, with the primary configured as the master name server for the secondary, which is sometimes called the slave name server.

See Also: *Domain Name System (DNS), master name server, name server, secondary name server, zone*

primary partition

A disk partition on which a bootable operating system can be installed.

Overview

Primary partitions cannot be subdivided into further segments, as extended partitions can. The partition table on a drive's master boot record can contain entries for up to four primary partitions or three primary and one extended partition. Only one primary partition at a time can be the active partition (contain the currently running operating system files). In Microsoft Windows NT, Windows 2000, Windows XP, and Windows .NET Server, the active partition is sometimes known as the system partition.

Primary partitions can also be used in multiboot systems to isolate the files of each operating system from one another.

See Also: *extended partition*

Primary Rate Interface ISDN (PRI-ISDN)

A high-speed version of Integrated Services Digital Network (ISDN).

Overview

In the United States and Japan, a Primary Rate Interface ISDN (PRI-ISDN) connection consists of 24 digital channels that are divided between 23 B channels and a single D channel. This flavor of PRI-ISDN is often referred to as 23B+D because of the types and numbers of channels that it uses. The B channels carry the voice or data between the customer premises and the telco's central office (CO), while the D channel is used for establishing and tearing down connections and for signaling. The bandwidth of each B channel and of the single D channel is 64 kilobits per second (Kbps), so the total bandwidth of PRI-ISDN is 1.544 megabits per second (Mbps), which is identical to that of a T1 circuit. By using the BONDING protocol, the 23 B channels can be combined to form a single 1.472-Mbps data channel.

The other flavor of PRI-ISDN, the European version, employs 30 B channels and one D channel, in other words 30B+D. The bandwidth of an E1 circuit is greater at 2.048 Mbps.

See Also: *Basic Rate Interface ISDN (BRI-ISDN), Integrated Services Digital Network (ISDN), T-carrier*

primary ring

The main ring used in the dual ring topology of a Fiber Distributed Data Interface (FDDI) network.

Overview

The primary ring is the only ring used unless it has a fault, in which case the network reconfigures itself to use the secondary ring with the data traveling in the opposite direction. This dual ring configuration provides FDDI with fault tolerance. It is usually a good idea to run the primary and secondary rings along different physical paths to make the FDDI network more fault-tolerant. An accident or disaster affecting one of the rings will thus not affect the other.

See Also: *fault tolerance, Fiber Distributed Data Interface (FDDI), secondary ring*

printing pool

A technique used to connect one printer to multiple print devices.

Overview

In Microsoft Windows printing terminology, a print device is the physical hardware that does the printing, but a printer is a software interface on a computer that enables jobs to be sent to a print device. Normally, a separate printer is configured for each individual print device. Using a printing pool, however, you can identify several print devices as a single printer to the operating system. Then, when a client sends a print job to the pool, the printer sends the job to the first available print device managed by the printer. Clients can thus print jobs without having to check to see which print device is actually free.

Printing pools are typically used in networks with high printing volume and are also used to provide a form of fault tolerance. Printing pools also simplify the administration of large numbers of print devices. Print devices that are pooled can, however, be a mix of local and network interface print devices. Note that the print devices in a printing pool must be the same make and model or at least be similar devices that use the same printer driver. If you do not have identical print devices and thus cannot create a printing pool, you can take other measures to meet the needs of increased printing volume:

- Share an existing printer that is currently not shared for network use
- Configure priorities between printers to enable critical documents to be printed before noncritical ones
- Institute company policies on how to use printers properly and audit printer usage

Be sure to place pooled print devices in close physical proximity to one another so that users do not have to search for the device that printed their job.

See Also: printing terminology

printing terminology

Terminology used to describe different aspects of printing.

Overview

In Microsoft Windows networking, the following are some important printing-related terms that administrators should know:

- **Print device:** A hardware device that produces printed output, such as a LaserJet, ink-jet, or dot-matrix print device. Most people loosely refer to these devices as printers, but the term *printer* has a specific meaning in the Windows operating system, as described below.
- **Printer:** A software interface on a Windows computer that allows users and applications to print to a print device. Microsoft uses the term *print device* to refer to the actual hardware device; *printer* refers to the software interface that controls that device. To create a printer, you use the Add Printer Wizard in the Printers folder.
- **Print server:** A computer with which a print device is associated. A print server receives print jobs from clients and sends them to the print device.
- **Printer driver:** A series of files that convert printing commands into machine-specific language for sending them to a print device. Each model and make of print device has its own specific printer driver.

In Microsoft Windows, print devices can be further subdivided into two types:

- **Local print device:** A print device that is locally attached to the parallel or serial port on the print server. If a local print device is being used only on the local machine, its software interface is called a local printer. If a local print device is shared, clients can access it over the network and its software interface is called a network printer from the clients' perspective.
- **Network-interface print device:** A print device that has its own built-in network interface card (NIC) and can be plugged into the network anywhere that a local area network (LAN) drop is free. A network-interface print device is not connected directly to the print server; it is managed remotely by the print server.

Notes

Keep network-interface print devices on the same network or subnet as their print server to minimize the extra network traffic. Be sure that your print server has sufficient RAM (random access memory) for processing documents and sufficient disk space for spooling print jobs. Dedicating a computer to the role of print server is usually recommended, especially if that computer will manage several print devices.

Print Operators group

A built-in group in Microsoft Windows 2000, Windows XP, and Windows .NET Server.

Overview

Print operators are users who can administer network printers. The Print Operators group is a domain local group whose initial membership is empty. This group has the following preassigned rights:

- Log on locally
- Shut down the system

Print operators also have the right to set up and configure network printers.

See Also: *built-in group*

print permissions

A set of permissions assigned to users and groups to control access to the printers on a Microsoft Windows print server.

Overview

Suitable print permissions are an important part of network administration, especially in enterprise-level networks with different administrative levels. There are four levels of print permissions in Windows, as described in the following table. You can permit or deny any of these permissions, and by clicking the Advanced button on the Printer Properties property page you can configure more granular customized sets of printer permissions if you like.

Print Permissions

Permission	*What It Allows Users To Do*
print	Connect to a printer Print a document Manage your own documents only
manage documents	Print permissions plus: Pause and restart any document Delete any document Manage job settings for all documents
manage printers	Manage documents permissions plus: Share a printer Change printer properties Delete a printer Change printer permissions

Notes

In Windows 2000, you can remotely administer printers over the Internet using a Web browser by accessing the following Uniform Resource Locator (URL):

```
http://Print_Server_Name/printers
```

Administrators can use this feature to configure printer permissions and settings, check the status of printers, and create real-time reports on printer usage.

See Also: *printing terminology, print server, Uniform Resource Locator (URL)*

print server

A server that manages a printer on a network.

Overview

A printer can either be directly connected to a port on the print server (called a local printer), or it can have its own built-in network interface card (NIC) and be connected directly to the network (called a network printer). Clients that want to print jobs send them to the print server, which queues or spools the jobs and then sends them to the printer.

Implementation

To deploy a print server on your network, you can use a Microsoft Windows 2000 or Windows .NET Server machine and configure it to be your print server. Alternatively, instead of dedicating a computer to managing a printer on a network, you can use a stand-alone print server device. These devices generally have a small footprint—some are even pocket-sized—and can be used to attach a printer anywhere in the network. Typically, an RJ-45 port on the device can be plugged directly into an Ethernet hub or into a wall plate in a work area, while an IEEE 1284 port on the device is connected to the printer. Stand-alone print server devices generally have built-in support for a variety of protocols (such as Transmission Control Protocol/Internet Protocol [TCP/IP], Internetwork Packet Exchange/Sequenced Packet Exchange [IPX/SPX], NetBIOS Enhanced User Interface [NetBEUI], and Data Link Control) and platforms (such as Windows 2000, Windows XP, Novell NetWare, and UNIX) and support a wide variety of makes and models of printers. Other features of stand-alone print server devices can include the following:

- Support for two or four parallel printer connections
- Support for Line Printer Daemon/Line Printer Remote (LPD/LPR) or Dynamic Host Configuration Protocol (DHCP)
- Support for Token Ring or AppleTalk networking architectures

See Also: *network interface card (NIC), printing terminology*

print sharer

Any hardware device that enables two or more computers to directly share one or more attached printers without using a network.

Overview

Print sharers are basically just switches and include the following types:

- **Manual switch boxes:** Here the user turns a rotary switch to select which computer controls the printer. The manual switch boxes are usually in a 2-to-1, 4-to-1, or 6-to-1 configuration. A special switch called an X-switch can allow either of two computers to print to either of two printers. Do not use manual switch boxes with laser printers, as the switching mechanism can cause voltage spikes that can seriously damage the printer.
- **Electronic print-sharing switches:** Here the user uses knobs or toggle switches to select a computer or printer. These switches have solid-state circuitry inside that performs the switching, unlike manual switch boxes, which have simple metallic contacts.
- **Port-contention or FIFO (first in, first out) switches:** These switches automatically monitor all input ports. When a signal enters an input port from a computer, the switch automatically assigns that port to the output printer port.
- **Code-operated switches:** These switches examine the input (computer) data ports for an ASCII string indicating which output (printer) port to switch the incoming printer data to.
- **Scanning switches:** These switches function like port-contention switches except that they sequentially scan the input ports instead of monitoring them all continuously.

Notes

If more than two computers need to share a printer, the best solution is to connect the computers to a local area network (LAN) and use a print server to set up a shared network printer. The print sharing devices listed previously are intended primarily for nonnetworked computers that must be directly connected to printers. In a small peer-to-peer networking setting, you can use a machine running Microsoft Windows XP. In larger networks, Windows 2000 or Windows .NET Server is a better choice.

See Also: *printing terminology, print server*

privacy

The concept that personal or business information should not be shared or accessed without authorization.

Overview

With the emergence of online shopping and business-to-business (B2B) e-commerce in the last few years, privacy has become a critical concern for both consumers and businesses. Privacy involves both ethical and legal issues, and building and maintaining trust is fundamental to its success.

Privacy in the United States generally uses the honor system, although the Federal Trade Commission (FTC) is beginning to establish itself as the privacy defender in the consumer arena. By contrast, the issue of employee privacy in corporations is basically an issue dealt with by state law. Corporations generally issue privacy policies to employees and customers, and many companies practice some form of online monitoring to ensure that employees are not misusing company resources. Examples of such monitoring including logging Web traffic and keeping copies of all e-mails sent and received. In the consumer arena, e-commerce companies sometimes sell customer information to other companies or use it for marketing purposes. Ideally, the privacy policy on the site should explain what the site does with your information and help you decide whether you will do business with the site.

The privacy situation in Europe is generally much stricter, and generally business cannot share a customer's personal information with a third party without the customer's explicit consent. This difference in privacy law can have a significant effect for large enterprises spanning the globe—solutions either involve adopting a strictest common denominator or partitioning company information.

Several independent organizations issue privacy compliance certifications, a popular one being eTrust. Another important development in the area of ensuring online privacy is the emergence of the Platform for Privacy Preferences (P3P), a standard specifying how Web sites communicate their privacy policy to visitors that is being developed by the World Wide Web Consortium (W3C) and is supported by major companies such as Microsoft Corporation, IBM, and America Online (AOL).

Notes

Before you shop online at an e-commerce Web site, be sure to read the privacy policy posted on the site (if you can find it!). Look for a seal from a privacy organization such as eTrust, and be sure not to use things such as your mother's birth name for privacy questions, such as those asked by your credit cards and bank. You should also make sure when making a purchase that the site is secure by looking for https:// in your browser's address field. You might also want to disable cookies on your browser if you are concerned about sites tracking your visits and spending habits, but be aware that this can affect your ability to access certain kinds of sites, such as e-commerce sites.

See Also: *B2B, cookie, e-business, network security, Platform for Privacy Preferences (P3P), World Wide Web Consortium (W3C)*

Privacy Enhanced Mail (PEM)

A specification for encrypting and securing e-mail.

Overview

Privacy Enhanced Mail (PEM) was developed by the Internet Engineering Task Force (IETF) as a standard method for encrypting e-mail messages and protecting their authenticity and integrity. PEM needs to be implemented only on the sending and receiving hosts and does not require any modification of the Internet's Simple Mail Transfer Protocol (SMTP) mail forwarding hosts.

PEM can work with a variety of encryption algorithms including

- MD2 and MD5 for message digests
- Data Encryption Standard (DES) for secret keys
- Rivest-Shamir-Adleman (RSA) for public keys

PEM is documented in RFCs 1421 through 1424.

Implementation

PEM modifies plain text SMTP e-mail messages by converting portions of the message to unintelligible blocks of ASCII code. Three different types of PEM blocks can be included in a message:

- **MIC-CLEAR:** PEM adds an integrity check block to the message but does not encrypt the message.
- **MIC-ONLY:** PEM first encrypts the message and then adds an integrity check.
- **ENCRYPTED:** PEM adds an integrity check to the message and then encrypts the message and the added block.

Issues

Although PEM can be used with either symmetric (secret) key cryptography or public key cryptography, it is mainly intended for use with public key cryptography and therefore requires a public key infrastructure (PKI) to be established before it can effectively be used. This has been the major stumbling block hindering the widespread adoption of PEM, since PKIs have been slow to emerge in the public arena. It has also given room for other schemes such as Pretty Good Privacy (PGP) to emerge and become popular in the market.

See Also: *cryptography, encryption, hashing algorithm, Internet Engineering Task Force (IETF), Pretty Good Privacy (PGP), public key cryptography, public key infrastructure (PKI), Simple Mail Transfer Protocol (SMTP)*

Private Branch Exchange (PBX)

A telephone switch at the customer premises that supports multiple independent telephone extensions.

Overview

Private Branch Exchanges (PBXs) can save businesses the cost of supplying an individual local loop connection for each employee because employees can share external trunk line connections. The PBX provides connectivity between the client's private telephone system that it supports and the telco's public trunk lines. In Europe a PBX is known as a Private Automatic Branch Exchange (PABX).

PBXs were originally switch consoles controlled by human operators, who would plug and unplug patch cords to establish connections for customers. The modern electronic PBX (also known simply as a switch) is a solid-state device that essentially establishes a private switching system that mimics the functions of a telco's much larger central office (CO) switching facility. PBXs allow businesses to have better control of their own telecommunications equipment, and they reduce costs by more effectively routing local telephone traffic.

PBXs support a number of features, including the following:

- **Direct Inward Dialing (DID):** A form of call routing that allows outside users to dial directly to any of the extensions
- **Direct Outward Dialing (DOD):** A form of call routing that allows extensions to dial directly to any outside phone number
- **Station-to-Station Dialing (SSD):** Allows any extension to call any other extension without using a business line

Most modern PBXs support digital phone extensions and T1 or multirate Integrated Services Digital Network (ISDN) for their telco connection and can handle data, fax, and other forms of traffic in addition to voice traffic. PBX boards can also be installed in servers to support computer-telephony integration (CTI). Many products and configurations are available.

Implementation

Typically, a telco or other service provider leases and installs a PBX in the main equipment room of a building or campus. The PBX handles all calls initiated and received in the building. If an outgoing call is directed to another line on the PBX, the PBX routes the call directly to its destination instead of forwarding it to the local CO. Outgoing calls directed to destinations outside the PBX are routed to the CO for handling.

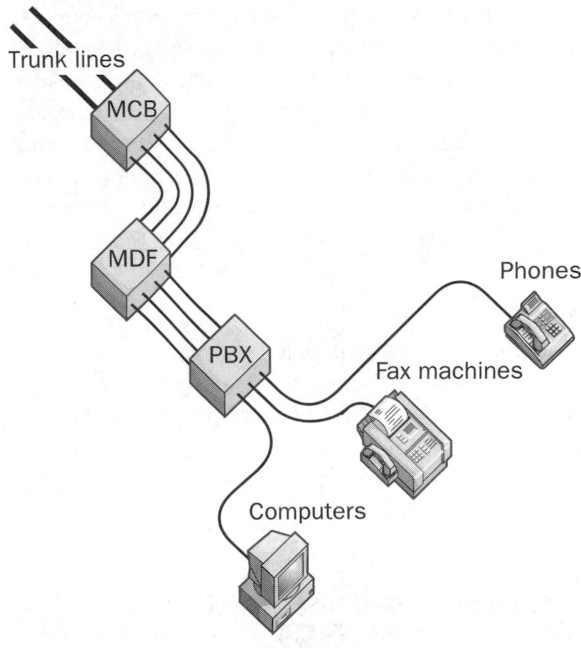

Private Branch Exchange (PBX). *Connecting customer premises equipment to a PBX.*

P

Telephones and other devices are connected by individual circuits directly to the PBX unit, and trunk lines coming in from the outside terminate at a multitrunk channel band (MCB) unit. The MCB interfaces with the main distribution frame (MDF), which provides the individual circuits that connect the outside world to the PBX unit. The more circuits that the MDF creates from the trunk lines, the more simultaneous outgoing calls can be initiated and received by users of the PBX system. Add-ons for the PBX unit can include call management systems (CMSs), which provide call notification and control services; call accounting services; and modem pools for remote dial-up access.

PBX switches come in various sizes. The smallest is a 3-by-8 switch that supports three business lines and eight extension lines. This configuration permits eight phones to be connected, but only three of them can make or receive calls at a time.

Prospects

The traditional PBX is generally expensive and proprietary. An alternative that is rapidly growing in popularity is the IP PBX, a PBX that uses a packet-switched Internet Protocol (IP) network as its transport instead of traditional circuit-switched telephone lines. IP PBXs are particularly useful for companies that need to support mobile knowledge workers or telecommuters, as they are more flexible and manageable than traditional PBXs. Some analysts predict the IP PBX market will pass the traditional PBX market in 2005.

Notes

An alternative to installing a PBX at the customer premises is to lease a Centrex service from the telco's CO. This service offers similar features to a PBX but from a remote location, and it is managed remotely by the telco.

See Also: *central office (CO), telco*

Private Communication Technology (PCT)

An encryption protocol similar to Secure Sockets Layer (SSL).

Overview

Private Communication Technology (PCT) is a security technology that was developed by Microsoft Corporation in response to certain weaknesses in version 2 of the SSL protocol. These issues were solved in version 3 of SSL and in its cousin, Transport Layer Security (TLS). As a result, PCT is now considered a legacy protocol and should generally not be used for securing transmissions over the Internet.

See Also: *encryption, Secure Sockets Layer (SSL), Transport Layer Security (TLS)*

private IP address

An Internet Protocol (IP) network ID that can be reused for different networks.

Overview

Because the pool of available IP addresses began to become exhausted in the 1990s, the Internet Engineering Task Force (IETF) came up with a way of reusing certain addresses. They designated three blocks of IP addresses for private use. In other words, any company can use any of these addresses for internal networking purposes. The caveat is that these addresses are not routable to the Internet and networks using them need to use network address translation (NAT) to establish connectivity with the Internet.

The three blocks of private IP addresses specified in FRC 1918 include

- 16,777,216 unique Class A addresses in the range 10.0.0.0 through 10.255.255.255
- 1,1048,576 unique Class B addresses in the range 172.16.0.0 through 172.31.255.255
- 65,536 unique Class C addresses in the range 192.168.0.0 through 192.168.255.255

See Also: *Class A, Class B, Class C, Internet Engineering Task Force (IETF), Internet Protocol (IP), IP address, network address translation (NAT)*

Project 802

An ongoing project of the Institute of Electrical and Electronics Engineers (IEEE) for defining local area network (LAN) and wide area network (WAN) standards and technologies.

Overview

The 802 specifications define the operation of the physical network components—cabling, network adapters, and connectivity devices such as hubs and switches. The Project 802 standards are constantly evolving, and new subcategories are being created to standardize new networking technologies.

Project 802 has a number of subsections, including the following:

- **802.1:** Internetworking standards
- **802.2:** The logical link control (LLC) layer of the Open Systems Interconnection (OSI) reference model data-link layer
- **802.3:** Ethernet (Carrier Sense Multiple Access with Collision Detection)
- **802.4:** Token Bus LAN
- **802.5:** Token Ring LAN
- **802.6:** Metropolitan area network (MAN)
- **802.7:** Broadband technologies
- **802.8:** Fiber-optic technologies
- **802.9:** Integrated voice/data networks
- **802.10:** Network security standards and technologies
- **802.11:** Wireless networking technologies and standards
- **802.12:** Demand priority access technologies
- **802.14:** Cable television access
- **802.15**: Wireless Personal Area Network (WPAN)
- **802.16**: Fixed broadband wireless networking
- **802.17**: Resilient Packet Ring (RPR)

See Also: *802.1, 802.2, 802.3, 802.4, 802.5, 802.6, 802.7, 802.8, 802.9, 802.10, 802.11, 802.12, 802.14, 802.15, 802.16, 802.17, Institute of Electrical and Electronics Engineers (IEEE), local area network (LAN), wide area network (WAN)*

promiscuous mode

A mode in which a network device listens to all traffic present on the local segment.

Overview

Devices such as network interface cards (NICs) typically listen only to traffic that is specifically addressed to the card and to broadcast traffic directed to every host. This is done to improve the card's performance, for if it had to process every frame or packet that arrived, the overhead could be great enough to cause errors or saturate the NIC.

Some NICs can be configured to operate in promiscuous mode, a mode of operation in which the NIC accepts all frames on the wire, including those not specifically directed to it. A NIC operating in promiscuous mode reads every frame it receives, whether the frames are broadcast, multicast, or unicast. In some networks, this can be a security problem because nodes that act "promiscuously" can be configured not only to read frames but also to store them and even retransmit them. Sensitive information can thus be intercepted on the network and retransmitted to remote stations. This problem can occur in both Ethernet and Token Ring networks when NICs are configured to act promiscuously.

Sometimes, however, a network device should act promiscuously. Examples include bridges, which must listen to all traffic in order to build their media access control (MAC) address tables; protocol analyzers; and other network troubleshooting devices that need to capture and analyze all traffic on a particular local area network (LAN) segment.

See Also: *bridge, MAC address, network interface card (NIC), network troubleshooting*

P

protocol

A set of rules or procedures for sending information over a network.

Overview

Protocols perform such functions as initializing and terminating communication sessions, addressing and routing packets, sending and broadcasting data, performing authentication or encryption, compressing data, and performing error correction. Some protocols have been developed by specific vendors and then accepted as de facto standards by the industry, but others were initially formulated by independent standards bodies and then accepted and implemented by vendors. The most widely implemented protocols are those relating to Transmission Control Protocol/Internet Protocol (TCP/IP) and the Internet.

Types

Protocols are usually classified according to the layer they correspond to in the Open Systems Interconnection (OSI) reference model for networking. Types of protocols include the following:

- **Data-link protocols:** Govern the framing of data, physical addressing of network nodes, and media access control methods. For local area networks (LANs), these primarily include Ethernet, Token Ring, and Fiber Distributed Data Interface (FDDI). For wide area networks (WANs), they include Point-to-Point Protocol (PPP), High-level Data Link Control (HDLC), frame relay, Asynchronous Transfer Mode (ATM), and X.25.
- **Network protocols:** Handle link services and are responsible for addressing, routing, and error checking. Examples include NetBEUI, Internetwork Packet Exchange (IPX), NWLink, and Internet Protocol (IP).
- **Transport protocols:** Enable the establishment of sessions and ensure reliable flow of data. Examples include NetBEUI, Sequenced Packet Exchange (SPX), NWLink, and Transmission Control Protocol (TCP).
- **Application layer protocols:** Enable applications to access network services. Examples include Hypertext Transfer Protocol (HTTP), File Transfer Protocol (FTP), Telnet, Simple Mail Transfer Protocol (SMTP), Simple Network Management Protocol (SNMP), Network News Transfer Protocol (NNTP), X.400, X.500, Server Message Block (SMB), and Network File System (NFS).

For More Information

Visit *www.protocols.com.*

See Also: *Open Systems Interconnection (OSI) reference model*

protocol converter

A device that emulates the behavior of another device.

Overview

Protocol converters are often used in mainframe computing environments where they enable one device to emulate the communication functions of another device. For this reason, a protocol converter is sometimes known as an "emulator," and such emulators can be either hardware-based or software-based. One common type of protocol converter lets you communicate asynchronously with a mainframe host from a PC over a synchronous communication link. This enables you to use the PC as the front end to the host instead of using expensive synchronous terminals. To support this synchronous/asynchronous conversion, the emulation hardware/software must perform several conversions:

- Connect the twinax or coax synchronous connection from the host to an asynchronous RS-232 connection for the PC. For a remote connection, the converter might include X.21 orV.35 serial interfaces as well.
- Take the Synchronous Data Link Control (SDLC) data stream from the host and convert it to an asynchronous format.
- Perform synchronous Extended Binary Coded Decimal Interchange Code (EBCDIC) to asynchronous ASCII conversion and translate standard input/output into appropriate screen/keyboard mappings.

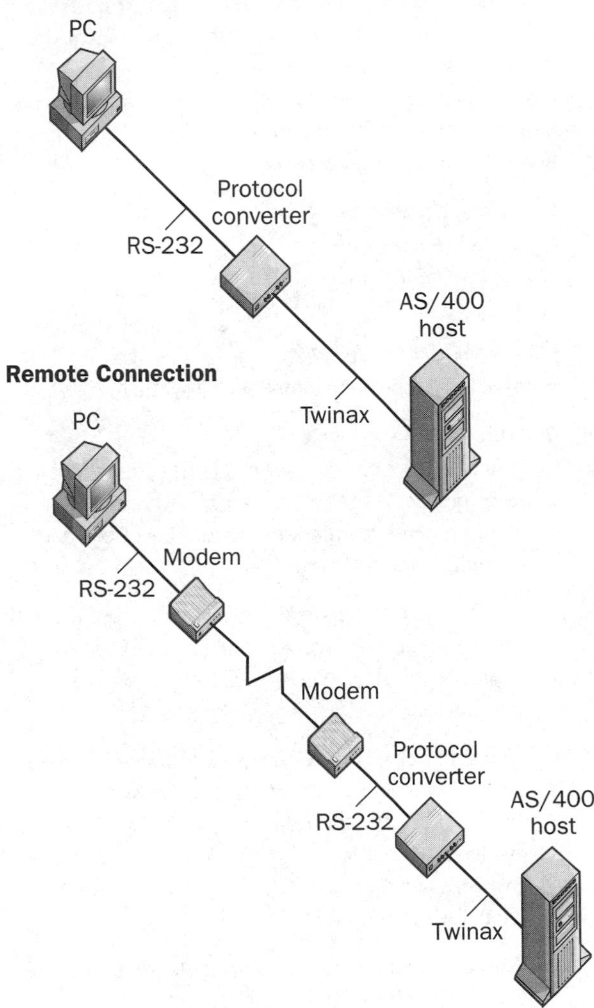

Protocol converter. *Two scenarios where you might use a protocol converter.*

For example, you can turn a PC into a 5250 terminal by installing a 5250 emulator card (a PC typically emulates a 3270 terminal for remote connections or a 5250 terminal for local connections). Here you might use twinax cabling to connect the port on the card directly to an AS/400 or System 390 mainframe. The 5250 emulator software running on the PC typically supports multiple concurrent 5250 sessions.

You can also use protocol converters to connect ASCII printers to AS/400 or System/3x mainframe hosts. A protocol converter for this purpose is sometimes called a printer emulation card.

See Also: *3270, 5250, mainframe, terminal emulator*

protocol file

A text file that provides resolution of protocol names into their respective RFC-defined protocol numbers on a Transmission Control Protocol/Internet Protocol (TCP/IP) network.

Overview

The entries in a protocol file include friendly names for TCP/IP protocol numbers and can be used for well-known service (WKS) records in Domain Name System (DNS) servers and other Windows Sockets applications.

The protocol file is in the following location on computers running Microsoft Windows:

- **Windows 2000, Windows XP, and Windows .NET Server:** %SystemRoot%\system32\drivers\etc\protocol
- **Windows Millennium Edition (Me):** \Windows\protocol

Each line in the protocol file contains the standard name for a protocol followed by the assigned number as defined in RFC 1060, an alias, and an optional comment prefixed with a pound sign (#). The following example comes from the sample protocol file included with Windows 95 and Windows 98:

```
ip      0  IP    # Internet protocol
icmp    1  ICMP  # Internet control message
                   protocol
ggp     3  GGP   # Gateway-gateway protocol
tcp     6  TCP   # Transmission control protocol
```

See Also: *hosts file, lmhosts file, Networks file, services file*

P

Protocol Independent Multicast-Dense Mode (PIM-DM)

A dense mode multicast routing protocol.

Overview

Protocol Independent Multicast-Dense Mode (PIM-DM) is a multicast routing protocol similar to Distance Vector Multicast Routing Protocol (DVMRP). PIM-DM shares the following similarities with DVMRP:

- Builds source-based trees using reverse-path forwarding
- Operates in dense mode to forward multicast traffic everywhere

The main difference between PIM-DM and DVMRP is that although DVMRP uses its own routing protocol for building its multicast routing tables, PIM-DM can utilize any underlying unicast routing protocol for this purpose, including Interior Gateway Routing Protocol (IGRP), Enhanced Interior Gateway Routing Protocol (EIGRP), Routing Information Protocol (RIP), or Open Shortest Path First (OSPF). This makes PIM-DM considerably more powerful and flexible than DVMRP, particularly for large internetworks.

See Also: *dense mode, Distance Vector Multicast Routing Protocol (DVMRP), Enhanced Interior Gateway Routing Protocol (EIGRP), Interior Gateway Routing Protocol (IGRP), multicasting, Open Shortest Path First (OSPF), Protocol Independent Multicast-Sparse Mode (PIM-SM), Routing Information Protocol (RIP), routing protocol, sparse mode, unicasting*

Protocol Independent Multicast-Sparse Mode (PIM-SM)

A sparse mode multicast routing protocol.

Overview

Protocol Independent Multicast-Sparse Mode (PIM-SM) is closely related to its dense mode cousin, Protocol Independent Multicast-Dense Mode (PIM-DM). Like PIM-DM, PIM-SM can also use a variety of underlying unicast routing protocols for building its routing tables. The differences are that PIM-SM is optimized for wide area network (WAN) usage where the distance between multicast source and receivers is assumed to be great and that there may be limited amounts of bandwidth available for communications between them. To optimize performance in a WAN environment, PIM-SM uses explicit join messages and builds a single shared tree for the entire multicast group instead of using source-based trees as in PIM-DM.

See Also: *dense mode, Protocol Independent Multicast-Dense Mode (PIM-DM), routing protocol, sparse mode, wide area network (WAN)*

protocol suite

A collection of protocols that work together as a group.

Overview

Most networking protocols are actually collections or suites of protocols that work together to perform various complementary functions. Examples of protocol suites include the following:

- NetWare's Internetwork Packet Exchange (IPX) and Sequenced Packet Exchange (SPX) and related protocols, such as NetWare Core Protocol (NCP) and Service Advertising Protocol (SAP)
- The Internet's TCP/IP protocol suite, which consists of Internet Protocol (IP), Transmission Control Protocol (TCP), and related protocols such as Address Resolution Protocol (ARP), Internet Control Message Protocol (ICMP), and Hypertext Transfer Protocol (HTTP)
- AppleTalk and its related protocols, such as AppleShare, EtherTalk, and LocalTalk

See Also: *protocol*

Provider Architecture for Differentiated Services and Traffic Engineering (PASTE)

An emerging standard for Internet service billing and traffic delivery.

Overview

The Internet Engineering Task Force (IETF) is developing Provider Architecture for Differentiated Services and Traffic Engineering (PASTE) as a way of defining how Internet service providers (ISPs) can deliver different traffic types to their clients and bill them accordingly. PASTE uses the Multiprotocol Label Switching (MPLS) protocol and the Resource Reservation Protocol (RSVP) to provide these differentiated services.

Existing traffic management technologies such as Cisco Systems' tag switching require that routers maintain state information for every virtual circuit they detect. PASTE eases this requirement by aggregating traffic flows that share a common path into a trunk. Routers need only maintain tables of trunks instead of tables for virtual circuits, which greatly reduces router overhead. Packets can then join or leave a trunk at any router. PASTE can thus be implemented without adding overhead to an ISP's routers, whose tables are often burdened by the rapidly expanding address space of the Internet.

See Also: *Internet Engineering Task Force (IETF), Internet service provider (ISP), Multiprotocol Label Switching (MPLS), Resource Reservation Protocol (RSVP), router*

provisioning

Delivering telecommunications services to the customer premises.

Overview

In enterprise networking, provisioning commonly refers to the process of requesting, obtaining, deploying, and configuring various telco services, mainly in order to build wide area networks (WANs) or to provide high-speed Internet access. For example, one could say "The provisioning of our T1 line took several weeks to complete."

Provisioning also has a more limited usage in terms of configuring various options for telco services. For example, an analog telephone line can be provisioned with only a few options, such as caller ID and call waiting. An Integrated Services Digital Network (ISDN) line can be provisioned with many more options, and the configuration of the ISDN equipment at the customer premises must match that at the telco's central office (CO) for communication to function properly. For example, the service profile identifier (SPID), which is a phone number with additional digits prefixed and appended to it, must be configured properly on the customer's ISDN equipment for the telco's ISDN switching equipment to recognize the type of equipment that is attached, recognize whether one or more devices is attached, and enable calls to be routed appropriately to the equipment.

See Also: *central office (CO), Integrated Services Digital Network (ISDN), T-carrier, telco, wide area network (WAN)*

proxy cache server

A type of proxy server that caches Web pages that users request on the Internet.

Overview

A proxy cache server can be used like a regular proxy server at the border of a private corporate network in order to cache the Web pages returned from the Internet when users in the private network request them. When users request these pages again, the pages are returned instantly from the cache; a new request need not be sent over the Internet. This speeds up browsing for frequently accessed Web sites and reduces the amount of bandwidth used on the corporate Internet link. Proxy cache servers can also be used at Internet service providers (ISPs) and at strategic locations on the Internet's high-speed backbone to provide relief to heavily accessed Web servers and to reduce overall backbone traffic. Another name for this kind of server is *caching proxy*.

Basically, proxy cache servers can perform two kinds of caching:

- **Passive caching:** Web pages that clients request are cached for later retrieval if requested.
- **Active caching:** The proxy server tries to anticipate which Web pages clients will request, and when the server has idle time and the network is sufficiently quiet, the proxy server requests the pages and stores them in the cache.

See Also: *caching, proxy server*

P

proxy server

An application that acts as an intermediary between a private network and the Internet.

Overview

Proxy servers act as secure gateways to the Internet for client computers, and are usually components of firewalls. They are transparent to client computers—a user interacting with the Internet through a proxy server is not aware that a proxy server is handling the requests unless the user tries to access a resource that the proxy server is configured to disallow. Similarly, the Web server receiving the requests from the proxy server interprets these requests as though they came directly from client computers.

Types

Two basic types of proxy servers are used in network firewall environments:

- **Circuit-level gateways:** These are used to establish virtual circuits (VCs) between machines on the internal private network and the proxy server on the border of the private network. The proxy server controls all connections between the internal private network and the external public network. If a client on the private network wants to access the Internet, for example, the Hypertext Transfer Protocol (HTTP) request packet generated by the client's Web browser traverses the virtual circuit to the proxy server; the proxy server then changes the source IP address of the packet to that of the external (public) network interface of the proxy server and forwards the packet onto the Internet. When a remote HTTP server on the Internet sends a response, the proxy server routes this response back through the virtual circuit to the client that made the request.

- **Application-level gateways:** These operate at Layer 7 (the application layer) and can be used to implement security policies for analyzing packets that reach the external (public) interface of the proxy server from distrusted public networks. These security policies can examine packet addresses and other header information, permit or deny packets on the basis of their contents, and modify the address, header, or contents of packets that they monitor in order to hide key information about the internal network's applications and services. Application-level gateways provide proxy services only for specifically configured applications and protocols such as HTTP, File Transfer Protocol (FTP), Simple Mail Transfer Protocol (SMTP), and Telnet. For each type of application for which you want to regulate access through the firewall, you must install and configure a related proxy service on the proxy server. Applications and protocols for which a proxy service is not installed cannot be accessed through the firewall.

Uses

Proxy servers are generally used to secure private networks connected to unsecured public networks such as the Internet. They have greater functionality than packet filtering routers because they operate at a higher level of the protocol stack and afford greater control over monitoring and managing network access. A proxy server functioning as a security agent for a private network is an essential part of a firewall.

Advantages and Disadvantages

The advantages of using a proxy server include the following:

- It provides a single, secure gateway to manage between your private corporate network and the public Internet.
- It can provide different types of access to the Internet for different groups of users as appropriate.
- It can monitor and track Internet usage for each user.
- It can enable multiple users to share a single high-speed Internet connection.

Instead of using a proxy server, you could provide modems for, and run telephone lines directly to, each user who needs Internet access, but this option is costly. You can also configure a physically separate network with several computers that have shared Internet access, but this is cumbersome for users.

See Also: *firewall, packet filtering, proxy cache server, virtual circuit*

P-series protocols

A group of protocols that are part of the X.400 messaging standards.

Overview

Five P-series protocols relate to messaging systems that support X.400, such as Microsoft Exchange Server:

- **P1:** Specifies the layout of messages transferred from one Message Transfer Agent (MTA) to another. This protocol specifies that X.400 messages consist of two parts: a P1 header, which acts as an envelope and must contain a globally unique recipient address for message routing and control purposes, and a P2 message, which is the actual content of the message.
- **P2:** Defines the format for transmitting the content of an X.400 message. This format includes a P2 header (which is not used because the P1 header provides the necessary routing information for the message) and a P2 body, which is the actual content of the message and consists of one or more body parts of various types (such as text, images, voice, or telex).
- **P3:** Specifies how a user agent (UA) communicates directly with an MTA for sending or receiving a message. This protocol is not used as often as the P7 Protocol for the same reason that Post Office Protocol version 3 (POP3) is used instead of Simple Mail Transfer Protocol (SMTP) to receive Internet mail.
- **P7:** Specifies how a UA communicates with a message store (MS) in order to selectively retrieve messages from the store and delete unwanted messages without downloading them.
- **P22:** A 1988 revision of the P2 Protocol that clarifies and extends certain features of P2.

See Also: *Post Office Protocol version 3 (POP3), Simple Mail Transfer Protocol (SMTP), X.400*

PSTN

Stands for Public Switched Telephone Network, the public telephone network managed by the local telco and long-distance carriers.

See: *Public Switched Telephone Network (PSTN)*

PTR

Stands for pointer record, a resource record for reverse name resolution.

See: *pointer (PTR) record*

public key cryptography

A popular method for encrypting data for transmission over a network.

Overview

Also known as asymmetric cryptography, public key cryptography is an encryption method developed by Martin Hellman and Whitfield Diffie in 1976 that is used for securing transmission of data over unsecure networks such as the Internet. Earliest forms of cryptography involve a private or secret key that was shared by the individuals involved in the transmission. The key is a mathematical entity that the sender can use to encrypt a message and the receiver can use to decrypt it. This form of cryptography is known as secret key cryptography or symmetric cryptography. The main problem with this form of cryptography is the question of how the owner of the key can securely transmit the key. In other words, the main problem is one of key management—how to create, store, and transmit the key to those who will need it to decrypt messages sent to them.

Public key cryptography solves this problem by creating a set of two different keys for anyone needing to transmit encrypted information. A precise mathematical relationship exists between the two keys, which together are called a key pair. Both keys are produced at the same time using a mathematical algorithm such as Rivest-Shamir-Adleman (RSA). As a result, when either one of the two keys is used to encrypt a message, the other can be used to decrypt it.

The two keys in a key pair are as follows:

- **Private key:** Held privately by the owner of the key pair and kept secret from anyone else. The responsibility for safe storage of the private key rests entirely with the key pair owner, who has no need to transmit the private key to others.

- **Public key:** Made available by the key pair owner to anyone who requests it. Because the public and private keys are related mathematically, in principle someone could take another person's public key, perform complex mathematical calculations on it, and extract the corresponding private key. The solution is to use keys sufficiently long and with a sufficiently complex mathematical relationship so that it is all but impossible to extract the private key from the public one.

Once a key pair is generated for someone, that person can use it to encrypt messages and to digitally sign messages so that the recipient can be sure of the sender's identity.

The entire public key cryptography system is ultimately founded on trust. All persons who are issued key pairs must trust the third-party authority who provided the key pairs. This trusted authority is called a certificate authority (CA). Someone who wants to obtain a key pair from a CA must contact the CA and present proof of identity. This could involve a face-to-face meeting, examination of a driver's license with photograph, or some other method of establishing a user's identity.

See Also: *cryptography, digital certificate, digital signature, encryption, public key infrastructure (PKI), Secure Sockets Layer (SSL)*

Public Key Cryptography Standards (PKCS)

A set of standards for cryptography.

Overview

The Public Key Cryptography Standards (PKCS) were developed by an industry consortium headed by RSA Laboratories and including Microsoft Corporation. PKCS specifies how a public key cryptography system should be implemented and operated. The following table shows the standards that are important to public key cryptography.

Public Key Cryptography Standards

Standard	*Description*
PKCS #1	Specifies how to encrypt and sign data using RSA encryption
PKCS #2	Now included in PKCS #1
PKCS #3	Describes the Diffie-Hellman key exchange protocol
PKCS #4	Now included in PKCS #1
PKCS #5	Specifies how to encrypt data using a secret key derived from a user's password
PKCS #6	Specifies the syntax standard for extended certificates
PKCS #7	Specifies the general syntax of messages that include cryptographic enhancements such as encryption and digital signatures
PKCS #8	Specifies the format for private key information
PKCS #9	Specifies various attribute types that are used in other PKCS standards
PKCS #10	Specifies the syntax for requesting digital certificates
PKCS #11	Specification for the Cryptoki application programming interface (API), which is used in smart cards
PKCS #12	Specifies a portable format for storing and transporting certificates, private keys, and so forth
PKCS #13	Specifies standards for elliptic curve cryptography (under development at the time of this writing)
PKCS #14	Specifies standards for generating pseudo-random numbers (under development at the time of this writing)
PKCS #15	Specifies the standard format for cryptographic token information (under development at the time of this writing)

See Also: *cryptography, PKCS #7, PKCS #12*

public key infrastructure (PKI)

An infrastructure to enable the use of public key cryptography in a corporate or public setting.

Overview

In order to implement public key cryptography, a public key infrastructure (PKI) must first be deployed. A PKI is essentially a group of services that enables key pairs to be generated, securely stored, and securely transmitted to users so that users can securely send encrypted transmissions and digital signatures over public networks such as the Internet. A PKI can be used to secure e-mail messages and World Wide Web (WWW) transactions, e-commerce and business-to-business (B2B) linkages, and corporate virtual private networks (VPNs).

Architecture

A public key infrastructure consists of a framework of coordinated services that are standardized to a degree by the Public Key Infrastructure X.509 (PKIX) working group of the Internet Engineering Task Force (IETF), although some work in this area still needs to be done. These coordinated services generally include

- A trusted certificate authority (CA) that can obtain a digital certificate and key pair that maps to their identity. This CA may be the enterprise itself, a trusted business party, or a trusted third party such as a government agency or vendor of public PKI services.
- A registration authority (RA) that can accept requests for digital certificates and cache them while the user's alleged identify is verified. Sometimes the verification of user identities is performed by a separate RA, but this service can also be integrated with the functions of the CA.
- A certificate store in which users can access the public keys of other users for encrypting messages or validating digital signatures. This store is usually based on the X.500 directory recommendations and must include a certificate revocation list (CRL) mechanism for identifying certificates that are compromised, expired, or otherwise no longer valid.
- A digital certificate and key management system for generating, storing, and securely transmitting certificates and key pairs to users who request them.

Implementation

Although companies can implement their own in-house PKI systems using software such as Microsoft Windows 2000's Certificate Services and other products, many enterprises employ the services of PKI vendors such as those discussed below to outsource their PKI needs. These vendors provide client software, plug-ins, and CA/RA/CRL services to help enterprises implement public key cryptography as their underlying security mechanism. Unfortunately, implementing PKI is usually easier said than done, and it can be time-consuming and costly (most PKI vendors charge on a per user basis, which adds up quickly for large enterprises). The net result is that PKI often suffers from the perception that it is difficult to implement and use, which has resulted in few large-scale PKI deployments being done so far.

Actually, the most difficult part of implementing PKI in the enterprise arena is usually application integration—getting all the various existing client software packages to recognize and utilize public key cryptography as the basis of their security. Many enterprises have backed away from PKI after an initial trial because of the difficulty of integrating PKI throughout their applications platforms. As an example of the kind of situation you want to avoid, consider the case of an employee who is leaving your company. You delete that person's information from your human resources database—but does your PKI system automatically revoke the employee's digital certificate? This is the sort of automated task that requires careful application integration to ensure your enterprise's security, and it can be difficult to achieve in enterprises with many legacy application packages. Rivest-Shamir-Adleman (RSA) has an innovative solution in this regard with its Web Passport, which uses a small downloadable plug-in module to bridge legacy applications to digital certificates without the need to build support for PKI into these applications.

Marketplace

Major vendors of PKI software and services include Baltimore Technologies, Entrust, RSA Security, and VeriSign. Products from these vendors vary greatly in manageability, application integration, and cost, so before settling on one solution, you should exercise due diligence in testing and piloting popular systems.

Before deciding to implement PKI in your enterprise, it is a good idea to consider first whether it is really needed. E-commerce and messaging are currently being successfully transacted in a relatively secure fashion without the need of PKI—for example, using the Secure Sockets Layer (SSL) protocol. Some startup companies are also developing products that sidestep some of the difficulties of implementing a PKI and provide innovative ways of securing corporate e-mail and Web transactions. Examples include SafeLoop, which sends encrypted electronic messages using Hypertext Transfer Protocol (HTTP) instead of Simple Mail Transport Protocol (SMTP), and Hilgraeve, which enables secure online document collaboration using online storage services instead of sending documents as e-mail attachments. P2P (peer-to-peer) technologies are also emerging as an alternative to traditional Internet messaging and collaboration protocols and may provide an additional option for enterprises seeking innovative solutions to secure electronic communications.

Prospects

Many industry analysts consider PKI's prospects of succeeding in the enterprise and in the larger public arena uncertain. The complexity and cost of implementing PKI has caused many enterprises to balk at the process, especially when funds are more urgently needed for putting out other security-related fires. Many IT (information technology) managers see e-mail filtering, antivirus software, firewalls, and intrusion detection systems as more of a priority than rolling out a complex PKI system. A few spectacular failures of large-scale PKI rollouts have also had a discouraging effect on the market. Another serious issue has been interoperability issues between software and platforms from different PKI vendors, a result of the effect of vendor politics on the standards process.

On the other hand, there have been many successful PKI implementations, even in the public arena. The U.S. Patent and Trademark Office has a PKI system that allows patent applications to be securely filed online, and the result has been considerable cost savings. But by and large the world is still years away from a time when digitally signed documents can be used as easily as paper ones for legal, medical, financial, and contractual transactions between individuals and companies.

One positive step occurred in October 2000 with the passing into U.S. law of the Electronic Signatures in Global and National Commerce (E-Sign) Act. However, this law recognizes the legal validity of digital certificates, but it also hedges bets by avoiding the task of defining exactly what a "digital certificate" is.

For More Information

Visit the PKI Forum at *www.pkiforum.org.*

See Also: *certificate authority (CA), cryptography, digital certificate, encryption, key pair, public key cryptography, Secure Sockets Layer (SSL)*

Public Switched Telephone Network (PSTN)

The public telephone network managed by the local telco and long-distance carriers.

Overview

The Public Switched Telephone Network (PSTN) consists of a digital Integrated Services Digital Network (ISDN) backbone of switched circuits together with the analog local loop wiring still found in many residences. The PSTN is sometimes referred to as the Plain Old Telephone Service (POTS), but this term actually refers to the older analog portion of the PSTN.

The PSTN provides the most popular basis for creating wide area networks (WANs) either through dial-up or leased lines. The PSTN is often used in wide area networking because of its ubiquitous nature since local loop connections to the service exist almost everywhere in the world. However, with the advent of alternative services such as high-speed cable modem services and passive optical networking (PON), the days of the slow, analog local loop connection may be approaching their end.

See Also: *analog, cable modem, digital, Integrated Services Digital Network (ISDN), local loop, passive optical network (PON), Plain Old Telephone Service (POTS), wide area network (WAN)*

publishing

In Active Directory directory service, the process of making directory objects accessible to users on the network.

Overview

Many objects created in Active Directory are automatically published or made available to users on the network. For example, when you create a new user object containing information about that user, such as the user's phone number and e-mail address, other users on the network can look up this information in Active Directory.

If an object that does not reside in Active Directory is published, Active Directory points to the object's location on the network. Most objects are automatically published in Active Directory if they reside on computers running Windows 2000, Windows XP, or Windows .NET Server, but you might have to manually publish the location of other objects, such as shared folders and printers on downlevel computers running Windows NT.

When you consider whether to publish an object in Active Directory, consider whether the information will be changed frequently. Published information should be relatively static. Information should be published when it will be useful to a large segment of the enterprise community. Structured information is more useful to publish than individual items such as files, which should be published instead in file systems accessed through share points. Applications can publish their connection points and application data in Active Directory.

See Also: *Active Directory*

pulse code modulation (PCM)

A common method for converting analog signals into digital ones used by telcos.

Overview

Pulse code modulation (PCM) is the standard method used by telephone companies and telecommunications providers for converting analog signals into digital ones that can be transmitted over the Integrated Services Digital Network (ISDN) and Asynchronous Transfer Mode (ATM) backbones of the Public Switched Telephone System (PSTN). Digital signaling has replaced analog in the PSTN backbone because digital signals can be transmitted long distances with little degradation in signal quality.

Implementation

The basis of PCM is the Nyquist Theorem from Information Theory, a branch of mathematics concerned with information and signaling. The Nyquist Theorem states that in order to accurately represent an analog signal as a digital one, the signal must be sampled at twice the maximum analog signal frequency. Since the maximum frequency used in analog voice communications in the local loop is 4 kilohertz (4000 hertz or 4000 cycles/second), the theorem indicates that analog signals must be sampled at twice that or 8 kHz. PCM does just this by taking analog signals with continually varying voltages and quantizing these signals into discrete voltages using an 8-bit (1 byte) representation for each sample. The voltage levels correspond to powers of 2 and represent a series of binary numbers so that the output of a PCM device is essentially a binary number. This sampling and quantization process results in a data transmission rate of 8 bits x 8 KHz = 64 Kbps, which explains why 64 Kbps DS-0 trunk lines form the basis of the PSTN's backbone.

A typical PCM converter consists of a sample-and-hold circuit that samples the analog voltage signal and holds it long enough so that an analog-to-digital converter can convert it into digital (binary) format. A single device plus its associated software that can perform both the analog-to-digital conversion and its reverse is known as a codec or coder/decoder.

See Also: *Asynchronous Transfer Mode (ATM), DS-0, Integrated Services Digital Network (ISDN), local loop, Public Switched Telephone Network (PSTN), telco*

PVC

Stands for permanent virtual circuit, a dedicated circuit between two nodes in a circuit-switched network.

See: *permanent virtual circuit (PVC)*

PVC cabling

Stands for polyvinyl chloride cabling, a grade of network cabling that uses polyvinyl chloride (PVC) plastic for its outer protective insulating jacket.

See: *polyvinyl chloride (PVC) cabling*

QIC

Stands for Quarter Inch Cartridge, the original tape format for tape backups.

See: *Quarter Inch Cartridge (QIC)*

QoS

Stands for quality of service, any network mechanism for ensuring that applications or services are able to operate as expected.

See: *quality of service (QoS)*

QoS ACS

Stands for QoS Admission Control Service, a feature of Microsoft Windows 2000 for implementing quality of service (QoS) on an Internet Protocol (IP) network.

See: *QoS Admission Control Service (QoS ACS)*

QoS Admission Control Service (QoS ACS)

A feature of Microsoft Windows 2000 for implementing quality of service (QoS) on an Internet Protocol (IP) network.

Overview

QoS Admission Control Service (QoS ACS) is a Windows 2000 service that can be used to centrally designate when, how, and by whom shared network segment resources will be used. QoS ACS is based on the Subnet Bandwidth Management (SBM) specification defined by the Internet Engineering Task Force (IETF). QoS ACS operates at the network layer and can service all transport protocols in the TCP/IP protocol suite, including Remote Display Protocol (RDP), User Datagram Protocol (UDP), and Transmission Control Protocol (TCP). A QoS ACS host (a server running Windows 2000 with the QoS ACS service installed and configured) uses the Resource Reservation Protocol (RSVP) as a message service for sending and receiving priority bandwidth requests.

Implementation

A QoS ACS host controls the bandwidth for the subnet to which it is connected. The QoS ACS host uses multicasting to send out messages called beacons to inform clients on the subnet that it is ready to receive bandwidth allocation requests. Clients on the subnet that desire access to shared network resources (such as multimedia servers) first submit their bandwidth request to the QoS ACS server so that it can determine whether sufficient bandwidth is available to allocate to the clients. Bandwidth is then allocated based on the current state of resource and bandwidth availability on the subnet and the requesting user's QoS ACS policy rights. These policy rights are defined in Active Directory directory service.

A client's request for bandwidth will be rejected if the QoS ACS host determines that the user does not have the right to reserve bandwidth on the subnetwork or if the subnetwork does not have sufficient resources to support the request at that time. If the client's request is rejected, the client must decide whether to try accessing the resource using a best-effort service level or wait until later, when priority bandwidth becomes available and can be allocated to the client. If the request is approved, the QoS ACS host logically allocates the requested bandwidth and forwards the client's resource request to the appropriate server on the network. No configuration is required for Windows clients, and non-Windows clients can request bandwidth, provided they are running suitable SBM client software.

See Also: *quality of service (QoS), Resource Reservation Protocol (RSVP)*

Q-series protocols

Also called Series Q protocols, a set of protocols developed by the International Telecommunication Union (ITU) that govern the operation of Integrated Services Digital Network (ISDN).

Overview

Some of the more important Q-series protocols include the following:

- **Q.920/921:** Specifies the User-Network Interface (UNI) data-link layer for ISDN, including the ISDN D channel's Link Access Protocol, D-channel (LAP-D) data-link layer protocol.
- **Q.922A:** Specifies the ITU encapsulation method for frame relay networks.
- **Q.931:** Specifies mechanisms for establishing, maintaining, and tearing down ISDN connections. This includes working with connections in the LAP-D data-link protocol, which runs on the ISDN D channel.
- **Q.93B:** The Asynchronous Transfer Mode (ATM) signaling protocol, which specifies mechanisms for establishing, maintaining, and tearing down broadband ISDN (B-ISDN) connections.

See Also: *Asynchronous Transfer Mode (ATM), Integrated Services Digital Network (ISDN), International Telecommunication Union (ITU), Link Access Protocol, D-channel (LAPD)*

quality of service (QoS)

Any network mechanism for ensuring that applications or services are able to operate as expected.

Overview

Network performance characteristics such as bandwidth, latency, and jitter (variation in delay) can have bad effects on some applications. For example, voice communications and streaming video can be frustrating when delivered over a network with insufficient bandwidth, unpredictable latency, or excessive jitter. Anyone who has used a cell phone has experienced the frustrating "dropouts" that occur from time to time, causing conversation to be difficult. Quality of service (QoS) is all about making sure that a network's bandwidth, latency, and jitter are predictable and suited to the needs of applications that use that network.

History

The general concept of network QoS originated in the telco market, where it represented a set of technologies and methods for ensuring that services provided to customers were above designated minimum levels of quality. For telephone service, this means, for example, reducing the latency of telephone line communications to less than 200 milliseconds even on long distance or overseas calls, as delays above this value result in frequent interruptions or awkward pauses in communications as callers wait for a response from the other end. It also meant reliable calls that were not accidentally disconnected, low levels of static and background noise, and minimal signal distortion as callers voices are modulated from analog to digital and back to analog again over the Public Switched Telephone Network (PSTN).

When enterprises began using telco services such as Integrated Services Digital Network (ISDN) and leased lines for connecting their geographically remote offices into a wide area network (WAN), QoS referred to the reliability of the carrier's WAN services for carrying network traffic, which was especially important for synchronous links between mainframes and remote terminals. However, QoS in its modern sense is associated with the emergence of Asynchronous Transfer Mode (ATM) networking, a technology that allows QoS parameters such as delay, jitter, and loss to be enforced for traffic traveling over the network. In essence, ATM allows "traffic contracts" to be established for different types of applications running on the network to ensure that applications that are sensitive to delay or hungry for bandwidth perform as users want them to. The fact that ATM employs fixed-size 53-byte cells is an advantage in implementing QoS on this technology, as ATM switches can generally process fixed-size cells faster than variable length ones. QoS as it refers to ATM networking basically means two things:

- **Prioritization:** Every cell is assigned a service class, and cells belonging to a specific service class are all handled the same way by switches on the ATM network. Prioritization allows different kinds of traffic to be treated differently onan ATM network. For example, voice traffic can be given higher priority than data to ensure that voice communications are always reliable. Different kinds of data traffic can be treated similarly. For example, traffic for an accounting application can be given high priority, while Web traffic can be assigned a lower priority.
- **Resource reservation:** An ATM connection can request and be assigned a given amount of bandwidth along the entire path between the two end nodes involved. This ensures that the application making the request will perform its function during the connection. Because ATM represents a homogeneous, tightly managed cell-switched system, resource reservation is achievable.

Although ATM remains the winner in the arena of network technologies that support QoS, the greatest interest today is in bringing QoS to Internet Protocol (IP) networks such as the Internet. IP was originally designed as a "best effort" delivery service with no guarantees of reliability, delay, or performance. As a result of the underlying operation of the Transmission Control Protocol (TCP) used to establish IP sessions, and because IP employs variable-length packets that are more complex for routers and local area network (LAN) switches to process than fixed-size ATM cells, it has been difficult to bring QoS to IP networks. Efforts have been underway in this regard for years and have resulted in complex protocols such as DiffServ, Resource Reservation Protocol (RSVP), and Multiprotocol Label Switching (MPLS). These efforts are not complete, and IP QoS generally remains a technology that is complex to implement and whose promises are not quite realized. Simple packet-based IP QoS prioritization schemes work well but are difficult to scale to the enterprise level, and more complex resource reservation-based IP QoS is difficult to achieve over networks with multiple subnets and combinations of hubs, switches, and routers. This is discussed further below.

Implementation

This section will cover the details of ATM QoS and examine the efforts underway to make IP QoS a reality. Beginning with ATM, the basic QoS parameters (or traffic parameters) that can be negotiated on an ATM network include the following:

- **Cell Transfer Delay (CTD):** The latency in seconds for a connection
- **Cell Delay Variation (CDV):** The tolerance per second for cells that should not exceed the peak cell rate
- **Cell Loss Ratio (CLR):** The acceptable ratio of cells delivered to cells lost in a transmission
- **Maximum Burst Size (MBS):** The maximum number of cells per burst
- **Peak Cell Rate (PCR):** The maximum number of cells that can be transmitted per second based on the specified peak bandwidth per second
- **Sustainable Cell Rate (SCR):** The maximum number of cells that can be transmitted per second based on the specified sustainable bandwidth per second

To implement QoS in an ATM network, the sending node signals the network using User to Network Interface (UNI) version 4 signaling to reserve bandwidth, restrict cell loss or delay, or similar QoS parameters. The ATM switches configure themselves accordingly to ensure that the requested QoS is achieved. ATM QoS is "hard state" QoS in that connections may be denied if they violate established QoS settings for the network. Some of the kinds of QoS behaviors that can be enforced on an ATM network include

- **Traffic contracts:** Each ATM end node in an ATM network negotiates a traffic contract with that network to specify data stream parameters such as peak bandwidth, average bandwidth, and maximum burst size. These parameters can be defined for the end node to control the type and amount of traffic that the host can send over an ATM circuit. If an ATM switch in the circuit cannot meet these requirements, it sends a message to the transmitting host indicating that the connection is refused. Each virtual channel or virtual path that is established by an ATM end node in an ATM network has its own traffic contract.

- **Traffic shaping:** This involves ATM devices using data queues to smooth out traffic bursts and limit the peak data rate so that the conditions of the negotiated traffic contracts are met. ATM switches can use several kinds of queuing, including first-in/first-out (FIFO) queuing, prioritized queuing, and weighted fair queuing.
- **Traffic policing:** ATM switches enforce traffic contracts so that the agreed-upon QoS conditions of each data stream are met. If these conditions are violated, ATM switches set the cell-loss priority (CLP) bit of each offending cell, which indicates that the offending cells may be dropped should congestion occur at the switch.

These mechanisms enable ATM QoS to support several different classes of QoS, such as

- **Constant Bit Rate (CBR):** The type of traffic under consideration requires a guaranteed rate of transport and does not tolerate cell loss. To implement CBR, an ATM end station informs the ATM network of the required QoS parameters during call setup. The network then performs admission control by reserving the necessary bandwidth or refusing the connection. The end station is responsible for complying with the agreed-upon peak data rate—if it exceeds this rate, the network drops the offending cells.
- **Variable Bit Rate (VBR):** Similar to CBR, except that maximum burst size and maximum sustainable rate are negotiated in addition to peak data rate.
- **Unspecified Bit Rate (UBR):** Used mainly for LAN emulation (LANE) mode—that is, running IP traffic over ATM backbones. In UBR, if a cell is dropped due to congestion, the entire IP packet to which the cell belongs is retransmitted. UBR does not reserve bandwidth or establish a cell-loss ratio.
- **Available Bit Rate (ABR):** Also used in LAN emulation mode, ABR implements periodic polling of the ATM network to adjust the data transmission rate as needed.

In the realm of IP networks, QoS can be implemented using the same basic approaches used in ATM, namely, prioritization and resource reservation. Prioritization means that the way a particular IP packet will be handled by QoS-enabled devices such as suitable routers and switches on the network is embedded within the packet itself. In other words, IP QoS prioritization works on a packet-by-packet basis, and as a packet traverses the network the various switches and routers handle the packet independently of one another (stateless QoS). Priority-based QoS is configured by setting packet-forwarding rules on the routers and switches on the network, so all such devices on the network must support this feature in order for it to work properly. Priority-based IP QoS schemes generally employ multiple queues on suitable routers and switches so that different types of traffic (packets having different priorities) are delivered to different queues on the device. The device then processes these queues in a way that ensures that traffic with high priority is processed first. Priority-based IP QoS is the basis of the IEEE 802.1p standard and is implemented at Layer 2 (the data link layer) of the Open Systems Interconnection (OSI) reference model, but there is also a Layer 3 approach to IP QoS prioritization called DiffServ, which is discussed later in this article.

By contrast, IP QoS resource reservation uses a stateful approach in which the receiving node (not the sending node) uses RSVP to contact all the various switches and routers along the path to be used, telling each device to reserve the required bandwidth for the traffic. This is complicated by the fact that the switches and routers must be able to adjust to changes in network performance should they occur. The network interface cards (NICs) of the sending and receiving hosts must also support QoS—in other words, the resource reservation type of QoS requires end-to-end support in order to work. The resource reservation approach to IP QoS using RSVP is the method utilized by the QoS Admission Control Service of Microsoft Windows 2000 to implement IP QoS on this platform.

RSVP is the basis of the integrated services (IntServ) approach to IP QoS because this feature must be "integrated" across all packet-forwarding devices on the network in order to work, including routers, switches, and NICs. The IntServ approach enables IP networks to be used as the backbone for applications ranging from voice, video, and real-time data to classical data traffic. By contrast, IP QoS prioritization employs differentiated services (DiffServ), which classifies traffic into different priority classes using the DS field in the IPv4 packet header to define how the packet will be forwarded. The DiffServ approach can be implemented on an IP network with only minor changes to routers but leaves the complexity of implementing QoS to the edges of the network. DiffServ provides only a statistically based QoS to IP networks with no firm guarantee of bandwidth or traffic handling—in contrast to IntServ, which provides guaranteed QoS, albeit in a much more complicated fashion. So it is a trade-off—DiffServ, with its statistical QoS capabilities but ease of configuration and use of existing routing and switching devices, or IntServ, with its guaranteed QoS capabilities but complex configuration and requirement of routing and switching devices that fully support RSVP.

Another approach to IP QoS is Multiprotocol Label Switching (MPLS), which was derived from Cisco's proprietary label switching technology. MPLS is designed to bring some of the advantages of circuit-switched networks to switched IP networks, including predictable delay and latency, the ability to reserve bandwidth, and QoS. All of the various approaches to IP QoS, including IntServ/RSVP, DiffServ, MPLS, and 802.1p are implemented to various degrees on routers and switches from Cisco Systems and other infrastructure vendors.

Prospects

IP QoS remains an elusive target and, in the opinion of some analysts, even an unnecessary one, considering the cost and complexity of implementing it in the enterprise. On the LAN side, the increasing availability and decreasing cost of Gigabit Ethernet (GbE) has made "throwing bandwidth at the problem" a cheaper and easier solution to network congestion than implementing IP QoS. In the WAN environment, where bandwidth is still scarce, IP

QoS makes more sense. On the other hand, prices for high-end WAN services such as T3 and OC-48 are likely to drop in the near future, since the speed at which Synchronous Optical Network (SONET) can run over fiber and the number of channels that can be carried by a single strand are doubling every year. Although the emergence of Voice over IP (VoIP) as a viable enterprise technology may seem to be a driving force for the implementation of IP QoS, some network architects contend that occasional dropouts or garbled transmissions are a small price to pay compared to overhauling their whole infrastructure to support IP QoS. The best solution may be to implement basic two-level traffic prioritization (high priority for voice and video, low for data), upgrade to GbE, and leave it at that for now until IP QoS technology matures and becomes cheaper and easier to manage.

See Also: *802.1p, Asynchronous Transfer Mode (ATM), bandwidth, cell (ATM), Gigabit Ethernet (GbE), Integrated Services Digital Network (ISDN), Internet Protocol (IP), jitter, latency, Multiprotocol Label Switching (MPLS), Public Switched Telephone Network (PSTN), Resource Reservation Protocol (RSVP), Transmission Control Protocol (TCP), wide area network (WAN)*

Quarter Inch Cartridge (QIC)

The original tape format for tape backups.

Overview

Quarter Inch Cartridge (QIC) is a cartridge-based tape format that was developed in the 1970s and became widely popular in the enterprise—in fact, it is still in use in many places. QIC employs serpentine recording to record several parallel tracks on the tape, switching directions at the end of each track. QIC tape cartridges come in two basic formats:

- **Data cartridge (DC):** A large 4 by 6 inch cassette 5/8 inch thick.

- **Mini cartridge (MC):** A smaller 3 ¼ by 2 ½ by 3/5 inch cassette.

There are dozens of different QIC formats based on tape capacity, transfer speed, and interface. Most QIC drives today employ Travan technology originally developed by 3M Corporation and now licensed by Imation Corporation.

For More Information

Get more information about QIC at *www.qic.org.*

See Also: *backup, tape format*

quartet signaling

A signaling method used by 100VG-AnyLAN.

Overview

Quartet signaling makes possible the transmission of data at a speed of 100 megabits per second (Mbps) while using the same transmission frequencies that are used on standard 10BaseT networks. Quartet signaling enables 100VG-AnyLan to leverage existing installations of Category 3, 4, and 5 unshielded twisted-pair (UTP) cabling for 100-Mbps transmission.

Implementation

100VG-AnyLan employs the demand priority method for controlling access to the media, which prevents collisions from occurring. Although 10BaseT Ethernet networks use only two pairs of wires in a four-pair UTP cabling—one pair for transmitting data and the other pair for receiving data and for detecting collisions on the network—100VG-AnyLAN transmits signals over all four pairs of wire in voice-grade UTP cabling, hence the term *quartet signaling*. In addition, quartet signaling uses a different line coding technique than the traditional Manchester coding method used in Ethernet networks. Quartet signaling uses the 5B/6B NRZ line coding method, but Manchester coding uses a 1B/2B scheme whereby 1 bit of data is encoded using two binary symbols. The 1B/2B algorithm is reliable and simple to implement but inefficient. The 5B/6B method encodes 5 bits using six binary symbols, which allows two and a half times as much information to be transmitted per wire compared to 10BaseT Ethernet (as shown in the following table).

Calculations for Line Coding Data Rates

	Manchester Coding	*Quartet Signaling*
Line coding	1B/2B	5B/6B
Line frequency	20 MHz	30 MHz
Data rate per pair	($^1/_2$) x 20 = 10 Mbps	($^5/_6$) x 30 = 25 Mbps
Number of pairs used	1	4
Total data rate	1 x 10 = 10 Mbps	4 x 25 = 100 Mbps

Notes

The 100BaseT4 form of Fast Ethernet also uses all four pairs of wire in twisted-pair cabling.

See Also: *10BaseT, 100VG-AnyLAN, demand priority, Ethernet, line coding, Manchester coding, unshielded twisted-pair (UTP) cabling*

queue

A collection of items waiting to be processed in a specific order.

Overview

Examples of queues in computer and networking technology are numerous and include the following:

- A print queue, which consists of print jobs waiting to be sent to a print device
- A messaging queue (on a mail server such as Microsoft Exchange Server), which consists of messages waiting to be sent
- A backlog of packets waiting to be forwarded over a specific interface by a router
- Information, function calls, or transactions sent by one application and forwarded to another by Microsoft Message Queuing (MSMQ)
- A collection of fax messages waiting to be processed and sent by a fax server
- A series of system messages, such as key presses and mouse clicks, sent by applications to an operating system for processing

queuing methods

Methods used by routers and local area network (LAN) switches for queuing incoming traffic.

Overview

Most LAN switches and routers implement some form of queuing to ensure that packets are not lost in times of heavy traffic. Certain forms of queuing also enable these devices to implement quality of service (QoS) through prioritizing different types of traffic by using different queues for each type. The most common queuing methods used in such devices include

- **First-in/first-out (FIFO) queuing:** Here, incoming packets are stored in the queue and forwarded in the order in which they arrived. FIFO queuing requires no configuration and helps routers handle traffic congestion, but they do not support QoS. On Cisco routers, FIFO queuing is the default queuing method for all interfaces unless configured otherwise.
- **Priority queuing:** Routers using this form of queuing employ multiple queues for different types of traffic, typically four queues for high, medium, normal, and low priority traffic. These traffic types can be distinguished according to incoming interface, packet size, source address, destination address, or network protocol. Queues are emptied in a fashion that ensures that higher priority traffic is given first attention, which enables these devices to support Internet Protocol (IP) QoS prioritization. Priority queuing is used by Asynchronous Transfer Mode (ATM) switches and is often used on wide area network (WAN) links to ensure that high-priority traffic such as Voice over IP (VoIP) and Enterprise Resource Planning (ERP) applications perform as expected.
- **Weighted fair queuing:** This is a flow-based form of queuing that allows interactive traffic to be moved ahead in the queue to ensure good performance. Weighted fair queuing implements QoS by ensuring that applications that require bandwidth get enough of it to function satisfactorily. Weighted fair queuing was introduced with release 11 of the Cisco Internetwork Operating System (IOS).

Queuing methods other than FIFO generally do not need to be configured for wide area network (WAN) access routers if the utilization rate of the WAN link is low. The interfaces that generally benefit most from queuing are subrate interfaces, that is, speeds slower than T1 (fractional T1 being the typical example).

See Also: *Asynchronous Transfer Mode (ATM), Ethernet switch, Internetwork Operating System (IOS), quality of service (QoS), router*

quota management

Managing disk storage for network users.

Overview

Quota management involves setting storage limits for individual users on file servers and other forms of network storage. Although disk space has become an inexpensive commodity over the last few years, managing large amounts of user files can become a nightmare from a management perspective. Setting quotas for users prevents them from accumulating unnecessary files and encourages them to manage their network workspace wisely. Quota management tools generally alert users when volumes are nearly full, which also frees administrators from the chore of intervening by locating and deleting unnecessary files or adding more disk space. Quotas also prevent volumes from becoming full, which can cause storage systems to crash under certain circumstances.

Marketplace

In addition to the disk quota management tools bundled with Microsoft Windows 2000, Windows XP, and Windows .NET Server, and, a number of third-party tools from different vendors are helpful for managing storage in an enterprise environment. Some popular examples include QuotaAdvisor from WQuinn, Quota Server from NORTHERN, Quota Sentinel from NTP Software, and SpaceGuard from Tools4ever.

See Also: *storage*

RA

Stands for registration authority, a company or organization that is responsible for receiving and validating requests for digital certificates and public/private key pairs.

See: registration authority (RA)

rack

Also called an equipment rack, a metal frame for holding and organizing networking devices.

Overview

Racks offer a way to organize equipment in a wiring closet. Racks can be either wall-mounted or freestanding and come in various heights and standard widths, with 19 inches being by far the most common width. This width is measured between the mounting holes on the rack where equipment is mounted—the actual width of the rack itself is usually several inches wider. The two most common heights for racks are 48 and 83 inches. On industry-standard racks, the holes on the frame are spaced 1.75 inches apart vertically, a distance symbolized as a "U" or "unit" of rack space. If a piece of networking equipment is described as 3U, it therefore occupies 3 x 1.75 = 5.25 inches of vertical space once it is mounted in the rack. A 48-inch rack is 21U in height, meaning it can hold a total of 21 1U devices (or some other combination of devices). An 83-inch rack is 42U in height.

Racks usually come with a variety of accessories. Cable organizers, for example, allow you to run bundled cabling down the side or back of the rack to avoid "spaghetti." You can use sliding shelves or drawers to incorporate odd-sized equipment in racks for easy access for configuration and wiring. Vented sides and fan trays help circulate air to keep equipment from overheating. By attaching a locking plastic or glass door, you can convert some racks into cabinets for more secure storage.

Wall-mounted racks allow you to organize equipment in areas with limited floor space. If your area is prone to earthquakes, it is a good idea to bolt the base of the rack to the floor to protect your equipment.

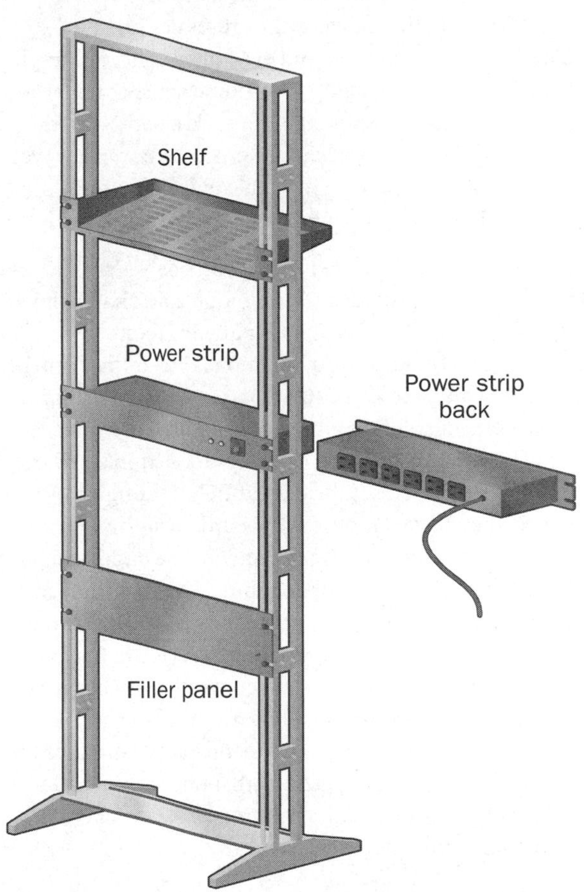

Rack. *Example of a typical equipment rack.*

R

Uses

A rack-mountable unit is a device designed to be mounted in a rack. Such rack-mountable devices include servers, hubs, routers, Ethernet switches, patch panels, and uninterruptible power supply (UPS) devices. Rack-mountable servers deserve special attention, as use of these devices in enterprise environments and Internet data centers has grown exponentially in recent years. Numerous manufacturers produce a variety of 1U and 2U rack-mount servers, including Compaq Computer Corporation, Dell Computer Corporation, Hewlett-Packard, and IBM. These servers often support hot-pluggable drives, dual 10/100 or 100/1000 network interface cards (NICs) with automatic failover, embedded hardware redundant array of independent disks (RAID), and other advanced features designed to enhance their reliability and ease of use. Storage appliances from many vendors also come in rack-mount format for easy interfacing with rack-mount servers. Another popular approach is to provide a complete Web server in a 1U appliance format, something widely used by Web hosting companies.

A novel approach is ClearCube Technology's C3 architecture, which provides a rack-mountable chassis into which up to eight fully functional CPU (central processing unit) blades (fully functional PCs in the form of a blade) can be inserted. C3 is essentially a desktop management solution where desktop PCs are replaced by C3 cage units that are centrally located in a server room or wiring closet. Instead of PCs residing on users' desks, they have a mouse, keyboard, monitor, and a small C/Port box that is connected to the cage using Category 5 (Cat5) network cabling. The C3 architecture allows these C/Port boxes to be located up to 600 feet (183 meters) from the cage. The advantage is that when a problem occurs with a user's computer, you can repair it in the server room instead of walking over to the user's work area. The C3 architecture also simplifies the process of operating system and application installations and upgrades, and it minimizes the potential of users damaging their workstations.

R

Notes

A ladder rack is a modular rack system for supporting cable runs in walls, false floors, and false ceilings, not a rack for mounting servers and other networking devices.

See Also: *cabinet, cabling*

RADIUS

Stands for Remote Authentication Dial-In User Service, an industry-standard security protocol for dial-up data networking services.

See: *Remote Authentication Dial-In User Service (RADIUS)*

RADSL

Stands for Rate-Adjusted Digital Subscriber Line, a Digital Subscriber Line (DSL) technology.

See: *Rate-Adjusted Digital Subscriber Line (RADSL)*

RAID

Stands for redundant array of independent disks, a group of technologies that enhance the performance and/or fault tolerance of disk storage systems.

See: *redundant array of independent disks (RAID)*

RAIT

Stands for redundant array of independent tapes, a technology that enhances the fault tolerance of tape backup systems.

See: *redundant array of independent tapes (RAIT)*

Rate-Adjusted Digital Subscriber Line (RADSL)

A Digital Subscriber Line (DSL) technology.

Overview

Rate-Adjusted Digital Subscriber Line (RADSL) is similar to Asymmetric Digital Subscriber Line (ADSL) but it also includes support for real-time allocation of bandwidth based on line quality. This makes RADSL more flexible and reliable than traditional ADSL, as it can accommodate changing line conditions to ensure that traffic is efficiently transported. Like ADSL, RADSL is an asymmetric technology that typically supports speeds up to 7 megabits per second (Mbps) in the downstream direction and up to 1.5 Mbps upstream.

See Also: *Asymmetric Digital Subscriber Line (ADSL), Digital Subscriber Line (DSL)*

RBOC

Stands for Regional Bell Operating Company, a large incumbent telco.

See: *Regional Bell Operating Company (RBOC)*

Rcp

A UNIX command for copying files to or from remote hosts.

Overview

Rcp is one of the popular r-commands available on all UNIX platforms. Rcp uses Transmission Control Protocol (TCP) to ensure reliable delivery of data between the client and the host. Rcp can be scripted in a batch file and does not require a password. The remote host must be running the rshd service, and the user's username must be configured in the remote host's .rhosts file.

Rcp is implemented on the Microsoft Windows 2000, Windows XP, and Windows .NET Server platforms, but this version includes only rcp client software and not rshd services.

See Also: *Transmission Control Protocol (TCP), UNIX*

RDP

Stands for Remote Desktop Protocol, a protocol for terminal-based computing.

See: *Remote Desktop Protocol (RDP)*

Recreational Software Advisory Council (RSAC)

A nonprofit organization with a content advisory system for Web sites on the Internet.

Overview

The system, known as RSACi (Recreational Software Advisory Council on the Internet), allows Web site administrators to rate their sites according to degrees of potentially objectionable content. There are four basic types of content, each with five levels, rated from 0 to 4. The content areas are Sex, Nudity, Violence, and Offensive Language.

By rating their Web sites according to the RSACi system, Web site administrators can help adults protect children from content that might be objectionable. Microsoft Internet Explorer has built-in client support for the RSACi system, which is administered using a password-protection scheme. Popular Internet portals such as America Online (AOL), Microsoft Network (MSN), and Yahoo! employ the RSACi system.

For More Information

Visit RSAC at *www.rsac.org.*

recursive query

A type of Domain Name System (DNS) query.

Overview

In a recursive query, the resolver contacts a name server to perform a name lookup, and the name server either returns a result or an error. The name server cannot refer the client to a different name server, but it can forward the query directly to another name server if it has a forwarder configured.

When a name lookup is performed on a name server, the resolver sends a recursive query to a nearby name server. If the name is outside the name server's zone of authority, the name server cannot resolve the name and returns an error unless it is also configured as a forwarder. If this is the case, the nearby name server performs an iterative query on a root name server, which then responds with the Internet Protocol (IP) address of a name server whose zone of authority includes the desired top-level domain. Further iterative queries are performed until the name is resolved into its IP address or an error is produced.

See Also: *inverse query, iterative query*

redirection

A process whereby a Web server forwards a request for a file to a different directory, Web site, or application.

Overview

Redirection enables client requests to always be fulfilled, even when content in a site is being updated or if the name of a virtual directory has been changed. For example, if you want to replace an old version of a page named old.htm with a newer version named new.htm, but you do not want to alter the navigational structure of your site or bother users with a notice of the change, you can enter a <META> tag in the <HEAD> section of the old.htm file to redirect browsers to the new page.

Examples

For example, the following tag in the <HEAD> section of the old page causes a browser accessing that page to be redirected to the new page after viewing the old page for 3 seconds:

```
<META HTTP-EQUIV="REFRESH"
CONTENT="3;URL=NEW.HTM">
```

You can place a notice on the old page such as, "This page will be redirected to its newer version after 3 seconds."

Notes

The term *redirection* is also used in printing. For example, if you are trying to print some documents but a print device has failed, Microsoft Windows 2000, Windows XP, and Windows .NET Server let you redirect all outstanding jobs for the print device to another print device that uses the same printer driver as the failed device. To redirect your pending documents, follow these steps:

1. Open the property sheet for the failed print device and select the Ports tab.
2. Click the Add Port button, select Local Port, select New Port, and enter the Universal Naming Convention (UNC) path for the second print device.
3. Click OK, and then click Apply.

See Also: *Web server*

redirector

A networking component on a client machine enabling the client to access shared network resources.

Overview

The function of a redirector is to make it appear to the client that shared network resources are located on the local machine instead of elsewhere on the network. On a machine running Microsoft Windows 2000, the Workstation service is the default redirector. However, you can install multiple redirectors in Windows 2000 if you need to provide users with connectivity to different file systems.

The Windows 2000 redirector is implemented in the form of a file system driver. When a client program requests a network resource, the request is handed to the I/O Manager, which calls the redirector. The redirector translates the request into Server Message Block (SMB) requests for transmission over the network to the Server service on the remote computer.

See Also: *Server Message Block (SMB)*

redundant array of independent disks (RAID)

A group of technologies that enhance the performance or fault tolerance, or both, of disk storage systems.

Overview

Redundant array of independent disks (RAID) technologies were conceived in the late 1980s as a way of preventing input/output (I/O) and disk storage from becoming the bottleneck in the emerging PC architecture. This was because at the time, processor and memory technologies were growing exponentially while capabilities and costs of disk storage were changing only incrementally. The original meaning of RAID was "redundant array of inexpensive disks," which

R

redundant array of independent disks (RAID)

highlighted the original purpose of RAID technologies as a means of utilizing the relatively low cost of commodity PC disk drives to provide storage solutions comparable to much more expensive mainframe disk storage platforms. By utilizing such technologies as mirroring, striping, and parity, RAID solutions soon emerged as the storage platform of choice for the PC server platform, a place which it still holds today, since RAID technologies have become integrated into network attached storage (NAS) and storage area network (SAN) technologies as well.

Types

The various levels of RAID that are currently defined include the following:

- **RAID 0:** Also called disk striping, this approach sees data written across the group of drives in stripes. Such "stripe sets" do not support any fault tolerance, but they do provide fast read/write performance. RAID 0 is most frequently employed in an environment where very large files (such as video or medical imaging files) need to be saved and read.
- **RAID 1:** Also called disk mirroring, this method has data written simultaneously to two (or more) disks, making one disk drive a mirror image of the other. Using mirror sets improves read performance slightly but has no effect on a single disk system for write performance. RAID 1 is frequently used for mission-critical servers such as authentication servers and e-commerce servers.
- **RAID 2:** Sometimes referred to as disk striping with error checking and correcting (ECC) or Hamming Code ECC, in this method information is striped (written across) bitwise across several disks and error checking information is calculated and written to a specially designated disk. RAID 2 has slow I/O and is rarely used.
- **RAID 3:** Sometimes known as disk striping with parity or parallel transfer with parity, in this approach data is striped to a disk set and parity information is written to a single disk for error recovery. I/O performance is not good and this method is rarely used nowadays.
- **RAID 4:** Sometimes referred to as disk striping with large stripes, here entire records are written to single drives, and parity information is stored on a single disk for error recovery. Write contention makes this method undesirable in most situations, and it is rarely used.
- **RAID 5:** Also known as disk striping with parity, here both the data and parity information are striped across all disks in stripes to provide full data recoverability in case any single drive fails. Disk striping with parity is an excellent way to protect data from the downtime caused by disk failures and is widely used in enterprises of all sizes. RAID 5 requires a minimum of three disks in order to work.
- **RAID 6:** Sometimes called disk striping with two parity schemes, this is an extension of RAID 5 that has additional fault tolerance built in and is designed to protect data against multiple simultaneous failed disk drives. Interest in this technology is growing in the enterprise networking arena, especially for high-availability e-commerce sites.
- **RAID 10:** Sometimes known as disk striping with disk mirroring, this is an expensive solution that has the same level of fault tolerance as RAID 1 together with the rapid I/O support of RAID 0. It is not commonly used due to the high cost of implementing it (every disk in the stripe set must be mirrored with a second disk). The "10" in RAID 10 is really 1+0 and the technology is sometimes called RAID 1+0 or RAID 0+1 to indicate more clearly what it is about.
- **RAID 53:** Sometimes called disk striping of stripe sets, this approach uses a stripe set (RAID 0) of individual RAID 3 disk arrays. RAID 53 has the same level of fault tolerance as RAID 3 and is very expensive and therefore not commonly used. The name RAID 53 is something of a misnomer, since one might more likely guess the designation to be RAID 30 = RAID 3+0.

Implementation

The two basic approaches to implementing RAID are

- **Software RAID:** This involves adding multiple Small Computer System Interface (SCSI) drives to the motherboard of a PC server and managing these drives as a RAID system using specialized software such as the built-in RAID support of Disk Management in Microsoft Windows 2000 Server, Windows XP, and Windows .NET Server.
- **Hardware RAID:** This utilizes separate storage units with dedicated I/O and integrated processing to provide better performance than software RAID but at a higher price. Popular hardware RAID 5 units often have hot-rebuild, hot-swap, and hot-spare capabilities to protect business-critical data and ensure high availability.

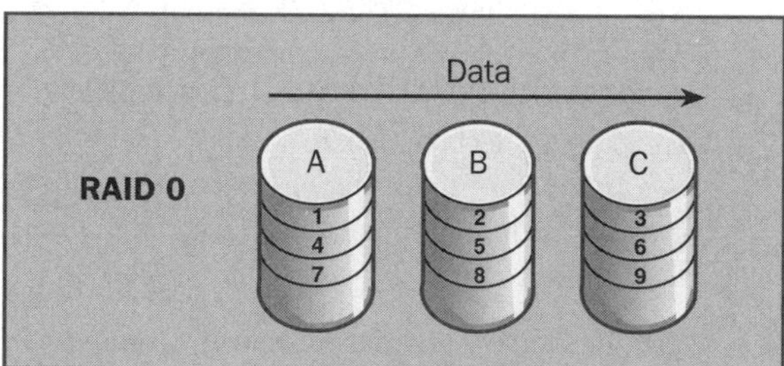

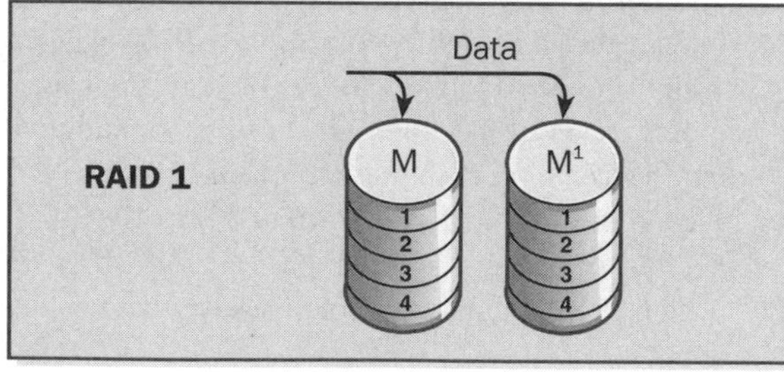

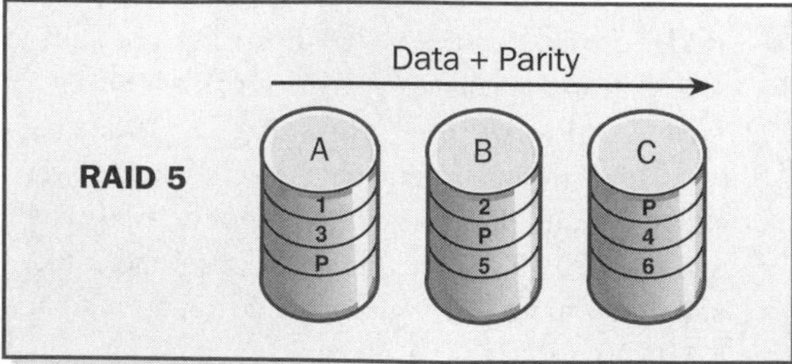

RAID. *The three common RAID technologies.*

Prospects

Different vendors have proposed a number of other RAID levels, including RAID 6, which employs high-speed caching and a real-time embedded operating system to support asynchronous transfers, and RAID 1+5, which combines the features of both mirroring and striping with parity. Land-5's RAIDn technology is one example of RAID 1+5, and this technology is expected to make inroads in the enterprise over the next few years. The most popular RAID levels, however, are still RAID 0, 1, and 5, and Windows 2000 Server supports all three of these storage technologies.

Another emerging approach is to integrate hardware RAID directly onto the motherboards of servers. This approach is expected to yield commodity PC servers costing less than $1,000 with built-in hardware RAID levels 0, 1, and 5 support.

For More Information

Visit the RAID Advisory Board at *www.raid-advisory.com.*

See Also: *fault tolerance, storage*

redundant array of independent tapes (RAIT)

A technology that enhances the fault tolerance of tape backup systems.

Overview

What redundant array of independent disks (RAID) is for disk storage technology, redundant array of independent tapes (RAIT) is for tape drives. RAIT employs multiple tape drives working together in synchronization to stripe incoming data across multiple backup tapes simultaneously. This provides a speed advantage for writing data to tape but poses some issues in the area of reading or modifying information stored on tapes. For example, the archived data is not accessible unless all of the tapes are available to be read. Furthermore, if even one byte of a large archived file needed to be modified, the entire file would need to be rewritten. However, data archived to tape rarely needs to be modified, but rather read for restore purposes.

To overcome this reading limitation, RAIT 5 was developed, the counterpart of RAID 5 stripe set with parity disk storage technology. RAIT 5 distributes parity information across multiple tapes in a RAIT system. Then, when data needs to be restored from tape, this can be done even if one tape is corrupt or missing. The restore process will be slow, but the fault-tolerant aspect of RAIT 5 is appealing to large enterprises that need to archive large amounts of data to tape.

See Also: *backup, redundant array of independent disks (RAID), tape drive*

Regional Bell Operating Company (RBOC)

A large incumbent telco.

Overview

Regional Bell Operating Companies (RBOCs) are regional telcos that were created as a result of the 1983 divestiture of the American Telephone and Telegraph (AT&T) telephone system, also known at the time as the "Bell System" or "Ma Bell." The divestiture divided the telephone company landscape into two parts:

- **Incumbent Local Exchange Carriers (ILECs):** These carriers owned the local loop in their particular coverage areas and provided local telephone services to their subscribers. The divestiture was done to end AT&T's monopoly over the U.S. telephone system. The company was broken up into several dozen smaller Bell Operating Companies (BOCs), each of which was to supply telephone services to local loop subscribers in a given geographical area. Seven larger Regional Bell Operating Companies (RBOCs) were also created, each consisting of two or more BOCs. In addition to the BOCs and RBOCs, dozens of small independent LECs also serviced different areas of the country. The seven original RBOCs were Ameritech, Bell Atlantic, BellSouth Corporation, Nynex, Pacific Bell Telephone Company (PacBell), Southwestern Bell Telephone Company, and US West.
- **Inter-exchange carriers (IXCs):** These companies provided long-distance services for subscribers through the ILECs' local loop. AT&T was left to function as the first IXC, and is joined today by Sprint Corporation and Worldcom to form the "big three" long-distance carriers.

The telephone systems landscape began to change with the passage of the Telecommunications Act of 1996. The act allowed RBOCs and independent LECs to compete with existing IXCs for long-distance carrier business, allowed mergers between telephone companies depending on FCC approval, and essentially opened up the telecommunications market to all kinds of companies, including cable television companies.

Of the seven original RBOCs, only four remain today:

- **SBC Communications:** This company merged with Ameritech and PacBell and is the largest RBOC.
- **Verizon Communications:** Formerly called Bell Atlantic, this company merged with Nynex and GTE and then renamed itself Verizon, and is the second largest RBOC.
- **Qwest Communications:** This company bought US West.
- **BellSouth:** This is the only remaining original RBOC.

Prospects

Some RBOCs—Verizon and SBC, in particular—are beginning to compete in the long-distance market long controlled by the IXCs, at least in their home states. Alignments between RBOCs are also occurring, such as the Cingular venture between BellSouth and SBC, which created the second largest wireless network in the United States. (Verizon, which bought Vodafone, has the largest such network, and AT&T is in third place).

Some industry analysts see the consolidation in the RBOC market as an indication of the failure of the Telecommunications Act of 1996, since the legislation was intended to foster competition and diversify the telecom landscape rather than lead to greater consolidation and fewer choices for consumers. However, the "Big Four" RBOCs are now large enough to be in a position to compete with the "Big Three" IXCs, and the eventual result will hopefully be a wider variety of services and lower prices for business and residential consumers.

The Competitive Local Exchange Carrier (CLEC) "bubble" of the late 1990s has largely burst, and many CLECs have been acquired by RBOCs, IXCs, or other communication companies. CLECs, which were mostly startups reselling Digital Subscriber Line (DSL) services obtained from RBOCs, depended upon the goodwill of RBOCs for obtaining access to telco central offices (COs) to colocate their switching equipment, and some RBOCs were frequently uncooperative in this regard, putting many CLECs in an untenable business position. The result is that the DSL market is now dominated by the RBOCs, with SBC, Verizon, and Qwest being the top three in this market. SBC partnered with CLEC Covad Communications to gain top position in the DSL market, and Verizon acquired NorthPoint Communications for similar purposes. Qwest (through US West) and SBC are also extending DSL services beyond their own home regions.

From an enterprise networking perspective, most large businesses have a kind of love-hate relationship with their RBOC. They love the reliability of RBOC telecommunication services that have matured over many years but hate the high prices and being locked into a single vendor. RBOCs are often slow to provision new high-speed data services, and offer services such as T1 (1.5 megabits per second [Mbps]) and T3 (45 Mbps) but provide few intermediate options between these services. Although the RBOCs will undoubtedly reign supreme in the residential consumer market for years to come, they face stiff competition to their control of the local loop from the new metropolitan Ethernet providers such as Yipes Communications, which has rolled out fiber-based Gigabit Ethernet (GbE) metropolitan area networks (MANs) in large urban areas around the United States.

See Also: *central office (CO), Competitive Local Exchange Carrier (CLEC), Incumbent Local Exchange Carrier (ILEC), inter-exchange carrier (IXC), metropolitan Ethernet, T-carrier, telco*

R

registration authority (RA)

A company or organization that is responsible for receiving and validating requests for digital certificates and public/private key pairs.

Overview

A registration authority is part of a public key infrastructure (PKI) for implementing public key cryptography. The RA receives a certificate request and verifies the identity of the requestor using acceptable forms of identification, which can be communicated face to face, over the telephone, by mail or courier, or in another secure fashion that is acceptable to the RA. Identification can include a driver's license, Social Security number, or another unique identifier for the requestor. If the RA approves the request, it contacts the certificate authority (CA) in the PKI and asks it to issue the requestor the desired digital certificate and key pair. The RA and CA are often different entities within the same company or organization.

See Also: *public key cryptography, public key infrastructure (PKI)*

registry

The database containing configuration information on Microsoft Windows platforms.

Overview

The registry is a hierarchical database in which Windows stores information such as configuration information for installed hardware and software, registered document types, user profiles, property settings for icons, and ports being used. The registry in 32-bit versions of Windows replaces the INI files, such as Win.ini and System.ini, that were used in the 16-bit versions Windows 3.1 and Windows for Workgroups 3.11.

Implementation

The registry in Windows 2000, Windows XP, and Windows .NET Server is logically divided into five subtrees, each containing a hierarchical collection of keys and subkeys (analogous to folders and subfolders in a file system) that themselves contain values (analogous to files). Physically, the registry consists of a series of hives and their associated transaction files located in %SystemRoot%\system32\config.

In Windows 98 and Windows Millennium Edition (Me), the logical structure is similar to that of Windows 2000, Windows XP, and Windows .NET Server, but the physical format is incompatible. A sixth subtree called HKEY_DYN_DATA is created dynamically and is used for performance measuring and Plug and Play configuration. The registry consists of dynamic information stored in RAM (random access memory) and two files in the %Win_Root% directory: system.dat, which stores computer-specific information, and user.dat, which stores user-specific information.

Notes

The main tool you should use to modify the registry is Control Panel, which provides a number of utilities for safely configuring different aspects of the system's hardware and installed software. If you want (or need) to dig deeper into the registry, use the registry editor. You can use the regedit or regedt32 tools instead, but do so carefully—a single wrong value can render your operating system unbootable!

relative path

The hierarchical path that locates a file or folder on a file system starting from the current directory.

Overview

The relative path is different from the absolute path, which locates the file or folder starting from the root of the file system. For example, if the current directory is C:\Windows, the relative path to the executable for the game of Solitaire, which is located in the current directory, is simply the name of the executable—sol.exe. If the current directory is C:\Windows\System, the relative path to Solitaire is ..\sol.exe.

In a UNIX file system, the syntax for relative paths is similar, except that it uses forward slashes instead of backslashes to separate levels in the file system hierarchy.

Notes

The idea of a relative path is also used in other naming contexts. For example, in Active Directory directory service of Microsoft Windows 2000 and Windows .NET Server, you can uniquely and globally specify directory objects using the object's distinguished name, which provides a kind of absolute path within the directory starting at the root and terminating at the desired object. For example, the object representing the user Mitch Tulloch in the domain northwind.expedia.com has this distinguished name:

```
DC=com,DC=expedia,DC=northwind,
OU=Users,CN=Mitch Tulloch
```

If a search context is established as the Users container within the northwind.expedia.com domain, the relative distinguished name of the Mitch Tulloch object is simply

```
CN=Mitch Tulloch
```

This relative distinguished name uniquely identifies the desired object within the Users container in Active Directory.

See Also: *absolute path*

remailer

A Web site that lets you forward e-mail messages anonymously.

Overview

Remailers can be used to ensure the privacy of your e-mail address when you send someone e-mail. This is because when a remailer is used to forward a message, all the original message header information is stripped away. The result is that the recipient has no way of determining who originally sent the message. You could use a remailer, for example, to keep recipients from adding your address to a mailing list. You can also use remailers to prevent yourself from being spammed when you voice an unpopular opinion on a mailing list or some other forum.

Another name for this kind of site is anonymous remailer. Yahoo! has a list of Web-based anonymous remailers.

See Also: *e-mail*

remote access

Technology that enables access to network resources from remote locations.

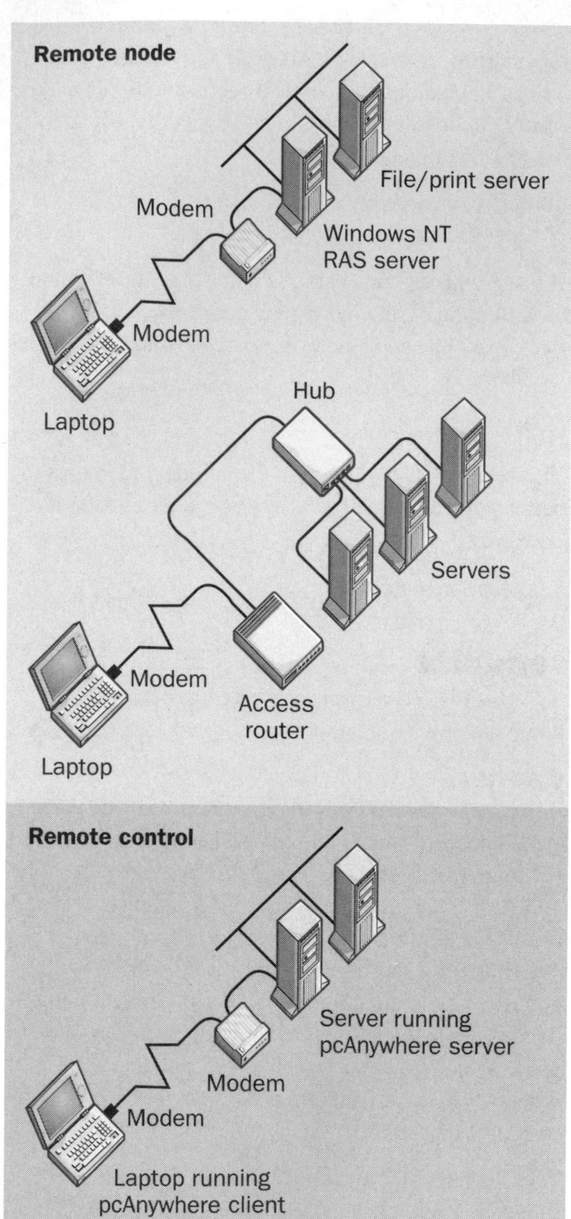

Remote access. *The two kinds of remote access.*

Overview

Remote access is an umbrella term for a group of technologies that enables

- administrators to manage servers, routers, and resources on a network from a remote location
- off-site and mobile users to securely access resources on their corporate networks

Types

There are two basic approaches to remote access:

- **Remote control:** Allows administrators to take control of remote computers and enter keystrokes, issue mouse clicks, and view display output as if they were sitting at the computer's local console. A popular software platform from Symantec Corporation called pcAnywhere is the leader in this category of the enterprise market; it enables administrators to remotely troubleshoot server problems, make configuration changes, and even demonstrate procedures to remote users—in other words, to perform all aspects of remote administration. Provided there is enough bandwidth in the connection, remote control technology usually works well, but when bandwidth is scarce, access to the remote console may be slow and jerky. Remote control access has high security, saves on hardware and licensing costs, and is relatively easy to implement on a network. Microsoft Windows 2000 Server, Windows XP, and Windows .NET Server have their own built-in remote control technology called Terminal Services (TS), which allows up to two concurrent connections for remote control.
- **Remote node:** This is the classic form of remote access and is usually simply referred to as "remote access." In this scenario, a remote access device, such as a router or remote access server (RAS), is used to provide a gateway for remote users to access file, print, and other services on a corporate network—for example, using a laptop and modem. Another remote node scenario is the situation in which a remote branch office accesses resources at company headquarters using a RAS over a leased line or dial-up Integrated Services Digital Line (ISDN) connection. Remote node devices are often computers running specialized remote access software such as the Routing and Remote Access

Service (RRAS) component of Microsoft Windows 2000 and Windows .NET Server. For supporting multiple remote dial-up users, servers can be fitted with a multiport serial board with 4, 8, 12, or more asynchronous communication ports that are connected to an analog modem bank or an ISDN terminal adapter. These machines are sometimes called RAS routers because they have at least one local area network (LAN) and one wide area network (WAN) interface and therefore function essentially as a router. Traditional software routers and LAN switches with ISDN or T1 capability are also frequently used as remote access devices, and these are also sometimes known as access servers. For additional security and ease of use, remote node devices can also include features such as network address translation (NAT), Dynamic Host Configuration Protocol (DHCP) server functionality, password-based authentication, callback, and basic firewall functionality.

Notes

A relatively new solution to the issue of remote access to corporate networks is the concept of the virtual private network (VPN). A VPN is generally a dial-up connection that is tunneled over the Internet to allow remote users to access resources on the corporate network or to allow administrators to remotely administer servers, routers, and other devices. The VPN solution has largely displaced traditional remote node services for mobile users because it allows users to dial in to a local Internet service provider (ISP) and save the long-distance costs associated with dialing in directly to a modem bank connected to a corporate RAS server from a remote location.

See Also: *Integrated Services Digital Network (ISDN), leased line, modem, remote administration, remote control, virtual private network (VPN)*

remote administration

Administering servers, routers, and other network resources from a remote location.

Overview

Remote administration technologies are widely used in today's 24x7 enterprise networks. The capability for administrators to connect to and remotely administer servers while off site when problems arise is essential. Also important is being able to step in and assist remote branch offices in administering their resources over wide area network (WAN) connections.

Types

There are two main approaches to remotely administering enterprise servers: software-based and hardware-based remote administration.

The software-based approach can employ a variety of tools and technologies that enable administrators to do everything from managing permissions on shared folders to actually taking control of a remote machine to configure applications or perform a reboot. Some of the popular platforms and products in this area include

- **Remote node software:** This software provides remote access capability to allow administrators to access shared resources on the remote network. An example here is the Routing and Remote Access Service (RRAS) component of Microsoft Windows 2000 or Windows .NET Server.
- **Remote control software:** This software allows users to actually take control of a remote machine and issue keystrokes or utilize the mouse pointer to do anything a user could do using the machine's local console. The most popular example in this category is Symantec Corporation's pcAnywhere platform, which is widely used in the enterprise for remote control and file transfer. Other popular choices include the Terminal Service (TS) component of Windows 2000 Server, Windows XP, Windows .NET Server, and Citrix Systems' MetaFrame platform. Even some platforms that were originally developed for hacking purposes, such as Back Orifice from Cult of the Dead Cow, have come to be considered legitimate and powerful tools for remote control and administration of servers.
- **Built-in tools:** Widely available tools such as Telnet and Secure Shell (SSH) enable administrators to log in and remotely configure servers, routers, and

R

local area network (LAN) switches from a command prompt window. Routers and switches, in particular, frequently support another form of remote administration called out-of-band management (OBM), which allows administrators to dial into these devices using a modem connected to an RS-232 serial port on the device and then configure the device using a terminal program such as Microsoft HyperTerminal.

- **Web-based administration:** Some software platforms include support for secure remote administration over the Internet using a standard Web browser. For example, Internet Information Services on Windows 2000 includes an Active Server Pages (ASP) application that allows administrators to remotely configure Internet Information Server (IIS) Web servers using a Web browser such as Microsoft Internet Explorer.

The other variety of remote administration technologies includes various hardware-based solutions such as

- **Access servers:** These are generally routers that provide remote access functionality to allow administrators to access resources on a remote network and manage them.
- **Vendor cards:** These are vendor-specific Peripheral Component Interconnect (PCI) cards that can be installed in the vendor's servers to provide remote control management capability. These cards are proprietary for the platform they are designed for and can be accessed even when the server is down or its operating system crashes. Such cards typically include keyboard and mouse ports that can be connected to the server's keyboard and mouse ports and an Ethernet port for connecting to the network. Examples include Hewlett-Packard's TopTools card and Compaq Computer Corporation's Remote Insight, Lights-Out Edition.
- **External keyboard video mouse (KVM) devices:** These range from stand-alone KVM switches to KVM cards that can be inserted into a separate server. This approach has the advantage over vendor cards in that a single KVM device can be used to control multiple servers.
- **Code-operated matrix switches:** These are useful if remote servers simply need to be rebooted. A switch is connected to a device's power supply and can be controlled from a remote location by means of a computer and a modem.

See Also: *Keyboard Video Mouse (KVM) switch, out-of-band management (OBM), remote access, remote control*

Remote Authentication Dial-In User Service (RADIUS)

An industry-standard security protocol for dial-up data networking services.

Overview

The Remote Authentication Dial-In User Service (RADIUS) is a client/server protocol used to securely authenticate dial-up users. RADIUS supports authentication, authorization, and accounting (AAA), a security infrastructure supported by Cisco Systems' Internetwork Operating System (IOS) and by other platforms, including Microsoft Windows 2000 and Windows .NET Server. RADIUS is defined in RFCs 2138 and 2139.

Uses

Internet service providers (ISPs) commonly use RADIUS to provide business customers with secure dial-up connections. RADIUS can also be used to enhance security for virtual private networking (VPN), typically using Point-to-Point Tunneling Protocol (PPTP).

Implementation

RADIUS is a client/server protocol that involves three components:

- **RADIUS client:** Software installed on the network access server (NAS) that allows the client to make a dial-up connection to the remote network.
- **RADIUS server:** Software installed on a separate server that is used to store the profile information of dial-up users in a central database.
- **Dial-up client:** Software used by remote users to dial in and be authenticated by a RADIUS-enabled network.

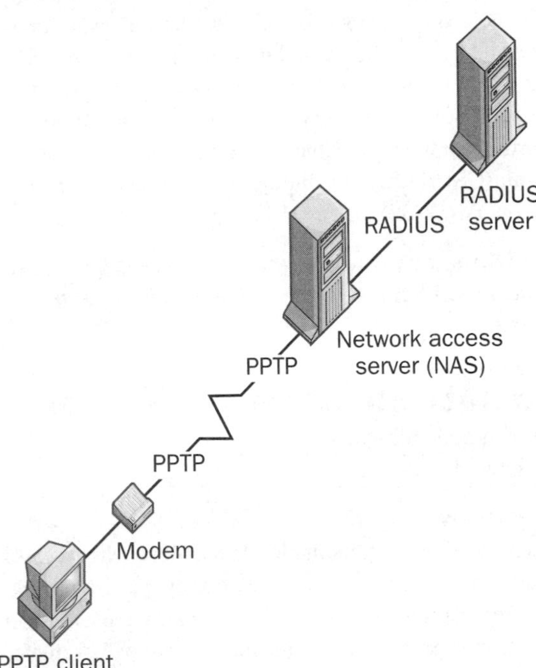

Remote Authentication Dial-In User Service (RADIUS). *A typical implementation of RADIUS for an ISP.*

In a typical scenario, a user dials in to a NAS at an Internet service provider (ISP). The NAS server is the RADIUS client, and it takes the user's credentials and reformats them as RADIUS packets, which it then forwards to the RADIUS server, also located at the ISP. The RADIUS server can then either authenticate the user directly from its user profile database or act as a proxy client to forward the authentication request to some other type of service or security device.

Once the RADIUS server has authenticated the client, it sends a RADIUS Access-Accept message to the NAS to inform it that the user connection attempt should be allowed. RADIUS messages are sent as user datagram protocol (UDP) packets using port 1812 for authentication and 1813 for accounting messages. All messages sent between the RADIUS client and the RADIUS server are unencrypted, except for user passwords, which are encrypted. Note that from the dial-up user's perspective, the RADIUS client is the user's dial-in server.

An RFC-compliant RADIUS server stores all user profile information in a flat-file ASCII database that is accessible to any NAS that needs it to authenticate users. Some RADIUS servers can also employ UNIX password files, Password Authentication Protocol (PAP), Challenge Handshake Authentication Protocol (CHAP), Microsoft Challenge Handshake Authentication Protocol (MS-CHAP), third-party security systems, or Network Information Services (NIS) for authenticating users. RADIUS servers are often used as well to provide connection statistics for billing purposes.

Marketplace

RADIUS is supported by access servers from Cisco and other router vendors. RADIUS is also supported by Windows 2000 and Windows .NET Server, where the Internet Authentication Service (IAS) supports RADIUS server functionality and the Routing and Remote Access Service (RRAS) operates as the RADIUS client.

Note that RADIUS implementations from different vendors are often incompatible. Despite the fact that RADIUS is an industry-standard security protocol, many vendors have added features to their implementation that are non-RFC compliant. As a result, when implementing RADIUS in your enterprise it is usually best to stick with solutions from a single vendor.

Notes

Cisco has a proprietary protocol called Terminal Access Controller Access Control System (TACACS) that is similar to RADIUS in operation but includes additional security features. Besides RADIUS and TACACS, the third commonly used security protocol on Cisco access servers is Kerberos.

See Also: *AAA, Challenge Handshake Authentication Protocol (CHAP), Internet service provider (ISP), Internetwork Operating System (IOS), Kerberos, Microsoft Challenge Handshake Authentication Protocol (MS-CHAP), network access server (NAS), Password Authentication Protocol (PAP), Point-to-Point Tunneling Protocol (PPTP), Terminal Access Controller Access Control System (TACACS), security protocols, User Datagram Protocol (UDP), virtual private network (VPN)*

remote bridge

A bridge that connects two geographically separated networks.

Overview

Remote bridges can be used to connect networks using a variety of means, including telephone lines, leased lines, or a circuit-switched service such as X.25. A remote bridge generally has at least one

- Local area network (LAN) port, typically an RJ-45 jack to support an unshielded twisted-pair (UTP) connection to an Ethernet switch or a hub.
- Serial port, such as an RS-232 port or V.35 interface, for connection to the telco service used to link the networks.

A synchronous serial port is employed for connections to digital leased lines, and an asynchronous serial port is used for modems. Some remote bridges even have synchronous and asynchronous serial ports. Remote bridges also commonly support Simple Network Management Protocol (SNMP) and have various other diagnostic and support features, including out-of-band management (OBM).

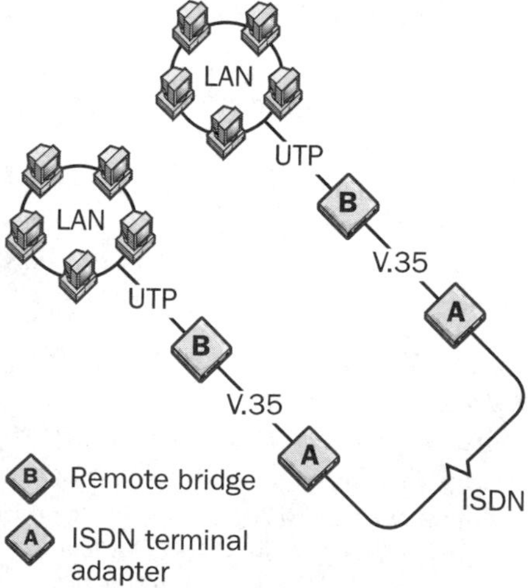

Remote bridge. *Using remote bridges to connect two distant LANs together.*

To use remote bridges to connect remote LANs, connect a bridge to the main hub or switch in each LAN, and then connect the serial port on each bridge to the modem, Integrated Services Digital Network (ISDN) terminal adapter, or Channel Service Unit/Data Service Unit (CSU/DSU), depending on the type of wide area network (WAN) link used.

See Also: *asynchronous transmission, bridge, leased line, RS-232, serial transmission, synchronous transmission, V.35*

remote client impersonation

A technique for attacking or gaining improper access to a network.

Overview

Remote client impersonation takes place when a third party monitors traffic on a network by using a packet sniffer, captures network traffic during the user authentication process, extracts the authentication parameters (such as username, password, and domain) from the captured frames, and then takes control of the authenticated connection. Authentication schemes in which the user's password is transmitted in clear text, such as the Password Authentication Protocol (PAP) supported by Point-to-Point Protocol (PPP), are most susceptible to remote client impersonation and replay attacks. More secure PPP authentication schemes, such as the Challenge Handshake Authentication Protocol (CHAP) or the Microsoft version of that protocol (MS-CHAP), are preferable. CHAP guards against remote client impersonation by using the user's password to create an encrypted hash of a challenge string instead of passing the actual password during the authentication process. It protects against replay attacks by using a different, arbitrarily selected challenge string for each authentication attempt.

Notes

A similar hacking technique called a replay attack takes place when a third party monitors network traffic, captures a connection during the authentication process, and then plays back the client's captured response to obtain a new authenticated connection.

See Also: *Challenge Handshake Authentication Protocol (CHAP), hacking, Microsoft Challenge Handshake Authentication Protocol (MS-CHAP), network security, network troubleshooting, Password Authentication Protocol (PAP), Point-to-Point Protocol (PPP)*

remote control

Controlling a remote server as if from a local console.

Overview

Remote control platforms allow you to control computers as if you were actually sitting at the local console and typing in keystrokes or clicking the mouse. Such platforms are widely used in the enterprise to

- Enable help desk personnel to step in and take control of a user's machine to fix a problem or demonstrate a procedure
- Allow training personnel to walk students through a procedure without having to sit beside the student
- Enable administrators who are offsite to respond to emergencies by configuring or troubleshooting servers using their laptop or even a Personal Digital Assistant (PDA)

Implementation

The most popular forms of remote control technology are software platforms such as pcAnywhere from Symantec Corporation or ReachOut from Previo Software. To utilize such platforms, a small-footprint remote control client must first be installed on the server that is to be controlled. Other software in this category include the Terminal Services (TS) component of Microsoft Windows 2000 Server, Windows XP, or Windows .NET Server, the Citrix Metaframe platform from Citrix Systems, and the open source Virtual Network Computing (VNC) platform from AT&T Laboratories Cambridge.

There are also a number of hardware-based remote control platforms, including proprietary Peripheral Component Interconnect (PCI) cards such as TopTools from Hewlett-Packard and keyboard video mouse (KVM) solutions such as Key-View from Cybex Computer Products Corporation. These solutions are generally more expensive than software-based tools, but they provide better performance and can also reboot servers when they crash.

See Also: *remote access, remote administration*

Remote Desktop Protocol (RDP)

A protocol for terminal-based computing.

Overview

Remote Desktop Protocol (RDP) is a terminal communications protocol based on the industry-standard T.120 multichannel conferencing protocol from the International Telecommunication Union (ITU). RDP is a proprietary protocol developed by Microsoft Corporation and is sometimes referred to as the Remote Display Protocol. It was formerly known as the T.SHARE protocol.

RDP forms the basis of Terminal Services (TS), a component of Microsoft Windows 2000 Server that supports terminal-based computing. RDP controls the transmission of keystrokes, mouse actions, and display information between Windows 2000 terminal clients and terminal servers. The version of RDP used in Windows 2000 and Windows XP is RDP 5.

Implementation

RDP is a multichannel-capable protocol that supports up to 64,000 separate channels. RDP supports multipoint transmission and employs separate virtual channels for transporting different information over serial transmission links, specifically:

- Mouse and keyboard signals sent from client to server
- Presentation data sent from server to client

RDP supports encryption of data using the RC4 encryption algorithm, and can use 40-bit, 56-bit, and 128-bit key sizes for varying degrees of security. Higher key sizes provide greater security but require greater processing overhead.

See Also: *remote control, T.120, terminal server*

R

Remote Network Monitoring (RMON)

Remote Network Monitoring (RMON)

An extension to Simple Network Management Protocol (SNMP).

Overview

Remote Network Monitoring (RMON) lets you monitor network traffic on a remote Ethernet segment from a central location on the network to detect problem conditions such as traffic congestion, dropped packets, and excessive collisions. You can also use RMON to set network traffic thresholds that trigger alarms so that you can correct network problems before they happen. Embedded RMON in Ethernet switches lets network administrators monitor switched Ethernet networks that cannot easily be monitored using traditional packet-sniffing network analyzers.

RMON was developed in 1992 and defined in RFC 1271. This was later superseded by RFC 1513 for Token Ring networks and RFC 1757 for Ethernet networks. The RMON Management Information Base (MIB) defined in RFC 1757 specifies nine groups of manageable objects (RMON monitoring elements) for various aspects of network traffic monitoring, totaling 204 objects and 2 events. These groups of objects, usually referred to as the RMON 1 groups, are as follows:

- **Statistics (1):** Records statistics for Ethernet network interfaces (ports), including packets sent and received, bytes sent and received, the number of each type of packet, packets dropped, errors, and collisions
- **History (2):** Specifies the types of data being sampled and the frequency at which data is sampled and records the sampled data for later analysis
- **Alarm (3):** Lets you set thresholds and sampling periods to trigger alarms when specified network conditions arise
- **Host (4):** Records MAC addresses; the number of packets sent and received for broadcast, unicast, and multicast packets; the number of bytes sent and received; and the number of error packets for all hosts on the subnet
- **HostTopN (5):** Lets you list hosts according to ranking parameters, such as amount of traffic generated or number of errors generated
- **Matrix (6):** Records statistics for communication between pairs of hosts, such as their source and destination addresses and the number of bytes and packets sent and received
- **Filter (7):** Controls which kinds of packets the agent should capture, such as all packets larger than a certain size, all packets that match a specific bit mask, or logical combinations of individual expressions
- **Capture (8):** Lets you capture packets for collecting network statistics and configure capture buffer sizes
- **Events (9):** Lets you generate SNMP traps and log entries

It is a good idea to ensure that your RMON-enabled device or probe supports at least groups 1, 2, 3, and 9 from the previous list. Probes that support only these four groups are said to support mini-RMON. Many network hardware vendors provide RMON-enabled devices that support only mini-RMON because these are generally considered the most useful RMON groups.

The original RMON specification (now called RMON 1) collected data only from the physical (Layer 1) and data-link (Layer 2) layers of the Open Systems Interconnection (OSI) reference model. To overcome this limitation, which hinders RMON from being useful in switched networks (the original RMON was designed for shared media networks), a newer version called RMON 2 was developed in 1997 and defined in RFC 2021. RMON 2 extends the original RMON specification with nine more Management Information Base (MIB) groups that specify the collection of statistics from the network layer (Layer 3) through the application layer (Layer 7). Using RMON 2, network administrators can remotely collect information about the flow of data in a switched enterprise networking environment. For example, using RMON 2–enabled routers or

Remote Network Monitoring (RMON)

switches, you could determine which workstations were accessing a specific client/server application on a specific server. RMON 2 is a superset of the original RMON MIB groups and extends them with an additional 268 manageable objects.

Comparison

RMON is similar in many ways to SNMP, for example:

- It employs the MIB format.
- It collects and reports network conditions to a network management station.

RMON differs from SNMP, however, in several significant ways, specifically:

- It supports caching of information gathered from supporting network devices.
- It provides much greater detail about the operation of network devices and the flow of traffic in and out of the device.
- It is more responsive to events occurring on the network. This is because RMON proactively sends the data it has collected instead of waiting to be polled by the network management station as SNMP generally does.
- It is an instrument-based network management protocol that utilizes specialized hardware, which can either be built into network devices or in stand-alone form as RMON probes.

Implementation

Like SNMP, RMON is implemented utilizing a MIB on RMON-enabled devices. These RMON-enabled devices may include

- Stand-alone devices called RMON probes that can be temporarily or permanently installed where desired on the network to study the flow of traffic on a local area network (LAN) segment. Such probes act much like traditional network protocol analyzers, except that they send the information they collect to a central location for analysis and display.
- Existing network devices such as repeaters, bridges, hubs, routers, or Ethernet switches that have RMON functionality embedded into their port circuitry in the form of RMON agent software.
- A stand-alone computer operating as an RMON probe.

An RMON probe consists of an SNMP agent for collecting information and communicating it to an SNMP management application, and one or more RMON MIBs defining the network objects to be managed. Typically, an SNMP-manageable device such as a hub or router only needs additional software installed on it to enable it to support RMON and turn it into a probe. Other devices called hosted probes are implemented as add-on hardware modules with built-in processing power and memory.

RMON is usually implemented on only one device or interface per network segment. For example, in a switched Ethernet environment, RMON agent software runs on each switch port to monitor and collect Ethernet network statistics for the attached segment. For RMON 1 these statistics relate only to the physical layer (Layer 1) and the data-link layer (Layer 2), but for RMON 2 they cover all layers of the OSI model.

When an SNMP management station wants to collect statistics to analyze and present them, the station contacts the RMON agents on the network. Alternatively (and more commonly), RMON agents are configured to send this information automatically when network traffic conditions on the device trigger the agent using SNMP traps.

Marketplace

The leading vendors of RMON probes and software include 3Com Corporation, Agilent Technologies, NetScout Systems, and Nortel Networks. Most vendors of Ethernet switch equipment also add RMON agent capability to the ports of their switches.

See Also: *Ethernet switch, Management Information Base (MIB), network management, Open Systems Interconnection (OSI) reference model, Simple Network Management Protocol (SNMP)*

remote procedure call (RPC)

A protocol that enables one computer to make a function call to another computer on the network.

Overview

Remote procedure call (RPC) is a message-passing programming technology developed by Sun Microsystems and later extended by the Open Software Foundation (OSF). RPC allows an application on one computer to execute procedures and interact with services on a remote computer over a network. RPCs are a common method of enabling client/server processing on the Microsoft Windows and on IBM AIX, HP-UX, Sun Solaris, and other UNIX platforms.

Although local procedure calls (LPCs) provide a mechanism for enabling the different components of an application located on a single computer to communicate with each other, RPCs enable message passing between the components of a distributed application that are located on different computers throughout a network. RPCs use a variety of other interprocess communication (IPC) mechanisms such as named pipes, mailslots, Windows Sockets, and NetBIOS to establish connections between the RPC client and RPC server components on different machines.

Notes

The remote procedure call service (RPC service), a component of the Windows 2000, Windows XP, and Windows .NET Server executive running in kernel mode, is responsible for message-passing between the client and server components of a distributed application—for example, between a client/server application such as Microsoft Outlook (client part) with Microsoft Exchange Server (server part). On a Windows 2000–based network, the server part of a distributed application first registers itself with the RPC Locator service. The client part of the application, which is on the local computer, can then query the RPC Locator service to determine the location of the required server part. A process called the remote procedure stub then packages the client's function call into a suitable RPC message and sends it to the remote computer using the RPC Run Time process. At the remote machine, a process called the application stub receives the RPC message, unpackages it into a function call, and executes it, returning any resulting values to the client part in a similar fashion. From the viewpoint of the client portion of the application, the server portion appears to be on the same computer.

repeater

A device that extends a network by boosting a signal so it can travel farther.

Overview

Digital signals traveling on cables weaken with distance—a phenomenon known as attenuation. A repeater is a kind of digital amplifier that works at the physical layer (Layer 1) of the Open Systems Interconnection (OSI) reference model to regenerate (amplify) a signal so that it can travel farther. Repeaters come in various types for different network architectures and data communication technologies. Repeaters can also perform other functions, such as filtering out noise caused by electromagnetic interference (EMI), reshaping the signal, and correcting timing to remove jitter so that the signal can travel farther.

Uses

Repeaters are used in Ethernet and Token Ring networking to extend signal transmission over long runs of fiber-optic cabling in order to connect remote local area networks (LANs). Repeaters are also be used in mainframe environments to boost signals for serial transmission to remote terminals. Repeaters can also be used to join dissimilar media such as unshielded twisted-pair (UTP) cabling and thinnet, but they cannot be used to join dissimilar network architectures such as Ethernet and Token Ring.

Repeaters are an inexpensive way to extend a network. Some specific examples of how repeaters could be used include

- Joining two 16-megabits per second (Mbps) Token Ring networks in different buildings over distances up to 1.85 miles (3 kilometers) over multimode fiber-optic cabling or up to 12.5 miles (20 kilometers) over single-mode fiber

- Increasing the lobe length between a Token Ring main ring and a remote node
- Joining dissimilar 10Base2 and 10Base5 segments to form a single Ethernet LAN
- Boosting signals from mainframe controllers to 3270 terminals over coaxial or UTP cabling to support distances up to 1.55 miles (2.5 kilometers)
- Extending the operating distance of T1 lines by placing G.703 repeaters at 1.35-mile (2.2-kilometer) intervals
- Extending backbone fiber-optic cable runs in campus-wide LANs or metropolitan area networks (MANs)

Repeaters are also used in fiber-optic networks to amplify and regenerate light signals for long-distance cable runs. Repeaters do not block broadcasts, so if you connect two Ethernet segments using a repeater, you increase the size of the collision domain, which degrades overall network performance. For this reason, bridges and routers are often preferable to repeaters.

Notes

Up to two Class II Ethernet repeaters can be cascaded together to connect remote nodes that are up to 670 feet (205 meters) apart.

See Also: *electromagnetic interference (EMI), hub, jitter, Open Systems Interconnection (OSI) reference model, physical layer, signal*

replay attack

Also known as remote client impersonation, a hacking technique for attacking or gaining improper access to a network.

See: *remote client impersonation*

Request for Comments (RFC)

A document that describes Internet standards, protocols, and technologies developed by the Internet Engineering Task Force (IETF).

Overview

Any interested party can submit an RFC to the IETF for consideration as an Internet standard. The process for ratifying such proposals as standards is based on consensus rather than by committee. Once proposed, an RFC is reviewed by various technical groups and given one of five classifications:

- Required
- Recommended
- Elective
- Limited Use
- Not Recommended

Once an RFC is classified, it is discussed and tested by research and technical groups and individuals. To become an accepted standard it must pass through three stages:

- **Proposed standard:** Stable, well understood, and generally considered useful
- **Draft standard:** Stable enough to develop implementations of the standard in applications and networking technology
- **Internet standard:** Technically mature, widely implemented, and significantly beneficial to the Internet community

RFCs are sequentially numbered and published by the RFC Editor at the Information Sciences Institute at the University of Southern California. Since 1969, over 3000 RFCs have been proposed and published on various networking protocols, procedures, applications, and concepts.

Note that old RFCs are not updated, so several RFCs might relate to the same Internet protocol or technology, and some of them might be obsolete. To find the current RFC for a protocol or technology, see the Internet Architecture Board (IAB) Official Protocol Standard published quarterly by the IAB.

Examples

The table shows some of the more important RFCs for commonly used Internet protocols.

Some Important RFCs for Internet Protocols

Protocol	*RFC(s)*
ARP	826
DHCP	2131, 2132
DNS	1034, 1035
FTP	959
HTTP-1.1	2068
ICMP	792
IGMP	1112
IMAP4	2060
IP	791, 919, 922, 950
IPv6	1883
Kerberos	1510
LDAPv3	2251
MIME	2045, 2046, 2047, 2049
NetBIOS	1001, 1002
NNTP	977
OSPFv2	2328
POP3	1939
PPP	1661, 1662
PPP-CHAP	1994
PPP-MP	1990
RADIUS	2138
RMON	1757
RSVP	2205
SMTP	821, 822, 974, 1869, 1870
SNMP	1157
SNMPv2	1441
TCP	793
Telnet	854, 855
UDP	768

For More Information

Visit the RFC Editor at *www.rfc-editor.org.*

See Also: Internet, Internet Engineering Task Force (IETF)

reservation

An Internet Protocol (IP) address that is reserved for a specific computer by a Dynamic Host Configuration Protocol (DHCP) server.

Overview

A DHCP reservation contains the IP address to be leased and the MAC address of the computer it will be leased to. Reservations are often used for servers on a network, which normally should all have the same IP address. An alternative procedure is to manually assign these servers a static IP address. The advantage of using a reservation is that the IP address of the server is centrally managed in the database of the DHCP server, which means there is less chance of an address conflict.

On Microsoft Windows networks, reservations (or static IP addresses) are always recommended for

- Domain controllers
- Domain Name System (DNS) and Windows Internet Name Service (WINS) servers
- Non-DHCP clients
- Router interfaces

Notes

To create a reservation for a computer, you must know the MAC address of its interface. On computers running Windows NT, Windows 2000, Windows XP, or Windows .NET Server, you can enter **ipconfig** at the command prompt to determine this value; on computers running Windows 95 or Windows 98, you can enter **winipcfg** in the Run dialog box (which you access from the Start menu).

See Also: Dynamic Host Configuration Protocol (DHCP), IP address, MAC address

residential gateway

A broadband device that acts as a front end for a home network.

Overview

The rapid growth of the broadband Internet market, together with the increase of teleworking, has provided a fertile market for the emergence of a new breed of broadband access device: the residential gateway. This device either connects to or replaces your Digital Subscriber Line (DSL) modem and enables you to network together PCs and peripherals (sometimes even telephones and fax machines) using a variety of technologies including Ethernet, home phone line networking, or 802.11b wireless networking. Connectivity to the network varies with the type of architecture used and may be standard RJ-45 jacks, universal serial bus (USB) connections, PC adapter cards, or Personal Computer Memory Card International Association (PCMCIA) cards. Features of residential gateways include ease of use, integrated firewall, and virtual private network (VPN) pass-through to support secure teleworking.

Marketplace

Emerging players in the residential gateway market include 2Wire, Cayman Systems, 3Com Corporation, and even the consumer electronics company Panasonic. Some analysts expect the residential gateway market to exceed $5 billion by 2005.

See Also: *Digital Subscriber Line (DSL), RJ connectors, universal serial bus (USB), virtual private network (VPN)*

resilient packet ring (RPR)

An emerging technology for Synchronous Optical Networking (SONET).

Overview

Resilient packet ring (RPR) is a new SONET technology designed for implementation by metropolitan Ethernet service providers. It is designed to make more efficient use of the underlying ring-based fiber-optic cabling infrastructure of existing SONET networks used by carriers.

RPR is based on earlier proprietary technologies developed by Cisco Systems, Nortel Networks, and other high-end infrastructure vendors. The Institute of Electrical and Electronics Engineers (IEEE) is working with the new Resilient Packet Ring Alliance to standardize this new technology and ensure interoperability between equipment from different vendors.

Implementation

Traditional SONET in the metropolitan marketplace employs a dual-ring architecture. One ring is active and carries traffic in one direction only, while the other ring is inactive and is used for redundancy purposes. Should the first ring fail, traffic is routed almost instantaneously to the second ring and then travels in the opposite direction to the first ring. This rapid failover makes SONET an ideal technology for delay-sensitive traffic such as voice and video, but it is not especially critical in transport of data, which is rapidly approaching becoming the dominant form of traffic carried by SONET networks.

RPR employs both rings of the SONET infrastructure to carry traffic simultaneously. Should one ring fail, its portion of traffic is automatically switched to the second ring. Since this switchover could result in sudden congestion of traffic, RPR employs quality of service (QoS) in order to differentiate between voice traffic, which needs high priority due to its sensitivity to delay, and Internet Protocol (IP) packet traffic, which can be assigned low priority since it is less sensitive to delay.

Marketplace

RPR technologies have been around for several years but have been based on proprietary implementations by SONET equipment vendors. The efforts of the Resilient Packet Ring Alliance, however, are guiding these vendors toward developing interoperable standards. Some of the significant vendors involved in producing RPR equipment include Cisco Systems, Dynarc, Lantern Communications, and Nortel Networks.

See Also: *Institute of Electrical and Electronics Engineers (IEEE), metropolitan Ethernet, quality of service (QoS), Synchronous Optical Network (SONET)*

resolver

A Domain Name System (DNS) client.

Overview

A resolver is software running on an Internet Protocol (IP) host that enables the host to query a DNS name server in order to resolve a host name into its associated IP address. The resolver software enables the host to formulate and send a query to the name server, interpret the response from the name server, and pass this information to the application on the client that initially called the resolver software (for example, a Web browser).

On UNIX platforms using Berkeley Internet Name Domain (BIND), a resolver is a set of library routines that are linked to the client programs that need to use them. On Microsoft Windows platforms the resolver is a component of Transmission Control Protocol/Internet Protocol (TCP/IP) software installed on the machine.

See Also: *Berkeley Internet Name Domain (BIND), Domain Name System (DNS), host name resolution, name server*

resource

Also called network resource, any volumes, folders, applications, or devices that users need access to.

Overview

Examples of network resources include the following:

- **Shared folders and volumes:** Contain files that users need to access. Users can be granted different levels of permissions on these shares. For example, users might be given read-only permission for shares that contain administrative documents, modify permission for shares that contain workgroup documents, and full control permission for their own personal shared folders.
- **Shared printers:** Allow many users to print to a single print device. You can control access to the printer by using print permissions and by setting priorities and times for accessing printers.
- **Applications:** Allow users to access back-end applications (such as databases) using front-end clients. These applications can be standard .exe executables or scripted Web server applications such as those developed using Microsoft Active Server Pages (ASP) technology.
- **Web servers:** Allow Hypertext Markup Language (HTML)–based documents and applications to be shared and accessed from any platform by using a standard Web browser such as Microsoft Internet Explorer.
- **File Transfer Protocol (FTP) servers:** Allow files to be shared between different operating system platforms such as UNIX and Microsoft Windows.

See Also: *shared folder*

resource domain

In Microsoft Windows NT, a domain containing network resources.

Overview

Resource domains are part of a master domain model or multiple master domain model enterprise-level implementation of Windows NT. Resource domains simplify resource administration by separating the administration of resources from the administration of user accounts.

In a master domain model implementation of Windows NT, an account domain—or master domain—contains user accounts for every user in the enterprise and is usually located at corporate headquarters. Servers and workstations at branch offices belong to other domains called resource domains. A trust relationship is established so that each resource domain in the enterprise trusts the account domain. Users at branch offices who want to log on to the network simply log on to the account domain even though their workstations are located within resource domains. Administrators at branch offices are responsible for managing only the resources (file and print shares, Web servers, database servers, and so forth) for their own domain and are usually not involved in centralized account management from a domain perspective.

See Also: *account domain, master domain, trust*

resource record (RR)

An entry in a Domain Name System (DNS) zone file.

Overview

Resource records (RRs) are individual records (lines) in a DNS database or zone file on a DNS name server. RRs provide information about hosts on a Transmission Control Protocol/Internet Protocol (TCP/IP) network—for example, the DNS domain name, IP address, and particular function of the host. Depending on the platform used, you may be able to edit the zone file using a simple text editor or a graphical user interface (GUI)–based name server administration tool.

A typical RR consists of a series of fields separated by spaces. The most common type of RR is the address record, or A record, which maps the IP address of an IP host to its domain name. Other common types of RRs include CNAME, NS, PTR, SOA, and SRV records. The following table describes some important types of RRs.

Commonly Used DNS Resource Records

Record Type	*Description*
A (address)	Maps the IP address to the host name
CNAME (canonical name)	Creates an alias for a host name
HINFO (host information)	Specifies information about the host, such as operating system and central processing unit (CPU) type
MX (mail exchanger)	Indicates a Simple Mail Transfer Protocol (SMTP) host (mail forwarder)
NS (name server)	Indicates a DNS name server that is authoritative for the domain
PTR (pointer)	Points to another location in the DNS namespace
SOA (start of authority)	Indicates the name server that is authoritative for the domain
SRV (server)	Locates a host that can provide a specific network service

See Also: *Domain Name System (DNS), IP address, name server, Transmission Control Protocol/Internet Protocol (TCP/IP)*

Resource Reservation Protocol (RSVP)

A signaling protocol used for conveying quality of service (QoS) requests.

Overview

Resource Reservation Protocol (RSVP) is part of the IntServ architecture developed by the Internet Engineering Task Force (IETF) to enable QoS on best-effort networks such as Internet Protocol (IP) networks. RSVP allows hosts to reserve bandwidth between two endpoints along a routed network. RSVP does this by sending special messages to RSVP-enabled routers along the path, which then give traffic sent between these endpoints the requested priority to ensure performance and reduce delay. Note that all routers on a network must be RSVP-enabled in order for the protocol to achieve its goals.

RSVP operates at Layer 3 (network layer) of the Open Systems Interconnection (OSI) reference model and is therefore independent of the type of networking media and network protocols used. RSVP is designed to operate in large heterogeneous routed internetworks such as the Internet to provide QoS for high-priority traffic.

RSVP supports both multicast and unicast transmissions and is a soft-state protocol that requires periodic refreshing to maintain its configured service levels. RSVP is defined in RFC 2205.

See Also: *bandwidth, heterogeneous network, Internet Engineering Task Force (IETF), network layer, Open Systems Interconnection (OSI) reference model, quality of service (QoS), routing*

reverse hosting

An extension to reverse proxying that is supported by Microsoft Internet and Acceleration (ISA) Server.

Overview

Using reverse hosting, a proxy server can simulate the virtual roots on a number of Web servers and redirect requests for a particular domain and root combination to a single Web server. This approach means that only a single hole needs to be opened through the proxy server to allow Hypertext Transfer Protocol (HTTP) requests to enter. Reverse proxying works as an application layer proxy service and supports HTTP only.

See Also: *Hypertext Transfer Protocol (HTTP), Internet Security and Acceleration Server (ISA Server), proxy server, reverse proxy*

reverse name lookup

The process of using a host's Internet Protocol (IP) address to look up its Domain Name System (DNS) name.

Overview
Reverse lookup occurs when a resolver queries a name server to resolve another host's IP address into its associated fully qualified domain name (FQDN). This is the reverse of the usual host name resolution process, in which a resolver queries a name server to resolve a host name into its associated IP address. Reverse name lookups use a special domain called in-addr.arpa.

Uses
Reverse name lookups are used in a variety of circumstances. For example, when a Web browser contacts a Web server, the Web server obtains the IP address of the computer the browser is running on. The Web server software often uses a reverse lookup to try to resolve the client's IP address into its associated FQDN, usually for purposes of logging the Hypertext Transfer Protocol (HTTP) session.

See Also: *Domain Name System (DNS), fully qualified domain name (FQDN), host name resolution, Hypertext Transfer Protocol (HTTP), in-addr.arpa, IP address, name lookup, name server*

reverse proxy
A form of proxying where the proxy server impersonates the Web server.

Overview
In reverse proxying, a proxy server is used to impersonate a Web server to the outside world. The proxy server receives client requests for Web content and fulfills these requests from its cache. It forwards Hypertext Transfer Protocol (HTTP) requests from clients to the actual Web server only if it cannot serve the requests from its own cache.

Reverse proxying offloads Web publishing responsibilities from Web servers and allows you to securely connect a company's internal Web servers to the Internet or to the rest of the company intranet. Microsoft Internet and Acceleration (ISA) Server supports reverse proxying so that you can publish to the Internet without compromising your internal network's security. ISA Server uses reverse proxying to send client requests downstream to a Web server or group of Web servers that are located behind the proxy server. This configuration results in improved Web server capacity planning, protects the security of data while allowing access to the Internet, and allows Web servers to access other servers on the internal network for publishing purposes.

See Also: *Hypertext Transfer Protocol (HTTP), Internet Security and Acceleration Server (ISA Server), proxy server, Web server*

Rexec
A UNIX command for running commands on remote hosts.

Overview
Rexec is one of the r-commands available on all UNIX systems. In order for the remote execution of the command to work, the remote host must be running the Rexec daemon (service). Rexec authenticates the username on the remote host before executing the command and prompts the client to enter a password.

Microsoft Windows 2000, Windows XP, and Windows .NET Server include a Rexec client but no Rexec service. Rexec provides functionality similar to that of Rsh, except Rexec uses clear-text password authentication.

Notes
You cannot use Rexec to run interactive commands such as Vi or Emacs. Instead, use Telnet or Secure Shell to run interactive commands on a remote host. Note also that Rexec forwards the user's password as clear text, which can pose a security risk in some environments.

See Also: *daemon, Rsh, Telnet, UNIX*

RFC
Stands for Request for Comments, a document that describes Internet standards, protocols, and technologies developed by the Internet Engineering Task Force (IETF).

See: *Request for Comments (RFC)*

RG

Stands for Radio Guide, a U.S. Army specification for grades of transmission lines.

Overview

The RG specifications refer to forms of coaxial cable used, many of which were popular in computer networking in the 1970s and 1980s. Examples of RG specifications for coax include

- **RG-8:** Also known as N series cable, which is a coaxial cable with an impedance of 50 ohms. RG-8 looks like thicknet Ethernet cabling but is actually a lower grade and does not perform as well. True thicknet cabling is labeled as IEEE 802.3 cabling, has a diameter of 3/8 inches, and is yellow or orange.
- **RG-58:** Often called thinnet, which is a form of coaxial cabling with an impedance of 50 ohms and a diameter of 3/16 inches used in 10Base2 Ethernet networking. Subdesignations of this standard include RG-58 /U, which has a solid copper core, and RG-58 A/U, which has a stranded copper core.
- **RG-59:** Another name for CATV or cable television cabling, which is a form of coaxial cabling with an impedance of 75 ohms.
- **RG-62:** A form of coaxial cabling with an impedance of 93 ohms that is used in Attached Resource Computer Network (ARCNET) networks.

See Also: coaxial cabling

Rijndael

The underlying cryptographic algorithm used in the Advanced Encryption Standard (AES).

Overview

The National Institute of Standards and Technology (NIST) selected Rijndael as the encryption algorithm to be used for the U.S. government encryption standard called AES, which replaces the Data Encryption Standard (DES). Rijndael was developed by Belgian computer scientists Vincent Rijmen and Joan Daemen, and it can employ 128-bit, 192-bit, or 256-bit key lengths, making it considerably stronger and more secure than the 56-bit DES. Rijndael also has a very small footprint (52 bytes), making it portable for cell phones, Personal Digital Assistants (PDAs), and other small devices.

Rijndael will likely take several years to completely displace DES in government use. Triple DES, a much stronger variant of DES, is likely to coexist alongside Rijndael for an even longer period of time where it has been deployed.

See Also: Advanced Encryption Standard (AES), Data Encryption Standard (DES), encryption

ring topology

A networking topology in which network stations are connected along a single path whose ends are joined to form a circle.

Overview

Ring topology is employed only in specialized networking technologies, as opposed to the star topology employed in basic structured wiring systems of enterprise Ethernet networks. Common examples of where ring topology is used include

- **Token Ring networks:** The ring of a Token Ring network is concentrated inside a device called a Multistation Access Unit (MAU).
- **Fiber Distributed Data Interface (FDDI) networks:** The ring in this case is both a physical and logical ring and usually runs around a campus or collection of buildings to form a high-speed backbone network. Usually a dual-ring approach is used to provide redundancy.
- **Synchronous Optical Network (SONET):** Used primarily by telcos for metropolitan area network (MAN) trunk rings, this technology also typically employs a dual-ring structure for redundancy.

In some ring topology networks such as Token Ring networks the circle is sometimes only logical—the actual physical arrangement of the cabling might be starlike, with a hub or concentrator at the center. A network based on ring topology is sometimes called a ring network.

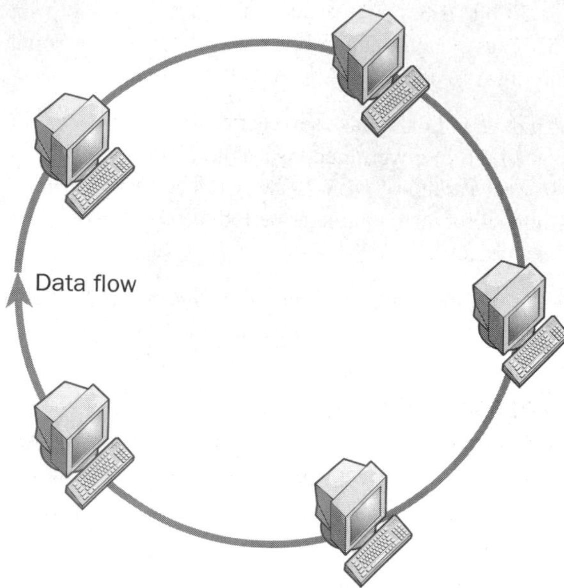

Ring topology. *Simple example of a ring network.*

See Also: *bus topology, mesh topology, star bus topology, star topology*

RIP

Stands for Routing Information Protocol, a popular distance vector routing protocol.

See: *Routing Information Protocol (RIP)*

RIPE

Stands for Réseaux IP Européens NCC, a nonprofit organization that administers the registration and allocation of numbers relating to the operation of the Internet in Europe, the Middle East, and parts of Africa.

See: *American Registry for Internet Numbers (ARIN)*

Rivest-Shamir-Adelman (RSA) algorithm

A popular algorithm for public key cryptography.

Overview

Rivest-Shamir-Adelman (RSA) is one of the most popular cryptographic algorithms in use today. Ron Rivest, Adi Shamir, and Leonard Adelman developed RSA in 1977 and RSA Security patented it in 1983. RSA is employed in many popular encryption technologies, such as Pretty Good Privacy (PGP), Transport Layer Security (TLS), Internet Protocol Security (IPsec), and for the Encrypting File System (EFS) in Microsoft Windows 2000, Windows XP, and Windows .NET Server.

Implementation

RSA employs a variable-length key, with typical key size being 512 bits. A longer key can be used to enhance security, or a shorter one can be used to increase the efficiency of the encryption process. RSA also employs a variable-length block size. Block size represents the chunk of plaintext that is encrypted in one application of the algorithm, and this block size must be smaller than the key's bit length. Encryption of a block of plaintext results in a corresponding block of ciphertext whose length is equal to the size of the key.

Marketplace

Until recently, RSA has been a patented technology owned by RSA Security. As of January 2000, however, RSA is now in the public domain. Some analysts suggest that the general growth and acceptance of public key infrastructure (PKI) systems has been hindered by the need for companies to license RSA technologies from RSA Security—if so, this obstacle has now been removed.

Issues

RSA is a relatively slow algorithm compared to other popular encryption algorithms such as the Data Encryption Standard (DES) used by the U.S. government (now replaced by Advanced Encryption Standard, or AES). As a result, RSA is usually not used for encrypting messages. Instead, it is typically used to encrypt a secret key, and the secret key is then used to encrypt the message.

Another issue is that while 512-bit keys are commonly used in e-commerce sites employing RSA encryption, in late 2000 a Swedish team of computer scientists cracked 512-bit RSA encryption using only a single workstation running a number field sieve algorithm. As a result, RSA with 512-bit encryption is no longer considered secure; however, 1024-bit length keys are probably secure for the foreseeable future.

See Also: *Advanced Encryption Standard (AES), Data Encryption Standard (DES), Encrypting File System (EFS), Internet Protocol Security (IPsec), Pretty Good Privacy (PGP), public key cryptography, public key infrastructure (PKI), Transport Layer Security (TLS)*

RJ connectors

A family of push-and-click connectors for twisted-pair wiring in telephone and computer network environments.

Overview

RJ stands for Registered Jack, and the RJ standards define both jacks or receptacles (female) and plugs (male) connectors for different purposes. Some common types of RJ connectors include

- **RJ-11:** A 4-wire or 6-wire telephone-type connector that connects telephones to wall plates. RJ-11 supports up to six wires, but usually only four are used with the two-pair twisted-pair cabling commonly found in telephone cabling.
- **RJ-45:** An 8-wire telephone-type connector used with twisted-pair cabling for connecting computers, wall plates, patch panels, and other networking components. RJ-45 is the standard type of connector for both unshielded twisted-pair (UTP) and shielded twisted-pair (STP) cabling in star-topology Ethernet networks such as 10BaseT and 100BaseT4. RJ-45 is defined in International Organization for Standardization (ISO) standard 8877.
- **RJ-48:** An 8-wire telephone-type connector used with twisted-pair cabling for connecting T1 and 56-kilobyte (KB) digital data service (DDS) lines. RJ-48 uses the same jack as RJ-45 but uses a different pinning, with one pair of wires to transmit signals, one pair to receive signals, one pair for drain, and one unused pair (reserved for future use). RJ-48 connectors come in three varieties: RJ-48C and RJ-48X for connecting T1 lines and RJ-48S for connecting 56-KB DDS lines.

Implementation

The diagram shows RJ-11 and RJ-45/48 connectors, which are used to terminate both ends of UTP cabling. Pins are labeled 1 through 4 or 1 through 6 for 4-wire and 6-wire RJ-11, and 1 through 8 for 8-wire (four-pair) RJ-45/48. Cables can be either straight-pinned or cross-pinned, depending on their use. For example, a straight-pinned RJ-45-terminated UTP cable is used to connect a computer to a 10BaseT hub, while a cross-pinned cable or crossover cable is used to connect two computers directly or to connect two hubs.

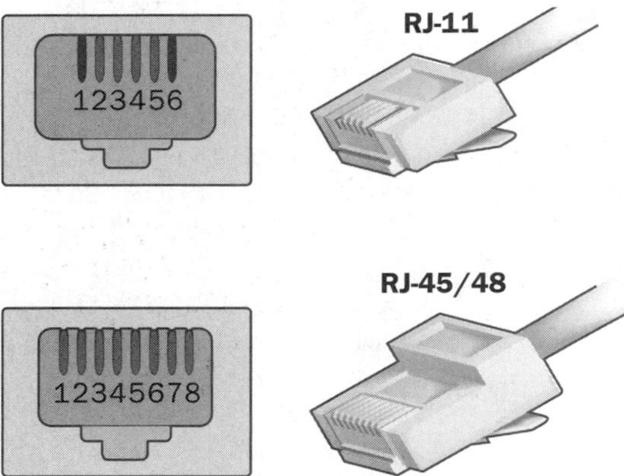

RJ connectors. *Two common types of RJ connectors.*

The following table shows the pinning for these various cables, with the colored wires coded as follows:

Y = yellow OR = orange

G = green BL = blue

R = red BK = black

W = white BN = brown

S = silver

If these colors are combined in striped cables, the coloring is coded OR/W for orange/white or orange with white striping, and so on. RJ-11 and RJ-45 cables generally use solid-color wires, and RJ-48 cables are usually striped. Note that RJ-45 has two types of cross-pinning: 568A/B and Universal Service Order Code (USOC). If the pinning of a wire is listed as Y (1–4), it means that the yellow wire is connected to pin 1 at one end and to pin 4 at the other.

R

Types of Cable Pinning

Connector/Cable	*Pinning*
RJ-11 straight (4-wire)	Y (1-1), G (2-2), R (3-3), BL (4-4)
RJ-11 crossed (4-wire)	Y (1-4), G (2-3), R (3-2), BL (4-1)
RJ-11 straight (6-wire)	BL (1-1), Y (2-2), G (3-3), R (4-4), BK (5-5), W (6-6)
RJ-11 crossed (6-wire)	BL (1-6), Y (2-5), G (3-4), R (4-3), BK (5-2), W (6-1)
RJ-45 straight (8-wire)	BL (1-1), OR (2-2), BK (3-3), R (4-4), G (5-5), Y (6-6), BN (7-7), S (8-8)
RJ-45 USOC crossed (8-wire)	BL (1-8), OR (2-7), BK (3-6), R (4-5), G (5-4), Y (6-3), BN (7-2), S (8-1)
RJ-45 568A/B crossed (8-wire)	BL (1-3), OR (2-6), BK (3-1), R (4-5), G (5-4), Y (6-2), BN (7-8), S (8-7)
RJ-48C straight (8-wire)	OR/W (1-1), W/OR (2-2), (3-3) unused, BL/W (4-4), W/BL (5-5), (6-6) unused, BL drain (7-7), OR drain (8-8)
RJ-48C crossed (8-wire)	OR/W (1-4), W/OR (2-5), (3-3) unused, BL/W (4-1), W/BL (5-2), (6-6) unused, BL drain (7-7), OR drain (8-8)

See Also: *connector (device), International Organization for Standardization (ISO), shielded twisted-pair (STP) cabling, unshielded twisted-pair (UTP) cabling*

RMON

Stands for Remote Network Monitoring, an extension to Simple Network Management Protocol (SNMP).

See: *Remote Network Monitoring (RMON)*

roaming user profile

A user profile stored on a network server so the user can access her desktop from any computer on the network.

Overview

Roaming user profiles are a feature of Microsoft Windows NT, Windows 2000, Windows XP, and Windows .NET Server that allow users to roam about the network and access their desktop settings and folders from any machine. This is done by storing such roaming profiles in a centralized location on the network, such as a file server or domain controller. If the server on which the profile is stored is unavailable when the user logs on to the network, the locally cached copy of the profile stored on his or her workstation will be used instead.

The system administrator enables roaming profiles for users. A roaming profile that cannot be modified by the user is known as a mandatory user profile. Windows 98 and Windows Millennium Edition (Me) also support roaming profiles, but these are not compatible with Windows 2000, Windows XP, and Windows .NET Server profiles.

See Also: *local user profile, mandatory user profile, user profile*

root

The base of a hierarchical file system.

Overview

The root is the first element in the absolute path of a file or directory on the file system. In other words, the root directory of a file system is the starting point for the tree of directories and files that comprise the file system. The symbol used to represent this directory depends on whether the file system is on a Microsoft Windows or UNIX platform: Windows designates the root directory with a backslash (\), but UNIX employs a forward slash (/).

The term *root* is also used to refer to the highest-level entity in a directory. For example, the root of Active Directory directory service in Windows 2000 is the RootDSE object.

R

Notes

The term *root* can also refer to the user with the highest level of administrative rights, particularly on UNIX platforms. Other names for this user are SuperUser (also UNIX platforms), Supervisor (NetWare platforms), and Administrator (Windows platforms).

See Also: *Active Directory, file system*

root certificate

A digital certificate that attests to the identity of a certificate authority (CA).

Overview

Every CA requires a root certificate so that it can be "trusted" by entities that request digital certificates from it. If a client trusts the root certificate of a CA, it automatically trusts any other certificates that are issued by that CA. Root certificates thus form one of the foundations of public key cryptography. The root certificate is either signed by the CA itself (self-signed) or by a higher authority in a hierarchy of CAs in a public key infrastructure (PKI).

See Also: *certificate authority (CA), public key infrastructure (PKI)*

root domain

The highest-level parent domain in a domain tree.

Overview

Root domains form the basis of domain trees in an Active Directory directory service implementation of Microsoft Windows 2000 and Windows .NET Server. All other domains in the tree derive their Domain Name System (DNS) name from the root domain and form a contiguous namespace with the root domain. An example of a root domain name for a company called Adventure Works might be adventure-works.com. The root domain is the first domain you create when you implement Active Directory in an enterprise. All other domains you create derive their DNS name from the root domain.

Notes

If you plan to connect your network directly to the Internet, you should register your root domain name with a domain name registration authority. You can use separate external and internal root domain names in your enterprise network if you want to separate network resources that will be accessible to outside users on the Internet from network resources intended for internal company use only. You should register both the internal and external root domain names to prevent future naming conflicts. You should also use a firewall to protect the private domain from the Internet.

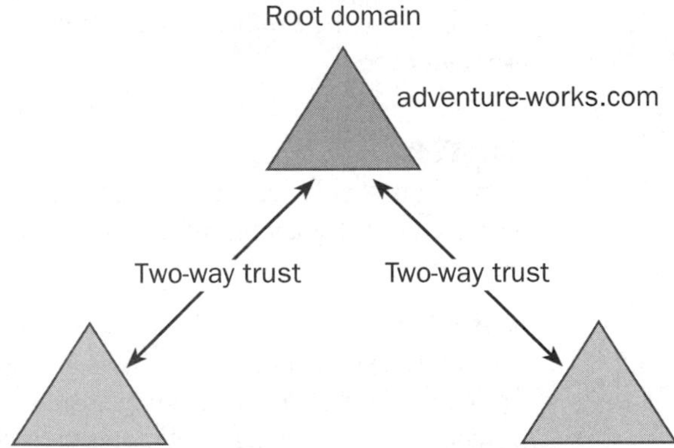

Root domain. *The root domain of a domain tree.*

You should select a root domain name before you implement Active Directory on your Windows 2000– or Windows .NET Server–based network. The name should be easily recognized by users in the outside world, and you should make sure that it is legally acceptable and does not violate existing trademarks or duplicate registered company names. Root domain names should be static and not subject to change.

See Also: *Active Directory, Domain Name System (DNS), domain tree*

root name server

A name server at the top of the Domain Name System (DNS).

Overview

Root name servers are those that can locate name servers that are authoritative for top-level domains such as .com, .org, and .net. Root name servers are the backbone of the DNS naming system and act as an ultimate authority when a local name server cannot resolve a name query. In fact, if all 13 root name servers on the Internet simultaneously failed, users would only be able to reach Web sites registered with local name servers. In other words, the Internet would no longer work and would essentially operate as thousands of small isolated islands. As a result, root name servers are spread out across the Internet for greater protection and are zealously guarded. Examples of root name servers include two belonging to the Military Network (MILNET), one to the National Aeronautics and Space Administration (NASA), several in Europe, one in Japan, and the remainder in the United States. More are likely to be deployed as the Internet grows in size and international reach.

See Also: *Domain Name System (DNS), name server*

routable protocol

A network protocol that can be routed.

Overview

Routable protocols are network protocols that use Layer 3 (network layer) addresses for forwarding packets to their destination. The most commonly used routable protocol today is the Transmission Control Protocol/Internet Protocol (TCP/IP), which is the protocol used on the Internet and in most enterprise networking environments.

Other routable protocols, now considered legacy protocols, include

- Internetwork Packet Exchange/Sequential Packet Exchange (IPX/SPX)
- Xerox Network Systems (XNS)
- DECnet
- AppleTalk
- Banyan VINES

Seldom-used network protocols that are not routable include

- NetBEUI
- Data Link Control (DLC)

Notes

A routable protocol is a network layer protocol that can be routed. A routing protocol, however, is something different: a protocol by which routers can communicate routing table information with one another. Do not get them confused!

See Also: *AppleTalk, Banyan VINES, Data Link Control (DLC), DECnet, NetBEUI, Transmission Control Protocol/Internet Protocol (TCP/IP), Xerox Network Systems (XNS)*

route

A path a packet travels across an internetwork and a command for displaying and configuring routing tables on routers.

Overview

The route a packet takes as it crosses an internetwork is the path, starting from the sending host to a neighboring router and then hopping from router to router until the packet reaches its destination host on some remote network. The process by which the best route to forward a packet is identified is known as routing.

Route is also a command that allows viewing and modification of entries in the internal routing table on an Internet Protocol (IP) host such as a Microsoft Windows 2000, Windows XP, or Windows .NET Server computer. This internal routing table contains routing information that determines how the computer delivers packets to local and remote hosts on the network.

Examples

Typing **route print** at the Windows command prompt displays the routing table of the local computer.

Typing **route add 172.16.25.0 mask 255.255.255.0 172.16.10.1 metric 2** adds a new route to the routing table, specifies that any packets destined for the network with network ID 172.16.25.0 should be forwarded to the router interface 172.16.10.1 in the local network, and specifies that packets sent along this route will traverse two hops on the network.

See Also: *hop count, router, routing, routing table*

router

A device used to connect or segment networks.

Overview

Routers are most often used in Transmission Control Protocol/Internet Protocol (TCP/IP) networks, the Internet being the prime example of a large routed network. Routers can be used either to connect many smaller networks into a larger network called an internetwork or to segment a large network into smaller subnetworks in order to improve performance or manageability. Routers are also sometimes used to join dissimilar media, such as unshielded twisted-pair (UTP) cabling and fiber-optic cabling, and different network architectures, such as Token Ring and Ethernet.

Routers can also be used to connect local area networks (LANs) to telecommunication services such as leased lines or Digital Subscriber Line (DSL). A router used to connect a LAN to a leased line such as a T1 line is often called an access server, and a router used to access DSL servers is known as a DSL router. These routers often support basic firewall functionality to filter out packets based on their source or destination network address. Such a device is sometimes called a packet-filtering router.

Routers generally block broadcast traffic and can thus prevent broadcast storms from slowing down the flow of traffic in a network. Routers are so complex that Cisco Systems, the major vendor of enterprise-level routers, has developed an operating system called Internetwork Operating System (IOS) that is devoted solely to managing routers.

Types

Routers can be either

- **Static routers:** These must have their routing tables configured manually with all network addresses and paths within the internetwork.

or

- **Dynamic routers:** These automatically create their routing tables by listening to network traffic and communicating with other routers.

Comparison

Routers are similar to bridges in that they both forward packets and can be used to either segment or join networks. However, routers use Layer 3 (network layer) addresses such as IP addresses to forward packets, but bridges employ Layer 2 addresses (MAC addresses) for this purpose. When should you use a bridge and when should you use a router? Use bridges to connect network segments that run the same network protocol—for example, to connect an IP segment to an IP segment. Also use bridges when you run legacy nonroutable network protocols such as NetBEUI on your network. On the other hand, use routers to connect network segments that run different network protocols—for example, to connect an IP segment to an Internetwork Packet Exchange (IPX) segment. Generally speaking, routers are more intelligent than bridges and improve network bandwidth by not forwarding broadcast packets to other networks. Finally, use routers when you want to connect your network to the Internet.

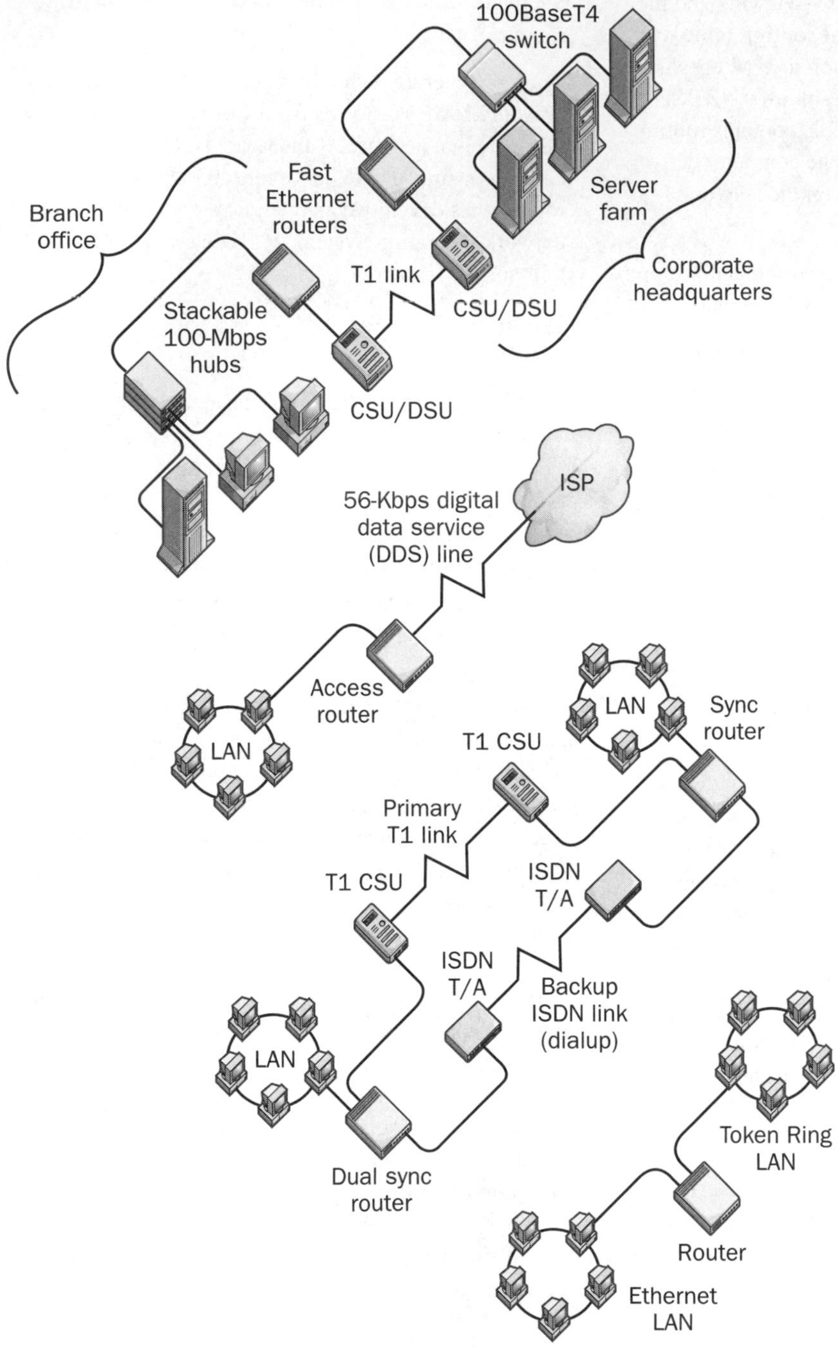

Router. *Some examples of typical uses for routers.*

Implementation

Routers work at the network layer (Layer 3) of the Open Systems Interconnection (OSI) reference model. They forward packets between networks on the basis of their destination logical addresses (IP addresses in the case of TCP/IP). Routers also route packets based on the available paths and their costs, thus taking advantage of redundant paths that can exist in a mesh topology network. To do this, routers contain internal tables called routing tables that keep track of the paths that packets can take as they move across the internetwork, along with the cost of reaching each remote network.

Because routers operate at a higher OSI level than bridges do, they have more powerful switching and filtering capabilities. They also generally require greater processing power, which results in routers usually costing more than bridges. Also, because routers use network addresses for routing packets, they can only work if the network protocol is a "routable protocol" such as TCP/IP or Internetwork Packet Exchange/Sequenced Packet Exchange (IPX/SPX). This is different from bridges, which are basically protocol-independent Layer 2 devices.

Marketplace

Cisco holds the dominant place in the high-end router marketplace, with over 88 percent of the market share. Cisco produces a wide variety of routers with varying capabilities for small, medium, and large enterprises. They also produce routers that are used to form the backbone of the Internet. Some common models of Cisco routers include

- **1600 and 1700 Series:** These are used primarily for small businesses to provide wide area network (WAN) access.
- **2600 Series:** These are standard routers for branch office access to corporate headquarters over WAN links.
- **3600 Series:** These are multifunction routers that can be used in branch/enterprise environments and are more powerful and flexible than the 2600 series.
- **7200 and 7500 Series:** These are high-end multiprotocol routers that support a wide variety of media and are used to build both collapsed backbones and WANs.
- **12000 Series:** These are heavy-duty router/switch combinations used in collapsed backbones and carrier networks.

Other popular router manufacturers include Nortel Networks, Juniper Networks, Ericsson, and 3Com Corporation.

Prospects

A few years ago it was thought that Layer 3 Ethernet switches (also simply called Layer 3 switches) would drive the router market out of existence. This has not entirely happened, despite the fact that such switches, being hardware-based, perform much better than traditional software routers. In the enterprise LAN arena, Layer 3 switches do indeed dominate now in collapsed backbones where routers once ruled in distributed backbones. But in the WAN access arena, routers are still going strong and it looks like they will be around for a long time, driven mainly by Internet service providers needing more routers to handle increased traffic.

Appearing on the horizon are terabit routers capable of forwarding 10^{12} bits per second (bps). These routers are intended mainly for use by telecommunications carriers in their backbone networks, and leading vendors include Cisco, Lucent Technologies, and Avici Systems. A startup called Hyperchip is even developing a petabit router capable of switching packets at 10^{15} bits per second, a speed equivalent to a million Gigabit Ethernet (GbE) ports! Such high-end routers are intended for the next generation of all-optical networks that are expected to emerge around 2005.

See Also: *dynamic routing, Ethernet switch, Internetwork Operating System (IOS), Layer 3 switch, Open Systems Interconnection (OSI) reference model, routable protocol, route, routing, routing algorithm, routing interface, routing metric, routing protocol, routing table, static routing*

router routing

Routing that occurs at the routers.

Overview

Routers are generally used to connect different networks together. Router routing is the process by which a router examines an incoming packet and determines which interface on the router to forward the packet to. This is different from host routing, which is routing that occurs at the host itself.

Usually the term *router routing* is simply abbreviated as *routing*. Whether this actually refers to host routing or router routing can usually be determined from the context of the discussion.

See Also: *host routing, router, routing*

routing

Forwarding packets from one network to another across an internetwork.

Overview

Routing is a method of joining multiple networks in a way that allows packets to travel from one network to the next. To do this, devices called routers are used to connect different networks. These routers accept packets destined to remote networks and forward them to the next step along the way.

Routing is only possible with network protocols that are "routable." Examples of routable protocols include

- **Transmission Control Protocol/Internet Protocol (TCP/IP):** The standard network protocol used on the Internet and in most enterprise networking environments today.
- **Internetwork Packet Exchange/Sequenced Packet Exchange (IPX/SPX):** A legacy protocol used in Novell Netware 2.x and 3.x platforms.

The rest of this article focuses on TCP/IP routing, which is the most common type.

Types

Routing can be classified in different ways depending on what is under consideration. For example, there is

- **Host routing:** This is routing that occurs at the host itself. Each host on an IP network normally maintains its own internal routing table. This table is used to determine whether to send a packet to the local network, to a specific router interface, or to the default gateway address.
- **Router routing:** This is routing that occurs at the routers that connect the various networks. Networks connected by routers are generally called subnets, although this term has a more precise meaning in the context of IP addressing. Most of the discussion below focuses on router routing, which is usually simply called routing.

Routing can also be classified according to how routers are configured to forward packets, specifically:

- **Static routing:** Administrators manually enter entries in router tables.
- **Dynamic routing:** Routing tables can be updated automatically when different routers communicate with one another using routing protocols.

Implementation

Routing takes place at the network layer (Layer 3) of the Open Systems Interconnection (OSI) reference model. In TCP/IP networking, this means that routing of packets is based on their destination IP addresses.

Routing takes place on a packet-by-packet basis and involves two steps:

- Determining the best route (path) over which the packet should travel to reach its destination host.
- Forwarding the packet to the appropriate remote network according to its destination IP address.

Forwarding of packets is handled independently by each router along the path the packet has to travel. In other words, the packet is forwarded across each successive "hop" until it arrives at its destination. Routers perform this forwarding using internal tables called routing tables, which contain information describing the potential paths that data can take to travel to remote networks. Between any two subnets on an internetwork there may be more than one route by which the packet can reach its destination. The information in the routing table, therefore, includes the metric (cost value) for each possible route to the destination, and the packet is usually sent along the path with the lowest cost. If two paths to the same destination have the same cost, the stream of packets can be load-balanced between the two routes. Each network traversed on a routed internetwork is called a subnet.

The value of the metric for a specific path depends on several factors. For example, the metric might be proportional to the number of routers that the packet stream must be switched through (the number of hops traversed), the delay or latency of packets when they are processed by each router, the amount of traffic congestion (load) at the router, the available bandwidth along a route, and even the relative reliability of the routers. For static routers, network administrators manually specify metrics for each path and enter them into routing tables, but for dynamic routers routing algorithms are used to automatically calculate metrics for each possible path. Dynamic routers do this by communicating with each other using special protocols called routing protocols. Examples of common routing protocols include the Routing Information Protocol (RIP) and the Open Shortest Path First (OSPF) protocol. Once the routing table for a static router has been properly configured (or once the tables of all dynamic routers have "converged" and stabilized), the router carries out its packet-forwarding function. The entire routing process works like this: if a local host wants to send a packet to a host on a remote network, the local host first checks its own internal routing table (host routing) to determine which nearby router to forward the packet to. The host then uses Address Resolution Protocol (ARP) to obtain the MAC address of the near-side interface of this router and sends the packet directly to this interface. This packet's header contains the destination host's logical network layer address (IP address). When the router receives the packet, it inspects this destination address and compares it to the information stored in its internal routing table to determine what to do with the packet. If the router cannot determine what to do with the packet, it simply drops the packet. Otherwise, it forwards the packet (router routing) to the destination host (if it is on a network connected to the router) or to a more distant router, which forwards the packet again until finally the packet reaches the network where its destination host resides. As the packet is forwarded from router to router across the internetwork, its network layer destination address remains the same, but its MAC address keeps changing to that of the next router interface along the path.

Issues

Routing in a network can suffer from a number of problems. One problem is the existence of routing loops, which occur when a packet passes through the same router more than once on a given trip. The result is that the packet loops until its lifetime decreases to zero and a router discards it. The originating host usually never knows that the packet was dropped and did not reach its destination. Routing loops occur most often in networks that use incorrectly configured static routers. Routing algorithms for dynamic routers can usually detect loops and reconfigure routing tables to eliminate them. Another problem is convergence. In a large internetwork using dynamic routers, it might take some time for a change in one router's tables to propagate to all other routers in the internetwork. In the meantime, temporary routing loops can occur and less efficient network paths might be chosen, resulting in more traffic congestion. Properly designed routing protocols and routers help avoid such issues and make routing a reliable process for building large internetworks from smaller networks.

See Also: *black hole, bridge, convergence, default gateway, dynamic routing, flooding, hop count, host routing, internetwork, Open Systems Interconnection (OSI) reference model, routable protocol, route, router, router routing, routing algorithm, routing interface, routing metric, routing protocol, routing table, static routing, subnet*

R

routing algorithm

A mathematical procedure that a dynamic router uses to calculate entries for its routing table.

Overview

Routing algorithms underlie the routing protocols that enable dynamic routers to exchange information with one another in order to calculate the metrics of various paths or routes throughout an internetwork. These algorithms generally operate using a combination of variables obtained either by inspecting header information in packets received by the router or manually specified by administrators. The routing algorithm processes the values of these variables to generate the internal routing table for the router. These variables are known as routing metrics and can include the following:

- **Hops:** The number of intermediate routers between a given network and the local router
- **Latency:** The time delay in processing a packet through the router or over a given route
- **Congestion:** The length of the packet queue at the incoming port of the router
- **Load:** The processor use at the router or the number of packets per second that it is currently processing
- **Bandwidth:** The available capacity of a route to support network traffic; decreases as network traffic increases
- **Reliability:** The relative amount of downtime that a particular router might experience because of malfunctions
- **Maximum Transmission Unit (MTU):** The largest packet size that the router can forward without needing to fragment the packet

Routing algorithms are usually implemented as a combination of dynamic (real-time calculated) and static (specified by the network administrator) factors, usually in a distributed fashion where each router independently calculates its own routing tables. In the case of dynamic routers, the exchange of routing information between routers is also part of this process. This provides a degree of fault tolerance for the routing network, for if one router goes down, the remaining routers can recalculate their routing tables to ensure they are able to route traffic around the failed router. Then, when the failed router is restored, the routing tables are recalculated a second time. Some routing algorithms support forwarding packets over several paths to a given destination (when such multiple paths exist) and thus better manage network traffic by load balancing packets accordingly.

Types

An important distinction between routing algorithms involves the space within which they operate. In a flat routing space, all routers are peers, but in a hierarchical routing space, different routing domains, areas, or autonomous systems are connected using a backbone routing network. The advantage of a hierarchical routing space is that it reduces the amount of intercommunication traffic that must take place between routers in order for them to calculate their routing tables. For example, routers that forward traffic only within their own routing table do not need to exchange routing information with routers in other domains. The downside, of course, is that a hierarchical system is much more difficult to implement and maintain than a flat routing space.

Based on this distinction, routing algorithms come in two basic types:

- **Distance vector routing algorithms:** These use a flat routing space, and an example of a routing protocol of this type is the Routing Information Protocol (RIP). Distance-vector routing is sometimes called Bellman-Ford routing or even "old ARPANET routing" by those who are familiar with this algorithm's origins.
- **Link state routing algorithms:** These employ a hierarchical routing space, and an example of a routing protocol of this type is the Open Shortest Path First (OSPF) protocol. Link state algorithms were developed later than distance-vector ones and have largely displaced them in enterprise networking.

From a network administrator's perspective, the differences between these algorithms are as follows:

A routing protocol based on the distance vector routing algorithm is simpler to implement than one based on the link state routing algorithm. Routing loops are less likely to occur when the link state algorithm is used, but link state algorithms require more processing power and routers that implement it are generally more costly. The two algorithms offer a trade-off with respect to network traffic between routers. Specifically, routers using the distance vector algorithm periodically send their entire routing table to other routers, but only to routers one hop away, while the link state algorithm floods the entire internetwork with information from each router, but only updated information is sent when needed.

See Also: *distance vector routing algorithm, dynamic routing, link state routing algorithm, Open Shortest Path First (OSPF), router, routing, Routing Information Protocol (RIP), routing protocol, routing table, static routing*

Routing Information Protocol (RIP)

A popular distance vector routing protocol.

Overview

Routing Information Protocol (RIP) is a dynamic routing protocol that is used to exchange routing table information between routers. Depending on the underlying network protocol being supported, this might be

- **RIP for IP:** Used on Internet Protocol (IP) networks
- **RIP for IPX:** Used on Internetwork Packet Exchange (IPX) networks

Both of these routing protocols are generally referred to simply as RIP. RIP was also adapted for the AppleTalk networking system to form the basis of the Routing Table Maintenance Protocol (RTMP).

History

RIP evolved from the Xerox Network Systems (XNS) protocol suite developed in the late 1970s and was designed in1980 as the first interior routing protocol, a protocol used to allow routers to communicate within an internetwork under a single administrative authority. RIP is implemented as a flat intradomain routing protocol, that is, an interior routing protocol with a flat routing space or routing domain.

RIP first became popular as a result of its inclusion in release 4.2 of the Berkeley Software Distribution UNIX (BSD UNIX) platform. RIP was commonly used throughout the enterprise in the 1980s, but it was supplanted in the 1990s in large enterprises by Open Shortest Path First (OSPF), a link-state interior routing protocol. Today RIP is viewed as a legacy protocol suitable mainly for small internetworks of fewer than 50 routers or so.

Types

There are two versions of RIP:

- **RIPv1:** This is the original version of RIP that was defined in RFC 1058.
- **RIPv2:** This is a newer version of RIP defined in RFC 1723. RIPv2 is fully backward compatible with the earlier RIPv1 but is enhanced to support optional multicasting of routing table information to the multicast address of 224.0.0.9, the inclusion of subnet mask values in RIP announcements, and simple password protection to prevent rogue RIP routers from hijacking network traffic.

Implementation

The metric used by RIP-enabled routers for calculated routing table entries is based on the number of hops it takes for packets to reach their destination networks. RIP routers do not employ other routing metrics used in link state routing protocols such as load, bandwidth, latency, or Maximum Transmission Unit (MTU) in calculating these routing costs. The routing table of a RIP router contains the cost in hops of every path to every destination network in the internetwork.

When a RIP router is first turned on, it broadcasts its presence using a General RIP Request message. This is done so that neighboring RIP routers can be alerted to send the original router advertisements of their routing tables. These RIP advertisements from neighboring RIP routers allow the original router to dynamically build its own routing tables. In addition, the original RIP router broadcasts to its neighbors all network IDs of locally attached networks so that they can update their own routing tables with this information.

RIP-enabled routers broadcast their complete routing tables every 30 seconds over User Datagram Protocol

(UDP) port 520. This adds some overhead to network traffic, but this information is information is propagated only throughout the local subnet and thus received only by routers that have a routing interface adjacent to this subnet. RIP does not support multipath routing. If a routing table has multiple routes for a single network ID, RIP stores the route with the lowest metric (number of hops to destination).

RIP supports a maximum metric of 15, in other words, networks that are more than 15 hops away from the local network are unreachable when using RIP. The RIP metric is also independent of the packet's Time to Live (TTL) value, so if two networks are separated by more than 15 routers, the packet is dropped even if the TTL value has not decremented to zero. When you try to send a packet to a network more than 15 hops away, a RIP router returns an Internet Control Message Protocol (ICMP) Destination Unreachable message.

Advantages and Disadvantages

RIP is a well-supported industry standard routing protocol, but its maximum of 15 hops, together with the use of broadcast announcements, limits the use of RIP to small internetworks. Another disadvantage is that the routing table of a RIP-enabled router can become quite large since it must contain information about all possible routes to all possible subnets on the internetwork.

Another weakness of RIP is that the routing table announcements are not synchronized over the internetwork and are sent without expectation of acknowledgments. In addition, routing entries in a RIP routing table time out 3 minutes after the last RIP announcement is received, so if a RIP router goes down, it takes time for this information to propagate throughout the internetwork, a problem known as slow convergence. This 3-minute timeout value exists so that information about routers that unexpectedly fail or go down can be propagated throughout the internetwork. If neighboring routers do not hear from a RIP router within 3 minutes, networks that are locally attached to the missing router are assigned a hop count of 16, making them unreachable. These factors can result in convergence problems and routing loops on large RIP-enabled internetworks.

Another factor is that RIP advertisement packets are only 512 bytes in length and can contain a maximum of 25 different routing table entries, so a large routing table with hundreds of entries means that dozens of RIP packets are broadcast every 30 seconds. This can result in a lot of extra broadcast traffic on the local subnet, making RIP unsuitable for large internetworks or for networks having slow wide area network (WAN) links.

Finally, RIP cannot take into account real-time network parameters such as congestion, latency, or router load when the RIP router determines whether to forward a packet along a specific route. An alternative to RIP is to use the Open Shortest Path First (OSPF) protocol, which can dynamically take into account such real-time network parameters, but implementing OSPF is fairly complex and may require you to upgrade existing routers.

Notes

RIP routers should be turned off properly so that they can advertise the fact that they are being turned off to their neighboring routers. This notification, called a triggered update, declares all locally attached networks to the router as having a hop count of 16, making them unreachable. These triggered changes then propagate throughout the internetwork.

If your RIP-enabled internetwork includes slower WAN links as well as fast local area network (LAN) links between networks, you can assign the WAN links hop values that are greater than 1 to compensate for their slower speed. For example, you can assign a T1 link between two networks a hop count of 3 or 4. However, the total hop count between any two networks must still be less than or equal to 15, and such a configuration makes sense only if the topology of the network is a complex mesh involving both fast LAN and slow WAN links.

A RIP-enabled router that can receive RIP broadcasts but cannot send them is called a "silent RIP router."

See Also: *AppleTalk, broadcasting, convergence, dynamic routing, interior gateway protocol (IGP), Internet Control Message Protocol (ICMP), Internet Protocol (IP), internetwork, Internetwork Packet Exchange (IPX), Open ShortestPath First (OSPF), router, routing, routing algorithm, subnet, User Datagram Protocol (UDP), Xerox Network Systems (XNS)*

routing interface

A port where a router connects to a network.

Overview

For any particular network, the port on the router that is directly connected to the local network is called the local interface, and any port on the router that is connected to a different network is called a remote interface. Each router interface has a unique MAC address burned into it, just like a network interface card (NIC) in a computer.

If only one router is connected to the local network, the local interface is the default gateway for all hosts on that network.

See Also: *default gateway, MAC address, router, routing*

routing metric

A variable used by a dynamic router to calculate its routing table entries.

Overview

Dynamic routers employ metrics to determine which routing interface the router should forward a packet to in order to route it to its destination. Routing metrics enable routers to make intelligent decisions about how to forward packets to ensure that

- Packets are delivered efficiently and quickly
- Congestion does not occur over links between networks
- Packets are not lost by being dropped by overloaded or dead routers

Implementation

The simplest metric used by routers to calculate routing table entries is the number of hops to a given destination network. This kind of metric is used by the Routing Information Protocol (RIP), an older routing protocol that enables dynamic routers to communicate with each other to share their routing information and synchronize the entries of their routing tables. On the other hand, if you need a more complicated metric that provides you with more control over the various paths that packets take across your network, you can use a routing protocol such as Open Shortest Path First (OSPF) instead. This protocol employs several variables in calculating its metric, including

- **Load:** Generally, the number of packets being processed per second by the router or its central processing unit (CPU) utilization. If the load on a router becomes high, the router can advise other routers to recalculate routing tables in order to divert traffic around it.
- **Latency:** The time interval needed to route a packet through the router or over a specific path through the internetwork. Latency can be increased by delays due to such factors as port congestion on the router, heavy router load, bandwidth utilization of links between networks, and physical distance between networks.

Some routing metrics are manually entered into a router's configuration by administrators who have a knowledge of the network's physical layout and performance. Such metrics can include

- **Bandwidth:** The total capacity of each network link to carry traffic between different networks in the internetwork.
- **Reliability:** The relative amount of anticipated downtime for a given link between two networks.
- **Cost:** A parameter roughly proportional to the actual cost in dollars of using each network link. Some wide area network (WAN) links might have more latency but cost much less.
- **Maximum Transmission Unit (MTU):** The largest size of packet that the router can forward without segmenting the packet into subpackets. Segmentation of network traffic by routers adds additional latency to network communication.

See Also: *dynamic routing, Open Shortest Path First (OSPF), routing, Routing Information Protocol (RIP), routing table, static routing*

routing protocol

A protocol that enables routers to communicate with each other.

Overview

Routing protocols are the software implementation of routing algorithms, mathematical procedures for determining the cost of various paths or routes through an internetwork so that traffic can be efficiently routed. Routing algorithms are used by dynamic routers, which exchange information with each other that enables them to build routing tables that accurately represent the possible paths on which packets may be routed through the network.

A good routing protocol should have the following characteristics:

- It should allow rapid convergence (recalculation) of routing table information when the network changes—for example, when a router goes down.
- It should prevent routing loops from occurring.
- It should select the optimal route for packets to be forwarded to reach their destination, based on routing metric information.

Types

Routing protocols can be classified in different ways. For example, you can classify them according to how they are affected by administrative boundaries in networks, which results in the following:

- **Interior Gateway Protocols (IGPs):** These routing protocols are used to exchange information between routers within a given administrative area or autonomous system (AS). Other names for this kind of routing protocol are interior routing protocol or intradomain routing protocol.
- **Exterior Gateway Protocols (EGPs):** These protocols are used to exchange information between routers in different administrative areas or autonomous systems (ASs). Other names for this kind of routing protocol are exterior routing protocol and interdomain routing protocol.

Routing protocols can also be classified according to the type of routing algorithm they use, specifically:

- **Distance-vector routing protocols:** These protocols employ the distance-vector routing algorithm to calculate their routing tables and send their entire routing table (or most of it) to other routers when updates are required. Because of their high overhead in communications, distance-vector routing protocols are useful only on relatively small networks with few routers.
- **Link-state routing protocols:** These protocols use the link-state routing algorithm for routing table calculation and send only the state of their own interfaces to other routers, minimizing communications overhead and making these protocols suitable for large networks with many routers.

Finally, routing protocols can be classified as either

- **Classful routing protocols:** These use Internet Protocol (IP) address class distinctions to derive subnet masks. They are essentially simple protocols that are limited in their scalability to large networks.

or

- **Classless routing protocols:** These protocols propagate subnet masks and do not consider IP address classes when routing packets. In other words, they employ classless interdomain routing (CIDR) in their operation.

Examples

Common examples of routing protocols include

- **Routing Information Protocol (RIP):** Based on the distance vector routing algorithm and used in small to medium-sized internetworks, RIP is an intradomain routing protocol that can function only within a given routing domain. Microsoft Windows NT Server, Windows 2000 Server, and Windows .NET Server support RIP; a multihomed machine running Windows NT, Windows 2000, or Windows .NET Server can be used as a RIP router.
- **Interior Gateway Routing Protocol (IGRP):** Based on the distance vector routing algorithm and used in medium-sized to large-sized internetworks, IGRP is an intradomain routing protocol that can function only within a given routing domain. IGRP uses a number of metrics to determine routing cost, including load, bandwidth, latency, reliability, and

R

Maximum Transmission Unit (MTU). The router determines some of these factors dynamically as it inspects incoming traffic, but others are specified by the network administrator. IGRP supports multipath routing for load balancing and fault tolerance.

- **Open Shortest Path First (OSPF):** Based on the link state routing algorithm and used in medium-sized to large-sized internetworks, OSPF is a hierarchical, intradomain routing protocol that is used within an autonomous system (AS). OSPF evolved from an earlier Open Systems Interconnection (OSI) routing protocol called intermediate-system-to-intermediate-system (IS-IS). OSPF supports multipath routing and uses one or more routing metrics, including bandwidth, reliability, load, latency, and MTU. If OSPF is configured to use more than one metric, it can also support type-of-service (TOS) requests for differentiating traffic.
- **Exterior Gateway Protocol (EGP):** An interdomain routing protocol for routing between different routing domains that are connected by a routing backbone such as the Internet. EGP was the first interdomain routing protocol and was designed in 1984 to enable communication between the core routers of the Internet. EGP does not use routing metrics—it simply keeps track of which networks are currently reachable through a given router.
- **Border Gateway Protocol (BGP):** Another interdomain routing protocol created specifically to enable the core or backbone routers of the Internet to communicate with each other. BGP is superior to EGP because it can detect routing loops and use routing metrics, and it has displaced EGP as the interdomain protocol of choice for the Internet.

Some less commonly used routing protocols include

- **NetWare Link Services Protocol (NLSP):** Used in Novell NetWare 4.*x* as part of its Multi-Protocol Router (MPR). NLSP is based on a combination of OSPF routing and Novell's Service Advertising Protocol (SAP) functions and is also based on the link state routing algorithm.
- **Routing Table Maintenance Protocol (RTMP):** Used in AppleTalk networks and based on the distance vector routing algorithm. RTMP is derived from RIP.

Notes

Remember that a routing protocol is different from a routable protocol. A routing protocol is used by routers to communicate with each other. A routable protocol, on the other hand, is a network protocol, such as Transmission Control Protocol/Internet Protocol (TCP/IP) or Internetwork Packet Exchange/Sequenced Packet Exchange (IPX/SPX), that allows packets to be routed across an internetwork.

See Also: *autonomous system (AS), Border Gateway Protocol (BGP), classful routing protocol, classless interdomain routing (CIDR), classless routing protocol, convergence, distance vector routing protocol, dynamic routing, Exterior Gateway Protocol (EGP), interior gateway protocol (IGP), Interior Gateway Routing Protocol (IGRP), link state routing algorithm, Open Shortest Path First (OSPF), Open Systems Interconnection (OSI) reference model, routable protocol, router, routing, routing algorithm, Routing Information Protocol (RIP), routing metric, routing table, static routing*

routing table

An internal table that determines which interface to send a packet to, based on its destination network addresses.

Overview

Routing tables enable both computers and routers to forward packets to their destinations. On Microsoft Windows platforms these routing tables are built automatically and are used to determine whether to forward specific packets to

- The local network for destination hosts on the local network segment
- A near-side router interface for destination hosts on a specific remote network segment
- The default gateway for hosts in unknown locations

R

Examples

To view the internal Transmission Control Protocol/Internet Protocol (TCP/IP) routing table on a computer running Windows, type **route print** at the command prompt. The result is a typical routing table that looks something like the following:

```
Active Routes:
                                 Gateway
Network Address Netmask          Address     Interface   Metric
127.0.0.0       255.0.0.0        127.0.0.1   127.0.0.1        1
172.16.8.0      255.255.255.0    172.16.8.50 172.16.8.50      1
172.16.8.50     255.255.255.255  127.0.0.1   127.0.0.1        1
172.16.255.255  255.255.255.255  172.16.8.50 172.16.8.50      1
224.0.0.0       224.0.0.0        172.16.8.50 172.16.8.50      1
255.255.255.255 255.255.255.255  172.16.8.50 172.16.8.50      1
```

This particular computer has a single network interface card (NIC) with the address 172.16.8.50. The columns of this table are interpreted as follows:

- **Network Address:** A destination network address on the network
- **Netmask:** The portion of the network address that must match in order for that route to be used
- **Gateway Address:** Where the packet needs to be forwarded (a local NIC or a local router interface)
- **Interface:** The address of the NIC through which the packet should be sent
- **Metric:** The number of hops to the destination network

See Also: *default gateway, routable protocol, route, router, routing, routing interface, routing metric, routing table*

RPC

Stands for remote procedure call, a protocol that enables one computer to make a function call to another computer on the network.

See: *remote procedure call (RPC)*

RPC Ping

A utility for testing for remote procedure call (RPC) connectivity over a network.

Overview

RPC Ping is included with Microsoft Exchange Server for testing RPC connectivity essential for the operation of an Exchange/Outlook messaging system. The server portion of RPC Ping runs on an Exchange server and responds to requests from the RPC Ping client on another station.

If an RPC-based mail client such as Microsoft Outlook cannot connect to an Exchange server in its site, perform the following tests:

- Check network connectivity between the client and the server to try to map a network drive to a shared folder on the server by typing the Net Use command at the command prompt on the client. If this fails, you might have a hardware failure such as a failed network interface card (NIC), a loose cable, or a configuration problem with your networking protocol (such as an erroneous Internet Protocol [IP] address).
- If network connectivity is successful, you might have a problem with the RPC binding order on the client. Try modifying this binding order in the registry.
- If the client still cannot connect to the server, run the server-side component of RPC Ping on the server to test which protocols RPC can bind with and which protocols can be accepted by the client. This server-side component of RPC Ping is called Rpings. Run the client-side component of RPC Ping called Rpingc32 to test RPC connectivity with the Exchange server. If Rpingc32 works for a specific protocol, rearrange the RPC binding order on the client so that this protocol is first.

See Also: *Exchange Server*

RPR

Stands for resilient packet ring, an emerging technology for Synchronous Optical Networking (SONET).

See: *resilient packet ring (RPR)*

RSA

Stands for Rivest-Shamir-Adelman, a popular algorithm for public key cryptography.

See: *Rivest-Shamir-Adelman (RSA) algorithm*

RS-232

A popular serial interface.

Overview

More properly known as RS-232C, RS-232 is a widely implemented serial transmission interface developed by the Electronic Industries Alliance (EIA) that is used for connecting data terminal equipment (DTE) such as computers or terminals to data communications equipment (DCE) such as modems, packet assembler/disassemblers (PADs), or serial printers.

RS-232 specifies the types of wires and connectors, the pinning of the connectors and the function of each wire, the voltage levels and their meanings, and control procedures such as handshaking. RS-232 is compatible with the V.24 and V.28 standards from the International Telecommunication Union (ITU).

Uses

On a PC, RS-232 is typically implemented in a universal asynchronous receiver-transmitter (UART) chip, which converts the internal parallel bus signal to a serial bit stream and vice versa, enabling communication between your system bus and serial devices. Even though the maximum speed of RS-232 is 115.2 kilobits per second (Kbps), older PCs support rates of up to only 56 or 64 Kbps. Newer PCs have a 16550 UART chip that supports serial throughput rates of up to 460.8 Kbps.

You can also use RS-232 with a null modem cable to connect two pieces of DTE (for example, to transfer files). If you are having trouble with an RS-232 connection, be sure that you are using a regular cable for DTE-DCE communication or a null modem cable for DTE-DTE communication—they look the same, but they are incompatible.

Architecture

The RS-232 specification uses unbalanced lines to provide full-duplex serial communication using baseband transmission. RS-232 provides a typical data rate of 19.2 Kbps over a maximum distance of 15 meters (49 feet), but the maximum data transfer rate is 115.2 Kbps. Up to two devices can be connected using RS-232. Devices cannot be daisy-chained together using RS-232. (Use RS-422/423 instead.)

RS-232 cables (cables designed to use the RS-232 serial interface specification) are typically 25-wire unshielded twisted-pair (UTP) cables with DB25 type connectors or 9-wire cables with DB9 connectors. The pin assignments are shown in the following table. Note that only pins 1 through 8 and pin 20 are required for most basic RS-232 functions, which means that 9-pin DB9 connectors can be used on RS-232 serial cables for most applications.

Pin Assignments for RS-232

Pin Number	*Function*
1	Equipment ground (for protection)
2	DTE transmit data
3	DTE receive data
4	Request-to-send (RTS), controlled by the DTE
5	Clear-to-send (CTS), controlled by the DCE
6	Data-set-ready (DSR), controlled by the DTE
7	Signal ground (common return path)
8	Carrier-detect (CD)
9	+ Voltage
10	- Voltage
11	Not used
12	Secondary received line signal indicator
13	Secondary CTS
14	Secondary DTE transmit data
15	DCE transmitter signal timing
16	Secondary DTE receive data
17	Receiver signal timing
18	Local loopback
19	Secondary RTS
20	Data-terminal-ready (DTR), controlled by the DTE
21	Signal quality detector
22	Ring indicator
23	Data signal rate selector
24	DTE transmitter signal timing
25	Test mode

See Also: *connector (device), data communications equipment (DCE), data terminal equipment (DTE),* *full-duplex, RS-422, serial transmission, unbalanced line*

RS-422

A high-speed serial interface.

Overview

RS-422 is a full-duplex serial interface that uses balanced lines and has more immunity from noise than the RS-232 interface. RS-422 was originally designed to supersede the earlier RS-232 standard, but they now coexist in networking environments. RS-422 transmits data at rates between 230 kilobits per second (Kbps) and 1 megabit per second (Mbps). RS-422 cables typically have 25 wires and use DB37 or DB9 connectors, and the maximum distance for an RS-422 link is typically 300 meters (985 feet).

An unbalanced version of RS-422 called RS-423 is defined but is less frequently implemented. RS-422 and RS-423 are compatible with the International Telecommunication Union (ITU) standards V.11 and V.10, respectively.

Uses

RS-422 is used in industrial environments with a lot of electromagnetic interference (EMI) or where more than two serial devices need to be chained together. It is typically used for high-speed synchronous communication between data terminal equipment (DTE) and multiple daisy-chained data communications equipment (DCE).

Notes

Some other related Electronic Industries Alliance (EIA) standards for serial transmission include

- **RS-449:** Specifies the pinning for RS-422 when DB37 connectors are used.
- **RS-485:** Expands RS-422 to include balanced multipoint serial communication using tristate drivers.
- **RS-530:** Specifies the pinning for RS-422 when DB25 connectors are used. Note that RS-530 cables look like RS-232 cables but are not compatible with them.

See Also: *connector (device), data communications equipment (DCE), data terminal equipment (DTE), full-duplex, RS-422, serial transmission, unbalanced line*

RSAC

Stands for Recreational Software Advisory Council, a nonprofit organization with a content advisory system for Web sites on the Internet.

See: *Recreational Software Advisory Council (RSAC)*

Rsh

A UNIX command that enables clients to run commands directly on remote hosts without having to log on to the remote host.

Overview

Rsh is one of the UNIX r-commands that are available on all UNIX systems. In order to use Rsh on a client machine,

- The remote host must be running the Rsh service or daemon.
- The Rsh user and client must have their computer name and username configured in the remote host's .rhosts file.

Rsh provides functionality similar to that of Rexec, another UNIX command that enables clients to run commands directly on remote hosts. The difference is that Rexec uses clear-text password authentication and does not prompt the client to enter a password upon connecting.

Notes

Microsoft Corporation's implementation of Rsh is client software only. If a user on a computer running Microsoft Windows 2000, Windows XP, or Windows .NET Server is logged on to a domain and tries to use Rsh to run a command on a remote UNIX server that is running the Rsh daemon, the domain controller must be available in order to authenticate the user, which is required by the Rsh client.

See Also: *Rexec*

RSVP

Stands for Resource Reservation Protocol, a signaling protocol used for conveying quality of service (QoS) requests.

See: *Resource Reservation Protocol (RSVP)*

runt

An undersized Ethernet frame.

Overview

A runt is an Ethernet frame that is smaller than the minimum 64-byte size. Runts are generally caused by malfunctioning interfaces on routers or malfunctioning network interface cards (NICs) in computers. Runts utilize network bandwidth in a hidden fashion when they are present and are therefore undesirable, but they are a less serious condition than jabbering, which occurs when an interface starts broadcasting frames without ceasing. Runts can slow down a network, but a jabbering card can bring everything to a standstill. To eliminate runts, identify the malfunctioning card or interface and replace it.

See Also: *Ethernet, jabber, network interface card (NIC), router*

SACL

Stands for system access control list, a form of access control list (ACL) used by Microsoft Windows 2000 for security control purposes.

See: *system access control list (SACL)*

safe mode

A mode of starting some versions of Microsoft Windows for troubleshooting purposes.

Overview

Safe mode bypasses startup files and runs a basic set of files and drivers including mouse, keyboard, video, mass storage, and basic system services. Safe mode is used for troubleshooting Windows when your system fails to boot properly—for example, when a device driver is corrupt or after you make an erroneous change to the registry. Safe mode bypasses the system startup files to allow you to start with a "clean" configuration.

To access safe mode when booting Windows 98 and Windows Millennium Edition (Me), press the F5 key when the screen shows the message "Starting Windows 98..." or "Starting Windows Me..." You can also start safe mode from the command prompt by typing **win/ d:m**. You can also press F6 to access safe mode with networking support. When you are in safe mode, you are informed of this by text displayed in all four corners of the screen.

To access safe mode while booting Windows 2000, Windows XP, or Windows .NET Server, press the F8 key when you see the message "Please select the operating system to start." You will then be presented with a list of options that includes three safe mode options: standard, networking-enabled, and safe mode with command prompt. Use the arrow keys to navigate the list. Press the Enter key to make your selection.

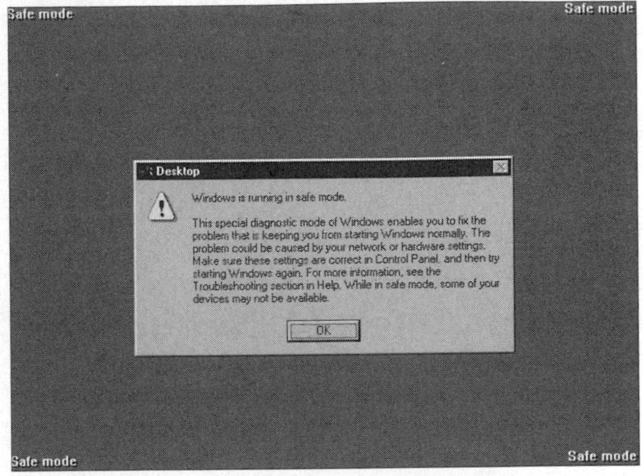

Safe mode. *Entering safe mode in Windows 2000.*

SAM database

Stands for Security Account Manager (SAM) database, which contains user and group account information on a Microsoft Windows NT domain controller.

See: *Security Account Manager (SAM) database*

SAN

Stands for storage area network, a dedicated storage network separate from the network where servers reside.

See: *storage area network (SAN)*

SAP

Stands for Service Advertising Protocol, a Novell NetWare protocol for advertising network resources.

See: *Service Advertising Protocol (SAP)*

SAS

Stands for secure attention sequence, the Ctrl+Alt+ Delete keystroke combination in Microsoft Windows NT, Windows 2000, Windows XP, and Windows .NET Server that displays the Windows Security dialog box.

See: *secure attention sequence (SAS)*

SATAN

Stands for Security Administrator Tool for Analyzing Networks, a popular network security analysis tool.

See: *Security Administrator Tool for Analyzing Networks (SATAN)*

Satellite Internet Backbone (SIBone)

A satellite-based network exchange point.

Overview

The Satellite Internet Backbone (SIBone) is the first network exchange point on the Internet that is located in outer space. SIBone uses a satellite deployed by eSAT, and Internet service providers (ISPs) can connect to this exchange point by colocating routers at eSAT's data centers (called teleports), where satellite links using radio telescopes connect the ground station with the satellite. eSAT's satellite employs a proprietary technology called Virtual Onboard Switching (VOS) to simulate a mesh-based technology.

SIBone provides Tier-2 ISPs with an alternative to buying transit services from larger Tier-1 ISPs. VOS allows Tier-2 ISPs to exchange Internet traffic with each other directly, potentially saving costs. SIBone's downside, however, is that the satellite's geosynchronous orbit means that it is 22,236 miles (35,785 kilometers) above the Earth's surface, which can increase the latency of connections by as much as 500 milliseconds (msec). This latency might be acceptable for general purpose Internet traffic but is too large for Voice over IP (VoIP) applications to work well.

See Also: *Internet, Internet service provider (ISP), latency, Voice over IP (VoIP)*

schema

A set of rules defining the structure of a directory.

Overview

In the Active Directory directory service of Microsoft Windows 2000 and Windows .NET Server, the schema defines which objects can be contained in the directory and what attributes those objects can have. The schema can also be considered a formal definition of Active Directory.

Active Directory comes with a default schema that is sufficient in most instances and that defines common network objects in the directory such as users, groups, domains, and computers. You can modify the schema by using the Active Directory Schema, a snap-in for the Microsoft Management Console (MMC). The schema is extensible in that new object classes and attribute types can be added to it. Members of the Schema Admins group have the necessary rights for modifying and extending the schema. The built-in Administrator account is included in this group. You can make the following types of modifications to the schema:

- Create new classes and attributes
- Modify existing classes and attributes
- Deactivate existing classes and attributes

Notes

The schema is actually stored in Active Directory itself in a container under the RootDSE object. Key attributes within the Active Directory schema that are prefixed with "System-" cannot be modified. This ensures consistency of the schema.

If you modify the schema, you should wait five minutes for the modifications to be written to the system, whereupon the changes are updated in Active Directory and replicated to all domain controllers. Therefore, if you modify the schema, you should wait until the changes have replicated throughout your entire enterprise before you create new objects that use these modifications.

As a safety measure, domain controllers by default have read-only permissions on the schema. If you want to write changes to the schema, you must first modify a registry setting on the domain controller on which you plan to make modifications. (Make modifications to the schema from only one domain controller at a time.) The Schema Manager MMC snap-in offers a check box that you can use to set or clear the key. To modify the registry manually, you add the parameter "Schema Update Allowed" with data type REG_DWORD and a nonzero value to the following registry key:

```
HKEY_LOCAL_MACHINE
      \System
          \CurrentControlSet
              \Services
                   \NTDS
                        \Parameters
```

See Also: *Active Directory*

scope

Short for Dynamic Host Configuration Protocol (DHCP) scope, a range of Internet Protocol (IP) addresses that a DHCP server can lease out to DHCP clients.

See: *DHCP scope*

scripting

Writing scripts for performing administration, building dynamic Web sites, and other tasks.

Overview

Scripting involves using scripting languages to write short programs called scripts. These scripts are then executed with the help of a scripting engine, an interpreter that is usually built in to the client or server where the script is executed.

Some uses for scripting in enterprise and e-business environments include

- Automating administrative tasks such as performing backups and unlocking user accounts
- Adding dynamic functionality to static Hypertext Markup Language (HTML) pages to create forms, shopping carts, and other features

Types

There are a wide variety of scripting languages used in enterprise and e-business environments today. Some of the more popular languages include

- **Batch file languages:** A batch file is a collection of Microsoft Windows or UNIX commands saved in a text file. On the Windows platform, for example, batch files are files that have the extension .bat. Batch files can be either manually executed by administrators or can be scheduled to run at specific times. In UNIX environments writing batch files is often called shell scripting.
- **Practical Extraction and Reporting Language (Perl):** This is a popular scripting language used in UNIX environments for writing common gateway interface (CGI) scripts that add dynamic functionality to static Web pages. There are also versions of Perl for the Windows platform.
- **Rexx:** This language originated in IBM's OS/2 computing environment, and is a scripting language that has powerful string manipulation features comparable to those found in Perl.
- **Python:** This is another scripting language that is popular in the UNIX environment. It includes support for object-oriented programming.
- **Visual Basic Scripting Edition (VBScript):** This is a subset of Visual Basic for Applications (VBA) and is a popular tool on Windows platforms for building dynamic Web sites.
- **JScript:** This is Microsoft Corporation's implementation of JavaScript and confirms to the European Computer Manufacturers Association (ECMA) 262 standard. JScript is a powerful tool for writing scripts that perform administrative tasks on the Windows platform.

Implementation

Looking specifically at Web scripting on the Windows platform, two basic approaches can be used:

- **Server-side scripting:** Here the script is executed on the Web server side of a Hypertext Transfer Protocol (HTTP) session. The client requests a page from the server, and the server processes the script and generates HTML, which is then sent to the client. Server-side scripting is popular and forms the basis of Microsoft Active Server Pages (ASP), a platform for building dynamic Web applications based on Microsoft Internet Information Services (IIS). Similar platforms include ColdFusion from Allaire Corporation, Java Server Pages (JSP) from Sun Microsystems, and PHP from the Apache Software Foundation.

- **Client-side scripting:** Here the script is embedded in the Web page downloaded by the client and is executed within the client browser to add dynamic functionality to the page.

Notes

The Windows Script Host (WSH) is a component of Windows that first appeared in Windows NT 4. The WSH enables scripts of various types to be run without the need of a separate container application, and it supports a wide range of ActiveX scripting engines.

See Also: *Active Server Pages (ASP), batch file, Hypertext Markup Language (HTML), Hypertext Transfer Protocol (HTTP), Internet Information Services (IIS), JScript, Practical Extraction and Reporting Language (Perl), VBScript, Windows commands, Windows Script Host (WSH)*

SCSI

Stands for Small Computer System Interface, a popular general-purpose input/output (I/O) bus.

See: *Small Computer System Interface (SCSI)*

S

SC/ST connectors

Connectors commonly used in fiber-optic networking.

Overview

The SC and ST connectors are the most widely used type of connectors for fiber-optic cabling. They are defined in the Electronic Industries Alliance/Telecommunications Industry Association (EIA/TIA) 568A cabling standard. Details of these connector types are as follows:

- **SC:** This stands for subscriber connector and is a duplex (two strand) fiber-optic connector having a square molded plastic body about twice the size of a standard RJ-45 copper wire connector and a push-pull locking interface. SC connectors are typically used in data communication, cable television (CATV), and telephony environments.
- **ST:** This stands for straight tip and is a simplex (one strand) fiber-optic connector with round ceramic ferrules and bayonet locking features. ST connectors are generally more common than SC connectors in fiber-optic networking environments.

Both SC and ST connectors can be used with either single-mode or multimode fiber-optic cabling. Coupling receptacles for these connectors come in either panel-mount or free-handing designs. For narrow space installations, you can even get 90-degree boot versions instead of straight versions.

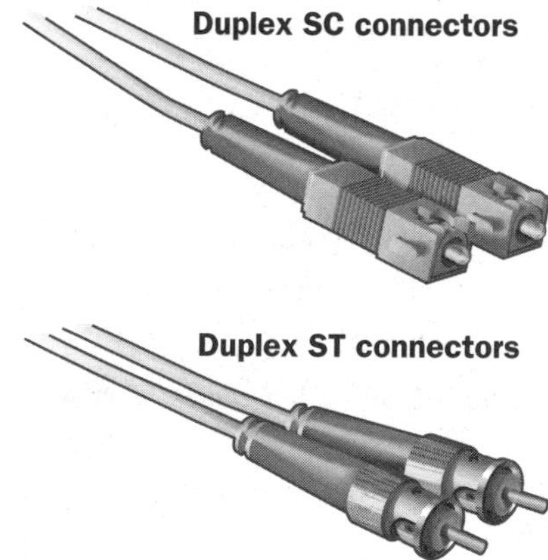

SC and ST connectors. *Fiber-optic SC and ST connectors.*

Issues

The main problem with SC and ST connectors is that they are expensive. To terminate a fiber-optic cable with one of these connectors you must splice the cable, polish the end of the fiber, and glue the connector onto the cable. The cost of these connectors plus installation labor means that about 35 percent of the cost of a fiber-optic patch cord is due to the connectors. As a result, fiber-optic cabling manufacturers have been developing new connector types that are easier to install and more compatible with writing panels for existing Category 5 (Cat5) cabling infrastructures. An early development in this regard was the SMA connector, a snap-in connector that features threaded-nut locking. Subtypes of this connector include SMA905 and SMA906.

A recent development has been the emergence of new fiber-optic connectors compatible with RJ-45 connectors. These new connectors allow existing Cat5 wiring panels to be used for optical interconnects instead of having to install special SC/ST/SMA patch panels in wiring closets. Some of the more popular versions of these new connectors include

- **MT-RJ:** Developed by Alcoa, AMP, and Siecor (now Corning Cable Systems)
- **LC:** Developed by Lucent Technologies
- **VF-45:** Developed by 3M Corporation
- **Opti-Jack:** Developed by Panduit Corporation

These different standards are inoperable with one another, and the TIA is essentially letting the market decide which will become the new market standard. The move to these smaller-footprint optical connectors means that SC/ST connectors are beginning to be viewed as legacy technology and might soon be on their way out.

Notes

For harsh environments, a good choice is the military-grade connector. These connectors satisfy the MIL-C-83522 (ST) specifications and are corrosion-proof; have isolated relief boots to reduce cable strain; and are heat, shock, vibration, fungus, and salt-spray resistant.

See Also: *Category 5 (Cat5) cabling, fiber-optic cabling, RJ connectors*

SDLC

Stands for Synchronous Data Link Control, a data-link layer protocol developed in the 1970s by IBM for its Systems Network Architecture (SNA) networking environment.

See: *Synchronous Data Link Control (SDLC)*

SDSL

Stands for Symmetric Digital Subscriber Line, a form of business-grade Digital Subscriber Line (DSL) service.

See: *Symmetric Digital Subscriber Line (SDSL)*

secondary name server

A type of name server in the Domain Name System (DNS).

Overview

A secondary name server is one that downloads its file of resource records from a master name server. The master name server can be either a primary name server or another secondary name server. Primary name servers get their resource records from local files called zone files. Secondary name servers do not maintain local zone files—they obtain their files from master name servers by means of a zone transfer, which occurs when a secondary name server polls a master name server and determines that there are updates to the DNS database that need to be downloaded. This primary/secondary (master/slave) architecture means that a DNS administrator has to maintain only a single set of DNS resource records (on the primary name server), which simplifies DNS administration.

A name server can be a primary name server for one zone and a secondary name server for a different zone. In other words, name servers are defined as primary or secondary on a per-zone basis. On Berkeley Internet Naming Domain (BIND) implementations of DNS, secondary name servers are often referred to as slave name servers.

Notes

Secondary name servers can be used to provide redundancy and load balancing for name resolution. On a corporate Internet Protocol (IP) network that uses DNS as its name resolution method, it is a good idea to have at least two name servers—a primary master name server, and a secondary name server for backup. Otherwise, if the primary goes down, users will not be able to resolve server names on the network and therefore will not be able to find and access any network resources.

BIND makes it possible for slave name servers to keep backup copies of zone files in case the master name server goes down. It is generally a good practice to keep such backup copies. You can also implement a list of up to 10 master name servers that can be tried successively by each slave name server in a very large DNS implementation. BIND v8 includes a feature whereby the primary notifies the slave when changes have been made to the primary's DNS database. This notification process causes BIND v8 name servers to be more up to date with each other than with the polling procedure of earlier BIND implementations.

See Also: *Berkeley Internet Name Domain (BIND), name server, zone, zone file*

secondary ring

The backup ring in Fiber Distributed Data Interface (FDDI) networking.

Overview

FDDI is a dual-ring topology networking architecture based on a token-passing access method. The secondary ring usually sits dark (unused), except when a fault occurs on the primary ring, in which case the network reconfigures itself to make use of the secondary ring to wrap around the fault. Because the data travels on the secondary ring in the opposite direction than it was traveling on the primary ring, when it's put to use, the secondary ring reroutes data back the way it came, thus avoiding the problem spot.

The dual-ring configuration provides FDDI with a degree of fault tolerance—if a computer or cable on the primary ring goes down, the secondary ring is put to use, working in conjunction with the portion of the primary ring that is not broken. This feature is known as a self-healing capability and is performed when the stations on both sides of the link concentrator reconfigure themselves when a failure occurs in the link (due to a cable break, a loose connector, or some device failure).

S

The FDDI specification allows the length of the two rings to reach up to 125 miles (200 kilometers), with up to 1000 attached stations. However, since the secondary ring is usually used for redundancy purposes, a maximum of 500 stations is allowed on an FDDI network. Repeaters are needed every 1.25 miles (2 kilometers) around the rings.

Notes

You can run the FDDI primary ring and secondary ring along different physical paths to make your FDDI network even more redundant. If an accident or disaster affects one of the rings, it might not affect the other.

See Also: *Fiber Distributed Data Interface (FDDI), primary ring*

secure attention sequence (SAS)

The Ctrl+Alt+Delete keystroke combination in Microsoft Windows NT, Windows 2000, Windows XP, and Windows .NET Server that displays the Windows Security dialog box.

Overview

Users can use the secure attention sequence keystroke combination to do the following:

- Log on to or log off of a Windows workstation
- Lock the console or unlock a locked workstation
- Change their passwords
- Invoke Task Manager
- Shut down, log off, or restart their systems

Notes

The secure attention sequence (SAS) offers protection against Trojan horse programs that masquerade as common system applications. For example, it is impossible to write a Trojan horse program that presents the user with a phony Windows Security dialog box in order to steal a user's credentials, because this program cannot be activated by the SAS. The most that a hacker can do is write a Trojan horse program that displays a Windows Security dialog box at random times while the user is already logged on. To guard against such an event, you should educate users to always use the SAS keystroke sequence even if the computer they are using already displays what appears to be the Windows Security dialog box.

The SAS also kills any logon scripts that are running and can be used to terminate scripts that have stopped responding.

Secure Hypertext Transfer Protocol (S-HTTP)

An Internet protocol for encryption of Hypertext Transfer Protocol (HTTP) traffic.

Overview

Secure Hypertext Transfer Protocol (S-HTTP) is an application-level protocol that extends the HTTP protocol by adding encryption to Web pages. It also provides mechanisms for authentication and signatures of messages. S-HTTP provides broad support for implementing different types of cryptographic algorithms and key management systems. Although S-HTTP systems can make use of digital certificates and public keys, messages can also be encrypted on a per-transaction basis using symmetric session keys.

S-HTTP was proposed as a draft standard in 1996 and is still under development. S-HTTP is not as widely implemented as Secure Sockets Layer (SSL), which is the most popular protocol for encrypting information sent over the Internet.

Notes

S-HTTP is also the name given to World Wide Web (WWW) server software that implements the S-HTTP protocol. This software was developed by Enterprise Integrations Technologies (EIT), the National Center for Supercomputing Applications (NCSA), and RSA Security.

See Also: *cryptography, Hypertext Transfer Protocol (HTTP), Secure Sockets Layer (SSL), security, security protocols, World Wide Web (WWW)*

Secure/Multipurpose Internet Mail Extensions (S/MIME)

A scheme for secure e-mail messaging.

Overview

RSA Security developed Secure/Multipurpose Internet Mail Extensions (S/MIME) as a mechanism for adding security to the Simple Mail Transfer Protocol (SMTP) e-mail messaging protocol. S/MIME adds support for digital signatures and encryption to SMTP to enable authentication of the sender and protect the privacy of the communication. S/MIME is defined in RFCs 2311 through 2315.

Implementation

S/MIME is basically an extension of the widely implemented Multipurpose Internet Mail Extensions (MIME) encoding standard, which defines how the body portion of an SMTP message is structured and formatted. S/MIME uses the RSA public key cryptography algorithm along with the Data Encryption Standard (DES) or Rivest-Shamir-Adleman (RSA) encryption algorithm. In an S/MIME message, the MIME body section consists of a message in PKCS #7 format that contains an encrypted form of the MIME body parts. The MIME content type for the encrypted data is application/pkcs7-mime.

Prospects

S/MIME has gained some popularity in the enterprise but its deployment has been hindered by the complexity and cost of implementing public key infrastructure (PKI) schemes. S/MIME is simpler to implement than the earlier Privacy Enhanced Mail (PEM) specification, but it has not achieved the same widespread use as the Pretty Good Privacy (PGP) scheme developed by Phil Zimmermann.

Notes

Note that since Hypertext Transfer Protocol (HTTP) messages can also transport MIME data, HTTP can also employ S/MIME for secure communications, although this is rarely implemented.

See Also: *Data Encryption Standard (DES), e-mail, encryption, Hypertext Transfer Protocol (HTTP), Multipurpose Internet Mail Extensions (MIME), PKCS #7, Privacy Enhanced Mail (PEM), public key infrastructure (PKI), Rivest-Shamir-Adelman (RSA) algorithm, Simple Mail Transfer Protocol (SMTP)*

Secure Sockets Layer (SSL)

A transport layer security protocol used on the Internet.

Overview

Secure Sockets Layer (SSL) is a security protocol used for securing communications performed over the Internet. SSL provides three things:

- **Authentication:** Ensures that the message received is from the individual it says it is from
- **Confidentiality:** Protects the message from being read by unintended recipients along the way
- **Integrity:** Ensures that the message has not been modified along the way

Netscape Communications developed SSL in 1996 to enable secure transmission of information over the Internet.

Implementation

SSL operates between the application and transport layers of the Open Systems Interconnection (OSI) reference model. SSL supports only those applications and application-layer protocols for which it has been explicitly implemented. In other words, SSL is not a transparent security protocol that can work automatically with any application-layer protocol. SSL commonly operates with the Hypertext Transfer Protocol (HTTP) and sometimes with the Simple Mail Transfer Protocol (SMTP) and Network News Transfer Protocol (NNTP). SSL has been implemented in a wide variety of applications including Web servers, Web browsers, and other Internet applications. Both the client and the server applications must support SSL in order for it to work.

SSL employs public-key encryption for secure authentication and symmetric key encryption for encryption of transmitted information. For public key encryption SSL employs the Rivest-Shamir-Adleman (RSA) encryption algorithm and therefore depends on the implementation of a supporting public key infrastructure (PKI). Message integrity is guaranteed by incorporating a message integrity check mechanism called a message authentication code (MAC).

S

An SSL session begins when an SSL-enabled client requests a connection with an SSL-enabled server over Transmission Control Protocol (TCP) port 443, the SSL port. This initiates the SSL handshake between the client and server. A Web page that uses SSL has a Uniform Resource Locator (URL) that begins with https instead of the standard http prefix. The server then sends the client its digital certificate and public key. The client and server then negotiate a mutually acceptable level of encryption, which is usually 40-bit, 56-bit, or 128-bit strength, depending on legal restrictions and availability. The client then generates a secret session key, encrypts it with the server's public key, and sends the encrypted session key to the server, which decrypts the session key using its private key. From that point on, the secret key cryptography is employed, and the session key is used to encrypt all data exchanged between the client and server, providing secure, private communication.

Issues

The main problems with SSL are

- Using SSL to secure Web transactions adds significant processing overhead to Web servers, sometimes as much as two orders of magnitude. In other words, a Web server that can support thousands of simultaneous unencrypted HTTP sessions might only be able to support a few dozen SSL sessions based on the same hardware configuration.
- SSL is difficult to implement in e-commerce environments that use Web server farms and server load balancers. This is because SSL is designed to use persistence, which means that the client must maintain the same Internet Protocol (IP) address during the entire session.

To address these issues, you can use specialized network devices called SSL Accelerators to offload SSL processing and session caching to other servers for enhanced performance and greater persistence.

Prospects

The Internet Engineering Task Force (IETF) has standardized a variant of SSL. This variant is known as Transport Layer Security (TLS), and it is similar to SSL 3 but is not interoperable with that protocol. Microsoft Windows 2000, Windows XP, and Windows .NET Server support both SSL and TLS security. As TLS becomes more widely implemented, use of the proprietary SSL protocol might fade, but this is likely to take place over many years due to wide industry support for SSL.

See Also: *Hypertext Transfer Protocol (HTTP), Internet, Internet Engineering Task Force (IETF), port, public key cryptography, Rivest-Shamir-Adelman (RSA) algorithm, Transmission Control Protocol (TCP), Transport Layer Security (TLS), Uniform Resource Locator (URL)*

security

Protection of computer, network, and business assets.

Overview

Security is an important concern in the field of IT (information technology), particularly since the Internet provided a ubiquitous method for connecting networks and systems all over the world. The rise in business on the Internet (e-business) in the 1990s resulted in an exponential increase in attacks on corporate networks, with an accompanying increasing awareness of the fundamental importance of security for protection of business assets such as financial data and confidential personnel information.

Security in general is difficult to achieve in any open system—that is, a system connected to other systems. E-businesses are by definition open systems, whether they involve business-to-client or business-to-consumer (B2C) relationships, as in e-commerce sites and online stores, or business-to-business (B2B) relationships, as in supply-chain and financial transaction systems. Some of the difficulties in securing open systems include

- Recognizing the importance of security and allocating staff and financial resources to implement it properly
- Finding and protecting the weakest point in your system
- Maintaining high security while keeping the system friendly and usable for those involved

In addition, even closed systems must consider the necessity of securing their assets from misuse by those working within the company or organization. In fact, many security analysts consider the "threat from within" to be the more serious one, despite the large amount of attention given to hackers in the mass media in the last few years.

Security encompasses a broad range of subjects that also includes:

- **Privacy:** Ensuring the confidentiality of information, usually through encryption
- **Integrity:** Ensuring the protection of information from being modified or deleted, again usually through encryption

Implementation

Fundamental to securing assets that are accessible through IT systems such as corporate networks and e-commerce sites are the three basic principles of security: authentication, authorization, and auditing. These three are often referred to as "golden rules" because Au is the chemical symbol for gold. These three principles are

- **Authentication:** The process by which a principal (a trusted, identified entity) identifies a user, consumer, or client. Authentication can employ passwords, signatures, smart cards, biometric identification, and other tools. The basis of authentication from an IT perspective is security protocols, which are protocols that enable users to be securely authenticated by network security principals. Examples of such security protocols include NTLM and Kerberos.
- **Authorization:** Once a user is authenticated, the next step is to ensure that the user can access only those resources for which the user is properly authorized. This is done through implementing access controls, permissions, privileges, and other elements, depending on the systems involved. The securest form of authorization is the mandatory or nondiscretionary access control, which enforces strict rules concerning resource access that affect even the resource's owners.
- **Auditing:** The third step is to ensure that access to resources and privileges is logged for purposes of later review. Audit logs help administrators determine when systems have been compromised and take steps to further secure them.

In addition to these golden rules, a number of other strategies are crucial for ensuring the security of business resources accessible through IT systems. These include

- **Murphy's Law:** If something can go wrong, it will. Therefore no system is completely secure and every system will fail at some point. Accept this fact and be prepared.

- **Do not trust technology:** Security is more about people than it is about technology. Systems will not be secure if administrators fail in their responsibilities to implement patches in a timely manner as new vulnerabilities are discovered for applications and operating systems. Likewise, a firewall is no help if the administrator has not taken the time to configure it properly. Similarly, users must be educated to be "security-conscious" and to avoid such mistakes as taping their passwords under their keyboards or opening executable attachments.
- **Least privilege:** Never give users more privileges than they need.
- **Multiple mechanisms:** Never trust a single security system such as a firewall—have multiple systems in place that redundantly protect your assets, including firewalls, virus scanners, intrusion detection devices, hostile content blockers, and virtual private networking (VPN). On the other hand, try to keep security systems as simple as possible, so you do not get overwhelmed with the job of managing security.
- **Comprehensiveness:** It is no use securing one part of a corporate network if another part is left unsecured. Any security solution must be a comprehensive one that hardens every aspect of the system from outside (or inside) attack.
- **Weakest link:** Identify the weakest point in your system and monitor it regularly. The weakest link of a system is different from the choke point, the narrowest part of the system through which an attacker must enter. However, you should also monitor choke points continuously, even if they are hardened.
- **Security policy:** Take the time to write and internally publish a comprehensive security policy that covers the management, use, and implementation of IT systems in a secure fashion. A security policy outlines your environment's basic security architecture, rules for accessing resources, and how these rules are enforced.
- **Security audit:** Having an independent organization check your network's security is a good idea to ensure that your security policy is comprehensive and implemented properly.
- **Standard deployment:** Have a standard process in place for deploying new IT resources such as Web servers on your network. For example, you should first create a standard "hardened" operating system image, then install additional applications needed, add a binary checksum to facilitate detection of modifications to your system, perform vulnerability analysis for your applications, and finally deploy your server on the network. Never deploy a server that is not properly hardened or that still has its default accounts and passwords in place unchanged.
- **Do not forget the obvious:** Most security breaches are caused by well-known vulnerabilities that have not been secured even though patches are readily available.
- **Know your enemy:** The best defense is a good knowledge about likely attackers. Familiarity with the procedures and tools used by hackers will help you identify, harden, and maintain your system's security. Good network security specialists usually have a collection of popular hacker tools in their arsenal, as many of these tools can be used for identifying vulnerabilities.
- **Regular assessment:** Periodically review your company's compliance with its security policy and ensure that your goals are being met.
- **Consider outsourcing:** Managed security providers (MSPs) are a new breed of company that has arisen in recent years to help small and medium-sized businesses secure their IT systems. You can save costs using these companies' services, but carefully evaluate their offerings first and remember that ultimately security is your own company's responsibility. Appointing a Chief Security Officer (CSO) is an important step in determining how best to implement your company's security requirements.

Finally, here are some tips on how to make your IT environment more secure:

- Use strong passwords and change them every 90 days. Be careful about telephone requests to change an employee's password in case someone is impersonating the employee.
- Teach employees how to choose and protect their passwords.
- Immediately disable the accounts of departing employees.
- Pay special attention to security for telecommuters (employees working from home) as you do not have direct management over their working environment. Ensure that they are using personal firewalls and remind them of the consequences of not complying with the company security policy.
- Disable all unnecessary services on servers.
- Apply new security patches released by vendors as soon as possible, but ensure that your systems are fully backed up first in case the patch causes unexpected problems.
- Ensure that your virus protection software has its signature updated regularly.
- Pay special attention to the security of your wireless networks. Most wireless networks are implemented with default security and the result is that anyone driving near your building with a laptop in their car can often access your network.

See Also: *access control, auditing, authentication protocol, business-to-business, encryption, firewall, hacking, intrusion detection system (IDS), Kerberos, network security, password, permissions, privacy, virtual private network (VPN)*

Security Account Manager (SAM) database

Contains user and group account information on a Microsoft Windows NT domain controller.

Overview

All user accounts, group accounts, and resource definitions such as shares and printers on a Windows NT–based network have their security principals defined in the Security Account Manager (SAM) database. The SAM database is also known as the domain directory database, or sometimes simply the directory database.

The master copy of the SAM database is stored on the primary domain controller (PDC) and occupies a portion of the Windows NT registry. Periodic directory synchronization ensures that backup domain controllers (BDCs) have an accurate replica of this master database, so BDCs can also be used for logons and for pass-through authentication of users attempting to access network resources.

Because the entire SAM database must reside in a domain controller's RAM, it cannot exceed about 40 megabytes (MB) in Windows NT, which works out to about 40,000 user accounts, or 26,000 users and Windows NT workstations combined. The following table lists the size of common objects in a SAM database.

Object Sizes in a SAM Database

Object	*Size in SAM Database*
User account	1 kilobyte (KB)
Computer account	0.5 KB
Global group account	0.5 KB plus 12 bytes per user
Local group account	0.5 KB plus 36 bytes per user

Notes

In Windows 2000 and Windows .NET Server, the functions of the SAM database have been migrated to the more powerful and scalable Active Directory directory service.

See Also: *Active Directory, backup domain controller (BDC), primary domain controller (PDC), registry*

S

Security Administrator Tool for Analyzing Networks (SATAN)

A popular network security analysis tool.

Overview

Security Administrator Tool for Analyzing Networks (SATAN) is a free tool developed by Dan Farmer and Wietse Venema in 1995 for remotely analyzing the security of networks. SATAN consists of a variety of routines that probe a network for security holes in ways that are similar to the ones hackers use. The tool tests the vulnerabilities of Transmission Control Protocol/Internet Protocol (TCP/IP) hosts using common TCP/IP protocols, such as File Transfer Protocol (FTP), Network File System (NFS), and Network Information System (NIS), and analyzes how the host responds to requests based on these protocols. The results are stored in a database and can be displayed using a Web browser.

SATAN runs on machines running UNIX and needs the Perl interpreter to operate. Typically, SATAN identifies weaknesses in the setup and configuration of network software; network administrators can use it to check the configuration of their network software. SATAN can also identify the network services that are running and provide information about the types of hardware and software and the topology of the network.

Issues

Because SATAN is free and can be downloaded from numerous places on the Internet, both network administrators and hackers can use it. If you are concerned about the possible misuse of SATAN against your network, you can obtain various types of free anti-SATAN software on the Internet that alert you to a SATAN attack so that you can take remedial action.

S

See Also: *File Transfer Protocol (FTP), Network File System (NFS), Network Information System (NIS), network security*

security descriptor

A unique header for an object stored in the Active Directory directory service of Microsoft Windows 2000 and Windows .NET Server.

Overview

Security descriptors contain security identifiers (SIDs), which are discretionary access control lists (DACLs) or system access control lists (SACLs) that specify the access permissions for the object. Specifically, the security descriptor for an object contains the following:

- **Owner SID:** Identifies the security principal (the owner of the object)
- **Group SID:** Used only by Services for Macintosh and the POSIX subsystem
- **DACL:** Contains the access permissions and rights for the object and its attributes, along with the SIDs of the security principals who can access the object
- **SACL:** Contains system-wide security policies such as the auditing policy

See Also: *Active Directory, discretionary access control list (DACL), security identifier (SID), system access control list (SACL)*

security group

A type of group in Microsoft Windows 2000 and Windows .NET Server.

Overview

Security groups are security principals that can contain other security principals such as user, group, and computer objects from the Active Directory directory service. They are one of two types of groups used in Windows 2000, the other being distribution groups. Security groups are used for grouping accounts and for controlling access to resources, much in the same way that global groups and local groups are used in Windows NT–based networks. (In other words, all groups in Windows NT are security groups.)

Types

Security groups come in three types:

- **Domain local groups:** Provide users with permissions to access resources; used only within the specific domain in which they are created
- **Global groups:** Logically group users for administrative purposes and have visibility in the current domain and trusted domains

- **Universal groups:** Similar to global groups but reduce global catalog replication traffic when they are used

See Also: *distribution group, group*

security identifier (SID)

An internal number used in Microsoft Windows 2000 and Windows .NET Server that uniquely identifies a user, group, or other object.

Overview

Security identifiers (SIDs) are used internally by Windows 2000 to provide user accounts with access to network resources. SIDs are guaranteed to be unique because they are created using a combination of user information, domain information, and time and date of account creation. The general format of a SID is a series of decimal numbers separated by dashes in the following form:

```
S-1-X-Y1-Y2-....
```

X is the value of the identifier authority, and Y1, Y2, and so on are values of subauthorities. The prefix S-1 means "SID revision 1."

Changing the name of a user, computer, or domain does not change the underlying SID for that account. Administrators cannot modify the SID for an account in Windows NT, and there is generally no need to know the SID assigned to a particular account. SIDs are primarily intended to be used internally by the operating system to ensure that accounts are uniquely identified to the system.

security log

A log in Microsoft Windows 2000, Windows XP, and Windows .NET Server that records auditing events.

Overview

Entries in the security log are either success entries, which are identified by a key symbol, or failure entries, which are identified by a padlock symbol. You can view and manage the security log by using the administrative tool Event Viewer, where you can view additional details by opening the property sheet for the particular event. You can also select events by filtering the security log. You can export the security log as a .csv file and import it into a spreadsheet or database program for further analysis.

Notes

In a high-security environment, you can enable a registry parameter named CrashOnAuditFail, which causes the system to display a Stop screen when the security log is full. This prevents unaudited system access on your server. When you restart the system, you must archive the current contents of the security log before continuing. See the *Microsoft Windows 2000 Server Resource Kit* from Microsoft Press for more information.

See Also: *application log, system log*

security principal

An object in the Active Directory directory service of Microsoft Windows 2000 and Windows .NET Server that can be assigned permissions and rights.

Overview

Three types of security principals are used in Windows 2000 networks:

- **User objects:** Represent individual user accounts
- **Group objects:** Can be used to group other security principals for assigning permissions and to ease administration
- **Computer objects:** Represent individual computers running Windows 2000 on the network

Security principals are uniquely identified by security identifiers (SIDs), which provide a unique, internal, alphanumeric identifier for the security principal.

See Also: *Active Directory, security identifier (SID)*

security protocols

Protocols used for authentication clients.

Overview

Security protocols are protocols that allow networks and systems to authenticate users, computers, and applications for purposes of accessing resources on these networks and systems. Security protocols use various forms of encryption to ensure the privacy, authenticity, and integrity of a user's credentials and of network communications.

Types

Some of the popular security protocols in use today include

- **NTLM:** Stands for Windows NT Lan Manager, the native security protocol on Microsoft Windows NT domain-based networks. NTLM is also known as Windows NT Challenge/Response Authentication protocol.
- **Kerberos:** Developed at the Massachusetts Institute of Technology (MIT) and used as the native security protocol by the Active Directory directory service on Windows 2000– and Windows .NET Server–based networks.
- **Remote Authentication Dial-In User Services (RADIUS):** A client/server protocol used to securely authenticate dial-up users for authentication, authorization, and accounting (AAA).
- **Terminal access controller access control system (TACACS):** A proprietary protocol developed by Cisco Systems and similar to RADIUS.
- **Secure Sockets Layer (SSL):** A protocol that secures Hypertext Transfer Protocol (HTTP) communications between users and Web servers.

See Also: *authentication protocol, Hypertext Transfer Protocol (HTTP), Kerberos, protocol, Remote Authentication Dial-In User Service (RADIUS), Secure Sockets Layer (SSL), Terminal Access Controller Access Control System (TACACS), Windows NT Challenge/ Response Authentication*

S

security provider

A server or device on a network that authenticates users trying to log on or access network resources.

Overview

In a Microsoft Windows 2000– or Windows .NET Server–based network, special servers called domain controllers act as security providers and handle tasks such as user logons and control of resource access. If all domain controllers are temporarily offline, users can still log on to their local computers and use local computer resources but cannot be authenticated for accessing resources elsewhere on the network.

Notes

Windows 98 and Windows Millennium Edition (Me) can operate as stand-alone computing environments or as part of a Windows 2000 domain. If files on a computer running Windows 98 or Windows Me will be shared by users on a Windows 2000– or Windows .NET Server–based network, be sure that you have configured Windows 98 or Windows Me networking to use user-level security instead of the more common share-level security used in workgroup environments.

See Also: *domain controller*

segmentation

The process of dividing a large network into smaller connected networks.

Overview

Segmentation improves the performance of Ethernet networks by reducing the size of collision domains. Because stations on an Ethernet network use contention to try to use the networking media, fewer stations in a given network segment means less contention and better network performance. Bridges or routers are generally used to segment an Ethernet network into smaller collision domains.

Notes

The term *segmentation* is also used to refer to the process by which routers break down oversized frames into smaller portions that are sequenced, forwarded, and then reassembled at the receiving station. Segmentation is usually a sign that the network is misconfigured because segmentation eats valuable CPU cycles on routers and produces greater latency in network communication.

See Also: *collision domain, Ethernet, frame*

separator page

A page that is printed between print jobs.

Overview

In the old days, separator pages indicated when one print job finished and the next one began. In Microsoft Windows NT, Windows 2000, Windows XP, and Windows .NET Server, separator pages can have two functions:

- Separating printed output in a multiuser environment so that users can more easily retrieve their print jobs
- Switching a print device between different print modes (if the device has this capability)—for example, switching between Printer Control Language (PCL) mode and PostScript mode

Windows 2000 includes several separator pages, which are located in the \Winnt\System32 directory:

- **Pcl.sep:** Switches the printing mode to PCL printing, typically for printers made by Hewlett-Packard. A separator page is also printed.
- **Pscript.sep:** Switches the printing mode to PostScript for supported printers. No separator page is printed.
- **Sysprint.sep:** Functions much as pscript.sep does but also prints a separator page.

Notes

You can use Notepad to edit any default separator page file to create a custom separator file. You can add new lines by using printer escape codes such as those shown in the following table.

Escape Codes for Custom Separator Pages

Code	*Function*
@D	Prints the date that the job was submitted. (Use Regional Settings in Control Panel to specify the format.)
@E	Ejects the page. (Use at the end of a separator page.)
@Fpathname	Prints the contents of the file specified by "pathname" without performing any processing of the file.
@Hnn	Sends escape code nn to the printer (device-specific functionality).
@I	Prints the job number.
@L	Prints the following characters as is until the next escape code is encountered.
@N	Prints the name of the user who submitted the job.
@T	Prints the time that the job was submitted.
@n	Skips n lines.
@0	Skips to the next line.

If a printer can auto-switch between printing modes (by identifying the type of the rendered file sent to it), you do not need to specify a separator page.

serial encapsulation protocols

Protocols used to encapsulate local area network (LAN) traffic for sending over a wide area network (WAN).

Overview

LAN traffic such as Ethernet frames cannot normally be sent over a WAN link without first encapsulating them in a format suitable for WAN serial transmission. This is accomplished through the use of special encapsulation protocols, with different protocols generally being used for different WAN technologies.

Types

Serial encapsulation protocols fall into two basic types:

- **Synchronous:** These protocols are used for synchronous serial links such as leased lines and packet-switching services, and include High-level Data-Link Control (HDLC), Link Access Control, B-channel (LAPB) used in X.25 networking, and Point-to-Point Protocol (PPP). HDLC is the default protocol used for synchronous serial connections on Cisco routers.
- **Asynchronous:** These protocols are used for asynchronous (dialup) serial links and include Serial Line Internet Protocol (SLIP) and Point-to-Point Protocol (PPP).

S

Notes

With the emergence of metropolitan Ethernet, the days of serial encapsulation might soon be over. Carriers such as Yipes Communications can now provision Gigabit Ethernet (GbE) directly to your demarc point, allowing you to connect your WAN as easily as you build your LAN.

See Also: *Gigabit Ethernet (GbE), High-level Data Link Control (HDLC), metropolitan Ethernet, Point-to-Point Protocol (PPP), Serial Line Internet Protocol (SLIP), serial transmission*

serial interface

An interface on a device that is used for serial transmission.

See: *serial transmission*

Serial Line Internet Protocol (SLIP)

A serial encapsulation protocol.

Overview

Serial Line Internet Protocol (SLIP) is a packet-framing protocol developed for sending Internet Protocol (IP) datagrams over point-to-point wide area networking (WAN) links. SLIP was developed in 1984 for UNIX environments as a simple protocol that provides only frame delimitation and has limited error recovery mechanisms. Later, a variant of SLIP called C-SLIP was developed that included support for data compression.

SLIP was used mainly in UNIX platforms to provide access to the Internet using low-speed dial-up links. SLIP is defined in RFC 1055 and C-SLIP in RFC 1144.

Comparison

SLIP is a legacy protocol that has now been replaced by the Point-to-Point Protocol (PPP) for the following reasons:

- Although SLIP supports only the Transmission Control Protocol/Internet Protocol (TCP/IP) network protocol, PPP is a multiprotocol encapsulation protocol that can also support Internetwork Packet Exchange (IPX) and AppleTalk. This is not really an issue if you are connecting to the Internet, however, since the Internet is strictly TCP/IP-based.
- SLIP generally requires that the host's TCP/IP parameters be configured manually, but PPP can negotiate the parameters during session establishment. These parameters include the host's IP address, the window size, and compression.
- SLIP might require the user to write a script for automating the logon process, but PPP supports both the Password Authentication Protocol (PAP) and the Challenge Handshake Authentication Protocol (CHAP), which let you automatically forward your credentials to the PPP server for authentication.

See Also: *Point-to-Point Protocol (PPP), wide area network (WAN)*

serial transmission

A form of signal transmission that sends information one bit at a time over a single data channel.

Overview

Serial transmission is performed over different kinds of electrical interfaces called serial interfaces. These serial interfaces are generally used to connect data communications equipment (DCE) such as modems to data terminal equipment (DTE) such as computers and terminals. The term *interface* indicates that these specifications describe how to establish an electrical (pinning) and mechanical (connector) shared boundary between devices. An interface specifies a series of protocols, an arrangement of pins, special control signals, and other functions that enable devices to communicate with each other.

Types

The common serial interfaces used in computer networking and telecommunications include the following:

- **RS-232:** The most commonly used serial interface in ordinary network communication, which supports transmission over a range of 0 to 20 kilobits per second (Kbps) at distances of up to 50 feet (15.24 meters). RS-232 can use either DB9 or DB25 connectors.
- **RS-422:** Specifies a balanced electrical interface but no specific mechanical interface for point-to-point serial communication. RS-422 typically uses either DB9 or DB37 connectors.

- **RS-423:** Similar to RS-422, except that unbalanced lines are used instead of balanced ones.
- **RS-449:** Specifies the mechanical interface for RS-422 and RS-423 and is used with these interfaces for high-speed serial communication with Channel Service Unit/Data Service Units (CSU/DSUs) and routers.
- **RS-485:** Defines a balanced, multipoint interface using tristate drivers to reduce noise. The combined interface RS-422/485 allows you to daisy-chain up to 31 serial devices to a single serial port and is typically used for interfacing industrial sensors and measuring equipment to a computer.
- **RS-530:** A successor to RS-232 and RS-449 that provides high-speed synchronous and asynchronous serial communication of up to 2 megabits per second (Mbps).
- **V.35:** An International Telecommunication Union (ITU) standard for data transmission at 48 Kbps that is typically used for connecting CSU/DSUs and routers for wide area network (WAN) communication over digital data service (DDS) lines. V.35 uses a block-shaped 34-pin connector.
- **X.21:** An ITU standard for synchronous communication between DTEs and DCEs on public X.25 packet-switched networks. X.21 typically uses a DB15 connector.

Notes

Serial interfaces such as RS-232 are the most commonly used protocol for devices called line drivers, which enable terminals and hosts to be connected over phone lines and extend the distance over which the serial interface can function by regenerating the signal.

Related terminology includes

- **Serial cable:** A cable used to connect pieces of DCE to pieces of DTE by using a serial interface
- **Serial port:** A plug or connector on pieces of DTE that can use serial transmission to send and receive data

See Also: *data communications equipment (DCE), data terminal equipment (DTE), line driver, parallel transmission, RS-232, V.35*

server

A computer whose role in a network is to provide services and resources to users.

Overview

Servers usually have one or more specific roles in a network, including:

- **Application servers:** These are used as the back end in a client/server environment. Examples include mail servers and database servers.
- **File and print servers:** These provide users with centralized locations for storing files and accessing print devices.
- **Authentication servers:** These servers validate users for logging on and accessing network resources. An example might be a Microsoft Windows 2000 domain controller.
- **Web servers:** These can be used to serve Web content ranging from static Hypertext Markup Language (HTML) pages to e-commerce sites.

See Also: *Web server*

server-based network

A network in which one or more servers centrally manage network security and storage.

Overview

In a server-based network, special computers called servers handle network tasks such as authenticating users, storing files, managing printers, and running applications such as database and e-mail programs. Security is generally centralized in a security provider, which allows users to have one user account for logging on to any computer in the network. Because files are stored centrally, they can be easily secured and backed up.

Server-based networks are more costly and complex to set up and administer than peer-to-peer networks, and they often require the services of a full-time network administrator. They are ideal for businesses that are concerned about security and file integrity and have more than 10 computers.

Examples

Microsoft Windows 2000 is a robust platform for server-based networking that offers centralized network administration, networking that is easy to set up and configure, NTFS file system (NTFS) security, file and print sharing, user profiles that allow multiple users to share one computer or allow one user to log on to many computers, Routing and Remote Access for supporting mobile users, and Internet Information Services (IIS) for establishing an intranet or Internet presence.

See Also: *peer-to-peer network*

server farm

A group of servers managed as a whole.

Overview

Server farms are typically used in large enterprises and e-commerce sites to group Web servers together for handling loads that would exceed the capacity of individual servers. Server farms are generally switched networks running Gigabit Ethernet (GbE) that are separate from the regular corporate network. They often employ load balancing and caching appliances at the front end to give users who are accessing the servers the illusion that they are accessing a single mega-server instead of many smaller servers grouped together. Server farms generally employ 1U or 2U rack-mounted servers that can be deployed by the hundreds or thousands in relatively small rooms.

Server farms come in all shapes and sizes and are often interconnected with storage area networks (SANs) to provide enterprise-level storage capacity and manageability that complements the farm's processing power.

S

See Also: *Gigabit Ethernet (GbE), rack, storage area network (SAN)*

serverless backup

A backup technology sometimes used in storage area networks (SANs).

Overview

Serverless backup is a new backup technology in which volumes are imaged and their images are stored for archival purposes. Serverless backup generally employs agents that create a "snapshot" of a database or file system and copies this snapshot to tape. Examples of vendors in this emerging market include Legato Systems, Computer Associates, VERITAS Software Corporation, and others. With the growing importance of SANs in enterprise environments, serverless backup is one technology enterprise networking architects might want to watch in the next few years.

See Also: *backup, storage area network (SAN)*

Server Message Block (SMB)

A general-purposes information-sharing protocol.

Overview

Server Message Block (SMB) is a client/server protocol developed jointly by Microsoft Corporation, IBM, and Intel Corporation for passing information between computers on a network. SMB employs NetBIOS for its transport protocol, and is widely used on Microsoft Windows networks and IBM's OS/2 platform for file and print sharing purposes. SMB can also be used on Transmission Control Protocol/Internet Protocol (TCP/IP) networks, in which case it uses NetBIOS over TCP/IP (NetBT) as its transport.

A popular open-source version of SMB called Samba is available for most UNIX platforms. Samba provides full-featured SMB servers which allow Windows clients access to file and print resources on UNIX networks and is a popular platform for Windows/UNIX interoperability.

Uses

SMB supports functions such as:

- Opening and closing connections between SMB clients (redirectors) and SMB servers (file and print servers) to allow clients to access shared network resources
- Locating, reading, and writing to files on a file server
- Locating and printing to shared print queues

SMB can also be used as a general message-passing protocol for performing remote transactions in a distributed applications environment. Remote procedure calls (RPCs) can be performed over SMB, and SMB also supports other interprocess communication (IPC) mechanisms, including named pipes and mailslots.

Implementation

SMB employs four basic types of messages:

- **Session control messages:** Open or close a redirector connection to a shared resource on the server. The SMB redirector packages the requests sent to remote servers in an SMB-enabled network.
- **File messages:** Used by the redirector to gain access to files on the server.
- **Printer messages:** Used by the redirector to send data to a print queue and get status information about the queue.
- **Message messages:** Let applications exchange messages with another computer.

SMB supports both share-level and user-level authentication, with user-level being preferred for greater security.

Notes

Common Internet File System (CIFS) is a standards-based version of the proprietary SMB protocol and runs directly on top of TCP/IP.

For More Information

You can find Samba at *www.samba.org.*

See Also: *Common Internet File System (CIFS), NetBIOS, NetBIOS over TCP/IP (NetBT), redirector, UNIX*

Server Operators

A built-in group in Microsoft Windows 2000 whose members have the rights to administer servers on the network.

Overview

Server Operators is a domain local group whose initial membership is empty. The Server Operators group has the following pre-assigned rights:

- Log on locally to the server console
- Change the system time
- Back up files and directories
- Restore files and directories
- Shut down the system
- Force shutdown from a remote system

Server Operators can also share and manage disk resources and printers on the network and lock the server.

See Also: *built-in group*

service

An operating system background process that provides some specific functionality for the network.

Overview

Services are processes that run in the background and provide functionality for other computers on the network. For example, the Server service enables a Microsoft Windows 2000 machine to act as a server and offer shared resources to other machines on the network. Similarly, the Workstation service enables machines to act as clients and access shared resources on servers. What are called services on Windows networks are referred to as daemons on UNIX networks.

In Windows NT, Windows 2000, Windows XP, and Windows .NET Server, services are remote procedure call (RPC)–enabled so that they can be called from remote computers over the network. Most services can be added and removed by using the Add/Remove Windows Components option in Add/Remove Programs and can be controlled and configured using the Services snap-in, which is accessible from Administrative Tools.

The following tables list the default services available for typical Windows 2000 Server and Windows NT 4 Server installations and indicates which services are normally installed and started automatically.

S

Common Windows 2000 Services

Service	Normally Installed	Automatically Started
Alerter	x	x
Application Management	x	
Boot Information Negotiation Layer		
Certificate Services		x
ClipBook	x	
COM+ Event System	x	
Computer Browser	x	x
DHCP Client		x
DHCP Server		x
Distributed File System	x	x
Distributed Link Tracking Client	x	x
Distributed Link Tracking Server	x	
Distributed Transaction Coordinator	x	x
DNS Client	x	x
DNS Server		x
Event Log	x	x
Fax Service	x	
File Replication	x	
File Server for Macintosh		x
FTP Publishing Service		x
IIS Admin Service	x	x
Indexing Service		x
Internet Authentication Service		x
Internet Connection Sharing	x	
Intersite Messaging	x	
IPsec Policy Agent	x	x
Kerberos Key Distribution Center	x	
License Logging Service	x	x
Logical Disk Manager	x	x
Logical Disk Manager Administrative Service	x	
Message Queuing		x
Messenger	x	x
Net Logon	x	x
NetMeeting Remote Desktop Sharing	x	
Network Connections	x	
Network DDE	x	

(continued)

Common Windows 2000 Services *continued*

Service	Normally Installed	Automatically Started
Network DDE DSDM	x	
Network News Transport Protocol (NNTP)		x
NT LM Security Support Provider	x	
On-line Presentation Broadcast		
Performance Logs and Alerts	x	
Plug and Play	x	x
Print Server for Macintosh		x
Print Spooler	x	x
Protected Storage	x	x
QoS Admission Control (RSVP)		x
QoS RSVP	x	
Remote Access Auto Connection Manager	x	
Remote Access Connection Manager	x	
Remote Procedure Call (RPC)	x	x
Remote Procedure Call (RPC) Locator	x	
Remote Registry Service	x	x
Remote Storage Engine		x
Remote Storage File		x
Remote Storage Media		x
Remote Storage Notification		
Removable Storage	x	x
Routing and Remote Access	x	
RunAs Service	x	x
Security Accounts Manager	x	x
Server	x	x
Simple Mail Transport Protocol (SMTP)	x	x
Simple TCP/IP Services		x
Single Instance Storage Groveler		
SiteServer ILS Service		x
Smart Card	x	
Smart Card Helper	x	
SNMP Service		x
SNMP Trap Service		
System Event Notification	x	x
Task Scheduler	x	x
TCP/IP NetBIOS Helper Service	x	x
TCP/IP Print Server		x

(continued)

Common Windows 2000 Services *continued*

Service	*Normally Installed*	*Automatically Started*
Telephony	x	
Telnet		
Terminal Services	x	
Terminal Services Licensing		x
Trivial FTP Daemon		
Uninterruptible Power Supply	x	
Utility Manager	x	
Windows Installer	x	
Windows Internet Name Service (WINS)		x
Windows Management Instrumentation	x	
Windows Management Instrumentation Driver Extensions	x	
Windows Media Monitor Service		x
Windows Media Program Service		x
Windows Media Station Service		x
Windows Media Unicast Service		x
Windows Time	x	x
Workstation	x	x
World Wide Web Publishing Service	x	x

Common Windows NT 4 Services

Service	*Normally Installed*	*Automatically Started*
Alerter	x	x
ClipBook Server	x	
Computer Browser	x	x
DHCP Client		x
Directory Replicator	x	
EventLog	x	x
File Server for Macintosh		x
FTP Publishing Service		x
Gateway Service for NetWare		x
Gopher Publishing Service		x
License Logging Service	x	x
Messenger	x	x
Microsoft DHCP Server		x
Microsoft DNS Server		x
Net Logon	x	x
Network DDE	x	
Network DDE DSDM	x	
Network Monitor Agent		
NT LM Security Support Provider	x	x
Plug and Play	x	x
Print Server for Macintosh		x
Protected Storage	x	x
Remote Access Autodial Manager		
Remote Access Connection Manager		
Remote Access Server		x
Remoteboot Service		
RIP for Internet Protocol		x
Remote Procedure Call (RPC) Locator	x	
Remote Procedure Call (RPC) Service	x	x
SAP Agent		x
Schedule	x	
Server	x	x
Simple TCP/IP Services		x
SNMP		x
SNMP Trap Service		
Spooler	x	x
TCP/IP NetBIOS Helper		
TCP/IP Print Server		
Telephony Service	x	
UPS	x	
Windows Internet Name Service (WINS)		x
Workstation	x	x
World Wide Web Publishing		x

See Also: *daemon*

Service Advertising Protocol (SAP)

A Novell NetWare protocol for advertising network resources.

Overview

Service Advertising Protocol (SAP) is used with Internetwork Packet Exchange (IPX) to enable file and print servers to advertise their availability to clients on a network. SAP periodically advertises the address of the server and the types of services it can provide to clients. It sends its advertisements by making frequent broadcasts to all machines on the local network. Routers generally forward the advertisements so that network services can be made available to machines throughout an IPX internetwork.

Issues

The use of SAP broadcasts on IPX internetworks creates effective limits on the size of a usable IPX internetwork. However, you can configure routers to reduce unnecessary SAP traffic by

- Filtering unnecessary SAP broadcasts using access lists on routers
- Using Cisco Systems IPX routers that allow SAP broadcasts to contain update information only, instead of the entire SAP table, and to forward SAP updates only when a change to the SAP table has occurred

See Also: *Internetwork Packet Exchange (IPX), NetWare protocols*

service-level agreement (SLA)

S

An agreement to provide services above a specified minimum level.

Overview

A service-level agreement (SLA) is a contractual agreement between a customer and a service provider that outlines what services will be provided and defines the acceptable range of performance and availability of those services. SLAs also generally indicate the costs and penalties that will be incurred when performance and availability fall below acceptable levels. SLAs are typically used in contracts with telecommunications service providers (telcos) that provision wide area networking (WAN) connections.

service pack

A collection of patches, fixes, and minor upgrades for a Microsoft product.

Overview

Service packs are typically identified with a number, such as Service Pack 2. Occasionally, interim releases of service packs are also issued, such as Service Pack 2a (SP2a) for Microsoft Transaction Server (MTS). Service packs for each product are generally cumulative. For example, if you apply Service Pack 3 to a product, you normally do not have to apply Service Packs 1 and 2 first, because Service Pack 3 includes the fixes and upgrades in Service Packs 1 and 2. Microsoft Office service packs are known as service releases and are numbered SR-n instead.

Service packs are usually included in Microsoft Developer Network (MSDN) and TechNet subscriptions and are also available for download from the Microsoft Web site. Check MSDN and TechNet for a list of current service packs and what they do for each product. Before you apply a service pack, read its documentation to determine whether you need to apply it. Occasionally, you must apply service packs in a specific order on a system that is running more than one BackOffice product. Check MSDN, TechNet, or the Microsoft Knowledge Base for information on this kind of situation.

Notes

A service pack is not the same as a decimal release, such as an upgrade from version 4 to version 4.01.

services file

A text file that assigns Transmission Control Protocol (TCP) and User Datagram Protocol (UDP) port numbers to Transmission Control Protocol/Internet Protocol (TCP/IP) protocols and services.

Overview

The entries in the services file are used for well-known service (WKS) records in Domain Name System (DNS) servers and other Windows Sockets applications. In addition, you can use the file to quickly determine which well-known TCP or UDP port number is assigned to a specific network service or protocol.

You will find the services file at the following location on a computer running Microsoft Windows:

- **Windows XP and Windows 2000:** %SystemRoot%\System32\drivers\etc\services
- **Windows 95 and Windows 98:** %WinDir%\Services

Each line in the services file contains the standard name for the service followed by the well-known port number as defined in RFC 1060, an alias, and an optional comment prefixed with a pound sign (#). The following example is part of the sample services file included with Windows:

```
# Format:
# <service name>  <port number>/<protocol>
[aliases...]  [#<comment>]
   ...
ftp-data  20/tcp          # FTP, data
ftp       21/tcp          # FTP. control
telnet    23/tcp
smtp      25/tcp  mail    # Simple Mail
                          Transfer Protocol
time      37/tcp  timeserver
time      37/udp  timeserver
```

Notes

You can change the default port number for a TCP/IP service by editing the services file—for example, if you need to run multiple Simple Network Management Protocol (SNMP) agents or if you want to change the default File Transfer Protocol (FTP) control port to make access more private.

See Also: hosts file, lmhosts file, Networks file, protocol file

Services for Macintosh

An optional set of services and protocols in Microsoft Windows 2000 and Windows .NET Server that enables file and print resources to be shared between Macintosh computers and computers running Windows 2000 or Windows .NET Server.

Overview

Services for Macintosh simplifies the administration of resources on heterogeneous networks containing a mix of Macintosh and Windows servers and clients. On the Windows 2000 and Windows .NET Server platforms, these services and protocols are sometimes known under the umbrella name AppleTalk network integration.

Services for Macintosh consists of three optional components:

- **AppleTalk protocol:** Apple's proprietary network protocol for Macintosh computers.
- **File Server for Macintosh (MacFile):** Lets you specify which volumes on your Windows 2000– or Windows .NET Server–based server you want to make available to Macintosh clients as Macintosh-accessible volumes, manages differences in permissions between the two platforms, and makes sure that Macintosh file names are legal NTFS file system (NTFS) names.
- **Print Server for Macintosh (MacPrint):** Enables Macintosh clients to spool their print jobs to a Windows 2000 or Windows .NET Server print server.

Macintosh client machines can access Windows 2000 or Windows .NET Server machines running Services for Macintosh in the same way that they access file and print resources on an AppleShare server. Services for Macintosh supports an unlimited number of client connections using the AppleTalk Filing Protocol (AFP), Apple's presentation-layer protocol for sharing files and applications over an AppleTalk network.

Implementation

On servers running Windows 2000 or Windows .NET Server, you can install File Server for Macintosh or Print Server for Macintosh by using the Windows Components Wizard from Add/Remove Programs in Control Panel, which automatically installs the AppleTalk protocol as well. You can also separately install the AppleTalk protocol by using Network and Dial-Up Connections. Services for Macintosh requires an NTFS-formatted volume in order to operate. When

Services for Macintosh is first installed, a Macintosh-accessible volume called Public Files is created on the server running Windows 2000 or Windows .NET Server. You can create other Macintosh-accessible volumes later using My Computer.

See Also: *AppleTalk*

session initiation protocol (SIP)

A signaling protocol used in Voice over IP (VoIP).

Overview

Session initiation protocol (SIP) is an Internet Engineering Task Force (IETF) initiative to replace part of the older H.323 conferencing protocol developed by the International Telecommunication Union (ITU). Using SIP, a VoIP client can initiate and terminate call sessions, invite members into a conferencing session, and perform other telephony tasks. SIP also enables Private Branch Exchanges (PBXs), VoIP gateways, and other communications devices to communicate with one another in a standardized way.

SIP is designed with simplicity in mind in order to avoid the heavy overhead of H.323. SIP employs ASCII text messages similar in format to Hypertext Transfer Protocol (HTTP) and Simple Mail Transfer Protocol (SMTP) messages. SIP operates at the application level of the Open Systems Interconnection (OSI) reference model.

SIP is defined in RFC 2543. 3Com Corporation has been the driving force behind the development of SIP.

See Also: *H.323, Hypertext Transfer Protocol (HTTP), Open Systems Interconnection (OSI) reference model, Private Branch Exchange (PBX), Simple Mail Transfer Protocol (SMTP), Voice over IP (VoIP)*

S

session layer

Layer 5 of the Open Systems Interconnection (OSI) reference model.

Overview

The session layer enables sessions to be established and terminated between computers on a network. The session layer does not concern itself with issues such as the reliability and efficiency of data transfer between stations because these functions are provided by the first four layers of the OSI reference model. The session layer is responsible for synchronizing data exchange between computers, structuring communication sessions, and other issues directly related to conversations between networked computers. The session layer is also responsible for name recognition functions at the level of logical network names and for assigning communication ports. For example, the NetBIOS protocol is considered to run at the session level.

The session layer of the OSI reference model is not widely implemented in common local area network (LAN) protocol suites such as Transmission Control Protocol/Internet Protocol (TCP/IP) and Internetwork Packet Exchange/Sequenced Packet Exchange (IPX/SPX). Instead, the top three layers of the OSI model—the application layer, presentation layer, and session layer—are often thought of best as a homogeneous whole subsumed within a generalized application layer.

See Also: *NetBIOS, Open Systems Interconnection (OSI) reference model*

share

Shared (or sharing of) network resources.

Overview

As a verb, the word *share* means to make resources on a computer available to other users on the network who have suitable permissions. Resources that can be shared include disk volumes, directories, and printers.

As a noun, the word *share* is typically another name for a folder or directory that allows users on the network who have suitable permissions to access its contents. The name of a share does not have to be the same as the local name of the object. A share usually contains such items as public data, network applications, and users' home folders.

In Microsoft Windows 98 and Windows Millennium Edition (Me), share access can take two forms:

- **Share-level security:** Controls access to a share using a password that is the same for all users. For example, a user who wants to connect to a share on a peer server running Windows 98 or Windows Me that uses share-level security must know only the password for the share in order to access it. Share-level security is commonly used in small workgroups.

- **User-level security:** Controls access to a share through user credentials and group membership. For example, one group of users can be assigned read-only access to the share, another group can be assigned full access, and a third group can be assigned custom access. In order for user-level security to work, the network must have a security provider (such as a Windows 2000 or Windows .NET Server domain controller).

In Windows 2000, shares are always based on user-level security. A network user's access to a shared folder on an NTFS file system (NTFS) volume is governed by a combination of NTFS permissions and shared folder permissions.

Notes

Share names that do not conform to the MS-DOS 8.3 naming convention cannot be accessed by MS-DOS–based workstations.

See Also: *NTFS permissions (Windows 2000, Windows XP, and Windows .NET Server)*

shared folder

A folder that has been shared to allow its contents to be accessed by users on the network (provided they have suitable permissions).

See: *share*

shared folder permissions

In Microsoft Windows, a set of permissions that can be assigned to a shared folder to control access by users and groups on the network.

Overview

Shared folder permissions can be applied only to the entire shared folder, not to its files and subfolders. If you want to control access to individual files and subfolders within a network share, you can use the more granular NTFS file system (NTFS) permissions on Windows NT, Windows 2000, Windows XP, and Windows .NET Server. In addition, shared folder permissions are effective only when a user accesses the folder over the network. If a user can log on locally to the console of the computer where the share is located, that user can always access the contents of the shared folder regardless of the shared folder permissions set (unless the folder is on an NTFS volume and the NTFS permissions restrict the user from accessing the resource). Finally, shared folder permissions are the only way to secure network resources that are stored on file allocation table (FAT) volumes.

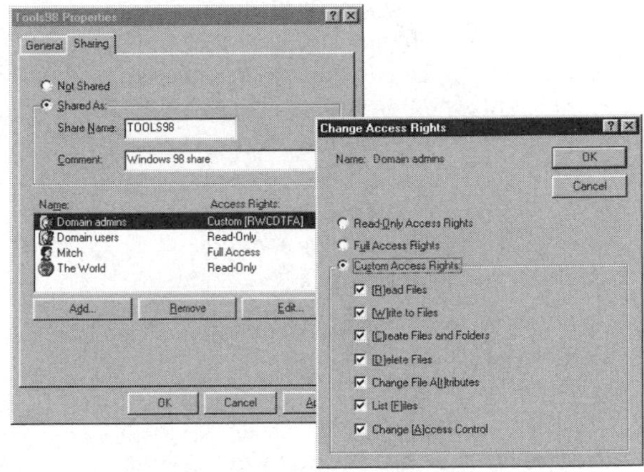

Shared folder permissions. *The Change Access Rights dialog box in Windows 98.*

If a user belongs to two or more groups, and these groups have different permissions on a given share, the user's ability to access the folder over the network can be calculated by two rules:

- The effective permission is the least restrictive (most permissive) permission, as in this example:

```
read + change = change permission
```

- No access or deny access overrides all other permissions, as in this example:

```
read + no access = no access
```

Different versions of Windows employ different mechanisms for assigning shared folder permissions to users and groups. The following tables show the permissions for each of these operating systems and lists what the permissions allow users to perform.

Windows 98 and Windows Me Shared Folder Permissions

Permission	*What It Allows Users to Do*
Read-Only Access Rights	List names of folders and files Browse hierarchies of folders Display the contents of folders and files Run executable files
Full Access Rights	Create and delete folders Add files to folders Create, modify, and delete files Change file attributes (Includes read permissions)
Custom Access Rights	Depending on the options specified, allows users to perform the following actions: Read files Write to files Create files and folders Delete files Change file attributes List files Change access control

Windows NT 4 Shared Folder Permissions

Permission	*What It Allows Users to Do*
No Access	Connect to a share without viewing its contents
Read	List names of folders and files Browse hierarchies of folders Display the contents of folders and files Run executable files
Change	Create and delete folders Create, modify, and delete files Change file attributes Includes read permissions
Full Control	Take ownership of files on NTFS volumes Change file permissions on NTFS volumes Includes read and change permissions

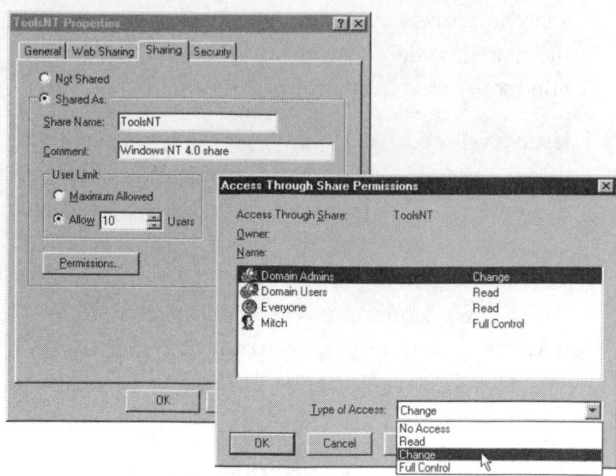

Shared folder permissions. *The Access Through Share Permissions dialog box in Windows NT 4.*

Windows 2000, Windows XP, and Windows .NET Server Shared Folder Permissions

Permission	*What It Allows Users to Do*
Read	List names of folders and files Browse hierarchies of folders Display the contents of folders and files Run executable files
Change	Create and delete folders Add files to folders Create, modify, and delete files Change file attributes Includes read permissions
Full Control	Take ownership of files on NTFS volumes Change file permissions Includes read and change permissions

Notes

When you first share a folder in Windows 2000, Windows XP, and Windows .NET Server, the default permissions are Full Control for the Everyone group. You should remove this default permission and assign more appropriate permissions to the share, such as change permission for Domain Users and full control for Administrators.

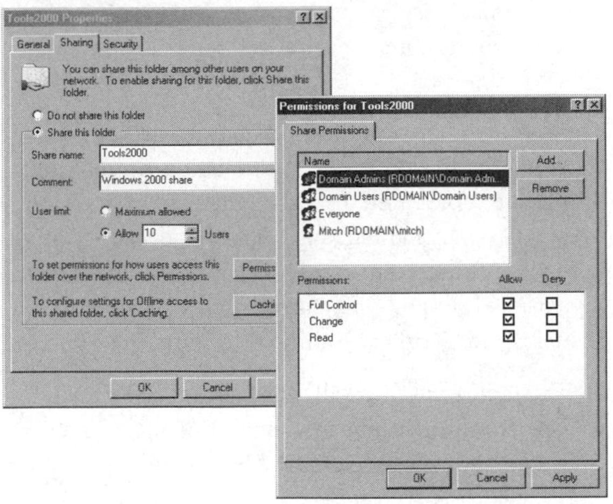

Shared folder permissions. *The Permissions dialog box in Windows 2000.*

When you assign permissions to shared folders, use group accounts instead of user accounts in order to simplify administration. Give users the most restrictive permissions that still enable them to perform the necessary tasks on the files in the share.

See Also: *NTFS permissions (Windows 2000, Windows XP, and Windows .NET Server), NTFS permissions (Windows NT), share*

shared SCSI bus

A Small Computer System Interface (SCSI) disk system shared between two nodes in a cluster.

Overview

Shared SCSI buses are used in clustering to allow multiple nodes in a cluster to access the same disk system. The shared SCSI bus logically represents the total interconnection between the cluster and the shared storage devices, but in practice this consists of a number of electrically separate SCSI bus segments. Each disk on a shared SCSI bus is owned by only one of the cluster's nodes. If the disk group fails over, ownership of the disk switches from the failed node to the other node.

Notes

When using a shared SCSI bus with Windows Clustering on Microsoft Windows 2000, you can remove the internal termination of the SCSI bus and use Y-cables or trilink connectors for terminating the external bus. In this way, you can remove the device if maintenance is required without affecting other devices on the bus.

See Also: *clustering, Small Computer System Interface (SCSI)*

share-level security

A mode of security on computers running Microsoft Windows 98 and Windows Millennium Edition (Me) that protects shared folders and printers using a password.

Overview

When using share-level security, all users use the same password to access the resource and any user who knows the password has permission to use the resource. The security options for protecting a shared folder using share-level security include

- Allowing read-only access, with or without a password
- Allowing full access, with or without a password
- Specifying one password for read-only access and another for full access

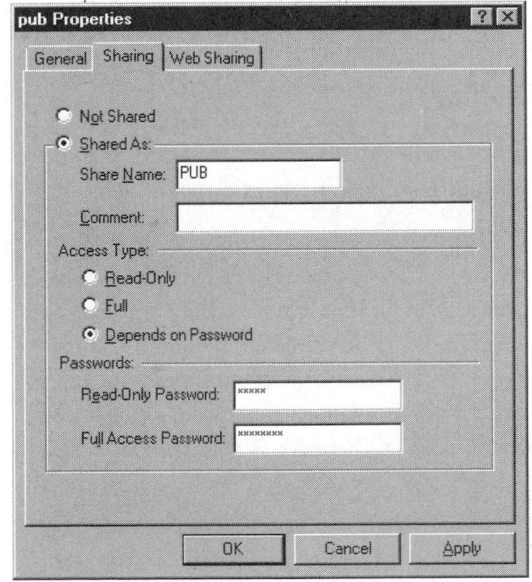

Share-level security. *The Sharing tab of a folder's Properties dialog box.*

Share-level security is often used in small peer-to-peer networks with computers running Windows 98 or Windows Me. Use the Network utility in Control Panel to enable share-level security.

See Also: *peer-to-peer network, user-level security*

shell

The user interface for an operating system.

Overview

The term *shell* refers to the external user-accessible portion of an operating system, and the term *kernel* refers to the part that is normally hidden from the user. On UNIX platforms *shell* usually refers to the command-line interface (also called the command interpreter), but on Microsoft Windows platforms the desktop graphical user interface (GUI) element can also be considered a type of shell.

In a UNIX command-line shell, when a user types a command such as ls (list directory contents), the shell executes the associated program called ls. When the shell executes the command, it typically starts a new process for the command and goes into a sleep state until the command finishes executing, at which time the shell wakes up and issues a prompt to indicate that it is ready to receive another command. The output of shell commands is directed by default to Standard Output, which is the screen, but you can redirect command outputs to files and other applications. One advantage of using a command-line shell is that shell scripts can be written for batch execution of a series of shell commands.

Various shells are available for different UNIX platforms, each tailored to a different administration and programming environment. One commonly used shell is the Bourne Shell, which functions as both a command interpreter and a high-level programming language in which shell scripts can be used to automate groups of processes. Other UNIX shells include the C Shell of System V UNIX, which includes job control and command history mechanisms, and the Korn shell, which supports command-line editing.

Notes

The command prompt in Windows provides similar functionality to UNIX shells, although scripting capabilities are more limited because they are based on the MS-DOS command language. The Windows Script Host (WSH) overcomes these limitations by supporting higher-level scripting languages such as Microsoft Visual Basic, Scripting Edition (VBScript), and JScript.

UNIX shell scripts are called batch files in Windows programming environments. In an IBM mainframe environment, they are called EXECs.

See Also: *kernel, UNIX, Windows Script Host (WSH)*

shielded twisted-pair (STP) cabling

Twisted-pair cabling that contains internal shielding.

Overview

The shielding in shielded twisted-pair (STP) cabling is designed to reduce crosstalk and other forms of electromagnetic interference (EMI). The outer insulating jacket contains an inner braided copper mesh to shield the pairs of twisted cables, which themselves are wrapped in foil.

STP cabling is more expensive than unshielded twisted-pair (UTP) cabling. It has an impedance of 150 ohms, has a maximum length of 295 feet (90 meters), and is used primarily in networking environments with a high amount of EMI due to motors, air conditioners, power lines, or other noisy electrical components. STP cabling is the default type of cabling for IBM Token Ring networks.

STP cabling comes in various grades or categories defined by the Electronic Industries Association/ Telecommunications Industry Associaiton (EIA/TIA) wiring standards, as shown in the following table.

STP Cabling Categories

Category	*Description*
IBM Type 1	Token Ring transmissions on AWG #22 wire up to 20 megabits per second (Mbps)
IBM Type 1A	Fiber Distributed Data Interface (FDDI), Copper Distributed Data Interface (CDDI), and Asynchronous Transfer Mode (ATM) transmission up to 300 Mbps
IBM Type 2A	Hybrid combination of STP data cable and Category 3 (Cat3) voice cable in one jacket
IBM Type 6A	AWG #26 patch cables

See Also: *crosstalk, electromagnetic interference (EMI), shielding, unshielded twisted-pair (UTP) cabling*

shielding

Metallic material added to cabling to reduce susceptibility to noise due to electromagnetic interference (EMI).

Overview

Shielding usually takes one of two forms:

- A braided copper or aluminum mesh enclosing the signal-carrying wires. This type of shielding offers superior performance and should be used in industrial areas where heavy machinery generates a lot of EMI.
- An aluminum foil sleeve that encloses individual wires or the entire wire bundle. This kind of shielding is more suitable for office environments to shield against noise due to air conditioners, fans, and other motors.

For best performance, you can combine both kinds of shielding. An additional uninsulated drain wire is sometimes used to terminate the shield; it runs the length of the wire in contact with the foil sleeve or mesh.

Shielded cabling is generally more expensive than unshielded cabling.

See Also: *coaxial cabling, shielded twisted-pair (STP) cabling*

short

A condition that occurs when signal-carrying conductors make contact.

Overview

The effect of a short is similar to having a break in the cable—network communication ceases. To find or isolate a short, use a cable tester or time domain reflectometer. Cable shorts can occur only in copper cables, not fiber-optic cables, although breaks can occur in fiber-optic cables.

See Also: *network troubleshooting*

Shortest Path First (SPF)

A routing algorithm used by the Open Shortest Path First (OSPF) protocol.

Overview

Also called the Dijkstra algorithm, Shortest Path First (SPF) is a routing algorithm in which a router computes the shortest path between each pair of nodes in the network. When an OSPF router is initialized, it sends a Hello message to determine whether it has any neighbors (routers that have an interface on the same network). Neighbors respond to the initiating router by using the same Hello packets. In fact, these Hello packets also serve to tell other routers that the transmitting router is still alive (keep-alive function). If more than two OSPF routers are on the internetwork, the Hello protocol causes one of the routers to be designated as the one to send out link state advertisements (LSAs) to all other routers on the network.

Neighbors then synchronize their topological databases with each other to become "adjacent" routers. Each router periodically floods the network with cost information for its adjacent nodes in the form of LSAs, allowing them to compile complete tables of network connections and calculate the path of least cost between any two nodes. Finally, each router analyzes its own database of network topology information and uses it to determine a shortest-path tree using itself as the root; from this tree, it derives a routing table for itself.

See Also: *Open Shortest Path First (OSPF)*

Short Message Service (SMS)

A protocol for sending short text messages over cellular communications systems.

Overview

Short Message Service (SMS) is a two-way text-based messaging service originally developed for the Global System for Mobile Communications (GSM) cellular telephone systems deployed across Europe. SMS allows messages to be sent or received simultaneously with voice, fax, or data transmission over GSM systems because it uses a separate signaling path instead of a dedicated channel. SMS thus works reliably even during peak usage periods of cellular systems. SMS offers an advantage over paging systems in that it notifies the sender using an alert when the recipient has received the message.

SMS can send short messages of up to 160 alphanumeric characters between two cellular users. SMS messages are typically charged to the senders, which encourages users to leave their cell phones on at all times in order to receive SMS messages and alerts.

Implementation

SMS works as a store-and-forward service in which messages that are sent are stored at an SMS messaging center until the recipient can connect and receive them. To use SMS, the user needs a subscription to a GSM bearer that supports SMS and a cell phone that supports SMS. The SMS function must be enabled for that user, typically through a subscription charge together with a per-message fee. Some SMS systems support compression to increase the amount of information that can be included in a message, and support concatenation of messages to create a single message from several message fragments.

Prospects

SMS has proven so popular in Europe that many non-GSM cellular systems around the world have also been implementing it in various degrees. Examples include Digital Advanced Mobile Phone System (D-AMPS) in the United States and Personal Digital Cellular (PDC) in Japan. The worldwide cdmaOne (IS-95b) system supports larger 256-byte two-way messages, but the analog Advanced Mobile Phone System (AMPS) still deployed in much of the United States supports 14-byte receive-only messaging.

SMS has also helped energize the drive toward deploying wireless application protocol (WAP) by creating consumer readiness for broadband wireless e-business.

See Also: *2G, 2.5G, cellular communications, Global System for Mobile Communications (GSM), Wireless Application Protocol (WAP)*

S-HTTP

Stands for Secure Hypertext Transfer Protocol, an Internet protocol for encryption of Hypertext Transfer Protocol (HTTP) traffic.

See: *Secure Hypertext Transfer Protocol (S-HTTP)*

SIBone

Stands for Satellite Internet Backbone, a satellite-based network exchange point.

See: *Satellite Internet Backbone (SIBone)*

SID

Stands for security identifier, an internal number that is used in Microsoft Windows 2000, Windows XP, and Windows .NET Server that uniquely identifies a user, group, or other object.

See: *security identifier (SID)*

signal

An electrical transmission that carries information.

Overview

In its simplest form, a signal is a form of alternating current (AC) running on network cabling that is generated by a networking component such as a network interface card (NIC). Signals are usually purposeful transmissions, as opposed to noise, which is an undesirable transmission generated randomly by networking components and the surrounding environment. Signals can be classified as:

- **Electrical:** Travel over copper wire as a medium
- **Optical:** Travel through fiber-optic cabling
- **Electromagnetic:** Travel through free space, as in wireless networking and cellular communications

In the computer networking environment, signals are generally square waves and thus digital in nature, carrying information in binary format. To accomplish this, information must be encoded into the signal using a line coding mechanism, a technique for representing binary information using a series of discrete voltages. The earliest digital signaling method to be used in computer networking is the unipolar nonreturn to zero (NRZ) mechanism, in which a binary 1 is represented by a positive voltage and a zero by no voltage. Ethernet uses a different method called Manchester coding, and other networking technologies employ other kinds of signaling methods.

See Also: *line coding, Manchester coding, network interface card (NIC), signaling*

signaling

The process in which control information is exchanged during establishment of a communication session.

Overview

In wide area network (WAN) technologies, signaling is the process by which the devices at either end of a WAN link communicate with each other to establish common timing and signal-flow settings. Signaling must occur before a communication session is established and before data is actually sent over the link. Session-establishment signaling between telecommunications devices generally has a certain degree of latency. That is, it takes time for sessions to be negotiated and established before data can be sent. For example, analog modems typically take 15 to 30 seconds from dial-up until the connection is established, and Integrated Services Digital Network (ISDN) dial-up services sometimes take only 1 to 2 seconds to establish a connection.

Implementation

Signaling between telecommunications devices generally takes place by one of two methods:

- **In-band signaling:** The signaling information is sent in the same communication channel as the data itself.
- **Out-of-band signaling:** The signaling happens on a separate channel, usually a separate pair of wires.

See Also: *analog modem, in-band signaling, Integrated Services Digital Network (ISDN), latency, out-of-band (OOB) signaling, wide area network (WAN)*

signal loss

The loss of strength of a signal as it propagates over a medium.

Overview

Signal loss generally refers to loss of signal strength in guided media such as copper cabling and fiber-optic cabling. Unguided media such as wireless networking technologies have signals that decrease in power per unit area primarily because of the inverse square law.

A number of mechanisms can cause signal loss in a wire or cable:

- **Attenuation:** Caused by resistive losses in the cable and affects only copper cabling
- **Absorption:** Causes signal loss in fiber cabling because the glass core material is not perfectly transparent
- **Fractures:** Can result in both attenuation and absorption of signal strength
- **Splices, connectors, and couplings:** Involve dissimilar materials joined together and generally produce some loss

Signal loss is usually expressed in units of decibels (dB) per source of the loss. The following table shows typical signal loss values for fiber-optic cabling. These rough values are useful for estimating total signal loss, which you can calculate by simply adding the loss for each element in the light path.

Signal Loss Values for Fiber-Optic Cabling

Source of Loss	*Approximate Signal Loss*
Connector loss	3 dB/termination
Coupling loss	2 dB/coupler
Intrinsic loss	6 dB/1000 meters
Microbending loss	Increases with decreasing bend radius
Splice loss	4 dB/splice

Notes

The total end-to-end signal loss of a light path through a fiber-optic cabling system is known as the optical power budget. If this value is greater than the power launch rating of your line driver, your system will not work.

Simple Mail Transfer Protocol (SMTP)

An application-layer protocol for delivery of e-mail over the Internet.

Overview

Simple Mail Transfer Protocol (SMTP) defines a message format and forwarding procedure to enable messages to be sent between hosts on the Internet. As such, SMTP is one of the most important protocols in use on the Internet. The basics of SMTP are defined in RFCs 821 and 822.

Implementation

To forward a message, an SMTP host first establishes a connection with a second SMTP host using Transmission Control Protocol (TCP) port 25. An SMTP session is then initiated by sending a HELO command and receiving an OK response. The first host then uses the following commands to forward messages to the second host:

- **MAIL FR:** Identifies the sending host to the receiving host
- **RCPT TO:** Identifies the targeted message recipient to the receiving host by using the Domain Name System (DNS) format user@DNSdomain
- **DATA:** Initiates the sending of the message body as a series of lines of ASCII text, ending with a single period (.) alone on a line
- **QUIT:** Closes the SMTP connection

SMTP uses plain 7-bit ASCII text to send e-mail messages and to issue SMTP commands to receiving hosts. Multipurpose Internet Mail Extensions (MIME) is typically used to encode multipart binary files including attachments into a form that SMTP can handle.

Notes

Note that SMTP only provides message transport only from one SMTP host to another. Support for storing messages in mailboxes is provided by Post Office Protocol version 3 (POP3) and Internet Mail Access Protocol version 4 (IMAP4).

See Also: ASCII, Internet Mail Access Protocol version 4 (IMAP4), Multipurpose Internet Mail Extensions (MIME), Post Office Protocol version 3 (POP3), Transmission Control Protocol (TCP)

Simple Network Management Protocol (SNMP)

A popular protocol for network management.

Overview

Simple Network Management Protocol (SNMP) is an Internet-standard Layer-7 (application layer) protocol for collecting information from and configuring network devices such as servers, printers, hubs, switches, and routers on an Internet Protocol (IP) network. SNMP can be used to collect information about network statistics from these devices and to relay this information to a central management console to monitor network health, trap errors, perform diagnostics, and generate reports. Typical statistical information might include the number of packets or frames sent or received per second and the number of errors per second. SNMP can also be used for reading and sometimes modifying device configuration information such as the IP address of an interface, or the version of the operating system running on the device.

S

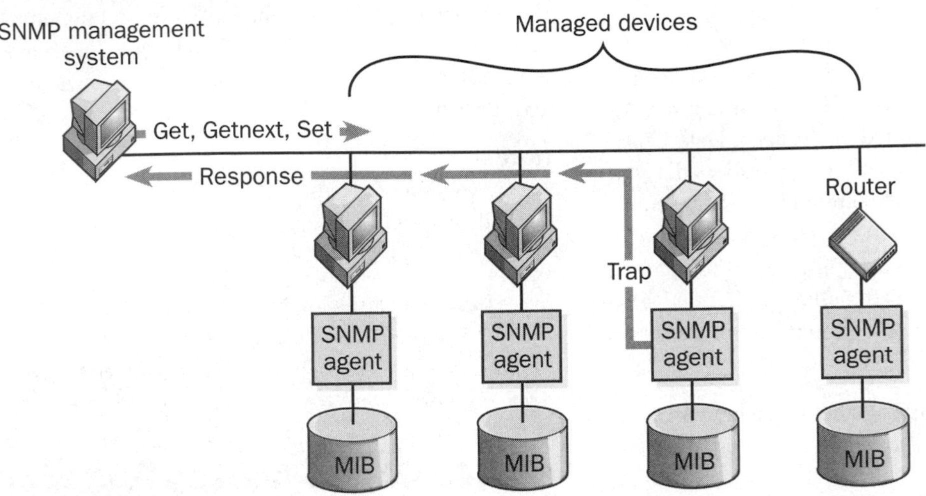

Simple Network Management Protocol (SNMP). *How SNMP can be used to manage devices on a network.*

SNMP was developed in the late 1980s and is still the most popular network management protocol in use. There are two versions of SNMP:

- **SNMPv1:** This is the original version of SNMP, which lacked security for ensuring the authenticity and integrity of SNMP messages.
- **SNMPv2:** This version has increased security that supports a simple authentication scheme based on SNMP communities.

SNMPv2 is defined in RFCs 1901 through 1908 and 2089.

Implementation

SNMP is a client/server protocol that consists of two components that work together:

- **SNMP agents:** These are programs that run on the network devices to be managed (called managed devices) and that collect Transmission Control Protocol/Internet Protocol (TCP/IP)–related configuration information and statistics about the operation of the device. Agents do not require heavy CPU usage to run. The types of information that an agent can collect are defined in a local database called a Management Information Base (MIB). MIB databases are hierarchical and contain managed objects that have uniquely assigned identifiers issued by the International Organization for Standardization (ISO). SNMP variables are specific instances of managed objects in MIBs. Agents running on managed devices monitor specific sets of SNMP variables and temporarily store this information until the agent is polled by a management system, whereupon the agent reports the values of the stored information to the management system. Most network devices have built-in SNMP agent software and associated MIBs.
- **SNMP management system:** Also called Network Management System (NMS), this is software that runs on an administrative console and can display data gathered from managed devices in a user-friendly form through a graphical user interface (GUI). SNMP Management Systems software can notify the administrator when certain conditions (such as errors) occur. Most SNMP management systems can also automatically determine the topology and components of a network with SNMP-enabled computers, routers, hubs, and switches and can display network topology, traffic, and conditions in graphical format. SNMP management systems regularly poll managed devices using SNMP messages for statistical and configuration information and then store this information in a central database, which can be used to present the information in a friendly way to users.

SNMP is a simple protocol that is message-based in operation. SNMP messages are sent between management consoles and managed devices over User Datagram Protocol (UDP) port 161. These messages contain a header and a payload called the Protocol Data Unit (PDU). The header contains information about the community being referenced. A community is a subset of agents that will be monitored using a specific management system and institutes a primitive level of security, acting as a primitive means of authentication. SNMP messages come in four types, three of which are issued by management stations and one by agents:

- **Get:** Issued by the management system to an agent on a managed device to read the value of a specific variable on the device.
- **Getnext:** Issued by the management system to determine which SNMP variables are supported by an agent running on a managed device and to traverse a series of variables to read their values sequentially.
- **Set:** Issued by the management system to an agent on a managed device to write a value for a specific variable on the device.
- **Trap:** Issued by an agent running on a managed device when an error or alert condition occurs. The trap message is sent to the management system to alert administrators of the situation.

SNMP version 2 adds additional security features, can be applied to network architectures other than TCP/IP, and supports additional data types. It is only partially backward compatible with SNMP 1. SNMP 2 also defines two additional types of messages:

S

- **Getbulk:** Similar to getnext but allows the retrieval of greater amounts of information in one data block
- **Inform:** Allows management systems to send information to other management systems using a trap-like message

The management station regularly sends get, getnext, and set messages to the SNMP agent on the managed device, in effect periodically polling the agent for the status of the device. The agent verifies the community name in the message, verifies the IP address or host name of the SNMP management system, processes the request, and sends the results to the management system.

Notes

A new version of SNMP called SNMPv3 is currently being developed to enhance the security of earlier versions.

See Also: *application layer, International Organization for Standardization (ISO), Internet Protocol (IP), Management Information Base (MIB), network management, port, User Datagram Protocol (UDP)*

Simple Object Access Protocol (SOAP)

A message-passing protocol used to enable distributed Web services.

Overview

Simple Object Access Protocol (SOAP) is a protocol developed by Microsoft Corporation, IBM, and other vendors to enable Web applications and services to communicate with one another over the Internet. SOAP enables these services to communicate regardless of the platform they are running on or the programming languages with which they were developed. SOAP is a cross-platform, standards-based solution that is easy to implement and that has broad industry support. SOAP has been proposed as a World Wide Web Consortium (W3C) standard.

Implementation

SOAP connects components of distributed applications using an XML–based RPC mechanism based on Extensible Markup Language (XML) and the Remote Procedure Call (RPC) architecture. Using SOAP, an application on one host can invoke object methods and functions on a remote host running a SOAP application. To perform this, the first application creates a block of XML text that contains the location of the remote object on the network and the data needed by the object to invoke the method. The application then passes the XML block to a SOAP server that encapsulates and transports the message block to the remote application using Hypertext Transfer Protocol (HTTP) or some other common Internet application layer protocol. Once the method has been invoked and execution is complete, the remote application returns a similar XML–based message to the initiating application.

SOAP is intended to complement existing distributed application platforms such as Microsoft's Distributed Component Object Model (DCOM) and the Open Group's Common Object Request Broker Architecture (CORBA). SOAP also forms the underlying transport mechanism for the Electronic Business Extensible Markup Language (ebXML) developed by the Organization for the Advancement of Structured Information Standards (OASIS).

See Also: *Common Object Request Broker Architecture (CORBA), Distributed Component Object Model (DCOM), Electronic Business Extensible Markup Language (ebXML), Hypertext Transfer Protocol (HTTP), remote procedure call (RPC), World Wide Web Consortium (W3C), XML*

simple volume

A type of disk volume in Microsoft Windows 2000, Windows XP, and Windows .NET Server.

Overview

In Windows 2000, Windows XP, and Windows .NET Server, a simple volume is one made up of one or more contiguous blocks of free disk space on a single physical disk. You can extend simple volumes to include additional free disk space from the initial drive or from other drives, forming a spanned volume. You can create simple volumes only on dynamic volumes created using Disk Management. Simple volumes have no fault tolerance but can be mirrored to form mirrored volumes.

See Also: *volume*

simplex

A form of communication in which signals are sent in only one direction.

Overview

Simplex is different from duplex, in which signals can simultaneously be sent and received by a station, and from half-duplex transmission, in which signals can be sent or received but not both at the same time. Simplex transmission occurs in many common communication applications, the most obvious being broadcast and cable television. It is not used in true network communication because stations on a network generally need to communicate both ways. Some forms of network communication might seem to be simplex in nature, such as streaming audio or video, but the communication actually takes place using bidirectional network traffic, usually Transmission Control Protocol (TCP) traffic. Simplex communication is not included in the V series recommendations of the International Telecommunication Union (ITU).

See Also: *duplex, half-duplex*

single domain model

A type of Microsoft Windows NT domain model used for small networks.

Overview

In the single domain model, all global users and group accounts reside in a single domain and all network resources reside in the same domain. The single domain model is simple to implement and offers centralized administration of accounts and resources. Although the model can theoretically work for as many as 40,000 accounts, it performs poorly with large numbers of accounts. The single domain model is, therefore, generally used only in small to mid-sized Windows NT–based networks.

When you upgrade a Windows NT–based network based on the single domain model to a Windows 2000–based network, you usually end up with a single domain in Active Directory directory service. You can then use Active Directory to create organizational units (OUs) to organize your network and assign administrative rights and permissions.

See Also: *complete trust model, master domain, multiple master domain model*

single master domain model

A type of Microsoft Windows NT domain model used for large networks.

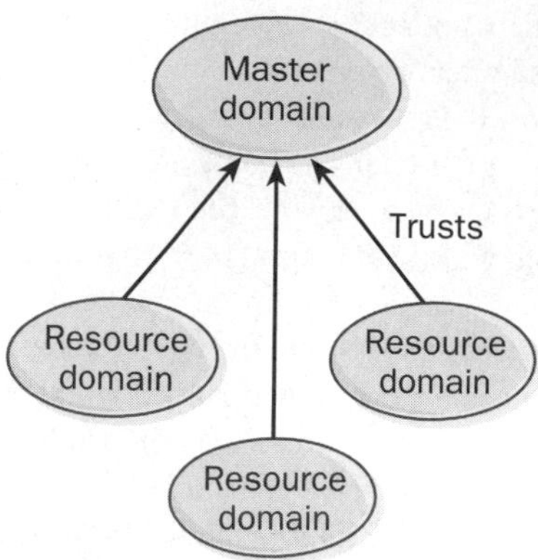

Single master domain model. *The structure of the single master domain model.*

Overview

In the single master domain model, all global users and group accounts reside in a single Windows NT domain called the accounts domain. Network resources reside in other domains are called resource domains. Each resource domain needs to have a trust relationship with the accounts domain. Users who log on to their accounts in the accounts domain can access shared network resources in any resource domain if they have the appropriate permissions. The advantages and disadvantages of using this model are shown in the following table.

Pros and Cons of the Single Master Domain Model

Pros	*Cons*
Not difficult to implement—one trust per resource domain	Poor performance when the number of accounts is large
Centralized administration of accounts	Local groups must be created in each resource domain
Resource domains manage their own resources	
Works for up to 40,000 accounts	

When you upgrade a Windows NT–based network based on the single master domain model to a Windows 2000–based network, you usually perform the upgrade from the top down. You first upgrade the master domain to a Windows 2000 domain based on Active Directory directory service. Then you upgrade resource domains to child domains within a directory tree whose root domain is the former master domain. You can move user accounts from the master domain to the domains where users actually work, because two-way transitive trusts enable users in any domain within the domain tree to access resources in any other domain.

Alternatively, companies with a centralized IT (information technology) department can upgrade both the master domain and the resource domains to a single Windows 2000 domain. Organizational units (OUs) can then be created within Active Directory to mirror the administrative structure of the former master domain model. Administrative rights and permissions can be assigned to users and groups based on the new OUs. Here are the advantages of using this approach:

- One domain to manage
- No trust relationships to create or manage
- Faster searching because all directory objects reside in a single domain

See Also: *complete trust model, multiple master domain model, single domain model*

single-mode fiber-optic cabling

A type of fiber-optic cabling that can carry only one signal at a time.

Overview

Single-mode fiber-optic cabling typically has a core that is only 5 or 10 micrometers in diameter—much smaller than the core of multimode fiber, which needs room to carry many different light signals simultaneously. Single-mode fiber uses light generated by a laser-emitting diode to carry signals. Such laser light is extremely stable and uniform and can be accurately focused, making it perfect for long-distance transmission. Single-mode fiber has extremely low signal attenuation and is typically used for long cable runs because it can generally carry signals up to 50 times farther than multimode fiber, which can carry many different signals simultaneously.

Uses

Use single-mode fiber-optic cabling for long cable runs or where extra bandwidth is required. The bandwidth of single-mode fiber is typically double that of multimode fiber. Be aware, however, that installing single-mode fiber requires more care and expertise to avoid signal loss, especially if you terminate the cable with connectors. Single-mode fiber is also more expensive than multimode because multimode systems use transmitters that have cheaper light-emitting diodes, but single-mode systems use more expensive laser-emitting diodes in their transmitters. Also, when you use single-mode fiber-optic cabling, the ancillary devices such as line drivers cost more.

See Also: *fiber-optic cabling, multimode fiber-optic cabling*

Single Sign On (SSO)

Any technology that requires users to have only one set of credentials to access network resources.

Overview

Single Sign On (SSO) has been an elusive goal in enterprise networking for many years. Enterprise networks are generally heterogeneous systems comprised of operating systems and applications from many vendors, and users on these networks often require different sets of credentials for each platform they need to access. As a result, different vendors have pursued the concept of SSO, whereby users employ only one set of credentials to log on to the network and access any applications or resources they might need.

SSO can be viewed as either a benefit or a hazard. From the benefit point of view, some analysts estimate that password maintenance costs the average enterprise hundreds of dollars per user each year—a cost that can be reduced through implementing SSO technologies. On the other hand, the complexity of implementing true SSO in a heterogeneous networking environment can be so great that many network administrators are loath to attempt it.

Marketplace

The foundation for Microsoft Windows 2000's SSO solution is the Kerberos authentication protocol, which can enable SSO to be implemented in a mixed Windows/UNIX environment. Novell has its own SSO solution called Novell Single Sign On (NSSO) that can be used in a mixed Novell/Windows environment. Security companies such as Entrust Technologies and RSA Security have offered SSO solutions based on public key cryptography systems. Third-party companies such as Axent Technologies also offer their own SSO systems for cross-platform authentication.

See Also: *authentication protocol, Kerberos, public key cryptography*

SIP

Stands for session initiation protocol, a signaling protocol used in Voice over IP (VoIP).

See: *session initiation protocol (SIP)*

SLA

Stands for service-level agreement, an agreement to provide services above a specified minimum level.

See: *service-level agreement (SLA)*

SLIP

Stands for Serial Line Internet Protocol, a serial encapsulation protocol.

See: *Serial Line Internet Protocol (SLIP)*

Small Business Server

A complete, integrated server solution from Microsoft Corporation for businesses with 25 or fewer PCs.

Overview

Microsoft BackOffice Small Business Server includes file, print, and application services; communication services; and Internet connection services.

Small Business Server integrates these applications from the BackOffice family of products:

- Microsoft Windows NT
- Microsoft Exchange Server
- Microsoft SQL Server
- Internet Information Services
- Microsoft Proxy Server

Small Business Server also extends this BackOffice functionality by including the following:

- Microsoft Fax Service
- Microsoft Modem Sharing Server
- Internet connectivity for small businesses

Small Business Server is easy to set up and manage, and it can grow with a business's needs. It includes the following features:

- Unified, integrated administration through the Small Business Server Console
- Simple, wizard-based installation and configuration (from creating users to installing printers and establishing Internet connectivity)
- Easy setup and configuration of client computers using the Set Up Computer Wizard
- Extensive online help and troubleshooting tips for the administrator and users
- An easy upgrade path to BackOffice Server when a business grows beyond 25 computers
- Support for e-mail, the Internet, and fax
- Scheduling and collaboration features through the Microsoft Outlook desktop information manager and Exchange Server

For More Information

Visit *www.microsoft.com/sbserver.*

Small Computer System Interface (SCSI)

A popular general-purpose input/output (I/O) bus.

Overview

Small Computer System Interface (SCSI) is a hardware bus specification for connecting storage devices and peripherals to a computer using a parallel transmission interface. SCSI was developed by Apple Computer and is widely used in the enterprise environment for servers and high-end workstations. Although SCSI is mainly used as a hard disk interface, it can also be used for connecting peripherals such as printers and scanners. The main competitor to SCSI is the Integrated Drive Electronics (IDE) interface, which is widely used in commodity PCs.

SCSI is defined by a number of American National Standards Institute (ANSI) standards that include the SCSI-1, SCSI-2, SCSI-3, and SCSI-5 specifications.

Advantages and Disadvantages

SCSI has two main advantages over IDE:

- SCSI supports daisy-chaining of multiple devices, making SCSI drives a more scalable solution for internal PC storage systems.
- SCSI drives generally have faster transfer speeds and better performance than IDE drives.

On the negative side, this extra performance comes at a significantly higher cost, and IDE drives have been closing in on SCSI speeds for the last few years. SCSI also has multiple versions that are incompatible with one another.

Types

SCSI standards and implementations can be classified in several ways. For example, SCSI devices differ depending on the width of the data path used, giving two categories:

- **Narrow SCSI:** One byte (8 bits) of data are transferred for each clock cycle. Narrow SCSI devices typically use the 50-pin Centronics SCSI interface.
- **Wide SCSI:** Two bytes (16 bits) are transferred each cycle. Wide SCSI devices usually employ a 68-pin parallel SCSI interface.

SCSI devices can also be classified according to their use of grounding:

- **Single-ended:** These use unbalanced transmission in which one data lead and one ground lead establish single-ended signal transmission over the bus. This type of device is more prone to the effects of noise and is less forgiving of cable lengths beyond specifications. Single-ended (SE) SCSI is generally considered obsolete.
- **Differential:** These use balanced transmission in which there are two data leads, neither of which are at ground potential. These devices are generally more expensive but are resistant to the effects of noise and can often function over distances that exceed the SCSI specifications. Differential SCSI is used in two common forms: high-voltage differential (HVD) and low-voltage differential (LVD) SCSI.

Finally, forms of SCSI are differentiated by the clock speed used:

- **SCSI:** This is the original 1986 SCSI-1 standard and supports transmission rates of 5 megabytes per second (MBps) over an 8-bit bus and supports up to seven daisy-chained devices. SCSI cables typically use Centronics 50 or Telco 50 connectors, and the chained bus length must not exceed 20 feet (6 meters).
- **Fast SCSI:** Sometimes referred to as Plain SCSI, the SCSI-2 standard supports transmission rates of 10 MBps over an 8-bit bus (called Fast Narrow SCSI) using Micro DB50 connectors or 20 MBps over a 16-bit bus (called Fast Wide SCSI). Fast SCSI supports up to seven daisy-chained devices and the bus length must not exceed 20 feet (6 meters) for Fast Narrow SCSI and 10 feet (3 meters) for Fast Wide SCSI.
- **Ultra SCSI:** Sometimes called Fast-20 SCSI, the SCSI-3 standard supports transmission rates of 20 MBps over an 8-bit bus (Narrow Ultra SCSI) or 40 MBps over a 16-bit bus (Wide Ultra SCSI). Ultra SCSI can support up to 15 daisy-chained devices and its cables typically use MicroD 68-pin or Mini 68 connectors. There are also variants of Ultra SCSI called Ultra2 SCSI, which supports 40 MBps (Narrow) or 80 MBps (Wide), and Ultra3 SCSI, which supports 80 MBps (Narrow) or 160 MBps (Wide).
- **SCSI-5:** Also called Very High Density Connector Interface (VHDCI), this form of SCSI is similar to SCSI-3 but uses a smaller 0.8 millimeter connector.

All these various forms of SCSI are incompatible with one another.

SCSI-1 (Centronics)

SCSI-2 (Mini 50)

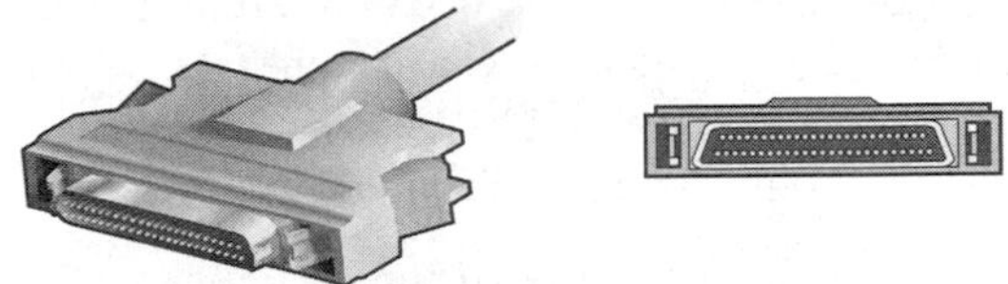

SCSI-3 (Mini 68)

SCSI-5 (MD 68)

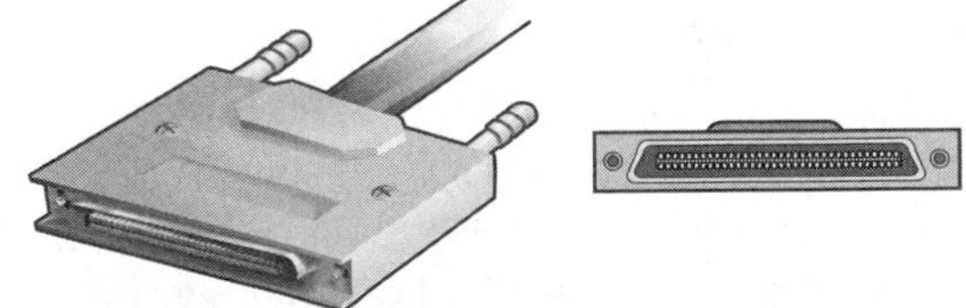

Small Computer System Interface (SCSI). *Four varieties of SCSI interface.*

Implementation

To implement SCSI on a system, use a SCSI adapter to interface with the system bus, suitable SCSI devices such as SCSI hard drives, SCSI cables to daisy-chain the devices, and SCSI terminators for the ends of the bus. Each device on a SCSI bus must have a SCSI device ID number assigned to it, allowing SCSI to be used for daisy-chaining a number of devices together on a single parallel bus. You can change SCSI IDs by using dip switches or jumpers or by using special SCSI configuration software.

SCSI cables must always be properly terminated in order for devices to be properly recognized; they should also use high-quality active terminators. Diagnostic terminators that help identify problems in signal quality are also available.

Always use the shortest cable possible for SCSI connections, because longer cables cause signals to weaken and are more affected by noise due to electromagnetic interference (EMI). When you calculate the total length of the SCSI bus, add the lengths of all the SCSI cable segments plus any internal SCSI cabling.

Be sure that all devices on a SCSI bus are configured for either single-ended or differential transmission—do not mix these methods on a single bus. You can connect single-ended devices to differential transmission devices only by using a signal converter. If you do not use a signal converter, your SCSI devices might be damaged by unexpected voltages.

See Also: *Fibre Channel, storage*

S

smart card

A plastic card with an embedded microchip used to authenticate the owner.

Overview

Smart cards have been around a long time, at least in concept. The first patent on "chip cards" was issued in 1974, but the technology of that day did not support implementation of the concept. By 1978, however, smart cards began to make their appearance, and their use spread rapidly, particularly in France and several other European countries.

Smart card technology was initially proprietary vendor-based technology that required cards, card readers, and software drivers to be used from a single vendor to ensure interoperability. To overcome this issue, the International Organization for Standards (ISO) developed the ISO 7816 standard that defined the operation of the physical and data-link layer of smart cards and readers. This standard was quickly adopted by financial credit institutions such as Visa International and MasterCard International and by the Global System for Mobile Communications (GSM) cellular phone system. In the last few years smart card readers have even become a built-in feature of high-end laptops from Acer America Corporation, Compaq Computer Corporation, and other PC vendors. Microsoft Windows 2000, Windows XP, and Windows .NET Server also have built-in support for smart card authentication, making the technology easy to implement in the enterprise desktop arena.

See Also: *authentication protocol, Global System for Mobile Communications (GSM)*

SMB

Stands for Server Message Block, a general-purposes information-sharing protocol.

See: *Server Message Block (SMB)*

SMDS

Stands for Switched Multimegabit Data Services, a high-speed metropolitan area network (MAN) data service offered by some telcos.

See: *Switched Multimegabit Data Services (SMDS)*

S/MIME

Stands for Secure/Multipurpose Internet Mail Extensions, a scheme for secure e-mail messaging.

See: *Secure/Multipurpose Internet Mail Extensions (S/MIME)*

SMS (Short Message Service)

Stands for Short Message Service, a protocol for sending short text messages over cellular communications systems.

See: *Short Message Service (SMS)*

SMS (System Management Server)

Stands for Systems Management Server, a server application from Microsoft Corporation for managing an organization's networked computers.

See: *Systems Management Server (SMS)*

SMTP

Stands for Simple Mail Transfer Protocol, an application-layer protocol for delivery of e-mail over the Internet.

See: *Simple Mail Transfer Protocol (SMTP)*

SNA

Stands for Systems Network Architecture, a set of IBM mainframe networking standards and protocols introduced in 1974.

See: *Systems Network Architecture (SNA)*

SNADS

Stands for SNA Distribution Services, the e-mail messaging transport protocol for IBM's Systems Network Architecture (SNA).

Overview

SNADS is a mainframe host-based messaging system that is commonly used in SNA networking environments. Microsoft Exchange Server includes a connector for enabling messaging connectivity between SNADS mail systems and Exchange servers. You can use Microsoft SNA Server to provide the underlying network connectivity for this connector to function. The SNADS connector allows Exchange Server to leverage the functionality of existing host-based messaging systems such as AS/400 and System 3x during migration to a distributed client/server-based environment.

See Also: *Exchange Server, SNA Server*

snap-in

A component that can be loaded into the Microsoft Management Console (MMC).

Overview

Snap-ins provide a specific management capability in Microsoft Windows 2000, Windows XP, Windows .NET Server, or Microsoft server applications. Numerous snap-ins are available for administering Windows 2000–based networks, including third-party snap-ins for managing installable third-party applications and services.

Snap-ins come in two types:

- Stand-alone snap-ins (or simply "snap-ins"), which provide an associated set of administrative functions
- Extensions, which provide additional functionality to stand-alone snap-ins

The following table shows some of the snap-ins that come with Windows 2000. Not all of them appear in the administrative tools program group accessed from the Start menu.

Windows 2000 Snap-Ins

Snap-In	*Function*
Active Directory Users and Computers	Configuring Active Directory, organizing a domain, creating user and group accounts, and configuring security for networking components
Active Directory Schema	Modifying the schema
Active Directory Sites and Services	Creating and managing sites
Active Directory Domains and Trusts	Administering a domain within a domain tree
Admission Control Services Manager	Configuring Admission Control Services

(continued)

S

Windows 2000 Snap-Ins *continued*

Snap-In	*Function*
Certificate Manager	Managing digital certificates and keys
Component Services	Manages COM+
Computer Management	Managing a computer and creating access to other useful snap-ins such as Disk Management and Event Viewer
Device Manager	Managing resources used by system devices
DHCP Manager	Creating and configuring Dynamic Host Configuration Protocol (DHCP) servers
Disk Defragmenter	Defragmenting disks
Disk Management	Configuring disks and volumes
DFS Manager	Configuring the Distributed file system (Dfs) for centralized management of network resources
DNS Manager	Creating and configuring Domain Name System (DNS) servers
Event Viewer	Viewing system, application, security, and other logs on local and remote computers
File Service Management	Creating shares on local and remote computers and monitoring and configuring network connections
Group Policy Editor	Creating group policy objects (GPOs) for configuring groups of computers centrally
Index Manager	Configuring indexing of directories
Internet Authentication Service	Configuring Internet Authentication Service (IAS) service and clients
Internet Information Services (IIS)	Creating and configuring World Wide Web (WWW) and File Transfer Protocol (FTP) sites
IP Security Policy Management	Configuring Internet Protocol Security (IPsec)
Local User Manager	Managing user accounts in a workgroup
Microsoft System Information	Viewing system component details

(continued)

Windows 2000 Snap-Ins *continued*

Snap-In	*Function*
Network Management	Managing network services and policies
Removable Storage Management	Managing removable storage devices
Routing and Remote Access Management	Configuring Routing and Remote Access Service (RRAS)
Security Configuration Editor	Creating and modifying security policies
Security Configuration Manager	Managing security policies
System Monitor Log Manager	Managing System Monitor logs
System Service Management	Monitoring, starting, and stopping services
Telephony Manager	Managing Telephony API (TAPI) applications

See Also: *Microsoft Management Console (MMC)*

SNA Server

A Microsoft Corporation server application for local area network (LAN)–host integration, now replaced by Microsoft Host Integration Server.

See: *Host Integration Server*

sniffing

Passively monitoring network traffic.

Overview

Sniffing is a term used to describe the process of nonintrusively capturing network traffic. Sniffing can be used for good or bad reasons. For example, network administrators might connect a packet analyzer ("sniffer") to a local area network (LAN) segment or Ethernet switch port to troubleshoot network problems. Hackers also employ sniffers to unobtrusively examine network traffic and look for weaknesses that might be exploited.

Sniffing makes use of network interfaces running in something called "promiscuous mode." In this mode the interface reads and examines every frame or packet on

S

the segment. This is in contrast to an interface working in normal mode, where only those frames addressed to the interface (or broadcast to every interface) are processed.

See Also: *hacking, interface, network troubleshooting*

SNMP

Stands for Simple Network Management Protocol, a popular protocol for network management.

See: *Simple Network Management Protocol (SNMP)*

SOAP

Stands for Simple Object Access Protocol, a message-passing protocol used to enable distributed Web services.

See: *Simple Object Access Protocol (SOAP)*

SOA record

Stands for start of authority record, the first record in a Domain Name System (DNS) zone file.

See: *start of authority (SOA) record*

socket

A logical endpoint for communication between two hosts on a Transmission Control Protocol/Internet Protocol (TCP/IP) network.

Overview

A socket is also an application programming interface (API) for establishing, maintaining, and tearing down communication between TCP/IP hosts. Sockets were first developed for the Berkeley UNIX platform as a way of providing support for creating virtual connections between different processes.

Sockets provide a mechanism for building distributed network applications such as client/server applications. Two sockets form a complete bidirectional communication path between processes on two different TCP/IP hosts. Network-aware applications and services can create and destroy sockets as needed.

Architecture

As an endpoint for network communication between hosts, a socket is uniquely identified by three attributes:

- The host's IP address
- The type of service needed—for example, a connectionless protocol such as User Datagram Protocol (UDP) or a connection-oriented protocol such as Transmission Control Protocol (TCP)
- The port number used by the application or service running on the host

For example, the following identifier would represent a socket for the Simple Mail Transfer Protocol (SMTP) mail service running on a host with the specified IP address. (Port 25 is the well-known port number for the SMTP service on a TCP/IP host.)

```
172.16.8.55 (TCP port 25)
```

Notes

In the Win32 programming environment, sockets are implemented using a programming interface called Windows Sockets. Windows Sockets on Microsoft Windows platforms supports most Internet protocols and services, such as Hypertext Transfer Protocol (HTTP), File Transfer Protocol (FTP), and Telnet.

See Also: *Windows Sockets*

SOCKS

A circuit-layer proxy used to securely send data over distrusted networks.

Overview

SOCKS is a protocol that can be used to establish a secure connection between two computers over the Internet. SOCKS was first developed in 1990, and its current version, SOCKSv5, originated in 1995. SOCKS is widely implemented in firewall, proxy server, and virtual private network (VPN) hardware and software. SOCKS is defined in RFCs 1928, 1929, and 1961.

Implementation

To use SOCKS, you must have SOCKS-enabled client software installed on the hosts that will be communicating over the proxy server. SOCKS lets hosts on each side of a proxy server communicate with each other by establishing a relay connection between the internal and external networks. Using SOCKS, these virtual circuits are set up and torn down between the two hosts on a session-by-session basis. When a SOCKS client wants to connect to a host on the other side of a firewall or proxy server to access network resources, SOCKS server software running on the proxy server authenticates the host's request, creates a circuit-level proxy connection to the target host, requests the necessary data, and relays the information back to the requesting host.

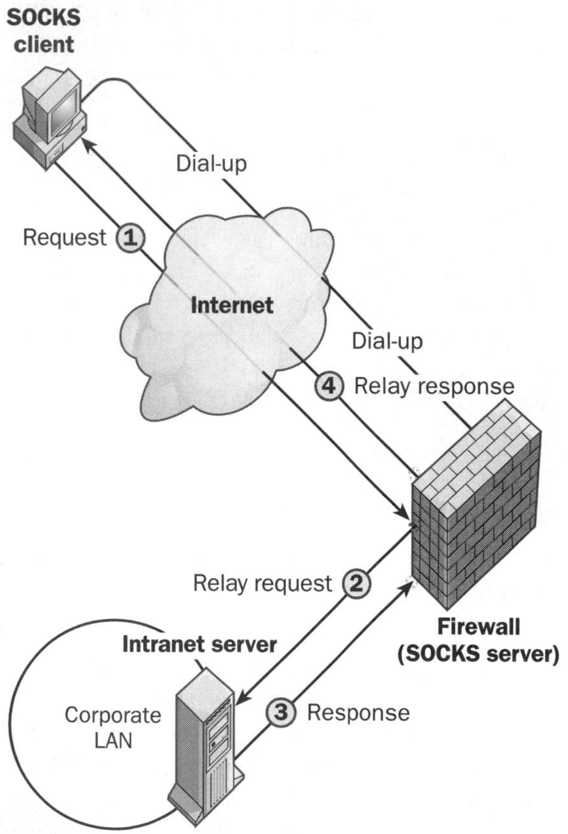

SOCKS. *How the SOCKS v5 protocol works.*

The SOCKS client on the requesting host must first negotiate an authentication method with the SOCKS server before it sends the user's credentials to the SOCKS server for authentication. SOCKS v5 supports a number of authentication methods, including Challenge Handshake Authentication Protocol (CHAP), and digital certificates based on a public key infrastructure (PKI). Once the user is authenticated, the SOCKS client sends a request message using the SOCKS protocol to the SOCKS server (the daemon or SOCKS service running on the firewall or proxy server). This request message contains the address of the target host, such as a Web server on a corporate intranet. The SOCKS server then establishes a Transmission Control Protocol (TCP) connection with the target host that functions as a proxy circuit between the requesting and target hosts. Once this "virtual circuit" is established, the SOCKS server notifies the SOCKS client and communication can begin between the two hosts, with the SOCKS server relaying each packet sent between them.

SOCKS servers usually include comprehensive logging functionality to analyze the flow of traffic between the trusted and distrusted networks.

Notes

The previous version of the protocol, SOCKS v4, was more difficult to configure on the client side and had no support for authentication of users or encryption of data. It also did not support User Datagram Protocol (UDP) traffic. SOCKS v5 is easier to configure, supports various authentication methods and encryption algorithms, and supports connectionless UDP traffic.

See Also: *Challenge Handshake Authentication Protocol (CHAP), firewall, proxy server, public key infrastructure (PKI), Transmission Control Protocol (TCP), virtual private network (VPN)*

softswitch

A media gateway controller for Voice over IP (VoIP).

Overview

Softswitches are part of the infrastructure that links VoIP implementations to the Public Switched Telephone Network (PSTN). They are used to set up telephone calls and coordinate the actions of other telephony devices such as media gateways and signaling gateways. Media gateways are used to translate traffic between Internet Protocol (IP) networks and a carrier's Asynchronous Transfer Mode (ATM) backbone network, and signaling gateways perform services similar to the Signaling System 7 (SS7) protocol used in the PSTN for call establishment, routing, and termination.

Softswitches are less expensive than traditional voice telephony switches. Many telcos are beginning to implement softswitches in their central office (CO) switching fabric to prepare for an eventual move to VoIP technologies, which will enable voice and data networks to converge.

See Also: *Asynchronous Transfer Mode (ATM), central office (CO), Public Switched Telephone Network (PSTN), telco, Voice over IP (VoIP)*

solid conductor wire

Wire that has a single solid copper core surrounded by insulation, as opposed to stranded conductor wire, which consists of many fine strands of wire woven into a conducting bundle.

Overview

Unshielded twisted-pair (UTP) cabling commonly comes in both solid and stranded forms. The solid conductor form is generally used for vertical backbone cabling between wiring closets on different floors and for horizontal runs from wiring closets to wall plates in work areas on each floor. Solid cabling is also used for permanently installed long cable runs inside and between buildings because it has less attenuation than stranded conductor wire and signals can travel farther without losing strength.

The following table compares the advantages of these two types of wire.

Solid Conductor Wire vs. Stranded Conductor Wire

Solid Conductor	*Stranded Conductor*
Less attenuation	More flexible
Better conductivity	Less likely to break or fracture
Easier to terminate	Longer lasting
Cheaper	

See Also: *stranded conductor wire, unshielded twisted-pair (UTP) cabling*

SONET

Stands for Synchronous Optical Network, a physical layer specification for broadband synchronous transmission used by telecommunications carriers.

See: *Synchronous Optical Network (SONET)*

source address

The address from which a frame or packet of data originates on a network.

Overview

The source address identifies the sending host to the receiving host and is used by the receiving host as a destination address for a response packet (such as an acknowledgment). Bridges also use the source address in building their internal routing tables of media access control (MAC) addresses for determining which packets should be forwarded to other network segments.

The source address refers to one of the following:

- The physical address, such as the MAC address of an Ethernet frame
- The logical address, such as the Internet Protocol (IP) address of an IP packet

Source addresses always identify the specific host that transmitted the packet or frame onto the network. This is in contrast to destination addresses, which sometimes direct packets to all hosts or to a specific group of hosts on the network.

Notes

You can see the source address of a packet or frame by using a network sniffer such as Network Monitor, a tool included with Microsoft Systems Management Server (SMS). Network Monitor displays source addresses in both ASCII and hexadecimal form.

See Also: *destination address*

spam

Unsolicited e-mail such as chain letters and advertising for services or products.

Overview
Spam is sometimes politely referred to as unsolicited commercial e-mail (UCE). To avoid getting spam, you can do the following:

- Avoid posting messages to Usenet newsgroups.
- Never reply to junk mail.
- Configure filters on your mail client to filter out mail containing certain keywords.
- Ask your Internet service provider (ISP) to configure its mail servers to reject spam.

If your e-mail address somehow gets on the mailing lists of spammers, you can usually configure rules on your e-mail program's Inbox to discard mail that comes from a specific address, uses words such as *sale* or *buy* in the subject header, or has specific words or phrases in the body of the message, but this is usually a tedious and losing game. A better solution is to use the Delete key. If the situation gets really bad, see whether your mail administrator or ISP can filter out spam.

See Also: *e-mail*

spanned volume
A type of disk volume in Microsoft Windows 2000 and Windows .NET Server.

Overview
A spanned volume is one made up of free space from more than one physical disk. You can extend spanned volumes by adding additional free space from other physical disks. Spanned volumes must be created on dynamic disks. They are not fault tolerant and cannot be mirrored.

Notes
In Windows NT, the equivalent to a spanned volume is a volume set.

See Also: *volume*

spanning tree algorithm (STA)
An algorithm that eliminates loops in a bridged or switched network.

Overview
The spanning tree algorithm (STA) has two main purposes:

- To establish a loop-free (tree-like) topology in a network containing bridges and switches. The elimination of loops in bridged (switched) networks is essential in order for communications to be reliable and to prevent traffic from endlessly looping around the network.
- To ensure that there is a path between each pair of network segments in a bridged network. In other words, to ensure that this loop-free tree actually "spans" the entire network.

The STA was created by Radia Perlman.

Implementation
To collect the network topology information needed to use the STA, bridges and switches periodically send to each other special data-link layer messages called bridge protocol data unit (BPDU) messages, which are based on the IEEE 802.1 specification. These messages allow a bridged/switched network to elect a root bridge for the entire network and designated bridges for each network segment, which form the basis of the spanning tree created by the algorithm. The STA determines which ports are redundant and form loops on the network and issues messages that cause those ports to be shut down (blocked) to eliminate the loops. Ports that are blocked are still active (receiving BPDU messages), however, so that if the network topology changes (for example, by a bridge going down or being moved) the port can be unblocked if required to ensure that the network is still fully spanned.

Issues
Implementing the STA on Ethernet switches can sometimes prevent Dynamic Host Configuration Protocol (DHCP) clients from renewing their leases with the DHCP server. For example, it could take a few seconds for the STA to check the ports on a switch for loops, and if a DHCP client tried to obtain a DHCP lease during this time, the DHCPREQUEST packet could be lost. Should this problem arise, you can work around it either by disabling the algorithm on switches or by manually

S

releasing and renewing the computer's Internet Protocol (IP) address using ipconfig.

See Also: *802.1, bridge, Ethernet switch*

sparse mode

One of two forms of the spanning tree algorithm (STA) used in multicasting.

Overview

Whereas dense mode routing is designed for large-scale multicasting where hosts are spread out across every corner of the network, sparse mode is intended to be efficient in routing multicast packets to clusters of hosts across a network. Sparse mode thus assumes that hosts are sparsely concentrated in small clusters or pockets scattered around a few areas of the network. An example of a situation where sparse mode multicasting might be required would be a corporate webcast originating at headquarters and targeted at a limited number of branch offices. Sparse mode is also more effective at dealing with heavy traffic congestion than dense mode when the number of intended recipients is small.

Implementation

Sparse mode multicasting creates a single multicast routing tree for all recipients. Unlike dense mode, where every corner of the network is first flooded with multicast packets and branches that are then pruned back, sparse mode relies on the recipient hosts to initiate the connection by sending a request to a nearby router.

Sparse mode multicasting can employ several different routing protocols to handle the flow:

- Core-Based Trees (CBT)
- Protocol Independent Multicast-Sparse Mode (PIM-SM)

See Also: *Core-Based Trees (CBT), dense mode, multicasting, Protocol Independent Multicast-Sparse Mode (PIM-SM), routing protocol, spanning tree algorithm (STA)*

special identity

Also known as a system group, a special group account in Microsoft Windows 2000 whose membership is controlled by the operating system itself, not by administrators or individual users.

Overview

User accounts become "members" of these special groups based on the type of system activity they participate in; you cannot modify the "membership" of these groups directly. Special identities on Windows 2000 systems include the following:

- **Creator Owner:** Consists of users who will create files or subdirectories within the current directory on an NTFS file system (NTFS) volume.
- **Everyone:** Consists of all network users, including guests and users from distrusted domains. Granting NTFS permissions to Everyone allows anyone to access the file or directory.
- **Interactive:** Consists of all users who log on interactively to the console of the machine or who access the NTFS file system on the machine from a local console.
- **Network:** Consists of all users who log on to the machine from over the network or who access the NTFS file system on the machine from over the network.
- **System:** Consists of the local operating system. System is not normally used when assigning permissions to files and directories on NTFS volumes.
- **Authenticated Users:** Consists of all users with a valid user account in the local directory database or in Active Directory directory service.
- **Anonymous Logon:** Consists of any user accounts that Windows 2000 did not authenticate.
- **Dialup:** Consists of any users who currently have a dial-up connection.

SPF

Stands for Shortest Path First, a routing algorithm used by the Open Shortest Path First (OSPF) protocol.

See: *Shortest Path First (SPF)*

SPM

Stands for statistical packet multiplexing, another name for statistical multiplexing (STM), a multiplexing technique used in frame relay and Asynchronous Transfer Mode (ATM) networking.

See: *statistical multiplexing (STM)*

spoofing

A tactic used by hackers that involves forging the identity of a packet source.

Overview

Spoofing is generally used to attempt to breach a network's security in order to compromise its systems. Spoofing is performed by altering packets' source addresses, making them appear as though they came from a trusted user within the network rather than from a distrusted outside user. Spoofing is one of the common methods used by hackers and is of particular concern when a network is connected to the Internet.

Because of limitations in the design of the current Internet Protocol (IP) standard, IPv4, spoofing of IP packets cannot be prevented, only protected against. One way to protect your network against IP address spoofing is to use the packet-filtering features of a router or firewall. Configure your packet-filtering router so that the input filter on the external router interface discards any packet coming from the external network whose source address makes it look as though it originated from your own internal network. Similarly, configure the output filter on your internal router interface to discard any outgoing packets that have a source address different from that of your internal network to protect against spoofing attacks from within your own network.

See Also: *hacking, Internet Protocol (IP), packet filtering*

spooling

The process of temporarily storing documents sent for printing on a hard disk and then sending them to the print device when it is ready (or when some other criterion has been met).

Overview

The application software that performs spooling is called a spooler. The spooler accepts and temporarily stores documents to be printed and then sends them to the printer according to predefined conditions such as print priority and schedule. Spooling of print jobs allows control to be returned more quickly to the application that generated the job. Spooling also allows jobs to be queued when the printer is unavailable so that the application does not have to generate the jobs again.

Notes

The term *spool* is actually an acronym for Simultaneous Peripheral Operation On Line.

See Also: *printing terminology*

spread spectrum

A wireless networking technology originally developed by the U.S. military for secure wireless communication.

Overview

Unlike other forms of wireless communication, spread spectrum technologies take advantage of a large portion of the electromagnetic spectrum, making it difficult for distrusted users to "listen in" on private conversations. Spread spectrum networking systems generally use very low power signals in the high radio or low microwave portion of the electromagnetic spectrum.

In the United States, spread spectrum communication can utilize three portions of the electromagnetic spectrum that have been allocated by the Federal Communications Commission (FCC) for wireless devices without special licensing:

- **Industrial band:** 902 to 928 megahertz (MHz)
- **Scientific band:** 2400 to 2483.5 MHz
- **Medical band:** 5725 to 5850 MHz

Types

Two basic mechanisms can be used to implement spread spectrum wireless communication: direct sequencing and frequency-hopping.

- **Direct sequencing:** This mechanism takes an individual binary bit from the transmission signal and converts it to a binary string. This string is then transmitted as a single wideband signal over an adjacent set of frequencies, with each bit in the string transmitted at a different frequency. The receiving station examines the bit pattern of the binary string and determines which single bit was originally transmitted by the sending station. This technology has built-in fault tolerance because electromagnetic interference (EMI) might degrade a portion of the binary string, but if the receiving station can recognize a different portion of the string, communication is assured. A typical example of direct sequencing technology might be to assign the string 10011011 to bit 1 and its inverse 01100100 to bit 0. Transmission of the bit sequence 110 would then consist of three transmitted strings: 10011011, 10011011, and 01100100.

- **Frequency-hopping:** This uses a continually changing carrier frequency. The pattern by which the carrier frequency is changed is programmed according to an algorithm known to both the sending and receiving stations. For communication to take place, the two stations must remain synchronized throughout the session. One station is designated the master station and the other the slave station. If particular frequencies within the spread spectrum communication band contain interference from other radio sources, frequency-hopping technology can avoid these frequencies by using adaptive techniques. To further enhance security, either station can also dynamically change the pattern of frequency hopping.

Uses

Spread spectrum technologies can have a variety of uses in networking, including point-to-point links between networks, wireless local area networks (LANs), and cellular-based roving network communication. One common use in networking environments is for connecting stations to a LAN when it is impractical or impossible to lay cabling. You can also use spread spectrum wireless bridge technologies to establish point-to-point or multipoint communication between buildings on a campus. These devices usually support line-of-sight connections that function to distances of 18.5 miles (30 kilometers) or more, with speed decreasing as the distance increases. Spread spectrum devices for wireless LAN stations generally have a much shorter range, usually no more than about 655 feet (200 meters).

See Also: *Direct Sequence Spread Spectrum (DSSS), direct sequencing, frequency hopping, Frequency Hopping Spread Spectrum (FHSS), wireless networking*

SQL

Stands for Structured Query Language, a standards-based language used by relational database management programs primarily for constructing queries.

See: *Structured Query Language (SQL)*

SQL Server

A high-performance client/server relational database management system (RDBMS) for the Microsoft Windows 2000 and Windows .NET Server operating systems.

Overview

A RDBMS is used in high-volume transaction-processing environments such as online order entry systems, data warehousing, decision-support applications, and e-commerce. Microsoft SQL Server includes the following advanced features:

- A distributed management framework for centrally managing all servers running SQL Server in an organization
- Built-in data replication to copy information throughout an enterprise—not only to SQL Server databases but also to Oracle, IBM DB2, Sybase, and other databases
- The Web Assistant for populating a Web server with structured query language (SQL) data for Internet or private intranet use
- Microsoft Distributed Transaction Coordinator for creating distributed transaction-based applications across multiple servers

S

- Integration with the security features of the Windows NT platform
- A high-performance, scalable, multithreaded parallel architecture
- Scalable dynamic locking architecture for page-level and row-level locking
- Data warehousing and online analytical processing (OLAP) enhancements
- Support for OLE Automation stored procedures
- Integration with Microsoft Exchange through the SQL Mail utility
- Support for Windows .NET Server, Windows 2000, Windows NT, Windows 98, and Windows 95
- A query processor that supports the complex queries used in decision support, data warehousing, and OLAP applications
- Wizards that ease tasks for administrators and programmers
- Support for Microsoft Management Console (MMC)
- Assorted tools for profiling and tuning a server's performance
- Integration with Microsoft Proxy Server and Microsoft Office 2000

SQL Server is a client/server database system. The server runs the SQL Server database software, which processes requests submitted by the database client software and sends the results back to the client. The SQL Executive and the SQL Server Database Engine service are examples of database services performed by SQL Server.

The SQL Server software is arranged in multiple layers. The Net-Library layer, which accepts connections from clients, hides the network connectivity details when a client communicates with a server running SQL Server. Net-Libraries use interprocess communication (IPC) mechanisms such as named pipes, remote procedure calls (RPCs), and Windows Sockets. Several Net-Libraries are included with SQL Server for both the server and the client. Net-Libraries on the server listen for client connection attempts.

A client computer runs the database client software, which is used to connect to the server running SQL Server, make requests, receive results, and display the results on the user's screen. Examples of database client software that can connect to SQL Server include SQL Server Enterprise Manager, ISQL/w, and Microsoft Access. The database client software is also made up of multiple layers. Users interact directly with the client application, which might present a form such as an order entry form. When the user submits the form, the client software interacts with the server running SQL Server using open database connectivity (ODBC) or DB-Library application programming interfaces (APIs). The server processes the request and returns information to the client.

For More Information
Visit *www.microsoft.com/sql.*

See Also: *database, Structured Query Language (SQL)*

SSL

Stands for Secure Sockets Layer, a transport layer security protocol used on the Internet.

See: *Secure Sockets Layer (SSL)*

SSO

Stands for Single Sign On, any technology that requires users to have only one set of credentials to access network resources.

See: *Single Sign On (SSO)*

SSP

Stands for storage service provider, a company offering outsourced storage services.

See: *storage service provider (SSP)*

STA

Stands for spanning tree algorithm, an algorithm that eliminates loops in a bridged or switched network.

See: *spanning tree algorithm (STA)*

stackable hubs

Hubs that can be connected to operate as a single hub.

Overview

Stackable hubs can be placed one above another on an equipment rack and connected using specialized short cables, generally ribbon cables. The reason for using stackable hubs is that the stacked hubs effectively create a single hub with a large number of ports and a single collision domain. This is generally superior to the older way of cascading hubs together by using uplink ports, a method which tends to generate crosstalk. Note that when you stack several hubs, the top and bottom hubs usually have a free connection that must be properly terminated in order for the stacked array to function properly.

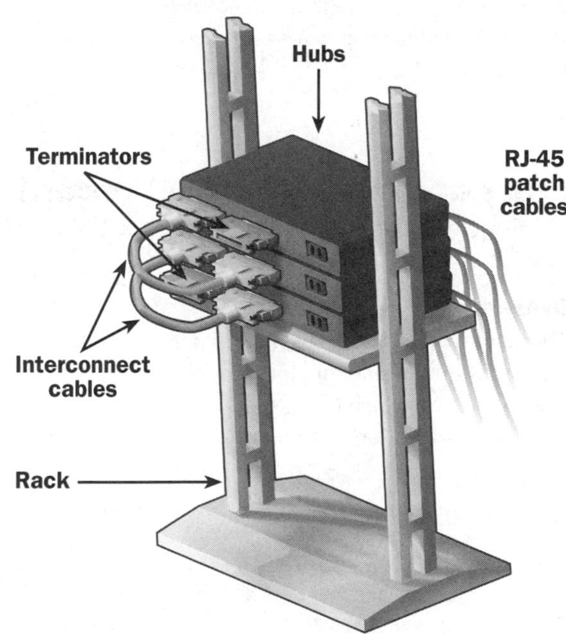

Stackable hubs. *How to connect stackable hubs.*

Besides hubs, Ethernet switches are often stackable as well. Switches are stacked mainly to provide greater scalability and increased manageability. Popular stackable Fast Ethernet switches for workgroup environments include 3Com Corporation's SuperStackII line of switches, Cisco Systems' Catalyst 2500 series, and Nortel Networks' BayStack 450 series.

See Also: *crosstalk, Ethernet switch, hub, rack*

stand-alone server

A server that does not perform logon authentication and is not part of a domain.

See: *member server*

standard Ethernet

The original Institute of Electrical and Electronics Engineers (IEEE) standard for implementing 10 megabits per second (Mbps) Ethernet over thick coaxial cabling.

See: *10Base5*

standards organizations

Organizations that help standardize technologies and practices.

Overview

Many standards organizations have contributed specifications and standards to the computer networking industry. Without these agencies, the networking world would be a nightmare of noninteroperable proprietary vendor-developed technologies. Some of the larger and more important standards bodies related to computer networking and Internet standards include

- American National Standards Institute (ANSI)
- European Computer Manufacturers Association (ECMA)
- Institute of Electrical and Electronics Engineers (IEEE)
- Internet Engineering Task Force (IETF)

S

- International Organization for Standards (ISO)
- International Telecommunication Union (ITU)
- Object Management Group (OMG)
- World Wide Web Consortium (W3C)

Many standards bodies are also devoted to specific technology areas, such as the ATM Forum and the Fibre Channel Alliance. The work of all these standards bodies is important to the long-term viability of the IT (information technology) sector and marketplace.

See Also: *American National Standards Institute (ANSI), Institute of Electrical and Electronics Engineers (IEEE), International Organization for Standardization (ISO), International Telecommunication Union (ITU), Internet Engineering Task Force (IETF), World Wide Web Consortium (W3C)*

star bus topology

A combination of star topology superimposed on a backbone bus topology.

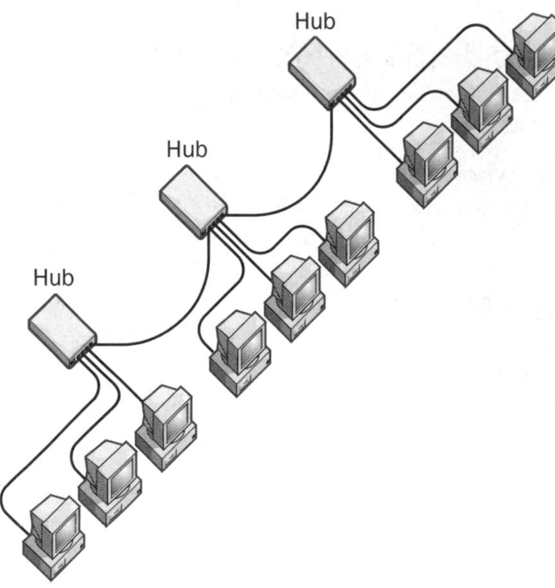

Star bus topology. *Example of a star bus topology.*

Overview

Star bus topology is a networking topology in which hubs for workgroups or departmental local area networks (LANs) are connected by using a network bus to form a single network. You can connect these hubs by using one of the following:

- Regular 10Base2 or 10BaseT cables with uplink ports on the hubs
- Crossover cables for regular (host) ports on the hub
- Special cables for stackable hubs

Notes

When you use this topology with standard Ethernet hubs, do not create an excessively large collision domain by adding too many stations. This will degrade network performance unless you segment the network by using bridges or routers.

See Also: *bus topology, star topology*

StarLAN

The popular name of 1Base5, an obsolete 1 megabit per second (Mbps) local area network (LAN) networking technology.

See: *1Base5*

start of authority (SOA) record

The first record in a Domain Name System (DNS) zone file.

Overview

The start of authority (SOA) record defines the general properties of the zone for a name server, such as the name server on which the zone file resides, the zone of authority, and the administrative contact for the domain.

Examples

Here is an example of a start of authority (SOA) record:

```
@    IN   SOA   nameserver.place.dom.
                postmaster.place.dom. (
1         ; serial number
3600      ; refresh   [1h]
600       ; retry     [10m]
86400     ; expire    [1d]
3600 )    ; min TTL   [1h]
```

This SOA record contains the following information:

- The name of the subdomain over which a particular name server has authority (nameserver.place.dom)
- The name of the host on which this zone file resides
- The e-mail address of the person who is responsible for administering the subdomain (postmaster@ place.dom)
- A serial number, which increases when the zone data is updated and which is used in zone transfers to determine whether the secondary name server needs a new version of the zone file
- A refresh interval, in seconds, that informs the secondary name server how frequently it should check with the master name server to see whether its zone information is current
- A retry interval, in seconds, that tells the secondary name server how often to contact the master name server if the initial contact is unsuccessful
- An expire interval, in seconds, that informs the secondary name server how long to keep trying to contact the master name server for a refresh of the zone data before the data expires and the secondary name server no longer responds to name queries
- The Time to Live (TTL), which is a value returned by the name server to resolvers when a name is resolved, informing the resolver how long it can cache the resolved name and Internet Protocol (IP) address

See Also: *Domain Name System (DNS), resource record (RR)*

star topology

A networking topology in which the components are connected by individual cables to a central unit, usually a hub.

Overview

Star topology is the most popular way to connect computers in a workgroup or departmental local area network (LAN), but it is slightly more expensive than using bus topology. When a computer or other networking component transmits a signal to the network, the signal travels to the hub, which forwards the signal simultaneously to all other components connected to the hub. One advantage of star topology is that the failure of a single computer or cable does not bring down the entire LAN. Another advantage is that topology centralizes networking equipment, which can reduce costs in the long run by making network management much easier.

Star topology is used mainly to

- Connect computers in a workgroup or departmental LAN using a hub.
- Connect workgroup or departmental hubs using a master hub or switch. This is a special star topology called either cascading hubs or star-wired topology.

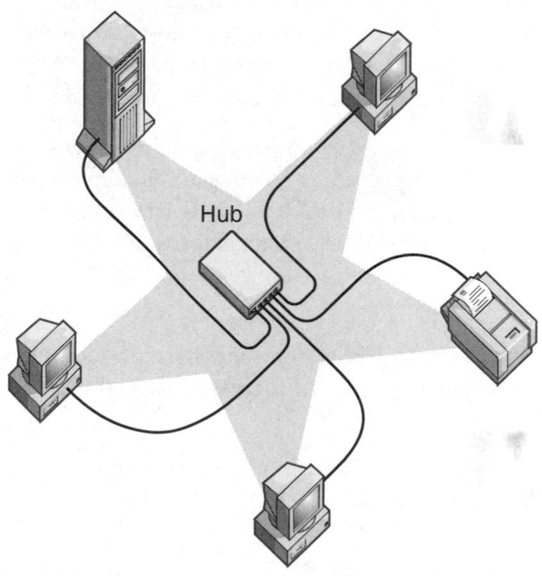

Star topology. *Example of a star topology network.*

Notes

If no one on a star network can access network resources, the hub might be down or overloaded. Try resetting the hub by using the reset switch, or try powering it off and then on. If a hub frequently needs to be reset, you might have a hardware malfunction or network bandwidth might be reaching capacity (which means that you should upgrade your components).

See Also: *bus topology, mesh topology, ring topology, star bus topology*

static address

An Internet Protocol (IP) address that is manually assigned to a host on a Transmission Control Protocol/Internet Protocol (TCP/IP) network.

Overview

Static IP addresses are usually used for

- Small workgroups whose machine configurations will not change often. Peer-to-peer networks that use either Microsoft Windows 95 or Windows 98 do not have a Dynamic Host Configuration Protocol (DHCP) server to assign IP addresses to stations on the network.
- Servers on a network, which should have an IP address that does not change. An alternative is to assign a DHCP reservation to these servers so that they receive their IP addresses automatically from a DHCP server but always receive the same reserved address.
- Windows NT–, Windows 2000–, and Windows .NET Server–based servers that are running certain services, such as DHCP, Windows Internet Name Service (WINS), or Domain Name System (DNS). Servers running these services normally require static IP addresses.

Computers running Windows support both static IP addressing and dynamic IP addressing through the DHCP.

See Also: *Dynamic Host Configuration Protocol (DHCP), IP address*

static mapping

On a Windows Internet Name Service (WINS) server, a manually entered NetBIOS name to Internet Protocol (IP) address mapping stored in the WINS database.

Overview

WINS servers normally create mappings dynamically when a WINS client performs NetBIOS name registration upon client initialization. Non-WINS clients do not register their names, so administrators must manually create WINS database entries. Once they do this, other hosts on the network can perform NetBIOS name discovery queries to resolve the NetBIOS name of non-WINS clients into their IP addresses.

See Also: *Windows Internet Name Service (WINS)*

static routing

A routing mechanism that depends on manually configured routing tables.

Overview

Static routing is generally used in smaller networks that contain only a couple of routers or when security is an issue. Routers that use static routing are sometimes called static routers. Each static router must be configured and maintained separately because static routers do not exchange routing information with each other.

For a static router to function properly, the routing table must contain a route for every network in the internetwork. Hosts on a network are configured so that their default gateway address matches the Internet Protocol (IP) address of the local router interface. When a host needs to send a packet to another network, it forwards the packet to the local router, which checks its routing table and determines which route to use to forward the packet.

Advantages and Disadvantages

Static routers are more difficult to administer than dynamic routers, but they can be more secure because the administrator controls the configuration of the router. They are therefore immune from attempts by hackers to spoof dynamic routing protocol packets in order to reconfigure the router and try to hijack network traffic.

Notes

You can configure a multihomed server as a static router in Microsoft Windows 2000 by first clicking the Advanced button on the Transmission Control Protocol/Internet Protocol (TCP/IP) property sheet. Select the Options tab, select TCP/IP Filtering and click Properties, then select Enable TCP/IP Filtering. You can then add static routes for each remote network by using the Route command.

See Also: *dynamic routing, routing table*

S

statistical multiplexing (STM)

A multiplexing technique used in frame relay and Asynchronous Transfer Mode (ATM) networking.

Overview

Statistical multiplexing (STM) enables information from a number of channels to be combined for transmission over a single channel. STM dynamically allocates bandwidth only to channels that are currently transmitting on an as-needed basis, without any bandwidth being allocated to quiet (non-transmitting) channels. This is in contrast to time-division multiplexing (TDM), where quiet devices still use up a portion of the multiplexed data stream, filling it with empty packets. STM usually packages the data from the active channels into packets and dynamically feeds them into the output channel on a first in, first out (FIFO) basis, but it can also allocate extra bandwidth to specific input channels on demand.

Switches and other devices that support statistical multiplexing usually include support for other features, such as:

- **Store-and-forward error detection and correction:** Identifies which channel sent each packet of data and corrects errors that occur
- **Data compression:** Increases the amount of data that can be sent per packet

A multiplexer that is capable of statistically multiplexing several data streams together is sometimes called a statmux. If you have a statmux at each end of a digital line, the receiving statmux can identify the channel of each packet sent by the sending statmux and demultiplex the data stream into its original data channels.

Notes

STM is sometimes referred to as statistical time-division multiplexing (STDM) or statistical packet multiplexing (SPM), but the shorter term is used more often.

See Also: *Asynchronous Transfer Mode (ATM), frame relay, multiplexer (MUX), multiplexing, time-division multiplexing (TDM)*

STDM

Stands for statistical time-division multiplexing, another name for statistical multiplexing, a multiplexing technique used in frame relay and Asynchronous Transfer Mode (ATM) networking.

See: *statistical multiplexing (STM)*

STM

Stands for statistical multiplexing, a multiplexing technique used in frame relay and Asynchronous Transfer Mode (ATM) networking.

See: *statistical multiplexing (STM)*

stop screen

A blue screen that appears whenever the Microsoft Windows NT, Windows 2000, Windows XP, or Windows .NET Server operating system experiences a fatal problem and terminates itself.

Overview

A stop screen includes the following information:

- The top of the screen shows the bugcheck information—the error code and a list of up to four developer-defined parameters.
- The middle portion of the screen lists all modules that have been successfully loaded and initialized by the operating system. This information is listed in three columns: preferred memory location, link time stamp, and driver name.
- The bottom portion shows the build number of the kernel and a stack dump that indicates the address range in which the driver might have failed.

The most important part of a stop screen is the bugcheck information in the first few lines, which gives a stop code and parameters that can help identify the source of the problem to Microsoft Corporation support technicians.

The table on the next page shows some common bugcheck codes and how to interpret them.

Common Bugcheck Codes

Code	*Description*
0x9	IRQL_NOT_GREATER_OR_EQUAL: An attempt was made to touch pageable memory at a process interrupt request level (IRQL) that was too high. This usually indicates that a driver is using improper addresses. A stack trace is usually helpful in debugging the problem.
0xA	IRQL_NOT_LESS_OR_EQUAL: Usually indicates a bad or corrupt pointer.
0x1E	KMODE_EXCEPTION_NOT_HANDLED: An exception (error) occurred with a driver or function. This is one of the most common bugcheck codes; you can often use the exception address to identify the driver or function involved.
0x20	KERNEL_APC_PENDING_DURING_EXIT: This usually indicates a problem with a third-party file system driver, such as a third-party redirector. Check with the manufacturer for an updated redirector.
0x2E	DATA_BUS_ERROR: This usually indicates a parity error in system memory. Try installing new RAM. It can also be caused by a driver accessing an address that does not exist; if swapping memory does not solve the problem, try swapping other hardware cards or install updated drivers for them.
0x3E	MULTIPROCESSOR_CONFIGURATION_NOT_SUPPORTED: This indicates mismatched CPUs in a symmetric multiprocessing (SMP) system.
0x4C	FATAL_UNHANDLED_HARD_ERROR: An error prevented the Windows NT operating system from booting properly. Common causes are missing or corrupt registry hives, a corrupt system dynamic-link library (DLL), a corrupt device driver, or an I/O problem with the disk subsystem.
0x51	REGISTRY_ERROR: This could mean corruption in the registry or an input/output (I/O) problem with the disk subsystem that prevents it from properly reading registry information. This error might also occur on a domain controller in which no more allocated space is available for storing the registry files.

(continued)

Common Bugcheck Codes *continued*

Code	*Description*
0x69	IO1_INITIALIZATION_FAILED: This indicates a failure in initializing the disk subsystem and usually means that you made an incorrect configuration decision during setup or have reconfigured the disk system incorrectly.
0x73	CONFIG_LIST_FAILED: This indicates corruption in the SAM, SOFTWARE, or SECURITY hive.
0x74	BAD_SYSTEM_CONFIG_INFO: This might indicate a corrupt SYSTEM hive in the registry, or it might mean that some critical registry keys in the hive are not present. Try LastKnownGood; if that fails, try the emergency repair disk (ERD).
0x75	CANNOT_WRITE_CONFIGURATION: This usually indicates that there are 0 bytes of free space on the system drive, so the SYSTEM hive of the registry cannot grow in size.
0x77	KERNEL_STACK_INPAGE_ERROR: This is usually caused by a bad block in the paging file or a disk controller error. If the paging file is on a Small Computer System Interface (SCSI) drive, check the cabling and termination.
0x7B	INACCESSIBLE_BOOT_DEVICE: If this occurs right after setup, it might mean that your disk controller is not supported by Windows NT. You might have to check the Windows Driver Library for a new device driver and do a custom installation. This error can also occur when you repartition the disk that contains the system partition. The solution is to edit the ARC paths in the boot.ini file. Another reason for this error is a Master Boot Record (MBR) or boot sector virus.
0x8B	MBR_CHECKSUM_MISMATCH: This usually indicates the presence of a Master Boot Record virus.
0x98	END_OF_NT_EVALUATION_PERIOD: Your evaluation copy of Windows NT has expired.

S

Notes

Sometimes you can compare the addresses of the parameters in the top portion of the stop screen with the addresses of drivers in the stack dump at the bottom and identify which driver might have caused the crash, but this will not always work. For more information on bugcheck codes and how to interpret them, check Microsoft TechNet.

See Also: *TechNet*

storage

Various technologies used to store information.

Overview

Advances in storage technologies and an explosion of enterprise storage needs have made the storage segment the hottest segment of the IT (information technology) market in the last few years. For example, demand for redundant array of independent disks (RAID) systems is doubling every year, and the overall storage utility market is expected to grow to $7 billion by 2003. New technologies such as solid state disks are eliminating the input/output (I/O) bottleneck in high-end servers, and the emergence of 10 Gigabit Ethernet (10GbE) makes storage over IP a promising technology that challenges the supremacy of Fibre Channel in the enterprise storage arena.

Types

Storage in the enterprise environment generally follows a hierarchical three-tier system:

- **Online storage:** This is the primary form of storage used by servers and is used to store data that needs to be easily accessible. The simplest form of online storage is disk storage—that is, disk drives housed within a PC server box. For additional storage other solutions might be used, including RAID 5 arrays, network attached storage (NAS) appliances, and storage area networks (SANs).
- **Nearline storage:** Also called secondary storage, this form is used to store data that infrequently needs to be accessed. Common forms of nearline storage include optical storage technologies such as CD-RW and DVD-RW drives, magneto-optical disks, and Write-Once Read-Many (WORM) disks.
- **Offline storage:** Also called tertiary storage, this form is used to store data that is archived and rarely needs to be accessed. Various forms of tape backup technologies are used for this type of storage.

The main problem with traditional disk drives, whose capacity has risen and footprint has fallen dramatically in recent years, is that the architecture of PC servers limits the amount of disk storage possible. Another issue is that free storage space inside one server cannot easily be allocated to another server. To get around these limitations, enhanced storage technologies have been developed in the last decade. The most popular of these storage technologies in the enterprise arena are currently

- **RAID-5 arrays:** These are external units that can be attached using Small Computer System Interface (SCSI) to servers to provide greater capacity than internal disk storage systems can provide. SCSI arrays are still the most popular form of storage in the enterprise arena, are easy to deploy and use, and can support many terabytes of storage.
- **Network attached storage (NAS):** These are generally stand-alone appliances that can be connected to your Ethernet network to quickly add storage capacity as needed. The main problem with NAS appliances is that they must be managed individually, so deploying a lot of them can become a management headache for administrators.
- **Storage area network (SAN):** This is a separate Fibre Channel or SCSI network containing storage appliances networked together and managed using an integrated set of tools. SANs are easier to manage than NASs but are also more expensive and complex to deploy.
- **Storage service provider (SSP):** These are companies that you can outsource your enterprise storage needs to, and they provide a managed storage environment for a wide range of business needs.

Marketplace

In the real world, different storage technologies generally overlap. Thus, an enterprise storage array such as IBM's Shark uses a combination of SAN and RAID technologies to provide up to 11 terabytes of storage. Shark connects to host servers through either UltraSCSI or Fibre Channel Enterprise Systems Connection (ESCON) links, can be deployed up to 60 miles (96 kilometers) away, supports snapshot backups, and can be used with Microsoft Windows, UNIX, and OS/390 mainframe systems. Besides IBM, the other heavyweight in the high-end storage market is EMC Corporation.

A popular vendor of NAS appliances is Snap Appliances, whose Snap Server line of storage devices can add up to 240 gigabytes (GB) of storage in minutes, support remote management through Simple Network Management Protocol (SNMP), and integrate with network management systems such as Hewlett-Packard Company's OpenView and Computer Associates' Unicentre/TNG. In addition to IBM and EMC, other popular SAN vendors include Connex and MTI Technology Corporation. Vendors of tertiary (offline) storage include VERITAS Software Corporation, EMC, and many others.

Prospects

Solid state disks are the hottest thing in storage nowadays. These disks are essentially multiple boards of synchronous dynamic random access memory (SDRAM) that are implemented in high-end servers to store most frequently used data such as pagefiles and swapfiles, temp files, log files, database tables and indexes, and logon credentials. These categories of data generally represent only about 5 percent of all stored data, but account for around 50 percent of all I/O generated by servers. Using solid state disks can eliminate the storage bottleneck from which enterprise servers have traditionally suffered.

S

See Also: *10G Ethernet, Fibre Channel, network attached storage (NAS), redundant array of independent disks (RAID), Small Computer System Interface (SCSI), storage area network (SAN), storage over IP, storage service provider (SSP), tape drive*

storage area network (SAN)

A dedicated storage network separate from the network where servers reside.

Overview

Storage area networks (SANs) currently represent the pinnacle of enterprise network storage. SANs are architectures rather than devices, and they provide a highly scalable and manageable storage solution for the needs of the largest enterprises. The idea of SANs originated in mainframe computing environments, but SANs have gained a significant foothold in distributed client/server environments in the last few years.

Typical applications that use a SAN include enterprise resource planning (ERP), Customer Relationship Management (CRM), enterprise data warehousing, and other high-availability applications that require significant amounts of storage. SANs can also be used as remote storage and archival facilities connected to corporate networks by Asynchronous Transfer Mode (ATM) or Synchronous Optical Network (SONET) connections.

Implementation

SANs use dedicated networks that contain a variety of storage technologies, including redundant array of independent disks (RAID) technologies such as disk mirroring and disk striping, magnetic and optical disk storage, and even tape libraries for archival purposes. SANs generally use high-speed Fibre Channel, a high-speed direct connection technology supporting data transfer rates of up to 1 gigabit per second (Gbps), for interconnections between SAN storage devices and server farms. The essence of the SAN idea is to have two separate networks connected: the corporate network with its servers and the storage network with its storage devices. In addition to Fibre Channel, other SAN interconnection technologies include Enterprise System Connection (ESCON) and variants of Small Computer System Interface (SCSI).

SANs can be implemented in three basic topologies:

- **Point-to-point:** Early SANs were direct physical connections between mainframe hosts and storage arrays, but this configuration is rarely used in a distributed client/server networking environment.

- **Arbitrated loop:** This approach employs Fibre Channel hubs to provide shared bandwidth with round-robin forwarding to enable multiple storage devices and servers to communicate with one another. Arbitrated loop SANs are best used in workgroup or departmental environments.
- **Fabric:** This is the most popular approach today, and it employs Fibre Channel switches to create a high-bandwidth any-to-any connection between storage devices and servers that use them. Fabric-based SANs are suitable for the largest enterprise environments.

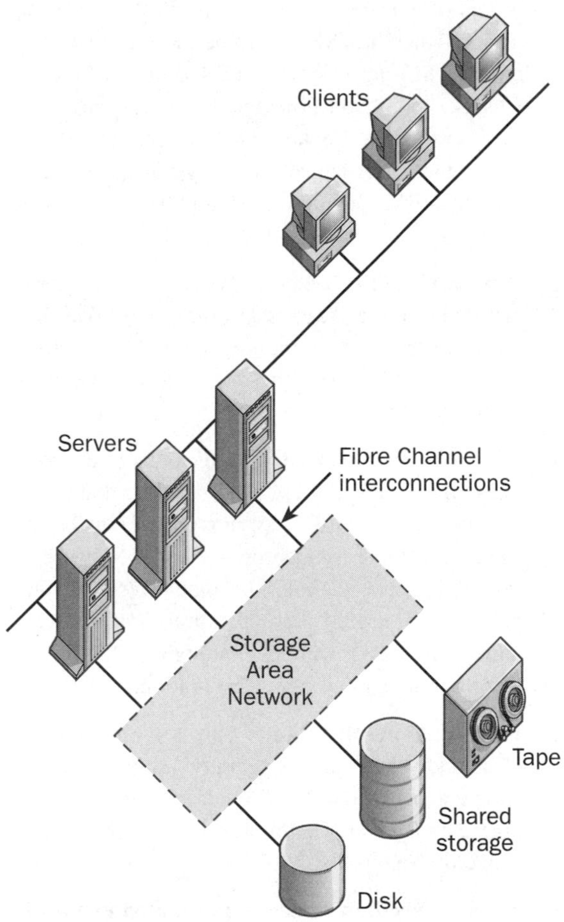

Storage area network (SAN). *Basic network architecture of a SAN.*

Marketplace

Some of the enterprise-level SAN vendors include Brocade Communications Systems, Compaq Computer Corporation, EMC Corporation, Hewlett-Packard, IBM, StorageTek, Sun Microsystems, and TrueSAN Networks. Less costly SAN solutions for mid-sized businesses are available from DotHill Systems, LSI Logic Corporation, MTI Corporation, nStor Technologies, and other vendors.

Issues

Despite the efforts of organizations such as the Storage Networking Industry Association (SNIA) and the Fibre Channel Alliance, SAN solutions from different vendors still suffer from some degree of interoperability problems, particularly in the area of Fibre Channel fabric switches. As a result, enterprise network architects who are thinking about implementing a SAN for their company are probably best off implementing a solution from a single SAN vendor.

Prospects

An emerging approach called storage over IP connects SANs to server farms using Internet Protocol (IP) running on Gigabit Ethernet (GbE). Other names for this technology are Storage over SAN (SoSAN) and Gigabit Ethernet SAN. Some analysts predict that storage over IP will eventually replace Fibre Channel as the dominant SAN technology in the enterprise, but this is likely to take a decade or so.

SAN management has traditionally used proprietary management tools, but an initiative of the FibreAlliance, which has the support of over 40 different storage vendors, is intended to change this situation. The FibreAlliance is working toward implementing a Fibre Channel Management Integration (FCMGMT-INT) Management Information Base (MIB) to allow Fibre Channel SANs to be managed using the open standard Simple Network Management Protocol (SNMP).

Notes

It is easy to get confused by the various buzzwords relating to external enterprise-level storage devices because standards in this area have not been developed and ratified by standards bodies. Here are two other related storage system concepts:

- **Direct-attached storage (DAS):** Involves a storage system connected to only a single computer using either Small Computer System Interface (SCSI) or Fibre Channel technology. DAS is usually the only solution if your servers are at different geographical locations around your enterprise or if the application that uses them can support only this form of storage—for example, Windows Clustering, which can use a shared SCSI bus.
- **Network-attached storage (NAS):** Involves data storage devices connected to computers using a standard network connection such as Ethernet. This is in contrast to SAN, in which a group of computers uses multipoint Fibre Channel technology. Another difference between NAS and SAN is that NAS involves the use of file servers similar to the Network File System (NFS) used in UNIX environments (from which the concept of NAS evolved), but SAN uses block-mode input/output (I/O) for applications such as clustering and database access. Use a SAN if your data can be centrally located within your enterprise and if your application needs to access data directly using block transfers instead of using shared files. Use NAS if your data needs to be shared between different operating system platforms or for file-based applications such as Web servers.

See Also: *Asynchronous Transfer Mode (ATM), Customer Relationship Management (CRM), enterprise resource planning (ERP), Fibre Channel, Gigabit Ethernet (GbE), redundant array of independent disks (RAID), Simple Network Management Protocol (SNMP), storage, storage over IP, Synchronous Optical Network (SONET)*

S

storage over IP

Various technologies used to transport storage data across Internet Protocol (IP) networks.

Overview

Storage over IP is an umbrella term for a group of emerging technologies intended mainly for connecting storage area networks (SANs) with server farms using IP networks. Storage over IP promises to simplify enterprise storage management by utilizing familiar networking technologies such as Fast Ethernet and Gigabit Ethernet (GbE) instead of Fibre Channel, the technology currently favored to connect SANs to server networks. Storage over IP also promises to allow SANs to grow beyond the current 6.2-mile (10-kilometer) limit imposed by Fibre Channel architecture.

Types

Some of the proposed standards for storage over IP include

- **ISCSI:** This specification allows Small Computer System Interface (SCSI) commands to be transported over Transmission Control Protocol (TCP). To implement iSCSI, you do not need to make changes to your network—the addition of Fibre Channel-to-Gigabit Ethernet switching gear is all that is required. Backers of the iSCSI specification include Adaptec, Cisco Systems, Hewlett-Packard, IBM, Quantum Corporation, and SANgate Systems.
- **EtherStorage:** A solution developed by Adaptec primarily for the lower end of the storage over IP market, EtherStorage employs Ultra-3 SCSI drives and standard GbE switches together with a proprietary IP-to-SCSI bridge.
- **Fibre Channel over IP:** This technology encapsulates Fibre Channel frames in IP packets that can be transported over GbE, Asynchronous Transfer Mode (ATM), or Synchronous Optical Network (SONET) networks. Fibre Channel over IP is supported by Brocade Communications Systems, Gadzoox Networks, Lucent Technologies, McData Corporation, and QLogic Corporation.
- **Fibre Channel Backbone:** This is similar to Fibre Channel over IP but is especially designed for the wide area network (WAN) environment and is supported by Brocade Communications Systems and Gadzoox Networks.
- **Service Specific Connection Oriented Protocol (SSCOP):** A specification developed by the International Telecommunication Union (ITU), which

employs a data-link Asynchronous Transfer Mode (ATM) protocol for sending storage data over IP.

- **Storage over IP (SOIP):** A specification developed Nishan Systems, which has patented the name "storage over IP" or "SOIP" for a technology that combines features of iSCSI and Fibre Channel over IP. SOIP is supported by Dell Computer Corporation, Quantum, Siemens, and Sun Microsystems.

See Also: *Fast Ethernet, Fibre Channel, Gigabit Ethernet (GbE), Small Computer System Interface (SCSI), storage area network (SAN), Transmission Control Protocol (TCP)*

storage service provider (SSP)

A company offering outsourced storage services.

Overview

Storage service providers (SSPs) are service providers modeled on the Application Service Provider (ASP) model that help companies manage their storage requirements. SSPs generally offer services in three areas:

- **Primary data storage:** Online storage residing either locally on your network or at a remote data center—in either case the SSP manages these devices.
- **Backup and restore:** Off-site archiving for greater security.
- **High availability:** Data is replicated off-site and is made available from anywhere.

Marketplace

Some of the popular players in the rapidly evolving SSP market include Arsenal Digital Solutions, Articulent, CreekPath Systems, ManagedStorage International, NaviSite, Nuclio Corporation, sanrise, Storability, StorageNetworks (a pioneer in this field), StorageProvider, StorageWay, and WorldStor.

See Also: *storage*

stored procedure

A precompiled set of Structured Query Language (SQL) statements that can be executed on demand as a single entity.

Overview

Stored procedures are generally stored in a database. They support features such as user-declared variables and conditional execution and can be run with a single call. They can accept parameters, and they can return parameters and status values. They can also call other stored procedures. You can create permanent stored procedures for global administrative tasks or temporary ones for a specific task.

In Microsoft SQL Server you create a stored procedure by creating a series of SQL statements. SQL Server parses and analyzes the stored procedure and stores it in various system tables. When you execute it for the first time, it is loaded into memory and compiled, storing the execution plan in the procedure cache. By preparsing and prenormalizing a stored procedure, you can achieve significant performance gains compared to using a simple SQL query.

You can use stored procedures with Microsoft SQL Server to

- Create devices and databases
- Access or update information in database tables
- Perform other administrative or user actions

A trigger is a special type of stored procedure that you can use to enforce referential integrity in a database. Other types of stored procedures supported by SQL Server include the following:

- **Extended stored procedures:** Dynamic-link libraries (DLLs) that can be loaded and run like stored procedures
- **Remote stored procedures:** Run from a remote client
- **System stored procedures:** Included with SQL Server to simplify common administrative tasks and to obtain information from system tables
- **User-defined stored procedures:** Created by users for a specific database
- **User-defined system stored procedures:** Created by users and runnable in any database

See Also: *Structured Query Language (SQL)*

S

STP cabling

Stands for shielded twisted-pair cabling, twisted-pair cabling that contains internal shielding.

See: *shielded twisted-pair (STP) cabling*

stranded conductor wire

Wire that has a core composed of many thin copper strands woven together and surrounded by insulation.

Overview

Stranded conductor wire is generally used for drop cables between computers and wall plates and for patch cables connecting patch panels with hubs and switches. Stranded conductor wire has more attenuation than solid conductor wire and should be used only for short cable runs. Stranded conductor wire is more durable and reliable than solid conductor wire because it can be bent numerous times without fracturing or breaking, and because damage to the wire has less impact on the surface area of the wire and hence on its capacity to carry alternating current.

Types

Stranded wire comes in two basic configuration types:

- **Bunch-stranded wire:** Uses a number of thin wires with the same diameter and twists them together in one direction.
- **Concentric-stranded wire:** Uses several layers of thin wires wrapped in alternating directions. These wires are generally easier to splice and terminate than bunch-stranded wires.

See Also: *solid conductor wire*

S

striped volume

A type of disk volume in Microsoft Windows 2000, Windows XP, and Windows .NET Server.

Overview

A striped volume is one that stores its data across two or more physical disks in stripes. Striping allocates data alternately and evenly across multiple physical disks. Striped volumes must be created on dynamic disks. They are not fault-tolerant and cannot be mirrored or extended. Striped volumes in Windows 2000, Windows XP, and Windows .NET Server are the equivalent of striped sets in Windows NT.

See Also: *volume*

stripe set

A type of disk volume in Microsoft Windows NT.

Overview

A stripe set is a single volume created using discontiguous free areas on two or more hard disks. Stripe sets are similar to volume sets but can give much faster read/write performance if segments reside on separately controlled drives. Use the Windows NT administrative tool Disk Administrator to create stripe sets by combining 2–32 free areas on two or more disk drives.

Notes

The Windows NT system partition and boot partition cannot be volume sets. Stripe sets also cannot be extended the way volume sets can.

stripe set with parity

A type of fault-tolerant disk volume in Microsoft Windows NT.

Overview

Stripe sets with parity are a fault tolerance technology whereby data is written simultaneously to two or more different disks. Parity information is distributed across the various disks so that if one disk drive fails, the lost data can be regenerated from the parity information. You can use the Windows NT administrative tool Disk Administrator to create, delete, and regenerate stripe sets with parity. Stripe sets with parity are often used to provide fault tolerance for application and data volumes in Windows NT. In Microsoft Windows 2000, Windows XP, and Windows .NET Server, a stripe set with parity is known as a RAID 5 volume.

See Also: *redundant array of independent disks (RAID)*

Structured Query Language (SQL)

A standards-based language used by relational database management programs primarily for constructing queries.

Overview

Structured Query Language (SQL) was originally developed by IBM for mainframe computing environments and is widely used in relational database management systems. The standard version of SQL is defined by the American National Standards Institute (ANSI), but many vendors have made enhancements to its syntax and command functions. The latest SQL standard is called SQL-92 but is more properly known as ANSI standard SQL X3.135-1992 or International Organization for Standardization (ISO) standard ISO/IEC 9075:1992. Microsoft SQL Server conforms to the ANSI SQL-92 standard and enhances this standard with additional statements for certain types of applications, such as data warehousing and Internet/intranet applications.

SQL includes a number of statements that you can use to perform different types of relational operations on the contents of a database, including creating databases and database objects, modifying these objects, and querying databases for information. The most basic SQL statement is the SELECT statement, which you can use to retrieve rows and columns of data from database tables and format the results set.

Examples

The typical format of a SELECT statement is

```
SELECT <columns> FROM <tables> WHERE <rows>
```

where a group of columns are retrieved from a table or tables in which data values are restricted to a particular row or rows. To return all the columns from a table, you can use a wildcard (but this is generally inefficient and should be avoided):

```
SELECT * FROM <tables>
```

Notes

If possible, include a WHERE clause in a SELECT statement to restrict the scope of your query and avoid unnecessary expenditure of system resources. The WHERE clause can include various comparison and logical operators, such as =, >, LIKE, BETWEEN, AND, and IS NULL.

See Also: *database, SQL Server*

structured wiring

Another name for the hierarchical system of unshielded twisted-pair (UTP) cabling used in the typical corporate network.

See: *cabling, infrastructure, premise cabling, unshielded twisted-pair (UTP) cabling*

subnet

A portion of a network that has been subnetted.

See Also: *subnetting*

subnet mask

A 32-bit number that is used to partition Internet Protocol (IP) addresses into a network ID and a host ID.

Overview

Subnet masks are used by Transmission Control Protocol/Internet Protocol (TCP/IP) services and applications to determine whether a given IP address on an internetwork is a local network address or a remote network address. Two types of subnet masks are used in TCP/IP networking:

- **Default subnet mask:** Partitions IP addresses into their network ID and host ID portions
- **Custom subnet mask:** Further partitions the network ID into a number of separate subnets by using a process called subnetting

The default subnet masks for IP address classes A, B, and C are shown in the following table. The table also shows how these subnet masks would partition an IP address such as *w.x.y.z* into a network ID and a host ID portion.

Default Subnet Masks for IP Addresses

Class	*Default Subnet Mask*	*Network ID*	*Host ID*
A	255.0.0.0	*w*	*x.y.z*
B	255.255.0.0	*w.x*	*y.z*
C	255.255.255.0	*w.x.y*	*z*

S

Implementation

Subnet masks are represented as four-octet dotted-decimal numbers, just as IP addresses are, except that the most common values for an octet in a subnet mask are 0 and 255. In binary notation, decimal 0 represents the octet 00000000, and decimal 255 represents 11111111. A subnet mask thus consists of 32 binary digits, the first n of which are 1s and the remaining of which are 0s.

When the subnet mask is logically ANDed with a 32-bit IP address of a TCP/IP host, the result is the network ID of the host—the portion of the host's IP address that identifies which network the host is on. When the inverse of the subnet mask (for example, the NOT mask) is logically ANDed with the IP address of the host, the result is the host ID of the host—the portion of the host's IP address that uniquely identifies the host on its network.

Examples

For example, consider the IP address 207.61.16.119 and the subnet mask 255.255.255.0. Converting these two numbers to binary and ANDing them gives the host's Network ID:

```
Host = 11001111 00111101 00010000 01110111
Mask = 11111111 11111111 11111111 00000000
AND  = 11001111 00111101 00010000 00000000
     = 207.61.16.0 = network ID
```

Taking the logical NOT of the subnet mask and ANDing it with the host's IP address gives the host's Host ID:

```
    Host = 11001111 00111101 00010000 01110111
NOT Mask = 00000000 00000000 00000000 11111111
     AND = 00000000 00000000 00000000 01110111
         = 0.0.0.119 = host ID
```

S

See Also: IP address, subnetting

subnetting

Partitioning a single Internet Protocol (IP) network into multiple subnets.

Overview

To subnet an IP network, you take the assigned network ID and borrow bits from the host ID to establish a group of subnet IDs (subnetted network IDs), one for each subnet. The more bits you borrow, the more subnets you produce, but the fewer the number of possible hosts for each subnet. The borrowing process also defines a unique custom subnet mask for the network. Subnets are then typically joined together using routers.

The advantages of subnetting include

- Reducing network congestion by limiting the range of broadcasts using routers
- Enabling different networking architectures to be joined

Implementation

To subnet your network, you first determine how many subnets you need and the maximum number of possible hosts on each subnet. Then use one of the three tables below, depending on whether you have a Class A, B, or C network ID assigned to your network.

Class A Subnetting Table

Subnet Mask	*Number of Subnets*	*Number of Hosts per Subnet*
255.0.0.0	1	16,777,214
255.128.0.0	2	8,388,608
255.192.0.0	4	4,194,302
255.224.0.0	8	2,097,150
255.240.0.0	16	1,048,574
255.248.0.0	32	524,286
255.252.0.0	64	262,142
255.254.0.0	128	131,070
255.255.0.0	256	65,534
255.255.128.0	512	32,766
255.255.192.0	1024	16,382
255.255.224.0	2048	8190
255.255.240.0	4096	4094
255.255.248.0	8192	2046
255.255.252.0	16,384	1022
255.255.254.0	32,768	510
255.255.255.0	65,536	254
255.255.255.128	131,072	126
255.255.255.192	262,144	62
255.255.255.224	524,288	30
255.255.255.240	1,048,576	14
255.255.255.248	2,097,152	6
255.255.255.252	4,194,304	2

Class B Subnetting Table

Subnet Mask	Number of Subnets	Number of Hosts per Subnet
255.255.0.0	1	65,534
255.255.128.0	2	32,766
255.255.192.0	4	16,382
255.255.224.0	8	8190
255.255.240.0	16	4094
255.255.248.0	32	2046
255.255.252.0	64	1022
255.255.254.0	128	510
255.255.255.0	256	254
255.255.255.128	512	126
255.255.255.192	1024	62
255.255.255.224	2048	30
255.255.255.240	4096	14
255.255.255.248	8192	6
255.255.255.252	16,384	2

Class C Subnetting Table

Subnet Mask	Number of Subnets	Number of Hosts per Subnet
255.255.255.0	1	254
255.255.255.128	2	126
255.255.255.192	4	62
255.255.255.224	8	30
255.255.255.240	16	14
255.255.255.248	32	6
255.255.255.252	64	2

Examples

For example, consider a class B network that uses the network ID 172.16.0.0. If this network needs to be subnetted into six subnets, you can accomplish this using a custom subnet mask of 255.255.224.0. Each subnet can be shown to support a maximum of 8190 hosts. The IP address blocks for these six subnets can be selected from the eight possible subnets:

- 172.16.0.1 to 172.16.31.254
- 172.16.32.1 to 172.16.63.254
- 172.16.64.1 to 172.16.95.254
- 172.16.96.1 to 172.16.127.254
- 172.16.128.1 to 172.16.159.254
- 172.16.160.1 to 172.16.191.254
- 172.16.192.1 to 172.16.223.254
- 172.16.224.1 to 172.16.255.254

See Also: *IP address, subnet mask, supernetting*

subtree

A major logical section of the Microsoft Windows 2000, Windows XP, and Windows .NET Server registries.

Overview

Subtrees are the root keys of the registry, and all other registry keys are subkeys of these root keys. The following table summarizes the functions of the five subtrees of the registry.

Subtrees of the Windows NT, Windows 2000, Windows XP, and Windows .NET Server Registries

Subtree	*Function*
HKEY_LOCAL_MACHINE	Contains configuration information for the local machine, including all hardware and software settings
HKEY_CLASSES_ROOT	Provides compatibility with Windows 3.*x* and points to the Classes subkey of HKEY_LOCAL_MACHINE
HKEY_CURRENT_CONFIG	Provides information about the active hardware profile
HKEY_CURRENT_USER	Contains the settings of the user who is currently logged on interactively and points to the SID_# of HKEY_USERS, in which SID_# is the security ID string of the current user

(continued)

S

Subtrees of the Windows NT, Windows 2000, Windows XP, and Windows .NET Server Registries *continued*

Subtree	*Function*
HKEY_USERS	Contains default system settings and the settings of the user who is currently logged on interactively, plus all previously logged on users

Notes

In Windows 98 and Windows Millennium Edition (Me), a sixth subtree called HKEY_DYN_DATA is generated dynamically and is used for performance measuring by means of System Monitor and plug and play configuration of devices. This subtree is also called the hardware tree.

Most registry troubleshooting takes place in the HKEY_LOCAL_MACHINE\System\Current ControlSet subkey.

See Also: *registry*

supernetting

The opposite of subnetting.

Overview

Subnetting involves creating a subnet mask that causes an Internet Protocol (IP) address to have more network ID bits than its default (classful) subnet mask. For example, the default subnet mask for a Class B address is 255.255.0.0, which identifies addresses for this network as having 16 network ID bits and 16 host ID bits. Subnetting is used to divide the default network into smaller networks. For example, a subnetted subnet mask of 255.255.128.0 identifies each Class B address as having 17 network ID bits and only 15 host ID bits.

Supernetting is the opposite procedure—instead of borrowing bits from the host ID to increase the bits for the network ID (thus increasing the number of networks), supernetting borrows bits from the network ID to increase bits for the host ID, thus combining smaller networks to create larger networks. For example, a supernetted subnet mask of 255.254.0.0 identifies each class B address as having 15 network ID bits and 17 host ID bits, thus creating fewer networks, each with more hosts, than when using the default subnet mask.

Implementation

Supernetting is needed because the number of available class B addresses is small. By using supernetting, contiguous blocks of class C addresses can be combined and used for networks larger than a single class C block can satisfy. For example, if a company needs to deploy 2000 hosts as an IP network that is directly connected to the Internet, it can assign IP addresses for these hosts by

- Using a single class B network ID. This approach is wasteful, as each class B network can support up to 65,534 different hosts, so most of these addresses would end up not being used. Also, it might be difficult or impossible to obtain a class B network ID from your Internet service provider (ISP), as they might have none available to assign.
- Using eight separate class C network IDs, each of which can support up to 254 different hosts, making a total of 8 x 254 = 2032 hosts. This method would work, but it would lead to poorer routing performance because each router would require eight entries in its routing table, one for each of the eight networks to which frames could be forwarded.
- Using supernetting to collapse the above block of eight class C network IDs into a single supernetted network ID. This is the best solution, as only one routing table entry will be required. The router must support classless interdomain routing (CIDR) for this procedure to work (most routers on the Internet support CIDR).

See Also: *classless interdomain routing (CIDR), IP address, subnet mask, subnetting*

surge protector

Also known as a surge suppressor, a device that protects sensitive data communications equipment (DCE) and data terminal equipment (DTE) from sudden rises in power line voltages called surges or spikes.

Overview

Surges occur only with copper cabling such as twisted-pair cabling or coaxial cabling—they do not occur with fiber-optic cabling, which is one advantage of using this more expensive type of cabling for networking applications. Surge protectors use various technologies for absorbing or deflecting unwanted electrical current, including avalanche diodes, metal oxide varistors, and chokes or filters. One of the best electrical protection methods, especially for copper wiring runs between different buildings, is to use opto isolators, which convert electrical signals to light and then back again, thus providing true electrical isolation between the connected buildings. However, opto isolation in itself does not provide surge protection; this is the responsibility of the other components described, the most common component being one of the various types of diodes.

Surge protectors for computer networking come in two main types:

- **Data-line surge protectors:** Connected to network cabling to prevent power surges from damaging networking components.
- **Alternating current (AC) outlet surge protectors:** Connected to AC outlets that provide power for networking components. These surge protectors prevent AC power spikes from damaging networking components.

See Also: *data communications equipment (DCE), data terminal equipment (DTE)*

SVC

Stands for switched virtual circuit, circuit-switching where switches are dynamically set up and torn down as needed.

See: *switched virtual circuit (SVC)*

switch

Any device that can control the flow of electrical signals.

Overview

A number of types of switches are used in computer networking for different purposes. For example, to control access by computers to printers, keyboards, and monitors you can use

- **Matrix switches:** Have a keypad for mapping input ports to output ports and are typically used to connect several printers to several workstations
- **Code-operated switches:** Use a data string sent by the PC to select the printer port to be used
- **Port-contention or scanning switches:** Use several input ports but only one output port and monitor the input ports continually for data to route to the output port
- **Keyboard Video Mouse (KVM) switches:** Allow one keyboard/video-monitor/mouse to be used for several servers

In the context of high-speed Ethernet networks, the term *switch* refers to an Ethernet switch, also called a local area network (LAN) switch or simply a switch. Thus, the phrase "routers and switches" is understood to mean "routers and Ethernet switches." In general, when referring to controlling data flow within a network, the term *switch* describes any data-link layer device that transfers frames between connected networks. Besides Ethernet, another popular networking technology that employs switches is Asynchronous Transfer Mode (ATM) networking.

Finally, the term *switch* is also used to refer to a device used at a telco central office (CO) for establishing connections in circuit-switched services or for forwarding packets in packet-switched services.

See Also: *Asynchronous Transfer Mode (ATM), central office (CO), circuit-switched services, data-link layer, Ethernet, Ethernet switch, Keyboard Video Mouse (KVM) switch, packet-switching services*

Switched 56

A digital switched-data communication technology that provides full-duplex dial-up connections at a speed of 56 kilobits per second (Kbps).

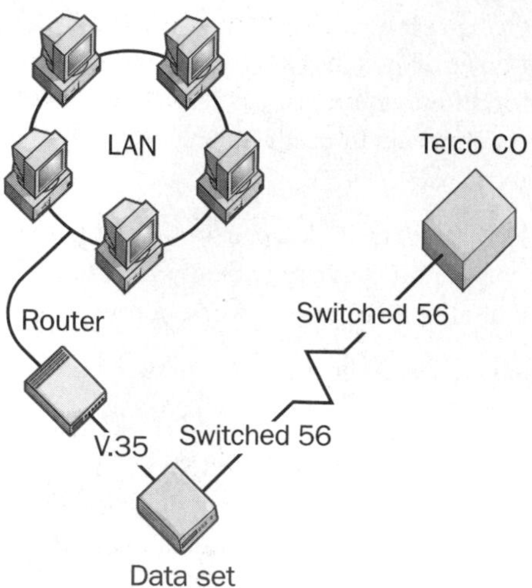

Switched 56. *Using the Switched 56 service.*

Overview

Switched 56 is essentially the dial-up version of digital data service (DDS) and is generally cheaper than leased-line services. A device called a data set, which is a type of Data Service Unit (DSU), provides Switched 56 services to customer premises. For a typical local area network (LAN) connection, a router on the LAN is attached to the data set by using a V.35 serial interface. The data set is then connected over the customer's local loop twisted-pair wiring to access equipment located at the telco's central office (CO).

Switched 56 uses the same communication channels as DS0. You can establish circuits by manually entering the destination number on a numeric keypad or (more typically) by using in-band signaling when connecting bridges or routers to the service. Depending on the wiring at the customer premises and the equipment at the CO, you can use one of three configurations for this service:

- **Type I service:** Uses a two-pair (4-wire) connection and is supported up to 3.5 miles (5.5 kilometers) from the CO over standard 26-gauge copper twisted-pair wiring.
- **Type II service:** Uses a one-pair (2-wire) connection with in-band signaling. This type is not widely implemented.
- **Type III service:** Uses a one-pair (2-wire) connection with out-of-band signaling and is supported to up to 3.5 miles (5.5 kilometers) from the CO on 22-gauge or 24-gauge copper twisted-pair wiring and includes forward error correction for enhanced data transmission. Although Type III service appears to be full-duplex, in reality time-compression multiplexing (TCM) rapidly switches half-duplex communication at 160 Kbps to simulate full-duplex at 56 Kbps.

Notes

Some carriers offer other higher speed versions of Switched 56. For example, some carriers offer Switched 56 as a 64-Kbps service under the name Switched 64. Other higher dial-up services include Switched 384 and Switched 1536, although these are not widely offered anymore.

Switched 56 is a data-only service that is often available where Integrated Services Digital Network (ISDN) is not available. However, Switched 56 does not support advanced ISDN features such as caller ID and has greater latency for establishing a connection. The cost is typically billed in the same way that ordinary telephone calls are—that is, local calls are free and long distance is billed by the minute.

Dial-up Switched 56 was originally used as a backup wide area network (WAN) link between two networks connected by expensive T1 lines, but it has been phased out by most carriers in favor of ISDN.

See Also: *telecommunications services*

Switched Multimegabit Data Services (SMDS)

A high-speed metropolitan area network (MAN) data service offered by some telcos.

Overview

Switched Multimegabit Data Services (SMDS) is a connectionless, shared-medium telecommunications service that can support data transfer speeds ranging from 56 kilobits per second (Kbps) to 34 megabits per second (Mbps). SMDS was developed by Bellcore in the late 1980s and was first deployed in 1992. SMDS was the first high-speed broadband networking technology offered to subscribers for high-speed wide area network

(WAN) communications and was a precursor to Asynchronous Transfer Mode (ATM) networking. SMDS never really caught on, however, and most carriers are now phasing it out, offering ATM and Synchronous Optical Networking (SONET) services instead. About the only place where SMDS is still provisioned in preference to ATM is Great Britain, where British Telecom (BT) continues to offer this service to customers.

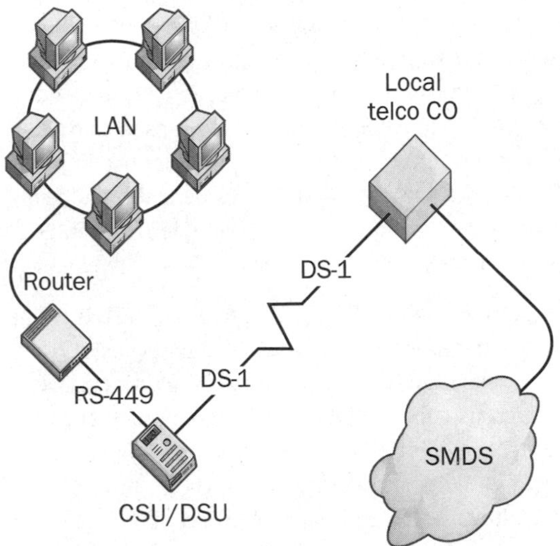

Switched Multimegabit Data Services (SMDS). *Connecting a LAN to an SMDS service.*

Implementation

SMDS is a packet-switching technology similar to Frame Relay and cell-switched ATM. SMDS cells are, in fact, almost identical to ATM cells but use an 8-bit access control field instead of a 4-bit generic flow control field as in ATM. In contrast to the connection-oriented switched-fabric of ATM, however, SMDS is a connectionless service that operates over a shared medium. SMDS and ATM are thus very different in operation and architecture.

The subscriber typically connects to the carrier's SMDS service through a switch or router using an integrated Channel Service Unit/Data Service Unit (CSU/DSU). The CSU/DSU demark point connects to the carrier's SMDS switches over a copper DS-1 connection (1.544 Mbps) for low-speed access or a fiber DS-3 connection (44.736 Mbps) to achieve the highest possible transmission speeds. This point of connection between the subscriber's LAN and the telco's central office (CO) is called the Subscriber Network Interface (SNI). The CO provides a gateway to the SMDS packet-switching network, which consists of high-speed switches joined by trunk lines connecting different telco COs.

An SMDS packet consists of a header with the source address, destination address, and a payload of up to 9188 bytes. The SMDS payload is large so that SMDS can easily encapsulate Ethernet, Token Ring, and Fiber Distributed Data Interface (FDDI) frames for WAN transmission. The E.164 addressing scheme uses decimal numbers up to 15 digits long and includes a country code, area code, and subscriber ID number (similar to ordinary telephone numbers). Different address classes support different data transfer speeds. The serial protocol used for communication between the customer premises equipment and SMDS equipment at the telco's CO is called the SMDS Interface Protocol (SIP), which is based on the IEEE 802.6 standard for MANs. The primary function of SIP is to provide encapsulation of the LAN protocol. (Internet Protocol, Internetwork Packet Exchange, AppleTalk, and just about anything else is supported.) Higher-layer protocols support processes such as address resolution and source address screening.

See Also: *802.6, Asynchronous Transfer Mode (ATM), Channel Service Unit/Data Service Unit (CSU/DSU), Ethernet, Fiber Distributed Data Interface (FDDI), frame relay, metropolitan area network (MAN), router, Synchronous Optical Network (SONET), telco, Token Ring, wide area network (WAN)*

switched virtual circuit (SVC)

Circuit-switching where switches are dynamically set up and torn down as needed.

Overview

Switched virtual circuits (SVCs) are used in circuit-switched services such as the Public Switched Telephone Network (PSTN) and Integrated Services Digital Network (ISDN). The PSTN employs a separate signaling network called Signaling System 7 (SS7) for establishing a communications session between two end nodes. The SS7 is used to configure switches in the telco switching fabric in order to establish a temporary path between the two end nodes. Once the call is finished, SS7 is used to tear down the connection, freeing up these switches to be used for other connections.

SVCs are also employed in certain wide area network (WAN) services such as Asynchronous Transfer Mode (ATM) and frame relay networking. Here different signaling methods are used to set up a temporary switched path through the ATM or frame relay cloud. For example, ATM can use the Interim Interswitch Signaling Protocol (IISP) or the Private Network-to-Network Interface (PNNI) signaling protocols to set up and tear down SVCs, and it can also use Multiprotocol Label Switching (MPLS) to route cells over ATM wide area network (WAN) links.

Comparison

SVCs might be contrasted with permanent virtual circuits (PVCs), which are more commonly used in ATM and frame relay WAN environments. PVCs are point-to-point connections between two end nodes that are permanently configured by the service provider and that utilize dedicated switches in the provider's switching fabric. PVCs are more expensive than SVCs because they need dedicated switching resources. In contrast, SVCs are temporary links in which the actual path over which frames are routed between the two end nodes varies from session to session. Each new session thus requires a new switching path to be established, with the result that SVCs are more flexible and cheaper than PVCs but often suffer from inconsistent connection quality between different sessions.

Notes

Most telcos still offer only PVCs for their wide-area ATM service offerings, mainly because SVCs are more difficult to implement due to the extra signaling protocols involved.

S

See Also: *Asynchronous Transfer Mode (ATM), circuit-switched services, frame relay, Integrated Services Digital Network (ISDN), Multiprotocol Label Switching (MPLS), permanent virtual circuit (PVC), Public Switched Telephone Network (PSTN), telco, wide area network (WAN)*

Symmetric Digital Subscriber Line (SDSL)

A form of business-grade Digital Subscriber Line (DSL) service.

Overview

Symmetric Digital Subscriber Line (SDSL) is used to provide business subscribers with permanent, high-speed data connections at speeds similar to dedicated T1 lines but at much lower prices. SDSL is based on High-bit-rate Digital Subscriber Line (HDSL) and provides data transfer speeds of 1.5 megabits per second (Mbps) in North America and 2.048 Mbps in Europe. Unlike its cousin Asymmetric Digital Subscriber Line (ADSL), which is popular in the residential broadband Internet access market, HDSL is a symmetric technology in which upstream and downstream speeds are equal.

SDSL employs the 2 Binary 1 Quaternary (2B1Q) line coding scheme used by the Basic Rate Services (BRI) form of Integrated Services Digital Network (ISDN). Although its cousin HDSL needs two pairs of copper wires (four wires), SDSL requires only one pair of wires (two wires) to work. Unlike ADSL, however, which allows a single phone line to carry both voice and data by using a splitter to "split off" frequencies above 26 kilohertz (KHz) for DSL signaling, SDSL takes complete control of the frequency spectrum of the wires, uses no splitter, and provides a data-only service.

SDSL maximum data rates vary with distance from the telco central office (CO). For distances up to 10,000 feet (3 kilometers), speeds of 1.5 Mbps are supported, which is equivalent to T1 speed. At farther distances speeds drop, until at 18,000 feet (5.5 kilometers) SDSL can only carry data at 416 kilobits per second (Kbps).

In the last few years, SDSL has became an attractive offering from competitive local exchange carriers (CLECs) who wanted to compete with high-priced T1 lines offered by incumbent local exchange carriers (ILECs), who generally used HDSL for provisioning these services.

Notes

SDSL is sometimes interpreted to stand for single-line DSL instead of symmetric DSL because it uses a single twisted-pair copper wire.

See Also: *Asymmetric Digital Subscriber Line (ADSL), Basic Rate Interface ISDN (BRI-ISDN), central office (CO), Competitive Local Exchange Carrier (CLEC), High-bit-rate Digital Subscriber Line (HDSL), Incumbent Local Exchange Carrier (ILEC), Integrated Services Digital Network (ISDN), line coding, T1, telco*

SYN attack

A popular form of denial of service (DoS) attack.

Overview

Also called SYN flooding, the SYN attack is a form of DoS attack directed at Transmission Control Protocol/ Internet Protocol (TCP/IP) networks connected to the Internet. A SYN attack is a protocol-level attack that can make a computer's network services unavailable to other users. SYN flooding is a DoS methodology specific that exploits the session establishment mechanism of the TCP. Using SYN flooding, an attacker can usurp control of all possible TCP/IP connections to a Web server or other Internet resource, making it impossible for legitimate users to access the resource. The *SYN* refers to the "**syn**chronize sequence **n**umber" message that is used to initialize a TCP connection.

Implementation

A malicious user initiates a SYN attack by sending a Transmission Control Protocol (TCP) connection request (SYN packet) to a targeted server in a network, usually a Web server. The attacker uses spoofing to alter the source IP address in the SYN packet. When the server receives the connection request, it allocates resources for handling and tracking the new connection and responds by sending a SYN-ACK packet to the nonexistent source address. Because there is no response to the SYN-ACK packet, the server continues to retransmit SYN-ACK several times (five times in Microsoft Windows NT) at increasingly longer time intervals. Finally, after the last retransmission, the server gives up and deallocates the resources previously allocated for the connection. For servers running Windows NT, the default time for this entire process is 189 seconds. The attacker configures software to automatically send large numbers of TCP SYNs in an attempt to tie up the server's TCP resources and prevent other users from connecting to the server.

Notes

SYN attacks against private networks are simple to prevent: you configure a firewall with access lists to accept only incoming IP addresses with known addresses. However, if you are running a Web server that needs to be accessible to anyone on the Internet, it is usually more difficult to defend the server against a SYN attack because if you configure an input filter, the attacker can simply modify the source IP address in the SYN packets. Ways to defend Web servers against SYN attacks include decreasing the time-out period for the TCP three-way handshake mechanism, increasing the size of the SYN-ACK queue, and applying various vendor-supplied patches to your Web server. For more information on configuring Internet Information Services (IIS) servers to withstand SYN attacks, consult the *Microsoft Internet Information Server Resource Kit* from Microsoft Press.

If you are running a Web server and your Web clients are receiving messages such as "The connection has been reset by the remote host," you might be the target of a SYN attack. If you are running IIS as your Web server, type **netstat –n –p tcp** at the command prompt to examine the number of TCP connections in a SYN_RECEIVED state. A large number of SYN_RECEIVED connections might indicate that your server is under attack.

See Also: *denial of service (DoS), hacking, TCP three-way handshake, Transmission Control Protocol (TCP)*

sync

Stands for synchronous transmission, serial transmission in which the sending and receiving nodes are synchronized together by a timing signal.

See: *synchronous transmission*

S

Synchronous Data Link Control (SDLC)

A data-link layer protocol developed in the 1970s by IBM for its Systems Network Architecture (SNA) networking environment.

Overview

Synchronous Data Link Control (SDLC) is primarily used in wide area networks (WANs) that use leased lines to connect mainframe SNA hosts and remote terminals. SDLC was the first bit-oriented synchronous transmission protocol developed by IBM. It quickly displaced the older, less efficient, character-oriented synchronous protocols such as Bisync and DDCMP. In a serial SDLC link, data is sent as a synchronous bit stream divided into frames that contain addressing and control information in addition to the payload of data.

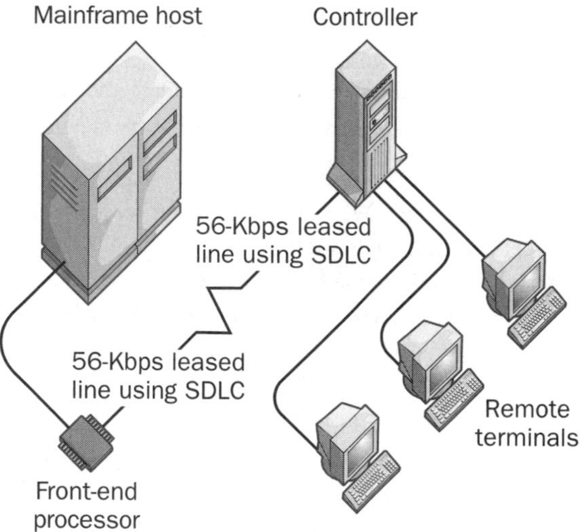

Synchronous Data Link Control (SDLC). *Connecting remote terminals to a mainframe host using SDLC.*

Implementation

SDLC uses a master/slave architecture in which one station is designated as primary (master) and the remaining stations are secondary (slaves). The primary station establishes and tears down SDLC connections, manages these connections, and polls each secondary station in a specific order to determine whether any secondary station wants to transmit data. You can use SDLC in a variety of connection topologies, including direct point-to-point connections between a primary and a secondary station and multipoint connections between a primary and a group of secondary stations. Ring topologies are also possible in which a primary controls a ring of secondary stations and is itself part of the ring.

Notes

A number of popular protocols have been derived from the SDLC protocol and standardized by various standards bodies. These include the following:

- **High-level Data Link Control (HDLC):** Developed by the International Organization for Standardization (ISO) and used by Cisco Systems routers for serial communication over leased lines as an alternative to the Point-to-Point Protocol (PPP)
- **Link Access Procedure Balanced (LAPB):** Part of the X.25 protocol stack
- **Logical Link Control (LLC) or IEEE 802.2:** The most popular data link protocol for local area networks (LANs)

See Also: *High-level Data Link Control (HDLC), Systems Network Architecture (SNA)*

Synchronous Optical Network (SONET)

A physical layer specification for broadband synchronous transmission used by telecommunications carriers.

Overview

Synchronous Optical Network (SONET) can simultaneously carry voice, video, and data over long distances of fiber-optic cabling at speeds in excess of 1 gigabit per second (Gbps). SONET was developed by Bellcore in the mid-1980s to carry high-volume voice traffic on the Public Switched Telephone System (PSTN). SONET was standardized by the American National Standards Institute (ANSI). A European version called Synchronous Digital Hierarchy (SDH), standardized by the International Telecommunication Union (ITU), is almost identical to the SONET specification.

S

Uses

SONET is primarily used by telecommunications carriers (telcos) as the underlying transport mechanism for Asynchronous Transfer Mode (ATM) networking. As such, SONET is widely deployed in both the internal telco switching networks and the trunk networks owned by long-distance carriers. SONET is used in the enterprise environment mainly as the underlying transport for high-speed ATM wide area network (WAN) connections. SONET is a reliable WAN technology that typically provides better than five-nines (99.999 percent) uptime.

Implementation

SONET transmission is generally built from multiplexed DS-0, DS-1, or DS-3 digital signal channels. SONET employs optical time-division multiplexing (TDM) technologies to form a single Synchronous Transport Signal (STS) link that is demultiplexed at the receiving end. The basic SONET transmission rate is 87 bytes transmitted every 125 microseconds, and these SONET frames are transmitted whether or not payload (data) is present. As a result, SONET tends to be somewhat wasteful of bandwidth, with utilizations in access networks often below 5 percent and in ATM backbones below 30 percent. SONET frames expand in size as the speed increases, with 16,704-byte frames being employed for OC-192 circuits. SONET transports local area network (LAN) traffic such as Gigabit Ethernet (GbE) frames by encapsulating them within SONET frames.

SONET capacity is measured in optical carrier (OC) units. A standard Synchronous Transport Signal (STS) SONET channel is equivalent to one OC unit and consists of 810 multiplexed 64 kilobit-per-second (Kbps) DS0 circuits forming a total capacity of 51.84 megabits per second (Mbps). Of these 810 circuits, 783 are used for payload and 27 are used for framing, error correction, format identification, and other forms of protocol overhead. The table below shows some of the currently defined SONET speeds.

SONET is usually implemented in telco networks as a dual-ring topology in order to provide redundancy and fault tolerance. One ring is the active ring and carries traffic in one direction only. The backup ring remains inactive unless a break in the primary ring occurs, in which case the backup ring takes over and carries traffic in the opposite direction. SONET rings utilize a self-healing technology called Automatic Protection Switching (APS) that can detect when the active ring is broken and switch traffic to the backup ring within 50 milliseconds.

SONET Speeds

Electrical Signal	*Optical Carrier*	*Speed*
STS-1	OC-1	51.48 Mbps
STS-3	OC-3	155.52 Mbps
STS-12	OC-12	622.08 Mbps
STS-24	OC-24	1.24 Gbps
STS-48	OC-48	2.48 Gbps
STS-192	OC-192	9.95 Gbps

Issues

Because SONET was originally designed as a circuit-switched TDM communications technology, it is ill-suited to carrying packet data and wasteful of bandwidth when used for this purpose. SONET was designed for carrying voice, a form of traffic that is highly sensitive to latency and jitter, and not packet data, which can tolerate high degrees of variation and delay.

SONET is also complex and expensive to deploy, which is why its implementation has been limited to telco networks. Due to the large installed base of telco SONET equipment, SONET is likely to remain around for many years despite the emergence of optical Ethernet in the metropolitan area network (MAN) as a viable alternative. SONET's main advantage over Gigabit Ethernet (GbE) and emerging 10 Gigabit Ethernet (10GbE) technologies is that it can transport data over much longer distances than these newer technologies can. Even if local exchange carriers (LECs) eventually migrate their systems entirely to 10GbE, SONET is likely to remain the technology of choice for inter-exchange carriers (IXCs) to carry data on their long-haul trunk lines.

Prospects

The trend with many carriers is to abandon SONET entirely except for use as a common communications interface passing traffic off to other carriers. Some newer carriers such as Yipes Communications are pursuing this route, using GbE instead of SONET within the remaining portion of their MANs.

A new SONET technology called resilient packet ring (RPR) enables SONET to simultaneously utilize both rings in a standard dual-ring system. If one ring fails, all traffic is routed to the remaining ring.

See Also: *American National Standards Institute (ANSI), Asynchronous Transfer Mode (ATM), DS-0, Gigabit Ethernet (GbE), inter-exchange carrier (IXC), local exchange carrier (LEC), multiplexing, optical carrier (OC-x) level, Public Switched Telephone Network (PSTN), resilient packet ring (RPR), telco, wide area network (WAN)*

synchronous transmission

Serial transmission in which the sending and receiving nodes are synchronized together by a timing signal.

Overview

Synchronous transmission is a form of serial transmission that uses clocking circuitry at both the transmitting station and the receiving station to ensure that communication is synchronized. This is in contrast to asynchronous transmission, in which start and stop bits are added to the beginning and end of each frame. Synchronous transmission is used in digital modems such as Integrated Services Digital Network (ISDN) terminal adapters, Channel Service Unit/Data Service Units (CSU/DSUs) for T-carrier services, and similar telecommunications services. Synchronous transmission interfaces are generally about 20 percent faster and somewhat more reliable than comparable asynchronous interfaces.

Implementation

Devices that communicate with each other synchronously use either separate clocking channels to ensure synchronization between them or some kind of special signal code embedded in the signal for self-clocking purposes. Separate clocking lines are generally used when the distance between the data terminal equipment (DTE) and data communications equipment (DCE) is fairly short. Typically, the receiving station (such as a modem, a common form of DCE) provides the clocking signal to the transmitting station (usually a computer or a terminal).

S

The alternative is to use signal preamble, a special group of bytes (usually 8 bytes) called a SYNC signal that alerts the receiver that data is coming, synchronizes the clocks at the two devices, and starts the transmission. Special predefined voltage transition patterns familiar to both the transmitting and receiving stations are contained within the signal and are used to maintain synchronization between the devices. The receiver must extract this embedded information from the signal and use it to maintain synchronization between it and the transmitting station.

See Also: *asynchronous transmission, serial transmission*

SYN flooding

Also known as SYN attack, a popular form of denial of service (DoS) attack.

See: *SYN attack*

system access control list (SACL)

A form of access control list (ACL) used by Microsoft Windows 2000 and Windows .NET Server for security control.

Overview

System access control lists (SACLs) are used for establishing systemwide security policies for actions such as logging or auditing resource access. SACLs should not be confused with the more familiar discretionary access control lists (DACLs) used by Windows 2000 and Windows .NET Server to control access to Active Directory directory service and NTFS file system (NTFS) objects by users and groups.

The SACL attached to a system, directory, or file object specifies

- Which security principals (users, groups, computers) should be audited when accessing the object
- Which access events should be audited for these principals

- Whether a Success or Failure attribute is generated for an access event, depending on the permissions granted in the DACL for the object

See Also: *access control, access control list (ACL), discretionary access control list (DACL)*

system group

Another name for special identity, a special group account in Microsoft Windows 2000 whose membership is controlled by the operating system itself, not by administrators or individual users.

See: *special identity*

system log

A log in Microsoft Windows NT, Windows 2000, Windows XP, and Windows .NET Server that records events generated by the operating system.

Overview

Events logged in the system log mainly consist of information about services starting, stopping, or failing and about system device drivers that fail. Administrators cannot alter the type of information logged in the system log. You can view and manage the system log by using the administrative tool Event Viewer.

The following are three types of events that can be logged to the system log:

- **Errors:** Identified by a white *X* in a red circle; indicates a significant problem that might have caused data loss or the loss of some aspect of system functionality (for example, a service failing to start properly)
- **Warnings:** Identified by an exclamation mark in a yellow triangle; indicates a problem that might not be critical but might have an impact later (such as low disk space)
- **Information:** Identified by a blue letter *i* in a speech balloon; indicates a significant but harmless event such as a service starting or device driver initializing

See Also: *application log, security log*

system partition

The partition on which Microsoft Windows 2000 and Windows .NET Server install hardware-specific files that are needed to start the operating system.

Overview

The files installed on the system partition include the boot loader file (ntldr), the hardware detector file (Ntdetect.com), and the Boot.ini file. The system partition is different from the boot partition, which contains the actual Windows 2000 operating system files and supporting files. During the boot process, the code in the Master Boot Record (MBR) locates the system partition by scanning the partition table.

The system partition must be on the first physical hard disk of the machine and must be an active partition (and hence a primary partition). In a default Windows 2000 installation, both the system partition and boot partition are on the C: drive.

See Also: *boot partition*

system policy

A file that applies a set of rules to a Microsoft Windows NT computer or set of computers to restrict what users or groups of users can see and do on their workstations.

Overview

System policies are included as an administrative feature on the Windows NT operating system platform for helping administrators lock down the desktop configuration of Microsoft Windows NT Workstation, Windows 98, and Windows 95 clients. On the Windows 2000 and Windows .NET Server platforms, a more advanced feature called Group Policy is implemented, which is integrated with Active Directory directory service.

System policies work by overwriting specific registry keys on the computers they are applied to. To apply a system policy to computers in a Windows NT domain, put the Ntconfig.pol file in the NetLogon Share on the primary domain controller (PDC) and use the Directory Replicator Service to replicate the file to other domain controllers. When users log on to the network, the system policy file is downloaded and applied to their Windows NT workstations.

You can create system policy files for Windows NT Workstation clients by using the administrative tool System Policy Editor. A system policy file created this way is usually named Ntconfig.pol.

Notes

If users have Windows 95 or Windows 98 clients, use Poledit.exe to create a Config.pol file and place this in the NetLogon Share, as just described. System policy files created for Windows 95 and Windows 98 clients are usually named Config.pol. If you have a mix of Windows NT, Windows 95, and Windows 98 clients on the network, you must create both an Ntconfig.pol file and a Config.pol file and store them in the NetLogon Share on the PDC.

See Also: Group Policy

Systems Management Server (SMS)

A server application from Microsoft Corporation for managing an organization's networked computers.

Overview

Microsoft Systems Management Server (SMS) lets network administrators

- Manage their hardware and software assets
- Distribute new software from a central location
- Manage shared applications loaded from network servers
- Perform network protocol analysis for planning and troubleshooting purposes
- Perform remote troubleshooting and remotely control individual PCs

For example, you can use SMS to determine which computers need updated drivers, which have sufficient free disk space to run new applications, or how many copies of Microsoft Office are installed in your organization. This simplifies maintenance and upgrading tasks for network administrators.

Using SMS, you can also manage, install, and control server-based applications from a central location. You can perform network protocol analysis to locate and resolve bottlenecks on your network. Using the administrative tools of the Microsoft Windows NT operating system, administrators have a single, consistent administrative environment for managing their network assets.

SMS organizes a company's network assets into hierarchical logical groupings of computers and domains called sites. Using the top site, an administrator can centrally manage the entire network. Sites can be designed so that sites without administrators can be managed by sites with administrators. This logical structure is scalable—as your company grows and your needs change, you can add sites and structure.

A typical SMS enterprise deployment might consist of the following tiers:

- A central SMS machine linked to a computer running Microsoft SQL Server that hosts the corporate inventory database, which includes centralized hardware and software inventory information on all your networked computers.
- Primary SMS servers for sharing the load of distribution to the logon servers. These are located so that the majority of network traffic generated by SMS is on local segments.
- Local area network (LAN) servers such as Windows NT and Windows 2000 domain controllers, file and print servers, and application servers.
- Clients such as Windows NT, Windows 2000, Windows 98, or Windows 95.

Software is distributed down the hierarchy, and inventory information is passed up the hierarchy. At each SMS site, inventory information is collected and forwarded to the site above it. Thus, the SMS database at the top site has complete inventory information for the entire network. From this top site, you can use the Systems Management Server Administrator program to query and view the inventory database for hardware, software, and configuration information about any computer on your network. Queries can be specific—for example, you can determine which computers in your network have Pentium processors or which systems have Office installed.

You can also use SMS to distribute and install software on clients and servers on your network, and you can schedule software distribution to minimize the impact on your system. The Systems Management Server Administrator program can

- Send software from one site to another.
- Move software to selected servers called distribution servers. Users can then access and install the software on their clients from these servers.
- Set up and configure network applications on servers for shared use by groups of users. SMS automatically creates a program item for the network application on users' computers.
- Install and configure software on clients and servers.

The following additional features of SMS 2 make it easy to use:

- Integrated setup with SQL Server
- Enhanced administration using wizards, taskpads, and Microsoft Management Console (MMC)
- Context-sensitive Hypertext Markup Language (HTML)–based help
- A nonintrusive 32-bit agent client that is invisible to the user except when distribution packages are available
- A status system that provides a common reporting mechanism for all components
- Support for the Common Information Model (CIM) specification
- Dynamic, discovery-based software inventory mechanisms
- The Network Topology Tracing Tool, which provides a graphical display of the network routes between servers within a site, including infrastructure devices such as routers and hubs
- Dynamic distribution lists for sending software to users automatically when they join a group

For More Information

Visit *www.microsoft.com/smsmgmt.*

Systems Network Architecture (SNA)

A set of IBM mainframe networking standards and protocols introduced in 1974.

Overview

Systems Network Architecture (SNA) includes services for configuring and managing system resources within an IBM mainframe networking environment. SNA originally defined a centralized architecture with mainframe hosts controlling terminals, but it has also been adapted for peer-to-peer communication and distributed client/server computing environments.

Architecture

SNA has seven protocol layers and is similar but not identical to the Open Systems Interconnection (OSI) reference model, whose development it influenced. The SNA protocol suite includes the following:

- **Synchronous Data Link Control (SDLC) protocol:** For data-link layer control of the flow of frames within an SNA network. SNA also supports IEEE 802.5 and 802.2 token passing with Logical Link Control (LLC).
- **Network Control Program (NCP):** For routing, segmentation, and framing functions. NCP usually runs on the host or on the front-end processor.
- **Virtual Telecommunications Access Method (VTAM):** For sequencing, flow control, error recovery, and session management functions. You use VTAM to implement Network Accessible Units (NAUs), which control the flow of data, in an SNA network.
- **Advanced Peer-to-Peer Networking (APPN):** Enables SNA connections between two hosts, such as a PC host accessing an application running on a mainframe host using Advanced Program-to-Program Communications (APPC) sessions. You use APPN to implement Physical Units (PUs) and Logical Units (LUs), which are forms of NAUs that control communication processes for hosts and terminals. LUs represent SNA end nodes such as connections by users or applications, and two LUs communicate by using associated PUs, which are

hardware devices or terminals. A number of types of LUs and PUs are used in an SNA networking environment.

- **NetView:** A network management program for configuring, controlling, troubleshooting, and usage accounting of SNA networks.

Before data can be transferred over SNA, a session must be established between an LU on the client and an LU on the host. For example, a Microsoft Windows NT– or Windows 2000–based server running Microsoft Host Integration Server can connect to a mainframe host by using SNA. Host Integration Server provides connectivity between Windows and SNA environments by providing an SNA gateway running on a Windows NT–, Windows 2000–, or Windows .NET–based server. Windows clients can then connect to the SNA mainframe host by going through the Host Integration Server gateway. By using LU 6.2, which is a peer-to-peer protocol, the Windows NT–based server running Host Integration Server or the mainframe host can initiate the user session. Clients on a Windows NT– or Windows 2000–based network can then access data stored on the host, including data stored in structured or unstructured AS/400 or Virtual Storage Access Method (VSAM) files, DB2 database tables, and transaction processing monitors.

Notes

Non-SNA architectures such as Token Ring networks can interface with SNA networks using Service Points (SPs).

See Also: *Advanced Peer-to-Peer Networking (APPN), Open Systems Interconnection (OSI) reference model, Synchronous Data Link Control (SDLC)*

S

SYSVOL share

An administrative share on Active Directory directory service–based installations of Microsoft Windows 2000 and Windows .NET Server.

Overview

The SYSVOL share is a shared directory on a domain controller on Windows 2000– and Windows .NET Server–based networks that contains the server's copy of the domain public files, such as group policy objects and scripts for the current domain and the entire enterprise. The contents of this share are replicated to all domain controllers in the Windows 2000 domain. The default path for the SYSVOL share is \%System_Root%\Sysvol\SYSVOL.

Notes

The SYSVOL share must be on an NTFS file system (NTFS) 5 volume because Active Directory uses the journaling function of NTFS 5 to track replication updates.

T

T1

The lowest level of theT-carrier hierarchy.

Overview

T1 is part of the T-carrier digital transmission architecture developed for the Public Switched Telephone Network (PSTN) in the 1960s. A T1 circuit (also called a T1 line) is formed from a combination of 24 DS-0 (Digital Signal Zero) channels, each having a bandwidth of 64 kilobits per second (Kbps), for a total bandwidth of 1.544 megabits per second (Mbps). These 24 DS-0 channels can either be used separately for carrying 24 separate voice circuits (called channelized T1) or aggregated into a single data stream (called unchannelized T1) for high-speed wide area network (WAN) connections.

T1 (sometimes called T-1) actually stands for T-carrier Level 1, but it is almost never referred to in this way.

Uses

T1 is the preferred technology used by enterprises for combining voice, fax, and data transmissions. This is because T1 is "trunking" technology that enables a single physical circuit to support as many as 24 separate virtual circuits, a process which is generally cheaper than provisioning 24 separate physical links. T1 lines are also typically used

- To provide enterprises with dedicated leased-line WAN links among remote locations—for example, to connect a branch office to corporate headquarters.
- To provide corporate users with high-speed access to the Internet.

Architecture

Like other members of the T-carrier family, T1 uses time-division multiplexing (TDM) to interleave multiple DS-0 channels into a single bit stream (called a DS-1 circuit). DS-0 generates 8 bits (1 byte) every 125 microseconds, or 8000 DS-0 frames per second. The bandwidth of a DS-0 channel is therefore

```
DS-0 = 8 bits x 8000 per second
     = 64,000 bits per second (bps)
     = 64 kilobits per second (Kbps)
```

Because T1 multiplexes 24 DS-0 channels together, a single T1 frame (or DS-1 frame) should equal 24 x 8 = 192 bps. The T1 specification, however, adds an extra bit to each frame to ensure that transceivers at each end of the line maintain their synchronization. This extra bit is added at the start of each DS-1 frame, which makes the length of a DS-1 frame equal to 192 + 1 = 193 bits. Using the same transmission rate of 8000 frames per second, this means that the total bandwidth of a T1 circuit is

```
T1 = 193 bits/frame x 8000 frames/sec
   = 1544000 bits/sec
   = 1.544 Mbps
```

TDM is applied to the individual DS-0 channels in such a way that each DS-0 channel is located at the same position of each DS-1 frame generated.

To package binary information into electrical signals, T1 originally used the Alternate Mark Inversion (AMI) line coding mechanism in which a voltage represents a binary 1 and no voltage represents zero. The problem with this mechanism was that it was hard to maintain synchronization between transceivers at opposite ends of the T1 circuit when a large number of successive 0s or 1s were transmitted. A scheme was therefore devised whereby bits were "robbed" from certain parts of each frame to ensure that synchronization could be maintained and to allow for control and signal maintenance information to be carried in-band within the circuit. The net result of this bit robbing was to reduce the data-carrying capacity of each DS-0 channel within DS-1 from 64 Kbps to only 56 Kbps. However, this bit-robbing scheme has no discernable effect on voice transmission.

You can work around the capacity-robbing effect of this bit robbing by replacing AMI line coding with Bipolar with 8-bit Zero Substitution (B8ZS) line coding. B8ZS substitutes a special byte if eight consecutive zero bits are detected to maintain a specific ones density to help maintain synchronization. This approach is called "ones density" and allows a T1 channel service unit/data service unit (CSU/DSU) at the customer premises to recover the data clock reliably when synchronization is lost with the T1 multiplexer at the telco central office (CO). The result of using B8ZS is that each DS-0 channel can carry the full 64 Kbps of data. An alternative scheme to B8ZS that is also commonly used is Zero Byte Time Slot Interface (ZBTSI) line coding.

Bellcore also developed an alternate scheme whereby a 2 Binary 1 Quaternary (2B1Q) line coding scheme was employed. 2B1Q is the same signal encoding mechanism employed by Integrated Services Digital Network (ISDN) and encodes 2 bits/baud instead of the 1 bit/baud supported by AMI. This new technology was called "repeaterless T1" because it eliminated the necessity of regenerating T1 signals every 6000 feet (1830 meters) using repeaters, a process that made original T1 deployments complex and expensive. Repeaterless T1 needed repeaters only every 12,000 feet (3660 meters) and transmitted data at only 784 Kbps over each twisted pair. Because two pairs of wires are used for T1, this new technology also carries data at T1 speed of 1.544 Mbps. This new technology is now commonly referred to as High bit-rate Digital Subscriber Line (HDSL). A telco will often provision customers with HDSL and call it T1 instead, because it is functionally equivalent in speed and framing to T1.

Implementation

T1 cannot operate over analog Plain Old Telephone Service (POTS) telephone lines. Instead, it must be deployed using specially conditioned copper twisted-pair lines, with two pairs of wires (four wires) being used for a single T1 circuit. To support full-duplex communication, two of these four wires are used for transmission (TX interface) and the other two for receiving (RX interface). T1 lines typically terminate at the customer premises with an RJ-48 connector, which looks like an RJ-45 connector but is pinned differently. T1 lines are generally unshielded twisted-pair (UTP) cabling but other media can be used, including coaxial cabling or fiber-optic cabling.

T1 usually cannot run over existing local loop wiring because:

- Bridge taps installed by telcos to trunk telephone traffic in neighborhood wiring causes distortion of T1 signals, so these must be removed to allow the circuit to carry T1 signals.
- Loading coils, which are used to reduce signal distortion for analog phone lines, have the opposite effect of increasing distortion of digital signals, and these also must be removed.

To deploy T1 as a solution for multiplexing voice traffic, a T1 channel bank is generally installed at the customer premises. This channel bank can be connected to a Private Branch Exchange (PBX), which then connects to digital telephone and fax equipment. For WAN data links the scenario is usually somewhat different, using customer premises equipment (CPE) such as

- A T1 CSU/DSU for connecting bridges or routers to T1 circuits
- T1 bridges and routers with integrated T1 CSU/DSUs
- A T1 multiplexer (MUX), a multiplexer for aggregating several T1 circuits for even higher-speed communication
- T1 access routers, which support multiple remote access links over a single T1 line

To test T1 equipment such as channel banks and CSU/DSUs, use a cable simulator, which is a passive device that simulates a standard 22-gauge twisted-pair T1 line that is 1310 feet (400 meters) long (the alternative is to use 1310 feet of actual 22-gauge twisted-pair wiring). Connect two cable simulators between your CPE and your T1 test equipment using the TX and RX interfaces to analyze your device's performance. A "wet" T1 line carries a small DC current of about 140 mA (milliamperes) at several hundred volts for powering the CSU/DSU at the customer premises. "Dry" lines carry no current, so CSU/DSUs must be powered from the customer premises. Do not touch a T1 line—a wet line can give you a serious shock!

Marketplace

The cost of provisioning T1 is complex and depends on whether you are using it for high-speed Internet access (T1 local loop connections between the customer premises and the telco CO) or for building a high-speed WAN (long-haul T1 lines crossing large geographical distances). A good rule of thumb for T1 WAN links is that the long-haul cost is about $2.50 per mile, which means a 2000-mile T1 leased line would cost about $5,000. These figures were for the year 2000, and the good news is that T1 prices have been falling about 10 percent per year for the last couple of years.

The cost for a T1 local loop connection to provide your company with dedicated high-speed Internet access is generally between $1,000 and $1,500 per month. These prices seem not to be changing much, despite forecasts that Digital Subscriber Line (DSL) technologies will cut into the T1 market, the main reason being the greater reliability of T1 compared to newcomer DSL.

The primary reason T1 lines are so expensive is that they are always "on" regardless of whether they are being used. This is characteristic of leased lines and provides both the benefit of availability and the cost of underutilization. A cheaper solution for many companies that do not require full T1 capacity is to lease a fractional T1 service such as 4 x DS0 = 256 Kbps from their carrier and then have them upgrade it to higher speeds as their WAN traffic grows. Fractional T1 is usually cheaper than using individual DS0 circuits multiplexed together.

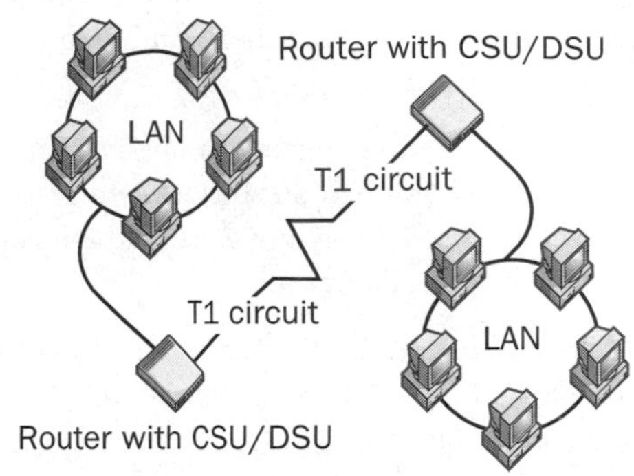

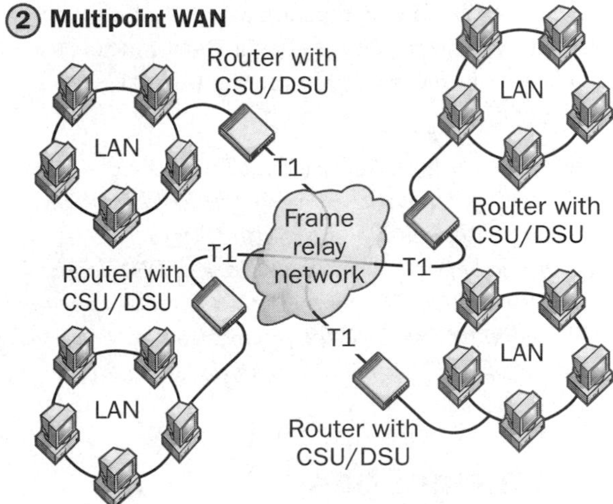

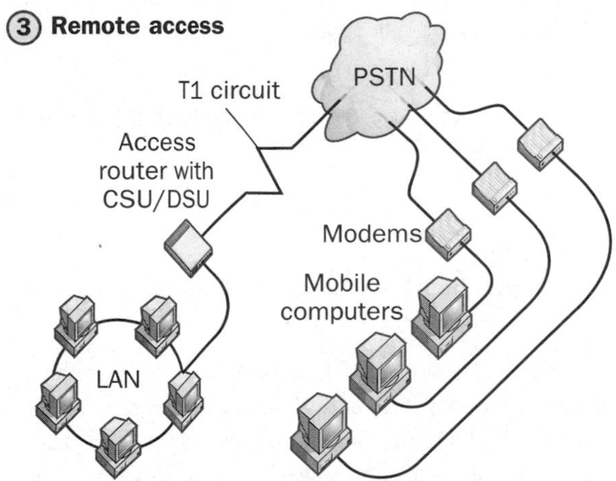

T1. Some different WAN scenarios using T1 lines.

Notes

T1 and PRI-ISDN both carry data at around 1.5 Mbps, but they are incompatible so far as their framing formats are concerned. For example:

- T1 multiplexes 24 DS-0 channels using TDM for carrying data and adds a control bit to each T1 frame (and may use bit robbing to gain additional bandwidth for control purposes)
- PRI-ISDN multiplexes 23 DS-0 channels for carrying data and adds a 24th DS-0 channel dedicated to carrying control information.

The European E1 specification avoids the bit robbing used in American T1 by adding a 16-bit control header to each E1 frame instead of the single bit added to T1 frames.

See Also: *Channel Service Unit/Data Service Unit (CSU/DSU), Digital Subscriber Line (DSL), DS-0, DS-1, High-bit-rate Digital Subscriber Line (HDSL), Integrated Services Digital Network (ISDN), leased line, line coding, PRI-ISDN, Private Branch Exchange (PBX), Public Switched Telephone Network (PSTN), T1 channel bank, T3, T-carrier, time-division multiplexing (TDM), trunking*

T1 channel bank

Customer premises equipment (CPE) used to terminate a T1 line and make it available across an organization.

Overview

T1 channel banks are typically used to enable T1 lines to connect to

- Data terminal equipment (DTE) such as routers and access servers
- Private Branch Exchange (PBX) units that provide integrated phone/fax services

A typical T1 channel bank consists of a modular chassis unit to which you can add various expansion cards to provide digital communication services for CPE. The modular chassis allows customers to add channels and upgrade fractional T1 services to full T1 or higher. It also allows customers to multiplex several channels to provide higher bandwidth for high-speed data connections to routers, Web servers, and other DTEs. The chassis typically includes a built-in T1 Channel Service Unit (CSU) for terminating the T1 circuit at the customer premises, plus a number of slots capable of holding expansion cards for various uses.

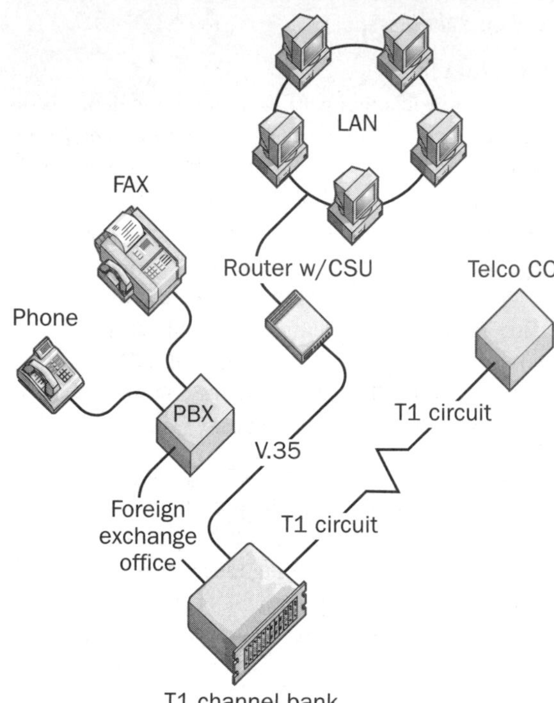

T1 channel bank. *Using a T1 channel bank to connect a router and PBX to a T1 line.*

Each expansion card in a T1 channel bank typically handles either one or two DS-0 channels, which means that different channels can supply different services (such as voice, fax, or data connections). Typical types of expansion cards include the following:

- **Data service cards:** These usually have a dual channel format that supports two DS-0 channels and employ a serial interface such as RS-232, RS-530, or V.35. These interfaces are then used for directly connecting the unit to bridges and routers having integrated Channel Service Unit/Data Service Units (CSU/DSUs).
- **High-speed data cards:** These support up to 1.544 megabits per second (Mbps) in 64-kilobits per

second (Kbps) or 56-Kbps increments (the speed depends on how DS-0 is provisioned by the carrier) by multiplexing DS-0 channels.

- **Voice cards:** These are used to connect the unit to a PBX or directly to a telephone using standard 4-wire connections.
- **Modem cards:** These convert the channel bank into a modem pool to support corporate remote access needs.

Some T1 channel banks can support as many as four T1 lines, which can be configured for both active and backup purposes to provide redundant wide area network (WAN) connections.

See Also: *Channel Service Unit (CSU), Channel Service Unit/Data Service Unit (CSU/DSU), customer premises equipment (CPE), data terminal equipment (DTE), Private Branch Exchange (PBX), T1, T-carrier*

T3

Part of the T-carrier hierarchy.

Overview

T3 represents the "next step up" for enterprises that want to build their wide area network (WAN) connections using dedicated leased lines. Although the commonly used and relatively inexpensive T1 lines used in enterprises carry traffic at 1.544 megabits per second (Mbps), T3 lines support a much faster speed of 44.736 Mbps, well above standard 10Base2 Ethernet speeds and almost comparable to Fast Ethernet. This huge jump in speed, however, comes at a significant cost and with some associated issues:

- T3 requires fiber-optic cabling to be provisioned from the telco central office (CO) to the customer premises, because T3 cannot run over existing copper local loop wiring even if it is properly conditioned. This up-front cost of laying fiber must be factored into the cost of deploying T3 in the enterprise.
- The cost of a dedicated T3 line is generally between $25,000 and $35,000 per month, a hefty price tag compared to the $1,000 to $1,500 cost of individual T1 lines. Many companies have a difficult time justifying the cost of upgrading from T1 to T3.
- Although T3 operates over fiber-optic cabling, there is no universal specification for how physical layer signaling occurs with this system. As a result, different telcos and telecommunications equipment vendors have developed many proprietary T3 signaling schemes, and most of these schemes cannot interoperate. This means that if you want to deploy T3 you must "buy in" to equipment from a single vendor (or lease equipment from your telco).

Despite these issues, T3 has grown in popularity in the last few years, particularly for large enterprises to connect their data centers to the Internet. The main problem faces companies whose WAN or Internet access needs are too great for a T1 line to satisfy yet do not require the capacity (or cannot afford the cost) of a full T3 line. The emerging solution to this problem is for telcos to provision services that bundle multiple T1 links for greater throughput. Cable and Wireless is one provider that offers a dedicated Internet access service called NxT1 that can aggregate from two to seven T1 lines into a single fat data pipe carrying up to 10 Mbps. This system employs Cisco 7500 routers running Multilink Point-to-Point Protocol (MPPP) for link aggregation. The disadvantage of this scheme is that customers must order additional T1 port connections to the provider's network, which adds to the cost. Nevertheless, the cost of this scheme is generally less than using fractional T3, which requires a full T3 interface at the customer premises.

See Also: *Multilink Point-to-Point Protocol (MPPP), T1, T-carrier*

T.120

A family of standards for multiuser conferencing and collaboration over a data network.

Overview

T.120 represents a series of eight International Telecommunication Union (ITU) standards that define real-time multipoint communication over a network such as the Internet. T.120 can be used for such tasks as video conferencing, data exchange, or interactive gaming. The T.120 standards define such things as

- Multipoint services for conferencing
- Standard network services
- Guidelines for defining data channels
- Whiteboard methodologies
- Application-sharing protocols
- File transfer methodologies

A related standard from the ITU is the H.323 standard for video and audio conferencing.

Architecture

The architecture of the T.120 standard follows that defined by the Open Systems Interconnection (OSI) reference model for networking. The T.120 architecture can be divided into two parts:

- **Network-layer and transport-layer standards (T.122 through T.125):** Allow data to be transmitted and received among conferencing nodes over a variety of supported network connections. These standards also provide platform independence and the capacity for simultaneously managing multiple participants running on different operating system platforms and conferencing software.
- **Application-layer standards (T.126 through T.128):** Support multiuser conferencing functions such as whiteboarding, file transfer, and application sharing across different platforms and networks.

The following table shows the details of the various standards included under the T.120 umbrella.

T.120 Suite of Conferencing Standards

Standard	*Description*
T.121	A required standard for T.120 applications that defines how conference nodes register themselves with a T.120 node controller. Also defines the generic application template (GAT) for building T.120 application protocols and management facilities.
T.122	Defines multipoint communication services (MCS) over various topologies to enable multiple participants to send data as part of a conference. The MCS defined by T.122 are implemented by T.125.
T.123	Defines flow control, error control, and sequencing mechanisms for connect, disconnect, send, and receive functions over different network connections.
T.124	Defines how multipoint conferences are initiated and administered and defines the generic conference control (GCC) that manages and monitors users, address lists, data flow, and MCS resources.
T.125	Defines how data is transmitted during a conference, specifying the private and broadcast channels that transport conference data. T.125 implements the MCS defined by T.122.
T.126	Defines mechanisms for transmitting and receiving whiteboard information among conference nodes and managing the multiuser whiteboard workspace.
T.127	Defines mechanisms for file transfer among conference nodes in either broadcast or directed mode.
T.128	Defines mechanisms for application sharing among conference nodes so that users can share their local programs with others for collaborative purposes.

Notes

T.120 also forms the basis of the Remote Desktop Protocol (RDP), which is used by the Terminal Services of Microsoft Windows 2000, Windows XP, and Windows .NET Server.

See Also: *H.323, International Telecommunication Union (ITU), Open Systems Interconnection (OSI) reference model, Remote Desktop Protocol (RDP), Terminal Services*

TACACS

Stands for Terminal Access Controller Access Control System, a security protocol supported by Cisco routers.

See: Terminal Access Controller Access Control System (TACACS)

taking ownership

Assuming the role of an object's creator, thus having the associated rights and privileges that this role incurs.

Overview

Ownership describes the highest level of permissions that can be granted to objects. On the Microsoft Windows 2000, Windows XP, and Windows .NET Server platforms, these objects can include files and folders, Active Directory directory service objects, and so on. For example, assuming ownership of an object such as a file on an NTFS file system (NTFS) volume gives one the right to share the object and assign permissions to it. Normally, the user who creates a file on an NTFS volume is the owner. Other users can take ownership of the file provided the user is either a member of the Administrators domain local group, has NTFS full control permission on the object, or has explicit permission to take ownership of the object.

Notes

Ownership can only be taken; it cannot be assigned.

See Also: NTFS permissions (Windows 2000, Windows XP, and Windows .NET Server), NTFS permissions (Windows NT), NTFS special permissions (Windows 2000, Windows XP, and Windows .NET Server), NTFS special permissions (Windows NT)

tape drive

A device used to back up data to magnetic tape.

Overview

Tape drives and their larger cousins, tape libraries, form the backbone of the disaster recovery plan for most enterprises. Tape drives are distinguished from one another by a variety of factors:

- **Recording technology:** There are several different ways in which data can be written to magnetic tape, including linear-scan, helical-scan, or hybrids of these two basic technologies. For more information about these various recording technologies and the tape formats from different vendors that support them, see the following article, "tape format."
- **Capacity:** The capacity of a tape drive is the amount of data it can store on a single tape cartridge. This capacity is usually measured in gigabytes (GB) and can be expressed as either native capacity for uncompressed data or compressed capacity. Tape drives for large enterprise networks may have capacities exceeding 50 GB, but drives for departmental or workgroup use may have capacities of only a few GB. Compressed capacity is usually specified as twice the native capacity—in other words, a tape drive with 50 GB native capacity would be rated as having a compressed capacity of 100 GB. The actual capacity when compression is used, however, depends on the type of data being backed up.
- **Transfer speed:** This is the speed at which data can be buffered by the tape drive and written to tape. For enterprise-class tape drives, transfer speeds exceeding 25 megabytes per second (MBps) are possible, but for workgroup or small business use the capacity is often measured in megabytes per minute (MB/min) instead and is considerably less.
- **Cost of media:** If you are backing up large amounts of data frequently, the cost of individual tape cartridges can be a significant expense that needs to be budgeted for accordingly. Cost for tapes range from about $10 to $100, depending on the tape format used.
- **Input/output (I/O) interface:** Most enterprise tape drives use Small Computer Systems Interface (SCSI) as their data interface, but some cheaper drives for small business use have ATAPI/IDE, parallel, or Universal Serial Bus (USB) interfaces.
- **Interoperability:** Usually a tape cartridge produced by one vendor will not work in a tape drive from a different vendor. The only difference is for tapes and drives that adhere to the new Linear Tape Open (LTO) standard developed by

Hewlett-Packard, IBM, and Seagate Technology. LTO drives and cartridges have only recently appeared on the market, but they are likely to become a dominant format in the years to come.

- **Software driver:** Before buying a tape drive for your servers, make sure that your backup software has a suitable driver for this hardware.

Marketplace

The tape drive market is basically divided into three categories:

- **Enterprise:** These drives have the largest capacities and best performance to meet the demanding backup needs of large companies. Some popular drives in this market include DLT 8000 drives from Quantum Corporation, which cost about $5,000 and have a native capacity of 40 GB; Exabyte Mammoth-2 and Sony AIT-2 drives, which are comparable in cost and capacity to the DLT 8000; and the new SuperDLT drives from Quantum and LTO Ultrium drives from IBM, which have higher capacity and cost.
- **Departmental:** These medium-capacity drives include the Tandberg SLR100, Benchmark DLT1, Ecrix VXA-1, and drives from other vendors. The cost for departmental drives is usually $1,000 or slightly higher, and capacity is measured in tens of GB.
- **Workgroup:** For small business settings, these are a wide range of popular drives, including digital audio tape (DAT) drives from a number of vendors, OnStream's ADR50 drives, and Ultrium 3580 from IBM. Drives for workgroup or desktop use typically have capacities of a few GB and cost several hundred dollars.

T

Notes

Here are some tips on getting the most from your tape drive:

- Make sure you clean your drive's read/write heads regularly, usually every 10 hours or so. Some newer drives automatically clean themselves as needed, while others display a light-emitting diode (LED) indicator when cleaning needs to be done.
- Avoid exposing both the tape drive and the tapes to stray magnetic fields such as those from computer monitors. When some tape formats are exposed to such fields, data can be lost—for others, the entire tape can be rendered unusable.
- Replace your tapes regularly according to the mean lifetime of the particular tape format you use. Most tapes can be used about 50 times before they wear out and become unreliable.

See Also: *backup, disaster recovery, tape format, tape library*

tape format

Techniques for storing digital data on magnetic tape for backup purposes.

Overview

Magnetic tape is the medium used by most companies for archiving valuable business information. No single standard exists, however, for how information is stored on tape. As a result, different vendors have developed a variety of tape formats for use by small, medium, and large businesses. These formats differ in capacity, format, and ease of use, and you need to weigh these factors when deciding which format is appropriate for your organization's needs.

The two main technologies used for storing data on magnetic tape are as follows:

- **Helical-scan:** This method pulls the magnetic tape out of the cartridge that houses it, tensions the exposed tape using capstans and rollers, and wraps the tape around a rotating drum that contains multiple read/write heads. Data is then written in diagonal stripes across the width of the tape, and the entire tape is filled in one pass. This technology is essentially the same used by common VCRs and was developed in the late 1980s. One problem with this technology is that the high speed of the drum rotation (7000 rpm or higher), coupled with the tensioning of the tape, can stretch the tape over time or even cause it to break, but most modern helical tape technologies are designed to minimize these effects.

- **Linear-scan:** This method leaves the tape in the cartridge while passing the small exposed portion of tape over stationary read/write heads. Data is written on one track until the end of the tape is reached, and then the tape reverses direction and the next track is written. This "serpentine" writing action continues until the entire tape is filled. Many linear tape formats use multiple heads to write several tracks simultaneously for greater throughput. The stationary heads and minimal tape tensioning make this approach more reliable than helical-scan technology, but helical-scan generally provides greater performance and supports higher capacity. Linear-scan is also an older technology than helical-scan and is better established, especially in the enterprise arena.

Marketplace

A number of vendors have developed both linear-scan and helical-scan tape technologies, with the result that numerous linear and several helical tape formats are on the market. The following are some of the popular linear-scan tape formats offered by different vendors:

- **Quarter-inch cartridge (QIC):** This is the oldest linear tape format, developed in the early 1980s by Tandberg Data. QIC cartridges have capacities up to 40 gigabytes (GB) with transfer speeds up to 10 megabytes per second (MBps). QIC cartridges originally had a large 4-by-6-by-5/8-inch form factor, but this is now considered obsolete and has been largely replaced by smaller minicartridges, especially those from Travan using technology developed by 3M Corporation/Imation Corporation.
- **Digital linear tape (DLT):** This linear tape technology was first developed by Conner in 1991 and acquired by Quantum Corporation in 1994. DLT has been the dominant tape format used in enterprise backup solutions for many years. DLT cartridges generally have a form factor of 5.25 inches and come in various types. For example, the Quantum DLT 8000 tape format is popular in the enterprise environment and has a native capacity of 40 GB per cartridge, supports transfer rates of 6 MBps, and costs about $100 each. The DLT 8000 format achieves its high transfer rate by writing four tracks of data simultaneously across the tape. Other popular DLT formats include DLT 7000 and DLT 4000.
- **Super DLT (S-DLT):** This format was recently developed by Quantum and uses a combination of magnetic-head and laser-guided technologies to improve on the earlier DLT architecture. Super DLT cartridges have a native capacity of 100 GB and support transfer speeds from 10 to 40 MBps.
- **9840:** This linear format uses half-inch tape and was developed by StorageTek for their tape automation market. The 9840 format is widely used in mainframe computing environments and has a native capacity of 20 GB and a transfer rate of 10 MBps.
- **Mammoth-2:** This linear tape format from Exabyte Corporation is a competitor of Quantum's DLT format and has a native capacity of 60 GB and a transfer rate of 12 MBps and costs about the same as comparable DLT tape.
- **SLR100:** This format from Tandberg Data has a native capacity of 50 GB and transfer speed of 5 MBps. SLR100 tapes cost about $100 each and are popular in the departmental backup arena.

The following are some of the popular helical-scan tape formats offered by different vendors:

- **Advanced Intelligent Tape (AIT):** This technology from Sony Corporation was the first helical-scan tape technology developed for tape backup. AIT has become a popular alternative to DLT in the enterprise and comes in several versions. AIT-2, for example, has a native capacity of 50 GB and a transfer speed of 6 MBps and costs about $100 per cartridge. The newer AIT-3 has a native capacity of 100 GB and a transfer speed of 11 MBps.
- **8-millimeter:** This helical tape format has the same width as standard videotape and supports native of 20 GB and higher, with transfer speeds of 3 MBps and higher. Sony and Exabyte are two popular manufacturers of 8-millimeter tapes.

- **Digital data storage (DDS):** Often wrongly called digital audio tape (DAT), this is a helical tape format based on technology originally developed for the professional audio market. DDS comes in several popular versions, including DDS-1 (2 GB native capacity) DDS-2 (4 GB), DDS-3 (12 GB), and DDS-4 (20 GB). Transfer rates range from 1.5 to 2.4 MBps. DAT cartridges use 4-millimeter tape in a 3.5-inch form factor and typically cost about $50 each.

Some other tape formats include

- **Advanced Digital Recording (ADR):** This is a technology originally developed by Phillips and now available from OnStream that combines aspects of both linear-scan (stationary heads) and helical-scan (multiple tracks written simultaneously). For example, the ADR50 format has a native capacity of 25 GB and a transfer rate of 2 MBps and is well-suited to the workgroup arena.
- **VXA:** This new format developed by Ecrix Corporation writes data to tape in packet form instead of the streaming method used by both linear-scan and helical-scan tape formats. It uses a variable tape speed in contrast to the fixed speed of the standard formats. VXA also employs a parity striping format called discrete packet format (DPF) to optimize data integrity. VXA-1 tapes have a capacity of 33 GB and a transfer speed of 3 MBps and cost less than $100.

Prospects

A new development in this field has been the emergence of an open standard for linear-scan tape media called Linear Tape Open (LTO). This standard was developed jointly by Hewlett-Packard, IBM, and Seagate Technology and is intended to bridge the interoperability gap that exists because of each tape vendor developing its own proprietary technology. The aim is that LTO tape from one vendor would work equally well on an LTO tape drive from a different vendor. There are actually two different LTO standards:

- **Accelis:** A fast data-access linear tape technology for small and mid-sized businesses.
- **Ultrium:** A high-capacity tape technology for large enterprises.

The Ultrium tape format has a native capacity of 100 GB and a transfer speed of 15 MBps and is likely to emerge as the main competitor to market leader DLT and its successor, Super DLT.

See Also: *backup, storage, tape drive*

tape library

A tape backup device that can retrieve and load tapes automatically.

Overview

When enterprises have hundreds of gigabytes (GB) to several terabytes of data that need to be regularly backed up, simple tape drives, even enterprise-class ones that have capacities of 100 GB or more, simply cannot do the job efficiently. That is where a tape library comes in. A tape library, also called a tape autoloader, is essentially a box with a robotic arm or other device that can store a number of tapes, select and load them, and unload and store them as needed. Tape libraries range from small boxes that can sit on a desk or be mounted in an equipment rack to large room-sized enclosures containing multiple tape drives and thousands of tapes.

Marketplace

One of the more popular vendors in the tape library market is Exabyte Corporation, whose tapes use a proprietary format called Mammoth (now Mammoth-2 or M2). IBM is another major player with its standards-based linear tape open (LTO) 3584 UltraScalable Tape Library, which can store as much as 240 TB of data. Other popular vendors of tape libraries include ADIC, Grau Data Storage, Spectra Logic Corporation, StorageTek, and several others.

See Also: *backup, disaster recovery, tape format, tape library*

TAPI

Stands for Telephony Application Programming Interface, a set of standard application programming interfaces (APIs) developed by Microsoft Corporation and Intel Corporation for accessing telephony services.

See: *Telephony Application Programming Interface (TAPI)*

T

T-carrier

A family of telco specifications for digital trunking, also used for high-speed wide area network (WAN) connections.

Overview

The original trunking (long-haul communications) architecture of the Plain Old Telephone System (POTS) was analog in nature. This L-carrier system allowed multiple analog local loop connections to be aggregated into trunk lines using frequency-division multiplexing (FDM). The main advantage of trunking was that it saved carriers the cost of having to deploy multiple long-haul lines between different geographical locations.

L-carrier services, however, suffered from distance limitations due to noise and signal distortion. As a result, Bell Laboratories developed T-carrier technology in the early 1960s to replace long-haul analog trunking lines with digital lines. This improved performance and made digital data services available to companies that needed to connect remote branch offices with mainframe computing centers. The first level of T-carrier, the T1 service, was first commercially deployed in the mid-1980s.

Uses

T-carrier services such as T1 and T3 lines have a variety of uses in the enterprise:

- To connect Private Branch Exchange (PBX) equipment at the customer premises with the telco central office (CO)
- To economically provide enterprises with integrated voice/fax/data services
- For building dedicated, high-speed WANs
- For providing users on corporate networks with reliable high-speed Internet access
- For connecting corporate Web servers to the Internet

Architecture

The T-carrier family of specifications basically outlines two considerations: physical media and signaling. As a physical media specification, various levels of the T-carrier hierarchy run over copper twisted-pair wiring, coaxial cabling, fiber-optic cabling, or wireless microwave transmission. For example, T1 lines employ two twisted pairs (four wires) to ensure efficient signaling (this is in contrast to traditional analog POTS lines, which employ only one pair of wires). By contrast, T3 uses fiber-optic cabling as its transmission medium. The table shows the various combinations allowed for physical media. Note that the exact specifications for T3 to run over fiber have never been standardized—as a result, different telcos have developed their own proprietary optical transmission schemes for T3.

T-Carrier Physical Media Combinations

T-Level	*Media*
T1	copper
T1C	copper
T2	copper/microwave
T3	fiber/microwave
T3C	fiber/microwave
T4	fiber/microwave

As far as signaling is concerned, the T-carrier system is based on the DS-0 signaling standard defined by AT&T for digital voice transmission. A single digitized voice channel (DS-0 or Digital Signal Zero channel) carries binary data at 64 kilobits per second (Kbps) and forms the building block of the T-carrier service hierarchy. For example, the T1 service consists of 24 DS-0 channels multiplexed to provide a total data rate of 1.55 megabits per second (Mbps). Note that no carrier is defined for DS-0 itself—that is, you cannot use a single DS-0 channel for digital data transmission, only multiple DS-0 channels aggregated together.

In T-carrier services, these DS-0 channels are multiplexed using time-division multiplexing (TDM) instead of the FDM scheme used in the older L-carrier services. For more details of the T-carrier multiplexing process, see the article "T1" earlier in this chapter. T-carrier services form a hierarchy of standard digital transmission speeds, as shown in the table below. In real life, however, only T1 and T3 services are implemented; T2 is rarely used and no real standard exists for T4

transmission. For digital transmission speeds faster than T-carrier services offer, a newer technology called Synchronous Optical Network (SONET) was developed. SONET now forms the basis of most long-haul and backbone transmission networks for telcos, with T1 and T3 used mainly for provisioning high-speed data services to the customer premises.

The following table shows the different T-carrier services that have been defined (there are no levels defined beyond T4, as SONET has taken over in this domain). Note that in common parlance T1 and DS-1 mean the same thing, but in fact T1 defines the physical specification and DS-1 defines the signaling method. Note also that T1C and T3C refer to "concatenating" (joining together) two T1 or T3 circuits to double aggregate bandwidth. Despite the number of different T-carrier levels defined, only T1 and T3 are commonly used, and T4 has never been implemented, as SONET covers that range. There is also a variant service called fractional T1 offered by most telcos, which essentially means a full T1 circuit is provisioned to the customer but transmission is limited (and charged) for only a portion of the circuit—for example, 4, 8, or 12 DS-0 channels instead of the full 24 channels.

T-Carrier Levels Currently Defined

T-Level	*DS-Level*	*Number of DS-0 Channels*	*Bandwidth*
T1	DS-1	24	1.544 Mbps
T1C	DS-1C	48	3.152
T2	DS-2	96	6.312
T3	DS-3	672	44.736
T3C	DS-3C	1344	91.053
T4	DS-4	4032	274.176

T

Implementation

T-carrier is usually provisioned as a leased line service from Incumbent Local Exchange Carriers (ILECs). Costs for these services are high, but their high level of reliability makes them a staple of enterprise telecommunications networks. T-carrier can be provisioned in two basic formats for customers:

- **Channelized:** Individual DS-0 channels can carry their own traffic. Channelized T1, for example, allows a single T1 line to carry 24 separate voice channels multiplexed together, which is cheaper for customers than ordering 24 separate local loop connections. Channelized T1 is often used to connect corporate Private Branch Exchanges (PBXs) to ILECs. A channelized T1 line is essentially a single line that is logically equivalent to 24 separate "virtual" telephone lines.
- **Unchannelized:** The DS-0 channels are essentially merged into a single fat pipe, primarily for carrying data for high-speed WAN links. Note the difference: channelized T1 is used for voice, unchannelized for data.

Often what is referred to as T-carrier is really a different service running over the T-carrier physical interface. For example, a 1.544 Mbps frame relay link is really a frame relay running over two-pair twisted wiring using the T1 physical layer specification.

Notes

In Europe a different digital carrier hierarchy called the E-carrier system evolved. For example, the European equivalent of the T1 line is the E1 line, which carries data at 2.048 Mbps. T-carrier and E-carrier systems are incompatible but can interface with each other by using special multiplexing equipment.

Japan calls its digital hierarchy the J-carrier system, but it is essentially the same as the AmericanT-carrier system.

See Also: *DS-0, DS-1, DS-3, frame relay, Incumbent Local Exchange Carrier (ILEC), Plain Old Telephone Service (POTS), Synchronous Optical Network (SONET), T1, T1 channel bank, T3, telco, time-division multiplexing (TDM), wide area network (WAN)*

TCP

Stands for Transmission Control Protocol, a transport layer protocol of the Transmission Control Protocol/Internet Protocol (TCP/IP) suite.

See: *Transmission Control Protocol (TCP)*

TCP/IP

Stands for Transmission Control Protocol/Internet Protocol, an industry-standard protocol suite forming the basis of the Internet.

***See:** Transmission Control Protocol/Internet Protocol (TCP/IP)*

TCP three-way handshake

The procedure used for establishing and terminating Transmission Control Protocol (TCP) sessions.

Overview

All TCP communications are connection-oriented in nature. In other words, a TCP session must be established before the hosts involved can engage in the exchange of data between them. The TCP three-way handshake does this by establishing a logical connection between the hosts to ensure reliable transmission can be achieved.

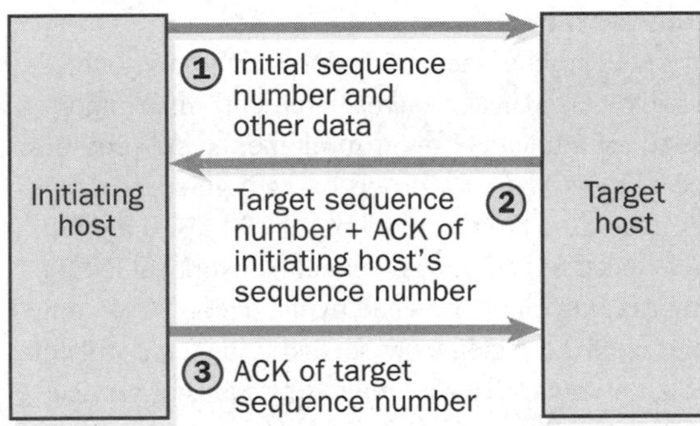

***TCP three-way handshake.** How the TCP three-way handshake procedure operates.*

The three stages of a TCP three-way handshake are the following:

1. The initiating host sends a TCP packet requesting a new session. This packet contains the initiating host's sequence number for the connection. The packet includes information such as a set SYN (synchronization) flag and data about the size of the window buffer on the initiating host.
2. The target host sends a TCP packet with its own sequence number and an ACK (acknowledgment) of the initiating host's sequence number.
3. The initiating host sends an ACK containing the target sequence number that it received.

A similar three-way process is used to terminate a TCP session between two hosts. Using the same type of handshake to end the connection ensures that the hosts have completed their transactions and that all data is accounted for.

***See Also:** ACK, connection-oriented protocol, Transmission Control Protocol (TCP)*

TDM

Stands for time-division multiplexing, a method for sending several data streams over a single communication path.

***See:** time-division multiplexing (TDM)*

TDMA

Stands for Time Division Multiple Access, a cellular communications technology based on time-division multiplexing (TDM).

***See:** Time Division Multiple Access (TDMA)*

TDR

Stands for time domain reflectometry, a cable testing technique for finding breaks or shorts in a cable.

***See:** time domain reflectometry (TDR)*

TechNet

An information resource program developed by Microsoft Corporation for IT (information technology) professionals who work with Microsoft products.

Overview

Microsoft TechNet is important to those who plan, deploy, maintain, support, and evaluate Microsoft business products, such as Microsoft Windows 2000 and members of the Microsoft BackOffice suite. The TechNet program includes a monthly CD subscription, a Web site, electronic newsletters, regular technical briefings at locations around the world, and special offers. Each month a collection of CDs updates your TechNet binder to ensure that you have the latest and most accurate information on all Microsoft products and services. The subscription includes four categories of CDs:

- Monthly issues of up-to-date technical information, which include the Technical Information, Supplementary Drivers and Patches, and full Microsoft Knowledge Base CDs. The Technical Information CD includes a large collection of manuals, resource kits, and other documentation on current versions of Microsoft products; you can either browse or search this CD to find the information you need. The Knowledge Base CD is a collection of thousands of articles written by Microsoft support professionals that answer technical questions, provide detailed how-to information, resolve bugs, list fixes, and document changes and corrections to Microsoft products.
- The Server Utilities, Client Utilities, and Software Library Archive CDs, as well as CDs that contain utilities from various Microsoft product resource kits.
- Service Pack CDs for all Microsoft products for which service packs are available. These service packs provide cumulative fixes and patches for bugs and known problems with Microsoft products and can include additional enhancements to the original product version.
- Extras, such as CDs for Microsoft Seminars Online and time-limited evaluation versions of Microsoft software.

An enhanced version of TechNet, called TechNet Plus, includes beta evaluation software for various upcoming Microsoft products.

For More Information

Visit Microsoft TechNet online at *www.microsoft.com/technet.*

telco

A local telephone company.

Overview

The term *telco* is generally used to refer to the local telephone company that owns the local loop connection between your customer premises and the telco central office (CO). The term is also sometimes used to mean any carrier or service provider that can provision voice or data services over your local loop, regardless of whether they actually own that loop.

In its strictest sense, your telco is your Incumbent Local Exchange Carrier (ILEC), typically one of the four Regional Bell Operating Companies (RBOCs), but sometimes an independent phone company, especially in rural areas. Other companies sometimes referred to as telcos include Competitive Local Exchange Carriers (CLECs), inter-exchange carriers (IXCs), and even metropolitan area network (MAN) service providers such as metropolitan Ethernet providers.

Architecture

From the point of view of business customers, who are usually located in dense urban areas, the most important aspect of a telco is how it implements and provides access to its MAN for provisioning high-speed data services. In a typical scenario, the MAN is a dual high-speed Synchronous Optical Network (SONET) ring running on fiber owned by the telco. OC-48 rings running at 2.5 gigabits per second (Gbps) are still common, but most telcos are upgrading to faster services such as OC-96 or OC-192. Business customers who need the highest performance can usually connect an Ethernet switch or router at their customer premises through a T3 line or trunked T1 lines to an Asynchronous Transfer Mode (ATM) switch residing at the periphery of the telco's network. The ATM switch then connects to the SONET ring to allow customers to establish wide area network (WAN) connections among different branch offices.

See Also: *Asynchronous Transfer Mode (ATM), central office (CO), Competitive Local Exchange Carrier (CLEC), Ethernet switch, Incumbent Local Exchange Carrier (ILEC), inter-exchange carrier*

T

(IXC), metropolitan Ethernet, optical carrier (OC-x) level, Regional Bell Operating Company (RBOC), router, Synchronous Optical Network (SONET), T1, T3, trunking

Telecommunications Industry Association (TIA)

A national trade organization representing all aspects of the telecommunications industry in the United States.

Overview

Working in conjunction with its subsidiary, the Multi-Media Telecommunications Association (MMTA), and its industry peer organization, the Electronic Industries Alliance (EIA), the Telecommunications Industry Association (TIA) represents its members in activities such as establishing public policies and government regulatory issues, developing standards for communication and networking, and organizing trade shows and other events. The TIA's goal is to provide member companies, which are drawn mostly from service providers and hardware vendors in the communication industry, with a forum for discussing industry issues and a voice for representing members' interests on the national and international level.

Active in telecommunications standards development, the TIA is endorsed and accredited by the American National Standards Institute (ANSI). The Standards and Technology Department consists of five divisions organized in more than 70 groups responsible for formulating new standards. These five divisions are

- Fiber Optics
- User Premises Equipment
- Network Equipment
- Wireless Communications
- Satellite Communications

For More Information

Visit the TIA at *www.tiaonline.org.*

See Also: *American National Standards Institute (ANSI), EIA/TIA wiring standards, Electronic Industries Alliance (EIA), standards organizations*

telecommunications services

Various services provided to customers by telcos.

Overview

In addition to standard voice services, telcos offer a wide variety of data transmission services. These services are provisioned to business customers by connecting switching and multiplexing devices located at the telco central office (CO) to customer premises equipment (CPE) such as access servers, routers, and Ethernet switches. These services may be provisioned over the ubiquitous copper local loop wiring, specially conditioned twisted-pair wiring, fiber-optic cabling, or even wirelessly, using microwave transmission or satellites. Using telco data services companies can deploy

- Dedicated leased lines for permanent, dedicated point-to-point wide area network (WAN) connections
- Packet-switched services such as frame relay and X.25 for building multipoint WANs
- Dial-up remote access solutions for mobile users using either analog modems over the circuit-switched Public Switched Telephone Network (PSTN) or using Integrated Services Digital Network (ISDN) services
- High-speed Internet access for corporate users using digital subscriber line (DSL) technologies such as Asymmetric Digital Subscriber Line (ADSL) and High-bit-rate Digital Subscriber Line (HDSL)

Other data communication technologies that telcos sometimes provide include

- Asynchronous Transfer Mode (ATM)
- digital data service (DDS)
- Switched 56
- Switched Multimegabit Data Services (SMDS)
- T-carrier services such as T1, T3, and fractional T1

See Also: *analog modem, Asynchronous Transfer Mode (ATM), central office (CO), digital data service (DDS), Digital Subscriber Line (DSL), frame relay,*

Integrated Services Digital Network (ISDN), Public Switched Telephone Network (PSTN), Switched 56, Switched Multimegabit Data Services (SMDS), T1, T3, T-carrier, telco, wide area network (WAN), X.25

telecommuting

Working from a location other than the office, usually from home.

Overview

Telecommuting has emerged as a phenomenon of the late 1990s as a new way of working. A knowledge worker who works from home may be called either a telecommuter or a teleworker. The empowering technology behind telecommuting is the Internet, a ubiquitous public network that provides cheap and easy network connectivity between home workers and the office. The negative side of this new technology is security—the Internet is a notoriously unsafe place with hackers, viruses, Trojan horses, and other threats to both home computers and office networks.

Some of the different ways companies can connect their teleworkers to their corporate networks include

- **Dial-up using 56K modems:** This method is more secure than a bare dedicated connection because a new Internet Protocol (IP) address is typically assigned to the home user for each session initiated with the user's Internet service provider (ISP). Speed is slow but cost is low also—typically $50 per month, including both an ISP account and a second phone line. Dial-up users should connect to their corporate local area network (LAN) using an encrypted virtual private network (VPN).
- **Digital Subscriber Line (DSL):** This is emerging as the technology of choice for teleworkers due to its high speed (at least 20 times that of dial-up), low cost (typically $50 per month over existing phone lines), and security (DSL is a dedicated point-to-point connection). Nevertheless, teleworkers using DSL need a firewall for full protection, and a VPN is required as well. The main problem with DSL is that it is usually available only in urban areas.
- **Cable modem:** This is usually not recommended for teleworkers due to the security issues concerning having your home computer on a LAN segment with other cable modem subscribers in your neighborhood. A firewall and VPN are definitely needed in this scenario.

Other less common teleworking scenarios include

- **Fixed wireless:** Availability is limited, coverage is usually in dense urban areas, and the service is costly.
- **Satellite:** The main issue here is the latency introduced by the long distances the signal must traverse between the subscriber and the service provider. Initial equipment is expensive and monthly costs are moderate.

See Also: *cable modem, Digital Subscriber Line (DSL), Internet, Internet service provider (ISP), modem, wireless networking*

Telephony Application Programming Interface (TAPI)

A set of standard application programming interfaces (APIs) developed by Microsoft Corporation and Intel Corporation for accessing telephony services.

Overview

Telephony Application Programming Interface (TAPI) receives programmatic telephony requests from applications and then forwards them to drivers for telephony devices such as telephones, modems, Integrated Services Digital Network (ISDN) equipment, and Private Branch Exchanges (PBXs). TAPI manages various telephony functions for these devices including

- Signaling
- Call hold and transfer
- Call conferencing and call parking
- Specialized PBX functions

See Also: *application programming interface (API), modem, Integrated Services Digital Network (ISDN), Private Branch Exchange (PBX)*

T

Telnet

An Internet standard protocol for executing commands on remote hosts.

Overview

Telnet is an application-layer protocol that is part of the Transmission Control Protocol/Internet Protocol (TCP/IP) suite of protocols. Using Telnet, a user on one IP host can connect to and run text-based commands on a different IP host, provided the user can be authenticated and has suitable privileges. The term *telnet* is also commonly used to refer to software that implements this protocol on a particular platform or system. The Telnet protocol is defined in RFC 854.

Uses

Telnet is widely used for remote administration of routers, Ethernet switches, and UNIX mail and Web servers. For example, you can use Telnet to connect to a Web server on port 80 to issue Hypertext Transfer Protocol (HTTP) commands to troubleshoot the server or to an Internet mail forwarding host on port 25 to issue Simple Mail Transfer Protocol (SMTP) commands to do the same.

Telnet is one of five common methods for remotely administering Cisco routers and access servers, the other four methods being

- Direct serial connection from a local terminal to the RS-232 console port
- Remote serial connection through a modem to the RS-343 auxiliary port
- Remote IP connection using HTTP from a Web browser
- Remote IP connection using Simple Network Management Protocol (SNMP) from an SNMP management console

Implementation

Telnet is a client/server protocol in which a Telnet client on the user's machine issues commands to a Telnet server (for example, a UNIX machine running the telnet daemon or a Microsoft Windows 2000 Server running the Telnet Server service). The Telnet client runs within a command-line window on the client machine; in other words, the user opens a command prompt and types **telnet** to start the Telnet client service. The user specifies the remote host's name or IP address, enters her credentials for authentication, and then issues commands. Any application that can be run from the command line on the remote Telnet server can also be remotely executed from the Telnet client machine. When the program or command is executed, its output (if any) is returned to the client and displayed within the command-prompt window.

Windows 2000 includes both a Telnet client implemented as a command-line utility and Telnet server software that supports as many as 63 simultaneous client connections but is licensed to provide only up to two simultaneous client connections. If you require support for additional client connections, you should obtain the Microsoft Windows Services for UNIX 2 add-on pack for Windows 2000 Server.

See Also: *Hypertext Transfer Protocol (HTTP), router, Simple Mail Transfer Protocol (SMTP), Transmission Control Protocol/Internet Protocol (TCP/IP), UNIX*

terminal

Traditionally, a device that provides user access to a mainframe computer.

Overview

Terminals originated in the mainframe computing environment, where they were used as front-end devices to allow users to access the processing power of these mainframes in an interactive way. Users would type commands and data into a terminal, and the information they typed would be sent over serial links to the mainframe for processing. Once the mainframe had completed the processing, it would return the results to the user's terminal and display it in the appropriate format.

The earliest terminals were called teletypes (abbreviated TTY) and were essentially electric typewriters through which users would send commands and data to a mainframe and the mainframe would then type the output returned to the user. A terminal that supports only text output is sometimes called an ASCII terminal.

Over the years a number of standards called terminal protocols have been developed that govern their use. The VT-100 terminal developed by Digital Equipment Corporation was a popular ASCII text-based terminal standard that is still used in some places, such as library online catalog systems, which remote users typically access by running a Telnet client over a dial-up connection. IBM's TN3270 terminal protocol is still widely used in IBM mainframe environments, and their TN5250 terminal protocol is popular with their AS/400 midrange computing environments. Other common terminal protocol standards include ANSI (American National Standards Institute), VT52, and VT220.

Implementation

Terminals generally have little or no inherent data-processing power and rely entirely on the back-end system to do the processing. The terminal is responsible only for processing and queuing input from the keyboard (and other additional input devices, such as a mouse), transmitting this information in a format recognized by the back-end host (typically a mainframe, midframe, or PC-based terminal server). The information the user enters on the keyboard is typically transmitted to the mainframe over an RS-232 or RS-423 asynchronous serial connection, but sometimes it is transmitted instead over an Ethernet or a Token Ring local area network (LAN) connection. Once the processing is completed, the output is sent back to the terminal and typically presented on a "green screen" monitor, which is usually in ASCII format on older systems, or by providing a graphical desktop environment in newer terminal server computing platforms. In other words, the application runs in one location (the mainframe) and the user interface is in a different location (the terminal).

That the mainframe traditionally does all the processing explains the origin of the term *dumb terminal*, which means that a terminal by itself is generally useless unless it is connected to a back-end processing system. However, there are also "smart" or "intelligent" terminals that have various degrees of inherent processing capability.

Terminals can be either local terminals, which are directly connected to their back-end mainframe host through a dedicated serial or shared/switched LAN connection; or remote terminals, which are typically connected over a telephone line using modems at both ends of the connection.

Prospects

The popularity of terminals declined in the late 1980s and early 1990s with the advent of distributed client/server environments and the eclipse of mainframe computing environments. In a client/server environment, data processing is shared between the front-end client computer, usually a full-featured PC with a graphical user interface (GUI) such as Microsoft Windows, and the back-end server, which can be a Windows NT–based server, a Novell NetWare server, an AS/400, or some other system. In the late 1990s, however, the pendulum started to swing back toward terminals with the rising popularity of terminal emulators and PC-based terminal servers. A terminal emulator is hardware or software, or both, that runs on a stripped-down PC with no operating system and causes the PC to function as a terminal, and a terminal server is a back-end server that generates and delivers the user desktop environment to the terminals and performs all the processing. This arrangement permits low-cost "thin clients" to be used and centralizes system administration at the back end, reducing deployment and management costs associated with a distributed client/server systems environment.

See Also: *RS-232, Telnet, terminal emulator, terminal server, Terminal Services, thin client*

Terminal Access Controller Access Control System (TACACS)

A security protocol supported by Cisco routers.

Overview

Terminal Access Controller Access Control System (TACACS) is a family of security protocols used for Authentication, Authorization, and Accounting (AAA). TACACS is similar to the industry standard Remote Authentication Dial-in User Services (RADIUS) security protocol but is more flexible and powerful. In particular, TACACS separates the AAA components and allows them to be used independently of one another.

For example, a common scenario employed by Internet service providers (ISPs) is to use RADIUS for authentication and TACACS for authorization and accounting.

The original version of TACACS was developed in the 1980s by the Defense Data Network for MILNET, the U.S. military portion of the Internet. A variation of this protocol called Extended TACACS (XTACACS) was developed in 1990 and standardized in RFC 1492. Cisco Systems then developed a third version called TACACS+ that is not compatible with earlier versions and has enhanced security features that make the earlier versions obsolete. The remainder of this article focuses on the Cisco version TACACS+ because it is the one in general use.

TACACS+ supports up to 16 different privilege levels and a variety of authentication methods, including standard logon, shell logon, Point-to-Point Protocol (PPP), Novell Asynchronous Services Interface (NASI), and AppleTalk Remote Access Protocol (ARAP).

Comparison

Although TACACS+ is similar to RADIUS, there are architectural differences in how the two protocols work. For example, RADIUS is a connectionless protocol that runs over User Datagram Protocol (UDP). In RADIUS the authentication and authorization features are integrated, and only passwords are encrypted. RADIUS also supports only Internet Protocol (IP) as a network transport and has no method for controlling access to which commands can be executed on a RADIUS-enabled router.

By contrast, TACACS+ is a connection-oriented protocol that runs over Transmission Control Protocol (TCP), separates the three components of AAA functionality, supports a wide variety of network transports, and uses packet encryption and router access lists for greater security. TACACS+ also includes more than 50 attribute/value pairs and supports secure virtual private networking (VPN). Despite these advantages, RADIUS is still the more widely deployed of the two protocols due to its being a vendor-independent industry standard, and TACACS+ is more commonly used in Cisco-only shops.

Implementation

In a typical ISP scenario using TACACS+, a dial-in user connects through the Public Switched Telephone Network (PSTN) to a Cisco access server (router) located at the ISP. The connection between the dial-in user and the router uses an authentication protocol such as Password Authentication Protocol (PAP), Challenge Handshake Authentication Protocol (CHAP), or Microsoft CHAP (MS-CHAP) for securely transmitting the user's credentials to the router.

During the authentication process, the access server forwards the user's credentials to a Cisco AAA server, which is also located at the ISP. The communication between the access server and the AAA server employs TACACS+ as its security protocol. Once the AAA server has authenticated the user, it informs the access server to allow the client connection attempt to be accepted and the user then accesses the Internet.

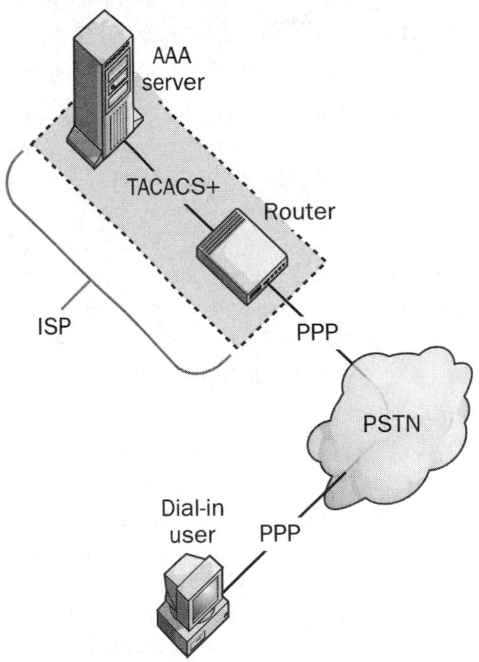

Terminal Access Controller Access Control System (TACACS). *How a TACACS+-enabled AAA server is used to authenticate dial-in users by an ISP.*

See Also: *AAA, Challenge Handshake Authentication Protocol (CHAP), Internet Protocol (IP), Internet* *service provider (ISP), Microsoft Challenge Handshake Authentication Protocol (MS-CHAP), Password Authentication Protocol (PAP), Point-to-Point Protocol (PPP), Public Switched Telephone Network (PSTN), Remote Authentication Dial-In User Service (RADIUS), Transmission Control Protocol (TCP), User Datagram Protocol (UDP), virtual private network (VPN)*

terminal emulator

Hardware or software, or both, that enables a PC to operate as a terminal.

Overview

Terminal emulators let you use a standard PC to connect to a back-end mainframe or terminal server. The rising popularity of terminal emulators led to the demise of older terminals with their chattery keyboards and green screens. Terminal emulators are typically software packages that run on standard PCs and may include accompanying interface cards to support different kinds of connections such as serial, Ethernet, or Token Ring.

Terminal emulators are often designed to emulate several terminal modes including American National Standards Institute (ANSI), VT52, VT100, VT220, TN3270, and TN5250. Terminal emulators also offer productivity features not supported by older terminals, such as keyboard remapping, support for using scripts and macros to automate tasks, hot-linking of emulator data with desktop applications such as Microsoft Excel, multiple session windows, and a Web browser interface.

Marketplace

Microsoft HyperTerminal is one popular terminal emulator that supports common terminal emulation modes and is included with 32-bit Microsoft Windows operating systems. Many other vendors offer terminal emulation products, including E-Term32 from DCSi, CRT from Van Dyke Technologies, HotVT from Datamission, and Softerm Modular TE from Softronics.

Notes

When running a terminal emulator, the emulation mode on the clients must match the terminal mode running on the back-end system for communication to work. If you are trying to connect to an unknown mainframe or other back-end system and your emulator cannot automatically detect the terminal mode needed, try using ANSI mode first. If that fails, try VT100 and other popular terminal modes.

See Also: *terminal, TN3270, TN5250*

terminal server

Generally, a server that provides the back-end support needed for terminals to function.

Overview

A terminal server can be a mainframe system, a UNIX host running X Windows, or a PC-based server running software such as the Terminal Services included with Microsoft Windows 2000 Server, Windows XP, and Windows .NET Server. The function of a terminal server is to generate the desktop environment that is presented to the user of the terminal and to perform all the processing of data submitted by the user.

The main advantages of terminal-based computing over a traditional client/server PC network are

- **Lower hardware costs:** "Thin clients" (special devices or stripped-down PCs) can be used instead of full-featured desktop PCs. For example, Terminal Services of Windows 2000 Server can present a 32-bit Windows user environment on older PCs that lack the hardware requirements for running a local copy of the latest versions of Windows operating systems.
- **Lower management costs:** Operating systems and applications are installed and run only on the back-end terminal servers, which simplifies deployment and troubleshooting and makes administration more centralized. For example, Terminal Services for Windows 2000 Server supports running applications such as Microsoft Office from centralized terminal servers instead of installing them on every desktop computer in the enterprise.
- **Multiplatform support:** Allows the same applications and desktop environments to be presented on a variety of client platforms, including Windows-based PCs, Macintosh computers, UNIX workstations, and other devices.

Notes

Single-port terminal servers are sometimes used in mainframe environments to allow users connected to different controllers to communicate over the corporate local area network (LAN) without needing a dedicated point-to-point communication link. In a typical configuration, the controller is connected to a terminal server by an RS-232 serial connection, and the terminal server is linked to the LAN by an Ethernet interface.

Some vendors produce rack-mountable terminal server devices with 8 or 16 RJ-45 ports that can be used to connect asynchronous terminals to an Ethernet local area network (LAN) running Transmission Control Protocol/Internet Protocol (TCP/IP) or some other network protocol. Such devices can be used to provide terminals (or PCs running terminal emulation software) with access to network file servers or dial-up access to the Internet. Windows-based management software allows these devices to be remotely managed from a PC for viewing and configuring port information. Built-in support for Password Authentication Protocol (PAP), Challenge Handshake Authentication Protocol (CHAP), and Remote Authentication Dial-In User Service (RADIUS) are often included to control user access. Users can dial in to the device, be authenticated, and select a desired host on the LAN they want to communicate with.

See Also: *terminal, terminal emulator, thin client*

Terminal Services

A component of Microsoft Windows 2000 Server, Windows XP, and Windows .NET Server that supports terminal-based computing.

Overview

Terminal Services enables users to access the Windows 2000, Windows XP, and Windows .NET Server desktop and run Microsoft Windows applications on remote computers and other terminal devices. Terminal Services enables each of these operating systems to function as a terminal server and provide terminal emulation for a wide range of client computers. By moving all processing to the server, Terminal Services reduces total cost of ownership by

- Simplifying system administration by centralizing the installation and management of all applications on the server and supporting full remote administration from a single desktop
- Extending the life of legacy hardware by enabling client computers with minimal processing power and memory to run standard Windows applications
- Extending the life of legacy operating systems by allowing applications designed for Windows 2000, Windows XP, or Windows .NET Server to run on legacy versions of Windows
- Increasing security by using encrypted sessions between clients and servers, by enabling administrators to fully monitor and control user operations by shadowing client sessions from another client computer, and by enabling administrators to input keyboard and mouse actions during client sessions for remote control purposes

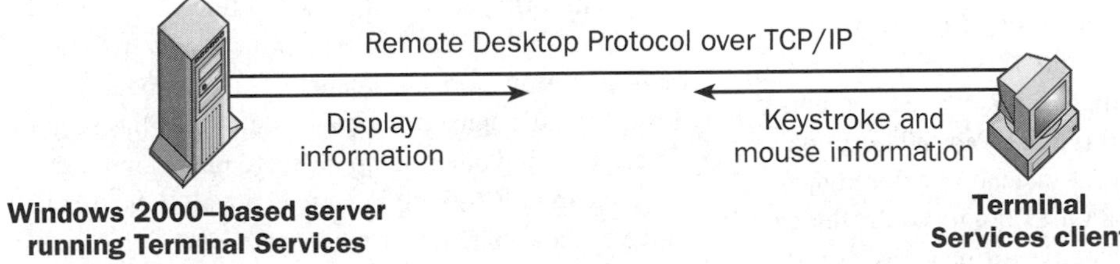

Terminal Services. *Underlying architecture of how Windows 2000 Terminal Services works.*

T

Implementation

Three components are required for Terminal Services to work:

- **Terminal server:** A Windows 2000, Windows XP, or Windows .NET Server running Terminal Services that provides each client computer with its own Windows desktop.
- **Terminal Services client:** A "thin client" application that displays the Windows 2000, Windows XP, or Windows .NET Server desktop and running applications within a window on the client computer. Terminal Services clients are provided for all versions of Windows, including 32-bit clients that can run on computers running Windows .NET Server, Windows XP, Windows 2000, Windows NT 4, Windows NT 3.51, Windows 98, or Windows 95 on either Intel or Alpha platforms, and a 16-bit client for Windows for Workgroups 3.11. Special client software can also be embedded in devices such as Windows-based terminals and handheld PCs.
- **Remote Desktop Protocol (RDP):** A protocol suite based on the T.120 standard from the International Telecommunication Union (ITU), which provides the basis for communication between the client and the terminal server. RDP takes all keystroke and mouse actions performed by the terminal client, transports them to the terminal server for processing, and returns the display output to the terminal client. RDP employs Transmission Control Protocol/Internet Protocol (TCP/IP) as its underlying network transport.

Notes

To use Terminal Services you must install both Terminal Services and Terminal Services Licensing, and you must specify the directory location of the licensing server database. You can install Terminal Services during setup or afterward using Add/Remove Programs in Control Panel (you should typically install Terminal Services on a member server instead of a domain controller because installation on a domain controller can affect the domain controller's performance as a result of the additional load that Terminal Services places on server processor, memory, and network interface). Once these services are installed, you can configure the terminal server's security to allow users to remotely run multiuser applications, configure user accounts to allow them to log on to the terminal server, create user profiles and home directories if desired, and install Terminal Services client software on client computers. You can install client software either by downloading it across the network or by creating client installation disks for manual installation.

By installing the Citrix MetaFrame add-on, non-Windows clients such as UNIX, Macintosh, and OS/2 Warp can also access a Windows 2000–, Windows XP–, or Windows .NET–based system running Terminal Services to run Windows 2000, Windows XP, or Windows .NET Server applications.

A good rule of thumb is that a terminal server needs an additional 4 to 8 MB of RAM for each additional client it supports. Also, do not run legacy MS-DOS or 16-bit Windows on the terminal server, because this can significantly reduce the number of concurrent users that the server can support and increase the memory requirements for each connected client.

See Also: *Remote Desktop Protocol (RDP), terminal, terminal server, thin client*

terminator

A device connected to one end of a bus or cable that absorbs signals.

Overview

In a bus-based system, a single wire or series of wire segments connects network components in a chain formation. If the ends of the cable are not terminated, a signal placed on the wire by one component will bounce back and forth between the ends of the cable, hogging the cable and preventing other components from signaling. Terminators eliminate this signal bounce by absorbing the signal after each component has seen it once, allowing other components to place their signals on the cable. By supplying a load equal to the impedance of the cable, the terminator prevents reflections or standing waves from developing on the cable. Terminators also prevent interference caused by signal reflection, which can lead to signal loss. Most communication systems such as networks and computer buses require some form of termination at the ends of the data path, although this is often provided internally by the devices at the ends of the data path.

Types

Terminators can be passive (simple resistors) or active (more complex electronics), depending on the type of bus being terminated. Passive terminators use resistors to provide this impedance matching, while active terminators generally use voltage regulators.

Examples of different types of terminators include the following:

- **Coaxial cabling terminators:** Passive terminators that come in various sizes and use Bayonet-Neill-Concelman (BNC) threading to terminate
  - RG-58 thinnet cabling for 10Base2 Ethernet networks with termination resistance of 50 ohms
  - RG-59 cable television terminators with resistance of 75 ohms
  - RG-62 ARCNET cabling terminators with resistance of 93 ohms
- **Small Computer System Interface (SCSI) terminators:** The ends of a SCSI cable must always be terminated in a chain of SCSI devices. The internal termination is usually supplied by the SCSI adapter card, and the external termination is supplied by the last device in the chain. SCSI terminators can be passive, active, differential, or forced-perfect. Forced-perfect terminators compensate for the differences in impedance along the length of a SCSI bus. Diagnostic terminators analyze and display the condition of the data paths within a SCSI bus and are useful for high-availability uses such as clustering.
- **Free connectors:** Connectors on the hubs at both ends of a series of stackable hubs. These terminators are specific to the type of hub sold by a vendor.

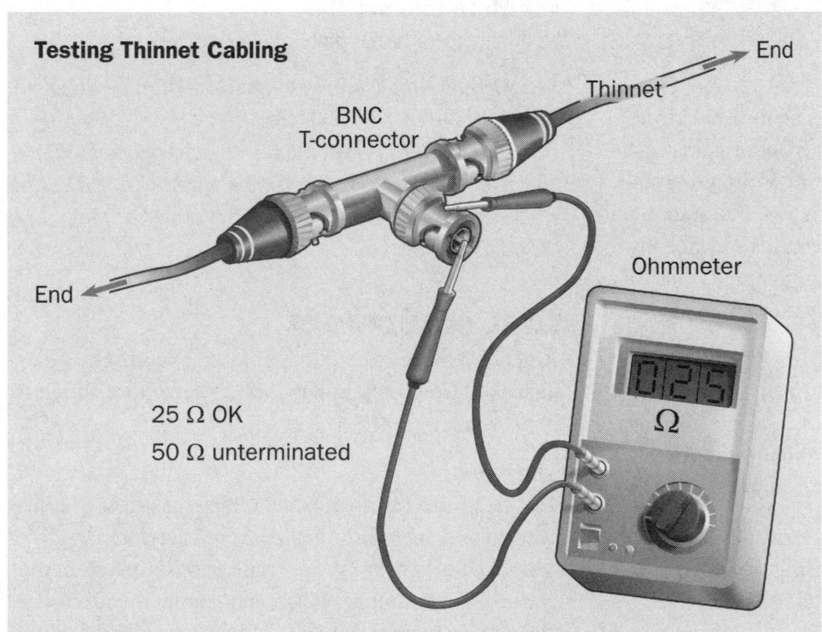

Terminator. *Using an ohmmeter to test if thinnet cabling is properly terminated.*

Notes

You can test the termination of a long 10Base2 network without having to hunt for the ends of the cable. Simply use an ohmmeter and test the resistance between the central conductor and the shield of any BNCT-connectors (after removing the cable from the network card to which it is attached). If the reading is about 25 ohms, the cable is properly terminated; if the reading is about 50 ohms, one of the terminators is loose or missing. If the cable appears to be properly terminated but network problems persist, remove one of the terminators and use the ohmmeter to test the connection to the T-connector that you exposed. If the result is less than 50 ohms, you probably have a short in the cable; if it is more than 56 ohms, there is probably a loose T-connector somewhere on the network.

See Also: *10Base2, coaxial cabling, Small Computer System Interface (SCSI), thinnet*

Terrestrial Trunked Radio (Tetra)

A European standard for digital mobile radio services.

Overview

Terrestrial Trunked Radio (Tetra) is an initiative from the European Telecommunications Standards Institute (ETSI) for a single standardized form of digital mobile communications. Tetra is defined in a memorandum of understanding among equipment vendors, service providers, testing bodies, and regulatory agencies that was laid out in 1994. Tetra consists of two complementary standards:

- A standard Time Division Multiple Access (TDMA) cellular communication system for voice and data communication on 25-kilohertz (kHz) channels
- A Packet Data Optimized (PDO) protocol for packet-switched data-only transmission at 36 kilobits per second (Kbps) on 25-kHz channels

Tetra includes support for security features such as multilevel authentication and encryption, allows voice and data communication to be combined using the same equipment, and supports multiplexing of up to four channels to provide data rates of up to 144 Kbps. Tetra complements the Global System for Mobile Communications (GSM) cellular communication standard: GSM itself can be considered an extension of the Integrated Services Digital Network (ISDN) to the wireless domain, and Tetra is an extension of ISDN Private Branch Exchange (PBX) systems to the same domain. Tetra thus provides additional communication functionality not built into GSM, such as direct mobile-to-mobile communication that bypasses the communication infrastructure, support for broadcast and group call features, fast call setup, and priority call.

Notes

Because of the recent growth of the Internet and wide demand for high-speed wireless mobile data services, a new high-speed wireless mobile packet-switching system called the Digital Advanced Wireless System (DAWS) is currently being developed by the ETSI to supercede the Tetra PDO standard.

For More Information

Visit the Tetra home page at *www.tetramou.com.*

See Also: *cellular communications, Digital Advanced Wireless System (DAWS), Global System for Mobile Communications (GSM), Integrated Services Digital Network (ISDN), Private Branch Exchange (PBX), standards organizations, Time Division Multiple Access (TDMA)*

test equipment

A general name for equipment used to configure, diagnose, and troubleshoot networking and telecommunications systems.

Overview

Test equipment is invaluable to busy network administrators for troubleshooting local area network (LAN) or wide area network (WAN) connections, to system integrators who install networks and communication services at customer premises, and to wiring and cabling installation service people. You can buy test equipment for dedicated, single-use testing purposes, but multifunction test equipment is more cost effective.

Test equipment comes in all shapes and sizes, from rack-mounted equipment for enterprise troubleshooting, to handheld scanners and packet sniffers, to laptops that run special software and use special Personal Computer Memory Card International Association (PCMCIA)–attached probes. Here are some examples:

- **Copper cable testers:** Typically handheld devices that can test installed copper cabling for compliance with Electronic Industries Association/Telecommunications Industry Association (EIA/TIA) standards for cabling system performance. These are usually multifunction devices that support both coaxial cabling and twisted-pair cabling. Two-way testers enable you to test a cable from both ends.
- **Fiber-optic cable testers:** Usually a separate category from coax/twisted-pair cable testers. These devices might support testing of single-mode fiber-optic cabling, multimode fiber-optic cabling, or both, and provide detailed measurements in decibels for optical link budget (OLB) calculations to ensure that a fiber installation will support the intended equipment layout. A typical fiber tester consists of two modules: a light source for injecting signals into the system at 850 or 1300 nanometers (depending on the type of fiber) and a power meter to measure what comes out the other end. Some devices include both functions and can be used to test fiber that is still on the spool.
- **Token Ring testers:** Test for shorts, opens, and grounds on shielded twisted-pair (STP) cabling in Token Ring installations.
- **LAN analyzers (sniffers):** For troubleshooting problems with LAN protocols at all levels of the Open Systems Interconnection (OSI) reference model protocol stack, from lower-level protocols such as Data Link Control (DLC), Internetwork Packet Exchange/Sequenced Packet Exchange (IPX/SPX), NetBIOS Enhanced User Interface (NetBEUI), and Transmission Control Protocol/Internet Protocol (TCP/IP) to higher-level protocols such as File Transfer Protocol (FTP), Hypertext Transfer Protocol (HTTP), NetBIOS, Server Message Block (SMB), and Simple Mail Transfer Protocol (SMTP). These devices basically capture LAN traffic and allow you to analyze and filter packets that use specific protocols, that are transmitted and received from specific computers, that are portions of a specific communication session between two computers, and so on. Microsoft Network Monitor, which is included with Microsoft Systems Management Server (SMS), Microsoft Windows 2000, Windows .NET Server, and Windows NT, is a software-based sniffer that runs on any PC with a network card and can capture and analyze most forms of LAN traffic.
- **SCSI testers:** Test Small Computer Systems Interface (SCSI) buses for shorts, opens, or improper termination. These are usually dedicated to a specific type of SCSI interface.
- **ISDN and T1 test equipment:** Includes continuity testers, channel testers, and line-quality analyzers for testing Integrated Services Digital Network (ISDN) and T-carrier circuits. They can sample frames to check for jitter and lack of synchronization.
- **WAN analyzers:** Test serial transmission protocols such as RS-232 and V.35, which are used to connect WAN devices such as routers and bridges to Channel Service Unit/Data Service Units (CSU/DSUs). They are typically used to troubleshoot frame relay, High-level Data Link Control (HDLC), Point-to-Point Protocol (PPP), Synchronous Data Link Control (SDLC), Serial Line Internet Protocol (SLIP), Systems Network Architecture (SNA), and X.25 connections. You can connect a WAN analyzer to a serial connection by using a Y-shaped connector called a data tap, which lets you monitor communication without interfering with the data being transmitted.

Notes

Cable testers can trace cables through walls, ceilings, and floors by measuring a cable's length and telling you whether the cable is terminated, has an open end, is connected to a port on a hub, and other data. You can plug two-way cable testers into a wall plate and test the patch panel to determine which cable connects to the wall plate.

Use a cable tester on a new enhanced Category 5 (Cat5e) cabling installation before you install and configure your Fast Ethernet network equipment. Good-quality cable testers typically test all four pairs of wires in unshielded twisted-pair (UTP) cabling over frequencies of up to 100 megahertz (MHz) or higher, checking cable integrity for shorts and opens, measuring cable segment lengths using time domain reflectometry (TDR), and allowing measurement of attenuation, near-end crosstalk (NEXT), and PowerSum NEXT to an accuracy of 0.1 decibels or better.

See Also: *cabling, Channel Service Unit/Data Service Unit (CSU/DSU), crosstalk, enhanced Category 5 (Cat5e) cabling, fiber-optic cabling, Integrated Services Digital Network (ISDN), network troubleshooting, Open Systems Interconnection (OSI) reference model, RS-232, shielded twisted-pair (STP) cabling, Small Computer System Interface (SCSI), T-carrier, time domain reflectometry (TDR), Token Ring, unshielded twisted-pair (UTP) cabling, V.35*

Tetra

Stands for Terrestrial Trunked Radio, a European standard for digital mobile radio services.

See: *Terrestrial Trunked Radio (Tetra)*

text file

Another name for an ASCII file, a file that contains unformatted ASCII text.

See: *ASCII file*

TFTP

Stands for Trivial File Transfer Protocol, a simple file transfer protocol for Transmission Control Protocol/Internet Protocol (TCP/IP).

See: *Trivial File Transfer Protocol (TFTP)*

thick coax

Another name for thicknet, the thick coaxial cabling used in Standard Ethernet (10Base5) networks.

See: *thicknet*

thicknet

The thick coaxial cabling used in Standard Ethernet (10Base5) networks.

Overview

Thicknet coaxial cabling is usually 3/8 inch in diameter, is fairly rigid, and has an impedance of 50 ohms. It can carry signals up to 500 meters (1640 feet)—hence the designation 10Base5 for "**10** megabits per second **Base**band transmission over **5** hundred meters." Thicknet was commonly used in the 1980s, mainly for Ethernet cabling, but it has been superceded by unshielded twisted-pair (UTP) cabling and fiber-optic cabling.

To connect a computer to a thicknet cable, you attach a vampire tap to the cable. The tap pierces the cable's insulation layers and makes contact with the signal-carrying copper core. The tap is connected to a transceiver, and a drop cable connects the transceiver to an attachment unit interface (AUI) connector on the computer's network interface card (NIC).

See Also: *10Base5, coaxial cabling, Ethernet, fiber-optic cabling, unshielded twisted-pair (UTP) cabling*

thin client

A client used for terminal-based computing.

Overview

A thin client is a device or stripped-down PC that has only the hardware necessary to support terminal client software. In terminal-based computing, the terminal client sends keystrokes and mouse movements over the network to a terminal server where actual applications reside. The server processes the client input and returns display data to the client, which displays the results for the user. In true terminal-based computing the server does the processing—the client is basically a "dumb" terminal that supports keyboard/mouse input and video output only. The thin clients used in terminal-based computing contrast with traditional "fat clients" in the form of standard PCs, which have greater hardware requirements, consume more network bandwidth, are more complex to manage, and cost more than thin clients.

The main difference between the newer generation of thin clients and the older mainframe-based dumb terminals is that today's thin clients can use an Ethernet network running Internet Protocol (IP) as their underlying network transport, but legacy dumb terminals ran over dedicated serial connections instead. The main advantage of thin clients over traditional fat clients is manageability—applications and user profiles can be securely and centrally managed on terminal servers locked away in back rooms, and practically nothing can go wrong with the machines on users' desktops other than a loose network connection.

History

The first thin client developed for the Microsoft Windows platform was WinFrame from Citrix Systems, a multiuser client/server terminal application developed in 1995 for the Windows NT 3.51 Server platform. To distinguish Citrix WinFrame clients from legacy dumb terminals, the term *Windows-Based Terminal (WBT)* was coined. Microsoft Corporation included its own terminal server platform in an edition of its next version of Windows NT, namely Terminal Server Edition for Windows NT 4 Server. Citrix then developed an enhanced version of its own product called MetaFrame. Citrix and Microsoft continue to be the two market leaders in thin-client computing platforms, with Microsoft including its Terminal Services as part of its Windows 2000, Windows XP, and Windows .NET Server platforms and Citrix MetaFrame supporting the Windows, Macintosh, UNIX, and Linux platforms.

Architecture

Despite the similar approach of the Citrix and Microsoft platforms, there are some underlying architectural differences between them. Most significantly, although Microsoft uses its proprietary Remote Desktop Protocol (RDP) for transporting keyboard, mouse, and video information over the network, Citrix uses its own Independent Computing Architecture (ICA) protocol for this purpose. Both of these protocols can operate over any IP network, including local area network (LAN) and dial-up or dedicated wide area network (WAN) connections. Both platforms also include ActiveX controls that allow the client to be any machine running the Microsoft Internet Explorer Web browser (Citrix also includes a plug-in for the Netscape Navigator browser), enabling Windows-based computing within a Web browser interface.

Marketplace

WBTs for enterprise markets come in a variety of formats, including compact desktop units, handheld devices, and even mobile devices such as wireless Personal Digital Assistants (PDAs). A wide variety of vendors produce WBTs that are compatible with Microsoft's RDP and Citrix's ICA architectures, including Wyse Technology, IBM, and many others. Boundless Technologies offers its Capio II terminal, which runs Windows CE, supports Super Video Graphics Array (SVGA) graphics, and has two universal serial bus (USB) ports and built-in 10/100BaseT Ethernet. Network Computing Devices has a similar entry called ThinSTAR. Wyse, which was the first to market with a WBT product, offers the Winterm 3200LE and many other models.

Web-based WBTs are increasingly popular as well, because they allow thin clients to run within standard Web browsers. Popular products in this category include Nfuse from Citrix, HobLink from Hob Software, and Microsoft's Windows 2000 Terminal Services Advanced Client (TSAC).

Prospects

Although thin clients reduce the management costs associated with managing desktop PCs, thin clients themselves require licensing and hence have only a small impact on software costs. Some vendors are trying to work around these licensing costs by providing innovative forms of terminal-based access to Windows 2000, Windows XP, and Windows .NET Server terminal servers. For example, Tarantella has a terminal server product called Tarantella that runs on UNIX platforms, emulates multiple WBT clients to a Windows 2000 terminal server, and supports both native 32-bit Windows applications and Java-based clients running within Web browsers.

Notes

Although the term *thin client* is usually used nowadays in the context of Windows terminal-based computing, other platforms have at times fallen under the banner of thin client, specifically:

- **Legacy-free PC:** Formerly known as the NetPC, this is a revised initiative from Microsoft and PC manufacturers whose aim is to simplify the PC architecture by removal of legacy features such as the Industry Standard Architecture (ISA) bus and to make systems more secure by removing expansion capabilities. Examples of legacy-free PCs in the marketplace include the Compaq iPaq, the IBM NetVista, and the Hewlett-Packard e-pc. Legacy-free PCs tend to be easier to manage than traditional PCs but cost about the same. Legacy-free PCs are not thin clients, however, because they run applications locally and hence need processor, memory, and storage to accomplish this.
- **Network computer (NC):** The NC architecture was created by IBM, Oracle Corporation, and Sun Microsystems as a terminal-based computing platform using a Java-based thin client. The NC architecture has recently re-emerged and scored some success with its new SunRay platform. The NC is a true "thin client" architecture, but it lags in popularity compared to the Windows-based Citrix and Windows 2000 Terminal Services platforms.

Note that the term *thin server* refers to a rack-mount server having a 1U or 2U format, not a terminal server for a thin client. See the article "rack," elsewhere in this book, for more information about thin servers.

See Also: *Independent Computing Architecture (ICA), Internet Protocol (IP), rack, Remote Desktop Protocol (RDP), terminal, terminal server, Terminal Services*

T

thin coax

Also called thinnet, the thin coaxial cabling used for 10Base2 Ethernet networks.

See: *thinnet*

thinnet

The thin coaxial cabling used for 10Base2 Ethernet networks.

Overview

Thinnet cabling is RG-58 coaxial cabling that is 3/16 inch in diameter, is relatively flexible, and has an impedance of 50 ohms. Thinnet uses Bayonet-Neill-Concelman (BNC) connectors to connect cable segments, computers, and concentrators (hubs) together in bus-style networks. Many older hubs, bridges, routers, and other networking devices still have at least one thinnet port for connecting to 10Base2 networks.

Thinnet was often used in the 1980s for workgroup or departmental local area networks (LANs). Thinnet has been superceded by the more popular unshielded twisted-pair (UTP) cabling used in structured wiring deployments for premise cabling. One place where thinnet is still used occasionally, however, is in electrically noisy environments such as shop floors in factories, where electromagnetic interference (EMI) caused by motors, generators, and other heavy equipment can disrupt communication over UTP. Coaxial cabling, with its internal shielding, can easily withstand this kind of noise.

Notes

Thinnet cables must be terminated at both ends. If communication on a thinnet network is down, check the termination points first, then check for loose BNC T-connectors attached to the computers on the network. Note that thinnet cabling can become damaged if it is sharply bent or twisted, so handle it carefully. (It is not nearly as fragile as fiber-optic cabling, however.)

See Also: *10Base2, BNC connector, bus topology, coaxial cabling, electromagnetic interference (EMI), terminator, unshielded twisted-pair (UTP) cabling*

TIA

Stands for Telecommunications Industry Association, a national trade organization representing all aspects of the telecommunications industry in the United States.

See: *Telecommunications Industry Association (TIA)*

Time Division Multiple Access (TDMA)

A cellular communications technology based on time-division multiplexing (TDM).

Overview

Time Division Multiple Access (TDMA) is used to refer to two systems:

- Any digital cellular communications system that employs TDM to enable a single channel to carry multiple conversations simultaneously.
- A specific cellular phone system in the United States that is operated byAT&T and is commonly called North American TDMA. More properly speaking, TDMA is the air interface for AT&T Wireless Services.

The first definition is the engineer's, and the second is the popular one from a consumer's point of view. This article will take the broader view of TDMA as a technology and consider the various popular implementations it has achieved.

History

The original analog cellular phone system developed by Bell Laboratories in the late 1970s and widely deployed in the United States was called Advanced Mobile Phone System (AMPS). This technology was based on Frequency Division Multiple Access (FDMA), which assigned one conversation to each channel. The main problems with this system were that FDMA systems supported only a limited number of concurrent users, and, because the channels were narrowly spaced with respect to each other, interference sometimes occurred. To overcome these problems, TDMA was used as the underlying technology for the first all-digital U.S. cellular communications system, called Digital Advanced Mobile Phone System (D-AMPS). The D-AMPS system operated in the same 800 megahertz (MHz) band of the frequency spectrum as AMPS but was able to handle greater numbers of simultaneous conversations and was more immune to interference between channels. D-AMPS is based on the IS-54 standard and is still used in parts of the United States, but newer Code Division Multiple Access (CDMA) cellular systems have become more widely deployed.

Other TDMA-based cellular systems eventually followed, including

- **Global System for Mobile Communications (GSM):** This is the world's most popular cellular communications system, but although it is prevalent in Europe and parts of Asia, it is still behind CDMA systems in the United States. GSM operates at 900 and 1800 MHz in Europe and at 1900 MHz in the United States.
- **Personal Digital Cellular (PDC):** This is the world's second most popular cellular system and is used exclusively in Japan.
- **Personal Communications Services (PCS):** This is an umbrella term for a variety of cellular communication systems that operate at 1900 MHz in the United States. One of the technologies used by PCS is TDMA.
- **Integrated Digital Enhanced Network (IDEN):** This TDMA-based system was developed by Motorola and is used in some parts of the United States.

Implementation

TDMA works by dividing a radio channel in time to create a series of short slots or time intervals, each a small fraction of a second. Signals from different subscribers are then assigned to specific slots, and the whole series of slots is repeated many times per second. The result is that small delays are introduced into conversations, but this happens so quickly that it cannot be noticed by the unaided ear.

Different TDMA-based cellular systems use different slot and cycle times. For example, North American TDMA (that is, D-AMPS) uses 30 kilohertz (KHz)–wide channels segmented into three time slots each 6.67 microseconds long and capable of carrying 320 bits of data per slot. The whole eight-slot frame repeats itself 50 times per second. By contrast, GSM uses eight slots each 0.577 microseconds long and carrying 156 bits of data, cycled at 217 times per second. The result is that a single D-AMPS channel can carry three simultaneous conversations and a GSM channel can carry eight conversations, and the quality of GSM communications is smoother than D-AMPS.

Prospects

Although TDMA systems based on the IS-54 are considered second generation (2G) cellular communication systems, a newer standard IS-136 has been developed as a 2.5G system capable of higher data transfer rates of 43.2 kilobits per second (Kbps).

See Also: *2G, 2.5G, Advanced Mobile Phone Service (AMPS), cellular communications, Code Division Multiple Access (CDMA), Digital Advanced Mobile Phone Service (D-AMPS), Frequency Division Multiple Access (FDMA), Global System for Mobile Communications (GSM), Personal Communications Services (PCS), time-division multiplexing (TDM)*

time-division multiplexing (TDM)

A method for sending several data streams over a single communication path.

Overview

In time-division multiplexing (TDM), data from different input channels is apportioned into fixed-length segments and then multiplexed in round-robin fashion into a single output data stream, which can then be transmitted over a single channel transmission system and then demultiplexed at the destination location. TDM segments can be created by the multiplexer itself or can be inherent in the input channel signals, such as fixed-length frames. For example, if input streams A, B, and C are divided into segments as shown here

```
A = A1, A2, A3,...
B = B1, B2, B3,...
C = C1, C2, C3,...
```

the time-division multiplexed output stream will look like this:

```
MUX(ABC) = A1, B1, C1, A2, B2, C2, A3, B3,
C3,...
```

One weakness in the TDM approach is that if an input channel does not have anything important to carry for a time, empty segments are inserted into the output stream regardless. For example, if channel A is not transmitting data, one-third of the output channel contains null data and is not being used. You can overcome this weakness by using a more sophisticated multiplexing technique called statistical multiplexing.

Uses

TDM is used in a variety of different networking and telecommunications technologies. In T-carrier transmission, for example, TDM enables a single T1 line to simultaneously carry 24 data channels by interleaving data into portions of a single 193-bit frame. For example, bits 1 through 8 represent channel 1, bits 9 through 16 represent channel 2, and so on to bits 185 through 192 for channel 24, plus one final bit number 193, which is used for link synchronization. This TDM-based framing process occurs 8000 times per second, producing a total throughput for T1 of 1.544 megabits per second (Mbps).

See Also: *multiplexing, statistical multiplexing (STM), T1, T-carrier*

time domain reflectometry (TDR)

A cable testing technique for finding breaks or shorts in a cable.

Overview

A time domain reflectometer is a device that sends a pulse onto a cable and measures the time that it takes for the reflection to return from a short or break in the cable. (This is analogous to the use of sonar to determine ocean depth.) The time interval between transmission and reception of the signal is called the signal delay; this delay can be used to determine the location of the short or break, typically within a few centimeters, even though the break might be hidden within the cable's jacket and not be visible. You can also use the reflectometer to determine the length of an undamaged cable and identify cables running through walls and false ceilings in a cabling installation.

Most high-quality cable testers can perform time domain reflectometry (TDR) tests in addition to their other functions. Time domain reflectometers are available for testing both copper cabling and fiber-optic cabling.

See Also: *cabling, network troubleshooting*

T

TLD

Stands for top-level domain, a domain that is directly beneath the root domain in the hierarchical Domain Name System (DNS).

See: *top-level domain (TLD)*

TLS

Stands for Transport Layer Security, a security protocol based on Secure Sockets Layer (SSL).

See: *Transport Layer Security (TLS)*

TN3270

A form of Telnet used for accessing mainframe hosts over an Internet Protocol (IP) network.

Overview

TN3270 was developed as an alternate to the regular Telnet service for accessing mainframe computers. TN3270 provides a better look and feel than standard Telnet, but its numeric field handling and keyboard interface are somewhat clumsy. TN3270 provides keyboard emulation and block-mode service at the client level, thus freeing the mainframe from translation functions. TN3270 supports workstation emulation only and does not include file-transfer or printer-emulation services. TN3270 originally stood for Telnet 3270 but is never referred to this way anymore.

By using Microsoft Host Integration Server, users running a TN3270 client can connect to mainframe computers using the TN3270 service included with Host Integration Server. TN3270 can also be used to connect clients to AS/400 systems, but the AS/400 systems must translate the 3270 data stream into 5250 format and provide keyboard mapping between the 3270 and 5250 key sequences, a process that consumes additional CPU resources on the AS/400.

See Also: *Telnet, TN5250*

TN5250

A form of Telnet used for accessing AS/400 systems over an Internet Protocol (IP) network.

Overview

TN5250 is to the AS/400 computing environment what TN3270 is to the mainframe world. TN5250 offers full 5250 terminal emulation, including hot backup and security features similar to those included with the TN3270 service. TN5250 provides workstation emulation only and does not include file-transfer or printer-emulation services. TN5250 originally stood for Telnet 5250 but is never referred to this way anymore.

A TN5250 service included with Microsoft Host Integration Server lets TN5250 clients connect to AS/400 systems without installing Transmission Control Protocol/Internet Protocol (TCP/IP) on the AS/400. Using Host Integration Server, TN5250 provides workstation emulation that supports almost all the field attributes and keyboard sequences of a "real" SNA 5250 except text assist.

See Also: *Telnet, TN3270*

Token Ring

A local area network (LAN) technology developed by IBM.

Overview

Token Ring was first developed by IBM in 1984 as an alternative to Ethernet. Token Ring originally operated at 4 megabits per second (Mbps). This speed was later extended to 16 Mbps, which enabled Token Ring to compete favorably for a while with the 10 Mbps speed of standard Ethernet. Over the years, the evolution of Token Ring, however, has not matched that of Ethernet. Fast Ethernet brought speeds of 100 Mbps, and an initiative called High-Speed Token Ring (HSTR) was undertaken jointly by Token Ring vendors IBM, Madge Networks, and Olicom to do the same. But in 1998, in the face of emerging Gigabit Ethernet (GbE) standards, IBM abandoned its HSTR efforts, which spelled the death knell for Token Ring and relegated it to the realm of a legacy technology. Despite this occurrence, there is still a large installed base in some shops, but it seems inevitable that they will have to consider migrating to Ethernet technologies in the near future.

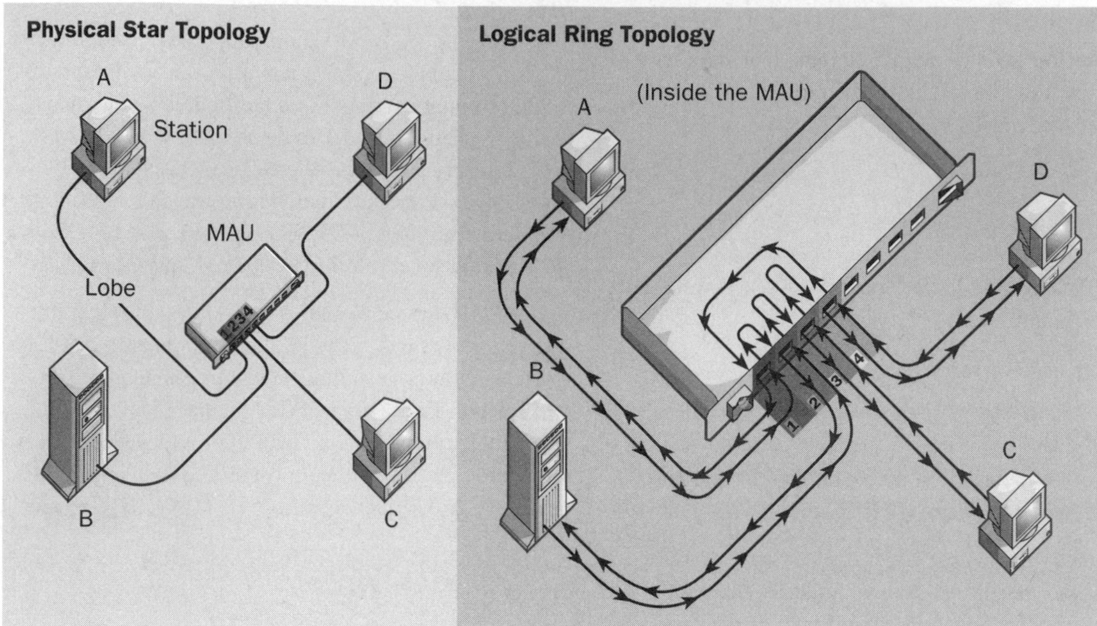

Token Ring. *The physical and logical topologies of a Token Ring network.*

Token Ring was standardized in the Institute of Electrical and Electronics Engineers (IEEE) 802.5 specifications, which describe a token-passing ring network configured as a physical star topology using structured wiring implemented with twisted-pair cabling and active hubs.

Implementation

In a Token Ring network, stations (computers) are wired in a star formation to a central wiring concentrating unit called a Multistation Access Unit (MAU). Note that the term *Multistation Access Unit* is sometimes abbreviated as MSAU instead of MAU to distinguish it from *media attachment unit*, a term used in older Ethernet networking technologies.

The MAU unit concentrates wiring in a star topology but internally forms a logical ring topology over which network traffic can travel. Lobes connect the individual stations to the MAU. The maximum cable length for a lobe is 74 feet (22.5 meters) or 328 feet (100 meters), depending on the cable type, but you can extend this distance up to 1.5 miles (2.4 kilometers) using repeaters designed for Token Ring networks. Note that distances between MAUs and attached stations are usually specified as lobe lengths, which refer to round-trip signal paths. Thus, a station with a lobe length of 655 feet (200 meters) actually uses a cable 328 feet (100 meters) long.

MAUs typically support 8 or 16 connections for attaching lobes. You can extend a Token Ring network by connecting the ring-out port of one MAU to the ring-in port of another MAU to form larger rings that can support larger numbers of stations (stackable MAUs simplify this interconnection process). The maximum number of MAUs that can be interconnected in this way is 33. Some MAUs also support interconnection using fiber-optic cabling to create networks that span a building or even a campus. Most MAUs also support in-band management by using Simple Network Management Protocol (SNMP) plus out-of-band management by using a serial interface.

Token Ring networks come in two types, both of which can operate at 4 or 16 Mbps:

- **Type 1 Token Ring:** Generally uses shielded twisted-pair (STP) cabling with a special data connector developed by IBM for Token Ring installations. However, 16-Mbps MAUs generally have ports for RJ-45 or DB9 connectors.

- **Type 3 Token Ring:** This type uses standard unshielded twisted-pair (UTP) cabling with RJ-45 connectors.

Type 1 Token Ring is often considered more reliable than Type 3, but the larger installed base of UTP cabling made Type 3 an attractive option for many Token Ring installations. Type 1 configurations support as many as 260 stations per ring, while Type 3 can support up to 72 stations per ring. Most MAUs and NICs are dual-speed and can run at either 4 or 16 Mbps, but not both. However, you can use bridges or routers to connect 4-Mbps Token Ring networks to 16-Mbps Token Ring networks.

STP cabling for Type 1 Token Ring comes in nine types, only two of which are common now:

- **Type 1 cable:** Uses two-pair 22-gauge shielded, grounded solid copper wire. Use this type for longer cable runs such as those between wiring closets and work areas. The maximum lobe length is 655 feet (200 meters).
- **Type 6 cable:** Uses two-pair 26-gauge stranded, shielded copper wire and is more flexible (and looks nicer!) than Type 1 cable. Use this type for work areas in which cables will be visible or where equipment will be moved frequently and especially for patch cables. The maximum lobe length is 148 feet (45 meters).

Token Ring stations pass a single data packet called a token from one computer to the next rather than let each node transmit independently, as in a contention-based network such as Ethernet. Only one token can be on the network at a time, so collisions do not occur in Token Ring networks as they do in Ethernet networks. This process is analogous to sending messages to a group of people by passing a hat. In order to pass a token in a Token Ring network, each station must know who its neighbors are and must perform a check to make sure that the circuit is unbroken. Messages containing this information are continually sent around the ring. The token circulates so long as this message is received. To generate the required information, the first station online in the ring assumes the role of Active Monitor Station. It creates the token and is responsible for taking action if the token is lost or damaged. The Active Monitor Station sends out an Active Monitor Present frame every seven seconds to the next node down the line. Each node in turn informs its downstream neighbor that it is its Nearest Active Upstream Neighbor. An error-detection process called beaconing occurs if the ring breaks and the token fails to circulate. If the Active Monitor Station fails, another station assumes its role of monitoring the status of the network and generating a new token if the existing one is lost.

If a station wants to transmit data over the network, it waits until the token comes by; if the token has not been claimed by another station, it claims the token and inverts the monitor setting bit to mark it "busy" so that no other station can claim the token for a predefined but variable amount of time. The originating station then removes the last byte from the token (called the delimiter byte), appends data to the token, and appends the delimiter byte to the end to form a frame of variable length (up to 8000 bytes). The token with data circulates around the ring in one direction from station to station. (Each station acts as a repeater to regenerate and forward the token.) When it returns to the originating station, the token and the data are removed and a new token is generated and placed onto the network.

Notes

You can get both types of cable in an adapter cable version (terminated at one end with an IBM data connector and at the other end with a DB9 male connector) or a patch-panel version (terminated at both ends with data connectors). Use patch panel cables to connect MAUs, and use adapter cables to connect stations to MAUs. You can also get baluns, which can convert Type 1 IBM cabling to UTP cabling to connect different Token Ring types, and you can get special adapters that allow data connectors to be connected to RJ-45 ports so that you can use installed UTP cabling with Type 1 MAUs.

Some network interface cards (NICs) for Token Ring networking support software-configurable physical layer addressing, but note that all Token Ring NICs must have unique MAC addresses for communications to work properly on a Token Ring network.

The following table provides suggestions for troubleshooting common Token Ring network problems.

Troubleshooting Tips for Token Ring Networks

Problem	*Suggestion*
Mismatched ring speed	Be sure that all connected stations use 4 Mbps or that all use 16 Mbps. Do not mix stations of different speeds.
Stations cannot receive	Check cables and reset the MAU.
Conflicting MAC addresses	Use NIC configuration software to change the MAC address on one of the conflicting computers.
Traffic congestion on the network	Segment the network by using a bridge or a router.

See Also: *Ethernet, Fast Ethernet, Gigabit Ethernet (GbE), local area network (LAN), MAC address, Multistation Access Unit (MAU or MSAU), network interface card (NIC), shielded twisted-pair (STP) cabling, unshielded twisted-pair (UTP) cabling*

top-level domain (TLD)

A domain that is directly beneath the root domain in the hierarchical Domain Name System (DNS).

Overview

Top-level domains (TLDs) are relatively few in number and are used to identify broad classes of Internet services. The number of TLDs is controlled by the Internet Corporation for Assigned Names and Numbers (ICANN), which keeps this number small to maintain the efficiency of the hierarchical DNS naming system. Name resolution for TLDs is provided by the Internet's 13 root name servers and 10 top-level domain servers.

The various TLDs are listed in the following table. Several additional TLDs, such as .name, .pro, .museum, .aero, and .coop, have been approved by ICANN. The first three TLDs are managed commercially by domain name registrars, and their use varies widely. For example, although .net was originally intended for networking companies only, even some personal home pages use this domain.

Top-Level Domains

Domain	*Description*
.com	Commercial businesses and miscellaneous other uses
.net	Networking and telecommunications companies
.org	Nonprofit organizations
.edu	Four-year degree-granting universities and colleges in North America
.gov	U.S. federal government
.mil	U.S. military use only
.int	Organizations established by international treaty
.biz	Businesses
.info	General purpose

In addition to the domains listed in the table, countries as well as states and provinces within countries are identified by two-letter country codes. For example, .uk is the top-level domain for the United Kingdom, .ca is the top-level domain for Canada, and mb.ca is the top-level domain for the province of Manitoba in Canada. Although the .com domain is by far the most popular one today due to the way it is marketed, many businesses are forced to use other domains such as .net, .biz, or their country domain because of the shortage of commercial top-level domains.

Notes

A special domain called in-addr.arpa is used for reverse DNS name lookups (resolving a host name given the host's Internet Protocol [IP] address).

See Also: *country code, Domain Name System (DNS), in-addr.arpa, Internet, Internet Corporation for Assigned Names and Numbers (ICANN), root name server*

topology

The physical layout of computers, cables, switches, routers, and other components of a network.

Overview

The term *topology* can refer to either a network's physical topology, which is the actual physical layout or pattern of the cabling, or its logical topology, which is the path that signals actually take around the network. This difference is most evident in Token Ring networks, whose cabling is physically arranged in a star but whose signal flows in a ring from one component to the next. The term *topology* without any further description is usually assumed to mean the physical layout. The term comes from topos, the Greek word for "place."

When you design a network, your choice of topology will be determined by the network's size, architecture, cost, and management. Basic network topologies include the following:

- **Bus topology:** The stations are connected in a linear fashion. An example is the 10Base2 form of Ethernet.
- **Star topology:** The stations are connected to a single concentrating device called a hub (Ethernet) or a Multistation Access Unit, or MAU (Token Ring physical topology).
- **Ring topology:** The stations are connected in a ring. Examples are Fiber Distributed Data Interface, or FDDI (logical and physical ring), and Token Ring (logical ring and physical star).
- **Mesh topology:** The stations are connected in a complex, redundant pattern. This topology is generally used only in wide area networks (WANs) in which different networks are connected using routers.

Variations of these basic topologies include the following:

- **Star bus topology:** Consists of many star networks whose concentrators (hubs) are connected in a linear bus fashion
- **Star-wired topology or cascaded-star topology:** Consists of star networks whose hubs are joined in star formation to other hubs, forming a kind of tree-shaped network with the main hub at the top

See Also: *bus topology, mesh topology, ring topology, star topology*

tracert

On Microsoft Windows platforms, a utility used for troubleshooting communication on routed Internet Protocol (IP) networks such as the Internet. The corresponding utility on UNIX platforms is known as traceroute.

Overview

Tracert (or traceroute) is used to "trace the route" across an IP internetwork from a local host to a remote one. Tracert uses Internet Control Message Protocol (ICMP) echo packets similar to the way ping operates. When an attempt is made to use tracert to trace the route to a remote IP host, a series of ICMP echo packets are assigned a steadily increasing Time to Live (TTL) to test network connectivity with routers and IP hosts that are farther away along the route. This continues until either connectivity fails or the target host is finally contacted and successfully responds.

Examples

If you run

```
tracert research.microsoft.com
```

from Winnipeg through your local Internet service provider (ISP), you might get a display similar to the following, depending on the route the packets take at that moment:

```
Tracing route to research.microsoft.com
[131.107.65.14] over a maximum of 30 hops:

  1   100 ms   100 ms   110 ms
wnpgas04.mts.net [205.200.55.1]

  2   100 ms    90 ms   100 ms  205.200.55.6

  3    90 ms   100 ms   110 ms
wnpgbr01-g11-102.mts.net [205.200.28.82]

  4   110 ms   100 ms   100 ms
dis4-winnipeg32-pos11-0.in.bellnexxia.net
[206.108.110.5]

  5   120 ms   100 ms   100 ms
core2-winnipeg32-pos6-2.in.bellnexxia.net
[206.108.102.129]
```

T

```
  6   120 ms   130 ms   120 ms
core2-toronto12-pos10-1.in.bellnexxia.net
[206.108.97.29]

  7   120 ms   130 ms   120 ms
core3-toronto12-pos6-0.in.bellnexxia.net
[64.230.242.201]

  8   180 ms   180 ms   181 ms
core2-vancouver-pos10-2.in.bellnexxia.net
[206.108.101.182]

  9   191 ms   180 ms   190 ms
core2-seattle-pos12-0.in.bellnexxia.net
[206.108.102.209]

 10   180 ms   190 ms   190 ms
bx3-seattle-pos5-0.in.bellnexxia.net
[206.108.102.202]

 11   180 ms   190 ms   190 ms
microsoft-gw.core1-seattle-pos6-2.in.
bellnexxia.net [206.108.108.134]

 12   180 ms   190 ms   190 ms  207.46.190.161

 13   180 ms  1042 ms   180 m  s
iuscixtukc1202-ge-5-0.msft.net [207.46.129.48]

 14   191 ms   190 ms   190 ms  207.46.168.122

 15   1 8 1m   s190ms190ms131.107.33.50

 16  1142 ms   1021 ms   191 ms
iusdinetdc7507-fe-0-1-0.msft.net
[131.107.34.135]

 17   190 ms   181 ms   190 ms  131.107.40.70

 18   190 ms   191 ms   190 ms
research.microsoft.com [131.107.65.14]

Trace complete.
```

Note that the destination host was finally reached after a distance of 18 hops, and note the gradually increasing response times.

See Also: *network troubleshooting, ping*

transaction

A method of coordinating a series of changes to a set of resources distributed over the network.

Overview

Transactions are units of work that must succeed or fail as a whole—a transaction can never partially succeed. If a transaction fails while only partially completed, the transaction is rolled back to the beginning. An example is a credit card purchase: The store requests the purchase amount from the credit card company, the company distributes the funds to the store, and the company bills the purchaser. If any part of the transaction fails, the entire transaction must fail to prevent money from being lost.

Component Services on Microsoft Windows 2000 (or Microsoft Transaction Server on Windows NT), a tool that provides the underlying support, or "plumbing," for creating scalable, distributed, transactional Web applications, provides failure isolations and mechanisms for recovering failed transactions and can run components of transactions as isolated processes for greater crash protection. Component Services uses the Distributed Component Object Model (DCOM) programming architecture for communication between components on Microsoft Windows networks.

See Also: *Distributed Component Object Model (DCOM)*

transaction log

A technology that provides fault tolerance and crash recovery for critical database files.

Overview

Transaction logs are used in products such as the Microsoft Exchange Server directory services database and information store and Microsoft SQL Server. Using Exchange Server as an example, data is written to transaction log files before it is applied to the directory or information store databases. This improves the performance of write operations to the Exchange databases. In Exchange, you might have several transaction logs in your database directory. When a database is backed up, the transaction logs are then purged.

Transaction logs also play an important role in providing fault tolerance and recoverability for databases. If a system crash corrupts the database files, you can use the transaction logs (if they are intact) to restore all changes to the database since the last backup. Transaction logs make online incremental and differential backups possible. Without transaction logs, you would be able to perform full backups only when backing up databases online.

Transact-SQL

Microsoft Corporation's version of Structured Query Language (SQL) used by Microsoft SQL Server.

Overview

Transact-SQL (sometimes called T-SQL) is a superset of the SQL-92 standard developed by the American National Standards Institute (ANSI) and the International Organization for Standards (ISO). Transact-SQL includes all the features of standard SQL plus several enhancements, including

- Conditional programming constructs such as IF and WHILE
- System stored procedures

Transact-SQL has continued to evolve with each new version of SQL Server released by Microsoft and is a powerful data manipulation language for relational database management systems (RDBMS).

See Also: *American National Standards Institute (ANSI), database, International Organization for Standardization (ISO), SQL Server, Structured Query Language (SQL)*

transceiver

An electronic device for connecting a computer to a baseband transmission network so that the computer can transmit and receive signals on the network.

Overview

In the 1980s transceivers were often separate devices attached to thicknet cabling using vampire taps, but today most network interface cards (NICs) have onboard transceivers built into them. Some Fast Ethernet NICs also have a media independent interface (MII) to which an external transceiver can be connected to provide different kinds of 100-megabits per second (Mbps) networking. This allows greater flexibility in your networking options. For example, 100BaseTX transceivers have an RJ-45 port for connecting unshielded twisted-pair (UTP) cabling, and 100BaseFX transceivers have an SC-type port for connecting fiber-optic cabling.

See Also: *baseband transmission, network interface card (NIC), thicknet*

transceiver cable

Also called a drop cable, a cable connecting a computer's network interface card (NIC) to a transceiver attached to a thicknet cable in Standard Ethernet.

See: *drop cable*

Transmission Control Protocol (TCP)

A transport layer protocol of the Transmission Control Protocol/Internet Protocol (TCP/IP) suite.

Overview

Transmission Control Protocol (TCP) is one of two transport layer protocols used by TCP/IP, the other being User Datagram Protocol (UDP). Although UDP supports only unreliable, connectionless network communications, TCP provides support for reliable, connection-oriented delivery of Internet Protocol (IP) packets. TCP supports only point-to-point communications between two hosts and does not support multipoint communications as UDP does.

Some of the features of TCP communications include

- **Byte stream:** TCP accepts a stream of bytes from application level protocols and apportions it into TCP packets without regard to application-level message boundaries within the stream.
- **Connection-oriented:** Before transferring packets, TCP negotiates a connection between sending and receiving hosts using a process called a TCP Three-Way Handshake. TCP connections are also closed using the same process, and connections are maintained using a keep-alive process to ensure that they do not unnecessarily time out. These procedures

T

enable TCP to guarantee that transmitted data will be delivered to its targeted destination.

- **Full-duplex:** A TCP connection consists of two logical pipes for transmitting packets in opposite directions.
- **Reliable:** All TCP packets within a particular byte stream (part of a specific communication session) are sequenced to ensure that the byte stream can be properly reconstructed at the destination. Packets that successfully arrive at their destination cause acknowledgements (ACKs) to be generated so the sending host will know that delivery has been successful. Packets that arrive out of order are buffered, and missing packets are retransmitted after a period of time when the sending host determines that no acknowledgements have been received for these packets. Sender-side and receiver-side flow control are implemented to prevent loss of packets when buffers are full and to eliminate subsequent unnecessary retransmissions. In addition, TCP checksums are included to enable the receiving host to verify the bit-level integrity of the transmission.

Notes

Microsoft Corporation's implementation of TCP on its Microsoft Windows 2000, Windows XP, and Windows .NET Server platforms include support for advanced features such as self-tuning to ensure that data is sent at a speed optimal for the receiving host, dead gateway detection to ensure that inoperative gateways do not hinder packet delivery, and checksums for ensuring error-free delivery.

See Also: ACK, connectionless protocol, connection-oriented protocol, Internet Protocol (IP), Transmission Control Protocol/Internet Protocol (TCP/IP), User Datagram Protocol (UDP)

T

Transmission Control Protocol/ Internet Protocol (TCP/IP)

An industry-standard protocol suite forming the basis of the Internet.

Overview

Transmission Control Protocol/Internet Protocol (TCP/IP) was developed in the 1970s and 1980s as a standard protocol for linking hosts and networks into wide area networks (WANs). TCP/IP is an open networking standard that is independent from underlying physical network transport mechanisms. It uses a simple addressing scheme called IP addresses that allow billions of individual hosts to communicate with one another on the Internet. TCP/IP is also a routable protocol that is suitable for connecting dissimilar systems (such as Microsoft Windows and UNIX hosts) in heterogeneous networks and is the most common network transport in use today.

TCP/IP is a constantly evolving protocol suite whose development is steered by such bodies as the Internet Society (ISOC), the Internet Architecture Board (IAB), and the Internet Engineering Task Force (IETF). The various protocols, addressing schemes, and concepts of TCP/IP are defined in a series of documents called Requests for Comments (RFCs) issued by the IETF under an open standards process.

The foundation of the TCP/IP protocol suite is the Internet Protocol (IP), which provides the addressing scheme and supports routing of traffic between networks. The current version of IP is called IPv4 (Internet Protocol version 4) and uses a 32-bit addressing scheme. Due to the explosion of popularity of the Internet in recent years, this addressing scheme is viewed as inadequate to handle the Internet's future growth. As a result, a new version called IPv6 is likely to be widely implemented over the next several years.

Architecture

As shown in the diagram, TCP/IP has a layered architecture consisting of four distinct operational layers. These four layers map loosely to the seven layers of the Open Systems Interconnection (OSI) reference model. The four-layer TCP/IP architecture is sometimes referred to as the DoD Model because TCP/IP was developed in connection with the ARPANET project of the U.S. Department of Defense (DoD). Each layer of the TCP/IP protocol suite has its associated component protocols, the most important of which are listed here:

- **Application layer protocols:** These are responsible for application-level access to TCP/IP networking services. These include Dynamic Host

Configuration Protocol (DHCP), Domain Name System (DNS), Hypertext Transfer Protocol (HTTP), File Transfer Protocol (FTP), Telnet, Simple Mail Transfer Protocol (SMTP), Simple Network Management Protocol (SNMP), and numerous others. In the Microsoft implementation of TCP/IP, application layer protocols interact with transport layer protocols by using either Windows Sockets or NetBIOS over TCP/IP (NetBT).

- **Transport layer protocols:** These establish communication through connection-oriented sessions and connectionless broadcasts. Protocols at this layer include Transmission Control Protocol (TCP) and User Datagram Protocol (UDP).
- **Internet layer protocols:** These are responsible for routing and encapsulation into IP packets. Protocols at this layer include Internet Protocol (IP), Address Resolution Protocol (ARP), Internet Control Message Protocol (ICMP), and Internet Group Management Protocol (IGMP).
- **Network layer protocols:** These place frames on the network. TCP/IP can operate over a wide variety of network transports include the various local area network (LAN) architectures (such as Ethernet and Token Ring) and WAN telecommunication service technologies, including dial-up modem connections over the Public Switched Telephone Network (PSTN), Integrated Services Digital Network (ISDN), and Asynchronous Transfer Mode (ATM) networks.

TCP/IP employs two naming schemes to identify hosts and networks on an internetwork:

- **IP addresses:** These are logical 32-bit (4-byte) numeric addresses usually written in the form *w.x.y.z*. Using an associated subnet mask, IP addresses are split into two portions, a network ID that uniquely identifies the local network on the internetwork and a host ID that uniquely identifies the host on the local network. For example, the IP address 205.116.8.44 is partitioned using the subnet mask 255.255.255.0 into the network ID 25.116.8.0 and the host ID 44. IP addresses are the basic or primary way of identifying hosts and networks on an internetwork; they can either be assigned to hosts manually as static addresses or automatically using DHCP as dynamic addresses.
- **Fully qualified domain names (FQDNs):** These are alphanumeric names generally expressed in the form <host_name>.<domain_name> where <domain_name> identifies the particular network to which the host belongs and <host_name> uniquely identifies the host on the specific network. FQDNs are based on a hierarchical worldwide naming system called the Domain Name System (DNS). As an example, the FQDN server12. microsoft.com represents a host named server12 that belongs to a network whose domain name is microsoft.com. This microsoft.com domain is a second-level domain that belongs to the top-level domain named .com, which itself belongs to the root DNS domain named "." (dot). FQDNs are essentially "friendly" names that are easier to remember than IP addresses. For TCP/IP communications to take place, however, FQDNs must first be resolved into their associated IP addresses by using either a DNS server called a name server or using a hosts file stored on the local machine.

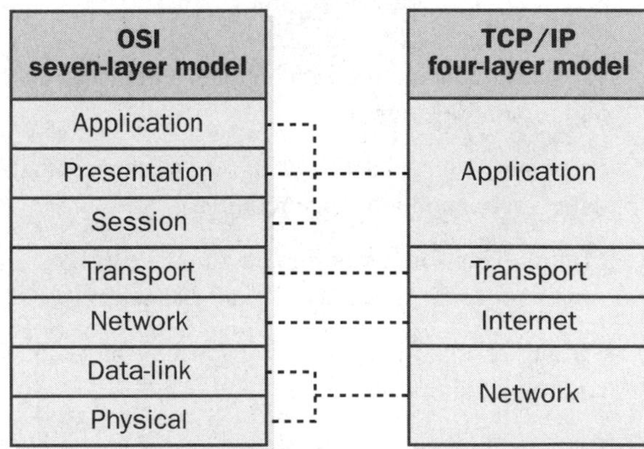

Transmission Control Protocol/Internet Protocol (TCP/IP). *How the four layers of the DoD TCP/IP model map to the seven-layer OSI reference model.*

See Also: *Address Resolution Protocol (ARP), Asynchronous Transfer Mode (ATM), Domain Name System (DNS), Dynamic Host Configuration Protocol (DHCP), Ethernet, File Transfer Protocol (FTP), fully qualified* *domain name (FQDN), hosts file, Hypertext Transfer Protocol (HTTP), Integrated Services Digital Network (ISDN), Internet, Internet Architecture Board (IAB), Internet Control Message Protocol (ICMP), Internet Engineering Task Force (IETF), Internet Group Management Protocol (IGMP), Internet Protocol (IP), Internet Society (ISOC), IP address, NetBIOS over TCP/IP (NetBT), Open Systems Interconnection (OSI) reference model, Public Switched Telephone Network (PSTN), Request for Comments (RFC), Simple Mail Transfer Protocol (SMTP), Simple Network Management Protocol (SNMP), subnet mask, Telnet, Token Ring, Transmission Control Protocol (TCP), User Datagram Protocol (UDP), Windows Sockets*

transport layer

Layer 4 of the Open Systems Interconnection (OSI) reference model.

Overview

The transport layer is responsible for providing reliable transport services to the upper-layer protocols. These services include:

- Flow control to ensure that the transmitting device does not send more data than the receiving device can handle
- Packet sequencing for segmentation of data packets and remote reassembly
- Error handling and acknowledgments to ensure that data is retransmitted when required
- Multiplexing for combining data from several sources for transmission over one data path
- Virtual circuits for establishing sessions between communicating stations

T

Notes

Transmission Control Protocol (TCP) resides at the equivalent of the OSI transport layer in the Transmission Control Protocol/Internet Protocol (TCP/IP) suite of protocols.

See Also: *Open Systems Interconnection (OSI) reference model, Transmission Control Protocol (TCP), Transmission Control Protocol/Internet Protocol (TCP/IP)*

Transport Layer Security (TLS)

A security protocol based on Secure Sockets Layer (SSL).

Overview

Transport Layer Security (TLS) is based on SSL 3 and is very similar in architecture and operation to that protocol. Netscape Communications originally developed SSL in 1993 to provide secure communications over the Internet for Hypertext Transfer Protocol (HTTP) traffic. SSL included support for public and symmetric key cryptography, two-way encrypted authentication, support for anonymous connections, client/server negotiation of the encryption algorithm to be used, and message integrity using digital certificates.

TLS supports all these features of SSL and provides services for secure authentication, data integrity, and confidentiality. TLS is used to secure HTTP, Simple Mail Transfer Protocol (SMTP), and other forms of Internet traffic.

TLS is defined in RFC 2246. A variant of TLS called EAP-TLS that uses the Extensible Authentication Protocol (EAP) extension to Point-to-Point Protocol (PPP) is defined in RFC 2716.

See Also: *Extensible Authentication Protocol (EAP), Hypertext Transfer Protocol (HTTP), Point-to-Point Protocol (PPP), public key cryptography, Secure Sockets Layer (SSL), Simple Mail Transfer Protocol (SMTP)*

tree

Also called a domain tree, a hierarchical grouping of Microsoft Windows 2000 or Windows .NET Server domains.

See: *domain tree*

Trivial File Transfer Protocol (TFTP)

A simple file transfer protocol for Transmission Control Protocol/Internet Protocol (TCP/IP).

Overview

Trivial File Transfer Protocol (TFTP) is a simple file transfer protocol that differs from the more popular File

Transfer Protocol (FTP) mainly in that it does not support any form of authentication. TFTP copies files to and from remote hosts by using the User Datagram Protocol (UDP). The remote host must be running the TFTP service or daemon for the TFTP client to be able to communicate with it. TFTP is defined in RFC 1350.

Uses

One place where TFTP is sometimes used is in UNIX environments where the bootstrap protocol (BOOTP) is used for booting diskless workstations. In this scenario, TFTP is used to download the boot disk image from the BOOTP server to the workstation. Another use for TFTP is in Cisco router networking where TFTP can be used to upload or download router configuration information or even perform a flash install of a new version of Cisco Systems' Internetwork Operating System (IOS).

Notes

The Microsoft Windows 2000 and Windows .NET Server platforms include both a command-line TFTP client and an optional TFTP service called the Trivial File Transfer Protocol Daemon (TFTPD) that is installed when the Remote Installation Services component is enabled.

See Also: *bootstrap protocol (BOOTP), File Transfer Protocol (FTP), Internetwork Operating System (IOS), router, User Datagram Protocol (UDP)*

trunking

Any method for aggregating multiple physical network links into a single logical link.

Overview

Trunking provides a way of overcoming the bandwidth limitations of a single physical network link. Trunking is generally employed in three contexts:

- In switched Ethernet networking, trunking can be used in either switch-switch or switch-server connections to relieve traffic congestion by providing increased bandwidth.
- In remote access and wide area networking, trunking is often used to aggregate multiple wide area network (WAN) links into a single fat pipe.
- In telecommunications, telcos sometimes use trunking to aggregate multiple Digital Subscriber Line (DSL) connections for transmission over T1 lines using Asynchronous Transfer Mode (ATM).

The Institute of Electrical and Electronics Engineers (IEEE) 802.3ad standard ensures interoperability among Fast Ethernet and Gigabit Ethernet (GbE) switches that support trunking.

Implementation

Looking specifically at trunking in switched Ethernet networks, trunking is essentially a form of inverse multiplexing that can be either hardware-based or software-based in its implementation. Trunking was originally developed to reduce congestion in switch-switch connections in switched local area network (LAN) environments. By aggregating several 100-megabit-per-second (Mbps) links between Fast Ethernet switches, for example, you can achieve data rates of 300 or 400 Mbps between the switches to accommodate network backbone traffic. In a full-duplex configuration, this means rates of 600 or 800 Mbps, which rivals the more expensive GbE technology and gives new life to old switches. Not only is it often more economical to trunk Fast Ethernet lines than to upgrade to GbE, but trunked Fast Ethernet cable runs can go farther than GbE cable runs. However, in certain situations trunking does not improve matters. For example, trunking cannot speed up server-to-server backups. GbE switches can be similarly joined for increased backbone capacity in congested enterprise networks. Note, however, that although the theoretical speed for quadruple-trunked full-duplex Fast Ethernet connections is 800 Mbps, in practice the maximum achievable rate is about 560 Mbps because of traffic overhead. Note that switches must be intelligent if they are to support trunked connections properly, so check your switch documentation before you attempt to implement trunking on your network.

Trunking can also be implemented in switch-server connections so that multiple connections to a single server can be aggregated. This form of trunking can be purely software based or can be implemented as a combination of both hardware and software. For example, trunking software installed on multiple network interface cards (NICs) in the server automatically handles load balancing across the various server interfaces and can remove an interface from the trunking group if the interface goes down. This provides increased bandwidth between the server and the switch and ensures fault-tolerant operation. Note that software-based trunking adds an overhead of up to 5 percent to the server's CPU, depending on the software and the NIC used. Look for special NICs from trunking software vendors with on-board processors that can run the trunking software and thus reduce the load on the CPU. Also, do not mix and match trunking software or hardware from different vendors in a single trunking group.

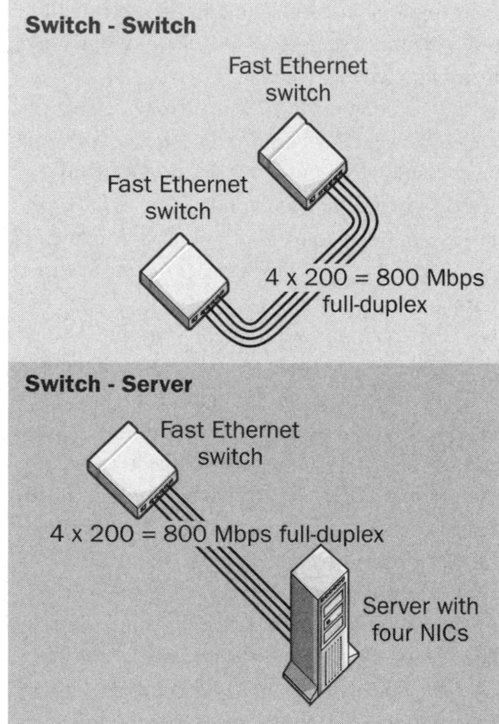

Trunking. *Two forms of trunking used in switched Ethernet networks.*

There are two basic approaches to how trunking can be implemented:

- **Symmetrical trunking:** Allows any port in a trunking group to transmit packets to any other port. Full-duplex connections are thus supported over all links in the group. For example, a server can both transmit and receive data at 400 Mbps in a trunked group of four interfaces and one switch.
- **Asymmetrical trunking:** Allows any port in a trunking group to transmit packets but allows only one port (the port on the switch) to receive packets. The server can transmit data at 400 Mbps but can receive data at only 100 Mbps.

Notes

Trunking by itself is limited to point-to-point connections between two switches or between a switch and a server. However, you can use the Multipoint Link Aggregation (MPLA) technology developed by 3Com Corporation to aggregate physical links connected to different switches into a single logical link. MPLA thus supports multipath trunking between multiple switches and servers, giving network administrators flexibility in configuring their hardware for optimal traffic servicing. Other vendors are working on similar multipath trunking technologies, but standards are still developing in this arena.

See Also: *802.3ad, Digital Subscriber Line (DSL), Ethernet, Ethernet switch, Fast Ethernet, Gigabit Ethernet (GbE), network interface card (NIC), T1*

trust

A secure communication channel between two domains in Microsoft Windows NT, Windows 2000, or Windows .NET Server.

Overview

Trust relationships allow users in one domain to access resources in another domain. Trusts work by having one domain trust the authority of the other domain to authenticate its user accounts.

Windows NT trusts, which are based on Windows NT Challenge/Response Authentication, are managed by the Windows NT Directory Services (NTDS). In Windows NT, trusts are one-way—the trusting domain (or resource domain) trusts the trusted domain (or accounts domain). This means that global users in the trusted domain can be authenticated for accessing resources in the trusting domain. Global users from the trusted domain can log on to any computer in either domain and can access resources in either domain if they have the appropriate permissions. Windows NT trusts are also nontransitive. In other words, if domain A trusts domain B and domain B trusts domain C, it is not true that domain A trusts domain C. If you want to establish a two-way trust between two Windows NT domains, you must create two trusts, one in each direction.

Administrators can set up trust relationships between domains by using the Policies menu in User Manager for Domains. The administrator on the accounts domain should permit the trust first, and then the administrator on the resource domain should complete the trust. Only global accounts (global users and global groups) can cross trusts. By using trusts, you can join Windows NT domains into a variety of domain models, including the complete trust model, the master domain model, and the multiple master domain model. You can join domains to support 100,000 or more users for enterprise-level networks.

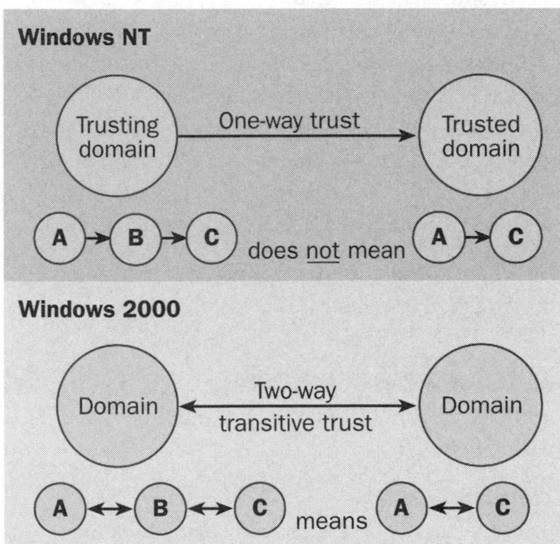

Trust. *How trust relationships work in Windows NT and Windows 2000.*

In Windows 2000 and Windows .NET Server, trusts are managed by Active Directory directory service and are based on the Kerberos v5 security protocol. These trusts are always two-way—in other words, if domain A trusts domain B, users in either domain can access resources in the other domain if they have the appropriate permissions. These trusts are also transitive—in other words, if domain A trusts domain B and domain B trusts domain C, domain A also trusts domain C. Trusts are much easier to manage on these platforms than earlier Windows NT trusts, primarily because there are far fewer trusts to manage. This is because Windows 2000 and Windows .NET Server domains are combined into hierarchical structures called domain trees. All users in a domain tree can access resources in any domain of the tree if they have suitable permissions. In Windows 2000 and Windows .NET Server, you can also use another type of trust called an explicit trust, which is a one-way trust similar to that implemented in Windows NT, to form a trust relationship between two domain forests.

See Also: *Active Directory, domain (DNS), domain tree, Kerberos, two-way transitive trust*

T-SHARE

The original name for Remote Desktop Protocol, a protocol for terminal-based computing.

See: *Remote Desktop Protocol (RDP)*

tunneling

A method for transporting packets of one network protocol over a different network protocol.

Overview

Tunneling is a way of using one network infrastructure (called the transit network) for carrying traffic for a different network. This is done by encapsulating the packets of the sending node in frames of the transit network and adding a suitable header to route the frame across the transit network to the receiving node. When the encapsulated frame arrives at the receiving node, it is de-encapsulated so the node can read it. The two nodes (sending and receiving) are called the tunnel endpoints, and the path over which encapsulated frames are routed

T

across the transit network is called the tunnel. In addition to encapsulating traffic, most tunneling technologies also encrypt traffic for greater security as it travels over the transit network, usually an intermediate public network such as the Internet.

Types

Tunneling is widely used as a wide-area networking (WAN) technology for connecting networks using an intermediate public network such as the Internet. Some common examples of tunneling technologies include the following:

- **IPX over IP:** Here Internetwork Packet Exchange (IPX) packets are encapsulated in Internet Protocol (IP) datagrams to enable them to be routed over an IP internetwork such as the Internet. This process allows legacy NetWare 3.x networks to communicate over IP.
- **SNA over IP:** Here Systems Network Architecture (SNA) traffic is encapsulated in IP using User Datagram Protocol (UDP) headers, a process described in RFC 1795 and also known as Data Link Switching (DLSw).
- **Point-to-Point Tunneling Protocol (PPTP):** This is a Microsoft Corporation protocol for tunneling IP, IPX, and NetBIOS Enhanced User Interface (NetBEUI) traffic over the Internet.
- **Layer-2 Tunneling Protocol (L2TP):** This protocol supports tunneling of IP, IPX, and NetBEUI traffic over any point-to-point datagram delivery service including X.25, frame relay, Asynchronous Transfer Mode (ATM), and IP.
- **IP Security (IPsec):** This protocol has a tunnel mode that allows IP traffic to be encapsulated and encrypted for transmission over a public IP network such as the Internet.

T

See Also: *Internet, Internet Protocol (IP), Internet Protocol Security (IPsec), Internetwork Packet Exchange (IPX), Layer 2 Tunneling Protocol (L2TP), Point-to-Point Tunneling Protocol (PPTP), Systems Network Architecture (SNA), wide area network (WAN)*

twinax cabling

A form of coaxial cabling with twin central conducting cores.

Overview

Twinax cabling typically uses 20 AWG stranded copper conductors, has an outside diameter of 1/3 inch, and comes with a polyvinyl chloride or plenum jacket. Twinax cabling typically has an impedance of 80 to 100 ohms. Twinax cabling is used primarily for connecting IBM System 3X or AS/400 systems to 5250 terminals.

Notes

To extend a twinax connection over long distances, use a repeater. Twinax repeaters can typically transmit signals up to 1 mile (1.6 kilometers) over unshielded twisted-pair (UTP) cabling and over longer distances using duplex fiber-optic cabling. One repeater is required at both ends of the connection.

Use a multiport repeater (hub) to connect several terminals over a single connection to an AS/400 or System 3X host. You can use twinax-to-RJ-45 baluns to connect the terminals and mainframe host to the hub by using UTP cabling. Some repeaters have RJ-11 ports for extending twinax connections over standard telephone cabling. Twinax cabling is traditionally used in a daisy-chained topology, but if you use a multiport repeater, you can also use a star topology configuration.

See Also: *cabling, coaxial cabling, repeater, unshielded twisted-pair (UTP) cabling*

twisted-pair cabling

Copper wire cabling consisting of multiple wires twisted together.

Overview

In computer networking and telecommunications, twisted-pair cabling may consist of from one to four pairs of color-coded insulated stranded copper wires that are twisted together in pairs and enclosed in a protective outer sheath. The twists in twisted-pair cabling help reduce frequency loss and improve signal transmission by reducing the effects of crosstalk. This is because twisting the wires together makes the cabling more resistant to electromagnetic interference (EMI), which helps maintain a high signal-to-noise ratio for reliable network communication to take place.

The earliest uses for twisted-pair cabling was for the Plain Old Telephone System (POTS), where the cabling was used for local loop wiring and was terminated with RJ-11 connectors. Twisted-pair cabling was developed in both shielded and unshielded configurations, with shielded cabling having better performance but costing more. Twisted-pair cabling is today the cabling medium of choice for building computer networks of all sizes from departmental local area networks (LANs) to structured wiring systems for office towers and campuses. Such twisted-pair cabling used for networking purposes employs RJ-45 connectors instead of the RJ-11 connectors used for telephony applications.

Twisted-pair cabling used in Ethernet networking is usually unshielded twisted-pair (UTP) cabling, but shielded twisted-pair (STP) cabling is typically used in Token Ring networks. UTP cabling comes in different grades for different purposes, the most common of which is Category 5 (Cat5) cabling.

Notes

In a telephone environment, one pair of wires is sufficient for ordinary telephone communication to take place. Most customer premises wiring established by telcos uses two-pair wiring in case a second line is later needed for fax or modem use.

See Also: *Category 5 (Cat5) cabling, crosstalk, electromagnetic interference (EMI), Ethernet, Plain Old Telephone Service (POTS), RJ connectors, shielded twisted-pair (STP) cabling, Token Ring, unshielded twisted-pair (UTP) cabling*

two-way transitive trust

A trust relationship between two domains in Microsoft Windows 2000 and Windows .NET Server.

Overview

By default, all Windows 2000 and Windows .NET Server trusts are two-way, meaning that each domain trusts the authority of the other domain for authentication. A Windows 2000 trust is also transitive—if domain A trusts domain B and domain B trusts domain C, domain A trusts domain C. Windows 2000 two-way transitive trusts are based on the Kerberos v5 security protocol.

Because of the two-way transitive nature of Windows 2000 and Windows .NET Server trusts, all domains in a domain tree implicitly trust one another. This means that resources of one domain are available to users in all other domains in the domain tree if they have suitable permissions.

Notes

You can also create one-way nontransitive trusts for Windows 2000– and Windows .NET Server–based networks. These one-way trusts are similar to the trust relationships formed by Windows NT domain controllers. A one-way trust between a domain and a domain tree provides users of the domain with access only to the domain in the tree to which it is joined. One-way trusts can be useful when domains require a less permanent relationship—for example, when two companies take part in a joint venture. Only the resources needed by the other company are made available to the trusted domain; the entire domain tree is not exposed.

See Also: *Active Directory, domain (DNS), Kerberos, trust*

T

UART

Stands for Universal Asynchronous Receiver/Transmitter, hardware used to translate between serial and parallel transmission.

See: *Universal Asynchronous Receiver/Transmitter (UART)*

UDA

Stands for Universal Data Access, a Microsoft Corporation technology for enabling access to any kind of data source.

See: *Universal Data Access (UDA)*

UDDI

Stands for Universal Description, Discovery, and Integration, a platform-independent framework for businesses to advertise and discover each other.

See: *Universal Description, Discovery, and Integration (UDDI)*

UDF (Uniqueness Database File)

Stands for Uniqueness Database File, a text file used to supplement answer files during unattended installations of Microsoft Windows NT, Windows 2000, Windows XP, and Windows .NET Server.

See: *Uniqueness Database File (UDF)*

UDF (Universal Disk Format)

Stands for Universal Disk Format, the successor to the CD-ROM File System (CDFS).

See: *Universal Disk Format (UDF)*

UDFS

Stands for Universal Disk File System, an older name for Universal Disk Format, the successor to the CD-ROM File System (CDFS).

See: *Universal Disk Format (UDF)*

UDP

Stands for User Datagram Protocol, a transport layer protocol of the Transmission Control Protocol/Internet Protocol (TCP/IP) suite.

See: *User Datagram Protocol (UDP)*

ULS

Stands for User Locator Service, an older name for Internet Locator Service, a Lightweight Directory Access Protocol (LDAP) directory service that enables Microsoft NetMeeting users to locate and contact other users for conferencing and collaboration over the Internet.

See: *Internet Locator Service (ILS)*

UM

Stands for Unified Messaging, technology that allows users to access their e-mail, telephone, and fax messages from a single mailbox.

See: *Unified Messaging (UM)*

UMTS

Stands for Universal Mobile Telecommunications System, another name for Wideband Code Division Multiple Access (W-CDMA), a third-generation (3G) cellular communications system deployed in Europe.

See: *Wideband Code Division Multiple Access (W-CDMA)*

unattended installation

Deploying software without administrative intervention.

Overview

Many Microsoft Corporation products, such as Microsoft Windows 2000, Windows XP, Windows .NET Server, BackOffice products, and .NET Server products, support various forms of automatic deployment methods in which direct involvement of the administrator at the target machine is not required. Unattended installation also enables administrators to perform mass deployments of operating system and application software on networked computers. For example, an administrator can install Windows 2000 Professional on multiple desktop client computers without having to remain at each desktop during the installation process and answer the prompts displayed during a normal CD-based installation.

One way of performing an unattended installation is to make use of a distribution server, a network file server that stores the shared source files for the software you want to install. To perform an installation, the Setup program is started on the target computer, which then automatically connects to the share point on the distribution server, downloads the necessary installation files, and installs the software. With Windows 2000 and Windows XP, for example, unattended installation makes use of a special file called an answer file (Unattend.txt) that provides a fixed set of responses to the prompts for information usually generated by the Setup program, thus freeing the administrator from having to remain at the target machine during installation answering prompts. These prompts include information about the computer name, the network protocol to employ, what optional components to install, and other data. You use the answer file by appending the filename to the /u switch when you run Setup from the command prompt. The answer file is a plaintext file that can be customized using either a simple text editor such as Notepad or using the wizard-based tool Setup Manager provided by Windows 2000 and Windows XP.

Another way of performing unattended installations is to use disk-image duplication (or disk cloning) software such as Symantec Corporation's Ghost or PowerQuest Corporation's DriveImage software. In order to use disk cloning as an installation method, however, the master and target systems must have identical hardware configurations. To create a clone, you install and configure the operating system and applications on the master machine and then use the disk imaging software to capture an exact bit-image of the master machine's hard drive, which you then duplicate to the hard drives on the other computers, producing exact clones of the master machine. When you use disk-image duplication software, you must be careful that incompatibilities do not result. For example, if you clone a computer running Windows 2000, the cloned version will have the same security identifier (SID) as the original, which means that the two computers cannot coexist on the same network. Makers of disk-image duplication software can provide utilities for modifying SIDs to work around this problem. Note also that the master and target computers must be stand-alone member servers and not part of a Windows 2000 domain.

Another tool used for unattended installations included with Windows 2000 Server is Remote Installation Services (RIS), which you can use to install Windows 2000 Professional or Windows XP on client computers from a distribution server share point. An image of the fully configured operating system with any locally installed applications that will be required is created and stored on the network share, and the RIS boot disk is used to boot the client computers, connect to the RIS server, download the image, and install the operating system on the client computers. If the client computers have ROM (read-only memory) that supports Pre-Boot Execution Environment (PXE) architecture and have remote boot–enabled network adapter cards, a remote boot disk is not required for each client.

Finally, if you need to perform mass installations of software on large numbers of networked computers, you might consider using desktop systems management software such as Microsoft Systems Management Server (SMS).

See Also: *answer file, disk imaging, Systems Management Server (SMS)*

Unattend.txt

Filename for an answer file, a text file that can be used to perform an unattended installation of Microsoft Windows 2000, Windows XP, and Windows .NET Server.

See: *answer file*

unbalanced line

An electrical cable in which the potential of the signal-carrying conductor is above ground while the return-path conductor is at ground potential.

Overview

An unbalanced line can be contrasted with a balanced line, in which both conductors carry a signal and have potentials that are equal in magnitude but 180 degrees out of phase. In computer networking, an example of an unbalanced line is coaxial cabling, in which the electrical signal is carried solely by the central conductor while the ground path (the internal wire-braid or mesh shielding inside the cable jacket, which is connected to the earth at one termination point of the cable) provides the unbalanced signal return path.

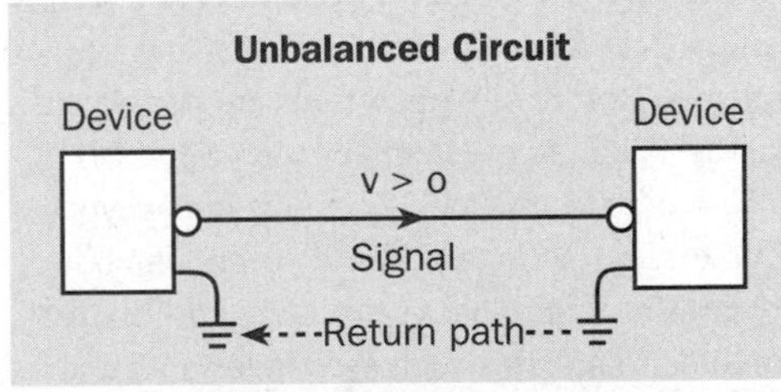

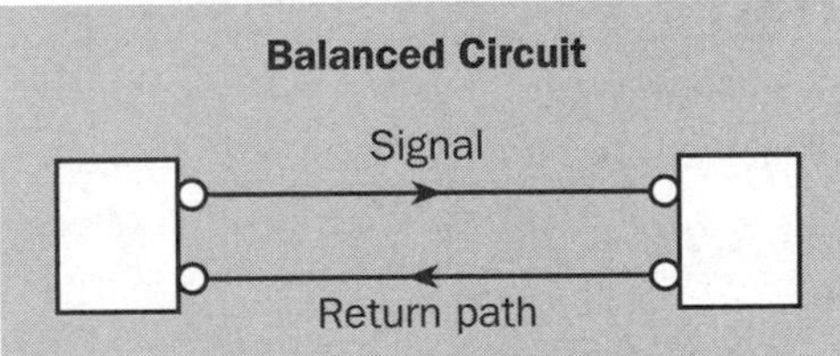

Unbalanced line. *The return-path conductor of the unbalanced line is at ground potential. The return-path conductor of the balanced line carries a signal.*

In contrast, an example of a balanced line is twisted-pair cabling, which comes in the shielded twisted-pair (STP) and the unshielded twisted-pair (UTP) varieties. Because of its electrical characteristics, unbalanced coaxial cabling is more susceptible to electromagnetic interference (EMI) than balanced STP cabling, but coaxial cabling is capable of higher transmission rates over longer distances.

See Also: *balanced line, coaxial cabling, electromagnetic interference (EMI), shielded twisted-pair (STP) cabling, unshielded twisted-pair (UTP) cabling*

UNC

Stands for Universal Naming Convention, a convention for naming shared network resources.

See: *Universal Naming Convention (UNC)*

unicasting

One-to-one communication between stations on a network.

Overview

Unicasting represents full-duplex, point-to-point communication using directed traffic sent between two hosts on a network. Unicasting is contrasted with broadcasting, which is point-to-multipoint in nature and directs information to all accessible hosts on the network, and multicasting, another form of multipoint communication in which information is directed only to hosts that request it. Most user-initiated network traffic is unicast or directed traffic, but broadcast traffic is mostly for clients and services to announce themselves on the network and multicast traffic is for streaming multimedia communication. In the Transmission Control Protocol/Internet Protocol (TCP/IP) protocol suite, the connection-oriented TCP supports unicasting of IP packets, and the connectionless User Datagram Protocol (UDP) provides broadcasting and multicasting of IP packets.

For a unicast packet to reach its destination host on the network, the packet header must contain the address of the destination host. In TCP/IP networking, this destination address is in the form of a logical address called an IP address. On an IP internetwork, routers (network devices that can forward packets to other networks) are usually configured to forward unicast packets (packets directed to a specific host on a destination network) and broadcast packets (packets directed to all users on a subnet, network, or internetwork).

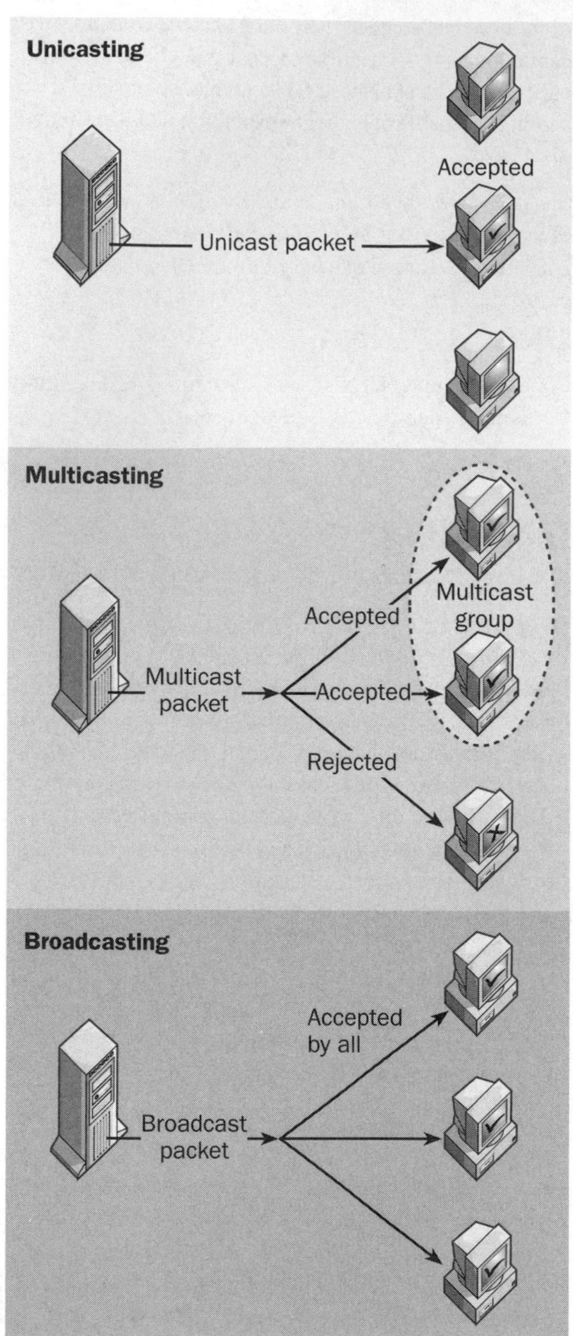

Unicasting. *Comparison of unicasting, multicasting, and broadcasting.*

See Also: *broadcasting, connectionless protocol, connection-oriented protocol, Internet Protocol (IP), multicasting, point-to-multipoint, point-to-point, routing, Transmission Control Protocol (TCP), Transmission Control Protocol/Internet Protocol (TCP/IP), User Datagram Protocol (UDP)*

Unicode

An international character set standard that is capable of representing characters in all written languages.

Overview

The American National Standards Institute (ANSI) character set, which employs a single byte (8 bits) to represent each character, can represent up to $2^8 = 256$ characters only. This is sufficient for most Western languages, but it is insufficient for languages such as Chinese or Arabic. In contrast, the Unicode character set employs two bytes (16 bits) per character and can thus represent a total of $2^{16} = 65,536$ characters—enough for every language in the world, plus punctuation and standard mathematical symbols.

Unicode is the native character encoding for file and object names in Microsoft Windows 2000, Windows XP, and Windows .NET Server. Filenames are also represented in the NTFS file system (NTFS) using Unicode characters. Before any operations are performed on strings, the Win32 subsystem converts all ANSI strings to Unicode. Many Win32 applications have entry points for both 8-bit ANSI and 16-bit Unicode string functions to ensure backward compatibility for running on older platforms such as Windows 95 and Windows 98.

For More Information

Visit the Unicode Consortium at *www.unicode.org.*

See Also: *ASCII*

Unified Messaging (UM)

Technology that allows users to access their e-mail, telephone, fax, and other forms of messages all from a single mailbox.

Overview

Unified Messaging (UM) has been a Holy Grail pursued by system and application vendors for years and which may finally be becoming a reality. The goal of UM is to make it easier for users to manage the various forms of personal communication they use in today's enterprise. For example, the typical knowledge worker might receive dozens of telephone calls, several faxes, a hundred or so e-mails, and numerous pager alerts and instant messaging (IM) communications in a single day. UM aims to simplify things by allowing users to access all these various forms of communication from a single interface, usually an Inbox of an e-mail program but also a telephone or even a Web browser.

Implementation

There are two basic approaches to implementing UM: unified and integrated. The unified solution stores all of a user's messages, regardless of their format, in a single message repository, usually the message store of a mail server. This approach best benefits companies that have not yet heavily invested in alternate messaging architectures such as voice mail and Private Branch Exchange (PBX) systems or network fax servers. Unified UM is typically implemented using third-party vendor add-on products for popular messaging and collaboration servers such as Microsoft Exchange Server or Lotus Notes. A new approach gaining some popularity is to replace traditional PBXs with PC-based PBXs—standard PCs configured with phone-line cards and specialized software to enable them to provide the functions of a traditional PBX together with advanced UM capabilities. Many of these PC-PBX systems are built on top of an Exchange architecture.

For companies that have already acquired voice mail systems and other legacy messaging systems, a better approach might be integrated UM, which makes use of existing messaging systems and ties them together using UM middleware. Integrated UM generally employs a peer-to-peer architecture that connects and synchronizes together various messaging systems such as e-mail, network fax, and voice mail. Integrated UM keeps each type of message stored in its own kind of repository and leverages the use of existing messaging hardware and software. The negative side is that the integrated UM solution generally requires some software customization to be performed to ensure that these various repositories replicate their message header information to one another to enable users to reliably access any form of message from any message interface, such as telephone, cell phone, or e-mail inbox.

Besides these above two solutions, which involve deploying hardware or software at the customer premises, a third approach to UM is gaining popularity, especially among small and mid-sized businesses. This third solution involves outsourcing UM needs to a third party or service provider. These subscription services are typically offered for a low monthly fee from telcos, cellular communication providers, Internet service providers (ISPs), or even portals such as Yahoo!. The user is typically assigned a telephone number, and others can telephone or send faxes to them using this number. Voice messages received are converted to .wav files and forwarded to the user's e-mail inbox, and faxes are converted to .tif files and similarly forwarded. Users then access their voice, fax, and e-mail messages either using their e-mail client or a standard Web browser.

Marketplace

Customer premises equipment (CPE) for implementing unified UM solutions are available from a number of infrastructure vendors including Avaya, Cisco Systems, Lucent Technologies, Mitel Networks, NEC Corporation, Nortel Networks, Siemens, and several others. In addition, many niche vendors specialize in unified and integrated UM solutions, including Active Voice and Captaris. Examples of some popular in-house UM systems include Unified Messenger from Avaya, OnePoint Messenger from Mitel, InternetPBX from COM2001.com (now Alexis), Telephony e-LinX from Esnatech, VoiXX from Intersis, MESSAGEmanager from System Solutions, and TOPCALL Communication Server ONE from TOPCALL International.

Examples of UM service providers include large carriers such as Bell Canada, Verizon Communications, MCI Worldcom, and many others. A number of companies also offer various forms of free UM services in exchange for advertising, including eFax.com, Hello Direct, JFAX.com, Verso Technologies, OneBox, ThinkLink, and uReach Technologies.

Prospects

The driving force behind the current wave of UM solutions is the proliferation of mobile workers using cell phones. Whether traditional UM infrastructure vendors will thrive in the face of the growing number of companies offering subscription-based UM solutions will be the big question to watch over the next few years.

For More Information

Visit the Unified Communications Consortium at *www.unified-msg.com.*

See Also: *e-mail, Internet service provider (ISP), portal, Private Branch Exchange (PBX), telco*

Uniform Resource Locator (URL)

An addressing scheme for locating resources on the Internet.

Overview

A Uniform Resource Locator (URL) is essentially an "address" of a file stored somewhere on the Internet. URLs enable Internet client software such as Hypertext Transfer Protocol (HTTP) clients (most commonly Web browsers) and File Transfer Protocol (FTP) clients to locate and access resources stored on Web servers, FTP servers, and other kinds of Internet hosts. URLs are to the Internet what absolute paths are to network file systems and what Universal Naming Convention (UNC) paths are to shared file and print resources on a Microsoft Windows network.

Architecture

A URL is a hierarchical, structured address based on the Domain Name System (DNS), although a URL can also use an Internet Protocol (IP) address to locate its targets. A URL adheres to the following standard form:

```
[protocol:]//[domain or IP address][:port]/
[path to target file]
```

The components of this syntax are:

- **Protocol:** This is an optional address element that describes the application layer Internet protocol on the server that must be used in order for the client to access the resource. Examples include HTTP:, FTP:, and Telnet:.
- **Domain name or IP address:** This represents the logical address of the server on which the resource resides and is a required element.
- **Port number:** This is required only if the port on the server to which the client must connect to access the resource differs from the default port for that type of protocol. In other words, if no port number is specified, the request is assumed to use the well-known port number for the protocol being used. For example, the well-known port number for HTTP is port 80.
- **Path:** This is required if the resource is not in the root of the server's directory that is mapped to the specified domain name or IP address. This path is usually a virtual path that is mapped to a hierarchical series of directories on the server or on the server's network.

Examples

The following are a few examples of URLs:

- *http://www.microsoft.com/train_cert/default.asp*
- *ftp://172.16.8.99:3355/usr/bin/frag.Z*
- *http://b12.sales.contoso.com/ Sales%20Department/Wigs/Colors/red.html*

The string *%20* in the third URL is an example of character encoding. Because some ASCII characters (such as spaces) are not allowed in URLs, they must be encoded using the form *%xx*, in which *xx* is the hexadecimal code for the character using the International Organization for Standardization (ISO) Latin-1 character set. The string *%20* represents a space character.

See Also: *absolute path, Domain Name System (DNS), File Transfer Protocol (FTP), Hypertext Transfer Protocol (HTTP), IP address, port number, Universal Naming Convention (UNC), Web browser*

uninterruptible power supply (UPS)

A device that can temporarily provide power to network components.

 uninterruptible power supply (UPS)

Overview

Downtime of computer networks and systems are the bane of today's 24x7 e-businesses, so guarding against such a condition is essential to the enterprise network architect. One of the key weapons in an administrator's arsenal is the uninterruptible power supply (UPS), which provides:

- Temporary power against brief power outages to prevent mission-critical data from being lost and against extended power failures to enable servers and other key networking components to be shut down in an orderly manner
- Power conditioning to eliminate harmful surges and brownouts that can corrupt data and damage equipment

The standard UPS is typically a device with rechargeable batteries and software drivers that can perform operations such as:

- Notifying users that a shutdown is imminent and that they should save their work
- Pausing services on servers to prevent new connections from being established
- Providing enough power to perform a soft shutdown of servers and other key network components
- Performing other actions as specified in a batch file that runs automatically
- Providing power line conditioning and smoothing out spikes and dips in the power flow

UPS devices range from small stand-alone boxes to rack-mountable units to room-sized devices having integrated diesel generators for extended power generation. UPS devices are generally rated according to two values:

- **Volt-amp (VA) or kilovolt-amp (kVA) rating:** This determines how much connected computer and networking equipment the UPS is capable of supporting. The larger the VA or kVA value, the greater the number and higher the power requirements of connected devices it can support. UPS devices range from small 1000 VA (1 kVA) units costing $100 or so and designed for Small Office/Home Office (SOHO) computer networks and servers to huge high-end 500-kVA units costing thousands of dollars and designed for mission-critical needs such as those of banks and hospitals. Note that UPS devices can also be rated in watts (W) since 1 VA is equal to 1 W and 1kVA equals 1 kilowatt (kW), but for some reason general usage is to rate them in VA and kVA instead.
- **Time@100%(min):** This is the amount of time that the unit can sustain maximum power generation. Small and mid-sized UPS devices can typically provide 100 percent power to network components and computers for between 5 and 15 minutes after a power failure. You can use additional battery packs with some UPS devices to extend uptime further.

Marketplace

Some of the larger vendors of UPS devices include American Power Conversion Corporation, Best Power, Clary Corporation, Exide Technologies, Falcon Electric, Liebert Corporation, ONEAC Corporation, OPTI-UPS, Powerware, Toshiba Corporation, Tripp Lite, and Tsi Power Corporation. An example of a high-end UPS is the Silcon DP300E from American Power Conversion, which comes in various models rated up to 1.6 megawatts (MW). Such high-end UPS devices are designed for the largest data centers.

Notes

Always test your UPS after installing it. Otherwise, you might be sorry when a power failure happens in your neighborhood! A good way of testing a UPS is simply to unplug a computer on your system and watch what happens. Some UPS units support Simple Network Management Protocol (SNMP), which lets you test the condition of the UPS at regular intervals and report the results to an SNMP management console.

Note also that the larger the load attached to a UPS unit, the shorter the time interval the unit can continue powering attached devices during a power outage. Be sure that your UPS unit can support your power needs for the time needed to properly shut down your system.

To determine what size UPS you need for your network, add the wattages of all the devices you want to connect and ensure that you buy a UPS unit whose VA rating exceeds this value by a good margin.

See Also: *disaster recovery*

Uniqueness Database File (UDF)

A text file used to supplement answer files during unattended installations of Microsoft Windows NT, Windows 2000, Windows XP, and Windows .NET Server.

Overview

Uniqueness Database Files (UDFs) are used to override the answer to prompts provided by answer files during unattended setup. These UDFs replace the general answers in the answer file with information that is specific to a given computer or small group of computers. UDFs typically supply information customized for individual computers such as computer name or username. By contrast, answer files specify more general setup options such as setup mode or time zone, which are the same for all computers on the network. Thus, although you might need only one answer file to deploy a number of Windows 2000 computers on your network, you would need a separate UDF for each computer to be deployed.

The way it works is that the UDF is merged into the answer file at the start of the graphical user interface (GUI) portion of setup. As a result, you can only use UDFs to define setup parameters for the GUI portion of setup, not the text portion. During the text portion of setup, only the answer file can specify parameters to use in response to setup prompts.

Notes

Windows XP and Windows .NET Server use Setup Manager to prepare unattended installation files for system deployment.

See Also: *answer file, unattended installation*

Universal Asynchronous Receiver/Transmitter (UART)

Hardware used to translate between serial and parallel transmission.

Overview

Universal Asynchronous Receiver/Transmitter (UART) chips are employed in the PC architecture to translate signals between a computer's internal bus and its COM ports. This is because although COM ports use serial transmission, which sends bits one at a time, a computer's internal bus is parallel and carries multiple bits of data simultaneously. Another function of the UART is to add start and stop bits when translating from parallel to serial transmission in order to ensure synchronization between the COM ports and connected remote serial devices and to strip off these bits when translating from serial back to parallel for incoming serial transmission.

UARTs employ their own internal clocking system that runs separately from the computer's internal clock, so the UART must be fast enough to handle data transferred to it from the internal bus or bits may be overwritten and communications may become garbled. Internal modems have their own UART chips because they bypass the computer's COM ports for their transmission.

See Also: *bus, modem, serial transmission*

Universal Data Access (UDA)

A Microsoft technology for enabling access to any kind of data source.

Overview

Universal Data Access (UDA) is part of Microsoft Corporation's Windows Distributed Network Architecture (Windows DNA) framework and enables applications to access data from all kinds of sources, including Structured Query Language (SQL) databases, Lightweight Directory Access Protocol (LDAP) directory services, e-mail repositories, spreadsheets, text files, and mainframe and other legacy data sources. UDA relies on three components to connect applications and data browsers with back-end data sources:

- **Open Database Connectivity (ODBC):** Used primarily to access SQL-compliant relational databases such as Microsoft SQL Server databases, Microsoft Jet databases, and Oracle databases.

- **OLE DB:** Specifies a series of extensible Component Object Model (COM) interfaces for accessing various kinds of data sources, including SQL databases (through ODBC), non-SQL structured data sources, and unstructured data such as text files.
- **ActiveX Data Objects (ADO):** Language-independent framework that enables applications to use OLE DB directly.

See Also: *ActiveX Data Objects (ADO), Component Object Model (COM), Joint Engine Technology (Jet), Lightweight Directory Access Protocol (LDAP), OLE DB, open database connectivity (ODBC), SQL Server, Structured Query Language (SQL), Windows Distributed interNet Applications Architecture (Windows DNA)*

Universal Description, Discovery, and Integration (UDDI)

A platform-independent framework for businesses to advertise and to discover one another.

Overview

Universal Description, Discovery, and Integration (UDDI) is an emerging platform used to simplify the process of companies locating and doing business-to-business (B2B) transactions with one another over the Internet. UDDI provides a standard way for businesses to code what they do and store this information in a directory that is publicly accessible to other businesses. The UDDI project is spearheaded by Ariba, IBM, and Microsoft Corporation and is in beta testing by more than 130 companies who have joined on to the initiative.

UDDI is built on a framework of other open standards, including Extensible Markup Language (XML), Hypertext Transfer Protocol (HTTP), and Simple Object Access Protocol (SOAP).

Implementation

UDDI uses a series of specialized servers called registries. Ariba, IBM, and Microsoft maintain beta versions of these registries, but the intention is to eventually turn UDDI over to an open standards body once testing is completed. UDDI registries store directory information about businesses in a centralized location in three formats:

- **White pages:** General information about businesses such as name, address, and description of business services.
- **Yellow pages:** Businesses organized by categories according to tags defined by government standards.
- **Green pages:** Information on the technical aspect of services which individual business systems expose for data exchange purposes using XML.

For More Information

Find out more about UDDI at *www.uddi.org.*

See Also: *B2B, directory, e-business, Hypertext Transfer Protocol (HTTP), Simple Object Access Protocol (SOAP), XML*

Universal Disk Format (UDF)

The successor to the CD-ROM File System (CDFS).

Overview

CDFS was a file system used in Microsoft Windows NT 4 and earlier versions for accessing information stored on CD-ROM disks. Universal Disk Format (UDF) is the successor to CDFS and is capable of both reading from and writing to removable media such as CD, CD-R, CD-RW, DVD, write-once read-many (WORM), and magneto-optical (MO) media. UDFS is an open industry standard based on the following standards:

- ISO 13346 from the International Organization for Standardization (ISO)
- ECMA 167 from the European Computer Manufacturers Organization (ECMA)
- OSTA UDF from the Optical Storage Technology Association (OSTA)

UDF supports a number of advanced features, including

- Access control lists (ACLs)
- Deep directory trees
- Large file sizes up to 64 gigabytes (GB) in size

- Long file names up to 255 characters long with a maximum path length of 1023 characters
- Named streams
- Sparse files
- Unicode file names

UDF is implemented on the Windows 2000, Windows XP, and Windows .NET Server platforms. Some versions of these platforms require special drivers in order to write to certain media.

See Also: *CD-ROM File System (CDFS), file system*

Universal DSL

Another name for G.Lite, a splitterless version of Asymmetric Digital Subscriber Line (ADSL).

See: *G.Lite*

universal group

A type of group in Microsoft Windows 2000 and Windows .NET Server.

Overview

Universal groups are one of three types of groups in Windows 2000 and Windows .NET Server, the other types being domain local groups and global groups. Universal groups differ from these other types in that they can include members from any domain in the forest and can be granted permissions for resources in any domain in the forest. Universal groups can contain user accounts, global groups, and even other universal groups, but they cannot contain domain local groups. Like global groups, all trusted domains have access to universal groups to grant them permission to access resources on the network.

Some typical uses for universal groups include

- You can use global groups nested inside universal groups to dramatically reduce network traffic due to global catalog replication in a Windows 2000–based network. Use universal groups only when their membership changes infrequently, because excessive replication traffic can occur in a domain tree if their membership changes frequently.
- You can also use universal groups to grant users access to resources that are located in multiple domains. Simply add global groups from each domain to a universal group and assign permissions for the resource to the universal group. This use of universal groups is similar to that of domain local groups, except that you can use domain local groups only to assign permissions for resources in a single domain.

Notes

You can create universal groups only when your Windows 2000 or Windows .NET Server domain is running in native mode, not when it is in mixed mode. In other words, you cannot use universal groups in a network that still has downlevel Microsoft Windows NT domain controllers. You can use them only in a network whose domain controllers are all running Windows 2000 or Windows .NET Server.

See Also: *domain local group, forest, global group, group, mixed mode, native mode*

Universal Mobile Telecommunications System (UMTS)

Another name for Wideband Code Division Multiple Access (W-CDMA), a third-generation (3G) cellular communications system being deployed in Europe.

See: *Wideband Code Division Multiple Access (W-CDMA)*

Universal Naming Convention (UNC)

A convention for naming shared network resources.

Overview

The syntax for a Universal Naming Convention (UNC) path to a network resource is as follows:

```
\\server_name\share_name[\path]
```

where "share_name" is a shared folder, and "path" is the (optional) path to the file within the shared folder.

The UNC path \\max\sales\1998\report.doc indicates that the document report.doc is located within the shared folder called sales on the file server called max. The document is in the 1998 subfolder of the sales shared folder.

See Also: *shared folder*

universal serial bus (USB)

A high-speed serial interface for connecting peripherals to computers.

Overview

Connecting peripherals to computer systems has traditionally suffered from two problems:

- Installing internal peripherals such as Peripheral Component Interconnect (PCI) modem cards involved opening the case, plugging the card into an available slot, screwing the card tight, and closing the case—a time-consuming and complicated process for the average user.
- Transmission speeds supported by standard RS-232 serial and Centronics parallel interfaces have been too slow for some external peripherals such as scanners and digital cameras to operate at an acceptable speed.

Universal serial bus (USB) was created to address these issues by providing a low-cost industry-standard high-speed serial interface for external peripherals and supporting Plug and Play (PnP). Installing a USB peripheral is as simple as connecting it to a USB port on the computer using a standard USB cable. Provided the computer is running an operating system that supports PnP and USB, such as Microsoft Windows 2000 or Windows XP, simply plugging in the peripheral causes it to be automatically recognized and configured for use. Since USB provides "hot plug-able" support, no rebooting of the computer is necessary when connecting or disconnecting USB devices. USB makes it easy to connect peripherals to computers and eliminates the need to configure interrupt request (IRQ) settings or dual inline package (DIP) switches since configuration of devices is automatic.

USB ports are included on most computer systems sold today, and USB peripherals are becoming popular, especially in the consumer market where USB-capable monitors, mice, keyboards, joysticks, scanners, digital cameras, printers, and other devices are now proliferating. Besides ease of use, another advantage of USB over legacy serial and parallel port communications is that USB carries up to 500 milliamps (mA) of power to connected peripherals, eliminating the need for bulky power supplies for many types of peripherals.

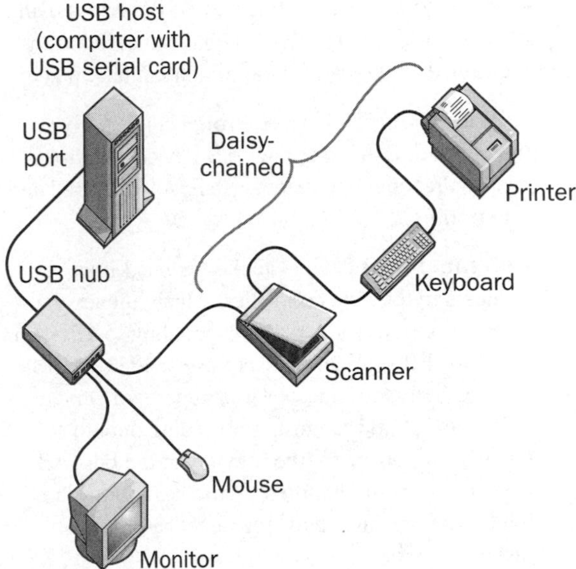

Universal serial bus (USB). *A typical example of using USB to connect peripherals to a computer system.*

Implementation

USB uses a master/slave architecture in which the computer (master) controls all communications between itself and attached peripherals (slave devices). There are several types of USB peripherals:

- **Input/output (I/O) device:** This is simply any peripheral that supports USB connectivity. Examples include USB keyboards, mice, scanners, and speakers.
- **Hub:** This is a device with multiple USB ports that allows several peripherals to share a single USB

port on the computer. USB hubs can be cascaded in a tiered star topology up to five levels deep to support greater numbers of peripherals.

- **Compound device:** This is a USB peripheral that acts as both an I/O device and a hub. An example is a USB monitor, which allows a keyboard or mouse to be connected through it to the computer.

The USB controller on the host system (a computer having a built-in USB port on the motherboard or an installed USB serial card) manages communication between the host and the connected USB devices using a packet-based token-passing mechanism called transfer queuing. Two kinds of communication take place:

- **Initialization:** The host controller continually polls the network to detect new USB devices and to ensure that connected devices are still attached and functioning.
- **Run time:** USB devices make various kinds of requests to the host controller, which queues the requests and respond to them according to a first-in, first-out (FIFO) manner. Requests made by USB devices include requests for or reports of status information, and requests for reading data to or writing data from another device on the bus. All USB requests are handled by the host controller, which obtains and sends the necessary control information or data to the device.

USB theoretically supports up to 126 peripherals connected together, but in practice it is best to keep the number to about a dozen for best performance and to simplify troubleshooting should incompatibilities arise. USB devices can be no more than 16.4 feet (5 meters) apart or the same distance from a hub or computer. The entire cabling arrangement of a computer and multiple USB peripherals is collectively referred to as the USB bus, even if the actual topology is star-like instead of bus-like in appearance.

USB cables are terminated differently at each end, depending on whether they connect to a computer (upstream connection) or I/O device (downstream connection). This is mainly done to prevent loops in the USB bus. The Type A (flat) connector plugs into the USB port on the computer or into the device ports on the hub, and the Type B (square) connector generally connects to the device.

USB supports two speeds, which depend basically on the type of media used to connect peripherals:

- 1.5-megabits per second (Mbps) transmission over unshielded USB cabling
- 12-Mbps transmission over shielded USB cabling

It is usually possible to combine these two types of media into a single arrangement, because USB hubs and host controllers are generally autosensing and can determine which transmission speed to use depending upon the attached cabling. USB cabling is typically 4-wire cabling and uses a 28-gauge twisted pair for data transmission and a 20-gauge untwisted pair for carrying power to the devices. The table shows the pinning types for USB cabling.

Pinning Types for USB Cabling

Pin	*Color*	*Function*
1	Red	+5 V power
2	White	Data -
3	Green	Data +
4	Black	Ground

Marketplace

For Small Office/Home Office (SOHO) users who want to network two computers, USB offers a simple way of doing this using USB direct cable networking. In this scenario, a USB port on one computer is connected directly to a USB port on another to provide Ethernet-like networking capability. Alternatively, more than two computers can be networked using a USB hub. Several companies offer the special USB cabling and software needed to implement USB direct cable networking, including ActionLink from ActionTec Electronics, EZLink USB from Anchor Chips, and USB Direct Connect from Belkin Components.

Prospects

USB is rapidly replacing serial and parallel interfaces as the most popular way of connecting peripherals to computer systems. A new specification called USB 2, or "high-speed USB," has been developed that is 40 times faster than USB 1.1, and USB 2–capable systems and software started becoming available toward the end of 2001 with support included in hardware from Intel Corporation, systems from Dell Computer Corporation, and in the Microsoft Windows XP operating system platform.

Notes

When you use shielded USB cabling, connect the shield to ground only at the USB host (computer), not at the USB devices (peripherals).

You can connect an Institute of Electrical and Electronics Engineers (IEEE) 1284–compliant printer that has a standard Centronics interface to a USB system by using a Centronics/USB adapter or patch cable.

See Also: IEEE 1284, IEEE 1394, parallel transmission, Plug and Play (PnP), RS-232, serial transmission

Universal Wireless Communications (UWC-136)

A standard for third-generation (3G) wireless cellular systems.

Overview

Universal Wireless Communications (UWC-136) is a standard developed by the Universal Wireless Communication Consortium (UWCC), a consortium of more than 85 telecommunications carriers and wireless product vendors.UWC-136 is part of the International Mobile Telecommunications-2000 (IMT-2000) initiative from the International Telecommunication Union (ITU), which promotes UWC-136 as a competing IMT-2000 standard.

UWC-136 is a pure Time Division Multiple Access (TDMA) cellular communication technology that is designed to be backward compatible with the existing IS-136 TDMA digital cellular phone system defined by the ANSI-136 and IS-41 standards and still widely used throughout North America. Implementation of UWC-136 is planned in phases by first upgrading existing IS-136 TDMA systems to IS-136+ to provide data rates of 43.2 kilobits per second (Kbps) over standard 30-kilohertz (kHz) channels. Then IS-136+ will be upgraded to IS-136HS, which is the high-speed component of UWC-136. Eventually, UWC-136 will provide packet-data services at speeds of up to 384 Kbps for wide-area coverage and up to 2 megabits per second (Mbps) for in-building coverage. Voice communication on this system will be high-fidelity wireline quality, comparable to that of Integrated Services Digital Network (ISDN).

For More Information

Visit the UWCC at *www.uwcc.org.*

See Also: 3G, cellular communications, IMT-2000, Integrated Services Digital Network (ISDN), International Telecommunication Union (ITU), Time Division Multiple Access (TDMA)

UNIX

A popular operating system widely deployed in today's enterprise networking environments.

Overview

UNIX is a multiprocessing, multitasking, multiuser operating system developed at AT&T Bell Laboratories in 1969. UNIX was the first operating system written entirely in the C programming language and consequently has close ties to C. Writing UNIX in C made UNIX a portable operating system—that is, by changing the source code slightly, UNIX could be "ported" (made to work on) any computer hardware platform including PowerPC, MIPS, Intel, Sparc, and various mainframe and midframe computing architectures.

UNIX has the stability and robustness of an operating system that has evolved over 25 years, but it has a reputation for being difficult to learn and administer, mainly due to its high degree of dependence on the command line. On the other hand, this emphasis makes UNIX easier to administer for those familiar with the platform, because it allows administrative tasks to be scripted, scheduled, and executed to make complex and repetitive tasks simple to perform. In fact, much of the original drive toward developing scripting languages came from the UNIX administration environment.

UNIX was designed as a time-sharing environment, in contrast to the batch environment of most computing systems of the time. Using UNIX, multiple users could simultaneously access the system and run their programs, communicating interactively with the system using remote terminals. UNIX users could thus collaborate in real time on computing projects by sharing files and resources.

UNIX has established strong roots for itself in academic computing environments, where it is still frequently used and taught today. UNIX also has its roots in the Internet environment where UNIX and Transmission Control Protocol/Internet Protocol (TCP/IP) evolved hand-in-hand in the 1980s. TCP/IP is the underlying network transport used by all UNIX systems.

Types

There are actually two main "branches" in the UNIX "family tree":

- **BSD:** Stands for Berkeley Software Distribution, an early variant of UNIX developed in the 1970s by students at the University of California at Berkeley, who licensed AT&T's version and added such new features as the C shell and vi editor to enhance the AT&T platform. BSD UNIX forms the basis of SunOS, a lightweight version of UNIX developed by Sun Microsystems that supports only a single processor. Another popular flavor of BSD is iXsystems (formerly BSDi) from Wind River Systems. There are also several free versions of BSD UNIX, including FreeBSD, OpenBSD, and NetBSD.
- **System V:** Developed by AT&T Bell Laboratories with UNIX Systems Laboratories, this version incorporates some features of BSD UNIX. The source code for System V UNIX was owned by Santa Cruz Operation (SCO), which is now called Tarantella and is part of Caldera International. System V forms the basis of Solaris, a popular version of UNIX from Sun Microsystems (Solaris also includes some features of BSD), and several other versions.

Based on evolution from these two branches, UNIX has evolved into a number of different "flavors" as vendors have adapted it to their own proprietary hardware platforms. These flavors include the following:

- **Solaris:** This version was developed by Sun Microsystems for its proprietary SPARC computing architecture and is the most popular version of UNIX in use today in the enterprise. Sun Enterprise Servers and Ultra Workstations running Solaris provide a powerful and reliable platform for high-performance computing. Solaris is based on SunOS 5.x, which itself was based on BSD with some features from System V R4 included. The current release of this product is Solaris 8, and it is compliant with the UNIX 98 standard.
- **AIX:** This version by IBM is for its midrange RS/6000 and PowerPC computing platforms. AIX is currently in distant second place in the commercial UNIX marketplace behind Sun's Solaris operating system. Efforts are underway to port AIX to Intel Corporation's new 64-bit Itanium processor architecture, which, when complete, should make AIX a viable competitor to Solaris in the high-end server market. The current release of this product is AIX 5L, and it is compliant with the UNIX 98 standard.
- **HP-UX:** This version was developed by Hewlett-Packard Company for its HP 9000 server line and is a close third-place finisher in the commercial UNIX market, behind Sun's Solaris and IBM's AIX platforms. HP-UX is based on System V but has some BSD features included. The current release of this product is HP-UX 11i, and it is compliant with the UNIX 95 standard.
- **Tru64 Unix:** This version was originally called Digital Unix and was developed by Digital Equipment Corporation (DEC) for its Alpha processor platform. It was renamed Tru64 when DEC was acquired by Compaq Computer Corporation. Tru64 runs only on the Alpha platform, which is now discontinued but still widely used in high-end computing environments by many companies. Tru64 Unix is compliant with System V R3.2 and R4. The current release of this product is Tru64 Unix 5.1, and it is compliant with the UNIX 95 standard.

- **UnixWare:** This version was developed by SCO (now Caldera) to port UNIX to the Intel PC platform. The current release is UnixWare 7, and it is compliant with the UNIX 95 standard.
- **IRIX:** This version was developed by Silicon Graphics, Inc. (SGI) for its high-end SGI MIPS servers and graphic workstations. IRIX is based on System V R3.2 and R4. The current release is IRIX 6.5, and it is compliant with the UNIX 95 standard.
- **Linux:** A UNIX-like operating system developed by Linus Torvalds which is rapidly growing in popularity for niche deployments in the enterprise.

Several attempts have been made to standardize the UNIX operating system. AT&T created a written standard called the System V Interface Definition (SVID) for its UNIX System V Release 4 (SVR4). In addition, an industry consortium created a standard called Portable Operating System Interface for UNIX (POSIX). The actual trademark *UNIX* is now owned by The Open Group, a consortium of software and hardware manufacturers.

Notes

Microsoft Windows 2000 and Windows .NET Server support interoperability with UNIX to support real-world heterogeneous enterprise networking environments. This interoperability is provided through built-in protocols, services, and tools in the Windows 2000 operating system and also through Microsoft Services for UNIX 2, an add-on product from Microsoft Corporation. Built-in Windows/UNIX interoperability on the Windows 2000 platform includes such features as:

- Common support for industry-standard protocols such as TCP/IP, Dynamic Host Configuration Protocol (DHCP), Domain Name System (DNS), and remote procedure call (RPC) functionality
- Support for File Transfer Protocol (FTP) and Hypertext Transfer Protocol (HTTP) for cross-platform file sharing
- Support for UNIX printing through Line Printer Daemon (LPD), Line Printer Queue (LPQ), and Line Printer Remote (LPR) utilities
- Support for remote terminal emulation using Telnet
- Support for cross-platform database access through open database connectivity (ODBC)
- Support for industry-standard network management through Simple Network Management Protocol (SNMP) and Remote Network Monitoring (RMON)

Services for UNIX 2 provides additional interoperability features with the following UNIX platforms: Solaris, HP-UX, Digital UNIX, IRIX, and Linux. Several third-party companies also offer Windows-compatible interoperability solutions such as:

- X Windows clients specifically designed for Windows-based PCs to support connectivity with UNIX servers
- X Windows servers for Windows such as that from Hummingbird International
- Server Message Block (SMB) to Network File System (NFS) protocol conversion for file sharing between platforms using products such as Samba

See Also: *AIX, Alpha platform, BSD, C++, HP-UX, Intel-based platform, Linux, POSIX, shell, Transmission Control Protocol/Internet Protocol (TCP/IP), UNIX commands*

UNIX commands

Commands for administering various aspects of the UNIX operating system.

Overview

UNIX commands are text-based commands executed from the command line to perform a wide variety of administrative tasks. Most of these commands can also be used in batch files to perform complex administrative tasks from a single command. You can create batch files with a text editor such as ed or vi and schedule their execution by using the Cron command.

The table shows some commonly used UNIX commands, listed in alphabetical order with brief descriptions. Some commands have a simple syntax, such as the cd command for changing the current directory.

Others are more complex and include scripting engines and even programming compilers, such as cc, the UNIX C compiler. Most versions of UNIX support most of these commands, but there are sometimes subtle differences from system to system. To see the exact syntax for any UNIX command, use the man command, which provides access to the UNIX online command reference. For example, to see the syntax for the cd command, type **man cd** at the UNIX command prompt. Note that that there are many UNIX commands not listed in this table—it would take many pages to list all the commands available on the various UNIX platforms.

Some of the commands below are asterisked (*), which indicates that they are specifically available on the Microsoft Windows 2000 platform when Microsoft Services for UNIX 2 is installed.

Some Common UNIX Commands

Command	*Description*
alias	Displays or sets aliases for long command strings
awk	Searches a file for a pattern and performs an action on the lines containing that pattern
basename*	Removes the path leaving only the file name
bg	Moves a stopped process into the background and restarts it
cal	Displays a calendar
cat*	Concatenates or displays files
cc	C language compiler
cd	Changes the current directory
chgrp	Changes group ownership of a file
chmod*	Changes access permissions for a file
chown*	Changes individual ownership of a file
chsh	Changes the default shell in a password file
clear	Clears the screen
cmp	Compares two files and returns the line numbers that differ
cp*	Copies a file
csh	C shell command interpreter
date	Displays the date and time

(continued)

Some Common UNIX Commands *continued*

Command	*Description*
df	Displays the amount of free disk space in a file system
diff	Displays differences between two files
dirname*	Delivers all but the last level of the path in string
du	Displays file system usage
echo	Echoes the text typed following the command to the screen
ed	Text editor
elm	Text-based e-mail
emacs	Text editor
f77	FORTRAN77 compiler
fg	Moves a stopped process to the foreground and restarts it
find*	Finds a file with specified characteristics
ftp	File Transfer Protocol (FTP) client
grep*	Searches a file for a text pattern
head*	Displays the beginning of a file (by default, displays the first 10 lines)
help	Displays help
hostname	Displays the name of the current host system
kill	Ends a running process
ksh	Korn shell command interpreter
ln*	Links files
lpq	Displays the print queue
lpr	Sends a print job to the spooler
ls*	Lists files in a directory and displays the file statistics
mail	Sends e-mail
man	Accesses the online manual
mkdir*	Creates a new directory
more*	Displays a file one screen at a time
mv*	Moves or renames a file
passwd	Changes your password
perl*	Interpretive scripting language
pico	Text editor
pine	Text-based e-mail program
ps	Displays the status of a process
pwd	Displays the name of the current directory
rm*	Deletes a file
rmdir*	Deletes a directory

(continued)

U

Some Common UNIX Commands *continued*

Command	*Description*
sed*	Stream line editor
sh*	Invokes the Korn shell command interpreter
sleep	Pauses a process
sort*	Sorts or merges files
split	Splits a file into multiple files
tail*	Copies name file to standard output starting at designated place
talk	Text-based chat
tee*	Transcribes standard input to standard output
telnet	Terminal emulator
touch*	Creates a new file of designated name
uniq*	Reports repeated lines in file
uucp	UNIX-to-UNIX system file copies
uudecode	Decodes a uuencoded file
uuencode	Encodes a binary file
vi*	Text editor
wc*	Displays line, word, or character count in file
who	Displays who else is logged on
whoami	Displays the name of the user currently logged on
whois	Finds remote users and sites
write	Sends a message to a user

See Also: *command, command interpreter, command line, UNIX*

UNIX-to-UNIX Copy (UUCP)

A command for transferring files between two UNIX hosts on a network.

Overview

UNIX-to-UNIX Copy (UUCP) is an early form of electronic messaging developed for UNIX platforms in the 1970s. UUCP was originally designed for transferring files over an asynchronous serial transmission interface such as RS-232. With UUCP, you can transfer files through a direct cable connection between serial ports on two computers by using a null modem cable or over telephone lines by using modems connected to the serial ports of each computer. A version of UUCP has been developed for transferring files over Ethernet as well. UUCP was also used for transferring electronic mail messages (e-mail) between hosts in the early days of the Internet. UNIX hosts used UUCP to transfer mail to a remote host simply by executing the MAIL program on the remote UNIX host and having it run on the local message file to be delivered.

UUCP uses the well-known port number 117 for its path service and number 540 for the UUCP daemon called UUCPD. UUCP has been eclipsed by File Transfer Protocol (FTP) as a general protocol for moving files between hosts and by Simple Mail Transfer Protocol (SMTP) for transferring e-mail messages.

Notes

Third-party vendors have created UUCP gateway connectors for Microsoft Exchange Server to enable Exchange to send and receive UUCP mail over the Internet.

See Also: *Ethernet, RS-232, serial transmission, Simple Mail Transfer Protocol (SMTP), UNIX, UNIX commands*

unshielded twisted-pair (UTP) cabling

Twisted-pair cabling with no internal shielding.

Overview

Unshielded twisted-pair (UTP) cabling is the most common form of network cabling for workgroups and departmental local area networks (LANs) because of its low cost, flexibility, and good performance. In UTP cabling the outer insulating jacket protects the cable from physical stress or damage but does not shield the cable from electromagnetic interference (EMI).

UTP cabling has an impedance of approximately 100 ohms and is available in various grades or categories based on data transmission capabilities, as shown in the table. Category 5 (Cat5) cabling and enhanced Category 5 (Cat5e) cabling are the most popular forms of UTP cabling in Ethernet networking. No agreed standards exist above Cat5e, but there is a proposed standard for Category 6 (Cat6) cabling and some manufacturers even offer UTP cabling they call Category 7 (Cat7) cabling.

UTP Cabling Categories

Category	*Use*
Category 1 (Cat1)	Analog voice grade
Category 2 (Cat2)	Digital voice transmissions up to 4 megabits per second (Mbps)
Category 3 (Cat3)	Digital transmissions up to 10 Mbps
Category 4 (Cat4)	Digital transmissions up to 16 Mbps
Category 5 (Cat5)	Digital transmissions up to 100 Mbps
enhanced Category 5 (Cat5e)	Digital transmission up to 250 Mbps

Notes

To ensure that Cat5e UTP cabling performs effectively, you should also use certified Cat5e wall plates, connectors, and patch panels. The patch panel or wall plate connections should be untwisted no more than 0.5 inch (1.3 cm); also try to keep cabling away from fluorescent lights, motors, and other sources of EMI. Do not bend the cable sharply—the radius of a bend should not be less than 10 times the diameter of the cable. Finally, avoid pulling cable wraps too tightly or crushing the cables in any way.

See Also: *Category 1 (Cat1) cabling, Category 2 (Cat2) cabling, Category 3 (Cat3) cabling, Category 4 (Cat4) cabling, Category 5 (Cat5) cabling, Category 6 (Cat6) cabling, Category 7 (Cat7) cabling, electromagnetic interference (EMI), enhanced Category 5 (Cat5e) cabling, Ethernet, shielded twisted-pair (STP) cabling, structured wiring*

update sequence number (USN)

A type of identifier used in directory replication in Microsoft Windows 2000 and Windows .NET Server.

Overview

Update sequence numbers (USNs) are used for controlling directory replication between domain controllers. When an object is changed in Active Directory directory service, that change must be replicated to all other domain controllers. To do this, Active Directory assigns a USN to each changed object, incrementing the values with time. Each domain controller uses a table to keep track of its own current USN and the highest USN it has received from each of the other domain controllers on the network.

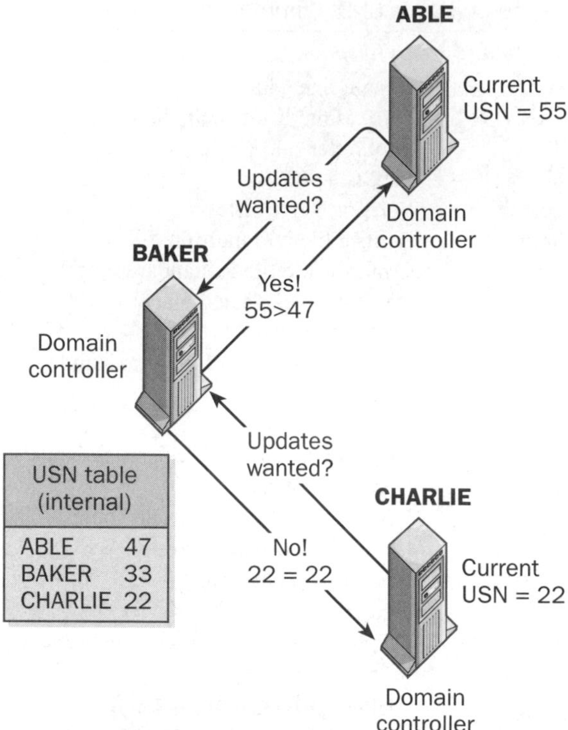

Update sequence number (USN). *How Active Directory uses USNs during directory replication between domain controllers.*

For example, if a domain controller called ABLE notifies a domain controller called BAKER of the updates it has for Active Directory, ABLE sends its own current USN number to BAKER, which compares the USN with the USN it recorded for ABLE in its internal table after the last directory update it received from ABLE. If the received USN is higher than the recorded USN, BAKER requests that ABLE send its updates for the directory. If the received USN is equal to or lower than the recorded one, BAKER knows that it has an up-to-date copy of ABLE's directory and does not request any updates.

USNs are more accurate than time stamps in controlling replication between domain controllers because time stamps depend on the clocks of domain controllers being exactly synchronized. However, time stamps are also employed if a tie-breaking mechanism is required for replication purposes. USNs also speed the recovery of Active Directory if a domain controller experiences a failure.

See Also: *Active Directory, domain controller*

uplink port

A port on an Ethernet hub used to connect the hub to another hub.

Overview

Uplink ports allow Ethernet hubs to be cascaded to form larger networks using standard unshielded twisted-pair (UTP) patch cables. This method of connecting hubs does not use up any of the hub's station ports, which are used to connect computers to the hub. An arrangement of hubs connected together is typically known as a cascaded star topology.

When cascading hubs together, be sure that the root or main hub of your cascaded star arrangement of hubs is a high-quality hub. Do not create collision domains larger than about 150 computers—network performance can degrade seriously due to too many collisions on the network. If hubs cannot meet your bandwidth requirements, consider replacing the main hub with an Ethernet switch.

Notes

If you do not have an uplink port on your hub, you can still connect a station port on the hub to a station port on another hub by using a crossover cable.

See Also: *crossover cable, Ethernet, hub, topology, unshielded twisted-pair (UTP) cabling*

UPN

Stands for User Principal Name, the logon name of a user on a Microsoft Windows 2000 or Windows .NET Server network.

See: *user principal name (UPN)*

UPS

Stands for uninterruptible power supply, a device that can temporarily provide power to network components.

See: *uninterruptible power supply (UPS)*

URL

Stands for Uniform Resource Locator, an addressing scheme for locating resources on the Internet.

See: *Uniform Resource Locator (URL)*

URL switching

A technology for load-balancing Hypertext Transfer Protocol (HTTP) traffic.

Overview

URL switching enables you to flexibly manage access to content stored on Web servers by load-balancing incoming HTTP requests. URL switching does this by directing these incoming requests to Web servers and caching servers based on the value of various substrings within the HTTP headers. For example, requests for static Web pages might be switched to a caching server, while requests for dynamic content are switched to a Web application server. Other criteria that can be used to switch requests include the size of the file requested and whether the content is multimedia in form. Once the switch determines the best server to service the request, it binds the request to that server for the duration of the session. Cookies can also be used with Uniform Resource Locators (URLs) to switch requests to specific Web servers in a server farm.

Other names sometimes used to describe URL switching include Web content switching and Layer-7 switching.

Marketplace

A leading vendor in URL switching devices arena is Alteon WebSystems (acquired by Nortel Networks). Other vendors of Web content switches include Cisco Systems, F5 Networks, Foundry Networks, and Intel Corporation.

See Also: *caching, Hypertext Transfer Protocol (HTTP), Layer 2 switch, Uniform Resource Locator (URL), Web server*

USB

Stands for universal serial bus, a high-speed serial interface for connecting peripherals to computers.

See: *universal serial bus (USB)*

Usenet

A global network of Internet hosts that supports tens of thousands of discussion groups covering every imaginable topic.

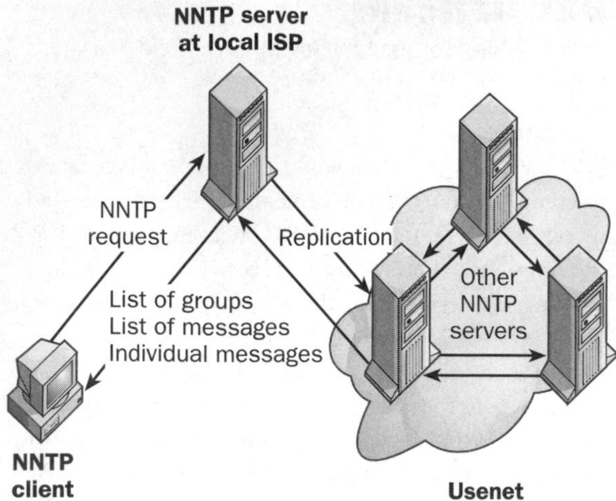

Usenet. *How the Usenet system works on the Internet.*

Overview

Usenet is part of the Internet's family of protocols and services and is typically used by individuals for such purposes as

- Asking questions or requesting assistance on a particular issue
- Distributing free information, including binary files such as images, sound clips, and multimedia files
- Advertising products and services
- Discussing issues of general, regional, local, or topical interest

Usenet currently consists of more than 60,000 newsgroups worldwide, and new groups are constantly being created as old ones disband. Most news servers do not carry the complete range of Usenet newsgroups because of the multigigabyte size of a full newsfeed. Other news servers exclude certain categories of groups, such as adult newsgroups. Some newsgroups are moderated, which means that new postings to the group must be approved by a moderator before they can appear in the newsgroup. This minimizes the "noise" or extraneous messages (mostly advertising).

Users typically gain access to the Usenet system by accessing a Usenet server running at their Internet service provider (ISP). Users typically must have an account and a password to connect to their ISP's news server to prevent unauthorized use, although free Usenet servers are also available across the Internet. Users employ Network News Transfer Protocol (NNTP) client software such as Microsoft Outlook Express to access newsgroups on the ISP's server and post new messages to them. Periodically, the ISP's news server replicates its newsgroup messages by pushing or pulling newsfeeds together with nearby Usenet servers on the Internet. As a result, within about 24 hours the messages posted by users are available on virtually every Usenet server in the world. A message typically remains on a news server for a few weeks or until enough new messages have been posted to the newsgroup to bump the old messages off the list.

Implementation

The Usenet system is based on NNTP, a standard Internet protocol defined in RFC 977. The architecture that supports Usenet has two components:

- **Client/server:** This component allows user desktop machines running NNTP client software such as Outlook Express to interact with Usenet servers (NNTP hosts) to perform actions such as downloading a list of available Usenet newsgroups on the server, reading existing messages in the newsgroups, replying to existing messages, or posting new messages.
- **Server/server:** This component allows NNTP hosts to communicate with each other, primarily for the purpose of replicating newsgroup messages between each other to ensure that each NNTP host has up-to-date messages in the newsgroups they host. An example of software that can function as an NNTP host is Microsoft Exchange Server, which fully supports NNTP and can be used to host newsgroup discussions.

The Usenet system of newsgroups is hierarchical in nature, similar to the Domain Name System (DNS). At the top level, Usenet consists of a number of top-level news hierarchies that identify either a range of topics (such as .rec for recreational topics) or a geographic location (such as .mn for Minnesota). Newsgroups are created hierarchically under these top-level categories, as in these examples:

- forsale.mn
- computers.forsale.mn
- macintosh.computers.forsale.mn

The following table shows some of the popular top-level categories.

Top-Level Usenet Categories

Category	*Description*
alt	Alternative, which is a collection of various topics
comp	Information on computer hardware, software, algorithms, and other topics
misc	Miscellaneous information
news	Information about Usenet itself
rec	Recreational topics such as hobbies and travel
sci	Scientific issues
soc	Social issues
talk	General discussion topics such as politics and religion

Notes

If you do not have an NNTP client program or if your company firewall will not allow you to access Usenet services using the well-known port number for NNTP (port 119), you can still access Usenet (if you can browse the Internet using a standard Web browser such as Microsoft Internet Explorer). Web sites such as Google (*www.google.com*) offer a Web interface for reading and posting to Usenet newsgroups. Before doing this at work, however, make sure that your company does not have any policies forbidding employees to access Usenet.

See Also: *Exchange Server, Internet, Internet service provider (ISP), Network News Transfer Protocol (NNTP)*

user account

Credentials assigned to a user to enable secure access to network resources.

Overview

User accounts allow users to log on to desktop computers to access network resources such as shared folders, shared printers, e-mail services, and databases. An administrator generally grants a user access to these resources by assigning the user a set of credentials (user name and password) called a user account. In Microsoft Windows 2000 and Windows .NET Server networks, there are two basic types of user accounts:

- **Domain user accounts:** These are created in Active Directory directory service and stored on domain controllers. You can log on to any computer on the network if you have a domain user account. Domain user accounts are usually referred to simply as user accounts.
- **Local user accounts:** These are stored within the local directory database of a stand-alone server or desktop workstation that belongs to a workgroup instead a domain. A user who has a local user account can log on only to the computer on which the account was actually created.

Notes

A group account (or simply group) essentially acts as a container for holding user accounts. Group accounts simplify network administration by allowing multiple users to be granted or denied access to network resources in a single step—by granting or denying access for the group account to the resource.

See Also: *account, domain user account, group, local user account*

User Datagram Protocol (UDP)

A transport layer protocol of the Transmission Control Protocol/Internet Protocol (TCP/IP) suite.

Overview

User Datagram Protocol (UDP) is one of two transport layer protocols within the TCP/IP protocol suite, the other being Transmission Control Protocol (TCP). Unlike TCP, which is intended for reliable, connection-oriented sessions between two hosts, UDP is a connectionless protocol in which packets are sent without first negotiating a connection between the sending and receiving hosts. UDP also does not include the segmentation, sequencing, flow control, acknowledgement, and retransmission features of TCP and is therefore an "unreliable" or "best-effort delivery" protocol in the same sense that ordinary mail ("snail mail") is

unreliable—that is, there is no guarantee that a packet (or letter) sent will reach its intended recipient (think of TCP as the equivalent of "registered mail" in this analogy). Reliable delivery of UDP packets is the responsibility of application layer protocols above it that use UDP as their underlying network transport. UDP packets do include a checksum header, however, to ensure the integrity of packets that reach their destination.

Because of these characteristics UDP is considered the more "lightweight" of the two TCP/IP transport layer protocols. Although TCP is used for one-to-one communication between two hosts—in other words, for unicasting—UDP is used for one-to-many communication, which includes both broadcasting and multicasting. The following table summarizes the various differences between UDP and TCP—as you can see, UDP is a much simpler protocol than TCP, mainly because it does not need to include mechanisms relating to establishing, maintaining, and tearing down sessions between hosts. Note that neither UDP nor TCP includes fields for source and destination address in their headers—this is because the underlying network layer protocol called Internet Protocol (IP) is responsible for such addressing.

Comparison of Features of UDP and TCP

Feature	*UDP*	*TCP*
Connection method	Connectionless	Connection-oriented
Communication model	One-to-one	One-to-many
Reliability	Best effort	Guaranteed
Header length	8 bytes	20 bytes
Header fields	Source and destination port, length, checksum	Source and destination port, sequence number, acknowledgement number, data offset, reserved, flags, window, checksum, urgent pointer, options, and padding

Uses

Some examples of where UDP is employed include applications and services where name queries are performed, such as

- Domain Name System (DNS)
- NetBIOS name resolution (but if Windows Internet Name Service [WINS] is employed, then TCP is used instead)

Other examples include protocols and services where reliability is provided by

- The application layer protocol itself—for example, Network File System (NFS) and Trivial File Transfer Protocol (TFTP)
- Periodic advertisements—for example, Routing Information Protocol (RIP)

Notes

UDP is defined by RFC 768.

See Also: *connectionless protocol, connection-oriented protocol, Domain Name System (DNS), Internet Protocol (IP), NetBIOS name resolution, Network File System (NFS), Routing Information Protocol (RIP), Transmission Control Protocol (TCP), Transmission Control Protocol/Internet Protocol (TCP/IP), Trivial File Transfer Protocol (TFTP), Windows Internet Name Service (WINS)*

user-level security

A mode of security on computers running Microsoft Windows 98 and Windows Me that protects shared folders and printers by requiring that users be authenticated by the network's security provider.

Overview

User-level security is more flexible and granular than share-level security, which protects shared resources using a password only. The security provider for enabling user-level security to be used on a Windows network can be a Windows 2000 or Windows .NET domain controller or a Novell NetWare server, depending on which network client the computer running Windows 98 or Windows Me has installed.

Windows 98 and Windows Me employ pass-through authentication for granting client requests for shared resources on the computer:

1. A remote client attempts to access a share on the computer running Windows 95 or Windows 98, passing it the user's credentials.

2 The computer forwards the user's credentials to the network security provider.

3 The security provider verifies the credentials and informs the computer.

4 The computer grants the user the specified level of access to the share, depending on the user's account and group memberships.

Notes

Use the Network utility in Control Panel to enable user-level security on a computer running Windows 98 or Windows Me.

See Also: *domain controller, share-level security*

User Locator Service (ULS)

Former name for Internet Locator Service, a Lightweight Directory Access Protocol (LDAP) directory service that enables Microsoft NetMeeting users to locate and contact other users for conferencing and collaboration over the Internet.

See: *Internet Locator Service (ILS)*

user mode

A restricted mode of operation for processes in Microsoft Windows NT, Windows 2000, Windows XP, and Windows .NET Server.

Overview

User mode processes include components of the operating system that directly support user applications and the applications that use those subsystems. User mode processes have lower priority and fewer privileges than kernel mode processes, and they cannot access hardware directly.

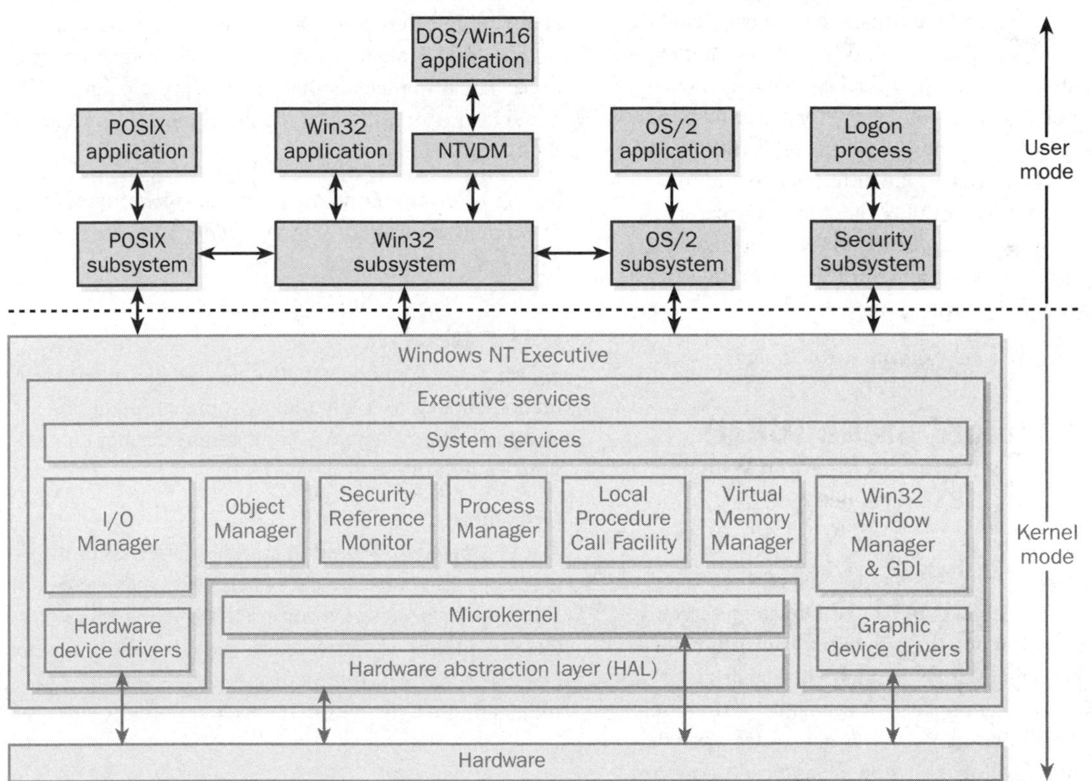

User mode. *Architecture of Windows 2000 user mode.*

U

User mode subsystems include

- Win32 subsystem, which supports Windows applications
- OS/2 subsystem, which supports OS/2 applications
- POSIX subsystem, which supports POSIX-compliant applications
- Security subsystem, which handles logon validation

See Also: *kernel mode*

username

A unique identifier that enables a user to log on to a computer or network.

Overview

Usernames are part of a user's credentials, which include the username, password, and domain name. Each user on the network must have a unique username so that his or her personal folders can be protected against unauthorized access and for administrative purposes such as auditing. A typical example of a username might be "jsmith" or "jeffs" for a user named Jeff Smith. On a network running Microsoft Windows 2000 or Windows .NET Server, an administrator or an account operator can employ the Active Directory Users and Computers console to create and manage user accounts, and account restrictions can be created and managed using group policies.

See Also: *naming convention, user account*

user principal name (UPN)

The logon name of a user on a Microsoft Windows 2000 or Windows .NET Server network.

Overview

User principal names (UPNs) are one of three types of names by which objects in Active Directory directory service can be known, the others being distinguished names (DNs) and relative distinguished names (RDNs). The UPN for a user consists of the name of the User object in Active Directory that is associated with that user's account, followed by the @ sign and then typically by the Domain Name System (DNS) name of the container in Active Directory in which the User object resides. The UPN must be unique for every User object stored in Active Directory.

Examples

If the User object in Active Directory for user Jeff Smith has the name jsmith and if this User object resides in the container with a DNS name of sales.microsoft.com, the default form of Jeff Smith's user principal name is as follows:

```
jsmith@sales.microsoft.com
```

An alternative form of the user principal name for Jeff Smith is

```
jsmith@microsoft.com
```

In other words, the suffix for the user principal name of a user can be either the name of the tree or the name of the domain that resides above the object named in the tree. Note the similarity between the user principal name for Jeff Smith and what you might expect his Simple Mail Transfer Protocol (SMTP) e-mail address to be. The difference is that the user principal name is merely a property that is assigned to the user and can be set to any value.

See Also: *Active Directory, distinguished name (DN), Domain Name System (DNS), Simple Mail Transfer Protocol (SMTP)*

user profile

On Microsoft Windows platforms, user-definable information about a user's work environment, including desktop settings, network connections, printer connections, and Start menu items.

Overview

A user's profile is stored in a folder named after the username and consists of a registry hive and a series of subfolders whose functions are listed in the following table. If additional software is installed on the computer (such as Microsoft Internet Explorer), additional subfolders might exist within the user's profile folder.

Typical User Profile Subfolders and Registry Hives

Subfolder or Hive	*Contents*
Application Data folder	Vendors' application-specific data
Desktop folder	Files and shortcuts on the Windows desktop
Favorites folder	Favorite locations
NetHood folder	Shortcuts to Network Neighborhood items
Personal folder	Users' personal documents
PrintHood folder	Shortcuts to Printer Folder items
Recent folder	Shortcuts to recently opened documents
SendTo folder	Shortcuts for the SendTo menu
Start Menu folder	Start menu shortcuts
Templates folder	Shortcuts to templates
ntuser.dat	Copy of the HKEY_CURRENT_USER hive
ntuser.dat.log	Transaction log for error recovery

Users group

A built-in group in Microsoft Windows 2000 and Windows .NET Server.

Overview

The Users group is a domain local group on domain controllers and a local group on stand-alone servers and computers running Windows 2000 or Windows XP. The initial membership of the Users group is the domain users global group, which consists of all ordinary users on the network. The Users group has no preassigned rights or permissions and should be assigned permissions to network resources that ordinary users will normally require.

See Also: *built-in group*

USN

Stands for update sequence number, a type of identifier used in directory replication in Microsoft Windows 2000 and Windows .NET Server.

See: *update sequence number (USN)*

UTP cabling

Stands for unshielded twisted-pair cabling, twisted-pair cabling with no internal shielding.

See: *unshielded twisted-pair (UTP) cabling*

UUCP

Stands for UNIX-to-UNIX Copy, a command for transferring files between two UNIX hosts on a network.

See: *UNIX-to-UNIX Copy (UUCP)*

uuencoding

A method of encoding binary files into 7-bit ASCII text.

Overview

Uuencoding was originally developed for UNIX platforms to enable binary files to be attached to e-mail messages and transmitted over the Internet using Simple Mail Transfer Protocol (SMTP). The sending program first "uuencodes" the attachments and sends them with the e-mail message, which the receiving program "uudecodes" into its original binary format.

Although still popular on some platforms, uuencoding has been largely superseded by Multipurpose Internet Mail Extensions (MIME), a more sophisticated scheme for encoding multipart e-mail messages. Uuencoding is still used in one context in Microsoft Windows, namely for Basic Authentication on Internet Information Services (IIS). Basic Authentication transmits the user's credentials between the Web browser client and the IIS computer in uuencoded form. This method is commonly referred to as cleartext transmission, although if you were to capture authentication traffic by using a network sniffer such as Microsoft Network Monitor, you would be unable to read the user's credentials without uudecoding the information. Uuencoding is not considered a cryptographic algorithm because it is extremely simple to crack.

An encoding method similar to uuencoding that is implemented on Apple Macintosh systems is called BinHex.

Notes

You can tell that a binary file has been uuencoded into an ASCII text file if the text of the file starts with "begin 644..."

See Also: *Basic authentication, Internet Information Services (IIS), Multipurpose Internet Mail Extensions (MIME), Simple Mail Transfer Protocol (SMTP), UNIX*

UWC-136

A standard for third-generation (3G) wireless cellular communication systems.

See: *Universal Wireless Communications (UWC-136)*

V.35

A popular serial transmission interface found on routers.

Overview

V.35 defines a high-speed physical interface for synchronous serial communication between data terminal equipment (DTE) and data communications equipment (DCE). V.35 is part of the V-series standards developed by the International Telecommunication Union (ITU) and is widely used in the networking industry.

V.35 uses balanced lines for signaling and unbalanced lines for sending control information. The standard supports transmission rates of up to 1.544 megabits per second (Mbps) over distances of up to 4000 feet (1200 meters). The V.35 interface is typically used to connect routers and other wide area network (WAN) access devices to Channel Service Unit/Data Service Units (CSU/DSUs) to build WANs using T1 lines.

V.35. *Typical V.35 connector format.*

V.35 uses a block-shaped 34-pin block connector for implementing these DTE-to-DCE connections, but you can also use V.35-to-RS-232 gender changers to connect V.35 equipment using 25-pin (DB25) serial cables.

Notes

Although the V.35 standard was replaced by the V.10 and V.11 standards in 1988, it remains one of the more popular DTE/DCE interfaces for local area network/wide area network (LAN/WAN) connectivity.

Notes

Although the V.35 specification tops out at speeds of 1.544 Mbps, routers from most vendors support higher speeds in their implementation of the V.35 interface, with some as high as 10 Mbps. Nevertheless, if you need WAN links faster than T1 speeds, you will probably need to use a router with a high-speed serial interface (HSSI) port instead of V.35.

See Also: *Channel Service Unit/Data Service Unit (CSU/DSU), data communications equipment (DCE), data terminal equipment (DTE), High-Speed Serial Interface (HSSI), International Telecommunication Union (ITU), router, serial transmission, T1, V-series, wide area network (WAN)*

V.90

A popular high-speed modem standard.

Overview

V.90 is part of the V-series standards developed by the International Telecommunication Union (ITU). V.90 evolved from two earlier modem standards: the x2 modem technology developed by U.S. Robotics (later bought by 3Com Corporation) and the K56flex modem technology developed by Rockwell. V.90 modems theoretically support downstream communication at 56 kilobits per second (Kbps) and upstream at 33.6 Kbps (upstream transmission is implemented using the same method as the older 33.6 Kbps V.34bis modem standard). V.90 downstream transmission is limited by several factors:

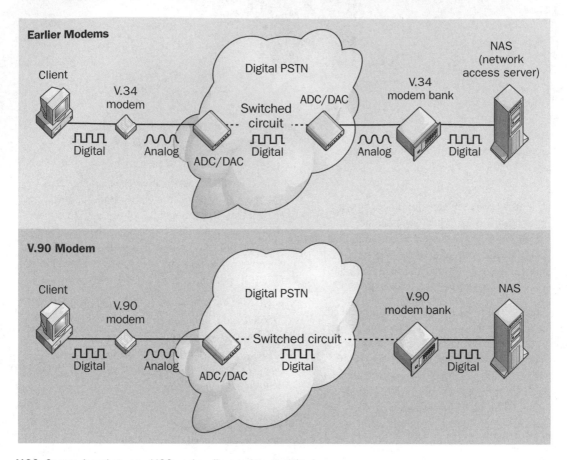

V.90. *Comparison between V.90 and earlier modem standards.*

- The downstream speed of 56 Kbps is achievable only when there is a digital phone line on one end of the connection, typically on the side of the telco or Internet service provider (ISP). In other words, V.90 is possible only on telephone networks that have only one analog segment in the communication path (the local loop at the subscriber end) instead of two analog segments (at both the subscriber and ISP/central office [CO] ends). The benefit of this scenario is that using a digital phone line on one end of the connection eliminates the quantization error that occurs during analog-to-digital conversion (ADC) that normally takes place with a modem. The digital connection at the telco is actually 64 Kbps, but due to digital-to-analog conversion (DAC) that takes place at the telco CO when the digital connection is switched to the analog local loop, some information loss results that reduces the possible downstream speed to 56 Kbps.
- Despite the fact thatV.90 can support 56 Kbps downloads, the actual top downstream speed is only 53 Kbps. This is because Federal Communications Commission (FCC) regulations governing signaling over telephone lines restricts the maximum signal power that can be transmitted over the Public Switched Telephone Network (PSTN) to levels that prevent crosstalk from degrading signal quality. The result of these regulations reduces the possible downstream speed of V.90 from 56 Kbps to 53 Kbps.

- Furthermore, in real life the achievable downstream speed is less than 53 Kbps if line distances between the customer premises and the telco CO exceed 3.5 miles (5.5 kilometers) or if line conditions are poor. In practice, typical downstream speeds for V.90 are usually between 40 to 50 Kbps and the speed is negotiated during call setup. The way this happens is that V.90 employs mechanisms whereby the client modem issues a request for a test tone during negotiation, which is then used to gauge the line quality to determine the optimal downstream transmission speed.

V.90 modems have proved enormously popular for dial-up Internet access. Some industry analysts estimate that there are almost 100 million V.90 modems in use around the world. Although use of broadband Internet using Digital Subscriber Line (DSL) and cable modems is increasing, analysts estimate that V.90 modems will continue to remain the dominant solution until around 2004.

See Also: *cable modem, crosstalk, Digital Subscriber Line (DSL), Internet access, modem, Public Switched Telephone Network (PSTN), serial transmission, V.92, V-series*

V.92

The latest high-speed modem standard from the International Telecommunication Union (ITU).

Overview

V.92 is an emerging standard that provides the same 56 kilobits per second (Kbps) theoretical downstream speeds as the earlier V.90 modem standard. V.92, however, offers some significant enhancements over V.90 modem technology, specifically:

- Upstream speed of 48 Kbps compared to only 33.6 Kbps for V.90 modems. This is accomplished by using the same transmission algorithm for upstream that is used for V.90 downstream communication—in contrast to V.90, which uses the older V.34bis standard for upstream communication.
- Faster call setup and handshaking, typically only 10 seconds compared to 30 seconds for V.90 modems.
- Support for call waiting, so that a user can interrupt a modem session to take a telephone call and then resume the modem session. This means that home users will need only one telephone line instead of two if they use V.92 modems for Internet access.

Marketplace

V.92 modems are being developed by a number of modem manufacturers, including U.S. Robotics, Lucent Technologies, Motorola, PCTEL, and several others.

Issues

Because of these features, V.92 appeals to enterprises using modem pools for remote access to corporate networks. Faster call setup and faster upstream speeds mean shorter remote access sessions and hence lower costs. This can be particularly significant when remote access is performed over long-distance telephone lines.

On the other hand, some Internet service providers (ISPs) may be reluctant to implement V.92, because users may leave their modems connected to the Internet all the time. This may mean greater costs for ISPs, who may have to add additional modem pools to handle the longer connection times (the average dial-up Internet access session is estimated by some analysts at 30 minutes).

See Also: *International Telecommunication Union (ITU), modem, remote access, V.90, V-series*

value entry

A data entry in the Microsoft Windows registry.

Overview

Value entries are contained in keys and are analogous to variables. They consist of three parts:

- **Name:** The name of the value entry (for example, MaintainServerList)

- **Data type:** The type of data stored in the value entry (for example, REG_SZ represents human-readable text)
- **Value:** The actual data contained in the value entry (for example, the string "Auto")

Some of the various data types supported by Windows 2000, Windows XP, and Windows .NET Server are shown in the table. Applications can also define other data types when required.

Examples of Value Entry Data Types

Data Type	*Description*
REG_BINARY	Raw binary data, usually displayed in the registry editor in hexadecimal format
REG_DWORD	Data represented by a number that is 4 bytes long and is displayed in the registry editor in binary, hexadecimal, or decimal format
REG_EXPAND_SZ	An expandable data string (text that contains a variable that is replaced when called by an application)
REG_MULTI_SZ	A multiple string, typically used for lists that are in human-readable text with entries separated by NULL characters
REG_SZ	A sequence of characters in human-readable text, typically used for descriptive information

See Also: *key (registry), registry*

variable-length subnet mask (VLSM)

A technique for conserving Internet Protocol (IP) addresses.

Overview

Variable-length subnet mask (VLSM) was developed in response to shortages in the available pool of IP addresses. Large IP internetworks consisting of multiple subnets typically use assigned IP address blocks inefficiently. This is because although different subnets often have different numbers of hosts, network architects usually design IP internetworks using a single "one size fits all" subnet mask.

For example, consider an enterprise assigned the class B network ID 181.63.0.0 that has hosts among four networks. The number of nodes on each network is 600 on network A, 400 on network B, 200 on network C, and 2 for network D (network D is a dedicated leased line, and because this is a form of point-to-point connection, only two nodes are on the network). The simplest scheme for subnetting the network into four parts would be to use the same subnet mask for each network, namely 255.255.252.0, which can support 1022 hosts per subnet. Because there are four subnets, this subnet mask means we are using 4088 IP addresses from the available pool of 65,534 associated with the class B address. But in fact we are only using 600+400+200+2=1202 of these 4088 addresses, and so 2886 addresses are essentially wasted.

VLSM reduces the amount of wasted addresses by selecting a subnet mask closest to the needs of each network. In the above scenario, this means:

- Network A will use subnet mask 255.255.252.0, which provides 1022 possible addresses of which only 600 are being used (therefore 422 are being wasted).
- Network B will use subnet mask 255.255.254.0, which provides 510 possible addresses of which only 400 are being used (therefore 110 are being wasted).
- Network C will use subnet mask 255.255.255.0, which provides 254 possible addresses of which only 200 are being used (therefore 54 are being wasted).
- Network D will use subnet mask 255.255.255.252, which provides two possible addresses of which both are being used and none are being wasted.

Using VLSM, we have reduced the number of wasted addresses from 2886 (when using a fixed subnet mask scheme) to only 522+110+54=686 addresses, a savings of 2200 addresses.

To use VLSM in the enterprise, a routing protocol supporting VLSM must be employed for communication between routers. Although some routing protocols exchange only network addresses with each other, routing protocols supporting VLSM also exchange subnet masks together with these network addresses. The routing protocols that support VLSM are:

- Enhanced Interior Gateway Routing Protocol (EIGRP)
- Open Shortest Path First (OSPF)
- Routing Information Protocol version 2 (RIPv2)

Issues

VSLM is most often used when OSPF is used to join pre-existing routing domains that use RIP within their domain boundaries. OSPF thus provides the backbone routing service to connect these "RIP islands," and each RIP island is defined as an OSPF area. The main problem with using VLSM, however, is that it requires careful planning to implement properly—you need to know all your subnets and the maximum possible hosts on each subnet before you start the process of subnetting your network using VLSM. For older networks, implementing VLSM basically means renumbering the network from the ground up, a time-consuming process.

A better alternative to resubnetting your internetwork using VLSM is simply resubnetting it using the private class A network ID 10.0.0.0 and a fixed subnet mask that provides enough addresses for your largest network. In this approach, you simply do not worry about wasting IP addresses because you have 16,777,214 to work with using this network ID. Of course, you can only use this approach if your IP internetwork is connected to the Internet using network address translation (NAT), but this is the standard approach anyway.

See Also: *Class A, Class B, Enhanced Interior Gateway Routing Protocol (EIGRP), IP address, Open Shortest Path First (OSPF), Routing Information Protocol (RIP), subnet mask, subnetting*

VBScript

Stands for Visual Basic Scripting Edition, a scripting language developed by Microsoft Corporation.

Overview

VBScript was designed primarily for use in Web applications running on the Internet Information Services (IIS) and Internet Explorer platforms. VBScript is a lightweight subset of the more powerful Visual Basic for Applications (VBA) programming language used in Microsoft Office and other Microsoft development platforms. VBScript omits features such as file input/output (I/O) and direct access to the operating system to provide a secure scripting platform for developing Web-based applications using server-side scripting technologies such as Active Server Pages (ASP). Internet Explorer includes a scripting engine for interpreting and running client-side scripts written in VBScript. VBScript can run on all versions of Microsoft Windows as well as on certain UNIX platforms.

Note that you cannot use VBScript to write stand-alone programs. Instead, you must embed script into standard Hypertext Markup Language (HTML) files. The script is executed when a Web browser opens the HTML file. Alternatively, ASP can use VBScript to generate HTML on the fly.

Examples

Script within an HTML page is enclosed within <SCRIPT> ... </SCRIPT> tags. For example, the following HTML segment displays a button that, when pressed, displays a message box that reads "Hello World!":

```
<INPUT TYPE=BUTTON VALUE="Click me"
NAME="BtnHello">
<SCRIPT LANGUAGE="VBScript">
   Sub BtnHello_OnClick
        MsgBox "Hello World!", 0, "An active
        document"
   End Sub
</SCRIPT>
```

In this code, the <INPUT> tag creates the command button and the <SCRIPT> tag contains the script for the event handler that handles the button click.

For More Information

Visit the Microsoft Windows Script Technologies site at *msdn.microsoft.com/scripting.*

See Also: *Active Server Pages (ASP), Hypertext Markup Language (HTML), Internet Information Services (IIS), JavaScript, JScript, scripting*

vCalendar

An Internet protocol for interoperability between scheduling programs running on different platforms.

Overview

vCalendar allows Personal Data Interchange (PDI) programs to exchange scheduling information over the Internet to book meetings, schedule events, and plan other activities. The vCalendar standards define the for mat by which scheduling information can be exchanged over the Internet. The basic units of scheduling information are the event, which consists of a scheduled activity and its time, date, and duration, and the to-do, a work item or assignment that is delegated to an individual.

vCalendar is defined in RFCs 2445 to 2447 and is broadly supported in the e-mail and groupware industry. The current version is vCalendar 1. Microsoft Outlook 98 and later can import and export information in vCalendar format.

For More Information

Visit the Internet Mail Consortium's PDI page at *www.imc.org/pdi.*

See Also: *vCard*

vCard

An Internet protocol for exchanging business information.

Overview

vCard enables users to exchange the kind of information found on business cards by using standard Internet applications such as e-mail clients and Web browsers. It can also be integrated into fax, cellular phone, pager, smart card, and other communication technologies. You can use vCard to electronically communicate information such as a user's name, title, business, address, telephone numbers, e-mail addresses, URLs (Uniform Resource Locators), company logo, photographic likeness, audio clip, and just about anything else. vCard specifies the format for encoding information for transmission over the Internet.

vCard is defined in RFCs 2425 and 2426. The current version is vCard 3. Microsoft Outlook 98 and later and Microsoft Outlook Express 5 support the vCard protocol.

See Also: *vCalendar*

VDSL

Stands for Very-high-rate Digital Subscriber Line, a high-speed flavor of Digital Subscriber Line (DSL).

See: *Very-high-rate Digital Subscriber Line (VDSL)*

Very-high-rate Digital Subscriber Line (VDSL)

A high-speed flavor of Digital Subscriber Line (DSL).

Overview

Very-high-rate Digital Subscriber Line (VDSL) was developed in the early 1990s as a high-speed version of Asymmetric Digital Subscriber Line (ADSL). Most existing VDSL implementations support speeds to 52 megabits per second (Mbps) in the upstream direction and 2.3 Mbps downstream over existing local loop copper wiring. A limiting factor is that VDSL operates over very short distances, typically only 1000 feet (300 meters) from the telco central office (CO). At longer distances, VDLS speeds drop sharply, and the service is difficult to provision beyond about 4500 feet (1400 meters).

VDSL is undergoing standardization by the International Telecommunication Union (ITU), so current VDSL services are vendor-specific. The plan is to standardize two different versions of VDSL:

- **Asymmetric:** This will support 52 Mbps upstream and 6.4 Mbps downstream.
- **Symmetric:** This will support 26 Mbps in both directions.

Marketplace

The VDSL marketplace is still growing, and not many carriers offer the technology to customers. VDSL Systems provides 16-port and 32-port VDSL multiplexers for the carrier market that can handle 26 Mbps traffic at distances up to 5000 feet (1500 meters). The company also provides VDSL customer premises equipment (CPE) in various form factors including access routers, PCI cards, and set-top boxes for the hotel industry.

Telco Systems has an innovative switching called CopperMax, which allows companies to use VDSL to link buildings together using existing telephone lines, provided they are less than 0.75 miles (0.5 kilometers) apart.

See Also: *Asymmetric Digital Subscriber Line (ADSL), Digital Subscriber Line (DSL), International Telecommunication Union (ITU), local loop*

virtual circuit

A logical path or connection between nodes in a network.

Overview

The path of a virtual circuit is composed of discrete segments of the network that are interconnected using switches. Before a transmission can be sent over the circuit, both end stations must agree on the path and its signaling characteristics, a process called establishing the circuit. Once the circuit has been established, the end stations communicate as if they were directly connected using physical wires, but it is the switches that actually establish the communication path throughout the network. To change the logical path the virtual circuit takes across the network, you simply reconfigure the switches—you do not need to reconnect any wires. This is called a virtual circuit because, like a real (physical) circuit, it connects two points for transmission purposes, but instead of being hard-wired it is configurable and therefore "virtual" in nature.

Virtual circuits are generally used in packet-switching networks such as Asynchronous Transfer Mode (ATM), frame relay, and X.25 networks. Virtual circuits are used in wide area networks (WANs) to increase efficiency by forwarding packets using circuit identifiers rather than routing packets using physical or logical addresses. The basic procedure is that once a circuit has been established between two stations, the circuit is assigned a circuit identifier (a number) that is then included in the header of every packet sent by the stations. All packets having this identifier are automatically forwarded by switches over the predefined circuit path without the need to add source or destination addresses to the packets (virtual circuits are point-to-point links and as a result do not need addressing). Using small circuit identifiers means less protocol overhead in packet headers and faster forwarding of packets.

Types

There are two basic types of virtual circuits:

- **Permanent virtual circuit (PVC):** Here the communication management station (the telco's central office) sets up the switches manually ahead of time and the circuit is always on. This type of virtual circuit provides performance comparable to dedicated (leased) telco lines, but it is generally a costly solution for building WANs because PVCs require carrier resources (switches) to be dedicated to a circuit, whether or not that particular circuit is being used.
- **Switched virtual circuit (SVC):** Here the switches are set up automatically when either end station attempts to establish a communication with the other. Once the session is finished, the circuit is torn down and the carrier switches are freed for other uses. Ordinary telephone communication on the circuit-switching Public Switched Telephone Network (PSTN) essentially functions in this fashion.

ATM networks can be implemented using either permanent or switched virtual circuits, as can older X.25 packet-switching networks. Frame relay generally supports only PVCs, although a few providers have begun to offer SVCs. Because an SVC does not require dedicated carrier resources, they can be billed according to usage, which can save companies money.

See Also: *Asynchronous Transfer Mode (ATM), circuit-switched services, frame relay, packet switching, Public Switched Telephone Network (PSTN), wide area network (WAN), X.25*

virtual directory

A directory that appears to Web browser users to be a subdirectory of a Web site's home directory.

Overview

Although a virtual directory behaves as if it were a subdirectory of the home directory, in fact it might be located in a different folder, drive, or server. The advantage of using virtual directories is that content does not need to be stored only on the Web server—it can be distributed on other servers throughout the Web provider's network. These servers can be located at secure, strategic locations for easy access by Web content developers. The disadvantage is a slight degradation in performance due to data being transmitted over the network.

Virtual directories are supported by Internet Information Services (IIS) on Microsoft Windows 2000, Windows XP, and Windows .NET Server.

Examples

For example, consider a user accessing a Web site by using the following Uniform Resource Locator (URL): *www.microsoft.com/otherstuff/file.htm.*

The directory *otherstuff* appears to the user to be a real subdirectory of the home directory *www.microsoft.com*, while in fact it could be a virtual directory that is mapped to a share on a different server on the Web provider's network.

See Also: *Internet Information Services (IIS), Web server*

virtual hosting

Also called reverse hosting, an extension to reverse proxying that is supported by Microsoft Internet and Acceleration (ISA) Server.

See: *reverse hosting*

V

virtual LAN (VLAN)

A group of ports on an Ethernet switch that behaves like a separate network segment.

Overview

The simplest form of a large Ethernet network is one built using only hubs arranged in a cascaded star topology. For example, in a building there might be one workgroup hub for each work area connected to a root hub in the wiring closet. Such a network has two drawbacks:

- The entire network is one collision domain, which causes the network to scale poorly as the number of hosts increases. Once a certain number of hosts are present on the network, collisions start to occur frequently and network bandwidth is wasted.
- The entire network is also one broadcast domain, which increases the probability of broadcast storms occurring and bringing down the network.

The first problem, that of collisions, is usually dealt with by replacing the main or root hub with an Ethernet switch, specifically a Layer 2 switch. This has the effect of partitioning the network into multiple smaller collision domains, which in this example means that each work area will be a separate collision domain. This reduces the overall effect of collisions on the network and isolates problems arising from too many collisions occurring in one area from other parts of the network.

Unfortunately, this simple solution does not solve the second problem, that of broadcasts. In a cascaded star topology where workgroup hubs are connected to a Layer 2 switch, the entire network is still one large broadcast domain, which increases the risk of broadcast storms. Furthermore, if network services are running that advertise themselves using broadcasts, then a significant amount of overall bandwidth might be consumed by these broadcasts, reducing the amount of available bandwidth for other forms of network communications.

The traditional solution to this problem has been to use routers to partition the network into multiple smaller broadcast domains, insofar as routers generally do not forward broadcasts between their interfaces. This works well, but as the network increases in size, the number of network devices (hubs, routers, and switches) increases also, which leads to greater infrastructure costs. Another problem with this traditional style of network is that when a user moves to a different work area and takes his or her computer along to the new area, then some recabling is usually necessary. For example, when the user connects the computer to the local area network (LAN) drop in the new work area, the administrator usually has to go to the wiring room and switch the ends of the old and new LAN drop plugs to make sure the user is connected to the right hub or switch. Because cabling is typically somewhat disorganized in wiring rooms, this task can be a nightmare and is prone to error.

Virtual LAN (VLAN) technologies were developed to solve all these problems. VLANs allow networks to be segmented logically without having to be physically rewired. Instead of having all ports on a switch be equal and belong to the same network, ports can be segregated into groups, each belonging to a separate logical network. For example, on a 3-port switch you could configure ports 1 and 2 as belonging to network 10 and port 3 as belonging to network 20 (see the illustration on the following page). Physically, all three ports seem to be on the same network, but in reality they are not—broadcasts sent to port 1 can only reach port 2 and not port 3. Administrators can easily make these port assignments indicating which VLANs are mapped to which ports by accessing the software for the switch. Note that VLAN ports do not have to be contiguous—for example, ports 1 and 3 could be on the same VLAN and port 2 on a different VLAN.

The benefits of using VLAN-enabled switches include

- The ability to segment networks into multiple smaller broadcast domains without needing additional network devices such as routers to do this. VLANs make switched Ethernet networks more bandwidth-efficient through this segmentation of broadcast domains.
- The ability to reconfigure ports logically without needing to unplug wires and move them around. If a user takes his or her computer to a new work area, no cables need to be swapped on the switch—just access the switch software and issue commands to change the VLAN assignments for the old and new ports. VLANs thus simplify the process of adding, moving, and deleting users on the network. They also improve network security by avoiding cabling mishaps that can arise when users are moved in traditional Ethernet networks.
- The ability to group users together according to function rather than physical location. In a traditional Ethernet network, all users in a given work area are on the same network segment regardless of their job description or department. Using VLANs, however, you could have one salesperson in each work area of the building sitting next to engineers in their work area, yet on a separate logical network segment.

Implementation

VLANs have the following characteristics:

- One switch may have several VLANs defined on it. A VLAN is identified using a special identification number called a VLAN ID. Stations attached to switch ports having the same VLAN ID act and function as though they are all on the same physical network segment. In other words, broadcasts sent by one host are received only by hosts connected to ports having the same VLAN ID as the sending host. Administrators typically assign VLAN IDs manually at the port level, although port assignments can also be managed dynamically for some switches (the switch does this by maintaining an internal table mapping the media access control [MAC] addresses of connected stations to their VLAN ID). When a host is moved to another department, the only change needed is the assignment of a different VLAN ID to the port to which the host is connected—no switching of patch cables is required.

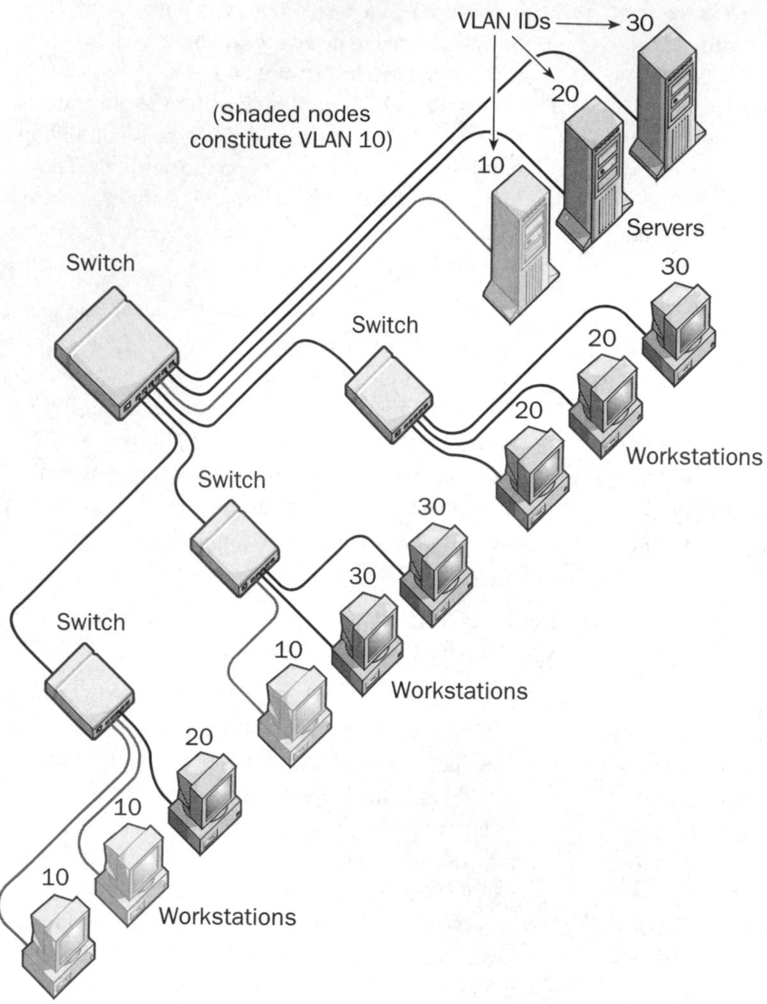

Virtual LAN (VLAN). *A simple example of a network designed using VLAN-enabled switches.*

- A single VLAN can span multiple switches connected together. By using a method called trunking, VLAN-enabled switches can be connected to form large VLANs spanning switches right across the enterprise. To do this, a port on the switch must be designated a trunk port, and trunk ports on different switches are connected using trunk lines. For example, when Fast Ethernet ports are used as trunk ports, trunking can be accomplished by connecting such ports on different switches using enhanced Category 5 (Cat5e) crossover cables.

Switch vendors have traditionally developed their own proprietary VLAN technologies, so implementing a VLAN typically means buying all your switching gear from a single vendor. Cisco Systems is the market leader in VLAN-enabled switches, and many of their Catalyst line of switches support VLANs. Cisco Catalyst switches employ several types of technologies in order to implement enterprise VLANs, namely:

- **Frame tagging:** When an Ethernet frame enters a port on a VLAN-enabled switch, the switch

V

encapsulates the frame by adding a special header or tag that contains the VLAN ID of the port at which the frame arrived. The switch uses the frame tag to determine which ports it can be forwarded to (ports having the same VLAN ID). The tag is then stripped off at the destination ports on the switch, or in the case of traffic moving across multiple switches using trunked connections, it is stripped off when it reaches the destination ports on other connected switches.

- **Inter-switch link (ISL):** This is a proprietary Cisco technology that enables a single port to belong to multiple VLANs—that is, to have multiple VLAN IDs assigned to it. ISL is used for trunking and is also available on special network interface cards (NICs) for servers. When a server has an ISL-supporting NIC installed, it behaves as if it had multiple physical NICs, one for each VLAN. This enables workstations on different VLANs to access the same server, eliminating the need to have separate servers for each VLAN.
- **VLAN Trunking Protocol (VTP):** This is a proprietary Cisco technology that simplifies the task of configuring VLANs across a network. By making any necessary configuration changes to settings on a VTP server, these changes are then propagated across the network to all VLAN-enabled switches that are defined as belonging to the same VTP management domain.

Issues

Three main issues have slowed the acceptance of VLANs in the enterprise: standards, Dynamic Host Configuration Protocol (DHCP), and Layer 3 switches. The problem of standards arises from the proprietary nature of VLAN implementations from different switch vendors. This has resulted in interoperability issues where equipment from one vendor fails to work with that from another vendor. There has been some progress toward standardizing VLAN technologies, however. One important step was the development of the 802.1Q standard from the Institute of Electrical and Electronics Engineers (IEEE), which replaces Cisco's proprietary ISL technology with a standards-based solution. Another development has been the adoption of RFC 2878 by the Internet Engineering Task Force (IETF), which standardizes VLAN frame tagging using the new VLAN Tagged Frame format. RFC 2878 also provides guidelines for switch vendors to improve interoperability with regard to signaling, link aggregation, and Layer 2 traffic prioritization.

The second issue is that of address management of stations on the network. VLANs were originally designed to simplify the management of hosts on the network by using their Layer 2 MAC addresses to identify them to switches. When a computer is unplugged from a LAN drop and moved to a different physical location and plugged in to a different drop, VLAN switches can automatically detect the computer's new location by its MAC address and reconfigure themselves dynamically. The problem is that DHCP was designed for the very same job of dynamic address management but uses Layer 3 (IP) addresses instead. Being a much simpler system, most network managers have chosen DHCP instead of VLANs to ensure that computers can be physically moved around the network if needed. As a result, most VLAN administration is performed manually by assigning VLAN IDs to ports using a command-line interface, a difficult chore in a large enterprise.

The third issue that has slowed the adoption of VLANs has been the emergence of Layer 3 switches, which can perform both bridging (Layer 2) and routing (Layer 3) functions in one box. Layer 3 switches have almost eliminated the need for VLANs in most enterprises. Instead of creating multiple VLANs to segment the network into smaller broadcast domains, the same thing can be accomplished by replacing the root Layer 2 switch with a Layer 3 switch. Each port on the Layer 3 switch represents a separate routed subnet, and the network is thus automatically partitioned into separate broadcast domains.

Prospects

Because of the above issues, the future of VLANs is cloudy. Most enterprise network architects see little point in deploying VLANs when Layer 3 switches can accomplish the same result with less effort. And DHCP manages addresses at Layer 3 more easily than VLANs do it at Layer 2, making it simple to move users around

the network. Nevertheless, there has been something of a resurgence of interest in VLANs recently, mainly in the service provider market where companies such as Yipes Communications that offer metropolitan Ethernet use VLAN-enabled switches from Extreme Networks to provision metropolitan area VLANs for their customers. Another growing use of VLANs is in the Web hosting arena, where these companies are using VLANs to help isolate traffic between different subscribers.

See Also: *802.1Q, broadcast domain, collision domain, Dynamic Host Configuration Protocol (DHCP), Ethernet switch, hub, Institute of Electrical and Electronics Engineers (IEEE), Internet Engineering Task Force (IETF), IP address, Layer 2 switch, Layer 3 switch, MAC address, router*

virtual memory

A mechanism by which applications function as though the system has more random access memory (RAM) than it actually does.

Overview

Virtual memory is designed to improve the performance of applications by providing them with greater effective memory than physical RAM provides. Virtual memory works by paging unneeded code from running applications to a file on the hard drive called the page file. In Microsoft Windows 2000, Windows XP, and Windows .NET Server, the Virtual Memory Manager maps the virtual addresses belonging to the address space of a running process to physical pages of memory in the computer. This ensures that each process has sufficient virtual memory to run efficiently and does not trespass on the memory of other processes. The Virtual Memory Manager handles paging between RAM and the page file, swapping pages by using a process called demand paging. The result is that each application has access to up to 4 gigabytes (GB) of memory. A similar process in Windows 98 and Windows Millennium Edition (Me) uses a comparable structure called the swap file.

Virtual memory is also supported by UNIX platforms and the Mac OS X platform.

virtual private network (VPN)

A technology for securely connecting a computer or network to a remote network over an intermediate network such as the Internet.

Overview

The term *virtual private network (VPN)* is used in various senses in the industry to describe a variety of technologies, but in essence it can have one of two meanings:

- Using an insecure public network such as the Internet to connect two networks (or to connect a network and a remote computer)
- Making this connection secure by employing technologies such as tunneling, authentication, and encryption

The two main types of VPNs are

- **Network-network:** A branch office network of an enterprise is connected by a VPN to corporate headquarters. Network-network VPNs offer a low-cost alternative to deploying expensive dedicated leased lines such as T1 lines at all branch offices (corporate headquarters still requires a leased line for its VPN gateway, however, to provide enough bandwidth for its branch office VPN connections). In spite of the cost advantage, however, network-network VPNs have been slow to gain a foothold in the enterprise due to the proven reliability of leased lines and the relative unreliability of the Internet in comparison.
- **Host-network:** A mobile knowledge worker uses his or her laptop or Personal Digital Assistant (PDA) and modem to dial in to a local Internet service provider (ISP) to connect securely to a company intranet or portal using an encrypted VPN connection. Using VPNs this way has proliferated in the enterprise as it is more cost-effective than traditional remote access solutions involving modem pools, dedicated phone lines, and toll-free numbers.

Architecture

VPNs are based on a client/server architecture:

- **VPN client:** This system initiates the VPN connection with the VPN server. For a typical host-network VPN scenario, the remote user first establishes a dial-up connection with a local ISP to connect to the Internet, and then once online, the client contacts the VPN server to connect to the corporate intranet.
- **VPN server:** This system authenticates the VPN client, negotiates which tunneling and encryption protocols to use, and establishes the secure VPN connection. The result is the formation of a secure encrypted tunnel that connects the VPN client to the VPN server. The effect is transparent—that is, as if both client and server were on the same local area network (LAN). For the connection to work, however, the VPN client must be assigned an Internet Protocol (IP) address that makes it appear to the VPN server as if it is on the same LAN as the server. VPN clients thus generally have two IP addresses, one for the VPN connection and one for the intermediate or transit network (the Internet).

Two VPN tunneling protocols are in use today: Microsoft Corporation's Point-to-Point Tunneling Protocol (PPTP) and Cisco Systems' Layer 2 Tunneling Protocol (L2TP). Both protocols are essentially extensions of the industry standard Point-to-Point Protocol (PPP) and are used to encapsulate PPP frames within IP datagrams for transmission over the Internet. In other words, VPNs employ two layers of encapsulation:

- First the IP datagrams from the client and server are encapsulated with PPP headers to form PPP frames for transmission through the serial interface to the modem or leased line.
- Then the PPP frames are encapsulated again with IP headers (and PPTP or L2TP headers) to form IP packets for routing over the Internet.

The result of using PPTP or L2TP is to create a virtual PPP connection between the VPN client and server. In short, the VPN connection behaves as if it were a dedicated point-to-point serial link but packets are actually routed across the Internet.

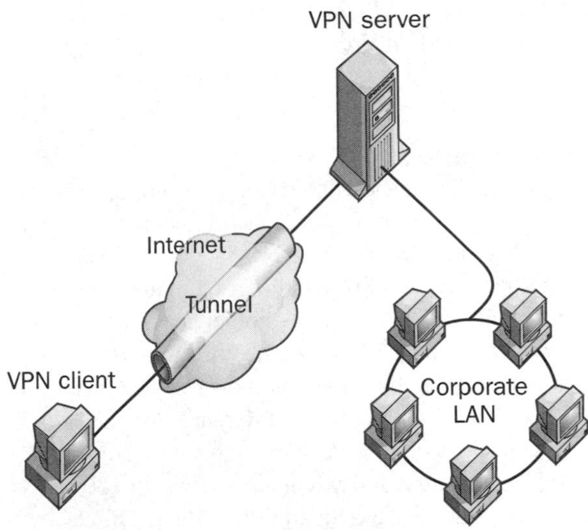

Virtual Private Network (VPN). *How a VPN connection works between a network and a remote host.*

Note that L2TP does not include a mechanism for encrypting VPN communications, so it must be combined with Internet Protocol Security (IPsec) when used to create a VPN connection.

Implementation

VPNs are typically implemented in one of two ways:

- **Customer premises equipment (CPE):** Here the VPN server is owned and operated by the private company and is located at the periphery of their corporate LAN. Such VPN servers may be routers, access servers, firewall appliances, or standard PC servers running VPN-enabled software such as Microsoft Windows 2000 Server.
- **Service provider:** Corporate VPN needs can also be outsourced to VPN service providers, typically telcos, ISPs, or application service providers (ASPs). The service provider maintains the VPN server at the edge of its own network and parcels out VPN services to companies on a monthly leased basis. In this scenario the customer only requires a standard "dumb" router for Internet access at its end, not a VPN-enabled router.

A third kind of VPN implementation involves using permanent virtual circuits (PVCs) carrying IP over public frame relay networks. This method is employed mainly for enterprise network-network VPNs.

Marketplace

A popular Linux-based VPN/firewall appliance is VelociRaptor from Cobalt Networks, which employs Cobalt's hardware and Raptor's firewall software to provide a secure VPN solution for the small business and remote office markets. Another popular VPN appliance is the Alcatel 7137 Secure VPN Gateway, originally developed by TimeStep (now part of Alcatel). Cisco Systems offers many different VPN-enabled routers and access servers, including the Cisco VPN 3005 Concentrator, which supports up to 100 concurrent users. For the Small Office/Home Office (SOHO) business environment, the Cisco PIX Firewall 506 is a small unit the size of a pocketbook that can support 10 simultaneous VPN connections. Another market contender is the VPN-1 Appliance from Check Point Software Technologies, which includes their widely used Firewall-1 product bundled in a Nokia appliance. Check Point also offers a VPN-1 Gateway for high-end corporate VPN connectivity. 3Com Corporation, Avaya, CoSine Communications, Data Fellows Corporation, Indus River Networks, Intel Corporation, Lucent Technologies, RadGuard, RedCreek Communications, and many other companies offer VPN solutions ranging from VPN gateways and appliances to software products.

Examples of service providers offering standard IP VPN services include Aventail Corporation, Genuity, UUNET, Qwest Communications International, and others. Providers of frame relay-based VPN services include AT&T, Equant, Infonet, MCI/Worldcom, Sprint Corporation, and others. Telera offers a nationwide Voice over IP (VOIP)-enabled managed VPN that employs VPN gateways stationed at colocation centers around the United States.

Prospects

The future of network-network VPNs and corporate host-network VPN gateways may be Digital Subscriber Line (DSL), a technology that provides high-speed Internet access at costs vastly lower than leased lines such as T1 lines. The main issue with most enterprises is that DSL has yet to prove itself as reliable a technology as the more costly leased lines, which are a mature technology that has been around for many years. Nevertheless, the combination of a DSL connection with VPN software to provide security is a tantalizing one for IT departments in times of shrinking budgets.

Notes

Although VPNs typically use the Internet as their transit network, it is also possible to run a VPN over a corporate IP LAN to create a "LAN within a LAN" for secure communications across the network.

For More Information

Visit the VPN Consortium at *www.vpnc.org.*

See Also: *application service provider (ASP), Digital Subscriber Line (DSL), firewall, frame relay, Internet, Internet Protocol Security (IPsec), Internet service provider (ISP), Layer 2 Tunneling Protocol (L2TP), permanent virtual circuit (PVC), Point-to-Point Protocol (PPP), Point-to-Point Tunneling Protocol (PPTP), T1, wide area network (WAN)*

virtual server

A technology that allows multiple independent Web sites to be hosted on a single Web server.

Overview

The term *virtual server* is another name for Web site. Internet Information Services (IIS) on Microsoft Windows 2000 and Windows .NET Server supports virtual servers to enable a single machine to host multiple Web sites. Virtual servers can be implemented three different ways in Windows 2000:

- By binding Internet Protocol (IP) addresses to the server's network interface card (NIC). Each virtual server can be assigned its own unique IP address. DNS servers can then resolve domain names into their respective IP addresses, allowing multiple companies to host their Web sites on a single IIS server. This is the preferred method if a large pool of available IP addresses exists for the server.

- By using a single IP address but assigning a unique port number to each virtual server. Clients must know the exact port number to connect to the server instead of using the default Hypertext Transfer Protocol (HTTP) port number 80.
- By enabling host headers on the IIS server. The server has only one IP address and uses the default HTTP port number 80. The client Web browser attempting to access a Web site on the IIS server must be HTTP 1.1–compliant to seamlessly access the site.

Notes

The term *virtual server* is also used in the Windows Clustering component of Microsoft Windows 2000 Server. In this context a virtual server is usually a resource group that contains all the resources necessary for running an application, including the network name and IP address resources.

See Also: *bindings, Hypertext Transfer Protocol (HTTP), Internet Information Services (IIS), IP address, virtual directory, Web server*

virus

A program designed to infect computer systems.

Overview

Viruses are generally malicious programs created to cause damage or annoyance to computer users. The effects of viruses range from harmless but annoying messages announcing the presence of an "infection" to malicious corruption or deletion of crucial operating system and data files.

Although the term *virus* is generally used to refer to any form of malicious code, technically viruses that infect computer systems do so by attaching themselves to executable files, and when these files are executed the virus spreads to other files or causes various forms of damage such as lost or corrupted data. Some other related forms of "malware" (malicious software) include

- **Worm:** Code that infects a machine and then spreads itself to other machines on the network. Worms do not need a host application to attach themselves to as viruses do. Some worms also multiply on host machines and cause various forms of damage to operating system or user files similar to that which viruses cause.
- **Logic bomb:** Code that executes when certain conditions occur—for example, on a specific date of the month or year. Logic bombs are really a form of virus or worm, depending on what actions they perform when the trigger.
- **Trojan:** Code that masquerades as a legitimate application, usually to trick users into divulging their credentials or other sensitive information.
- **Hoaxes:** These are not viruses at all but simply threats of viruses. This might seem innocuous, but many industry analysts say that enterprise administrators often spend more time dealing with these hoaxes than in eradicating actual viruses, and in a business environment any time wasted is money wasted.

Viruses have many entry points in today's enterprise networks, including Internet connections, remote access connections, electronic mail, and users downloading and saving software from the Internet onto floppy disks and taking these disks to work to install the software on their office machines.

History

The first recorded PC virus was the Pakistani Brain virus detected in 1987. Since then tens of thousands of different "strains" of viruses have been detected over the years, and the rate at which new viruses are appearing is accelerating, mainly as a result of the widespread availability over the Internet of scripts that can be easily assembled to form new types of viruses. Some of the better-known viruses in the history of malware include

- **Jerusalem virus:** This virus, which appeared in 1990, was an .exe file that trashed the boot sector of machines it infected. It was widespread for almost five years before being eradicated and is estimated to have caused more than $50 million in damage during its lifetime.

- **Concept virus:** This macro virus for Microsoft Word caused about $50 million in damage before it was eradicated about four months after its appearance in 1995.
- **Melissa virus:** This Word macro virus appeared in 1999, was spread by e-mail, and caused an estimated $300 million in damage worldwide.
- **"I Love You" virus:** This VBScript virus appeared in 2000 and was also propagated by e-mail and caused an estimated $700 million in damage in less than a week.

Types

Common categories of viruses include the following:

- **File virus:** These are standard viruses that reproduce by attaching themselves to executable files such as .exe, .cmd, and .bat files. When the executable file is run, the virus code is executed, causing the virus to reproduce itself and inflict whatever form of damage the virus developer intends.
- **Boot-sector virus:** These are viruses that infect the boot sector of a floppy or hard disk and execute when the operating system is booted. They can cause various types of damage, including the total disabling of computer systems. Notorious boot viruses have included the Michelangelo virus and the Stoned virus. A related type of virus is the Master Boot Record (MBR) virus, which infects the system's MBR.
- **Polymorphic virus:** This type of virus modifies itself as it reproduces, causing its signature to change and making it difficult to detect by standard virus protection software unless the specific evolution algorithm is known.
- **Macro virus:** This is an increasingly popular form of virus consisting of a macro writing in Visual Basic for Applications (VBA) or some other scripting language and designed to execute within a word processing or spreadsheet applications such as those included in Microsoft Office. The malicious macro is inserted into a harmless document, the document is sent as an e-mail attachment to a user, and when the user opens the document the macro is executed and the virus infects the system, typically with the result that data is lost or corrupted.

Implementation

Viruses generally consist of two components:

- **Propagation mechanism:** This is code that, when executed, causes the virus to copy itself to other files on the system.
- **Payload:** This code generates the virus's effect, which may range from harmless messages appearing on the system to the entire operating system being wiped out.

Virus protection software guards enterprise computer systems from the danger of viruses by scanning potential virus-bearing files and prompting the deletion of these files. Virus protection software consists of two components:

- **Virus signature:** This is a file containing small portions of every known virus, and is used as a template for comparison with files for detection of virus infection. Virus signature files for virus protection software must be updated frequently, otherwise new types of viruses will not be detected and will cause damage to the system.
- **Search engine:** This software compares the signature file with other files on the computer to determine which files might be infected with a virus.

Marketplace

The market leaders in virus protection software include Computer Associates, McAfee, Sophos, Symantec Corporation, and Trend Micro. Popular products include Norton AntiVirus from Symantec and VirusScan from McAfee.

Prospects

Viruses seem to be an inevitable fact of life for computer users, and protecting against them is essential for any enterprise connected to the Internet. The earliest viruses were spread from user to user by swapping floppy disks. In the mid-1990s, Word and Microsoft Excel macro viruses became the bane of the office productivity worker, and many enterprises disable macros for these applications to prevent users who open e-mail attachments containing macro viruses from infecting the network. The trend at the beginning of the new millennium seems to be that e-mail viruses are the ones to fear most—many companies have had their messaging systems brought to their knees for days as a results of infections by the Melissa and I Love You viruses, and some have even shut down their in-house mail systems and begun outsourcing their messaging needs from application service providers (ASPs) or Internet service providers (ISPs) who have dedicated resources for combating such viruses when they appear. Some of the more popular ASPs offering virus-protected messaging services include Critical Path and MessageClick.

Some of the newer developments in the virus realm include

- Viruses spread by nonstandard means, such as through multimedia files. By simply visiting a Web site that automatically starts a media player application to play the file, it is possible to infect your machine with a virus. Be sure to download the latest patches from your media application vendor to reduce the chance of infection through this method.
- Viruses that target wireless devices such as cell phones and wireless Personal Digital Assistants (PDAs). The first known example was a Trojan called Liberty Crack, which infected wireless Palm Pilot systems, causing applications to be deleted on the systems. A number of vendors are working to address this critical area, including F-Secure, Finjan Software, McAfee, Symantec, and Trend Micro.

Notes

To keep viruses from proliferating on your network, you can take the following measures:

- Install virus protection software on each computer in your network and keep their virus signature files up to date at all times. This applies especially to desktop computers, file servers, and mail servers, as these types of machines are the most vulnerable. Enterprise virus protection software usually includes mechanisms for automatically updating signature files on machines across a network.
- If you have Internet connectivity, be sure that your virus protection software scans for viruses in Web content downloaded from the Internet and in attachments to Simple Mail Transfer Protocol (SMTP) e-mail messages. Many newer viruses can be downloaded from Web sites or received as attachments to e-mail messages. When the attachments are opened, the machine is infected and the virus begins to spread.
- Regularly perform backups of all-important servers and include periodic archives in your backup schedule, because many viruses do not activate for weeks or months after infection.
- Scan new computers for infection before bringing them onto the network.
- Issue a company policy prohibiting users from installing any personal programs on their desktop computers. You might even disable their floppy drives, because infection by means of a floppy is a common route to virus infection. Some companies go so far as to prevent or prohibit users from sending or receiving attachments to their e-mail, a draconian but effective measure in curbing the spread of viruses.

For More Information

You can visit the McAfee Virus Information Center at *www.mcafee.com/centers/anti-virus.*

See Also: *application service provider (ASP), e-mail, hacking, Internet service provider (ISP), network security, Personal Digital Assistant (PDA), security, Simple Mail Transfer Protocol (SMTP)*

VLAN

Stands for virtual LAN, a group of ports on an Ethernet switch that behaves like a separate network segment.

See: *virtual LAN (VLAN)*

VLSM

Stands for variable-length subnet mask, a technique for conserving Internet Protocol (IP) addresses.

See: variable-length subnet mask (VLSM)

Voice over IP (VoIP)

An umbrella term for a set of technologies that allow voice traffic to be carried over Internet Protocol (IP) networks such as the Internet.

Overview

Voice over IP (VoIP) is one of the driving forces behind convergence in the networking and telecommunications industry. The term *convergence* refers to the goal of combining all forms of enterprise communications (voice telephony, fax, and data) into a single IP data stream and managing this through a single integrated system. The goal of convergence is twofold:

- To reduce costs by eliminating redundant infrastructures. For example, the typical corporate office building has two separate wiring infrastructures: voice telephony wiring and Category 5 (Cat5) or enhanced Category 5 (Cat5e) twisted-pair network wiring. Similarly, large enterprises spanning several geographical locations often have two communication infrastructures as well: Private Branch Exchanges (PBXs) linked by dedicated tie lines and leased lines for wide area networking (WAN). VoIP enables an enterprise to consolidate these two systems into a single communications infrastructure running on an IP data network, with resultant cost savings.
- To simplify management of all forms of business communication (such as e-mail, voice mail, and faxes) by consolidating all messages into a single user interface, typically in the user's e-mail Inbox.

To achieve these two goals of convergence, VoIP addresses the first issue and unified messaging (UM) addresses the second. These systems may be deployed separately or together in the enterprise, depending on business needs and goals.

Advantages and Disadvantages

Although VoIP promises to save enterprises money by avoiding costly long-distance toll charges, the expertise needed to implement VoIP and the cost of new equipment is often seen as a barrier to embracing this new technology. Other concerns often voiced by network managers include

- **Latency:** Because of the best effort nature of IP communications, voice communications sometimes sound garbled and contain undesirable pauses due to high jitter and latency. This is probably the number one issue that companies consider when choosing a VoIP solution. The problem is especially bad when IP traffic is routed over the public Internet, where VoIP conversations can sound like old CB radio sessions in quality. Improvements in IP quality of service (QoS) discussed below are reducing the importance of this issue, but these IP QoS solutions are complex and difficult to implement.
- **Interoperability:** Because there are competing VoIP standards and vendors have developed their own proprietary solutions, when a company adopts a VoIP plan it must essentially use equipment from only one vendor. Even simple IP phones with RJ-45 Ethernet jacks from one vendor usually do not work with VoIP systems from another vendor. In contrast, traditional PBXs and digital telephones from different vendors interoperate seamlessly. If a dominant VoIP standard emerges over the next few years, however, this interoperability problem might finally be resolved.
- **Cost:** Companies that have already invested heavily in legacy PBXs, digital phone systems, and "dumb" routers might be reluctant to abandon them to deploy all-new VoIP switching, routing, telephones, and call control equipment. The cost of the expertise needed to implement and maintain VoIP solutions must also be considered.

Despite these concerns, VoIP is encroaching steadily into large companies and will probably overtake the legacy PBX market in the next five years if trends continue.

Architecture

Most VoIP solutions developed by different vendors are still proprietary solutions that require all customer premises equipment (CPE) to be purchased or leased from a single vendor, but recently there have been moves toward standards-based VoIP solutions that should eventually allow equipment from different vendors to interoperate in a plug and play (PnP) fashion.

The main problem at this point is that competing standards have evolved in the VoIP arena, and it is still unclear which standards will dominate in the emerging VoIP industry. The main standards and protocols of relevance to VoIP are:

- **H.323:** The earliest VoIP systems were based on the H.323 and T.120 of protocols developed by the International Telecommunication Union (ITU) for audio, video, and data communication and conferencing over IP networks. H.323 works well but is complex to implement—a typical H.323 VoIP system includes end-user stations known as VoIP terminals, gateways for translating between IP networks and telephony networks, gatekeepers for handling calling functions, and multipoint control units (MCUs) for handling multipoint conferencing. In addition to its complexity, H.323 also suffers from considerable protocol overhead because it was originally designed to support video communications. Nevertheless, most VoIP vendors have built their systems around H.323, and it is still considered the primary standard for interoperability between different VoIP systems.
- **Session Initiation Protocol (SIP):** This is an application-layer control protocol defined in RFC 2543 that is designed to allow different telephony, data networking, and VoIP equipment to communicate with one another. SIP is a lightweight protocol with much less overhead than H.323 and is seen by some industry analysts as the logical successor to H.323.
- **Media Gateway Control Protocol (MGCP):** This protocol is defined in RFC 2705 and is designed to translate between the voice traffic carried on the Public Switched Telephone Network (PSTN) and IP traffic carried on the Internet. MGCP is a master/slave protocol that enables media gateway controllers and media gateways to communicate with each other and to control IP telephony terminal equipment. MGCP has been implemented in some VoIP systems but is being phased out in favor of the newer Megaco/H.248 standard.
- **Megaco/H.248:** This protocol is a joint effort of the Megaco working group of the Internet Engineering Task Force (IETF) and the ITU-T Study Group 16. Megaco/H.248 is the successor to MGCP and includes additional features that support peer-to-peer communication and simplified implementation of media gateways and controllers.

For more information on the different VoIP protocols, see the individual entries about them elsewhere in this book.

Implementation

VoIP is all about saving cost for companies, and there are a variety of ways in which it can be implemented using the various architectures outlined previously. One important scenario is for linking offices to eliminate long-distance calling costs. The traditional way for companies to do this has been to connect the PBXs in two offices using tie lines. A tie line is a dedicated connection used for both signaling and call transfer between PBXs. This approach is called a "toll bypass" solution because it bypasses the tolls levied for traditional long-distance traffic, in effect emulating a "toll-free" solution.

Tie lines are usually implemented over T1 lines. For offices relatively near each other, the monthly cost of leasing T1 lines for this purpose can be less than the accumulated cost of a month's long-distance calls between the offices, but when the distance between offices is great, the T1 line costs become excessive as they are billed by the mile for most U.S. telcos. Another problem is that a separate tie line must be deployed between each pair of offices—calls cannot be routed across multiple call lines.

Voice over IP (VoIP)

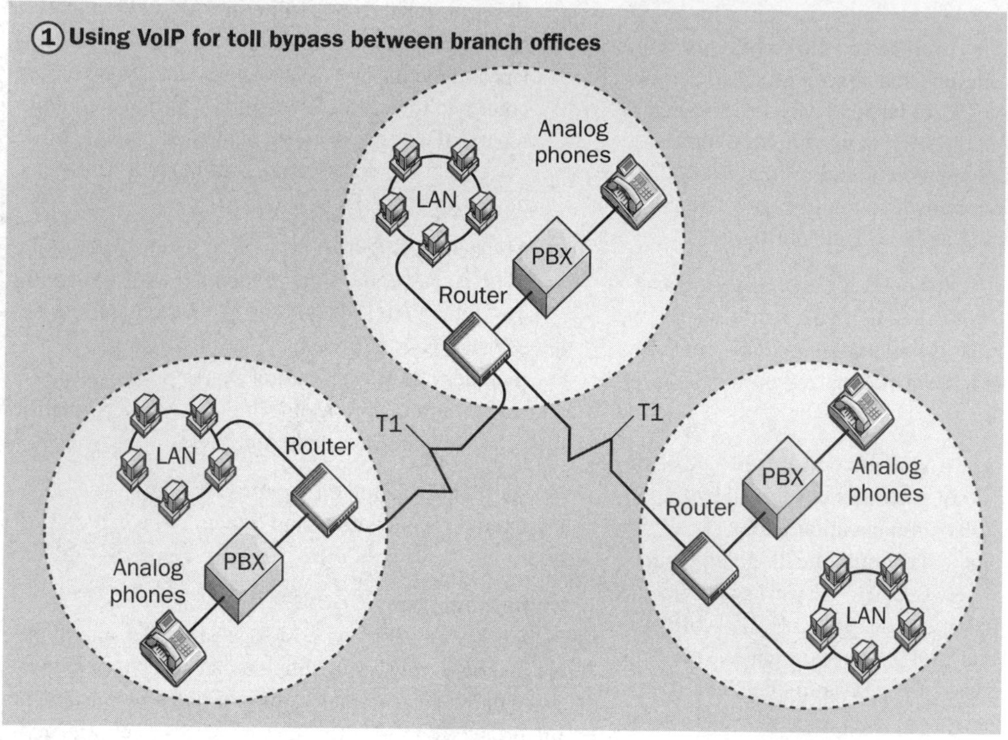

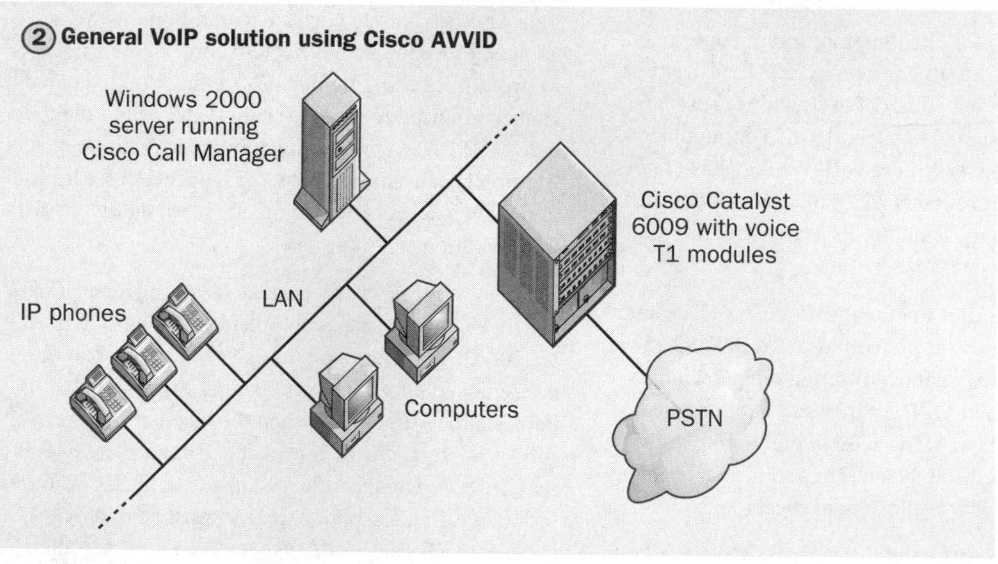

V

Voice over IP (VoIP). *Two common types of VoIP solutions.*

VoIP can save costs in this situation by routing voice traffic over existing data lines between offices, also typically T1 lines for large companies. This means instead of needing two T1 lines between offices (one for data and one for tying PBXs together) companies need only one line (voice and data combined). In addition, companies do not need T1 lines between every pair of offices (full mesh topology), as IP packets can be routed across the enterprise provided there is at least one path between each pair of offices (partial mesh).

A more general VoIP solution is to replace existing PBXs with VoIP-enabled routers that perform gateway and gatekeeper functions to handle call setup and routing. One hidden cost in this "all-IP" approach is that traditional digital phones costing about $50 must be replaced by special IP phones often costing hundreds of dollars. This approach to VoIP, championed by Cisco Systems, is sometimes called an IP PBX approach since it completely replaces existing legacy PBX systems. Companies that have invested heavily in legacy PBX equipment may be reluctant to follow this route also and may instead prefer to useVoIP for replacing PBX tie lines to continue leveraging their investment in legacy equipment. Alternatively, some VoIP vendors such as Nortel Networks offer a VoIP gateway approach that let the legacy PBXs continue to handle call processing while line-provisioning is performed by specialized VoIP routers and servers.

Marketplace

Cisco has been the dominant player in the high-end enterprise VoIP market for some time. In fact, Cisco itself uses VoIP across its company, and with more than 10,000 IP phones deployed around the organization, this is still probably one of the largest and most successful VoIP implementations around. Cisco has developed a special architecture for VoIP solutions called Architecture for Voice, Video, and Integrated Data (AVVID) that consisting of three layers: switching and routing infrastructure for routing IP traffic, applications such as Cisco Call Manager running Microsoft Windows 2000 servers for implementing call control, and wired or wireless IP telephones. In the infrastructure area, for example, Cisco 2600, 3600, and AS5300 routers and Cisco Catalyst 6009 switches all support the H.323 standards and can function as H.323 gateways and gatekeepers for building highly scalable VoIP solutions. Cisco's AVVID architecture is straightforward in concept and can effectively scale to more than 100,000 users to meet the needs of the largest enterprise.

The approach taken by Avaya, which, together with Nortel, represents the two dominant players in the legacy PBX market in the United States, is adapted specifically to its own proprietary line of PBX equipment, and scales to 10,000 users for large VoIP deployments. The advantage here is that Avaya offers a clear upgrade path from using its legacy PBXs to move to an all-IP telephony solution. Nortel's Call Pilot solution also supports up to 10,000 users and is popular in Europe but just emerging in the U.S. market. Another large player is Alcatel, whose VoIP solution supports legacy PBX connections and whose call control applications run on UNIX platforms. Alcatel even offers an IP Telephony Starter Kit to enable small companies to quickly and painlessly roll out a VoIP solution. This kit includes an Alcatel OmniStack 6024 Ethernet switch, an OmniPXC 4400 IP PBX, and 10 IP Reflex telephones.

Some larger telecommunication carriers such as AT&T and WorldCom are now offering their own VoIP solutions using Cisco 2600 and 3600 routers deployed at the customer premises in a VoIP gateway approach. AT&T integrates its VoIP solution with Internet access and virtual private network (VPN) support to provide an all-in-one communications infrastructure solution for its customers.

Notes

Despite the great attention garnered by VoIP in the press, other technologies also can serve well for various needs in the enterprise, namely:

- **Voice over frame relay (VoFR):** Standards for this technology are more mature than for VoIP, and VoFR is a good option to consider for replacing tie lines between PBXs in branch offices. Instead of connecting branch offices in pairs using dedicated point-to-point T1 lines, frame relay assembler/ disassemblers (FRADs) are used to connect all the

offices using the carrier's frame relay cloud. VoFR then multiplexes voice traffic and compresses them into packets and routes them between each pair of offices using permanent virtual circuits (PVCs) preconfigured by the carrier to simulate point-to-point links.

- **Voice over High-level Data Link Control (VoHDLC):** This is another good solution for point-to-point connections, and, like VoFR, it supports multiplexing and compression of voice traffic. The downside here is that HDLC is a Cisco proprietary Layer 2 protocol, so implementing it means you have to go with only one vendor.

The main advantage VoIP has over both of these alternative technologies is scalability—both VoFR and VoHDLC require that voice traffic be encoded and decoded multiple times in transit, and this adds overhead that limits the scalability of these technologies. In contrast, VoIP can be used on IP networks of any size, including the largest of networks, the Internet. The downside of VoIP, of course, is that IP is a best effort packet delivery service with no intrinsic quality of service (QoS). As a result, the quality of voice communications can be poor when using VoIP, especially over a large network such as the Internet, and can result in unacceptable levels of latency, jitter, and dropouts. However, by employing special standards and protocols such as 802.1p, 802.1Q, Resource Reservation Protocol (RSVP), and Multiprotocol Label Switching (MPLS), QoS can be added to IP to the point where voice quality approaches that offered by VoFR, VoHDSL, or even the PSTN.

Another alternative that is used by only a few large companies is Voice over Asynchronous Transfer Mode (VoATM), which provides excellent voice quality since ATM technology has built-in support for QoS. The problem is that to implement VoATM you already need an underlying ATM network connecting branch offices, and only a limited number of large enterprises have implemented ATM across the WAN due to the high cost and complexity of this solution.

An emerging technology gaining a lot of attention is Voice over Digital Subscriber Line (VoDSL), which enables carriers to provision multichannel voice and data communications over Symmetric Digital Subscriber Line (SDSL). Since SDSL is relatively cheap compared to T1 lines, this is an attractive option for certain IP telephony solutions. A typical VoDSL solution involves placing an integrated access device (IAD) at the customer premises, which is connected to both telephone equipment and the computer network. Most VoDSL IADs currently support only 16 voice channels, so this solution is currently marketed mainly toward small and mid-sized businesses. One difficulty is that VoDSL works only with SDSL and does not support the more commonly available Asymmetric Digital Subscriber Line (ADSL) technology. This limits its availability in some areas, but this will still be a technology to watch in the next few years. Vendors of first-generation VoDSL equipment include Copper Mountain Networks, Jetstream Communications, and Tollbridge Technologies.

See Also: *802.1p, 802.1Q, Asynchronous Transfer Mode (ATM), Digital Subscriber Line (DSL), frame relay, Frame Relay Access Device (FRAD), H.323, High-level Data Link Control (HDLC), Internet Protocol (IP), IP PBX, IP telephony, jitter, latency, Megaco, Multiprotocol Label Switching (MPLS), permanent virtual circuit (PVC), Private Branch Exchange (PBX), Public Switched Telephone Network (PSTN), Resource Reservation Protocol (RSVP), session initiation protocol (SIP), Unified Messaging (UM)*

voice profile for Internet mail (VPIM)

An Internet Engineering Task Force (IETF) specification that defines a unified way of transmitting voice mail and fax messages over the Internet.

Overview

Voice profile for Internet mail (VPIM) uses e-mail systems that support Multipurpose Internet Mail Extensions (MIME) and Simple Mail Transfer Protocol Service Extensions (ESMTP) standards for Internet messaging. VPIM can also be deployed over corporate

V

intranets for integrated business messaging solutions. VPIM includes a proposed directory service that enables lookup of routable addresses and includes a mapping specification to support interoperability with other voice messaging systems.

VPIM defines the mechanisms by which voice mail and fax messages can be exchanged between Simple Mail Transfer Protocol (SMTP) mail servers on a Transmission Control Protocol/Internet Protocol (TCP/IP) internetwork. However, VPIM leaves open the way in which specific mail clients interface with these SMTP servers to send and receive voice and fax messages, which will initially be accomplished by implementing VPIM helper applications. VPIM is implemented as a MIME profile, which allows voice and fax information to be encoded using any SMTP mail server that supports MIME. You can implement VPIM by running additional VPIM software on existing SMTP mail servers or by installing VPIM-SMTP gateways on the TCP/IP internetwork. VPIM gateways support messaging between telephones, cell phones, fax machines, pagers, and computers. VPIM will be able to use Lightweight Directory Access Protocol (LDAP) or X.500-based directories for white pages lookup to address messages to users.

Notes

VPIM is supported by the popular UNIX mail forwarder software called Sendmail; other vendors are also implementing VPIM. The current standard, VPIM v2, can be found in RFC 2421, and VPIM v3 is under development.

For More information

Find our more about VPIM at *www.ema.org/vpimdir.*

See Also: *ESMTP, Internet Engineering Task Force (IETF), Lightweight Directory Access Protocol (LDAP), Multipurpose Internet Mail Extensions (MIME), Simple Mail Transfer Protocol (SMTP), X.500*

VoIP

Stands for Voice over IP, an umbrella term for a set of technologies that allow voice traffic to be carried over Internet Protocol (IP) networks such as the Internet.

See: *Voice over IP (VoIP)*

VoIP gateway

A device used in Voice over IP (VoIP) systems.

Overview

A VoIP gateway is a device that allows telephone calls to be transmitted over Internet Protocol (IP) backbone networks by converting voice signals into IP packets and transmitting them over the network. The reverse process then takes place at the other end of the call.

Most VoIP gateways are chassis-based units that have either digital or analog built-in Private Branch Exchange (PBX) interfaces. A device called a gatekeeper keeps track of IP address to phone number mappings for routing calls between different gateways. Built-in local area network (LAN) or wide area network (WAN) interfaces, or both, are included for connecting the gateway to the IP backbone. Some gateways also have built-in routing capabilities. The LAN interface is usually Ethernet, but some gateways support Token Ring. The WAN interface is typically T1 or E1, but smaller gateways designed for Small Office/Home Office (SOHO) environments support Integrated Services Digital Network (ISDN) interfaces. The number of voice interfaces per chassis typically ranges from 72 to 960, depending on the vendor. Voice interfaces are typically the digital signal cross-connect level (DSX-1) type, but some gateways also support the foreign exchange station (FXS) type interfaces for direct attachment of analog telephones.

Notes

When shopping for a VoIP gateway, consider the following points:

- Audio quality should be your primary consideration. The audio quality with low traffic congestion should be close to that of a digital PBX. With heavy traffic congestion, latency and jitter should remain low enough that voice quality is acceptable to average users. A packet loss of 15 percent or more results in transmission with borderline intelligibility; delays of over 700 milliseconds are unacceptable to most users.

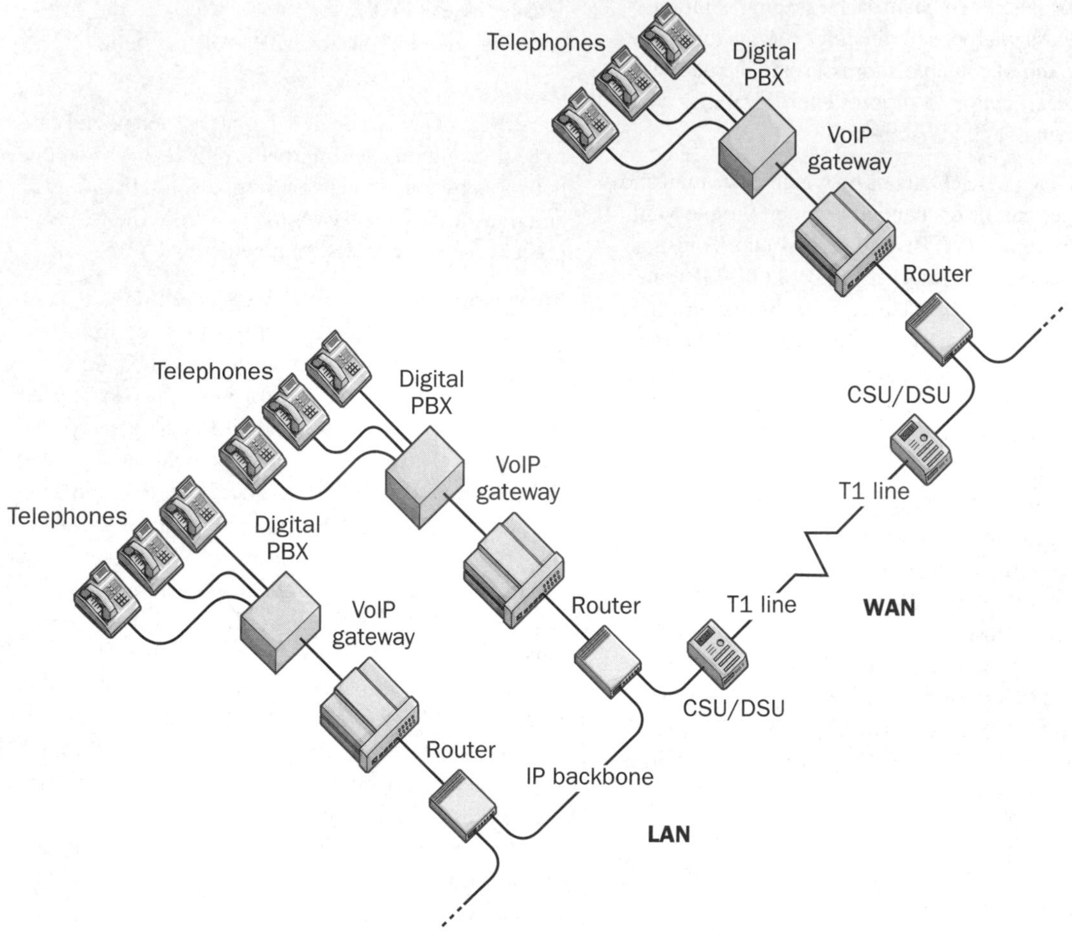

VoIP gateway. *Using a VoIP gateway to implement Voice over IP.*

- Find out what extra features are supported by the gateway, such as dialed number identification service (DNIS) for call routing, automatic number identification (ANI) and caller ID for identifying the incoming caller, and interactive voice response (IVR) for creating telephone menus.
- VoIP gateway technologies are still evolving, so equipment from different vendors might not interoperate, even if the vendors claim to support the H.323 standards of the International Telecommunication Union (ITU). You should therefore buy VoIP from a single vendor, especially if you have an enterprise implementation with many gateways.
- If you are concerned about eavesdropping on voice conversations on IP networks such as the Internet, be sure that your gateways support the H.245 encryption standard. The alternative practice of using a virtual private network (VPN) gateway to encrypt VoIP traffic usually results in additional incompatibility problems. Also be aware that it is difficult to configure a VoIP gateway to operate across a firewall that hides network IP addresses using network address translation (NAT), especially if the traffic is encrypted.

See Also: *Integrated Services Digital Network (ISDN), Internet Protocol (IP), Private Branch Exchange (PBX), Voice over IP (VoIP)*

V

volume

A bounded amount of disk storage.

Overview

In MS-DOS and early Microsoft Windows platforms, a volume is a portion of a hard disk that can be formatted with a file system and can have a unique drive letter assigned to it. In Windows 2000, Windows XP, and Windows .NET Server, a volume is a logical storage entity composed of portions of one or more physical disks. Volumes can be formatted using the NTFS file system (NTFS) or file allocation table (FAT) and can be assigned a drive letter.

Windows 2000, Windows XP, and Windows .NET Server support two different types of disk storage:

- **Basic storage:** Supported for backwards compatibility with Windows NT version 4 or earlier and can include primary partitions, extended partitions, logical drives, volume sets, mirror sets, stripe sets, or stripe sets with parity
- **Dynamic storage:** Volumes created using the Computer Management snap-in for the Microsoft Management Console (MMC) that can include simple volumes, spanned volumes, striped volumes, mirrored volumes, or RAID 5 volumes

See Also: *basic volume, dynamic volume, storage*

volume set

A single volume created using discontiguous free areas on hard disks.

Overview

Volume sets can be created in Microsoft Windows NT by combining between 2 and 32 free areas on your disk drives. You can extend a volume set formatted with the NTFS file system (NTFS) without having to reformat the entire volume. In Windows 2000, Windows XP, and Windows .NET Server, volume sets are instead called spanned volumes and are created using the Computer Management snap-in for the Microsoft Management Console (MMC).

Notes

Note that in Windows NT the system and boot partitions cannot be on volume sets.

See Also: *stripe set, volume*

VPIM

Stands for voice profile for Internet mail, an Internet Engineering Task Force (IETF) specification that defines a unified way of transmitting voice mail and fax messages over the Internet.

See: *voice profile for Internet mail (VPIM)*

VPN

Stands for virtual private network, a technology for securely connecting a computer or network to a remote network over an intermediate network such as the Internet.

See: *virtual private network (VPN)*

V-series

A series of communication standards developed by the International Telecommunication Union (ITU).

Overview

V-series protocols define methodologies for exchanging data over digital telephone networks. Standards below V.100 define:

- Signaling methods used by serial communication interfaces used in telephony.
- Techniques such as flow control and error control used in communication between data terminal equipment (DTE) such as computers and data communications equipment (DCE) such as modems and multiplexers.

Standards V.100 and higher deal with issues relating to internetworking the telephone system with other types of networks such as packet-switching networks such as X.25.

The following table describes some of the more popular V-series standards relating to modems and other serial interface standards.

Popular Serial Transmission Standards

V Standard	*Description*
V.22	Early standard for full-duplex serial transmission over one pair of wires at 1200 bits per second (bps).
V.22bis	Same as V.22 but supports 2400 bps.
V.24	The ITU equivalent of the RS-232 serial interface.
V.32	Industry standard for 9600-bps serial transmission.
V.32bis	Same as V.32 but supports 14.4 kilobits per second (Kbps).
V.32ter	Same as V.32 but supports 19.2 Kbps.
V.33	Protocol for full-duplex synchronous serial communication over leased lines with two pairs of wires; supports speeds of up to 14.4 Kbps and is used primarily in IBM mainframe environments.
V.34	Supports 28.8-Kbps serial transmission over dial-up (one wire pair) or leased (one or two wire pairs) lines.
V.34bis	Same as V.34 but supports 33.6 Kbps.
V.35	Protocol for synchronous serial communication at speeds of up to 48 Kbps; typically used for DTE/DCE communication between Channel Service Unit/Data Service Units (CSU/DSUs) and bridges/routers. V.35 has technically been replaced by V.10/11 but is still widely implemented in equipment such as routers, switches, and other wide area network (WAN) access devices.
V.42	Same as V.32 but enhances error correction mechanisms using LAPM (link access procedures for modems) and MNP (Microcom Networking Protocol).
V.42bis	Adds 4-to-1 data compression to V.42 and V.90.
V.44	Adds 6-to-1 data compression to V.42, V.90, and V.92.
V.90	High-speed modem standard that supports asymmetric communication with a maximum downstream data rate of 56 Kbps and an upstream rate of 33.6 Kbps.
V.92	High-speed modem standard that supports asymmetric communication with a maximum downstream data rate of 56 Kbps and an upstream rate of 48 Kbps.

See Also: *Channel Service Unit/Data Service Unit (CSU/DSU), International Telecommunication Union (ITU), modem, RS-232, serial transmission, V.35, V.90, V.92*

W3C

Stands for World Wide Web Consortium, a vendor-neutral organization created in 1994 that develops common, interoperable standards and protocols for the World Wide Web (WWW).

See: *World Wide Web Consortium (W3C)*

wall plate

Also called a faceplate, a cabling fixture attached to a wall in a work area for connecting computers to the network.

Overview

Wall plates are generally used in work areas to enable desktop computers to be connected to the network. The wall plates connect to the building's structured wiring system, and the computers connect to the wall plate by a short unshielded twisted-pair (UTP) cable called a drop cable.

Wall plates come in mono-port, dual-port, and quad-port configurations, generally with RJ-45 jacks, which resemble household RJ-11 telephone wall jacks but are larger and have more wires. These RJ-45 jacks are typically used when networks are running Ethernet or Fast Ethernet. Other less common types of jacks include SC jacks for networks that use fiber-optic cabling, and BNC jacks for legacy 10Base2 networks.

The back end of the jacks in a wall plate typically connect to a horizontal cable that runs inside the wall or through a false ceiling or floor. This horizontal table terminates at a patch panel in the wiring closet on that floor, and vertical cabling running through elevator shafts or vertical rises connects wiring on different floors to switches in the main equipment room in the basement.

Implementation

Wall plates are an important feature of a permanent networking installation because they enable stations to be easily disconnected and reconnected to the network and protect network cables from damage caused by physical handling. The most common type are flush wall plates, which are flat like AC outlets, but angled wall plates are often a better choice because they offer better protection from excessive cable bending and protect drop cables from damage by contact with heavy or sharp-edged furniture.

Be sure to label or number wall plates so that you can easily identify the port on the patch panel to which they connect. If you cannot run cabling inside walls and must instead tack cabling directly onto the interior wall surface, use surface-mount boxes instead of wall plates. These are box-shaped adapters that screw onto the wall and have side or face jacks for connecting cables.

Flush

Angled

Wall plate. *Examples of flush and angled wall plates.*

Notes

You can also get special wall plates for serial interfaces that use DB connectors such as DB9 or DB25. These wall plates are used in mainframe computing environments in which dumb terminals are connected to mainframe hosts by using RS-232 serial lines.

See Also: *cabling, drop cable, premise cabling, RJ connectors, structured wiring, wiring closet*

WAN

Stands for wide area network, a geographically distributed network composed of multiple local area networks (LANs) joined into a single large network using services provided by telecommunication carriers.

See: wide area network (WAN)

WAN services

Services offered by telecommunication carriers to enable companies to build wide area networks (WANs).

Overview

WAN services are generally provided to enterprises by telcos, usually either by Regional Bell Operating Companies (RBOCs) or inter-exchange carriers (IXCs). The range of different types of WAN services that telcos can offer includes

- **Dedicated or leased lines:** These services establish a permanent point-to-point connection between two locations. They are always "on" and ready to carry network traffic. Leased lines are typically expensive because telco switches must be dedicated to the customer even when they are not being used. Examples of leased line services include T-carrier services such as T1, fractional T1, and T3. Leased lines are most popular with large enterprises that need reliable, high-bandwidth WAN links between branch offices.
- **Circuit-switched services:** These services establish a temporary path through the carrier's network, usually only lasting as long as the call. When the session is terminated, the carrier's switches are then freed up for other customers to use. Examples of circuit-switched services include Integrated Services Digital Network (ISDN) and dial-up modem connections using the Public Switched Telephone Network (PSTN). One problem with using circuit-switched services is that the quality of transmission depends on the switches and trunk lines used and therefore varies from call to call. For this reason, circuit-switched services are typically used for backup in case a leased line goes down. Because circuit-switched services also cost much less than leased lines, they are frequently used in low-traffic WAN networking environments.
- **Packet-switched services:** These services use virtual circuits instead of end-to-end physical connections. Data is transmitted in packets across a public data network (PDN) owned by the carrier (which is really a misnomer, as the network is owned privately). Examples of packet-switching services include frame relay and X.25.
- **Cell-switched services:** This is similar to packet-switching but employs small fixed-size cells instead of variable-size packets. Asynchronous Transfer Mode (ATM) is a popular cell-switching technology used in high-end enterprise WAN services. Connectivity at the customer premises is usually provided using an integrated access device (IAD) or router.

The WAN environment has been changing radically in recent years. Although enterprises have traditionally relied on T1 or frame relay for most branch-office connectivity solutions, several new solutions have emerged that can offer considerable cost savings and ease of use over standard WAN solutions. These new technologies include

- **Digital Subscriber Line (DSL):** A family of different technologies for transmitting data over existing copper local loop wiring at T1 speeds or higher. DSL circumvents the cost of deploying expensive conditioned T1 lines and is a much cheaper solution than T1, but it has not yet achieved the same degree of reliability. Nevertheless, many enterprises are eying this new technology carefully in consideration of future WAN deployments.
- **Virtual private network (VPN):** Using the public Internet for securely carrying private Internet Protocol (IP) traffic between different locations. Any kind of Internet connection can be used for a VPN, including dial-up, DSL, and T1. The advantage here is that data can be carried long distances without any added cost since a public network carries the traffic instead of a carrier's private network.

- **IP over ATM over SONET:** This technology transports Internet Protocol (IP) traffic using ATM as the Layer 2 (data link layer) protocol and Synchronous Optical Network (SONET) as the underlying Layer 1 (physical layer) transport. The main problem with this solution is the "cell tax," the intrinsic overhead involved in translating IP packets into ATM cells, which can be as high as 13 percent of the throughput—or even higher.
- **Packet over SONET:** Also known as IP over SONET or IP over PPP over SONET, this technology replaces Layer-2 ATM with Point-to-Point Protocol (PPP) encapsulation.
- **Metropolitan Ethernet:** Here carriers run Gigabit Ethernet (GbE) connections right to the customer premises using fiber-optic cabling, which are then typically connected to a metropolitan area network (MAN) dual SONET ring.
- **Fixed wireless:** Buildings too far from a telco central office (CO) to deploy fiber for high-speed WAN links can find an alternative in fixed wireless networking technologies such as Local Multipoint Distribution System (LMDS), Multichannel Multipoint Distribution System (MMDS), microwave systems, or even point-to-point infrared laser transmission. Satellite networking is another emerging option, but its use is limited due to the high latencies involved.

See Also: *Asynchronous Transfer Mode (ATM), circuit-switched services, Digital Subscriber Line (DSL), frame relay, Gigabit Ethernet (GbE), Integrated Access Device (IAD), Integrated Services Digital Network (ISDN), inter-exchange carrier (IXC), Internet Protocol (IP), leased line, Local Multipoint Distribution Service (LMDS), metropolitan Ethernet, Multipoint Multichannel Distribution Service (MMDS), packet-switching services, Point-to-Point Protocol (PPP), Public Switched Telephone Network (PSTN), Regional Bell Operating Company (RBOC), Synchronous Optical Network (SONET), T-carrier, telco, virtual private network (VPN), wide area network (WAN), X.25*

WAP

Stands for Wireless Application Protocol, a technology for implementing mobile devices with the Web.

See: *Wireless Application Protocol (WAP)*

wavelength division multiplexing (WDM)

Transmitting multiple bitstreams down a single strand of fiber-optic cabling using different colors (wavelengths) for each stream.

Overview

Wavelength division multiplexing (WDM) was developed in the late 1980s as a way of increasing the carrying capacity of fiber-optic cabling. Inter-exchange carriers (IXCs) such as AT&T, Sprint Corporation, and Worldcom began implementing WDM in the mid-1990s when it became apparent that the rapid growth of the Internet would soon stress the carrying capacity of long-haul trunk lines. Telcos now turn to WDM as a standard solution when traffic congestion grows on backbone carrier networks.

WDM allows two or more separate bitstreams to be beamed down a strand of fiber using lasers of different frequencies, usually 10 nanometers or more apart in frequency. Each data stream itself can carry multiple data sessions by dividing the stream into different time slots using time-division multiplexing (TDM). WDM thus employs two forms of multiplexing: frequency-division multiplexing (FDM) to create different light paths and TDM to enable each light path to carry multiple data streams.

WDM supports common physical layer technologies used by telcos, including Synchronous Optical Network (SONET) and Asynchronous Transfer Mode (ATM). Although early WDM systems only supported 2 light channels, versions have been developed that support 4, 8, 16, and even 32 or more separate channels. WDM can operate over distances up to about 30 miles (50 kilometers), and this can be extended to hundreds of miles using optical repeaters.

Notes

A newer version of this technology called dense wavelength division multiplexing (DWDM) is essentially WDM on steroids and is basically WDM where the wavelength separation between adjacent channels is 2 nanometers or less, potentially resulting in hundreds of channels being carried over a single strand of fiber and throughput in excess of 1 terabit per second.

See Also: *Asynchronous Transfer Mode (ATM), dense wavelength division multiplexing (DWDM), fiber-optic cabling, frequency-division multiplexing (FDM), inter-exchange carrier (IXC), Synchronous Optical Network (SONET), time-division multiplexing (TDM)*

WBEM

Stands for Web-Based Enterprise Management, a set of technologies for developing standards-based network management platforms.

See: *Web-Based Enterprise Management (WBEM)*

W-CDMA

Stands for Wideband Code Division Multiple Access and known as Universal Mobile Telecommunications System (UMTS) in Europe, a worldwide standard for a third-generation (3G) cellular communications system.

See: *Wideband Code Division Multiple Access (W-CDMA)*

WDM

Stands for wavelength division multiplexing, transmitting multiple data streams down a single strand of fiber-optic cabling using different colors (wavelengths) for each stream.

See: *wavelength division multiplexing (WDM)*

Web

Short for World Wide Web, the popular Internet service that is rapidly changing the way we live and work.

See: *World Wide Web (WWW)*

Web application

A collection of elements on a Web site that performs a task programmatically.

Overview

Web applications are applications that are designed to run on Web servers and are accessed through Web browsers. Web applications may be implemented as client/server, multi-tier, or peer-to-peer applications. A common example of a Web application is the ordering mechanism or "shopping cart" on an e-commerce site such as Amazon.com.

Web applications can be developed by using a variety of technologies, including the following:

- Active Server Pages (ASP)
- ActiveX components or Java applets
- Internet Server API (ISAPI)
- Perl scripting using Common Gateway Interface (CGI)

See Also: *Active Server Pages (ASP), ActiveX, Common Gateway Interface (CGI), Internet Server API (ISAPI), Java, Web page*

Web-Based Enterprise Management (WBEM)

A set of technologies for developing standards-based network management platforms.

Overview

Web-Based Enterprise Management (WBEM) was developed by the Distributed Management Task Force (DMTF), which originated in 1996 as a joint initiative of companies headed by Microsoft Corporation, Intel Corporation, Cisco Systems, Compaq Computer Corporation, and BMC Software. WBEM was designed to help bring order to the chaos of the enterprise network management marketplace with its proprietary solutions and platforms. WBEM provides a framework of application programming interfaces (APIs), an object model, and a syntax for developing network management solutions that are interoperable between vendors.

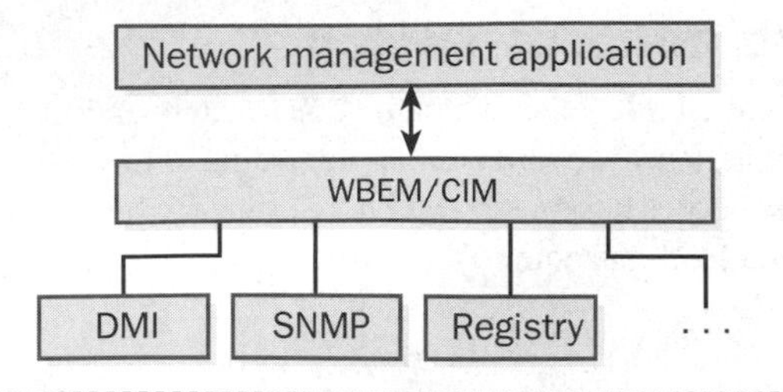

Web-Based Enterprise Management. *The architecture of the WBEM framework.*

WBEM is designed to work in heterogeneous enterprise networking environments to collect diagnostic and management data relating to hardware from multiple vendors, different operating systems, different network protocols, and distributed applications. WBEM enables information such as the amount of RAM in a computer, the capacity of a hard disk, the type of process, and the version of the operating system or firmware to be extracted from computers, routers, switches, and other network devices. This information can be used to detect potential problems before they occur, for remote management purposes, and for planning and other decision-making purposes.

WBEM simplifies management by providing a common model and data source that can be extended to function with existing protocols, networking components, and applications. An important part of the WBEM framework for WBEM is the Common Information Model (CIM), a set of schemas for cross-platform network management also developed by the DMTF. Once network management information is collected and stored in the CIM repository, it can be shared across an enterprise and displayed using WBEM management systems. Using CIM, a WBEM management application can access network information using Simple Network Management Protocol (SNMP), Desktop Management Interface (DMI), and other sources such as the Windows registry.

Microsoft has built the WBEM architecture into its Windows 2000, Windows XP, and Windows .NET Server platforms in the form of Windows Management Instrumentation (WMI), Microsoft's implementation of WBEM for 32-bit Microsoft Windows platforms.

For More Information

Find out more about WBEM at *www.dmtf.org/wbem.*

See Also: *Common Information Model (CIM), Desktop Management Interface (DMI), Distributed Management Task Force (DMTF), Simple Network Management Protocol (SNMP), Windows Management Instrumentation (WMI)*

Web browser

A client-side Hypertext Transfer Protocol (HTTP) application.

Overview

Web browsers enable users to access content published on Web servers that reside on the Internet or corporate intranets. Web browsers request and receive content hosted on Web servers using HTTP, the standard application layer protocol for the World Wide Web (WWW). Such content can be static, meaning it consists of text files formatted using Hypertext Markup Language (HTML), or the content can be dynamic, meaning it is generated on demand using server-side or client-side scripting technologies such as Microsoft Active Server Pages (ASP) and JavaScript.

Web browsers typically include features that make "browsing" (locating and accessing resources on) the Web simple, such as

- Toolbar buttons for navigating forward and backward through the tree of previously displayed pages, for stopping the download process, and for manually refreshing a page that loaded incompletely.
- Lists of favorites or bookmarks that store Uniform Resource Locators (URLs) of frequently accessed sites as well as tools for organizing and accessing those URLs.
- Options for specifying a default home page from which to begin browsing, a default search engine for searching the Web, and other default browsing options.

- Security options for handling such concerns as whether to allow scripts, ActiveX components, or Java applets to run on the browser.
- Facilities for displaying a page's underlying source code or HTML and even for editing and publishing Web content.
- Integration with other Internet software such as mail, news, or chat applications. Some Web browsers are packaged as stand-alone applications, while others are part of an overall suite of Internet tools that are integrated at various levels.

History

The first graphical Web browser was developed in 1993 by a group of students headed by Marc Andreessen at the National Center for Supercomputing Applications (NCSA). This browser was known as Mosaic and was distributed free. In 1994, Andreessen left NCSA to help found Netscape Communications, which developed the Netscape Navigator browser. The popularity of this browser helped foster the explosive growth of the Internet in the mid-1990s.

Microsoft quickly entered the arena with its Internet Explorer browser, which has since become the most widely used browser in the marketplace. Starting with Microsoft Windows 95, Microsoft began integrating Internet Explorer into its Windows operating systems, with the result that users running Windows can access Internet resources as easily as files on their own hard drives.

Web browsers have now become a standard interface for a wide range of platforms and services, including messaging, network management, mainframe access, and many other enterprise applications. The Web browser can be thought of a kind of "universal client" that is simple to learn and use, yet powerful enough to handle the most complex programming environments.

See Also: *Active Server Pages (ASP), ActiveX, Hypertext Markup Language (HTML), Hypertext Transfer Protocol (HTTP), Internet Explorer, Java, JavaScript, Web server, World Wide Web (WWW)*

Web content switch

Also called a Layer 7 switch or URL switch, an Ethernet switch that forwards frames according to Layer 4 or higher header information and used primarily for directing and load-balancing Web traffic.

See: *Layer 7 switch*

Web hosting

Hosting of Web content by service providers.

Overview

Companies offering Web hosting services range from local Internet service providers (ISPs) who provide businesses with a few dozen megabytes of server space and access to Perl scripting engines to global companies with server farms that offer dedicated servers, e-mail accounts, domain name holding, Microsoft FrontPage support, open database connectivity (ODBC) support, domain name hosting and holding services, and other services. Some industry analysts estimate that about two-thirds of all corporate Web sites are hosted by Web hosting service providers.

Web hosting started to become big business around 1998 and service providers offering Web hosting services reached their heyday in early 2000. Since then Web hosting providers have been rapidly supplanted by "content hosting" providers that offer an even greater range of services, which can include back-end system integration, custom programming, security management, and site mirroring. However, the distinction between the terms *Web hosting* and *content hosting* is often blurred in this rapidly evolving market.

Web hosting providers generally offer three different kinds of hosting services:

- **Shared hosting:** Your site is running on a Web server owned by the hosting provider, but the server hosts other people's sites as well.
- **Dedicated hosting:** Your site is running on a Web server owned by the hosting provider and your company has exclusive use of that server.

- **Colocated hosting:** You configure your Web server and then bring it in to the hosting provider's data center and they connect it to their high-speed Internet backbone.

When shopping for a Web hosting or content hosting service provider, it is a good idea to find out what degree of availability they guarantee. Many providers offer 99.99 percent availability with no downtime and give clients a refund if any downtime occurs, even if it is only a few minutes. They ensure such levels of availability by hosting sites on multiple redundant servers and scheduling maintenance so that one server is always online. It is also a good idea to make sure that the provider offers the full range of services that you require (or might soon require), such as database access and site mirroring. Find out the size of the pipe that connects the provider with the Internet backbone and at which point of presence (POP) the provider is connected to the Internet. For business hosting purposes, a minimum dual OC3 connection with guaranteed 155-megabits per second (Mbps) throughput is recommended. Decide whether you want dedicated or shared hosting—that is, whether you are willing to share a server and its network bandwidth with other companies or whether you require the stability, reliability, and throughput of your own dedicated Web server.

See Also: *Internet service provider (ISP), Web server*

Web page

A file of text information formatted using Hypertext Markup Language (HTML).

Overview

Web pages are sent by Web servers in response to requests from Web browsers and can contain formatted text, images, scripts, and various forms of active content. Web pages are generally of two types:

- **Static:** Stored as files on the server in the same form that they are delivered to the client. These files usually have the extension .htm or .html.
- **Dynamic:** Pages that include scripts, ActiveX components, Java applets, Dynamic HTML (DHTML), and other forms of active content to make static pages more interesting or useful. Dynamic pages often do not actually exist on the server until the client requests them, whereupon they are generated by the server using Active Server Pages (ASP) or some other server-side scripting technology.

See Also: *Active Server Pages (ASP), ActiveX, Dynamic HTML (DHTML), Hypertext Markup Language (HTML), Internet, Java, scripting, Web browser, Web server*

Web server

A server-side Hypertext Transfer Protocol (HTTP) application.

Overview

Web servers enable the publishing content on the Internet or on corporate intranets. Web servers host Web pages and other content that can be delivered using HTTP to Web browsers and other clients.

The first Web servers were originally developed for the UNIX platform and were used for publishing static Web content consisting of text files formatted using Hypertext Markup Language (HTML). To enhance static Web pages, dynamic features such as forms were later added using scripts written in interpretive languages such as Perl that ran within the UNIX Common Gateway Interface (CGI) execution environment. Other technologies developed later for delivering dynamic Web content include Java applets, ActiveX controls, Microsoft Active Server Pages (ASP) server-side scripting, and many others.

Marketplace

Some of the big players in the Web server arena include

- **Microsoft Internet Information Server (IIS):** A component of the Windows 2000 and Windows .NET Server platforms, IIS is a popular development platform for Internet applications that supports HTTP, File Transfer Protocol (FTP), Simple Mail Transfer Protocol (SMTP), Network News Transfer Protocol (NNTP), Secure Sockets Layer (SSL), Secure/Multipurpose Internet Mail

Extensions (S/MIME), and other Internet standard protocols. IIS also supports Microsoft FrontPage, a popular Web site development tool.

- **iPlanet Web Server:** Formerly Netscape Enterprise Server, iPlanet is a robust Web platform that runs on a variety of platforms and is widely used in enterprise environments.
- **Apache:** An open source application developed originally for the UNIX platform, Apache is popular with the Internet service provider (ISP) community that originated within the academic environment where the Internet originated.
- **Lotus Domino:** The Web server component of IBM's Lotus Notes messaging and collaboration platform.

Industry surveys have indicated that Apache is the predominant player when it comes to hosting public Internet sites, but an industry survey in 2001 indicated that IIS was the most popular Web server platform in Fortune 1000 companies, with 48 percent of respondents using IIS, 24 percent using iPlanet, 18 percent using Apache, and the rest using Domino or other platforms. The iPlanet platform is also used by 7 of the top 10 Fortune 1000 companies.

See Also: *Active Server Pages (ASP), ActiveX, Apache, Common Gateway Interface (CGI), Hypertext Transfer Protocol (HTTP), Internet, Internet Information Services (IIS), Java, Web browser, World Wide Web (WWW)*

Web-to-host

Providing access to legacy mainframe and midframe host systems to client systems using a standard Web browser interface.

Overview

Web-to-host technologies enable large companies to leverage their existing investment in IBM S/390 mainframe and AS/400 midframe host systems to gain advantage in the e-business and e-commerce arena. Host systems are widely used in enterprises for database hosting and transactional processing, and providing easy access to resources on host systems can give companies a competitive edge in the Internet economy.

In the client/server computing era, special host client software displaced legacy "dumb terminals" by providing 3270 and 5250 terminal emulation on standard PCs. Web-to-host takes this process a step further by providing ActiveX or Java applets that allow terminal emulation sessions to run within a standard Web browser interface, making it as easy to access host resources as it is to browse the Web.

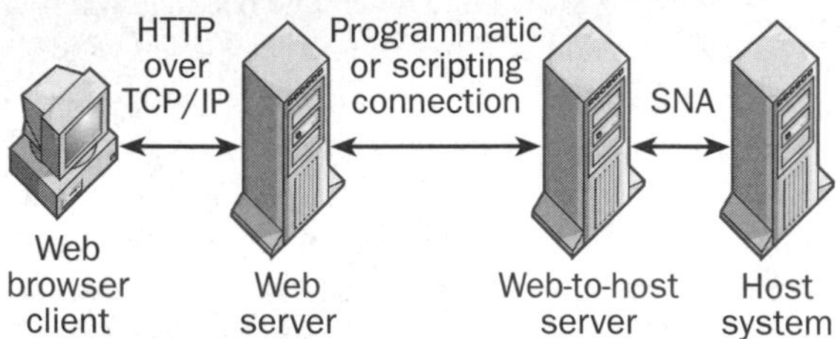

Web-to-host. *Example of how Web-to-host integration can be implemented.*

Implementation

Web-to-host platforms work in two basic ways:

- **Direct connection:** These platforms provide a direct connection between resources on the host and client Web browsers. Session security is usually provided by the host itself. This security is needed as traditional 3270 and 5250 terminal emulation clients communicate with hosts in clear-text data streams, and this is unacceptable when using the public Internet as the transmission medium.
- **Web server:** Here a Web server acts as a gateway between the host and browser client. The gateway typically provides security by encrypting the data stream, usually using Secure Sockets Layer (SSL) encryption.

In the second approach, the Web-to-host product, such as Microsoft Host Integration Server, communicates with the host system using Systems Network Architecture (SNA) and with the Web server using a programmatic technology such as Microsoft Corporation's Internet Server API (ISAPI) or various scripting technologies. The Web server then communicates with the browser client using standard Hypertext Transfer Protocol (HTTP), which is typically augmented with ActiveX controls or Java applets for greater display functionality.

Marketplace

Besides Microsoft's own Host Integration Server platform, a number of popular Web-to-host integration products are available in the marketplace. A popular solution is WebSphere Host OnDemand from IBM, which provides advanced display and printer emulation, integrated security, and enhanced database support. Some other popular products include WEB-ifier by Anota, e-Vantage Host Access Server by Attachmate Corporation, HostExplorer by Hummingbird International, HostFront by Farabi Technology Corporation, Novation by GT Software, WebConnect by OpenConnect Systems, Rumba by NetManage, WinSurf Mainframe Access by ICOM Infomatics, and Reflection by WRQ.

Notes

When shopping for a Web-to-host solution, look for the following features:

- Enhanced input and display features such as resizable terminal windows, custom screen colors, keyboard mapping, and macros
- 3270 and 5250 printer emulation to enable jobs run on hosts to print to local printers instead of remote host-connected ones
- Centralized deployment and management of host-client connections
- SSL encryption for data stream security

See Also: *3270, 5250, ActiveX, AS/400, Host Integration Server, Hypertext Transfer Protocol (HTTP), Internet Server API (ISAPI), Java, mainframe, scripting, Secure Sockets Layer (SSL), Systems Network Architecture (SNA), terminal emulator, Web browser, Web server*

well-known port numbers

Transmission Control Protocol (TCP) or User Datagram Protocol (UDP) port numbers that have been assigned to specific Transmission Control Protocol/Internet Protocol (TCP/IP) applications or services by the Internet Assigned Numbers Authority (IANA).

Overview

Well-known port numbers are assigned from the range 0 through 1023 from a total possible range of port numbers 0 through 65535. The following table lists many of the well-known port numbers.

Well-Known Port Numbers

Port Number	*Keyword*	*Description*
0/tcp, udp		Reserved
1/tcp, udp	tcpmux	TCP Port Service Multiplexer
2/tcp, udp	compressnet	Management Utility
3/tcp, udp	compressnet	Compression Process
4/tcp, udp		Unassigned
5/tcp, udp	rje	Remote Job Entry
6/tcp, udp		Unassigned
7/tcp, udp	echo	Echo
8/tcp, udp		Unassigned
9/tcp, udp	discard	Discard; alias = sink null
10/tcp, udp		Unassigned
11/tcp, udp	systat	Active Users; alias = users
12/tcp, udp		Unassigned
13/tcp, udp	daytime	Daytime
14/tcp, udp		Unassigned
15/tcp, udp		Unassigned (was netstat)
16/tcp, udp		Unassigned
17/tcp, udp	qotd	Quote of the Day; alias = quote
18/tcp, udp	msp	Message Send Protocol
19/tcp, udp	chargen	Character Generator; alias = ttytst source
20/tcp, udp	ftp-data	File Transfer (default data)
21/tcp, udp	ftp	File Transfer (control), connection dialog
22/tcp, udp		Unassigned
23/tcp, udp	telnet	Telnet
24/tcp, udp		Any private mail system
25/tcp, udp	smtp	Simple Mail Transfer; alias = mail
26/tcp, udp		Unassigned
27/tcp, udp	nsw-fe	NSW User System FE
28/tcp, udp		Unassigned
29/tcp, udp	msg-icp	MSG ICP
30/tcp, udp		Unassigned
31/tcp, udp	msg-auth	MSG Authentication
32/tcp, udp		Unassigned

(continued)

Well-Known Port Numbers *continued*

Port Number	*Keyword*	*Description*
33/tcp, udp	dsp	Display Support Protocol
34/tcp, udp		Unassigned
35/tcp, udp		Any private printer server
36/tcp, udp		Unassigned
37/tcp, udp	time	Time; alias = timeserver
38/tcp, udp		Unassigned
39/tcp, udp	rlp	Resource Location Protocol; alias = resource
40/tcp, udp		Unassigned
41/tcp, udp	graphics	Graphics
42/tcp, udp	nameserver	Host Name Server; alias = nameserver
43/tcp, udp	nicname	Who Is; alias = nicname
44/tcp, udp	mpm-flags	MPM FLAGS Protocol
45/tcp, udp	mpm	Message Processing Module
46/tcp, udp	mpm-snd	MPM (default send)
47/tcp, udp	ni-ftp	NI FTP
48/tcp, udp		Unassigned
49/tcp, udp	login	Login Host Protocol
50/tcp, udp	re-mail-ck	Remote Mail Checking Protocol
51/tcp, udp	la-maint	IMP Logical Address Maintenance
52/tcp, udp	xns-time	XNS Time Protocol
53/tcp, udp	domain	Domain Name Server
54/tcp, udp	xns-ch	XNS Clearinghouse
55/tcp, udp	isi-gl	ISI Graphics Language
56/tcp, udp	xns-auth	XNS Authentication
57/tcp, udp		Any private terminal access
58/tcp, udp	xns-mail	XNS Mail
59/tcp, udp		Any private file service
60/tcp, udp		Unassigned
61/tcp, udp	ni-mail	NI MAIL
62/tcp, udp	acas	ACA Services
63/tcp, udp	via-ftp	VIA Systems – FTP
64/tcp, udp	covia	Communications Integrator (CI)
65/tcp, udp	tacacs-ds	TACACS-Database Service
66/tcp, udp	sql*net	Oracle SQL*NET
67/tcp, udp	bootpc	DHCP/BOOTP Protocol Server
68/tcp, udp	bootpc	DHCP/BOOTP Protocol Server

(continued)

Well-Known Port Numbers *continued*

Port Number	*Keyword*	*Description*
69/tcp, udp	tftp	Trivial File Transfer
70/tcp, udp	gopher	Gopher
71/tcp, udp	netrjs-1	Remote Job Service
72/tcp, udp	netrjs-2	Remote Job Service
73/tcp, udp	netrjs-3	Remote Job Service
74/tcp, udp	netrjs-4	Remote Job Service
75/udp		Any private dial-out service
76/tcp, udp		Unassigned
77/tcp, udp		Any private RJE service
78/tcp, udp	vettcp	Vettcp
79/tcp, udp	finger	Finger
80/tcp, udp	www	World Wide Web HTTP
81/tcp, udp	hosts2-ns	HOSTS2 Name Server
82/tcp, udp	xfer	XFER Utility
83/tcp, udp	mit-ml-dev	MIT ML Device
84/tcp, udp	ctf	Common Trace Facility
85/tcp, udp	mit-ml-dev	MIT ML Device
86/tcp, udp	mfcobol	Micro Focus Cobol
87/tcp, udp		Any private terminal link; alias = ttylink
88/tcp, udp	kerberos	Kerberos
89/tcp, udp	su-mit-tg	SU/MIT Telnet Gateway
90/tcp, udp		DNSIX Security Attribute Token Map
91/tcp, udp	mit-dov	MIT Dover Spooler
92/tcp, udp	npp	Network Printing Protocol
93/tcp, udp	dcp	Device Control Protocol
94/tcp, udp	objcall	Tivoli Object Dispatcher
95/tcp, udp	supdup	SUPDUP
96/tcp, udp	dixie	DIXIE Protocol Specification
97/tcp, udp	swift-rvf	Swift Remote Virtual File Protocol
98/tcp, udp	tacnews	TAC News
99/tcp, udp	metagram	Metagram Relay
100/tcp	newacct	(unauthorized use)
101/tcp, udp	hostname	NIC Host Name Server; alias = hostname
102/tcp, udp	iso-tsap	ISO-TSAP
103/tcp, udp	gppitnp	Genesis Point-to-Point Trans Net; alias = webster
104/tcp, udp	acr-nema	ACR-NEMA Digital Imag. & Comm. 300

(continued)

W

Well-Known Port Numbers *continued*

Port Number	*Keyword*	*Description*
105/tcp, udp	csnet-ns	Mailbox Name Nameserver
106/tcp, udp	3com-tsmux	3COM-TSMUX
107/tcp, udp	rtelnet	Remote Telnet Service
108/tcp, udp	snagas	SNA Gateway Access Server
109/tcp, udp	pop2	Post Office Protocol version 2 (POP2); alias = postoffice
110/tcp, udp	pop3	Post Office Protocol version 3 (POP3); alias = postoffice
111/tcp, udp	sunrpc	SUN Remote Procedure Call
112/tcp, udp	mcidas	McIDAS Data Transmission Protocol
113/tcp, udp	auth	Authentication Service; alias = authentication
114/tcp, udp	audionews	Audio News Multicast
115/tcp, udp	sftp	Simple File Transfer Protocol
116/tcp, udp	ansanotify	ANSA REX Notify
117/tcp, udp	uucp-path	UUCP Path Service
118/tcp, udp	sqlserv	SQL Services
119/tcp, udp	nntp	Network News Transfer Protocol (NNTP); alias = usenet
120/tcp, udp	cfdptkt	CFDPTKT
121/tcp, udp	erpc	Encore Expedited Remote Pro. Call
122/tcp, udp	smakynet	SMAKYNET
123/tcp, udp	ntp	Network Time Protocol; alias = ntpd ntp
124/tcp, udp	ansatrader	ANSA REX Trader
125/tcp, udp	locus-map	Locus PC-Interface Net Map Server
126/tcp, udp	unitary	Unisys Unitary Login
127/tcp, udp	locus-con	Locus PC-Interface Conn Server
128/tcp, udp	gss-xlicen	GSS X License Verification
129/tcp, udp	pwdgen	Password Generator Protocol
130/tcp, udp	cisco-fna	Cisco FNATIVE

(continued)

Well-Known Port Numbers *continued*

Port Number	*Keyword*	*Description*
131/tcp, udp	cisco-tna	Cisco TNATIVE
132/tcp, udp	cisco-sys	Cisco SYSMAINT
133/tcp, udp	statsrv	Statistics Service
134/tcp, udp	ingres-net	INGRES-NET Service
135/tcp, udp	loc-srv	Location Service
136/tcp, udp	profile	PROFILE Naming System
137/tcp, udp	netbios-ns	NetBIOS Name Service
138/tcp, udp	netbios-dgm	NetBIOS Datagram Service
139/tcp, udp	netbios-ssn	NetBIOS Session Service
140/tcp, udp	emfis-data	EMFIS Data Service
141/tcp, udp	emfis-cntl	EMFIS Control Service
142/tcp, udp	bl-idm	Britton-Lee IDM
143/tcp, udp	imap2	Interim Mail Access Protocol v2
144/tcp, udp	news	NewS; alias = news
145/tcp, udp	uaac	UAAC Protocol
146/tcp, udp	iso-ip0	ISO-IP0
147/tcp, udp	iso-ip	ISO-IP
148/tcp, udp	cronus	CRONUS-SUPPORT
149/tcp, udp	aed-512	AED 512 Emulation Service
150/tcp, udp	sql-net	SQL-NET
151/tcp, udp	hems	HEMS
152/tcp, udp	bftp	Background File Transfer Program
153/tcp, udp	sgmp	SGMP; alias = sgmp
154/tcp, udp	netsc-prod	Netscape
155/tcp, udp	netsc-dev	Netscape
156/tcp, udp	sqlsrv	SQL Service
157/tcp, udp	knet-cmp	KNET/VM Command/ Message Protocol
158/tcp, udp	pcmail-srv	PCMail Server; alias = repository
159/tcp, udp	nss-routing	NSS-Routing
160/tcp, udp	sgmp-traps	SGMP-TRAPS
161/tcp, udp	snmp	SNMP; alias = snmp
162/tcp, udp	snmptrap	SNMPTRAP
163/tcp, udp	cmip-man	CMIP/TCP Manager
164/tcp, udp	cmip-agent	CMIP/TCP Agent
165/tcp, udp	xns-courier	Xerox
166/tcp, udp	s-net	Sirius Systems
167/tcp, udp	namp	NAMP

(continued)

Well-Known Port Numbers *continued*

Port Number	*Keyword*	*Description*
168/tcp, udp	rsvd	RSVD
169/tcp, udp	send	SEND
170/tcp, udp	print-srv	Network PostScript
171/tcp, udp	multiplex	Network Innovations Multiplex
172/tcp, udp	cl/1	Network Innovations CL/1
173/tcp, udp	xyplex-mux	Xyplex
174/tcp, udp	mailq	MAILQ
175/tcp, udp	vmnet	VMNET
176/tcp, udp	genrad-mux	GENRAD-MUX
177/tcp, udp	xdmcp	X Display Manager Control Protocol
178/tcp, udp	nextstep	NextStep Window Server
179/tcp, udp	bgp	Border Gateway Protocol (BGP)
180/tcp, udp	ris	Intergraph
181/tcp, udp	unify	Unify
182/tcp, udp	audit	Unisys Audit SITP
183/tcp, udp	ocbinder	OCBinder
184/tcp, udp	ocserver	OCServer
185/tcp, udp	remote-kis	Remote-KIS
186/tcp, udp	kis	KIS Protocol
187/tcp, udp	aci	Application Communication Interface
188/tcp, udp	mumps	Plus Five's MUMPS
189/tcp, udp	qft	Queued File Transport
190/tcp, udp	gacp	Gateway Access Control Protocol
191/tcp, udp	prospero	Prospero
192/tcp, udp	osu-nms	OSU Network Monitoring System
193/tcp, udp	srmp	Spider Remote Monitoring Protocol
194/tcp, udp	irc	Internet Relay Chat (IRC) Protocol
195/tcp, udp	dn6-nlm-aud	DNSIX Network Level Module Audit
196/tcp, udp	dn6-smm-red	DNSIX Session Mgt Module Audit Redir
197/tcp, udp	dls	Directory Location Service

(continued)

Well-Known Port Numbers *continued*

Port Number	*Keyword*	*Description*
198/tcp, udp	dls-mon	Directory Location Service Monitor
199/tcp, udp	smux	SMUX
200/tcp, udp	src	IBM System Resource Controller
201/tcp, udp	at-rtmp	AppleTalk Routing Maintenance
202/tcp, udp	at-nbp	AppleTalk Name Binding
203/tcp, udp	at-3	AppleTalk Unused
204/tcp, udp	at-echo	AppleTalk Echo
205/tcp, udp	at-5	AppleTalk Unused
206/tcp, udp	at-zis	AppleTalk Zone Information
207/tcp, udp	at-7	AppleTalk Unused
208/tcp, udp	at-8	AppleTalk Unused
209/tcp, udp	tam	Trivial Authenticated Mail Protocol
210/tcp, udp	z39.50	ANSI Z39.50
211/tcp, udp	914c/g	Texas Instruments 914C/G Terminal
212/tcp, udp	anet	ATEXSSTR
213/tcp, udp	ipx	Internetwork Packet Exchange (IPX)
214/tcp, udp	vmpwscs	VM PWSCS
215/tcp, udp	softpc	Insignia Solutions
216/tcp, udp	atls	Access Technology License Server
217/tcp, udp	dbase	dBASE UNIX
218/tcp, udp	mpp	Netix Message Posting Protocol
219/tcp, udp	uarps	Unisys ARPs
220/tcp, udp	imap3	Interactive Mail Access Protocol v3
221/tcp, udp	fln-spx	Berkeley rlogind with SPX auth
222/tcp, udp	fsh-spx	Berkeley rshd with SPX auth
223/tcp, udp	cdc	Certificate Distribution Center
224–241		Reserved
243/tcp, udp	sur-meas	Survey Measurement
245/tcp, udp	link	LINK
246/tcp, udp	dsp3270	Display Systems Protocol

(continued)

W

Well-Known Port Numbers *continued*

Port Number	*Keyword*	*Description*
247–255		Reserved
345/tcp, udp	pawserv	Perf Analysis Workbench
346/tcp, udp	zserv	Zebra server
347/tcp, udp	fatserv	Fatmen Server
371/tcp, udp	clearcase	Clearcase
372/tcp, udp	ulistserv	UNIX Listserv
373/tcp, udp	legent-1	Legent Corporation
374/tcp, udp	legent-2	Legent Corporation
512/tcp	print	Microsoft Windows NT Server and Windows NT Workstation 4 can send LPD client print jobs from any available reserved port between 512 and 1023; see also the description for ports 721 to 731
512/udp	biff	Used by the mail system to notify users of new mail received; currently receives messages only from processes on the same computer; alias = comsat
513/tcp	login	Remote logon such as Telnet; automatic authentication performed based on privileged port numbers and distributed databases that identify "authentication domains"
513/udp	who	Maintains databases showing who's logged on to the computers on a local net and the load average of the computer; alias = whod
514/tcp	cmd	Like exec, but automatic authentication is performed as for logon server
514/udp	syslog	

(continued)

Well-Known Port Numbers *continued*

Port Number	*Keyword*	*Description*
515/tcp, udp	printer	Spooler; the print server LPD service listens on tcp port 515 for incoming connections; alias = spooler
517/tcp, udp	talk	Like tenex link, but across computers; unfortunately, does not use link protocol (actually just a rendezvous port from which a TCP connection is established)
518/tcp, udp	ntalk	
519/tcp, udp	utime	Unixtime
520/tcp	efs	Extended filename server
520/udp	router	Local routing process (on site); uses variant of Xerox NS routing information protocol; alias = router routed
525/tcp, udp	timed	Timeserver
526/tcp, udp	tempo	Newdate
530/tcp, udp	courier	RPC
531/tcp	conference	Chat
531/udp	rvd-control	MIT disk
532/tcp, udp	netnews	Readnews
533/tcp, udp	netwall	For emergency broadcasts
540/tcp, udp	uucp	Uucpd
543/tcp, udp	klogin	
544/tcp, udp	kshell	Krcmd; alias = cmd
550/tcp, udp	new-rwho	New-who
555/tcp, udp	dsf	
556/tcp, udp	remotefs	Rfs server; alias = rfs_server rfs
560/tcp, udp	rmonitor	Rmonitord
561/tcp, udp	monitor	
562/tcp, udp	chshell	Chcmd
564/tcp, udp	9pfs	Plan 9 file service
565/tcp, udp	whoami	Whoami
570/tcp, udp	meter	Demon

(continued)

Well-Known Port Numbers *continued*

Port Number	*Keyword*	*Description*
571/tcp, udp	meter	Udemon
600/tcp, udp	ipcserver	Sun IPC server
607/tcp, udp	nqs	Nqs
666/tcp, udp	doom	Reserved for Id software
704/tcp, udp	elcsd	Errlog copy/server daemon
721–731/tcp	printer	In Windows NT 3.5, all TCP/IP print jobs sent from a computer running Windows NT were sourced from TCP ports 721 through 731; Windows NT 4 and Windows 2000 source LPD client print jobs from any available reserved port between 512 and 1023
740/tcp, udp	netcp	NETscout Control Protocol
741/tcp, udp	netgw	NetGW
742/tcp, udp	netrcs	Network-based Rev. Cont. Sys.
744/tcp, udp	flexlm	Flexible License Manager
747/tcp, udp	fujitsu-dev	Fujitsu Device Control
748/tcp, udp	ris-cm	Russell Info Sci Calendar Manager
749/tcp, udp	kerberos-adm	Kerberos administration
750/tcp	rfile	Kerberos authentication; alias = kdc
750/udp	loadav	
751/tcp, udp	pump	Kerberos authentication
752/tcp, udp	qrh	Kerberos password server
753/tcp, udp	rrh	Kerberos userreg server
754/tcp, udp	tell	Send; Kerberos slave propagation
758/tcp, udp	nlogin	
759/tcp, udp	con	
760/tcp, udp	ns	

Well-Known Port Numbers *continued*

Port Number	*Keyword*	*Description*
761/tcp, udp	rxe	
762/tcp, udp	quotad	
763/tcp, udp	cycleserv	
764/tcp, udp	omserv	
765/tcp, udp	webster	
767/tcp, udp	phonebook	Phone
769/tcp, udp	vid	
770/tcp, udp	cadlock	
771/tcp, udp	rtip	
772/tcp, udp	cycleserv2	
773/tcp	submit	
773/udp	notify	
774/tcp	rpasswd	
774/udp	acmaint_dbd	
775/tcp	entomb	
775/udp	acmaint_transd	
776/tcp, udp	wpages	
780/tcp, udp	wpgs	
781/tcp, udp	hp-collector	HP performance data collector
782/tcp, udp	hp-managed-node	HP performance data managed node
783/tcp, udp	hp-alarm-mgr	HP performance data alarm manager
800/tcp, udp	mdbs_daemon	
801/tcp, udp	device	
888/tcp	erlogin	Logon and environment passing
996/tcp, udp	xtreelic	XTREE License Server
997/tcp, udp	maitrd	
998/tcp	busboy	
998/udp	puparp	
999/tcp	garcon	
999/udp	applix	Applix ac
999/tcp, udp	puprouter	
1000/tcp	cadlock	
1000/udp	ock	

(continued)

Notes

Registered ports are port numbers that are not controlled by IANA but that IANA registers to indicate to the Internet community which vendor applications use them. Registered ports range from 1024 through 65535 and can be used by any process or program requesting it if the operating system has not already allocated it for a specific use. Programs and processes that communicate using remote procedure calls (RPCs) often randomly select a registered port for each RPC communication session.

See Also: *Internet Assigned Numbers Authority (IANA), port, port number, Transmission Control Protocol (TCP), User Datagram Protocol (UDP)*

WEP

Stands for Wired Equivalent Privacy, a data encryption scheme for securing 802.11b wireless local area networks (WLANs).

See: *Wired Equivalent Privacy (WEP)*

wide area network (WAN)

A geographically distributed network composed of multiple local area networks (LANs) joined into a single large network using services provided by telecommunication carriers.

Overview

Wide area networks (WANs) are commonly deployed in enterprise networking environments having company offices locating in different cities, states, regions, countries, or continents. A WAN is needed wherever offices are too far apart to be connected by local area network (LAN) technologies such as Ethernet, Fast Ethernet, and Gigabit Ethernet.

A company can build a WAN in two basic ways:

- Leasing WAN services such as T1 lines or frame relay from telecommunication carriers such as local exchange carriers (LECs) or inter-exchange carriers (IXCs). This is the typical approach used by most enterprises, and it usually incurs installation plus monthly usage costs paid to the carrier.
- Purchase or lay their own long-haul fiber to connect remote locations. This solution is expensive to deploy but can save money in the long run by eliminating monthly leasing costs for carrier services.

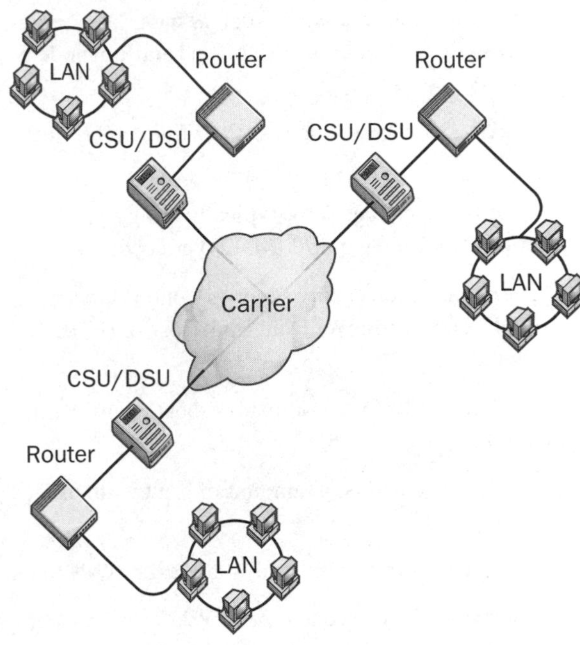

Wide area network (WAN). *Example of how a typical WAN is built.*

Implementation

In a typical carrier-based WAN, company LANs are connected to the carrier's services using special customer services equipment (CPE) deployed at the demarc point, the point where the company's LAN ends the and the carrier's network begins. The boundary of each LAN might be a router, bridge, access server, or other form of data terminal equipment (DTE), which connects through data communication equipment (DCE) such as a modem or channel service unit/data service unit (CSU/DSU) to the termination point of the carrier's line. From the point of view of the company LANs, the carrier's network appears as a "cloud" whose structure is unimportant and whose job is simply to get data from one LAN to another. Configuration of DCE at the customer premises is typically the responsibility of

the carrier, who must ensure that these devices are configured properly to be able to access carrier services.

Routers and access servers typically support several types of WAN service connections including

- Circuit-switched services such as Integrated Services Digital Network (ISDN) and dial-up modem connections
- Packet-switched services such as frame relay and X.25
- Mainframe connections, typically using Synchronous Data Link Control (SDLC) protocol
- Peer connections using Point-to-Point Protocol (PPP) and High-level Data Link Control (HDLC) protocol

When planning a WAN, companies should consider the following:

- The average and peak amount of bandwidth usage anticipated
- The types of traffic that will travel over WAN links
- The availability of each type of WAN services from different carriers

See Also: *bridge, Channel Service Unit/Data Service Unit (CSU/DSU), data communications equipment (DCE), data terminal equipment (DTE), demarc, frame relay, High-level Data Link Control (HDLC), Integrated Services Digital Network (ISDN), inter-exchange carrier (IXC), local area network (LAN), local exchange carrier (LEC), modem, Point-to-Point Protocol (PPP), router, Synchronous Data Link Control (SDLC), T1, WAN services, X.25*

Wideband Code Division Multiple Access (W-CDMA)

Known as Universal Mobile Telecommunications System (UMTS) in Europe, a worldwide standard for a third-generation (3G) cellular communications system.

Overview

Wideband Code Division Multiple Access (W-CDMA) is a cellular communication technology that is based on existing second generation (2G) Code Division Multiple Access (CDMA) technology but offering much higher speeds. The term *Wideband* in W-CDMA is used because it uses wider frequency bands than regular CDMA, allowing higher throughput and enabling downward compatibility with existing Global System for Mobile Communication (GSM) systems widely used in Europe and many other parts of the world.

The UMTS standard was proposed by the European Telecommunications Standards Institute (ETSI) and has been incorporated into the International Mobile Telecommunications-2000 (IMT-2000) initiative, a 3G roadmap from the International Telecommunication Union (ITU). W-CDMA is currently being deployed in dense urban areas in Europe as an upgrade to GSM and in Japan by NTT DoCoMo and J-Phone.

Architecture

W-CDMA uses a newly licensed part of the 2-gigahertz (GHz) band of the electromagnetic spectrum, which causes some problems because this frequency band is already used in the United States for other purposes. As a result, W-CDMA may not take hold in the United States, where a competing standard called CDMA2000, based upon QUALCOMM's cdmaOne technology, is the emerging candidate for a 3G standard. W-CDMA is not fully compatible with air and network interfaces of CDMA2000 standards, as CDMA2000 uses synchronous base station transmissions with 20-millisecond frames and W-CDMA uses asynchronous base station transmissions with 10-millisecond frames. This probably means that cellular phone manufacturers will need to build phones that support both the W-CDMA and CDMA2000 standards in order to provide customers with true worldwide roaming service.

W-CDMA chipsets run at 4.096 megahertz (MHz), which provides a maximum transmission speed of 4 megabits per second (Mbps). Because of protocol overhead and other operational considerations, however, W-CDMA is likely to support a real capacity of only 1.1 Mbps and this only with stationary users. The channel bandwidth for W-CDMA is 5 MHz, much wider than the 1.25 MHz channels of CDMA2000.

For More Information

Visit the UMTS Forum at *www.umts-forum.org.*

See Also: *2G, 3G, CDMA2000, Code Division Multiple Access (CDMA), International Mobile Telecommunications-2000 (IMT-2000)*

WiFi

A seal of approval from the Wireless Ethernet Compatibility Alliance (WECA) certifying that wireless networking devices such as access points and network cards are fully compliant with the 802.11b wireless networking standard.

Overview

The WiFi seal of approval guarantees 802.11b wireless devices from one vendor will interoperate with similar devices from any other wireless vendor. WECA is composed of major wireless networking vendors and software developers and its goal is to promote the 802.11 standards by ensuring interoperability between equipment from different vendors.

For More Information

Find out more about WiFi at *www.wirelessethernet.org.*

See Also: *wireless networking*

Windows 3.1

The original 16-bit version of Microsoft Windows that made personal computers easier to use and more productive.

Overview

This original version of Windows went through several earlier versions, but the first widely used version was Windows 3.0, which was released in 1990 and provided users with a graphical user interface (GUI) environment that was easier to learn and use than the command-line environment of Microsoft's earlier MS-DOS operating system. In 1992, Microsoft Corporation released Windows 3.1, which included additional enhancements and utilities and became widely popular with both consumers and business. Windows 3.1 is now considered a legacy operating system and has largely been replaced by Windows 98, Windows Millennium Edition (Me), and Windows XP in the consumer market and by Windows NT and Windows 2000 in the business arena.

Some of the unique features of Windows 3.1 that distinguished it from the earlier MS-DOS operating system include

- A GUI that displays applications in separate windows that can be resized and arranged in any fashion
- Virtual memory, a technique for swapping between RAM and disk space that increases the number of applications that can be run simultaneously
- Customizable user interface elements, including the color scheme, fonts, arrangement of windows, and mouse settings
- Data sharing by applications using Dynamic Data Exchange (DDE) and object linking and embedding (OLE)
- TrueType fonts, which are displayed in What You See Is What You Get (WYSIWYG) fashion and can be scaled to any size
- Device independence, which makes it easier for manufacturers to write device drivers for their hardware
- Network-aware File Manager and Print Manager utilities, which enable access to shared network drives and printers

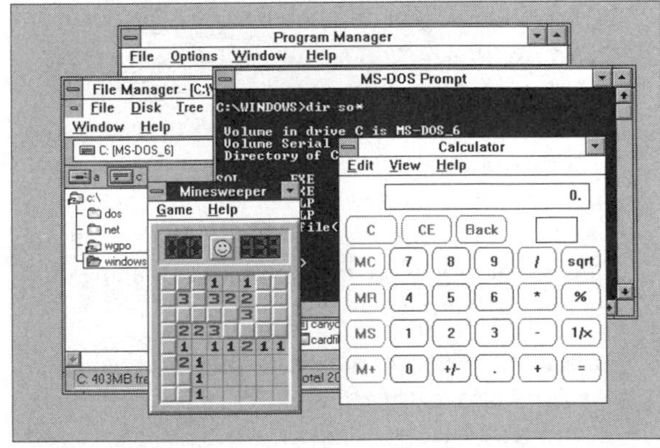

Windows 3.1. *The graphical user interface of Windows 3.1.*

Architecture

Windows 3.1 was a 16-bit cooperative multitasking graphical operating system that ran on top of MS-DOS and shared some architectural similarities with MS-DOS. Windows 3.1 used a layered architecture (see the figure) consisting of three main components:

- A top-layer Windows application programming interface (API) that allows software developers to write 16-bit Windows programs without needing to understand the details of how the operating system routines work internally or how device drivers are implemented and communicate with underlying hardware.
- A middle layer consisting of Windows core components and extensions. The core components make up the kernel of the operating system and consist of three subcomponents:
    - **Krnl386.exe:** Handles basic operating system tasks such as memory management, process and thread scheduling, and file input/output (I/O)
    - **User.exe:** Manages user I/O devices such as the keyboard and mouse, manages communication ports, and keeps track of Windows user interface elements such as windows, dialog boxes, icons, and menus
    - **Gdi.exe:** Manages drawing screen graphics and printing

  The middle layer also includes extensions to the core operating system components that are supplied in the form of dynamic-link libraries (DLLs) that add extra functionality to the Windows environment, such as multimedia support and DDE. Windows DLLs make the Windows operating system environment extensible, allowing software manufacturers to add basic functionality to Windows by creating their own custom DLLs. Windows optimizes memory usage by dynamically loading only the DLLs that it needs at a given time.
- A bottom layer, consisting of Windows drivers, that provides device drivers for different hardware devices managed by Windows, such as the keyboard, mouse, video display, and communication ports.

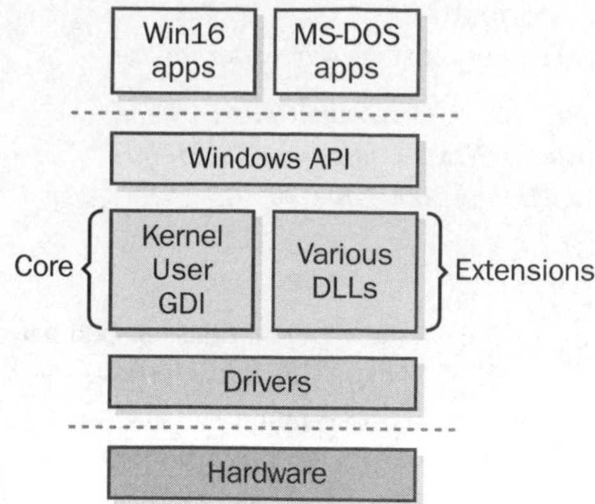

Windows 3.1. *The architecture of Windows 3.1.*

Windows 3.1 had two modes of operation:

- **Standard Mode:** Does not use virtual memory and cannot multitask with MS-DOS applications. In Standard Mode, MS-DOS applications can run only full-screen.
- **386 Enhanced Mode:** Requires an Intel 386 or higher processor, uses virtual memory, and supports multitasking of MS-DOS applications in separate windows. (See the diagram.) This mode includes the Virtual Machine Manager (VMM), which creates and manages separate virtual machines (VMs) running on a single CPU. Each VM functions as though it has access to and control over the entire system's resources. Windows 3.1 and all 16-bit Windows applications run in a single system VM, while each additional MS-DOS application runs in its own separate DOS VM. Virtual device drivers (VxDs) are 32-bit protected-mode DLLs that allow more than one process to share a system resource simultaneously in order to support multitasking. Windows applications are multitasked cooperatively—that is, they must be written to properly relinquish control to other applications to allow them to share system resources. Running Win.com at the MS-DOS prompt invokes the 386 Enhanced Mode system loader (Win386.exe).

Windows 3.1 stored its system and operating system configuration information in a series of text files accessed during the boot process. These included the following:

- Config.sys and Autoexec.bat, which have the same function as in MS-DOS
- Win.ini, which configures the Windows desktop and working environment
- System.ini, which stores the Windows system configuration, including device drivers and mode settings
- Other INI files such as Progman.ini, Protocol.ini, Control.ini, and Lanman.ini

See Also: *Microsoft Windows, Windows for Workgroups*

Windows 3.11

Also called Windows for Workgroups, a version of Microsoft Windows 3.1 released in 1994 that included integrated networking components.

See: *Windows for Workgroups*

Windows 95

Microsoft Corporation's popular desktop operating system and successor to the earlier Microsoft Windows 3.1 and Windows for Workgroups platforms.

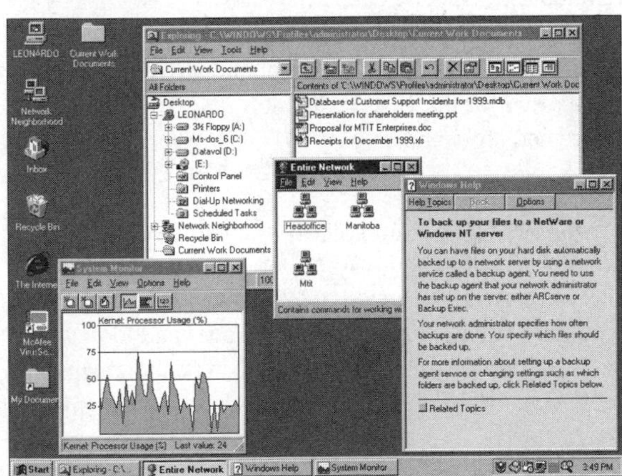

Windows 95. *The Windows 95 desktop.*

Overview

Windows 95 was designed as a desktop operating system for home, office, and business use that preserves full backward compatibility with applications for legacy operating systems such as MS-DOS, Windows 3.1, and Windows for Workgroups. Windows 95 proved wildly popular with both consumers and businesses. It has since been succeeded by several later generations of consumer Windows, including Windows 98, Windows Millennium Edition (Me), and Windows XP.

Windows 95 includes the following enhanced and new features over earlier versions of Microsoft Windows:

- A completely redesigned graphical user interface (GUI) with advanced features such as a configurable desktop, taskbar, Start button, and context menus
- Compatibility with legacy hardware and with MS-DOS and 16-bit Windows applications
- 32-bit virtual device drivers (VxDs) for protected-mode management of devices and services
- Preemptive multitasking kernel that multitasks Win32 and MS-DOS-based applications, replacing the cooperative multitasking approach used by Windows 3.1
- Fully integrated 32-bit disk, network, and print subsystems
- Integrated built-in networking software for Microsoft Networks, Novell NetWare, and Banyan Vines
- Support for long filenames
- Support for plug and play automatic hardware installation and configuration
- Advanced Power Management (APM) support for mobile users
- Integrated Windows Messaging for e-mail
- Integrated dial-up networking for Internet connectivity and for Remote Access Service (RAS) connectivity

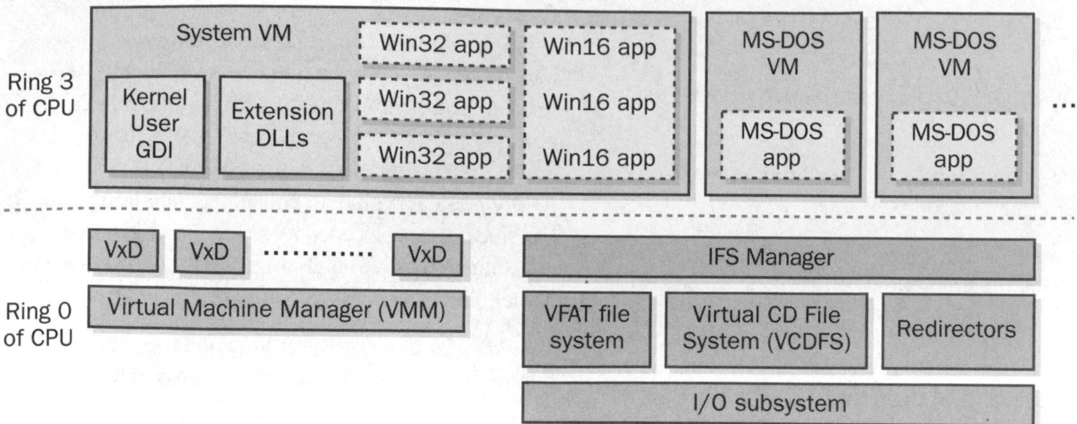

Windows 95. *The Windows 95 architecture.*

- Integrated support for multimedia sound and video applications
- Microsoft Internet Explorer, an integrated Web browser
- Support for advanced features for network administrators, including hardware profiles, user profiles, and system policies

Architecture

The Windows 95 architecture evolved from Windows 3.1 and Windows for Workgroups, but in contrast to these 16-bit versions of Windows, which ran on top of MS-DOS, Windows 95 is a 32-bit operating system with a 32-bit kernel, VxDs, and an Installable File System (IFS) manager, and it does not require that MS-DOS be loaded on the computer. However, Windows 95 includes some 16-bit code and 16-bit components to ensure backward compatibility with MS-DOS, Windows 3.1, and Windows for Workgroups. Windows 95 also supports multithreaded operation and preemptive multitasking operation and manages system resources more effectively than earlier versions of Windows, allowing more and larger applications to be multitasked.

For added protection against application crashes, Windows 95 supports virtual machines (VMs). VMs in Windows 95 are similar to those implemented in Windows 3.1 except for two differences: in Windows 95, 32-bit Windows applications (Win32 apps) can run within their own protected memory address space within the system VM, and 16-bit Windows applications (Win16 apps) also run in the system VM but share their own address space (since they must be cooperatively multitasked). MS-DOS applications run in individual VMs of their own.

Another change in Windows 95 is that system configuration information that was formerly stored in boot files (Config.sys and Autoexec.bat) and INI files is stored in a database structure called the registry. The registry is the central repository for all hardware and software configuration information. Boot and INI files are still supported for backward compatibility with legacy hardware and software.

Notes

Windows 95 went through several incremental releases, each with additional features and enhancements. To determine which version of Windows 95 you are using, run the System utility in Control Panel and look at the version number on the General tab. The incremental versions are described in the table on the following page.

Windows 95 Incremental Releases

Version Number	*Release*
4.00.950	Original full retail version and upgrade from Windows 3.1.
4.00.950A	Windows 95 with Service Pack 1, also called OEM Service Release 1 (OSR1).
4.00.950B	OEM Service Release 2 (OSR2) or OEM Service Release 2.1 (OSR2.1). If "USB Supplement to OSR2" shows up as an installed program when you use the Add/Remove Programs utility in Control Panel, you have OSR2.1 installed.
4.00.950C	OEM Service Release 2.5 (OSR2.5).

If your 20-digit product ID number has *OEM* in it, you have an original equipment manufacturer (OEM) version of Windows 95 that was probably preinstalled on your computer.

See Also: *Microsoft Windows, Windows 3.1, Windows 98, Windows Me (Windows Millennium Edition), Windows XP*

Windows 98

An upgrade for Microsoft Windows 95 and earlier versions of Windows operating systems.

Overview

Windows 98 includes the following features and enhancements over Windows 95:

- A Web-aware user interface that allows Web-like views of local resources and a single tool for browsing local, network, and Internet resources
- Integrated Internet software including Microsoft Internet Explorer, Outlook Express, NetMeeting, Personal Web Server, FrontPad, and NetShow
- Windows Update Manager for accessing the Internet to download enhancements and fixes to Windows 98
- Improved networking support, including a faster Transmission Control Protocol/Internet Protocol (TCP/IP) protocol stack, improved dial-up networking, and support for virtual private networking
- Support for FAT32 drives and a FAT32 conversion utility
- Maintenance Wizard for scheduling system maintenance utilities and other new utilities that simplify administration of computers running Windows 98, including the Microsoft System Information utility, System File Checker, Registry Checker, and Windows Scripting Host (for running administrative scripts from the desktop)
- Support for DVD drives and for multiple monitors on a single computer
- Support for universal serial bus (USB), FireWire (IEEE 1394), and infrared wireless connectivity based on Infrared Data Association (IrDA) standards
- Support for DirectX 5 and OnNow instant-on technology
- Built-in Remote Access Service (RAS) for remote dial-up clients
- Hypertext Markup Language (HTML)-based online help
- Improved versions of many Windows 95 tools and utilities

See Also: *Windows 95, Windows Me (Windows Millennium Edition), Windows XP*

Windows 2000

A powerful 32-bit operating system family from Microsoft Corporation and the successor to the earlier Microsoft Windows NT platform.

Overview

The Windows 2000 operating system is designed as a secure, robust, and highly scalable platform for both desktop and server business applications. There are four members of the Windows 2000 family—the Professional, Server, Advanced Server, and Datacenter Server

versions—and each has a place in the corporate enterprise.

- **Windows 2000 Professional** is a powerful desktop operating system that replaces Windows NT Workstation 4. It builds on both the ease-of-use of Windows 98 and the power and reliability of Windows NT. Windows 2000 Professional includes the following features:
  - Wizards for simplifying system configuration and common system maintenance tasks, and time-saving improvements for the user interface, including Microsoft Internet Explorer 5, an integrated Web browser
  - Features for mobile users, including Advanced Configuration and Power Interface (ACPI) support for laptop power management and offline files, and Synchronization Manager for remote use of network resources
  - Support for 4-gigabyte (GB) RAM, two-way symmetric multiprocessing (SMP), universal serial bus (USB) and IEEE 1394 interfaces, Microsoft DirectX 7, OpenGL 1.2, video port extensions, DVD and smart card technologies
  - IntelliMirror client for deployment and maintenance in conjunction with Windows 2000 Server
  - Local data protection using the Encrypting File System (EFS)
  - Support for Transmission Control Protocol/Internet Protocol (TCP/IP) virtual private networking using Point-to-Point Tunneling Protocol (PPTP), Layer 2 Tunneling Protocol (L2TP), and Internet Protocol Security (IPsec)
  - Add-on Windows Services for UNIX components for interoperability with UNIX networking environments, including a Network File System (NFS) client and server, Telnet client and server, scripting tools, and password synchronization features
- **Windows 2000 Server, Standard Edition**, is a comprehensive application, file, print, and Internet services platform that replaces Windows NT Server 4 and provides increased reliability, scalability, management, and applications support. Its features include the following:
  - Active Directory directory service, a directory service based on the X.500 directory specifications that simplifies centralized, one-point management of distributed network resources.
  - Windows Management Tools, which are snap-ins for the Microsoft Management Console (MMC). MMC provides a unified interface for managing enterprise-level network resources.
  - Enhanced Internet services, including Hypertext Transfer Protocol (HTTP), File Transfer Protocol (FTP), Simple Mail Transfer Protocol (SMTP), and Network News Transfer Protocol (NNTP) server support through Internet Information Services (IIS).
  - Windows Terminal Services for running terminal emulation on thin clients, replacing Windows NT Server, Terminal Server Edition.
  - Four-way SMP support.
  - Enhanced COM+ component services.
  - Support for Kerberos and public key infrastructure (PKI) security services.
- **Windows 2000 Advanced Server** is a powerful server operating system that replaces Windows NT Server 4, Enterprise Edition. Windows 2000 Advanced Server is designed for enterprise-level networking environments that require high availability and scalability. Its features include all the ones in Windows 2000 Server, Standard Edition, plus the following:
  - Support for up to 64-GB RAM (through Intel Corporation's Physical Address Extensions) and eight-way SMP
  - Network-based and component-based load balancing with failover clustering
- **Windows 2000 Datacenter Server** is the high end of the Windows 2000 Server family. It supports all the features of Windows 2000 Advanced Server plus advanced clustering and 16-way SMP, with 32-way SMP available through original equipment manufacturers (OEMs).

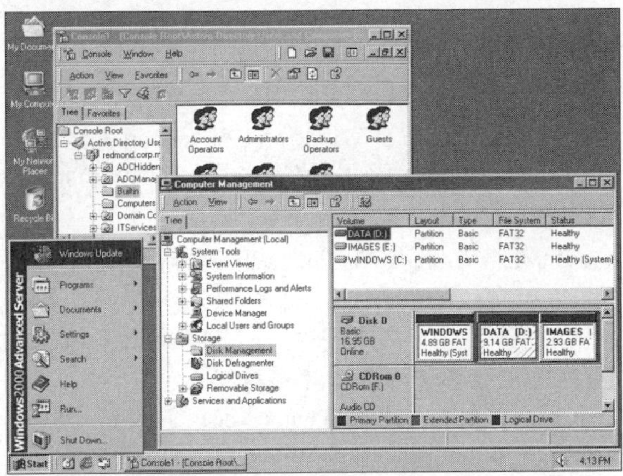

Windows 2000. *The Windows 2000 desktop.*

Architecture

The architecture of Windows 2000 is similar to that of Windows NT with a few exceptions:

- The kernel is modified to include support for Terminal Services.
- Kernel Mode includes two new modules: Plug and Play Manager and Power Manager.
- I/O Manager includes additional drivers for Asynchronous Transfer Mode (ATM), quality of service (QoS), and other functions.

Notes

If you are a Windows NT system administrator who is moving to the more powerful and scalable Windows 2000 operating system platform, you might be confused at first by the differences between the administrative tools on the two platforms. The following table can help you get up to speed quickly on Windows 2000 system administration by highlighting some of the differences between the basic administrative tools on the Windows NT and Windows 2000 platforms. Note that there is usually no one-to-one correspondence between tools on the two platforms; what can be done with one tool on Windows NT might require several on Windows 2000, and vice versa. The tools listed in the second column are therefore not exact equivalents of those in the first column. Unless otherwise indicated, all Windows 2000 tools referred to are in the Administrative Tools program group, which can be accessed either from the Start menu or from Control Panel.

Comparison of Administrative Tools in Windows 2000 and Windows NT

Windows NT Administrative Tool	*Windows 2000 Equivalent(s)*
Administrative Wizards	Configure Your Server (Various consoles also have integrated wizards.)
Backup	Backup (in System Tools in Accessories)
Disk Administrator	Computer Management
Event Viewer	Event Viewer
License Manager	Licensing
Network Client Administrator	No equivalent
Performance Monitor	Performance
Remote Access Admin	Routing and Remote Access
Server Manager	Computer Management
System Policy Editor	Active Directory Users and Computers Group Policy
User Manager for Domains	Active Directory Users and Computers Active Directory Domains and Trusts Local Security Policy
Windows NT Diagnostics	Computer Management

See Also: *Microsoft Windows, Windows .NET Server, Windows NT, Windows XP*

Windows CE

A version of Microsoft Windows designed for a broad range of handheld and mobile products, including handheld computers, Personal Digital Assistants (PDAs), Windows terminals, smart phones, digital pagers, and industrial controllers.

Overview

Windows CE is primarily intended for handheld PCs that provide portable messaging and Internet capability

and for embedded systems in which the operating system is hard-coded by a vendor into a device's ROM. Windows CE is based on a subset of the standard Win32 application programming interface (API), which means that original equipment manufacturer (OEM) developers can use all of the standard Win32 development tools to create custom-based Windows CE solutions for their Windows CE–based products. Windows CE is a component-based operating system that you can use to create "mix-and-match" operating systems that provide only the functionality needed for an embedded system, thus minimizing the memory requirements of such a system. For example, a Windows CE–based industrial sensor might contain the Windows CE kernel and communication modules but not the graphical user interface (GUI). Modules include the following:

- Operating system kernel (32-bit, multitasking, multithreaded, executes in ROM), graphical device interface (GDI), and USER components
- Device drivers, including keyboard, touch panel, notification light-emitting diode (LED), display, audio, battery, Personal Computer Memory Card International Association (PCMCIA), serial devices, and file allocation table (FAT)/FAT32 volumes
- Communication components, including support for both wired and wireless local area network (LAN) connectivity, Transmission Control Protocol/Internet Protocol (TCP/IP) with Windows Sockets, Point-to-Point Protocol (PPP), Serial Line Internet Protocol (SLIP), Infrared Data Association (IrDA) standards, and Telephony Application Programming Interface (TAPI)
- Windows CE Embedded Shell support, which allows developers to create custom shells for providing a user interface for their CE devices
- Win32-like registry for storing configuration information

Windows CE is implemented on a specific hardware platform using a thin layer of code between the kernel and the hardware called the OEM adaptation layer (OAL), which isolates device-specific features of hardware from the operating system kernel, enabling developers to ignore specific hardware functionality.

The current version of Windows CE, version 3, is the basis of the popular PocketPC handheld computing platform.

See Also: *Microsoft Windows, Personal Digital Assistant (PDA)*

Windows commands

Text-based commands that can be issued at the command prompt of Microsoft Windows NT, Windows 2000, Windows XP, or Windows .NET Server for performing administrative and housekeeping tasks.

Overview

Most Windows services are managed using graphical user interface (GUI)–based administrative tools, but you can also perform many administrative tasks at the command prompt either by issuing Windows commands interactively in real time or by saving a series of commands in a text file and running them as a batch file. Windows commands are grouped into several categories:

- **Common Windows commands:** Include commands for performing routing administration tasks. Some of the more frequently used commands are listed in the first table below.
- **Net commands:** For starting, stopping, and configuring networking services.
- **TCP/IP commands:** Commands associated with managing Transmission Control Protocol/Internet Protocol (TCP/IP) networking. These frequently used commands are listed in the second table in this article.
- **MS-DOS configuration commands:** For configuring an MS-DOS environment to run MS-DOS applications. These commands include buffers, country, device, devichigh, dos, dosonly, driveparm, echoconfig, fcbs, files, install, lastdrive, ntcmdprompt, shell, stacks, and switches.

- **MS-DOS subsystem commands:** For backward compatibility with MS-DOS applications. These commands include append, backup, debug, edit, edlin, exe2bin, expand, fastopen, graphics, loadfix, loadhigh, mem, nlsfunc, qbasic, setver, and share.
- **Batch commands:** Used only within batch files for automating system tasks. These commands include call, echo, endlocal, for, goto, if, pause, rem, setlocal, and shift.
- **Filter commands:** For sorting, viewing, and selecting portions of a command's output. These commands include find, more, and sort.
- **Redirection symbols:** For redirecting the input or output of a command to something other than standard input or output. These symbols include >, <, >>, and |.
- **Conditional processing symbols:** Allow you to issue multiple commands from the same command prompt and to act based on the results of the commands' execution. These symbols include &, &&, ||, ( ), and ^.
- **OS/2 configuration commands:** For configuring the operating system environment for applications that run using the OS/2 subsystem of Windows NT. These commands include codepage, devinfo, libpath, and protshell.

The following table lists some of the most frequently used Windows and TCP/IP commands and provides a brief description of what they do.

Common Windows Commands for Windows NT, Windows 2000, Windows XP, and Windows .NET Server

Command	*Description*
Assoc	Displays or modifies file extension associations
At	Schedules commands and programs to run on a system at a specified time and date
Attrib	Displays or changes file attributes
Cacls	Displays or modifies the access control lists (ACLs) of files

(continued)

Common Windows Commands for Windows NT, Windows 2000, Windows XP, and Windows .NET Server *continued*

Command	*Description*
Chdir (Cd)	Displays the name of the current directory or changes the current directory
Chkdsk	Displays a disk status report and corrects errors on the disk
Cls	Clears the screen
Cmd	Starts a new instance of the Windows command interpreter
Compact	Displays and alters the compression of files or directories
Convert	Converts file allocation table (FAT) volumes to NTFS file system (NTFS)
Copy	Copies one or more files to another location
Date	Displays the date or allows you to change the date
Del (Erase)	Deletes specified files
Dir	Displays a list of a directory's files and subdirectories
Diskcopy	Copies a floppy disk
Diskperf	Starts and stops system disk performance counters
Doskey	Calls the doskey program, which recalls Windows commands, edits command lines, and creates macros
Exit	Quits the command interpreter and returns to the program that started it
Format	Formats a disk to accept Windows NT files
Help	Provides online information about Windows NT commands
Mkdir (Md)	Creates a directory or subdirectory
Move	Moves one or more files to a specified directory
Ntbooks	Accesses online Windows NT manuals
Prompt	Changes the Windows NT command prompt
Rename (Ren)	Changes the name of a file or files
Rmdir (Rd)	Deletes (removes) a directory
Start	Opens a separate window to run a program or a command

(continued)

Common Windows Commands for Windows NT, Windows 2000, Windows XP, and Windows .NET Server *continued*

Command	*Description*
Time	Displays the system time or sets the computer's internal clock
Tree	Displays the directory structure of a path or disk
Type	Displays the contents of a text file
Ver	Displays the Windows NT version number
Vol	Displays the disk volume label and serial number
Winnt	Performs an installation or upgrade of Windows NT 4
Winnt32	Performs an installation or upgrade of Windows NT 4
Xcopy	Copies files and directories, including subdirectories

TCP/IP Commands

Command	*Description*
Arp	Displays or modifies the IP–to–MAC address translation tables
Finger	Displays user information on a system running the finger service
Ftp	Transfers files to or from a File Transfer Protocol (FTP) server
Hostname	Prints the name of the current computer (host)
Ipconfig	Displays current TCP/IP network configuration values
Lpq	Obtains status of a print queue of a Line Printer Daemon (LPD) server
Lpr	Prints a file to an LPD server
Nbtstat	Displays protocol statistics and current NetBIOS over TCP/IP (NBT) connections
Netstat	Displays TCP/IP protocol statistics and connections
Nslookup	Displays information from Domain Name System (DNS) name servers
Ping	Verifies connections to a remote computer
Rcp	Copies files to or from a system running rshd
Rexec	Runs commands on remote computers running rexec
Route	Displays or modifies network routing tables
Rsh	Runs commands on remote computers running rsh
Tftp	Transfers files to or from a system running tftp
Tracert	Displays the route taken to a remote host on an internetwork

(continued)

TCP/IP Commands *continued*

See Also: *command, command interpreter, command line, command prompt, Net commands*

Windows Distributed interNet Applications Architecture (Windows DNA)

An application development framework from Microsoft Corporation.

Overview

Windows Distributed interNet Applications Architecture (Windows DNA) is a programming architecture for rapidly and easily developing highly scalable networked applications that can be accessed from a wide variety of clients including traditional desktop "fat" clients, standard Web browsers, and Internet appliances. Windows DNA is based on Microsoft's "digital nervous system" paradigm for connecting applications, data sources, Web services, and users in new and dynamic ways. Windows DNA leverages the integrated services of Microsoft Windows platforms using an enhanced version of the Component Object Model (COM) framework called COM+.

Microsoft first introduced its Windows DNA strategy in September 1997 as a framework that would both embrace the existing Win32 application programming interface (API) client/server model for application development and also extend this model to include Web services and Internet-based clients. Windows DNA is being superseded by Microsoft's newer .NET Framework.

Architecture

Windows DNA services is based on a tiered architecture as follows:

- **Presentation services:** This is the level at which applications interact with users. Presentation services in Windows DNA include support for Hypertext Markup Language (HTML), Dynamic HTML (DHTML) scripting, and the Win32 API. The key enabler for Windows DNA at the presentation level is Internet Explorer, Microsoft's universal Web client application.
- **Application services:** Handles the core logic of distributed applications. Services at this level include Web services running on Microsoft Internet Information Services (IIS), Microsoft Message Queuing (MSMQ) services, transaction services, and component services provided by the COM+ object model.
- **Data services:** Provides access to data sources using ActiveX Data Objects (ADO) and OLE DB for implementing Microsoft's Universal Data Access (UDA) strategy.
- **System services:** Include services for security, management, directory, networking, and communication provided by the Microsoft Windows 2000 operating system and other Microsoft products such as SQL Server 2000 and Exchange Server 2000.

Implementation

To use the Windows DNA paradigm for distributed application development, you can take the following approach:

1. Separate your application into three logical tiers—presentation, business logic, and data.
2. Select the Windows components and technologies for your presentation level that provide your client with a suitable interface.
3. Write COM components to implement your business logic using the application services of Windows 2000 or Windows NT.
4. Use ADO to access data and use OLE DB to expose data for your third tier.

See Also: *ActiveX Data Objects (ADO), application programming interface (API), COM+, Dynamic HTML (DHTML), Hypertext Markup Language (HTML), Internet Information Services (IIS), .NET Framework, OLE DB, scripting, Universal Data Access (UDA)*

Windows DNA

Stands for Windows Distributed interNet Applications Architecture, an application development framework based on the Microsoft Windows 2000 operating system platform.

See: *Windows Distributed interNet Applications Architecture (Windows DNA)*

Windows Explorer

The primary tool for accessing file systems in 32-bit Microsoft Windows platforms.

Overview

You can use Windows Explorer to perform tasks such as

- Create, move, copy, open, edit, and delete files or folders
- Search for files using complex queries
- Map and disconnect network drives to shared folders on network servers
- View and manipulate properties of files and other file system objects
- Share folders and printers for use on the network
- Configure NTFS file system (NTFS) permissions, auditing, and ownership (only in Windows NT, Windows 2000, Windows XP, and Windows .NET Server)

Windows Explorer displays a hierarchical window-based view of file system and network resources in two panes. The left pane shows a hierarchical view of all available file system resources, including the desktop, local drives, mapped network drives, printers, and

My Network Places. In Windows 2000, the left pane can also show search tools or a history of recently accessed resources. The right pane shows the files and folders or other objects within the currently selected drive or folder in the left pane.

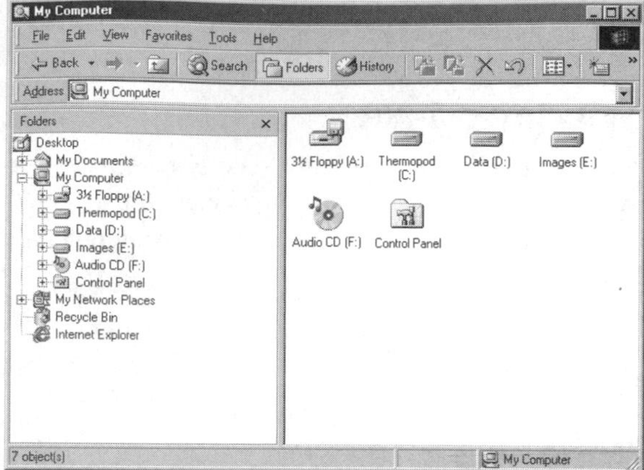

Windows Explorer. *The graphical user interface (GUI) of Windows Explorer.*

See Also: *file system, My Computer, My Network Places*

Windows for Workgroups

A version of Microsoft Windows 3.1 released in 1994 that included integrated networking components.

Overview

Windows for Workgroups used the same graphical user interface (GUI) as Windows 3.1 but included the following enhancements and new features:

- Integrated networking including support for the NetBIOS Enhanced User Interface (NetBEUI) and Internetwork Packet Exchange/Sequenced Packet Exchange (IPX/SPX) network protocols
- Add-on support for Transmission Control Protocol/Internet Protocol (TCP/IP) including Dynamic Host Configuration Protocol (DHCP), Telnet, and File Transfer Protocol (FTP) through the Microsoft TCP/IP-32 for Windows for Workgroups add-on
- Improved performance with 32-bit networking software that provides support for the Network Driver Interface Specification (NDIS) 3 standard, plus backward compatibility with the NDIS 2 standard of the 16-bit Windows 3.1 operating system
- Password-protected logon
- Low 4-kilobyte (KB) footprint in conventional memory for use with 32-bit network drivers, enabling large MS-DOS applications to be multitasked in a Windows environment
- Compatibility with Microsoft Windows NT Advanced Server, Novell NetWare, and Banyan VINES
- Autodetection of many network interface cards (NICs)
- Integrated mail and fax software
- Workgroup version of Microsoft Mail for e-mail connectivity, and the Schedule+ utility for keeping track of appointments and tasks
- Additional network utilities such as Chat, Net Watcher, WinPopup, and WinMeter

The first version of Windows for Workgroups was version 3.10, but version 3.11 soon followed, adding high-performance 32-bit networking access. Windows for Workgroups quickly became the default desktop operating system for many companies until it was superseded by Windows 95.

Architecture

The architecture of Windows for Workgroups is essentially the same as that of Windows 3.1 except for the networking subsystem, which supports the newer NDIS 3 standard. Windows for Workgroups also includes enhancements to 32-bit disk access, which is implemented as two Windows virtual device drivers (VxDs): Virtual File Allocation Table (VFAT), which is a 32-bit, protected-mode replacement for the MS-DOS file allocation table (FAT) file system; and VCACHE, which replaces the MS-DOS SmartDrive disk-caching utility and improves disk input/output (I/O). The network redirector (VREDIR) is implemented as a file system driver as well. The Installable File System (IFS) manager maintains a table that identifies which type of file

system device is associated with each disk volume and forwards all I/O calls to the appropriate device.

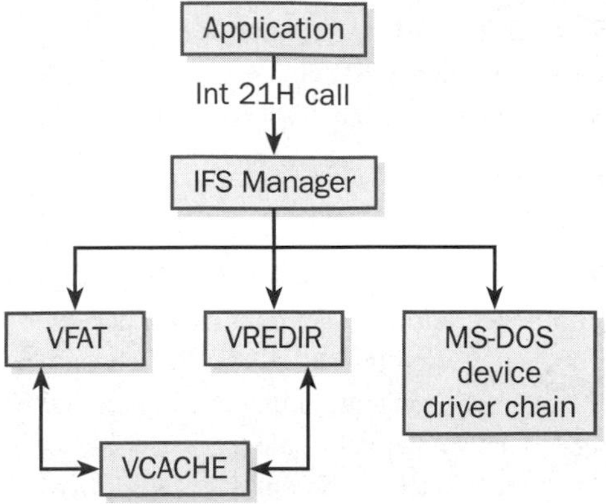

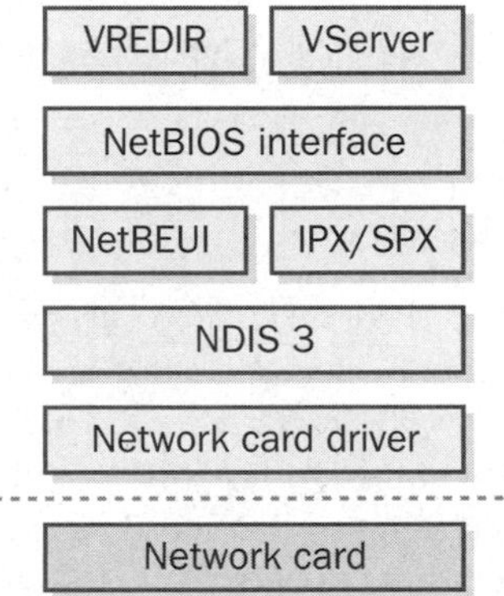

Windows for Workgroups 3.11. *The architecture of Windows for Workgroups 3.11.*

See Also: *Microsoft Windows, Windows 3.1*

Windows Internet Name Service (WINS)

A service in Microsoft Windows NT, Windows 2000, and Windows .NET Server dynamically registering, managing, and resolving NetBIOS names.

Overview

Windows Internet Name Service (WINS) was a popular name resolution service on Windows NT networks because it provided a dynamic means of managing NetBIOS name resolution on networks. WINS provided a central location for registering and resolving the NetBIOS names of computers into their associated Internet Protocol (IP) addresses, simplifying the task of finding and accessing resources on a network.

WINS worked by requiring each NetBIOS host (computer) to register its NetBIOS name and IP address with a WINS server using a procedure called NetBIOS name registration. These NetBIOS name-to-IP address mappings were stored in a database called the WINS database and needed to be renewed periodically through NetBIOS name registration renewal messages. If the computer's IP address changed, the WINS database was automatically updated to reflect this, making WINS a totally automatic procedure for managing these mappings. And when a computer shut down, a name release occurred, removing the computer's mapping from the WINS database.

When a WINS client (that is, a computer running Windows) wanted to connect to a shared network resource, it first queried the designated WINS server by issuing a NetBIOS name query message, providing the WINS server with the NetBIOS name of the computer it wanted to connect to. The WINS server responded by checking its WINS database and returning the IP address of the desired computer to the client, enabling the client to locate and connect to the resource.

WINS replaced an earlier form of NetBIOS name resolution based on network broadcasts and had several advantages over this previous approach:

- Traffic directed to WINS servers consumes less network bandwidth than broadcasts.
- WINS enables the browsing of network resources across multiple domains and subnets.
- The WINS database of NetBIOS name-to-IP address mappings is dynamically maintained, eliminating the need for maintaining lmhosts files on clients.

On the newer Windows 2000 and Windows .NET Server platforms, WINS has been replaced by the Domain Name System (DNS) as the primary method for name resolution and resource location. WINS is still available as an option, however, for supporting downlevel

(Windows NT, Windows 98, Windows 95, and Windows for Workgroups) servers and clients on the network.

Notes

A single WINS server can support up to about 5000 clients. However, it is a good idea to always use at least two WINS servers in order to provide fault tolerance for NetBIOS name resolution. WINS servers maintain their own separate WINS databases, but they can be configured to replicate their NetBIOS name to IP address mappings by way of a process called WINS database replication.

See Also: *Domain Name System (DNS), lmhosts file, NetBIOS, NetBIOS name resolution*

Windows Management Instrumentation (WMI)

Microsoft Corporation's implementation of the Web-Based Enterprise Management (WBEM) architecture for enterprise-level network management.

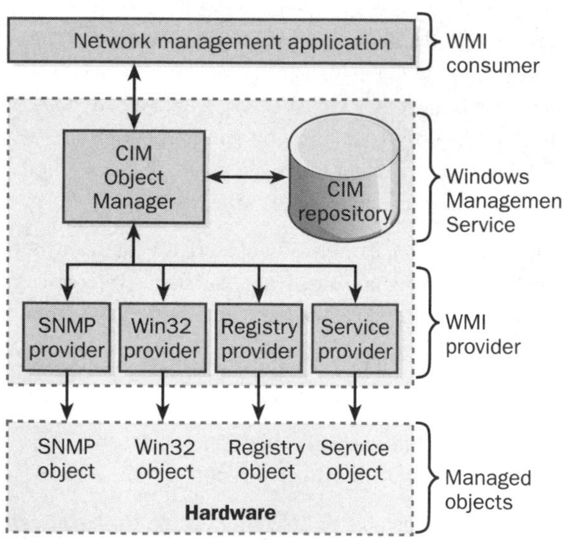

Windows Management Instrumentation (WMI). *The WMI architecture.*

Overview

Windows Management Instrumentation (WMI) is a layer of services in 32-bit Microsoft Windows platforms that lets network management applications track, monitor, and control computers, networking devices, and applications. WMI is based on the WBEM framework developed by the Desktop Management Task Force (DMTF) and uses the Common Information Model (CIM) for describing manageable network objects. Support for WMI is built into Windows 98, Windows 2000, Windows XP, and Windows .NET Server and is available as an add-on for Windows NT 4.

Architecture

WMI has two main components:

- **Windows Management Service (WinMgmt.exe):** This component brokers communication between WMI consumers and providers. A WMI consumer is a management application that can interact with or query managed network objects. The Windows Management Service itself consists of
  - **CIM repository:** An object repository that is used for storing information collected from WMI-manageable hardware and software. This repository is compliant with the CIM standard.
  - **CIM Object Manager:** This component collects information from WMI providers and stores it in the repository.
- **WMI providers:** These function as intermediaries between the network object being managed and WMI. There are WMI providers for Simple Network Management Protocol (SNMP), Win32 objects, the Registry, and Service objects. For example, the Registry provider allows information to be collected from the registries of remote computers and stored in the repository. Similarly, if SNMP information needs to be collected from SNMP-manageable devices, the SNMP provider translates this information into a format suitable for WMI. WMI is also used by Microsoft Systems Management Server (SMS), and the SMS client includes WMI providers that interact with hardware on computers.

See Also: *Common Information Model (CIM), network management, Simple Network Management Protocol (SNMP), Systems Management Server (SMS), Web-Based Enterprise Management (WBEM)*

Windows Me (Windows Millennium Edition)

An upgrade to the Microsoft Windows 98 operating system.

Overview

Windows Me (Windows Millennium Edition) offers many new features and enhancements to the popular Windows 98 operating system, including

- Better ways to manage digital photos, movies, and music
- Protection of critical system files and System Restore for rolling back your system back to a previous working state
- Improved Help and Support areas
- Support for existing and upcoming universal serial bus (USB) devices
- Easier ways of networking your computers together
- Enhancements in networking, messaging, and Internet connectivity

See Also: *Windows 98, Windows XP*

Windows Millennium Edition (Windows Me)

An upgrade to the Microsoft Windows 98 operating system.

See: *Windows Me (Windows Millennium Edition)*

Windows .NET Server

The upcoming version of Microsoft Windows server operating systems that forms the basis of Microsoft Corporation's .NET Framework.

Overview

Microsoft's Windows .NET Server family will be the foundation of the next generation of Internet-enabled businesses. It includes all the features customers expect from a Windows operating system platform, including reliability, scalability, and security, plus additional features that enable businesses to experience the full functionality of the .NET Framework.

Currently, Microsoft plans to release four different editions of Windows .NET Server:

- **Windows .NET Standard Server:** A reliable network operating system for building business solutions quickly and easily. Standard Server supports two-way symmetric multiprocessing (SMP) and up to 4 gigabytes (GB) of memory.
- **Windows .NET Enterprise Server:** An enhanced server platform for building hosting applications, infrastructure, and Web services. Enterprise Server supports four-way SMP and up to 32 GB of memory and will also be available for Intel Corporation's 64-bit Itanium processor platform.
- **Windows .NET Datacenter Server:** A platform for building mission-critical enterprise solutions. Datacenter Server supports 32-way SMP and up to 64 GB of memory on the Intel x86 platform and 128 GB of memory on the 64-bit Itanium platform.
- **Windows .NET Web Server:** Optimized for the job of Web applications hosting, Web Server is easy to deploy and manage and can be used in conjunction with Microsoft's ASP.NET Web application technology and managed from a browser-based interface.

At the time of writing, Windows .NET Server is in beta 3. As a result, the information in this article is subject to change.

See Also: *.NET platform*

Windows NT

Microsoft Corporation's original 32-bit business operating system family.

Overview

Microsoft Windows NT is the basis of Microsoft's BackOffice suite of server applications and provides a secure, scalable, and reliable platform for running enterprise line-of-business (LOB) applications. Windows NT was first released in 1993 in two editions, Windows NT Advanced Server (formerly called LAN Manager for Windows NT) and a client edition, Windows NT 3.1. In 1994 the platform was enhanced and released as Windows NT Server 3.5 and Windows NT

Workstation 3.5, which were both soon upgraded to Windows NT 3.51. Windows NT 3.51 included innovative networking and security features such as

- NTFS file system for advanced local and remote file system security
- Windows NT domains, which are implemented using domain controllers for secure logons in a networking environment
- Trust relationships for building enterprise-level multidomain networks
- Centralized storage of user profiles to support roaming users on the network
- Remote Access Service (RAS) for supporting remote users
- Support for both the server and client sides of Dynamic Host Configuration Protocol (DHCP) and Windows Internet Name Service (WINS)
- Support for the software implementation of redundant array of independent disks (RAID) levels 0, 1, and 5
- Integrated support for the Transmission Control Protocol/Internet Protocol (TCP/IP) protocol suite and associated utilities
- Support for Portable Operating System Interface for UNIX (POSIX) and Operating System/2 (OS/2) text-based applications
- Services for Apple Macintosh
- Support for Novell NetWare migration

In 1996 the Windows NT platform was upgraded to version 4, its final version, and included new features and enhancements such as

- An easy-to-use Windows 95–style desktop interface
- Administrative wizards
- Integrated Internet services and tools, including Internet Information Server (IIS)
- Administrative tools such as System Policy Editor, Network Monitor, and Task Manager

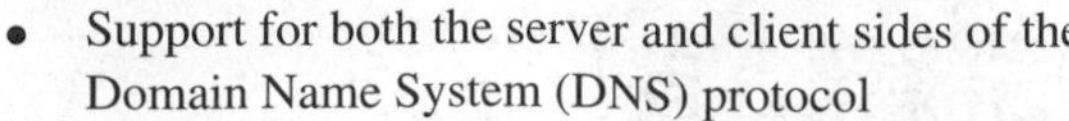

- Support for both the server and client sides of the Domain Name System (DNS) protocol
- Support for the Distributed Component Object Model (DCOM)
- Improvements to the core operating system services and components

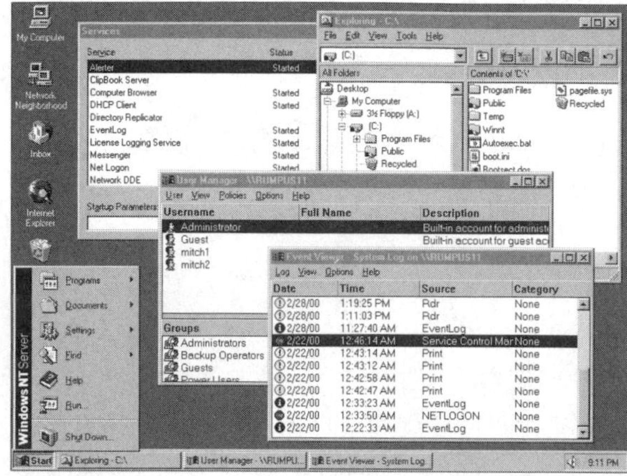

Windows NT. *The Windows NT 4 user interface.*

The Windows NT 4 family included four editions:

- **Windows NT Server 4:** A fast 32-bit multitasking server operating system for networking environments. It can run as a file and print server, an application server, or an authentication and access control server (domain controller), and it can support as many concurrent connections as licenses purchased and up to 256 concurrent RAS sessions.
- **Windows NT Workstation 4:** A fast 32-bit multitasking desktop operating system that supported 10 incoming concurrent sessions and one RAS session.
- **Windows NT Server 4, Enterprise Edition:** Included Microsoft Cluster Server (MSCS) for two-node clustering, Windows NT Load Balancing Service (WLBS) for load balancing up to 32 servers, eight-way symmetric multiprocessing (and support for up to 32 processors from selected vendors), 4-GB Memory Tuning (4GT), and additional tools and enhancements.

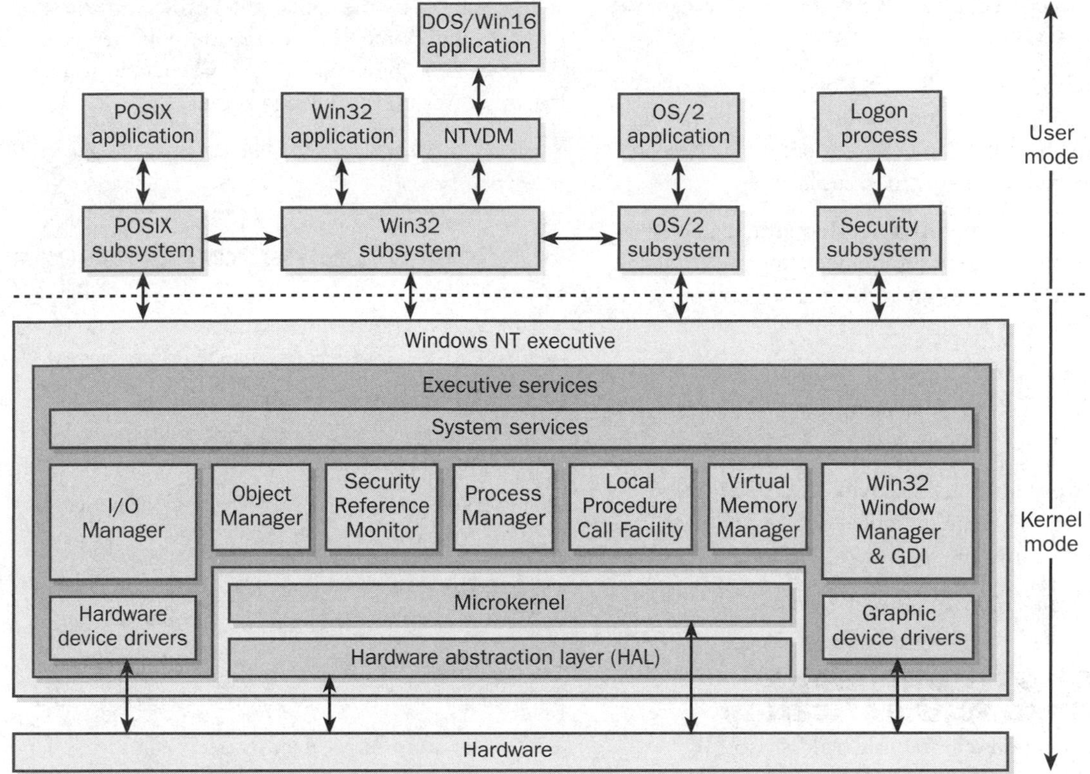

Windows NT. *Windows NT 4 architecture.*

- **Windows NT Server 4, Terminal Server Edition:** Included Terminal Services to present the familiar 32-bit Windows user interface on Windows terminal devices and on earlier versions of Windows desktop operating systems, including those running on legacy hardware.

Microsoft's Windows NT platform is still widely used in business and industry, but it has been superseded by Microsoft's newer and more powerful Windows 2000 platform.

Architecture

Windows NT processes run in one of two modes: user mode and kernel mode. User mode provides an execution environment for user applications as well as the various Windows NT subsystems that support them, which included:

- **Win32 subsystem:** Supports Win32 applications. (All other subsystems depend on this subsystem.)
- **Security subsystem:** Responsible for authentication, access control, and implementing security and audit policies.
- **OS/2 subsystem:** Responsible for running text-based OS/2 1.x applications.
- **POSIX subsystem:** Responsible for running POSIX-compliant UNIX applications.

Windows NT processes that run in user mode are limited to an assigned portion of the system's overall address space but can use virtual memory as needed. User mode processes run at a lower priority than kernel mode processes and have no direct access to system hardware functions. User mode processes must issue all

hardware access requests to the Windows NT executive for fulfillment.

The other mode of Windows NT operation is kernel mode, used for running underlying operating system processes, which run at a higher priority than those in user mode. Kernel mode processes include

- **Windows NT executive services:** Implemented in various modules specific to operating system functions. All managers and device drivers are implemented at this level.
- **Microkernel:** Handles core operating system functions such as thread scheduling and interrupt handling.
- **Hardware abstraction layer (HAL):** Makes Windows NT more portable between platforms by isolating hardware-specific differences.

See Also: *Microsoft Windows, Windows 2000*

Windows NT Challenge/ Response Authentication

The authentication scheme used by Microsoft Windows NT–based networks.

Overview

Windows NT Challenge/Response Authentication, also commonly known as NTLM (which stands for Windows NT LAN Manager) authentication, enables user on Windows NT networks to be securely authenticated without the transmission of actual passwords across the network.

When a client attempts to log on to a Windows NT network, the domain controller challenges the client to perform a complex mathematical calculation on the user's password. The domain controller also performs the same calculation on the user's password, obtaining the password from its Security Account Manager (SAM) database. If the two calculations agree, the client is authenticated and allowed to log on to the network and access resources.

Notes

Windows 2000 uses a different authentication scheme based on the Kerberos security protocol, but NTLM authentication is still supported for backward compatibility with Windows NT domain controllers. On Windows 2000, however, NTLM is known instead as Integrated Windows Authentication.

See Also: *authentication protocol, network security, security protocols*

Windows NT Directory Services (NTDS)

The directory services used by Microsoft Windows NT to locate, manage, and organize network resources.

Overview

Windows NT Directory Services (NTDS) utilizes domains, trusts, and directory synchronization to provide users of enterprise-level Windows NT networks with the following capabilities:

- **Single-logon capability:** Users can log on anywhere in the enterprise using only one account.
- **Centralized administration:** Administrators can manage the entire network from a single location.
- **Universal resource access:** Users can access resources anywhere in the enterprise if they have the appropriate permissions.

To build effective enterprise-level directory services using Windows NT domains, you should consider the following factors:

- The number of domains needed (the domain model used)
- The number of domain controllers needed to support the number of users
- The placement of backup domain controllers (BDCs) to assure efficient directory synchronization of directory services
- The placement of BDCs to assure effective logon and resource authentication over slow wide area network (WAN) links

See Also: *domain controller, domain (DNS), trust, Windows NT*

Windows NT LAN Manager Authentication

Also called Windows NT Challenge/Response Authentication, the authentication scheme used by Microsoft Windows NT–based networks.

See: *Windows NT Challenge/Response Authentication*

Windows Script Host (WSH)

A language-independent scripting environment supported by recent versions of Microsoft Windows.

Overview

Scripting is a powerful tool that administrators can use to automate the execution of complex tasks such as performing system administration, installing software components, and managing files and network resources. The original MS-DOS and Windows 3.1 platforms from Microsoft Corporation supported only limited scripting ability using the DOS batch file language. Microsoft developed the Windows Script Host (WSH) to provide the Windows platform with a more powerful scripting environment based on the Component Object Model (COM).

WSH supports any scripting language that can be implemented using COM. Although Visual Basic, Scripting Edition (VBScript) is the most popular language for writing WSH scripts, other languages that can be used include JScript, Perl, TCL, REXX, Python, and even the legacy DOS batch file language. WSH provides two separate execution environments within which scripts can run:

- **Wscript.exe:** Runs scripts from the Windows desktop environment—for example, by double-clicking on a desktop shortcut for the script.
- **Cscript.exe:** Runs scripts from the command-line console.

The manner in which scripts are run is configured using .wsh files, which act somewhat like the legacy INI files from the Windows 3.1 environment and enable administrators to configure settings such as how long a script should be allowed to run before being terminated. To execute the script associated with a particular .wsh file, simply double-click on the file in the Windows desktop environment or use Cscript.exe at the command-line. You can even create several different .wsh files for a single script and use these in different situations.

The original version of WSH was included in the Windows NT 4 Option Pack and was supported by Windows 98 through an optional download. WSH version 2 is included with Windows 2000 and later.

See Also: *batch file, Component Object Model (COM), scripting*

Windows Sockets

Also called Winsock, an application programming interface (API) for interprocess communication (IPC) on Microsoft Windows platforms.

Overview

Windows Sockets provides an IPC mechanism for implementing both reliable, connection-oriented two-way communication and unreliable connectionless communication between processes running on two different computers. Windows Sockets is Microsoft Corporation's implementation of the Berkeley Sockets interface developed on UNIX platforms for Transmission Control Protocol/Internet Protocol (TCP/IP) networks.

Windows Sockets is implemented as a dynamic-link library (DLL) for Windows operating systems. The current implementation of Windows Sockets on Windows platforms is version 2, which supports multicasting, multiple network protocols (including TCP/IP, NWLink, and AppleTalk), and offers better performance than the previous version 1.1. Examples of applications that use Windows Sockets include File Transfer Protocol (FTP), Telnet, Microsoft Internet Explorer, and many others.

See Also: *application programming interface (API), dynamic-link library (DLL), interprocess communication (IPC), Transmission Control Protocol/Internet Protocol (TCP/IP)*

Windows Update

A Web site for updating Microsoft Windows platforms with new features and enhancements.

Overview

Windows Update can be thought of as an online extension of Windows that helps you keep your version of Windows up-to-date with the latest features and security enhancements. To use Windows Update, select its shortcut from the Start menu (Windows Update requires Internet connectivity to work). This action opens Microsoft Internet Explorer and takes you to the site *www.windowsupdate.microsoft.com*. Once you have connected to the site, ActiveX controls scan your system for outdated system files and determine which new versions of these files should be installed. These system files can include drivers, patches, help files, or new Windows components you can download to keep your computer up-to-date. Note that you must be an administrator or a member of the Administrators group to access the Product Updates section of the Windows Update Web site.

Notes

You also have the option of restoring previous versions of system files that have been changed by Windows Update.

Windows XP

The current desktop version of the Microsoft Windows platform.

Overview

Windows XP is the most recent Windows desktop operating system platform and is intended to be the successor to Windows 2000 Professional. Windows XP comes in two editions:

- Windows XP Home Edition for consumers
- Windows XP Professional for business and professional users

Windows XP is built upon an enhanced version of the Windows 2000 code base and integrates the strengths of the Windows 2000 platform (standards-based security, reliability, and manageability) with the flexibility and

ease of use of the Windows 98 and Windows Millennium Edition (Me) line of products, which provide full Plug and Play (PnP) support and have an easy-to-use interface). Windows XP offers dramatically improved application response times and faster boot and resume times compared to previous versions, and it is tuned to provide users with a powerful and compelling "experience" of the Windows paradigm.

Windows XP is also the associated desktop client operating system for the upcoming Windows .NET Family of server operating systems. There is also a version of Windows XP called Windows XP Embedded that is designed for handheld and mobile devices having limited processing, memory, storage, and display capacities.

See Also: *Windows 2000, Windows .NET Server*

WINS

Stands for Windows Internet Name Service, a service in Microsoft Windows NT, Windows 2000, and Windows .NET Server for dynamically registering, managing, and resolving NetBIOS names.

See: *Windows Internet Name Service (WINS)*

Winsock

Properly called Windows Sockets, an application programming interface (API) for interprocess communication (IPC) on Microsoft Windows platforms.

See: *Windows Sockets*

WINS proxy agent

A computer that enables non-WINS clients to perform NetBIOS name resolution using the Windows Internet Name Service (WINS).

Overview

A WINS client is an operating system that can register its NetBIOS name with a WINS server. All Microsoft operating systems that are network-capable are (or can be configured to be) WINS clients. An example of a non-WINS client would be a Macintosh computer or a UNIX host.

A WINS proxy agent is a proxy for (acts on behalf of) non-WINS clients to allow them to communicate with WINS servers. WINS proxy agents work by listening for NetBIOS name registration broadcasts from non-WINS clients and then forwarding these broadcasts directly to a WINS server. The WINS server then checks its WINS database to see whether the NetBIOS name received is already being used on the network. If the name is in use, the WINS server returns a negative registration response to the proxy agent, and the proxy server then forwards this response back to the non-WINS client indicating that the name is already in use on the network. If the name is still available, the WINS server registers the NetBIOS name of the non-WINS client and informs the proxy agent to tell the client that registration was successful.

Non-WINS clients typically use broadcasts to perform NetBIOS name registration and resolution and are sometimes called B-node clients. A similar process to the above occurs when a B-node client tries to perform NetBIOS name discovery.

For example, if a non-WINS or B-node client wants to register its name on the network, it broadcasts a NetBIOS name registration request. The proxy agent detects this broadcast request and forwards it directly to the WINS server, which checks its WINS database to see whether the NetBIOS name is already being used on the network. If the name is in use, the WINS server responds to the proxy agent with a negative registration response, and the proxy server forwards this response back to the B-node client indicating that the name is already in use on the network.

Notes

WINS proxy agents are needed only on those subnets that have no WINS server and have non-WINS clients that need to be able to resolve the names of NetBIOS computers on other subnets. WINS proxy agents must be WINS clients but cannot be WINS servers.

See Also: *B-node, NetBIOS, NetBIOS name resolution, Windows Internet Name Service (WINS)*

WINS record

A Domain Name System (DNS) resource record that identifies a host as a Windows Internet Name Service (WINS) server.

Overview

WINS records are used in Microsoft Windows NT–based networks to enable Domain Name System (DNS) servers to refer name lookups to WINS servers. On Windows NT–based networks, WINS uses a dynamically updated database, while the DNS database is static and needs to be manually configured. DNS is thus harder to manage than WINS on Windows NT. So by configuring DNS to use WINS wherever possible, you simplify administration of name resolution on the network.

WINS records are specific to Microsoft Corporation's implementation of DNS on Windows NT and are not used with the new dynamic update of Windows 2000 or in non–Microsoft Windows networks such as those using Berkeley Internet Name Domain (BIND) running on UNIX servers.

See Also: *Domain Name System (DNS), resource record (RR)*

WINS server

A Microsoft Windows NT, Windows 2000, or Windows .NET Server machine running the Windows Internet Name Service (WINS).

Overview

WINS servers accept NetBIOS name registrations and queries from WINS clients and WINS proxy agents and then automatically create and maintain a database of NetBIOS name-to-Internet Protocol (IP) address mappings for clients on the network to speed up NetBIOS name resolution. Client computers periodically renew their name registrations for all its NetBIOS-enabled services to keep the WINS database fresh, and when a client is shut down properly or when a NetBIOS-related service is stopped on the host, the registered NetBIOS names for the client are released from the WINS database. In addition, WINS servers maintain their database

through replication with other WINS servers. To do this, you can configure WINS servers in one of two roles:

- **Push partners:** These WINS servers send notices to their pull partners, notifying them of a certain threshold number of changes to their WINS database. You can configure this number on the push partners by using the Windows NT administrative tool WINS Manager or the WINS console in both Windows 2000 and Windows .NET Server. The pull partners respond by requesting the changes, which the push partners then send.
- **Pull partners:** These periodically send requests to their push partners, asking if any changes have been made to their WINS databases. You can configure the time interval for sending these requests on the pull partner. The push partners respond by sending the changes.

WINS servers play a crucial role in supporting efficient NetBIOS name resolution on a network by eliminating NetBIOS broadcasts. When one computer tries to contact another using NetBIOS over Transmission Control/Internet Protocol (TCP/IP), a NetBIOS name query request is first sent directly to a WINS server, which then returns the IP address of the target host and thus enables network communication to take place.

Notes

For fault tolerance on large networks, you should consider using a second WINS server, with WINS replication configured between the primary WINS server and secondary WINS server. One primary and one secondary WINS server are recommended for every 10,000 WINS clients on the network.

WINS servers must have static IP addresses assigned. To enable non-WINS clients to be resolved, create static mappings for them in the WINS database. To enable non-WINS clients to perform NetBIOS name resolution, use WINS proxy agents.

When you configure WINS replication, you should consider the following:

- You can configure WINS servers to be both push and pull partners with other WINS servers.
- WINS servers replicate only changes, not the full WINS database.
- On Windows NT WINS servers, you can manually force WINS replication by clicking the Replicate Now button in WINS Manager. On Windows 2000 WINS servers, you use the Action menu in the WINS console.

Over local area network (LAN) or high-speed wide area network (WAN) links, you should configure all WINS servers as both push and pull partners to keep the WINS database up-to-date on all WINS servers. Over slow WAN links, however, you should configure WINS servers as pull partners only so that you can schedule replication when WAN traffic is light.

See Also: NetBIOS name resolution, Windows Internet Name Service (WINS)

Wired Equivalent Privacy (WEP)

A data encryption scheme for securing 802.11b wireless local area networks (WLANs).

Overview

Wired Equivalent Privacy (WEP) provides Layer-2 (data-link layer) security for WLANs based on the popular 802.11b standard. To perform encryption, WEP uses a shared-key algorithm from RSA Security called RC4 Pseudo Random Number Generator (PRNG), which encrypts all data being sent and received between a wireless client and an access point (AP). Key strength for WEP encryption can be configured as either 40-bit or 128-bit, with 40-bit encryption adding approximately 10 percent overhead to 802.11b transmission.

Issues

WEP has recently been shown to be a flawed protocol that can be cracked using inexpensive off-the-shelf WLAN equipment. The problem lies in the fact that WEP integrates encryption and authentication functions so that a group of users share a common key. The

Institute of Electrical and Electronics Engineers (IEEE) 802.11b working group is working on a new version of WEP that will provide stronger security.

Meanwhile, many wireless vendors are offering additional layers of security to their products, which render WEP superfluous to a degree. For example, Cisco Systems' Aironet 350 Series of products include a proprietary encryption scheme that is separated from authentication and adds support for Remote Access Dial-In User Service (RADIUS). Other vendors offer their own similar proprietary schemes for enhancing WLAN security. The problem is that WEP was intended as an industry standard, while proprietary schemes do not work with each other. For now, enterprises concerned about WLAN security are probably best off buying all their equipment from a single vendor and implementing extra layers of security on top of WEP.

See Also: 802.11b, encryption, Institute of Electrical and Electronics Engineers (IEEE), wireless networking

Wireless Application Protocol (WAP)

A technology for implementing mobile devices with the Web.

Overview

Wireless Application Protocol (WAP) is a set of standards, protocols, and technologies designed to bring Web content to mobile handheld communication devices such as cellular phones and Personal Digital Assistants (PDAs). Such devices generally have limited data input and display features, making it difficult for users to access regular Web content written in Hypertext Markup Language (HTML). To overcome this, the WAP standards include Wireless Markup Language (WML) and WMLScript, offshoots of HTML that can be used to create content custom designed for mobile devices that have small displays and limited bandwidth.

WAP was developed by Ericsson, Motorola, Nokia, and Phone.com (acquired by Openwave Systems) based on technology originally developed in 1995 by Unwired Planet (which became Phone.com). Together these four companies formed the WAP Forum in 1997 to steer the development of WAP standards and technologies. Typical uses for WAP include accessing stock market information, performing online banking, and accessing corporate inventory and sales information.

WAP enables Web content to be delivered over cellular communication systems, which are characterized by a number of issues that make then unsuitable for accessing traditional HTML Web content over Transmission Control Protocol/Internet Protocol (TCP/IP). These issues include

- **Low speed:** WAP is designed to deliver useful content at second-generation (2G) cellular speeds of 9.6 kilobits per second (Kbps) or less. Such limited bandwidth would make it difficult to use TCP/IP with its high protocol overhead.
- **High latency:** Cellular communications can experience latency as high as several seconds on occasion, which could lead to time-outs if TCP/IP were used.
- **Unreliability:** Because cell phone users sometimes go through tunnels or otherwise have their transmissions drop out, using TCP/IP would lead to excessive retransmissions.

The current WAP standard is version 1.2. Version 2 of WAP will include support for animation, color graphics, location-specific content, music downloads, streaming media, and synchronization with content stored on desktop computers.

Architecture

WAP uses a layered protocol stack loosely based on the Open Systems Interconnection (OSI) reference model. The layers of the WAP stack, starting from the bottom, are

- **Bearer layer:** This represents the underlying cellular communications physical and data-link layers, which govern how signals are transmitted and received. WAP is designed to operate with any cellular bearer system, including Time-Division

Wireless Application Protocol (WAP)

Multiple Access (TDMA), Code-Division Multiple Access (CDMA), and Global System for Mobile Communication (GSM).

- **Transport layer:** The Wireless Datagram Protocol (WDP) operates at this level. WDP provides a consistent interface between upper layers and the various cellular bearer systems.
- **Security layer:** The Wireless Transport Layer Security (WTLS) protocol operates at this level, providing authentication, privacy, and data integrity functions. WTLS is based on the Internet standard Transport Layer Security (TLS) protocol, which itself is based on Secure Sockets Layer (SSL).
- **Transaction layer:** The Wireless Transaction Protocol (WTP) operates at this level, providing three types of datagram delivery services: unreliable one-way requests, reliable two-way requests, and reliable two-way request-reply transactions.
- **Session layer:** The Wireless Session Protocol (WSP) operates at this level, providing connectionless (using WDP) and connection-oriented (using WDP and WTP) communication services. WSP also functions in a similar role to Hypertext Transfer Protocol (HTTP) in traditional Web systems.
- **Application layer:** The Wireless Application Environment (WAE) resides at this level and includes a microbrowser that interprets and displays WML and WMLScript content for the user.

Implementation

A WAP system consists of three basic components:

- **WAP client:** This is a WAP-enabled mobile device such as a cell phone or wireless PDA. Display on such devices may range from two lines of text to a small graphical display.
- **Web server:** This is a standard Web server on which content that WAP clients can access resides. This content is typically formatted in WML.
- **WAP gateway:** This acts as an intermediary between WAP clients and Web servers and fulfills three roles:

  - Translates requests from WAP clients into a form understandable by Web servers hosting WML content.
  - Translates WML content served up by Web servers into a binary format for transmission to the WAP client, which then displays the content (binary transmission is used instead of text to minimize bandwidth usage)
  - Performs authentication of WAP clients and encryption of WAP transmissions to ensure privacy

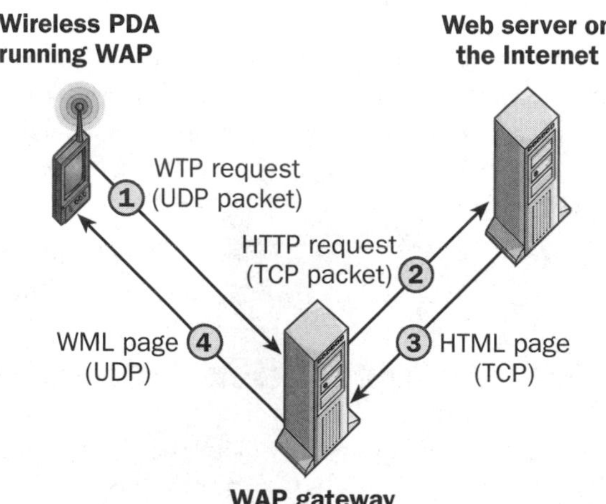

Wireless Application Protocol (WAP). *How WAP works.*

A disadvantage of WAP's gateway approach is that content providers must develop redundant versions of their Web content in WML and HTML. The emerging WAP 2 standard may solve this problem by storing content as XHTML instead, since standard PC Web browsers can translate XHTML into HTML while WAP 2 gateways can convert XHTML into WML.

Prospects

WAP has provided widely popular in Europe, thanks to its implementation by such major cellular communication companies as Ericsson and Nokia, who were involved in the development of WAP. WAP usage in Western Europe topped 7 million users in 2000, and that almost doubled in 2001. Critics have disparaged WAP as being painfully slow—in one test it took users almost two minutes just to find out what was on a certain TV channel using a WAP TV guide. In reality, WAP's limitations are really the limitations of cell phones and PDAs, with their small displays and slow wireless connections. It may be that when true third-generation (3G) cellular finally arrives with its megabit speeds, vendors will increase the display sizes on mobile devices to the point where delivering standard HTML Web pages to cell phones might succeed. If this happens, WAP will clearly be an interim technology, but one that more and more people are finding uses for every day.

Notes

The earlier Handheld Device Markup Language (HDML) was a precursor to WAP and formed the initial foundation from which WML was developed.

For More Information

Visit the WAP Forum at *www.wapforum.org.*

See Also: *2G, 3G, bandwidth, cellular communications, Handheld Device Markup Language (HDML), Hypertext Markup Language (HTML), Hypertext Transfer Protocol (HTTP), latency, Open Systems Interconnection (OSI) reference model, Web browser, Web server, Wireless Markup Language (WML), XHTML*

wireless local area network (WLAN)

A set of technologies used to replace traditional wired Ethernet local area networks (LANs) with wireless ones.

Overview

WLAN technologies can be used to replace or enhance traditional wired Ethernet LANs and are increasing in popularity in networking environments at many large companies. Popular WLAN technologies include

- **802.11b.** This operates in the unlicensed 2.4 gigahertz (GHz) band and provides speeds up to 11 megabits per second (Mbps).
- **802.11a.** This is a high-speed version of 802.11b that offers speeds up to 54 Mbps.
- **HiperLAN.** This is a high-speed wireless technology developed by the European Telecommunications Standards Institute (ETSI) that offers speeds up to 25 Mbps (a newer version, HiperLAN/2, provides speeds up to 54 Mbps).
- **HomeRF.** This is a low-speed frequency-hopping wireless technology (most wireless technologies now use direct sequencing instead) that offers speeds of only 1 Mbps.

See Also: *802.11a, 802.11b, HiperLAN/2, HomeRF, WiFi, wireless networking*

Wireless Markup Language (WML)

A language used to create content for the Wireless Application Protocol (WAP) platform.

Overview

Wireless Markup Language (WML) is a formatting language similar to Hypertext Markup Language (HTML) used on the Web. WML is implemented as an Extensible Markup Language (XML) application and is designed to produce content readable from WAP-enabled cell phones and Personal Digital Assistants (PDAs).

WML is both more and less powerful than HTML. WML lacks many of the formatting features of HTML, since these features are hard to implement on the small displays offered by mobile devices. In fact, the only styles supported by WML are emphasis, strong emphasis, boldface, italics, and underlining. WML also has limited support for tables, images, and other advanced HTML features. On the other hand, WML supports features not found in HTML, including tags for:

- Organizing content into decks of cards. WAP phones display only one WML card of information at a time. Cards are organized into decks, and when a card is accessed the entire deck is downloaded and cached for speedier access.
- Linking cards together to facilitate navigating through a deck.
- Providing dynamic interaction between user and content based on events, input forms, and selection lines.

Examples

A simple WML "Hello World" application might look like this:

```
<?xml version="1.0">
<!DOCTYPE wml PUBLIC "-//WAPFORUM//DTD WML
1.1//EN" "http://www.wapforum.org/DTD/
wml_1.1.xml">
<wml>
   <card title="WML Sample">
      <p>Hello World</p>
   </card>
</wml>
```

The first three lines are the XML Prolog and must appear at the start of all WML files. The <wml>…</wml> tags define the deck, and each card is defined by <card>…
</card> delimiters. The output of this application on a WAP phone would be to display the title "WML Sample" at the top of the screen with "Hello World" underneath.

WML is displayed on a WAP phone using a microbrowser, which is similar to a Web browser but adapted to devices with small displays and minimal processing power. The most popular microbrowser is that from Phone.com (acquired by Openwave Systems), who originally developed their browser for the earlier Handheld Device Markup Language (HDML). Nokia has developed its own microbrowser and has made the source code available for developers to use.

Marketplace

Some vendors have produced platforms that can transcode (translate) existing HTML content into WML for delivery to WAP devices. An example is IBM, whose WebSphere Everyplace Suite, Service Provider Edition, functions as middleware between cellular providers and Web content providers.

See Also: Hypertext Markup Language (HTML), Wireless Application Protocol (WAP), XML

wireless networking

Networking that uses electromagnetic waves traveling through free space to connect stations on a network.

Overview

In the broadest sense, wireless networking is composed of all forms of network communication that use electromagnetic waves of any wavelength or frequency, which includes the following portions of the electromagnetic spectrum:

- **Infrared (IR) laser:** Also called optical wireless, this point-to-point wireless technology ranges in frequency from about 300 gigahertz (GHz) to 200 terahertz (THz) and is used primarily in confined areas where line-of-sight communication is possible. IR cannot penetrate buildings or structures, but it can reflect off light-colored surfaces. Unfortunately, IR is absorbed by water vapor, so fog or rain can disrupt network communications.
- **Microwave:** Ranging from 2 GHz to 40 GHz, this point-to-point wireless technology is widely used for both terrestrial and satellite communication. Microwave also suffers from signal degradation when weather conditions are poor, but not as much as IR.
- **Broadcast radio:** Ranging from 30 megahertz (MHz) to 1 GHz, this technology can be used in both point-to-point and multipoint topologies and can travel through most buildings and structures, but it suffers from multipath interference when traveling over long distances.

When most people talk about wireless networking, they are talking about one of three things:

- **Fixed wireless:** These are services used to connect two fixed stations, typically an office building with a service provider's access point. Fixed wireless is mainly used for metropolitan area network (MAN) communications between different locations within an urban area. Examples of fixed wireless services include Local Multipoint Distribution System (LMDS) and Multichannel Multipoint Distribution System (MMDS).

- **Wireless local area network (WLAN):** WLAN technologies are used to replace or enhance traditional wired Ethernet local area networks (LANs) and are extremely popular in the enterprise. The most popular WLAN technology is 802.11b, which operates in the unlicensed 2.4 GHz band and provides speeds up to 11 megabits per second (Mbps). Other WLAN technologies include
  - HomeRF, a slower frequency-hopping wireless technology (most wireless technologies now use direct sequencing instead) offering speeds of only 1 Mbps. A wideband version of HomeRF offers speeds up to 10 Mbps, but it looks as though 802.11b has eclipsed HomeRF on the low-speed WLAN front.
  - 802.11a, a high-speed version of 802.11b that offers speeds up to 54 Mbps. 802.11a has the most momentum at present to be the high-speed successor of 802.11b, but unfortunately it is not backward compatible with 802.11b.
  - HiperLAN, a high-speed wireless technology developed by the European Telecommunications Standards Institute (ETSI) and offering speeds up to 25 Mbps. HiperLAN/2 can provide speeds up to 54 Mbps. HiperLAN is a compelling alternative to 802.11a with its built-in support for quality of service (QoS) and robust performance in dispersive environments due to its implementation of orthogonal frequency division multiplexing (OFDM).
- **Wireless personal area network (WPAN):** This is a wireless network used to connect devices that are worn or carried by users over short distances. Bluetooth is an emerging standard for WPANs that bi-directional data communications at 432.6 Kbps over distances up to 33 feet (10 meters).

The rest of this article focuses on WLAN technologies, as these are the most popular form of wireless networks used in enterprise environments.

History

Wireless networking first came to the attention of enterprise users in the mid-1990s when early proprietary products appeared offering speeds under 1 Mbps. In 1997 the Institute of Electrical and Electronics Engineers (IEEE) ratified the first WLAN standard, the 802.11 specification, which supported speeds up to 2 Mbps. In 1999 the IEEE ratified a new standard, the 802.11b High Rate specification, which brought wireless speeds up to 11 Mbps, making them comparable to Ethernet and, for the first time, an attractive alternative to traditional wired Ethernet LANs. Early 802.11b equipment from different vendors proved incompatible due to implementation differences, so the Wireless Ethernet Compatibility Alliance (WECA) was formed to promote interoperability between different vendors. WECA provides a certification called WiFi, which, if it appears on an 802.11b wireless device, virtually guarantees interoperability with devices from any other wireless vendor.

In 2000 the IEEE ratified a standard called 802.11a, which provides even faster speeds of up to 54 Mbps, and access points and PC cards for this technology are now beginning to appear in the marketplace. WECA has also developed a certification for 802.11a interoperability called WiFi5 (802.11a is five times faster than 802.11b). Currently, the IEEE is developing another standard called 802.11g, which runs at 22 Mbps and is backward compatible with 802.11b. It is uncertain at present whether this new technology will succeed in the marketplace.

802.11b currently rules the market in the WLAN arena, but enterprise network architects are beginning to look at 802.11a as an option when higher speed is required. Another recent development is the move toward integrating 802.11b WLAN technology with General Packet Radio Service (GPRS), a 2.5G cellular communication technology. This integration will enable cell phones and similar devices connect to corporate WLANs to send and retrieve data, taking us one step further into a wired world.

Uses

Wireless networks are typically used for

- Communication with mobile stations, which precludes the use of fixed cabling, or for mobile users

such as workers moving about in large warehouses or knowledge workers at convention centers for conferences

- Work areas in which it is impractical or expensive to run cabling, such as older buildings that are costly to renovate
- Rapid deployment and reconfiguration of networks in companies that evolve quickly
- Networking buildings together on a campus using wireless bridges or fixed wireless services from a telco
- Sitting in a rubber tire in your swimming pool working on your laptop while sipping margaritas (do not try this if you value your laptop!)

Implementation

Wireless LANs (WLANs) are the simplest and most popular forms of wireless networking technology. To connect wireless stations to a traditional wired LAN, you need just two components:

- **Access point (AP):** This is basically a bridge that has an Ethernet port and a wireless transceiver. The Ethernet port connects to the wired LAN, and the transceiver transmits signals to and receives signals from the wireless stations. The effective reception range from an access point is defined by a circular area called a cell or Basic Service Set. A typical access point might provide up to 32,290 square feet (3000 square meters) of coverage in open areas (or less when obstacles are present) and support data transmission rates of 1 to 10 Mbps. However, the number of wireless stations that an access point can effectively handle is inversely proportional to the average traffic generated by each station. In other words, wireless networks are shared networks not switched ones. When multiple access point have overlapping cells, the access points hand off communication as stations roam from one cell to another.
- **PC card:** This is typically a card having an integrated antenna that connects the computer to the access point. There are also external devices that plug into an RJ-45 port of an Ethernet card or RS-232 serial port to provide similar connectivity. Some PC cards have an external or detachable antenna for greater distance reception. The card turns the computer in which it is installed into a wireless station on the network. The typical power output of a PC card is around 100 milliwatts (mW), which provides a coverage range of about 1000 feet (305 meters) in open areas, or less when obstacles such as walls or buildings are present.

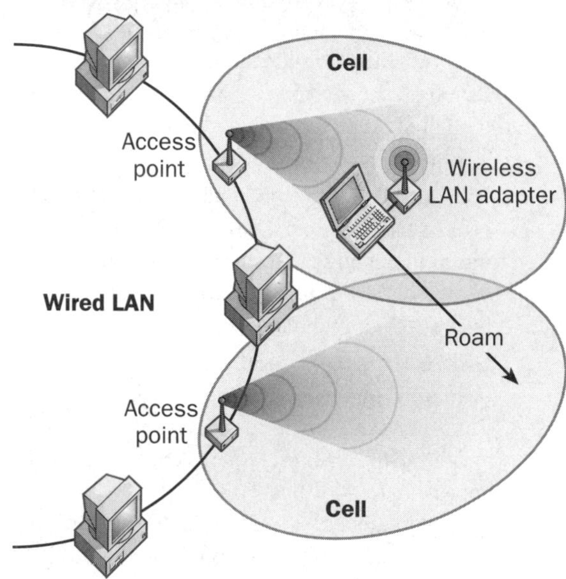

Wireless networking. *A simple wireless LAN (WLAN) in operation.*

Most wireless systems use the Carrier Sense Multiple Access with Collision Avoidance (CSMA/CA) media access method, in contrast to the Carrier Sense Multiple Access with Collision Detection (CSMA/CD) method used in wired Ethernet networks. The primary reason for this is that it is difficult to detect collisions between unguided electromagnetic waves.

Marketplace

Dozens of vendors offer WLAN access points and PC cards, some of the more popular being 3Com Corporation with its AirConnect series of products, Apple Computer with its AirPort line, Enterasys Networks with its RoamAbout AP and PC card, Cisco Systems with its Aironet 340 Series Wireless products, and Agere

Systems with its ORiNOCO line. Prices have fallen rapidly in the last year, and access points are now typically less than $1000 and PC cards may cost less than $200.

Issues

The biggest issue relating to wireless networking is security. Initiatives such as Wired Equivalent Privacy (WEP) from the IEEE have proven insufficient to guarantee the security of wireless networks. In addition, many products from wireless vendors are provided with security turned off by default, and if users do not enable security features their precious data will be broadcast to the world for anyone to intercept. Simply by driving around a downtown area with an 802.11b-enabled laptop, a user can often establish connections with numerous corporate wireless networks and view shared resources on these networks. As a result some wireless vendors are introducing their own proprietary solutions to ensure security for their wireless networking products.

Another issue is the susceptibility of WLANs to electromagnetic interference (EMI). For example, a microwave oven can degrade or sometimes disrupt 802.11b communication since it operates in the same microwave portion of the electromagnetic spectrum. Wireless networks also can have their speed limited by obstacles such as iron girders in buildings, concrete walls, and other signal-absorbing obstacles.

See Also: *802.11, 802.11a, 802.11b, access point (AP), Bluetooth, Carrier Sense Multiple Access with Collision Avoidance (CSMA/CA), Carrier Sense Multiple Access with Collision Detection (CSMA/CD), electromagnetic interference (EMI), General Packet Radio Service (GPRS), HiperLAN/2, HomeRF, Institute of Electrical and Electronics Engineers (IEEE), Local Multipoint Distribution Service (LMDS), Multipoint Multichannel Distribution Service (MMDS), Orthogonal Frequency Division Multiplexing (OFDM), quality of service (QoS), Wired Equivalent Privacy (WEP)*

wiring closet

A room on the floor of a building that contains hubs, switches, and other network components for that floor.

Overview

Also called an equipment room or server room (and various other names), wiring closets generally serve networks on individual floors of a building and are connected using vertical backbone cabling running down the elevator shaft to the main equipment room, which is usually in the basement. The wiring closet on each floor is the termination point for horizontal cabling running from wall plates in work areas on the floor. This horizontal wiring typically terminates in a series of patch panels in the wiring closet. Patch cables are used to connect jacks on the patch panels to ports on hubs and switches to establish network connectivity between computers on the floor and with other floors. In a single-floor building, the wiring closet and the main equipment room are the same and are sometimes called the telecommunications closet because telecommunications services typically terminate in that room as well.

Notes

The standards of the Electronic Industries Association/Telecommunications Industry Association (EIA/TIA) recommend one wiring closet per floor, with a minimum size of 9.8 feet by 6.6 feet (3 meters by 2 meters) per 4898 square feet (455 square meters) of floor space. When stations must be located more than 300 feet (91 meters) from the wiring closet, additional wiring closets are recommended. Wiring closets should be well lit and have an adequate power supply. Equipment should be mounted on racks for greater security and efficiency. "Spaghetti" should be minimized—keep everything accurately labeled to save yourself hours of troubleshooting time when things go wrong. Keep access to the wiring closet clear and secure, and include fire protection devices.

See Also: *infrastructure, premise cabling, structured wiring, wall plate*

WLAN

Stands for wireless local area network, a set of technologies used to replace traditional wired Ethernet local area networks (LANs) with wireless ones.

See: *wireless local area network (WLAN)*

WMI

Stands for Windows Management Instrumentation, Microsoft Corporation's implementation of the Web-Based Enterprise Management (WBEM) architecture for enterprise-level network management.

See: *Windows Management Instrumentation (WMI)*

WML

Stands for Wireless Markup Language, a language used to create content for the Wireless Application Protocol (WAP) platform.

See: *Wireless Markup Language (WML)*

workgroup

A logical grouping of networked peer computers that can share resources with one another.

Overview

Workgroups are usually established to share resources, including files, printers, and other devices. A workgroup is sometimes called a peer-to-peer network because all computers in a workgroup are equally important. In other words, no single computer "runs the network," as in a domain-based model.

Each computer in a workgroup handles security separately using its own local security database, which tracks who can log on to the computer and what rights or permissions users have to resources on the computer. A user who wants to log on to a computer must have an account in that computer's local security database. A user with an account on one computer does not necessarily have any permissions or rights to resources on other computers.

If a computer in a workgroup is used to provide file, print, or other resources to other computers in the workgroup, that computer is generally called a peer server or a stand-alone server. Because security is local to each computer in a workgroup, a peer server can share resources using share-level security only, which uses passwords to protect access to each resource. Users who know this password can access the resources at the level of access with which it is shared (such as read-only access or full access).

Workgroups are simple to implement but hard to maintain. Administrators must create accounts on each computer for the users who need access to them. As a result, workgroups are generally used for small networks of 10 or fewer computers in which security and centralized administration are not an issue.

See Also: *domain (DNS), server-based network*

World Wide Web (WWW)

The popular Internet service that is rapidly changing the way we live and work.

Overview

The World Wide Web Consortium (W3C) defines the World Wide Web (WWW, or Web) as "the universe of network-accessible information, the embodiment of human knowledge." The WWW began as a project for sharing hypertext information over a network that was developed by Tim Berners-Lee at CERN (Conseil Européen pour la Recherche Nucleaire), a physics research center in Geneva, Switzerland.

The Web consists of Web sites hosted on Web servers around the world and connected to the Internet. Users access the Web using Web browsers and similar client applications that use the Web's client/server protocol called Hypertext Transfer Protocol (HTTP). Web sites range from collections of text files formatted with Hypertext Markup Language (HTML) and their associated image, sound, multimedia, and script files to dynamic Web applications that can perform virtually every function imaginable. Individual HTML files within a Web site are called Web pages, and pages can be linked to other pages in the same or different sites, which explains why the word "web" is used, since this conjures up pictures of spider webs.

The Web contains a vast amount of information that is growing exponentially. Of all the interesting things that one could say about the Web (it would take a million books to exhaust the subject), we will focus on one interesting study done by IBM in 2000 that showed that "hyperspace" (another name for the Web) is actually divided into four different "regions" roughly equal in size, as follows:

- **Core:** This comprises 30 percent of the Web and consists of highly visible public Web sites such as Yahoo! and MSN. It is possible to browse from one point in the core to any other point in the core simply by following enough hyperlinks.
- **Origination node:** This comprises 24 percent of the Web and consists of sites that contain links that enable you to reach sites in the Core, but which cannot be traversed in the opposite direction. An example might be a personal home page with a link to MSN on it.
- **Termination node:** This comprises another 24 percent of the Web and consists of sites that you can reach from the Core but which do not link back to the Core. In other words, these are dead-end sites and pages containing various kinds of content but usually with no hyperlinks on them.
- **Disconnected pages:** This comprises 22 percent of the Web and consists of a number of "islands" of Web content that are completely disconnected from the Core. Broken links are often the cause of this condition.

As a result of this fascinating study, one might deduce that if you chose two Web pages at random, you have about one chance in four of being able to browse from one to the other by following links, perhaps hundreds of them! The average "link distance" between two randomly selected pages, however, was determined to be only about 16 clicks.

See Also: Hypertext Markup Language (HTML), Hypertext Transfer Protocol (HTTP), World Wide Web Consortium (W3C)

World Wide Web Consortium (W3C)

A vendor-neutral organization created in 1994 that develops common, interoperable standards and protocols for the World Wide Web (WWW).

Overview

Represented by the Massachusetts Institute of Technology (MIT) in the United States and a number of international research centers, the World Wide Web Consortium (W3C) provides a variety of services to its member organizations, including the following:

- Discussion groups and meetings on issues relating to the evolution of the WWW
- Repositories of information, reference documents, and code relating to WWW protocols, services, and applications
- The creation and testing of applications that demonstrate new types of WWW technologies

The process by which the W3C develops new standards and protocols involves four steps:

1. **Note:** An initial idea or comment is submitted as a document for discussion.
2. **Working draft:** Presents work in progress toward a possible standard by the W3C working group involved.
3. **Proposed recommendation:** Issued when a consensus has been reached within the working group.
4. **Recommendation:** Receives the director's stamp of approval as a W3C recommendation.

The director of the W3C is Tim Berners-Lee, the creator of the WWW. Membership in the W3C is tailored to organizations, but private individuals can also join as affiliate members.

For More Information

Visit the W3C at *www.w3c.org.*

See Also: Internet, standards organizations, World Wide Web (WWW)

WOW

Stands for "Win16 on Win32," a component of the Microsoft Windows NT operating system that enables 16-bit Windows applications (such as those designed to

run on Windows 3.1 and Windows for Workgroups 3.11) to run properly on Windows NT's 32-bit operating system.

Overview

Like MS-DOS applications, 16-bit Windows applications (Win16 applications) also run on Windows NT within the context of a Windows NT Virtual DOS Machine (NTVDM), which simulates the 16-bit environment necessary for these applications to run. However, although MS-DOS applications each require their own separate NTVDMs in which to run, Win16 applications run within a single NTVDM called WOW, which corresponds to the system process Wowexec.exe. And although NTVDMs hosting MS-DOS applications are single-threaded, WOW is a multithreaded NTVDM in which each Win16 application runs as a separate thread using the same shared address space. WOW also simulates the cooperative multitasking environment for which applications written for Windows 3.1 and Windows for Workgroups 3.11 are designed. WOW allows only one Win16 application to run at a time, blocking the threads of all other Win16 applications until the running application relinquishes control. If the Windows NT kernel needs to preempt the Win16 application (by preempting WOW), it always resumes with the same Win16 application.

WOW also handles the translation of 16-bit Windows application programming interfaces (APIs) and messages to their corresponding 32-bit APIs and messages, enabling interoperability and data sharing between 16-bit and 32-bit Windows applications operating on the Windows NT platform.

Windows NT also includes an option for running Win16 applications in their own separate NTVDMs, which enables Win16 applications to function as a process within Windows NT's preemptive, multitasking environment. You can run a Win16 application in a separate NTVDM by opening the Run box from the Start menu, typing the path to the Win16 executable, and selecting the Run In Separate Memory Space check box. Note that doing this can have negative effects on Win16 applications that need to share data with each other by using legacy data-sharing mechanisms such as Dynamic Data Exchange (DDE).

WSH

Stands for Windows Script Host, a language-independent scripting environment supported by recent versions of Microsoft Windows.

See: *Windows Script Host (WSH)*

WWW

Stands for World Wide Web, the popular Internet service that is rapidly changing the way we live and work.

See: *World Wide Web (WWW)*

X.25

A legacy packet-switching protocol.

Overview

X.25 is the earliest example of a packet-switching protocol designed to provide wide area network (WAN) connectivity. It was developed in the early 1970s and standardized in 1976 by the Comité Consultatif International Télégraphique et Téléphonique (CCITT), the precursor of the International Telecommunication Union (ITU). X.25 is a synchronous, connection-oriented, bidirectional, full-duplex packet-switching protocol originally designed for connecting "dumb terminals" (character-based terminals) to remote mainframe hosts.

X.25 was designed to be a reliable WAN service that compensated for the fact that dumb terminals lacked the processing power to include an X.25 protocol stack. To ensure this reliability of communication, X.25 includes extra protocol overhead in packet headers. In addition, because X.25 was designed when analog transmission over noisy copper telephone wire was the norm, X.25 packets have additional overhead for error correction. The result of these two factors is the comparatively low overall bandwidth of X.25, which originally operated at only 19.2 kilobits per second (Kbps) (although this was generally sufficient for character-based communication between mainframes and terminals). The current X.25 standard supports speeds up to 2 megabits per second (Mbps) over two pairs of wires, but most implementations are 64-Kbps connections through a standard DS-0 link. The X.25 standard is updated every four years, and versions after 1984 are backward compatible with the 1984 version.

Architecture

The X.25 standard roughly corresponds in its functionality to the first three layers of the Open Systems Interconnection (OSI) reference model. The reason this correspondence is only rough is that X.25 was actually developed before the OSI model was created. Specifically, X.25 defines the following:

- **Physical layer:** Also called the physical layer in X.25 terminology, this layer defines the physical interface for connecting routers or terminals at the customer premises with X.25 switches at the carrier's facilities. The physical layer interface of X.25 is defined by the X.21 standard, which was originally derived from the RS-232 interface for serial transmission. The original X.21 connector was a 15-pin connector, but a newer standard called X.21bis uses a more common 25-pin connector. In general, RS-232 and V.35 serial interfaces have largely replaced X.21 interfaces on X.25 equipment.
- **Data-link layer:** Called the link access layer in X.25 terminology, this layer defines the encapsulation (framing) and error-correction methods used by X.25 and also enables X.25 equipment to initiate or terminate a communication session or initiate data transfer using the Link Access Procedure, Balanced (LAPB), which was derived from the earlier High-level Data Link Control (HDLC) protocol.
- **Network layer:** Called the packet layer in X.25 terminology, this layer defines the way to deliver X.25 packets reliably between end nodes on an X.25 network using the Packet Layer Protocol (PLP) and is also responsible for call setup and termination and for X.25 addressing using the X.121 standard.

Implementation

An X.25 network consists of four elements:

- **Data terminal equipment (DTE):** These include routers and computers at the customer premises that need to communicate using X.25.

- **Data communications equipment (DCE):** These include modems and Channel Service Unit/Data Service Units (CSU/DSUs) that connect the customer's DTE to the X.25 network. You can also connect multiple DTEs to a single DCE by using the multiplexing methods inherent in the X.25 protocol. Similarly, a single X.25 end node can establish several virtual circuits simultaneously with remote nodes.
- **Packet assembler/disassembler (PAD)**: This is a device that you can use to connect a dumb terminal to an X.25 network. The dumb terminal is DTE, and the PAD resides between the DTE and the DCE. Note that a PAD is not required for a router having built-in X.25 support—PADs are only required to connect dumb terminals that have no processing power to implement X.25 directly. The X.3 standard defines the various parameters used for configuring a PAD, the X.28 standard defines the data transmission interface between the DTE and the PAD, and the X.29 standard defines the control protocol between the DTE and the PAD.
- **Public data network (PDN):** This is the X.25 "cloud" of circuits and packet-switching exchanges (PSEs) (switches) at the carrier facility that you can use to connect DTE at different locations together and carry the X.25 packets from one DTE to another. These PDNs typically run parallel to the carrier's Public Switched Telephone Network (PSTN) voice network, and each carrier typically operates its own PDN. Different carriers' PDNs can be interconnected to form larger X.25 networks using the X.75 standard.

X.25 supports two different types of connection-oriented communications:

- **Permanent virtual circuit (PVC):** Here the carrier sets up the switches for the connection ahead of time, emulating a dedicated point-to-point communications link for the connected nodes. PVCs are used when large amounts of data regularly need to be transferred over PDNs, such as for connections between banks and credit agencies.
- **Switched virtual circuit (SVC):** The switches are set up when the call is initiated and are torn down afterward. SVCs are used when only small amounts of information need to be occasionally sent over PDNs.

In typical SVC communications, a DTE initiates a communication session with another DTE by dialing its X.121 address and establishing a virtual circuit. Packets are then forwarded through the PDN by using the ID number of the virtual circuit established for that particular communication session. This ID number is called the logical channel identifier (LCI) and is a 12-bit address that identifies the virtual circuit. X.25 packets are generally 128, 256, or 512 bytes in size, although actual size can range from 64 to 4096 bytes depending on the implementation.

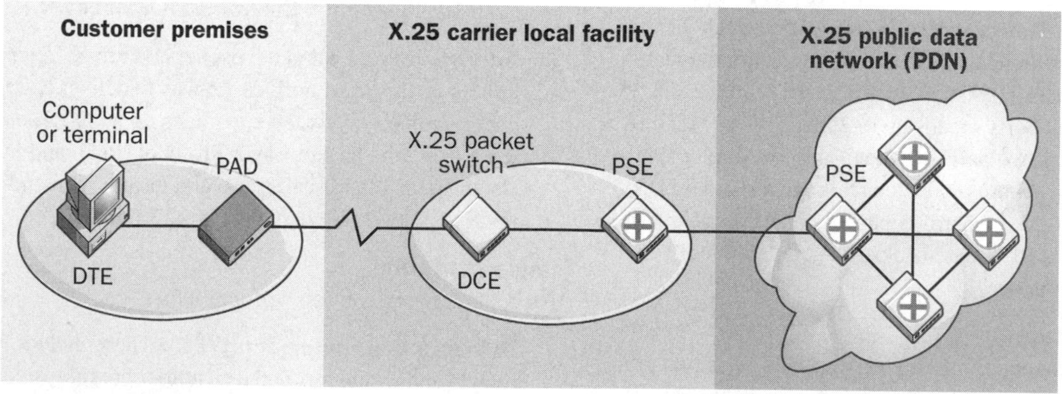

X.25. *Anatomy of a simple X.25 network.*

Issues

X.25 is efficient for batch file transfer but not for interactive communication such as Telnet sessions, in which Transmission Control Protocol/Internet Protocol (TCP/IP) is run over X.25. If you often use Telnet from your X.25 terminal, you can improve efficiency by employing VanJacobsen TCP/IP Header Compression to reduce the overhead of the TCP/IP packet header from 40 bytes to 5 bytes (if your TCP/IP stack supports this feature). Another cause of X.25's inefficiency for interactive communication is the typical half-second latency in communication due to the store-and-forward nature of the packet-switching network. Frame relay does not use store-and-forward packet switching and hence has much less latency. In general, X.25 is not a good communication medium for applications that use TCP/IP because the high latency and low speed can sometimes cause TCP/IP applications to time out.

Prospects

Newer WAN technologies such as frame relay, Integrated Services Digital Network (ISDN), and T-carrier services are now generally preferred to X.25. However, X.25 networks still have applications in areas such as credit card verification, automatic teller machine transactions, and other dedicated business and financial uses. A striking example of how X.25 is still used is offered by the U.S. federal government's Automated Clearing House (ACH) network, a 30-year-old nationwide X.25 network used for collections payments between U.S. banks. Businesses use ACH to perform direct deposit of employee payroll, to credit and debit bank and credit institution funds transfers, and many other tasks. The U.S. Department of the Treasury has created a Web-based front end called *www.pay.gov* to this legacy X.25 system to allow ordinary citizens to pay taxes and other government fees such as those for National Parks permits.

See Also: *Channel Service Unit/Data Service Unit (CSU/DSU), connection-oriented protocol, data communications equipment (DCE), data terminal equipment (DTE), DS-0, frame relay, High-level Data Link Control (HDLC), Integrated Services Digital Network (ISDN), International Telecommunication Union (ITU), Open Systems Interconnection (OSI) reference model, packet assembler/ disassembler (PAD), packet-switching services, permanent virtual circuit (PVC), Public Switched Telephone Network (PSTN), router, RS-232, switched virtual circuit (SVC), T-carrier, Telnet, terminal, Transmission Control Protocol/Internet Protocol (TCP/IP), V.35, wide area network (WAN), X-series*

x86 platform

A PC hardware platform whose processor is based on the Intel 386 architecture microprocessor.

Overview

The x86, or Intel, platform is one of the two processor platforms supported by Microsoft Windows NT (the other being the Alpha platform) and the only processor platform supported by Microsoft Windows 2000. Intel-based systems have essentially caught up with Alpha in terms of speed and functionality and are used for everything from mobile laptop computers to desktop workstations to high-performance symmetric multiprocessing (SMP) servers.

The x86 family is based on the 386 processor and includes the 486, Pentium, Pentium Pro, Pentium II, Pentium III, and Pentium IV processors. Intel processors are based on the complex instruction set computing (CISC) architecture, which uses a large set of basic processor instructions to simplify code compilation. The CISC architecture differs from the reduced instruction set computing (RISC) architecture of the Alpha platform, which uses fewer processor instructions and offers better performance.

Notes

The Windows .NET Server platform also supports the new Itanium 64-bit architecture from Intel Corporation.

See Also: *64-bit architecture, Alpha platform*

X.121 address

An address of an end node connected to an X.25 public data network.

Overview

Also called international data numbers (IDNs), X.121 addresses are similar to long-distance telephone numbers

and are used by X.25 end nodes to call each other to set up communication sessions. X.121 addresses are used during the call setup phase of X.25 communication and are used to establish a switched virtual circuit (SVC) between the source node and destination node on the network.

X.121 addresses are typically 14 decimal digits in length, unless fewer can suffice to uniquely determine the address of the destination node being called. The first four digits form the data network identification code (DNIC), with the first three digits indicating the country or region and the fourth digit indicating the carrier that owns the common packet-switching network being used to make the call. The remaining digits form the national terminal number (NTN) and identify the end node being called. An additional 1-byte header indicates the number of digits of both the source and destination nodes.

Once an X.25 communication session is established, a 12-bit logical channel identifier (LCI) is assigned to the two hosts as the identification number of the virtual circuit that is established between them. The X.25 network uses the LCI in the headers of the X.25 packets for routing data between the nodes. The X.121 address is used only at call setup to establish the virtual circuit.

See Also: X.25, X-series

X.400

A set of electronic messaging standards defined in 1984 and 1988 by the International Telecommunication Union (ITU).

Overview

The X.400 standards are based on the Open Systems Interconnection (OSI) reference model developed by the International Organization for Standardization (ISO). X.400 defines global standards to enable users to send e-mail between X.400-compliant messaging systems.

X.400 was originally intended to be the uniform, worldwide standard for global messaging, but the Internet's Simple Mail Transfer Protocol (SMTP) has far eclipsed it in popularity. X.400 is still used, however, in some parts of Europe by post, telephone, and telegraph (PTT) authorities.

Implementation

X.400 defines a global Message Handling System (MHS) that consists of a number of messaging components. From an administrative point of view, the primary building blocks of the MHS are management domains (MDs). Note that these management domains are not the same as DNS domains—the Domain Name System (DNS) is used by SMTP messaging services, not X.400. A management domain is a collection of X.400 messaging systems having at least one Message Transfer Agent (MTA) managed by a specific organization. X.400 management domains come in two varieties:

- **Administrative Management Domains (ADMDs):** Messaging systems managed by an administrator or a registered private agency. These are the top-level management domains that handle third-party messaging traffic. An example is a telephone carrier service company such as AT&T.
- **Private Management Domains (PRMDs):** Unique subscriptions to an ADMD, such as telephone numbers of users. PRMDs can send or receive messages from an ADMD, but PRMDs cannot communicate directly with each other.

An X.400 MHS consists of the following five kinds of messaging components:

- **Message Transfer Systems (MTSs):** Collections of one or more MTAs that function together to provide message-forwarding services for a particular X.400 domain.
- **Message Transfer Agents (MTAs):** Route and deliver transport messages to and from User Agents (UAs) and with other MTAs. An MTA corresponds to a mail server in a typical local area network (LAN)–based messaging system. MTAs maintain a database of all UAs registered in their domain and routing tables that indicate how messages should be forwarded to other domains.
- **Message Stores (MSs):** Temporarily store messages that an MTA has received until they can be processed and forwarded for delivery. X.400 thus uses a store-and-forward method of message delivery.

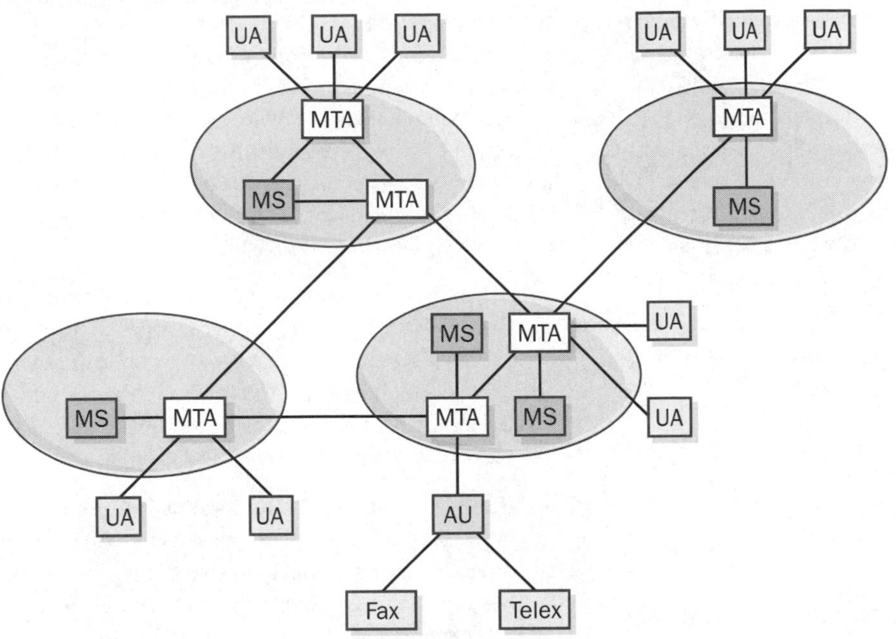

X.400. *Architecture of an X.400 Message Handling System (MHS).*

- **User Agents (UAs):** Provide messaging functionality directly to users. From a practical point of view, a UA can be identified as the e-mail client software that a user is running; from an abstract point of view, a UA is a domain belonging to a user and consisting of additional subcomponents. The goal of an X.400 MHS is to facilitate exchange of messages between different UAs.
- **Access Units (AUs):** Gateways between an X.400 MHS and another messaging system such as a telex or fax system.

Each UA in an X.400 MTS is identified by a special X.400 address called an Originator/Recipient (O/R) address. The O/R address is the e-mail address of the X.400 user and can be quite complex compared to an SMTP e-mail address, which is one reason that SMTP has overtaken X.400 in popularity as a global messaging standard. An O/R address consists of a series of VALUE=ATTRIBUTE pairs separated by semicolons. Not all fields need to be complete—only those that uniquely identify the recipient are required. Here is an example of an X.400 address:

```
C=US;A=MCI;P=MICROSOFT;O=SALES;S=SMITH;G=JEFF;
```

The individual address fields are as follows:

- Country (C) is United States
- ADMD (A) is MCI
- PRMD (P) is Microsoft (company name)
- Organization (O) is Sales Department of Microsoft
- Surname (S) is Smith
- Given name (G) is Jeff

An X.400 message consists of a P1 envelope and its P2/22 message contents. The envelope contains the e-mail address information needed for routing the message to its destination. The X.400 protocol for a message envelope includes support for message tracking and delivery priority features. The X.400 protocol for the message content includes a header and body part for the message.

What typically happens in the message transfer process is that a UA sends a message addressed to another UA in the MHS. The message is forwarded to an MTA in the local MTS, which either delivers the message locally or forwards it to a remote MTA for handling, depending on where the destination UA is located. The message is passed from MTA to MTA until it reaches the MTS of the destination UA, whereupon it is either delivered if the destination UA is connected or stored in an MS until the UA can retrieve it.

See Also: e-mail, P-series protocols, Simple Mail Transfer Protocol (SMTP), X-series

X.500

An International Telecommunication Union (ITU) recommendation for a global directory.

Overview

A directory is a tool designed to provide a single source for locating, organizing, and managing a network's resources within a business or enterprise. The X.500 recommendations define a global, hierarchical directory that includes the following features:

- A vendor-neutral standards-based directory based on ITU recommendations
- A single, global, hierarchical namespace of objects and their attributes
- Data management functions for viewing, adding, modifying, and deleting directory objects
- Search capabilities for customizing complete data queries

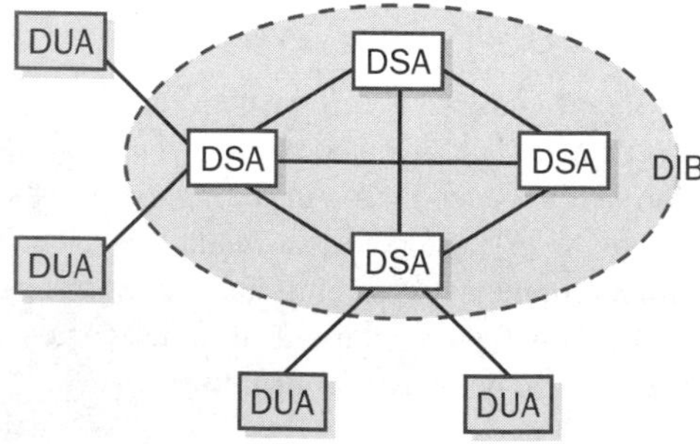

X.500. *Architecture of an X.500 directory.*

Implementation

From an administrative point of view, the building blocks of the X.500 directory service are Directory Management Domains (DMDs). An X.500 DMD is a collection of X.500 components that includes at least one Directory System Agent (DSA) and is managed by a Domain Management Organization (DMO). There are two types of DMDs:

- **Administrative Directory Management Domains (ADDMDs):** Directory services managed by a registered private agency that provide public directory services. Examples of ADDMDs are Four11 and Bigfoot, which provide public X.500 directory services over the Internet.
- **Private Directory Management Domains (PRDMDs):** Directory services that provide private directory access. An example is a domain controller hosting Active Directory directory service on a network running Microsoft Windows 2000.

The three main components of an X.500 directory are

- **Directory Information Base (DIB):** The actual hierarchical database that contains all the information in the directory. X.500 uses a distributed directory hierarchy in which different subsets of the DIB are found on different servers at different locations. From the user's point of view, however, the entire global X.500 directory appears to be accessible from the local directory server that the Directory User Agent (DUA) connects to. A schema is used to define the various classes of objects and their attributes, which can be stored in the directory. The Directory Information Tree (DIT) is the naming hierarchy that describes the hierarchical structure of the DIB.
- **Directory System Agent (DSA):** A particular server that maintains a subset of the DIB and provides an access point to the directory for DUAs to connect. Each DSA is responsible for a subset of the DIB and includes a set of naming contexts that define objects that are near each other in the DIT. DSAs also communicate with each other for directory replication purposes. This ensures that each DSA's subset of the DIB is current and complete and helps maintain the integrity of the whole X.500 directory system.

- **Directory User Agents (DUAs):** The client software that accesses the X.500 directory on behalf of the user. DUAs can perform such actions as searching, reading, updating, and deleting information in the directory, depending on the level of functionality of the client and the level of access granted to the user. The functionality of a DUA can be built into any type of software, including e-mail clients, Web browsers, or even the operating system itself.

To access information in the directory, a DUA connects to a local DSA and queries the directory by using the Directory Access Protocol (DAP), the standard X.500 protocol for locating, accessing, and modifying information in an X.500 directory. Various attribute-based search methods are possible using X.500-based directory services, including the following:

- White pages searches, for name-to-address lookups
- Yellow pages searches, for looking up a category
- Browsing, for listings related to a given attribute

When a DUA issues a query, the query travels through a chain of DSAs and a result set travels back along the same chain. These queries use DAP, while DSAs communicate with each other using the Directory System Protocol (DSP).

Marketplace

X.500 forms the architectural basis of Active Directory in Windows 2000 and Windows .NET Server, Novell Networks' Novell Directory Services (NDS) eDirectory, Oracle Corporation's Internet Directory (OID), and other popular directory services. Neither Active Directory nor NDS are full X.500 directories, however, although full X.500 directories are offered by a few vendors, including Global Directory Server from Critical Path, eTrust from Computer Associates, and DirX from Siemens.

Prospects

Despite the compelling features of X.500, it is not widely used for several reasons:

- It is a complex directory that was originally based on network protocols used by the Open Systems Interconnection (OSI) reference model and incurs considerable protocol overhead on Transmission Control Protocol/Internet Protocol (TCP/IP) networks.
- It has no native global name registration facility such as the Internet's Domain Name System (DNS), which makes it difficult to implement it as a truly global standard.

The feature-heavy Directory Access Protocol (DAP) used by X.500 is particularly complex and has been widely replaced by the Lightweight Directory Access Protocol (LDAP) developed by the University of Michigan and standardized by the Internet Engineering Task Force (IETF). LDAP directories such as iPlanet's Directory Server and InnoSoft's IDDS are generally more popular than full X.500 ones and much easier to manage, though offering fewer features.

See Also: *Active Directory, directory, Directory Access Protocol (DAP), Lightweight Directory Access Protocol (LDAP), Novell Directory Services (NDS), X-series*

xDSL

Refers to different "flavors" of Digital Subscriber Line (DSL), a group of broadband telecommunications technologies supported over copper local loop connections.

See Also: *Digital Subscriber Line (DSL)*

Xerox Network Systems (XNS)

A suite of networking protocols developed by Xerox Corporation's Palo Alto Research Center (PARC) in the early 1980s.

Overview

Xerox Network Systems (XNS) is based on a five-layer model, in contrast to the seven-layer Open Systems Interconnection (OSI) reference model for networking. The layers of the XNS protocol stack are as follows:

- **Level 0 (media access layer):** Maps to the OSI physical layer and data-link layer and performs similar functions. XNS does not tie into any one media access protocol and supports the Ethernet,

High-level Data Link Control (HDLC), Token Ring, and X.25 protocols, among others.

- **Level 1 (network layer):** Maps to the OSI network layer and defines the Internet Datagram Protocol (IDP). IDP functions similarly to the Internet Protocol (IP) of Transmission Control Protocol/Internet Protocol (TCP/IP) and uses a logical addressing scheme that requires four-byte network numbers, four-byte host numbers, and two-byte socket numbers for both source and destination addresses. IDP is responsible for delivering datagrams by using unicast, multicast, and broadcast methods. Level 1 also defines the Routing Information Protocol (RIP), which handles dynamic routing and has evolved into later versions for use in Internetwork Packet Exchange/Sequenced Packet Exchange (IPX/SPX) and TCP/IP networks.
- **Level 2 (transport layer):** Maps to the OSI transport layer and defines the Sequenced Packet Protocol (SPP). SPP functions similarly to the Transmission Control Protocol (TCP) of TCP/IP and is responsible for providing reliable transmission of IDP packets, including sequence numbers and acknowledgments. Level 2 also defines the Packet Exchange Protocol (PEP), which functions similarly to the User Datagram Protocol (UDP) of TCP/IP. For troubleshooting purposes, the Echo Protocol (EP) functions similarly to the ping utility of TCP/IP.
- **Level 3:** Maps to the OSI presentation layer and includes the Filing Protocol (FP), Clearinghouse Protocol (CP), Printing Protocol (PP), and others.
- **Level 4:** Maps to the OSI application layer (XNS has no level that maps to the OSI session layer).

XNS is little used today, but it was important in the evolution of other networking protocols, such as IPX/SPX and TCP/IP.

***See Also:** IPX/SPX-Compatible Protocol, protocol, Transmission Control Protocol/Internet Protocol (TCP/IP)*

XHTML

An enhanced version of Hypertext Markup Language (HTML) developed by the World Wide Web Consortium (W3C).

Overview

XHTML is basically a reformulation of HTML 4.01 in Extensible Markup Language (XML) using an XML document type definition (DTD). In other words, XHTML is HTML defined in terms of XML. XHTML thus includes all the functionality of HTML while being fully compliant with XML and including the extensibility and portability of XML.

XHTML is expected to smooth the migration from HTML to XML by allowing developers to create HTML documents that contain XML functionality and are compliant with XML applications. Some of the advantages of using XHTML instead of HTML for Web content development include

- Easier portability to nonstandard user interfaces
- The ability to create new DTDs

Web sites can be developed in or migrated to XHTML without worry of browser incompatibility because XHTML conforms to the operation of existing HTTP user agents. Migrating HTML sites to XHTML ensures that site content is XML-conforming, which is advantageous because it is likely that XML will eventually become the paradigm for developing all Web content.

The current standard is XHTML 1, which was released in January 2000.

For More Information

Find out more about XHTML at *www.w3.org/TR/xhtml1.*

***See Also:** Hypertext Markup Language (HTML), World Wide Web Consortium (W3C), XML*

XML

A meta-language used as a universal standard for electronic data exchange. The acronym stands for Extensible Markup Language.

Overview

XML is a derivative of Standardized Generalized Markup Language (SGML), an International Organization for Standardization (ISO) standard developed in 1986. SGML allows you to programmatically describe the structure and content of an electronic document. XML is basically a subset of SGML and is a language that can be used for creating other languages. Numerous XML "dialects" have been developed in the last few years for different sectors of industry. These dialects allow companies within each sector to exchange business information electronically and perform such business transactions as ordering, invoicing, and payment.

The goals of the designers of XML were to create a meta-language for developing business dialects that

- Supports a wide range of applications and processing schemes including client/server, distributed, and multi-tier
- Is easy to implement and use over the Internet
- Creates documents that are human-readable
- Is formal, concise, easy to understand, and has few optional features

History

Electronic business communication emerged in the 1970s when companies such as Kmart and Sears developed proprietary electronic processes for simplifying communication between stores and suppliers. Using these processes, large companies were able to reduce the amount of paperwork involved in their business transactions and save costs because of the reduced amount of labor involved in processing electronic communications over paper ones. Toward the end of the 1970s the U.S. government and companies from the transportation and manufacturing sectors worked with the American National Standards Institute (ANSI) to develop uniform standards for the electronic exchange of business information. The result of this effort was the ANSI X12 standard, which formed the basis of electronic data interchange (EDI). EDI basically defines the format and protocols for electronic exchange of invoices, purchase orders, receipts, and other documents.

EDI has been widely used by business, industry, and government, but its complexity and high cost have tended to limit its implementation in large enterprises. The high cost of EDI is mainly because it uses dedicated leased lines for exchange of business information between companies. To overcome the limitations of EDI, the World Wide Web Consortium (W3C) began developing XML in 1996 as an alternative to EDI, leveraging the popularity of Hypertext Markup Language (HTML) and the ubiquity of the Internet as a communication medium. Although EDI is intrinsically secure because it uses dedicated leased lines, XML requires an additional mechanism for ensuring secure transmission of electronic documents over the unsecure public Internet—for example, by employing a virtual private network (VPN).

The initial XML standard called XML 1 was published in 1998, and the XML Working Group of the W3C steers further development of the language. XML standards continue to evolve, and the most important ones are outlined in the "Architecture" section later in this article.

Uses

One of the earliest implementations of XML was by Microsoft Corporation in their Channel Definition Format (CDF) push technology for the Web. Since then XML has been embraced by all sectors of industry and is supported by software from major vendors such as Microsoft, Oracle Corporation, SAP, and PeopleSoft and by application service providers such as Ariba and Commerce One. Hundreds of different dialects (schemas) have been developed for different industry sectors—for example, to name a few:

- **ACORD XML:** An XML schema developed by the insurance industry for electronic exchange of life insurance information
- **ADPr:** Stands for Active Digital Profile; used for exchanging provisioning information for IT (information technology) products and services
- **AgXML:** Schema for the agricultural products sector developed by Monsanto, Archer Daniels Midland, and other members of this sector and managed by an independent nonprofit organization called AgXML LLC

- **BizTalk:** An XML framework from Microsoft for general e-commerce
- **BPML:** Stands for Business Process Modeling Language, a schema developed by a consortium of 80 companies to standardize how business processes are modeled
- **CDA:** Stands for Clinical Document Architecture, a schema for health care companies to share clinical and patient information electronically
- **CXML:** An XML schema developed by Commerce One for e-commerce
- **MathML:** Used by the academic sector for formatting documents containing mathematical expressions
- **RosettaNet:** XML schema for the high-tech manufacturing industry that has been embraced by over 300 different vendors
- **XKMS:** Stands for XML Key Management Specification, an XML specification developed by the financial and credit sector for secure electronic banking and credit transactions

Comparison

XML resembles HTML in many ways—for example, both languages use plain text files that are marked up using tags. But there are significant differences between XML and HTML, namely the following:

- XML markup describes the data itself, but HTML markup determines how the data is displayed in a Web browser. In other words, although HTML is a markup language, XML is a language for creating new markup languages. Note that unlike HTML, XML itself does not control how data is displayed. Instead, this feature is supported in XML through an associated standard called Extensible Stylesheet Language (XSL).
- HTML uses a fixed set of tags, but XML allows users to create their own tags to describe any kind of data.
- XML documents are easier to search than HTML ones because each kind of data has its own unique type of tags associated with it.
- HTML documents are basically designed for display in Web browsers, but XML can be used as a general language that allows all types of applications to communicate with one another.

Architecture

XML actually embraces a whole series of standards for different language and protocols, and it is still evolving as new pieces are developed and come into play. Some of the important parts of the XML specification include

- **Extensible Stylesheet Language (XSL):** Specifies how XML documents are displayed in a Web browser or other standard interface and allows XML documents to be translated into other types of documents such as HTML Web pages. Although XML documents contain the content (data) used by an application, XSL style sheets format the content of these documents to make them visually understandable. For example, an XSL style sheet could specify how an electronic invoice is displayed in HTML. Microsoft Internet Explorer includes a default XSL style sheet that can be used to display the contents of XML documents in the browser window.
- **Extensible Stylesheet Language Transformations (XSLT):** Allows XML documents to be translated into other types of documents regardless of whether they ever need to be human-readable. XSLT is essentially one-half of XSL, the "translation" part, without any consideration of the "display" part.
- **XPath:** Provides a programmatic syntax for querying XML documents to locate and select specific types of data within them. For example, an XML-enabled application could use XPath to extract pricing information from invoice documents.
- **Xpointer:** Complements XPath by allowing you to identify a portion within an XML document for further processing.
- **XML Query:** Like XPath, XML Query also lets you search for and extract specific kinds of information from an XML document, but XML Query offers a more database-like approach to this process. XML Query is currently still under development by the W3C.

- **XLink:** Provides a standard way of representing hyperlinks within XML documents.
- **Xinclude:** Copies a portion of an XML document into the current document. Compared to Microsoft's Object Linking and Embedding (OLE) technology, XLink is like Linking and XInclude is like Embedding. XInclude is also currently under development by the W3C.
- **Xbase:** Provides a method of coding relative hyperlinks within XML documents.
- **Document type definition (DTD):** A language that allows you to define an XML dialect. Each dialect requires an associated DTD that specifies the structure and syntax of valid and well-formed documents for that dialect. DTD is a complex language that is different from XML and much harder to read and is expected to be superceded by XML Schema, which is described next.
- **XML Schema:** A newer method for defining XML dialects than the older DTD specification. XML Schema uses XML itself to create special documents called schemas that describe the structure and syntax of a particular XML dialect. Hundreds of XML schemas have been developed (see the Implementation section below).
- **Resource Description Framework (RDF):** Specifies how document metadata such as copyright and search keywords can be embedded in XML documents. RDF makes it easier to manage large numbers of XML documents in a collection or repository.
- **Document Object Model (DOM):** Allows XML documents to be parsed into the native object format of a standard programming language. DOM makes it easier for developers to XML-enable their applications.
- **SAX:** Similar to DOM, but instead of reading the entire XML document into memory to process it (as DOM does), SAX allows applications to read through XML documents in real time and trigger events when certain conditions arise. Unlike the other XML standards described above, which are standardized by the W3C, SAX is an open-source project.
- **Simple Object Access Protocol (SOAP):** Enables applications to access remote objects using XML. SOAP is a specification developed by IBM and Microsoft.
- **Uniform Description, Discovery, and Integration (UDDI):** Enables vendors to expose their proprietary XML schemas to each other through a distributed directory service.
- **XAML:** Developed by IBM, Oracle, Hewlett-Packard, and Sun Microsystems, this emerging XML standard is designed to simplify the process of coordinating complex business transactions between multiple parties.

Implementation

XML requires much stricter adherence to formatting rules than HTML does. Specifically, XML documents must be

- **Well-formed:** Complies with the general rules and syntax of XML. For example, in an XML document every opening tag requires a corresponding closing tag. In HTML you can get away with omitting closing tags (omitting the </p> in a <p>…</p> expression, for example), but not so in XML—the rules must be strictly followed. Another example is that all attributes within tags must be enclosed in quotes. For example, in HTML you could have either <font size=4> or <font size="4">, and both would be interpreted correctly by most browsers. In XML only the second of these statements would be considered acceptable in a well-formed document. Other essential aspects of XML formatting include case sensitivity (HTML is not case sensitive) and proper nesting of elements (HTML lets you get away with coding <b><p>…</p></b> instead of <p><b>…</b></p>).
- **Valid:** Complies with the rules specified in the documents corresponding DTD or schema. In other words, the vocabulary of a particular XML dialect is limited to what is defined in that dialect's "dictionary."

Examples

A simple example of an XML document is the following, which contains the name and phone number for a sales contact person:

```
<?xml version "1.0"?>
<contact_book>
    <contact type="sales">
        <name>
            <first_name>Jeff</first_name>
            <last_name>Smith</last_name>
        </name>
        <phone>555-1212</phone>
    </contact>
</contact_book>
```

The first line of this document (required) is called the prolog, and it informs the XML parser within an application that it is parsing an XML document and other relevant information. The rest of the document is called the document element and contains the data to be used by the application. Note how you can use XML to define tags that are used to describe what the data is about. The "extensible" nature of XML lies in the fact that you can create custom tags to describe different kinds of data as needed. For example, you could create an <im> tag to include the Instant Messaging (IM) identifier for the contact above.

Prospects

Although XML has captured the minds of industry and software vendors alike as a way to simplify and reduce the cost of doing business electronically, few businesses have actually implemented full XML-based business-to-business (B2B) solutions. The reasons for this include

- XML standards have evolved considerably in the few years since XML originated, and they are still evolving. As a result, before implementing XML solutions, many businesses are adopting a "wait-and-see" approach until XML becomes a mature standard.
- Although EDI is expensive and complex, those who have implemented EDI solutions often see little incentive to change, taking an "if it ain't broke, don't fix it" approach.

Despite these issues, it seems almost inevitable that XML will eventually succeed in dominating the electronic business marketplace due to its flexibility, power, and ease of use. A number of vendors are developing workaround approaches to help companies migrate from EDI to XML. For example, Vitria Technology, PaperFree Corporation, and several other companies have created Web-based applications that allow businesses to access EDI documents using a standard Web browser interface and to translate EDI messages into XML.

For More Information

Visit the W3C's XML site at *www.w3.org/xml.* Other useful sites to visit include *www.xml.org* and *www.xml.com.*

See Also: *B2B, Electronic Business Extensible Markup Language (ebXML), electronic data interchange (EDI), Hypertext Markup Language (HTML), Simple Object Access Protocol (SOAP), Universal Description, Discovery, and Integration (UDDI), virtual private network (VPN), World Wide Web Consortium (W3C)*

XNS

Stands for Xerox Network Systems, a suite of networking protocols developed by Xerox Corporation's Palo Alto Research Center (PARC) in the early 1980s.

See: *Xerox Network Systems (XNS)*

X-series

A series of standards and recommendations from the International Telecommunication Union (ITU) dealing with data communication over computer networks and telecommunication services.

Overview

Some of the more important X-series standards and recommendations include the following:

- **X.25:** Defines a protocol for a global packet-switching network for wide area network (WAN) connectivity. Related X-series protocols include X.3, X.28, X.29, X.92, X.96, X.110, and X.121.

- **X.400:** Defines a standard for a global message handling system for e-mail. Related protocols include X.402, X.403, X.407 (ANS.1), X.408, X.411, X.413, X.420, and the P-series protocols.
- **X.500:** Defines a recommendation for a global directory service. Related protocols include X.501, X.509, X.511, and X.518 through X.521.

See Also: *X.25, X.121 address, X.400, X.500*

xSP

Represents the various "flavors" of service providers that emerged in the late 1990s.

Overview

The earliest of the new breed of service providers that emerged in the 1990s was the Internet service provider (ISP), which originally meant a company that provided connectivity with the Internet, usually dial-up for home users and T1 or fractional T1 lines for businesses. As the number of ISPs on the market exploded in the late 1990s, many of the larger ones began to offer additional services to customers including Web hosting, custom Web application development, and e-commerce storefronts. Soon many players in the Internet marketplace began to refer to themselves as different types of service providers in an effort to differentiate themselves from one another according to the services they specialized in offering. Today a growing number of service providers have emerged, often overlapping in the services they offer and changing their focus to adjust to the market. Currently the list includes

- **Application service provider (ASP):** A company that offers software services to business customers across the Internet, particularly services involving outsourcing of Web and e-business applications. ASPs were the next to occur after ISPs, and the late 1990s saw hundreds of them appear—and most of them disappear a year or two later.
- **Business service provider (BSP):** Basically an ASP that provides a wide range of online business services that include not just Web hosting and e-commerce services typical of ASPs but also customer relations management, desktop maintenance support, system integration and consulting services, and other value-added business services.
- **Caching service provider (CSP):** A company that maintains caching servers that speed the transfer of information across the Internet's infrastructure and offers managed access to these servers for a fee.
- **Commercial service provider (also CSP):** This broad term typically includes ISPs, online service providers, telephone and cable network operators, and similar companies.
- **Content service provider (again CSP):** Helps organizations maintain fresh content on their portals without the need or cost of creating their own internal publishing house.
- **Full-service provider (FSP):** Really just another name for BSP.
- **Hosting service provider (HSP):** Basically an ISP that concentrates on Web hosting.
- **Management service provider (MSP):** A company that manages the (IT) information technology infrastructure for other businesses.
- **Storage service provider (SSP):** A company offering outsourced storage services to businesses.
- **Security service provider (also SSP):** A company offering outsourced security services to businesses.
- **Wireless application service provider (WASP):** An ASP that supports wireless business applications.

Together, all these different types of service providers are generally grouped under the acronym *xSP*, where *x* represents a variable that can be replaced by other letters, such as *I* for Internet or *A* for Application.

See Also: *application service provider (ASP), caching service provider (CSP), commercial service provider (CSP), Management Service Provider (MSP), outsourcing, storage service provider (SSP)*

X Window System

A multiuser client/server graphical user interface (GUI) for UNIX environments.

Overview

The X Window System, also known simply as X, provides a multitasking GUI windowing environment for network-attached UNIX workstations and terminals. The Massachusetts Institute of Technology (MIT), Stanford, and IBM jointly developed X starting in 1984. The first popular release of the platform was X version 11, which came out in 1987. In 1988 the X Consortium was formed to steer development of the system, and Release Six of X, usually called X11R6, appeared in 1996 and remains the most popular version of X. In 1997 the X Consortium turned over responsibility for overseeing further development of X to The Open Group.

Elements of X include the following:

- **X servers:** These form the server portion of the X Window System and are typically UNIX servers but can also be mainframe computers running UNIX.
- **X clients:** These are typically UNIX desktop workstations running the X Window System client software. The client software enables the workstations to display a windowed GUI in the X Window System environment. An alternative to using workstations is using X terminals, which are dumb terminals that have no operating system and use a ROM routine to implement X client software. X terminal machines always must be connected to X servers by using local area network (LAN) connections, in contrast to character-based dumb terminals, which usually use serial connections such as RS-232 or X.21.
- **X protocol:** This is the protocol used for communication between X clients and X servers, and it enables the client to send keyboard and mouse data to the server and display the GUI on the client.
- **X window manager:** Examples include OSF/Motif and K Desktop Environment (KDE), which implement windowing features such as menus, toolbars, and gadgets that provide the look and feel of a windowing GUI environment that allows X applications to run.

X is available on all UNIX platforms and on Linux distributions, and there are even versions for Microsoft Windows, OS/2, and the Macintosh platform.

For More Information

Visit X.Org at *www.x.org.*

See Also: *K Desktop Environment (KDE), UNIX*

Y2K

Also called the year 2000 problem or the millennium bug (even though it is not actually a bug), a computer problem that was expected to affect older hardware and software on January 1, 2000. Similar problems were expected to arise on other dates, particularly September 9, 1999, and February 28, 2000.

Overview

The Y2K problem represented a family of problems that were anticipated at the turn of the millennium. These problems were expected to arise from three primary sources: internal representation of dates, incorrect programming of leap years, and specialized use of certain key dates.

The issue of internal representation of dates in computer software was expected to be the most critical Y2K-related issue. This is because until recently, most software had been written to store date information in a format that used only the last two digits of a year to represent the year. For example, the year 1960 was internally represented as 60. In the early days of programming, system and disk memory were expensive and had to be carefully optimized, and saving 2 bytes by representing the date 1954 internally as the two-digit number 54 yielded significant savings on a system with limited RAM. This type of "good programming practice" continued even into the mid-1990s. And even though some programmers were aware of potential Y2K problems early on, no one expected programs developed in the 1970s and 1980s to continue being used into the next millennium. This date representation issue was the most commonly identified version of the year 2000 problem because the year 2000 would have been represented internally as 00, which is the same representation for the date 1900. In fact, most older software did interpret the internal date 00 as 1900 instead of 2000, which was expected to lead to problems when calculations were performed using dates. For example, many analysts predicted that financial software might calculate that an employee born in 1954 was actually 00 - 54 = -54 years old in the year 2000, and that such negative ages could lead to such problems as missed paychecks or pension contributions—which on a large scale could have had disastrous social consequences.

This date-representation issue was not just a software application problem but also involved PC hardware, specifically in relation to the real-time clock (RTC) chip, which in most PCs uses only two digits to represent a year, and the basic input/output system (BIOS) routing, which is stored in flash ROM. If the BIOS did not contain code to roll over the century from 19xx to 20xx on January 1, 2000, the operating system would see the date 1900 when the user first turned on his or her PC in the year 2000. In some systems this problem could be fixed with a BIOS upgrade, but other systems had to be replaced with Y2K-compliant hardware.

Another Y2K-related issue was that the year 2000 was a leap year because it was divisible by 4, but some older software applications and hardware BIOS programs were expected to not recognize this fact and would therefore produce dates that were off by one day after February 28, 2000.

Finally, many older software applications used special dates to represent special situations. For example, many older COBOL applications gave the date 9/9/99 a special meaning such as "this item is to be saved forever" or "this item is to be deleted after 30 days." Such applications, therefore, had the potential to produce unpredictable results after September 9, 1999.

Fortunately, the IT (information technology) industry was well aware of these problems years in advance and publicized the potential loss of business that could arise should these issues not be fixed in time. Hardware vendors released new versions of BIOS and other system code to ensure Y2K compliance, and software vendors issued new versions of applications or fixed Y2K issues using service packs and hotfixes. Similarly, IT departments around the world addressed Y2K concerns by allocating resources to upgrading legacy hardware such as PCs built before 1996, upgrading software and applying service packs to eliminate Y2K-related issues, and debugging and rewriting custom software to eliminate other possible date-related bugs. This turned out to be an enormous task—for example, an estimated 180 billion lines of COBOL code had been written for mainframe environments in business, industry, and government, and much, if not most, of this code had the potential to be affected. Y2K problems were not limited to the mainframe arena but also affected server and desktop operating systems and applications on UNIX, Macintosh, and Microsoft Windows platforms, which in turn affected hardware BIOS programming, operating systems, application software, custom code, macros, and data files. The problem was enormous and well publicized, but government and public agencies, enterprise-level businesses, and software and hardware vendors had devoted extensive resources to ensure that systems functioned properly on and after January 1, 2000. The result of these efforts was that instead of the end of the electronic world occurring at the beginning of the new millennium, virtually all government agencies and businesses around the world experienced little more than hiccups in their operation. The Y2K problem, which threatened to be one of humanity's greatest disasters, turned out to be one of IT's greatest triumphs.

Y-connector

A type of connector that can be used to connect a single device or cable to two devices or cables.

Overview

Y-connectors are used in several places in computer networking and systems interconnection. Some examples of different types of Y-connectors include the following:

- **RJ-11 Y-connector:** Allows two or more telephone devices to be plugged into a single RJ-11 wall plate. Some vendors call these adapters modular coupler splitters. This arrangement allows only one of the devices to work at any given time.

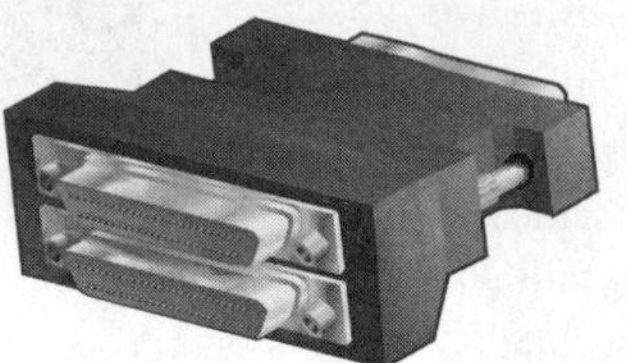

Y-connector. *A typical SCSI Y-connector.*

- **SCSI Y-connector:** Allows a Small Computer Systems Interface (SCSI) device to be added to the middle of a chain of SCSI devices. A typical SCSI Y-connector has one 50-pin Centronics male connector and two 50-pin Centronics female connectors. One use for a SCSI Y-connector is the connection of a single RAID 5 SCSI array to two nodes of a Microsoft Windows 2000 server cluster.

See Also: *RJ connectors, Small Computer System Interface (SCSI), Y-splitter*

Y-splitter

Also called a Y-cable, a type of cable adapter that is arranged in a Y-shaped formation and is used to connect one device to a pair of other devices.

Overview

Y-splitters are used in a number of scenarios in computer networking and systems interconnection. Some examples of where Y-splitters may be used include the following:

- **PS/2 Y-splitter:** Typically used to connect an external keyboard and mouse to a single PS/2 port on a laptop such as the IBM ThinkPad. This type of splitter typically has cables that are about 1 foot (30 centimeters) long. PS/2 Y-splitters should use shielded cabling for best operation in noisy electrical environments.
- **Internal power Y-splitter:** An adapter used inside a PC to connect additional internal drives to the internal power supply of the PC. This type of splitter comes in various arrangements for connecting different combinations of hard disk, CD-ROM, and floppy disk.

- **External power Y-splitter:** An adapter commonly used with high-end Ethernet switches to connect them to two redundant external power supplies. If one power supply fails, the other immediately takes over the load, and the failed power supply can be hot-swapped with a replacement.
- **RS-366 Y-splitter:** Used for some videoconferencing systems running in dual port mode over Integrated Services Digital Network (ISDN) connections.

PS/2 Y-splitter

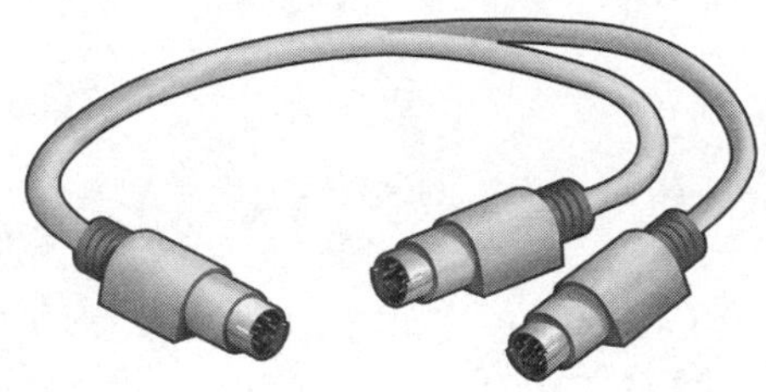

Internal power Y-splitter

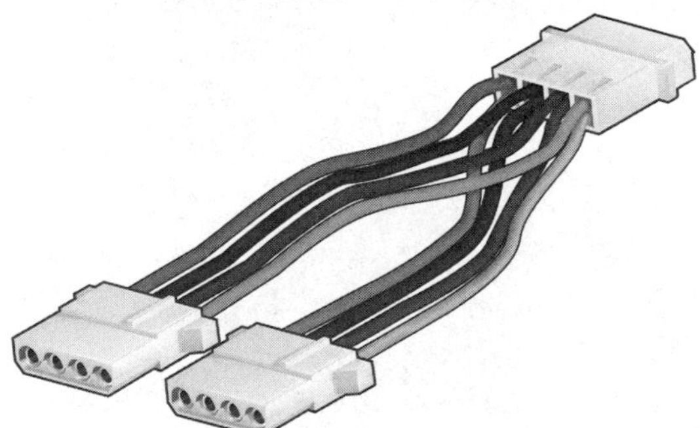

Y-splitter. *Examples of two kinds of Y-splitters.*

See Also: *Integrated Services Digital Network (ISDN), Y-connector*

Z

ZAK

Stands for Zero Administration Kit, a collection of tools, methodologies, and guidelines developed for Microsoft Windows 95, Windows 98, and Windows NT 4 that network administrators can use to implement policy-based management of Windows NT–based networks.

See: *Zero Administration Kit (ZAK)*

Zero Administration Kit (ZAK)

A collection of tools, methodologies, and guidelines developed for Microsoft Windows 95, Windows 98, and Windows NT 4 that network administrators can use to implement policy-based management of Windows NT–based networks.

Overview

Microsoft Corporation developed the Zero Administration Kit (ZAK) as part of their Zero Administration Initiative for Microsoft Windows (ZAW), a multifaceted approach designed to reduce the cost and effort of installing, configuring, and managing desktop workstations. ZAW was intended to provide tools and procedures that would simplify the administration of logons, security, applications, and other functions. The ZAK was the first result of the ZAW initiative, and it enabled administrators of Windows 95–, Windows 98–, and Windows NT 4–based networks to

- Manage the configuration of users' desktops from a central location without having to visit each computer. For example, you can specify exactly which applications the user can run, the appearance of the desktop, and where user data might be saved.
- Restrict local access to users' desktops. For example, you could lock down the desktops to prevent users from performing actions that might result in costly help desk calls, such as installing unapproved applications or modifying critical system files.
- Configure applications and data to be stored on network servers. This facilitated upgrading of applications, enabled centralized backup, and provided improved security by enabling administrators to download applications from the network and use local hard drives for caching.

Implementation

The ZAK employed the security of the NTFS file system (NTFS) along with Windows NT system policies and user profiles. Administrators could use the predefined set of system policies to override default local settings and use standard user profiles to configure and manage users' desktops from a central location. The ZAK included two preconfigured modes of operation, though advanced administrators could also create their own custom network configurations. The default modes were:

- **TaskStation Mode:** A desktop configuration that is designed for a "task-oriented" user such as a bank teller or a data entry person. This mode was ideal for users who required access to only one line-of-business application. TaskStation Mode completely locked down users' desktops and booted directly into Microsoft Internet Explorer or some other specified application. The user had no access to the Microsoft Windows Start button, taskbar, Task Manager, Control Panel, file system, or context menus in this mode of operation.
- **AppStation Mode:** A desktop configuration that is designed for typical "knowledge workers" who might use three or four business applications every day but may lack the knowledge and experience to configure or troubleshoot the system or install other applications. This mode provided users with a constrained Windows interface that allowed them access to only those applications they needed in order to perform their jobs. The user had no access to Task Manager, Control Panel, the file system, or context menus in this mode.

Notes

The Windows NT 4 ZAK has now been superseded by Intellimirror and Group Policy features in Windows 2000, Windows XP, and Windows .NET Server. These features provide greater management and control of user desktops and applications than ZAK provided.

For More Information

You can find ZAK at *www.microsoft.com/windows/zak.*

See Also: *Group Policy, IntelliMirror*

zone

In AppleTalk networking, a logical grouping of computers on a network.

Overview

A zone is to legacy AppleTalk networks of Apple Macintosh computers what a virtual LAN (VLAN) is to Ethernet networks. In other words, a zone is a logical way of grouping computers on a network regardless of the physical network segment they each reside upon. For example, a single zone may span several network segments, and multiple zones can be assigned to the same physical network.

Information concerning which zone a particular computer is on is propagated throughout an AppleTalk network using a protocol called the Zone Information Protocol (ZIP). Each computer maintains information about the zones other machines reside in using a local zone information table (ZIT). Administrators can configure which zone a computer belongs to by using the Choose utility on that machine.

Computers that belong to the same zone have access to the same set of shared resources on the network. If a user moves to a different physical network, the user can still belong to the same zone provided the router interface in the user's new location belongs to that zone.

Notes

The term *zone* is also used to refer to a zone of authority, a portion of the Domain Name System (DNS) namespace that is managed by a particular name server.

See Also: *AppleTalk, zone of authority*

zone file

A file on a name server that contains information about a zone in which the name server is authoritative.

Overview

A zone file is a text file consisting of a series of resource records that form the Domain Name System (DNS) database of the name server. These records identify the domain and subdomains that the name server is responsible for managing, Internet Protocol (IP) address to host name mappings for hosts within these domains and subdomains, timing parameters for zone transfers between primary and secondary name servers, and other data.

A name server typically has at least three zone files:

- **<root_domain>.dns:** The forward lookup zone file that is used to resolve host names into IP addresses for Transmission Control Protocol/Internet Protocol (TCP/IP) hosts over which the name server has authority. In the example that follows, the root domain is microsoft.com, and therefore the zone file is microsoft.com.dns.
- **z.y.x.w.in-addr.arpa:** The reverse lookup zone file for the forward lookup zone, which is used to resolve IP addresses into host names for TCP/IP hosts over which the name server has authority. In the example that follows, the network ID is 192.250.100.0, so the reverse lookup zone file is 100.250.192.in-addr.arpa.dns.
- **cache.dns:** A standard file that exists on all name servers and that contains the host names and IP addresses of name servers on the Internet that maintain the root domain of the entire DNS namespace.

Examples

A typical zone file might look like this:

```
; Database file microsoft.com.dns for
microsoft.com. zone.
@                IN      SOA
dns1.microsoft.com.      admin.microsoft.com.
                 12      ; serial number
                 3600    ; refresh
                 600     ; retry
                 86400   ; expire
                 3600    ; minimum TTL
```

```
; Zone NS records
@           IN    NS     dns1
@           IN    NS     dns2
; Zone A records
dns1        IN    A      192.250.100.10
dns2        IN    A      192.250.100.11
proxy1      IN    A      192.250.100.101
fred        IN    A      192.250.100.102
wilma       IN    A      192.250.100.103
localhost   IN    A      127.0.0.1
www         IN    CNAME  fred
ftp         IN    CNAME  wilma
```

Notes

Microsoft Windows 2000 gives you the option of integrating DNS with Active Directory directory service. This results in zone information being stored in Active Directory, which has several advantages over traditional implementations of DNS such as Berkeley Internet Name Domain (BIND), in which zone data is stored in text files:

- It provides a more efficient mechanism for zone transfers through the domain replication process of Active Directory. This eliminates the chore of manually configuring zone transfers between primary and secondary DNS servers.
- It provides additional fault tolerance for the DNS information because all Active Directory integrated zones are primary zones and therefore contain a copy of the zone data.

See Also: Active Directory, Berkeley Internet Name Domain (BIND), Domain Name System (DNS), IP address, name server, resource record (RR), zone of authority, zone transfer

zone of authority

A portion of the Domain Name System (DNS) namespace that is managed by a particular name server.

Overview

A zone of authority (often simply called a zone) is an administrative unit of DNS namespace and can consist of a single DNS domain or a domain combined with some of its subdomains. An example of a domain might be microsoft.com, which might contain the subdomains sales.microsoft.com, support.microsoft.com, and tech.microsoft.com. The name server that administers the microsoft.com domain is said to be authoritative for that domain. The zone of authority for such a name server might be, for example:

- **Microsoft.com and all three of its subdomains:** The name server contains information about all the hosts in Microsoft.com and in each of its three subdomains. This is not a particularly efficient approach, as it concentrates name resolution within a single name server and may place an undue burden upon the DNS administrator of the zone.
- **Microsoft.com and the two subdomains sales.microsoft.com and support.microsoft.com:** Authority for the subdomain tech.microsoft.com would be delegated to a different name server. This approach is useful if the tech.microsoft.com subdomain needs to be managed as a separate entity from the rest of microsoft.com.
- **Microsoft.com only, with none of its subdomains:** Authority for the subdomains is delegated to one or more name servers, and the name server for microsoft.com contains only delegation information about the other name servers and about hosts in the microsoft.com domain. This approach reduces the burden of administering hosts in the microsoft.com domain by distributing it to administrators in one or more delegated zones.

Note that the concepts of a zone and a domain are related: each zone is anchored in a specific domain known as the zone's root domain. However, not all of the subdomains of the domain necessarily belong to that same zone; those that have been delegated belong to different zones. Another way of saying this is to say that zones are bounded from one another by delegation—that is, each act of delegation creates a new zone.

Each name server must either

- Have its own local zone file, which contains the mappings between Internet Protocol (IP) addresses and host names for hosts found in that zone. A primary name server is one that has its own locally stored zone file called a primary zone file, which is implemented on Berkeley Internet Name Domain (BIND) name servers as a text file called a zone file.

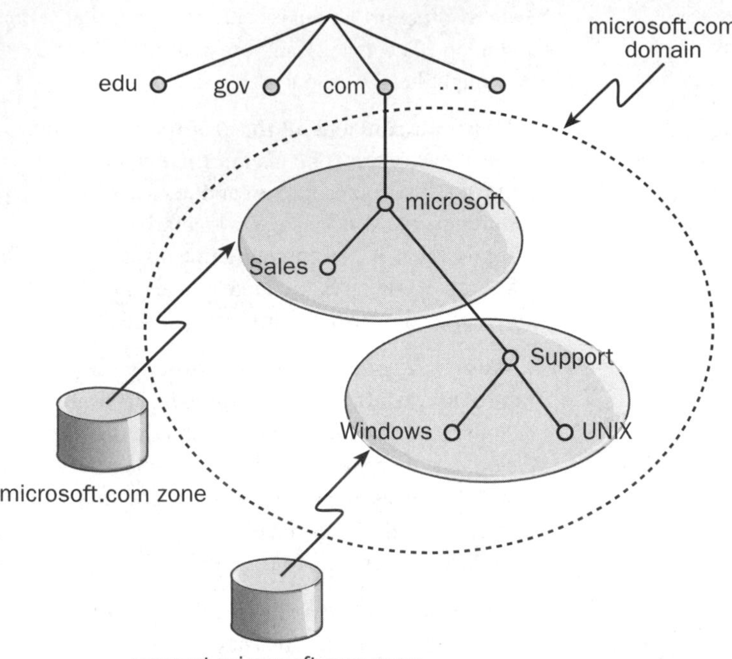

Zone of authority. *Examples of zones delegated on the domain name system (DNS) namespace.*

or

- Download its zone file from another name server using a process known as zone transfer. A secondary name server has no local zone file but downloads it from the primary name server authoritative over the particular zone. This secondary zone file is a read-only file that can only be modified in its original version on the primary name server from which it has been downloaded. Secondary name servers are used in the DNS system mainly to provide redundancy.

A single name server can manage one or more zones, depending on how it is configured. For example, a name server might have one zone for the domain microsoft.com and another zone for the domain adventure.expedia.com.

In networks that use Microsoft Windows 2000 and Windows .NET Server, a zone can take yet a third form, called an Active Directory directory–integrated zone. In this type of zone, the zone information is stored in Active Directory directory service instead of in a text file, and it is replicated across the network using the standard directory replication method employed by domain controllers. Windows 2000 DNS also supports dynamic DNS (DDNS) to ease the administrative burden of manually maintaining zone files.

Notes

Do not confuse DNS zones with AppleTalk zones, discussed in the article "zone" elsewhere in this chapter.

See Also: *Active Directory, Berkeley Internet Name Domain (BIND), domain (DNS), Domain Name System (DNS), dynamic DNS (DDNS), IP address, name server, zone file, zone transfer*

zone transfer

The process of transferring zone information from a primary name server to a secondary name server.

Overview

Zone transfers are an essential part of the operation of the Domain Name System (DNS). Primary name servers maintain the master copy of the zone information for a particular DNS zone of authority, usually in the form of a text file called a zone file. Secondary name servers then download this information from the primary name server authoritative over their zone using the method of zone transfer. The advantages of this approach are that:

- If the primary name server goes down, the secondary name server has a complete, up-to-date copy of the zone file and can handle name resolution requests by DNS clients on the network.
- If a large number of DNS clients on the local network are making name resolution requests from a particular zone, these requests can be load balanced between the primary and secondary name servers for that zone.
- If the primary name server is located on the remote side of a slow wide area network (WAN) link, placing a secondary name server on the local side reduces bandwidth usage for the WAN link by allowing name resolution requests to be handled locally. In this scenario the only network traffic created by DNS is the occasional zone transfers that take place over the link.

Implementation

Zone transfers generally occur in three circumstances:

- When a secondary name server is rebooted.
- When the refresh interval for a secondary name server expires. This interval is defined in the start of authority (SOA) record at the beginning of the zone file on the primary name server.
- When changes have been made to the zone file on the primary name server and a notify list has been configured on the primary name server. A notify list is a list of Internet Protocol (IP) addresses that specify which secondary name servers are allowed to access zone information on the primary name server for purposes of zone transfer. The primary name server immediately notifies the secondary name server that the zone file has been modified and instructs it to initiate a zone transfer without waiting for the refresh interval to expire.

The secondary name server always initiates a zone transfer. Typically, the secondary name server periodically contacts the primary name server to determine whether any changes have been made to the primary name server's zone file. If so, it initiates a request for a zone transfer. Specifically, when the refresh interval expires on the secondary name server, the following occurs:

1. The secondary name server requests and receives the SOA record from the primary name server.
2. The secondary name server compares the version number in the primary name server's SOA record with its own current version number. If they differ, the secondary name server requests a zone transfer from the primary name server.
3. In standard DNS operation, the entire zone file is then transferred during this process.

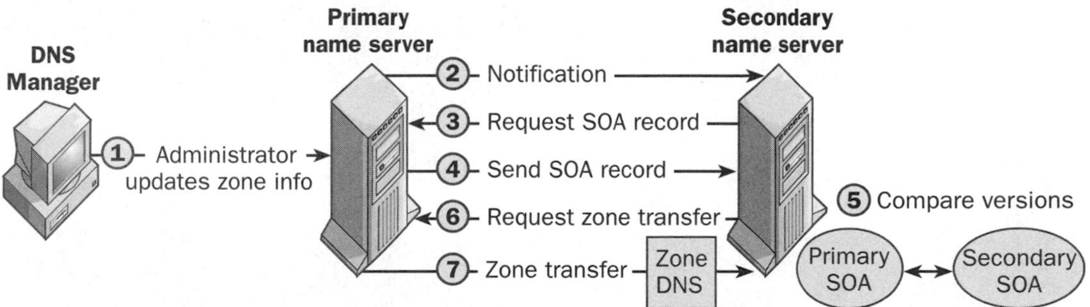

Zone transfer. *How a typical zone transfer works.*

Notes

DNS as implemented on the Microsoft Windows 2000 and Windows .NET Server platforms allows zone information to be transferred incrementally using updates. In other words, the entire contents of the zone file are not sent when a small change is made to a resource record in the zone file. This method is called incremental zone transfer and is defined in RFC 1995.

An advantage of using directory-integrated DNS zones on Windows 2000 and Windows .NET Server is that the dnsZone object container in Active Directory can be secured using Windows 2000 access control lists (ACLs) for greater security.

See Also: *Domain Name System (DNS), incremental zone transfer, name server, zone file, zone of authority*

Index

Numbers and Symbols

A

B

C

D

E

F

G

I

J

K

L

M

N

O

P

S

U

V

W

X

Y

Z

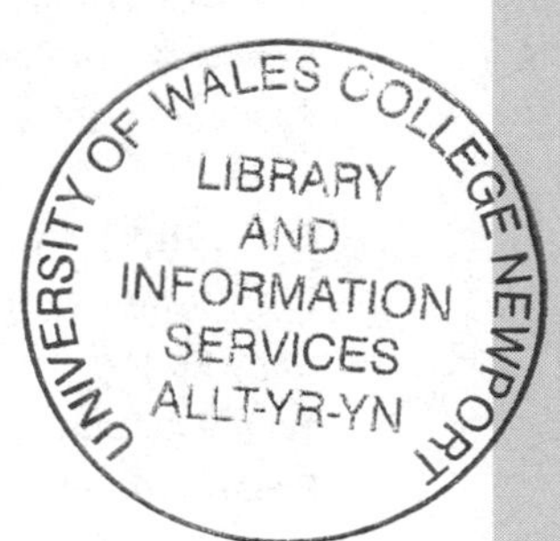

Drill and Wire Gauge

Drill bits and wires come in a variety of diameters, depending on the job. How do you measure their diameters? With a drill and wire gauge. Simply insert the drill or wire into a hole of the same size on the gauge to discover its diameter—often marked in metric equivalents.

At Microsoft Press, we use tools to illustrate our books for software developers and IT professionals. Tools are an elegant symbol of human inventiveness and a powerful metaphor for how people can extend their capabilities, precision, and reach. From basic calipers and pliers to digital micrometers and lasers, our stylized illustrations of tools give each book a visual identity and each book series a personality. With tools and knowledge, there are no limits to creativity and innovation. Our tag line says it all: *The tools you need to put technology to work.*

The manuscript for this book was prepared using Microsoft Word 2000 and submitted to Microsoft Press in electronic form. The contents was structured using XML. The majority of the pages were composed using Adobe FrameMaker+SGML 6.0, with text type in Times and display type in ITC Franklin Gothic. Composed pages were sent to the printer as electronic prepress files. The CD was created using XML output from FrameMaker.

Cover Designer:	Methodologie, Inc.
Interior Graphic Design:	James D. Kramer
Principal Graphic Artist:	Rob Nance
Production Information Analyst:	Barbara Norfleet

For nSight, Inc. (www.nSightWorks.com)

Project Manager:	Susan H. McClung
Copy Editor:	Joseph Gustaitis
Technical Editors:	Ari Globerman, John Panzarella
Proofreaders:	Sarah Campbell, Rebecca Merz, Robert Saley
Desktop Production Specialist:	Donald Cowan
Indexer:	James Minkin

About the Authors

Mitch Tulloch is the author of 10 books, including the *Microsoft Encyclopedia of Networking, 1st Edition* (Microsoft Press); *Windows 2000 Administration in a Nutshell* (O'Reilly and Associates); and *Administering IIS4* (Osborne/McGraw-Hill). Mitch also has written articles for such industry magazines as *NetworkWorld* and is a regular contributor to myITforum.com and Swynk.com.

Mitch holds B.Sc. and Cert.Ed. degrees from the University of Manitoba and is a Microsoft Certified Systems Engineer (MCSE). He has more than 20 years of experience teaching and training in technical subjects and currently works as an independent consultant and writer. Mitch is also an accomplished keyboardist and is currently working on several CD projects. You can find out more about Mitch at his Web site, *www.mtit.com.*

Ingrid Tulloch is an experienced researcher who has contributed her skill and expertise to both the first and second editions of the *Microsoft Encyclopedia of Networking*. She is also a professional artist who has exhibited in several North American cities and holds B.A. and Cert.Ed. degrees from the University of Manitoba. You can find out more about Ingrid and view her art online at *www.mtit.com*.

MICROSOFT LICENSE AGREEMENT

Book Companion CD

IMPORTANT—READ CAREFULLY: This Microsoft End-User License Agreement ("EULA") is a legal agreement between you (either an individual or an entity) and Microsoft Corporation for the Microsoft product identified above, which includes computer software and may include associated media, printed materials, and "online" or electronic documentation ("SOFTWARE PRODUCT"). Any component included within the SOFTWARE PRODUCT that is accompanied by a separate End-User License Agreement shall be governed by such agreement and not the terms set forth below. By installing, copying, or otherwise using the SOFTWARE PRODUCT, you agree to be bound by the terms of this EULA. If you do not agree to the terms of this EULA, you are not authorized to install, copy, or otherwise use the SOFTWARE PRODUCT; you may, however, return the SOFTWARE PRODUCT, along with all printed materials and other items that form a part of the Microsoft product that includes the SOFTWARE PRODUCT, to the place you obtained them for a full refund.

SOFTWARE PRODUCT LICENSE

The SOFTWARE PRODUCT is protected by United States copyright laws and international copyright treaties, as well as other intellectual property laws and treaties. The SOFTWARE PRODUCT is licensed, not sold.

1. **GRANT OF LICENSE.** This EULA grants you the following rights:
   - a. **Software Product.** You may install and use one copy of the SOFTWARE PRODUCT on a single computer. The primary user of the computer on which the SOFTWARE PRODUCT is installed may make a second copy for his or her exclusive use on a portable computer.
   - b. **Storage/Network Use.** You may also store or install a copy of the SOFTWARE PRODUCT on a storage device, such as a network server, used only to install or run the SOFTWARE PRODUCT on your other computers over an internal network; however, you must acquire and dedicate a license for each separate computer on which the SOFTWARE PRODUCT is installed or run from the storage device. A license for the SOFTWARE PRODUCT may not be shared or used concurrently on different computers.
   - c. **License Pak.** If you have acquired this EULA in a Microsoft License Pak, you may make the number of additional copies of the computer software portion of the SOFTWARE PRODUCT authorized on the printed copy of this EULA, and you may use each copy in the manner specified above. You are also entitled to make a corresponding number of secondary copies for portable computer use as specified above.
   - d. **Sample Code.** Solely with respect to portions, if any, of the SOFTWARE PRODUCT that are identified within the SOFTWARE PRODUCT as sample code (the "SAMPLE CODE"):
     - i. **Use and Modification.** Microsoft grants you the right to use and modify the source code version of the SAMPLE CODE, *provided* you comply with subsection (d)(iii) below. You may not distribute the SAMPLE CODE, or any modified version of the SAMPLE CODE, in source code form.
     - ii. **Redistributable Files.** Provided you comply with subsection (d)(iii) below, Microsoft grants you a nonexclusive, royalty-free right to reproduce and distribute the object code version of the SAMPLE CODE and of any modified SAMPLE CODE, other than SAMPLE CODE, or any modified version thereof, designated as not redistributable in the Readme file that forms a part of the SOFTWARE PRODUCT (the "Non-Redistributable Sample Code"). All SAMPLE CODE other than the Non-Redistributable Sample Code is collectively referred to as the "REDISTRIBUTABLES."
     - iii. **Redistribution Requirements.** If you redistribute the REDISTRIBUTABLES, you agree to: (i) distribute the REDISTRIBUTABLES in object code form only in conjunction with and as a part of your software application product; (ii) not use Microsoft's name, logo, or trademarks to market your software application product; (iii) include a valid copyright notice on your software application product; (iv) indemnify, hold harmless, and defend Microsoft from and against any claims or lawsuits, including attorney's fees, that arise or result from the use or distribution of your software application product; and (v) not permit further distribution of the REDISTRIBUTABLES by your end user. Contact Microsoft for the applicable royalties due and other licensing terms for all other uses and/or distribution of the REDISTRIBUTABLES.

2. **DESCRIPTION OF OTHER RIGHTS AND LIMITATIONS.**
   - **Limitations on Reverse Engineering, Decompilation, and Disassembly.** You may not reverse engineer, decompile, or disassemble the SOFTWARE PRODUCT, except and only to the extent that such activity is expressly permitted by applicable law notwithstanding this limitation.
   - **Separation of Components.** The SOFTWARE PRODUCT is licensed as a single product. Its component parts may not be separated for use on more than one computer.
   - **Rental.** You may not rent, lease, or lend the SOFTWARE PRODUCT.
   - **Support Services.** Microsoft may, but is not obligated to, provide you with support services related to the SOFTWARE PRODUCT ("Support Services"). Use of Support Services is governed by the Microsoft policies and programs described in the

user manual, in "online" documentation, and/or in other Microsoft-provided materials. Any supplemental software code provided to you as part of the Support Services shall be considered part of the SOFTWARE PRODUCT and subject to the terms and conditions of this EULA. With respect to technical information you provide to Microsoft as part of the Support Services, Microsoft may use such information for its business purposes, including for product support and development. Microsoft will not utilize such technical information in a form that personally identifies you.

- **Software Transfer.** You may permanently transfer all of your rights under this EULA, provided you retain no copies, you transfer all of the SOFTWARE PRODUCT (including all component parts, the media and printed materials, any upgrades, this EULA, and, if applicable, the Certificate of Authenticity), **and** the recipient agrees to the terms of this EULA.
- **Termination.** Without prejudice to any other rights, Microsoft may terminate this EULA if you fail to comply with the terms and conditions of this EULA. In such event, you must destroy all copies of the SOFTWARE PRODUCT and all of its component parts.

3. **COPYRIGHT.** All title and copyrights in and to the SOFTWARE PRODUCT (including but not limited to any images, photographs, animations, video, audio, music, text, SAMPLE CODE, REDISTRIBUTABLES, and "applets" incorporated into the SOFTWARE PRODUCT) and any copies of the SOFTWARE PRODUCT are owned by Microsoft or its suppliers. The SOFTWARE PRODUCT is protected by copyright laws and international treaty provisions. Therefore, you must treat the SOFTWARE PRODUCT like any other copyrighted material **except** that you may install the SOFTWARE PRODUCT on a single computer provided you keep the original solely for backup or archival purposes. You may not copy the printed materials accompanying the SOFTWARE PRODUCT.

4. **U.S. GOVERNMENT RESTRICTED RIGHTS.** The SOFTWARE PRODUCT and documentation are provided with RESTRICTED RIGHTS. Use, duplication, or disclosure by the Government is subject to restrictions as set forth in subparagraph (c)(1)(ii) of the Rights in Technical Data and Computer Software clause at DFARS 252.227-7013 or subparagraphs (c)(1) and (2) of the Commercial Computer Software—Restricted Rights at 48 CFR 52.227-19, as applicable. Manufacturer is Microsoft Corporation/One Microsoft Way/Redmond, WA 98052-6399.

5. **EXPORT RESTRICTIONS.** You agree that you will not export or re-export the SOFTWARE PRODUCT, any part thereof, or any process or service that is the direct product of the SOFTWARE PRODUCT (the foregoing collectively referred to as the "Restricted Components"), to any country, person, entity, or end user subject to U.S. export restrictions. You specifically agree not to export or re-export any of the Restricted Components (i) to any country to which the U.S. has embargoed or restricted the export of goods or services, which currently include, but are not necessarily limited to, Cuba, Iran, Iraq, Libya, North Korea, Sudan, and Syria, or to any national of any such country, wherever located, who intends to transmit or transport the Restricted Components back to such country; (ii) to any end user who you know or have reason to know will utilize the Restricted Components in the design, development, or production of nuclear, chemical, or biological weapons; or (iii) to any end user who has been prohibited from participating in U.S. export transactions by any federal agency of the U.S. government. You warrant and represent that neither the BXA nor any other U.S. federal agency has suspended, revoked, or denied your export privileges.

DISCLAIMER OF WARRANTY

NO WARRANTIES OR CONDITIONS. MICROSOFT EXPRESSLY DISCLAIMS ANY WARRANTY OR CONDITION FOR THE SOFTWARE PRODUCT. THE SOFTWARE PRODUCT AND ANY RELATED DOCUMENTATION ARE PROVIDED "AS IS" WITHOUT WARRANTY OR CONDITION OF ANY KIND, EITHER EXPRESS OR IMPLIED, INCLUDING, WITHOUT LIMITATION, THE IMPLIED WARRANTIES OF MERCHANTABILITY, FITNESS FOR A PARTICULAR PURPOSE, OR NONINFRINGEMENT. THE ENTIRE RISK ARISING OUT OF USE OR PERFORMANCE OF THE SOFTWARE PRODUCT REMAINS WITH YOU.

LIMITATION OF LIABILITY. TO THE MAXIMUM EXTENT PERMITTED BY APPLICABLE LAW, IN NO EVENT SHALL MICROSOFT OR ITS SUPPLIERS BE LIABLE FOR ANY SPECIAL, INCIDENTAL, INDIRECT, OR CONSEQUENTIAL DAMAGES WHATSOEVER (INCLUDING, WITHOUT LIMITATION, DAMAGES FOR LOSS OF BUSINESS PROFITS, BUSINESS INTERRUPTION, LOSS OF BUSINESS INFORMATION, OR ANY OTHER PECUNIARY LOSS) ARISING OUT OF THE USE OF OR INABILITY TO USE THE SOFTWARE PRODUCT OR THE PROVISION OF OR FAILURE TO PROVIDE SUPPORT SERVICES, EVEN IF MICROSOFT HAS BEEN ADVISED OF THE POSSIBILITY OF SUCH DAMAGES. IN ANY CASE, MICROSOFT'S ENTIRE LIABILITY UNDER ANY PROVISION OF THIS EULA SHALL BE LIMITED TO THE GREATER OF THE AMOUNT ACTUALLY PAID BY YOU FOR THE SOFTWARE PRODUCT OR US$5.00; PROVIDED, HOWEVER, IF YOU HAVE ENTERED INTO A MICROSOFT SUPPORT SERVICES AGREEMENT, MICROSOFT'S ENTIRE LIABILITY REGARDING SUPPORT SERVICES SHALL BE GOVERNED BY THE TERMS OF THAT AGREEMENT. BECAUSE SOME STATES AND JURISDICTIONS DO NOT ALLOW THE EXCLUSION OR LIMITATION OF LIABILITY, THE ABOVE LIMITATION MAY NOT APPLY TO YOU.

MISCELLANEOUS

This EULA is governed by the laws of the State of Washington USA, except and only to the extent that applicable law mandates governing law of a different jurisdiction.

Should you have any questions concerning this EULA, or if you desire to contact Microsoft for any reason, please contact the Microsoft subsidiary serving your country, or write: Microsoft Sales Information Center/One Microsoft Way/Redmond, WA 98052-6399.

PN 097-0002296

System Requirements

Here are the system requirements for running the *Microsoft Encyclopedia of Networking, Second Edition* electronic book on compact disc.

Minimum System Requirements

This eBook requires a system running:

- Pentium class with 166-megahertz (MHz) or higher processor
- Operating System required:
  Microsoft Windows 95 or
  Microsoft Windows 98 or
  Microsoft Windows NT 4 SP3 or later
  Microsoft Windows 2000 Professional or
  Microsoft Windows 2000 Server or
  Microsoft Windows Millennium Edition or
  Microsoft Windows XP
- Memory required:
  Microsoft Windows 95: 12 MB RAM or
  Microsoft Windows 98: 16 MB RAM or
  Microsoft Windows NT 4 SP6: 16 MB RAM
  Microsoft Windows 2000 Professional: 64 MB RAM
  Microsoft Windows 2000 Server: 64 MB RAM
  Microsoft Windows Millennium Edition: 64 MB RAM
  Microsoft Windows XP: 64 MB RAM

- Disk Space required:
  -To install and run an eBook from a network (network installation): 10 MB
  -To install and run an eBook to the hard drive (local installation): 20–31 MB
  -To install Microsoft Internet Explorer to the hard drive (local installation) and install and run an eBook from a network (network installation): 121 MB
  -To install Microsoft Internet Explorer to the hard drive (local installation) and install and run an eBook from a hard drive (local installation): 140–160 MB, depending on the size of the sample files, if locally installed.

Microsoft Internet Explorer 5.5 is included on the CD and will be installed on the user's machine automatically if necessary. The Internet Explorer setup has been configured to install the minimum necessary files and will not change the user's current settings or associations.

Recommended System Requirements

The following system configuration is recommended for the best viewing experience of Microsoft Press eBooks:

- Pentium II (or similar) with 266-MHz or higher processor
- Windows 98 or later
- 64 MB RAM
- 8x CD-ROM drive or faster
- 800x600 with high color (16-bit) display settings